The National Hockey League

Official Guide & Record Book

1991-92

Running Press
Philadelphia, Pennsylvania

THE NATIONAL HOCKEY LEAGUE
Official Guide & Record Book/1991-92

Staff:
Senior editors: Stu Hackel, Gary Meagher; Statisticians: Benny Ercolani, Greg Inglis; Editorial Staff: Brian Albert, Michael Berger, Sam Esposito, Jane Freer, Suzanne Unger.

Managing Editors: Ralph Dinger, James Duplacey

Contributing Editor: Igor Kuperman

European Editor: Tom Ratschunas

Contributors:
Bill Benswanger, Nonny Daly (Hockey East), Luca Del-Vita, Mike Emrick (NHLBA), Manon Gagnon (QMJHL), John Garner (ECAC), Stu Judge (WHL), Neil McDonald, Carol McLaughlin, Mike Meyers (IHL), Herb Morell (OHL), Marc Nathan, Renato Rossi, Hellen M. Schroeder (AHL), Doug Spencer (WCHA), Steven Steinsaltz, Jeff Weiss (CCHA).

Consulting Publisher: Dan Diamond

Photo Credits:
Historical and special event photos: Bruce Bennett, David Bier, New York Rangers, Rice Studio, Robert Shaver, Imperial Oil Turofsky Collection, Hockey Hall of Fame.

Current photos: Graig Abel, Toronto; Joe Angeles, St. Louis; Steve Babineau, Boston; Sol Benjamin, Chicago; Bruce Bennett, NY Islanders; Tony Biegun, Winnipeg, Denis Brodeur, Montreal; Mark Buckner, St. Louis; Denny Cavanaugh, Pittsburgh; Steve Crandall, New Jersey; Bill Cunningham, Vancouver; Willie Dagenais, Montreal; Bob Fisher, Montreal; Ray Grabowski, Chicago; John Hartman, Detroit; The Ice Age, Toronto; George Kalinsky, NY Rangers; Deborah King, Washington; Jim Mackey, Detroit; Rob McFarland, Minnesota; Bill McKeown, Edmonton; Jack Murray, Vancouver; Photography Ink, Los Angeles; Andre Pichette, Quebec; Richard Pilling, New Jersey; Protography, Minnesota; Wen Roberts, Los Angeles, Al Ruelle, Boston; Harry Scull, Jr., Buffalo; Don Smith, San Jose; Diane Sobolewski, Hartford; Gerry Thomas, Edmonton; Jim Turner, New Jersey; Brad Watson, Calgary; Westfile, Edmonton; Rocky Widner, San Jose; Bill Wippert, Buffalo.

Canadian representatives: Cannon Book Distribution Ltd., Toronto 416/252-5207

International representatives: Worldwide Media Services, Inc., 115 East Twenty-third Street, New York, NY 10010.

Typesetting: Compeer Typographic Services Limited, Toronto
Printing: The Alger Press Limited, Oshawa and Toronto

9 8 7 6 5 4 3 2 1
Digit on the right indicates the number of this printing.

ISBN 1-56138-068-7

ISSN 0-8286647

This book may be ordered by mail from the publisher.
Please add $2.50 for postage and handling.
But try your bookstore first!
Running Press Book Publishers
125 South Twenty-second Street
Philadelphia, Pennsylvania 19103

Running Press
Philadelphia, Pennsylvania

Table of Contents

Table of Contents *continued*

(1991-92 NHL Schedule begins inside front cover)

Introduction

A Double Anniversary

WELCOME TO THE 1991-92 EDITION OF THE *NHL OFFICIAL GUIDE & RECORD BOOK*. LIKE THE NATIONAL Hockey League, this book has expanded and now encompasses 416 pages of accurate and up to date information about the league and the talent pool that supplies it with players.

On page 7 you will find a special feature that describes league-wide plans for a season of celebration to mark the NHL's 75th season of play in 1991-92. From classic uniforms to celebrity captains, from fine art to a commemorative book, the NHL's 75th anniversary season provides the league with an opportunity to acknowledge the fans and players that have sustained the NHL since its founding in 1917.

Simultaneous to the NHL's 75th, the *NHL Official Guide & Record Book* is celebrating an anniversary of its own. The book you are reading now is the 60th annual edition of hockey's leading statistical guide.

Its earliest predecessor, the *National Hockey Guide & Record Book* of 1932-33, is shown full-size on this page. This vest-pocket book of 140 pages was edited by Jim Hendy, a member of the Hockey Hall of Fame who is acknowledged to be the father of modern record keeping in hockey. Despite its modest size, the 1932-33 Guide takes four pages to debate the merits of two of the game's glittering superstars, the Listowel Thunderbolt (Fred "Cyclone" Taylor) and the Mitchell Meteor (Howie Morenz). It also lists the complete career records of the "Big Six," hockey's highest-scoring half-dozen active players at the end of the 1931-32 season: Bill Cook, Morenz, Frank Boucher, Aurel Joliat, Harry Oliver, and Nels Stewart. Contrast this list with the six leading scorers among today's players: Wayne Gretzky, Bryan Trottier, Peter Stastny, Denis Savard, Paul Coffey, and Jari Kurri.

Several new features and enhancements have been added to the 1991-92 edition of the *NHL Official Guide & Record Book*. Full information on the NHL's newest franchise, the San Jose Sharks, begins on page 81. The Expansion and Dispersal Drafts that provided the Sharks with the majority of their player personnel can be found on page 168. An analysis of the 1991 Entry Draft by player source, country of origin, year of birth and position can be found on pages 166 and 167. As well, the upcoming tour of NHL clubs by the Canadian and U.S. Olympic Teams is listed on page 183.

More than 360 new players from junior, college, and European hockey have been added to our player register, which begins on page 213 for forwards and defenseman and on page 391 for goaltenders. The retired players and retired goaltenders sections have been enhanced by the addition of a new statistic which lists the number of NHL Stanley Cup wins by each player.

As always, our thanks to readers and members of the media who take the time to comment on the Guide & Record Book. Thanks as well to the people working in the communications departments of the NHL's member clubs and to their counterparts in the AHL, IHL, junior leagues and college conferences.

Best wishes for an enjoyable NHL 75th Anniversary Season in 1991-92.

ACCURACY REMAINS THE *GUIDE & RECORD BOOK*'S TOP PRIORITY, We appreciate comments and clarification from our readers. Please direct these to the editors:

Stu Hackel — 33rd floor, 650 Fifth Avenue, New York, NY 10019-6108 … or

Gary Meagher — 75 International Blvd., suite 300, Rexdale, Ontario M9W 6L9.

Your involvement makes a better book.

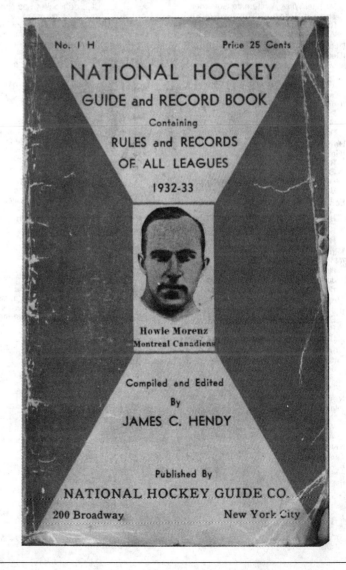

No. I H — Price 25 Cents

NATIONAL HOCKEY GUIDE and RECORD BOOK

Containing RULES and RECORDS OF ALL LEAGUES 1932-33

Howie Morenz
Montreal Canadiens

Compiled and Edited By JAMES C. HENDY

Published By NATIONAL HOCKEY GUIDE CO.

200 Broadway — New York City

National Hockey League

Organized November 22, 1917

Board of Governors

BOARD OF GOVERNORS — Officers
Chairman — William W. Wirtz
Vice-Chairman — Ronald Corey
Secretary — Robert O. Swados

Boston Bruins
(Boston Professional Hockey Association, Inc.)
Jeremy Jacobs — Governor
Harry Sinden — Alternate Governor
Louis Jacobs — Alternate Governor

Buffalo Sabres
(Niagara Frontier Limited Partnership)
Seymour H. Knox III — Governor
Robert O. Swados — Alternate Governor
Gerry Meehan — Alternate Governor
Seymour Knox IV — Alternate Governor

Calgary Flames
(Calgary Flames Hockey Club)
Harley Hotchkiss — Governor
Byron Seaman — Alternate Governor
William Hay — Alternate Governor

Chicago Blackhawks
(Chicago Blackhawk Hockey Team, Inc.)
William W. Wirtz — Governor
Michael Wirtz — Alternate Governor
Thomas N. Ivan — Alternate Governor
Robert Pulford — Alternate Governor
W. Rockwell Wirtz — Alternate Governor

Detroit Red Wings
(Detroit Red Wings, Inc.)
Michael Ilitch — Governor
James Devellano — Alternate Governor
James Lites — Alternate Governor

Edmonton Oilers
(Edmonton Oilers Hockey, Limited)
Peter Pocklington — Governor
Glen Sather — Alternate Governor
Robert Lloyd — Alternate Governor

Hartford Whalers
(Hartford Whalers Hockey Club Limited Partnership)
Richard Gordon — Governor
Emile Francis — Alternate Governor
Don Conrad — Alternate Governor
Ben Sisti — Alternate Governor

Los Angeles Kings
(L.A. Kings, Ltd.)
Bruce McNall — Governor
Rogatien Vachon — Alternate Governor
Roy Mlakar — Alternate Governor

Minnesota North Stars
(Northstar Hockey Partnership)
Norman N. Green — Governor
James Erickson — Alternate Governor
Bob Clarke — Alternate Governor

Montreal Canadiens
(Le Club de Hockey Canadien, Inc.)
Ronald Corey — Governor
Ron Bowman — Alternate Governor
Serge Savard — Alternate Governor

New Jersey Devils
(Meadowlanders, Inc.)
John J. McMullen — Governor
John C. Whitehead — Alternate Governor
Louis A. Lamoriello — Alternate Governor

New York Islanders
(Nassau Sports)
John O. Pickett — Governor
William Torrey — Alternate Governor
William Skehan — Alternate Governor
John H. Krumpe — Alternate Governor

New York Rangers
(New York Rangers Hockey Club — a division of Madison Square Garden Center, Inc.)
Stanley Jaffe — Governor
Kevin Billet — Alternate Governor
Thomas A. Conway — Alternate Governor
Neil Smith — Alternate Governor

Philadelphia Flyers
(Philadelphia Flyers Limited Partnership)
Jay T. Snider — Governor
Edward M. Snider — Alternate Governor
Ron Ryan — Alternate Governor
Russ Farwell — Alternate Governor

Pittsburgh Penguins
(Pittsburgh Penguins, Inc.)
Marie Denise DeBartolo York — Governor
J. Paul Martha — Alternate Governor
Craig Patrick — Alternate Governor

Quebec Nordiques
(Club de Hockey Les Nordiques de Québec)
Société en commandite)
Marcel Aubut — Governor
Maurice Filion — Alternate Governor
Gilles Leger — Alternate Governor

St. Louis Blues
(St. Louis Blues Hockey Club, L.P.)
Michael F. Shanahan — Governor
Ron Caron — Alternate Governor
Jack Quinn — Alternate Governor
Thomas Guilfoil — Alternate Governor

San Jose Sharks
(The San Jose Sharks)
George Gund — Governor
Gordon Gund — Alternate Governor
Art Savage — Alternate Governor
Jack Ferreira — Alternate Governor
Irwin Leonard — Alternate Governor

Toronto Maple Leafs
(Maple Leafs Gardens Limited)
Cliff Fletcher — Governor
Donald P. Giffen — Alternate Governor
Blair Cowper-Smith — Alternate Governor

Vancouver Canucks
(Vancouver Hockey Club, Limited)
Arthur R. Griffiths — Governor
Frank A. Griffiths — Alternate Governor
Frank W. Griffiths — Alternate Governor
Pat Quinn — Alternate Governor

Washington Capitals
(Washington Hockey Limited Partnership)
Abe Pollin — Governor
David Poile — Alternate Governor
Richard M. Patrick — Alternate Governor

Winnipeg Jets
(8 Hockey Ventures, Inc.)
Barry L. Shenkarow — Governor
Bill Davis — Alternate Governor
Michael A. Smith — Alternate Governor

League Offices

MONTREAL
960 Sun Life Building,
1155 Metcalfe Street,
Montreal, Que. H3B 2W2
Phone: 514/871-9220

ENVOY ID	
Accounting	NHLMTL.ACTG
Auto-delivery station	NHLMTL.AUTO
Central Registry	BON
Information Systems	NHLMTL.MIS
General	NHLMTL.GNRL

Telex via CCI NY 7601297
FAX 514/871-1663

NEW YORK
33rd Floor, 650 Fifth Avenue,
New York, N.Y., 10019-6108
Phone: 212/398-1100

ENVOY ID	
Accounting	NHLNY.ACTG
Broadcasting	NHLNY.TV
General	NHLNY.GNRL
Marketing	NHLNY.MKTG

Telex via CCI NY 7601278
FAX 212/245-8221

TORONTO
75 International Blvd., Suite 300
Rexdale, Ont., M9W 6L9
Phone: 416/798-0809

ENVOY ID	
Auto-delivery station	NHLTOR.AUTO
Central Scouting	NHLTOR.SCTG
General	NHLTOR.GNRL
Jim Gregory	HOCKEY.OPERATIONS
Officiating	OFFICIATING.TOR
Communications	NHL.COMM

Telex via CCI NY 7601296
General FAX 416/798-0819
Communications FAX 416/798-0852

OFFICERS
President — John A. Ziegler, Jr.
Executive Vice-President — Brian F. O'Neill
Vice-President/General Counsel — Gilbert Stein
Vice-President of Finance and Treasurer — Kenneth G. Sawyer
Vice-President, Hockey Operations — Jim Gregory
Vice-President, NHL Project Development — Ian "Scotty" Morrison
Vice-President, Broadcasting — Joel Nixon
Vice-President, Marketing/Public Relations — Steve Ryan

League Departments

MONTREAL
Administration
Brian O'Neill — Executive Vice President
Madeleine Supino — Secretary
Phil Scheuer — Director of Administration
Steve Hatzepetros — Assistant Director of Administration
Nancy Starnino — Secretary
Robert Bouchard — Administrative Assistant

Central Registry
Garry Lovegrove — Director of Central Registry
Madeleine Supino — Assistant Director
Audrey Harari — Assistant
Steve Pellegrini — Assistant

Information Systems
Mario Carangi — Director, Information Systems
Miranda Ishak — Assistant Director
Luc Coulombe — Assistant Director, Planning & Development
Tony Borsellino — Planning & Development
John Sullivan — Programmer/Analyst
Guylene Mercier — Programmer
Johanne Hinds — Operations
Peggy Spracklin — Operations

Finance
Joseph DeSousa — Controller
Rosa Troiano — Secretary
Mary Skiadopoulos — Assistant Controller
Steve Hatzepetros — Manager, Finance
Lynne Blagrave — Manager, Pension Administration
Donna Gillman — Accounting Supervisor
Doris Long — Secretary
Vivianne Chen — Secretary
Jocelyne Comeau — Accountant
Vicki Sciortino — Accountant

Pension
Jacques Bourgeois — Director, Pension
Lynne Blagrave — Manager, Pension Administration
Mary Skiadopoulos — Controller, Pension
Susan Lee — Pension Assistant
Vivianne Chen — Secretary

Office Services
Jean Huard — Printer
Darrin Burke — Office Assistant
Marcia Golding — Receptionist

NEW YORK

Broadcasting
Joel Nixon — Vice-President, Broadcasting
Stu Hackel — Director of Broadcasting
Suzanne Unger — Project Manager
Lois Cutler — Administrative Assistant

Legal Department
Gilbert Stein — Vice-President/General Counsel
Pat Honig — Assistant

NHL Services, Inc.
Steve Ryan — President
Lucia Ripi — Assistant
Tina Lalama — Secretary
Walter Luby — Controller
Patricia Cassell-Cooper — Assistant Controller
Mary McCarthy — Assistant Controller
Evelyn Torres — Accounts Payable
Ivonne Merchant — Secretary
Steve Flatow — Executive Director, Marketing Division
Kathleen Dober — Secretary
Jim Ryan — General Manager, Promotional Licensing
Maria Pace Buettel — Manager, Client and Team Services
Mike Humes — General Manager,
  NHL All-Star Weekend (215) 569-1883
Karen Hovsepian — Director of Special Events
Krista Lizzi — Special Events Coordinator
Fred Scalera — General Manager, Retail Licensing Division
Ann Kiely — Secretary
Brian Jennings — Regional Sales Manager
Bill Tighe — Regional Sales Manager
Stu Hackel — General Manager, Publishing & Video Division
Michael A. Berger — Executive Editor, Goal Magazine
John Karr — Executive Director,
  NHL Anniversaries (612) 854-1069
John Halligan — Director of Communications,
  NHL Anniversaries (212) 532-7673

Office Administration
Janet Meyers — Director, Administration
Andy Crawford — Administrative Assistant
Lola Skaro — Receptionist

President's Staff
Darcy Rota — Special Assistant to the President
Susan K. Rudin-Leonard — Assistant to the President
Scott Shanes — Presidential Liaison Officer
Karen Falco — Secretary

Finance
Ken Sawyer — Vice-President, Finance and Treasurer

Security
Frank Torpey — Director of Security

TORONTO

Jim Gregory — Vice-President of Hockey Operations
Bryan Lewis — Director of Officiating
Wally Harris — Assistant Director of Officiating
Will Norris — Coordinator of Development
Dave Newell — Officiating Coach
Frank Bonello — Director of Central Scouting
John Andersen — Central Scouting Administration
Al Wiseman — Assistant Director of Security
Chris Edwards — Video Coordinator

Secretarial Staff
Mary Keenan, Kelley Rosset

Officiating Supervisory Staff
Dave Newell, Matt Pavelich, Lou Maschio, Jim Christison,
John D'Amico, Bob Nadin, Sam Sisco, Charlie Banfield

Central Scouting Staff
Mike Abbamont, Tim Bernhardt, Jack Birch, Pat
Carmichael, Mike Donaldson, Gary Eggleston, Laurence
Ferguson, Ralph Goldhirsch, Paul Goulet, Ron Harris, Tom
Martin, Dan Reinisch, Jack Timmins, Barry Trapp,
Rolland Faubert

Communications
Gary Meagher — Executive Director of Communications
Susan Elliott — Director, Editorial and Information Systems
Benny Ercolani — Statistician/Information Officer
Greg Inglis — Information Officer

Receptionist
Dorothy Reaves

Hockey Hall of Fame
Exhibition Place
Toronto, Ont. M6K 3C3
Phone: 416/595-1345
FAX 416/971-5828
Ian Morrison — President
Esther Richards — Executive Secretary
Jeff Denomme — Director of Administration and Finance
Ray Paquet — Director of Exhibits
Philip Pritchard — Director of Information and Acquisitions
M.H. (Lefty) Reid — Historical Consultant
Marilyn Robbins — Receptionist
Raymond Bruce — Security Coordinator
Jefferson Davis — Collections Manager
Scott North — Operations Manager
Barry Eversley — Exhibit Maintenance Manager
Sylvia Lau — Accounting Clerk
Doug MacLellan — Photographer
Support Staff — Tom Gaston, Rey Sandre, Craig Campbell,
  Jim Hughes

**National Hockey League
Players' Association**
37 Maitland St.
Toronto, Ont. M4Y 1C8
Phone: 416/924-7800
FAX 416/924-3005
Envoy ID NHLPA.TOR
Alan Eagleson — Executive Director
Bob Goodenow — Deputy Executive Director
Sam Simpson — Director of Operations

SPECIAL FEATURE

*The NHL's Anniversary Ambassadors: clockwise from top left, Guy Lafleur, Ted Lindsay,
Lanny McDonald, and Stan Mikita combined for twenty-four All-Star Team selections.*

1991-92:
The NHL's 75th Anniversary Season

WHEN THE OWNERS OF FIVE HOCKEY CLUBS MET IN MONTREAL'S WINDSOR HOTEL TO form the National Hockey League in November of 1917, it is likely that no one in the room even dreamed of the possibility that the league they were forming would last three-quarters of a century.

This season – 1991-92 – is the NHL's seventy-fifth, and the resulting anniversary provides the league and its member clubs with an opportunity to celebrate hockey's rich history by saying "thank you" to the game's many fans.

Many special events and activities are planned to commemorate the 75th Anniversary Season.

Each player, referee, and linesman will wear a uniform patch bearing the 75th Anniversary logo depicted above. This logo will also be reproduced on the ice surface in each NHL arena.

On Thursday, October 3, 1991 – the season's opening night – the three games scheduled commemorate long-standing rivalries between the league's six oldest teams. The Rangers visit Boston, Toronto plays in Montreal and

continued overleaf

The NHL's 75th Anniversary Season
continued

Detroit journeys to Chicago. Each "original six" team will wear classic old-style jerseys in these opening games. The Rangers, Maple Leafs and Red Wings – who begin the season on the road – also face "original six" opponents in their home openers and will wear their retro-look jerseys for these games as well. This vintage look also will be seen on other occasions during the season as team general managers can schedule games in which classic jerseys are worn at any time during the season.

The opening night match-up between the Maple Leafs and Canadiens – the NHL's two remaining charter franchises – will feature a return to the Pullman-car hockey that characterized the NHL until the end of the 1950s. The Maple Leafs, their fans, and members of the media covering the club will journey to Montreal by special train in a style reminiscent of the league's six-team era.

Later in the season, hockey fans will also have an opportunity to participate in the selection of an All-Time NHL All-Star Team. This "dream team" will be featured in next year's *NHL Official Guide & Record Book*.

Some of these all-time greats will also by featured in a limited-edition set of fine art prints being produced for release in 1991-92.

A comprehensive history of the NHL has been produced as both a book and a video cassette. *The Official NHL 75th Anniversary Commemorative Book* combines three hundred photographs with a detailed depiction of seventy-five years of NHL play. The book's text is supplemented by fifteen special essays by some of the game's most distinguished chroniclers, each of whom is writing on a topic about which he has first-hand knowledge.

Hockey, Heroes and History, the NHL's official anniversary video, combines rare footage with knowledgeable commentary in an 87-minute presentation hosted by Lanny McDonald and narrated by Dick Irvin and Brian McFarlane of *Hockey Night in Canada*.

Lanny McDonald is also one of four distinguished former players who will serve as anniversary ambassadors and league-wide spokespeople for the NHL. McDonald is joined by Guy Lafleur, Ted Lindsay, and Stan Mikita to give the NHL's ambassadors a combined 2,188 goals scored in seventy-two years of regular-season and playoff competition.

In addition to these anniversary ambassadors, each club has appointed a celebrity captain to help promote its own activities during the 75th anniversary season. Celebrity captains range from athletes (Yogi Berra, David Wheaton, Jim Kelly) to entertainers (Jim Belushi, John Candy, Michael J. Fox, Susan Saint James) to broadcasters (Marv Albert, Larry King).

These activities and many more that will take place in each of the league's twenty-two cities combine to make 1991-92 a season of celebration throughout the NHL.

Snoopy, the world's most popular beagle, is the official mascot of the NHL's 75th Anniversary.

Celebrity Captains, NHL 75th Anniversary

Marv Albert, *New York Rangers;*
Jim Belushi, *Chicago Blackhawks*
Yogi Berra, *New Jersey Devils*
Kurt Browning, *Edmonton Oilers*
John Candy, *Los Angeles Kings*
Dave Coulier, *Detroit Red Wings*
Burton Cummings, *Winnipeg Jets*
Michael J. Fox, *Boston Bruins*
John Goodman, *St. Louis Blues*
Gordie Howe, *Hartford Whalers*
Jim Kelly, *Buffalo Sabres*
Larry King, *Washington Capitals*
Gordon Lightfoot, *Toronto Maple Leafs*
Ralph Macchio, *New York Islanders*
Willie McCovey, *San Jose Sharks*
Terry O'Reilly, *Boston Bruins*
Maurice Richard, *Montreal Canadiens*
Fred (Mr.) Rogers, *Pittsburgh Penguins*
Susan Saint James, *Hartford Whalers*
Ian Tyson, *Calgary Flames*
David Wheaton, *Minnesota North Stars*

Original-era photos showing the classic jerseys of the NHL's "original six" clubs which will be featured at the 1991-92 home openers of each of these teams and at various games in other NHL cities throughout the season. Clockwise from top left: Lionel Hitchman, Boston (circa 1933), Doug Bentley, Chicago, and Max Bentley, Toronto (circa 1948), Howie Morenz, Montreal (circa 1933), the 1931-32 Detroit Falcons, Lester Patrick (silver hair, standing at center of back row) and the rest of the 1928 New York Rangers.

Referees and Linesmen

BLAINE ANGUS . . . Referee . . . Born: Sept. 5, 1961 in Shawville, Que. . . . Hired by the NHL in 1991, Angus has been an NHL trainee since 1988 . . . refereed in the OHL and OHA last season . . . enjoys golf, running and carpentry in the off-season . . . is a registered x-ray technologist . . . resides in Barrie, Ontario with his wife and two children.

RON ASSELSTINE . . . Linesman . . . Born: Nov. 6, 1946 in Toronto, Ont. . . . First NHL Game: Oct. 10, 1979 . . . Total NHL Games: 960 . . . In 1989, was selected to work in three NHL-Soviet Super Series games and the 40th NHL All-Star Game in Edmonton. Ron is very active in his community as chairman of the "Make-A-Wish" Foundation and as an Ontario Provincial Police "Auxiliary" Officer. He is married and has two children.

WAYNE BONNEY . . . Linesman . . . Born: May 27, 1953 in Ottawa, Ont. . . . First NHL Game: Oct. 10, 1979 . . . Total NHL Games: 919 . . . Joined the NHL in 1979. Bonney worked the 1989 All-Star Game in Edmonton and made his first career appearance in the Stanley Cup Championship series in 1991. He currently resides in Kirkland, Que., with his wife and daughter and is an avid baseball player.

RYAN BOZAK . . . Linesman . . . Born: Jan. 3, 1947 in Swift Current, Sask. . . . First NHL Game: 1972 . . . Total NHL Games: 1,390 . . . Joined the NHL in 1972 and worked his 1,300th NHL game in 1989-90. He was selected to officiate in the 1983 NHL All-Star Game on Long Island. During the off-season he enjoys golf and tennis and resides in San Diego, CA. Bozak has two children.

GORD BROSEKER . . . Linesman . . . Born: July 8, 1950 in Baltimore, MD . . . First NHL Game: Jan 14, 1975 . . . Total NHL Games: 1,214 . . . Joined the NHL in 1973 and officiated in his 1,200th NHL game in 1990-91. Before beginning his officiating career, he played baseball in the Texas Rangers' organization. Broseker was selected to officiate in the 1991 Stanley Cup championship series. He currently resides in Richmond, VA, with his wife and daughter.

PIERRE CHAMPOUX . . . Linesman . . . Born: Apr. 18, 1963 in Ville St. Pierre, Que. . . . First NHL Game: Oct. 8, 1988 . . . Total NHL Games: 165 . . . Began officiating minor league games at the age of 12 in the Quebec pee wee league. Since then he has worked in two international competitions, having officiated in an exhibition game between the United States and Canada at the Forum and in Canada Cup 1987. During the off-season, Champoux assists the Quebec Hockey Federation in the development of new officials and enjoys golf, tennis and cycling. Champoux is single.

KEVIN COLLINS . . . Linesman . . . Born: Dec. 15,1950 in Springfield, MA . . . First NHL Game: Oct. 13, 1977 . . . Total NHL Games: 1,126 . . . Joined the NHL in 1971. He was selected to officiate in the 1988 NHL All-Star Game in St. Louis and officiated in 1991 Stanley Cup championship series. Currently residing in Springfield, MA, Collins is married and has three children.

MICHAEL CVIK . . . Linesman . . . Born: July 6, 1962 in Calgary, Alta. . . . First NHL Game: Oct. 8, 1987 . . . Total NHL Games: 279 . . . The tallest of the officials at 6'9", began his officiating career in the AAHA in 1978. After working his way through the WHL, he joined the NHL in 1987. During the off-season, Mike participates in the Annual Child Find Bike Ride for Child Find Alberta. He is an avid cyclist and enjoys reading and golf. He is single.

PAT DAPUZZO . . . Linesman . . . Born: Dec. 29, 1958 in Hoboken, NJ . . . First NHL Game: Dec. 5, 1984 . . . Total NHL Games: 498 . . . Officiated in his first NHL game on Dec. 5, 1984, in Madison Square Garden. In 1989, he was selected to officiate in the 88-89 Super Series when the New Jersey Devils faced the Central Red Army on January 2. Pat resides in Bergen, NJ and is single. He is an avid weightlifter and karate enthusiast.

PAUL DEVORSKI . . . Referee . . . Born: Aug. 18, 1958 in Guelph, Ont. . . . Joined the NHL in 1987 . . . Total NHL Games: 47 . . . Devorski is a part owner of Gold's Gym in Guelph and enjoys golf, fastball and water skiing. He is single.

MARK FAUCETTE . . . Referee . . . Born: June 9, 1958 in Springfield, MA . . . First NHL Game: 1985 . . . Total NHL Games: 131 . . . Joined the NHL in 1985. A resident of Agawam, MA during the off-season, Faucette organizes softball tournaments to raise funds for Boston Children Hospital's "Jimmy Fund". He is married.

RON FINN . . . Linesman . . . Born: Dec. 1, 1940 in Toronto, Ont. . . . First NHL Game: October 11, 1969 . . . Total NHL Games: 1,698 . . . Has worked in more games than any other active official. . . . A resident of Brampton, Ont. He has worked in two All-Star Games including 1977 (Vancouver) and 1982 (Washington, D.C.). He also worked during Rendez-Vous '87 in Quebec City. Finn set an NHL playoff record for officials by working in his 252nd career playoff game on April 23, 1991. He is active in his community during the off-season, working with the Canadian Special Olympics and is an instructor at various officiating schools in Ontario and New Brunswick. Ron is married and has four children.

KERRY FRASER . . . Referee . . . Born: June 30, 1952 in Sarnia, Ont. . . . Total NHL Games: 678 . . . After playing minor league hockey as a youngster, attended the NHL training camp for officials in 1972. Fraser has become one of the League's most experienced and respected referees, as proven by his selection to referee five Stanley Cup championship series (1985, 1986, 1989-91). During the off-season, Fraser assists in numerous charitable fundraisers, attends public speaking engagements to service clubs and works with amateur hockey officials' groups. Fraser enjoys sailing and golf. He is married and has seven children.

GERARD GAUTHIER . . . Linesman . . . Born: Sept. 5, 1948 in Montreal, Que. . . . First NHL Game: Oct. 16, 1971 . . . Total NHL Games: 1,526 . . . Attended his first NHL training camp in 1971 after two years in junior hockey. He has been selected to work at two NHL All-Star Games in his career; Los Angeles (1981) and Calgary (1985). In addition, he has worked in the 1984 Canada Cup and in two Stanley Cup Championship series — 1982 and 1983. On January 25, 1991, Gauthier became the fifth linesman in NHL history to reach 1,500 career games. During the off-season, Gauthier enjoys golfing and tennis. He is married and has two children.

TERRY GREGSON . . . Referee . . . Born: Nov. 7 1953 in Guelph, Ont. . . . First NHL Game: Dec. 19, 1981 . . . Total NHL Games: 553 . . . Joined the NHL in 1979. Gregson was selected to officiate his second career All-Star Game in 1991 at Chicago. President of the National Hockey League Officials Association, Gregson is also Co-Chairman of the NHLOA's Children's Wish Foundation. During the off-season he is an avid traveller and photographer and participates in charity golf tournaments. Gregson is married.

SHANE HEYER . . . Referee . . . Born: Feb. 7,1964 in Summerland, B.C. . . . First NHL Game: Oct. 5, 1988 . . . Total NHL Games: 233 . . . Began officiating in Penticton, B.C., at the age of 10 and was invited to join the NHL program in 1988. In his first year of service, Heyer was selected to work in the December 31 game between the Los Angeles Kings and the Dynamo Riga club during Super Series '88-89. Heyer is single and enjoys softball, cycling and golf.

BOB HODGES . . . Linesman . . . Born: Aug. 16, 1944 in Galt, Ont. . . . First NHL Game: Oct. 14, 1972 . . . Total NHL Games: 1,365 . . . Hired by the NHL in 1972-73 season at the age of 28, Hodges is one of the NHL's senior officials. He has been chosen to work in the Stanley Cup Finals three times (1982, 1986 and 1987) and officiated at the All-Star Game in Calgary (1985) and Pittsburgh (1990). During the off-season he works with the Royal Canadian Legion and enjoys hunting, fishing and baseball. Hodges is married and has two children.

RON HOGGARTH . . . Referee . . . Born: Apr. 12, 1948 in Barrie, Ont. . . . First NHL Game: Oct. 16, 1971 . . . Total NHL Games: 968 . . . Began officiating while still a student at McMaster University. He joined the NHL in 1971. In addition to officiating in several Soviet-NHL matches, Hoggarth was selected to referee the 1989 NHL All-Star Game in Edmonton. During the summer, Hoggarth owns and operates KoHo pools in Barrie and is active in golf and tennis. He is married and has two daughters.

DAVE JACKSON . . . Referee . . . Born: Nov. 28, 1964 in Montreal, Que. . . . One of two officials to join the NHL in 1989, he was an NHL trainee at the age of 21. He made one NHL appearance in 1990-91, working mostly in the AHL. During the off-season, he works in lawn equipment sales and volunteers as a tutor at a local high school. Jackson is married and is an avid golfer and softball player.

SWEDE KNOX . . . Linesman . . . Born: Mar. 2, 1948 in Edmonton, Alta. . . . First NHL Game: Oct. 14, 1972 . . . Total NHL Games: 1,491 . . . Joined the NHL in 1971. In 1982, he was selected to work in the NHL All-Star Game in Washington, D.C. He has also worked in numerous Stanley Cup championship series. A full-time resident of Edmonton, Swede is married and has two children. He enjoys carpentry during the off-season.

DON KOHARSKI . . . Referee . . . Born: Dec. 2, 1955 in Halifax, N.S. . . . First NHL Game: Oct. 14, 1977 . . . Total NHL Games: 678 (163 as a linesman) . . . Hired as an official in the WHA at the age of 18. He joined the NHL in 1977 as a linesman, becoming a referee after 163 games. Koharski gained international experience in Canada Cup 1987 and has worked in five Stanley Cup Finals (1986-88, 1990 and 1991). During the off-season, Koharski is active in the Make-A-Wish Foundation of Burlington, Ont. He is married and has two sons.

DENNIS LARUE . . . Referee . . . Born: July 14, 1959 in Savannah, GA . . . Attended the USA Hockey Referee Development Camp in 1983 and joined the NHL in 1988. He made his NHL debut on March 26, 1991, spending most of the season in the AHL. During the off-season he is involved in summer camp programs for children and in an instructor at the USA Hockey Select Officials Camp. He is an avid water-skiier and golfer. Dennis is married and has two children.

BRAD LAZAROWICH . . . Linesman . . . Born: Aug. 4, 1962 in Vancouver, B.C. . . . First NHL Game: Oct. 9, 1986 . . . Total NHL Games: 372 . . . Joined the NHL in 1986. In 1988, he was chosen to officiate in Super Series '88-89 (Dynamo Riga vs. Vancouver). During the off-season, Brad is employed by the Delta Corporation in the Water Works division and is an avid bicyclist, golfer and weightlifter. He is married and has a daughter.

DAN MAROUELLI . . . Referee . . . Born: July 16, 1955 in Edmonton, Alta. . . . First NHL Game: Nov. 2, 1984 . . . Total NHL Games: 407 . . . Began his officiating career at the age of 13 with the Knights of Columbus. He joined the NHL in 1982. During the summer, Marouelli works at a number of refereeing schools and owns a small construction business in addition to participating in many charity fundraising events. He is an avid golfer. Dan is married and has three children.

DAN McCOURT . . . Linesman . . . Born: Aug. 14, 1954 . . . First NHL Game: Dec. 27, 1980 . . . Total NHL Games: 738 . . . Joined the NHL in 1979. . . . Worked the 1990 All-Star Game in Pittsburgh. During the off-season, he instructs at various officiating schools and is involved with local charities. He enjoys golf, baseball and raquetball. McCourt is married and has two daughters.

BILL McCREARY . . . Referee . . . Born: Nov. 17, 1955 in Guelph, Ont. . . . First NHL Game: Nov. 3, 1984 . . . Total NHL Games: 419 . . . Joined the NHL in 1982. He was selected to referee the Red Army vs. Buffalo Sabres game on January 9 in Super Series '88-89. During the off-season, McCreary is active in charity events for the Make-a-Wish Foundation and Special Olympics and coaches minor baseball and hockey. He also enjoys hunting and fishing. He is married and has two sons and a daughter.

MIKE McGEOUGH . . . Referee . . . Born: June 20, 1957 in Regina, Sask. . . . Total NHL Games: 55 . . . Began his NHL career in 1987. During the off-season, McGeough enjoys golf and bicycling. He instructs at various refereeing schools. He is married and has three children.

RANDY MITTON . . . Linesman . . . Born: Sept. 22, 1950 in Fredericton, N.B. . . . First NHL Game: Dec. 26, 1973 . . . Total NHL Games: 1,289 . . . Became involved in NHL officiating in 1972 after working in the WHL and AHL for two years. He gained international experience as a linesman for the 1987 Canada Cup and was selected to officiate in the 1988 NHL All-Star Game in St. Louis. During the off-season, Mitton is active with the Elks Club and teaches at a number of officiating schools in Western Canada. He is married and has two children.

DENIS MOREL . . . Referee . . . Born: Dec. 13, 1948 in Quebec City, Que. . . . First NHL Game: Jan. 18, 1976 . . . Total NHL Games: 937 . . . Began officiating in Quebec minor leagues before joining the NHL in 1976. Morel has worked in two Stanley Cup Championship series — 1988 and 1989. During the summer, he is active in the Trois-Rivieres Special Olympics Program and hosts an annual charity golf tournament. He enjoys swimming and golf and is an avid reader. He is married and has two children.

BRIAN MURPHY . . . Linesman . . . Born: Dec. 13, 1964 in Dover, NH . . . First NHL Game: Oct. 7, 1988 . . . Total NHL Games: 172 . . . The youngest NHL official. Joined the League in 1988-89 after graduating from the University of New Hampshire with a degree in Business Administration. During his years at University, he worked in the NCAA officiating ranks, including the 1988 NCAA Division I National Championship Game in Lake Placid. During the off-season, Murphy works as a part-time accountant and is an instructor at AHAUS Officiating Development Camps.

MARK PARE . . . Linesman . . . Born: July 26, 1957 in Windsor, Ont. . . . First NHL Game: Oct. 11, 1979 . . . Total NHL Games: 943 . . . Joined the NHL in 1979 after working minor leagues in Windsor. During the off-season, he is a salesman for a food products company. He enjoys golfing. Pare is married and has two children.

JERRY PATEMAN . . . Linesman . . . Born: Jan. 12, 1958 in The Hague, Netherlands . . . First NHL Game: Nov. 10, 1982 . . . Total NHL Games: 355 . . . The only NHL official not born in North America, Pateman started refereeing minor hockey in Chatham, Ont. at the age of 14. He joined the NHL in 1982 and officiated in the 1991 All-Star Game in Chicago. During the summer, Pateman works part-time at a food products company and instructs at officiating schools in the area. Pateman now resides in Tecumseh, Ont. with his wife and two children.

LANCE ROBERTS . . . Referee . . . Born: May 28, 1957 in Edmonton, Alta. . . . Joined the NHL in 1987, working eight games in 1989-90 . . . Began his career at the age of 15 in the minor leagues of Alberta. Roberts takes college courses during the summer and also works with young offenders at a detention center. He is married with two daughters and enjoys golf and fastball.

RAY SCAPINELLO . . . Linesman . . . Born: Nov. 5, 1946 in Guelph, Ont. . . . First NHL Game in 1971 in Buffalo . . . Total NHL Games: 1,617. . . . Joined NHL in 1971 . . . Has worked three All-Star Games, ten consecutive Stanley Cup Finals plus the Canada Cup, Challenge Cup and Rendez-Vous 87 . . . In the off-season, Ray is a two-handicap golfter and works with the ''Make-A-Wish'' chapter in Guelph . . . He is married and has a son.

DAN SCHACHTE . . . Linesman . . . Born: July 13, 1958 in Madison, WI . . . First NHL Game: October 8, 1982 . . . Total NHL Games: 605 . . . Joined the NHL in 1982. He was chosen to officiate in the 1991 All-Star Game in Chicago. During the off-season, Schachte owns and operates a construction business in Madison, WI where he lives with his wife and two sons. He enjoys hunting, fishing and boating.

JAY SHARRERS . . . Linesman . . . Born: July 3, 1967 in New Westminster, B.C.. . . . New to NHL staff in 1990 . . . Worked 42 NHL games in 1990-91 . . . Has also worked Canadian college games and, in 1985-86, a tournament involving college teams from the U.S., Canada and Japan . . . Enjoys weightlifting, cycling, baseball and golf.

ROB SHICK . . . Referee . . . Born: Dec. 4, 1957, in Port Alberni, B.C. . . . First NHL Game: Apr. 6, 1986 . . . Total NHL Games: 242 . . . Joined the NHL in 1984. He is married. During the off-season, he is an avid fastball player and runs a landscaping business in Lethbridge, Alta.

PAUL STEWART . . . Referee . . . Born: Mar. 21, 1955 in Boston, MA . . . First NHL Game: Mar. 27, 1987 . . . Total NHL Games: 236 . . . Joined the NHL in 1985. Shortly after joining the League, he was asked to officiate in the 1987 Canada Cup. Stewart is the only former NHL player on the active officiating staff. During the off-season, Stewart continues his graduate studies at Northeastern University and is employed in estate planning. Stewart is married and enjoys landscaping, gardening and golf.

LEON STICKLE . . . Linesman . . . Born: Apr. 20, 1948 in Toronto, Ont. . . . First NHL Game: Oct. 17, 1970 . . . Total NHL Games: 1,597 . . . Joined the NHL in 1969 after four years in the minor leagues. In his career, he has worked in three NHL All-Star Games (Montreal, 1975; Buffalo,1978 and Long Island, 1983). He also was selected as an official for the Canada Cup tournament in 1981 and 1984. He has worked in the Stanley Cup Finals six times (1977, 1978, 1980, 1981, 1984 and 1985). During the off-season, Stickle is active with the Ontario and Canadian Special Olympics and coaches minor league baseball. He also enjoys golf. He is married and has three children.

RICHARD TROTTIER . . . Referee . . . Born: Feb. 28, 1957 in Laval, Que. . . . Total NHL Games: 25 . . . He worked in both the NHL and AHL last season. During his career, he has served as the executive vice-president for the Quebec Esso Cup in 1987-88 and 1988-89 and has been the referee-in-chief for the Quebec Ice Hockey Federation since 1986. During the off-season, he enjoys golf and fitness training.

ANDY vanHELLEMOND . . . Referee . . . Born: Feb. 16, 1948 in Winnipeg, Man. . . . First NHL Game: Nov. 22, 1972 . . . Total NHL Games: 1,198 . . . Joined the NHL in 1971 and has become one of the senior NHL officials. He worked in the NHL All-Star contest in Calgary (1985) and Rendez-Vous '87 in Quebec City. He has been selected to work in the Stanley Cup Final series 15 consecutive years since 1977. During the off-season, vanHellemond enjoys golfing, gardening and baseball.

MARK VINES . . . Linesman . . . Born: Dec. 3, 1960 in Elmira, Ont. . . . First NHL Game: Oct. 13, 1984 . . . Total NHL Games: 564 . . . Joined the NHL in 1984. He attends university during the off-season and is single.

STEPHEN WALKOM . . . Referee . . . Born: Aug. 8, 1963 in North Bay, Ontario. . . . NHL officiating trainee since 1989-90, working OHL and minor pro games . . . Has also worked Canadian college, Northern OHA, senior and junior B . . . Honors degree in Commerce from Laurentian U . . . Lives in Kitchener, Ont. . . . Enjoys running, cycling, racquet sports . . . Power-skating instructor.

NHL Attendance

| Season | Regular Season | | Playoffs | | Total |
	Games	Attendance	Games	Attendance	Attendance
1960-61	210	2,317,142	17	242,000	2,559,142
1961-62	210	2,435,424	18	277,000	2,712,424
1962-63	210	2,590,574	16	220,906	2,811,480
1963-64	210	2,732,642	21	309,149	3,041,791
1964-65	210	2,822,635	20	303,859	3,126,494
1965-66	210	2,941,164	16	249,000	3,190,184
1966-67	210	3,084,759	16	248,336	3,333,095
1967-68[1]	444	4,938,043	40	495,089	5,433,132
1968-69	456	5,550,613	33	431,739	5,982,352
1969-70	456	5,992,065	34	461,694	6,453,759
1970-71[2]	546	7,257,677	43	707,633	7,965,310
1971-72	546	7,609,368	36	582,666	8,192,034
1972-73[3]	624	8,575,651	38	624,637	9,200,288
1973-74	624	8,640,978	38	600,442	9,241,420
1974-75[4]	720	9,521,536	51	784,181	10,305,717
1975-76	720	9,103,761	48	726,279	9,830,040
1976-77	720	8,563,890	44	646,279	9,210,169
1977-78	720	8,526,564	45	686,634	9,213,198
1978-79	680	7,758,053	45	694,521	8,452,574
1979-80[5]	840	10,533,623	63	976,699	11,510,322
1980-81	840	10,726,198	68	966,390	11,692,588
1981-82	840	10,710,894	71	1,058,948	11,769,842
1982-83	840	11,020,610	66	1,088,222	12,028,832
1983-84	840	11,359,386	70	1,107,400	12,466,786
1984-85	840	11,633,730	70	1,107,500	12,741,230
1985-86	840	11,621,000	72	1,152,503	12,773,503
1986-87	840	11,855,880	87	1,383,967	13,239,847
1987-88	840	12,117,512	83	1,336,901	13,454,413
1988-89	840	12,417,969	83	1,327,214	13,745,183
1989-90	840	12,579,651	85	1,355,593	13,935,244
1990-91	840	12,343,897	92	1,442,203	13,786,100

[1] First expansion: Los Angeles, Pittsburgh, California (Cleveland), Philadelphia, St. Louis and Minnesota
[2] Second expansion: Buffalo and Vancouver
[3] Third expansion: Atlanta (Calgary) and New York Islanders
[4] Fourth expansion: Kansas City (Colorado, New Jersey) and Washington
[5] Fifth expansion: Edmonton, Hartford, Quebec and Winnipeg

League Presidents

Top: The NHL's first president, Frank Calder, at left, presents the Calder trophy to Boston goaltender Frank Brimsek as the outstanding rookie of 1938-39. Middle: Mervyn "Red" Dutton, president from 1943-46, at right, congratulates Clarence S. Campbell who served as NHL president from 1946 to 1977. Bottom: John A. Ziegler, Jr., president from 1977 to date.

Frank Calder
President, 1917-1943

After an illustrious tenure as secretary of the National Hockey Association, Frank Calder was elected as the first president of the National Hockey League when the League was formed in 1917. He served in this capacity until his death on February 4, 1943.

Born in England in 1877, Calder came to Canada at the turn of the century as a school teacher, but turned to sports writing in 1909. His forthright writing style won him the attention and respect of Montreal Canadiens' owner George Kennedy whose support helped Calder to the position of NHL president.

For nearly 26 years, Calder worked hard to change the League from a small-time circuit to a grand international sports organization. Among his many achievements, Calder guided the NHL through its first expansion into the U.S., including the addition of the Boston Bruins in 1924 and the Chicago Blackhawks, Detroit Cougars and New York Rangers in 1926.

To commemorate his years of service, the League established the Calder Memorial Trophy to honor the rookie of the year at the conclusion of each season. Additionally, Calder was elected to the Hockey Hall of Fame in 1945 as one of its first inductees.

Mervyn "Red" Dutton
President, 1943-46

Born on July 23, 1898 in Russell, Manitoba, Mervyn "Red" Dutton succeeded Frank Calder as the second president of the NHL. For two seasons, 1943-44 and 1944-45, Dutton remained at the head of the League before resuming his career in private business. Most remembered for his rugged playing style, Dutton overcame severe war injuries to skate as a professional for over a decade. After anchoring the defense for Calgary in the Western Hockey League from 1921 to 1925, Dutton signed with the NHL's Montreal Maroons. He stayed with the Maroons through 1930 when he joined the New York Americans. In 1936, he took over coaching and managing that club and remained there until 1942 when the team disbanded.

Upon Frank Calder's death in 1943, Dutton became president of the NHL, a position he maintained until Clarence Campbell assumed the role in 1946. Dutton was elected to the Hockey Hall of Fame in 1958.

Clarence Campbell
President, 1946-77

Clarence Campbell was a Rhodes Scholar who was born July 9, 1905 in Fleming, Saskatchewan. In 1926, a 20-year-old Campbell graduated from the University of Alberta with bachelor of arts and bachelor of law degrees.

Following his studies at Oxford, England, Campbell returned to Canada to begin his law practise. Forever active in sports, he also became an NHL referee, working 155 regular-season games and twelve Stanley Cup playoff contests through 1939 when he joined the Canadian Armed Forces for the duration of World War II.

On September 5, 1946, Campbell became the NHL's third president succeeding Mervyn "Red" Dutton. Within a year of his appointment, he established the NHL Players' Pension Plan which has since become the prototype for other professional sports leagues.

Campbell led the League through its greatest era of expansion in 1967 when the NHL doubled in size from six to twelve teams. In 1972, he also succeeded in breaking ground in a new era of international competition, when, for the first time in hockey history, Canada's finest NHL talent faced-off against the Soviet Union's elite in an eight-game challenge series.

Elected to the Hockey Hall of Fame in 1966, Campbell also received the Lester Patrick Trophy for "outstanding service to hockey in the United States" in 1972. He retired from the NHL in 1977, but continued to stay close to the League until his death in 1984.

John A. Ziegler, Jr.
President, 1977 to date

John A. Ziegler, Jr., President and Chief Executive Officer of the National Hockey League, was born in Grosse Pointe, Michigan, on February 9, 1934.

He graduated from the University of Michigan in 1957, earning a bachelor of arts and *juris doctor* degrees. Upon graduation he joined the Detroit law firm of Dickinson, Wright, McKean and Cudlip and became a partner in the firm in 1964. In 1969 he left the firm and in September of 1970 he set up his own firm, Ziegler, Dykhouse & Wise. He continued as senior partner in the firm until assuming his present position in September, 1977.

In 1959 he began to do legal work for Olympia Stadium, the Detroit Red Wings and Mr. Bruce Norris. He continued to serve these clients in various capacities until his election as president of the National Hockey League. In 1966 he joined the NHL Board of Governors as an alternate governor for the Detroit Red Wings and, as such, worked many of the NHL's committees and was involved in various aspects of the League's litigation as well as relations and negotiations with the Players' Association.

In June of 1976, he succeeded William Wirtz as Chairman of the National Hockey League Board of Governors. He was inducted into the Hockey Hall of Fame as a Builder in June, 1987.

An ardent sports fan, Ziegler played amateur hockey in the Detroit area from 1949 to 1969. He as continued to make his home in the Detroit area (Ortonville, Michigan) while maintaining ces in Montreal and New York.

Boston Bruins

1990-91 Results: 44w-24L-12t 100pts. First, Adams Division

In addition to earning his 12th consecutive All-Star berth in 1990-91, Ray Bourque captured his fourth Norris Trophy.

Schedule

Home				Away			
Oct.	Thur.	3	NY Rangers	**Oct.**	Mon.	7	NY Rangers
	Sat.	5	NY Islanders		Wed.	9	Buffalo
	Sat.	12	Montreal		Thur.	17	Vancouver
	Thur.	31	Los Angeles		Sat.	19	San Jose
Nov.	Sat.	2	Detroit		Thur.	24	St Louis
	Thur.	7	Calgary		Sat.	26	Minnesota
	Sat.	9	New Jersey		Sun.	27	Chicago
	Thur.	14	Quebec	**Nov.**	Mon.	4	NY Islanders
	Sat.	23	Buffalo		Tues.	5	Pittsburgh
	Fri.	29	Montreal*		Sat.	16	Hartford
Dec.	Sun.	1	Hartford		Wed.	20	Buffalo
	Thur.	5	Quebec		Fri.	22	Washington
	Sat.	7	Philadelphia		Mon.	25	Montreal
	Thur.	12	Montreal		Wed.	27	NY Islanders
	Sat.	14	Toronto	**Dec.**	Sun.	8	NY Rangers
	Thur.	19	Pittsburgh		Tues.	10	Quebec
	Sat.	21	Edmonton		Sun.	22	Montreal
	Thur.	26	Hartford		Fri.	27	Buffalo
Jan.	Thur.	2	Winnipeg		Sun.	29	Winnipeg
	Sat.	4	Buffalo		Tues.	31	Detroit
	Thur.	9	Quebec	**Jan.**	Wed.	8	Montreal
	Sat.	11	Philadelphia		Wed.	15	Hartford
	Thur.	16	Hartford		Wed.	22	Toronto
	Thur.	23	Montreal		Sat.	25	Hartford*
	Mon.	27	Minnesota		Tues.	28	Quebec
	Thur.	30	Calgary	**Feb.**	Tues.	4	Winnipeg
Feb.	Sat.	1	Buffalo		Thur.	6	Philadelphia
	Sat.	8	New Jersey*		Thur.	13	St Louis
	Sun.	9	Pittsburgh*		Mon.	17	Los Angeles*
	Thur.	27	Toronto		Wed.	19	Calgary
	Sat.	29	Washington*		Fri.	21	Edmonton
Mar.	Thur.	5	Vancouver		Sun.	23	Vancouver*
	Sat.	7	Chicago*	**Mar.**	Sun.	1	Washington*
	Sun.	15	Los Angeles		Tues.	3	Hartford
	Thur.	19	St Louis		Sun.	8	Chicago*
	Sat.	21	Edmonton*		Wed.	11	Buffalo
	Mon.	23	San Jose		Sat.	14	Quebec
	Sat.	28	Buffalo*		Thur.	26	New Jersey
Apr.	Thur.	2	Quebec		Tues.	31	Quebec
	Sun.	5	Hartford	**Apr.**	Sat.	4	Montreal

* Denotes afternoon game.

Home Starting Times:

Weeknights .... 7:35 p.m.
Saturdays and Sundays .... 7:05 p.m.
Matinees .... 1:35 p.m.

Franchise date: November 1, 1924

68th NHL Season

Year-by-Year Record

Season	GP	Home W	L	T	Road W	L	T	Overall W	L	T	GF	GA	Pts.	Finished	Playoff Result
1990-91	80	26	9	5	18	15	7	44	24	12	299	264	100	1st, Adams Div.	Lost Conf. Championship
1989-90	80	23	13	4	23	12	5	46	25	9	289	232	101	1st, Adams Div.	Lost Final
1988-89	80	17	15	8	20	14	6	37	29	14	289	256	88	2nd, Adams Div.	Lost Div. Final
1987-88	80	24	13	3	20	17	3	44	30	6	300	251	94	2nd, Adams Div.	Lost Final
1986-87	80	25	11	4	14	23	3	39	34	7	301	276	85	3rd, Adams Div.	Lost Div. Semi-Final
1985-86	80	24	9	7	13	22	5	37	31	12	311	288	86	3rd, Adams Div.	Lost Div. Semi-Final
1984-85	80	21	15	4	15	19	6	36	34	10	303	287	82	4th, Adams Div.	Lost Div. Semi-Final
1983-84	80	25	12	3	24	13	3	49	25	6	336	261	104	1st, Adams Div.	Lost Div. Semi-Final
1982-83	80	28	6	6	22	14	4	50	20	10	327	228	110	1st, Adams Div.	Lost Conf. Championship
1981-82	80	24	12	4	19	15	6	43	27	10	323	285	96	2nd, Adams Div.	Lost Div. Final
1980-81	80	26	10	4	11	20	9	37	30	13	316	272	87	2nd, Adams Div.	Lost Prelim. Round
1979-80	80	27	9	4	19	12	9	46	21	13	310	234	105	2nd, Adams Div.	Lost Quarter-Final
1978-79	80	25	10	5	18	13	9	43	23	14	316	270	100	1st, Adams Div.	Lost Semi-Final
1977-78	80	29	6	5	22	12	6	51	18	11	333	218	113	1st, Adams Div.	Lost Final
1976-77	80	27	7	6	22	16	2	49	23	8	312	240	106	1st, Adams Div.	Lost Final
1975-76	80	27	5	8	21	10	9	48	15	17	313	237	113	1st, Adams Div.	Lost Semi-Final
1974-75	80	29	5	6	11	21	8	40	26	14	345	245	94	2nd, Adams Div.	Lost Prelim. Round
1973-74	78	33	4	2	19	13	7	52	17	9	349	221	113	1st, East Div.	Lost Final
1972-73	78	27	10	2	24	12	3	51	22	5	330	235	107	2nd, East Div.	Lost Quarter-Final
1971-72	78	28	4	7	26	9	4	**54**	**13**	**11**	**330**	**204**	**119**	**1st, East Div.**	**Won Stanley Cup**
1970-71	78	33	4	2	24	10	5	57	14	7	399	207	121	1st, East Div.	Lost Quarter-Final
1969-70	76	27	3	8	13	14	11	**40**	**17**	**19**	**277**	**216**	**99**	**2nd, East Div.**	**Won Stanley Cup**
1968-69	76	29	3	6	13	15	10	42	18	16	303	221	100	2nd, East Div.	Lost Semi-Final
1967-68	74	22	9	6	15	18	4	37	27	10	259	216	84	3rd, East Div.	Lost Quarter-Final
1966-67	70	10	21	4	7	22	6	17	43	10	182	253	44	6th,	Out of Playoffs
1965-66	70	15	17	3	6	26	3	21	43	6	174	275	48	5th,	Out of Playoffs
1964-65	70	12	17	6	9	26	0	21	43	6	166	253	48	6th,	Out of Playoffs
1963-64	70	13	15	7	5	25	5	18	40	12	170	212	48	6th,	Out of Playoffs
1962-63	70	7	18	10	7	21	7	14	39	17	198	281	45	6th,	Out of Playoffs
1961-62	70	9	22	4	6	25	4	15	47	8	177	306	38	6th,	Out of Playoffs
1960-61	70	13	17	5	2	25	8	15	42	13	176	254	43	6th,	Out of Playoffs
1959-60	70	21	11	3	7	23	5	28	34	8	220	241	64	5th,	Out of Playoffs
1958-59	70	21	11	3	11	18	6	32	29	9	205	215	73	2nd,	Lost Semi-Final
1957-58	70	15	14	6	12	14	9	27	28	15	199	194	69	4th,	Lost Final
1956-57	70	20	9	6	14	15	6	34	24	12	195	174	80	3rd,	Lost Final
1955-56	70	16	14	7	7	20	6	23	34	13	147	185	59	5th,	Out of Playoffs
1954-55	70	16	10	9	7	16	12	23	26	21	169	188	67	4th,	Lost Semi-Final
1953-54	70	22	8	5	10	20	5	32	28	10	177	181	74	4th,	Lost Semi-Final
1952-53	70	19	10	6	9	19	7	28	29	13	152	172	69	3rd,	Lost Final
1951-52	70	15	12	8	10	17	8	25	29	16	162	176	66	4th,	Lost Semi-Final
1950-51	70	13	12	10	9	18	8	22	30	18	178	197	62	4th,	Lost Semi-Final
1949-50	70	15	12	8	7	20	8	22	32	16	198	228	60	5th,	Out of Playoffs
1948-49	60	18	10	2	11	13	6	29	23	8	178	163	66	2nd,	Lost Semi-Final
1947-48	60	12	8	10	11	16	3	23	24	13	167	168	59	3rd,	Lost Semi-Final
1946-47	60	18	7	5	8	16	6	26	23	11	190	175	63	3rd,	Lost Semi-Final
1945-46	50	16	5	4	8	13	4	24	18	8	167	156	56	2nd,	Lost Final
1944-45	50	11	12	2	5	18	2	16	30	4	179	219	36	4th,	Lost Semi-Final
1943-44	50	14	8	3	5	18	2	19	26	5	223	268	43	5th,	Out of Playoffs
1942-43	50	17	3	5	7	14	4	24	17	9	195	176	57	2nd,	Lost Final
1941-42	48	17	4	3	8	13	3	25	17	6	160	118	56	3rd,	Lost Semi-Final
1940-41	48	15	4	5	12	4	8	**27**	**8**	**13**	**168**	**102**	**67**	**1st,**	**Won Stanley Cup**
1939-40	48	20	3	1	11	9	4	31	12	5	170	98	67	1st,	Lost Final
1938-39	48	20	2	2	16	8	0	**36**	**10**	**2**	**156**	**76**	**74**	**1st,**	**Won Stanley Cup**
1937-38	48	18	3	3	12	8	4	30	11	7	142	89	67	1st, Amn. Div.	Lost Semi-Final
1936-37	48	14	4	6	9	14	1	23	18	7	120	110	53	2nd, Amn. Div.	Lost Quarter-Final
1935-36	48	15	8	1	7	12	5	22	20	6	92	83	50	2nd, Amn. Div.	Lost Quarter-Final
1934-35	48	17	7	0	9	9	6	26	16	6	129	112	58	1st, Amn. Div.	Lost Semi-Final
1933-34	48	11	11	2	7	14	3	18	25	5	111	130	41	4th, Amn. Div.	Out of Playoffs
1932-33	48	20	2	3	5	13	5	25	15	8	124	88	58	1st, Amn. Div.	Lost Semi-Final
1931-32	48	11	10	3	4	11	9	15	21	12	122	117	42	4th, Amn. Div.	Out of Playoffs
1930-31	44	17	1	5	11	9	1	28	10	6	143	90	62	1st, Amn. Div.	Lost Semi-Final
1929-30	44	23	1	0	15	4	1	38	5	1	179	98	77	1st, Amn. Div.	Lost Final
1928-29	44	16	6	1	10	7	4	**26**	**13**	**5**	**89**	**52**	**57**	**1st, Amn. Div.**	**Won Stanley Cup**
1927-28	44	13	4	5	7	9	6	20	13	11	77	70	51	1st, Amn. Div.	Lost Semi-Final
1926-27	44	15	7	0	6	13	3	21	20	3	97	89	45	2nd, Amn. Div.	Lost Final
1925-26	36	10	7	1	7	8	3	17	15	4	92	85	38	4th,	Out of Playoffs
1924-25	30	3	12	0	3	12	0	6	24	0	49	119	12	6th,	Out of Playoffs

1991-92 Player Personnel

FORWARDS	HT	WT	S	Place of Birth	Date	1990-91 Club
BARAHONA, Ralph	5-10	180	L	Long Beach, CA	11/16/65	Boston-Maine
BRICKLEY, Andy	5-11	200	L	Melrose, MA	8/9/61	Boston-Maine
BYCE, John	6-1	180	L	Madison, WI	8/9/67	Boston-Maine
BYERS, Lyndon	6-1	200	R	Nipawin, Sask.	2/29/64	Boston
CARPENTER, Bob	6-0	190	L	Beverly, MA	7/13/63	Boston
CRAWFORD, Lou	6-0	185	L	Belleville, Ont.	11/5/62	Maine
DONATO, Ted	5-10	170	L	Dedham, MA	4/28/68	Harvard
DOURIS, Peter	6-1	195	R	Toronto, Ont.	2/19/66	Boston-Maine
FERREIRA, Brian	6-0	175	R	Falmouth, MA	1/2/68	Maine-Johnstown
GLENNON, Matt	6-0	185	L	Hull, MA	9/20/68	Boston College
HODGE, Ken	6-1	200	L	Windsor, Ont.	4/13/66	Boston-Maine
JANNEY, Craig	6-1	190	L	Hartford, CT	9/26/67	Boston
JUNEAU, Joe	6-0	175	R	Pont-Rouge, Que.	1/5/68	R.P.I.
LAZARO, Jeff	5-10	180	L	Waltham, MA	3/21/68	Boston-Maine
LEACH, Steve	5-11	200	R	Cambridge, MA	1/16/66	Washington
MARKWART, Nevin	5-10	180	L	Toronto, Ont.	12/9/64	Boston
MISKOLCZI, Ted	6-3	180	R	Port Colborne, Ont.	8/5/70	Owen Sound
MURRAY, Glen	6-2	200	R	Bridgewater, N.S.	11/1/72	Sudbury
NEELY, Cam	6-1	210	R	Comox, B.C.	6/6/65	Boston
NILAN, Chris	6-0	205	R	Boston, MA	2/9/58	Boston
POULIN, Dave	5-11	190	L	Timmins, Ont.	12/17/58	Boston
ROSENBLATT, Howard	6-0	195	R	Pawtucket, RI	1/3/69	Merrimack
RUZICKA, Vladimir	6-3	210	L	Most, Czechoslovakia	6/6/63	Boston
SKRIKO, Petri	5-10	175	L	Lapeenranta, Finland	3/12/62	Vancouver-Boston
STEVENSON, Shayne	6-1	190	R	Newmarket, Ont.	10/26/70	Boston-Maine
STUMPEL, Josef	6-1	190	R	Nitra, Czech	6/20/72	Nitra
SWEENEY, Bob	6-3	200	R	Concord, MA	1/25/64	Boston
THOMLINSON, Dave	6-1	195	L	Edmonton, Alta.	10/22/66	St. Louis-Peoria
VESEY, Jim	6-1	200	R	Boston, MA	9/29/65	Peoria
WALZ, Wes	5-10	180	R	Calgary, Alta.	5/15/70	Boston-Maine
WINNES, Chris	6-0	170	R	Ridgefield, CT	2/12/68	Maine-New Hampshire

DEFENSEMEN:	HT	WT	S	Place of Birth	Date	1990-91 Club
ALLAIN, Rick	6-0	190	L	Guelph, Ont.	5/20/69	Maine-Johnstown
BANCROFT, Steve	6-1	215	L	Toronto, Ont.	1/16/67	Maine-Newmarket
BEERS, Bob	6-2	200	R	Pittsburgh, PA	5/20/67	Boston-Maine
BOURQUE, Ray	5-11	210	L	Montreal, Que.	12/28/60	Boston
CAPUANO, Jack	6-2	210	L	Cranston, R.I.	7/7/66	Vancouver-Milw.
FEATHERSTONE, Glen	6-4	215	L	Toronto, Ont.	7/8/68	St. Louis
GALLEY, Garry	6-0	190	L	Montreal, Que.	4/16/63	Boston
GORMAN, Sean	6-3	180	L	Cambridge, MA	2/1/69	Princeton
KRYS, Mark	6-0	185	R	Timmins, Ont.	5/29/69	Boston U.
PRATSLER, Petr	6-2	200	L	Hradec Kralove, Czech.	9/22/65	Phoenix
QUINTAL, Stephane	6-3	215	R	Boucherville, Que.	10/22/68	Boston-Maine
REISMAN, Eric	6-2	220	L	New York, NY	5/19/68	Ohio State
SMITH, Dennis	5-11	190	L	Detroit, MI	7/27/64	L.A.-New Haven
SWEENEY, Don	5-10	185	L	St. Stephen, N.B.	8/17/66	Boston
TILEY, Brad	6-1	185	L	Markdale, Ont.	7/5/71	Sault Ste. Marie
WESLEY, Glen	6-1	195	L	Red Deer, Alta.	10/2/68	Boston
WIEMER, Jim	6-4	210	L	Sudbury, Ont.	1/9/61	Boston

GOALTENDERS	HT	WT	C	Place of Birth	Date	1990-91 Club
BLUE, John	5-10	185	L	Huntington Beach, CA	2/19/66	K'zoo-Knox.-Alb.-Peoria-Maine
COUSINEAU, Marcel	5-10	175	L	Lachine, Que.	4/30/73	Beauport
DelGUIDICE, Matt	5-9	170	R	West Haven, CT	3/5/67	Boston-Maine
FOSTER, Norm	5-9	175	L	Vancouver, B.C.	2/10/65	Boston-Maine-Cape Breton
HARVEY, Chris	6-1	180	L	Cambridge, MA	12/8/67	Maine-Johnstown
LEMELIN, Reggie	5-11	170	L	Quebec City, Que.	11/19/54	Boston
MOOG, Andy	5-8	170	L	Penticton, B.C.	2/18/60	Boston
PARSON, Mike	6-0	170	L	Listowel, Ont.	3/12/70	Maine-Johnstown

General Managers' History

Arthur H. Ross, 1924-25 to 1953-54; Lynn Patrick, 1954-55 to 1964-65; Leighton "Hap" Emms, 1965-66 to 1966-67; Milt Schmidt, 1967-68 to 1971-72; Harry Sinden, 1972-73 to date.

Coaching History

Arthur H. Ross, 1924-25 to 1927-28; Cy Denneny, 1928-29; Arthur H. Ross, 1929-30 to 1933-34; Frank Patrick, 1934-35 to 1935-36; Arthur H. Ross, 1936-37 to 1938-39; Ralph (Cooney) Weiland, 1939-40 to 1940-41; Arthur H. Ross, 1941-42 to 1944-45; Aubrey V. (Dit) Clapper, 1945-46 to 1948-49; George (Buck) Boucher, 1949-50; Lynn Patrick, 1950-51 to 1953-54; Lynn Patrick and Milt Schmidt, 1954-55; Milt Schmidt, 1955-56 to 1960-61; Phil Watson, 1961-62; Phil Watson and Milt Schmidt, 1962-63; Milt Schmidt, 1963-64 to 1965-66; Harry Sinden, 1966-67 to 1969-70; Tom Johnson, 1970-71 to 1971-72; Tom Johnson and Bep Guidolin, 1972-73; Bep Guidolin, 1973-74; Don Cherry, 1974-75 to 1978-79; Fred Creighton and Harry Sinden, 1979-80; Gerry Cheevers, 1980-81 to 1983-84; Gerry Cheevers and Harry Sinden, 1984-85; Butch Goring, 1985-86; Butch Goring and Terry O'Reilly, 1986-87; Terry O'Reilly, 1987-88 to 1988-89; Mike Milbury, 1989-90 to 1990-91; Rick Bowness, 1991-92.

1990-91 Scoring

Regular Season

* rookie

Pos	#	Player	Team	GP	G	A	Pts	+/-	PIM	PP	SH	GW	GT	S	%
D	77	Ray Bourque	BOS	76	21	73	94	33	75	7	0	3	1	323	6.5
C	23	Craig Janney	BOS	77	26	66	92	15	8	9	1	5	0	133	19.5
R	8	Cam Neely	BOS	69	51	40	91	26	98	18	1	8	0	262	19.5
C	10	*Ken Hodge	BOS	70	30	29	59	11	20	12	2	4	0	137	21.9
L	27	Dave Christian	BOS	78	32	21	53	8	41	9	0	2	0	173	18.5
C	20	Bob Sweeney	BOS	80	15	33	48	12	115	0	1	2	0	116	12.9
D	26	Glen Wesley	BOS	80	11	32	43	0	78	5	1	1	0	199	5.5
L	12	Randy Burridge	BOS	62	15	13	28	17	40	1	0	4	0	108	13.9
R	18	Petri Skriko	VAN	20	4	4	8	9-	8	0	1	2	0	47	8.5
			BOS	28	5	14	19	4	9	1	0	3	0	73	6.8
			TOTAL	48	9	18	27	5-	17	1	1	5	0	120	7.5
D	28	Garry Galley	BOS	70	6	21	27	0	84	1	0	0	0	128	4.7
D	36	Jim Wiemer	BOS	61	4	19	23	3	62	0	0	1	0	86	4.7
D	32	Don Sweeney	BOS	77	8	13	21	2	67	0	1	3	0	102	7.8
C	19	Dave Poulin	BOS	31	8	12	20	5	25	0	2	0	0	60	13.3
L	14	*Jeff Lazaro	BOS	49	5	13	18	7	67	1	1	1	0	73	6.8
L	11	Bob Carpenter	BOS	29	8	8	16	2	22	2	0	0	1	54	14.8
C	38	Vladimir Ruzicka	BOS	29	8	8	16	1	19	4	0	0	0	51	15.7
C	13	*Wes Walz	BOS	56	8	8	16	14-	32	1	0	1	0	57	14.0
R	30	Chris Nilan	BOS	41	6	9	15	4	277	0	0	2	0	41	14.6
L	31	John Carter	BOS	50	4	7	11	13-	68	1	1	2	0	61	6.6
L	25	Andy Brickley	BOS	40	2	9	11	4-	8	0	0	0	0	28	7.1
D	21	Stephane Quintal	BOS	45	2	6	8	2	89	1	0	0	0	54	3.7
D	41	Allen Pedersen	BOS	57	2	6	8	15	107	0	0	0	0	34	5.9
R	16	Peter Douris	BOS	39	5	2	7	12-	9	1	0	1	0	46	10.9
L	48	*Graeme Townshend	BOS	18	2	5	7	1	12	0	0	0	0	10	20.0
L	17	Nevin Markwart	BOS	23	3	3	6	0	36	0	0	0	1	13	23.1
L	44	*Ron Hoover	BOS	15	4	0	4	0	31	0	0	1	0	17	23.5
R	34	Lyndon Byers	BOS	19	2	2	4	2-	82	0	0	0	0	20	10.0
R	42	*John Byce	BOS	18	1	3	4	1	6	0	0	0	0	13	7.7
C	37	*Ralph Barahona	BOS	3	2	1	3	2	0	0	0	0	0	5	40.0
L	29	*Jarmo Kekalainen	BOS	16	2	1	3	0	6	0	0	0	0	12	16.7
G	35	Andy Moog	BOS	51	0	2	2	0	20	0	0	0	0	0	.0
D	55	Ken Hammond	BOS	1	1	0	1	2	2	0	0	0	0	3	33.3
D	43	*Bob Beers	BOS	16	0	1	1	8-	10	0	0	0	0	9	.0
G	33	*Matt Delguidice	BOS	1	0	0	0	0	0	0	0	0	0	0	.0
D	40	Bruce Shoebottom	BOS	1	0	0	0	1-	5	0	0	0	0	0	.0
D	6	Gord Kluzak	BOS	2	0	0	0	2	0	0	0	0	0	3	.0
G	39	*Norm Foster	BOS	3	0	0	0	0	0	0	0	0	0	0	.0
R	49	*Shayne Stevenson	BOS	14	0	0	0	4-	26	0	0	0	0	8	.0
G	1	Rejean Lemelin	BOS	33	0	0	0	0	10	0	0	0	0	0	.0

Goaltending

No.	Goaltender	GPI	Mins	Avg	W	L	T	EN	SO	GA	SA	S%
33	*Matt Delguidice	1	10	.00	0	0	0	0	0	0	7	1.000
35	Andy Moog	51	2844	2.87	25	13	9	1	4	136	1307	.896
1	Rejean Lemelin	33	1829	3.64	17	10	3	2	1	111	841	.868
39	Norm Foster	3	184	4.57	2	1	0	0	0	14	82	.829
	Totals	**80**	**4872**	**3.25**	**44**	**24**	**12**	**3**	**5**	**264**	**2240**	**.882**

Playoffs

Pos	#	Player	Team	GP	G	A	Pts	+/-	PIM	PP	SH	GW	OT	S	%
D	77	Ray Bourque	BOS	19	7	18	25	4-	12	3	0	0	0	84	8.3
C	23	Craig Janney	BOS	18	4	18	22	4-	11	4	0	0	0	26	15.4
R	8	Cam Neely	BOS	19	16	4	20	3-	36	9	0	4	0	72	22.2
C	38	Vladimir Ruzicka	BOS	17	2	11	13	2	0	1	0	2	1	32	6.3
L	27	Dave Christian	BOS	19	8	4	12	2-	4	0	0	2	0	39	20.5
D	26	Glen Wesley	BOS	19	2	9	11	8-	19	2	0	0	0	47	4.3
C	10	*Ken Hodge	BOS	15	4	6	10	2-	6	1	0	1	0	24	16.7
C	19	Dave Poulin	BOS	16	0	9	9	3	20	0	0	0	0	17	.0
R	18	Petri Skriko	BOS	18	4	4	8	2-	4	3	0	0	0	33	12.1
C	20	Bob Sweeney	BOS	17	4	2	6	5-	45	0	0	1	0	25	16.0
D	28	Garry Galley	BOS	16	1	5	6	2-	17	0	0	0	0	20	5.0
L	14	*Jeff Lazaro	BOS	19	3	2	5	2-	30	0	0	0	0	28	10.7
D	36	Jim Wiemer	BOS	16	1	3	4	5	14	1	0	0	0	24	4.2
D	32	Don Sweeney	BOS	19	3	0	3	3-	25	0	0	0	0	31	9.7
L	12	Randy Burridge	BOS	19	0	3	3	5-	39	0	0	0	0	20	.0
R	30	Chris Nilan	BOS	19	0	2	2	2-	62	0	0	0	0	10	.0
L	17	Nevin Markwart	BOS	12	1	0	1	2-	22	0	0	0	0	7	14.3
L	11	Bob Carpenter	BOS	1	0	1	1	1	2	0	0	0	0	1	.0
D	21	Stephane Quintal	BOS	3	0	1	1	0	7	0	0	0	0	1	.0
R	16	Peter Douris	BOS	7	0	1	1	1	6	0	0	0	0	7	.0
R	34	Lyndon Byers	BOS	1	0	0	0	1-	10	0	0	0	0	0	.0
R	40	*Chris Winnes	BOS	1	0	0	0	1-	0	0	0	0	0	3	.0
G	1	Rejean Lemelin	BOS	2	0	0	0	0	0	0	0	0	0	0	.0
C	13	*Wes Walz	BOS	2	0	0	0	3-	0	0	0	0	0	2	.0
D	43	*Bob Beers	BOS	6	0	0	0	1-	4	0	0	0	0	4	.0
D	55	Ken Hammond	BOS	8	0	0	0	5-	10	0	0	0	0	4	.0
L	44	*Ron Hoover	BOS	8	0	0	0	2-	18	0	0	0	0	5	.0
D	41	Allen Pedersen	BOS	8	0	0	0	0	10	0	0	0	0	2	.0
G	35	Andy Moog	BOS	19	0	0	0	0	4	0	0	0	0	0	.0

Goaltending

No.	Goaltender	GPI	Mins	Avg	W	L	EN	SO	GA	SA	S%
1	Rejean Lemelin	2	32	.00	0	0	0	0	0	18	1.000
35	Andy Moog	19	1133	3.18	10	9	2	0	60	569	.895
	Totals	19	1166	3.19	10	9	2	0	62	589	.895

Club Records

Team

(Figures in brackets for season records are games played; records for fewest points, wins, ties, losses, goals, goals against are for 70 or more games)

Most Points	121	1970-71 (78)
Most Wins	57	1970-71 (78)
Most Ties	21	1954-55 (70)
Most Losses	47	1961-62 (70)
Most Goals	399	1970-71 (78)
Most Goals Against	306	1961-62 (70)
Fewest Points	38	1961-62 (70)
Fewest Wins	14	1962-63 (70)
Fewest Ties	5	1972-73 (78)
Fewest Losses	13	1971-72 (78)
Fewest Goals	147	1955-56 (70)
Fewest Goals Against	172	1952-53 (70)

Longest Winning Streak
Over-all . . . . 14 Dec. 3/29-
Jan. 9/30
Home . . . . *20 Dec. 3/29-
Mar. 18/30
Away . . . . 8 Feb. 17-
Mar. 8/72

Longest Undefeated Streak
Over-all . . . . 23 Dec. 22/40-
Feb. 23/41
(15 wins, 8 ties)
Home . . . . 27 Nov. 22/70-
Mar. 20/71
(26 wins, 1 tie)
Away . . . . 15 Dec. 22/40-
Mar. 16/41
(9 wins, 6 ties)

Longest Losing Streak
Over-all . . . . 11 Dec. 3/24-
Jan. 5/25
Home . . . . *11 Dec. 8/24-
Feb. 17/25
Away . . . . 14 Dec. 27/64-
Feb. 21/65

Longest Winless Streak
Over-all . . . . 20 Jan. 28-
Mar. 11/62
(16 losses, 4 ties)
Home . . . . 11 Dec. 8/24-
Feb. 17/25
(11 losses)

Away . . . . 14 Three times
Most Shutouts, Season . . . 15 1927-28 (44)
Most PIM, Season 2,443 1987-88 (80)
Most Goals, Game . . . . 14 Jan. 21/45
(NYR 3 at Bos. 14)

Individual

Most Seasons	21	John Bucyk
Most Games	1,436	John Bucyk
Most Goals, Career	545	John Bucyk
Most Assists, Career	794	John Bucyk
Most Points, Career	1,339	John Bucyk
		(545 goals, 794 assists)
Most PIM, Career	2,095	Terry O'Reilly
Most Shutouts, Career	74	Tiny Thompson

Longest Consecutive
Games Streak . . . . 418 John Bucyk
(Jan. 23/69-Mar. 2/75)

Most Goals, Season . . . . . . 76 Phil Esposito
(1970-71)
Most Assists, Season . . . . 102 Bobby Orr
(1970-71)
Most Points, Season . . . . . 152 Phil Esposito
(1970-71)
(76 goals, 76 assists)
Most PIM, Season . . . . 304 Jay Miller
(1987-88)

Most Points, Defenseman
Season . . . . *139 Bobby Orr
(1970-71)
(37 goals, 102 assists)

Most Points, Center
Season . . . . 152 Phil Esposito
(1970-71)
(76 goals, 76 assists)

Most Points, Right Wing
Season . . . . 105 Ken Hodge
(1970-71)
(43 goals, 62 assists)
Ken Hodge
(1973-74)
(50 goals, 55 assists)
Rick Middleton
(1983-84)
(47 goals, 58 assists)

Most Points, Left Wing
Season . . . . 116 John Bucyk
(1970-71)
(51 goals, 65 assists)

Most Points, Rookie
Season . . . . 92 Barry Pederson
(1981-82)
(44 goals, 48 assists)
Most Shutouts, Season . . . . 15 Hal Winkler
(1927-28)
Most Goals, Game . . . . 4 Several players
Most Assists, Game . . . . 6 Ken Hodge
(Feb. 9/71)
Bobby Orr
(Jan. 1/73)
Most Points, Game . . . . 7 Bobby Orr
(Nov. 15/73)
Phil Esposito
(Dec. 19/74)
Barry Pederson
(Apr. 4/82)
Cam Neely
(Oct. 16/88)

* NHL Record.

Captains' History

No Captain, 1924-25 to 1926-27; Lionel Hitchman, 1927-28 to 1930-31; George Owen, 1931-32; Dit Clapper, 1932-33 to 1937-38; Cooney Weiland, 1938-39; Dit Clapper, 1939-40 to 1945-46; Dit Clapper, John Crawford, 1946-47; John Crawford 1947-48 to 1949-50; Milt Schmidt, 1950-51 to 1953-54; Milt Schmidt, Ed Sanford, 1954-55; Fern Flaman, 1955-56 to 1960-61; Don McKenney, 1961-62, 1962-63; Leo Boivin, 1963-64 to 1965-66; John Bucyk, 1966-67; no captain, 1967-68 to 1972-73; John Bucyk, 1973-74 to 1976-77; Wayne Cashman, 1977-78 to 1982-83; Terry O'Reilly, 1983-84, 1984-85; Ray Bourque, Rick Middleton (co-captains) 1985-86 to 1987-88; Ray Bourque, 1988-89 to date.

Retired Numbers

2	Eddie Shore	1926-1940
3	Lionel Hitchman	1925-1934
4	Bobby Orr	1966-1976
5	Dit Clapper	1927-1947
7	Phil Esposito	1967-1975
9	John Bucyk	1957-1978
15	Milt Schmidt	1936-1955

All-time Record vs. Other Clubs

Regular Season

		At Home							On Road							Total					
	GP	W	L	T	GF	GA	PTS	GP	W	L	T	GF	GA	PTS	GP	W	L	T	GF	GA	PTS
Buffalo	72	42	22	8	303	225	92	71	24	34	13	232	266	61	143	66	56	21	535	491	153
Calgary	35	21	10	4	120	96	46	35	19	14	2	129	133	40	70	40	24	6	249	229	86
Chicago	273	159	82	32	996	768	350	274	91	139	44	732	883	226	547	250	221	76	1728	1651	576
Detroit	276	150	83	43	976	728	343	275	75	148	52	692	915	202	551	225	231	95	1668	1643	545
Edmonton	19	15	2	2	90	51	32	19	8	11	0	62	69	19	38	23	10	5	152	120	51
Hartford	44	29	11	4	171	111	62	44	17	21	6	158	161	40	88	46	32	10	329	272	102
Los Angeles	50	38	9	3	240	137	79	50	29	16	5	191	169	63	100	67	25	8	431	306	142
Minnesota	50	37	6	7	231	118	81	50	28	11	11	192	136	67	100	65	17	18	423	254	148
Montreal	298	136	110	52	879	799	324	297	82	172	43	679	1013	207	595	218	282	95	1558	1812	531
New Jersey	29	19	7	3	131	89	41	29	17	4	8	112	78	42	58	36	11	11	243	167	83
NY Islanders	35	19	8	8	137	96	46	35	18	14	3	119	112	39	70	37	22	11	256	211	85
NY Rangers	274	149	87	38	1000	764	336	276	103	119	54	773	838	260	550	252	206	92	1773	1602	596
Philadelphia	49	33	10	6	205	142	72	48	22	20	6	145	159	50	97	55	30	12	350	301	122
Pittsburgh	50	38	6	6	234	139	82	50	26	14	10	201	155	62	100	64	20	16	435	294	144
Quebec	44	23	15	6	182	142	52	44	25	15	4	200	169	54	88	48	30	10	382	311	106
St. Louis	48	32	9	7	219	129	71	48	21	18	9	169	149	51	96	53	27	16	388	278	122
Toronto	276	149	80	47	915	0	345	277	85	146	46	717	943	216	553	234	226	93	1632	943	561
Vancouver	40	34	3	3	186	88	71	40	21	12	7	174	136	49	80	55	15	10	360	224	120
Washington	31	19	5	7	128	86	41	31	16	7	8	122	92	40	62	35	12	15	250	178	81
Winnipeg	19	14	3	2	93	61	31	19	10	8	1	66	66	21	38	24	11	3	159	127	52
Defunct Club	164	112	39	13	525	306	237	164	79	67	18	496	440	176	328	191	106	31	1021	746	413

Totals 2176 1268 610 298 7961 5078 2834 2176 816 1007 353 6361 7082 1985 4352 2084 1617 651 14322 12160 4819

Playoffs

	Series	W	L	GP	W	L	T	GF	GA	Last Mtg.	Round	Result
Buffalo	4	4	0	22	15	7	0	94	70	1989	DSF	W 4-1
Chicago	6	5	1	22	16	5	1	97	63	1978	QF	W 4-0
Detroit	7	4	3	33	19	14	0	96	98	1957	SF	W 4-1
Edmonton	2	0	2	9	1	8	0	20	41	1990	F	L 1-4
Hartford	2	2	0	13	8	5	0	24	17	1991	DSF	W 4-2
Los Angeles	2	2	0	13	8	5	0	56	38	1977	QF	W 4-2
Minnesota	1	0	1	3	0	3	0	13	20	1981	PR	L 0-3
Montreal	26	5	21	128	44	84	0	303	402	1991	DF	W 4-3
New Jersey	1	1	0	7	4	3	0	30	19	1988	DF	W 4-3
NY Islanders	2	0	2	11	3	8	0	35	49	1983	CF	L 2-4
NY Rangers	9	6	3	42	22	18	2	114	104	1973	QF	L 1-4
Philadelphia	4	2	2	20	11	9	0	60	57	1978	SF	W 4-1
Pittsburgh	3	2	1	15	9	6	0	55	48	1991	CF	L 2-4
Quebec	2	1	1	11	6	5	0	37	36	1983	DSF	W 3-1
St. Louis	2	2	0	8	8	0	0	48	15	1972	SF	W 4-0
Toronto	13	5	8	62	30	31	1	153	150	1974	QF	W 4-0
Washington	1	1	0	4	4	0	0	5	6	1990	CF	W 4-0
Defunct Clubs	3	1	2	11	4	5	2	20	20			
Totals	90	43	47	434	212	216	6	1293	1274			

Playoff Results 1991-87

Year	Round	Opponent	Result	GF	GA
1991	CF	Pittsburgh	L 2-4	18	27
	DF	Montreal	W 4-3	18	18
	DSF	Hartford	W 4-2	24	17
1990	F	Edmonton	L 1-4	8	20
	CF	Washington	W 4-0	15	6
	DF	Montreal	W 4-1	16	12
	DSF	Hartford	W 4-3	23	21
1989	DF	Montreal	L 1-4	13	16
	DSF	Buffalo	W 4-1	16	14
1988	F	Edmonton	L 0-4	12	21
	CF	New Jersey	W 4-3	30	19
	DF	Montreal	W 4-1	15	10
	DSF	Buffalo	W 4-2	28	22
1987	DSF	Montreal	L 0-4	11	19

Abbreviations: Round: F – Final;
CF – conference final; **DF** – division final;
DSF – division semi-final; **SF** – semi-final;
QF – quarter-final; **PR** – preliminary round.
GA – goals against; **GF** – goals for.

1990-91 Results

	Home				Away	
Oct.	4 Philadelphia	4-1	Oct.	7 Quebec		5-2
	6 Quebec	7-1		10 Winnipeg		4-2
	25 Vancouver	4-2		11 Minnesota		3-3
	27 Chicago	5-4		13 Los Angeles		1-7
Nov.	1 St Louis	3-2		17 Vancouver		1-3
	8 Buffalo	1-4		19 Edmonton		1-8
	10 Pittsburgh	3-3		20 Calgary		1-8
	15 Quebec	6-0		31 Buffalo		3-3
	17 Montreal	1-1	Nov.	5 NY Rangers		3-2
	23 Hartford*	3-4		7 Montreal		2-0
	29 Edmonton	4-2		11 Washington		5-3
Dec.	1 NY Rangers	4-5		14 Hartford		1-3
	6 Montreal	4-6		19 Toronto		5-2
	13 Hartford	8-2		24 Hartford		4-3
	15 New Jersey	1-1	Dec.	4 Detroit		5-4
	20 Buffalo	4-1		8 Montreal		1-7
	22 Minnesota	6-2		9 Buffalo		3-2
Jan.	3 Vancouver	8-3		12 Hartford		5-1
	5 Washington	3-5		18 New Jersey		3-8
	7 Winnipeg	5-2		23 NY Rangers		5-5
	10 Quebec	5-3		26 Buffalo		3-3
	12 Philadelphia	1-3		28 Winnipeg		0-6
	14 Detroit	6-1		30 Minnesota		4-4
	17 Los Angeles	5-3	Jan.	8 Quebec		2-4
	24 Hartford	3-0		15 NY Islanders		5-4
	26 Calgary*	5-2		22 Buffalo		4-6
	31 Montreal	5-2		27 Montreal*		2-7
Feb.	2 Pittsburgh	6-3	Feb.	2 Pittsburgh*		2-6
	5 Edmonton	6-5		10 Quebec*		7-4
	7 Calgary	1-4		13 Montreal		7-4
	9 Chicago*	5-3		16 Los Angeles		5-4
	28 NY Islanders	5-0		21 Chicago		1-4
Mar.	2 Buffalo*	4-7		23 St Louis		2-9
	7 St Louis	5-5	Mar.	3 New Jersey		3-1
	9 Toronto*	2-0		5 Toronto		3-6
	14 Montreal	3-2		17 Philadelphia		3-1
	16 Detroit*	3-5		19 Hartford		1-1
	21 Quebec	3-3		24 Washington*		3-3
	23 Buffalo*	6-3		26 Quebec		7-4
	31 Hartford	7-3		30 NY Islanders		3-5

* Denotes afternoon game.

Entry Draft Selections 1991-77

1991
Pick
18	Glen Murray
40	Jozef Stumpel
62	Marcel Cousineau
84	Brad Tiley
106	Marivsz Czerkawski
150	Gary Golczewski
172	John Moser
194	Daniel Hodge
216	Steve Norton
238	Stephen Lombardi
260	Torsten Kienass

1990
Pick
21	Bryan Sholinski
63	Cameron Stewart
84	Jerome Buckley
105	Mike Bales
126	Mark Woolf
147	Jim Mackey
168	John Gruden
189	Darren Wetherill
210	Dean Capuano
231	Andy Bezeau
252	Ted Miskolczi

1989
Pick
17	Shayne Stevenson
38	Mike Parson
57	Wes Walz
80	Jackson Penney
101	Mark Montanari
122	Stephen Foster
143	Otto Hascak
164	Rick Allain
185	James Lavish
206	Geoff Simpson
227	David Franzosa

1988
Pick
18	Robert Cimetta
60	Stephen Heinze
81	Joe Juneau
102	Daniel Murphy
123	Derek Geary
165	Mark Krys
186	Jon Rohloff
228	Eric Reisman
249	Doug Jones

1987
Pick
3	Glen Wesley
14	Stephane Quintal
56	Todd Lalonde
67	Darwin McPherson
77	Matt Delguidice
98	Ted Donato
119	Matt Glennon
140	Rob Cheevers
161	Chris Winnes
182	Paul Ohman
203	Casey Jones
224	Eric Lemarque
245	Sean Gorman

1986
Pick
13	Craig Janney
34	Pekka Tirkkonen
76	Dean Hall
97	Matt Pesklewis
118	Garth Premak
139	Paul Beraldo
160	Brian Ferreira
181	Jeff Flaherty
202	Greg Hawgood
223	Steffan Malmquist
244	Joel Gardner

1985
Pick
31	Alain Cote
52	Bill Ranford
73	Jaime Kelly
94	Steve Moore
115	Gord Hynes
136	Per Martinele
157	Randy Burridge
178	Gord Cruickshank
199	Dave Buda
210	Bob Beers
220	John Byce
241	Marc West

1984
Pick
19	Dave Pasin
40	Ray Podloski
61	Jeff Cornelius
82	Robert Joyce
103	Mike Bishop
124	Randy Oswald
145	Mark Thietke
166	Don Sweeney
186	Kevin Heffernan
207	J.D. Urbanic
227	Bill Kopecky
248	Jim Newhouse

1983
Pick
21	Nevin Markwart
42	Greg Johnston
62	Greg Puhalski
82	Alain Larochelle
102	Allen Pederson
122	Terry Taillefor
142	Ian Armstrong
162	Francois Olivier
182	Harri Laurilla
202	Paul Fitzsimmons
222	Norm Foster
242	Greg Murphy

1982
Pick
1	Gord Kluzak
22	Brian Curran
39	Lyndon Byers
60	Dave Reid
102	Bob Nicholson
123	Bob Sweeney
144	John Meulenbrooks
165	Tony Fiore
186	Doug Kostynski
207	Tony Gilliard
228	Tommy Lehmann
249	Bruno Campese

1981
Pick
14	Normand Leveille
35	Luc Dufour
77	Scott McLellan
98	Joe Mantione
119	Bruce Milton
140	Mats Thelin
161	Armel Parisee
182	Don Sylvester
203	Richard Bourque

1980
Pick
18	Barry Pederson
60	Tom Fergus
81	Steve Kasper
102	Randy Hillier
123	Steve Lyons
144	Tony McMurchy
165	Mike Moffat
186	Michael Thelven
207	Jens Ohling

1979
Pick
8	Ray Bourque
15	Brad McCrimmon
36	Doug Morrison
57	Keith Crowder
78	Larry Melnyk
99	Marco Baron
120	Mike Krushelnyski

1978
Pick
16	Al Secord
35	Graeme Nicolson
52	Brad Knelson
68	George Buat
85	Darryl MacLeod
102	Jeff Brubaker
119	Murray Skinner
136	Robert Hehir
153	Craig MacTavish

1977
Pick
16	Dwight Foster
34	Dave Parro
52	Mike Forbes
70	Brian McGregor
88	Doug Butler
106	Keith Johnson
122	Ralph Cox
138	Mario Claude

General Manager

SINDEN, HARRY JAMES
President and General Manager, Boston Bruins.
Born in Collins Bay, Ont., September 14, 1932.

Harry Sinden never played a game in the NHL but stepped into the Bruins' organization with an impressive coaching background in minor professional hockey and his continued excellence has earned him a place in the Hockey Hall of Fame as one of the true builders in hockey history. In 1965-66 as playing-coach of Oklahoma City Blazers in the CPHL, Sinden led the club to second place in the regular standings and then to eight straight playoff victories for the Jack Adams Trophy. After five years in OHA Senior hockey — including 1958 with the World Amateur Champion Whitby Dunlops — Sinden was named playing-coach in the old Eastern Professional League and its successor, the Central Professional League. Under his guidance, the Bruins of 1967-68 made the playoffs for the first time in nine seasons, finishing third in the East Division, and were nosed out of first place in 1968-69 by Montreal. In 1969-70, Sinden led the Bruins to their first Stanley Cup win since 1940-41. The following season he went into private business but returned to the hockey scene in the summer of 1972 when he was appointed coach of Team Canada. He moulded that group of NHL stars into a powerful unit and led them into an exciting eight-game series against the Soviet national team in September of 1972. Team Canada emerged the winner by a narrow margin with a record of four wins, three losses and one tie. Sinden then returned to the Bruins organization early in the 1972-73 season. Sinden took over as the Bruins' coach in February 1985, after replacing Gerry Cheevers. Boston finished 11-10-3 with Sinden behind the bench before being defeated by Montreal in five games in the Adams Division semi-finals.

NHL Coaching Record

Season	Team	Games	Regular Season W	L	T	%	Playoffs Games	W	L	%
1966-67	Boston	70	17	43	10	.314				
1967-68	Boston	74	37	27	10	.568	4	0	4	.000
1968-69	Boston	76	42	18	16	.658	10	6	4	.600
1969-70	Boston	76	40	17	19	.651	14	12	2	.857*
1979-80	Boston	10	4	6	0	.400	9	4	5	.444
1984-85	Boston	24	11	10	3	.521	5	2	3	.400
	NHL Totals	330	151	121	58	.545	42	24	18	.571

* Stanley Cup win.

Club Directory

Boston Garden
150 Causeway Street
Boston, Massachusetts 02114
Phone 617/227-3206
FAX 617/523-7184
ENVOY ID
Front Office: BRUINS. GM
Public
Relations: BRUINS. PR
Capacity: 14,448

Executive
Owner and Governor	Jeremy M. Jacobs
Alternative Governor	Louis Jacobs
Alternative Governor, President and General Manager	Harry Sinden
Vice President	Tom Johnson
Ass't General Manager	Mike Milbury
Assistant to the President	Nate Greenberg
General Counsel	Barbara Macon
Director of Administration	Dale Hamilton
Administrative Assistant	Carol Gould
Receptionist	Karen Leonard

Coaching Staff
Coach	Rick Bowness
Assistant Coaches	Gordie Clark, Mike O'Connell
Coach, Maine Mariners (AHL)	E.J. McGuire

Scouting Staff
Coordinator of Minor League Player Personnel/Scouting	Bob Tindall
Director of Player Evaluation	Bart Bradley
Scouting Staff	Jim Morrison (Ontario), Andre Lachapelle (Quebec), Joe Lyons (New England), Don Saatzer (Minnesota), Lars Waldner (Europe), Marcel Pelletier (Pro Consultant), Jean Ratelle (College & High School), Harvey Keck (Western Canada), Svenvake Svensson (Europe)

Communications Staff
Director of Media Relations	Heidi Holland
Director of Community Relations, Marketing Services	Sue Byrne
Public Relations Ass't	Kevin Lyons
Director of Player & Alumni Community Relations	John Bucyk
Administrative Assistant	Marilyn Viola
Video Producer	Joe Curnane

Medical and Training Staff
Athletic Trainer	Jim Narrigan
Athletic Therapist	Don Worden
Equipment Manager	Ken Fleger
Assistant Equipment Manager	Eric Anderson
Team Physicians	Dr. Bertram Zarins, Dr. John J. Boyle, Dr. Ashby Moncure
Team Dentists	Dr. Robert Thomas and Dr. Richard Miner
Team Psychologist	Dr. Fred Neff

Ticketing and Finance Staff
Director of Ticket Operations	Matt Brennan
Assistant Director of Ticket Operations	Jim Foley
Receptionist	Linda Bartlett
Controller	John J. Dionne
Accounting Manager	Richard McGlinchey
Accounts Payable	Barbara Johnson

Television and Radio
Broadcasters (TV-38)	Fred Cusick and Derek Sanderson
Broadcasters (NESN)	Fred Cusick, Derek Sanderson and Dave Shea
Broadcasters (Radio)	Bob Wilson and John Bucyk
TV Channels	New England Sports Network (Home Games) and WSBK TV-38 (Road Games)
Radio Station	WEEI (590 AM) and Bruins Radio Network
Dimensions of Rink	191 feet by 83 feet
Club Colors	Gold, Black and White
Training Camp Site	Wilmington, MA.

Coach

BOWNESS, RICK
Coach, Boston Bruins. Born in Moncton, N.B., January 25, 1955.

Rick Bowness was named the 19th head coach in Boston Bruins history on June 4, 1991, succeeding Mike Milbury who ascended to the position of assistant general manager. Bowness, 36, comes to Boston after two seasons at the helm of the Maine Mariners, the Bruins' American Hockey League affiliate; 21 of the players in a Bruins uniform during the 1990-91 season had also played for Bowness in Maine. His two-season record with the Mariners was 65-72-23.

Bowness began his coaching career in 1982 as a player/assistant coach with the AHL's Sherbrooke Jets. He retired as a player in 1983 to become an assistant coach in Winnipeg under Barry Long, and also served in that capacity under John Ferguson and Dan Maloney. In 1987-88 he was named general manager and coach of the Moncton Hawks, Winnipeg's AHL affiliate. He remained with Moncton until February 7, 1989, when he was summoned to the parent Winnipeg club to serve as interim head coach. Bowness joined the Bruins organization on June 7, 1989.

Bowness, a right wing, enjoyed a nine-year playing career after being drafted by the Atlanta Flames in the second round of the 1975 Amateur Draft, playing for the Atlanta, Detroit, St. Louis and Winnipeg organizations.

Coaching Record

Season	Team	Games	Regular Season W	L	T	%	Playoffs Games	W	L	%
1987-88	Moncton (AHL)	80	27	45	8	.388	...	...	...	...
1988-89	Moncton (AHL)	53	28	20	5	.576	...	...	...	...
	Winnipeg (NHL)	28	8	17	3	.340	...	...	...	...
1989-90	Maine (AHL)	80	31	38	11	.457	...	...	...	...
1990-91	Maine (AHL)	80	34	34	12	.500	2	0	2	0.00
	NHL Totals	28	8	17	3	.340	...	...	...	...

Buffalo Sabres
1990-91 Results: 31w-30L-19T 81PTS. Third, Adams Division

Schedule

	Home			Away
Oct.	Fri. 4 Pittsburgh		**Oct.**	Sat. 5 Washington
	Wed. 9 Boston			Sat. 12 Quebec
	Sun. 13 Vancouver			Wed. 16 Montreal
	Fri. 18 Montreal			Sat. 19 Hartford
	Fri. 25 San Jose			Wed. 30 Detroit
	Sun. 27 Hartford		**Nov.**	Sat. 2 Montreal
Nov.	Fri. 1 Montreal			Thur. 7 Philadelphia
	Fri. 8 Philadelphia			Tues. 12 San Jose
	Wed. 20 Boston			Thur. 14 Los Angeles
	Fri. 22 Chicago			Sat. 16 Calgary
	Wed. 27 Quebec			Sat. 23 Boston
	Fri. 29 NY Rangers			Sat. 30 Quebec
Dec.	Sun. 8 Calgary		**Dec.**	Wed. 4 Winnipeg
	Wed. 11 St Louis			Sat. 7 Hartford
	Fri. 13 Hartford			Sat. 14 Montreal
	Wed. 18 Washington			Sat. 21 Toronto
	Fri. 20 Edmonton			Mon. 23 Hartford
	Fri. 27 Boston			Sat. 28 New Jersey
	Tues. 31 St Louis		**Jan.**	Sat. 4 Boston
Jan.	Fri. 3 NY Islanders			Tues. 7 Philadelphia
	Wed. 8 Quebec			Tues. 14 NY Rangers
	Fri. 10 Edmonton			Wed. 15 New Jersey
	Sun. 12 NY Rangers			Tues. 21 St Louis
	Sun. 26 Winnipeg*			Thur. 23 Pittsburgh
	Fri. 31 Montreal			Sat. 25 Montreal*
Feb.	Tues. 4 Washington			Wed. 29 Detroit
	Fri. 7 Minnesota		**Feb.**	Sat. 1 Boston
	Sun. 9 Los Angeles			Tues. 11 Hartford
	Wed. 12 Detroit			Wed. 19 Vancouver
	Fri. 14 San Jose			Sun. 23 Edmonton
	Sun. 16 Hartford			Tues. 25 Calgary
Mar.	Sun. 1 Chicago			Sat. 29 Pittsburgh*
	Fri. 6 New Jersey		**Mar.**	Tues. 3 Quebec
	Sun. 8 NY Islanders			Sat. 14 NY Islanders*
	Wed. 11 Boston			Tues. 17 Minnesota
	Sun. 15 Quebec			Thur. 19 Los Angeles
	Wed. 25 Toronto			Sun. 22 Chicago
	Sun. 29 Hartford			Sat. 28 Boston*
Apr.	Thur. 2 Montreal			Tues. 31 Minnesota
	Sun. 5 Quebec		**Apr.**	Sat. 4 Quebec

* Denotes afternoon game.

Home Starting Times:
Weeknights . . . . 7:35 p.m.
Sundays . . . . 7:05 p.m.
Except Jan. 26 . . . . 1:35 p.m.

Franchise date: May 22, 1970

22nd NHL Season

Alexander Mogilny had a fine sophomore campaign for the Sabres, connecting for 30 goals in 1990-91.

Year-by-Year Record

Season	GP	Home W	L	T	Road W	L	T	Overall W	L	T	GF	GA	Pts.	Finished	Playoff Result
1990-91	80	15	13	12	16	17	7	31	30	19	292	278	81	3rd, Adams Div.	Lost Div. Semi-Final
1989-90	80	27	11	2	18	16	6	45	27	8	286	248	98	2nd, Adams Div.	Lost Div. Semi-Final
1988-89	80	25	12	3	13	23	4	38	35	7	291	299	83	3rd, Adams Div.	Lost Div. Semi-Final
1987-88	80	19	14	7	18	18	4	37	32	11	283	305	85	3rd, Adams Div.	Lost Div. Semi-Final
1986-87	80	18	18	4	10	26	4	28	44	8	280	308	64	5th, Adams Div.	Out of Playoffs
1985-86	80	23	16	1	14	21	5	37	37	6	296	291	80	5th, Adams Div.	Out of Playoffs
1984-85	80	23	10	7	15	18	7	38	28	14	290	237	90	3rd, Adams Div.	Lost Div. Semi-Final
1983-84	80	25	9	6	23	16	1	48	25	7	315	257	103	2nd, Adams Div.	Lost Div. Semi-Final
1982-83	80	25	7	8	13	22	5	38	29	13	318	285	89	3rd, Adams Div.	Lost Div. Final
1981-82	80	23	8	9	16	18	6	39	26	15	307	273	93	3rd, Adams Div.	Lost Div. Semi-Final
1980-81	80	21	7	12	18	13	9	39	20	21	327	250	99	1st, Adams Div.	Lost Quarter-Final
1979-80	80	27	5	8	20	12	8	47	17	16	318	201	110	1st, Adams Div.	Lost Semi-Final
1978-79	80	19	13	8	17	15	8	36	28	16	280	263	88	2nd, Adams Div.	Lost Prelim. Round
1977-78	80	25	7	8	19	12	9	44	19	17	288	215	105	2nd, Adams Div.	Lost Quarter-Final
1976-77	80	27	8	5	21	16	3	48	24	8	301	220	105	2nd, Adams Div.	Lost Quarter-Final
1975-76	80	28	7	5	18	14	8	46	21	13	339	240	105	2nd, Adams Div.	Lost Quarter-Final
1974-75	80	28	6	6	21	10	9	49	16	15	354	240	113	1st, Adams Div.	Lost Final
1973-74	78	23	10	6	9	24	6	32	34	12	242	250	76	5th, East Div.	Out of Playoffs
1972-73	78	30	6	3	7	21	11	37	27	14	257	219	88	4th, East Div.	Lost Quarter-Final
1971-72	78	11	19	9	5	24	10	16	43	19	203	289	51	6th, East Div.	Out of Playoffs
1970-71	78	16	13	10	8	26	5	24	39	15	217	291	63	5th, East Div.	Out of Playoffs

1991-92 Player Personnel

FORWARDS	HT	WT	S	Place of Birth	Date	1990-91 Club
AMBROZIAK, Peter	6-0	191	L	Toronto, Ont.	9/15/71	Ottawa
ANDREYCHUK, Dave	6-3	225	R	Hamilton, Ont.	9/29/63	Buffalo
AUDETTE, Donald	5-8	182	R	Laval, Que.	9/23/69	Rochester-Buffalo
BOYCE, Ian	5-8	175	R	St. Laurent, Que.	1/24/68	Rochester
CIAVAGLIA, Peter	5-10	175	L	Albany, NY	7/16/69	Harvard
CORKUM, Bob	6-2	212	R	Salisbury, MA	12/18/67	Rochester-Buffalo
DAWE, Jason	5-10	185	L	Scarborough, Ont.	5/29/73	Peterborough
FRANCESCHETTI, Lou	6-0	190	L	Toronto, Ont.	3/28/58	Toronto-Buffalo
FRAWLEY, Dan	6-1	196	R	Sturg. Falls, Ont.	6/2/62	Rochester
GAGE, Jody	6-0	190	R	Toronto, Ont.	11/29/59	Rochester
HARTMAN, Mike	6-0	192	L	Detroit, MI	2/7/67	Buffalo
HAWERCHUK, Dale	5-11	190	L	Toronto, Ont.	4/4/63	Buffalo
HOGUE, Benoit	5-10	197	L	Repentigny, Que.	10/28/66	Buffalo
IOB, Tony	5-11	202	L	Renfrew, Ont.	1/2/71	King.-SSM
LAMBERT, Danny	5-11	195	L	Wawa, Ont.	1/7/70	S.S.Marie
LOEWEN, Darcy	5-10	192	L	Calgary, Alta.	2/26/69	Rochester
LUDZIK, Steve	5-11	195	L	Toronto, Ont.	4/3/62	Rochester
MARSHALL, Chris	5-10	170	L	Quincy, MA	12/12/68	Cincinnati
MAY, Brad	6-0	209	L	Toronto, Ont.	11/29/71	Niagara Falls
MOGILNY, Alexander	5-11	195	L	Khabarovsk, USSR	2/18/69	Buffalo
PALMER, Chris	5-11	180	R	Bancroft, Ont.	5/14/66	Utica
PERGOLA, David	6-1	185	R	Waltham, MA	3/4/69	Boston Coll.
PRITCHARD, Andy	5-11	185	R	Oakville, Ont.	5/12/67	St. Lawrence
RAY, Rob	6-0	208	L	Stirling, Ont.	6/8/68	Buffalo
ROBERTS, Tim	6-2	180	L	Boston, MA	3/6/69	R.P.I.
RUHACHUK, Brad	5-11	180	L	Winnipeg, Man.	6/11/70	Lethbridge
RUUTTU, Christian	5-11	192	L	Lappeen, Finland	2/20/64	Buffalo
SAVAGE, Joel	5-11	205	R	Surrey, B.C.	12/25/69	Rochester
SEJHA, Jiri	5-10	185	L	Pardubice, Czech.	7/22/62	Rochester
SHANNON, Darrin	6-2	205	L	Barrie, Ont.	12/8/69	Buffalo
SNUGGERUD, Dave	6-0	192	L	Minnetonka, MN	6/20/66	Buffalo
TANTI, Tony	5-9	190	L	Toronto, Ont.	9/7/63	Pittsburgh-Buffalo
TURGEON, Pierre	6-1	202	L	Rouyn, Que.	8/29/69	Buffalo
VAIVE, Rick	6-1	198	R	Ottawa, Ont.	5/14/59	Buffalo
WALLWORK, Bob	5-11	180	L	Boston, MA	3/15/68	Cincinnati
WINCH, Jason	6-1	216	L	Listowel, Ont.	5/23/71	Niagara Falls
YOUNG, Jason	5-10	182	L	Sudbury, Ont.	12/16/72	Sudbury
DEFENSEMEN						
BASSEGIO, Dave	6-3	180	L	Niagara Falls, Ont.	10/28/67	Rochester
BODGER, Doug	6-2	213	L	Chemainus, B.C.	6/18/66	Buffalo
BOUCHER, Phillippe	6-2	189	R	St. Apoll., Que.	3/24/73	Granby
BROWN, Greg	5-11	185	R	Hartford, CT	3/7/68	Rochester
CURRAN, Brian	6-4	200	L	Toronto, Ont.	11/5/63	Toronto-Buffalo
DI VITA, David	6-2	205	L	S.C. Shores, MI	2/3/69	Lake Superior
HALLER, Kevin	6-2	191	L	Trochu, Alta.	12/5/70	Rochester
HOULDER, Bill	6-3	210	L	Thunder Bay, Ont.	3/11/67	Rochester
KENNEDY, Dean	6-2	205	R	Redver, Sask.	1/18/63	Buffalo
KRUPP, Uwe	6-6	235	R	Cologne, Germany	6/24/65	Buffalo
KUMMU, Ryan	6-3	205	L	Kitchener, Ont.	5/5/67	Erie
LEDYARD, Grant	6-2	200	L	Winnipeg, Man.	11/19/61	Buffalo
McSWEEN, Don	5-11	197	L	Detroit, MI	6/9/64	Rochester
MILLER, Brad	6-4	225	L	Edmonton, Alta.	7/23/69	Rochester
O'DONNELL, Sean	6-2	214	L	Ottawa, Ont.	10/13/71	Sudbury
RAMSEY, Mike	6-3	195	L	Minneapolis, MN	12/3/60	Buffalo
ROONEY, Larry	5-11	165	L	Boston, MA	1/30/68	Providence Coll.
SMITH, Steve	5-9	215	L	Trenton, Ont.	4/4/63	Rochester
SNELL, Chris	5-10	198	L	Regina, Sask.	5/12/71	Ottawa
SUTTON, Ken	6-0	190	L	Edmonton, Alta.	5/11/69	Rochester
WELLS, Jay	6-1	215	L	Paris, Ont.	5/18/59	Buffalo

GOALTENDERS	HT	WT	C	Place of Birth	Date	1990-91 Club
BRADLEY, John	6-0	165	L	Pawtucket, R.I.	2/6/68	Boston U.
DRAPER, Tom	5-11	180	L	Outremont, Que.	11/20/66	Moncton
LITTMAN, David	6-0	183	L	Cranston, RI	6/13/67	Rochester
MALARCHUK, Clint	6-0	185	L	Grande Prairie, Alta.	5/1/61	Buffalo
PUPPA, Daren	6-3	205	R	Kirkland Lake, Ont.	3/23/65	Buffalo
PYE, Bill	5-9	170	L	Canton, MI	4/9/69	N. Michigan
VITUCCI, Nick	5-8	182	L	Welland, Ont.	6/16/67	Greensboro
WEEKS, Steve	5-11	165	L	Scarborough, Ont.	6/30/58	Milwaukee

Coaching History

"Punch" Imlach, 1970-71; "Punch" Imlach, Floyd Smith and Joe Crozier, 1971-72; Joe Crozier, 1972-73 to 1973-74; Floyd Smith, 1974-75 to 1976-77; Marcel Pronovost, 1977-78; Marcel Pronovost and Bill Inglis, 1978-79; Scott Bowman, 1979-80; Roger Neilson, 1980-81; Jim Roberts and Scott Bowman, 1981-82; Scott Bowman 1982-83 to 1984-85; Jim Schoenfeld and Scott Bowman, 1985-86; Scott Bowman, Craig Ramsay and Ted Sator, 1986-87; Ted Sator, 1987-88 to 1988-89; Rick Dudley, 1989-90 to date.

Captains' History

Floyd Smith, 1970-71; Gerry Meehan, 1971-72 to 1973-74; Jim Schoenfeld, 1974-75 to 1976-77; Danny Gare, 1977-78 to 1980-81; Gil Perreault, 1981-82 to 1985-86; Gil Perreault and Lindy Ruff, 1986-87; Lindy Ruff, 1987-88; Lindy Ruff and Mike Foligno, 1988-89; Mike Foligno, 1989-90. Mike Foligno and Mike Ramsey, 1990-91; Mike Ramsey, 1991-92.

1990-91 Scoring

Regular Season

* rookie

Pos	#	Player	Team	GP	G	A	Pts	+/−	PIM	PP	SH	GW	GT	S	%
C	10	Dale Hawerchuk	BUF	80	31	58	89	2	32	12	0	1	1	194	16.0
C	77	Pierre Turgeon	BUF	78	32	47	79	14	26	13	2	3	0	174	18.4
L	25	Dave Andreychuk	BUF	80	36	33	69	11	32	13	0	4	3	234	15.4
L	89	Alexander Mogilny	BUF	62	30	34	64	14	16	3	3	5	0	201	14.9
R	22	Rick Vaive	BUF	71	25	27	52	11	74	9	0	3	1	155	16.1
C	21	Christian Ruuttu	BUF	77	16	34	50	6−	96	2	3	1	1	155	10.3
C	33	Benoit Hogue	BUF	76	19	28	47	8−	76	1	0	2	2	134	14.2
D	4	Uwe Krupp	BUF	74	12	32	44	14	66	6	0	0	2	138	8.7
D	3	Grant Ledyard	BUF	60	8	23	31	13	46	2	1	1	1	118	6.8
D	8	Doug Bodger	BUF	58	5	23	28	8−	54	2	0	0	0	139	3.6
R	19	Tony Tanti	PIT	46	6	12	18	1	44	3	0	0	0	74	8.1
			BUF	10	1	7	8	2	6	0	0	0	0	19	5.3
			TOTAL	56	7	19	26	3	50	3	0	0	0	93	7.5
R	18	Dave Snuggerud	BUF	80	9	15	24	13−	32	0	4	2	0	128	7.0
L	42	Mikko Makela	BUF	60	15	7	22	2−	25	2	2	1	1	62	24.2
R	12	Greg Paslawski	WPG	43	9	10	19	6−	10	1	0	1	0	66	13.6
			BUF	12	2	1	3	0	4	0	0	1	0	9	22.2
			TOTAL	55	11	11	22	6−	14	1	0	2	0	75	14.7
D	5	Mike Ramsey	BUF	71	6	14	20	14	46	0	0	1	0	87	6.9
L	32	Rob Ray	BUF	66	8	8	16	11−	350	0	0	1	0	54	14.8
L	16	*Darrin Shannon	BUF	34	8	6	14	11−	12	1	0	0	1	56	14.3
L	20	Mike Hartman	BUF	60	9	3	12	10−	204	2	0	1	0	65	13.8
D	26	Dean Kennedy	BUF	64	4	8	12	5	119	0	0	2	0	46	8.7
R	15	Lou Franceschetti	TOR	16	1	1	2	2−	30	0	0	0	0	7	14.3
			BUF	35	1	7	8	2	28	0	0	1	0	20	5.0
			TOTAL	51	2	8	10	0	58	0	0	1	0	27	7.4
D	41	*Ken Sutton	BUF	15	3	6	9	2	13	2	0	0	0	26	11.5
D	7	*Kevin Haller	BUF	21	1	8	9	9	20	1	0	0	0	42	2.4
R	28	*Donald Audette	BUF	8	4	3	7	1−	4	2	0	1	0	17	23.5
G	30	Clint Malarchuk	BUF	37	0	4	4	0	19	0	0	0	0	0	.0
G	31	Daren Puppa	BUF	38	0	4	4	0	6	0	0	0	0	0	.0
D	9	*Greg Brown	BUF	39	1	2	3	20−	35	0	0	0	0	26	3.8
D	24	Jay Wells	BUF	43	1	2	3	18−	86	0	0	0	0	36	2.8
D	37	Bill Houlder	BUF	7	0	2	2	2−	4	0	0	0	0	7	.0
L	23	Jiri Sejba	BUF	11	0	2	2	5−	8	0	0	0	0	10	.0
R	38	Joel Savage	BUF	3	0	1	1	2−	0	0	0	0	0	2	.0
D	39	Brian Curran	TOR	4	0	0	0	2−	7	0	0	0	0	0	.0
			BUF	17	0	1	1	3−	43	0	0	0	0	7	.0
			TOTAL	21	0	1	1	5−	50	0	0	0	0	7	.0
G	34	*Dave Littman	BUF	1	0	0	0	0	0	0	0	0	0	0	.0
L	36	*Darcy Loewen	BUF	6	0	0	0	4−	8	0	0	0	0	2	.0
D	44	*Brad Miller	BUF	13	0	0	0	1−	67	0	0	0	0	4	.0
G	35	*Darcy Wakaluk	BUF	16	0	0	0	0	2	0	0	0	0	0	.0

Goaltending

No.	Goaltender	GPI	Mins	Avg	W	L	T	EN	SO	GA	SA	S%
35	*Darcy Wakaluk	16	630	3.33	4	5	3	2	0	35	292	.880
30	Clint Malarchuk	37	2131	3.35	12	14	10	1	1	119	1090	.891
31	Daren Puppa	38	2092	3.38	15	11	6	0	2	118	1029	.885
34	*Dave Littman	1	36	5.00	0	0	0	0	0	3	18	.833
	Totals	**80**	**4902**	**3.40**	**31**	**30**	**19**	**3**	**3**	**278**	**2432**	**.886**

Playoffs

Pos	#	Player	Team	GP	G	A	Pts	+/−	PIM	PP	SH	GW	OT	S	%
D	3	Grant Ledyard	BUF	6	3	3	6	1−	10	0	0	0	0	11	27.3
C	10	Dale Hawerchuk	BUF	6	2	4	6	3−	10	1	0	0	0	19	10.5
L	89	Alexander Mogilny	BUF	6	0	6	6	1−	2	0	0	0	0	20	.0
D	7	*Kevin Haller	BUF	6	1	4	5	1−	10	0	0	0	0	13	7.7
C	33	Benoit Hogue	BUF	5	3	1	4	1−	10	0	0	0	0	13	23.1
C	77	Pierre Turgeon	BUF	6	3	1	4	1−	6	1	0	0	0	13	23.1
L	25	Dave Andreychuk	BUF	6	2	2	4	2−	8	1	0	0	0	21	9.5
C	21	Christian Ruuttu	BUF	6	1	3	4	3	29	0	1	0	0	7	14.3
R	18	Dave Snuggerud	BUF	6	1	3	4	2	4	0	1	0	0	10	10.0
L	16	*Darrin Shannon	BUF	6	1	2	3	2−	4	0	0	0	0	5	20.0
R	22	Rick Vaive	BUF	6	1	2	3	0	6	1	0	0	0	3	33.3
R	19	Tony Tanti	BUF	5	2	0	2	3−	8	1	0	0	0	8	25.0
D	4	Uwe Krupp	BUF	6	1	1	2	2−	6	1	0	0	0	13	7.7
L	32	Rob Ray	BUF	6	1	1	2	1	56	0	0	1	0	6	16.7
D	5	Mike Ramsey	BUF	5	1	0	1	0	12	0	0	1	0	8	12.5
R	15	Lou Franceschetti	BUF	6	1	0	1	2−	2	0	0	0	0	1	100.0
D	24	Jay Wells	BUF	1	0	1	1	0	0	0	0	0	0	0	.0
D	26	Dean Kennedy	BUF	2	0	1	1	2	17	0	0	0	0	0	.0
D	8	Doug Bodger	BUF	4	0	1	1	3	0	0	0	0	0	5	.0
G	30	Clint Malarchuk	BUF	4	0	1	1	0	0	0	0	0	0	0	.0
D	41	*Ken Sutton	BUF	6	0	1	1	4−	2	0	0	0	0	13	.0
L	20	Mike Hartman	BUF	2	0	0	0	0	17	0	0	0	0	0	.0
G	31	Daren Puppa	BUF	2	0	0	0	0	0	0	0	0	0	0	.0
G	35	*Darcy Wakaluk	BUF	2	0	0	0	0	2	0	0	0	0	0	.0

Goaltending

No.	Goaltender	GPI	Mins	Avg	W	L	EN	SO	GA	SA	S%
35	*Darcy Wakaluk	2	37	3.24	0	1	0	0	2	22	.909
30	Clint Malarchuk	4	246	4.15	2	2	0	0	17	116	.853
31	Daren Puppa	2	81	7.41	0	1	0	0	10	46	.783
	Totals	6	366	4.75	2	4	0	0	29	184	.842

General Managers' History

George "Punch" Imlach, 1970-71 to 1977-78; John Anderson (acting), 1978-79; Scott Bowman, 1979-80 to 1985-86; Scott Bowman and Gerry Meehan, 1986-87; Gerry Meehan, 1987-88 to date.

Retired Numbers

11	Gilbert Perreault	1970-1987

Club Records

Team

(Figures in brackets for season records are games played; records for fewest points, wins, ties, losses, goals, goals against are for 70 or more games)

Most Points	113	1974-75 (80)	
Most Wins	49	1974-75 (80)	
Most Ties	21	1980-81 (80)	
Most Losses	44	1986-87 (80)	
Most Goals	354	1974-75 (80)	
Most Goals Against	308	1986-87 (80)	
Fewest Points	51	1971-72 (78)	
Fewest Wins	16	1971-72 (78)	
Fewest Ties	6	1985-86 (80)	
Fewest Losses	16	1974-75 (80)	
Fewest Goals	203	1971-72 (78)	
Fewest Goals Against	201	1979-80 (80)	

Longest Winning Streak

Over-all	10	Jan. 4-23/84
Home	12	Nov. 12/72- Jan. 7/73 Oct. 13- Dec. 10/89
Away	10	Dec. 10/83- Jan. 23/84

Longest Undefeated Streak

Over-all	14	March 6- April 6/80 (8 wins, 6 ties)
Home	21	Oct. 8/72- Jan. 7/73 (18 wins, 3 ties)
Away	10	Dec. 10/83- Jan. 23/84 (10 wins)

Longest Losing Streak

Over-all	7	Oct. 25- Nov. 8/70
Home	5	Feb. 15-Mar. 3/85 Dec. 29/89- Jan. 26/90
Away	7	Oct. 14- Nov. 7/70 Feb. 6-27/71

Longest Winless Streak

Over-all	10	Nov. 7- Dec. 1/71 (8 losses, 2 ties)

Home	12	Jan. 27- Mar. 10/91 (7 losses, 5 ties)
Away	23	Oct. 30/71- Feb. 19/72 (15 losses, 8 ties)
Most Shutouts, Season	7	1974-75 (80)
Most PIM, Season	2,277	1987-88 (80)
Most Goals, Game	14	Jan. 21/75 (Wsh. 2 at Buf. 14) Mar. 19/81 (Tor. 4 at Buf. 14)

Individual

Most Seasons	17	Gilbert Perreault
Most Games	1,191	Gilbert Perreault
Most Goals, Career	512	Gilbert Perreault
Most Assists, Career	814	Gilbert Perreault
Most Points, Career	1,326	Gilbert Perreault
Most PIM, Career	1,390	Larry Playfair
Most Shutouts, Career	14	Don Edwards
Longest Consecutive Games Streak	776	Craig Ramsay (Mar. 27/73-Feb. 10/83)
Most Goals, Season	56	Danny Gare (1979-80)
Most Assists, Season	69	Gilbert Perreault (1975-76)
Most Points, Season	113	Gilbert Perreault (1975-76) (44 goals, 69 assists)
Most PIM, Season	350	Rob Ray (1990-91)
Most Points, Defenseman Season	81	Phil Housley (1989-90) (21 goals, 60 assists)
Most Points, Center Season	113	Gilbert Perreault (1975-76) (44 goals, 69 assists)
Most Points, Right Wing Season	100	Reńe Robert (1974-75) (40 goals, 60 assists)

Most Points, Left Wing Season	95	Richard Martin (1974-75) (52 goals, 43 assists)
Most Points, Rookie Season	74	Richard Martin (1971-72) (44 goals, 30 assists)
Most Shutouts, Season	5	Don Edwards (1977-78) Tom Barrasso (1984-85)
Most Goals, Game	5	Dave Andreychuk (Feb. 6/86)
Most Assists, Game	5	Gilbert Perreault (Feb. 1/76; Mar. 9/80; Jan. 4/84)
Most Points, Game	7	Gilbert Perreault (Feb. 1/76)

* NHL Record.

All-time Record vs. Other Clubs

Regular Season

			At Home							On Road							Total				
	GP	W	L	T	GF	GA	PTS	GP	W	L	T	GF	GA	PTS	GP	W	L	T	GF	GA	PTS
Boston	71	34	24	13	266	232	81	72	22	42	8	225	303	52	143	56	66	21	491	535	133
Calgary	35	20	11	4	147	106	44	34	11	13	10	115	125	32	69	31	24	14	262	231	76
Chicago	41	26	9	6	166	109	58	40	12	22	6	103	130	30	81	38	31	12	269	239	88
Detroit	42	30	5	7	191	102	67	43	17	22	4	132	161	38	85	47	27	11	323	263	105
Edmonton	19	8	8	3	78	78	19	19	3	14	2	49	86	8	38	11	22	5	127	164	27
Hartford	44	23	15	6	183	145	52	44	23	16	5	140	133	51	88	46	31	11	323	278	103
Los Angeles	42	21	13	8	175	132	50	42	19	16	7	145	146	45	84	40	29	15	320	278	95
Minnesota	42	23	9	10	162	113	56	42	19	17	6	135	131	44	84	42	26	16	297	244	100
Montreal	67	29	20	18	207	199	76	67	18	41	8	201	279	44	134	47	61	26	408	478	120
New Jersey	29	22	3	4	142	81	48	29	19	5	5	122	87	43	58	41	8	9	264	168	91
NY Islanders	35	19	12	4	121	99	42	36	17	13	6	107	102	40	71	36	25	10	228	201	82
NY Rangers	42	26	10	6	190	136	58	41	14	17	10	117	144	38	83	40	27	16	307	280	96
Philadelphia	40	20	14	6	144	119	46	41	9	26	6	103	151	24	81	29	40	12	247	270	70
Pittsburgh	42	22	6	14	192	112	58	42	14	16	12	151	160	40	84	36	22	26	343	272	98
Quebec	44	26	12	6	183	145	58	44	15	22	7	135	166	37	88	41	34	13	318	311	95
St. Louis	40	26	10	4	168	121	56	40	11	24	5	104	156	27	80	37	34	9	272	277	83
Toronto	47	29	16	2	199	136	60	46	21	18	7	172	147	49	93	50	34	9	371	283	109
Vancouver	41	22	11	8	155	116	52	41	12	19	10	134	155	34	82	34	30	18	289	271	86
Washington	31	23	5	3	139	84	49	31	21	4	6	134	82	48	62	44	9	9	273	166	97
Winnipeg	19	16	1	2	91	50	34	19	10	7	2	70	61	22	38	26	8	4	161	111	56
Defunct Club	23	13	5	5	94	63	31	23	12	8	3	97	76	27	46	25	13	8	191	139	58
Totals	**836**	**478**	**219**	**139**	**3393**	**2478**	**1095**	**836**	**319**	**382**	**135**	**2691**	**2981**	**773**	**1672**	**797**	**601**	**274**	**6084**	**5459**	**1868**

Playoffs

	Series	W	L	GP	W	L	T	GF	GA	Last Mtg.	Round	Result
Boston	4	0	4	22	7	15	0	70	94	1989	DSF	L 1-4
Chicago	2	2	0	9	8	1	0	36	17	1980	QF	W 4-0
Minnesota	2	1	1	7	3	4	0	28	26	1981	QF	L 1-4
Montreal	5	2	3	27	13	14	0	82	98	1991	DSF	L 2-4
NY Islanders	3	0	3	16	4	12	0	45	59	1980	SF	L 2-4
NY Rangers	1	1	0	3	2	1	0	11	6	1978	PR	W 2-1
Philadelphia	2	0	2	11	3	8	0	23	35	1978	QF	L 1-4
Pittsburgh	1	0	1	3	1	2	0	9	7	1979	PR	L 1-2
Quebec	2	0	2	8	2	6	0	27	35	1985	DSF	L 2-3
St. Louis	1	1	0	3	2	1	0	8	7	1976	PR	W 2-1
Vancouver	2	2	0	7	6	1	0	28	14	1981	PR	W 3-0
Totals	**25**	**9**	**16**	**116**	**51**	**65**	**0**	**366**	**401**			

Playoff Results 1991-87

Year	Round	Opponent	Result	GF	GA
1991	DSF	Montreal	L 2-4	24	29
1990	DSF	Montreal	L 2-4	13	17
1989	DSF	Boston	L 1-4	14	16
1988	DSF	Boston	L 2-4	22	28

Abbreviations: Round: F – Final; CF – conference final; DF – division final; DSF – division semi-final; PR – preliminary round. **GA** – goals against; **GF** – goals for.

			1990-91 Results				
		Home				**Away**	
Oct.	4	Montreal	3-3	Oct.	6	Montreal	5-6
	12	Quebec	2-4		10	Hartford	3-4
	17	Montreal	3-4		13	Quebec	4-4
	19	Pittsburgh	4-4		20	NY Islanders	3-1
	28	Hartford	5-0		25	New Jersey	1-5
	31	Boston	3-3		27	Toronto	3-1
Nov.	4	Calgary	2-1	Nov.	3	Boston	4-1
	9	Vancouver	7-1		7	NY Rangers	2-6
	21	NY Rangers	5-5		10	Washington	4-2
	23	Edmonton	3-2		14	Los Angeles	2-4
Dec.	2	Detroit	3-3		16	Edmonton	2-4
	7	Hartford	3-4		17	Calgary	3-3
	9	Boston	2-3		26	NY Rangers	0-5
	14	Pittsburgh	3-4		28	Montreal	2-1
	16	St Louis	3-5	Dec.	1	Quebec	2-4
	23	Quebec	10-3		6	Philadelphia	4-3
	26	Boston	3-3		11	Detroit	3-8
	28	Chicago	5-0		18	Hartford	4-3
	31	Philadelphia	5-2		20	Boston	1-4
Jan.	2	NY Islanders	5-4		29	New Jersey	4-4
	4	Winnipeg	4-1	Jan.	8	Vancouver	3-3
	16	Detroit	5-3		10	Los Angeles	2-5
	22	Boston	6-4		12	Minnesota	5-3
	27	Calgary*	4-5		14	Toronto	9-3
	31	Quebec	1-4		24	Chicago	5-4
Feb.	3	Edmonton	2-3		26	Montreal*	1-4
	6	St Louis	4-5		29	St Louis	3-8
	8	Los Angeles	4-4	Feb.	10	Winnipeg*	2-0
	13	Minnesota	6-6		12	Quebec	4-4
	15	Montreal	2-2		19	Pittsburgh	3-6
	17	Toronto	0-3		23	Hartford	5-4
	24	Hartford	5-5		26	NY Islanders	1-1
Mar.	6	New Jersey	3-3		28	Quebec	5-1
	8	Chicago	3-5	Mar.	2	Boston*	7-4
	10	Vancouver	5-7		12	Minnesota	2-5
	17	Hartford	6-1		14	Winnipeg	6-2
	20	Montreal	3-2		16	Montreal	4-6
	24	Philadelphia*	6-2		23	Boston*	3-6
	28	Quebec	4-4		26	Washington	4-2
	31	Washington	5-2		30	Hartford	5-5

* Denotes afternoon game.

Entry Draft
Selections 1991-77

1991
Pick
13 Philippe Boucher
35 Jason Dawe
57 Jason Young
72 Peter Ambroziak
101 Steve Shields
123 Sean O'Donnell
124 Brian Holzinger
145 Chris Snell
162 Jiri Kuntos
189 Tony Iob
211 Spencer Meany
233 Mihail Volkov
255 Michael Smith

1990
Pick
14 Brad May
82 Brian McCarthy
97 Richard Smehlik
100 Todd Bojcun
103 Brad Pascall
142 Viktor Gordijuk
166 Milan Nedoma
187 Jason Winch
208 Sylvain Naud
229 Kenneth Martin
250 Brad Rubachuk

1989
Pick
14 Kevin Haller
56 John (Scott) Thomas
77 Doug MacDonald
98 Ken Sutton
107 Bill Pye
119 Mike Barkley
161 Derek Plante
183 Donald Audette
194 Mark Astley
203 John Nelson
224 Todd Henderson
245 Michael Bavis

1988
Pick
13 Joel Savage
55 Darcy Loewen
76 Keith E. Carney
89 Alexander Mogilny
97 Robert Ray
106 David DiVita
118 Mike McLaughlin
139 Mike Griffith
160 Daniel Ruoho
181 Wade Flaherty
223 Thomas Nieman
244 Robert Wallwork

1987
Pick
1 Pierre Turgeon
22 Brad Miller
53 Andrew MacVicar
84 John Bradley
85 David Pergola
106 Chris Marshall
127 Paul Flanagan
148 Sean Dooley
153 Tim Roberts
169 Grant Tkachuk
190 Ian Herbers
211 David Littman
232 Allan MacIsaac

1986
Pick
5 Shawn Anderson
26 Greg Brown
47 Bob Corkum
56 Kevin Kerr
68 David Baseggio
89 Larry Rooney
110 Miguel Baldris
131 Mike Hartman
152 Francois Guay
173 Shawn Whitham
194 Kenton Rein
215 Troy Arndt

1985
Pick
14 Calle Johansson
35 Benoit Hogue
56 Keith Gretzky
77 Dave Moylan
98 Ken Priestlay
119 Joe Reekie
140 Petri Matikainen
161 Trent Kaese
182 Jiri Sejba
203 Boyd Sutton
224 Guy Larose
245 Ken Baumgartner

1984
Pick
18 Mikael Andersson
39 Doug Trapp
60 Ray Sheppard
81 Bob Halkidis
102 Joey Rampton
123 James Gasseau
144 Darcy Wakaluk
165 Orwar Stambert
207 Brian McKinnon
228 Grant Delcourt
249 Sean Baker

1983
Pick
5 Tom Barrasso
10 Normand Lacombe
11 Adam Creighton
31 John Tucker
34 Richard Hajdu
74 Daren Puppa
94 Jayson Meyer
114 Jim Hofford
134 Christian Ruutlu
154 Don McSween
174 Tim Hoover
194 Mark Ferner
214 Uwe Krupp
234 Marc Hamelin
235 Kermit Salfi

1982
Pick
6 Phil Housley
9 Paul Cyr
16 Dave Andreychuk
26 Mike Anderson
30 Jens Johansson
68 Timo Jutila
79 Jeff Hamilton
100 Bob Logan
111 Jeff Parker
121 Jacob Gustavsson
142 Allen Bishop
163 Claude Verrett
184 Rob Norman
205 Mike Craig
226 Jim Plankers

1981
Pick
17 Jiri Dudacek
38 Hannu Virta
59 Jim Aldred
60 Colin Chisholm
80 Jeff Eatough
83 Anders Wikberg
101 Mauri Eivola
122 Ali Butorac
143 Haikki Leime
164 Gates Orlando
185 Venci Sebeck
206 Warren Harper

1980
Pick
20 Steve Patrick
41 Mike Moller
56 Sean McKenna
62 Jay North
83 Jim Wiemer
104 Dirk Reuter
125 Daniel Naud
146 Jari Paavola
167 Randy Cunneyworth
188 Dave Beckon
209 John Bader

1979
Pick
11 Mike Ramsey
32 Lindy Ruff
53 Mark Robinson
55 Jacques Cloutier
74 Gilles Hamel
95 Alan Haworth
116 Rick Knickle

1978
Pick
13 Larry Playfair
32 Tony McKegney
49 Rob McClanahan
66 Mike Gazdic
82 Randy Ireland
99 Cam MacGregor
116 Dan Eastman
133 Eric Strobel
150 Eugene O'Sullivan

1977
Pick
14 Ric Seiling
32 Ron Areshenkoff
68 Bill Stewart
86 Richard Sirois
104 Wayne Ramsey

Coach
DUDLEY, RICK
Coach, Buffalo Sabres. Born in Toronto, Ont., January 31, 1949.

Rick Dudley was named head coach of the Sabres on June 16, 1989, marking his return to a club for which he played 279 games between 1972-73 and 1980-81. Dudley's NHL playing career included stints in Buffalo and Winnipeg. He tallied 174 points (75-99-174) in 309 NHL games before ending his playing career in 1981-82.

Dudley's coaching career began in 1982-83 when he assumed the head coaching duties for the Carolina Thunderbirds of the ACHL. He met with instant success as he led his club to the title in his first season. In 1983-84 and 1984-85, Dudley led his team to a first-place finish during the regular-season, before winning another title in 1985-86. Dudley joined the Flint Generals (IHL) in 1986-87 and led them to the Turner Cup Finals in 1987-88. In 1988-89, he was the head coach for the New Haven Nighthawks (AHL) where he again led his club to the Final series. In seven years, Dudley compiled a minor league coaching record of 315-157-38 for a .655 winning percentage.

Coaching Record

Season	Team	Games	W	L	T	%	Games	W	L	%
		Regular Season					**Playoffs**			
1982-83	Carolina (ACHL)	68	51	10	7	.619	8	8	0	1.000
1983-84	Carolina (ACHL)	72	43	24	5	.632	10	5	5	.500
1984-85	Carolina (ACHL)	64	53	11	0	.828	10	8	2	.800
1985-86	Carolina (ACHL)	63	49	14	0	.778	11	8	3	.727
1986-87	Flint (IHL)	82	42	33	7	.555	6	2	4	.333
1987-88	Flint (IHL)	82	42	31	9	.567	16	10	6	.625
1988-89	New Haven (AHL)	80	35	35	10	.500	17	9	8	.529
1989-90	Buffalo (NHL)	80	45	27	8	.613	6	2	4	.333
1990-91	Buffalo (NHL)	80	31	30	19	.506	6	2	4	.333
	NHL Totals	160	76	57	27	.559	12	4	8	.333

Club Directory

Memorial Auditorium
Buffalo, N.Y. 14202
Phone **716/856-7300**
Outside Buffalo: **800/333-PUCK**
GM FAX 716/856-7350
FAX 716/856-2104
ENVOY ID
Front Office: SABRES. GM
Public
Relations: SABRES. PR
Capacity: 16,433

Board of Directors
Chairman of the Board and President . . . . Seymour H. Knox, III
Vice-Chairman of the Board and Counsel . . . . . . Robert O. Swados
Vice-Chairman of the Board . . . . Robert E. Rich, Jr.
Treasurer . . . . Joseph T.J. Stewart
Board of Directors . . . . Edwin C. Andrews
  Niagara Frontier Hockey L.P.   Peter C. Andrews
  (includes above listed officers)   George L. Collins, Jr. M.D.
                                    John B. Fisher
                                    John Houghton
                                    Richard Rupp
                                    Howard T. Saperston, Jr.
                                    Paul A. Schoellkopf
                                    George Strawbridge, Jr.
Consultant . . . . Northrup R. Knox
Assistant to the President . . . . Seymour H. Knox, IV
Senior Vice-President/Administration . . . . Mitchell Owen
Senior Vice-President/Finance . . . . Robert W. Pickel
Vice-President/Marketing . . . . George Bergantz
Vice-President/General Manager . . . . Gerry Meehan
Director of Hockey Operations . . . . John Muckler
Assistant to the General Manager . . . . Craig Ramsay
Director of Player Personnel . . . . Don Luce
Head Coach . . . . Rick Dudley
Associate Coach . . . . John Van Boxmeer
Assistant Coach . . . . John Tortorella
Director of Scouting . . . . Rudy Migay
Coordinator of Minor League Pro. Development   Joe Crozier
Administrative Assistant to the General
  Manager . . . . Debbie Bonner
Scouting Staff . . . . Don Barrie, Jack Bowman, Larry Carriere, Boris Janicek, Dennis McIvor, Paul Merritt, Mike Racicot, Frank Zywiec
Information Manager – Hockey Dept. . . . . Ken Bass
Head Athletic Trainer . . . . Jim Pizzutelli
Trainer . . . . Rip Simonick
Equipment Supervisor . . . . John Allaway
Administrative Assistants . . . . Carol McHugh, Verna B. Wojcik
Controller . . . . Dan DiPofi
Exec. Director of Sales & Marketing Services . . Steve Donner
Director of Amateur Hockey Development . . . . . John Mickler
Director of Communications . . . . Paul Wieland
Director of Community Relations and
  Promotions . . . . Stan Makowski
Director of Event Sales . . . . Jeffrey Pickel
Director of Information . . . . Budd Bailey
Director of Media Relations . . . . Steve Rossi
Director of Public Relations . . . . John Gurtler
Director of Sales . . . . John Livsey
Director of Special Events . . . . Larry Playfair
Local Advertising Sales Manager . . . . Bob Russell
Sales Representatives . . . . Jeff Hall, Tom Pokel
Assistant Ticket Manager . . . . John Sinclair
Promotion Manager . . . . Matt Rabinowitz
Manager – Sabreland . . . . Cliff Smith
Director of Television Sales . . . . Don Angelo
Local Television Sales Manager . . . . Jim DiMino
Voice of the Sabres . . . . Ted Darling
Club Doctor . . . . John L. Butsch, M.D.
Orthopedic Consultant . . . . Peter James, M.D.
Club Dentist . . . . Donald DeRose, D.D.S.
Club Staff: Olive Anticola, Evelyn Battleson, Barbara Blendowski, Elaine Burzynski, Shirley Curry, Robert M. Dahar, Jim DiMino, Cyndi Dyll, Carm Glebe, Birgid Haensel, Chris Ivansitz, Mary Jones, Mike Kaminska, Sally Lippert, Gerry Magill, Melissa Nitkowski, Anne Robillard, Mary Beth Romano, Cheryl Schoenthaler, Ann Marie Seaman, Cheryl Smith, Bruce Wawrzyniak
Dimensions of Rink . . . . 193 feet by 84 feet
Location of Press Box . . . . Suspended from ceiling on west side
Club Colors . . . . Blue, White, Gold
Off-Ice Officials: Hank Olejniczak (Supervisor and Offical Scorer), Tony Caggiano, Sam Costello, Richard Costolnick, Dale Guynn, Robert Kalenik, Don Kwak, Walter Mendel, Duke Morettin, Jim Murdoch, Clifford Smith, Bill Truman
Photographer . . . . Bill Wippert
Public Address Announcer . . . . Milt Ellis

General Manager
MEEHAN, GERARD MARCUS (GERRY)
General Manager, Buffalo Sabres. Born in Toronto, Ont., September 3, 1946.

Gerry Meehan became general manager of the Sabres midway through the 1986-87 season. He retired as a player in 1979 after ten NHL seasons as a center with six different clubs. He played in Buffalo from 1970 to 1974 and, after his playing career, remained in the Buffalo area, earning an undergraduate degree from Canisius College and a law degree from the University of Buffalo. He practiced law in Buffalo before accepting the post of assistant GM for the Sabres in 1984-85 when he became the first former Buffalo player to move into the club's front office.

Calgary Flames

1990-91 Results: 46w-26l-8t 100pts. Second, Smythe Division

Year-by-Year Record

Season	GP	Home W	Home L	Home T	Road W	Road L	Road T	Overall W	Overall L	Overall T	GF	GA	Pts.	Finished	Playoff Result
1990-91	80	29	8	3	17	18	5	46	26	8	344	263	100	2nd, Smythe Div.	Lost Div. Semi-Final
1989-90	80	28	7	5	14	16	10	42	23	15	348	265	99	1st, Smythe Div.	Lost Div. Semi-Final
1988-89	**80**	**32**	**4**	**4**	**22**	**13**	**5**	**54**	**17**	**9**	**354**	**226**	**117**	**1st, Smythe Div.**	**Won Stanley Cup**
1987-88	80	26	11	3	22	12	6	48	23	9	397	305	105	1st, Smythe Div.	Lost Div. Final
1986-87	80	25	13	2	21	18	1	46	31	3	318	289	95	2nd, Smythe Div.	Lost Div. Semi-Final
1985-86	80	23	11	6	17	20	3	40	31	9	354	315	89	2nd, Smythe Div.	Lost Final
1984-85	80	23	11	6	18	16	6	41	27	12	363	302	94	3rd, Smythe Div.	Lost Div. Final
1983-84	80	22	11	7	12	21	7	34	32	14	311	314	82	2nd, Smythe Div.	Lost Div. Final
1982-83	80	21	12	7	11	22	7	32	34	14	321	317	78	2nd, Smythe Div.	Lost Div. Final
1981-82	80	20	11	9	9	23	8	29	34	17	334	345	75	3rd, Smythe Div.	Lost Div. Semi-Final
1980-81	80	25	5	10	14	22	4	39	27	14	329	298	92	3rd, Patrick Div.	Lost Semi-Final
1979-80	80	18	15	7	17	17	6	35	32	13	282	269	83	4th, Patrick Div.	Lost Prelim. Round
1978-79	80	25	11	4	16	20	4	41	31	8	327	280	90	4th, Patrick Div.	Lost Prelim. Round
1977-78	80	20	13	7	14	14	12	34	27	19	274	252	87	3rd, Patrick Div.	Lost Prelim. Round
1976-77	80	22	11	7	12	23	5	34	34	12	264	265	80	3rd, Patrick Div.	Lost Prelim. Round
1975-76	80	19	14	7	16	19	5	35	33	12	262	237	82	3rd, Patrick Div.	Lost Prelim. Round
1974-75	80	24	9	7	10	22	8	34	31	15	243	233	83	4th, Patrick Div.	Out of Playoffs
1973-74	78	17	15	7	13	19	7	30	34	14	214	238	74	4th, West Div.	Lost Quarter-Final
1972-73	78	16	16	7	9	22	8	25	38	15	191	239	65	7th, West Div.	Out of Playoffs

Schedule

Home			Away		
Oct.	Fri.	4 Edmonton	Oct.	Sun.	6 Winnipeg
	Tues.	15 Minnesota		Tues.	8 San Jose
	Thur.	17 Toronto		Thur.	10 Los Angeles
	Wed.	30 New Jersey		Sat.	12 Edmonton
Nov.	Tues.	12 Detroit		Sat.	19 Vancouver
	Thur.	14 Vancouver		Tues.	22 Minnesota
	Sat.	16 Buffalo		Thur.	24 Chicago
	Thur.	21 Vancouver		Sat.	26 St Louis
	Mon.	25 Winnipeg	Nov.	Fri.	1 Winnipeg
	Thur.	28 Los Angeles		Mon.	4 NY Rangers
	Sat.	30 San Jose		Wed.	6 Hartford
Dec.	Sat.	14 Detroit		Thur.	7 Boston
	Tues.	17 Winnipeg		Sat.	9 Toronto
	Thur.	19 Quebec		Fri.	22 Vancouver
	Sat.	28 Philadelphia	Dec.	Tues.	3 Detroit
	Sun.	29 Los Angeles		Thur.	5 New Jersey
	Tues.	31 Montreal		Sat.	7 Montreal
Jan.	Sat.	4 Edmonton		Sun.	8 Buffalo
	Wed.	8 San Jose		Tues.	10 Washington
	Fri.	10 Pittsburgh		Sat.	21 Winnipeg
	Wed.	22 NY Rangers		Mon.	23 Edmonton
	Mon.	27 Chicago	Jan.	Sun.	5 Edmonton
Feb.	Wed.	5 Quebec		Mon.	13 Montreal
	Tues.	11 NY Islanders		Tues.	14 Quebec
	Thur.	13 Washington		Thur.	16 NY Rangers
	Wed.	19 Boston		Fri.	24 San Jose
	Fri.	21 Los Angeles		Sat.	25 Los Angeles
	Tues.	25 Buffalo		Thur.	30 Boston
	Thur.	27 Philadelphia	Feb.	Sat.	1 Washington
Mar.	Tues.	3 Pittsburgh		Sun.	2 NY Islanders
	Thur.	5 Toronto		Fri.	7 Winnipeg
	Sat.	7 St Louis		Sat.	15 St Louis
	Sat.	14 Vancouver		Sun.	16 Chicago
	Mon.	16 Hartford		Sun.	23 San Jose*
	Thur.	19 San Jose	Mar.	Sun.	1 Vancouver*
	Tues.	24 Edmonton		Sun.	10 Pittsburgh
	Thur.	26 Los Angeles		Thur.	12 Philadelphia
	Sat.	28 Minnesota		Sat.	21 Los Angeles*
	Tues.	31 Edmonton	Apr.	Thur.	2 Vancouver
Apr.	Sun.	5 Winnipeg		Fri.	3 San Jose

* Denotes afternoon game.

Home Starting Times:
Weeknights .... 7:35 p.m.
Saturdays, Sundays and Dec. 31 .... 6:05 p.m.

Franchise date: June 24, 1980.
Transferred from Atlanta

20th NHL Season

Doug Gilmour had his fifth straight season with at least 50 assists, setting up his teammates 62 times in 1990-91.

1991-92 Player Personnel

FORWARDS	HT	WT	S	Place of Birth	Date	1990-91 Club
BANKS, Darren	6-2	215	L	Toronto, Ont.	3/18/66	Salt Lake
CHERNOMAZ, Rick	5-8	185	R	Selkirk, Man.	9/1/63	Salt Lake
CLARK, Kerry	6-1	190	R	Kelvington, Sask.	8/21/68	Salt Lake
DEASLEY, Bryan	6-3	205	L	Toronto, Ont.	11/26/68	Salt Lake
FLEURY, Theoren	5-6	160	R	Oxbow, Sask.	6/29/68	Calgary
FORSLUND, Tomas	6-0	185	L	Falund, Sweden	11/24/68	Leksand
GILLINGHAM, Todd	6-2	200	L	Labrador City, Nfld.	1/31/70	Trois Rivieres
GILMOUR, Doug	5-11	170	L	Kingston, Ont.	6/25/63	Calgary
HABSCHEID, Marc	6-0	185	R	Swift Current, Sask.	3/1/63	Detroit
HARKINS, Todd	6-3	210	R	Cleveland, OH	10/8/68	Salt Lake
HARRIS, Tim	6-2	190	R	Uxbridge, Ont.	10/16/67	Lake Superior
HEAPHY, Shawn	5-8	180	L	Sudbury, Ont.	1/27/68	Michigan State
HOFFMAN, Matt	6-1	200	R	Saginaw, MI	7/6/71	Oshawa
HUNTER, Tim	6-2	202	R	Calgary, Alta.	9/10/60	Calgary
KRUSE, Paul	6-0	202	L	Merritt, B.C.	3/15/70	Calgary-Salt Lake
LINDBERG, Chris	6-1	185	L	Ft. Francis, Ont.	4/16/67	Cdn. National Team
LYONS, Corey	5-10	186	L	Calgary, Alta.	6/18/68	Salt Lake
MAKAROV, Sergei	5-11	185	R	Chelyabinsk, USSR	6/19/58	Calgary
MATTEAU, Stephane	6-3	195	L	Rouyn-Noranda, Que.	9/2/69	Calgary
McCARTHY, Sandy	6-3	224	R	Toronto, Ont.	6/15/72	Laval
NIEUWENDYK, Joe	6-1	195	L	Oshawa, Ont.	9/10/66	Calgary
OTTO, Joel	6-4	220	R	Elk River, MN	10/29/61	Calgary
PATTERSON, Colin	6-2	195	R	Rexdale, Ont.	5/11/60	Calgary
RANHEIM, Paul	6-0	195	R	St. Louis, MO	1/25/66	Calgary
REICHEL, Robert	5-10	185	L	Most, Czech.	6/25/71	Calgary
ROBERTS, Gary	6-1	190	L	North York, Ont.	5/23/66	Calgary
SIMARD, Martin	6-3	215	R	Montreal, Que.	6/25/66	Salt Lake-Calgary
STERN, Ronnie	6-0	195	R	Ste. Agathe, Que.	1/11/67	Van.-Milw.-Cgy.
ST. PIERRE, David	6-0	180	R	Montreal, Que.	3/22/72	Longueuil
STRUCH, David	5-10	180	L	Flin Flon, Man.	2/11/71	Saskatoon
SUNDBLAD, Nikolas	6-1	196	R	Stockholm, Sweden	1/3/73	AIK
SWEENEY, Tim	5-11	180	L	Boston, MA	4/12/67	Calgary-Salt Lake
WILSON, Carey	6-2	205	R	Winnipeg, Man.	5/19/62	Hartford-Calgary
YOUNG, C.J.	5-10	180	R	Waban, MA	1/1/68	Salt Lake
ZEMLAK, Richard	6-2	190	R	Wynard, Sask.	3/3/63	Salt Lake

DEFENSEMEN	HT	WT	S	Place of Birth	Date	1990-91 Club
DAHL, Kevin	5-11	190	R	Regina, Sask.	12/30/68	Fredericton
GRANT, Kevin	6-3	210	R	Toronto, Ont.	1/9/69	Salt Lake
GUY, Kevan	6-3	202	R	Edmonton, Alta.	7/16/65	Vancouver-Calgary
JOHANSSON, Roger	6-3	185	L	Ljungby, Sweden	4/17/67	Calgary
KYTE, Jim	6-5	220	L	Ottawa, Ont.	3/21/64	Pittsburgh-Calgary
MacINNIS, Al	6-2	196	R	Inverness, N.S.	7/11/63	Calgary
MACOUN, Jamie	6-2	197	L	Newmarket, Ont.	8/17/61	Calgary
MELROSE, Kevan	5-10	185	L	Calgary, Alta.	3/28/66	Salt Lake
MUSIL, Frank	6-3	215	L	Pardubice, Czech.	12/17/64	Minnesota-Calgary
NATTRESS, Ric	6-2	210	R	Hamilton, Ont.	5/25/62	Calgary
OLSEN, Darryl	6-0	180	L	Calgary, Alta.	10/7/66	Salt Lake
OSIECKI, Mark	6-2	200	R	St. Paul, MN	7/23/68	Salt Lake
STOLK, Darren	6-4	205	L	Taber, Alta.	7/22/68	Muskegon
SUTER, Gary	6-0	190	L	Madison, WI	6/24/64	Calgary

GOALTENDERS	HT	WT	C	Place of Birth	Date	1990-91 Club
KIDD, Trevor	6-2	185	L	Dugald, Man.	3/29/72	Spokane
MUZZATTI, Jason	6-1	190	L	Toronto, Ont.	2/3/70	Michigan State
SHARPLES, Warren	6-0	180	L	Montreal, Que.	3/1/68	Salt Lake
VERNON, Mike	5-9	170	L	Calgary, Alta.	2/24/63	Calgary
WAMSLEY, Rick	5-11	185	L	Simcoe, Ont.	5/25/59	Calgary

Mike Vernon, right, ranked second among goaltenders with 31 wins in 1990-91.

1990-91 Scoring

Regular Season

* rookie

Pos	#	Player	Team	GP	G	A	Pts	+/–	PIM	PP	SH	GW	GT	S	%
R	14	Theo Fleury	CGY	79	51	53	104	48	136	9	7	9	0	249	20.5
D	2	Al MacInnis	CGY	78	28	75	103	42	90	17	0	1	1	305	9.2
C	25	Joe Nieuwendyk	CGY	79	45	40	85	19	36	22	4	1	0	222	20.3
C	39	Doug Gilmour	CGY	78	20	61	81	27	144	2	2	5	0	135	14.8
R	42	Sergei Makarov	CGY	78	30	49	79	15	44	9	0	5	0	93	32.3
D	20	Gary Suter	CGY	79	12	58	70	26	102	6	0	1	0	258	4.7
L	10	Gary Roberts	CGY	80	22	31	53	15	252	0	0	3	0	132	16.7
C	26	*Robert Reichel	CGY	66	19	22	41	17	22	3	0	3	0	131	14.5
C	29	Joel Otto	CGY	76	19	20	39	4 –	183	7	1	4	1	109	17.4
L	12	Paul Fenton	WPG	17	4	4	8	4 –	18	1	0	1	0	28	14.3
			TOR	30	5	10	15	3	0	1	1	0	0	46	10.9
			CGY	31	5	7	12	2	10	0	1	0	0	59	8.5
			TOTAL	78	14	21	35	5 –	28	2	2	2	0	133	10.5
R	23	*Stephane Matteau	CGY	78	15	19	34	17	93	0	1	1	0	114	13.2
L	28	Paul Ranheim	CGY	39	14	16	30	20	4	2	0	2	0	108	13.0
C	33	Carey Wilson	HFD	45	8	15	23	14 –	16	4	0	1	0	59	13.6
			CGY	12	3	3	6	1	2	0	0	1	0	20	15.0
			TOTAL	57	11	18	29	13 –	18	4	0	2	0	79	13.9
L	27	Brian MacLellan	CGY	57	13	14	27	15	55	5	0	2	0	74	17.6
D	3	Frantisek Musil	MIN	8	0	2	2	0	23	0	0	0	0	5	.0
			CGY	67	7	14	21	12	160	2	0	1	0	68	10.3
			TOTAL	75	7	16	23	12	183	2	0	1	0	73	9.6
D	34	Jamie Macoun	CGY	79	7	15	22	29	84	1	1	0	0	117	6.0
D	6	Ric Nattress	CGY	58	5	13	18	1 –	63	0	0	1	0	81	6.2
D	21	Roger Johansson	CGY	38	4	13	17	9	47	0	0	0	0	41	9.8
L	7	*Tim Sweeney	CGY	42	7	9	16	1	8	0	0	4	0	40	17.5
R	22	Ronnie Stern	VAN	31	2	3	5	14 –	171	0	0	1	0	30	6.7
			CGY	13	1	3	4	0	69	0	0	0	0	15	6.7
			TOTAL	44	3	6	9	14 –	240	0	0	1	0	45	6.7
D	4	Jim Kyte	PIT	1	0	0	0	0	2	0	0	0	0	0	.0
			CGY	42	0	9	9	10	153	0	0	0	0	29	.0
			TOTAL	43	0	9	9	10	155	0	0	0	0	29	.0
R	19	Tim Hunter	CGY	34	5	2	7	1	143	0	0	1	0	29	17.2
R	16	Sergei Priakin	CGY	24	1	6	7	3 –	0	0	0	0	0	26	3.8
D	5	Kevan Guy	VAN	39	1	6	7	6 –	39	0	0	1	0	37	2.7
			CGY	4	0	0	0	1	4	0	0	0	0	6	.0
			TOTAL	43	1	6	7	5 –	43	0	0	1	0	43	2.3
G	30	Mike Vernon	CGY	54	0	4	4	0	8	0	0	0	0	0	.0
R	13	*Martin Simard	CGY	16	0	2	2	0	53	0	0	0	0	7	.0
D	32	Rick Lessard	CGY	1	0	1	1	1 –	0	0	0	0	0	0	.0
G	31	Rick Wamsley	CGY	29	0	1	1	0	0	0	0	0	0	0	.0
G	1	Steve Guenette	CGY	1	0	0	0	0	0	0	0	0	0	0	.0
L	18	Paul Kruse	CGY	1	0	0	0	1 –	7	0	0	0	0	0	.0

Goaltending

No.	Goaltender	GPI	Mins	Avg	W	L	T	EN	SO	GA	SA	S%
31	Rick Wamsley	29	1670	3.05	14	7	5	0	0	85	762	.888
30	Mike Vernon	54	3121	3.31	31	19	3	2	1	172	1406	.878
1	Steve Guenette	1	60	4.00	1	0	0	0	0	4	30	.867
	Totals	80	4859	3.25	46	26	8	2	1	263	2200	.880

Playoffs

Pos	#	Player	Team	GP	G	A	Pts	+/–	PIM	PP	SH	GW	OT	S	%
R	14	Theo Fleury	CGY	7	2	5	7	1	14	0	0	1	1	20	10.0
D	20	Gary Suter	CGY	7	1	6	7	0	12	1	0	0	0	11	9.1
C	25	Joe Nieuwendyk	CGY	7	4	1	5	4 –	10	2	0	0	0	27	14.8
D	2	Al MacInnis	CGY	7	2	3	5	5	8	2	0	0	0	25	8.0
L	28	Paul Ranheim	CGY	7	2	2	4	0	0	0	0	0	0	16	12.5
C	33	Carey Wilson	CGY	7	2	2	4	2	0	1	0	0	0	9	22.2
L	10	Gary Roberts	CGY	7	1	3	4	1	18	0	0	0	0	9	11.1
R	22	Ronnie Stern	CGY	7	1	3	4	0	14	0	0	0	0	12	8.3
C	29	Joel Otto	CGY	7	1	2	3	0	8	0	0	0	0	9	11.1
C	26	*Robert Reichel	CGY	6	1	1	2	0	0	0	0	1	0	15	6.7
C	39	Doug Gilmour	CGY	7	1	1	2	1	0	0	0	0	0	11	9.1
R	42	Sergei Makarov	CGY	3	1	0	1	1 –	0	0	0	0	0	2	50.0
D	6	Ric Nattress	CGY	7	1	0	1	2 –	0	1	0	0	0	9	11.1
R	23	*Stephane Matteau	CGY	5	0	1	1	1 –	0	0	0	0	0	8	.0
D	34	Jamie Macoun	CGY	7	0	1	1	1	4	0	0	0	0	8	.0
L	27	Brian MacLellan	CGY	1	0	0	0	0	0	0	0	0	0	1	.0
R	11	Colin Patterson	CGY	1	0	0	0	1 –	0	0	0	0	0	2	.0
G	31	Rick Wamsley	CGY	1	0	0	0	0	0	0	0	0	0	0	.0
L	12	Paul Fenton	CGY	5	0	0	0	3 –	2	0	0	0	0	5	.0
D	3	Frantisek Musil	CGY	7	0	0	0	5 –	12	0	0	0	0	4	.0
R	19	Tim Hunter	CGY	7	0	0	0	2 –	10	0	0	0	0	6	.0
D	4	Jim Kyte	CGY	7	0	0	0	2 –	4	0	0	0	0	1	.0
G	30	Mike Vernon	CGY	7	0	0	0	0	2	0	0	0	0	0	.0

Goaltending

No.	Goaltender	GPI	Mins	Avg	W	L	EN	SO	GA	SA	S%
30	Mike Vernon	7	427	2.95	3	4	0	0	21	204	.897
31	Rick Wamsley	1	2	30.00	0	0	0	0	1	2	.500
	Totals	7	432	3.06	3	4	0	0	22	206	.893

Captains' History

Keith McCreary, 1972-73 to 1974-75; Pat Quinn, 1975-76, 1976-77; Tom Lysiak, 1977-78, 1978-79; Jean Pronovost, 1979-80; Brad Marsh, 1980-81; Phil Russell, 1981-82, 1982-83; Lanny McDonald, Doug Risebrough (co-captains), 1983-84; Lanny McDonald, Doug Risebrough, Jim Peplinski (tri-captains), 1984-85 to 1986-87; Lanny McDonald, Jim Peplinski (co-captains), 1987-88; Lanny McDonald, Jim Peplinski, Tim Hunter (tri-captains), 1988-89; Brad McCrimmon, 1989-90. Rotating, 1990-91.

Club Records

Team

(Figures in brackets for season records are games played; records for fewest points, wins, ties, losses, goals, goals against are for 70 or more games)

Most Points 117 1988-89 (80)
Most Wins 54 1988-89 (80)
Most Ties 19 1977-78 (80)
Most Losses 38 1972-73 (78)
Most Goals 397 1987-88 (80)
Most Goals Against 345 1981-82 (80)
Fewest Points 65 1972-73 (78)
Fewest Wins 25 1972-73 (78)
Fewest Ties 3 1986-87 (80)
Fewest Losses 17 1988-89 (80)
Fewest Goals 191 1972-73 (78)
Fewest Goals Against 226 1988-89 (80)

Longest Winning Streak
Overall ....10 Oct. 14-
Nov. 3/78
Home .... 9 Oct. 17-
Nov. 15/78
Jan. 3-
Feb. 5/89
Mar. 3-
Apr. 1/90
Feb. 21-
Mar. 14/91
Away .... 7 Nov. 10-
Dec. 4/88

Longest Undefeated Streak
Over-all ....13 Nov. 10-
Dec. 8/88
(12 wins, 1 tie)
Home .... 18 Dec. 29/90-
Mar. 14/91
(17 wins, 1 tie)
Away .... 9 Feb. 20-
Mar. 21/88
(6 wins, 3 ties)
Nov. 11-
Dec. 16/90
(6 wins, 3 ties)

Longest Losing Streak
Over-all .... 11 Dec. 14/85-
Jan. 7/86

Home .... 4 Five times
Away .... 9 Dec. 1/85-
Jan. 12/86

Longest Winless Streak
Over-all .... 11 Dec. 14/85-
Jan. 7/86
(11 losses)

Home .... 6 Nov. 25-Dec. 18/82
(5 losses, 1 tie)

Away ....13 Feb. 3-
Mar. 29/73
(10 losses, 3 ties)

Most Shutouts, Season 8 1974-75 (80)
Most PIM, Season 2,431 1987-88 (80)
Most Goals, Game ....12 Mar. 21/75
(Van. 4 at Atl. 12)
Feb. 22/90
(Tor. 2 at Cgy. 12)

Individual

Most Seasons........... 10 Jim Peplinski
Most Games ....705 Jim Peplinski
Most Goals, Career .....229 Kent Nilsson
Most Assists, Career ....455 Al MacInnis
Most Points, Career.....609 Al MacInnis
(154 goals, 455 assists)
Most PIM, Career ......2,238 Tim Hunter
Most Shutouts, Career ...20 Dan Bouchard
Longest Consecutive
Games Streak ....257 Brad Marsh
(Oct. 11/78-
Nov. 10/81)
Most Goals, Season ......66 Lanny McDonald
(1982-83)
Most Assists, Season.....82 Kent Nilsson
(1980-81)
Most Points, Season .....131 Kent Nilsson
(1980-81)
(49 goals, 82 assists)
Most PIM, Season ....375 Tim Hunter
(1988-89)

Most Points, Defenseman
Season ....103 Al MacInnis
(1990-91)
(28 goals, 75 assists)
Most Points, Center
Season ....131 Kent Nilsson
(1980-81)
(49 goals, 82 assists)
Most Points, Right Wing
Season ....110 Joe Mullen
(1988-89)
(51 goals, 59 assists)
Most Points, Left Wing
Season ....83 Eric Vail
(1978-79)
(35 goals, 48 assists)
Most Points, Rookie
Season ....92 Joe Nieuwendyk
(1987-88)
(51 goals, 41 assists)
Most Shutouts, Season .....5 Dan Bouchard
(1973-74)
Phil Myre
(1974-75)
Most Goals, Game ....5 Joe Nieuwendyk
(Jan. 11/89)
Most Assists, Game ....6 Guy Chouinard
(Feb. 25/81)
Gary Suter
(Apr. 4/86)
Most Points, Game ....7 Sergei Makarov
(Feb. 25/90)

All-time Record vs. Other Clubs

Regular Season

	At Home							On Road							Total						
	GP	W	L	T	GF	GA	PTS	GP	W	L	T	GF	GA	PTS	GP	W	L	T	GF	GA	PTS
Boston	35	14	19	2	133	129	30	35	10	21	4	96	120	24	70	24	40	6	229	249	54
Buffalo	34	13	11	10	125	115	36	35	11	20	4	106	147	26	69	24	31	14	231	262	62
Chicago	38	20	11	7	132	113	47	36	11	17	8	108	132	30	74	31	28	15	240	245	77
Detroit	34	22	7	5	159	101	49	34	11	18	5	115	137	27	68	33	25	10	274	238	76
Edmonton	44	21	18	5	203	175	47	44	12	24	8	160	202	32	88	33	42	13	363	377	79
Hartford	19	15	3	1	107	67	31	19	9	7	3	77	67	21	38	24	10	4	184	134	52
Los Angeles	60	36	16	8	285	203	80	59	23	31	5	226	241	51	119	59	47	13	511	444	131
Minnesota	36	22	4	10	149	95	54	37	14	18	5	121	141	33	73	36	22	15	270	236	87
Montreal	34	9	20	5	110	125	23	34	10	19	5	85	120	25	68	19	39	10	195	245	48
New Jersey	33	26	3	4	164	83	56	34	22	9	3	133	93	47	67	48	12	7	297	176	103
NY Islanders	40	18	11	11	148	126	47	40	10	21	9	107	158	29	80	28	32	20	255	284	76
NY Rangers	40	24	10	6	184	122	54	40	18	17	5	149	145	41	80	42	27	11	333	267	95
Philadelphia	40	20	12	8	126	137	48	41	11	29	1	108	170	23	81	31	41	9	274	307	71
Pittsburgh	34	20	7	7	145	96	47	35	10	16	9	119	129	29	69	30	23	16	264	225	76
Quebec	19	11	4	4	88	60	26	19	8	7	4	76	81	20	38	19	11	8	164	141	46
St. Louis	37	19	15	3	133	108	41	37	18	14	5	125	131	41	74	37	29	8	258	239	82
Toronto	36	22	11	3	167	120	47	35	14	14	7	139	143	35	71	36	25	10	306	263	82
Vancouver	61	43	10	8	280	169	94	61	28	21	12	209	209	68	122	71	31	20	489	378	162
Washington	29	21	5	3	132	68	45	29	12	13	4	108	110	28	58	33	18	7	240	178	73
Winnipeg	42	31	7	4	209	129	66	41	15	18	8	150	168	38	83	46	25	12	359	297	104
Defunct Club	13	8	4	1	51	34	17	13	7	3	3	43	33	17	26	15	7	4	94	67	34
Totals	**758**	**435**	**208**	**115**	**3270**	**2375**	**985**	**758**	**284**	**357**	**117**	**2560**	**2877**	**685**	**1516**	**719**	**565**	**232**	**5830**	**5252**	**1670**

Playoffs

	Series	W	L	GP	W	L	T	GF	GA	Last Mtg.	Round	Result
Chicago	2	2	0	8	7	1	0	30	17	1989	CF	W 4-1
Detroit	1	0	1	2	0	2	0	5	8	1978	PR	L 0-2
Edmonton	5	1	4	30	11	19	0	96	132	1991	DSF	L 3-4
Los Angeles	5	2	3	20	11	9	0	74	72	1990	DSF	L 2-4
Minnesota	1	0	1	6	2	4	0	18	25	1981	SF	L 2-4
Montreal	2	1	1	11	5	6	0	32	31	1989	F	W 4-2
NY Rangers	1	0	1	4	1	3	0	8	14	1980	PR	L 1-3
Philadelphia	2	1	1	11	4	7	0	28	43	1981	QF	W 4-3
St. Louis	1	1	0	7	4	3	0	28	22	1986	CF	W 4-3
Toronto	1	0	1	2	0	2	0	5	9	1979	PR	L 0-2
Vancouver	4	3	1	18	10	8	0	62	57	1989	DSF	W 4-3
Winnipeg	3	1	2	13	6	7	0	43	45	1987	DSF	L 2-4
Totals	**28**	**12**	**16**	**132**	**61**	**71**	**0**	**439**	**475**			

Playoff Results 1991-87

Year	Round	Opponent	Result	GF	GA
1991	DSF	Edmonton	L 3-4	20	22
1990	DSF	Los Angeles	L 2-4	24	29
1989	**F**	**Montreal**	**W 4-2**	**19**	**16**
	CF	Chicago	W 4-1	15	8
	DF	Los Angeles	W 4-0	22	11
	DSF	Vancouver	W 4-3	26	20
1988	DF	Edmonton	L 0-4	11	18
	DSF	Los Angeles	W 4-1	30	18
1987	DSF	Winnipeg	L 2-4	15	22

Abbreviations: Round: F Final; **CF** conference final; **DF** division final; **DSF** division semi-final; **SF** semi-final; **QF** quarter-final. **PR** preliminary round. **GA** goals against; **GF** goals for.

1990-91 Results

	Home				Away		
Oct.	4	Vancouver	3-2	Oct.	8	Winnipeg	4-3
	6	Toronto	4-1		10	Detroit	5-6
	18	St Louis	3-4		13	New Jersey	3-5
	20	Boston	8-1		14	Chicago*	3-1
	25	Edmonton	4-2		21	Edmonton	2-1
	27	Washington	9-4		23	Los Angeles	4-6
	30	New Jersey	6-3	Nov.	3	Toronto	7-3
Nov.	1	Winnipeg	2-1		4	Buffalo	1-2
	15	NY Islanders	3-4		6	Pittsburgh	5-6
	17	Buffalo	3-3		8	Philadelphia	8-2
	22	Los Angeles	6-3		10	NY Islanders	1-5
	24	Chicago	3-5		11	NY Rangers	4-4
Dec.	5	NY Rangers	4-1		19	Vancouver	6-4
	7	Quebec	3-5		28	Winnipeg	2-2
	18	Vancouver	2-3	Dec.	1	Montreal	5-3
	20	Los Angeles	3-4		2	Quebec	5-5
	22	Edmonton	2-6		9	Edmonton	3-2
	29	Hartford	8-2		11	Minnesota	4-1
	31	Montreal	7-2		13	Los Angeles	4-1
Jan.	5	Detroit	7-0		16	Vancouver*	5-2
	15	Winnipeg	7-5		27	Edmonton	1-4
	30	NY Rangers	5-1	Jan.	2	Winnipeg	3-3
Feb.	2	Chicago	3-1		3	Toronto	5-3
	15	Washington	8-2		10	Pittsburgh	1-5
	17	St Louis	7-4		11	Washington	2-4
	19	Detroit	4-4		13	Winnipeg	3-4
	21	Vancouver	6-4		22	Philadelphia	3-4
	23	Quebec	10-8		23	Hartford	4-5
	27	Edmonton	4-2		26	Boston*	2-5
Mar.	1	Pittsburgh	6-2		27	Buffalo*	5-4
	2	Minnesota	5-1	Feb.	5	New Jersey	1-2
	4	Montreal	3-2		7	Boston	4-4
	7	Philadelphia	4-2		9	Hartford	5-2
	12	Winnipeg	5-3		12	Los Angeles	4-4
	14	NY Islanders	4-2		25	Vancouver	2-4
	16	Los Angeles	3-4	Mar.	9	St Louis	8-4
	18	Winnipeg	4-3		10	Minnesota	3-7
	26	Vancouver	7-2		20	Vancouver	3-2
	28	Edmonton	3-3		23	Los Angeles*	4-8
	31	Los Angeles*	5-3		29	Edmonton	5-6

* Denotes afternoon game.

Entry Draft
Selections 1991-77

1991
Pick
19 Niklas Sundblad
41 Francois Groleau
52 Sandy McCarthy
63 Brian Caruso
85 Steven Magnusson
107 Jerome Butler
129 Bobby Marshall
140 Matt Hoffman
151 Kelly Harper
173 David St. Pierre
195 David Struch
217 Sergei Zolotov
239 Marko Jantunen
261 Andrei Trefilov

1990
Pick
11 Trevor Kidd
26 Nicolas P. Perreault
32 Vesa Viitakoski
41 Etienne Belzile
62 Glen Mears
83 Paul Kruse
125 Chris Tschupp
146 Dimitri Frolov
167 Shawn Murray
188 Mike Murray
209 Rob Sumner
230 invalid claim
251 Leo Gudas

1989
Pick
24 Kent Manderville
42 Ted Drury
50 Veli-Pekka Kautonen
63 Corey Lyons
70 Robert Reichel
84 Ryan O'Leary
105 Francis (Toby) Kearney
147 Alex Nikolic
168 Kevin Wortman
189 Sergei Gomolyakov
210 Dan Sawyer
231 Alexander Yudin
252 Kenneth Kennholt

1988
Pick
21 Jason Muzzatti
42 Todd Harkins
84 Gary Socha
85 Thomas Forslund
90 Scott Matusovich
126 Jonas Bergqvist
147 Stefan Nilsson
168 Troy Kennedy
189 Brett Peterson
210 Guy Darveau
231 Dave Tretowicz
252 Sergei Priakin

1987
Pick
19 Bryan Deasley
25 Stephane Matteau
40 Kevin Grant
61 Scott Mahoney
70 Tim Harris
103 Tim Corkery
124 Joe Aloi
145 Peter Ciavaglia
166 Theoren Fleury
187 Mark Osiecki
208 William Sedergren
229 Peter Hasselblad
250 Magnus Svensson

1986
Pick
16 George Pelawa
37 Brian Glynn
79 Tom Quinlan
100 Scott Bloom
121 John Parker
142 Rick Lessard
163 Mark Olsen
184 Warren Sharples
205 Doug Pickell
226 Anders Lindstrom
247 Antonin Stavjana

1985
Pick
17 Chris Biotti
27 Joe Nieuwendyk
38 Jeff Wenaas
59 Lane MacDonald
80 Roger Johansson
101 Esa Keskinen
122 Tim Sweeney
143 Stu Grimson
164 Nate Smith
185 Darryl Olsen
206 Peter Romberg
227 Alexandr Koznevniko
248 Bill Gregoire

1984
Pick
12 Gary Roberts
33 Ken Sabourin
38 Paul Ranheim
75 Peter Rosol
96 Joel Paunio
117 Brett Hull
138 Kevan Melrose
159 Jiri Hrdina
180 Gary Suter
200 Peter Rucka
221 Stefan Jonsson
241 Rudolf Suchanek

1983
Pick
13 Dan Quinn
51 Brian Bradley
55 Perry Berezan
66 John Bekkers
71 Kevan Guy
77 Bill Claviter
91 Igor Liba
111 Grant Blair
131 Jeff Hogg
151 Chris MacDonald
171 Rob Kivell
191 Tom Pratt
211 Jaroslav Benak
231 Sergei Makarov

1982
Pick
29 Dave Reierson
37 Richard Kromm
51 Jim Laing
65 Dave Meszaros
72 Mark Lamb
93 Lou Kiriakou
114 Jeff Vaive
118 Mats Kihlstrom
135 Brad Ramsden
156 Roy Myllari
177 Ted Pearson
198 Jim Uens
219 Rick Erdall
240 Dale Thompson

1981
Pick
15 Allan MacInnis
56 Mike Vernon
78 Peter Madach
99 Mario Simioni
120 Todd Hooey
141 Rick Heppner
162 Dale Degray
183 George Boudreau
204 Bruce Eakin

1980
Pick
13 Denis Cyr
31 Tony Curtale
32 Kevin LaVallee
39 Steve Konroyd
76 Marc Roy
97 Randy Turnbull
118 John Multan
139 Dave Newsom
160 Claude Drouin
181 Hakan Loob
202 Steve Fletcher

1979
Pick
12 Paul Reinhart
23 Mike Perovich
33 Pat Riggin
54 Tim Hunter
75 Jim Peplinski
96 Brad Kempthorne
117 Glenn Johnson

1978
Pick
11 Brad Marsh
47 Tim Bernhardt
64 Jim MacRae
80 Gord Wappel
97 Greg Meredith
114 Dave Hindmarch
131 Dave Morrison
148 Doug Todd
165 Mark Green
180 Robert Sullivan
196 Bernhard Englbrecht

1977
Pick
20 Miles Zaharko
28 Red Laurence
31 Brian Hill
72 Jim Craig
82 Curt Christofferson
100 Bernard Harbec
118 Bob Gould
133 Jim Bennett
148 Tim Harrer

Club Directory

Olympic Saddledome
P.O. Box 1540 Station M
Calgary, Alberta T2P 3B9
Phone **403/261-0475**
FAX 403/261-0470
ENVOY ID
Public
    Relations: FLAMES. PR
Capacity: 20,133

Owners
Harley N. Hotchkiss
Norman L. Kwong
Sonia Scurfield
Byron J. Seaman
Daryl K. Seaman

President/Alternate Governor .... W.C. (Bill) Hay
General Manager/Head Coach .... Doug Risebrough
Vice-President, Business and Finance .... Clare Rhyasen
Vice-President, Hockey Operations .... Al MacNeil
Vice-President, Marketing .... Leo Ornest
Vice-President, Corporate &
      Community Relations .... Lanny McDonald
Assistant General Manager .... Al Coates
Controller .... Lynne Tosh
Director of Public Relations .... Rick Skaggs
Assistant Coaches .... Paul Baxter, Guy Charron, Jamie Hislop
Goaltending Consultant .... Glenn Hall
Salt Lake City Head Coach .... Bob Francis
Salt Lake City Assistant Coach .... Jim Leavins
Chief Scout .... Gerry Blair
Co-ordinator of Scouting .... Ian McKenzie
Scouts .... Ray Clearwater, Al Godfrey, Guy Lapointe,
                   Gerry McNamara, Lou Reycroft
Scouting Staff .... David Mayville, Lars Norrman, Larry Popein,
                   Pekka Rautakallio, Tom Thompson
Executive Secretaries .... Bernie Doenz, Brenda Koyich, Yvette
                   Mutcheson, June Yeates
Ticket Manager....................... Ann-Marie Malarchuk
Assistant Ticket Manager .... Linda Forrest
Assistant Public Relations Director .... Mike Burke
Assistant Controller .... Dorothy Stuart
Assistant to Vice-President, Marketing .... Judy Shupe
Marketing and Advertising .... Pat Halls
Manager, Retail Operations .... Mark Mason
Accounting Clerk .... Lynn Horton
Trainer .... Jim "Bearcat" Murray
Equipment Manager .... Bobby Stewart
Assistant Trainer .... Al Murray
Director of Medicine .... Dr. Terry Groves
Orthopedic Surgeon .... Dr. Lowell Van Zuiden
Team Dentist........................ Dr. Bill Blair
Consulting Psychologists .... Hap Davis, Ph.D.
                   and Robert Offenberger, Ph.D.
Location of Press Boxes .... Print/TV—North side; Radio—South Side
Dimensions of Rink .... 200 feet by 85 feet
Ends of Rink .... Tempered Glass
Club Colours .... White, Red and Gold
Club Trains at .... Olympic Saddledome
TV Channels .... CKKX-TV (Channels 2 & 7)
                   CBC-TV (Channels 6 & 9)
Radio .... CFR Radio (660 AM)

Coach and General Manager

RISEBROUGH, DOUG
Coach and General Manager, Calgary Flames. Born in Guelph, Ont., January 29, 1954

The second-year Flames head coach enters his first full NHL season as Calgary's general manager. Already the club's assistant general manager, Risebrough ascended to the general manager's post on May 16, 1991. Risebrough was appointed head coach of the Flames on May 18, 1990. After ending his 14-year NHL playing career with the Flames in 1987, Risebrough was named an assistant coach and joined Terry Crisp behind the bench.

During his first season as an NHL head coach, Risebrough led the Flames to a fourth place overall finish in the NHL standings. Risebrough was Montreal's first selection, seventh overall, in the 1974 Amateur Draft. During his nine years with the Canadiens, he helped his club to four consecutive Stanley Cup championships between 1976 and 1979. He joined the Flames just prior to the start of the club's 1982 training camp. During his NHL career, his clubs have won five Stanley Cups (1976-1979 and 1989 with Calgary) and two Presidents' Trophies (1987-88 and 1988-89).

Coaching Record

Season	Team	Games	Regular Season				Games	Playoffs			
			W	L	T	%		W	L	%
1990-91	Calgary (NHL)	80	46	26	8	.625	7	3	4	.429

Coaching History
Bernie Geoffrion, 1972-73 to 1973-74; Bernie Geoffrion and Fred Creighton, 1974-75; Fred Creighton, 1975-76 to 1978-79; Al MacNeil, 1979-80 (Atlanta); 1980-81 to 1981-82 (Calgary); Bob Johnson, 1982-83 to 1986-87; Terry Crisp, 1987-88 to 1989-90; Doug Risebrough, 1990-91 to date.

General Manager's History
Cliff Fletcher, 1972-73 to 1990-91. Doug Risebrough, 1991-92.

Retired Numbers
9   Lanny McDonald   1981-1989

Chicago Blackhawks

1990-91 Results: 49w-23L-8T 106PTS. First, Norris Division

Year-by-Year Record

Season	GP	Home W	L	T	Road W	L	T	Overall W	L	T	GF	GA	Pts.	Finished	Playoff Result
1990-91	80	28	8	4	21	15	4	49	23	8	284	211	106	1st, Norris Div.	Lost Div. Semi-Final
1989-90	80	25	13	2	16	20	4	41	33	6	316	294	88	1st, Norris Div.	Lost Conf. Championship
1988-89	80	16	14	10	11	27	2	27	41	12	297	335	66	4th, Norris Div.	Lost Conf. Championship
1987-88	80	21	17	2	9	24	7	30	41	9	284	326	69	3rd, Norris Div.	Lost Div. Semi-Final
1986-87	80	18	13	9	11	24	5	29	37	14	290	310	72	3rd, Norris Div.	Lost Div. Semi-Final
1985-86	80	23	12	5	16	21	3	39	33	8	351	349	86	1st, Norris Div.	Lost Div. Semi-Final
1984-85	80	22	16	2	16	19	5	38	35	7	309	299	83	2nd, Norris Div.	Lost Conf. Championship
1983-84	80	25	13	2	5	29	6	30	42	8	277	311	68	4th, Norris Div.	Lost Div. Semi-Final
1982-83	80	29	8	3	18	15	7	47	23	10	338	268	104	1st, Norris Div.	Lost Conf. Championship
1981-82	80	20	13	7	10	25	5	30	38	12	332	363	72	4th, Norris Div.	Lost Conf. Championship
1980-81	80	21	11	8	10	22	8	31	33	16	304	315	78	2nd, Smythe Div.	Lost Prelim. Round
1979-80	80	21	12	7	13	15	12	34	27	19	241	250	87	1st, Smythe Div.	Lost Quarter-Final
1978-79	80	18	12	10	11	24	5	29	36	15	244	277	73	1st, Smythe Div.	Lost Quarter-Final
1977-78	80	20	9	11	12	20	8	32	29	19	230	220	83	1st, Smythe Div.	Lost Quarter-Final
1976-77	80	19	16	5	7	27	6	26	43	11	240	298	63	3rd, Smythe Div.	Lost Prelim. Round
1975-76	80	17	15	8	15	15	10	32	30	18	254	261	82	1st, Smythe Div.	Lost Quarter-Final
1974-75	80	24	12	4	13	23	4	37	35	8	268	241	82	3rd, Smythe Div.	Lost Quarter-Final
1973-74	78	20	6	13	21	8	10	41	14	23	272	164	105	2nd, West Div.	Lost Semi-Final
1972-73	78	26	9	4	16	18	5	42	27	9	284	225	93	1st, West Div.	Lost Final
1971-72	78	28	3	8	18	14	7	46	17	15	256	166	107	1st, West Div.	Lost Semi-Final
1970-71	78	30	6	3	19	14	6	49	20	9	277	184	107	1st, West Div.	Lost Final
1969-70	76	26	7	5	19	15	4	45	22	9	250	170	99	1st, East Div.	Lost Semi-Final
1968-69	76	20	14	4	14	19	5	34	33	9	280	246	77	6th, East Div.	Out of Playoffs
1967-68	74	20	13	4	12	13	12	32	26	16	212	222	80	4th, East Div.	Lost Semi-Final
1966-67	70	24	5	6	17	12	6	41	17	12	264	170	94	1st,	Lost Semi-Final
1965-66	70	21	8	6	16	17	2	37	25	8	240	187	82	2nd,	Lost Semi-Final
1964-65	70	20	13	2	14	15	6	34	28	8	224	176	76	3rd,	Lost Final
1963-64	70	26	4	5	10	18	7	36	22	12	218	169	84	2nd,	Lost Semi-Final
1962-63	70	17	9	9	15	12	8	32	21	17	194	178	81	2nd,	Lost Semi-Final
1961-62	70	20	10	5	11	16	8	31	26	13	217	186	75	3rd,	Lost Final
1960-61	70	20	6	9	9	18	8	29	24	17	198	180	75	3rd,	**Won Stanley Cup**
1959-60	70	18	11	6	10	18	7	28	29	13	191	180	69	3rd,	Lost Semi-Final
1958-59	70	14	12	9	14	17	4	28	29	13	197	208	69	3rd,	Lost Semi-Final
1957-58	70	15	17	3	9	22	4	24	39	7	163	202	55	5th,	Out of Playoffs
1956-57	70	12	15	8	4	24	7	16	39	15	169	225	47	6th,	Out of Playoffs
1955-56	70	9	19	7	10	20	5	19	39	12	155	216	50	6th,	Out of Playoffs
1954-55	70	6	21	8	7	19	9	13	40	17	161	235	43	6th,	Out of Playoffs
1953-54	70	8	21	6	4	30	1	12	51	7	133	242	31	6th,	Out of Playoffs
1952-53	70	14	11	10	13	17	5	27	28	15	169	175	69	4th,	Lost Semi-Final
1951-52	70	9	19	7	8	25	2	17	44	9	158	241	43	6th,	Out of Playoffs
1950-51	70	8	22	5	5	25	5	13	47	10	171	280	36	6th,	Out of Playoffs
1949-50	70	13	18	4	9	20	6	22	38	10	203	244	54	6th,	Out of Playoffs
1948-49	60	13	12	5	8	19	3	21	31	8	173	211	50	5th,	Out of Playoffs
1947-48	60	10	17	3	10	17	3	20	34	6	195	225	46	6th,	Out of Playoffs
1946-47	60	10	17	3	9	20	1	19	37	4	193	274	42	6th,	Out of Playoffs
1945-46	50	15	5	5	8	15	2	23	20	7	200	178	53	3rd,	Lost Semi-Final
1944-45	50	9	14	2	4	16	5	13	30	7	141	194	33	5th,	Out of Playoffs
1943-44	50	15	6	4	7	17	1	22	23	5	178	187	49	4th,	Lost Final
1942-43	50	14	3	8	3	15	7	17	18	15	179	180	49	5th,	Out of Playoffs
1941-42	48	15	8	1	7	15	2	22	23	3	145	155	47	4th,	Lost Quarter-Final
1940-41	48	11	10	3	5	15	4	16	25	7	112	139	39	5th,	Lost Semi-Final
1939-40	48	15	7	2	8	12	4	23	19	6	112	120	52	4th,	Lost Quarter-Final
1938-39	48	5	13	6	7	15	2	12	28	8	91	132	32	7th,	Out of Playoffs
1937-38	48	10	10	4	4	15	5	14	25	9	97	139	37	3rd, Amn. Div.	**Won Stanley Cup**
1936-37	48	8	13	3	6	14	4	14	27	7	99	131	35	4th, Amn. Div.	Out of Playoffs
1935-36	48	15	7	2	6	12	6	21	19	8	93	92	50	3rd, Amn. Div.	Lost Quarter-Final
1934-35	48	12	9	3	14	8	2	26	17	5	118	88	57	2nd, Amn. Div.	Lost Quarter-Final
1933-34	48	13	4	7	7	13	4	20	17	11	88	83	51	2nd, Amn. Div.	**Won Stanley Cup**
1932-33	48	12	7	5	4	13	7	16	20	12	88	101	44	4th, Amn. Div.	Out of Playoffs
1931-32	48	13	5	6	5	14	5	18	19	11	86	101	47	2nd, Amn. Div.	Lost Quarter-Final
1930-31	44	14	7	1	10	10	2	24	17	3	108	78	51	2nd, Amn. Div.	Lost Final
1929-30	44	12	9	1	9	9	4	21	18	5	117	111	47	2nd, Amn. Div.	Lost Quarter-Final
1928-29	44	3	13	6	4	16	2	7	29	8	33	85	22	5th, Amn. Div.	Out of Playoffs
1927-28	44	2	18	2	5	16	1	7	34	3	68	134	17	5th, Amn. Div.	Out of Playoffs
1926-27	44	12	8	2	7	14	1	19	22	3	115	116	41	3rd, Amn. Div.	Lost Quarter-Final

Schedule

	Home			Away
Oct.	Thur. 3 Detroit	**Oct.**	Sat. 5 Minnesota
	Sun. 6 New Jersey		Sat. 12 Washington
	Thur. 10 Vancouver		Sat. 19 St Louis
	Sun. 13 San Jose		Tues. 22 Pittsburgh
	Thur. 17 Edmonton		Sat. 26 Hartford
	Sun. 20 St Louis	**Nov.**	Sat. 2 Minnesota
	Thur. 24 Calgary		Sat. 9 Montreal
	Sun. 27 Boston		Sat. 16 Toronto
	Thur. 31 NY Islanders		Tues. 19 Detroit
Nov.	Sun. 3 Minnesota		Fri. 22 Buffalo
	Thur. 7 Quebec		Wed. 27 Edmonton
	Sun. 10 Hartford		Fri. 29 Vancouver
	Thur. 14 Toronto	**Dec.**	Sun. 1 Winnipeg
	Sun. 17 St Louis		Sat. 7 NY Islanders
Dec.	Thur. 5 Los Angeles		Tues. 10 Detroit
	Sun. 8 Minnesota		Sat. 14 Philadelphia*
	Sun. 15 Philadelphia		Sat. 21 New Jersey
	Thur. 19 Montreal		Thur. 26 St Louis
	Sun. 22 St Louis		Tues. 31 Minnesota
	Fri. 27 Winnipeg	**Jan.**	Sat. 4 Toronto
	Sun. 29 Detroit		Fri. 10 Winnipeg
Jan.	Thur. 2 NY Rangers		Tues. 14 Philadelphia
	Sun. 5 Minnesota		Sat. 25 Minnesota*
	Thur. 9 Toronto		Mon. 27 Calgary
	Sun. 12 Washington		Wed. 29 Edmonton
	Thur. 16 Toronto		Thur. 30 Vancouver
	Thur. 23 Quebec	**Feb.**	Sat. 1 Los Angeles
Feb.	Thur. 13 Los Angeles		Wed. 5 San Jose
	Sun. 16 Calgary		Sat. 8 St Louis
	Thur. 20 New Jersey		Sat. 22 Detroit*
	Sun. 23 St Louis		Tues. 25 NY Rangers
	Thur. 27 Detroit		Sat. 29 Toronto
Mar.	Thur. 5 NY Islanders	**Mar.**	Sun. 1 Buffalo
	Sun. 8 Boston*		Sat. 7 Boston*
	Tues. 10 San Jose		Wed. 11 NY Rangers
	Sun. 15 Pittsburgh		Sat. 21 Toronto
	Thur. 19 Minnesota		Thur. 26 Quebec
	Sun. 22 Buffalo		Sat. 28 Hartford
	Sun. 29 Toronto		Tues. 31 Detroit
Apr.	Sun. 5 Detroit	**Apr.**	Sat. 4 St Louis

* Denotes afternoon game.

Home Starting Times:
All Games . . . . 7:35 p.m.
Except Matinees . . . . 1:35 p.m.

Franchise date: September 25, 1926

66th NHL Season

Coaching History

Pete Muldoon, 1926-27; Barney Stanley and Hugh Lehman, 1927-28; Herb Gardiner, 1928-29; Tom Shaughnessy and Bill Tobin, 1929-30; Dick Irvin, 1930-31; Dick Irvin and Bill Tobin, 1931-32; Godfrey Matheson, Emil Iverson and Tommy Gorman, 1932-33; Tommy Gorman, 1933-34; Clem Loughlin, 1934-35 to 1936-37; Bill Stewart, 1937-38; Bill Stewart and Paul Thompson, 1938-39; Paul Thompson, 1939-40 to 1943-44; Paul Thompson and Johnny Gottselig, 1944-45; Johnny Gottselig, 1945-46 to 1946-47; Johnny Gottselig and Charlie Conacher, 1947-48; Charlie Conacher, 1948-49 to 1949-50; Ebbie Goodfellow, 1950-51 to 1951-52; Sid Abel, 1952-53 to 1953-54; Frank Eddolls, 1954-55; Dick Irvin, 1955-56; Tommy Ivan, 1956-57; Tommy Ivan and Rudy Pilous, 1957-58; Rudy Pilous, 1958-59 to 1962-63; Billy Reay, 1963-64 to 1975-76; Billy Reay and Bill White, 1976-77; Bob Pulford, 1977-78 to 1978-79; Eddie Johnston, 1979-80; Keith Magnuson, 1980-81; Keith Magnuson and Bob Pulford, 1981-82; Orval Tessier, 1982-83 to 1983-84; Orval Tessier and Bob Pulford, 1984-85; Bob Pulford, 1985-86 to 1986-87; Bob Murdoch, 1987-88; Mike Keenan, 1988-89 to date.

Captains' History

Dick Irvin, 1926-27 to 1928-29; Duke Dutkowski, 1929-30; Ty Arbour, 1930-31; Cy Wentworth, 1931-32; Helge Bostrom, 1932-33; Chuck Gardiner, 1933-34; no captain, 1934-35; Johnny Gottselig, 1935-36 to 1939-40; Earl Seibert, 1940-41, 1941-42; Doug Bentley, 1942-43, 1943-44; Clint Smith 1944-45; John Mariucci, 1945-46; Red Hamill, 1946-47; John Mariucci, 1947-48; Gaye Stewart, 1948-49; Doug Bentley, 1949-50; Jack Stewart, 1950-51, 1951-52; Bill Gadsby, 1952-53, 1953-54; Gus Mortson, 1954-55 to 1956-57; no captain, 1957-58; Eddie Litzenberger, 1958-59 to 1960-61; Pierre Pilote, 1961-62 to 1967-68, no captain, 1968-69; Pat Stapleton, 1969-70; no captain, 1970-71 to 1974-75; Stan Mikita, Pit Martin, 1975-76; Stan Mikita, Pit Martin, Keith Magnuson, 1976-77; Keith Magnuson, 1977-78, 1978-79; Keith Magnuson, Terry Ruskowski, 1979-80; Terry Ruskowski, 1980-81, 1981-82; Darryl Sutter, 1982-83 to 1986-87; Keith Brown, Troy Murray, Denis Savard, 1987-88; Dirk Graham, 1988-89 to date.

1991-92 Player Personnel

FORWARDS	HT	WT	S	Place of Birth	Date	1990-91 Club
ANDRIJEVSKI, Andrei	5-10	180	R	Soviet Union	2/4/73	Dynamo Minsk
BELANGER, Hugo	6-1	190	L	St. Herbert, Que.	5/28/70	Clarkson
BOYER, Zac	6-1	185	R	Inuvik, N.W.T.	10/25/71	Kamloops
BYRAM, Shawn	6-2	204	L	Neepawa, Man.	9/12/68	Capital Dist.
CONN, Rob	6-2	200	R	Calgary, Alta.	9/3/68	U. Alaska-Anch.
CREIGHTON, Adam	6-5	214	L	Burlington, Ont.	6/2/65	Chicago
DAM, Trevor	5-10	208	R	Scarborough, Ont.	4/20/70	London
DUBINSKY, Steve	6-0	180	L	Montreal, Que.	7/9/70	Clarkson
EDGERLY, Derek	6-1	190	L	Malden, MA	4/3/71	Northeastern U.
EGELAND, Tracy	6-1	180	R	Lethbridge, Alta.	8/20/70	Indianapolis
ELVENAS, Stefan	6-1	183	L	Lund, Sweden	3/30/70	Rogle
GILBERT, Greg	6-1	192	L	Mississauga, Ont.	1/22/62	Chicago
GILLIS, Paul	5-11	198	L	Toronto, Ont.	12/31/63	Quebec-Chicago
GOULET, Michel	6-1	195	L	Peribonka, Que.	4/21/60	Chicago
GRAHAM, Dirk	5-11	190	R	Regina, Sask.	7/29/59	Chicago
GRAVELLE, Dan	5-11	190	L	Montreal, Quebec	3/10/70	Merrimac
GREYERBIEHL, Jason	6-0	175	L	Bramalea, Ont.	3/24/70	Colgate
GRIMSON, Stu	6-5	225	L	Pengilly, B.C.	5/20/65	Chicago
GROSSI, Dino	6-0	190	R	Toronto, Ont.	6/25/70	Northeastern
HOUSE, Bobby	6-1	200	R	Whitehorse, Yukon	1/7/73	Spokane-Brandon
HUDSON, Mike	6-1	185	L	Guelph, Ont.	2/6/67	Chicago
JOHANNSON, Jim	6-2	200	L	Rochester, MN	3/10/64	Indianapolis
KIRTON, Scott	6-4	215		Penetang'ene, Ont.	10/4/71	Powell River, T-2/Jr.A.
KOZAK, Mike	6-2	200	R	Toronto, Ont.	3/14/69	Clarkson
LAFAYETTE, Justin	6-6	220	L	Vancouver, B.C.	1/23/70	Ferris State
LAPPIN, Mike	5-10	175	L	Chicago, IL	1/1/69	St. Lawrence
LARMER, Steve	5-10	189	L	Peterborough, Ont.	6/16/61	Chicago
LEMIEUX, Jocelyn	5-10	200	L	Mont-Laurier, Que.	11/18/67	Chicago
LESSARD, Owen	6-1	196	L	Sudbury, Ont.	1/11/70	Indianapolis
LUPZIG, Andreas	6-2	185	L	West Germany	8/5/68	Koln
MATTHEWS, Jamie	6-1	190	R	Amherst, N. Scotia	5/25/73	Sudbury
McAMMOND, Dean	5-11	185	L	Grand Catch, B.C.	6/15/73	Prince Albert
NOONAN, Brian	6-1	180	R	Boston, MA	5/29/65	Indianapolis-Chicago
PELUSO, Mike	6-4	225	L	Pengilly, Minn.	11/8/65	Chicago-Indianapolis
PETERSON, Erik	6-0	185	L	Boston, MA	4/31/72	Providence
POJAR, Jon	6-0	190	L	St. Paul, MN	5/5/70	St. Cloud State
POMICHTER, Mike	6-1	200	L	New Haven, Conn.	9/10/73	Springfield Jr.B
PRESLEY, Wayne	5-11	172	R	Detroit, MI	3/23/65	Chicago
PULLOLA, Tommi	6-5	202	L	Vaasa, Finland	5/18/71	Lukko
ROENICK, Jeremy	5-11	170	R	Boston, MA	1/17/70	Chicago
SANDSTROM, Ulf	5-10	180	R	Fagerstad, Sweden	4/24/67	Lulea
SAUNDERS, Matt	6-0	180	L	Ottawa, Ont.	7/17/70	Northeastern
STAPLETON, Mike	5-10	183	R	Sarnia, Ont.	5/5/66	Indianapolis-Chicago
STICKNEY, Brett	6-5	205	L	Hanover, N.H.	5/26/72	St. Paul's Prep.
ST. JACQUES, Kevin	5-11	190	R	Edmonton, Alta.	2/25/71	Lethbridge
TEPPER, Stephen	6-4	215	R	Santa Ana, Calif.	3/10/69	U. of Maine
THOMAS, Steve	5-10	185	L	Stockport, England	7/15/63	Chicago
TONELLI, John	6-1	200	L	Milton, Ontario	3/23/57	Los Angeles
TOPOROWSKI, Kerry	6-2	212	R	Prince Albert, Sask.	4/9/71	Spokane
TUCKER, Chris	5-11	183	L	White Plains, NY	2/9/72	U. of Wisconsin
VINCELETTE, Dan	6-1	200	L	Verdun, Que.	8/1/67	Quebec-Halifax
WILLIAMS, Sean	6-1	182	L	Oshawa, Ont.	1/28/68	Indianapolis
WOODCROFT, Craig	6-1	195	L	Toronto, Ont.	12/3/69	Colgate

DEFENSEMEN						
AUGER, Jacques	6-1	215	R	Levis, Quebec	4/20/72	U. of Wisconsin
BALKOVEC, Maco	6-2	190	L	N.Westminster, B.C.	1/17/71	Merritt T2/Jr.A
BENNETT, Adam	6-4	206	R	Georgetown, Ont.	3/30/71	Sudbury-Indianapolis
BROWN, Keith	6-1	191	R	Cornerbrook, Nfld.	5/6/60	Chicago
CHELIOS, Chris	6-1	192	R	Chicago, IL	1/25/62	Chicago
CLEARY, Joe	5-11	190	R	Buffalo, NY	1/17/70	Boston College
DAGENAIS, Mike	6-3	198	L	Gloucester, Ont.	7/22/69	Indianapolis
DEAN, Scott	5-11	200	R	Lake Forest, ILL.	6/12/72	Lake Forest
DROPPA, Ivan	6-2	209	L	Czechoslovakia	2/1/72	Kosice
DYKHUIS, Karl	6-2	200	L	Sept-Iles, Que.	7/8/72	Cdn. National Team
HEED, Jonas	6-0	180	L	Sodertalje, Sweden	1/3/67	Frolunda
HENTGES, Mathew	6-5	220	L	St. Paul, MN	12/19/69	Merrimac
KELLOG, Bob	6-4	210	L	Springfield, MA	2/16/71	Northeastern
KONROYD, Steve	6-1	203	L	Scarborough, Ont.	2/10/61	Chicago
KRAVCHUK, Igor	6-1	200	L	UFA, Soviet Union	9/13/66	CSKA
KUCERA, Frantisek	6-2	205	R	Prague, Czech.	2/3/68	Chicago-Indianapolis
LANZ, Rick	6-2	195	R	Karlouyvary, Czech.	9/16/61	Indianapolis
LARKIN, Mike	6-1	180	R	Boston, Mass.	3/15/73	Rice Memorial H.S.
MANSON, Dave	6-2	190	L	Prince Albert, Sask.	1/27/67	Chicago
MacDONALD, Scott	6-3	202	R	Brockton, Mass.	9/13/72	Choate
MARCHMENT, Bryan	6-1	198	L	Scarborough, Ont.	5/1/69	Moncton-Winnipeg
NORTON, Chris	6-2	200	R	London, Ont.	3/11/65	Moncton
PLAYFAIR, Jim	6-4	200	L	Ft. St. James, B.C.	5/22/64	Indianapolis
RUSSELL, Cam	6-4	175	L	Halifax, N.S.	1/12/69	Indianapolis-Chicago
SIRKKA, Jeff	6-1	205	L	Copper Cliff, Ont.	6/17/68	Indianapolis
SPEER, Michael	6-2	202	L	Toronto, Ont.	3/26/71	Owen Sound-Windsor-Indianapolis
TENZER, Dirk	6-2	200	R	New York, NY	7/26/70	Hamilton College
TICHY, Milan	6-3	198	L	Czechoslovakia	9/22/69	Trencin
YAWNEY, Trent	6-3	183	L	Hudson Bay, Sask.	9/29/65	Chicago

GOALTENDERS	HT	WT	C	Place of Birth	Date	1990-91 Club
BELFOUR, Ed	5-11	182	L	Carman, Man.	4/21/65	Chicago
BELLEY, Roch	5-10	170	L	Hull, Quebec	8/12/71	Niagara Falls
DONEGHEY, Michael	6-0	165	L	Boston, MA	7/28/70	Merrimac
HASEK, Dominik	5-11	165	L	Pardubice, Czech.	1/29/65	Indianapolis-Chicago
LeBLANC, Ray	5-10	170	R	Fitchburg, MA	10/24/64	Indy-Ft. Wayne
MILLEN, Greg	5-9	175	R	Toronto, Ont.	6/25/57	Chicago
WAITE, Jim	6-0	163	R	Sherbrooke, Que.	4/15/69	Indianapolis-Chicago

1990-91 Scoring

Regular Season

* rookie

Pos	#	Player	Team	GP	G	A	Pts	+/−	PIM	PP	SH	GW	GT	S	%
R	28	Steve Larmer	CHI	80	44	57	101	37	79	17	2	9	0	231	19.0
C	27	Jeremy Roenick	CHI	79	41	53	94	38	80	15	4	10	1	194	21.1
R	16	Michel Goulet	CHI	74	27	38	65	27	65	9	0	1	1	167	16.2
D	7	Chris Chelios	CHI	77	12	52	64	23	192	5	2	2	0	187	6.4
L	32	Steve Thomas	CHI	69	19	35	54	8	129	2	0	3	0	192	9.9
C	22	Adam Creighton	CHI	72	22	29	51	0	135	10	2	6	0	127	17.3
R	33	Dirk Graham	CHI	80	24	21	45	12	88	4	6	7	0	189	12.7
D	24	Doug Wilson	CHI	51	11	29	40	25	32	6	1	1	0	162	6.8
C	19	Troy Murray	CHI	75	14	23	37	13	74	4	0	2	0	130	10.8
L	11	Tony Mckegney	QUE	50	17	16	33	25−	44	7	0	2	1	111	15.3
			CHI	9	0	1	1	2−	4	0	0	0	0	10	.0
			TOTAL	59	17	17	34	27−	48	7	0	2	1	121	14.0
R	17	Wayne Presley	CHI	71	15	19	34	11	122	1	0	3	0	141	10.6
D	3	Dave Manson	CHI	75	14	15	29	20	191	6	1	2	0	154	9.1
L	14	Greg Gilbert	CHI	72	10	15	25	6	58	1	0	0	0	98	10.2
C	20	Mike Hudson	CHI	55	7	9	16	5	62	0	0	1	0	53	13.2
D	8	Trent Yawney	CHI	61	3	13	16	6	77	3	0	0	0	52	5.8
C	12	Paul Gillis	QUE	49	3	8	11	19−	91	0	1	0	0	57	5.3
			CHI	13	0	5	5	1	53	0	0	0	0	9	.0
			TOTAL	62	3	13	16	18−	144	0	1	0	0	66	4.5
D	6	*Frantisek Kucera	CHI	40	2	12	14	3	32	1	0	0	0	65	3.1
R	26	Jocelyn Lemieux	CHI	67	6	7	13	7−	119	1	1	2	0	89	6.7
D	5	Steve Konroyd	CHI	70	0	12	12	11	40	0	0	0	0	93	.0
D	4	Keith Brown	CHI	45	1	10	11	9	55	0	0	0	0	71	1.4
D	25	Bob McGill	CHI	77	4	5	9	8	151	0	0	0	0	69	5.8
L	44	*Mike Peluso	CHI	53	6	1	7	3−	320	2	0	0	0	29	20.7
C	10	Brian Noonan	CHI	7	0	4	4	1−	2	0	0	0	0	12	.0
G	30	*Ed Belfour	CHI	74	0	3	3	0	34	0	0	0	0	0	.0
C	12	Mike Stapleton	CHI	7	0	1	1	0	2	0	0	0	0	6	.0
L	23	*Stu Grimson	CHI	35	0	1	1	3−	183	0	0	0	0	14	.0
G	36	Jim Waite	CHI	1	0	0	0	0	0	0	0	0	0	0	.0
G	29	Greg Millen	CHI	3	0	0	0	0	0	0	0	0	0	0	.0
D	52	*Cam Russell	CHI	3	0	0	0	1	5	0	0	0	0	0	.0
G	34	*Dominic Hasek	CHI	5	0	0	0	0	0	0	0	0	0	0	.0

Goaltending

No.	Goaltender	GPI	Mins	Avg	W	L	T	EN	SO	GA	SA	S%
36	Jim Waite	1	60	2.00	1	0	0	0	0	2	28	.929
34	*Dominic Hasek	5	195	2.46	3	0	1	0	0	8	93	.914
30	*Ed Belfour	74	4127	2.47	43	19	7	3	4	170	1883	.910
31	Jaques Cloutier	10	403	3.57	2	3	0	0	0	24	175	.863
29	Greg Millen	3	58	4.14	0	1	0	0	0	4	32	.875
	Totals	**80**	**4846**	**2.61**	**49**	**23**	**8**	**3**	**4**	**211**	**2214**	**.905**

Playoffs

Pos	#	Player	Team	GP	G	A	Pts	+/−	PIM	PP	SH	GW	OT	S	%
C	27	Jeremy Roenick	CHI	6	3	5	8	2	4	1	0	1	0	13	23.1
D	7	Chris Chelios	CHI	6	1	7	8	2	46	1	0	0	0	11	9.1
R	28	Steve Larmer	CHI	6	5	1	6	2	4	1	0	0	0	16	31.3
L	42	*Warren Rychel	CHI	3	1	3	4	1	2	1	0	1	0	7	14.3
D	24	Doug Wilson	CHI	5	2	1	3	1	2	2	0	0	0	18	11.1
R	33	Dirk Graham	CHI	6	1	2	3	2	17	0	0	0	0	5	20.0
L	32	Steve Thomas	CHI	6	1	2	3	3	15	0	0	0	0	17	5.9
C	20	Mike Hudson	CHI	6	0	2	2	1	8	0	0	0	0	5	.0
D	4	Keith Brown	CHI	6	1	0	1	0	8	0	0	0	0	9	11.1
D	5	Steve Konroyd	CHI	6	1	0	1	1	8	0	0	0	0	5	20.0
G	34	*Dominic Hasek	CHI	3	0	1	1	0	0	0	0	0	0	0	.0
L	14	Greg Gilbert	CHI	5	0	1	1	1	2	0	0	0	0	2	.0
C	22	Adam Creighton	CHI	6	0	1	1	0	10	0	0	0	0	10	.0
D	3	Dave Manson	CHI	6	0	1	1	2	36	0	0	0	0	11	.0
C	19	Troy Murray	CHI	6	0	1	1	0	12	0	0	0	0	5	.0
R	17	Wayne Presley	CHI	6	0	1	1	0	38	0	0	0	0	11	.0
D	52	*Cam Russell	CHI	1	0	0	0	1−	0	0	0	0	0	0	.0
D	8	Trent Yawney	CHI	1	0	0	0	0	0	0	0	0	0	1	.0
C	12	Paul Gillis	CHI	2	0	0	0	1	2	0	0	0	0	0	.0
L	11	Tony McKegney	CHI	2	0	0	0	0	4	0	0	0	0	2	.0
L	44	*Mike Peluso	CHI	3	0	0	0	1−	2	0	0	0	0	0	.0
R	26	Jocelyn Lemieux	CHI	4	0	0	0	2−	0	0	0	0	0	4	.0
L	23	*Stu Grimson	CHI	5	0	0	0	1−	46	0	0	0	0	2	.0
D	25	Bob McGill	CHI	5	0	0	0	1	2	0	0	0	0	5	.0
G	30	*Ed Belfour	CHI	6	0	0	0	0	6	0	0	0	0	0	.0

Goaltending

No.	Goaltender	GPI	Mins	Avg	W	L	EN	SO	GA	SA	S%
34	*Dominic Hasek	3	69	2.61	0	0	0	0	3	39	.923
30	*Ed Belfour	6	295	4.07	2	4	0	0	20	183	.891
	Totals	6	364	3.79	2	4	0	0	23	222	.896

General Managers' History

Major Frederic McLaughlin, 1926-27 to 1941-42; Bill Tobin, 1942-43 to 1953-54; Tommy Ivan, 1954-55 to 1976-77; Bob Pulford, 1977-78 to 1989-90; Mike Keenan, 1990-91 to date.

Retired Numbers

1	Glenn Hall	1957-1967
9	Bobby Hull	1957-1972
21	Stan Mikita	1958-1980
35	Tony Esposito	1969-1984

Club Records

Team

(Figures in brackets for season records are games played; records for fewest points, wins, ties, losses, goals, goals against are for 70 or more games)

Most Points 107 1970-71 (78)
                            1971-72 (78)
Most Wins 49   1970-71 (78)
                            1990-91 (80)
Most Ties 23   1973-74 (78)
Most Losses 51   1953-54 (70)
Most Goals 351   1985-86 (80)
Most Goals Against ...363   1981-82 (80)
Fewest Points 31   1953-54 (70)
Fewest Wins 12   1953-54 (70)
Fewest Ties 6   1989-90 (80)
Fewest Losses 14   1973-74 (78)
Fewest Goals *133   1953-54 (70)
Fewest Goals Against ...164 1973-74 (78)
Longest Winning Streak
  Over-all..............8   Dec. 9-26/71
                            Jan. 4-21/81
  Home 13   Nov. 11-
                            Dec. 20/70
  Away 7   Dec. 9-29/64
Longest Undefeated Streak
  Over-all.............15   Jan. 14-
                            Feb. 16/67
                            (12 wins, 3 ties)
  Home 18   Oct. 11-
                            Dec. 20/70
                            (16 wins, 2 ties)
  Away 12   Oct. 29-
                            Dec. 3/75
                            (6 wins, 9 ties)
Longest Losing Streak
  Over-all.............13   Feb. 25-
                            Oct. 11/51
  Home 11   Feb. 8-
                            Nov. 22/28
  Away 17   Jan. 2-
                            Oct. 7/54
Longest Winless Streak
  Over-all.............21   Dec. 17/50-
                            Jan. 28/51
                            (18 losses, 3 ties)

Home ....*15   Dec. 16/28-
                          Feb. 28/29
                          (11 losses, 4 ties)
Away 23   Dec. 19/50-
                          Oct. 11/51
                          (15 losses, 8 ties)
Most Shutouts, Season 15 1969-70 (76)
Most PIM, Season 2,496   1988-89 (80)
Most Goals, Game 12   Jan. 30/69
                             (Chi. 12 at Phil. 0)

Individual

Most Seasons ....22 Stan Mikita
Most Games ....1,394 Stan Mikita
Most Goals, Career .....604 Bobby Hull
Most Assists, Career ....926 Stan Mikita
Most Points, Career ..1,467 Stan Mikita
                            (541 goals, 926 assists)
Most PIM, Career ....1,442 Keith Magnuson
Most Shutouts, Career ...74 Tony Esposito
Longest Consecutive
  Games Streak ....720 Steve Larmer
                           (1982-83 to present)
Most Goals, Season ....58 Bobby Hull
                              (1968-69)
Most Assists, Season .....87 Denis Savard (81-82, 87-88)
Most Points, Season ....131 Denis Savard
                             (1987-88)
                             (44 goals, 87 assists)
Most PIM, Season ....352 Dave Manson
                             (1988-89)
Most Points, Defenseman
  Season ....85 Doug Wilson
                           (1981-82)
                           (39 goals, 46 assists)
Most Points, Center,
  Season ....131 Denis Savard
                           (1987-88)
                           (44 goals, 87 assists)

Most Points, Right Wing,
  Season ....101 Steve Larmer
                            (1990-91)
                            (44 goals, 57 assists)
Most Points, Left Wing,
  Season ....107 Bobby Hull
                            (1968-69)
                            (58 goals, 49 assists)
Most Points, Rookie,
  Season ....90 Steve Larmer
                            (1982-83)
                            (43 goals, 47 assists)
Most Shutouts, Season ...15 Tony Esposito
                            (1969-70)
Most Goals, Game ....5 Grant Mulvey
                            (Feb. 3/82)
Most Assists, Game ....6 Pat Stapleton
                            (Mar. 30/69)
Most Points, Game ....7 Max Bentley
                            (Jan. 28/43)
                            Grant Mulvey
                            (Feb. 3/82)

* NHL Record.

All-time Record vs. Other Clubs

Regular Season

			At Home							On Road							Total				
	GP	W	L	T	GF	GA	PTS	GP	W	L	T	GF	GA	PTS	GP	W	L	T	GF	GA	PTS
Boston	274	139	91	44	883	732	322	273	82	159	32	768	996	196	547	221	250	76	1651	1728	518
Buffalo	40	22	12	6	130	103	50	41	9	26	6	109	166	24	81	31	38	12	239	269	74
Calgary	36	17	11	8	132	108	42	38	11	20	7	113	132	29	74	28	31	15	245	240	71
Detroit	298	141	110	47	903	817	329	297	87	183	27	732	1024	201	595	228	293	74	1635	1841	530
Edmonton	19	10	7	2	86	88	22	19	5	13	1	68	96	11	38	15	20	3	154	184	33
Hartford	19	11	5	3	91	58	25	19	8	9	2	65	72	18	38	19	14	5	156	130	43
Los Angeles	48	25	17	6	187	147	56	49	23	21	5	174	173	51	97	48	38	11	361	320	107
Minnesota	77	50	18	9	324	206	109	77	32	34	11	266	276	75	154	82	52	20	590	482	184
Montreal	264	89	121	54	709	738	232	264	51	165	48	622	1022	150	528	140	286	102	1331	1760	382
New Jersey	35	23	7	5	151	97	51	35	14	15	6	111	110	34	70	37	22	11	262	207	85
NY Islanders	37	17	16	4	118	131	38	36	9	16	11	105	133	29	73	26	32	15	223	264	67
NY Rangers	275	125	108	42	843	764	292	275	106	115	54	778	812	266	550	231	223	96	1621	1576	558
Philadelphia	50	24	10	16	176	132	64	50	15	27	8	140	171	38	100	39	37	24	316	303	102
Pittsburgh	49	33	7	9	207	137	75	48	22	22	4	162	169	48	97	55	29	13	369	306	123
Quebec	19	11	7	1	80	65	23	19	7	8	4	76	81	18	38	18	15	5	156	146	41
St. Louis	80	48	21	11	328	250	107	78	26	38	14	248	276	66	158	74	59	25	576	526	173
Toronto	288	143	106	39	868	758	325	289	84	156	49	737	1001	217	577	227	262	88	1626	1759	542
Vancouver	46	29	12	5	169	106	63	46	15	20	11	134	137	41	92	44	32	16	303	243	104
Washington	29	18	6	5	121	87	41	29	9	17	3	91	115	21	58	27	23	8	212	202	62
Winnipeg	21	15	4	2	111	68	32	21	9	9	3	83	87	21	42	24	13	5	194	155	53
Defunct Club	139	79	40	20	408	267	178	140	52	67	21	316	345	125	279	131	107	41	724	612	303
Totals	2143	1069	736	338	7046	5859	2476	2143	676	1140	327	5898	7394	1679	4286	1745	1876	665	12944	13253	4155

Playoffs

	Series	W	L	GP	W	L	T	GF	GA	Last Mtg.	Round	Result
Boston	6	1	5	22	5	16	1	63	97	1978	QF	L 0-4
Buffalo	2	0	2	9	1	8	0	17	36	1980	QF	L 0-4
Calgary	2	0	2	8	1	7	0	17	30	1989	CF	L 1-4
Detroit	12	7	5	60	33	27	0	187	171	1989	DSF	W 4-2
Edmonton	3	0	3	16	4	12	0	56	94	1990	CF	L 2-4
Los Angeles	1	1	0	5	4	1	0	10	7	1974	QF	W 4-1
Minnesota	6	4	2	33	19	14	0	119	119	1991	DSF	L 2-4
Montreal	17	5	12	81	29	50	2	185	261	1976	QF	L 0-4
NY Islanders	2	0	2	6	0	6	0	6	21	1979	QF	L 0-4
NY Rangers	5	4	1	24	14	10	0	66	54	1973	SF	W 4-1
Philadelphia	1	1	0	4	4	0	0	20	8	1971	QF	W 4-0
Pittsburgh	1	1	0	4	4	0	0	14	8	1972	QF	W 4-0
St. Louis	7	6	1	35	23	12	0	137	97	1990	DF	W 4-3
Toronto	7	2	5	25	9	15	1	57	76	1986	DSF	L 0-3
Vancouver	1	0	1	5	1	4	0	13	18	1982	CF	L 1-4
Defunct Clubs	4	2	2	9	5	3	1	16	15			
Totals	77	34	43	346	156	185	5	983	1112			

Abbreviations: Round: F Final; CF conference final; **DF** division final; **DSF** division semi-final; **SF** semi-final; **QF** quarter-final. **GA** goals against; **GF** goals for.

Playoff Results 1991-87

Year	Round	Opponent	Result	GF	GA
1991	DSF	Minnesota	L 2-4	16	23
1990	CF	Edmonton	L 2-4	20	25
	DF	St. Louis	W 4-3	28	22
	DSF	Minnesota	W 4-3	21	18
1989	CF	Calgary	L 1-4	8	15
	DF	St. Louis	W 4-1	19	12
	DSF	Detroit	W 4-2	25	18
1988	DSF	St. Louis	L 4-1	17	21
1987	DSF	Detroit	L 0-4	6	15

1990-91 Results

		Home					Away	
Oct.	4	NY Rangers	4-3	Oct.	6	St Louis	5-2
	7	NY Islanders	2-4		13	Minnesota	4-1
	11	Pittsburgh	4-1		16	Detroit	2-3
	14	Calgary*	1-3		20	Toronto	2-6
	18	Toronto	3-0		27	Boston	4-5
	21	Minnesota	7-1	Nov.	3	Philadelphia*	3-1
	25	Washington	3-2		6	Hartford	1-1
	28	Montreal	2-1		10	Toronto	5-1
Nov.	1	Quebec	6-2		14	Detroit	3-2
	4	Los Angeles	0-2		16	Washington	4-3
	8	Edmonton	5-3		17	Quebec	7-2
	11	Winnipeg	3-3		20	Edmonton	3-1
	29	Detroit	1-5		21	Vancouver	1-4
Dec.	2	St Louis	3-2		24	Calgary	5-3
	6	NY Islanders	5-2	Dec.	1	Detroit*	3-4
	9	Philadelphia	4-5		8	Toronto	2-1
	13	Winnipeg	5-4		11	Pittsburgh	4-1
	16	Minnesota*	5-2		15	Minnesota*	1-5
	19	Washington	3-2		22	St Louis	0-5
	23	Detroit	3-2		28	Buffalo	0-5
	26	St Louis	6-6		29	NY Islanders	3-1
Jan.	3	New Jersey	5-3		31	Detroit	4-0
	6	Los Angeles	1-3	Jan.	11	Winnipeg	3-1
	10	Toronto	7-2		16	New Jersey	2-2
	13	Minnesota	5-3		17	NY Rangers	3-2
	24	Buffalo	4-5		28	Vancouver	1-0
	26	Toronto	5-1	Feb.	1	Edmonton	3-4
Feb.	14	Quebec	2-1		2	Calgary	1-3
	17	Detroit*	3-3		6	Montreal	8-3
	21	Boston	4-1		9	Boston*	3-5
	24	St Louis	6-2		10	Hartford	1-3
	28	Hartford	6-3		18	Philadelphia*	3-5
Mar.	3	Vancouver	8-0		23	Minnesota	3-3
	6	Montreal	3-5		26	St Louis	1-3
	10	NY Rangers	5-2	Mar.	8	Buffalo	5-3
	17	St Louis	6-4		14	Los Angeles	6-3
	21	New Jersey	3-3		16	St Louis	3-2
	24	Minnesota*	5-4		23	Pittsburgh*	7-5
	28	Toronto	5-3		26	Toronto	2-2
	31	Detroit	5-1		30	Minnesota	1-2

* Denotes afternoon game.

Entry Draft Selections 1991-77

1991
Pick
22 Dean McAmmond
39 Michael Pomichter
44 Jamie Matthews
66 Bobby House
71 Igor Kravchuk
88 Zac Boyer
110 Maco Balkovec
112 Kevin St. Jacques
132 Jacques Auger
154 Scott Kirton
176 Roch Belley
198 Scott MacDonald
220 Alexander Andrijevski
242 Mike Larkin
264 Scott Dean

1990
Pick
16 Karl Dykhuis
37 Ivan Droppa
79 Chris Tucker
121 Brett Stickney
124 Derek Edgerly
163 Hugo Belanger
184 Owen Lessard
205 Erik Peterson
226 Steve Dubinsky
247 Dino Grossi

1989
Pick
6 Adam Bennett
27 Michael Speer
48 Bob Kellogg
111 Tommi Pullola
132 Tracy Egeland
153 Milan Tichy
174 Jason Greyerbiehl
195 Matt Saunders
216 Mike Kozak
237 Michael Doneghey

1988
Pick
8 Jeremy Roenick
50 Trevor Dam
71 Stefan Elvenas
92 Joe Cleary
113 Justin Lafayette
134 Craig Woodcroft
155 Jon Pojar
176 Mathew Hentges
197 Daniel Maurice
218 Dirk Tenzer
239 Lupzig Andreas

1987
Pick
8 Jimmy Waite
29 Ryan McGill
50 Cam Russell
60 Mike Dagenais
92 Ulf Sandstrom
113 Mike McCormick
134 Stephen Tepper
155 John Reilly
176 Lance Werness
197 Dale Marquette
218 Bill Lacouture
239 Mike Lappin

1986
Pick
14 Everett Sanipass
35 Mark Kurzawski
77 Kucera Frantisek
98 Lonnie Loach
119 Mario Doyon
140 Mike Hudson
161 Marty Nanne
182 Geoff Benic
203 Glen Lowes
224 Chris Thayer
245 Sean Williams

1985
Pick
11 Dave Manson
53 Andy Helmuth
74 Dan Vincellette
87 Rick Herbert
95 Brad Belland
116 Jonas Heed
137 Victor Posa
158 John Reid
179 Richard LaPlante
200 Brad Hamilton
221 Ian Pound
237 Rick Braccia

1984
Pick
3 Ed Olczyk
45 Trent Yawney
66 Tommy Eriksson
90 Timo Lehkonen
101 Darin Sceviour
111 Chris Clifford
132 Mike Stapleton
153 Glen Greenough
174 Ralph Di Fiorie
195 Joakim Persson
216 Bill Brown
224 David Mackey
237 Dan Williams

1983
Pick
18 Bruce Cassidy
39 Wayne Presley
59 Marc Bergevin
79 Tarek Howard
99 Kevin Robinson
115 Jari Torkki
119 Mark Lavarre
139 Scott Birnie
159 Kevin Paynter
179 Brian Noonan
199 Dominik Hasek
219 Steve Pepin

1982
Pick
7 Ken Yaremchuk
28 Rene Badeau
49 Tom McMurchy
70 Bill Watson
91 Brad Beck
112 Mark Hatcher
133 Jay Ness
154 Jeff Smith
175 Phil Patterson
196 Jim Camazzola
217 Mike James
238 Bob Andrea

1981
Pick
12 Tony Tanti
25 Kevin Griffin
54 Darrell Anholt
75 Perry Pelensky
96 Doug Chessell
117 Bill Schafhauser
138 Marc Centrone
159 Johan Mellstrom
180 John Benns
201 Sylvain Roy

1980
Pick
3 Denis Savard
15 Jerome Dupont
28 Steve Ludzik
30 Ken Solheim
36 Len Dawes
57 Troy Murray
58 Marcel Frere
67 Carey Wilson
78 Brian Shaw
99 Kevin Ginnell
120 Steve Larmer
141 Sean Simpson
162 Jim Ralph
183 Don Dietrich
204 Dan Frawley

1979
Pick
7 Keith Brown
28 Tim Trimper
49 Bill Gardner
70 Louis Begin
91 Lowell Loveday
112 Doug Crossman

1978
Pick
10 Tim Higgins
29 Doug Lecuyer
46 Rick Paterson
63 Brian Young
79 Mark Murphy
96 Dave Feamster
113 Dave Mancuso
130 Sandy Ross
147 Mark Locken
164 Glenn Van
179 Darryl Sutter

1977
Pick
6 Doug Wilson
19 Jean Savard
60 Randy Ireland
78 Gary Platt
96 Jack O'Callahan
114 Floyd Lahache
129 Jeff Geiger
144 Stephen Ough

Club Directory

Chicago Stadium
1800 W. Madison St.
Chicago, IL. 60612
Phone **312/733-5300**
FAX 312/733-5356
ENVOY ID
Front Office: HAWKS. GM
Public
Relations: HAWKS. PR
Capacity: 17,317

President	William W. Wirtz
Executive Vice-President	Arthur Michael Wirtz, Jr.
Vice-President & Assistant to the President	Thomas N. Ivan
Senior Vice President	Robert J. Pulford
General Manager/Head Coach	Mike Keenan
Assistant General Manager	Jack Davison
Director of Player Personnel	Bob Murray
Associate Coach	Darryl Sutter
Assistant Coaches	Rich Preston, Dave McDowall
Scouts	Kerry Davison, Michel Dumas, Dave Lucas, Jim Pappin, Jan Spieczny, Jim Walker, Russ Huston, Steve Lyons, Duane Sutter, Brian DeBruyn, Dan Maloney
Director of Team Services	Steve Williams
Executive Secretary	Cindy Bodnarchuk
Receptionist/Secretary	Vicki Littleton

Medical Staff

Club Doctors	Louis W. Kolb Howard Baim
Club Dentist	Robert Duresa
Head Trainer	Michael Gapski
Equipment Manager/Asst. Trainer	Randy Lacey, Lou Varga
Team Psychologist	Cal Botterill

Finance

Controller	Robert Rinkus
Assistant to the Controller	Penny Swenson
Accounting Secretary	Pat Dema

Public Relations/Marketing

Director of Marketing	Peter Wirtz
Director of Public Relations	Jim DeMaria
Asst. PR & Director of Community Relations	Tom Finks
Public Relations Secretary	Barbara Davidson

Ticketing

Ticket Manager	John Stroth
Season Ticket Coordinator	Mildred Hornik
Switchboard Operators	Esther Middleton, Mary Joiner
Team Photographers	Sol Benjamin, Ray Grabowski
Organist	Frank Pellico
Soloist	Wayne Messmer
Public Address Announcer	Harvey Wittenberg
Executive Offices	Chicago Stadium
Home Ice	Chicago Stadium
Largest Hockey Crowd	20,960 on April 10, 1982 vs. Minnesota
Location of Press Box	West end of Stadium
Dimensions of Rink	185 feet by 85 feet
Ends of Rink	Plexi-glass extends above boards all around rink
Club Colors	Red, Black & White
Uniforms	Home – Base color white, trimmed with black & red; Away – Base color red trimmed with black & white
Radio Station	WBBM (AM 780)
Television Station	Sports Channel
Broadcasters	Pat Foley, Dale Tallon

Coach and General Manager

KEENAN, MICHAEL (MIKE)
Coach and General Manager, Chicago Blackhawks.
Born in Toronto, Ont., October 21, 1949.

In his third season as coach of the Blackhawks, Mike Keenan's club won the Presidents' Trophy for best overall League finish. The Blackhawks' 106-point season not only paced the NHL but was also Chicago's best regular-season finish in 20 years, and the club's 49 wins tied the record for most wins in franchise history. Named coach of the Blackhawks on June 9, 1988, Keenan assumed the post of general manager on June 5, 1990.

Keenan spent four years as head coach of the Philadelphia Flyers (1984-85 to 1987-88) before being hired by the Blackhawks on June 9, 1988. While with the Flyers, he led his team to the Stanley Cup Final twice in four years and distinguished himself as the first coach in League history to register 40-or-more wins in each of his first three seasons. Keenan was the head coach for Team Canada in the 1987 Canada Cup and led his club to a 2-1 series victory over the Soviet Union in the final.

A former team captain of the St. Lawrence University Saints, Keenan began coaching at the Junior B level, winning back-to-back championships in the Metro Toronto League. After leading the OHL's Peterborough Petes to the 1979-80 Memorial Cup Finals, he joined the AHL's Rochester Americans, carrying that team to the 1982-83 Calder Cup title. The following season, 1983-84, immediately preceding his tenure with the Flyers, Keenan posted yet another championship, this time taking the CIAU Canadian college title with the University of Toronto Blues.

Coaching Record

Season	Team	Games	Regular Season W	L	T	%	Playoffs Games	W	L	%
1979-80	Peterborough (OHL)	68	47	20	1	.699	18	15	3	.833
1980-81	Rochester (AHL)	80	30	42	8	.425	...	...	...	...
1981-82	Rochester (AHL)	80	40	31	9	.556	9	4	5	.444
1982-83	Rochester (AHL)	80	46	25	9	.631	16	12	4	.750
1983-84	U. of Toronto (CIAU)	49	41	5	3	.867	...	...	...	...
1984-85	Philadelphia (NHL)	80	53	20	7	.706	19	12	7	.632
1985-86	Philadelphia (NHL)	80	53	23	4	.688	5	2	3	.400
1986-87	Philadelphia (NHL)	80	46	26	8	.625	26	15	11	.577
1987-88	Philadelphia (NHL)	80	38	33	9	.531	7	3	4	.429
1988-89	Chicago (NHL)	80	27	41	12	.413	16	9	7	.563
1989-90	Chicago (NHL)	80	41	33	6	.550	20	10	10	.500
1990-91	Chicago (NHL)	80	49	23	8	.663	6	2	4	.333
	NHL Totals	560	307	199	54	.596	99	53	46	.535

Detroit Red Wings

1990-91 Results: 34w-38L-8T 76PTS. Third, Norris Division

Johan Garpenlov, one of the NHL's "young guns", fired 18 goals for the Wings in his first season.

Schedule

Home			Away		
Oct.	Thur.	10 Montreal	**Oct.**	Thur.	3 Chicago
	Tues.	15 Edmonton		Sat.	5 Toronto
	Thur.	17 St Louis		Sat.	12 Minnesota
	Wed.	23 Winnipeg		Sat.	19 Quebec
	Fri.	25 Toronto		Sat.	26 Toronto
	Mon.	28 Los Angeles	**Nov.**	Sat.	2 Boston
	Wed.	30 Buffalo		Fri.	8 Washington
Nov.	Fri.	1 Hartford		Tues.	12 Calgary
	Tues.	5 Minnesota		Thur.	14 San Jose
	Thur.	7 St Louis		Sat.	16 Los Angeles
	Tues.	19 Chicago		Sat.	23 Minnesota
	Fri.	22 Minnesota		Sat.	30 St Louis
	Mon.	25 Washington	**Dec.**	Sat.	7 New Jersey
	Wed.	27 St Louis		Sat.	14 Calgary
Dec.	Tues.	3 Calgary		Sun.	15 Edmonton
	Fri.	6 NY Rangers		Tues.	17 Vancouver
	Tues.	10 Chicago		Sat.	21 Los Angeles
	Thur.	12 Quebec		Sat.	28 Toronto
	Tues.	31 Boston		Sun.	29 Chicago
Jan.	Fri.	3 Toronto	**Jan.**	Sat.	4 St Louis
	Tues.	7 NY Islanders		Tues.	14 NY Islanders
	Thurs.	9 Minnesota		Sat.	25 New Jersey
	Sat.	11 Edmonton	**Feb.**	Sat.	1 Montreal
	Thur.	16 Pittsburgh		Mon.	3 Pittsburgh
	Tues.	21 Philadelphia		Sun.	9 NY Rangers
	Thur.	23 Vancouver		Tues.	11 Toronto
	Wed.	29 Buffalo		Wed.	12 Buffalo
	Fri.	31 New Jersey		Sun.	23 Hartford*
Feb.	Wed.	5 Washington		Thur.	27 Chicago
	Fri.	7 Toronto		Sat.	29 St Louis
	Sat.	15 San Jose	**Mar.**	Sat.	7 Quebec
	Mon.	17 St Louis		Sun.	8 Montreal
	Thur.	20 Toronto		Thur.	12 St Louis
	Sat.	22 Chicago*		Sat.	14 Minnesota*
Mar.	Tues.	3 Winnipeg		Sun.	15 Winnipeg*
	Thur.	5 Minnesota		Tues.	17 San Jose
	Fri.	20 NY Rangers		Sun.	22 Philadelphia
	Tues.	24 Pittsburgh		Sun.	29 NY Islanders
	Sat.	28 Vancouver*	**Apr.**	Sat.	4 Minnesota
	Tues.	31 Chicago		Sun.	5 Chicago

* Denotes afternoon game.

Home Starting Times:
All games .... 7:35 p.m.
Except Matinees .... 1:05 p.m.

Franchise date: September 25, 1926

66th NHL Season

Year-by-Year Record

		Home			Road			Overall							
Season	GP	W	L	T	W	L	T	W	L	T	GF	GA	Pts.	Finished	Playoff Result
1990-91	80	26	14	0	8	24	8	34	38	8	273	298	76	3rd, Norris Div.	Lost Div. Semi-Final
1989-90	80	20	14	6	8	24	8	28	38	14	288	323	70	5th, Norris Div.	Out of Playoffs
1988-89	80	20	14	6	14	20	6	34	34	12	313	316	80	1st, Norris Div.	Lost Div. Semi-Final
1987-88	80	24	10	6	17	18	5	41	28	11	322	269	93	1st, Norris Div.	Lost Conf. Championship
1986-87	80	20	14	6	14	22	4	34	36	10	260	274	78	2nd, Norris Div.	Lost Conf. Championship
1985-86	80	10	26	4	7	31	2	17	57	6	266	415	40	5th, Norris Div.	Out of Playoffs
1984-85	80	19	14	7	8	27	5	27	41	12	313	357	66	3rd, Norris Div.	Lost Div. Semi-Final
1983-84	80	18	20	2	13	22	5	31	42	7	298	323	69	3rd, Norris Div.	Lost Div. Semi-Final
1982-83	80	14	19	7	7	25	8	21	44	15	263	344	57	5th, Norris Div.	Out of Playoffs
1981-82	80	15	19	6	6	28	6	21	47	12	270	351	54	6th, Norris Div.	Out of Playoffs
1980-81	80	16	15	9	3	28	9	19	43	18	252	339	56	5th, Norris Div.	Out of Playoffs
1979-80	80	14	21	5	12	22	6	26	43	11	268	306	63	5th, Norris Div.	Out of Playoffs
1978-79	80	15	17	8	8	24	8	23	41	16	252	295	62	5th, Norris Div.	Out of Playoffs
1977-78	80	22	11	7	10	23	7	32	34	14	252	266	78	2nd, Norris Div.	Lost Quarter-Final
1976-77	80	12	22	6	4	33	3	16	55	9	183	309	41	5th, Norris Div.	Out of Playoffs
1975-76	80	17	15	8	9	29	2	26	44	10	226	300	62	4th, Norris Div.	Out of Playoffs
1974-75	80	17	17	6	6	28	6	23	45	12	259	335	58	4th, Norris Div.	Out of Playoffs
1973-74	78	21	12	6	8	27	4	29	39	10	255	319	68	6th, East Div.	Out of Playoffs
1972-73	78	22	12	5	15	17	7	37	29	12	265	243	86	5th, East Div.	Out of Playoffs
1971-72	78	25	11	3	8	24	7	33	35	10	261	262	76	5th, East Div.	Out of Playoffs
1970-71	78	17	15	7	5	30	4	22	45	11	209	308	55	7th, East Div.	Out of Playoffs
1969-70	76	20	11	7	20	10	8	40	21	15	246	199	95	3rd, East Div.	Lost Quarter-Final
1968-69	76	23	8	7	10	23	5	33	31	12	239	221	78	5th, East Div.	Out of Playoffs
1967-68	74	18	15	4	9	20	8	27	35	12	245	257	66	6th, East Div.	Out of Playoffs
1966-67	70	21	11	3	6	28	1	27	39	4	212	241	58	5th,	Out of Playoffs
1965-66	70	20	8	7	11	19	5	31	27	12	221	194	74	4th,	Lost Final
1964-65	70	25	7	3	15	16	4	40	23	7	224	175	87	1st,	Lost Semi-Final
1963-64	70	23	9	3	7	20	8	30	29	11	191	204	71	4th,	Lost Final
1962-63	70	19	10	6	13	15	7	32	25	13	200	194	77	4th,	Lost Final
1961-62	70	17	11	7	6	22	7	23	33	14	184	219	60	5th,	Out of Playoffs
1960-61	70	15	13	7	10	16	9	25	29	16	195	215	66	4th,	Lost Final
1959-60	70	18	14	3	8	15	12	26	29	15	186	197	67	4th,	Lost Semi-Final
1958-59	70	13	17	5	12	20	3	25	37	8	167	218	58	6th,	Out of Playoffs
1957-58	70	16	11	8	13	18	4	29	29	12	176	207	70	3rd,	Lost Semi-Final
1956-57	70	23	7	5	15	13	7	38	20	12	198	157	88	1st,	Lost Semi-Final
1955-56	70	21	6	8	9	18	8	30	24	16	183	148	76	2nd,	Lost Final
1954-55	**70**	**25**	**5**	**5**	**17**	**12**	**6**	**42**	**17**	**11**	**204**	**134**	**95**	**1st,**	**Won Stanley Cup**
1953-54	**70**	**24**	**4**	**7**	**13**	**15**	**7**	**37**	**19**	**14**	**191**	**132**	**88**	**1st,**	**Won Stanley Cup**
1952-53	70	20	5	10	16	11	8	36	16	18	222	133	90	1st,	Lost Semi-Final
1951-52	**70**	**24**	**7**	**4**	**20**	**7**	**8**	**44**	**14**	**12**	**215**	**133**	**100**	**1st,**	**Won Stanley Cup**
1950-51	70	25	3	7	19	10	6	44	13	13	236	139	101	1st,	Lost Semi-Final
1949-50	**70**	**19**	**9**	**7**	**18**	**10**	**7**	**37**	**19**	**14**	**229**	**164**	**88**	**1st,**	**Won Stanley Cup**
1948-49	60	21	6	3	13	13	4	34	19	7	195	145	75	1st,	Lost Final
1947-48	60	16	9	5	14	9	7	30	18	12	187	148	72	2nd,	Lost Final
1946-47	60	14	10	6	8	17	5	22	27	11	190	193	55	4th,	Lost Semi-Final
1945-46	50	16	5	4	4	15	6	20	20	10	146	159	50	4th,	Lost Semi-Final
1944-45	50	19	5	1	12	9	4	31	14	5	218	161	67	2nd,	Lost Final
1943-44	50	18	5	2	8	13	4	26	18	6	214	177	58	2nd,	Lost Semi-Final
1942-43	**50**	**16**	**4**	**5**	**9**	**10**	**6**	**25**	**14**	**11**	**169**	**124**	**61**	**1st,**	**Won Stanley Cup**
1941-42	48	14	7	3	5	18	1	19	25	4	140	147	42	5th,	Lost Final
1940-41	48	14	5	5	7	11	6	21	16	11	112	102	53	3rd,	Lost Final
1939-40	48	11	10	3	5	16	3	16	26	6	91	126	38	5th,	Lost Semi-Final
1938-39	48	14	8	2	4	16	4	18	24	6	107	128	42	5th,	Lost Semi-Final
1937-38	48	8	10	6	4	15	5	12	25	11	99	133	35	4th, Amn. Div.	Out of Playoffs
1936-37	**48**	**14**	**5**	**5**	**11**	**9**	**4**	**25**	**14**	**9**	**128**	**102**	**59**	**1st, Amn. Div.**	**Won Stanley Cup**
1935-36	**48**	**14**	**5**	**5**	**10**	**11**	**3**	**24**	**16**	**8**	**124**	**103**	**56**	**1st, Amn. Div.**	**Won Stanley Cup**
1934-35	48	11	8	5	8	14	2	19	22	7	127	114	45	4th, Amn. Div.	Out of Playoffs
1933-34	48	15	5	4	9	9	6	24	14	10	113	98	58	1st,	Lost Final
1932-33*	48	15	3	6	10	12	2	25	15	8	111	93	58	2nd,	Lost Semi-Final
1931-32	48	15	8	1	3	12	9	18	20	10	95	108	46	3rd,	Lost Quarter-Final
1930-31**	44	10	7	5	6	14	2	16	21	7	102	105	39	4th,	Out of Playoffs
1929-30	44	9	9	3	5	15	3	14	24	6	117	133	34	4th,	Out of Playoffs
1928-29	44	11	6	5	8	10	4	19	16	9	72	63	47	3rd,	Lost Quarter-Final
1927-28	44	12	6	4	7	13	2	19	19	6	88	79	44	4th,	Out of Playoffs
1926-27***	44	6	15	1	6	13	3	12	28	4	76	105	28	5th, Amn. Div.	Out of Playoffs

* Team name changed to Red Wings. ** Team name changed to Falcons. *** Team named Cougars.

1991-92 Player Personnel

FORWARDS	HT	WT	S	Place of Birth	Date	1990-91 Club
AIVAZOFF, Micah	6-0	185	L	Powell River, B.C.	5/4/69	New Haven
BERMINGHAM, Jim	6-3	201	L	Montreal, Que.	11/12/71	Laval
BURR, Shawn	6-1	195	L	Sarnia, Ont.	7/1/66	Detroit
CARSON, Jimmy	6-0	200	R	Southfield, MI	7/20/68	Detroit
CASSELMAN, Mike	5-11	180	L	Morrisburg, Ont.	8/23/68	Clarkston
CROWDER, Troy	6-4	215	R	Sudbury, Ont.	5/3/68	New Jersey
CUMMINS, Jim	6-2	200	L	Dearborn, MI	5/17/70	Michigan State
FEDOROV, Sergei	6-1	191	L	Pskow, USSR	12/13/69	Detroit
FEDYK, Brent	6-0	195	R	Yorkton, Sask.	3/8/67	Detroit
FIRTH, Jason	5-11	175	L	Dartmouth, N.S.	3/29/71	Kitchener
FLANAGAN, Dave	6-1	210	R	Charlottetown, PEI	12/13/67	Hampton Roads
GALLANT, Gerard	5-10	185	L	Summerside, P.E.I.	9/2/63	Detroit
GARPENLOV, Johan	5-11	185	L	Stockholm, Sweden	3/21/68	Detroit
GOBER, Mike	6-0	192	L	St. Louis, MO	4/10/67	San Diego
HOLLAND, Dennis	5-10	165	L	Vernon, B.C.	1/30/69	Adirondack-San Diego
HURD, Kelly	5-10	170	R	Castlegar, B.C.	5/13/68	Michigan Tech
JONES, Bob	5-11	196	L	Sault Ste. Marie, Ont.	1/13/69	San Diego
KENNEDY, Sheldon	5-10	170	R	Brandon, Man.	6/15/69	Adirondack-Detroit
KERR, Alan	5-11	195	R	Hazelton, B.C.	3/28/64	NY Islanders-Capital District
KOCUR, Kory	5-11	188	R	Kelvington, Sask.	3/6/69	Adirondack
KREICK, Brad	6-3	190	L	Ann Arbor, MI	5/6/68	Brown
LAPOINTE, Martin	5-11	197	R	Villa St. Pierre, Que.	9/12/73	Laval
LOACH, Lonnie	5-10	180	L	New Liskeard, Ont.	4/14/68	Ft. Wayne
MacLELLAN, Brian	6-3	215	L	Guelph, Ont.	10/27/58	Calgary
McDOUGALL, Bill	6-0	185	R	Mississauga, Ont.	8/10/66	Detroit-Adirondack
McRAE, Chris	6-0	200	L	Beaverton, Ont.	8/26/65	Adirondack
MERKOSKY, Glenn	5-10	175	L	Edmonton, Alta.	4/8/59	Adirondack
MILLER, Kevin	5-9	170	R	Lansing, MI	9/2/65	NY Rangers-Detroit
OLIVER, Don	5-11	175	L	London, Ont.	11/9/69	Ohio State
POTVIN, Marc	6-1	200	R	Ottawa, Ont.	1/29/67	Adirondack-Detroit
PRIMEAU, Keith	6-4	220	L	Toronto, Ont.	11/24/71	Detroit-Adirondack
PROBERT, Bob	6-3	215	L	Windsor, Ont.	6/5/65	Detroit
QUINNEY, Ken	5-10	186	R	New Westminster, B.C.	5/23/65	Quebec-Halifax
SHANK, Daniel	5-10	190	R	Montreal, Que.	5/12/67	Adirondack-Detroit
SHEPPARD, Ray	6-1	187	R	Pembrook, Ont.	5/27/66	NY Rangers
SHUCHUK, Gary	5-10	185	R	Edmonton, Alta.	2/17/67	Adirondack-Detroit
SILLINGER, Mike	5-10	191	R	Regina, Sask.	6/29/71	Regina-Detroit
STAUBER, Pete	5-11	185	L	Duluth, MN	5/10/66	Adirondack
TOMLINSON, Kirk	5-11	190	L	Tottenham, Ont.	5/5/68	Nashville-Adirondack
WIEBE, Dan	6-4	190	L	Manning, Alta.	4/3/69	U. of Alberta
YSEBAERT, Paul	6-1	190	L	Sarnia, Ont.	5/15/66	New Jersey-Detroit
YZERMAN, Steve	5-11	185	R	Cranbrook, B.C.	5/9/65	Detroit
DEFENSEMEN						
ANGLEHART, Serge	6-2	190	R	Hull, Que.	4/10/70	Adirondack
BANNISTER, Darin	6-0	185	R	Calgary, Alta.	1/16/67	San Diego
BIGNELL, Greg	6-0	180	L	Kitchener, Ont.	5/9/69	Hampton
BOUGHNER, Bob	5-11	201	R	Windsor, Ont.	3/8/71	Sault Ste. Marie
CHIASSON, Steve	6-1	205	L	Barrie, Ont.	4/14/67	Detroit
CROSSMAN, Doug	6-2	190	L	Peterborough, Ont.	6/30/60	NY Islanders-Hartford-Detroit
DOLLAS, Bobby	6-2	212	L	Montreal, Que.	1/31/65	Detroit
DUPUIS, Guy	6-2	199	R	Moncton, N.B.	5/10/70	Adirondack
KRAUSE, Rob	6-2	210	L	Prairie, Alta.	10/28/69	Cincinnati-Adirondack
KRUPPKE, Gord	6-1	200	R	Slave Lake, Alta.	4/2/69	Adirondack-Detroit
LIDSTROM, Niklas	6-2	180	L	Vasteras, Sweden	4/28/70	Vasteras (Swe)
LUONGO, Chris	6-0	190	R	Detroit, MI	3/17/67	Adirondack-Phoenix
MALGUNAS, Stewart	5-11	180	L	Prince George, B.C.	4/21/70	Adirondack
MARSH, Brad	6-3	220	L	London, Ont.	3/31/58	Toronto-Detroit
MAYER, Derek	6-0	185	R	Rossland, B.C.	5/21/67	Adirondack-San Diego
McCRIMMON, Brad	5-11	197	L	Dodsland, Sask.	3/29/59	Detroit
PRAZNIK, Jody	6-1	180	L	Winnipeg, Man.	6/28/69	Hampton
PUSHER, Jamie	6-3	192	R	Lethbridge, Alta.	2/11/73	Lethbridge
RACINE, Yves	6-0	185	L	Matane, Que.	2/7/69	Adirondack-Detroit
SCHENA, Rob	6-1	190	L	Saugess, MA	2/5/67	San Diego
VIAL, Dennis	6-1	200	L	Sault Ste. Marie, Ont.	4/10/69	Binghamton-NY Rangers-Detroit
WILKIE, Bob	6-2	200	R	Calgary, Alta.	2/11/69	Adirondack-Detroit
YORK, Jason	6-1	192	R	Ottawa, Ont.	5/20/70	Windsor
ZOMBO, Rick	6-1	195	R	DesPlaines, IL	5/8/63	Detroit

GOALTENDERS	HT	WT	C	Place of Birth	Date	1990-91 Club
BESTER, Alan	5-7	155	L	Hamilton, Ont.	3/26/64	Toronto-Newmarket-Detroit
CHEVELDAE, Tim	5-10	175	L	Melville, Sask.	2/15/68	Detroit
GAGNON, Dave	6-0	185		Windsor, Ont.	10/31/67	Adir.-Hampt.-Detroit
KING, Scott	6-1	185		Thunder Bay, Ont.	6/25/67	Hampton-Adir.-Detroit
OSGOOD, Chris	5-10	156	L	Peace River, Alta.	11/26/72	Medicine Hat
REIMER, Mark	5-11	170	L	Calgary, Alta.	3/23/67	Adirondack-San Diego

General Managers' History

Art Duncan, 1926-27; Jack Adams, 1927-28 to 1962-63; Sidney Abel, 1963-64 to 1969-70; Sidney Abel and Ned Harkness, 1970-71; Ned Harkness, 1971-72 to 1973-74; Alex Delvecchio, 1974-75 to 1975-76; Alex Delvecchio and Ted Lindsay, 1976-77; Ted Lindsay, 1977-78 to 1979-80; Jimmy Skinner, 1980-81 to 1981-82; Jim Devellano, 1982-83 to 1989-90; Bryan Murray, 1990-91 to date.

1990-91 Scoring

Regular Season

* rookie

Pos	#	Player	Team	GP	G	A	Pts	+/-	PIM	PP	SH	GW	GT	S	%
C	19	Steve Yzerman	DET	80	51	57	108	2–	34	12	6	4	1	326	15.6
C	91	*Sergei Fedorov	DET	77	31	48	79	11	66	11	3	5	1	259	12.0
C	23	Kevin Miller	NYR	63	17	27	44	1	63	1	2	3	0	113	15.0
			DET	11	5	2	7	4–	4	0	1	0	0	23	21.7
			TOTAL	74	22	29	51	3–	67	1	3	3	0	136	16.2
L	11	Shawn Burr	DET	80	20	30	50	14	112	6	0	4	0	164	12.2
D	33	Yves Racine	DET	62	7	40	47	1	33	2	0	1	1	131	5.3
C	10	Jimmy Carson	DET	64	21	25	46	3	28	5	1	4	2	175	12.0
L	21	*Paul Ysebaert	N.J.	11	4	3	7	1	6	1	0	0	0	14	28.6
			DET	51	15	18	33	8–	16	5	0	1	0	114	13.2
			TOTAL	62	19	21	40	7–	22	6	0	1	0	128	14.8
R	22	Dave Barr	DET	70	18	22	40	20	55	2	2	2	1	98	18.4
L	15	*Johan Garpenlov	DET	71	18	22	40	4–	18	2	0	3	0	91	19.8
R	24	Bob Probert	DET	55	16	23	39	3–	315	4	0	3	0	88	18.2
D	39	Doug Crossman	NYI	16	1	6	7	4–	12	1	0	0	0	30	3.3
			HFD	41	4	19	23	13–	19	2	0	0	0	62	6.5
			DET	17	3	4	7	6–	17	1	0	0	0	16	18.8
			TOTAL	74	8	29	37	23–	48	4	0	0	0	108	7.4
R	14	Brent Fedyk	DET	67	16	19	35	20	38	0	0	1	0	74	21.6
L	17	Gerard Gallant	DET	45	10	16	26	6	111	3	0	1	0	82	12.2
D	4	Rick Zombo	DET	77	4	19	23	2–	55	0	0	0	0	68	5.9
D	3	Steve Chiasson	DET	42	3	17	20	0	80	1	0	1	0	101	3.0
C	25	Marc Habscheid	DET	46	9	8	17	10–	22	0	4	1	0	54	16.7
D	5	Rick Green	DET	65	2	14	16	10	24	0	0	0	0	36	5.6
C	55	*Keith Primeau	DET	58	3	12	15	12–	106	0	0	1	0	33	9.1
D	2	Brad McCrimmon	DET	64	0	13	13	7	81	0	0	0	0	43	.0
D	36	*Per Djoos	DET	26	0	12	12	2–	16	0	0	0	0	23	.0
C	16	John Chabot	DET	27	5	5	10	6	4	2	0	1	0	26	19.2
D	8	Bobby Dollas	DET	56	3	5	8	6	20	0	0	1	0	59	5.1
R	29	Randy McKay	DET	47	1	7	8	15–	183	0	0	0	0	22	4.5
G	32	Tim Cheveldae	DET	65	0	5	5	0	2	0	0	0	0	0	.0
D	20	Brad Marsh	TOR	22	0	0	0	6–	15	0	0	0	0	18	.0
			DET	20	1	3	4	3–	16	0	0	0	0	16	6.3
			TOTAL	42	1	3	4	9–	31	0	0	0	0	34	2.9
R	48	*Gary Shuchuk	DET	6	1	2	3	1	6	0	0	0	0	8	12.5
D	28	*Bob Wilkie	DET	8	1	2	3	2–	2	0	0	0	0	9	11.1
R	12	*Sheldon Kennedy	DET	7	1	0	1	1–	12	0	0	0	0	11	9.1
C	43	*Bill McDougall	DET	2	0	1	1	0	0	0	0	0	0	3	.0
C	21	*Mike Sillinger	DET	3	0	1	1	2–	0	0	0	0	0	6	.0
D	37	*Chris Luongo	DET	4	0	1	1	0	4	0	0	0	0	4	.0
R	34	Daniel Shank	DET	7	0	1	1	0	14	0	0	0	0	4	.0
G	38	*Scott King	DET	1	0	0	0	0	0	0	0	0	0	0	.0
G	35	*David Gagnon	DET	2	0	0	0	0	0	0	0	0	0	0	.0
G	31	Alain Chevrier	DET	3	0	0	0	0	0	0	0	0	0	0	.0
R	18	Kevin McClelland	DET	3	0	0	0	4–	7	0	0	0	0	1	.0
D	40	*Gord Kruppke	DET	4	0	0	0	1	0	0	0	0	0	0	.0
L	7	*Tom Bissett	DET	5	0	0	0	4–	0	0	0	0	0	2	.0
G	35	Allan Bester	TOR	6	0	0	0	0	0	0	0	0	0	0	.0
			DET	3	0	0	0	0	0	0	0	0	0	0	.0
			TOTAL	9	0	0	0	0	0	0	0	0	0	0	.0
R	46	*Marc Potvin	DET	9	0	0	0	4–	55	0	0	0	0	13	.0
G	1	Glen Hanlon	DET	19	0	0	0	0	4	0	0	0	0	0	.0
D	36	*Dennis Vial	NYR	21	0	0	0	4–	61	0	0	0	0	5	.0
			DET	9	0	0	0	3–	16	0	0	0	0	3	.0
			TOTAL	30	0	0	0	7–	77	0	0	0	0	8	.0

Goaltending

No.	Goaltender	GPI	Mins	Avg	W	L	T	EN	SO	GA	SA	S%
38	*Scott King	1	45	2.67	0	0	0	0	0	2	11	.818
1	Glen Hanlon	19	862	3.20	4	6	3	0	0	46	438	.895
32	Tim Cheveldae	65	3615	3.55	30	26	5	5	2	214	1716	.875
35	Allan Bester	3	178	4.38	0	3	0	1	0	13	99	.869
31	Alain Chevrier	3	108	6.11	0	2	0	0	0	11	55	.800
35	*David Gagnon	2	35	10.29	0	1	0	0	0	6	28	.786
	Totals	**80**	**4854**	**3.68**	**34**	**38**	**8**	**6**	**2**	**298**	**2353**	**.873**

Playoffs

Pos	#	Player	Team	GP	G	A	Pts	+/-	PIM	PP	SH	GW	OT	S	%
C	19	Steve Yzerman	DET	7	3	3	6	1–	4	1	0	0	0	27	11.1
C	91	*Sergei Fedorov	DET	7	1	5	6	1–	4	0	0	1	0	22	4.5
C	23	Kevin Miller	DET	7	3	2	5	0	20	0	1	0	0	11	27.3
D	39	Doug Crossman	DET	6	0	5	5	0	6	0	0	0	0	6	.0
D	3	Steve Chiasson	DET	5	3	1	4	1–	19	1	0	0	0	12	25.0
L	11	Shawn Burr	DET	7	0	4	4	3–	15	0	0	0	0	17	.0
C	10	Jimmy Carson	DET	7	2	1	3	2–	4	0	0	1	0	6	33.3
R	24	Bob Probert	DET	6	1	2	3	2–	50	0	0	0	0	4	25.0
D	33	Yves Racine	DET	7	2	0	2	6–	0	2	0	0	0	15	13.3
C	55	*Keith Primeau	DET	5	1	1	2	3	25	0	0	0	0	2	50.0
D	2	Brad McCrimmon	DET	7	1	1	2	3	21	0	0	0	0	7	14.3
L	21	*Paul Ysebaert	DET	2	0	2	2	2	0	0	0	0	0	5	.0
R	14	Brent Fedyk	DET	6	1	0	1	3–	2	0	0	1	0	3	33.3
D	8	Bobby Dollas	DET	7	1	0	1	2–	13	0	0	0	0	3	33.3
D	4	Rick Zombo	DET	7	1	0	1	4–	10	0	0	0	0	6	16.7
C	7	*Mike Sillinger	DET	3	0	1	1	0	0	0	0	0	0	3	.0
R	29	Randy Mckay	DET	5	0	1	1	0	41	0	0	0	0	4	.0
L	15	*Johan Garpenlov	DET	6	0	1	1	1–	4	0	0	0	0	7	.0
G	35	Allan Bester	DET	1	0	0	0	0	0	0	0	0	0	0	.0
D	20	Brad Marsh	DET	1	0	0	0	0	0	0	0	0	0	1	.0
C	43	*Bill McDougall	DET	1	0	0	0	1–	0	0	0	0	0	0	.0
D	5	Rick Green	DET	3	0	0	0	0	0	0	0	0	0	0	.0
R	48	*Gary Shuchuk	DET	3	0	0	0	2–	0	0	0	0	0	1	.0
C	25	Marc Habscheid	DET	5	0	0	0	2–	0	0	0	0	0	3	.0
R	46	*Marc Potvin	DET	6	0	0	0	3–	32	0	0	0	0	2	.0
G	32	Tim Cheveldae	DET	7	0	0	0	0	0	0	0	0	0	0	.0

Goaltending

No.	Goaltender	GPI	Mins	Avg	W	L	EN	SO	GA	SA	S%
35	Allan Bester	1	20	3.00	0	0	0	0	1	12	.917
32	Tim Cheveldae	7	398	3.32	3	4	1	0	22	208	.894
	Totals	7	420	3.43	3	4	1	0	24	221	.891

Club Records

Team

(Figures in brackets for season records are games played; records for fewest points, wins, ties, losses, goals, goals against are for 70 or more games)

Most Points	101	1950-51 (70)	
Most Wins	44	1950-51 (70)	
		1951-52 (70)	
Most Ties	18	1952-53 (70)	
		1980-81 (80)	
Most Losses	57	1985-86 (80)	
Most Goals	322	1987-88 (80)	
Most Goals Against	415	1985-86 (80)	
Fewest Points	40	1985-86 (80)	
Fewest Wins	16	1976-77 (80)	
Fewest Ties	4	1966-67 (70)	
Fewest Losses	13	1950-51 (70)	
Fewest Goals	167	1958-59 (70)	
Fewest Goals Against	132	1953-54 (70)	

Longest Winning Streak
Over-all ... 9 Mar. 3-21/51;
Feb. 27-
Mar. 20/55
Home ... 14 Jan. 21-
Mar. 25/65
Away ... 5 Four times

Longest Undefeated Streak
Over-all ... 15 Nov. 27-
Dec. 28/52
(8 wins, 7 ties)
Home ... 18 Dec. 26/54-
Mar. 20/55
(13 wins, 5 ties)
Away ... 15 Oct. 18-
Dec. 20/51
(10 wins, 5 ties)

Longest Losing Streak
Over-all ... 14 Feb. 24-
Mar. 25/82
Home ... 7 Feb. 20-
Mar. 25/82
Away ... 14 Oct. 19-
Dec. 21/66

Longest Winless Streak
Over-all ... 19 Feb. 26-
Apr. 3/77
(18 losses, 1 tie)
Home ... 10 Dec. 11/85-
Jan. 18/86
(9 losses, 1 tie)

Away ... 26 Dec. 15/76-
Apr. 3/77
(23 losses, 3 ties)
Most Shutouts, Season ... 13 1953-54 (70)
Most. PIM, Season ... 2,393 1985-86 (80)
Most Goals, Game ... 15 Jan. 23/44
(NYR at Det. 15)

Individual

Most Seasons	25	Gordie Howe
Most Games	1,687	Gordie Howe
Most Goals, Career	786	Gordie Howe
Most Assists, Career	1,023	Gordie Howe
Most Points, Career	1,809	Gordie Howe (786 goals, 1,023 assists)
Most PIM, Career	1,643	Gordie Howe
Most Shutouts, Career	85	Terry Sawchuk

Longest Consecutive
Games Streak ... 548 Alex Delvecchio
(Dec. 13/56-
Nov. 11/64)
Most Goals, Season ... 65 Steve Yzerman
(1988-89)
Most Assists, Season ... 90 Steve Yzerman
(1988-89)
Most Points, Season ... 155 Steve Yzerman
(1988-89)
(65 goals, 90 assists)
Most PIM, Season ... 398 Bob Probert
(1987-88)
Most Points, Defenseman
Season ... 74 Reed Larson
(1982-83)
(22 goals, 52 assists)
Most Points, Center,
Season ... 155 Steve Yzerman
(1988-89)
(65 goals, 90 assists)
Most Points, Right Wing,
Season ... 103 Gordie Howe
(1968-69)
(44 goals, 59 assists)
Most Points, Left Wing,
Season ... 105 John Ogrodnick
(1984-85)
(55 goals, 50 assists)

Most Points, Rookie,
Season ... 87 Steve Yzerman
(1983-84)
(39 goals, 48 assists)
Most Shutouts, Season ... 12 Terry Sawchuk
(1951-52; 1954-55);
Glenn Hall
(1955-56)
Most Goals, Game ... 6 Syd Howe
(Feb. 3/44)
Most Assists, Game ... *7 Billy Taylor
(Mar. 16/47)
Most Points, Game ... 7 Carl Liscombe
(Nov. 5/42)
Don Grosso
(Feb. 3/44)
Billy Taylor
(Mar. 16/47)

* NHL Record

Captains' History

Art Duncan, 1926-27; Reg Noble, 1927-28 to 1929-30; George Hay, 1930-31; Carson Cooper, 1931-32; Larry Aurie, 1932-33; Herbie Lewis, 1933-34; Ebbie Goodfellow, 1934-35; Doug Young, 1935-36 to 1937-38; Ebbie Goodfellow, 1938-39 to 1941-42; Sid Abel, 1942-43; Mud Bruneteau, Bill Hollett (co-captains), 1943-44; Bill Hollett, 1944-45; Bill Hollett, Sid Abel, 1945-46; Sid Abel, 1946-47 to 1951-52; Ted Lindsay, 1952-53 to 1955-56; Red Kelly, 1957-58; Gordie Howe, 1958-59 to 1961-62; Alex Delvecchio, 1962-63 to 1973-74; Marcel Dionne, 1974-75; Danny Grant, Terry Harper, 1975-76; Danny Grant, Dennis Polonich, 1976-77; Dan Maloney, Dennis Hextall, 1977-78; Dennis Hextall, Nick Libett, Paul Woods, 1978-79; Dale McCourt, 1979-80; Errol Thompson, Reed Larson, 1980-81; Reed Larson, 1981-82; Danny Gare, 1982-83 to 1985-86; Steve Yzerman, 1986-87 to date.

All-time Record vs. Other Clubs

Regular Season

	At Home							On Road							Total						
	GP	W	L	T	GF	GA	PTS	GP	W	L	T	GF	GA	PTS	GP	W	L	T	GF	GA	PTS
Boston	275	148	75	52	915	692	348	276	83	150	43	728	976	209	551	231	225	95	1643	1668	557
Buffalo	43	22	17	4	161	132	48	42	5	30	7	102	191	17	85	27	47	11	263	323	65
Calgary	34	18	11	5	137	115	41	34	7	22	5	101	159	19	68	25	33	10	238	274	60
Chicago	297	183	87	27	1024	732	393	298	110	141	47	817	903	267	595	293	228	74	1841	1635	660
Edmonton	19	6	12	1	73	94	13	19	5	11	3	81	106	13	38	11	23	4	154	200	26
Hartford	19	6	7	6	66	59	18	19	5	13	1	51	80	11	38	11	20	7	117	139	29
Los Angeles	54	23	24	7	217	200	53	54	12	32	10	157	233	34	108	35	56	17	374	433	87
Minnesota	72	34	26	12	283	248	80	73	20	41	12	209	290	52	145	54	67	24	492	538	132
Montreal	271	124	94	53	769	695	301	270	62	165	43	602	957	167	541	186	259	96	1371	1652	468
New Jersey	29	17	10	2	125	96	36	29	8	14	7	79	107	23	58	25	24	9	204	203	59
NY Islanders	34	18	14	2	125	113	38	34	12	20	2	95	136	26	68	30	34	4	220	249	64
NY Rangers	274	156	74	44	962	674	356	273	86	130	57	696	839	229	547	242	204	101	1658	1513	585
Philadelphia	48	21	18	9	167	160	51	48	10	28	10	138	196	30	96	31	46	19	305	356	81
Pittsburgh	54	34	10	10	214	152	78	54	13	38	3	152	238	29	108	47	48	13	366	390	107
Quebec	19	11	7	1	80	68	23	19	5	12	2	64	86	12	38	16	19	3	144	154	35
St. Louis	73	28	34	11	253	241	67	72	18	44	10	189	272	46	145	46	78	21	442	513	113
Toronto	291	169	79	43	857	707	347	291	93	154	44	762	962	230	582	245	250	87	1619	1669	577
Vancouver	40	23	11	6	172	121	52	41	13	25	4	127	173	30	81	35	34	12	299	294	82
Washington	35	14	11	10	128	103	38	35	12	19	4	105	137	28	70	26	30	14	233	240	66
Winnipeg	21	11	7	3	86	81	25	21	7	7	7	69	73	21	42	18	14	10	155	154	46
Defunct Club	141	76	40	25	429	307	177	141	49	63	29	363	375	127	282	125	103	54	792	682	304

Totals 2143 1125 685 333 7243 5790 2583 2143 634 1157 352 5687 7489 1620 4286 1759 1842 685 12930 13279 4203

Playoffs

	Series	W	L	GP	W	L	T	GF	GA	Last Mtg.	Round	Result
Boston	7	3	4	33	14	19	0	98	96	1957	SF	L 1-4
Calgary	1	1	0	2	2	0	0	8	5	1978	PR	W 2-0
Chicago	12	5	7	60	27	33	0	171	187	1989	DSF	L 2-4
Edmonton	2	0	2	10	2	8	0	26	39	1988	CF	L 1-4
Montreal	12	5	7	62	29	33	0	149	161	1978	QF	L 1-4
NY Rangers	5	4	1	23	13	10	0	57	49	1950	F	W 4-3
St. Louis	3	1	2	16	8	8	0	53	51	1991	DF	L 3-4
Toronto	22	11	11	110	56	54	0	291	287	1988	DSF	W 4-2
Defunct Clubs	4	3	1	10	7	2	1	21	13			
Totals	68	35	33	326	158	167	1	874	888			

Abbreviations: Round: F Final; **CF** conference final; **DF** division final; **DSF** division semi-final; **SF** semi-final; **QF** quarter-final. **PR** preliminary round. **GA** goals against; **GF** goals for.

Playoff Results 1991-87

Year	Round	Opponent	Result	GF	GA
1991	DSF	St. Louis	L 3-4	20	24
1989	DSF	Chicago	L 2-4	18	25
1988	CF	Edmonton	L 1-4	16	23
	DF	St. Louis	W 4-1	21	14
	DSF	Toronto	W 4-2	32	20
1987	CF	Edmonton	L 1-4	10	16
	DF	Toronto	W 4-3	20	18
	DSF	Chicago	W 4-0	15	6

1990-91 Results

		Home				Away	
Oct.	10	Calgary	6-5	Oct.	4	New Jersey	3-3
	12	Hartford	4-2		6	Washington	4-6
	16	Chicago	3-2		7	Philadelphia	2-7
	18	Montreal	5-2		13	Toronto	3-3
	23	Vancouver	6-0		20	Quebec*	3-5
	26	Minnesota	8-6		27	Minnesota	2-2
	30	St Louis	2-5	Nov.	3	Montreal	2-5
Nov.	1	Toronto	5-4		6	Vancouver	3-6
	14	Chicago	2-3		8	Los Angeles	1-5
	19	Washington	2-3		10	St Louis	1-6
	21	Minnesota	4-3		17	Toronto	8-4
	23	St Louis	5-3		29	Chicago	5-1
	27	Los Angeles	4-3	Dec.	2	Buffalo	3-3
Dec.	1	Chicago*	4-3		8	St Louis	1-2
	4	Boston	4-5		15	Philadelphia*	3-1
	7	St Louis	3-6		16	Pittsburgh	1-4
	11	Buffalo	8-3		22	Winnipeg	5-2
	13	Quebec	5-2		23	Chicago	2-3
	18	Philadelphia	3-1		28	Pittsburgh	0-5
	20	Winnipeg	3-1	Jan.	4	Edmonton	2-3
	31	Chicago	0-4		5	Calgary	0-7
Jan.	2	Minnesota	6-2		12	NY Islanders	2-2
	9	Edmonton	5-3		14	Boston	1-6
	11	NY Rangers	6-3		16	Buffalo	3-5
	22	Washington	1-2		26	St Louis	4-5
	25	St Louis	4-9		30	Minnesota	2-5
	28	New Jersey	2-6	Feb.	2	Toronto	5-2
Feb.	1	Toronto	4-1		9	Minnesota	5-6
	4	Los Angeles	4-6		13	Hartford	2-6
	8	NY Islanders	8-4		17	Chicago*	3-3
	12	Winnipeg	6-1		19	Calgary	4-4
	16	Minnesota*	0-3		22	Edmonton	5-5
	25	Toronto	5-4		23	Vancouver	2-5
	27	Montreal	5-4	Mar.	9	Minnesota*	2-6
Mar.	1	New Jersey	1-6		10	St Louis	4-1
	5	Quebec	6-3		13	NY Rangers	4-1
	7	NY Islanders	2-0		14	Hartford	2-4
	22	Toronto	1-3		16	Boston*	5-3
	27	Pittsburgh	4-7		23	Toronto	1-4
	30	NY Rangers*	6-5		31	Chicago	1-5

* Denotes afternoon game.

Entry Draft Selections
1991-77

1991
Pick
10 Martin Lapointe
32 Jamie Pushor
54 Chris Osgood
76 Michael Knuble
98 Dimitri Motkov
142 Igor Malykhin
186 Jim Bermingham
208 Jason Firth
230 Bart Turner
252 Andrew Miller

1990
Pick
3 Keith Primeau
45 Viacheslav Kozlov
66 Stewart Malgunas
87 Tony Burns
108 Claude Barthe
129 Jason York
150 Wes McCauley
171 Anthony Gruba
192 Travis Tucker
213 Brett Larson
234 John Hendry

1989
Pick
11 Mike Sillinger
32 Bob Boughner
53 Niklas Lidstrom
74 Sergei Fedorov
95 Shawn McCosh
116 Dallas Drake
137 Scott Zygulski
158 Andy Suhy
179 Bob Jones
200 Greg Bignell
204 Rick Judson
221 Vladimir Konstantivov
242 Joseph Frederick
246 Jason Glickman

1988
Pick
17 Kory Kocur
38 Serge Anglehart
47 Guy Dupuis
59 Petr Hrbek
80 Sheldon Kennedy
143 Kelly Hurd
164 Brian McCormack
185 Jody Praznik
206 Glen Goodall
227 Darren Colbourne
248 Donald Stone

1987
Pick
11 Yves Racine
32 Gordon Kruppke
41 Bob Wilkie
52 Dennis Holland
74 Mark Reimer
95 Radomir Brazda
116 Sean Clifford
137 Mike Gober
158 Kevin Scott
179 Mikko Haapakoski
200 Darin Bannister
221 Craig Quinlan
242 Tomas Jansson

1986
Pick
1 Joe Murphy
22 Adam Graves
43 Derek Mayer
64 Tim Cheveldae
85 Johan Garpenlov
106 Jay Stark
127 Per Djoos
148 Dean Morton
169 Marc Potvin
190 Scott King
211 Tom Bissett
232 Peter Ekroth

1985
Pick
8 Brent Fedyk
29 Jeff Sharples
50 Steve Chiasson
71 Mark Gowans
92 Chris Luongo
113 Randy McKay
134 Thomas Bjur
155 Mike Luckraft
176 Rob Schenna
197 Eerik Hamalainen
218 Bo Svanberg
239 Mikael Lindman

1984
Pick
7 Shawn Burr
28 Doug Houda
49 Milan Chalupa
91 Mats Lundstrom
112 Randy Hansch
133 Stefan Larsson
152 Lars Karlsson
154 Urban Nordin
175 Bill Shibicky
195 Jay Rose
216 Tim Kaiser
236 Tom Nickolau

1983
Pick
4 Steve Yzerman
25 Lane Lambert
46 Bob Probert
68 David Korol
86 Petr Klima
88 Joey Kocur
106 Chris Pusey
126 Bob Pierson
146 Craig Butz
166 Dave Sikorski
186 Stuart Grimson
206 Jeff Frank
226 Charles Chiatto

1982
Pick
17 Murray Craven
23 Yves Courteau
44 Carmine Vani
66 Craig Coxe
86 Brad Shaw
107 Claude Vilgrain
128 Greg Hudas
149 Pat Lahey
170 Gary Cullen
191 Brent Meckling
212 Mike Stern
233 Shaun Reagan

1981
Pick
23 Claude Loiselle
44 Corrado Micalef
86 Larry Trader
107 Gerard Gallant
128 Greg Stefan
149 Rick Zombo
170 Don Leblanc
191 Robert Nordmark

1980
Pick
11 Mike Blaisdell
46 Mark Osborne
88 Mike Corrigan
109 Wayne Crawford
130 Mike Braun
151 John Beukeboom
172 Dave Miles
193 Brian Rorabeck

1979
Pick
3 Mike Foligno
45 Jody Gage
46 Boris Fistric
66 John Ogrodnick
87 Joe Paterson
108 Carmen Cirella

1978
Pick
9 Willie Huber
12 Brent Peterson
28 Glenn Hicks
31 Al Jensen
53 Doug Derkson
62 Bjorn Skaare
78 Ted Nolan
95 Sylvain Locas
112 Wes George
129 John Barrett
146 Jim Malazdrewicz
163 Goeff Shaw
178 Carl Van Harrewyn
194 Ladislav Svozil
208 Tom Bailey
219 Larry Lozinski
224 Randy Betty
226 Brian Crawley
228 Doug Feasby

1977
Pick
1 Dale McCourt
37 Rick Vasko
55 John Hilworth
73 Jim Korn
91 Jim Baxter
109 Randy Wilson
125 Raymond Roy
141 Kip Churchill
155 Lance Gatoni
163 Robert Plumb
170 Alain Belanger
175 Dean Willers
178 Roland Cloutier
181 Edward Hill
184 Val James
185 Grant Morin

Club Directory

Joe Louis Sports Arena
600 Civic Center Drive
Detroit, Michigan 48226
Phone **(313) 567-7333**
GM: (313) 567-7301
FAX PR: 313/567-0296
ENVOY ID
Front Office: DRW. GM
Public
Relations: DRW. PR
Capacity: 19,275

Owner and President	Michael Ilitch
Owner and Secretary-Treasurer	Marian Ilitch
Executive Vice-President	James Lites
General Counsel	Denise Ilitch Lites
Sr. Vice-President	Jim Devellano
General Manager and Head Coach	Bryan Murray
Asst. General Manager & Hockey Operations Director	Nick Polano
Associate Coach	Doug MacLean
Assistant Coach	Dave Lewis
Goaltending Consultant	Phil Myre
Director of Pro Scouting	Dan Belisle
Director of Amateur Scouting	Ken Holland
Director of U.S. Scouting	Billy Dea
Western Hockey League Scout	Wayne Meier
Western U.S. Scout	Chris Coury
Eastern U.S. Scout	Mike Addesa
Northern Ontario Scout	Dave Polano
Eastern Canada Scout	John Stanton
European Scouts	Hakan Andersson, Vladimir Havluj
Controller	Scott Fisher
Director of Marketing	Jeff Cogen
Director of Advertising Sales	Terry Murphy
Director of Corporate Sales	Gary Vitto
Director of Broadcast Sales	Tony Nagorsen
Director of Public Relations	Bill Jamieson
Secretary to General Manager	Nancy Beard
Box Office Manager	Bob Kerlin
Public Relations Coordinator	Howard Berlin
P.R. Assistants	Marilyn Rowe, Kathy Best
Athletic Therapist	John Wharton
Athletic Trainer	Mark Brennan
Assistant Trainer	Larry Wasylon
Team Physicians	Dr. John Finley, D.O., Dr. David Collon, M.D.
Team Dentist	Dr. C.J. Regula, D.M.D.
Team Opthamologist	Dr. Charles Slater, M.D.
Accounting Assistant	Cathy Witzke
Largest crowd	21,019* Nov. 25, 1983; Detroit 5, Pittsburgh 2
Location of Press Box, Radio-TV Booths	Jefferson Ave. side of Arena, top of seats
Location of Media Hospitality Lounge	First floor, in hallway, near Red Wings' dressing room, Atwater St. side of Arena.
Dimensions of Rink	200 feet by 85 feet; S.A.R. Plastic extends above boards all around rink
Club Colors	Red and White
Radio Flagship Station	WJR-AM, 760
TV Stations	Pro-Am Sports System (PASS-Cable) WKBD-TV (Channel 50)
Radio Announcer	Bruce Martyn, Paul Woods
TV Announcers	Dave Strader, Mickey Redmond

*NHL Record

Retired Numbers

6	Larry Aurie	1927-1939
9	Gordie Howe	1946-1971

Coaching History

Art Duncan, 1926-27; Jack Adams, 1927-28 to 1946-47; Tommy Ivan, 1947-48 to 1953-54; Jimmy Skinner, 1954-55 to 1956-57; Jimmy Skinner and Sid Abel, 1957-58; Sid Abel, 1958-59 to 1967-68; Bill Gadsby, 1968-69; Bill Gadsby and Sid Abel, 1969-70; Ned Harkness and Doug Barkley, 1970-71; Doug Barkley and John Wilson, 1971-72; John Wilson, 1972-73; Ted Garvin and Alex Delvecchio, 1973-74; Alex Delvecchio, 1974-75; Doug Barkley and Alex Delvecchio, 1975-76; Alex Delvecchio and Larry Wilson, 1976-77; Bobby Kromm, 1977-78 to 1978-79; Bobby Kromm and Ted Lindsay, 1979-80; Ted Lindsay and Wayne Maxner, 1980-81; Wayne Maxner and Billy Dea, 1981-82; Nick Polano, 1982-83 to 1984-85; Harry Neale and Brad Park, 1985-86; Jacques Demers, 1986-87 to 1989-90; Bryan Murray, 1990-91 to date.

Coach and General Manager

MURRAY, BRYAN CLARENCE
Coach and General Manager, Detroit Red Wings.
Born in Shawville, Que., December 5, 1942.

Appointed coach and G.M. of the Red Wings in the summer of 1990, Bryan Murray came to Detroit after nine seasons behind the bench in Washington.

A graduate of McGill, his first major coaching experience came in junior hockey when he took over the last-place Regina Pats and carried the team to the WHL championship in 1979-80. His one-year success in Regina translated into a professional coaching job in 1980-81 with the Capitals' AHL farm team, the Hershey Bears, whom he guided to their best season in over 40 years. That first-year effort netted him the Hockey News Minor League Coach-of-the-Year honors. Although he began the 1981-82 campaign in Hershey, Murray was promoted to Washington and the NHL on November 11, 1981.

Coaching Record

Season	Team	Games	Regular Season W	L	T	%	Playoffs Games	W	L	%
1979-80	Regina (WHL)	72	47	24	1	.660	22	16	6	.727
1980-81	Hershey (AHL)	80	47	24	9	.644	10	6	4	.600
1981-82	Washington (NHL)	76	25	28	13	.477	....			
1982-83	Washington (NHL)	80	39	25	16	.588	4	1	3	.250
1983-84	Washington (NHL)	80	48	27	5	.631	8	4	4	.500
1984-85	Washington (NHL)	80	46	25	9	.631	5	2	3	.400
1985-86	Washington (NHL)	80	50	23	7	.669	9	5	4	.556
1986-87	Washington (NHL)	80	38	32	10	.538	7	3	4	.429
1987-88	Washington (NHL)	80	38	33	9	.531	14	7	7	.500
1988-89	Washington (NHL)	80	41	29	10	.575	6	2	4	.333
1989-90	Washington (NHL)	46	18	24	4	.435	....			
1990-91	Detroit (NHL)	80	34	38	8	.475	7	3	4	.429
	NHL Totals	752	377	284	91	.562	60	27	33	.450

Edmonton Oilers

1990-91 Results: 37w-37L-6T 80PTS. Third, Smythe Division

Year-by-Year Record

Season	GP	Home W	L	T	Road W	L	T	Overall W	L	T	GF	GA	Pts.	Finished	Playoff Result
1990-91	80	22	15	3	15	22	3	37	37	6	272	272	80	3rd, Smythe Div.	Lost Conference Final
1989-90	**80**	**23**	**11**	**6**	**15**	**17**	**8**	**38**	**28**	**14**	**315**	**283**	**90**	**2nd, Smythe Div.**	**Won Stanley Cup**
1988-89	80	21	16	3	17	18	5	38	34	8	325	306	84	3rd, Smythe Div.	Lost Div. Semi-Final
1987-88	**80**	**28**	**8**	**4**	**16**	**17**	**7**	**44**	**25**	**11**	**363**	**288**	**99**	**2nd, Smythe Div.**	**Won Stanley Cup**
1986-87	**80**	**29**	**6**	**5**	**21**	**18**	**1**	**50**	**24**	**6**	**372**	**284**	**106**	**1st, Smythe Div.**	**Won Stanley Cup**
1985-86	80	32	6	2	24	11	5	56	17	7	426	310	119	1st, Smythe Div.	Lost Div. Final
1984-85	**80**	**26**	**7**	**7**	**23**	**13**	**4**	**49**	**20**	**11**	**401**	**298**	**109**	**1st, Smythe Div.**	**Won Stanley Cup**
1983-84	**80**	**31**	**5**	**4**	**26**	**13**	**1**	**57**	**18**	**5**	**446**	**314**	**119**	**1st, Smythe Div.**	**Won Stanley Cup**
1982-83	80	25	9	6	22	12	6	47	21	12	424	315	106	1st, Smythe Div.	Lost Final
1981-82	80	31	5	4	17	12	11	48	17	15	417	295	111	1st, Smythe Div.	Lost Div. Semi-Final
1980-81	80	17	13	10	12	22	6	29	35	16	328	327	74	4th, Smythe Div.	Lost Quarter-Final
1979-80	80	17	14	9	11	25	4	28	39	13	301	322	69	4th, Smythe Div.	Lost Prelim. Round

Schedule

	Home			Away	
Oct.	Sun.	6 Los Angeles	**Oct.**	Fri.	4 Calgary
	Sat.	12 Calgary		Tues.	8 Los Angeles
	Wed.	23 Washington		Thur.	10 St Louis
	Sat.	26 Vancouver		Tues.	15 Detroit
	Wed.	30 St Louis		Thur.	17 Chicago
Nov.	Fri.	1 New Jersey		Sat.	19 NY Islanders
	Wed.	6 NY Islanders		Sun.	20 NY Rangers
	Sat.	23 Winnipeg		Sun.	27 Vancouver
	Wed.	27 Chicago	**Nov.**	Sun.	3 Vancouver*
	Fri.	29 San Jose		Fri.	8 San Jose
Dec.	Sun.	1 Vancouver*		Sat.	9 Los Angeles
	Tues.	3 Pittsburgh		Wed.	13 Pittsburgh
	Sun.	8 San Jose		Thur.	14 Philadelphia
	Sat.	14 Winnipeg		Sat.	16 Quebec
	Sun.	15 Detroit		Mon.	18 Montreal
	Mon.	23 Calgary	**Dec.**	Fri.	6 Winnipeg
	Sat.	28 Los Angeles		Tues.	10 Vancouver
	Sun.	29 Montreal		Thur.	12 San Jose
Jan.	Sun.	5 Calgary		Wed.	18 Toronto
	Wed.	15 Vancouver		Fri.	20 Buffalo
	Tues.	21 San Jose		Sat.	21 Boston
	Thur.	23 NY Rangers	**Jan.**	Thur.	2 Los Angeles
	Wed.	29 Chicago		Sat.	4 Calgary
	Fri.	31 Hartford		Wed.	8 Winnipeg
Feb.	Sun.	2 Quebec*		Fri.	10 Buffalo
	Wed.	5 Montreal		Sat.	11 Detroit
	Fri.	7 NY Islanders		Mon.	13 Minnesota
	Wed.	19 Los Angeles		Sat.	25 San Jose
	Fri.	21 Boston		Tues.	28 Vancouver
	Sun.	23 Buffalo	**Feb.**	Tues.	11 Minnesota
	Wed.	26 Winnipeg		Thur.	13 Hartford
	Fri.	28 Philadelphia		Sat.	15 Philadelphia*
Mar.	Wed.	4 Toronto		Sun.	16 Toronto
	Fri.	6 St Louis	**Mar.**	Sun.	1 Winnipeg*
	Wed.	11 New Jersey		Tues.	17 Pittsburgh
	Sat.	14 Hartford		Thur.	19 New Jersey
	Fri.	27 Minnesota		Sat.	21 Boston*
	Sun.	29 Los Angeles		Sun.	22 Washington*
Apr.	Fri.	3 Winnipeg		Tues.	24 Calgary
	Sun.	5 San Jose*		Tues.	31 Calgary

* Denotes afternoon game.

Home Starting Times:
Weeknights . . . . 7:35 p.m.
Saturdays and Sundays . . . . 6:05 p.m.
Matinees . . . . 2:05 p.m.

Franchise date: June 22, 1979

 13th NHL Season

Esa Tikkanen, Edmonton's specialty-teams sparkplug, led all Oilers in scoring in 1990-91.

1991-92 Player Personnel

FORWARDS	HT	WT	S	Place of Birth	Date	1990-91 Club
ALLISON, Scott	6-4	194	L	St. Boniface, Man.	4/22/72	P'Albert-Portland
ANDERSON, Glenn	6-1	190	L	Vancouver, B.C.	10/2/60	Edmonton
ANTOS, Dean	5-11	175	L	Killam, Alta.	5/20/67	Northern Michigan
BEAULIEU, Nicolas	6-2	200	L	Rimouski, Que.	8/19/68	Albany-Phoenix
BERUBE, Craig	6-1	205	L	Calahoo, Alta.	12/17/65	Philadelphia
BLAIN, Joel	6-0	195	L	Malartic, Que.	10/12/71	Hull
BORGO, Richard	5-11	190	R	Thunder Bay, Ont.	9/25/70	Kitchener
BUCHBERGER, Kelly	6-2	210	L	Langenburg, Sask.	12/2/66	Edmonton
CROWLEY, Joe	6-2	195	L	Concord, MA	2/29/72	Boston College
CURRIE, Dan	6-2	195	L	Burlington, Ont.	3/15/68	Edmonton-C. Breton
FISHER, Craig	6-3	180	L	Oshawa, Ont.	6/30/70	Philadelphia-Hershey
GELINAS, Martin	5-11	195	L	Shawinigan, Que.	6/5/70	Edmonton
HAAS, David	6-2	196	L	Toronto, Ont.	6/23/68	Edmonton-Cape Breton
KAPUSTA, Tomas	6-0	187	L	Zlin, Czech.	2/23/67	Cape Breton
KLIMA, Petr	6-0	190	L	Chaomutov, Czech.	12/23/64	Edmonton
LAFORGE, Marc	6-2	210	L	Sudbury, Ont.	1/3/68	Cape Breton
LAMB, Mark	5-9	180	L	Ponteix, Sask.	8/3/64	Edmonton
LINSEMAN, Ken	5-11	190	L	Kingston, Ont.	8/11/58	Edmonton
MacTAVISH, Craig	6-1	195	L	London, Ont.	8/15/58	Edmonton
MELLANBY, Scott	6-1	205	R	Montreal, Que.	6/11/66	Philadelphia
MESSIER, Mark	6-1	210	L	Edmonton, Alta.	1/18/61	Edmonton
MIDDENDORF, Max	6-4	210	R	Syracuse, NY	8/18/67	Edm.-C. Breton-F. Wayne
MURPHY, Joe	6-1	190	L	London, Ont.	10/16/67	Edmonton
PODEIN, Shjon	6-2	200	L	Rochester, MN	3/5/68	Cape Breton
SEMENOV, Anatoli	6-2	190	L	Moscow, USSR	3/5/62	Edmonton
SIM, Trevor	6-2	192	L	Calgary, Alta.	6/9/70	Cape Breton
SIMPSON, Craig	6-2	195	L	London, Ont.	2/15/67	Edmonton
SOBERLAK, Peter	6-2	195	L	Kamloops, B.C.	5/12/69	Cape Breton
SRSEN, Tomas	5-11	180	L	Olomouc, Czech.	8/26/66	Edm.-C. Breton
TIKKANEN, Esa	6-1	200	L	Helsinki, Finland	1/25/65	Edmonton
TISDALE, Tim	6-1	186	L	Shaunavon, Sask.	5/28/68	Cape Breton
VAN ALLEN, Shaun	6-1	200	L	Shaunavon, Sask.	8/29/67	Edmonton-Cape Breton
VIAZMIKIN, Igor	6-1	195	L	Moscow, USSR	1/8/66	Edmonton-Cape Breton-Khimik
WARE, Mike	6-5	208	R	York, Ont.	3/22/67	Cape Breton-Edm.
WRIGHT, Tyler	5-11	175	R	Canora, Sask.	4/6/73	Swift Current

DEFENSEMEN	HT	WT	S	Place of Birth	Date	1990-91 Club
BARBE, Mario	6-1	204	L	Cadillac, Que.	3/17/67	Cape Breton
BAUER, Collin	6-1	180	L	Edmonton, Alta.	9/6/70	Cape Breton
BEUKEBOOM, Jeff	6-4	215	R	Ajax, Ont.	3/28/65	Edmonton
HAWGOOD, Greg	5-10	190	L	Edmonton, Alta.	8/10/68	Maine-Edm.-C. Breton
JOSEPH, Chris	6-2	210	R	Burnaby, B.C.	9/10/69	Cape Breton-Edm.
LEGAULT, Alexandre	6-1	205	R	Chicoutimi, Que.	12/27/71	Boston U-Drummondville
LEROUX, Francois	6-6	221	L	Ste-Adele, Que.	4/18/70	Edm.-Cape Breton
LOWE, Kevin	6-2	195	L	Lachute, Que.	4/15/59	Edmonton
MACIVER, Norm	5-11	180	L	Thunder Bay, Ont.	9/8/64	Bing.-C. Breton-Edm.
MUNI, Craig	6-3	200	L	Toronto, Ont.	7/19/62	Edmonton
SMITH, Geoff	6-3	200	L	Edmonton, Alta.	3/7/69	Edmonton
SMITH, Steve	6-4	215	L	Glasgow, Scotland	4/30/63	Edmonton
SOULES, Jason	6-2	212	L	Hamilton, Ont.	3/14/71	Belleville-Cape Breton
WERENKA, Brad	6-2	204	L	Two Hills, Alta.	2/12/69	Northern Michigan

GOALTENDERS	HT	WT	C	Place of Birth	Date	1990-91 Club
BELOSHEIKIN, Evgeny	5-10	185	L	Sakhalin, USSR	4/17/66	Central Red Army
FUHR, Grant	5-10	186	R	Spruce Grove, Alta.	9/28/62	Edm.-Cape Breton
GREENLAY, Mike	6-3	200	L	Vitoria, Brazil	9/15/68	C. Breton-K'ville
RANFORD, Bill	5-10	170	L	Brandon, Man.	12/14/66	Edmonton
REDDICK, Eldon	5-8	170	L	Halifax, N.S.	10/6/64	Edm.-C. Breton

General Manager's History
Glen Sather, 1979-80 to date.

Coaching History
Glen Sather, 1979-80; Bryan Watson and Glen Sather, 1980-81; Glen Sather, 1981-82 to 1988-89; John Muckler, 1989-90 to 1990-91; Ted Green, 1991-92.

Captains' History
Ron Chipperfield, 1979-80; Lee Fogolin, 1980-81 to 1982-83; Wayne Gretzky, 1983-84 to 1987-88; Mark Messier, 1988-89 to date.

Retired Numbers
3   Al Hamilton   1972-1980

1990-91 Scoring

Regular Season
* rookie

Pos	#	Player	Team	GP	G	A	Pts	+/-	PIM	PP	SH	GW	GT	S	%
L	10	Esa Tikkanen	EDM	79	27	42	69	22	85	3	2	6	0	235	11.5
L	85	Petr Klima	EDM	70	40	28	68	24	113	7	1	5	0	204	19.6
C	11	Mark Messier	EDM	53	12	52	64	15	34	3	1	2	0	109	11.0
R	8	Joe Murphy	EDM	80	27	35	62	2	35	4	1	4	1	141	19.1
L	18	Craig Simpson	EDM	75	30	27	57	8-	66	15	0	5	0	143	21.0
R	9	Glenn Anderson	EDM	74	24	31	55	7-	59	8	0	4	0	193	12.4
D	5	Steve Smith	EDM	77	13	41	54	14	193	4	0	2	0	114	11.4
L	20	Martin Gelinas	EDM	73	20	20	40	7-	34	4	0	1	0	124	16.1
C	13	Ken Linseman	EDM	56	7	29	36	15	94	2	1	0	0	49	14.3
C	14	Craig MacTavish	EDM	80	17	15	32	1-	76	2	6	1	0	113	15.0
L	19	Anatoli Semenov	EDM	57	15	16	31	17	26	3	1	1	0	101	14.9
D	22	Charlie Huddy	EDM	53	5	22	27	4	32	2	0	0	0	90	5.6
C	12	Adam Graves	EDM	76	7	18	25	21-	127	2	0	1	0	126	5.6
D	2	Chris Joseph	EDM	49	5	17	22	3	59	2	0	0	0	74	6.8
D	4	Kevin Lowe	EDM	73	3	13	16	9-	113	0	0	0	0	51	5.9
D	25	Geoff Smith	EDM	59	1	12	13	13	55	0	0	0	0	66	1.5
C	7	Mark Lamb	EDM	37	4	8	12	2-	25	1	0	1	0	41	9.8
D	6	Jeff Beukeboom	EDM	67	3	7	10	6	150	0	0	0	0	48	6.3
D	28	Craig Muni	EDM	76	1	9	10	10	77	0	0	0	0	47	2.1
R	32	Dave Brown	EDM	58	3	4	7	7-	160	0	0	0	0	32	9.4
D	36	Norm Maciver	EDM	21	2	5	7	1	14	1	0	0	0	25	8.0
L	16	Kelly Buchberger	EDM	64	3	1	4	6-	160	0	0	2	0	54	5.6
G	30	Bill Ranford	EDM	60	0	4	4	0	0	0	0	0	0	0	.0
D	35	Francois Leroux	EDM	1	0	2	2	1	0	0	0	0	0	1	.0
L	24	*Brad Aitken	PIT	6	0	1	1	2-	25	0	0	0	0	3	.0
			EDM	3	0	1	1	1-	0	0	0	0	0	0	.0
			TOTAL	9	0	2	2	3-	25	0	0	0	0	3	.0
R	26	*Max Middendorf	EDM	3	1	0	1	0	2	0	0	0	0	1	100.0
R	29	*Igor Vyazmikin	EDM	4	1	0	1	0	0	0	0	1	0	5	20.0
L	26	*David Haas	EDM	5	1	0	1	2-	0	0	0	0	0	4	25.0
C	23	Greg Hawgood	EDM	6	0	1	1	2-	6	0	0	0	0	9	.0
G	1	Kari Takko	MIN	2	0	0	0	0	0	0	0	0	0	0	.0
			EDM	11	0	1	1	0	0	0	0	0	0	0	.0
			TOTAL	13	0	1	1	0	0	0	0	0	0	0	.0
G	33	Eldon Reddick	EDM	2	0	0	0	0	0	0	0	0	0	0	.0
L	15	*Tomas Srsen	EDM	2	0	0	0	0	0	0	0	0	0	0	.0
C	26	*Shaun Van Allen	EDM	2	0	0	0	0	0	0	0	0	0	0	.0
L	15	*Dan Currie	EDM	5	0	0	0	0	0	0	0	0	0	5	.0
G	31	Grant Fuhr	EDM	13	0	0	0	0	0	0	0	0	0	0	.0

Goaltending

No.	Goaltender	GPI	Mins	Avg	W	L	T	EN	SO	GA	SA	S%
31	Grant Fuhr	13	778	3.01	6	4	3	0	1	39	380	.897
30	Bill Ranford	60	3415	3.20	27	27	3	5	0	182	1705	.893
1	Kari Takko	11	529	4.20	4	4	0	0	0	37	279	.867
33	Eldon Reddick	2	120	4.50	0	2	0	0	0	9	59	.847
	Totals	80	4850	3.36	37	37	6	5	1	272	2428	.888

Playoffs

Pos	#	Player	Team	GP	G	A	Pts	+/-	PIM	PP	SH	GW	OT	S	%
L	10	Esa Tikkanen	EDM	18	12	8	20	3	24	3	0	3	2	76	15.8
L	18	Craig Simpson	EDM	18	5	11	16	1	12	1	0	0	0	21	23.8
C	11	Mark Messier	EDM	18	4	11	15	2	16	1	0	0	0	41	9.8
L	85	Petr Klima	EDM	18	7	6	13	1-	16	1	0	3	1	51	13.7
R	9	Glenn Anderson	EDM	18	6	7	13	2-	41	3	0	0	0	43	14.0
L	19	Anatoli Semenov	EDM	12	5	5	10	7-	6	0	0	0	0	28	17.9
D	22	Charlie Huddy	EDM	18	3	7	10	9	10	1	0	0	0	35	8.6
L	20	Martin Gelinas	EDM	18	3	6	9	4	25	0	0	1	0	29	10.3
R	8	Joe Murphy	EDM	15	2	5	7	3	14	1	0	1	0	22	9.1
C	14	Craig MacTavish	EDM	18	3	3	6	3-	20	0	0	1	1	24	12.5
C	12	Adam Graves	EDM	18	2	4	6	7	22	0	0	0	0	48	4.2
C	7	Mark Lamb	EDM	15	0	5	5	4-	20	0	0	0	0	14	.0
D	6	Jeff Beukeboom	EDM	18	1	3	4	5-	28	0	0	0	0	15	6.7
D	36	Norm Maciver	EDM	18	0	4	4	10	18	0	0	0	0	18	.0
L	16	Kelly Buchberger	EDM	12	2	1	3	3-	25	0	0	0	0	12	16.7
D	5	Steve Smith	EDM	18	1	2	3	8-	45	1	0	0	0	30	3.3
D	28	Craig Muni	EDM	18	0	3	3	5	20	0	0	0	0	10	.0
D	4	Kevin Lowe	EDM	14	1	0	1	14	0	0	0	0	0	5	20.0
G	31	Grant Fuhr	EDM	17	0	2	2	0	2	0	0	0	0	0	.0
C	13	Ken Linseman	EDM	2	0	1	1	4-	2	0	0	0	0	3	.0
R	32	Dave Brown	EDM	16	0	1	1	2-	30	0	0	0	0	11	.0
G	30	Bill Ranford	EDM	3	0	0	0	0	0	0	0	0	0	0	.0
D	25	Geoff Smith	EDM	4	0	0	0	0	0	0	0	0	0	0	.0
Pos	**#**	**Player**	**Team**	**GP**	**G**	**A**	**Pts**	**+/-**	**PIM**	**PP**	**SH**	**GW**	**OT**	**S**	**%**

Goaltending

No.	Goaltender	GPI	Mins	Avg	W	L	EN	SO	GA	SA	S%
31	Grant Fuhr	17	1019	3.00	8	7	1	0	51	488	.895
30	Bill Ranford	3	135	3.56	1	2	0	0	8	78	.897
	Totals	18	1156	3.11	9	9	1	0	60	567	.894

Club Records

Team

(Figures in brackets for season records are games played; records for fewest points, wins, ties, losses, goals, goals against are for 70 or more

Most Points .... 119 — 1983-84 (80), 1985-86 (80)
Most Wins .... 57 — 1983-84 (80)
Most Ties .... 16 — 1980-81 (80)
Most Losses .... 39 — 1979-80 (80)
Most Goals .... *446 — 1983-84 (80)
Most Goals Against ...... 327 — 1980-81 (80)
Fewest Points .... 69 — 1979-80 (80)
Fewest Wins .... 28 — 1979-80 (80)
Fewest Ties .... 5 — 1983-84 (80)
Fewest Losses .... 17 — 1981-82 (80), 1985-86 (80)
Fewest Goals .... 272 — 1990-91 (80)
Fewest Goals Against .... 272 — 1990-91 (80)

Longest Winning Streak
- **Over-all** .... 8 — Five times
- **Home** .... 8 — Jan. 19/85-Feb. 22/85; Feb. 24-Apr. 2/86
- **Away** .... 8 — Dec. 9/86-Jan. 17/87

Longest Undefeated Streak
- **Over-all** .... 15 — Oct. 11/84-Nov. 9/84 (12 wins, 3 ties)
- **Home** .... 12 — Oct. 5-Dec. 3/83 (10 wins, 2 ties)
- **Away** .... 9 — Jan. 17-Mar. 2/82 (6 wins, 3 ties); Nov. 23/82-Jan. 18/83 (7 wins, 2 ties)

Longest Losing Streak
- **Over-all** .... 9 — Oct. 21-Nov. 10/90
- **Home** .... 4 — Oct. 21-Nov. 3/90
- **Away** .... 9 — Nov. 25-Dec. 30/80

Longest Winless Streak
- **Over-all** .... 9 — Oct. 21-Nov. 10/90
- **Home** .... 7 — Oct. 24-Nov. 19/80 (3 losses, 4 ties)
- **Away** .... 9 — Nov. 25-Dec. 30/80 (9 losses)

Most Shutouts, Season ..... 4 — 1987-88 (80)
Most PIM, Season ..... 2,173 — 1987-88 (80)
Most Goals, Game .... 13 — Nov. 19/83 (NJ 4 at Edm. 13); Nov. 8/85 (Van. 0 at Edm. 13)

Individual

Most Seasons .... 12 — Kevin Lowe, Mark Messier
Most Games .... 911 — Kevin Lowe
Most Goals, Career ...... 583 — Wayne Gretzky
Most Assists, Career ... 1,086 — Wayne Gretzky
Most Points, Career .... 1,669 — Wayne Gretzky (583 goals, 1,086 assists)
Most PIM, Career ...... 1,278 — Kevin McClelland
Most Shutouts, Career ...... 9 — Grant Fuhr
Longest Consecutive Games Streak .... 420 — Kevin Lowe (Jan. 24/81-Mar. 7/86)
Most Goals, Season ...... *92 — Wayne Gretzky (1981-82)
Most Assists, Season ... *163 — Wayne Gretzky (1985-86)
Most Points, Season .... *215 — Wayne Gretzky (1985-86) (52 goals, 163 assists)
Most PIM, Season .... 286 — Steve Smith (1987-88)
Most Points, Defenseman, Season .... 138 — Paul Coffey (1985-86) (48 goals, 90 assists)
Most Points, Center, Season .... *215 — Wayne Gretzky (1985-86) (52 goals, 163 assists)
Most Points, Right Wing, Season .... 135 — Jari Kurri (1984-85) (71 goals, 64 assists)
Most Points, Left Wing, Season .... 106 — Mark Messier (1982-83) (48 goals, 58 assists)
Most Points, Rookie, Season .... 75 — Jari Kurri (1980-81) (32 goals, 43 assists)
Most Shutouts, Season ..... 4 — Grant Fuhr (1987-88)
Most Goals, Game .... 5 — Wayne Gretzky (Feb. 18/81, Dec. 30/81, Dec. 15/84, Dec. 6/87); Jari Kurri (Nov. 19/83); Pat Hughes (Feb. 3/84)
Most Assists, Game .... *7 — Wayne Gretzky (Feb. 15/80; Dec. 11/85; Feb. 14/86)
Most Points, Game .... 8 — Wayne Gretzky (Nov. 19/83); Paul Coffey (Mar. 14/86); Wayne Gretzky (Jan. 4/84)

* NHL Record.

All-time Record vs. Other Clubs

Regular Season

	At Home							On Road							Total						
	GP	W	L	T	GF	GA	PTS	GP	W	L	T	GF	GA	PTS	GP	W	L	T	GF	GA	PTS
Boston	19	8	8	3	69	62	19	19	2	15	2	51	90	6	38	10	23	5	120	152	25
Buffalo	19	14	3	2	86	49	30	19	8	8	3	78	78	19	38	22	11	5	164	127	49
Calgary	44	24	12	8	202	160	56	44	18	21	5	175	203	41	88	42	33	13	377	363	97
Chicago	19	13	5	1	96	68	27	19	7	10	2	88	86	16	38	20	15	3	184	154	43
Detroit	19	11	5	3	106	81	25	19	12	6	1	94	73	25	38	23	11	4	200	154	50
Hartford	19	14	2	3	90	59	31	19	8	8	3	73	82	19	38	22	10	6	163	141	50
Los Angeles	44	26	9	9	245	174	61	44	20	16	8	211	189	48	88	46	25	17	456	363	109
Minnesota	19	12	1	6	99	61	30	19	9	6	4	69	70	22	38	21	7	10	168	131	52
Montreal	19	11	8	0	70	58	22	19	6	10	3	63	71	15	38	17	18	3	133	129	37
New Jersey	21	12	6	3	112	85	27	22	11	9	2	80	75	24	43	23	15	5	192	160	51
NY Islanders	19	11	5	3	74	59	25	19	4	8	7	81	82	15	38	15	13	10	155	141	40
NY Rangers	19	10	8	1	82	68	21	19	10	6	3	81	80	23	38	20	14	4	163	148	44
Philadelphia	19	11	5	3	74	58	25	19	5	13	1	59	86	11	38	16	18	4	133	144	36
Pittsburgh	19	15	3	1	109	67	31	19	11	7	1	93	71	23	38	26	10	2	202	138	54
Quebec	19	15	4	0	109	57	30	19	11	6	2	93	77	24	38	26	10	2	202	134	54
St. Louis	19	12	5	2	94	76	26	19	10	6	3	88	74	23	38	22	11	5	182	150	49
Toronto	19	13	2	4	108	61	30	19	11	7	1	97	75	23	38	24	9	5	205	136	53
Vancouver	44	33	7	4	237	139	70	44	24	14	6	197	157	54	88	57	21	10	434	296	124
Washington	19	8	7	4	77	67	20	19	8	10	1	74	84	17	38	16	17	5	151	151	37
Winnipeg	42	29	10	3	203	134	61	41	24	14	3	203	168	51	83	53	24	6	406	302	112
Totals	**480**	**302**	**115**	**63**	**2342**	**1643**	**667**	**480**	**219**	**200**	**61**	**2048**	**1971**	**499**	**960**	**521**	**315**	**124**	**4390**	**3614**	**1166**

Playoffs

	Series	W	L	GP	W	L	T	GF	GA	Last Mtg.	Round	Result
Boston	2	2	0	9	8	1	0	41	20	1990	F	W 4-1
Calgary	5	4	1	30	19	11	0	132	96	1991	DSF	W 4-3
Chicago	3	3	0	16	12	4	0	94	56	1990	CF	W 4-2
Detroit	2	2	0	10	8	2	0	39	26	1988	CF	W 4-1
Los Angeles	6	4	2	30	20	10	0	131	109	1991	DF	W 4-2
Minnesota	2	1	1	9	5	4	0	36	30	1991	CF	L 1-4
Montreal	1	1	0	3	3	0	0	15	6	1981	PR	W 3-0
NY Islanders	3	1	2	15	6	9	0	47	58	1984	F	W 4-1
Philadelphia	3	2	1	15	8	7	0	49	44	1987	F	W 4-3
Vancouver	1	1	0	3	3	0	0	17	5	1986	DSF	W 3-0
Winnipeg	6	6	0	26	22	4	0	120	75	1990	DSF	W 4-3
Totals	**34**	**27**	**7**	**164**	**112**	**52**	**0**	**721**	**525**			

Playoff Results 1991-87

Year	Round	Opponent	Result	GF	GA
1991	CF	Minnesota	L 1-4	14	20
	DF	Los Angeles	W 4-2	21	20
	DSF	Calgary	W 4-3	22	20
1990	**F**	**Boston**	**W 4-1**	**20**	**8**
	CF	Chicago	W 4-2	25	20
	DF	Los Angeles	W 4-0	24	10
	DSF	Winnipeg	W 4-3	24	22
1989	DSF	Los Angeles	L 3-4	20	25
1988	**F**	**Boston**	**W 4-0**	**21**	**12**
	CF	Detroit	W 4-1	23	16
	DF	Calgary	W 4-0	18	11
	DSF	Winnipeg	W 4-1	25	17
1987	**F**	**Philadelphia**	**W 4-3**	**22**	**18**
	CF	Detroit	W 4-1	16	10
	DF	Winnipeg	W 4-0	17	9
	DSF	Los Angeles	W 4-1	32	20

Abbreviations: Round: F Final; **CF** conference final; **DF** division final; **DSF** division semi-final; **PR** preliminary round. **GA** goals against; **GF** goals for.

1990-91 Results

Home				Away			
Oct.	6	Winnipeg	3-3	Oct.	11	Los Angeles	5-5
	7	Toronto	3-2		14	Vancouver*	4-5
	16	St Louis	2-5		24	Winnipeg	1-3
	19	Boston	8-1		25	Calgary	2-4
	21	Calgary	1-2	Nov.	6	St Louis	1-2
	28	Washington	0-1		8	Chicago	3-5
	31	Winnipeg	0-1		10	Los Angeles	4-7
Nov.	3	New Jersey	2-5		23	Buffalo	2-3
	14	Vancouver	5-3		24	Toronto	4-1
	16	Buffalo	4-2		27	Pittsburgh	7-3
	18	NY Islanders	3-1		29	Boston	2-4
	20	Chicago	1-3	Dec.	1	Hartford	4-2
Dec.	5	Quebec	3-2		2	Philadelphia	6-3
	7	NY Rangers	4-3		15	Los Angeles	3-8
	9	Calgary	2-3		20	Vancouver	4-7
	12	Vancouver	5-4		22	Calgary	6-2
	18	Los Angeles	4-3		28	Vancouver	5-2
	23	Vancouver	4-3	Jan.	8	Pittsburgh	1-6
	27	Calgary	4-1		9	Detroit	3-5
	30	Hartford	4-3		12	New Jersey*	5-4
Jan.	2	Montreal	0-3		13	Philadelphia	5-3
	4	Detroit	3-2		15	NY Rangers	2-2
	22	Los Angeles	4-2		17	NY Islanders	6-1
	25	NY Rangers	3-4		23	Vancouver	5-6
	30	Vancouver	9-4		27	Winnipeg*	3-2
Feb.	1	Chicago	4-3	Feb.	3	Buffalo	3-2
	11	Pittsburgh	7-5		5	Boston	5-6
	12	St Louis	2-4		6	Hartford	1-5
	14	Los Angeles	2-4		8	Washington	3-6
	22	Detroit	5-5		16	Toronto	2-3
	24	Quebec	6-3		18	New Jersey	4-0
Mar.	1	Minnesota	1-1		20	Minnesota	1-5
	2	Montreal	1-3		27	Calgary	2-4
	8	Philadelphia	5-4	Mar.	5	Winnipeg	5-4
	10	Washington	3-5		6	Minnesota	1-5
	13	NY Islanders	2-1		15	Winnipeg	3-4
	23	Winnipeg	0-3		17	Montreal	4-2
	24	Los Angeles	3-4		19	Quebec	7-6
	29	Calgary	6-5		26	Los Angeles	0-2
	31	Winnipeg	6-3		28	Calgary	4-4

* Denotes afternoon game.

Entry Draft
Selections 1991-79

1991
Pick
12	Tyler Wright
20	Martin Rucinsky
34	Andrew Verner
56	George Breen
78	Mario Nobili
93	Ryan Haggerty
144	David Oliver
166	Gary Kitching
210	Vegar Barlie
232	Evgeny Belosheiken
254	Juha Riihijarvi

1990
Pick
17	Scott Allison
38	Alexandre Legault
59	Joe Crowley
67	Joel Blain
101	Greg Louder
122	Keijo Sailynoja
143	Mike Power
164	Roman Mejzlik
185	Richard Zemlicka
206	Petr Korinek
227	invalid claim
248	Sami Nuutinen

1989
Pick
15	Jason Soules
36	Richard Borgo
78	Josef Beranek
92	Peter White
120	Anatoli Semenov
140	Davis Payne
141	Sergei Yashin
162	Darcy Martini
225	Roman Bozek

1988
Pick
19	Francois Leroux
39	Petro Koivunen
53	Trevor Sim
61	Collin Bauer
82	Cam Brauer
103	Don Martin
124	Len Barrie
145	Mike Glover
166	Shjon Podein
187	Tom Cole
208	Vladimir Zubkov
229	Darin MacDonald
250	Tim Tisdale

1987
Pick
21	Peter Soberlak
42	Brad Werenka
63	Geoff Smith
64	Peter Eriksson
105	Shaun Van Allen
126	Radek Toupal
147	Tomas Srsen
168	Age Ellingsen
189	Gavin Armstrong
210	Mike Tinkham
231	Jeff Pauletti
241	Jesper Duus
252	Igor Viazmikin

1986
Pick
21	Kim Issel
42	Jamie Nichols
63	Ron Shudra
84	Dan Currie
105	David Haas
126	Jim Ennis
147	Ivan Matulik
168	Nicolas Beaulieu
189	Mike Greenlay
210	Matt Lanza
231	Mojmir Bozik
252	Tony Hand

1985
Pick
20	Scott Metcalfe
41	Todd Carnelley
62	Mike Ware
104	Thomas Kapusta
125	Brian Tessier
146	Shawn Tyers
167	Tony Fairfield
188	Kelly Buchberger
209	Mario Barbe
230	Peter Headon
251	John Haley

1984
Pick
21	Selmar Odelein
42	Daryl Reaugh
63	Todd Norman
84	Rich Novak
105	Richard Lambert
106	Emanuel Viveiros
126	Ivan Dornic
147	Heikki Riihijarvi
168	Todd Ewen
209	Joel Curtis
229	Simon Wheeldon
250	Darren Gani

1983
Pick
19	Jeff Beukeboom
40	Mike Golden
60	Mike Flanagan
80	Esa Tikkanen
120	Don Barber
140	Dale Derkatch
160	Ralph Vos
180	Dave Roach
200	Warren Yadlowski
220	John Miner
240	Steve Woodburn

1982
Pick
20	Jim Playfair
41	Steve Graves
62	Brent Loney
83	Jaroslav Pouzar
104	Dwayne Boettger
125	Raimo Summanen
146	Brian Small
167	Dean Clark
188	Ian Wood
209	Grant Dion
230	Chris Smith
251	Jeff Crawford

1981
Pick
8	Grant Fuhr
29	Todd Strueby
71	Paul Houck
92	Phil Drouillard
111	Steve Smith
113	Marc Habscheid
155	Mike Sturgeon
176	Miloslav Horava
197	Gord Sherven

1980
Pick
6	Paul Coffey
48	Shawn Babcock
69	Jari Kurri
90	Walt Poddubny
111	Mike Winther
132	Andy Moog
153	Rob Polmantuin
174	Lars-Gunnar Petersson

1979
Pick
21	Kevin Lowe
48	Mark Messier
69	Glenn Anderson
84	Max Kostovich
105	Mike Toal
126	Blair Barnes

Club Directory

Northlands Coliseum
Edmonton, Alberta T5B 4M9
Phone **403/474-8561**
Ticketing 403/471-2191
FAX 403/477-9625
ENVOY ID   OILERS.GM
             OILERS.PR

Capacity: 17,313 (standing 190)

Owner/Governor	Peter Pocklington
Alternate Governor	Glen Sather
General Counsel	Bob Lloyd, Gary Frohlich
President/General Manager	Glen Sather
Exec. Vice-President/Assistant G.M.	Bruce MacGregor
Coach	Ted Green
Assistant Coaches	Ron Low, Kevin Primeau
Director of Player Personnel/Chief Scout	Barry Fraser
Hockey Operations	Kevin Prendergast
Scouting Staff	Ace Bailey, Ed Chadwick, Lorne Davis, Bob Freeman, Harry Howell, Jan Slepicka
Executive Secretary	Betsy Dolinsky
Receptionist/Secretary	Lori Willoughby

Medical and Training Staff
Athletic Trainer/Therapist	Ken Lowe
Athletic Trainer	Barrie Stafford
Assistant Trainer	Lyle Kulchisky
Massage Therapist	Stewart Poirier
Team Medical Chief of Staff	Dr. Gordon Cameron
Team Orthopedic Surgeon/Director of Glen Sather Sports Medicine Clinic	Dr. David C. Reid
Team Physician	Dr. Don Groot
Team Dentists	Dr. A.H. Sneazwell, Dr. B. Nord
Fitness Consultant	Dr. Art Quinney
Physical Therapy Consultant	Dr. Dave Magee
Sports Psychologist	Dr. Murray Smith

Finance
Vice-President, Finance	Werner Baum
Accountants	Ellie Merrick, Allison Coward, Sandy Westergaard
Executive Secretary	Lisa Colby

Public Relations
Director of Public Relations	Bill Tuele
Coordinator of Publications and Statistics	Steve Knowles
Director of Community Relations/Special Events	Trish Kerr
Public Relations Secretary	Fiona Liew

Marketing
Director of Marketing	Stew MacDonald
Marketing Representative/Properties Mgr.	Darrell Holowaychuk
Marketing Representative	Brad MacGregor
Sales Representative	Dave Semenko
Marketing Secretary	Heather Hansch
Merchandising Clerk	Julia Slade
Warehouse Supervisor	Ray MacDonald

Ticketing
Director of Ticketing Operations	Sheila Stock
Ticketing Operations	Marcia Godwin, Marcella Kinsman, Sheila McCaskill

Retail Sales
Manager – Champions Retail Stores	Skip Krake
Location of Press Boxes	East Side at top (Radio/TV) West Side at top (Media)
Dimensions of Rink	200 feet by 85 feet
Ends of Rink	Herculite extends above boards around rink
Club Colors	Blue, Orange and White
Training Camp Site	Northlands Coliseum, Edmonton, Alberta
Television Channel	CITV (Channel 13) (Cable 8) CBXT TV (Channel 5) (Cable 4)
Radio Station	CFRN (1260 AM)

General Manager

SATHER, GLEN CAMERON
President and General Manager, Edmonton Oilers. Born in High River, Alta., Sept. 2, 1943.

A journeyman left-winger who played for six different teams during his nine-year NHL career, 48-year-old Glen Sather was one of the League's most successful coaches ever before relinquishing his coaching duties on June 12, 1989. He was the 1985-86 Jack Adams Award winner, led his club to four Stanley Cup championships and had a ten-year winning percentage of .629 (442-241-99). His 442 wins place him sixth on the all-time list in regular season wins. In addition, Sather led his team to 89 play-off victories, fourth on the all-time list. His .706 winning percentage in the playoffs ranks him first.

After closing out his NHL playing career in 1975-76 with an 80-113-193 scoring mark in 660 games, Sather jumped to the Oilers in the World Hockey Association, where he enjoyed his best and last season as a player with totals of 19-34-53 in 81 games. Midway through that 1976-77 campaign, on January 27, 1977, he also assumed the Edmonton coaching duties and led his team to the first of its 11 straight WHA and NHL playoff appearances. Three years later, when the club entered the NHL, Sather took on the added responsibilities of Oilers' president and general manager, which he currently maintains.

NHL Coaching Record

			Regular Season				Playoffs			
Season	Team	Games	W	L	T	%	Games	W	L	%
1979-80	Edmonton (NHL)	80	28	39	13	.431	3	0	3	.000
1980-81	Edmonton (NHL)	62	25	26	11	.492	9	5	4	.555
1981-82	Edmonton (NHL)	80	48	17	15	.694	5	2	3	.400
1982-83	Edmonton (NHL)	80	47	21	12	.663	16	11	5	.687
1983-84	Edmonton (NHL)	80	57	18	5	.744	19	15	4	.789*
1984-85	Edmonton (NHL)	80	49	20	11	.681	18	15	3	.833*
1985-86	Edmonton (NHL)	80	56	17	7	.744	10	6	4	.600
1986-87	Edmonton (NHL)	80	50	24	6	.663	21	16	5	.762*
1987-88	Edmonton (NHL)	80	44	25	11	.619	18	16	2	.889*
1988-89	Edmonton (NHL)	80	38	34	8	.538	7	3	4	.429
	NHL Totals	**782**	**442**	**241**	**99**	**.629**	**126**	**89**	**37**	**.706**

* Stanley Cup win

Coach

GREEN, TED
Coach, Edmonton Oilers. Born in Eriksdale, Man., March 23, 1940.

Ted Green became the fourth coach of the Edmonton Oilers on June 27, 1991, succeeding John Muckler behind the bench of the five-time Stanley Cup champions. In his playing/coaching career, Green has played a vital role on twelve championship teams. A member of the Memorial Cup-winning Winnipeg Braves in 1959, Green established himself as a steady, "stay-at-home" defenseman in the NHL with the Boston Bruins, earning two All-Star berths and winning the Stanley Cup in 1972.

In 1973, Green joined the WHA, where he added three Avco Cup championship rings to his collection. After retiring as a player, Green coached the Carman Hornets to the Manitoba Intermediate championship. In 1981, Green joined the Oilers' organization as an assistant coach and has been a part of each of the Oilers' Stanley Cup victories. Green also served as an assistant coach for the Team Canada squad that captured the Canada Cup in 1984. Following a one-year sabbatical from the Oilers in 1986, Green rejoined the team in 1987 and was named co-coach in the 1989-90 season.

Hartford Whalers

1990-91 Results: 31w-38L-11T 73PTS. Fourth, Adams Division

Schedule

Home		Away	
Oct.	Tues. 8 Montreal	**Oct.**	Sat. 5 Quebec
	Sat. 12 NY Rangers		Mon. 14 Montreal
	Sat. 19 Buffalo		Wed. 16 Winnipeg
	Wed. 23 San Jose		Sun. 27 Buffalo
	Sat. 26 Chicago	**Nov.**	Fri. 1 Detroit
	Wed. 30 Los Angeles		Sat. 2 Pittsburgh
Nov.	Wed. 6 Calgary		Sat. 9 St Louis
	Tues. 12 Quebec		Sun. 10 Chicago
	Thur. 14 Montreal		Sun. 17 Toronto
	Sat. 16 Boston		Fri. 22 New Jersey
	Sat. 23 Washington		Mon. 25 Quebec
	Sat. 30 Montreal		Wed. 27 Philadelphia
Dec.	Wed. 4 Toronto	**Dec.**	Sun. 1 Boston
	Sat. 7 Buffalo		Fri. 13 Buffalo
	Sat. 14 NY Rangers		Sat. 21 Montreal
	Tues. 17 NY Islanders		Thur. 26 Boston
	Thur. 19 New Jersey		Sat. 28 Quebec
	Mon. 23 Buffalo	**Jan.**	Thur. 9 NY Islanders
	Sun. 29 NY Islanders		Sat. 11 Montreal
Jan.	Thur. 2 Quebec		Thur. 16 Boston
	Sat. 4 Washington		Sun. 26 Montreal*
	Wed. 15 Boston		Fri. 31 Edmonton
	Tues. 21 Winnipeg	**Feb.**	Sat. 1 Vancouver
	Sat. 25 Boston*		Tues. 4 San Jose
	Tues. 28 Minnesota		Thur. 6 Los Angeles
Feb.	Sun. 9 Minnesota*		Sat. 15 New Jersey*
	Tues. 11 Buffalo		Sun. 16 Buffalo
	Thur. 13 Edmonton		Thur. 27 Pittsburgh
	Wed. 19 Montreal		Sat. 29 Minnesota*
	Sat. 22 Quebec*	**Mar.**	Sun. 1 NY Rangers
	Sun. 23 Detroit*		Mon. 9 Quebec
	Tues. 25 St Louis		Fri. 13 Winnipeg
Mar.	Tues. 3 Boston		Sat. 14 Edmonton
	Thur. 5 Quebec		Mon. 16 Calgary
	Sat. 7 Vancouver		Wed. 18 Vancouver
	Wed. 11 Los Angeles		Tues. 24 Washington
	Sat. 21 San Jose		Thur. 26 St Louis
	Sun. 22 Pittsburgh		Sun. 29 Buffalo
	Sat. 28 Chicago	**Apr.**	Thur. 2 Philadelphia
Apr.	Sat. 4 Philadelphia*		Sun. 5 Boston

* Denotes afternoon game.

Home Starting Times:
Weeknights and Saturdays .... 7:35 p.m.
Sundays .... 7:05 p.m.
Matinees .... 1:35 p.m.
Except Nov. 30 .... 8:05 p.m.

Franchise date: June 22, 1979

13th NHL Season

Paul Cyr rebounded from a serious knee injury that kept him out of action for two seasons to appear in 70 games for the Whalers.

Year-by-Year Record

Season	GP	Home W	Home L	Home T	Road W	Road L	Road T	Overall W	Overall L	Overall T	GF	GA	Pts.	Finished	Playoff Result
1990-91	80	18	16	6	13	22	5	31	38	11	238	276	73	4th, Adams Div.	Lost Div. Semi-Final
1989-90	80	17	18	5	21	15	4	38	33	9	275	268	85	4th, Adams Div.	Lost Div. Semi-Final
1988-89	80	21	17	2	16	21	3	37	38	5	299	290	79	4th, Adams Div.	Lost Div. Semi-Final
1987-88	80	21	14	5	14	24	2	35	38	7	249	267	77	4th, Adams Div.	Lost Div. Semi-Final
1986-87	80	26	9	5	17	21	2	43	30	7	287	270	93	1st, Adams Div.	Lost Div. Semi-Final
1985-86	80	21	17	2	19	19	2	40	36	4	332	302	84	4th, Adams Div.	Lost Div. Final
1984-85	80	17	18	5	13	23	4	30	41	9	268	318	69	5th, Adams Div.	Out of Playoffs
1983-84	80	19	16	5	9	26	5	28	42	10	288	320	66	5th, Adams Div.	Out of Playoffs
1982-83	80	13	22	4	6	32	2	19	54	7	261	403	45	5th, Adams Div.	Out of Playoffs
1981-82	80	13	17	10	8	24	8	21	41	18	264	351	60	5th, Adams Div.	Out of Playoffs
1980-81	80	14	17	9	7	24	9	21	41	18	292	372	60	4th, Norris Div.	Out of Playoffs
1979-80	80	22	12	6	5	22	13	27	34	19	303	312	73	4th, Norris Div.	Lost Prelim. Round

1991-92 Player Personnel

FORWARDS	HT	WT	S	Place of Birth	Date	1990-91 Club
ANDERSSON, Mikael	5-11	185	L	Malmo, Sweden	5/10/66	Hartford-Springfield
ATCHEYNUM, Blair	6-2	190	R	Estevan, Sask.	4/20/69	Springfield
BLACK, James	5-11	185	L	Regina, Sask.	8/15/69	Hartford-Springfield
BRIGHT, Chris	6-0	187	L	Guelph, Ont.	10/14/70	Springfield
BROWN, Rob	5-11	185	L	Kingston, Ont.	4/10/68	Pittsburgh-Hartford
CHALIFOUX, Denis	5-8	165	R	Laval, Que.	2/21/71	Laval
CORRIVEAU, Yvon	6-1	195	L	Welland, Ont.	2/8/67	Hartford-Springfield
CULLEN, John	5-10	185	R	Puslinch, Ont.	8/2/64	Pittsburgh-Hartford
CUNNEYWORTH, Randy	6-0	180	L	Etobicoke, Ont.	5/10/61	Hartford-Springfield
CYR, Paul	5-10	180	L	Port Alberni, B.C.	10/31/63	Hartford
DANIELS, Scott	6-3	200	L	Prince Albert, B.C.	9/19/69	Springfield-Louisville
DAY, Joe	5-11	180	L	Chicago, IL	5/11/68	Springfield
DINEEN, Kevin	5-11	190	R	Quebec City, Que.	10/28/63	Hartford
ENS, Kelly	6-2	194	L	Saskatoon, Sask.		Springfield-Louisville
EVASON, Dean	5-10	180	R	Flin Flon, Man.	8/22/64	Hartford
FENTON, Paul	5-11	195	L	Springfield, MA	12/22/59	Wpg.-Tor.-Cgy.
GOVEDARIS, Chris	6-0	200	L	Toronto, Ont.	2/2/70	Hartford-Springfield
GREIG, Mark	5-11	190	R	High River, Atla.	1/25/70	Hartford-Springfield
HOLIK, Robert	6-3	210	L	Jihlava, Czech.	1/1/71	Hartford
HUNTER, Mark	6-0	205	R	Petrolia, Ont.	11/12/62	Calgary-Hartford
KASTELIC, Ed	6-4	215	R	Toronto, Ont.	1/29/64	Hartford
KRYGIER, Todd	5-11	180	L	Northville, MI	10/12/65	Hartford
McKENZIE, Jim	6-3	205	L	Gull Lake, Sask.	11/3/69	Hartford-Springfield
NYLANDER, Mikael	5-11	176	L	Stockholm, Sweden	10/3/72	Huddinge
PARKER, Jeff	6-3	205	L	St. Paul, MN	9/7/64	Hartford-Muskegon
PEDERSON, Barry	5-11	185	R	Big River, Sask.	3/13/61	Pittsburgh
PICARD, Michel	5-11	190	L	Beauport, Que.	11/7/69	Springfield-Hartford
POULIN, Patrick	6-1	208	L	Vanier, Que.	4/23/73	St. Hyacinthe
RUSSELL, Kerry	5-11	165	R	Kamloops, B.C.	6/23/69	Michigan State
SANDERSON, Geoff	6-0	185	L	St. Albert, Alta.	2/1/72	Swift Current-Hartford
TANCILL, Chris	5-10	185	R	Livonia, MI	2/7/68	Hartford-Springfield
TOMLAK, Mike	6-3	205	L	Thunder Bay, Ont.	10/17/64	Hartford-Springfield
VERBEEK, Pat	5-9	190	R	Sarnia, Ont.	5/24/64	Hartford
YAKE, Terry	5-11	185	R	N. Westmin'r, B.C.	10/22/68	Hartford-Springfield

DEFENSEMEN	HT	WT	S	Place of Birth	Date	1990-91 Club
BACA, Jergus	6-2	211	L	Kosice, Czech.	1/4/65	Hartford-Springfield
BEAULIEU, Corey	6-1	210	L	Winnipeg, Man.	9/10/69	Binghamton DNP
BERGEVIN, Corey	6-1	210	L	Montreal, Que.	8/11/65	Cap. District-Springfield
BOE, Vincent	5-11	188	L	Ft. Saskatchewan, Sask.	12/23/70	Seattle
BRAUER, Cam	6-3	200	L	Calgary, Alta.	1/4/70	Springfield-Louisville
BURKE, Jim	6-2	200	R	Newtown, Mass.	1/3/68	Springfield
BURT, Adam	6-0	190	L	Detroit, MI	1/15/69	Hartford
CHAPMAN, Brian	6-0	195	L	Brockville, Ont.	2/10/68	Hartford-Springfield
COTE, Sylvain	5-11	185	R	Duberger, Que.	1/19/66	Hartford
EVANS, Shawn	6-3	195	L	Kingston, Ont.	9/7/65	Switzerland-Maine
HAMRLICK, Martin	5-11	176	R	Zlin, Czech.	5/6/73	Zlin
HOUDA, Doug	6-2	200	R	Blairmore, Alta.	6/3/66	Det.-Adirondack-Hfd.
HUMENIUK, Scott	6-0	190	R	Saskatoon, Sask.	9/10/69	Springfield
LADOUCEUR, Randy	6-2	220	L	Brockville, Ont.	6/30/60	Hartford
RICHARDS, Todd	6-0	194	R	Robinsdale, MN	10/20/66	Fred.-Spring.-Hartford
SHAW, Brad	6-0	190	R	Cambridge, Ont.	4/28/64	Hartford
STEVENS, John	6-1	195	L	Campbelton, N.B.	5/1/66	Hartford-Springfield
YULE, Steve	6-1	210	R	Gleichen, Alta.	5/27/72	Kamloops
ZALAPSKI, Zarley	6-1	210	L	Edmonton, Alta.	4/22/68	Pittsburgh-Hartford

GOALTENDERS	HT	WT	C	Place of Birth	Date	1990-91 Club
CROZIER, Jim	5-9	160	L	North Bay, Ont.	2/9/68	Cornell
GOSSELIN, Mario	5-8	160	L	Thetford Mines, Que.	6/15/63	Phoenix
IMOO, Dusty	5-8	155	L	New Westminister, B.C.	7/18/70	Regina
LENARDUZZI, Mike	6-0	165	L	Mississauga, Ont.	9/14//72	S.S. Marie
MADSEN, Lance	6-1	190	L	Minneapolis, MN	2/17/68	Louisville
REAUGH, Daryl	6-4	200	L	Prince George, B.C.	2/13/65	Springfield-Hartford
SIDORKIEWICZ, Peter	5-9	180	L	D. Bialostocka, Pol.	6/29/63	Hartford
WHITMORE, Kay	5-11	175	L	Sudbury, Ont.	4/10/67	Hartford-Springfield

General Managers' History

Jack Kelly, 1979-80 to 1981-82; Emile Francis, 1982-83 to 1988-89; Ed Johnston, 1989-90 to date.

Coaching History

Don Blackburn, 1979-80; Don Blackburn and Larry Pleau, 1980-81; Larry Pleau, 1981-82; Larry Kish and Larry Pleau, 1982- 83; Jack "Tex" Evans, 1983-84 to 1986-87; Jack "Tex" Evans and Larry Pleau, 1987-88; Larry Pleau, 1988-89; Rick Ley, 1989-90 to 1990-91; Jim Roberts, 1991-92.

Captains' History

Rick Ley, 1979-80; Rick Ley, Mark Howe and Mike Rogers, 1980-81. Dave Keon, 1981-82; Russ Anderson, 1982-83; Mark Johnson, 1983-84; Mark Johnson and Ron Francis, 1984-85; Ron Francis, 1985-86 to 1990-91.

1990-91 Scoring

Regular Season

* rookie

Pos	#	Player	Team	GP	G	A	Pts	+/−	PIM	PP	SH	GW	GT	S	%
C	15	John Cullen	PIT	65	31	63	94	0	83	10	0	2	1	171	18.1
			HFD	13	8	8	16	6−	18	4	0	1	0	34	23.5
			TOTAL	78	39	71	110	6−	101	14	0	3	1	205	19.0
R	16	Pat Verbeek	HFD	80	43	39	82	0	246	15	0	5	1	247	17.4
R	4	Rob Brown	PIT	25	6	10	16	0	31	2	0	0	0	32	18.8
			HFD	44	18	24	42	7−	101	10	0	2	0	94	19.1
			TOTAL	69	24	34	58	7−	132	12	0	2	0	126	19.0
D	3	Zarley Zalapski	PIT	66	12	36	48	15	59	5	1	1	0	135	8.9
			HFD	11	3	3	6	7−	6	3	0	0	0	21	14.3
			TOTAL	77	15	39	54	8	65	8	1	1	0	156	9.6
R	11	Kevin Dineen	HFD	61	17	30	47	15−	104	4	0	2	0	161	10.6
L	24	*Bobby Holik	HFD	78	21	22	43	3−	113	8	0	3	0	173	12.1
R	26	Mark Hunter	CGY	57	10	15	25	1−	125	6	0	0	0	90	11.1
			HFD	11	4	3	7	3	40	1	0	0	0	20	20.0
			TOTAL	68	14	18	32	2	165	7	0	0	0	110	12.7
D	32	Brad Shaw	HFD	72	4	28	32	10−	29	2	0	1	0	129	3.1
L	17	Todd Krygier	HFD	72	13	17	30	1	95	3	0	2	3	113	11.5
C	12	Dean Evason	HFD	75	6	23	29	6−	170	1	0	0	0	85	7.1
L	18	Paul Cyr	HFD	70	12	13	25	8−	107	0	1	2	0	128	9.4
D	21	Sylvain Cote	HFD	73	7	12	19	17−	17	1	0	0	0	154	4.5
L	28	Mike Tomlak	HFD	64	8	8	16	9−	55	0	1	0	0	69	11.6
L	7	Randy Cunneyworth	HFD	32	9	5	14	6−	49	0	0	1	0	56	16.1
L	34	Mikael Andersson	HFD	41	4	7	11	0	8	0	0	0	0	57	7.0
D	6	Adam Burt	HFD	42	2	7	9	4−	63	1	0	1	0	43	4.7
L	33	*Jim McKenzie	HFD	41	4	3	7	7−	108	0	0	0	0	16	25.0
D	27	Doug Houda	DET	22	0	4	4	2−	43	0	0	0	0	21	.0
			HFD	19	1	2	3	3−	41	0	0	0	1	21	4.8
			TOTAL	41	1	6	7	5−	84	0	0	0	1	42	2.4
D	44	Dave Babych	HFD	8	0	6	6	4−	4	0	0	0	0	15	.0
C	38	*Terry Yake	HFD	19	1	4	5	3−	10	0	0	1	0	19	5.3
R	22	Ed Kastelic	HFD	45	2	2	4	7−	211	0	0	0	0	15	13.3
L	14	*Chris Govedaris	HFD	14	1	3	4	4−	4	0	0	1	0	10	10.0
D	29	Randy Ladouceur	HFD	67	1	3	4	10−	118	0	0	0	0	44	2.3
D	46	*Todd Richards	HFD	2	0	4	4	4−	2	0	0	0	0	4	.0
G	30	Peter Sidorkiewicz	HFD	52	0	4	4	0	6	0	0	0	0	0	.0
C	37	*Chris Tancill	HFD	9	1	1	2	2	4	0	1	0	0	6	16.7
L	20	Yvon Corriveau	HFD	23	1	1	2	8−	18	0	0	0	0	21	4.8
D	40	*Jergus Baca	HFD	9	0	2	2	3−	14	0	0	0	0	15	.0
C	13	Geoff Sanderson	HFD	2	1	0	1	2−	0	0	0	0	0	2	50.0
L	47	*Michel Picard	HFD	5	1	0	1	2−	2	0	0	0	0	7	14.3
D	45	John Stevens	HFD	14	0	1	1	0	11	0	0	0	0	7	.0
G	35	*Kay Whitmore	HFD	18	0	1	1	0	4	0	0	0	0	0	.0
C	23	*James Black	HFD	1	0	0	0	0	0	0	0	0	0	0	.0
G	49	*Ross McKay	HFD	1	0	0	0	0	0	0	0	0	0	0	.0
D	42	Brian Chapman	HFD	3	0	0	0	0	29	0	0	0	0	0	.0
D	36	Marc Bergevin	HFD	4	0	0	0	3−	4	0	0	0	0	2	.0
R	8	*Mark Greig	HFD	4	0	0	0	1−	0	0	0	0	0	1	.0
R	25	Jeff Parker	HFD	4	0	0	0	2−	2	0	0	0	0	4	.0
G	31	*Daryl Reaugh	HFD	20	0	0	0	0	4	0	0	0	0	0	.0

Goaltending

No.	Goaltender	GPI	Mins	Avg	W	L	T	EN	SO	GA	SA	S%
31	*Daryl Reaugh	20	1010	3.15	7	7	1	0	1	53	479	.889
30	Peter Sidorkiewicz	52	2953	3.33	21	22	7	4	1	164	1284	.872
35	*Kay Whitmore	18	850	3.67	3	9	3	0	0	52	379	.863
49	Ross McKay	1	35	5.14	0	0	0	0	0	3	15	.800
	Totals	**80**	**4867**	**3.40**	**31**	**38**	**11**	**4**	**2**	**276**	**2161**	**.872**

Playoffs

Pos	#	Player	Team	GP	G	A	Pts	+/−	PIM	PP	SH	GW	OT	S	%
C	15	John Cullen	HFD	6	2	7	9	0	10	0	0	0	0	10	20.0
R	26	Mark Hunter	HFD	6	5	1	6	3	17	3	0	0	0	14	35.7
R	16	Pat Verbeek	HFD	6	3	2	5	0	40	2	0	0	0	15	20.0
D	29	Randy Ladouceur	HFD	6	1	4	5	4	6	0	0	0	0	10	10.0
D	3	Zarley Zalapski	HFD	6	1	3	4	3−	8	0	0	1	0	17	5.9
C	12	Dean Evason	HFD	6	0	4	4	1−	29	0	0	0	0	6	.0
D	32	Brad Shaw	HFD	6	1	2	3	4−	2	0	0	0	0	5	20.0
C	38	*Terry Yake	HFD	6	1	1	2	0	16	0	1	0	0	5	20.0
D	21	Sylvain Cote	HFD	6	0	2	2	2	2	0	0	0	0	10	.0
L	17	Todd Krygier	HFD	6	0	2	2	1−	0	0	0	0	0	8	.0
R	4	Rob Brown	HFD	5	1	0	1	2	7	1	0	1	0	10	10.0
L	18	Paul Cyr	HFD	6	1	0	1	2−	10	0	0	0	0	14	7.1
R	11	Kevin Dineen	HFD	6	1	0	1	3−	16	0	0	0	0	11	9.1
G	30	Peter Sidorkiewicz	HFD	6	0	1	1	0	2	0	0	0	0	0	.0
L	7	Randy Cunneyworth	HFD	1	0	0	0	0	0	0	0	0	0	0	.0
L	28	Mike Tomlak	HFD	3	0	0	0	3−	2	0	0	0	0	0	.0
C	13	*Geoff Sanderson	HFD	3	0	0	0	0	0	0	0	0	0	4	.0
L	24	*Bobby Holik	HFD	6	0	0	0	3−	7	0	0	0	0	15	.0
D	27	Doug Houda	HFD	6	0	0	0	4−	8	0	0	0	0	6	.0
L	33	*Jim McKenzie	HFD	6	0	0	0	2−	8	0	0	0	0	2	.0
D	46	*Todd Richards	HFD	6	0	0	0	1−	2	0	0	0	0	6	.0

Goaltending

No.	Goaltender	GPI	Mins	Avg	W	L	EN	SO	GA	SA	S%
30	Peter Sidorkiewicz	6	359	4.01	2	4	0	0	24	174	.862
	Totals	**6**	**360**	**4.00**	**2**	**4**	**0**	**0**	**24**	**174**	**.862**

Club Records

Team

(Figures in brackets for season records are games played; records for fewest points, wins, ties, losses, goals, goals against are for 70 or more games.)

Most Points	93	1986-87 (80)
Most Wins	43	1986-87 (80)
Most Ties	19	1979-80 (80)
Most Losses	54	1982-83 (80)
Most Goals	332	1985-86 (80)
Most Goals Against	403	1982-83 (80)
Fewest Points	45	1982-83 (80)
Fewest Wins	19	1982-83 (80)
Fewest Ties	4	1985-86 (80)
Fewest Losses	30	1986-87 (80)
Fewest Goals	238	1990-91 (80)
Fewest Goals Against	267	1987-88 (80)

Longest Winning Streak
Over-all ....7 Mar. 16-29/85
Home ....5 Mar. 17-29/85
Away ....6 Nov. 10-
Dec. 7/90

Longest Undefeated Streak
Over-all ....10 Jan. 20-
Feb. 10/82
(6 wins, 4 ties)
Home ....7 Mar. 15-
Apr. 5/86
(5 wins, 2 ties)
Away ....6 Jan. 23-Feb. 10/82
(3 wins, 3 ties)
Nov. 30-
Dec. 26/89
(5 wins, 1 tie)
Nov. 10-
Dec. 7/90

Longest Losing Streak
Over-all ....9 Feb. 19/83-
Mar. 8/83
Home ....6 Feb. 19/83-
Mar. 12/83
Feb. 10-
Mar. 3/85
Away ....13 Dec. 18/82-
Feb. 5/83

Longest Winless Streak
Over-all ....12 Dec. 18/82-
Jan. 11/83
(11 losses, 1 tie)
Home ....13 Jan. 15-
Mar. 10/85
(11 losses, 2 ties)
Away ....15 Nov. 11/79-
Jan. 9/80
(11 losses, 4 ties)

Most Shutouts, Season 5 1986-87 (80)
Most PIM, Season 2,209 1990-91 (80)
Most Goals, Game ....11 Feb. 12/84
(Edm. 0 at Hfd. 11)
Oct. 19/85
(Mtl. 6 at Hfd. 11)
Jan. 17/86
(Que. 6 at Hfd. 11)
Mar. 15/86
(Chi. 4 at Hfd. 11)

Individual

Most Seasons ....10 Ron Francis
Most Games ....714 Ron Francis
Most Goals, Career ....264 Ron Francis
Most Assists, Career ....557 Ron Francis
Most Points, Career ....821 Ron Francis
(264 goals, 557 assists)
Most PIM, Career ......1,368 Torrie Robertson
Most Shutouts, Career ....13 Mike Liut
Longest Consecutive
Games Streak ....419 Dave Tippett
(Mar. 3/84-Oct. 7/89)
Most Goals, Season ....56 Blaine Stoughton
(1979-80)
Most Assists, Season .....69 Ron Francis
(1989-90)
Most Points, Season .....105 Mike Rogers
(1979-80)
(44 goals, 61 assists)
(1980-81)
(40 goals, 65 assists)
Most PIM, Season ......358 Torrie Robertson
(1985-86)
Most Points, Defenseman
Season ....69 Dave Babych
(1985-86)
(14 goals, 55 assists)
Most Points, Center,
Season ....105 Mike Rogers
(1979-80)
(44 goals, 61 assists)
Mike Rogers
(1980-81)
(40 goals, 65 assists)
Most Points, Right Wing,
Season ....100 Blaine Stoughton
(1979-80)
(56 goals, 44 assists)
Most Points, Left Wing,
Season ....80 Pat Boutette
(1980-81)
(28 goals, 52 assists)

Most Points, Rookie,
Season ....72 Sylvain Turgeon
(1983-84)
(40 goals, 32 assists)
Most Shutouts, Season .....4 Mike Liut
(1986-87)
Peter Sidorkiewicz
(1988-89)
Most Goals, Game ....4 Jordy Douglas
(Feb. 3/80)
Ron Francis
(Feb. 12/84)
Most Assists, Game ....6 Ron Francis
(Mar. 5/87)
Most Points, Game ....6 Paul Lawless
(Jan. 4/87)
Ron Francis
(Mar. 5/87,
Oct. 8/89)

Retired Numbers

2	Rick Ley	1979-1981
9	Gordie Howe	1979-1980
19	John McKenzie	1976-1979

All-time Record vs. Other Clubs

Regular Season

	At Home							On Road							Total					
	GP	W	L	T	GF	GA	PTS	GP	W	L	T	GF	GA	PTS	GP	W	L	T	GF	GA	PTS
Boston	44	21	17	6	161	158	48	44	11	29	4	114	183	26	88	32	46	10	275	341	74
Buffalo	44	16	23	5	133	140	37	44	15	23	6	145	183	36	88	31	46	11	278	323	73
Calgary	19	7	9	3	67	77	17	19	3	15	1	67	107	7	38	10	24	4	134	184	24
Chicago	19	9	8	2	72	65	20	19	5	11	3	58	91	13	38	14	19	5	130	156	33
Detroit	19	13	5	1	80	51	27	19	7	6	6	59	66	20	38	20	11	7	139	117	47
Edmonton	19	8	8	3	82	73	19	19	2	14	3	59	90	7	38	10	22	6	141	163	26
Los Angeles	19	11	6	2	80	79	24	19	6	11	2	75	82	14	38	17	17	4	155	161	38
Minnesota	19	9	10	0	69	71	18	19	7	11	1	64	83	15	38	16	21	1	133	154	33
Montreal	44	16	23	5	142	169	37	44	7	31	6	130	209	20	88	23	54	11	272	378	57
New Jersey	19	11	4	4	75	56	26	19	9	8	2	84	68	20	38	20	12	6	159	124	46
NY Islanders	19	7	9	3	62	75	17	19	6	11	2	50	76	14	38	13	20	5	112	151	31
NY Rangers	19	11	6	2	78	68	24	19	6	11	2	58	81	14	38	17	17	4	136	149	38
Philadelphia	19	8	7	4	81	80	20	19	4	14	1	48	81	9	38	12	21	5	129	161	29
Pittsburgh	19	12	7	0	90	76	24	19	7	9	3	77	83	17	38	19	16	3	167	159	41
Quebec	44	18	16	10	155	155	46	44	13	24	7	147	195	33	88	31	40	17	302	350	79
St. Louis	19	8	9	2	63	60	18	19	7	10	2	66	71	16	38	15	19	4	129	131	34
Toronto	19	12	4	3	97	64	27	19	11	6	2	82	69	24	38	23	10	5	179	133	51
Vancouver	19	8	7	4	66	69	20	19	7	7	5	53	65	19	38	15	14	9	119	134	39
Washington	19	7	10	2	63	78	16	19	7	11	1	53	68	15	38	14	21	3	116	146	31
Winnipeg	19	10	5	4	82	62	24	19	8	11	0	69	72	16	38	18	16	4	151	134	40
Totals	**480**	**222**	**193**	**65**	**1798**	**1726**	**509**	**480**	**148**	**273**	**59**	**1558**	**2023**	**355**	**960**	**370**	**466**	**124**	**3356**	**3749**	**864**

Playoffs

	Series	W	L	GP	W	L	T	GF	GA	Last Mtg.	Round	Result
Boston	2	0	2	13	5	8	0	38	47	1991	DSF	L 2-4
Montreal	4	1	4	20	5	15	0	52	75	1989	DSF	L 0-4
Quebec	2	1	1	9	5	4	0	35	34	1987	DSF	L 2-4
Totals	**8**	**1**	**7**	**42**	**15**	**27**	**0**	**125**	**156**			

Playoff Results 1991-87

Year	Round	Opponent	Result	GF	GA
1991	DSF	Boston	L 3-4	24	24
1990	DSF	Boston	L 3-4	21	23
1989	DSF	Montreal	L 0-4	11	18
1988	DSF	Montreal	L 2-4	20	23
1987	DSF	Quebec	L 2-4	19	27

Abbreviations: Round: F Final; **CF** conference final; **DF** division final; **DSF** division semi-final; **GA** goals against; **GF** goals for.

1990-91 Results

		Home				Away	
Oct.	4	Quebec	3-3	Oct.	8	Montreal	3-5
	6	NY Rangers	5-4		12	Detroit	2-4
	10	Buffalo	4-3		16	Quebec	1-1
	13	Montreal	5-2		17	Toronto	3-1
	27	Vancouver	2-4		19	Los Angeles	2-5
	31	Montreal	2-4		24	Minnesota	0-3
Nov.	3	St Louis	1-4		28	Buffalo	0-5
	6	Chicago	1-1	Nov.	9	Winnipeg	4-5
	14	Boston	3-1		10	Minnesota	3-2
	17	Washington	4-2		15	New Jersey	4-2
	21	Quebec	4-4		23	Boston*	4-3
	24	Boston	3-4		29	Pittsburgh	6-4
	28	Quebec	3-4	Dec.	3	Montreal	4-2
Dec.	1	Edmonton	2-4		7	Buffalo	4-3
	5	Montreal	3-4		13	Boston	2-8
	8	Pittsburgh	3-1		15	Washington	3-2
	12	Boston	1-5		20	NY Islanders	2-4
	18	Buffalo	3-4		26	Quebec	4-1
	22	Philadelphia	1-0		29	Calgary	2-8
	23	Philadelphia	2-5		30	Edmonton	3-4
Jan.	2	Vancouver	5-2	Jan.	8	Los Angeles	3-4
	5	Winnipeg	4-3		10	Vancouver	5-4
	16	Los Angeles	4-3		12	Toronto	2-2
	23	Calgary	5-4		13	NY Rangers	3-4
	26	Philadelphia	5-3		24	Boston	0-3
	29	NY Islanders	1-8		31	St Louis	3-4
Feb.	6	Edmonton	5-1	Feb.	2	Philadelphia*	2-0
	9	Calgary	2-5		3	NY Islanders	1-1
	10	Chicago	3-1		15	NY Rangers	3-5
	13	Detroit	6-2		16	Montreal	2-1
	20	Montreal	5-3		24	Buffalo	5-5
	23	Buffalo	4-5		26	Winnipeg	4-5
Mar.	3	Toronto	4-4		28	Chicago	3-6
	5	St Louis	1-4	Mar.	2	Quebec	3-3
	9	Pittsburgh	2-5		12	Washington	3-2
	10	Quebec	1-2		17	Buffalo	1-6
	14	Detroit	4-2		23	Quebec	3-7
	16	New Jersey	6-2		25	Montreal	2-3
	19	Boston	1-1		27	New Jersey	3-4
	30	Buffalo	5-5		31	Boston	3-7

* Denotes afternoon game.

Entry Draft
Selections 1991-79

1991
Pick
- 9 Patrick Poulin
- 31 Martin Hamrlik
- 53 Todd Hall
- 59 Mikael Nylander
- 75 Jim Storm
- 119 Mike Harding
- 141 Brian Mueller
- 163 Steve Yule
- 185 Chris Belanger
- 207 Jason Currie
- 229 Mike Santonelli
- 251 Rob Peters

1990
Pick
- 15 Mark Greig
- 36 Geoff Sanderson
- 57 Mike Lenarduzzi
- 78 Chris Bright
- 120 Cory Keenan
- 141 Jergus Baca
- 162 Martin D'Orsonnens
- 183 Corey Osmak
- 204 Espen Knutsen
- 225 Tommie Eriksen
- 246 Denis Chalifoux

1989
Pick
- 10 Robert Holik
- 52 Blair Atcheynum
- 73 Jim McKenzie
- 94 James Black
- 115 Jerome Bechard
- 136 Scott Daniels
- 157 Raymond Saumier
- 178 Michel Picard
- 199 Trevor Buchanan
- 220 John Battice
- 241 Peter Kasowski

1988
Pick
- 11 Chris Govedaris
- 32 Barry Richter
- 74 Dean Dyer
- 95 Scott Morrow
- 116 Corey Beaulieu
- 137 Kerry Russell
- 158 Jim Burke
- 179 Mark Hirth
- 200 Wayde Bucsis
- 221 Rob White
- 242 Dan Slatalla

1987
Pick
- 18 Jody Hull
- 39 Adam Burt
- 81 Terry Yake
- 102 Marc Rousseau
- 123 Jeff St. Cyr
- 144 Greg Wolf
- 165 John Moore
- 186 Joe Day
- 228 Kevin Sullivan
- 249 Steve Laurin

1986
Pick
- 11 Scott Young
- 32 Marc Laforge
- 74 Brian Chapman
- 95 Bill Horn
- 116 Joe Quinn
- 137 Steve Torrel
- 158 Ron Hoover
- 179 Robert Glasgow
- 200 Sean Evoy
- 221 Cal Brown
- 242 Brian Verbeek

1985
Pick
- 5 Dana Murzyn
- 26 Kay Whitmore
- 68 Gary Callaghan
- 110 Shane Churla
- 131 Chris Brant
- 152 Brian Puhalsky
- 173 Greg Dornbach
- 194 Paul Tory
- 215 Jerry Pawlowski
- 236 Bruce Hill

1984
Pick
- 11 Sylvain Cote
- 110 Mike Millar
- 131 Mike Vellucci
- 173 John Devereaux
- 194 Brent Regan
- 215 Jim Culhane
- 236 Pete Abric

1983
Pick
- 2 Sylvain Turgeon
- 20 David Jensen
- 23 Ville Siren
- 61 Leif Karlsson
- 64 Dave MacLean
- 72 Ron Chyzowski
- 104 Brian Johnson
- 124 Joe Reekie
- 143 Chris Duperron
- 144 James Falle
- 164 Bill Fordy
- 193 Reine Karlsson
- 204 Allan Acton
- 224 Darcy Kaminski

1982
Pick
- 14 Paul Lawless
- 35 Mark Paterson
- 56 Kevin Dineen
- 67 Ulf Samuelsson
- 88 Ray Ferraro
- 109 Randy Gilhen
- 130 Jim Johannson
- 151 Mickey Kramptoich
- 172 Kevin Skilliter
- 214 Martin Linse
- 235 Randy Cameron

1981
Pick
- 4 Ron Francis
- 61 Paul MacDermid
- 67 Michael Hoffman
- 93 Bill Maguire
- 103 Dan Bourbonnais
- 130 John Mokosak
- 151 Denis Dore
- 172 Jeff Poeschl
- 193 Larry Power

1980
Pick
- 8 Fred Arthur
- 29 Michel Galarneau
- 50 Mickey Volcan
- 71 Kevin McClelland
- 100 Darren Jensen
- 113 Mario Cerri
- 134 Mike Martin
- 155 Brent Denat
- 176 Paul Fricker
- 197 Lorne Bokshowan

1979
Pick
- 18 Ray Allison
- 39 Stuart Smith
- 60 Don Nachbaur
- 81 Ray Neufeld
- 102 Mark Renaud
- 123 Dave McDonald

Pat Verbeek had 43 goals for the Whalers in 1990-91.

Club Directory

Hartford Whalers
242 Trumbull Street
Eighth Floor
Hartford, Connecticut 06103
Phone **203/728-3366**
GM FAX 203/247-1274
FAX 203/522-7707
TWX 710-425-8732
ENVOY ID

Front Office: WHALERS. GM
Public
Relations: WHALERS. PR
Capacity: 15,635

Managing General Partner/Governor	Richard Gordon
General Partner/Alternate Governor	Ben J. Sisti

Hockey Department

Vice President/General Manager	Ed Johnston
Assistant General Manager	Ken Schinkel
Special Assistant to the General Manager	Tom Rowe
Head Coach	Jim Roberts
Assistant Coaches	Darcy Regier, Claude Larose
Goaltending Coach	Jacques Caron
Strength and Conditioning Coach	Doug McKerney
Scouting Staff	Leo Boivin, Steve Brklacich, Bruce Haralson, Fred Gore, Claude Larose, Jiri Crha, Willy Lindstrom
Executive Secretary	Ann Sullivan
Secretary	Karen Stansfield
Head Trainer	Frank "Bud" Gouvela
Assistant Trainer/Equipment Manager	Skip Cunningham
Assistant Equipment Manager	Keith Parker
Club Doctor	Dr. John Falkerson
Club Dentist	Dr. Walter Kunisch

Administration

President/Alternate Governor	Emile Francis
Special Assistant to the Managing General Partner	Gordie Howe
Executive Vice President of Finance & Administration	W. David Andrews III
Vice President of Marketing & Sales	Rick Francis
Treasurer	Mike Amendola
Advertising Sales Manager	Richard Chmura
Director of Public Relations	John H. Forslund
Public/Community Relations Assistant	Mary Lynn Gorman
Chief Statistician	Frank Polnaszek
Advertising Sales Manager	Richard Chmura
Ticket Sales Manager	Jim Baldwin
Ticket Office Supervisors	Mike Barnes, Chris O'Connor

General Information

Radio Play-By-Play	Chuck Kaiton
TV/Cable Play-By-Play	Rick Peckham
TV/Cable Commentator	Gerry Cheevers
Commercial TV Outlet	TBA
Cable TV Outlet	SportsChannel
Radio Network Flagship Station	WTIC-AM (1080)
Home Ice	Hartford Civic Center, Veterans Memorial Coliseum

General Manager

JOHNSTON, ED
Vice-President and General Manager, Hartford Whalers.
Born in Montreal, Que., November 24, 1935.

Ed Johnston was named vice-president and general manager of the Whalers on May 11, 1989 after serving in the Pittsburgh Penguins' organization for six years. He was the general manager of the Penguins from 1982-83 to 1987-88 before being named assistant general manager in 1988-89.

Johnston's coaching career began with the Chicago Blackhawks organization. He coached Moncton of the AHL in 1978-79 before taking over as Blackhawks head coach for the 1979-80 campaign. He was head coach of the Penguins for three years (1980-81 to 1982-83). His NHL coaching record is 113-156-54.

Johnston played 11 years with the Boston Bruins and was a member of two NHL Stanley Cup championship teams. He also played with Toronto, St. Louis and Chicago during his 16-year NHL career and had a 3.25 career goals-against-average and 32 shutouts. Johnston owns the distinction of being the last goaltender to play an entire NHL regular season—having played all 70 games during the 1963-64 season.

NHL Coaching Record

			Regular Season				Playoffs			
Season	Team	Games	W	L	T	%	Games	W	L	%
1979-80	Chicago	80	34	27	19	.544	4	0	4	.000
1980-81	Pittsburgh	80	30	37	13	.456	5	2	3	.400
1981-82	Pittsburgh	80	31	36	13	.469	5	2	3	.400
1982-83	Pittsburgh	80	18	53	9	.281	....	....	....	....
NHL Totals		320	113	156	54	.438	14	4	10	.286

Coach

ROBERTS, JIM
Coach, Hartford Whalers. Born in Toronto, Ont., April 9, 1940.

Jim Roberts was appointed head coach of the Hartford Whalers on June 7, 1991. He is the seventh man in franchise history to hold the position. Roberts comes to the Whalers after three seasons—and two Calder Cup Championships— at the helm of the American Hockey League's Springfield Indians.

Roberts, a 16-season National Hockey League forward and defenseman with Montreal and St. Louis, joined the Buffalo Sabres as an associate coach in 1979-80. His five-year tenure with the Sabres included a 45-game stint as interim head coach during the 1981-82 season; Buffalo posted a 21-16-8 record. In 1984, Roberts joined the Pittsburgh Penguins as an assistant to head coach Bob Berry, and he remained with the club until joining the New York Islanders organization— as head coach in Springfield—in 1988.

Coaching Record

			Regular Season				Playoffs			
Season	Team	Games	W	L	T	%	Games	W	L	%
1981-82	Buffalo (NHL)	45	21	16	8	.556	....	....	....	....
1988-89	Springfield Indians (AHL)	80	32	44	4	.425	....	....	....	....
1989-90	Springfield Indians (AHL)	80	38	38	4	.500	18	12	6	.666
1990-91	Springfield Indians (AHL)	80	43	27	10	.600	18	12	6	.666
NHL Totals		45	21	16	8	.556	....	....	....	....

Los Angeles Kings

1990-91 Results: 46W-24L-10T 102PTS. First, Smythe Division

Year-by-Year Record

Season	GP	Home W	Home L	Home T	Road W	Road L	Road T	Overall W	Overall L	T	GF	GA	Pts.	Finished	Playoff Result
1990-91	80	26	9	5	20	15	5	46	24	10	340	254	102	1st, Smythe Div.	Lost Div. Final
1989-90	80	21	16	3	13	23	4	34	39	7	338	337	75	4th, Smythe Div.	Lost Div. Final
1988-89	80	25	12	3	17	19	4	42	31	7	376	335	91	2nd, Smythe Div.	Lost Div. Final
1987-88	80	19	18	3	11	24	5	30	42	8	318	359	68	4th, Smythe Div.	Lost Div. Semi-Final
1986-87	80	20	17	3	11	24	5	31	41	8	318	341	70	4th, Smythe Div.	Lost Div. Semi-Final
1985-86	80	9	27	4	14	22	4	23	49	8	284	389	54	5th, Smythe Div.	Out of Playoffs
1984-85	80	20	14	6	14	18	8	34	32	14	339	326	82	4th, Smythe Div.	Lost Div. Semi-Final
1983-84	80	13	19	8	10	25	5	23	44	13	309	376	59	5th, Smythe Div.	Out of Playoffs
1982-83	80	20	13	7	7	28	5	27	41	12	308	365	66	5th, Smythe Div.	Out of Playoffs
1981-82	80	19	15	6	5	26	9	24	41	15	314	369	63	4th, Smythe Div.	Lost Div. Final
1980-81	80	22	11	7	21	13	6	43	24	13	337	290	99	2nd, Norris Div.	Lost Prelim. Round
1979-80	80	18	13	9	12	23	5	30	36	14	290	313	74	2nd, Norris Div.	Lost Prelim. Round
1978-79	80	20	13	7	14	21	5	34	34	12	292	286	80	3rd, Norris Div.	Lost Prelim. Round
1977-78	80	18	16	6	13	18	9	31	34	15	243	245	77	3rd, Norris Div.	Lost Prelim. Round
1976-77	80	20	13	7	14	18	8	34	31	15	271	241	83	2nd, Norris Div.	Lost Quarter-Final
1975-76	80	22	13	5	16	20	4	38	33	9	263	265	85	2nd, Norris Div.	Lost Quarter-Final
1974-75	80	22	7	11	20	10	10	42	17	21	269	185	105	2nd, Norris Div.	Lost Prelim. Round
1973-74	78	22	13	4	11	20	8	33	33	12	233	231	78	3rd, West Div.	Lost Quarter-Final
1972-73	78	21	11	7	10	25	4	31	36	11	232	245	73	6th, West Div.	Out of Playoffs
1971-72	78	14	23	2	6	26	7	20	49	9	206	305	49	7th, West Div.	Out of Playoffs
1970-71	78	17	14	8	8	26	5	25	40	13	239	303	63	5th, West Div.	Out of Playoffs
1969-70	76	12	22	4	2	30	6	14	52	10	168	290	38	6th, West Div.	Out of Playoffs
1968-69	76	19	14	5	5	28	5	24	42	10	185	260	58	4th, West Div.	Lost Semi-Final
1967-68	74	20	13	4	11	20	6	31	33	10	200	224	72	2nd, West Div.	Lost Quarter-Final

Schedule

Home

Oct.	Tues.	8	Edmonton
	Thur.	10	Calgary
	Sat.	12	Winnipeg
	Wed.	16	San Jose
	Sat.	19	Minnesota
Nov.	Thur.	7	Vancouver
	Sat.	9	Edmonton
	Thur.	14	Buffalo
	Sat.	16	Detroit
	Thur.	21	NY Rangers
	Sat.	23	San Jose
	Tues.	26	Toronto
	Sat.	30	New Jersey
Dec.	Thur.	12	Winnipeg
	Sat.	14	Vancouver
	Tues.	17	Minnesota
	Sat.	21	Detroit
	Thur.	26	San Jose
	Tues.	31	Vancouver
Jan.	Thur.	2	Edmonton
	Sat.	4	Philadelphia
	Tues.	14	San Jose
	Thur.	16	Washington
	Sat.	25	Calgary
	Tues.	28	St Louis
	Thur.	30	NY Rangers
Feb.	Sat.	1	Chicago
	Tues.	4	NY Islanders
	Thur.	6	Hartford
	Sat.	15	Washington
	Mon.	17	Boston*
	Thur.	27	Quebec
	Sat.	29	Montreal
Mar.	Tues.	3	Philadelphia
	Sat.	7	Pittsburgh
	Mon.	9	Toronto
	Tues.	17	Winnipeg
	Thur.	19	Buffalo
	Sat.	21	Calgary*
Apr.	Sat.	4	Vancouver*

Away

Oct.	Fri.	4	Winnipeg
	Sun.	6	Edmonton
	Tues.	22	New Jersey
	Wed.	23	NY Rangers
	Sat.	26	NY Islanders
	Mon.	28	Detroit
	Wed.	30	Hartford
	Thur.	31	Boston
Nov.	Sat.	2	Toronto
	Mon.	11	Winnipeg*
	Tues.	12	Vancouver
	Tues.	19	San Jose
	Thur.	28	Calgary
Dec.	Tues.	3	San Jose
	Thur.	5	Chicago
	Sat.	7	Quebec
	Sat.	28	Edmonton
	Sun.	29	Calgary
Jan.	Tues.	7	Pittsburgh
	Thur.	9	Philadelphia
	Fri.	10	Washington
	Sun.	12	New Jersey
	Wed.	22	Minnesota
	Thur.	23	St Louis
Feb.	Sat.	8	Pittsburgh*
	Sun.	9	Buffalo
	Tues.	11	St Louis
	Thur.	13	Chicago
	Wed.	19	Edmonton
	Fri.	21	Calgary
	Sun.	23	Winnipeg
	Tues.	25	Vancouver
Mar.	Wed.	4	San Jose
	Wed.	11	Hartford
	Sat.	14	Montreal
	Sun.	15	Boston
	Thur.	26	Calgary
	Fri.	27	Winnipeg
	Sun.	29	Edmonton
Apr.	Sun.	5	Vancouver*

* Denotes afternoon game.

Home Starting Times:

All Games	7:35 p.m.
Except Dec. 14, Dec. 31	6:05 p.m.
Feb. 17, Mar. 21, Apr. 4	1:05 p.m.

Franchise date: June 5, 1967

25th NHL Season

The Great One, who became the first NHL player to reach the 2,000 point mark, won his ninth Art Ross Trophy in 1990-91.

1991-92 Player Personnel

LEFT WINGS	HT	WT	S	Place of Birth	Date	1990-91 Club
BECHARD, Jerome	5-11	187	L	Regina, Sask.	3/30/69	New Haven-Phoenix
BERG, Bob	6-2	190	L	Beamsville, Ont.	7/2/70	New Haven-Sudbury
BROWNE, David	5-11	185		Hampstead, Que.	2/28/68	Vermont
DONNELLY, Mike	5-11	185	L	Detroit, MI	10/10/63	Los Angeles
GRANATO, Tony	5-10	185	R	Downers Grove, IL	7/25/64	Los Angeles
LAPRADE, Doug	6-0	190	R	Port Arthur, Ont.	10/9/68	Lake Superior
LEMARQUE, Eric	5-10	185	R	Paris, France	7/1/69	Briancon
MILLER, Jay	6-2	210	L	Wellesley, Mass.	7/16/60	Los Angeles
ROBITAILLE, Luc	6-1	190	L	Montreal, Que.	2/17/66	Los Angeles
SIP, Radek	6-1	205		Duchov, Czech.	9/10/71	Lethbridge-Cal. Tier 2
WILLIAMS, Darryl	5-11	185	L	Mt. Pearl, Nfld.	2/9/68	New Haven-Phoenix
CENTERS						
BALLANTINE, Jim	5-11	185		Rockford, IL	11/5/67	U. of Michigan
COUTURIER, Sylvain	6-2	205	L	Greenfield Pk. Que.	4/23/68	Phoenix-Los Angeles
GILHEN, Randy	5-10	190	L	Zweibrucken, W. Ger.	6/13/63	Pittsburgh
GRETZKY, Wayne	6-0	170	L	Brantford, Ont.	1/26/61	Los Angeles
KUDELSKI, Bob	6-1	200	R	Springfield, MA	3/3/64	Los Angeles
LeBLANC, Denis	6-0	207	L	Montreal, Que.	1/18/70	St. Hyacinthe
LEVEQUE, Guy	5-11	166	L	Kingston, Ont.	2/28/72	Cornwall
McCOSH, Shawn	6-0	188	R	Oshawa, Ont.	6/5/69	New Haven
McINTYRE, John	6-1	175	L	Ravenswood, Ont.	4/29/69	Toronto-Los Angeles
MILLER, Colin	6-0	190		Grimsby, Ont.	8/21/71	Sault Ste. Marie
ROHLICEK, Jeff	6-0	180	L	Park Ridge, IL	1/27/66	New Haven-Phoenix
RYDMARK, Daniel	5-10	176	L	Vasteras, Sweden	2/23/70	Malmo
SAUMIER, Marc	5-10	190	L	Hull, Quebec	4/18/67	Phoenix
SEGUIN, Brett	5-9	199		Rochester, NY	2/20/72	Ottawa
VUKONICH, Mike	6-1	185	L	Duluth, MN	5/11/68	Harvard
WILLETT, Paul	5-9	175		New Richmond, Que.	5/10/69	New Haven-Roanoke
RIGHT WINGS						
BJUGSTAD, Scott	6-1	185	L	St. Paul, MN	6/2/61	Los Angeles-Phoenix
BREAULT, Francois	5-11	185	L	Acton Vale, Que.	5/11/67	Los Angeles
HEISE, Kevin	6-2	195	R	Regina, Sask.	9/9/68	U. of Calgary
KARJALAINEN, Kyosti	6-1	190	L	Gavle, Sweden	6/19/67	Phoenix
KURRI, Jari	6-1	195	R	Helsinki, Finland	5/18/60	Milan
SANDSTROM, Tomas	6-2	200	L	Jakobstad, Finland	9/4/64	Los Angeles
SEMCHUK, Brandy	6-1	187	R	Calgary, Alta.	9/22/71	New Haven-Lethbridge
SINSALO, Ilkke	6-1	200	L	Valeakoski, Finland	7/10/58	Minnesota-L.A.
TAYLOR, Dave	6-0	195	R	Levack, Ont.	12/4/55	Los Angeles
THOMSON, Jim	6-1	205	R	Edmonton, Alta.	10/30/65	Los Angeles-New Haven
VAN KESSEL, John	6-4	193	R	Bridgewater, Ont.	12/19/69	Phoenix
WHITE, Kevin	6-1	192		Charlotown, P.E.I.	6/22/70	North Bay
WHYTE, Sean	6-0	198	R	Sudbury, Ont.	5/4/70	Phoenix
WILSON, Ross	6-3	197	R	The Pas, Man.	6/26/69	New Haven
DEFENSEMEN						
AHOLA, Peter	6-3	205	L	Espoo, Finland	5/14/68	Boston U.
BENNING, Brian	6-0	195	L	Edmonton, Alta.	6/10/66	Los Angeles
BLAKE, Rob	6-3	215	R	Simcoe, Ont.	12/10/69	Los Angeles
BUSKAS, Rod	6-2	195	R	Wetaskiwin, Alta.	1/7/61	Los Angeles
CHAPDELAINE, Rene	6-1	195	R	Weyburn, Sask.	9/27/66	New Haven-Phoenix
CHYCHRUN, Jeff	6-4	215	L	LaSalle, Que.	5/3/66	Philadelphia
HOLDEN, Paul	6-3	210	L	Kitchener, Ont.	3/15/70	New Haven
HUDDY, Charlie	6-0	210	L	Oshawa, Ont.	6/2/59	Edmonton
JAQUES, Steve	5-11	180	L	Burnaby, B.C.	2/21/69	Phoenix
JOHNSON, Luke	5-9	175		Minneapolis, MN	11/9/69	U. Minnesota
LAIDLAW, Tom	6-2	205	L	Brampton, Ont.	4/15/58	Phoenix
MacDONALD, Kevin	6-0	195	L	Prescott, Ont.	2/24/66	Phoenix
McSORLEY, Marty	6-1	225	R	Hamilton, Ont.	5/18/63	Los Angeles
MILLER, Kris	6-0	200	L	Bemidji, MN	3/30/69	Minn.-Duluth
MINOR, Doug	6-2	195		Kenora, Ont.	3/2/71	Ottawa
POCHIPINSKI, Trevor	6-2	190	R	Saskatoon, Sask.	7/8/68	Colorado-New Haven
RICARD, Eric	6-4	200	R	St. Cesaire, Que.	2/16/69	New Haven-Phoenix
ROBINSON, Larry	6-3	220	L	Winchester, Ont.	6/2/51	Los Angeles
RUARK, Mike	6-2	190		Calgary, Alta.	4/18/71	Medicine Hat-Spokane-Portland
SYDOR, Darryl	6-0	205	L	Edmonton, Alta.	5/13/72	Kamloops
THOMPSON, Brent	6-2	175	L	Calgary, Alta.	1/9/71	Medicine Hat
WATTERS, Tim	5-11	185	L	Kamloops, B.C.	7/25/59	Los Angeles

GOALTENDERS	HT	WT	C	Place of Birth	Date	1990-91 Club
BASILIO, Sean	6-3	195		Stoney Creek, Ont.	9/21/71	London
BERTHIAUME, Daniel	5-9	150	L	Longueuil, Que.	1/26/66	Los Angeles
BOULIANE, Andre	5-10	165		Hull, Que.	7/2/71	Longueuil
GILMOUR, Darryl	6-0	171	L	Winnipeg, Man.	2/13/67	New Haven-Nashville
GOVERDE, Dave	6-0	210	L	Toronto, Ont.	4/9/70	Sudbury
HRUDEY, Kelly	5-10	185	L	Edmonton, Alta.	1/13/61	Los Angeles
MARION, Wayne				Pembroke, Ont.	2/18/71	Kanata
STAUBER, Robb	6-0	170	L	Duluth, MN	11/25/67	New Haven-L.A.

1990-91 Scoring

Regular Season

* rookie

Pos	#	Player	Team	GP	G	A	Pts	+/-	PIM	PP	SH	GW	GT	S	%
C	99	Wayne Gretzky	L.A.	78	41	122	163	30	16	8	0	5	2	212	19.3
L	20	Luc Robitaille	L.A.	76	45	46	91	28	68	11	0	5	1	229	19.7
R	7	Tomas Sandstrom	L.A.	68	45	44	89	27	106	16	0	6	1	221	20.4
L	21	Tony Granato	L.A.	68	30	34	64	22	154	11	1	3	0	197	15.2
D	28	Steve Duchesne	L.A.	78	21	41	62	19	66	8	0	3	0	171	12.3
C	6	Todd Elik	L.A.	74	21	37	58	20	58	2	0	4	0	153	13.7
R	18	Dave Taylor	L.A.	73	23	30	53	27	148	6	0	2	1	122	18.9
D	4	*Rob Blake	L.A.	75	12	34	46	3	125	9	0	2	0	150	8.0
D	33	Marty McSorley	L.A.	61	7	32	39	48	221	1	1	1	0	100	7.0
R	37	Robert Kudelski	L.A.	72	23	13	36	9	46	2	3	3	0	137	16.8
D	2	Brian Benning	L.A.	61	7	24	31	12	127	2	0	1	0	120	5.8
L	27	John Tonelli	L.A.	71	14	16	30	3	49	2	0	5	0	84	16.7
C	11	Steve Kasper	L.A.	67	9	19	28	3	33	0	1	1	0	70	12.9
D	19	Larry Robinson	L.A.	62	1	22	23	22	16	0	0	0	0	70	1.4
L	47	Brad Jones	L.A.	53	9	11	20	11	57	0	1	1	0	47	19.1
L	29	Jay Miller	L.A.	66	8	12	20	9	259	1	0	0	0	35	22.9
R	9	Ilkka Sinisalo	MIN	46	5	12	17	10–	24	1	1	1	0	68	7.4
			L.A.	7	0	0	0	4	2	0	0	0	0	4	.0
			TOTAL	53	5	12	17	6–	26	1	1	1	0	72	6.9
C	44	John McIntyre	TOR	13	0	3	3	0	25	0	0	0	0	7	.0
			L.A.	56	8	5	13	6	115	0	1	0	0	26	30.8
			TOTAL	69	8	8	16	6	140	0	1	0	0	33	24.2
L	23	Mike Donnelly	L.A.	53	7	5	12	3	41	0	0	2	0	76	9.2
D	77	Rod Buskas	L.A.	57	3	8	11	14	182	0	0	0	0	60	5.0
L	8	Scott Bjugstad	L.A.	31	2	4	6	5–	12	0	0	1	0	39	5.1
R	24	*Frank Breault	L.A.	17	1	4	5	1–	6	0	0	0	0	12	8.3
D	22	Bob Halkidis	L.A.	34	1	3	4	8	133	0	0	0	0	25	4.0
D	5	Tim Watters	L.A.	45	0	4	4	7	92	0	0	0	0	29	.0
R	17	Jim Thomson	L.A.	8	1	0	1	0	19	0	0	1	0	6	16.7
D	63	*Rene Chapdelaine	L.A.	3	0	1	1	1	10	0	0	0	0	1	.0
C	12	*Sylvain Couturier	L.A.	3	0	1	1	0	0	0	0	0	0	2	.0
D	26	*Rick Hayward	L.A.	4	0	0	0	0	5	0	0	0	0	0	.0
D	10	*Dennis Smith	L.A.	4	0	0	0	3	4	0	0	0	0	1	.0
G	36	Daniel Berthiaume	L.A.	37	0	0	0	0	10	0	0	0	0	0	.0
G	32	Kelly Hrudey	L.A.	47	0	0	0	0	14	0	0	0	0	0	.0

Goaltending

No.	Goaltender	GPI	Mins	Avg	W	L	T	EN	SO	GA	SA	S%
32	Kelly Hrudey	47	2730	2.90	26	13	6	4	3	132	1321	.900
36	Daniel Berthiaume	37	2119	3.31	20	11	4	1	1	117	1086	.892
	Totals	**80**	**4863**	**3.13**	**46**	**24**	**10**	**5**	**4**	**254**	**2412**	**.895**

Playoffs

Pos	#	Player	Team	GP	G	A	Pts	+/-	PIM	PP	SH	GW	OT	S	%
L	20	Luc Robitaille	LA	12	12	4	16	2–	22	5	0	2	1	44	27.3
C	99	Wayne Gretzky	LA	12	4	11	15	0	2	1	0	2	1	26	15.4
D	28	Steve Duchesne	LA	12	4	8	12	7	8	1	0	0	0	39	10.3
C	11	Steve Kasper	LA	10	4	6	10	4	8	0	1	0	0	11	36.4
L	23	Mike Donnelly	LA	12	5	4	9	6	6	0	0	0	0	29	17.2
C	6	Todd Elik	LA	12	2	7	9	0	6	0	0	0	0	32	6.3
R	7	Tomas Sandstrom	LA	10	4	4	8	1	14	3	0	0	0	32	12.5
L	27	John Tonelli	LA	12	2	4	6	1	12	1	0	0	0	16	12.5
R	37	Robert Kudelski	LA	8	3	2	5	4	2	0	0	0	0	13	23.1
D	4	*Rob Blake	LA	12	1	4	5	1–	26	1	0	0	0	19	5.3
L	21	Tony Granato	LA	12	1	4	5	1	28	0	0	0	0	32	3.1
D	19	Larry Robinson	LA	12	1	4	5	7	15	0	0	0	0	15	6.7
D	2	Brian Benning	LA	12	0	5	5	1	6	0	0	0	0	19	.0
R	18	Dave Taylor	LA	12	2	1	3	3–	12	0	0	1	0	25	8.0
L	47	Brad Jones	LA	8	1	1	2	2	2	0	0	1	0	6	16.7
D	77	Rod Buskas	LA	2	0	2	2	2	22	0	0	0	0	2	.0
R	9	Ilkka Sinisalo	LA	2	0	1	1	1	0	0	0	0	0	2	.0
C	44	John Mcintyre	LA	12	0	1	1	2–	24	0	0	0	0	5	.0
L	8	Scott Bjugstad	LA	2	0	0	0	0	0	0	0	0	0	5	.0
D	22	Bob Halkidis	LA	3	0	0	0	2–	0	0	0	0	0	2	.0
D	5	Tim Watters	LA	7	0	0	0	4–	12	0	0	0	0	4	.0
L	29	Jay Miller	LA	8	0	0	0	1–	17	0	0	0	0	2	.0
G	32	Kelly Hrudey	LA	12	0	0	0	0	2	0	0	0	0	0	.0
D	33	Marty McSorley	LA	12	0	0	0	1–	58	0	0	0	0	30	.0

Goaltending

No.	Goaltender	GPI	Mins	Avg	W	L	EN	SO	GA	SA	S%
32	Kelly Hrudey	12	798	2.78	6	6	0	0	37	382	.903
	Totals	12	799	2.78	6	6	0	0	37	382	.903

General Managers' History

Larry Regan, 1967-68 to 1972-73; Larry Regan and Jake Milford, 1973-74; Jake Milford, 1974-75 to 1976-77; George Maguire, 1977-78 to 1982-83; George Maguire and Rogatien Vachon, 1983-84; Rogatien Vachon, 1984-85 to date.

Coaching History

Leonard "Red" Kelly, 1967-68 to 1968-69; Hal Laycoe and John Wilson, 1969-70; Larry Regan, 1970-71; Larry Regan and Fred Glover, 1971-72; Bob Pulford, 1972-73 to 1976-77; Ron Stewart, 1977-78; Bob Berry, 1978-79 to 1980-81; Parker MacDonald and Don Perry, 1981-82; Don Perry, 1982-83; Don Perry, Rogatien Vachon and Roger Neilson, 1983-84; Pat Quinn, 1984-85 to 1985-86; Pat Quinn and Mike Murphy 1986-87; Mike Murphy and Robbie Ftorek, 1987-88; Robbie Ftorek, 1988-89; Tom Webster, 1989-90 to date.

Captains' History

Bob Wall, 1967-68, 1968-69; Larry Cahan, 1969-70, 1970-71; Bob Pulford, 1971-72, 1972-73; Terry Harper, 1973-74, 1974-75; Mike Murphy, 1975-76 to 1980-81; Dave Lewis, 1981-82, 1982-83; Terry Ruskowski, 1983-84, 1984-85; Dave Taylor, 1985-86 to 1988-89; Wayne Gretzky, 1989-90 to date.

Club Records

Team

(Figures in brackets for season records are games played; records for fewest points, wins, ties, losses, goals, goals against are for 70 or more games)

Most Points	105	1974-75 (80)
Most Wins	46	1990-91 (80)
Most Ties	21	1974-75 (80)
Most Losses	52	1969-70 (76)
Most Goals	376	1988-89 (80)
Most Goals Against	389	1985-86 (80)
Fewest Points	38	1969-70 (76)
Fewest Wins	14	1969-70 (76)
Fewest Ties	7	1988-89 (80)
		1989-90 (80)
Fewest Losses	17	1974-75 (80)
Fewest Goals	168	1969-70 (76)
Fewest Goals Against	185	1974-75 (80)

Longest Winning Streak
Over-all .... 8 Oct. 21-Nov. 7/72
Home .... 10 Oct. 13-Nov. 20/90
Away .... 8 Dec. 18/74-Jan. 16/75

Longest Undefeated Streak
Over-all .... 11 Feb. 28-Mar. 24/74 (9 wins, 2 ties)
Home .... 11 Oct. 11-Nov. 20/90 (10 wins, 1 tie)
Away .... 11 Oct. 10-Dec. 11/74 (6 wins, 5 ties)

Longest Losing Streak
Over-all .... 10 Feb. 22-Mar. 9/84
Home .... 9 Feb. 8-Mar. 12/86
Away .... 12 Jan. 11-Feb. 15/70

Longest Winless Streak
Over-all .... 17 Jan. 29-Mar. 5/70 (13 losses, 4 ties)

Home .... 9 Jan. 29-Mar. 5/70 (8 losses, 1 tie) Feb. 8-Mar. 12/86 (9 losses)
Away .... 21 Jan. 11-Apr. 3/70 (17 losses, 4 ties)

Most Shutouts, Season 9 1974-75 (80)
Most PIM, Season 2,228 1990-91 (80)
Most Goals, Game ....12 Nov. 28/84 (Van. 1 at L.A. 12)

Individual

Most Seasons	14	Dave Taylor
Most Games	953	Dave Taylor
Most Goals, Career	550	Marcel Dionne
Most Assists, Career	757	Marcel Dionne
Most Points Career	1,307	Marcel Dionne
Most PIM, Career	1,449	Dave Taylor
Most Shutouts, Career	32	Rogie Vachon

Longest Consecutive Games Streak ....324 Marcel Dionne (Jan. 7/78-Jan. 9/82)
Most Goals, Season ......70 Bernie Nicholls (1988-89)
Most Assists, Season ....122 Wayne Gretzky (1990-91)
Most Points, Season ....168 Wayne Gretzky (1988-89) (54 goals, 114 assists)
Most PIM, Season ......358 Dave Williams (1986-87)
Most Points, Defenseman Season ....76 Larry Murphy (1980-81) (16 goals, 60 assists)
Most Points, Center, Season ....168 Wayne Gretzky (1988-89) (54 goal, 114 assists)

Most Points, Right Wing, Season ....112 Dave Taylor (1980-81) (47 goals, 65 assists)
Most Points, Left Wing, Season ....111 Luc Robitaille (1987-88) (53 goals, 58 assists)
Most Points, Rookie, Season ....84 Luc Robitaille (1986-87) (45 goals, 39 assists)
Most Shutouts, Season .....8 Rogie Vachon (1976-77)
Most Goals, Game ....4 Several players
Most Assists, Game ....6 Bernie Nicholls (Dec. 1/88)
Most Points, Game ....8 Bernie Nicholls (Dec. 1/88)

Retired Numbers

30	Rogatien Vachon	1971-1978
16	Marcel Dionne	1975-1987

All-time Record vs. Other Clubs

Regular Season

	At Home							On Road							Total						
	GP	W	L	T	GF	GA	PTS	GP	W	L	T	GF	GA	PTS	GP	W	L	T	GF	GA	PTS
Boston	50	16	29	5	169	191	37	50	9	38	3	137	240	21	100	25	67	8	306	431	58
Buffalo	42	16	19	7	146	145	39	42	13	21	8	132	175	34	84	29	40	15	278	320	73
Calgary	59	31	23	5	241	226	67	60	16	36	8	203	285	40	119	47	59	13	444	511	107
Chicago	49	21	23	5	173	174	47	48	17	25	6	147	187	40	97	38	48	11	320	361	87
Detroit	54	32	12	10	233	157	74	54	24	23	7	200	217	55	108	56	35	17	433	374	129
Edmonton	44	16	20	8	189	211	40	44	9	26	9	174	245	27	88	25	46	17	363	456	67
Hartford	19	11	6	2	82	75	24	19	6	11	2	79	80	14	38	17	17	4	161	155	38
Minnesota	53	25	14	14	204	165	64	54	14	33	7	143	218	35	107	39	47	21	347	383	99
Montreal	54	14	34	6	160	218	34	54	7	36	11	143	249	25	108	21	70	17	303	467	59
New Jersey	32	24	2	6	180	99	54	31	14	12	5	120	101	33	63	38	14	11	300	200	87
NY Islanders	34	14	13	7	117	114	35	34	11	19	4	100	128	26	68	25	32	11	217	242	61
NY Rangers	48	19	20	9	160	169	47	48	15	28	5	143	193	35	96	34	48	14	303	362	82
Philadelphia	54	15	32	7	155	186	37	53	14	32	7	138	206	35	107	29	64	14	293	392	72
Pittsburgh	59	37	14	8	227	152	82	60	17	35	8	189	230	42	119	54	49	16	416	382	124
Quebec	19	11	7	1	89	69	23	19	9	7	3	78	76	21	38	20	14	4	167	145	44
St. Louis	53	27	19	7	191	155	61	53	13	34	6	142	204	32	106	40	53	13	333	359	93
Toronto	50	29	15	6	181	138	64	50	13	0	9	164	213	35	100	42	15	15	345	351	99
Vancouver	65	38	18	9	276	198	85	65	23	30	12	229	252	58	130	61	48	21	505	450	143
Washington	35	22	10	3	147	102	47	35	15	14	6	130	146	36	70	37	24	9	277	248	83
Winnipeg	41	14	20	7	171	174	35	42	15	20	7	158	186	37	83	29	40	14	329	360	72
Defunct Club	35	27	6	2	141	76	56	34	11	14	9	91	109	31	69	38	20	11	232	185	87
Totals	949	459	356	134	3632	3194	1052	949	285	494	142	3040	3940	712	1898	744	850	276	6672	7134	1764

Playoffs

	Series	W	L	GP	W	L	T	GF	GA	Last Mtg.	Round	Result
Boston	2	0	2	13	5	8	0	38	56	1977	QF	L 2-4
Calgary	5	3	2	20	9	11	0	72	84	1990	DSF	W 4-2
Chicago	1	0	1	5	1	4	0	7	10	1974	QF	L 1-4
Edmonton	6	2	4	30	10	20	0	20	21	1991	DF	L 2-4
Minnesota	1	0	1	7	3	4	0	21	26	1968	QF	L 3-4
NY Islanders	1	0	1	4	1	3	0	10	21	1980	PR	L 1-3
NY Rangers	2	0	2	6	1	5	0	14	32	1981	PR	L 1-3
St. Louis	1	0	1	4	0	4	0	5	16	1969	SF	L 0-4
Toronto	2	0	2	5	1	4	0	9	18	1978	PR	L 0-2
Vancouver	2	1	1	11	5	6	0	40	35	1991	DSF	W 4-2
Defunct Clubs	1	1	0	7	4	3	0	23	25			
Totals	24	7	17	112	40	72	0	348	454			

Playoff Results 1991-87

Year	Round	Opponent	Result	GF	GA
1991	DF	Edmonton	L 2-4	20	21
	DSF	Vancouver	W 4-2	26	16
1990	DF	Edmonton	L 0-4	10	24
	DSF	Calgary	W 4-2	29	24
1989	DF	Calgary	L 0-4	11	22
	DSF	Edmonton	W 4-3	25	20
1988	DSF	Calgary	L 4-1	18	30
1987	DSF	Edmonton	L 1-4	20	32

Abbreviations: Round: F Final; **CF** conference final; **DF** division final; **DSF** division semi-final; **SF** semi-final; **QF** quarter-final. **PR** preliminary round. **GA** goals against; **GF** goals for.

1990-91 Results

		Home				Away	
Oct.	4	NY Islanders	4-1	Oct.	9	Vancouver	6-2
	6	Vancouver	3-6		26	Winnipeg	2-6
	11	Edmonton	5-5		28	Winnipeg	6-2
	13	Boston	7-1		30	NY Islanders	4-1
	14	St Louis	4-1		31	NY Rangers	4-9
	17	Minnesota	5-2	Nov.	2	Washington	3-4
	19	Hartford	5-2		4	Chicago	2-0
	23	Calgary	6-4		22	Calgary	3-6
Nov.	8	Detroit	5-1		24	Montreal	4-2
	10	Edmonton	7-4		25	Quebec	4-4
	14	Buffalo	4-2		27	Detroit	3-4
	17	Pittsburgh	2-1		29	St Louis	4-4
	20	New Jersey	5-4	Dec.	18	Edmonton	3-4
Dec.	1	Toronto	3-4		20	Calgary	4-3
	5	Winnipeg	3-3		22	Vancouver	3-4
	8	Winnipeg	4-4		31	Minnesota	4-2
	11	NY Rangers	4-6	Jan.	2	NY Rangers	1-4
	13	Calgary	1-4		3	NY Islanders	6-3
	15	Edmonton	8-3		5	Toronto	4-2
	27	Philadelphia	5-7		6	Chicago	3-1
	29	Montreal	2-3		14	New Jersey	6-1
Jan.	8	Hartford	4-3		16	Hartford	3-4
	10	Buffalo	5-2		17	Boston	3-5
	12	Vancouver	6-2		22	Edmonton	2-4
	26	Vancouver	5-4		25	Vancouver	5-1
	30	New Jersey	2-4	Feb.	4	Detroit	6-4
Feb.	2	Vancouver	9-1		5	Philadelphia	3-2
	12	Calgary	4-4		8	Buffalo	4-4
	16	Boston	4-5		9	St Louis	4-5
	18	Washington*	5-2		14	Edmonton	4-2
	20	Quebec	6-1		22	Winnipeg	6-4
	26	Pittsburgh	8-2		24	Winnipeg*	5-3
	28	Winnipeg	4-2	Mar.	5	Washington	3-3
Mar.	2	Winnipeg	6-3		7	Pittsburgh	2-3
	12	Philadelphia	6-0		9	Quebec	3-0
	14	Chicago	3-6		10	Montreal	4-4
	20	Toronto	4-4		16	Calgary	4-3
	23	Calgary*	8-4		17	Vancouver	4-5
	26	Edmonton	2-0		24	Edmonton	4-3
	28	Minnesota	6-5		31	Calgary*	3-5

* Denotes afternoon game.

Entry Draft
Selections 1991-76

1991
Pick
- 42 Guy Leveque
- 79 Keith Redmond
- 81 Alexei Zhitnik
- 108 Pauli Jaks
- 130 Brett Seguin
- 152 Kelly Fairchild
- 196 Craig Brown
- 218 Mattias Olsson
- 240 Andre Bouliane
- 262 Michael Gaul

1990
Pick
- 7 Darryl Sydor
- 28 Brandy Semchuk
- 49 Bob Berg
- 91 David Goverde
- 112 Erik Andersson
- 133 Robert Lang
- 154 Dean Hulett
- 175 Denis Leblanc
- 196 Patrik Ross
- 217 K.J. (Kevin) White
- 238 Troy Mohns

1989
Pick
- 39 Brent Thompson
- 81 Jim Maher
- 102 Eric Ricard
- 103 Thomas Newman
- 123 Daniel Rydmark
- 144 Ted Kramer
- 165 Sean Whyte
- 182 Jim Giacin
- 186 Martin Maskarinec
- 207 Jim Hiller
- 228 Steve Jaques
- 249 Kevin Sneddon

1988
Pick
- 7 Martin Gelinas
- 28 Paul Holden
- 49 John Van Kessel
- 70 Rob Blake
- 91 Jeff Robison
- 109 Micah Aivazoff
- 112 Robert Larsson
- 133 Jeff Kruesel
- 154 Timo Peltomaa
- 175 Jim Larkin
- 196 Brad Hyatt
- 217 Doug Laprade
- 238 Joe Flanagan

1987
Pick
- 4 Wayne McBean
- 27 Mark Fitzpatrick
- 43 Ross Wilson
- 90 Mike Vukonich
- 111 Greg Batters
- 132 Kyosti Karjalainen
- 174 Jeff Gawlicki
- 195 John Preston
- 216 Rostislav Vlach
- 237 Mikael Lindholm

1986
Pick
- 2 Jimmy Carson
- 44 Denis Larocque
- 65 Sylvain Couturier
- 86 Dave Guden
- 107 Robb Stauber
- 128 Sean Krakiwsky
- 149 Rene Chapdelaine
- 170 Trevor Pochipinski
- 191 Paul Kelly
- 212 Russ Mann
- 233 Brian Hayton

1985
Pick
- 9 Craig Duncanson
- 10 Dan Gratton
- 30 Par Edlund
- 72 Perry Florio
- 93 Petr Prajzler
- 135 Tim Flannigan
- 156 John Hyduke
- 177 Steve Horner
- 219 Trent Ciprick
- 240 Marion Howarth

1984
- 6 Craig Redmond
- 24 Brian Wilks
- 48 John English
- 69 Tom Glavine
- 87 Dave Grannis
- 108 Greg Strome
- 129 Tim Hanley
- 150 Shannon Deegan
- 171 Luc Robitaille
- 192 Jeff Crossman
- 213 Paul Kenny
- 234 Brian Martin

1983
Pick
- 47 Bruce Shoebottom
- 67 Guy Benoit
- 87 Bob LaForest
- 100 Garry Galley
- 107 Dave Lundmark
- 108 Kevin Stevens
- 127 Tim Burgess
- 147 Ken Hammond
- 167 Bruce Fishback
- 187 Thomas Ahlen
- 207 Jan Blaha
- 227 Chad Johnson

1982
Pick
- 27 Mike Heidt
- 48 Steve Seguin
- 64 Dave Gans
- 82 Dave Ross
- 90 Darcy Roy
- 95 Ulf Issakson
- 132 Victor Nechaev
- 153 Peter Helander
- 174 Dave Chartier
- 195 John Franzosa
- 216 Ray Shero
- 237 Mats Ulander

1981
Pick
- 2 Doug Smith
- 39 Dean Kennedy
- 81 Marty Dallman
- 123 Brad Thompson
- 134 Craig Hurley
- 144 Peter Sawkins
- 165 Dan Brennan
- 186 Allan Tuer
- 207 Jeff Baikie

1980
Pick
- 4 Larry Murphy
- 10 Jim Fox
- 33 Greg Terrion
- 34 Dave Morrison
- 52 Steve Bozek
- 73 Bernie Nicholls
- 94 Alan Graves
- 115 Darren Eliot
- 136 Mike O'Connor
- 157 Bill O'Dwyer
- 178 Daryl Evans
- 199 Kim Collins

1979
Pick
- 16 Jay Wells
- 29 Dean Hopkins
- 30 Mark Hardy
- 50 J.P. Kelly
- 71 John Gibson
- 92 Jim Brown
- 113 Jay MacFarlane

1978
Pick
- 77 Paul Mancini
- 94 Doug Keans
- 111 Don Waddell
- 128 Rob Mierkains
- 145 Ric Scully
- 162 Brad Thiessen
- 177 Jim Armstrong
- 193 Claude Larochelle

1977
Pick
- 84 Julian Baretta
- 85 Warren Holmes
- 103 Randy Rudnyk
- 121 Bob Suter

1976
Pick
- 21 Steve Clippingdale
- 49 Don Moores
- 67 Bob Mears
- 85 Rob Palmer
- 103 Larry McRae

Club Directory

The Great Western Forum
3900 West Manchester Blvd.
P.O. Box 17013
Inglewood, California 90308
Phone 213/419-3160
FAX 213/673-8927
ENVOY ID
  Front Office: KINGS.GM
  Public Relations: KINGS.PR
Capacity: 16,005

Executive
Governor/President	Bruce McNall
Alternate Governors	Roy A. Mlakar, Rogatien Vachon
Executive Vice-President	Roy A. Mlakar
Executive Secretary to Vice-President	Susie Pulkkila
Vice-President	Steven H. Nesenblatt
Vice-President	Suzan A. Waks
Vice-President	Bruce Bargmann
Vice President, Adminstration	Robert Moor
Vice-President, Special Projects	Nora J. Rothrock
Vice President, Communications	Scott Carmichael
Executive Director, Marketing	Greg McElroy
Executive Director, Finance	Martin Greenspun

Hockey Operations
General Manager	Rogatien Vachon
Assistant General Manager	Nick Beverley
Administrative Assistant to General Manager	John Wolf
Executive Secretary to General Manager	Marcia Galloway
Head Coach	Tom Webster
Assistant Coaches	Rick Wilson, Cap Raeder
Director of Scouting and Development	Bob Owen
Scouting Staff	Jim Anderson, Ron Ansell, Serge Aubry, Serge Blanchard, John Bymark, Gary Harker, Jan Lindgren, Mark Miller, Al Murray, Vaclav Nedomansky, Don Perry, Alex Smart

Medical Staff
Head Trainer	Peter Demers
Equipment Manager	Peter Millar
Assistant Equipment Manager	Mark O'Neill
Massage Therapist	Juergen Merz
Team Physicians	Dr. Steve Lombardo, Dr. Ron Kvitne
Internist	Dr. Michael Mellman
Team Dentist	Dr. Gordon Knuth
Team Opthalmologist	Dr. Howard Lazerson
Team Hospital	Centinela Hospital Medical Centre

Communications/Marketing/Finance
Media Relations	Susan Carpenter
Media Relations, Assistant	Adam Fell
Director of Team Services	Ron Muniz
Director of Community and Player Relations	Jim Fox
Director of Publications	Nick Salata
Director of Merchandising	Harvey Boles
Director of Sales	Dennis Metz
Administrative Assistants	Kelley Clark, Angela Ladd
Play-by-Play Announcer/T.V.	Bob Miller
Color Commentator – Television	Jim Fox
Play-by-Play Announcer/Radio	Nick Nickson
Color Commentator – Radio	Brian Engblom
Video Coordinator	Bill Gurney
Radio Station	XTRA (690 AM)
Television	Prime Ticket Cable Network
Home ice	The Great Western Forum
Dimensions of Rink	200 feet by 85 feet
Supervisor of Off-Ice Officials	Bill Meuris
Public Address Announcer	David Courtney
Colors	Black, White and Silver
Training Camp	Lake Arrowhead, CA & The Forum
Location of Press Box	Westside Colonnade, Sec. 28, Row 1-10

Coach

WEBSTER, TOM
Coach, Los Angeles Kings. Born in Kirkland Lake, Ont., October 4, 1948.

In his second full season with Los Angeles, Tom Webster coached the Kings to their first-ever division title, their best ever overall finish and most wins in franchise history. In recognition of his accomplishment Webster was named a finalist for the 1991 Jack Adams Trophy as the NHL's Coach of the Year. Named on May 31, 1989 as the 16th head coach in Kings history, Webster joined Los Angeles after a two-year stint with the Windsor Spitfires of the OHL. While with Windsor he led his club to the OHL Championship in 1988.

In 1981, Webster led the Adirondack Red Wings of the AHL to a Calder Cup Championship and in 1984 he coached the Tulsa Oilers to the CHL Championship. Webster was the head coach of the New York Rangers for 14 games in 1986-87 before stepping down due to an ear ailment. Webster coached Canada's national junior team to a fourth-place finish at the 1989 World Championships in Alaska.

Drafted by the Boston Bruins in 1967, Webster spent two seasons in the NHL with the Detroit Red Wings (1970-71) and Oakland Seals (1971-72) before joining the New England Whalers of the WHA for seven seasons (1972-79). He completed his NHL career with the Red Wings in 1979-80.

Coaching Record
Season	Team	Games	Regular Season W	L	T	%	Playoffs Games	W	L	%
1979-80	Adirondack (AHL)	80	32	37	11	.469	5	1	4	.200
1980-81	Adirondack (AHL)	80	35	40	5	.469	18	12	6	.667
1981-82	Springfield (AHL)	80	32	43	5	.431	....	....	....	....
1982-83	Tulsa (CHL)	80	32	47	1	.406	....	....	....	....
1983-84	Tulsa (CHL)	68	36	27	5	.566	9	8	1	.889
1984-85	Salt lake (IHL)	82	35	39	8	.476	7	3	4	.429
1986-87	NY Rangers (NHL)	14	5	7	2	.429	....	....	....	....
1987-88	Windsor (OHL)	66	50	14	2	.773	12	12	0	1.000
1988-89	Windsor (OHL)	66	25	37	4	.409	4	0	4	.000
1989-90	Los Angeles (NHL)	80	34	39	7	.469	10	4	6	.400
1990-91	Los Angeles (NHL)	80	46	24	10	.638	12	6	6	.500
	NHL Totals	174	85	70	19	.543	22	10	12	.455

General Manager

VACHON, ROGATIEN
General Manager, Los Angeles Kings. Born in Palmorelle, Que., September 8, 1945.

Rogie Vachon was named general manager of the Kings on Jan. 30, 1984 after spending the first half of the 1983-84 season as an assistant coach to Don Perry. In his first year as GM of the club, Los Angeles improved from 59 points in 1983-84 to 82 points in 1984-85. A veteran of 16 NHL seasons, Vachon spent seven years in a Los Angeles uniform, in addition to Montreal, Detroit and Boston. While with the Canadiens in 1967-68, Vachon shared the Vezina Trophy with Lorne "Gump" Worsley. During his seven-year stint in Los Angeles from 1971 to 1978, Vachon helped the club emerge as one of the NHL's top defensive teams. In 1974-75, his finest season, Vachon was named *Hockey News'* Player of the Year after compiling a 2.24 average and a 27-14-13 record while leading the Kings to their highest point total in team history (105). Following his retirement in 1982, he returned to Los Angeles to instruct the Kings' young goaltenders.

Minnesota North Stars

1990-91 Results: 27w-39L-14T 68PTS. Fourth, Norris Division

Year-by-Year Record

Season	GP	Home W	L	T	Road W	L	T	Overall W	L	T	GF	GA	Pts.	Finished		Playoff Result
1990-91	80	19	15	6	8	24	8	27	39	14	256	266	68	4th,	Norris Div.	Lost Final
1989-90	80	26	12	2	10	28	2	36	40	4	284	291	76	4th,	Norris Div.	Lost Div. Semi-Final
1988-89	80	17	15	8	10	22	8	27	37	16	258	278	70	3rd,	Norris Div.	Lost Div. Semi-Final
1987-88	80	10	24	6	9	24	7	19	48	13	242	349	51	5th,	Norris Div.	Out of Playoffs
1986-87	80	17	20	3	13	20	7	30	40	10	296	314	70	5th,	Norris Div.	Out of Playoffs
1985-86	80	21	15	4	17	18	5	38	33	9	327	305	85	2nd,	Norris Div.	Lost Div. Semi-Final
1984-85	80	14	19	7	11	24	5	25	43	12	268	321	62	4th,	Norris Div.	Lost Div. Final
1983-84	80	22	14	4	17	17	6	39	31	10	345	344	88	1st,	Norris Div.	Lost Conf. Championship
1982-83	80	23	6	11	17	18	5	40	24	16	321	290	96	2nd,	Norris Div.	Lost Div. Final
1981-82	80	21	7	12	16	16	8	37	23	20	346	288	94	1st,	Norris Div.	Lost Div. Semi-Final
1980-81	80	23	10	7	12	18	10	35	28	17	291	263	87	3rd,	Adams Div.	Lost Final
1979-80	80	25	8	7	11	20	9	36	28	16	311	253	88	3rd,	Adams Div.	Lost Semi-Final
1978-79	80	19	15	6	9	25	6	28	40	12	257	289	68	4th,	Adams Div.	Out Of Playoffs
1977-78	80	12	24	4	6	29	5	18	53	9	218	325	45	5th,	Smythe Div.	Out of Playoffs
1976-77	80	17	14	9	6	25	9	23	39	18	240	310	64	2nd,	Smythe Div.	Lost Prelim. Round
1975-76	80	15	22	3	5	31	4	20	53	7	195	303	47	4th,	Smythe Div.	Out of Playoffs
1974-75	80	17	20	3	6	30	4	23	50	7	221	341	53	4th,	Smythe Div.	Out of Playoffs
1973-74	78	18	15	6	5	23	11	23	38	17	235	275	63	7th,	West Div.	Out of Playoffs
1972-73	78	26	8	5	11	22	6	37	30	11	254	230	85	3rd,	West Div.	Lost Quarter-Final
1971-72	78	22	11	6	15	18	6	37	29	12	212	191	86	2nd,	West Div.	Lost Quarter-Final
1970-71	78	16	15	8	12	19	8	28	34	16	191	223	72	4th,	West Div.	Lost Semi-Final
1969-70	76	11	16	11	8	19	11	19	35	22	224	257	60	3rd,	West Div.	Lost Quarter-Final
1968-69	76	11	21	6	7	22	9	18	43	15	189	270	51	6th,	West Div.	Out of Playoffs
1967-68	74	17	12	8	10	20	7	27	32	15	191	226	69	4th,	West Div.	Lost Semi-Final

Schedule

Home			Away		
Oct.	Sat.	5 Chicago	**Oct.**	Tues.	15 Calgary
	Thur.	10 Quebec		Thur.	17 San Jose
	Sat.	12 Detroit		Sat.	19 Los Angeles
	Tues.	22 Calgary		Tues.	29 NY Rangers
	Thur.	24 Philadelphia		Thur.	31 Pittsburgh
	Sat.	26 Boston	**Nov.**	Sun.	3 Chicago
Nov.	Sat.	2 Chicago		Tues.	5 Detroit
	Sat.	9 Pittsburgh		Wed.	6 Toronto
	Tues.	12 Toronto		Sat.	16 St Louis
	Tues.	19 NY Islanders		Fri.	22 Detroit
	Sat.	23 Detroit		Sat.	30 Toronto
	Fri.	29 Toronto	**Dec.**	Sun.	8 Chicago
Dec.	Tues.	3 St Louis		Thur.	12 Vancouver
	Wed.	4 St Louis		Sat.	14 San Jose
	Sat.	7 Washington		Tues.	17 Los Angeles
	Tues.	10 New Jersey		Thur.	26 Winnipeg
	Sat.	21 Philadelphia	**Jan.**	Thur.	2 St Louis
	Sat.	28 St Louis		Sun.	5 Chicago
	Tues.	31 Chicago		Tues.	7 Washington
Jan.	Sat.	4 Vancouver		Thur.	9 Detroit
	Sat.	11 San Jose		Mon.	27 Boston
	Mon.	13 Edmonton		Tues.	28 Hartford
	Wed.	15 Montreal		Thur.	30 Philadelphia
	Wed.	22 Los Angeles	**Feb.**	Wed.	5 Toronto
	Sat.	25 Chicago*		Fri.	7 Buffalo
Feb.	Sat.	1 NY Rangers		Sun.	9 Hartford*
	Mon.	3 Toronto		Mon.	17 Montreal
	Tues.	11 Edmonton		Tues.	18 Quebec
	Thur.	13 Winnipeg		Fri.	21 NY Rangers
	Sat.	15 Pittsburgh		Sat.	22 NY Islanders
	Wed.	26 Montreal		Mon.	24 New Jersey
	Sat.	29 Hartford*	**Mar.**	Sun.	1 Toronto
Mar.	Sun.	8 Winnipeg		Tues.	3 Washington
	Wed.	11 Toronto		Thur.	5 Detroit
	Sat.	14 Detroit*		Tues.	10 St Louis
	Tues.	17 Buffalo		Thur.	19 Chicago
	Tues.	24 Vancouver		Sat.	21 Quebec
	Tues.	31 Buffalo		Fri.	27 Edmonton
Apr.	Thur.	2 St Louis		Sat.	28 Calgary
	Sat.	4 Detroit	**Apr.**	Sun.	5 St Louis

* Denotes afternoon game.

Home Starting Times:
All Games .... 7:05 p.m.
Except Matinees .... 1:05 p.m.

Franchise date: June 5, 1967

25th NHL Season

Dave Gagner's second consecutive 40-goal season helped him lead the Stars in scoring in 1990-91.

1991-92 Player Personnel

FORWARDS	HT	WT	S	Place of Birth	Date	1990-91 Club
BARNETT, Brett	6-3	185	L	Toronto, Ont.	10/12/67	Cincinnati-Roanoke
BARRAULT, Doug	6-2	205	R	Golden, B.C.	4/21/70	Lethbridge-Seattle
BELLOWS, Brian	5-11	195	L	St. Catharines, Ont.	9/1/64	Minnesota
BEREZAN, Perry	6-2	190	R	Edmonton, Alta.	12/5/64	Minnesota
BLUM, Ken	6-1	185	R	Hackensack, N.J.	6/8/71	Hamilton
BUREAU, Marc	6-0	190	R	Trois Rivieres, Que.	5/19/66	Minnesota-Calgary
CHURLA, Shane	6-1	200	R	Fernie, B.C.	6/24/65	Minnesota
CRAIG, Mike	6-1	180	R	St. Mary's, Ont.	6/6/71	Minnesota
DAHLEN, Ulf	6-2	195	L	Ostersund, Sweden	1/12/67	Minnesota
DUCHESNE, Gaetan	5-11	200	L	Les Saulles, Que.	7/11/62	Minnesota
ELIK, Todd	6-2	190	L	Brampton, Ont.	4/15/66	Los Angeles
GAGNER, Dave	5-10	180	L	Chatham, Ont.	12/11/64	Minnesota
GAVIN, Stewart	6-0	190	L	Ottawa, Ont.	3/15/60	Minnesota
GOTAAS, Steve	5-10	180	R	Camrose, Alta.	5/10/67	Kalamazoo
HAWORTH, Alan	5-10	185	R	Drummondville, Que.	9/1/60	Bern
KOVACS, Frank	6-2	205	L	Regina, Sask.	6/6/71	Regina
LARTER, Tyler	5-10	185	L	Charlottetown, P.E.I.	3/12/68	Baltimore
LENARDON, Tim	6-2	185	L	Trail, B.C.	5/11/62	Fiemme
MALTAIS, Steve	6-2	210	L	Arvida, Que.	1/25/69	Baltimore
McGOWAN, Cal	6-1	185	L	Sydny, Nebraska	6/19/70	Kamloops
McRAE, Basil	6-2	205	L	Beaverton, Ont.	1/5/61	Minnesota
MESSIER, Mitch	6-2	200	R	Regina, Sask.	8/21/65	K-zoo-Minnesota
MODANO, Mike	6-3	190	L	Livonia, MI	6/7/70	Minnesota
PENNEY, Jackson	5-10	180	L	Edmonton, Alta.	2/5/69	Kalamazoo
PROPP, Brian	5-10	195	L	Lanigan, Sask.	2/15/59	Minnesota
ROBINSON, Scott	6-2	180	L	100 Mile House, B.C.	3/29/64	Kalamazoo
SMITH, Bobby	6-4	210	L	North Sydney, N.S.	2/12/58	Montreal
SPENRATH, Greg	6-1	210	L	Edmonton, Alta.	9/27/69	Erie
THYER, Mario	5-11	170	L	Montreal, Que.	9/29/66	Kalamazoo
DEFENSEMEN						
BILLECK, Laurie	6-3	210	R	Dauphin, Man.	2/2/71	Prince Albert
CICCONE, Enrico	6-4	200	L	Montreal, Que.	4/10/70	Kalamazoo
DAHLQUIST, Chris	6-1	190	L	Fridley, MN	12/14/62	Minnesota-Pittsburgh
GILES, Curt	5-8	175	L	The Pas, Man.	11/30/58	Minnesota
GLYNN, Brian	6-4	215	L	Iserlohn, Germany	11/23/67	Minnesota-Salt Lake
HATCHER, Derian	6-5	205	L	Sterling Hts., MI	6/4/72	North Bay
JERRARD, Paul	5-10	185	R	Winnipeg, Man.	4/20/65	Kalamazoo
JOHNSON, Jim	6-1	190	L	New Hope, MN	8/9/62	Minnesota-Pittsburgh
LUDWIG, Craig	6-3	217	L	Rhinelander, WI	3/15/61	NY Islanders
MARSHALL, Paul	6-2	185	L	Quincy, MA	10/22/66	Albany-San Diego
MITCHELL, Roy	6-1	200	R	Edmonton, Alta.	3/14/69	Fredericton
MOYLAN, Dave	6-1	195	L	Tilsonburg, Ont.	8/13/67	Kalamazoo
PEDERSON, Allen	6-4	205	L	Edmonton, Alta.	1/13/65	Boston-Maine
RAMAGE, Rob	6-2	195	R	Byron, Ont.	1/11/59	Toronto
SANDELIN, Scott	6-0	200	R	Hibbing, MN	8/8/64	Hershey
STRAUB, Brian	6-2	195	L	Bozeman, MT	7/2/68	U. of Maine
TINORDI, Mark	6-4	205	L	Red Deer, Alta.	5/9/66	Minnesota

GOALTENDERS	HT	WT	C	Place of Birth	Date	1990-91 Club
CASEY, Jon	5-10	155	L	Grand Rapids, MN	3/29/62	Minnesota
DYCK, Larry	5-11	180	L	Winkler, Man.	12/15/65	Kalamazoo
GUENETTE, Steve	5-10	175	L	Gloucester, Ont.	11/13/65	Calgary-Salt Lake
HOUK, Rod	5-8	170	L	Regina, Sask.	2/2/68	U. of Regina
STOLP, Jeff	6-0	180	L	Nashwak, MN	6/20/70	U. of Minnesota
WAKALUK, Darcy	5-11	180	L	Pincher Creek, Alta.	3/14/66	Buffalo

General Managers' History

Wren A. Blair, 1967-68 to 1973-74; Jack Gordon, 1974-75 to 1976-77; Lou Nanne, 1977-78 to 1987-88; Jack Ferreira, 1988-89 to 1989-90; Bob Clarke 1990-91 to date.

Coaching History

Wren Blair, 1967-68; John Muckler and Wren Blair, 1968-69; Wren Blair and Charlie Bruns, 1969-70; Jackie Gordon, 1970-71 to 1972-73; Jackie Gordon and Parker MacDonald, 1973-74; Jackie Gordon and Charlie Burns, 1974-75; Ted Harris, 1975-76 to 1976-77; Ted Harris, Andŕe Beaulieu, Lou Nanne, 1977-78; Harry Howell and Glen Sonmor, 1978-79; Glen Sonmor, 1979-80 to 1981-82; Glen Sonmor and Murray Oliver, 1982-83; Bill Mahoney, 1983-84 to 1984-85; Lorne Henning, 1985-86; Lorne Henning and Glen Sonmor, 1986-87; Herb Brooks, 1987-88; Pierre Page, 1988-89 to 1989-90; Bob Gainey, 1990-91 to date.

Captains' History

Bob Woytowich, 1967-68; Elmer Vasko, 1968-69; Claude Larose, 1969-70; Ted Harris, 1970-71 to 1973-74; Bill Goldsworthy, 1974-75, 1975-76; Bill Hogaboam, 1976-77; Nick Beverly, 1977-78; J.P. Parise, 1978-79; Paul Shmyr, 1979-80, 1980-81; Tim Young, 1981-82; Craig Hartsburg, 1982-83; Brian Bellows, Craig Hartsburg, 1983-84; Craig Hartsburg, 1984-85 to 1987-88; Curt Fraser, Bob Rouse and Curt Giles, 1988-89; Curt Giles, 1989-90 to 1990-91.

1990-91 Scoring

Regular Season

* rookie

Pos	#	Player	Team	GP	G	A	Pts	+/−	PIM	PP	SH	GW	GT	S	%
C	15	Dave Gagner	MIN	73	40	42	82	9	114	20	0	5	2	223	17.9
L	23	Brian Bellows	MIN	80	35	40	75	13−	43	17	0	4	0	296	11.8
L	16	Brian Propp	MIN	79	26	47	73	7	58	9	0	1	0	171	15.2
C	7	Neal Broten	MIN	79	13	56	69	3−	26	1	2	0	1	191	6.8
R	9	Mike Modano	MIN	79	28	36	64	2	61	9	0	2	2	232	12.1
C	18	Bobby Smith	MIN	73	15	31	46	9−	60	7	0	2	1	121	12.4
R	22	Ulf Dahlen	MIN	66	21	18	39	7	6	4	0	3	0	133	15.8
D	24	Mark Tinordi	MIN	69	5	27	32	1	189	1	0	2	0	92	5.4
L	14	Doug Smail	WPG	15	1	2	3	6−	10	0	0	0	0	18	5.6
			MIN	57	7	13	20	2−	38	0	2	0	0	89	7.9
			TOTAL	72	8	15	23	8−	48	0	2	0	0	107	7.5
D	6	Brian Glynn	MIN	66	8	11	19	5−	83	3	0	0	0	111	7.2
L	10	Gaetan Duchesne	MIN	68	9	9	18	4	18	0	0	1	0	100	9.0
C	21	Perry Berezan	MIN	52	11	6	17	2−	30	1	3	1	0	73	15.1
D	8	Jim Johnson	PIT	24	0	5	5	3−	23	0	0	0	0	22	.0
			MIN	44	1	9	10	9	100	0	0	0	0	61	1.6
			TOTAL	68	1	14	15	6	123	0	0	0	0	83	1.2
D	2	Curt Giles	MIN	70	4	10	14	3	48	0	0	0	0	53	7.5
R	20	*Mike Craig	MIN	39	8	4	12	11−	32	1	0	2	0	59	13.6
D	4	Chris Dahlquist	PIT	22	1	2	3	0	30	0	0	0	0	15	6.7
			MIN	42	2	6	8	1−	33	0	0	0	0	37	5.4
			TOTAL	64	3	8	11	1−	63	0	0	0	0	52	5.8
D	5	Neil Wilkinson	MIN	50	2	9	11	5−	117	0	0	0	0	55	3.6
L	12	Stewart Gavin	MIN	38	4	4	8	3−	36	0	1	0	0	56	7.1
C	11	*Marc Bureau	CGY	5	0	0	0	4−	2	0	0	0	0	4	.0
			MIN	9	0	6	6	3−	4	0	0	0	0	8	.0
			TOTAL	14	0	6	6	7−	6	0	0	0	0	12	.0
D	3	Rob Zettler	MIN	47	1	4	5	10−	119	0	0	0	0	30	3.3
R	27	Shane Churla	MIN	40	2	2	4	1	286	0	0	0	0	32	6.3
D	26	Shawn Chambers	MIN	29	1	3	4	2	24	0	0	0	0	55	1.8
L	17	Basil McRae	MIN	40	1	3	4	8−	224	0	0	0	0	44	2.3
L	31	Larry DePalma	MIN	14	3	0	3	5−	26	1	0	1	0	18	16.7
G	30	Jon Casey	MIN	55	0	2	2	0	22	0	0	0	0	0	.0
L	29	*Warren Babe	MIN	1	0	1	1	1	0	0	0	0	0	0	.0
D	32	*Pat MacLeod	MIN	1	0	1	1	1	0	0	0	0	0	1	.0
D	46	*Dan Keczmer	MIN	9	0	1	1	0	6	0	0	0	0	6	.0
C	34	Steve Gotaas	MIN	1	0	0	0	1−	2	0	0	0	0	2	.0
R	37	*Mitch Messier	MIN	2	0	0	0	2−	0	0	0	0	0	0	.0
G	35	Jarmo Myllys	MIN	2	0	0	0	0	2	0	0	0	0	0	.0
L	44	*Kevin Evans	MIN	4	0	0	0	3−	19	0	0	0	0	2	.0
D	40	*Dean Kolstad	MIN	5	0	0	0	2−	15	0	0	0	0	9	.0
L	45	*Mike McHugh	MIN	6	0	0	0	3−	0	0	0	0	0	4	.0
G	1	Brian Hayward	MTL	0	0	0	0	0	0	0	0	0	0	0	.0
			MIN	26	0	0	0	0	2	0	0	0	0	0	.0
			TOTAL	26	0	0	0	0	2	0	0	0	0	0	.0

Goaltending

No.	Goaltender	GPI	Mins	Avg	W	L	T	EN	SO	GA	SA	S%
30	Jon Casey	55	3185	2.98	21	20	11	5	3	158	1450	.891
1	Brian Hayward	26	1473	3.14	6	15	3	4	2	77	674	.886
1	Kari Takko	2	119	6.05	0	2	0	1	0	12	74	.838
35	Jarmo Myllys	2	78	6.15	0	2	0	1	0	8	57	.860
	Totals	**80**	**4876**	**3.27**	**27**	**39**	**14**	**11**	**5**	**266**	**2266**	**.883**

Playoffs

Pos	#	Player	Team	GP	G	A	Pts	+/−	PIM	PP	SH	GW	OT	S	%
L	23	Brian Bellows	MIN	23	10	19	29	6−	30	6	0	1	0	68	14.7
C	15	Dave Gagner	MIN	23	12	15	27	4−	28	6	1	1	0	78	15.4
L	16	Brian Propp	MIN	23	8	15	23	4−	28	8	0	3	1	52	15.4
C	7	Neal Broten	MIN	23	9	13	22	2	6	2	1	0	0	55	16.4
R	9	Mike Modano	MIN	23	8	12	20	3−	16	3	0	1	0	59	13.6
C	18	Bobby Smith	MIN	23	8	8	16	5−	56	2	0	5	0	60	13.3
L	12	Stewart Gavin	MIN	21	3	10	13	9	20	0	1	1	0	40	7.5
D	24	Mark Tinordi	MIN	23	5	6	11	1−	78	4	0	0	0	54	9.3
R	22	Ulf Dahlen	MIN	15	2	6	8	4−	4	0	0	0	0	26	7.7
D	6	Brian Glynn	MIN	23	2	6	8	8−	18	2	0	0	0	43	4.7
D	4	Chris Dahlquist	MIN	23	1	6	7	4	20	0	0	0	0	21	4.8
D	26	Shawn Chambers	MIN	23	0	7	7	7−	16	0	0	0	0	44	.0
D	5	Neil Wilkinson	MIN	22	3	3	6	1	12	1	0	0	0	31	9.7
C	11	*Marc Bureau	MIN	23	3	2	5	4−	20	0	1	0	0	19	15.8
L	10	Gaetan Duchesne	MIN	23	2	3	5	0	34	0	0	0	0	26	7.7
R	27	Shane Churla	MIN	22	2	1	3	2−	90	0	0	1	0	14	14.3
R	20	*Mike Craig	MIN	10	1	1	2	2−	20	1	0	1	0	12	8.3
L	17	Basil McRae	MIN	22	1	1	2	3−	94	0	0	0	0	15	6.7
D	2	Curt Giles	MIN	10	1	0	1	4−	16	0	0	0	0	7	14.3
D	8	Jim Johnson	MIN	14	0	1	1	8	52	0	0	0	0	12	.0
G	30	Jon Casey	MIN	23	0	1	1	0	12	0	0	0	0	0	.0
C	21	Perry Berezan	MIN	1	0	0	0	1−	0	0	0	0	0	2	.0
L	14	Doug Smail	MIN	1	0	0	0	1−	0	0	0	0	0	0	.0
G	1	Brian Hayward	MIN	6	0	0	0	0	0	0	0	0	0	0	.0

Goaltending

No.	Goaltender	GPI	Mins	Avg	W	L	EN	SO	GA	SA	S%
30	Jon Casey	23	1205	3.04	14	7	2	1	61	571	.893
1	Brian Hayward	6	171	3.86	0	2	1	0	11	75	.853
	Totals	23	1384	3.25	14	9	3	1	75	649	.884

Retired Numbers

19 Bill Masterton 1967-1968

Club Records

Team

(Figures in brackets for season records are games played; records for fewest points, wins, ties, losses, goals, goals against are for 70 or more games)

Most Points	96	1982-83 (80)
Most Wins	40	1982-83 (80)
Most Ties	22	1969-70 (76)
Most Losses	53	1975-76, 1977-78 (80)
Most Goals	346	1981-82 (80)
Most Goals Against	349	1987-88 (80)
Fewest Points	45	1977-78 (80)
Fewest Wins	18	1968-69 (76)
		1977-78 (80)
Fewest Ties	4	1989-90 (80)
Fewest Losses	23	1981-82 (80)
Fewest Goals	189	1968-69 (76)
Fewest Goals Against	191	1971-72 (78)

Longest Winning Streak
Over-all .... 7 — Mar. 16-28/80
Home .... 11 — Nov. 4-Dec. 27/72
Away .... 5 — Dec. 2-16/67
                          Feb. 5-Mar. 5/83

Longest Undefeated Streak
Over-all .... 12 — Feb. 18-Mar. 15/82
                          (9 wins, 3 ties)
Home .... 13 — Oct. 28-Dec. 27/72
                          (12 wins, 1 tie)
                          Nov. 21-Jan. 9/80
                          (10 wins, 3 ties)
                          Jan. 17-Mar. 17/91
                          (11 wins, 2 ties)
Away .... 6 — Nov. 30-Dec. 16/67
                          (5 wins, 1 tie)
                          Nov. 7-27/71
                          (5 wins, 1 tie)
                          Nov. 9-Dec. 3/83
                          (5 wins, 1 tie)

Longest Losing Streak
Over-all .... 10 — Feb. 1-20/76
Home .... 6 — Jan. 17-Feb. 4/70

Away .... 8 — Oct. 19-Nov. 13/75; Jan. 28-Mar. 3/88

Longest Winless Streak
Over-all .... 20 — Jan. 15-Feb. 28/70
                          (15 losses, 5 ties)
Home .... 12 — Jan. 17-Feb. 25/70
                          (8 losses, 4 ties)
Away .... 23 — Oct. 25/74-Jan. 28/75
                          (19 losses, 4 ties)

Most Shutouts, Season ... 7 — 1972-73 (78)
Most PIM, Season ..... 2,313 — 1987-88 (80)
Most Goals, Game .... 15 — Nov. 11/81 (Wpg. 2 at Minn. 15)

Individual

Most Seasons	12	Curt Giles
Most Games	760	Curt Giles
Most Goals, Career	332	Dino Ciccarelli
Most Assists, Career	500	Neal Broten
Most Points Career	729	Neal Broten (229 goals, 500 assists)
Most PIM, Career	1,322	Basil McRae
Most Shutouts, Career	26	Cesare Maniago

Longest Consecutive
Games Streak .... 442 — Danny Grant (Dec. 4/68-Apr. 7/74)
Most Goals, Season ...... 55 — Dino Ciccarelli (1981-82)
                              Brian Bellows (1989-90)
Most Assists, Season ...... 76 — Neal Broten (1985-86)
Most Points, Season ..... 114 — Bobby Smith (1981-82) (43 goals, 71 assists)
Most PIM, Season .... 382 — Basil McRae (1987-88)
Most Points, Defenseman Season .... 77 — Craig Hartsburg (1981-82) (17 goals, 60 assists)

Most Points, Center, Season ... 114 — Bobby Smith (1981-82) (43 goals, 71 assists)
Most Points, Right Wing, Season ... 107 — Dino Ciccarelli (1981-82) (55 goals, 52 assists)
Most Point, Left Wing, Season ... 99 — Brian Bellows (1989-90) (55 goals, 44 assists)
Most Points, Rookie, Season ... 98 — Neal Broten (1981-82) (38 goals, 60 assists)
Most Shutouts, Season ... 6 — Cesare Maniago (1967-68)
Most Goals, Game ... 5 — Tim Young (Jan. 15/79)
Most Assists, Game ... 5 — Murray Oliver (Oct. 24/71) Larry Murphy (Oct. 17/89)
Most Points, Game ... 7 — Bobby Smith (Nov. 11/81)

All-time Record vs. Other Clubs

Regular Season

			At Home							On Road							Total					
	GP	W	L	T	GF	GA	PTS	GP	W	L	T	GF	GA	PTS	GP	W	L	T	GF	GA	PTS
Boston	50	11	28	11	136	192	33	50	6	37	7	118	231	19	100	17	65	18	254	423	52
Buffalo	42	17	19	6	131	135	40	42	9	23	10	113	162	28	84	26	42	16	244	297	68
Calgary	37	18	14	5	141	121	41	36	4	22	10	95	149	18	73	22	36	15	236	270	59
Chicago	77	34	32	11	276	266	79	77	18	50	9	206	324	45	154	52	82	20	482	590	124
Detroit	73	41	20	12	290	209	94	72	26	34	12	248	283	64	145	67	54	24	538	492	158
Edmonton	19	6	9	4	70	69	16	19	1	12	6	61	99	8	38	7	21	10	131	168	24
Hartford	19	11	7	1	83	64	23	19	10	9	0	71	69	20	38	21	16	1	154	133	43
Los Angeles	54	33	14	7	218	143	73	53	14	25	14	165	204	42	107	47	39	21	383	347	115
Montreal	48	12	26	10	123	175	34	48	9	32	7	122	209	25	96	21	58	17	245	384	59
New Jersey	34	20	8	6	140	89	46	34	15	16	3	111	113	33	68	35	24	9	251	202	79
NY Islanders	36	13	18	5	105	139	31	36	9	19	8	107	144	26	72	22	37	13	212	283	57
NY Rangers	50	15	28	7	154	198	37	50	10	30	10	138	181	30	100	25	58	17	292	379	67
Philadelphia	55	22	20	13	182	186	57	56	8	38	10	126	223	26	111	30	58	23	308	409	83
Pittsburgh	53	30	18	5	207	181	65	53	15	33	5	142	202	35	106	45	51	10	349	383	100
Quebec	19	11	6	2	76	62	24	19	4	13	2	51	92	10	38	15	19	4	127	154	34
St. Louis	81	35	31	15	280	246	85	83	24	42	17	238	294	65	164	59	73	32	518	540	150
Toronto	74	38	27	9	289	249	85	75	26	35	14	250	276	66	149	64	62	23	539	525	151
Vancouver	45	28	10	7	193	129	63	45	14	23	8	140	182	36	90	42	33	15	333	311	99
Washington	29	13	8	8	112	85	34	29	9	13	7	86	95	25	58	22	21	15	198	180	59
Winnipeg	21	12	7	2	98	67	26	21	10	10	1	73	74	21	42	22	17	3	171	141	47
Defunct Club	33	19	8	6	123	86	44	32	10	16	6	84	105	26	65	29	24	12	207	191	70
Totals	949	439	358	152	3427	3091	1030	949	251	532	166	2745	3711	668	1898	690	890	318	6172	6802	1698

Playoffs

	Series	W	L	GP	W	L	T	GF	GA	Last Mtg.	Round	Result
Boston	1	1	0	3	3	0	0	20	13	1981	PR	W 3-0
Buffalo	2	1	1	7	4	3	0	26	28	1981	QF	W 4-1
Calgary	1	1	0	6	4	2	0	25	18	1981	SF	W 4-2
Chicago	6	2	4	33	14	19	0	119	119	1991	DSF	W 4-2
Edmonton	2	1	1	9	4	5	0	30	36	1991	CF	W 4-1
Los Angeles	1	1	0	7	4	3	0	26	21	1968	QF	W 4-3
Montreal	2	1	1	13	6	7	0	37	48	1980	QF	W 4-3
NY Islanders	1	0	1	5	1	4	0	16	26	1981	F	L 1-4
Philadelphia	2	0	2	11	3	8	0	26	41	1980	SF	L 1-4
Pittsburgh	1	0	1	6	2	4	0	16	28	1991	F	L 2-4
St. Louis	9	4	5	52	26	26	0	158	152	1991	DF	W 4-2
Toronto	2	2	0	7	6	1	0	35	26	1983	DSF	W 3-1
Totals	30	14	16	159	77	82	0	534	556			

Playoff Results 1991-87

Year	Round	Opponent	Result	GF	GA
1991	F	Pittsburgh	L 2-4	16	28
	CF	Edmonton	W 4-1	20	14
	DF	St. Louis	W 4-2	22	17
	DSF	Chicago	W 4-2	23	16
1990	DSF	Chicago	L 3-4	18	21
1989	DSF	St. Louis	L 1-4	15	23

Abbreviations: Round: F Final; **CF** conference final; **DF** division final; **DSF** division semi-final; **SF** semi-final; **QF** quarter-final. **PR** preliminary round. **GA** goals against; **GF** goals for.

1990-91 Results

		Home				Away	
Oct.	4	St Louis	2-3	Oct.	8	NY Rangers	3-6
	6	NY Islanders	4-2		9	New Jersey	2-5
	11	Boston	3-3		17	Los Angeles	2-5
	13	Chicago	1-4		20	St Louis	2-2
	24	Hartford	3-0		21	Chicago	1-7
	27	Detroit	2-2		26	Detroit	6-8
Nov.	8	Quebec	3-2		30	Toronto	4-5
	10	Hartford	2-3	Nov.	1	Philadelphia	3-6
	13	Pittsburgh	1-4		3	Quebec	2-0
	15	NY Rangers	2-4		4	Montreal	2-2
	17	St Louis	2-3		19	NY Rangers	2-2
	23	Vancouver	6-4		21	Detroit	3-4
	24	New Jersey	3-5		27	Vancouver	1-1
Dec.	1	Pittsburgh	6-3		30	Winnipeg	4-2
	6	Toronto	1-2	Dec.	5	Toronto	3-2
	8	Philadelphia	7-0		13	St Louis	2-4
	11	Calgary	4-5		16	Chicago*	2-5
	15	Chicago*	5-1		20	Pittsburgh	3-4
	26	Winnipeg	4-6		22	Boston	2-6
	29	Boston	4-4		23	Hartford	5-2
	31	Los Angeles	2-4	Jan.	2	Detroit	2-6
Jan.	3	Toronto	3-3		8	NY Islanders	3-0
	5	Vancouver	5-6		13	Chicago	3-5
	12	Buffalo	3-5		21	Winnipeg	0-2
	15	Montreal	1-5		25	Washington	2-2
	17	Washington	5-2		26	New Jersey	3-1
	22	St Louis	7-3		28	Toronto	0-4
	30	Detroit	5-2	Feb.	2	Quebec	6-4
Feb.	7	Toronto	4-2		4	Montreal	3-5
	9	Detroit	6-5		12	NY Islanders	4-5
	20	Edmonton	5-1		13	Buffalo	6-6
	23	Chicago	3-3		16	Detroit*	3-0
	26	Philadelphia	2-2	Mar.	1	Edmonton	1-1
Mar.	6	Edmonton	5-1		2	Calgary	1-5
	9	Detroit*	6-2		14	St Louis	2-2
	10	Calgary	7-3		16	Toronto	3-4
	12	Buffalo	5-2		22	Washington	1-3
	17	Toronto	4-3		24	Chicago*	4-5
	25	St Louis	4-5		28	Los Angeles	5-6
	30	Chicago	2-1		31	St Louis	1-2

* Denotes afternoon game.

Entry Draft Selections 1991-77

1991
Pick
- 8 Richard Matvichuk
- 74 Mike Torchia
- 97 Mike Kennedy
- 118 Mark Lawrence
- 137 Geoff Finch
- 174 Michael Burkett
- 184 Derek Herlofsky
- 206 Tom Nemeth
- 228 Shayne Green
- 250 Jukka Suomalainen

1990
Pick
- 8 Derian Hatcher
- 50 Laurie Billeck
- 70 Cal McGowan
- 71 Frank Kovacs
- 92 Enrico Ciccone
- 113 Roman Turek
- 134 Jeff Levy
- 155 Doug Barrault
- 176 Joe Biondi
- 197 Troy Binnie
- 218 Ole Dahlstrom
- 239 John McKersie

1989
Pick
- 7 Doug Zmolek
- 28 Mike Craig
- 60 Murray Garbutt
- 75 Jean-François Quintin
- 87 Pat MacLeod
- 91 Bryan Schoen
- 97 Rhys Hollyman
- 112 Scott Cashman
- 154 Jonathan Pratt
- 175 Kenneth Blum
- 196 Artur Irbe
- 217 Tom Pederson
- 238 Helmut Balderis

1988
Pick
- 1 Mike Modano
- 40 Link Gaetz
- 43 Shaun Kane
- 64 Jeffrey Stolp
- 148 Ken MacArthur
- 169 Travis Richards
- 190 Ari Matilainen
- 211 Grant Bischoff
- 232 Trent Andison

1987
Pick
- 6 David Archibald
- 35 Scott McCrady
- 48 Kevin Kaminski
- 73 John Weisbrod
- 88 Teppo Kivela
- 109 D'Arcy Norton
- 130 Timo Kulonen
- 151 Don Schmidt
- 172 Jarmo Myllys
- 193 Larry Olimb
- 214 Mark Felicio
- 235 Dave Shields

1986
Pick
- 12 Warren Babe
- 30 Neil Wilkinson
- 33 Dean Kolstad
- 54 Eric Bennett
- 55 Rob Zettler
- 58 Brad Turner
- 75 Kirk Tomlinson
- 96 Jari Gronstand
- 159 Scott Mathias
- 180 Lance Pitlick
- 201 Dan Keczmer
- 222 Garth Joy
- 243 Kurt Stahura

1985
Pick
- 51 Stephane Roy
- 69 Mike Berger
- 90 Dwight Mullins
- 111 Mike Mullowney
- 132 Mike Kelfer
- 153 Ross Johnson
- 174 Tim Helmer
- 195 Gordon Ernst
- 216 Ladislav Lubina
- 237 Tommy Sjodin

1984
Pick
- 13 David Quinn
- 46 Ken Hodge
- 76 Miroslav Maly
- 89 Jiri Poner
- 97 Kari Takko
- 118 Gary McColgan
- 139 Vladimir Kyhos
- 160 Darin MacInnis
- 181 Duane Wahlin
- 201 Mike Orn
- 222 Tom Terwilliger
- 242 Mike Nightengale

1983
Pick
- 1 Brian Lawton
- 36 Malcolm Parks
- 38 Frantisek Musil
- 56 Mitch Messier
- 76 Brian Durand
- 96 Rich Geist
- 116 Tom McComb
- 136 Sean Toomey
- 156 Don Biggs
- 176 Paul Pulis
- 196 Milos Riha
- 212 Oldrich Valek
- 236 Paul Roff

1982
Pick
- 2 Brian Bellows
- 59 Wally Chapman
- 80 Rob Rouse
- 81 Dusan Pasek
- 101 Marty Wiitala
- 122 Todd Carlile
- 143 Victor Zhluktov
- 164 Paul Miller
- 185 Pat Micheletti
- 206 Arnold Kadlec
- 227 Scott Knutson

1981
Pick
- 13 Ron Meighan
- 27 Dave Donnelly
- 31 Mike Sands
- 33 Tom Hirsch
- 34 Dave Preuss
- 41 Jali Wahlsten
- 69 Terry Tait
- 76 Jim Malwitz
- 97 Kelly Hubbard
- 118 Paul Guay
- 139 Jim Archibald
- 160 Kari Kanervo
- 181 Scott Bjugstad
- 202 Steve Kudebeh

1980
Pick
- 16 Brad Palmer
- 32 Don Beaupre
- 53 Randy Velischek
- 79 Mark Huglen
- 100 Dave Jensen
- 121 Dan Zavarise
- 142 Bill Stewart
- 163 Jeff Walters
- 184 Bob Lakso
- 205 Dave Richter

1979
Pick
- 6 Craig Hartsburg
- 10 Tom McCarthy
- 42 Neal Broten
- 63 Kevin Maxwell
- 90 Jim Dobson
- 111 Brian Gualazzi

1978
Pick
- 1 Bobby Smith
- 19 Steve Payne
- 24 Steve Christoff
- 54 Curt Giles
- 70 Roy Kerling
- 87 Bob Bergloff
- 104 Kim Spencer
- 121 Mike Cotter
- 138 Brent Gogol
- 155 Mike Seide

1977
Pick
- 7 Brad Maxwell
- 25 Dave Semenko
- 61 Kevin McCloskey
- 79 Bob Parent
- 97 Jamie Gallimore
- 115 J.P. Sanvido
- 133 Greg Tebbutt
- 151 Keith Hanson

Club Directory

Met Sports Center
7901 Cedar Avenue South
Bloomington, Minnesota
55425
Phone 612/853-9333
PR: 612/853-9378/380
FAX 612/853-9467
GM FAX 612/853-9408
ENVOY ID
Front Office: STARS. GM
Public
Relations: STARS. PR
Capacity: 15,274

Governor	Norman N. Green
Alternate Governors	Bob Clarke, Jim Erickson

Owner
Norman N. Green

Executive

President & CEO	Norman N. Green
Vice-President/General Manager	Bob Clarke
Sr. Vice President of Sales and Properties	John Thomas
Vice President of Communications and Operations	Pat Forciea
Vice-President of Finance and Administration	Pat Hoffman
Legal Counsel	Jim Erickson

Hockey

Head Coach	Bob Gainey
Assistant Coaches	Doug Jarvis, Andy Murray
Director of Player Personnel	Les Jackson
Team Services	Doug Armstrong
Chief Scout	Dennis Patterson
Scouts	Craig Button, Doug Overton, Wayne Simpson
Head Athletic Trainer	Dave Surprenant
Assistant Trainer	Dave Smith
Equipment Manager	Mark Baribeau
Team Physicians	Dr. William Simonet, Dr. John Schaefer, Dr. Jim Schaffausen
Team Dentists	Dr. Paul Belvedere, Dr. Doug Lambert
Team Physical Therapist	Tom Coplin

Administration

Group Sales Manager	Murray Cohn
Director of Merchandising	Peter Jocketty
Director of Communications & Media Relations	Joan St. Peter
Assistant Director of Communications	Dan Stuchal
Director of Ticket Sales	Tom Vannelli
Director of Public Relations & Advertising	Elaine Waddell

Team and Building Information

Location of Press Boxes	North Side — Press and Radio / South Side — Television
Dimensions of Rink	200 feet by 85 feet
Ends of Rink	Unbreakable glass extends above boards around rink
Uniforms	White base at home, Black base on the road
Radio	KSTP-AM 1500; Al Shaver
Television	KMSP-TV, Channel 9;

Coach

GAINEY, BOB
Coach, Minnesota North Stars. Born in Peterborough, Ont., December 13, 1953.

In his first season as an NHL head coach, Bob Gainey led the Minnesota North Stars through stunning playoff upsets of the League's top two teams and all the way to the Stanley Cup Finals. After surprising the League's top finishing Chicago Blackhawks in the Norris Division Semi-Finals, Gainey's Stars went on to eliminate the League's second place finishers—the St. Louis Blues—in the Norris Division Finals. The North Stars then defeated the defending Stanley Cup Champion Edmonton Oilers before bowing in six games to the Pittsburgh Penguins in the 1991 Stanley Cup Finals.

Gainey, who was appointed head coach of the North Stars on June 19, 1990 following a 16-year NHL career and a one-season coaching stint in Epinal, France, was Montreal's first choice (eighth overall) in the 1973 Amateur Draft. During his 16-year career with the Canadiens, Gainey was a member of five Stanley Cup-winning teams and was named the Conn Smythe Trophy winner in 1979. He was a four-time recipient of the Frank Selke Trophy (1978-81), awarded to the League's top defensive forward, and participated in four NHL All-Star Games (1977, 1978, 1980 and 1981). He served as team captain for eight seasons (1981-89). During his career, he played in 1,160 regular-season games, registering 239 goals and 262 assists for 501 points. In addition, he tallied 73 points (25-48-73) in 182 post-season games. He retired in July of 1989 and served as player/coach for Epinal, a second division French team.

Coaching Record

Season	Team	Games	Regular Season W	L	T	%	Games	Playoffs W	L	%
1989-90	Epinal	....	....	....	....	....				
1990-91	Minnesota (NHL)	80	27	39	14	.425	23	14	9	.643
	NHL Totals	80	27	39	14	.425	23	14	9	.643

General Manager

CLARKE, ROBERT EARLE (BOB)
General Manager, Minnesota North Stars. Born in Flin Flon, Man., August 13, 1949.

In his first season as general manager of the Minnesota North Stars, Bob Clarke oversaw the club's rise from 1989-90's first round playoff elimination to 1990-91 Stanley Cup Finalists. After 21 seasons with the Philadelphia Flyers, Bob Clarke joined the Minnesota North Stars on June 8, 1990. Clarke, 42, spent the previous six seasons as general manager of the Flyers, for whom he played 15 seasons (1969-84). During his tenure as Flyers' general manager, Clarke's team compiled a record of 256-177-47.

As a player, the former Philadelphia captain led his club to Stanley Cup championships in 1974 and 1975 and captured numerous individual awards, including the Hart Trophy as the League's most valuable player in 1973, 1975 and 1976. The four-time All-Star also received the Masterton Memorial Trophy (perserverance and dedication) in 1972 and the Frank J. Selke Trophy (top defensive forward) in 1983. He appeared in nine All-Star Games and was elected to the Hockey Hall of Fame in 1987. He was awarded the Lester Patrick Trophy in 1979-80 in recognition of his contribution to hockey in the United States. Clarke appeared in 1,144 regular-season games, recording 358 goals and 852 assists for 1,210 points. He also added 119 points in 136 playoff games.

Montreal Canadiens

1990-91 Results: 39W-30L-11T 89PTS. Second, Adams Division

Smooth skating Russ Courtnall led the Habs in scoring in 1990-91 with a career-high 76 points.

Schedule

Home			Away		
Oct.	Thur.	3 Toronto	**Oct.**	Tues.	8 Hartford
	Sat.	5 NY Rangers		Thur.	10 Detroit
	Mon.	14 Hartford		Sat.	12 Boston
	Wed.	16 Buffalo		Fri.	18 Buffalo
	Wed.	23 Quebec		Sat.	19 Philadelphia
	Sat.	26 Pittsburgh		Thur.	24 Quebec
	Wed.	30 Winnipeg	**Nov.**	Fri.	1 Buffalo
Nov.	Sat.	2 Buffalo		Wed.	6 NY Rangers
	Mon.	4 New Jersey		Fri.	8 New Jersey
	Sat.	9 Chicago		Thur.	14 Hartford
	Mon.	11 Washington		Thur.	21 Quebec
	Sat.	16 Philadelphia		Wed.	27 Washington
	Mon.	18 Edmonton		Fri.	29 Boston*
	Sat.	23 Quebec		Sat.	30 Hartford
	Mon.	25 Boston	**Dec.**	Thur.	5 NY Islanders
Dec.	Wed.	4 Vancouver		Mon.	9 Toronto
	Sat.	7 Calgary		Thur.	12 Boston
	Sat.	14 Buffalo		Thur.	19 Chicago
	Mon.	16 St Louis		Thur.	26 Quebec
	Sat.	21 Hartford		Sun.	29 Edmonton
	Sun.	22 Boston		Tues.	31 Calgary
Jan.	Wed.	8 Boston	**Jan.**	Sat.	4 San Jose
	Sat.	11 Hartford		Wed.	15 Minnesota
	Mon.	13 Calgary		Thur.	16 St Louis
	Sat.	25 Buffalo*		Thur.	23 Boston
	Sun.	26 Hartford*		Fri.	31 Buffalo
	Wed.	29 New Jersey	**Feb.**	Tues.	4 Vancouver
Feb.	Sat.	1 Detroit		Wed.	5 Edmonton
	Mon.	10 Vancouver		Sat.	8 Toronto
	Wed.	12 San Jose		Wed.	19 Hartford
	Sat.	15 Quebec		Wed.	26 Minnesota
	Mon.	17 Minnesota		Fri.	28 San Jose
	Sat.	22 Pittsburgh		Sat.	29 Los Angeles
	Sun.	23 Quebec	**Mar.**	Tues.	3 NY Islanders
Mar.	Sat.	7 NY Islanders		Wed.	11 Quebec
	Sun.	8 Detroi		Mon.	16 NY Rangers
	Sat.	14 Los Angeles		Wed.	25 Winnipeg
	Wed.	18 Philadelphia		Fri.	27 Washington
	Sat.	21 St Louis		Sat.	28 Pittsburgh
Apr.	Sat.	4 Boston	**Apr.**	Thur.	2 Buffalo

* Denotes afternoon game.

Home Starting Times:

Weeknights .... 7:35 p.m.
Saturdays .... 8:05 p.m.
Sundays .... 7:05 p.m.
Matinees .... 1.05 p.m.

Franchise date: November 22, 1917

75th NHL Season

Year-by-Year Record

		Home			Road			Overall							
Season	GP	W	L	T	W	L	T	W	L	T	GF	GA	Pts.	Finished	Playoff Result
1990-91	80	23	12	5	16	18	6	39	30	11	273	249	89	2nd, Adams Div.	Lost Div. Final
1989-90	80	26	8	6	15	20	5	41	28	11	288	234	93	3rd, Adams Div.	Lost Div. Final
1988-89	80	30	6	4	23	12	5	53	18	9	315	218	115	1st, Adams Div.	Lost Final
1987-88	80	26	8	6	19	14	7	45	22	13	298	238	103	1st, Adams Div.	Lost Div. Final
1986-87	80	27	9	4	14	20	6	41	29	10	277	241	92	2nd, Adams Div.	Lost Conf. Championship
1985-86	**80**	25	11	4	15	22	3	**40**	**33**	**7**	**330**	**280**	**87**	**2nd, Adams Div.**	**Won Stanley Cup**
1984-85	80	24	10	6	17	17	6	41	27	12	309	262	94	1st, Adams Div.	Lost Div. Final
1983-84	80	19	19	2	16	21	3	35	40	5	286	295	75	4th, Adams Div.	Lost Conf. Championship
1982-83	80	25	6	9	17	18	5	42	24	14	350	286	98	2nd, Adams Div.	Lost Div. Semi-Final
1981-82	80	25	6	9	21	11	8	46	17	17	360	223	109	1st, Adams Div.	Lost Div. Semi-Final
1980-81	80	31	7	2	14	15	11	45	22	13	332	232	103	1st, Norris Div.	Lost Prelim. Round
1979-80	80	30	7	3	17	13	10	47	20	13	328	240	107	1st, Norris Div.	Lost Quarter-Final
1978-79	**80**	29	6	5	23	11	6	**52**	**17**	**11**	**337**	**204**	**115**	**1st, Norris Div.**	**Won Stanley Cup**
1977-78	**80**	32	4	4	27	6	7	**59**	**10**	**11**	**359**	**183**	**129**	**1st, Norris Div.**	**Won Stanley Cup**
1976-77	**80**	33	1	6	27	7	6	**60**	**8**	**12**	**387**	**171**	**132**	**1st, Norris Div.**	**Won Stanley Cup**
1975-76	**80**	32	3	5	26	8	6	**58**	**11**	**11**	**337**	**174**	**127**	**1st, Norris Div.**	**Won Stanley Cup**
1974-75	80	27	8	5	20	6	14	47	14	19	374	225	113	1st, Norris Div.	Lost Semi-Final
1973-74	78	24	12	3	21	12	6	45	24	9	293	240	99	2nd, East Div.	Lost Quarter-Final
1972-73	**78**	29	4	6	23	6	10	**52**	**10**	**16**	**329**	**184**	**120**	**1st, East Div.**	**Won Stanley Cup**
1971-72	78	29	3	7	17	13	9	46	16	16	307	205	108	3rd, East Div.	Lost Quarter-Final
1970-71	**78**	29	7	3	13	16	10	**42**	**23**	**13**	**291**	**216**	**97**	**3rd, East Div.**	**Won Stanley Cup**
1969-70	76	21	9	8	17	13	8	38	22	16	244	201	92	5th, East Div.	Out of Playoffs
1968-69	**76**	26	7	5	20	12	6	**46**	**19**	**11**	**271**	**202**	**103**	**1st, East Div.**	**Won Stanley Cup**
1967-68	**74**	26	5	6	16	17	4	**42**	**22**	**10**	**236**	**167**	**94**	**1st, East Div.**	**Won Stanley Cup**
1966-67	70	19	9	7	13	16	6	32	25	13	202	188	77	2nd,	Lost Final
1965-66	**70**	23	11	1	18	10	7	**41**	**21**	**8**	**239**	**173**	**90**	**1st,**	**Won Stanley Cup**
1964-65	**70**	20	8	7	16	15	4	**36**	**23**	**11**	**211**	**185**	**83**	**2nd,**	**Won Stanley Cup**
1963-64	70	22	7	6	14	14	7	36	21	13	209	167	85	1st,	Lost Semi-Final
1962-63	70	15	10	10	13	9	13	28	19	23	225	183	79	3rd,	Lost Semi-Final
1961-62	70	26	2	7	16	12	7	42	14	14	259	166	98	1st,	Lost Semi-Final
1960-61	70	24	6	5	17	13	5	41	19	10	254	188	92	1st,	Lost Semi-Final
1959-60	**70**	23	4	8	17	14	4	**40**	**18**	**12**	**255**	**178**	**92**	**1st,**	**Won Stanley Cup**
1958-59	**70**	21	8	6	18	10	7	**39**	**18**	**13**	**258**	**158**	**91**	**1st,**	**Won Stanley Cup**
1957-58	**70**	23	8	4	20	9	6	**43**	**17**	**10**	**250**	**158**	**96**	**1st,**	**Won Stanley Cup**
1956-57	**70**	23	6	6	12	17	6	**35**	**23**	**12**	**210**	**155**	**82**	**2nd,**	**Won Stanley Cup**
1955-56	**70**	29	5	1	16	10	9	**45**	**15**	**10**	**222**	**131**	**100**	**1st,**	**Won Stanley Cup**
1954-55	70	26	5	4	15	13	7	41	18	11	228	157	93	2nd,	Lost Final
1953-54	70	27	5	3	8	19	8	35	24	11	195	141	81	2nd,	Lost Final
1952-53	**70**	18	12	5	10	11	14	**28**	**23**	**19**	**155**	**148**	**75**	**2nd,**	**Won Stanley Cup**
1951-52	70	22	8	5	12	18	5	34	26	10	195	164	78	2nd,	Lost Final
1950-51	70	17	10	8	8	20	7	25	30	15	173	184	65	3rd,	Lost Final
1949-50	70	17	8	10	12	14	9	29	22	19	172	150	77	2nd,	Lost Semi-Final
1948-49	60	19	8	3	9	15	6	28	23	9	152	126	65	3rd,	Lost Semi-Final
1947-48	60	13	13	4	7	16	7	20	29	11	147	169	51	5th,	Out of Playoffs
1946-47	60	19	6	5	15	10	5	34	16	10	189	138	78	1st,	Lost Final
1945-46	**50**	16	6	3	12	11	2	**28**	**17**	**5**	**172**	**134**	**61**	**1st,**	**Won Stanley Cup**
1944-45	50	21	2	2	17	6	2	38	8	4	228	121	80	1st,	Lost Semi-Final
1943-44	**50**	22	0	3	16	5	4	**38**	**5**	**7**	**234**	**109**	**83**	**1st,**	**Won Stanley Cup**
1942-43	50	14	4	7	5	15	5	19	19	12	181	191	50	4th,	Lost Semi-Final
1941-42	48	12	10	2	6	17	1	18	27	3	134	173	39	6th,	Lost Quarter-Final
1940-41	48	11	9	4	5	17	2	16	26	6	121	147	38	6th,	Lost Quarter-Final
1939-40	48	5	14	5	5	19	0	10	33	5	90	168	25	7th,	Out of Playoffs
1938-39	48	8	11	5	7	13	4	15	24	9	115	146	39	6th,	Lost Quarter-Final
1937-38	48	13	4	7	5	13	6	18	17	13	123	128	49	3rd, Cdn. Div.	Lost Quarter-Final
1936-37	48	16	8	0	8	10	6	24	18	6	115	111	54	1st, Cdn. Div.	Lost Semi-Final
1935-36	48	5	11	8	6	15	3	11	26	11	82	123	33	4th, Cdn. Div.	Out of Playoffs
1934-35	48	11	11	2	8	12	4	19	23	6	110	145	44	3rd, Cdn. Div.	Lost Quarter-Final
1933-34	48	16	6	2	6	14	4	22	20	6	99	101	50	2nd, Cdn. Div.	Lost Quarter-Final
1932-33	48	15	5	4	3	20	1	18	25	5	92	115	41	3rd, Cdn. Div.	Lost Quarter-Final
1931-32	48	18	3	3	7	13	4	25	16	7	128	111	57	1st, Cdn. Div.	Lost Semi-Final
1930-31	**44**	15	3	4	11	7	4	**26**	**10**	**8**	**129**	**89**	**60**	**1st, Cdn. Div.**	**Won Stanley Cup**
1929-30	**44**	13	5	4	8	9	5	**21**	**14**	**9**	**142**	**114**	**51**	**2nd, Cdn. Div.**	**Won Stanley Cup**
1928-29	44	12	4	6	10	3	9	22	7	15	71	43	59	1st, Cdn. Div.	Lost Semi-Final
1927-28	44	12	7	3	14	4	4	26	11	7	116	48	59	1st, Cdn. Div.	Lost Semi-Final
1926-27	44	15	5	2	13	9	0	28	14	2	99	67	58	2nd, Cdn. Div.	Lost Semi-Final
1925-26	36	5	12	1	6	12	0	11	24	1	79	108	23	7th,	Out of Playoffs
1924-25	30	10	5	0	7	6	2	17	11	2	93	56	36	3rd,	Lost Final
1923-24	**24**	10	2	0	3	9	0	**13**	**11**	**0**	**59**	**48**	**26**	**2nd,**	**Won Stanley Cup**
1922-23	24	10	2	0	3	7	2	13	9	2	73	61	28	2nd,	Lost NHL Final
1921-22	24	8	3	1	4	8	0	12	11	1	88	94	25	3rd,	Out of Playoffs
1920-21	24	9	3	0	4	8	0	13	11	0	112	99	26	3rd and 2nd*	Out of Playoffs
1919-20	24	8	4	0	5	7	0	13	11	0	129	113	26	2nd and 3rd*	Out of Playoffs
1918-19	18	7	2	0	3	6	0	10	8	0	88	78	20	1st and 2nd*	Cup Final but no Decision
1917-18	22	8	3	0	5	6	0	13	9	0	115	84	26	1st and 3rd*	Lost NHL Final

* Season played in two halves with no combined standing at end.
From 1917-18 through 1925-26, NHL champions played against PCHL champions for Stanley Cup.

1991-92 Player Personnel

FORWARDS	HT	WT	S	Place of Birth	Date	1990-91 Club
BÉLANGER, Jesse	6-0	170	R	St-Georges de Beauce, Qué.	6/15/69	Fredericton
BOBYCK, Brent	5-10	174	L	Regina, Sask.	4/26/68	Fred.-Albany-W. Salem
BRUNET, Benoit	5-11	184	L	Ste-Anne de Bellevue, Qué.	8/24/68	Montreal-Fredericton
CARBONNEAU, Guy	5-11	184	R	Sept-Iles, Qué.	3/18/60	Montréal
CASSELS, Andrew	6-0	192	L	Bramalea, Ont.	7/23/69	Montréal
CHORSKE, Tom	6-1	204	L	Minneapolis, MN	9/18/66	Montréal
CORSON, Shayne	6-0	201	L	Barrie, Ont.	8/13/66	Montréal
COURTNALL, Russ	5-11	183	R	Duncan, B.C.	6/2/65	Montréal
DESJARDINS, Norman	5-10	184	R	Montréal, Qué.	3/25/68	Fredericton
DIONNE, Gilbert	6-0	194	L	Drummondville, Que.	9/19/70	Montreal-Fredericton
DIPIETRO, Paul	5-9	181	R	Sault Ste-Marie, Ont.	9/8/70	Fredericton
EWEN,Todd	6-2	220	R	Saskatoon, Sask.	3/22/66	Montreal
FERGUSON, John Jr.	6-0	192	L	Winnipeg, Man.	7/7/67	Fredericton
FLEETWOOD, Brent	6-1	180	L	Edmonton, Alta.	6/4/70	Fredericton-W. Salem
GILCHRIST, Brent	5-11	181	L	Moose Jaw, Sask.	4/3/67	Montréal
KEANE, Mike	5-10	178	R	Winnipeg, Man.	5/28/67	Montréal
KJELLBERG, Patrik	6-2	196	L	Falun, Sweden	6/17/69	AIK (Sweden)
LABELLE, Marc	6-1	215	L	Maniwaki, Que.	12/20/69	Fredericton
LAROUCHE, Steve	5-11	180	R	Rouyn, Que.	4/14/71	Chicoutimi
LEBEAU, Patrick	5-10	172	L	St-Jérôme, Qué.	3/17/70	Montreal-Fredericton
LEBEAU, Stéphan	5-10	172	R	St-Jérôme, Qué.	2/28/68	Montreal
LeCLAIR, John	6-1	185	L	St. Albans, VT	7/5/69	U. of Vermont-Mtl.
McPHEE, Mike	6-1	203	L	Sydney, N.S.	7/14/60	Montréal
RICHER, Stéphane J.J.	6-2	212	R	Ripon, Qué.	6/7/66	Montréal
ROBERGE, Mario	5-11	185	L	Québec, Qué.	1/23/64	Montreal-Fredericton
RONAN, Edward	6-0	197	R	Quincy, MA	3/21/68	Boston University
SAGISSOR, Tom	5-11	202	R	Hastings, MN	9/12/67	Fredericton
SAVARD, Denis	5-10	175	R	Pt. Gatineau, Qué.	2/4/61	Montreal
SEVIGNY, Pierre	6-0	189	L	Trois-Rivières, Que.	9/8/71	St-Hyacinthe
SKRUDLAND, Brian	6-0	196	L	Peace River, Alta.	7/31/63	Montréal
St. AMOUR, Martin	6-3	194	L	Montréal, Qué.	1/30/70	Fredericton
TURGEON, Sylvain	6-0	195	L	Noranda, Que.	1/17/65	Montreal
VALLIS, Lindsay	6-3	207	R	Winnipeg, Man.	1/12/71	Seattle
WOODLEY, Dan	5-11	185	R	Oklahoma, OK	12/29/67	Fred.-K.C.-Albany

DEFENSEMEN	HT	WT	S	Place of Birth	Date	1990-91 Club
BRISEBOIS, Patrice	6-2	175	R	Montréal, Que.	1/27/71	Mtl.-Drum'ville
CHARRON, Eric	6-3	192	L	Verdun, Qué.	1/14/70	Fredericton
COTE, Alain	6-0	200	R	Montmagny, Qué.	4/14/67	Montreal-Fredericton
DAIGNEAULT, J.J.	5-11	185	L	Montréal, Que.	10/12/65	Montréal
DESJARDINS, Eric	6-1	200	R	Rouyn, Qué.	6/14/69	Montréal
DUFRESNE, Donald	6-1	206	R	Québec, Qué.	4/10/67	Montréal-Fredericton
GAUTHIER, Luc	5-9	195	R	Longueuil, Qué.	4/19/64	Montreal-Fredericton
HILL, Sean	6-0	195	R	Duluth, MN	2/14/70	U. of Wisconsin
LEFEBVRE, Sylvain	6-2	204	L	Richmond, Qué.	10/14/67	Montréal
ODELEIN, Lyle	5-10	206	L	Quill Lake, Sask.	7/21/68	Montréal
SCHNEIDER, Mathieu	5-11	189	L	New York, NY	6/12/69	Montréal
SIMON, Darcy	6-1	200	R	N. Battleford, Sask.	1/21/70	Fredericton
SVOBODA, Petr	6-1	174	L	Most, Czech.	2/14/66	Montréal
UNIAC, John	5-11	210	R	Stratford, Ont.	3/29/71	Kitchener
VEILLEUX, Steve	6-0	190	R	Lachenaie, Que.	3/9/69	Milwaukee

GOALTENDERS	HT	WT	C	Place of Birth	Date	1990-91 Club
BERGERON, J.C.	6-2	192	L	Hauterive, Qué.	10/14/68	Montreal-Fredericton
CHABOT, Frederic	5-11	175	R	Hebertville-Stn., Qué.	2/12/68	Montreal-Fredericton
KUNTAR, Les	6-2	195	L	Elma, N.Y.	7/28/69	St. Lawrence
RACICOT, Andre	5-11	165	L	Rouyn-Noranda, Qué.	6/9/69	Montréal-Fredericton
ROY, Patrick	6-0	182	L	Québec, Qué.	10/5/65	Montréal

1990-91 Scoring

Regular Season

* rookie

Pos	#	Player	Team	GP	G	A	Pts	+/–	PIM	PP	SH	GW	GT	S	%
R	6	Russ Courtnall	MTL	79	26	50	76	5	29	5	1	5	1	279	9.3
R	44	Stephane Richer	MTL	75	31	30	61	0	53	9	0	4	1	221	14.0
C	18	Denis Savard	MTL	70	28	31	59	1–	52	7	2	0	0	187	15.0
C	47	Stephan Lebeau	MTL	73	22	31	53	4	24	8	0	2	0	108	20.4
L	27	Shayne Corson	MTL	71	23	24	47	9	138	7	0	2	1	164	14.0
C	21	Guy Carbonneau	MTL	78	20	24	44	1–	63	4	1	3	1	131	15.3
L	35	Mike McPhee	MTL	64	22	21	43	6	56	2	0	4	0	123	17.9
R	12	Mike Keane	MTL	73	13	23	36	6	50	2	1	2	0	109	11.9
C	39	Brian Skrudland	MTL	57	15	19	34	12	85	1	1	2	0	71	21.1
D	8	Matt Schneider	MTL	69	10	20	30	7	63	5	0	3	0	164	6.1
D	25	Petr Svoboda	MTL	60	4	22	26	5	52	3	0	1	0	67	6.0
D	28	Eric Desjardins	MTL	62	7	18	25	7	27	0	0	1	0	114	6.1
C	15	*Andrew Cassels	MTL	54	6	19	25	2	20	1	0	3	1	55	10.9
D	3	Sylvain Lefebvre	MTL	63	5	18	23	11–	30	1	0	1	0	76	6.6
L	31	*Tom Chorske	MTL	57	9	11	20	8–	32	3	0	1	0	82	11.0
D	48	J.J. Daigneault	MTL	51	3	16	19	2–	31	2	0	0	0	68	4.4
C	41	Brent Gilchrist	MTL	51	6	9	15	3–	10	1	0	1	0	81	7.4
D	34	Donald Dufresne	MTL	53	2	13	15	5	55	0	0	0	0	32	6.3
L	20	Sylvain Turgeon	MTL	19	5	7	12	2–	20	1	0	1	0	41	12.2
C	17	*John LeClair	MTL	10	2	5	7	1	2	0	0	1	0	12	16.7
D	5	Alain Cote	MTL	28	0	6	6	8	26	0	0	0	0	24	.0
R	36	Todd Ewen	MTL	28	3	2	5	4	128	0	0	0	0	13	23.1
L	22	*Benoit Brunet	MTL	17	1	3	4	1–	0	0	0	0	0	12	8.3
L	29	*Patrick Lebeau	MTL	2	1	1	2	0	0	0	0	0	0	3	33.3
D	43	*Patrice Brisebois	MTL	10	0	2	2	1	4	0	0	0	0	11	.0
G	33	Patrick Roy	MTL	48	0	2	2	0	6	0	0	0	0	0	.0
D	24	*Lyle Odelein	MTL	52	0	2	2	7	259	0	0	0	0	25	.0
G	37	*J.C. Bergeron	MTL	18	0	1	1	0	0	0	0	0	0	0	.0
G	40	*Andre Racicot	MTL	21	0	1	1	0	0	0	0	0	0	0	.0
C	11	Ryan Walter	MTL	25	0	1	1	3–	12	0	0	0	0	14	.0
L	45	*Gilbert Dionne	MTL	2	0	0	0	2–	0	0	0	0	0	0	.0
G	1	*Frederic Chabot	MTL	3	0	0	0	0	0	0	0	0	0	0	.0
D	49	Luc Gauthier	MTL	3	0	0	0	1	2	0	0	0	0	0	.0
L	32	Mario Roberge	MTL	5	0	0	0	2–	21	0	0	0	0	2	.0

Goaltending

No.	Goaltender	GPI	Mins	Avg	W	L	T	EN	SO	GA	SA	S%
33	Patrick Roy	48	2835	2.71	25	15	6	3	1	128	1362	.906
53	*Andre Racicot	21	975	3.20	7	9	2	1	1	52	479	.891
1	*Frederic Chabot	3	108	3.33	0	0	1	0	0	6	45	.867
37	*J.C. Bergeron	18	941	3.76	7	6	2	0	0	59	426	.862
	Totals	**80**	**4869**	**3.07**	**39**	**30**	**11**	**4**	**2**	**249**	**2316**	**.892**

Playoffs

Pos	#	Player	Team	GP	G	A	Pts	+/–	PIM	PP	SH	GW	OT	S	%
L	27	Shayne Corson	MTL	13	9	6	15	5	36	4	1	3	1	42	21.4
R	44	Stephane Richer	MTL	13	9	5	14	0	6	1	0	1	1	44	20.5
C	39	Brian Skrudland	MTL	13	3	10	13	7	42	1	0	0	0	15	20.0
C	18	Denis Savard	MTL	13	2	11	13	1–	35	1	0	0	0	33	6.1
R	6	Russ Courtnall	MTL	13	8	3	11	3	7	2	2	1	1	51	15.7
D	8	Matt Schneider	MTL	13	2	7	9	2	18	1	0	0	0	33	6.1
C	41	Brent Gilchrist	MTL	13	5	3	8	3	6	0	0	1	0	21	23.8
L	35	Mike McPhee	MTL	13	1	7	8	5–	12	1	0	0	0	31	3.2
C	21	Guy Carbonneau	MTL	13	1	5	6	2–	10	0	0	1	0	21	4.8
R	12	Mike Keane	MTL	12	3	2	5	3	6	0	0	0	0	19	15.8
D	28	Eric Desjardins	MTL	13	1	4	5	5	8	1	0	0	0	23	4.3
C	47	Stephan Lebeau	MTL	7	2	1	3	1	2	1	0	0	0	11	18.2
C	15	*Andrew Cassels	MTL	8	0	2	2	3–	2	0	0	0	0	5	.0
D	5	Alain Cote	MTL	11	0	2	2	4	26	0	0	0	0	14	.0
D	3	Sylvain Lefebvre	MTL	11	1	0	1	6–	6	0	0	0	0	8	12.5
D	25	Petr Svoboda	MTL	2	0	1	1	1–	2	0	0	0	0	5	.0
D	48	J.J. Daigneault	MTL	5	0	1	1	4	0	0	0	0	0	2	.0
D	34	Donald Dufresne	MTL	10	0	1	1	2	21	0	0	0	0	8	.0
D	38	*Sean Hill	MTL	1	0	0	0	1	0	0	0	0	0	0	.0
G	40	*Andre Racicot	MTL	2	0	0	0	0	0	0	0	0	0	0	.0
C	17	*John LeClair	MTL	3	0	0	0	2	0	0	0	0	0	3	.0
L	20	Sylvain Turgeon	MTL	5	0	0	0	0	2	0	0	0	0	7	.0
C	11	Ryan Walter	MTL	5	0	0	0	0	2	0	0	0	0	2	.0
D	24	*Lyle Odelein	MTL	12	0	0	0	5–	54	0	0	0	0	4	.0
L	32	Mario Roberge	MTL	12	0	0	0	1–	24	0	0	0	0	3	.0
G	33	Patrick Roy	MTL	13	0	0	0	0	2	0	0	0	0	0	.0

Goaltending

No.	Goaltender	GPI	Mins	Avg	W	L	EN	SO	GA	SA	S%
33	Patrick Roy	13	785	3.06	7	5	0	0	40	394	.898
40	*Andre Racicot	2	12	10.00	0	1	0	0	2	14	.857
	Totals	13	804	3.13	7	6	0	0	42	408	.897

General Managers' History

Joseph Cattarinich, 1909-1910; George Kennedy, 1910-11 to 1919-20; Leo Dandurand, 1920-21 to 1934-35; Ernest Savard, 1935-36; Cecil Hart, 1936-37 to 1938-39; Jules Dugal, 1939-40; Tom P. Gorman, 1941-42 to 1945-46; Frank J. Selke, 1946-47 to 1963-64; Sam Pollock, 1964-65 to 1977-78; Irving Grundman, 1978-79 to 1982-83; Serge Savard, 1983-84 to date.

Coaching History

George Kennedy, 1917-18 to 1919-20; Leo Dandurand, 1920-21 to 1924-25; Cecil Hart, 1925-26 to 1931-32; Newsy Lalonde, 1932-33 to 1933-34; Newsy Lalonde and Leo Dandurand, 1934-35; Sylvio Mantha, 1935-36; Cecil Hart, 1936-37 to 1937-38; Cecil Hart and Jules Dugal, 1938-39; "Babe" Siebert, 1939*; Pit Lepine, 1939-40; Dick Irvin 1940-41 to 1954-55; Toe Blake, 1955-56 to 1967-68; Claude Ruel, 1968-69 to 1969-70; Claude Ruel and Al MacNeil, 1970-71; Scott Bowman, 1971-72 to 1978-79; Bernie Geoffrion and Claude Ruel, 1979-80; Claude Ruel, 1980-81; Bob Berry, 1981-82 to 1982-83; Bob Berry and Jacques Lemaire, 1983-84; Jacques Lemaire, 1984-85; Jean Perron, 1985-86 to 1987-88; Pat Burns, 1988-89 to date.

* Named coach in summer but died before 1939-40 season began.

Captains' History

Newsy Lalonde, 1917-18 to 1920-21; Sprague Cleghorn, 1921-22 to 1924-25; Bill Couture, 1925-26; Sylvio Mantha, 1926-27 to 1931-32; George Hainsworth, 1932-33; Sylvio Mantha, 1933-34 to 1935-36; Babe Seibert, 1936-37 to 1938-39; Walter Buswell, 1939-40; Toe Blake, 1940-41 to 1946-47; Toe Blake, Bill Durnan (co-captains) 1947-48; Emile Bouchard, 1948-49 to 1955-56; Maurice Richard, 1956-57 to 1959-60; Doug Harvey, 1960-61; Jean Beliveau, 1961-62 to 1970-71; Henri Richard, 1971-72 to 1974-75; Yvan Cournoyer, 1975-76 to 1978-79; Serge Savard, 1979-80, 1980-81; Bob Gainey, 1981-82 to 1988-89, Guy Carbonneau and Chris Chelios (co-captains), 1989-90; Guy Carbonneau, 1990-91 to date.

Retired Numbers

2	Doug Harvey	1947-1961
4	Aurèle Joliat	1922-1938
	Jean Béliveau	1950-1971
7	Howie Morenz	1923-1937
9	Maurice Richard	1942-1960
10	Guy Lafleur	1971-1984
16	Elmer Lach	1942-1954
	Henri Richard	1955-1975

Club Records

Team

(Figures in brackets for season records are games played; records for fewest points, wins, ties, losses, goals, goals against are for 70 or more games)

Most Points	*132	1976-77 (80)
Most Wins	*60	1976-77 (80)
Most Ties	23	1962-63 (70)
Most Losses	40	1983-84 (80)
Most Goals	387	1976-77 (80)
Most Goals Against	295	1983-84 (80)
Fewest Points	65	1950-51 (70)
Fewest Wins	25	1950-51 (70)
Fewest Ties	5	1983-84 (80)
Fewest Losses	*8	1976-77 (80)
Fewest Goals	155	1952-53 (70)
Fewest Goals Against	*131	1955-56 (70)

Longest Winning Streak

Over-all .... 12 Jan. 6-
Feb. 3/68

Home .... 13 Nov. 2/43-
Jan. 8/44
Jan. 30-
Mar. 26/77

Away .... 8 Dec. 18/77-
Jan. 18/78
Jan. 21-
Feb. 21/82

Longest Undefeated Streak

Over-all .... 28 Dec. 12/77-
Feb. 23/78
(23 wins, 5 ties)

Home .... *34 Nov. 1/76-
Apr. 2/77
(28 wins, 6 ties)

Away .... *23 Nov. 27/74-
Mar. 12/75
(14 wins, 9 ties)

Longest Losing Streak

Over-all .... 12 Feb. 13/26-
Mar. 13/26

Home .... 7 Dec. 16/39-
Jan. 18/40

Away .... 10 Dec. 1/25-
Feb. 2/26

Longest Winless Streak

Over-all .... 12 Feb. 13-
Mar. 13/26
(12 losses)
Nov. 28-
Dec. 29/35
(8 losses, 4 ties)

Home .... *15 Dec. 16/39-
Mar. 7/40
(12 losses, 3 ties)

Away .... 12 Oct. 20-
Dec. 13/51
(8 losses, 4 ties)

Most Shutouts, Season	**22	1928-29 (44)
Most PIM, Season	1,840	1987-88 (80)
Most Goals, Game	*16	Mar. 3/20 (Mtl. 16 at Que. 3)

Individual

Most Seasons	20	Henri Richard
Most Games	1,256	Henri Richard
Most Goals Career	544	Maurice Richard
Most Assists, Career	728	Guy Lafleur
Most Points Career	1,246	Guy Lafleur (518 goals, 728 assists)
Most PIM, Career	2,174	Chris Nilan
Most Shutouts, Career	75	George Hainsworth

Longest Consecutive Games Streak .... 560 Doug Jarvis
(Oct. 8/75-Apr. 4/82)

Most Goals, Season ...... 60 Steve Shutt
(1976-77)
Guy Lafleur
(1977-78)

Most Assists, Season	82	Peter Mahovlich (1974-75)
Most Points, Season	136	Guy Lafleur (1976-77) (56 goals, 80 assists)
Most PIM, Season	358	Chris Nilan (1984-85)
Most Points, Defenseman Season	85	Larry Robinson (1976-77) (19 goals, 66 assists)
Most Points, Center, Season	117	Peter Mahovlich (1974-75) (35 goals, 82 assists)
Most Points, Right Wing, Season	136	Guy Lafleur (1976-77) (56 goals, 80 assists)
Most Points, Left Wing, Season	110	Mats Naslund (1985-86) (43 goals, 67 assists)
Most Points, Rookie, Season	71	Mats Naslund (1982-83) (26 goals, 45 assists) Kjell Dahlin (1985-86) (32 goals, 39 assists)
Most Shutouts, Season	*22	George Hainsworth (1928-29)
Most Goals, Game	6	Newsy Lalonde (Jan. 10/20)
Most Assists, Game	6	Elmer Lach (Feb. 6/43)
Most Points, Game	8	Maurice Richard 5G-3A (Dec. 28/44) Bert Olmstead 4G-4A (Jan. 9/54)

* NHL Record.

All-time Record vs. Other Clubs

Regular Season

		At Home							On Road							Total						
	GP	W	L	T	GF	GA	PTS	GP	W	L	T	GF	GA	PTS	GP	W	L	T	GF	GA	PTS
Boston	297	172	82	43	1013	679	387	298	110	136	52	799	879	272	595	282	218	95	1812	1558	659
Buffalo	67	41	18	8	279	201	90	67	20	29	18	199	207	58	134	61	47	26	478	408	148
Calgary	34	19	10	5	120	85	43	34	20	9	5	125	110	45	68	39	19	10	245	195	88
Chicago	264	165	51	48	1022	622	378	264	121	89	54	738	709	296	528	286	140	102	1760	1331	674
Detroit	270	165	62	43	957	602	373	271	94	124	53	695	769	241	541	259	186	96	1652	1371	614
Edmonton	19	10	6	0	71	63	20	19	8	11	0	58	70	16	38	18	17	0	129	133	36
Hartford	44	31	7	6	209	130	68	44	23	16	5	169	142	51	88	54	23	11	378	272	119
Los Angeles	54	39	7	11	249	143	83	54	34	14	6	218	160	74	108	70	21	17	467	303	157
Minnesota	48	32	9	7	209	122	71	48	26	12	10	175	123	62	96	58	21	17	384	245	133
New Jersey	29	21	4	4	127	74	46	29	22	7	0	143	77	44	58	43	11	4	270	151	90
NY Islanders	34	20	8	6	133	104	46	35	15	16	4	106	117	34	69	35	24	10	239	221	80
NY Rangers	265	177	54	34	1051	613	388	264	108	106	50	769	756	266	529	285	160	84	1820	1369	654
Philadelphia	48	27	11	10	187	136	64	48	19	17	12	145	131	50	96	46	28	22	332	267	114
Pittsburgh	54	45	4	5	283	133	95	54	29	16	9	204	159	67	108	74	20	14	487	292	162
Quebec	44	30	8	6	199	130	66	44	19	23	2	156	158	40	88	49	31	8	355	288	106
St. Louis	48	35	8	5	215	125	75	48	25	10	13	167	120	63	96	60	18	18	382	245	138
Toronto	311	189	82	40	1106	764	418	311	109	158	44	813	942	262	622	298	240	84	1919	1706	680
Vancouver	41	33	6	2	209	105	68	40	27	5	8	164	95	62	81	60	11	10	373	200	130
Washington	35	26	4	5	170	69	57	35	17	12	6	126	91	40	70	43	16	11	296	160	97
Winnipeg	19	17	2	0	107	47	34	19	8	7	4	78	64	20	38	25	9	4	185	111	54
Defunct Club	231	148	58	25	779	469	321	230	98	97	35	586	606	231	461	246	155	60	1365	1075	552
Totals	**2256**	**1439**	**501**	**313**	**8695**	**5416**	**3191**	**2256**	**952**	**914**	**390**	**6633**	**6485**	**2294**	**4512**	**2391**	**1415**	**703**	**15328**	**11901**	**5485**

Playoffs

	Series	W	L	GP	W	L	T	GF	GA	Last Mtg.	Round	Result
Boston	26	21	5	128	84	44	0	402	303	1991	DF	L 3-4
Buffalo	5	3	2	27	14	13	0	98	82	1991	DSF	W 4-2
Calgary	2	1	1	11	6	5	0	31	32	1989	F	L 2-4
Chicago	17	12	5	81	50	29	2	261	185	1976	QF	W 4-0
Detroit	12	5	7	62	33	29	0	161	149	1978	QF	W 4-1
Edmonton	1	0	1	3	0	3	0	6	15	1981	PR	L 0-3
Hartford	4	4	0	20	15	5	0	75	52	1989	DSF	W 4-0
Minnesota	2	1	1	13	7	6	0	48	37	1980	QF	L 3-4
NY Islanders	3	2	1	17	10	7	0	44	44	1984	CF	L 2-4
NY Rangers	13	7	6	55	32	21	2	171	139	1986	CF	W 4-1
Philadelphia	4	3	1	21	14	7	0	72	52	1989	CF	W 4-2
Quebec	4	2	2	25	13	12	0	86	69	1987	DF	W 4-3
St. Louis	3	3	0	12	12	0	0	42	14	1977	QF	W 4-0
Toronto	13	7	6	67	39	28	0	203	148	1979	QF	W 4-0
Vancouver	1	1	0	5	4	1	0	20	9	1975	QF	W 4-1
Defunct Clubs	12	7	5	32	18	10	4	82	83			
Totals	**123***	**79**	**43**	**579**	**351**	**220**	**8**	**1806**	**1413**			

* 1919 Final incomplete due to influenza epidemic.

Abbreviations: Round: F – Final; **CF** – conference final; **DF** – division final; **DSF** – division semi-final; **PR** – preliminary round. **QF** – quarter-final; **GA** – goals against; **GF** – goals for.

Playoff Results 1991-87

Year	Round	Opponent	Result	GF	GA
1991	DF	Boston	L 3-4	18	18
	DSF	Buffalo	W 4-2	29	24
1990	DF	Boston	L 1-4	12	16
	DSF	Buffalo	W 4-2	17	13
1989	F	Calgary	L 2-4	16	19
	CF	Philadelphia	W 4-2	17	8
	DF	Boston	W 4-1	16	13
	DSF	Hartford	W 4-0	18	11
1988	DF	Boston	L 1-4	10	15
	DSF	Hartford	W 4-2	23	20
1987	CF	Philadelphia	L 2-4	22	22
	DF	Quebec	W 4-3	26	21
	DSF	Boston	W 4-0	19	11

1990-91 Results

	Home			Away	
Oct. 6	Buffalo	6-5	Oct. 4 Buffalo	3-3
8	Hartford	5-3	12 NY Rangers	0-3
15	Washington	3-1	13 Hartford	2-5
20	Philadelphia	3-5	17 Buffalo	4-3
24	NY Islanders	8-2	18 Detroit	2-5
Nov. 3	Detroit	5-2	23 Pittsburgh	5-4
4	Minnesota	2-2	27 St Louis	0-3
7	Boston	0-2	28 Chicago	1-2
10	New Jersey	3-1	31 Hartford	4-2
11	Quebec	5-4	Nov. 13 New Jersey	3-6
24	Los Angeles	2-4	15 Philadelphia	1-4
25	Winnipeg	4-3	17 Boston	1-1
28	Buffalo	1-2	19 Quebec	5-2
Dec. 1	Calgary	3-5	30 Washington	4-3
3	Hartford	2-4	Dec. 5 Hartford	4-3
8	Boston	7-1	6 Boston	6-4
19	Quebec	1-1	12 Toronto	1-4
22	NY Rangers	3-1	15 Winnipeg	2-4
Jan. 5	Quebec	3-0	18 Quebec	4-6
6	Pittsburgh	6-3	23 Philadelphia	4-4
9	NY Islanders	4-3	27 Vancouver	7-5
12	Washington	4-1	29 Los Angeles	3-2
13	St Louis	1-3	31 Calgary	2-7
23	Toronto	7-3	Jan. 2 Edmonton	3-0
26	Buffalo*	4-1	15 Minnesota	5-1
27	Boston*	1-3	17 St Louis	4-2
30	Winnipeg	8-4	31 Boston	2-5
Feb. 4	Minnesota	5-3	Feb. 2 NY Islanders	3-3
6	Chicago	3-8	7 Quebec	5-1
9	NY Rangers	6-4	15 Buffalo	2-2
13	Boston	4-7	20 Hartford	3-5
16	Hartford	1-2	27 Detroit	3-5
23	Toronto	3-3	Mar. 1 Vancouver	7-1
Mar. 9	Vancouver	4-2	2 Edmonton	3-1
10	Los Angeles	4-4	4 Calgary	2-3
16	Buffalo	6-4	6 Chicago	5-3
17	Edmonton	2-4	12 Pittsburgh	4-4
23	New Jersey	3-3	14 Boston	2-3
25	Hartford	3-2	20 Buffalo	3-3
30	Quebec	4-3	31 Quebec	1-4

* Denotes afternoon game.

Coach

BURNS, PAT
Coach, Montreal Canadiens. Born in St-Henri, Que., April 4, 1952.

Despite juggling a youthful lineup that featured 11 newcomers to the NHL, Pat Burns' Montreal Canadiens recorded their third straight .500-plus season of the coach's three-year tenure. In 1988-89, after leading his club to the Stanley Cup Finals, Burns was named recipient of the Jack Adams Award, only the third rookie coach in League history to receive that honor. Following 17 years of service with the Gatineau (Quebec) and Ottawa Police Departments, Burns began his rise to the NHL coaching ranks by assuming the head coaching position with the Hull Olympiques of the Quebec Major Hockey League in 1983-84. In 1985-86, his best year at Hull, he led the Olympiques to the Memorial Cup Final after finishing the regular-season with a 54-18-0 record. Later that year he served as an assistant coach to Bert Templeton for Team Canada at the 1986 World Junior Hockey Championships in Czechoslovkia. Burns' pro coaching career began in 1987-88 when he guided the Canadiens' top minor league affiliate, the AHL Sherbrooke Canadiens, to a 42-34-4 regular-season record.

Coaching Record

			Regular Season				Playoffs			
Season	Team	Games	W	L	T	%	Games	W	L	%
1983-84	Hull (QMJHL)	70	25	45	0	.357	....	....	....	....
1984-85	Hull (QMJHL)	68	33	34	1	.493	5	1	4	.200
1985-86	Hull (QMJHL)	72	54	18	0	.750	15	15	0	1.000
1986-87	Hull (QMJHL)	70	26	39	5	.407	8	4	4	.500
1987-88	Sherbrooke (AHL)	80	42	34	4	.550	6	2	4	.333
1988-89	Montreal (NHL)	80	53	18	9	.719	21	14	7	.667
1989-90	Montreal (NHL)	80	41	28	11	.581	11	5	6	.455
1990-91	Montreal (NHL)	80	39	30	11	.556	13	7	6	.538
	NHL Totals	240	133	76	31	.619	45	26	19	.578

General Manager

SAVARD, SERGE A.
Managing Director, Montreal Canadiens. Born in Montreal, Que., January 22, 1946.

When Serge Savard was named managing director of the Montreal Canadiens on April 28, 1983, he took over a club that finished in fourth place with 75 points. In 1984-85, the Canadiens were vastly improved, finishing first with 94 points. Evidence of Savard's front office efforts were visible throughout the organization where he spent 14 of his 16 NHL seasons as a standout defenseman and an important part of eight Stanley Cup winning teams. As a player, Savard captured the Conn Smythe Trophy as the most valuable player in the 1969 Stanley Cup playoffs and was recipient of the Bill Masterton Trophy in 1978-79 for his dedication, perseverance and sportsmanship to the game of hockey. He was acquired by the Winnipeg Jets in the 1981 Waiver Draft and closed out his playing career with two seasons as a leader and teacher to the young Jets' team which showed remarkable improvement during Savard's term. In the 1960's, Savard twice suffered multiple leg fractures and most experts doubted he would ever play again. He was named to the NHL's Second All-Star Team in 1978-79.

Entry Draft Selections 1991-77

1991
Pick
17 Brent Bilodeau
28 Jim Campbell
43 Craig Darby
61 Yves Sarault
73 Vladimir Vujtek
83 Sylvain Lapointe
100 Brad Layzell
105 Tony Prpic
127 Oleg Petrov
149 Brady Kramer
171 Brian Savage
193 Scott Fraser
215 Greg MacEachern
237 Paul Lepler
259 Dale Hooper

1990
Pick
12 Turner Stevenson
39 Ryan Kuwabara
58 Charles Poulin
60 Robert Guillet
81 Gilbert Dionne
102 Paul Dipietro
123 Craig Conroy
144 Stephen Rohr
165 Brent Fleetwood
186 Derek Maguire
207 Mark Kettelhut
228 John Uniac
249 Sergei Martinyuk

1989
Pick
13 Lindsay Vallis
30 Patrice Brisebois
41 Steve Larouche
51 Pierre Sevigny
83 Andre Racicot
104 Marc Deschamps
146 Craig Ferguson
167 Patrice Lebeau
188 Roy Mitchell
209 Ed Henrich
230 Justin Duberman
251 Steve Cadieux

1988
Pick
20 Eric Charron
34 Martin St. Amour
46 Neil Carnes
83 Patrik Kjellberg
93 Peter Popovic
104 Jean-Claude Bergeron
125 Patrik Carnback
146 Tim Chase
167 Sean Hill
188 Haris Vitolinis
209 Juri Krivohija
230 Kevin Dahl
251 Dave Kunda

1987
Pick
17 Andrew Cassels
33 John Leclair
38 Eric Desjardins
44 Mathieu Schneider
58 Francois Gravel
80 Kris Miller
101 Steve McCool
122 Les Kuntar
143 Rob Kelley
164 Will Geist
185 Eric Tremblay
206 Barry McKinlay
227 Ed Ronan
248 Bryan Herring

1986
Pick
15 Mark Pederson
27 Benoit Brunet
57 Jyrkki Lumme
78 Brent Bobyck
94 Eric Aubertin
99 Mario Milani
120 Steve Bisson
141 Lyle Odelin
162 Rick Hayward
183 Antonin Routa
204 Eric Bohemier
225 Charlie Moore
246 Karel Svoboda

1985
Pick
12 Jose Charbonneau
16 Tom Chorske
33 Todd Richards
47 Rockey Dundas
75 Martin Desjardins
79 Brent Gilchrist
96 Tom Sagissor
117 Donald Dufresne
142 Ed Cristofoli
163 Mike Claringbull
184 Roger Beedon
198 Maurice Mansi
205 Chad Arthur
226 Mike Bishop
247 John Ferguson Jr.

1984
Pick
5 Peter Svoboda
9 Shayne Corson
29 Stephane Richer
51 Patrick Roy
54 Graeme Bonar
65 Lee Brodeur
95 Gerald Johannson
116 Jim Nesich
137 Scott MacTavish
158 Brad McCaughey
179 Eric Demers
199 Ron Annear
220 Dave Tanner
240 Troy Crosby

1983
Pick
17 Alfie Turcotte
26 Claude Lemieux
27 Sergio Momesso
35 Todd Francis
45 Daniel Letendre
78 John Kordic
98 Dan Wurst
118 Arto Javanainen
138 Vladislav Tretiak
158 Rob Bryden
178 Grant MacKay

198 Thomas Rundquist
218 Jeff Perpich
238 Jean Guy Bergeron

1982
Pick
19 Alain Heroux
31 Jocelyn Gauvreau
32 Kent Carlson
33 David Maley
40 Scott Sandelin
61 Scott Harlow
69 John Devoe
103 Kevin Houle
117 Ernie Vargas
124 Michael Dark
145 Hannu Jarvenpaa
150 Steve Smith
166 Tom Kolioupoulos
187 Brian Williams
208 Bob Emery
229 Darren Acheson
250 Bill Brauer

1981
Pick
7 Mark Hunter
18 Gilbert Delorme
19 Jan Ingman
32 Lars Eriksson
40 Chris Chelios
46 Dieter Hegen
82 Kjell Dahlin
88 Steve Rooney
124 Tom Anastos
145 Tom Kurvers
166 Paul Gess
187 Scott Ferguson
208 Danny Burrows

1980
Pick
1 Doug Wickenheiser
27 Ric Nattress
40 John Chabot
45 John Newberry
61 Craig Ludwig
82 Jeff Teal
103 Remi Gagne
124 Mike McPhee
145 Bill Norton
166 Steve Penney
187 John Schmidt
208 Scott Robinson

1979
Pick
27 Gaston Gingras
37 Mats Naslund
43 Craig Levie
44 Guy Carbonneau
58 Rick Wamsley
79 Dave Orleski
100 Yvon Joly
121 Greg Moffatt
124 Mike McPhee
145 Bill Norton
166 Steve Penney
187 John Schmidt
208 Scott Robinson

1978
Pick
8 Dan Geoffrion
17 Dave Hunter
30 Dale Yakiwchuk
36 Ron Carter
42 Richard David
69 Kevin Reeves
86 Mike Boyd
103 Keith Acton
120 Jim Lawson
137 Larry Landon
154 Kevin Constantine
171 John Swan
186 Daniel Metivier

201 Vjacselev Fetisov
212 Jeff Mars
222 Greg Tignanelli
225 George Goulakos
227 Ken Moodie
229 Serge Leblanc
230 Bob Magnuson
231 Chris Nilan
232 Rick Wilson
233 Louis Sleigher
234 Doug Robb

1977
Pick
10 Mark Napier
18 Normand Dupont

36 Rod Langway
43 Alain Cote
46 Pierre Lagace
49 Moe Robinson
54 Gord Roberts
64 Bob Holland
90 Gaetan Rochette
108 Bill Himmelright
124 Richard Sevigny
137 Keith Hendrickson
140 Mike Reilly
152 Barry Barrett
154 Sid Tanchak
160 Mark Holden
162 Craig Laughlin
167 Daniel Poulin

Club Directory

Montreal Forum
2313 St. Catherine Street West
Montreal, Quebec H3H 1N2
Phone 514/932-2582
FAX (Hockey) 514/932-8736
P.R. 514/932-8285
ENVOY ID
Front Office: CANADIEN. GM

Public
Relations: CANADIEN. PR
Capacity: 16,197

Owner: The Molson Companies Limited

Chairman of the Board, President and Governor — Ronald Corey
Vice-President Hockey. Managing Director and Alternate Governor — Serge Savard
Senior Vice-President, Corporate Affairs — Jean Béliveau
Vice-President, Forum Operations — Aldo Giampaolo
Vice-President, Finance and Administration — Fred Steer
Assistant to the Managing Director & Managing Director of Fredericton Canadiens — Jacques Lemaire
Assistant to the Managing Director, Director of Recruitment — André Boudrias
Head Coach — Pat Burns
Assistant Coaches — Jacques Laperrière, Charles Thiffault
Goaltending Instructor — François Allaire
Director of Player Development and Scout — Claude Ruel
Chief Scout — Doug Robinson
Scouting Staff — Neil Armstrong, Scott Baker, Pat Flannery, Pierre Mondou, Gerry O'Flaherty, Richard Scammell, Eric Taylor, Jean-Claude Tremblay, Del Wilson
Farm Team (AHL) — Fredericton Canadiens
Head Coach — Paulin Bordeleau
Director of Operations — Wayne Gamble

Medical and Training Staff
Club Physician — Dr. D.G. Kinnear
Athletic Trainer — Gaétan Lefebvre
Assistant to the Athletic Trainer — John Shipman
Equipment Manager — Eddy Palchak
Assistants to the Equipment Manager — Pierre Gervais, Sylvain Toupin

Marketing
EFFIX Inc. — François-Xavier Seigneur
Director of Advertising Sales — Floyd Curry

Communications
Director of Public Relations — Claude Mouton
Director of Press Relations — Michèle Lapointe
Computer Supervisor — Sylvain Roy

Finance
Controller — Dennis McKinley
Administrative Supervisor — Dave Poulton
Accountants — Françoise Brault, Gilles Viens

Forum
Forum Superintendent — Alain Gauthier
Director of Security — Pierre Sauvé
Director of Events — Louise Laliberté
Director of Concessions — Yvon Gosselin
Director of Purchasing — Robert Loiseau

Ticketing
Box Office Manager — TBA
Assistant to the Box Office Manager — Doug Foster

Executive Secretaries
President (Lise Beaudry)/Managing Director (Donna Stuart)/Senior V.P., C.A. (Louise Richer)/V.P. Forum Operations (Vicky Mercuri)/V.P. Finance (Susan Cryans)/Public Rel. (Normande Herget)/Press Rel. (Frédérique Cardinal)

Location of Press Box — suspended above ice — west side
Location of Radio and TV booth — suspended above ice — east side
Dimensions of rink — 200 feet by 85 feet
Ends of rink — Herculite extends above boards all around rink
Club colors — Red, White and Blue
Club trains at — Montreal Forum

Play-by-Play — Radio/TV — Dick Irvin (English), Richard Garneau, Claude Quenneville, René Pothier (French)
TV Channels — CBMT (6), CFTM (10), CBFT (2)
Radio Stations — CBF (690) (French), CJAD (800) (English)

New Jersey Devils

1990-91 Results: 32w-33L-15T 79PTS. Fourth, Patrick Division

Tenth Anniversary

Year-by-Year Record

Season	GP	Home W	Home L	Home T	Road W	Road L	Road T	Overall W	Overall L	Overall T	GF	GA	Pts.	Finished	Playoff Result
1990-91	80	23	10	7	9	23	8	32	33	15	272	264	79	4th, Patrick Div.	Lost Div. Semi-Final
1989-90	80	22	15	3	15	19	6	37	34	9	295	288	83	2nd, Patrick Div.	Lost Div. Semi-Final
1988-89	80	17	18	5	10	23	7	27	41	12	281	325	66	5th, Patrick Div.	Out of Playoffs
1987-88	80	23	16	1	15	20	5	38	36	6	295	296	82	4th, Patrick Div.	Lost Conf. Championship
1986-87	80	20	17	3	9	28	3	29	45	6	293	368	64	6th, Patrick Div.	Out of Playoffs
1985-86	80	17	21	2	11	28	1	28	49	3	300	374	59	6th, Patrick Div.	Out of Playoffs
1984-85	80	13	21	6	9	27	4	22	48	10	264	346	54	5th, Patrick Div.	Out of Playoffs
1983-84	80	10	28	2	7	28	5	17	56	7	231	350	41	5th, Patrick Div.	Out of Playoffs
1982-83	80	11	20	9	6	29	5	17	49	14	230	338	48	5th, Patrick Div.	Out of Playoffs
1981-82	80	14	21	5	4	28	8	18	49	13	241	362	49	5th, Smythe Div.	Out of Playoffs
1980-81	80	15	16	9	7	29	4	22	45	13	258	344	57	5th, Smythe Div.	Out of Playoffs
1979-80	80	12	20	8	7	28	5	19	48	13	234	308	51	6th, Smythe Div.	Out of Playoffs
1978-79	80	8	24	8	7	29	4	15	53	12	210	331	42	4th, Smythe Div.	Out of Playoffs
1977-78	80	17	14	9	2	26	12	19	40	21	257	305	59	2nd, Smythe Div.	Lost Prelim. Round
1976-77	80	12	20	8	8	26	6	20	46	14	226	307	54	5th, Smythe Div.	Out of Playoffs
1975-76	80	8	24	8	4	32	4	12	56	12	190	351	36	5th, Smythe Div.	Out of Playoffs
1974-75	80	12	20	8	3	34	3	15	54	11	184	328	41	5th, Smythe Div.	Out of Playoffs

Schedule

	Home			Away
Oct.	Sat. 5 St Louis		**Oct.**	Sun. 6 Chicago
	Tues. 8 Quebec			Sun. 13 Philadelphia
	Sat. 12 Pittsburgh*			Wed. 16 NY Rangers
	Sat. 19 Washington			Fri. 18 Washington
	Tues. 22 Los Angeles			Thur. 24 Pittsburgh
	Sat. 26 San Jose			Tues. 29 Vancouver
Nov.	Fri. 8 Montreal			Wed. 30 Calgary
	Tues. 12 Philadelphia		**Nov.**	Fri. 1 Edmonton
	Thur. 14 NY Islanders			Mon. 4 Montreal
	Sat. 16 Winnipeg*			Sat. 9 Boston
	Wed. 20 Washington			Sat. 23 Philadelphia
	Fri. 22 Hartford			Wed. 27 Pittsburgh
Dec.	Thur. 5 Calgary			Sat. 30 Los Angeles
	Sat. 7 Detroit		**Dec.**	Sun. 8 Philadelphia
	Fri. 13 Pittsburgh			Tues. 10 Minnesota
	Sat. 21 Chicago			Sat. 14 NY Islanders
	Sat. 28 Buffalo			Thur. 19 Hartford
	Sun. 29 Washington			Mon. 23 NY Rangers
Jan.	Thur. 2 Pittsburgh			Thur. 26 NY Islanders
	Sat. 4 NY Rangers			Tues. 31 Pittsburgh
	Thur. 9 St Louis		**Jan.**	Fri. 24 Washington
	Sat. 11 Toronto			Wed. 29 Montreal
	Sun. 12 Los Angeles			Fri. 31 Detroit
	Wed. 15 Buffalo		**Feb.**	Sat. 1 Toronto
	Sat. 25 Detroit			Thur. 6 St Louis
Feb.	Tues. 4 Philadelphia			Sat. 8 Boston*
	Thur. 13 Vancouver			Sun. 9 Quebec*
	Sat. 15 Hartford*			Thur. 20 Chicago
	Sun. 16 NY Rangers*			Fri. 21 Winnipeg
	Tues. 18 Philadelphia			Tues. 25 Toronto
	Mon. 24 Minnesota			Sat. 29 NY Islanders
	Fri. 28 NY Islanders		**Mar.**	Wed. 4 NY Rangers
Mar.	Mon. 2 NY Rangers			Fri. 6 Buffalo
	Thur. 19 Edmonton			Sat. 7 Washington
	Sat. 21 NY Islanders*			Wed. 11 Edmonton
	Tues. 24 San Jose			Thur. 12 Vancouver
	Thur. 26 Boston			Sat. 14 San Jose
	Sat. 28 Quebec*			Sun. 22 NY Rangers*
Apr.	Wed. 1 Washington			Sun. 29 Philadelphia*
	Sun. 5 Pittsburgh		**Apr.**	Sat. 4 NY Islanders*

* Denotes afternoon game.

Home Starting Times:

All Games	7:35 p.m.
Matinees	1:35 p.m.
Except Oct. 5 and Apr. 5	5:05 p.m.

Franchise date: June 30, 1982. Transferred from Denver to New Jersey. Previously transferred from Kansas City to Denver, Colorado.

18th NHL Season

Chris Terreri appeared in 53 games in 1990-91, recording a goals-against average of 2.91.

1991-92 Player Personnel

FORWARDS	HT	WT	S	Place of Birth	Date	1990-91 Club
BARR, David	6-1	190	R	Toronto, Ont.	11/30/60	Detroit
BODNARCHUK, Mike	6-1	175	R	Bramalea, Ont.	3/26/70	Utica
BOSCHMAN, Laurie	6-0	185	L	Major, Sask.	6/4/60	New Jersey
BRADY, Neil	6-2	200	L	Montreal, Que.	4/12/68	New Jersey-Utica
BROWN, Doug	5-10	180	R	Southborough, MA	6/12/64	New Jersey
CHRISTIAN, Jeff	6-1	195	L	Burlington, Ont.	7/30/70	Utica
CIGER, Zdeno	6-1	190	L	Martin, Czech.	10/19/69	New Jersey-Utica
CONACHER, Pat	5-8	190	L	Edmonton, Alt.	5/1/59	New Jersey-Utica
DOWD, Jim	6-1	185	R	Brick, NJ	12/25/68	Lake Superior
HANKINSON, Ben	6-2	180	R	Edina, MN	1/5/69	U. Minnesota
HEXTALL, Donevan	6-2	190	L	Wolseley, Sask.	2/24/72	Prince Albert
LEMIEUX, Claude	6-1	215	R	Buckingham, Que.	7/16/65	New Jersey
LUIK, Scott	6-1	210	L	Scarborough, Ont.	1/15/70	Oshawa
MacLEAN, John	6-0	200	R	Oshawa, Ont.	11/20/64	New Jersey
MALEY, David	6-2	195	L	Beaver Dam, WI	4/24/63	New Jersey
McKAY, Randy	6-1	185	R	Montreal, Que.	1/25/67	Detroit
MILLER, Jason	6-1	190	L	Edmonton, Alta.	3/1/71	Medicine Hat-N.J.
MORRIS, Jon	6-0	175	R	Lowell, MA	5/6/66	New Jersey-Utica
MULLER, Kirk	6-0	205	L	Kingston, Ont.	2/8/66	New Jersey
PODDUBNY, Walt	6-1	210	L	Thunder Bay, Ont.	2/14/60	New Jersey
REGNIER, Curt	6-2	220	L	Prince Albert, Sask.	1/24/72	Prince Albert
RIEHL, Kevin	5-10	180	L	Leader, Sask.	3/11/71	Medicine Hat
RUCHTY, Matt	6-1	210	L	Kitchener, Ont.	11/27/69	Bowling Green
SIMON, Jason	6-1	190	L	Sarnia, Ont.	3/21/69	Utica-Johnstown
SKALDE, Jarrod	6-0	170	L	Niagara Falls, Ont.	2/26/71	Oshawa-Belleville-Utica
STASTNY, Peter	6-1	200	L	Bratislava, Czech.	9/18/56	New Jersey
STEWART, Alan	6-0	195	L	Fort St. John, B.C.	1/31/64	Utica-New Jersey
SULLIVAN, Brian	6-4	195	R	S. Windsor, CT	4/23/69	Northeastern U.
SUNDSTROM, Patrik	6-1	200	L	Skelleftea, Sweden	12/14/61	New Jersey
TODD, Kevin	5-10	175	L	Winnipeg, Man.	5/4/63	Utica-New Jersey
VILGRAIN, Claude	6-1	205	R	Port-au-Prince, Haiti	3/1/63	Utica
DEFENSEMEN						
ALBELIN, Tommy	6-1	190	L	Stockholm, Sweden	5/21/64	New Jersey-Utica
COPELAND, Todd	6-2	210	L	Ridgewood, N.J.	5/18/67	Utica
CRAIEVICH, David	6-1	210	R	Chatham, Ont.	5/3/71	Oshawa
DANEYKO, Ken	6-0	210	L	Windsor, Ont.	4/17/64	New Jersey
DEAN, Kevin	6-2	195	L	Madison, WI	4/1/69	N. Hampshire
DRIVER, Bruce	6-0	185	L	Toronto, Ont.	4/29/62	New Jersey
FETISOV, Viacheslav	6-1	220	L	Moscow, USSR	5/20/58	New Jersey-Utica
HUSCROFT, Jamie	6-2	200	L	Creston, B.C.	1/9/67	Utica, New Jersey
KASATONOV, Alexei	6-1	215	L	Leningrad, USSR	10/14/59	New Jersey
KIENE, Chris	6-5	220	L	S. Windsor, CT	3/16/66	Johnstown
KUCHYNA, Petr	6-3	180	R	Jihlava, Czech.	1/14/70	Dukla Jihlava, Czech.
MALKOC, Dean	6-3	200	L	Vancouver, B.C.	1/26/70	Kamloops-Swift Current-Utica
MODRY, Jaroslav	6-2	195	L	Budajovice, Czech.	2/7/71	Dukla Trencin, Czech.
NIEDERMAYER, Scott	6-0	200	L	Edmonton, Alta.	8/31/71	Kamloops
NORWOOD, Lee	6-1	200	L	Oakland, CA	2/2/60	Detroit-New Jersey
O'CONNOR, Myles	5-11	185	L	Calgary, Alta.	4/2/67	Utica-New Jersey
SEVERYN, Brent	6-2	210	L	Vegreville, Alta.	2/22/66	Halifax
SHARPLES, Jeff	6-1	195	L	Terrace, B.C.	7/28/67	Utica
STEVENS, Scott	6-2	215	L	Kitchener, Ont.	4/1/64	St. Louis
WEINRICH, Eric	6-1	210	L	Roanoke, VA	12/19/66	New Jersey
WOLANSKI, Paul	6-1	210	R	Kitchener, Ont.	3/22/71	Niagara Falls
GOALTENDERS	**HT**	**WT**	**C**	**Place of Birth**	**Date**	**1990-91 Club**
BILLINGTON, Craig	5-10	170	L	London, Ont.	9/11/66	Cdn. National Team
BRODEUR, Martin	6-1	190	L	Montreal, Que.	5/6/72	St. Hyacinthe
BURKE, Sean	6-4	210	L	Windsor, Ont.	1/29/67	New Jersey
MELANSON, Roland	5-10	185	L	Moncton, N.B.	6/28/60	Utica-New Jersey
SCHWAB, Corey	6-0	180	L	N. Battleford, Sask.	11/4/70	Seattle
TERRERI, Chris	5-8	155	L	Providence, RI	11/15/64	New Jersey

General Manager

LAMORIELLO, LOU
President and General Manager, New Jersey Devils.
Born in Providence, Rhode Island, October 21, 1942.

Lou Lamoriello is entering his fourth season as president and general manager of the Devils following a more than 20-year association with Providence College as a player, coach and administrator. A member of the varsity hockey Friars during his undergraduate days, he became an assistant coach with the college club after graduating in 1963. Lamoriello was later named head coach and in the ensuing 15 years, led his teams to a 248-179-13 record, a .578 winning percentage and appearances in 10 post-season tournaments, including the 1983 NCAA Final Four. Lamoriello also served a five-year term as athletic director at Providence and was a co-founder of Hockey East, one of the strongest collegiate hockey conferences in the U.S. He remained as athletic director until he was hired as president of the Devils on April 30, 1987. He assumed the dual responsibility of general manager on September 10, 1987.

1990-91 Scoring

Regular Season

* rookie

Pos	#	Player	Team	GP	G	A	Pts	+/-	PIM	PP	SH	GW	GT	S	%
R	15	John MacLean	N.J.	78	45	33	78	8	150	19	2	7	2	292	15.4
L	9	Kirk Muller	N.J.	80	19	51	70	1	76	7	0	3	1	221	8.6
R	11	Brendan Shanahan	N.J.	75	29	37	66	4	141	7	0	2	3	195	14.9
C	26	Peter Stastny	N.J.	77	18	42	60	0	53	4	0	3	0	117	15.4
R	22	Claude Lemieux	N.J.	78	30	17	47	8–	105	10	0	2	0	271	11.1
C	17	Patrik Sundstrom	N.J.	71	15	31	46	7	48	4	1	1	0	96	15.6
D	23	Bruce Driver	N.J.	73	9	36	45	11	62	7	0	2	0	195	4.6
D	7	Alexei Kasatonov	N.J.	78	10	31	41	23	76	1	0	3	0	122	8.2
D	5	*Eric Weinrich	N.J.	76	4	34	38	10	48	1	0	0	0	96	4.2
R	24	Doug Brown	N.J.	58	14	16	30	18	4	0	2	2	1	122	11.5
C	20	*Jon Morris	N.J.	53	9	19	28	9	27	1	0	1	0	44	20.5
L	33	*Zdeno Ciger	N.J.	45	8	17	25	3	8	2	0	1	0	82	9.8
L	8	David Maley	N.J.	64	8	14	22	9	151	1	0	3	0	67	11.9
C	16	Laurie Boschman	N.J.	78	11	9	20	1–	79	0	1	1	0	91	12.1
D	3	Ken Daneyko	N.J.	80	4	16	20	10–	249	1	2	1	0	106	3.8
D	2	Viacheslav Fetisov	N.J.	67	3	16	19	5	62	1	0	0	0	71	4.2
L	32	Pat Conacher	N.J.	49	5	11	16	9	27	0	0	0	0	45	11.1
D	28	Lee Norwood	DET	21	3	7	10	6	50	1	0	0	0	36	8.3
			N.J.	28	3	2	5	1–	87	1	0	0	1	27	11.1
			TOTAL	49	6	9	15	5	137	2	0	0	1	63	9.5
D	6	Tommy Albelin	N.J.	47	2	12	14	1	44	1	0	0	0	66	3.0
L	12	Walt Poddubny	N.J.	14	4	6	10	8	10	0	0	0	0	22	18.2
R	25	*Troy Crowder	N.J.	59	6	3	9	10–	182	0	0	0	0	46	13.0
L	10	Alan Stewart	N.J.	41	5	2	7	6–	159	0	0	0	0	33	15.2
R	21	*Jeff Madill	N.J.	14	4	0	4	1–	46	0	0	0	0	24	16.7
D	4	*Myles O'Connor	N.J.	22	3	1	4	3	41	0	0	0	0	14	21.4
G	31	Chris Terreri	N.J.	53	0	3	3	0	2	0	0	0	0	0	.0
C	21	*Jarrod Skalde	N.J.	1	0	1	1	0	0	0	0	0	0	2	.0
D	18	Jamie Huscroft	N.J.	8	0	1	1	1	27	0	0	0	0	3	.0
D	27	*Dave Marcinyshyn	N.J.	9	0	1	1	1–	21	0	0	0	0	4	.0
L	27	Perry Anderson	N.J.	1	0	0	0	0	5	0	0	0	0	1	.0
G	30	Roland Melanson	N.J.	1	0	0	0	0	0	0	0	0	0	0	.0
C	19	*Jason Miller	N.J.	1	0	0	0	1	0	0	0	0	0	0	.0
C	18	*Kevin Todd	N.J.	1	0	0	0	1–	0	0	0	0	0	0	.0
C	19	*Neil Brady	N.J.	3	0	0	0	0	0	0	0	0	0	6	.0
G	1	Sean Burke	N.J.	35	0	0	0	0	18	0	0	0	0	0	.0

Goaltending

No.	Goaltender	GPI	Mins	Avg	W	L	T	EN	SO	GA	SA	S%
31	Chris Terreri	53	2970	2.91	24	21	7	3	1	144	1348	.893
1	Sean Burke	35	1870	3.59	8	12	8	3	0	112	875	.872
30	Roland Melanson	1	20	6.00	0	0	0	0	0	2	7	.714
	Totals	**80**	**4876**	**3.25**	**32**	**33**	**15**	**6**	**1**	**264**	**2236**	**.882**

Playoffs

Pos	#	Player	Team	GP	G	A	Pts	+/-	PIM	PP	SH	GW	OT	S	%
R	15	John MacLean	NJ	7	5	3	8	2	20	1	0	0	0	31	16.1
R	11	Brendan Shanahan	NJ	7	3	5	8	3	12	2	0	0	0	20	15.0
C	26	Peter Stastny	NJ	7	3	4	7	2–	2	1	0	2	0	7	42.9
R	22	Claude Lemieux	NJ	7	4	0	4	3–	34	2	0	1	0	24	16.7
R	24	Doug Brown	NJ	7	2	2	4	1	2	0	1	0	0	14	14.3
D	7	Alexei Kasatonov	NJ	7	1	3	4	1–	10	0	0	0	0	12	8.3
C	20	*Jon Morris	NJ	5	0	4	4	3	2	0	0	0	0	1	.0
D	23	Bruce Driver	NJ	7	1	2	3	1	12	1	0	0	0	21	4.8
D	5	*Eric Weinrich	NJ	7	1	2	3	2–	6	1	0	0	0	12	8.3
C	16	Laurie Boschman	NJ	7	1	1	2	1–	16	0	0	0	0	8	12.5
L	33	*Zdeno Ciger	NJ	6	0	2	2	1–	4	0	0	0	0	13	.0
L	32	Pat Conacher	NJ	7	0	2	2	1–	2	0	0	0	0	9	.0
R	21	*Jeff Madill	NJ	7	0	2	2	0	8	0	0	0	0	13	.0
L	9	Kirk Muller	NJ	7	0	2	2	3–	10	0	0	0	0	16	.0
D	6	Tommy Albelin	NJ	3	0	1	1	1	2	0	0	0	0	6	.0
L	27	Perry Anderson	NJ	4	0	1	1	1–	10	0	0	0	0	3	.0
D	3	Ken Daneyko	NJ	7	0	1	1	2	10	0	0	0	0	4	.0
C	14	*Kevin Todd	NJ	1	0	0	0	1–	6	0	0	0	0	0	.0
C	17	Patrik Sundstrom	NJ	2	0	0	0	0	0	0	0	0	0	2	.0
D	18	Jamie Huscroft	NJ	3	0	0	0	0	6	0	0	0	0	0	.0
D	28	Lee Norwood	NJ	4	0	0	0	0	18	0	0	0	0	4	.0
D	2	Viacheslav Fetisov	NJ	7	0	0	0	3–	15	0	0	0	0	7	.0
G	31	Chris Terreri	NJ	7	0	0	0	0	2	0	0	0	0	0	.0

Goaltending

No.	Goaltender	GPI	Mins	Avg	W	L	EN	SO	GA	SA	S%
31	Chris Terreri	7	428	2.94	3	4	0	0	21	216	.903
	Totals	7	429	2.94	3	4	0	0	21	216	.903

General Managers' History

(Kansas City) Sidney Abel, 1974-75 to 1975-76; (Colorado) Ray Miron, 1976-77 to 1980-81; Billy MacMillan, 1981-82 to 1982-83; Billy MacMillan and Max McNab, 1983-84; Max McNab 1984-85 to 1986-87; Lou Lamoriello, 1987-88 to date.

Coaching History

(Kansas City) Bep Guidolin, 1974-75; Bep Guidolin, Sid Abel, and Eddie Bush, 1975-76; (Colorado) John Wilson, 1976-77; Pat Kelly, 1977-78; Pat Kelly, Aldo Guidolin, 1978-79; Don Cherry, 1979-80; Bill MacMillan, 1980-81; Bert Marshall and Marshall Johnston, 1981-82; (New Jersey) Bill MacMillan, 1982-83; Bill MacMillan and Tom McVie, 1983-84; Doug Carpenter, 1984-85 to 1986-87; Doug Carpenter and Jim Schoenfeld, 1987-88; Jim Schoenfeld, 1988-89; Jim Schoenfeld and John Cunniff, 1989-90; John Cunniff and Tom McVie, 1990-91; Tom McVie, 1991-92.

Captains' History

Simon Nolet, 1974-75 to 1976-77; Wilf Paiement, 1977-78; Gary Croteau, 1978-79; Mike Christie, Rene Robert, Lanny McDonald, 1979-80; Lanny McDonald, 1980-81, Lanny McDonald, Rob Ramage, 1981-82; Don Lever, 1982-83; Don Lever, Mel Bridgman, 1983-84; Mel Bridgman, 1984-85, 1985-86; Kirk Muller, 1987-88 to date.

Club Records

Team

(Figures in brackets for season records are games played; records for fewest points, wins, ties, losses, goals, goals against are for 70 or more games)

Most Points	83	1989-90 (80)
Most Wins	38	1987-88 (80)
Most Ties	21	1977-78 (80)
Most Losses	56	1983-84 (80)
		1975-76 (80)
Most Goals	300	1985-86 (80)
Most Goals Against	374	1985-86
Fewest Points	*36	1975-76 (80)
	41	1983-84 (80)
Fewest Wins	*12	1975-76 (80)
	17	1982-83 (80)
		1983-84 (80)
Fewest Ties	3	1985-86 (80)
Fewest Losses	33	1990-91 (80)
Fewest Goals	*184	1974-75 (80)
	230	1982-83 (80)
Fewest Goals Against	264	1990-91 (80)

Longest Winning Streak

Over-all . . . . 5 Mar. 27-Apr. 3/88

Home . . . . 8 Oct. 9-Nov. 7/87

Away . . . . 4 Oct. 5-23/89

Longest Undefeated Streak

Over-all . . . . 8 Mar. 20-Apr. 3/88
(7 wins, 1 tie)
Dec. 15-30/90
(3 wins, 5 ties)

Home . . . . 9 Oct. 9-Nov. 12/87
(8 wins, 1 tie)
Nov. 17-Dece. 29/90
(5 wins, 4 ties)

Away . . . . 6 Jan. 20-Feb. 9/89
(3 wins, 3 ties)
Mar. 12-Apr. 3/88
(5 wins, 1 tie)

Longest Losing Streak

Over-all . . . . *14 Dec. 30/75-Jan. 29/76

. . . . 10 Oct. 14-Nov. 4/83

Home . . . . 9 Dec. 22/85-Feb. 6/86

Away . . . . 12 Oct. 19/83-Dec. 1/83

Longest Winless Streak

Over-all . . . . *27 Feb. 12-Apr. 4/76
(21 losses, 6 ties)

. . . . 18 Oct. 20-Nov. 26/82
(14 losses 4 ties)

Home . . . . *14 Feb. 12-Mar. 30/76
(10 losses, 4 ties)
Feb. 4-Mar. 31/79
(12 losses, 2 ties)

. . . . 9 Dec. 22/85-Feb. 6/86
(9 losses)

Away . . . . *32 Nov. 12/77-Mar. 15/78
(22 losses, 10 ties)

. . . . 14 Dec. 26/82-Mar. 5/83
(13 losses, 1 tie)

Most Shutouts, Season	3	1988-89 (80)
Most PIM, Season	2,494	1988-89 (80)
Most Goals, Game	9	Apr. 1/79

(St.L. 5 at Col. 9)
Feb. 12/82
(Que. 2 at Col. 9)
Apr. 6/86
(NYI 7 at N.J. 9)
Mar. 10/90
(Que. 3 at N.J. 9)
Dec. 5/90
(Van. 4 at N.J. 9)

Individual

Most Seasons	9	Aaron Broten
Most Games	641	Aaron Broten
Most Goals, Career	217	John MacLean
Most Assists, Career	335	Kirk Muller
Most Points, Career	520	Kirk Muller

(185 goals, 335 assists)

Most PIM, Career	1,048	Ken Daneyko
Most Shutouts, Career	4	Sean Burke

Longest Consecutive

Games Streak . . . . 321 Kirk Muller
(Apr. 5/87-Mar. 31/91)

Most Goals, Season . . . . . . 46 Pat Verbeek
(1987-88)

Most Assists, Season . . . . . 57 Aaron Broten,
Kirk Muller
(1987-88)

Most Points, Season . . . . . 94 Kirk Muller
(1987-88)
(37 goals, 57 assists)

Most PIM, Season . . . . . . 283 Ken Daneyko
(1988-89)

Most Points, Defenseman

Season . . . . 66 Tom Kurvers
(1988-89)
(16 goals, 50 assists)

Most Points, Center

Season . . . . 94 Kirk Muller
(1987-88)
(37 goals, 57 assists)

Most Points, Right Wing,

Season . . . . *87 Wilf Paiement
(1977-78)
(31 goals, 56 assists)

. . . . 87 John MacLean
(1988-89)
(42 goals, 45 assists)

Most Points, Left Wing,

Season . . . . 86 Kirk Muller
(1989-90)
(30 goals, 56 assists)

Most Points, Rookie,

Season . . . . *60 Barry Beck
(1977-78)
(22 goals, 38 assists)

. . . . 54 Kirk Muller
(1984-85)
(17 goals, 37 assists)

Most Shutouts, Season . . . . . 3 Sean Burke
(1988-89)

Most Goals, Game . . . . 4 Bob MacMillan
(Jan. 8/82)
Pat Verbeek
(Feb. 28/88)

Most Assists, Game . . . . 5 Kirk Muller
(Mar. 25/87)
Greg Adams
(Oct. 10/86)
Tom Kurvers
(Feb. 13/89)

Most Points, Game . . . . 6 Kirk Muller
(Nov. 29/86)
(3 goals, 3 assists)

* – Record includes Kansas City Scouts and Colorado Rockies from 1974-75 through 1981-82

1990-91 Results

	Home				Away	
Oct.	4	Detroit	3-3	**Oct.**	7	Pittsburgh	4-7
	6	Philadelphia	3-1		11	Philadelphia	4-7
	9	Minnesota	5-2		20	Washington	0-4
	13	Calgary	5-3		23	NY Islanders	8-1
	17	Washington	3-2		30	Calgary	3-6
	19	NY Rangers	3-2	**Nov.**	1	Vancouver	1-2
	25	Buffalo	5-1		3	Edmonton	5-2
	27	Pittsburgh	7-5		10	Montreal	1-3
Nov.	7	NY Islanders	3-6		18	Philadelphia	4-1
	9	NY Rangers	2-3		20	Los Angeles	4-5
	13	Montreal	6-3		24	Minnesota	5-3
	15	Hartford	2-4	**Dec.**	1	St Louis	4-1
	17	Philadelphia*	3-2		3	Winnipeg	4-4
	28	Philadelphia	5-5		7	Washington	2-5
	30	NY Islanders	5-5		11	NY Islanders	2-3
Dec.	5	Vancouver	9-4		13	Pittsburgh	5-9
	8	Washington	4-2		15	Boston	1-1
	18	Boston	8-3		20	Philadelphia	3-3
	23	Toronto	4-2		22	Quebec	4-1
	27	NY Islanders	1-1		30	NY Rangers	3-3
	29	Buffalo	4-4	**Jan.**	1	Washington*	3-4
Jan.	8	St Louis	3-5		3	Chicago	3-5
	12	Edmonton*	4-5		5	Pittsburgh*	2-5
	14	Los Angeles	1-6		22	Philadelphia	3-5
	16	Chicago	2-2		28	Detroit	6-2
	24	Quebec	6-1		30	Los Angeles	4-2
	26	Minnesota	1-3	**Feb.**	2	St Louis	4-5
Feb.	5	Calgary	2-1		9	Quebec*	1-3
	10	Vancouver*	2-0		13	NY Rangers	3-6
	14	Winnipeg	3-3		24	NY Rangers*	2-5
	16	Philadelphia*	3-2		27	Toronto	3-7
	18	Edmonton	0-4	**Mar.**	1	Detroit	6-1
	22	Pittsburgh	5-2		3	NY Islanders	3-4
	25	Washington	5-1		6	Buffalo	3-3
Mar.	3	Boston	1-3		10	Winnipeg*	3-4
	13	Toronto	3-2		16	Hartford	2-6
	15	NY Rangers	5-2		21	Chicago	2-2
	19	Pittsburgh	5-4		23	Montreal	3-3
	27	Hartford	4-3		26	NY Rangers	3-3
	31	NY Islanders	2-3		30	Washington	0-4

* Denotes afternoon game.

All-time Record vs. Other Clubs

Regular Season

		At Home							On Road							Total					
	GP	W	L	T	GF	GA	PTS	GP	W	L	T	GF	GA	PTS	GP	W	L	T	GF	GA	PTS
Boston	29	4	17	8	78	112	16	29	7	19	3	89	131	17	58	11	36	11	167	243	33
Buffalo	29	5	19	5	87	122	15	29	3	22	4	81	142	10	58	8	41	9	168	264	25
Calgary	34	9	22	3	93	133	21	33	3	26	4	83	164	10	67	12	48	7	176	297	31
Chicago	35	15	14	6	110	111	36	35	7	23	5	97	151	19	70	22	37	11	207	262	55
Detroit	29	14	8	7	102	79	35	29	10	17	2	96	125	22	58	24	25	9	203	204	57
Edmonton	22	9	11	2	75	80	20	21	6	12	3	85	112	15	43	15	23	5	160	192	35
Hartford	19	8	9	2	68	84	18	19	4	11	4	56	75	12	38	12	20	6	124	159	30
Los Angeles	31	13	14	5	101	120	29	32	2	24	6	99	180	10	63	14	38	11	200	300	39
Minnesota	34	16	15	3	113	111	35	34	8	20	6	89	140	22	68	24	35	9	202	251	57
Montreal	29	7	22	0	77	143	14	29	4	21	4	74	127	12	58	11	43	4	151	270	26
NY Islanders	50	16	26	8	164	208	40	49	3	40	6	134	238	12	99	19	66	14	298	446	52
NY Rangers	50	20	26	4	177	199	44	49	13	29	7	161	219	33	99	33	55	11	338	418	77
Philadelphia	49	20	25	4	173	204	44	49	8	36	5	109	216	21	98	28	61	9	282	420	65
Pittsburgh	46	23	15	8	182	167	54	48	16	29	3	174	210	35	94	39	44	11	356	377	89
Quebec	19	9	9	1	85	71	19	19	6	11	2	64	87	14	38	15	20	3	149	158	33
St. Louis	35	13	15	7	108	105	33	35	8	24	3	109	160	19	70	21	39	10	217	265	52
Toronto	29	11	9	9	106	94	31	29	6	21	2	97	137	14	58	17	30	11	203	231	45
Vancouver	38	15	16	7	115	129	36	37	6	20	11	109	141	23	75	21	37	17	224	270	59
Washington	47	19	22	6	152	148	44	47	8	36	3	133	219	19	94	27	58	9	285	367	63
Winnipeg	18	5	8	5	57	63	15	20	3	14	3	50	82	9	38	8	22	8	107	145	24
Defunct Club	8	4	2	2	25	19	10	8	2	3	3	19	27	7	16	6	5	5	44	46	17
Totals	**680**	**254**	**325**	**101**	**2253**	**2502**	**609**	**680**	**133**	**458**	**89**	**2008**	**3083**	**355**	**1360**	**387**	**783**	**190**	**4261**	**5585**	**964**

Playoffs

	Series	W	L	GP	W	L	T	GF	GA	Last Mtg.	Round	Result
Boston	1	0	1	7	3	4	0	19	30	1988	CF	L 3-4
NY Islanders	1	1	0	6	4	2	0	23	18	1988	DSF	W 4-2
Philadelphia	1	0	1	2	0	2	0	3	6	1978	PR	L 0-2
Pittsburgh	1	0	1	7	3	4	0	17	25	1991	DSF	L 3-4
Washington	2	1	1	13	6	7	0	43	44	1990	DSF	L 2-4
Totals	**6**	**2**	**4**	**35**	**16**	**19**	**0**	**105**	**123**			

Abbreviations: Round: F – Final; **CF** – conference final; **DF** – division final; **DSF** – division semi-final; **PR** – preliminary round. **GA** – goals against; **GF** – goals for.

Playoff Results 1991-87

Year	Round	Opponent	Result	GF	GA
1991	DSF	Pittsburgh	L 3-4	17	25
1990	DSF	Washington	L 2-4	18	21
1988	CF	Boston	L 3-4	19	30
	DF	Washington	W 4-3	25	23
	DSF	NY Islanders	W 4-2	23	18

Entry Draft
Selections 1991-77

1991
Pick
3 Scott Niedermayer
11 Brian Rolston
33 Donevan Hextall
55 Fredrik Lindquist
77 Bradley Willner
121 Curt Regnier
143 David Craievich
165 Paul Wolanski
187 Daniel Reimann
231 Kevin Riehl
253 Jason Hehr

1990
Pick
20 Martin Brodeur
24 David Harlock
29 Chris Gotziaman
53 Michael Dunham
56 Brad Bombardir
64 Mike Bodnarchuk
95 Dean Malkoc
104 Peter Kuchyna
116 Lubomir Kolnik
137 Chris McAlpine
179 Jaroslav Modry
200 Corey Schwab
221 Valeri Zelepukin
242 Todd Reirden

1989
Pick
5 Bill Guerin
18 Jason Miller
26 Jarrod Skalde
47 Scott Pellerin
89 Mike Heinke
110 David Emma
152 Sergei Starikov
173 Andre Faust
215 Jason Simon
236 Peter Larsson

1988
Pick
12 Corey Foster
23 Jeff Christian
54 Zdenek Ciger
65 Matt Ruchty
75 Scott Luik
96 Chris Nelson
117 Chad Johnson
138 Chad Erickson
159 Bryan Lafort
180 Sergei Svetlov
201 Bob Woods
207 Alexander Semak
222 Charles Hughes
243 Michael Pohl

1987
Pick
2 Brendan Shanahan
23 Rickard Persson
65 Brian Sullivan
86 Kevin Dean
107 Ben Hankinson
128 Tom Neziol
149 Jim Dowd
170 John Blessman
191 Peter Fry
212 Alain Charland

1986
Pick
3 Neil Brady
24 Todd Copeland
45 Janne Ojanen
62 Marc Laniel
66 Anders Carlsson
108 Troy Crowder
129 Kevin Todd
150 Ryan Pardoski
171 Scott McCormack
192 Frederic Chabot
213 John Andersen
236 Doug Kirton

1985
Pick
3 Craig Wolanin
24 Sean Burke
32 Eric Weinrich
45 Myles O'Connor
66 Gregg Polak
108 Bill McMillan
129 Kevin Schrader
150 Ed Krayer
171 Jamie Huscroft
192 Terry Shold
213 Jamie McKinley
234 David Williams

1984
Pick
2 Kirk Muller
23 Craig Billington
44 Neil Davey
74 Paul Ysebaert
86 Jon Morris
107 Kirk McLean
128 Ian Ferguson
149 Vladimir Kames
170 Mike Roth
190 Mike Peluso
211 Jarkko Piiparinen
231 Chris Kiene

1983
Pick
6 John MacLean
24 Shawn Evans
87 Chris Terreri
108 Gordon Mark
129 Greg Evtushevski
150 Viacheslav Fetisov
171 Jay Octeau
192 Alexi Chernykh
213 Allan Stewart
234 Alexei Kasatonov

1982
Pick
8 Rocky Trottier
18 Ken Daneyko
43 Pat Verbeek
54 Dave Kasper
85 Scott Brydges
106 Mike Moher
127 Paul Fulcher
148 John Hutchings
169 Alan Hepple
190 Brent Shaw
207 Tony Gilliard
211 Scott Fusco
232 Dan Dorian

1981
Pick
5 Joe Cirella
26 Rich Chernomaz
48 Uli Hiemer
66 Gus Greco
87 Doug Speck
108 Bruce Driver
129 Jeff Larmer
150 Tony Arima
171 Tim Army
192 John Johannson

1980
Pick
19 Paul Gagne
22 Joe Ward
64 Rick LaFerriere
85 Ed Cooper
106 Aaron Broten
127 Dan Fascinato
148 Andre Hidi
169 Shawn MacKenzie
190 Bob Jansch

1979
Pick
1 Rob Ramage
64 Steve Peters
85 Gary Dillon
106 Bob Attwell

1978
Pick
4 Mike Gillis
27 Merlin Malinowski
41 Paul Messier
58 Dave Watson
73 Tim Thomlison
74 Rod Guimont
91 John Hynes
108 Andy Clark
125 John Oliver
142 Kevin Krook
159 Jeff Jensen
174 Bo Ericsson
190 Jari Viitala
204 Ulf Zetterstrom

1977
Pick
2 Barry Beck
38 Doug Berry
47 Randy Pierce
92 Daniel Lempe
110 Rick Doyle
126 Joe Contini
142 Jack Hughes

Tenth Anniversary

Club Directory

Byrne Meadowlands Arena
P.O. Box 504
East Rutherford, N.J. 07073
Phone 201/935-6050
GM FAX 201/507-0711
FAX 201/935-2127
ENVOY ID
Front Office: DEVILS. GM
Public
Relations: DEVILS. PR
Capacity: 19,040

Chairman	John J. McMullen
President & General Manager	Louis A. Lamoriello
Executive Vice President	Max McNab
Senior Vice President, Finance	Chris Modrzynski
Vice President, Community Development	Jerry Dailey
Vice President, Operations & Human Resources	Peter McMullen
Vice President, Administration	Mike O'Neil
Vice President, Marketing	Brian Petrovek

Hockey Club Personnel

Director of Player Personnel	Marshall Johnston
Head Coach	Tom McVie
Assistant Coaches	Robbie Ftorek, Doug Sulliman
Goaltending Coach	Warren Strelow
Assistant Director of Player Personnel	David Conte
Scouting Staff	Claude Carrier, Glen Dirk, Milt Fisher, Frank Jay, Dan Labraaten, Marcel Pronovost, Joe Mahoney, Ed Thomlinson, Les Widdifield, Fernie Flaman
Special Assignment Scouts	John Cunniff, Bob Sauve
Athletic Trainer	Ted Schuch
Equipment Managers	J.P. Mattingly, Dave Baglio
Physical Conditioning Coach	Dimitri Lopuchin
Massage Therapist	Bob Huddleston
Team Orthopedists	Dr. Barry Fisher, Dr. Len Jaffe
Team Internist	Dr. Richard Commentucci
Team Cardiologist	Dr. Joseph Niznik
Team Dentist	Dr. H. Hugh Gardy
Exercise Physiologist	Dr. Garret Caffrey
Administrative Assistants to the President/GM	Marie Carnevale, Charlotte Smaldone
Staff Assistant	Angela Gorgone

Communications Department

Director, Public & Media Relations	David Freed
Director of Broadcast Operations	Chris Moore
Assistant Director, Media Relations	Mike Levine
Public & Media Relations Assistant	George Moreira
Receptionist	Jelsa Belotta
Staff Assistants	David Perricone, Ted Vincent

Finance Department

Assistant Controller	Scott Struble
Staff Accountants	Dominic Russomagno, Mark Spinelli
Accounts Payable Clerk	Michelle Zhang
Secretary	Eileen Musikant

Marketing Department

Director, Promotional Marketing	Ken Ferriter
Group Sales Manager	Don Gleeson
Sales Managers	Neil Desormeaux, Holly Meyer, Matt Zanelli
Secretary	Karen Lynch

Ticketing Department

Director, Ticket Operations	Terry Farmer
Assistant Director, Ticket Operations	Scott Tanfield
Team Photographers	Steve Crandall, Jim Turner
Video Consultant	Mitch Kaufman
Location of Press Box	Section 108, center ice
Location of Broadcast Booth	Front, Section 234
Dimensions of Rink	200 feet by 85 feet
Club Colors	Red, Green and White
Television Outlet	SportsChannel
Flagship Radio Station	WABC (770 AM)

Coach

McVIE, TOM
Coach, New Jersey Devils. Born in Trail, B.C., June 6, 1935.

The 1991-92 NHL season marks the beginning of Tom McVie's first full stint as head coach of the New Jersey Devils. Previously coach of the Devils for 60 games during the 1983-84 season (taking over for Bill MacMillan), the 56-year-old British Columbia native replaced John Cunniff behind the Devils bench on March 4, 1991. McVie is no stranger to the National Hockey League, having also served as head coach for the Washington Capitals (1975-76 to 1977-78) and Winnipeg Jets (1979-80 to 1980-81).

McVie began his professional coaching career in 1973-74 with the Dayton Gems of the International Hockey League, and has compiled more than 500 professional coaching victories. Before rejoining the Devils last March, McVie served seven seasons as the general manager/coach of the Devils American Hockey League affiliates in Utica and Maine. His 14-year playing career included stints in Seattle, Portland, Los Angeles and Phoenix of the Western Hockey League.

Coaching Record

Season	Team	Regular Season					Playoffs			
		Games	W	L	T	%	Games	W	L	%
1973-74	Dayton (IHL)	76	38	35	3	.520	4	1	3	.250
1974-75	Dayton (IHL)	75	46	26	3	.633	14	7	7	.500
1975-76	Dayton (IHL)	34	21	10	3	.662	....	....	....	.....
	Washington (NHL)	44	8	31	5	.239	....	....	....	.....
1976-77	Washington (NHL)	80	24	42	14	.388	....	....	....	.....
1977-78	Washington (NHL)	80	17	49	14	.294	....	....	....	.....
1978-79	Winnipeg (WHA)	19	11	8	0	.579	12	10	2	.833
1979-80	Winnipeg (NHL)	77	19	47	11	.318	....	....	....	.....
1980-81	Winnipeg (NHL)	31	1	23	7	.145	....	....	....	.....
1981-82	Oklahoma City (CHL)	80	25	54	1	.319	4	1	3	.250
1982-83	Maine (AHL)	80	39	33	8	.538	17	8	9	.471
1983-84	Maine (AHL)	17	9	6	2	.588	....	....	....	.....
	New Jersey (NHL)	60	15	38	7	.308	....	....	....	.....
1984-85	Maine (AHL)	80	38	32	10	.538	11	5	6	.454
1985-86	Maine (AHL)	80	40	31	9	.556	5	1	4	.200
1986-87	Maine (AHL)	80	35	40	5	.469	....	....	....	.....
1987-88	Utica (AHL)	80	34	35	11	.506	....	....	....	.....
1988-89	Utica (AHL)	80	37	34	9	.531	5	1	4	.200
1989-90	Utica (AHL)	80	44	32	4	.575	5	1	4	.200
1990-91	Utica (AHL)	65	33	30	2	.523	....	....	....	.....
	New Jersey (NHL)	13	4	5	4	.462	7	3	4	.429
	NHL Totals	385	88	235	62	.309	7	3	4	.429

New York Islanders
1990-91 Results: 25w-45L-10T 60PTS. Sixth, Patrick Division

Year-by-Year Record

Season	GP	Home W	L	T	Road W	L	T	Overall W	L	T	GF	GA	Pts.	Finished		Playoff Result
1990-91	80	15	19	6	10	26	4	25	45	10	223	290	60	6th,	Patrick Div.	Out of Playoffs
1989-90	80	15	17	8	16	21	3	31	38	11	281	288	73	4th,	Patrick Div.	Lost Div. Semi-Final
1988-89	80	19	18	3	9	29	2	28	47	5	265	325	61	6th,	Patrick Div.	Out of Playoffs
1987-88	80	24	10	6	15	21	4	39	31	10	308	267	88	1st,	Patrick Div.	Lost Div. Semi-Final
1986-87	80	20	15	5	15	18	7	35	33	12	279	281	82	3rd,	Patrick Div.	Lost Div. Final
1985-86	80	22	11	7	17	18	5	39	29	12	327	284	90	3rd,	Patrick Div.	Lost Div. Semi-Final
1984-85	80	26	11	3	14	23	3	40	34	6	345	312	86	3rd,	Patrick Div.	Lost Div. Final
1983-84	80	28	11	1	22	15	3	50	26	4	357	269	104	1st,	Patrick Div.	Lost Final
1982-83	**80**	**26**	**11**	**3**	**16**	**15**	**9**	**42**	**26**	**12**	**302**	**226**	**96**	**2nd,**	**Patrick Div.**	**Won Stanley Cup**
1981-82	**80**	**33**	**3**	**4**	**21**	**13**	**6**	**54**	**16**	**10**	**385**	**250**	**118**	**1st,**	**Patrick Div.**	**Won Stanley Cup**
1980-81	**80**	**23**	**6**	**11**	**25**	**12**	**3**	**48**	**18**	**14**	**355**	**260**	**110**	**1st,**	**Patrick Div.**	**Won Stanley Cup**
1979-80	**80**	**26**	**9**	**5**	**13**	**19**	**8**	**39**	**28**	**13**	**281**	**247**	**91**	**2nd,**	**Patrick Div.**	**Won Stanley Cup**
1978-79	80	31	3	6	20	12	8	51	15	14	358	214	116	1st,	Patrick Div.	Lost Semi-Final
1977-78	80	29	3	8	19	14	7	48	17	15	334	210	111	1st,	Patrick Div.	Lost Quarter-Final
1976-77	80	24	11	5	23	10	7	47	21	12	288	193	106	2nd,	Patrick Div.	Lost Semi-Final
1975-76	80	24	8	8	18	13	9	42	21	17	297	190	101	2nd,	Patrick Div.	Lost Semi-Final
1974-75	80	22	6	12	11	19	10	33	25	22	264	221	88	3rd,	Patrick Div.	Lost Semi-Final
1973-74	78	13	17	9	6	24	9	19	41	18	182	247	56	8th,	East Div.	Out of Playoffs
1972-73	78	10	25	4	2	35	2	12	60	6	170	347	30	8th,	East Div.	Out of Playoffs

Schedule

Home
Oct. Sat. 12 Philadelphia; Tues. 15 Pittsburgh; Sat. 19 Edmonton; Tues. 22 Winnipeg; Sat. 26 Los Angeles; Tues. 29 San Jose
Nov. Sat. 2 Washington; Mon. 4 Boston; Sat. 16 NY Rangers; Wed. 27 Boston; Sat. 30 Washington
Dec. Thur. 5 Montreal; Sat. 7 Chicago; Tues. 10 St Louis; Sat. 14 New Jersey; Mon. 23 Pittsburgh; Thur. 26 New Jersey; Sat. 28 NY Rangers
Jan. Sat. 4 Quebec; Thur. 9 Hartford; Sat. 11 St Louis; Tues. 14 Detroit; Thur. 16 Philadelphia; Thur. 23 Toronto; Sat. 25 Pittsburgh*
Feb. Sat. 1 Philadelphia; Sun. 2 Calgary; Sat. 15 Vancouver; Mon. 17 Winnipeg*; Thur. 20 NY Rangers; Sat. 22 Minnesota; Sun. 23 Washington; Sat. 29 New Jersey
Mar. Tues. 3 Montreal; Tues. 10 Philadelphia; Sat. 14 Buffalo*; Thur. 26 San Jose; Sat. 28 NY Rangers; Sun. 29 Detroit
Apr. Sat. 4 New Jersey*

Away
Oct. Sat. 5 Boston; Wed. 9 NY Rangers; Sun. 13 Quebec; Thur. 17 Pittsburgh; Thur. 31 Chicago
Nov. Wed. 6 Edmonton; Sat. 9 San Jose; Sun. 10 Vancouver; Thur. 14 New Jersey; Tues. 19 Minnesota; Wed. 20 Winnipeg; Sat. 23 Pittsburgh; Fri. 29 Washington
Dec. Wed. 11 Toronto; Tues. 17 Hartford; Thur. 19 Philadelphia; Sat. 21 St Louis; Sun. 29 Hartford
Jan. Wed. 1 Washington*; Fri. 3 Buffalo; Tues. 7 Detroit; Sun. 12 Philadelphia; Thur. 30 Pittsburgh
Feb. Tues. 4 Los Angeles; Thur. 6 Vancouver; Fri. 7 Edmonton; Tues. 11 Calgary; Fri. 14 NY Rangers; Tues. 25 Philadelphia; Fri. 28 New Jersey
Mar. Thur. 5 Chicago; Sat. 7 Montreal; Sun. 8 Buffalo; Thur. 12 Pittsburgh; Sun. 15 Washington*; Wed. 18 NY Rangers; Sat. 21 New Jersey*; Tues. 24 Quebec
Apr. Wed. 1 Toronto; Sun. 5 Washington*

* Denotes afternoon game.

Home Starting Times:
All Games .... 7:35 p.m.
Except Matinees .... 2:05 p.m.
Dec. 28, Feb. 1, Feb. 2, Feb. 22, Feb. 23, Mar. 28, Mar. 29 .... 5:05 p.m.

Franchise date: June 6, 1972

20th NHL Season

Brent Sutter, captain of Islanders since 1987-88, is entering his 12th season with the four-time Stanley Cup champions.

1991-92 Player Personnel

FORWARDS	HT	WT	Place of Birth	Date	1990-91 Club
BERG, Bill	6-1	190	St. Catharines, Ont.	10/21/67	NY Islanders
CHYZOWSKI, David	6-1	190	Edmonton, Alta.	7/11/71	NYI-Capital District
DALGARNO, Brad	6-3	215	Vancouver, B.C.	8/11/67	NYI-Capital District
DIMAIO, Rob	5-8	175	Calgary, Alta.	2/19/68	NYI-Capital District
DOUCET, Wayne	6-2	203	Etobicoke, Ont.	6/19/70	Capital District
EWEN, Dean	6-1	185	St. Albert, Alta.	2/28/69	Capital District
FERRARO, Ray	5-10	185	Trail, B.C.	8/23/64	NYI-Hartford
FITZGERALD, Tom	6-1	193	Melrose, MA	8/28/68	NYI-Capital District
FLATLEY, Patrick	6-2	197	Toronto, Ont.	10/3/63	NY Islanders
FLEURY, Sylvain	5-11	189	Drummondville, Que.	4/30/70	Longueuil
FRASER, Iain	5-10	175	Scarborough, Ont.	8/10/69	Cap. Dist.-Richmond
GREEN, Travis	6-0	196	Creston, B.C.	12/20/70	Capital District
GRIEVE, Brent	6-1	205	Oshawa, Ont.	5/9/69	Capital District
HUBER, Phil	5-11	196	Calgary, Alta.	1/10/69	Cap. Dist.-Richmond
JABLONSKI, Jeff	6-1	185	Toledo, OH	6/20/67	Capital District
JOHNSON, John	5-10	185	Kirkfield, Ont.	2/22/71	Niagara Falls
JUNKAR, Steve	6-0	184	Castlegar, B.C.	6/26/72	Spokane
KING, Derek	6-1	210	Hamilton, Ont.	2/11/67	NY Islanders
KROMM, Rich	5-11	180	Trail, B.C.	3/29/64	NYI-Capital District
LaFONTAINE, Pat	5-10	177	St. Louis, MO	2/22/65	NY Islanders
LAUER, Brad	6-0	195	Humboldt, Sask.	10/27/66	NYI-Capital District
LAXDAL, Derek	6-1	175	St. Boniface, Man.	2/21/66	NYI-Capital District
LeBRUN, Sean	6-2	200	Prince George, B.C.	5/2/69	Capital District
McDONOUGH, Hubie	5-9	180	Manchester, NH	7/8/63	NYI-Capital District
PALFFY, Zigmund	5-11	180	Skalica, Czech.	5/5/72	Nitra
PARKS, Greg	5-9	180	Edmonton, Alta.	3/25/67	NYI-Capital District
RUTHERFORD, Paul	6-1	195	Sudbury, Ont.	1/1/69	Ohio State
SCISSONS, Scott	6-1	195	Saskatoon, Sask.	10/29/71	NYI-Saskatoon
SPARKS, Todd	6-0	187	Edmonston, N.B.	6/9/71	Hull
SUTTER, Brent	5-11	180	Viking, Alta.	6/10/62	NY Islanders
TAYLOR, Chris	6-0	190	Stratford, Ont.	3/6/72	London
TOWNSHEND, Graeme	6-2	225	Kingston, Jamaica	10/2/65	Boston-Maine
VANDERYDT, Rob	6-1	177	Bleuheim, Ont.	6/8/68	Miami-Ohio
VOLEK, David	6-0	185	Prague, Czech.	8/16/66	NY Islanders
VUKOTA, Mick	6-2	195	Saskatoon, Sask.	9/14/66	NYI-Capital District
WOOD, Randy	6-1	195	Princeton, NJ	10/12/63	NY Islanders

DEFENSEMEN	HT	WT	Place of Birth	Date	
BAUMGARTNER, Ken	6-1	200	Flin Flon, Man.	3/11/66	NY Islanders
CALHANE, Jim	6-0	195	Haileybury, Ont.	3/13/65	Cap. District-K.C.
CHEVELDAYOFF, Kevin	6-0	202	Saskatoon, Sask.	2/4/70	Capital District
CHYNOWETH, Dean	6-2	190	Calgary, Alta.	10/30/68	NYI-Capital District
FINLEY, Jeff	6-2	185	Edmonton, Alta.	4/14/67	NYI-Capital District
HAYWARD, Rick	6-0	180	Toledo, OH	2/25/66	L.A.-Phoenix
HILLIER, Randy	6-1	192	Toronto, Ont.	3/30/60	Pittsburgh
KURVERS, Tom	6-0	205	Minneapolis, MN	9/14/62	Toronto-Vancouver
LACHANCE, Scott	6-2	197	Chadottesville, VA	10/22/72	Boston U.
LAMMENS, Hank	6-2	210	Brockville, Ont.	2/21/66	Capital District
LEHTO, Joni	6-0	195	Turku, Finland	7/15/70	Ottawa
McBEAN, Wayne	6-2	185	Calgary, Alta.	2/21/69	NYI-Capital District
NORTON, Jeff	6-2	190	Acton, MA	11/25/65	NY Islanders
NYLUND, Gary	6-4	210	Surrey, B.C.	10/28/63	NY Islanders
PILON, Richard	6-0	202	Saskatoon, Sask.	4/30/68	NY Islanders
PRYOR, Chris	5-11	210	St. Paul, MN	1/31/61	Capital District
REEKIE, Joe	6-3	215	Victoria, B.C.	2/22/65	NYI-Capital District
TURNER, Brad	6-2	190	Winnipeg, Man.	5/25/68	Cap. Dist.-Richmond
VASKE, Dennis	6-2	210	Rockford, IL	10/11/67	NYI-Capital District

GOALTENDERS	HT	WT	Place of Birth	Date	1990-91 Club
CAPPRINI, Jon	6-2	140	Pingree, MA	2/26/68	Babson Coll.
FITZPATRICK, Mark	6-2	190	Toronto, Ont.	11/13/68	NYI-Capital District
HEALY, Glenn	5-10	175	Pickering, Ont.	8/23/62	NY Islanders
LORENZ, Danny	5-10	170	Murrayeville, B.C.	12/12/69	NYI-Capital District
MANELUK, George	5-11	185	Winnipeg, Man.	7/25/67	NYI-Capital District
McLENNAN, Jamie	6-0	140	Edmonton, Alta.	6/30/71	Lethbridge

1990-91 Scoring

Regular Season

* rookie

Pos	#	Player	Team	GP	G	A	Pts	+/-	PIM	PP	SH	GW	GT	S	%
C	16	Pat LaFontaine	NYI	75	41	44	85	6-	42	12	2	5	1	225	18.2
L	25	Dave Volek	NYI	77	22	34	56	10-	57	6	0	1	1	224	9.8
C	21	Brent Sutter	NYI	75	21	32	53	8-	49	6	2	4	1	186	11.3
R	26	Patrick Flatley	NYI	56	20	25	45	2-	74	8	0	4	0	137	14.6
L	27	Derek King	NYI	66	19	26	45	1	44	2	0	2	0	130	14.6
L	11	Randy Wood	NYI	76	24	18	42	12-	45	6	1	3	1	186	12.9
C	33	Ray Ferraro	HFD	15	2	5	7	1-	18	1	0	0	0	18	11.1
			NYI	61	19	16	35	11-	52	5	0	1	1	91	20.9
			TOTAL	76	21	21	42	12-	70	6	0	1	1	109	19.3
D	8	Jeff Norton	NYI	44	3	25	28	13-	16	2	1	0	0	87	3.4
L	4	*Bill Berg	NYI	78	9	14	23	3-	67	0	0	0	0	95	9.5
D	36	Gary Nylund	NYI	72	2	21	23	8-	105	0	0	0	0	102	2.0
D	6	Wayne McBean	NYI	52	5	14	19	21-	47	2	0	0	0	93	5.4
D	29	Joe Reekie	NYI	66	3	16	19	17	96	0	0	2	0	70	4.3
R	15	Brad Dalgarno	NYI	41	3	12	15	10-	24	0	0	1	0	34	8.8
L	9	Dave Chyzowski	NYI	56	5	9	14	19-	61	0	0	0	0	66	7.6
C	39	Hubie McDonough	NYI	52	6	6	12	14-	10	0	1	0	0	47	12.8
L	32	Brad Lauer	NYI	44	4	8	12	6-	45	0	1	0	0	70	5.7
C	7	John Tucker	BUF	18	1	3	4	0	4	0	0	0	0	16	6.3
			NYI	20	3	4	7	1-	4	1	0	0	0	19	15.8
			TOTAL	38	4	7	11	1-	8	1	0	0	0	35	11.4
R	14	Tom Fitzgerald	NYI	41	5	5	10	9-	24	0	0	2	0	60	8.3
D	17	Craig Ludwig	NYI	75	1	8	9	24-	77	0	0	0	0	46	2.2
L	24	Ken Baumgartner	NYI	78	1	6	7	14-	282	0	0	0	0	41	2.4
R	12	Mick Vukota	NYI	60	2	4	6	13-	238	0	0	0	0	39	5.1
D	47	Richard Pilon	NYI	60	1	4	5	12-	126	0	0	0	0	33	3.0
L	28	Don Maloney	NYI	12	0	5	5	3-	6	0	0	0	0	10	.0
C	20	*Greg Parks	NYI	20	1	2	3	0	4	0	0	0	0	10	10.0
D	2	Dean Chynoweth	NYI	25	1	1	2	6-	59	0	0	0	0	14	7.1
R	28	Paul Guay	NYI	3	0	2	2	2	2	0	0	0	0	5	.0
G	35	Glenn Healy	NYI	53	0	2	2	0	14	0	0	0	0	0	.0
L	37	Rich Kromm	NYI	6	1	0	1	2-	0	0	1	0	0	6	16.7
D	44	Jari Gronstrand	NYI	3	0	1	1	2-	2	0	0	0	0	1	.0
C	34	Rob Dimaio	NYI	1	0	0	0	0	0	0	0	0	0	0	.0
C	50	Scott Scissons	NYI	1	0	0	0	0	0	0	0	0	0	1	.0
G	30	Mark Fitzpatrick	NYI	2	0	0	0	0	0	0	0	0	0	0	.0
R	10	Alan Kerr	NYI	2	0	0	0	0	5	0	0	0	0	2	.0
G	45	*Danny Lorenz	NYI	2	0	0	0	0	0	0	0	0	0	0	.0
L	42	*Shawn Byram	NYI	4	0	0	0	2-	14	0	0	0	0	3	.0
R	38	Derek Laxdal	NYI	4	0	0	0	1-	0	0	0	0	0	3	.0
G	40	*George Maneluk	NYI	4	0	0	0	0	0	0	0	0	0	0	.0
D	71	*Dennis Vaske	NYI	5	0	0	0	4	2	0	0	0	0	3	.0
D	3	Jeff Finley	NYI	11	0	0	0	1-	4	0	0	0	0	0	.0
G	1	Jeff Hackett	NYI	30	0	0	0	0	0	0	0	0	0	0	.0

Goaltending

No.	Goaltender	GPI	Mins	Avg	W	L	T	EN	SO	GA	SA	S%
30	Mark Fitzpatrick	2	120	3.00	1	1	0	0	0	6	60	.900
35	Glenn Healy	53	2999	3.32	18	24	9	4	0	166	1557	.893
1	Jeff Hackett	30	1508	3.62	5	18	1	3	0	91	741	.877
45	*Danny Lorenz	2	80	3.75	0	1	0	0	0	5	36	.861
40	*George Maneluk	4	140	6.43	1	0	0	0	0	15	94	.840
	Totals	80	4867	3.58	25	45	10	7	0	290	2495	.884

David Volek finished second in team scoring for the Islanders in 1990-91.

General Managers' History

William A. Torrey, 1972-73 to date.

Coaching History

Phil Goyette and Earl Ingarfield, 1972-73; Al Arbour, 1973-74 to 1985-86; Terry Simpson, 1986-87 to 1987-88; Terry Simpson and Al Arbour, 1988-89; Al Arbour, 1989-90 to date.

Captains' History

Ed Westfall, 1972-73 to 1975-76; Ed Westfall, Clark Gillies, 1976-77; Clark Gillies, 1977-78, 1978-79; Denis Potvin, 1979-80 to 1986-87; Brent Sutter, 1987-88 to date.

Club Records

Team

(Figures in brackets for season records are games played; records for fewest points, wins, ties, losses, goals, goals against are for 70 or more games)

Most Points	118	1981-82 (80)
Most Wins	54	1981-82 (80)
Most Ties	22	1974-75 (80)
Most Losses	60	1972-73 (78)
Most Goals	385	1981-82 (80)
Most Goals Against	347	1972-73 (78)
Fewest Points	30	1972-73 (78)
Fewest Wins	12	1972-73 (78)
Fewest Ties	4	1983-84 (80)
Fewest Losses	15	1978-79 (80)
Fewest Goals	170	1972-73 (78)
Fewest Goals Against	190	1975-76 (80)

Longest Winning Streak
Over-all .... *15   Jan. 21/82-Feb. 20/82
Home 14   Jan. 2/82-Feb. 27/82
Away 8   Feb. 27/81-Mar. 31/81

Longest Undefeated Streak
Over-all 15   Jan. 21-Feb. 21/82 (15 wins)
Nov. 4-Dec. 4/80 (13 wins, 2 ties)
Home 23   Oct. 17/78-Jan. 27/79 (19 wins, 4 ties)
Jan. 2/82-Apr. 3/82 (21 wins, 2 ties)
Away 8   Four times

Longest Losing Streak
Over-all 12   Dec. 27/72-Jan. 18/73
Nov. 22-Dec. 17/88

Home 5   Jan. 2-23/73
Feb. 28-Mar. 19/74
Nov. 22-Dec. 17/88
Away 15   Jan. 20-Apr. 1/73

Longest Winless Streak
Over-all 15   Nov. 22-Dec. 23/72 (12 losses, 3 ties)
Oct. 14-Nov. 21/72 (6 losses, 1 tie)
Nov. 28-Dec. 23/72 (5 losses, 2 ties)
Home 7   Feb. 13-Mar. 13/90 (4 losses, 3 ties)
Away 20   Nov. 3/72-Jan. 13/73 (19 losses, 1 tie)

Most Shutouts, Season 10   1975-76 (80)
Most PIM, Season 1,857   1986-87 (80)
Most Goals, Game 11   Dec. 20/83 (Pit. 3 at NYI 11)
Mar. 3/84 (NYI 11 at Tor. 6)

Individual

Most Seasons 17   Billy Smith
Most Games 1,123   Bryan Trottier
Most Goals, Career 573   Mike Bossy
Most Assists, Career 853   Bryan Trottier
Most Points, Career 1,353   Bryan Trottier (500 goals, 853 assists)
Most PIM, Career 1,466   Garry Howatt
Most Shutouts, Career 25   Glenn Resch
Longest Consecutive Games Streak 576   Bill Harris (Oct. 7/72-Nov. 30/79)

Most Goals, Season 69   Mike Bossy (1978-79)
Most Assists, Season 87   Bryan Trottier (1978-79)
Most Points, Season 147   Mike Bossy (1981-82) (64 goals, 83 assists)
Most PIM, Season 356   Brian Curran (1986-87)
Most Points, Defenseman, Season 101   Denis Potvin (1978-79) (31 goals, 70 assists)
Most Points, Center, Season 134   Bryan Trottier (1978-79) (47 goals, 87 assists)
Most Points, Right Wing, Season .... *147   Mike Bossy (1981-82) (64 goals, 83 assists)
Mot Points, Left Wing, Season 100   John Tonelli (1984-85) (42 goals, 58 assists)
Most Points, Rookie, Season 95   Bryan Trottier (1975-76) (32 goals, 63 assists)
Most Shutouts, Season 7   Glenn Resch (1975-76)
Most Goals, Game 5   Bryan Trottier (Dec. 23/78; Feb. 13/82) John Tonelli (Jan. 6/81)
Most Assists, Game 6   Mike Bossy (Jan. 6/81)
Most Points, Game 8   Bryan Trottier (Dec. 23/78)

* NHL Record.

All-time Record vs. Other Clubs

Regular Season

	At Home						On Road						Total					
	GP	W	L	T	GF	GA	PTS	GP	W	L	T	GF	GA	PTS	GP	W	L	T	GF	GA	PTS
Boston	35	14	18	3	112	119	31	35	8	19	8	99	137	24	70	22	37	11	211	256	55
Buffalo	36	13	17	6	102	107	32	35	12	19	4	99	121	28	71	25	36	10	201	228	60
Calgary	40	21	10	9	158	107	51	40	11	18	11	126	148	33	80	32	28	20	284	255	84
Chicago	36	16	9	11	133	105	43	37	16	17	4	131	118	36	73	32	26	15	264	223	79
Detroit	34	20	12	2	136	95	42	34	14	18	2	113	125	30	68	34	30	4	249	220	72
Edmonton	19	8	4	7	82	81	23	19	5	11	3	59	74	13	38	13	15	10	141	155	36
Hartford	19	11	6	2	76	50	24	19	9	7	3	75	62	21	38	20	13	5	151	112	45
Los Angeles	34	19	11	4	128	100	42	34	14	13	7	114	117	33	68	32	25	11	242	217	75
Minnesota	36	19	9	8	144	107	46	36	18	13	5	139	105	41	72	37	22	13	283	212	87
Montreal	35	16	15	4	117	106	36	34	8	20	6	104	133	22	69	24	35	10	221	239	58
New Jersey	49	40	3	6	238	134	86	50	26	16	8	208	164	60	99	66	19	14	446	298	146
NY Rangers	60	39	16	5	256	185	83	62	18	39	5	189	249	41	122	57	55	10	445	434	124
Philadelphia	61	30	21	10	237	182	70	60	17	35	8	181	224	42	121	47	56	18	418	406	112
Pittsburgh	55	33	14	8	241	170	74	54	19	25	10	184	206	48	109	52	39	18	425	376	122
Quebec	19	12	6	1	88	69	25	19	9	9	1	67	74	19	38	21	15	2	155	143	44
St. Louis	37	22	6	9	145	79	53	36	16	14	6	122	127	38	73	38	20	15	267	206	91
Toronto	35	21	11	3	155	108	45	36	16	17	3	132	123	37	71	38	27	6	287	231	82
Vancouver	36	21	7	8	142	94	50	37	18	16	3	122	118	39	73	39	23	11	264	212	89
Washington	50	34	15	1	215	151	69	49	22	20	7	170	154	51	99	56	35	8	385	305	120
Winnipeg	19	10	4	5	76	57	25	19	12	6	1	76	62	25	38	22	10	6	152	119	50
Defunct Club	13	11	0	2	75	33	24	13	4	5	4	35	41	12	26	15	5	6	110	74	36
Totals	758	430	214	114	3056	2239	974	758	292	357	109	2545	2682	693	1516	722	571	223	5601	4921	1667

Playoffs

	Series	W	L	GP	W	L	T	GF	GA	Last Mtg.	Round	Result
Boston	2	2	0	11	8	3	0	49	35	1983	CF	W 4-2
Buffalo	3	3	0	16	12	4	0	59	45	1980	SF	W 4-2
Chicago	2	2	0	6	6	0	0	21	6	1979	QF	W 4-0
Edmonton	3	2	1	15	9	6	0	58	47	1984	F	L 1-4
Los Angeles	1	1	0	4	3	1	0	21	10	1980	PR	W 3-1
Minnesota	1	1	0	5	4	1	0	26	16	1981	F	W 4-1
Montreal	3	1	2	17	7	10	0	44	48	1984	CF	W 4-2
New Jersey	1	0	1	6	2	4	0	18	23	1988	DSF	L 2-4
NY Rangers	7	5	2	35	20	15	0	126	110	1990	DSF	L 1-4
Philadelphia	4	1	3	25	11	14	0	69	83	1987	DF	L 3-4
Pittsburgh	2	2	0	12	7	5	0	43	31	1982	DSF	W 3-2
Quebec	1	1	0	4	4	0	0	18	9	1982	CF	W 4-0
Toronto	2	1	1	10	6	4	0	33	20	1981	PR	W 3-0
Vancouver	2	2	0	6	6	0	0	26	14	1982	F	W 4-0
Washington	5	4	1	24	14	10	0	76	66	1987	DSF	W 4-3
Totals	39	28	11	196	119	77	0	687	563			

Abbreviations: Round: F – Final; **CF** – conference final; **DF** – division final; **DSF** – division semi-final; **SF** – semi-final; **QF** – quarter-final; **PR** – preliminary round; **GA** – goals against; **GF** – goals for.

Playoff Results 1991-87

Year	Round	Opponent	Result	GF	GA
1990	DSF	NY Rangers	L 1-4	13	22
1988	DSF	New Jersey	L 2-4	18	23
1987	DF	Philadelphia	L 3-4	16	23
	DSF	Washington	W 4-3	19	19

1990-91 Results

	Home				Away	
Oct.	13 Pittsburgh	4-6	Oct.	4 Los Angeles	1-4
	16 Winnipeg	4-1		6 Minnesota	2-4
	20 Buffalo	1-3		7 Chicago	4-2
	23 New Jersey	1-8		19 Washington	3-4
	27 Philadelphia	5-2		24 Montreal	2-8
	30 Los Angeles	1-4		28 Pittsburgh	3-8
Nov.	3 Washington	2-5	Nov.	2 NY Rangers	3-2
	6 Toronto	4-3		7 New Jersey	6-3
	10 Calgary	5-1		15 Calgary	4-3
	22 Winnipeg	3-1		16 Vancouver	2-3
	24 NY Rangers*	2-2		18 Edmonton	1-3
	27 Philadelphia	1-5		25 Philadelphia	1-4
Dec.	1 Washington	1-3		30 New Jersey	5-5
	4 Vancouver	2-4	Dec.	6 Chicago	2-5
	11 New Jersey	3-2		13 Philadelphia	2-2
	18 Toronto	2-2		15 Quebec	7-2
	20 Hartford	4-2		23 Pittsburgh	4-3
	22 Pittsburgh	3-4		27 New Jersey	1-1
	29 Chicago	1-3	Jan.	2 Buffalo	4-5
	31 Quebec*	6-3		9 Montreal	3-4
Jan.	3 Los Angeles	3-6		13 Quebec	4-3
	5 Philadelphia	3-2		25 Winnipeg	1-8
	8 Minnesota	0-3		27 Washington*	4-5
	12 Detroit	2-2		29 Hartford	8-1
	17 Boston	4-5	Feb.	6 NY Rangers	2-5
	17 Edmonton	1-6		8 Detroit	4-8
	22 NY Rangers	3-2		9 Toronto	2-3
	31 Washington	3-4		14 Pittsburgh	2-5
Feb.	2 Montreal	3-3		18 NY Rangers*	5-4
	3 Hartford	1-1		21 St Louis	2-7
	12 Minnesota	5-4		24 Philadelphia	3-4
	16 Pittsburgh	4-3		28 Boston	0-5
	23 Philadelphia	3-5	Mar.	2 Washington	2-3
	26 Buffalo	1-1		7 Detroit	0-2
Mar.	5 New Jersey	4-3		13 Edmonton	1-2
	9 NY Rangers	6-4		14 Calgary	2-4
	10 Pittsburgh	3-4		16 Vancouver	4-4
	21 Washington	2-6		24 NY Rangers	1-3
	23 St Louis	2-3		28 St Louis	0-3
	30 Boston	5-3		31 New Jersey	3-2

* Denotes afternoon game.

Entry Draft
Selections 1991-77

1991
Pick
4	Scott Lachance
26	Zigmund Palffy
48	Jamie McLennan
70	Milan Hnilicka
92	Steve Junker
114	Robert Valicevic
136	Andreas Johansson
158	Todd Sparks
180	John Johnson
202	Robert Canavan
224	Marcus Thuresson
246	Marty Schriner

1990
Pick
6	Scott Scissons
27	Chris Taylor
48	Dan Plante
90	Chris Marinucci
111	Joni Lehto
132	Michael Guilbert
153	Sylvain Fleury
174	John Joyce
195	Richard Enga
216	Martin Lacroix
237	Andy Shier

1989
Pick
2	Dave Chyzowski
23	Travis Green
44	Jason Zent
65	Brent Grieve
86	Jace Reed
90	Steve Young
99	Kevin O'Sullivan
128	Jon Larson
133	Brett Harkins
149	Phil Huber
170	Matthew Robbins
191	Vladimir Malakhov
212	Kelly Ens
233	Iain Fraser

1988
Pick
16	Kevin Cheveldayoff
29	Wayne Doucet
37	Sean Le Brun
58	Danny Lorenz
79	Andre Brassard
100	Paul Rutherford
111	Pavel Gross
121	Jason Rathbone
142	Yves Gaucher
163	Marty McInnis
184	Jeff Blumer
205	Jeff Kampersal
226	Phillip Neururer
247	Joe Capprini

1987
Pick
13	Dean Chynoweth
34	Jeff Hackett
55	Dean Ewen
76	George Maneluk
97	Petr Vlk
118	Rob Dimaio
139	Knut Walbye
160	Jeff Saterdalen
181	Shawn Howard
202	John Herlihy
223	Michael Erickson
244	Will Averill

1986
Pick
17	Tom Fitzgerald
38	Dennis Vaske
59	Bill Berg
80	Shawn Byram
101	Dean Sexsmith
104	Todd McLellan
122	Tony Schmalzbauer
138	Will Anderson
143	Richard Pilon
164	Peter Harris
185	Jeff Jablonski
206	Kerry Clark
227	Dan Beaudette
248	Paul Thompson

1985
Pick
6	Brad Dalgarno
13	Derek King
34	Brad Lauer
55	Jeff Finley
76	Kevin Herom
89	Tommy Hedlund
97	Jeff Sveen
118	Rod Dallman
139	Kurt Lackten
160	Hank Lammens
181	Rich Wiest
202	Real Arsenault
223	Mike Volpe
244	Tony Grenier

1984
Pick
20	Duncan MacPherson
41	Bruce Melanson
62	Jeff Norton
70	Doug Wieck
83	Ari Eerik Haanpaa
104	Mike Murray
125	Jim Wilharm
146	Kelly Murphy
167	Franco Desantis
187	Tom Warden
208	David Volek
228	Russ Becker
249	Allister Brown

1983
Pick
3	Pat LaFontaine
16	Gerald Diduck
37	Garnet McKechney
57	Mike Neill
65	Mikko Makela
84	Bob Caulfield
97	Ron Viglasi
117	Darin Illikainen
137	Jim Sprenger
157	Dale Henry
177	Kevin Vescio
197	Dave Shellington
217	John Bjorkman
237	Peter McGeough

1982
Pick
21	Patrick Flatley
42	Vern Smith
63	Garry Lacey
84	Alan Kerr
105	Rene Breton
126	Roger Kortko
147	John Tiano
168	Todd Okerlund
189	Gord Paddock
210	Eric Faust
231	Pat Goff
252	Jim Koudys

1981
Pick
21	Paul Boutilier
42	Gord Dineen
57	Ron Handy
63	Neal Coulter
84	Todd Lumbard
94	Jacques Sylvestre
126	Chuck Brimmer
147	Teppo Virta
168	Bill Dowd
189	Scott MacLellan
210	Dave Randerson

1980
Pick
17	Brent Sutter
38	Kelly Hrudey
59	Dave Simpson
68	Monty Trottier
80	Greg Gilbert
101	Ken Leiter
122	Dan Revell
143	Mark Hamway
164	Morrison Gare
185	Peter Steblyk
206	Glen Johannesen

1979
Pick
17	Duane Sutter
25	Tomas Jonsson
38	Bill Carroll
59	Roland Melanson
80	Tom Lockridge
101	Glen Duncan
122	John Gibb

1978
Pick
15	Steve Tambellini
34	Randy Johnston
51	Dwayne Lowdermilk
84	Greg Hay
101	Kelly Davis
118	Richard Pepin
135	David Cameron
152	Paul Joswiak
169	Scott Cameron
184	Chris Lowdall
199	Gunnar Persson

1977
Pick
15	Mike Bossy
33	John Tonelli
50	Hector Marini
51	Bruce Andres
69	Steve Stoyanovich
87	Markus Mattsson
105	Steve Letzgus
121	Harold Luckner

General Manager
TORREY, WILLIAM ARTHUR (BILL)
President and General Manager, New York Islanders.
Born in Montreal, Que., June 23, 1934.

Although he never played professionally, Bill Torrey has been a valuable addition to professional hockey and was named winner of the 1983 Lester Patrick Trophy for his contribution to hockey in the United States. He attended St. Lawrence University in Canton, N.Y. where he played for the varsity team and graduated in 1957 with a Bachelor of Science degree. He joined the Pittsburgh Hornets of the American Hockey League in 1960 and served with that club until 1965, first as director of public relations and later as business manager. In September 1968, Torrey moved to the California Seals of the NHL as executive vice-president and during his tenure, the Seals went from last place in the West Division to playoff berths the following two seasons. On February 15, 1972, he was appointed general manager of the New York Islanders and has moulded the franchise into one of the greatest in the history of professional sports. His most satisfying season was 1979-80 when the Islanders won their first of four consecutive Stanley Cup titles.

Club Directory

**Nassau Veterans'
Memorial Coliseum**
Uniondale, N.Y. 11553
Phone **516/794-4100**
GM FAX 516/542-9350
FAX 516/542-9348
ENVOY ID
  Front Office: ISLANDERS. GM
  Public
  Relations: ISLANDERS. PR
Capacity: 16,297

Owner	John O. Pickett, Jr.
Chairman of the Board and General Manager	William A. Torrey
President	John H. Krumpe
General Counsel	William M. Skehan
Vice-President/Admin. & CFO	Arthur J. McCarthy
Vice-President/Sales & Marketing	William E. Barnes
Vice-President	Joseph H. Dreyer
Head Coach	Al Arbour
Assistant Coaches	Lorne Henning, Ken Morrow
Assistant General Manager/Director of Scouting	Gerry Ehman
Scouting Staff	Harry Boyd, Richard Green, Earl Ingarfield, Hal Laycoe, Bert Marshall, Mario Saraceno, Jack Vivian, Anders Kallur
Publicity Director	Greg Bouris
Assistant Publicity Director	Catherine Schutte
Publicity Assistant	Kevin Dessart
Editor, Islander News	Chris Botta
Controller	Ralph Sellitti
Director of Public Affairs	Jill Knee
Director of Sales	Jim Johnson
Director of Community Relations	Bob Nystrom
Director of Executive Suite Sales & Corporate Affairs	Taylor Baldwin
Administrative Assistants:	
Owner	Rosemarie LaNasa, Grace Hare
Chairman of the Board and General Manager	Joanne Holewa, Jill Murphy
Athletic Trainer	Ed Tyburski
Equipment Manager	John Doolan
Assistant Equipment Manager	Terry Murphy
Team Orthopedists	Jeffrey Minkoff, M.D., Barry Fisher, M.D.
Team Internist	Gerald Cordani, M.D.
Physical Therapist	Steve Wirth
Team Dentist	Bruce Michnick, D.D.S., Jan Sherman, D.D.S.
Photographer	Bruce Bennett
Location of Press Box	East Side of Building
Dimensions of Rink	200 feet by 85 feet
Ends of Rink	Herculite extends above boards around rink
Club Colors	Blue, Orange and White
Training Camp Site/Practice Facilities	Cantiague Park, Hicksville, NY
Television Announcers	Jiggs McDonald, Ed Westfall, Stan Fischler
Television Station	SportsChannel
Radio Announcers	Barry Landers, Bob Nystrom
Islanders Radio Network	WPAT (930 AM), WGBB (1240 AM), WRHD (1570 AM), WFAS (1230 AM)

Coach

ARBOUR, AL
Coach, New York Islanders. Born in Sudbury, Ont., November 1, 1932.

The 1990-91 season saw Al Arbour increase his regular-season NHL games coached mark to 1,358, the second highest total in League history behind Dick Irvin. His total of 671 wins leaves him just 20 victories away from passing Irvin for second place on the all-time NHL coaching win list. Arbour was named as the Islanders head coach on June 26, 1989 after serving as vice president in charge of player development for three years.

Arbour, 58, began his coaching career with the St. Louis Blues in 1970 and coached parts of three seasons there before joining the Islanders at the start of the 1973-74 season. Arbour has coached 1,198 regular-season games and has a career record of 615-386-197 with a winning percentage of .596. In the playoffs, Arbour has coached 182 games, posting a record of 113-69 with a .621 winning percentage. Arbour enters the 1991-92 season ranking third on the NHL's all-time regular season wins list and is only one win behind Scotty Bowman on the NHL's all-time playoff win list.

Coaching Record

Season	Team		Regular Season					Playoffs			
		Games	W	L	T	%		Games	W	L	%
1970-71	St. Louis (NHL)	50	21	15	14	.560		....			
1971-72	St. Louis (NHL)	44	19	19	6	.500		11	4	7	.364
1972-73	St. Louis (NHL)	13	2	6	5	.346		....			
1973-74	NY Islanders (NHL)	78	19	41	18	.358		....			
1974-75	NY Islanders (NHL)	80	33	25	22	.550		....			
1975-76	NY Islanders (NHL)	80	42	21	17	.631		13	7	6	.538
1976-77	NY Islanders (NHL)	80	47	21	12	.663		12	8	4	.666
1977-78	NY Islanders (NHL	80	48	17	15	.694		7	3	4	.429
1978-79	NY Islanders (NHL)	80	51	15	14	.725		10	6	4	.600
1979-80	NY Islanders (NHL)	80	39	28	13	.589		21	15	6	.714*
1980-81	NY Islanders (NHL)	80	48	18	14	.600		18	15	3	.833*
1981-82	NY Islanders (NHL)	80	54	16	10	.738		19	15	4	.789*
1982-83	NY Islanders (NHL)	80	42	26	12	.600		20	15	5	.750*
1983-84	NY Islanders (NHL)	80	50	26	4	.650		21	12	9	.571
1984-85	NY Islanders (NHL)	80	40	34	6	.538		10	4	6	.400
1985-86	NY Islanders (NHL)	80	39	29	12	.563		3	0	3	.000
1988-89	NY Islanders (NHL)	53	21	29	3	.425		....			
1989-90	NY Islanders (NHL)	80	31	38	11	.456		5	1	4	.200
1990-91	NY Islanders (NHL)	80	25	45	10	.375		....			
	NHL Totals	1349	671	469	218	.578		187	114	73	.610

*Stanley Cup win

New York Rangers

1990-91 Results: 36W-31L-13T 85PTS. Second, Patrick Division

Darren Turcotte picked up 34 of his 67 points on the power-play in 1990-91.

Schedule

Home

Oct.
Mon. 7 Boston
Wed. 9 NY Islanders
Mon. 14 Washington
Wed. 16 New Jersey
Sun. 20 Edmonton
Wed. 23 Los Angeles
Tues. 29 Minnesota
Thur. 31 Quebec

Nov.
Mon. 4 Calgary
Wed. 6 Montreal
Fri. 8 Toronto
Mon. 11 Pittsburgh
Wed. 13 Washington

Dec.
Mon. 2 Philadelphia
Sun. 8 Boston
Mon. 16 San Jose
Wed. 18 Philadelphia
Mon. 23 New Jersey
Sun. 29 Pittsburgh

Jan.
Mon. 6 Winnipeg
Wed. 8 St Louis
Tues. 14 Buffalo
Thur. 16 Calgary

Feb.
Wed. 5 Pittsburgh
Sun. 9 Detroit
Wed. 12 Vancouver
Fri. 14 NY Islanders
Mon. 17 Vancouver*
Fri. 21 Minnesota
Sun. 23 Philadelphia
Tues. 25 Chicago

Mar.
Sun. 1 Hartford
Wed. 4 New Jersey
Mon. 9 Washington
Wed. 11 Chicago
Mon. 16 Montreal
Wed. 18 NY Islanders
Sun. 22 New Jersey*
Wed. 25 Philadelphia

Apr.
Thur. 2 Pittsburgh

Away

Oct.
Thur. 3 Boston
Sat. 5 Montreal
Fri. 11 Washington
Sat. 12 Hartford
Sat. 19 Pittsburgh
Sat. 26 Quebec

Nov.
Sat. 2 Philadelphia*
Sat. 16 NY Islanders
Tues. 19 Vancouver
Thur. 21 Los Angeles
Sat. 23 St Louis
Wed. 27 Winnipeg
Fri. 29 Buffalo

Dec.
Fri. 6 Detroit
Tues. 10 Pittsburgh
Fri. 13 Washington
Sat. 14 Hartford
Sat. 21 Pittsburgh
Thur. 26 Washington
Sat. 28 NY Islanders
Tues. 31 Winnipeg*

Jan.
Thur. 2 Chicago
Sat. 4 New Jersey
Sat. 11 Quebec
Sun. 12 Buffalo
Wed. 22 Calgary
Thur. 23 Edmonton
Tues. 28 San Jose
Thur. 30 Los Angeles

Feb.
Sat. 1 Minnesota
Fri. 7 Washington

Mar.
Mon. 2 New Jersey
Sat. 7 Philadelphia*
Sat. 14 St Louis
Fri. 20 Detroit
Tues. 24 Philadelphia
Sat. 28 NY Islanders

Apr.
Sat. 4 Toronto

* Denotes afternoon game.

Home Starting Times:
All Games .... 7:35 p.m.
Matinees .... 1:35 p.m.

Franchise date: May 15, 1926

66th NHL Season

Year-by-Year Record

Season	GP	Home			Road			Overall						Finished		Playoff Result
		W	L	T	W	L	T	W	L	T	GF	GA	Pts.			
1990-91	80	22	11	7	14	20	6	36	31	13	297	265	85	2nd,	Patrick Div.	Lost Div. Semi-Final
1989-90	80	20	11	9	16	20	4	36	31	13	279	267	85	1st,	Patrick Div.	Lost Div. Final
1988-89	80	21	17	2	16	18	6	37	35	8	310	307	82	3rd,	Patrick Div.	Lost Div. Semi-Final
1987-88	80	22	13	5	14	21	5	36	34	10	300	283	82	5th,	Patrick Div.	Out of Playoffs
1986-87	80	18	18	4	16	20	4	34	38	8	307	323	76	4th,	Patrick Div.	Lost Div. Semi-Final
1985-86	80	20	18	2	16	20	4	36	38	6	280	276	78	4th,	Patrick Div.	Lost Conf. Championship
1984-85	80	16	18	6	10	26	4	26	44	10	295	345	62	4th,	Patrick Div.	Lost Div. Semi-Final
1983-84	80	27	12	1	15	17	8	42	29	9	314	304	93	4th,	Patrick Div.	Lost Div. Semi-Final
1982-83	80	24	13	3	11	22	7	35	35	10	306	287	80	4th,	Patrick Div.	Lost Div. Final
1981-82	80	19	15	6	20	12	8	39	27	14	316	306	92	2nd,	Patrick Div.	Lost Div. Final
1980-81	80	17	13	10	13	23	4	30	36	14	312	317	74	4th,	Patrick Div.	Lost Semi-Final
1979-80	80	22	10	8	16	22	2	38	32	10	308	284	86	3rd,	Patrick Div.	Lost Quarter-Final
1978-79	80	19	13	8	21	16	3	40	29	11	316	292	91	3rd,	Patrick Div.	Lost Final
1977-78	80	18	15	7	12	22	6	30	37	13	279	280	73	4th,	Patrick Div.	Lost Prelim. Round
1976-77	80	17	18	5	12	19	9	29	37	14	272	310	72	4th,	Patrick Div.	Out of Playoffs
1975-76	80	16	16	8	13	26	1	29	42	9	262	333	67	4th,	Patrick Div.	Out of Playoffs
1974-75	80	21	11	8	16	18	6	37	29	14	319	276	88	2nd,	Patrick Div.	Lost Prelim. Round
1973-74	78	26	6	7	14	17	8	40	24	14	300	251	94	3rd,	East Div.	Lost Semi-Final
1972-73	78	26	8	5	21	15	3	47	23	8	297	208	102	3rd,	East Div.	Lost Semi-Final
1971-72	78	26	6	7	22	11	6	48	17	13	317	192	109	2nd,	East Div.	Lost Final
1970-71	78	30	2	7	19	16	4	49	18	11	259	177	109	2nd,	East Div.	Lost Semi-Final
1969-70	76	22	8	8	16	14	8	38	22	16	246	189	92	4th,	East Div.	Lost Quarter-Final
1968-69	76	27	7	4	14	19	5	41	26	9	231	196	91	3rd,	East Div.	Lost Quarter-Final
1967-68	74	22	8	7	17	15	5	39	23	12	226	183	90	2nd,	East Div.	Lost Quarter-Final
1966-67	70	18	12	5	12	16	7	30	28	12	188	189	72	4th,		Lost Semi-Final
1965-66	70	12	16	7	6	25	4	18	41	11	195	261	47	6th,		Out of Playoffs
1964-65	70	8	19	4	12	19	4	20	38	12	179	246	52	5th,		Out of Playoffs
1963-64	70	14	13	8	8	25	2	22	38	10	186	242	54	5th,		Out of Playoffs
1962-63	70	12	17	6	10	19	6	22	36	12	211	233	56	5th,		Out of Playoffs
1961-62	70	16	11	8	10	21	4	26	32	12	195	207	64	4th,		Lost Semi-Final
1960-61	70	15	15	5	7	23	5	22	38	10	204	248	54	5th,		Out of Playoffs
1959-60	70	10	15	10	7	23	5	17	38	15	187	247	49	6th,		Out of Playoffs
1958-59	70	14	14	6	12	16	7	26	32	12	201	217	64	5th,		Out of Playoffs
1957-58	70	14	15	6	18	10	7	32	25	13	195	188	77	2nd,		Lost Semi-Final
1956-57	70	15	12	8	11	18	6	26	30	14	184	227	66	4th,		Lost Semi-Final
1955-56	70	20	7	8	12	21	2	32	28	10	204	203	74	3rd,		Lost Semi-Final
1954-55	70	10	12	13	7	23	5	17	35	18	150	210	52	5th,		Out of Playoffs
1953-54	70	18	12	5	11	19	5	29	31	10	161	182	68	5th,		Out of Playoffs
1952-53	70	11	14	10	6	23	6	17	37	16	152	211	50	6th,		Out of Playoffs
1951-52	70	16	16	3	7	21	7	23	34	13	192	219	59	5th,		Out of Playoffs
1950-51	70	14	11	10	6	18	11	20	29	21	169	201	61	5th,		Out of Playoffs
1949-50	70	19	12	4	9	19	7	28	31	11	170	189	67	4th,		Lost Final
1948-49	60	13	12	5	5	19	6	18	31	11	133	172	47	6th,		Out of Playoffs
1947-48	60	11	12	7	10	14	6	21	26	13	176	201	55	4th,		Lost Semi-Final
1946-47	60	11	14	5	11	18	1	22	32	6	167	186	50	5th,		Out of Playoffs
1945-46	50	8	12	5	5	16	4	13	28	9	144	191	35	6th,		Out of Playoffs
1944-45	50	7	11	7	4	18	3	11	29	10	154	247	32	6th,		Out of Playoffs
1943-44	50	4	17	4	2	22	1	6	39	5	162	310	17	6th,		Out of Playoffs
1942-43	50	7	13	5	4	18	3	11	31	8	161	253	30	6th,		Out of Playoffs
1941-42	48	15	8	1	14	9	1	29	17	2	177	143	60	1st,		Lost Semi-Final
1940-41	48	13	7	4	8	12	4	21	19	8	143	125	50	4th,		Lost Quarter-Final
1939-40	48	17	4	3	10	7	7	**27**	**11**	**10**	**136**	**77**	**64**	**2nd,**		**Won Stanley Cup**
1938-39	48	13	8	3	13	8	3	26	16	6	149	105	58	2nd,		Lost Semi-Final
1937-38	48	15	5	4	12	10	2	27	15	6	149	96	60	2nd,	Amn. Div.	Lost Quarter-Final
1936-37	48	9	7	8	10	13	1	19	20	9	117	106	47	3rd,	Amn. Div.	Lost Final
1935-36	48	11	6	7	8	11	5	19	17	12	91	96	50	4th,	Amn. Div.	Out of Playoffs
1934-35	48	11	7	6	11	12	1	22	20	6	137	139	50	3rd,	Amn. Div.	Lost Semi-Final
1933-34	48	11	7	6	10	12	2	21	19	8	120	113	50	3rd,	Amn. Div.	Lost Quarter-Final
1932-33	48	12	7	5	11	10	3	**23**	**17**	**8**	**135**	**107**	**54**	**3rd,**	**Amn. Div.**	**Won Stanley Cup**
1931-32	48	13	7	4	10	10	4	23	17	8	134	112	54	1st,		Lost Final
1930-31	44	11	5	6	8	7	6	19	16	9	106	87	47	3rd,	Amn. Div.	Lost Semi-Final
1929-30	44	11	5	6	6	12	4	17	17	10	136	143	44	3rd,	Amn. Div.	Lost Semi-Final
1928-29	44	12	6	4	9	7	6	21	13	10	72	65	52	2nd,	Amn. Div.	Lost Final
1927-28	44	10	8	4	9	8	5	**19**	**16**	**9**	**94**	**79**	**47**	**2nd,**	**Amn. Div.**	**Won Stanley Cup**
1926-27	44	13	5	4	12	8	2	25	13	6	95	72	56	1st,	Amn. Div.	Lost Quarter-Final

1991-92 Player Personnel

FORWARDS	HT	WT	S	Place of Birth	Date	1990-91 Club
AMONTE, Tony	6-0	180	L	Hingham, MA	8/2/70	Boston U.
BENNETT, Rick	6-3	215	L	Springfield, MA	7/24/67	NYR-Binghamton
BROTEN, Paul	5-11	190	R	Roseau, MN	10/27/65	NYR-Binghamton
CICHOCKI, Chris	5-11	185	R	Detroit, MI	9/7/63	Binghamton
DeBRUSK, Louie	6-1	225	L	Cambridge, Ont.	3/19/71	London-Binghamton
DOMI, Tahir	5-10	200	R	Windsor, Ont.	11/1/69	NYR-Binghamton
ERIXON, Jan	6-0	196	L	Skelleftea, Sweden	7/8/62	NY Rangers
GARTNER, Mike	6-0	190	R	Ottawa, Ont.	10/29/59	NY Rangers
GOODALL, Glen	5-8	170	R	Fort Nelson, B.C.	1/22/70	Adirondack
GRAVES, Adam	5-11	185	L	Toronto, Ont.	4/12/68	Edmonton
HULL, Jody	6-2	200	R	Cambridge, Ont.	2/2/69	NY Rangers
JANSSENS, Mark	6-3	216	L	Surrey, B.C.	5/19/68	NY Rangers
KERR, Tim	6-3	230	R	Windsor, Ont.	1/5/60	Philadelphia
KING, Kris	5-11	210	L	Bracebridge, Ont.	2/18/66	NY Rangers
KING, Steven	6-0	190	R	E. Greenwich, RI	7/22/69	Brown University
KOCUR, Joe	6-0	195	R	Kelvington, Sask.	12/21/64	Detroit-NYR
LACROIX, Daniel	6-2	188	L	Montreal, Que	3/11/69	Binghamton
LAROSE, Guy	5-9	175	L	Hull, Que.	8/31/67	Moncton-Binghamton
MALLETTE, Troy	6-2	210	L	Sudbury, Ont.	2/25/70	NY Rangers
McREYNOLDS, Brian	6-1	192	L	Penetang'ene, Ont.	1/5/65	NYR-Binghamton
MILLEN, Corey	5-7	168	R	Cloquet, MN	4/29/64	NYR-Binghamton
NEMCHINOV, Sergei	6-0	200	L	Moscow, USSR	1/14/64	Soviet Wings
NICHOLLS, Bernie	6-0	185	R	Haliburton, Ont.	6/24/61	L.A.-NY Rangers
OGRODNICK, John	6-0	205	L	Ottawa, Ont.	6/20/59	NY Rangers
PATERSON, Joe	6-2	207	L	Toronto, Ont.	6/25/60	Binghamton
PROSOFSKY, Jason	6-4	220	R	Medicine Hat, Alta.	5/4/71	Medicine Hat
RICE, Steven	6-0	215	R	Kitchener, Ont.	5/26/71	London-Bing.-NYR
ROB, Lubos	5-11	183	L	Budejovice, Czech.	8/5/70	Motor
TURCOTTE, Darren	6-0	185	L	Boston, MA	3/2/68	NY Rangers
WEIGHT, Doug	5-11	185	L	Warren, MI	1/12/71	Lake Superior State
ZAMUNER, Rob	6-2	202	L	Oakville, Ont.	9/17/69	Binghamton

DEFENSEMEN	HT	WT	S	Place of Birth	Date	1990-91 Club
ANDERSSON, Peter	6-0	187	R	Orebro, Sweden	8/29/65	Malmo
BLOEMBERG, Jeff	6-2	205	R	Listowel, Ont.	1/31/68	NYR-Binghamton
CIRELLA, Joe	6-3	210	R	Hamilton, Ont.	5/9/63	Quebec-NYR
DJOOS, Per	5-11	175	R	Mora, Sweden	5/11/68	Adir.-Bing.
DUVAL, Murray	6-1	205	L	Thompson, Man.	1/22/70	Kamloops
FIORENTINO, Peter	6-1	200	R	Niagara Falls, Ont.	12/22/68	Binghamton
HARDY, Mark	5-11	195	L	Semaden, Switz.	2/1/59	NY Rangers
LAVIOLETTE, Peter	6-2	200	L	Norwood, MA	12/7/64	Binghamton
LEETCH, Brian	5-11	185	L	Corpus Christi, TX	3/3/68	NY Rangers
MOLLER, Randy	6-2	207	R	Red Deer, Alta.	8/23/63	NY Rangers
PATRICK, James	6-2	204	R	Winnipeg, Man.	6/14/63	NY Rangers
ROCHEFORT, Normand	6-1	214	L	Trois Rivieres, Que.	1/28/61	NY Rangers
SHAW, David	6-2	204	R	St. Thomas, Ont.	5/25/64	NY Rangers
VARY, John	6-1	207	R	Owen Sound, Ont.	5/13/73	Kingston
WERENKA, Darcy	6-1	210	R	Edmonton, Alta.	5/13/73	Lethbridge
YOUNG, Barry	6-2	202	L	Belfast, Ireland	8/07/72	Sudbury

GOALTENDERS	HT	WT	C	Place of Birth	Date	1990-91 Club
HIRSCH, Corey	5-9	150	L	Medicine Hat, Alta.	7/1/72	Kamloops
LaFOREST, Mark	5-11	190	L	Welland, Ont.	7/10/62	Binghamton
RICHTER, Mike	5-10	185	L	Abington, PA	9/22/66	NY Rangers
ROUSSON, Boris	6-1	200	L	Valdor, Que.	6/14/70	Granby
ST. LAURENT, Sam	5-10	190	L	Arvida, Que.	2/16/59	Binghamton
VANBIESBROUCK, John	5-8	172	L	Detroit, MI	9/4/63	NY Rangers

1990-91 Scoring

Regular Season

* rookie

Pos	#	Player	Team	GP	G	A	Pts	+/−	PIM	PP	SH	GW	GT	S	%
D	2	Brian Leetch	NYR	80	16	72	88	2	42	6	0	4	1	206	7.8
C	9	Bernie Nicholls	NYR	71	25	48	73	5	96	8	0	2	0	163	15.3
R	22	Mike Gartner	NYR	79	49	20	69	9−	53	22	1	4	2	262	18.7
C	8	Darren Turcotte	NYR	74	26	41	67	5−	37	15	2	3	1	212	12.3
R	19	Brian Mullen	NYR	79	19	43	62	12	44	4	0	3	0	188	10.1
D	3	James Patrick	NYR	74	10	49	59	5−	58	6	0	2	0	138	7.2
L	25	John Ogrodnick	NYR	79	31	23	54	15	10	12	0	4	0	250	12.4
R	23	Ray Sheppard	NYR	59	24	23	47	8	21	7	0	5	0	129	18.6
C	11	Kelly Kisio	NYR	51	15	20	35	3	58	7	1	2	0	74	20.3
L	12	Kris King	NYR	72	11	14	25	1−	154	0	0	0	1	107	10.3
L	20	Jan Erixon	NYR	53	7	18	25	13	8	0	3	0	0	40	17.5
D	24	Randy Moller	NYR	61	4	19	23	13	161	1	0	0	1	75	5.3
L	16	Troy Mallette	NYR	71	12	10	22	8−	252	0	0	2	0	91	13.2
C	15	Mark Janssens	NYR	67	9	7	16	1−	172	0	0	1	0	45	20.0
R	21	Jody Hull	NYR	47	5	8	13	2	10	0	0	0	0	57	8.8
D	18	Joe Cirella	QUE	39	2	10	12	28−	59	0	0	0	0	60	3.3
			NYR	19	1	0	1	1	52	0	0	0	0	22	4.5
			TOTAL	58	3	10	13	27−	111	0	0	0	0	82	3.7
D	27	David Shaw	NYR	77	2	10	12	8	89	0	0	1	0	61	3.3
R	37	Paul Broten	NYR	28	4	6	10	7	18	0	0	0	0	34	11.8
D	5	Normand Rochefort	NYR	44	3	7	10	10	35	0	0	0	0	34	8.8
R	26	Joey Kocur	DET	52	5	4	9	6−	253	0	0	0	0	67	7.5
			NYR	5	0	0	0	1−	36	0	0	0	0	6	.0
			TOTAL	57	5	4	9	7−	289	0	0	0	0	73	6.8
D	6	Miloslav Horava	NYR	29	1	6	7	2	12	0	0	0	0	27	3.7
D	14	Mark Hardy	NYR	70	1	5	6	1−	89	0	0	0	0	63	1.6
C	32	*Corey Millen	NYR	4	3	1	4	1	0	2	0	0	0	8	37.5
G	34	John Vanbiesbrouck	NYR	40	0	3	3	0	18	0	0	0	0	0	.0
R	10	*Steven Rice	NYR	11	1	1	2	2	4	0	0	0	0	12	8.3
D	38	Jeff Bloemberg	NYR	3	0	2	2	3	0	0	0	0	0	4	.0
R	28	*Tie Domi	NYR	28	1	0	1	5−	185	0	0	0	0	5	20.0
D	44	Lindy Ruff	NYR	14	0	1	1	2−	27	0	0	0	0	10	.0
G	35	*Mike Richter	NYR	45	0	1	1	0	4	0	0	0	0	0	.0
C	16	*Brian McReynolds	NYR	1	0	0	0	1−	0	0	0	0	0	0	.0
L	17	Eric Bennett	NYR	6	0	0	0	2−	6	0	0	0	0	3	.0

Goaltending

No.	Goaltender	GPI	Mins	Avg	W	L	T	EN	SO	GA	SA	S%
35	*Mike Richter	45	2596	3.12	21	13	7	3	0	135	1392	.903
34	John Vanbiesbrouck	40	2257	3.35	15	18	6	1	3	126	1154	.891
	Totals	**80**	**4872**	**3.26**	**36**	**31**	**13**	**4**	**3**	**265**	**2550**	**.896**

Playoffs

Pos	#	Player	Team	GP	G	A	Pts	+/−	PIM	PP	SH	GW	OT	S	%
C	9	Bernie Nicholls	NYR	5	4	3	7	0	8	0	0	1	0	24	16.7
D	2	Brian Leetch	NYR	6	1	3	4	2−	0	0	0	0	0	13	7.7
C	15	Mark Janssens	NYR	6	3	0	3	1	6	0	0	0	0	6	50.0
R	10	*Steven Rice	NYR	2	2	1	3	2	6	1	0	0	0	4	50.0
L	20	Jan Erixon	NYR	6	1	2	3	1−	0	0	0	0	0	7	14.3
C	32	*Corey Millen	NYR	6	1	2	3	0	0	1	0	0	0	11	9.1
C	8	Darren Turcotte	NYR	6	1	2	3	2−	0	1	0	0	0	19	5.3
L	12	Kris King	NYR	6	2	0	2	2	36	0	0	1	0	15	13.3
R	22	Mike Gartner	NYR	6	1	1	2	4−	0	1	0	0	0	22	4.5
R	31	*Tony Amonte	NYR	2	0	2	2	1	2	0	0	0	0	5	.0
D	18	Joe Cirella	NYR	6	0	2	2	2	26	0	0	0	0	4	.0
R	26	Joey Kocur	NYR	6	0	2	2	3−	21	0	0	0	0	6	.0
D	24	Randy Moller	NYR	6	0	2	2	2	11	0	0	0	0	11	.0
R	19	Brian Mullen	NYR	6	0	2	2	1−	0	0	0	0	0	9	.0
D	14	Mark Hardy	NYR	6	0	1	1	2−	30	0	0	0	0	7	.0
G	34	John Vanbiesbrouck	NYR	1	0	0	0	0	0	0	0	0	0	0	.0
C	39	*Doug Weight	NYR	1	0	0	0	0	0	0	0	0	0	0	.0
L	25	John Ogrodnick	NYR	4	0	0	0	2−	0	0	0	0	0	5	.0
R	37	Paul Broten	NYR	5	0	0	0	1	2	0	0	0	0	5	.0
L	16	Troy Mallette	NYR	5	0	0	0	3−	18	0	0	0	0	1	.0
D	3	James Patrick	NYR	6	0	0	0	1−	6	0	0	0	0	7	.0
G	35	*Mike Richter	NYR	6	0	0	0	0	0	0	0	0	0	0	.0
D	27	David Shaw	NYR	6	0	0	0	2−	11	0	0	0	0	4	.0

Goaltending

No.	Goaltender	GPI	Mins	Avg	W	L	EN	SO	GA	SA	S%
34	John Vanbiesbrouck	1	52	1.15	0	0	0	0	1	22	.955
35	*Mike Richter	6	313	2.68	2	4	1	1	14	182	.923
	Totals	6	367	2.62	2	4	1	1	16	205	.922

Coaching History

Lester Patrick, 1926-27 to 1938-39; Frank Boucher, 1939-40 to 1947-48; Frank Boucher and Lynn Patrick, 1948-49; Lynn Patrick, 1949-50; Neil Colville, 1950-51; Neil Colville and Bill Cook, 1951-52; Bill Cook, 1952-53; Frank Boucher and Murray Patrick, 1953-54; Murray Patrick, 1954-55; Phil Watson, 1955-56 to 1958-59; Phil Watson and Alf Pike, 1959-60; Alf Pike, 1960-61; Doug Harvey, 1961-62; Murray Patrick and George Sullivan, 1962-63; George Sullivan, 1963-64 to 1964-65; George Sullivan and Emile Francis, 1965-66; Emile Francis, 1966-67 to 1967-68; Bernie Geoffrion and Emile Francis, 1968-69; Emile Francis, 1969-70 to 1972-73; Larry Popein and Emile Francis, 1973-74; Emile Francis, 1974-75; Ron Stewart and John Ferguson, 1975-76; John Ferguson, 1976-77; Jean-Guy Talbot, 1977-78; Fred Shero, 1978-79 to 1979-80; Fred Shero and Craig Patrick, 1980-81; Herb Brooks, 1981-82 to 1983-84; Herb Brooks and Craig Patrick, 1984-85; Ted Sator, 1985-86; Ted Sator, Tom Webster, Phil Esposito 1986-87; Michel Bergeron, 1987-88; Michel Bergeron and Phil Esposito, 1988-89; Roger Neilson, 1989-90 to date.

Retired Numbers

1	Eddie Giacomin	1965-1976
7	Rod Gilbert	1960-1978

Captains' History

Bill Cook, 1926-27 to 1936-37; Art Coulter, 1937-38 to 1941-42; Ott Heller, 1942-43 to 1944-45; Neil Colville 1945-46 to 1948-49; Buddy O'Connor, 1949-50; Frank Eddolls, 1950-51; Frank Eddolls, Allan Stanley, 1951-52; Allan Stanley, 1952-53; Allan Stanley, Don Raleigh, 1953-54; Don Raleigh, 1954-55; Harry Howell, 1955-56, 1956-57; George Sullivan, 1957-58 to 1960-61; Andy Bathgate, 1961-61, 1962-63; Andy Bathgate, Camille Henry, 1963-64; Camille Henry, Bob Nevin, 1964-65; Bob Nevin 1965-66 to 1970-71; Vic Hadfield, 1971-72 to 1973-74; Brad Park, 1974-75; Brad Park, Phil Esposito, 1975-76; Phil Esposito, 1976-77, 1977-78; Dave Maloney, 1978-79, 1979-80; Dave Maloney, Walt Tkaczuk, Barry Beck, 1980-81; Barry Beck, 1981-82 to 1985-86; Ron Greschner, 1986-87; Ron Greschner and Kelly Kisio, 1987-88; Kelly Kisio, 1988-89 to 1990-91.

General Managers' History

Lester Patrick, 1927-28 to 1945-46; Frank Boucher, 1946-47 to 1954-55; Murray "Muzz" Patrick, 1955-56 to 1963-64; Emile Francis, 1964-65 to 1974-75; Emile Francis and John Ferguson, 1975-76; John Ferguson, 1976-77 to 1977-78; John Ferguson and Fred Shero, 1978-79; Fred Shero, 1979-80; Fred Shero and Craig Patrick, 1980-81; Craig Patrick, 1981-82 to 1985-86; Phil Esposito, 1986-87 to 1988-89; Neil Smith, 1989-90 to date.

Club Records

Team

(Figures in brackets for season records are games played; records for fewest points, wins, ties, losses, goals, goals against are for 70 or more games)

Most Points	109	1970-71 (78)
		1971-72 (78)
Most Wins	49	1970-71 (78)
Most Ties	21	1950-51 (70)
Most Losses	44	1984-85 (80)
Most Goals	319	1974-75 (80)
Most Goals Against	345	1984-85 (80)
Fewest Points	47	1965-66 (70)
Fewest Wins	17	1952-53; 54-55; 59-60 (70)
Fewest Ties	6	1985-86 (80)
Fewest Losses	17	1971-72 (78)
Fewest Goals	150	1954-55 (70)
Fewest Goals Against	177	1970-71 (78)

Longest Winning Streak

Over-all	10	Dec. 19/39-Jan. 13/40
		Jan. 19-Feb. 10/73
Home	14	Dec. 19/39-Feb. 25/40
Away	7	Jan. 12-Feb. 12/35
		Oct. 28-Nov. 29/78

Longest Undefeated Streak

Over-all	19	Nov. 23/39-Jan. 13/40 (14 wins, 5 ties)
Home	26	Mar. 29/70-Feb. 2/71 (19 wins, 7 ties)
Away	11	Nov. 5/39-Jan. 13/40 (6 wins, 5 ties)

Longest Losing Streak

Over-all	11	Oct. 30-Nov. 27/43
Home	7	Oct. 20-Nov. 14/76
Away	10	Oct. 30-Dec. 23/43

Longest Winless Streak

Over-all	21	Jan. 23-Mar. 19/44 (17 losses, 4 ties)
Home	10	Jan. 30-Mar. 19/44 (7 losses, 3 ties)
Away	16	Oct. 9-Dec. 20/52 (12 losses, 4 ties)

Most Shutouts, Season	13	1928-29 (44)
Most PIM, Season	2,018	1989-90 (80)
Most Goals, Game	12	Nov. 21/71 (Cal. 1 at NYR 12)

Individual

Most Seasons	17	Harry Howell
Most Games	1,160	Harry Howell
Most Goals, Career	406	Rod Gilbert
Most Assists, Career	615	Rod Gilbert
Most Points, Career	1,021	Rod Gilbert (406 goals, 615 assists)
Most PIM, Career	1,226	Ron Greschner
Most Shutouts, Career	49	Ed Giacomin
Longest Consecutive Games Streak	560	Andy Hebenton (Oct. 7/55-Mar. 24/63)
Most Goals, Season	50	Vic Hadfield (1971-72)
Most Assists, Season	72	Brian Leetch (1990-91)
Most Points, Season	109	Jean Ratelle (1971-72) (46 goals, 63 assists)
Most PIM, Season	305	Troy Mallette (1989-90)
Most Points, Defenseman Season	88	Brian Leetch (1990-91) (16 goals, 72 assists)
Most Points, Center, Season	109	Jean Ratelle (1971-72) (46 goals, 63 assists)
Most Points, Right Wing, Season	97	Rod Gilbert (1971-72) (43 goals, 54 assists) Rod Gilbert (1974-75) (36 goals, 61 assists)
Most Points, Left Wing, Season	106	Vic Hadfield (1971-72) (50 goals, 56 assists)
Most Points, Rookie, Season	76	Mark Pavelich (1981-82) (33 goals, 43 assists)
Most Shutouts, Season	13	John Ross Roach (1928-29)
Most Goals, Game	5	Don Murdoch (Oct. 12/76) Mark Pavelich (Feb. 23/83)
Most Assists, Game	5	Walt Tkaczuk (Feb. 12/72) Rod Gilbert (Mar. 2/75; Mar. 30/75; Oct. 8/76) Don Maloney (Jan. 3/87)
Most Points, Game	7	Steve Vickers (Feb. 18/76)

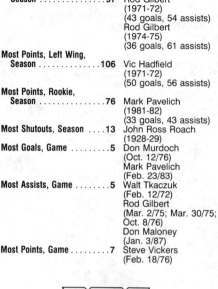

1990-91 Results

		Home				Away	
Oct.	8	Minnesota	6-3	Oct.	4	Chicago	3-4
	10	Washington	4-2		6	Hartford	4-5
	12	Montreal	3-0		13	Washington	5-2
	17	Winnipeg	5-3		19	New Jersey	2-3
	22	Toronto	5-1		20	Pittsburgh	4-3
	25	Philadelphia	5-3		27	Quebec	4-1
	29	Quebec	5-0	Nov.	3	Pittsburgh	1-3
	31	Los Angeles	9-4		9	New Jersey	3-2
Nov.	2	NY Islanders	2-3		13	Philadelphia	1-1
	5	Boston	2-3		15	Minnesota	2-3
	7	Buffalo	6-2		16	Winnipeg	6-4
	11	Calgary	4-4		21	Buffalo	5-5
	19	Minnesota	2-2		24	NY Islanders*	2-2
	26	Buffalo	5-0		30	Philadelphia	1-5
	28	Washington	3-6	Dec.	1	Boston	5-4
Dec.	3	Pittsburgh	4-9		5	Calgary	1-4
	17	Washington	5-3		7	Edmonton	3-4
	19	Toronto	1-4		11	Los Angeles	6-4
	23	Boston	5-5		14	Vancouver	5-3
	30	New Jersey	2-2		22	Montreal	1-3
Jan.	2	Los Angeles	4-1		30	New Jersey	5-3
	7	Philadelphia	3-2	Jan.	3	Pittsburgh	7-5
	9	St Louis	2-3		5	St Louis	3-2
	13	Hartford	4-3		11	Detroit	3-6
	15	Edmonton	2-2		22	NY Islanders	2-3
	17	Chicago	2-3		25	Edmonton	4-3
Feb.	3	Winnipeg	3-4		30	Calgary	1-5
	6	NY Islanders	5-2		31	Vancouver	3-3
	8	Vancouver	8-1	Feb.	9	Montreal	4-6
	13	New Jersey	6-3		21	Philadelphia	4-4
	15	Hartford	5-3		22	Washington	2-3
	18	NY Islanders*	4-5		28	St Louis	4-4
	24	New Jersey*	5-2	Mar.	2	Toronto	2-4
	27	Washington	4-4		7	Quebec	2-4
Mar.	4	Philadelphia	6-2		9	NY Islanders	4-6
	13	Detroit	1-4		10	Chicago	2-5
	17	Pittsburgh*	2-4		15	New Jersey	2-5
	24	NY Islanders	3-1		21	Pittsburgh	2-5
	26	New Jersey	3-3		23	Philadelphia*	4-7
	31	Pittsburgh	6-3		30	Detroit*	5-6

* Denotes afternoon game.

All-time Record vs. Other Clubs

Regular Season

			At Home							On Road							Total				
	GP	W	L	T	GF	GA	PTS	GP	W	L	T	GF	GA	PTS	GP	W	L	T	GF	GA	PTS
Boston	276	119	103	54	838	773	292	274	87	149	38	764	1000	212	550	206	252	92	1602	1773	504
Buffalo	41	17	14	10	144	117	44	42	10	26	6	136	190	26	83	27	40	16	280	307	70
Calgary	40	17	18	5	145	149	39	40	10	24	6	122	184	26	80	27	42	11	267	333	65
Chicago	275	115	106	54	812	778	284	275	108	125	42	764	843	258	550	223	231	96	1576	1621	542
Detroit	273	130	86	57	839	696	317	274	74	156	44	674	962	192	547	204	242	101	1513	1658	509
Edmonton	19	6	10	3	80	81	15	19	8	10	1	68	82	17	38	14	20	4	148	163	32
Hartford	19	11	6	2	81	58	24	19	6	11	2	68	78	14	38	17	17	4	149	136	38
Los Angeles	48	28	15	5	193	143	61	48	20	19	9	169	160	49	96	48	34	14	362	303	110
Minnesota	50	30	10	10	181	138	70	50	28	15	7	198	154	63	100	58	25	17	379	292	133
Montreal	264	106	108	50	756	769	262	265	54	177	34	613	1051	142	529	160	285	84	1369	1820	404
New Jersey	49	29	13	7	219	161	65	50	26	20	4	199	177	56	99	55	33	11	418	338	121
NY Islanders	62	39	18	5	249	189	83	60	16	39	5	185	256	37	122	55	57	10	434	445	120
Philadelphia	74	31	25	18	241	222	80	75	26	36	13	218	262	65	149	57	61	31	459	484	145
Pittsburgh	68	35	26	7	285	237	77	69	33	25	11	255	243	77	137	68	51	18	540	480	154
Quebec	19	13	3	3	82	47	29	19	6	10	3	81	85	15	38	19	13	6	163	132	44
St. Louis	50	40	5	5	217	133	85	51	22	21	8	166	157	52	101	62	26	13	383	270	137
Toronto	265	109	101	55	807	779	273	264	77	149	38	685	910	192	529	186	250	93	1492	1689	465
Vancouver	43	33	7	3	198	106	69	42	29	10	3	174	134	61	85	62	17	6	372	240	130
Washington	50	26	18	6	218	181	58	49	17	24	8	167	194	42	99	43	42	14	385	375	100
Winnipeg	19	9	8	2	93	84	20	19	10	7	2	74	72	22	38	19	15	4	167	156	42
Defunct Club	139	87	30	22	460	290	196	139	82	34	23	441	291	187	278	169	64	45	901	581	383
Totals	2143	1030	730	383	7138	6111	2443	2143	749	1087	307	6221	7485	1805	4286	1779	1817	690	13359	13596	4248

Playoffs

	Series	W	L	GP	W	L	T	GF	GA	Last Mtg.	Round	Result
Boston	9	3	6	42	18	22	2	104	114	1973	QF	W 4-1
Buffalo	1	0	1	3	1	2	0	6	11	1978	PR	L 1-2
Calgary	1	1	0	4	3	1	0	14	8	1980	PR	W 3-1
Chicago	5	1	4	24	10	14	0	54	66	1973	SF	L 1-4
Detroit	5	1	4	23	10	13	0	49	57	1950	F	L 3-4
Los Angeles	2	2	0	6	5	1	0	32	14	1981	PR	W 3-1
Montreal	13	6	7	55	21	32	2	139	171	1986	CF	L 1-4
NY Islanders	7	2	5	35	15	20	0	110	126	1990	DSF	W 4-1
Philadelphia	8	4	4	38	19	19	0	130	119	1987	DSF	L 2-4
Pittsburgh	1	0	1	4	0	4	0	11	19	1989	DSF	L 0-4
St. Louis	1	1	0	6	4	2	0	29	22	1981	QF	W 4-2
Toronto	8	5	3	35	19	16	0	86	86	1971	QF	W 4-2
Washington	3	1	2	17	7	10	0	51	63	1991	DSF	L 2-4
Defunct	9	6	3	22	11	7	4	43	29			
Totals	73	33	40	314	143	163	8	858	905			

Playoff Results 1991-87

Year	Round	Opponent	Result	GF	GA
1991	DSF	Washington	L 2-4	16	16
1990	DF	Washington	L 1-4	15	22
	DSF	NY Islanders	W 4-1	22	13
1989	DSF	Pittsburgh	L 0-4	11	19
1987	DSF	Philadelphia	L 2-4	13	22

Abbreviations: Round: F Final; **CF** conference final; **DF** division final; **DSF** division semi-final; **SF** semi-final; **QF** quarter-final. **PR** preliminary round. **GA** goals against; **GF** goals for.

Entry Draft Selections 1991-77

1991
Pick
15 Alexei Kovalev
37 Darcy Werenka
96 Corey Machanic
125 Fredrik Jax
128 Barry Young
147 John Rushin
169 Corey Hirsch
191 Vjateslav Uvayev
213 Jamie Ram
235 Vitali Chinakov
257 Brian Wiseman

1990
Pick
13 Michael Stewart
34 Doug Weight
55 John Vary
69 Jeff Nielsen
76 Rick Willis
85 Sergei Zubov
99 Lubos Rob
118 Jason Weinrich
139 Bryan Lonsinger
160 Todd Hedlund
181 Andrew Silverman
202 Jon Hillebrandt
223 Brett Lievers
244 Sergei Nemchinov

1989
Pick
20 Steven Rice
40 Jason Prosofsky
45 Rob Zamuner
49 Louie Debrusk
67 Jim Cummins
88 Aaron Miller
118 Joby Messier
139 Greg Leahy
160 Greg Spenrath
181 Mark Bavis
202 Roman Oksyuta
223 Steve Locke
244 Ken MacDermid

1988
Pick
22 Troy Mallette
26 Murray Duval
68 Tony Amonte
99 Martin Bergeron
110 Dennis Vial
131 Mike Rosati
152 Eric Couvrette
173 Shorty Forrest

194 Paul Cain
202 Eric Fenton
215 Peter Fiorentino
236 Keith Slifstien

1987
Pick
10 Jayson More
31 Daniel Lacroix
46 Simon Gagne
69 Michael Sullivan
94 Eric O'Borsky
115 Ludek Cajka
136 Clint Thomas
157 Charles Wiegand
178 Eric Burrill
199 David Porter
205 Brett Barnett
220 Lance Marciano

1986
Pick
9 Brian Leetch
51 Bret Walter
53 Shawn Clouston
72 Mark Janssens
93 Jeff Bloemberg
114 Darren Turcotte
135 Robb Graham
156 Barry Chyzowski
177 Pat Scanlon
198 Joe Ranger
219 Russell Parent
240 Soren True

1985
Pick
7 Ulf Dahlen
28 Mike Richter
49 Sam Lindstahl
70 Pat Janostin
91 Brad Stephan
112 Brian McReynolds
133 Neil Pilon
154 Lary Bernard
175 Stephane Brochu
196 Steve Nemeth
217 Robert Burakovski
238 Rudy Poeschek

1984
Pick
14 Terry Carkner
35 Raimo Helminen
77 Paul Broten
98 Clark Donatelli
119 Kjell Samuelsson
140 Thomas Hussey
161 Brian Nelson
182 Ville Kentala
188 Heinz Ehlers
202 Kevin Miller
223 Tom Lorentz
243 Scott Brower

1983
Pick
12 Dave Gagner
33 Randy Heath
49 Vesa Salo
53 Gordie Walker
73 Peter Andersson
93 Jim Andonoff
113 Bob Alexander
133 Steve Orth
153 Peter Marcov
173 Paul Jerrard
213 Bryan Walker
233 Ulf Nilsson

1982
Pick
15 Chris Kontos
36 Tomas Sandstrom
57 Corey Millen
78 Chris Jensen
120 Tony Granato
141 Sergei Kapustin
160 Brian Glynn
162 Jan Karlsson
183 Kelly Miller
193 Simo Saarinen
204 Bob Lowes
225 Andy Otto
246 Dwayne Robinson

1981
Pick
9 James Patrick
30 Jan Erixon
50 Peter Sundstrom
51 Mark Morrison
72 John Vanbiesbrouck
114 Eric Magnuson
135 Mike Guentzel
156 Ari Lahtenmaki
177 Paul Reifenberger
198 Mario Proulx

1980
Pick
14 Jim Malone
35 Mike Allison
77 Kurt Kleinendorst
98 Scot Kleinendorst
119 Reijo Ruotsalainen
140 Bob Scurfield
161 Bart Wilson
182 Chris Wray
203 Anders Backstrom

1979
Pick
13 Doug Sulliman
34 Ed Hospodar
76 Pat Conacher
97 Dan Makuch
118 Stan Adams

1978
Pick
26 Don Maloney
43 Ray Markham
44 Dean Turner
59 Dave Silk
60 Andre Dore
76 Mike McDougall
93 Tom Laidlaw
110 Dan Clark
127 Greg Kostenko
144 Brian McDavid
161 Mark Rodrigues
176 Steve Weeks
192 Pierre Daigneault
206 Chris McLaughlin
217 Todd Johnson
223 Dan McCarthy

1977
Pick
8 Lucien DeBlois
13 Ron Duguay
26 Mike Keating
44 Steve Baker
62 Mario Marois
80 Benoit Gosselin
98 John Bethel
116 Robert Sullivan
131 Lance Nethery
146 Alex Jeans
157 Peter Raps
164 Mike Brown
171 Mark Miller

General Manager

SMITH, NEIL
General Manager, New York Rangers. Born in Toronto, Ont., January 9, 1954.

Smith, 37-years-old, joined the Rangers on July 17, 1989 after seven seasons with the Detroit Red Wings and two with the New York Islanders. After serving as a scout for the Islanders in 1980-81 and 1981-82, Smith joined the Red Wings. While with the Red Wings, Smith held several positions including director of scouting and player development. He also served as general manager of the Adirondack Red Wings (AHL), leading that club to two Calder Cups (1985-86 and 1988-89).

A former All-American defenseman from Western Michigan University, Smith was drafted in 1974 by the New York Islanders. After receiving his degree in communications and business, Smith played two seasons in the IHL–1978-79 with the Kalamazoo Wings and Saginaw Gears and 1979-80 with the Dayton Gems, Milwaukee Admirals and Muskegon Mohawks.

Coach

NEILSON, ROGER PAUL
Coach, New York Rangers. Born in Toronto, Ont., June 16, 1934.

Roger Neilson began his coaching career as a 17-year-old with a neighborhood baseball team in his native Toronto. He began scouting Ontario prospects for the Montreal Canadiens before becoming coach of the Peterborough Petes of the OHA in 1966. He remained in Peterborough for ten seasons, winning one OHA championship while finishing lower than third in regular-season play only twice. He made his pro coaching debut with the Dallas Black Hawks of the CHL in 1976-77 and moved up to the NHL with the Toronto Maple Leafs in 1977-78. He joined the Buffalo Sabres in 1979-80 as associate coach under Scotty Bowman. He acted as the Sabres' bench coach for part of this campaign and for all of 1980-81. He became associate coach of the Vancouver Canucks under Harry Neale in 1981-82 and coached five games late in the season when Neale was serving a suspension. He also guided the Canucks in the 1982 playoffs and in 1982-83. In 1983-84, he coached the Los Angeles Kings for the last 28 games of the regular season. He served as co-coach of the Chicago Blackhawks from 1984-85 through 1986-87 before taking on special scouting assignments for the Blackhawks. He also has provided television commentary on Canadian NHL telecasts.

Club Directory

Madison Square Garden
4 Pennsylvania Plaza
New York, New York 10001
Phone **212/465-6000**
PR FAX 212/465-6494
ENVOY ID
  Front Office: RANGERS. GM
  Public
  Relations: RANGERS. PR
Capacity: 17,842

Executive Management
Governor .... Stanley R. Jaffe
Alternate Governors .... Neil Smith, Kevin Billet, Thomas A. Conway
Vice-President & General Manager .... Neil Smith
Vice-President & General Counsel .... Kenneth W. Munoz
Vice-President, Legal Affairs .... Kevin Billet
Director of Communications .... Barry Watkins
Director of Marketing .... Kevin Kennedy
Director of Community Relations .... Maureen Brady

Team Management
Assistant General Manager/Player Development ... Larry Pleau
Coach .... Roger Neilson
Assistant Coaches .... Wayne Cashman, Colin Campbell
Development Coach .... Ron Smith
Scouting Staff .... Tony Feltrin, Herb Hammond, Lou Jankowski, Martin Madden, David McNab, Christer Rockstrom
Director of Administration .... Mark Piazza
Manager of Team Services .... Matthew Loughran
Scouting Coordinator .... Bill Short

Medical/Training Staff
Team Physician/Ortho Surgeon .... Barton Nisonson, M.D.
Assistant Team Physician.................. Anthony Maddalo
Medical Consultants .... Howard Chester, James A. Nicholas, Ronald Weissman
Trainer/Medical .... Dave Smith
Trainer/Equipment .... Joe Murphy
Assistant Trainers........................ Larry Nastasi, Tim Paris
Locker-room Assistant .... Benny Petrizzi

Communications Staff
Assistant to the Director of Communications ... Kevin McDonald
Administrative Assistant .... Ann Marie Gilmartin

Home Ice .... Madison Square Garden
Press Facilities .... 33rd Street
Television Facilities .... 31st Street
Radio Facilities .... 33rd Street
Rink Dimensions .... 200 feet by 85 feet
Ends and Sides of Rink .... Plexiglass (8 feet)
Club Colors .... Blue, Red and White
Training Camp .... Rye, New York
TV Announcers .... Bruce Beck, John Davidson, Sam Rosen
Radio Announcers .... Marv Albert, Sal Messina, Howie Rose
Television Outlets .... Madison Square Garden Cable Network
Radio Outlet .... MSG Radio—WFAN (66 AM), WEVD (1050 AM), WXPS (107.1 FM)

The New York Rangers Hockey Club is part of the
Madison Sqaure Garden Corporation
A Paramount Communications Company

Coaching Record

| Season | Team | Games | Regular Season | | | | Playoffs | | | |
			W	L	T	%	Games	W	L	%
1966-67	Peterborough (OHA)					UNAVAILABLE				
1967-68	Peterborough (OHA)	54	13	30	11	.342	....	....	....	
1968-69	Peterborough (OHA)	54	27	18	9	.583	10	4	6	.400
1969-70	Peterborough (OHA)	54	29	13	12	.648	....	....	....	
1970-71	Peterborough (OHA)	62	41	13	8	.726	....	....	....	
1971-72	Peterborough (OHA)	63	34	20	9	.611	....	....	....	
1972-73	Peterborough (OHA)	63	42	13	8	.730	....	....	....	
1973-74	Peterborough (OHA)	70	35	21	14	.600	....	....	....	
1974-75	Peterborough (OHA)	70	37	20	13	.621	....	....	....	
1975-76	Peterborough (OHA)	66	18	37	11	.356	....	....	....	
1976-77	Dallas (CHL)	76	35	25	16	.566	....	....	....	
1977-78	Toronto (NHL)	80	41	29	10	.575	13	6	7	.462
1978-79	Toronto (NHL)	80	34	33	13	.506	6	2	4	.333
1979-80	Buffalo (NHL)	26	14	6	6	.654	....	....	....	
1980-81	Buffalo (NHL)	80	39	20	21	.619	8	4	4	.500
1981-82	Vancouver (NHL)	5	4	0	1	.900	17	11	6	.647
1982-83	Vancouver (NHL)	80	30	35	15	.469	4	1	3	.250
1983-84	Los Angeles (NHL)	28	8	17	3	.339	....	....	....	
1989-90	NY Rangers (NHL)	80	36	31	13	.531	10	5	5	.500
1990-91	NY Rangers (NHL)	80	36	31	13	.531	6	2	4	.333
	NHL Totals	587	259	228	100	.526	64	31	33	.484

Philadelphia Flyers

1990-91 Results: 33w-37L-10T 76PTS. Fifth, Patrick Division

Schedule

Home		Away	
Oct. Thur. 10 Pittsburgh		**Oct.** Fri. 4 Washington	
Sun. 13 New Jersey		Sun. 6 Pittsburgh*	
Thur. 17 Quebec		Sat. 12 NY Islanders	
Sat. 19 Montreal		Thur. 24 Minnesota	
Thur. 31 San Jose		Fri. 25 Winnipeg	
Nov. Sat. 2 NY Rangers*		**Nov.** Tues. 5 St Louis	
Thur. 7 Buffalo		Fri. 8 Buffalo	
Thur. 14 Edmonton		Tues. 12 New Jersey	
Sun. 17 Winnipeg		Sat. 16 Montreal	
Sat. 23 New Jersey		Wed. 20 Pittsburgh	
Wed. 27 Hartford		Sat. 30 Pittsburgh	
Fri. 29 Pittsburgh*		**Dec.** Mon. 2 NY Rangers	
Dec. Thur. 5 Washington		Sat. 7 Boston	
Sun. 8 New Jersey		Sun. 15 Chicago	
Thur. 12 Toronto		Wed. 18 NY Rangers	
Sat. 14 Chicago*		Sat. 21 Minnesota	
Thur. 19 NY Islanders		Fri. 27 Vancouver	
Sun. 22 Washington		Sat. 28 Calgary	
Jan. Tues. 7 Buffalo		**Jan.** Fri. 3 San Jose	
Thur. 9 Los Angeles		Sat. 4 Los Angeles	
Sun. 12 NY Islanders		Sat. 11 Boston	
Tues. 14 Chicago		Thur. 16 NY Islanders	
Thur. 23 Winnipeg		Tues. 21 Detroit	
Tues. 28 Washington		Sat. 25 Toronto	
Thur. 30 Minnesota		**Feb.** Sat. 1 NY Islanders	
Feb. Sun. 2 St Louis		Tues. 4 New Jersey	
Thur. 6 Boston		Sat. 8 Quebec*	
Thur. 13 Quebec		Tues. 18 New Jersey	
Sat. 15 Edmonton*		Sat. 22 Washington	
Sun. 16 Pittsburgh		Sun. 23 NY Rangers	
Tues. 25 NY Islanders		Thur. 27 Calgary	
Mar. Sat. 7 NY Rangers*		Fri. 28 Edmonton	
Sun. 8 Vancouver		**Mar.** Sun. 1 San Jose*	
Thur. 12 Calgary		Tues. 3 Los Angeles	
Sat. 14 Washington*		Tues. 10 NY Islanders	
Sun. 22 Detroit		Wed. 18 Montreal	
Tues. 24 NY Rangers		Fri. 20 Washington	
Sun. 29 New Jersey*		Wed. 25 NY Rangers	
Apr. Thur. 2 Hartford		Tues. 31 Pittsburgh	
Sun. 5 Toronto		**Apr.** Sat. 4 Hartford*	

* Denotes afternoon game.

Home Starting Times:
- Weeknights .... 7:35 p.m.
- Sundays .... 7:05 p.m.
- Matinees .... 1:05 p.m.
- Except Oct. 19 .... 8:05 p.m.
- Mar. 14 .... 11:05 a.m.
- Mar. 29 .... 1:35 p.m.

Franchise date: June 5, 1967

25th NHL Season

Ken Wregget appeared in 30 games for the Flyers in 1990-91, compiling a goals-against average of 3.56.

Year-by-Year Record

		Home			Road			Overall							
Season	GP	W	L	T	W	L	T	W	L	T	GF	GA	Pts.	Finished	Playoff Result
1990-91	80	18	16	6	15	21	4	33	37	10	252	267	76	5th, Patrick Div.	Out of Playoffs
1989-90	80	17	19	4	13	20	7	30	39	11	290	297	71	6th, Patrick Div.	Out of Playoffs
1988-89	80	22	15	3	14	21	5	36	36	8	307	285	80	4th, Patrick Div.	Lost Conf. Championship
1987-88	80	20	14	6	18	19	3	38	33	9	292	292	85	3rd, Patrick Div.	Lost Div. Semi-Final
1986-87	80	29	9	2	17	17	6	46	26	8	310	245	100	1st, Patrick Div.	Lost Final
1985-86	80	33	6	1	20	17	3	53	23	4	335	241	110	1st, Patrick Div.	Lost Div. Semi-Final
1984-85	80	32	4	4	21	16	3	53	20	7	348	241	113	1st, Patrick Div.	Lost Final
1983-84	80	25	10	5	19	16	5	44	26	10	350	290	98	3rd, Patrick Div.	Lost Div. Semi-Final
1982-83	80	29	8	3	20	15	5	49	23	8	326	240	106	1st, Patrick Div.	Lost Div. Semi-Final
1981-82	80	25	10	5	13	21	6	38	31	11	325	313	87	3rd, Patrick Div.	Lost Div. Semi-Final
1980-81	80	23	9	8	18	15	7	41	24	15	313	249	97	2nd, Patrick Div.	Lost Quarter-Final
1979-80	80	27	5	8	21	7	12	48	12	20	327	254	116	1st, Patrick Div.	Lost Final
1978-79	80	26	10	4	14	15	11	40	25	15	281	248	95	2nd, Patrick Div.	Lost Quarter-Final
1977-78	80	29	6	5	16	14	10	45	20	15	296	200	105	2nd, Patrick Div.	Lost Semi-Final
1976-77	80	33	6	1	15	10	15	48	16	16	323	213	112	1st, Patrick Div.	Lost Semi-Final
1975-76	80	36	2	2	15	11	14	51	13	16	348	209	118	1st, Patrick Div.	Lost Final
1974-75	**80**	**32**	**6**	**2**	**19**	**12**	**9**	**51**	**18**	**11**	**293**	**181**	**113**	**1st, Patrick Div.**	**Won Stanley Cup**
1973-74	**78**	**28**	**6**	**5**	**22**	**10**	**7**	**50**	**16**	**12**	**273**	**164**	**112**	**1st, West Div.**	**Won Stanley Cup**
1972-73	78	27	8	4	10	22	7	37	30	11	296	256	85	2nd, West Div.	Lost Semi-Final
1971-72	78	19	13	7	7	25	7	26	38	14	200	236	66	5th, West Div.	Out of Playoffs
1970-71	78	20	10	9	8	23	8	28	33	16	207	225	73	3rd, West Div.	Lost Quarter-Final
1969-70	76	11	14	13	6	21	11	17	35	24	197	225	58	5th, West Div.	Out of Playoffs
1968-69	76	14	16	8	6	19	13	20	35	21	174	225	61	3rd, West Div.	Lost Quarter-Final
1967-68	74	17	13	7	14	19	4	31	32	11	173	179	73	1st, West Div.	Lost Quarter-Final

1991-92 Player Personnel

FORWARDS

	HT	WT	S	Place of Birth	Date	1990-91 Club
ACTON, Keith	5-8	170	L	Stouffville, Ont.	4/15/58	Flyers
ARMSTRONG, Bill	6-2	195	L	London, Ont.	6/25/66	Hershey-Flyers
BARRIE, Len	6-0	200	R	Kimberley, B.C.	6/4/69	Hershey
BOIVIN, Claude	6-2	200	L	Ste. Foy, Que.	3/1/70	Hershey
BROWN, Dave	6-5	205	R	Saskatoon, Sask.	10/12/62	Edmonton
COOKE, Jamie	6-2	205	R	Toronto, Ont.	11/5/68	Colgate
CRAVEN, Murray	6-2	185	L	Medicine Hat, Alta.	7/20/64	Flyers
DALLMAN, Rod	5-11	185	L	Prince Albert, Sask.	1/26/67	Hershey-San Diego
DANIELS, Kimbi	5-10	175	R	Brandon, Man.	1/19/72	Swift Current-Flyers
DOBBIN, Brian	5-11	205	R	Petrolia, Ont.	8/18/66	Hershey
DUPRE, Yannick	6-0	189	L	Montreal, Que.	11/20/72	Drummondville
EKLUND, Pelle	5-10	175	L	Stockholm, Sweden	3/22/63	Flyers
FREER, Mark	5-10	180	L	Peterborough, Ont.	7/14/68	Hershey
HORACEK, Tony	6-4	210	L	Vancouver, B.C.	2/3/67	Flyers-Hershey
HOSTAK, Martin	6-3	198	L	Hradec Kral., Czech.	11/11/67	Hershey-Flyers
JENSEN, Chris	5-10	170	R	Fort St. John, B.C.	10/28/63	Flyers-Hershey
JONES, Brad	6-0	195	L	Sterling Heights, MI	6/28/65	Los Angeles
KASPER, Steve	5-8	170	L	Montreal, Que.	9/28/61	Los Angeles
KINISKY, Al	6-4	220	L	Pt. Coquitlam, B.C.	5/31/72	Seattle
KUSHNER, Dale	6-1	195	L	Terrace, B.C.	6/13/66	Flyers-Hershey
LACOMBE, Normand	6-0	205	R	Pierrefonds, Que.	10/18/64	Flyers
MURRAY, Pat	6-2	185	L	Stratford, Ont.	8/20/69	Hershey-Flyers
NORRIS, Clayton	6-2	205	R	Edmonton, Alberta	3/8/72	Medicine Hat
PEDERSON, Mark	6-2	196	L	Prelate, Sask.	1/14/68	Montreal-Flyers
RICCI, Mike	6-0	190	L	Scarborough, Ont.	10/27/71	Flyers
SIMON, Chris	6-3	220	L	Wawa, Ont.	1/30/72	Ottawa
SIMPSON, Reid	6-1	211	L	Flin Flon, Man.	5/21/69	Hershey
SMITH, Derrick	6-2	215	L	Scarborough, Ont.	1/22/65	Flyers
SUTTER, Ron	6-0	180	R	Viking, Alta.	12/2/63	Flyers
TOCCHET, Rick	6-0	205	R	Scarborough, Ont.	4/9/64	Flyers
TOOKEY, Tim	5-11	190	L	Edmonton, Alta.	8/29/60	Hershey

DEFENSEMEN

	HT	WT	S	Place of Birth	Date	1990-91 Club
ARMSTRONG, Bill	6-4	215	L	Richmond Hill, Ont.	5/18/70	Hershey
BARON, Murray	6-3	210	L	Prince George, B.C.	6/1/67	Hershey-Flyers
BEADLE, Steve	5-11	190	L	Lansing, MI	5/30/68	Hershey
CARKNER, Terry	6-3	212	L	Smiths Falls, Ont.	3/7/66	Flyers
DUCHESNE, Steve	5-11	195	L	Sept-Iles, Que.	6/30/65	Los Angeles
FENYVES, Dave	5-11	192	L	Dunnville, Ont.	4/29/60	Hershey-Flyers
FOSTER, Corey	6-3	200	L	Ottawa, Ont.	10/27/69	Cape Breton
HOWE, Mark	5-11	185	L	Detroit, MI	5/28/55	Flyers
HUFFMAN, Kerry	6-2	200	L	Peterborough, Ont.	1/3/68	Flyers-Hershey
KORDIC, Daniel	6-5	220	L	Edmonton, Alta.	4/18/71	Medicine Hat
LATAL, Jiri	6-0	190	L	Olomouc, Czech.	2/2/67	Flyers
MORROW, Steve	6-2	212	L	Plano, TX	4/3/68	U. of New Hampshire
MURPHY, Gord	6-2	190	R	Willowdale, Ont.	2/23/67	Flyers
PITLICK, Lance	6-0	185	R	Minneapolis, MN	11/5/67	Hershey
PORKKA, Toni	6-2	190	R	Rauma, Finland	2/4/70	Lukko
RUMBLE, Darren	6-1	200	L	Barrie, Ont.	1/23/69	Hershey-Flyers
SAMUELSSON, Kjell	6-6	235	R	Tyringe, Sweden	10/18/58	Flyers
SANDWITH, Terran	6-4	210	L	Stoney Plain, Alta.	4/17/72	Tri-City
STOTHERS, Mike	6-4	212	L	Toronto, Ont.	2/22/62	Hershey

GOALTENDERS

	HT	WT	C	Place of Birth	Date	1990-91 Club
D'AMOUR, Marc	5-9	192	L	Sudbury, Ont.	4/29/61	Hershey
DEGRACE, Yanick	5-11	167	L	Lameque, N.B.	4/16/71	Trois-Rivieres
HEXTALL, Ron	6-3	192	L	Brandon, Man.	5/3/64	Flyers
HOFFORT, Bruce	5-10	185	L	N. Battleford, Sask.	7/30/66	Hershey-Flyers
LETOURNEAU, Ray	5-11	185	L	Penacook, N.H.	1/14/69	Yale
PEETERS, Pete	6-1	195	L	Edmonton, Alta.	8/17/57	Flyers-Hershey
ROUSSEL, Dominic	6-1	185	L	Hull, Que.	2/22/70	Hershey
WREGGET, Ken	6-1	195	L	Brandon, Man.	3/25/64	Flyers

1990-91 Scoring

Regular Season

* rookie

Pos	#	Player	Team	GP	G	A	Pts	+/−	PIM	PP	SH	GW	GT	S	%
R	22	Rick Tocchet	PHI	70	40	31	71	2 −	150	8	0	5	1	217	18.4
C	9	Per-Erik Eklund	PHI	73	19	50	69	2 −	14	8	0	4	1	131	14.5
L	32	Murray Craven	PHI	77	19	47	66	2 −	53	6	0	0	0	170	11.2
C	14	Ron Sutter	PHI	80	17	28	45	2	92	2	0	1	0	149	11.4
D	3	Gordon Murphy	PHI	80	11	31	42	7 −	58	6	0	2	0	203	5.4
C	18	*Mike Ricci	PHI	68	21	20	41	8 −	64	9	0	4	0	121	17.4
R	19	Scott Mellanby	PHI	74	20	21	41	8	155	5	0	6	0	165	12.1
C	25	Keith Acton	PHI	76	14	23	37	9 −	131	2	1	1	1	120	11.7
D	29	Terry Carkner	PHI	79	7	25	32	15 −	204	6	0	1	0	97	7.2
R	20	Normand Lacombe	PHI	74	11	20	31	1 −	27	1	0	1	0	91	12.1
D	28	Kjell Samuelsson	PHI	78	9	19	28	4	82	1	0	3	1	101	8.9
L	41	*Mark Pederson	MTL	47	8	15	23	3	18	4	0	2	1	62	12.9
			PHI	12	2	1	3	8 −	5	1	0	0	0	14	14.3
			TOTAL	59	10	16	26	5 −	23	5	0	2	1	76	13.2
D	11	Jiri Latal	PHI	50	5	21	26	19 −	14	1	0	0	0	81	6.2
R	12	Tim Kerr	PHI	27	10	14	24	8 −	8	6	0	0	0	74	13.5
L	24	Derrick Smith	PHI	72	11	10	21	0	37	0	1	2	0	100	11.0
L	10	*Dale Kushner	PHI	63	7	11	18	4 −	195	1	0	0	0	59	11.9
L	17	Craig Berube	PHI	74	8	9	17	6 −	293	0	0	0	0	46	17.4
D	8	*Murray Baron	PHI	67	8	8	16	3 −	74	0	0	1	0	86	9.3
C	26	*Martin Hostak	PHI	50	3	10	13	1	22	1	0	0	0	64	4.7
D	2	Mark Howe	PHI	19	0	10	10	9	8	0	0	0	0	40	.0
L	21	Tony Horacek	PHI	34	3	6	9	6	49	0	0	1	0	35	8.6
D	6	Jeff Chychrun	PHI	36	0	6	6	1	105	0	0	0	0	25	.0
D	39	Dave Fenyves	PHI	40	1	4	5	1	28	0	0	0	0	32	3.1
L	23	*Pat Murray	PHI	16	2	1	3	5 −	15	1	0	0	0	16	12.5
R	45	Chris Jensen	PHI	18	2	1	3	5 −	2	0	0	0	0	22	9.1
D	5	Kerry Huffman	PHI	10	1	2	3	1	10	0	0	1	0	14	7.1
D	50	*Scott Sandelin	PHI	15	0	3	3	3 −	0	0	0	0	0	4	.0
D	36	*Darren Rumble	PHI	3	1	0	1	1	0	0	0	0	0	2	50.0
L	58	*Bill Armstrong	PHI	1	0	1	1	0	0	0	0	0	0	1	.0
C	46	*Kimbi Daniels	PHI	2	0	1	1	2 −	0	0	0	0	0	2	.0
G	33	Pete Peeters	PHI	26	0	1	1	0	0	0	0	0	0	0	.0
G	27	Ron Hextall	PHI	36	0	1	1	0	10	0	0	0	0	0	.0
C	15	*Craig Fisher	PHI	2	0	0	0	0	0	0	0	0	0	2	.0
G	30	*Bruce Hoffort	PHI	2	0	0	0	0	0	0	0	0	0	0	.0
G	35	Ken Wregget	PHI	30	0	0	0	0	6	0	0	0	0	0	.0

Goaltending

No.	Goaltender	GPI	Mins	Avg	W	L	T	EN	SO	GA	SA	S%
33	Pete Peeters	26	1270	2.88	9	7	1	2	1	61	623	.902
27	Ron Hextall	36	2035	3.13	13	16	5	4	0	106	982	.892
35	Ken Wregget	30	1484	3.56	10	14	3	3	0	88	660	.867
30	*Bruce Hoffort	2	39	4.62	1	0	1	0	0	3	20	.850
	Totals	80	4853	3.30	33	37	10	9	1	267	2294	.884

Mike Ricci led all Flyers' freshman in scoring in 1990-91 with 21 goals and 20 assists.

General Managers' History

Normand Robert Poile, 1967-68 to 1969-70; Keith Allen, 1970-71 to 1982-83; Bob McCammon, 1983-84; Bobby Clarke, 1984-85 to 1989-90; Russ Farwell, 1990-91 to date.

Coaching History

Keith Allen, 1967-68 to 1968-69; Vic Stasiuk, 1969-70 to 1970-71; Fred Shero, 1971-72 to 1977-78; Bob McCammon and Pat Quinn, 1978-79; Pat Quinn, 1979-80 to 1980-81; Pat Quinn and Bob McCammon, 1981-82; Bob McCammon, 1982-83 to 1983-84; Mike Keenan, 1984-85 to 1987-88; Paul Holmgren, 1988-89 to date.

Captains' History

Lou Angotti, 1967-68; Ed Van Impe, 1968-69 to 1971-72; Ed Van Impe, Bob Clarke, 1972-73; Bob Clarke, 1973-74 to 1978-79; Mel Bridgman, 1979-80, 1980-81; Bill Barber, 1981-82; Bill Barber, Bob Clarke, 1982-83; Bob Clarke, 1983-84; Dave Poulin, 1984-85 to 1988-89; Dave Poulin and Ron Sutter, 1989-90; Ron Sutter, 1990-91 to date.

Retired Numbers

1	Bernie Parent	1967-1971 and 1973-1979
4	Barry Ashbee	1970-1974
9	Bill Barber	1972-1985
16	Bobby Clarke	1969-1984

Club Records

Team

(Figures in brackets for season records are games played; records for fewest points, wins, ties, losses, goals, goals against are for 70 or more games)

Most Points	118	1975-76 (80)	
Most Wins	53	1984-85 (80)	
		1985-86 (80)	
Most Ties	........*24	1969-70 (76)	
Most Losses	38	1971-72 (78)	
Most Goals	350	1983-84 (80)	
Most Goals Against	313	1981-82 (80)	
Fewest Points	58	1969-70 (76)	
Fewest Wins	17	1969-70 (76)	
Fewest Ties	4	1985-86 (80)	
Fewest Losses	12	1979-80 (80)	
Fewest Goals	173	1967-68 (74)	
Fewest Goals Against	164	1973-74 (78)	

Longest Winning Streak
Over-all 13   Oct. 19-Nov. 17/85
Home . . . .*20   Jan. 4-
Apr. 3/76
Away 8   Dec. 22/82-
Jan. 16/83

Longest Undefeated Streak
Over-all . . . .*35   Oct. 14/79-
Jan. 6/80
(25 wins, 10 ties)
Home 26   Oct. 11/79-
Feb. 3/80
(19 wins, 7 ties)
Away 16   Oct. 20/79-
Jan. 6/80
(11 wins, 5 ties)

Longest Losing Streak
Over-all 6   Mar. 25-
Apr. 4/70
Home 5   Jan. 30-
Feb. 15/69
Away 8   Oct. 25-
Nov. 26/72

Longest Winless Streak
Over-all 11   Nov. 21-
Dec. 14/69
(9 losses, 2 ties)
Dec. 10/70-
Jan. 3/71
(9 losses, 2 ties)
Home 8   Dec. 19/68-
Jan. 18/69
(4 losses, 4 ties)
Away 19   Oct. 23/71-
Jan. 27/72
(15 losses, 4 ties)
Most Shutouts, Season 13   1974-75 (80)
Most PIM, Season 2,621   1980-81 (80)
Most Goals, Game 13   Mar. 22/84
(Pit. 4 at Phi. 13)
Oct. 18/84
(Van. 2 at Phil. 13)

Individual

Most Seasons	15	Bobby Clarke
Most Games	1,144	Bobby Clarke
Most Goals, Career	420	Bill Barber
Most Assists, Career	852	Bobby Clarke
Most Points, Career	...1,210	Bobby Clarke
		(358 goals, 852 assists)
Most PIM, Career	1,600	Paul Holmgren
Most Shutouts, Career	50	Bernie Parent

Longest Consecutive
Game Streak 287   Rick MacLeish
(Oct. 6/72-Feb. 5/76)
Most Goals, Season 61   Reggie Leach
(1975-76)
Most Assists, Season 89   Bobby Clarke
(1974-75; 1975-76)
Most Points, Season 119   Bobby Clarke
(1975-76)
(30 goals, 89 assists)

Most PIM, Season . . . . . .*472   Dave Schultz
(1974-75)
Most Points, Defenseman,
Season 82   Mark Howe
(1985-86)
(24 goals, 58 assists)
Most Points, Center,
Season 119   Bobby Clarke
(1975-76)
(30 goals, 89 assists)
Most Points, Right Wing,
Season 98   Tim Kerr
(1984-85)
(54 goals, 44 assists)
Most Points, Left Wing,
Season 112   Bill Barber
(1975-76)
(50 goals, 62 assists)
Most Points, Rookie,
Season 76   Dave Poulin
(1983-84)
(31 goals, 45 assists)
Most Shutouts, Season 12   Bernie Parent
(1973-74; 1974-75)
Most Goals, Game 4   Rick MacLeish
(Feb. 13/73; Mar. 4/73)
Tom Bladon
(Dec. 11/77)
Tim Kerr
(Oct. 25/84, Jan. 17/85,
Feb. 9/85, Nov. 20/86)
Brian Propp
(Dec. 2/86)
Rick Tocchet
(Feb. 27/88;
Jan. 25/90)
Most Assists, Game 5   Bobby Clarke
(Apr. 1/76)
Most Points, Game 8   Tom Bladon
(Dec. 11/77)

* NHL Record.

All-time Record vs. Other Clubs

Regular Season

		At Home							On Road							Total						
	GP	W	L	T	GF	GA	PTS	GP	W	L	T	GF	GA	PTS	GP	W	L	T	GF	GA	PTS
Boston	48	20	22	6	159	145	46	49	10	33	6	142	205	26	97	30	55	12	301	350	72
Buffalo	41	26	9	6	151	103	58	40	14	20	6	119	144	34	81	40	29	12	270	247	92
Calgary	41	29	11	1	170	108	59	40	12	20	8	137	166	32	81	41	31	9	307	274	91
Chicago	50	27	15	8	171	140	62	50	10	24	16	132	176	36	100	37	39	24	303	316	98
Detroit	48	28	10	10	196	138	66	48	18	21	9	160	167	45	96	46	31	19	356	305	111
Edmonton	19	13	5	1	86	59	27	19	5	11	3	58	74	13	38	18	16	4	144	133	40
Hartford	19	14	4	1	81	48	29	19	7	8	0	80	81	14	38	21	12	1	161	129	43
Los Angeles	53	32	14	7	206	138	71	54	32	15	7	186	155	71	107	64	29	14	392	293	142
Minnesota	56	38	8	10	223	126	86	55	20	22	13	186	182	53	111	58	30	23	409	308	139
Montreal	48	17	19	12	131	145	46	48	11	27	10	136	187	32	96	28	46	22	267	332	78
New Jersey	49	36	8	5	216	109	77	49	25	20	4	204	173	54	98	61	28	9	420	282	131
NY Islanders	60	35	17	8	224	181	78	61	21	30	10	182	237	52	121	56	47	18	406	418	130
NY Rangers	75	36	26	13	262	218	85	74	25	31	18	222	241	68	149	61	57	31	484	459	153
Pittsburgh	75	59	10	6	338	177	124	73	31	28	14	239	231	76	148	90	38	20	577	408	200
Quebec	19	15	2	2	82	48	32	19	7	5	7	72	66	21	38	22	7	9	154	114	53
St. Louis	56	37	10	9	220	129	83	56	27	22	7	169	161	61	112	64	32	16	389	290	144
Toronto	48	31	10	7	196	115	69	49	19	17	13	166	169	51	97	50	27	20	362	284	120
Vancouver	42	30	12	0	193	119	60	42	22	10	10	164	125	54	84	52	22	10	357	244	114
Washington	49	29	16	4	193	134	62	50	22	20	8	178	180	52	99	51	36	12	371	314	114
Winnipeg	19	16	3	0	95	53	32	19	10	8	1	72	66	21	38	26	11	1	167	119	53
Defunct Club	34	24	4	6	137	67	54	35	13	14	8	102	89	34	69	37	18	14	239	156	88
Totals	**949**	**592**	**235**	**122**	**3730**	**2500**	**1306**	**949**	**361**	**406**	**178**	**3106**	**3275**	**900**	**1898**	**953**	**641**	**300**	**6836**	**5775**	**2206**

Playoffs

	Series	W	L	GP	W	L	T	GF	GA	Last Mtg.	Round	Result
Boston	4	2	2	20	9	11	0	57	60	1978	QF	L 1-4
Buffalo	2	2	0	11	8	3	0	35	23	1978	QF	W 4-1
Calgary	2	1	1	11	7	4	0	43	28	1981	QF	L 3-4
Chicago	1	0	1	4	0	4	0	8	20	1971	QF	L 0-4
Edmonton	3	1	2	15	5	7	8	0	44	49	1987	F	L 3-4
Minnesota	2	2	0	11	8	3	0	41	26	1980	SF	W 4-1
Montreal	4	1	3	21	6	15	0	52	72	1989	CF	L 2-4
New Jersey	1	1	0	2	2	0	0	6	3	1978	PR	W 2-0
NY Islanders	4	3	1	25	14	11	0	83	69	1987	DF	W 4-3
NY Rangers	8	4	4	38	19	19	0	119	130	1987	DSF	W 4-3
Pittsburgh	1	1	0	7	4	3	0	31	24	1989	DF	W 4-3
Quebec	2	2	0	11	7	4	0	39	29	1985	CF	W 4-2
St. Louis	2	0	2	11	3	8	0	20	34	1969	QF	L 0-4
Toronto	3	3	0	17	12	5	0	67	47	1977	QF	W 4-2
Vancouver	1	1	0	3	2	1	0	15	9	1979	PR	W 2-1
Washington	3	1	2	16	7	9	0	55	65	1989	DSF	W 4-2
Totals	**43**	**25**	**18**	**223**	**116**	**107**	**0**	**715**	**688**			

Playoff Results 1991-87

Year	Round	Opponent	Result	GF	GA
1989	CF	Montreal	L 2-4	8	17
	DF	Pittsburgh	W 4-3	31	24
	DSF	Washington	W 4-2	25	19
1988	DSF	Washington	L 3-4	25	31
1987	F	Edmonton	L 3-4	18	22
	CF	Montreal	W 4-2	22	22
	DF	NY Islanders	W 4-3	23	16
	DSF	NY Rangers	W 4-2	22	13

Abbreviations: Round: F Final; **CF** conference final; **DF** division final; **DSF** division semi-final; **SF** semi-final; **QF** quarter-final. **PR** preliminary round. **GA** goals against; **GF** goals for.

1990-91 Results

		Home					Away	
Oct.	7	Detroit	7-2	Oct.	4	Boston	1-4
	11	New Jersey	7-4		6	New Jersey	1-3
	13	Winnipeg	4-3		16	Pittsburgh	5-1
	18	Quebec	5-4		20	Montreal	5-3
	23	Washington	2-6		25	NY Rangers	3-5
	30	Pittsburgh	2-6		27	NY Islanders	2-5
Nov.	1	Minnesota	6-3	Nov.	4	Toronto	7-1
	3	Chicago*	1-3		6	Winnipeg	4-2
	8	Calgary	2-8		10	Quebec	5-2
	11	Vancouver	2-0		17	New Jersey*	2-3
	13	NY Rangers	1-1		21	Pittsburgh	5-4
	15	Montreal	4-1		27	NY Islanders	5-1
	18	New Jersey	1-4		28	New Jersey	5-5
	23	Toronto*	4-1	Dec.	8	Minnesota	0-7
	25	NY Islanders	4-1		9	Chicago	5-4
	30	NY Rangers	5-1		11	Washington	1-4
Dec.	2	Edmonton	3-6		16	Winnipeg	4-2
	6	Buffalo	3-4		18	Detroit	1-3
	13	NY Islanders	2-2		22	Hartford	0-1
	15	Detroit*	1-3		27	Los Angeles	7-5
	20	New Jersey	3-3		29	St Louis	3-1
	23	Montreal	4-4		31	Buffalo	2-5
Jan.	13	Edmonton	3-5	Jan.	4	Washington	3-3
	15	Pittsburgh	5-4		5	NY Islanders	2-3
	17	Quebec	5-1		7	NY Rangers	2-3
	22	Calgary	4-3		12	Boston	3-1
	24	Washington	6-1		26	Hartford	3-5
	31	Pittsburgh	4-2	Feb.	10	Washington*	2-5
Feb.	2	Hartford*	0-2		13	Toronto	6-3
	5	Los Angeles	2-3		16	New Jersey*	2-3
	7	Vancouver	1-2		23	NY Islanders	5-3
	18	Chicago*	5-3		25	Minnesota	2-3
	21	NY Rangers	4-4	Mar.	4	NY Rangers	2-6
	24	NY Islanders	4-3		7	Calgary	2-4
Mar.	2	St Louis	4-4		8	Edmonton	4-5
	17	Boston	1-3		12	Los Angeles	0-6
	21	St Louis	1-4		13	Vancouver	5-4
	23	NY Rangers*	7-4		16	Washington	0-6
	26	Pittsburgh	1-3		24	Buffalo*	2-6
	28	Washington	0-3		30	Pittsburgh*	4-4

* Denotes afternoon game.

Entry Draft Selections 1991-77

1991	**1987**	**1983**	**1979**
Pick	Pick	Pick	Pick
6 Peter Forsberg	20 Darren Rumble	41 Peter Zezel	14 Brian Propp
50 Yanic Dupre	30 Jeff Harding	44 Derrick Smith	22 Blake Wesley
86 Aris Brimanis	62 Martin Hostak	81 Alan Bourbeau	35 Pelle Lindbergh
94 Yanick Degrace	83 Tomaz Eriksson	101 Jerome Carrier	56 Lindsay Carson
116 Clayton Norris	104 Bill Gall	121 Rick Tocchet	77 Don Gillen
122 Dimitri Yushkevich	125 Tony Link	141 Bobby Mormina	98 Thomas Eriksson
138 Andrei Lomakin	146 Mark Strapon	161 Per-Erik Eklund	119 Gord Williams
182 James Bode	167 Darryl Ingham	181 Rob Nichols	**1978**
204 Josh Bartell	188 Bruce McDonald	201 William McCormick	Pick
226 Neil Little	209 Steve Morrow	221 Brian Jopling	6 Behn Wilson
248 John Porco	230 Darius Rusnak	241 Harold Duvall	7 Ken Linseman
1990	251 Dale Roehl	**1982**	14 Dan Lucas
Pick	**1986**	Pick	33 Mike Simurda
4 Mike Ricci	Pick	4 Ron Sutter	37 Gord Salt
25 Chris Simon	20 Kerry Huffman	46 Miroslav Dvorak	50 Glen Cochrane
40 Mikael Renberg	23 Jukka Seppo	47 Bill Campbell	67 Russ Wilderman
42 Terran Sandwith	28 Kent Hawley	77 Mikael Hjalm	83 Brad Tamblyn
46 Kimbi Daniels	83 Mark Bar	98 Todd Bergen	100 Mark Taylor
46 Bill Armstrong	125 Steve Scheifele	119 Ron Hextall	117 Mike Ewanouski
47 Chris Therien	146 Sami Wahlsten	140 Dave Brown	126 Jerry Price
52 Al Kinisky	167 Murray Baron	161 Alain Lavigne	134 Darren Switzer
88 Dan Kordic	188 Blaine Rude	182 Magnus Roupe	151 Greg Francis
109 Vjateslav Butsayev	209 Shawn Sabol	203 Tom Allen	167 Rick Berard
151 Patrik Englund	230 Brett Lawrence	224 Rick Gal	168 Don Lucia
172 Toni Porkka	251 Daniel Stephano	245 Mark Vichorek	182 Mark Berge
193 Greg Hanson	**1985**	**1981**	183 Ken Moore
214 Tommy Soderstrom	Pick	Pick	195 Jim Olson
235 William Lund	21 Glen Seabrooke	16 Steve Smith	198 Anton Stastny
1989	42 Bruce Rendall	37 Rich Costello	**1977**
Pick	48 Darryl Gilmour	47 Ken Strong	Pick
33 Greg Johnson	63 Shane Whelan	58 Ken Strong	17 Kevin McCarthy
34 Patrik Juhlin	84 Paul Marshall	65 David Michayluk	35 Tom Gorence
72 Reid Simpson	105 Daril Holmes	79 Ken Latta	53 Dave Hoyda
117 Niklas Eriksson	126 Ken Alexander	100 Justin Hanley	67 Yves Guillemette
138 John Callahan Jr.	147 Tony Horacek	121 Andre Villeneuve	71 Rene Hamelin
159 Sverre Sears	168 Mike Cusack	137 Vladimir Svitek	89 Dan Clark
180 Glen Wisser	189 Gordon Murphy	142 Gil Hudon	107 Alain Chaput
201 Al Kummu	231 Rod Williams	163 Steve Taylor	123 Richard Dalpe
222 Matt Brait	252 Paul Maurice	184 Len Hachborn	135 Pete Peeters
243 James Pollio	**1984**	205 Steve Tsujiura	136 Clint Eccles
1988	Pick	**1980**	139 Mike Greeder
Pick	22 Greg Smyth	Pick	150 Tom Bauer
14 Claude Boinvin	27 Scott Mellanby	21 Mike Stothers	151 Mike Bauman
35 Pat Murray	37 Jeff Chychrun	42 Jay Fraser	153 Bruce Crowder
56 Craig Fisher	43 Dave McLay	63 Paul Mercier	158 Bob Nicholson
63 Dominic Roussel	47 John Stevens	84 Taras Zytynsky	159 Dave Isherwood
77 Scott Lagrand	79 Dave Hanson	105 Daniel Held	161 Steve Jones
98 Edward O'Brien	100 Brian Dobbin	126 Brian Tutt	165 Jim Trainor
119 Gordie Frantti	121 John Dzikowski	147 Ross Fitzpatrick	166 Barry Duench
140 Jamie Cooke	142 Tom Allen	168 Mark Botell	168 Rob McNais
161 Johan Salle	163 Luke Vitale	189 Peter Dineen	172 Mike Laycock
182 Brian Arthur	184 Bill Powers	195 Bob O'Brien	
203 Jeff Dandreta	205 Daryn Fersovitch	210 Andy Brickley	
224 Scott Billey	247 Juraj Bakos		
245 Drahomir Kadlec			

Club Directory

The Spectrum
Pattison Place
Philadelphia, PA 19148
Phone **215/465-4500**
PR FAX 215/389-9403
Pres. & GM FAX 215/389-9409
TWX 910-997-2239
ENVOY ID
  Front Office: FLYERS. GM
  Public
  Relations: FLYERS. PR
Capacity: 17,378

Board of Directors
Ed Snider, Jay Snider, Joe Scott, Keith Allen, Fred Shabel,
Sylvan Tobin, Carl Hirsh, Sanford Lipstein, Ron Ryan

Majority Ownership	Ed Snider and family
Limited Partners	Sylvan and Fran Tobin
President	Jay Snider
Chairman of the Board Emeritus	Joe Scott
Executive Vice-Presidents	Keith Allen, Ron Ryan
General Manager	Russ Farwell
Head Coach	Paul Holmgren
Assistant General Manager	John Blackwell
Assistant Coaches	Craig Hartsburg, Ken Hitchcock
Goaltending Instructor	Bernie Parent
Head Coach, Hershey Bears (AHL)	Mike Eaves
Physical Conditioning Coach	Pat Croce, LPT, ATC
Director of Pro Scouting	Bill Barber
Pro Scout & Player Development Coordinator	Kevin McCarthy
Chief Scout	Jerry Melnyk
Scouts	Bill Dineen, Inge Hammarstrom, Kevin Maxwell, Simon Nolet, Glen Sonmor, Red Sullivan
Vice-President, Sales	Jack Betson
Vice-President, Communications	John Brogan
Accounting Manager	Jeff Niessen
Accountant	Susann Schaffer
Accounting Clerk	Karen Rehm
Accounts Payable Clerk	Michelle Stanek
Marketing Assistant	Lynn McGoldrick
Director of Public Relations	Rodger Gottlieb
Assistant Director of Public Relations	Jill Vogel
Public Relations Assistant	Suzann Waters
Director of Community Relations	Linda Panasci
Vice-President, Finance	Bob Baer
Director of Team Services	Joe Kadlec
Computer Analyst	David Gelberg
Video Coordinator	Leon Friedrich
Executive Assistants/Secretaries	Ileen Forcine, Dianna Taylor, Robin Walther, Kellie O'Neill
Ticket Manager	Cecilia Baker
Ticket Office Assistant	Carmen Moses
Merchandising	Marci Sorkin
Archivist	Mott Linn
Office Coordinator	Joan Kadlec
Receptionist	Aggie Preston
P.A. Announcer	Lou Nolan
Team Physician	Jeff Hartzell, M.D.
Orthopedic Surgeon	Arthur Bartolozzi, M.D.
Oral Surgeon	Everett Borghesani, D.D.S.
Team Dentist	Jim Larson, D.D.S.
Athletic Therapist	Gary Smith
Trainers	Jim Evers, Harry Bricker
Manager, Practice Facility	Anthony Tomasco
Dimensions of rink	200 feet by 85 feet
Location of Press Box	Mid-ice, North side, concourse level
Club colors	Orange, Black and White
Training camp site and Practice Facility	The Coliseum, Voorhees, NJ
TV Announcers	Mike Emrick, Bill Clement
Radio Announcers	Gene Hart, Bobby Taylor
TV Stations	PRISM, SportsChannel Philadelphia, WPHL TV-17
Radio Station	610 WIP All Sports Radio

Coach

HOLMGREN, PAUL
Coach, Philadelphia Flyers. Born in St. Paul, MN., December 2, 1955.

After serving as an assistant coach for the Flyers for three years, Holmgren assumed the head coaching duties on June 1, 1988. In his first NHL season, he led the Flyers to a 36-36-8 record (80 points) and the Wales Conference Championship series where they lost to Montreal.

Always a Philadelphia fan favorite, the St. Paul native played 500 of his 527 career NHL games in a Flyers' uniform, accumulating 138-171-309 scoring totals and setting an all-time club record with 1,600 penalty minutes. Holmgren was traded to the North Stars on February 23, 1984, where he played a total of 27 games over two years before retiring following the 1984-85 season. On July 22, 1985, he rejoined the Flyers as an assistant coach.

Coaching Record

		Regular Season					Playoffs			
Season	Team	Games	W	L	T	%	Games	W	L	%
1988-89	Philadelphia (NHL)	80	36	36	8	.500	19	10	9	.526
1989-90	Philadelphia (NHL)	80	30	39	11	.444	....	....	....	....
1990-91	Philadelphia (NHL)	80	33	37	10	.475	....	....	....	....
	NHL Totals	**240**	**99**	**112**	**29**	**.473**	**19**	**10**	**9**	**.526**

General Manager

FARWELL, RUSS
General Manager, Philadelphia Flyers. Born in Peace River, Alta., April 20, 1956.

Before being appointed to his position on June 6, 1990, Russ Farwell, 35, spent eight seasons in the Western Hockey League. He served as general manager of the Seattle Thunderbirds from 1988-90 and was named the WHL and CHL Executive of the Year in 1990. In two seasons under Farwell's leadership, the Thunderbirds were 85-52-7, including a 52-17-3 mark last year. Prior to his position with Seattle, Farwell spent six seasons as general manager of the Medicine Hat Tigers. During that time, the Tigers were 281-135-16, participated in the WHL's Eastern Division Finals five times and won consecutive Memorial Cup titles in 1986-87 and 1987-88.

Farwell is the first individual to be named an NHL general manager directly from junior hockey since Wren Blair went from Oshawa to Minnesota in 1967-68. The only other man to do so was Leighton "Hap" Emms, who went from Barrie to Boston in 1965-66.

Pittsburgh Penguins

1990-91 Results: 41w-33l-6t 88pts. First, Patrick Division

Year-by-Year Record

Season	GP	Home W	L	T	Road W	L	T	Overall W	L	T	GF	GA	Pts.	Finished	Playoff Result
1990-91	80	25	12	3	16	21	3	41	33	6	342	305	88	1st, Patrick Div.	Won Stanley Cup
1989-90	80	22	15	3	10	25	5	32	40	8	318	359	72	5th, Patrick Div.	Out of Playoffs
1988-89	80	24	13	3	16	20	4	40	33	7	347	349	87	2nd, Patrick Div.	Lost Div. Final
1987-88	80	22	12	6	14	23	3	36	35	9	319	316	81	6th, Patrick Div.	Out of Playoffs
1986-87	80	19	15	6	11	23	6	30	38	12	297	290	72	5th, Patrick Div.	Out of Playoffs
1985-86	80	20	15	5	14	23	3	34	38	8	313	305	76	5th, Patrick Div.	Out of Playoffs
1984-85	80	17	20	3	7	31	2	24	51	5	276	385	53	6th, Patrick Div.	Out of Playoffs
1983-84	80	7	29	4	9	29	2	16	58	6	254	390	38	6th, Patrick Div.	Out of Playoffs
1982-83	80	14	22	4	4	31	5	18	53	9	257	394	45	6th, Patrick Div.	Out of Playoffs
1981-82	80	21	11	8	10	25	5	31	36	13	310	337	75	4th, Patrick Div.	Lost Div. Semi-Final
1980-81	80	21	16	3	9	21	10	30	37	13	302	345	73	3rd, Norris Div.	Lost Prelim. Round
1979-80	80	20	13	7	10	24	6	30	37	13	251	303	73	3rd, Norris Div.	Lost Prelim. Round
1978-79	80	23	12	5	13	19	8	36	31	13	281	279	85	2nd, Norris Div.	Lost Quarter-Final
1977-78	80	16	15	9	9	22	9	25	37	18	254	321	68	4th, Norris Div.	Out of Playoffs
1976-77	80	22	12	6	12	21	7	34	33	13	240	252	81	3rd, Norris Div.	Lost Prelim. Round
1975-76	80	23	11	6	12	22	6	35	33	12	339	303	82	3rd, Norris Div.	Lost Prelim. Round
1974-75	80	25	5	10	12	23	5	37	28	15	326	289	89	3rd, Norris Div.	Lost Quarter-Final
1973-74	78	15	18	6	13	23	3	28	41	9	242	273	65	5th, West Div.	Out of Playoffs
1972-73	78	24	11	4	8	26	5	32	37	9	257	265	73	5th, West Div.	Out of Playoffs
1971-72	78	18	15	6	8	23	8	26	38	14	220	258	66	4th, West Div.	Lost Quarter-Final
1970-71	78	18	12	9	3	25	11	21	37	20	221	240	62	6th, West Div.	Out of Playoffs
1969-70	76	17	13	8	9	25	4	26	38	12	182	238	64	2nd, West Div.	Lost Semi-Final
1968-69	76	12	20	6	8	25	5	20	45	11	189	252	51	5th, West Div.	Out of Playoffs
1967-68	74	15	12	10	12	22	3	27	34	13	195	216	67	5th, West Div.	Out of Playoffs

Schedule

Home	Away
Oct. Sun. 6 Philadelphia*	**Oct.** Fri. 4 Buffalo
Thur. 17 NY Islanders	Thur. 10 Philadelphia
Sat. 19 NY Rangers	Sat. 12 New Jersey*
Tues. 22 Chicago	Tues. 15 NY Islanders
Thur. 24 New Jersey	Sat. 26 Montreal
Tues. 29 Washington	**Nov.** Fri. 8 Winnipeg
Thur. 31 Minnesota	Sat. 9 Minnesota
Nov. Sat. 2 Hartford	Mon. 11 NY Rangers
Tues. 5 Boston	Fri. 15 Washington
Wed. 13 Edmonton	Mon. 18 Quebec
Wed. 20 Philadelphia	Fri. 29 Philadelphia*
Sat. 23 NY Islanders	**Dec.** Tues. 3 Edmonton
Wed. 27 New Jersey	Thur. 5 San Jose
Sat. 30 Philadelphia	Sat. 7 St Louis
Dec. Tues. 10 NY Rangers	Fri. 13 New Jersey
Sat. 14 Washington	Thur. 19 Boston
Tues. 17 San Jose	Mon. 23 NY Islanders
Sat. 21 NY Rangers	Sat. 28 Washington
Thur. 26 Toronto	Sun. 29 NY Rangers
Tues. 31 New Jersey	**Jan.** Thur. 2 New Jersey
Jan. Sat. 4 Winnipeg*	Fri. 10 Calgary
Tues. 7 Los Angeles	Sun. 12 Vancouver*
Thur. 23 Buffalo	Thur. 16 Detroit
Tues. 28 Winnipeg	Sat. 25 NY Islanders*
Thur. 30 NY Islanders	Sun. 26 Washington*
Feb. Sat. 1 St Louis	**Feb.** Wed. 5 NY Rangers
Mon. 3 Detroit	Sun. 9 Boston*
Sat. 8 Los Angeles*	Sat. 15 Minnesota
Tues. 18 Toronto	Sun. 16 Philadelphia
Thur. 20 Quebec	Sat. 22 Montreal
Thur. 27 Hartford	Tues. 25 Washington
Sat. 29 Buffalo*	**Mar.** Tues. 3 Calgary
Mar. Tues. 10 Calgary	Fri. 6 San Jose
Thur. 12 NY Islanders	Sat. 7 Los Angeles
Tues. 17 Edmonton	Sat. 14 Toronto
Thur. 19 Quebec	Sun. 15 Chicago
Thur. 26 Vancouver	Sun. 22 Hartford
Sat. 28 Montreal	Tues. 24 Detroit
Tues. 31 Philadelphia	**Apr.** Thur. 2 NY Rangers
Apr. Sat. 4 Washington*	Sun. 5 New Jersey

* Denotes afternoon game.

Home Starting Times:

All Games	7:35 p.m.
Matinees	1:35 p.m.
Except Oct. 6	4:05 p.m.
Dec. 31	6:05 p.m.
Feb. 8	2:05 p.m.
Mar. 28	8:05 p.m.

Franchise date: June 5, 1967

25th NHL Season

Kevin Stevens had his finest professional season in 1990-91, registering 86 points on 40 goals and 46 assists.

1991-92 Player Personnel

FORWARDS	HT	WT	S	Place of Birth	Date	1990-91 Club
BLOUIN, Jean	6-0	197	L	Beauport, Que.	2/26/71	Laval
BODDEN, Jim	5-11	180	R	Dundas, Ont.	10/26/67	U. of Miami-Ohio
BOURQUE, Phil	6-1	196	L	Chelmsford, MA	6/8/62	Pittsburgh
CALLANDER, Jock	6-1	188	R	Regina, Sask.	4/23/61	Muskegon
CAUFIELD, Jay	6-4	235	R	Philadelphia, PA	7/17/60	Pittsburgh
DANIELS, Jeff	6-1	200	L	Oshawa, Ont.	6/24/68	Muskegon-Pittsburgh
ERREY, Bob	5-10	182	L	Montreal, Que.	9/21/64	Pittsburgh
FRANCIS, Ron	6-2	200	L	Sault Ste. Marie, Ont.	3/1/63	Hartford
GARDNER, Joal	6-0	175	L	Petrolia, Ont.	9/16/67	Muskegon
GAUTHIER, Daniel	6-1	190	L	Charlemagne, Que.	5/17/70	Knoxville-Albany
HEWARD, Jamie	6-2	194	R	Regina, Sask.	3/30/71	Regina
HRDINA, Jiri	6-0	190	L	Miada Boleslav, Czech.	1/5/58	Calgary
JAGR, Jaromir	6-2	208	L	Kladno, Czech.	2/12/72	Pittsburgh
KACHOWSKI, Mark	5-10	200	L	Edmonton, Alta.	2/20/65	Muskegon
LALONDE, Christian	6-1	210	L	LaSalle, Que.	5/3/66	Alb.-Musk.-Knox.
LEACH, Jamie	6-1	205	R	Winnipeg, Man.	8/25/69	Pittsburgh-Muskegon
LEMIEUX, Mario	6-4	210	R	Montreal, Que.	10/5/65	Pittsburgh
LONEY, Troy	6-3	210	L	Bow Island, Alta.	9/21/63	Pittsburgh-Muskegon
MAJOR, Mark	6-3	223	L	Toronto, Ont.	3/20/70	Muskegon
MICHAYLUK, Dave	5-10	189	L	Wakaw, Sask.	5/18/62	Muskegon
MICK, Troy	5-11	192	L	Barnaby, B.C.	3/30/69	Knoxville-Albany
MULLEN, Joe	5-9	180	R	New York, NY	2/26/57	Pittsburgh
MULVENA, Glenn	5-11	187	L	Calgary, Alta.	2/18/67	Muskegon
NEEDHAM, Mike	5-10	185	R	Calgary, Alta.	4/4/70	Muskegon
PATTERSON, Ed	6-2	210	R	Delta, B.C.	11/14/72	Sw. Current-Kam.
PRIESTLAY, Ken	5-10	190	L	Richmond, B.C.	8/24/67	Cdn. Nats-Pit.
PURDY, Brian	6-0	180	L	Kelowna, B.C.	3/30/71	Brandon
RECCHI, Mark	5-10	185	L	Kamloops, B.C.	2/1/68	Pittsburgh
ROHLIK, Steve	6-0	180	L	St. Paul, MN	5/15/68	Did Not Play
SHUTE, Dave	5-11	188	L	Carlisle, PA	2/10/71	Medicine Hat
SMART, Jason	6-4	212	L	Prince George, B.C.	1/23/70	Muskegon-Albany
SMITH, Sandy	5-11	200	R	Brainerd, MN	10/23/67	Muskegon
STEVENS, Kevin	6-3	215	L	Brockton, MA	4/15/65	Pittsburgh
TROTTIER, Bryan	5-11	195	L	Val Marie, Sask.	7/17/56	Pittsburgh
YOUNG, Scott	6-0	190	R	Clinton, MA	10/1/67	Hartford-Pittsburgh

DEFENSEMEN	HT	WT	S	Place of Birth	Date	1990-91 Club
ANDRINGA, Rob	5-10	175	L	Madison, WI	10/26/68	U. of Wisconsin
BRULE, Eric	5-10	200	L	Victoriaville, Que.	1/17/70	Chicoutimi
COFFEY, Paul	6-1	205	L	Weston, Ont.	6/1/61	Pittsburgh
DELORME, Gilbert	6-1	200	R	Boucherville, Que.	11/25/62	Did Not Play
DINEEN, Gord	6-0	195	R	Quebec City, Que.	9/21/62	Pittsburgh-Muskegon
DYCK, Paul	6-1	192	L	Steinbach, Man.	4/15/71	Moose Jaw
JENNINGS, Grant	6-3	200	L	Hudson Bay, Sask.	5/5/65	Hartford-Pittsburgh
LAUS, Paul	6-1	212	R	Beamsville, Ont.	9/26/70	Musk.-Alb.-Knox.
MELANSON, Robert	6-1	202	L	Antigonish, N.S.	3/5/71	Hull
MURPHY, Larry	6-1	210	R	Scarborough, Ont.	3/8/61	Minnesota-Pittsburgh
NELSON, Todd	6-0	201	L	Prince Albert, Sask.	5/11/69	Muskegon
PAEK, Jim	6-1	194	L	Seoul, Korea	4/7/67	Cdn. Nats.-Pit.
PEACOCK, Shane	5-10	198	R	Winterburn, Alta.	7/7/73	Lethbridge
ROBERTS, Gord	6-1	195	L	Detroit, MI	10/2/57	St. L.-Peoria-Pit.
ROCHETTE, Eric	6-2	207	L	Montreal, Que.	7/17/71	Chicoutimi
SAMUELSSON, Ulf	6-1	195	L	Fagersta, Sweden	3/26/64	Hartford-Pittsburgh
STANTON, Paul	6-0	193	R	Boston, MA	6/22/67	Pittsburgh
TAGLIANETTI, Peter	6-2	195	L	Framingham, MA	8/15/63	Minnesota-Pittsburgh

GOALTENDERS	HT	WT	C	Place of Birth	Date	1990-91 Club
BARRASSO, Tom	6-3	212	R	Boston, MA	3/31/65	Pittsburgh
BLISHEN, Don	5-10	180	L	Calgary, Alta.	8/24/71	Brandon
DOPSON, Rob	6-0	200	L	Smith Falls, Ont.	8/21/67	Muskegon
MORRISETTE, Alain	5-9	160	L	Rimouski, Que.	8/26/69	Fredericton
PIETRANGELO, Frank	5-9	185	L	Niagara Falls, Ont.	12/17/64	Pittsburgh
RACINE, Bruce	6-0	178	L	Cornwall, Ont.	8/9/66	Muskegon-Albany
YOUNG, Wendell	5-9	183	L	Halifax, N.S.	8/1/63	Pittsburgh

General Managers' History

Jack Riley, 1967-68 to 1969-70; Leonard "Red" Kelly, 1970-71 to 1971-72; Jack Riley, 1972-73 to 1973-74; Jack Button, 1974-75; Wren A. Blair, 1975-76 to 1976-77; Baz Bastien, 1977-78 to 1982-83; Ed Johnston, 1983-84 to 1987-88; Tony Esposito, 1988-89; Tony Esposito and Craig Patrick, 1989-90; Craig Patrick, 1990-91 to date.

Coaching History

George Sullivan, 1967-68 to 1968-69; Red Kelly, 1969-70 to 1971-72; Red Kelly and Ken Schinkel, 1972-73; Ken Schinkel and Marc Boileau, 1973-74; Marc Boileau, 1974-75; Marc Boileau and Ken Schinkel, 1975-76; Ken Schinkel, 1976-77; John Wilson, 1977-78 to 1979-80; Eddie Johnston, 1980-81 to 1982-83; Lou Angotti, 1983-84; Bob Berry, 1984-85 to 1986-87; Pierre Creamer, 1987-88; Gene Ubriaco, 1988-89; Gene Ubriaco and Craig Patrick, 1989-90. Bob Johnson, 1990-91 to date.

Captains' History

Ab McDonald, 1967-68; no captain, 1968-69 to 1972-73; Ron Schock, 1973-74 to 1976-77; Jean Pronovost, 1977-78; Orest Kindrachuk, 1978-79 to 1980-81; Randy Carlyle, 1981-82 to 1983-84; Mike Bullard, 1984-85, 1985-86; Mike Bullard and Terry Ruskowski, 1986-87; Dan Frawley and Mario Lemieux, 1987-88; Mario Lemieux, 1988-89 to date.

1990-91 Scoring

Regular Season

* rookie

Pos	#	Player	Team	GP	G	A	Pts	+/-	PIM	PP	SH	GW	GT	S	%
R	8	Mark Recchi	PIT	78	40	73	113	0	48	12	0	9	0	184	21.7
D	77	Paul Coffey	PIT	76	24	69	93	18–	128	8	0	3	0	240	10.0
C	9	Ron Francis	HFD	67	21	55	76	2–	51	10	1	6	0	149	14.1
			PIT	14	2	9	11	0	21	0	0	1	0	25	8.0
			TOTAL	81	23	64	87	2–	72	10	1	7	0	174	13.2
L	25	Kevin Stevens	PIT	80	40	46	86	1–	133	18	0	6	2	253	15.8
R	68	*Jaromir Jagr	PIT	80	27	30	57	4–	42	7	0	4	0	136	19.9
C	66	Mario Lemieux	PIT	26	19	26	45	8	30	6	1	2	0	89	21.3
D	55	Larry Murphy	MIN	31	4	11	15	8–	38	1	0	2	0	103	3.9
			PIT	44	5	23	28	2	30	2	0	0	0	85	5.9
			TOTAL	75	9	34	43	6–	68	3	0	2	0	188	4.8
L	12	Bob Errey	PIT	79	20	22	42	11	115	0	1	2	0	131	15.3
R	34	Scott Young	HFD	34	6	9	15	9–	8	3	1	2	0	94	6.4
			PIT	43	11	16	27	3	33	3	1	3	0	116	9.5
			TOTAL	77	17	25	42	6–	41	6	2	5	0	210	8.1
R	7	Joe Mullen	PIT	47	17	22	39	9	6	8	0	2	0	85	20.0
L	29	Phil Bourque	PIT	78	20	14	34	7	106	1	4	0	0	122	16.4
C	19	Bryan Trottier	PIT	52	9	19	28	5	24	0	1	0	0	68	13.2
D	5	Ulf Samuelsson	HFD	62	3	18	21	13	174	0	0	0	0	110	2.7
			PIT	14	1	4	5	4	37	0	0	0	0	15	6.7
			TOTAL	76	4	22	26	17	211	0	0	0	0	125	3.2
C	15	Randy Gilhen	PIT	72	15	10	25	3	51	1	2	1	0	112	13.4
C	38	Jiri Hrdina	CGY	14	0	3	3	4–	4	0	0	0	0	8	.0
			PIT	37	6	14	20	2–	13	1	1	0	0	58	10.3
			TOTAL	51	6	17	23	6–	17	1	1	0	0	66	9.1
D	22	*Paul Stanton	PIT	75	5	18	23	11	40	1	0	1	0	72	6.9
L	24	Troy Loney	PIT	44	7	9	16	10	85	0	0	2	0	51	13.7
D	28	Gordie Roberts	STL	3	0	1	1	1–	8	0	0	0	0	2	.0
			PIT	61	3	12	15	18	70	0	0	0	0	22	13.6
			TOTAL	64	3	13	16	17	78	0	0	0	0	24	12.5
C	10	Barry Pederson	PIT	46	6	8	14	2	21	1	0	1	0	26	23.1
D	32	Peter Taglianetti	MIN	16	0	1	1	0	14	0	0	0	0	15	.0
			PIT	39	3	8	11	16	93	0	0	0	0	25	12.0
			TOTAL	55	3	9	12	16	107	0	0	0	0	40	7.5
D	3	Grant Jennings	HFD	44	1	4	5	13–	82	0	0	0	0	28	3.6
			PIT	13	1	3	4	2	26	0	0	0	0	8	12.5
			TOTAL	57	2	7	9	11–	108	0	0	0	0	36	5.6
G	35	Tom Barrasso	PIT	48	0	5	5	0	40	0	0	0	0	0	.0
D	23	Randy Hillier	PIT	31	2	2	4	3–	32	0	0	0	0	14	14.3
R	20	*Jamie Leach	PIT	7	2	0	2	1–	0	0	0	0	0	8	25.0
R	16	Jay Caufield	PIT	23	1	1	2	2–	71	0	0	1	0	5	20.0
L	18	*Jeff Daniels	PIT	11	0	2	2	0	2	0	0	0	0	6	.0
C	18	Ken Priestlay	PIT	2	0	1	1	0	0	0	0	0	0	2	.0
G	1	Wendell Young	PIT	18	0	1	1	0	0	0	0	0	0	0	.0
G	40	Frank Pietrangelo	PIT	25	0	1	1	0	24	0	0	0	0	0	.0
D	2	*Jim Paek	PIT	3	0	0	0	2	9	0	0	0	0	0	.0
D	5	Gord Dineen	PIT	9	0	0	0	4–	6	0	0	0	0	6	.0

Goaltending

No.	Goaltender	GPI	Mins	Avg	W	L	T	EN	SO	GA	SA	S%
35	Tom Barrasso	48	2754	3.59	27	16	3	2	1	165	1579	.896
40	Frank Pietrangelo	25	1311	3.94	10	11	1	0	0	86	714	.880
1	Wendell Young	18	773	4.04	4	6	2	0	0	52	428	.879
	Totals	**80**	**4843**	**3.78**	**41**	**33**	**6**	**2**	**1**	**305**	**2723**	**.888**

Playoffs

Pos	#	Player	Team	GP	G	A	Pts	+/-	PIM	PP	SH	GW	OT	S	%
C	66	Mario Lemieux	PIT	23	16	28	44	14	16	6	2	0	0	93	17.2
R	8	Mark Recchi	PIT	24	10	24	34	6	33	5	0	2	0	60	16.7
L	25	Kevin Stevens	PIT	24	17	16	33	14	53	7	0	4	1	83	20.5
D	55	Larry Murphy	PIT	23	5	18	23	17	44	4	0	0	0	66	7.6
R	7	Joe Mullen	PIT	22	8	9	17	17	4	1	0	1	0	44	18.2
C	9	Ron Francis	PIT	24	7	10	17	13	24	0	0	4	0	48	14.6
L	29	Phil Bourque	PIT	24	6	7	13	6	16	0	0	0	0	39	15.4
R	68	*Jaromir Jagr	PIT	24	3	10	13	2	6	1	0	1	1	57	5.3
D	77	Paul Coffey	PIT	12	2	9	11	1–	6	0	0	0	0	37	5.4
L	12	Bob Errey	PIT	24	5	2	7	5	29	0	1	0	0	40	12.5
C	19	Bryan Trottier	PIT	23	3	4	7	1–	49	0	0	2	0	16	18.8
R	34	Scott Young	PIT	17	1	6	7	1	2	1	0	0	0	21	4.8
D	5	Ulf Samuelsson	PIT	20	3	2	5	7	34	1	0	1	0	21	14.3
C	38	Jiri Hrdina	PIT	14	2	2	4	1	6	0	0	1	0	7	28.6
L	24	Troy Loney	PIT	24	2	2	4	3–	41	0	0	0	0	38	5.3
D	22	*Paul Stanton	PIT	22	1	2	3	6	24	0	0	0	0	18	5.6
D	28	Gordie Roberts	PIT	24	1	2	3	13	63	0	0	0	0	12	8.3
D	32	Peter Taglianetti	PIT	19	0	3	3	7	49	0	0	0	0	10	.0
D	3	Grant Jennings	PIT	13	1	1	2	3	16	0	0	0	0	9	11.1
D	2	*Jim Paek	PIT	8	1	0	1	2	2	0	0	0	0	8	12.5
C	15	Randy Gilhen	PIT	16	1	0	1	4–	14	0	0	0	0	10	10.0
G	40	Frank Pietrangelo	PIT	5	0	1	1	0	2	0	0	0	0	0	.0
G	35	Tom Barrasso	PIT	20	0	1	1	0	2	0	0	0	0	0	.0
D	23	Randy Hillier	PIT	8	0	0	0	1	24	0	0	0	0	2	.0

Goaltending

No.	Goaltender	GPI	Mins	Avg	W	L	EN	SO	GA	SA	S%
35	Tom Barrasso	20	1175	2.60	12	7	1	1	51	629	.919
40	Frank Pietrangelo	5	288	3.13	4	1	1	1	15	148	.899
	Totals	24	1465	2.78	16	8	2	2	68	779	.913

Retired Numbers

21	Michel Briere	1969-1970

Club Records

Team

(Figures in brackets for season records are games played; records for fewest points, wins, ties, losses, goals, goals against are for 70 or more games)

Most Points	89	1974-75 (80)
Most Wins	41	1990-91 (80)
Most Ties	20	1970-71 (78)
Most Losses	58	1983-84 (80)
Most Goals	347	1988-89 (80)
Most Goals Against	394	1982-83 (80)
Fewest Points	38	1983-84 (80)
Fewest Wins	16	1983-84 (80)
Fewest Ties	5	1984-85 (80)
Fewest Losses	28	1974-75 (80)
Fewest Goals	182	1969-70 (76)
Fewest Goals Against	216	1967-68 (74)

Longest Winning Streak
Over-all ... 7 Oct. 9-Oct. 22/86
Home ... 11 Jan. 5-Mar. 7/91
Away ... 4 Oct. 14-Nov. 2/83; Jan. 16-Jan. 23/88

Longest Undefeated Streak
Over-all ... 11 Feb. 7-28/76 (7 wins, 4 ties)
Home ... 20 Nov. 30/74-Feb. 22/75 (12 wins, 8 ties)
Away ... 7 Mar. 13-27/79 (5 wins, 2 ties)

Longest Losing Streak
Over-all ... 11 Jan. 22/83-Feb. 10/83
Home ... 7 Oct. 8-29/83
Away ... 18 Dec. 23/82-Mar. 4/83

Longest Winless Streak
Over-all ... 18 Jan. 2-Feb. 10/83 (17 losses, 1 tie)
Home ... 11 Oct. 8-Nov. 19/83 (9 losses, 2 ties)

Away ... 18 Oct. 25/70-Jan. 14/71 (11 losses, 7 ties) Dec. 23/82-Mar. 4/83 (18 losses)

Most Shutouts, Season ... 6 1967-68 (74) 1976-77 (80)
Most PIM, Season ... *2,670 1988-89 (80)
Most Goals, Game ... 12 Mar. 15/75 (Wash. 1 at Pit. 12)

Individual

Most Seasons	11	Rick Kehoe
Most Games	753	Jean Pronovost
Most Goals, Career	364	Mario Lemieux
Most Assists, Career	519	Mario Lemieux
Most Points, Career	883	Mario Lemieux (364 goals, 519 assists)
Most PIM, Career	959	Rod Buskas
Most Shutouts, Career	11	Les Binkley

Longest Consecutive Games Streak ... 320 Ron Schock (Oct. 24/73-Apr. 3/77)
Most Goals, Season ... 85 Mario Lemieux (1988-89)
Most Assists, Season ... 114 Mario Lemieux (1988-89)
Most Points, Season ... 199 Mario Lemieux (1988-89)
Most PIM, Season ... 409 Paul Baxter (1981-82)
Most Points, Defenseman, Season ... 113 Paul Coffey (1988-89) (30 goals, 83 assists)
Most Points, Center, Season ... 199 Mario Lemieux (1988-89) (85 goals, 114 assists)
Most Points, Right Wing, Season ... 115 Rob Brown (1988-89) (49 goals, 66 assists)

Most Points, Left Wing, Season ... 86 Kevin Stevens (1990-91) (40 goals, 46 assists)
Most Points, Rookie, Season ... 100 Mario Lemieux (1984-85) (43 goals, 57 assists)
Most Shutouts, Season ... 6 Les Binkley (1967-68)
Most Goals, Game ... 5 Mario Lemieux (Dec. 31/88)
Most Assists, Game ... 6 Ron Stackhouse (Mar. 8/75) Greg Malone (Nov. 28/79) Mario Lemieux (Oct. 15/88)
Most Points, Game ... 8 Mario Lemieux (Oct. 15/88, Dec. 31/88)

* NHL Record.

All-time Record vs. Other Clubs

Regular Season

		At Home							On Road							Total					
	GP	W	L	T	GF	GA	PTS	GP	W	L	T	GF	GA	PTS	GP	W	L	T	GF	GA	PTS
Boston	50	14	26	10	155	201	38	50	6	38	6	139	234	18	100	20	64	16	294	435	56
Buffalo	42	16	14	12	160	151	44	42	6	22	14	112	192	26	84	22	36	26	272	343	70
Calgary	35	16	10	9	129	119	41	34	7	20	7	96	145	21	69	23	30	16	225	264	62
Chicago	48	22	22	4	169	162	48	49	7	33	9	137	207	23	97	29	55	13	306	369	71
Detroit	54	38	13	3	238	152	79	54	10	34	10	152	214	30	108	48	47	13	390	366	109
Edmonton	19	7	11	1	71	93	15	19	3	15	1	67	109	7	38	10	26	2	138	202	22
Hartford	19	9	7	3	83	77	21	19	7	12	0	76	90	14	38	16	19	3	159	167	35
Los Angeles	60	35	17	8	230	189	78	59	14	37	8	152	227	36	119	49	54	16	382	416	114
Minnesota	53	33	15	5	202	142	71	53	18	30	5	181	207	41	106	51	45	10	383	349	112
Montreal	54	16	29	9	159	204	41	54	4	45	5	133	283	13	108	20	74	14	292	487	54
New Jersey	48	29	16	3	210	174	61	46	15	23	8	167	182	38	94	44	39	11	377	356	99
NY Islanders	54	25	19	10	206	184	60	55	14	33	8	170	241	36	109	39	52	18	376	425	96
NY Rangers	69	25	33	11	243	255	61	68	26	35	7	237	285	59	137	51	68	18	480	540	120
Philadelphia	73	28	31	14	231	239	70	75	10	59	6	177	338	26	148	38	90	20	408	577	96
Quebec	19	11	6	2	85	78	24	19	9	10	0	73	87	18	38	20	16	2	158	165	42
St. Louis	53	23	19	11	194	164	57	54	13	36	5	146	213	31	107	36	55	16	340	377	88
Toronto	50	26	19	5	199	167	57	50	17	23	10	169	206	44	100	43	42	15	368	373	101
Vancouver	40	25	8	7	177	136	57	40	17	20	3	153	153	37	80	42	28	10	330	289	94
Washington	55	27	22	6	226	186	60	56	23	29	4	216	250	50	111	50	51	10	442	436	110
Winnipeg	19	13	6	0	83	58	26	19	10	8	1	73	76	21	38	23	14	1	156	134	47
Defunct Club	35	22	6	7	148	93	51	34	13	10	11	108	101	37	69	35	16	18	256	194	88
Totals	949	460	349	140	3598	3224	1060	949	249	572	128	2934	4040	626	1898	709	921	268	6532	7264	1686

Playoffs

	Series	W	L	GP	W	L	T	GF	GA	Last Mtg.	Round	Result
Boston	3	1	2	15	6	9	0	48	55	1991	CF	W 4-2
Buffalo	1	1	0	3	2	1	0	9	9	1979	PR	W 2-1
Chicago	1	0	1	4	0	4	0	8	14	1972	QF	L 0-4
Minnesota	1	1	0	6	4	2	0	28	16	1991	F	W 4-2
New Jersey	1	1	0	7	4	3	0	25	17	1991	DSF	W 4-3
NY Islanders	2	0	2	12	5	7	0	31	43	1982	DSF	L 2-3
NY Rangers	1	1	0	4	4	0	0	19	11	1989	DSF	W 4-0
Philadelphia	1	0	1	7	3	4	0	24	31	1989	DF	L 3-4
St. Louis	3	1	2	13	6	7	0	40	45	1981	PR	L 2-3
Toronto	2	0	2	6	2	4	0	13	21	1977	PR	L 1-2
Washington	1	1	0	5	4	1	0	19	13	1991	DF	W 4-1
Defunct Clubs	1	1	0	4	4	0	0	13	6			
Totals	18	8	10	86	44	42	0	277	281			

Playoff Results 1991-87

Year	Round	Opponent	Result	GF	GA
1991	F	**Minnesota**	**W 4-2**	28	16
	CF	Boston	W 4-2	27	18
	DF	Washington	W 4-1	19	13
	DSF	New Jersey	W 4-3	25	17
1989	DF	Philadelphia	L 3-4	24	31
	DSF	NY Rangers	W 4-0	19	11

Abbreviations: Round: F Final; **CF** conference final; **DF** division final; **DSF** division semi-final; **QF** quarter-final. **PR** preliminary round. **GA** goals against; **GF** goals for.

1990-91 Results

		Home				Away	
Oct.	7	New Jersey	7-4	Oct.	5	Washington	7-4
	16	Philadelphia	1-5		9	St Louis	3-4
	20	NY Rangers	3-4		11	Chicago	1-4
	23	Montreal	4-5		13	NY Islanders	6-4
	25	Quebec	6-3		19	Buffalo	4-4
	28	NY Islanders	8-3		27	New Jersey	5-7
Nov.	3	NY Rangers	3-1		30	Philadelphia	6-2
	6	Calgary	6-5	Nov.	10	Boston	3-3
	8	St Louis	2-3		13	Minnesota	4-1
	21	Philadelphia	4-5		14	Winnipeg	6-4
	24	Washington	3-2		17	Los Angeles	1-2
	27	Edmonton	3-7		23	Washington	3-7
	29	Hartford	4-6	Dec.	1	Minnesota	3-6
Dec.	5	Washington	1-3		3	NY Rangers	9-4
	7	Vancouver	2-2		8	Hartford	1-3
	11	Chicago	1-4		14	Buffalo	4-3
	13	New Jersey	9-5		22	NY Islanders	4-3
	16	Detroit	4-1		26	Washington	7-3
	18	Winnipeg	9-2		29	Toronto	3-6
	20	Minnesota	4-3	Jan.	6	Montreal	3-6
	23	NY Islanders	3-4		15	Philadelphia	4-5
	28	Detroit	5-0		17	Toronto	6-5
	31	St Louis	4-3		26	Quebec	6-5
Jan.	3	NY Rangers	5-7		31	Philadelphia	2-4
	5	New Jersey*	5-2	Feb.	3	Boston	3-6
	8	Edmonton	6-1		8	Winnipeg	2-6
	10	Calgary	5-1		11	Edmonton	5-7
	22	New Jersey	5-3		16	NY Islanders	3-4
	29	Washington	3-2		22	New Jersey	2-5
Feb.	2	Boston*	6-2		24	Washington*	5-5
	14	NY Islanders	5-2		26	Los Angeles	2-8
	19	Buffalo	5-2		27	Vancouver	3-4
	21	Toronto	11-4	Mar.	1	Calgary	2-6
Mar.	5	Vancouver	4-1		9	Hartford	5-2
	7	Los Angeles	3-2		10	NY Islanders	4-3
	12	Montreal	4-4		17	NY Rangers*	4-2
	16	Quebec*	6-3		19	New Jersey	4-5
	21	NY Rangers	5-4		26	Philadelphia	3-1
	23	Chicago*	5-7		27	Detroit	7-4
	30	Philadelphia*	4-4		31	NY Rangers	3-6

* Denotes afternoon game.

Entry Draft
Selections 1991-77

1991
Pick
16 Markus Naslund
38 Rusty Fitzgerald
60 Shane Peacock
82 Joe Tamminen
104 Robert Melanson
126 Brian Clifford
148 Ed Patterson
170 Peter McLaughlin
192 Jeff Lembke
214 Chris Tok
236 Paul Dyck
258 Pasi Huura

1990
Pick
5 Jaromir Jagr
61 Joe Dziedzic
68 Chris Tamer
89 Brian Farrell
107 Ian Moran
110 Denis Casey
130 Mika Valila
131 Ken Plaquin
145 Pat Neaton
152 Petteri Koskimaki
173 Ladislav Karabin
194 Timothy Fingerhut
215 Michael Thompson
236 Brian Bruininks

1989
Pick
16 Jamie Heward
37 Paul Laus
58 John Brill
79 Todd Nelson
100 Tom Nevers
121 Mike Markovich
126 Mike Needham
142 Patrick Schafhauser
163 Dave Shute
184 Andrew Wolf
205 Greg Hagen
226 Scott Farrell
247 Jason Smart

1988
Pick
4 Darrin Shannon
25 Mark Major
62 Daniel Gauthier
67 Mark Recchi
88 Greg Andrusak
130 Troy Mick
151 Jeff Blaeser
172 Rob Gaudreau
193 Donald Pancoe
214 Cory Laylin
235 Darren Stolk

1987
Pick
5 Chris Joseph
26 Richard Tabaracci
47 Jamie Leach
68 Risto Kurkinen
89 Jeff Waver
110 Shawn McEachern
131 Jim Bodden
152 Jiri Kucera
173 Jack MacDougall
194 Daryn McBride
215 Mark Carlson
236 Ake Lilljebjorn

1986
Pick
4 Zarley Zalapski
25 Dave Capuano
46 Brad Aitken
67 Rob Brown
88 Sandy Smith
109 Jeff Daniels
130 Doug Hobson
151 Steve Rohlik
172 Dave McLlwain
193 Kelly Cain
214 Stan Drulia
235 Rob Wilson

1985
Pick
2 Craig Simpson
23 Lee Giffin
58 Bruce Racine
86 Steve Gotaas
107 Kevin Clemens
114 Stuart Marston
128 Steve Titus
149 Paul Stanton
170 Jim Paek
191 Steve Shaunessy
212 Doug Greschuk
233 Gregory Choules

1984
Pick
1 Mario Lemieux
9 Doug Bodger
16 Roger Belanger
64 Mark Teevens
85 Arto Javanainen
127 Tom Ryan
169 John Del Col
189 Steve Hurt
210 Jim Steen
250 Mark Ziliotto

1983
Pick
15 Bob Errey
22 Todd Charlesworth
58 Mike Rowe
63 Frank Pietrangelo
103 Patrick Emond
123 Paul Ames
163 Marty Ketola
183 Alec Haidy
203 Garth Hildebrand
223 Dave Goertz

1982
Pick
10 Rich Sutter
38 Tim Hrynewich
52 Troy Loney
94 Grant Sasser
136 Grant Couture
157 Peter Derkson
178 Greg Gravel
199 Stu Wenaas
220 Chris McCauley
241 Stan Bautch

1981
Pick
28 Steve Gatzos
49 Tom Thornbury
70 Norm Schmidt
109 Paul Edwards
112 Rod Buskas
133 Geoff Wilson
154 Mitch Lamoureaux
175 Dean Defazio
196 David Hannan

1980
Pick
9 Mike Bullard
51 Randy Boyd
72 Tony Feltrin
93 Doug Shedden
114 Pat Graham
156 Robert Geale
177 Brian Lundberg
198 Steve McKenzie

1979
Pick
31 Paul Marshall
52 Bennett Wolf
73 Brian Cross
94 Nick Ricci
115 Marc Chorney

1978
Pick
25 Mike Meeker
61 Shane Pearsall
75 Rob Garner

1977
Pick
30 Jim Hamilton
48 Kim Davis
66 Mark Johnson
102 Greg Millen

Club Directory

Civic Arena
Pittsburgh, PA 15219
Phone **412/642-1800**
FAX 412/261-0382
ENVOY ID
Front Office: PENS. GM.
Public
Relations   PENS. PR
Capacity: 16,164

Chairman of the Board	Edward J. DeBartolo, Sr.
President	Marie Denise DeBartolo York
Secretary & Treasurer	Anthony W. Liberati
Vice-President & General Counsel	Paul Martha
General Manager	Craig Patrick
Director of Player Development & Recruitment	Scott Bowman
Head Coach	Bob Johnson
Assistant Coaches	Rick Kehoe, Rick Paterson, Barry Smith
Trainer	Skip Thayer
Conditioning Coach	John Welday
Equipment Manager	Steve Latin
Scouts	Greg Malone, Les Binkley, John Gill, Charlie Hodge, Ralph Cox, Pierre Maguire, Gilles Meloche
Vice President, Communications & Sales	Bill Strong
Vice President, Marketing	Tinsy Labrie
Business Manager	Ed Walter
Vice President, Building Operations	Jimmy Sacco
Purchasing Agent	Dana Backstrom
Director of Press Relations	Cindy Himes
Assistant Director of Press Relations	Harry Sanders
Director of Ticket Sales	Jeff Mercer
Box Office Manager	Carol Coulson
Team Physician	Dr. Charles Burke
Team Dentists	Dr. Ronald Linaburg, Dr. Raymond Rainka, Dr. David Donatelli
Executive Office	Civic Arena, Gate 2
Location of Press Box	East Side of Building
Dimensions of Rink	200 feet by 85 feet
Club Colors	Black, Gold and White
Club Trains at	Pittsburgh, PA
Radio Station	KDKA (1020 AM)
Television Station	KDKA-TV (Channel 2)
Cable	KBL Sports Network
Play-by-Play Announcer	Mike Lange
Color Commentator	Paul Steigerwald

General Manager

PATRICK, CRAIG
General Manger, Pittsburgh Penguins. Born in Detroit, MI, May 20, 1946.

Craig Patrick is the latest member of hockey's royal family to have his name inscribed on the Stanley Cup. Appointed general manager of the Penguins on December 5, 1989, Patrick laid the groundwork for Pittsburgh's successful Stanley Cup march through shrewd acquisitions and drafts; his trade for Ulf Samuelsson and Ron Francis, his signing of free agent Bryan Trottier and the drafting of Jaromir Jagr are all moves considered crucial to Pittsburgh's Stanley Cup win. Patrick also hired Coach Bob Johnson, who piloted the Penguins during last season's championship run.

A 1969 graduate of the University of Denver, Patrick was captain of the Pioneers' NCAA Championship hockey team that year. He returned to his alma mater in 1986 where he served as director of athletics and recreation for two years. Patrick served as administrative assistant to the president of the Amateur Hockey Association of the United States in 1980 and as an assistant coach/assistant general manager for the 1980 gold-medal winning U.S. Olympic hockey team. Before pursuing a coaching career, Patrick played professional hockey with Washington, Kansas City, St. Louis, Minnesota and California from 1971-79. In eight seasons, Patrick tallied 163 points (72-91-163) in 401 games.

NHL Coaching Record

Season	Team	Games	Regular Season				Games	Playoffs			
			W	L	T	%		W	L		%
1980-81	NY Rangers (NHL)	59	26	23	10	.525	14	7	7		.500
1984-85	NY Rangers (NHL)	35	11	22	2	.343	3	0	3		.000
1989-90	Pittsburgh (NHL)	54	22	26	6	.463	....	....	....		....
	NHL Totals	148	59	71	18	.459	17	10	7		.412

Coach

JOHNSON, BOB
Coach, Pittsburgh Penguins. Born in Minneapolis, MN, March 4, 1931.

In his first season as head coach for the Pittsburgh Penguins, Bob Johnson led the team to a Stanley Cup title. Johnson took over head coaching duties for the Penguins on June 12, 1990 after spending the past three years as Executive Director of USA Hockey in Colorado. Johnson began his coaching career in 1956 at Warroad High School in Minnesota before advancing to the college level with Colorado College in 1963. He was appointed the first hockey coach at the University of Wisconsin where he compiled a 367-175-23 record through 15 seasons. He led the Badgers to three NCAA Championships in 1973, 1977 and 1981 and earned NCAA Coach of the Year honors in 1977. Johnson coached the U.S. National Team in 1973, 1974, 1975 and 1981. He moved to the NHL ranks in 1982 where he served as the head coach of the Calgary Flames for five seasons, leading that team to its first Campbell Conference Championship in 1986 and a berth in the Stanley Cup Finals.

Coaching Record

Season	Team	Games	Regular Season				%	Games	Playoffs		%
			W	L	T				W	L	
1966-67	U. Wisconsin (WCHA)	26	16	10	0		.615	....	....	....	....
1967-68	U. Wisconsin (WCHA)	31	21	10	0		.677	....	....	....	....
1968-69	U. Wisconsin (WCHA)	34	22	10	2		.676	....	....	....	....
1969-70	U. Wisconsin (WCHA)	34	23	11	0		.676	....	....	....	....
1970-71	U. Wisconsin (WCHA)	34	20	13	1		.603	....	....	....	....
1971-72	U. Wisconsin (WCHA)	38	27	10	1		.724	....	....	....	....
1972-73	U. Wisconsin (WCHA)	40	29	9	2		.750	....	....	....	....
1973-74	U. Wisconsin (WCHA)	36	18	13	5		.569	....	....	....	....
1974-75	U. Wisconsin (WCHA)	38	24	12	2		.658	....	....	....	....
1976-77	U. Wisconsin (WCHA)	45	37	7	1		.833	....	....	....	....
1977-78	U. Wisconsin (WCHA)	43	28	12	3		.686	....	....	....	....
1978-79	U. Wisconsin (WCHA)	40	24	13	3		.638	....	....	....	....
1979-80	U. Wisconsin (WCHA)	36	15	20	1		.431	....	....	....	....
1980-81	U. Wisconsin (WCHA)	42	27	14	1		.655	....	....	....	....
1981-82	U. Wisconsin (WCHA)	47	35	11	1		.755	....	....	....	....
1982-83	Calgary (NHL)	80	32	34	14		.487	9	4	5	.444
1983-84	Calgary (NHL)	80	34	32	14		.512	11	6	5	.545
1984-85	Calgary (NHL)	80	41	27	12		.587	4	1	3	.250
1985-86	Calgary (NHL)	80	40	31	9		.556	22	12	10	.545
1986-87	Calgary (NHL)	80	46	31	3		.594	6	2	4	.333
1990-91	Pittsburgh (NHL)	80	41	33	6		.550	24	16	8	.666
	NHL Totals	480	234	188	58		.548	76	41	35	.540

Quebec Nordiques

1990-91 Results: 16w-50L-14T 46PTS. Fifth, Adams Division

Year-by-Year Record

		Home			Road			Overall							
Season	GP	W	L	T	W	L	T	W	L	T	GF	GA	Pts.	Finished	Playoff Result
1990-91	80	9	23	8	7	27	6	16	50	14	236	354	46	5th, Adams Div.	Out of Playoffs
1989-90	80	8	26	6	4	35	1	12	61	7	240	407	31	5th, Adams Div.	Out of Playoffs
1988-89	80	16	20	4	11	26	3	27	46	7	269	342	61	5th, Adams Div.	Out of Playoffs
1987-88	80	15	23	2	17	20	3	32	43	5	271	306	69	5th, Adams Div.	Out of Playoffs
1986-87	80	20	13	7	11	26	3	31	39	10	267	276	72	4th, Adams Div.	Lost Div. Final
1985-86	80	23	13	4	20	18	2	43	31	6	330	289	92	1st, Adams Div.	Lost Div. Semi-Final
1984-85	80	24	12	4	17	18	5	41	30	9	323	275	91	2nd, Adams Div.	Lost Conf. Championship
1983-84	80	24	11	5	18	17	5	42	28	10	360	278	94	3th, Adams Div.	Lost Div. Final
1982-83	80	23	10	7	11	24	5	34	34	12	343	336	80	4th, Adams Div.	Lost Div. Semi-Final
1981-82	80	24	13	3	9	18	13	33	31	16	356	345	82	4th, Adams Div.	Lost Conf. Championship
1980-81	80	18	11	11	12	21	7	30	32	18	314	318	78	4th, Adams Div.	Lost Prelim. Round
1979-80	80	17	16	7	8	28	4	25	44	11	248	313	61	5th, Adams Div.	Out of Playoffs

Schedule

	Home			Away	
Oct.	Sat. 5 Hartford		Oct.	Tues. 8 New Jersey	
	Sat. 12 Buffalo			Thur. 10 Minnesota	
	Sun. 13 NY Islanders			Thur. 17 Philadelphia	
	Sat. 19 Detroit			Wed. 23 Montreal	
	Thur. 24 Montreal			Thur. 31 NY Rangers	
	Sat. 26 NY Rangers		Nov.	Thur. 7 Chicago	
	Tues. 29 Winnipeg			Tues. 12 Hartford	
Nov.	Sat. 2 San Jose			Thur. 14 Boston	
	Sun. 10 Washington*			Sat. 23 Montreal	
	Sat. 16 Edmonton			Wed. 27 Buffalo	
	Mon. 18 Pittsburgh			Thur. 28 St Louis	
	Thur. 21 Montreal		Dec.	Thur. 5 Boston	
	Mon. 25 Hartford			Thur. 12 Detroit	
	Sat. 30 Buffalo			Tues. 17 Washington	
Dec.	Tues. 3 Vancouver			Thur. 19 Calgary	
	Sat. 7 Los Angeles			Sat. 21 San Jose	
	Tues. 10 Boston			Sun. 22 Vancouver	
	Sat. 14 St Louis		Jan.	Thur. 2 Hartford	
	Thur. 26 Montreal			Sat. 4 NY Islanders	
	Sat. 28 Hartford			Wed. 8 Buffalo	
	Mon. 30 Toronto			Thur. 9 Boston	
Jan.	Sat. 11 NY Rangers			Thur. 23 Chicago	
	Tues. 14 Calgary			Wed. 29 Toronto	
	Tues. 21 Vancouver			Fri. 31 Winnipeg	
	Sat. 25 Winnipeg*		Feb.	Sun. 2 Edmonton*	
	Tues. 28 Boston			Wed. 5 Calgary	
Feb.	Sat. 8 Philadelphia*			Thur. 13 Philadelphia	
	Sun. 9 New Jersey*			Sat. 15 Montreal	
	Tues. 11 Washington			Thur. 20 Pittsburgh	
	Tues. 18 Minnesota			Sat. 22 Hartford*	
Mar.	Tues. 3 Buffalo			Sun. 23 Montreal	
	Sat. 7 Detroit			Wed. 26 San Jose	
	Mon. 9 Hartford			Thur. 27 Los Angeles	
	Wed. 11 Montreal		Mar.	Thur. 5 Hartford	
	Sat. 14 Boston			Sun. 15 Buffalo	
	Sat. 21 Minnesota			Tues. 17 Toronto	
	Tues. 24 NY Islanders			Thur. 19 Pittsburgh	
	Thur. 26 Chicago			Sat. 28 New Jersey*	
	Tues. 31 Boston		Apr.	Thur. 2 Boston	
Apr.	Sat. 4 Buffalo			Sun. 5 Buffalo	

* Denotes afternoon game.

Home Starting Times:
All Games .... 7:35 p.m.
Except Matinees .... 2:05 p.m.

Franchise date: June 22, 1979

13th NHL Season

Mats Sundin led all Nordique rookies in scoring, compiling 59 points in 80 games.

1991-92 Player Personnel

FORWARDS	HT	WT	Place of Birth	Date	1990-91 Club
ANDERSON, Niclas	5-9	175	Kungalv, Sweden	5/20/71	Frolunda
BAKER, Jamie	6-0	190	Ottawa, Ont.	8/31/66	Québec-Halifax
CHARBONNEAU, Stéphane	195		Ste-Adèle, Qué.	6/27/70	Chicoutimi-Shawinigan
	6-2				
CHASSÉ, Denis	6-2	190	Montréal, Qué.	2/7/70	Drummondville
COOK, Brian	6-2	205	Waterloo, IA	1/2/67	St. Cloud State
DORE, Daniel	6-3	202	Ferme-Neuve, Qué.	4/9/70	Québec-Halifax
FORTIER, Marc	6-0	192	Windsor, Qué.	2/26/66	Québec-Halifax
HOUGH, Mike	6-1	192	Montréal, Qué.	2/6/63	Québec
IHNACAK, Miroslav	5-11	175	Poprad, Czech.	11/19/62	Halifax
JACKSON, Jeff	6-1	195	Dresden, Ont.	4/24/65	Québec-Halifax
KAMENSKY, Valeri	6-2	198	Voskresensk, USSR	4/18/66	Central Red Army
KAMINSKI, Kevin	5-9	170	Churchbridge, Sask.	3/13/69	Halifax-Ft. Wayne
LAPOINTE, Claude	5-9	173	Lachine, Qué.	10/11/68	Québec-Halifax
McRAE, Ken	6-1	195	Winchester, Ont.	4/23/68	Québec-Halifax
MAJOR, Bruce	6-3	180	Vernon, B.C.	1/3/67	Hfx.-Qué.-Ft. Wayne
McGILL, Ryan	6-2	195	Sherwood Park, Alta.	2/28/69	Hfx.-Indianapolis
MILLER, Kip	5-10	160	Lansing, MI	6/11/69	Québec-Halifax
MORIN, Stephane	6-0	175	Montréal, Qué.	3/27/69	Québec-Halifax
NOLAN, Owen	6-1	194	Belfast, Ireland	2/12/72	Québec-Halifax
NOREN, Darryl	5-10	180	Livonia, MI	8/7/68	Albany-Greensboro
PASLAWSKI, Greg	5-11	190	Kindersley, Sask.	8/25/61	Buffalo-Winnipeg
PEARSON, Scott	6-1	205	Cornwall, Ont.	12/19/69	Qué.-Tor.-Hfx.
RAGLAN, Herb	6-0	205	Peterborough, Ont.	8/5/67	Québec-St. Louis
REIMER, Robert	5-11	190	Swift Current, Sask.	2/11/70	Moose Jaw
ROBERGE, Serge	6-1	195	Quebec, Que.	3/31/65	Québec-Halifax
SAKIC, Joe	5-11	185	Burnaby, B.C.	7/7/69	Québec
SANIPASS, Everett	6-2	204	Big Cove, N.B.	2/13/68	Québec-Halifax
SMAIL, Doug	5-9	175	Moose Jaw, Sask.	9/2/57	Wpg.-Minnesota
STIENBURG, Trevor	6-1	200	Kingston, Ont.	5/13/66	Halifax
SUNDIN, Mats	6-2	190	Stockholm, Swe.	2/13/71	Québec
TWIST, Tony	6-1	212	Sherwood Park, Sask.	5/9/68	Québec-Peoria
VAN DORP, Wayne	6-4	225	Vancouver, B.C.	5/19/61	Québec
VERMETTE, Mark	6-1	203	Cochenour, Ont.	10/3/67	Québec-Halifax
WARD, Ed	6-3	190	Edmonton, Alta.	11/10/69	N. Michigan U.
ZAVISHA, Brad	6-2	195	Hines Creek, Alta.	1/4/72	Portland-Seattle

DEFENSEMEN					
ANDERSON, Shawn	6-1	200	Montréal, Qué.	2/7/68	Québec-Halifax
BZDEL, Gérald	6-1	196	Wynyard, Sask.	3/13/68	Halifax
DAVIS, Scott	6-0	188	Winnipeg, Man.	5/25/71	Seattle
DOYON, Mario	6-0	174	Québec, Qué.	8/27/68	Québec-Halifax
DUBOIS, Eric	6-0	193	Montréal, Qué.	5/9/70	Laval
ESPE, David	6-0	185	St. Paul, MI	11/3/66	Halifax
FINN, Steven	6-0	198	Laval, Qué.	8/20/66	Québec
FOGARTY, Brian	6-2	198	Brantford, Ont.	6/11/69	Québec-Halifax
FOOTE, Adam	6-1	180	Toronto, Ont.	7/10/71	Sault Ste. Marie
GUSAROV, Alexei	6-2	170	Leningrad, USSR	7/8/64	Québec-Halifax-CSKA
KLEMM, Jon	6-3	200	Cranbrook, B.C.	1/8/70	Spokane
LAMBERT, Dan	5-8	177	St. Boniface, Man.	1/12/70	Qué.-Hfx.-Ft. Wayne
LESCHYSHYN, Curtis	6-1	205	Thompson, Man.	9/21/69	Québec
MARCINYSHYN, David	6-3	210	Edmonton, Alta.	2/4/67	N.J.-Utica
McNEILL, Mike	6-1	175	Winona, MN	7/22/66	Que.-Chi.-Indy
RYMSHA, Andy	6-3	210	St. Catharines, Ont.	12/10/68	Halifax-Peoria
SMYTH, Greg	6-3	212	Oakville, Ont.	4/23/66	Québec-Halifax
SPROTT, Jim	6-1	200	Oakville, Ont.	4/11/69	Halifax-Peoria
TATARINOV, Mikhail	5-10	194	Irkutsk, USSR	7/16/66	Wsh.-Moscow Dynamo
VELISCHEK, Randy	6-0	200	Montréal, Qué.	2/10/62	Québec
WOLANIN, Craig	6-3	205	Grosse Pointe, MI	7/27/67	Québec

GOALTENDERS	HT	WT	Place of Birth	Date	1990-91 Club
CLOUTIER, Jacques	5-7	168	Noranda, Qué.	1/3/60	Québec-Chicago
FISET, Stephane	6-0	175	Montréal, Qué.	6/17/70	Québec-Halifax
GORDON, Scott	5-10	175	Brockton, MA	2/6/63	Québec-Halifax
TANNER, John	6-3	182	Cambridge, Ont.	3/17/71	Qué.-Sud.-Lon.
TUGNUTT, Ron	5-11	155	Scarborough, Ont.	10/22/67	Québec-Halifax

General Managers' History

Maurice Filion, 1979-80 to 1987-88; Martin Madden 1988-89; Martin Madden and Maurice Filion, 1989-90; Pierre Page, 1990-91 to date.

Coaching History

Jacques Demers, 1979-80; Maurice Filion and Michel Bergeron, 1980-81; Michel Bergeron, 1981-82 to 1986-87; Andre Savard and Ron Lapointe, 1987-88; Ron Lapointe, and Jean Perron, 1988-89; Michel Bergeron, 1989-90; Dave Chambers, 1990-91 to date.

Captains' History

Marc Tardif, 1979-80, 1980-81; Robbie Ftorek and Andre Dupont, 1981-82; Mario Marois, 1982-83 to 1984-85; Mario Marois, Peter Stastny, 1985-86; Peter Stastny, 1986-87 to 1989-90; Joe Sakic and Steven Finn, 1990-91 to date.

Retired Numbers

3	J.C. Tremblay	1972-1979
8	Marc Tardif	1979-1983

1990-91 Scoring

Regular Season

* rookie

Pos	#	Player	Team	GP	G	A	Pts	+/-	PIM	PP	SH	GW	GT	S	%
C	19	Joe Sakic	QUE	80	48	61	109	26 —	24	12	3	7	1	245	19.6
R	13	*Mats Sundin	QUE	80	23	36	59	24 —	58	4	0	1	155		14.8
C	40	Tony Hrkac	QUE	70	16	32	48	22 —	16	6	0	0	122		13.1
C	25	*Stephane Morin	QUE	48	13	27	40	6	30	3	1	2	0	63	20.6
R	18	Mike Hough	QUE	63	13	20	33	7 —	111	3	1	1	0	106	12.3
D	43	Bryan Fogarty	QUE	45	9	22	31	11 —	24	3	0	2	0	107	8.4
R	10	Guy Lafleur	QUE	59	12	16	28	10 —	2	3	0	0	0	90	13.3
D	29	Steven Finn	QUE	71	6	13	19	26 —	228	0	0	1	0	91	6.6
D	6	Craig Wolanin	QUE	80	5	13	18	13 —	89	0	1	0	0	109	4.6
L	22	Scott Pearson	TOR	12	0	0	0	5 —	20	0	0	0	0	13	.0
			QUE	35	11	4	15	4 —	86	0	0	0	0	61	18.0
			TOTAL	47	11	4	15	9 —	106	0	0	0	0	74	14.9
D	37	Shawn Anderson	QUE	31	3	10	13	2	21	2	0	0	0	44	6.8
R	11	*Owen Nolan	QUE	59	3	10	13	19 —	109	0	0	0	0	54	5.6
D	5	Alexei Gusarov	QUE	36	3	9	12	4 —	12	1	0	0	0	36	8.3
D	27	Randy Velischek	QUE	79	2	10	12	19 —	42	0	0	0	0	47	4.3
C	20	*Mike McNeill	CHI	23	2	2	4	1 —	6	0	1	0	0	20	10.0
			QUE	14	2	5	7	5	4	1	0	0	0	11	18.2
			TOTAL	37	4	7	11	4	10	1	1	0	0	31	12.9
L	21	Everett Sanipass	QUE	29	5	5	10	15 —	41	1	0	0	0	38	13.2
R	14	Herb Raglan	STL	32	3	6	4	5	52	0	0	1	0	29	10.3
			QUE	15	1	3	4	1	30	0	0	0	0	19	5.3
			TOTAL	47	4	6	10	5	82	0	0	1	0	48	8.3
D	7	Curtis Leschyshyn	QUE	55	3	7	10	19 —	49	2	0	1	0	57	5.3
C	49	*Kip Miller	QUE	13	4	2	6	1 —	7	0	0	1	1	16	25.0
R	36	Ken Quinney	QUE	19	3	4	7	2 —	2	1	0	0	0	19	15.8
R	45	Mark Vermette	QUE	34	3	4	7	15 —	10	0	0	0	0	42	7.1
L	32	Jeff Jackson	QUE	10	3	1	4	3 —	4	0	0	0	0	13	23.1
C	47	*Claude Lapointe	QUE	13	2	2	4	3	4	0	0	0	0	7	28.6
C	9	Marc Fortier	QUE	14	0	4	4	3 —	6	0	0	0	0	13	.0
C	28	*Jamie Baker	QUE	18	2	0	2	4 —	8	0	1	0	1	18	11.1
L	5	Wayne Van Dorp	QUE	4	1	0	1	1	30	0	0	0	0	2	50.0
L	17	Dan Vincelette	QUE	16	0	1	1	10 —	38	0	0	0	0	16	.0
R	33	*Daniel Dore	QUE	1	0	0	0	1	0	0	0	0	0	0	.0
L	38	Dave Latta	QUE	1	0	0	0	0	0	0	0	0	0	1	.0
D	2	Greg Smyth	QUE	1	0	0	0	0	0	0	0	0	0	0	.0
D	50	Dan Lambert	QUE	1	0	0	0	0	0	0	0	0	0	0	.0
G	31	*Stephane Fiset	QUE	3	0	0	0		0	0	0	0	0	0	.0
L	42	Bruce Major	QUE	4	0	0	0	1 —	0	0	0	0	0	0	.0
G	34	*John Tanner	QUE	6	0	0	0		2	0	0	0	0	0	.0
R	39	Serge Roberge	QUE	9	0	0	0		24	0	0	0	0	0	.0
D	58	*Mario Doyon	QUE	12	0	0	0	3 —	4	0	0	0	0	12	.0
C	12	Ken McRae	QUE	12	0	0	0	7 —	36	0	0	0	0	6	.0
G	30	*Scott Gordon	QUE	13	0	0	0		0	0	0	0	0	0	.0
D	15	Tony Twist	QUE	24	0	0	0	4 —	104	0	0	0	0	2	.0
G	32	Jacques Cloutier	CHI	10	0	0	0		0	0	0	0	0	0	.0
			QUE	15	0	0	0		0	0	0	0	0	0	.0
			TOTAL	25	0	0	0		0	0	0	0	0	0	.0
G	1	Ron Tugnutt	QUE	56	0	0	0		0	0	0	0	0	0	.0

Goaltending

No.	Goaltender	GPI	Mins	Avg	W	L	T	EN	SO	GA	SA	S%
31	*Stephane Fiset	3	186	3.87	0	2	1	0	0	12	123	.902
1	Ron Tugnutt	56	3144	4.05	12	29	10	3	0	212	1851	.885
34	*John Tanner	6	228	4.21	1	3	1	0	0	16	133	.880
32	Jacques Cloutier	15	829	4.41	3	8	2	0	0	61	526	.884
30	*Scott Gordon	13	485	5.94	0	8	0	2	0	48	225	.787
	Totals	**80**	**4883**	**4.35**	**16**	**50**	**14**	**5**	**0**	**354**	**2863**	**.876**

Scott Pearson, a hard-working two-way winger, was acquired from Toronto in mid-season.

Club Records

Team

(Figures in brackets for season records are games played; records for fewest points, wins, ties, losses, goals, goals against are for 70 or more games)

Most Points	94	1983-84 (80)
Most Wins	43	1985-86 (80)
Most Ties	18	1980-81 (80)
Most Losses	61	1989-90 (80)
Most Goals	360	1983-84 (80)
Most Goals Against	407	1989-90 (80)
Fewest Points	31	1989-90 (80)
Fewest Wins	12	1989-90 (80)
Fewest Ties	5	1987-88 (80)
Fewest Losses	28	1983-84 (80)
Fewest Goals	236	1990-91 (80)
Fewest Goals Against	275	1984-85 (80)

Longest Winning Streak
Over-all 7   Nov. 24-
Dec. 10/83
Oct. 10-21/85
Dec. 31/85-
Jan. 11/86
Home 10   Nov. 26/83-
Jan. 10/84
Away 5   Feb. 28-
Mar. 24, 1986

Longest Undefeated Streak
Over-all 11   Mar. 10-31/81
(7 wins, 4 ties)
Home 14   Nov. 19/83
Jan. 21/84
(11 wins, 3 ties)
Away 8   Feb. 17/81-
Mar. 22/81
(6 wins, 2 ties)

Longest Losing Streak
Over-all 14   Oct. 21-
Nov. 19/90
Home 8   Oct. 21-
Nov. 24/90
Away 18   Jan. 18-
Apr. 1/90

Longest Winless Streak
Over-all 17   Oct. 21-
Nov. 25/90
(15 losses, 2 ties)
Home 11   Nov. 14-
Dec. 26/89
(7 losses, 4 ties)

Away 18   Jan. 18-
Apr. 1/90
(18 losses)
Most Shutouts, Season 6   1985-86 (80)
Most PIM, Season 2,104   1989-90 (80)
Most Goals, Game 12   Feb. 1/83
(Hfd. 3 at Que. 12)
Oct. 20/84
(Que. 12 at Tor. 3)

Individual

Most Seasons	11	Michel Goulet
Most Games	813	Michel Goulet
Most Goals, Career	456	Michel Goulet
Most Assists, Career	668	Peter Stastny
Most Points, Career	1,048	Peter Stastny (380 goals, 668 assists)
Most PIM, Career	1,545	Dale Hunter
Most Shutouts, Career	6	Mario Gosselin

**Longest Consecutive
Games Streak** 312   Dale Hunter
(Oct. 9/80-Mar. 13/84)
Most Goals, Season 57   Michel Goulet
(1982-83)
Most Assists, Season 93   Peter Stastny
(1981-82)
Most Points, Season 139   Peter Stastny
(1981-82)
(46 goals, 93 assists)
Most PIM, Season 301   Gord Donnelly
(1987-88)

**Most Points, Defenseman,
Season** 68   Jeff Brown
(1988-89)
(21 goals, 47 assists)

**Most Points, Center,
Season** 139   Peter Stastny
(1981-82)
(46 goals, 93 assists)

**Most Points, Right Wing,
Season** 103   Jacques Richard
(1980-81)
(52 goals, 51 assists)

**Most Points, Left Wing,
Season** .... *121   Michel Goulet
(1983-84)
(56 goals, 65 assists)

**Most Points, Rookie,
Season** .... *109   Peter Stastny
(1980-81)
(39 goals, 70 assists)
Most Shutouts, Season 4   Clint Malarchuk
(1985-86)
Most Goals, Game 4   Michel Goulet
(Dec. 14/85;
Mar. 17/86)
Peter Stastny
(Feb. 22/81;
Feb. 11/89)
Most Assists, Game 5   Anton Stastny
(Feb. 22/81)
Michel Goulet
(Jan. 3/84)
Most Points, Game 8   Peter Stastny
(Feb. 22/81)
Anton Stastny
(Feb. 22/81)

* NHL Record.

All-time Record vs. Other Clubs

Regular Season

		At Home							On Road							Total					
	GP	W	L	T	GF	GA	PTS	GP	W	L	T	GF	GA	PTS	GP	W	L	T	GF	GA	PTS
Boston	44	15	25	4	169	200	34	44	15	23	6	142	182	36	88	30	48	10	311	382	70
Buffalo	44	22	15	7	166	135	51	44	12	26	6	145	183	30	88	34	41	13	311	318	81
Calgary	19	7	8	4	81	76	18	19	4	11	4	60	88	12	38	11	19	8	141	164	30
Chicago	19	8	7	4	81	76	20	19	7	11	1	65	80	15	38	15	18	5	146	156	35
Detroit	19	12	5	2	86	64	26	19	7	11	1	68	80	15	38	19	16	3	154	144	41
Edmonton	19	6	11	2	77	93	14	19	4	15	0	57	109	8	38	10	26	2	134	202	22
Hartford	44	24	13	7	195	147	55	44	16	18	10	155	155	42	88	40	31	17	350	302	97
Los Angeles	19	7	9	3	76	78	17	19	7	11	1	69	89	15	38	14	20	4	145	167	32
Minnesota	19	13	4	2	92	51	28	19	6	11	2	62	76	14	38	19	15	4	154	127	42
Montreal	44	23	19	2	158	156	48	44	8	30	6	130	199	22	88	31	49	8	288	355	70
New Jersey	19	11	6	2	87	64	24	19	9	9	1	71	85	19	38	20	15	3	158	149	43
NY Islanders	19	9	9	1	74	67	19	19	6	12	1	69	88	13	38	15	21	2	143	155	32
NY Rangers	19	10	6	3	85	81	23	19	3	13	3	47	82	9	38	13	19	6	132	163	32
Philadelphia	19	5	7	7	66	72	17	19	2	15	2	48	82	6	38	7	22	9	114	154	23
Pittsburgh	19	10	9	0	87	73	20	19	6	11	2	78	85	14	38	16	20	2	165	158	34
St. Louis	19	9	7	3	69	64	21	19	3	15	1	63	92	7	38	12	22	4	132	156	28
Toronto	19	9	5	5	78	67	23	19	9	8	2	86	65	20	38	18	13	7	164	132	43
Vancouver	19	9	6	4	57	57	18	19	7	10	2	76	80	16	38	16	16	6	133	137	34
Washington	19	7	8	4	62	71	18	19	8	9	2	76	81	18	38	15	17	6	132	152	36
Winnipeg	19	7	10	2	76	85	16	19	6	9	4	74	81	16	38	13	19	6	150	166	32
Totals	**480**	**221**	**191**	**68**	**1922**	**1777**	**510**	**480**	**145**	**278**	**57**	**1635**	**2062**	**347**	**960**	**366**	**469**	**125**	**3557**	**3839**	**857**

Playoffs

	Series	W	L	GP	W	L	T	GF	GA	Last Mtg.	Round	Result
Boston	2	1	1	11	5	6	0	36	37	1983	DSF	L 1-3
Buffalo	2	2	0	8	6	2	0	35	27	1985	DSF	W 3-2
Hartford	2	1	1	9	4	5	0	34	35	1987	DSF	W 4-2
Montreal	4	2	2	25	12	13	0	69	86	1987	DF	L 3-4
NY Islanders	1	0	1	4	0	4	0	9	18	1982	CF	L 0-4
Philadelphia	2	0	2	11	4	7	0	29	39	1985	CF	L 2-4
Totals	**13**	**6**	**7**	**68**	**31**	**37**	**0**	**212**	**242**			

Playoff Results 1991-87

Year	Round	Opponent	Result	GF	GA
1987	DF	Montreal	L 3-4	21	26
	DSF	Hartford	W 4-2	27	19

Abbreviations: Round: F Final; **CF** conference final; **DF** division final; **DSF** division semi-final; **GA** goals against; **GF** goals for.

1990-91 Results

		Home					Away	
Oct.	7	Boston	2-5	**Oct.**	4	Hartford	3-3
	13	Buffalo	4-4		6	Boston	1-7
	16	Hartford	1-1		10	Toronto	8-5
	20	Detroit*	5-3		12	Buffalo	4-2
	21	Vancouver*	2-3		18	Philadelphia	4-5
	27	NY Rangers	1-4		25	Pittsburgh	3-6
Nov.	3	Minnesota	0-2		29	NY Rangers	0-5
	6	Washington	1-4	**Nov.**	1	Chicago	2-6
	10	Philadelphia	2-5		8	Minnesota	2-3
	17	Chicago	2-7		11	Montreal	4-5
	19	Montreal	2-5		13	St Louis	2-4
	24	Winnipeg	4-11		15	Boston	0-6
	25	Los Angeles	4-4		21	Hartford	4-4
Dec.	1	Buffalo	4-2		28	Hartford	4-3
	2	Calgary	5-5	**Dec.**	5	Edmonton	2-3
	15	NY Islanders	2-7		7	Calgary	5-3
	18	Montreal	6-4		10	Vancouver	3-2
	22	New Jersey	1-4		13	Detroit	2-5
	26	Hartford	1-4		19	Montreal	1-1
	29	Washington	4-3		23	Buffalo	3-10
Jan.	8	Boston	4-2		31	NY Islanders*	3-6
	12	St Louis	4-4	**Jan.**	3	St Louis	7-8
	13	NY Islanders	3-4		5	Montreal	0-3
	22	Toronto	4-4		10	Boston	3-5
	26	Pittsburgh	5-6		17	Philadelphia	1-5
	29	Winnipeg	2-5		24	New Jersey	1-6
Feb.	2	Minnesota	4-6		31	Buffalo	4-1
	7	Montreal	1-5	**Feb.**	14	Chicago	1-2
	9	New Jersey*	3-1		17	Winnipeg*	0-6
	10	Boston*	4-7		18	Vancouver	3-3
	12	Buffalo	4-4		20	Los Angeles	1-6
	28	Buffalo	1-5		23	Calgary	8-10
Mar.	2	Hartford	3-3		24	Edmonton	3-6
	7	NY Rangers	4-2	**Mar.**	5	Detroit	3-6
	9	Los Angeles	0-3		10	Hartford	2-1
	12	Toronto	3-4		14	Washington	3-5
	19	Edmonton	6-7		16	Pittsburgh*	3-6
	23	Hartford	7-3		21	Boston	3-3
	26	Boston	4-7		28	Buffalo	4-4
	31	Montreal	4-1		30	Montreal	3-4

* Denotes afternoon game.

Entry Draft
Selections 1991-79

1991
Pick
1 Eric Lindros
24 Rene Corbet
46 Richard Brennan
68 Dave Karpa
90 Patrick Labrecque
103 Bill Lindsay
134 Mikael Johansson
156 Janne Laukkanen
157 Aaron Asp
178 Adam Bartell
188 Brent Brekke
200 Paul Koch
222 Doug Friedman
244 Eric Meloche

1990
Pick
1 Owen Nolan
22 Ryan Hughes
43 Bradley Zavisha
106 Jeff Parrott
127 Dwayne Norris
148 Andrei Kovalenko
158 Alexander Karpovtsev
169 Pat Mazzoli
190 Scott Davis
211 Mika Stromberg
232 Wade Klippenstein

1989
Pick
1 Mats Sundin
22 Adam Foote
43 Stephane Morin
54 John Tanner
68 Niclas Andersson
76 Eric Dubois
85 Kevin Kaiser
106 Dan Lambert
127 Sergei Mylnikov
148 Paul Krake
169 Viacheslav Bykov
190 Andrei Khumutov
211 Byron Witkowski
232 Noel Rahn

1988
Pick
3 Curtis Leschyshyn
5 Daniel Dore
24 Stephane Fiset
45 Petri Aaltonen
66 Darin Kimble
87 Stephane Venne
108 Ed Ward
129 Valeri Kamensky
150 Sakari Lindfors
171 Dan Wiebe
213 Alexei Gusarov
234 Claude Lapointe

1987
Pick
9 Bryan Fogarty
15 Joe Sakic
51 Jim Sprott
72 Kip Miller
93 Rob Mendel
114 Garth Snow
135 Tim Hanus
156 Jake Enebak
177 Jaroslav Sevcik
183 Ladislav Tresl
198 Darren Nauss
219 Mike Williams

1986
Pick
18 Ken McRae
39 Jean-M Routhier
41 Stephane Guerard
81 Ron Tugnutt
102 Gerald Bzdel
117 Scott White
123 Morgan Samuelsson
134 Mark Vermette
144 Jean-Francois Nault
165 Keith Miller
186 Pierre Millier
207 Chris Lappin
228 Martin Latreille
249 Sean Boudreault

1985
Pick
15 David Latta
36 Jason Lafreniere
57 Max Middendorf
65 Peter Massey
78 David Espe
99 Bruce Major
120 Andy Akervik
141 Mike Oliverio
162 Mario Brunetta
183 Brit Peer
204 Tom Sasso
225 Gary Murphy
246 Jean Bois

1984
Pick
15 Trevor Stienburg
36 Jeff Brown
57 Steve Finn
78 Terry Perkins
120 Darren Cota
141 Henrik Cedergren
162 Jyrki Maki
183 Guy Ouellette
203 Ken Quinney
244 Peter Loob

1983
Pick
32 Yves Heroux
52 Bruce Bell
54 Iiro Jarvi
92 Luc Guenette
112 Brad Walcott
132 Craig Mack
152 Tommy Albelin
172 Wayne Groulx
192 Scott Shaunessy
232 Bo Berglund
239 Dinorich Kokrement

1982
Pick
13 David Shaw
34 Paul Gillis
55 Mario Gosselin
76 Jiri Lala
97 Phil Stanger
131 Daniel Poudrier
181 Mike Hough
202 Vincent Lukac
223 Andre Martin
244 Jozef Lukac
248 Jan Jasko

1981
Pick
11 Randy Moller
53 Jean-Marc Gaulin
74 Clint Malarchuk
95 Ed Lee
116 Mike Eagles
158 Andre Cote
179 Marc Brisebois
200 Kari Takko

1980
Pick
24 Normand Rochefort
66 Jay Miller
108 Mark Kumpel
129 Gaston Therrien
150 Michel Bolduc
171 Christian Tanguay
192 William Robinson

1979
Pick
20 Michel Goulet
41 Dale Hunter
62 Lee Norwood
83 Anton Stastny
104 Pierre Lacroix
125 Scott McGeown

Club Directory

Colisée de Québec
2205 Ave du Colisée
Québec City, Quebec
G1L 4W7
Phone 418/529-8441
FAX 418/529-1052
ENVOY ID
Front Office: NORDIQUES. GM
Public
Relations: NORDIQUES. PR
NORDIQUES.
Marketing: MKTG
Capacity: 15,399

President and Governor . . . . Marcel Aubut
Alternate Governors . . . . Pierre Pagé, Gilles Léger
Senior Vice-President . . . . Maurice Filion
Executive Secretaries to the President . . . . Louise Marois, Nicole Vandal

Hockey Club Personnel
General Manager . . . . Pierre Pagé
Assistant to the General Manager . . . . Gilles Léger
Head Coach . . . . Dave Chambers
Associate Coach . . . . Jacques Martin
Assistant Coach . . . . Don Jackson
Goaltending Coach . . . . Daniel Bouchard
Scouts – Professional hockey
and special assignments . . . . André Savard, Dave Draper, Orval Tessier
Chief Scout . . . . Pierre Gauthier
Assistant to the Chief Scout . . . . Darwin Bennett
Scouts . . . . Ross Ainsworth, Don Boyd, Michel Georges,
Mark Kelley, Frank Moberg, Don Paarup,
Yvon Gendron, Bengt Lundholm, Jacques
Noël
Physiotherapist . . . . Jacques Lavergne
Trainers . . . . René Lacasse, René Lavigueur,
Brian Turpin
Team Physician . . . . Dr. Pierre Beauchemin
Executive Secretary – hockey department . . . . . . Theresa O'Connor
Secretary – hockey department and Travel
Coordinator . . . . Lynn-Ann Ferguson

Administration and Finance
Vice President/Administration and Finance . . . . . Jean Laflamme
Controller . . . . Francois Giguère
Assistant to the Controller . . . . Remi Bolduc
Executive Secretary . . . . Josette Gagné

Sales and Marketing
Vice-President/Sales and Marketing . . . . Gilles Lépine
Director of Sales & Promotions . . . . André Lestourneau
Supervisor of Marketing . . . . Bernard Thiboutot
Supervisors – Sales and Promotions . . . . Alain Desmarteau, Diane Thivierge
Supervisor of Novelties & Souvenirs . . . . Tom Maguire
Coordinator – Promotions . . . . Marc Bourassa
Executive Secretaries – Marketing and
Promotions . . . . Marie Godin, Julienne Bois
Executive Secretary – Sales . . . . Marie-Josée Aubin

Communications and Special Projects
Vice-President/Communications and Special
Programs . . . . Jean-D. Legault
Director of Public Relations . . . . Richard Thibault
Director of Corporate and Community Affairs . . . Guy Lafleur
Supervisor of Press Relations . . . . Jean Martineau
Coordinator of Public Relations . . . . Nicole Bouchard
Graphic Communications Coordinator . . . . Pierre Masson
Executive Secretary – Public Relations . . . . Christiane Huard
Team Photographer . . . . Jean-Yves Michaud

Location of Press Boxes . . . . East & West side of building, upper level
Dimensions of Rink . . . . 200 feet by 85 feet
Club Colors . . . . Blue, White and Red
Training Camp Site . . . . Quebec City
Radio Station . . . . CJRP 1060
Radio Announcers . . . . Alain Crête, Jacques Demers
TV Station . . . . CFAP (2) Quatre-Saisons
TV Announcers . . . . André Côté, Claude Bédard

Coach

CHAMBERS, DAVE
Coach, Quebec Nordiques. Born in Leaside, Ont., May 7, 1940.

In 1990-91, Dave Chambers' first season as head coach of the Quebec Nordiques, the Nordiques posted a 15-point improvement over the previous season, recorded 11 fewer losses and allowed 53 fewer goals. Chambers was appointed head coach of the Nordiques on June 5, 1990 after serving as an assistant coach with the Minnesota North Stars in 1989-90. Prior to joining the North Stars, Chambers' coaching career spanned 20 seasons in the amateur ranks.

He began his collegiate coaching career in 1967 at the University of Saskatchewan. He coached three more seasons at the University of Guelph and Ohio State University before landing at York University in Toronto. During a five-year stay at York, he led his club to three division titles and earned coach of the year honors twice — 1975 and 1977. Chambers coached the Toronto Marlboros of the OHL from 1978-79 until 1979-80 and earned Emms Division coach of the year honors in 1980. After serving as a coaching consultant for the Oshawa Generals in 1983-84, Chambers returned to York where he led his team to the OUAA and CIAU Championship in 1984-85 and the regional championship in 1985-86. Chambers was involved with the Canadian national junior team and Team Canada for five years, leading the Canadian junior team to the national title at the World Junior Championships in Moscow in 1987-88.

Coaching Record

			Regular Season				Playoffs			
Season	Team	Games	W	L	T	%	Games	W	L	%
1967-68	U. Sask. (CIAU)						....			
1968-69	U. Sask. (CIAU)						....			
1969-70	U. Guelph (CIAU)	29	14	14	1	.500	....			
1970-71	Ohio State (CCHA)	29	20	9	0	.690	....			
1971-72	Ohio State (CCHA)	29	24	5	0	.828	....			
1972-73	York Univ. (CIAU)						....			
1973-74	York Univ. (CIAU)						....			
1974-75	York Univ. (CIAU)						....			
1975-76	York Univ. (CIAU)						....			
1976-77	York Univ. (CIAU)						....			
1977-78	Italy	43	29	11	3	.709	....			
1978-79	Toronto (OHL)	68	32	31	5	.507	....			
1979-80	Italy						....			
1980-81	Italy						....			
1985-86	York Univ. (CIAU)						....			
1986-87	York Univ. (CIAU)						....			
1987-88	York Univ. (CIAU)						....			
1990-91	**Quebec (NHL)**	80	16	50	14	.288	....			
	NHL Totals	**80**	**16**	**50**	**14**	**.288**	....			

General Manager

PAGE, PIERRE
General Manager, Quebec Nordiques. Born in St. Hermas, Que., April 30, 1948.

Pierre Page was named general manager of the Nordiques on May 4, 1990 after two seasons as head coach of the Minnesota North Stars. In his rookie season with Minnesota, the club posted a 27-37-16 record for 70 points, a 19-point improvement over the previous year and earned its first playoff berth since 1985-86. In 1989-90, the North Stars continued improving, finishing the season with 76 points (36-40-4).

Page, 43, joined the Calgary Flames in 1980-81 as an assistant coach to Al MacNeil. He served in that capacity through the 1981-82 season before accepting a position as coach and general manager of the Flames' top minor league affiliate in Denver (two seasons) and, later, Moncton (one season). In 1985-86, Page returned to Calgary as an assistant to head coach Bob Johnson and remained in that capacity through the 1987-88 season under Terry Crisp.

Before joining the Flames, Page was head coach of the Dalhousie University Tigers of the CIAU where in 1978-79, he guided his club to a second place finish in the national final. He also served as an assistant coach with the 1980 Canadian Olympic Team and the 1981 Team Canada entry in the Canada Cup.

NHL Coaching Record

			Regular Season				Playoffs			
Season	Team	Games	W	L	T	%	Games	W	L	%
1988-89	Minnesota (NHL)	80	27	37	16	.438	5	1	4	.200
1989-90	Minnesota (NHL)	80	36	40	4	.475	7	3	4	.429
	NHL Totals	**160**	**63**	**77**	**20**	**.456**	**12**	**4**	**8**	**.333**

St. Louis Blues

1990-91 Results: 47W-22L-11T 105PTS. Second, Norris Division

25 YEARS

St. Louis BLUES ™ ®

Year-by-Year Record

Season	GP	Home W	L	T	Road W	L	T	Overall W	L	T	GF	GA	Pts.	Finished	Playoff Result
1990-91	80	24	9	7	23	13	4	47	22	11	310	250	105	2nd, Norris Div.	Lost Div. Final
1989-90	80	20	15	5	17	19	4	37	34	9	295	279	83	2nd, Norris Div.	Lost Div. Final
1988-89	80	22	11	7	11	24	5	33	35	12	275	285	78	2nd, Norris Div.	Lost Div. Final
1987-88	80	18	17	5	16	21	3	34	38	8	278	294	76	2nd, Norris Div.	Lost Div. Final
1986-87	80	21	12	7	11	21	8	32	33	15	281	293	79	1st, Norris Div.	Lost Div. Semi-Final
1985-86	80	23	11	6	14	23	3	37	34	9	302	291	83	3rd, Norris Div.	Lost Conf. Championship
1984-85	80	21	12	7	16	19	5	37	31	12	299	288	86	1st, Norris Div.	Lost Div. Semi-Final
1983-84	80	23	14	3	9	27	4	32	41	7	293	316	71	2nd, Norris Div.	Lost Div. Semi-Final
1982-83	80	16	16	8	9	24	7	25	40	15	285	316	65	4th, Norris Div.	Lost Div. Semi-Final
1981-82	80	22	14	4	10	26	4	32	40	8	315	349	72	3rd Norris Div.	Lost Div. Final
1980-81	80	29	7	4	16	11	13	45	18	17	352	281	107	1st, Smythe Div.	Lost Quarter-Final
1979-80	80	20	13	7	14	21	5	34	34	12	266	278	80	2nd, Smythe Div.	Lost Prelim. Round
1978-79	80	14	20	6	4	30	6	18	50	12	249	348	48	3rd, Smythe Div.	Out of Playoffs
1977-78	80	12	20	8	8	27	5	20	47	13	195	304	53	4th, Smythe Div.	Out of Playoffs
1976-77	80	22	13	5	10	26	4	32	39	9	239	276	73	1st, Smythe Div.	Lost Quarter-Final
1975-76	80	20	12	8	9	25	6	29	37	14	249	290	72	3rd, Smythe Div.	Lost Prelim. Round
1974-75	80	23	13	4	12	18	10	35	31	14	269	267	84	2nd, Smythe Div.	Lost Prelim. Round
1973-74	78	16	16	7	10	24	5	26	40	12	206	248	64	6th, West Div.	Out of Playoffs
1972-73	78	21	11	7	11	23	5	32	34	12	233	251	76	4th, West Div.	Lost Quarter-Final
1971-72	78	17	17	5	11	22	6	28	39	11	208	247	67	3rd, West Div.	Lost Semi-Final
1970-71	78	23	7	9	11	18	10	34	25	19	223	208	87	2nd, West Div.	Lost Quarter-Final
1969-70	76	24	9	5	13	18	7	37	27	12	224	179	86	1st, West Div.	Lost Final
1968-69	76	21	8	9	16	17	5	37	25	14	204	157	88	1st, West Div.	Lost Final
1967-68	74	18	12	7	9	19	9	27	31	16	177	191	70	3rd, West Div.	Lost Final

Schedule

Home		Away	
Oct. Thur. 10 Edmonton		**Oct.** Sat. 5 New Jersey	
Sat. 12 San Jose		Mon. 7 Toronto	
Tues. 15 Toronto		Thur. 17 Detroit	
Sat. 19 Chicago		Sun. 20 Chicago	
Thur. 24 Boston		Mon. 28 Toronto	
Sat. 26 Calgary		Wed. 30 Edmonton	
Nov. Tues. 5 Philadelphia		**Nov.** Fri. 1 Vancouver	
Sat. 9 Hartford		Sun. 3 Winnipeg	
Thur. 14 Winnipeg		Thur. 7 Detroit	
Sat. 16 Minnesota		Sun. 10 Chicago	
Wed. 20 Toronto		Wed. 27 Detroit	
Sat. 23 NY Rangers		**Dec.** Tues. 3 Minnesota	
Thur. 28 Quebec		Wed. 4 Minnesota	
Sat. 30 Detroit		Tues. 10 NY Islanders	
Dec. Sat. 7 Pittsburgh		Wed. 11 Buffalo	
Thur. 19 San Jose		Sat. 14 Quebec	
Sat. 21 NY Islanders		Mon. 16 Montreal	
Thur. 26 Chicago		Sun. 22 Chicago	
Jan. Thur. 2 Minnesota		Sat. 28 Minnesota	
Sat. 4 Detroit		Tues. 31 Buffalo	
Tues. 14 Washington		**Jan.** Mon. 6 Toronto	
Thur. 16 Montreal		Wed. 8 NY Rangers	
Tues. 21 Buffalo		Thur. 9 New Jersey	
Thur. 23 Los Angeles		Sat. 11 NY Islanders	
Sat. 25 Vancouver		Tues. 28 Los Angeles	
Feb. Thur. 6 New Jersey		Thur. 30 San Jose	
Sat. 8 Chicago		**Feb.** Sat. 1 Pittsburgh	
Tues. 11 Los Angeles		Sun. 2 Philadelphia	
Thur. 13 Boston		Mon. 17 Detroit	
Sat. 15 Calgary		Wed. 19 Winnipeg	
Sat. 22 Toronto		Sun. 23 Chicago	
Thur. 27 Washington		Tues. 25 Hartford	
Sat. 29 Detroit		**Mar.** Mon. 2 Vancouver	
Mar. Tues. 10 Minnesota		Fri. 6 Edmonton	
Thur. 12 Detroit		Sat. 7 Calgary	
Sat. 14 NY Rangers		Tues. 17 Washington	
Thur. 26 Hartford		Thur. 19 Boston	
Sat. 28 Toronto		Sat. 21 Montreal	
Apr. Sat. 4 Chicago		Mon. 23 Toronto	
Sun. 5 Minnesota		**Apr.** Thur. 2 Minnesota	

* Denotes afternoon game.

Home Starting Times:
Weeknights & Saturdays .... 7:35 p.m.
Sundays .... 6:05 p.m.

Franchise date: June 5, 1967.

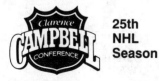

25th
NHL
Season

Jeff Brown led all Blues' rearguards in scoring with 59 points.

1991-92 Player Personnel

FORWARDS

	HT	WT	S	Place of Birth	Date	1990-91 Club
BASSEN, Bob	5-10	180	L	Calgary, Alta.	5/6/65	St. Louis
BRIND'AMOUR, Rod	6-1	202	L	Ottawa, Ont.	8/9/70	St. Louis
CAVALLINI, Gino	6-1	218	L	Toronto, Ont.	11/24/62	St. Louis
CHASE, Kelly	5-11	195	R	Porcupine, Sask.	10/25/67	St. Louis-Peoria
EMERSON, Nelson	5-11	178	R	Hamilton, Ont.	8/17/67	Peoria
HAWLEY, Joe	5-10	186	R	Peterborough, Ont.	3/13/71	Peterborough
HEJNA, Tony	6-0	190	R	Buffalo, NY	1/8/68	Peoria
HEROUX, Yves	5-11	200	R	Terrebonne, Que.	4/27/65	Peoria-Albany
HOOVER, Ron	6-0	190	L	Oakville, Ont.	10/28/66	Boston-Maine
HULL, Brett	5-10	203	R	Belleville, Ont.	8/9/64	St. Louis
KIMBLE, Darin	6-02	205	R	Lucky Lake, Sask.	11/22/68	St. Louis-Quebec
LOWRY, Dave	6-1	195	L	Sudbury, Ont.	2/14/65	St. Louis
MACKEY, Dave	6-4	200	L	Richmond, B.C.	7/24/66	Milwaukee
MIEHM, Kevin	6-2	197	L	Kitchener, Ont.	9/10/69	Peoria
MONGEAU, Michel	5-9	190	L	Nun's Island, Que.	2/9/65	St. Louis-Peoria
OATES, Adam	5-11	189	R	Weston, Ont.	8/27/62	St. Louis
O'BRIEN, David	6-1	188	R	Brighton, MA	9/13/66	Peoria
PELLERIN, Brian	5-10	185	R	Hinton, Alta.	2/20/70	Pr. Albert
PION, Richard	5-10	165	R	Montreal, Que.	7/20/65	Peoria
QUINN, Dan	5-10	175	L	Ottawa, Ont.	6/1/65	St. Louis-Vancouver
RUFF, Jason	6-03	192	L	Kelowna, B.C.	1/27/70	Lethbridge
SHANAHAN, Brendan	6-3	210	R	Mimico, Ont.	1/23/69	New Jersey
SUTTER, Rich	5-11	188	R	Viking, Alta.	12/2/63	St. Louis
TUTTLE, Steve	6-1	190	R	Vancouver, BC.	1/5/66	St. Louis-Peoria
WILSON, Ron	5-9	180	L	Toronto, Ont.	5/13/56	St. Louis

DEFENSEMEN

	HT	WT	S	Place of Birth	Date	1990-91 Club
BROWN, Jeff	6-1	204	R	Ottawa, Ont.	4/30/66	St. Louis
BUTCHER, Garth	6-00	204	R	Regina, Sask.	1/8/63	St. Louis-Vancouver
CAVALLINI, Paul	6-1	202	L	Toronto, Ont.	10/13/65	St. Louis
CORKERY, Tim	6-04	210	R	Ponoka, Alta.	2/17/67	Nashville
FRENETTE, Derek	6-01	205	L	Montreal, Que.	7/13/71	Hull
LAVOIE, Dominic	6-2	205	R	Montreal, Que.	11/21/67	St. Louis-Peoria
MAROIS, Mario	5-11	197	R	Anc. Lorette, Que.	12/15/57	St. Louis
MARSHALL, Jason	6-02	185	R	Cranbrook, B.C.	2/22/71	Tri-City
McKEE, Brian	5-11	185	L	Willowdale, Ont.	12/13/64	Fort Wayne
ROBINSON, Rob	6-1	214	L	St. Catharines, Ont.	4/19/67	Peoria
SKARDA, Randy	6-1	205	R	St. Paul, MN	5/5/68	Peoria
VEITCH, Darren	6-00	190	R	Saskatoon, Sask.	4/24/60	Peoria-Newmarket

GOALTENDERS

	HT	WT	C	Place of Birth	Date	1990-91 Club
HEBERT, Guy	5-11	180	L	Troy, NY	1/7/67	Peoria
JABLONSKI, Pat	6-0	178	R	Toledo, OH	6/20/67	St. Louis-Peoria
JOSEPH, Curtis	5-10	182	L	Keswick, Ont.	4/29/67	St. Louis
MAY, Darrell	6-00	175	L	Edmonton, Alta.	3/6/62	Did Not Play
RAYMOND, Alain	5-10	177	L	Rimouski, Que.	6/24/65	Nashville
RIENDEAU, Vincent	5-10	181	L	St. Hyacinthe, Que.	4/20/66	St. Louis

General Managers' History

Lynn Patrick, 1967-68 to 1968-69; Scotty Bowman, 1969-70 to 1970-71; Lynn Patrick, 1971-72; Sid Abel, 1972-73; Charles Catto, 1973-74; Gerry Ehman, 1974-75; Dennis Ball, 1975-76; Emile Francis, 1976-77 to 1982-83; Ron Caron, 1983-84 to date.

Coaching History

Lynn Patrick and Scott Bowman, 1967-68; Scott Bowman, 1968-69 to 1969-70; Al Arbour and Scott Bowman, 1970-71; Sid Abel, Bill McCreary, Al Arbour, 1971-72; Al Arbour and Jean-Guy Talbot, 1972-73; Jean-Guy Talbot and Lou Angotti, 1973-74; Lou Angotti, Lynn Patrick and Garry Young, 1974-75; Garry Young, Lynn Patrick and Leo Boivin, 1975-76; Emile Francis, 1976-77; Leo Boivin and Barclay Plager, 1977-78; Barclay Plager, 1978-79; Barclay Plager and Red Berenson, 1979-80; Red Berenson, 1980-81; Red Berenson and Emile Francis, 1981-82; Barclay Plager and Emile Francis, 1982-83; Jacques Demers, 1983-84 to 1985-86; Jacques Martin, 1986-87 to 1987-88. Brian Sutter, 1988-89 to date.

Captains' History

Al Arbour, 1967-68 to 1969-70; Red Berenson, Barclay Plager, 1970-71; Barclay Plager, 1971-72 to 1975-76; no captain, 1976-77; Red Berenson, 1977-78; Barry Gibbs, 1978-79; Brian Sutter, 1979-80 to 1987-88; Bernie Federko, 1988-89; Rick Meagher, 1989-90; Scott Stevens, 1990-91 to date.

1990-91 Scoring

Regular Season

* rookie

Pos	#	Player	Team	GP	G	A	Pts	+/-	PIM	PP	SH	GW	GT	S	%
R	16	Brett Hull	STL	78	86	45	131	23	22	29	0	11	1	389	22.1
C	12	Adam Oates	STL	61	25	90	115	15	29	3	1	3	0	139	18.0
C	7	Dan Quinn	VAN	64	18	31	49	28−	46	8	0	3	1	157	11.5
			STL	14	4	7	11	5−	20	4	0	2	0	26	15.4
			TOTAL	78	22	38	60	33−	66	12	0	5	1	183	12.0
D	21	Jeff Brown	STL	67	12	47	59	4	39	6	1	0	2	176	6.8
C	19	Rod Brind'Amour	STL	78	17	32	49	2	93	4	0	3	0	169	10.1
D	2	Scott Stevens	STL	78	5	44	49	23	150	1	0	1	0	160	3.1
L	10	Dave Lowry	STL	79	19	21	40	19	168	0	2	5	0	123	15.4
C	18	Ron Wilson	STL	73	10	27	37	1	54	1	2	1	0	101	9.9
D	14	Paul Cavallini	STL	67	10	25	35	19	89	3	0	0	0	116	8.6
L	17	Gino Cavallini	STL	78	8	27	35	4	81	3	0	2	0	131	6.1
C	28	Bob Bassen	STL	79	16	18	34	17	183	0	2	1	0	117	13.7
R	23	Rich Sutter	STL	77	16	11	27	6	122	0	2	2	0	130	12.3
D	5	Garth Butcher	VAN	69	6	12	18	18−	257	1	0	1	0	70	8.6
			STL	13	0	4	4	4	32	0	0	0	0	5	.0
			TOTAL	82	6	16	22	14−	289	1	0	1	0	75	8.0
D	36	Glen Featherstone	STL	68	5	15	20	19	204	1	0	1	0	59	8.5
R	15	Paul MacLean	STL	37	6	11	17	2−	24	0	0	2	0	53	11.3
D	44	Mario Marois	STL	64	2	14	16	17	81	0	0	0	0	59	3.4
R	35	Steve Tuttle	STL	20	3	6	9	2	2	0	0	0	0	16	18.8
R	29	Darin Kimble	QUE	35	2	5	7	5−	114	0	0	0	0	14	14.3
			STL	26	1	1	2	2	128	0	0	1	0	14	7.1
			TOTAL	61	3	6	9	3−	242	0	0	1	0	28	10.7
D	20	Tom Tilley	STL	22	2	4	6	5	4	0	0	0	0	28	7.1
D	27	Harold Snepsts	STL	54	1	4	5	3	50	0	0	1	0	33	3.0
R	22	Rick Meagher	STL	24	3	1	4	0	6	0	0	0	0	21	14.3
D	38	*Dominic Lavoie	STL	6	1	2	3	4	2	0	0	0	0	11	9.1
R	26	David Bruce	STL	12	1	2	3	1	14	0	0	0	0	23	4.3
C	32	*Nelson Emerson	STL	4	0	3	3	2−	2	0	0	0	0	6	.0
C	41	*Michel Mongeau	STL	7	1	2	3	1	0	1	0	0	0	13	7.7
G	30	Vincent Riendeau	STL	44	0	2	2	0	0	0	0	0	0	0	.0
G	39	Kelly Chase	STL	2	1	0	1	1	15	0	0	1	0	1	100.0
G	1	*Pat Jablonski	STL	8	0	1	1	0	0	0	0	0	0	0	.0
G	31	*Curtis Joseph	STL	30	0	1	1	0	0	0	0	0	0	0	.0
L	40	*Dave Thomlinson	STL	3	0	0	0	3−	0	0	0	0	0	0	.0

Goaltending

No.	Goaltender	GPI	Mins	Avg	W	L	T	EN	SO	GA	SA	S%
30	Vincent Riendeau	44	2671	3.01	29	9	6	1	3	134	1241	.892
1	*Pat Jablonski	8	492	3.05	2	3	3	1	0	25	228	.890
31	*Curtis Joseph	30	1710	3.12	16	10	2	0	0	89	874	.898
	Totals	**80**	**4877**	**3.08**	**47**	**22**	**11**	**2**	**3**	**250**	**2345**	**.893**

Playoffs

Pos	#	Player	Team	GP	G	A	Pts	+/-	PIM	PP	SH	GW	OT	S	%
C	12	Adam Oates	STL	13	7	13	20	7	10	2	0	1	0	39	17.9
R	16	Brett Hull	STL	13	11	8	19	5	4	3	0	2	0	58	19.0
D	21	Jeff Brown	STL	13	3	9	12	6	6	0	0	0	0	42	7.1
C	7	Dan Quinn	STL	13	4	7	11	2−	32	2	0	1	0	27	14.8
C	19	Rod Brind'amour	STL	13	2	5	7	0	10	1	0	0	0	24	8.3
R	23	Rich Sutter	STL	13	4	2	6	2	16	0	0	1	0	21	19.0
D	14	Paul Cavallini	STL	13	2	3	5	0	20	1	0	0	0	33	6.1
L	10	Dave Lowry	STL	13	1	4	5	6−	35	0	0	0	0	21	4.8
L	40	*Dave Thomlinson	STL	3	3	1	4	2	4	1	0	1	0	12	25.0
C	28	Bob Bassen	STL	13	1	3	4	1	24	0	0	0	0	16	6.3
L	17	Gino Cavallini	STL	13	1	3	4	2	2	0	0	0	0	29	3.4
D	5	Garth Butcher	STL	13	2	1	3	1	54	0	0	0	0	21	9.5
R	35	Steve Tuttle	STL	6	0	3	3	2−	0	0	0	0	0	5	.0
D	2	Scott Stevens	STL	13	0	3	3	8	36	0	0	0	0	17	.0
R	22	Rick Meagher	STL	9	1	1	0	2	0	0	0	0	0	8	.0
R	26	David Bruce	STL	3	0	0	0	0	2	0	0	0	0	1	.0
G	1	*Pat Jablonski	STL	3	0	0	0	0	0	0	0	0	0	0	.0
R	39	Kelly Chase	STL	9	0	0	0	1−	18	0	0	0	0	0	.0
C	18	Ron Wilson	STL	7	0	0	0	0	28	0	0	0	0	0	.0
D	27	Harold Snepsts	STL	8	0	0	0	1−	12	0	0	0	0	3	.0
D	36	Glen Featherstone	STL	5	0	0	0	1−	31	0	0	0	0	6	.0
D	44	Mario Marois	STL	9	0	0	0	0	37	0	0	0	0	4	.0
R	29	Darin Kimble	STL	13	0	0	0	0	38	0	0	0	0	3	.0
G	30	Vincent Riendeau	STL	13	0	0	0	0	0	0	0	0	0	0	.0

Goaltending

No.	Goaltender	GPI	Mins	Avg	W	L	EN	SO	GA	SA	S%
30	Vincent Riendeau	13	687	3.06	6	7	2	1	35	294	.881
1	*Pat Jablonski	3	90	3.33	0	0	0	0	5	35	.857
	Totals	**13**	**780**	**3.23**	**6**	**7**	**2**	**1**	**42**	**331**	**.873**

Retired Numbers

3	Bob Gassoff	1973-1977
8	Barclay Plager	1967-1977
11	Brian Sutter	1976-1988
24	Bernie Federko	1976-1989

Club Records

Team

(Figures in brackets for season records are games played; records for fewest points, wins, ties, losses, goals, goals against are for 70 or more games)

Most Points	107	1980-81 (80)
Most Wins	47	1990-91 (80)
Most Ties	19	1970-71 (78)
Most Losses	50	1978-79 (80)
Most Goals	352	1980-81 (80)
Most Goals Against	349	1981-82 (80)
Fewest Points	48	1978-79 (80)
Fewest Wins	18	1978-79 (80)
Fewest Ties	7	1983-84 (80)
Fewest Losses	18	1980-81 (80)
Fewest Goals	177	1967-68 (74)
Fewest Goals Against	157	1968-69 (76)

Longest Winning Streak
Over-all ... 7 Jan. 21-
Feb. 3/88
Mar. 19-31/91
Home ... 9 Jan. 26-
Feb. 26/91
Away ... 4 Four times

Longest Undefeated Streak
Over-all ... 12 Nov. 10-
Dec. 8/68
(5 wins, 7 ties)
Home ... 11 Feb. 12-
Mar. 19/69
(5 wins, 6 ties)
Feb. 7-
Mar. 29/75
(9 wins, 2 ties)
Away ... 7 Dec. 9-26/87
(4 wins, 3 ties)

Longest Losing Streak
Over-all ... 7 Nov. 12-26/67;
Feb. 12-25/89
Home ... 5 Nov. 19-
Dec. 6/77
Away ... 10 Jan. 20/82-
Mar. 8/82

Longest Winless Streak
Over-all ... 12 Jan. 17-
Feb. 15/78
(10 losses, 2 ties)

Home ... 7 Dec. 28/82-
Jan. 25/83
(5 losses, 2 ties)
Away ... 17 Jan. 23-
Apr. 7/74
(14 losses, 3 ties)

Most Shutouts, Season ... 13 1968-69 (76)
Most PIM, Season ... 1,987 1990-91 (80)
Most Goals, Game ... 10 Feb. 2/82
(Wpg. 6 at St. L. 10)
Dec. 1/84
(Det. 5 at St. L. 10)
Jan. 15/86
(Tor. 1 at St. L. 10)

Individual

Most Seasons	13	Bernie Federko
Most Games	927	Bernie Federko
Most Goals, Career	352	Bernie Federko
Most Assists, Career	721	Bernie Federko
Most Points, Career	1,073	Bernie Federko
Most PIM, Career	1,786	Brian Sutter
Most Shutouts, Career	16	Glenn Hall

Longest Consecutive
Games Streak ... 662 Garry Unger
(Feb. 7/71-Apr. 8/79)
Most Goals, Season ... 86 Brett Hull
(1990-91)
Most Assists, Season ... 90 Adam Oates
(1990-91)
Most Points, Season ... 131 Brett Hull
(1990-91)
(86 goals, 45 assists)
Most PIM, Season ... 306 Bob Gassoff
(1975-76)
Most Points, Defenseman
Season ... 66 Rob Ramage
(1985-86)
(10 goals, 56 assists)
Most Points, Center,
Season ... 115 Adam Oates
(1990-91)
(25 goals, 90 assists)

Most Points, Right Wing,
Season ... 131 Brett Hull
(1990-91)
(86 goals, 45 assists)
Most Points, Left Wing,
Season ... 85 Chuck Lefley
(1975-76)
(43 goals, 42 assists)
Most Points, Rookie,
Season ... 73 Jorgen Pettersson
(1980-81)
(37 goals, 36 assists)
Most Shutouts, Season ... 8 Glenn Hall
(1968-69)
Most Goals, Game ... 6 Red Berenson
(Nov. 7/68)
Most Assists, Game ... 5 Brian Sutter
(Nov. 22/88)
Bernie Federko
(Feb. 27/88)
Most Points, Game ... 7 Red Berenson
(Nov. 7/68)
Garry Unger
(Mar. 13/71)

All-time Record vs. Other Clubs

Regular Season

		At Home						On Road						Total					
	GP	W	L	T	GF	GA	PTS	GP	W	L	T	GF	GA	PTS	GP	W	L	T	GF	GA	PTS
Boston	48	18	21	9	149	169	45	48	9	32	7	129	219	25	96	27	53	16	278	388	70
Buffalo	40	24	11	5	156	104	53	40	10	26	4	121	168	24	80	34	37	9	277	272	77
Calgary	37	14	18	5	131	125	33	37	15	19	3	108	133	33	74	29	37	8	239	258	66
Chicago	78	38	26	14	276	248	90	80	21	48	11	250	328	53	158	59	74	25	526	576	143
Detroit	72	44	18	10	272	189	98	73	34	28	11	241	253	79	145	78	46	21	513	442	177
Edmonton	19	6	10	3	74	88	15	19	5	12	2	76	94	12	38	11	22	5	150	182	27
Hartford	19	10	7	2	71	66	22	19	9	8	2	60	63	20	38	19	15	4	131	129	42
Los Angeles	53	34	13	6	204	142	74	53	19	27	7	155	191	45	106	53	40	13	359	333	119
Minnesota	83	42	24	17	294	238	101	81	31	35	15	246	280	77	164	73	59	32	540	518	178
Montreal	48	10	25	13	120	167	33	48	8	35	5	125	215	21	96	18	60	18	245	382	54
New Jersey	35	24	8	3	160	109	51	35	15	13	7	105	108	37	70	39	21	10	265	217	88
NY Islanders	36	14	16	6	127	122	34	37	6	22	9	79	145	21	73	20	38	15	206	267	55
NY Rangers	51	21	22	8	157	166	50	50	5	40	5	113	217	15	101	26	62	13	270	383	65
Philadelphia	56	22	27	7	161	169	51	56	10	37	9	129	220	29	112	32	64	16	290	389	80
Pittsburgh	54	36	13	5	213	146	77	53	19	23	11	164	194	49	107	55	36	16	377	340	126
Quebec	19	15	3	1	92	63	31	19	7	9	3	64	69	17	38	22	12	4	156	132	48
Toronto	73	44	19	10	261	208	98	72	20	45	7	221	292	47	145	64	64	17	482	500	145
Vancouver	46	27	12	7	185	137	61	46	20	21	5	143	148	45	92	47	33	12	328	285	106
Washington	29	13	8	8	122	88	34	29	12	14	3	90	102	27	58	25	22	11	212	190	61
Winnipeg	21	9	4	8	91	69	26	21	4	12	5	66	79	13	42	13	16	13	157	148	39
Defunct Club	32	25	4	3	131	55	53	33	11	10	12	95	100	34	65	36	14	15	226	155	87
Totals	949	490	309	150	3447	2868	1130	949	290	516	143	2780	3618	723	1898	780	825	293	6227	6486	1853

Playoffs

	Series	W	L	GP	W	L	T	GF	GA	Last Mtg.	Round	Result
Boston	2	0	2	8	0	8	0	15	48	1972	SF	L 0-4
Buffalo	1	0	1	3	1	2	0	8	7	1976	PR	L 1-2
Calgary	1	0	1	7	3	4	0	22	28	1986	CF	L 3-4
Chicago	7	1	6	35	12	23	0	97	137	1990	DF	L 3-4
Detroit	3	2	1	16	8	8	0	51	53	1991	DSF	W 4-3
Los Angeles	1	1	0	4	4	0	0	16	5	1969	SF	W 4-0
Minnesota	9	5	4	52	26	26	0	152	158	1991	DF	L 2-4
Montreal	3	0	3	12	0	12	0	14	42	1977	QF	L 0-4
NY Rangers	1	0	1	6	2	4	0	22	29	1981	QF	L 2-4
Philadelphia	2	2	0	11	8	3	0	34	20	1969	QF	W 4-0
Pittsburgh	3	2	1	13	7	6	0	45	40	1981	PR	W 3-2
Toronto	3	2	1	18	10	8	0	56	53	1990	DSF	W 4-1
Winnipeg	1	1	0	4	3	1	0	20	13	1982	DSF	W 3-1
Totals	37	16	21	189	84	105	0	552	633			

Playoff Results 1991-87

Year	Round	Opponent	Result	GF	GA
1991	DF	Minnesota	L 2-4	17	22
	DSF	Detroit	W 4-3	24	20
1990	DF	Chicago	L 3-4	22	28
	DSF	Toronto	W 4-1	20	16
1989	DF	Chicago	L 1-4	12	19
	DSF	Minnesota	W 4-1	23	15
1988	DF	Detroit	L 1-4	14	21
	DSF	Chicago	W 4-1	21	17
1987	DSF	Toronto	L 2-4	12	15

Abbreviations: Round: F Final; **CF** conference final; **DF** division final; **DSF** division semi-final; **SF** semi-final; **QF** quarter-final. **PR** preliminary round. **GA** goals against; **GF** goals for.

1990-91 Results

		Home				Away	
Oct.	6	Chicago	2-5	Oct.	4	Minnesota	3-2
	9	Pittsburgh	4-3		12	Vancouver	0-4
	20	Minnesota	2-2		14	Los Angeles	1-4
	25	Toronto	8-5		16	Edmonton	5-2
	27	Montreal	3-0		18	Calgary	4-3
Nov.	6	Edmonton	2-1		24	Toronto	8-3
	10	Detroit	6-1		30	Detroit	5-2
	13	Quebec	4-2	Nov.	1	Boston	2-3
	20	Winnipeg	4-2		3	Hartford	4-1
	24	Vancouver	3-3		8	Pittsburgh	3-2
	27	Toronto	3-4		17	Minnesota	3-2
	29	Los Angeles	4-4		18	Winnipeg	3-4
Dec.	1	New Jersey	1-4		23	Detroit	3-5
	8	Detroit	2-1	Dec.	2	Chicago	2-3
	11	Winnipeg	3-3		7	Detroit	6-3
	13	Minnesota	4-2		15	Toronto	4-2
	20	Washington	3-3		16	Buffalo	5-3
	22	Chicago	5-0		26	Chicago	6-6
	29	Philadelphia	1-3		27	Toronto	4-6
Jan.	3	Quebec	8-7		31	Pittsburgh	3-4
	5	NY Rangers	2-3	Jan.	8	New Jersey	5-3
	15	Washington	7-3		9	NY Rangers	3-2
	17	Hartford	2-4		12	Quebec	4-4
	26	Detroit	5-4		13	Montreal	3-1
	29	Buffalo	8-3		22	Minnesota	3-7
	31	Hartford	4-3		25	Detroit	9-4
Feb.	2	New Jersey	5-4	Feb.	4	Toronto	5-6
	9	Los Angeles	5-4		6	Buffalo	5-4
	19	Toronto	3-2		12	Edmonton	4-2
	21	NY Islanders	7-2		14	Vancouver	3-2
	23	Boston	9-2		17	Calgary	4-7
	26	Chicago	3-1		24	Chicago	2-6
	28	NY Rangers	4-4	Mar.	2	Philadelphia	4-4
Mar.	9	Calgary	4-8		5	Hartford	4-1
	10	Detroit	1-4		7	Boston	5-5
	14	Minnesota	2-2		17	Chicago	4-6
	16	Chicago	2-3		19	Washington	2-1
	28	NY Islanders	3-0		21	Philadelphia	4-1
	30	Toronto	5-2		23	NY Islanders	3-2
	31	Minnesota	2-1		25	Minnesota	5-4

* Denotes afternoon game.

Entry Draft Selections 1991-77

1991
Pick
27 Steve Staios
64 Kyle Reeves
65 Nathan Lafayette
87 Grayden Reid
109 Jeff Callinan
131 Bruce Gardiner
153 Terry Hollinger
175 Christopher Kenady
197 Jed Fiebelkorn
219 Chris Mackenzie
241 Kevin Rappana
263 Mike Veisor

1990
Pick
33 Craig Johnson
54 Patrice Tardif
96 Jason Ruff
117 Kurtis Miller
138 Wayne Conlan
180 Parris Duffus
201 Steve Widmeyer
222 Joe Hawley
243 Joe Fleming

1989
Pick
9 Jason Marshall
31 Rick Corriveau
55 Denny Felsner
93 Daniel Laperriere
114 David Roberts
124 Derek Frenette
135 Jeff Batters
156 Kevin Plager
177 John Roderick
198 John Valo
219 Brian Lukowski

1988
Pick
9 Rod Brind' Amour
30 Adrien Plavsic
51 Rob Fournier
72 Jaan Luik
105 Dave Lacouture
114 Dan Fowler
135 Matt Hayes
156 John McCoy
177 Tony Twist
198 Bret Hedican
219 Heath Deboer
240 Michael Francis

1987
Pick
12 Keith Osborne
54 Kevin Miehm
59 Robert Nordmark
75 Darin Smith
82 Andy Rymsha
117 Rob Robinson
138 Tobb Crabtree
159 Guy Hebert
180 Robert Dumas
201 David Marvin
207 Andy Cesarski
222 Dan Rolfe
243 Ray Savard

1986
Pick
10 Jocelyn Lemieux
31 Mike Posma
52 Tony Hejna
73 Glen Featherstone
87 Michael Wolak
115 Mike O'Toole
136 Andy May
157 Randy Skarda
178 Martyn Ball
199 Rod Thacker
220 Terry MacLean
234 Bill Butler
241 David Obrien

1985
Pick
37 Herb Raglan
44 Nelson Emerson
54 Ned Osmond
100 Dan Brooks
121 Rick Burchill
138 Pat Jablonski
159 Scott Brickey
180 Jeff Urban
201 Vince Guidotti
222 Ron Saatzer
243 Dave Jecha

1984
Pick
26 Brian Benning
32 Tony Hrkac
50 Toby Ducolon
53 Robert Dirk
56 Alan Perry
71 Graham Herring
92 Scott Paluch
113 Steve Tuttle
134 Cliff Ronning
148 Don Porter
155 Jim Vesey
176 Daniel Jomphe
196 Tom Tilley
217 Mark Cupolo
237 Mark Lanigan

1983
DID NOT DRAFT

1982
Pick
50 Mike Posavad
92 Scott Machej
113 Perry Ganchar
134 Doug Gilmour
155 Chris Delaney
176 Matt Christensen
197 John Shumski
218 Brian Ahern
239 Peter Smith

1981
Pick
20 Marty Ruff
36 Hakin Nordin
62 Gordon Donnelly
104 Mike Hickey
125 Peter Aslin
146 Erik Holmberg
167 Alain Vigneault
188 Dan Wood
209 Richard Zemlak

1980
Pick
12 Rik Wilson
54 Jim Pavese
75 Bob Brooke
96 Alain Lemieux
117 Perry Anderson
138 Roger Hagglund
159 Par Rabbitt
180 Peter Lindberg
201 John Smyth

1979
Pick
2 Perry Turnbull
65 Bob Crawford
86 Mark Reeds
107 Gilles Leduc

1978
Pick
3 Wayne Babych
39 Steve Harrison
72 Kevin Willison
89 Jim Nill
106 Steve Stockman
109 Paul MacLean
123 Denis Houle
140 Tony Meagher
143 Rick Simpson
157 Jim Lockhurst
160 Bob Froese
170 Dan Lerg
173 Risto Siltanen
175 Dan Hermansson
181 Jean-Francois Boutin
185 John Sullivan
188 Serge Menard
191 Don Boyd
197 Paul Stasiuk
200 Gerhard Truntschka
203 Victor Shkurdjuk
205 Carl Bloomberg
207 Terry Kitching
209 Brian O'Connor
210 Brian Crombeen
211 Mike Pidgeon
214 John Cochrane
216 Joe Casey
218 Jim Farrell
221 Blair Wheeler

1977
Pick
9 Scott Campbell
27 Neil Labatte
45 Tom Roulston
63 Tony Currie
81 Bruce Hamilton
99 Gary McMonagle
117 Matti Forss
132 Raimo Hirvonen
147 Bjorn Olsson

Club Directory

St. Louis Arena
5700 Oakland Avenue
St. Louis, MO 63110
Phone 314/781-5300
GM FAX 314/645-1573
FAX 314/645-1340
ENVOY ID
Front Office: BLUES. GM
Public
Relations: BLUES. PR
Capacity: 17,188

Board of Directors
Michael F. Shanahan, Mark Sauer, Ed Trusheim, Andy Craig, Larry Alexander

Advisor to Board
Lewis N. Wolff

Management

Chairman of the Board	Michael F. Shanahan
President	Jack J. Quinn
Vice-President/General Manager	Ronald Caron
Vice-President/Director of Sales	Bruce Affleck
Vice-President/Director of Player Personnel and Scouting	Ted Hampson
Vice-President/Director of Broadcast Sales	Matt Hyland
Vice-President/Director of Finance and Administration	Jerry Jasiek
Vice-President/Director of Marketing and Public Relations	Susie Mathieu
Vice-President/Director of Player Development	Bob Plager
Secretary and General Counsel	Timothy R. Wolf
Head Coach	Brian Sutter
Assistant Coach	Wayne Thomas
Assistant Coach	Bob Berry
Coach, Peoria Rivermen	Harold Snepsts
Assistant Director of Scouting	Jack Evans
Western Canada/U.S. Scout	Pat Ginnell
Scouts	Matt Keator, Paul MacLean
Director of Alumni Services	Norm Mackie
Director of Promotions & Community Relations	Tracy Lovasz
Assistant Director of Public Relations	Jeff Trammel
Assistant Director of Public Relations	Michael Caruso
Controller	Margaret Steinmeyer
Accountant	Rita Russell
Accountant	Marsha McBride
Sales Staff	John Casson, Wes Edwards, Tammy Iuli, Jill Mann
Merchandise Manager	George Pavlik
Head Trainer	Mike Folga
Assistant Trainer	Jim Pickard
Equipment Manager	Frank Burns
Conditioning Consultant	Mackie Shilstone
Executive Secretary	Lynn Diederichsen
Hockey Secretary	Sue Profeta
Marketing/Public Relations Secretary	Donna Quirk
Receptionist	Pam Barrett
Orthopedic Surgeon	Dr. Jerome Gilden
Internist	Dr. Aaron Birenbaum
Dentist	Dr. Les Rich
Optometrist	Dr. N. Rex Ghormley
Largest Hockey Attendance	20,009 (March 31/73)
Location of Press Box	East side of building, upper level
Club Colors	Blue, Gold, Red and White
Training Camp	Brentwood Ice Rink, St. Louis Mo.
Radio Station	KMOX Radio
Television Station	KPLR-TV (Channel 11)
Broadcasters	Bruce Affleck, John Kelly, Ken Wilson

Coach

SUTTER, BRIAN
Coach, St. Louis Blues. Born in Viking, Alta., October 7, 1956.

Led by Brian Sutter in his third season behind the bench, the 1990-91 St. Louis Blues posted the highest win total in franchise history. That mark keyed the Blues' second place overall League finish; their 105-point season was also the second-best finish in franchise history. For his efforts, Sutter was named the Jack Adams Trophy winner as the NHL's Coach of the Year. In his three seasons, the Blues have never finished lower than second place in the Norris Division.

The Blues' second choice, 20th overall, in the 1976 Amateur Draft, Brian was the first of a record six brothers to play in the NHL. After a junior career with Lethbridge of the Western Junior League, Sutter turned pro in 1976 and played in only 38 games in the minor leagues (Kansas City, CHL) before making his NHL debut with the Blues. From 1979-80 until his retirement last season, Sutter served as captain of the St. Louis club. He also appeared in three NHL All-Star Games (1982, 1983 and 1985) and ranks second on the Blues' all-time list in games played (779), goals (303), assists (333) and points (636).

Coaching Record

Team	Seasons	Regular Season					Playoffs			
		Games	W	L	T	%	Games	W	L	%
1988-89	St. Louis (NHL)	80	33	35	12	.488	10	5	5	.500
1989-90	St. Louis (NHL)	80	37	34	9	.519	12	7	5	.583
1990-91	St. Louis (NHL)	80	47	22	11	.656	13	6	7	.462
NHL Totals		**240**	**117**	**91**	**32**	**.554**	**35**	**18**	**17**	**.514**

General Manager

CARON, RON
Vice-President General Manager and Alternate Governor, St. Louis Blues.
Born in Hull, Que., December 19, 1929

Ron Caron joined the St. Louis Blues on August 13, 1983 after a 26-year association with the Montreal Canadiens' organization. He joined the Canadiens in 1957 on a part-time scouting basis after coaching in the amateur ranks. In 1966, Caron was promoted to a full-time position as chief scout of the Montreal Junior Canadiens and was instrumental in assembling two Memorial Cup championship teams. In 1968, he was named chief scout of the parent club and served as an assistant to former manager Sam Pollock. In 1969 he added the responsibilities of general manager of the Montreal Voyageurs of the AHL and maintained that role until 1978 when he was named director of scouting and player personnel for the Canadiens. Caron remained with the Montreal organization until the conclusion of the 1982-83 campaign.

San Jose Sharks

Neil Wilkinson was a key acquistion by the Sharks in the 1990-91 Dispersal Draft.

1991-92 Player Personnel

FORWARDS	HT	WT	S	Place of Birth	Date	1990-91 Club
AKERVIK, Andy	6-4	215	R	Duluth, MN	8/11/67	Kansas City
ANDERSON, Perry	6-1	225	L	Barrie, Ont.	10/14/61	Utica
BEAUFAIT, Mark	5-9	165	R	Livonia, MI	5/13/70	Northern Michigan U.
— BOZEK, Steve	5-11	180	L	Kelowna, B.C.	1126/60	Vancouver
BRUCE, David	5-11	190	R	Thunder Bay, Ont.	10/7/64	Peoria
— CARTER, John	5-10	170	L	Winchester, MA	5/3/63	Boston
COURTENAY, Ed	6-4	200	R	Verdun, Qué.	2/2/68	Kalamazoo
COXE, Craig	6-4	220	L	Chula Vista, CA	1/21/64	Vancouver
CRAIGWELL, Dale	5-11	180	L	Toronto, Ont.	4/24/71	Oshawa
DePALMA, Larry	6-0	200	L	Trenton, MI	10/27/65	Min.-Kalamazoo
EVANS, Kevin	5-9	185	L	Peterborough, OH	7/10/65	Kalamazoo
FALLOON, Pat	5-11	192	R	Foxwarren, Man.	9/22/72	Spokane
FREDERICK, Troy	6-5	226	L	Virden, Manitoba	4/4/69	Kansas City
GARBUTT, Murray	6-1	205	L	Hanna, Alta.	7/29/71	Spokane
GAUDREAU, Robert	5-11	185	R	Lincoln, R.I.	1/20/70	Providence Coll.
GRILLO, Dean	6-2	210	R	Bemidji, MN	12/8/72	Warroad
HILTNER, Mike	6-1	194	R	St. Cloud, MN	3/22/66	Kansas City
— HRKAC, Tony	5-11	175	L	Thunder Bay, Ont.	7/7/66	Quebec
— KISIO, Kelly	5-9	183	R	Peace River, Alta.	9/18/59	N.Y. Rangers
KRAVETS, Mikhail	5-10	176	L	Leningrad, USSR	11/12/63	SKA Leningrad
LAPPIN, Peter	5-11	180	R	St. Charles, IL	12/31/65	Kalamazoo
LAWTON, Brian	6-0	190	L	New Brunswick, N.J.	6/29/65	Phoenix
MADILL, Jeff	5-11	195	R	Oshawa, Ont.	6/21/65	Utica
McHUGH, Mike	5-10	190	L	Philadelphia, PA	8/16/65	Kalamazoo
McLEAN, Jeff	5-10	186	L	Port Moody, B.C.	9/6/69	U. of North Dakota
— MULLEN, Brian	5-10	180	L	New York, N.Y.	3/16/62	N.Y. Rangers
NILSSON, Frederick	6-1	198	L	Vasteras, Sweden	4/16/71	Vasteras
ODGERS, Jeff	6-0	195	R	Spy Hill, Sask.	5/31/69	Kansas City
OLIMB, Larry	5-10	155	L	Warroad, MN	8/11/69	U. of Minnesota
OTEVREL, Jaroslav	6-2	185	L	Czechoslovakia	9/16/68	Zlin
PAVELICH, Mark	5-8	170	R	Eveleth, MN	2/28/58	Did Not Play
QUINTIN, J.F.	6-0	187	L	St. Jean, Quebec	5/28/69	Kalamazoo
SULLIVAN, Kevin	6-3	200	R	Hartford, CT	5/16/68	Nashville
SULLIVAN, Mike	6-2	185	L	Marshfield,MA	2/27/68	San Diego
WEISBROD, John	6-3	215	R	Syosset, N.Y.	10/8/68	Harvard
WHITNEY, Ray	5-9	160	R	Fort Sask., Alta.	5/8/72	Spokane
WOOD, Dody	5-11	180	L	Chetwynd, B.C.	3/10/72	Seattle

DEFENSEMEN						
COLMAN, Mike	6-3	225	R	Stoneham, MA	8/4/68	Kansas City
GAETZ, Link	6-2	210	L	Vancouver, B.C.	10/2/68	Kansas City
HAMMOND, Ken	6-1	190	L	Port Credit, Ontario	8/22/63	Maine
KANE, Shaun	6-3	195	L	Holyoke, MA	2/24/70	Providence Coll.
JOYCE, Duane	6-2	203	R	Pembroke, MA	6/25/68	Kalamazoo
KECZMER, Dan	6-1	175	L	Mount Clemens, MI	5/25/68	Kalamazoo
KOLSTAD, Dean	6-6	210	L	Edmonton, Alta.	6/16/68	Kalamazoo
KRISS, Aaron	6-2	185	L	Parma, OH	9/17/72	Cranbrook
LESSARD, Rick	6-2	200	L	Timmins, Ont.	1/9/68	Salt Lake City
MacLEOD, Pat	5-11	190	L	Melfort, Sask.	6/15/69	Kalamazoo
— McGILL, Bob	6-1	193	R	Edmonton, Alta.	4/27/62	Chicago
MORE, Jayson	6-1	190	L	Souris, Man.	1/12/69	Fredericton
OZOLISH, Sandis	6-1	189	L	Riga, Latvia	3/8/72	Dynamo Riga
PEDERSON, Tom	5-9	165	R	Bloomington, MN	1/1/70	U. of Minnesota
SCREMIN, Claudio	6-2	205	R	Burnaby, B.C.	5/28/68	Kansas City
— WILKINSON, Neil	6-3	180	R	Selkirk, Man.	8/15/67	Minnesota
WILLIAMS, Dave	6-2	195	R	Plainfield, N.J.	8/25/67	Knoxville
— WILSON, Doug	6-1	187	L	Ottawa, Ont.	7/5/57	Chicago
— ZETTLER, Rob	6-3	190	L	Sept Iles, Que.	3/8/68	Minnesota
ZMOLEK, Doug	6-1	195	L	Rochester, MN	11/3/70	U. of Minnesota

GOALTENDERS	HT	WT	C	Place of Birth	Date	1990-91 Club
CASHMAN, Scott	6-2	186	L	Ottawa, Ont.	9/20/69	Boston U.
FLAHERTY, Wade	6-0	170	L	Terrace, B.C.	1/11/68	Kansas City
— HACKETT, Jeff	6-1	175	L	London, Ont.	6/1/68	N.Y. Islanders
— HAYWARD, Brian	5-10	180	L	Toronto, Ont.	6/25/60	Minnesota
IRBE, Artur	5-7	180	L	Riga, Latvia	2/2/67	Dynamo Riga
MYLLYS, Jarmo	5-8	150	R	Sovanlinna, Finland	5/29/65	Kalamazoo
RYDER, Dan	6-1	184	L	Kitchener, Ont.	10/24/72	Sudbury
SAURDIFF, Corwin	5-11	168	L	Warroad, MN	10/17/72	Waterloo
SCHOEN, Bryan	6-2	180	L	St. Paul, MN	9/9/70	Denver U.

Schedule

	Home			Away	
Oct.	Sat. 5 Vancouver		**Oct.**	Fri. 4 Vancouver	
	Tues. 8 Calgary			Sat. 12 St Louis	
	Thur. 10 Winnipeg			Sun. 13 Chicago	
	Thur. 17 Minnesota			Wed. 16 Los Angeles	
	Sat. 19 Boston			Wed. 23 Hartford	
Nov.	Fri. 8 Edmonton			Fri. 25 Buffalo	
	Sat. 9 NY Islanders			Sat. 26 New Jersey	
	Tues. 12 Buffalo			Tues. 29 NY Islanders	
	Thur. 14 Detroit			Thur. 31 Philadelphia	
	Tues. 19 Los Angeles		**Nov.**	Sat. 2 Quebec	
	Fri. 22 Toronto			Mon. 4 Toronto	
	Tues. 26 Vancouver			Sat. 16 Vancouver	
Dec.	Tues. 3 Los Angeles			Sat. 23 Los Angeles	
	Thur. 5 Pittsburgh			Fri. 29 Edmonton	
	Tues. 10 Winnipeg			Sat. 30 Calgary	
	Thur. 12 Edmonton		**Dec.**	Sun. 8 Edmonton	
	Sat. 14 Minnesota			Mon. 16 NY Rangers	
	Sat. 21 Quebec			Tues. 17 Pittsburgh	
	Sat. 28 Vancouver			Thur. 19 St Louis	
Jan.	Fri. 3 Philadelphia			Thur. 26 Los Angeles	
	Sat. 4 Montreal		**Jan.**	Tues. 7 Vancouver	
	Fri. 24 Calgary			Wed. 8 Calgary	
	Sat. 25 Edmonton			Sat. 11 Minnesota	
	Tues. 28 NY Rangers			Sun. 12 Winnipeg	
	Thur. 30 St Louis			Tues. 14 Los Angeles	
Feb.	Tues. 4 Hartford			Tues. 21 Edmonton	
	Wed. 5 Chicago		**Feb.**	Sun. 2 Winnipeg*	
	Tues. 18 Washington			Sun. 9 Washington*	
	Fri. 21 Vancouver			Wed. 12 Montreal	
	Sun. 23 Calgary*			Fri. 14 Buffalo	
	Wed. 26 Quebec			Sat. 15 Detroit	
	Fri. 28 Montreal		**Mar.**	Tues. 10 Chicago	
Mar.	Sun. 1 Philadelphia*			Wed. 11 Winnipeg	
	Wed. 4 Los Angeles			Thur. 19 Calgary	
	Fri. 6 Pittsburgh			Sat. 21 Hartford	
	Sun. 8 Toronto*			Mon. 23 Boston	
	Sat. 14 New Jersey			Tues. 24 New Jersey	
	Tues. 17 Detroit			Thur. 26 NY Islanders	
Apr.	Wed. 1 Winnipeg			Sun. 29 Winnipeg*	
	Fri. 3 Calgary		**Apr.**	Sun. 5 Edmonton*	

* Denotes afternoon game.

Home Starting Times:
All Games . . . . 7:30 p.m.
Except Oct. 5 . . . . 8:00 p.m.
Feb. 23, Mar. 1, Mar. 8 . . . . 1:30 p.m.

Franchise date: May 9, 1990

**1st
NHL
Season**

General Manager

FERREIRA, JACK
Executive Vice President and General Manager, San Jose Sharks.
Born in Providence, R.I., June 9, 1944.

Jack Ferreira takes on the role of general manager and head of all hockey operations for the Sharks, the same position he held from 1988 to 1990 with the Minnesota North Stars.

A former all-American goaltender at Boston University, Ferreira was an assistant coach on the collegiate level at Brown, Princeton and the U.S. Military Academy. Ferreira's player development and management background began in 1972. He spent five years as assistant general manager of the New England Whalers of the World Hockey Association. He spent 1977 to 1980 as a member of the NHL's Central Scouting Bureau before joining the Calgary Flames scouting staff from 1980 to 1986. He followed this with a two-year stint as director of player development for the New York Rangers.

Ferreira was named general manager of the North Stars in June, 1988 and initiated a major restructuring of the hockey operation which proved to be instrumental in significant on-ice gains during his two seasons with the club. Inheriting a team which had failed to make the playoffs in two consecutive seasons, the North Stars became one of the most improved clubs in the NHL, qualifying for post-season play in 1988-89 and 1989-90. In addition, the organization's top minor league affiliate in Kalamazoo, Michigan, posted a 100-point season.

Ferreira is a member of the USA Hockey Committee for the 1992 Winter Olympics and served as general manager for the fourth-place USA squad at the 1991 World Hockey Championship in Finland.

Coach

KINGSTON, GEORGE
Head Coach, San Jose Sharks.
Born in Biggar, Sask., August 20, 1939.

George Kingston was named Sharks head coach on April 12, 1991, bringing to the job more than 30 years of hockey experience on the professional, amateur and international levels.

Prior to joining the Sharks, Kingston spent two years as sport director of the Norwegian Ice Hockey Federation and coach of Norway's national team. A native of Biggar, Saskatchewan, Kingston has spent most of his coaching career in Canada, including 19 years as head coach at the University of Calgary. While there, he also worked as a part-time assistant with the Calgary Flames from 1980-82. His other NHL experience came in 1988-89 as an assistant coach with the Minnesota North Stars.

Kingston has a wealth of experience on the international level including various positions with the Canadian Olympic and national programs. Among his involvement: serving as an assistant coach on the 1984 Olympic squad and head coach for the gold medal-winning Team Canada in the 1987 Spengler Cup. Kingston was chairman of the hockey tournament during the 1988 Winter Olympics in Calgary.

After starting his coaching career with six years at the high school level, Kingston guided the program at the University of Calgary from 1968-88 posting a 245-128 (.657) record over 15 seasons. During his tenure he took four one-year leaves of absence to pursue advanced degrees or work with the Canadian National program. He led the Calgary Dinosaurs to the playoffs 14 times and won five conference titles. Kingston was named Canadian college coach of the year in 1974 and 1981.

After one season at Minnesota, Kingston accepted an offer in 1989 to develop the national program in Norway. He coached Norway to the country's best-ever finish in three prestigious international tournaments: the 1990 World Junior Championships (6th place), the "A" Pool of the 1990 International Ice Hockey Federation World Championships (relegated to the 1991 "B" Pool by just one goal); and, the "B" pool of the 1991 World Championships. The latter qualified Norway for the 1992 "A" Pool competition and the 1992 Winter Olympics. Along with his coaching duties, Kingston also worked with the country's coaching, player development and referee education programs, and served as a consultant to the organizing committee for the 1994 Winter Olympics, hosted by the city of Lillehammer, Norway.

Kingston also sports an impressive background as an educator. A former teacher and department head with the Edmonton Public School Board, he spent 21 years as a professor at the University of Calgary, where he was Associate Academic Dean from 1975-88. Kingston has a doctorate in philosophy from the University of Alberta at Edmonton, where he also completed a master's program and two bachelor's degrees. Kingston has combined his education and coaching background to author well over 100 presentations, journals and video narrations on hockey.

Coaching Record

Season	Team	Games	Regular Season W	L	T	%	Playoffs Games	W	L	%
1968-69	U. of Calgary (CIAU)	20	11	9	0	.550	....	....	....	....
1969-70	U. of Calgary (CIAU)	14	11	3	0	.786	....	....	....	....
1970-71	U. of Calgary (CIAU)	20	13	7	0	.650	....	....	....	....
1971-72	U. of Calgary (CIAU)	20	15	5	0	.750	....	....	....	....
1972-73	U. of Calgary (CIAU)	24	16	8	0	.667	....	....	....	....
1973-74	U. of Calgary (CIAU)	18	14	4	0	.778	....	....	....	....
1975-76	U. of Calgary (CIAU)	24	17	7	0	.708	....	....	....	....
1978-79	U. of Calgary (CIAU)	24	15	9	0	.625	....	....	....	....
1979-80	U. of Calgary (CIAU)	29	18	11	0	.629	....	....	....	....
1980-81	U. of Calgary (CIAU)	24	18	6	0	.750	....	....	....	....
1981-82	U. of Calgary (CIAU)	24	14	10	0	.583	....	....	....	....
1982-83	U. of Calgary (CIAU)	24	10	14	0	.417	....	....	....	....
1984-85	U. of Calgary (CIAU)	24	8	16	0	.333	....	....	....	....
1985-86	U. of Calgary (CIAU)	28	19	9	0	.679	....	....	....	....
1986-87	U. of Calgary (CIAU)	28	23	5	0	.821	....	....	....	....
1987-88	U. of Calgary (CIAU)	28	23	5	0	.821	....	....	....	....

General Managers' History

Jack Ferreira, 1991-92.

Coaching History

George Kingston, 1991-92.

Club Directory

Cow Palace in Daly City, California

10 Almaden Boulevard
Suite 600
P.O. Box 1240
San Jose, California 95113
Phone **408/287-7070**
General FAX 408/999-5797
Hockey/PR FAX 408/999-5707
ENVOY ID
 Front Office: SHARKS. GM
 Media
 Relations: SHARKS. PR
Capacity: 10,800

Executive
Co-Owner & Chairman	George Gund III
Co-Owner & Vice Chairman	Gordon Gund
President & CEO	Arthur L. Savage
Exec. Vice President/General Manager	Jack Ferreira
Exec. Vice President, Building Operations	Frank Jirik
Exec. Vice President, Business Operations	Matt Levine
Exec. Vice President, Finance	Grant Rollin
Exec. Assistant to President	Dianna Carthew

Hockey Operations
Assistant General Manger	Dean Lombardi
Director of Player Personnel	Chuck Grillo
Head Coach	George Kingston
Associate Coach	Bob Murdoch
Assistant Coach	Drew Remenda
Strength Coach	George Kinnear
Scouting Coordinator	Joe Will
Exec. Assistant to General Manager	Brenda Knight
Director of Media Relations	Tim Bryant
Assistant Director of Media Relations	Ken Arnold
Media Relations Assistant	Jill Freeman
Scouting Staff	Bob Gernander, Ray Payne, Bill Goldsworthy, Larry Ross, Bob Friedlander, Ben Hays, Sakari Pietila, Pat Funk, Jack Morganstern
Head Trainer	Tom Woodcock
Equipment Manager	Bob Crocker, Jr.
Assistant Equipment Manager	Howard Baldwin, Jr.
Team Physician	Arthur J. Ting, M.D.
Medical Staff	Warren King, M.D.; Steven Sullivan, M.D.; John A. Selling, M.D.
Team Dentist	Robert Bonahoom, D.D.S.
Travel Coordinator	Dawn Beres

Finance
Controller	Peggy Ferguson
Accountant	Glen Rice
Payroll	Bonita Tanner
Executive Assistant	Cecilia Briones

Business Operations
Vice Pres., Broadcast & Media Marketing	Chuck Prewitt
Director of Production & Video Operations	Mark Stulberger
Director of Executive Sales	Ted Atlee
Director of Ticket Sales	Rich Muschell
Director of Merchandise Marketing	Mary Keen Meulman
Director of Community Development	Alysse Soll
Director of Special Projects	Herb Briggin
Manager of Event Services	Kris Van Giesen
Group Account Service Manager	Mary Lewis
Account Service Managers	Wanda Mae Colson, Bob Fitzgerald, Andy Hawkes, Paul Solby, Gene Wiggins
Senior Account Executive	M. Aurelius Sofia
Publications Adv. Sales Acct. Executive	Jim Josel
Merchandise Manager	Scott Howard
Asst. Merchandise Manager	Brad Porteus
Executive Assistant	Joyce Coppola
Media Marketing Assistant	Valerie Bigelow
Assistant to Community Development	Diane Bloom
Sales Assistant	Annie Chan
Merchandise Sales Assistant	Julie Burns
Retail Store Manger	Jannette Scott

Building Operations
Director of Ticket Operations	Daniel DeBoer
Assistant to Ticket Operations	Mary Enriquez
Executive Assistant	Chris Palmer
Office Management	Alfred Lazar
Receptionist	Marcia Thomas

Miscellaneous
Team Colors	Pacific Teal, Gray, Black, White
Home Ice	Cow Palace
Dimensions of Rink	185' × 85'
Television Station	KICU-TV 36
Radio Station	KNEW (910 AM)
Play-By-Play (Radio)	Dan Rusanowsky
Play-By-Play (Television)	Joe Starkey
Color Commentator	Dennis Hull

Entry Draft Selections 1991

1991

Pick		Pick	
2	Pat Falloon	111	Fredrik Nilsson
23	Ray Whitney	133	Jaroslav Otevrel
30	Sandis Ozolnich	155	Dean Grillo
45	Dody Wood	177	Corwin Saurdiff
67	Kerry Toporowski	199	Dale Craigdell
89	Dan Ryder	221	Aaron Kriss
		243	Mikhail Kravets

Toronto Maple Leafs

1990-91 Results: 23w-46L-11T 57PTS. Fifth, Norris Division

Dave Ellett finished second in team scoring for the Leafs, leading all defensemen with 49 points.

Schedule

Home				Away		
Oct.	Sat.	5	Detroit	Oct.	Thur. 3	Montreal
	Mon.	7	St Louis		Tues. 15	St Louis
	Wed.	9	Washington		Thur. 17	Calgary
	Sat.	12	Vancouver		Sat. 19	Winnipeg
	Sat.	26	Detroit		Mon. 21	Vancouver
	Mon.	28	St Louis		Fri. 25	Detroit
Nov.	Sat.	2	Los Angeles	Nov.	Fri. 1	Washington
	Mon.	4	San Jose		Fri. 8	NY Rangers
	Wed.	6	Minnesota		Tues. 12	Minnesota
	Sat.	9	Calgary		Thur. 14	Chicago
	Sat.	16	Chicago		Wed. 20	St Louis
	Sun.	17	Hartford		Fri. 22	San Jose
	Sat.	30	Minnesota		Tues. 26	Los Angeles
Dec.	Sat.	7	Vancouver		Fri. 29	Minnesota
	Mon.	9	Montreal	Dec.	Wed. 4	Hartford
	Wed.	11	NY Islanders		Thur. 12	Philadelphia
	Wed.	18	Edmonton		Sat. 14	Boston
	Sat.	21	Buffalo		Fri. 20	Washington
	Mon.	23	Winnipeg		Thur. 26	Pittsburgh
	Sat.	28	Detroit		Mon. 30	Quebec
Jan.	Sat.	4	Chicago	Jan.	Fri. 3	Detroit
	Mon.	6	St Louis		Thur. 9	Chicago
	Wed.	22	Boston		Sat. 11	New Jersey
	Sat.	25	Philadelphia		Thur. 16	Chicago
	Wed.	29	Quebec		Thur. 23	NY Islanders
Feb.	Sat.	1	New Jersey	Feb.	Mon. 3	Minnesota
	Wed.	5	Minnesota		Fri. 7	Detroit
	Sat.	8	Montreal		Tues. 18	Pittsburgh
	Tues.	15	Detroit		Thur. 20	Detroit
	Sat.	15	Winnipeg		Sat. 22	St Louis
	Sun.	16	Edmonton		Thur. 27	Boston
	Tues.	25	New Jersey	Mar.	Wed. 4	Edmonton
	Sat.	29	Chicago		Thur. 5	Calgary
Mar.	Sun.	1	Minnesota		Sun. 8	San Jose*
	Sat.	14	Pittsburgh		Mon. 9	Los Angeles
	Tues.	17	Quebec		Wed. 11	Minnesota
	Sat.	21	Chicago		Wed. 25	Buffalo
	Mon.	23	St Louis		Sat. 28	St Louis
Apr.	Wed.	1	NY Islanders		Sun. 29	Chicago
	Sat.	4	NY Rangers	Apr.	Sun. 5	Philadelphia

* Denotes afternoon game.

Home Starting Times:
Weeknights .... 7:35 p.m.
Saturdays .... 8:05 p.m.
Sundays .... 7:05 p.m.

Franchise date: November 22, 1917

75th NHL Season

Year-by-Year Record

Season	GP	Home W	L	T	Road W	L	T	Overall W	L	T	GF	GA	Pts.	Finished	Playoff Result
1990-91	80	15	21	4	8	25	7	23	46	11	241	318	57	5th, Norris Div.	Out of Playoffs
1989-90	80	24	14	2	14	24	2	38	38	4	337	358	80	3rd, Norris Div.	Lost Div. Semi-Final
1988-89	80	15	20	5	13	26	1	28	46	6	259	342	62	5th, Norris Div.	Out of Playoffs
1987-88	80	14	20	6	7	29	4	21	49	10	273	345	52	4th, Norris Div.	Lost Div. Semi-Final
1986-87	80	22	14	4	10	28	2	32	42	6	286	319	70	4th, Norris Div.	Lost Div. Final
1985-86	80	16	21	3	9	27	4	25	48	7	311	386	57	4th, Norris Div.	Lost Div. Final
1984-85	80	10	28	2	10	24	6	20	52	8	253	358	48	5th, Norris Div.	Out of Playoffs
1983-84	80	17	16	7	9	29	2	26	45	9	303	387	61	5th, Norris Div.	Out of Playoffs
1982-83	80	20	15	5	8	25	7	28	40	12	293	330	68	3rd, Norris Div.	Lost Div. Semi-Final
1981-82	80	12	20	8	8	24	8	20	44	16	298	380	56	5th, Norris Div.	Out of Playoffs
1980-81	80	14	21	5	14	16	10	28	37	15	322	367	71	5th, Adams Div.	Lost Prelim. Round
1979-80	80	17	19	4	18	21	1	35	40	5	304	327	75	4th, Adams Div.	Lost Prelim. Round
1978-79	80	20	12	8	14	21	5	34	33	13	267	252	81	3rd, Adams Div.	Lost Quarter-Final
1977-78	80	21	13	6	20	16	4	41	29	10	271	237	92	3rd, Adams Div.	Lost Semi-Final
1976-77	80	18	13	9	15	19	6	33	32	15	301	285	81	3rd, Adams Div.	Lost Quarter-Final
1975-76	80	23	12	5	11	19	10	34	31	15	294	276	83	3rd, Adams Div.	Lost Quarter-Final
1974-75	80	19	12	9	12	21	7	31	33	16	280	309	78	3rd, Adams Div.	Lost Quarter-Final
1973-74	78	21	11	7	14	16	9	35	27	16	274	230	86	4th, East Div.	Lost Quarter-Final
1972-73	78	20	12	7	7	29	3	27	41	10	247	279	64	6th, East Div.	Out of Playoffs
1971-72	78	21	11	7	12	20	7	33	31	14	209	208	80	4th, East Div.	Lost Quarter-Final
1970-71	78	24	9	6	13	24	2	37	33	8	248	211	82	4th, East Div.	Lost Quarter-Final
1969-70	76	18	13	7	11	21	6	29	34	13	222	242	71	6th, East Div.	Out of Playoffs
1968-69	76	20	8	10	15	18	5	35	26	15	234	217	85	4th, East Div.	Lost Quarter-Final
1967-68	74	24	9	4	9	22	6	33	31	10	209	176	76	5th, East Div.	Out of Playoffs
1966-67	70	24	8	6	8	19	5	32	27	11	204	211	75	3rd,	Won Stanley Cup
1965-66	70	22	9	4	12	16	7	34	25	11	208	187	79	3rd,	Lost Semi-Final
1964-65	70	17	15	3	13	11	11	30	26	14	204	173	74	4th,	Lost Semi-Final
1963-64	70	22	7	6	11	18	6	33	25	12	192	172	78	3rd,	Won Stanley Cup
1962-63	70	21	8	6	14	15	6	35	23	12	221	180	82	1st,	Won Stanley Cup
1961-62	70	25	5	5	12	17	6	37	22	11	232	180	85	2nd,	Won Stanley Cup
1960-61	70	21	6	8	18	13	4	39	19	12	234	176	90	2nd,	Lost Semi-Final
1959-60	70	20	9	6	15	17	3	35	26	9	199	195	79	2nd,	Lost Final
1958-59	70	17	13	5	10	19	6	27	32	11	189	201	65	4th,	Lost Final
1957-58	70	12	16	7	9	22	4	21	38	11	192	226	53	6th,	Out of Playoffs
1956-57	70	12	16	7	9	18	8	21	34	15	174	192	57	5th,	Out of Playoffs
1955-56	70	19	10	6	5	23	7	24	33	13	153	181	61	4th,	Lost Semi-Final
1954-55	70	14	10	11	10	14	11	24	24	22	147	135	70	3rd,	Lost Semi-Final
1953-54	70	22	6	7	10	18	7	32	24	14	152	131	78	3rd,	Lost Semi-Final
1952-53	70	17	12	6	10	18	7	27	30	13	156	167	67	5th,	Out of Playoffs
1951-52	70	17	10	8	12	15	8	29	25	16	168	157	74	3rd,	Lost Semi-Final
1950-51	70	25	5	8	16	13	6	41	16	13	212	138	95	2nd,	Won Stanley Cup
1949-50	70	18	9	8	13	18	4	31	27	12	176	173	74	3rd,	Lost Semi-Final
1948-49	60	22	8	10	10	17	3	22	25	13	147	161	57	4th,	Won Stanley Cup
1947-48	60	22	3	5	10	12	8	32	15	13	182	143	77	1st,	Won Stanley Cup
1946-47	60	20	8	2	11	11	8	31	19	10	209	172	72	2nd,	Won Stanley Cup
1945-46	50	10	13	2	9	11	5	19	24	7	174	185	45	5th,	Out of Playoffs
1944-45	50	13	9	3	11	13	1	24	22	4	183	161	52	3rd,	Won Stanley Cup
1943-44	50	13	11	1	10	12	3	23	23	4	214	174	50	3rd,	Lost Semi-Final
1942-43	50	17	6	2	5	13	7	22	19	9	198	159	53	3rd,	Lost Semi-Final
1941-42	48	18	6	0	9	12	3	27	18	3	158	136	57	2nd,	Won Stanley Cup
1940-41	48	16	5	3	12	9	3	28	14	6	145	99	62	2nd,	Lost Semi-Final
1939-40	48	15	3	6	10	14	0	25	17	6	134	110	56	3rd,	Lost Final
1938-39	48	13	6	5	6	12	6	19	20	9	114	107	47	3rd,	Lost Final
1937-38	48	13	6	5	11	9	4	24	15	9	151	127	57	1st, Cdn. Div.	Lost Final
1936-37	48	14	9	1	8	12	4	22	21	5	119	115	49	3rd, Cdn. Div.	Lost Quarter-Final
1935-36	48	15	4	5	8	15	1	23	19	6	126	106	52	2nd, Cdn. Div.	Lost Final
1934-35	48	16	4	4	14	8	2	30	14	4	157	111	64	1st, Cdn. Div.	Lost Final
1933-34	48	19	2	3	7	11	6	26	13	9	174	119	61	1st, Cdn. Div.	Lost Semi-Final
1932-33	48	16	4	4	8	14	2	24	18	6	119	111	54	1st, Cdn. Div.	Lost Final
1931-32	48	17	4	3	6	14	4	23	18	7	155	127	53	2nd, Cdn. Div.	Won Stanley Cup
1930-31	44	15	4	3	7	9	6	22	13	9	118	99	53	2nd, Cdn. Div.	Lost Quarter-Final
1929-30	44	10	8	4	7	13	2	17	21	6	116	124	40	4th, Cdn. Div.	Out of Playoffs
1928-29	44	15	5	2	6	13	3	21	18	5	85	69	47	3rd, Cdn. Div.	Lost Semi-Final
1927-28	44	9	8	5	9	10	3	18	18	8	89	88	44	4th, Cdn. Div.	Out of Playoffs
1926-27*	44	10	10	2	5	14	3	15	24	5	79	94	35	5th, Cdn. Div.	Out of Playoffs
1925-26	36	11	5	2	1	16	1	12	21	3	92	114	27	6th,	Out of Playoffs
1924-25	30	10	5	0	9	11	0	19	11	0	90	84	38	2nd,	Lost NHL S-Final
1923-24	24	7	5	0	3	9	0	10	14	0	59	85	20	3rd,	Out of Playoffs
1922-23	24	10	1	1	3	10	1	13	10	1	82	88	27	3rd,	Out of Playoffs
1921-22	24	8	4	0	5	6	1	13	10	1	98	97	27	2nd,	Won Stanley Cup
1920-21	24	9	3	0	6	6	0	15	9	0	105	100	30	2nd and 1st***	Lost NHL Final
1919-20**	24	9	3	0	4	8	0	12	12	0	119	106	24	3rd and 2nd***	Lost NHL Final
1918-19	18	5	4	0	0	9	0	5	13	0	64	92	10	3rd and 3rd***	Out of Playoffs
1917-18	22	10	1	0	3	8	0	13	9	0	108	109	26	2nd and 1st***	Won Stanley Cup

* Name changed from St. Patricks to Maple Leafs. ** Name changed from Arenas to St. Patricks.
*** Season played in two halves with no combined standing at end.

1991-92 Player Personnel

FORWARDS	HT	WT	S	Place of Birth	Date	1990-91 Club
AITKEN, Brad	6-3	200	L	Scarborough, Ont.	10/30/67	K.C.-Muskegon
BRADLEY, Brian	5-10	170	R	Kitchener, Ont.	1/21/65	Vancouver-Toronto
BROTEN, Aaron	5-10	180	L	Roseau, Mn.	11/14/60	Quebec-Toronto
BULLARD, Mike	5-10	185	L	Ottawa, Ont.	3/10/61	Ambri Piotta
CHITARONI, Terry	5-11	200	R	Haileybury, Ont.	9/12/72	Sudbury
CLARK, Wendel	5-11	194	L	Kelvington, Sask.	10/25/66	Toronto
CIMETTA, Robert	6-0	190	L	Toronto, Ont.	2/15/70	Newmarket-Toronto
DAMPHOUSSE, Vince	6-1	190	L	Montreal, Que.	12/17/67	Toronto
DEBLOIS, Lucien	5-11	200	R	Joliette, Que.	6/21/57	Quebec-Toronto
DOERS, Michael	6-0	175	R	Madison, WI	6/17/71	U. of Vermont
EASTWOOD, Michael	6-2	190	R	Ottawa, Ont.	7/1/67	Western Michigan
ELVENAS, Roger	6-1	185	L	Lund, Sweden	5/29/68	Rogle (Sweden)
FERGUS, Tom	6-3	210	L	Chicago, IL	6/16/62	Toronto
FOLIGNO, Mike	6-2	195	L	Sudbury, Ont.	1/29/59	Buffalo-Toronto
HANNAN, David	5-10	185	L	Sudbury, Ont.	11/26/61	Toronto
HAWKINS, Todd	6-1	195	R	Kingston, Ont.	8/2/66	Milw.-Newmarket
HENDRICKSON, Darby	6-0	175	L	Richfield, MN	8/28/72	Richfield H.S.
HULST, Kent	6-0	180	L	St. Thomas, Ont.	4/8/68	Newmarket
JACKSON, Mike	6-0	192	R	Mississauga, Ont.	2/4/69	Newmarket
JOHNSTON, Greg	6-1	190	R	Barrie, Ont.	1/14/65	Newmarket-Toronto
KRUSHELNYSKI, Mike	6-1	180	R	Montreal, Que.	4/27/60	L.A.-Toronto
KUCHARCIK, Thomas	6-2	200	L	Mlada Boleslav	10/5/70	Dukla Jihlava
KRUDASHOV, Alexei	6-0	180	R	Soviet Union	21/7/71	Soviet Wings
KUZMINSKY, Alex	5-11	175	L	Kiev, U.S.S.R.	12/7/72	Sokol Kiev
LACROIX, Eric	6-1	200	L	Montreal, Que.	7/15/71	Gov. Dummer H.S.
LEEMAN, Gary	5-11	175	R	Toronto, Ont.	2/19/64	Toronto
LOISELLE, Claude	5-11	195	L	Ottawa, Ont.	5/29/63	Quebec-Toronto
MacWILLIAM, Mike	6-1	195	L	Burnaby, B.C.	2/14/67	Greensboro
MAGUIRE, Kevin	6-2	200	R	Toronto, Ont.	1/5/63	Toronto
MALLGRAVE, Matt	6-0	180	R	Washington, D.C.	5/3/70	Harvard
MAROIS, Daniel	6-1	190	R	Montreal, Que.	10/3/68	Toronto
McCARTHY, Joe	6-1	200	L			Vermont
McCLELLAND, Kevin	6-2	205	R	Oshawa, Ont.	7/4/62	Det.-Adirondack
McINTYRE, Robb	6-0	180	L	Royal Oak, MI	27/4/72	Dubuque
MERKLER, Keith	6-2	205	L	Syosset, NY	4/23/71	Princeton
MILLAR, Mike	5-10	170	L	St. Catharines, Ont.	4/28/65	Newmarket-Toronto
MOES, Mike	5-11	185	L	Burlington, Ont.	3/30/67	Newmarket
OSBORNE, Keith	6-1	180	R	Toronto, Ont.	4/2/69	Peoria-Newmarket
PEARSON, Rob	6-1	180	R	Oshawa, Ont.	8/3/71	Bell.-Osh.-Newmkt.
PERREAULT, Yanic	5-11	182	L	Sherbrooke, Que.	4/4/71	Trois-Rivieres
PERRY, Jeff	6-0	192	L	Sarnia, Ont.	12/4/71	Owen Sound
PROCHAZKA, Martin	5-11	176	R	Slany, Czech.	3/3/72	Poldi Kladno
REID, Dave	6-0	205	L	Toronto, Ont.	5/15/64	Toronto
ROBITAILLE, Martin	5-10	165	R	Medford, MA	7/31/70	U. of Maine
SACCO, Joe	6-1	180	R	Medford, MA	2/4/69	Newmarket-Toronto
STEVENS, Mike	5-11	195	R	Kitchener, Ont.	12/30/65	Newmarket
STIVER, Dan	6-0	185	R	Chicoutimi, Que.	9/14/71	U. of Michigan
ST. LAURENT, Jeffrey	6-2	175	R	Sanford, MA	5/16/71	U. of New Hampshire
THORNTON, Scott	6-2	200	L	London, Ont.	1/9/71	Bell.-Newmkt.-Tor.
TOMBERLIN, Justin	6-0	191	L	Grand Rapids, MN	11/15/70	U. of Maine
TOMLINSON, David	5-11	180	L	N. Vancouver, B.C.	5/8/68	Boston U.
VACHON, Nick	5-10	190	L	Montreal, Que.	9/20/72	Gov. Dummer H.S.
WALTERS, Greg	6-1	195	R	Calgary, Alta.	8/12/70	Newmarket
ZEZEL, Peter	4-9	200	L	Toronto, Ont.	4/22/65	Washington-Toronto

DEFENSEMEN	HT	WT	S	Place of Birth	Date	1990-91 Club
BEREHOWSKY, Drake	6-1	211	R	Toronto, Ont.	1/3/72	Kingston-N. Bay-Tor.
BURKE, David	6-1	185	L	Detroit, MI	10/15/70	Cornell
CARNEY, Keith	6-1	180	L	Cumberland, RI	2/7/71	U. of Lowell
CHEBATOR, Rob	6-0	170	L	Arlington, MA	12/1/70	Arlington H.S.
CROWLEY, Edward	6-2	190	R	Concord, MA	5/3/70	Boston College
DELAY, Mike	6-0	190	L	Boston, MA	8/31/69	Boston College
ELLETT, Dave	6-1	200	L	Cleveland, OH.	3/30/64	Winnipeg-Toronto
ESAU, Leonard	6-3	195	R	Meadow Lake, Sask.	3/16/68	Newmarket
GODYNYUK, Alexander	6-0	210	L	Soviet Union	1/27/70	Sokol Kiev-N'mkt.-Tor.
GILL, Todd	6-1	185	L	Brockville, Ont.	11/9/65	Toronto
JENSEN, Chris	6-2	190	R	Wilmette, IL	6/29/68	U. of New Hampshire
LANGILLE, Derek	6-0	185	L	Toronto, Ont.	6/25/69	Newmarket
LEHOUX, Guy	5-11	205	L	Disraeli, Que.	19/10/71	Drummondville
MALONE, Scott	6-1	195	L	Boston, MA	1/16/71	Baltimore-Newmarket
MILLER, Gary	6-1	202	L	Midland, Ont.	19/3/72	North Bay
MIRONOV, Dimitri	6-2	191	R	Moscow, U.S.S.R.	25/12/65	Soviet Wings
O'ROURKE, Chris	6-2	195	R	Sherwood Park, Alta.	6/1/71	Alaska-Fairbanks
PETIT, Michel	6-1	205	R	St. Malo, Que.	2/12/64	Quebec-Toronto
QUEENEVILLE, Joel	6-1	200	L	Windsor, Ont.	9/15/58	Washington-Baltimore
RICHARDSON, Luke	6-4	210	L	Ottawa, Ont.	3/26/69	Toronto
ROUSE, Bob	6-1	210	R	Surrey, B.C.	6/18/64	Washington-Toronto
SACCO, David	6-0	190	R	Malden, MA	7/31/70	Newmarket
SHANNON, Darryl	6-2	190	L	Barrie, Ont.	6/21/68	Newmarket-Toronto
WEINRICH, Alex	6-0	180	R	Lewiston, MA	3/12/69	Merrimack

GOALTENDERS	HT	WT	C	Place of Birth	Date	1990-91 Club
HORYNA, Robert	5-11	185	L	Hradec, Czech.	9/10/70	Newmarket
ING, Peter	6-2	165	L	Toronto, Ont.	4/28/69	Toronto
POTVIN, Felix	6-0	185	L	Anjou, Que.	6/23/71	Chicoutimi
REESE, Jeff	5-9	170	L	Brantford, Ont.	3/24/66	Toronto-Newmarket
RHODES, Damian	6-0	170	L	St. Paul, MN	5/28/69	Newmarket-Toronto

General Managers' History

Conn Smythe, 1927-28 to 1956-57; Hap Day, 1957-58; George "Punch" Imlach, 1958-59 to 1968-69; Jim Gregory, 1969-70 to 1978-79; Punch Imlach, 1979-80 to 1980-81; Punch Imlach and Gerry McNamara, 1981-82; Gerry McNamara, 1982-83 to 1987-88; Gord Stellick, 1988-89; Floyd Smith, 1989-90 to 1990-91; Cliff Fletcher, 1991-92.

Retired Numbers

5	Bill Barilko	1946-1951
6	Irwin "Ace" Bailey	1927-1934

1990-91 Scoring

Regular Season

* rookie

Pos	#	Player	Team	GP	G	A	Pts	+/-	PIM	PP	SH	GW	GT	S	%
L	10	Vince Damphousse	TOR	79	26	47	73	31–	65	10	1	4	0	247	10.5
D	4	Dave Ellett	WPG	17	4	7	11	4–	6	1	1	0	0	41	9.8
			TOR	60	8	30	38	4–	69	5	0	1	1	154	5.2
			TOTAL	77	12	37	49	8–	75	6	1	1	1	195	6.2
C	26	Mike Krushelnyski	L.A.	15	1	5	6	7	10	1	0	0	0	11	9.1
			TOR	59	17	22	39	6–	48	2	2	1	1	98	17.3
			TOTAL	74	18	27	45	1	58	3	2	1	1	109	16.5
C	44	Brian Bradley	VAN	44	11	20	31	2–	42	3	0	3	0	84	13.1
			TOR	26	0	11	11	7–	20	0	0	0	0	32	.0
			TOTAL	70	11	31	42	9–	62	3	0	3	0	116	9.5
C	25	Peter Zezel	WSH	20	7	5	12	13–	10	6	0	0	0	21	33.3
			TOR	32	14	14	28	7–	4	6	0	5	0	69	20.3
			TOTAL	52	21	19	40	20–	14	12	0	5	0	90	23.3
D	22	Michel Petit	QUE	19	4	7	11	15–	47	3	0	0	0	39	10.3
			TOR	54	9	19	28	19–	132	3	1	2	0	95	9.5
			TOTAL	73	13	26	39	34–	179	6	1	2	0	134	9.7
D	8	Rob Ramage	TOR	80	10	25	35	2	173	5	0	2	0	169	5.9
L	17	Wendel Clark	TOR	63	18	16	34	5–	152	4	0	2	0	181	9.9
C	9	Dave Hannan	TOR	74	11	23	34	9–	82	0	1	2	0	72	15.3
R	32	Dan Marois	TOR	78	21	9	30	16–	112	6	0	1	1	152	13.8
R	11	Gary Leeman	TOR	52	17	12	29	25–	39	4	0	1	1	135	12.6
L	14	Dave Reid	TOR	69	15	13	28	10–	18	1	8	0	0	110	13.6
C	27	Lucien Deblois	QUE	14	2	2	4	1	13	0	0	1	0	8	25.0
			TOR	38	10	12	22	4–	30	0	1	0	0	57	17.5
			TOTAL	52	12	14	26	3–	43	0	1	1	0	65	18.5
D	28	Bob Rouse	WSH	47	5	15	20	7–	65	1	0	0	0	50	10.0
			TOR	13	2	4	6	11–	10	1	0	0	0	15	13.3
			TOTAL	60	7	19	26	18–	75	2	0	0	0	65	10.8
R	71	Mike Foligno	BUF	31	4	5	9	4	42	0	0	0	1	27	14.8
			TOR	37	8	7	15	3–	65	1	0	0	0	56	14.3
			TOTAL	68	12	12	24	1	107	1	0	0	1	83	14.5
D	23	Todd Gill	TOR	72	2	22	24	4–	113	0	0	0	0	90	2.2
C	21	Aaron Broten	QUE	20	5	4	9	3–	6	1	0	0	0	40	12.5
			TOR	27	6	4	10	12	32	0	0	1	0	45	13.3
			TOTAL	47	11	8	19	9	38	1	0	1	0	85	12.9
C	12	Doug Shedden	TOR	23	8	10	18	2	10	4	0	0	1	35	22.9
C	15	Claude Loiselle	QUE	59	5	10	15	20–	86	0	2	0	0	79	6.3
			TOR	7	1	1	2	0	2	0	0	0	0	10	10.0
			TOTAL	66	6	11	17	20–	88	0	2	0	0	89	6.7
R	18	Kevin Maguire	TOR	63	9	5	14	10–	180	1	0	0	0	52	17.3
D	2	Luke Richardson	TOR	78	1	9	10	28–	238	0	0	0	0	68	1.5
C	19	Tom Fergus	TOR	14	5	4	9	5–	8	2	0	0	0	17	29.4
C	7	Gilles Thibaudeau	TOR	20	2	7	9	7–	4	0	0	0	0	36	5.6
L	34	Rob Cimetta	TOR	25	2	4	6	5–	21	2	0	1	0	18	11.1
L	20	*Joe Sacco	TOR	20	0	5	5	5–	2	0	0	0	0	20	.0
R	36	Mike Millar	TOR	7	2	2	4	1–	2	0	0	0	0	11	18.2
C	24	*Scott Thornton	TOR	33	1	3	4	15–	30	0	0	0	0	31	3.2
D	93	*Alexander Godynuk	TOR	18	0	3	3	3–	16	0	0	0	0	15	.0
D	26	Darren Veitch	TOR	2	0	1	1	4–	0	0	0	0	0	2	.0
D	29	*Drake Berehowsky	TOR	8	0	1	1	6–	25	0	0	0	0	4	.0
D	29	*Darryl Shannon	TOR	10	0	1	1	1	0	0	0	0	0	3	.0
G	35	Jeff Reese	TOR	30	0	1	1	0	0	0	0	0	0	0	.0
R	16	Greg Johnston	TOR	1	0	0	0	0	0	0	0	0	0	0	.0
D	34	*Jeff Serowik	TOR	1	0	0	0	0	0	0	0	0	0	1	.0
G	31	*Damian Rhodes	TOR	1	0	0	0	0	0	0	0	0	0	0	.0
G	1	*Peter Ing	TOR	56	0	0	0	0	6	0	0	0	0	0	.0

Goaltending

No.	Goaltender	GPI	Mins	Avg	W	L	T	EN	SO	GA	SA	S%
31	*Damian Rhodes	1	60	1.00	1	0	0	0	0	1	26	.962
1	*Peter Ing	56	3126	3.84	16	29	8	3	1	200	1716	.883
35	Jeff Reese	30	1430	3.86	6	13	3	3	1	92	695	.868
30	Allan Bester	6	247	4.37	0	4	0	1	0	18	129	.860
	Totals	**80**	**4874**	**3.91**	**23**	**46**	**11**	**7**	**2**	**318**	**2573**	**.876**

Coaching History

Conn Smythe, 1927-28 to 1929-30; Conn Smythe and Art Duncan, 1930-31; Art Duncan and Dick Irvin, 1931-32; Dick Irvin, 1932-33 to 1939-40; Hap Day, 1940-41 to 1949-50; Joe Primeau, 1950-51 to 1952-53; "King" Clancy, 1953-54 to 1955-56; Howie Meeker, 1956-57; Billy Reay, 1957-58; Billy Reay and "Punch" Imlach, 1958-59; "Punch" Imlach, 1959-60 to 1968-69; John McLellan, 1969-70 to 1970-71; John McLellan and "King" Clancy, 1971-72; John McLellan, 1972-73; Red Kelly, 1973-74 to 1976-77; Roger Neilson, 1977-78 to 1978-79; Floyd Smith, Dick Duff and "Punch" Imlach, 1979-80; "Punch" Imlach, Joe Crozier and Mike Nykoluk, 1980-81; Mike Nykoluk, 1981-82 to 1983-84; Dan Maloney, 1984-85 to 1985-86; John Brophy, 1986-87 to 1987-88; John Brophy and George Armstrong, 1988-89; Doug Carpenter, 1989-90; Doug Carpenter and Tom Watt, 1990-91; Tom Watt, 1991-92.

Club Records

Team
(Figures in brackets for season records are games played; records for fewest points, wins, ties, losses, goals, goals against are for 70 or more games)

Most Points	95	1950-51 (70)
Most Wins	41	1950-51 (70)
		1977-78 (80)
Most Ties	22	1954-55 (70)
Most Losses	52	1984-85 (80)
Most Goals	337	1989-90 (80)
Most Goals Against	387	1983-84 (80)
Fewest Points	48	1984-85 (80)
Fewest Wins	20	1981-82, 1984-85 (80)
Fewest Ties	4	1989-90 (80)
Fewest Losses	16	1950-51 (70)
Fewest Goals	147	1954-55 (70)
Fewest Goals Against	*131	1953-54 (70)

Longest Winning Streak
Over-all	9	Jan. 30-Feb. 28/25
Home	9	Nov. 11-Dec. 26/53
Away	7	Nov. 14-Dec. 15/40
		Dec. 4/60-Jan. 5/61

Longest Undefeated Streak
Over-all	11	Oct. 15-Nov. 8/50 (8 wins, 3 ties)
Home	18	Nov. 28/33-Mar. 10/34 (15 wins, 3 ties)
		Oct. 31/53-Jan. 23/54 (16 wins, 2 ties)
Away	9	Nov. 30/47-Jan. 11/48 (4 wins, 5 ties)

Longest Losing Streak
Over-all	10	Jan. 15-Feb. 8/67
Home	7	Nov. 10-Dec. 5/84
		Jan. 26-Feb. 25/85
Away	11	Feb. 20/-Apr. 1/88

Longest Winless Streak
Over-all	15	Dec. 26/87-Jan. 25/88 (11 losses, 4 ties)
Home	11	Dec. 19/87-Jan. 25/88 (7 losses, 4 ties)
Away	18	Oct. 6/82-Jan. 5/83 (13 losses, 5 ties)

Most Shutouts, Season	13	1953-54 (70)
Most PIM, Season	2,419	1989-90 (80)
Most Goals, Game	14	Mar. 16/57 (NYR 1 at Tor. 14)

Individual
Most Seasons	21	George Armstrong
Most Games	1,187	George Armstrong
Most Goals, Career	389	Darryl Sittler
Most Assists, Career	620	Borje Salming
Most Points, Career	916	Darryl Sittler (389 goals, 527 assists)
Most PIM, Career	1,670	Dave Williams
Most Shutouts, Career	62	Turk Broda
Longest Consecutive Games Streak	486	Tim Horton (Feb. 11/61-Feb. 4/68)
Most Goals, Season	54	Rick Vaive (1981-82)
Most Assists, Season	72	Darryl Sittler (1977-78)
Most Points, Season	117	Darryl Sittler (1977-78) (45 goals, 72 assists)
Most PIM, Season	351	Dave Williams (1977-78)
Most Points, Defenseman Season	79	Ian Turnbull (1976-77) (22 goals, 57 assists)
Most Points, Center Season	117	Darryl Sittler (1977-78) (45 goals, 72 assists)
Most Points, Right Wing, Season	97	Wilf Paiement (1980-81) (40 goals, 57 assists)
Most Points, Left Wing, Season	94	Vince Damphousse (1989-90) (33 goals, 61 assists)
Most Points, Rookie, Season	66	Peter Ihnacak (1982-83) (28 goals, 38 assists)
Most Shutouts, Season	13	Harry Lumley (1953-54)
Most Goals, Game	6	Corb Denneny (Jan. 26/21) Darryl Sittler (Feb. 7/76)
Most Assists, Game	6	Babe Pratt (Jan. 8/44)
Most Points, Game	*10	Darryl Sittler (Feb. 7/76)

* NHL Record.

Captains' History
Hap Day, 1927-28 to 1936-37; Charlie Conacher, 1937-38; Red Horner, 1938-39, 1939-40; Syl Apps, 1940-41 to 1942-43; Bob Davidson, 1943-44, 1944-45; Syl Apps, 1945-46 to 1947-48; Ted Kennedy, 1948-49 to 1954-55; Sid Smith, 1955-56; Ted Kennedy, Jim Thomson, 1956-57; George Armstrong, 1957-58 to 1968-69; Dave Keon, 1969-70 to 1974-75; Darryl Sittler, 1975-76 to 1980-81; Rick Vaive, 1981-82 to 1985-86; no captain, 1986-87 to 1988-89; Rob Ramage, 1989-90 to 1990-91; Wendel Clark, 1991-92.

All-time Record vs. Other Clubs

Regular Season

	At Home GP	W	L	T	GF	GA	PTS	On Road GP	W	L	T	GF	GA	PTS	Total GP	W	L	T	GF	GA	PTS
Boston	277	146	85	46	943	717	338	276	80	149	47	737	915	207	553	226	234	93	1680	1632	545
Buffalo	46	18	21	7	147	172	43	47	16	29	2	136	199	34	93	34	50	9	283	371	77
Calgary	35	14	14	7	143	139	35	36	11	22	3	120	167	25	71	25	36	10	263	306	60
Chicago	289	156	84	49	1001	737	361	288	106	143	39	758	889	251	577	262	227	88	1759	1626	612
Detroit	291	154	93	44	962	762	352	291	96	152	43	707	857	235	582	250	245	87	1669	1619	587
Edmonton	19	7	11	1	75	97	15	19	2	13	4	61	108	8	38	9	24	5	136	205	23
Hartford	19	6	11	2	69	82	14	19	4	12	3	64	97	11	38	10	23	5	133	179	25
Los Angeles	50	28	13	9	213	164	65	50	15	29	6	138	181	36	100	43	42	15	351	345	101
Minnesota	75	35	26	14	276	250	84	74	27	38	9	249	289	63	149	62	64	23	525	539	147
Montreal	311	158	109	44	942	813	360	311	82	189	40	764	1106	204	622	240	298	84	1706	1919	564
New Jersey	29	21	6	2	137	97	44	29	9	11	9	94	106	27	58	30	17	11	231	203	71
NY Islanders	36	16	17	3	123	132	35	35	11	21	3	108	155	25	71	27	38	6	231	287	60
NY Rangers	264	149	77	38	910	685	336	265	101	109	55	779	807	257	529	250	186	93	1689	1492	593
Philadelphia	49	17	19	13	169	166	47	48	10	31	7	115	196	27	97	27	50	20	284	362	74
Pittsburgh	50	23	17	10	206	169	56	50	19	26	5	167	199	43	100	42	43	15	373	368	99
Quebec	19	8	9	2	65	86	18	19	5	9	5	67	78	15	38	13	18	7	132	164	33
St. Louis	72	45	20	7	292	221	97	73	9	44	10	208	261	48	145	64	64	17	500	482	145
Vancouver	41	17	15	9	157	146	43	41	12	22	7	131	144	31	82	29	37	16	288	290	74
Washington	31	18	9	4	148	110	40	31	11	18	2	90	120	24	62	29	27	6	238	230	64
Winnipeg	21	6	14	1	82	103	13	21	7	11	3	92	104	17	42	13	25	4	174	207	30
Defunct Club	232	158	53	21	860	515	337	233	84	120	29	607	745	197	465	242	173	50	1467	1260	534
Totals	2256	1200	723	333	7920	6363	2733	2256	727	1198	331	6192	7723	1785	4512	1927	1921	664	14112	14086	4518

Playoffs

	Series	W	L	GP	W	L	T	GF	GA	Last Mtg.	Round	Result
Boston	13	8	5	62	31	30	1	150	153	1974	QF	L 0-4
Calgary	1	1	0	2	2	0	0	9	5	1979	PR	W 2-0
Chicago	7	5	2	25	15	9	1	76	57	1986	DSF	W 3-0
Detroit	22	11	11	110	54	56	0	287	291	1988	DSF	L 2-4
Los Angeles	2	2	0	5	4	1	0	18	9	1978	PR	W 2-0
Minnesota	2	0	2	7	1	6	0	26	35	1983	DSF	L 1-3
Montreal	13	6	7	67	28	39	0	148	203	1979	QF	L 0-4
NY Islanders	2	1	1	10	4	6	0	33	35	1981	PR	L 0-3
NY Rangers	8	3	5	35	16	19	0	86	86	1971	QF	L 2-4
Philadelphia	3	0	3	15	5	12	0	47	67	1977	QF	L 2-4
Pittsburgh	2	2	0	6	4	2	0	21	13	1977	PR	W 2-1
St. Louis	3	1	2	18	8	10	0	53	56	1990	DSF	L 1-4
Defunct	4	3	1	10	5	4	1	20	16			
Totals	82	43	39	374	177	194	3	961	1024			

Playoff Results 1991-87

Year	Round	Opponent	Result	GF	GA
1990	DSF	St. Louis	L 1-4	16	20
1988	DSF	Detroit	L 2-4	20	32
1987	DF	Detroit	L 3-4	18	20
	DSF	St. Louis	W 4-2	15	12

Abbreviations: Round: F Final; **CF** conference final; **DF** division final; **DSF** division semi-final; **QF** quarter-final. **PR** preliminary round. **GA** goals against; **GF** goals for.

1990-91 Results

	Home				Away	
Oct.	10 Quebec	5-8	Oct.	4 Winnipeg	1-7
	13 Detroit	3-3		6 Calgary	1-4
	17 Hartford	1-3		7 Edmonton	2-3
	20 Chicago	6-2		18 Chicago	0-3
	24 St Louis	3-8		22 NY Rangers	1-5
	27 Buffalo	1-3		25 St Louis	5-8
	30 Minnesota	5-4	Nov.	1 Detroit	4-5
Nov.	3 Calgary	3-7		6 NY Islanders	3-4
	4 Philadelphia	1-7		21 Washington	3-5
	8 Vancouver	3-5		23 Philadelphia*	1-4
	10 Chicago	1-5		27 St Louis	4-3
	12 Winnipeg	5-2		29 Vancouver	1-2
	14 Washington	5-3	Dec.	1 Los Angeles	4-3
	17 Detroit	4-8		6 Minnesota	2-1
	19 Boston	2-5		18 NY Islanders	2-2
	24 Edmonton	1-4		19 NY Rangers	4-1
Dec.	5 Minnesota	2-3		22 Washington*	5-2
	8 Chicago	1-2		23 New Jersey	2-4
	12 Montreal	4-1	Jan.	3 Minnesota	3-3
	15 St Louis	2-4		10 Chicago	2-7
	27 St Louis	6-4		22 Quebec	4-4
	29 Pittsburgh	6-3		23 Montreal	3-7
Jan.	5 Los Angeles	2-4		26 Chicago	1-5
	8 Calgary	3-5	Feb.	1 Detroit	1-4
	12 Hartford	2-2		6 Winnipeg	5-5
	14 Buffalo	3-9		7 Minnesota	2-4
	17 Pittsburgh	5-6		17 Hartford	3-0
	28 Minnesota	4-0		19 St Louis	2-3
Feb.	2 Detroit	2-5		21 Pittsburgh	4-11
	4 St Louis	6-5		23 Montreal	3-3
	9 NY Islanders	3-2		25 Detroit	4-5
	13 Philadelphia	3-6	Mar.	3 Hartford	4-4
	16 Edmonton	3-2		9 Boston*	0-2
	27 New Jersey	7-3		12 Quebec	4-3
Mar.	2 NY Rangers	2-5		13 New Jersey	2-3
	5 Boston	6-3		17 Minnesota	3-4
	7 Vancouver	3-3		20 Los Angeles	4-4
	16 Minnesota	4-3		22 Detroit	3-1
	23 Detroit	4-1		28 Chicago	3-5
	26 Chicago	2-2		30 St Louis	2-5

* Denotes afternoon game.

Entry Draft
Selections 1991-77

1991		1987		1983		1979	
Pick		**Pick**		**Pick**		**Pick**	
47	Yanic Perreault	7	Luke Richardson	7	Russ Courtnall	9	Laurie Boschman
69	Terry Chitaroni	28	Daniel Marois	28	Jeff Jackson	51	Normand Aubin
102	Alexei Kudashov	49	John McIntyre	48	Allan Bester	72	Vincent Tremblay
113	Jeff Perry	71	Joe Sacco	83	Dan Hodgson	93	Frank Nigro
120	Alexander Kuzminsky	91	Mike Eastwood	128	Cam Plante	114	Bill McCreary
135	Martin Prochazka	112	Damian Rhodes	148	Paul Bifano		
160	Dimitri Mironov	133	Trevor Jobe	168	Cliff Albrecht	**1978**	
164	Robb McIntyre	154	Chris Jensen	184	Greg Rolston	**Pick**	
167	Thomas Kucharcik	175	Brian Blad	188	Brian Ross	21	Joel Quenneville
179	Guy Lehoux	196	Ron Bernacci	208	Mike Tomlak	48	Mark Kirton
201	Gary Miller	217	Ken Alexander	228	Ron Choules	65	Bob Parent
223	Jonathan Kelley	238	Alex Weinrich			81	Jordy Douglas
245	Chris O'Rourke	**1986**		**1982**		92	Mel Hewitt
1990		**Pick**		**Pick**		98	Normand Lefebvre
Pick		6	Vincent Damphousse	3	Gary Nylund	115	John Scammell
10	Drake Berehowsky	36	Darryl Shannon	24	Gary Leeman	132	Kevin Reinhart
31	Felix Potvin	48	Sean Boland	25	Peter Ihnacak	149	Mike Waghorne
73	Darby Hendrickson	69	Kent Hulst	45	Ken Wregget	166	Laurie Cuvelier
80	Greg Walters	90	Scott Taylor	73	Vaclav Ruzicka	**1977**	
115	Alexander Godynyuk	111	Stephane Giguere	87	Eduard Uvara	**Pick**	
136	Eric Lacroix	132	Danny Hie	99	Sylvain Charland	11	John Anderson
157	Dan Stiver	153	Stephen Brennan	108	Ron Dreger	12	Trevor Johansen
178	Robert Horyna	174	Brian Bellefeuille	115	Craig Kales	24	Bob Gladney
199	Rob Chebator	195	Sean Davidson	129	Dom Campedelli	29	Rockey Saganiuk
220	Scott Malone	216	Mark Holick	139	Jeff Triano	65	Dan Eastman
241	Nick Vachon	237	Brian Hoard	171	Miroslav Ihnacak	83	John Wilson
1989		**1985**		192	Leigh Verstraete	101	Roy Sommer
Pick		**Pick**		213	Tim Loven	119	Lynn Jorgenson
3	Scott Thornton	1	Wendel Clark	234	Jim Appleby	**1976**	
12	Rob Pearson	22	Ken Spangler	**1981**		**Pick**	
21	Steve Bancroft	43	Dave Thomlinson	**Pick**		30	Randy Carlyle
66	Matt Martin	64	Greg Vey	6	Jim Benning	48	Alain Belanger
96	Keith Carney	85	Jeff Serowik	24	Gary Yaremchuk	52	Gary McFayden
108	David Burke	106	Jiri Latal	55	Ernie Godden	66	Tim Williams
125	Michael Doers	127	Tim Bean	90	Normand LeFrancois	84	Greg Hotham
129	Keith Merkler	148	Andy Donahue	102	Barry Brigley	102	Dan Dkjakalovic
150	Derek Langille	169	Todd Whittemore	132	Andrew Wright		
171	Jeffrey St. Laurent	190	Bob Reynolds	153	Richard Turmel		
192	Justin Tomberlin	211	Tim Armstrong	174	Greg Barber		
213	Mike Jackson	232	Mitch Murphy	195	Marc Magnan		
234	Steve Chartrand	**1984**		**1980**			
1988		**Pick**		**Pick**			
Pick		4	Al Iafrate	25	Craig Muni		
6	Scott Pearson	25	Todd Gill	26	Bob McGill		
27	Tie Domi	67	Jeff Reese	43	Fred Boimistruck		
48	Peter Ing	88	Jack Capuano	74	Stewart Gavin		
69	Ted Crowley	109	Joe Fabian	95	Hugh Larkin		
87	Leonard Esau	130	Joe McInnis	116	Ron Dennis		
132	Matt Mallgrave	151	Derek Laxdal	137	Russ Adam		
153	Roger Elvenas	172	Dan Turner	158	Fred Perlini		
174	Mike Delay	192	David Buckley	179	Darwin McCutcheon		
195	David Sacco	213	Mikael Wurst	200	Paul Higgins		
216	Mike Gregorio	233	Peter Slanina				
237	Peter Deboer						

Club Directory

Maple Leaf Gardens
60 Carlton Street
Toronto, Ontario M5B 1L1
Phone **416/977-1641**
FAX 416/977-5364
ENVOY ID
Front Office: LEAFS. GM
Public
Relations: LEAFS. PR
Capacity: 15,642 (standing 200)

Board of Directors

Thor Eaton	Fredrick G. McDowell	J. Douglas Crump
Donald P. Giffin	Edward S. Rogers	Steve A. Stavro
Edward Lawrence		

Chairman of the Board & C.E.O.	Donald P. Giffin
President, Chief Operating Officer and General Manager	Cliff Fletcher
Secretary–Treasurer	J. Donald Crump
Vice-President	Steve A. Stavro
Alternate Governor	Cliff Fletcher
Alternate Governor & Counsel	Blair Cowper-Smith
Executive Secretary to the Chairman & C.E.O.	Martina Hegemer
Director of Business Operations and Communications	Bob Stellick
Director of Player Development	Floyd Smith
Special Consultant to the President	Darryl Sittler
Head Coach	Tom Watt
Assistant Coach	Mike Kitchen
Assistant Coach	Mike Murphy
Director of Scouting	Pierre Dorion
Scouts	George Armstrong, Dick Duff, Garth Malarchuk, Dan Marr, Jim Bzdel, Peter Johnson, Anders Hedberg, Bob Johnson, Jack Gardiner, Doug Woods
Public Relations Coordinator	Pat Park
Public Relations Assistant	Mark Hillier
Administrative Assistants	Mary Speck, Ellen Salnek
Executive Secretary to the President	Martina Hegemer
Athletic Therapist	Chris Broadhurst
Trainers	Dan "Smokey" Lemelin, Brian Papineau
Controller	Ian Clarke
Assistant Controller	Paul Franck
Director of Marketing and Advertising	Bill Cluff
Marketing Assistant	Dennis Cordick
Box Office Manager	Irwin "Patty" Patoff
Assistant Box Office Manager	Dave Allen
Building Superintendent	Wayne Gillespie
Team Doctors	Dr. Michael Clarfield, Dr. Darrell Olgilvie-Harris, Dr. Leith Douglas, Dr. Michael Easterbrook, Dr. Simon McGrail
Team Dentist	Dr. Ernie Lewis
Head Off Ice Official	Joe Lamantia
Computer Scoreboard Operator	Glenn Gold
Farm Club	St. John's Maple Leafs (AHL)
Head Coach	Marc Crawford
Player Assistant Coach	Joel Quenneville
Trainer	Brent Smith
Equipment Manager	Rob McLean

Coach

WATT, TOM
Coach, Toronto Maple Leafs. Born in Toronto, Ont., June 17, 1935.
Tom Watt enters his first full season as head coach of the Maple Leafs, after replacing Doug Carpenter on October 29, 1990; the appointment marks Watt's third stint as an NHL head coach. Born in Toronto, Watt joined the hometown Leafs on June 8, 1990 as an assistant coach. Immediately prior to joining Toronto, Watt served as an assistant coach to the Stanley Cup Champion Calgary Flames for two seasons.

Watt began his NHL coaching career as an assistant coach with the Vancouver Canucks in 1980-81. He became head coach of the Winnipeg Jets for the 1981-82 season and guided the club to a 48-point improvement over its previous season, in recognition of which Watt was named the Jack Adams Trophy winner as the NHL's Coach of the Year. Watt spent two more seasons with the Jets before returning to the University of Toronto, where he had earlier won 11 conference championships and nine CIAU titles. Watt rejoined the NHL in 1985 as head coach and assistant to the general manager of the Vancouver Canucks, where he remained through the 1986-87 season.

NHL Coaching Record

			Regular Season				Playoffs			
Season	Team	Games	W	L	T	%	Games	W	L	%
1981-82	Winnipeg	80	33	33	14	.500	4	1	3	.250
1982-83	Winnipeg	80	33	39	8	.463	3	0	3	.000
1983-84	Winnipeg	21	6	13	2	.333	....			
1985-86	Vancouver	80	23	44	13	.369	3	0	3	.000
1986-87	Vancouver	80	29	43	8	.413	....			
1990-91	Toronto	69	22	37	10	.391	....			
	NHL Totals	410	146	209	55	.423	10	1	9	.100

General Manager

FLETCHER, CLIFF
President, General Manager and Chief Operating Officer, Toronto Maple Leafs. Born in Montreal, Que., August 16, 1935.
Cliff Fletcher joined the Maple Leafs on July 1, 1991 after 19 years with the Flames franchise. Fletcher's tenure with the Flames was highlighted by the club's 1989 Stanley Cup Championship, but their success was not limited to that championship. In the Flames' eleven seasons under Fletcher after the move from Atlanta to Calgary, the club won one Stanley Cup, two Presidents' Trophies (for top overall finish), two Campbell Conference Championships and three division titles. Over the last seven seasons, the Flames have posted a 317-178-65 record for a .624 winning percentage.

A native of Montreal, Fletcher joined the Flames franchise in Atlanta in September, 1972. In the summer of 1980 he organized the successful transfer of the franchise to Calgary. He began his hockey career with the Montreal Junior Canadiens, where he served for 10 years as a scout for Sam Pollock. In 1967 he became the eastern Canada scout for the St. Louis Blues, and two seasons later was promoted to assistant general manager.

During his 24-year NHL career, Fletcher has been involved in five Stanley Cup Finals. His teams have been involved in the last 16 consecutive playoffs and have missed post-season play only twice in the past 24 years.

Vancouver Canucks
1990-91 Results: 28w-43L-9T 65pts. Fourth, Smythe Division

Year-by-Year Record

Season	GP	Home W	L	T	Road W	L	T	Overall W	L	T	GF	GA	Pts.	Finished		Playoff Result
1990-91	80	18	17	5	10	26	4	28	43	9	243	315	65	4th,	Smythe Div.	Lost Div. Semi-Final
1989-90	80	13	16	11	12	25	3	25	41	14	245	306	64	5th,	Smythe Div.	Out of Playoffs
1988-89	80	19	15	6	14	24	2	33	39	8	251	253	74	4th,	Smythe Div.	Lost Div. Semi-Final
1987-88	80	15	20	5	10	26	4	25	46	9	272	320	59	5th,	Smythe Div.	Out of Playoffs
1986-87	80	17	19	4	12	24	4	29	43	8	282	314	66	5th,	Smythe Div.	Out of Playoffs
1985-86	80	17	18	5	6	26	8	23	44	13	282	333	59	4th,	Smythe Div.	Lost Div. Semi-Final
1984-85	80	15	21	4	10	25	5	25	46	9	284	401	59	5th,	Smythe Div.	Out of Playoffs
1983-84	80	20	16	4	12	23	5	32	39	9	306	328	73	3rd,	Smythe Div.	Lost Div. Semi-Final
1982-83	80	20	12	8	10	23	7	30	35	15	303	309	75	3rd,	Smythe Div.	Lost Div. Semi-Final
1981-82	80	20	8	12	10	25	5	30	33	17	290	286	77	2nd,	Smythe Div.	Lost Final
1980-81	80	17	12	11	11	20	9	28	32	20	289	301	76	3rd,	Smythe Div.	Lost Prelim. Round
1979-80	80	14	17	9	13	20	7	27	37	16	256	281	70	3rd,	Smythe Div.	Lost Prelim. Round
1978-79	80	15	18	7	10	24	6	25	42	13	217	291	63	2nd,	Smythe Div.	Lost Prelim. Round
1977-78	80	13	15	12	7	28	5	20	43	17	239	320	57	3rd,	Smythe Div.	Out of Playoffs
1976-77	80	13	21	6	12	21	7	25	42	13	235	294	63	4th,	Smythe Div.	Out of Playoffs
1975-76	80	22	11	7	11	21	8	33	32	15	271	272	81	2nd,	Smythe Div.	Lost Prelim. Round
1974-75	80	23	12	5	15	20	5	38	32	10	271	254	86	1st,	Smythe Div.	Lost Quarter-Final
1973-74	78	14	18	7	10	25	4	24	43	11	224	296	59	7th,	East Div.	Out of Playoffs
1972-73	78	17	18	4	5	29	5	22	47	9	233	339	53	7th,	East Div.	Out of Playoffs
1971-72	78	14	20	5	6	30	3	20	50	8	203	297	48	7th,	East Div.	Out of Playoffs
1970-71	78	17	18	4	7	28	4	24	46	8	229	296	56	6th,	East Div.	Out of Playoffs

Schedule

Home				Away			
Oct.	Fri.	4	San Jose	Oct.	Sat.	5	San Jose
	Thur.	17	Boston		Tues.	8	Winnipeg
	Sat.	19	Calgary		Thur.	10	Chicago
	Mon.	21	Toronto		Sat.	12	Toronto
	Thur.	24	Washington		Sun.	13	Buffalo
	Sun.	27	Edmonton		Sat.	26	Edmonton
	Tues.	29	New Jersey	Nov.	Thur.	7	Los Angeles
Nov.	Fri.	1	St Louis		Thur.	14	Calgary
	Sun.	3	Edmonton*		Thur.	21	Calgary
	Tues.	5	Winnipeg		Tues.	26	San Jose
	Sun.	10	NY Islanders	Dec.	Sun.	1	Edmonton*
	Tues.	12	Los Angeles		Tues.	3	Quebec
	Sat.	16	San Jose		Wed.	4	Montreal
	Tues.	19	NY Rangers		Sat.	7	Toronto
	Fri.	22	Calgary		Sat.	14	Los Angeles
	Fri.	29	Chicago		Sat.	28	San Jose
Dec.	Tues.	10	Edmonton		Tues.	31	Los Angeles
	Thur.	12	Minnesota	Jan.	Fri.	3	Washington
	Tues.	17	Detroit		Sat.	4	Minnesota
	Thur.	19	Winnipeg		Tues.	14	Winnipeg
	Sun.	22	Quebec		Wed.	15	Edmonton
	Fri.	27	Philadelphia		Tues.	21	Quebec
Jan.	Tues.	7	San Jose		Thur.	23	Detroit
	Sun.	12	Pittsburgh*		Sat.	25	St Louis
	Tues.	28	Edmonton	Feb.	Mon.	10	Montreal
	Thur.	30	Chicago		Wed.	12	NY Rangers
Feb.	Sat.	1	Hartford		Thur.	13	New Jersey
	Tues.	4	Montreal		Sat.	15	NY Islanders
	Thur.	6	NY Islanders		Mon.	17	NY Rangers*
	Wed.	19	Buffalo		Fri.	21	San Jose
	Sun.	23	Boston*	Mar.	Thur.	5	Boston
	Tues.	25	Los Angeles		Sat.	7	Hartford
	Fri.	28	Winnipeg		Sun.	8	Philadelphia
Mar.	Sun.	1	Calgary*		Sat.	14	Calgary
	Mon.	2	St Louis		Sun.	22	Winnipeg*
	Thur.	12	New Jersey		Tues.	24	Minnesota
	Wed.	18	Hartford		Thur.	26	Pittsburgh
	Fri.	20	Winnipeg		Sat.	28	Detroit*
Apr.	Thur.	2	Calgary		Sun.	29	Washington*
	Sun.	5	Los Angeles*	Apr.	Sat.	4	Los Angeles*

* Denotes afternoon game.

Home Starting Times:
Weeknights .... 7:35 p.m.
Saturdays .... 5:05 p.m.
Sundays and Holidays .... 7:05 p.m.
Matinees .... 2:05 p.m.

Franchise date: May 22, 1970.

22nd NHL Season

Troy Gamble

1991-92 Player Personnel

FORWARDS

	HT	WT	S	Place of Birth	Date	1990-91 Club
ADAMS, Greg	6-3	190	L	Nelson, B.C.	8/1/63	Vancouver
ANTOSKI, Shawn	6-4	240	L	Brantford, Ont.	3/25/70	Vancouver-Milwaukee
BADER, Darin	6-0	202	L	Edmonton, AB	4/1/71	Saskatoon
BAKOVIC, Peter	6-2	200	R	Thunder Bay, Ont.	1/31/65	Milwaukee
BAWA, Robin	6-2	214	R	Chemanius, B.C.	3/26/66	Fort Wayne
BROWN, Cam	6-1	205	L	Saskatoon, Sask.	5/15/69	Vancouver-Milwaukee
CAPUANO, Dave	6-2	190	L	Warwick, R.I.	7/27/68	Vancouver
CIPRIANO, Mark	5-11	195	R	Delta, B.C.	6/1/71	Victoria
COURTNALL, Geoff	6-1	190	L	Victoria, B.C.	8/18/62	Van.-St. Loius
KRON, Robert	5-10	174	R	Brno, Czech.	2/27/67	Vancouver
LARIONOV, Igor	5-9	165	L	Voskresensk, USSR	12/3/60	Vancouver
LINDEN, Trevor	6-4	205	R	Medicine Hat, Alta.	4/11/70	Vancouver
MAZUR, Jay	6-2	205	R	Hamilton, Ont.	1/22/65	Vancouver-Milwaukee
McBAIN, Andrew	6-1	205	R	Scarborough, Ont.	1/18/65	Vancouver-Milwaukee
MOMESSO, Sergio	6-3	215	L	Montreal	9/4/65	Van.-St. Louis
MURANO, Eric	6-0	200	R	LaSalle, Que.	5/4/67	Milwaukee
MURPHY, Rob	6-3	210	L	Hull, Que.	4/7/69	Vancouver
NEDVED, Petr	6-3	185	L	Liberec, Czech.	12/9/71	Vancouver
ODJICK, Gino	6-3	220	L	Maniwaki, PQ	9/7/70	Vancouver-Milwaukee
RONNING, Cliff	5-8	175	L	Burnaby, B.C.	10/1/65	Van.-St. Louis
SANDLAK, Jim	6-3	220	R	Kitchener, Ont.	12/12/66	Vancouver
STOJANOV, Alex	6-4	225	L	Windsor, Ont.	4/25/73	Hamilton
VALK, Garry	6-1	190	L	Edmonton, Alta.	11/27/67	Vancouver
WALTER, Ryan	6-0	200	L	Burnaby, B.C.	4/23/58	Montreal

DEFENSEMEN

	HT	WT	S	Place of Birth	Date	
AGNEW, Jim	6-1	190	L	Hartney, Man.	3/21/66	Milwaukee-Vancouver
BABYCH, Dave	6-2	215	L	Edmonton, Alta.	5/23/61	Hartford
BLAD, Brian	6-2	202	L	Brockville, Ont.	7/22/67	Milwaukee
DIDUCK, Gerald	6-2	207	R	Edmonton, Alta.	4/6/65	Van.-Montreal
DIRK, Robert	6-4	218	L	Regina, Sask.	8/20/66	Van.-St. Louis
GIBSON, Don	6-1	210	R	Deloriane, Man.	12/29/67	Vancouver-Milwaukee
HERTER, Jason	6-1	190	R	Hafford, Sask.	1/15/71	N. Dakota
LIDSTER, Doug	6-1	200	L	Kamloops, B.C.	10/18/60	Vancouver
LUMME, Jyrki	6-1	207	L	Tampere, Finland	7/16/66	Vancouver
MURZYN, Dana	6-2	200	L	Calgary, Alta.	12/9/66	Van.-Calgary
NEUMEIER, Troy	6-2	195	L	Langenburg, Sask.	9/3/60	Pr. Albert-Milw.
PLAVSIC, Adrien	6-1	190	L	Montreal, Que.	1/13/70	Vancouver
VALIMONT, Carl	6-1	200	L	Southington, CT	3/1/66	Milwaukee

GOALTENDERS

	HT	WT	C	Place of Birth	Date	1990-91 Club
D'ALESSIO, Corrie	5-11	155	L	Cornwall, Ont.	12/9/69	Cornell
GAMBLE, Troy	5-11	195	L	New Glasgow, N.S.	4/7/67	Vancouver
McLEAN, Kirk	6-0	185	L	Willowdale, Ont.	6/26/66	Vancouver
MASON, Bob	6-1	180	R	Int'l Falls, Ont.	4/22/61	Vancouver-Milwaukee

General Managers' History

Normand Robert Poile, 1970-71 to 1972-73; Hal Laycoe, 1973-74; Phil Maloney, 1974-75 to 1976-77; Jake Milford, 1977-78 to 1981-82; Harry Neale, 1982-83 to 1984-85; Jack Gordon, 1985-86 to 1986-87; Pat Quinn, 1987-88 to date.

Coaching History

Hal Laycoe, 1970-71 to 1971-72; Vic Stasiuk, 1972-73; Bill McCreary and Phil Maloney, 1973-74; Phil Maloney, 1974-75 to 1975-76; Phil Maloney and Orland Kurtenbach, 1976-77; Orland Kurtenbach, 1977-78; Harry Neale, 1978-79 to 1980-81; Harry Neale and Roger Neilson, 1981-82; Roger Neilson 1982-83; Roger Neilson and Harry Neale, 1983-84; Bill Laforge, 1984-85; Tom Watt, 1985-86, 1986-87; Bob McCammon, 1987-88 to 1989-90. Bob McCammon and Pat Quinn, 1990-91; Pat Quinn, 1991-92.

Captains' History

Orland Kurtenbach, 1970-71 to 1973-74; no captain, 1974-75; Andre Boudrias, 1975-76; Chris Oddleifson, 1976-77; Don Lever, 1977-78; Don Lever, Kevin McCarthy, 1978-79; Kevin McCarthy, 1979-80 to 1981-82; Stan Smyl, 1982-83 to 1989-90; Dan Quinn, Doug Lidster and Trevor Linden, 1990-91; Doug Lidster and Trevor Linden, 1991-92.

Retired Numbers

11	Wayne Maki	1971-1973

1990-91 Scoring

Regular Season

* rookie

Pos	#	Player	Team	GP	G	A	Pts	+/-	PIM	PP	SH	GW	GT	S	%
R	16	Trevor Linden	VAN	80	33	37	70	25–	65	16	2	4	1	229	14.4
L	10	Geoff Courtnall	STL	66	27	30	57	19	56	9	0	6	0	216	12.5
			VAN	11	6	2	8	3–	8	3	0	2	0	47	12.8
			TOTAL	77	33	32	65	16	64	12	0	8	0	263	12.5
L	8	Greg Adams	VAN	55	21	24	45	16–	10	5	1	2	2	148	14.2
C	7	Cliff Ronning	STL	48	14	18	32	2	10	5	0	2	0	81	17.3
			VAN	11	6	6	12	2–	0	2	0	0	0	32	18.8
			TOTAL	59	20	24	44	0	10	7	0	2	0	113	17.7
L	28	Dave Capuano	VAN	61	13	31	44	1	42	5	0	1	0	77	16.9
D	3	Doug Lidster	VAN	78	6	32	38	6–	77	4	0	1	0	157	3.8
L	27	Sergio Momesso	STL	59	10	18	28	12	131	0	0	1	1	86	11.6
			VAN	11	6	2	8	1	43	3	0	2	0	33	18.2
			TOTAL	70	16	20	36	13	174	3	0	3	1	119	13.4
C	18	Igor Larionov	VAN	64	13	21	34	3–	14	1	1	0	0	66	19.7
L	14	Steve Bozek	VAN	62	15	17	32	6–	22	0	1	2	1	126	11.9
L	58	*Robert Kron	VAN	76	12	20	32	11–	21	2	3	0	0	124	9.7
D	21	Jyrki Lumme	VAN	80	5	27	32	15–	59	1	0	0	0	157	3.2
D	24	Tom Kurvers	TOR	19	0	3	3	12–	8	0	0	0	0	23	.0
			VAN	32	4	23	27	13–	20	3	0	0	0	76	5.3
			TOTAL	51	4	26	30	25–	28	3	0	0	0	99	4.0
R	23	*Garry Valk	VAN	59	10	11	21	23–	67	1	0	1	0	90	11.1
R	33	*Jay Mazur	VAN	36	11	7	18	3	14	1	1	2	0	59	18.6
C	19	*Petr Nedved	VAN	61	10	6	16	21–	20	1	0	0	0	97	10.3
R	12	Stan Smyl	VAN	45	2	12	14	5–	87	0	0	0	0	45	4.4
R	25	Jim Sandlak	VAN	59	7	6	13	20–	125	4	0	0	0	88	8.0
D	4	Gerald Diduck	MTL	32	1	2	3	3	39	0	0	0	0	34	2.9
			VAN	31	3	7	10	8–	66	0	0	0	0	66	4.5
			TOTAL	63	4	9	13	5–	105	0	0	1	0	100	4.0
D	15	*Adrien Plavsic	VAN	48	2	10	12	23–	62	0	0	0	0	69	2.9
L	29	*Gino Odjick	VAN	45	7	1	8	6–	296	0	0	0	1	39	17.9
D	6	Robert Nordmark	VAN	45	2	6	8	10–	63	1	0	0	0	65	3.1
C	44	Rob Murphy	VAN	42	5	1	6	11–	90	0	0	0	0	19	26.3
D	22	Robert Dirk	STL	41	1	3	4	2	100	0	0	0	0	20	5.0
			VAN	11	1	0	1	7–	20	0	0	0	0	9	11.1
			TOTAL	52	2	3	5	5–	120	0	0	0	0	29	6.9
R	9	Andrew McBain	VAN	13	0	5	5	3–	32	0	0	0	0	8	.0
D	5	Dana Murzyn	CGY	19	0	2	2	4–	30	0	0	0	0	25	.0
			VAN	10	1	0	1	3–	8	0	0	0	0	15	6.7
			TOTAL	29	1	2	3	7–	38	0	0	0	0	40	2.5
D	24	*Don Gibson	VAN	14	0	3	3	1–	20	0	0	0	0	9	.0
G	35	*Troy Gamble	VAN	47	0	1	1	0	14	0	0	0	0	0	.0
L	48	*Cam Brown	VAN	1	0	0	0	0	7	0	0	0	0	0	.0
G	30	*Steve McKichan	VAN	1	0	0	0	0	0	0	0	0	0	0	.0
G	33	Steve Weeks	VAN	1	0	0	0	0	0	0	0	0	0	0	.0
L	27	*Shawn Antoski	VAN	2	0	0	0	2–	0	0	0	0	0	2	.0
C	24	*Jack Capuano	VAN	3	0	0	0	1–	0	0	0	0	0	4	.0
G	31	Bob Mason	VAN	6	0	0	0	0	0	0	0	0	0	0	.0
C	22	Craig Coxe	VAN	7	0	0	0	3–	27	0	0	0	0	5	.0
D	36	Jim Agnew	VAN	20	0	0	0	11–	81	0	0	0	0	12	.0
G	1	Kirk McLean	VAN	41	0	0	0	0	0	0	0	0	0	0	.0

Goaltending

No.	Goaltender	GPI	Mins	Avg	W	L	T	EN	SO	GA	SA	S%
35	*Troy Gamble	47	2433	3.45	16	16	6	4	1	140	1156	.879
1	Kirk McLean	41	1969	3.99	10	22	3	3	0	131	983	.867
31	Bob Mason	6	353	4.93	2	4	0	0	0	29	188	.846
31	*Steve McKichan	1	20	6.00	0	0	0	0	0	2	8	.750
35	Steve Weeks	1	59	6.10	0	1	0	0	0	6	29	.793
	Totals	80	4856	3.89	28	43	9	7	1	315	2371	.867

Playoffs

Pos	#	Player	Team	GP	G	A	Pts	+/-	PIM	PP	SH	GW	OT	S	%
C	7	Cliff Ronning	VAN	6	6	3	9	1	12	2	0	2	1	22	27.3
L	10	Geoff Courtnall	VAN	6	3	5	8	2	4	0	0	0	0	26	11.5
R	16	Trevor Linden	VAN	6	3	4	7	3	2	0	0	0	0	12	.0
D	21	Jyrki Lumme	VAN	6	2	3	5	4–	0	1	1	0	0	7	28.6
D	24	Tom Kurvers	VAN	6	2	2	4	4–	12	1	0	0	0	13	15.4
L	27	Sergio Momesso	VAN	6	2	1	3	3	25	0	0	0	0	10	.0
L	28	Dave Capuano	VAN	6	1	1	2	4–	0	0	0	0	0	11	9.1
D	3	Doug Lidster	VAN	6	1	1	2	3–	6	0	0	0	0	9	.0
D	4	Gerald Diduck	VAN	6	1	0	1	1–	11	0	0	0	0	10	10.0
C	18	Igor Larionov	VAN	6	1	0	1	5–	0	0	0	0	0	8	12.5
R	33	*Jay Mazur	VAN	6	1	0	1	5–	8	0	0	0	0	6	.0
D	5	Dana Murzyn	VAN	6	0	1	1	1–	8	0	0	0	0	6	.0
C	19	*Petr Nedved	VAN	6	0	1	1	1–	0	0	0	0	0	8	.0
G	1	Kirk Mclean	VAN	6	0	1	1	0	0	0	0	0	0	0	.0
L	14	Steve Bozek	VAN	3	0	1	1	1–	0	0	0	0	0	4	.0
G	35	*Troy Gamble	VAN	4	0	1	1	0	2	0	0	0	0	0	.0
C	44	Rob Murphy	VAN	5	0	1	1	1–	0	0	0	0	0	8	.0
L	8	Greg Adams	VAN	5	0	0	0	2–	2	0	0	0	0	8	.0
R	23	*Garry Valk	VAN	6	0	0	0	4–	20	0	0	0	0	6	.0
D	22	Robert Dirk	VAN	6	0	0	0	4–	13	0	0	0	0	6	.0
L	29	*Gino Odjick	VAN	6	0	0	0	2–	18	0	0	0	1	1	.0

Goaltending

No.	Goaltender	GPI	Mins	Avg	W	L	EN	SO	GA	SA	S%
1	Kirk McLean	2	123	3.41	1	1	0	0	7	66	.894
35	*Troy Gamble	4	249	3.86	1	3	3	0	16	133	.880
	Totals	6	374	4.17	2	4	3	0	26	202	.871

Club Records

Team

(Figures in brackets for season records are games played; records for fewest points, wins, ties, losses, goals, goals against are for 70 or more games)

Most Points	86	1974-75 (80)
Most Wins	38	1974-75 (80)
Most Ties	20	1980-81 (80)
Most Losses	50	1971-72 (78)
Most Goals	306	1983-84 (80)
Most Goals Against	401	1984-85 (80)
Fewest Points	48	1971-72 (78)
Fewest Wins	20	1971-72 (78)
		1977-78 (80)
Fewest Ties	8	1970-71 (78)
		1971-72 (78)
		1986-87 (80)
		1988-89 (80)
Fewest Losses	32	1974-75 (80)
		1975-76 (80)
		1980-81 (80)
Fewest Goals	203	1971-72 (78)
Fewest Goals Against	253	1988-89 (80)

Longest Winning Streak
Over-all ....7 Feb. 10-23/89
Home ....8 Feb. 27/83-
                   Mar. 21/83
                   Jan. 31-
                   Mar. 10/89
Away ....3 Ten times

Longest Undefeated Streak
Over-all ....10 Mar. 5-25/77
                       (5 wins, 5 ties)
Home ....12 Oct. 29-
                    Dec. 17/74
                    (11 wins, 1 tie)
                    Jan. 29-
                    Mar. 18/89
                    (10 wins, 2 ties)
Away ....5 Three times

Longest Losing Streak
Over-all ....9 Four times
Home ....6 Dec. 18/70-
                   Jan. 20/71
                   Nov. 3-18/78
Away ....12 Nov. 28/81-
                     Feb. 6/82

Longest Winless Streak
Over-all ....13 Nov. 9-
                       Dec. 7/73
                       (10 losses, 3 ties)
Home ....11 Dec. 18/70-
                    Feb. 6/71
                    (10 losses, 1 tie)

Away ....20 Jan. 2/86-
                       Apr. 2/86
                       (14 losses, 6 ties)
Most Shutouts, Season 8 1974-75 (80)
Most PIM, Season 2,196 1987-88 (80)
Most Goals, Game ....11 Mar. 28/71
                            (Cal. 5 at Van. 11)
                            Nov. 25/86
                            (L.A. 5 at Van. 11)

Individual

Most Seasons	13	Stan Smyl
Most Games	896	Stan Smyl
Most Goals, Career	262	Stan Smyl
Most Assists, Career	411	Stan Smyl
Most Points, Career	673	Stan Smyl
		(262 goals, 411 assists)
Most PIM, Career	1,556	Stan Smyl
Most Shutouts, Career	11	Gary Smith

Longest Consecutive
  Games Streak ....437 Don Lever
                           (Oct. 7/72-Jan. 14/78)
Most Goals, Season ....45 Tony Tanti
                              (1983-84)
Most Assists, Season ......62 André Boudrias
                               (1974-75)
Most Points, Season ......91 Patrik Sundstrom
                              (1983-84)
                              (38 goals, 53 assists)
Most PIM, Season ....343 Dave Williams
                             (1980-81)
Most Points, Defenseman,
  Season ....63 Doug Lidster
                          (1986-87)
                          (12 goals, 51 assists)
Most Points, Center,
  Season ....91 Patrik Sundstrom
                          (1983-84)
                          (38 goals, 53 assists)
Most Points, Right Wing,
  Season ....88 Stan Smyl
                          (1982-83)
                          (38 goals, 50 assists)
Most Points, Left Wing,
  Season ....81 Darcy Rota
                          (1982-83)
                          (42 goals, 39 assists)
Most Points, Rookie,
  Season ....60 Ivan Hlinka
                          (1981-82)
                          (23 goals, 37 assists)

Most Shutouts, Season .....6 Gary Smith
                              (1974-75)
Most Goals, Game ....4 Several players
Most Assists, Game ....6 Patrik Sundstrom
                             (Feb. 29/84)
Most Points, Game ....7 Patrik Sundstrom
                            (Feb. 29/84)

All-time Record vs. Other Clubs

Regular Season

				At Home							On Road							Total				
	GP	W	L	T	GF	GA	PTS	GP	W	L	T	GF	GA	PTS	GP	W	L	T	GF	GA	PTS
Boston	40	12	21	7	136	174	31	40	3	34	3	88	186	9	80	15	55	10	224	360	40
Buffalo	41	19	12	10	155	134	48	41	11	22	8	116	155	30	82	30	34	18	271	289	78
Calgary	61	21	28	12	209	209	54	61	10	43	8	169	280	28	122	31	71	20	378	489	82
Chicago	46	20	15	11	137	134	51	46	12	29	5	106	169	29	92	32	44	16	243	303	80
Detroit	41	23	12	6	173	127	52	40	11	23	6	121	172	28	81	34	35	12	294	299	80
Edmonton	44	14	24	6	157	197	34	44	7	33	4	139	237	18	88	21	57	10	296	434	52
Hartford	19	7	7	5	65	53	19	19	7	6	4	69	66	18	38	14	15	9	134	119	37
Los Angeles	65	30	23	12	252	229	72	65	18	38	9	198	276	45	130	48	61	21	450	505	117
Minnesota	45	23	14	8	182	140	54	45	10	28	7	129	193	27	90	33	42	15	311	333	81
Montreal	40	5	27	8	95	164	18	41	6	33	2	105	209	14	81	11	60	10	200	373	32
New Jersey	37	20	6	11	141	109	51	38	17	15	6	129	115	40	75	37	21	17	270	224	91
NY Islanders	37	16	18	3	118	122	35	36	7	21	8	94	142	22	73	23	39	11	212	264	57
NY Rangers	42	10	29	3	134	174	23	43	7	33	3	106	198	17	85	17	62	6	240	372	40
Philadelphia	42	10	22	10	125	164	30	42	12	30	0	119	193	24	84	22	52	10	244	357	54
Pittsburgh	40	20	17	3	153	153	43	40	8	25	7	136	177	23	80	28	42	10	289	330	66
Quebec	19	10	7	2	80	76	22	19	8	7	4	57	57	20	38	18	14	6	137	133	42
St. Louis	46	21	20	5	148	143	47	46	12	27	7	137	185	31	92	33	47	12	285	328	78
Toronto	41	22	12	7	144	131	51	41	15	17	9	146	157	39	82	37	29	16	290	288	90
Washington	29	13	12	4	100	95	30	29	11	16	2	91	95	24	58	24	28	6	191	190	54
Winnipeg	42	23	13	6	162	132	52	41	11	23	7	151	168	29	83	34	36	13	313	300	81
Defunct Club	19	14	3	2	82	48	30	19	10	8	1	71	68	21	38	24	11	3	153	116	51
Totals	**836**	**353**	**342**	**141**	**2948**	**2908**	**847**	**836**	**213**	**513**	**110**	**2477**	**3498**	**536**	**1672**	**566**	**855**	**251**	**5425**	**6406**	**1383**

Playoffs

	Series	W	L	GP	W	L	T	GF	GA	Last Mtg.	Round	Result
Buffalo	2	0	2	7	1	6	0	14	28	1981	PR	L 0-3
Calgary	4	1	3	18	8	10	0	57	62	1989	DSF	L 3-4
Chicago	1	1	0	5	4	1	0	18	13	1982	CF	W 4-1
Edmonton	1	0	1	3	0	3	0	5	17	1986	DSF	L 0-3
Los Angeles	2	1	1	11	6	5	0	35	40	1991	DSF	L 2-4
Montreal	1	0	1	5	1	4	0	9	20	1975	QF	L 1-4
NY Islanders	2	0	2	6	0	6	0	14	26	1982	F	L 0-4
Philadelphia	1	0	1	3	1	2	0	9	15	1979	PR	L 1-2
Totals	**14**	**3**	**11**	**58**	**21**	**37**	**0**	**161**	**221**			

Playoff Results 1991-87

Year	Round	Opponent	Result	GF	GA
1991	DSF	Los Angeles	L 2-4	16	26
1989	DSF	Calgary	L 3-4	20	26

Abbreviations: Round: F – Final; **CF** – conference final; **DF** – division final; **DSF** – division semi-final; **PR** – preliminary round. **QF** – quarter-final. **GA** – goals against; **GF** – goals for.

1990-91 Results

		Home					Away	
Oct.	9	Los Angeles	2-6	Oct.	4	Calgary	2-3
	12	St Louis	4-0		6	Los Angeles	6-3
	14	Edmonton*	5-4		19	Winnipeg	5-7
	17	Boston	3-1		21	Quebec*	3-2
	30	Washington	1-2		23	Detroit	0-6
Nov.	1	New Jersey	2-1		25	Boston	2-4
	3	Winnipeg	3-5		27	Hartford	4-2
	6	Detroit	6-3	Nov.	8	Toronto	5-3
	16	NY Islanders	3-2		9	Buffalo	1-7
	19	Calgary	4-6		11	Philadelphia	0-2
	21	Chicago	4-1		14	Edmonton	3-5
	27	Minnesota	1-1		23	Minnesota	4-6
	29	Toronto	2-1		24	St Louis	3-3
Dec.	10	Quebec	2-3	Dec.	2	Winnipeg	5-1
	14	NY Rangers	3-5		4	NY Islanders	4-2
	16	Calgary*	2-5		5	New Jersey	4-9
	20	Edmonton	7-4		7	Pittsburgh	2-2
	22	Los Angeles	4-3		12	Edmonton	4-5
	27	Montreal	5-7		18	Calgary	3-2
	28	Edmonton	2-5		23	Edmonton	3-4
Jan.	8	Buffalo	3-3		31	Winnipeg	1-2
	10	Hartford	4-5	Jan.	2	Hartford	2-5
	16	Winnipeg	1-2		3	Boston	3-8
	23	Edmonton	6-5		5	Minnesota	6-5
	25	Los Angeles	1-5		12	Los Angeles	2-6
	28	Chicago	0-1		26	Los Angeles	4-5
	31	NY Rangers	3-3		30	Edmonton	4-9
Feb.	14	St Louis	2-3	Feb.	2	Los Angeles	1-9
	16	Washington	4-2		5	Washington	3-5
	18	Quebec	3-3		7	Philadelphia	2-1
	23	Detroit	5-2		8	NY Rangers	1-8
	25	Calgary	4-2		10	New Jersey*	0-2
	27	Pittsburgh	4-3		20	Winnipeg	5-5
Mar.	1	Montreal	1-7		21	Calgary	4-6
	13	Philadelphia	4-5	Mar.	3	Chicago	0-8
	16	NY Islanders	4-4		5	Pittsburgh	1-4
	17	Los Angeles	5-4		7	Toronto	3-3
	20	Calgary	2-3		9	Montreal	2-4
	22	Winnipeg	3-1		10	Buffalo	7-5
	28	Winnipeg	3-2		26	Calgary	2-7

* Denotes afternoon game.

Entry Draft
Selections 1991-77

1991
Pick
7	Alex Stojanov
29	Jassen Cullimore
51	Sean Pronger
95	Danny Kesa
117	Jevgeni Namestnikov
139	Brent Thurston
161	Eric Johnson
183	David Neilson
205	Brad Barton
227	Jason Fitzsimmons
249	Xavier Majic

1989
Pick
2	Petr Nedved
18	Shawn Antoski
23	Jiri Slegr
65	Darin Bader
86	Gino Odjick
128	Daryl Filipek
149	Paul O'Hagan
170	Mark Cipriano
191	Troy Neumier
212	Tyler Ertel
233	Karri Kivi

1989
Pick
8	Jason Herter
29	Robert Woodward
71	Brett Hauer
113	Pavel Bure
134	James Revenberg
155	Rob Sangster
176	Sandy Moger
197	Gus Morschauser
218	Hayden O'Rear
239	Darcy Cahill
248	Jan Bergman

1988
Pick
2	Trevor Linden
33	Leif Rohlin
44	Dane Jackson
107	Corrie D'Alessio
122	Phil Von Stefenelli
128	Dixon Ward
149	Greg Geldart
170	Roger Akerstorm
191	Paul Constantin
212	Chris Wolanin
233	Steffan Nilsson

1987
Pick
24	Rob Murphy
45	Steve Veilleux
66	Doug Torrel
87	Sean Fabian
108	Gary Valk
129	Todd Fanning
150	Viktor Tuminev
171	Craig Daly
192	John Fletcher
213	Roger Hansson
233	Neil Eisenhut
234	Matt Evo

1986
Pick
7	Dan Woodley
49	Don Gibson
70	Ronnie Stern
91	Eric Murano
112	Steve Herniman
133	Jon Helgeson
154	Jeff Noble
175	Matt Merton
196	Marc Lyons
217	Todd Hawkins
238	Vladimir Krutov

1985
Pick
4	Jim Sandlak
25	Troy Gamble
46	Shane Doyle
67	Randy Siska
88	Robert Kron
109	Martin Hrstka
130	Brian McFarlane
151	Hakan Ahlund
172	Curtis Hunt
193	Carl Valimont
214	Igor Larionov
235	Darren Taylor

1984
Pick
10	J.J. Daigneault
31	Jeff Rolicek
52	Dave Saunders
55	Landis Chaulk
58	Mike Stevens
73	Brian Bertuzzi
94	Brett MacDonald
115	Jeff Korchinski
136	Blaine Chrest
157	Jim Agnew
178	Rex Grant
198	Ed Lowney
219	Doug Clarke
239	Ed Kister

1983
Pick
9	Cam Neely
30	Dave Bruce
50	Scott Tottle
70	Tim Lorentz
90	Doug Quinn
110	Dave Lowry
130	Terry Maki
150	John Labatt
170	Allan Measures
190	Roger Grillo
210	Steve Kayser
230	Jay Mazur

1982
Pick
11	Michel Petit
53	Yves Lapointe
71	Shawn Kilroy
116	Taylor Hall
137	Parie Proft
158	Newell Brown
179	Don McLaren
200	Al Raymond
221	Steve Driscoll
242	Shawn Green

1981
Pick
10	Garth Butcher
52	Jean-Marc Lanthier
73	Wendell Young
105	Moe Lemay
115	Stu Kulak
136	Bruce Holloway
157	Petri Skriko
178	Frank Caprice
199	Rejean Vignola

1980
Pick
7	Rick Lanz
49	Andy Schliebener
70	Marc Crawford
91	Darrel May
112	Ken Berry
133	Doug Lidster
154	John O'Connor
175	Patrik Sundstrom
196	Grant Martin

1979
Pick
5	Rick Vaive
26	Brent Ashton
47	Ken Ellacott
68	Art Rutland
89	Dirk Graham
110	Shane Swan

1978
Pick
4	Bill Derlago
22	Curt Fraser
40	Stan Smyl
56	Harold Luckner
57	Brad Smith
90	Gerry Minor
107	Dave Ross
124	Steve O'Neill
141	Charlie Antetomaso
158	Richard Martens

1977
Pick
4	Jere Gillis
22	Jeff Bandura
40	Glen Hanlon
56	Dave Morrow
58	Murray Bannerman
76	Steve Hazlett
94	Brian Drumm
112	Ray Creasey

Club Directory

Pacific Coliseum
100 North Renfrew Street
Vancouver, B.C. V5K 3N7
Phone **604/254-5141**
FAX 604/251-5123
GM FAX 604/251-5514
ENVOY ID
Front Office: CANUCKS. GM
Public
Relations: CANUCKS. PR
Capacity: 16,123

Northwest Sports Enterprises Ltd.
Board of Directors

J. Lawrence Dampier	Senator E.M. Lawson	Andrew E. Saxton
Arthur R. Griffiths	W.L. McEwen	Peter W. Webster
Frank A. Griffiths, C.A.	David S. Owen	Sydney W. Welsh
F.W. Griffiths	Senator Ray Perrault	D.A. Williams, C.A.
Coleman E. Hall	J. Raymond Peters	D. Alexander Farac (Sec.)
Douglas Holtby	Peter Paul Saunders	

Chairman	Frank A. Griffiths, C.A.
Vice-Chairman and Governor	Arthur R. Griffiths
President and General Manager/Head Coach	Pat Quinn
Vice-President and	
Director of Hockey Operations	Brian Burke
Vice-President and Director of	
Marketing and Communications	Glen Ringdal
Vice-President of Finance/Administration	Carlos Mascarenhas
Senior Advisor	Jack Gordon
Assistant Coaches	Rick Ley, Ron Wilson, Stan Smyl
Trainers	Larry Ashley, Pat O'Neill, Ed Georgica
Strength Coach	Wayne Wilson
Massage Therapist	TBA
Director of Public and Media Relations	Steve Tambellini
Director of Scouting	Mike Penny
Director of Pro Scouting	Murray Oliver
Scouting Staff	Scott Carter, Ron Delorme, Ron Lapointe, Paul MacIntosh, Jack McCartan, Ed McColgan, Noel Price, Ken Slater, Ernie Vargas
Director of Publishing	Norm Jewison
Director of Special Events	Lynn Harrison
Director of Corporate Sales	Dave Nonis
Director of Hockey Information	Steve Frost
Public Relations Assistant	Gail Nishi
Box Office Manager	Fiona Hayes
Executive Secretary, Pres. & GM	Jette Sandeford
Executive Secretary, Vice-President and Director of Hockey Operations	Patti Timms
Executive Secretary, Vice-President and Director of Marketing and Communications	Jane Dutka
Manager of Food and Beverage Operations	John Faris
Director of Retail Operations	Larry Donen
General Manager Farm Team (Milwaukee Admirals)	Phil Wittliff
Milwaukee Head Coach	Jack McIlhargey
Milwaukee Assistant Coach	Curt Fraser
Club Doctors	Dr. Gord Matheson, Dr. Ross Davidson
Club Dentist	Dr. David Lawson
Club Colors	White, Black, Red and Gold
Press Box	West Side, Renfrew St. Entrance
Dimensions of rink	200 feet by 85 feet
Club Trains at:	Victoria, B.C.
Play-by-Play Broadcaster	Jim Robson (radio and TV)
Radio Station	CKNW (980 AM) and Western Information Network
TV Channel	CBC (2), BCTV (8), CHEK (6)

General Manager

QUINN, PAT
President and General Manager, Vancouver Canucks.
Born in Hamilton, Ont., January 29, 1943.

Pat Quinn took up management responsibilities with the Vancouver Canucks in 1987-88 after coaching in Los Angeles from 1984 to 1987 and in Philadelphia from 1978 to 1982. In Philadelphia, Quinn was awarded the Jack Adams award for leading the Flyers to the Stanley Cup finals in 1979-80. He started his coaching career with the Maine Mariners of the AHL and eventually was promoted to the head coaching job with Philadelphia. An NHL defenseman himself, Quinn played in more than 600 games over nine years.

NHL Coaching Record

			Regular Season				Playoffs			
Season	Team	Games	W	L	T	%	Games	W	L	%
1978-79	Philadelphia	30	18	8	4	.667	8	3	5	.375
1979-80	Philadelphia	80	48	12	20	.725	19	13	6	.684
1980-81	Philadelphia	80	41	24	15	.606	12	6	6	.500
1981-82	Philadelphia	72	34	29	9	.535	....	....	....	....
1984-85	Los Angeles	80	34	32	14	.513	3	0	3	.000
1985-86	Los Angeles	80	23	49	8	.338	....	....	....	....
1986-87	Los Angeles	42	18	20	4	.476	....	....	....	....
1990-91	Vancouver	26	9	13	4	.423	6	2	4	.333
	NHL Totals	**490**	**225**	**187**	**78**	**.539**	**48**	**24**	**24**	**.500**

Trevor Linden had 16 powerplay goals for the Canucks in 1990-91.

Washington Capitals

1990-91 Results: 37w-36L-7T 81PTS. Third, Patrick Division

Schedule

Home			Away		
Oct.	Fri.	4 Philadelphia	Oct.	Wed.	9 Toronto
	Sat.	5 Buffalo		Mon.	14 NY Rangers
	Fri.	11 NY Rangers		Sat.	19 New Jersey
	Sat.	12 Chicago		Wed.	23 Edmonton
	Fri.	18 New Jersey		Thur.	24 Vancouver
Nov.	Fri.	1 Toronto		Sun.	27 Winnipeg
	Fri.	8 Detroit		Tues.	29 Pittsburgh
	Fri.	15 Pittsburgh	Nov.	Sat.	2 NY Islanders
	Fri.	22 Boston		Sun.	10 Quebec*
	Wed.	27 Montreal		Mon.	11 Montreal
	Fri.	29 NY Islanders		Wed.	13 NY Rangers
Dec.	Tues.	10 Calgary		Wed.	20 New Jersey
	Fri.	13 NY Rangers		Sat.	23 Hartford
	Tues.	17 Quebec		Mon.	25 Detroit
	Fri.	20 Toronto		Sat.	30 NY Islanders
	Thur.	26 NY Rangers	Dec.	Thur.	5 Philadelphia
	Sat.	28 Pittsburgh		Sat.	7 Minnesota
Jan.	Wed.	1 NY Islanders*		Sun.	8 Winnipeg
	Fri.	3 Vancouver		Sat.	14 Pittsburgh
	Tues.	7 Minnesota		Wed.	18 Buffalo
	Fri.	10 Los Angeles		Sun.	22 Philadelphia
	Fri.	24 New Jersey		Sun.	29 New Jersey
	Sun.	26 Pittsburgh*	Jan.	Sat.	4 Hartford
Feb.	Sat.	1 Calgary		Sun.	12 Chicago
	Fri.	7 NY Rangers		Tues.	14 St Louis
	Sun.	9 San Jose*		Thur.	16 Los Angeles
	Sat.	22 Philadelphia		Tues.	28 Philadelphia
	Tues.	25 Pittsburgh	Feb.	Tues.	4 Buffalo
Mar.	Sun.	1 Boston*		Wed.	5 Detroit
	Tues.	3 Minnesota		Tues.	11 Quebec
	Fri.	6 Winnipeg		Thur.	13 Calgary
	Sat.	7 New Jersey		Sat.	15 Los Angeles
	Sun.	15 NY Islanders*		Tues.	18 San Jose
	Tues.	17 St Louis		Sun.	23 NY Islanders
	Fri.	20 Philadelphia		Thur.	27 St Louis
	Sun.	22 Edmonton*		Sat.	29 Boston*
	Tues.	24 Hartford	Mar.	Mon.	9 NY Rangers
	Fri.	27 Montreal		Sat.	14 Philadelphia*
	Sun.	29 Vancouver*	Apr.	Wed.	1 New Jersey
Apr.	Sun.	5 NY Islanders*		Sat.	4 Pittsburgh*

* Denotes afternoon game.

Home Starting Times:
Weeknights and Saturdays .... 7:35 p.m.
Sundays .... 1:35 p.m.
Except Jan. 26 .... 12:05 p.m.

Franchise date: June 11, 1974

18th
NHL
Season

Michal Pivonka had his finest season in 1990-91, scoring 20 goals and setting up 50 others for 70 points.

Year-by-Year Record

Season	GP	Home W	Home L	Home T	Road W	Road L	Road T	Overall W	L	T	GF	GA	Pts.	Finished	Playoff Result
1990-91	80	21	14	5	16	22	2	37	36	7	284	211	81	3rd, Patrick Div.	Lost Div. Final
1989-90	80	19	18	3	17	20	3	36	38	6	284	275	78	3rd, Patrick Div.	Lost Conf. Championship
1988-89	80	25	12	3	16	17	7	41	29	10	305	259	92	1st, Patrick Div.	Lost Div. Semi-Final
1987-88	80	22	14	4	16	19	5	38	33	9	281	249	85	2nd, Patrick Div.	Lost Div. Final
1986-87	80	22	15	3	16	17	7	38	32	10	285	278	86	2nd, Patrick Div.	Lost Div. Semi-Final
1985-86	80	30	8	2	20	15	5	50	23	7	315	272	107	2nd, Patrick Div.	Lost Div. Final
1984-85	80	27	11	2	19	14	7	46	25	9	322	240	101	2nd, Patrick Div.	Lost Div. Semi-Final
1983-84	80	26	11	3	22	16	2	48	27	5	308	226	101	2nd, Patrick Div.	Lost Div. Final
1982-83	80	22	12	6	17	13	10	39	25	16	306	283	94	3rd, Patrick Div.	Lost Div. Semi-Final
1981-82	80	16	16	8	10	25	5	26	41	13	319	338	65	5th, Patrick Div.	Out of Playoffs
1980-81	80	16	17	7	10	19	11	26	36	18	286	317	70	5th, Patrick Div.	Out of Playoffs
1979-80	80	20	14	6	7	26	7	27	40	13	261	293	67	5th, Patrick Div.	Out of Playoffs
1978-79	80	15	15	9	9	22	9	24	41	15	273	338	63	4th, Norris Div.	Out of Playoffs
1977-78	80	10	23	7	7	26	7	17	49	14	195	321	48	5th, Norris Div.	Out of Playoffs
1976-77	80	17	15	8	7	27	6	24	42	14	221	307	62	4th, Norris Div.	Out of Playoffs
1975-76	80	6	26	8	5	33	2	11	59	10	224	394	32	5th, Norris Div.	Out of Playoffs
1974-75	80	7	28	5	1	39	0	8	67	5	181	446	21	5th, Norris Div.	Out of Playoffs

1991-92 Player Personnel

FORWARDS	HT	WT	S	Place of Birth	Date	1990-91 Club
BERGLAND, Tim	6-2	194	R	Crookston, MN	1/11/65	Wsh.-Balt.
BONDRA, Peter	5-11	180	L	Kosice, Czech.	2/7/68	Washington
BURRIDGE, Randy	5-9	180	L	Fort Erie, Ont.	1/7/66	Boston
CICCARELLI, Dino	5-10	175	R	Sarnia, Ont.	2/8/60	Washington
DRUCE, John	6-1	200	L	Peterborough, Ont.	2/23/66	Washington
DUHAIME, Trevor	6-0	185	R	Toronto, Ont.	8/2/71	St. Jean
DUNCANSON, Craig	6-0	190	L	Sudbury, Ont.	3/17/67	Winnipeg-Moncton
GERVAIS, Victor	5-9	172	L	Prince George, B.C.	3/13/69	Balt.-Hampton Roads
GREENLAW, Jeff	6-1	230	L	Toronto, Ont.	2/28/68	Baltimore-Wsh.
HALVERSON, Trevor	6-1	205	L	White River, Ont.	4/6/71	North Bay
HLUSHKO, Todd	5-11	180	L	Toronto, Ont.	2/7/70	Baltimore
HUGHES, Brent	5-11	180	L	New Westmin'er, B.C.	4/5/66	Balt.-Moncton
HUNTER, Dale	5-10	198	L	Petrolia, Ont.	7/31/60	Washington
KHRISTICH, Dmitri	6-2	190	R	Kiev, USSR	7/23/69	Sokol Kiev-Wsh.-Balt.
KONOWALCHUK, Steve	6-0	180	L	Salt Lake City, UT	11/11/72	Portland
KOVACS, Bill	6-4	235	L	Hamilton, Ont.	5/11/71	Sudbury
KYPREOS, Nick	6-0	195	L	Toronto, Ont.	6/4/66	Washington
LONGO, Chris	5-10	180	R	Belleville, Ont.	1/5/72	Peterborough
MARTELL, Steve	5-10	185	R	Sydney, N.S.	3/3/70	London
MARTIN, Brian	6-1	205	R	St. Catharines, Ont.	3/27/67	Hampton Rds.-Utica
MAY, Alan	6-1	200	R	Barrhead, Alta.	1/14/65	Washington
MEWS, Harry	5-10	175	L	Nepean, Ont.	2/9/67	Balt.-Hampton Roads
MILLER, Kelly	5-11	196	L	Detroit, MI.	3/3/63	Washington
MORISSETTE, Dave	6-1	198	R	Quebec City, Que.	12/24/72	Shawinigan
MORRISON, Justin	5-10	180	R	Newmarket, Ont.	2/9/72	Kingston
NELSON, Jeff	6-0	180	L	Prince Albert, Sask.	12/18/72	Prince Albert
PEAKE, Pat	6-0	195	R	Rochester, MI	5/28/73	Detroit
PEARCE, Randy	5-11	203	L	Kitchener, Ont.	2/23/70	Kitchener
PIVONKA, Michal	6-2	198	L	Kladno, Czech.	1/28/66	Washington
PURVES, John	6-0	201	R	Toronto, Ont.	2/12/68	Baltimore-Washington
REYNOLDS, Bobby	5-11	175	L	Flint, MI	7/14/67	Newmarket-Baltimore
RIDLEY, Mike	6-1	200	L	Winnipeg, Man.	7/8/63	Washington
SAKIC, Brian	5-10	179	L	Burnaby, B.C.	4/9/71	Tri-Cities
SAVAGE, Reggie	5-10	187	L	Montreal, Que.	5/1/70	Baltimore-Washington
SEFTEL, Steve	6-2	210	L	Kitchener, Ont.	5/14/68	Baltimore-Washington
TAYLOR, Rod	5-8	175	L	Pontiac, MI	12/1/68	Ferris State
TAYLOR, Tim	6-0	180	L	Stratford, Ont.	2/6/69	Baltimore
TIPPETT, Dave	5-10	180	L	Moosomin, Sask.	8/25/61	Washington
WALCOTT, Richie	6-2	216	R	Grand Cache, Alta.	5/17/70	Halifax Jr.B
WHEELDON, Simon	5-11	170	L	Vancouver, B.C.	8/30/66	Moncton-Winnipeg

DEFENCEMEN	HT	WT	S	Place of Birth	Date	1990-91 Club
BABCOCK, Bobby	6-1	222	L	Toronto, Ont.	8/3/68	Baltimore-Washington
BARTLEY, Wade	6-0	190	R	Killarney, Man.	5/16/70	Sudbury-Baltimore
BLESSMAN, John	6-3	210	L	Toronto, Ont.	4/27/67	Greensboro
CHAMBERS, Shawn	6-2	200	L	Sterling Heights, MI	10/11/66	Minnesota
CLARKE, Chris	6-0	180	L	Arnprior, Ont.	8/6/67	W. Michigan
CORRIVEAU, Rick	6-0	200	L	Welland, Ont.	1/6/71	London
FERNER, Mark	6-0	193	L	Regina, Sask.	9/5/65	Washington-Baltimore
HATCHER, Kevin	6-4	225	R	Detroit, MI	9/9/66	Washington
IAFRATE, Al	6-3	220	L	Dearborn, MI	3/21/66	Toronto-Washington
JOHANSSON, Calle	5-11	205	L	Goteberg, Sweden	2/14/67	Washington
LALOR, Mike	6-0	200	L	Buffalo, NY	3/8/63	Washington
LANGWAY, Rod	6-3	224	L	Formosa, Taiwan	5/3/57	Washington
LAVIGNE, Eric	6-3	215	L	Victoriaville, Que.	11/4/72	Hull
LEASK, Rob	6-2	210	L	Toronto, Ont.	6/9/72	Hamilton
LEBLANC, Carl	6-0	210	L	Drummondville, Que.	6/9/72	Granby
LOVSIN, Ken	6-0	195	R	Peace River, Alta.	12/3/66	Washington-Baltimore
MATHIESON, Jim	6-1	209	R	Kindersley, Sask.	1/24/70	Baltimore
PASMA, Rod	6-4	207	L	Brampton, Ont.	2/26/72	Cornwall-Kingston
PUCHNIAK, Rob	6-2	210	L	Winnipeg, Man.	3/10/72	Brandon-Lethbridge
SABOURIN, Ken	6-3	205	L	Scarborough, Ont.	4/28/66	S. Lake-Cgy.-Wsh.
SLANEY, John	6-0	186	L	St. John's, Nfld.	2/7/72	Cornwall
SORENSON, Mark	6-0	180	L	Newmarket, Ont.	3/27/69	U. Michigan
VYKOUKAL, Jiri	5-11	175	R	Olomouc, Czech.	3/11/71	Baltimore

GOALTENDERS	HT	WT	C	Place of Birth	Date	1990-91 Club
BEAUPRE, Don	5-9	165	L	Waterloo, Ont.	9/19/61	Washington-Baltimore
DAFOE, Byron	5-11	175	L	Duncan, B.C.	2/25/71	Portland-Pr. Albert
HARVEY, Alain	6-2	190	L	Les Escoumins, Que.	5/9/69	Richmond-Cap. Dist.
HRIVNAK, Jim	6-2	185	L	Montreal, Que.	5/28/68	Washington-Baltimore
KOLZIG, Olaf	6-3	207	L	Jo'burg, S. Africa	4/9/70	Balt.-Hampton Rds.
LIUT, Mike	6-2	195	L	Weston, Ont.	1/7/56	Washington
SIMPSON, Shawn	5-11	183	R	Gloucester, Ont.	8/10/68	Baltimore

General Managers' History

Milt Schmidt, 1974-75 to 1975-76; Max McNab, 1976-77 to 1980-81; Roger Crozier, 1981-82; David Poile, 1982-83 to date.

Coaching History

Jim Anderson, George Sullivan, Milt Schmidt, 1974-75; Milt Schmidt and Tom McVie, 1975-76; Tom McVie, 1976-77 to 1977-78; Danny Belisle, 1978-79; Danny Belisle and Gary Green, 1979-80; Gary Green, 1980-81; Gary Green and Bryan Murray, 1981-82; Bryan Murray, 1982-83 to 1988-89; Bryan Murray and Terry Murray, 1989-90; Terry Murray, 1990-91 to date.

1990-91 Scoring

Regular Season

* rookie

Pos	#	Player	Team	GP	G	A	Pts	+/-	PIM	PP	SH	GW	GT	S	%
D	4	Kevin Hatcher	WSH	79	24	50	74	10–	69	9	2	3	0	267	9.0
C	17	Mike Ridley	WSH	79	23	48	71	9	26	6	5	4	0	155	14.8
C	20	Michal Pivonka	WSH	79	20	50	70	3	34	6	0	4	0	172	11.6
R	19	John Druce	WSH	80	22	36	58	4	46	7	1	4	0	209	10.5
D	6	Calle Johansson	WSH	80	11	41	52	2–	23	2	1	2	0	128	8.6
L	10	Kelly Miller	WSH	80	24	26	50	10	29	4	2	3	1	155	15.5
C	32	Dale Hunter	WSH	76	16	30	46	22–	234	9	0	2	0	106	15.1
R	22	Dino Ciccarelli	WSH	54	21	18	39	17–	66	2	0	2	3	186	11.3
D	34	Al Iafrate	TOR	42	3	15	18	15–	113	2	0	0	0	51	5.9
			WSH	30	6	8	14	1–	124	0	1	1	0	55	10.9
			TOTAL	72	9	23	32	16–	237	2	1	1	0	106	8.5
R	21	Stephen Leach	WSH	68	11	19	30	9–	99	4	0	1	0	134	8.2
R	12	*Peter Bondra	WSH	54	12	16	28	10–	47	4	0	1	0	95	12.6
L	29	*Dimitri Khristich	WSH	40	13	14	27	1–	21	1	0	0	1	77	16.9
D	3	*Mikhail Tatarinov	WSH	65	8	15	23	4–	82	3	1	1	0	145	5.5
L	9	Nick Kypreos	WSH	79	9	9	18	4–	196	0	0	3	0	60	15.0
C	14	Dave Tippett	WSH	61	6	9	15	13–	24	0	0	2	0	68	8.8
C	11	Tim Bergland	WSH	47	5	9	14	1–	21	0	0	0	0	41	12.2
L	16	Alan May	WSH	67	4	6	10	10–	264	0	0	0	0	66	6.1
D	8	*Ken Sabourin	CGY	16	1	3	4	9	36	0	0	0	0	9	11.1
			WSH	28	1	4	5	6	81	0	0	0	0	14	7.1
			TOTAL	44	2	7	9	15	117	0	0	0	0	23	8.7
D	5	Rod Langway	WSH	56	1	7	8	12	24	0	0	0	0	32	3.1
L	27	Bob Joyce	WSH	17	3	3	6	3	8	0	0	1	0	30	10.0
D	26	Mike Lalor	WSH	68	1	5	6	23–	61	0	0	0	0	49	2.0
D	28	Chris Felix	WSH	8	0	4	4	0	0	0	0	0	0	7	.0
C	23	Rob Murray	WSH	17	0	3	3	0	19	0	0	0	0	8	.0
L	24	*Jeff Greenlaw	WSH	10	2	0	2	1	10	0	0	1	0	9	22.2
C	37	Alfie Turcotte	WSH	6	1	1	2	1–	0	0	0	1	0	8	12.5
R	37	*John Purves	WSH	7	1	0	1	3–	0	0	0	1	0	8	12.5
D	2	Joel Quenneville	WSH	9	1	0	1	8–	0	0	0	0	0	3	33.3
D	36	*Mark Ferner	WSH	7	0	1	1	2–	4	0	0	0	0	3	.0
D	38	*Bob Babcock	WSH	1	0	0	0	0	0	0	0	0	0	0	.0
D	37	*Ken Lovsin	WSH	1	0	0	0	2–	0	0	0	0	0	2	.0
D	37	*Kent Paynter	WSH	1	0	0	0	0	15	0	0	0	0	0	.0
C	38	*Reggie Savage	WSH	1	0	0	0	1–	0	0	0	0	0	2	.0
L	40	*Steve Seftel	WSH	4	0	0	0	2–	2	0	0	0	0	2	.0
L	18	*Steve Maltais	WSH	7	0	0	0	1–	2	0	0	0	0	3	.0
G	39	*Jim Hrivnak	WSH	9	0	0	0	0	0	0	0	0	0	0	.0
R	25	John Kordic	TOR	3	0	0	0	0	9	0	0	0	0	1	.0
			WSH	7	0	0	0	1	101	0	0	0	0	0	.0
			TOTAL	10	0	0	0	1	110	0	0	0	0	1	.0
G	1	Mike Liut	WSH	35	0	0	0	0	0	0	0	0	0	0	.0
G	33	Don Beaupre	WSH	45	0	0	0	0	18	0	0	0	0	0	.0

Goaltending

No.	Goaltender	GPI	Mins	Avg	W	L	T	EN	SO	GA	SA	S%
33	Don Beaupre	45	2572	2.64	20	18	3	3	5	113	1095	.897
39	*Jim Hrivnak	9	432	3.61	4	2	1	0	0	26	226	.885
1	Mike Liut	35	1834	3.73	13	16	3	2	0	114	786	.855
	Totals	**80**	**4850**	**3.19**	**37**	**36**	**7**	**5**	**5**	**258**	**2112**	**.878**

Playoffs

Pos	#	Player	Team	GP	G	A	Pts	+/-	PIM	PP	SH	GW	OT	S	%
C	32	Dale Hunter	WSH	11	1	9	10	2	41	0	0	0	0	16	6.3
R	22	Dino Ciccarelli	WSH	11	5	4	9	3–	22	3	0	2	1	44	11.4
D	6	Calle Johansson	WSH	10	2	7	9	3–	8	1	0	0	0	24	8.3
C	17	Mike Ridley	WSH	11	3	4	7	2–	8	1	0	1	0	34	8.8
L	10	Kelly Miller	WSH	11	4	2	6	0	6	0	1	0	0	27	14.8
D	4	Kevin Hatcher	WSH	11	3	3	6	3–	8	2	0	0	0	54	5.6
C	14	Dave Tippett	WSH	10	2	3	5	0	8	0	0	0	0	17	11.8
C	20	Michal Pivonka	WSH	11	2	3	5	6–	8	0	0	0	0	26	7.7
D	34	Al Iafrate	WSH	10	1	3	4	3	22	0	0	1	0	26	3.8
L	29	*Dimitri Khristich	WSH	11	1	3	4	2–	6	0	0	0	0	15	6.7
R	21	Stephen Leach	WSH	9	1	2	3	3	8	0	0	0	0	17	5.9
D	26	Mike Lalor	WSH	10	1	2	3	1–	22	0	0	0	0	12	8.3
C	11	Tim Bergland	WSH	11	1	1	2	2–	12	0	0	0	0	5	20.0
R	19	John Druce	WSH	11	1	1	2	4–	7	1	0	0	0	22	4.5
L	16	Alan May	WSH	11	1	1	2	2–	37	0	0	1	0	11	9.1
D	5	Rod Langway	WSH	11	0	2	2	1	6	0	0	0	0	12	.0
R	12	*Peter Bondra	WSH	4	0	1	1	1	2	0	0	0	0	7	.0
L	9	Nick Kypreos	WSH	9	0	1	1	1–	38	0	0	0	0	3	.0
G	33	Don Beaupre	WSH	11	0	1	1	0	2	0	0	0	0	0	.0
L	24	*Jeff Greenlaw	WSH	1	0	0	0	0	2	0	0	0	0	1	.0
D	37	*Kent Paynter	WSH	1	0	0	0	1–	0	0	0	0	0	1	.0
G	1	Mike Liut	WSH	2	0	0	0	0	0	0	0	0	0	0	.0
D	15	Neil Sheehy	WSH	2	0	0	0	2–	19	0	0	0	0	0	.0
D	8	*Ken Sabourin	WSH	11	0	0	0	4–	34	0	0	0	0	4	.0

Goaltending

No.	Goaltender	GPI	Mins	Avg	W	L	EN	SO	GA	SA	S%
33	Don Beaupre	11	624	2.79	5	5	2	1	29	294	.901
1	Mike Liut	2	48	5.00	0	1	0	0	4	30	.867
	Totals	11	675	3.11	5	6	2	1	35	326	.893

Captains' History

Doug Mohns, 1974-75; Bill Clement, Yvon Labre, 1975-76; Yvon Labre, 1976-77, 1977-78; Guy Charron, 1978-79; Ryan Walter, 1979-80 to 1981-82; Rod Langway, 1982-83 to date.

Retired Numbers

7	Yvon Labre	1973-1981

Club Records

Team

(Figures in brackets for season records are games played; records for fewest points, wins, ties, losses, goals, goals against are for 70 or more games)

Most Points	107	1985-86 (80)
Most Wins	50	1985-86 (80)
Most Ties	18	1980-81 (80)
Most Losses	*67	1974-75 (80)
Most Goals	322	1984-85 (80)
Most Goals Against	*446	1974-75 (80)
Fewest Points	*21	1974-75 (80)
Fewest Wins	*8	1974-75 (80)
Fewest Ties	5	1974-75 (80) 1983-84 (80)
Fewest Losses	23	1985-86 (80)
Fewest Goals	181	1974-75 (80)
Fewest Goals Against	226	1983-84 (80)

Longest Winning Streak
Over-all .... 10 Jan. 27-Feb. 18/84
Home .... 8 Feb. 1-Mar. 11/86 Mar. 3-April 1/89
Away .... 6 Feb. 26-Apr. 1/84

Longest Undefeated Streak
Over-all .... 14 Nov. 24-Dec. 23/82 (9 wins, 5 ties)
Home .... 12 Nov. 7/82-Dec. 14/82 (9 wins, 3 ties)
Away .... 10 Nov. 24/82-Jan. 8/83 (6 wins, 4 ties)

Longest Losing Streak
Over-all .... *17 Feb. 18-Mar. 26/75
Home .... *11 Feb. 18-Mar. 30/75
Away .... *37 Oct. 9/74-Mar. 26/75

Longest Winless Streak
Over-all .... 25 Nov. 29/75-Jan. 21/76 (22 losses, 3 ties)
Home .... 14 Dec. 3/75-Jan. 21/76 (11 losses, 3 ties)

Away .... *37 Oct. 9/74-Mar. 26/75 (37 losses)
Most Shutouts, Season 8 1983-84 (80)
Most PIM, Season 2,204 1989-90 (80)
Most Goals, Game .... 11 Dec. 11/81 (Tor. 2 at Wash. 11)

Individual

Most Seasons	10	Mike Gartner
Most Games	756	Mike Gartner
Most Goals, Career	397	Mike Gartner
Most Assists, Career	392	Mike Gartner
Most Points, Career	789	Mike Gartner (397 goals, 392 assists)
Most PIM, Career	1,630	Scott Stevens
Most Shutouts, Career	8	Al Jensen Don Beaupre

Longest Consecutive Games Streak .... 422 Bob Carpenter
Most Goals, Season .... 60 Dennis Maruk (1981-82)
Most Assists, Season ..... 76 Dennis Maruk (1981-82)
Most Points, Season .... 136 Dennis Maruk (1981-82) (60 goals, 76 assists)
Most PIM, Season .... 339 Alan May (1989-90)
Most Points, Defenseman, Season .... 81 Larry Murphy (1986-87) (23 goals, 58 assists)
Most Points, Center, Season .... 136 Dennis Maruk (1981-82) (60 goals, 76 assists)
Most Points, Right Wing, Season .... 102 Mike Gartner (1984-85) (50 goals, 52 assists)
Most Points, Left Wing, Season .... 87 Ryan Walter (1981-82) (38 goals, 49 assists)

Most Points, Rookie, Season .... 67 Bobby Carpenter (1981-82) (32 goals, 35 assists) Chris Valentine (1981-82) (30 goals, 37 assists)
Most Shutouts, Season ..... 5 Don Beaupre (1990-91)
Most Goals, Game .... 5 Bengt Gustafsson (Jan. 8/84)
Most Assists, Game .... 6 Mike Ridley (Jan. 7/89)
Most Points, Game .... 7 Dino Ciccarelli (Mar. 18/89)

* NHL Record.

All-time Record vs. Other Clubs

Regular Season

			At Home							On Road							Total				
	GP	W	L	T	GF	GA	PTS	GP	W	L	T	GF	GA	PTS	GP	W	L	T	GF	GA	PTS
Boston	31	7	16	8	92	122	22	31	9	19	3	86	128	21	62	16	35	11	178	250	43
Buffalo	31	4	21	6	82	134	14	31	5	23	3	84	139	13	62	9	44	9	166	273	27
Calgary	29	13	12	4	110	108	30	29	5	21	3	68	132	13	58	18	33	7	178	240	43
Chicago	29	17	9	3	115	91	37	29	6	18	5	87	121	17	58	23	27	8	202	212	54
Detroit	35	19	12	4	137	105	42	35	11	14	10	103	128	32	70	30	26	14	240	233	74
Edmonton	19	10	8	1	84	74	21	19	7	8	4	67	77	18	38	17	16	5	151	151	39
Hartford	19	11	7	1	68	53	23	19	10	7	2	78	63	22	38	21	14	3	146	116	45
Los Angeles	35	14	15	6	146	130	34	35	10	22	3	102	147	23	70	24	37	9	248	277	57
Minnesota	29	13	9	7	95	86	33	29	8	13	8	85	112	24	58	21	22	15	180	198	57
Montreal	35	12	17	6	91	126	30	35	4	26	5	69	170	13	70	16	43	11	160	296	43
New Jersey	47	36	8	3	219	133	75	47	22	19	6	148	152	50	94	58	27	9	367	285	125
NY Islanders	49	20	22	7	154	170	47	50	15	34	1	151	215	31	99	35	56	8	305	385	78
NY Rangers	49	24	17	8	194	167	56	50	18	26	6	181	218	42	99	42	43	14	375	385	98
Philadelphia	50	20	22	8	180	178	48	49	16	29	4	134	193	36	99	36	51	12	314	371	84
Pittsburgh	56	29	23	4	250	216	62	55	22	27	6	186	226	50	111	51	50	10	436	442	112
Quebec	19	9	8	2	81	70	20	19	8	7	4	71	62	20	38	17	15	6	152	132	40
St. Louis	29	14	12	3	102	90	31	29	8	13	8	88	122	24	58	22	25	11	190	212	55
Toronto	31	18	11	2	120	90	38	31	9	18	4	110	148	22	62	27	29	6	230	238	60
Vancouver	29	16	11	2	95	91	34	29	12	13	4	95	100	28	58	28	24	6	190	191	62
Winnipeg	19	13	5	1	89	58	27	19	6	8	5	69	68	17	38	19	13	6	158	126	44
Defunct Club	10	2	8	0	28	42	4	10	4	5	1	30	39	9	20	6	13	1	58	81	13
Totals	**680**	**321**	**273**	**86**	**2532**	**2334**	**728**	**680**	**215**	**370**	**95**	**2092**	**2760**	**525**	**1360**	**536**	**643**	**181**	**4624**	**5094**	**1253**

Playoffs

	Series	W	L	GP	W	L	T	GF	GA	Last Mtg.	Round	Result
Boston	1	0	1	4	0	4	0	6	15	1990	CF	L 0-4
New Jersey	2	1	1	13	7	6	0	44	43	1990	DSF	W 4-2
NY Islanders	5	1	4	24	10	14	0	66	76	1987	DSF	L 3-4
NY Rangers	3	2	1	17	10	7	0	63	51	1991	DSF	W 4-2
Philadelphia	3	2	1	16	9	7	0	65	55	1989	DSF	L 2-4
Pittsburgh	1	0	1	5	1	4	0	13	19	1991	DF	L 1-4
Totals	**15**	**6**	**9**	**79**	**37**	**42**	**0**	**257**	**259**			

Playoff Results 1991-87

Year	Round	Opponent	Result	GF	GA
1991	DF	Pittsburgh	L 1-4	13	19
	DSF	NY Rangers	W 4-2	16	16
1990	CF	Boston	L 0-4	6	15
	DF	NY Rangers	W 4-1	22	15
	DSF	New Jersey	W 4-2	21	18
1989	DSF	Philadelphia	L 2-4	19	25
1988	DF	New Jersey	L 3-4	23	25
	DSF	Philadelphia	W 4-3	31	25
1987	DSF	NY Islanders	L 3-4	19	19

Abbreviations: Round: F Final; **CF** conference final; **DF** division final; **DSF** division semi-final; **GA** goals against; **GF** goals for.

1990-91 Results

		Home				Away	
Oct.	5	Pittsburgh	4-7	Oct.	10	NY Rangers	2-4
	6	Detroit	6-4		15	Montreal	1-3
	12	Winnipeg	3-1		17	New Jersey	2-3
	13	NY Rangers	2-5		23	Philadelphia	6-2
	19	NY Islanders	4-3		25	Chicago	2-3
	20	New Jersey	4-0		27	Calgary	4-9
Nov.	2	Los Angeles	4-3		28	Edmonton	1-0
	10	Buffalo	2-4		30	Vancouver	2-1
	11	Boston	3-5	Nov.	3	NY Islanders	5-2
	16	Chicago	3-4		6	Quebec	4-1
	21	Toronto	5-3		14	Toronto	3-5
	23	Pittsburgh	7-3		17	Hartford	2-4
	30	Montreal	3-4		19	Detroit	3-2
Dec.	7	New Jersey	5-2		24	Pittsburgh	2-3
	11	Philadelphia	4-1		28	NY Rangers	6-3
	15	Hartford	2-3	Dec.	1	NY Islanders	3-1
	22	Toronto*	2-5		5	Pittsburgh	3-1
	26	Pittsburgh	3-7		8	New Jersey	2-4
	28	NY Rangers	3-5		17	NY Rangers	3-5
Jan.	1	New Jersey*	4-3		19	Chicago	2-3
	4	Philadelphia	3-3		20	St Louis	3-3
	11	Calgary	4-2		29	Quebec	3-4
	25	Minnesota	2-2	Jan.	5	Boston	5-3
	27	NY Islanders*	5-4		12	Montreal	1-4
Feb.	2	Winnipeg	2-4		15	St Louis	3-7
	5	Vancouver	5-3		17	Minnesota	2-5
	8	Edmonton	6-3		22	Detroit	2-1
	10	Philadelphia*	5-2		24	Philadelphia	1-6
	22	NY Rangers	3-2		29	Pittsburgh	2-3
	24	Pittsburgh*	5-5		31	NY Islanders	4-3
Mar.	2	NY Islanders	3-2	Feb.	15	Calgary	2-8
	5	Los Angeles	3-3		16	Vancouver	2-4
	12	Hartford	2-3		18	Los Angeles*	2-5
	14	Quebec	5-3		25	New Jersey	1-5
	16	Philadelphia	6-0		27	NY Rangers	4-4
	19	St Louis	1-2	Mar.	8	Winnipeg	2-1
	22	Minnesota	3-1		10	Edmonton	5-3
	24	Boston*	3-3		21	NY Islanders	6-2
	26	Buffalo	2-4		28	Philadelphia	3-0
	30	New Jersey	4-0		31	Buffalo	2-5

* Denotes afternoon game.

Entry Draft
Selections 1991-77

1991
Pick
14 Pat Peake
21 Trevor Halverson
25 Eric Lavigne
36 Jeff Nelson
58 Steve Konowalchuk
80 Justin Morrison
146 Dave Morissette
168 Rick Corriveau
190 Trevor Duhaime
209 Rob Leask
212 Carl Leblanc
234 Rob Puchniak
256 Bill Kovacs

1990
Pick
9 John Slaney
30 Rod Pasma
51 Chris Longo
72 Randy Pearce
93 Brian Sakic
94 Mark Ouimet
114 Andrei Kovalev
135 Roman Kontsek
156 Peter Bondra
159 Steve Martell
177 Ken Klee
198 Michael Boback
219 Alan Brown
240 Todd Hlushko

1989
Pick
19 Olaf Kolzig
35 Byron Dafoe
59 Jim Mathieson
61 Jason Woolley
82 Trent Klatt
145 Dave Lorentz
166 Dean Holoien
187 Victor Gervais
208 Andri Sidorov
229 Andri Sidorov
250 Ken House

1988
Pick
15 Reginald Savage
36 Tim Taylor
41 Wade Bartley
57 Duane Derksen
78 Rob Krauss

120 Dimitri Khristich
141 Keith Jones
144 Brad Schlegal
162 Todd Hilditch
183 Petr Pavlas
192 Mark Sorensen
204 Claudio Scremin
225 Chris Venkus
246 Ron Pascucci

1987
Pick
36 Jeff Ballantyne
57 Steve Maltais
78 Tyler Larter
99 Pat Beauchesne
120 Rich Defreitas
141 Devon Oleniuk
162 Thomas Sjogren
204 Chris Clarke
225 Milos Vanik
240 Dan Brettschneider
246 Ryan Kummu

1986
Pick
19 Jeff Greenlaw
40 Steve Seftel
60 Shawn Simpson
61 Jimmy Hrivnak
82 Erin Ginnell
103 John Purves
124 Stefan Nilsson
145 Peter Choma
166 Lee Davidson
187 Tero Toivola
208 Bobby Bobcock
229 John Schratz
250 Scott McCrory

1985
Pick
19 Yvon Corriveau
40 John Druce
61 Robert Murray
82 Bill Houlder
83 Larry Shaw
103 Claude Dumas
124 Doug Stromback
145 Jamie Nadjiwan
166 Mark Haarmann
187 Steve Hollett
208 Dallas Eakins
229 Steve Hrynewich
250 Frank DiMuzio

1984
Pick
17 Kevin Hatcher
34 Steve Leach
59 Michal Pivonka
80 Kris King
122 Vito Cramarossa
143 Timo Iijima
164 Frank Joo
185 Jim Thomson
205 Paul Cavallini
225 Mikhail Tatarinov
246 Per Schedrin

1983
Pick
75 Tim Bergland
95 Martin Bouliane
135 Dwaine Hutton
155 Marty Abrams
175 David Cowan
195 Yves Beaudoin
215 Alain Raymond
216 Anders Huss

1982
Pick
5 Scott Stevens
58 Milan Novy
89 Dean Evason
110 Ed Kastelic
152 Wally Schreiber
173 Jamie Reeves
194 Juha Nurmi
215 Wayne Prestage
236 John Holden
247 Marco Kallas

1981
Pick
3 Bob Carpenter
45 Eric Calder
68 Tony Kellin
89 Mike Siltala
91 Peter Sidorkiewicz
110 Jim McGeough
131 Risto Jalo
152 Gaetan Duchesne
173 George White
194 Chris Valentine

1980
Pick
5 Darren Veitch
47 Dan Miele
55 Torrie Robertson
89 Timo Blomqvist
110 Todd Bidner
131 Frank Perkins
152 Bruce Raboin
173 Peter Andersson
194 Tony Camazzola

1979
Pick
4 Mike Gartner
24 Errol Rausse
67 Harvie Pocza
88 Tim Tookey
109 Greg Theberge

1978
Pick
2 Ryan Walter
18 Tim Coulis
20 Paul Mulvey
23 Paul MacKinnon
38 Glen Currie
45 Jay Johnston
55 Bengt Gustafsson
71 Lou Franceschetti
88 Vince Magnan
105 Mats Hallin
122 Rick Sirois
139 Denis Pomerleau
156 Barry Heard
172 Mark Toffolo
187 Paul Hogan
189 Steve Barger
202 Rod Pacholsuk
213 Wes Jarvis
215 Ray Irwin

1977
Pick
3 Robert Picard
21 Mark Lofthouse
39 Eddy Godin
57 Nelson Burton
75 Denis Turcotte
93 Perry Schnarr
111 Rollie Bouton
127 Brent Tremblay
143 Don Micheletti
165 Archie Henderson

Coach

MURRAY, TERRY RODNEY
Coach, Washington Capitals. Born in Shawville, Que., July 20, 1950.

With nearly 20 years of professional hockey experience, Terry Murray was named head coach of the Washington Capitals on January 15, 1990. Murray spent six seasons as an assistant coach with the Capitals. He was then named head coach of the Baltimore Skipjacks in June, 1988 where he led his club to a 64-point season in 1988-89 and was 26-17-1 during his 1989-90 tenure.

Murray was selected 88th overall by California in the 1970 Amateur Draft. He enjoyed a successful playing career with the Maine Mariners, leading that club to two Calder Cup championships in 1977-78 and 1978-79. He was awarded the Eddie Shore Trophy as the AHL's outstanding defenseman in 1978 and 1979. In addition he was an AHL First Team All-Star in 1975-76, 1977-78 and 1978-79. While serving as an assistant coach with the Capitals, they compiled a 259-165-66 record. His AHL coaching record stands at 56-63-5.

Coaching Record

Team		Games	Regular Season W	L	T	%	Games	Playoffs W	L	%
1988-89	Baltimore (AHL)	80	30	46	4	.400	....	....	....	....
1989-90	Baltimore (AHL)	44	26	17	1	.603	....	....	....	....
1989-90	**Washington (NHL)**	34	18	14	2	.559	15	8	7	.533
1990-91	**Washington (NHL)**	80	37	36	7	.506	11	5	6	.455
	NHL Totals	114	55	50	9	.522	26	13	13	.500

General Manager

POILE, DAVID
Vice-President and General Manager, Washington Capitals.
Born in Toronto, Ont., February 14, 1949.

David Poile was named to the position of general manager of the Capitals on August 30, 1982 and quickly built the franchise into a solid Stanley Cup contender. During his inaugural campaign (1982-83), he led the Caps to their first winning season (39-25-16) and a first-time berth in the Stanley Cup playoffs. He received *The Sporting News* "Executive of the Year" award in 1982-83 for his efforts and duplicated the feat in 1983-84 following the Capitals' 48-27-5 season. Poile, a graduate of Northeastern University with a degree in business administration, began his professional hockey management career in 1972 as an administrative assistant for the Atlanta Flames organization where he served until joining the Washington franchise. A former collegiate hockey star at Northeastern, he won MVP and scoring honors during his senior year.

Club Directory

Capital Centre
Landover, Maryland 20785
Phone 301/386-7000
TWX 710/600-7017
PR FAX 301/386-7012
GM FAX 301/386-7082
ENVOY ID
Front Office: CAPS. GM
Public
Relations: CAPS. PR
Capacity: 18,130

Board of Directors

Abe Pollin — Chairman	Albert Cohen	Arthur K. Mason
David P. Bindeman	J. Martin Irving	Dr. Jack Meshel
Stuart L. Bindeman	James T. Lewis	David M. Osnos
James E. Cafritz	R. Robert Linowes	Richard M. Patrick
A. James Clark		

Management
Chairman & Governor .... Abe Pollin
President & Alternate Governor ...... Richard M. Patrick
Vice-President and General Manager .. David Poile
Legal Counsel and Alternate Governors ...... David M. Osnos, Peter O'Malley
Vice-President and Comptroller .... Edmund Stelzer

Coaching Staff
Head Coach .... Terry Murray
Assistant Coach .... John Perpich
Head Coach, Baltimore (AHL) ...... Rob Laird
Assistant Coach, Baltimore (AHL) .... Barry Trotz
Video Coordinator & Director of Team Services . Tod Button

Scouting Staff
Director of Player Personnel and Recruitment .. Jack Button
Professional Scout .... Paul Gardner
Chief U.S. Scout .... Jack Barzee
Chief Eastern Scout .... Hugh Rogers
Chief Western Scout .... Craig Channell
Chief Quebec Scout .... Gilles Cote
Scouts .... Keith Allain, Rudy Crha, Fred Devereaux, Michel Goulet, Mike Humitz, Eje Johansson, Kelly Pratt, Bud Quinn, Richard Rothermel, Bob Schmidt, Dan Sylvester, Darrell Young

Training Staff
Head Trainer .... Stan Wong
Assistant Trainer/Head Equipment Mgr. ..... Doug Shearer
Assistant Equipment Mgr. .... Craig Leydig
Assistant to the Equipment Manager .... Rick Harper
Strength and Conditioning Coach ...... Frank Costello
Team Nutritionist .... Dr. Pat Mann

Front Office Staff
Vice-President/Marketing .... Lew Strudler
Director of Public Relations .... Lou Corletto
Assistant Director of Marketing .... Debi Angus
Director of Community Relations .... Yvon Labre
Director of Promotions .... Charles Copeland
Director of Season Subscriptions .... Joanne Kowalski
Assistant Comptroller .... Aggie Ballard
Public Relations Assistant .... Dan Kaufman
Administrative Assistant to the
  General Manager .... Pat Young
Administrative Assistant to the
  V.P./Marketing .... Paula Bogley
Administrative Assistant to the PR Director .. Julie Hensley
Administrative Assistant to the Sales Dept. .. Janice Toepper
Partial Plans Administrator .... Stephanie Rhine
Corporate Sales Manager .... Kerry Gregg
Coordinator of Printing Services and Special
Projects .... Karen Merewitz
Regional Sales Managers .... Jerry Murphy, John Oakes, Ron Potter, Bryan Maust
Accounting Assistants .... David Berman, Crystal Coffren, Melanie Loveless, Kathleen Brady
Souvenir Coordinator .... Kim Fagnilli
Receptionist .... Nancy Woodall
Assistant to the Hockey Dept. .... Todd Warren
Sales Representatives .... Darren Bruening, Chris Garinger, Don Gore, Phil Kessel, Brian Rupp

Operations Staff
Director of Telescreen .... Brad Froman
Director of Television .... Ernie Fingers
Director of Production .... Bill Harpole
Manager of Production .... Mike Long

Medical Team
Team Physicians .... Dr. Stephen S. Haas, Dr. Carl C. MacCartee, Jr., Dr. Frank S. Melograna, Dr. Richard Grossman
Team Dentist .... Dr. Howard Salob
Organist .... Chris Mitchell
Public Address Announcer .... Marv Brooks
Dimensions of Rink .... 200 feet by 85 feet
Team Nickname .... Capitals
Club Colors .... Red, White and Blue
Training Camp .... Piney Orchard Ice Arena, Odenton, Maryland
Radio Station .... WMAL (630 AM), WCAO (600 AM)
TV Stations .... WDCA-TV (Channel 20), Home Team Sports (Cable)

Winnipeg Jets

1990-91 Results: 26w-43L-11T 63PTS. Fifth, Smythe Division

Year-by-Year Record

Season	GP	Home			Road			Overall						Finished	Playoff Result
		W	L	T	W	L	T	W	L	T	GF	GA	Pts.		
1990-91	80	17	18	5	9	25	6	26	43	11	260	288	63	5th, Smythe Div.	Out of Playoffs
1989-90	80	22	13	5	15	19	6	37	32	11	298	290	85	3rd, Smythe Div.	Lost Div. Semi-Final
1988-89	80	17	18	5	9	24	7	26	42	12	300	355	64	5th, Smythe Div.	Out of Playoffs
1987-88	80	20	14	6	13	22	5	33	36	11	292	310	77	3rd, Smythe Div.	Lost Div. Semi-Final
1986-87	80	25	12	3	15	20	5	40	32	8	279	271	88	3rd, Smythe Div.	Lost Div. Final
1985-86	80	18	19	3	8	28	4	26	47	7	295	372	59	3rd, Smythe Div.	Lost Div. Semi-Final
1984-85	80	21	13	6	22	14	4	43	27	10	358	332	96	2nd, Smythe Div.	Lost Div. Final
1983-84	80	17	15	8	14	23	3	31	38	11	340	374	73	4th, Smythe Div.	Lost Div. Semi-Final
1982-83	80	22	16	2	11	23	6	33	39	8	311	333	74	4th, Smythe Div.	Lost Div. Semi-Final
1981-82	80	18	13	9	15	20	5	33	33	14	319	332	80	2nd, Norris Div.	Lost Div. Semi-Final
1980-81	80	7	25	8	2	32	6	9	57	14	246	400	32	6th, Smythe Div.	Out of Playoffs
1979-80	80	13	19	8	7	30	3	20	49	11	214	314	51	5th, Smythe Div.	Out of Playoffs

Schedule

Home			Away		
Oct.	Fri.	4 Los Angeles	**Oct.**	Thur.	10 San Jose
	Sun.	6 Calgary		Sat.	12 Los Angeles
	Tues.	8 Vancouver		Tues.	22 NY Islanders
	Wed.	16 Hartford		Wed.	23 Detroit
	Sat.	19 Toronto		Tues.	29 Quebec
	Fri.	25 Philadelphia		Wed.	30 Montreal
	Sun.	27 Washington	**Nov.**	Tues.	5 Vancouver
Nov.	Fri.	1 Calgary		Thur.	14 St Louis
	Sun.	3 St Louis		Sat.	16 New Jersey*
	Fri.	8 Pittsburgh		Sun.	17 Philadelphia
	Mon.	11 Los Angeles*		Sat.	23 Edmonton
	Wed.	20 NY Islanders		Mon.	25 Calgary
	Wed.	27 NY Rangers	**Dec.**	Tues.	10 San Jose
Dec.	Sun.	1 Chicago		Thur.	12 Los Angeles
	Wed.	4 Buffalo		Sat.	14 Edmonton
	Fri.	6 Edmonton		Tues.	17 Calgary
	Sun.	8 Washington		Thur.	19 Vancouver
	Sat.	21 Calgary		Mon.	23 Toronto
	Thur.	26 Minnesota		Fri.	27 Chicago
	Sun.	29 Boston	**Jan.**	Thur.	2 Boston
	Tues.	31 NY Rangers*		Sat.	4 Pittsburgh*
Jan.	Wed.	8 Edmonton		Mon.	6 NY Rangers
	Fri.	10 Chicago		Tues.	21 Hartford
	Sun.	12 San Jose		Thur.	23 Philadelphia
	Tues.	14 Vancouver		Sat.	25 Quebec*
	Fri.	31 Quebec		Sun.	26 Buffalo*
Feb.	Sun.	2 San Jose*		Tues.	28 Pittsburgh
	Tues.	4 Boston	**Feb.**	Thur.	13 Minnesota
	Fri.	7 Calgary		Sat.	15 Toronto
	Wed.	19 St Louis		Mon.	17 NY Islanders*
	Fri.	21 New Jersey		Wed.	26 Edmonton
	Sun.	23 Los Angeles		Fri.	28 Vancouver
Mar.	Sun.	1 Edmonton*	**Mar.**	Tues.	3 Detroit
	Wed.	11 San Jose		Fri.	6 Washington
	Fri.	13 Hartford		Sun.	8 Minnesota
	Sun.	15 Detroit*		Tues.	17 Los Angeles
	Sun.	22 Vancouver*		Fri.	20 Vancouver
	Wed.	25 Montreal	**Apr.**	Wed.	1 San Jose
	Fri.	27 Los Angeles		Fri.	3 Edmonton
	Sun.	29 San Jose*		Sun.	5 Calgary

* Denotes afternoon game.

Home Starting Times:

Weeknights	7:35 p.m.
Saturdays & Sundays	7:05 p.m.
Matinees	2:05 p.m.
Except Dec 31.	4:35 p.m.

Franchise date: June 22, 1979

13th NHL Season

Ed Olczyk, who had his fourth consecutive season with at least 30 goals, finished second in team scoring with the Jets in 1990-91.

1991-92 Player Personnel

FORWARDS	HT	WT	S	Place of Birth	Date	1990-91 Club
AMUNDSON, Darrin	6-02	175	R	Duluth, MN	11/9/68	Minn-Duluth
ARNIEL, Scott	6-1	188	L	Kingston, Ont.	7/17/62	Buffalo-Winnipeg
ASHTON, Brent	6-1	210	L	Saskatoon, Sask.	5/18/60	Winnipeg
BARBER, Don	6-01	205	L	Victoria, B.C.	12/2/64	Moncton-Minnesota
BARNES, Stu	5-10	175	R	Edmonton, Alta.	12/25/70	Cdn. National Team
BORSATO Luciano	5-10	165	R	Richmond Hill, Ont.	1/7/66	Moncton-Winnipeg
CIRONE, Jason	5-9	184	L	Toronto, Ont.	2/21/71	Cornwall-Windsor
COLE, Danton	5-11	189	R	Lansing, MI	1/10/67	Moncton-Winnipeg
DAVIDSON, Lee	5-11	165	L	Winnipeg, Man.	6/30/68	Moncton
DRAPER, Kris	5-11	188	L	Toronto, Ont.	5/24/71	Ottawa-Winnipeg
EAGLES, Mike	5-10	180	L	Sussex, N.B.	3/7/63	Winnipeg
ELYNUIK, Pat	6-0	185	R	Foam Lake, Sask.	10/30/67	Winnipeg
ERIKSSON, Bryan	5-9	175	R	Roseau, MN	7/3/60	Moncton-Winnipeg
EVANS, Doug	5-9	185	L	Peterborough, Ont.	6/2/63	Winnipeg
GERNANDER, Ken	5-10	175	L	Coleraine, MN	6/30/69	U. Minnesota
HANKINSON, Peter	5-9	175	R	Edina, MN	11/24/67	Moncton
HARTJE, Tod	6-01	180	L	Anoka, MN	2/27/68	Sokol Kiev
JOSEPH, Tony	6-4	203	R	Cornwall, Ont.	3/1/69	Moncton
JOYCE, Bob	6-00	195	L	St. John, N.B.	7/11/66	Baltimore
KHARIN, Sergei	5-11	180	R	Odintsovo, USSR	2/20/63	Moncton-Winnipeg
KUMPEL, Mark	6-0	190	R	Wakefield, MA	3/7/61	Winnipeg
LEBEAU, Benoit	6-01	190	L	Montreal, PQ	6/4/68	Merrimack U.
LEBLANC, John	6-01	190	L	Cambellton, N.B.	1/21/64	Did Not Play
LEVINS, Scott	6-3	200	R	Portland, OR	1/30/70	Moncton
MacDERMID, Paul	6-1	205	R	Chesley, Ont.	4/14/63	Winnipeg
MARTIN, Craig	6-2	219	R	Amherst, N.S.	1/21/71	Hull-St. Hyacinthe
McLLWAIN, Dave	6-0	190	R	Seaforth, Ont.	1/9/67	Winnipeg
MURRAY, Rob	6-01	180	R	Toronto, Ont.	4/4/67	Washington-Baltimore
MURRAY, Troy	6-01	195	R	Calgary, Alta.	7/31/62	Chicago
OLCZYK, Eddie	6-01	200	L	Chicago, IL.	8/16/66	Toronto-Winnipeg
OSBORNE, Mark	6-02	205	L	Toronto, Ont.	8/31/61	Toronto-Winnipeg
ROMANIUK, Russ	6-00	185	L	Winnipeg, Man.	6/9/70	U. of North Dakota
RYCHEL, Warren	6-00	185	L	Tecumseh, Ont.	5/12/67	Indianapolis-Chicago
SCHNEIDER, Scott	6-1	180	R	Rochester, MN	5/18/65	Moncton
STEEN, Thomas	5-10	195	L	Grums, Sweden	6/8/60	Winnipeg
SYKES, Phil	6-0	175	L	Dawson Creek, B.C.	3/18/59	Winnipeg

DEFENSEMEN	HT	WT	S	Place of Birth	Date	
CARLYLE, Randy	5-10	200	L	Sudbury, Ont.	4/19/56	Winnipeg
COWIE, Rob	6-00	195	L	Toronto, Ont.	11/3/67	Northeastern U.
CRONIN, Shawn	6-2	210	R	Flushing, MI	8/20/63	Winnipeg
DONNELLY, Gord	6-1	202	R	Montreal, Que.	2/2/62	Winnipeg
EAKINS, Dallas	6-2	195	L	Dade City, FL	2/27/67	Moncton
GALLOWAY, Kyle	5-11	170	L	Winnipeg, Man.	11/10/69	U. of Manitoba
HOUSLEY, Phil	5-10	179	L	St. Paul, MN	3/9/64	Winnipeg
LANGILLE, Derek	6-00	185	L	Toronto, Ont.	6/25/69	Newmarket
MANTHA, Moe	6-2	210	R	Lakewood, OH	1/21/61	Winnipeg
MARTTILA, Jukka	6-0	185	L	Tampere, Finland	4/15/60	Tappara
NUMMINEN, Teppo	6-1	190	R	Tampere, Finland	7/3/68	Winnipeg
OLAUSSON, Fredrik	6-2	200	R	Vaxsjo, Sweden	10/5/66	Winnipeg
PAYNTER, Kent	6-00	185	L	Summerside, PEI	4/17/65	Baltimore-Washington
POESCHEK, Rudy	6-02	210	R	Terrace, B.C.	9/29/66	Binghamton-Moncton
RICCIARDI, Jeff	5-10	203	L	Thunder Bay, Ont.	6/22/71	Ottawa
SEBASTIAN, Jeff	6-02	198	R	Vancouver, B.C.	11/21/71	Seattle
SOROKIN, Sergei	5-11	187	L	Gorky, USSR	10/2/69	Dynamo Moscow

GOALTENDERS	HT	WT	C	Place of Birth	Date	1990-91 Club
BEAUREGARD, Stephane	5-11	182	R	Cowansville, Que.	1/10/68	Ft. Wayne-Wpg.-Mctn.
ESSENSA, Bob	6-0	160	L	Toronto, Ont.	1/14/65	Moncton-Winnipeg
GAUTHIER, Sean	5-11	202	L	Sudbury, Ont.	3/28/71	Kingston
O'NEILL, Mike	5-7	160	L	Montreal, Que.	11/3/67	Moncton
TABARACCI, Rich	5-10	186	L	Toronto, Ont.	1/2/69	Winnipeg-Moncton

General Managers' History

John Ferguson, 1979-80 to 1987-88; John Ferguson and Mike Smith, 1988-89; Mike Smith, 1989-90 to date.

Coaching History

Tom McVie, 1979-80; Tom McVie and Bill Sutherland, 1980-81; Tom Watt, 1981-82 to 1982-83; Tom Watt, John Ferguson and Barry Long, 1983-84; Barry Long, 1984-85; Barry Long and John Ferguson, 1985-86. Dan Maloney, 1986-87 to 1987-88; Dan Maloney and Rick Bowness 1988-89; Bob Murdoch, 1989-90 to 1990-91; John Paddock, 1991-92.

Captains' History

Lars-Erik Sjoberg, 1979-80; Morris Lukowich, 1980-81; Dave Christian, 1981-82; Dave Christian, Lucien DeBlois, 1982-83; Lucien DeBlois, 1983-84; Dale Hawerchuk, 1984-85 to 1988-89; Randy Carlyle, Dale Hawerchuk and Thomas Steen, 1989-90; Thomas Steen, 1990-91 to date.

1990-91 Scoring

Regular Season

* rookie

Pos	#	Player	Team	GP	G	A	Pts	+/-	PIM	PP	SH	GW	GT	S	%
D	6	Phil Housley	WPG	78	23	53	76	13–	24	12	1	3	0	206	11.2
C	16	Ed Olczyk	TOR	18	4	10	14	7–	13	0	0	0	0	45	8.9
			WPG	61	26	31	57	20–	69	14	0	2	2	181	14.4
			TOTAL	79	30	41	71	27–	82	14	0	2	2	226	13.3
C	25	Thomas Steen	WPG	58	19	48	67	3–	49	7	0	3	0	125	15.2
R	15	Pat Elynuik	WPG	80	31	34	65	13–	73	16	0	4	1	150	20.7
D	4	Fredrik Olausson	WPG	71	12	29	41	22–	24	5	0	0	0	168	7.1
R	23	Paul MacDermid	WPG	69	15	21	36	6–	128	3	0	1	0	94	16.0
L	7	Brent Ashton	WPG	61	12	24	36	10–	58	1	0	2	0	107	11.2
L	39	Doug Evans	WPG	70	7	27	34	1–	108	1	0	0	1	70	10.0
D	27	Teppo Numminen	WPG	80	8	25	33	15–	28	3	0	0	0	151	5.3
D	8	Randy Carlyle	WPG	52	9	19	28	6	44	2	0	1	0	89	10.1
R	20	Dave McLlwain	WPG	60	14	11	25	13–	46	2	2	2	0	104	13.5
C	24	*Danton Cole	WPG	66	13	11	24	14–	24	1	1	1	1	109	11.9
D	22	Moe Mantha	WPG	57	9	15	24	20–	33	4	1	2	0	102	8.8
L	17	Phil Sykes	WPG	70	12	10	22	9–	59	0	2	0	1	65	18.5
L	12	Mark Osborne	TOR	18	3	3	6	10–	4	1	1	0	0	32	9.4
			WPG	37	8	8	16	1–	59	0	0	2	1	55	14.5
			TOTAL	55	11	11	22	11–	63	1	1	2	1	87	12.6
C	11	Scott Arniel	WPG	75	5	17	22	12–	87	0	0	1	1	91	5.5
R	21	Mark Kumpel	WPG	53	7	3	10	10–	10	0	0	1	0	65	10.8
R	36	Mike Eagles	WPG	44	0	9	9	10–	79	0	0	0	0	51	.0
D	34	Gord Donnelly	WPG	57	3	4	7	13–	265	0	0	0	0	35	8.6
R	18	Bryan Erickson	WPG	6	0	7	7	1	0	0	0	0	0	16	.0
R	44	Shawn Cronin	WPG	67	1	5	6	10–	189	0	0	0	0	40	2.5
R	26	Sergei Kharin	WPG	7	2	3	5	2	2	0	0	0	0	13	15.4
D	3	*Bryan Marchment	WPG	28	2	2	4	5–	91	0	0	0	0	24	8.3
			MIN	7	0	0	0	3–	4	0	0	0	0	10	.0
L	32	Don Barber	WPG	16	1	2	3	3–	14	0	0	0	0	19	5.3
			TOTAL	23	1	2	3	6–	18	0	0	0	0	29	3.4
G	35	Bob Essensa	WPG	55	0	3	3	0	6	0	0	0	0	0	.0
L	45	Craig Duncanson	WPG	7	2	0	2	5–	0	0	0	0	0	6	33.3
C	19	Kris Draper	WPG	3	1	0	1	0	5	0	0	0	1	1	100.0
C	38	*Luciano Borsato	WPG	1	0	1	1	0	0	0	0	0	0	0	.0
G	30	*Steph Beauregard	WPG	16	0	1	1	0	2	0	0	0	0	0	.0
G	31	*Rick Tabaracci	WPG	24	0	1	1	0	0	0	0	0	0	0	.0
R	29	Rudy Poeschek	WPG	1	0	0	0	0	0	0	0	0	0	0	.0
L	19	Iain Duncan	WPG	2	0	0	0	1–	0	0	0	0	0	2	.0
C	33	*Simon Wheeldon	WPG	4	0	0	0	0	0	0	0	0	0	4	.0
C	38	*Guy Larose	WPG	7	0	0	0	1–	8	0	0	0	0	7	.0

Goaltending

No.	Goaltender	GPI	Mins	Avg	W	L	T	EN	SO	GA	SA	S%
35	Bob Essensa	55	2916	3.15	19	24	6	5	4	153	1496	.898
31	*Rick Tabaracci	24	1093	3.90	4	9	4	4	1	71	570	.875
30	*Steph Beauregard	16	836	3.95	3	10	1	0	0	55	423	.870
	Totals	80	4860	3.56	26	43	11	9	5	288	2498	.885

Bob Essensa set a single-season franchise record by recording four shutouts in 1990-91.

Club Records

Team

(Figures in brackets for season records are games played; records for fewest points, wins, ties, losses, goals, goals against are for 70 or more games)

Most Points 96 1984-85 (80)
Most Wins 43 1984-85 (80)
Most Ties 14 1980-81 (80)
                           1981-82 (80)
Most Losses 57 1980-81 (80)
Most Goals............358 1984-85 (80)
Most Goals Against 400 1980-81 (80)
Fewest Points 32 1980-81 (80)
Fewest Wins 9 1980-81 (80)
Fewest Ties 7 1985-86 (80)
Fewest Losses 27 1984-85 (80)
Fewest Goals 214 1979-80 (80)
Fewest Goals Against ...271 1986-87 (80)

Longest Winning Streak
Over-all ....9 Mar. 8-27/85
Home ....7 Jan. 23-Mar. 1/87
Away ....8 Feb. 25-Apr. 6/85

Longest Undefeated Streak
Over-all.............13 Mar. 8-Apr. 7/85
                        (10 wins, 3 ties)
Home ....11 Dec. 23/83
                        Feb. 5/84
                        (6 wins, 5 ties)
Away ....9 Feb. 25-Apr. 7/85 (8
                        wins, 1 tie)

Longest Losing Streak
Over-all.............10 Nov. 30-
                        Dec. 20/80
Home ....4 Four times
Away ....9 Dec. 26/79-
                        Jan. 22/80

Longest Winless Streak
Over-all.............*30 Oct. 19-
                        Dec. 20/80
                        (23 losses, 7 ties)
Home ....14 Oct. 19-
                        Dec. 14/80
                        (9 losses, 5 ties)
Away ....18 Oct. 10-
                        Dec. 20/80
                        (16 losses, 2 ties)

Most Shutouts, Season 5 1990-91 (80)
Most PIM, Season 2,278 1987-88 (80)
Most Goals, Game ....12 Feb. 25/85
                            (Wpg. 12 at NYR. 5)

Individual

Most Seasons ....10 Doug Smail
                            Thomas Steen
Most Games ....725 Thomas Steen
Most Goals, Career .....379 Dale Hawerchuk
Most Assists, Career ....550 Dale Hawerchuk
Most Points, Career ....929 Dale Hawerchuk
                            (379 goals, 550 assists)
Most PIM, Career ......1,338 Laurie Boschman
Most Shutouts, Career ......6 Bob Essensa
Longest Consecutive
  Games Streak ....475 Dale Hawerchuk
                            (Dec. 19/82-Dec. 10/89)
Most Goals, Season ......53 Dale Hawerchuk
                            (1984-85)
Most Assists, Season .....77 Dale Hawerchuk
                            (1984-85, 1987-88)
Most Points, Season .....130 Dale Hawerchuk
                            (1984-85)
                            (53 goals, 77 assists)
Most PIM, Season ....287 Jimmy Mann
                            (1979-80)
Most Points, Defenseman
  Season ....76 Phil Housley
                            (1990-91)
                            (23 goals, 53 assists)
Most Points, Center,
  Season ....130 Dale Hawerchuk
                            (1984-85)
                            (53 goals, 77 assists)
Most Points, Right Wing,
  Season ....101 Paul Maclean
                            (1984-85)
                            (41 goals, 60 assists)
Most Points, Left Wing,
  Season ....92 Morris Lukowich
                            (1981-82)
                            (43 goals, 49 assists)
Most Points, Rookie,
  Season ....103 Dale Hawerchuk
                            (1981-82)
                            (45 goals, 58 assists)
Most Shutouts, Season .....4 Bob Essensa
                            (1990-91)
Most Goals, Game ....5 Willy Lindstrom
                            (Mar. 2/82)
Most Assists, Game ....5 Dale Hawerchuk
                            (Mar. 6/84,
                            Mar. 18/89,
                            Mar. 4/90)

Most Points, Game ....6 Willy Lindstrom
                            (Mar. 2/82)
                            Dale Hawerchuk
                            (Dec. 14/83,
                            Mar. 18/89)
                            Thomas Steen
                            (Oct. 24/84)

* NHL Record.

Retired Numbers

9   Bobby Hull   1972-1980

All-time Record vs. Other Clubs

Regular Season

	At Home							On Road							Total						
	GP	W	L	T	GF	GA	PTS	GP	W	L	T	GF	GA	PTS	GP	W	L	T	GF	GA	PTS
Boston	19	8	10	1	66	66	17	19	2	14	3	61	93	7	38	10	24	4	127	159	24
Buffalo	19	7	10	2	61	70	16	19	1	16	2	50	91	4	38	8	26	4	111	161	20
Calgary	41	18	15	8	168	150	44	42	7	31	4	129	209	18	83	25	46	12	297	359	62
Chicago	21	9	9	3	87	83	21	21	4	15	2	68	111	10	42	13	24	5	155	194	31
Detroit	21	7	7	7	73	69	21	21	7	11	3	81	86	17	42	14	18	10	154	155	38
Edmonton	41	14	24	3	168	203	31	42	10	29	3	134	203	23	83	24	53	6	302	406	54
Hartford	19	11	8	0	72	69	22	19	5	10	4	62	82	14	38	16	18	4	134	151	36
Los Angeles	42	20	15	7	186	158	47	41	20	14	7	174	171	47	83	40	29	14	360	329	94
Minnesota	21	10	10	1	74	73	21	21	7	12	2	67	98	16	42	17	22	3	141	171	37
Montreal	19	7	8	4	64	78	18	19	2	17	0	47	107	4	38	9	25	4	111	185	22
New Jersey	20	14	3	3	82	50	31	18	8	5	5	63	57	21	38	22	8	8	145	107	52
NY Islanders	19	6	12	1	62	76	13	19	4	10	5	57	76	13	38	10	22	6	119	152	26
NY Rangers	19	7	10	2	72	74	16	19	8	9	2	84	93	18	38	15	19	4	156	167	34
Philadelphia	19	8	10	1	66	72	17	19	6	13	0	53	95	6	38	14	23	1	119	167	23
Pittsburgh	19	8	10	1	76	73	17	19	6	13	0	58	83	12	38	14	23	1	134	156	29
Quebec	19	9	6	4	81	74	22	19	10	7	2	85	96	22	38	19	13	6	166	150	44
St. Louis	21	12	4	5	79	66	29	21	4	9	7	69	91	16	42	16	13	13	148	157	45
Toronto	21	11	7	3	104	92	25	21	14	6	1	103	82	29	42	25	13	4	207	174	54
Vancouver	41	23	11	7	168	151	53	42	13	23	6	132	162	32	83	36	34	13	300	313	85
Washington	19	8	6	5	68	69	21	19	5	13	1	58	89	11	38	13	19	6	126	158	32
Totals	480	217	195	68	1877	1816	502	480	140	280	60	1635	2155	340	960	357	475	128	3512	3971	842

Playoffs

	Series	W	L	GP	W	L	T	GF	GA	Last Mtg.	Round	Result
Calgary	3	2	1	13	7	6	0	45	43	1987	DSF	W 4-2
Edmonton	6	0	6	26	4	22	0	75	120	1990	DSF	L 3-4
St. Louis	1	0	1	4	1	3	0	13	20	1982	DSF	L 1-3
Totals	10	2	8	43	12	31	0	133	183			

Playoff Results 1991-87

Year	Round	Opponent	Result	GF	GA
1990	DSF	Edmonton	L 3-4	22	24
1988	DSF	Edmonton	L 1-4	17	25
1987	DF	Edmonton	L 0-4	9	17
	DSF	Calgary	W 4-2	22	15

Abbreviations: Round: F – Final; CF – conference final; DF – division final; DSF – division semi-final; GA – goals against; GF – goals for.

1990-91 Results

	Home				Away	
Oct.	4	Toronto	7-1	Oct.	6 Edmonton	3-3
	8	Calgary	3-4		12 Washington	1-3
	10	Boston	2-4		13 Philadelphia	3-4
	19	Vancouver	7-5		16 NY Islanders	1-4
	24	Edmonton	3-1		17 NY Rangers	3-5
	26	Los Angeles	6-2		31 Edmonton	1-0
	28	Los Angeles	2-6	Nov.	1 Calgary	1-2
Nov.	6	Philadelphia	2-4		3 Vancouver	5-3
	9	Hartford	5-4		11 Chicago	3-3
	14	Pittsburgh	4-6		12 Toronto	2-5
	16	NY Rangers	4-6		20 St Louis	2-4
	18	St Louis	4-3		22 NY Islanders	1-3
	28	Calgary	2-2		24 Quebec	11-4
	30	Minnesota	2-4		25 Montreal	3-4
Dec.	2	Vancouver	1-5	Dec.	5 Los Angeles	3-3
	3	New Jersey	4-4		8 Los Angeles	4-4
	15	Montreal	4-2		11 St Louis	3-3
	16	Philadelphia	2-4		13 Chicago	4-5
	22	Detroit	2-5		18 Pittsburgh	2-9
	28	Boston	6-0		20 Detroit	1-3
	31	Vancouver	2-1		26 Minnesota	6-4
Jan.	2	Calgary	3-3	Jan.	4 Buffalo	1-4
	11	Chicago	1-3		5 Hartford	3-4
	13	Calgary	4-3		7 Boston	2-5
	21	Minnesota	2-0		15 Calgary	5-7
	25	NY Islanders	8-1		16 Vancouver	2-1
	27	Edmonton*	2-3		29 Quebec	3-2
Feb.	6	Toronto	5-5		30 Montreal	4-8
	8	Pittsburgh	6-2	Feb.	2 Washington	4-3
	10	Buffalo*	0-2		3 NY Rangers	4-3
	17	Quebec*	6-0		12 Detroit	1-6
	20	Vancouver	5-5		14 New Jersey	3-3
	22	Los Angeles	4-6		28 Los Angeles	2-4
	24	Los Angeles*	3-5	Mar.	2 Los Angeles	3-6
	26	Hartford	5-4		12 Calgary	3-5
Mar.	5	Edmonton	4-5		18 Calgary	3-4
	8	Washington	1-2		22 Vancouver	1-3
	10	New Jersey*	4-3		23 Edmonton	3-0
	13	Buffalo	2-6		28 Vancouver	2-3
	15	Edmonton	4-3		31 Edmonton	3-6

* Denotes afternoon game.

Entry Draft
Selections 1991-79

1991		1988		1985		1982	
Pick		**Pick**		**Pick**		**Pick**	
5	Aaron Ward	10	Teemu Selanne	18	Ryan Stewart	12	Jim Kyte
49	Dimitri Filimonov	31	Russell Romaniuk	39	Roger Ohman	74	Tom Martin
91	Juha Ylonen	52	Stephane Beauregard	60	Dan Berthiaume	75	Dave Ellett
99	Jan Kaminsky	73	Brian Hunt	81	Fredrik Olausson	96	Tim Mishler
115	Jeff Sebastian	94	Anthony Joseph	102	John Borrell	138	Derek Ray
159	Jeff Ricciardi	101	Benoit Lebeau	123	Danton Cole	159	Guy Gosselin
181	Sean Gauthier	115	Ronald Jones	144	Brent Mowery	180	Tom Ward
203	Igor Ulanov	127	Markus Akerblom	165	Tom Draper	201	Mike Savage
225	Jason Jennings	136	Jukka Marttila	186	Nevin Kardum	222	Bob Shaw
247	Sergei Sorokin	157	Mark Smith	207	Dave Quigley	243	Jan Urban Ericson
		178	Mike Helber	228	Chris Norton		
1990		199	Pavel Kostichkin	249	Anssi Melametsa	**1981**	
Pick		220	Kevin Heise			**Pick**	
19	Keith Tkachuk	241	Kyle Galloway	**1984**		1	Dale Hawerchuk
35	Mike Muller			**Pick**		22	Scott Arniel
74	Roman Meluzin	**1987**		30	Peter Douris	43	Jyrki Seppa
75	Scott Levins	**Pick**		68	Chris Mills	64	Kirk McCaskill
77	Alexei Zhamnov	16	Bryan Marchment	72	Sean Clement	85	Marc Behrend
98	Craig Martin	37	Patrik Eriksson	93	Scott Schneider	106	Bob O'Connor
119	Daniel Jardemyr	79	Don McLennan	114	Gary Lorden	127	Peter Nilsson
140	John Lilley	96	Ken Gernander	135	Luciano Borsato	148	Dan McFaul
161	Henrik Andersson	100	Darrin Amundson	156	Brad Jones	169	Greg Dick
182	Rauli Raitanen	121	Joe Harwell	177	Gord Whitaker	190	Vladimir Kadlec
203	Mika Alatalo	142	Todd Hartje	197	Rick Forst	211	Dave Kirwin
224	Sergei Selyanin	163	Markku Kyllonen	218	Mike Warus		
245	Keith Morris	184	Jim Fernholz	238	Jim Edmonds	**1980**	
		226	Roger Rougelot			**Pick**	
1989		247	Hans Goran Elo	**1983**		2	David Babych
Pick				**Pick**		23	Moe Mantha
4	Stu Barnes	**1986**		8	Andrew McBain	44	Murray Eaves
25	Dan Ratushny	**Pick**		14	Bobby Dollas	65	Guy Fournier
46	Jason Cirone	8	Pat Elynuik	29	Brad Berry	86	Glen Ostir
62	Kris Draper	29	Teppo Numminen	43	Peter Taglianetti	107	Ron Loustel
64	Mark Brownschidle	50	Esa Palosaari	69	Bob Essensa	128	Brian Mullen
69	Allain Roy	71	Hannu Jarvenpaa	89	Harry Armstrong	135	Mike Lauen
109	Dan Bylsma	92	Craig Endean	109	Joel Baillargeon	149	Sandy Beadle
130	Pekka Peltola	113	Robertson Bateman	129	Iain Duncan	170	Ed Christian
131	Doug Evans	155	Frank Furlan	149	Ron Pessetti	191	Dave Chartier
151	Jim Solly	176	Mark Green	169	Todd Flichel		
172	Stephane Gauvin	197	John Blue	189	Cory Wright	**1979**	
193	Joe Larson	218	Matt Cote	209	Eric Cormier	**Pick**	
214	Bradley Podiak	239	Arto Blomsten	229	Jamie Husgen	19	Jimmy Mann
235	Genneyna Davydov					40	Dave Christian
240	Sergei Kharin					61	Bill Whelton
						82	Pat Daley
						103	Thomas Steen
						124	Tim Watters

Coach

PADDOCK, JOHN
Coach, Winnipeg Jets. Born in Brandon, Man., June 9, 1954.

John Paddock was named head coach of the Jets on June 17, 1991, the 10th head coach in the club's history. Paddock joins the Jets after serving one season as head coach of the Binghamton Rangers of the American Hockey League, the league where he got his coaching start in 1983. Paddock, then playing for the Maine Mariners, succeeded Tom McVie behind the Mariners bench when McVie was summoned to New Jersey; the Mariners won the AHL Calder Cup Championship that season. Paddock later joined the Hershey Bears, where he won another Calder Cup and two Coach of the Year awards. Paddock served one season as assistant general manager for the Philadelphia Flyers before joining the New York Rangers organization last season.

Paddock played 87 NHL games as a right wing, drafted by the Washington Capitals, and recorded eight goals and 14 assists during his career.

Coaching Record

			Regular Season				Playoffs			
Season	**Team**	**Games**	**W**	**L**	**T**	**%**	**Games**	**W**	**L**	**%**
1983-84	Maine (AHL)	80	33	36	11	.481	17	12	5	.706
1984-85	Maine (AHL)	80	38	32	10	.538	11	5	6	.454
1985-86	Hershey (AHL)	80	48	29	3	.619	18	10	8	.555
1986-87	Hershey (AHL)	80	43	36	1	.544	5	1	4	.200
1987-88	Hershey (AHL)	80	50	27	3	.644	12	12	0	1.000
1988-89	Hershey (AHL)	80	40	30	10	.563	12	7	5	.583
1990-91	Binghamton (AHL)	80	44	30	6	.588	10	4	6	.400

Club Directory

Winnipeg Arena
15-1430 Maroons Road
Winnipeg, Manitoba R3G 0L5
Phone **204/783-5387**
Mktg., PR FAX 204/788-4668
ENVOY ID
General
Manager: JETS. GM
Public
Relations: JETS. PR
Marketing: JETS, MAR
Capacity: 15,393

Board of Directors

Barry L. Shenkarow	Marvin Shenkarow	Dick Archer
Bob Chipman	Don Binda	Bill Davis
Dick Archer	Steve Bannatyne	Jerry Kruk

President & Governor .... Barry L. Shenkarow
Alternate Governors .... Michael Smith, Bill Davis

Hockey Operations

Vice-President & General Manager .... Michael Smith
Assistant General Manager/Director of Hockey
Operations .... Dennis McDonald
Coach .... John Paddock
Assistant Coaches .... Terry Simpson, Glen Williamson
Goaltending Coach .... Dave Prior
Special Consultant .... Ken Buna
Director of Scouting .... Bill Lesuk
Assistant Director of Scouting .... Joe Yannetti
Scouts .... Connie Broden, Mike Antonovitch,
Sean Coady, Tom Savage, Larry Hornung
Director of Hockey Operations, Moncton ... Dave Farrish
Executive Ass't. to Vice-President & G.M. ... Pat MacDonald
Administrative Ass't - Hockey Operations ... Loris Enns

Finance and Administration

Director of Finance & Administration .... Don Binda
Director of Team Services .... Murray Harding
Controller .... Glenda Leiske
Ticket Manager .... Dianne Gabbs
Accounting/Ticketing Assistants .... Trish Benson
Accounting Assistants .... Bryan Braun, Doug Bergman
Administrative Assistant/Team Services/
Communications .... Heather Reynolds
Administrative Assistant/Novelty Operations ... Lynda Sweetland
Receptionists .... Sherri Wilson/Trish Benson
Jets' All Sports Store Manager .... Gavin Shipley

Communications

Director of Communications .... Mike O'Hearn
Director of Community Relations .... Lori Summers
Statistician/Communications Assistant .... Bruce Barton
Administrative Ass't., Community Relations .... Sherri Wilson
Administrative Ass't., Goals for Kids .... Michelle McCrea
Communications Assistant .... Igor Kuperman

Marketing

Vice-President of Marketing .... Madeline Hanson
Director of Sales .... Val Overwater
Marketing Assistant .... Val Kuhn
Senior Account Executive .... Gord Dmytriw
Merchandising Manager .... Chris Newman
Administrative Assistant/Sales .... Teresa Bastian
Account Executive .... Hartley Miller

Dressing Room

Athletic Therapist .... Jim Ramsay
Athletic Trainer .... Phil Walker
Equipment Manager .... Craig Heisinger, Stan Wilson
Team Physician .... Dr. Wayne Hildahl
Team Dentist .... Dr. Gene Solmundson
Team Colors .... Blue, Red and White
Training Camp .... Winnipeg Arena
Press Box Location .... East Side
TV Channel .... CKY-TV
Radio Station .... CKY AM 580
Play-by-Play .... Curt Keilback (Radio)
Color Commentary .... Don Wittman/Bob Irving (Radio)

General Manager

MIKE SMITH
General Manager, Winnipeg Jets. Born on August 31, 1945 in Potsdam, New York.

Mike Smith was appointed general manager of the club on December 3, 1988 after ten years of service within the Jets organization. He had held the position of assistant general manager and director of scouting since 1984.

Smith began his NHL career in 1976-77 when he was an assistant coach with the New York Rangers under John Ferguson. After two seasons in New York, he assumed the same coaching duties with the Colorado Rockies. When the Jets entered the League in 1979-80, Smith was hired as general manager of their CHL franchise in Tulsa. In 1980-81, midway through the season, Smith was asked to come to Winnipeg to be head coach. In 1981-82 he became the team's director of recruiting.

1990-91 Final Statistics

Standings

Abbreviations: GA – goals against; **GF** – goals for; **GP** – games played; **L** – losses; **PTS** – points; **T** – ties; **W** – wins; **%** – percentage of games won.

CLARENCE CAMPBELL CONFERENCE
Norris Division

	GP	W	L	T	GF	GA	PTS	%
Chicago	80	49	23	8	284	211	106	.663
St. Louis	80	47	22	11	310	250	105	.656
Detroit	80	34	38	8	273	298	76	.475
Minnesota	80	27	39	14	256	266	68	.425
Toronto	80	23	46	11	241	318	57	.356

Smythe Division

	GP	W	L	T	GF	GA	PTS	%
Los Angeles	80	46	24	10	340	254	102	.638
Calgary	80	46	26	8	344	263	100	.625
Edmonton	80	37	37	6	272	272	80	.500
Vancouver	80	28	43	9	243	315	65	.406
Winnipeg	80	26	43	11	260	288	63	.394

PRINCE OF WALES CONFERENCE
Adams Division

	GP	W	L	T	GF	GA	PTS	%
Boston	80	44	24	12	299	264	100	.625
Montreal	80	39	30	11	273	249	89	.556
Buffalo	80	31	30	19	292	278	81	.506
Hartford	80	31	38	11	238	276	73	.456
Quebec	80	16	50	14	236	354	46	.288

Patrick Division

	GP	W	L	T	GF	GA	PTS	%
Pittsburgh	80	41	33	6	342	305	88	.550
NY Rangers	80	36	31	13	297	265	85	.531
Washington	80	37	36	7	258	258	81	.506
New Jersey	80	32	33	15	272	264	79	.494
Philadelphia	80	33	37	10	252	267	76	.475
NY Islanders	80	25	45	10	223	290	60	.375

Dirk Graham, who led the Blackhawks with six short-handed goals, was awarded the Frank Selke Trophy as the league's best defensive forward for 1990-91.

INDIVIDUAL LEADERS

Goal Scoring

Player	Team	GP	G
Brett Hull	St. L.	78	86
Cam Neely	Bos.	69	51
Theo Fleury	Cgy.	79	51
Steve Yzerman	Det.	80	51
Mike Gartner	NYR	79	49
Joe Sakic	Que.	80	48
Tomas Sandstrom	L.A.	68	45
Luc Robitaille	L.A.	76	45

Assists

Player	Team	GP	A
Wayne Gretzky	L.A.	78	122
Adam Oates	St. L.	61	90
Al MacInnis	Cgy.	78	75
Ray Bourque	Bos.	76	73
Mark Recchi	Pit.	78	73
Brian Leetch	NYR	80	72

Power-Play Goals

Player	Team	GP	PP
Brett Hull	St. L.	78	29
Mike Gartner	NYR	79	22
Joe Nieuwendyk	Cgy.	79	22
Dave Gagner	Min.	73	20
John MacLean	N.J.	78	19
Cam Neely	Bos.	69	18

Short-Hand Goals

Player	Team	GP	SH
Dave Reid	Tor.	69	8
Theo Fleury	Cgy.	79	7
Dirk Graham	Chi.	80	6
Craig MacTavish	Edm.	80	6
Steve Yzerman	Det.	80	6
Mike Ridley	Wsh.	79	5

Game-Winning Goals

Player	Team	GP	GW
Brett Hull	St. L.	78	11
Jeremy Roenick	Chi.	79	10
Mark Recchi	Pit.	78	9
Theo Fleury	Cgy.	79	9
Steve Larmer	Chi.	80	9

Game-Tying Goals

Player	Team	GP	GT
Dino Ciccarelli	Wsh.	54	3
Todd Krygier	Hfd.	72	3
Brendan Shanahan	N.J.	75	3
Dave Andreychuk	Buf.	80	3

Shots

Player	Team	GP	S
Brett Hull	St. L.	78	389
Steve Yzerman	Det.	80	326
Ray Bourque	Bos.	76	323
Al MacInnis	Cgy.	78	305
Brian Bellows	Min.	80	296
John MacLean	N.J.	78	292
Russ Courtnall	Mtl.	79	279
Claude Lemieux	N.J.	78	271

First Goals

Player	Team	GP	FG
Brett Hull	St. L.	78	19
Luc Robitaille	L.A.	76	10
Wayne Gretzky	L.A.	78	10
Murray Craven	Phi.	77	9
Mike Gartner	NYR	79	9
Kevin Hatcher	Wsh.	79	9

Shooting Percentage
(minimum 80 shots)

Player	Team	GP	G	S	%
Sergei Makarov	Cgy.	78	30	93	32.3
Peter Zezel	Wsh.–Tor.	52	21	90	23.3
Brett Hull	St. L.	78	86	389	22.1
*Ken Hodge	Bos.	70	30	137	21.9
Mark Recchi	Pit.	78	40	184	21.7

Plus/Minus

Player	Team	GP	+/–
Marty McSorley	L.A.	61	48
Theo Fleury	Cgy.	79	48
Al MacInnis	Cgy.	78	42
Jeremy Roenick	Chi.	79	38
Steve Larmer	Chi.	80	37
Ray Bourque	Bos.	76	33
Wayne Gretzky	L.A.	78	30
Jamie Macoun	Cgy.	79	29

Individual Leaders

Abbreviations: * – rookie eligible for Calder Trophy; **A** – assists; **G** – goals; **GP** – games played; **GT** – game-tying goals; **GW** – game-winning goals; **PIM** – penalties in minutes; **PP** – power play goals; **Pts** – points; **S** – shots on goal; **SH** – short-handed goals; **%** – percentage of shots resulting in goals; **+/–** – difference between Goals For (GF) scored when a player is on the ice with his team at even strength or short-handed and Goals Against (GA) scored when the same player is on the ice with his team at even strength or on a power play.

Individual Scoring Leaders for Art Ross Trophy

Player	Team	GP	G	A	Pts	+/–	PIM	PP	SH	GW	GT	S	%
Wayne Gretzky	Los Angeles	78	41	122	163	30	16	8	0	5	2	212	19.3
Brett Hull	St. Louis	78	86	45	131	23	22	29	0	11	1	389	22.1
Adam Oates	St. Louis	61	25	90	115	15	29	3	1	3	0	139	18.0
Mark Recchi	Pittsburgh	78	40	73	113	0	48	12	0	9	0	184	21.7
John Cullen	Pit.–Hfd.	78	39	71	110	6–	101	14	0	3	1	205	19.0
Joe Sakic	Quebec	80	48	61	109	26–	24	12	3	7	1	245	19.6
Steve Yzerman	Detroit	80	51	57	108	2–	34	12	6	4	1	326	15.6
Theo Fleury	Calgary	79	51	53	104	48	136	9	7	9	0	249	20.5
Al MacInnis	Calgary	78	28	75	103	42	90	17	0	1	1	305	9.2
Steve Larmer	Chicago	80	44	57	101	37	79	17	2	9	0	231	19.0
Jeremy Roenick	Chicago	79	41	53	94	38	80	15	4	10	1	194	21.1
Ray Bourque	Boston	76	21	73	94	33	75	7	0	3	1	323	6.5
Paul Coffey	Pittsburgh	76	24	69	93	18–	128	8	0	3	0	240	10.0
Craig Janney	Boston	77	26	66	92	15	8	9	1	5	0	133	19.5
Cam Neely	Boston	69	51	40	91	26	98	18	1	8	0	262	19.5
Luc Robitaille	Los Angeles	76	45	46	91	28	68	11	0	5	1	229	19.7
Tomas Sandstrom	Los Angeles	68	45	44	89	27	106	16	0	6	1	221	20.4
Dale Hawerchuk	Buffalo	80	31	58	89	2	32	12	0	1	1	194	16.0
Brian Leetch	NY Rangers	80	16	72	88	2	42	6	0	4	1	206	7.8
Ron Francis	Hfd.–Pit.	81	23	64	87	2–	72	10	1	7	0	174	13.2
Kevin Stevens	Pittsburgh	80	40	46	86	1–	133	18	0	6	2	253	15.8
Joe Nieuwendyk	Calgary	79	45	40	85	19	36	22	4	1	0	222	20.3
Pat LaFontaine	NY Islanders	75	41	44	85	6–	42	12	2	5	1	225	18.2
Pat Verbeek	Hartford	80	43	39	82	0	246	15	0	5	1	247	17.4
Dave Gagner	Minnesota	73	40	42	82	9	114	20	0	5	2	223	17.9
Doug Gilmour	Calgary	78	20	61	81	27	144	2	2	5	0	135	14.8

Defensemen Scoring Leaders

Player	Team	GP	G	A	Pts	+/–	PIM	PP	SH	GW	GT	S	%
Al MacInnis	Calgary	78	28	75	103	42	90	17	0	1	1	305	9.2
Ray Bourque	Boston	76	21	73	94	33	75	7	0	3	1	323	6.5
Paul Coffey	Pittsburgh	76	24	69	93	18–	128	8	0	3	0	240	10.0
Brian Leetch	NY Rangers	80	16	72	88	2	42	6	0	4	1	206	7.8
Phil Housley	Winnipeg	78	23	53	76	13–	24	12	1	3	0	206	11.2
Kevin Hatcher	Washington	79	24	50	74	10–	69	9	2	3	0	267	9.0
Gary Suter	Calgary	79	12	58	70	26	102	6	0	1	0	258	4.7
Chris Chelios	Chicago	77	12	52	64	23	192	5	2	2	0	187	6.4
Steve Duchesne	Los Angeles	78	21	41	62	19	66	6	0	3	0	171	12.3
Jeff Brown	St Louis	67	12	47	59	4	39	6	1	0	2	176	6.8
James Patrick	NY Rangers	74	10	49	59	5–	58	6	0	2	0	138	7.2
Zarley Zalapski	Pit.–Hfd.	77	15	39	54	3	65	8	1	0	0	156	9.6
Steve Smith	Edmonton	77	13	41	54	14	193	4	0	2	0	114	11.4
Calle Johansson	Washington	80	11	41	52	2–	23	2	1	2	0	128	8.6
Dave Ellett	Wpg.–Tor.	77	12	37	49	8–	75	6	1	1	1	195	6.2
Scott Stevens	St. Louis	78	5	44	49	23	150	1	0	1	0	160	3.1
Yves Racine	Detroit	62	7	40	47	1	33	2	0	1	1	131	5.3
*Rob Blake	Los Angeles	75	12	34	46	3	125	9	0	2	0	150	8.0
Bruce Driver	New Jersey	73	9	36	45	11	62	7	0	2	0	195	4.6
Uwe Krupp	Buffalo	74	12	32	44	14	66	6	0	0	2	138	8.7
Glen Wesley	Boston	80	11	32	43	0	78	5	1	1	0	199	5.5
Larry Murphy	Min.–Pit.	75	9	34	43	6–	68	3	0	2	0	188	4.8
Gordon Murphy	Philadelphia	80	11	31	42	7–	58	6	0	2	0	203	5.4
Fredrik Olausson	Winnipeg	71	12	29	41	22–	24	5	0	0	0	168	7.1
Alexei Kasatonov	New Jersey	78	10	31	41	23	76	1	0	3	0	122	8.2
Doug Wilson	Chicago	51	11	29	40	25	32	6	1	1	0	162	6.8

CONSECUTIVE SCORING STREAKS

Goals

Games	Player	Team	G
10	Brett Hull	St. Louis	16
9	Denis Savard	Montreal	9
8	Cam Neely	Boston	9
7	Brett Hull	St. Louis	10
7	Mike Gartner	NY Rangers	7

13 players tied with five each

Assists

Games	Player	Team	A
23	Wayne Gretzky	Los Angeles	48
11	Al MacInnis	Calgary	19
10	Ray Bourque	Boston	16
9	Wayne Gretzky	Los Angeles	14
9	Vincent Damphousse	Toronto	13
8	Darren Turcotte	NY Rangers	11
8	Adam Oates	St. Louis	23
8	Wayne Gretzky	Los Angeles	15
8	John Cullen	Pittsburgh	14
8	Murray Craven	Philadelphia	13
8	Mark Recchi	Pittsburgh	13
8	Doug Wilson	Chicago	10
8	Pat Elynuik	Winnipeg	9
8	Scott Stevens	St. Louis	9

Points

Games	Player	Team	G	A	Pts
25	Wayne Gretzky	Los Angeles	8	49	57
16	Wayne Gretzky	Los Angeles	11	21	32
15	Adam Oates	St. Louis	8	36	44
13	John Cullen	Pittsburgh	7	20	27
13	Mike Ridley	Washington	6	12	18
12	Theo Fleury	Calgary	15	11	26
11	Al MacInnis	Calgary	6	19	25
11	Dave Gagner	Minnesota	7	16	23
11	Pat LaFontaine	NY Islanders	13	10	23
11	Mark Recchi	Pittsburgh	6	15	21
11	Darren Turcotte	NY Rangers	6	13	19
11	Denis Savard	Chicago	10	2	12

Al MacInnis who led all rearguards with 103 points, became only the fourth defenseman in NHL history to register 100 points in a season.

Joe Sakic, who finished in sixth place on the NHL scoring ladder, scored 24 goals at home and 24 on the road.

Mark Recchi, in only his second full season in the NHL, led the Penguins in scoring with 113 points.

Sergei Fedorov, who led all freshmen scorers in goals, assists, points, and game-winning goals, was named to the Upper Deck/NHL All-Rookie Team.

Individual Rookie Scoring Leaders

Scoring Leaders

Rookie	Team	GP	G	A	Pts	+/-	PIM	PP	SH	GW	GT	S	%
Sergei Fedorov	Detroit	77	31	48	79	11	66	11	3	5	1	259	12.0
Ken Hodge	Boston	70	30	29	59	11	20	12	2	4	0	137	21.9
Mats Sundin	Quebec	80	23	36	59	24 –	58	4	0	1	1	155	14.8
Jaromir Jagr	Pittsburgh	80	27	30	57	4 –	42	7	0	4	0	136	19.9
Rob Blake	Los Angeles	75	12	34	46	3	125	9	0	2	0	150	8.0
Bobby Holik	Hartford	78	21	22	43	3 –	113	8	0	3	0	173	12.1
Mike Ricci	Philadelphia	68	21	20	41	8 –	64	9	0	4	0	121	17.4
Robert Reichel	Calgary	66	19	22	41	17	22	3	0	3	0	131	14.5
Paul Ysebaert	N.J.–Det.	62	19	21	40	7 –	22	6	0	1	0	128	14.8
Johan Garpenlov	Detroit	71	18	22	40	4 –	18	2	0	3	0	91	19.8
Stephane Morin	Quebec	48	13	27	40	6	30	3	1	2	0	63	20.6

Shooting Percentage
(minimum 80 shots)

Rookie	Team	GP	G	S	%
Ken Hodge	Bos.	70	30	137	21.9
Jaromir Jagr	Pit.	80	27	136	19.9
Johan Garpenlov	Det.	71	18	91	19.8
Mike Ricci	Phi.	68	21	121	17.4
Mats Sundin	Que.	80	23	155	14.8
Paul Ysebaert	N.J.–Det.	62	19	128	14.8

Goal Scoring

Rookie	Team	GP	S
Sergei Fedorov	Det.	77	31
Ken Hodge	Bos.	70	30
Jaromir Jagr	Pit.	80	27
Mats Sundin	Que.	80	23
Mike Ricci	Phi	68	21
Bobby Holik	Hfd.	78	21

Assists

Rookie	Team	GP	S
Sergei Fedorov	Det.	77	48
Mats Sundin	Que.	80	36
Rob Blake	L.A.	75	34
Eric Weinrich	N.J.	76	34
Jaromir Jagr	Pit.	80	30

Power-Play Goals

Rookie	Team	GP	S
Ken Hodge	Bos.	70	12
Sergei Fedorov	Det.	77	11
Mike Ricci	Phi	68	9
Rob Blake	L.A.	75	9

Short-Hand Goals

Rookie	Team	GP	S
Robert Kron	Van.	76	3
Sergei Fedorov	Det.	77	3
Ken Hodge	Bos.	70	2

Plus/Minus

Rookie	Team	GP	+/-
Robert Reichel	Cgy.	66	17
Stephane Matteau	Cgy.	78	17
Ken Sabourin	Cgy.–Wsh.	44	15
Ken Hodge	Bos.	70	11
Paul Stanton	Pit.	75	11
Sergei Fedorov	Det.	77	11

Game-Winning Goals

Rookie	Team	GP	S
Sergei Fedorov	Det.	77	5
Tim Sweeny	Cgy.	42	4
Mike Ricci	Phi.	68	4
Ken Hodge	Bos.	70	4
Jaromir Jagr	Pit.	80	4

Game-Tying Goals
10 players tied with 1 each

Shots

Rookie	Team	GP	S
Sergei Fedorov	Det.	77	259
Bobby Holik	Hfd.	78	173
Mats Sundin	Que.	80	155
Rob Blake	L.A.	75	150
Mikhail Tatarinov	Wsh.	65	145

First Goals

Rookie	Team	GP	FG
Ken Hodge	Bos.	70	6
Mike Ricci	Phi.	68	5
Troy Crowder	N.J.	59	4

Ken Hodge led all rookie scorers in the second half of the 1990-91 season with 25 goals and 18 assists.

Three-or-More-Goal Games

Player	Team	Date		Final		Score		G
Brian Bellows	Minnesota	Nov. 23	VAN	4	MIN	6		3
*Peter Bondra	Washington	Nov. 28	WSH	6	NYR	3		3
Phil Bourque	Pittsburgh	Dec. 03	PIT	9	NYR	4		3
Jimmy Carson	Detroit	Mar. 05	QUE	3	DET	6		3
Dino Ciccarelli	Washington	Feb. 08	EDM	3	WSH	6		3
John Cullen	Pittsburgh	Jan. 17	PIT	6	TOR	5		3
Ulf Dahlen	Minnesota	Mar. 09	DET	2	MIN	6		3
Per-Erik Eklund	Philadelphia	Mar. 23	NYR	4	PHI	7		3
Patrick Flatley	NY Islanders	Dec. 23	NYI	4	PIT	3		3
Theo Fleury	Calgary	Dec. 05	NYR	1	CGY	4		3
Theo Fleury	Calgary	Feb. 17	STL	4	CGY	7		3
Theo Fleury	Calgary	Feb. 23	QUE	8	CGY	10		3
Theo Fleury	Calgary	Mar. 09	CGY	8	STL	4		3
Theo Fleury	Calgary	Mar. 26	VAN	2	CGY	7		3
Bryan Fogarty	Quebec	Dec. 01	BUF	2	QUE	4		3
Ron Francis	Hartford	Feb. 13	DET	2	HFD	4		3
Dave Gagner	Minnesota	Dec. 23	MIN	5	HFD	2		3
*Johan Garpenlov	Detroit	Nov. 23	STL	3	DET	5		4
Michel Goulet	Chicago	Feb. 23	CHI	3	MIN	3		3
Wayne Gretzky	Los Angeles	Jan. 03	L.A.	6	NYI	3		3
Wayne Gretzky	Los Angeles	Jan. 26	VAN	4	L.A.	5		3
Dale Hawerchuk	Buffalo	Mar. 13	BUF	4	WPG	4		3
*Ken Hodge	Boston	Feb. 05	EDM	5	BOS	6		3
*Ken Hodge	Boston	Feb. 28	NYI	0	BOS	5		3
Brett Hull	St Louis	Oct. 24	STL	8	TOR	3		3
Brett Hull	St Louis	Oct. 25	TOR	5	STL	8		3
Brett Hull	St Louis	Feb. 23	BOS	2	STL	9		3
Brett Hull	St Louis	Mar. 07	STL	5	BOS	5		3
Jeff Jackson	Quebec	Jan. 03	QUE	7	STL	8		3
*Jaromir Jagr	Pittsburgh	Feb. 02	BOS	2	PIT	6		3
Derek King	NY Islanders	Dec. 31	QUE	6	NYI	6		4
Petr Klima	Edmonton	Jan. 30	VAN	4	EDM	9		3
Petr Klima	Edmonton	Feb. 05	EDM	5	BOS	6		3
Petr Klima	Edmonton	Mar. 31	WPG	3	EDM	6		3
Robert Kudelski	Los Angeles	Jan. 12	VAN	2	L.A.	6		3
Pat LaFontaine	NY Islanders	Oct. 27	PHI	2	NYI	5		3
Steve Larmer	Chicago	Oct. 13	CHI	4	MIN	1		3
Claude Lemieux	New Jersey	Dec. 05	VAN	4	N.J.	9		3
Claude Lemieux	New Jersey	Jan. 24	QUE	1	N.J.	6		3
Mario Lemieux	Pittsburgh	Mar. 26	PIT	3	PHI	1		3
Trevor Linden	Vancouver	Dec. 20	EDM	4	VAN	7		3
Craig MacTavish	Edmonton	Dec. 22	EDM	6	CGY	2		3
Sergei Makarov	Calgary	Jan. 05	DET	0	CGY	7		3
Sergei Makarov	Calgary	Jan. 15	WPG	5	CGY	7		3
Mike McPhee	Montreal	Feb. 04	MIN	3	MTL	5		3
John MacLean	New Jersey	Jan. 28	N.J.	6	DET	2		3
John MacLean	New Jersey	Feb. 25	WSH	1	N.J.	5		3
Alexander Mogilny	Buffalo	Mar. 31	WSH	2	BUF	5		3
Cam Neely	Boston	Jan. 17	L.A.	3	BOS	5		3
Cam Neely	Boston	Feb. 09	CHI	3	BOS	5		3
Stephane Richer	Montreal	Mar. 06	MTL	5	CHI	3		3
Mike Ridley	Washington	Dec. 07	N.J.	2	WSH	5		3
Jeremy Roenick	Chicago	Oct. 11	PIT	1	CHI	4		3
Jeremy Roenick	Chicago	Dec. 16	MIN	2	CHI	5		3
Joe Sakic	Quebec	Mar. 19	EDM	7	QUE	6		3
Tomas Sandstrom	Los Angeles	Nov. 20	N.J.	4	L.A.	5		3
Tomas Sandstrom	Los Angeles	Nov. 24	L.A.	4	MTL	2		3
Tomas Sandstrom	Los Angeles	Jan. 14	L.A.	6	N.J.	1		3
Kevin Stevens	Pittsburgh	Oct. 25	QUE	3	PIT	6		3
*Mats Sundin	Quebec	Nov. 24	WPG	11	QUE	4		3
*Mats Sundin	Quebec	Feb. 23	QUE	8	CGY	10		3
Steve Thomas	Chicago	Nov. 17	CHI	7	QUE	2		3
Esa Tikkanen	Edmonton	Oct. 14	EDM	4	VAN	5		3
Rick Tocchet	Philadelphia	Jan. 24	WSH	1	PHI	6		3
Pierre Turgeon	Buffalo	Oct. 28	HFD	0	BUF	5		3
Darren Turcotte	NY Rangers	Mar. 30	NYR	5	DET	6		3
Dave Volek	NY Islanders	Dec. 20	HFD	4	NYI	4		3
Doug Wilson	Chicago	Jan. 26	TOR	1	CHI	5		3
Steve Yzerman	Detroit	Nov. 17	DET	8	TOR	4		3
Steve Yzerman	Detroit	Dec. 22	DET	5	WPG	2		3
Steve Yzerman	Detroit	Jan. 26	DET	4	STL	5		3

NOTE: 88 Three-or-more-goal games recorded in 1989-90.

Detroit's Steve Yzerman fired three hat-tricks during the 1990-91 campaign.

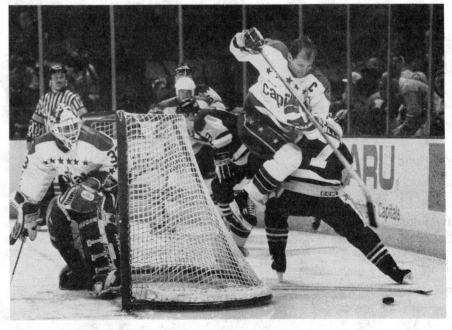

Rod Langway performs some on-ice magic behind the Caps' net as Don Beaupre hugs the post. Beaupre set a franchise record with five shutouts in the 1990-91 campaign.

Goaltending Leaders

Minimum 25 games

Goals Against Average

Goaltender	Team	GPI	MINS	GA	AVG
*Ed Belfour	Chicago	74	4127	170	2.47
Don Beaupre	Washington	45	2572	113	2.64
Patrick Roy	Montreal	48	2835	128	2.71
Andy Moog	Boston	51	2844	136	2.87
Pete Peeters	Philadelphia	26	1270	61	2.88

Wins

Goaltender	Team	GPI	MINS	W	L	T
*Ed Belfour	Chicago	74	4127	43	19	7
Mike Vernon	Calgary	54	3121	31	19	3
Tim Cheveldae	Detroit	65	3615	30	26	5
Vincent Riendeau	St. Louis	44	2671	29	9	6
Tom Barrasso	Pittsburgh	48	2754	27	16	3
Bill Ranford	Edmonton	60	3415	27	27	3

Save Percentage

Goaltender	Team	GPI	MINS	GA	SA	S%	W	L	T
*Ed Belfour	Chicago	74	4127	170	1883	.910	43	19	7
Patrick Roy	Montreal	48	2835	128	1362	.906	25	15	6
*Mike Richter	NY Rangers	45	2596	135	1392	.903	21	13	7
Pete Peeters	Philadelphia	26	1270	61	623	.902	9	7	1
Kelly Hrudey	Los Angeles	47	2730	132	1321	.900	26	13	6

Shutouts

Goaltender	Team	GPI	MINS	SO	W	L	T
Don Beaupre	Washington	45	2572	5	20	18	3
Andy Moog	Boston	51	2844	4	25	13	9
Bob Essensa	Winnipeg	55	2916	4	19	24	6
*Ed Belfour	Chicago	74	4127	4	43	19	7

4 goaltenders tied with three each.

Team-by-Team Point Totals

1986-87 to 1990-91

(Ranked by five-year average)

	90-91	89-90	88-89	87-88	86-87	Average
Calgary	100	99	117	105	95	103.2
Montreal	89	93	115	103	92	98.4
Boston	100	101	88	94	85	93.6
Edmonton	80	90	84	99	106	91.8
Washington	81	78	92	85	86	84.4
St. Louis	105	83	78	76	79	84.2
Philadelphia	76	71	80	85	100	82.4
Buffalo	81	98	83	85	64	82.2
NY Rangers	85	85	82	82	76	82.0
Hartford	73	85	79	77	93	81.4
Los Angeles	102	75	91	68	70	81.2
Chicago	106	88	66	69	72	80.2
Pittsburgh	88	72	87	81	72	80.0
Detroit	76	70	80	93	78	79.4
Winnipeg	63	85	64	77	88	75.4
New Jersey	79	83	66	82	64	74.8
NY Islanders	60	73	61	88	82	72.8
Minnesota	68	76	70	51	70	67.0
Vancouver	65	64	74	59	66	65.6
Toronto	57	80	62	52	70	64.2
Quebec	46	31	61	69	72	55.8

Team Record When Scoring First Goal of a Game

Team	GP	FG	W	L	T
Boston	80	54	38	8	8
Buffalo	80	39	20	11	8
Calgary	80	33	20	8	5
Chicago	80	45	34	6	5
Detroit	80	40	25	11	4
Edmonton	80	37	25	9	3
Hartford	80	32	23	6	3
Los Angeles	80	53	35	10	8
Minnesota	80	39	21	12	6
Montreal	80	39	27	7	5
New Jersey	80	40	25	9	6
NY Islanders	80	35	18	13	4
NY Rangers	80	41	25	12	4
Philadelphia	80	45	27	10	8
Pittsburgh	80	37	24	11	2
Quebec	80	28	9	11	8
St. Louis	80	50	31	11	8
Toronto	80	41	14	20	7
Vancouver	80	36	20	15	1
Washington	80	41	25	11	5
Winnipeg	80	35	18	13	4

Team Plus/Minus Differential

Team	GF	PPGF	Net GF	GA	PPGA	Net GA	Goal Differential
Los Angeles	340	80	260	254	63	191	+69
Calgary	344	91	253	263	77	186	+67
Chicago	284	87	197	211	68	143	+54
St. Louis	310	70	240	250	55	195	+45
Boston	299	74	225	264	64	200	+25
Pittsburgh	342	89	253	305	73	232	+21
New Jersey	272	69	203	264	80	184	+19
Edmonton	272	63	209	272	80	192	+17
NY Rangers	297	91	206	265	73	192	+14
Montreal	273	66	207	249	54	195	+12
Detroit	273	57	216	298	89	209	+7
Buffalo	292	73	219	278	62	216	+3
Philadelphia	252	68	184	267	72	195	−11
Minnesota	256	76	180	266	75	191	−11
Washington	258	64	194	258	44	214	−20
Hartford	238	73	165	276	72	204	−39
NY Islanders	223	51	172	290	78	212	−40
Winnipeg	260	74	186	288	57	231	−45
Toronto	241	61	180	318	83	235	−55
Vancouver	243	65	178	315	76	239	−61
Quebec	236	51	185	354	98	256	−71

Team Record when Leading, Trailing, Tied

Team	Leading after 1 period W	L	T	Leading after 2 periods W	L	T	Trailing after 1 period W	L	T	Trailing after 2 periods W	L	T	Tied after 1 period W	L	T	Tied after 2 periods W	L	T
Boston	27	4	7	36	2	3	5	14	3	3	19	3	12	6	2	5	3	6
Buffalo	17	5	2	23	4	3	5	19	9	1	21	9	9	6	8	7	5	7
Calgary	19	3	5	31	3	6	13	15	3	3	19	1	14	8	0	12	4	1
Chicago	25	2	3	41	3	5	7	13	2	2	17	2	17	8	3	6	3	1
Detroit	19	3	2	24	2	2	5	27	3	3	33	5	10	8	3	7	3	1
Edmonton	21	7	1	26	3	3	9	17	2	5	28	2	7	13	3	6	6	1
Hartford	14	4	3	21	4	3	6	27	5	3	31	1	11	7	3	7	3	7
Los Angeles	26	5	6	39	2	4	3	9	2	2	17	3	17	10	2	5	5	3
Minnesota	15	9	3	24	4	4	3	15	7	0	25	4	9	15	4	3	10	6
Montreal	19	5	5	28	0	1	7	15	1	7	20	5	13	10	5	4	10	5
New Jersey	22	9	3	23	1	3	6	16	8	4	27	6	4	8	4	5	5	6
NY Islanders	13	9	1	19	4	3	5	27	4	2	34	2	7	9	5	4	7	5
NY Rangers	21	7	5	27	5	3	4	14	4	1	22	3	11	10	4	8	4	7
Philadelphia	22	5	6	24	2	6	5	20	2	1	27	2	6	12	2	8	8	2
Pittsburgh	25	10	0	31	3	2	8	19	3	3	23	1	8	4	3	7	3	5
Quebec	7	6	5	12	5	5	5	33	3	1	37	4	4	11	6	3	8	5
St. Louis	29	5	5	30	2	5	9	13	1	6	18	2	9	4	5	11	2	4
Toronto	12	8	4	16	3	3	5	23	3	4	36	5	6	15	4	3	7	3
Vancouver	13	8	1	13	3	1	7	23	2	4	30	3	8	12	6	11	10	5
Washington	19	9	4	25	4	5	11	19	1	4	24	3	7	8	2	8	8	2
Winnipeg	14	9	2	18	3	2	4	21	5	3	23	3	8	13	4	5	17	6

Team Statistics

TEAMS' HOME-AND-ROAD RECORD

Norris Division

	GP	W	L	T	GF	GA	PTS	%	GP	W	L	T	GF	GA	PTS	%
				Home								Road				
CHI	40	28	8	4	162	103	60	.750	40	21	15	4	122	108	46	.575
ST.L.	40	24	9	7	155	114	55	.688	40	23	13	4	155	136	50	.625
DET	40	26	14	0	162	137	52	.650	40	8	24	8	111	161	24	.300
MIN	40	19	15	6	149	120	44	.550	40	8	24	8	107	146	24	.300
TOR	40	15	21	4	134	160	34	.425	40	8	25	7	107	158	23	.288
Total	200	112	67	21	762	634	245	.613	200	68	101	31	602	709	167	.418

Smythe Division

	GP	W	L	T	GF	GA	PTS	%	GP	W	L	T	GF	GA	PTS	%
L.A.	40	26	9	5	189	122	57	.713	40	20	15	5	151	132	45	.563
CGY	40	29	8	3	194	115	61	.763	40	17	18	5	150	148	39	.488
EDM	40	22	15	3	134	119	47	.588	40	15	22	3	138	153	33	.413
VAN	40	18	17	5	127	130	41	.513	40	10	26	4	116	185	24	.300
WPG	40	17	18	5	143	134	39	.488	40	9	25	6	117	154	24	.300
Total	200	112	67	21	787	620	245	.613	200	71	106	23	672	772	165	.413

Adams Division

	GP	W	L	T	GF	GA	PTS	%	GP	W	L	T	GF	GA	PTS	%
BOS	40	26	9	5	170	108	57	.713	40	18	15	7	129	156	43	.538
MTL	40	23	12	5	149	118	51	.638	40	16	18	6	124	131	38	.475
BUF	40	15	13	12	157	129	42	.525	40	16	17	7	135	149	39	.488
HFD	40	18	16	6	128	128	42	.525	40	13	22	5	110	148	31	.388
QUE	40	9	23	8	123	170	26	.325	40	7	27	6	113	184	20	.250
Total	200	91	73	36	727	653	218	.545	200	70	99	31	611	768	171	.428

Patrick Division

	GP	W	L	T	GF	GA	PTS	%	GP	W	L	T	GF	GA	PTS	%
PIT	40	25	12	3	184	132	53	.663	40	16	21	3	158	173	35	.438
NYR	40	22	11	7	161	114	51	.638	40	14	20	6	136	151	34	.425
WSH	40	21	14	5	145	123	47	.588	40	16	22	2	113	135	34	.425
N.J.	40	23	10	7	147	115	53	.663	40	9	23	8	125	149	26	.325
PHI	40	18	16	6	130	124	42	.525	40	15	21	4	122	143	34	.425
NYI	40	15	19	6	113	134	36	.450	40	10	26	4	110	156	24	.300
Total	240	124	82	34	880	742	282	.588	240	80	133	27	764	907	187	.390
Total	**840**	**439**	**289**	**112**	**3156**	**2649**	**990**	**.589**	**840**	**289**	**439**	**112**	**2649**	**3156**	**690**	**.411**

TEAMS' DIVISIONAL RECORD

Norris Division

	GP	W	L	T	GF	GA	PTS	%	GP	W	L	T	GF	GA	PTS	%
			Against Own Division								Against Other Divisions					
CHI	32	20	8	4	116	83	44	.688	48	29	15	4	168	128	62	.646
ST.L.	32	18	11	3	127	106	39	.609	48	29	11	8	183	144	66	.688
DET	32	13	16	3	105	119	29	.453	48	21	22	5	168	179	47	.490
MIN	32	10	17	5	98	109	25	.391	48	17	22	9	158	157	43	.448
TOR	32	10	19	3	96	125	23	.359	48	13	27	8	145	193	34	.354
Total	160	71	71	18	542	542	160	.500	240	109	97	34	822	801	252	.525

Smythe Division

	GP	W	L	T	GF	GA	PTS	%	GP	W	L	T	GF	GA	PTS	%
L.A.	32	19	9	4	145	110	42	.656	48	27	15	6	195	144	60	.625
CGY	32	18	10	4	122	107	40	.625	48	28	16	4	222	156	60	.625
EDM	32	13	16	3	114	117	29	.453	48	24	21	3	158	155	51	.531
VAN	32	11	20	1	108	141	23	.359	48	17	23	8	135	174	42	.438
WPG	32	10	16	6	99	113	26	.406	48	16	27	5	161	175	37	.385
Total	160	71	71	18	588	588	160	.500	240	112	102	26	871	804	250	.521

Adams Division

	GP	W	L	T	GF	GA	PTS	%	GP	W	L	T	GF	GA	PTS	%
BOS	32	19	8	5	128	90	43	.672	48	25	16	7	171	174	57	.594
MTL	32	15	13	4	103	96	34	.531	48	24	17	7	170	153	55	.573
BUF	32	11	12	9	120	110	31	.484	48	20	18	10	172	168	50	.521
HFD	32	9	16	7	91	117	25	.391	48	22	22	4	147	159	48	.500
QUE	32	9	14	9	95	124	27	.422	48	7	36	5	141	230	19	.198
Total	160	63	63	34	537	537	160	.500	240	98	109	33	801	884	229	.477

Patrick Division

	GP	W	L	T	GF	GA	PTS	%	GP	W	L	T	GF	GA	PTS	%
PIT	35	19	14	2	155	134	40	.571	45	22	19	4	187	171	48	.533
NYR	35	15	14	6	125	121	36	.514	45	21	17	7	172	144	49	.544
WSH	35	20	12	3	129	105	43	.614	45	17	24	4	129	153	38	.422
N.J.	35	13	16	6	117	126	32	.457	45	19	17	9	155	138	47	.522
PHI	35	12	16	7	109	119	31	.443	45	21	21	3	143	148	45	.500
NYI	35	12	19	4	103	133	28	.400	45	13	26	6	120	157	32	.356
Total	210	91	91	28	738	738	210	.500	270	113	124	33	906	911	259	.480

TEAM STREAKS

Consecutive Wins

Games	Team	From	To
7	Los Angeles	Jan. 3	Jan. 14
7	Los Angeles	Feb. 18	Mar. 2
7	St. Louis	Mar. 19	Mar. 31
6	Philadelphia	Oct. 7	Oct. 20
6	NY Rangers	Oct. 20	Oct. 31
6	St Louis	Nov. 3	Nov. 17
6	Los Angeles	Nov. 4	Nov. 20
6	Pittsburgh	Dec. 13	Dec. 22
6	Calgary	Feb. 27	Mar. 9

Consecutive Home Wins

Games	Team	From	To
11	Pittsburgh	Jan. 5	Mar. 7
10	Los Angeles	Oct. 13	Nov. 20
9	St Louis	Jan. 26	Feb. 26
9	Calgary	Feb. 21	Mar. 14
8	NY Rangers	Oct. 8	Oct. 31
8	Calgary	Dec. 29	Feb. 17
7	New Jersey	Oct. 6	Oct. 27
7	Boston	Jan. 14	Feb. 5
6	Detroit	Oct. 10	Oct. 26
6	St Louis	Oct. 25	Nov. 20
6	Buffalo	Dec. 28	Jan. 22
6	Minnesota	Jan. 17	Feb. 20
6	Los Angeles	Feb. 18	Mar. 12

Consecutive Road Wins

Games	Team	From	To
6	Hartford	Nov. 10	Dec. 7
5	Chicago	Nov. 10	Nov. 20
4	St Louis	Oct. 16	Oct. 30
4	Washington	Oct. 28	Nov. 6
4	Montreal	Nov. 19	Dec. 6
4	Calgary	Dec. 9	Dec. 16
4	Los Angeles	Jan. 3	Jan. 14
4	Chicago	Mar. 8	Mar. 23
4	Washington	Mar. 8	Mar. 28
4	St Louis	Mar. 19	Mar. 25

Consecutive Undefeated

Games	Team	W	T	From	To
10	NY Rangers	5	5	Nov. 7	Nov. 26
10	Chicago	8	2	Mar. 8	Mar. 28
9	St Louis	6	3	Dec. 7	Dec. 26
8	Chicago	6	2	Nov. 6	Nov. 20
8	New Jersey	3	5	Dec. 15	Dec. 30
8	Buffalo	5	3	Dec. 23	Jan. 8
8	Calgary	6	2	Feb. 7	Feb. 23
8	Los Angeles	7	1	Feb. 18	Mar. 5

Consecutive Home Undefeated

Games	Team	W	T	From	To
18	Calgary	17	1	Dec. 29	Mar. 14
14	Pittsburgh	13	1	Jan. 5	Mar. 21
13	Minnesota	11	2	Jan. 17	Mar. 17
11	Los Angeles	10	1	Oct. 11	Nov. 20
10	St Louis	9	1	Jan. 26	Feb. 28
9	St Louis	7	2	Oct. 9	Nov. 24
9	New Jersey	5	4	Nov. 17	Dec. 29
8	New Jersey	7	1	Oct. 4	Oct. 27
8	NY Rangers	8	0	Oct. 8	Oct. 31
8	Buffalo	4	4	Oct. 19	Dec. 2
8	Buffalo	7	1	Dec. 23	Jan. 22
7	Montreal	6	1	Dec. 8	Jan. 12
7	Boston	7	0	Jan. 14	Feb. 5
7	Chicago	6	1	Jan. 26	Mar. 3
7	Washington	5	2	Feb. 5	Mar. 5

Consecutive Road Undefeated

Games	Team	W	T	From	To
9	Calgary	6	3	Nov. 11	Dec. 16
7	Chicago	6	1	Nov. 3	Nov. 20
6	NY Rangers	3	3	Nov. 9	Nov. 24
6	Hartford	6	0	Nov. 10	Dec. 7
6	Chicago	5	1	Dec. 29	Jan. 28
5	Montreal	4	1	Nov. 17	Dec. 6
5	Toronto	4	1	Dec. 1	Dec. 22
5	Washington	4	1	Feb. 27	Mar. 28
5	Chicago	4	1	Mar. 8	Mar. 26

Joe Nieuwendyk clicked for 22 goals while the Flames enjoyed a manpower advantage in 1990-91, helping the Flames lead the league with a power-play percentage of 23.7.

Team Penalties

Abbreviations: GP - games played; **PEN** - total penalty minutes, including bench penalties; **BMI** - total bench minor minutes; **AVG** - average penalty minutes per game calculated by dividing total penalty minutes by games played.

Team	GP	PEN	BMI	AVG
MTL	80	1425	18	17.8
PIT	80	1641	8	20.5
WPG	80	1675	10	20.9
BOS	80	1694	28	21.2
NYI	80	1723	8	21.5
BUF	80	1733	28	21.7
QUE	80	1741	22	21.8
EDM	80	1823	22	22.8
WSH	80	1839	14	23.0
NYR	80	1893	18	23.7
DET	80	1940	18	24.3
PHI	80	1945	20	24.3
TOR	80	1962	10	24.5
MIN	80	1964	18	24.6
ST.L.	80	1987	16	24.8
N.J.	80	2024	10	25.3
VAN	80	2063	16	25.8
CGY	80	2201	32	27.5
HFD	80	2209	24	27.6
L.A.	80	2228	24	27.9
CHI	80	2412	20	30.2
TOTAL	**840**	**40122**	**384**	**47.8**

TEAMS' POWER-PLAY RECORD

Abbreviations: ADV – total advantages; **PPGF** – power-play goals for; **%** – calculated by dividing number of power-play goals by total advantages.

			Home					Road						Overall		
	Team	GP	ADV	PPGF	%		Team	GP	ADV	PPGF	%		Team	GP	ADV	PPGF	%
1	CHI	40	206	55	26.7		ST.L.	40	172	38	22.1		CGY	80	384	91	23.7
2	CGY	40	195	52	26.7		PIT	40	186	41	22.0		NYR	80	389	91	23.4
3	NYR	40	209	55	26.3		N.J.	40	169	36	21.3		PIT	80	388	89	22.9
4	BOS	40	195	49	25.1		PHI	40	164	34	20.7		CHI	80	393	87	22.1
5	PIT	40	202	48	23.8		CGY	40	189	39	20.6		BOS	80	351	74	21.1
6	WSH	40	182	43	23.6		NYR	40	180	36	20.0		L.A.	80	391	80	20.5
7	MTL	40	174	41	23.6		L.A.	40	168	33	19.6		PHI	80	338	68	20.1
8	MIN	40	188	40	21.3		HFD	40	190	37	19.5		ST.L.	80	348	70	20.1
9	L.A.	40	223	47	21.1		MIN	40	194	36	18.6		N.J.	80	347	69	19.9
10	WPG	40	203	41	20.2		WPG	40	178	33	18.5		MIN	80	382	76	19.9
11	PHI	40	174	34	19.5		EDM	40	165	30	18.2		WPG	80	381	74	19.4
12	TOR	40	176	34	19.3		BUF	40	182	33	18.1		WSH	80	340	64	18.8
13	N.J.	40	178	33	18.5		VAN	40	179	31	17.3		MTL	80	357	66	18.5
14	BUF	40	218	40	18.3		QUE	40	157	27	17.2		BUF	80	400	73	18.3
15	ST.L.	40	176	32	18.2		CHI	40	187	32	17.1		HFD	80	403	73	18.1
16	DET	40	172	30	17.4		NYI	40	163	27	16.6		TOR	80	346	61	17.6
17	HFD	40	213	36	16.9		BOS	40	156	25	16.0		EDM	80	361	63	17.5
18	EDM	40	196	33	16.8		TOR	40	170	27	15.9		VAN	80	391	65	16.6
19	VAN	40	212	34	16.0		DET	40	175	27	15.4		DET	80	347	57	16.4
20	NYI	40	154	24	15.6		MTL	40	183	25	13.7		NYI	80	317	51	16.1
21	QUE	40	171	24	14.0		WSH	40	158	21	13.3		QUE	80	328	51	15.5
TOTAL		**840**	**4017**	**825**	**20.5**			**840**	**3665**	**668**	**18.2**			**840**	**7682**	**1493**	**19.4**

TEAMS' PENALTY KILLING RECORD

Abbreviations: TSH – times short-handed; **PPGA** – power-play goals against; **%** – calculated by dividing times short minus power-play goals against by times short.

			Home					Road						Overall		
	Team	GP	TSH	PPGA	%		Team	GP	TSH	PPGA	%		Team	GP	TSH	PPGA	%
1	ST.L.	40	167	22	86.8		WSH	40	151	18	88.1		WSH	80	314	44	86.0
2	BOS	40	179	24	86.6		CHI	40	226	32	85.8		CHI	80	425	68	84.0
3	L.A.	40	195	28	85.6		BUF	40	195	31	84.1		WPG	80	351	57	83.8
4	WPG	40	150	22	85.3		WPG	40	201	35	82.6		ST.L.	80	339	55	83.8
5	CGY	40	196	30	84.7		MTL	40	152	28	81.6		BUF	80	368	62	83.2
6	WSH	40	163	26	84.0		DET	40	207	39	81.2		L.A.	80	370	63	83.0
7	HFD	40	164	28	82.9		ST.L.	40	172	33	80.8		BOS	80	368	64	82.6
8	N.J.	40	185	32	82.7		L.A.	40	175	35	80.0		CGY	80	420	77	81.7
9	BUF	40	173	31	82.1		PHI	40	204	41	79.9		PHI	80	376	72	80.9
10	PHI	40	172	31	82.0		CGY	40	224	47	79.0		MTL	80	282	54	80.9
11	CHI	40	199	36	81.9		EDM	40	195	41	79.0		HFD	80	369	72	80.5
12	MIN	40	190	35	81.6		BOS	40	189	40	78.8		MIN	80	378	75	80.2
13	PIT	40	160	30	81.3		MIN	40	188	40	78.7		NYR	80	362	73	79.8
14	NYR	40	196	37	81.1		HFD	40	205	44	78.5		N.J.	80	394	80	79.7
15	TOR	40	181	36	80.1		NYR	40	166	36	78.3		EDM	80	388	80	79.4
16	MTL	40	130	26	80.0		PIT	40	191	42	77.5		PIT	80	351	73	79.2
17	NYI	40	154	31	79.9		N.J.	40	209	48	77.0		NYI	80	353	78	77.9
18	EDM	40	193	39	79.8		NYI	40	199	47	76.4		DET	80	399	89	77.7
19	VAN	40	161	34	78.9		VAN	40	178	42	76.4		VAN	80	339	76	77.6
20	QUE	40	165	35	78.8		TOR	40	187	47	74.9		TOR	80	368	83	77.4
21	DET	40	192	50	74.0		QUE	40	203	58	71.4		QUE	80	368	98	73.4
TOTAL		**840**	**3665**	**668**	**81.8**			**840**	**4017**	**825**	**79.5**			**840**	**7682**	**1493**	**80.6**

SHORT HAND GOALS FOR

		Home			Road			Overall	
	Team	GP	SHGF	Team	GP	SHGF	Team	GP	SHGF
1	CHI	40	11	CHI	40	9	CHI	80	20
2	TOR	40	11	VAN	40	8	DET	80	17
3	CGY	40	10	EDM	40	8	CGY	80	17
4	DET	40	10	DET	40	7	TOR	80	16
5	BUF	40	8	BUF	40	7	BUF	80	15
6	WSH	40	8	CGY	40	7	WSH	80	13
7	PIT	40	7	NYI	40	6	EDM	80	13
8	BOS	40	6	QUE	40	5	PIT	80	12
9	ST.L.	40	6	TOR	40	5	BOS	80	11
10	N.J.	40	5	PIT	40	5	QUE	80	10
11	MIN	40	5	WPG	40	5	ST.L.	80	10
12	EDM	40	5	BOS	40	5	VAN	80	10
13	QUE	40	5	WSH	40	5	NYI	80	9
14	NYR	40	5	NYR	40	4	NYR	80	9
15	L.A.	40	4	ST.L.	40	4	MIN	80	9
16	HFD	40	3	MIN	40	4	L.A.	80	8
17	WPG	40	3	L.A.	40	4	N.J.	80	8
18	MTL	40	3	MTL	40	3	WPG	80	8
19	NYI	40	3	N.J.	40	3	MTL	80	6
20	VAN	40	2	HFD	40	2	HFD	80	5
21	~~PIT~~ PHI	40	1	PHI	40	1	PHI	80	2
TOTAL		**840**	**121**		**840**	**107**		**840**	**228**

SHORT HAND GOALS AGAINST

		Home			Road			Overall	
	Team	GP	SHGA	Team	GP	SHGA	Team	GP	SHGA
1	BUF	40	1	HFD	40	2	EDM	80	4
2	MIN	40	2	EDM	40	2	DET	80	5
3	EDM	40	2	DET	40	3	TOR	80	6
4	NYR	40	2	TOR	40	3	MIN	80	7
5	DET	40	2	PHI	40	4	BOS	80	8
6	BOS	40	3	MTL	40	4	BUF	80	8
7	CHI	40	3	CGY	40	4	CGY	80	8
8	TOR	40	3	QUE	40	5	HFD	80	9
9	CGY	40	4	WPG	40	5	MTL	80	10
10	WSH	40	5	BOS	40	5	CHI	80	10
11	PIT	40	5	MIN	40	5	NYR	80	10
12	N.J.	40	6	NYI	40	6	QUE	80	11
13	MTL	40	6	PIT	40	7	NYI	80	12
14	QUE	40	6	BUF	40	7	WPG	80	12
15	VAN	40	6	CHI	40	7	PIT	80	12
16	NYI	40	6	N.J.	40	7	N.J.	80	13
17	HFD	40	7	L.A.	40	7	WSH	80	15
18	WPG	40	7	NYR	40	8	PHI	80	16
19	ST.L.	40	8	ST.L.	40	10	VAN	80	18
20	L.A.	40	11	VAN	40	10	L.A.	80	18
21	PHI	40	12	WSH	40	10	ST.L.	80	18
TOTAL		**840**	**107**		**840**	**121**		**840**	**228**

Overtime Results

Team	1990-91 GP	W	L	T	1989-90 GP	W	L	T	1988-89 GP	W	L	T	1987-88 GP	W	L	T	1986-87 GP	W	L	T	1985-86 GP	W	L	T	1984-85 GP	W	L	T	1983-84 GP	W	L	T
Boston	17	5	0	12	14	3	2	9	19	3	2	14	14	4	4	6	12	2	3	7	17	2	3	12	18	4	4	10	7	1	0	6
Buffalo	24	3	2	19	15	4	3	8	13	2	4	7	12	0	1	11	13	1	4	8	9	1	2	6	17	0	3	14	13	5	1	7
Calgary	15	3	4	8	21	3	3	15	17	5	3	9	15	2	4	9	4	1	0	3	12	1	2	9	14	1	1	12	18	4	0	14
Chicago	12	3	1	8	10	2	2	6	17	2	3	12	15	4	2	9	15	1	0	14	12	3	1	8	12	2	3	7	9	0	1	8
Detroit	14	2	4	8	17	2	1	14	16	3	1	12	16	2	3	11	17	2	5	10	13	2	5	6	14	0	2	12	11	3	1	7
Edmonton	15	4	5	6	20	5	1	14	15	4	3	8	16	3	2	11	14	5	3	6	14	5	2	7	12	0	1	11	9	4	0	5
Hartford	18	2	5	11	9	0	0	9	10	1	4	5	12	3	2	7	9	2	0	7	7	1	2	4	17	4	4	9	15	2	3	10
Los Angeles	16	4	2	10	12	3	2	7	14	6	1	7	12	1	3	8	12	2	2	8	14	3	3	8	19	3	2	14	17	1	3	13
Minnesota	17	0	3	14	11	3	4	4	17	0	1	16	16	1	2	13	14	2	2	10	15	4	2	9	15	1	2	12	18	5	3	10
Montreal	17	3	3	11	17	4	2	11	11	2	0	9	16	1	2	13	16	2	4	10	14	1	6	7	18	3	3	12	7	1	1	5
New Jersey	17	1	1	15	16	3	4	9	17	1	4	12	12	4	2	6	13	3	4	6	10	4	3	3	12	0	2	10	15	1	7	7
NY Islanders	15	2	3	10	16	3	2	11	11	3	3	5	13	3	0	10	20	5	3	12	17	4	1	12	15	1	8	6	10	3	3	4
NY Rangers	16	1	2	13	17	2	2	13	10	1	1	8	11	0	1	10	19	5	6	8	13	0	7	6	17	2	5	10	17	5	3	9
Philadelphia	11	1	0	10	18	2	5	11	14	1	5	8	13	1	3	9	10	1	1	8	9	4	1	4	9	1	1	7	14	3	1	10
Pittsburgh	12	4	2	6	14	3	3	8	10	2	1	7	16	5	2	9	21	5	4	12	14	3	3	8	8	3	0	5	12	1	5	6
Quebec	18	1	3	14	8	0	1	7	10	2	1	7	9	2	2	5	14	0	4	10	11	4	1	6	14	3	2	9	15	0	5	10
St. Louis	18	3	4	11	15	2	4	9	16	3	1	12	14	2	4	8	21	4	2	15	17	5	3	9	15	2	1	12	11	3	1	7
Toronto	17	4	2	11	11	3	4	4	11	1	4	6	13	1	2	10	13	3	4	6	17	4	6	7	15	5	2	8	13	1	3	9
Vancouver	15	3	3	9	21	2	5	14	14	2	4	8	11	0	2	9	10	2	0	8	16	1	2	13	17	7	1	9	16	3	4	9
Washington	14	4	3	7	9	2	1	6	16	2	4	10	15	2	4	9	17	5	2	10	11	4	0	7	12	3	0	9	9	1	3	5
Winnipeg	14	1	2	11	19	4	4	11	20	6	2	12	21	8	2	11	11	2	1	8	8	0	1	7	14	3	1	10	24	7	6	11
Totals	166	54		112	155	55		100	149	52		97	146	49		97	148	55		93	135	56		79	152	48		104	140	54		86

1990-91
Home Team Wins: 31
Visiting Team Wins: 23

Rookie Peter Ing blanked Wayne Gretzky on a penalty shot on January 5, 1991.

1990-91 Penalty Shots

Scored

Pierre Turgeon (Buffalo) scored against Patrick Roy (Montreal), October 17. Final score: Montreal 4 at Buffalo 3.

Joey Kocur (Detroit) scored against Jacques Cloutier (Chicago), November 29. Final score: Detroit 5 at Chicago 1.

Bob Sweeney (Boston) scored against Peter Sidorkiewicz (Hartford), December 12. Final score: Boston 5 at Hartford 1.

Murray Craven (Philadelphia) scored against Andre Racicot (Montreal), December 23. Final score: Montreal 4 at Philadelphia 4.

Bob Errey (Pittsburgh) scored against Chris Terreri (New Jersey), January 5. Final score: New Jersey 2 at Pittsburgh 5.

Normand Lacombe (Philadelphia) scored against Kelly Hrudey (Los Angeles), February 5. Final score: Los Angeles 3 at Philadelphia 2.

Wayne Presley (Chicago) scored against Rejean Lemelin (Boston), February 9. Final score: Chicago 3 at Boston 5.

Theoren Fleury (Calgary) scored against Jacques Cloutier (Quebec), February 23. Final score: Quebec 8 at Calgary 10.

Scott Pearson (Quebec) scored against Tom Barrasso (Pittsburgh), March 16. Final score: Quebec 3 at Pittsburgh 6.

Stopped

Rick Tabaracci (Winnipeg) stopped Jeff Beukeboom (Edmonton), October 6. Final score: Winnipeg 3 at Edmonton 3.

Pete Peeters (Philadelphia) stopped Gary Leeman (Toronto), November 4. Final score: Philadelphia 7 at Toronto 1.

Chris Terreri (New Jersey) stopped Mike Ricci (Philadelphia), November 17. Final score: Philadelphia 2 at New Jersey 3.

Tim Cheveldae (Detroit) stopped Rich Sutter (St. Louis), November 23. Final score: St. Louis 3 at Detroit 5.

Peter Ing (Toronto) stopped Wayne Gretzky (Los Angeles), January 5. Final score: Los Angeles 4 at Toronto 2.

Tim Cheveldae (Detroit) stopped Ken Linseman (Edmonton), January 9. Final score: Edmonton 3 at Detroit 5.

Bob Essensa (Winnipeg) stopped Mike Craig (Minnesota), January 21. Final score: Minnesota 0 at Winnipeg 2.

Darcy Wakaluk (Buffalo) stopped Dave Manson (Chicago), January 24. Final score: Buffalo 5 at Chicago 4.

Vincent Riendeau (St. Louis) stopped Brent Fedyk (Detroit). January 15. Final score: St. Louis 9 at Detroit 4.

Pat Jablonski (St. Louis) stopped Michel Goulet (Chicago), February 26. Final score: Chicago 1 at St. Louis 3.

Kay Whitmore (Hartford) stopped Randy Burridge (Boston), March 31. Final score: Hartford 3 at Boston 7.

Summary

20 penalty shots resulted in 9 goals.

NHL Record Book

All-Time Standings of NHL Teams

(ranked by percentage)

Team	Games	Won	Lost	Tied	Goals For	Goals Against	Points	%
Montreal	4512	2391	1415	706	15328	11901	5488	.608
Edmonton	960	521	315	124	4390	3614	1166	.607
Philadelphia	1898	953	641	304	6836	5775	2210	.582
Buffalo	1672	797	601	274	6084	5459	1868	.559
Boston	4352	2084	1617	651	14334	12900	4819	.554
**Calgary	1516	719	565	232	5830	5252	1670	.551
NY Islanders	1516	722	571	223	5601	4921	1667	.550
Toronto	4512	1927	1921	664	14112	14086	4518	.501
NY Rangers	4286	1779	1817	690	13359	13596	4248	.496
Detroit	4286	1759	1842	685	12932	13279	4203	.490
St Louis	1898	780	825	293	6227	6486	1853	.488
Chicago	4286	1745	1876	665	12944	13244	4155	.485
Los Angeles	1898	744	878	276	6672	7134	1764	.465
Washington	1360	536	643	181	4624	5094	1253	.461
Hartford	960	370	466	124	3356	3749	864	.450
Minnesota	1898	690	890	318	6172	6802	1698	.447
Quebec	960	366	469	125	3557	3839	857	.446
Pittsburgh	1898	709	921	268	6532	7264	1686	.444
Winnipeg	960	357	475	128	3512	3971	842	.439
Vancouver	1672	566	855	251	5425	6408	1383	.414
*New Jersey	1360	387	782	191	4233	5567	965	.355

* Totals included those of Kansas City (1974-75, 1975-76) and Colorado (1976-77 through 1981-82)
** Totals include those of Atlanta (1972-73 through 1979-80)

Year-By-Year Final Standings & Leading Scorers

*Stanley Cup winner.

1917-18

Team	GP	W	L	T	GF	GA	PTS
Montreal	22	13	9	0	115	84	26
*Toronto	22	13	9	0	108	109	26
Ottawa	22	9	13	0	102	114	18
**Mtl. Wanderers	6	1	5	0	17	35	2

**Montreal Arena burned down and Wanderers forced to withdraw from League. Canadiens and Toronto each counted a win for defaulted games with Wanderers.

Leading Scorers

Player	Club	GP	G	A	PTS
Malone, Joe	Montreal	20	44	—	44
Denneny, Cy	Ottawa	22	36	—	36
Noble, Reg	Toronto	20	28	—	28
Lalonde, Newsy	Montreal	14	23	—	23
Denneny, Corbett	Toronto	21	20	—	20
Pitre, Didier	Montreal	19	17	—	17
Cameron, Harry	Toronto	20	17	—	17
Darragh, Jack	Ottawa	18	14	—	14
Hyland, Harry	Mtl.W., Ott.	16	14	—	14
Skinner, Alf	Toronto	19	13	—	13
Gerard, Eddie	Ottawa	21	13	—	13

1918-19

Team	GP	W	L	T	GF	GA	PTS
Ottawa	18	12	6	0	71	53	24
Montreal	18	10	8	0	88	78	20
Toronto	18	5	13	0	64	92	10

Leading Scorers

Player	Club	GP	G	A	PTS	PIM
Lalonde, Newsy	Montreal	17	21	9	30	40
Cleghorn, Odie	Montreal	17	23	6	29	33
Denneny, Cy	Ottawa	18	18	4	22	43
Nighbor, Frank	Ottawa	18	18	4	22	27
Pitre, Didier	Montreal	17	14	4	18	9
Skinner, Alf	Toronto	17	12	3	15	26
Cameron, Harry	Tor., Ott.	14	11	3	14	35
Noble, Reg	Toronto	17	11	3	14	35
Darragh, Jack	Ottawa	14	12	1	13	27
Randall, Ken	Toronto	14	7	6	13	27

1919-20

Team	GP	W	L	T	GF	GA	PTS
*Ottawa	24	19	5	0	121	64	38
Montreal	24	13	11	0	129	113	26
Toronto	24	12	12	0	119	106	24
Quebec	24	4	20	0	91	177	8

Leading Scorers

Player	Club	GP	G	A	PTS	PIM
Malone, Joe	Quebec	24	39	9	48	12
Lalonde, Newsy	Montreal	23	36	6	42	33
Denneny, Corbett	Toronto	23	23	12	35	18
Nighbor, Frank	Ottawa	23	26	7	33	18
Noble, Reg	Toronto	24	24	7	31	51
Darragh, Jack	Ottawa	22	22	5	27	22
Arbour, Amos	Montreal	20	22	4	26	10
Wilson, Cully	Toronto	23	21	5	26	79
Broadbent, Punch	Ottawa	20	19	4	23	39
Cleghorn, Odie	Montreal	21	19	3	22	30
Pitre, Didier	Montreal	22	15	7	22	6

The Toronto Arenas' Reg Noble scored 28 goals in 20 games during the NHL's innagural season of 1917-18.

1920-21

Team	GP	W	L	T	GF	GA	PTS
Toronto	24	15	9	0	105	100	30
*Ottawa	24	14	10	0	97	75	28
Montreal	24	13	11	0	112	99	26
Hamilton	24	6	18	0	92	132	12

Leading Scorers

Player	Club	GP	G	A	PTS	PIM
Lalonde, Newsy	Montreal	24	33	8	41	36
Denneny, Cy	Ottawa	24	34	5	39	0
Dye, Babe	Ham., Tor.	24	35	2	37	32
Malone, Joe	Hamilton	20	30	4	34	2
Cameron, Harry	Toronto	24	18	9	27	35
Noble, Reg	Toronto	24	20	6	26	54
Prodgers, Goldie	Hamilton	23	18	8	26	8
Denneny, Corbett	Toronto	20	17	6	23	27
Nighbor, Frank	Ottawa	24	18	3	21	10
Berlinquette, Louis	Montreal	24	12	9	21	24

1921-22

Team	GP	W	L	T	GF	GA	PTS
Ottawa	24	14	8	2	106	84	30
*Toronto	24	13	10	1	98	97	27
Montreal	24	12	11	1	88	94	25
Hamilton	24	7	17	0	88	105	14

Leading Scorers

Player	Club	GP	G	A	PTS	PIM
Broadbent, Punch	Ottawa	24	32	14	46	24
Denneny, Cy	Ottawa	22	27	12	39	18
Dye, Babe	Toronto	24	30	7	37	18
Malone, Joe	Hamilton	24	25	7	32	4
Cameron, Harry	Toronto	24	19	8	27	18
Denneny, Corbett	Toronto	24	19	7	26	28
Noble, Reg	Toronto	24	17	8	25	10
Cleghorn, Odie	Montreal	23	21	3	24	26
Cleghorn, Sprague	Montreal	24	17	7	24	63
Reise, Leo	Hamilton	24	9	14	23	8

1922-23

Team	GP	W	L	T	GF	GA	PTS
*Ottawa	24	14	9	1	77	54	29
Montreal	24	13	9	2	73	61	28
Toronto	24	13	10	1	82	88	27
Hamilton	24	6	18	0	81	110	12

Leading Scorers

Player	Club	GP	G	A	PTS	PIM
Dye, Babe	Toronto	22	26	11	37	19
Denneny, Cy	Ottawa	24	21	10	31	20
Adams, Jack	Toronto	23	19	9	28	42
Boucher, Billy	Montreal	24	23	4	27	52
Cleghorn, Odie	Montreal	24	19	7	26	14
Roach, Mickey	Hamilton	23	17	8	25	8
Boucher, George	Ottawa	23	15	9	24	44
Joliat, Aurel	Montreal	24	13	9	22	31
Noble, Reg	Toronto	24	12	10	22	41
Wilson, Cully	Hamilton	23	16	3	19	46

1923-24

Team	GP	W	L	T	GF	GA	PTS
Ottawa	24	16	8	0	74	54	32
*Montreal	24	13	11	0	59	48	26
Toronto	24	10	14	0	59	85	20
Hamilton	24	9	15	0	63	68	18

Leading Scorers

Player	Club	GP	G	A	PTS	PIM
Denneny, Cy	Ottawa	21	22	1	23	10
Boucher, Billy	Montreal	23	16	6	22	33
Joliat, Aurel	Montreal	24	15	5	20	19
Dye, Babe	Toronto	19	17	2	19	23
Boucher, George	Ottawa	21	14	5	19	28
Burch, Billy	Hamilton	24	16	2	18	4
Clancy, King	Ottawa	24	9	8	17	18
Adams, Jack	Toronto	22	13	3	16	49
Morenz, Howie	Montreal	24	13	3	16	20
Noble, Reg	Toronto	23	12	3	15	23

1924-25

Team	GP	W	L	T	GF	GA	PTS
Hamilton	30	19	10	1	90	60	39
Toronto	30	19	11	0	90	84	38
Montreal	30	17	11	2	93	56	36
Ottawa	30	17	12	1	83	66	35
Mtl. Maroons	30	9	19	2	45	65	20
Boston	30	6	24	0	49	119	12

Leading Scorers

Player	Club	GP	G	A	PTS	PIM
Dye, Babe	Toronto	29	38	6	44	41
Denneny, Cy	Ottawa	28	27	15	42	16
Joliat, Aurel	Montreal	24	29	11	40	85
Morenz, Howie	Montreal	30	27	7	34	31
Boucher, Billy	Montreal	30	18	13	31	92
Adams, Jack	Toronto	27	21	8	29	66
Burch, Billy	Hamilton	27	20	4	24	10
Green, Red	Hamilton	30	19	4	23	63
Herberts, Jimmy	Boston	30	17	5	22	50
Day, Hap	Toronto	26	10	12	22	27

1925-26

Team	GP	W	L	T	GF	GA	PTS
Ottawa	36	24	8	4	77	42	52
*Mtl. Maroons	36	20	11	5	91	73	45
Pittsburgh	36	19	16	1	82	70	39
Boston	36	17	15	4	92	85	38
NY Americans	36	12	20	4	68	89	28
Toronto	36	12	21	3	92	114	27
Montreal	36	11	24	1	79	108	23

Leading Scorers

Player	Club	GP	G	A	PTS	PIM
Stewart, Nels	Mtl. Maroons	36	34	8	42	119
Denneny, Cy	Ottawa	36	24	12	36	18
Cooper, Carson	Boston	36	28	3	31	10
Herberts, Jimmy	Boston	36	26	5	31	47
Morenz, Howie	Montreal	31	23	3	26	39
Adams, Jack	Toronto	36	21	5	26	52
Joliat, Aurel	Montreal	35	17	9	26	52
Burch, Billy	NY Americans	36	22	3	25	33
Smith, Hooley	Ottawa	28	16	9	25	53
Nighbor, Frank	Ottawa	35	12	13	25	40

1926-27

Canadian Division

Team	GP	W	L	T	GF	GA	PTS
*Ottawa	44	30	10	4	86	69	64
Montreal	44	28	14	2	99	67	58
Mtl. Maroons	44	20	20	4	71	68	44
NY Americans	44	17	25	2	82	91	36
Toronto	44	15	24	5	79	94	35

American Division

Team	GP	W	L	T	GF	GA	PTS
New York	44	25	13	6	95	72	56
Boston	44	21	20	3	97	89	45
Chicago	44	19	22	3	115	116	41
Pittsburgh	44	15	26	3	79	108	33
Detroit	44	12	28	4	76	105	28

Leading Scorers

Player	Club	GP	G	A	PTS	PIM
Cook, Bill	New York	44	33	4	37	58
Irvin, Dick	Chicago	43	18	18	36	34
Morenz, Howie	Montreal	44	25	7	32	49
Fredrickson, Frank	Det., Bos.	41	18	13	31	46
Dye, Babe	Chicago	41	25	5	30	14
Bailey, Ace	Toronto	42	15	13	28	82
Boucher, Frank	New York	44	13	15	28	17
Burch, Billy	NY Americans	43	19	8	27	40
Oliver, Harry	Boston	42	18	6	24	17
Keats, Gordon	Bos., Det.	42	16	8	24	52

Nels Stewart, the first NHL sharpshooter to score 300 career goals, won the scoring championship for the Maroons in 1925-26.

A two-time Stanley Cup winner with the NY Rangers, Frank Boucher later coached the Broadway Blues to the Cup in 1939.

1927-28

Canadian Division

Team	GP	W	L	T	GF	GA	PTS
Montreal	44	26	11	7	116	48	59
Mtl. Maroons	44	24	14	6	96	77	54
Ottawa	44	20	14	10	78	57	50
Toronto	44	18	18	8	89	88	44
NY Americans	44	11	27	6	63	128	28

American Division

Team	GP	W	L	T	GF	GA	PTS
Boston	44	20	13	11	77	70	51
*New York	44	19	16	9	94	79	47
Pittsburgh	44	19	17	8	67	76	46
Detroit	44	19	19	6	88	79	44
Chicago	44	7	34	3	68	134	17

Leading Scorers

Player	Club	GP	G	A	PTS	PIM
Morenz, Howie	Montreal	43	33	18	51	66
Joliat, Aurel	Montreal	44	28	11	39	105
Boucher, Frank	New York	44	23	12	35	15
Hay, George	Detroit	42	22	13	35	20
Stewart, Nels	Mtl. Maroons	41	27	7	34	104
Gagne, Art	Montreal	44	20	10	30	75
Cook, Fred	New York	44	14	14	28	45
Carson, Bill	Toronto	32	20	6	26	36
Finnigan, Frank	Ottawa	38	20	5	25	34
Cook, Bill	New York	43	18	6	24	42
Keats, Gordon	Chi., Det.	38	14	10	24	60

1928-29

Canadian Division

Team	GP	W	L	T	GF	GA	PTS
Montreal	44	22	7	15	71	43	59
NY Americans	44	19	13	12	53	53	50
Toronto	44	21	18	5	85	69	47
Ottawa	44	14	17	13	54	67	41
Mtl. Maroons	44	15	20	9	67	65	39

American Division

Team	GP	W	L	T	GF	GA	PTS
*Boston	44	26	13	5	89	52	57
New York	44	21	13	10	72	65	52
Detroit	44	19	16	9	72	63	47
Pittsburgh	44	9	27	8	46	80	26
Chicago	44	7	29	8	33	85	22

Leading Scorers

Player	Club	GP	G	A	PTS	PIM
Bailey, Ace	Toronto	44	22	10	32	78
Stewart, Nels	Mtl. Maroons	44	21	8	29	74
Cooper, Carson	Detroit	43	18	9	27	14
Morenz, Howie	Montreal	42	17	10	27	47
Blair, Andy	Toronto	44	12	15	27	41
Boucher, Frank	New York	44	10	16	26	8
Oliver, Harry	Boston	43	17	6	23	24
Cook, Bill	New York	43	15	8	23	41
Ward, Jimmy	Mtl. Maroons	43	14	8	22	46

Seven players tied with 19 points

1929-30

Canadian Division

Team	GP	W	L	T	GF	GA	PTS
Mtl. Maroons	44	23	16	5	141	114	51
*Montreal	44	21	14	9	142	114	51
Ottawa	44	21	15	8	138	118	50
Toronto	44	17	21	6	116	124	40
NY Americans	44	14	25	5	113	161	33

American Division

Team	GP	W	L	T	GF	GA	PTS
Boston	44	38	5	1	179	98	77
Chicago	44	21	18	5	117	111	47
New York	44	17	17	10	136	143	44
Detroit	44	14	24	6	117	133	34
Pittsburgh	44	5	36	3	102	185	13

Leading Scorers

Name	Club	GP	G	A	PTS	PIM
Weiland, Cooney	Boston	44	43	30	73	27
Boucher, Frank	New York	42	26	36	62	16
Clapper, Dit	Boston	44	41	20	61	48
Cook, Bill	New York	44	29	30	59	56
Kilrea, Hec	Ottawa	44	36	22	58	72
Stewart, Nels	Mtl. Maroons	44	39	16	55	81
Morenz, Howie	Montreal	44	40	10	50	72
Himes, Norm	NY Americans	44	28	22	50	15
Lamb, Joe	Ottawa	44	29	20	49	119
Gainor, Norm	Boston	42	18	31	49	39

1930-31

Canadian Division

Team	GP	W	L	T	GF	GA	PTS
*Montreal	44	26	10	8	129	89	60
Toronto	44	22	13	9	118	99	53
Mtl. Maroons	44	20	18	6	105	106	46
NY Americans	44	18	16	10	76	74	46
Ottawa	44	10	30	4	91	142	24

American Division

Team	GP	W	L	T	GF	GA	PTS
Boston	44	28	10	6	143	90	62
Chicago	44	24	17	3	108	78	51
New York	44	19	16	9	106	87	47
Detroit	44	16	21	7	102	105	39
Philadelphia	44	4	36	4	76	184	12

Leading Scorers

Player	Club	GP	G	A	PTS	PIM
Morenz, Howie	Montreal	39	28	23	51	49
Goodfellow, Ebbie	Detroit	44	25	23	48	32
Conacher, Charlie	Toronto	37	31	12	43	78
Cook, Bill	New York	43	30	12	42	39
Bailey, Ace	Toronto	40	23	19	42	46
Primeau, Joe	Toronto	38	9	32	41	18
Stewart, Nels	Mtl. Maroons	42	25	14	39	75
Boucher, Frank	New York	44	12	27	39	20
Weiland, Cooney	Boston	44	25	13	38	14
Cook, Fred	New York	44	18	17	35	72
Joliat, Aurel	Montreal	43	13	22	35	73

1931-32

Canadian Division

Team	GP	W	L	T	GF	GA	PTS
Montreal	48	25	16	7	128	111	57
*Toronto	48	23	18	7	155	127	53
Mtl. Maroons	48	19	22	7	142	139	45
NY Americans	48	16	24	8	95	142	40

American Division

Team	GP	W	L	T	GF	GA	PTS
New York	48	23	17	8	134	112	54
Chicago	48	18	19	11	86	101	47
Detroit	48	18	20	10	95	108	46
Boston	48	15	21	12	122	117	42

Leading Scorers

Player	Club	GP	G	A	PTS	PIM
Jackson, Harvey	Toronto	48	28	25	53	63
Primeau, Joe	Toronto	46	13	37	50	25
Morenz, Howie	Montreal	48	24	25	49	46
Conacher, Charlie	Toronto	44	34	14	48	66
Cook, Bill	New York	48	34	14	48	33
Trottier, Dave	Mtl. Maroons	48	26	18	44	94
Smith, Reg	Mtl. Maroons	43	11	33	44	49
Siebert, Albert	Mtl. Maroons	48	21	18	39	64
Clapper, Dit	Boston	48	17	22	39	21
Joliat, Aurel	Montreal	48	15	24	39	46

Lionel Conacher won back-to-back Cups with Chicago and the Montreal Maroons.

1932-33
Canadian Division
Team	GP	W	L	T	GF	GA	PTS
Toronto	48	24	18	6	119	111	54
Mtl. Maroons	48	22	20	6	135	119	50
Montreal	48	18	25	5	92	115	41
NY Americans	48	15	22	11	91	118	41
Ottawa	48	11	27	10	88	131	32

American Division
Team	GP	W	L	T	GF	GA	PTS
Boston	48	25	15	8	124	88	58
Detroit	48	25	15	8	111	93	58
*New York	48	23	17	8	135	107	54
Chicago	48	16	20	12	88	101	44

Leading Scorers
Player	Club	GP	G	A	PTS	PIM
Cook, Bill	New York	48	28	22	50	51
Jackson, Harvey	Toronto	48	27	17	44	43
Northcott, Lawrence	Mtl. Maroons	48	22	21	43	30
Smith, Reg	Mtl. Maroons	48	20	21	41	66
Haynes, Paul	Mtl. Maroons	48	16	25	41	18
Joliat, Aurel	Montreal	48	18	21	39	53
Barry, Marty	Boston	48	24	13	37	40
Cook, Fred	New York	48	22	15	37	35
Stewart, Nels	Boston	47	18	18	36	62
Morenz, Howie	Montreal	46	14	21	35	32
Gagnon, Johnny	Montreal	48	12	23	35	64
Shore, Eddie	Boston	48	8	27	35	102
Boucher, Frank	New York	47	7	28	35	4

1933-34
Canadian Division
Team	GP	W	L	T	GF	GA	PTS
Toronto	48	26	13	9	174	119	61
Montreal	48	22	20	6	99	101	50
Mtl. Maroons	48	19	18	11	117	122	49
NY Americans	48	15	23	10	104	132	40
Ottawa	48	13	29	6	115	143	32

American Division
Team	GP	W	L	T	GF	GA	PTS
Detroit	48	24	14	10	113	98	58
*Chicago	48	20	17	11	88	83	51
New York	48	21	19	8	120	113	50
Boston	48	18	25	5	111	130	41

Leading Scorers
Player	Club	GP	G	A	PTS	PIM
Conacher, Charlie	Toronto	42	32	20	52	38
Primeau, Joe	Toronto	45	14	32	46	8
Boucher, Frank	New York	48	14	30	44	4
Barry, Marty	Boston	48	27	12	39	12
Dillon, Cecil	New York	48	13	26	39	10
Stewart, Nels	Boston	48	21	17	38	68
Jackson, Harvey	Toronto	38	20	18	38	38
Joliat, Aurel	Montreal	48	22	15	37	27
Smith, Reg	Mtl. Maroons	47	18	19	37	58
Thompson, Paul	Chicago	48	20	16	36	17

1934-35
Canadian Division
Team	GP	W	L	T	GF	GA	PTS
Toronto	48	30	14	4	157	111	64
*Mtl. Maroons	48	24	19	5	123	92	53
Montreal	48	19	23	6	110	145	44
NY Americans	48	12	27	9	100	142	33
St. Louis	48	11	31	6	86	144	28

American Division
Team	GP	W	L	T	GF	GA	PTS
Boston	48	26	16	6	129	112	58
Chicago	48	26	17	5	118	88	57
New York	48	22	20	6	137	139	50
Detroit	48	19	22	7	127	114	45

Leading Scorers
Player	Club	GP	G	A	PTS	PIM
Conacher, Charlie	Toronto	47	36	21	57	24
Howe, Syd	St.L., Det.	50	22	25	47	34
Aurie, Larry	Detroit	48	17	29	46	24
Boucher, Frank	New York	48	13	32	45	2
Jackson, Harvey	Toronto	42	22	22	44	27
Lewis, Herb	Detroit	47	16	27	43	26
Chapman, Art	NY Americans	47	9	34	43	4
Barry, Marty	Boston	48	20	20	40	33
Schriner, Sweeney	NY Americans	48	18	22	40	6
Stewart, Nels	Boston	47	21	18	39	45
Thompson, Paul	Chicago	48	16	23	39	20

1935-36
Canadian Division
Team	GP	W	L	T	GF	GA	PTS
Mtl. Maroons	48	22	16	10	114	106	54
Toronto	48	23	19	6	126	106	52
NY Americans	48	16	25	7	109	122	39
Montreal	48	11	26	11	82	123	33

American Division
Team	GP	W	L	T	GF	GA	PTS
*Detroit	48	24	16	8	124	103	56
Boston	48	22	20	6	92	83	50
Chicago	48	21	19	8	93	92	50
New York	48	19	17	12	91	96	50

Leading Scorers
Player	Club	GP	G	A	PTS	PIM
Schriner, Sweeney	NY Americans	48	19	26	45	8
Barry, Marty	Detroit	48	21	19	40	16
Thompson, Paul	Chicago	45	17	23	40	19
Thoms, Bill	Toronto	48	23	15	38	29
Conacher, Charlie	Toronto	44	23	15	38	74
Smith, Reg	Mtl. Maroons	47	19	19	38	75
Romnes, Doc	Chicago	48	13	25	38	6
Chapman, Art	NY Americans	47	10	28	38	14
Lewis, Herb	Detroit	45	14	23	37	25
Northcott, Lawrence	Mtl. Maroons	48	15	21	36	41

1936-37
Canadian Division
Team	GP	W	L	T	GF	GA	PTS
Montreal	48	24	18	6	115	111	54
Mtl. Maroons	48	22	17	9	126	110	53
Toronto	48	22	21	5	119	115	49
NY Americans	48	15	29	4	122	161	34

American Division
Team	GP	W	L	T	GF	GA	PTS
*Detroit	48	25	14	9	128	102	59
Boston	48	23	18	7	120	110	53
New York	48	19	20	9	117	106	47
Chicago	48	14	27	7	99	131	35

Leading Scorers
Player	Club	GP	G	A	PTS	PIM
Schriner, Sweeney	NY Americans	48	21	25	46	17
Apps, Syl	Toronto	48	16	29	45	10
Barry, Marty	Detroit	48	17	27	44	6
Aurie, Larry	Detroit	45	23	20	43	20
Jackson, Harvey	Toronto	46	21	19	40	12
Gagnon, Johnny	Montreal	48	20	16	36	38
Gracie, Bob	Mtl. Maroons	47	11	25	36	18
Stewart, Nels	Bos., NYA	43	23	12	35	37
Thompson, Paul	Chicago	47	17	18	35	28
Cowley, Bill	Boston	46	13	22	35	4

Syl Apps finished second in league scoring as a rookie in 1936-37.

1937-38

Canadian Division

Team	GP	W	L	T	GF	GA	PTS
Toronto	48	24	15	9	151	127	57
NY Americans	48	19	18	11	110	111	49
Montreal	48	18	17	13	123	128	49
Mtl. Maroons	48	12	30	6	101	149	30

American Division

Team	GP	W	L	T	GF	GA	PTS
Boston	48	30	11	7	142	89	67
New York	48	27	15	6	149	96	60
*Chicago	48	14	25	9	97	139	37
Detroit	48	12	25	11	99	133	35

Leading Scorers

Player	Club	GP	G	A	PTS	PIM
Drillon, Gord	Toronto	48	26	26	52	4
Apps, Syl	Toronto	47	21	29	50	9
Thompson, Paul	Chicago	48	22	22	44	14
Mantha, Georges	Montreal	47	23	19	42	12
Dillon, Cecil	New York	48	21	18	39	6
Cowley, Bill	Boston	48	17	22	39	8
Schriner, Sweeney	NY Americans	49	21	17	38	22
Thoms, Bill	Toronto	48	14	24	38	14
Smith, Clint	New York	48	14	23	37	0
Stewart, Nels	NY Americans	48	19	17	36	29
Colville, Neil	New York	45	17	19	36	11

1938-39

Team	GP	W	L	T	GF	GA	PTS
*Boston	48	36	10	2	156	76	74
New York	48	26	16	6	149	105	58
Toronto	48	19	20	9	114	107	47
NY Americans	48	17	21	10	119	157	44
Detroit	48	18	24	6	107	128	42
Montreal	48	15	24	9	115	146	39
Chicago	48	12	28	8	91	132	32

Leading Scorers

Player	Club	GP	G	A	PTS	PIM
Blake, Hector	Montreal	48	24	23	47	10
Schriner, Sweeney	NY Americans	48	13	31	44	20
Cowley, Bill	Boston	34	8	34	42	2
Smith, Clint	New York	48	21	20	41	2
Barry, Marty	Detroit	48	13	28	41	4
Apps, Syl	Toronto	44	15	25	40	4
Anderson, Tom	NY Americans	48	13	27	40	14
Gottselig, Johnny	Chicago	48	16	23	39	15
Haynes, Paul	Montreal	47	5	33	38	27
Conacher, Roy	Boston	47	26	11	37	12
Carr, Lorne	NY Americans	46	19	18	37	16
Colville, Neil	New York	48	18	19	37	12
Watson, Phil	New York	48	15	22	37	42

1939-40

Team	GP	W	L	T	GF	GA	PTS
Boston	48	31	12	5	170	98	67
*New York	48	27	11	10	136	77	64
Toronto	48	25	17	6	134	110	56
Chicago	48	23	19	6	112	120	52
Detroit	48	16	26	6	91	126	38
NY Americans	48	15	29	4	106	140	34
Montreal	48	10	33	5	90	168	25

Leading Scorers

Player	Club	GP	G	A	PTS	PIM
Schmidt, Milt	Boston	48	22	30	52	37
Dumart, Woody	Boston	48	22	21	43	16
Bauer, Bob	Boston	48	17	26	43	2
Drillon, Gord	Toronto	43	21	19	40	13
Cowley, Bill	Boston	48	13	27	40	24
Hextall, Bryan	New York	48	24	15	39	52
Colville, Neil	New York	48	19	19	38	22
Howe, Syd	Detroit	46	14	23	37	17
Blake, Hector	Montreal	48	17	19	36	48
Armstrong, Murray	NY Americans	48	16	20	36	12

1940-41

Team	GP	W	L	T	GF	GA	PTS
*Boston	48	27	8	13	168	102	67
Toronto	48	28	14	6	145	99	62
Detroit	48	21	16	11	112	102	53
New York	48	21	19	8	143	125	50
Chicago	48	16	25	7	112	139	39
Montreal	48	16	26	6	121	147	38
NY Americans	48	8	29	11	99	186	27

Leading Scorers

Player	Club	GP	G	A	PTS	PIM
Cowley, Bill	Boston	46	17	45	62	16
Hextall, Bryan	New York	48	26	18	44	16
Drillon, Gord	Toronto	42	23	21	44	2
Apps, Syl	Toronto	41	20	24	44	6
Patrick, Lynn	New York	48	20	24	44	12
Howe, Syd	Detroit	48	20	24	44	8
Colville, Neil	New York	48	14	28	42	28
Wiseman, Eddie	Boston	48	16	24	40	-10
Bauer, Bobby	Boston	48	17	22	39	2
Schriner, Sweeney	Toronto	48	24	14	38	6
Conacher, Roy	Boston	40	24	14	38	7
Schmidt, Milt	Boston	44	13	25	38	23

1941-42

Team	GP	W	L	T	GF	GA	PTS
New York	48	29	17	2	177	143	60
*Toronto	48	27	18	3	158	136	57
Boston	48	25	17	6	160	118	56
Chicago	48	22	23	3	145	155	47
Detroit	48	19	25	4	140	147	42
Montreal	48	18	27	3	134	173	39
Brooklyn	48	16	29	3	133	175	35

Leading Scorers

Player	Club	GP	G	A	PTS	PIM
Hextall, Bryan	New York	48	24	32	56	30
Patrick, Lynn	New York	47	32	22	54	18
Grosso, Don	Detroit	48	23	30	53	13
Watson, Phil	New York	48	15	37	52	48
Abel, Sid	Detroit	48	18	31	49	45
Blake, Hector	Montreal	47	17	28	45	19
Thoms, Bill	Chicago	47	15	30	45	8
Drillon, Gord	Toronto	48	23	18	41	6
Apps, Syl	Toronto	38	18	23	41	0
Anderson, Tom	Brooklyn	48	12	29	41	54

1942-43

Team	GP	W	L	T	GF	GA	PTS
*Detroit	50	25	14	11	169	124	61
Boston	50	24	17	9	195	176	57
Toronto	50	22	19	9	198	159	53
Montreal	50	19	19	12	181	191	50
Chicago	50	17	18	15	179	180	49
New York	50	11	31	8	161	253	30

Leading Scorers

Player	Club	GP	G	A	PTS	PIM
Bentley, Doug	Chicago	50	33	40	73	18
Cowley, Bill	Boston	48	27	45	72	10
Bentley, Max	Chicago	47	26	44	70	2
Patrick, Lynn	New York	50	22	39	61	28
Carr, Lorne	Toronto	50	27	33	60	15
Taylor, Billy	Toronto	50	18	42	60	2
Hextall, Bryan	New York	50	27	32	59	28
Blake, Hector	Montreal	48	23	36	59	28
Lach, Elmer	Montreal	45	18	40	58	14
O'Connor, Herb	Montreal	50	15	43	58	2

1943-44

Team	GP	W	L	T	GF	GA	PTS
*Montreal	50	38	5	7	234	109	83
Detroit	50	26	18	6	214	177	58
Toronto	50	23	23	4	214	174	50
Chicago	50	22	23	5	178	187	49
Boston	50	19	26	5	223	268	43
New York	50	6	39	5	162	310	17

Leading Scorers

Player	Club	GP	G	A	PTS	PIM
Cain, Herb	Boston	48	36	46	82	4
Bentley, Doug	Chicago	50	38	39	77	22
Carr, Lorne	Toronto	50	36	38	74	9
Liscombe, Carl	Detroit	50	36	37	73	17
Lach, Elmer	Montreal	48	24	48	72	23
Smith, Clint	Chicago	50	23	49	72	4
Cowley, Bill	Boston	36	30	41	71	12
Mosienko, Bill	Chicago	50	32	38	70	10
Jackson, Art	Boston	49	28	41	69	8
Bodnar, Gus	Toronto	50	22	40	62	18

1944-45

Team	GP	W	L	T	GF	GA	PTS
Montreal	50	38	8	4	228	121	80
Detroit	50	31	14	5	218	161	67
*Toronto	50	24	22	4	183	161	52
Boston	50	16	30	4	179	219	36
Chicago	50	13	30	7	141	194	33
New York	50	11	29	10	154	247	32

Leading Scorers

Player	Club	GP	G	A	PTS	PIM
Lach, Elmer	Montreal	50	26	54	80	37
Richard, Maurice	Montreal	50	50	23	73	36
Blake, Hector	Montreal	49	29	38	67	15
Cowley, Bill	Boston	49	25	40	65	2
Kennedy, Ted	Toronto	49	29	25	54	14
Mosienko, Bill	Chicago	50	28	26	54	0
Carveth, Joe	Detroit	50	26	28	54	6
DeMarco, Albert	New York	50	24	30	54	10
Smith, Clint	Chicago	50	23	31	54	0
Howe, Syd	Detroit	46	17	36	53	6

Maurice Richard led the league in goals scored five times and captured the Hart Trophy in 1947.

1945-46

Team	GP	W	L	T	GF	GA	PTS
*Montreal	50	28	17	5	172	134	61
Boston	50	24	18	8	167	156	56
Chicago	50	23	20	7	200	178	53
Detroit	50	20	20	10	146	159	50
Toronto	50	19	24	7	174	185	45
New York	50	13	28	9	144	191	35

Leading Scorers

Player	Club	GP	G	A	PTS	PIM
Bentley, Max	Chicago	47	31	30	61	6
Stewart, Gaye	Toronto	50	37	15	52	8
Blake, Hector	Montreal	50	29	21	50	2
Smith, Clint	Chicago	50	26	24	50	2
Richard, Maurice	Montreal	50	27	21	48	50
Mosienko, Bill	Chicago	40	18	30	48	12
DeMarco, Albert	New York	50	20	27	47	20
Lach, Elmer	Montreal	50	13	34	47	34
Kaleta, Alex	Chicago	49	19	27	46	17
Taylor, Billy	Toronto	48	23	18	41	14
Horeck, Pete	Chicago	50	20	21	41	34

1946-47

Team	GP	W	L	T	GF	GA	PTS
Montreal	60	34	16	10	189	138	78
*Toronto	60	31	19	10	209	172	72
Boston	60	26	23	11	190	175	63
Detroit	60	22	27	11	190	193	55
New York	60	22	32	6	167	186	50
Chicago	60	19	37	4	193	274	42

Leading Scorers

Player	Club	GP	G	A	PTS	PIM
Bentley, Max	Chicago	60	29	43	72	12
Richard, Maurice	Montreal	60	45	26	71	69
Taylor, Billy	Detroit	60	17	46	63	35
Schmidt, Milt	Boston	59	27	35	62	40
Kennedy, Ted	Toronto	60	28	32	60	27
Bentley, Doug	Chicago	52	21	34	55	18
Bauer, Bob	Boston	58	30	24	54	4
Conacher, Roy	Detroit	60	30	24	54	6
Mosienko, Bill	Chicago	59	25	27	52	2
Dumart, Woody	Boston	60	24	28	52	12

1947-48

Team	GP	W	L	T	GF	GA	PTS
*Toronto	60	32	15	13	182	143	77
Detroit	60	30	18	12	187	148	72
Boston	60	23	24	13	167	168	59
New York	60	21	26	13	176	201	55
Montreal	60	20	29	11	147	169	51
Chicago	60	20	34	6	195	225	46

Leading Scorers

Player	Club	GP	G	A	PTS	PIM
Lach, Elmer	Montreal	60	30	31	61	72
O'Connor, Buddy	New York	60	24	36	60	8
Bentley, Doug	Chicago	60	20	37	57	16
Stewart, Gaye	Tor., Chi.	61	27	29	56	83
Bentley, Max	Chi., Tor.	59	26	28	54	14
Poile, Bud	Tor., Chi.	58	25	29	54	17
Richard, Maurice	Montreal	53	28	25	53	89
Apps, Syl	Toronto	55	26	27	53	12
Lindsay, Ted	Detroit	60	33	19	52	95
Conacher, Roy	Chicago	52	22	27	49	4

1948-49

Team	GP	W	L	T	GF	GA	PTS
Detroit	60	34	19	7	195	145	75
Boston	60	29	23	8	178	163	66
Montreal	60	28	23	9	152	126	65
*Toronto	60	22	25	13	147	161	57
Chicago	60	21	31	8	173	211	50
New York	60	18	31	11	133	172	47

Leading Scorers

Player	Club	GP	G	A	PTS	PIM
Conacher, Roy	Chicago	60	26	42	68	8
Bentley, Doug	Chicago	58	23	43	66	38
Abel, Sid	Detroit	60	28	26	54	49
Lindsay, Ted	Detroit	50	26	28	54	97
Conacher, Jim	Det., Chi.	59	26	23	49	43
Ronty, Paul	Boston	60	20	29	49	11
Watson, Harry	Toronto	60	26	19	45	0
Reay, Billy	Montreal	60	22	23	45	33
Bodnar, Gus	Chicago	59	19	26	45	14
Peirson, John	Boston	59	22	21	43	45

1949-50

Team	GP	W	L	T	GF	GA	PTS
*Detroit	70	37	19	14	229	164	88
Montreal	70	29	22	19	172	150	77
Toronto	70	31	27	12	176	173	74
New York	70	28	31	11	170	189	67
Boston	70	22	32	16	198	228	60
Chicago	70	22	38	10	203	244	54

Leading Scorers

Player	Club	GP	G	A	PTS	PIM
Lindsay, Ted	Detroit	69	23	55	78	141
Abel, Sid	Detroit	69	34	35	69	46
Howe, Gordie	Detroit	70	35	33	68	69
Richard, Maurice	Montreal	70	43	22	65	114
Ronty, Paul	Boston	70	23	36	59	8
Conacher, Roy	Chicago	70	25	31	56	16
Bentley, Doug	Chicago	64	20	33	53	28
Peirson, John	Boston	57	27	25	52	49
Prystai, Metro	Chicago	65	29	22	51	31
Guidolin, Bep	Chicago	70	17	34	51	42

1950-51

Team	GP	W	L	T	GF	GA	PTS
Detroit	70	44	13	13	236	139	101
*Toronto	70	41	16	13	212	138	95
Montreal	70	25	30	15	173	184	65
Boston	70	22	30	18	178	197	62
New York	70	20	29	21	169	201	62
Chicago	70	13	47	10	171	280	36

Leading Scorers

Player	Club	GP	G	A	PTS	PIM
Howe, Gordie	Detroit	70	43	43	86	74
Richard, Maurice	Montreal	65	42	24	66	97
Bentley, Max	Toronto	67	21	41	62	34
Abel, Sid	Detroit	69	23	38	61	30
Schmidt, Milt	Boston	62	22	39	61	33
Kennedy, Ted	Toronto	63	18	43	61	32
Lindsay, Ted	Detroit	67	24	35	59	110
Sloan, Tod	Toronto	70	31	25	56	105
Kelly, Red	Detroit	70	17	37	54	24
Smith, Sid	Toronto	70	30	21	51	10
Gardner, Cal	Toronto	66	23	28	51	42

Frank Mahovlich set a Leafs' team record with 48 goals in 1960-61.

1951-52

Team	GP	W	L	T	GF	GA	PTS
*Detroit	70	44	14	12	215	133	100
Montreal	70	34	26	10	195	164	78
Toronto	70	29	25	16	168	157	74
Boston	70	25	29	16	162	176	66
New York	70	23	34	13	192	219	59
Chicago	70	17	44	9	158	241	43

Leading Scorers

Player	Club	GP	G	A	PTS	PIM
Howe, Gordie	Detroit	70	47	39	86	78
Lindsay, Ted	Detroit	70	30	39	69	123
Lach, Elmer	Montreal	70	15	50	65	36
Raleigh, Don	New York	70	19	42	61	14
Smith, Sid	Toronto	70	27	30	57	6
Geoffrion, Bernie	Montreal	67	30	24	54	66
Mosienko, Bill	Chicago	70	31	22	53	10
Abel, Sid	Detroit	62	17	36	53	32
Kennedy, Ted	Toronto	70	19	33	52	33
Schmidt, Milt	Boston	69	21	29	50	57
Peirson, John	Boston	68	20	30	50	30

1952-53

Team	GP	W	L	T	GF	GA	PTS
Detroit	70	36	16	18	222	133	90
*Montreal	70	28	23	19	155	148	75
Boston	70	28	29	13	152	172	69
Chicago	70	27	28	15	169	175	69
Toronto	70	27	30	13	156	167	67
New York	70	17	37	16	152	211	50

Leading Scorers

Player	Club	GP	G	A	PTS	PIM
Howe, Gordie	Detroit	70	49	46	95	57
Lindsay, Ted	Detroit	70	32	39	71	111
Richard, Maurice	Montreal	70	28	33	61	112
Hergesheimer, Wally	New York	70	30	29	59	10
Delvecchio, Alex	Detroit	70	16	43	59	28
Ronty, Paul	New York	70	16	38	54	20
Prystai, Metro	Detroit	70	16	34	50	12
Kelly, Red	Detroit	70	19	27	46	8
Olmstead, Bert	Montreal	69	17	28	45	83
Mackell, Fleming	Boston	65	27	17	44	63
McFadden, Jim	Chicago	70	23	21	44	29

1953-54

Team	GP	W	L	T	GF	GA	PTS
*Detroit	70	37	19	14	191	132	88
Montreal	70	35	24	11	195	141	81
Toronto	70	32	24	14	152	131	78
Boston	70	32	28	10	177	181	74
New York	70	29	31	10	161	182	68
Chicago	70	12	51	7	133	242	31

Leading Scorers

Player	Club	GP	G	A	PTS	PIM
Howe, Gordie	Detroit	70	33	48	81	109
Richard, Maurice	Montreal	70	37	30	67	112
Lindsay, Ted	Detroit	70	26	36	62	110
Geoffrion, Bernie	Montreal	54	29	25	54	87
Olmstead, Bert	Montreal	70	15	37	52	85
Kelly, Red	Detroit	62	16	33	49	18
Reibel, Earl	Detroit	69	15	33	48	18
Sandford, Ed	Boston	70	16	31	47	42
Mackell, Fleming	Boston	67	15	32	47	60
Mosdell, Ken	Montreal	67	22	24	46	64
Ronty, Paul	New York	70	13	33	46	18

1954-55

Team	GP	W	L	T	GF	GA	PTS
*Detroit	70	42	17	11	204	134	95
Montreal	70	41	18	11	228	157	93
Toronto	70	24	24	22	147	135	70
Boston	70	23	26	21	169	188	67
New York	70	17	35	18	150	210	52
Chicago	70	13	40	17	161	235	43

Leading Scorers

Player	Club	GP	G	A	PTS	PIM
Geoffrion, Bernie	Montreal	70	38	37	75	57
Richard, Maurice	Montreal	67	38	36	74	125
Beliveau, Jean	Montreal	70	37	36	73	58
Reibel, Earl	Detroit	70	25	41	66	15
Howe, Gordie	Detroit	64	29	33	62	68
Sullivan, George	Chicago	69	19	42	61	51
Olmstead, Bert	Montreal	70	10	48	58	103
Smith, Sid	Toronto	70	33	21	54	14
Mosdell, Ken	Montreal	70	22	32	54	82
Lewicki, Danny	New York	70	29	24	53	8

1955-56

Team	GP	W	L	T	GF	GA	PTS
*Montreal	70	45	15	10	222	131	100
Detroit	70	30	24	16	183	148	76
New York	70	32	28	10	204	203	74
Toronto	70	24	33	13	153	181	61
Boston	70	23	34	13	147	185	59
Chicago	70	19	39	12	155	216	50

Leading Scorers

Player	Club	GP	G	A	PTS	PIM
Beliveau, Jean	Montreal	70	47	41	88	143
Howe, Gordie	Detroit	70	38	41	79	100
Richard, Maurice	Montreal	70	38	33	71	89
Olmstead, Bert	Montreal	70	14	56	70	94
Sloan, Tod	Toronto	70	37	29	66	100
Bathgate, Andy	New York	70	19	47	66	59
Geoffrion, Bernie	Montreal	59	29	33	62	66
Reibel, Earl	Detroit	68	17	39	56	10
Delvecchio, Alex	Detroit	70	25	26	51	24
Creighton, Dave	New York	70	20	31	51	43
Gadsby, Bill	New York	70	9	42	51	84

1956-57

Team	GP	W	L	T	GF	GA	PTS
Detroit	70	38	20	12	198	157	88
*Montreal	70	35	23	12	210	155	82
Boston	70	34	24	12	195	174	80
New York	70	26	30	14	184	227	66
Toronto	70	21	34	15	174	192	57
Chicago	70	16	39	15	169	225	47

Leading Scorers

Player	Club	GP	G	A	PTS	PIM
Howe, Gordie	Detroit	70	44	45	89	72
Lindsay, Ted	Detroit	70	30	55	85	103
Beliveau, Jean	Montreal	69	33	51	84	105
Bathgate, Andy	New York	70	27	50	77	60
Litzenberger, Ed	Chicago	70	32	32	64	48
Richard, Maurice	Montreal	63	33	29	62	74
McKenney, Don	Boston	69	21	39	60	31
Moore, Dickie	Montreal	70	29	29	58	56
Richard, Henri	Montreal	63	18	36	54	71
Ullman, Norm	Detroit	64	16	36	52	47

1957-58

Team	GP	W	L	T	GF	GA	PTS
*Montreal	70	43	17	10	250	158	96
New York	70	32	25	13	195	188	77
Detroit	70	29	29	12	176	207	70
Boston	70	27	28	15	199	194	69
Chicago	70	24	39	7	163	202	55
Toronto	70	21	38	11	192	226	53

Leading Scorers

Player	Club	GP	G	A	PTS	PIM
Moore, Dickie	Montreal	70	36	48	84	65
Richard, Henri	Montreal	67	28	52	80	56
Bathgate, Andy	New York	65	30	48	78	42
Howe, Gordie	Detroit	64	33	44	77	40
Horvath, Bronco	Boston	67	30	36	66	71
Litzenberger, Ed	Chicago	70	32	30	62	63
Mackell, Fleming	Boston	70	20	40	60	72
Beliveau, Jean	Montreal	55	27	32	59	93
Delvecchio, Alex	Detroit	70	21	38	59	22
McKenney, Don	Boston	70	28	30	58	22

1958-59

Team	GP	W	L	T	GF	GA	PTS
*Montreal	70	39	18	13	258	158	91
Boston	70	32	29	9	205	215	73
Chicago	70	28	29	13	197	208	69
Toronto	70	27	32	11	189	201	65
New York	70	26	32	12	201	217	64
Detroit	70	25	37	8	167	218	58

Leading Scorers

Player	Club	GP	G	A	PTS	PIM
Moore, Dickie	Montreal	70	41	55	96	61
Beliveau, Jean	Montreal	64	45	46	91	67
Bathgate, Andy	New York	70	40	48	88	48
Howe, Gordie	Detroit	70	32	46	78	57
Litzenberger, Ed	Chicago	70	33	44	77	37
Geoffrion, Bernie	Montreal	59	22	44	66	30
Sullivan, George	New York	70	21	42	63	56
Hebenton, Andy	New York	70	33	29	62	8
McKenney, Don	Boston	70	32	30	62	20
Sloan, Tod	Chicago	59	27	35	62	79

1959-60

Team	GP	W	L	T	GF	GA	PTS
*Montreal	70	40	18	12	255	178	92
Toronto	70	35	26	9	199	195	79
Chicago	70	28	29	13	191	180	69
Detroit	70	26	29	15	186	197	67
Boston	70	28	34	8	220	241	64
New York	70	17	38	15	187	247	49

Leading Scorers

Player	Club	GP	G	A	PTS	PIM
Hull, Bobby	Chicago	70	39	42	81	68
Horvath, Bronco	Boston	68	39	41	80	60
Beliveau, Jean	Montreal	60	34	40	74	57
Bathgate, Andy	New York	70	26	48	74	28
Richard, Henri	Montreal	70	30	43	73	66
Howe, Gordie	Detroit	70	28	45	73	46
Geoffrion, Bernie	Montreal	59	30	41	71	36
McKenney, Don	Boston	70	20	49	69	28
Stasiuk, Vic	Boston	69	29	39	68	121
Prentice, Dean	New York	70	32	34	66	43

1960-61

Team	GP	W	L	T	GF	GA	PTS
Montreal	70	41	19	10	254	188	92
Toronto	70	39	19	12	234	176	90
*Chicago	70	29	24	17	198	180	75
Detroit	70	25	29	16	195	215	66
New York	70	22	38	10	204	248	54
Boston	70	15	42	13	176	254	43

Leading Scorers

Player	Club	GP	G	A	PTS	PIM
Geoffrion, Bernie	Montreal	64	50	45	95	29
Beliveau, Jean	Montreal	69	32	58	90	57
Mahovlich, Frank	Toronto	70	48	36	84	131
Bathgate, Andy	New York	70	29	48	77	22
Howe, Gordie	Detroit	64	23	49	72	30
Ullman, Norm	Detroit	70	28	42	70	34
Kelly, Red	Toronto	64	20	50	70	12
Moore, Dickie	Montreal	57	35	34	69	62
Richard, Henri	Montreal	70	24	44	68	91
Delvecchio, Alex	Detroit	70	27	35	62	26

1961-62

Team	GP	W	L	T	GF	GA	PTS
Montreal	70	42	14	14	259	166	98
*Toronto	70	37	22	11	232	180	85
Chicago	70	31	26	13	217	186	75
New York	70	26	32	12	195	207	64
Detroit	70	23	33	14	184	219	60
Boston	70	15	47	8	177	306	38

Leading Scorers

Player	Club	GP	G	A	PTS	PIM
Hull, Bobby	Chicago	70	50	34	84	35
Bathgate, Andy	New York	70	28	56	84	44
Howe, Gordie	Detroit	70	33	44	77	54
Mikita, Stan	Chicago	70	25	52	77	97
Mahovlich, Frank	Toronto	70	33	38	71	87
Delvecchio, Alex	Detroit	70	26	43	69	18
Backstrom, Ralph	Montreal	66	27	38	65	29
Ullman, Norm	Detroit	70	26	38	64	54
Hay, Bill	Chicago	60	11	52	63	34
Provost, Claude	Montreal	70	33	29	62	22

1962-63

Team	GP	W	L	T	GF	GA	PTS
*Toronto	70	35	23	12	221	180	82
Chicago	70	32	21	17	194	178	81
Montreal	70	28	19	23	225	183	79
Detroit	70	32	25	13	200	194	77
New York	70	22	36	12	211	233	56
Boston	70	14	39	17	198	281	45

Leading Scorers

Player	Club	GP	G	A	PTS	PIM
Howe, Gordie	Detroit	70	38	48	86	100
Bathgate, Andy	New York	70	35	46	81	54
Mikita, Stan	Chicago	65	31	45	76	69
Mahovlich, Frank	Toronto	67	36	37	73	56
Richard, Henri	Montreal	67	23	50	73	57
Beliveau, Jean	Montreal	69	18	49	67	68
Bucyk, John	Boston	69	27	39	66	36
Delvecchio, Alex	Detroit	70	20	44	64	8
Hull, Bobby	Chicago	65	31	31	62	27
Oliver, Murray	Boston	65	22	40	62	38

1963-64

Team	GP	W	L	T	GF	GA	PTS
Montreal	70	36	21	13	209	167	85
Chicago	70	36	22	12	218	169	84
*Toronto	70	33	25	12	192	172	78
Detroit	70	30	29	11	191	204	71
New York	70	22	38	10	186	242	54
Boston	70	18	40	12	170	212	48

Leading Scorers

Player	Club	GP	G	A	PTS	PIM
Mikita, Stan	Chicago	70	39	50	89	146
Hull, Bobby	Chicago	70	43	44	87	50
Beliveau, Jean	Montreal	68	28	50	78	42
Bathgate, Andy	NYR, Tor.	71	19	58	77	34
Howe, Gordie	Detroit	69	26	47	73	70
Wharram, Ken	Chicago	70	39	32	71	18
Oliver, Murray	Boston	70	24	44	68	41
Goyette, Phil	New York	67	24	41	65	15
Gilbert, Rod	New York	70	24	40	64	62
Keon, Dave	Toronto	70	23	37	60	6

1964-65

Team	GP	W	L	T	GF	GA	PTS
Detroit	70	40	23	7	224	175	87
*Montreal	70	36	23	11	211	185	83
Chicago	70	34	28	8	224	176	76
Toronto	70	30	26	14	204	173	74
New York	70	20	38	12	179	246	52
Boston	70	21	43	6	166	253	48

Leading Scorers

Player	Club	GP	G	A	PTS	PIM
Mikita, Stan	Chicago	70	28	59	87	154
Ullman, Norm	Detroit	70	42	41	83	70
Howe, Gordie	Detroit	70	29	47	76	104
Hull, Bobby	Chicago	61	39	32	71	32
Delvecchio, Alex	Detroit	68	25	42	67	16
Provost, Claude	Montreal	70	27	37	64	28
Gilbert, Rod	New York	70	25	36	61	52
Pilote, Pierre	Chicago	68	14	45	59	162
Bucyk, John	Boston	68	26	29	55	24
Backstrom, Ralph	Montreal	70	25	30	55	41
Esposito, Phil	Chicago	70	23	32	55	44

1965-66

Team	GP	W	L	T	GF	GA	PTS
*Montreal	70	41	21	8	239	173	90
Chicago	70	37	25	8	240	187	82
Toronto	70	34	25	11	208	187	79
Detroit	70	31	27	12	221	194	74
Boston	70	21	43	6	174	275	48
New York	70	18	41	11	195	261	47

Leading Scorers

Player	Club	GP	G	A	PTS	PIM
Hull, Bobby	Chicago	65	54	43	97	70
Mikita, Stan	Chicago	68	30	48	78	58
Rousseau, Bobby	Montreal	70	30	48	78	20
Beliveau, Jean	Montreal	67	29	48	77	50
Howe, Gordie	Detroit	70	29	46	75	83
Ullman, Norm	Detroit	70	31	41	72	35
Delvecchio, Alex	Detroit	70	31	38	69	16
Nevin, Bob	New York	69	29	33	62	10
Richard, Henri	Montreal	62	22	39	61	47
Oliver, Murray	Boston	70	18	42	60	30

1966-67

Team	GP	W	L	T	GF	GA	PTS
Chicago	70	41	17	12	264	170	94
Montreal	70	32	25	13	202	188	77
*Toronto	70	32	27	11	204	211	75
New York	70	30	28	12	188	189	72
Detroit	70	27	39	4	212	241	58
Boston	70	17	43	10	182	253	44

Leading Scorers

Player	Club	GP	G	A	PTS	PIM
Mikita, Stan	Chicago	70	35	62	97	12
Hull, Bobby	Chicago	66	52	28	80	52
Ullman, Norm	Detroit	68	26	44	70	26
Wharram, Ken	Chicago	70	31	34	65	21
Howe, Gordie	Detroit	69	25	40	65	53
Rousseau, Bobby	Montreal	68	19	44	63	58
Esposito, Phil	Chicago	69	21	40	61	40
Goyette, Phil	New York	70	12	49	61	6
Mohns, Doug	Chicago	61	25	35	60	58
Richard, Henri	Montreal	65	21	34	55	28
Delvecchio, Alex	Detroit	70	17	38	55	10

1967-68

East Division

Team	GP	W	L	T	GF	GA	PTS
*Montreal	74	42	22	10	236	167	94
New York	74	39	23	12	226	183	90
Boston	74	37	27	10	259	216	84
Chicago	74	32	26	16	212	222	80
Toronto	74	33	31	10	209	176	76
Detroit	74	27	35	12	245	257	66

West Division

Team	GP	W	L	T	GF	GA	PTS
Philadelphia	74	31	32	11	173	179	73
Los Angeles	74	31	33	10	200	224	72
St. Louis	74	27	31	16	177	191	70
Minnesota	74	27	32	15	191	226	69
Pittsburgh	74	27	34	13	195	216	67
Oakland	74	15	42	17	153	219	47

Leading Scorers

Player	Club	GP	G	A	PTS	PIM
Mikita, Stan	Chicago	72	40	47	87	14
Esposito, Phil	Boston	74	35	49	84	21
Howe, Gordie	Detroit	74	39	43	82	53
Ratelle, Jean	New York	74	32	46	78	18
Gilbert, Rod	New York	73	29	48	77	12
Hull, Bobby	Chicago	71	44	31	75	39
Ullman, Norm	Det., Tor.	71	35	37	72	28
Delvecchio, Alex	Detroit	74	22	48	70	14
Bucyk, John	Boston	72	30	39	69	8
Wharram, Ken	Chicago	74	27	42	69	18

1968-69

East Division

Team	GP	W	L	T	GF	GA	PTS
*Montreal	76	46	19	11	271	202	103
Boston	76	42	18	16	303	221	100
New York	76	41	26	9	231	196	91
Toronto	76	35	26	15	234	217	85
Detroit	76	33	31	12	239	221	78
Chicago	76	34	33	9	280	246	77

West Division

Team	GP	W	L	T	GF	GA	PTS
St. Louis	76	37	25	14	204	157	88
Oakland	76	29	36	11	219	251	69
Philadelphia	76	20	35	21	174	225	61
Los Angeles	76	24	42	10	185	260	58
Pittsburgh	76	20	45	11	189	252	51
Minnesota	76	18	43	15	189	270	51

Leading Scorers

Player	Club	GP	G	A	PTS	PIM
Esposito, Phil	Boston	74	49	77	126	79
Hull, Bobby	Chicago	74	58	49	107	48
Howe, Gordie	Detroit	76	44	59	103	58
Mikita, Stan	Chicago	74	30	67	97	52
Hodge, Ken	Boston	75	45	45	90	75
Cournoyer, Yvan	Montreal	76	43	44	87	31
Delvecchio, Alex	Detroit	72	25	58	83	8
Berenson, Red	St. Louis	76	35	47	82	43
Beliveau, Jean	Montreal	69	33	49	82	55
Mahovlich, Frank	Detroit	76	49	29	78	38
Ratelle, Jean	New York	75	32	46	78	26

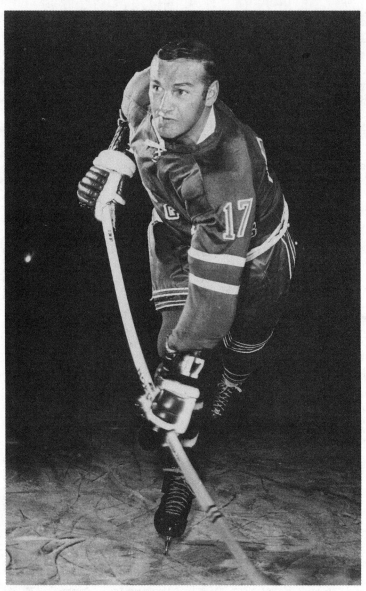

Dave Balon had the finest season of his career in 1969-70, registering 70 points for the New York Rangers, a 39 point improvement on his 1968-69 statistics.

Andy Bathgate (9) finished among the NHL's top ten scorers for nine straight seasons.

1969-70

East Division

Team	GP	W	L	T	GF	GA	PTS
Chicago	76	45	22	9	250	170	99
*Boston	76	40	17	19	277	216	99
Detroit	76	40	21	15	246	199	95
New York	76	38	22	16	246	189	92
Montreal	76	38	22	16	244	201	92
Toronto	76	29	34	13	222	242	71

West Division

Team	GP	W	L	T	GF	GA	PTS
St. Louis	76	37	27	12	224	179	86
Pittsburgh	76	26	38	12	182	238	64
Minnesota	76	19	35	22	224	257	60
Oakland	76	22	40	14	169	243	58
Philadelphia	76	17	35	24	197	225	58
Los Angeles	76	14	52	10	168	290	38

Leading Scorers

Player	Club	GP	G	A	PTS	PIM
Orr, Bobby	Boston	76	33	87	120	125
Esposito, Phil	Boston	76	43	56	99	50
Mikita, Stan	Chicago	76	39	47	86	50
Goyette, Phil	St. Louis	72	29	49	78	16
Tkaczuk, Walt	New York	76	27	50	77	38
Ratelle, Jean	New York	75	32	42	74	28
Berenson, Red	St. Louis	67	33	39	72	38
Parise, Jean-Paul	Minnesota	74	24	48	72	72
Howe, Gordie	Detroit	76	31	40	71	58
Mahovlich, Frank	Detroit	74	38	32	70	59
Balon, Dave	New York	76	33	37	70	100
McKenzie, John	Boston	72	29	41	70	114

1970-71

East Division

Team	GP	W	L	T	GF	GA	PTS
Boston	78	57	14	7	399	207	121
New York	78	49	18	11	259	177	109
*Montreal	78	42	23	13	291	216	97
Toronto	78	37	33	8	248	211	82
Buffalo	78	24	39	15	217	291	63
Vancouver	78	24	46	8	229	296	56
Detroit	78	22	45	11	209	308	55

West Division

Team	GP	W	L	T	GF	GA	PTS
Chicago	78	49	20	9	277	184	107
St. Louis	78	34	25	19	223	208	87
Philadelphia	78	28	33	17	207	225	73
Minnesota	78	28	34	16	191	223	72
Los Angeles	78	25	40	13	239	303	63
Pittsburgh	78	21	37	20	221	240	62
California	78	20	53	5	199	320	45

Leading Scorers

Player	Club	GP	G	A	PTS	PIM
Esposito, Phil	Boston	78	76	76	152	71
Orr, Bobby	Boston	78	37	102	139	91
Bucyk, John	Boston	78	51	65	116	8
Hodge, Ken	Boston	78	43	62	105	113
Hull, Bobby	Chicago	78	44	52	96	32
Ullman, Norm	Toronto	73	34	51	85	24
Cashman, Wayne	Boston	77	21	58	79	100
McKenzie, John	Boston	65	31	46	77	120
Keon, Dave	Toronto	76	38	38	76	4
Beliveau, Jean	Montreal	70	25	51	76	40
Stanfield, Fred	Boston	75	24	52	76	12

1971-72

East Division

Team	GP	W	L	T	GF	GA	PTS
*Boston	78	54	13	11	330	204	119
New York	78	48	17	13	317	192	109
Montreal	78	46	16	16	307	205	108
Toronto	78	33	31	14	209	208	80
Detroit	78	33	35	10	261	262	76
Buffalo	78	16	43	19	203	289	51
Vancouver	78	20	50	8	203	297	48

West Division

Team	GP	W	L	T	GF	GA	PTS
Chicago	78	46	17	15	256	166	107
Minnesota	78	37	29	12	212	191	86
St. Louis	78	28	39	11	208	247	67
Pittsburgh	78	26	38	14	220	258	66
Philadelphia	78	26	38	14	200	236	66
California	78	21	39	18	216	288	60
Los Angeles	78	20	49	9	206	305	49

Leading Scorers

Player	Club	GP	G	A	PTS	PIM
Esposito, Phil	Boston	76	66	67	133	76
Orr, Bobby	Boston	76	37	80	117	106
Ratelle, Jean	New York	63	46	63	109	4
Hadfield, Vic	New York	78	50	56	106	142
Gilbert, Rod	New York	73	43	54	97	64
Mahovlich, Frank	Montreal	76	43	53	96	36
Hull, Bobby	Chicago	78	50	43	93	24
Cournoyer, Yvan	Montreal	73	47	36	83	15
Bucyk, John	Boston	78	32	51	83	4
Clarke, Bobby	Philadelphia	78	35	46	81	87
Lemaire, Jacques	Montreal	77	32	49	81	26

1972-73

East Division

Team	GP	W	L	T	GF	GA	PTS
*Montreal	78	52	10	16	329	184	120
Boston	78	51	22	5	330	235	107
NY Rangers	78	47	23	8	297	208	102
Buffalo	78	37	27	14	257	219	88
Detroit	78	37	29	12	265	243	86
Toronto	78	27	41	10	247	279	64
Vancouver	78	22	47	9	233	339	53
NY Islanders	78	12	60	6	170	347	30

West Division

Team	GP	W	L	T	GF	GA	PTS
Chicago	78	42	27	9	284	225	93
Philadelphia	78	37	30	11	296	256	85
Minnesota	78	37	30	11	254	230	85
St. Louis	78	32	34	12	233	251	76
Pittsburgh	78	32	37	9	257	265	73
Los Angeles	78	31	36	11	232	245	73
Atlanta	78	25	38	15	191	239	65
California	78	16	46	16	213	323	48

Leading Scorers

Player	Club	GP	G	A	PTS	PIM
Esposito, Phil	Boston	78	55	75	130	87
Clarke, Bobby	Philadelphia	78	37	67	104	80
Orr, Bobby	Boston	63	29	72	101	99
MacLeish, Rick	Philadelphia	78	50	50	100	69
Lemaire, Jacques	Montreal	77	44	51	95	16
Ratelle, Jean	NY Rangers	78	41	53	94	12
Redmond, Mickey	Detroit	76	52	41	93	24
Bucyk, John	Boston	78	40	53	93	12
Mahovlich, Frank	Montreal	78	38	55	93	51
Pappin, Jim	Chicago	76	41	51	92	82

1973-74

East Division

Team	GP	W	L	T	GF	GA	PTS
Boston	78	52	17	9	349	221	113
Montreal	78	45	24	9	293	240	99
NY Rangers	78	40	24	14	300	251	94
Toronto	78	35	27	16	274	230	86
Buffalo	78	32	34	12	242	250	76
Detroit	78	29	39	10	255	319	68
Vancouver	78	24	43	11	224	296	59
NY Islanders	78	19	41	18	182	247	56

West Division

Team	GP	W	L	T	GF	GA	PTS
*Philadelphia	78	50	16	12	273	164	112
Chicago	78	41	14	23	272	164	105
Los Angeles	78	33	33	12	233	231	78
Atlanta	78	30	34	14	214	238	74
Pittsburgh	78	28	41	9	242	273	65
St. Louis	78	26	40	12	206	248	64
Minnesota	78	23	38	17	235	275	63
California	78	13	55	10	195	342	36

Leading Scorers

Player	Club	GP	G	A	PTS	PIM
Esposito, Phil	Boston	78	68	77	145	58
Orr, Bobby	Boston	74	32	90	122	82
Hodge, Ken	Boston	76	50	55	105	43
Cashman, Wayne	Boston	78	30	59	89	111
Clarke, Bobby	Philadelphia	77	35	52	87	113
Martin, Rick	Buffalo	78	52	34	86	38
Apps, Syl	Pittsburgh	75	24	61	85	37
Sittler, Darryl	Toronto	78	38	46	84	55
MacDonald, Lowell	Pittsburgh	78	43	39	82	14
Park, Brad	NY Rangers	78	25	57	82	148
Hextall, Dennis	Minnesota	78	20	62	82	138

1974-75

PRINCE OF WALES CONFERENCE

Norris Division

Team	GP	W	L	T	GF	GA	PTS
Montreal	80	47	14	19	374	225	113
Los Angeles	80	42	17	21	269	185	105
Pittsburgh	80	37	28	15	326	289	89
Detroit	80	23	45	12	259	335	58
Washington	80	8	67	5	181	446	21

Adams Division

Team	GP	W	L	T	GF	GA	PTS
Buffalo	80	49	16	15	354	240	113
Boston	80	40	26	14	345	245	94
Toronto	80	31	33	16	280	309	78
California	80	19	48	13	212	316	51

CLARENCE CAMPBELL CONFERENCE

Patrick Division

Team	GP	W	L	T	GF	GA	PTS
*Philadelphia	80	51	18	11	293	181	113
NY Rangers	80	37	29	14	319	276	88
NY Islanders	80	33	25	22	264	221	88
Atlanta	80	34	31	15	243	233	83

Smythe Division

Team	GP	W	L	T	GF	GA	PTS
Vancouver	80	38	32	10	271	254	86
St. Louis	80	35	31	14	269	267	84
Chicago	80	37	35	8	268	241	82
Minnesota	80	23	50	7	221	341	53
Kansas City	80	15	54	11	184	328	41

Leading Scorers

Player	Club	GP	G	A	PTS	PIM
Orr, Bobby	Boston	80	46	89	135	101
Esposito, Phil	Boston	79	61	66	127	62
Dionne, Marcel	Detroit	80	47	74	121	14
Lafleur, Guy	Montreal	70	53	66	119	37
Mahovlich, Pete	Montreal	80	35	82	117	64
Clarke, Bobby	Philadelphia	80	27	89	116	125
Robert, Rene	Buffalo	74	40	60	100	75
Gilbert, Rod	NY Rangers	76	36	61	97	22
Perreault, Gilbert	Buffalo	68	39	57	96	36
Martin, Rick	Buffalo	68	52	43	95	72

Bobby Orr became the first defenseman to win the scoring title in 1969-70.

1975-76

PRINCE OF WALES CONFERENCE

Norris Division

Team	GP	W	L	T	GF	GA	PTS
*Montreal	80	58	11	11	337	174	127
Los Angeles	80	38	33	9	263	265	85
Pittsburgh	80	35	33	12	339	303	82
Detroit	80	26	44	10	226	300	62
Washington	80	11	59	10	224	394	32

Adams Division

Boston	80	48	15	17	313	237	113
Buffalo	80	46	21	13	339	240	105
Toronto	80	34	31	15	294	276	83
California	80	27	42	11	250	278	65

CLARENCE CAMPBELL CONFERENCE

Patrick Division

Philadelphia	80	51	13	16	348	209	118
NY Islanders	80	42	21	17	297	190	101
Atlanta	80	35	33	12	262	237	82
NY Rangers	80	29	42	9	262	333	67

Smythe Division

Chicago	80	32	30	18	254	261	82
Vancouver	80	33	32	15	271	272	81
St. Louis	80	29	37	14	249	290	72
Minnesota	80	20	53	7	195	303	47
Kansas City	80	12	56	12	190	351	36

Leading Scorers

Player	Club	GP	G	A	PTS	PIM
Lafleur, Guy	Montreal	80	56	69	125	36
Clarke, Bobby	Philadelphia	76	30	89	119	136
Perreault, Gilbert	Buffalo	80	44	69	113	36
Barber, Bill	Philadelphia	80	50	62	112	104
Larouche, Pierre	Pittsburgh	76	53	58	111	33
Ratelle, Jean	Bos., NYR	80	36	69	105	18
Mahovlich, Pete	Montreal	80	34	71	105	76
Pronovost, Jean	Pittsburgh	80	52	52	104	24
Sittler, Darryl	Toronto	79	41	59	100	90
Apps, Syl	Pittsburgh	80	32	67	99	24

1976-77

PRINCE OF WALES CONFERENCE

Norris Division

Team	GP	W	L	T	GF	GA	PTS
*Montreal	80	60	8	12	387	171	132
Los Angeles	80	34	31	15	271	241	83
Pittsburgh	80	34	33	13	240	252	81
Washington	80	24	42	14	221	307	62
Detroit	80	16	55	9	183	309	41

Adams Division

Boston	80	49	23	8	312	240	106
Buffalo	80	48	24	8	301	220	104
Toronto	80	33	32	15	301	285	81
Cleveland	80	25	42	13	240	292	63

CLARENCE CAMPBELL CONFERENCE

Patrick Division

Philadelphia	80	48	16	16	323	213	112
NY Islanders	80	47	21	12	288	193	106
Atlanta	80	34	34	12	264	265	80
NY Rangers	88	29	37	14	272	310	72

Smythe Division

St. Louis	80	32	39	9	239	276	73
Minnesota	80	23	39	18	240	310	64
Chicago	80	26	43	11	240	298	63
Vancouver	80	25	42	13	235	294	63
Colorado	80	20	46	14	226	307	54

Leading Scorers

Player	Club	GP	G	A	PTS	PIM
Lafleur, Guy	Montreal	80	56	80	136	20
Dionne, Marcel	Los Angeles	80	53	69	122	12
Shutt, Steve	Montreal	80	60	45	105	28
MacLeish, Rick	Philadelphia	79	49	48	97	42
Perreault, Gilbert	Buffalo	80	39	56	95	30
Young, Tim	Minnesota	80	29	66	95	58
Ratelle, Jean	Boston	78	33	61	94	22
McDonald, Lanny	Toronto	80	46	44	90	77
Sittler, Darryl	Toronto	73	38	52	90	89
Clarke, Bobby	Philadelphia	80	27	63	90	71

1977-78

PRINCE OF WALES CONFERENCE

Norris Division

Team	GP	W	L	T	GF	GA	PTS
*Montreal	80	59	10	11	359	183	129
Detroit	80	32	34	14	252	266	78
Los Angeles	80	31	34	15	243	245	77
Pittsburgh	80	25	37	18	254	321	68
Washington	80	17	49	14	195	321	48

Adams Division

Boston	80	51	18	11	333	218	113
Buffalo	80	44	19	17	288	215	105
Toronto	80	41	29	10	271	237	92
Cleveland	80	22	45	13	230	325	57

CLARENCE CAMPBELL CONFERENCE

Patrick Division

NY Islanders	80	48	17	15	334	210	111
Philadelphia	80	45	20	15	296	200	105
Atlanta	80	34	27	19	274	252	87
NY Rangers	80	30	37	13	279	280	73

Smythe Division

Chicago	80	32	29	19	230	220	83
Colorado	80	19	40	21	257	305	59
Vancouver	80	20	43	17	239	320	57
St. Louis	80	20	47	13	195	304	53
Minnesota	80	18	53	9	218	325	45

Leading Scorers

Player	Club	GP	G	A	PTS	PIM
Lafleur, Guy	Montreal	79	60	72	132	26
Trottier, Bryan	NY Islanders	77	46	77	123	46
Sittler, Darryl	Toronto	80	45	72	117	100
Lemaire, Jacques	Montreal	76	36	61	97	14
Potvin, Denis	NY Islanders	80	30	64	94	81
Bossy, Mike	NY Islanders	73	53	38	91	6
O'Reilly, Terry	Boston	77	29	61	90	211
Perreault, Gilbert	Buffalo	79	41	48	89	20
Clarke, Bobby	Philadelphia	71	21	68	89	83
McDonald, Lanny	Toronto	74	47	40	87	54
Paiement, Wilf	Colorado	80	31	56	87	114

1978-79

PRINCE OF WALES CONFERENCE

Norris Division

Team	GP	W	L	T	GF	GA	PTS
*Montreal	80	52	17	11	337	204	115
Pittsburgh	80	36	31	13	281	279	85
Los Angeles	80	34	34	12	292	286	80
Washington	80	24	41	15	273	338	63
Detroit	80	23	41	16	252	295	62

Adams Division

Boston	80	43	23	14	316	270	100
Buffalo	80	36	28	16	280	263	88
Toronto	80	34	33	13	267	252	81
Minnesota	80	28	40	12	257	289	68

CLARENCE CAMPBELL CONFERENCE

Patrick Division

NY Islanders	80	51	15	14	358	214	116
Philadelphia	80	40	25	15	281	248	95
NY Rangers	80	40	29	11	316	292	91
Atlanta	80	41	31	8	327	280	90

Smythe Division

Chicago	80	29	36	15	244	277	73
Vancouver	80	25	42	13	217	291	63
St. Louis	80	18	50	12	249	348	48
Colorado	80	15	53	12	210	331	42

Leading Scorers

Player	Club	GP	G	A	PTS	PIM
Trottier, Bryan	NY Islanders	76	47	87	134	50
Dionne, Marcel	Los Angeles	80	59	71	130	30
Lafleur, Guy	Montreal	80	52	77	129	28
Bossy, Mike	NY Islanders	80	69	57	126	25
MacMillan, Bob	Atlanta	79	37	71	108	14
Chouinard, Guy	Atlanta	80	50	57	107	14
Potvin, Denis	NY Islanders	73	31	70	101	58
Federko, Bernie	St. Louis	74	31	64	95	14
Taylor, Dave	Los Angeles	78	43	48	91	124
Gillies, Clark	NY Islanders	75	35	56	91	68

Dealt to the Bruins in 1975, Jean Ratelle became the first player to be traded in mid-season and finish among the league's top ten scorers since Norm Ullman in 1967-68.

1979-80

PRINCE OF WALES CONFERENCE

Norris Division

Team	GP	W	L	T	GF	GA	PTS
Montreal	80	47	20	13	328	240	107
Los Angeles	80	30	36	14	290	313	74
Pittsburgh	80	30	37	13	251	303	73
Hartford	80	27	34	19	303	312	73
Detroit	80	26	43	11	268	306	63

Adams Division

Team	GP	W	L	T	GF	GA	PTS
Buffalo	80	47	17	16	318	201	110
Boston	80	46	21	13	310	234	105
Minnesota	80	36	28	16	311	253	88
Toronto	80	35	40	5	304	327	75
Quebec	80	25	44	11	248	313	61

CLARENCE CAMPBELL CONFERENCE

Patrick Division

Team	GP	W	L	T	GF	GA	PTS
Philadelphia	80	48	12	20	327	254	116
*NY Islanders	80	39	28	13	281	247	91
NY Rangers	80	38	32	10	308	284	86
Atlanta	80	35	32	13	282	269	83
Washington	80	27	40	13	261	293	67

Smythe Division

Team	GP	W	L	T	GF	GA	PTS
Chicago	80	34	27	19	241	250	87
St. Louis	80	34	34	12	266	278	80
Vancouver	80	27	37	16	256	281	70
Edmonton	80	28	39	13	301	322	69
Winnipeg	80	20	49	11	214	314	51
Colorado	80	19	48	13	234	308	51

Leading Scorers

Player	Club	GP	G	A	PTS	PIM
Dionne, Marcel	Los Angeles	80	53	84	137	32
Gretzky, Wayne	Edmonton	79	51	86	137	21
Lafleur, Guy	Montreal	74	50	75	125	12
Perreault, Gilbert	Buffalo	80	40	66	106	57
Rogers, Mike	Hartford	80	44	61	105	10
Trottier, Bryan	NY Islanders	78	42	62	104	68
Simmer, Charlie	Los Angeles	64	56	45	101	65
Stoughton, Blaine	Hartford	80	56	44	100	16
Sittler, Darryl	Toronto	73	40	57	97	62
MacDonald, Blair	Edmonton	80	46	48	94	6
Federko, Bernie	St. Louis	79	38	56	94	24

1980-81

PRINCE OF WALES CONFERENCE

Norris Division

Team	GP	W	L	T	GF	GA	PTS
Montreal	80	45	22	13	332	232	103
Los Angeles	80	43	24	13	337	290	99
Pittsburgh	80	30	37	13	302	345	73
Hartford	80	21	41	18	292	372	60
Detroit	80	19	43	18	252	339	56

Adams Division

Team	GP	W	L	T	GF	GA	PTS
Buffalo	80	39	20	21	327	250	99
Boston	80	37	30	13	316	272	87
Minnesota	80	35	28	17	291	263	87
Quebec	80	30	32	18	314	318	78
Toronto	80	28	37	15	322	367	71

CLARENCE CAMPBELL CONFERENCE

Patrick Division

Team	GP	W	L	T	GF	GA	PTS
*NY Islanders	80	48	18	14	355	260	110
Philadelphia	80	41	24	15	313	249	97
Calgary	80	39	27	14	329	298	92
NY Rangers	80	30	36	14	312	317	74
Washington	80	26	36	18	286	317	70

Smythe Division

Team	GP	W	L	T	GF	GA	PTS
St. Louis	80	45	18	17	352	281	107
Chicago	80	31	33	16	304	315	78
Vancouver	80	28	32	20	289	301	76
Edmonton	80	29	35	16	328	327	74
Colorado	80	22	45	13	258	344	57
Winnipeg	80	9	57	14	246	400	32

Leading Scorers

Player	Club	GP	G	A	PTS	PIM
Gretzky, Wayne	Edmonton	80	55	109	164	28
Dionne, Marcel	Los Angeles	80	58	77	135	70
Nilsson, Kent	Calgary	80	49	82	131	26
Bossy, Mike	NY Islanders	79	68	51	119	32
Taylor, Dave	Los Angeles	72	47	65	112	130
Stastny, Peter	Quebec	77	39	70	109	37
Simmer, Charlie	Los Angeles	65	56	49	105	62
Rogers, Mike	Hartford	80	40	65	105	32
Federko, Bernie	St. Louis	78	31	73	104	47
Richard, Jacques	Quebec	78	52	51	103	39
Middleton, Rick	Boston	80	44	59	103	16
Trottier, Bryan	NY Islanders	73	31	72	103	74

Mike Bossy became the first NHL player to score 50 goals in his rookie season, firing 53 in 1977-78.

1981-82

CLARENCE CAMPBELL CONFERENCE

Norris Division

Team	GP	W	L	T	GF	GA	PTS
Minnesota	80	37	23	20	346	288	94
Winnipeg	80	33	33	14	319	332	80
St. Louis	80	32	40	8	315	349	72
Chicago	80	30	38	12	332	363	72
Toronto	80	20	44	16	298	380	56
Detroit	80	21	47	12	270	351	54

Smythe Division

Team	GP	W	L	T	GF	GA	PTS
Edmonton	80	48	17	15	417	295	111
Vancouver	80	30	33	17	290	286	77
Calgary	80	29	34	17	334	345	75
Los Angeles	80	24	41	15	314	369	63
Colorado	80	18	49	13	241	362	49

PRINCE OF WALES CONFERENCE

Adams Division

Team	GP	W	L	T	GF	GA	PTS
Montreal	80	46	17	17	360	223	109
Boston	80	43	27	10	323	285	96
Buffalo	80	39	26	15	307	273	93
Quebec	80	33	31	16	356	345	82
Hartford	80	21	41	18	264	351	60

Patrick Division

Team	GP	W	L	T	GF	GA	PTS
*NY Islanders	80	54	16	10	385	250	118
NY Rangers	80	39	27	14	316	306	92
Philadelphia	80	38	31	11	325	313	87
Pittsburgh	80	31	36	13	310	337	75
Washington	80	26	41	13	319	338	65

Leading Scorers

Player	Club	GP	G	A	PTS	PIM
Gretzky, Wayne	Edmonton	80	92	120	212	26
Bossy, Mike	NY Islanders	80	64	83	147	22
Stastny, Peter	Quebec	80	46	93	139	91
Maruk, Dennis	Washington	80	60	76	136	128
Trottier, Bryan	NY Islanders	80	50	79	129	88
Savard, Denis	Chicago	80	32	87	119	82
Dionne, Marcel	Los Angeles	78	50	67	117	50
Smith, Bobby	Minnesota	80	43	71	114	82
Ciccarelli, Dino	Minnesota	76	55	51	106	138
Taylor, Dave	Los Angeles	78	39	67	106	130

1982-83

CLARENCE CAMPBELL CONFERENCE

Norris Division

Team	GP	W	L	T	GF	GA	PTS
Chicago	80	47	23	10	338	268	104
Minnesota	80	40	24	16	321	290	96
Toronto	80	28	40	12	293	330	68
St. Louis	80	25	40	15	285	316	65
Detroit	80	21	44	15	263	344	57

Smythe Division

Team	GP	W	L	T	GF	GA	PTS
Edmonton	80	47	21	12	424	315	106
Calgary	80	32	34	14	321	317	78
Vancouver	80	30	35	15	303	309	75
Winnipeg	80	33	39	8	311	333	74
Los Angeles	80	27	41	12	308	365	66

PRINCE OF WALES CONFERENCE

Adams Division

Team	GP	W	L	T	GF	GA	PTS
Boston	80	50	20	10	327	228	110
Montreal	80	42	24	14	350	286	98
Buffalo	80	38	29	13	318	285	89
Quebec	80	34	34	12	343	336	80
Hartford	80	19	54	7	261	403	45

Patrick Division

Team	GP	W	L	T	GF	GA	PTS
Philadelphia	80	49	23	8	326	240	106
*NY Islanders	80	42	26	12	302	226	96
Washington	80	39	25	16	306	283	94
NY Rangers	80	35	35	10	306	287	80
New Jersey	80	17	49	14	230	338	48
Pittsburgh	80	18	53	9	257	394	45

Leading Scorers

Player	Club	GP	G	A	PTS	PIM
Gretzky, Wayne	Edmonton	80	71	125	196	59
Stastny, Peter	Quebec	75	47	77	124	78
Savard, Denis	Chicago	78	35	86	121	99
Bossy, Mike	NY Islanders	79	60	58	118	20
Dionne, Marcel	Los Angeles	80	56	51	107	22
Pederson, Barry	Boston	77	46	61	107	47
Messier, Mark	Edmonton	77	48	58	106	72
Goulet, Michel	Quebec	80	57	48	105	51
Anderson, Glenn	Edmonton	72	48	56	104	70
Nilsson, Kent	Calgary	80	46	58	104	10
Kurri, Jari	Edmonton	80	45	59	104	22

Mike Rogers had three consecutive 100-point seasons from 1979-80 to 1981-82.

1985-86
CLARENCE CAMPBELL CONFERENCE
Norris Division

Team	GP	W	L	T	GF	GA	PTS
Chicago	80	39	33	8	351	349	86
Minnesota	80	38	33	9	327	305	85
St. Louis	80	37	34	9	302	291	83
Toronto	80	25	48	7	311	386	57
Detroit	80	17	57	6	266	415	40

Smythe Division

Team	GP	W	L	T	GF	GA	PTS
Edmonton	80	56	17	7	426	310	119
Calgary	80	40	31	9	354	315	89
Winnipeg	80	26	47	7	295	372	59
Vancouver	80	23	44	13	282	333	59
Los Angeles	80	23	49	8	284	389	54

PRINCE OF WALES CONFERENCE
Adams Division

Team	GP	W	L	T	GF	GA	PTS
Quebec	80	43	31	6	330	289	92
*Montreal	80	40	33	7	330	280	87
Boston	80	37	31	12	311	288	86
Hartford	80	40	36	4	332	302	84
Buffalo	80	37	37	6	296	291	80

Patrick Division

Team	GP	W	L	T	GF	GA	PTS
Philadelphia	80	53	23	4	335	241	110
Washington	80	50	23	7	315	272	107
NY Islanders	80	39	29	12	327	284	90
NY Rangers	80	36	38	6	280	276	78
Pittsburgh	80	34	38	8	313	305	76
New Jersey	80	28	49	3	300	374	59

Leading Scorers

Player	Club	GP	G	A	PTS	PIM
Gretzky, Wayne	Edmonton	80	52	163	215	52
Lemieux, Mario	Pittsburgh	79	48	93	141	43
Coffey, Paul	Edmonton	79	48	90	138	120
Kurri, Jari	Edmonton	78	68	63	131	22
Bossy, Mike	NY Islanders	80	61	62	123	14
Stastny, Peter	Quebec	76	41	81	122	60
Savard, Denis	Chicago	80	47	69	116	111
Naslund, Mats	Montreal	80	43	67	110	16
Hawerchuk, Dale	Winnipeg	80	46	59	105	44
Broten, Neal	Minnesota	80	29	76	105	47

1986-87
CLARENCE CAMPBELL CONFERENCE
Norris Division

Team	GP	W	L	T	GF	GA	PTS
St. Louis	80	32	33	15	281	293	79
Detroit	80	34	36	10	260	274	78
Chicago	80	29	37	14	290	310	72
Toronto	80	32	42	6	286	319	70
Minnesota	80	30	40	10	296	314	70

Smythe Division

Team	GP	W	L	T	GF	GA	PTS
*Edmonton	80	50	24	6	372	284	106
Calgary	80	46	31	3	318	289	95
Winnipeg	80	40	32	8	279	271	88
Los Angeles	80	31	41	8	318	341	70
Vancouver	80	29	43	8	282	314	66

PRINCE OF WALES CONFERENCE
Adams Division

Team	GP	W	L	T	GF	GA	PTS
Hartford	80	43	30	7	287	270	93
Montreal	80	41	29	10	277	241	92
Boston	80	39	34	7	301	276	85
Quebec	80	31	39	10	267	276	72
Buffalo	80	28	44	8	280	308	64

Patrick Division

Team	GP	W	L	T	GF	GA	PTS
Philadelphia	80	46	26	8	310	245	100
Washington	80	38	32	10	285	278	86
NY Islanders	80	35	33	12	279	281	82
NY Rangers	80	34	38	8	307	323	76
Pittsburg	80	30	38	12	297	290	72
New Jersey	80	29	45	6	293	368	64

Leading Scorers

Player	Club	GP	G	A	PTS	PIM
Gretzky, Wayne	Edmonton	79	62	121	183	28
Kurri, Jari	Edmonton	79	54	54	108	41
Lemieux, Mario	Pittsburgh	63	54	53	107	57
Messier, Mark	Edmonton	77	37	70	107	73
Gilmour, Doug	St. Louis	80	42	63	105	58
Ciccarelli, Dino	Minnesota	80	52	51	103	92
Hawerchuk, Dale	Winnipeg	80	47	53	100	54
Goulet, Michel	Quebec	75	49	47	96	61
Kerr, Tim	Philadelphia	75	58	37	95	57
Bourque, Ray	Boston	78	23	72	95	36

1983-84
CLARENCE CAMPBELL CONFERENCE
Norris Division

Team	GP	W	L	T	GF	GA	PTS
Minnesota	80	39	31	10	345	344	88
St. Louis	80	32	41	7	293	316	71
Detroit	80	31	42	7	298	323	69
Chicago	80	30	42	8	277	311	68
Toronto	80	26	45	9	303	387	61

Smythe Division

Team	GP	W	L	T	GF	GA	PTS
*Edmonton	80	57	18	5	446	314	119
Calgary	80	34	32	14	311	314	82
Vancouver	80	32	39	9	306	328	73
Winnipeg	80	31	38	11	340	374	73
Los Angeles	80	23	44	13	309	376	59

PRINCE OF WALES CONFERENCE
Adams Division

Team	GP	W	L	T	GF	GA	PTS
Boston	80	49	25	6	336	261	104
Buffalo	80	48	25	7	315	257	103
Quebec	80	42	28	10	360	278	94
Montreal	80	35	40	5	286	295	75
Hartford	80	28	42	10	288	320	66

Patrick Division

Team	GP	W	L	T	GF	GA	PTS
NY Islanders	80	50	26	4	357	269	104
Washington	80	48	27	5	308	226	101
Philadelphia	80	44	26	10	350	290	98
NY Rangers	80	42	29	9	314	304	93
New Jersey	80	17	56	7	231	350	41
Pittsburgh	80	16	58	6	254	390	38

Leading Scorers

Player	Club	GP	G	A	PTS	PIM
Gretzky, Wayne	Edmonton	74	87	118	205	39
Coffey, Paul	Edmonton	80	40	86	126	104
Goulet, Michel	Quebec	75	56	65	121	76
Stastny, Peter	Quebec	80	46	73	119	73
Bossy, Mike	NY Islanders	67	51	67	118	8
Pederson, Barry	Boston	80	39	77	116	64
Kurri, Jari	Edmonton	64	52	61	113	14
Trottier, Bryan	NY Islanders	68	40	71	111	59
Federko, Bernie	St. Louis	79	41	66	107	43
Middleton, Rick	Boston	80	47	58	105	14

1984-85
CLARENCE CAMPBELL CONFERENCE
Norris Division

Team	GP	W	L	T	GF	GA	PTS
St. Louis	80	37	31	12	299	288	86
Chicago	80	38	35	7	309	299	83
Detroit	80	27	41	12	313	357	66
Minnesota	80	25	43	12	268	321	62
Toronto	80	20	52	8	253	358	48

Smythe Division

Team	GP	W	L	T	GF	GA	PTS
*Edmonton	80	49	20	11	401	298	109
Winnipeg	80	43	27	10	358	332	96
Calgary	80	41	27	12	363	302	94
Los Angeles	80	34	32	14	339	326	82
Vancouver	80	25	46	9	284	401	59

PRINCE OF WALES CONFERENCE
Adams Division

Team	GP	W	L	T	GF	GA	PTS
Montreal	80	41	27	12	309	262	94
Quebec	80	41	30	9	323	275	91
Buffalo	80	38	28	14	290	237	90
Boston	80	36	34	10	303	287	82
Hartford	80	30	41	9	268	318	69

Patrick Division

Team	GP	W	L	T	GF	GA	PTS
Philadelphia	80	53	20	7	348	241	113
Washington	80	46	25	9	322	240	101
NY Islanders	80	40	34	6	345	312	86
NY Rangers	80	26	44	10	295	345	62
New Jersey	80	22	48	10	264	346	54
Pittsburgh	80	24	51	5	276	385	53

Leading Scorers

Player	Club	GP	G	A	PTS	PIM
Gretzky, Wayne	Edmonton	80	73	135	208	52
Kurri, Jari	Edmonton	73	71	64	135	30
Hawerchuk, Dale	Winnipeg	80	53	77	130	74
Dionne, Marcel	Los Angeles	80	46	80	126	46
Coffey, Paul	Edmonton	80	37	84	121	97
Bossy, Mike	NY Islanders	76	58	59	117	38
Ogrodnick, John	Detroit	79	55	50	105	30
Savard, Denis	Chicago	79	38	67	105	56
Federko, Bernie	St. Louis	76	30	73	103	27
Gartner, Mike	Washington	80	50	52	102	7

1987-88

CLARENCE CAMPBELL CONFERENCE

Norris Division

Team	GP	W	L	T	GF	GA	PTS
Detroit	80	41	28	11	322	269	93
St. Louis	80	34	38	8	278	294	76
Chicago	80	30	41	9	284	326	69
Toronto	80	21	49	10	273	345	52
Minnesota	80	19	48	13	242	349	51

Smythe Division

	GP	W	L	T	GF	GA	PTS
Calgary	80	48	23	9	397	305	105
*Edmonton	80	44	25	11	363	288	99
Winnipeg	80	33	36	11	292	310	77
Los Angeles	80	30	42	8	318	359	68
Vancouver	80	25	46	9	272	320	59

PRINCE OF WALES CONFERENCE

Adams Division

	GP	W	L	T	GF	GA	PTS
Montreal	80	45	22	13	298	238	103
Boston	80	44	30	6	300	251	94
Buffalo	80	37	32	11	283	305	85
Hartford	80	35	38	7	249	267	77
Quebec	80	32	43	5	271	306	69

Patrick Division

	GP	W	L	T	GF	GA	PTS
NY Islanders	80	39	31	10	308	267	88
Washington	80	38	33	9	281	249	85
Philadelphia	80	38	33	9	292	282	85
New Jersey	80	38	36	6	295	296	82
NY Rangers	80	36	34	10	300	283	82
Pittsburgh	80	36	35	9	319	316	81

Leading Scorers

Player	Club	GP	G	A	PTS	PIM
Lemieux, Mario	Pittsburgh	76	70	98	168	92
Gretzky, Wayne	Edmonton	64	40	109	149	24
Savard, Denis	Chicago	80	44	87	131	95
Hawerchuk, Dale	Winnipeg	80	44	77	121	59
Robitaille, Luc	Los Angeles	80	53	58	111	82
Stastny, Peter	Quebec	76	46	65	111	69
Messier, Mark	Edmonton	77	37	74	111	103
Carson, Jimmy	Los Angeles	80	55	52	107	45
Loob, Hakan	Calgary	80	50	56	106	47
Goulet, Michel	Quebec	80	48	58	106	56

Joe Mullen had the finest season of his career in 1988-89, registering 51 goals and 59 assists.

1988-89

CLARENCE CAMPBELL CONFERENCE

Norris Division

Team	GP	W	L	T	GF	GA	PTS
Detroit	80	34	34	12	313	316	80
St. Louis	80	33	35	12	275	285	78
Minnesota	80	27	37	16	258	278	70
Chicago	80	27	41	12	297	335	66
Toronto	80	28	46	6	259	342	62

Smythe Division

	GP	W	L	T	GF	GA	PTS
*Calgary	80	54	17	9	354	226	117
Los Angeles	80	42	31	7	376	335	91
Edmonton	80	38	34	8	325	306	84
Vancouver	80	33	39	8	251	253	74
Winnipeg	80	26	42	12	300	355	64

PRINCE OF WALES CONFERENCE

Adams Division

	GP	W	L	T	GF	GA	PTS
Montreal	80	53	18	9	315	218	115
Boston	80	37	29	14	289	256	88
Buffalo	80	38	35	7	291	299	83
Hartford	80	37	38	5	299	290	79
Quebec	80	27	46	7	269	342	61

Patrick Division

	GP	W	L	T	GF	GA	PTS
Washington	80	41	29	10	305	259	92
Pittsburgh	80	40	33	7	347	349	87
NY Rangers	80	37	35	8	310	307	82
Philadelphia	80	36	36	8	307	285	80
New Jersey	80	27	41	12	281	325	66
NY Islanders	80	28	47	5	265	325	61

Leading Scorers

Player	Club	GP	G	A	PTS	PIM
Lemieux, Mario	Pittsburgh	76	85	114	199	100
Gretzky, Wayne	Los Angeles	78	54	114	168	26
Yzerman, Steve	Detroit	80	65	90	155	61
Nicholls, Bernie	Los Angeles	79	70	80	150	96
Brown, Rob	Pittsburgh	68	49	66	115	118
Coffey, Paul	Pittsburgh	75	30	83	113	193
Mullen, Joe	Calgary	79	51	59	110	16
Kurri, Jari	Edmonton	76	44	58	102	69
Carson, Jimmy	Edmonton	80	49	51	100	36
Robitaille, Luc	Los Angeles	78	46	52	98	65

1989-90

CLARENCE CAMPBELL CONFERENCE

Norris Division

Team	GP	W	L	T	GF	GA	PTS
Chicago	80	41	33	6	316	294	88
St. Louis	80	37	34	9	295	279	83
Toronto	80	38	38	4	337	358	80
Minnesota	80	36	40	4	284	291	76
Detroit	80	28	38	14	288	323	70

Smythe Division

	GP	W	L	T	GF	GA	PTS
Calgary	80	42	23	15	348	265	99
*Edmonton	80	38	28	14	315	283	90
Winnipeg	80	37	32	11	298	290	85
Los Angeles	80	34	39	7	338	337	75
Vancouver	80	25	41	14	245	306	64

PRINCE OF WALES CONFERENCE

Adams Division

	GP	W	L	T	GF	GA	PTS
Boston	80	46	25	9	289	232	101
Buffalo	80	45	27	8	286	248	98
Montreal	80	41	28	11	288	234	93
Hartford	80	38	33	9	275	268	85
Quebec	80	12	61	7	240	407	31

Patrick Division

	GP	W	L	T	GF	GA	PTS
NY Rangers	80	36	31	13	279	267	85
New Jersey	80	37	34	9	295	288	83
Washington	80	36	38	6	284	275	78
NY Islanders	80	31	38	11	281	288	73
Pittsburgh	80	32	40	8	318	359	72
Philadelphia	80	30	39	11	290	297	71

Leading Scorers

Player	Club	GP	G	A	PTS	PIM
Gretzky, Wayne	Los Angeles	73	40	102	142	42
Messier, Mark	Edmonton	79	45	84	129	79
Yzerman, Steve	Detroit	79	62	65	127	79
Lemieux, Mario	Pittsburgh	59	45	78	123	78
Hull, Brett	St. Louis	80	72	41	113	24
Nicholls, Bernie	L.A., NYR	79	39	73	112	86
Turgeon, Pierre	Buffalo	80	40	66	106	29
LaFontaine, Pat	NY Islanders	74	54	51	105	38
Coffey, Paul	Pittsburgh	80	29	74	103	95
Sakic, Joe	Quebec	80	39	63	102	27
Oates, Adam	St. Louis	80	23	79	102	30

1990-91

CLARENCE CAMPBELL CONFERENCE

Norris Division

Team	GP	W	L	T	GF	GA	PTS
Chicago	80	49	23	8	284	211	106
St. Louis	80	47	22	11	310	250	105
Detroit	80	34	38	8	273	298	76
Minnesota	80	27	39	14	256	266	68
Toronto	80	23	46	11	241	318	57

Smythe Division

	GP	W	L	T	GF	GA	PTS
Los Angeles	80	46	24	10	340	254	102
Calgary	80	46	26	8	344	263	100
Edmonton	80	37	37	6	272	272	80
Vancouver	80	28	43	9	243	315	65
Winnipeg	80	26	43	11	260	288	63

PRINCE OF WALES CONFERENCE

Adams Division

	GP	W	L	T	GF	GA	PTS
Boston	80	44	24	12	299	264	100
Montreal	80	39	30	11	273	249	89
Buffalo	80	31	30	19	292	278	81
Hartford	80	31	38	11	238	276	73
Quebec	80	16	50	14	236	354	46

Patrick Division

	GP	W	L	T	GF	GA	PTS
*Pittsburgh	80	41	33	6	342	305	88
NY Rangers	80	36	31	13	297	265	85
Washington	80	37	36	7	258	258	81
New Jersey	80	32	33	15	272	264	79
Philadelphia	80	33	37	10	252	267	76
NY Islanders	80	25	45	10	223	290	60

Leading Scorers

Player	Club	GP	G	A	PTS	PIM
Gretzky, Wayne	Los Angeles	78	41	122	163	16
Hull, Brett	St. Louis	78	86	45	131	22
Oates, Adam	St. Louis	61	25	90	115	29
Recchi, Mark	Pittsburgh	78	40	73	113	48
Cullen, John	Pit., Hfd.	78	39	71	110	101
Sakic, Joe	Quebec	80	48	61	109	24
Yzerman, Steve	Detroit	80	51	57	108	34
Fleury, Theo	Calgary	79	51	53	104	136
MacInnis, Al	Calgary	78	28	75	103	90
Larmer, Steve	Chicago	80	44	57	101	79

Note: Detailed statistics for 1991-92 are listed in the Final Statistics, 1991-92 section of the **NHL Guide & Record Book**.

NHL History

1917 — National Hockey League organized November 22 in Montreal following suspension of operations by the National Hockey Association of Canada Limited (NHA). Montreal Canadiens, Montreal Wanderers, Ottawa Senators and Quebec Bulldogs attended founding meeting. Delegates decided to use NHA rules.

Toronto Arenas were later admitted as fifth team; Quebec decided not to operate during the first season. Quebec players allocated to remaining four teams.

Frank Calder elected president and secretary-treasurer.

First NHL games played December 19, with Toronto only arena with artificial ice. Clubs played 22-game split schedule.

1918 — Emergency meeting held January 3 due to destruction by fire of Montreal Arena which was home ice for both Canadiens and Wanderers.

Wanderers withdrew, reducing the NHL to three teams; Canadiens played remaining home games at 3,250-seat Jubilee rink.

Quebec franchise sold to P.J. Quinn of Toronto on October 18 on the condition that the team operate in Quebec City for 1918-19 season. Quinn did not attend the November League meeting and Quebec did not play in 1918-19.

1919-20 — NHL reactivated Quebec Bulldogs franchise. Former Quebec players returned to the club. New Mount Royal Arena became home of Canadiens. Toronto Arenas changed name to St. Patricks. Clubs played 24-game split schedule.

1920-21 — H.P. Thompson of Hamilton, Ontario made application for the purchase of an NHL franchise. Quebec franchise shifted to Hamilton with other NHL teams providing players to strengthen the club.

1921-22 — Split schedule abandoned. First and second place teams at the end of full schedule to play for championship.

1922-23 — Clubs agreed that players could not be sold or traded to clubs in any other league without first being offered to all other clubs in the NHL. In March, Foster Hewitt broadcast radio's first hockey game.

1923-24 — Ottawa's new 10,000-seat arena opened. First U.S. franchise granted to Boston for following season.

Dr. Cecil Hart Trophy donated to NHL to be awarded to the player judged most useful to his team.

1924-25 — Canadian Arena Company of Montreal granted a franchise to operate Montreal Maroons. NHL now six team league with two clubs in Montreal. Inaugural game in new Montreal Forum played November 29, 1924 as Canadiens defeated Toronto 7-1. Forum was home rink for the Maroons, but no ice was available in the Canadiens arena November 29, resulting in shift to Forum.

Hamilton finished first in the standings, receiving a bye into the finals. But Hamilton players, demanding $200 each for additional games in the playoffs, went on strike. The NHL suspended all players, fining them $200 each. Stanley Cup finalist to be the winner of NHL semi-final between Toronto and Canadiens.

Prince of Wales and Lady Byng trophies donated to NHL.

Clubs played 30-game schedule.

1925-26 — Hamilton club dropped from NHL. Players signed by new New York Americans franchise. Franchise granted to Pittsburgh.

Clubs played 36-game schedule.

1926-27 — New York Rangers granted franchise May 15, 1926. Chicago Black Hawks and Detroit Cougars granted franchises September 25, 1926. NHL now ten-team league with an American and a Canadian Division.

Stanley Cup came under the control of NHL. In previous seasons, winners of the now-defunct Western or Pacific Coast leagues would play NHL champion in Cup finals.

Toronto franchise sold to a new company controlled by Hugh Aird and Conn Smythe. Name changed from St. Patricks to Maple Leafs.

Clubs played 44-game schedule.

The Montreal Canadiens donated the Vezina Trophy to be awarded to the team allowing the fewest goals-against in regular season play. The winning team would, in turn, present the trophy to the goaltender playing in the greatest number of games during the season.

1929-30 — Detroit franchise changed name from Cougars to Falcons.

1930-31 — Pittsburgh transferred to Philadelphia for one season. Pirates changed name to Philadelphia Quakers. Trading deadline for teams set at February 15 of each year. NHL approved operation of farm teams by Rangers, Americans, Falcons and Bruins. Four-sided electric arena clock first demonstrated.

1931-32 — Philadelphia dropped out. Ottawa withdrew for one season. New Maple Leaf Gardens completed.

Clubs played 48-game schedule

1932-33 — Detroit franchise changed name from Falcons to Red Wings. Franchise application received from St. Louis but refused because of additional travel costs. Ottawa team resumed play.

1933-34 — First All-Star game played as a benefit for injured player Ace Bailey. Stanley Cup champion Leafs defeated All-Stars 7-3 in Toronto.

1934-35 — Ottawa franchise transferred to St. Louis. Team called St. Louis Eagles and consisted largely of Ottawa's players.

1935-36 — Ottawa-St. Louis franchise terminated. Montreal Canadiens finished season with very poor record. To strengthen the club, NHL gave Canadiens first call on the services of all French-Canadian players for three seasons.

1937-38 — Second benefit all-star game staged November 2 in Montreal in aid of the family of the late Canadiens star Howie Morenz.

Montreal Maroons withdrew from the NHL on June 22, 1938, leaving seven clubs in the League.

1938-39 — Expenses for each club regulated at $5 per man per day for meals and $2.50 per man per day for accommodation.

1939-40 — Benefit All-Star Game played October 29, 1939 in Montreal for the children of the late Albert (Babe) Siebert.

1940-41 — Ross-Tyer puck adopted as the official puck of the NHL. Early in the season it was apparent that this puck was too soft. The Spalding puck was adopted in its place.

After the playoffs, Arthur Ross, NHL governor from Boston, donated a perpetual trophy to be awarded annually to the player voted outstanding in the league.

1941-42 — New York Americans changed name to Brooklyn Americans.

1942-43 — Brooklyn Americans withdrew from NHL, leaving six teams: Boston, Chicago, Detroit, Montreal, New York and Toronto. Playoff format saw first-place team play third-place team and second play fourth.

Clubs played 50-game schedule.

Frank Calder, president of the NHL since its inception, died in Montreal. Mervyn "Red" Dutton, former manager of the New York Americans, became president. The NHL commissioned the Calder Memorial Trophy to be awarded to the League's outstanding rookie each year.

1945-46 — Philadelphia, Los Angeles and San Francisco applied for NHL franchises.

The Philadelphia Arena Company of the American Hockey League applied for an injunction to prevent the possible operation of an NHL franchise in that city.

1946-47 — Mervyn Dutton retired as president of the NHL prior to the start of the season. He was succeeded by Clarence S. Campbell.

Individual trophy winners and all-star team members to receive $1,000 awards.

Playoff guarantees for players introduced.

Clubs played 60-game schedule.

1947-48 — The first annual All-Star Game for the benefit of the players' pension fund was played when the All-Stars defeated the Stanley Cup Champion Toronto Maple Leafs 4-3 in Toronto on October 13, 1947.

Ross Trophy, awarded to the NHL's outstanding player since 1941, to be awarded annually to the League's scoring leader.

Philadelphia and Los Angeles franchise applications refused.

National Hockey League Pension Society formed.

1949-50 — Clubs played 70-game schedule.

First intra-league draft held April 30, 1950. Clubs allowed to protect 30 players. Remaining players available for $25,000 each.

1951-52 — Referees included in the League's pension plan.

1952-53 — In May of 1952, City of Cleveland applied for NHL franchise. Application denied. In March of 1953, the Cleveland Barons of the AHL challenged the NHL champions for the Stanley Cup. The NHL governors did not accept this challenge.

1953-54 — The James Norris Memorial Trophy presented to the NHL for annual presentation to the League's best defenseman.

Intra-league draft rules amended to allow teams to protect 18 skaters and two goaltenders, claiming price reduced to $15,000.

1954-55 — Each arena to operate an "out-of-town" scoreboard. Referees and linesmen to wear shirts of black and white vertical stripes. Teams agree to wear white uniforms at home and colored uniforms on the road.

1956-57 — Standardized signals for referees and linesmen introduced.

The NHL's first All-Star Game was held on February 14, 1934 to raise money for injured Toronto defenseman Ace Bailey and his family. In this game, the Leafs played the All-Stars who utilized Howie Morenz, Jr. (seated in front) as team mascot.

1960-61 — Canadian National Exhibition, City of Toronto and NHL reach agreement for the construction of a Hockey Hall of Fame on the CNE grounds. Hall opens on August 26, 1961.

1963-64 — Player development league established with clubs operated by NHL franchises located in Minneapolis, St. Paul, Indianapolis, Omaha and, beginning in 1964-65, Tulsa. First universal amateur draft took place. All players of qualifying age (17) unaffected by sponsorship of junior teams available to be drafted.

1964-65 — Conn Smythe Trophy presented to the NHL to be awarded annually to the outstanding player in the Stanley Cup playoffs.
 Minimum age of players subject to amateur draft changed to 18.

1965-66 — NHL announced expansion plans for a second six-team division to begin play in 1967-68.

1966-67 — Fourteen applications for NHL franchises received.
 Lester Patrick Trophy presented to the NHL to be awarded annually for outstanding service to hockey in the United States.
 NHL sponsorship of junior teams ceased, making all players of qualifying age not already on NHL-sponsored lists eligible for the amateur draft.

1967-68 — Six new teams added: California Seals, Los Angeles Kings, Minnesota North Stars, Philadelphia Flyers, Pittsburgh Penguins, St. Louis Blues. New teams to play in West Division. Remaining six teams to play in East Division.
 Minimum age of players subject to amateur draft changed to 20.
 Clubs played 74-game schedule.
 Clarence S. Campbell Trophy awarded to team finishing the regular season in first place in West Division.
 California Seals changed name to Oakland Seals on December 8, 1967.

1968-69 — Clubs played 76-game schedule.
 Amateur draft expanded to cover any amateur player of qualifying age throughout the world.

1970-71 — Two new teams added: Buffalo Sabres and Vancouver Canucks. These teams joined East Division; Chicago switched to West Division.
 Clubs played 78-game schedule.

1971-72 — Playoff format amended. In each division, first to play fourth; second to play third.

1972-73 — Soviet Nationals and Canadian NHL stars play eight-game pre-season series. Canadians win 4-3-1.
 Two new teams added. Atlanta Flames join West Division; New York Islanders join East Division.

1974-75 — Two new teams added: Kansas City Scouts and Washington Capitals. Teams realigned into two nine-team conferences, the Prince of Wales made up of the Norris and Adams Divisions, and the Clarence Campbell made up of the Smythe and Patrick Divisions.
 Clubs played 80-game schedule.

1976-77 — California franchise transferred to Cleveland. Team named Cleveland Barons. Kansas City franchise transferred to Denver. Team named Colorado Rockies.

1977-78 — Clarence S. Campbell retires as NHL president. Succeeded by John A. Ziegler, Jr.

1978-79 — Cleveland and Minnesota franchises merge, leaving NHL with 17 teams. Merged team placed in Adams Division, playing home games in Minnesota.
 Minimum age of players subject to amateur draft changed to 19.

1979-80 — Four new teams added: Edmonton Oilers, Hartford Whalers, Quebec Nordiques and Winnipeg Jets.
 Minimum age of players subject to entry draft changed to 18.

1980-81 — Atlanta franchise shifted to Calgary, retaining "Flames" name.

1981-82 — Unbalanced schedule adopted.

1982-83 — Colorado Rockies franchise shifted to East Rutherford, New Jersey. Team named New Jersey Devils.

1991-92 — San Jose Sharks added, making the NHL a 22-team league. NHL celebrates 75th Anniversary Season.

Major Rule Changes

1910-11 — Game changed from two 30-minute periods to three 20-minute periods.

1911-12 — National Hockey Association (forerunner of the NHL) originated six-man hockey, replacing seven-man game.

1917-18 — Goalies permitted to fall to the ice to make saves. Previously a goaltender was penalized for dropping to the ice.

1918-19 — Penalty rules amended. For minor fouls, substitutes not allowed until penalized player had served three minutes. For major fouls, no substitutes for five minutes. For match fouls, no substitutes allowed for the remainder of the game.
 With the addition of two lines painted on the ice twenty feet from center, three playing zones were created, producing a forty-foot neutral center ice area in which forward passing was permitted in this neutral zone. Kicking the puck was permitted in this neutral zone.
 Tabulation of assists began.

1921-22 — Goaltenders allowed to pass the puck forward up to their own blue line.
 Overtime limited to twenty minutes.
 Minor penalties changed from three minutes to two minutes.

1923-24 — Match foul defined as actions deliberately injuring or disabling an opponent. For such actions, a player was fined not less than $50 and ruled off the ice for the balance of the game. A player assessed a match penalty may be replaced by a substitute at the end of 20 minutes. Match penalty recipients must meet with the League president who can assess additional punishment.

1925-26 — Delayed penalty rules introduced. Each team must have a minimum of four players on the ice at all times.
 Two rules were amended to encourage offense: No more than two defensemen permitted to remain inside a team's own blue line when the puck has left the defensive zone. A faceoff to be called for ragging the puck unless short-handed.
 Team captains only players allowed to talk to referees.
 Goaltender's leg pads limited to 12-inch width.
 Timekeeper's gong to mark end of periods rather than referee's whistle. Teams to dress a maximum of 12 players for each game from a roster of no more than 14 players.

1926-27 — Blue lines repositioned to sixty feet from each goal-line, thereby enlarging the neutral zone and standardizing distance from blueline to goal.
 Uniform goal nets adopted throughout NHL with goal posts securely fastened to the ice.

1927-28 — To further encourage offense, forward passes allowed in defending and neutral zones and goaltender's pads reduced in width from 12 to 10 inches.
 Game standardized at three twenty-minute periods of stop-time separated by ten-minute intermissions.
 Teams to change ends after each period.
 Ten minutes of sudden-death overtime to be played if the score is tied after regulation time.
 Minor penalty to be assessed to any player other than a goaltender for deliberately picking up the puck while it is in play. Minor penalty to be assessed for deliberately shooting the puck out of play.
 The Art Ross goal net adopted as the official net of the NHL.
 Maximum length of hockey sticks limited to 53 inches measured from heel of blade to end of handle. No minimum length stipulated.
 Home teams given choice of goals to defend at start of game.

1928-29 — Forward passing permitted in defensive and neutral zones and into attacking zone if pass receiver is in neutral zone when pass is made. No forward passing allowed inside attacking zone.
 Minor penalty to be assessed to any player who delays the game by passing the puck back into his defensive zone.
 Ten-minute overtime without sudden-death provision to be played in games tied after regulation time. Games tied after this overtime period declared a draw.
 Exclusive of goaltenders, team to dress at least 8 and no more than 12 skaters.

The Los Angeles Kings were one of half dozen new teams added when the NHL expanded from six to twelve teams in 1967-68.

The New York Rangers and Detroit Red Wings met in the 1950 Stanley Cup finals, the only final series that required double overtime in the seventh game to determine the Cup winner.

1929-30 — Forward passing permitted inside all three zones but not permitted across either blue line.

Kicking the puck allowed, but a goal cannot be scored by kicking the puck in.

No more than three players including the goaltender may remain in their defensive zone when the puck has gone up ice. Minor penalties to be assessed for the first two violations of this rule in a game; major penalties thereafter.

Goaltenders forbidden to hold the puck. Pucks caught must be cleared immediately. For infringement of this rule, a faceoff to be taken ten feet in front of the goal with no player except the goaltender standing between the faceoff spot and the goal-line.

Highsticking penalties introduced.

Maximum number of players in uniform increased from 12 to 15.

December 21, 1929 — Forward passing rules instituted at the beginning of the 1929-30 season more than doubled number of goals scored. Partway through the season, these rules were further amended to read, ''No attacking player allowed to precede the play when entering the opposing defensive zone.'' This is similar to modern offside rule.

1930-31 — A player without a complete stick ruled out of play and forbidden from taking part in further action until a new stick is obtained. A player who has broken his stick must obtain a replacement at his bench.

A further refinement of the offside rule stated that the puck must first be propelled into the attacking zone before any player of the attacking side can enter that zone; for infringement of this rule a faceoff to take place at the spot where the infraction took place.

1931-32 — Though there is no record of a team attempting to play with two goaltenders on the ice, a rule was instituted which stated that each team was allowed only one goaltender on the ice at one time. Attacking players forbidden to impede the movement or obstruct the vision of opposing goaltenders.

Defending players with the exception of the goaltender forbidden from falling on the puck within 10 feet of the net.

1932-33 — Each team to have captain on the ice at all times.

If the goaltender is removed from the ice to serve a penalty, the manager of the club to appoint a substitute.

Match penalty with substitution after five minutes instituted for kicking another player.

1933-34 — Number of players permitted to stand in defensive zone restricted to three including goaltender.

Visible time clocks required in each rink.

Two referees replace one referee and one linesman.

1934-35 — Penalty shot awarded when a player is tripped and thus prevented from having a clear shot on goal, having no player to pass to other than the offending player. Shot taken from inside a 10-foot circle located 38 feet from the goal. The goaltender must not advance more than one foot from his goal-line when the shot is taken.

1937-38 — Rules introduced governing icing the puck.

Penalty shot awarded when a player other than a goaltender falls on the puck within 10 feet of the goal.

1938-39 — Penalty shot modified to allow puck carrier to skate in before shooting.

One referee and one linesman replace two referee system.

Blue line widened to 12 inches.

Maximum number of players in uniform increased from 14 to 15.

1939-40 — A substitute replacing a goaltender removed from ice to serve a penalty may use a goaltender's stick and gloves but no other goaltending equipment.

1940-41 — Flooding ice surface between periods made obligatory.

1941-42 — Penalty shots classified as minor and major. Minor shot to be taken from a line 28 feet from the goal. Major shot, awarded when a player is tripped with only the goaltender to beat, permits the player taking the penalty shot to skate right into the goalkeeper and shoot from point-blank range.

One referee and two linesmen employed to officiate games.

For playoffs, standby minor league goaltenders employed by NHL as emergency substitutes.

1942-43 — Because of wartime restrictions on train scheduling, regular-season overtime was discontinued on November 21, 1942.

Player limit reduced from 15 to 14. Minimum of 12 men in uniform abolished.

1943-44 — Red line at center ice introduced to speed up the game and reduce offside calls. This rule is considered to mark the beginning of the modern era in the NHL.

Delayed penalty rules introduced.

1945-46 — Goal indicator lights synchronized with official time clock required at all rinks.

1946-47 — System of signals by officials to indicate infractions introduced.

Linesmen from neutral cities employed for all games.

1947-48 — Goal awarded when a player with the puck has an open net to shoot at and a thrown stick prevents the shot on goal. Major penalty to any player who throws his stick in any zone other than defending zone. If a stick is thrown by a player in his defending zone but the thrown stick is not considered to have prevented a goal, a penalty shot is awarded.

All playoff games played until a winner determined, with 20-minute sudden-death overtime periods separated by 10-minute intermissions.

1949-50 — Ice surface painted white.

Clubs allowed to dress 17 players exclusive of goaltenders.

Major penalties incurred by goaltenders served by a member of the goaltender's team instead of resulting in a penalty shot.

1950-51 — Each team required to provide an emergency goaltender in attendance with full equipment at each game for use by either team in the event of illness or injury to a regular goaltender.

1951-52 — Visiting teams to wear basic white uniforms; home teams basic colored uniforms.

Goal crease enlarged from 3 × 7 feet to 4 × 8 feet.

Number of players in uniform reduced to 15 plus goaltenders.

Faceoff circles enlarged from 10-foot to 15-foot radius.

1952-53 — Teams permitted to dress 15 skaters on the road and 16 at home.

1953-54 — Number of players in uniform set at 16 plus goaltenders.

1954-55 — Number of players in uniform set at 18 plus goaltenders up to December 1 and 16 plus goaltenders thereafter.

1956-57 — Player serving a minor penalty allowed to return to ice when a goal is scored by opposing team.

1959-60 — Players prevented from leaving their benches to enter into an altercation. Substitutions permitted providing substitutes do not enter into altercation.

1960-61 — Number of players in uniform set at 16 plus goaltenders.

1961-62 — Penalty shots to be taken by the player against whom the foul was committed. In the event of a penalty shot called in a situation where a particular player hasn't been fouled, the penalty shot to be taken by any player on the ice when the foul was called.

1964-65 — No bodily contact on faceoffs.

In playoff games, each team to have its substitute goaltender dressed in his regular uniform except for leg pads and body protector. All previous rules governing standby goaltenders terminated.

1965-66 — Teams required to dress two goaltenders for each regular-season game.

1966-67 — Substitution allowed on coincidental major penalties.

Between-periods intermissions fixed at 15 minutes.

1967-68 — If a penalty incurred by a goaltender is a co-incident major, the penalty to be served by a player of the goaltender's team on the ice at the time the penalty was called.

1970-71 — Home teams to wear basic white uniforms; visiting teams basic colored uniforms.

Limit of curvature of hockey stick blade set at $1/2$ inch.

Minor penalty for deliberately shooting the puck out of the playing area.

1971-72 — Number of players in uniform set at 17 plus 2 goaltenders.

Third man to enter an altercation assessed an automatic game misconduct penalty.

1972-73 — Minimum width of stick blade reduced to 2 inches from $2\text{-}1/2$ inches.

1974-75 — Bench minor penalty imposed if a penalized player does not proceed directly and immediately to the penalty box.

1976-77 — Rule dealing with fighting amended to provide a major and game misconduct penalty for any player who is clearly the instigator of a fight.

1977-78 — Teams requesting a stick measurement to be assessed a minor penalty in the event that the measured stick does not violate the rules.

1981-82 — If both of a team's listed goaltenders are incapacitated, the team can dress and play any eligible goaltender who is available.

1982-83 — Number of players in uniform set at 18 plus 2 goaltenders.

1983-84 — Five-minute sudden-death overtime to be played in regular-season games that are tied at the end of regulation time.

1985-86 — Substitutions allowed in the event of co-incidental minor penalties.

1986-87 — Delayed off-side is no longer in effect once the players of the offending team have cleared the opponents' defensive zone.

1991-92 — Video replays employed to assist referees in goal–no goal situations. Number of players in uniform set at 17 plus 2 goaltenders.

Team Records

BEST WINNING PERCENTAGE, ONE SEASON:
.875 — **Boston Bruins,** 1929-30. 38W-5L-1T. 77PTS in 44GP.
.830 — Montreal Canadiens, 1943-44. 38W-5L-7T. 83PTS in 50GP
.825 — Montreal Canadiens, 1976-77. 60W-8L-12T. 132PTS in 80GP
.806 — Montreal Canadiens, 1977-78. 59W-10L-11T. 129PTS in 80GP
.800 — Montreal Canadiens, 1944-45. 38W-8L-4T. 80PTS in 50GP

MOST POINTS, ONE SEASON:
132 — **Montreal Canadiens,** 1976-77. 60W-8L-12T. 80GP
129 — Montreal Canadiens, 1977-78. 59W-10L-11T. 80GP
127 — Montreal Canadiens, 1975-76. 58W-11L-11T. 80GP

FEWEST POINTS, ONE SEASON:
8 — **Quebec Bulldogs,** 1919-20. 4W-20L-0T. 24GP
10 — Toronto Arenas, 1918-19. 5W-13L-0T. 18GP
12 — Hamilton Tigers, 1920-21. 6W-18L-0T. 24GP
— Hamilton Tigers, 1922-23. 6W-18L-0T. 24GP
— Boston Bruins, 1924-25. 6W-24L-0T. 30GP
— Philadelphia Quakers, 1930-31. 4W-36L-4T. 44GP

FEWEST POINTS, ONE SEASON (MINIMUM 70-GAME SCHEDULE):
21 — **Washington Capitals,** 8W-67L-5T. 80GP
30 — NY Islanders, 1972-73. 12W-60L-6T. 78GP
31 — Chicago Blackhawks, 1953-54. 12W-51L-7T. 70GP
— Quebec Nordiques, 1989-90. 12W-61L-7T. 80GP

MOST WINS, ONE SEASON:
60 — **Montreal Canadiens,** 1976-77. 80GP
59 — Montreal Canadiens, 1977-78. 80GP
58 — Montreal Canadiens, 1975-76. 80GP

FEWEST WINS, ONE SEASON:
4 — **Quebec Bulldogs,** 1919-20. 24GP
— **Philadelphia Quakers,** 1930-31. 44GP
5 — Toronto Arenas, 1918-19. 18GP
— Pittsburgh Pirates, 1929-30. 44GP

FEWEST WINS, ONE SEASON (MINIMUM 70-GAME SCHEDULE):
8 — **Washington Capitals,** 1974-75. 80GP
9 — Winnipeg Jets, 1980-81 80GP
11 — Washington Capitals, 1975-76. 80GP

MOST LOSSES, ONE SEASON:
67 — **Washington Capitals,** 1974-75. 80GP
61 — Quebec Nordiques, 1989-90. 80GP
60 — NY Islanders, 1972-73. 78GP
59 — Washington Capitals, 1975-76. 80GP

FEWEST LOSSES, ONE SEASON:
5 — **Ottawa Senators,** 1919-20. 24GP
— **Boston Bruins,** 1929-30. 44GP
— **Montreal Canadiens,** 1943-44. 50GP

FEWEST LOSSES, ONE SEASON (MINIMUM 70-GAME SCHEDULE):
8 — **Montreal Canadiens,** 1976-77. 80GP
10 — Montreal Canadiens, 1972-73. 78GP
— Montreal Canadiens, 1977-78. 80GP
11 — Montreal Canadiens, 1975-76. 80GP

MOST TIES, ONE SEASON:
24 — **Philadelphia Flyers,** 1969-70. 76GP
23 — Montreal Canadiens, 1962-63. 70GP
— Chicago Blackhawks, 1973-74. 78GP

FEWEST TIES, ONE SEASON (Since 1926-27):
1 — **Boston Bruins,** 1929-30. 44GP
2 — NY Americans, 1926-27. 44GP
— Montreal Canadiens, 1926-27. 44GP
— Boston Bruins, 1938-39. 48GP
— NY Rangers, 1941-42. 48GP

FEWEST TIES, ONE SEASON (MINIMUM 70-GAME SCHEDULE):
3 — **New Jersey Devils,** 1985-86. 80GP
— **Calgary Flames,** 1986-87. 80GP
4 — Detroit Red Wings, 1966-67. 70GP
— NY Islanders, 1983-84. 80GP
— Hartford Whalers, 1985-86. 80GP
— Philadelphia Flyers, 1985-86. 80GP
— Minnesota North Stars, 1989-90. 80GP
— Toronto Maple Leafs, 1989-90. 80GP

MOST HOME WINS, ONE SEASON:
36 — **Philadelphia Flyers,** 1975-76. 40GP
33 — Boston Bruins, 1970-71. 39GP
— Boston Bruins, 1973-74. 39GP
— Montreal Canadiens, 1976-77. 40GP
— Philadelphia Flyers, 1976-77. 40GP
— NY Islanders, 1981-82. 40GP
— Philadelphia Flyers,1985-86. 40GP

MOST ROAD WINS, ONE SEASON:
27 — **Montreal Canadiens,** 1976-77. 40GP
— **Montreal Canadiens,** 1977-78. 40GP
26 — Boston Bruins, 1971-72. 39GP
— Montreal Canadiens, 1975-76. 40GP
— Edmonton Oilers, 1983-84. 40GP

MOST HOME LOSSES, ONE SEASON:
29 — **Pittsburgh Penguins,** 1983-84. 40GP
28 — Washington Capitals, 1974-75. 40GP
— New Jersey Devils, 1983-84. 40GP
— Toronto Maple Leafs, 1984-85. 40GP
27 — Los Angeles Kings, 1985-86. 40GP

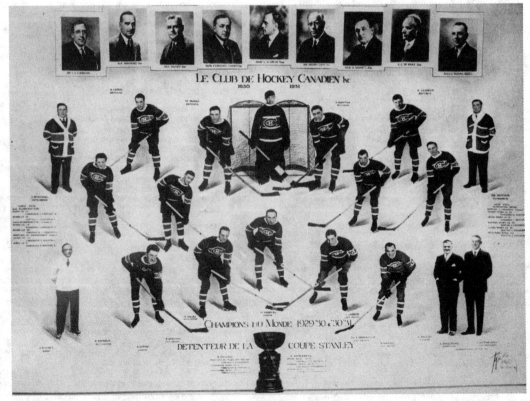

The Montreal Canadiens won back-to-back Stanley Cups in 1929-30 and 1930-31.

Charlie Conacher, Busher Jackson and Joe Primeau formed the Maple Leafs' famed ''Kid Line'' and were key components in Toronto's record eight-game winning streak to start the 1934-35 season.

MOST ROAD LOSSES, ONE SEASON:
39 — **Washington Capitals**, 1974-75. 40GP
37 — California Seals, 1973-74. 39GP
35 — NY Islanders, 1972-73. 39GP
— Quebec Nordiques, 1989-90. 40GP

MOST HOME TIES, ONE SEASON:
13 — **NY Rangers,** 1954-55. 35GP
— **Philadelphia Flyers,** 1969-70. 38GP
— **California Seals,** 1971-72. 39GP
— **California Seals,** 1972-73. 39GP
— **Chicago Blackhawks,** 1973-74. 39GP
12 — NY Islanders, 1974-75. 40GP
— Vancouver Canucks, 1977-78. 40GP
— Buffalo Sabres, 1980-81. 40GP
— Minnesota North Stars, 1981-82. 40GP
— Vancouver Canucks, 1981-82. 40GP
— Buffalo Sabres, 1990-91. 40GP

MOST ROAD TIES, ONE SEASON:
15 — **Philadelphia Flyers,** 1976-77. 40GP
14 — Montreal Canadiens, 1952-53. 35GP
— Montreal Canadiens, 1974-75. 40GP
— Philadelphia Flyers, 1975-76. 40GP

FEWEST HOME WINS, ONE SEASON:
2 — **Chicago Blackhawks,** 1927-28. 22GP
3 — Boston Bruins, 1924-25. 15GP
— Chicago Blackhawks, 1928-29. 22GP
— Philadelphia Quakers, 1930-31. 22GP

FEWEST HOME WINS, ONE SEASON (MINIMUM 70-GAME SCHEDULE):
6 — **Chicago Blackhawks,** 1954-55. 35GP
— **Washington Capitals,** 1975-76. 40GP
7 — Boston Bruins, 1962-63. 35GP
— Washington Capitals, 1974-75. 40GP
— Winnipeg Jets, 1980-81. 40GP
— Pittsburgh Penguins, 1983-84. 40GP

FEWEST ROAD WINS, ONE SEASON:
0 — **Toronto Arenas,** 1918-19. 9GP
— **Quebec Bulldogs,** 1919-20. 12GP
— **Pittsburgh Pirates,** 1929-30. 22GP
1 — Hamilton Tigers, 1921-22. 12GP
— Toronto St. Patricks, 1925-26. 18GP
— Philadelphia Quakers, 1930-31. 22GP
— NY Americans, 1940-41. 24GP
— Washington Capitals, 1974-75. 40GP

FEWEST ROAD WINS, ONE SEASON (MINIMUM 70-GAME SCHEDULE):
1 — **Washington Capitals,** 1974-75. 40GP
2 — Boston Bruins, 1960-61. 35GP
— Los Angeles Kings, 1969-70. 38GP
— NY Islanders, 1972-73. 39GP
— California Seals, 1973-74. 39GP
— Colorado Rockies, 1977-78. 40GP
— Winnipeg Jets, 1980-81. 40GP

FEWEST HOME LOSSES, ONE SEASON:
0 — **Ottawa Senators,** 1922-23. 12GP
— **Montreal Canadiens,** 1943-44. 25GP
1 — Toronto Arenas, 1917-18. 11GP
— Ottawa Senators, 19. 9GP
— Ottawa Senators, 1919-20. 12GP
— Toronto St. Patricks, 1922-23. 12GP
— Boston Bruins, 1929-30 and 1930-31. 22GP
— Montreal Canadiens, 1976-77. 40GP

FEWEST HOME LOSSES, ONE SEASON (MINIMUM 70-GAME SCHEDULE):
1 — **Montreal Canadiens,** 1976-77. 40GP
2 — Montreal Canadiens, 1961-62. 35GP
— NY Rangers, 1970-71. 39GP
— Philadelphia Flyers, 1975-76. 40GP

FEWEST ROAD LOSSES, ONE SEASON:
3 — **Montreal Canadiens,** 1928-29. 22GP
4 — Ottawa Senators, 1919-20. 12GP
— Montreal Canadiens, 1927-28. 22GP
— Boston Bruins, 1929-30. 20GP
— Boston Bruins, 1940-41. 24GP

FEWEST ROAD LOSSES, ONE SEASON (MINIMUM 70-GAME SCHEDULE):
6 — **Montreal Canadiens,** 1972-73. 39GP
— **Montreal Canadiens,** 1974-75. 40GP
— **Montreal Canadiens,** 1977-78. 40GP
7 — Detroit Red Wings, 1951-52. 35GP
— Montreal Canadiens, 1976-77. 40GP
— Philadelphia Flyers, 1979-80. 40GP

LONGEST WINNING STREAK:
15 Games — NY Islanders, Jan. 21, 1982 - Feb. 20, 1982.
14 Games — Boston Bruins, Dec. 3, 1929 - Jan. 9, 1930.
13 Games — Boston Bruins, Feb. 23, 1971 - March 20, 1971.
— Philadelphia Flyers, Oct. 19, 1985 - Nov. 17, 1985.

LONGEST WINNING STREAK FROM START OF SEASON:
8 Games — **Toronto Maple Leafs,** 1934-35.
— **Buffalo Sabres,** 1975-76.
7 Games — Edmonton Oilers, 1983-84.
— Quebec Nordiques, 1985-86.
— Pittsburgh Penguins, 1986-87.

LONGEST HOME WINNING STREAK FROM START OF SEASON:
11 Games — **Chicago Blackhawks,** 1963-64
10 Games — Ottawa Senators, 1925-26
9 Games — Montreal Canadiens, 1953-54
— Chicago Blackhawks, 1971-72
8 Games — Boston Bruins, 1983-84
— Philadelphia Flyers, 1986-87
— New Jersey Devils, 1987-88

LONGEST WINNING STREAK, INCLUDING PLAYOFFS:
15 Games — **Detroit Red Wings,** Feb. 27, 1955 - April 5, 1955. Nine regular-season games, six playoff games.

LONGEST HOME WINNING STREAK (ONE SEASON):
20 Games — **Boston Bruins,** Dec. 3, 1929 - Mar. 18, 1930.
— **Philadelphia Flyers,** Jan. 4, 1976 - April 3, 1976.

LONGEST HOME WINNING STREAK, INCLUDING PLAYOFFS:
24 Games — Philadelphia Flyers, Jan. 4, 1976 - April 25, 1976. 20 regular-season games, 4 playoff games.

LONGEST ROAD WINNING STREAK (ONE SEASON):
10 Games — Buffalo Sabres, Dec. 10, 1983 - Jan. 23, 1984.
  8 Games — Boston Bruins, Feb. 17, 1972 - Mar. 8, 972.
      — Los Angeles Kings, Dec. 18, 1974 - Jan. 16, 1975.
      — Montreal Canadiens, Dec. 18, 1977 - Jan. 18. 1978.
      — NY Islanders, Feb. 27, 1981 - March 29, 1981.
      — Montreal Canadiens, Jan. 21, 1982 - Feb. 21, 1982.
      — Philadelphia Flyers, Dec. 22, 1982 - Jan. 16, 1983.
      — Winnipeg Jets, Feb. 25, 1985 - Apr. 6, 1985.
      — Edmonton Oilers, Dec. 9, 1986 - Jan. 17, 1987.

LONGEST UNDEFEATED STREAK (ONE SEASON):
35 Games — Philadelphia Flyers, Oct. 14, 1979 - Jan. 6, 1980. 25w-10т.
 28 Games — Montreal Canadiens, Dec. 18, 1977 - Feb. 23, 1978. 23w-5т.
 23 Games — Boston Bruins, Dec. 22, 1940 - Feb. 23, 1941. 15w-8т.
      — Philadelphia Flyers, Jan. 29, 1976 - Mar. 18, 1976. 17w-6т.

LONGEST UNDEFEATED STREAK FROM START OF SEASON:
15 Games — Edmonton Oilers, 1984-85. 12w-3т.
 14 Games — Montreal Canadiens, 1943-44. 11w-3т.
 13 Games — Montreal Canadiens, 1972-73. 9w-4т.

LONGEST HOME UNDEFEATED STREAK (ONE SEASON):
34 Games — Montreal Canadiens, Nov. 1, 1976 - Apr. 2, 1977. 28w-6т.
 27 Games — Boston Bruins, Nov. 22, 1970 - Mar. 20, 1971. 26w-1т.

LONGEST HOME UNDEFEATED STREAK, INCLUDING PLAYOFFS:
38 Games — Montreal Canadiens, Nov. 1, 1976 - April 26, 1977. 28w-6т in regular season and 4w in playoffs).

LONGEST ROAD UNDEFEATED STREAK (ONE SEASON):
23 Games — Montreal Canadiens, Nov. 27, 1974 - Mar. 12, 1975. 14w-9т.
 17 Games — Montreal Canadiens, Dec. 18, 1977 - March 1, 1978. 14w-3т.
 16 Games — Philadelphia Flyers, Oct. 20, 1979 - Jan. 6, 1980. 11w-5т.

LONGEST LOSING STREAK (ONE SEASON):
17 Games — Washington Capitals, Feb. 18, 1975 - Mar. 26, 1975.
 15 Games — Philadelphia Quakers, Nov. 29, 1930 - Jan. 8, 1931.

LONGEST LOSING STREAK FROM START OF SEASON:
11 Games — NY Rangers, 1943-44.
  7 Games — Montreal Canadiens, 1938-39.
      — Chicago Blackhawks, 1947-48.
      — Washington Capitals, 1983-84.

LONGEST HOME LOSING STREAK (ONE SEASON):
11 Games — Boston Bruins, Dec. 8, 1924 - Feb. 17, 1925.
      — Washington Capitals, Feb. 18, 1975 - Mar. 30, 1975.

LONGEST ROAD LOSING STREAK (ONE SEASON):
37 Games — Washington Capitals, Oct. 9, 1974 - Mar. 26, 1975.

LONGEST WINLESS STREAK (ONE SEASON):
30 Games — Winnipeg Jets, Oct. 19, 1980 - Dec. 20, 1980. 23L-7т.
 27 Games — Kansas City Scouts, Feb. 12, 1976 - April 4, 1976. 21L-6т.
 25 Games — Washington Capitals, Nov. 29, 1975 - Jan. 21, 1976. 22L-3т.

LONGEST WINLESS STREAK FROM START OF SEASON:
15 Games — NY Rangers, 1943-44. 14L-1т.
 12 Games — Pittsburgh Pirates, 1927-28. 9L-3т.
 11 Games — Minnesota North Stars, 1973-74. 5L-6т.

LONGEST HOME WINLESS STREAK (ONE SEASON):
15 Games — Chicago Blackhawks, Dec. 16, 1928 - Feb. 28, 1929. 11L-4т.
      — Montreal Canadiens, Dec. 16, 1939 - Mar. 7, 1940. 12L-3т.

LONGEST ROAD WINLESS STREAK (ONE SEASON):
37 Games — Washington Capitals, Oct. 9, 1974 - Mar. 26, 1975. 37L-0т.

LONGEST NON-SHUTOUT STREAK:
264 Games — Calgary Flames, Nov. 12, 1981 - Jan. 9, 1985.
 262 Games — Los Angeles Kings, Mar. 15, 1986 - Oct. 25, 1989.
 230 Games — Quebec Nordiques, Feb. 10, 1980 - Jan. 13, 1983.
 229 Games — Edmonton Oilers, Mar. 15, 1981 - Feb. 11, 1984.
 228 Games — Chicago Blackhawks, Mar. 14, 1970 - Feb. 21, 1973.

LONGEST NON-SHUTOUT STREAK INCLUDING PLAYOFFS:
264 Games — Los Angeles Kings, Mar. 15 1986 - Apr. 6, 1989. (5 playoff games in 1987; 5 in 1988; 2 in 1989)
 262 Games — Chicago Blackhawks, Mar. 14, 1970 - Feb. 21, 1973. (8 playoff games in 1970; 18 in 1971; 8 in 1972).
 251 Games — Quebec Nordiques, Feb. 10, 1980 - Jan. 13, 1983. (5 playoff games in 1981; 16 in 1982).
 235 Games — Boston Bruins, Oct. 26, 1977 - Feb. 20, 1980. (15 playoff games in 1978; 11 in 1979).
      — Pittsburgh Penguins, Jan. 7, 1989 - May 25, 1991. (11 playoff games in 1989; 23 in 1991).

MOST CONSECUTIVE GAMES SHUT OUT:
8 — Chicago Blackhawks, 1928-29.

MOST SHUTOUTS, ONE SEASON:
22 — Montreal Canadiens, 1928-29. All by George Hainsworth. 44GP
 16 — NY Americans, 1928-29. Roy Worters had 13; Flat Walsh 3. 44GP
 15 — Ottawa Senators, 1925-26. All by Alex Connell. 36GP
      — Ottawa Senators, 1927-28. All by Alex Connell. 44GP
      — Boston Bruins, 1927-28. All by Hal Winkler. 44GP
      — Chicago Blackhawks, 1969-70. All by Tony Esposito. 76GP

MOST GOALS, ONE SEASON:
446 — Edmonton Oilers, 1983-84. 80GP
 426 — Edmonton Oilers, 1985-86. 80GP
 424 — Edmonton Oilers, 1982-83. 80GP
 417 — Edmonton Oilers, 1981-82. 80GP
 401 — Edmonton Oilers, 1984-85. 80GP

HIGHEST GOALS-PER-GAME AVERAGE, ONE SEASON:
5.58 — Edmonton Oilers, 1983-84. 446G in 80GP.
 5.38 — Montreal Canadiens, 1919-20. 129G in 24GP.
 5.33 — Edmonton Oilers, 1985-86. 426G in 80GP.
 5.30 — Edmonton Oilers, 1982-83. 424G in 80GP.
 5.23 — Montreal Canadiens, 1917-18. 115G in 22GP.

FEWEST GOALS, ONE SEASON:
33 — Chicago Blackhawks, 1928-29. 44GP
 45 — Montreal Maroons, 1924-25. 30GP
 46 — Pittsburgh Pirates, 1928-29. 44GP

FEWEST GOALS, ONE SEASON (MINIMUM 70-GAME SCHEDULE):
133 — Chicago Blackhawks, 1953-54. 70GP
 147 — Toronto Maple Leafs, 1954-55. 70GP
      — Boston Bruins, 1955-56. 70GP
 150 — NY Rangers, 1954-55. 70GP

LOWEST GOALS-PER-GAME AVERAGE, ONE SEASON:
.75 — Chicago Blackhawks, 1928-29, 33G in 44GP.
 1.05 — Pittsburgh Pirates, 1928-29. 46G in 44GP.
 1.20 — NY Americans, 1928-29. 53G in 44GP.

MOST GOALS AGAINST, ONE SEASON:
446 — Washington Capitals, 1974-75. 80GP
 415 — Detroit Red Wings, 1985-86. 80GP
 407 — Quebec Nordiques, 1989-90. 80GP
 403 — Hartford Whalers, 1982-83. 80GP
 401 — Vancouver Canucks, 1984-85. 80GP

HIGHEST GOALS-AGAINST-PER-GAME AVERAGE, ONE SEASON:
7.38 — Quebec Bulldogs, 1919-20, 177GA vs. in 24GP.
 6.20 — NY Rangers, 1943-44, 310GA vs. in 50GP.
 5.58 — Washington Capitals, 1974-75, 446GA vs. in 80GP.

The diminutive Roy "Shrimp" Worters helped the New York Americans rack up 16 shutouts in the 1928-29 campaign, the second-highest team total in league history.

FEWEST GOALS AGAINST, ONE SEASON:
42 — Ottawa Senators, 1925-26. 36GP
43 — Montreal Canadiens, 1928-29. 44GP
48 — Montreal Canadiens, 1923-24. 24GP
— Montreal Canadiens, 1927-28. 44GP

FEWEST GOALS AGAINST, ONE SEASON (MINIMUM 70-GAME SCHEDULE):
131 — Toronto Maple Leafs, 1953-54. 70GP
— Montreal Canadiens, 1955-56. 70GP
132 — Detroit Red Wings, 1953-54. 70GP
133 — Detroit Red Wings, 1951-52. 70GP
— Detroit Red Wings, 1952-53. 70GP

LOWEST GOALS-AGAINST-PER-GAME AVERAGE, ONE SEASON:
.98 — Montreal Canadiens, 1928-29. 43GA vs. in 44GP.
1.09 — Montreal Canadiens, 1927-28. 48GA vs. in 44GP.
1.17 — Ottawa Senators, 1925-26. 42GA vs. in 36GP.

MOST POWER-PLAY GOALS, ONE SEASON:
120 — Pittsburgh Penguins, 1988-89. 80GP
111 — NY Rangers, 1987-88. 80GP
110 — Pittsburgh Penguins, 1987-88. 80GP
— Winnipeg Jets, 1987-88, 80GP
109 — Calgary Flames, 1987-88. 80GP

MOST POWER-PLAY GOALS AGAINST, ONE SEASON:
122 — Chicago Blackhawks, 1988-89. 80GP
120 — Pittsburgh Penguins, 1987-88. 80GP
115 — New Jersey Devils, 1988-89. 80GP
111 — Detroit Red Wings, 1985-86. 80GP
— Pittsburgh Penguins, 1988-89. 80GP
110 — Pittsburgh Penguins, 1982-83. 80GP

MOST SHORTHAND GOALS, ONE SEASON:
36 — Edmonton Oilers, 1983-84. 80GP
28 — Edmonton Oilers, 1986-87. 80GP
27 — Edmonton Oilers, 1985-86. 80GP
— Edmonton Oilers, 1988-89. 80GP

MOST SHORTHAND GOALS AGAINST, ONE SEASON:
22 — Pittsburgh Penguins, 1984-85. 80GP
21 — Calgary Flames, 1984-85. 80GP
— Pittsburgh Penguins, 1989-90. 80GP
20 — Minnesota North Stars, 1982-83. 80GP
— Quebec Nordiques, 1985-86. 80GP

MOST ASSISTS, ONE SEASON:
737 — Edmonton Oilers, 1985-86. 80GP
736 — Edmonton Oilers, 1983-84. 80GP
706 — Edmonton Oilers, 1981-82. 80GP

FEWEST ASSISTS, ONE SEASON:
45 — NY Rangers, 1926-27. 44GP

FEWEST ASSISTS, ONE SEASON (MINIMUM 70-GAME SCHEDULE):
206 — Chicago Blackhawks, 1953-54. 70GP

MOST SCORING POINTS, ONE SEASON:
1,182 — Edmonton Oilers, 1983-84. 80GP
1,163 — Edmonton Oilers, 1985-86. 80GP
1,123 — Edmonton Oilers, 1981-82. 80GP

MOST 50-OR-MORE-GOAL SCORERS, ONE SEASON:
3 — **Edmonton Oilers,** 1983-84. Wayne Gretzky, 87; Glenn Anderson, 54; Jari Kurri, 52 80GP.
— **Edmonton Oilers,** 1985-86. Jari Kurri, 68; Glenn Anderson, 54; Wayne Gretzky, 52. 80GP.
2 — Boston Bruins, 1970-71. Phil Esposito, 76; John Bucyk, 51. 78GP
— Boston Bruins, 1973-74. Phil Esposito, 68; Ken Hodge, 50. 78GP
— Philadelphia Flyers, 1975-76. Reggie Leach, 61; Bill Barber, 50. 80GP
— Pittsburgh Penguins, 1975-76. Pierre Larouche, 53; Jean Pronovost, 52. 80GP
— Montreal Canadiens, 1976-77. Steve Shutt, 60; Guy Lafleur, 56. 80GP
— Los Angeles Kings, 1979-80. Charlie Simmer, 56; Marcel Dionne, 53. 80GP
— Montreal Canadiens, 1979-80. Pierre Larouche, 50; Guy Lafleur, 50. 80GP
— Los Angeles Kings, 1980-81. Marcel Dionne, 58; Charlie Simmer, 56. 80GP
— Edmonton Oilers, 1981-82. Wayne Gretzky, 92; Mark Messier, 50. 80GP
— NY Islanders, 1981-82. Mike Bossy, 64; Bryan Trottier, 50. 80GP
— Edmonton Oilers, 1984-85. Wayne Gretzky, 73; Jari Kurri, 71. 80GP
— Washington Capitals, 1984-85. Bob Carpenter, 53; Mike Gartner, 50. 80GP
— Edmonton Oilers, 1986-87. Wayne Gretzky, 62; Jari Kurri, 54. 80GP
— Calgary Flames, 1987-88. Joe Nieuwendyk, 51; Hakan Loob, 50. 80GP
— Los Angeles Kings, 1987-88. Jimmy Carson, 55; Luc Robitaille, 53. 80GP
— Los Angeles Kings, 1988-89. Bernie Nicholls, 70; Wayne Gretzky, 54. 80GP
— Calgary Flames, 1988-89. Joe Nieuwendyk, 51; Joe Mullen, 51. 80GP

MOST 40-OR-MORE-GOAL SCORERS, ONE SEASON:
4 — **Edmonton Oilers,** 1982-83. Wayne Gretzky, 71; Glenn Anderson, 48; Mark Messier, 48; Jari Kurri, 45. 80GP
— **Edmonton Oilers,** 1983-84. Wayne Gretzky, 87; Glenn Anderson, 54; Jari Kurri, 52; Paul Coffey, 40. 80GP
— **Edmonton Oilers,** 1984-85. Wayne Gretzky, 73; Jari Kurri, 71; Mike Krushelnyski, 43; Glenn Anderson, 42. 80GP
— **Edmonton Oilers,** 1985-86. Jari Kurri, 68; Glenn Anderson, 54; Wayne Gretzky, 52; Paul Coffey, 48. 80GP
— **Calgary Flames,** 1987-88. Joe Nieuwendyk, 51; Hakan Loob, 50; Mike Bullard, 48; Joe Mullen, 40. 80GP
3 — Boston Bruins, 1970-71. Phil Esposito, 76; John Bucyk, 51; Ken Hodge, 43. 78GP
— NY Rangers, 1971-72. Vic Hadfield, 50; Jean Ratelle, 46; Rod Gilbert, 43. 78GP
— Buffalo Sabres, 1975-76. Danny Gare, 50; Rick Martin, 49; Gilbert Perreault, 44. 80GP
— Montreal Canadiens, 1979-80. Guy Lafleur, 50; Pierre Larouche, 50; Steve Shutt, 47. 80GP
— Buffalo Sabres, 1979-80. Danny Gare, 56; Rick Martin, 45; Gilbert Perreault, 40. 80GP
— Los Angeles Kings, 1980-81. Marcel Dionne, 58; Charlie Simmer, 56; Dave Taylor, 47. 80GP
— Los Angeles Kings, 1984-85. Marcel Dionne, 46; Bernie Nicholls, 46; Dave Taylor, 41. 80GP
— NY Islanders, 1984-85. Mike Bossy, 58; Brent Sutter, 42; John Tonelli; 42. 80GP
— Chicago Blackhawks, 1985-86. Denis Savard, 47; Troy Murray, 45; Al Secord, 40. 80GP
— Chicago Blackhawks, 1987-88. Denis Savard, 44; Rick Vaive, 43; Steve Larmer, 41. 80GP
— Edmonton Oilers, 1987-88. Craig Simpson, 43; Jari Kurri, 43; Wayne Gretzky, 40. 80GP
— Los Angeles Kings, 1988-89. Bernie Nicholls, 70; Wayne Gretzky 54; Luc Robitaille, 46. 80GP
— Los Angeles Kings, 1990-91. Luc Robitaille, 45; Tomas Sandstrom, 45; Wayne Gretzky 41. 80GP

Mike Bullard was one of four Calgary Flames to score at least 40 goals in 1987-88.

Glenn Anderson hit the 40-goal plateau in four consecutive seasons from 1982-83 to 1985-86.

MOST 30-OR-MORE GOAL SCORERS, ONE SEASON:
6 — **Buffalo Sabres,** 1974-75. Rick Martin, 52; Reńe Robert, 40; Gilbert Perreault, 39; Don Luce, 33; Rick Dudley, Danny Gare, 31 each. 80GP
— **NY Islanders,** 1977-78, Mike Bossy, 53; Bryan Trottier, 46; Clark Gillies, 35; Denis Potvin, Bob Nystrom, Bob Bourne, 30 each. 80GP
— **Winnipeg Jets,** 1984-85. Dale Hawerchuk, 53; Paul MacLean, 41; Laurie Boschman, 32; Brian Mullen, 32; Doug Smail, 31; Thomas Steen, 30. 80GP
5 — Chicago Blackhawks, 1968-69. 76GP
— Boston Bruins, 1970-71. 78GP
— Montreal Canadiens, 1971-72. 78GP
— Philadelphia Flyers, 1972-73. 78GP
— Boston Bruins, 1973-74. 78GP
— Montreal Canadiens, 1974-75. 80GP
— Montreal Canadiens, 1975-76. 80GP
— Pittsburgh Penguins, 1975-76. 80GP
— NY Islanders, 1978-79. 80GP
— Detroit Red Wings, 1979-80. 80GP
— Philadelphia Flyers, 1979-80. 80GP
— NY Islanders, 1980-81. 80GP
— St. Louis Blues, 1980-81. 80GP
— Chicago Blackhawks, 1981-82. 80GP
— Edmonton Oilers, 1981-82. 80GP
— Montreal Canadiens, 1981-82. 80GP
— Quebec Nordiques, 1981-82. 80GP
— Washington Capitals, 1981-82. 80GP
— Edmonton Oilers, 1982-83. 80GP
— Edmonton Oilers, 1983-84. 80GP
— Edmonton Oilers, 1984-85. 80GP
— Los Angeles Kings, 1984-85. 80GP
— Edmonton Oilers, 1985-86. 80GP
— Edmonton Oilers, 1986-87. 80GP
— Edmonton Oilers, 1987-88. 80GP
— Edmonton Oilers, 1988-89. 80GP

MOST 20-OR-MORE GOAL SCORERS, ONE SEASON:
11 — **Boston Bruins,** 1977-78; Peter McNab, 41; Terry O'Reilly, 29; Bobby Schmautz, Stan Jonathan, 27 each; Jean Ratelle, Rick Middleton, 25 each; Wayne Cashman, 24; Gregg Sheppard, 23; Brad Park, 22; Don Marcotte, Bob Miller, 20 each. 80GP
10 — Boston Bruins, 1970-71. 78GP
— Montreal Canadiens, 1974-75. 80GP
— St. Louis Blues, 1980-81. 80GP

MOST 100 OR-MORE-POINT SCORERS, ONE SEASON:
4 — **Boston Bruins,** 1970-71, Phil Esposito, 76G-76A-152PTS; Bobby Orr, 37G-102A-139PTS; John Bucyk, 51G-65A-116PTS; Ken Hodge, 43G-62A-105PTS. 78GP
— **Edmonton Oilers,** 1982-83, Wayne Gretzky, 71G-125A-196PTS; Mark Messier, 48G-58A-106PTS; Glenn Anderson, 48G-56A-104PTS; Jari Kurri, 45G-59A-104PTS. 80GP.
— **Edmonton Oilers,** 1983-84, Wayne Gretzky, 87G-118A-205PTS; Paul Coffey, 40G-86A-126PTS; Jari Kurri, 52G-61A-113PTS; Mark Messier, 37G-64A-101PTS. 80GP.
— **Edmonton Oilers,** 1985-86, Wayne Gretzky, 52G-163A-215PTS; Paul Coffey, 48G-90A-138PTS; Jari Kurri, 68G-63A-131PTS; Glenn Anderson, 54G-48A-102PTS. 80GP
3 — Boston Bruins, 1973-74, Phil Esposito, 68G-77A-145PTS; Bobby Orr, 32G-90A-122PTS; Ken Hodge, 50G-55A-105PTS. 78GP
— NY Islanders, 1978-79, Bryan Trottier, 47G-87A-134PTS; Mike Bossy, 69G-57A-126PTS; Denis Potvin, 31G-70A-101PTS. 80GP
— Los Angeles Kings, 1980-81, Marcel Dionne, 58G-77A-135PTS; Dave Taylor, 47 G-65A-112PTS; Charlie Simmer, 56G-49A-105PTS. 80GP
— Edmonton Oilers, 1984-85, Wayne Gretzky, 73G-135A-208PTS; Jari Kurri, 71G-64A-135PTS; Paul Coffey, 37G-84A-121PTS. 80GP
— NY Islanders, 1984-85, Mike Bossy, 58G-59A-117PTS; Brent Sutter, 42G-60A-102PTS; John Tonelli, 42G-58A-100PTS. 80GP
— Edmonton Oilers, 1986-87, Wayne Gretzky, 62G-121A-183PTS; Jari Kurri, 54G-54A-108PTS; Mark Messier, 37G-70A-107PTS. 80GP
— Pittsburgh Penguins, 1988-89, Mario Lemieux, 85G-114A-199PTS; Rob Brown, 49G-66A-115PTS; Paul Coffey, 30G-83A-113PTS. 80GP

MOST PENALTY MINUTES, ONE SEASON:
2,670 – Pittsburgh Penguins, 1988-89. 80GP
2,621 – Philadelphia Flyers, 1980-81. 80GP
2,499 – New Jersey Devils, 1988-89. 80GP
2,496 – Chicago Blackhawks, 1988-89. 80GP

MOST GOALS, BOTH TEAMS, ONE GAME:
21 — **Montreal Canadiens, Toronto St. Patricks,** at Montreal, Jan. 10, 1920. Montreal won 14-7.
— **Edmonton Oilers, Chicago Blackhawks,** at Chicago, Dec. 11, 1985. Edmonton won 12-9.
20 — Edmonton Oilers, Minnesota North Stars, at Edmonton, Jan. 4, 1984. Edmonton won 12-8.
— Toronto Maple Leafs, Edmonton Oilers, at Toronto, Jan. 8, 1986. Toronto won 11-9.
19 — Montreal Wanderers, Toronto Arenas, at Montreal, Dec. 19, 1917. Montreal won 10-9.
— Montreal Canadiens, Quebec Bulldogs, at Quebec, March 3, 1920, Montreal won 16-3.
— Montreal Canadiens, Hamilton Tigers, at Montreal, Feb. 26, 1921. Canadiens won 13-6.
— Boston Bruins, NY Rangers, at Boston, March 4, 1944, Boston won 10-9.
— Boston Bruins, Detroit Red Wings, at Detroit, March 16, 1944. Detroit won 10-9.
— Vancouver Canucks, Minnesota North Stars, at Vancouver, Oct. 7, 1983. Vancouver won 10-9.

MOST GOALS, ONE TEAM, ONE GAME:
16 — **Montreal Canadiens,** March 3, 1920, at Quebec. Defeated Quebec Bulldogs 16-3.

MOST CONSECUTIVE GOALS, ONE TEAM, ONE GAME:
15 — **Detroit Red Wings,** Jan. 23, 1944, at Detroit. Defeated NY Rangers 15-0.

MOST POINTS, BOTH TEAMS, ONE GAME:
62 — **Edmonton Oilers, Chicago Blackhawks,** at Chicago, Dec. 11, 1985. Edmonton won 12-9. Edmonton had 24A, Chicago, 17.
53 — Quebec Nordiques, Washington Capitals, at Washington, Feb. 22, 1981. Quebec won 11-7. Quebec had 22A, Washington, 13.
— Edmonton Oilers, Minnesota North Stars, at Edmonton, Jan. 4, 1984. Edmonton won 12-8. Edmonton had 20A, Minnesota 13.
— Minnesota North Stars, St. Louis Blues, at St. Louis, Jan. 27, 1984. Minnesota won 10-8. Minnesota had 19A, St. Louis 16.
— Toronto Maple Leafs, Edmonton Oilers, at Toronto, Jan. 8, 1986. Toronto won 11-9. Toronto had 17A, Edmonton 16.
52 — Mtl. Maroons, NY Americans, at New York, Feb. 18, 1936. 8-8 tie. New York had 20A, Montreal 16. (3A allowed for each goal.)
— Vancouver Canucks, Minnesota North Stars, at Vancouver, Oct. 7, 1983. Vancouver won 10-9. Vancouver had 16A, Minnesota 17.

MOST POINTS, ONE TEAM, ONE GAME:
40 — **Buffalo Sabres,** Dec. 21, 1975, at Buffalo. Buffalo defeated Washington 14-2, receiving 26A.
39 — Minnesota North Stars, Nov. 11, 1981, at Minnesota. Minnesota defeated Winnipeg 15-2, receiving 24A.
37 — Detroit Red Wings, Jan. 23, 1944, at Detroit. Detroit defeated NY Rangers 15-0, receiving 22A.
— Toronto Maple Leafs, March 16, 1957, at Toronto. Toronto defeated NY Rangers 14-1, receiving 23A.
— Buffalo Sabres, Feb. 25, 1978, at Cleveland. Buffalo defeated Cleveland 13-3, receiving 24A.
36 — Edmonton Oilers, Dec. 11, 1985, at Chicago. Edmonton defeated Chicago 12-9, receiving 24A.

MOST SHOTS, BOTH TEAMS, ONE GAME:
141 — **NY Americans, Pittsburgh Pirates,** Dec. 26, 1925, at New York. NY Americans, who won game 3-1, had 73 shots; Pit. Pirates, 68 shots.

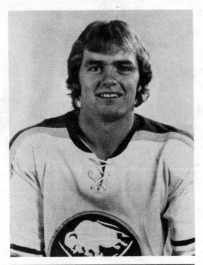

Danny Gare was one of six Buffalo Sabres to score at least 30 goals in 1974-75.

Paul Coffey, one of three Penguins to compile 100 points during the 1988-89 season.

MOST SHOTS, ONE TEAM, ONE GAME:
83 — **Boston Bruins,** March 4, 1941, at Boston. Boston defeated Chicago 3-2.
73 — NY Americans, Dec. 26, 1925, at New York. NY Americans defeated Pit. Pirates 3-1.
— Boston Bruins, March 21, 1991, at Boston. Boston tied Quebec 3-3.
72 — Boston Bruins, Dec. 10, 1970, at Boston. Boston defeated Buffalo 8-2.

MOST PENALTIES, BOTH TEAMS, ONE GAME:
85 Penalties — **Edmonton Oilers (44), Los Angeles Kings (41)** at Los Angeles, Feb. 28, 1990. Edmonton received 26 minors, 7 majors, 6 10-minute misconducts, 4 game misconducts and 1 match penalty; Los Angeles received 26 minors, 9 majors, 3 10-minute misconducts and 3 game misconducts.

MOST PENALTY MINUTES, BOTH TEAMS, ONE GAME:
406 Minutes — **Minnesota North Stars, Boston Bruins** at Boston, Feb. 26, 1981. Minnesota received 18 minors, 13 majors, 4 10-minute misconducts a 7 game misconducts; a total of 211PIM. Boston received 20 minors, 13 majors, 3 10-minute misconducts and six game misconducts; a total of 195PIM.

MOST PENALTIES, ONE TEAM, ONE GAME:
44 — **Penalties — Edmonton Oilers,** Feb. 28, 1990, at Los Angeles. Edmonton received 26 minors, 7 majors, 6 10-minute misconducts, 4 game misconducts and 1 match penalty.
42 — Minnesota North Stars, Feb. 26, 1981, at Boston. Minnesota received 18 minors, 13 majors, 4 10-minute misconducts and 7 game misconducts.
— Boston Bruins, Feb. 26, 1981, at Boston vs. Minnesota. Boston received 20 minors, 13 majors, 3 10-minute misconducts and 7 game misconducts.

MOST PENALTY MINUTES, ONE TEAM, ONE GAME:
211 — **Minnesota North Stars,** Feb. 26, 1981, at Boston. Minnesota received 18 minors, 13 majors, 4 10-minute misconducts and 7 game misconducts.

MOST GOALS, BOTH TEAMS, ONE PERIOD:
12 — **Buffalo Sabres, Toronto Maple Leafs,** at Buffalo, March 19, 1981, second period. Buffalo scored 9 goals, Toronto 3. Buffalo won 14-4.
— **Edmonton Oilers, Chicago Blackhawks,** at Chicago, Dec. 11, 1985, second period. Edmonton scored 6 goals, Chicago 6. Edmonton won 12-9.
10 — NY Rangers, NY Americans, at NY Americans, March 16, 1939, third period. NY Rangers scored 7 goals, NY Americans 3. NY Rangers won 11-5.
— Toronto Maple Leafs, Detroit Red Wings, at Detroit, March 17, 1946, third period. Toronto scored 6 goals, Detroit 4. Toronto won 11-7.
— Vancouver Canucks, Buffalo Sabres, at Buffalo, Jan. 8, 1976, third period. Buffalo scored 6 goals, Vancouver 4. Buffalo won 8-5.
— Buffalo Sabres, Montreal Canadiens, at Montreal, Oct. 26, 1982, first period. Montreal scored 5 goals, Buffalo 5. 7-7 tie.
— Boston Bruins, Quebec Nordiques, at Quebec, Dec. 7, 1982, second period. Quebec scored 6 goals, Boston 4. Quebec won 10-5.
— Calgary Flames, Vancouver Canucks, at Vancouver, Jan. 16, 1987, first period. Vancouver scored 6 goals, Calgary 4. Vancouver won 9-5.
— Winnipeg Jets, Detroit Red Wings, at Detroit, Nov. 25, 1987, third period. Detroit scored 7 goals, Winnipeg 3. Detroit won 10-8.
— Chicago Blackhawks, St. Louis Blues, at St. Louis, Mar. 15, 1988, third period. Chicago scored 5 goals, St. Louis 5. 7-7 tie.

MOST GOALS, ONE TEAM, ONE PERIOD:
9 — **Buffalo Sabres,** March 19, 1981, at Buffalo, second period during 14-4 win over Toronto.
8 — Detroit Red Wings, Jan. 23, 1944, at Detroit, third period during 15-0 win over NY Rangers.
— Boston Bruins, March 16, 1969, at Boston, second period during 11-3 win over Toronto.
— NY Rangers, Nov. 21, 1971, at New York, third period during 12-1 win over California.
— Philadelphia Flyers, March 31, 1973, at Philadelphia, second period during 10-2 win over NY Islanders.
— Buffalo Sabres, Dec. 21, 1975, at Buffalo, third period during 14-2 win over Washington.
— Minnesota North Stars, Nov. 11, 1981, at Minnesota, second period during 15-2 win over Winnipeg.

MOST POINTS, BOTH TEAMS, ONE PERIOD:
35 — **Edmonton, Oilers, Chicago Blackhawks,** at Chicago, Dec. 11, 1985, second period. Edmonton had 6G, 12A; Chicago, 6G, 11A. Edmonton won 12-9.
31 — Buffalo Sabres, Toronto Maple Leafs, at Buffalo, March 19, 1981, second period. Buffalo had 9G, 14A; Toronto, 3G, 5A. Buffalo won 14-4.
29 — Winnipeg Jets, Detroit Red Wings, at Detroit, Nov. 25, 1987, third period. Detroit had 7G, 13A; Winnipeg had 3G, 6A. Detroit won 10-8.
— Chicago Blackhawks, St. Louis Blues, at St. Louis, Mar. 15, 1988, third period. St. Louis had 5G, 10A; Chicago had 5G, 9A. 7-7 tie.

MOST POINTS, ONE TEAM, ONE PERIOD:
23 — **NY Rangers,** Nov. 21, 1971, at New York, third period during 12-1 win over California. NY Rangers scored 8G and 15A.
— **Buffalo Sabres,** Dec. 21, 1975, at Buffalo, third period during 14-2 win over Washington. Buffalo scored 8G and 15A.
— **Buffalo Sabres,** March 19, 1981, at Buffalo, second period, during 14-4 win over Toronto. Buffalo scored 9G and 14A.
22 — Detroit Red Wings, Jan. 23, 1944, at Detroit, third period during 15-0 win over NY Rangers. Detroit scored 8G and 14A.
— Boston Bruins, March 16, 1969, at Boston, second period during 11-3 win over Toronto Maple Leafs. Boston scored 8G and 14A.
— Minnesota North Stars, Nov. 11, 1981, at Minnesota, second period during 15-2 win over Winnipeg. Minnesota scored 8G and 14A.

MOST SHOTS, ONE TEAM, ONE PERIOD:
33 — **Boston Bruins,** March 4, 1941, at Boston, second period. Boston defeated Chicago 3-2.

MOST PENALTIES, BOTH TEAMS, ONE PERIOD:
67 — **Minnesota North Stars, Boston Bruins,** at Boston, Feb. 26, 1981, first period. Minnesota received 15 minors, 8 majors, 4 10-minute misconducts and 7 game misconducts, a total 34 penalties. Boston had 16 minors, 8 majors, 3 10-minute misconducts and 6 game misconducts, a total 33 penalties.

Bryan Hextall, Phil Watson and Lynn Patrick helped the Rangers score seven third period goals on March 16, 1939.

Ron Tugnutt turned in 1990-91's most sensational performance, stopping 70 of 73 shots in a 3-3 tie with Boston.

MOST PENALTY MINUTES, BOTH TEAMS, ONE PERIOD:
372 — **Los Angeles Kings, Philadelphia Flyers** at Philadelphia, March 11, 1979, first period. Philadelphia received 4 minors, 8 majors, 6 10-minute misconducts and 8 game misconducts for 188 minutes. Los Angeles received 2 minors, 8 majors, 6 10-minute misconducts and 8 game misconducts for 184 minutes.

MOST PENALTIES, ONE TEAM, ONE PERIOD:
34 — **Minnesota North Stars,** Feb. 26, 1981, at Boston, first period. 15 minors, 8 majors, 4 10-minute misconducts, 7 game misconducts.

MOST PENALTY MINUTES, ONE TEAM, ONE PERIOD:
188 — **Philadelphia Flyers,** March 11, 1979, at Philadelphia vs. Los Angeles, first period. Flyers received 4 minors, 8 majors, 6 10-minute misconducts and 8 game misconducts.

FASTEST SIX GOALS, BOTH TEAMS
3 Minutes, 15 Seconds — **Montreal Canadiens, Toronto Maple Leafs,** at Montreal, Jan. 4, 1944, first period. Montreal scored 4G, Toronto 2. Montreal won 6-3.

FASTEST FIVE GOALS, BOTH TEAMS:
1 Minute, 24 Seconds — **Chicago Blackhawks, Toronto Maple Leafs,** at Toronto, Oct. 15, 1983, second period. Scorers were: Gaston Gingras, Toronto, 16:49; Denis Savard, Chicago, 17:12; Steve Larmer, Chicago, 17:27; Savard, 17:42; and John Anderson, Toronto, 18:13. Toronto won 10-8.
1 Minute, 39 Seconds — Detroit Red Wings, Toronto Maple Leafs, at Toronto, Nov. 15, 1944, third period. Scorers were: Ted Kennedy, Toronto, 10:36 and 10:55; Hal Jackson, Detroit, 11:48; Steve Wochy, Detroit, 12:02; Don Grosso, Detroit, 12:15. Detroit won 8-4.

FASTEST FIVE GOALS, ONE TEAM:
2 Minutes, 7 Seconds — **Pittsburgh Penguins,** at Pittsburgh, Nov. 22, 1972, third period. Scorers: Bryan Hextall, 12:00; Jean Pronovost, 12:18; Al McDonough, 13:40; Ken Schinkel, 13:49; Ron Schock, 14:07. Pittsburgh defeated St. Louis 10-4.
2 Minutes, 37 seconds — NY Islanders at New York, Jan. 26, 1982, first period. Scorers: Duane Sutter, 1:31; John Tonelli, 2:30; Bryan Trottier, 2:46; Bryan Trottier, 3:31; Duane Sutter, 4:08. NY Islanders defeated Pittsburgh 9-2.
2 Minutes, 55 Seconds — Boston Bruins, at Boston, Dec. 19, 1974. Scorers: Bobby Schmautz, 19:13 (first period); Ken Hodge, 0:18; Phil Esposito, 0:43; Don Marcotte, 0:58; John Bucyk, 2:08 (second period). Boston defeated NY Rangers 11-3.

FASTEST FOUR GOALS, BOTH TEAMS:
53 Seconds — **Chicago Blackhawks, Toronto Maple Leafs,** at Toronto, Oct. 15, 1983, second period. Scorers were: Gaston Gingras, Toronto, 16:49; Denis Savard, Chicago, 17:12; Steve Larmer, Chicago, 17:27; and Savard at 17:42. Toronto won 10-8.
57 Seconds — Quebec Nordiques, Detroit Red Wings, at Quebec, Jan. 27, 1990, first period. Scorers were: Paul Gillis, Quebec, 18:01; Claude Loiselle, Quebec, 18:12; Joe Sakic, Quebec, 18:27; and Jimmy Carson, Detroit, 18:58. Detroit won 8-6.
1 Minute, 1 Second — Colorado Rockies, NY Rangers, at New York, Jan. 15, 1980, first period. Scorers were: Doug Sulliman, NY Rangers, 7:52; Ed Johnstone, NY Rangers, 7:57; Warren Miller, NY Rangers, 8:20; Rob Ramage, Colorado, 8:53. 6-6 tie.
— Chicago Blackhawks, Toronto Maple Leafs, at Toronto, Oct. 15, 1983, second period. Scorers were: Denis Savard, Chicago, 17:12; Steve Larmer, Chicago, 17:27; Savard, 17:42; John Anderson, Toronto, 18:13. Toronto won 10-8.

FASTEST FOUR GOALS, ONE TEAM:
1 Minute, 20 Seconds — **Boston Bruins,** at Boston, Jan. 21, 1945, second period. Scorers were: Bill Thoms at 6:34; Frank Mario at 7:08 and 7:27; and Ken Smith at 7:54. Boston defeated NY Rangers 14-3.

FASTEST THREE GOALS, BOTH TEAMS:
15 Seconds — **Minnesota North Stars, NY Rangers,** at Minnesota, Feb. 10, 1983, second period. Scorers were: Mark Pavelich, NY Rangers, 19:18; Ron Greschner, NY Rangers, 19:27; Willi Plett, Minnesota, 19:33. Minnesota won 7-5.
18 Seconds — Montreal Canadiens, NY Rangers, at Montreal, Dec. 12, 1963, first period. Scorers were: Dave Balon, Montreal, 0:58; Gilles Tremblay, Montreal, 1:04; Camille Henry, NY Rangers, 1:16. Montreal won 6-4.
18 Seconds — California Golden Seals, Buffalo Sabres, at California, Feb. 1, 1976, third period. Scorers were: Jim Moxey, California, 19:38; Wayne Merrick, California, 19:45; Danny Gare, Buffalo, 19:56. Buffalo won 9-5.

FASTEST THREE GOALS, ONE TEAM:
20 Seconds — **Boston Bruins,** at Boston, Feb. 25, 1971, third period. John Bucyk scored at 4:50, Ed Westfall at 5:02 and Ted Green at 5:10. Boston defeated Vancouver 8-3.
21 Seconds — Chicago Blackhawks, at New York, Mar. 23, 1952, third period. Bill Mosienko scored all three goals, at 6:09, 6:20 and 6:30. Chicago defeated NY Rangers 7-6.
21 Seconds — Washington Capitals, at Washington, Nov. 23, 1990, first period. Michal Pivonka scored at 16:18 and Stephen Leach scored at 16:29 and 16:39. Washington defeated Pittsburgh 7-3.

FASTEST THREE GOALS FROM START OF PERIOD, BOTH TEAMS:
1 Minute, 5 seconds — **Hartford Whalers, Montreal Canadiens,** at Montreal, March 11, 1989, second period. Scorers were: Kevin Dineen, Hartford, 0:11; Guy Carbonneau, Montreal, 0:36; Petr Svoboda, Montreal, 1:05. Montreal won 5-3.

FASTEST TWO GOALS, BOTH TEAMS:
2 Seconds — **St. Louis Blues, Boston Bruins,** at Boston, Dec. 19, 1987, third period. Scorers were: Ken Linseman, Boston, at 19:50; Doug Gilmour, St. Louis, at 19:52. St. Louis won 7-5.
3 Seconds — Chicago Blackhawks, Minnesota North Stars, at Minnesota, November 5, 1988, third period. Scorers were: Steve Thomas, Chicago, at 6:03; Dave Gagner, Minnesota, at 6:06. 5-5 tie.

FASTEST TWO GOALS, ONE TEAM:
4 Seconds — **Montreal Maroons,** at Montreal, Jan. 3, 1931, third period. Nels Stewart scored both goals, at 8:24 and 8:28. Mtl. Maroons defeated Boston 5-3.
— **Buffalo Sabres,** at Buffalo, Oct. 17, 1974, third period. Scorers were: Lee Fogolin at 14:55 and Don Luce at 14:59. Buffalo defeated California 6-1.
— **Toronto Maple Leafs,** at Quebec, December 29, 1988, third period. Scorers were: Ed Olczyk at 5:24 and Gary Leeman at 5:28. Toronto defeated Quebec 6-5.
— **Calgary Flames,** at Quebec, October 17, 1989, third period. Scorers were: Doug Gilmour at 19:45 and Paul Ranheim at 19:49. Calgary and Quebec tied 8-8.

FASTEST TWO GOALS FROM START OF PERIOD, BOTH TEAMS:
14 Seconds — **NY Rangers, Quebec Nordiques,** at Quebec, Nov. 5, 1983, third period. Scorers: Andre Savard, Quebec, 0:08; Pierre Larouche, NY Rangers, 0:14. 4-4 tie.
28 Seconds — Boston Bruins, Montreal Canadiens, at Montreal, Oct. 11, 1989, third period. Scorers: Jim Wiemer, Boston 0:10, Tom Chorske, Montreal 0:28. Montreal won 4-2.
35 Seconds — Boston Bruins, Pittsburgh Penguins, at Boston, Feb. 10, 1973, second period. Scorers: Lowell MacDonald, Pittsburgh, 0:07; Phil Esposito, Boston, 0:35. Boston won 6-3.

FASTEST TWO GOALS FROM START OF GAME, ONE TEAM:
24 Seconds — **Edmonton Oilers,** March 28, 1982, at Los Angeles. Mark Messier, at 0:14 and Dave Lumley, at 0:24, scored in first period. Edmonton defeated Los Angeles 6-2.
29 Seconds — Pittsburgh Penguins, Dec. 6, 1981, at Pittsburgh. George Ferguson, at 0:17, and Greg Malone, at 0:29, scored in first period. Pittsburgh defeated Chicago 6-4.
32 Seconds — Calgary Flames, Mar. 11, 1987, at Hartford. Doug Risebrough scored at 0:09 and Colin Patterson, at 0:32, in first period. Calgary defeated Hartford 6-1.

FASTEST TWO GOALS FROM START OF PERIOD, ONE TEAM:
21 Seconds — **Chicago Blackhawks,** Nov. 5, 1983, at Minnesota, second period. Ken Yaremchuk scored at 0:12 and Darryl Sutter at 0:21. Minnesota defeated Chicago 10-5.
30 Seconds — Washington Capitals, Jan. 27, 1980, at Washington, second period. Mike Gartner scored at 0:08 and Bengt Gustafsson at 0:30. Washington defeated NY Islanders 7-1.
31 Seconds — Buffalo Sabres, Jan. 10, 1974, at Buffalo, third period. Rene Robert scored at 0:21 and Rick Martin at 0:30. Buffalo defeated NY Rangers 7-2.
— NY Islanders, Feb. 22, 1986, at New York, third period. Roger Kortko scored at 0:10 and Bob Bourne at 0:31. NY Islanders defeated Detroit 5-2.

Gary Leeman, at left, combined with Ed Olcyzk to score goals four seconds apart in the third period of a 6-5 Toronto victory over Quebec on December 29, 1988.

Individual Records

Career

MOST SEASONS:
- **26 — Gordie Howe,** Detroit, 1946-47 – 1970-71; Hartford, 1979-80.
- 24 — Alex Delvecchio, Detroit, 1950-51 – 1973-74.
- — Tim Horton, Toronto, NY Rangers, Pittsburgh, Buffalo, 1949-50, 1951-52 – 1973-74.
- 23 — John Bucyk, Detroit, Boston, 1955-56 – 1977-78.
- 22 — Dean Prentice, NY Rangers, Boston, Detroit, Pittsburgh, Minnesota, 1952-53 – 1973-74.
- — Doug Mohns, Boston, Chicago, Minnesota, Atlanta, Washington, 1953-54 – 1974-75.
- — Stan Mikita, Chicago, 1958-59 – 1979-80.

MOST GAMES:
- **1,767 — Gordie Howe,** Detroit, 1946-47 – 1970-71; Hartford, 1979-80.
- 1,549 — Alex Delvecchio, Detroit, 1950-51 – 1973-74.
- 1,540 — John Bucyk, Detroit, Boston, 1955-56 – 1977-78.

MOST GOALS:
- **801 — Gordie Howe,** Detroit, Hartford, in 26 seasons, 1,767GP.
- 731 — Marcel Dionne, Detroit, Los Angeles, NY Rangers, in 18 seasons, 1,348GP.
- 718 — Wayne Gretzky, Edmonton, Los Angeles, in 12 seasons, 952GP.
- 717 — Phil Esposito, Chicago, Boston, NY Rangers, in 18 seasons, 1,282GP.
- 610 — Bobby Hull, Chicago, Winnipeg, Hartford, in 16 seasons, 1,063GP.

HIGHEST GOALS-PER-GAME AVERAGE, CAREER
(AMONG PLAYERS WITH 200 OR MORE GOALS):
- **.804 — Mario Lemieux,** Pittsburgh, 364G, 453GP, from 1984-85 – 1990-91.
- .776 — Wayne Gretzky, Edmonton, Los Angeles, 718G, 925GP, from 1979-80 – 1990-91.
- .771 — Brett Hull, Calgary, St. Louis, 236G, 306GP, from 1986-87 – 1990-91.
- .767 — Cy Denneny, Ottawa, Boston, 250G, 326GP, from 1917-18 – 1928-29.
- .762 — Mike Bossy, NY Islanders, 573G, 752GP, from 1977-78 – 1986-87.

MOST ASSISTS:
- **1,424 — Wayne Gretzky,** Edmonton, Los Angeles, in 12 seasons, 925GP.
- 1,049 — Gordie Howe, Detroit, Hartford in 26 seasons, 1,767GP.
- 1,040 — Marcel Dionne, Detroit, Los Angeles, NY Rangers in 18 seasons, 1,348GP.
- 926 — Stan Mikita, Chicago, in 22 seasons, 1,394GP.
- 873 — Phil Esposito, Chicago, Boston, NY Rangers in 18 seasons, 1,282GP.

HIGHEST ASSIST-PER-GAME AVERAGE, CAREER
(AMONG PLAYERS WITH 300 OR MORE ASSISTS):
- **1.539 — Wayne Gretzky,** Edmonton, Los Angeles, 1,424A, 925GP from 1979-80 – 1990-91.
- 1.146 — Mario Lemieux, Pittsburgh, 519A, 453GP from 1984-85 – 1990-91.
- .982 — Bobby Orr, Boston, Chicago, 645A, 657GP from 1966-67 – 1978-79.
- .912 — Paul Coffey, Edmonton, Pittsburgh, 738A, 809GP from 1980-81 – 1990-91.
- .867 — Peter Stastny, Quebec, New Jersey, 716A, 826GP from 1980-81 – 1990-91.
- .860 — Denis Savard, Chicago, Montreal, 693A, 806GP from 1980-81 – 1990-91.

MOST POINTS:
- **2,142 — Wayne Gretzky,** Edmonton, Los Angeles, in 12 seasons, 925GP (718G-1,424A).
- 1,850 — Gordie Howe, Detroit, Hartford, in 26 seasons, 1,767GP (801G-1049A).
- 1,771 — Marcel Dionne, Detroit, Los Angeles, NY Rangers, in 18 seasons, 1,348GP (731G-1,040A).
- 1,590 — Phil Esposito, Chicago, Boston, NY Rangers in 18 seasons, 1,282GP (717G-873A).
- 1,467 — Stan Mikita, Chicago in 22 seasons, 1,394GP (541G-926A).

MOST GOALS BY A CENTER, CAREER
- **731 — Marcel Dionne,** Detroit, Los Angeles, NY Rangers, in 18 seasons
- 718 — Wayne Gretzky, Edmonton, Los Angeles, in 12 seasons.
- 717 — Phil Esposito, Chicago, Boston, NY Rangers, in 18 seasons.
- 541 — Stan Mikita, Chicago, in 22 seasons.
- 512 — Gilbert Perreault, Buffalo, in 17 seasons.
- 509 — Bryan Trottier, NY Islanders, Pittsburgh, in 16 seasons.

MOST ASSISTS BY A CENTER, CAREER;
- **1,424 — Wayne Gretzky,** Edmonton, Los Angeles, in 11 seasons.
- 1,040 — Marcel Dionne, Detroit, Los Angeles, NY Rangers, in 18 seasons.
- 926 — Stan Mikita, Chicago, in 22 seasons.
- 873 — Phil Esposito, Chicago, Boston, NY Rangers, in 18 seasons.
- 872 — Bryan Trottier, NY Islanders, Pittsburgh, in 16 seasons.

MOST POINTS BY A CENTER, CAREER:
- **2,142 — Wayne Gretzky,** Edmonton, Los Angeles, in 12 seasons.
- 1,771 — Marcel Dionne, Detroit, Los Angeles, NY Rangers, in 18 seasons.
- 1,590 — Phil Esposito, Chicago, Boston, NY Rangers, in 18 seasons.
- 1,467 — Stan Mikita, Chicago, in 22 seasons
- 1,381 — Bryan Trottier, NY Islanders, Pittsburgh, in 16 seasons.
- 1,326 — Gilbert Perreault, Buffalo, in 17 seasons.

MOST GOALS BY A LEFT WING, CAREER:
- **610 — Bobby Hull,** Chicago, Winnipeg, Hartford, in 16 seasons.
- 556 — John Bucyk, Detroit, Boston, in 23 seasons.
- 533 — Frank Mahovlich, Toronto, Detroit, Montreal, in 18 seasons.
- 487 — Michel Goulet, Quebec, Chicago, in 12 seasons.
- 424 — Steve Shutt, Montreal, Los Angeles, in 13 seasons.
- 420 — Bill Barber, Philadelphia, in 12 seasons.

MOST ASSISTS BY A LEFT WING, CAREER:
- **813 — John Bucyk,** Detroit, Boston, in 23 seasons.
- 570 — Frank Mahovlich, Toronto, Detroit, Montreal, in 18 seasons.
- 560 — Bobby Hull, Chicago, Winnipeg, Hartford, in 16 seasons.
- 535 — Brian Propp, Philadelphia, Boston, Minnesota, in 12 seasons.
- 528 — Michel Goulet, Quebec, Chicago, in 12 seasons.
- 516 — Wayne Cashman, Boston, in 17 seasons.
- 500 — John Tonelli, NY Islanders, Calgary, Los Angeles, in 13 seasons.

MOST POINTS BY A LEFT WING, CAREER:
- **1,369 — John Bucyk,** Detroit, Boston, in 23 seasons.
- 1,170 — Bobby Hull, Chicago, Winnipeg, Hartford, in 16 seasons.
- 1,103 — Frank Mahovlich, Toronto, Detroit, Montreal, in 18 seasons.
- 1,015 — Michel Goulet, Quebec, Chicago, in 12 seasons.
- 933 — Brian Propp, Philadelphia, Boston, MInnesota, in 12 seasons.
- 883 — Bill Barber, Philadelphia, in 12 seasons.
- 860 — Dean Prentice, NY Rangers, Boston, Detroit, Pittsburgh, Minnesota, in 22 seasons.

MOST GOALS BY A RIGHT WING, CAREER:
- **801 — Gordie Howe,** Detroit, Hartford, in 26 seasons.
- 573 — Mike Bossy, NY Islanders, in 10 seasons.
- 560 — Guy Lafleur, Montreal, NY Rangers, Quebec, in 17 seasons.
- 544 — Maurice Richard, Montreal, in 18 seasons.

MOST ASSISTS BY A RIGHT WING, CAREER:
- **1,049 — Gordie Howe,** Detroit, Hartford, in 26 seasons.
- 793 — Guy Lafleur, Montreal, NY Rangers, Quebec, in 17 seasons.
- 624 — Andy Bathgate, NY Rangers, Toronto, Detroit, Pittsburgh in 17 seasons.
- 615 — Rod Gilbert, NY Rangers, in 18 seasons.

MOST POINTS BY A RIGHT WING, CAREER:
- **1,850 — Gordie Howe,** Detroit, Hartford, in 26 seasons.
- 1,353 — Guy Lafleur, Montreal, NY Rangers, Quebec, in 17 seasons.
- 1,126 — Mike Bossy, NY Islanders, in 10 seasons.
- 1,043 — Jari Kurri, Edmonton in 10 seasons.
- 1,021 — Rod Gilbert, NY Rangers, in 18 seasons.

Dean Prentice registered 860 points as a left winger in his 22-year career in the NHL.

MOST GOALS BY A DEFENSEMAN, CAREER:

- 310 — **Denis Potvin,** NY Islanders, in 15 seasons.
- 307 — Paul Coffey, Edmonton, Pittsburgh, in 11 seasons.
- 270 — Bobby Orr, Boston, Chicago, in 12 seasons.
- 251 — Ray Bourque, Boston, in 12 seasons.
- 248 — Doug Mohns, Boston, Chicago, Minnesota, Atlanta, Washington, in 22 seasons.

MOST ASSISTS BY A DEFENSEMAN, CAREER:

- 742 — **Denis Potvin,** NY Islanders, in 15 seasons.
- 740 — Larry Robinson, Montreal, Los Angeles, in 19 seasons.
- 738 — Paul Coffey, Edmonton, Pittsburgh, in 11 seasons.
- 683 — Ray Bourque, Boston, in 12 seasons.
- — Brad Park, NY Rangers, Boston, Detroit, in 17 seasons.
- 645 — Bobby Orr, Boston, Chicago, in 12 seasons.

MOST POINTS BY A DEFENSEMAN, CAREER:

- 1,052 — **Denis Potvin,** NY Islanders, in 15 seasons.
- 1,045 — Paul Coffey, Edmonton, Pittsburgh, in 11 seasons.
- 945 — Larry Robinson, Montreal, Los Angeles, in 19 seasons.
- 934 — Ray Bourque, Boston, in 12 seasons.
- 915 — Bobby Orr, Boston, Chicago, in 12 seasons.
- 896 — Brad Park, NY Rangers, Boston, Detroit, in 17 seasons.

MOST OVERTIME GOALS, CAREER:

- 7 — **Mario Lemieux,** Pittsburgh.
- — **Jari Kurri,** Edmonton.
- 6 — Paul MacLean, Winnipeg, Detroit, St. Louis.
- 5 — Greg Paslawski, St. Louis, Winnipeg.
- — Bernie Nicholls, Los Angeles, NY Rangers.
- — Tomas Sandstrom, NY Rangers, Los Angeles.
- — Bob Sweeney, Boston.

MOST OVERTIME ASSISTS, CAREER:

- 10 — **Wayne Gretzky,** Edmonton, Los Angeles.
- 9 — Bernie Federko, St. Louis.
- 8 — Dale Hawerchuk, Winnipeg.
- 7 — Mario Lemieux, Pittsburgh.
- — Paul MacLean, Winnipeg, Detroit, St. Louis.

MOST OVERTIME POINTS, CAREER:

- 14 — **Mario Lemieux,** Pittsburgh, 7G-7A
- 13 — Paul MacLean, Winnipeg, Detroit, St. Louis. 6G-7A
- 12 — Dale Hawerchuk, Winnipeg. 4G-8A
- — Wayne Gretzky, Edmonton, Los Angeles. 2G-10A
- 11 — Jari Kurri, Edmonton. 7G-4A

HIGHEST POINTS-PER-GAME AVERAGE, CAREER:
(AMONG PLAYERS WITH 500 OR MORE POINTS):

- 2.316 — **Wayne Gretzky,** Edmonton, Los Angeles, 2,142PTS (718G-1,424A), 925GP from 1979-80 – 1990-91.
- 1.949 — Mario Lemieux, Pittsburgh, 883PTS (364G-519A), 453GP from 1984-85 – 1990-91.
- 1.497 — Mike Bossy, NY Islanders, 1,126PTS (573G-553A), 752GP from 1978-79 – 1986-87.
- 1.393 — Bobby Orr, Boston, Chicago, 915PTS (270G-645A), 657GP from 1966-67 – 1978-79.
- 1.383 — Jari Kurri, Edmonton, 1,043PTS (474G-569A), 754GP from 1980-81 – 1989-90.

MOST PENALTY MINUTES:

- 3,966 — **Dave Williams,** Toronto, Vancouver, Detroit, Los Angeles, Hartford, in 14 seasons, 962GP.
- 2,783 — Chris Nilan, Monteal, NY Rangers, Boston, in 12 seasons, 632GP.
- 2,572 — Willi Plett, Atlanta, Calgary, Minnesota, Boston, in 12 seasons, 834GP.
- 2,471 — Dale Hunter, Quebec, Washington, in 10 seasons, 838GP.
- 2,294 — Dave Schultz, Philadelphia, Los Angeles, Pittsburgh, Buffalo, in 9 seasons, 535GP.

MOST GAMES, INCLUDING PLAYOFFS:

- 1,924 — **Gordie Howe,** Detroit, Hartford, 1,767 regular-season and 157 playoff games.
- 1,670 — Alex Delvecchio, Detroit, 1,549 regular-season and 121 playoff games.
- 1,664 — John Bucyk, Detroit, Boston, 1,540 regular-season and 124 playoff games.

MOST GOALS, INCLUDING PLAYOFFS:

- 869 — **Gordie Howe,** Detroit, Hartford, 801 regular-season goals and 68 playoff goals.
- 811 — Wayne Gretzky, Edmonton, Los Angeles, 718 regular-season and 93 playoff goals.
- 778 — Phil Esposito, Chicago, Boston, NY Rangers, 717 regular-season and 61 playoff goals.
- 752 — Marcel Dionne, Detroit, Los Angeles, NY Rangers, 731 regular-season and 21 playoff goals.

MOST ASSISTS, INCLUDING PLAYOFFS:

- 1,630 — **Wayne Gretzky,** Edmonton, Los Angeles, 1,424 regular-season and 206 playoff assists.
- 1,141 — Gordie Howe, Detroit, Hartford, 1,049 regular-season and 92 playoff assists.
- 1,064 — Marcel Dionne, Detroit, Los Angeles, NY Rangers, 1,040 regular-season and 24 playoff assists.
- 1,017 — Stan Mikita, Chicago, 926 regular-season and 91 playoff assists.
- 982 — Bryan Trottier, NY Islanders, 872 regular-season and 110 playoff assists.

MOST POINTS, INCLUDING PLAYOFFS:

- 2,441 — **Wayne Gretzky,** Edmonton, Los Angeles, 2,142 regular-season and 299 playoff points.
- 2,010 — Gordie Howe, Detroit, Hartford, 1,850 regular-season and 160 playoff assists.
- 1,816 — Marcel Dionne, Detroit, Los Angeles, NY Rangers, 1,771 regular-season and 45 playoff points.
- 1,727 — Phil Esposito, Chicago, Boston, NY Rangers, 1,590 regular-season and 137 playoff points.
- 1,617 — Stan Mikita, Chicago, 1,467 regular-season and 150 playoff points.

MOST PENALTY MINUTES, INCLUDING PLAYOFFS:

- 4,421 — **Dave Williams,** Toronto, Vancouver, Los Angeles, 3,966 in regular season; 455 in playoffs.
- 3,309 — Chris Nilan, Montreal, NY Rangers, Boston, 2,783 in regular-season; 526 in playoffs.
- 3,038 — Willi Plett, Atlanta, Calgary, Minnesota, Boston, 2,572 in regular-season; 466 in playoffs.
- 3,019 — Dale Hunter, Quebec, Washington, 2,471 in regular-season; 548 in playoffs.
- 2,706 — Dave Schultz, Philadelphia, Los Angeles, Pittsburgh, Buffalo, 2,294 regular-season; 412 in playoffs.

Rod Gilbert was the second right-winger in NHL history to reach the 1000-point plateau.

Andy Hebenton, the NHL's original "iron man," played nine straight seasons without missing a game before being sent to the minors by the Bruins at the start of the 1964-65 season.

Gordie Howe scored 20-or-more goals in 22 of his 26 NHL seasons.

MOST CONSECUTIVE GAMES:
964 — Doug Jarvis, Montreal, Washington, Hartford, from Oct. 8, 1975 – Oct. 10, 1987.
914 — Garry Unger, Toronto, Detroit, St. Louis, Atlanta from Feb. 24, 1968, – Dec. 21, 1979.
776 — Craig Ramsay, Buffalo, from March 27, 1973, – Feb. 10, 1983.
720 — Steve Larmer, Chicago, from Oct. 6, 1982 to March 31, 1991.
630 — Andy Hebenton, NY Rangers, Boston, nine complete 70-game seasons from 1955-56 – 1963-64.

MOST GAMES APPEARED IN BY A GOALTENDER, CAREER:
971 — Terry Sawchuk, Detroit, Boston, Toronto, Los Angeles, NY Rangers from 1949-50 – 1969-70.
906 — Glenn Hall, Detroit, Chicago, St. Louis from 1952-53 – 1970-71.
886 — Tony Esposito, Montreal, Chicago from 1968-69 – 1983-84.
860 — Lorne "Gump" Worsley, NY Rangers, Montreal, Minnesota from 1952-53 – 1973-74.

MOST CONSECUTIVE COMPLETE GAMES BY A GOALTENDER:
502 — Glenn Hall, Detroit, Chicago. Played 502 games from beginning of 1955-56 season - first 12 games of 1962-63. In his 503rd straight game, Nov. 7, 1962, at Chicago, Hall was removed from the game against Boston with a back injury in the first period.

MOST SHUTOUTS BY A GOALTENDER, CAREER:
103 — Terry Sawchuk, Detroit, Boston, Toronto, Los Angeles, NY Rangers in 20 seasons.
94 — George Hainsworth, Montreal Canadiens, Toronto in 10 seasons.
84 — Glenn Hall, Detroit, Chicago, St. Louis in 16 seasons.

MOST GAMES SCORING THREE-OR-MORE GOALS:
48 — Wayne Gretzky, Edmonton, Los Angeles, in 12 seasons, 35 three-goal games, 9 four-goal games, 4 five-goal games.
39 — Mike Bossy, NY Islanders, in 10 seasons, 30 three-goal games, 9 four-goal games.
32 — Phil Esposito, Chicago, Boston, NY Rangers, In 18 seasons, 27 three-goal games, 5 four-goal games.
28 — Bobby Hull, Chicago, Winnipeg, Hartford, in 16 seasons, 24 three-goal games, 4 four-goal games.
  — Marcel Dionne, Detroit, Los Angeles, NY Rangers, in 18 seasons, 25 three-goal games, 3 four-goal games.
26 — Cy Denneny, Ottawa in 12 seasons, 20 three-goal games, 5 four-goal games, 1 six-goal game.
  — Maurice Richard, Montreal, in 18 seasons, 23 three-goal games, 2 four-goal games, 1 five-goal game.
  — Mario Lemieux, Pittsburgh, in 7 seasons, 19 three-goal games, 6 four-goal games and 1 five-goal game.

MOST 20-OR-MORE GOAL SEASONS:
22 — Gordie Howe, Detroit, Hartford in 26 seasons.
17 — Marcel Dionne, Detroit, Los Angeles, NY Rangers, in 18 seasons.
16 — Phil Esposito, Chicago, Boston, NY Rangers, in 18 seasons.
  — Norm Ullman, Detroit, Toronto, in 19 seasons.
  — John Bucyk, Detroit, Boston, in 22 seasons.
15 — Frank Mahovlich, Toronto, Detroit, Montreal in 17 seasons.
  — Gilbert Perreault, Buffalo, in 17 seasons.

MOST CONSECUTIVE 20-OR-MORE GOAL SEASONS:
22 — Gordie Howe, Detroit, 1949-50 – 1970-71.
17 — Marcel Dionne, Detroit, Los Angeles, NY Rangers, 1971-72 – 1987-88.
16 — Phil Esposito, Chicago, Boston, NY Rangers, 1964-65 – 1979-80.
14 — Maurice Richard, Montreal, 1943-44 – 1956-57.
  — Stan Mikita, Chicago, 1961-62 – 1974-75.
13 — Bobby Hull, Chicago, 1959-60 – 1971-72.
  — Guy Lafleur, Montreal, 1971-72 – 1983-84.
  — Bryan Trottier, NY Islanders, 1975-76 – 1987-88.

MOST 30-OR-MORE GOAL SEASONS:
14 — Gordie Howe, Detroit, Hartford in 26 seasons.
  — **Marcel Dionne,** Detroit, Los Angeles, NY Rangers, in 18 seasons.
13 — Bobby Hull, Chicago, Winnipeg, Hartford in 16 seasons.
  — Phil Esposito, Chicago, Boston, NY Rangers, in 18 seasons.

MOST CONSECUTIVE 30-OR-MORE GOAL SEASONS:
13 — Bobby Hull, Chicago, 1959-60 – 1971-72.
  — **Phil Esposito,** Boston, NY Rangers, 1967-68 – 1979-80.
12 — Marcel Dionne, Detroit, Los Angeles,1974-75 – 1985-86.
  — Mike Gartner, Washington, Minnesota, NY Rangers, 1979-80 – 1990-91.
  — Wayne Gretzky, Edmonton, Los Angeles, 1979-80 – 1990-91.
10 — Darryl Sittler, Toronto, Philadelphia, 1973-74 – 1982-83.
  — Mike Bossy, NY Islanders, 1977-78 – 1986-87.

MOST 40-OR-MORE GOAL SEASONS:
12 — Wayne Gretzky, Edmonton, Los Angeles, in 12 seasons.
10 — Marcel Dionne, Detroit, Los Angeles, NY Rangers, in 18 seasons.
9 — Mike Bossy, NY Islanders, in 10 seasons.
8 — Bobby Hull, Chicago, Winnipeg, Hartford, in 16 seasons.
  — Phil Esposito, Chicago, Boston, NY Rangers, in 18 seasons.
7 — Michel Goulet, Quebec, Chicago, in 11 seasons.
  — Jari Kurri, Edmonton, in 10 seasons.
  — Dale Hawerchuk, Winnipeg, Buffalo, in 10 seasons.
  — Mike Gartner, Washington, Minnesota, NY Rangers, in 12 seasons.

MOST CONSECUTIVE 40-OR-MORE GOAL SEASONS:
12 — Wayne Gretzky, Edmonton, Los Angeles, 1979-80 – 1990-91.
9 — Mike Bossy, NY Islanders, 1977-78 – 1985-86.
7 — Phil Esposito, Boston, 1968-69 – 1974-75.
  — Michel Goulet, Quebec, 1981-82 – 1987-88.
  — Jari Kurri, Edmonton, 1982-83 – 1988-89.
6 — Guy Lafleur, Montreal, 1974-75 – 1979-80.
  — Joe Mullen, St. Louis, Calgary, 1983-84 – 1988-89.
  — Mario Lemieux, Pittsburgh, 1984-85 – 1989-90.

MOST 100-OR-MORE POINT SEASONS:
12 — **Wayne Gretzky,** Edmonton, Los Angeles, 1979-80 – 1990-91.
8 — Marcel Dionne, Detroit, 1974-75; Los Angeles, 1976-77; 1978-79 – 1982-83; 1984-85.
7 — Mike Bossy, NY Islanders, 1978-79; 1980-81 – 1985-86.
— Peter Stastny, Quebec, 1980-81 – 1985-86; 1987-88.
6 — Phil Esposito, Boston, 1968-69; 1970-71 – 1974-75.
— Bobby Orr, Boston, 1969-70 – 1974-75.
— Guy Lafleur, Montreal, 1974-75 – 1979-80.
— Bryan Trottier, NY Islanders, 1977-78 – 1981-82; 1983-84.
— Dale Hawerchuk, Winnipeg, 1981-82; 1983-84 – 1987-88.
— Jari Kurri, Edmonton, 1982-83 – 1986-87; 1988-89.
— Mario Lemieux, Pittsburgh, 1984-85 – 1989-90.

MOST CONSECUTIVE 100-OR-MORE POINT SEASONS:
12 — **Wayne Gretzky,** Edmonton, Los Angeles, 1979-80 – 1990-91.
6 — Bobby Orr, Boston, 1969-70 – 1974-75.
— Guy Lafleur, Montreal, 1974-75 – 1979-80.
— Mike Bossy, NY Islanders, 1980-81 – 1985-86.
— Peter Stastny, Quebec, 1980-81 – 1985-86.
— Mario Lemieux, Pittsburgh, 1984-85 – 1989-90.

MOST 50-OR-MORE GOAL SEASONS:
9 — **Mike Bossy,** NY Islanders, in 11 seasons.
— Wayne Gretzky, Edmonton, Los Angeles, in 12 seasons.
6 — Guy Lafleur, Montreal, NY Rangers, Quebec, in 17 seasons.
— Marcel Dionne, Detroit, Los Angeles, NY Rangers, in 18 seasons.
5 — Bobby Hull, Chicago, Winnipeg, Hartford, in 16 seasons.
— Phil Esposito, Chicago, Boston, NY Rangers, in 18 seasons.

MOST CONSECUTIVE 50-OR-MORE GOAL SEASONS:
9 — **Mike Bossy,** NY Islanders, 1977-78 – 1985-86.
8 — Wayne Gretzky, Edmonton, 1979-80 – 1986-87.
6 — Guy Lafleur, Montreal, 1974-75 – 1979-80.
5 — Phil Esposito, Boston, 1970-71 – 1974-75.
— Marcel Dionne, Los Angeles, 1978-79 – 1982-83.

MOST 60-OR-MORE GOAL SEASONS:
5 — **Mike Bossy,** NY Islanders, in 10 seasons.
— Wayne Gretzky, Edmonton, Los Angeles, in 12 seasons.
4 — Phil Esposito, Chicago, Boston, NY Rangers, in 18 seasons.

MOST CONSECUTIVE 60-OR-MORE GOAL SEASONS:
4 — **Wayne Gretzky,** Edmonton, 1981-82 – 1984-85.
3 — Mike Bossy, NY Islanders, 1980-81 – 1982-83.
2 — Phil Esposito, Boston, 1970-71 – 1971-72; 1973-74 – 1974-75.
— Jari Kurri, Edmonton, 1984-85 – 1985-86.
— Mario Lemieux, Pittsburgh, 1987-88 – 1988-89.
— Steve Yzerman, Detroit, 1988-89 – 1989-90.
— Brett Hull, St. Louis, 1989-90 – 1990-91.

Single Season

MOST GOALS, ONE SEASON:
92 — **Wayne Gretzky,** Edmonton, 1981-82. 80 game schedule.
87 — Wayne Gretzky, Edmonton, 1983-84. 80 game schedule.
86 — Brett Hull, St. Louis, 1990-91. 80 game schedule.
85 — Mario Lemieux, Pittsburgh, 1988-89. 80 game schedule.
76 — Phil Esposito, Boston, 1970-71. 78 game schedule.
73 — Wayne Gretzky, Edmonton, 1984-85. 80 game schedule.
72 — Brett Hull, St. Louis, 1989-90. 80 game schedule.
71 — Jari Kurri, Edmonton, 1984-85 80 game schedule.
— Wayne Gretzky, Edmonton, 1982-83. 80 game schedule.
70 — Mario Lemieux, Pittsburgh, 1987-1988. 80 game schedule.
— Bernie Nicholls, Los Angeles, 1988-89. 80 game schedule.
69 — Mike Bossy, NY Islanders, 1978-79. 80 game schedule.
68 — Phil Esposito, Boston, 1973-74. 78 game schedule.
— Mike Bossy, NY Islanders, 1980-81. 80 game schedule.
— Jari Kurri, Edmonton, 1985-86. 80 game schedule.

MOST ASSISTS, ONE SEASON:
163 — **Wayne Gretzky,** Edmonton , 1985-86. 80 game schedule.
135 — Wayne Gretzky, Edmonton, 1984-85. 80 game schedule.
125 — Wayne Gretzky, Edmonton, 1982-83. 80 game schedule.
122 — Wayne Gretzky, Los Angeles, 1990-91. 80 game schedule.
121 — Wayne Gretzky, Edmonton, 1986-87. 80 game schedule.
120 — Wayne Gretzky, Edmonton, 1981-82. 80 game schedule.
118 — Wayne Gretzky, Edmonton, 1983-84. 80 game schedule.
114 — Wayne Gretzky, Los Angeles, 1988-89. 80 game schedule.
— Mario Lemieux, Pittsburgh, 1988-89. 80 game schedule.
109 — Wayne Gretzky, Edmonton, 1980-81. 80 game schedule.
— Wayne Gretzky, Edmonton, 1987-88. 80 game schedule.
102 — Bobby Orr, Boston, 1970-71. 78 game schedule.
— Wayne Gretzky, Los Angeles, 1989-90. 80 game schedule.

MOST POINTS, ONE SEASON:
215 — **Wayne Gretzky,** Edmonton, 1985-86. 80 game schedule.
212 — Wayne Gretzky, Edmonton, 1981-82. 80 game schedule.
208 — Wayne Gretzky, Edmonton, 1984-85. 80 game schedule.
205 — Wayne Gretzky, Edmonton, 1983-84. 80 game schedule.
199 — Mario Lemieux, Pittsburgh, 1988-89. 80 game schedule.
196 — Wayne Gretzky, Edmonton, 1982-83. 80 game schedule.
183 — Wayne Gretzky, Edmonton, 1986-87. 80 game schedule.
168 — Mario Lemieux, Pittsburgh, 1987-88. 80 game schedule.
— Wayne Gretzky, Los Angeles, 1988-89. 80 game schedule.
164 — Wayne Gretzky, Edmonton, 1980-81. 80 game schedule.
163 — Wayne Gretzky, Los Angeles, 1990-91. 80 game schedule.
155 — Steve Yzerman, Detroit, 1988-89. 80 game schedule.
152 — Phil Esposito, Boston, 1970-71. 78 game schedule.
150 — Bernie Nicholls, Los Angeles, 1988-89. 80 game schedule.

MOST GAMES SCORING AT LEAST THREE GOALS, ONE SEASON:
10 — **Wayne Gretzky,** Edmonton, 1981-82. 6 three-goal games, 3 four-goal games, 1 five-goal game.
— **Wayne Gretzky,** Edmonton, 1983-84. 6 three-goal games, 4 four-goal games.
9 — Mike Bossy, NY Islanders, 1980-81. 6 three-goal games, 3 four-goal games.
— Mario Lemieux, Pittsburgh, 1988-89. 7 three-goal games, 1 four-goal game, 1 five-goal game.
7 — Joe Malone, Montreal, 1917-18. 2 three-goal games, 2 four-goal games, 3 five-goal games.
— Phil Esposito, Boston, 1970-71. 7 three-goal games.
— Rick Martin, Buffalo, 1975-76. 6 three-goal games, 1 four-goal game.

HIGHEST GOALS-PER-GAME AVERAGE, ONE SEASON (AMONG PLAYERS WITH 20-OR-MORE GOALS):
2.20 — **Joe Malone,** Montreal, 1917-18, with 44G in 20GP.
1.64 — Cy Denneny, Ottawa, 1917-18, with 36G in 22GP.
— Newsy Lalonde, Montreal, 1917-18, with 23G in 14GP.
1.63 — Joe Malone, Quebec, 1919-20, with 39G in 24GP.
1.57 — Newsy Lalonde, Montreal, 1919-20, with 36G in 23GP.
1.50 — Joe Malone, Hamilton, 1920-21, with 30G in 20GP.

HIGHEST GOALS-PER-GAME AVERAGE, ONE SEASON (AMONG PLAYERS WITH 50-OR-MORE GOALS):
1.18 — **Wayne Gretzky,** Edmonton, 1983-84, with 87G in 74GP.
1.15 — Wayne Gretzky, Edmonton, 1981-82, with 92G in 80GP.
1.12 — Mario Lemieux, Pittsburgh, 1988-89, with 85G in 76GP.
1.10 — Brett Hull, St. Louis, 1990-91, with 86G in 78GP.
1.00 — Maurice Richard, Montreal, 1944-45, with 50G in 50GP.
.97 — Phil Esposito, Boston, 1970-71, with 76G in 78GP.
— Jari Kurri, Edmonton, 1984-85, with 71G in 73GP.
.91 — Wayne Gretzky, Edmonton, 1984-85, with 73G in 80GP.
— Mario Lemieux, Pittsburgh, 1987-88, with 70G in 77GP.
.90 — Brett Hull, St. Louis, 1989-90, with 72G in 80GP.

HIGHEST ASSISTS-PER-GAME AVERAGE, ONE SEASON (AMONG PLAYERS WITH 35-OR-MORE ASSISTS):
2.04 — **Wayne Gretzky,** Edmonton, 1985-86, with 163A in 80GP.
1.70 — Wayne Gretzky, Edmonton, 1987-88, with 109A in 64GP.
1.69 — Wayne Gretzky, Edmonton, 1984-85, with 135A in 80GP.
1.59 — Wayne Gretzky, Edmonton, 1983-84, with 118A in 74GP.
1.56 — Wayne Gretzky, Edmonton, 1982-83, with 125A in 80GP.
1.56 — Wayne Gretzky, Los Angeles, 1990-91, with 122A in 78GP.
1.53 — Wayne Gretzky, Edmonton, 1986-87, with 121A in 79GP.
1.50 — Wayne Gretzky, Edmonton, 1981-82, with 120A in 80GP.
1.50 — Mario Lemieux, Pittsburgh, 1988-89, with 114A in 76GP.
1.48 — Adam Oates, St. Louis, 1990-91, with 90A in 61GP.

HIGHEST POINTS-PER-GAME AVERAGE, ONE SEASON (AMONG PLAYERS WITH 50-OR-MORE POINTS):
2.77 — **Wayne Gretzky,** Edmonton, 1983-84, with 205PTS in 74GP.
2.69 — Wayne Gretzky, Edmonton, 1985-86, with 215PTS in 80GP.
2.65 — Wayne Gretzky, Edmonton, 1981-82, with 212PTS in 80GP.
2.62 — Mario Lemieux, Pittsburgh, 1988-89, with 199PTS in 78GP.
2.60 — Wayne Gretzky, Edmonton, 1984-85, with 208PTS in 80GP.
2.45 — Wayne Gretzky, Edmonton, 1982-83, with 196PTS in 80GP.
2.33 — Wayne Gretzky, Edmonton, 1987-88, with 149PTS in 64GP.
2.32 — Wayne Gretzky, Edmonton, 1986-87, with 183PTS in 79GP.
2.18 — Mario Lemieux, Pittsburgh, 1987-88 with 168PTS in 77GP.
2.15 — Wayne Gretzky, Los Angeles, 1988-89, with 168PTS in 78GP.
2.09 — Wayne Gretzky, Los Angeles, 1990-91, with 163 PTS in 78GP.
2.08 — Mario Lemieux, Pittsburgh, 1989-90, with 123 PTS in 59GP.
2.05 — Wayne Gretzky, Edmonton, 1980-81, with 164PTS in 80GP.

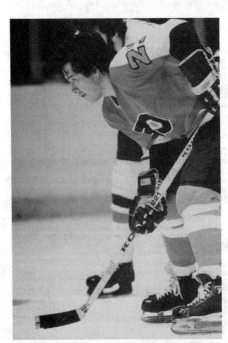

Reggie Leach scored 61 goals in the regular season and added 19 in the playoffs to become the first player to score 80 goals in a season in 1975-76.

MOST GOALS, ONE SEASON, INCLUDING PLAYOFFS:

100 — Wayne Gretzky, Edmonton, 1983-84, 87G in 74 regular-season games and 13G in 19 playoff games.
97 — Wayne Gretzky, Edmonton, 1981-82, 92G in 80 regular-season games and 5G in 5 playoff games.
— Mario Lemieux, Pittsburgh, 1988-89, 85G in 76 regular-season games and 12G in 11 playoff games.
— Brett Hull, St. Louis, 1990-91, 86G in 78 regular-season games and 11G in 13 playoff games.
90 — Wayne Gretzky, Edmonton, 1984-85, 73G in 80 regular-season games and 17G in 18 playoff games.
— Jari Kurri, Edmonton, 1984-85, 71G in 80 regular season games and 19G in 18 playoff games.
85 — Mike Bossy, NY Islanders, 1980-81, 68G in 79 regular-season games and 17G in 18 playoff games.
— Brett Hull, St. Louis, 1989-90, 72G in 80 regular season games and 13G in 12 playoff games.
83 — Wayne Gretzky, Edmonton, 1982-83, 71G in 73 regular-season games and 12G in 16 playoff games.
81 — Mike Bossy, NY Islanders, 1981-82, 64G in 80 regular-season games and 17G in 19 playoff games.
80 — Reggie Leach, Philadelphia, 1975-76, 61G in 80 regular-season games and 19G in 16 playoff games.

MOST ASSISTS, ONE SEASON, INCLUDING PLAYOFFS:

174 — Wayne Gretzky, Edmonton, 1985-86, 163A in 80 regular-season games and 11A in 10 playoff games.
165 — Wayne Gretzky, Edmonton, 1984-85, 135A in 80 regular-season games and 30A in 18 playoff games.
151 — Wayne Gretzky, Edmonton, 1982-83, 125A in 80 regular-season games and 26A in 16 playoff games.
150 — Wayne Gretzky, Edmonton, 1986-87, 121A in 79 regular-season games and 29A in 21 playoff games.
140 — Wayne Gretzky, Edmonton, 1983-84, 118A in 74 regular-season games and 22A in 19 playoff games.
— Wayne Gretzky, Edmonton, 1987-88, 109A in 64 regular-season games and 31A in 19 playoff games.
133 — Wayne Gretzky, Los Angeles, 1990-91, 122A in 78 regular-season games and 11A in 12 playoff games.
131 — Wayne Gretzky, Los Angeles, 1988-89, 114A in 78 regular-season games and 17A in 11 playoff games.
127 — Wayne Gretzky, Edmonton, 1981-82, 120A in 80 regular-season games and 7A in 5 playoff games.
123 — Wayne Gretzky, Edmonton, 1980-81, 109A in 80 regular-season games and 14A in 9 playoff games.
121 — Mario Lemieux, Pittsburgh, 1988-89, 114A in 76 regular-season games and 7A in 11 playoff games.

MOST POINTS, ONE SEASON, INCLUDING PLAYOFFS:

255 — Wayne Gretzky, Edmonton, 1984-85, 208PTS in 80 regular-season games and 47PTS in 18 playoff games.
240 — Wayne Gretzky, Edmonton, 1983-84, 205PTS in 74 regular-season games and 35PTS in 19 playoff games.
234 — Wayne Gretzky, Edmonton, 1982-83, 196PTS in 80 regular-season games and 38PTS in 16 playoff games.
— Wayne Gretzky, Edmonton, 1985-86, 215PTS in 80 regular-season games and 19PTS in 10 playoff games.
224 — Wayne Gretzky, Edmonton, 1981-82, 212PTS in 80 regular-season games and 12PTS in 5 playoff games.
218 — Mario Lemieux, Pittsburgh, 1988-89, 199PTS in 76 regular-season games and 19PTS in 11 playoff games.
217 — Wayne Gretzky, Edmonton, 1986-87, 183PTS in 79 regular-season games and 34PTS in 21 playoff games.
192 — Wayne Gretzky, Edmonton, 1987-88, 149PTS in 64 regular-season games and 43PTS in 19 playoff games.
190 — Wayne Gretzky, Los Angeles, 1988-89, 168PTS in 78 regular-season games and 22PTS in 11 playoff games.
185 — Wayne Gretzky, Edmonton, 1980-81, 164PTS in 80 regular-season games and 21PTS in 9 playoff games.

MOST GOALS, ONE SEASON, BY A DEFENSEMAN:

48 — Paul Coffey, Edmonton, 1985-86. 80 game schedule.
46 — Bobby Orr, Boston, 1974-75. 80 game schedule.
40 — Paul Coffey, Edmonton, 1983-84. 80 game schedule.
39 — Doug Wilson, Chicago, 1981-82. 80 game schedule.
37 — Bobby Orr, Boston, 1970-71. 78 game schedule.
— Bobby Orr, Boston, 1971-72. 78 game schedule.
— Paul Coffey, Edmonton, 1984-85 80 game schedule..
33 — Bobby Orr, Boston, 1969-70. 76 game schedule.
32 — Bobby Orr, Boston, 1973-74. 78 game schedule.
31 — Denis Potvin, NY Islanders, 1975-76. 80 game schedule.
— Denis Potvin, NY Islanders, 1978-79. 80 game schedule.
— Raymond Bourque, Boston, 1983-84. 80 game schedule.
— Phil Housley, Buffalo, 1983-84. 80 game schedule.
30 — Denis Potvin, NY Islanders, 1979-80. 80 game schedule.
— Paul Coffey, Pittsburgh, 1988-89. 80 game schedule.

MOST GOALS, ONE SEASON, BY A CENTER:

92 — Wayne Gretzky, Edmonton, 1981-82. 80 game schedule.
87 — Wayne Gretzky, Edmonton, 1983-84. 80 game schedule.
85 — Mario Lemieux, Pittsburgh, 1988-89. 80 game schedule.
76 — Phil Esposito, Boston, 1970-71. 78 game schedule.
73 — Wayne Gretzky, Edmonton, 1984-85. 80 game schedule.
71 — Wayne Gretzky, Edmonton, 1982-83. 80 game schedule.
70 — Mario Lemieux, Pittsburgh, 1987-88. 80 game schedule.
— Bernie Nicholls, Los Angeles, 1988-89. 80 game schedule.

MOST GOALS, ONE SEASON, BY A RIGHT WINGER:

86 — Brett Hull, St. Louis, 1990-91. 80 game schedule.
72 — Brett Hull, St. Louis, 1989-90. 80 game schedule.
71 — Jari Kurri, Edmonton, 1984-85. 80 game schedule.
69 — Mike Bossy, NY Islanders, 1978-79. 80 game schedule.
68 — Jari Kurri, Edmonton, 1985-86. 80 game schedule..
— Mike Bossy, NY Islanders, 1980-81. 80 game schedule.
66 — Lanny McDonald, Calgary, 1982-83. 80 game schedule.
64 — Mike Bossy, NY Islanders, 1981-82. 80 game schedule.
61 — Reggie Leach, Philadelphia, 1975-76. 80 game schedule.
— Mike Bossy, NY Islanders, 1985-86. 80 game schedule.
60 — Guy Lafleur, Montreal, 1977-78. 80 game schedule.
— Mike Bossy, NY Islanders, 1982-83. 80 game schedule.

MOST GOALS, ONE SEASON, BY A LEFT WINGER:

60 — Steve Shutt, Montreal, 1976-77. 80 game schedule.
58 — Bobby Hull, Chicago, 1968-69. 76 game schedule.
57 — Michel Goulet, Quebec, 1982-83. 80 game schedule.
56 — Charlie Simmer, Los Angeles, 1979-80. 80 game schedule.
— Charlie Simmer, Los Angeles, 1980-81. 80 game schedule.
— Michel Goulet, Quebec, 1983-84. 80 game schedule.
55 — Michel Goulet, Quebec, 1984-85. 80 game schedule.
— John Ogrodnick, Detroit, 1984-85. 80 game schedule.
54 — Bobby Hull, Chicago, 1965-66. 70 game schedule.
— Al Secord, Chicago, 1982-83. 80 game schedule.

Steve Shutt is the NHL's only left-winger to score 60 goals in a single season.

MOST GOALS, ONE SEASON, BY A ROOKIE:
53 — **Mike Bossy,** NY Islanders, 1977-78. 80 game schedule.
51 — Joe Nieuwendyk, Calgary, 1987-88. 80 game schedule.
45 — Dale Hawerchuk, Winnipeg, 1981-82. 80 game schedule.
— Luc Robitaille, Los Angeles, 1986-87. 80 game schedule.
44 — Richard Martin, Buffalo, 1971-72. 80 game schedule.
— Barry Pederson, Boston, 1981-82. 80 game schedule.
43 — Steve Larmer, Chicago, 1982-83. 80 game schedule.
— Mario Lemieux, Pittsburgh, 1984-85. 80 game schedule.
40 — Darryl Sutter, Chicago, 1980-81. 80 game schedule.
— Sylvain Turgeon, Hartford, 1983-84. 80 game schedule.
— Warren Young, Pittsburgh, 1984-85. 80 game schedule.

MOST GOALS, ONE SEASON, BY A ROOKIE DEFENSEMAN:
23 — **Brian Leetch,** NY Rangers, 1988-89. 80 game schedule.
22 — Barry Beck, Colorado, 1977-78. 80 game schedule.
19 — Reed Larson, Detroit, 1977-78. 80 game schedule.
— Phil Housley, Buffalo, 1982-83. 80 game schedule.

MOST ASSISTS, ONE SEASON, BY A DEFENSEMAN:
102 — **Bobby Orr,** Boston, 1970-71. 78 game schedule.
90 — Paul Coffey, Edmonton, 1985-86. 80 game schedule.
90 — Bobby Orr, Boston, 1973-74. 78 game schedule.
89 — Bobby Orr, Boston, 1974-75. 80 game schedule.

MOST ASSISTS, ONE SEASON, BY A CENTER:
163 — **Wayne Gretzky,** Edmonton, 1985-86. 80 game schedule.
135 — Wayne Gretzky, Edmonton, 1984-85. 80 game schedule.
125 — Wayne Gretzky, Edmonton, 1982-83. 80 game schedule.
122 — Wayne Gretzky, Los Angeles, 1990-91. 80 game schedule.
121 — Wayne Gretzky, Edmonton, 1986-87. 80 game schedule.
120 — Wayne Gretzky, Edmonton, 1981-82. 80 game schedule.
118 — Wayne Gretzky, Edmonton, 1983-84. 80 game schedule.
114 — Wayne Gretzky, Edmonton, 1988-89. 80 game schedule.
— Mario Lemieux, Pittsburgh, 1988-89. 80 game schedule.
109 — Wayne Gretzky, Edmonton, 1980-81. 80 game schedule.
— Wayne Gretzky, Edmonton, 1987-88. 80 game schedule.

MOST ASSISTS, ONE SEASON, BY A RIGHT WINGER:
83 — **Mike Bossy,** NY Islanders, 1981-82. 80 game schedule.
80 — Guy Lafleur, Montreal, 1976-77. 80 game schedule.
77 — Guy Lafleur, Montreal, 1978-79. 80 game schedule.

MOST ASSISTS, ONE SEASON, BY A LEFT WINGER:
67 — **Mats Naslund,** Montreal, 1985-86. 80 game schedule.
65 — John Bucyk, Boston, 1970-71. 78 game schedule.
— Michel Goulet, Quebec, 1983-84. 80 game schedule.
64 — Mark Messier, Edmonton, 1983-84. 80 game schedule.
62 — Bill Barber, Philadelphia, 1975-76. 80 game schedule.
61 — Vincent Damphousse, Toronto, 1989-90. 80 game schedule.
60 — Anton Stastny, Quebec, 1982-83. 80 game schedule.

MOST ASSISTS, ONE SEASON, BY A ROOKIE:
70 — **Peter Stastny,** Quebec, 1980-81. 80 game schedule.
63 — Bryan Trottier, NY Islanders, 1975-76. 80 game schedule.
62 — Sergei Makarov, Calgary, 1989-90. 80 game schedule.
60 — Larry Murphy, Los Angeles, 1980-81. 80 game schedule.

MOST ASSISTS, ONE SEASON, BY A ROOKIE DEFENSEMAN:
60 — **Larry Murphy,** Los Angeles, 1980-81. 80 game schedule.
55 — Chris Chelios, Montreal, 1984-85. 80 game schedule.
50 — Stefan Persson, NY Islanders, 1977-78. 80 game schedule.
— Gary Suter, Calgary, 1985-86, 80 game schedule..
48 — Raymond Bourque, Boston, 1979-80. 80 game schedule.
— Brian Leetch, NY Rangers, 1988-89. 80 game schedule.

MOST POINTS, ONE SEASON, BY A DEFENSEMAN:
139 — **Bobby Orr,** Boston, 1970-71. 78 game schedule.
138 — Paul Coffey, Edmonton,1985-86. 80 game schedule.
135 — Bobby Orr, Boston, 1974-75. 80 game schedule.
126 — Paul Coffey, Edmonton, 1983-84. 80 game schedule.
122 — Bobby Orr, Boston, 1973-74. 78 game schedule.

MOST POINTS, ONE SEASON, BY A CENTER:
215 — **Wayne Gretzky,** Edmonton, 1985-86. 80 game schedule.
212 — Wayne Gretzky, Edmonton, 1981-82. 80 game schedule.
208 — Wayne Gretzky, Edmonton, 1984-85. 80 game schedule.
205 — Wayne Gretzky, Edmonton, 1983-84. 80 game schedule.
199 — Mario Lemieux, Pittsburgh, 1988-89. 80 game schedule.
196 — Wayne Gretzky, Edmonton, 1982-83. 80 game schedule.
183 — Wayne Gretzky, Edmonton, 1986-87. 80 game schedule.
168 — Mario Lemieux, Pittsburgh, 1987-88. 80 game schedule.
— Wayne Gretzky, Los Angeles, 1988-89. 80 game schedule.
164 — Wayne Gretzky, Edmonton, 1980-81. 80 game schedule.
163 — Wayne Gretzky, Los Angeles, 1990-91. 80 game schedule.

MOST POINTS, ONE SEASON, BY A RIGHT WINGER:
147 — **Mike Bossy,** NY Islanders, 1981-82. 80 game schedule.
136 — Guy Lafleur, Montreal, 1976-77. 80 game schedule.
135 — Jari Kurri, Edmonton, 1984-85. 80 game schedule.
132 — Guy Lafleur, Montreal, 1977-78. 80 game schedule.

MOST POINTS, ONE SEASON, BY A LEFT WINGER:
121 — **Michel Goulet,** Quebec, 1983-84. 80 game schedule.
116 — John Bucyk, Boston, 1970-71. 78 game schedule.
112 — Bill Barber, Philadelphia, 1975-76. 80 game schedule.
111 — Luc Robitaille, Los Angeles, 1987-88. 80 game schedule.
110 — Mats Naslund, Montreal, 1985-86. 80 game schedule.
107 — Bobby Hull, Chicago, 1968-69. 76 game schedule.

MOST POINTS, ONE SEASON, BY A ROOKIE:
109 — **Peter Stastny,** Quebec, 1980-81. 80 game schedule.
103 — Dale Hawerchuk, Winnipeg, 1981-82. 80 game schedule.
100 — Mario Lemieux, Pittsburgh, 1984-85. 80 game schedule.
98 — Neal Broten, Minnesota, 1981-82. 80 game schedule.

MOST POINTS, ONE SEASON, BY A ROOKIE DEFENSEMAN:
76 — **Larry Murphy,** Los Angeles, 1980-81. 80 game schedule.
71 — Brian Leetch, NY Rangers, 1988-89. 80 game schedule.
68 — Gary Suter, Calgary, 1985-86. 80 game schedule.
66 — Phil Housley, Buffalo, 1982-83. 80 game schedule.
65 — Raymond Bourque, Boston, 1979-80. 80 game schedule.
64 — Chris Chelios, Montreal, 1984-85. 80 game schedule.

MOST POINTS, ONE SEASON, BY A GOALTENDER:
14 — **Grant Fuhr,** Edmonton, 1983-84. (14A)
8 — Mike Palmateer, Washington, 1980-81. (8A)
— Grant Fuhr, Edmonton, 1987-88. (8A)
— Ron Hextall, Philadelphia, 1988-89. (8A)
7 — Ron Hextall, Philadelphia, 1987-88. (1G-6A)
— Mike Vernon, Calgary, 1987-88. (7A)
6 — Gilles Meloche, California, 1974-75. (6A)
— Grant Fuhr, Edmonton, 1981-82. (6A)
— Tom Barraso, Buffalo, 1985-86. (6A)
— Ron Hextall, Philadelphia, 1986-87. (6A)
— Roland Melanson, Los Angeles, 1986-87. (6A)
— Patrick Roy, Montreal, 1988-89. (6A)

*Neal Broten, who scored 98 points as a rookie
in 1980-81, is the Stars' all-time points leader.*

MOST POWER-PLAY GOALS, ONE SEASON:
- **34 — Tim Kerr,** Philadelphia, 1985-86. 80 game schedule.
- 31 — Joe Nieuwendyk, Calgary, 1987-88. 80 game schedule.
- — Mario Lemieux, Pittsburgh, 1988-89. 80 game schedule.
- 29 — Michel Goulet, Quebec, 1987-88. 80 game schedule.
- — Brett Hull, St. Louis, 1990-91. 80 game schedule.
- 28 — Phil Esposito, Boston, 1971-72. 78 game schedule.
- — Mike Bossy, NY Islanders, 1980-81. 80 game schedule.
- — Michel Goulet, Quebec, 1985-86. 80 game schedule.

MOST SHORTHAND GOALS, ONE SEASON:
- **13 — Mario Lemieux,** Pittsburgh, 1988-89. 80 game schedule.
- 12 — Wayne Gretzky, Edmonton, 1983-84. 80 game schedule.
- 11 — Wayne Gretzky, Edmonton, 1984-85. 80 game schedule.
- 10 — Marcel Dionne, Detroit, 1974-75. 80 game schedule.
- — Mario Lemieux, Pittsburgh, 1987-88. 80 game schedule.
- — Dirk Graham, Chicago, 1988-89. 80 game schedule.

MOST SHOTS ON GOAL, ONE SEASON:
- **550 — Phil Esposito, Boston,** 1970-71. 78 game schedule.
- 426 — Phil Esposito, Boston, 1971-72. 78 game schedule.
- 414 — Bobby Hull, Chicago, 1968-69. 76 game schedule.

MOST PENALTY MINUTES, ONE SEASON:
- **472 — Dave Schultz,** Philadelphia, 1974-75.
- 409 — Paul Baxter, Pittsburgh, 1981-82.
- 405 — Dave Schultz, Los Angeles, Pittsburgh, 1977-78.

MOST SHUTOUTS, ONE SEASON:
- **22 — George Hainsworth,** Montreal, 1928-29. 44GP
- 15 — Alex Connell, Ottawa, 1925-26. 36GP
- — Alex Connell, Ottawa, 1927-28. 44GP
- — Hal Winkler, Boston, 1927-28. 44GP
- — Tony Esposito, Chicago, 1969-70. 63GP
- 14 — George Hainsworth, Montreal, 1926-27. 44GP

LONGEST UNDEFEATED STREAK BY A GOALTENDER:
- **32 Games — Gerry Cheevers,** Boston, 1971-72. 24w-8T.
- 31 Games — Pete Peeters, Boston, 1982-83. 26w-5T.
- 27 Games — Pete Peeters, Philadelphia, 1979-80. 22w-5T.
- 23 Games — Frank Brimsek, Boston, 1940-41. 15w-8T.
- — Glenn Resch, NY Islanders, 1978-79. 15w-8T.
- — Grant Fuhr, Edmonton, 1981-82. 15w-8T.

MOST GAMES, ONE SEASON, BY A GOALTENDER:
- **75 — Grant Fuhr,** Edmonton, 1987-88.
- 74 — Ed Belfour, Chicago, 1990-91.
- 73 — Bernie Parent, Philadelphia, 1973-74.
- 72 — Gary Smith, Vancouver, 1974-75.
- — Don Edwards, Buffalo, 1977-78.
- 71 — Gary Smith, California, 1970-71.
- — Tony Esposito, Chicago, 1974-75.

MOST WINS, ONE SEASON, BY A GOALTENDER:
- **47 — Bernie Parent,** Philadelphia, 1973-74.
- 44 — Bernie Parent, Philadelphia, 1974-75.
- — Terry Sawchuk, Detroit, 1950-51.
- — Terry Sawchuk, Detroit, 1951-52.

LONGEST WINNING STREAK, ONE SEASON, BY A GOALTENDER:
- **17 — Gilles Gilbert,** Boston, 1975-76.
- 14 — Don Beaupre, Minnesota, 1985-86.
- — Ross Brooks, Boston, 1973-74.
- — Tiny Thompson, Boston, 1929-30.

MOST GOALS, 50 GAMES FROM START OF SEASON:
- **61 — Wayne Gretzky,** Edmonton, 1981-82. Oct. 7, 1981 - Jan. 22, 1982. (80-game schedule)
- — **Wayne Gretzky,** Edmonton, 1983-84. Oct. 5, 1983 - Jan. 25, 1984. (80-game schedule)
- 54 — Mario Lemieux, Pittsburgh, 1988-89. Oct. 7, 1988 - Jan. 31, 1989. (80-game schedule)
- 53 — Wayne Gretzky, Edmonton, 1984-85. Oct. 11, 1984 - Jan. 28, 1985. (80-game schedule)
- 52 — Brett Hull, St. Louis, 1990-91. Oct. 4, 1990 - Jan. 26, 1991. (80-game schedule).
- 50 — Maurice Richard, Montreal, 1944-45. Oct. 28, 1944 - March 18, 1945. (50-game schedule)
- — Mike Bossy, NY Islanders, 1980-81. Oct. 11, 1980 - Jan. 24, 1981. (80-game schedule)

LONGEST CONSECUTIVE POINT-SCORING STREAK FROM START OF SEASON:
- **51 Games — Wayne Gretzky,** Edmonton, 1983-84. 61G-92A-153PTS during streak which was stopped by goaltender Markus Mattsson and Los Angeles on Jan. 28, 1984.

LONGEST CONSECUTIVE POINT SCORING STREAK:
- **51 Games — Wayne Gretzky,** Edmonton, 1983-84. 61G-92A-153PTS during streak.
- 46 Games — Mario Lemieux, Pittsburgh, 1989-90. 39G-64A-103PTS during streak.
- 39 Games — Wayne Gretzky, Edmonton, 1985-86. 33G-75A-108PTS during streak.
- 30 Games — Wayne Gretzky, Edmonton, 1982-83. 24G52A76PTS during streak.
- 28 Games — Guy Lafleur, Montreal, 1976-77. 19G-42A-61PTS during streak.
- — Wayne Gretzky, Edmonton, 1984-85. 20G-43A-63PTS during streak.
- — Mario Lemieux, Pittsburgh, 1985-86. 21G-38A-59PTS during streak.
- — Paul Coffey, Edmonton, 1985-86. 16G-39A-55PTS during a streak.
- — Steve Yzerman, Detroit, 1988-89. 29G-36A-65PTS during streak.

LONGEST CONSECUTIVE POINT-SCORING STREAK BY A DEFENSEMAN:
- **28 Games — Paul Coffey,** Edmonton, 1985-86. 16G-39A-55PTS during streak.
- 19 Games — Ray Bourque, Boston, 1987-88. 6G-21A-27PTS during streak.
- 17 Games — Ray Bourque, Boston, 1984-85. 4G-24A-28PTS during streak.
- 16 Games — Gary Suter, Calgary, 1987-88. 8G-17A-25PTS during streak.
- 15 Games — Bobby Orr, Boston, 1973-74. 8G-15A-23PTS during streak.
- 15 Games — Bobby Orr, Boston, 1970-71. 10G-23A-33PTS during streak.

LONGEST CONSECUTIVE GOAL-SCORING STREAK:
- **16 Games — Harry (Punch) Broadbent,** Ottawa, 1921-22. 25 goals during streak.
- 14 Games — Joe Malone, Montreal, 1917-18. 35 goals during streak.
- 13 Games — Newsy Lalonde, Montreal, 1920-21. 24 goals during streak.
- — Charlie Simmer, Los Angeles, 1979-80. 17 goals during streak.
- 12 Games — Cy Denneny, Ottawa, 1917-18. 23 goals during streak.
- — Dave Lumley, Edmonton, 1981-82. 15 goals during streak.
- 11 Games — Babe Dye, Toronto, Hamilton, 1920-21. 22 goals during streak.
- — Babe Dye, Toronto, 1921-22. 15 goals during streak.
- — Marcel Dionne, Los Angeles, 1982-83. 14 goals during streak.
- — Pat LaFontaine, NY Islanders, 1989-90. 18 goals during streak.

Gerry Cheevers went undefeated in 32 consecutive contests in 1971-72, winning 24 games and tying eight.

LONGEST CONSECUTIVE ASSIST-SCORING STREAK:
23 Games — Wayne Gretzky, Los Angeles, 1990-91. 48A during streak.
17 Games — Wayne Gretzky, Edmonton, 1983-84. 38A during streak.
— Paul Coffey, Edmonton, 1985-86. 27A during streak.
— Wayne Gretzky, Los Angeles, 1989-90. 35A during streak.
15 Games — Jari Kurri, Edmonton, 1983-84. 21A during streak.
14 Games — Stan Mikita, Chicago, 1967-68. 18A during streak.
— Bobby Orr, Boston, 1970-71. 23A during streak.
— Jude Drouin, Minnesota, 1971-72. 21A during streak.
— Wayne Gretzky, Edmonton, 1981-82. 26A during streak.
— Wayne Gretzky, Edmonton, 1985-86. 39A during streak.
— Mario Lemieux, Pittsburgh, 1985-86. 23A during streak.

LONGEST SHUTOUT SEQUENCE BY A GOALTENDER:
461 Minutes, 29 Seconds — Alex Connell, Ottawa, 1927-28, six consecutive shutouts. (Forward passing not permitted in attacking zones in 1927-1928.)
343 Minutes, 5 Seconds — George Hainsworth, Montreal, 1928-29, four consecutive shutouts.
324 Minutes, 40 Seconds — Roy Worters, NY Americans, 1930-31, four consecutive shutouts.
309 Minutes, 21 Seconds — Bill Durnan, Montreal, 1948-49, four consecutive shutouts.

Single Game

MOST GOALS, ONE GAME:
7 — **Joe Malone,** Quebec Bulldogs, Jan. 31, 1920, at Quebec. Quebec 10, Toronto 6.
6 — Newsy Lalonde, Montreal, Jan. 10, 1920, at Montreal. Montreal 14, Toronto 7.
— Joe Malone, Quebec Bulldogs, March 10, 1920, at Quebec. Quebec 10, Ottawa 4.
— Corb Denneny, Toronto, Jan. 26, 1921, at Toronto. Toronto 10, Hamilton 3.
— Cy Denneny, Ottawa, March 7, 1921, at Ottawa. Ottawa 12, Hamilton 5.
— Syd Howe, Detroit, Feb. 3, 1944, at Detroit. Detroit 12, NY Rangers 2.
— Red Berenson, St. Louis, Nov. 7, 1968, at Philadelphia. St. Louis 8, Philadelphia 0.
— Darryl Sittler, Toronto, Feb. 7, 1976, at Toronto. Toronto 11, Boston 4.

MOST GOALS, ONE ROAD GAME:
6 — **Red Berenson,** St. Louis, Nov. 7, 1968, at Philadelphia. St. Louis 8, Philadelphia 0.
5 — Joe Malone, Montreal, Dec. 19, 1917, at Ottawa. Montreal 9, Ottawa 4.
— Redvers Green, Hamilton, Dec. 5, 1924, at Toronto. Hamilton 10, Toronto 3.
— Babe Dye, Toronto, Dec. 22, 1924, at Boston. Toronto 10, Boston 2.
— Harry Broadbent, Mtl. Maroons, Jan. 7, 1925, at Hamilton. Mtl. Maroons 6, Hamilton 2.
— Don Murdoch, NY Rangers, Oct. 12, 1976, at Minnesota. NY Rangers 10, Minnesota 4.
— Tim Young, Minnesota, Jan. 15, 1979, at NY Rangers. Minnesota 8, NY Rangers 1.
— Willy Lindstrom, Winnipeg, March 2, 1982, at Philadelphia. Winnipeg 7, Philadelphia 6.
— Bengt Gustafsson, Washington, Jan. 8, 1984, at Philadelphia. Washington 7, Philadelphia 1.
— Wayne Gretzky, Edmonton, Dec. 15, 1984, at St. Louis. Edmonton 8, St. Louis 2.
— Dave Andreychuk, Buffalo, Feb. 6, 1986, at Boston. Buffalo 8, Boston 6.

Charlie Simmer set a modern-day NHL record by scoring in 13 consecutive games in 1979-80.

Alex Connell holds the NHL mark for the longest shutout sequence, blanking the opposition for 461 minutes, 29 seconds over eight games.

MOST ASSISTS, ONE GAME:
7 — **Billy Taylor,** Detroit, March 16, 1947, at Chicago. Detroit 10, Chicago 6.
— **Wayne Gretzky,** Edmonton, Feb. 15, 1980, at Edmonton. Edmonton 8, Washington 2.
— **Wayne Gretzky,** Edmonton, Dec. 11, 1985, at Chicago. Edmonton 12, Chicago 9.
— **Wayne Gretzky,** Edmonton, Feb. 14, 1986, at Edmonton. Edmonton 8, Quebec 2.
6 — Elmer Lach, Montreal, Feb. 6, 1943, at Montreal. Montreal 8, Boston 3.
— Walter (Babe) Pratt, Toronto, Jan. 8, 1944, at Toronto. Toronto 12, Boston 3.
— Don Grosso, Detroit, Feb. 3, 1944, at Detroit. Detroit 12, NY Rangers 2.
— Pat Stapleton, Chicago, March 30, 1969, at Chicago. Chicago 9, Detroit 5.
— Ken Hodge, Boston, Feb. 9, 1971, at Boston. Boston 6, NY Rangers 3.
— Bobby Orr, Boston, Jan. 1, 1973, at Vancouver. Boston 8, Vancouver 2.
— Ron Stackhouse, Pittsburgh, March 8, 1975, at Pittsburgh. Pittsburgh 8, Philadelphia 2.
— Greg Malone, Pittsburgh, Nov. 28, 1979, at Pittsburgh. Pittsburgh 7, Quebec 2.
— Mike Bossy, NY Islanders, Jan. 6, 1981, at New York. NY Islanders 6, Toronto 3.
— Guy Chouinard, Calgary, Feb. 25, 1981, at Calgary. Calgary 11, NY Islanders 4.
— Mark Messier, Edmonton, Jan. 4, 1984, at Edmonton. Edmonton 12, Minnesota 8.
— Patrik Sundstrom, Vancouver, Feb 29, 1984, at Pittsburgh. Vancouver 9, Pittsburgh 5.
— Wayne Gretzky, Edmonton, Dec. 20, 1985, at Edmonton. Edmonton 9, Los Angeles 4.
— Paul Coffey, Edmonton, March 14, 1986 at Edmonton. Edmonton 12, Detroit 3.
— Gary Suter, Calgary, Apr. 4, 1986 at Calgary. Calgary 9, Edmonton 3.
— Ron Francis, Hartford, March 5, 1987 at Hartford. Hartford 10, Boston 2.
— Mario Lemieux, Pittsburgh, Oct. 15, 1988, at Pittsburgh. Pittsburgh 9, St. Louis 2.
— Bernie Nicholls, Los Angeles, Dec. 1, 1988, at Los Angeles. Los Angeles 9, Toronto 3.
— Mario Lemieux, Pittsburgh, Dec. 31, 1988 at Pittsburgh. Pittsburgh 8, New Jersey 6.

MOST ASSISTS, ONE ROAD GAME:
   7 — **Billy Taylor,** Detroit, March 16, 1947, at Chicago. Detroit 10, Chicago 6.
    — **Wayne Gretzky,** Edmonton, Dec. 11, 1985, at Chicago. Edmonton 12, Chicago 9.
   6 — Bobby Orr, Boston, Jan. 1, 1973, at Vancouver. Boston 8, Vancouver 2.
    — Patrik Sundstrom, Vancouver, Feb. 29, 1984, at Pittsburgh. Vancouver 9, Pittsburgh 5.

MOST POINTS, ONE GAME:
  10 — **Darryl Sittler,** Toronto, Feb. 7, 1976, at Toronto, 6G-4A. Toronto 11, Boston 4.
   8 — Maurice Richard, Montreal, Dec. 28, 1944, at Montreal, 5G-3A. Montreal 9, Detroit 1.
    — Bert Olmstead, Montreal, Jan. 9, 1954, at Montreal, 4G-4A. Montreal 12, Chicago 1.
    — Tom Bladon, Philadelphia, Dec. 11, 1977, at Philadelphia, 4G-4A. Philadelphia 11, Cleveland 1.
    — Bryan Trottier, NY Islanders, Dec. 23, 1978, at New York, 5G-3A. NY Islanders 9, NY Rangers 4.
    — Peter Stastny, Quebec, Feb. 22, 1981, at Washington, 4G-4A. Quebec 11, Washington 7.
    — Anton Stastny, Quebec, Feb. 22, 1981, at Washington, 3G-5A. Quebec 11, Washington 7.
    — Wayne Gretzky, Edmonton, Nov. 19, 1983, at Edmonton, 3G-5A. Edmonton 13, New Jersey 4.
    — Wayne Gretzky, Edmonton, Jan. 4, 1984, at Edmonton, 4G-4A. Edmonton 12 Minnesota 8.
    — Paul Coffey, Edmonton, March 14, 1986, at Edmonton, 2G-6A. Edmonton 12, Detroit 3.
    — Mario Lemieux, Pittsburgh, Oct. 15, 1988, at Pittsburgh, 2G-6A. Pittsburgh 9, St. Louis 2.
    — Mario Lemieux, Pittsburgh, Dec. 31, 1988, at Pittsburgh, 5G-3A. Pittsburgh 8, New Jersey 6.
    — Bernie Nicholls, Los Angeles, Dec. 1, 1988, at Los Angeles, 2G-6A. Los Angeles 9, Toronto 3.
   7 — Seven points have been scored by one player in one game on 33 occasions. Most recently, Sergei Makarov of Calgary (Feb 28, 1990 vs. Edmonton) and Stephane Richer of Montreal (Feb 14, 1990 vs. Vancouver) had 7-point games.
    Joe Malone had the first 7-point game in the NHL on Jan. 31, 1920 when his Quebec Bulldogs defeated Toronto St. Patrick's 10-6 in Quebec. All of Malone's 7 points were goals.
    Wayne Gretzky recorded seven 7-point games in the 1980s.

MOST POINTS, ONE ROAD GAME:
   8 — **Peter Stastny,** Quebec, Feb. 22, 1981, at Washington, 4G-4A. Quebec 11, Washington 7.
    — **Anton Stastny,** Quebec, Feb. 22, 1981, at Washington, 3G-5A. Quebec 11, Washington 7.
   7 — Billy Taylor, Detroit, March 16, 1947, at Chicago, 7A. Detroit 10, Chicago. 6.
    — Red Berenson, St. Louis, Nov. 7, 1968, at Philadelphia, 6G-1A. St. Louis 8, Philadelphia 0.
    — Gilbert Perreault, Buffalo, Feb. 1, 1976, at California, 2G-5A. Buffalo 9, California 5.
    — Peter Stastny, Quebec, April 1, 1982, at Boston, 3G-4A. Quebec 8, Boston 5.
    — Wayne Gretzky, Edmonton, Nov. 6, 1983, at Winnipeg, 4G-3A. Edmonton 8, Winnipeg 5.
    — Patrik Sundstrom, Vancouver, Feb. 29, 1984, at Pittsburgh, 1G-6A. Vancouver 9, Pittsburgh 5.
    — Wayne Gretzky, Edmonton, Dec. 11, 1985, at Chicago. 7A, Edmonton 12, Chicago 9.
    — Mario Lemieux, Pittsburgh, Jan. 21, 1989, at Edmonton, 2G, 5A. Pittsburgh 7, Edmonton 4.
    — Cam Neely, Boston, Oct. 16, 1988, at Chicago, 3G, 4A. Boston 10, Chicago 3.
    — Dino Ciccarelli, Washington, March 18, 1989, at Hartford, 4G, 3A. Washington 8, Hartford 2.

MOST GOALS, ONE GAME, BY A DEFENSEMAN:
   5 — **Ian Turnbull,** Toronto, Feb. 2, 1977, at Toronto. Toronto 9, Detroit 1.
   4 — Harry Cameron, Toronto, Dec. 26, 1917, at Toronto. Toronto 7, Montreal 5.
    — Harry Cameron, Montreal, March 3, 1920, at Quebec City. Montreal 16, Que. Bulldogs 3.
    — Sprague Cleghorn, Montreal, Jan. 14, 1922, at Montreal. Montreal 10, Hamilton 6.
    — Johnny McKinnon, Pit. Pirates, Nov. 19, 1929, at Pittsburgh. Pit. Pirates 10, Toronto 5.
    — Hap Day, Toronto, Nov. 19, 1929, at Pittsburgh. Pit. Pirates 10, Toronto 5.
    — Tom Bladon, Philadelphia, Dec. 11, 1977, at Philadelphia. Philadelphia 11, Cleveland 1.
    — Ian Turnbull, Los Angeles, Dec. 12, 1981, at Los Angeles. Los Angeles 7, Vancouver 5.
    — Paul Coffey, Edmonton, Oct. 26, 1984, at Calgary. Edmonton 6, Calgary 5.

MOST GOALS BY ONE PLAYER IN HIS FIRST NHL GAME:
   3 — **Alex Smart,** Montreal, Jan. 14, 1943, at Montreal. Montreal 5, Chicago 1.
    — **Real Cloutier,** Quebec, Oct. 10, 1979, at Quebec. Atlanta 5, Quebec 3.

MOST GOALS, ONE GAME, BY A PLAYER IN HIS FIRST NHL SEASON:
   5 — **Howie Meeker,** Toronto, Jan. 8, 1947, at Toronto. Toronto 10, Chicago 4.
    — **Don Murdoch,** NY Rangers, Oct. 12, 1976, at Minnesota. NY Rangers 10, Minnesota 4.

MOST ASSISTS, ONE GAME, BY A DEFENSEMAN:
   6 — **Babe Pratt,** Toronto, Jan. 8, 1944, at Toronto. Toronto 12, Boston 3.
    — **Pat Stapleton,** Chicago, March 30, 1969, at Chicago. Chicago 9, Detroit 5.
    — **Bobby Orr,** Boston, Jan. 1, 1973, at Vancouver, Boston 8, Vancouver 2.
    — **Ron Stackhouse,** Pittsburgh, March 8, 1975, at Pittsburgh. Pittsburgh 8, Philadelphia 2.
    — **Paul Coffey,** Edmonton, Mar. 14, 1986, at Edmonton. Edmonton 12, Detroit 3.
    — **Gary Suter,** Calgary, Apr. 4, 1986, at Calgary. Calgary 9, Edmonton 3.

MOST ASSISTS BY ONE PLAYER IN HIS FIRST NHL GAME:
   4 — **Earl (Dutch) Reibel,** Detroit, Oct. 8, 1953, at Detroit. Detroit 4, NY Rangers 1.
    — **Roland Eriksson,** Minnesota, Oct. 6, 1976, at New York. NY Rangers 6, Minnesota 5.
   3 — Al Hill, Philadelphia, Feb. 14, 1977, at Philadelphia. Philadelphia 6, St. Louis 4.

MOST ASSISTS, ONE GAME, BY A PLAYER IN HIS FIRST NHL SEASON:
   7 — **Wayne Gretzky,** Edmonton, Feb. 15, 1980, at Edmonton. Edmonton 8, Washington 2.
   6 — Gary Suter, Calgary, Apr. 4, 1986, at Calgary. Calgary 9, Edmonton 3.
   5 — Jim McFadden, Detroit, Nov. 23, 1947, at Chicago. Detroit 9, Chicago 3.
    — Mark Howe, Hartford, Jan. 30, 1980, at Hartford. Hartford 8, Boston 2.
    — Anton Stastny, Quebec, Feb. 22, 1981, at Washington. Quebec 11, Washington 7.
    — Mark Osborne, Detroit, Feb. 7, 1982, at Detroit. Detroit 8, St. Louis 5.
    — Sergei Makarov, Calgary, Feb. 25, 1990, at Calgary. Calgary 10, Edmonton 4.

MOST POINTS, ONE GAME, BY A DEFENSEMAN:
   8 — **Tom Bladon,** Philadelphia, Dec. 11, 1977, at Philadelphia. 4G-4A. Philadelphia 11, Cleveland 1.
    — **Paul Coffey,** Edmonton, Mar. 14, 1986, at Edmonton. 2G-6A. Edmonton 12, Detroit 3.
   7 — Bobby Orr, Boston, Nov. 15, 1973, at Boston, 3G-4A. Boston 10, NY Rangers 2.

MOST POINTS BY ONE PLAYER IN HIS FIRST NHL GAME:
   5 — **Al Hill,** Philadelphia, Feb. 14, 1977, at Philadelphia. 2G-3A. Philadelphia 6, St. Louis 4.
   4 — Alex Smart, Montreal, Jan. 14, 1943, at Montreal, 3G-1A. Montreal 5, Chicago 1.
    — Earl (Dutch) Reibel, Detroit, Oct. 8, 1953, at Detroit. 4A. Detroit 4, NY Rangers 1.
    — Roland Eriksson, Minnesota, Oct. 6, 1976 at New York. 4A. NY Rangers 6, Minnesota 5.

MOST POINTS, ONE GAME, BY A PLAYER IN HIS FIRST NHL SEASON:
   8 — **Peter Stastny,** Quebec, Feb. 22, 1981, at Washington. 4G-4A. Quebec 11, Washington 7.
    — **Anton Stastny,** Quebec, Feb. 22, 1981, at Washington. 3G-5A. Quebec 11, Washington 7.
   7 — Wayne Gretzky, Edmonton, Feb. 15, 1980, at Edmonton. 7A. Edmonton 8, Washington 2.
    — Sergei Makarov, Calgary, Feb. 25, 1990, at Calgary. 2G-5A. Calgary 10, Edmonton 4.
   6 — Wayne Gretzky, Edmonton, March 29, 1980, at Toronto. 2G-4A. Edmonton 8, Toronto 5.
    — Gary Suter, Calgary, Apr. 4, 1986, at Calgary. 6A. Calgary 9, Edmonton 3.

MOST PENALTIES, ONE GAME:
  10 — **Chris Nilan,** Boston, March 31, 1991, at Boston against Hartford. 6 minors, 2 majors, 1 10-minute misconduct, 1 game misconduct.
   9 — Jim Dorey, Toronto, Oct. 16, 1968, at Toronto against Pittsburgh. 4 minors, 2 majors, 2 10-minute misconducts, 1 game misconduct.
    — Dave Schultz, Pittsburgh, Apr. 6, 1978, at Detroit. 5 minors, 2 majors, 2 10-minute misconducts.
    — Randy Holt, Los Angeles, Mar. 11, 1979, at Philadelphia. 1 minor, 3 majors, 2 10-minute misconducts, 3 game misconducts.
    — Russ Anderson, Pittsburgh, Jan. 19, 1980, at Pittsburgh. 3 minors, 3 majors, 3 game misconducts.
    — Kim Clackson, Quebec, March 8, 1981, at Quebec. 4 minors, 3 majors, 2 game misconducts.
    — Terry O'Reilly, Boston, Dec. 19, 1984 at Hartford. 5 minors, 3 majors, 1 game misconduct.
    — Larry Playfair, Los Angeles, Dec. 9, 1986, at NY Islanders. 6 minors, 2 majors, 1 10-minute misconduct.

MOST PENALTY MINUTES, ONE GAME:
  67 — **Randy Holt,** Los Angeles, Mar. 11, 1979, at Philadelphia. 1 minor, 3 majors, 2 10-minute misconducts, 3 game misconducts.
  55 — Frank Bathe, Philadelphia, March 11, 1979, at Philadelphia. 3 majors, 2 10-minute misconducts, 2 game misconducts.
  51 — Russ Anderson, Pittsburgh, Jan. 19, 1980, at Pittsburgh. 3 minors, 3 majors, 3 game misconducts.

MOST GOALS, ONE PERIOD:
4 — **Harvey (Busher) Jackson,** Toronto, Nov. 20, 1934, at St. Louis, third period. Toronto 5, St. Louis Eagles 2.
— **Max Bentley,** Chicago, Jan. 28, 1943, at Chicago, third period. Chicago 10, NY Rangers 1.
— **Clint Smith,** Chicago, March 4, 1945, at Chicago, third period. Chicago 6, Montreal 4.
— **Red Berenson,** St. Louis, Nov. 7, 1968, at Philadelphia, second period. St. Louis 8, Philadelphia 0.
— **Wayne Gretzky,** Edmonton, Feb. 18, 1981, at Edmonton, third period. Edmonton 9, St. Louis 2.
— **Grant Mulvey,** Chicago, Feb. 3, 1982, at Chicago, first period. Chicago 9, St. Louis 5.
— **Bryan Trottier,** NY Islanders, Feb 13, 1982, at New York, second period. NY Islanders 8, Philadelphia 2.
— **Al Secord,** Chicago, Jan. 7, 1987 at Chicago, second period. Chicago 6, Toronto 4.
— **Joe Nieuwendyk,** Calgary, Jan. 11, 1989, at Calgary, second period. Calgary 8, Winnipeg 3.

MOST ASSISTS, ONE PERIOD:
5 — **Dale Hawerchuk,** Winnipeg, Mar. 6, 1984, at Los Angeles, second period. Winnipeg 7, Los Angeles 3.
4 — Four assists have been recorded in one period on 39 occasions since Buddy O'Connor of Montreal first accomplished the feat vs. NY Rangers on Nov. 8, 1942. Wayne Gretzky (Edmonton, Los Angeles) has recorded four assists in one period on 10 occasions including the NHL's most recent equalling of this mark on Mar. 4, 1989 vs. Philadelphia at Los Angeles.

MOST POINTS, ONE PERIOD:
6 — **Bryan Trottier,** NY Islanders, Dec. 23, 1978, at NY Islanders, second period. 3G, 3A. NY Islanders 9, NY Rangers 4.
5 — Les Cunningham, Chicago, Jan. 28, 1940, at Chicago, third period. 2G, 3A. Chicago 8, Montreal 1.
— Max Bentley, Chicago, Jan. 28, 1943, at Chicago, third period. 4G, 1A. Chicago 10, NY Rangers 1.
— Leo Labine, Boston, Nov. 28, 1954, at Boston, second period, 3G, 2A. Boston 6, Detroit 2.
— Darryl Sittler, Toronto, Feb. 7, 1976, at Toronto, second period. 3G, 2A. Toronto 11, Boston 4.
— Dale Hawerchuk, Winnipeg, Mar. 6, 1984, at Los Angeles, second period. 5A. Winnipeg 7 Los Angeles 3.
— Jari Kurri, Edmonton, October 26, 1984 at Edmonton, second period. Edmonton 8, Los Angeles 2.
— Pat Elynuik, Winnipeg, Jan. 20, 1989, at Winnipeg, second period. 2G, 3A. Winnipeg 7, Pittsburgh 3.
— Ray Ferraro, Hartford, Dec. 9, 1989, at Hartford, first period. 3G, 2A. Hartford 7, New Jersey 3.
— Stephane Richer, Montreal, Feb. 14, 1990, at Montreal, first period. 2G, 3A. Montreal 10, Vancouver 1.

MOST PENALTIES, ONE PERIOD:
9 — **Randy Holt,** Los Angeles, Mar. 11, 1979, at Philadelphia, first period. 1 minor, 3 majors, 2 10-minute misconducts, 3 game misconducts.

MOST PENALTY MINUTES, ONE PERIOD:
67 — **Randy Holt,** Los Angeles, Mar. 11, 1979, at Philadelphia, first period. 1 minor, 3 majors, 2 10-minute misconducts, 3 game misconducts.

FASTEST GOAL BY A ROOKIE IN HIS FIRST NHL GAME:
15 Seconds — **Gus Bodnar,** Toronto, Oct. 30, 1943. Toronto 5, NY Rangers 2.
18 Seconds — Danny Gare, Buffalo, Oct. 10, 1974. Buffalo 9, Boston 5.
36 Seconds — Al Hill, Philadelphia, Feb. 14, 1977. Philadelphia 6, St. Louis 4.

FASTEST GOAL FROM START OF A GAME:
5 Seconds — **Doug Smail,** Winnipeg, Dec. 20, 1981, at Winnipeg. Winnipeg 5, St. Louis 4.
— **Bryan Trottier,** NY Islanders, Mar. 22, 1984, at Boston. NY Islanders 3, Boston 3.
6 Seconds — Henry Boucha, Detroit, Jan. 28, 1973, at Montreal. Detroit 4, Montreal 2.
— Jean Pronovost, Pittsburgh, March 25, 1976, at St. Louis. St. Louis 5, Pittsburgh 2.
7 Seconds — Charlie Conacher, Toronto, Feb. 6, 1932, at Toronto. Toronto 6, Boston 0.
— Danny Gare, Buffalo, Dec. 17, 1978, at Buffalo. Buffalo 6, Vancouver 3.
— Dave Williams, Los Angeles, Feb. 14, 1987 at Los Angeles. Los Angeles 5, Harford 2.
8 Seconds — Ron Martin, NY Americans, Dec. 4, 1932, at New York. NY Americans 4, Montreal 2.
— Chuck Arnason, Colorado, Jan. 28, 1977, at Atlanta. Colorado 3, Atlanta 3.
— Wayne Gretzky, Edmonton, Dec. 14, 1983, at New York. Edmonton 9, NY Rangers 4.
— Gaetan Duchesne, Washington, Mar. 14, 1987, at St. Louis. Washington 3, St. Louis 3.
— Tim Kerr, Philadelphia, March 7, 1989, at Philadelphia. Philadelphia 4, Edmonton 4.

FASTEST GOAL FROM START OF A PERIOD:
4 Seconds — **Claude Provost,** Montreal, Nov. 9, 1957, at Montreal, second period. Montreal 4, Boston 2.
— **Denis Savard,** Chicago, Jan. 12, 1986, at Chicago, third period. Chicago 4, Hartford 2.

FASTEST TWO GOALS:
4 Seconds — **Nels Stewart,** Mtl. Maroons, Jan. 3, 1931, at Montreal at 8:24 and 8:28, third period. Mtl. Maroons 5, Boston 3.
5 Seconds — Pete Mahovlich, Montreal, Feb. 20, 1971, at Montreal at 12:16 and 12:21, third period. Montreal 7, Chicago 1.
6 Seconds — Jim Pappin, Chicago, Feb. 16, 1972, at Chicago at 2:57 and 3:03, third period. Chicago 3, Philadelphia 3.
— Ralph Backstrom, Los Angeles, Nov. 2, 1972, at Los Angeles at 8:30 and 8:36, third period. Los Angeles 5, Boston 2.
— Lanny McDonald, Calgary, Mar. 22, 1984, at Calgary at 16:23 and 16:29, first period. Detroit 6, Calgary 4.
— Sylvain Turgeon, Hartford, Mar. 28, 1987, at Hartford at 13:59 and 14:05, second period. Hartford 5, Pittsburgh 4.

FASTEST THREE GOALS:
21 Seconds — **Bill Mosienko,** Chicago, March 23, 1952, at New York, against goaltender Lorne Anderson. Mosienko scored at 6:09, 6:20 and 6:30 of third period, all with both teams at full strength. Chicago 7, NY Rangers 6.
44 Seconds — Jean Béliveau, Montreal, Nov. 5, 1955 at Montreal against goaltender Terry Sawchuk. Béliveau scored at :42, 1:08 and 1:26 of second period, all with Montreal holding a 6-4 man advantage. Montreal 4, Boston 2.

FASTEST THREE ASSISTS:
21 Seconds — **Gus Bodnar,** Chicago, March 23, 1952, at New York, Bodnar assisted on Bill Mosienko's three goals at 6:09, 6:20, 6:30 of third period. Chicago 7, NY Rangers 6.
44 Seconds — Bert Olmstead, Montreal, Nov. 5, 1955, at Montreal against Boston. Olmstead assisted on Jean Beliveau's three goals at :42, 1:08 and 1:26 of second period. Montreal 4, Boston 2.

Bill Mosienko scored three goals in 21 seconds in the final game of the 1951-52 season.

Top 100 All-Time Goal-Scoring Leaders

* active player

(figures in parentheses indicate ranking of top 10 by goals per game)

	Player	Seasons	Games	Goals	Goals per game
1.	Gordie Howe, Det., Hfd.	26	1,767	801	.453
2.	Marcel Dionne, Det., L.A., NYR	18	1,348	731	.542
*3.	Wayne Gretzky, Edm., L.A.	12	925	718	.776 (2)
4.	Phil Esposito, Chi., Bos., NYR	18	1,282	717	.559 (9)
5.	Bobby Hull, Chi., Wpg., Hfd.	16	1,063	610	.574 (7)
6.	Mike Bossy, NYI	10	752	573	.762 (3)
7.	Guy Lafleur, Mtl., NYR, Que.	17	1,126	560	.497
8.	John Bucyk, Det., Bos.	23	1,540	556	.361
9.	Maurice Richard, Mtl.	18	978	544	.556(10)
10.	Stan Mikita, Chi.	22	1,394	541	.388
11.	Frank Mahovlich, Tor., Det., Mtl.	18	1,181	533	.451
12.	Gilbert Perreault, Buf.	17	1,191	512	.430
*13.	Bryan Trottier, NYI, Pit.	16	1,175	509	.433
14.	Jean Beliveau, Mtl.	20	1,125	507	.451
15.	Lanny McDonald, Tor., Col., Cgy.	16	1,111	500	.450
*16.	Mike Gartner, Wsh., Min., NYR	12	929	498	.536
17.	Jean Ratelle, NYR, Bos.	21	1,281	491	.383
18.	Norm Ullman, Det., Tor.	20	1,410	490	.348
*19.	Michel Goulet, Que., Chi.	12	895	487	.544
20.	Darryl Sittler, Tor., Phi., Det.	15	1,096	484	.442
*21.	Jari Kurri, Edm.	10	754	474	.629 (4)
22.	Alex Delvecchio, Det.	24	1,549	456	.294
23.	Rick Middleton, NYR, Bos.	14	1,005	448	.446
*24.	Rick Vaive, Van., Tor., Chi., Buf.	12	856	440	.514
25.	Yvan Cournoyer, Mtl.	16	968	428	.442
26.	Steve Shutt, Mtl., L.A.	13	930	424	.456
27.	Bill Barber, Phi.	12	903	420	.465
*28.	Glenn Anderson, Edm.	11	828	413	.499
29.	Garry Unger, Tor., Det., St. L., Atl., L.A., Edm.	16	1,105	413	.374
*30.	Dave Taylor, L.A.	14	953	411	.431
*31.	Dale Hawerchuk, Wpg., Buf.	10	793	410	.517
*32.	Dino Ciccarelli, Min., Wsh.	11	747	406	.544
33.	Rod Gilbert, NYR	18	1,065	406	.381
*34.	Peter Stastny, Que., N.J.	11	826	403	.488
*35.	Brian Propp, Phi., Bos., Min.	12	883	398	.451
36.	Dave Keon, Tor., Hfd.	18	1,296	396	.306
37.	Pierre Larouche, Pit., Mtl., Hfd., NYR	14	812	395	.486
38.	Bernie Geoffrion, Mtl., NYR	16	883	393	.445
*39.	Mark Messier, Edm.	12	851	392	.461
40.	Jean Pronovost, Pit., Atl., Wsh.	14	998	391	.392
41.	Dean Prentice, NYR, Bos., Det., Pit., Min.	22	1,378	391	.284
42.	Richard Martin, Buf., L.A.	11	685	384	.561 (8)
43.	Reggie Leach, Bos., Cal., Phi., Det.	13	934	381	.408
*44.	Denis Savard, Chi., Mtl.	11	806	379	.470
*45.	John Ogrodnick, Det., Que., NYR	12	854	379	.444
46.	Ted Lindsay, Det., Chi.	17	1,068	379	.355
47.	Butch Goring, L.A., NYI, Bos.	16	1,107	375	.339
48.	Rick Kehoe, Tor., Pit.	14	906	371	.409
49.	Bernie Federko, St. L., Det.	14	1,000	369	.369
50.	Jacques Lemaire, Mtl.	12	853	366	.429
*51.	Mario Lemieux, Pit.	7	453	364	.804 (1)
*52.	Bernie Nicholls, L.A., NYR	10	705	364	.516
53.	Peter McNab, Buf., Bos., Van., N.J.	14	954	363	.381
54.	Ivan Boldirev, Bos., Cal., Chi., Atl., Van., Det.	15	1,052	361	.343
*55.	Tim Kerr, Phi.	11	601	358	.596 (5)
*56.	Joey Mullen, St. L., Cgy., Pit.	10	693	358	.517
57.	Bobby Clarke, Phi.	15	1,144	358	.313
58.	Henri Richard, Mtl.	20	1,256	358	.285
59.	Dennis Maruk, Cal., Cle., Wsh., Min.	13	882	356	.404
60.	Wilf Paiement, K.C., Col., Tor., Que., NYR, Buf., Pit.	14	946	356	.376
61.	Danny Gare, Buf., Det., Edm.	13	827	354	.428
62.	Rick MacLeish, Phi., Hfd., Pit., Det.	14	846	349	.413
63.	Andy Bathgate, NYR, Tor., Det., Pit.	17	1,069	349	.326
*64.	Bobby Smith, Min., Mtl.	13	964	343	.356
*65.	Steve Yzerman, Det.	8	594	342	.576 (6)
66.	Charlie Simmer, Cal., Cle., L.A., Bos., Pit.	14	712	342	.480
*67.	Steve Larmer, Chi.	11	727	342	.470
*68.	Mike Foligno, Det., Buf., Tor.	12	887	332	.374
69.	Ron Ellis, Tor.	16	1,034	332	.321
70.	Ken Hodge, Chi., Bos., NYR	13	881	328	.372
71.	Nels Stewart, Mtl. M., Bos., NYA	15	654	324	.495
72.	Pit Martin, Det., Bos., Chi., Van.	17	1,101	324	.294
73.	Vic Hadfield, NYR, Pit.	16	1,002	323	.322
*74.	John Tonelli, NYI, Cgy., L.A.	13	976	322	.330
*75.	Tony McKegney, Buf., Que., Min., St. L., Det., Chi.	14	912	320	.351

"Terrible" Ted Lindsay had a wonderful career, firing 379 goals for the Wings and Black Hawks.

	Player	Seasons	Games	Assists	Assists per game
76.	Clark Gillies, NYI, Buf.	14	958	319	.333
77.	Paul MacLean, St. L., Wpg., Det.	9	677	318	.470
*78.	Dave Christian, Wsh., Bos.	12	862	316	.367
79.	Mike Bullard, Pit., Cgy., St. L., Phi.	10	662	315	.476
80.	Don Lever, Van., Atl., Cgy., Col., N.J., Buf.	15	1,020	313	.307
*81.	Brian Bellows, Min.	9	673	312	.464
82.	Denis Potvin, NYI	15	1,060	310	.292
*83.	Paul Coffey, Edm., Pit.	11	809	307	.379
84.	Bob Nevin, Tor., NYR, Min., L.A.	18	1,128	307	.272
85.	Brian Sutter, St. L.	12	779	303	.389
86.	Dennis Hull, Chi., Det.	14	959	303	.316
87.	George Armstrong, Tor.	21	1,187	296	.249
88.	Tom Lysiak, Atl., Chi.	13	919	292	.318
89.	Peter Mahovlich, Det., Mtl., Pit.	16	884	288	.326
*90.	Pat Lafontaine, NYI	8	530	287	.542
91.	Rene Robert, Pit., Buf., Col., Tor.	12	744	284	.382
*92.	Brent Sutter, NYI	11	686	283	.413
93.	Bill Goldsworthy, Bos., Min., NYR	14	771	283	.367
94.	Dick Duff, Tor., NYR, Mtl., L.A., Buf.	18	1,030	283	.275
95.	John Anderson, Tor., Que., Hfd.	12	814	282	.346
96.	Bob Pulford, Tor., L.A.	16	1,079	281	.260
97.	Red Kelly, Det., Tor.	20	1,316	281	.214
98.	Camille Henry, NYR, Chi., St. L.	12	727	279	.384
*99.	Dave Andreychuk, Buf.	9	631	278	.441
	Jim Pappin, Tor., Chi., Cal., Cle.	14	767	278	.362
	Ralph Backstrom, Mtl., L.A., Chi.	17	1,032	278	.269

Top 100 All-Time Assist Leaders

* active player

(figures in parentheses indicate ranking of top 10 in order of assists per game)

Player	Seasons	Games	Assists	Assists per game
*1. Wayne Gretzky, Edm., L.A.	12	925	1,424	1.539 (1)
2. Gordie Howe, Det., Hfd.	26	1,767	1,049	.594
3. Marcel Dionne, Det., L.A., NYR	18	1,348	1,040	.772 (9)
4. Stan Mikita, Chi.	22	1,394	926	.664
5. Phil Esposito, Chi., Bos., NYR	18	1,282	873	.681
*6. Bryan Trottier, NYI, Pit.	16	1,175	872	.742
7. Bobby Clarke, Phi.	15	1,144	852	.745
8. Alex Delvecchio, Det.	24	1,549	825	.533
9. Gilbert Perreault, Buf.	17	1,191	814	.683
10. John Bucyk, Det., Bos.	23	1,540	813	.528
11. Guy Lafleur, Mtl., NYR, Que.	17	1,126	793	.704
12. Jean Ratelle, NYR, Bos.	21	1,281	776	.606
13. Bernie Federko, St. L., Det.	14	1,000	761	.761
14. Denis Potvin, NYI	15	1,060	742	.700
*15. Larry Robinson, Mtl. L.A.	18	1,328	740	.557
16. Norm Ullman, Det., Tor.	20	1,410	739	.524
*17. Paul Coffey, Edm., Pit.	11	809	738	.912 (4)
*18. Peter Stastny, Que., N.J.	11	826	716	.867 (5)
19. Jean Beliveau, Mtl.	20	1,125	712	.633
*20. Denis Savard, Chi., Mtl.	11	806	693	.860 (6)
21. Henri Richard, Mtl.	20	1,256	688	.548
*22. Ray Bourque, Bos.	12	870	683	.785 (7)
23. Brad Park, NYR, Bos., Det.	17	1,113	683	.614
24. Bobby Orr, Bos., Chi.	12	657	645	.982 (3)
*25. Mark Messier, Edm.	12	851	642	.754
26. Darryl Sittler, Tor., Phi., Det. ..	15	1,096	637	.581
27. Borje Salming, Tor., Det.	17	1,148	637	.555
*28. Bobby Smith, Min., Mtl.	13	964	635	.659
29. Andy Bathgate, NYR, Tor., Det., Pit. .	17	1,069	624	.584
30. Rod Gilbert, NYR	18	1,065	615	.577
*31. Dale Hawerchuk, Wpg., Buf. ...	10	793	608	.767
*32. Dave Taylor, L.A.	14	953	607	.637
33. Dave Keon, Tor., Hfd.	18	1,296	590	.455
34. Frank Mahovlich, Tor., Det., Mtl. .	18	1,181	570	.483
*35. Jari Kurri, Edm.	10	754	569	.755
*36. Ron Francis, Hfd., Pit.	10	728	566	.777 (8)
37. Bobby Hull, Chi., Wpg., Hfd. ...	16	1,063	560	.527
*38. Doug Wilson, Chi.	13	938	554	.591
39. Mike Bossy, NYI	10	752	553	.735
*40. Ken Linseman, Phi., Edm., Bos. .	13	858	551	.642
41. Tom Lysiak, Atl., Chi.	13	919	551	.600
42. Red Kelly, Det., Tor.	20	1,316	542	.412
43. Rick Middleton, NYR, Bos.	14	1,005	540	.537
*44. Brian Propp, Phi., Bos., Min. ..	12	883	535	.606
*45. Michel Goulet, Que., Chi.	12	895	528	.590
46. Dennis Maruk, Cal., Cle., Wsh., Min.	13	882	521	.591
*47. Mario Lemieux, Pit.	7	453	519	1.146 (2)
48. Wayne Cashman, Bos.	17	1,027	516	.502
49. Butch Goring, L.A., NYI, Bos. ..	16	1,107	513	.463
*50. Larry Murphy, L.A., Wsh., Min., Pit. .	11	860	512	.595
51. Lanny McDonald, Tor., Col., Cgy. ...	16	1,111	506	.455
52. Ivan Boldirev, Bos., Cal., Chi., Atl., Van., Det.	15	1,052	505	.480
*53. Bernie Nicholls, L.A., NYR	10	705	504	.715
*54. Neal Broten, Min.	11	718	500	.696
*55. John Tonelli, NYI, Cgy., L.A. ...	13	976	500	.512
*56. Randy Carlyle, Tor., Pit., Wpg. ...	15	967	489	.506
57. Peter Mahovlich, Det., Mtl., Pit. ...	16	884	485	.549
58. Pit Martin, Det., Bos., Chi., Van. ...	17	1,101	485	.441
*59. Glenn Anderson, Edm.	11	828	483	.583
60. Ken Hodge, Chi., Bos., NYR ...	13	881	472	.536
61. Ted Lindsay, Det., Chi.	17	1068	472	.442
*62. Mark Howe, Hfd., Phi.	12	765	471	.616
63. Jacques Lemaire, Mtl.	12	853	469	.550
64. Dean Prentice, NYR, Bos., Det., Pit., Min.	22	1,378	469	.340
65. Phil Goyette, Mtl., NYR, St. L., Buf. ..	16	941	467	.496
66. Bill Barber, Phi.	12	903	463	.513
67. Reed Larson, Det., Bos., Edm., NYI, Min., Buf.	14	904	463	.512
68. Doug Mohns, Bos., Chi., Min., Atl., Wsh.	22	1,390	462	.332
*69. Dale Hunter, Que., Wsh.	11	838	461	.550
*70. Mike Gartner, Wsh., Min., NYR ...	12	929	460	.495
*71. Steve Yzerman, Det.	8	594	458	.771
72. Bobby Rousseau, Mtl., Min., NYR ...	15	942	458	.486
73. Wilf Paiement, K.C., Col., Tor., Que., NYR, Buf., Pit.	14	946	458	.484
*74. Al MacInnis, Cgy.	10	606	455	.751
75. Murray Oliver, Det., Bos., Tor., Min. .	17	1,127	454	.403
76. Doug Harvey, Mtl., NYR, Det., St. L. .	19	1,113	452	.406
77. Guy Lapointe, Mtl., St. L., Bos. ...	16	884	451	.510
78. Walt Tkachuk, NYR	14	945	451	.477
79. Peter McNab, Buf., Bos., Van., N.J. .	14	954	450	.472
80. Mel Bridgman, Phi., Cgy., N.J., Det., Van.	14	977	449	.460
*81. Dave Babych, Wpg., Hfd.	11	739	444	.601
*82. Steve Larmer, Chi.	11	727	437	.601

Red Kelly delivered 542 passes that his teammates converted for goals in his 20 seasons in the NHL.

Player	Seasons	Games	Assists	Assists per game
83. Bill Gadsby, NYR, Det.	20	1,248	437	.350
*84. Thomas Steen, Wpg.	10	725	436	.601
85. Yvan Cournoyer, Mtl.	16	968	435	.449
*86. Phil Housley, Buf., Wpg.	9	686	433	.631
87. Ron Greschner, NYR	16	982	431	.439
88. Bernie Geoffrion, Mtl., NYR	16	883	429	.486
89. Pierre Larouche, Pit., Mtl., Hfd., NYR	14	812	427	.526
90. Paul Reinhart, Atl., Cgy., Van.	11	648	426	.657
91. Syl Apps, Jr., NYR, Pit., L.A.	10	727	423	.582
92. Kent Nilsson, Atl., Cgy., Min., Edm. .	8	547	422	.771(10)
93. Bert Olmstead, Chi., Mtl., Tor.	14	848	421	.496
94. Maurice Richard, Mtl.	18	978	421	.430
95. Craig Ramsay, Buf.	14	1,070	420	.393
96. Bob Nevin, Tor., NYR, Min., L.A. ...	18	1,128	419	.371
97. Rene Robert, Pit., Buf., Col., Tor. ...	12	744	418	.562
98. Pierre Pilote, Chi., Tor.	14	890	418	.470
99. Carol Vadnais, Mtl., Oak., Cal., Bos., NYR, N.J.	17	1,087	418	.385
100. George Armstrong, Tor.	21	1,187	417	.351

Top 100 All-Time Point Leaders

* active player

(figures in parentheses indicate ranking of top 10 by points per game)

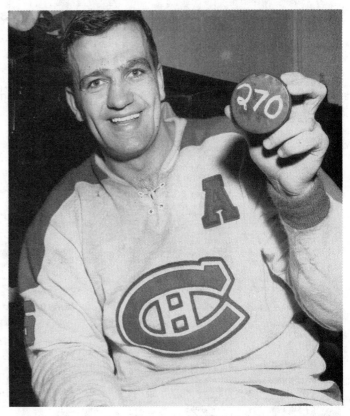

Bernie "Boom Boom" Geoffrion averaged .931 points-per-game in his 16-year career, compiling 822 points in 883 games.

	Player	Seasons	Games	Goals	Assists	Points	Points per game	
*1.	Wayne Gretzky, Edm., L.A. .	12	925	718	1,424	**2,142**	2.316	(1)
2.	Gordie Howe, Det., Hfd.	26	1,767	801	1,049	**1,850**	1.047	
3.	Marcel Dionne, Det., L.A., NYR	18	1,348	731	1,040	**1,771**	1.314	(9)
4.	Phil Esposito, Chi., Bos., NYR	18	1,282	717	873	**1,590**	1.240	
5.	Stan Mikita, Chi.	22	1,394	541	926	**1,467**	1.052	
*6.	Bryan Trottier, NYI, Pit.	16	1,175	509	872	**1,381**	1.175	
7.	John Bucyk, Det., Bos.	23	1.540	556	813	**1,369**	.889	
8.	Guy Lafleur, Mtl., NYR, Que.	17	1,126	560	793	**1,353**	1.202	
9.	Gilbert Perreault, Buf.	17	1,191	512	814	**1,326**	1.113	
10.	Alex Delvecchio, Det.	24	1,549	456	825	**1,281**	.827	
11.	Jean Ratelle, NYR, Bos. ...	21	1,281	491	776	**1,267**	.989	
12.	Norm Ullman, Det., Tor.	20	1,410	490	739	**1,229**	.872	
13.	Jean Beliveau, Mtl.	20	1,125	507	712	**1,219**	1.084	
14.	Bobby Clarke, Phi.	15	1,144	358	852	**1,210**	1.058	
15.	Bobby Hull, Chi., Wpg., Hfd.	16	1,063	610	560	**1,170**	1.101	
16.	Bernie Federko, St. L., Det. .	14	1,000	369	761	**1,130**	1.130	
17.	Mike Bossy, NYI	10	752	573	553	**1,126**	1.497	(3)
18.	Darryl Sittler, Tor., Phi., Det.	15	1,096	484	637	**1,121**	1.023	
*19.	Peter Stastny, Que., N.J. ...	11	826	403	716	**1,119**	1.355	(6)
20.	Frank Mahovlich, Tor., Det., Mtl.	18	1181	533	570	**1,103**	.934	
*21.	Denis Savard, Chi., Mtl.	11	806	379	693	**1,072**	1.330	(8)
22.	Denis Potvin, NYI	15	1,060	310	742	**1,052**	.992	
23.	Henri Richard, Mtl.	20	1,256	358	688	**1,046**	.833	
*24.	Paul Coffey, Edm., Pit.	11	809	307	738	**1,045**	1.292	(10)
*25.	Jari Kurri, Edm.	10	754	474	569	**1,043**	1.383	(5)
*26.	Mark Messier, Edm.	12	851	392	642	**1,034**	1.215	
27.	Rod Gilbert, NYR	18	1,065	406	615	**1,021**	.959	
*28.	Dale Hawerchuk, Wpg., Buf. .	10	793	410	608	**1,018**	1.284	
*29.	Dave Taylor, L.A.	14	953	411	607	**1,018**	1.068	
*30.	Michel Goulet, Que., Chi. ...	12	895	487	528	**1,015**	1.134	
31.	Lanny McDonald, Tor., Col., Cgy.	16	1,111	500	506	**1,006**	.905	
32.	Rick Middleton, NYR, Bos. .	14	1,005	448	540	**988**	.983	
33.	Dave Keon, Tor., Hfd.	18	1,296	396	590	**986**	.761	
*34.	Bobby Smith, Min., Mtl.	13	964	343	635	**978**	1.015	
35.	Andy Bathgate, NYR, Tor., Det., Pit.	17	1,069	349	624	**973**	.910	
36.	Maurice Richard, NYR, Tor., Det., Pit.	18	978	544	421	**965**	.987	
*37.	Mike Gartner, Wsh., Min., NYR	12	929	498	460	**958**	1.031	
*38.	Larry Robinson, Mtl., L.A. ..	18	1,328	205	740	**945**	.712	
*39.	Ray Bourque, Bos.	12	870	251	683	**934**	1.074	
*40.	Brian Propp, Phi., Bos., Min.	12	883	398	535	**933**	1.057	
41.	Bobby Orr, Bos., Chi.	12	657	270	645	**915**	1.393	(4)
*42.	Glenn Anderson, Edm.	11	828	413	483	**896**	1.082	
43.	Brad Park, NYR, Bos., Det. .	17	1,113	213	683	**896**	.805	
44.	Butch Goring, L.A., NYI, Bos.	16	1,107	375	513	**888**	.802	
*45.	Mario Lemieux, Pit.	7	453	364	519	**883**	1.949	(2)
46.	Bill Barber, Phi.	12	903	420	463	**883**	.978	
47.	Dennis Maruk, Cal., Cle., Wsh., Min.	13	882	356	521	**877**	.994	
*48.	Bernie Nicholls, L.A., NYR .	10	705	364	504	**868**	1.231	
49.	Ivan Boldirev, Bos., Cal., Chi., Atl., Van., Det.	15	1,052	361	505	**866**	.823	
50.	Yvan Cournoyer, Mtl.	16	968	428	435	**863**	.892	
51.	Dean Prentice, NYR, Bos., Det., Pit., Min.	22	1,378	391	469	**860**	.624	
52.	Ted Lindsay, Det., Chi.	17	1,068	379	472	**851**	.797	
53.	Tom Lysiak, Atl., Chi.	13	919	292	551	**843**	.917	
54.	Jacques Lemaire, Mt.	12	853	366	469	**835**	.979	
*55.	Ron Francis, Hfd., Pit.	10	728	266	566	**832**	1.143	
56.	Red Kelly, Det., Tor.	20	1,316	281	542	**823**	.625	
57.	Pierre Larouche, Pit., Mtl., Hfd., NYR	14	812	395	427	**822**	1.012	
58.	Bernie Geoffrion, Mtl., NYR .	16	883	393	429	**822**	.931	
*59.	John Tonelli, NYI, Cgy., L.A.	13	976	322	500	**822**	.842	
60.	Steve Shutt, Mtl., L.A.	13	930	424	393	**817**	.878	
61.	Wilf Paiement, K.C., Col., Tor., Que., NYR, Buf., Pit. .	14	946	356	458	**814**	.860	
62.	Peter McNab, Buf., Bos., Van., N.J.	14	954	363	450	**813**	.852	
63.	Pit Martin, Det., Bos., Chi., Van.	17	1101	324	485	**809**	.735	
*64.	Ken Linseman, Phi., Edm., Bos.	12	858	256	551	**807**	.941	
65.	Garry Unger, Tor., Det., St. L., Atl., L.A., Edm.	16	1,105	413	391	**804**	.728	
*66.	Steve Yzerman, Det.	8	594	342	458	**800**	1.347	(7)
67.	Ken Hodge, Chi., Bos., NYR	13	881	328	472	**800**	.908	
68.	Wayne Cashman, Bos.	17	1,027	277	516	**793**	.772	
69.	Borje Salming, Tor., Det. ...	17	1,148	150	637	**787**	.686	
*70.	John Ogrodnick, Det., Que., NYR	12	854	379	406	**785**	.919	
*71.	Dino Ciccarelli, Min., Wsh. .	11	747	406	378	**784**	1.050	
*72.	Rick Vaive, Van., Tor., Chi., Buf.	12	856	440	344	**784**	.916	
*73.	Steve Larmer, Chi.	11	727	342	437	**779**	1.072	
*74.	Doug Wilson, Chi.	14	938	225	554	**779**	.830	
75.	Jean Pronovost, Pit., Atl., Wsh	14	998	391	383	**774**	.776	
76.	Peter Mahovlich, Det., Mtl., Pit.	16	884	288	485	**773**	.874	
77.	Rick Kehoe, Tor., Pit.	14	906	371	396	**767**	.847	
*78.	Joey Mullen, St. L., Cgy., Pit.	10	693	358	404	**762**	1.100	
79.	Rick MacLeish, Phi., Hfd., Pit., Det.	14	846	349	410	**759**	.897	
*80.	Neal Broten, Min.	11	718	229	500	**729**	1.015	
81.	Murray Oliver, Det., Bos., Tor., Min.	17	1,127	274	454	**728**	.646	
82.	Bob Nevin, Tor., NYR, Min., L.A.	18	1,128	307	419	**726**	.644	
83.	George Armstrong, Tor.	21	1,187	296	417	**713**	.601	
84.	Vic Hadfield, NYR, Pit.	16	1,002	323	389	**712**	.711	
85.	Charlie Simmer, Cal., Cle., L.A., Bos., Pit.	14	712	342	369	**711**	.999	
86.	Doug Mohns, Bos., Chi., Min., Atl., Wsh.	22	1,390	248	462	**710**	.511	
*87.	Dave Christian, Wpg., Wsh., Bos.	12	862	316	392	**708**	.821	
88.	Bobby Rousseau, Mtl., Min., NYR	15	942	245	458	**703**	.746	
89.	Rene Robert, Pit., Buf., Col., Tor.	12	744	284	418	**702**	.944	
90.	Richard Martin, Buf., L.A. ...	11	685	384	317	**701**	1.023	
91.	Mel Bridgman, Phi., Chi., N.J., Det., Van.	14	977	252	449	**701**	.718	
92.	Clark Gillies, NYI, Buf.	14	958	319	378	**697**	.728	
*93.	Mike Foligno, Det., Buf., Tor.	12	887	332	354	**686**	.773	
94.	Kent Nilsson, Atl., Cgy., Min., Edm.	8	547	263	422	**685**	1.252	
95.	Danny Gare, Buf., Det., Edm.	13	827	354	331	**685**	.828	
96.	Reed Larson, Det., Bos., Edm., NYI, Min., Buf.	14	904	222	463	**685**	.758	
*97.	Dale Hunter, Que., Wsh.	11	838	221	461	**682**	.814	
98.	Don Lever, Van., Atl., Cgy., Col., N.J., Buf.	15	1,020	313	367	**680**	.667	
99.	Walt Tkaczuk, NYR	14	945	227	451	**678**	.717	
100.	Phil Goyette, Mtl., NYR, St. L., Buf.	16	941	207	467	**674**	.716	

All-Time Games Played Leaders

Regular Season

* active player

#	Player	Team	Seasons	GP
1.	Gordie Howe	Detroit	25	1,687
		Hartford	1	80
		Total	**26**	**1,767**
2.	Alex Delvecchio	Detroit	24	1,549
3.	John Bucyk	Detroit	2	104
		Boston	21	1,436
		Total	**23**	**1,540**
4.	Tim Horton	Toronto	$19\frac{3}{4}$	1,185
		NY Rangers	$1\frac{1}{4}$	93
		Pittsburgh	1	44
		Buffalo	2	124
		Total	**24**	**1,446**
5.	Harry Howell	NY Rangers	17	1,160
		California	$1\frac{1}{2}$	83
		Los Angeles	$2\frac{1}{2}$	168
		Total	**21**	**1,411**
6.	Norm Ullman	Detroit	$12\frac{1}{2}$	875
		Toronto	$7\frac{1}{2}$	535
		Total	**20**	**1,410**
7.	Stan Mikita	Chicago	22	1,394
8.	Doug Mohns	Boston	11	710
		Chicago	$6\frac{1}{2}$	415
		Minnesota	$2\frac{1}{2}$	162
		Atlanta	1	28
		Washington	1	75
		Total	**22**	**1,390**
9.	Dean Prentice	NY Rangers	$10\frac{1}{2}$	666
		Boston	3	170
		Detroit	$3\frac{1}{2}$	230
		Pittsburgh	2	144
		Minnesota	3	168
		Total	**22**	**1,378**
10.	Ron Stewart	Toronto	13	838
		Boston	2	126
		St. Louis	$\frac{1}{2}$	19
		NY Rangers	4	306
		Vancouver	1	42
		NY Islanders	$\frac{1}{2}$	22
		Total	**21**	**1,353**
11.	Marcel Dionne	Detroit	4	309
		Los Angeles	$11\frac{3}{4}$	921
		NY Rangers	$2\frac{1}{4}$	118
		Total	**18**	**1,348**
* 12.	Larry Robinson	Montreal	17	1,202
		Los Angeles	2	126
		Total	**19**	**1,328**
13.	Red Kelly	Detroit	$12\frac{1}{2}$	846
		Toronto	$7\frac{1}{2}$	470
		Total	**20**	**1,316**
14.	Dave Keon	Toronto	15	1,062
		Hartford	3	234
		Total	**18**	**1,296**
15.	Phil Esposito	Chicago	4	235
		Boston	$8\frac{1}{4}$	625
		NY Rangers	$5\frac{3}{4}$	422
		Total	**18**	**1,282**
16.	Jean Ratelle	NY Rangers	$15\frac{1}{4}$	862
		Boston	$5\frac{3}{4}$	419
		Total	**21**	**1,281**
17.	Henri Richard	Montreal	20	1,256
18.	Bill Gadsby	Chicago	$8\frac{1}{2}$	468
		NY Rangers	$6\frac{1}{2}$	457
		Detroit	5	323
		Total	**20**	**1,248**
19.	Allan Stanley	NY Rangers	$6\frac{1}{2}$	307
		Chicago	$1\frac{3}{4}$	111
		Boston	2	129
		Toronto	9	633
		Philadelphia	1	64
		Total	**21**	**1,244**
20.	Eddie Westfall	Boston	11	734
		NY Islanders	7	493
		Total	**18**	**1,227**
21.	Eric Nesterenko	Toronto	5	206
		Chicago	16	1,013
		Total	**21**	**1,219**
22.	Marcel Pronovost	Detroit	16	983
		Toronto	5	223
		Total	**21**	**1,206**
23.	Gilbert Perreault	Buffalo	17	1,191
24.	George Armstrong	Toronto	21	1,187
25.	Frank Mahovlich	Toronto	$11\frac{3}{4}$	720
		Detroit	$2\frac{3}{4}$	198
		Montreal	$3\frac{1}{2}$	263
		Total	**18**	**1,181**
26.	Don Marshall	Montreal	10	585
		NY Rangers	7	479
		Buffalo	1	62
		Toronto	1	50
		Total	**19**	**1,176**
* 27.	Bryan Trottier	NY Islanders	15	1,123
		Pittsburgh	1	52
		Total	**16**	**1,175**
28.	Bob Gainey	Montreal	16	1,160
29.	Leo Boivin	Toronto	$3\frac{1}{4}$	137
		Boston	$11\frac{1}{2}$	717
		Detroit	$1\frac{1}{4}$	85
		Pittsburgh	$1\frac{1}{2}$	114
		Minnesota	$1\frac{1}{2}$	97
		Total	**19**	**1,150**
30.	Borje Salming	Toronto	16	1,099
		Detroit	1	49
		Total	**17**	**1,148**
31.	Bobby Clarke	Philadelphia	15	1,144
32.	Bob Nevin	Toronto	$5\frac{3}{4}$	250
		NY Rangers	$7\frac{1}{4}$	505
		Minnesota	2	138
		Los Angeles	3	235
		Total	**18**	**1,128**
33.	Murray Oliver	Detroit	$2\frac{1}{2}$	101
		Boston	$6\frac{1}{2}$	429
		Toronto	3	226
		Minnesota	5	371
		Total	**17**	**1,127**
34.	Guy Lafleur	Montreal	14	961
		NY Rangers	1	67
		Quebec	2	98
		Total	**17**	**1,126**
35.	Jean Beliveau	Montreal	20	1,125
36.	Doug Harvey	Montreal	14	890
		NY Rangers	3	151
		Detroit	1	2
		St. Louis	1	70
		Total	**19**	**1,113**
37.	Brad Park	NY Rangers	$7\frac{1}{2}$	465
		Boston	$7\frac{1}{2}$	501
		Detroit	2	147
		Total	**17**	**1,113**
38.	Lanny McDonald	Toronto	$6\frac{1}{2}$	477
		Colorado	$1\frac{3}{4}$	142
		Calgary	$7\frac{3}{4}$	441
		Total	**16**	**1,111**
39.	Butch Goring	Los Angeles	$10\frac{3}{4}$	736
		NY Islanders	$4\frac{3}{4}$	332
		Boston	$\frac{1}{2}$	39
		Total	**16**	**1,107**
40.	Garry Unger	Toronto	$\frac{1}{2}$	15
		Detroit	3	216
		St. Louis	$8\frac{1}{2}$	662
		Atlanta	1	79
		Los Angeles	$\frac{3}{4}$	58
		Edmonton	$2\frac{1}{4}$	75
		Total	**16**	**1,105**
41.	Pit Martin	Detroit	$3\frac{1}{4}$	119
		Boston	$1\frac{3}{4}$	111
		Chicago	$10\frac{1}{4}$	740
		Vancouver	$1\frac{3}{4}$	131
		Total	**17**	**1,101**
42.	Darryl Sittler	Toronto	$11\frac{1}{2}$	844
		Philadelphia	$2\frac{1}{2}$	191
		Detroit	1	61
		Total	**15**	**1,096**
43.	Carol Vadnais	Montreal	2	42
		Oakland	2	152
		California	$1\frac{3}{4}$	94
		Boston	$3\frac{1}{4}$	263
		NY Rangers	$6\frac{3}{4}$	485
		New Jersey	1	51
		Total	**17**	**1,087**
44.	Bob Pulford	Toronto	14	947
		Los Angeles	2	132
		Total	**16**	**1,079**
45.	Craig Ramsay	Buffalo	14	1,070
46.	Andy Bathgate	NY Rangers	$11\frac{3}{4}$	719
		Toronto	$1\frac{1}{4}$	70
		Detroit	2	130
		Pittsburgh	2	150
		Total	**17**	**1,069**
47.	Ted Lindsay	Detroit	14	862
		Chicago	3	206
		Total	**17**	**1,068**
48.	Terry Harper	Montreal	10	554
		Los Angeles	3	234
		Detroit	4	252
		St. Louis	1	11
		Colorado	1	15
		Total	**19**	**1,066**
49.	Rod Gilbert	NY Rangers	18	1,065
50.	Bobby Hull	Chicago	15	1,036
		Winnipeg	$\frac{2}{3}$	18
		Hartford	$\frac{1}{3}$	9
		Total	**16**	**1,063**
51.	Denis Potvin	NY Islanders	15	1,060
52.	Jean Guy Talbot	Montreal	13	791
		Minnesota	$\frac{1}{4}$	4
		Detroit	$\frac{1}{2}$	32
		St. Louis	$2\frac{1}{2}$	172
		Buffalo	$\frac{3}{4}$	57
		Total	**17**	**1,056**
53.	Ivan Boldirev	Boston	$1\frac{1}{4}$	13
		California	$2\frac{3}{4}$	191
		Chicago	$4\frac{3}{4}$	384
		Atlanta	1	65
		Vancouver	$2\frac{3}{4}$	216
		Detroit	$2\frac{1}{2}$	183
		Total	**15**	**1,052**
54.	Eddie Shack	NY Rangers	$2\frac{1}{4}$	141
		Toronto	$8\frac{3}{4}$	504
		Boston	2	120
		Los Angeles	$1\frac{1}{4}$	84
		Buffalo	$1\frac{1}{2}$	111
		Pittsburgh	$1\frac{1}{4}$	87
		Total	**17**	**1,047**
55.	Serge Savard	Montreal	15	917
		Winnipeg	2	123
		Total	**17**	**1,040**
56.	Ron Ellis	Toronto	16	1,034
57.	Harold Snepsts	Vancouver	$11\frac{3}{4}$	781
		Minnesota	1	71
		Detroit	3	120
		St. Louis	$1\frac{1}{4}$	61
		Total	**17**	**1,033**
58.	Ralph Backstrom	Montreal	$14\frac{1}{4}$	844
		Los Angeles	$2\frac{1}{4}$	172
		Chicago	$\frac{1}{4}$	16
		Total	**17**	**1,032**
59.	Dick Duff	Toronto	$9\frac{3}{4}$	582
		NY Rangers	$\frac{3}{4}$	43
		Montreal	5	305
		Los Angeles	$\frac{3}{4}$	39
		Buffalo	$1\frac{3}{4}$	61
		Total	**18**	**1,030**
60.	Wayne Cashman	Boston	17	1,027
61.	Jim Neilson	NY Rangers	12	810
		California	2	98
		Cleveland	2	115
		Total	**16**	**1,023**
62.	Don Lever	Vancouver	$7\frac{2}{3}$	593
		Atlanta	$\frac{1}{3}$	28
		Calgary	$1\frac{1}{4}$	85
		Colorado	$\frac{3}{4}$	59
		New Jersey	3	216
		Buffalo		39
		Total	**15**	**1,020**
63.	Phil Russell	Chicago	$6\frac{3}{4}$	504
		Atlanta	$1\frac{1}{4}$	93
		Calgary	3	229
		New Jersey	$2\frac{3}{4}$	172
		Buffalo	$1\frac{1}{4}$	18
		Total	**15**	**1,016**
64.	Dave Lewis	NY Islanders	$6\frac{3}{4}$	514
		Los Angeles	$3\frac{1}{4}$	221
		New Jersey	3	209
		Detroit	2	64
		Total	**15**	**1,008**
65.	Bob Murray	Chicago	15	1,008
66.	Jim Roberts	Montreal	$9\frac{2}{3}$	611
		St. Louis	$5\frac{1}{3}$	395
		Total	**15**	**1,006**
67.	Claude Provost	Montreal	15	1,005
68.	Rick Middleton	NY Rangers	2	124
		Boston	12	881
		Total	**14**	**1,005**
69.	Vic Hadfield	NY Rangers	13	839
		Pittsburgh	3	163
		Total	**16**	**1,002**
70.	Bernie Federko	St. Louis	14	927
		Detroit	1	73
		Total	**15**	**1,000**

Goaltending Records

* active player

All-Time Shutout Leaders

Goaltender	Team	Seasons	Games	Shutouts
Terry Sawchuk	Detroit	14	734	85
(1949-1970)	Boston	2	102	11
	Toronto	3	91	4
	Los Angeles	1	36	2
	NY Rangers	1	8	1
	Total	**21**	**971**	**103**
George Hainsworth	Montreal	7½	318	75
(1926-1937)	Toronto	3½	146	19
	Total	**11**	**464**	**94**
Glenn Hall	Detroit	4	148	17
(1952-1971)	Chicago	10	618	51
	St. Louis	4	140	16
	Total	**18**	**906**	**84**
Jacques Plante	Montreal	11	556	58
(1952-1973)	NY Rangers	2	98	5
	St. Louis	2	69	10
	Toronto	2¾	106	7
	Boston	¼	8	2
	Total	**18**	**837**	**82**
Tiny Thompson	Boston	10¼	468	74
(1928-1940)	Detroit	1¾	85	7
	Total	**12**	**553**	**81**
Alex Connell	Ottawa	8	293	64
(1925-1937)	Detroit	1	48	6
	NY Americans	1	1	0
	Mtl. Maroons	2	75	11
	Total	**12**	**417**	**81**
Tony Esposito	Montreal	1	13	2
(1968-1984)	Chicago	15	873	74
	Total	**16**	**886**	**76**
Lorne Chabot	NY Rangers	2	80	21
(1926-1937)	Toronto	5	214	33
	Montreal	1	47	8
	Chicago	1	48	8
	Mtl. Maroons	1	16	2
	NY Americans	1	6	1
	Total	**11**	**411**	**73**
Harry Lumley	Detroit	6½	324	26
(1943-1960)	NY Rangers	½	1	0
	Chicago	2	134	5
	Toronto	4	267	34
	Boston	3	78	6
	Total	**16**	**804**	**71**

Goaltender	Team	Seasons	Games	Shutouts
Roy Worters	Pittsburgh Pirates	3	123	22
(1925-1937)	NY Americans	9	360	44
	*Montreal		1	0
	Total	**12**	**484**	**66**
Turk Broda	Toronto	14	629	62
(1936-1952)				
John Roach	Toronto	7	223	13
(1921-1935)	NY Rangers	4	89	30
	Detroit	3	180	15
	Total	**14**	**492**	**58**

Goaltender	Team	Seasons	Games	Shutouts
Clint Benedict	Ottawa	7	158	19
(1917-1930)	Mtl. Maroons	6	204	38
	Total	**13**	**362**	**57**
Bernie Parent	Boston	2	57	1
(1965-1979)	Philadelphia	9½	486	50
	Toronto	1½	65	4
	Total	**13**	**608**	**55**
Ed Giacomin	NY Rangers	10¼	539	49
(1965-1978)	Detroit	2¾	71	5
	Total	**13**	**610**	**54**
David Kerr	Mtl. Maroons	3	101	11
(1930-1941)	NY Americans	1	1	0
	NY Rangers	7	324	40
	Total	**11**	**426**	**51**
Rogie Vachon	Montreal	5¼	206	13
(1966-1982)	Los Angeles	6¾	389	32
	Detroit	2	109	4
	Boston	2	91	2
	Total	**16**	**795**	**51**
Ken Dryden	Montreal	8	397	46
(1970-1979)				
Gump Worsley	NY Rangers	10	583	24
(1952-1974)	Montreal	6½	172	16
	Minnesota	4½	107	3
	Total	**21**	**862**	**43**
Chuck Gardiner	Chicago	7	316	42
(1927-1934)				
Frank Brimsek	Boston	9	444	35
(1938-1950)	Chicago	1	70	5
	Total	**10**	**514**	**40**
Johnny Bower	NY Rangers	3	77	5
(1953-1970)	Toronto	12	475	32
	Total	**15**	**552**	**37**
Bill Durnan	Montreal	7	383	34
(1943-1950)				
Eddie Johnston	Boston	11	444	27
(1962-1978)	Toronto	1	26	1
	St. Louis	3⅔	118	4
	Chicago	⅓	4	0
	Total	**16**	**592**	**32**
Roger Crozier	Detroit	7	313	20
(1963-1977)	Buffalo	6	202	10
	Washington	1	3	0
	Total	**14**	**518**	**30**
Cesare Maniago	Toronto	1	7	0
(1960-1978)	Montreal	1	14	0
	NY Rangers	2	34	2
	Minnesota	9	420	26
	Vancouver	2	93	2
	Total	**15**	**568**	**30**

*Played 1 game for Canadiens in 1929-30.

Ten or More Shutouts, One Season

Number of Shutouts	Goaltender	Team	Season	Length of Schedule
22	George Hainsworth	Montreal	1928-29	44
15	Alex Connell	Ottawa	1925-26	36
	Alex Connell	Ottawa	1927-28	44
	Hal Winkler	Boston	1927-28	44
	Tony Esposito	Chicago	1969-70	76
14	George Hainsworth	Montreal	1926-27	44
13	Clint Benedict	Mtl. Maroons	1926-27	44
	Alex Connell	Ottawa	1926-27	44
	George Hainsworth	Montreal	1927-28	44
	Roy Worters	NY Americans	1927-28	44
	John Roach	NY Rangers	1928-29	44
	Roy Worters	NY Americans	1928-29	44
	Harry Lumley	Toronto	1953-54	70
12	Tiny Thompson	Boston	1928-29	44
	Lorne Chabot	Toronto	1928-29	44
	Chuck Gardiner	Chicago	1930-31	44
	Terry Sawchuk	Detroit	1951-52	70
	Terry Sawchuk	Detroit	1953-54	70
	Terry Sawchuk	Detroit	1954-55	70
	Glenn Hall	Detroit	1955-56	70
	Bernie Parent	Philadelphia	1973-74	78
	Bernie Parent	Philadelphia	1974-75	80

Number of Shutouts	Goaltender	Team	Season	Length of Schedule
11	Lorne Chabot	NY Rangers	1927-28	44
	Harry Holmes	Detroit	1927-28	44
	Clint Benedict	Mtl. Maroons	1928-29	44
	Joe Miller	Pittsburgh Pirates	1928-29	44
	Tiny Thompson	Boston	1932-33	48
	Terry Sawchuk	Detroit	1950-51	70
10	Lorne Chabot	NY Rangers	1926-27	44
	Roy Worters	Pittsburgh Pirates	1927-28	44
	Clarence Dolson	Detroit	1928-29	44
	John Roach	Detroit	1932-33	48
	Chuck Gardiner	Chicago	1933-34	48
	Tiny Thompson	Boston	1935-36	48
	Frank Brimsek	Boston	1938-39	48
	Bill Durnan	Montreal	1948-49	60
	Gerry McNeil	Montreal	1952-53	70
	Harry Lumley	Toronto	1952-53	70
	Tony Esposito	Chicago	1973-74	78
	Ken Dryden	Montreal	1976-77	80

All-Time Win Leaders

(Minimum 200 Wins)

Wins	Goaltender	GP	Decisions	Mins.	Losses	Ties	%
435	Terry Sawchuk	971	960	57,154	337	188	.551
434	Jacques Plante	837	817	49,553	246	137	.615
423	Tony Esposito	886	881	52,585	307	151	.566
407	Glenn Hall	906	899	53,484	327	165	.544
355	Rogie Vachon	795	761	46,298	291	115	.542
335	Gump Worsley	862	838	50,232	353	150	.489
332	Harry Lumley	804	799	48,097	324	143	.505
305	Billy Smith	680	643	38,431	233	105	.556
302	Turk Broda	629	627	38,173	224	101	.562
289	Ed Giacomin	610	592	35,693	206	97	.570
286	Dan Bouchard	655	631	37,919	232	113	.543
284	Tiny Thompson	553	553	34,174	194	75	.581
283	*Mike Liut	642	632	37,032	264	72	.505
270	Bernie Parent	608	588	35,136	197	121	.562
270	Gilles Meloche	788	752	45,401	351	131	.446
258	Ken Dryden	397	389	23,352	57	74	.758
252	Frank Brimsek	514	514	31,210	182	80	.568
251	Johnny Bower	549	537	32,016	196	90	.551
247	George Hainsworth	464	467	29,415	146	74	.608
246	*Pete Peeters	489	461	27,699	155	51	.589
236	Eddie Johnston	592	579	34,209	256	87	.483
231	Glenn Resch	571	537	32,279	224	82	.507
230	Gerry Cheevers	418	398	24,394	94	74	.671
226	*Grant Fuhr	423	403	23,910	117	54	.628
226	*Rejean Lemelin	489	453	27,057	147	63	.568
218	John Roach	491	491	30,423	204	69	.514
214	*Andy Moog	379	351	21,123	92	45	.674
212	*Greg Millen	594	580	34,890	282	86	.440
208	Bill Durnan	383	382	22,945	112	62	.626
208	Don Edwards	459	440	26,181	155	77	.560
206	Lorne Chabot	411	411	25,309	140	65	.580
206	Roger Crozier	518	477	28,566	197	74	.509
203	David Kerr	426	426	26,519	148	75	.565

Active Shutout Leaders

Goaltender	Teams	Seasons	Games	Shutouts
Mike Liut	St. L., Hfd., Wsh.	12	642	24
Pete Peeters	Phi., Bos., Wsh.	13	489	21
Greg Millen	Pit., Hfd., St. L., Que., Chi.	12	594	17
Tom Barrasso	Buffalo, Pittsburgh	8	382	14
Bob Froese	Philadelphia, NY Rangers	8	242	13
Patrick Roy	Montreal	7	289	13
Andy Moog	Edmonton, Boston	11	379	13
Glen Hanlon	Van., St. L., NYR, Det.	14	477	13
Clint Malarchuk	Que., Wsh., Buf.	9	309	12
Kelly Hrudey	NY Islanders, Los Angeles	8	356	12
Rick Wamsley	Mtl., St. L., Cgy.	11	387	12
Rejean Lemelin	Atl., Cgy., Bos.	13	489	12
Don Beaupre	Minnesota, Washington	11	420	11
John Vanbiesbrouck	NY Rangers	9	356	10
Grant Fuhr	Edmonton	10	423	9

Active Goaltending Leaders

(Ranked by winning percentage; minimum 250 games played)

Goaltender	Teams	Seasons	GP	Decisions	W	L	T	Winning %
Andy Moog	Edmonton, Boston	11	379	351	214	92	45	.674
Mike Vernon	Calgary	8	292	275	169	82	24	.658
Patrick Roy	Montreal	7	289	275	158	82	35	.638
Grant Fuhr	Edmonton	10	423	397	226	117	54	.637
Pete Peeters	Phi., Bos., Wsh.	13	489	452	246	155	51	.601
Rick Wamsley	Mtl., St. L., Cgy.	11	387	367	197	124	46	.599
Rejean Lemelin	Atl., Cgy., Bos.	13	489	436	226	147	63	.591
Kelly Hrudey	NYI, L.A.	8	356	332	164	128	40	.554
Tom Barrasso	Buffalo, Pittsburgh	8	382	362	176	145	41	.543
Rollie Melanson	NYI, L.A., N.J.	10	282	260	124	103	33	.540
Clint Malarchuk	Que., Wsh., Buf.	9	309	290	131	117	42	.524
Mike Liut	St. L., Hfd., Wsh.	12	642	619	283	264	72	.515
Don Beaupre	Minnesota, Washington	11	420	392	174	165	53	.511
J. Vanbiesbrouck	NY Rangers	9	356	336	153	146	37	.510
Brian Hayward	Wpg., Mtl., Min.	9	332	314	140	138	36	.503
Steve Weeks	NYR, Hfd., Van.	11	254	240	102	107	31	.490
Greg Stefan	Detroit	9	299	272	115	127	30	.478
Glen Hanlon	Van., St. L., NYR, Det.	14	477	430	167	202	61	.459
Greg Millen	Pit., Hfd., St. L., Que., Chi.	13	594	580	212	282	86	.440
Ken Wreggett	Toronto, Philadelphia	8	284	262	88	151	23	.380

Goals Against Average Leaders

(minimum 25 games played, 1926–27 to date; 15 games, 1917–18 to 1925–26)

Season	Goaltender and Club	GP	Mins.	GA	SO	AVG.
1990-91	Ed Belfour, Chicago	74	4,127	170	4	2.47
1989-90	Patrick Roy, Montreal	54	3,173	134	3	2.53
	Mike Liut, Hartford, Washington	37	2,161	91	4	2.53
1988-89	Patrick Roy, Montreal	48	2,744	113	4	2.47
1987-88	Pete Peeters, Washington	35	1,896	88	2	2.78
1986-87	Brian Hayward, Montreal	37	2,178	102	1	2.81
1985-86	Bob Froese, Philadelphia	51	2,728	116	5	2.55
1984-85	Tom Barrasso, Buffalo	54	3,248	144	5	2.66
1983-84	Pat Riggin, Washington	41	2,299	102	4	2.66
1982-83	Pete Peeters, Boston	62	3,611	142	8	2.36
1981-82	Denis Herron, Montreal	27	1,547	68	3	2.64
1980-81	Richard Sevigny, Montreal	33	1,777	71	2	2.40
1979-80	Bob Sauve, Buffalo	32	1,880	74	4	2.36
1978-79	Ken Dryden, Montreal	47	2,814	108	5	2.30
1977-78	Ken Dryden, Montreal	52	3,071	105	5	2.05
1976-77	Michel Larocque, Montreal	26	1,525	53	4	2.09
1975-76	Ken Dryden, Montreal	62	3,580	121	8	2.03
1974-75	Bernie Parent, Philadelphia	68	4,041	137	12	2.03
1973-74	Bernie Parent, Philadelphia	73	4,314	136	12	1.89
1972-73	Ken Dryden, Montreal	54	3,165	119	6	2.26
1971-72	Tony Esposito, Chicago	48	2,780	82	9	1.77
1970-71	Jacques Plante, Toronto	40	2,329	73	4	1.88
1969-70	Ernie Wakely, St. Louis	30	1,651	58	4	2.11
1968-69	Jacques Plante, St. Louis	37	2,139	70	5	1.96
1967-68	Gump Worsley, Montreal	40	2,213	73	6	1.98
1966-67	Glenn Hall, Chicago	32	1,664	66	2	2.38
1965-66	Johnny Bower, Toronto	35	1,998	75	3	2.25
1964-65	Johnny Bower, Toronto	34	2,040	81	3	2.38
1963-64	Johnny Bower, Toronto	51	3,009	106	5	2.11
1962-63	Jacques Plante, Montreal	56	3,320	138	5	2.49
1961-62	Jacques Plante, Montreal	70	4,200	166	4	2.37
1960-61	Johnny Bower, Toronto	58	3,480	145	2	2.50
1959-60	Jacques Plante, Montreal	69	4,140	175	3	2.54
1958-59	Jacques Plante, Montreal	67	4,000	144	9	2.16
1957-58	Jacques Plante, Montreal	57	3,386	119	9	2.11
1956-57	Jacques Plante, Montreal	61	3,660	123	9	2.02
1955-56	Jacques Plante, Montreal	64	3,840	119	7	1.86
1954-55	Harry Lumley, Toronto	69	4,140	134	8	1.94
	Terry Sawchuk, Detroit	68	4,080	132	12	1.94

Season	Goaltender and Club	GP	Mins.	GA	SO	AVG.
1953-54	Harry Lumley, Toronto	69	4,140	128	13	1.86
1952-53	Terry Sawchuk, Detroit	63	3,780	120	9	1.90
1951-52	Terry Sawchuk, Detroit	70	4,200	133	12	1.90
1950-51	Al Rollins, Toronto	40	2,367	70	5	1.77
1949-50	Bill Durnan, Montreal	64	3,840	141	8	2.20
1948-49	Bill Durnan, Montreal	60	3,600	126	10	2.10
1947-48	Turk Broda, Toronto	60	3,600	143	5	2.38
1946-47	Bill Durnan, Montreal	60	3,600	138	4	2.30
1945-46	Bill Durnan, Montreal	40	2,400	104	4	2.60
1944-45	Bill Durnan, Montreal	50	3,000	121	1	2.42
1943-44	Bill Durnan, Montreal	50	3,000	109	2	2.18
1942-43	Johnny Mowers, Detroit	50	3,010	124	6	2.47
1941-42	Frank Brimsek, Boston	47	2,930	115	3	2.35
1940-41	Turk Broda, Toronto	48	2,970	99	5	2.00
1939-40	Dave Kerr, NY Rangers	48	3,000	77	8	1.54
1938-39	Frank Brimsek, Boston	43	2,610	68	10	1.56
1937-38	Tiny Thompson, Boston	48	2,970	89	7	1.80
1936-37	Normie Smith, Detroit	48	2,980	102	6	2.05
1935-36	Tiny Thompson, Boston	48	2,930	82	10	1.68
1934-35	Lorne Chabot, Chicago	48	2,940	88	8	1.80
1933-34	Wilf Cude, Detroit, Montreal	30	1,920	47	5	1.47
1932-33	Tiny Thompson, Boston	48	3,000	88	11	1.76
1931-32	Chuck Gardiner, Chicago	48	2,989	92	4	1.85
1930-31	Roy Worters, NY Americans	44	2,760	74	8	1.61
1929-30	Tiny Thompson, Boston	44	2,680	98	3	2.19
1928-29	George Hainsworth, Montreal	44	2,800	43	22	0.92
1927-28	George Hainsworth, Montreal	44	2,730	48	13	1.05
1926-27	Clint Benedict, Mtl. Maroons	43	2,748	65	13	1.42
1925-26	Alex Connell, Ottawa	36	2,251	42	15	1.12
1924-25	Georges Vezina, Montreal	30	1,860	56	5	1.81
1923-24	Georges Vezina, Montreal	24	1,459	48	3	1.97
1922-23	Clint Benedict, Ottawa	24	1,478	54	4	2.19
1921-22	Clint Benedict, Ottawa	24	1,508	84	2	3.34
1920-21	Clint Benedict, Ottawa	24	1,457	75	2	3.09
1919-20	Clint Benedict, Ottawa	24	1,444	64	5	2.66
1918-19	Clint Benedict, Ottawa	18	1,113	53	2	2.86
1917-18	Georges Vezina, Montreal	21	1,282	84	1	3.93

Coaching Records

(Minimum 600 regular-season games. Ranked by number of games coached.)

Coach	Team	Seasons	Games	Wins	Losses	Ties	%*
Dick Irvin	Chicago	1930-31; 55-56	114	43	56	15	.443
	Toronto	1931-40	427	216	152	59	.575
	Montreal	1940-55	896	431	313	152	.566
	Total		**1,437**	**690**	**521**	**226**	**.559**
Al Arbour	St. Louis	1970-73	107	42	40	25	.509
	NY Islanders	1973-86; 88-91	1,251	629	429	193	.580
	Total		**1,358**	**671**	**469**	**218**	**.574**
Scott Bowman	St. Louis	1967-71	238	110	83	45	.557
	Montreal	1971-79	634	419	110	105	.744
	Buffalo	1979-87	404	210	134	60	.594
	Total		**1,276**	**739**	**327**	**210**	**.661**
Billy Reay	Toronto	1957-59	90	26	50	14	.367
	Chicago	1963-77	1,012	516	335	161	.589
	Total		**1,102**	**542**	**385**	**175**	**.571**
Jack Adams	Detroit	1927-44	964	413	390	161	.512
Sid Abel	Chicago	1952-54	140	39	79	22	.357
	Detroit	1957-68; 69-70	810	340	338	132	.501
	St. Louis	1971-72	10	3	6	1	.350
	Kansas City	1975-76	3	0	3	0	.000
	Total		**963**	**382**	**426**	**155**	**.477**
Punch Imlach	Toronto	1958-69; 79-81	840	391	311	138	.548
	Buffalo	1970-72	119	32	62	25	.374
	Total		**959**	**423**	**373**	**163**	**.526**
Toe Blake	Montreal	1955-68	914	500	255	159	.634
Michel Bergeron	Quebec	1980-87; 89-90	634	265	283	86	.486
	NY Rangers	1987-89	158	73	67	18	.519
	Total		**792**	**338**	**350**	**104**	**.492**
Glen Sather	Edmonton	1979-89	782	442	241	99	.629
Emile Francis	NY Rangers	1965-75	654	347	209	98	.606
	St. Louis	1976-77, 81-83	124	46	64	14	.427
	Total		**778**	**393**	**273**	**112**	**.577**
Bob Pulford	Los Angeles	1972-77	396	178	150	68	.535
	Chicago	1977-79 1981-82; 84-87	375	158	155	62	.504
	Total		**771**	**336**	**305**	**130**	**.520**
Milt Schmidt	Boston	1954-61; 62-66	726	245	360	121	.421
	Washington	1974-76	43	5	33	5	.174
	Total		**769**	**250**	**393**	**126**	**.407**
Bryan Murray	Washington	1981-90	672	343	246	83	.572
	Detroit	1990-91	80	34	38	8	.475
	Total		**752**	**377**	**284**	**91**	**.562**
Red Kelly	Los Angeles	1967-69	150	55	75	20	.433
	Pittsburgh	1969-73	274	90	132	52	.423
	Toronto	1973-77	318	133	123	62	.516
	Total		**742**	**278**	**330**	**134**	**465**
Fred Shero	Philadelphia	1971-78	554	308	151	95	.642
	NY Rangers	1978-81	180	82	74	24	.522
	Total		**734**	**390**	**225**	**119**	**.612**
Art Ross	Boston	1924-45	728	361	277	90	.558
Bob Berry	Los Angeles	1978-81	240	107	94	39	.527
	Montreal	1981-84	223	116	71	36	.601
	Pittsburgh	1984-87	240	88	127	25	.419
	Total		**703**	**311**	**292**	**100**	**.514**
Jacques Demers	Quebec	1979-80	80	25	44	11	.381
	St.Louis	1983-86	240	106	106	28	.500
	Detroit	1986-90	320	137	136	47	.502
	Total		**640**	**268**	**286**	**86**	**.486**
Jack Evans	California	1975-76	80	27	42	11	.406
	Cleveland	1976-78	160	47	87	26	.375
	Hartford	1983-88	374	163	174	37	.485
	Total		**614**	**237**	**303**	**74**	**.446**
Tommy Ivan	Detroit	1947-54	470	262	118	90	.653
	Chicago	1956-58	140	40	78	22	.364
	Total		**610**	**302**	**196**	**112**	**.587**
Lester Patrick	NY Rangers	1926-39	604	281	216	107	.554

* % arrived at by dividing possible points into actual points.

Sid Abel coached Chicago, Detroit, St. Louis, and Kansas City in 16 years behind the bench in the NHL.

All-Time Penalty-Minute Leaders

* active player

(Regular season. Minimum 1,500 minutes)

Player	Teams	Seasons	Games	Penalty Minutes	Mins. per game
Dave Williams,	Tor., Van., Det., L.A., Hfd.	13	962	3,966	4.12
*Chris Nilan,	Mtl., NYR, Bos.	12	632	2,783	4.40
Willi Plett,	Atl., Cgy., Minn., Bos.	12	834	2,572	3.08
*Dale Hunter,	Que., Wsh.	10	838	2,469	2.95
Dave Schultz,	Phi., L.A., Pit., Buf.	9	535	2,294	4.29
*Tim Hunter,	Calgary	9	515	2,238	4.35
Bryan Watson,	Mtl., Det., Cal., Pit., St. L., Wsh.	16	878	2,212	2.52
Terry O'Reilly,	Boston	14	891	2,095	2.35
Al Secord,	Chi., Tor., Phi.	11	766	2,093	2.73
*Laurie Boschman,	Tor., Edm., Wpg., N.J.	12	864	2,043	2.36
Phil Russell,	Chi., Atl., Cgy., N.J., Buf.	15	1,016	2,038	2.01
Harold Snepsts,	Van., Min., Det., St. L.	17	1,033	2,009	1.94
*Rob Ramage,	Col., St. L., Cgy., Tor.	12	915	1,995	2.18
Andre Dupont,	NYR, St. L., Phi., Que.	13	810	1,986	2.45
*Mike Foligno,	Det., Buf., Tor.	12	887	1,862	2.10
*Jay Wells,	L.A., Phi., Buf.	12	774	1,845	2.38
Garry Howatt,	NYI, Hfd., N.J.	12	720	1,836	2.55
Carol Vadnais,	Mtl., Oak., Cal., Bos., NYR, N.J.	17	1,087	1,813	1.67
*Basil McRae,	Que., Tor., Det., Min.	10	383	1,812	4.73
Larry Playfair,	Buf., L.A.	11	688	1,812	2.63
Ted Lindsay,	Det., Chi.	17	1,068	1,808	1.69
Brian Sutter,	St. Louis	12	779	1,786	2.29
*Marty McSorley,	Pit., Edm., L.A.	8	449	1,779	3.96
*Scott Stevens,	Wsh. St. L.	9	679	1,778	2.62
Wilf Paiment,	K.C., Col., Tor., Que., NYR, Buf., Pit.	14	946	1,757	1.86
Torrie Robertson,	Wsh., Hfd., Det.	9	442	1,751	3.96
*Joey Kocur,	Det., NYR	7	404	1,750	4.33
Jim Korn,	Det., Tor., Buf., N.J., Cgy.	10	597	1,750	2.93
*Ken Linseman,	Phi., Edm., Bos.	13	858	1,725	2.01
*Garth Butcher,	Van., St. L.	10	623	1,700	2.73
Gordie Howe,	Det., Hfd.	26	1,767	1,685	0.95
Paul Holmgren,	Phi., Min.	9	527	1,684	3.20
*Mario Marois,	NYR, Van., Que., Win., St. L.	14	904	1,674	1.85
Jerry Korab,	Chi., Van., Buf., L.A.	15	975	1,629	1.67
Mel Bridgman,	Phi., Cgy., N.J., Det., Van.	14	977	1,625	1.66
*Kevin McClelland,	Pit., Edm., Det.	10	564	1,620	2.87
Tim Horton,	Tor., NYR, Pit., Buf.	24	1,446	1,611	1.11
*Bob McGill,	Tor., Chi.	10	579	1,595	2.75
*Rick Tocchet,	Phi.	7	489	1,583	3.24
Paul Baxter,	Que., Pit., Cgy.	8	472	1,564	3.31
Glen Cochrane,	Phi., Van., Chi., Edm.	9	411	1,556	3.79
Stan Smyl,	Van.	13	896	1,556	1.74
Mike Milbury,	Boston	12	754	1,552	2.06
Dave Hutchison,	L.A., Tor., Chi., N.J.	10	584	1,550	2.65
Doug Risebrough,	Mtl., Cal.	13	740	1,542	2.08
Bill Gadsby,	Chi., NYR, Det.	20	1,248	1,539	1.23

One Season Scoring Records

Goals-Per-Game Leaders, One Season

(Among players with 20 goals or more in one season)

Player	Team	Season	Games	Goals	Average
Joe Malone	Montreal	1917-18	20	44	2.20
Cy Denneny	Ottawa	1917-18	22	36	1.64
Newsy Lalonde	Montreal	1917-18	14	23	1.64
Joe Malone	Quebec	1919-20	24	39	1.63
Newsy Lalonde	Montreal	1919-20	23	36	1.57
Joe Malone	Hamilton	1920-21	20	30	1.50
Babe Dye	Ham., Tor.	1920-21	24	35	1.46
Cy Denneny	Ottawa	1920-21	24	34	1.42
Reg Noble	Toronto	1917-18	20	28	1.40
Newsy Lalonde	Montreal	1920-21	24	33	1.38
Odie Cleghorn	Montreal	1918-19	17	23	1.35
Harry Broadbent	Ottawa	1921-22	24	32	1.33
Babe Dye	Toronto	1924-25	29	38	1.31
Babe Dye	Toronto	1921-22	24	30	1.25
Newsy Lalonde	Montreal	1918-19	17	21	1.24
Cy Denneny	Ottawa	1921-22	22	27	1.23
Aurel Joliat	Montreal	1924-25	24	29	1.21
Wayne Gretzky	Edmonton	1983-84	74	87	1.18
Babe Dye	Toronto	1922-23	22	26	1.18
Wayne Gretzky	Edmonton	1981-82	80	92	1.15
Frank Nighbor	Ottawa	1919-20	23	26	1.13
Mario Lemieux	Pittsburgh	1988-89	76	85	1.12
Brett Hull	St. Louis	**1990-91**	78	86	1.10
Amos Arbour	Montreal	1919-20	20	22	1.10
Cy Denneny	Ottawa	1923-24	21	22	1.05
Joe Malone	Hamilton	1921-22	24	25	1.04
Billy Boucher	Montreal	1922-23	24	25	1.04
Maurice Richard	Montreal	1944-45	50	50	1.00
Howie Morenz	Montreal	1924-25	30	30	1.00
Reg Noble	Toronto	1919-20	24	24	1.00
Corbett Denneny	Toronto	1919-20	23	23	1.00
Jack Darragh	Ottawa	1919-20	22	22	1.00
Cooney Weiland	Boston	1929-30	44	43	.98
Phil Esposito	Boston	1970-71	78	76	.97
Jari Kurri	Edmonton	1984-85	73	71	.97

Assists-Per-Game Leaders, One Season

(Among players with 35 assists or more in one season)

Player	Team	Season	Games	Assists	Average
Wayne Gretzky	Edmonton	1985-86	80	163	2.04
Wayne Gretzky	Edmonton	1987-88	64	109	1.70
Wayne Gretzky	Edmonton	1984-85	80	135	1.69
Wayne Gretzky	Edmonton	1983-84	74	118	1.59
Wayne Gretzky	Edmonton	1982-83	80	125	1.56
Wayne Gretzky	Los Angeles	**1990-91**	78	122	1.56
Wayne Gretzky	Edmonton	1986-87	79	121	1.53
Wayne Gretzky	Edmonton	1981-82	80	120	1.50
Mario Lemieux	Pittsburgh	1988-89	76	114	1.50
Adam Oates	St. Louis	**1990-91**	61	90	1.48
Wayne Gretzky	Los Angeles	1988-89	78	114	1.46
Wayne Gretzky	Los Angeles	1989-90	73	102	1.40
Wayne Gretzky	Edmonton	1980-81	80	109	1.36
Mario Lemieux	Pittsburgh	1989-90	59	78	1.32
Bobby Orr	Boston	1970-71	78	102	1.31
Mario Lemieux	Pittsburgh	1987-88	77	98	1.27
Bobby Orr	Boston	1973-74	74	90	1.22
Mario Lemieux	Pittsburgh	1985-86	79	93	1.18
Bobby Clarke	Philadelphia	1975-76	76	89	1.17
Peter Stastny	Quebec	1981-82	80	93	1.16
Paul Coffey	Edmonton	1985-86	79	90	1.14
Bobby Orr	Boston	1969-70	76	87	1.14
Bryan Trottier	NY Islanders	1978-79	76	87	1.14
Bobby Orr	Boston	1972-73	63	72	1.14
Bill Cowley	Boston	1943-44	36	41	1.14
Steve Yzerman	Detroit	1988-89	80	90	1.13
Paul Coffey	Pittsburgh	1987-88	46	52	1.13
Bobby Orr	Boston	1974-75	80	89	1.11
Bobby Clarke	Philadelphia	1974-75	80	89	1.11
Paul Coffey	Pittsburgh	1988-89	75	83	1.11
Denis Savard	Chicago	1982-83	78	86	1.10
Denis Savard	Chicago	1981-82	80	87	1.09
Denis Savard	Chicago	1987-88	80	87	1.09
Wayne Gretzky	Edmonton	1979-80	79	86	1.09
Paul Coffey	Edmonton	1983-84	80	86	1.08
Elmer Lach	Montreal	1944-45	50	54	1.08
Peter Stastny	Quebec	1985-86	76	81	1.07
Mark Messier	Edmonton	1989-90	79	84	1.06
Paul Coffey	Edmonton	1984-85	80	84	1.05
Marcel Dionne	Los Angeles	1979-80	80	84	1.05
Bobby Orr	Boston	1971-72	76	80	1.05
Mike Bossy	NY Islanders	1981-82	80	83	1.04
Phil Esposito	Boston	1968-69	74	77	1.04
Bryan Trottier	NY Islanders	1983-84	68	71	1.04
Pete Mahovlich	Montreal	1974-75	80	82	1.03
Kent Nilsson	Calgary	1980-81	80	82	1.03
Peter Stastny	Quebec	1982-83	75	77	1.03
Bernie Nicholls	Los Angeles	1988-89	79	80	1.01
Guy Lafleur	Montreal	1979-80	74	75	1.01
Guy Lafleur	Montreal	1976-77	80	80	1.00
Marcel Dionne	Los Angeles	1984-85	80	80	1.00
Bryan Trottier	NY Islanders	1977-78	77	77	1.00
Mike Bossy	NY Islanders	1983-84	67	67	1.00
Jean Ratelle	NY Rangers	1971-72	63	63	1.00
Ron Francis	Hartford	1985-86	53	53	1.00
Guy Chouinard	Calgary	1980-81	52	52	1.00
Elmer Lach	Montreal	1943-44	48	48	1.00

Penalty Leaders

* Match Misconduct penalty not included in total penalty minutes.
** Three Match Misconduct penalties not included in total penalty minutes.

1946-47 was the first season that a Match penalty was automatically written into the player's total penalty minutes as 20 minutes. Now all penalties, Match, Game Misconduct, and Misconduct, are written as 10 minutes. Penalty minutes not calculated in 1917-18.

Season	Player and Club	GP	PIM	Season	Player and Club	GP	PIM	Season	Player and Club	GP	PIM
1990-91	Rob Ray, Buffalo	66	350	1966-67	John Ferguson, Montreal	67	177	1942-43	Jimmy Orlando, Detroit	40	89*
1989-90	Basil McRae, Minnesota	66	351	1965-66	Reg Fleming, Bos., NYR	69	166	1941-42	Jimmy Orlando, Detroit	48	81**
1988-89	Tim Hunter, Calgary	75	375	1964-65	Carl Brewer, Toronto	70	177	1940-41	Jimmy Orlando, Detroit	48	99
1987-88	Bob Probert, Detroit	74	398	1963-64	Vic Hadfield, NY Rangers	69	151	1939-40	Red Horner, Toronto	30	87
1986-87	Tim Hunter, Calgary	73	361	1962-63	Howie Young, Detroit	64	273	1938-39	Red Horner, Toronto	48	85
1985-86	Joey Kocur, Detroit	59	377	1961-62	Lou Fontinato, Montreal	54	167	1937-38	Red Horner, Toronto	47	82*
1984-85	Chris Nilan, Montreal	77	358	1960-61	Pierre Pilote, Chicago	70	165	1936-37	Red Horner, Toronto	48	124
1983-84	Chris Nilan, Montreal	76	338	1959-60	Carl Brewer, Toronto	67	150	1935-36	Red Horner, Toronto	43	167
1982-83	Randy Holt, Washington	70	275	1958-59	Ted Lindsay, Chicago	70	184	1934-35	Red Horner, Toronto	46	125
1981-82	Paul Baxter, Pittsburgh	76	409	1957-58	Lou Fontinato, NY Rangers	70	152	1933-34	Red Horner, Toronto	42	126*
1980-81	Dave Williams, Vancouver	77	343	1956-57	Gus Mortson, Chicago	70	147	1932-33	Red Horner, Toronto	48	144
1979-80	Jimmy Mann, Winnipeg	72	287	1955-56	Lou Fontinato, NY Rangers	70	202	1931-32	Red Dutton, NY Americans	47	107
1978-79	Dave Williams, Toronto	77	298	1954-55	Fern Flaman, Boston	70	150	1930-31	Harvey Rockburn, Detroit	42	118
1977-78	Dave Schultz, L.A., Pit.	74	405	1953-54	Gus Mortson, Chicago	68	132	1929-30	Joe Lamb, Ottawa	44	119
1976-77	Dave Williams, Toronto	77	338	1952-53	Maurice Richard, Montreal	70	112	1928-29	Red Dutton, Mtl. Maroons	44	139
1975-76	Steve Durbano, Pit., K.C.	69	370	1951-52	Gus Kyle, Boston	69	127	1927-28	Eddie Shore, Boston	44	165
1974-75	Dave Schultz, Philadelphia	76	472	1950-51	Gus Mortson, Toronto	60	142	1926-27	Nels Stewart, Mtl. Maroons	44	133
1973-74	Dave Schultz, Philadelphia	73	348	1949-50	Bill Ezinicki, Toronto	67	144	1925-26	Bert Corbeau, Toronto	36	121
1972-73	Dave Schultz, Philadelphia	76	259	1948-49	Bill Ezinicki, Toronto	52	145	1924-25	Billy Boucher, Montreal	30	92
1971-72	Bryan Watson, Pittsburgh	75	212	1947-48	Bill Barilko, Toronto	57	147	1923-24	Bert Corbeau, Toronto	24	55
1970-71	Keith Magnuson, Chicago	76	291	1946-47	Gus Mortson, Toronto	60	133	1922-23	Billy Boucher, Montreal	24	52
1969-70	Keith Magnuson, Chicago	76	213	1945-46	Jack Stewart, Detroit	47	73	1921-22	Sprague Cleghorn, Montreal	24	63
1968-69	Forbes Kennedy, Phi., Tor.	77	219	1944-45	Pat Egan, Boston	48	86	1920-21	Bert Corbeau, Toronto	24	86
1967-68	Barclay Plager, St. Louis	49	153	1943-44	Mike McMahon, Montreal	42	98	1919-20	Cully Wilson, Toronto	23	79
								1918-19	Joe Hall, Montreal	17	85

Points-Per-Game Leaders, One Season

(Among players with 50 points or more in one season)

Player	Team	Season	Games	Points	Average
Wayne Gretzky	Edmonton	1983-84	74	205	2.77
Wayne Gretzky	Edmonton	1985-86	80	215	2.69
Wayne Gretzky	Edmonton	1981-82	80	212	2.65
Mario Lemieux	Pittsburgh	1988-89	76	199	2.62
Wayne Gretzky	Edmonton	1984-85	80	208	2.60
Wayne Gretzky	Edmonton	1982-83	80	196	2.45
Wayne Gretzky	Edmonton	1987-88	64	149	2.33
Wayne Gretzky	Edmonton	1986-87	79	183	2.32
Mario Lemieux	Pittsburgh	1987-88	77	168	2.18
Wayne Gretzky	Los Angeles	1988-89	78	168	2.15
Wayne Gretzky	Los Angeles	**1990-91**	78	163	2.09
Mario Lemieux	Pittsburgh	1989-90	59	123	2.08
Wayne Gretzky	Edmonton	1980-81	80	164	2.05
Bill Cowley	Boston	1943-44	36	71	1.97
Phil Esposito	Boston	1970-71	78	152	1.95
Wayne Gretzky	Los Angeles	1989-90	73	142	1.95
Steve Yzerman	Detroit	1988-89	80	155	1.94
Bernie Nicholls	Los Angeles	1988-89	79	150	1.90
Adam Oates	St. Louis	**1990-91**	61	115	1.89
Phil Esposito	Boston	1973-74	78	145	1.86
Jari Kurri	Edmonton	1984-85	73	135	1.85
Mike Bossy	NY Islanders	1981-82	80	147	1.84
Mario Lemieux	Pittsburgh	1985-86	79	141	1.78
Bobby Orr	Boston	1970-71	78	139	1.78
Jari Kurri	Edmonton	1983-84	64	113	1.77
Bryan Trottier	NY Islanders	1978-79	76	134	1.76
Mike Bossy	NY Islanders	1983-84	67	118	1.76
Paul Coffey	Edmonton	1985-86	79	138	1.75
Phil Esposito	Boston	1971-72	76	133	1.75
Peter Stastny	Quebec	1981-82	80	139	1.74
Wayne Gretzky	Edmonton	1979-80	79	137	1.73
Jean Ratelle	NY Rangers	1971-72	63	109	1.73
Marcel Dionne	Los Angeles	1979-80	80	137	1.71
Herb Cain	Boston	1943-44	48	82	1.71
Guy Lafleur	Montreal	1976-77	80	136	1.70
Dennis Maruk	Washington	1981-82	80	136	1.70
Phil Esposito	Boston	1968-69	74	126	1.70
Guy Lafleur	Montreal	1974-75	70	119	1.70
Mario Lemieux	Pittsburgh	1986-87	63	107	1.70
Bobby Orr	Boston	1974-75	80	135	1.69
Marcel Dionne	Los Angeles	1980-81	80	135	1.69
Guy Lafleur	Montreal	1977-78	78	132	1.69
Guy Lafleur	Montreal	1979-80	74	125	1.69
Rob Brown	Pittsburgh	1988-89	68	115	1.69
Jari Kurri	Edmonton	1985-86	78	131	1.68
Brett Hull	St. Louis	**1990-91**	78	131	1.68
Phil Esposito	Boston	1972-73	78	130	1.67
Cooney Weiland	Boston	1929-30	44	73	1.66
Peter Stastny	Quebec	1982-83	75	124	1.65
Bobby Orr	Boston	1973-74	74	122	1.65
Kent Nilsson	Calgary	1980-81	80	131	1.64
Marcel Dionne	Los Angeles	1978-79	80	130	1.63
Dale Hawerchuk	Winnipeg	1984-85	80	130	1.63
Mark Messier	Edmonton	1989-90	79	129	1.63
Bryan Trottier	NY Islanders	1983-84	68	111	1.63
Charlie Simmer	Los Angeles	1980-81	65	105	1.62
Guy Lafleur	Montreal	1978-79	80	129	1.61
Bryan Trottier	NY Islanders	1981-82	80	129	1.61
Phil Esposito	Boston	1974-75	79	127	1.61
Steve Yzerman	Detroit	1989-90	79	127	1.61
Peter Stastny	Quebec	1985-86	76	122	1.61
Michel Goulet	Quebec	1983-84	75	121	1.61
Bryan Trottier	NY Islanders	1977-78	77	123	1.60
Bobby Orr	Boston	1972-73	63	101	1.60
Guy Chouinard	Calgary	1980-81	52	83	1.60
Elmer Lach	Montreal	1944-45	50	80	1.60
Steve Yzerman	Detroit	1987-88	64	102	1.59
Mike Bossy	NY Islanders	1978-79	80	126	1.58
Paul Coffey	Edmonton	1983-84	80	126	1.58
Marcel Dionne	Los Angeles	1984-85	80	126	1.58
Bobby Orr	Boston	1969-70	76	120	1.58
Charlie Simmer	Los Angeles	1979-80	64	101	1.58
Bobby Clarke	Philadelphia	1975-76	76	119	1.57
Guy Lafleur	Montreal	1975-76	80	125	1.56
Dave Taylor	Los Angeles	1980-81	72	112	1.56
Denis Savard	Chicago	1982-83	78	121	1.55
Mike Bossy	NY Islanders	1985-86	80	123	1.54
Bobby Orr	Boston	1971-72	76	117	1.54
Mike Bossy	NY Islanders	1984-85	76	117	1.54
Doug Bentley	Chicago	1943-44	50	77	1.54
Marcel Dionne	Los Angeles	1976-77	80	122	1.53
Paul Coffey	Pittsburgh	1988-89	75	113	1.51

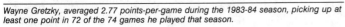

Wayne Gretzky, averaged 2.77 points-per-game during the 1983-84 season, picking up at least one point in 72 of the 74 games he played that season.

Cooney Weiland averaged 1.66 points-per-game during the 1929-30 campaign.

Active NHL Players' Three-or-More-Goal Games

Regular Season

Teams named are the ones the players were with at the time of their multiple-scoring games. Players listed alphabetically.

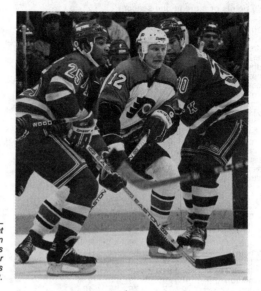

Tim Kerr has scored at least three goals in a game 17 times in his career. He will play for the New York Rangers in 1991-92.

Player	Team	3-Goals	4-Goals	5-Goals
Acton, Keith	Mtl., Min.	3	—	—
Adams, Greg	Vancouver	1	—	—
Allison, Mike	NY Rangers	1	—	—
Anderson, Glenn	Edmonton	17	3	—
Anderson, Perry	New Jersey	1	—	—
Andreychuk, Dave	Buffalo	5	—	1
Arniel, Scott	Winnipeg	1	—	—
Ashton, Brent	Que., Wpg.	6	—	—
Barber, Don	Minnesota	1	—	—
Barr, Dave	St. L., Det.	2	—	—
Bellows, Brian	Minnesota	4	1	—
Bjugstad, Scott	Minnesota	3	—	—
Bondra, Peter	Washington	1	—	—
Boschman, Laurie	Winnipeg	1	—	—
Bourque, Phil	Pittsburgh	1	—	—
Bourque, Ray	Boston	1	—	—
Bozek, Steve	Los Angeles	2	—	—
Brickley, Andy	Pit., Bos.	2	—	—
Brooke, Bob	NY Rangers	1	—	—
Broten, Aaron	New Jersey	1	—	—
Broten, Neal	Minnesota	6	—	—
Brown, Rob	Pittsburgh	7	—	—
Bullard, Mike	Pittsburgh	7	—	—
Burr, Shawn	Detroit	2	—	—
Burridge, Randy	Boston	2	—	—
Carbonneau, Guy	Montreal	—	1	—
Carpenter, Bob	Wsh., Bos.	2	1	—
Carson, Jimmy	L.A., Edm., Det.	7	1	—
Cavallini, Gino	St. Louis	1	—	—
Chabot, John	Pittsburgh	1	—	—
Christian, Dave	Wpg., Wsh.	2	—	—
Ciccarelli, Dino	Min., Wsh.	14	3	1
Clark, Wendel	Toronto	2	1	—
Coffey, Paul	Edmonton	4	1	—
Carson, Shayne	Montreal	2	—	—
Courtnall, Geoff	Bos., Wsh.	2	—	—
Courtnall, Russ	Tor., Mtl.	2	—	—
Craven, Murray	Philadelphia	2	—	—
Creighton, Adam	Buf., Chi.	2	—	—
Crowder, Keith	Boston	2	—	—
Cullen, John	Pittsburgh	2	—	—
Cunneyworth, R.	Pittsburgh	1	1	—
Cyr, Paul	Buffalo	1	—	—
Dahlen, Ulf	NYR, Min.	2	—	—
Damphousse, V.	Toronto	3	—	—
Daoust, Dan	Toronto	1	—	—
DeBlois, Lucien	Winnipeg	1	—	—
Dineen, Kevin	Hartford	5	—	—
Duchesne, Steve	Los Angeles	1	—	—
Duncan, Iain	Winnipeg	1	—	—
Eklund, Pelle	Philadelphia	1	—	—
Evason, Dean	Hartford	1	—	—
Federko, Bernie	St. Louis	11	—	—
Fergus, Tom	Toronto	4	—	—
Ferraro, Ray	Hartford	5	—	—
Flatley, Patrick	NY Islanders	1	1	—
Fleury, Theo	Calgary	5	—	—
Fogarty, Bryan	Quebec	1	—	—
Foligno, Mike	Det., Buf.	8	—	—
Francis, Ron	Hartford	8	1	—
Fraser, Curt	Chicago	1	—	—
Gagne, Paul	New Jersey	1	—	—
Gagner, Dave	Minnesota	3	—	—
Gallant, Gerard	Detroit	4	—	—
Garpenlov, Johan	Detroit	—	1	—
Gartner, Mike	Wsh., Min.	12	2	—
Gelinas, Martin	Edmonton	1	—	—
Gilbert, Greg	NY Islanders	2	—	—
Gillis, Paul	Quebec	1	—	—
Gilmour, Doug	St. Louis	2	—	—
Gould, Bobby	Calgary	1	—	—
Goulet, Michel	Que., Chi.	12	2	—
Graham, Dirk	Minnesota	1	—	—
Granato, Tony	NY Rangers	2	1	—
Graves, Adam	Edmonton	1	—	—
Gretzky, Wayne	Edm., L.A.	35	9	4
Gustafsson, Bengt	Washington	1	—	1
Hamel, Gilles	Buffalo	1	—	—
Hannan, Dave	Edmonton	1	—	—
Hawerchuk, Dale	Wpg., Buf.	12	—	—
Hodge, Ken	Boston	2	—	—
Horacek, Tony	Philadelphia	1	—	—
Housley, Phil	Buffalo	2	—	—
Howe, Mark	Hartford	1	—	—
Hrdina, Jiri	Calgary	1	1	—
Hull, Brett	Cgy., St. L.	10	—	—
Hull, Jody	Hartford	1	—	—
Hunter, Dale	Quebec	3	—	—
Hunter, Mark	St. L., Cgy.	5	1	—
Ihnacak, Peter	Toronto	1	—	—
Jackson, Jeff	Quebec	1	—	—
Jagr, Jaromir	Pittsburgh	1	—	—
Janney, Craig	Boston	1	—	—
Johnson, Mark	Hfd., NJ	5	—	—
Kasper, Steve	Boston	3	—	—
Kerr, Tim	Philadelphia	13	4	—
King, Derek	NY Islanders	1	1	—
Klima, Petr	Det., Edm.	6	—	—
Korn, Jim	Toronto	1	—	—
Krushelnyski, Mike	Edmonton	1	—	—
Kudelski, Robert	Los Angeles	1	—	—
Kurri, Jari	Edmonton	18	1	1
Lacombe, Normand	Edmonton	1	—	—
LaFontaine, Pat	NY Islanders	7	—	—
Lambert, Lane	Detroit	2	—	—
Larmer, Steve	Chicago	5	—	—
Lawless, Paul	Hartford	1	—	—
Lawton, Brian	Minnesota	2	—	—
Leeman, Gary	Toronto	4	—	—
Lemieux, Claude	Mtl., N.J.	3	—	—
Lemieux, Jocelyn	Chicago	1	—	—
Lemieux, Mario	Pittsburgh	19	6	1
Linden, Trevor	Vancouver	3	—	—
Linseman, Ken	Phi., Edm., Bos.	3	—	—
Loob, Hakan	Calgary	5	1	—
Ludzik, Steve	Chicago	1	—	—
MacLean, John	New Jersey	6	—	—
MacLean, Paul	Wpg., St. L.	7	1	—
MacLellan, Brian	L.A., NYR, Min., Cgy.	2	2	—
MacTavish, Craig	Edmonton	2	—	—
Makarov, Sergei	Calgary	1	—	—
Makela, Mikko	NY Islanders	1	—	—
Marois, Daniel	Toronto	3	—	—
McBain, Andrew	Winnipeg	1	—	—
McKegney, Tony	Buf., Que., Min., St. L.	7	1	—
McKenna, Sean	Buffalo	1	—	—
McPhee, Mike	Montreal	3	—	—
Meagher, Rick	Hartford	2	—	—
Messier, Mark	Edmonton	10	3	—
Modano, Mike	Minnesota	1	—	—
Mogilny, Alexander	Buffalo	1	—	—
Momesso, Sergio	Montreal	1	—	—
Mullen, Brian	Wpg., NYR	2	—	—
Mullen, Joe	St. L., Cgy.	5	2	—
Muller, Kirk	New Jersey	3	—	—
Murray, Troy	Chicago	1	—	—
Murzyn, Dana	Calgary	1	—	—
Naslund, Mats	Montreal	4	1	—
Neely, Cam	Boston	8	—	—
Neufeld, Ray	Winnipeg	4	—	—
Nicholls, Bernie	Los Angeles	12	2	—
Nieuwendyk, Joe	Calgary	4	2	1
Ogrodnick, John	Detroit	6	—	—
Olczyk, Ed	Toronto	2	—	—
Osborne, Mark	Detroit	1	—	—
Otto, Joel	Calgary	1	—	—
Paslawski, Greg	St. Louis	2	—	—
Pederson, Barry	Boston	6	1	—
Poddubny, Walt	Tor., Que.	4	1	—
Poulin, Dave	Philadelphia	5	—	—
Presley, Wayne	Chicago	1	—	—
Probert, Bob	Detroit	1	—	—
Propp, Brian	Philadelphia	3	1	—
Quinn, Dan	Pit., Van.	4	—	—
Reeds, Mark	St. Louis	1	—	—
Reinhart, Paul	Calgary	1	—	—
Richer, Stephane	Montreal	5	1	—
Ridley, Mike	NYR, Wsh.	3	1	—
Roberts, Gary	Calgary	1	—	—
Robinson, Larry	Montreal	1	—	—
Robitaille, Luc	Los Angeles	7	—	—
Roenick, Jeremy	Chicago	3	—	—
Ronning, Cliff	St. Louis	1	—	—
Ruff, Lindy	Buffalo	1	1	—
Sakic, Joe	Quebec	4	—	—
Sandlak, Jim	Vancouver	1	—	—
Sandstrom, Tomas	NYR, L.A.	6	1	—
Savard, Denis	Chicago	11	—	—
Secord, Al	Chicago	4	2	—
Shanahan, Brendan	New Jersey	1	—	—
Shedden, Doug	Pittsburgh	2	—	—
Sheppard, Ray	Buffalo	2	—	—
Sinisalo, Ilkka	Philadelphia	3	—	—
Simpson, Craig	Pit., Edm.	3	—	—
Skriko, Petri	Vancouver	4	1	—
Smail, Doug	Winnipeg	2	—	—
Smith, Derrick	Philadelphia	1	—	—
Smith, Bobby	Minnesota	5	1	—
Stastny, Peter	Quebec	14	2	—
Steen, Thomas	Winnipeg	3	—	—
Stevens, Kevin	Pittsburgh	2	—	—
Sulliman, Doug	Hartford	2	—	—
Sundin, Mats	Quebec	2	—	—
Sundstrom, Patrik	Vancouver	2	—	—
Sundstrom, Peter	NY Rangers	2	—	—
Sutter, Brent	NY Islanders	6	—	—
Sutter, Rich	Vancouver	1	—	—
Sweeney, Bob	Boston	1	—	—
Tanti, Tony	Van., Pit.	10	1	—
Taylor, Dave	Los Angeles	7	1	—
Thomas, Steve	Chicago	3	1	—
Tikkanen, Esa	Edmonton	3	—	—
Tocchet, Rick	Philadelphia	6	2	—
Tonelli, John	NYI, L.A.	4	—	1
Trottier, Bryan	NY Islanders	13	1	2
Tucker, John	Buffalo	1	—	—
Turcotte, Darren	NY Rangers	2	—	—
Turgeon, Pierre	Buffalo	2	—	—
Turgeon, Sylvain	Hfd., N.J.	4	—	—
Vaive, Rick	Tor., Chi.	10	3	—
Verbeek, Pat	New Jersey	4	1	—
Volek, Dave	NY Islanders	1	—	—
Vukota, Mick	NY Islanders	1	—	—
Walter, Ryan	Montreal	1	—	—
Wickenheiser, Doug	Mtl., St. L.	2	—	—
Wilson, Carey	Calgary	1	—	—
Wilson, Doug	Chicago	2	—	—
Wood, Randy	NY Islanders	1	—	—
Yzerman, Steve	Detroit	11	1	—
Zezel, Peter	Philadelphia	1	—	—

Daniel Marois scored 31 goals as a rookie with Toronto in 1988-89.

As a freshman, Denis Savard had 75 points in 76 games during the 1980-81 season.

Rookie Scoring Records

All-Time Top 50 Goal-Scoring Rookies

	Rookie	Team	Position	Season	GP	G	A	PTS
1.	*Mike Bossy	NY Islanders	Right wing	1977-78	73	53	38	91
2.	*Joe Niewendyk	Calgary	Center	1987-88	75	51	41	92
3.	*Dale Hawerchuk	Winnipeg	Center	1981-82	80	45	58	103
	*Luc Robitaille	Los Angeles	Left wing	1986-87	79	45	39	84
5.	Rick Martin	Buffalo	Left wing	1971-72	73	44	30	74
	Barry Pederson	Boston	Center	1981-82	80	44	48	92
7.	*Steve Larmer	Chicago	Right wing	1982-83	80	43	47	90
	*Mario Lemieux	Pittsburgh	Center	1984-85	73	43	57	100
9.	Darryl Sutter	Chicago	Left wing	1980-81	76	40	22	62
	Sylvain Turgeon	Hartford	Left wing	1983-84	76	40	32	72
	Warren Young	Pittsburgh	Left wing	1984-85	80	40	32	72
12.	*Eric Vail	Atlanta	Left wing	1974-75	72	39	21	60
	Anton Stastny	Quebec	Left wing	1980-81	80	39	46	85
	*Peter Stastny	Quebec	Center	1980-81	77	39	70	109
	Steve Yzerman	Detroit	Center	1983-84	80	39	48	87
16.	*Gilbert Perreault	Buffalo	Center	1970-71	78	38	34	72
	Neal Broten	Minnesota	Center	1981-82	73	38	60	98
	Ray Sheppard	Buffalo	Right wing	1987-88	74	38	27	65
19.	Jorgen Pettersson	St. Louis	Left wing	1980-81	62	37	36	73
	Jimmy Carson	Los Angeles	Centre	1986-87	80	37	42	79
21.	Mike Foligno	Detroit	Right wing	1979-80	80	36	35	71
	Mike Bullard	Pittsburgh	Center	1981-82	75	36	27	63
	Paul MacLean	Winnipeg	Right wing	1981-82	74	36	25	61
	Tony Granato	NY Rangers	Right wing	1988-89	78	36	27	63
25.	Marian Stastny	Quebec	Right wing	1981-82	74	35	54	89
	Brian Bellows	Minnesota	Right wing	1982-83	78	35	30	65
27.	Nels Stewart	Mtl. Maroons	Center	1925-26	36	34	8	42
	*Danny Grant	Minnesota	Left wing	1968-69	75	34	31	65
	Norm Ferguson	Oakland	Right wing	1968-69	76	34	20	54
	Brian Propp	Philadelphia	Left wing	1979-80	80	34	41	75
	Wendel Clark	Toronto	Left wing	1985-86	66	34	11	45
32.	*Willi Plett	Atlanta	Right wing	1976-77	64	33	23	56
	Dale McCourt	Detroit	Center	1977-78	76	33	39	72
	Mark Pavelich	NY Rangers	Center	1981-82	79	33	43	76
	Ron Flockhart	Philadelphia	Center	1981-82	72	33	39	72
	Steve Bozek	Los Angeles	Center	1981-82	71	33	23	56
37.	Bill Mosienko	Chicago	Right wing	1943-44	50	32	38	70
	Michel Bergeron	Detroit	Right wing	1975-76	72	32	27	59
	*Bryan Trottier	NY Islanders	Center	1975-76	80	32	63	95
	Don Murdoch	NY Rangers	Right wing	1976-77	59	32	24	56
	Jari Kurri	Edmonton	Left wing	1980-81	75	32	43	75
	Bobby Carpenter	Washington	Center	1981-82	80	32	35	67
	Kjell Dahlin	Montreal	Right wing	1985-86	77	32	39	71
	Petr Klima	Detroit	Left wing	1985-86	74	32	24	56
	Darren Turcotte	NY Rangers	Right wing	1989-90	76	32	34	66
46.	Danny Gare	Buffalo	Right wing	1974-75	78	31	31	62
	Pierre Larouche	Pittsburgh	Center	1974-75	79	31	37	68
	Dave Poulin	Philadelphia	Center	1983-84	73	31	45	76
	Daniel Marois	Toronto	Right wing	1988-89	76	31	23	54
	*Sergei Fedorov	Detroit	Center	1990-91	77	31	48	79

* Calder Trophy Winner.

All-Time Top 50 Point-Scoring Rookies

	Rookie	Team	Position	Season	GP	G	A	PTS
1.	*Peter Stastny	Quebec	Center	1980-81	77	39	70	109
2.	*Dale Hawerchuk	Winnipeg	Center	1981-82	80	45	58	103
3.	*Mario Lemieux	Pittsburgh	Center	1984-85	73	43	57	100
4.	Neal Broten	Minnesota	Center	1981-82	73	38	60	98
5.	*Bryan Trottier	NY Islanders	Center	1975-76	80	32	63	95
6.	Barry Pederson	Boston	Center	1981-82	80	44	48	92
	*Joe Nieuwendyk	Calgary	Center	1987-88	75	51	41	92
8.	*Mike Bossy	NY Islanders	Right wing	1977-78	73	53	38	91
9.	*Steve Larmer	Chicago	Right wing	1982-83	80	43	47	90
10.	Marian Stastny	Quebec	Right wing	1981-82	74	35	54	89
11.	Steve Yzerman	Detroit	Center	1983-84	80	39	48	87
12.	*Sergei Makarov	Calgary	Right wing	1989-90	80	24	62	86
13.	Anton Stastny	Quebec	Left wing	1980-81	80	39	46	85
14.	*Luc Robitaille	Los Angeles	Left wing	1986-87	79	45	39	84
15.	Jimmy Carson	Los Angeles	Center	1986-87	80	37	42	79
	*Sergei Fedorov	Detroit	Center	1990-91	77	31	48	79
17.	Marcel Dionne	Detroit	Center	1971-72	78	28	49	77
18.	Larry Murphy	Los Angeles	Defense	1980-81	80	16	60	76
	Mark Pavelich	NY Rangers	Center	1981-82	79	33	43	76
	Dave Poulin	Philadelphia	Center	1983-84	73	31	45	76
21.	Brian Propp	Philadelphia	Left wing	1979-80	80	34	41	75
	Jari Kurri	Edmonton	Left wing	1980-81	75	32	43	75
	Denis Savard	Chicago	Center	1980-81	76	28	47	75
	Mike Modano	Minnesota	Center	1989-90	80	29	46	75
25.	Rick Martin	Buffalo	Left wing	1971-72	73	44	30	74
	*Bobby Smith	Minnesota	Center	1978-79	80	30	44	74
27.	Jorgen Pettersson	St. Louis	Left wing	1980-81	62	37	36	73
28.	*Gilbert Perreault	Buffalo	Center	1970-71	78	38	34	72
	Dale McCourt	Detroit	Center	1977-78	76	33	39	72
	Ron Flockhart	Philadelphia	Center	1981-82	72	33	39	72
	Sylvain Turgeon	Hartford	Left wing	1983-84	76	40	32	72
	Warren Young	Pittsburgh	Left wing	1984-85	80	40	32	72
	Carey Wilson	Calgary	Center	1984-85	74	24	48	72
34.	Mike Foligno	Detroit	Right wing	1979-80	80	36	35	71
	Dave Christian	Winnipeg	Center	1980-81	80	28	43	71
	Mats Naslund	Montreal	Left wing	1982-83	74	26	45	71
	Kjell Dahlin	Montreal	Right wing	1985-86	77	32	39	71
	*Brian Leetch	NY Rangers	Defense	1988-89	68	23	48	71
39.	Bill Mosienko	Chicago	Right wing	1943-44	50	32	38	70
40.	Roland Eriksson	Minnesota	Center	1976-77	80	25	44	69
41.	Jude Drouin	Minnesota	Center	1970-71	75	16	52	68
	Pierre Larouche	Pittsburgh	Center	1974-75	79	31	37	68
	Ron Francis	Hartford	Center	1981-82	59	25	43	68
	*Gary Suter	Calgary	Defense	1985-86	80	18	50	68
45.	Tom Webster	Detroit	Right wing	1970-71	78	30	37	67
	Bobby Carpenter	Washington	Center	1981-82	80	32	35	67
	Chris Valentine	Washington	Center	1981-82	60	30	37	67
	Mark Osborne	Detroit	Left wing	1981-82	80	26	41	67
	Mark Recchi	Pittsburgh	Right wing	1989-90	74	30	37	67
50.	Peter Ihnacak	Toronto	Center	1982-83	80	28	38	66
	Phil Housley	Buffalo	Defense	1982-83	77	19	47	66
	Pelle Eklund	Philadelphia	Center	1985-86	70	15	51	66
	Darren Turcotte	NY Rangers	Center	1989-90	76	32	34	66
	Jeremy Roenick	Chicago	Center	1989-90	78	26	40	66

* Calder Trophy Winner.

50-Goal Seasons

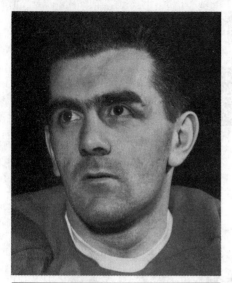

Maurice Richard

Vic Hadfield

Rick Kehoe

Player	Team	Date of 50th Goal	Score		Goaltender	Player's Game No.	Team Game No.	Total Goals	Total Games	Age When First 50th Scored (Yrs. & Mos.)
Maurice Richard	Mtl.	18-3-45	Mtl. 4	at Bos. 2	Harvey Bennett	50	50	50	50	23.7
Bernie Geoffrion	Mtl.	16-3-61	Tor. 2	at Mtl. 5	Cesare Maniago	62	68	50	64	30.1
Bobby Hull	Chi.	25-3-62	Chi. 1	at NYR 4	Gump Worsley	70	70	50	70	23.2
Bobby Hull	Chi.	2-3-66	Det. 4	at Chi. 5	Hank Bassen	52	57	54	65	
Bobby Hull	Chi.	18-3-67	Chi. 5	at Tor. 9	Bruce Gamble	63	66	52	66	
Bobby Hull	Chi.	5-3-69	NYR 4	at Chi. 4	Ed Giacomin	64	66	58	74	
Phil Esposito	Bos.	20-2-71	Bos. 4	at L.A. 5	Denis DeJordy	58	58	76	78	29.0
John Bucyk	Bos.	16-3-71	Bos. 11	at Det. 4	Roy Edwards	69	69	51	78	35.1
Phil Esposito	Bos.	20-2-72	Bos. 3	at Chi. 1	Tony Esposito	60	60	66	76	
Bobby Hull	Chi.	2-4-72	Det. 1	at Chi. 6	Andy Brown	78	78	50	78	
Vic Hadfield	NYR	2-4-72	Mtl. 6	at NYR 5	Denis DeJordy	78	78	50	78	31.6
Phil Esposito	Bos.	25-3-73	Buf. 1	at Bos. 6	Roger Crozier	75	75	55	78	
Mickey Redmond	Det.	27-3-73	Det. 8	at Tor. 1	Ron Low	73	75	52	76	25.3
Rick MacLeish	Phi.	1-4-73	Phi. 4	at Pit. 5	Cam Newton	78	78	50	78	23.2
Phil Esposito	Bos.	20-2-74	Bos. 5	at Min. 5	Cesare Maniago	56	56	68	78	
Mickey Redmond	Det.	23-3-74	NYR 3	at Det. 5	Ed Giacomin	69	71	51	76	
Ken Hodge	Bos.	6-4-74	Bos. 2	at Mtl. 6	Michel Larocque	75	77	50	76	29.10
Rick Martin	Buf.	7-4-74	St.L. 2	at Buf. 5	Wayne Stephenson	78	78	52	78	22.9
Phil Esposito	Bos.	8-2-75	Bos. 8	at Det. 5	Jim Rutherford	54	54	61	79	
Guy Lafleur	Mtl.	29-3-75	K.C. 1	at Mtl. 4	Denis Herron	66	76	53	70	23.6
Danny Grant	Det.	2-4-75	Wsh. 3	at Det. 8	John Adams	78	78	50	80	29.2
Rick Martin	Buf.	3-4-75	Bos. 2	at Buf. 4	Ken Broderick	67	79	52	68	
Reggie Leach	Phi.	14-3-76	Atl. 1	at Phi. 6	Daniel Bouchard	69	69	61	80	25.11
Jean Pronovost	Pit.	24-3-76	Bos. 5	at Pit. 5	Gilles Gilbert	74	74	52	80	31.3
Guy Lafleur	Mtl.	27-3-76	K.C. 2	at Mtl. 8	Denis Herron	76	76	56	80	
Bill Barber	Phi.	3-4-76	Buf. 2	at Phi. 5	Al Smith	79	79	50	80	23.9
Pierre Larouche	Pit.	3-4-76	Wash. 5	at Pit. 4	Ron Low	75	79	53	76	20.5
Danny Gare	Buf.	4-4-76	Tor. 2	at Buf. 5	Gord McRae	79	80	50	79	21.11
Steve Shutt	Mtl.	1-3-77	Mtl. 5	at NYI 4	Glenn Resch	65	65	60	80	24.8
Guy Lafleur	Mtl.	6-3-77	Mtl. 1	at Buf. 4	Don Edwards	68	68	56	80	
Marcel Dionne	L.A.	2-4-77	Min. 2	at L.A. 7	Pete LoPresti	79	79	53	80	25.8
Guy Lafleur	Mtl.	8-3-78	Wsh. 3	at Mtl. 4	Jim Bedard	63	65	60	78	
Mike Bossy	NYI	1-4-78	Wsh. 2	at NYI 3	Bernie Wolfe	69	76	53	73	21.2
Mike Bossy	NYI	24-2-79	Det. 1	at NYI 3	Rogie Vachon	58	58	69	80	
Marcel Dionne	L.A.	11-3-79	L.A. 3	at Phi. 6	Wayne Stephenson	68	68	59	80	
Guy Lafleur	Mtl.	31-3-79	Pit. 3	at Mtl. 5	Denis Herron	76	76	52	80	
Guy Chouinard	Atl.	6-4-79	NYR 2	at Atl. 9	John Davidson	79	79	50	80	22.5
Marcel Dionne	L.A.	12-3-80	L.A. 2	at Pit. 4	Nick Ricci	70	70	53	80	
Mike Bossy	NYI	16-3-80	NYI 6	at Chi. 1	Tony Esposito	68	71	51	75	
Charlie Simmer	L.A.	19-3-80	Det. 3	at L.A. 4	Jim Rutherford	57	73	56	64	26.0
Pierre Larouche	Mtl.	25-3-80	Chi. 4	at Mtl. 8	Tony Esposito	72	75	50	73	
Danny Gare	Buf.	27-3-80	Det. 1	at Buf. 10	Jim Rutherford	71	75	56	76	
Blaine Stoughton	Hfd.	28-3-80	Hfd. 4	at Van. 4	Glen Hanlon	75	75	56	80	27.0
Guy Lafleur	Mtl.	2-4-80	Mtl. 7	at Det. 2	Rogie Vachon	72	78	50	74	
Wayne Gretzky	Edm.	2-4-80	Min. 1	at Edm. 1	Gary Edwards	78	79	51	79	19.2
Reggie Leach	Phi.	3-4-80	Wsh. 2	at Phi. 4	(empty net)	75	79	50	76	
Mike Bossy	NYI	24-1-81	Que. 3	at NYI 7	Ron Grahame	50	50	68	79	
Charlie Simmer	L.A.	26-1-81	L.A. 7	at Que. 5	Michel Dion	51	51	56	65	
Marcel Dionne	L.A.	8-3-81	L.A. 4	at Wpg. 1	Markus Mattsson	68	68	58	80	
Wayne Babych	St.L.	12-3-81	St.L. 3	at Mtl. 4	Richard Sevigny	70	68	54	78	22.9
Wayne Gretzky	Edm.	15-3-81	Edm. 3	at Cgy. 3	Pat Riggin	69	69	55	80	
Rick Kehoe	Pit.	16-3-81	Pit. 7	at Edm. 6	Eddie Mio	70	70	55	80	29.7
Jacques Richard	Que.	29-3-81	Mtl. 0	at Que. 4	Richard Sevigny	76	75	52	78	28.6
Dennis Maruk	Wsh.	5-4-81	Det. 2	at Wsh. 7	Larry Lozinski	80	80	50	80	25.3
Wayne Gretzky	Edm.	30-12-81	Phi. 5	at Edm. 7	(empty net)	39	39	92	80	
Dennis Maruk	Wsh.	21-2-82	Wpg. 3	at Wsh. 6	Doug Soetaert	61	61	60	80	
Mike Bossy	NYI	4-3-82	Tor. 1	at NYI 10	Michel Larocque	66	66	64	80	
Dino Ciccarelli	Min.	8-3-82	St.L. 1	at Min. 8	Mike Liut	67	68	55	76	21.7
Rick Vaive	Tor.	24-3-82	St.L. 3	at Tor. 4	Mike Liut	72	75	54	77	22.10
Rick Middleton	Bos.	28-3-82	Bos. 5	at Buf. 9	Paul Harrison	72	77	51	75	
Blaine Stoughton	Hfd.	28-3-82	Min. 5	at Hfd. 2	Gilles Meloche	76	76	52	80	28.3
Marcel Dionne	L.A.	30-3-82	Cgy. 7	at L.A. 5	Pat Riggin	75	77	50	78	
Mark Messier	Edm.	31-3-82	L.A. 3	at Edm. 7	Mario Lessard	78	79	50	78	21.3
Bryan Trottier	NYI	3-4-82	Phi. 3	at NYI 6	Pete Peeters	79	79	50	80	25.9
Lanny McDonald	Cgy.	18-2-83	Cgy. 1	at Buf. 5	Bob Sauve	60	60	66	80	30.0
Wayne Gretzky	Edm.	19-2-83	Edm. 10	at Pit. 7	Nick Ricci	60	60	71	80	
Michel Goulet	Que.	5-3-83	Que. 7	at Hfd. 3	Mike Veisor	67	67	57	80	22.11
Mike Bossy	NYI	12-3-83	Wsh. 2	at NYI 6	Al Jensen	70	71	60	79	
Marcel Dionne	L.A.	17-3-83	Que. 3	at L.A. 4	Daniel Bouchard	71	71	56	80	
Al Secord	Chi.	20-3-83	Tor. 3	at Chi. 7	Mike Palmateer	73	73	54	80	25.0
Rick Vaive	Tor.	30-3-83	Tor. 4	at Det. 2	Gilles Gilbert	76	78	51	78	

Player	Team	Date of 50th Goal		Score		Goaltender	Player's Game No.	Team Game No.	Total Goals	Total Games	Age When First 50th Scored (Yrs. & Mos.)
Wayne Gretzky	Edm.	7-1-84	Hfd. 3	at	Edm. 5	Greg Millen	42	42	87	74	
Michel Goulet	Que.	8-3-84	Que. 8	at	Pit. 6	Denis Herron	63	69	56	75	
Rick Vaive	Tor.	14-3-84	Min. 3	at	Tor. 3	Gilles Meloche	69	72	52	76	
Mike Bullard	Pit.	14-3-84	Pit. 6	at	L.A. 7	Markus Mattsson	71	72	51	76	23.0
Jari Kurri	Edm.	15-3-84	Edm. 2	at	Mtl. 3	Rick Wamsley	57	73	52	64	23.10
Glenn Anderson	Edm.	21-3-84	Hfd. 3	at	Edm. 5	Greg Millen	76	76	54	80	23.6
Tim Kerr	Phi.	22-3-84	Pit. 4	at	Phi. 13	Denis Herron	74	75	54	79	24.3
Mike Bossy	NYI	31-3-84	NYI 3	at	Wsh. 1	Pat Riggin	67	79	51	67	
Wayne Gretzky	Edm.	26-1-85	Pit. 3	at	Edm. 6	Denis Herron	49	49	73	80	
Jari Kurri	Edm.	3-2-85	Hfd. 3	at	Edm. 6	Greg Millen	50	53	71	73	
Mike Bossy	NYI	5-3-85	Phi. 5	at	NYI 4	Bob Froese	61	65	58	76	
Tim Kerr	Phi.	7-3-85	Wsh. 6	at	Phi. 9	Pat Riggin	63	65	54	74	
John Ogrodnick	Det.	13-3-85	Det. 6	at	Edm. 7	Grant Fuhr	69	69	55	79	25.9
Bob Carpenter	Wsh.	21-3-85	Wsh. 2	at	Mtl. 3	Steve Penney	72	72	53	80	21.9
Michel Goulet	Que.	26-3-85	Buf. 3	at	Que. 4	Tom Barrasso	62	73	55	69	
Dale Hawerchuk	Wpg.	29-4-85	Chi. 5	at	Wpg. 5	W. Skorodenski	77	77	53	80	21.1
Mike Gartner	Wsh.	7-4-85	Pit. 3	at	Wsh. 7	Brian Ford	80	80	50	80	25.5
Jari Kurri	Edm.	4-3-86	Edm. 6	at	Van. 2	Richard Brodeur	63	65	68	78	
Mike Bossy	NYI	11-3-86	Cgy. 4	at	NYI 8	Rejean Lemelin	67	67	61	80	
Glenn Anderson	Edm.	14-3-86	Det. 3	at	Edm. 12	Greg Stefan	63	71	54	72	
Michel Goulet	Que.	17-3-86	Que. 8	at	Mtl. 6	Patrick Roy	67	72	53	75	
Wayne Gretzky	Edm.	18-3-86	Wpg. 2	at	Edm. 6	Brian Hayward	72	72	52	80	
Tim Kerr	Phi.	20-3-86	Pit. 1	at	Phi. 5	Roberto Romano	68	72	58	76	
Wayne Gretzky	Edm.	2-4-87	Edm. 6	at	Min. 5	Don Beaupre	55	55	62	79	
Tim Kerr	Phi.	3-17-87	NYR 1	at	Phi. 4	J. Vanbiesbrouck	67	71	58	75	
Jari Kurri	Edm.	3-17-87	N.J. 4	at	Edm. 7	Craig Billington	69	70	54	79	
Mario Lemieux	Pit.	3-12-87	Que. 3	at	Pit. 6	Mario Gosselin	53	70	54	63	21.5
Dino Ciccarelli	Min.	3-7-87	Pit. 7	at	Min. 3	Gilles Meloche	66	66	52	80	
Mario Lemieux	Pit.	2-2-88	Wsh. 2	at	Pit. 3	Pete Peeters	51	54	70	77	
Steve Yzerman	Det.	1-3-88	Buf. 0	at	Det. 4	Tom Barrasso	64	64	50	64	22.10
Joe Nieuwendyk	Cgy.	12-3-88	Buf. 4	at	Cgy. 10	Tom Barrasso	66	70	51	75	21.5
Craig Simpson	Edm.	15-3-88	Buf. 4	at	Edm. 6	Jacques Cloutier	71	71	56	80	21.1
Jimmy Carson	L.A.	26-3-88	Chi. 5	at	L.A. 9	Darren Pang	77	77	55	88	19.7
Luc Robitaille	L.A.	1-4-88	L.A. 6	at	Cgy. 3	Mike Vernon	79	79	53	80	21.10
Hakan Loob	Cgy.	3-4-88	Min. 1	at	Cgy. 4	Don Beaupre	80	80	50	80	27.9
Stephane Richer	Mtl.	3-4-88	Mtl. 4	at	Buf. 4	Tom Barrasso	72	80	50	72	21.10
Mario Lemieux	Pit.	20-1-89	Pit. 3	at	Wpg. 7	Eldon Reddick	44	46	85	76	
Bernie Nicholls	L.A.	28-1-89	Edm. 7	at	L.A. 6	Grant Fuhr	51	51	70	79	27.7
Steve Yzerman	Det.	5-2-89	Det. 6	at	Wpg. 2	Eldon Reddick	55	55	65	80	
Wayne Gretzky	L.A.	4-3-89	Phi. 2	at	L.A. 6	Ron Hextall	66	67	54	78	
Joe Nieuwendyk	Cgy.	21-3-89	NYI 1	at	Cgy. 4	Mark Fitzpatrick	72	74	51	77	
Joe Mullen	Cgy.	31-3-89	Wpg. 1	at	Cgy. 4	Bob Essensa	78	79	51	79	32.1
Brett Hull	St.L.	6-2-90	Tor. 4	at	St.L. 6	Jeff Reese	54	54	72	80	25.6
Steve Yzerman	Det.	24-2-90	Det. 3	at	NYI 3	Glenn Healy	63	63	62	79	
Cam Neely	Bos.	10-3-90	Bos. 3	at	NYI 3	Mark Fitzpatrick	69	71	55	76	24.9
Brian Bellows	Min.	22-3-90	Min. 5	at	Det. 1	Tim Cheveldae	75	75	55	80	25.6
Pat LaFontaine	NYI	24-3-90	NYI 5	at	Edm. 5	Bill Ranford	71	77	54	74	25.1
Stephane Richer	Mtl.	24-3-90	Mtl. 4	at	Hfd. 7	Peter Sidorkiewicz	75	77	51	75	
Gary Leeman	Tor.	28-3-90	NYI 6	at	Tor. 3	Mark Fitzpatrick	78	78	51	80	26.1
Luc Robitaille	L.A.	21-3-90	L.A. 3	at	Van. 6	Kirk McLean	79	79	52	80	
Brett Hull	St. L.	25-1-91	St. L. 9	at	Det. 4	Dave Gagnon	49	49	86	78	
Cam Neely	Bos.	26-3-91	Bos. 7	at	Que. 4	empty net	67	78	51	69	
Theoren Fleury	Cgy.	26-3-91	Van. 2	at	Cgy. 7	Bob Mason	77	77	51	79	22.9

Rick Vaive

Craig Simpson

Players' 500th Goals

Player	Team	Date	Game No.	Score		Opposing Goaltender	Total Goals	Total Games
Maurice Richard	Montreal	Oct. 19/57	863	Chi. 1	at Mtl. 3	Glenn Hall	544	978
Gordie Howe	Detroit	Mar. 14/62	1,045	Det. 2	at NYR 3	Gump Worsley	801	1,767
Bobby Hull	Chicago	Feb. 21/70	861	NYR. 2	at Chi. 4	Ed Giacomin	610	1,063
Jean Béliveau	Montreal	Feb. 11/71	1,101	Min. 2	at Mtl. 6	Gilles Gilbert	507	1,125
Frank Mahovlich	Montreal	Mar. 21/73	1,105	Van. 2	at Mtl. 3	Dunc Wilson	533	1,181
Phil Esposito	Boston	Dec. 22/74	803	Det. 4	at Bos. 5	Jim Rutherford	717	1,282
John Bucyk	Boston	Oct. 30/75	1,370	St. L. 2	at Bos. 3	Yves Belanger	556	1,540
Stan Mikita	Chicago	Feb. 27/77	1,221	Van. 4	at Chi. 3	Cesare Maniago	541	1,394
Marcel Dionne	Los Angeles	Dec. 14/82	887	L.A. 2	at Wsh. 7	Al Jensen	731	1,348
Guy Lafleur	Montreal	Dec. 20/83	918	Mtl. 6	at N.J. 0	Glenn Resch	560	1,126
Mike Bossy	NY Islanders	Jan. 2/86	647	Bos. 5	at NYI 7	empty net	573	752
Gilbert Perreault	Buffalo	Mar. 9/86	1,159	NJ 3	at Buf. 4	Alain Chevrier	512	1,191
*Wayne Gretzky	Edmonton	Nov. 22/86	575	Van. 2	at Edm. 5	empty net	718	925
Lanny McDonald	Calgary	Mar. 21/89	1,107	NYI 1	at Cgy. 4	Mark Fitzpatrick	500	1,111
*Bryan Trottier	NY Islanders	Feb. 13/90	1,104	Cgy. 4	at NYI 2	Rick Wamsley	509	1,175

* Active

Lanny McDonald

Gordie Howe

Gilbert Perreault

Peter Mahovlich

100-Point Seasons

Player	Team	Date of 100th Point	G or A	Score		Player's Game No.	Team Game No.	Points G-A PTS		Total Games	Age when first 100th point scored (Yrs. & Mos.)
Phil Esposito	Bos.	2-3-69	(G)	Pit. 0	at Bos. 4	60	62	49-77 —	126	74	27.1
Bobby Hull	Chi.	20-3-69	(G)	Chi. 5	at Det. 5	71	71	58-49 —	107	76	30.2
Gordie Howe	Det.	30-3-69	(G)	Det. 5	at Chi. 9	76	76	44-59 —	103	76	41.0
Bobby Orr	Bos.	15-3-70	(G)	Det. 5	at Bos. 5	67	67	33-87 —	120	76	22.11
Phil Esposito	Bos.	6-2-71	(A)	Buf. 3	at Bos. 4	51	51	76-76 —	152	78	
Bobby Orr	Bos.	22-2-71	(A)	Bos. 4	at L.A. 5	58	58	37-102 —	139	78	
John Bucyk	Bos.	13-3-71	(A)	Bos. 6	at Van. 3	68	68	51-65 —	116	78	35.10
Ken Hodge	Bos.	21-3-71	(A)	Buf. 7	at Bos. 5	72	72	43-62 —	105	78	26.9
Jean Ratelle	NYR	18-2-72	(A)	NYR 2	at Cal. 2	58	58	46-63 —	109	63	31.4
Phil Esposito	Bos.	19-2-72	(A)	Bos. 6	at Min. 4	59	59	66-67 —	133	76	
Bobby Orr	Bos.	2-3-72	(A)	Van. 3	at Bos. 7	64	64	37-80 —	117	76	
Vic Hadfield	NYR	25-3-72	(A)	NYR 3	at Mtl. 3	74	74	50-56 —	106	78	31.5
Phil Esposito	Bos.	3-3-73	(A)	Bos. 1	at Mtl. 5	64	64	55-75 —	130	78	
Bobby Clarke	Phi.	29-3-73	(G)	Atl. 2	at Phi. 4	76	76	37-67 —	104	78	23.7
Bobby Orr	Bos.	31-3-73	(G)	Bos. 3	at Tor. 7	62	77	29-72 —	101	63	
Rick MacLeish	Phi.	1-4-73	(G)	Phi. 4	at Pit. 5	78	78	50-50 —	100	78	23.3
Phil Esposito	Bos.	13-2-74	(A)	Bos. 9	at Cal. 6	53	53	68-77 —	145	78	
Bobby Orr	Bos.	12-3-74	(A)	Buf. 0	at Bos. 4	62	66	32-90 —	122	74	
Ken Hodge	Bos.	24-3-74	(A)	Mtl. 3	at Bos. 6	72	72	50-55 —	105	76	
Phil Esposito	Bos.	8-2-75	(A)	Bos. 8	at Det. 5	54	54	61-66 —	127	79	
Bobby Orr	Bos.	13-2-75	(A)	Bos. 1	at Buf. 3	57	57	46-89 —	135	80	
Guy Lafleur	Mtl.	7-3-75	(G)	Wsh. 4	at Mtl. 8	56	66	53-66 —	119	70	24.6
Pete Mahovlich	Mtl.	9-3-75	(G)	Mtl. 5	at NYR 3	67	67	35-82 —	117	80	29.5
Marcel Dionne	Det.	9-3-75	(G)	Det. 5	at Phi. 8	67	67	47-74 —	121	80	23.7
Bobby Clarke	Phi.	22-3-75	(A)	Min. 0	at Phi. 4	72	72	27-89 —	116	80	
Rene Robert	Buf.	5-4-75	(A)	Buf. 4	at Tor. 2	74	80	40-60 —	100	74	26.4
Guy Lafleur	Mtl.	10-3-76	(G)	Mtl. 5	at Chi. 1	69	69	56-69 —	125	80	
Bobby Clarke	Phi.	11-3-76	(A)	Buf. 1	at Phi. 6	64	68	30-89 —	119	76	
Bill Barber	Phi.	18-3-76	(A)	Van. 2	at Phi. 3	71	71	50-62 —	112	80	23.8
Gilbert Perreault	Buf.	21-3-76	(A)	K.C. 1	at Buf. 3	73	73	44-69 —	113	80	25.4
Pierre Larouche	Pit.	24-3-76	(G)	Bos. 5	at Pit. 5	70	74	53-58 —	111	76	20.4
Pete Mahovlich	Mtl.	28-3-76	(A)	Mtl. 2	at Bos. 2	77	77	34-71 —	105	80	
Jean Ratelle	Bos.	30-3-76	(G)	Buf. 4	at Bos. 4	77	77	36-69 —	105	80	
Jean Pronovost	Pit.	3-4-76	(A)	Wsh. 5	at Pit. 4	79	79	52-52 —	104	80	30.4
Darryl Sittler	Tor.	3-4-76	(A)	Bos. 4	at Tor. 2	78	79	41-59 —	100	79	26.7
Guy Lafleur	Mtl.	26-2-77	(A)	Clev. 3	at Mtl. 5	63	63	56-80 —	136	80	
Marcel Dionne	L.A.	5-3-77	(G)	Pit. 3	at L.A. 3	67	67	53-69 —	122	80	
Steve Shutt	Mtl.	27-3-77	(A)	Mtl. 6	at Det. 0	77	77	60-45 —	105	80	24.9
Bryan Trottier	NYI	25-2-78	(A)	Chi. 1	at NYI 7	59	60	46-77 —	123	77	21.7
Guy Lafleur	Mtl.	28-2-78	(G)	Det. 3	at Mtl. 9	59	61	60-72 —	132	78	
Darryl Sittler	Tor.	12-3-78	(A)	Tor. 7	at Pit. 1	67	67	45-72 —	117	80	
Guy Lafleur	Mtl.	27-2-79	(A)	Mtl. 3	at NYI 7	61	61	52-77 —	129	80	
Bryan Trottier	NYI	6-3-79	(A)	Buf. 3	at NYI 2	59	63	47-87 —	134	76	
Marcel Dionne	L.A.	8-3-79	(G)	L.A. 4	at Buf. 6	66	66	59-71 —	130	80	
Mike Bossy	NYI	11-3-79	(G)	NYI 4	at Bos. 4	66	66	69-57 —	126	80	22.2
Bob MacMillan	Atl.	15-3-79	(A)	Atl. 4	at Phi. 5	66	69	37-71 —	108	79	26.6
Guy Chouinard	Atl.	30-3-79	(A)	L.A. 3	at Atl. 5	75	75	50-57 —	107	80	22.5
Denis Potvin	NYI	8-4-79	(A)	NYI 5	at NYR 2	73	80	31-70 —	101	73	25.5
Marcel Dionne	L.A.	6-2-80	(A)	L.A. 3	at Hfd. 7	53	53	53-84 —	137	80	
Guy Lafleur	Mtl.	10-2-80	(A)	Mtl. 3	at Bos. 2	55	55	50-75 —	125	74	
Wayne Gretzky	Edm.	24-2-80	(A)	Bos. 4	at Edm. 2	61	62	51-86 —	137	79	19.2
Bryan Trottier	NYI	30-3-80	(A)	NYI 9	at Que. 6	75	77	42-62 —	104	78	
Gilbert Perreault	Buf.	1-4-80	(A)	Buf. 5	at Atl. 2	77	77	40-66 —	106	80	
Mike Rogers	Hfd.	4-4-80	(A)	Hfd. 9	at Que. 2	79	79	44-61 —	105	80	25.5
Charlie Simmer	L.A.	5-4-80	(A)	Van. 5	at L.A. 3	64	80	56-45 —	101	64	26.0
Blaine Stoughton	Hfd.	6-4-80	(A)	Det. 3	at Hfd. 5	80	80	56-44 —	100	80	27.0
Wayne Gretzky	Edm.	6-2-81	(G)	Wpg. 4	at Edm. 10	53	53	55-109 —	164	80	
Marcel Dionne	L.A.	12-2-81	(A)	L.A. 5	at Chi. 5	58	58	58-77 —	135	80	
Charlie Simmer	L.A.	14-2-81	(A)	Bos. 5	at L.A. 4	59	59	56-49 —	105	65	
Kent Nilsson	Cgy.	27-2-81	(G)	Hfd. 1	at Cgy. 5	64	64	49-82 —	131	80	24.6
Mike Bossy	NYI	3-3-81	(G)	Edm. 8	at NYI 8	65	66	68-51 —	119	79	
Dave Taylor	L.A.	14-3-81	(G)	Min. 4	at L.A. 10	63	70	47-65 —	112	72	25.3
Mike Rogers	Hfd.	22-3-81	(G)	Tor. 3	at Hfd. 3	74	74	40-65 —	105	80	
Bernie Federko	St.L.	28-3-81	(A)	Buf. 4	at St.L. 7	74	76	31-73 —	104	80	24.10
Rick Middleton	Bos.	28-3-81	(A)	Chi. 2	at Bos. 5	76	76	44-59 —	103	80	27.4
Jacques Richard	Que.	29-3-81	(G)	Mtl. 0	at Que. 4	75	76	52-51 —	103	78	28.6
Bryan Trottier	NYI	29-3-81	(G)	NYI 5	at Wsh. 4	69	76	31-72 —	103	73	
Peter Stastny	Que.	29-3-81	(G)	Mtl. 0	at Que. 4	73	76	39-70 —	109	77	24.6
Wayne Gretzky	Edm.	27-12-81	(A)	L.A. 3	at Edm. 10	38	38	92-120 —	212	80	
Mike Bossy	NYI	13-2-82	(A)	Phi. 2	at NYI 8	55	55	64-83 —	147	80	
Peter Stastny	Que.	16-2-82	(A)	Wpg. 3	at Que. 7	60	60	46-93 —	139	80	
Dennis Maruk	Wsh.	20-2-82	(A)	Wsh. 3	at Min. 7	60	60	60-76 —	136	80	26.3
Bryan Trottier	NYI	23-2-82	(G)	Chi. 1	at NYI 5	61	61	50-79 —	129	80	
Denis Savard	Chi.	27-2-82	(A)	Chi. 5	at L.A. 3	64	64	32-87 —	119	80	21.1
Bobby Smith	Min.	3-3-82	(A)	Det. 4	at Min. 6	66	66	43-71 —	114	80	24.1
Marcel Dionne	L.A.	6-3-82	(G)	L.A. 6	at Hfd. 7	64	66	50-67 —	117	78	
Dave Taylor	L.A.	20-3-82	(A)	Pit. 5	at L.A. 7	71	72	39-67 —	106	78	
Dale Hawerchuk	Wpg.	24-3-82	(A)	L.A. 3	at Wpg. 5	74	74	45-58 —	103	80	18.11
Dino Ciccarelli	Min.	27-3-82	(A)	Min. 6	at Bos. 5	72	76	55-52 —	107	76	21.8
Glenn Anderson	Edm.	28-3-82	(G)	Edm. 6	at L.A. 2	78	78	38-67 —	105	80	21.7
Mike Rogers	NYR	2-4-82	(G)	Pit. 7	at NYR 5	79	79	38-65 —	103	80	

Player	Team	Date of 100th Point	G or A	Score	Player's Game No.	Team Game No.	Points G-A PTS	Total Games	Age when first 100th point scored (Yrs. & Mos.)
Wayne Gretzky	Edm.	5-1-83	(A)	Edm. 8 at Wpg. 3	42	42	71-125 - 196	80	
Mike Bossy	NYI	3-3-83	(A)	Tor. 1 at NYI. 5	66	67	60-58 — 118	79	
Peter Stastny	Que.	5-3-83	(A)	Hfd. 3 at Que. 10	62	67	47-77 — 124	75	
Denis Savard	Chi.	6-3-83	(A)	Mtl. 4 at Chi. 5	65	67	35-86 — 121	78	
Mark Messier	Edm.	23-3-83	(G)	Edm. 4 at Wpg. 7	73	76	48-58 — 106	77	22.2
Barry Pederson	Bos.	26-3-83	(A)	Hfd. 4 at Bos. 7	73	76	46-61 — 107	77	22.0
Marcel Dionne	L.A.	26-3-83	(A)	Edm. 9 at L.A. 3	75	75	56-51 — 107	80	
Michel Goulet	Que.	27-3-83	(A)	Que. 6 at Buf. 6	77	77	57-48 — 105	80	22.11
Glenn Anderson	Edm.	29-3-83	(A)	Edm. 7 at Van. 4	70	78	48-56 — 104	72	
Jari Kurri	Edm.	29-3-83	(A)	Edm. 7 at Van. 4	78	78	45-59 — 104	80	22.10
Kent Nilsson	Cgy.	29-3-83	(G)	L.A. 3 at Cgy. 5	78	78	46-58 — 104	80	
Wayne Gretzky	Edm.	18-12-83	(G)	Edm. 7 at Wpg. 5	34	34	87-118 — 205	74	
Paul Coffey	Edm.	4-3-84	(A)	Mtl. 1 at Edm. 6	68	68	40-86 — 126	80	22.9
Michel Goulet	Que.	4-3-84	(A)	Que. 1 at Buf. 1	62	67	56-65 — 121	75	
Jari Kurri	Edm.	7-3-84	(G)	Chi. 4 at Edm. 7	53	69	52-61 — 113	64	
Peter Stastny	Que.	8-3-84	(A)	Que. 8 at Pit. 6	69	69	46-73 — 119	80	
Mike Bossy	NYI	8-3-84	(G)	Tor. 5 at NYI 9	56	68	51-67 — 118	67	
Barry Pederson	Bos.	14-3-84	(A)	Bos. 4 at Det. 2	71	71	39-77 — 116	80	
Bryan Trottier	NYI	18-3-84	(G)	NYI 4 at Hfd. 5	62	73	40-71 — 111	68	
Bernie Federko	St.L.	20-3-84	(A)	Wpg. 3 at St.L. 9	75	76	41-66 — 107	79	
Rick Middleton	Bos.	27-3-84	(G)	Bos. 6 at Que. 4	77	77	47-58 — 105	80	
Dale Hawerchuk	Wpg.	27-3-84	(A)	Wpg. 3 at L.A. 3	77	77	37-65 — 102	80	
Mark Messier	Edm.	27-3-84	(G)	Edm. 9 at Cgy. 2	72	79	37-64 — 101	73	
Wayne Gretzky	Edm.	29-12-84	(A)	Det. 3 at Edm. 6	35	35	73-135 — 208	80	
Jari Kurri	Edm.	29-1-85	(G)	Edm. 4 at Cgy. 2	48	51	71-64 — 135	73	
Mike Bossy	NYI	23-2-85	(G)	Bos. 1 at NYI 7	56	60	58-59 — 117	76	
Dale Hawerchuk	Wpg.	25-2-85	(A)	Wpg. 12 at NYR 5	64	64	53-77 — 130	80	
Marcel Dionne	L.A.	5-3-85	(A)	Pit. 0 at L.A. 6	66	66	46-80 — 126	80	
Brent Sutter	NYI	12-3-85	(A)	NYI 6 at St. L. 5	68	68	42-60 — 102	72	22.10
John Ogrodnick	Det.	22-3-85	(A)	NYR 3 at Det. 5	73	73	55-50 — 105	79	25.9
Paul Coffey	Edm.	26-3-85	(G)	Edm. 7 at NYI 5	74	74	37-84 — 121	80	
Denis Savard	Chi.	29-3-85	(A)	Chi. 5 at Wpg. 5	75	76	38-67 — 105	79	
Peter Stastny	Que.	2-4-85	(A)	Bos. 4 at Que. 6	74	77	32-68 — 100	75	
Bernie Federko	St.L.	4-4-85	(A)	NYR 5 at St.L. 4	74	78	30-73 — 103	76	
John Tonelli	NYI	6-4-85	(G)	NJ 5 at NYI 5	80	80	42-58 — 100	80	28.1
Paul MacLean	Wpg.	6-4-85	(A)	Wpg. 6 at Edm. 5	78	79	41-60 — 101	79	27.1
Mike Gartner	Wsh.	7-4-85	(G)	Pit. 3 at Wsh. 7	80	80	50-52 — 102	80	25.6
Bernie Nicholls	L.A.	6-4-85	(A)	Van. 4 at L.A. 4	80	80	46-54 — 100	80	22.9
Mario Lemieux	Pit.	7-4-85	(G)	Pit. 3 at Wsh. 7	73	80	43-57 — 100	73	19.6
Wayne Gretzky	Edm.	4-1-86	(A)	Hfd. 3 at Edm. 4	39	39	52-163 — 215	80	
Mario Lemieux	Pit.	15-2-86	(G)	Van. 4 at Pit. 9	55	56	48-93 — 141	79	
Paul Coffey	Edm.	19-2-86	(G)	Tor. 5 at Edm. 9	59	60	48-90 — 138	79	
Jari Kurri	Edm.	2-3-86	(G)	Phi. 1 at Edm. 2	62	64	68-63 — 131	78	
Peter Stastny	Que.	1-3-86	(A)	Buf. 8 at Que. 4	66	68	41-81 — 122	76	
Mike Bossy	NYI	8-3-86	(G)	Wsh. 6 at NYI 2	65	65	61-62 — 123	80	
Denis Savard	Chi.	12-3-86	(A)	Buf. 7 at Chi. 6	69	69	47-69 — 116	80	
Mats Naslund	Mtl.	13-3-86	(A)	Mtl. 2 at Bos. 3	70	70	43-67 — 110	80	26.4
Michel Goulet	Que.	24-3-86	(A)	Que. 1 at Min. 0	70	75	53-50 — 103	75	
Glenn Anderson	Edm.	25-3-86	(G)	Edm. 7 at Det. 2	66	74	54-48 — 102	72	
Neal Broten	Min.	26-3-86	(A)	Min. 6 at Tor. 1	76	76	29-76 — 105	80	26.4
Dale Hawerchuk	Wpg.	31-3-86	(A)	Wpg. 5 at L.A. 2	78	78	46-59 — 105	80	
Bernie Federko	St.L.	5-4-86	(G)	Chi. 5 at St.L. 7	79	79	34-68 — 102	80	
Wayne Gretzky	Edm.	1-11-87	(A)	Cgy. 3 at Edm. 5	42	42	62-121 — 183	79	
Jari Kurri	Edm.	3-14-87	(A)	Buf. 3 at Edm. 5	67	68	54-54 — 108	79	
Mario Lemieux	Pit.	3-18-87	(A)	St.L. 3 at Pit. 5	55	72	54-53 — 107	63	
Mark Messier	Edm.	3-19-87	(A)	Edm. 4 at Cgy. 5	71	71	37-70 — 107	77	
Doug Gilmour	St.L.	4-2-87	(A)	Buf. 3 at St.L. 5	78	78	42-63 — 105	80	23.10
Dino Ciccarelli	Min.	3-30-87	(A)	NYR 6 at Min. 5	78	78	52-51 — 103	80	
Dale Hawerchuk	Wpg.	4-5-87	(A)	Wpg. 3 at Cgy. 1	80	80	47-53 — 100	80	
Mario Lemieux	Pit.	20-1-88	(G)	Pit. 8 at Chi. 3	45	48	70-98 — 168	77	
Wayne Gretzky	Edm.	11-2-88	(A)	Edm. 7 at Van. 2	43	56	40-109 — 149	64	
Denis Savard	Chi.	12-2-88	(A)	St.L. 3 at Chi. 4	57	57	44-87 — 131	80	
Dale Hawerchuk	Wpg.	23-2-88	(G)	Wpg. 4 at Pit. 3	61	61	44-77 — 121	80	
Steve Yzerman	Det.	27-2-88	(A)	Det. 4 at Que. 5	63	63	50-52 — 102	64	22.10
Peter Stastny	Que.	8-3-88	(A)	Hfd. 4 at Que. 6	63	67	46-65 — 111	76	
Mark Messier	Edm.	15-3-88	(A)	Buf. 4 at Edm. 6	68	71	37-74 — 111	77	
Jimmy Carson	L.A.	26-3-88	(A)	Chi. 5 at L.A. 9	77	77	55-52 — 107	80	19.8
Hakan Loob	Cgy.	26-3-88	(A)	Van. 1 at Cgy. 6	76	76	50-56 — 106	80	27.9
Mike Bullard	Cgy.	26-3-88	(A)	Van. 1 at Cgy. 6	76	76	48-55 — 103	79	27.1
Michel Goulet	Que.	27-3-88	(A)	Pit. 6 at Que. 3	76	76	48-58 — 106	80	
Luc Robitaille	L.A.	30-3-88	(G)	Cgy. 7 at L.A. 9	78	78	53-58 — 111	80	22.1
Mario Lemieux	Pit.	31-12-88	(A)	N.J. 6 at Pit. 8	36	38	85-114-199	76	
Wayne Gretzky	L.A.	21-1-89	(A)	L.A. 4 at Hfd. 5	47	48	54-114-168	78	
Steve Yzerman	Det.	27-1-89	(G)	Tor. 1 at Det. 8	50	50	65-90-155	80	
Bernie Nicholls	L.A.	21-1-89	(A)	L.A. 4 at Hfd. 5	48	48	70-80-150	79	
Rob Brown	Pit.	16-3-89	(A)	Pit. 2 at N.J. 1	60	72	49-66-115	68	20.11
Paul Coffey	Pit.	20-3-89	(A)	Pit. 2 at Min. 7	69	74	30-83-113	75	
Joe Mullen	Cgy.	23-3-89	(G)	L.A. 2 at Cgy. 4	74	75	51-59-110	79	32.1
Jari Kurri	Edm.	29-3-89	(A)	Edm. 5 at Van. 2	75	79	44-58-102	76	
Jimmy Carson	Edm.	2-4-89	(A)	Edm. 2 at Cgy. 4	80	80	49-51-100	80	
Mario Lemieux	Pit.	28-1-90	(G)	Pit. 2 at Buf. 7	50	50	45-78-123	59	
Wayne Gretzky	L.A.	30-1-90	(G)	N.J. 2 at L.A. 5	51	51	40-102-142	73	
Steve Yzerman	Det.	19-2-90	(A)	Mtl. 5 at Det. 5	61	61	62-65-127	79	
Mark Messier	Edm.	20-2-90	(A)	Edm. 4 at Van. 2	62	62	45-84-129	79	
Brett Hull	St.L.	3-3-90	(A)	NYI 4 at St.L. 5	67	67	72-41-113	80	25.7
Bernie Nicholls	NYR	12-3-90	(A)	L.A. 6 at NYR 2	70	71	39-73-112	79	
Pierre Turgeon	Buf.	25-3-90	(G)	N.J. 4 at Buf. 3	76	76	40-66-106	80	20.7
Paul Coffey	Pit.	25-3-90	(A)	Pit. 2 at Hfd. 4	77	77	29-74-103	80	
Pat LaFontaine	NYI	27-3-90	(G)	Cgy. 4 at NYI 2	72	78	54-51-105	74	25.1
Adam Oates	St.L.	29-3-90	(A)	St.L. 3 at St.L. 5	79	79	23-79-102	80	27.7
Joe Sakic	Que.	31-3-90	(G)	Hfd. 3 at Que. 2	79	79	39-63-102	80	20.8
Ron Francis	Hfd.	31-3-90	(G)	Hfd. 3 at Que. 2	79	79	32-69-101	80	27.0
Luc Robitaille	L.A.	1-4-90	(A)	L.A. 4 at Cgy. 8	80	80	52-49-101	80	

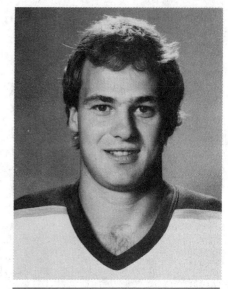

Dale Hawerchuk

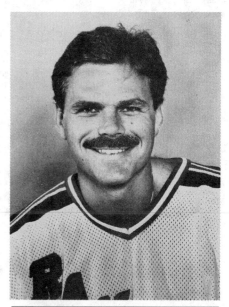

Mike Gartner

Pat LaFontaine

100-Point Seasons *continued*

Player	Team	Date of 100th Point	G or A		Score	Player's Game No.	Team Game No.	Points G-A PTS	Total Games	Age when first 100th point scored (Yrs. & Mos.)
Wayne Gretzky	L.A.	30-1-91	(A)	N.J. 4	at L.A. 2	50	51	41-122-163	78	
Brett Hull	St.L.	23-2-91	(G)	Bos. 2	at St.L. 9	60	62	86-45-131	78	
Mark Recchi	Pit.	5-3-91	(G)	Van. 1	at Pit. 4	66	67	40-73-113	78	23.1
Steve Yzerman	Det.	10-3-91	(A)	Det. 4	at St.L. 1	72	72	51-57-108	80	
John Cullen	Hfd.	16-3-91	(G)	N.J. 2	at Hfd. 6	71	71	39-71-110	78	26.7
Adam Oates	St.L.	17-3-91	(A)	St.L. 4	at Chi. 6	54	73	25-90-115	61	
Joe Sakic	Que.	19-3-91	(G)	Edm. 7	at Que. 6	74	74	48-61-109	80	
Steve Larmer	Chi.	24-3-91	(A)	Min. 4	at Chi. 5	76	76	44-57-101	80	29.9
Theoren Fleury	Cgy.	26-3-91	(G)	Van. 2	at Cgy. 7	77	77	51-53-104	79	22.9
Al MacInnis	Cgy.	28-3-91	(A)	Edm. 4	at Cgy. 4	78	78	28-75-103	78	27.8

Five-or-more-Goal Games

Player	Team	Date	Score		Opposing Goaltender
SEVEN GOALS					
Joe Malone	Quebec Bulldogs	Jan. 31/20	Tor. 6	at Que. 10	Ivan Mitchell
SIX GOALS					
Newsy Lalonde	Montreal	Jan. 10/20	Tor. 7	at Mtl. 14	Ivan Mitchell
Joe Malone	Quebec Bulldogs	Mar. 10/20	Ott. 4	at Que. 10	Clint Benedict
Corb Denneny	Toronto St. Pats	Jan. 26/21	Ham. 3	at Tor. 10	Howard Lockhart
Cy Denneny	Ottawa Senators	Mar. 7/21	Ham. 5	at Ott. 12	Howard Lockhart
Syd Howe	Detroit	Feb. 3/44	NYR 2	at Det. 12	Ken McAuley
Red Berenson	St. Louis	Nov. 7/68	St. L. 8	at Phil 0	Doug Favell
Darryl Sittler	Toronto	Feb. 7/76	Bos. 4	at Tor. 11	Dave Reece
FIVE GOALS					
Joe Malone	Montreal	Dec. 19/17	Mtl. 9	at Ott. 4	Clint Benedict
Harry Hyland	Mtl. Wanderers	Dec. 19/17	Tor. 9	at Mtl. 10	Arthur Brooks
Joe Malone	Montreal	Jan. 12/18	Ott. 4	at Mtl. 9	Clint Benedict
Joe Malone	Montreal	Feb. 2/18	Tor. 2	at Mtl. 11	Harry Holmes
Mickey Roach	Toronto St. Pats	Mar. 6/20	Que. 2	at Tor. 11	Frank Brophy
Newsy Lalonde	Montreal	Feb. 16/21	Ham. 5	at Mtl. 10	Howard Lockhart
Babe Dye	Toronto St. Pats	Dec. 16/22	Mtl. 2	at Tor. 7	Georges Vezina
Redvers Green	Hamilton Tigers	Dec. 5/24	Ham. 10	at Tor. 3	John Roach
Babe Dye	Toronto St. Pats	Dec. 22/24	Tor. 10	at Bos. 2	Charlie Stewart
Harry Broadbent	Mtl. Maroons	Jan. 7/25	Mtl. 6	at Ham. 2	Vernon Forbes
Pit Lepine	Montreal	Dec. 14/29	Ott. 4	at Mtl. 6	Alex Connell
Howie Morenz	Montreal	Mar. 18/30	NYA 3	at Mtl. 8	Roy Worters
Charlie Conacher	Toronto	Jan. 19/32	NYA 3	at Tor. 11	Roy Worters
Ray Getliffe	Montreal	Feb. 6/43	Bos. 3	at Mtl. 8	Frank Brimsek
Maurice Richard	Montreal	Dec. 28/44	Det. 1	at Mtl. 9	Harry Lumley
Howie Meeker	Toronto	Jan. 8/47	Chi. 4	at Tor. 10	Paul Bibeault
Bernie Geoffrion	Montreal	Feb. 19/55	NYR 2	at Mtl. 10	Gump Worsley
Bobby Rousseau	Montreal	Feb. 1/64	Det. 3	at Mtl. 9	Roger Crozier
Yvan Cournoyer	Montreal	Feb. 15/75	Chi. 3	at Mtl. 12	Mike Veisor
Don Murdoch	NY Rangers	Oct. 12/76	NYR 10	at Min. 4	Gary Smith
Ian Turnbull	Toronto	Feb. 2/77	Det. 1	at Tor. 9	Ed Giacomin (2) Jim Rutherford (3)

Player	Team	Date	Score		Opposing Goaltender
FIVE GOALS					
Bryan Trottier	NY Islanders	Dec. 23/78	NYR 4	at NYI 9	Wayne Thomas (4) John Davidson (1)
Tim Young	Minnesota	Jan. 15/79	Min. 8	at NYR 1	Doug Soetaert (3) Wayne Thomas (2)
John Tonelli	NY Islanders	Jan. 6/81	Tor. 3	at NYI 6	Jiri Crha
Wayne Gretzky	Edmonton	Feb. 18/81	St.L. 2	at Edm. 9	Mike Liut (3) Ed Staniowski (2)
Wayne Gretzky	Edmonton	Dec. 30/81	Phi. 5	at Edm. 7	Pete Peeters (4) Empty Net (1)
Grant Mulvey	Chicago	Feb. 3/82	St.L. 5	at Chi. 9	Mike Liut (4) Gary Edwards (1)
Bryan Trottier	NY Islanders	Feb. 13/82	Phi. 2	at NYI 8	Pete Peeters
Willy Lindstrom	Winnipeg	Mar. 2/82	Wpg. 7	at Phi. 6	Pete Peeters
Mark Pavelich	NY Rangers	Feb. 23/83	Hfd. 3	at NYR 11	Greg Millen
Jari Kurri	Edmonton	Nov. 19/83	NJ. 4	at Edm. 13	Glenn Resch (3) Ron Low (2)
Bengt Gustafsson	Washington	Jan. 8/84	Wsh. 7	at Phi. 1	Pelle Lindbergh
Pat Hughes	Edmonton	Feb. 3/84	Cgy. 5	at Edm. 10	Don Edwards (3) Rejean Lemelin (2)
Wayne Gretzky	Edmonton	Dec. 15/84	Edm. 8	at St. L. 2	Rick Wamsley (4) Mike Liut(1)
Dave Andreychuk	Buffalo	Feb. 6/86	Buf. 8	at Bos. 6	Pat Riggin (1) Doug Keans (4)
Wayne Gretzky	Edmonton	Dec. 6/87	Min. 4	at Edm. 10	Kari Takko (1)
Mario Lemieux	Pittsburgh	Dec. 31/88	N.J. 6	at Pit. 8	Bob Sauve (3) Chris Terreri (2)
Joe Nieuwendyk	Calgary	Jan. 11/89	Wpg. 3	at Cgy. 8	Daniel Berthiaume

Players' 1,000th Points

Player	Team	Date	Game No.	G or A		Score	Total Points G A PTS	Total Games
Gordie Howe	Detroit	Nov. 27/60	938	(A)	Tor. 0	at Det. 2	801-1,049–1,850	1,767
Jean Beliveau	Montreal	Mar. 3/68	911	(G)	Mtl. 2	at Det. 5	507-712–1,219	1,125
Alex Delvecchio	Detroit	Feb. 16/69	1,143	(A)	LA 3	at Det. 6	456-825–1,281	1,549
Norm Ullman	Toronto	Oct. 16/71	1,113	(A)	NYR 5	at Tor. 3	490-739–1,229	1,410
Bobby Hull	Chicago	Dec. 12/71	909	(A)	Minn. 3	at Chi. 5	610-560–1,170	1,063
Stan Mikita	Chicago	Oct. 15/72	924	(A)	St.L. 3	at Chi. 1	541-926–1,467	1,394
John Bucyk	Boston	Nov. 9/72	1,144	(A)	Det. 3	at Bos. 8	556-813–1,369	1,540
Frank Mahovlich	Montreal	Feb. 13/73	1,090	(A)	Phi. 7	at Mtl. 6	533-570–1,103	1,181
Henri Richard	Montreal	Dec. 20/73	1,194	(A)	Mtl. 2	at Buf. 2	358-688–1,046	1,256
Phil Esposito	Boston	Feb. 15/74	745	(A)	Bos. 4	at Van. 2	717-873–1,590	1,282
Rod Gilbert	NY Rangers	Feb. 19/77	1,027	(A)	NYR 2	at NYI 5	406-615–1,021	1,065
Jean Ratelle	Boston	Apr. 3/77	1,007	(A)	Tor. 4	at Bos. 7	491-776–1,267	1,281
Bobby Clarke	Philadelphia	Mar. 19/81	922	(G)	Bos. 3	at Phi. 5	358-852–1,210	1,144
Marcel Dionne	Los Angeles	Jan. 7/81	740	(G)	L.A. 5	at Hfd. 3	731-1,040–1,771	1,348
Guy Lafleur	Montreal	Mar. 4/81	720	(G)	Mtl. 9	at Wpg. 3	560-793–1,353	1,126
Gilbert Perreault	Buffalo	Apr. 3/82	871	(A)	Buf. 5	at Mtl. 4	512-814–1,326	1,191
Darryl Sittler	Philadelphia	Jan. 20/83	927	(A)	Cgy 2	at Phi. 5	484-637–1,121	1,096
*Wayne Gretzky	Edmonton	Dec. 19/84	424	(A)	L.A. 3	at Edm. 7	718-1,424–2,142	925
*Bryan Trottier	NY Islanders	Jan. 29/85	726	(A)	Min. 4	at NYI 4	509-872–1,381	1,175
Mike Bossy	NY Islanders	Jan. 24/86	656	(G)	NYI 7	at Tor. 5	573-553–1,126	752
Denis Potvin	NY Islanders	Apr. 4/87	987	(G)	Buf. 6	at NYI 6	310-742–1,052	1,060
Bernie Federko	St. Louis	Mar. 19/88	855	(A)	Hfd. 5	at St.L. 3	369-761–1,130	1,000
Lanny McDonald	Calgary	Mar. 7/89	1,101	(A)	Wpg. 5	at Cgy. 9	500-506–1,006	1,111
*Peter Stastny	Quebec	Oct. 19/89	682	(G)	Que. 5	at Chi. 3	403-716–1,119	826
*Jari Kurri	Edmonton	Jan. 2/90	716	(A)	Edm. 6	at St.L. 4	474-569–1,043	754
*Denis Savard	Chicago	Mar. 11/90	727	(A)	St.L. 6	at Chi. 4	379-693–1,072	806
*Paul Coffey	Pittsburgh	Dec. 22/90	770	(A)	Pit. 4	at NYI 3	307-738–1,045	809
*Mark Messier	Edmonton	Jan. 13/91	822	(A)	Edm. 5	at Phi. 3	392-642–1,034	851
*Dave Taylor	Los Angeles	Feb. 5/91	930	(A)	L.A. 3	at Phi. 2	411-607–1,018	953
*Michel Goulet	Chicago	Feb. 23/91	878	(G)	Chi. 3	at Min. 3	487-528–1,015	895
*Dale Hawerchuk	Buffalo	Mar. 8/91	781	(G)	Chi. 5	at Buf. 3	410-608–1,018	793

* Active

Darryl Sittler

Individual Awards

Hart Memorial Trophy

Art Ross Trophy

Calder Memorial Trophy

James Norris Memorial Trophy

HART MEMORIAL TROPHY

An annual award "to the player adjudged to be the most valuable to his team". Winner selected in poll by Professional Hockey Writers' Association in the 21 NHL cities at the end of the regular schedule. The winner receives $3,000 and the runner-up $1,000.

History: The Hart Memorial Trophy was presented by the National Hockey League in 1960 after the original Hart Trophy was retired to the Hockey Hall of Fame. The original Hart Trophy was donated to the NHL in 1923 by Dr. David A. Hart, father of Cecil Hart, former manager-coach of the Montreal Canadiens.

1990-91 Winner: Brett Hull, St. Louis Blues
Runners-up: Wayne Gretzky, Los Angeles Kings
Ed Belfour, Chicago Blackhawks

St. Louis Blues' right wing Brett Hull captured the Hart Memorial Trophy, awarded annually "to the player adjudged to be the most valuable to his team", by edging out Los Angeles center Wayne Gretzky in the voting.

Hull, who is the first St. Louis player to win the award, received 277 of a possible 330 points, while Gretzky received 220. Hull received 44 first place votes and was named on 65 of the 66 ballots, while Gretzky was named on all 66 of the ballots. Ed Belfour of the Chicago Blackhawks placed third in the voting with 63 points.

Hull, in his third full season with the Blues, led the League in goal-scoring with 86. The only player to have scored more goals in a season is Wayne Gretzky (92 in 1981-82 and 87 in 1983-84). Hull also led the League in power-play goals (29), game-winning goals (11), shots (389) and first goals (19). The St. Louis Blues finished second in the League's overall standings with a 47-22-11 record (105 points), their best record since 1980-81. Hull, whose shooting percentage was 22.1, was the leading vote-getter in All-Star Fan Balloting this season.

He is only the third player (Mario Lemieux, 1987-88 and Mark Messier, 1989-90), other than Gretzky to win the award since 1979-80. He wins the award 25 years after his father, Bobby Hull of the Chicago Blackhawks, won it for the second consecutive season (1964-65 and 1965-66).

ART ROSS TROPHY

An annual award "to the player who leads the league in scoring points at the end of the regular season." Overall winner receives $3,000 and the overall runner-up $1,000.

History: Arthur Howie Ross, former manager-coach of Boston Bruins, presented the trophy to the National Hockey League in 1947. If two players finish the schedule with the same number of points, the trophy is awarded in the following manner: 1. Player with most goals. 2. Player with fewer games played. 3. Player scoring first goal of the season.

1990-91 Winner: Wayne Gretzky, Los Angeles Kings
Runners-up: Brett Hull, St. Louis Blues
Adam Oates, St. Louis Blues

Wayne Gretzky of the Los Angeles Kings won his second consecutive Art Ross Trophy in 1990-91. Gretzky had 41 goals and 122 assists for 163 points in 78 games en route to the ninth Art Ross Trophy of his 12 year NHL career.

CALDER MEMORIAL TROPHY

An annual award "to the player selected as the most proficient in his first year of competition in the National Hockey League". Winner selected in poll by Professional Hockey Writers' Association at the end of the regular schedule. The winner receives $3,000 and the runner-up $1,000.

History: From 1936-37 until his death in 1943, Frank Calder, NHL President, bought a trophy each year to be given permanently to the outstanding rookie. After Calder's death, the NHL presented the Calder Memorial Trophy in his memory and the trophy is to be kept in perpetuity. To be eligible for the award, a player cannot have played more than 25 games in any single preceding season nor in six or more games in each of any two preceding seasons in any major professional league. Beginning in 1990-91, to be eligible for this award a player must not have attained his twenty-sixth birthday by September 15th of the season in which he is eligible.

1990-91 Winner: Ed Belfour, Chicago Blackhawks
Runners-up: Sergei Fedorov, Detroit Red Wings
Ken Hodge, Boston Bruins

Ed Belfour of the Chicago Blackhawks was awarded the Calder Memorial Trophy as the "player adjudged to be the most proficient in his first season". He is the first goaltender since 1984 (Tom Barrasso, Buffalo) to capture both the Calder and Vezina Trophies in the same season. (Please note that prior to 1981-82, the Vezina was awarded to the goaltender(s) whose team allowed the fewest goals).

Belfour received 313 points in the voting, including 59 first-place votes. He was named on 65 of the 66 ballots. Fedorov placed second in the voting with 197 points and was named on all 66 ballots. Ken Hodge of the Boston Bruins (24 points) edged Mike Richter of the New York Rangers for the third place finish.

Belfour, a rookie goaltender for the Blackhawks, led the League in wins (43), goals-against-average (2.47) and save percentage (.910) in 1990-91. He played 74 games in nets for the Blackhawks, breaking an NHL rookie record previously held by Don Edwards (72 games in 1977-78).

JAMES NORRIS MEMORIAL TROPHY

An annual award "to the defense player who demonstrates throughout the season the greatest all-round ability in the position." Winner selected in poll by Professional Hockey Writers' Association at the end of the regular schedule. The winner receives $3,000 and the runner-up $1,000.

History: The James Norris Memorial Trophy was presented in 1953 by the four children of the late James Norris in memory of the former owner-president of the Detroit Red Wings.

1990-91 Winner: Ray Bourque, Boston Bruins
Runners-up: Al MacInnis, Calgary Flames
Chris Chelios, Chicago Blackhawks

Veteran Boston Bruins' defenseman Ray Bourque received 257 points and appeared on 63 of the 66 ballots en route to winning his fourth James Norris Trophy as the defenseman demonstrating "the greatest all-around ability in the position".

Bourque edged out Calgary's Al MacInnis, who received 228 points and finished second in the voting for the second consecutive season. Chris Chelios of the Chicago Blackhawks was third in the voting with 56 points.

Bourque, the captain of the Bruins, is a four-time winner of the Norris Trophy (1986-87, 1987-88, 1989-90 and 1990-91). In 1990-91 he led the Bruins in scoring for the fourth time in his 12-year career, recording 94 points (21-73-94) in 76 games. A 12-time NHL All-Star, Bourque led his club in plus-minus with a plus-33 rating. He scored seven power-play goals and three game-winners en route to leading the Bruins to their second straight Adams Division Championship. In addition to his Norris Trophy honors, Bourque also received the Calder Trophy in 1980 as the League's top rookie and was runner-up to Mark Messier for the 1989-90 Hart Trophy.

Bourque is the first four-time winner of the Norris Trophy since 1971, when Bobby Orr captured his fourth consecutive trophy with the Boston Bruins. Only two players – Bobby Orr (1967-75, Boston) and Doug Harvey (1955-58 and 1960-62, Montreal and NY Rangers) – have been awarded the Norris Trophy more than Bourque.

Vezina Trophy

Lady Byng Memorial Trophy

Frank J. Selke Trophy

Conn Smythe Trophy

VEZINA TROPHY

An annual award "to the goalkeeper adjudged to be the best at his position" as voted by the general managers of each of the 21 clubs. Over-all winner receives $3,000, runner-up $1,000.

History: Leo Dandurand, Louis Letourneau and Joe Cattarinich, former owners of the Montreal Canadiens, presented the trophy to the National Hockey League in 1926-27 in memory of Georges Vezina, outstanding goalkeeper of the Canadiens who collapsed during an NHL game November 28, 1925, and died of tuberculosis a few months later. Until the 1981-82 season, the goalkeeper(s) of the team allowing the fewest number of goals during the regular-season were awarded the Vezina Trophy.

1990-91 Winner: Ed Belfour, Chicago Blackhawks
Runners-up: Patrick Roy, Montreal Canadiens
Mike Richter, NY Rangers

Ed Belfour of the Chicago Blackhawks was awarded the Vezina Trophy as the "goalkeeper adjudged to be the best at his position". He is the first goaltender since 1984 (Tom Barrasso, Buffalo) to capture both the Calder and Vezina Trophies in the same season. (Please note that prior to 1981-82, the Vezina was awarded to the goaltender(s) whose team allowed the fewest goals).

Belfour received 101 of a possible 105 points in the voting, including 19 first-place votes, to outdistance two-time Vezina Trophy winner Patrick Roy of the Montreal Canadiens, who received 44 points. Rookie Mike Richter of the New York Rangers was third with 12 points.

Belfour, the rookie goaltender for the Blackhawks, led the League in wins (43), goals-against-average (2.47) and save percentage (.910) in 1990-91. He played 74 games in nets for the Blackhawks, one game shy of an NHL record set by Grant Fuhr in 1987-88. In addition to winning the Presidents' Trophy for the League's best overall record during the regular-season (49-23-8), the Blackhawks finished 1990-91 with the best defensive record, allowing only 211 goals. He registered four shutouts during the year, second only to Don Beaupre of the Washington Capitals (5).

LADY BYNG MEMORIAL TROPHY

An annual award "to the player adjudged to have exhibited the best type of sportsmanship and gentlemanly conduct combined with a high standard of playing ability." Winner selected in poll by Professional Hockey Writers' Association at the end of the regular schedule. The winner receives $3,000 and the runner-up $1,000.

History: Lady Byng, wife of Canada's Governor-General at the time, presented the Lady Byng Trophy in 1925. After Frank Boucher of New York Rangers won the award seven times in eight seasons, he was given the trophy to keep and Lady Byng donated another trophy in 1936. After Lady Byng's death in 1949, the National Hockey League presented a new trophy, changing the name to Lady Byng Memorial Trophy.

1990-91 Winner: Wayne Gretzky, Los Angeles Kings
Runners-up: Brett Hull, St. Louis Blues
Joe Sakic, Quebec Nordiques

Los Angeles' Wayne Gretzky captured the Lady Byng Trophy, awarded annually "to the player adjudged to have exhibited the best type of sportsmanship and gentlemanly conduct combined with a high standard of playing ability", for the second time in his illustrious career.

Gretzky, a seven-time nominee and two-time winner of the Lady Byng Trophy, received 159 points, including 20 first-place votes, to edge St. Louis right wing Brett Hull. Hull, the 1989-90 recipient of the Lady Byng Trophy, captured 151 points in the voting. Joe Sakic of the Quebec Nordiques, a first-time NHL award nominee, placed third with 90 points.

Gretzky, the captain of the Los Angeles Kings, was a 1989-90 runner-up for the Lady Byng Trophy. En route to capturing his ninth Art Ross Trophy as the League's leading scorer with 163 points (41-122-163) in 78 games, Gretzky registered only 16 penalty minutes. He has never recorded more than 59 minutes in a season, 16 being the lowest. He won the Lady Byng in his first NHL season (1979-80) with the Edmonton Oilers and has been a runner-up five times (1981 and 1987-1990).

FRANK J. SELKE TROPHY

An annual award "to the forward who best excels in the defensive aspects of the game." Winner selected in poll by Professional Hockey Writers' Association at the end of the regular schedule. The winner receives $3,000 and the runner-up $1,000.

History: Presented to the National Hockey League in 1977 by the Board of Governors of the NHL in honour of Frank J. Selke, one of the great architects of NHL championship teams.

1990-91 Winner: Dirk Graham, Chicago Blackhawks
Runners-up: Esa Tikkanen, Edmonton Oilers
Steve Larmer, Chicago Blackhawks

Dirk Graham of the Chicago Blackhawks was awarded the Frank J. Selke Trophy in recognition of "the forward who best excels in the defensive aspects of the game". Graham is a first-time NHL award winner.

Graham captured 157 of a possible 330 points in the voting, to narrowly edge Esa Tikkanen of the Edmonton Oilers (33). Graham's teammate Steve Larmer placed third in the voting with 74 points.

Graham, the captain of the Blackhawks, recorded 45 points (24-21-45) in 80 games this season. He tallied four power-play and seven game-winning goals. His six shorthanded goals led the team, third best in the League. The Blackhawks had the second best penalty-killing record in the League, allowing only 68 goals in 425 opportunities, 84%. They led the League in shorthanded goals with 20. The Blackhawks allowed only 211 goals during the season, fewest among the 21 clubs.

CONN SMYTHE TROPHY

An annual award "to the most valuable player for his team in the playoffs." Winner selected by the Professional Hockey Writers' Association at the conclusion of the final game in the Stanley Cup Finals. The winner receives $3,000.

History: Presented by Maple Leaf Gardens Limited in 1964 to honor Conn Smythe, the former coach, manager, president and owner-governor of the Toronto Maple Leafs.

1990-91 Winner: Mario Lemieux, Pittsburgh Penguins

Mario Lemieux of the Pittsburgh Penguins won the Conn Smythe Trophy as playoff MVP in '91 as he led the Penguins to their first Stanley Cup win in team history. Pittsburgh won series over New Jersey, Washington, Boston and Minnesota. Lemieux led all scorers in the '91 playoffs, registering 16 goals and 28 assists for 44 points, the second highest total in Stanley Cup playoff history.

William M. Jennings
Trophy

Jack Adams
Award

Bill Masterton
Trophy

Lester Patrick
Trophy

Alka-Seltzer
Plus Award

WILLIAM M. JENNINGS TROPHY

An annual award "to the goalkeeper(s) having played a minimum of 25 games for the team with the fewest goals scored against it." Winners selected on regular-season play. Overall winner receives $3,000, runner-up $1,000. Leader at end of first half of season and leader in second half each receive $250.

History: The Jennings Trophy was presented in 1981-82 by the National Hockey League's Board of Governors to honor the late William M. Jennings, longtime governor and president of the New York Rangers and one of the great builders of hockey in the United States.

1990-91 Winner: Ed Belfour, Chicago Blackhawks
Runner-up: Patrick Roy, Montreal Canadiens

Chicago's Ed Belfour was the workhorse of a Blackhawks goaltending contingent that combined for a league-leading 2.61 goals-against-average. Belfour saw action in 74 of the Blackhawks' 80 games and recorded four shutouts while compiling a league-leading 2.47 goals-against-average.

JACK ADAMS AWARD

An annual award presented by the National Hockey League Broadcasters' Association to "the NHL coach adjudged to have contributed the most to his team's success." Winner selected by poll among members of the NHL Broadcasters' Association at the end of the regular season. The winner receives $1,000 from the NHLBA.

History: The award was presented by the NHL Broadcasters' Association in 1974 to commemorate the late Jack Adams, coach and general manager of the Detroit Red Wings, whose lifetime dedication to hockey serves as an inspiration to all who aspire to further the game.

1990-91 Winner: Brian Sutter, St. Louis Blues
Runners-up: Tom Webster, Los Angeles Kings
Mike Keenan, Chicago Blackhawks

Brian Sutter, head coach of the St. Louis Blues, captured the Jack Adams Award as "the NHL coach adjudged to have contributed the most to his team's success". Sutter, a first-time NHL award winner, edged Tom Webster of Los Angeles and Mike Keenan of Chicago.

Sutter became the youngest head coach in the NHL on June 20, 1988 when he joined the Blues. In his three seasons behind the bench, Sutter had led his club to three consecutive second-place division finishes. In 1990-91, the Blues finished second in the League's overall standings with a 47-22-11 record (105 pts) and a .656 winning percentage, their best regular-season record since 1980-81 (45-18-17) and the second best in their 24-year history.

BILL MASTERTON MEMORIAL TROPHY

An annual award under the trusteeship of the Professional Hockey Writers' Association to "the National Hockey League player who best exemplifies the qualities of perseverance, sportsmanship and dedication to hockey." Winner selected by poll among the 21 chapters of the PHWA at the end of the regular season. A $2,500 grant from the PHWA is awarded annually to the Bill Masterton Scholarship Fund, based in Bloomington, MN, in the name of the Masterton Trophy winner.

History: The trophy was presented by the NHL Writers' Association in 1968 to commemorate the late William Masterton, a player of the Minnesota North Stars, who exhibited to a high degree the qualities of perseverance, sportsmanship and dedication to hockey, and who died January 15, 1968.

1990-91 Winner: Dave Taylor, Los Angeles Kings

Taylor, an alternate captain in his 14th season with the Kings, scored his 400th career goal on December 29, 1990 and became only the 29th player in NHL history to score 1,000 points on February 5, 1991. He has been named to three NHL All-Star Teams (1979-80, 1980-81 and 1981-82). He currently ranks 29th on the NHL's all-time point scoring list with 1,018. He has been honored with the Kings' Most Inspirational Player Award five times (1978-79, 1980-81, 1981-82, 1984-85 and 1986-87), as well as winning the Unsung Hero and Community Service Awards in 1989-90.

In addition to his outstanding career, Taylor plays an active role in his community. He spearheaded "Tip a King", a one-night charity event which in its third year raised over $225,000 for the Children's Cancer Research Fund. He participates in many summertime charity events including Carl's Jr. "King for a Day" promotion, which allows children to become an honourary clubhouse attendant for a game.

LESTER PATRICK TROPHY

An annual award "for outstanding service to hockey in the United States." Eligible recipients are players, officials, coaches, executives and referees. Winner selected by an award committee consisting of the President of the NHL, an NHL Governor, a representative of the New York Rangers, a member of the Hockey Hall of Fame Builder's section, a member of the Hockey Hall of Fame Player's section, a member of the U.S. Hockey Hall of Fame, a member of the NHL Broadcasters' Association and a member of the Professional Hockey Writers' Association. Each except the League President is rotated annually. The winner receives a miniature of the trophy.

History: Presented by the New York Rangers in 1966 to honor the late Lester Patrick, longtime general manager and coach of the New York Rangers, whose teams finished out of the playoffs only once in his first 16 years with the club.

1990-91 Winners: Rod Gilbert
Mike Ilitch

Mike Ilitch, owner and president of the Detroit Red Wings, and Rod Gilbert, record-setting right wing and Hockey Hall of Famer formerly of the New York Rangers, are the 1991 Lester Patrick Trophy winners for outstanding service to hockey in the United States.

A Detroit native, Ilitch realized a lifelong dream when he purchased the Red Wings in 1982, but his commitment to hockey extends far beyond his NHL ownership. Ilitch, owner of Little Caesars Pizza, is one of the country's primary supporters of youth hockey through the Little Caesars youth hockey program. More than 6,000 youngsters participate in sports annually through Ilitch's programs, and graduates of the Little Caesars hockey program include New York Rangers' goaltender John Vanbiesbrouck, Chicago Blackhawks' right wing Wayne Presley and, interestingly, Cincinatti Reds' third baseman Chris Sabo.

Gilbert, the Rangers' all-time leader in goals (406), assists (615) and points (1,021), has long been recognized as the premier right wing in the franchise's history. He holds many of the club's other scoring records, and his tenure in New York sparked a regional interest in hockey that equalled that of any professional sports franchise. Such was Gilbert's magnetism that the New York City area saw a growth in hockey participation – especially at the youth level – that remains continuing and unparalleled today. Gilbert continues his work within the game currently as Manager of Community Relations for the Rangers, as an active member of the Rangers' Alumni Association, and as an enthusiastic instructor at numerous youth hockey clinics.

ALKA-SELTZER PLUS AWARD

An annual award "to the player, having played a minimum of 60 games, who leads the League in plus/minus statistics" at the end of the regular season. Miles, Inc. will contribute $3,000 on behalf of the winner to the charity of his choice and $1000 on behalf of each individual team winner.

History: The award was presented to the NHL in 1989-90 by Miles, Inc., to recognize the League leader in plus-minus statistics. Plus-minus statistics are calculated by giving a player a "plus" when on-ice for an even-strength or shorthand goal scored by his team. He receives a "minus" when on-ice for an even-strength or shorthand goal scored by the opposing team. A plus-minus award has been presented since the 1982-83 season.

1990-91 Winners: Marty McSorley, Los Angeles Kings
Theoren Fleury, Calgary Flames

Los Angeles Kings' defenseman Marty McSorley and Calgary Flames' center Theoren Fleury, co-holders of the NHL's leading plus/minus ratings of plus-48, captured the 1990-91 Alka-Seltzer Plus Award. For both McSorley and Fleury, plus-48 represents a career high in the category. McSorley also posted career marks for assists (32) and points (39) in 61 games. Fleury achieved his plus-48 rating in 79 games, finishing the season with 104 points, including his first 50-goal season. Individual team leaders were: Ray Bourque, Boston; Uwe Krupp, Alexander Mogilny, Mike Ramsey, Pierre Turgeon, Buffalo; Jeremy Roenick, Chicago; Dave Barr, Brent Fedyk, Detroit; Petr Klima, Edmonton; Todd Krygier, Hartford; Dave Gagner, Minnesota; Shayne Corson, Montreal; Alexei Kasatonov, New Jersey; Joe Reekie, NY Islanders; John Ogrodnick, NY Rangers; Scott Mellanby, Philadelphia; Gordie Roberts, Pittsburgh; Mike Hough, Quebec; Brett Hull, Scott Stevens, St. Louis; Rob Ramage, Toronto; Dave Capuano, Vancouver; Kelly Miller, Washington; Doug Evans, Winnipeg.

King Clancy
Memorial Trophy

Lester B. Pearson
Award

Budweiser/NHL
Man of The Year

Trico Goaltender
Award

Presidents'
Trophy

KING CLANCY MEMORIAL TROPHY

An annual award "to the player who best exemplifies leadership qualities on and off the ice and has made a noteworthy humanitarian contribution in his community". The winner receives $3,000 and the runner-up $1,000.

History: The King Clancy Memorial Trophy was presented to the National Hockey League by the Board of Governors in 1988 to honor the late Frank "King" Clancy.

1990-91 Winner: Dave Taylor, Los Angeles Kings

Taylor, an alternate captain in his 14th season with the Kings, scored his 400th career goal on December 29, 1990 and became only the 29th player in NHL history to score 1,000 points on February 5, 1991. He has been named to three NHL All-Star Teams (1979-80, 1980-81 and 1981-82). He currently ranks 29th on the NHL's all-time point scoring list with 1,018. He has been honored with the Kings' Most Inspirational Player Award five times (1978-79, 1980-81, 1981-82, 1984-85 and 1986-87), as well as winning the Unsung Hero and Community Service Awards in 1989-90.

In addition to his outstanding career, Taylor plays an active role in his community. He spearheaded "Tip a King," a one-night charity event which in its third year raised over $225,000 for the Children's Cancer Research Fund. He participates in many summertime charity events.

After his first season with the Kings, Taylor enrolled in a UCLA class to correct a lifelong speech impediment. For the past 12 years, he had devoted his time to working with men and women in Southern California with similar speech problems.

LESTER B. PEARSON AWARD

An annual award presented to the NHL's outstanding player as selected by the members of the National Hockey League Players' Association. The winner receives $3,000 and the runner-up $1,500.

History: The award was presented in 1970-71 by the NHLPA in honor of the late Lester B. Pearson, former Prime Minister of Canada.

1990-91 Winner: Brett Hull, St. Louis Blues
Runners-up: Wayne Gretzky, Los Angeles Kings
Ed Belfour, Chicago Blackhawks

Brett Hull's spectacular 1990-91 season was recognized by his peers as he captured the Lester B. Pearson Award. Hull fired 86 goals in '90-91, leading the league in that category for the second year in a row. Hull also led the league in power-play goals (29), game-winning goals (11) and shots on net (389).

NHL AWARD MONEY BREAKDOWN

(All team awards are based on units of 21 per team except Presidents' Trophy which is based on 20 units.)

Stanley Cup Playoffs		Individual Shares	Total
Division Semi-Final Losers	(8 teams)	$ 3,000	$ 504,000
Division Final Losers	(4 teams)	6,000	504,000
Conference Championship Losers	(2 teams)	11,000	462,000
Stanley Cup Championship Losers		18,000	378,000
Stanley Cup Winners		25,000	525,000
TOTAL PLAYOFF AWARD MONEY			$2,373,000
Final Standings, Regular Season			
Presidents' Trophy (Team's share $100,000)		$5,000	$200,000
Division Winners	(4 teams)	5,000	420,000
Second Place	(4 teams)	2,500	210,000
TOTAL CHAMPIONSHIP POOL			$830,000
Individual Awards			
First Team All-Stars		$5,000	$30,000
Second Team All-Stars		2,000	12,000
All-Star Game winners' share		1,000	20,000
All-Star Game losers' share		750	15,000
Individual Award Winners		3,000	30,000
Individual Award Runners-up		1,000	9,000
TOTAL INDIVIDUAL AWARD MONEY			$116,000

BUD LIGHT/NHL MAN OF THE YEAR

An annual award to the player recognized in the local community as a positive role model through his conduct on and off the ice. This includes involvement with local youth groups, charities and causes, as well as recognition among his peers and fans as a player who extols sportsmanlike qualities while maximizing his efforts toward improving his play and that of the team. The winner is selected by a special committee of distinguished NHL officials and management executives. The Bud Light/NHL Man of the Year recognizes one player from each of the local media representatives. Each nominated player receives a check for $1,000 to be given to his favorite charity. The winner receives $21,000 to be distributed to his favorite charities.

1990-91 Winner: Kevin Dineen, Hartford Whalers

Veteran forward Kevin Dineen of the Hartford Whalers was named recipient of the 1991 Bud Light/NHL Man of the Year Award.

Dineen's intense style of play and his off-ice involvement with several charities has made him one of the most highly regarded individuals in Connecticut sports history.

As Honorary Chairman of the Crohn's & Colitis Foundation and the Arthritis Foundation, Dineen has lent more than his name to these causes. Dineen donates countless hours to both of these organizations. In addition to these charities, Dineen spends many hours representing the Whalers in their anti-drug program as well as trying to bring hope to the sick through numerous hospital visits.

Dineen's accomplishments on and off the ice are even more magnificent if one considers his well-documented battle with Crohn's Disease. Despite this affliction, Dineen has always performed to the best of his abilities on the ice and has remained committed to those less fortunate off the ice.

Six charities will benefit from Dineen's $20,000 award. Those charities are: The Crohn's & Colitis Foundation of America ($15,000), UConn Children's Cancer Fund ($1,000), Arthritis Foundation – Hartford Chapter ($1,000), South End Community Services Inc. ($1,000), Juvenile Inflammatory Disease Center ($1,000), and Foodshare of Greater Hartford ($1,000).

Dineen previously donated $1,000 to the House of Bread charitable organization which he earned for being a nominee for the award.

TRICO GOALTENDER AWARD

An annual award to the goaltender with the best save percentage during the regular schedule. The winner receives $10,000 to benefit the charitable organization of his choice. The runners-up each receive $1,000 to be presented in their names to the charity of their choice.

History: The award was presented to the National Hockey League in 1988-89 by Trico to recognize the goaltender with the best save percentage during the regular schedule.

1990-91 Winner: Ed Belfour, Chicago Blackhawks
Runners-up: Patrick Roy, Montreal Canadiens
Mike Richter, NY Rangers

Chicago Blackhawks goaltender Ed Belfour, the NHL's 1991 Calder Memorial Trophy as Rookie of the Year and Vezina Trophy winner as the League's best goaltender, was the 1990-91 winner of the Trico Goaltender Award.

Belfour stopped better than nine of every ten shots taken at him, during the 1990-91 NHL regular season, posting a .910 save percentage. The Carman, Manitoba native edged two-time Trico Goaltender Award winner Patrick Roy of the Montreal Canadiens (.906) and Mike Richter of the New Year Rangers (.903).

To capture the award Belfour pushed aside 1,713 of the 1,883 shots he faced during the regular season. The 26-year-old led the League in games played (74, second highest in NHL History to Grant Fuhr's 75 games, 1987-88), wins (43) and goals-against-average (2.47). Belfour also notched four shutouts.

Roy, 25 years old, appeared in 48 games, posting the second best save percentage (.906) and third best goals-against-average (2.71). The Canadiens' netminder allowed only 128 goals this season, stopping 1,234 of 1,362 shots faced.

New York Rangers rookie Mike Richter finished third with a .903 save percentage in 45 games played. The Philadelphia, Pennsylvania native stopped 1,257 of the 1,392 shots he faced.

Tom Barrasso returned to top form in 1990-91, winning the Pro-Set Player of the Month Award for December.

PRESIDENTS' TROPHY

An annual award to the club finishing the regular-season with the best overall record. The winner receives $200,000, to be split evenly between the team and its players. Based on 20 players in each game during the regular-season, a player who appears in all 80 games receives $5,000. Players appearing in less than 80 games receive pro-rated amounts.

History: Presented to the National Hockey League in 1985-86 by the NHL Board of Governors to recognize the team compiling the top regular-season record.

1990-91 Winner: Chicago Blackhawks
Runners-up: St. Louis Blues
Los Angeles Kings

The Chicago Blackhawks won the 1990-91 Presidents' Trophy with the NHL's best regular-season record of 49–23–8 for 106 points. The St. Louis Blues finished second at 47–22–11 for 105 points, while the Los Angeles Kings had the third best regular-season mark of 46–24–10 for 102 points.

PRO SET NHL PLAYER OF THE YEAR AWARD

An annual award presented by Pro Set to the National Hockey League's most valuable player in the regular-season. The winner is awarded $7,500 to benefit youth hockey.

History: In 1990, Pro Set initiated its relationship with the National Hockey League by sponsoring the Player of the Year Award. Pro Set also sponsors the Player of the Week and Player of the Month awards, donating $500 and $1,000, respectively, to youth hockey organizations chosen by the award recipient.

1990-91 Winner: Brett Hull, St. Louis Blues
Hull, who scored 86 goals during the 1990-91 season and helped lead the Blues to a second-place overall finish, is the first winner of the Pro Set NHL Player of the Year Award. Hull, whose 86 goals were a record for goals scored by a right wing (surpassing his own record of 72 goals set during the 1989-90 season), finished first in the NHL last season in goals and second overall in points (86-45-131).

Hull also posted a 10-game goal scoring streak (during which he scored 16 times) – tops in the League – as well as a mini-streak of seven games (10 goals). Among his 86 goals were four three-goal games, including back-to-back hat tricks during Blues' wins versus the Toronto Maple Leafs on October 24 and 25.

In addition to being named the Pro Set Player of the Year, Hull also garnered two Player of the Week honors, and one Player of the Month award.

In Hull's name, Pro Set will donate $7,500 to a St. Louis pee wee team representing the St. Louis Blues in the annual Quebec International Pee Wee Tournament.

1990-91 Pro Set/NHL Award Winners

Player of the Week

Week Ending	Player	Team	Youth Hockey Organization
October 14	**Kevin Stevens**	Pittsburgh	Pembroke Youth Hockey (MA)
October 21	**Ken Wregget**	Philadelphia	Nova Scotia "AAA" Hockey League (N.S.)
October 28	**Brett Hull**	St. Louis	Webster Groves Amateur Hockey Association (MO)
November 4	**Bob Essensa**	Winnipeg	Winnipeg Minor Hockey Association (Man.)
November 11	**Glenn Healy**	NY Islanders	Pickering Hockey Assocation (Ont.)
November 18	**Steve Yzerman**	Detroit	Detroit Hockey Association (MI)
November 25	**Tomas Sandstrom**	Los Angeles	Los Angeles Kings Hockey School (CA)
December 2	**John MacLean**	New Jersey	Navesink Hockey Club (NJ)
December 9	**Brian Hayward**	Minnesota	Georgetown Youth Hockey Organization (Ont.)
December 16	**Ray Bourque**	Boston	Danvers Youth Hockey Association (MA)
December 23	**Steve Yzerman**	Detroit	Detroit Hockey Association (MI)
December 30	**Bill Ranford**	Edmonton	Red Deer Minor Hockey Association (Alta.)
January 6	**Daniel Berthiaume**	Los Angeles	Los Angeles Kings Hockey School (CA)
January 13	**Jeremy Roenick**	Chicago	Maryville Academy (IL)
January 20	**Alexander Mogilny**	Buffalo	Saints Hockey Club (NY)
January 27	**Adam Oates**	St. Louis	Troy Amateur Hockey Association (NY)
February 3	**Thomas Steen**	Winnipeg	Grums Minor Hockey (Sweden)
February 10	**Mike McPhee**	Montreal	Strait Area Minor Hockey Association (N.S.)
February 17	**Brett Hull**	St. Louis	Affton Youth Hockey Association (MO)
February 24	**Wayne Gretzky**	Los Angeles	Hockey Ministries Camp (Que.)
March 3	**Joe Nieuwendyk**	Calgary	Whitby Ontario Minor Hockey Association (Ont.)
March 10	**Tim Cheveldae**	Detroit	Melville Youth Hockey Assocation (Sask.)
March 17	**Dale Hawerchuk**	Buffalo	Oshawa Minor Hockey Association (Ont.)
March 24	**Joe Sakic**	Quebec	Burnaby Minor Hockey Association (B.C.)
March 31	**Vincent Riendeau**	St. Louis	Drummondville Minor Hockey League (Que.)

Player of the Month

Month	Player	Team	Youth Hockey Recipient
October	**John Vanbiesbrouck**	NY Rangers	Island Blades Hockey Club (NY)
November	**Pete Peeters**	Philadelphia	Moranville N. District Minor Hockey Association (Alta.)
December	**Tom Barrasso**	Pittsburgh	Assabet Valley Minor Hockey Association (MA)
January	**Wayne Gretzky**	Los Angeles	Brantford Minor Hockey Association (Ont.)
February	**Brett Hull**	St. Louis	Kirkwood Youth Hockey Association (MO)
March	**Kelly Hrudey**	Los Angeles	Elmwod Community League (Alta.)

Player of the Year

Year	Player	Team	Youth Hockey Recipient
1990-91	**Brett Hull**	St. Louis	St. Louis Blues Peewees (MO)

NATIONAL HOCKEY LEAGUE INDIVIDUAL AWARD WINNERS

ART ROSS TROPHY

	Winner	Runner-up
1991	Wayne Gretzky, L.A.	Brett Hull, St.L.
1990	Wayne Gretzky, L.A.	Mark Messier, Edm.
1989	Mario Lemieux, Pit.	Wayne Gretzky, L.A.
1988	Mario Lemieux, Pit.	Wayne Gretzky, Edm.
1987	Wayne Gretzky, Edm.	Jari Kurri, Edm.
1986	Wayne Gretzky, Edm.	Mario Lemieux, Pit.
1985	Wayne Gretzky, Edm.	Jari Kurri, Edm.
1984	Wayne Gretzky, Edm.	Paul Coffey, Edm.
1983	Wayne Gretzky, Edm.	Peter Stastny, Que.
1982	Wayne Gretzky, Edm.	Mike Bossy, NYI
1981	Wayne Gretzky, Edm.	Marcel Dionne, L.A.
1980	Marcel Dionne, L.A.	Wayne Gretzky, Edm.
1979	Bryan Trottier, NYI	Marcel Dionne, L.A.
1978	Guy Lafleur, Mtl.	Bryan Trottier, NYI
1977	Guy Lafleur, Mtl.	Marcel Dionne, L.A.
1976	Guy Lafleur, Mtl.	Bobby Clarke, Phi.
1975	Bobby Orr, Bos.	Phil Esposito, Bos.
1974	Phil Esposito, Bos.	Bobby Orr, Bos.
1973	Phil Esposito, Bos.	Bobby Clarke, Phi.
1972	Phil Esposito, Bos.	Bobby Orr, Bos.
1971	Phil Esposito, Bos.	Bobby Orr, Bos.
1970	Bobby Orr, Bos.	Phil Esposito, Bos.
1969	Phil Esposito, Bos.	Bobby Hull, Chi.
1968	Stan Mikita, Chi.	Phil Esposito, Bos.
1967	Stan Mikita, Chi.	Bobby Hull, Chi.
1966	Bobby Hull, Chi.	Stan Mikita, Chi.
1965	Stan Mikita, Chi.	Norm Ullman, Det.
1964	Stan Mikita, Chi.	Bobby Hull, Chi.
1963	Gordie Howe, Det.	Andy Bathgate, NYR
1962	Bobby Hull, Chi.	Andy Bathgate, NYR
1961	Bernie Geoffrion, Mtl.	Jean Beliveau, Mtl.
1960	Bobby Hull, Chi.	Bronco Horvath, Bos.
1959	Dickie Moore, Mtl.	Jean Beliveau, Mtl.
1958	Dickie Moore, Mtl.	Henri Richard, Mtl.
1957	Gordie Howe, Det.	Ted Lindsay, Det.
1956	Jean Beliveau, Mtl.	Gordie Howe, Det.
1955	Bernie Geoffrion, Mtl.	Maurice Richard, Mtl.
1954	Gordie Howe, Det.	Maurice Richard, Mtl.
1953	Gordie Howe, Det.	Ted Lindsay, Det.
1952	Gordie Howe, Det.	Ted Lindsay, Det.
1951	Gordie Howe, Det.	Maurice Richard, Mtl.
1950	Ted Lindsay, Det.	Sid Abel, Det.
1949	Roy Conacher, Chi.	Doug Bentley, Chi.
1948	Elmer Lach, Mtl.	Buddy O'Connor, NYR
1947*	Max Bentley, Chi.	Maurice Richard, Mtl.
1946	Max Bentley, Chi.	Gaye Stewart, Tor.
1945	Elmer Lach, Mtl.	Maurice Richard, Mtl.
1944	Herbie Cain, Bos.	Doug Bentley, Chi.
1943	Doug Bentley, Chi.	Bill Cowley, Bos.
1942	Bryan Hextall, NYR	Lynn Patrick, NYR
1941	Bill Cowley, Bos.	Bryan Hextall, NYR
1940	Milt Schmidt, Bos.	Woody Dumart, Bos.
1939	Toe Blake, Mtl.	Dave Schriner, NYA
1938	Gordie Drillon, Tor.	Syl Apps, Tor.
1937	Dave Schriner, NYA	Syl Apps, Tor.
1936	Dave Schriner, NYA	Marty Barry, Det.
1935	Charlie Conacher, Tor.	Syd Howe, St.L-Det.
1934	Charlie Conacher, Tor.	Joe Primeau, Tor
1933	Bill Cook, NYR	Harvey Jackson, Tor.
1932	Harvey Jackson, Tor.	Joe Primeau, Tor.
1931	Howie Morenz, Mtl.	Ebbie Goodfellow, Det.
1930	Cooney Weiland, Bos.	Frank Boucher, NYR
1929	Ace Bailey, Tor.	Nels Stewart, Mtl.M
1928	Howie Morenz, Mtl.	Aurel Joliat, Mtl.
1927	Bill Cook, NYR	Dick Irvin, Chi.
1926	Nels Stewart, Mtl.M.	Cy Denneny, Ott.
1925	Babe Dye, Tor.	Cy Denneny, Ott.
1924	Cy Denneny, Ott.	Billy Boucher, Mtl.
1923	Babe Dye, Tor.	Cy Denneny, Ott.
1922	Punch Broadbent, Ott.	Cy Denneny, Ott.
1921	Newsy Lalonde, Mtl.	Cy Denneny, Ott.
1920	Joe Malone, Que.	Newsy Lalonde, Mtl.
1919	Newsy Lalonde, Mtl.	Odie Cleghorn, Mtl.
1918	Joe Malone, Mtl.	Cy Denneny, Ott.

* Scoring leader prior to inception of Art Ross Trophy in 1947-48

HART TROPHY

	Winner	Runner-up
1991	Brett Hull, St.L.	Wayne Gretzky, L.A.
1990	Mark Messier, Edm.	Ray Bourque, Bos.
1989	Wayne Gretzky, L.A.	Mario Lemieux, Pit.
1988	Mario Lemieux, Pit.	Grant Fuhr, Edm.
1987	Wayne Gretzky, Edm.	Ray Bourque, Bos.
1986	Wayne Gretzky, Edm.	Mario Lemieux, Pit.
1985	Wayne Gretzky, Edm.	Dale Hawerchuk, Wpg.
1984	Wayne Gretzky, Edm.	Rod Langway, Wsh.
1983	Wayne Gretzky, Edm.	Pete Peeters, Bos.
1982	Wayne Gretzky, Edm.	Bryan Trottier, NYI
1981	Wayne Gretzky, Edm.	Mike Liut, St.L.
1980	Wayne Gretzky, Edm.	Marcel Dionne, L.A.
1979	Bryan Trottier, NYI	Guy Lafleur, Mtl
1978	Guy Lafleur, Mtl.	Bryan Trottier, NYI
1977	Guy Lafleur, Mtl.	Bobby Clarke, Phi.
1976	Bobby Clarke, Phi.	Denis Potvin, NYI
1975	Bobby Clarke, Phi.	Rogatien Vachon, L.A.
1974	Phil Esposito, Bos.	Bernie Parent, Phi.
1973	Bobby Clarke, Phi.	Phil Esposito, Bos.
1972	Bobby Orr, Bos.	Ken Dryden, Mtl.
1971	Bobby Orr, Bos.	Phil Esposito, Bos.
1970	Bobby Orr, Bos.	Tony Esposito, Chi.
1969	Phil Esposito, Bos.	Jean Beliveau, Mtl.
1968	Stan Mikita, Chi.	Jean Beliveau, Mtl.
1967	Stan Mikita, Chi.	Ed Giacomin, NYR
1966	Bobby Hull, Chi.	Jean Beliveau, Mtl.
1965	Bobby Hull, Chi.	Norm Ullman, Det.
1964	Jean Beliveau, Mtl.	Bobby Hull, Chi.
1963	Gordie Howe, Det.	Stan Mikita, Chi.
1962	Jacques Plante, Mtl.	Doug Harvey, NYR
1961	Bernie Geoffrion, Mtl.	Johnny Bower, Tor.
1960	Gordie Howe, Det.	Bobby Hull, Chi.
1959	Andy Bathgate, NYR	Gordie Howe, Det.
1958	Gordie Howe, Det.	Andy Bathgate, NYR
1957	Gordie Howe, Det.	Jean Beliveau, Mtl.
1956	Jean Beliveau, Mtl.	Tod Sloan, Tor.
1955	Ted Kennedy, Tor.	Harry Lumley, Tor.
1954	Al Rollins, Chi.	Red Kelly, Det.
1953	Gordie Howe, Det.	Al Rollins, Chi.
1952	Gordie Howe, Det.	Elmer Lach, Mtl.
1951	Milt Schmidt, Bos.	Maurice Richard, Mtl.
1950	Charlie Rayner, NYR	Ted Kennedy, Tor.
1949	Sid Abel, Det.	Bill Durnan, Mtl.
1948	Buddy O'Connor, NYR	Frank Brimsek, Bos.
1947	Maurice Richard, Mtl.	Milt Schmidt, Bos.
1946	Max Bentley, Chi.	Gaye Stewart, Tor.
1945	Elmer Lach, Mtl.	Maurice Richard, Mtl.
1944	Babe Pratt, Tor.	Bill Cowley, Bos.
1943	Bill Cowley, Bos.	Doug Bentley, Chi.
1942	Tom Anderson, Bro.	Syl Apps, Tor.
1941	Bill Cowley, Bos.	Dit Clapper, Bos.
1940	Ebbie Goodfellow, Det.	Syl Apps, Tor.
1939	Toe Blake, Mtl.	Syl Apps, Tor.
1938	Eddie Shore, Bos.	Paul Thompson, Chi.
1937	Babe Siebert, Mtl.	Lionel Conacher, Mtl.M
1936	Eddie Shore, Bos.	Hooley Smith, Mtl.M
1935	Eddie Shore, Bos.	Charlie Conacher, Tor.
1934	Aurel Joliat, Mtl.	Lionel Conacher, Chi.
1933	Eddie Shore, Bos.	Bill Cook, NYR
1932	Howie Morenz, Mtl.	Ching Johnson, NYR
1931	Howie Morenz, Mtl.	Eddie Shore, Bos.
1930	Nels Stewart, Mtl.M.	Lionel Hitchman, Bos.
1929	Roy Worters, NYA	Ace Bailey, Tor.
1928	Howie Morenz, Mtl.	Roy Worters, Pit.
1927	Herb Gardiner, Mtl.	Bill Cook, NYR
1926	Nels Stewart, Mtl.M.	Sprague Cleghorn, Bos.
1925	Billy Burch, Ham.	Howie Morenz, Mtl.
1924	Frank Nighbor, Ott.	Sprague Cleghorn, Mtl.

LADY BYNG TROPHY

	Winner	Runner-up
1991	Wayne Gretzky, L.A.	Brett Hull, St.L.
1990	Brett Hull, St.L.	Wayne Gretzky, L.A.
1989	Joe Mullen, Cgy.	Wayne Gretzky, L.A.
1988	Mats Naslund, Mtl.	Wayne Gretzky, Edm.
1987	Joe Mullen, Cgy.	Wayne Gretzky, Edm.
1986	Mike Bossy, NYI	Jari Kurri, Edm.
1985	Jari Kurri, Edm.	Joe Mullen, St.L.
1984	Mike Bossy, NYI	Rick Middleton, Bos.
1983	Mike Bossy, NYI	Rick Middleton, Bos.
1982	Rick Middleton, Bos.	Mike Bossy, NYI
1981	Rick Kehoe, Pit.	Wayne Gretzky, Edm.
1980	Wayne Gretzky, Edm.	Marcel Dionne, L.A.
1979	Bob MacMillan, Atl.	Marcel Dionne, L.A.
1978	Butch Goring, L.A.	Peter McNab, Bos.
1977	Marcel Dionne, L.A.	Jean Ratelle, Bos.
1976	Jean Ratelle, NYR-Bos.	Jean Pronovost, Pit.
1975	Marcel Dionne, Det.	John Bucyk, Bos.
1974	John Bucyk, Bos.	Lowell MacDonald, Pit.
1973	Gilbert Perreault, Buf.	Jean Ratelle, NYR
1972	Jean Ratelle, NYR	John Bucyk, Bos.
1971	John Bucyk, Bos.	Dave Keon, Tor.
1970	Phil Goyette, St.L.	John Bucyk, Bos.
1969	Alex Delvecchio, Det.	Ted Hampson, Oak.
1968	Stan Mikita, Chi.	John Bucyk, Bos.
1967	Stan Mikita, Chi.	Dave Keon, Tor.
1966	Alex Delvecchio, Det.	Bobby Rousseau, Mtl.
1965	Bobby Hull, Chi.	Alex Delvecchio, Det.
1964	Ken Wharram, Chi.	Dave Keon, Tor.
1963	Dave Keon, Tor.	Camille Henry, NYR
1962	Dave Keon, Tor.	Claude Provost, Mtl.
1961	Red Kelly, Tor.	Norm Ullman, Det.
1960	Don McKenney, Bos.	Andy Hebenton, NYR
1959	Alex Delvecchio, Det.	Andy Hebenton, NYR
1958	Camille Henry, NYR	Don Marshall, Mtl.
1957	Andy Hebenton, NYR	Earl Reibel, Det.
1956	Earl Reibel, Det.	Floyd Curry, Mtl.
1955	Sid Smith, Tor.	Danny Lewicki, NYR
1954	Red Kelly, Det.	Don Raleigh, NYR
1953	Red Kelly, Det.	Wally Hergesheimer, NYR
1952	Sid Smith, Tor.	Red Kelly, Det.
1951	Red Kelly, Det.	Woody Dumart, Bos.
1950	Edgar Laprade, NYR	Red Kelly, Det.
1949	Bill Quackenbush, Det.	Harry Watson, Tor.
1948	Buddy O'Connor, NYR	Syl Aps, Tor.
1947	Bobby Bauer, Bos.	Syl Apps, Tor.
1946	Toe Blake, Mtl.	Clint Smith, Chi.
1945	Bill Mosienko, Chi.	Syd Howe, Det.
1944	Clint Smith, Chi.	Herb Cain, Bos.
1943	Max Bentley, Chi.	Buddy O'Connor, Mtl.
1942	Syl Apps, Tor.	Gordie Drillon, Tor.
1941	Bobby Bauer, Bos.	Gordie Drillon, Tor.
1940	Bobby Bauer, Bos.	Clint Smith, NYR
1939	Clint Smith, NYR	Marty Barry, Det.
1938	Gordie Drillon, Tor.	Clint Smith, NYR
1937	Marty Barry, Det.	Gordie Drillon, Tor.
1936	Doc Romnes, Chi.	Dave Schriner, NYA
1935	Frank Boucher, NYR	Russ Blinco, Mtl.M
1934	Frank Boucher, NYR	Joe Primeau, Tor.
1933	Frank Boucher, NYR	Joe Primeau, Tor.
1932	Joe Primeau, Tor.	Frank Boucher, NYR
1931	Frank Boucher, NYR	Normie Himes, NYA
1930	Frank Boucher, NYR	Normie Himes, NYA
1929	Frank Boucher, NYR	Harry Darragh, Pit.
1928	Frank Boucher, NYR	George Hay, Det.
1927	Billy Burch, NYA	Dick Irvin, Chi.
1926	Frank Nighbor, Ott.	Billy Burch, NYA
1925	Frank Nighbor, Ott.	none

CONN SMYTHE TROPHY WINNERS

1991	Mario Lemieux	Pittsburgh
1990	Bill Ranford	Edmonton
1989	Al MacInnis	Calgary
1988	Wayne Gretzky	Edmonton
1987	Ron Hextall	Philadelphia
1986	Patrick Roy	Montreal
1985	Wayne Gretzky	Edmonton
1984	Mark Messier	Edmonton
1983	Bill Smith	NY Islanders
1982	Mike Bossy	NY Islanders
1981	Butch Goring	NY Islanders
1980	Bryan Trottier	NY Islanders
1979	Bob Gainey	Montreal
1978	Larry Robinson	Montreal
1977	Guy Lafleur	Montreal
1976	Reggie Leach	Philadelphia
1975	Bernie Parent	Philadelphia
1974	Bernie Parent	Philadelphia
1973	Yvan Cournoyer	Montreal
1972	Bobby Orr	Boston
1971	Ken Dryden	Montreal
1970	Bobby Orr	Boston
1969	Serge Savard	Montreal
1968	Glenn Hall	St. Louis
1967	Dave Keon	Toronto
1966	Roger Crozier	Detroit
1965	Jean Beliveau	Montreal

LESTER B. PEARSON AWARD WINNERS

1991	Brett Hull	St. Louis
1990	Mark Messier	Edmonton
1989	Steve Yzerman	Detroit
1988	Mario Lemieux	Pittsburgh
1987	Wayne Gretzky	Edmonton
1986	Mario Lemieux	Pittsburgh
1985	Wayne Gretzky	Edmonton
1984	Wayne Gretzky	Edmonton
1983	Wayne Gretzky	Edmonton
1982	Wayne Gretzky	Edmonton
1981	Mike Liut	St. Louis
1980	Marcel Dionne	Los Angeles
1979	Marcel Dionne	Los Angeles
1978	Guy Lafleur	Montreal
1977	Guy Lafleur	Montreal
1976	Guy Lafleur	Montreal
1975	Bobby Orr	Boston
1974	Phil Esposito	Boston
1973	Bobby Clarke	Philadelphia
1972	Jean Ratelle	NY Rangers
1971	Phil Esposito	Boston

FRANK J. SELKE TROPHY WINNERS

	Winner	Runner-up
1991	Dirk Graham, Chi.	Esa Tikkanen, Edm.
1990	Rick Meagher, St.L.	Guy Carbonneau, Mtl.
1989	Guy Carbonneau, Mtl.	Esa Tikkanen, Edm.
1988	Guy Carbonneau, Mtl.	Steve Kasper, Bos.
1987	Dave Poulin, Phi.	Guy Carbonneau, Mtl.
1986	Troy Murray, Chi.	Ron Sutter, Phi.
1985	Craig Ramsay, Buf.	Doug Jarvis, Wsh.
1984	Doug Jarvis, Wsh.	Bryan Trottier, NYI
1983	Bobby Clarke, Phi.	Jari Kurri, Edm.
1982	Steve Kasper, Bos.	Bob Gainey, Mtl.
1981	Bob Gainey, Mtl.	Craig Ramsay, Buf.
1980	Bob Gainey, Mtl.	Craig Ramsay, Buf.
1979	Bob Gainey, Mtl.	Don Marcotte, Bos.
1978	Bob Gainey, Mtl.	Craig Ramsay, Buf.

VEZINA TROPHY

	Winner	Runner-up
1991	Ed Belfour, Chi.	Patrick Roy, Mtl.
1990	Patrick Roy, Mtl.	Daren Puppa, Buf.
1989	Patrick Roy, Mtl.	Mike Vernon, Cgy.
1988	Grant Fuhr, Edm.	Tom Barrasso, Buf.
1987	Ron Hextall, Phi.	Mike Liut, Hfd.
1986	John Vanbiesbrouck, NYR	Bob Froese, Phi.
1985	Pelle Lindbergh, Phi.	Tom Barrasso, Buf.
1984	Tom Barrasso, Buf.	Rejean Lemelin, Cgy.
1983	Pete Peeters, Bos.	Roland Melanson, NYI
1982	Bill Smith, NYI	Grant Fuhr, Edm.
1981	Richard Sevigny, Mtl. Denis Herron, Mtl. Michel Larocque, Mtl.	Pete Peeters, Phi. Rick St. Croix, Phi.
1980	Bob Sauve, Buf. Don Edwards, Buf.	Gerry Cheevers, Bos. Gilles Gilbert, Bos.
1979	Ken Dryden, Mtl. Michel Larocque, Mtl.	Glenn Resch, NYI Bill Smith, NYI
1978	Ken Dryden, Mtl. Michel Larocque	Bernie Parent, Phi. Wayne Stephenson, Phi.
1977	Ken Dryden, Mtl. Michel Larocque, Mtl.	Glenn Resch, NYI Bill Smith, NYI
1976	Ken Dryden, Mtl.	Glenn Resch, NYI Bill Smith, NYI
1975	Bernie Parent, Phi.	Rogie Vachon, L.A. Gary Edwards, L.A.
1974	Bernie Parent, Phi. (tie) Tony Esposito, Chi. (tie)	Gilles Gilbert, Bos.
1973	Ken Dryden, Mtl.	Ed Giacomin, NYR Gilles Villemure, NYR
1972	Tony Esposito, Chi. Gary Smith, Chi.	Cesare Maniago, Min. Lorne Worsley, Min.
1971	Ed Giacomin, NYR Gilles Villemure, NYR	Tony Esposito, Chi.
1970	Tony Esposito, Chi.	Jacques Plante, St.L. Ernie Wakely, St.L.
1969	Jacques Plante, St.L. Glenn Hall, St.L.	Ed Giacomin, NYR
1968	Lorne Worsley, Mtl. Rogatien Vachon, Mtl.	Johnny Bower, Tor. Bruce Gamble, Tor.
1967	Glenn Hall, Chi. Denis Dejordy, Chi.	Charlie Hodge, Mtl.
1966	Lorne Worsley, Mtl. Charlie Hodge, Mtl.	Glenn Hall, Chi.
1965	Terry Sawchuk, Tor. Johnny Bower, Tor.	Roger Crozier, Det.
1964	Charlie Hodge, Mtl.	Glenn Hall, Chi.
1963	Glenn Hall, Chi.	Johnny Bower, Tor. Don Simmons, Tor.
1962	Jacques Plante, Mtl.	Johnny Bower, Tor.
1961	Johnny Bower, Tor.	Glenn Hall, Chi.
1960	Jacques Plante, Mtl.	Glenn Hall, Chi.
1959	Jacques Plante, Mtl.	Johnny Bower, Tor. Ed Chadwick, Tor.
1958	Jacques Plante, Mtl.	Lorne Worsley, NYR Marcel Paille, NYR
1957	Jacques Plante, Mtl.	Glenn Hall, Det.
1956	Jacques Plante, Mtl.	Glenn Hall, Det.
1955	Terry Sawchuk, Det.	Harry Lumley, Tor.
1954	Harry Lumley, Tor.	Terry Sawchuk, Det.
1953	Terry Sawchuk, Det.	Gerry McNeil, Mtl.
1952	Terry Sawchuk, Det.	Al Rollins, Tor.
1951	Al Rollins, Tor.	Terry Sawchuk, Det.
1950	Bill Durnan, Mtl.	Harry Lumley, Det.
1949	Bill Durnan, Mtl.	Harry Lumley, Det.
1948	Turk Broda, Tor.	Harry Lumley, Det.
1947	Bill Durnan, Mtl.	Turk Broda, Tor.
1946	Bill Durnan, Mtl.	Frank Brimsek, Bos.
1945	Bill Durnan, Mtl.	Frank McCool, Tor. (tie) Harry Lumley, Det. (tie)
1944	Bill Durnan, Mtl.	Paul Bibeault, Tor.
1943	Johnny Mowers, Det.	Turk Broda, Tor.
1942	Frank Brimsek, Bos.	Turk Broda, Tor.
1941	Turk Broda, Tor.	Frank Brimsek, Bos. (tie) Johnny Mowers, Det. (ti
1940	Dave Kerr, NYR	Frank Brimsek, Bos.
1939	Frank Brimsek, Bos.	Dave Kerr, NYR
1938	Tiny Thompson, Bos.	Dave Kerr, NYR
1937	Normie Smith, Det.	Dave Kerr, NYR
1936	Tiny Thompson, Bos.	Mike Karakas, Chi.
1935	Lorne Chabot, Chi.	Alex Connell, Mtl.M
1934	Charlie Gardiner, Chi.	Wilf Cude, Det.
1933	Tiny Thompson, Bos.	John Roach, Det.
1932	Charlie Gardiner, Chi.	Alex Connell, Det.
1931	Roy Worters, NYA	Charlie Gardiner, Chi.
1930	Tiny Thompson, Bos.	Charlie Gardiner, Chi.
1929	George Hainsworth, Mtl.	Tiny Thompson, Bos.
1928	George Hainsworth, Mtl.	Alex Connell, Ott.
1927	George Hainsworth, Mtl.	Clint Benedict, Mtl.M

KING CLANCY MEMORIAL TROPHY WINNERS

1991	Dave Taylor	Los Angeles
1990	Kevin Lowe	Edmonton
1989	Bryan Trottier	NY Islanders
1988	Lanny McDonald	Calgary

Derek Sanderson, the Calder Trophy winner in 1968, flips the puck past the 1965 rookie of the year, Roger Crozier.

CALDER MEMORIAL TROPHY WINNERS

	Winner	Runner-up
1991	Ed Belfour, Chi.	Sergei Fedorov, Det.
1990	Sergei Makarov, Cgy.	Mike Modano, Min.
1989	Brian Leetch, NYR	Trevor Linden, Van.
1988	Joe Nieuwendyk, Cgy.	Ray Sheppard, Buf.
1987	Luc Robitaille, L.A.	Ron Hextall, Phi.
1986	Gary Suter, Cgy.	Wendel Clark, Tor.
1985	Mario Lemieux, Pit.	Chris Chelios, Mtl.
1984	Tom Barrasso, Buf.	Steve Yzerman, Det.
1983	Steve Larmer, Chi.	Phil Housley, Buf.
1982	Dale Hawerchuk, Wpg.	Barry Pederson, Bos.
1981	Peter Stastny, Que.	Larry Murphy, L.A.
1980	Ray Bourque, Bos.	Mike Foligno, Det.
1979	Bobby Smith, Min	Ryan Walter, Wsh.
1978	Mike Bossy, NYI	Barry Beck, Col.
1977	Willi Plett, Atl.	Don Murdoch, NYR
1976	Bryan Trottier, NYI	Glenn Resch, NYI
1975	Eric Vail, Atl.	Pierre Larouche, Pit.
1974	Denis Potvin, NYI	Tom Lysiak, Atl.
1973	Steve Vickers, NYR	Bill Barber, Phi.
1972	Ken Dryden, Mtl.	Rick Martin, Buf.
1971	Gilbert Perreault, Buf.	Jude Drouin, Min.
1970	Tony Esposito, Chi.	Bill Fairbairn, NYR
1969	Danny Grant, Min.	Norm Ferguson, Oak.
1968	Derek Sanderson, Bos.	Jacques Lemaire, Mtl.
1967	Bobby Orr, Bos.	Ed Van Impe, Chi.
1966	Brit Selby, Tor.	Bert Marshall, Det.
1965	Roger Crozier, Det.	Ron Ellis, Tor.
1964	Jacques Laperriere, Mtl.	John Ferguson, Mtl.
1963	Kent Douglas, Tor.	Doug Barkley, Det.
1962	Bobby Rousseau, Mtl.	Cliff Pennington, Bos.
1961	Dave Keon, Tor.	Bob Nevin, Tor.
1960	Bill Hay, Chi.	Murray Oliver, Det.
1959	Ralph Backstrom, Mtl.	Carl Brewer, Tor.
1958	Frank Mahovlich, Tor.	Bobby Hull, Chi.
1957	Larry Regan, Bos.	Ed Chadwick, NYR
1956	Glenn Hall, Det.	Andy Hebenton, NYR
1955	Ed Litzenberger, Chi.	Don McKenney, Bos.
1954	Camille Henry, NYR	Earl Reibel, Det.
1953	Lorne Worsley, NYR	Gordie Hannigan, Tor.
1952	Bernie Geoffrion, Mtl.	Hy Buller, NYR
1951	Terry Sawchuk, Det.	Al Rollins, Tor.
1950	Jack Gelineau, Bos.	Phil Maloney, Bos.
1949	Pentti Lund, NYR	Allan Stanley, NYR
1948	Jim McFadden, Det.	Pete Babando, Bos.
1947	Howie Meeker, Tor.	Jimmy Conacher, Det.
1946	Edgar Laprade, NYR	George Gee, Chi.
1945	Frank McCool, Tor.	Ken Smith, Bos.
1944	Gus Bodnar, Tor.	Bill Durnan, Mtl.
1943	Gaye Stewart, Tor.	Glen Harmon, Mtl.
1942	Grant Warwick, NYR	Buddy O'Connor, Mtl.
1941	Johnny Quilty, Mtl.	Johnny Mowers, Det.
1940	Kilby MacDonald, NYR	Wally Stanowski, Tor.
1939	Frank Brimsek, Bos.	Roy Conacher, Bos.
1938	Cully Dahlstrom, Chi.	Murph Chamberlain, Tor
1937	Syl Apps, Tor.	Gordie Drillon, Tor.
1936	Mike Karakas, Chi.	Bucko McDonald, Det.
1935	Dave Schriner, NYA	Bert Connolly, NYR
1934	Russ Blinko, Mtl.M.	
1933	Carl Voss, Det.	

JAMES NORRIS TROPHY WINNERS

	Winner	Runner-up
1991	Ray Bourque, Bos.	Al MacInnis, Cgy.
1990	Ray Bourque, Bos.	Al MacInnis, Cgy.
1989	Chris Chelios, Mtl	Paul Coffey, Pit.
1988	Ray Bourque, Bos.	Scott Stevens, Wsh.
1987	Ray Bourque, Bos.	Mark Howe, Phi.
1986	Paul Coffey, Edm.	Mark Howe, Phi.
1985	Paul Coffey, Edm.	Ray Bourque, Bos.
1984	Rod Langway, Wsh.	Paul Coffey, Edm.
1983	Rod Langway, Wsh.	Mark Howe, Phi.
1982	Doug Wilson, Chi.	Ray Bourque, Bos.
1981	Randy Carlyle, Pit.	Denis Potvin, NYI
1980	Larry Robinson, Mtl.	Borje Salming, Tor.
1979	Denis Potvin, NYI	Larry Robinson, Mtl.
1978	Denis Potvin, NYI	Brad Park, Bos.
1977	Larry Robinson, Mtl.	Borje Salming, Tor.
1976	Denis Potvin, NYI	Brad Park, NYR-Bos.
1975	Bobby Orr, Bos.	Denis Potvin, NYI
1974	Bobby Orr, Bos.	Brad Park, NYR
1973	Bobby Orr, Bos.	Guy Lapointe, Mtl.
1972	Bobby Orr, Bos.	Brad Park, NYR
1971	Bobby Orr, Bos.	Brad Park, NYR
1970	Bobby Orr, Bos.	Brad Park, NYR
1969	Bobby Orr, Bos.	Tim Horton, Tor.
1968	Bobby Orr, Bos.	J.C. Tremblay, Mtl
1967	Harry Howell, NYR	Pierre Pilote, Chi.
1966	Jacques Laperriere, Mtl.	Pierre Pilote, Chi.
1965	Pierre Pilote, Chi.	Jacques Laperriere, Mtl.
1964	Pierre Pilote, Chi.	Tim Horton, Tor.
1963	Pierre Pilote, Chi.	Carl Brewer, Tor.
1962	Doug Harvey, NYR	Pierre Pilote, Chi.
1961	Doug Harvey, Mtl.	Marcel Pronovost, Det.
1960	Doug Harvey, Mtl.	Allan Stanley, Tor.
1959	Tom Johnson, Mtl.	Bill Gadsby, NYR
1958	Doug Harvey, Mtl.	Bill Gadsby, NYR
1957	Doug Harvey, Mtl.	Red Kelly, Det.
1956	Doug Harvey, Mtl.	Bill Gadsby, NYR
1955	Doug Harvey, Mtl.	Red Kelly, Det.
1954	Red Kelly, Det.	Doug Harvey, Mtl.

JACK ADAMS AWARD WINNERS

	Winner	Runner-up
1991	Brian Sutter, St.L.	Tom Webster, L.A.
1990	Bob Murdoch, Wpg.	Mike Milbury, Bos.
1989	Pat Burns, Mtl.	Bob McCammon, Van.
1988	Jacques Demers, Det.	Terry Crisp, Cgy.
1987	Jacques Demers, Det.	Jack Evans, Hfd.
1986	Glen Sather, Edm.	Jacques Demers, St.L.
1985	Mike Keenan, Phi.	Barry Long, Wpg.
1984	Bryan Murray, Wsh.	Scott Bowman, Buf.
1983	Orval Tessier, Chi.	
1982	Tom Watt, Wpg.	
1981	Red Berenson, St.L.	Bob Berry, L.A.
1980	Pat Quinn, Phi.	
1979	Al Arbour, NYI	Fred Shero, NYR
1978	Bobby Kromm, Det.	Don Cherry, Bos.
1977	Scott Bowman, Mtl.	Tom McVie, Wsh.
1976	Don Cherry, Bos.	
1975	Bob Pulford, L.A.	
1974	Fred Shero, Phi.	

LESTER PATRICK TROPHY WINNERS

1991	Rod Gilbert
	Mike Illitch
1990	Len Ceglarski
1989	Dan Kelly
	Lou Nanne
	*Lynn Patrick
	Bud Poile
1988	Keith Allen
	Fred Cusick
	Bob Johnson
1987	*Hobey Baker
	Frank Mathers
1986	John MacInnes
	Jack Riley
1985	Jack Butterfield
	Arthur M. Wirtz
1984	John A. Ziegler Jr.
	*Arthur Howie Ross
1983	Bill Torrey
1982	Emile P. Francis
1981	Charles M. Schulz
1980	Bobby Clarke
	Edward M. Snider
	Frederick A. Shero
	1980 U.S. Olympic Hockey Team
1979	Bobby Orr
1978	Philip A. Esposito
	Tom Fitzgerald
	William T. Tutt
	William W. Wirtz
1977	John P. Bucyk
	Murray A. Armstrong
	John Mariucci
1976	Stanley Mikita
	George A. Leader
	Bruce A. Norris
1975	Donald M. Clark
	William L. Chadwick
	Thomas N. Ivan
1974	Alex Delvecchio
	Murray Murdoch
	*Weston W. Adams, Sr.
	*Charles L. Crovat
1973	Walter L. Bush, Jr.
1972	Clarence S. Campbell
	John Kelly
	Ralph "Cooney" Weiland
	*James D. Norris
1971	William M. Jennings
	*John B. Sollenberger
	*Terrance G. Sawchuk
1970	Edward W. Shore
	*James C. V. Hendy
1969	Robert M. Hull
	*Edward J. Jeremiah
1968	Thomas F. Lockhart
	*Walter A. Brown
	*Gen. John R. Kilpatrick
1967	Gordon Howe
	*Charles F. Adams
	*James Norris, Sr.
1966	J.J. "Jack" Adams
	* awarded posthumously

PRO SET NHL PLAYER OF THE YEAR

1991	Brett Hull	St. Louis

DODGE RAM TOUGH AWARD WINNERS

1991	Brett Hull	St. Louis
1990	Brett Hull	St. Louis
1989	Mario Lemieux	Pittsburgh
1988	Joe Nieuwendyk	Calgary

BUD MAN OF THE YEAR AWARD WINNERS

1991	Kevin Dineen	Hartford
1990	Kevin Lowe	Edmonton
1989	Lanny McDonald	Calgary
1988	Bryan Trottier	NY Islanders

TRICO GOALTENDER AWARD WINNERS

1991	Ed Belfour	Chicago
1990	Patrick Roy	Montreal
1989	Patrick Roy	Montreal

ALKA-SELTZER PLUS AWARD WINNER

1991	Marty McSorley	Los Angeles
	Theoren Fleury	Calgary
1990	Paul Cavallini	St. Louis

BILL MASTERTON TROPHY WINNERS

1991	Dave Taylor	Los Angeles
1990	Gord Kluzak	Boston
1989	Tim Kerr	Philadelphia
1988	Bob Bourne	Los Angeles
1987	Doug Jarvis	Hartford
1986	Charlie Simmer	Boston
1985	Anders Hedberg	NY Rangers
1984	Brad Park	Detroit
1983	Lanny McDonald	Calgary
1982	Glenn Resch	Colorado
1981	Blake Dunlop	St. Louis
1980	Al MacAdam	Minnesota
1979	Serge Savard	Montreal
1978	Butch Goring	Los Angeles
1977	Ed Westfall	NY Islanders
1976	Rod Gilbert	NY Rangers
1975	Don Luce	Buffalo
1974	Henri Richard	Montreal
1973	Lowell MacDonald	Pittsburgh
1972	Bobby Clarke	Philadelphia
1971	Jean Ratelle	NY Rangers
1970	Pit Martin	Chicago
1969	Ted Hampson	Oakland
1968	Claude Provost	Montreal

WILLIAM M. JENNINGS TROPHY WINNERS

	Winner	Runner-up
1991	Ed Belfour, Chi.	Patrick Roy, Mtl.
1990	Andy Moog, Bos.	Patrick Roy, Mtl.
	Rejean Lemelin	Brian Hayward
1989	Patrick Roy, Mtl.	Mike Vernon, Cgy.
	Brian Hayward	Rick Wamsley
1988	Patrick Roy, Mtl.	Clint Malarchuk,
	Brian Hayward	Wsh.
		Pete Peeters
1987	Patrick Roy, Mtl.	Ron Hextall, Phi.
	Brian Hayward	
1986	Bob Froese, Phi.	Al Jensen, Wsh.
	Darren Jensen	Pete Peeters
1985	Tom Barrasso, Buf.	Pat Riggin, Wsh.
	Bob Sauve	
1984	Al Jensen, Wsh.	Tom Barrasso,
	Pat Riggin	Buf.
		Bob Sauve
1983	Roland Melanson, NYI	Pete Peeters, Bos.
	Bill Smith	
1982	Rick Wamsley, Mtl.	Billy Smith, NYI
	Denis Herron	Roland Melanson

Ken Dryden, the Conn Smythe Trophy winner in 1971.

NHL Amateur and Entry Draft
History

Year	Site	Date	Total Players Drafted
1963	Queen Elizabeth Hotel	June 5	21
1964	Queen Elizabeth Hotel	June 11	24
1965	Queen Elizabeth Hotel	April 27	11
1966	Mount Royal Hotel	April 25	24
1967	Queen Elizabeth Hotel	June 7	18
1968	Queen Elizabeth Hotel	June 13	24
1969	Queen Elizabeth Hotel	June 12	84
1970	Queen Elizabeth Hotel	June 11	115
1971	Queen Elizabeth Hotel	June 10	117
1972	Queen Elizabeth Hotel	June 8	152
1973	Mount Royal Hotel	May 15	168
1974	NHL Montreal Office	May 28	247
1975	NHL Montreal Office	June 3	217
1976	NHL Montreal Office	June 1	135
1977	NHL Montreal Office	June 14	185
1978	Queen Elizabeth Hotel	June 15	234
1979	Queen Elizabeth Hotel	August 9	126
1980	Montreal Forum	June 11	210
1981	Montreal Forum	June 10	211
1982	Montreal Forum	June 9	252
1983	Montreal Forum	June 8	242
1984	Montreal Forum	June 9	250
1985	Toronto Convention Centre	June 15	252
1986	Montreal Forum	June 21	252
1987	Joe Louis Sports Arena	June 13	252
1988	Montreal Forum	June 11	252
1989	Metropolitan Sports Center	June 17	252
1990	B. C. Place	June 16	250
1991	Memorial Auditorium	June 9	264

* The NHL Amateur Draft became the NHL Entry Draft in 1979

Wendel Clark was chosen first overall by Toronto in the 1985 Entry Draft.

First Selections

Year	Player	Pos	Drafted By	Drafted From	Age
1969	Rejean Houle	LW	Montreal	Jr. Canadiens	19.8
1970	Gilbert Perreault	C	Buffalo	Jr. Canadiens	19.7
1971	Guy Lafleur	RW	Montreal	Quebec Remparts	19.9
1972	Billy Harris	RW	NY Islanders	Toronto Marlboros	20.4
1973	Denis Potvin	D	NY Islanders	Ottawa 67's	19.7
1974	Greg Joly	D	Washington	Regina Pats	20.0
1975	Mel Bridgman	C	Philadelphia	Victoria Cougars	20.1
1976	Rick Green	D	Washington	London Knights	20.3
1977	Dale McCourt	C	Detroit	St. Catharines Fincups	20.4
1978	Bobby Smith	C	Minnesota	Ottawa 67's	20.4
1979	Bob Ramage	D	Colorado	London Knights	20.5
1980	Doug Wickenheiser	C	Montreal	Regina Pats	19.2
1981	Dale Hawerchuk	C	Winnipeg	Cornwall Royals	18.2
1982	Gord Kluzak	D	Boston	Nanaimo Islanders	18.3
1983	Brian Lawton	C	Minnesota	Mount St. Charles HS	18.11
1984	Mario Lemieux	C	Pittsburgh	Laval Voisins	18.8
1985	Wendel Clark	LW/D	Toronto	Saskatoon Blades	18.7
1986	Joe Murphy	C	Detroit	Michigan State	18.8
1987	Pierre Turgeon	C	Buffalo	Granby Bisons	17.10
1988	Mike Modano	C	Minnesota	Prince Albert Raiders	18.0
1989	Mats Sundin	RW	Quebec	Nacka (Sweden)	18.4
1990	Owen Nolan	RW	Quebec	Cornwall Royals	18.4
1991	Eric Lindros	C	Quebec	Oshawa Generals	18.3

Draft Summary

Following is a summary of the number of players drafted from the Ontario Hockey League (OHL), Western Hockey League (WHL), Quebec Major Junior Hockey League (QMJHL), United States Colleges, United States High Schools, European Leagues and other Leagues throughout North America since 1969:

	OHL	WHL	QMJHL	US Coll.	US HS	International	Other
1969	36	20	11	7	0	1	9
1970	51	22	13	16	0	0	13
1971	41	28	13	22	0	0	13
1972	46	44	30	21	0	0	11
1973	56	49	24	25	0	0	14
1974	69	66	40	41	0	6	25
1975	45	54	28	59	0	6	25
1976	47	33	18	26	0	8	3
1977	42	44	40	49	0	5	5
1978	59	48	22	73	0	15	17
1979	48	37	19	15	0	6	1
1980	73	41	24	42	7	13	10
1981	59	37	28	21	17	32	17
1982	60	55	17	20	47	35	18
1983	57	41	24	14	35	34	37
1984	55	37	16	22	44	40	36
1985	59	48	15	20	48	30	32
1986	66	32	22	22	40	28	42
1987	32	36	17	40	69	38	20
1988	32	30	22	48	56	39	25
1989	39	44	16	48	47	38	20
1990	39	33	14	38	57	53	16
1991	43	40	25	43	37	55	21
Total	1154	919	498	732	503	482	433

Ontario Hockey League

Club	'69	'70	'71	'72	'73	'74	'75	'76	'77	'78	'79	'80	'81	'82	'83	'84	'85	'86	'87	'88	'89	'90	'91	Total
Peterborough	5	5	4	5	9	4	3	1	4	6	9	10	3	5	7	3	9	2	5	2	2	4	3	110
Kitchener	1	6	2	8	4	13	3	1	3	4	4	4	5	5	8	4	6	3	2	1	7	5	3	102
Oshawa	5	4	3	5	5	7	6	6	1	3	2	9	5	5	6	6	6	3	2	4	2	4		102
Toronto	3	7	6	5	6	8	4	4	7	5	4	10	2	6	4	4	3	4	1	2	2	–		97
London	4	9	1	5	6	6	3	5	4	3	6	2	5	5	3	7	1	3	2	6	3	3	1	93
Ottawa	2	4	3	4	6	5	6	5	5	5	3	8	4	9	2	2	3	3	2	1	–	5	5	92
S.S. Marie	–	–	–	4	5	2	5	1	5	3	3	8	1	6	4	5	7	1	2	3	1	2		68
Sudbury	–	–	–	6	6	4	5	4	4	3	7	2	4	–	2	5	3	1	–	1	2	8		67
Hamilton	2	3	5	4	6	4	7	3	–	8	1	–	–	–	–	3	6	4	4	–	–	2		62
Kingston	–	–	–	–	4	4	6	4	9	2	8	5	2	1	3	3	4	1	1	–	2	2		61
Niagara Falls	4	2	1	4	–	–	–	2	3	5	8	6	6	–	–	–	–	–	–	–	4	4	4	53
St. Catharines	5	5	8	5	4	7	3	4	6	–	–	–	–	–	–	–	–	–	–	–	–	–	–	47
Windsor	–	–	–	–	2	1	4	2	3	5	3	2	2	3	7	–	5	2	1	–				42
Cornwall	–	–	–	–	–	–	–	–	–	–	7	4	3	2	2	3	3	2	3	3				32
Brantford	–	–	–	–	–	–	–	3	8	5	2	7	2	–	–	–								27
North Bay	–	–	–	–	–	–	–	–	–	4	4	3	3	3	1	4	2							25
Belleville	–	–	–	–	–	–	–	–	–	3	4	4	5	2	–	4	2	1						24
Guelph	–	–	–	–	–	–	–	–	–	1	5	3	8	2	–	4	–	–						23
Montreal	5	6	8	1	–	–	–	–	–	–	–	–	–	–	–	–	–	–	–					20
Owen Sound	–	–	–	–	–	–	–	–	–	–	–	–	–	–	–	–	–	1	1					2
Detroit	–	–	–	–	–	–	–	–	–	–	–	–	–	–	–	–	–	–	2					2

Year	Total Ontario Drafted	Total Players Drafted	Ontario %
1969	36	84	42.9
1970	51	115	44.3
1971	41	117	35.0
1972	46	152	30.3
1973	56	168	33.3
1974	69	247	27.9
1975	45	217	20.7
1976	47	135	34.8
1977	42	185	22.7
1978	59	234	25.2
1979	48	126	38.1
1980	73	210	34.8
1981	59	211	28.0
1982	60	252	23.8
1983	57	242	23.6
1984	55	250	22.0
1985	59	252	23.4
1986	66	252	26.2
1987	32	252	12.7
1988	32	252	12.7
1989	39	252	15.5
1990	39	250	15.6
1991	43	264	16.3
Total	**1154**	**4719**	**24.5**

Western Hockey League

Club	'69	'70	'71	'72	'73	'74	'75	'76	'77	'78	'79	'80	'81	'82	'83	'84	'85	'86	'87	'88	'89	'90	'91	Total
Regina	–	–	5	5	1	8	5	3	1	4	1	3	5	6	8	4	4	3	2	–	5	1	–	74
Saskatoon	1	–	1	3	8	4	5	3	4	1	2	2	3	5	1	5	4	4	3	2	2			71
Portland	–	–	–	–	4	8	7	8	6	7	7	5	2	4	3	1	4	1	1					68
Calgary	3	5	2	7	4	8	4	4	4	3	–	2	5	4	3	3	3	2	–	–	–	–		66
Victoria	–	–	–	2	2	5	7	4	3	3	1	8	6	2	3	4	2	1	2	4	4	2	–	65
Medicine Hat	–	–	4	6	4	5	3	5	4	–	4	2	1	2	1	6	2	5	1	4	1	3		63
New Westm'r	–	–	–	6	8	7	9	5	8	6	5	1	–	–	2	1	1	2	1	–	–	–		62
Brandon	–	3	1	5	2	7	4	–	3	1	10	5	2	2	1	3	2	1	3	3	–	1	1	60
Kamloops	–	–	–	–	4	4	4	4	–	–	2	4	4	4	4	3	1	5	4	6				53
Lethbridge	–	–	–	–	–	2	3	5	4	1	4	7	2	1	5	1	–	3	3	4	7			52
Flin Flon	4	4	5	2	4	7	4	3	1	5	–	–	–	–	–	–	–							39
Seattle	–	–	–	–	–	4	2	3	–	6	–	1	3	1	2	4	2	6	3					37
Prince Albert	–	–	–	–	–	–	–	–	4	2	2	6	6	1	3	3	4	6						37
Winnipeg	3	2	4	2	5	4	4	–	4	–	–	1	4	1	–									34
Edmonton	4	4	5	6	6	2	3	2	–	2	–													34
Swift Current	1	–	1	3	6	–	–	–	–	–	–	–	5	2	2	2	1							23
Moose Jaw	–	–	–	–	–	–	–	–	–	–	4	1	3	–	3	1	2							14
Billings	–	–	–	–	–	4	3	4	2	–	–													13
Estevan	4	4	4	–	–	–	–																	12
Kelowna	–	–	–	–	–	–	–	–	2	4	5	–												11
Spokane	–	–	–	–	–	–	–	–	–	–	1	3	2	1	5									12
Tri-Cities	–	–	–	–	–	–	–	–	–	–	–	4	3	3										10
Nanaimo	–	–	–	–	–	–	5	1	–	–														6
Vancouver	–	–	2	–	–	–	–	–	–															2

Year	Total Western Drafted	Total Players Drafted	Western %
1969	20	84	23.8
1970	22	115	19.1
1971	28	117	23.9
1972	44	152	28.9
1973	49	168	29.2
1974	66	247	26.7
1975	54	217	24.9
1976	33	135	24.4
1977	44	185	23.8
1978	48	234	20.5
1979	37	126	29.4
1980	41	210	19.5
1981	37	211	17.5
1982	55	252	21.8
1983	41	242	16.9
1984	37	250	14.8
1985	48	252	19.0
1986	32	252	12.7
1987	36	252	14.3
1988	30	252	11.9
1989	44	252	17.5
1990	33	250	13.2
1991	40	264	15.2
Total	**919**	**4719**	**19.5**

Quebec Major Junior Hockey League

Club	'69	'70	'71	'72	'73	'74	'75	'76	'77	'78	'79	'80	'81	'82	'83	'84	'85	'86	'87	'88	'89	'90	'91	Total
Quebec	1	1	2	4	6	1	3	7	1	3	2	2	1	2	2	3	–	–	–	–	–			47
Shawinigan	3	2	1	6	1	5	3	–	3	–	2	2	5	5	–	2	1	–	2	–	2			47
Trois Rivieres	–	1	2	2	2	3	2	6	3	2	2	2	1	3	–	3	–	1	3	3	1	2		46
Cornwall	2	1	2	6	4	8	1	3	1	6	1	5	5	–	–	–	–	–	–					45
Sherbrooke	–	–	2	2	4	3	7	5	6	3	4	1	5	2	–	–	–	–						44
Laval	–	–	–	1	–	2	1	1	4	2	1	–	2	1	2	–	5	3	1	3	3	4		36
Hull	–	–	–	–	–	3	2	2	3	–	3	1	–	3	1	–	4	3	2	2	3	3		35
Montreal	–	–	–	4	4	8	1	3	2	4	3	–	3	–	–									32
Chicoutimi	–	–	–	–	1	–	5	1	1	3	6	1	3	–	3	1	2	2	1	1	–			31
Drummondville	2	4	1	2	7	–	–	–	–	–	–	1	2	2	2	4	1	–	4					30
Sorel	2	3	1	3	1	8	1	1	3	–	5	–	–	–	–									28
Verdun	–	1	1	2	–	–	1	3	3	–	3	3	–	3	0	3	1	–	–					24
Granby	–	–	–	–	–	–	–	2	1	3	2	2	4	–	2	–	2	–						18
Longueuil	–	–	–	–	–	–	–	1	2	1	2	1	–	2	3									12
St. Jean	–	–	–	–	–	–	2	–	1	1	0	3	1	–	3									11
Victoriaville	–	–	–	–	–	–	–	–	–	4	–	1	–											5
St. Hyacinthe	–	–	–	–	–	–	–	–	–	–	3	1												4
St. Jerome	1	–	1	–	–	–	–	–	–	–	–													2
Beauport	–	–	–	–	–	–	–	–	–	–	1													1

Year	Total Quebec Drafted	Total Players Drafted	Quebec %
1969	11	84	13.1
1970	13	115	11.3
1971	13	117	11.1
1972	30	152	19.7
1973	24	168	14.3
1974	40	247	16.2
1975	28	217	12.9
1976	18	135	13.3
1977	40	185	21.6
1978	22	234	9.4
1979	19	126	15.1
1980	24	210	11.4
1981	28	211	13.3
1982	17	252	6.7
1983	24	242	9.9
1984	16	250	6.4
1985	15	252	5.9
1986	22	252	8.7
1987	17	252	6.7
1988	22	252	8.7
1989	16	252	6.3
1990	14	250	5.6
1991	25	264	9.5
Total	**498**	**4719**	**10.6**

International

Country	'69	'70	'71	'72	'73	'74	'75	'76	'77	'78	'79	'80	'81	'82	'83	'84	'85	'86	'87	'88	'89	'90	'91	Total
Sweden	–	–	–	–	–	5	2	5	2	8	5	9	13	14	10	14	15	9	15	14	9	8	11	168
Czechoslovakia	–	–	–	–	–	–	–	–	–	1	1	–	4	13	9	13	8	6	11	5	8	21	9	109
Finland	1	–	–	–	–	1	3	2	3	2	–	4	13	5	9	10	4	10	6	7	3	8	6	97
Soviet Union	–	–	–	–	–	–	–	–	1	–	2	–	–	3	5	1	2	1	2	11	18	14	25	85
Germany	–	–	–	–	–	–	–	–	–	–	2	–	–	2	1	2	1	–	1	2	–	–	1	12
Norway	–	–	–	–	–	–	–	–	–	–	–	–	–	–	–	–	–	–	2	–	–	2	1	5
Denmark	–	–	–	–	–	–	–	–	–	–	–	–	–	–	–	–	–	1	1	–	–	–	–	2
Switzerland	–	–	–	–	–	1	–	–	–	–	–	–	–	–	–	–	–	–	–	–	–	–	1	2
Scotland	–	–	–	–	–	–	–	–	–	–	–	–	–	–	–	–	–	–	–	–	–	–	1	1
Poland	–	–	–	–	–	–	–	–	–	–	–	–	–	–	–	–	–	–	–	–	–	1	–	1

Year	Total International Drafted	Total Players Drafted	International %
1969	1	84	1.2
1970	0	115	0
1971	0	117	0
1972	0	152	0
1973	0	168	0
1974	6	247	2.4
1975	6	217	2.8
1976	8	135	5.9
1977	5	185	2.7
1978	15	234	6.4
1979	6	126	4.8
1980	13	210	6.2
1981	32	211	15.2
1982	35	252	13.9
1983	34	242	14.0
1984	40	250	17.6
1985	30	252	12.0
1986	28	252	11.1
1987	38	252	15.1
1988	39	252	15.5
1989	38	252	15.1
1990	53	250	21.2
1991	55	264	20.8
Total	**483**	**4719**	**10.2**

United States Colleges

Club	'69	'70	'71	'72	'73	'74	'75	'76	'77	'78	'79	'80	'81	'82	'83	'84	'85	'86	'87	'88	'89	'90	'91	Total
Minnesota	1	3	2	–	–	9	4	4	5	5	2	3	1	1	1	–	2	1	1	1	–	–	–	46
Michigan Tech	–	–	3	1	2	5	4	4	1	2	1	4	–	1	–	2	2	2	1	1	2	1	2	41
Michigan	1	–	–	–	2	2	3	3	1	6	–	4	–	–	–	1	1	–	1	2	3	5	4	39
Wisconsin	–	1	2	4	5	4	4	2	3	–	1	–	3	2	–	1	1	–	1	–	1	–	1	36
Denver	1	3	2	4	2	3	1	2	2	2	2	1	–	1	–	1	2	4	1	1	–	–	–	35
Boston U.	–	4	–	–	1	1	1	1	1	4	5	1	–	1	–	1	1	2	2	3	1	2	1	33
North Dakota	2	3	3	1	4	2	1	–	1	2	3	3	1	–	1	–	–	–	2	1	1	–	–	31
Michigan State	–	–	–	1	–	1	1	1	1	–	–	2	–	2	–	2	–	1	1	4	4	5	4	30
Providence	–	–	–	–	–	3	2	3	4	–	5	4	1	2	–	1	1	–	–	–	–	1	–	27
New Hampshire	–	–	–	1	1	3	6	–	4	1	1	2	1	1	1	2	–	–	1	–	–	–	–	25
Clarkson	–	2	2	1	–	2	–	2	2	1	1	1	1	1	–	1	1	1	3	2	–	–	–	25
Cornell	–	–	2	1	1	–	1	1	1	–	1	1	1	–	1	2	–	1	2	5	2	–	–	23
Colorado	2	1	–	–	1	3	1	2	2	–	–	–	3	–	1	–	1	–	2	–	–	–	–	20
Bowling Green	–	–	–	–	1	3	2	1	1	1	–	1	–	–	–	3	2	1	3	–	–	–	–	20
Notre Dame	–	2	3	–	7	2	–	3	1	–	–	–	–	–	–	–	–	–	–	–	–	–	–	19
Lake Superior	–	–	–	1	1	1	–	3	–	–	–	1	–	3	–	3	2	3	1	–	–	–	–	19
St. Lawrence	–	–	–	–	1	–	1	4	–	–	3	–	1	1	1	1	1	1	2	–	–	–	–	18
RPI	–	–	–	1	–	–	1	3	–	1	2	1	1	–	1	–	2	2	–	3	–	–	–	18
W. Michigan	–	–	–	–	–	–	2	–	2	–	2	2	2	1	1	1	1	4	–	–	–	–	–	18
Boston College	–	1	–	–	1	1	–	5	–	2	1	1	–	–	1	2	–	2	–	–	–	–	–	17
Harvard	–	2	–	–	2	–	2	2	–	–	1	1	–	2	–	1	2	–	–	–	–	–	–	16
Northern Mich.	–	–	–	–	–	4	–	1	2	1	–	–	–	4	1	2	–	1	–	–	–	–	–	16
Vermont	–	–	–	1	–	4	–	1	1	–	1	1	–	1	1	2	–	1	–	–	–	–	–	15
Minn.-Duluth	–	–	2	1	–	–	1	1	–	1	–	–	–	–	2	1	2	1	–	–	–	–	–	12
Brown	–	–	1	2	1	–	3	2	–	–	–	–	–	–	–	–	1	–	–	–	–	–	–	11
Miami of Ohio	–	–	–	–	–	–	–	–	–	–	–	–	–	1	2	4	2	–	2	–	–	–	–	11
Ohio State	–	–	–	–	–	–	–	2	1	–	1	–	–	2	2	–	1	1	–	–	–	–	–	10
Colgate	–	–	–	–	1	–	2	1	–	–	1	1	2	2	–	–	–	–	–	–	–	–	–	10
Yale	–	1	–	1	–	2	1	–	1	2	1	–	–	–	–	–	–	–	–	–	–	–	–	9
Maine	–	–	–	–	–	–	–	1	1	–	1	3	2	1	–	–	–	–	–	–	–	–	–	9
Northeastern	–	1	–	–	1	1	–	1	1	1	–	1	1	–	–	–	–	–	–	–	–	–	–	8
Princeton	–	1	–	1	–	1	1	–	1	–	1	–	–	–	–	–	–	–	–	–	–	–	–	7
Ferris State	–	–	–	–	–	–	–	–	–	–	–	–	–	2	1	1	1	2	–	–	–	–	–	7
St. Louis	–	–	–	–	1	2	1	2	–	–	–	–	–	–	–	–	–	–	–	–	–	–	–	6
U. of Ill.-Chi.	–	–	–	–	–	–	–	–	–	–	–	–	1	–	2	1	2	–	–	–	–	–	–	6
Pennsylvania	–	–	1	2	1	–	–	–	–	–	–	–	–	–	–	–	–	–	–	–	–	–	–	5
Dartmouth	–	–	1	–	1	–	1	1	–	–	–	–	–	–	–	–	–	–	–	–	–	–	–	4
Union College	–	–	–	–	–	–	–	4	–	–	–	–	–	–	–	–	–	–	–	–	–	–	–	4
Lowell	–	–	–	–	–	–	1	1	–	–	1	–	–	–	–	1	–	–	–	–	–	–	–	4
Merrimack	–	–	–	–	–	–	1	–	–	–	–	–	–	1	–	1	1	–	–	–	–	–	–	4
Babson College	–	–	–	–	–	–	–	–	–	–	–	–	–	–	–	1	1	1	–	–	–	–	–	3
Alaska-Anchorage	–	–	–	–	–	–	–	–	–	–	–	–	–	–	–	–	–	–	2	1	–	–	–	3
Alaska-Fairbanks	–	–	–	–	–	–	–	–	–	–	–	–	–	–	–	–	–	–	–	–	1	1	–	2
Salem State	–	–	–	–	–	1	–	–	–	–	–	–	–	–	–	–	–	–	–	–	–	–	–	1
Bemidji State	–	–	1	–	–	–	–	–	–	–	–	–	–	–	–	–	–	–	–	–	–	–	–	1
San Diego U.	–	–	–	–	–	–	–	–	–	–	–	–	–	–	–	–	–	1	–	–	–	–	–	1
Greenway	–	–	–	–	–	–	–	–	–	–	–	–	–	–	–	–	–	–	1	–	–	–	–	1
St. Anselen College	–	–	–	–	–	–	–	–	–	–	–	–	–	–	–	–	–	–	1	–	–	–	–	1
Hamilton College	–	–	–	–	–	–	–	–	–	–	–	–	–	–	–	–	–	–	1	–	–	–	–	1
St. Thomas	–	–	–	–	–	–	–	–	–	–	–	–	–	–	–	–	–	–	–	–	1	–	–	1
St. Cloud State	–	–	–	–	–	–	–	–	–	–	–	–	–	–	–	–	–	–	–	–	1	–	–	1
Amer. Int'l College	–	–	–	–	–	–	–	–	–	–	–	–	–	–	–	–	–	–	–	–	1	–	–	1

Year	Total College Drafted	Total Players Drafted	College %
1969	7	84	8.3
1970	16	115	13.9
1971	22	117	18.8
1972	21	152	13.8
1973	25	168	14.9
1974	41	247	16.6
1975	59	217	26.7
1976	26	135	19.3
1977	49	185	26.5
1978	73	234	31.2
1979	15	126	11.9
1980	42	210	20.0
1981	21	211	10.0
1982	20	252	7.9
1983	14	242	5.8
1984	22	250	8.8
1985	20	252	7.9
1986	22	252	8.7
1987	40	252	15.9
1988	48	252	19.0
1989	48	252	19.0
1990	38	250	15.2
1991	43	264	16.3
Total	**732**	**4719**	**15.5**

1991 Entry Draft Analysis

Country of Origin

Country	Players Drafted
Canada	138
United States	68
Soviet Union	25
Sweden	12
Czechoslovakia	10
Finland	6
Germany	1
Norway	1
Poland	1
United Kingdom	1

Position

Position	Players Drafted
Defense	89
Center	63
Right Wing	43
Left Wing	39
Goaltender	29
unstated	1

Birth Year

Year	Players Drafted
1972	94
1971	92
1973	60
unstated	5
1966	4
1969	3
1968	2
1970	2
1964	1
1965	1

1991 Dispersal Draft

The following players were selected by the San Jose Sharks in the 1991 Dispersal Draft.

Player	Position	1990-91 Club	League
Shane Churla	Right Wing	Minnesota	NHL
Brian Hayward	Goaltender	Minnesota	NHL
Neil Wilkinson	Defense	Minnesota	NHL
Rob Zettler	Defense	Minnesota	NHL
Ed Courtenay	Right Wing	Kalamazoo	IHL
Kevin Evans	Left Wing	Kalamazoo	IHL
Link Gaetz	Defense	Kalamazoo	IHL
Dan Keczmer	Defense	Kalamazoo	IHL
Dean Kolstad	Defense	Kalamazoo	IHL
Peter Lappin	Right Wing	Kalamazoo	IHL
Pat MacLeod	Defense	Kalamazoo	IHL
Mike McHugh	Left Wing	Kalamazoo	IHL
Jarmo Myllys	Goaltender	Kalamazoo	IHL
J.F. Quintin	Left Wing	Kalamazoo	IHL
Scott Cashman	Goaltender	Boston University	H.E.
Murray Garbutt	Center	Spokane	WHL
Rob Gaudreau	Right Wing	Providence College	H.E.
Artur Irbe	Goaltender	Dynamo Riga	USSR
Shaun Kane	Defense	Providence College	H.E.
Larry Olimb	Defense	U. of Minnesota	WCHA
Tom Pederson	Defense	U. of Minnesota	WCHA
Bryan Schoen	Goaltender	Denver University	WCHA
John Weisbrod	Center	Harvard	ECAC
Doug Zmolek	Defense	U.of Minnesota	WCHA

San Jose also obtained Minnesota's 2nd round choice (30th overall) in 1991 Entry Draft, and Minnesota's 1st round choice in 1992 Entry Draft.

1991 Expansion Draft

The San Jose Sharks and Minnesota North Stars each selected 10 players in the 1991 Expansion Draft, conducted via telephone conference call on May 30, 1991. Following is a list of the players chosen in order of selection:

Pick	Claimed by	Claimed from	Player	Position
1	San Jose	NY Islanders	Jeff Hackett	G
2	Minnesota	Toronto	Rob Ramage	D
3	San Jose	Montreal	Jayson More	D
4	Minnesota	Hartford	David Babych	D
5	San Jose	Calgary	Rick Lessard	D
6	Minnesota	Boston	Allen Pedersen	D
7	San Jose	Chicago	Bob McGill	D
8	Minnesota	Edmonton	Charlie Huddy	D
9	San Jose	Philadelphia	Tim Kerr	C/RW
10	Minnesota	NY Rangers	Kelly Kisio	C
11	San Jose	New Jersey	Jeff Madill	RW
12	Minnesota	Pittsburgh	Randy Gilhen	C
13	San Jose	St. Louis	David Bruce	C/RW
14	Minnesota	Washington	Rob Murray	C
15	San Jose	Buffalo	Greg Paslawski	RW
16	Minnesota	Winnipeg	Tyler Larter	C
17	San Jose	Detroit	Bengt Gustafsson	C
18	Minnesota	Los Angeles	Jim Thomson	RW
19	San Jose	Vancouver	Craig Coxe	C
20	Minnesota	Quebec	Guy Lafleur	RW

 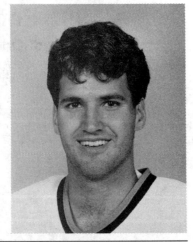

Shane Churla, left, was the first player chosen by the San Jose Sharks in the 1991 Dispersal Draft. Goaltender Jeff Hackett, right, was the Sharks' first choice in the 1991 Expansion Draft.

1991 Entry Draft

Transferred draft choice notation:
Example: S.J.-Det. represents a draft choice transferred from San Jose to Detroit.

Pick	Player	Claimed By	Amateur Club	Position
ROUND # 1				
1	LINDROS, Eric	Que.	Oshawa	C
2	FALLOON, Pat	S.J.	Spokane	RW
3	NIEDERMAYER, Scott	Tor.-N.J.	Kamloops	D
4	LACHANCE, Scott	NYI	Boston University	D
5	WARD, Aaron	Wpg.	Michigan	D
6	FORSBERG, Peter	Phi.	Modo	C
7	STOJANOV, Alex	Van.	Hamilton	RW
8	MATVICHUK, Richard	Min.	Saskatoon	D
9	POULIN, Patrick	Hfd.	St.-Hyacinthe	LW
10	LAPOINTE, Martin	Det.	Laval	RW
11	ROLSTON, Brian	N.J.	Detroit Comp. Jr. A	C
12	WRIGHT, Tyler	Edm.	Swift Current	C
13	BOUCHER, Philippe	Buf.	Granby	D
14	PEAKE, Pat	Wsh.	Detroit	C
15	KOVALEV, Alexei	NYR	Dynamo Moscow	RW
16	NASLUND, Markus	Pit.	Modo	RW
17	BILODEAU, Brent	Mtl.	Seattle	D
18	MURRAY, Glen	Bos.	Sudbury	RW
19	SUNDBLAD, Niklas	Cgy.	AIK	RW
20	RUCINSKY, Martin	L.A.-Edm.	Litvinov	LW
21	HALVERSON, Trevor	St. L.-Wsh.	North Bay	LW
22	McAMMOND, Dean	Chi.	Prince Albert	C
ROUND # 2				
23	WHITNEY, Ray	S.J.	Spokane	C
24	CORBET, Rene	Que.	Drummondville	LW
25	LAVIGNE, Eric	Tor.-Que.-Wsh.	Hull	D
26	PALFFY, Zigmund	NYI	Nitra	LW
27	STAIOS, Steve	Wpg.-St. L.	Niagara Falls	D
28	CAMPBELL, Jim	Phi.-Mtl.	Northwood Prep	C
29	CULLIMORE, Jassen	Van.	Peterborough	D
30	OZOLNICH, Sandis	Min.-S.J.	Dynamo Riga	D
31	HAMRLIK, Martin	Hfd.	TJ Zlin	D
32	PUSHOR, Jamie	Det.	Lethbridge	D
33	HEXTALL, Donevan	N.J.	Prince Albert	LW
34	VERNER, Andrew	Edm.	Peterborough	G
35	DAWE, Jason	Buf.	Peterborough	LW
36	NELSON, Jeff	Wsh.	Prince Albert	C
37	WERENKA, Darcy	NYR	Lethbridge	D
38	FITZGERALD, Rusty	Pit.	Duluth East H.S.	C
39	POMICHTER, Michael	Mtl.-Chi.	Springfield Jr. B	C
40	STUMPEL, Jozef	Bos.	Nitra	RW
41	GROLEAU, Francois	Cgy.	Shawinigan	D
42	LEVEQUE, Guy	L.A.	Cornwall	C
43	DARBY, Craig	St. L.-Mtl.	Albany Academy	C
44	MATTHEWS, Jamie	Chi.	Sudbury	C
ROUND # 3				
45	WOOD, Dody	S.J.	Seattle	C
46	BRENNAN, Richard	Que.	Tabor Academy	D
47	PERREAULT, Yanic	Tor.	Trois-Rivieres	C
48	McLENNAN, Jamie	NYI	Lethbridge	G
49	FILIMONOV, Dimitri	Wpg.	Dynamo Moscow	D
50	DUPRE, Yanic	Phi.	Drummondville	LW
51	PRONGER, Sean	Van.	Bowling Green	C
52	McCARTHY, Sandy	Min.-Cgy.	Laval	RW
53	HALL, Todd	Hfd.	Hamden H.S.	D
54	OSGOOD, Chris	Det.	Medicine Hat	G
55	LINDQUIST, Fredrik	N.J.	Djurgarden	C
56	BREEN, George	Edm.	Cushing Academy	RW
57	YOUNG, Jason	Buf.	Sudbury	LW
58	KONOWALCHUK, Steve	Wsh.	Portland	C
59	NYLANDER, Mikael	NYR-Hfd.	Huddinge	C
60	PEACOCK, Shane	Pit.	Lethbridge	D
61	SARAULT, Yves	Mtl.	St-Jean	LW
62	COUSINEAU, Marcel	Bos.	Beauport	G
63	CARUSO, Brian	Cgy.	U. Minn.-Duluth	LW
64	REEVES, Kyle	L.A.-St. L.	Tri-City	RW
65	LAFAYETTE, Nathan	St. L.	Cornwall	C
66	HOUSE, Bobby	Chi.	Brandon	RW
ROUND # 4				
67	TOPOROWSKI, Kerry	S.J.	Spokane	D
68	KARPA, Dave	Que.	Ferris State	D
69	CHITARONI, Terry	Tor.	Sudbury	C
70	HNILICKA, Milan	NYI	Poldi Kladno	G
71	KRAVCHUK, Igor	Wpg.-Chi.	CSKA	D
72	AMBROZIAK, Peter	Phi.-Buf.	Ottawa	LW
73	VUJTEK, Vladimir	Van.-Mtl.	Tri-City	LW
74	TORCHIA, Mike	Min.	Kitchener	G
75	STORM, Jim	Hfd.	Michigan Tech	LW
76	KNUBLE, Michael	Det.	Kalamazoo Jr. A	RW
77	WILLNER, Bradley	N.J.	Richfield H.S.	D
78	NOBILI, Mario	Edm.	Longueuil	LW
79	REDMOND, Keith	Buf.-L.A.	Bowling Green	LW
80	MORRISON, Justin	Wsh.	Kingston	C
81	ZHITNIK, Alexei	NYR-Min.-L.A.	Sokol Kiev	D
82	TAMMINEN, Joe	Pit.	Virginia H.S.	C
83	LAPOINTE, Sylvain	Mtl.	Clarkson University	D
84	TILEY, Brad	Bos.	Sault-Ste-Marie	D
85	MAGNUSSON, Steven	Cgy.	Anoka H.S.	C
86	BRIMANIS, Aris	L.A.-Phi.	Bowling Green	D
87	REID, Grayden	St. L.	Owen Sound	C
88	BOYER, Zac	Chi.	Kamloops	RW

Pick	Player	Claimed By	Amateur Club	Position
ROUND # 5				
89	RYDER, Dan	S.J.	Sudbury	G
90	LABRECQUE, Patrick	Que.	St-Jean	G
91	YLONEN, Juha	Tor.-Wpg.	Espoo	C
92	JUNKER, Steve	NYI	Spokane	LW
93	HAGGERTY, Ryan	Wpg.-Edm.	Westminster H.S.	C
94	DEGRACE, Yanick	Phi.	Trois-Rivieres	G
95	KESA, Danny	Van.	Prince Albert	RW
96	MACHANIC, Corey	Min.-NYR	U. of Vermont	D
97	KENNEDY, Mike	Hfd.-Min.	University of B.C.	LW
98	MOTKOV, Dimitri	Det.	CSKA	D
99	KAMINSKY, Jan	N.J.-Wpg.	Dynamo Moscow	LW
100	LAYZELL, Brad	Edm.-Mtl.	R.P.I.	D
101	SHIELDS, Steve	Buf.	Michigan	G
102	KUDASHOV, Alexei	Wsh.-Tor.	Soviet Wings	C
103	LINDSAY, Bill	NYR-Que.	Tri-City	LW
104	MELANSON, Robert	Pit.	Hull	D
105	PRPIC, Tony	Mtl.	Culver Academy	RW
106	CZERKAWSKI, Marivsz	Bos.	GKS Tychy	RW
107	BUTLER, Jerome	Cgy.	Roseau	G
108	JAKS, Pauli	L.A.	Ambri Piotta	G
109	CALLINAN, Jeff	St. L.	Minnetonka H.S.	G
110	BALKOVEC, Maco	Chi.	Merritt T-II Jr. A	D
ROUND # 6				
111	NILSSON, Fredrik	S.J.	Vasteras	C
112	ST. JACQUES, Kevin	Que.-Chi.	Lethbridge	LW
113	PERRY, Jeff	Tor.	Owen Sound	LW
114	VALICEVIC, Robert	NYI	Detroit R.W. Jr. A	RW
115	SEBASTIAN, Jeff	Wpg.	Seattle	D
116	NORRIS, Clayton	Phi.	Medicine Hat	RW
117	NAMESTNIKOV, Van.	Van.	Novgorod	D
118	LAWRENCE, Mark	Min.	Detroit	RW
119	HARDING, Mike	Hfd.	Northern Michigan	RW
120	KUZMINSKY, Alexander	Det.-Tor.	Sokol Kiev	C
121	REGNIER, Curt	N.J.	Prince Albert	RW
122	YUSHKEVICH, Dimitri	Edm.-Phi.	Torpedo Jaroslav	D
123	O'DONNELL, Sean	Buf.	Sudbury	D
124	HOLZINGER, Brian	Wsh.-Buf.	Detroit R.W. Jr. A	C
125	JAX, Fredrik	NYR	Leksand	RW
126	CLIFFORD, Brian	Pit.	Nichols H.S.	C
127	PETROV, Oleg	Mtl.	CSKA	RW
128	YOUNG, Barry	Bos.-NYR	Sudbury	D
129	MARSHALL, Bobby	Cgy.	Miami-Ohio	D
130	SEGUIN, Brett	L.A.	Ottawa	C
131	GARDINER, Bruce	St. L.	Colgate	C
132	AUGER, Jacques	Chi.	U. of Wisconsin	D
ROUND # 7				
133	OTEVREL, Jaroslav	S.J.	TJ Zlin	
134	JOHANSSON, Mikael	Que.	Djurgarden	C
135	PROCHAZKA, Martin	Tor.	Poldi Kladno	C
136	JOHANSSON, Andreas	NYI	Falun	C
137	FINCH, Geoff	Wpg.-Min.	Brown	
138	LOMAKIN, Andrei	Phi.	Moscow Dynamo	RW
139	THURSTON, Brent	Van.	Spokane	LW
140	HOFFMAN, Matt	Min.-Cgy.	Oshawa	LW
141	MUELLER, Brian	Hfd.	South Kent H.S.	D
142	MALYKHIN, Igor	Det.	CSKA	D
143	CRAIEVICH, David	N.J.	Oshawa	D
144	OLIVER, David	Edm.	Michigan	RW
145	SNELL, Chris	Buf.	Ottawa	D
146	MORISSETTE, Dave	Wsh.	Shawinigan	LW
147	RUSHIN, John	NYR	Kennedy H.S.	C
148	PATTERSON, Ed	Pit.	Kamloops	RW
149	KRAMER, Brady	Mtl.	Haverford H.S.	C
150	GOLCZEWSKI, Gary	Bos.	Trinity-Pawling H.S.	LW
151	HARPER, Kelly	Cgy.	Michigan State	C
152	FAIRCHILD, Kelly	L.A.	Grand Rapids H.S.	D
153	HOLLINGER, Terry	St. L.	Lethbridge	D
154	KIRTON, Scott	Chi.	Powell River T-II	RW
ROUND # 8				
155	GRILLO, Dean	S.J.	Warroad H.S.	RW
156	LAUKKANEN, Janne	Que.	Reipas	D
157	ASP, Aaron	Tor.-Que.	Ferris State	C
158	SPARKS, Todd	NYI	Hull	LW
159	RICCIARDI, Jeff	Wpg.	Ottawa	D
160	MIRONOV, Dimitri	Phi.-Tor.	Soviet Wings	D
161	JOHNSON, Eric	Van.	Armstrong H.S.	RW
162	KUNTOS, Jiri	Min.-Buf.	Dukla Jihlava	D
163	YULE, Steve	Hfd.	Kamloops	D
164	McINTYRE, Robb	Det.-Tor.	Dubuque Jr. A	LW
165	WOLANSKI, Paul	N.J.	Niagara Falls	D
166	KITCHING, Gary	Edm.	Thunder Bay Jr. A	C
167	KUCHARCIK, Thomas	Buf.-Tor.	Dukla Jihlava	C
168	CORRIVEAU, Rick	Wsh.	London	D
169	HIRSCH, Corey	NYR	Kamloops	G
170	McLAUGHLIN, Peter	Pit.	Belmont Hill H.S.	D
171	SAVAGE, Brian	Mtl.	Miami-Ohio	C
172	MOSER, John	Bos.	Park H.S.	D
173	ST. PIERRE, David	Cgy.	Longueuil	C
174	BURKETT, Michael	L.A.-Min.	Michigan State	LW
175	KENADY, Christopher	St. L.	St. Paul Jr. A	RW
176	BELLEY, Roch	Chi.	Niagara Falls	G
ROUND # 9				
177	SAURDIFF, Corwin	S.J.	Waterloo Jr. A	G
178	BARTELL, Adam	Que.	Niagara Falls	D
179	LEHOUX, Guy	Tor.	Drummondville	D
180	JOHNSON, John	NYI	Niagara Falls	G
181	GAUTHIER, Sean	Wpg.	Kingston	G
182	BODE, James	Phi.	Armstrong H.S.	RW
183	NEILSON, David	Van.	Prince Albert	LW
184	HERLOFSKY, Derek	Min.	St. Paul Jr. A	G
185	BELANGER, Chris	Hfd.	Western Michigan	D
186	BERMINGHAM, Jim	Det.	Laval	C
187	REIMANN, Daniel	N.J.	Anoka H.S.	D
188	BREKKE, Brent	Edm.-Que.	Western Michigan	D
189	IOB, Tony	Buf.	Sault-Ste-Marie	LW
190	DUHAIME, Trevor	Wsh.	St-Jean	RW
191	UVAYEV, Vjateslav	NYR	Spartak Moscow	D
192	LEMBKE, Jeff	Pit.	Omaha Jr. A	G
193	FRASER, Scott	Mtl.	Dartmouth	C
194	HODGE, Daniel	Bos.	Merrimack	D
195	STRUCH, David	Cgy.	Saskatoon	C
196	BROWN, Craig	L.A.	Western Michigan	G
197	FIEBELKORN, Jed	St. L.	Osseo H.S.	RW
198	MacDONALD, Scott	Chi.	Choate H.S.	D
ROUND # 10				
199	CRAIGWELL, Dale	S.J.	Oshawa	C
200	KOCH, Paul	Que.	Omaha Jr. A	D
201	MILLER, Gary	Tor.	North Bay	D
202	CANAVAN, Robert	NYI	Hingham H.S.	LW
203	ULANOV, Igor	Wpg.	Khimik	D
204	BARTELL, Josh	Phi.	Rome Free Academy	D
205	BARTON, Brad	Van.	Kitchener	D
206	NEMETH, Tom	Min.	Cornwall	LW
207	CURRIE, Jason	Hfd.	Clarkson	G
208	FIRTH, Jason	Det.	Kitchener	C
209	LEASK, Rob	N.J.-Wsh.	Hamilton	D
210	BARLIE, Vegar	Edm.	Valerengen	RW
211	MEANY, Spencer	Buf.	St. Lawrence	RW
212	LeBLANC, Carl	Wsh.	Granby	D
213	RAM, Jamie	NYR	Michigan Tech	G
214	TOK, Chris	Pit.	Greenway H.S.	D
215	MacEACHERN, Greg	Mtl.	Laval	D
216	NORTON, Steve	Bos.	Michigan State	D
217	ZOLOTOV, Sergei	Cgy.	Soviet Wings	LW
218	OLSSON, Mattias	L.A.	Farjestad	D
219	MacKENZIE, Chris	St. L.	Colgate	LW
220	ANDRIJEVSKI, Alex	Chi.	Dynamo Moscow	RW
ROUND # 11				
221	KRISS, Aaron	S.J.	Cranbrook H.S.	D
222	FRIEDMAN, Doug	Que.	Boston University	LW
223	KELLEY, Jonathan	Tor.	Arlington H.S.	C
224	THURESSON, Marcus	NYI	Leksand	C
225	JENNINGS, Jason	Wpg.	Western Michigan	RW
226	LITTLE, Neil	Phi.	R.P.I.	G
227	FITZSIMMONS, Jason	Van.	Moose Jaw	G
228	GREEN, Shayne	Min.	Kamloops	RW
229	SANTONELLI, Mike	Hfd.	Matignon H.S.	C
230	TURNER, Bart	Det.	Michigan State	LW
231	RIEHL, Kevin	N.J.	Medicine Hat	C
232	BELOSHEIKEN, Evgeny	Edm.	CSKA	G
233	VOLKOV, Mihail	Buf.	Soviet Wings	RW
234	MORRIS, Rob	Wsh.	Lethbridge	D
235	CHINAKOV, Vitali	NYR	Torpedo Jaroslav	C
236	DYCK, Paul	Pit.	Moose Jaw	D
237	LEPLER, Paul	Mtl.	Rochester Jr. A	D
238	LOMBARDI, Stephen	Bos.	Deerfield H.S.	C
239	JANTUNEN, Marko	Cgy.	Reipas	C
240	BOULIANE, Andre	L.A.	Longueuil	G
241	RAPPANA, Kevin	St. L.	Duluth East H.S.	D
242	LARKIN, Mike	Chi.	Rice Memorial H.S.	D
ROUND # 12				
243	KRAVETS, Mikhail	S.J.	SKA Leningrad	LW
244	MELOCHE, Eric	Que.	Drummondville	RW
245	O'ROURKE, Chris	Tor.	Alaska-Fairbanks	D
246	SCHRINER, Marty	NYI	North Dakota	C
247	SOROKIN, Sergei	Wpg.	Dynamo Moscow	D
248	PORCO, John	Phi.	Belleville	C
249	MAJIC, Xavier	Van.	R.P.I.	C
250	SUOMALAINEN, Jukka	Min.	GrIFK	D
251	PETERS, Rob	Hfd.	Ohio State	D
252	MILLER, Andrew	Det.	Wexford Jr. B	RW
253	HEHR, Jason	N.J.	Kelowna T-II Jr. A	D
254	RIIHIJARVI, Juha	Edm.	Karpat	RW
255	SMITH, Michael	Buf.	Lake Superior	D
256	KOVACS, Bill	Wsh.	Sudbury	LW
257	WISEMAN, Brian	NYR	Michigan	C
258	HUURA, Pasi	Pit.	Ilves	D
259	HOOPER, Dale	Mtl.	Springfield Jr. B	D
260	KIENASS, Torsten	Bos.	Dynamo Berlin	D
261	TREFILOV, Andrei	Cgy.	Dynamo Moscow	G
262	GAUL, Michael	L.A.	St. Lawrence	D
263	VEISOR, Mike	St. L.	Springfield Jr. B	G
264	DEAN, Scott	Chi.	Lake Forest H.S.	D

Draft Choices, 1990-69

1990

FIRST ROUND

Selection	Claimed By	Amateur Club
1. NOLAN, Owen	Que.	Cornwall
2. NEDVED, Petr	Van.	Seattle
3. PRIMEAU, Keith	Det.	Niagara Falls
4. RICCI, Mike	Phi.	Peterborough
5. JAGR, Jaromir	Pit.	Poldi Kladno
6. SCISSONS, Scott	NYI	Saskatoon
7. SYDOR, Darryl	L.A.	Kamloops
8. HATCHER, Derian	Min.	North Bay
9. SLANEY, John	Wsh.	Cornwall
10. BEREHOWSKY, Drake	Tor.	Kingston
11. KIDD, Trevor	Cgy.	Brandon
12. STEVENSON, Turner	Mtl.	Seattle
13. STEWART, Michael	NYR	Michigan State
14. MAY, Brad	Buf.	Niagara Falls
15. GREIG, Mark	Hfd.	Lethbridge
16. DYKHUIS, Karl	Chi.	Hull
17. ALLISON, Scott	Edm.	Prince Albert
18. ANTOSKI, Shawn	Van.	North Bay
19. TKACHUK, Keith	Wpg.	Malden Catholic
20. BRODEUR, Martin	N.J.	St. Hyacinthe
21. SMOLINSKI, Bryan	Bos.	Michigan State

SECOND ROUND

Selection	Claimed By	Amateur Club
22. HUGHES, Ryan	Que.	Cornell
23. SLEGR, Jiri	Van.	Litvinov
24. HARLOCK, David	N.J.	Michigan
25. SIMON, Chris	Phi.	Ottawa
26. PERREAULT, Nicolas P.	Cgy.	Hawkesbury T-II Jr. A
27. TAYLOR, Chris	NYI	London
28. SEMCHUK, Brandy	L.A.	Canadian Olympic
29. GOTZIAMAN, Chris	N.J.	Roseau
30. PASMA, Rod	Wsh.	Cornwall
31. POTVIN, Felix	Tor.	Chicoutimi
32. VIITAKOSKI, Vesa	Cgy.	Saipa
33. JOHNSON, Craig	St. L.	Hill-Murray H.S.
34. WEIGHT, Doug	NYR	Lake Superior
35. MULLER, Mike	Wpg.	Wayzata
36. SANDERSON, Geoff	Hfd.	Swift Current
37. DROPPA, Ivan	Chi.	L. Mikulas
38. LEGAULT, Alexandre	Edm.	Boston University
39. KUWABARA, Ryan	Mtl.	Ottawa
40. RENBERG, Mikael	Phi.	Pitea
41. BELZILE, Etienne	Cgy.	Cornell
42. SANDWITH, Terran	Phi.	Tri-Cities

Bobby Holik was the Hartford Whalers' first selection in the 1989 Entry Draft.

1989

FIRST ROUND

Selection	Claimed By	Amateur Club
1. SUNDIN, Mats	Que.	Nacka (Sweden)
2. CHYZOWSKI, Dave	NYI	Kamloops
3. THORNTON, Scott	Tor.	Belleville
4. BARNES, Stu	Wpg.	Tri-Cities
5. GUERIN, Bill	N.J.	Springfield Jr. B
6. BENNETT, Adam	Chi.	Sudbury
7. ZMOLEK, Doug	Min.	John Marshall
8. HERTER, Jason	Van.	U. of North Dakota
9. MARSHALL, Jason	St. L.	Vernon T-II Jr. A
10. HOLIK, Robert	Hfd.	Jihlava (Czech.)
11. SILLINGER, Mike	Det.	Regina
12. PEARSON, Rob	Tor.	Belleville
13. VALLIS, Lindsay	Mtl.	Seattle
14. HALLER, Kevin	Buf.	Regina
15. SOULES, Jason	Edm.	Niagara Falls
16. HEWARD, Jamie	Pit.	Regina
17. STEVENSON, Shayne	Bos.	Kitchener
18. MILLER, Jason	N.J.	Medicine Hat
19. KOLZIG, Olaf	Wsh.	Tri-Cities
20. RICE, Steven	NYR	Kitchener
21. BANCROFT, Steve	Tor.	Belleville

SECOND ROUND

Selection	Claimed By	Amateur Club
22. FOOTE, Adam	Que.	Sault Ste. Marie
23. GREEN, Travis	NYI	Spokane
24. MANDERVILLE, Kent	Cgy.	Notre Dame T-II Jr. A
25. RATUSHNY, Dan	Wpg.	Cornell
26. SKALDE, Jarrod	N.J.	Oshawa
27. SPEER, Michael	Chi.	Guelph
28. CRAIG, Mike	Min.	Oshawa
29. WOODWARD, Robert	Van.	Deerfield
30. BRISEBOIS, Patrice	Mtl.	Laval
31. CORRIVEAU, Rick	St. L.	London
32. BOUGHNER, Bob	Det.	Sault-Ste. Marie
33. JOHNSON, Greg	Phi.	Thunder Bay Jr. A
34. JUHLIN, Patrik	Phi.	Vasteras (Sweden)
35. DAFOE, Byron	Wsh.	Portland
36. BORGO, Richard	Edm.	Kitchener
37. LAUS, Paul	Pit.	Niagara Falls
38. PARSON, Mike	Bos.	Guelph
39. THOMPSON, Brent	L.A.	Medicine Hat
40. PROSOFSKY, Jason	NYR	Medicine Hat
41. LAROUCHE, Steve	Mtl.	Trois-Rivieres
42. DRURY, Ted	Cgy.	Fairfield Prep

1988

FIRST ROUND

Selection	Claimed By	Amateur Club
1. MODANO, Mike	Min.	Prince Albert
2. LINDEN, Trevor	Van.	Medicine Hat
3. LESCHYSHYN, Curtis	Que.	Saskatoon
4. SHANNON, Darrin	Pit.	Windsor
5. DORE, Daniel	Que.	Drummondville
6. PEARSON, Scott	Tor.	Kingston
7. GELINAS, Martin	L.A.	Hull
8. ROENICK, Jeremy	Chi.	Thayer Academy
9. BRIND'AMOUR, Rod	St.L.	Notre Dame Jr.A
10. SELANNE, Teemu	Wpg.	Jokerit (Finland)
11. CIMETTA, Chris	Hfd.	Toronto
12. FOSTER, Corey	N.J.	Peterborough
13. SAVAGE, Joel	Buf.	Victoria
14. BOIVIN, Claude	Phi.	Drummondville
15. SAVAGE, Reginald	Wsh.	Victoriaville
16. CHEVELDAYOFF, Kevin	NYI	Brandon
17. KOCUR, Kory	Det.	Saskatoon
18. CIMETTA, Robert	Bos.	Toronto
19. LEROUX, Francois	Edm.	St. Jean
20. CHARRON, Eric	Mtl.	Trois-Rivieres
21. MUZZATTI, Jason	Cgy.	Michigan State

SECOND ROUND

Selection	Claimed By	Amateur Club
22. MALLETTE, Troy	NYR	Sault Ste. Marie
23. CHRISTIAN, Jeff	N.J.	London
24. FISET, Stephane	Que.	Victoriaville
25. MAJOR, Mark	Pit.	North Bay
26. DUVAL, Murray	NYR	Spokane
27. DOMI, Tie	Tor.	Peterborough
28. HOLDEN, Paul	L.A.	London
29. DOUCET, Wayne	NYI	Hamilton
30. PLAVSIC, Adrien	St.L.	U. of New Hampshire
31. ROMANIUK, Russell	Wpg.	St. Boniface Jr. A
32. RICHTER, Barry	Hfd.	Culver Academy
33. ROHLIN, Leif	Van.	VIK (Sweden)
34. ST. AMOUR, Martin	Mtl.	Verdun
35. PLANTE, Dan	Phi.	Michigan State
36. TAYLOR, Tim	Wsh.	London
37. LE BRUN, Sean	NYI	New Westminster
38. ANGLEHART, Serge	Det.	Drummondville
39. KOIVUNEN, Petro	Edm.	K-Espoo (Finland)
40. GAETZ, Link	Min.	Spokane
41. BARTLEY, Wade	Wsh.	Dauphin Jr. A
42. HARKINS, Todd	Cgy.	Miami-Ohio

1987

FIRST ROUND

Selection	Claimed By	Amateur Club
1. TURGEON, Pierre	Buf.	Granby
2. SHANAHAN, Brendan	N.J.	London
3. WESLEY, Glen	Bos.	Portland
4. McBEAN, Wayne	L.A.	Medicine Hat
5. JOSEPH, Chris	Pit.	Seattle
6. ARCHIBALD, David	Min.	Portland
7. RICHARDSON, Luke	Tor.	Peterborough
8. WAITE, Jimmy	Chi.	Chicoutimi
9. FOGARTY, Bryan	Que.	Kingston
10. MORE, Jayson	NYR	New Westminster
11. RACINE, Yves	Det.	Longueuil
12. OSBORNE, Keith	St.L.	North Bay
13. CHYNOWETH, Dean	NYI	Medicine Hat
14. QUINTAL, Stephane	Bos.	Granby
15. SAKIC, Joe	Que.	Swift Current
16. MARCHMENT, Bryan	Wpg.	Belleville
17. CASSELS, Andrew	Mtl.	Ottawa
18. HULL, Jody	Hfd.	Peterborough
19. DEASLEY, Bryan	Cgy.	U. of Michigan
20. RUMBLE, Darren	Phi.	Kitchener
21. SOBERLAK, Peter	Edm.	Swift Current

SECOND ROUND

Selection	Claimed By	Amateur Club
22. MILLER, Brad	Buf.	Regina
23. PERSSON, Rickard	N.J.	Ostersund, Sweden
24. MURPHY, Rob	Van.	Laval
25. MATTEAU, Stephane	Cgy.	Hull
26. TABARACCI, Richard	Pit.	Cornwall
27. FITZPATRICK, Mark	L.A.	Medicine Hat
28. MAROIS, Daniel	Tor.	Chicoutimi
29. McGILL, Ryan	Chi.	Swift Current
30. HARDING, Jeff	Phi.	St. Michael's Jr. B
31. LACROIX, Daniel	NYR	Granby
32. KRUPPKE, Gordon	Det.	Prince Albert
33. LECLAIR, John	Mtl.	Bellows Academy
34. HACKETT, Jeff	NYI	Oshawa
35. McCRADY, Scott	Min.	Medicine Hat
36. BALLANTYNE, Jeff	Wsh.	Ottawa
37. ERIKSSON, Patrik	Wpg.	Brynas, Sweden
38. DESJARDINS, Eric	Mtl.	Granby
39. BURT, Adam	Hfd.	North Bay
40. GRANT, Kevin	Cgy.	Kitchener
41. WILKIE, Bob	Det.	Swift Current
42. WERENKA, Brad	Edm.	N. Michigan

1986

FIRST ROUND

Selection	Claimed By	Amateur Club
1. MURPHY, Joe	Det.	Michigan State
2. CARSON, Jimmy	L.A.	Verdun Juniors
3. BRADY, Neil	N.J.	Medicine Hat Tigers
4. ZALAPSKI, Zarley	Pit.	Team Canada
5. ANDERSON, Shawn	Buf.	Team Canada
6. DAMPHOUSSE, Vincent	Tor.	Laval Olympiques
7. WOODLEY, Dan	Van.	Portland Winterhawks
8. ELYNUIK, Pat	Wpg.	Prince Albert Raiders
9. LEETCH, Brian	NYR	Avon Old Farms HS
10. LEMIEUX, Jocelyn	St.L.	Laval Olympiques
11. YOUNG, Scott	Hfd.	Boston University
12. BABE, Warren	Min.	Lethbridge Broncos
13. JANNEY, Craig	Bos.	Boston College
14. SANIPASS, Everett	Chi.	Verdun Juniors
15. PEDERSON, Mark	Mtl.	Medicine Hat Tigers
16. PELAWA, George	Cgy.	Bemidji HS
17. FITZGERALD, Tom	NYI	Austin Prep
18. McRAE, Ken	Que.	Sudbury Wolves
19. GREENLAW, Jeff	Wsh.	Team Canada
20. HUFFMAN, Kerry	Phi.	Guelph Platers
21. ISSEL, Kim	Edm.	Prince Albert Raiders

SECOND ROUND

Selection	Claimed By	Amateur Club
22. GRAVES, Adam	Det.	Windsor Spitfires
23. SEPPO, Jukka	Phi.	Vasa Sport, (Finland)
24. COPELAND, Todd	N.J.	Belmont Hill HS
25. CAPUANO, Dave	Pit.	Mt. St. Charles HS
26. BROWN, Greg	Buf.	St. Mark's
27. BRUNET, Benoit	Mtl.	Hull Olympiques
28. HAWLEY, Kent	Phi.	Ottawa 67's
29. NUMMINEN, Teppo	Wpg.	Tappara, (Finland)
30. WILKINSON, Neil	Min.	Selkirk Settlers
31. POSMA, Mike	St.L.	Buffalo Jr. Sabres
32. LaFORGE, Marc	Hfd.	Kingston Canadians
33. KOLSTAD, Dean	Min.	Prince Albert Raiders
34. TIRKKONEN, Pekka	Bos.	Sapko, (Finland)
35. KURZAWSKI, Mark	Chi.	Windsor Spitfires
36. SHANNON, Darryl	Tor.	Windsor Spitfires
37. GLYNN, Brian	Cgy.	Saskatoon Blades
38. VASKE, Dennis	NYI	Armstrong HS
39. ROUTHIER, Jean-M	Que.	Hull Olympiques
40. SEFTEL, Steve	Wsh.	Kingston Canadians
41. GUERARD, Stephane	Que.	Shawinigan Cataractes
42. NICHOLS, Jamie	Edm.	Portland Winter Hawks

1985

FIRST ROUND

Selection	Claimed By	Amateur Club
1. CLARK, Wendel	Tor.	Saskatoon Blades
2. SIMPSON, Craig	Pit.	Michigan State
3. WOLANIN, Craig	N.J.	Kitchener Rangers
4. SANDLAK, Jim	Van.	London Knights
5. MURZYN, Dana	Hfd.	Cgy. Wranglers
6. DALGARNO, Brad	NYI	Hamilton Steelhawks
7. DAHLEN, Ulf	NYR	Ostersund (Sweden)
8. FEDYK, Brent	Det.	Regina Pats
9. DUNCANSON, Craig	L.A.	Sudbury Wolves
10. GRATTON, Dan	L.A.	Oshawa Generals
11. MANSON, David	Chi.	Prince Albert Raiders
12. CHARBONNEAU, Jose	Mtl.	Drummondville
13. KING, Derek	NYI	Sault Greyhounds
14. JOHANSSON, Carl	Buf.	V. Frolunda (Sweden)
15. LATTA, Dave	Que.	Kitchener Rangers
16. CHORSKE, Tom	Mtl.	Minneapolis HS
17. BIOTTI, Chris	Cgy.	Belmont Hill HS
18. STEWART, Ryan	Wpg.	Kamloops Blazers
19. CORRIVEAU, Yvon	Wsh.	Tor. Marlboros
20. METCALFE, Scott	Edm.	Kingston Canadians
21. SEABROOKE, Glen	Phi.	Peterborough Petes

SECOND ROUND

Selection	Claimed By	Amateur Club
22. SPANGLER, Ken	Tor.	Cgy. Wranglers
23. GIFFIN, Lee	Pit.	Oshawa Generals
24. BURKE, Sean	N.J.	Tor. Marlboros
25. GAMBLE, Troy	Van.	Medicine Hat Tigers
26. WHITMORE, Kay	Hfd.	Peterborough Petes
27. NIEUWENDYK, Joe	Cgy.	Cornell Big Red
28. RICHTER, Mike	NYR	Northwood Prep
29. SHARPLES, Jeff	Det.	Kelowna Wings
30. EDLUND, Par	L.A.	Bjorkloven (Sweden)
31. COTE, Alain	Bos.	Que. Remparts
32. WEINRICH, Eric	N.J.	North Yarmouth
33. RICHARD, Todd	Mtl.	Armstrong HS
34. LAUER, Brad	NYI	Regina Pats
35. HOGUE, Benoit	Buf.	St Jean Castors
36. LAFRENIERE, Jason	Que.	Hamilton Steelhawks
37. RAGLAN, Herb	St.L.	Kingston Canadians
38. WENAAS, Jeff	Cgy.	Medicine Hat Tigers
39. OHMAN, Roger	Wpg.	Leksand Jr. (Sweden)
40. DRUCE, John	Wsh.	Peterborough Petes
41. CARNELLEY, Todd	Edm.	Kamloops Blazers
42. RENDALL, Bruce	Phi.	Chatham Maroons

1984

FIRST ROUND

Selection	Claimed By	Amateur Club
1. LEMIEUX, Mario	Pit.	Laval Voisins
2. MULLER, Kirk	N.J.	Team Canada-Guelph
3. OLCZYK, Ed	Chi.	Team USA
4. IAFRATE, Al	Tor.	Team USA-Belleville
5. SVOBODA, Petr	Mtl.	Czechoslovakia Jr.
6. REDMOND, Craig	L.A.	Team Canada
7. BURR, Shawn	Det.	Kitchener Rangers
8. CORSON, Shayne	Mtl.	Brantford Alexanders
9. BODGER, Doug	Pit.	Kamloops Jr. Oilers
10. DAIGNEAULT, J.J.	Van.	Canada-Longueuil
11. COTE, Sylvain	Hfd.	Que. Remparts
12. ROBERTS, Gary	Cgy.	Ottawa 67's
13. QUINN, David	Min.	Kent High School
14. CARKNER, Terry	NYR	Peterborough Petes
15. STIENBURG, Trevor	Que.	Guelph Platers
16. BELANGER, Roger	Pit.	Kingston Canadians
17. HATCHER, Kevin	Wsh.	North Bay Centennials
18. ANDERSSON, Bo Mikael	Buf.	V. Frolunda (Sweden)
19. PASIN, Dave	Bos.	Prince Albert Raiders
20. MACPHERSON, Duncan	NYI	Saskatoon Blades
21. ODELEIN, Selmar	Edm.	Regina Pats

SECOND ROUND

Selection	Claimed By	Amateur Club
22. SMYTH, Greg	Phi.	London Knights
23. BILLINGTON, Craig	N.J.	Belleville Bulls
24. WILKS, Brian	L.A.	Kitchener Rangers
25. GILL, Todd	Tor.	Windsor Spitfires
26. BENNING, Brian	St.L.	Portland Winter Hawks
27. MELLANBY, Scott	Phi.	Henry Carr Jr. B
28. HOUDA, Doug	Det.	Cgy. Wranglers
29. RICHER, Stephane	Mtl.	Granby Bisons
30. DOURIS, Peter	Wpg.	U. of N. Hampshire
31. ROHLICEK, Jeff	Van.	Portland Winter Hawks
32. HRKAC, Anthony	St.L.	Orillia Jr. A
33. SABOURIN, Ken	Cgy.	Sault Greyhounds
34. LEACH, Stephen	Wsh.	Matignon High School
35. HELMINEN, Raimo Ilmari	NYR	Ilves (Finland)
36. BROWN, Jeff	Que.	Sudbury Wolves
37. CHYCHRUN, Jeff	Phi.	Kingston Canadians
38. RANHEIM, Paul	Cgy.	Edina Hornets HS
39. TRAPP, Doug	Buf.	Regina Pats
40. PODLOSKI, Ray	Bos.	Portland Winter Hawks
41. MELANSON, Bruce	NYI	Oshawa Generals
42. REAUGH, Daryl	Edm.	Kamloops Jr. Oilers

1983

FIRST ROUND

Selection	Claimed By	Amateur Club
1. LAWTON, Brian	Min.	Mount St. Charles HS
2. TURGEON, Sylvain	Hfd.	Hull Olympiques
3. LAFONTAINE, Pat	NYI	Verdun Juniors
4. YZERMAN, Steve	Det.	Peterborough Petes
5. BARRASSO, Tom	Buf.	Acton-Boxboro HS
6. MacLEAN, John	N.J.	Oshawa Generals
7. COURTNALL, Russ	Tor.	Victoria Cougars
8. McBAIN, Andrew	Wpg.	North Bay Centennials
9. NEELY, Cam	Van.	Portland Winter Hawks
10. LACOMBE, Normand	Buf.	University of New Hampshire
11. CREIGHTON, Adam	Buf.	Ottawa 67's
12. GAGNER, Dave	NYR	Brantford Alexanders
13. QUINN, Dan	Cgy.	Belleville Bulls
14. DOLLAS, Bobby	Wpg.	Laval Voisins
15. ERREY, Bob	Pit.	Peterborough Petes
16. DIDUCK, Gerald	NYI	Lethbridge Broncos
17. TURCOTTE, Alfie	Mtl.	Portland Winter Hawks
18. CASSIDY, Bruce	Chi.	Ottawa 67's
19. BEUKEBOOM, Jeff	Edm.	Sault Greyhounds
20. JENSEN, David	Hfd.	Lawrence Academy
21. MARKWART, Nevin	Bos.	Regina Pats

SECOND ROUND

Selection	Claimed By	Amateur Club
22. CHARLESWORTH, Todd	Pit.	Oshawa Generals
23. SIREN, Ville	Hfd.	Ilves (Finland)
24. EVANS, Shawn	N.J.	Peterborough Petes
25. LAMBERT, Lane	Det.	Saskatoon Blades
26. LEMIEUX, Claude	Mtl.	Trois Rivieres Draveurs
27. MOMESSO, Sergio	Mtl.	Shawinigan Cataractes
28. JACKSON, Jeff	Tor.	Brantford Alexanders
29. BERRY, Brad	Wpg.	St. Albert Saints
30. BRUCE, Dave	Van.	Kitchener Rangers
31. TUCKER, John	Buf.	Kitchener Rangers
32. HEROUX, Yves	Que.	Chicoutimi Sagueneens
33. HEATH, Randy	NYR	Portland Winter Hawks
34. HAJDU, Richard	Buf.	Kamloops Jr. Oilers
35. FRANCIS, Todd	Mtl.	Brantford Alexanders
36. PARKS, Malcolm	Min.	St. Albert Saints
37. McKECHNEY, Grant	NYI	Kitchener Rangers
38. MUSIL, Frantisek	Min.	Czech. National Team
39. PRESLEY, Wayne	Chi.	Kitchener Rangers
40. GOLDEN, Mike	Edm.	Reading High School
41. ZEZEL, Peter	Phi.	Tor. Malboros
42. JOHNSTON, Greg	Bos.	Tor. Malboros

1982

FIRST ROUND

Selection	Claimed By	Amateur Club
1. KLUZAK, Gord	Bos.	Nanaimo Islanders
2. BELLOWS, Brian	Min.	Kitchener Rangers
3. NYLUND, Gary	Tor.	Portland Winter Hawks
4. SUTTER, Ron	Phi.	Lethbridge Broncos
5. STEVENS, Scott	Wsh.	Kitchener Rangers
6. HOUSLEY, Phil	Buf.	S. St. Paul High School
7. YAREMCHUK, Ken	Chi.	Portland Winter Hawks
8. TROTTIER, Rocky	N.J.	Nanaimo Islanders
9. CYR, Paul	Buf.	Victoria Cougars
10. SUTTER, Rich	Pit.	Lethbridge Broncos
11. PETIT, Michel	Van.	Sherbrooke Castors
12. KYTE, Jim	Wpg.	Cornwall Royals
13. SHAW, David	Que.	Kitchener Rangers
14. LAWLESS, Paul	Hfd.	Windsor Spitfires
15. KONTOS, Chris	NYR	Tor. Marlboros
16. ANDREYCHUK, Dave	Buf.	Oshawa Generals
17. CRAVEN, Murray	Det.	Medicine Hat Tigers
18. DANEYKO, Ken	N.J.	Seattle Breakers
19. HEROUX, Alain	Mtl.	Chicoutimi Sagueneens
20. PLAYFAIR, Jim	Edm.	Portland Winter Hawks
21. FLATLEY, Pat	NYI	University of Wisconsin

SECOND ROUND

Selection	Claimed By	Amateur Club
22. CURRAN, Brian	Bos.	Portland Winter Hawks
23. COURTEAU, Yves	Det.	Laval Voisins
24. LEEMAN, Gary	Tor.	Regina Pats
25. IHNACAK, Peter	Tor.	Czech National Team
26. ANDERSON, Mike	Buf.	N. St. Paul High School
27. HEIDT, Mike	L.A.	Cgy. Wranglers
28. BADEAU, Rene	Chi.	Que. Remparts
29. REIERSON, Dave	Cgy.	Prince Albert Raiders
30. JOHANSSON, Jens	Buf.	Pitea (Sweden)
31. GAUVREAU, Jocelyn	Mtl.	Granby Bisons
32. CARLSON, Kent	Mtl.	St. Lawrence University
33. MALEY, David	Mtl.	Edina High School
34. GILLIS, Paul	Que.	Niagara Falls Flyers
35. PATERSON, Mark	Hfd.	Ottawa 67's
36. SANDSTROM, Tomas	NYR	Farjestads (Sweden)
37. KROMM, Richard	Cgy.	Portland Winter Hawks
38. HRYNEWICH, Tim	Pit.	Sudbury Wolves
39. BYERS, Lyndon	Bos.	Regina Pats
40. SANDELIN, Scott	Mtl.	Hibbing High School
41. GRAVES, Steve	Edm.	Sault Greyhounds
42. SMITH, Vern	NYI	Lethbridge Broncos

1981

FIRST ROUND

Selection	Claimed By	Amateur Club
1. HAWERCHUK, Dale	Wpg.	Cornwall Royals
2. SMITH, Doug	L.A.	Ottawa 67's
3. CARPENTER, Bobby	Wsh.	St. John's High School
4. FRANCIS, Ron	Hfd.	Sault Greyhounds
5. CIRELLA, Joe	Col.	Oshawa Generals
6. BENNING, Jim	Tor.	Portland Winter Hawks
7. HUNTER, Mark	Mtl.	Brantford Alexanders
8. FUHR, Grant	Edm.	Victoria Cougars
9. PATRICK, James	NYR	U. of North Dakota
10. BUTCHER, Garth	Van.	Regina Pats
11. MOLLER, Randy	Que.	Lethbridge Broncos
12. TANTI, Tony	Chi.	Oshawa Generals
13. MEIGHAN, Ron	Min.	Niagara Falls Flyers
14. LEVEILLE, Normand	Bos.	Chicoutimi Sagueneens
15. MacINNIS, Allan	Cgy.	Kitchener Rangers
16. SMITH, Steve	Phi.	Sault Greyhounds
17. DUDACEK, Jiri	Buf.	Kladno (Czech.)
18. DELORME, Gilbert	Mtl.	Chicoutimi Sagueneens
19. INGMAN, Jan	Mtl.	Sweden
20. RUFF, Marty	St.L.	Lethbridge Broncos
21. BOUTILIER, Paul	NYI	Sherbrooke Castors

SECOND ROUND

Selection	Claimed By	Amateur Club
22. ARNIEL, Scott	Wpg.	Cornwall Royals
23. LOISELLE, Claude	Det.	Windsor Spitfires
24. YAREMCHUK, Gary	Tor.	Portland Winter Hawks
25. GRIFFIN, Kevin	Chi.	Portland Winter Hawks
26. CHERNOMAZ, Rich	Col.	Victoria Cougars
27. DONNELLY, Dave	Min.	St. Albert Saints
28. GATZOS, Steve	Pit.	Sault Greyhounds
29. STRUEBY, Todd	Edm.	Regina Pats
30. ERIXON, Jan	NYR	Skellleftea (Sweden)
31. SANDS, Mike	Min.	Sudbury Wolves
32. ERIKSSON, Lars	Mtl.	Brynas (Sweden)
33. HIRSCH, Tom	Min.	Patrick Henry HS
34. PREUSS, Dave	Min.	St. Thomas Academy
35. DUFOUR, Luc	Bos.	Chicoutimi Sagueneens
36. NORDIN, Hakan	St.L.	Farjestads (Sweden)
37. COSTELLO, Rich	Phi.	Natick High School
38. VIRTA, Hannu	Buf.	TPS Finland
39. KENNEDY, Dean	L.A.	Brandon Wheat Kings
40. CHELIOS, Chris	Mtl.	Moose Jaw Canucks
41. WAHLSTEN, Jali	Min.	TPS Finland
42. DINEEN, Gord	NYI	Sault Greyhounds

Entry Draft *continued*

1980

FIRST ROUND

Selection	Claimed By	Amateur Club
1. WICKENHEISER, Doug	Mtl.	Regina Pats
2. BABYCH, Dave	Wpg.	Portland Winter Hawks
3. SAVARD, Denis	Chi.	Mtl. Juniors
4. MURPHY, Larry	L.A.	Peterborough Petes
5. VEITCH, Darren	Wsh.	Regina Pats
6. COFFEY, Paul	Edm.	Kitchener Rangers
7. LANZ, Rick	Van.	Oshawa Generals
8. ARTHUR, Fred	Hfd.	Cornwall Royals
9. BULLARD, Mike	Pit.	Brantford Alexanders
10. FOX, Jimmy	L.A.	Ottawa 67's
11. BLAISDELL, Mike	Det.	Regina Pats
12. WILSON, Rik	St.L.	Kingston Canadians
13. CYR, Denis	Cgy.	Mtl. Juniors
14. MALONE, Jim	NYR	Tor. Marlboros
15. DUPONT, Jerome	Chi.	Tor. Marlboros
16. PALMER, Brad	Min.	Victoria Cougars
17. SUTTER, Brent	NYI	Red Deer Rustlers
18. PEDERSON, Barry	Bos.	Victoria Cougars
19. GAGNE, Paul	Col.	Windsor Spitfires
20. PATRICK, Steve	Buf.	Brandon Wheat Kings
21. STOTHERS, Mike	Phi.	Kingston Canadians

SECOND ROUND

Selection	Claimed By	Amateur Club
22. WARD, Joe	Col.	Seattle Breakers
23. MANTHA, Moe	Wpg.	Tor. Marlboros
24. ROCHEFORT, Normand	Que.	Que. Remparts
25. MUNI, Craig	Tor.	Kingston Canadians
26. McGILL, Bob	Tor.	Victoria Cougars
27. NATTRESS, Ric	Mtl.	Brantford Alexanders
28. LUDZIK, Steve	Chi.	Niagara Falls Flyers
29. GALARNEAU, Michel	Hfd.	Hull Olympiques
30. SOLHEIM, Ken	Chi.	Medicine Hat Tigers
31. CURTALE, Tony	Cgy.	Brantford Alexanders
32. LaVALLEE, Kevin	Cgy.	Brantford Alexanders
33. TERRION, Greg	L.A.	Brantford Alexanders
34. MORRISON, Dave	L.A.	Peterborough Petes
35. ALLISON, Mike	NYR	Sudbury Wolves
36. DAWES, Len	Chi.	Victoria Cougars
37. BEAUPRE, Don	Min.	Sudbury Wolves
38. HRUDEY, Kelly	NYI	Medicine Hat Tigers
39. KONROYD, Steve	Cgy.	Oshawa Generals
40. CHABOT, John	Mtl.	Hull Olympiques
41. MOLLER, Mike	Buf.	Lethbridge Broncos
42. FRASER, Jay	Phi.	Ottawa 67's

1979

FIRST ROUND

Selection	Claimed By	Amateur Club
1. RAMAGE, Rob	Col.	London Knights
2. TURNBULL, Perry	St.L.	Portland Winter Hawks
3. FOLIGNO, Mike	Det.	Sudbury Wolves
4. GARTNER, Mike	Wsh.	Niagara Falls Flyers
5. VAIVE, Rick	Van.	Sherbrooke Castors
6. HARTSBURG, Craig	Min.	Sault Greyhounds
7. BROWN, Keith	Chi.	Portland Winter Hawks
8. BOURQUE, Raymond	Bos.	Verdun Black Hawks
9. BOSCHMAN, Laurie	Tor.	Brandon Wheat Kings
10. McCARTHY, Tom	Min.	Oshawa Generals
11. RAMSEY, Mike	Buf.	University of Min.
12. REINHART, Paul	Atlanta	Kitchener Rangers
13. SULLIMAN, Doug	NYR	Kitchener Rangers
14. PROPP, Brian	Phi.	Brandon Wheat Kings
15. McCRIMMON, Brad	Bos.	Brandon Wheat Kings
16. WELLS, Jay	L.A.	Kingston Canadians
17. SUTTER, Duane	NYI	Lethbridge Broncos
18. ALLISON, Ray	Hfd.	Brandon Wheat Kings
19. MANN, Jimmy	Wpg.	Sherbrooke Beavers
20. GOULET, Michel	Que.	Que. Remparts
21. LOWE, Kevin	Edm.	Que. Remparts

SECOND ROUND

Selection	Claimed By	Amateur Club
22. WESLEY, Blake	Phi.	Portland Winter Hawks
23. PEROVICH, Mike	Atlanta	Brandon Wheat Kings
24. RAUSSE, Errol	Wsh.	Seattle Breakers
25. JONSSON, Tomas	NYI	MoDo AIK (Sweden)
26. ASHTON, Brent	Van.	Saskatoon Blades
27. GINGRAS, Gaston	Mtl.	Hamilton Fincups
28. TRIMPER, Tim	Chi.	Peterborough Petes
29. HOPKINS, Dean	L.A.	London Knights
30. HARDY, Mark	L.A.	Mtl. Juniors
31. MARSHALL, Paul	Pit.	Brantford Alexanders
32. RUFF, Lindy	Buf.	Lethbridge Broncos
33. RIGGIN, Pat	Atlanta	London Knights
34. HOSPODAR, Ed	NYR	Ottawa 67's
35. LINDBERGH, Pelle	Phi.	Solna (Sweden)
36. MORRISON, Doug	Bos.	Lethbridge Broncos
37. NASLUND, Mats	Mtl.	Brynas IFK (Sweden)
38. CARROLL, Billy	NYI	London Knights
39. SMITH, Stuart	Hfd.	Peterborough Petes
40. CHRISTIAN, Dave	Wpg.	U. of North Dakota
41. HUNTER, Dale	Que.	Sudbury Wolves
42. BROTEN, Neal	Min.	University of Min.

1978

FIRST ROUND

Selection	Claimed By	Amateur Club
1. SMITH, Bobby	Min.	Ottawa 67's
2. WALTER, Ryan	Wsh.	Seattle Breakers
3. BABYCH, Wayne	St.L.	Portland Winter Hawks
4. DERLAGO, Bill	Van.	Brandon Wheat Kings
5. GILLIS, Mike	Col.	Kingston Canadians
6. WILSON, Behn	Phi.	Kingston Canadians
7. LINSEMAN, Ken	Phi.	Kingston Canadians
8. GEOFFRION, Danny	Mtl.	Cornwall Royals
9. HUBER, Willie	Det.	Hamilton Fincups
10. HIGGINS, Tim	Chi.	Ottawa 67's
11. MARSH, Brad	Atl.	London Knights
12. PETERSON, Brent	Det.	Portland Winter Hawks
13. PLAYFAIR, Larry	Buf.	Portland Winter Hawks
14. LUCAS, Danny	Phi.	Sault Greyhounds
15. TAMBELLINI, Steve	NYI	Lethbridge Broncos
16. SECORD, Al	Bos.	Hamilton Fincups
17. HUNTER, Dave	Mtl.	Sudbury Wolves
18. COULIS, Tim	Wsh.	Hamilton Fincups

SECOND ROUND

Selection	Claimed By	Amateur Club
19. PAYNE, Steve	Min.	Ottawa 67's
20. MULVEY, Paul	Wsh.	Portland Winter Hawks
21. QUENNEVILLE, Joel	Tor.	Windsor Spitfires
22. FRASER, Curt	Van.	Victoria Cougars
23. MacKINNON, Paul	Wsh.	Peterborough Petes
24. CHRISTOFF, Steve	Min.	University of Min.
25. MEEKER, Mike	Pit.	Peterborough Petes
26. MALONEY, Don	NYR	Kitchener Rangers
27. MALINOWSKI, Merlin	Col.	Medicine Hat Tigers
28. HICKS, Glenn	Det.	Flin Flon Bombers
29. LECUYER, Doug	Chi.	Portland Winter Hawks
30. YAKIWCHUK, Dale	Mtl.	Portland Winter Hawks
31. JENSEN, Al	Det.	Hamilton Fincups
32. McKEGNEY, Tony	Buf.	Kingston Canadians
33. SIMURDA, Mike	Phi.	Kingston Canadians
34. JOHNSTON, Randy	NYI	Peterborough Petes
35. NICOLSON, Graeme	Bos.	Cornwall Royals
36. CARTER, Ron	Mtl.	Sherbrooke Castors

1977

FIRST ROUND

Selection	Claimed By	Amateur Club
1. McCOURT, Dale	Det.	St. Catharines Fincups
2. BECK, Barry	Col.	New Westminster
3. PICARD, Robert	Wsh.	Mtl. Jrs.
4. GILLIS, Jere	Van.	Sherbrooke Castors
5. CROMBEEN, Mike	Cle.	Kingston Canadians
6. WILSON, Doug	Chi.	Ottawa 67's
7. MAXWELL, Brad	Min.	New Westminster
8. DEBLOIS, Lucien	NYR	Sorel Black Hawks
9. CAMPBELL, Scott	St.L.	London Knights
10. NAPIER, Mark	Mtl.	Tor. Marlboros
11. ANDERSON, John	Tor.	Tor. Marlboros
12. JOHANSON, Trevor	Tor.	Tor. Marlboros
13. DUGUAY, Ron	NYR	Sudbury Wolves
14. SEILING, Ric	Buf.	St. Catharines Fincups
15. BOSSY, Mike	NYI	Laval Nationales
16. FOSTER, Dwight	Bos.	Kitchener Rangers
17. McCARTHY, Kevin	Phi.	Wpg. Monarchs
18. DUPONT, Norm	Mtl.	Montreal Jrs.

SECOND ROUND

Selection	Claimed By	Amateur Club
19. SAVARD, Jean	Chi.	Que. Remparts
20. ZAHARKO, Miles	Atl.	New Westminister
21. LOFTHOUSE, Mark	Wsh.	New Westminster
22. BANDURA, Jeff	Van.	Portland Winter Hawks
23. CHICOINE, Daniel	Cle.	Sherbrooke Castors
24. GLADNEY, Bob	Tor.	Oshawa Generals
25. SEMENKO, Dave	Min.	Brandon Wheat Kings
26. KEATING, Mike	NYR	St. Catharines Fincups
27. LABATTE, Neil	St.L.	Tor. Marlboros
28. LAURENCE, Don	Atl.	Kitchener Rangers
29. SAGANIUK, Rocky	Tor.	Lethbridge Broncos
30. HAMILTON, Jim	Pit.	London Knights
31. HILL, Brian	Atl.	Medicine Hat Tigers
32. ARESHENKOFF, Ron	Buf.	Medicine Hat Tigers
33. TONELLI, John	NYI	Tor. Marlboros
34. PARRO, Dave	Bos.	Saskatoon Blades
35. GORENCE, Tom	Phi.	U. of Minnesota
36. LANGWAY, Rod	Mtl.	U. of N. Hampshire

1976

FIRST ROUND

Selection	Claimed By	Amateur Club
1. GREEN, Rick	Wsh.	London Knights
2. CHAPMAN, Blair	Pit.	Saskatoon Blades
3. SHARPLEY, Glen	Min.	Hull Festivals
4. WILLIAMS, Fred	Det.	Saskatoon Blades
5. JOHANSSON, Bjorn	Cal.	Sweden
6. MURDOCH, Don	NYR	Medicine Hat Tigers
7. FEDERKO, Bernie	St.L.	Saskatoon Blades
8. SHAND, Dave	Atl.	Peterborough Petes
9. CLOUTIER, Real	Chi.	Que. Remparts
10. PHILLIPOFF, Harold	Atl.	New Westminster
11. GARDNER, Paul	K.C.	Oshawa Generals
12. LEE, Peter	Mtl.	Ottawa 67's
13. SCHUTT, Rod	Mtl.	Sudbury Wolves
14. McKENDRY, Alex	NYI	Sudbury Wolves
15. CARROLL, Greg	Wsh.	Medicine Hat Tigers
16. PACHAL, Clayton	Bos.	New Westminster
17. SUZOR, Mark	Phi.	Kingston Canadians
18. BAKER, Bruce	Mtl.	Ottawa 67's

SECOND ROUND

Selection	Claimed By	Amateur Club
19. MALONE, Greg	Pit.	Oshawa Generals
20. SUTTER, Brian	St.L.	Lethbridge Broncos
21. CLIPPINGDALE, Steve	L.A.	New Westminster
22. LARSON, Reed	Det.	University of Min.
23. STENLUND, Vern	Cal.	London Knights
24. FARRISH, Dave	NYR	Sudbury Wolves
25. SMRKE, John	St.L.	Tor. Marlboros
26. MANNO, Bob	Van.	St. Catharines Hawks
27. McDILL, Jeff	Chi.	Victoria Cougars
28. SIMPSON, Bobby	Atl.	Sherbrooke Castors
29. MARSH, Peter	Pit.	Sherbrooke Castors
30. CARLYLE, Randy	Tor.	Sudbury Wolves
31. ROBERTS, Jim	Min.	Ottawa 67's
32. KASZYCKI, Mike	NYI	Sault Greyhounds
33. KOWAL, Joe	Buf.	Hamilton Fincups
34. GLOECKNER, Larry	Bos.	Victoria Cougars
35. CALLANDER, Drew	Phi.	Regina Pats
36. MELROSE, Barry	Mtl.	Kamloops Chiefs

1975

FIRST ROUND

Selection	Claimed By	Amateur Club
1. BRIDGMAN, Mel	Phi.	Victoria Cougars
2. DEAN, Barry	K.C.	Medicine Hat Tigers
3. KLASSEN, Ralph	Cal.	Saskatoon Blades
4. MAXWELL, Brian	Min.	Medicine Hat Tigers
5. LAPOINTE, Rick	Det.	Victoria Cougars
6. ASHBY, Don	Tor.	Cgy. Centennials
7. VAYDIK, Greg	Chi.	Medicine Hat Tigers
8. MULHERN, Richard	Atl.	Sherbrooke Beavers
9. SADLER, Robin	Mtl.	Edm. Oil Kings
10. BLIGHT, Rick	Van.	Brandon Wheat Kings
11. PRICE, Pat	NYI	Saskatoon Blades
12. DILLON, Wayne	NYR	Tor. Marlboros
13. LAXTON, Gord	Pit.	New Westminster
14. HALWARD, Doug	Bos.	Peterborough Petes
15. MONDOU, Pierre	Mtl.	Montreal Juniors
16. YOUNG, Tim	L.A.	Ottawa 67's
17. SAUVE, Bob	Buf.	Laval Nationales
18. FORSYTH, Alex	Wsh.	Kingston Canadians

SECOND ROUND

Selection	Claimed By	Amateur Club
19. SCAMURRA, Peter	Wsh.	Peterborough Petes
20. CAIRNS, Don	K.C.	Victoria Cougars
21. MARUK, Dennis	Cal.	London Knights
22. ENGBLOM, Brian	Mtl.	University of Wisconsin
23. ROLLINS, Jerry	Det.	Wpg. Jr. Jets
24. JARVIS, Doug	Tor.	Peterborough Petes
25. ARNDT, Daniel	Chi.	Saskatoon Blades
26. BOWNASS, Rick	Atl.	Montreal Juniors
27. STANIOWSKI, Ed	St.L.	Regina Pats
28. GASSOFF, Brad	Van.	Kamloops Chiefs
29. SALVIAN, David	NYI	St. Catharines Hawks
30. SOETAERT, Doug	NYR	Edm. Oil Kings
31. ANDERSON, Russ	Pit.	U. of Minnesota
32. SMITH, Barry	Bos.	New Westminster
33. BUCYK, Terry	L.A.	Lethbridge Broncos
34. GREENBANK, Kelvin	Mtl.	Wpg. Jr. Jets
35. BREITENBACH, Ken	Buf.	St. Catharines Hawks
36. MASTERS, Jamie	St.L.	Ottawa 67's

1974

FIRST ROUND

Selection	Claimed By	Amateur Club
1. JOLY, Greg	Wsh.	Regina Pats
2. PAIEMENT, Wilfred	K.C.	St. Catharines Hawks
3. HAMPTON, Rick	Cal.	St. Catharines Hawks
4. GILLIES, Clark	NYI	Regina Pats
5. CONNOR, Cam	Mtl.	Flin Flon Bombers
6. HICKS, Doug	Min.	Flin Flon Bombers
7. RISEBROUGH, Doug	Mtl.	Kitchener Rangers
8. LAROUCHE, Pierre	Pit.	Sorel Black Hawks
9. LOCHEAD, Bill	Det.	Oshawa Generals
10. CHARTRAW, Rick	Mtl.	Kitchener Rangers
11. FOGOLIN, Lee	Buf.	Oshawa Generals
12. TREMBLAY, Mario	Mtl.	Montreal Juniors
13. VALIQUETTE, Jack	Tor.	Sault Greyhounds
14. MALONEY, Dave	NYR	Kitchener Rangers
15. McTAVISH, Gord	Mtl.	Sudbury Wolves
16. MULVEY, Grant	Chi.	Cgy. Centennials
17. CHIPPERFIELD, Ron	Cal.	Brandon Wheat Kings
18. LARWAY, Don	Bos.	Swift Current Broncos

SECOND ROUND

Selection	Claimed By	Amateur Club
19. MARSON, Mike	Wsh.	Sudbury Wolves
20. BURDON, Glen	K.C.	Regina Pats
21. AFFLECK, Bruce	Cal.	University of Denver
22. TROTTIER, Bryan	NYI	Swift Current Broncos
23. SEDLBAUER, Ron	Van.	Kitchener Rangers
24. NANTAIS, Rick	Min.	Que. Remparts
25. HOWE, Mark	Bos.	Tor. Marlboros
26. HESS, Bob	St.L.	New Westminster
27. COSSETTE, Jacques	Pit.	Sorel Black Hawks
28. CHOUINARD, Guy	Atl.	Que. Remparts
29. GARE, Danny	Buf.	Cgy. Centennials
30. MacGREGOR, Gary	Mtl.	Cornwall Royals
31. WILLIAMS, Dave	Tor.	Swift Current Broncos
32. GRESCHNER, Ron	NYR	New Westminster
33. LUPIEN, Gilles	Mtl.	Montreal Juniors
34. DAIGLE, Alain	Chi.	Trois Rivieres Draveurs
35. McLEAN, Don	Phi.	Sudbury Wolves
36. STURGEON, Peter	Bos.	Kitchener Rangers

1973

FIRST ROUND

Selection	Claimed By	Amateur Club
1. POTVIN, Denis	NYI	Ottawa 67's
2. LYSIAK, Tom	Atl.	Medicine Hat Tigers
3. VERVERGAERT, Dennis	Van.	London Knights
4. McDONALD, Lanny	Tor.	Medicine Hat Tigers
5. DAVIDSON, John	St.L.	Cgy. Centennials
6. SAVARD, Andre	Bos.	Que. Remparts
7. STOUGHTON, Blaine	Pit.	Flin Flon Bombers
8. GAINEY, Bob	Mtl.	Peterborough Petes
9. DAILEY, Bob	Van.	Tor. Marlboros
10. NEELEY, Bob	Tor.	Peterborough Petes
11. RICHARDSON, Terry	Det.	New Westminster
12. TITANIC, Morris	Buf.	Sudbury Wolves
13. ROTA, Darcy	Chi.	Edm. Oil Kings
14. MIDDLETON, Rick	NYR	Oshawa Generals
15. TURNBULL, Ian	Tor.	Ottawa 67's
16. MERCREDI, Vic	Atl.	New Westminster

SECOND ROUND

Selection	Claimed By	Amateur Club
17. GOLDUP, Glen	Mtl.	Tor. Marlboros
18. DUNLOP, Blake	Min.	Ottawa 67's
19. BORDELEAU, Paulin	Van.	Tor. Marlboros
20. GOODENOUGH, Larry	Phi.	London Knights
21. VAIL, Eric	Atl.	Sudbury Wolves
22. MARRIN, Peter	Mtl.	Tor. Marlboros
23. BIANCHIN, Wayne	Pit.	Flin Flon Bombers
24. PESUT, George	St.L.	Saskatoon Blades
25. ROGERS, John	Min.	Edm. Oil Kings
26. LEVINS, Brent	Phi.	Swift Current Broncos
27. CAMPBELL, Colin	Pit.	Peterborough Petes
28. LANDRY, Jean	Buf.	Que. Remparts
29. THOMAS, Reg	Chi.	London Knights
30. HICKEY, Pat	NYR	Hamilton Red Wings
31. JONES, Jim	Bos.	Peterborough Petes
32. ANDRUFF, Ron	Mtl.	Flin Flon Bombers

1972

FIRST ROUND

Selection	Claimed By	Amateur Club
1. HARRIS, Billy	NYI	Tor. Marlboros
2. RICHARD, Jacques	Atl.	Que. Remparts
3. LEVER, Don	Van.	Niagara Falls Flyers
4. SHUTT, Steve	Mtl.	Tor. Marlboros
5. SCHOENFELD, Jim	Buf.	Niagara Falls Flyers
6. LAROCQUE, Michel	Mtl.	Ottawa 67's
7. BARBER, Bill	Phi.	Kitchener Rangers
8. GARDNER, Dave	Mtl.	Tor. Marlboros
9. MERRICK, Wayne	St.L.	Ottawa 67's
10. BLANCHARD, Albert	NYR	Kitchener Rangers
11. FERGUSON, George	Tor.	Tor. Marlboros
12. BYERS, Jerry	Min.	Kitchener Rangers
13. RUSSELL, Phil	Chi.	Edm. Oil Kings
14. VAN BOXMEER, John	Mtl.	Guelph Juniors
15. MacMILLAN, Bobby	NYR	St. Catharines Hawks
16. BLOOM, Mike	Bos.	St. Catharines Hawks

SECOND ROUND

Selection	Claimed By	Amateur Club
17. HENNING, Lorne	NYI	New Westminster
18. BIALOWAS, Dwight	Atl.	Regina Pats
19. McSHEFFREY, Brian	Van.	Ottawa 67's
20. KOZAK, Don	L.A.	Edm. Oil Kings
21. SACHARUK, Larry	NYR	Saskatoon Blades
22. CASSIDY, Tom	Cal.	Kitchener Rangers
23. BLADON, Tom	Phi.	Edm. Oil Kings
24. LYNCH, Jack	Pit.	Oshawa Generals
25. CARRIERE, Larry	Buf.	Loyola College
26. GUITE, Pierre	Det.	St. Catharines Hawks
27. OSBURN, Randy	Tor.	London Knights
28. WEIR, Stan	Cal.	Medicine Hat Tigers
29. OGILVIE, Brian	Chi.	Edm. Oil Kings
30. LUKOWICH, Bernie	Pit.	New Westminster
31. VILLEMURE, Rene	NYR	Shawinigan Bruins
32. ELDER, Wayne	Bos.	London Knights

1971

FIRST ROUND

Selection	Claimed By	Amateur Club
1. LAFLEUR, Guy	Mtl.	Que. Remparts
2. DIONNE, Marcel	Det.	St. Catharines Hawks
3. GUEVREMONT, Jocelyn	Van.	Mtl. Junior Canadiens
4. CARR, Gene	St.L.	Flin Flon Bombers
5. MARTIN, Rick	Buf.	Mtl. Junior Canadiens
6. JONES, Ron	Bos.	Edm. Oil Kings
7. ARNASON, Chuck	Mtl.	Flinflon Bombers
8. WRIGHT, Larry	Phi.	Regina Pats
9. PLANTE, Pierre	Phi.	Drummondville Rangers
10. VICKERS, Steve	NYR	Tor. Marlboros
11. WILSON, Murray	Mtl.	Ottawa 67's
12. SPRING, Dan	Chi.	Edm. Oil Kings
13. DURBANO, Steve	NYR	Tor. Marlboros
14. O'REILLY, Terry	Bos.	Oshawa Generals

SECOND ROUND

Selection	Claimed By	Amateur Club
15. BAIRD, Ken	Cal.	Flin Flon Bombers
16. BOUCHA, Henry	Det.	U.S. Nationals
17. LALONDE, Bobby	Van.	Mtl. Junior Canadiens
18. McKENZIE, Brian	Pit.	St. Catharines Hawks
19. RAMSAY, Craig	Buf.	Peterborough Petes
20. ROBINSON, Larry	Mtl.	Kitchener Rangers
21. NORRISH, Rod	Min.	Regina Pats
22. KEHOE, Rick	Tor.	Hamilton Red Wings
23. FORTIER, Dave	Tor.	St. Catharines Hawks
24. DEGUISE, Michel	Mtl.	Sorel Eperviers
25. FRENCH, Terry	Mtl.	Ottawa 67's
26. KRYSKOW, Dave	Chi.	Edm. Oil Kings
27. WILLIAMS, Tom	NYR	Hamilton Red Wings
28. RIDLEY, Curt	Bos.	Portage Terriers

1970

FIRST ROUND

Selection	Claimed By	Amateur Club
1. PERREAULT, Gilbert	Buf.	Mtl. Junior Canadiens
2. TALLON, Dale	Van.	Tor. Marlboros
3. LEACH, Reg	Bos.	Flin Flon Bombers
4. MacLEISH, Rick	Bos.	Peterborough Petes
5. MARTINIUK, Ray	Mtl.	Flin Flon Bombers
6. LEFLEY, Chuck	Mtl.	Canadian Nationals
7. POLIS, Greg	Pit.	Estevan Bruins
8. SITTLER, Darryl	Tor.	London Knights
9. PLUMB, Ron	Bos.	Peterborough Petes
10. ODDLEIFSON, Chris	Oak.	Wpg. Jets
11. WILSON, Norm	NYR	Mtl. Junior Canadiens
12. LAJEUNESSE, Serge	Det.	Mtl. Junior Canadiens
13. STEWART, Bob	Bos.	Oshawa Generals
14. MALONEY, Dan	Chi.	London Knights

SECOND ROUND

Selection	Claimed By	Amateur Club
15. DEADMARSH, Butch	Buf.	Brandon Wheat Kings
16. HARGREAVES, Jim	Van.	Wpg. Jets
17. HARVEY, Fred	Min.	Hamilton Red Wings
18. CLEMENT, Bill	Phi.	Ottawa 67's
19. LAFRAMBOISE, Pete	Oak.	Ottawa 67's
20. BARRETT, Fred	Min.	Tor. Marlboros
21. NORRISH, Rod	Pit.	Flin Flon Bombers
22. THOMPSON, Errol	Tor.	Charlottetown Royals
23. KEOGAN, Murray	St.L.	U. of Minnesota
24. McDONOUGH, Al	L.A.	St. Catharines Hawks
25. MURPHY, Mike	NYR	Tor. Marlboros
26. GUINDON, Bobby	Det.	Mtl. Junior Canadiens
27. BOUCHARD, Dan	Bos.	London Knights
28. ARCHAMBAULT, Mike	Chi.	Drummondville Rangers

1969

FIRST ROUND

Selection	Claimed By	Amateur Club
1. HOULE, Rejean	Mtl.	Mon. Junior Canadiens
2. TARDIF, Marc	Mtl.	Mon. Junior Canadiens
3. TANNAHILL, Don	Bos.	Niagara Falls Flyers
4. SPRING, Frank	Bos.	Edm. Oil Kings
5. REDMOND, Dick	Min.	St. Catharines Hawks
6. CURRIER, Bob	Phi.	Cornwall Royals
7. FEATHERSTONE, Tony	Oak.	Peterborough Petes
8. DUPONT, Andre	NYR	Mtl. Junior Canadiens
9. MOSER, Ernie	Tor.	Estevan Bruins
10. RUTHERFORD, Jim	Det.	Hamilton Red Wings
11. BOLDIREV, Ivan	Bos.	Oshawa Generals
12. JARRY, Pierre	NYR	Ottawa 67's
13. BORDELEAU, J.-P.	Chi.	Mtl. Junior Canadiens
14. O'BRIEN, Dennis	Min.	St. Catharines Hawks

SECOND ROUND

Selection	Claimed By	Amateur Club
15. KESSELL, Rick	Pit.	Oshawa Generals
16. HOGANSON, Dale	L.A.	Estevan Bruins
17. CLARKE, Bobby	Phi.	Flin Flon Bombers
18. STACKHOUSE, Ron	Oak.	Peterborough Petes
19. LOWE, Mike	St.L.	Loyola College
20. BRINDLEY, Doug	Tor.	Niagara Falls Flyers
21. GARWASIUK, Ron	Det.	Regina Pats
22. QUOQUOCHI, Art	Bos.	Mtl. Junior Canadiens
23. WILSON, Bert	NYR	London Knights
24. ROMANCHYCH, Larry	Chi.	Flin Flon Bombers
25. GILBERT, Gilles	Min.	London Knights
26. BRIERE, Michel	Pit.	Shawinigan Falls
27. BODDY, Greg	L.A.	Edm. Oil Kings
28. BROSSART, Bill	Phi.	Estevan Bruins

NHL All-Stars

Active Players' All-Star Selection Records

GOALTENDERS

Player	First Team Selections		Second Team Selections		Total
Patrick Roy	(2)	1988-89; 1989-90.	(2)	1987-88; 1990-91.	4
Tom Barrasso	(1)	1983-84.	(1)	1984-85.	2
Grant Fuhr	(1)	1987-88.	(1)	1981-82.	2
Mike Liut	(1)	1980-81.	(1)	1986-87.	2
Pete Peeters	(1)	1982-83.	(0)		1
J. Vanbiesbrouck	(1)	1985-86.	(0)		1
Ron Hextall	(1)	1986-87.	(0)		1
Ed Belfour	(1)	1990-91.	(0)		1
R. Melanson	(0)		(1)	1982-83.	1
Bob Froese	(0)		(1)	1985-86.	1
Mike Vernon	(0)		(1)	1988-89.	1
Darren Puppa	(0)		(1)	1989-90.	1

DEFENSEMEN

Player	First Team Selections		Second Team Selections		Total
Ray Bourque	(8)	1979-80; 1981-82; 1983-84; 1984-85; 1986-87; 1987-88; 1989-90; 1990-91.	(4)	1980-81; 1982-83; 1985-86; 1988-89.	12
Paul Coffey	(3)	1984-85; 1985-86; 1988-89.	(4)	1981-82; 1982-83; 1983-84; 1989-90.	7
Larry Robinson	(3)	1976-77; 1978-79; 1979-80.	(3)	1977-78; 1980-81; 1985-86.	6
Al MacInnis	(2)	1989-90; 1990-91.	(2)	1986-87; 1988-89.	4
Mark Howe	(3)	1982-83; 1985-86; 1986-87.	(0)		3
Rod Langway	(2)	1982-83; 1983-84.	(1)	1984-85.	3
Doug Wilson	(1)	1981-82.	(2)	1984-85; 1989-90.	3
Chris Chelios	(1)	1988-89.	(1)	1990-91.	2
Randy Carlyle	(1)	1980-81.	(0)		1
Scott Stevens	(1)	1987-88.	(0)		1
Larry Murphy	(0)		(1)	1986-87.	1
Gary Suter	(0)		(1)	1987-88.	1
Brad McCrimmon	(0)		(1)	1987-88.	1
Brian Leetch	(0)		(1)	1990-91.	1

CENTERS

Player	First Team Selections		Second Team Selections		Total
Wayne Gretzky	(8)	1980-81; 1981-82; 1982-83; 1983-84; 1984-85; 1985-86; 1986-87; 1990-91.	(4)	1979-80; 1987-88; 1988-89; 1989-90.	12
Bryan Trottier	(2)	1977-78; 1978-79.	(2)	1981-82; 1983-84.	4
Mario Lemieux	(2)	1987-88; 1988-89.	(2)	1985-86; 1986-87.	4
Mark Messier	(1)	1989-90.	(0)		1
Denis Savard	(0)		(1)	1982-83.	1
Dale Hawerchuk	(0)		(1)	1984-85.	1
Adam Oates	(0)		(1)	1990-91.	1

RIGHT WING

Player	First Team Selections		Second Team Selections		Total
Jari Kurri	(2)	1984-85; 1986-87.	(3)	1983-84; 1985-86; 1988-89.	5
Cam Neely	(0)		(3)	1987-88; 1989-90; 1990-91.	3
Brett Hull	(2)	1989-90; 1990-91.	(0)		2
Joe Mullen	(1)	1988-89.	(0)		1
Dave Taylor	(0)		(1)	1980-81.	1
Tim Kerr	(0)		(1)	1986-87.	1

LEFT WING

Player	First Team Selections		Second Team Selections		Total
Luc Robitaille	(4)	1987-88; 1988-89; 1989-90; 1990-91.	(1)	1986-87.	5
Michel Goulet	(3)	1983-84; 1985-86; 1986-87.	(2)	1982-83; 1987-88.	5
Mark Messier	(2)	1981-82; 1982-83.	(1)	1983-84.	3
John Tonelli	(0)		(2)	1981-82; 1984-85.	2
John Ogrodnick	(1)	1984-85.	(0)		1
Mats Naslund	(0)		(1)	1985-86.	1
Gerard Gallant	(0)		(1)	1988-89.	1
Brian Bellows	(0)		(1)	1989-90.	1
Kevin Stevens	(0)		(1)	1990-91.	1

Leading NHL All-Stars 1930-91

Player	Pos	Team	NHL Seasons	First Team Selections	Second Team Selections	Total Selections
Howe, Gordie	RW	Detroit	26	12	9	21
Richard, Maurice	RW	Montreal	18	8	6	14
Hull, Bobby	LW	Chicago	16	10	2	12
*Gretzky, Wayne	C	Edm., L.A.	12	8	4	12
*Bourque, Ray	D	Boston	12	8	4	12
Harvey, Doug	D	Mtl., NYR	19	10	1	11
Hall, Glenn	G	Chi., St.L.	18	7	4	11
Beliveau, Jean	C	Montreal	20	6	4	10
Seibert, Earl	D	NYR., Chi	15	4	6	10
Orr, Bobby	D	Boston	12	8	1	9
Lindsay, Ted	LW	Detroit	17	8	1	9
Mahovlich, Frank	LW	Tor., Det., Mtl.	18	3	6	9
Shore, Eddie	D	Boston	14	7	1	8
Mikita, Stan	C	Chicago	22	6	2	8
Kelly, Red	D	Detroit	20	6	2	8
Esposito, Phil	C	Boston	18	6	2	8
Pilote, Pierre	D	Chicago	14	5	3	8
Brimsek, Frank	G	Boston	10	2	6	8
Bossy, Mike	RW	NY Islanders	10	5	3	8
Potvin, Denis	D	NY Islanders	15	5	2	7
Park, Brad	D	NYR, Bos.	17	5	2	7
*Coffey, Paul	D	Edm., Pit.	11	3	4	7
Plante, Jacques	G	Mtl-Tor	18	3	4	7
Gadsby, Bill	D	Chi., NYR, Det.	20	3	4	7
Sawchuk, Terry	G	Detroit	21	3	4	7
Durnan, Bill	G	Montreal	7	6	0	6
Lafleur, Guy	RW	Montreal	16	6	0	6
Dryden, Ken	G	Montreal	8	5	1	6
*Robinson, Larry	D	Montreal	19	3	3	6
Horton, Tim	D	Toronto	24	3	3	6
Salming, Borje	D	Toronto	17	1	5	6
*Robitaille, Luc	LW	Los Angeles	5	4	1	5
Cowley, Bill	C	Boston	13	4	1	5
Jackson, Harvey	LW	Toronto	15	4	1	5
*Goulet, Michel	LW	Quebec	12	3	2	5
Conacher, Charlie	RW	Toronto	12	3	2	5
Stewart, Jack	D	Detroit	12	3	2	5
Lach, Elmer	C	Montreal	14	3	2	5
Quackenbush, Bill	D	Det., Bos.	14	3	2	5
Blake, Toe	LW	Montreal	15	3	2	5
Esposito, Tony	G	Chicago	16	3	2	5
Reardon, Ken	D	Montreal	7	2	3	5
*Kurri, Jari	RW	Edmonton	10	2	3	5
Apps, Syl	C	Toronto	10	2	3	5
Giacomin, Ed	G	NY Rangers	13	2	3	5

* Active

Position Leaders in All-Star Selections

Position	Player	First Team	Second Team	Total
GOAL	Glenn Hall	7	4	11
	Frank Brimsek	2	6	8
	Jacques Plante	3	4	7
	Terry Sawchuk	3	4	7
	Bill Durnan	6	0	6
	Ken Dryden	5	1	6
DEFENSE	*Ray Bourque	8	4	12
	Doug Harvey	10	1	11
	Earl Seibert	4	6	10
	Bobby Orr	8	1	9
	Eddie Shore	7	1	8
	Red Kelly	6	2	8
	Pierre Pilote	5	3	8

Position	Player	First Team	Second Team	Total
LEFT WING	Bobby Hull	10	2	12
	Ted Lindsay	8	1	9
	Frank Mahovlich	3	6	9
	Harvey Jackson	4	1	5
	*Michel Goulet	3	2	5
	Toe Blake	3	2	5
	Luc Robitaille	4	1	5
RIGHT WING	Gordie Howe	12	9	21
	Maurice Richard	8	6	14
	Mike Bossy	5	3	8
	Guy Lafleur	6	0	6
	Charlie Conacher	3	2	5
CENTER	*Wayne Gretzky	8	4	12
	Jean Beliveau	6	4	10
	Stan Mikita	6	2	8
	Phil Esposito	6	2	8
	Bill Cowley	4	1	5
	Elmer Lach	3	2	5
	Syl Apps	2	3	5

* active player

All-Star Teams

1930-91

Voting for the NHL All-Star Team is conducted among the representatives of the Professional Hockey Writers' Association at the end of the season.

Following is a list of the First and Second All-Star Teams since their inception in 1930-31.

First Team		Second Team
1990-91		
Belfour, Ed, Chi.	G	Roy, Patrick, Mtl.
Bourque, Ray, Bos.	D	Chelios, Chris, Chi.
MacInnis, Al, Cgy.	D	Leetch, Brian, NYR
Gretzky, Wayne, L.A.	C	Oates, Adam, St. L.
Hull, Brett, St. L.	RW	Neely, Cam, Bos.
Robitaille, Luc, L.A.	LW	Stevens, Kevin, Pit.
1989-90		
Roy, Patrick, Mtl.	G	Puppa, Darren, Buf.
Bourque, Ray, Bos.	D	Coffey, Paul, Pit.
MacInnis, Al, Cgy.	D	Wilson, Doug, Chi.
Messier, Mark, Edm.	C	Gretzky, Wayne, L.A.
Hull, Brett, St. L.	RW	Neely, Cam, Bos.
Robitaille, Luc, L.A.	LW	Bellows, Brian, Min.
1988-89		
Roy, Patrick, Mtl.	G	Vernon, Mike, Cgy.
Chelios, Chris, Mtl.	D	MacInnis, Al, Cgy.
Coffey, Paul, Pit.	D	Bourque, Ray, Bos.
Lemieux, Mario, Pit.	C	Gretzky, Wayne, L.A.
Mullen, Joe, Cgy.	RW	Kurri, Jari, Edm.
Robitaille, Luc, L.A.	LW	Gallant, Gerard, Det.
1987-88		
Fuhr, Grant, Edm.	G	Roy, Patrick, Mtl.
Bourque, Ray, Bos.	D	Suter, Gary, Cgy.
Stevens, Scott, Wsh.	D	McCrimmon, Brad, Cgy.
Lemieux, Mario, Pit.	C	Gretzky, Wayne, Edm.
Loob, Hakan, Cgy.	RW	Neely, Cam, Bos.
Robitaille, Luc, L.A.	LW	Goulet, Michel, Que.
1986-87		
Hextall, Ron, Phi.	G	Liut, Mike, Hfd.
Bourque, Ray, Bos.	D	Murphy, Larry, Wsh.
Howe, Mark, Phi.	D	MacInnis, Al, Cgy.
Gretzky, Wayne, Edm.	C	Lemieux, Mario, Pit.
Kurri, Jari, Edm.	RW	Kerr, Tim, Phi.
Goulet, Michel, Que.	LW	Robitaille, Luc, L.A.
1985-86		
Vanbiesbrouck, J., NYR	G	Froese, Bob Phi.
Coffey, Paul, Edm.	D	Robinson, Larry, Mtl.
Howe, Mark, Phi.	D	Bourque, Ray, Bos.
Gretzky, Wayne, Edm.	C	Lemieux, Mario, Pit.
Bossy, Mike, NYI	RW	Kurri, Jari, Edm.
Goulet, Michel, Que.	LW	Naslund, Mats, Mtl.
1984-85		
Lindbergh, Pelle, Phi.	G	Barrasso, Tom Buf.
Coffey, Paul, Edm.	D	Langway, Rod, Wsh.
Bourque, Ray, Bos.	D	Wilson, Doug, Chi.
Gretzky, Wayne, Edm.	C	Hawerchuk, Dale, Wpg.
Kurri, Jari, Edm.	RW	Bossy, Mike, NYI
Ogrodnick, John, Det.	LW	Tonelli, John, NYI
1983-84		
Barrasso, Tom, Buf.	G	Riggin, Pat Wsh.
Langway, Rod, Wsh.	D	Coffey, Paul, Edm.
Bourque, Ray, Bos.	D	Potvin, Denis, NYI
Gretzky, Wayne, Edm.	C	Trottier, Bryan, NYI
Bossy, Mike, NYI	RW	Kurri, Jari, Edm.
Goulet, Michel, Que.	LW	Messier, Mark, Edm.

First Team		Second Team
1982-83		
Peeters, Pete, Bos.	G	Melanson, Roland, NYI
Howe, Mark, Phi.	D	Bourque, Ray, Bos.
Langway, Rod, Wsh.	D	Coffey, Paul, Edm.
Gretzky, Wayne, Edm.	C	Savard, Denis, Chi.
Bossy, Mike, NYI	RW	McDonald, Lanny, Cgy.
Messier, Mark, Edm.	LW	Goulet, Michel, Que.

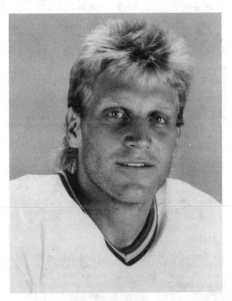

Brett Hull, top, who scored 86 goals in 1990-91, earned a berth on the First All-Star Team. Luc Robitaille has been a First Team All-Star for the past four seasons.

First Team		Second Team
1981-82		
Smith, Bill, NYI	G	Fuhr, Grant, Edm.
Wilson, Doug, Chi.	D	Coffey, Paul, Edm.
Bourque, Ray, Bos.	D	Engblom, Brian, Mtl.
Gretzky, Wayne, Edm.	C	Trottier, Bryan, NYI
Bossy, Mike, NYI	RW	Middleton, Rick, Bos.
Messier, Mark, Edm.	LW	Tonelli, John, NYI
1980-81		
Liut, Mike, St.L.	G	Lessard, Mario, L.A.
Potvin, Denis, NYI	D	Robinson, Larry, Mtl.
Carlyle, Randy, Pit.	D	Bourque, Ray, Bos.
Gretzky, Wayne, Edm.	C	Dionne, Marcel, L.A.
Bossy, Mike, NYI	RW	Taylor, Dave, L.A.
Simmer, Charlie, L.A.	LW	Barber, Bill, Phi.
1979-80		
Esposito, Tony, Chi.	G	Edwards, Don, Buf.
Robinson, Larry, Mtl.	D	Salming, Borje, Tor.
Bourque, Ray, Bos.	D	Schoenfeld, Jim, Buf.
Dionne, Marcel, L.A.	C	Gretzky, Wayne, Edm.
Lafleur, Guy, Mtl.	RW	Gare, Danny, Buf.
Simmer, Charlie, L.A.	LW	Shutt, Steve, Mtl.
1978-79		
Dryden, Ken, Mtl.	G	Resch, Glenn, NYI
Potvin, Denis, NYI	D	Salming, Borje, Tor.
Robinson, Larry, Mtl.	D	Savard, Serge, Mtl.
Trottier, Bryan, NYI	C	Dionne, Marcel, L.A.
Lafleur, Guy, Mtl.	RW	Bossy, Mike, NYI
Gillies, Clark, NYI	LW	Barber, Bill, Phi.
1977-78		
Dryden, Ken, Mtl.	G	Edwards, Don, Buf.
Potvin, Denis, NYI	D	Robinson, Larry, Mtl.
Park, Brad, Bos.	D	Salming, Borje, Tor.
Trottier, Bryan, NYI	C	Sittler, Darryl, Tor.
Lafleur, Guy, Mtl.	RW	Bossy, Mike, NYI
Gillies, Clark, NYI	LW	Shutt, Steve, Mtl.
1976-77		
Dryden, Ken, Mtl.	G	Vachon, Rogatien, L.A.
Robinson, Larry, Mtl.	D	Potvin, Denis, NYI
Salming, Borje, Tor.	D	Lapointe, Guy, Mtl.
Dionne, Marcel, L.A.	C	Perreault, Gilbert, Buf.
Lafleur, Guy, Mtl.	RW	McDonald, Lanny, Tor.
Shutt, Steve, Mtl.	LW	Martin, Richard, Buf.
1975-76		
Dryden, Ken, Mtl.	G	Resch, Glenn, NYI
Potvin, Denis, NYI	D	Salming, Borje, Tor.
Park, Brad, Bos.	D	Lapointe, Guy, Mtl.
Clarke, Bobby, Phi.	C	Perreault, Gilbert, Buf.
Lafleur, Guy, Mtl.	RW	Leach, Reggie, Phi.
Barber, Bill, Phi.	LW	Martin, Richard, Buf.
1974-75		
Parent, Bernie, Phi.	G	Vachon, Rogie, L.A.
Orr, Bobby, Bos.	D	Lapointe, Guy, Mtl.
Potvin, Denis, NYI	D	Salming, Borje, Tor.
Clarke, Bobby, Phi.	C	Esposito, Phil, Bos.
Lafleur, Guy, Mtl.	RW	Robert, René, Buf.
Martin, Richard, Buf.	LW	Vickers, Steve, NYR

First Team		Second Team

1973-74

First Team		Second Team
Parent, Bernie, Phi.	G	Esposito, Tony, Chi.
Orr, Bobby, Bos.	D	White, Bill, Chi.
Park, Brad, NYR	D	Ashbee, Barry, Phi.
Esposito, Phil, Bos.	C	Clarke, Bobby, Phi.
Hodge, Ken, Bos.	RW	Redmond, Mickey, Det.
Martin, Richard, Buf.	LW	Cashman, Wayne, Bos.

1972-73

First Team		Second Team
Dryden, Ken, Mtl.	G	Esposito, Tony, Chi.
Orr, Bobby, Bos.	D	Park, Brad, NYR
Lapointe, Guy, Mtl.	D	White, Bill, Chi.
Esposito, Phil, Bos.	C	Clarke, Bobby, Phi.
Redmond, Mickey, Det.	RW	Cournoyer, Yvan, Mtl.
Mahovlich, Frank, Mtl.	LW	Hull, Dennis, Chi.

1971-72

First Team		Second Team
Esposito, Tony, Chi.	G	Dryden, Ken, Mtl.
Orr, Bobby, Bos.	D	White, Bill, Chi.
Park, Brad, NYR	D	Stapleton, Pat, Chi.
Esposito, Phil, Bos.	C	Ratelle, Jean, NYR
Gilbert, Rod, NYR	RW	Cournoyer, Yvan, Mtl.
Hull, Bobby, Chi.	LW	Hadfield, Vic, NYR

1970-71

First Team		Second Team
Giacomin, Ed, NYR	G	Plante, Jacques, Tor.
Orr, Bobby, Bos.	D	Park, Brad, NYR
Tremblay, J.C., Mtl.	D	Stapleton, Pat, Chi.
Esposito, Phil, Bos.	C	Keon, Dave, Tor.
Hodge, Ken, Bos.	RW	Cournoyer, Yvan, Mtl.
Bucyk, John, Bos.	LW	Hull, Bobby, Chi.

1969-70

First Team		Second Team
Esposito, Tony, Chi.	G	Giacomin, Ed, NYR
Orr, Bobby, Bos.	D	Brewer, Carl, Det.
Park, Brad, NYR	D	Laperriere, Jacques, Mtl.
Esposito, Phil, Bos.	C	Mikita, Stan, Chi.
Howe, Gordie, Det.	RW	McKenzie, John, Bos.
Hull, Bobby, Chi.	LW	Mahovlich, Frank, Det.

1968-69

First Team		Second Team
Hall, Glenn, St.L.	G	Giacomin, Ed, NYR
Orr, Bobby, Bos.	D	Green, Ted, Bos.
Horton, Tim, Tor.	D	Harris, Ted, Mtl.
Esposito, Phil, Bos.	C	Beliveau, Jean, Mtl.
Howe, Gordie, Det.	RW	Cournoyer, Yvan, Mtl.
Hull, Bobby, Chi.	LW	Mahovlich, Frank, Det.

1967-68

First Team		Second Team
Worsley, Lorne, Mtl.	G	Giacomin, Ed, NYR
Orr, Bobby, Bos.	D	Tremblay, J.C., Mtl.
Horton, Tim, Tor.	D	Neilson, Jim, NYR
Mikita, Stan, Chi.	C	Esposito, Phil, Bos.
Howe, Gordie, Det.	RW	Gilbert, Rod, NYR
Hull, Bobby, Chi.	LW	Bucyk, John, Bos.

1966-67

First Team		Second Team
Giacomin, Ed, NYR	G	Hall, Glenn, Chi.
Pilote, Pierre, Chi.	D	Horton, Tim, Tor.
Howell, Harry, NYR	D	Orr, Bobby, Bos.
Mikita, Stan, Chi.	C	Ullman, Norm, Det.
Wharram, Ken, Chi.	RW	Howe, Gordie, Det.
Hull, Bobby, Chi.	LW	Marshall, Don, NYR

1965-66

First Team		Second Team
Hall, Glenn, Chi.	G	Worsley, Lorne, Mtl.
Laperriere, Jacques, Mtl.	D	Stanley, Allan, Tor.
Pilote, Pierre, Chi.	D	Stapleton, Pat, Chi.
Mikita, Stan, Chi.	C	Beliveau, Jean, Mtl.
Howe, Gordie, Det.	RW	Rousseau, Bobby, Mtl.
Hull, Bobby, Chi.	LW	Mahovlich, Frank, Tor.

1964-65

First Team		Second Team
Crozier, Roger, Det.	G	Hodge, Charlie, Mtl.
Pilote, Pierre, Chi.	D	Gadsby, Bill, Det.
Laperriere, Jacques, Mtl.	D	Brewer, Carl, Tor.
Ullman, Norm, Det.	C	Mikita, Stan, Chi.
Provost, Claude, Mtl.	RW	Howe, Gordie, Det.
Hull, Bobby, Chi.	LW	Mahovlich, Frank, Tor.

1963-64

First Team		Second Team
Hall, Glenn, Chi.	G	Hodge, Charlie, Mtl.
Pilote, Pierre, Chi.	D	Vasko, Elmer, Chi.
Horton, Tim, Tor.	D	Laperriere, Jacques, Mtl.
Mikita, Stan, Chi.	C	Beliveau, Jean, Mtl.
Wharram, Ken, Chi.	RW	Howe, Gordie, Det.
Hull, Bobby, Chi.	LW	Mahovlich, Frank, Tor.

1962-63

First Team		Second Team
Hall, Glenn, Chi.	G	Sawchuk, Terry, Det.
Pilote, Pierre, Chi.	D	Horton, Tim, Tor.
Brewer, Carl, Tor.	D	Vasko, Elmer, Chi.
Mikita, Stan, Chi.	C	Richard, Henri, Mtl.
Howe, Gordie, Det.	RW	Bathgate, Andy, NYR
Mahovlich, Frank, Tor.	LW	Hull, Bobby, Chi.

1961-62

First Team		Second Team
Plante, Jacques, Mtl.	G	Hall, Glenn, Chi.
Harvey, Doug, NYR	D	Brewer, Carl, Tor.
Talbot, Jean-Guy, Mtl.	D	Pilote, Pierre, Chi.
Mikita, Stan, Chi.	C	Keon, Dave, Tor.
Bathgate, Andy, NYR	RW	Howe, Gordie, Det.
Hull, Bobby, Chi.	LW	Mahovlich, Frank, Tor.

1960-61

First Team		Second Team
Bower, Johnny, Tor.	G	Hall, Glenn, Chi.
Harvey, Doug, Mtl.	D	Stanley, Allan, Tor.
Pronovost, Marcel, Det.	D	Pilote, Pierre, Chi.
Beliveau, Jean, Mtl.	C	Richard, Henri, Mtl.
Geoffrion, Bernie, Mtl.	RW	Howe, Gordie, Det.
Mahovlich, Frank, Tor.	LW	Moore, Dickie, Mtl.

1959-60

First Team		Second Team
Hall, Glenn, Chi.	G	Plante, Jacques, Mtl.
Harvey, Doug, Mtl.	D	Stanley, Allan, Tor.
Pronovost, Marcel, Det.	D	Pilote, Pierre, Chi.
Beliveau, Jean, Mtl.	C	Horvath, Bronco, Bos.
Howe, Gordie, Det.	RW	Geoffrion, Bernie, Mtl.
Hull, Bobby, Chi.	LW	Prentice, Dean, NYR

1958-59

First Team		Second Team
Plante, Jacques, Mtl.	G	Sawchuk, Terry, Det.
Johnson, Tom, Mtl.	D	Pronovost, Marcel, Det.
Gadsby, Bill, NYR	D	Harvey, Doug, Mtl.
Beliveau, Jean, Mtl.	C	Richard, Henri, Mtl.
Bathgate, Andy, NYR	RW	Howe, Gordie, Det.
Moore, Dickie, Mtl.	LW	Delvecchio, Alex, Det.

1957-58

First Team		Second Team
Hall, Glenn, Chi.	G	Plante, Jacques, Mtl.
Harvey, Doug, Mtl.	D	Flaman, Fern, Bos.
Gadsby, Bill, NYR	D	Pronovost, Marcel, Det.
Richard, Henri, Mtl.	C	Beliveau, Jean, Mtl.
Howe, Gordie, Det.	RW	Bathgate, Andy, NYR
Moore, Dickie, Mtl.	LW	Henry, Camille, NYR

1956-57

First Team		Second Team
Hall, Glenn, Det.	G	Plante, Jacques, Mtl.
Harvey, Doug, Mtl.	D	Flaman, Fern, Bos.
Kelly, Red, Det.	D	Gadsby, Bill, NYR
Beliveau, Jean, Mtl.	C	Litzenberger, Eddie, Chi.
Howe, Gordie, Det.	RW	Richard, Maurice, Mtl.
Lindsay, Ted, Det.	LW	Chevrefils, Real, Bos.

1955-56

First Team		Second Team
Plante, Jacques, Mtl.	G	Hall, Glenn, Det.
Harvey, Doug, Mtl.	D	Kelly, Red, Det.
Gadsby, Bill, NYR	D	Johnson, Tom, Mtl.
Beliveau, Jean, Mtl.	C	Sloan, Tod, Tor.
Richard, Maurice, Mtl.	RW	Howe, Gordie, Det.
Lindsay, Ted, Det.	LW	Olmstead, Bert, Mtl.

1954-55

First Team		Second Team
Lumley, Harry, Tor.	G	Sawchuk, Terry, Det.
Harvey, Doug, Mtl.	D	Goldham, Bob, Det.
Kelly, Red, Det.	D	Flaman, Fern, Bos.
Beliveau, Jean, Mtl.	C	Mosdell, Ken, Mtl.
Richard, Maurice, Mtl.	RW	Geoffrion, Bernie, Mtl.
Smith, Sid, Tor.	LW	Lewicki, Danny, NYR

1953-54

First Team		Second Team
Lumley, Harry, Tor.	G	Sawchuk, Terry, Det.
Kelly, Red, Det.	D	Gadsby, Bill, Chi.
Harvey, Doug, Mtl.	D	Horton, Tim, Tor.
Mosdell, Ken, Mtl.	C	Kennedy, Ted, Tor.
Howe, Gordie, Det.	RW	Richard, Maurice, Mtl.
Lindsay, Ted, Det.	LW	Sandford, Ed, Bos.

1952-53

First Team		Second Team
Sawchuk, Terry, Det.	G	McNeil, Gerry, Mtl.
Kelly, Red, Det.	D	Quackenbush, Bill, Bos.
Harvey, Doug, Mtl.	D	Gadsby, Bill, Chi.
Mackell, Fleming, Bos.	C	Delvecchio, Alex, Det.
Howe, Gordie, Det.	RW	Richard, Maurice, Mtl.
Lindsay, Ted, Det.	LW	Olmstead, Bert, Mtl.

1951-52

First Team		Second Team
Sawchuk, Terry, Det.	G	Henry, Jim, Bos.
Kelly, Red, Det.	D	Buller, Hy, NYR
Harvey, Doug, Mtl.	D	Thomson, Jim, Tor.
Lach, Elmer, Mtl.	C	Schmidt, Milt, Bos.
Howe, Gordie, Det.	RW	Richard, Maurice, Mtl.
Lindsay, Ted, Det.	LW	Smith, Sid, Tor.

1950-51

First Team		Second Team
Sawchuk, Terry, Det.	G	Rayner, Chuck, NYR
Kelly, Red, Det.	D	Thomson, Jim, Tor.
Quackenbush, Bill, Bos.	D	Reise, Leo, Det.
Schmidt, Milt, Bos.	C	Abel, Sid, Det.
	(tied)	Kennedy, Ted, Tor.
Howe, Gordie, Det.	RW	Richard, Maurice, Mtl.
Lindsay, Ted, Det.	LW	Smith, Sid, Tor.

1949-50

First Team		Second Team
Durnan, Bill, Mtl.	G	Rayner, Chuck, NYR
Mortson, Gus, Tor.	D	Reise, Leo, Det.
Reardon, Kenny, Mtl.	D	Kelly, Red, Det.
Abel, Sid, Det.	C	Kennedy, Ted, Tor.
Richard, Maurice, Mtl.	RW	Howe, Gordie, Det.
Lindsay, Ted, Det.	LW	Leswick, Tony, NYR

1948-49

First Team		Second Team
Durnan, Bill, Mtl.	G	Rayner, Chuck, NYR
Quackenbush, Bill, Det.	D	Harmon, Glen, Mtl.
Stewart, Jack, Det.	D	Reardon, Kenny, Mtl.
Abel, Sid, Det.	C	Bentley, Doug, Chi.
Richard, Maurice, Mtl.	RW	Howe, Gordie, Det.
Conacher, Roy, Chi.	LW	Lindsay, Ted, Det.

1947-48

First Team		Second Team
Broda, W. "Turk", Tor.	G	Brimsek, Frank, Bos.
Quackenbush, Bill, Det.	D	Reardon, Kenny, Mtl.
Stewart, Jack, Det.	D	Colville, Neil, NYR
Lach, Elmer, Mtl.	C	O'Connor, "Buddy", NYR
Richard, Maurice, Mtl.	RW	Poile, "Bud", Chi.
Lindsay, Ted, Det.	LW	Stewart, Gaye, Chi.

First Team		Second Team
1946-47		
Durnan, Bill, Mtl.	G	Brimsek, Frank, Bos.
Reardon, Kenny, Mtl.	D	Stewart, Jack, Det.
Bouchard, Emile, Mtl.	D	Quackenbush, Bill, Det.
Schmidt, Milt, Bos.	C	Bentley, Max, Chi.
Richard, Maurice, Mtl.	RW	Bauer, Bobby, Bos.
Bentley, Doug, Chi.	LW	Dumart, Woody, Bos.

1945-46		
Durnan, Bill, Mtl.	G	Brimsek, Frank, Bos.
Crawford, Jack, Bos.	D	Reardon, Kenny, Mtl.
Bouchard, Emile, Mtl.	D	Stewart, Jack, Det.
Bentley, Max, Chi.	C	Lach, Elmer, Mtl.
Richard, Maurice, Mtl.	RW	Mosienko, Bill, Chi.
Stewart, Gaye, Tor.	LW	Blake, "Toe", Mtl.
Irvin, Dick, Mtl.	Coach	Gottselig, John, Chi.

1944-45		
Durnan, Bill, Mtl.	G	Karakas, Mike, Chi.
Bouchard, Emile, Mtl.	D	Harmon, Glen, Mtl.
Hollett, Bill, Det.	D	Pratt, "Babe", Tor.
Lach, Elmer, Mtl.	C	Cowley, Bill, Bos.
Richard, Maurice, Mtl.	RW	Mosienko, Bill, Chi.
Blake, "Toe", Mtl.	LW	Howe, Syd, Det.
Irvin, Dick, Mtl.	Coach	Adams, Jack, Det.

1943-44		
Durnan, Bill, Mtl.	G	Bibeault, Paul, Tor.
Seibert, Earl, Chi.	D	Bouchard, Emile, Mtl.
Pratt, "Babe", Tor.	D	Clapper, "Dit", Bos.
Cowley, Bill, Bos.	C	Lach, Elmer, Mtl.
Carr, Lorne, Tor.	RW	Richard, Maurice, Mtl.
Bentley, Doug, Chi.	LW	Cain, Herb, Bos.
Irvin, Dick, Mtl.	Coach	Day, C.H., "Hap", Tor.

1942-43		
Mowers, Johnny, Det.	G	Brimsek, Frank, Bos.
Seibert, Earl, Chi.	D	Crawford, Johnny, Bos.
Stewart, Jack, Det.	D	Hollett, Bill, Bos.
Cowley, Bill, Bos.	C	Apps, Syl, Tor.
Carr, Lorne, Tor.	RW	Hextall, Bryan, NYR
Bentley, Doug, Chi.	LW	Patrick, Lynn, NYR
Adams, Jack, Det.	Coach	Ross, Art, Bos.

1941-42		
Brimsek, Frank, Bos.	G	Broda, W. "Turk", Tor.
Seibert, Earl, Chi.	D	Egan, Pat, NYA
Anderson, Tommy, NYA	D	McDonald, Bucko, Tor.
Apps, Syl, Tor.	C	Watson, Phil, NYR
Hextall, Bryan, NYR	RW	Drillon, Gord, Tor.
Patrick, Lynn, NYR	LW	Abel, Sid, Det.
Boucher, Frank, NYR	Coach	Thompson, Paul, Chi.

1940-41		
Broda, W. "Turk", Tor.	G	Brimsek, Frank, Bos.
Clapper, "Dit", Bos.	D	Seibert, Earl, Chi.
Stanowski, Wally, Tor.	D	Heller, Ott, NYR
Cowley, Bill, Bos.	C	Apps, Syl, Tor.
Hextall, Bryan, NYR	RW	Bauer, Bobby, Bos.
Schriner, Dave, Tor.	LW	Dumart, Woody, Bos.
Weiland, "Cooney", Bos.	Coach	Irvin, Dick, Mtl.

1939-40		
Kerr, Dave, NYR	G	Brimsek, Frank, Bos.
Clapper, "Dit", Bos.	D	Coulter, Art, NYR
Goodfellow, Ebbie, Det.	D	Seibert, Earl, Chi.
Schmidt, Milt, Bos.	C	Colville, Neil, NYR
Hextall, Bryan, NYR	RW	Bauer, Bobby, Bos.
Blake, "Toe", Mtl.	LW	Dumart, Woody, Bos.
Thompson, Paul, Chi.	Coach	Boucher, Frank, NYR

First Team		Second Team
1938-39		
Brimsek, Frank, Bos.	G	Robertson, Earl, NYA
Shore, Eddie, Bos.	D	Seibert, Earl, Chi.
Clapper, "Dit", Bos.	D	Coulter, Art, NYR
Apps, Syl, Tor.	C	Colville, Neil, NYR
Drillon, Gord, Tor.	RW	Bauer, Bobby, Bos.
Blake, "Toe", Mtl.	LW	Gottselig, Johnny, Chi.
Ross, Art, Bos.	Coach	Dutton, "Red", NYA

1937-38		
Thompson, "Tiny", Bos.	G	Kerr, Dave, NYR
Shore, Eddie, Bos.	D	Coulter, Art, NYR
Seibert, "Babe", Mtl.	D	Seibert, Eart, Chi.
Cowley, Bill, Bos.	C	Apps, Syl, Tor.
Dillon, Cecil, NYR	RW	Dillon, Cecil, NYR
Drillon, Gord, Tor.	(tied)	Drillon, Gord, Tor.
Thompson, Paul, Chi.	LW	Blake, Toe, Mtl.
Patrick, Lester, NYR	Coach	Ross, Art, Bos.

1936-37		
Smith, Norm, Det.	G	Cude, Wilf, Mtl.
Siebert, "Babe", Mtl.	D	Seibert, Earl, Chi.
Goodfellow, Ebbie, Det.	D	Conacher, Lionel, Mtl. M.
Barry, Marty, Det.	C	Chapman, Art, NYA
Aurie, Larry, Det.	RW	Dillon, Cecil, NYR
Jackson, Harvey, Tor.	LW	Schriner, Dave, NYA
Adams, Jack, Det.	Coach	Hart, Cecil, Mtl.

1935-36		
Thompson, "Tiny", Bos.	G	Cude, Wilf, Mtl.
Shore, Eddie, Bos.	D	Seibert, Earl, Chi.
Seibert, "Babe", Bos.	D	Goodfellow, Ebbie, Det.
Smith, "Hooley", Mtl. M.	C	Thoms, Bill, Tor.
Conacher, Charlie, Tor.	RW	Dillon, Cecil, NYR
Schriner, Dave, NYA	LW	Thompson, Paul, Chi.
Patrick, Lester, NYR	Coach	Gorman, T.P., Mtl. M.

1934-35		
Chabot, Lorne, Chi.	G	Thompson, "Tiny", Bos.
Shore, Eddie, Bos.	D	Wentworth, Cy, Mtl. M.
Seibert, Earl, NYR	D	Coulter, Art, Chi.
Boucher, Frank, NYR	C	Weiland, "Cooney", Det.
Conacher, Charlie, Tor.	RW	Clapper, "Dit", Bos.
Jackson, Harvey, Tor.	LW	Joliat, Aurel, Mtl.
Patrick, Lester, NYR	Coach	Irvin, Dick, Tor.

First Team		Second Team
1933-34		
Gardiner, Charlie, Chi.	G	Worters, Roy, NYA
Clancy, "King", Tor.	D	Shore, Eddie, Bos.
Conacher, Lionel, Chi.	D	Johnson, "Ching", NYR
Boucher, Frank, NYR	C	Primeau, Joe, Tor.
Conacher, Charlie, Tor.	RW	Cook, Bill, NYR
Jackson, Harvey, Tor.	LW	Joliat, Aurel, Mtl.
Patrick, Lester, NYR	Coach	Irvin, Dick, Tor.

1932-33		
Roach, John Ross, Det.	G	Gardiner, Charlie, Chi.
Shore, Eddie, Bos.	D	Clancy, "King", Tor.
Johnson, "Ching", NYR	D	Conacher, Lionel, Mtl. M.
Boucher, Frank, NYR	C	Morenz, Howie, Mtl.
Cook, Bill, NYR	RW	Conacher, Charlie, Tor.
Northcott, "Baldy", Mtl M.	LW	Jackson, Harvey, Tor.
Patrick, Lester, NYR	Coach	Irvin, Dick, Tor.

First Team		Second Team
1931-32		
Gardiner, Charlie, Chi.	G	Worters, Roy, NYA
Shore, Eddie, Bos.	D	Mantha, Sylvio, Mtl.
Johnson, "Ching", NYR	D	Clancy, "King", Tor.
Morenz, Howie, Mtl.	C	Smith, "Hooley", Mtl. M.
Cook, Bill, NYR	RW	Conacher, Charlie, Tor.
Jackson, Harvey, Tor.	LW	Joliat, Aurel, Mtl.
Patrick, Lester, NYR	Coach	Irvin, Dick, Tor.

1930-31		
Gardiner, Charlie, Chi.	G	Thompson, "Tiny", Bos.
Shore, Eddie, Bos.	D	Mantha, Sylvio, Mtl.
Clancy, "King", Tor.	D	Johnson, "Ching", NYR
Morenz, Howie, Mtl.	C	Boucher, Frank, NYR
Joliet, Aurel, Mtl.	RW	Clapper, "Dit", Bos.
Patrick, Lester, NYR	LW	Cook, "Bun", NYR
	Coach	Irvin, Dick, Chi.

Howie Morenz, pictured here at the Ace Bailey Benefit Game, earned a berth on the initial NHL All-Star Team in 1930-31.

All-Star Game Results

Year	Venue	Score	Coaches	Attendance
1991	Chicago	Campbell 11, Wales 5	John Muckler, Mike Milbury	18,472
1990	Pittsburgh	Wales 12, Campbell 7	Pat Burns, Terry Crisp	16,236
1989	Edmonton	Campbell 9, Wales 5	Glen Sather, Terry O'Reilly	17,503
1988	St. Louis	Wales 6, Campbell 5 OT	Mike Keenan, Glen Sather	17,878
1986	Hartford	Wales 4, Campbell 3 OT	Mike Keenan, Glen Sather	15,100
1985	Calgary	Wales 6, Campbell 4	Al Arbour, Glen Sather	16,825
1984	New Jersey	Wales 7, Campbell 6	Al Arbour, Glen Sather	18,939
1983	NY Islanders	Campbell 9, Wales 3	Roger Neilson, Al Arbour	15,230
1982	Washington	Wales 4, Campbell 2	Al Arbour, Glen Sonmor	18,130
1981	Los Angeles	Campbell 4, Wales 1	Pat Quinn, Scott Bowman	15,761
1980	Detroit	Wales 6, Campbell 3	Scott Bowman, Al Arbour	21,002
1978	Buffalo	Wales 3, Campbell 2 OT	Scott Bowman, Fred Shero	16,433
1977	Vancouver	Wales 4, Campbell 3	Scott Bowman, Fred Shero	15,607
1976	Philadelphia	Wales 7, Campbell 5	Floyd Smith, Fred Shero	16,436
1975	Montreal	Wales 7, Campbell 1	Bep Guidolin, Fred Shero	16,080
1974	Chicago	West 6, East 4	Billy Reay, Scott Bowman	16,426
1973	New York	East 5, West 4	Tom Johnson, Billy Reay	16,986
1972	Minnesota	East 3, West 2	Al MacNeil, Billy Reay	15,423
1971	Boston	West 2, East 1	Scott Bowman, Harry Sinden	14,790
1970	St. Louis	East 4, West 1	Claude Ruel, Scott Bowman	16,587
1969	Montreal	East 3, West 3	Toe Blake, Scott Bowman	16,260
1968	Toronto	Toronto 4, All-Stars 3	Punch Imlach, Toe Blake	15,753
1967	Montreal	Montreal 3, All-Stars 0	Toe Blake, Sid Abel	14,284
1965	Montreal	All-Stars 5, Montreal 2	Billy Reay, Toe Blake	13,529
1964	Toronto	All-Stars 3, Toronto 2	Sid Abel, Punch Imlach	14,232
1963	Toronto	All-Stars 3, Toronto 3	Sid Abel, Punch Imlach	14,034
1962	Toronto	Toronto 4, All-Stars 1	Punch Imlach, Rudy Pilous	14,236
1961	Chicago	All-Stars 3, Chicago 1	Sid Abel, Rudy Pilous	14,534
1960	Montreal	All-Stars 2, Montreal 1	Punch Imlach, Toe Blake	13,949
1959	Montreal	Montreal 6, All-Stars 1	Toe Blake, Punch Imlach	13,818
1958	Montreal	Montreal 6, All-Stars 3	Toe Blake, Milt Schmidt	13,989
1957	Montreal	All-Stars 5, Montreal 3	Milt Schmidt, Toe Blake	13,003
1956	Montreal	All-Stars 1, Montreal 1	Jim Skinner, Toe Blake	13,095
1955	Detroit	Detroit 3, All-Stars 1	Jim Skinner, Dick Irvin	10,111
1954	Detroit	All-Stars 2, Detroit 2	King Clancy, Jim Skinner	10,689
1953	Montreal	All-Stars 3, Montreal 1	Lynn Patrick, Dick Irvin	14,153
1952	Detroit	1st team 1, 2nd team 1	Tommy Ivan, Dick Irvin	10,680
1951	Toronto	1st team 2, 2nd team 2	Joe Primeau, Hap Day	11,469
1950	Detroit	Detroit 7, All-Stars 1	Tommy Ivan, Lynn Patrick	9,166
1949	Toronto	All-Stars 3, Toronto 1	Tommy Ivan, Hap Day	13,541
1948	Chicago	All-Stars 3, Toronto 1	Tommy Ivan, Hap Day	12,794
1947	Toronto	All-Stars 4, Toronto 3	Dick Irvin, Hap Day	14,169

There was no All-Star contest during the calendar year of 1966 since the game was moved from the start of season to mid-season. In 1979, the Challenge Cup series between the Soviet Union and Team NHL replaced the All-Star Game. In 1987, Rendez-Vous '87, two games between the Soviet Union and Team NHL replaced the All-Star Game.

1990-91 All-Star Game Summary

January 19, 1991 at Chicago   Campbell 11, Wales 5

PLAYERS ON ICE: **Campbell Conference** — Vernon, Ranford, MacInnis, S. Stevens, S. Smith, Housley, Chelios, Suter, Messier, Oates, Fleury, Gagner, B. Smith, Yzerman, Roenick, Gretzky, Sandstrom, Linden, Larmer, Robitaille, Damphousse

Wales Conference — Roy, Moog, Leetch, Hatcher, Krupp, Coffey, Galley, Bourque, Turcotte, Cullen, LaFontaine, Savard, Sakic, Neely, Lafleur, Recchi, MacLean, Tocchet, Verbeek, K. Stevens, Christian

GOALTENDERS				
	Campbell:	Vernon	30 minutes	2 goals against
		Ranford	30 minutes	3 goals against
	Wales:	Roy	30 minutes	5 goals against
		Moog	30 minutes	6 goals against

SUMMARY
First Period

1. Campbell	Gagner	(Larmer, Roenick)	6.17	
2. Wales	LaFontaine	(Turcotte)	9:17	
3. Campbell	Damphousse	(Oates)	11:36	

PENALTIES: None.

Second Period

4. Wales	LaFontaine	(Hatcher)	1:33	
5. Campbell	Suter		5:23	
6. Campbell	Gretzky	(Sandstrom)	9:10	
7. Campbell	Oates	(Yzerman)	9:48	
8. Campbell	Fleury	(Messier, Chelios)	14:40	
9. Wales	Tocchet	(Verbeek, Sakic)	15:36	
10. Campbell	Roenick	(S. Smith, Oates)	17:07	

PENALTIES: None.

Third Period

11. Wales	MacLean	(Cullen, Bourque)	2:29	PPG
12. Campbell	Chelios	(Larmer, Roenick)	5:23	
13. Campbell	Damphousse	(Oates, Housley)	8:54	
14. Campbell	Damphousse	(Housley, Oates)	11:40	
15. Wales	K. Stevens	(Tocchet)	13:56	PPG
16. Campbell	Damphousse		17:14	

PENALTIES: Housley (C) 0:57, Housley (C) 12:26.

SHOTS ON GOAL BY:				
Campbell Conference	15	15	11	41
Wales Conference	10	9	22	41

Attendance: 18,472

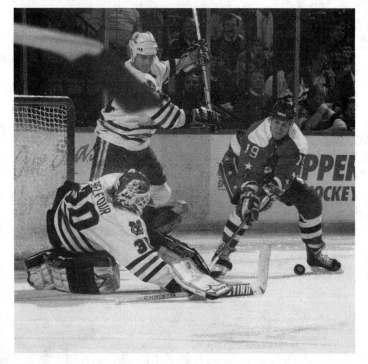

Goaltender Ed Belfour, winner of the Calder, Vezina, Jennings and Trico awards, also earned a berth on the NHL/Upper Deck All-Rookie Team in 1990-91.

NHL/UPPER DECK ALL-ROOKIE TEAM

Voting for the NHL/Upper Deck All-Rookie Team is conducted among the representatives of the Professional Hockey Writers' Association at the end of the season. The rookie all-star team was first selected for the 1982-83 season.

1990-91
Ed Belfour, Chicago	Goal
Eric Weinrich, New Jersey	Defense
Rob Blake, Los Angeles	Defense
Sergei Fedorov, Detroit	Center
Ken Hodge, Boston	Right Wing
Jaromir Jagr, Pittsburgh	Left Wing

1989-90
Bob Essensa, Winnipeg	Goal
Brad Shaw, Hartford	Defense
Geoff Smith, Edmonton	Defense
Mike Modano, Minnesota	Center
Sergei Makarov, Calgary	Right Wing
Rod Brind'Amour, St. Louis	Left Wing

1988-89
Peter Sidorkiewicz, Hartford	
Brian Leetch, NY Rangers	
Zarley Zalapski, Pittsburgh	
Trevor Linden, Vancouver	
Tony Granato, NY Rangers	
David Volek, NY Islanders	

1987-88
Darren Pang, Chicago	Goal
Glen Wesley, Boston	Defense
Calle Johansson, Buffalo	Defense
Joe Nieuwendyk, Calgary	Center
Ray Sheppard, Buffalo	Right Wing
Iain Duncan, Winnipeg	Left Wing

1986-87
Ron Hextall, Philadelphia	
Steve Duchesne, Los Angeles	
Brian Benning, St. Louis	
Jimmy Carson, Los Angeles	
Jim Sandlak, Vancouver	
Luc Robitaille, Los Angeles	

1985-86
Patrick Roy, Montreal	Goal
Gary Suter, Calgary	Defense
Dana Murzyn, Hartford	Defense
Mike Ridley, NY Rangers	Center
Kjell Dahlin, Montreal	Right Wing
Wendel Clark, Toronto	Left Wing

1984-85
Steve Penney, Montreal	
Chris Chelios, Montreal	
Bruce Bell, Quebec	
Mario Lemieux, Pittsburgh	
Tomas Sandstrom, NY Rangers	
Warren Young, Pittsburgh	

1983-84
Tom Barrasso, Buffalo	Goal
Thomas Eriksson, Philadelphia	Defense
Jamie Macoun, Calgary	Defense
Steve Yzerman, Detroit	Center
Hakan Loob, Calgary	Right Wing
Sylvain Turgeon, Hartford	Left Wing

1982-83
Pelle Lindbergh, Philadelphia	
Scott Stevens, Washington	
Phil Housley, Buffalo	
Dan Daoust, Montreal/Toronto	
Steve Larmer, Chicago	
Mats Naslund, Montreal	

All-Star Game Records
1947 through 1991

TEAM RECORDS

MOST GOALS, BOTH TEAMS, ONE GAME:
19 — Wales 12, Campbell 7, 1990 at Pittsburgh
16 — Campbell 11, Wales 5, 1991 at Chicago
14 — Campbell 9, Wales 5, 1989 at Edmonton
13 — Wales 7, Campbell 6, 1984 at New Jersey
12 — Campbell 9, Wales 3, 1983 at NY Islanders
  — Wales 7, Campbell 5, 1976 at Philadelphia
11 — Wales 6, Campbell 5, 1988 at St. Louis
10 — West 6, East 4, 1974 at Chicago
  — Wales 6, Campbell 4, 1985 at Calgary

FEWEST GOALS, BOTH TEAMS, ONE GAME:
2 — NHL All-Stars 1, Montreal Canadiens 1, 1956 at Montreal
  — First Team All-Stars 1, Second Team All-Stars 1, 1952 at Detroit
3 — West 2, East 1, 1971 at Boston
  — Montreal Canadiens 3, NHL All-Stars 0, 1967 at Montreal
  — NHL All-Stars 2, Montreal Canadiens 1, 1960 at Montreal

MOST GOALS, ONE TEAM, ONE GAME:
12 — Wales 12, Campbell 7, 1990 at Pittsburgh
11 — Campbell 11, Wales 5, 1991 at Chicago
9 — Wales 9, Wales 3, 1983 at NY Islanders
  Campbell 9, Wales 5, 1989 at Edmonton
7 — Wales 7, Campbell 5, 1976 at Philadelphia
  — Wales 7, Campbell 1, 1975 at Montreal
  — Detroit Red Wings 7, NHL All-Stars 1, 1950 at Detroit
  — Wales 7, Campbell 6, 1984 at New Jersey
  — Campbell 7, Wales 12, 1990 at Pittsburgh

FEWEST GOALS, ONE TEAM, ONE GAME:
0 — NHL All-Stars 0, Montreal Canadiens 3, 1967 at Montreal
1 — 17 times (1981, 1975, 1971, 1970, 1962, 1961, 1960, 1959, both teams 1956, 1955, 1953, both teams 1952, 1950, 1949, 1948)

MOST SHOTS, BOTH TEAMS, ONE GAME (SINCE 1955):
87 — 1990 at Pittsburgh — Wales (45 shots),
  Campbell 7 (42 shots)
82 — 1991 at Chicago — Campbell 11 (41 shots),
  Wales 5 (41 shots)
81 — 1968 at Toronto — NHL All-Stars 3 (40 shots),
  Toronto Maple Leafs 4 (41 shots)
75 — 1955 at Detroit — NHL All-Stars 1 (31 shots),
  Detroit Red Wings 3 (44 shots)
  — 1989 at Edmonton — Campbell 9 (37 shots),
  Wales 5 (38 shots)

FEWEST SHOTS, BOTH TEAMS, ONE GAME (SINCE 1955):
52 — 1978 at Buffalo — Campbell 2 (12 shots)
  Wales 3 (40 shots)
53 — 1960 at Montreal — NHL All-Stars 2 (27 shots)
  Montreal Canadiens 1 (26 shots)
55 — 1956 at Montreal — NHL All-Stars 1 (28 shots)
  Montreal Canadiens 1 (27 shots)
  — 1971 at Boston — West 2 (28 shots)
  East 1 (27 shots)

MOST SHOTS, ONE TEAM, ONE GAME (SINCE 1955):
45 — 1990 at Pittsburgh — Wales (12-7 vs. Campbell)
44 — 1955 at Detroit — Detroit Red Wings (3-1 vs. NHL All-Stars)
  — 1970 at St. Louis — East (4-1 vs. West)
43 — 1981 at Los Angeles — Campbell (4-1 vs. Wales)
42 — 1976 at Philadelphia — Wales (7-5 vs. Campbell)
  — 1990 at Pittsburgh — Campbell (7-12 vs. Wales)

FEWEST SHOTS, ONE TEAM, ONE GAME (SINCE 1955):
12 — 1978 at Buffalo — Campbell (2-3 vs. Wales)
17 — 1970 at St. Louis — West (1-4 vs. East)
23 — 1961 at Chicago — Chicago Black Hawks (1-3 vs. NHL All-Stars)
24 — 1976 at Philadelphia — Campbell (5-7 vs. Wales)

MOST POWER-PLAY GOALS, BOTH TEAMS, ONE GAME (SINCE 1950):
3 — 1953 at Montreal — NHL All-Stars 3 (2 power-play goals),
  Montreal Canadiens 1 (1 power-play goal)
  — 1954 at Detroit — NHL All-Stars 2 (1 power-play goal)
  Detroit Red Wings 2 (2 power-play goals)
  — 1958 at Montreal — NHL All-Stars 3 (1 power-play goal)
  Montreal Canadiens 6 (2 power-play goals)

FEWEST POWER-PLAY GOALS, BOTH TEAMS, ONE GAME (SINCE 1950):
0 — 13 times (1952, 1959, 1960, 1967, 1968, 1969, 1972, 1973, 1976, 1980, 1981, 1984, 1985)

FASTEST TWO GOALS, BOTH TEAMS, FROM START OF GAME:
37 seconds — 1970 at St. Louis — Jacques Laperriere of East scored at 20 seconds and Dean Prentice of West scored at 37 seconds. Final score: East 4, West 1.
4:08 — 1963 at Toronto — Frank Mahovlich scored for Toronto Maple Leafs at 2:22 of first period and Henri Richard scored at 4:08 for NHL All-Stars. Final score: NHL All-Stars 3, Toronto Maple Leafs 3.
4:19 — 1980 at Detroit — Larry Robinson scored at 3:58 for Wales and Steve Payne scored at 4:19 for Wales. Final score: Wales 6, Campbell 3.

FASTEST TWO GOALS, BOTH TEAMS:
10 seconds — 1976 at Philadelphia — Dennis Ververgaert scored at 4:33 and at 4:43 of third period for Campbell. Final score: Wales 7, Campbell 5.
14 seconds — 1989 at Edmonton. Steve Yzerman and Gary Leeman scored at 17:21 and 17:35 of second period for Campbell. Final score: Campbell 9, Wales 5.
16 seconds — 1990 at Pittsburgh. Kirk Muller of Wales scored at 8:47 of second period and Al MacInnis of Campbell scored at 9:03. Final score: Wales 12, Campbell 7.

FASTEST THREE GOALS, BOTH TEAMS:
1:32 — 1980 at Detroit — all by Wales — Ron Stackhouse scored at 11:40 of third period, Craig Hartsburg scored at 12:40; and Reed Larson scored at 13:12. Final score: Wales 6, Campbell 3.
1:57 — 1990 at Pittsburgh — all by Wales – Rick Tocchet scored at 16:55 of first period, Mario Lemieux scored at 17:37; Pierre Turgeon scored at 18:52. Final score: Wales 12, Campbell 7.
2:01 — 1976 at Philadelphia — Curt Bennett scored at 16:59 of first period for Campbell; Pete Mahovlich scored at 18:31 for Wales; Brad Park scored at 19:00 for Wales. Final score: Wales 7, Campbell 5.

FASTEST FOUR GOALS, BOTH TEAMS:
4:21 — 1990 at Pittsbrugh — Steve Yzerman scored at 14:31 of first period for Campbell; Rick Tocchet scored at 16:55 for Wales; Mario Lemieux scored at 17:37 for Wales. Final score: Wales 12, Campbell 7.
4:26 — 1990 at Pittsbrugh — Luc Robitaille scored at 15:09 and 16:11 of third period for Campbell; Kirk Muller scored at 17:50 for Wales; Doug Smail scored at 19:35 Campbell. Final score: Wales 12, Campbell 7.
4:26 — 1980 at Detroit — all by Wales; Ron Stackhouse scored at 11:40 of third period; Craig Hartsburg scored at 12:40; Reed Larson scored at 13:12; Real Cloutier scored at 16:06. Final score: Wales 6, Campbell 3.

FASTEST TWO GOALS, ONE TEAM, FROM START OF GAME:
4:19 — 1980 at Detroit — Wales — Larry Robinson scored at 3:58 and Steve Payne scored at 4:19. Final score: Wales 6, Campbell 3.
4:38 — 1971 at Boston — West — Chico Maki scored at 36 seconds and Bobby Hull scored at 4:38. Final score: West 2, East 1.
5:13 — 1990 at Pittsburgh — Mario Lemieux scored at :21 and Dave Andreychuk scored at 5:13. Final score: Wales 12, Campbell 7.
5:25 — 1953 at Montreal — NHL All-Stars — Wally Hergesheimer scored at 4:06 and 5:25. Final score: NHL All-Stars 3, Montreal Canadiens 1.

FASTEST TWO GOALS, ONE TEAM:
10 seconds — 1976 at Philadelphia — Campbell — Dennis Ververgaert scored at 4:33 and at 4:43 of third period. Final score: Wales 7, Campbell 5.
14 seconds — 1989 at Edmonton — Campbell — Steve Yzerman and Gary Leeman scored at 17:21 and 17:35 of second period. Final score: Campbell 9, Wales 5.
21 seconds — 1980 at Detroit — Wales — Larry Robinson scored at 3:58 of first period and Steve Payne scored at 4:19. Final score: Wales 6, Campbell 3.
29 seconds — 1976 at Philadelphia — Campbell — Denis Potvin scored at 14:17 of third period and Steve Vickers scored at 14:46. Final score: Wales 7, Campbell 5.
29 seconds — 1976 at Philadelphia — Wales — Pete Mahovlich scored at 18:31 of first period and Brad Park scored at 19:00. Final score: Wales 7, Campbell 5.

FASTEST THREE GOALS, ONE TEAM:
1:32 — 1980 at Detroit — Wales — Ron Stackhouse scored at 11:40 of third period; Craig Hartsburg scored at 12:40; Reed Larson scored at 13:12. Final score: Wales 6, Campbell 3.
1:57 — 1990 at Pittsburgh — Wales — Rick Tocchett scored at 16:55 of first period; Mario Lemieux scored at 17:37; Pierre Turgeon scored at 18:52. Final score: Wales 12, Campbell 7.
2:25 — 1984 at New Jersey — Wales — Rick Middleton scored at 14:49 of first period; Mats Naslund at 16:40; Pierre Larouche at 17:14. Final score: Wales 7, Campbell 6.
3:26 — 1980 at Detroit — Wales — Craig Hartsburg scored at 12:40 of third period; Reed Larson scored at 13:12; Real Cloutier scored at 16:06. Final score: Wales 6, Campbell 3.

FASTEST FOUR GOALS, ONE TEAM:

4:26 — 1980 at Detroit — Wales — Ron Stackhouse scored at 11:40 of third period; Craig Hartsburg scored at 12:40; Reed Larson scored at 13:12; Real Cloutier scored at 16:06. Final score: Wales 6, Campbell 3.

5:52 — 1990 at Pittsburgh — Wales — Mario Lemieux scored at 13:00 of first period; Rick Tocchett scored at 16:55; Mario Lemieux scored at 17:37; Pierre Turgeon scored at 18:52. Final score: Wales 12, Campbell 7.

7:25 — 1976 at Philadelphia — Wales — Al MacAdam scored at 9:34 of second period; Guy Lafleur scored at 11:54; Marcel Dionne scored at 13:51; Dan Maloney scored at 16:59. Final score: Wales 7, Campbell 5.

MOST GOALS, BOTH TEAMS, ONE PERIOD:

9 — 1990 at Pittsburgh — First Period — Wales (7), Campbell (2). Final score: Wales 12, Campbell 7.

7 — 1983 at NY Islanders — Third period — Campbell (6), Wales (1) Final score: Campbell 9, Wales 3.

— 1991 at Chicago — Second Period — Campbell (5), Wales (2). Final score: Campbell 11, Wales 5.

MOST GOALS, ONE TEAM, ONE PERIOD:

7 — 1990 at Pittsburgh — First period — Wales. Final score: Wales 12, Campbell 7.

6 — 1983 at NY Islanders — Third period — Campbell. Final score: Campbell 9, Wales 3.

5 — 1984 at New Jersey — First period — Wales. Final score: Wales 7, Campbell 6.

— 1991 at Chicago — Second period — Campbell. Final score: Campbell 11, Wales 5.

MOST SHOTS, BOTH TEAMS, ONE PERIOD:

36 — 1990 at Pittsburgh — Third period — Campbell (22), Wales (14). Final score: Wales 12, Campbell 7.

30 — 1959 at Montreal — Second period — NHL All-Stars (16), Montreal (14). Final score: Montreal Canadiens 6, NHL All-Stars 1.

29 — 1955 at Detroit — Third period — Detroit Red Wings (18), NHL All-Stars (11). Final score: Detroit Red Wings 3, NHL All-Stars 1.

— 1968 at Toronto — Second period — Toronto Maple Leafs (18), NHL All-Stars (11). Final score: Toronto Maple Leafs 4, NHL All-Stars 3.

— 1980 at Detroit — Third period — Wales (17), Campbell (12). Final score: Wales 6, Campbell 3.

— 1989 at Edmonton — Third period — Wales (15). Campbell (14). Final score: Campbell 9, Wales 5.

MOST SHOTS, ONE TEAM, ONE PERIOD:

22 — 1990 at Pittsburgh — Third period — Campbell. Final score: Wales 12, Campbell 7.

— 1991 at Chicago — Third Period — Wales. Final score: Campbell 11, Wales 5.

20 — 1970 at St. Louis — Third period — East. Final score: East 4, West 1.

18 — 1955 at Detroit — Third period — Detroit Red Wings. Final score: Detroit Red Wings 3, NHL All-Stars 1.

— 1968 at Toronto — Second period — Toronto Maple Leafs. Final score: Toronto Maple Leafs 4, NHL All-Stars 3.

— 1981 at Los Angeles — First period — Campbell. Final score: Campbell 4, Wales 1.

FEWEST SHOTS, BOTH TEAMS, ONE PERIOD:

9 — 1971 at Boston — Third period — East (2), West (7). Final score: West 2, East 1.

— 1980 at Detroit — Second period — Campbell (4), Wales (5). Final score: Wales 6, Campbell 3.

13 — 1982 at Washington — Third period — Campbell (6), Wales (7). Final score: Wales 4, Campbell 2.

14 — 1978 at Buffalo — First period — Campbell (7), Wales (7). Final score: Wales 3, Campbell 2.

— 1986 at Hartford — First period — Campbell (6), Wales (8). Final score: Wales 4, Campbell 3.

FEWEST SHOTS, ONE TEAM, ONE PERIOD:

2 — 1971 at Boston   Third period   East
Final score: West 2, East 1

2 — 1978 at Buffalo   Second period   Campbell
Final score: Wales 3, Campbell 2

3 — 1978 at Buffalo   Third period   Campbell
Final score: Wales 3, Campbell 2

4 — 1955 at Detroit   First period   NHL All-Stars
Final score: Detroit Red Wings 3, NHL All-Stars 1

4 — 1980 at Detroit   Second period   Campbell
Final score: Wales 6, Campbell 3

INDIVIDUAL RECORDS
Career

MOST GAMES PLAYED:
23 — **Gordie Howe** from 1948 through 1980
15 — Frank Mahovlich from 1959 through 1974
13 — Jean Beliveau from 1953 through 1969
— Alex Delvecchio from 1953 through 1967
— Doug Harvey from 1951 through 1969
— Maurice Richard from 1947 through 1959

MOST GOALS:
11 — **Wayne Gretzky** in 11GP
10 — Gordie Howe in 23GP
9 — Mario Lemieux in 5 GP
8 — Frank Mahovlich in 15GP
7 — Maurice Richard in 13GP
5 — Bobby Hull in 12GP
— Ted Lindsay in 11GP
— Denis Potvin in 8GP
— Luc Robitaille in 4GP

MOST ASSISTS:
9 — **Gordie Howe** in 23GP
8 — Ray Bourque in 10GP
7 — Doug Harvey in 13GP
— Guy Lafleur in 5GP
6 — Red Kelly in 11GP
— Norm Ullman in 11GP
— Mats Naslund in 3GP
— Paul Coffey in 9GP

MOST POINTS:
19 — **Gordie Howe** (10G-9A in 23GP)
14 — Mario Lemieux (9G-5A in 5GP)
— Wayne Gretzky (11G-3A in 11GP)
13 — Frank Mahovlich (8G-5A in 15GP)
10 — Bobby Hull (5G-5A in 12GP)
— Ted Lindsay (5G-5A in 11GP)
— Ray Bourque (2G-8A in 10GP)
9 — Maurice Richard (7G-2A in 13GP)
— Henri Richard (4G-5A in 10GP)
— Denis Potvin (5G-4A in 8GP)

MOST PENALTY MINUTES:
27 — **Gordie Howe** in 23GP
21 — Gus Mortson in 9GP
16 — Harry Howell in 7GP

MOST POWER-PLAY GOALS:
6 — **Gordie Howe** in 23GP
3 — Bobby Hull in 12GP
2 — Maurice Richard in 13GP

Vincent Damphousse tied an All-Star Game record with four goals in the 1991 mid-season classic.

Game

MOST GOALS, ONE GAME:
4 — **Wayne Gretzky**, Campbell, 1983
— **Mario Lemieux**, Wales, 1990
— **Vince Damphousse**, Campbell, 1991
3 — Ted Lindsay, Detroit Red Wings, 1950
— Mario Lemieux, Wales, 1988
2 — Wally Hergesheimer, NHL All-Stars, 1953
— Earl Reibel, Detroit Red Wings, 1955
— Andy Bathgate, NHL All-Stars, 1958
— Maurice Richard, Montreal Canadiens, 1958
— Frank Mahovlich, Toronto Maple Leafs, 1963
— Gordie Howe, NHL All-Stars, 1965
— John Ferguson, Montreal Canadiens, 1967
— Frank Mahovlich, East All-Stars, 1969
— Greg Polis, West All-Stars, 1973
— Syl Apps, Wales, 1975
— Dennis Ververgaert, Campbell, 1976
— Richard Martin, Wales, 1977
— Lanny McDonald, Wales, 1977
— Mike Bossy, Wales, 1982
— Pierre Larouche, Wales, 1984
— Mario Lemieux, Wales, 1985
— Brian Propp, Wales, 1986
— Luc Robitaille, Campbell, 1988
— Joe Mullen, Campbell, 1989
— Pierre Turgeon, Wales, 1990
— Kirk Muller, Wales, 1990
— Luc Robitaille, Campbell, 1990
— Pat LaFontaine, Wales, 1991

MOST ASSISTS, ONE GAME:
5 — **Mats Naslund**, Wales, 1988
4 — Ray Bourque, Wales, 1985
— Adam Oates, Campbell, 1991
3 — Dickie Moore, Montreal Canadiens, 1958
— Doug Harvey, Montreal Canadiens, 1959
— Guy Lafleur, Wales, 1975
— Pete Mahovlich, Wales, 1976
— Mark Messier, Campbell, 1983
— Rick Vaive, Campbell, 1984
— Mark Johnson, Wales, 1984
— Don Maloney, Wales, 1984
— Mike Krushelnyski, Campbell, 1985
— Brett Hull, Campbell, 1990

MOST POINTS, ONE GAME:
6 — **Mario Lemieux**, Wales, 1988 (3G-3A)
5 — Mats Naslund, Wales, 1988 (5A)
— Adam Oates, Campbell, 1991 (1G-4A)
4 — Ted Lindsay, Detroit Red Wings, 1950 (3G-1A)
— Gordie Howe, NHL All-Stars, 1965 (2G-2A)
— Pete Mahovlich, Wales, 1976 (1G-3A)
— Wayne Gretzky, Campbell, 1983 (4G)
— Don Maloney, Wales, 1984 (1G-3A)
— Ray Bourque, Wales, 1985 (4A)
— Mario Lemieux, Wales, 1990 (4G)
— Vince Damphousse, Campbell, 1991 (4G)

MOST GOALS, ONE PERIOD:
4 — **Wayne Gretzky**, Campbell, Third period, 1983
3 — Mario Lemieux, Wales, First period, 1990
— Vince Damphousse, Campbell, Third period, 1991
2 — Ted Lindsay, Detroit Red Wings, First period, 1950
— Wally Hergesheimer, NHL All-Stars, First period, 1953
— Andy Bathgate, NHL All-Stars, Third period, 1958
— Frank Mahovlich, Toronto Maple Leafs, First period, 1963
— Dennis Ververgaert, Campbell, Third period, 1976
— Richard Martin, Wales, Third period, 1977
— Pierre Turgeon, Wales, First period, 1990
— Luc Robitaille, Campbell, Third period, 1990

MOST ASSISTS, ONE PERIOD:
3 — **Mark Messier**, Clarence Campbell, Third period, 1983
2 — By several players

MOST POINTS, ONE PERIOD:
4 — **Wayne Gretzky**, Campbell, Third period, 1983 (4G)
3 — Gordie Howe, NHL All-Stars, Second period, 1965 (1G-2A)
— Pete Mahovlich, Wales, First period, 1976 (1G-2A)
— Mark Messier, Campbell, Third period, 1983 (3A)
— Mario Lemieux, Wales, Second period, 1988 (1G-2A)
— Mario Lemieux, Wales, First period, 1990 (3G)
— Vince Damphousse, Campbell, Third period, 1991 (3G)

FASTEST GOAL FROM START OF GAME:
19 seconds — **Ted Lindsay**, Detroit Red Wings, 1950
20 seconds — Jacques Laperriere, East All-Stars, 1970
21 seconds — Mario Lemieux, Wales, 1990
36 seconds — Chico Maki, West All-Stars, 1971
37 seconds — Dean Prentice, West All-Star, 1970

FASTEST GOAL FROM START OF A PERIOD:
19 seconds — **Ted Lindsay**, Detroit Red Wings, 1950 (first period)
20 seconds — Jacques Laperriere, East, 1970 (first period)
21 seconds — Mario Lemieux, Wales, 1990 (first period)
26 seconds — Wayne Gretzky, Campbell, 1982 (second period)
28 seconds — Maurice Richard, NHL All-Stars, 1947 (third period)
33 seconds — Bert Olmstead, Montreal Canadiens, 1957 (second period)

FASTEST TWO GOALS FROM START OF GAME:
5:25 — **Wally Hergesheimer**, NHL All-Stars, 1953, at 4:06 and 5:25 of first period.
12:11 — Frank Mahovlich, Toronto, 1963, at 2:22 and 12:11 of first period.
13:00 — Mario Lemieux, Wales, 1990, at :21 and 13:00 of first period.

FASTEST TWO GOALS FROM START OF A PERIOD:
4:43 — **Dennis Ververgaert**, Campbell, 1976, at 4:33 and 4:43 of third period.
5:25 — Wally Hergesheimer, NHL All-Stars, 1953, at 4:06 and 5:25 of first period.
12:11 — Frank Mahovlich, Toronto, 1963. Scored at 2:22 and 12:11 of first period.
13:00 — Mario Lemieux, Wales, 1990, Scored at :21 and 13:00 of first period.

FASTEST TWO GOALS:
10 seconds — **Dennis Ververgaert**, Campbell, 1976. Scored at 4:33 and 4:43 of third period.
1:02 — Luc Robitaille, Campbell, 1990. Scored at 15:09 and 16:11 of third period.
1:19 — Wally Hergesheimer, NHL All-Stars, 1953. Scored at 4:06 and 5:25 of first period.
2:46 — Vince Damphousse, Campbell, 1991. Scored at 8:54 and 11:40 of third period.

Goaltenders

MOST GAMES PLAYED:
13 — **Glenn Hall** from 1955-1969
11 — Terry Sawchuk from 1950-1968
8 — Jacques Plante from 1956-1970
6 — Tony Esposito from 1970-1980
— Ed Giacomin from 1967-1973

MOST GOALS AGAINST:
22 — **Glenn Hall** in 13GP
19 — Terry Sawchuk in 11GP
18 — Jacques Plante in 8GP
15 — Mike Vernon in 4GP
14 — Turk Broda in 4GP

BEST GOALS-AGAINST-AVERAGE AMONG THOSE WITH AT LEAST TWO GAMES PLAYED:
0.68 — **Gilles Villemure** in 3GP
1.02 — Frank Brimsek in 2GP
1.59 — Johnny Bower in 4GP
1.64 — Lorne "Gump" Worsley in 4GP
1.98 — Gerry McNeil in 3GP
2.03 — Don Edwards in 2GP
2.44 — Terry Sawchuk in 11GP

MOST MINUTES PLAYED:
467 — **Terry Sawchuk** in 11GP
421 — Glenn Hall in 13GP
370 — Jacques Plante in 8GP
209 — Turk Broda in 4GP
182 — Ed Giacomin in 6GP
165 — Tony Esposito in 6GP

Phil Esposito was selected to the NHL All-Star Team on eight occasions during his 18-year NHL career.

NHL Soviet Game Record, 1972-1991

The second Canada Cup tournament, held in 1981, featured a Canadian team with an abundance of scoring power. From left to right, Guy Lafleur, Mike Bossy and Wayne Gretzky.

Date	Venue	Score	Goaltenders
9/2/72	Montreal	Soviet Union 7, Team Canada 3	Tretiak – Dryden
9/4/72	Toronto	Team Canada 4, Soviet Union 1	Esposito – Tretiak
9/6/72	Winnipeg	Soviet Union 4, Team Canada 4	Tretiak – Esposito
9/8/72	Vancouver	Soviet Union 5, Team Canada 4	Tretiak – Dryden
9/22/72	Moscow	Soviet Union 5, Team Canada 4	Tretiak – Esposito
9/24/72	Moscow	Team Canada 3, Soviet Union 2	Dryden – Tretiak
9/26/72	Moscow	Team Canada 4, Soviet Union 3	Esposito – Tretiak
9/28/72	Moscow	Team Canada 6, Soviet Union 5	Dryden – Tretiak
12/28/75	New York	Red Army 7, NY Rangers 3	Tretiak – Davidson
12/29/75	Pittsburgh	Soviet Wings 7, Pittsburgh 4	Sidelnikov – Plasse
12/31/75	Montreal	Montreal 3, Red Army 3	Dryden – Tretiak
1/4/76	Buffalo	Buffalo 12, Soviet Wings 6	Desjardins – Kylikov, Sidelnikov
1/7/76	Chicago	Soviet Wings 4, Chicago 2	Sidelnikov – Esposito
1/8/76	Boston	Red Army 5, Boston 2	Tretiak – Gilbert
1/10/76	New York	Soviet Wings 2, NY Islanders 1	Sidelnikov – Resch
1/11/76	Philadelphia	Philadelphia 4, Red Army 1	Stephenson – Tretiak
9/9/76	Philadelphia	Soviet Union 5, Team U.S.A. 0	Tretiak – Curran
9/11/76	Toronto	Team Canada 3, Soviet Union 1	Vachon – Tretiak
12/28/77	Vancouver	Vancouver 2, Spartak 0	Ridley – Pashkov
1/3/78	Denver	Spartak 8, Colorado 3	Pashkov – Favell, McKenzie
1/5/78	St. Louis	Spartak 2, St. Louis 1	Doroshenko – Johnston, Myre
1/6/78	Montreal	Montreal 5, Spartak 2	Dryden, Larocque – Pashkov
1/8/78	Atlanta	Spartak 2, Atlanta 1	Doroshenko – Belanger
12/31/78	Minnesota	Soviet Wings 8, Minnesota 5	Myshkin – Edwards, LoPresti
1/2/79	Philadelphia	Philadelphia 4, Soviet Wings 4	Parent – Myshkin
1/4/79	Detroit	Detroit 6, Soviet Wings 5	Rutherford, Vachon – Myshkin
1/9/79	Boston	Soviet Wings 4, Boston 1	Sidelnikov – Cheevers, Pettie
2/8/79	New York	Team NHL 4, Soviet Union 2	Dryden – Tretiak
2/10/79	New York	Soviet Union 5, Team NHL 4	Tretiak – Dryden
2/11/79	New York	Soviet Union 6, Team NHL 0	Myshkin – Cheevers
12/26/79	Vancouver	Vancouver 6, Dynamo 2	Ridley – Myshkin
12/27/79	New York	Red Army 5, NY Rangers 2	Tretiak – Baker, Davidson
12/29/79	New York	Red Army 3, NY Islanders 2	Tretiak – Smith
12/31/79	Montreal	Montreal 4, Red Army 2	Sevigny – Tretiak
1/2/80	Winnipeg	Dynamo 7, Winnipeg 0	Myshkin – Hamel, Middlebrook
1/3/80	Buffalo	Buffalo 6, Red Army 1	Edwards – Tretiak
1/4/80	Edmonton	Dynamo 4, Edmonton 1	Myshkin – Mio
1/6/80	Quebec	Red Army 6, Quebec 4	Tretiak – Dion
1/8/80	Washington	Washington 5, Dynamo 5	Inness – Myshkin
9/5/81	Edmonton	Soviet Union 4, Team U.S.A. 1	Tretiak – Esposito
9/9/81	Montreal	Team Canada 7, Soviet Union 3	Liut – Myshkin
9/13/81	Montreal	Soviet Union 8, Team Canada 1	Tretiak – Liut
12/28/82	Edmonton	Edmonton 4, Soviet Union 3	Moog – Myshkin
12/30/82	Quebec	Soviet Union 3, Quebec 0	Tretiak – Bouchard
12/31/82	Montreal	Soviet Union 5, Montreal 0	Tretiak – Sevigny
1/2/83	Calgary	Calgary 3, Soviet Union 2	Edwards, Lemelin – Myshkin
1/4/83	Minnesota	Soviet Union 6, Minnesota 3	Tretiak – Mattson, Beaupre
1/6/83	Philadelphia	Soviet Union 5, Philadelphia 1	Tretiak – Lindbergh
9/8/84	Edmonton	Soviet Union 2, Team U.S.A. 1	Myshkin – Barrasso
9/10/84	Edmonton	Soviet Union 6, Team Canada 3	Tyzhnykh – Lemelin
9/13/84	Calgary	Team Canada 3, Soviet Union 2	Peeters – Myshkin
12/26/85	Los Angeles	Red Army 5, Los Angeles 2	Mylnikov – Janecyk
12/27/85	Edmonton	Red Army 6, Edmonton 3	Mylnikov – Moog
12/29/85	Quebec	Quebec 5, Red Army 1	Malarchuk – Mylnikov
12/29/85	Calgary	Calgary 4, Dynamo 3	Vernon – Myshkin
12/31/85	Montreal	Red Army 6, Montreal 1	Mylnikov – Soetaert, Roy
1/2/86	St. Louis	Red Army 4, St. Louis 2	Mylnikov – Millen, Wamsley
1/4/86	Minnesota	Red Army 4, Minnesota 3	Mylnikov – Casey
1/4/86	Pittsburgh	Dynamo 3, Pittsburgh 3	Myshkin – Herron
1/6/86	Boston	Dynamo 6, Boston 4	Myshkin – Keans
1/8/86	Buffalo	Dynamo 7, Buffalo 4	Myshkin – Cloutier
2/11/87	Quebec	NHL All-Stars 4, Soviet Union 3	Fuhr – Belosheykin
2/13/87	Quebec	Soviet Union 5, NHL All-Stars 3	Belosheykin – Fuhr
9/4/87	Hartford	Soviet Union 5, Team USA 1	Mylnikov – Barrasso
9/6/87	Hamilton, Ont.	Team Canada 3, Soviet Union 3	Fuhr – Belosheykin
9/11/87	Montreal	Soviet Union 6, Team Canada 5	Mylnikov – Fuhr
9/13/87	Hamilton, Ont.	Team Canada 6, Soviet Union 5	Fuhr – Belosheykin
9/15/87	Hamilton, Ont.	Team Canada 6, Soviet Union 5	Fuhr – Mylnikov
12/26/88	Quebec	Red Army 5, Quebec 5	Mylnikov – Mason
12/27/88	Calgary	Dynamo Riga 2, Calgary 2	Irbe – Wamsley
12/28/88	Edmonton	Edmonton 2, Dynamo Riga 1	Irbe – Fuhr
12/29/88	NY Islanders	Red Army 5, NY Islanders 3	Mylnikov – Smith, Hrudey
12/30/88	Vancouver	Vancouver 6, Dynamo Riga 1	Irbe – McLean
12/31/88	Boston	Red Army 5, Boston 4	Mylnikov – Lemelin
12/31/88	Los Angeles	Dynamo Riga 5, Los Angeles 2	Irbe – Fitzpatrick
1/2/89	New Jersey	Red Army 5, New Jersey 0	Mylnikov – Terreri
1/4/89	Pittsburgh	Pittsburgh 4, Red Army 2	Mylnikov, Goloshumov – Pietrangelo, Young
1/4/89	Chicago	Chicago 4, Dynamo Riga 1	Irbe – Belfour
1/5/89	St. Louis	St. Louis 5, Dynamo Riga 0	Irbe – Jablonski
1/7/89	Minnesota	Dynamo Riga 2, Minnesota 1	Irbe – Myllys
1/7/89	Hartford	Red Army 6, Hartford 3	Goloshumov – Liut
1/9/89	Buffalo	Buffalo 6, Red Army 5	Goloshumov, Mylnikov – Cloutier, Puppa
9/14/89	Leningard	Calgary 4, Khimik 2	Vernon, Wamsley – Chervyakov
9/15/89	Moscow	Washington 8, Spartak 7	Mason, Kolzig – Goloshumov
9/16/89	Kiev	Calgary 5, Sokol 2	Wamsley, Guenette – Shundrov, Samoilov
9/17/89	Moscow	Dynamo Moscow 7, Washington 2	Myshkin, Shtalenkov – Dafoe, Beaupre

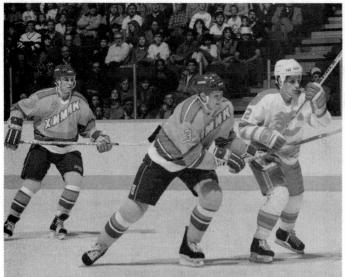

Calgary defeated Khimik Voskresensk of the Soviet National League 6-3 in this international exhibition game on December 8, 1989.

U.S. and Canadian Olympic Teams to play NHL Clubs in 1991-92

Beginning on October 8, 1991 and running until January 22, 1992, the U.S. and Canadian Olympic hockey teams will begin a 22-game exhibition tour against NHL opponents.

The U.S. Olympic Team will play fifteen games, one against each U.S.-based NHL club. The Canadian Olympic Team will play seven games, one against each NHL team based in Canada.

These games mark the first tour of NHL cities by North American Olympic teams and will serve to prepare both the U.S. and Canadian Olympic teams for competition at the 1992 Winter Olympics in Albertville, France.

Date	Location	Result	Goaltenders
9/18/89	Moscow	Calgary 3, Soviet Wings 2	Vernon – Bratash
9/19/89	Riga	Washington 2, Dynamo Riga 1	Dafoe, Kolzig – Irbe
9/20/89	Moscow	Red Army 2, Calgary 1	Mikhailovsky – Vernon, Wamsley
9/21/89	Leningrad	Washington 5, SKA Leningrad 4	Mason – Belosheykin
12/4/89	Los Angeles	Khimik 6, Los Angeles 3	Chervyakov – Gosselin
12/6/89	Edmonton	Edmonton 6, Khimik 2	Fuhr – Chervyakov
12/8/89	Calgary	Calgary 6, Khimik 3	Wamsley – Chervyakov
12/11/89	Detroit	Khimik 4, Detroit 2	Chervyakov – Cheveldae
12/12/89	Washington	Washington 5, Khimik 2	Mason – Chervyakov
12/14/89	St. Louis	Khimik 6, St. Louis 3	Chervyakov – Hebert
12/26/89	NY Islanders	NY Islanders 5, Soviet Wings 4	Fitzpatrick, Healy – Bratash
12/27/89	Hartford	Hartford 4, Soviet Wings 3	Whitmore – Drozdov
12/27/89	Winnipeg	Winnipeg 4, Red Army 1	Beauregard – Irbe
12/29/89	Pittsburgh	Dynamo Moscow 5, Pittsburgh 2	Karpin – Young
12/29/89	Vancouver	Red Army 6, Vancouver 0	Irbe – Weeks
12/31/89	Quebec	Soviet Wings 4, Quebec 4	Bratash – Tugnutt, Millen
12/31/89	Toronto	Dynamo Moscow 7, Toronto 4	Karpin – Laforest
1/1/90	NY Rangers	Soviet Wings 3, NY Rangers 1	Drozdov – Richter
1/2/90	Minnesota	Red Army 4, Minnesota 2	Irbe – Myllys
1/3/90	Montreal	Montreal 2, Soviet Wings 1	Hayward – Drozdov
1/3/90	Buffalo	Buffalo 4, Dynamo Moscow 2	Malarchuk – Karpin
1/6/90	New Jersey	New Jersey 7, Dynamo Moscow 1	Terreri – Karpin, Myshkin
1/7/90	Chicago	Red Army 6, Chicago 4	Irbe – Waite
1/9/90	Philadelphia	Red Army 5, Philadelphia 4	Mikhailovsky – Peeters
1/9/90	Boston	Dynamo Moscow 3, Boston 1	Myshkin – Foster
9/12/90	Leningrad	Montreal 5, SKA Leningrad – Torpedo Yaroslavl 3	Hayward, Racicot – Saprykin
9/13/90	Moscow	Spartak 8, Minnesota 5	Marjin, Goloshumov – Casey, Takko
9/14/90	Riga	Montreal 4, Dynamo Riga 2	Roy, Bergeron – Irbe
9/15/90	Moscow	Soviet Wings 3, Minnesota 2	Bratash, Zvyagin – Casey, Myllys
9/16/90	Moscow	Dynamo Moscow 4, Montreal 1	Shtalenkov – Hayward, Racicot
9/17/90	Voskresensk	Minnesota 3, Khimik 2	Myllys, Takko – Chervyakov
9/18/90	Moscow	Red Army 3, Montreal 2	Drozdov, Mikhailovsky – Roy, Bergeron
9/19/90	Kiev	Sokol, 5, Minnesota 0	Samoilov, Tkachenko – Casey, Myllys
12/3/90	Los Angeles	Los Angeles 5, Khimik 1	Hrudey, Berthiaume – Chervyakov
12/5/90	St. Louis	St. Louis 4, Khimik 2	Joseph – Chervyakov, Kapkaikin
12/8/90	NY Islanders	Khimik 2, NY Islanders 2	Chervyakov – Healy
12/10/90	Montreal	Khimik 6, Montreal 3	Chervyakov – Bergeron
12/12/90	Buffalo	Khimik 5, Buffalo 4	Chervyakov – Puppa, Wakaluk
12/16/90	Boston	Khimik 5, Boston 2	Chervyakov – Lemelin, Delguidice
12/18/90	Minnesota	Minnesota 6, Khimik 4	Casey, Hayward – Chervyakov, Kapkaikin
12/26/90	Detroit	Red Army 5, Detroit 2	Mikhailovsky – Gagnon
12/31/90	NY Rangers	Red Army 6, NY Rangers 1	Mikhailovsky – Vanbiesbrouck, Richter
1/1/91	Toronto	Toronto 7, Dynamo Moscow 4	Bester, Reese – Shtalenkov
1/1/91	Chicago	Red Army 4, Chicago 2	Mikhailovsky – Cloutier, Millen
1/3/91	Hartford	Dynamo Moscow 0, Hartford 0	Trefilov – Sidorkiewicz
1/4/91	Calgary	Red Army 6, Calgary 4	Mikhailovsky – Wamsley
1/6/91	New Jersey	Dynamo Moscow 2, New Jersey 2	Trefilov – Burke, Terreri
1/6/91	Edmonton	Edmonton 4, Red Army 2	Takko – Mikhailovsky
1/8/91	Washington	Washington 3, Dynamo Moscow 2	Hrivnak – Trefilov
1/9/91	Winnipeg	Red Army 6, Winnipeg 4	Mikhailovsky – Beauregard
1/10/91	Philadelphia	Dynamo Moscow 4, Philadelphia 1	Shtalenkov – Wregget
1/12/91	Pittsburgh	Dynamo Moscow 4, Pittsburgh 3	Shtalenkov, Trefilov – Young, Pietrangelo
1/13/91	Vancouver	Red Army 4, Vancouver 3	Ivashkin – Gamble
1/15/91	Quebec	Dynamo Moscow 4, Quebec 1	Trefilov – Gordon

U.S. and Canadian Olympic Series 1991-1992 Schedule

U.S. OLYMPIC TEAM

Tues.	**Oct. 8, 1991**	at	Minnesota
Wed.	**Oct. 23**	at	Buffalo
Thurs.	**Oct. 24**	at	New York Islanders
Wed.	**Nov. 6**	at	New Jersey
Sun.	**Nov. 10**	at	Philadelphia
Mon.	**Nov. 11**	at	Boston
Sun.	**Nov. 17**	at	San Jose
Wed.	**Nov. 20**	at	Hartford
Mon.	**Nov. 25**	at	St. Louis
Sun.	**Dec. 1**	at	Detroit
Wed.	**Dec. 4**	at	New York Rangers
Tues.	**Dec. 10**	at	Los Angeles
Thurs.	**Dec. 12**	at	Chicago
Tues.	**Jan. 21, 1992**	at	Pittsburgh
Wed.	**Jan. 22**	at	Washington

CANADIAN OLYMPIC TEAM

Thurs.	**Nov. 21, 1991**	at	Edmonton
Sun.	**Nov. 24**	at	Vancouver
Sun.	**Dec. 8**	at	Quebec
Tues.	**Dec. 10**	at	Montreal
Thurs.	**Dec. 12**	at	Calgary
Tues.	**Jan. 14, 1992**	at	Toronto
Thurs.	**Jan. 16**	at	Winnipeg

Hockey Hall of Fame

Location: Toronto's Exhibition Park, on the shore of Lake Ontario, adjacent to Ontario Place and Exhibition Stadium. The Hockey Hall of Fame building is in the middle of Exhibition Place, directly north of the stadium. The Hockey Hall of Fame is relocating to a site at the corner of Front and Yonge Streets in downtown Toronto. Projected opening date for the new Hall of Fame is October, 1992.

Telephone: (416) 595-1345.

Hours: Mid-May to mid-August - 10 am to 5 pm Monday through Thursday; 10 am to 7 pm Friday through Sunday. Mid-August to Labor Day - Hours vary during annual Exhibition. September after Labor Day to mid-May - 10 am to 4:30 pm. Also closed Christmas Day, New Year's Day and the day prior to the annual Exhibition.

Admission: Adults $3.25, Seniors & Students $2.25 Group rates, and reduced rate during Exhibition.

History: The Hockey Hall of Fame building was completed May 1, 1961, and officially opened August 26, 1961, by the Prime Minister of Canada, John G. Diefenbaker, and U.S. ambassador to Canada, Livingston T. Merchant. The six member clubs of the NHL operating at the time provided the funds required for construction. The City of Toronto, owner of the grounds, provided an ideal site, and the Canadian National Exhibition Association, as administrator of the park area, agreed to service and maintain the building in perpetuity for the purposes of the Hockey Hall of Fame. Hockey exhibits are provided and financed by the NHL with co-operative support of the Canadian Amateur Hockey Association. Staff and most administration costs are underwritten by the NHL.

Eligibility Requirements: Any person who is, or has been distinguished in hockey as a player, executive or referee/linesman, shall be eligible for election. Player and referee/linesman candidates will normally have completed their active participating careers three years prior to election, but in exceptional cases this period may be shortened by the Hockey Hall of Fame Board of Directors. Veteran player candidates must have concluded their careers as active players in the sport of hockey for at least 25 years. Candidates for election as executives and referees/linesmen shall be nominated only by the Board of Directors and upon election shall be known as Builders or referees/linesmen. Candidates for election as players shall be chosen on the basis of "playing ability, integrity, character and their contribution to their team and the game of hockey in general."

Honor Roll: There are 281 Honored Members of the Hockey Hall of Fame. Of the total, 195 are listed as players, 74 as Builders and 12 as Referees/Linesmen. Ian (Scotty) Morrison is President of the Hall.

(Year of election to the Hall is indicated in brackets after the Members' names).

Denis Potvin, the highest scoring defenseman in NHL history, was inducted into the Hall of Fame in 1991.

PLAYERS

Abel, Sidney Gerald (1969)
*Adams, John James "Jack" (1959)
Apps, Charles Joseph Sylvanus "Syl" (1961)
Armstrong, George Edward (1975)
Bailey, Irvine Wallace "Ace" (1975)
*Bain, Donald H. "Dan" (1945)
*Baker, Hobart "Hobey" (1945)
Barber, William Charles "Bill" (1990)
*Barry, Martin J. "Marty" (1965)
Bathgate, Andrew James "Andy" (1978)
Beliveau, Jean Arthur (1972)
*Benedict, Clinton S. (1965)
*Bentley, Douglas Wagner (1964)
*Bentley, Maxwell H. L. (1966)
Blake, Hector "Toe" (1966)
Boivin, Leo Joseph (1986)
*Boon, Richard R. "Dickie" (1952)
Bossy, Michael (1991)
Bouchard, Emile Joseph "Butch" (1966)
*Boucher, Frank (1958)
*Boucher, George "Buck" (1960)
Bower, John William (1976)
*Bowie, Russell (1945)
Brimsek, Francis Charles (1966)
*Broadbent, Harry L. "Punch" (1962)
*Broda, Walter Edward "Turk" (1967)
Bucyk, John Paul (1981)
*Burch, Billy (1974)
*Cameron, Harold Hugh "Harry" (1962)
Cheevers, Gerald Michael "Gerry" (1985)
*Clancy, Francis Michael "King" (1958)
*Clapper, Aubrey "Dit" (1947)
Clarke, Robert "Bobby" (1987)
*Cleghorn, Sprague (1958)
*Colville, Neil MacNeil (1967)
*Conacher, Charles W. (1961)
*Connell, Alex (1958)
*Cook, William Osser (1952)
Coulter, Arthur Edmund (1974)
Cournoyer, Yvan Serge (1982)
Cowley, William Mailes (1968)
*Crawford, Samuel Russell "Rusty" (1962)
*Darragh, John Proctor "Jack" (1962)
*Davidson, Allan M. "Scotty" (1950)
*Day, Clarence Henry "Hap" (1961)
Delvecchio, Alex (1977)
*Denneny, Cyril "Cy" (1959)
*Drillon, Gordon Arthur (1975)
*Drinkwater, Charles Graham (1950)

Dryden, Kenneth Wayne (1983)
*Dunderdale, Thomas (1974)
*Durnan, William Ronald (1964)
*Dutton, Mervyn A. "Red" (1958)
*Dye, Cecil Henry "Babe" (1970)
Esposito, Anthony James "Tony" (1988)
Esposito, Philip Anthony (1984)
Farrell, Arthur F. (1965)
Flaman, Ferdinand Charles "Fern" (1990)
Foyston, Frank (1958)
*Frederickson, Frank (1958)
Gadsby, William Alexander (1970)
*Gardiner, Charles Robert "Chuck" (1945)
*Gardiner, Herbert Martin "Herb" (1958)
*Gardner, James Henry "Jimmy" (1962)
Geoffrion, Jos. A. Bernard "Boom Boom" (1972)
*Gerard, Eddie (1945)
Giacomin, Edward "Eddie" (1987)
*Gilbert, Rodrigue Gabriel "Rod" (1982)
*Gilmour, Hamilton Livingstone "Billy" (1962)
*Goheen, Frank Xavier "Moose" (1952)
*Goodfellow, Ebenezer R. "Ebbie" (1963)
*Grant, Michael "Mike" (1950)
*Green, Wilfred "Shorty" (1962)
*Griffis, Silas Seth "Si" (1950)
*Hainsworth, George (1961)
Hall, Glenn Henry (1975)
*Hall, Joseph Henry (1961)
*Harvey, Douglas Norman (1973)
*Hay, George (1958)
*Hern, William Milton "Riley" (1962)
Hextall, Bryan Aldwyn (1969)
*Holmes, Harry "Hap" (1972)
*Hooper, Charles Thomas "Tom" (1962)
Horner, George Reginald "Red" (1965)
*Horton, Miles Gilbert "Tim" (1977)
Howe, Gordon (1972)
*Howe, Sydney Harris (1965)
Howell, Henry Vernon "Harry" (1979)
Hull, Robert Marvin (1983)
*Hutton, John Bower "Bouse" (1962)
*Hyland, Harry M. (1962)
*Irvin, James Dickenson "Dick" (1958)
*Jackson, Harvey "Busher" (1971)
*Johnson, Ernest "Moose" (1952)
*Johnson, Ivan "Ching" (1958)
Johnson, Thomas Christian (1970)
*Joliat, Aurel (1947)
*Keats, Gordon "Duke" (1958)

Kelly, Leonard Patrick "Red" (1969)
Kennedy, Theodore Samuel "Teeder" (1966)
Keon, David Michael (1986)
Lach, Elmer James (1966)
Lafleur, Guy Damien (1988)
*Lalonde, Edouard Charles "Newsy" (1950)
Laperriere, Jacques (1987)
*Laviolette, Jean Baptiste "Jack" (1962)
*Lehman, Hugh (1958)
Lemaire, Jacques Gerard (1984)
*LeSueur, Percy (1961)
*Lewis, Herbert A. (1989)
Lindsay, Robert Blake Theodore "Ted" (1966)
Lumley, Harry (1980)
*MacKay, Duncan "Mickey" (1952)
Mahovlich, Frank William (1981)
*Malone, Joseph "Joe" (1950)
Mantha, Sylvio (1960)
*Marshall, John "Jack" (1965)
*Maxwell, Fred G. "Steamer" (1962)
*McGee, Frank (1945)
*McGimsie, William George "Billy" (1962)
*McNamara, George (1958)
Mikita, Stanley (1983)
*Moore, Richard Winston (1974)
*Moran, Patrick Joseph "Paddy" (1958)
*Morenz, Howie (1945)
*Mosienko, William "Billy" (1965)
*Nighbor, Frank (1947)
*Noble, Edward Reginald "Reg" (1962)
*O'Connor, Herbert William "Buddy" (1988)
*Oliver, Harry (1967)
Olmstead, Murray Bert "Bert" (1985)
Orr, Robert Gordon (1979)
Parent, Bernard Marcel (1984)
Park, Douglas Bradford "Brad" (1988)
*Patrick, Joseph Lynn (1980)
*Patrick, Lester (1947)
Perreault, Gilbert (1990)
*Phillips, Tommy (1945)
Pilote, Joseph Albert Pierre Paul (1975)
*Pitre, Didier "Pit" (1962)
*Plante, Joseph Jacques Omer (1978)
Potvin, Denis (1991)
*Pratt, Walter "Babe" (1966)
*Primeau, A. Joseph (1963)
Pronovost, Joseph René Marcel (1978)
Pulford, Bob (1991)
*Pulford, Harvey (1945)

Quackenbush, Hubert George "Bill" (1976)
*Rankin, Frank (1961)
Ratelle, Joseph Gilbert Yvan Jean "Jean" (1985)
Rayner, Claude Earl "Chuck" (1973)
Reardon, Kenneth Joseph (1966)
Richard, Joseph Henri (1979)
Richard, Joseph Henri Maurice "Rocket" (1961)
*Richardson, George Taylor (1950)
*Roberts, Gordon (1971)
*Ross, Arthur Howie (1945)
*Russel, Blair (1965)
*Russell, Ernest (1965)
*Ruttan, J.D. "Jack" (1962)
Savard, Serge A. (1986)
*Sawchuk, Terrance Gordon "Terry" (1971)
*Scanlan, Fred (1965)
Schmidt, Milton Conrad "Milt" (1961)
*Schriner, David "Sweeney" (1962)
*Seibert, Earl Walter (1963)
*Seibert, Oliver Levi (1961)
*Shore, Edward W. "Eddie" (1947)
*Siebert, Albert C. "Babe" (1964)
*Simpson, Harold Edward "Bullet Joe" (1962)
Sittler, Darryl Glen (1989)
*Smith, Alfred E. (1962)
Smith, Clint (1991)
*Smith, Reginald "Hooley" (1972)
*Smith, Thomas James (1973)
Stanley, Allan Herbert (1981)
*Stanley, Russell "Barney" (1962)
*Stewart, John Sherratt "Black Jack" (1964)
*Stewart, Nelson "Nels" (1962)
*Stuart, Bruce (1961)
*Stuart, Hod (1945)
*Taylor, Frederic "Cyclone" (O.B.E.) (1947)
*Thompson, Cecil R. "Tiny" (1959)
Tretiak, Vladislav (1989)
*Trihey, Col. Harry J. (1950)
Ullman, Norman Victor Alexander "Norm" (1982)
*Vezina, Georges (1945)
*Walker, John Phillip "Jack" (1960)
Walsh, Martin "Marty" (1962)
*Watson, Harry E. (1962)
*Weiland, Ralph "Cooney" (1971)
*Westwick, Harry (1962)
*Whitcroft, Fred (1962)
*Wilson, Gordon Allan "Phat" (1962)
Worsley, Lorne John "Gump" (1980)
*Worters, Roy (1969)

BUILDERS
*Adams, Charles Francis (1960)
*Adams, Weston W. (1972)
*Aheam, Thomas Franklin "Frank" (1962)
*Ahearne, John Francis "Bunny" (1977)
*Allan, Sir Montagu (C.V.O.) (1945)
*Ballard, Harold Edwin (1977)
*Bauer, Father David (1989)
*Bickell, John Paris (1978)
 Bowman, Scott (1991)
*Brown, George V. (1961)
*Brown, Walter A. (1962)
*Buckland, Frank (1975)
 Butterfield, Jack Arlington (1980)
*Calder, Frank (1947)
*Campbell, Angus D. (1964)
*Campbell, Clarence Sutherland (1966)
*Cattarinich, Joseph (1977)
*Dandurand, Joseph Viateur "Leo" (1963)
 Dilio, Francis Paul (1964)
*Dudley, George S. (1958)
*Dunn, James A. (1968)
 Eagleson, Robert Alan (1989)
 Francis, Emile (1982)
*Gibson, Dr. John L. "Jack" (1976)
*Gorman, Thomas Patrick "Tommy" (1963)
*Hanley, William (1986)
*Hay, Charles (1974)
*Hendy, James C. (1968)
*Hewitt, Foster (1965)
*Hewitt, William Abraham (1947)
*Hume, Fred J. (1962)
*Imlach, George "Punch" (1984)
 Ivan, Thomas N. (1974)
*Jennings, William M. (1975)
 Juckes, Gordon W. (1979)
*Kilpatrick, Gen. John Reed (1960)
*Leader, George Alfred (1969)
 LeBel, Robert (1970)
*Lockhart, Thomas F. (1965)
*Loicq, Paul (1961)
*Mariucci, John (1985)
*McLaughlin, Major Frederic (1963)
*Milford, John "Jake" (1984)
 Molson, Hon. Hartland de Montarville (1973)
*Nelson, Francis (1947)
*Norris, Bruce A. (1969)
*Norris, Sr., James (1958)
*Norris, James Dougan (1962)
*Northey, William M. (1947)
*O'Brien, John Ambrose (1962)
*Patrick, Frank (1958)
*Pickard, Allan W. (1958)
 Pilous, Rudy (1985)
 Poile, Norman "Bud" (1990)
 Pollock, Samuel Patterson Smyth (1978)
*Raymond, Sen. Donat (1958)
*Robertson, John Ross (1947)
*Robinson, Claude C. (1947)
*Ross, Philip D. (1976)
*Selke, Frank J. (1960)
 Sinden, Harry James (1983)
*Smith, Frank D. (1962)
*Smythe, Conn (1958)
 Snider, Edward M. (1988)
*Stanley of Preston, Lord (G.C.B.) (1945)
*Sutherland, Cap. James T. (1947)
 Tarasov, Anatoli V. (1974)
*Turner, Lloyd (1958)
*Tutt, William Thayer (1978)
 Voss, Carl Potter (1974)
*Waghorn, Fred C. (1961)
*Wirtz, Arthur Michael (1971)
 Wirtz, William W. "Bill" (1976)
 Ziegler, John A. Jr. (1987)

REFEREES/LINESMEN
 Armstrong, Neil (1991)
 Ashley, John George (1981)
 Chadwick, William L. (1964)
*Elliott, Chaucer (1961)
*Hayes, George William (1988)
*Hewitson, Robert W. (1963)
*Ion, Fred J. "Mickey" (1961)
 Pavelich, Matt (1987)
*Rodden, Michael J. "Mike" (1962)
*Smeaton, J. Cooper (1961)
 Storey, Roy Alvin "Red" (1967)
 Udvari, Frank Joseph (1973)
*Deceased

United States Hockey Hall of Fame

The United States Hockey Hall of Fame is located in Eveleth, Minnesota, 60 miles north of Duluth, on Highway 53. The facility is open Monday to Saturday 9 a.m. to 5 p.m. and Sundays 11 a.m to 5 p.m.; Adult $2.50; Seniors $2.25; Juniors $1.50; and Children 7-12 $1.25; Children under 6 free. Group rates available.

The Hall was dedicated and opened on June 21, 1973, largely as the result of the work of D. Kelly Campbell, Chairman of the Eveleth Civic Association's Project H Committee. The National Hockey League contributed $100,000 towards the construction of the building. There are now 75 enshrinees consisting of 47 players, 13 coaches, 14 administrators, and one referee. New members are inducted annually in October and must have made a significant contribution toward hockey in the United States through the vehicle of their careers.

PLAYERS
*Abel, Clarence "Taffy"
*Baker, Hobart "Hobey"
Bartholome, Earl
Bessone, Peter
Blake, Robert
Brimsek, Frank
*Chaisson, Ray
Chase, John P.
Christian, Roger
Christian, William "Bill"
Cleary, Robert
Cleary, William
*Conroy, Anthony
Dahlstrom, Carl "Cully"
DesJardins, Victor
Desmond, Richard
Dill, Robert
Everett, Doug
Ftorek, Robbie
*Garrison, John B.
Garrity, Jack
*Goheen, Frank "Moose"
Harding, Austin "Austie"
Iglehart, Stewart
Johnson, Virgil
Karakas, Mike
Kirrane, Jack
Lane, Myles J.
*Linder, Joseph
*LoPresti, Sam L.
*Mariucci, John
Matchefts, John
Mayasich, John
McCartan, Jack
Moe, William
Moseley, Fred
*Murray, Hugh "Muzz" Sr.
*Nelson, Hubert "Hub"
Olson , Eddie
*Owen, Jr., George
*Palmer, Winthrop
Paradise, Robert
Purpur, Clifford "Fido"
Riley, William
*Romnes, Elwin "Doc"
Rondeau, Richard
Williams, Thomas
*Winters, Frank "Coddy"
*Yackel, Ken

COACHES
*Almquist, Oscar
Brooks, Herbert
*Gordon, Malcolm K.
Heyliger, Victor
Ikola, Willard
*Jeremiah, Edward J.
Johnson, Bob
*Kelley, John "Snooks"
Pleban, John "Connie"
Riley, Jack
Ross, Larry
*Thompson, Clifford, R.
*Stewart, William
*Winsor, Alfred "Ralph"

ADMINISTRATORS
*Brown, George V.
*Brown, Walter A.
Bush, Walter
Clark, Donald
*Gibson, J.C. "Doc"
*Jennings, William M.
*Kahler, Nick
*Lockhart, Thomas F.
Marvin, Cal
Ridder, Robert
Trumble, Harold
*Tutt, William Thayer
Wirtz, William W. "Bill"
*Wright, Lyle Z.

REFEREE
Chadwick, William
*Deceased

Bill Chadwick is the only referee to have been inducted into both the Hockey Hall of Fame and the U.S. Hockey Hall of Fame.

Results

Prince of Wales Conference   **Clarence Campbell Conference**

1991 Stanley Cup Playoffs

Mario Lemieux, whose 44 points was the second-highest total in post-season history, won the Conn Smythe Trophy in 1991.

DIVISION SEMI-FINALS
(Best-of-seven series)

Series 'A'

Wed. Apr. 3	Hartford 5	at Boston 2
Fri. Apr. 5	Hartford 3	at Boston 4
Sun. Apr. 7	Boston 6	at Hartford 3
Tue. Apr. 9	Boston 3	at Hartford 4
Thu. Apr. 11	Hartford 1	at Boston 6
Sat. Apr. 13	Boston 3	at Hartford 1

Boston won series 4-2

Series 'B'

Wed. Apr. 3	Buffalo 5	at Montreal 7
Fri. Apr. 5	Buffalo 4	at Montreal 5
Sun. Apr. 7	Montreal 4	at Buffalo 5
Tue. Apr. 9	Montreal 4	at Buffalo 6
Thu. Apr. 11	Buffalo 3	at Montreal 4*
Sat. Apr. 13	Montreal 5	at Buffalo 1

* Russ Courtnall scored at 5:56 of overtime
Montreal won series 4-2

Series 'C'

Wed. Apr. 3	New Jersey 3	at Pittsburgh 1
Fri. Apr. 5	New Jersey 4	at Pittsburgh 5*
Sun. Apr. 7	Pittsburgh 4	at New Jersey 3
Tue. Apr. 9	Pittsburgh 1	at New Jersey 4
Thu. Apr. 11	New Jersey 4	at Pittsburgh 2
Sat. Apr. 13	Pittsburgh 4	at New Jersey 3
Mon. Apr. 15	New Jersey 1	at Pittsburgh 4

* Jaromir Jagr scored at 8:52 of overtime
Pittsburgh won series 4-3

Series 'D'

Wed. Apr. 3	Washington 1	at NY Rangers 2
Fri. Apr. 5	Washington 3	at NY Rangers 0
Sun. Apr. 7	NY Rangers 0	at Washington 0
Tue. Apr. 9	NY Rangers 2	at Washington 3
Thu. Apr. 11	Washington 5	at NY Rangers 4*
Sat. Apr. 13	NY Rangers 2	at Washington 4

* Dino Ciccarelli scored at 6:44 of overtime
Washington won series 4-2

DIVISION FINALS
(Best-of-seven series)
Prince of Wales Conference

Series 'I'

Wed. Apr. 17	Montreal 1	at Boston 2
Fri. Apr. 19	Montreal 4	at Boston 3*
Sun. Apr. 21	Boston 3	at Montreal 2
Tue. Apr. 23	Boston 2	at Montreal 6
Thu. Apr. 25	Montreal 1	at Boston 4
Sat. Apr. 27	Boston 2	at Montreal 3**
Mon. Apr. 29	Montreal 1	at Boston 2

* Stephane Richer scored at 0:27 of overtime
** Shayne Corson scores at 17:47 of overtime
Boston won series 4-3

Series 'J'

Wed. Apr. 17	Washington 4	at Pittsburgh 2
Fri. Apr. 19	Washington 6	at Pittsburgh 7*
Sun. Apr. 21	Pittsburgh 3	at Washington 1
Tue. Apr. 23	Pittsburgh 3	at Washington 1
Thu. Apr. 25	Washington 1	at Pittsburgh 4

* Kevin Stevens scored at 8:10 of overtime
Pittsburgh won series 4-1

CONFERENCE CHAMPIONSHIPS
(Best-of-seven series)

Series 'M'

Wed. May 1	Pittsburgh 3	at Boston 6
Fri. May 3	Pittsburgh 4	at Boston 5*
Sun. May 5	Boston 1	at Pittsburgh 4
Tue. May 7	Boston 1	at Pittsburgh 4
Thu. May 9	Pittsburgh 7	at Boston 2
Sat. May 11	Boston 3	at Pittsburgh 5

* Vladimir Ruzicka scored at 8:14 of overtime
Pittsburgh won series 4-2

Clarence Campbell Conference

Series 'E'

Thu. Apr. 4	Minnesota 4	at Chicago 3*
Sat. Apr. 6	Minnesota 2	at Chicago 5
Mon. Apr. 8	Chicago 6	at Minnesota 5
Wed. Apr. 10	Chicago 1	at Minnesota 3
Fri. Apr. 12	Minnesota 6	at Chicago 0
Sun. Apr. 14	Chicago 1	at Minnesota 3

* Brian Propp scored at 4:14 of overtime
Minnesota won series 4-2

Series 'F'

Thu. Apr. 4	Detroit 6	at St Louis 3
Sati. Apr. 6	Detroit 2	at St Louis 4
Mon. Apr. 8	St Louis 5	at Detroit 5
Wed. Apr. 10	St Louis 3	at Detroit 4
Fri. Apr. 12	Detroit 1	at St Louis 6
Sun. Apr. 14	St Louis 3	at Detroit 0
Tue. Apr. 16	Detroit 2	at St Louis 3

St Louis won series 4-3

Series 'G'

Thu. Apr. 4	Vancouver 6	at Los Angeles 5
Sat. Apr. 6	Vancouver 2	at Los Angeles 3*
Mon. Apr. 8	Los Angeles 1	at Vancouver 2**
Wed. Apr. 10	Los Angeles 6	at Vancouver 1
Fri. Apr. 12	Vancouver 4	at Los Angeles 7
Sun. Apr. 14	Los Angles 4	at Vancouver 1

* Wayne Gretzky scored at 11:08 of overtime
** Cliff Ronning scored at 3:12 of overtime
Los Angeles won series 4-2

Series 'H'

Thu. Apr. 4	Edmonton 3	at Calgary 1
Sat. Apr. 6	Edmonton 1	at Calgary 3
Mon. Apr. 8	Calgary 3	at Edmonton 4
Wed. Apr. 10	Calgary 2	at Edmonton 5
Fri. Apr. 12	Edmonton 3	at Calgary 5
Sun. Apr. 14	Calgary 2	at Edmonton 1*
Tue. Apr. 16	Edmonton 5	at Calgary 4**

* Theo Fleury scored at 4:40 of overtime
** Esa Tikkanen scored at 6:58 of overtime
Edmonton won series 4-3

Clarence Campbell Conference

Series 'K'

Thu. Apr. 18	Minnesota 2	at St Louis 1
Sat. Apr. 20	Minnesota 2	at St Louis 5
Mon. Apr. 22	St Louis 1	at Minnesota 5
Wed. Apr. 24	St Louis 4	at Minnesota 8
Fri. Apr. 26	Minnesota 2	at St Louis 4
Sun. Apr. 28	St Louis 2	at Minnesota 3

Minnesota won series 4-2

Series 'L'

Thu. Apr. 18	Edmonton 3	at Los Angeles 4*
Sat. Apr. 20	Edmonton 4	at Los Angeles 3**
Mon. Apr. 22	Los Angeles 3	at Edmonton 4***
Wed. Apr. 24	Los Angeles 3	at Edmonton 4
Fri. Apr. 26	Edmonton 2	at Los Angeles 5
Sun. Apr. 28	Los Angeles 3	at Edmonton 4****

* Luc Robitaille scored at 2:13 of overtime
** Petr Klima scored at 24:48 of overtime
*** Esa Tikkanen scored at 20:48 of overtime
**** Craig MacTavish scored at 16:57 of overtime
Edmonton won series 4-2

Series 'N'

Thu. May 2	Minnesota 3	at Edmonton 1
Sat. May 4	Minnesota 2	at Edmonton 7
Mon. May 6	Edmonton 3	at Minnesota 7
Wed. May 8	Edmonton 1	at Minnesota 5
Fri. May 10	Minnesota 3	at Edmonton 2

Minnesota won series 4-1

STANLEY CUP CHAMPIONSHIP
(Best-of-seven series)

Series 'O'

Wed. May 15	Minnesota 5	at Pittsburgh 4
Fri. May 17	Minnesota 1	at Pittsburgh 4
Sun. May 19	Pittsburgh 1	at Minnesota 3
Tue. May 21	Pittsburgh 5	at Minnesota 3
Thu. May 23	Minnesota 4	at Pittsburgh 6
Sat. May 25	Pittsburgh 8	at Minnesota 0

Pittsburgh won series 4-2

Team Playoff Records

	GP	W	L	GF	GA	%
Pittsburgh	24	16	8	95	68	.667
Minnesota	23	14	9	81	75	.609
Boston	19	10	9	60	62	.526
Edmonton	18	9	9	57	60	.500
Montreal	13	7	6	47	42	.538
Los Angles	12	6	6	46	37	.500
St Louis	13	6	7	41	42	.462
Washinton	11	5	6	29	35	.455
New Jersey	7	3	4	21	21	.429
Detroit	7	3	4	20	24	.429
Calgary	7	3	4	20	22	.429
Buffalo	6	2	4	24	29	.333
Hartford	6	2	4	17	24	.333
NY Rangers	6	2	4	16	16	.333
Chicago	6	2	4	16	23	.333
Vancouver	6	2	4	16	26	.333

STANLEY CUP CHAMPIONSHIP 1991

Individual Leaders

Abbreviations: * – rookie eligible for Calder Trophy; **A** – assists; **G** – goals; **GP** – games played; **GW** – game-winning goals; **OT** – overtime goals; **PIM** – penalties in minutes; **PP** – power play goals; **PTS** – points; **S** – shots on goal; **SH** – short-handed goals; **%** – percentage of shots resulting in goals; +/− – difference between Goals For (**GF**) scored when a player is on the ice with his team at even strength or short-handed and Goals Against (**GA**) scored when the same player is on the ice with his team at even strength or on a power play.

Playoff Scoring Leaders

Player	Team	GP	G	A	Pts	+/−	PIM	PP	SH	GW	OT	S	%
Mario Lemieux	Pittsburgh	23	16	28	44	14	16	6	2	0	0	93	17.2
Mark Recchi	Pittsburgh	24	10	24	34	6	33	5	0	2	0	60	16.7
Kevin Stevens	Pittsburgh	24	17	16	33	14	53	7	0	4	1	83	20.5
Brian Bellows	Minnesota	23	10	19	29	6−	30	6	0	1	0	68	14.7
Dave Gagner	Minnesota	23	12	15	27	4−	28	6	1	1	0	78	15.4
Ray Bourque	Boston	19	7	18	25	4−	12	3	0	0	0	84	8.3
Brian Propp	Minnesota	23	8	15	23	4−	28	8	0	3	1	52	15.4
Larry Murphy	Pittsburgh	23	5	18	23	17	44	4	0	0	0	66	7.6
Neal Broten	Minnesota	23	9	13	22	2	6	2	1	0	0	55	16.4
Craig Janney	Boston	18	4	18	22	4−	11	4	0	0	0	26	15.4

Playoff Defensemen Scoring Leaders

Player	Team	GP	G	A	Pts	+/−	PIM	PP	SH	GW	OT	S	%
Ray Bourque	Boston	19	7	18	25	4−	12	3	0	0	0	84	8.3
Larry Murphy	Pittsburgh	23	5	18	23	17	44	4	0	0	0	66	7.6
Steve Duchesne	Los Angeles	12	4	8	12	7	8	1	0	0	0	39	10.3
Jeff Brown	St Louis	13	3	9	12	6	6	0	0	0	0	42	7.1
Mark Tinordi	Minnesota	23	5	6	11	1−	78	4	0	0	0	54	9.3
Paul Coffey	Pittsburgh	12	2	9	11	1−	6	0	0	0	0	37	5.4
Glen Wesley	Boston	19	2	9	11	8−	19	2	0	0	0	47	4.3
Charlie Huddy	Edmonton	18	3	7	10	9	10	1	0	0	0	35	8.6
Calle Johansson	Washington	10	2	7	9	3−	8	1	0	0	0	24	8.3
Matt Schneider	Montreal	13	2	7	9	2	18	1	0	0	0	33	6.1

GOALTENDING LEADERS

Goals Against Average

Goaltender	Team	GPI	Mins.	GA	AVG
John Vanbiesbrouck	NY Rangers	1	52	1	1.15
Tom Barrasso	Pittsburgh	20	1175	51	2.60
*Dominic Hasek	Chicago	3	69	3	2.61
*Mike Richter	NY Rangers	6	313	14	2.68
Kelly Hrudey	Los Angeles	12	798	37	2.78

Wins

Goaltender	Team	GPI	Mins.	W	L
Jon Casey	Minnesota	23	1205	14	7
Tom Barrasso	Pittsburgh	20	1175	12	7
Andy Moog	Boston	19	1133	10	9
Grant Fuhr	Edmonton	17	1019	8	7
Patrick Roy	Montreal	13	785	7	5

Save Percentage

Goaltender	Team	GPI	Mins.	GA	SA	S%	W	L
Rejean Lemelin	Boston	2	32	0	18	1.000	0	0
John Vanbiesbrouck	NY Rangers	1	52	1	22	.955	0	0
*Mike Richter	NY Rangers	6	313	14	182	.923	2	4
Dominic Hasek	Chicago	3	69	3	39	.923	0	0
Tom Barrasso	Pittsburgh	20	1175	51	629	.919	12	7

Shutouts

Goaltender	Team	GPI	Mins.	SO
Frank Pietrangelo	Pittsburgh	5	288	1
*Mike Richter	NY Rangers	6	313	1
Don Beaupre	Washington	11	624	1
Vincent Riendeau	St Louis	13	687	1
Tom Barrasso	Pittsburgh	20	1175	1
Jon Casey	Minnesota	23	1205	1

Goal Scoring

Name	Team	GP	G
Kevin Stevens	Pittsburgh	24	17
Cam Neely	Boston	19	16
Mario Lemieux	Pittsburgh	23	16
Luc Robitaille	Los Angeles	12	12
Esa Tikkanen	Edmonton	18	12
Dave Gagner	Minnesota	23	12
Brett Hull	St Louis	13	11
Brian Bellows	Minnesota	23	10
Mark Recchi	Pittsburgh	24	10
Shayne Corson	Montreal	13	9

Assists

Name	Team	GP	A
Mario Lemieux	Pittsburgh	23	28
Mark Recchi	Pittsburgh	24	24
Brian Bellows	Minnesota	23	19
Craig Janney	Boston	18	18
Ray Bourque	Boston	19	18
Larry Murphy	Pittsburgh	23	18
Kevin Stevens	Pittsburgh	24	16
Dave Gagner	Minnesota	23	15
Brian Propp	Minnesota	23	15
Adam Oates	St Louis	13	13

Power-Play Goals

Name	Team	GP	PP
Cam Neely	Boston	19	9
Brian Propp	Minnesota	23	8
Kevin Stevens	Pittsburgh	24	7
Brian Bellows	Minnesota	23	6
Dave Gagner	Minnesota	23	6
Mario Lemieux	Pittsburgh	23	6
Luc Robitaille	Los Angeles	12	5
Mark Recchi	Pittsburgh	24	5
Shayne Corson	Montreal	13	4
Craig Janney	Boston	18	4

Short-Hand Goals

Name	Team	GP	SH
Russ Courtnall	Montreal	13	2
Mario Lemieux	Pittsburgh	23	2
Jyrki Lumme	Vancouver	6	1
Christian Ruuttu	Buffalo	6	1
Dave Snuggerud	Buffalo	6	1
*Terry Yake	Hartford	6	1
Doug Brown	New Jersey	7	1
Kevin Miller	Detroit	7	1
Steve Kasper	Los Angeles	10	1
Kelly Miller	Washington	11	1

Game-Winning Goals

Name	Team	GP	GW
Bobby Smith	Minnesota	23	5
Cam Neely	Boston	19	4
Ron Francis	Pittsburgh	24	4
Kevin Stevens	Pittsburgh	24	4
Shayne Corson	Montreal	13	3
Petr Klima	Edmonton	18	3
Esa Tikkanen	Edmonton	18	3
Brian Propp	Minnesota	23	3
Cliff Ronning	Vancouver	6	2

Plus/Minus

Name	Team	GP	+/−
Joe Mullen	Pittsburgh	22	17
Larry Murphy	Pittsburgh	23	17
Mario Lemieux	Pittsburgh	23	14
Kevin Stevens	Pittsburgh	24	14
Ron Francis	Pittsburgh	24	13
Gordie Roberts	Pittsburgh	24	13
Norm MacIver	Edmonton	18	10
Charlie Huddy	Edmonton	18	9
Stewart Gavin	Minnesota	21	9
Scott Stevens	St Louis	13	8

First Goals

Name	Team	GP	FG
John MacLean	New Jersey	7	3
Cam Neely	Boston	19	3
Dave Gagner	Minnesota	23	3
Mario Lemieux	Pittsburgh	23	3
Al MacInnis	Calgary	7	2
Joe Nieuwendyk	Calgary	7	2
Steve Kasper	Los Angeles	10	2
Mike Keane	Montreal	12	2
Craig Simpson	Edmonton	18	2
Petri Skriko	Boston	18	2

Shots

Name	Team	GP	S
Mario Lemieux	Pittsburgh	23	93
Ray Bourque	Boston	19	84
Kevin Stevens	Pittsburgh	24	83
Dave Gagner	Minnesota	23	78
Esa Tikkanen	Edmonton	18	76
Cam Neely	Boston	19	72
Brian Bellows	Minnesota	23	68
Larry Murphy	Pittsburgh	23	66
Bobby Smith	Minnesota	23	60
Mark Recchi	Pittsburgh	24	60

Overtime Goals

Name	Team	GP	OT
Esa Tikkanen	Edmonton	18	2
Cliff Ronning	Vancouver	6	1
Theo Fleury	Calgary	7	1
Dino Ciccarelli	Washington	11	1
Wayne Gretzky	Los Angeles	12	1
Luc Robitaille	Los Angeles	12	1
Shayne Corson	Montreal	13	1
Russ Courtnall	Montreal	13	1
Stephane Richer	Montreal	13	1

Team Statistics

TEAMS' HOME-AND-ROAD RECORD

	Home						Road					
	GP	W	L	GF	GA	%	GP	W	L	GF	GA	%
PIT	13	9	4	52	37	.692	11	7	4	43	31	.636
MIN	11	8	3	45	33	.727	12	6	6	36	42	.500
BOS	10	7	3	36	30	.700	9	3	6	24	32	.333
EDM	9	6	3	32	23	.667	9	3	6	25	37	.333
MTL	6	5	1	27	19	.833	7	2	5	20	23	.286
L.A.	6	4	2	27	21	.667	6	2	4	19	16	.333
STL	7	5	2	26	17	.714	6	1	5	15	25	.167
WSH	5	2	3	9	16	.400	6	3	3	20	19	.500
N.J.	3	1	2	10	9	.333	4	2	2	11	12	.500
DET	3	2	1	9	8	.667	4	1	3	11	16	.250
CGY	4	2	2	13	12	.500	3	1	2	7	10	.333
BUF	3	2	1	12	13	.667	3	0	3	12	16	.000
HFD	3	1	2	8	12	.333	3	1	2	9	12	.333
NYR	3	1	2	6	9	.333	3	1	2	10	7	.333
CHI	3	1	2	8	12	.333	3	1	2	8	11	.333
VAN	3	1	2	4	11	.333	3	1	2	12	15	.333
TOTAL	92	57	35	324	282	.620	92	35	57	282	324	.380

TEAMS' POWER PLAY RECORD

Abbreviations: **ADV**-total advantages; **PPGF**-power play goals for; **%** arrived by dividing number of power-play goals by total advantages.

		Home					Road					Overall		
	Team	GP	ADV	PPGF	%	Team	GP	ADV	PPGF	%	Team	GP	ADV	PPGF	%
1	HFD	3	10	3	30.0	VAN	3	8	3	37.5	HFD	6	23	6	26.1
2	BOS	10	58	16	27.6	N.J.	4	14	4	28.6	N.J.	7	33	8	24.2
3	MIN	11	69	19	27.5	BUF	3	15	4	26.7	BOS	19	100	24	24.0
4	CGY	4	23	6	26.1	WSH	6	30	7	23.3	MIN	23	152	35	23.0
5	L.A.	6	28	7	25.0	HFD	3	13	3	23.1	L.A.	12	53	12	22.6
6	MTL	6	32	7	21.9	CHI	3	15	3	20.0	VAN	6	23	5	21.7
7	N.J.	3	19	4	21.1	L.A.	6	25	5	20.0	CGY	7	35	7	20.0
8	CHI	3	16	3	18.8	PIT	11	66	13	19.7	CHI	6	31	6	19.4
9	PIT	13	71	13	18.3	MIN	12	83	16	19.3	MTL	13	68	13	19.1
10	EDM	9	49	8	16.3	BOS	9	42	8	19.0	PIT	24	137	26	19.0
11	VAN	3	15	2	13.3	NYR	3	17	3	17.6	BUF	6	36	6	16.7
12	STL	7	43	5	11.6	MTL	7	36	6	16.7	WSH	11	50	8	16.0
13	BUF	3	21	2	9.5	DET	4	21	3	14.3	EDM	18	91	12	13.2
14	DET	3	12	1	8.3	STL	3	37	5	13.5	STL	13	80	10	12.5
15	NYR	3	19	1	5.3	EDM	9	42	4	9.5	DET	7	33	4	12.1
16	WSH	5	20	1	5.0	CGY	3	12	1	8.3	NYR	6	36	4	11.1
TOTAL		92	505	98	19.4		92	476	88	18.5		92	981	186	19.0

TEAMS' PENALTY KILLING RECORD

Abbreviations: **TSH**-Total times short-handed; **PPGA**-power play goals against; **%** arrived by dividing-times short minus power-play goals against-by times short.

		Home					Road					Overall		
	Team	GP	TSH	PPGA	%	Team	GP	TSH	PPGA	%	Team	GP	TSH	PPGA	%
1	DET	3	15	1	93.3	NYR	3	10	0	100.0	NYR	6	28	2	92.9
2	VAN	3	12	1	91.7	DET	4	24	2	91.7	DET	7	39	3	92.3
3	NYR	3	18	2	88.9	L.A.	6	32	4	87.5	L.A.	12	56	8	85.7
4	CGY	4	16	2	87.5	MTL	7	40	6	85.0	WSH	11	59	9	84.7
5	WSH	5	27	4	85.2	WSH	6	32	5	84.4	CGY	7	32	5	84.4
6	STL	7	38	6	84.2	N.J.	4	19	3	84.2	MTL	13	68	12	82.4
7	L.A.	6	24	4	83.3	MIN	12	74	13	82.4	MIN	23	136	24	82.4
8	BOS	10	52	9	82.7	CGY	3	16	3	81.3	N.J.	7	38	7	81.6
9	MIN	11	62	11	82.3	BOS	9	40	8	80.0	BOS	19	92	17	81.5
10	EDM	9	45	8	82.2	PIT	11	64	13	79.7	VAN	6	24	5	79.2
11	N.J.	3	19	4	78.9	BUF	3	18	4	77.8	PIT	24	120	25	79.2
12	MTL	6	28	6	78.6	CHI	3	26	6	76.9	STL	13	67	14	79.1
13	PIT	13	56	12	78.6	EDM	9	50	13	74.0	EDM	18	95	21	77.9
14	HFD	3	17	4	76.5	STL	6	29	8	72.4	BUF	6	37	9	75.7
15	BUF	3	19	5	73.7	HFD	3	19	6	68.4	HFD	6	36	10	72.2
16	CHI	3	28	9	67.9	VAN	3	12	4	66.7	CHI	6	54	15	72.7
TOTAL		92	476	88	81.5		92	505	98	80.6		92	981	186	81.0

SHORT-HANDED GOALS

	For			Against	
Team	Games	Goals	Team	Games	Goals
MIN	23	4	WSH	11	0
MTL	13	3	N.J.	7	0
PIT	24	3	DET	7	0
BUF	6	2	CGY	7	0
HFD	6	1	HFD	6	0
VAN	6	1	CHI	6	0
N.J.	7	1	VAN	6	0
DET	7	1	STL	13	1
WSH	11	1	L.A.	12	1
L.A.	12	1	BUF	6	1
NYR	6	0	NYR	6	1
CHI	6	0	EDM	18	2
CGY	7	0	MTL	13	2
STL	13	0	MIN	23	3
EDM	18	0	BOS	19	3
BOS	19	0	PIT	24	4
TOTAL	92	18	**TOTAL**	92	18

Team Penalties

Abbreviations: **GP** – games played; **PEN** – total penalty minutes, including bench penalites; **BMI** – total bench penalty minutes; **AVG** – average penalty minutes per game.

Team	Games	PEN	BMI	AVG
CGY	7	125	4	17.9
EDM	18	400	2	22.2
BOS	19	439	2	23.1
PIT	24	571	12	23.8
L.A.	12	306	2	25.5
MTL	13	333	4	25.6
VAN	6	154	0	25.7
MIN	23	674	4	29.3
WSH	11	328	2	29.8
N.J.	7	211	2	30.1
NYR	6	183	0	30.5
HFD	6	192	0	32.0
STL	13	421	0	32.4
BUF	6	221	0	36.8
DET	7	272	2	38.9
CHI	6	278	4	46.3
TOTAL	92	5108	40	55.5

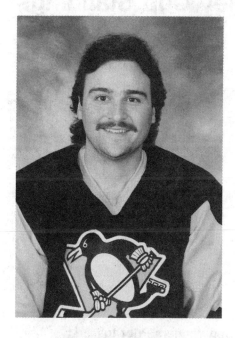

Goaltender Frank Pietrangelo (top) came off the bench to win four games for the Penguins in the 1991 playoffs. Mark Tinordi (bottom) established himself as one of the league's finest rearguards with his strong post-season play in 1991.

Stanley Cup Record Book

History: The Stanley Cup, the oldest trophy competed for by professional athletes in North America, was donated by Frederick Arthur, Lord Stanley of Preston and son of the Earl of Derby, in 1893. Lord Stanley purchased the trophy for 10 guineas ($50 at that time) for presentation to the amateur hockey champions of Canada. Since 1910, when the National Hockey Association took possession of the Stanley Cup, the trophy has been the symbol of professional hockey supremacy. It has been competed for by only NHL teams since 1926 and has been under the exclusive control of the NHL since 1946.

Stanley Cup Standings

1918-91

Team	Yrs.	Series	Won	Lost	Games	Won	Lost	Tied	GF	GA	Cup Wins	Winning %
Montreal	66	123*	79	43	579	351	220	8	1806	1413	22**	.606
Toronto	54	82	43	39	374	177	194	3	961	1024	13	.477
Boston	52	90	43	47	434	212	216	6	1293	1274	5	.488
Chicago	46	77	34	43	346	156	185	5	983	1112	3	.451
NY Rangers	43	73	33	40	314	143	163	8	858	905	3	.455
Detroit	40	68	35	33	326	158	167	1	874	888	7	.485
St. Louis	21	37	16	21	189	84	105	0	552	633	0	.444
Philadelphia	20	43	25	18	223	116	107	0	715	688	2	.520
Calgary***	17	28	12	16	132	61	71	0	439	475	1	.462
Los Angeles	17	24	7	17	112	40	72	0	348	454	0	.357
Minnesota	16	30	14	16	159	77	82	0	534	556	0	.484
Buffalo	16	25	9	16	116	51	65	0	366	401	0	.440
NY Islanders	15	39	28	11	196	119	77	0	687	563	4	.607
Edmonton	12	34	27	7	164	112	52	0	721	525	5	.683
Pittsburgh	11	18	8	10	86	44	42	0	273	285	1	.512
Vancouver	11	14	3	11	58	21	37	0	161	221	0	.362
Washington	9	15	6	9	79	37	42	0	257	259	0	.468
Winnipeg	8	10	2	8	43	12	31	0	133	183	0	.279
Quebec	7	13	6	7	68	31	37	0	212	242	0	.456
Hartford	7	8	1	7	42	15	27	0	125	156	0	.357
New Jersey****	4	6	2	4	35	16	19	0	109	119	0	.457

* 1919 final incomplete due to influenza epidemic.
** Montreal also won the Stanley Cup in 1916.
*** Includes totals of Atlanta 1972-80.
**** Includes totals of Colorado 1976-82.

Stanley Cup Winners Prior to Formation of NHL in 1917

Season	Champions	Manager	Coach
1916-17	Seattle Metropolitans	Pete Muldoon	Pete Muldoon
1915-16	Montreal Canadiens	George Kennedy	George Kennedy
1914-15	Vancouver Millionaires	Frank Patrick	Frank Patrick
1913-14	Toronto Blueshirts	Jack Marshall	Scotty Davidson*
1912-13**	Quebec Bulldogs	M.J. Quinn	Joe Malone*
1911-12	Quebec Bulldogs	M.J. Quinn	C. Nolan
1910-11	Ottawa Senators		Bruce Stuart*
1909-10	Montreal Wanderers	R. R. Boon	Pud Glass*
1908-09	Ottawa Senators		Bruce Stuart*
1907-08	Montreal Wanderers	R. R. Boon	Cecil Blachford
1906-07	Montreal Wanderers (March)	R. R. Boon	Cecil Blachford
1906-07	Kenora Thistles (January)	F.A. Hudson	Tommy Phillips*
1905-06	Montreal Wanderers		Cecil Blachford*
1904-05	Ottawa Silver Seven		A. T. Smith
1903-04	Ottawa Silver Seven		A. T. Smith
1902-03	Ottawa Silver Seven		A. T. Smith
1901-02	Montreal A.A.A.		C. McKerrow
1900-01	Winnipeg Victoria		D. H. Bain
1899-1900	Montreal Shamrocks		H.J. Trihey*
1898-99	Montreal Shamrocks		H.J. Trihey*
1897-98	Montreal Victorias		F. Richardson
1896-97	Montreal Victorias		Mike Grant*
1895-96	Montreal Victorias (December, 1896)		Mike Grant*
1895-96	Winnipeg Victorias (February)		J.C. G. Armytage
1894-95	Montreal Victorias		Mike Grant*
1893-94	Montreal A.A.A.		
1892-93	Montreal A.A.A.		

** Victoria defeated Quebec in challenge series. No official recognition.
* In the early years the teams were frequently run by the Captain. *Indicates Captain

Stanley Cup Winners

Season	Champions	Manager	Coach
1990-91	Pittsburgh Penguins	Craig Patrick	Bob Johnson
1989-90	Edmonton Oilers	Glen Sather	John Muckler
1988-89	Calgary Flames	Cliff Fletcher	Terry Crisp
1987-88	Edmonton Oilers	Glen Sather	Glen Sather
1986-87	Edmonton Oilers	Glen Sather	Glen Sather
1985-86	Montreal Canadiens	Serge Savard	Jean Perron
1984-85	Edmonton Oilers	Glen Sather	Glen Sather
1983-84	Edmonton Oilers	Glen Sather	Glen Sather
1982-83	New York Islanders	Bill Torrey	Al Arbour
1981-82	New York Islanders	Bill Torrey	Al Arbour
1980-81	New York Islanders	Bill Torrey	Al Arbour
1979-80	New York Islanders	Bill Torrey	Al Arbour
1978-79	Montreal Canadiens	Irving Grundman	Scotty Bowman
1977-78	Montreal Canadiens	Sam Pollock	Scotty Bowman
1976-77	Montreal Canadiens	Sam Pollock	Scotty Bowman
1975-76	Montreal Canadiens	Sam Pollock	Scotty Bowman
1974-75	Philadelphia Flyers	Keith Allen	Fred Shero
1973-74	Philadelphia Flyers	Keith Allen	Fred Shero
1972-73	Montreal Canadiens	Sam Pollock	Scotty Bowman
1971-72	Boston Bruins	Milt Schmidt	Tom Johnson
1970-71	Montreal Canadiens	Sam Pollock	Al MacNeil
1969-70	Boston Bruins	Milt Schmidt	Harry Sinden
1968-69	Montreal Canadiens	Sam Pollock	Claude Ruel
1967-68	Montreal Canadiens	Sam Pollock	Toe Blake
1966-67	Toronto Maple Leafs	Punch Imlach	Punch Imlach
1965-66	Montreal Canadiens	Sam Pollock	Toe Blake
1964-65	Montreal Canadiens	Sam Pollock	Toe Blake
1963-64	Toronto Maple Leafs	Punch Imlach	Punch Imlach
1962-63	Toronto Maple Leafs	Punch Imlach	Punch Imlach
1961-62	Toronto Maple Leafs	Punch Imlach	Punch Imlach
1960-61	Chicago Black Hawks	Tommy Ivan	Rudy Pilous
1959-60	Montreal Canadiens	Frank Selke	Toe Blake
1958-59	Montreal Canadiens	Frank Selke	Toe Blake
1957-58	Montreal Canadiens	Frank Selke	Toe Blake
1956-57	Montreal Canadiens	Frank Selke	Toe Blake
1955-56	Montreal Canadiens	Frank Selke	Toe Blake
1954-55	Detroit Red Wings	Jack Adams	Jimmy Skinner
1953-54	Detroit Red Wings	Jack Adams	Tommy Ivan
1952-53	Montreal Canadiens	Frank Selke	Dick Irvin
1951-52	Detroit Red Wings	Jack Adams	Tommy Ivan
1950-51	Toronto Maple Leafs	Conn Smythe	Joe Primeau
1949-50	Detroit Red Wings	Jack Adams	Tommy Ivan
1948-49	Toronto Maple Leafs	Conn Smythe	Hap Day
1947-48	Toronto Maple Leafs	Conn Smythe	Hap Day
1946-47	Toronto Maple Leafs	Conn Smythe	Hap Day
1945-46	Montreal Canadiens	Tommy Gorman	Dick Irvin
1944-45	Toronto Maple Leafs	Conn Smythe	Hap Day
1943-44	Montreal Canadiens	Tommy Gorman	Dick Irvin
1942-43	Detroit Red Wings	Jack Adams	Jack Adams
1941-42	Toronto Maple Leafs	Conn Smythe	Hap Day
1940-41	Boston Bruins	Art Ross	Cooney Weiland
1939-40	New York Rangers	Lester Patrick	Frank Boucher
1938-39	Boston Bruins	Art Ross	Art Ross
1937-38	Chicago Black Hawks	Bill Stewart	Bill Stewart
1936-37	Detroit Red Wings	Jack Adams	Jack Adams
1935-36	Detroit Red Wings	Jack Adams	Jack Adams
1934-35	Montreal Maroons	Tommy Gorman	Tommy Gorman
1933-34	Chicago Black Hawks	Tommy Gorman	Tommy Gorman
1932-33	New York Rangers	Lester Patrick	Lester Patrick
1931-32	Toronto Maple Leafs	Conn Smythe	Dick Irvin
1930-31	Montreal Canadiens	Cecil Hart	Cecil Hart
1929-30	Montreal Canadiens	Cecil Hart	Cecil Hart
1928-29	Boston Bruins	Art Ross	Cy Denneny
1927-28	New York Rangers	Lester Patrick	Lester Patrick
1926-27	Ottawa Senators	Dave Gill	Dave Gill
1925-26	Montreal Maroons	Eddie Gerard	Eddie Gerard
1924-25	Victoria Cougars	Lester Patrick	Lester Patrick
1923-24	Montreal Canadiens	Leo Dandurand	Leo Dandurand
1922-23	Ottawa Senators	Tommy Gorman	Pete Green
1921-22	Toronto St. Pats	Charlie Querrie	Eddie Powers
1920-21	Ottawa Senators	Tommy Gorman	Pete Green
1919-20	Ottawa Senators	Tommy Gorman	Pete Green
1918-19	No decision.*		
1917-18	Toronto Arenas	Charlie Querrie	Dick Carroll

* In the spring of 1919 the Montreal Canadiens travelled to Seattle to meet Seattle, PCHL champions. After five games had been played — teams were tied at 2 wins and 1 tie — the series was called off by the local Department of Health because of the influenza epidemic and the death from influenza of Joe Hall.

Championship Trophies

PRINCE OF WALES TROPHY

Beginning with the 1981-82 season, the club which advances to the Stanley Cup Finals as the winner of the Wales Conference Championship is presented with the Prince of Wales Trophy.

History: His Royal Highness, the Prince of Wales, donated the trophy to the National Hockey League in 1924. From 1927-28 through 1937-38, the award was presented to the team finishing first in the American Division of the NHL. From 1938-39, when the NHL reverted to one section, to 1966-67, it was presented to the team winning the NHL championship. With expansion in 1967-68, it again became a divisional trophy, awarded to the champions of the East Division through to the end of the 1973-74 season. Beginning in 1974-75, it was awarded to the regular-season winner of the conference bearing the name of the trophy. Starting with the 1981-82 season, the trophy has been presented to the playoff champion in the Wales Conference.

1990-91 Winner: Pittsburgh Penguins

The Pittsburgh Penguins captured their first Prince of Wales Trophy on May 11, 1991, after defeating the Boston Bruins in game six of the Prince of Wales Conference Championship series. Prior to facing the Bruins, Pittsburgh had series wins over New Jersey and Washington.

PRINCE OF WALES TROPHY WINNERS

1990-91	**Pittsburgh Penguins**	1956-57	Detroit Red Wings
1989-90	Boston Bruins	1955-56	Montreal Canadiens
1988-89	Montreal Canadiens	1954-55	Detroit Red Wings
1987-88	Boston Bruins	1953-54	Detroit Red Wings
1986-87	Philadelphia Flyers	1952-53	Detroit Red Wings
1985-86	Montreal Canadiens	1951-52	Detroit Red Wings
1984-85	Philadelphia Flyers	1950-51	Detroit Red Wings
1983-84	New York Islanders	1949-50	Detroit Red Wings
1982-83	New York Islanders	1948-49	Detroit Red Wings
1981-82	New York Islanders	1947-48	Toronto Maple Leafs
1980-81	Montreal Canadiens	1946-47	Montreal Canadiens
1979-80	Buffalo Sabres	1945-46	Montreal Canadiens
1978-79	Montreal Canadiens	1944-45	Montreal Canadiens
1977-78	Montreal Canadiens	1943-44	Montreal Canadiens
1976-77	Montreal Canadiens	1942-43	Detroit Red Wings
1975-76	Montreal Canadiens	1941-42	New York Rangers
1974-75	Buffalo Sabres	1940-41	Boston Bruins
1973-74	Boston Bruins	1939-40	Boston Bruins
1972-73	Montreal Canadiens	1938-39	Boston Bruins
1971-72	Boston Bruins	1937-38	Boston Bruins
1970-71	Boston Bruins	1936-37	Detroit Red Wings
1969-70	Chicago Blackhawks	1935-36	Detroit Red Wings
1968-69	Montreal Canadiens	1934-35	Boston Bruins
1967-68	Montreal Canadiens	1933-34	Detroit Red Wings
1966-67	Chicago Blackhawks	1932-33	Boston Bruins
1965-66	Montreal Canadiens	1931-32	New York Rangers
1964-65	Detroit Red Wings	1930-31	Boston Bruins
1963-64	Montreal Canadiens	1929-30	Boston Bruins
1962-63	Toronto Maple Leafs	1928-29	Boston Bruins
1961-62	Montreal Canadiens	1927-28	Boston Bruins
1960-61	Montreal Canadiens	1926-27	Ottawa Senators
1959-60	Montreal Canadiens	1925-26	Montreal Maroons
1958-59	Montreal Canadiens	1924-25	Montreal Canadiens
1957-58	Montreal Canadiens		

Prince of Wales Trophy

Clarence S. Campbell Bowl

Stanley Cup

CLARENCE S. CAMPBELL BOWL

Beginning with the 1981-82 season, the club which advances to the Stanley Cup Finals as the winner of the Campbell Conference championship is presented with the Clarence S. Campbell Bowl.

History: Presented by the member clubs in 1968 for perpetual competition by the National Hockey League in recognition of the services of Clarence S. Campbell, President of the NHL from 1946 to 1977. From 1967-68 through 1973-74, the trophy was awarded to the champions of the West Division. Beginning in 1974-75, it was awarded to the regular-season winner of the conference bearing the name of the trophy. Starting with the 1981-82 season, the trophy has been presented to the playoff champion in the Campbell Conference. The trophy itself is a hallmark piece made of sterling silver and was crafted by a British silversmith in 1878.

1990-91 Winner: Minnesota North Stars

The Minnesota North Stars won their first Clarence S. Campbell Bowl in team history after a four games to one series victory over the defending Stanley Cup champion Edmonton Oilers. Before defeating the Oilers, the North Stars had series wins over Chicago and St. Louis.

CLARENCE S. CAMPBELL BOWL WINNERS

1990-91	**Minnesota North Stars**		
1989-90	Edmonton Oilers	1978-79	New York Islanders
1988-89	Calgary Flames	1977-78	New York Islanders
1987-88	Edmonton Oilers	1976-77	Philadelphia Flyers
1986-87	Edmonton Oilers	1975-76	Philadelphia Flyers
1985-86	Calgary Flames	1974-75	Philadelphia Flyers
1984-85	Edmonton Oilers	1973-74	Philadelphia Flyers
1983-84	Edmonton Oilers	1972-73	Chicago Blackhawks
1982-83	Edmonton Oilers	1971-72	Chicago Blackhawks
1981-82	Vancouver Canucks	1970-71	Chicago Blackhawks
1980-81	New York Islanders	1969-70	St. Louis Blues
1979-80	Philadelphia Flyers	1968-69	St. Louis Blues
		1967-68	Philadelphia Flyers

Stanley Cup Winners:

Rosters and Final Series Scores

1990-91 — Pittsburgh Penguins — Mario Lemieux (Captain), Paul Coffey, Randy Hillier, Bob Errey, Tom Barrasso, Phil Bourque, Jay Caufield, Ron Francis, Randy Gilhen, Jiri Hrdina, Jaromir Jagr, Grant Jennings, Troy Loney, Joe Mullen, Larry Murphy, Jim Paek, Frank Pietrangelo, Barry Pederson, Mark Recchi, Gordie Roberts, Ulf Samuelsson, Paul Stanton, Kevin Stevens, Peter Taglianetti, Bryan Trottier, Scott Young, Wendell Young, Edward J. DeBartolo, Sr. (Owner), Marie D. DeBartolo York (President), Paul Martha (Vice-President & General Counsel), Craig Patrick (General Manager), Scotty Bowman (Director of Player Development & Recruitment), Bob Johnson (Coach), Rick Kehoe (Assistant Coach), Gilles Meloche (Goaltending Coach & Scout), Rick Paterson (Assistant Coach), Barry Smith (Assistant Coach), Steve Latin (Equipment Manager), Skip Thayer (Trainer), John Welday (Strength & Conditioning Coach), Greg Malone (Scout).
Scores: May 15 at Pittsburgh — Minnesota 5, Pittsburgh 4; May 17 at Pittsburgh — Pittsburgh 4, Minnesota 1; May 19 at Minnesota — Minnesota 3, Pittsburgh 1; May 21 at Minnesota — Pittsburgh 5, Minnesota 3; May 23 at Pittsburgh — Pittsburgh 6, Minnesota 4; May 25 at Minnesota — Pittsburgh 8, Minnesota 0.

1989-90 — Edmonton Oilers — Kevin Lowe, Steve Smith, Jeff Beukeboom, Mark Lamb, Joe Murphy, Glenn Anderson, Mark Messier, Adam Graves, Craig MacTavish, Kelly Buchberger, Jari Kurri, Craig Simpson, Martin Gelinas, Randy Gregg, Charlie Huddy, Geoff Smith, Reijo Ruotsalainen, Craig Muni, Bill Ranford, Dave Brown, Eldon Reddick, Petr Klima, Esa Tikkanen, Grant Fuhr, Peter Pocklington (Owner), Glen Sather (President/General Manager), John Muckler (Coach), Ted Green (Co-Coach), Ron Low (Ass't Coach), Bruce MacGregor (Ass't General Manager), Barry Fraser (Director of Player Personnel), John Blackwell (Director of Operations, AHL), Ace Bailey, Ed Chadwick, Lorne Davis, Harry Howell, Matti Vaisanen and Albert Reeves (Scouts), Bill Tuele (Director of Public Relations), Werner Baum (Controller), Dr. Gordon Cameron (Medical Chief of Staff), Dr. David Reid (Team Physician), Barrie Stafford (Athletic Trainer), Ken Lowe (Athletic Therapist), Stuart Poirier (Massage Therapist), Lyle Kulchisky (Ass't Trainer).
Scores: May 15 at Boston — Edmonton 3, Boston 2; May 18 at Boston — Edmonton 7, Boston 2; May 20 at Edmonton — Boston 2, Edmonton 1; May 22 at Edmonton — Edmonton 5, Boston 1; May 24 at Boston — Edmonton 4, Boston 1.

1988-89 — Calgary Flames — Mike Vernon, Rick Wamsley, Al MacInnis, Brad McCrimmon, Dana Murzyn, Ric Nattress, Joe Mullen, Lanny McDonald (Co-captain), Gary Roberts, Colin Patterson, Hakan Loob, Theoren Fleury, Tim Hunter (Ass't. captain), Gary Suter, Mark Hunter, Jim Peplinski (Co-captain), Joe Nieuwendyk, Brian MacLellan, Joel Otto, Jamie Macoun, Doug Gilmour, Rob Ramage. Norman Green, Harley Hotchkiss, Norman Kwong, Sonia Scurfield, B.J. Seaman, D.K. Seaman (Owners), Cliff Fletcher (President and General Manager), Al MacNeil (Ass't General Manager), Al Coates (Ass't to the President), Terry Crisp (Head Coach), Doug Risebrough, Tom Watt (Ass't Coaches), Glenn Hall (Goaltending Consultant), Jim Murray (Trainer), Bob Stewart (Equipment Manager), Al Murray (Ass't Trainer).
Scores: May 14 at Calgary — Calgary 3, Montreal 2; May 17 at Calgary — Montreal 4, Calgary 2; May 19 at Montreal — Montreal 4, Calgary 3; May 21 at Montreal — Calgary 4, Montreal 2; May 23 at Calgary — Calgary 3, Montreal 2; May 25 at Montreal — Calgary 4, Montreal 2.

1987-88 — Edmonton Oilers — Keith Acton, Glenn Anderson, Jeff Beukeboom, Geoff Courtnall, Grant Fuhr, Randy Gregg, Wayne Gretzky, Dave Hannan, Charlie Huddy, Mike Krushelnyski, Jari Kurri, Normand Lacombe, Kevin Lowe, Craig MacTavish, Kevin McClelland, Marty McSorley, Mark Messier, Craig Muni, Bill Ranford, Craig Simpson, Steve Smith, Esa Tikkanen, Peter Pocklington (Owner), Glen Sather (General Manager/Coach), John Muckler (Co-Coach), Ted Green (Ass't Coach), Barry Fraser (Director of Player Personnel), Bill Tuele (Director of Public Relations), Dr. Gordon Cameron (Team Physician), Peter Millar (Athletic Therapist), Barrie Stafford (Trainer), Juergen Mers (Massage Therapist), Lyle Kulchisky (Ass't Trainer).
Scores: May 18 at Edmonton — Edmonton 2, Boston 1; May 20 at Edmonton — Edmonton 4, Boston 2; May 22 at Boston — Edmonton 6, Boston 3; May 24 at Boston — Boston 3, Edmonton 3 (suspended due to power failure); May 26 at Edmonton — Edmonton 6, Boston 3.

Kevin Lowe has played a vital role in all five Stanley Cup wins by the Edmonton Oilers.

1986-87 — Edmonton Oilers — Glenn Anderson, Jeff Beukeboom, Kelly Buchberger, Paul Coffey, Grant Fuhr, Randy Gregg, Wayne Gretzky, Charlie Huddy, Dave Hunter, Mike Krushelnyski, Jari Kurri, Moe Lemay, Kevin Lowe, Craig MacTavish, Kevin McClelland, Marty McSorley, Mark Messier, Andy Moog, Craig Muni, Kent Nilsson, Jaroslav Pouzar, Reijo Ruotsalainen, Steve Smith, Esa Tikkanen, Peter Pocklington (Owner), Glen Sather (General Manager/Coach), John Muckler (Co-Coach), Ted Green (Ass't. Coach), Ron Low (Ass't. Coach), Bruce MacGregor (Ass't. General Manager), Barry Fraser (Director of Player Personnel), Peter Millar (Athletic Therapist), Barrie Stafford (Trainer), Lyle Kulchisky (Ass't Trainer).
Scores: May 17 at Edmonton — Edmonton 4, Philadelphia 3; May 20 at Edmonton — Edmonton 3, Philadelphia 2; May 22 at Philadelphia — Philadelphia 5, Edmonton 3; May 24 at Philadelphia — Edmonton 4, Philadelphia 1; May 26 at Edmonton — Philadelphia 4, Edmonton 3; May 28 at Philadelphia — Philadelphia 3, Edmonton 2; May 31 at Edmonton — Edmonton 3, Philadelphia 1.

1985-86 — Montreal Canadiens — Bob Gainey, Doug Soetaert, Patrick Roy, Rick Green, David Maley, Ryan Walter, Serge Boisvert, Mario Tremblay, Bobby Smith, Craig Ludwig, Tom Kurvers, Kjell Dahlin, Larry Robinson, Guy Carbonneau, Chris Chelios, Petr Svoboda, Mats Naslund, Lucien DeBlois, Steve Rooney, Gaston Gingras, Mike Lalor, Chris Nilan, John Kordic, Claude Lemieux, Mike McPhee, Brian Skrudland, Stephane Richer, Ronald Corey (President), Serge Savard (General Manager), Jean Perron (Coach), Jacques Laperriere (Ass't. Coach), Jean Beliveau (Vice President), Francois-Xavier Seigneur (Vice President), Fred Steer (Vice President), Jacques Lemaire (Ass't. General Manager), Andre Boudrias (Ass't. General Manager), Claude Ruel, Yves Belanger (Athletic Therapist), Gaetan Lefebvre (Ass't. Athletic Therapist), Eddy Palchek (Trainer), Sylvain Toupin (Ass't. Trainer).
Scores: May 16 at Calgary — Calgary 5, Montreal 3; May 18 at Calgary — Montreal 3, Calgary 2; May 20 at Montreal — Montreal 5, Calgary 3; May 22 at Montreal — Montreal 1, Calgary 0; May 24 at Calgary — Montreal 4, Calgary 3.

1984-85 — Edmonton Oilers — Glenn Anderson, Bill Carroll, Paul Coffey, Lee Fogolin, Grant Fuhr, Randy Gregg, Charlie Huddy, Pat Hughes, Dave Hunter, Don Jackson, Mike Krushelnyski, Jari Kurri, Willy Lindstrom, Kevin Lowe, Dave Lumley, Kevin McClelland, Larry Melnyk, Mark Messier, Andy Moog, Mark Napier, Jaroslav Pouzar, Dave Semenko, Esa Tikkanen, Peter Pocklington (Owner), Glen Sather (General Manager/Coach), John Muckler (Ass't. Coach), Ted Green (Ass't. Coach), Bruce MacGregor (Ass't. General Manager), Barry Fraser (Director of Player Personnel/Chief Scout), Peter Millar (Athletic Therapist), Barrie Stafford, Lyle Kulchisky (Trainers).
Scores: May 21 at Philadelphia — Philadelphia 4, Edmonton 1; May 23 at Philadelphia — Edmonton 3, Philadelphia 1; May 25 at Edmonton — Edmonton 4, Philadelphia 3; May 28 at Edmonton — Edmonton 5, Philadelphia 3; May 30 at Edmonton — Edmonton 8, Philadelphia 3.

1983-84 — Edmonton Oilers — Glenn Anderson, Paul Coffey, Pat Conacher, Lee Fogolin, Grant Fuhr, Randy Gregg, Wayne Gretzky, Charlie Huddy, Pat Hughes, Dave Hunter, Don Jackson, Jari Kurri, Willy Lindstrom, Ken Linseman, Kevin Lowe, Dave Lumley, Kevin McClelland, Mark Messier, Andy Moog, Jaroslav Pouzar, Dave Semenko, Peter Pocklington (Owner), Glen Sather (General Manager/Coach), John Muckler (Ass't. Coach), Ted Green (Ass't. Coach), Bruce MacGregor (Ass't. General Manager), Barry Fraser (Director of Player Personnel/Chief Scout), Peter Millar (Athletic Therapist), Barrie Stafford (Trainer).
Scores: May 10 at New York — Edmonton 1, NY Islanders 0; May 12 at New York — NY Islanders 6, Edmonton 1; May 15 at Edmonton — Edmonton 7, NY Islanders 2; May 17 at Edmonton — Edmonton 7, NY Islanders 2; May 19 at Edmonton — Edmonton 5, NY Islanders 2.

1982-83 — New York Islanders — Mike Bossy, Bob Bourne, Paul Boutilier, Bill Carroll, Greg Gilbert, Clark Gillies, Butch Goring, Mats Hallin, Tomas Jonsson, Anders Kallur, Gord Lane, Dave Langevin, Mike McEwen, Roland Melanson, Wayne Merrick, Ken Morrow, Bob Nystrom, Stefan Persson, Denis Potvin, Bill Smith, Brent Sutter, Duane Sutter, John Tonelli, Bryan Trottier, Al Arbour (coach), Lorne Henning (ass't coach), Bill Torrey (general manager), Ron Waske, Jim Pickard (trainers).
Scores: May 10 at Edmonton — NY Islanders 2, Edmonton 0; May 12 at Edmonton — NY Islanders 6, Edmonton 3; May 14 at New York — NY Islanders 5, Edmonton 1; May 17 at New York — NY Islanders 4, Edmonton 2

1981-82 — New York Islanders — Mike Bossy, Bob Bourne, Bill Carroll, Butch Goring, Greg Gilbert, Clark Gillies, Tomas Jonsson, Anders Kallur, Gord Lane, Dave Langevin, Hector Marini, Mike McEwen, Roland Melanson, Wayne Merrick, Ken Morrow, Bob Nystrom, Stefan Persson, Denis Potvin, Bill Smith, Brent Sutter, Duane Sutter, John Tonelli, Bryan Trottier, Al Arbour (coach), Lorne Henning (ass't coach), Bill Torrey (general manager), Ron Waske, Jim Pickard (trainers)
Scores: May 8 at New York — NY Islanders 6, Vancouver 5; May 11 at New York — NY Islanders 6, Vancouver 4; May 13 at Vancouver — NY Islanders 3, Vancouver 0; May 16 at Vancouver — NY Islanders 3, Vancouver 1

1980-81 — New York Islanders — Denis Potvin, Mike McEwen, Ken Morrow, Gord Lane, Bob Lorimer, Stefan Persson, Dave Langevin, Mike Bossy, Bryan Trottier, Butch Goring, Wayne Merrick, Clark Gillies, John Tonelli, Bob Nystrom, Bill Carroll, Bob Bourne, Hector Marini, Anders Kallur, Duane Sutter, Garry Howatt, Lorne Henning, Bill Smith, Roland Melanson, Al Arbour (coach), Bill Torrey (general manager), Ron Waske, Jim Pickard (trainers).
Scores: May 12 at New York — NY Islanders 6, Minnesota 3; May 14 at New York — NY Islanders 6, Minnesota 3; May 17 at Minnesota — NY Islanders 7, Minnesota 5; May 19 at Minnesota — Minnesota 4, NY Islanders 2; May 21 at New York — NY Islanders 5, Minnesota 1.

1979-80 — New York Islanders — Gord Lane, Jean Potvin, Bob Lorimer, Denis Potvin, Stefan Persson, Ken Morrow, Dave Langevin, Duane Sutter, Garry Howatt, Clark Gillies, Lorne Henning, Wayne Merrick, Bob Bourne, Steve Tambellini, Bryan Trottier, Mike Bossy, Bob Nystrom, John Tonelli, Anders Kallur, Butch Goring, Alex McKendry, Glenn Resch, Billy Smith, Al Arbour (coach), Bill Torrey (general manager), Ron Waske, Jim Pickard (trainers).
Scores: May 13 at Philadelphia — NY Islanders 4, Philadelphia 3; May 15 at Philadelphia — Philadelphia 8, NY Islanders 3; May 17 at Long Island — NY Islanders 6, Philadelphia 2; May 19 at Long Island — NY Islanders 5, Philadelphia 2; May 22 at Philadelphia — Philadelphia 6, NY Islanders 3; May 24 at Long Island — NY Islanders 5, Philadelphia 4.

1978-79 — Montreal Canadiens — Ken Dryden, Larry Robinson, Serge Savard, Guy Lapointe, Brian Engblom, Gilles Lupien, Rick Chartraw, Guy Lafleur, Steve Shutt, Jacques Lemaire, Yvan Cournoyer, Rejean Houle, Pierre Mondou, Bob Gainey, Doug Jarvis, Yvon Lambert, Doug Risebrough, Pierre Larouche, Mario Tremblay, Cam Connor, Pat Hughes, Rod Langway, Mark Napier, Michel Larocque, Richard Sevigny, Scotty Bowman (coach), Irving Grundman (managing director), Eddy Palchak, Pierre Meilleur (trainers).
Scores: May 13 at Montreal — NY Rangers 4, Montreal 1; May 15 at Montreal — Montreal 6, NY Rangers 2; May 17 at New York — Montreal 4, NY Rangers 1; May 19 at New York — Montreal 4, NY Rangers 3; May 21 at Montreal — Montreal 4, NY Rangers 1.

1977-78 — Montreal Canadiens — Ken Dryden, Larry Robinson, Serge Savard, Guy Lapointe, Bill Nyrop, Pierre Bouchard, Brian Engblom, Gilles Lupien, Rick Chartraw, Guy Lafleur, Steve Shutt, Jacques Lemaire, Yvan Cournoyer, Rejean Houle, Pierre Mondou, Bob Gainey, Doug Jarvis, Yvon Lambert, Doug Risebrough, Pierre Larouche, Mario Tremblay, Michel Larocque, Scotty Bowman (coach), Sam Pollock (general manager), Eddy Palchak, Pierre Meilleur (trainers).
Scores: May 13 at Montreal — Montreal 4, Boston 1; May 16 at Montreal — Montreal 3, Boston 2; May 18 at Boston — Boston 4, Montreal 0; May 21 at Boston — Boston 4, Montreal 3; May 23 at Montreal — Montreal 4, Boston 1; May 25 at Boston — Montreal 4, Boston 1.

1976-77 — Montreal Canadiens — Ken Dryden, Guy Lapointe, Larry Robinson, Serge Savard, Jimmy Roberts, Rick Chartraw, Bill Nyrop, Pierre Bouchard, Brian Engblom, Yvan Cournoyer, Guy Lafleur, Jacques Lemaire, Steve Shutt, Pete Mahovlich, Murray Wilson, Doug Jarvis, Yvon Lambert, Bob Gainey, Doug Risebrough, Mario Tremblay, Rejean Houle, Pierre Mondou, Mike Polich, Michel Larocque, Scotty Bowman (coach), Sam Pollock (general manager), Eddy Palchak, Pierre Meilleur (trainers).
Scores: May 7 at Montreal — Montreal 7, Boston 3; May 10 at Montreal — Montreal 3, Boston 0; May 12 at Boston — Montreal 4, Boston 2; May 14 at Boston — Montreal 2, Boston 1.

1975-76 — Montreal Canadiens — Ken Dryden, Serge Savard, Guy Lapointe, Larry Robinson, Bill Nyrop, Pierre Bouchard, Jim Roberts, Guy Lafleur, Steve Shutt, Pete Mahovlich, Yvan Cournoyer, Jacques Lemaire, Yvon Lambert, Bob Gainey, Doug Jarvis, Doug Risebrough, Murray Wilson, Mario Tremblay, Rick Chartraw, Michel Larocque, Scotty Bowman (coach), Sam Pollock (general manager), Eddy Palchak, Pierre Meilleur (trainers).
Scores: May 9 at Montreal — Montreal 4, Philadelphia 3; May 11 at Montreal — Montreal 2, Philadelphia 1; May 13 at Philadelphia — Montreal 3, Philadelphia 2; May 16 at Philadelphia — Montreal 5, Philadelphia 3.

1974-75 — Philadelphia Flyers — Bernie Parent, Wayne Stephenson, Ed Van Impe, Tom Bladon, André Dupont, Joe Watson, Jim Watson, Ted Harris, Larry Goodenough, Rick MacLeish, Bobby Clarke, Bill Barber, Reggie Leach, Gary Dornhoefer, Ross Lonsberry, Bob Kelly, Terry Crisp, Don Saleski, Dave Schultz, Orest Kindrachuk, Bill Clement, Fred Shero (coach), Keith Allen (general manager), Frank Lewis, Jim McKenzie (trainers).
Scores: May 15 at Philadelphia — Philadelphia 4, Buffalo 1; May 18 at Philadelphia — Philadelphia 2, Buffalo 1; May 20 at Buffalo — Buffalo 5, Philadelphia 4; May 22 at Buffalo — Buffalo 4, Philadelphia 2; May 25 at Philadelphia — Philadelphia 5, Buffalo 1; May 27 at Buffalo — Philadelphia 2, Buffalo 0.

1973-74 — Philadelphia Flyers — Bernie Parent, Ed Van Impe, Tom Bladon, André Dupont, Joe Watson, Jim Watson, Barry Ashbee, Bill Barber, Dave Schultz, Don Saleski, Gary Dornhoefer, Terry Crisp, Bobby Clarke, Simon Nolet, Ross Lonsberry, Rick MacLeish, Bill Flett, Orest Kindrachuk, Bill Clement, Bob Kelly, Bruce Cowick, Al MacAdam, Bobby Taylor, Fred Shero (coach), Keith Allen (general manager), Frank Lewis, Jim McKenzie (trainers).
Scores: May 7 at Boston — Boston 3, Philadelphia 2; May 9 at Boston — Philadelphia 3, Boston 2; May 12 at Philadelphia — Philadelphia 4, Boston 1; May 14 at Philadelphia — Philadelphia 4, Boston 2; May 16 at Boston — Boston 5, Philadelphia 1; May 19 at Philadelphia — Philadelphia 1, Boston 0.

1972-73 — Montreal Canadiens — Ken Dryden, Guy Lapointe, Serge Savard, Larry Robinson, Jacques Laperriere, Bob Murdoch, Pierre Bouchard, Jim Roberts, Yvan Cournoyer, Frank Mahovlich, Jacques Lemaire, Pete Mahovlich, Marc Tardif, Henri Richard, Rejean Houle, Guy Lafleur, Chuck Lefley, Claude Larose, Murray Wilson, Steve Shutt, Michel Plasse, Scotty Bowman (coach), Sam Pollock (general manager), Ed Palchak, Bob Williams (trainers).
Scores: April 29 at Montreal — Montreal 8, Chicago 3; May 1 at Montreal — Montreal 4, Chicago 1; May 3 at Chicago — Chicago 7, Montreal 4; May 6 at Chicago — Montreal 4, Chicago 0; May 8 at Montreal — Chicago 8, Montreal 7; May 10 at Chicago — Montreal 6, Chicago 4.

1971-72 — Boston Bruins — Gerry Cheevers, Ed Johnston, Bobby Orr, Ted Green, Carol Vadnais, Dallas Smith, Don Awrey, Phil Esposito, Ken Hodge, John Bucyk, Mike Walton, Wayne Cashman, Garnet Bailey, Derek Sanderson, Fred Stanfield, Ed Westfall, John McKenzie, Don Marcotte, Garry Peters, Chris Hayes, Tom Johnson (coach), Milt Schmidt (general manager), Dan Canney, John Forristall (trainers).
Scores: April 30 at Boston — Boston 6, NY Rangers 5; May 2 at Boston — Boston 2, NY Rangers 1; May 4 at New York — NY Rangers 5, Boston 2; May 7 at New York — Boston 3, NY Rangers 2; May 9 at Boston — NY Rangers 3, Boston 2; May 11 at New York — Boston 3, NY Rangers 0.

1970-71 — Montreal Canadiens — Ken Dryden, Rogatien Vachon, Jacques Laperriere, Jean-Claude Tremblay, Guy Lapointe, Terry Harper, Pierre Bouchard, Jean Beliveau, Marc Tardif, Yvan Cournoyer, Rejean Houle, Claude Larose, Henri Richard, Phil Roberto, Pete Mahovlich, Leon Rochefort, John Ferguson, Bobby Sheehan, Jacques Lemaire, Frank Mahovlich, Bob Murdoch, Chuck Lefley, Al MacNeil (coach), Sam Pollock (general manager), Yvon Belanger, Ed Palchak (trainers).
Scores: May 4 at Chicago — Chicago 2, Montreal 1; May 6 at Chicago — Chicago 5, Montreal 3; May 9 at Montreal — Montreal 4, Chicago 2; May 11 at Montreal — Montreal 5, Chicago 2; May 13 at Chicago — Chicago 2, Montreal 0; May 16 at Montreal — Montreal 4, Chicago 3; May 18 at Chicago — Montreal 3, Chicago 2.

1969-70 — Boston Bruins — Gerry Cheevers, Ed Johnston, Bobby Orr, Rick Smith, Dallas Smith, Bill Speer, Gary Doak, Don Awrey, Phil Esposito, Ken Hodge, John Bucyk, Wayne Carleton, Wayne Cashman, Derek Sanderson, Fred Stanfield, Ed Westfall, John McKenzie, Jim Lorentz, Don Marcotte, Bill Lesuk, Dan Schock, Harry Sinden (coach), Milt Schmidt (general manager), Dan Canney, John Forristall (trainers).
Scores: May 3 at St. Louis — Boston 6, St. Louis 1; May 5 at St. Louis — Boston 6, St. Louis 2; May 7 at Boston — Boston 4, St. Louis 1; May 10 at Boston — Boston 4, St. Louis 3.

1968-69 — Montreal Canadiens — Lorne Worsley, Rogatien Vachon, Jacques Laperriere, Jean-Claude Tremblay, Ted Harris, Serge Savard, Terry Harper, Larry Hillman, Jean Beliveau, Ralph Backstrom, Dick Duff, Yvan Cournoyer, Claude Provost, Bobby Rousseau, Henri Richard, John Ferguson, Christian Bordeleau, Mickey Redmond, Jacques Lemaire, Lucien Grenier, Tony Esposito, Claude Ruel (coach), Sam Pollock (general manager), Larry Aubut, Eddy Palchak (trainers).
Scores: April 27 at Montreal — Montreal 3, St. Louis 1; April 29 at Montreal — Montreal 3, St. Louis 1; May 1 at St. Louis — Montreal 4, St. Louis 0; May 4 at St. Louis — Montreal 2, St. Louis 1.

1967-68 — Montreal Canadiens — Lorne Worsley, Rogatien Vachon, Jacques Laperriere, Jean-Claude Tremblay, Ted Harris, Serge Savard, Terry Harper, Carol Vadnais, Jean Beliveau, Gilles Tremblay, Ralph Backstrom, Dick Duff, Claude Larose, Yvan Cournoyer, Claude Provost, Bobby Rousseau, Henri Richard, John Ferguson, Danny Grant, Jacques Lemaire, Mickey Redmond, Toe Blake (coach), Sam Pollock (general manager), Larry Aubut, Eddy Palchak (trainers).
Scores: May 5 at St. Louis — Montreal 3, St. Louis 2; May 7 at St. Louis — Montreal 1, St. Louis 0; May 9 at Montreal — Montreal 4, St. Louis 3; May 11 at Montreal — Montreal 3, St. Louis 2.

1966-67 — Toronto Maple Leafs — Johnny Bower, Terry Sawchuk, Larry Hillman, Marcel Pronovost, Tim Horton, Bob Baun, Aut Erickson, Allan Stanley, Red Kelly, Ron Ellis, George Armstrong, Pete Stemkowski, Dave Keon, Mike Walton, Jim Pappin, Bob Pulford, Brian Conacher, Eddie Shack, Frank Mahovlich, Milan Marcetta, Larry Jeffrey, Bruce Gamble, Punch Imlach (manager-coach), Bob Haggart (trainer).
Scores: April 20 at Montreal — Toronto 2, Montreal 6; April 22 at Montreal — Toronto 3, Montreal 0; April 25 at Toronto — Toronto 3, Montreal 2; April 27 at Toronto — Toronto 2, Montreal 6; April 29 at Montreal — Toronto 4, Montreal 1; May 2 at Toronto — Toronto 3, Montreal 1.

1965-66 — Montreal Canadiens — Lorne Worsley, Charlie Hodge, Jean-Claude Tremblay, Ted Harris, Jean-Guy Talbot, Terry Harper, Jacques Laperriere, Noel Price, Jean Beliveau, Ralph Backstrom, Dick Duff, Gilles Tremblay, Claude Larose, Yvan Cournoyer, Claude Provost, Bobby Rousseau, Henri Richard, Dave Balon, John Ferguson, Leon Rochefort, Jim Roberts, Toe Blake (coach), Sam Pollock (general manager), Larry Aubut, Andy Galley (trainers).
Scores: April 24 at Montreal — Detroit 3, Montreal 2; April 26 at Montreal — Detroit 5, Montreal 2; April 28 at Detroit — Montreal 4, Detroit 2; May 1 at Detroit — Montreal 2, Detroit 1; May 3 at Montreal — Montreal 5, Detroit 1; May 5 at Detroit — Montreal 3, Detroit 2.

1964-65 — Montreal Canadiens — Lorne Worsley, Charlie Hodge, Jean-Claude Tremblay, Ted Harris, Jean-Guy Talbot, Terry Harper, Jacques Laperriere, Jean Gauthier, Noel Picard, Jean Beliveau, Ralph Backstrom, Dick Duff, Claude Larose, Yvan Cournoyer, Claude Provost, Bobby Rousseau, Henri Richard, Dave Balon, John Ferguson, Red Berenson, Jim Roberts, Toe Blake (coach), Sam Pollock (general manager), Larry Aubut, Andy Galley (trainers).
Scores: April 17 at Montreal — Montreal 3, Chicago 2; April 20 at Montreal — Montreal 2, Chicago 0; April 22 at Chicago — Montreal 1, Chicago 3; April 25 at Chicago — Montreal 1, Chicago 5; April 27 at Montreal — Montreal 6, Chicago 0; April 29 at Chicago — Montreal 1, Chicago 2; May 1 at Montreal — Montreal 4, Chicago 0.

1963-64 — Toronto Maple Leafs — Johnny Bower, Carl Brewer, Tim Horton, Bob Baun, Allan Stanley, Larry Hillman, Al Arbour, Red Kelly, Gerry Ehman, Andy Bathgate, George Armstrong, Ron Stewart, Dave Keon, Billy Harris, Don McKenney, Jim Pappin, Bob Pulford, Eddie Shack, Frank Mahovlich, Eddie Litzenberger, Punch Imlach (manager-coach), Bob Haggert (trainer).
Scores: April 11 at Toronto — Toronto 3, Detroit 2; April 14 at Toronto — Toronto 3, Detroit 4; April 16 at Detroit — Toronto 3, Detroit 4; April 18 at Detroit — Toronto 4, Detroit 2; April 21 at Toronto — Toronto 1, Detroit 2; April 23 at Detroit — Toronto 4, Detroit 3; April 25 at Toronto — Toronto 4, Detroit 0.

1962-63 — Toronto Maple Leafs — Johnny Bower, Don Simmons, Carl Brewer, Tim Horton, Kent Douglas, Allan Stanley, Bob Baun, Larry Hillman, Red Kelly, Dick Duff, George Armstrong, Bob Nevin, Ron Stewart, Dave Keon, Billy Harris, Bob Pulford, Eddie Shack, Ed Litzenberger, Frank Mahovlich, John MacMillan, Punch Imlach (manager-coach), Bob Haggert (trainer).
Scores: April 9 at Toronto — Toronto 4, Detroit 2; April 11 at Toronto — Toronto 4, Detroit 2; April 14 at Detroit — Toronto 2, Detroit 3; April 16 at Detroit — Toronto 4, Detroit 2; April 18 at Toronto — Toronto 3, Detroit 1.

1961-62 — Toronto Maple Leafs — Johnny Bower, Don Simmons, Carl Brewer, Tim Horton, Bob Baun, Allan Stanley, Al Arbour, Larry Hillman, Red Kelly, Dick Duff, George Armstrong, Frank Mahovlich, Bob Nevin, Ron Stewart, Bill Harris, Bert Olmstead, Bob Pulford, Eddie Shack, Dave Keon, Ed Litzenberger, John MacMillan, Punch Imlach (manager-coach), Bob Haggert (trainer).
Scores: April 10 at Toronto — Toronto 4, Chicago 1; April 12 at Toronto — Toronto 3, Chicago 2; April 15 at Chicago — Toronto 0, Chicago 3; April 17 at Chicago — Toronto 1, Chicago 4; April 19 at Toronto — Toronto 8, Chicago 4; April 22 at Chicago — Toronto 2, Chicago 1.

1960-61 — Chicago Blackhawks — Glenn Hall, Al Arbour, Pierre Pilote, Elmer Vasko, Jack Evans, Dollard St. Laurent, Reg Fleming, Tod Sloan, Ron Murphy, Eddie Litzenberger, Bill Hay, Bobby Hull, Ab McDonald, Eric Nesterenko, Ken Wharram, Earl Balfour, Stan Mikita, Murray Balfour, Chico Maki, Wayne Hicks, Tommy Ivan (manager), Rudy Pilous (coach), Nick Garen (trainer).
Scores: April 6 at Chicago — Chicago 3, Detroit 2; April 8 at Detroit — Detroit 3, Chicago 1; April 10 at Chicago — Chicago 3, Detroit 1; April 12 at Detroit — Detroit 2, Chicago 1; April 14 at Chicago — Chicago 6, Detroit 3; April 16 at Detroit — Chicago 5, Detroit 1.

1959-60 — Montreal Canadiens — Jacques Plante, Charlie Hodge, Doug Harvey, Tom Johnson, Bob Turner, Jean-Guy Talbot, Albert Langlois, Ralph Backstrom, Jean Beliveau, Marcel Bonin, Bernie Geoffrion, Phil Goyette, Bill Hicke, Don Marshall, Ab McDonald, Dickie Moore, André Pronovost, Claude Provost, Henri Richard, Maurice Richard, Frank Selke (manager), Toe Blake (coach), Hector Dubois, Larry Aubut (trainers).
Scores: April 7 at Montreal — Montreal 4, Toronto 2; April 9 at Montreal — Montreal 2, Toronto 1; April 12 at Toronto — Montreal 5, Toronto 2; April 14 at Toronto — Montreal 4, Toronto 0.

1958-59 — Montreal Canadiens — Jacques Plante, Charlie Hodge, Doug Harvey, Tom Johnson, Bob Turner, Jean-Guy Talbot, Albert Langlois, Bernie Geoffrion, Ralph Backstrom, Bill Hicke, Maurice Richard, Dickie Moore, Claude Provost, Ab McDonald, Henri Richard, Marcel Bonin, Phil Goyette, Don Marshall, André Pronovost, Jean Beliveau, Frank Selke (manager), Toe Blake (coach), Hector Dubois, Larry Aubut (trainers).
Scores: April 9 at Montreal — Montreal 5, Toronto 3; April 11 at Montreal — Montreal 3, Toronto 1; April 14 at Toronto — Toronto 3, Montreal 2; April 16 at Toronto — Montreal 3, Toronto 2; April 18 at Montreal — Montreal 5, Toronto 3.

1957-58 — Montreal Canadiens — Jacques Plante, Gerry McNeil, Doug Harvey, Tom Johnson, Bob Turner, Dollard St-Laurent, Jean-Guy Talbot, Albert Langlois, Jean Beliveau, Bernie Geoffrion, Maurice Richard, Dickie Moore, Claude Provost, Floyd Curry, Bert Olmstead, Henri Richard, Marcel Bonin, Phil Goyette, Don Marshall, Andre Pronovost, Connie Broden, Frank Selke (manager), Toe Blake (coach), Hector Dubois, Larry Aubut (trainers).
Scores: April 8 at Montreal — Montreal 2, Boston 1; April 10 at Montreal — Boston 5, Montreal 2; April 13 at Boston — Montreal 3, Boston 0; April 15 at Boston — Boston 3, Montreal 1; April 17 at Montreal — Montreal 3, Boston 2; April 20 at Boston — Montreal 5, Boston 3.

1956-57 — Montreal Canadiens — Jacques Plante, Gerry McNeil, Doug Harvey, Tom Johnson, Bob Turner, Dollard St. Laurent, Jean-Guy Talbot, Jean Beliveau, Bernie Geoffrion, Floyd Curry, Dickie Moore, Maurice Richard, Claude Provost, Bert Olmstead, Henri Richard, Phil Goyette, Don Marshall, Andre Pronovost, Connie Broden, Frank Selke (manager), Toe Blake (coach), Hector Dubois, Larry Aubut (trainers).
Scores: April 6, at Montreal — Montreal 5, Boston 1; April 9, at Montreal — Montreal 1, Boston 0; April 11, at Boston — Montreal 4, Boston 2; April 14, at Boston — Boston 2, Montreal 0; April 16, at Montreal — Montreal 5, Boston 1.

1955-56 — Montreal Canadiens — Jacques Plante, Doug Harvey, Emile Bouchard, Bob Turner, Tom Johnson, Jean-Guy Talbot, Dollard St. Laurent, Jean Beliveau, Bernie Geoffrion, Bert Olmstead, Floyd Curry, Jackie Leclair, Maurice Richard, Dickie Moore, Henri Richard, Ken Mosdell, Don Marshall, Claude Provost, Frank Selke (manager), Toe Blake (coach), Hector Dubois (trainer).
Scores: March 31, at Montreal — Montreal 6, Detroit 4; April 3, at Montreal — Montreal 5, Detroit 1; April 5, at Detroit — Detroit 3, Montreal 1; April 8, at Detroit — Montreal 3, Detroit 0; April 10, at Montreal — Montreal 3, Detroit 1.

1954-55 — Detroit Red Wings — Terry Sawchuk, Red Kelly, Bob Goldham, Marcel Pronovost, Ben Woit, Jim Hay, Larry Hillman, Ted Lindsay, Tony Leswick, Gordie Howe, Alex Delvecchio, Marty Pavelich, Glen Skov, Earl Reibel, John Wilson, Bill Dineen, Vic Stasiuk, Marcel Bonin, Jack Adams (manager), Jimmy Skinner (coach), Carl Mattson (trainer).
Scores: April 3, at Detroit — Detroit 4, Montreal 2; April 5, at Detroit — Detroit 7, Montreal 1, April 7 at Montreal — Montreal 4, Detroit 2; April 9, at Montreal — Montreal 5, Detroit 3; April 10, at Detroit — Detroit 5, Montreal 1; April 12, at Montreal — Montreal 6, Detroit 3; April 14, at Detroit — Detroit 3, Montreal 1

1953-54 — Detroit Red Wings — Terry Sawchuk, Red Kelly, Bob Goldham, Ben Woit, Marcel Pronovost, Al Arbour, Keith Allen, Ted Lindsay, Tony Leswick, Gordie Howe, Marty Pavelich, Alex Delvecchio, Metro Prystai, Glen Skov, John Wilson, Bill Dineen, Jim Peters, Earl Reibel, Vic Stasiuk, Jack Adams (manager), Tommy Ivan (coach), Carl Mattson (trainer).
Scores: April 4, at Detroit — Detroit 3, Montreal 1; April 6, at Detroit — Montreal 3, Detroit 1; April 8, at Montreal — Detroit 5, Montreal 2; April 10, at Montreal — Detroit 2, Montreal 0; April 11, at Detroit — Montreal 1, Detroit 0; April 13, at Montreal — Montreal 4, Detroit 1; April 16, at Detroit — Detroit 2, Montreal 1.

1952-53 — Montreal Canadiens — Gerry McNeil, Jacques Plante, Doug Harvey, Emile Bouchard, Tom Johnson, Dollard St. Laurent, Bud MacPherson, Maurice Richard, Elmer Lach, Bert Olmstead, Bernie Geoffrion, Floyd Curry, Paul Masnick, Billy Reay, Dickie Moore, Ken Mosdell, Dick Gamble, Johnny McCormack, Lorne Davis, Calum McKay, Eddie Mazur, Frank Selke (manager), Dick Irvin (coach), Hector Dubois (trainer).
Scores: April 9, at Montreal — Montreal 4, Boston 2; April 11, at Montreal — Boston 4, Montreal 1; April 12, at Boston — Montreal 3, Boston 0; April 14, at Boston — Montreal 7, Boston 3; April 16, at Montreal — Montreal 1, Boston 0.

1951-52 — Detroit Red Wings — Terry Sawchuk, Bob Goldham, Ben Woit, Red Kelly, Leo Reise, Marcel Pronovost, Ted Lindsay, Tony Leswick, Gordie Howe, Metro Prystai, Marty Pavelich, Sid Abel, Glen Skov, Alex Delvecchio, John Wilson, Vic Stasiuk, Larry Zeidel, Jack Adams (manager) Tommy Ivan (coach), Carl Mattson (trainer).
Scores: April 10, at Montreal — Detroit 3, Montreal 1; April 12 at Montreal — Detroit 2, Montreal 1; April 13, at Detroit — Detroit 3, Montreal 0; April 15, at Detroit — Detroit 3, Montreal 0.

1950-51 — Toronto Maple Leafs — Turk Broda, Al Rollins, Jim Thomson, Gus Mortson, Bill Barilko, Bill Juzda, Fern Flaman, Hugh Bolton, Ted Kennedy, Sid Smith, Tod Sloan, Cal Gardner, Howie Meeker, Harry Watson, Max Bentley, Joe Klukay, Danny Lewicki, Ray Timgren, Fleming Mackell, Johnny McCormack, Bob Hassard, Conn Smythe (manager), Joe Primeau (coach), Tim Daly (trainer).
Scores: April 11, at Toronto — Toronto 3, Montreal 2; April 14, at Toronto — Montreal 3, Toronto 2; April 17, at Montreal — Toronto 2, Montreal 1; April 19, at Montreal — Toronto 3, Montreal 2; April 21, at Toronto — Toronto 3, Montreal 2.

1949-50 — Detroit Red Wings — Harry Lumley, Jack Stewart, Leo Reise, Clare Martin, Al Dewsbury, Lee Fogolin, Marcel Pronovost, Red Kelly, Ted Lindsay, Sid Abel, Gordie Howe, George Gee, Jimmy Peters, Marty Pavelich, Jim McFadden, Pete Babando, Max McNab, Gerry Couture, Joe Carveth, Steve Black, John Wilson, Larry Wilson, Jack Adams (manager), Tommy Ivan (coach), Carl Mattson (trainer).
Scores: April 11, at Detroit — Detroit 4, NY Rangers 1; April 13, at Toronto* — NY Rangers 3, Detroit 1; April 15, at Toronto — Detroit 4, NY Rangers 0; April 18, at Detroit — NY Rangers 4, Detroit 3; April 20, at Detroit — NY Rangers 2, Detroit 1; April 22, at Detroit — Detroit 5, NY Rangers 4; April 23, at Detroit — Detroit 4, NY Rangers 3.

* Ice was unavailable in Madison Square Garden and Rangers elected to play second and third games on Toronto ice.

1948-49 — Toronto Maple Leafs — Turk Broda, Jim Thomson, Gus Mortson, Bill Barilko, Garth Boesch, Bill Juzda, Ted Kennedy, Howie Meeker, Vic Lynn, Harry Watson, Bill Ezinicki, Cal Gardner, Max Bentley, Joe Klukay, Sid Smith, Don Metz, Ray Timgren, Fleming Mackell, Harry Taylor, Bob Dawes, Tod Sloan, Conn Smythe (manager), Hap Day (coach), Tim Daly (trainer).

Scores: April 8, at Detroit — Toronto 3, Detroit 2; April 10, at Detroit — Toronto 3, Detroit 1; April 13, at Toronto — Toronto 3, Detroit 1; April 16, at Toronto — Toronto 3, Detroit 1.

1947-48 — Toronto Maple Leafs — Turk Broda, Jim Thomson, Wally Stanowski, Garth Boesch, Bill Barilko. Gus Mortson, Phil Samis, Syl Apps, Bill Ezinicki, Harry Watson, Ted Kennedy, Howie Meeker, Vic Lynn, Nick Metz, Max Bentley, Joe Klukay, Les Costello, Don Metz, Sid Smith, Conn Smythe (manager), Hap Day (coach), Tim Daly (trainer).
Scores: April 7, at Toronto — Toronto 5, Detroit 3; April 10, at Toronto — Toronto 4, Detroit 2; April 11, at Detroit — Toronto 2, Detroit 0; April 14, at Detroit — Toronto 7, Detroit 2.

1946-47 — Toronto Maple Leafs — Turk Broda, Garth Boesch, Gus Mortson, Jim Thomson, Wally Stanowski, Bill Barilko, Harry Watson, Bud Poile, Ted Kennedy, Syl Apps, Don Metz, Nick Metz, Bill Ezinicki, Vic Lynn, Howie Meeker, Gaye Stewart, Joe Klukay, Gus Bodnar, Bob Goldham, Conn Smythe (manager), Hap Day (coach), Tim Daly (trainer).
Scores: April 8, at Montreal — Montreal 6, Toronto 0; April 10, at Montreal — Toronto 4, Montreal 0; April 12, at Toronto — Toronto 4, Montreal 2; April 15, at Toronto — Toronto 2, Montreal 1; April 17, at Montreal — Montreal 3, Toronto 1; April 19, at Toronto — Toronto 2, Montreal 1.

1945-46 — Montreal Canadiens — Elmer Lach, Toe Blake, Maurice Richard, Bob Fillion, Dutch Hiller, Murph Chamberlain, Ken Mosdell, Buddy O'Connor, Glen Harmon, Jim Peters, Emile Bouchard, Bill Reay, Ken Reardon, Leo Lamoureux, Frank Eddolls, Gerry Plamondon, Bill Durnan, Tommy Gorman (manager), Dick Irvin (coach), Ernie Cook (trainer).
Scores: March 30, at Montreal — Montreal 4, Boston 3; April 2, at Montreal — Montreal 3, Boston 2; April 4, at Boston — Montreal 4, Boston 2; April 7, at Boston — Boston 3, Montreal 2; April 9, at Montreal — Montreal 6, Boston 3.

1944-45 — Toronto Maple Leafs — Don Metz, Frank McCool, Wally Stanowski, Reg Hamilton, Elwyn Morris, Johnny McCreedy, Tommy O'Neill, Ted Kennedy, Babe Pratt, Gus Bodnar, Art Jackson, Jack McLean, Mel Hill, Nick Metz, Bob Davidson, Dave Schriner, Lorne Carr, Conn Smythe (manager), Frank Selke (business manager), Hap Day (coach), Tim Daly (trainer).
Scores: April 6, at Detroit — Toronto 1, Detroit 0; April 8, at Detroit — Toronto 2, Detroit 0; April 12, at Toronto — Toronto 1, Detroit 0; April 14, at Toronto — Detroit 5, Toronto 3; April 19, at Detroit — Detroit 2, Toronto 0; April 21, at Toronto — Detroit 1, Toronto 0; April 22, at Detroit — Toronto 2, Detroit 1.

1943-44 — Montreal Canadiens — Toe Blake, Maurice Richard, Elmer Lach, Ray Getliffe, Murph Chamberlain, Phil Watson, Emile Bouchard, Glen Harmon, Buddy O'Connor, Jerry Heffernan, Mike McMahon, Leo Lamoureux, Fernand Majeau, Bob Fillion, Bill Durnan, Tommy Gorman (manager), Dick Irvin (coach), Ernie Cook (trainer).
Scores: April 4, at Montreal — Montreal 5, Chicago 1; April 6, at Chicago — Montreal 3, Chicago 1; April 9, at Chicago — Montreal 3, Chicago 2; April 13, at Montreal — Montreal 5, Chicago 4.

1942-43 — Detroit Red Wings — Jack Stewart, Jimmy Orlando, Sid Abel, Alex Motter, Harry Watson, Joe Carveth, Mud Bruneteau, Eddie Wares, Johnny Mowers, Cully Simon, Don Grosso, Carl Liscombe, Connie Brown, Syd Howe, Les Douglas, Hal Jackson, Joe Fisher, Jack Adams (manager), Ebbie Goodfellow (playing-coach), Honey Walker (trainer).
Scores: April 1, at Detroit — Detroit 6, Boston 2; April 4, at Detroit — Detroit 4, Boston 3; April 7, at Boston — Detroit 4, Boston 0; April 8, at Boston — Detroit 2, Boston 0.

1941-42 — Toronto Maple Leafs — Wally Stanowski, Syl Apps, Bob Goldham, Gord Drillon, Hank Goldup, Ernie Dickens, Dave Schriner, Bucko McDonald, Bob Davidson, Nick Metz, Bingo Kampman, Don Metz, Gaye Stewart, Turk Broda, Johnny McCreedy, Lorne Carr, Pete Langelle, Billy Taylor, Conn Smythe (manager), Hap Day (coach), Frank Selke (business manager), Tim Daly (trainer).
Scores: April 4, at Toronto — Detroit 3, Toronto 2; April 7, at Toronto — Detroit 4, Toronto 2; April 9, at Detroit — Detroit 5, Toronto 2; April 12, at Detroit — Toronto 4, Detroit 3; April 14, at Toronto — Toronto 9, Detroit 3; April 16, at Detroit — Toronto 3, Detroit 0; April 18, at Toronto — Toronto 3, Detroit 1.

1940-41 — Boston Bruins — Bill Cowley, Des Smith, Dit Clapper, Frank Brimsek, Flash Hollett, John Crawford, Bobby Bauer, Pat McCreavy, Herb Cain, Mel Hill, Milt Schmidt, Woody Dumart, Roy Conacher, Terry Reardon, Art Jackson, Eddie Wiseman, Art Ross (manager), Cooney Weiland (coach), Win Green (trainer).
Scores: April 6, at Boston — Detroit 2, Boston 3; April 8, at Boston — Detroit 1, Boston 2; April 10, at Detroit — Boston 4, Detroit 2; April 12, at Detroit — Boston 3, Detroit 1.

1939-40 — New York Rangers — Dave Kerr, Art Coulter, Ott Heller, Alex Shibicky, Mac Colville, Neil Colville, Phil Watson, Lynn Patrick, Clint Smith, Muzz Patrick, Babe Pratt, Bryan Hextall, Kilby Macdonald, Dutch Hiller, Alf Pike, Sanford Smith, Lester Patrick (manager), Frank Boucher (coach), Harry Westerby (trainer).
Scores: April 2, at New York — NY Rangers 2, Toronto 1; April 3, at New York — NY Rangers 6, Toronto 2; April 6, at Toronto — NY Rangers 1, Toronto 2; April 9, at Toronto — NY Rangers 0, Toronto 3; April 11, at Toronto — NY Rangers 2, Toronto 1; April 13, at Toronto — NY Rangers 3, Toronto 2.

1938-39 — Boston Bruins — Bobby Bauer, Mel Hill, Flash Hollett, Roy Conacher, Gord Pettinger, Milt Schmidt, Woody Dumart, Jack Crawford, Ray Getliffe, Frank Brimsek, Eddie Shore, Dit Clapper, Bill Cowley, Jack Portland, Red Hamill, Cooney Weiland, Art Ross (manager-coach), Win Green (trainer).
Scores: April 6, at Boston — Toronto 1, Boston 2; April 9, at Boston — Toronto 3, Boston 2; April 11, at Toronto — Toronto 1, Boston 3; April 13 at Toronto — Toronto 0, Boston 2; April 16, at Boston — Toronto 1, Boston 3.

1937-38 — Chicago Blackhawks — Art Wiebe, Carl Voss, Hal Jackson, Mike Karakas, Mush March, Jack Shill, Earl Seibert, Cully Dahlstrom, Alex Levinsky, Johnny Gottselig, Lou Trudel, Pete Palangio, Bill MacKenzie, Doc Romnes, Paul Thompson, Roger Jenkins, Alf Moore, Bert Connolly, Virgil Johnson, Paul Goodman, Bill Stewart (manager-coach), Eddie Froelich (trainer).
Scores: April 5, at Toronto — Chicago 3, Toronto 1; April 7, at Toronto — Chicago 1, Toronto 5; April 10 at Chicago — Chicago 2, Toronto 1; April 12, at Chicago — Chicago 4, Toronto 1.

1936-37 — Detroit Red Wings — Normie Smith, Pete Kelly, Larry Aurie, Herbie Lewis, Hec Kilrea, Mud Bruneteau, Syd Howe, Wally Kilrea, Jimmy Franks, Bucko McDonald, Gordon Pettinger, Ebbie Goodfellow, Johnny Gallagher, Scotty Bowman, Johnny Sorrell, Marty Barry, Earl Robertson, Johnny Sherf, Howard Mackie, Jack Adams (manager-coach), Honey Walker (trainer).
Scores: April 6, at New York — Detroit 1, NY Rangers 5; April 8, at Detroit — Detroit 4, NY Rangers 2; April 11, at Detroit — Detroit 0, NY Rangers 1; April 13, at Detroit — Detroit 1, NY Rangers 0; April 15, at Detroit — Detroit 3, NY Rangers 0.

1935-36 — Detroit Red Wings — Johnny Sorrell, Syd Howe, Marty Barry, Herbie Lewis, Mud Bruneteau, Wally Kilrea, Hec Kilrea, Gordon Pettinger, Bucko McDonald, Scotty Bowman, Pete Kelly, Doug Young, Ebbie Goodfellow, Normie Smith, Jack Adams (manager-coach), Honey Walker (trainer).
Scores: April 5, at Detroit — Detroit 3, Toronto 1; April 7, at Detroit — Detroit 9, Toronto 4; April 9, at Toronto — Detroit 3, Toronto 4; April 11, at Toronto — Detroit 3, Toronto 1.

1934-35 — Montreal Maroons — Marvin (Cy) Wentworth, Alex Connell, Toe Blake, Stew Evans, Earl Robinson, Bill Miller, Dave Trottier, Jimmy Ward, Larry Northcott, Hooley Smith, Russ Blinco, Allan Shields, Sammy McManus, Gus Marker, Bob Gracie, Herb Cain, Tommy Gorman (manager), Lionel Conacher (coach), Bill O'Brien (trainer).
Scores: April 4, at Toronto — Mtl. Maroons 3, Toronto 2; April 6, at Toronto — Mtl. Maroons 3, Toronto 1; April 9, at Montreal — Mtl. Maroons 4, Toronto 1.

1933-34 — Chicago Blackhawks — Taffy Abel, Lolo Couture, Lou Trudel, Lionel Conacher, Paul Thompson, Leroy Goldsworthy, Art Coulter, Roger Jenkins, Don McFayden, Tommy Cook, Doc Romnes, Johnny Gottselig, Mush March, Johny Sheppard, Chuck Gardiner (captain), Bill Kendall, Tommy Gorman (manager-coach), Eddie Froelich (trainer).
Scores: April 3, at Detroit — Chicago 1, Detroit 2; April 5, at Detroit — Chicago 4, Detroit 1; April 8, at Chicago — Detroit 5, Chicago 2; April 10, at Chicago — Chicago 1, Detroit 0.

1932-33 — New York Rangers — Ching Johnson, Butch Keeling, Frank Boucher, Art Somers, Babe Siebert, Bun Cook, Andy Aitkinhead, Ott Heller, Ozzie Asmundson, Gord Pettinger, Doug Brennan, Cecil Dillon, Bill Cook (captain), Murray Murdoch, Earl Seibert, Lester Patrick (manager-coach), Harry Westerby (trainer).
Scores: April 4, at New York — NY Rangers 5, Toronto 1; April 8, at Toronto — NY Rangers 3, Toronto 1; April 11, at Toronto — Toronto 3, NY Rangers 2; April 13, at Toronto — NY Rangers 1, Toronto 0.

1931-32 — Toronto Maple Leafs — Charlie Conacher, Harvey Jackson, King Clancy, Andy Blair, Red Horner, Lorne Chabot, Alex Levinsky, Joe Primeau, Hal Darragh, Hal Cotton, Frank Finnigan, Hap Day, Ace Bailey, Bob Gracie, Fred Robertson, Earl Miller, Conn Smythe (manager), Dick Irvin (coach), Tim Daly (trainer).
Scores: April 5 at New York — Toronto 6, NY Rangers 4; April 7, at Boston* — Toronto 6, NY Rangers 2; April 9, at Toronto — Toronto 6, NY Rangers 4.

* Ice was unavailable in Madison Square Garden and Rangers elected to play the second game on neutral ice.

1930-31 — Montreal Canadiens — George Hainsworth, Wildor Larochelle, Marty Burke, Sylvio Mantha, Howie Morenz, Johnny Gagnon, Aurel Joliat, Armand Mondou, Pit Lepine, Albert Leduc, Georges Mantha, Art Lesieur, Nick Wasnie, Bert McCaffrey, Gus Rivers, Jean Pusie, Leo Dandurand (manager), Cecil Hart (coach), Ed Dufour (trainer).
Scores: April 3, at Chicago — Montreal 2, Chicago 1; April 5, at Chicago — Chicago 2, Montreal 1; April 9, at Montreal — Chicago 3, Montreal 2; April 11, at Montreal — Montreal 4, Chicago 2; April 14, at Montreal — Montreal 2, Chicago 0.

1929-30 — Montreal Canadiens — George Hainsworth, Marty Burke, Sylvio Mantha, Howie Morenz, Bert McCaffrey, Aurel Joliat, Albert Leduc, Pit Lepine, Wildor Larochelle, Nick Wasnie, Gerald Carson, Armand Mondou, Georges Mantha, Gus Rivers, Leo Dandurand (manager), Cecil Hart (coach), Ed Dufour (trainer).
Scores: April 1 at Boston — Montreal 3, Boston 0; April 3 at Montreal — Montreal 4, Boston 3.

1928-29 — Boston Bruins — Cecil (Tiny) Thompson, Eddie Shore, Lionel Hitchman, Perk Galbraith, Eric Pettinger, Frank Fredrickson, Mickey Mackay, Red Green, Dutch Gainor, Harry Oliver, Eddie Rodden, Dit Clapper, Cooney Weiland, Lloyd Klein, Cy Denneny, Bill Carson, George Owen, Myles Lane, Art Ross (manager-coach), Win Green (trainer).
Scores: March 28 at Boston — Boston 2, NY Rangers 0; March 29 at New York — Boston 2, NY Rangers 1.

Frankie Brimsek backstopped the Bruins to Cup wins in 1939 and 1941.

1927-28 — New York Rangers — Lorne Chabot, Taffy Abel, Leon Bourgault, Ching Johnson, Bill Cook, Bun Cook, Frank Boucher, Billy Boyd, Murray Murdoch, Paul Thompson, Alex Gray, Joe Miller, Patsy Callighen, Lester Patrick (manager-coach), Harry Westerby (trainer).
Scores: April 5 at Montreal — Mtl. Maroons 2, NY Rangers 0; April 7 at Montreal — NY Rangers 2, Mtl. Maroons 1; April 10 at Montreal — Mtl. Maroons 2, NY Rangers 1; April 12 at Montreal — NY Rangers 1, Mtl. Maroons 0; April 14 at Montreal — NY Rangers 2, Mtl. Maroons 1.

1926-27 — Ottawa Senators — Alex Connell, King Clancy, George (Buck) Boucher, Ed Gorman, Frank Finnigan, Alex Smith, Hec Kilrea, Hooley Smith, Frank Nighbor, Jack Adams, Milt Halliday, Dave Gil (manager-coach).
Scores: April 7 at Boston — Ottawa 0, Boston 0; April 9 at Boston — Ottawa 3, Boston 1; April 11 at Ottawa — Boston 1, Ottawa 1; April 13 at Ottawa — Ottawa 3, Boston 1.

1925-26 — Montreal Maroons — Clint Benedict, Reg Noble, Frank Carson, Dunc Munro, Nels Stewart, Harry Broadbent, Babe Siebert, Dinny Dinsmore, Bill Phillips, Hobart (Hobie) Kitchen, Sammy Rothschiel, Albert (Toots) Holway, Shorty Horne, Bern Brophy, Eddie Gerard (manager-coach), Bill O'Brien (trainer).
Scores: March 30 at Montreal — Mtl. Maroons 3, Victoria 0; April 1 at Montreal — Mtl. Maroons 3, Victoria 0; April 3 at Montreal — Victoria 3, Mtl. Maroons 2; April 6 at Montreal — Mtl. Maroons 2, Victoria 0.

The series in the spring of 1926 ended the annual playoffs between the champions of the east and the champions of the west. The west coast league disbanded, selling its players to Chicago, Detroit and New York Rangers. Since 1926-27 the annual playoffs in the National Hockey League have decided the Stanley Cup champions.

1924-25 — Victoria Cougars — Harry (Happy) Holmes, Clem Loughlin, Gordie Fraser, Frank Fredrickson, Jack Walker, Harold (Gizzy) Hart, Harold (Slim) Halderson, Frank Foyston, Wally Elmer, Harry Meeking, Jocko Anderson, Lester Patrick (manager-coach).
Scores: March 21 at Victoria — Victoria 5, Montreal 2; March 23 at Vancouver — Victoria 3, Montreal 1; March 27 at Victoria — Montreal 4, Victoria 2; March 30 at Victoria — Victoria 6, Montreal 1.

1923-24 — Montreal Canadiens — Georges Vezina, Sprague Cleghorn, Billy Couture, Howie Morenz, Aurel Joliat, Billy Boucher, Odie Cleghorn, Sylvio Mantha, Bobby Boucher, Billy Bell, Billy Cameron, Joe Malone, Fortier, Leo Dandurand (manager-coach).
Scores: March 18 at Montreal — Montreal 3, Van. Maroons 2; March 20 at Montreal — Montreal 2, Van. Maroons 1. March 22 at Montreal — Montreal 6, Cgy. Tigers 1; March 25 at Ottawa* — Montreal 3, Cgy. Tigers 0. (Because of an agreement between the NHL and the two western leagues WCHL and PCHA, Montreal had to play the champions of each league during the Stanley Cup series of 1924.)

*Game transferred to Ottawa to benefit from an artificial ice surface.

1922-23 — Ottawa Senators — George (Buck) Boucher, Lionel Hitchman, Frank Nighbor, King Clancy, Harry Helman, Clint Benedict, Jack Darragh, Eddie Gerard, Cy Denneny, Harry Broadbent, Tommy Gorman (manager), Pete Green (coach), F. Dolan (trainer).
Scores: March 16 at Vancouver — Ottawa 1, Van. Maroons 0; March 19 at Vancouver — Van. Maroons 4, Ottawa 1; March 23 at Vancouver — Ottawa 3, Van. Maroons 2; March 26 at Vancouver — Ottawa 5, Van. Maroons 1; March 29 at Vancouver — Ottawa 2, Edm. Eskimos 1; March 31 at Vancouver — Ottawa 1, Edm. Eskimos 0. (Because of an agreement between the NHL and the two western leagues, WCHL and PCHA, Ottawa had to play the champions of each league during the Stanley Cup series of 1923.)

1921-22 — Toronto St. Pats — Ted Stackhouse, Corb Denneny, Rod Smylie, Lloyd Andrews, John Ross Roach, Harry Cameron, Bill (Red) Stuart, Cecil (Babe) Dye, Ken Randall, Reg Noble, Eddie Gerard (borrowed for one game from Ottawa), Stan Jackson, Nolan Mitchell, Charlie Querrie (manager), Eddie Powers (coach).
Scores: March 17 at Toronto — Van. Millionaires 4, Toronto 3; March 20 at Toronto — Toronto 2, Van. Millionaires 1; March 23 at Toronto — Van. Millionaires 3, Toronto 0; March 25 at Toronto — Toronto 6, Van. Millionaires 0; March 28 at Toronto — Toronto 5, Van. Millionaires 1.

1920-21 — Ottawa Senators — Jack McKell, Jack Darragh, Morley Bruce, George (Buck) Boucher, Eddie Gerard, Clint Benedict, Sprague Cleghorn, Frank Nighbor, Harry Broadbent, Cy Denneny, Leth Graham, Tommy Gorman (manager), Pete Green (coach), F. Dolan (trainer).
Scores: March 21 at Vancouver — Van. Millionaires 2, Ottawa 1; March 24 at Vancouver — Ottawa 4, Van. Millionaires 3; March 28 at Vancouver — Ottawa 3, Van. Millionaires 2; March 31 at Vancouver — Van. Millionaires 3, Ottawa 2; April 4 at Vancouver — Ottawa 2, Van. Millionaires 1

1919-20 — Ottawa Senators — Jack McKell, Jack Darragh, Morley Bruce, Horrace Merrill, George (Buck) Boucher, Eddie Gerard, Clint Benedict, Sprague Cleghorn, Frank Nighbor, Harry Broadbent, Cy Denneny, Price, Tommy Gorman (manager), Pete Green (coach).
Scores: March 22 at Ottawa — Ottawa 3, Seattle 2; March 24 at Ottawa — Ottawa 3, Seattle 0; March 27 at Ottawa — Seattle 3, Ottawa 1; March 30 at Toronto* — Seattle 5, Ottawa 2; April 1 at Toronto* — Ottawa 6, Seattle 1.

*Games transferred to Toronto to benefit from artificial ice surface.

1918-19 — No decision, Series halted by Spanish influenza epidemic, illness of several players and death of Joe Hall of Montreal Canadiens from flu. Five games had been played when the series was halted, each team having won two and tied one. The results are shown:
Scores: March 19 at Seattle — Seattle 7, Montreal 0; March 22 at Seattle — Montreal 4, Seattle 2; March 24 at Seattle — Seattle 7, Montreal 2; March 26 at Seattle — Montreal 0, Seattle 0; March 30 at Seattle — Montreal 4, Seattle 3.

1917-18 — Toronto Arenas — Rusty Crawford, Harry Meeking, Ken Randall, Corb Denneny, Harry Cameron, Jack Adams, Alf Skinner, Harry Mummery, Harry (Happy) Holmes, Reg Noble, Sammy Hebert, Jack Marks, Jack Coughlin, Neville, Charlie Querrie (manager), Dick Carroll (coach), Frank Carroll (trainer).
Scores: March 20 at Toronto — Toronto 5, Van. Millionaires 3; March 23 at Toronto — Van. Millionaires 6, Toronto 4; March 26 at Toronto — Toronto 6, Van. Millionaires 3; March 28 at Toronto — Van. Millionaires 8, Toronto 1; March 30 at Toronto — Toronto 2, Van. Millionaires 1.

1916-17 — Seattle Metropolitans — Harry (Happy) Holmes, Ed Carpenter, Cully Wilson, Jack Walker, Bernie Morris, Frank Foyston, Roy Rickey, Jim Riley, Bobby Rowe (captain), Peter Muldoon (manager).
Scores: March 17 at Seattle — Montreal 8, Seattle 4; March 20 at Seattle — Seattle 6, Montreal 1; March 23 at Seattle — Seattle 4, Montreal 1; March 25 at Seattle — Seattle 9, Montreal 1.

1915-16 — Montreal Canadiens — Georges Vezina, Bert Corbeau, Jack Laviolette, Newsy Lalonde, Louis Berlinguette, Goldie Prodgers, Howard McNamara, Didier Pitre, Skene Ronan, Amos Arbour, Skinner Poulin, Jack Fournier, George Kennedy (manager).
Scores: March 20 at Montreal — Portland 2, Montreal 0; March 22 at Montreal — Montreal 2, Portland 1; March 25 at Montreal — Montreal 6, Portland 3; March 28 at Montreal — Portland 6, Montreal 5; March 30 at Montreal — Montreal 2, Portland 1.

1914-15 — Vancouver Millionaires — Kenny Mallen, Frank Nighbor, Fred (Cyclone) Taylor, Hughie Lehman, Lloyd Cook, Mickey MacKay, Barney Stanley, Jim Seaborn, Si Griffis (captain), Jean Matz, Frank Patrick (playing manager).
Scores: March 22 at Vancouver — Van. Millionaires 6, Ottawa 2; March 24 at Vancouver — Van. Millionaires 8, Ottawa 3; March 26 at Vancouver — Van. Millionaires 12, Ottawa 3.

1913-14 — Toronto Blueshirts — Con Corbeau, F. Roy McGiffen, Jack Walker, George McNamara, Cully Wilson, Frank Foyston, Harry Cameron, Harry (Happy) Holmes, Alan M. Davidson (captain), Harriston, Jack Marshall (playing-manager), Frank and Dick Carroll (trainers).
Scores: March 7 at Montreal — Montreal 2, Toronto 0; March 11 at Toronto — Toronto 6, Montreal 0; Total goals: Toronto 6, Montreal 2. March 14 at Toronto — Toronto 5, Victoria 2; March 17 at Toronto — Toronto 6, Victoria 5; March 19 at Toronto — Toronto 2, Victoria 1.

1912-13 — Quebec Bulldogs — Joe Malone, Joe Hall, Paddy Moran, Harry Mummery, Tommy Smith, Jack Marks, Russell Crawford, Billy Creighton, Jeff Malone, Rocket Power, M.J. Quinn (manager), D. Beland (trainer).
Scores: March 8 at Quebec — Que. Bulldogs 14, Sydney 3; March 10 at Quebec — Que. Bulldogs 6, Sydney 2.

Victoria challenged Quebec but the Bulldogs refused to put the Stanley Cup in competition so the two teams played an exhibition series with Victoria winning two games to one by scores of 7-5, 3-6, 6-1. It was the first meeting between the Eastern champions and the Western champions. The following year, and until the Western Hockey League disbanded after the 1926 playoffs, the Cup went to the winner of the series between East and West.

1911-12 — Quebec Bulldogs — Goldie Prodgers, Joe Hall, Walter Rooney, Paddy Moran, Jack Marks, Jack MacDonald, Eddie Oatman, Leonard, Joe Malone (captain), C. Nolan (coach), M.J. Quinn (manager), D. Beland (trainer).
Scores: March 11 at Quebec — Que. Bulldogs 9, Moncton 3; March 13 at Quebec — Que. Bulldogs 8, Moncton 0.

Prior to 1912, teams could challenge the Stanley Cup champions for the title, thus there was more than one Championship Series played in most of the seasons between 1894 and 1911.

1910-11 — Ottawa Senators — Hamby Shore, Percy LeSueur, Jack Darragh, Bruce Stuart, Marty Walsh, Bruce Ridpath, Fred Lake, Albert (Dubby) Kerr, Alex Currie, Horace Gaul.
Scores: March 13 at Ottawa — Ottawa 7, Galt 4; March 16 at Ottawa — Ottawa 13, Port Arthur 4.

1909-10 — Montreal Wanderers — Cecil W. Blackford, Ernie (Moose) Johnson, Ernie Russell, Riley Hern, Harry Hyland, Jack Marshall, Frank (Pud) Glass (captain), Jimmy Gardner, R. R. Boon (manager).
Scores: March 12 at Montreal — Mtl. Wanderers 7, Berlin (Kitchener) 3.

1908-09 — Ottawa Senators — Fred Lake, Percy LeSueur, Fred (Cyclone) Taylor, H.L. (Billy) Gilmour, Albert Kerr, Edgar Dey, Marty Walsh, Bruce Stuart (captain).
Scores: Ottawa, as champions of the Eastern Canada Hockey Association took over the Stanley Cup in 1909 and, although a challenge was accepted by the Cup trustees from Winnipeg Shamrocks but could not be arranged because of the lateness of the season, no other challenges were made in 1909. The following season — 1909-10 — however, the Senators accepted two challenges as defending Cup Champions. The first was against Galt in a two-game, total-point series, and the second against Edmonton, also a two-game, total-point series. Results: January 5 at Ottawa — Ottawa 12, Galt 3; January 7 at Ottawa — Ottawa 3, Galt 1. January 18 at Ottawa — Ottawa 8, Edm. Eskimos 4; January 20 at Ottawa — Ottawa 13, Edm. Eskimos 7.

1907-08 — Montreal Wanderers — Riley Hern, Art Ross, Walter Small, Frank (Pud) Glass, Bruce Stuart, Ernie Russell, Ernie (Moose) Johnson, Cecil Blachford (captain), Tom Hooper, Larry Gilmour, Ernie Liffiton, R.R. Boon (manager).
Scores: Wanderers accepted four challenges for the Cup: January 9 at Montreal — Mtl. Wanderers 9, Ott. Victorias 3; January 13 at Montreal — Mtl. Wanderers 13, Ott. Victorias 1; March 10 at Montreal — Mtl. Wanderers 11, Wpg. Maple Leafs 5; March 12 at Montreal — Mtl. Wanderers 9, Wpg. Maple Leafs 3; March 14 at Montreal — Mtl. Wanderers 6, Tor. Maple Leafs 4. Note: Toronto played in the Ontario Professional Hockey League (1908, 1909). This club was not associated with the current NHL franchise. At start of following season, 1908-09, Wanderers were challenged by Edmonton. Results: December 28 at Montreal — Mtl. Wanderers 7, Edm. Eskimos 3; December 30 at Montreal — Edm. Eskimos 7, Mtl. Wanderers 6. Total goals: Mtl. Wanderers 13, Edm. Eskimos 10.

1906-07 — (March) — Montreal Wanderers — W. S. (Billy) Strachan, Riley Hern, Lester Patrick, Hod Stuart, Frank (Pud) Glass, Ernie Russell, Cecil Blachford (captain), Ernie (Moose) Johnson, Rod Kennedy, Jack Marshall, R. R. Boon (manager).
Scores: March 23 at Winnipeg — Mtl. Wanderers 7, Kenora 2; March 25 at Winnipeg — Kenora 6, Mtl. Wanderers 5. Total goals: Mtl. Wanderers 12, Kenora 8.

1906-07 — (January) — Kenora Thistles — Eddie Geroux, Art Ross, Si Griffis, Tom Hooper, Billy McGimsie, Roxy Beaudro, Tom Phillips.
Scores: January 17 at Montreal — Kenora 4, Mtl. Wanderers 2; Jan. 21 at Montreal — Kenora 8, Mtl. Wanderers 6.

1905-06 — (March) — Montreal Wanderers — H. Menard, Billy Strachan, Rod Kennedy, Lester Patrick, Frank (Pud) Glass, Ernie Russell, Ernie (Moose) Johnson, Cecil Blachford (captain), Josh Arnold, R. R. Boon (manager).
Scores: March 14 at Montreal — Mtl. Wanderers 9, Ottawa 1; March 17 at Ottawa — Ottawa 9, Mtl. Wanderers 3. Total goals: Mtl. Wanderers 12, Ottawa 10. Wanderers accepted a challenge from New Glasgow, N.S., prior to the start of the 1906-07 season. Results: December 27 at Montreal — Mtl. Wanderers 10, New Glasgow 3; December 29 at Montreal — Mtl. Wanderers 7, New Glasgow 2.

1905-06 — (February) — Ottawa Silver Seven — Harvey Pulford (captain), Arthur Moore, Harry Westwick, Frank McGee, Alf Smith (playing coach), Billy Gilmour, Billy Hague, Percy LeSueur, Harry Smith, Tommy Smith, Dion, Ebbs.
Scores: February 27 at Ottawa — Ottawa 16, Queen's University 7; February 28 at Ottawa — Ottawa 12, Queen's University 7; March 6 at Ottawa — Ottawa 6, Smith's Falls 5; March 8 at Ottawa — Ottawa 8, Smith's Falls 2.

1904-05 — Ottawa Silver Seven — Dave Finnie, Harvey Pulford (captain), Arthur Moore, Harry Westwick, Frank McGee, Alf Smith (playing coach), Billy Gilmour, Frank White, Horace Gaul, Hamby Shore, Allen.
Scores: January 13 at Ottawa — Ottawa 9, Dawson City 2; January 16 at Ottawa — Ottawa 23, Dawson City 2; March 7 at Ottawa — Rat Portage 9, Ottawa 3; March 9 at Ottawa — Ottawa 4, Rat Portage 2; March 11 at Ottawa — Ottawa 5, Rat Portage 4.

1903-04 — Ottawa Silver Seven — S. C. (Suddy) Gilmour, Arthur Moore, Frank McGee, J.B. (Bouse) Hutton, H.L. (Billy) Gilmour, Jim McGee, Harry Westwick, E. H. (Harvey) Pulford (captain), Scott, A. T. (Alf) Smith (playing coach).
Scores: December 30 at Ottawa — Ottawa 9, Wpg. Rowing Club 1; January 1 at Ottawa — Wpg. Rowing Club 6, Ottawa 2; January 4 at Ottawa — Ottawa 2, Wpg. Rowing Club 0. February 23 at Ottawa — Ottawa 6, Tor. Malboros 3; February 25 at Ottawa — Ottawa 11, Tor. Marlboros 2; March 2 at Montreal — Ottawa 5, Mtl. Wanderers 5. Following the tie game, a new two-game series was ordered to be played in Ottawa but Wanderers refused unless the tie-game was replayed in Montreal. When no settlement could be reached, the series was abandoned and Ottawa retained the Cup and accepted a two-game challenge from Brandon. Results: (both games at Ottawa), March 9, Ottawa 6, Brandon 3; March 11, Ottawa 9, Brandon 3.

1902-03 — (March) — Ottawa Silver Seven — S. C. (Suddy) Gilmour, P.T. (Percy) Sims, J. B. (Bouse) Hutton, D. J. (Dave) Gilmour, H. L. (Billy) Gilmour, Harry Westwick, Frank McGee, F. H. Wood, A. A. Fraser, Charles D. Spittal, E. H. (Harvey) Pulford (captain), Arthur Moore, A. T. (Alf) Smith (coach.)
Scores: March 7 at Montreal — Ottawa 1, Mtl. Victorias 1; March 10 at Ottawa — Ottawa 8, Mtl. Victorias 0. Total goals: Ottawa 9, Mtl. Victorias 1; March 12 at Ottawa — Ottawa 6, Rat Portage 2; March 14 at Ottawa — Ottawa 4, Rat Portage 2.

1902-03 — (February) — Montreal AAA — Tom Hodge, R.R. (Dickie) Boon, W.C. (Billy) Nicholson, Art Hooper, W.J. (Billy) Bellingham, Charles A. Liffiton, Jack Marshall, Jim Gardner, Cecil Blachford, George Smith.
Scores: January 29 at Montreal — Mtl. AAA 8, Wpg. Victorias 1; January 31 at Montreal — Wpg. Victorias 2, Mtl. AAA 2; February 2 at Montreal — Wpg. Victorias 4, Mtl. AAA 2; February 4 at Montreal — Mtl. AAA 5, Wpg. Victorias 1.

1901-02 — (March) — Montreal AAA — Tom Hodge, R. R. (Dickie) Boon, W.C. (Billy) Nicholson, Art Hooper, W. J. (Billy) Bellingham, Charles A. Liffiton, Jack Marshall, Roland Elliott, Jim Gardner.
Scores: March 13 at Winnipeg — Wpg. Victorias 1, Mtl. AAA 0; March 15 at Winnipeg — Mtl. AAA 5, Wpg. Victorias 0; March 17 at Winnipeg — Mtl. AAA 2, Wpg. Victorias 1.

1901-02 — (January) — Winnipeg Victorias — Burke Wood, A.B. (Tony) Gingras, Charles W. Johnstone, R.M. (Rod) Flett, Magnus L. Flett, Dan Bain (captain), Fred Scanlon, F. Cadham, G. Brown.
Scores: January 21 at Winnipeg — Wpg. Victorias 5, Tor Wellingtons 3; January 23 at Winnipeg — Wpg. Victorias 5, Tor. Wellingtons 3.

1900-01 — Winnipeg Victorias — Burke Wood, Jack Marshall, A.B. (Tony) Gingras, Charles W. Johnstone, R. M. (Rod) Flett, Magnus L. Flett, Dan Bain (captain), G. Brown.
Scores: January 29 at Montreal — Wpg. Victorias 4, Mtl. Shamrocks 3; January 31 at Montreal — Wpg. Victorias 2, Mtl. Shamrocks 1.

1899-1900 — Montreal Shamrocks — Joe McKenna, Frank Tansey, Frank Wall, Art Farrell, Fred Scanlon, Harry Trihey (captain), Jack Brannen.
Scores: February 12 at Montreal — Mtl. Shamrocks 4, Wpg. Victorias 3; February at Montreal — Wpg. Victorias 3, Mtl. Shamrocks 2; February 16 at Montreal — Mtl. Shamrocks 5, Wpg. Victorias 4; March 5 at Montreal — Mtl. Shamrocks 10, Halifax 2; March 7 at Montreal — Mtl. Shamrocks 11, Halifax 0.

1898-99 — (March) — Montreal Shamrocks — Joe McKenna, Frank Tansey, Frank Wall, Harry Trihey (captain), Art Farrell, Fred Scanlon, Jack Brannen, Dalby, Hoerner.
Scores: March 14 at Montreal — Mtl. Shamrocks 6, Queen's University 2.

1898-99 — (February) — Montreal Victorias — Gordon Lewis, Mike Grant, Graham Drinkwater, Cam Davidson, Bob McDougall, Ernie McLea, Frank Richardson, Jack Ewing, Russell Bowie, Douglas Acer, Fred McRobie.
Scores: February 15 at Montreal — Mtl. Victorias 2, Wpg. Victorias 1; February 18 at Montreal — Mtl. Victorias 3, Wpg. Victorias 2.

1897-98 — Montreal Victorias — Gordon Lewis, Hartland McDougall, Mike Grant, Graham Drinkwater, Cam Davidson, Bob McDougall, Ernie McLea, Frank Richardson (captain), Jack Ewing.
The Victorias as champions of the Amateur Hockey Association, retained the Cup and were not called upon to defend it.

1896-97 — Montreal Victorias — Gordon Lewis, Harold Henderson, Mike Grant (captain), Cam Davidson, Graham Drinkwater, Robert McDougall, Ernie McLea, Shirley Davidson, Hartland McDougall, Jack Ewing, Percy Molson, David Gillilan, McLellan.
Scores: December 27 at Montreal — Mtl. Victorias 15, Ott. Capitals 2.

1895-96 — (December) — Montreal Victorias — Gordon Lewis, Harold Henderson, Mike Grant (captain), Robert McDougall, Graham Drinkwater, Shirley Davidson, Ernie McLea, Robert Jones, Cam Davidson, Hartland McDougall, David Gillilan, Reg Wallace, Stanley Willett.
Scores: December 30 at Winnipeg — Mtl. Victorias 6, Wpg. Victorias 5.

1895-96 — (February) — Winnipeg Victorias — G.H. Merritt, Rod Flett, Fred Higginbotham, Jack Armitage (captain), C.J. (Tote) Campbell, Dan Bain, Charles Johnstone, H. Howard.
Scores: February 14 at Montreal — Wpg. Victorias 2, Mtl. Victorias 0.

1894-95 — Montreal Victorias — Robert Jones, Harold Henderson, Mike Grant (captain), Shirley Davidson, Bob McDougall, Norman Rankin, Graham Drinkwater, Roland Elliot, William Pullan, Hartland McDougall, Arthur Fenwick, A. McDougall. Montreal Victorias as champions of the Amateur Hockey Association were prepared to defend the Stanley Cup. However, the Stanley Cup trustees had already accepted a challenge match between the 1894 champion Montreal AAA and Queen's University. It was declared that if Montreal AAA defeated Queen's University, Montreal Victorias would be declared Stanley Cup champions. If Queen's University won, the Cup would go to the university club. In a game played March 9, 1895, Montreal AAA defeated Queen's University 5-1. As a result, Montreal Victorias were awarded the Stanley Cup.

1893-94 — Montreal AAA — Herbert Collins, Allan Cameron, George James, Billy Barlow, Clare Mussen, Archie Hodgson, Haviland Routh, Alex Irving, James Stewart, A.C. (Toad) Waud, A. Kingan, E. O'Brien.
Scores: March 17 at Mtl. Victorias — Mtl. AAA 3, Mtl. Victorias 2; March 22 at Montreal — Mtl. AAA 3, Ott. Generals 1.

1892-93 — Montreal AAA — Tom Paton, James Stewart, Allan Cameron, Alex Irving, Haviland Routh, Archie Hodgson, Billy Barlow, A.B. Kingan, J. Lowe.
In accordance with the terms governing the presentation of the Stanley Cup, it was awarded for the first time to the Montreal AAA as champions of the Amateur Hockey Association in 1893. Once Montreal AAA had been declared holders of the Stanley Cup, any Canadian hockey team could challenge for the trophy.

All-Time NHL Playoff Formats

1917-18 — The regular-season was split into two halves. The winners of both halves faced each other in a two-game, total-goals series for the NHL championship and the right to meet the PCHA champion in the best-of-five Stanley Cup Finals.

1918-19 — Same as 1917-18, except that the Stanley Cup Finals was extended to a best-of-seven series.

1919-20 — Same as 1917-1918, except that Ottawa won both halves of the split regular-season schedule to earn an automatic berth into the best-of-five Stanley Cup Finals against the PCHA champions.

1921-22 — The top two teams at the conclusion of the regular-season faced each other in a two-game, total-goals series for the NHL championship. The NHL champion then moved on to play the winner of the PCHA-WCHL playoff series in the best-of-five Stanley Cup Finals.

1922-23 — The top two teams at the conclusion of the regular-season faced each other in a two-game, total-goals series for the NHL championship. The NHL champion then moved on to play the PCHA champion in the best-of-three Stanley Cup Semi-Finals, and the winner of the Semi-Finals played the WCHL champion, which had been given a bye, in the best-of-three Stanley Cup Finals.

1923-24 — The top two teams at the conclusion of the regular-season faced each other in a two-game, total-goals series for the NHL championship. The NHL champion then moved on to play the loser of the PCHA-WCHL playoff (the winner of the PCHA-WCHL playoff earned a bye into the Stanley Cup Finals) in the best-of-three Stanley Cup Semi-Finals. The winner of this series met the PCHA-WCHL playoff winner in the best-of-three Stanley Cup Finals.

1924-25 — The first place team (Hamilton) at the conclusion of the regular-season was supposed to play the winner of a two-game, total goals series between the second (Toronto) and third (Montreal) place clubs. However, Hamilton refused to abide by this new format, demanding greater compensation than offered by the League. Thus, Toronto and Montreal played their two-game, total-goals series, and the winner (Montreal) earned the NHL title and then played the WCHL champion (Victoria) in the best-of-five Stanley Cup Finals.

1925-26 — The format which was intended for 1924-25 went into effect. The winner of the two-game, total-goals series between the second and third place teams squared off against the first place team in the two-game, total-goals NHL championship series. The NHL champion then moved on to play the WHL champion in the best-of-five Stanley Cup Finals.

After the 1925 season, the NHL was the only major professional hockey league still in existence and consequently took over sole control of the Stanley Cup competition.

1926-27 — The 10-team league was divided into two divisions — Candian and American — of five teams apiece. In each division, the winner of the two-game, total-goals series between the second and third place teams faced the first place team in a two-game, total-goals series for the division title. The two division title winners then met in the best-of-five Stanley Cup Finals.

1928-29 — Both first place teams in the two divisions played each other in a best-of-five series. Both second place teams in the two divisions played each other in a two-game, total-goals series as did the two third place teams. The winners of these latter two series then played each other in a best-of-three series for the right to meet the winner of the series between the two first place clubs. This Stanley Cup Finals was a best-of-three.

Series A: First in Canadian Division versus first in American (best-of-five)
Series B: Second in Canadian Division versus second in American (two-game, total-goals)
Series C: Third in Canadian Division versus third in American (two-game, total-goals)
Series D: Winner of Series B versus winner of Series C (best-of-three)
Series E: Winner of Series A versus winner of Series D (best of three) for Stanley Cup

1931-32 — Same as 1928-29, except that Series D was changed to a two-game, total-goals series.

1936-37 — Same as 1928-29, except that Series A and E were both best-of-five and Series B, C, and D were each best-of-three.

1938-39 — With the NHL reduced to seven teams, the two-division system was replaced by one seven-team league. Based on final regular-season standings, the following playoff format was adopted:

Series A: First versus Second (best-of-seven)
Series B: Third versus Fourth (best-of-three)
Series C: Fifth versus Sixth (best-of-three)
Series D: Winner of Series B versus winner of Series C (best-of-three)
Series E: Winner of Series A versus winner of Series D (best-of-seven)

1942-43 — With the NHL reduced to six teams (the "original six"), only the top four finishers qualified for playoff action. The best-of-seven Semi-Finals pitted Team #1 vs Team #3 and Team #2 vs Team #4. The winners of each Semi-Final series met in the best-of-seven Stanley Cup Finals.

1967-68 — When it doubled in size from 6 to 12 teams, the NHL once again was divided into two divisions — East and West — of six teams apiece. The top four clubs in each division qualified for the playoffs (all series were best-of-seven):

Series A: Team #1 (East) vs Team #3 (East)
Series B: Team #2 (East) vs Team #4 (East)
Series C: Team #1 (West) vs Team #3 (West)
Series D: Team #2 (West) vs Team #4 (West)

Series E: Winner of Series A vs winner of Series B
Series F: Winner of Series C vs winner of Series D
Series G: Winner of Series E vs Winner of Series F

1970-71 — Same as 1967-68 except that Series E matched the winners of Series A and D, and Series F matched the winners of Series B and C.

1971-72 — Same as 1970-71, except that Series A and C matched Team #1 vs Team #4, and Series B and D matched Team #2 vs Team #3.

1974-75 — With the League now expanded to 18 teams in four divisions, a completely new playoff format was introduced. First, the #2 and #3 teams in each of the four divisions were pooled together in the Preliminary round. These eight (#2 and #3) clubs were ranked #1 to #8 based on regular-season record:

Series A: Team #1 vs Team #8 (best-of-three)
Series B: Team #2 vs Team #7 (best-of-three)
Series C: Team #3 vs Team #6 (best-of-three)
Series D: Team #4 vs Team #5 (best-of-three)
The winners of this Preliminary round then pooled together with the four division winners, which had received byes into this Quarter-Final round. These eight teams were again ranked #1 to #8 based on regular-season record:

Series E: Team #1 vs Team #8 (best-of-seven)
Series F: Team #2 vs Team #7 (best-of-seven)
Series G: Team #3 vs Team #6 (best-of-seven)
Series H: Team #4 vs Team #5 (best-of-seven)
The four Quarter-Finals winners, which moved on to the Semi-Finals, were then ranked #1 to #4 based on regular season record:

Series I: Team #1 vs Team #4 (best-of-seven)
Series J: Team #2 vs Team #3 (best-of-seven)
Series K: Winner of Series I vs winner of Series J (best-of-seven)

1977-78 — Same as 1974-75, except that the Preliminary round consisted of the #2 teams in the four divisions and the next four teams based on regular-season record (not their standings within their divisions).

1979-80 — With the addition of four WHA franchises, the League expanded its playoff structure to include 16 of its 21 teams. The four first place teams in the four divisions automatically earned playoff berths. Among the 17 other clubs, the top 12, according to regular-season record, also earned berths. All 16 teams were then pooled together and ranked #1 to #16 based on regular-season record:

Series A: Team #1 vs Team #16 (best-of-five)
Series B: Team #2 vs Team #15 (best-of-five)
Series C: Team #3 vs Team #14 (best-of-five)
Series D: Team #4 vs Team #13 (best-of-five)
Series E: Team #5 vs Team #12 (best-of-five)
Series F: Team #6 vs Team #11 (best-of-five)
Series G: Team #7 vs Team #10 (best-of-five)
Series H: Team #8 vs Team # 9 (best-of-five)
The eight Preliminary round winners, ranked #1 to #8 based on regular-season record, moved on to the Quarter-Finals:

Series I: Team #1 vs Team #8 (best-of-seven)
Series J: Team #2 vs Team #7 (best-of-seven)
Series K: Team #3 vs Team #6 (best-of-seven)
Series L: Team #4 vs Team #5 (best-of-seven)
The eight Quarter-Finals winners, ranked #1 to #4 based on regular-season record, moved on to the semi-finals:

Series M: Team #1 vs Team #4 (best-of-seven)
Series N: Team #2 vs Team #3 (best-of-seven)
Series O: Winner of Series M vs winner of Series N (best-of-seven)

1981-82 — The first four teams in each division earn playoff berths. In each division, the first-place team opposes the fourth-place team and the second-place team opposes the third-place team in a best-of-five Division Semi-Final series (DSF). In each division, the two winners of the DSF meet in a best-of-seven Division Final series (DF). The two winners in each conference meet in a best-of-seven Conference Final series (CF). In the Prince of Wales Conference, the Adams Division winner opposes the Patrick Division winner; in the Clarence Campbell Conference, the Smythe Division winner opposes the Norris Division winner. The two CF winners meet in a best-of-seven Stanley Cup Final (F) series.

1986-87 to date — Division Semi-Final series changed from best-of-five to best-of-seven.

Team Records

1918-1991

MOST STANLEY CUP CHAMPIONSHIPS:
22 — Montreal Canadiens 1924-30-31-44-46-53-56-57-58-59-60-65-66-68-69-71-73-76-77-78-79-86
13 — Toronto Maple Leafs 1918-22-32-42-45-47-48-49-51-62-63-64-67
7 — Detroit Red Wings 1936-37-43-50-52-54-55

MOST FINAL SERIES APPEARANCES:
32 — Montreal Canadiens in 73-year history.
21 — Toronto Maple Leafs in 73-year history.
18 — Detroit Red Wings in 64-year history.

MOST YEARS IN PLAYOFFS:
66 — Montreal Canadiens in 74-year history.
54 — Toronto Maple Leafs in 74-year history.
52 — Boston Bruins in 67-year history.

MOST CONSECUTIVE STANLEY CUP CHAMPIONSHIPS:
5 — Montreal Canadiens (1956-57-58-59-60)
4 — Montreal Canadiens (1976-77-78-79)
— NY Islanders (1980-81-82-83)

MOST CONSECUTIVE FINAL SERIES APPEARANCES:
10 — Montreal Canadiens (1951-60, inclusive)

MOST CONSECUTIVE PLAYOFF APPEARANCES:
24 — Boston Bruins (1968-91, inclusive)
22 — Chicago Blackhawks (1970-91, inclusive)
21 — Montreal Canadiens (1949-69, inclusive)
— Montreal Canadiens (1971-91, inclusive)
20 — Detroit Red Wings (1939-58, inclusive)

MOST GOALS BOTH TEAMS, ONE PLAYOFF SERIES:
69 — Edmonton Oilers, Chicago Blackhawks in 1985 CF. Edmonton won best-of-seven series 4-2, outscoring Chicago 44-25.
62 — Chicago Blackhawks, Minnesota North Stars in 1985 DF. Chicago won best-of-seven series 4-2, outscoring Minnesota 33-29.
60 — Edmonton Oilers, Calgary Flames in 1984 DF. Edmonton won best-of-seven series 4-3, outscoring Calgary 33-27.

MOST GOALS ONE TEAM, ONE PLAYOFF SERIES:
44 — Edmonton Oilers in 1985 CF. Edmonton won best-of-seven series 4-2, outscoring Chicago 44-25.
35 — Edmonton Oilers in 1983 DF. Edmonton won best-of-seven series 4-1, outscoring Calgary 35-13.

MOST GOALS, BOTH TEAMS, TWO-GAME SERIES:
17 — Toronto St. Patricks, Montreal Canadiens in 1918 NHL F. Toronto won two-game total goal series 10-7.
15 — Boston Bruins, Chicago Blackhawks in 1927 QF. Boston won two-game total goal series 10-5.
— Pittsburgh Penguins, St. Louis Blues in 1975 PR. Pittsburgh won best-of-three series 2-0, outscoring St. Louis 9-6.

MOST GOALS, ONE TEAM, TWO-GAME SERIES:
11 — Buffalo Sabres in 1977 PR. Buffalo won best-of-three series 2-0, outscoring Minnesota 11-3.
— **Toronto Maple Leafs** in 1978 PR. Toronto won best-of-three series 2-0, outscoring Los Angeles 11-3.
10 — Boston Bruins in 1927 QF. Boston won two-game total goal series 10-5.

MOST GOALS, BOTH TEAMS, THREE-GAME SERIES:
33 — Minnesota North Stars, Boston Bruins in 1981 PR. Minnesota won best-of-five series 3-0, outscoring Boston 20-13.
31 — Chicago Blackhawks, Detroit Red Wings in 1985 DSF. Chicago won best-of-five series 3-0, outscoring Detroit 23-8.
28 — Toronto Maple Leafs, NY Rangers in 1932 F. Toronto won best-of-five series 3-0, outscoring New York 18-10.

MOST GOALS, ONE TEAM, THREE-GAME SERIES:
23 — Chicago Blackhawks in 1985 DSF. Chicago won best-of-five series 3-0, outscoring Detroit 23-8.
20 — Minnesota North Stars in 1981 PR. Minnesota won best-of-five series 3-0, outscoring Boston 20-13.
— NY Islanders in 1981 PR. New York won best-of-five series 3-0, outscoring Toronto 20-4.

MOST GOALS, BOTH TEAMS, FOUR-GAME SERIES:
36 — Boston Bruins, St. Louis Blues in 1972 SF. Boston won best-of-seven series 4-0, outscoring St. Louis 28-8.
— **Edmonton Oilers, Chicago Blackhawks** in 1983 CF. Edmonton won best-of-seven series 4-0, outscoring Chicago 25-11.
— **Minnesota North Stars, Toronto Maple Leafs** in 1983 DSF. Minnesota won best-of-seven series 3-1; teams tied in scoring 18-18.
35 — NY Rangers, Los Angeles Kings in 1981 PR. NY Rangers won best-of-five series 3-1, outscoring Los Angeles 23-12.

MOST GOALS, ONE TEAM, FOUR-GAME SERIES:
28 — Boston Bruins in 1972 SF. Boston won best-of-seven series 4-0, outscoring St. Louis 28-8.

MOST GOALS, BOTH TEAMS, FIVE-GAME SERIES:
52 — Edmonton Oilers, Los Angeles Kings in 1987 DSF. Edmonton won best-of-seven series 4-1, outscoring Los Angeles 32-20.
50 — Los Angeles Kings, Edmonton Oilers in 1982 DSF. Los Angeles won best-of-five series 3-2, outscoring Edmonton 27-23.
48 — Edmonton Oilers, Calgary Flames in 1983 DF. Edmonton won best-of-seven series 4-1, outscoring Calgary 35-13.
— Calgary Flames, Los Angeles Kings in 1988 DSF. Calgary won best-of-seven series 4-1, outscoring Los Angeles 30-18.

MOST GOALS, ONE TEAM, FIVE-GAME SERIES:
35 — Edmonton Oilers in 1983 DF. Edmonton won best-of-seven series 4-1, outscoring Calgary 35-13.
32 — Edmonton Oilers in 1987 DSF. Edmonton won best-of-seven series 4-1, outscoring Los Angeles 32-20.
28 — NY Rangers in 1979 QF. NY Rangers won best-of-seven series 4-1, outscoring Philadelphia 28-8.
27 — Philadelphia Flyers in 1980 SF. Philadelphia won best-of-seven series 4-1, outscoring Minnesota 27-14.
— Los Angeles Kings, in 1982 DSF. Los Angeles won best-of-five series 3-2, outscoring Edmonton 27-23.

MOST GOALS, BOTH TEAMS, SIX-GAME SERIES:
69 — Edmonton Oilers, Chicago Blackhawks in 1985 CF. Edmonton won best-of-seven series 4-2, outscoring Chicago 44-25.
62 — Chicago Blackhawks, Minnesota North Stars in 1985 DF. Chicago won best-of-seven series 4-2, outscoring Minnesota 33-29.
56 — Montreal Canadiens, Chicago Blackhawks in 1973 F. Montreal won best-of-seven series 4-2, outscoring Chicago 33-23.

MOST GOALS, ONE TEAM, SIX-GAME SERIES:
44 — Edmonton Oilers in 1985 CF. Edmonton won best-of-seven series 4-2, outscoring Chicago 44-25.
33 — Chicago Blackhawks in 1985 DF. Chicago won best-of-seven series 4-2, outscoring Minnesota 33-29.
— Montreal Canadiens in 1973 F. Montreal won best-of-seven series 4-2, outscoring Chicago 33-23.

MOST GOALS, BOTH TEAMS, SEVEN-GAME SERIES:
60 — Edmonton Oilers, Calgary Flames in 1984 DF. Edmonton won best-of-seven series 4-3, outscoring Calgary 33-27.

MOST GOALS, ONE TEAM, SEVEN-GAME SERIES:
33 — Philadelphia Flyers in 1976 QF. Philadelphia won best-of-seven series 4-3, outscoring Toronto 33-23.
— **Boston Bruins** in 1983 DF. Boston won best-of-seven series 4-3, outscoring Buffalo 33-23.
— **Edmonton Oilers** in 1984 DF. Edmonton won best-of-seven series 4-3, outscoring Calgary 33-27.

FEWEST GOALS, BOTH TEAMS, TWO-GAME SERIES:
1 — NY Rangers, NY Americans, in 1929 SF. NY Rangers defeated NY Americans 1-0 in two-game, total-goal series.
— **Mtl. Maroons, Chicago Blackhawks** in 1935 SF. Mtl. Maroons defeated Chicago 1-0 in two-game, total-goal series.

FEWEST GOALS, ONE TEAM, TWO-GAME SERIES:
0 — Mtl. Maroons in 1937 SF. Lost best-of-three series 2-0 to NY Rangers while being outscored 5-0.
— **NY Americans** in 1939 QF. Lost best-of-three series 2-0 to Toronto while being outscored 6-0.
— **NY Americans** in 1929 SF. Lost two-game total-goal series 1-0 against NY Rangers.
— **Chicago Blackhawks** in 1935 SF. Lost two-game total-goal series 1-0 against Mtl. Maroons.

FEWEST GOALS, BOTH TEAMS, THREE-GAME SERIES:
7 — Boston Bruins, Montreal Canadiens in 1929 SF. Boston won best-of-five series 3-0, outscoring Montreal 5-2.
— **Detroit Red Wings, Mtl. Maroons** in 1936 SF. Detroit won best-of-five series 3-0, outscoring Mtl. Maroons 6-1.

FEWEST GOALS, ONE TEAM, THREE-GAME SERIES:
1 — Mtl. Maroons in 1936 SF. Lost best-of-five series 3-0 to Detroit and were outscored 6-1.

FEWEST GOALS, BOTH TEAMS, FOUR-GAME SERIES:
9 — Toronto Maple Leafs, Boston Bruins in 1935 SF. Toronto won best-of-five series 3-1, outscoring Boston 7-2.

FEWEST GOALS, ONE TEAM, FOUR-GAME SERIES:
2 — Boston Bruins in 1935 SF. Toronto won best-of-five series 3-1, outscoring Boston 7-2.
— **Montreal Canadiens** in 1952 F. Detroit won best-of-seven series 4-0, outscoring Montreal 11-2.

FEWEST GOALS, BOTH TEAMS, FIVE-GAME SERIES:
11 — NY Rangers, Mtl. Maroons in 1928 F. NY Rangers won best-of-five series 3-2 , while outscored by Mtl. Maroons 6-5.

FEWEST GOALS, ONE TEAM, FIVE-GAME SERIES:
5 — NY Rangers in 1928 F. NY Rangers won best-of-five series 3-2, while outscored by Mtl. Maroons 6-5.

FEWEST GOALS, BOTH TEAMS, SIX-GAME SERIES:
22 — Toronto Maple Leafs, Boston Bruins in 1951 SF. Toronto won best-of-seven series 4-1 with 1 tie, outscoring Boston 17-5.

FEWEST GOALS, ONE TEAM, SIX-GAME SERIES:
5 — Boston Bruins in 1951 SF. Toronto won best-of-seven series 4-1 with 1 tie, outscoring Boston 17-5.

FEWEST GOALS, BOTH TEAMS, SEVEN-GAME SERIES:
18 — **Toronto Maple Leafs, Detroit Red Wings** in 1945 F. Toronto won best-of-seven series 4-3; teams tied in scoring 9-9.

FEWEST GOALS, ONE TEAM, SEVEN-GAME SERIES:
9 — **Toronto Maple Leafs,** in 1945 F. Toronto won best-of- seven series 4-3; teams tied in scoring 9-9.
— **Detroit Red Wings,** in 1945 F. Toronto won best-of-seven series 4-3; teams tied in scoring 9-9.

MOST GOALS, BOTH TEAMS, ONE GAME:
18 — **Los Angeles Kings, Edmonton Oilers** at Edmonton, April 7, 1982. Los Angeles 10, Edmonton 8. Los Angeles won best-of-five DSF 3-2.
17 — Pittsburgh Penguins, Philadelphia Flyers at Pittsburgh, April 25, 1989. Pittsburgh 10, Philadelphia 7. Philadelphia won best-of-seven DF 4-3.
16 — Edmonton Oilers, Los Angeles Kings at Edmonton, April 9, 1987. Edmonton 13, Los Angeles 3. Edmonton won best-of-seven DSF 4-1.
— Los Angeles Kings, Calgary Flames at Los Angeles, April 10, 1990. Los Angeles 12, Calgary 4. Los Angeles won best-of-seven DF 4-2.

MOST GOALS, ONE TEAM, ONE GAME:
13 — **Edmonton Oilers** at Edmonton, April 9, 1987. Edmonton 13, Los Angeles 3. Edmonton won best-of-seven DSF 4-1.
12 — Los Angeles Kings at Los Angeles, April 10, 1990. Los Angeles 12, Calgary 4. Los Angeles won best-of-seven DSF 4-2.
11 — Montreal Canadiens at Montreal, March 30, 1944. Montreal 11, Toronto 0. Canadiens won best-of-seven SF 4-1.
— Edmonton Oilers at Edmonton May 4, 1985. Edmonton 11, Chicago 2. Edmonton won best-of-seven CF 4-2.

MOST GOALS, BOTH TEAMS, ONE PERIOD:
9 — **NY Rangers, Philadelphia Flyers,** April 24, 1979, at Philadelphia, third period. NY Rangers won 8-3 scoring six of nine third-period goals.
— **Los Angeles Kings, Calgary Flames** at Los Angeles, April 10, 1990, second period. Los Angeles won game 12-4, scoring five of nine second-period goals.
8 — Chicago Blackhawks, Montreal Canadiens at Montreal, May 8, 1973, in the second period. Chicago won 8-7 scoring five of eight second-period goals.
— Chicago Blackhawks, Edmonton Oilers at Chicago, May 12, 1985 in the first period. Chicago won 8-6, scoring five of eight first-period goals.
— Edmonton Oilers, Winnipeg Jets at Edmonton, April 6, 1988 in the third period. Edmonton won 7-4, scoring six of eight third period goals.
— Hartford Whalers, Montreal Canadiens at Hartford, April 10, 1988 in the third period. Hartford won 7-5, scoring five of eight third period goals.

MOST GOALS, ONE TEAM, ONE PERIOD:
7 — **Montreal Canadiens,** March 30, 1944, at Montreal in third period, during 11-0 win against Toronto.

LONGEST OVERTIME:
116 Minutes, 30 Seconds — Detroit Red Wings, Mtl. Maroons at Montreal, March 24, 25, 1936. Detroit 1, Mtl. Maroons 0. Mud Bruneteau scored, assisted by Hec Kilrea, at 16:30 of sixth overtime period, or after 176 minutes, 30 seconds from start of game, which ended at 2:25 a.m. Detroit won best-of-five SF 3-0.

SHORTEST OVERTIME:
9 Seconds — **Montreal Canadiens, Calgary Flames,** at Calgary, May 18, 1986. Montreal won 3-2 on Brian Skrudland's goal and captured the best-of-seven F 4-1.
11 Seconds — **NY Islanders, NY Rangers,** at NY Rangers, April 11, 1975. NY Islanders won 4-3 on Jean-Paul Parise's goal and captured the best-of-three PR 2-1.

MOST OVERTIME GAMES, ONE PLAYOFF YEAR:
16 — **1982.** Of 71 games played, 16 went into overtime.

FEWEST OVERTIME GAMES, ONE PLAYOFF YEAR:
0 — **1963.** None of the 16 games went into overtime, the only year since 1926 that no overtime was required in any playoff series.

MOST OVERTIME-GAME VICTORIES, ONE TEAM, ONE PLAYOFF YEAR:
6 — **NY Islanders,** 1980. One against Los Angeles in the PR; two against Boston in the QF; one against Buffalo in the SF; and two against Philadelphia in the F. Islanders played 21 games.

MOST OVERTIME GAMES, FINAL SERIES:
5 — **Toronto Maple Leafs,, Montreal Canadiens** in 1951. Toronto defeated Montreal 4-1 in best-of-seven series.

MOST OVERTIME GAMES, SEMI-FINAL SERIES:
4 — **Toronto Maple Leafs, Boston Bruins** in 1933. Toronto won best-of-five series 3-2.
— **Boston Bruins, NY Rangers** in 1939. Boston won best-of-seven series 4-3.
— **St. Louis Blues, Minnesota North Stars** in 1968. St. Louis won best-of-seven series 4-3.

MOST GAMES PLAYED BY ALL TEAMS, ONE PLAYOFF YEAR:
92 — 1991. There were 51 DSF, 24 DF, 11 CF and 6 F games.
87 — 1987. There were 44 DSF, 25 DF, 11 CF and 7 F games.
85 — 1990. There were 49 DSF, 21 DF, 10 CF and 5 F games.
83 — 1988. There were 46 DSF, 27 DF, 12 CF and 4 F games.
82 — 1989. There were 44 DSF, 21 DF, 11 CF and 6 F games.

MOST GAMES PLAYED, ONE TEAM, ONE PLAYOFF YEAR:
26 — **Philadelphia Flyers,** 1987. Won DSF 4-2 against NY Rangers, DF 4-3 against NY Islanders, CF 4-2 against Montreal, and lost F 4-3 against Edmonton.
24 — Pittsburgh Penguins,1991. Won DSF 4-3 against New Jersey, DF 4-1 against Washington, CF 4-2 against Boston, and F 4-2 against Minnesota.
23 — Minnesota North Stars, 1991. Won DSF 4-2 against Chicago, DF 4-2 against St. Louis, CF 4-1 against Edmonton, and lost F 4-2 against Pittsburgh.

MOST ROAD VICTORIES, ONE TEAM, ONE PLAYOFF YEAR:
8 — **NY Islanders,** 1980. Won two at Los Angeles in PR; three at Boston in QF; two at Buffalo in SF; and one at Philadelphia in F series.
Philadelphia Flyers, 1987. Won two at NY Rangers in DSF; two at NY Islanders in DF; three at Montreal in CF; and one at Edmonton in F series.
— Edmonton Oilers, 1990. Won one at Winnipeg in DSF; two at Los Angeles in DF; two at Chicago in CF and three at Boston in F series.

MOST HOME VICTORIES, ONE TEAM, ONE PLAYOFF YEAR:
11 — **Edmonton Oilers,** 1988
10 — Edmonton Oilers, 1985 in 10 home-ice games.
— Montreal Canadiens, 1986
9 — Philadelphia Flyers, 1974
— Philadelphia Flyers, 1980
— NY Islanders, 1981
— NY Islanders, 1983
— Edmonton Oilers, 1984
— Edmonton Oilers, 1987
— Calgary Flames, 1989
— Pittsburgh Penguins, 1991

MOST ROAD VICTORIES, ALL TEAMS, ONE PLAYOFF YEAR:
46 — **1987.** Of 87 games played, road teams won 46 (22 DSF, 14 DF, 8 CF and 2 Stanley Cup).

MOST CONSECUTIVE PLAYOFF GAME VICTORIES:
12 — **Edmonton Oilers.** Streak began May 15, 1984 at Edmonton with a 7-2 win over NY Islanders in third game of F series, and ended May 9, 1985 when Chicago defeated Edmonton 5-2 at Chicago. Included in the streak were three wins over the NY Islanders, in 1984, three over Los Angeles, four over Winnipeg and two over Chicago, all in 1985.
11 — Montreal Canadiens. Streak began April 16, 1959, at Toronto with 3-2 win in fourth game of F series, won by Montreal 4-1, and ended March 23, 1961, when Chicago defeated Montreal 4-3 in second game of SF series. Included in streak were eight straight victories in 1960.
— Montreal Canadiens. Streak began April 28, 1968, at Montreal with 4-3 win in fifth game of SF series, won by Montreal 4-1, and ended April 17, 1969, at Boston when Boston defeated them 5-0 in third game of SF series. Included in the streak were four straight wins over St. Louis in the 1968 F and four straight wins over NY Rangers in a 1969 QF series.
— Boston Bruins. Streak began April 14, 1970, at Boston with 3-2 victory over NY Rangers in fifth game of a QF series, won by Boston 4-2. It continued with a four-game victory over Chicago in the 1970 SF and a four-game win over St. Louis in the 1970 F. Boston then won the first game of a 1971 QF series against Montreal. Montreal ended the streak April 8, 1971, at Boston with a 7-5 victory.
— Montreal Canadiens. Streak started May 6, 1976, at Montreal with 5-2 win in fifth game of a SF series against Philadelphia, won by Montreal 4-1. Continued with a four-game sweep over Philadelphia in the 1976 F and a four-game win against St. Louis in the 1977 QF. Montreal won the first two games of a 1977 SF series against the NY Islanders before NY Islanders ended the streak, April 2, 1977 at New York with a 5-3 victory.

MOST CONSECUTIVE VICTORIES, ONE PLAYOFF YEAR:
10 — **Boston Bruins** in 1970. Boston won last two games of best-of-seven QF against NY Rangers to win series 4-2 and then defeated Chicago 4-0 in best-of-seven SF and St. Louis 4-0 in best-of-seven F.

LONGEST PLAYOFF LOSING STREAK:
16 Games — **Chicago Blackhawks.** Streak started in 1975 QF against Buffalo when Chicago lost last two games. Then Chicago lost four games to Montreal in 1976 QF; two games to NY Islanders in 1977 PR; four games to Boston in 1978 QF and four games to NY Islanders in 1979 QF. Streak ended on April 8, 1980 when Chicago defeated St. Louis 3-2 in the opening game of their 1980 PR series.
12 Games — Toronto Maple Leafs. Streak started on April 16, 1979 as Toronto lost four straight games in a QF series against Montreal. Continued with three-game PR defeats versus Philadelphia and NY Islanders in 1980 and 1981 respectively. Toronto failed to qualify for the 1982 playoffs and lost the first two games of a 1983 DSF against Minnesota. Toronto ended the streak with a 6-3 win against the North Stars on April 9, 1983.
10 Games — NY Rangers. Streak started in 1968 QF against Chicago when NY Rangers lost last four games and continued through 1969 (four straight losses to Montreal in QF) and 1970 (two straight losses to Boston in QF) before ending with a 4-3 win against Boston, at New York, April 11, 1970.
— Philadelphia Flyers. Streak started on April 18, 1968, the last game in the 1968 QF series against St. Louis, and continued through 1969 (four straight losses to St. Louis in QF), 1971 (four straight losses to Chicago in QF) and 1973 (opening game loss to Minnesota in QF) before ending with a 4-1 win against Minnesota, at Philadelphia, April 5, 1973.

MOST SHUTOUTS, ONE PLAYOFF YEAR, ALL TEAMS:
8 — **1937.** Of 17 games played, NY Rangers had 4. Detroit 3, Boston 1.
— **1975.** Of 51 games played, Philadelphia had 5, Montreal 2, NY Islanders 1.
— **1980.** Of 67 games played, Buffalo had 3, Philadelphia 2, Montreal, NY Islanders and Minnesota 1 each.
— **1984.** Of 70 games played, Montreal had 3, Edmonton, Minnesota, NY Rangers, St. Louis and Vancouver 1 each.

FEWEST SHUTOUTS, ONE PLAYOFF YEAR, ALL TEAMS:
0 — **1959.** 18 games played.

MOST SHUTOUTS, BOTH TEAMS, ONE SERIES:
5 — **1945 F, Toronto Maple Leafs, Detroit Red Wings.** Toronto had 3 shutouts, Detroit 2. Toronto won best-of-seven series 4-3.
— **1950 SF, Toronto Maple Leafs, Detroit Red Wings.** Toronto had 3 shutouts, Detroit 2. Detroit won best-of-seven series 4-3.

MOST PENALTIES, BOTH TEAMS, ONE SERIES:
219 — **New Jersey Devils, Washington Capitals** in 1988 DF won by New Jersey 4-3. New Jersey received 98 minors, 11 majors, 9 misconducts and 1 match penalty. Washington received 80 minors, 11 majors, 8 misconducts and 1 match penalty.

MOST PENALTY MINUTES, BOTH TEAMS, ONE SERIES:
656 — **New Jersey Devils, Washington Capitals** in 1988 DF won by New Jersey 4-3. New Jersey had 351 minutes; Washington 305.

MOST PENALTIES, ONE TEAM, ONE SERIES:
119 — **New Jersey Devils** in 1988 DF versus Washington. New Jersey received 98 minors, 11 majors, 9 misconducts and 1 match penalty.

MOST PENALTY MINUTES, ONE TEAM, ONE SERIES:
351 — **New Jersey Devils** in 1988 DF versus Washington. Series won by New Jersey 4-3.

MOST PENALTY MINUTES, BOTH TEAMS, ONE GAME:
298 Minutes — **Detroit Red Wings, St. Louis Blues,** at St. Louis, April 12, 1991. Detroit received 33 penalties for 152 minutes; St. Louis 33 penalties for 146 minutes. St. Louis won 6-1.
267 Minutes — NY Rangers, Los Angeles Kings, at Los Angeles, April 9, 1981. NY Rangers received 31 penalties for 142 minutes; Los Angeles 28 penalties for 125 minutes. Los Angeles won 5-4.

MOST PENALTIES, BOTH TEAMS, ONE GAME:
66 — **Detroit Red Wings, St. Louis Blues,** at St. Louis, April 12, 1991. Detroit received 33 penalties; St. Louis 33. St. Louis won 6-1.
62 — New Jersey Devils, Washington Capitals, at New Jersey, April 22, 1988. New Jersey received 32 penalties; Washington 30. New Jersey won 10-4.

MOST PENALTIES, ONE TEAM, ONE GAME:
33 — **Detroit Red Wings,** at St. Louis, April 12,1991. St. Louis won 6-1.
— **St. Louis Blues,** at St. Louis, April 12, 1991. St. Louis won 6-1.
32 — New Jersey Devils, at Washington, April 22,1988. New Jersey won 10-4.
31 — NY Rangers, at Los Angeles, April 9, 1981. Los Angeles won 5-4.
30 — Philadelphia Flyers, at Toronto, April 15, 1976. Toronto won 5-4.

MOST PENALTY MINUTES, ONE TEAM, ONE GAME:
152 — **Detroit Red Wings,** at St. Louis, April 12, 1991. St. Louis won 6-1.
146 — St. Louis Blues, at St. Louis, April 12, 1991. St. Louis won 6-1.
142 — NY Rangers, at Los Angeles, April 9, 1981. Los Angeles won 5-4.

MOST PENALTIES, BOTH TEAMS, ONE PERIOD:
43 — **NY Rangers, Los Angeles Kings,** April 9, 1981, at Los Angeles, first period. NY Rangers had 24 penalties; Los Angeles 19. Los Angeles won 5-4.

MOST PENALTY MINUTES, BOTH TEAMS, ONE PERIOD:
248 — **NY Islanders, Boston Bruins,** April 17, 1980, first period, at Boston. Each team received 124 minutes. Islanders won 5-4.

MOST PENALTIES, ONE TEAM, ONE PERIOD: (AND) MOST PENALTY MINUTES, ONE TEAM, ONE PERIOD:
24 Penalties; 125 Minutes — **NY Rangers,** April 9, 1981, at Los Angeles, first period. Los Angeles won 5-4.

FEWEST PENALTIES, BOTH TEAMS, BEST-OF-SEVEN SERIES:
19 — **Detroit Red Wings, Toronto Maple Leafs** in 1945 F, won by Toronto 4-3. Detroit received 10 minors. Toronto 9 minors.

FEWEST PENALTIES, ONE TEAM, BEST-OF-SEVEN SERIES:
9 — **Toronto Maple Leafs** in 1945 F, won by Toronto 4-3 against Detroit.

MOST POWER-PLAY GOALS BY ALL TEAMS, ONE PLAYOFF YEAR:
199 — **1988** in 83 games.

MOST POWER-PLAY GOALS, ONE TEAM, ONE PLAYOFF YEAR:
35 — **Minnesota North Stars,** 1991 in 23 games.
32 — Edmonton Oilers, 1988 in 18 games.
31 — NY Islanders, 1981, in 18 games.

MOST POWER-PLAY GOALS, BOTH TEAMS, ONE SERIES:
21 — **NY Islanders, Philadelphia Flyers** in 1980 F, won by NY Islanders 4-2. NY Islanders had 15 and Flyers 6.
— **NY Islanders, Edmonton Oilers** in 1981 QF, won by NY Islanders 4-2. NY Islanders had 13 and Edmonton 8.
— **Philadelphia Flyers, Pittsburgh Penguins** in 1989 DF, won by Philadelphia 4-3. Philadelphia had 11 and Pittsburgh 10.
— **Minnesota North Stars, Chicago Blackhawks** in 1991 DSF, won by Minnesota 4-2. Minnesota had 15 and Chicago 6.
20 — Toronto Maple Leafs, Philadelphia Flyers in 1976 QF series won by Philadelphia 4-3. Toronto had 12 power-play goals; Philadelphia 8.

MOST POWER-PLAY GOALS, ONE TEAM, ONE SERIES:
15 — **NY Islanders** in 1980 F against Philadelphia. NY Islanders won series 4-2.
— **Minnesota North Stars** in 1991 DSF against Chicago. Minnesota won series 4-2.
13 — NY Islanders in 1981 QF against Edmonton. NY Islanders won series 4-2.
— Calgary Flames in 1986 CF against St. Louis. Calgary won series 4-3.
12 — Toronto Maple Leafs in 1976 QF series won by Philadelphia 4-3.

MOST POWER-PLAY GOALS, BOTH TEAMS, ONE GAME:
8 — **Minnesota North Stars, St. Louis Blues,** April 24, 1991 at Minnesota. Minnesota had 4, St. Louis 4. Minnesota won 8-4.
7 — **Minnesota North Stars, Edmonton Oilers,** April 28, 1984 at Minnesota. Minnesota had 4, Edmonton 3. Edmonton won 8-5.
— Philadelphia Flyers, NY Rangers, April 13, 1985 at New York. Philadelphia had 4, NY Rangers 3. Philadelphia won 6-5.
— Edmonton Oilers, Chicago Blackhawks, May 14, 1985 at Edmonton. Chicago had 5, Edmonton 2. Edmonton won 10-5.
— Edmonton Oilers, Los Angeles Kings, April 9, 1987 at Edmonton. Edmonton had 5, Los Angeles 2. Edmonton won 13-3.
— Vancouver Canucks, Calgary Flames, April 9, 1989 at Vancouver. Vancouver had 4, Calgary 3. Vancouver won 5-3.

MOST POWER-PLAY GOALS, ONE TEAM, ONE GAME:
6 — **Boston Bruins,** April 2, 1969, at Boston against Toronto. Boston won 10-0.

MOST POWER-PLAY GOALS, BOTH TEAMS, ONE PERIOD:
5 — **Minnesota North Stars, Edmonton Oilers,** April 28, 1984, second period, at Minnesota. Minnesota had 4 and Edmonton 1. Edmonton won 8-5.
— **Vancouver Canucks, Calgary Flames,** April 9, 1989, third period at Vancouver. Vancouver had 3 and Calgary 2. Vancouver won 5-3.
— **Minnesota North Stars, St. Louis Blues,** April 24, 1991, second period, at Minnesota. Minnesota had 4 and St. Louis 1. Minnesota won 8-4.

MOST POWER-PLAY GOALS, ONE TEAM, ONE PERIOD:
4 — **Toronto Maple Leafs,** March 26, 1936, second period against Boston at Toronto. Toronto won 8-3.
— **Minnesota North Stars,** April 28, 1984, second period against Edmonton at Minnesota. Edmonton won 8-5.
— **Boston Bruins,** April 11, 1991, third period against Hartford at Boston. Boston won 6-1.
— **Minnesota North Stars,** April 24, 1991, second period against St. Louis at Minnesota. Minnesota won 8-4.

MOST SHORTHAND GOALS BY ALL TEAMS, ONE PLAYOFF YEAR:
33 — **1988,** in 83 games.

Dave Keon scored one of the Leafs' two short-handed goals in the first period of game six of the 1965 semi-finals.

MOST SHORTHAND GOALS, ONE TEAM, ONE PLAYOFF YEAR:
10 — Edmonton Oilers 1983, in 16 games.
  9 — NY Islanders, 1981, in 19 games.
  8 — Philadelphia Flyers, 1989, in 19 games.
  7 — NY Islanders, 1980, in 21 games.
  7 — Chicago Blackhawks, 1989, in 16 games.

MOST SHORTHAND GOALS, BOTH TEAMS, ONE SERIES:
  7 — **Boston Bruins** (4), **NY Rangers** (3), in 1958 SF, won by Boston 4-2.
    — **Edmonton Oilers** (5), **Calgary Flames** (2), in 1983 DF won by Edmonton 4-1.

MOST SHORTHAND GOALS, ONE TEAM, ONE SERIES:
  5 — **Edmonton Oilers** in 1983 against Calgary in best-of-seven DF won by Edmonton 4-1.
    — **NY Rangers** in 1979 against Philadelphia in best-of-seven QF, won by NY Rangers 4-1.
  4 — Boston Bruins in 1958 against NY Rangers in best-of-seven SF series, won by Boston 4-2.
    — Minnesota North Stars in 1981 against Calgary in best-of-seven SF, won by Minnesota 4-2.
    — Chicago Blackhawks in 1989 against Detroit in best-of-seven DSF won by Chicago 4-2.
    — Philadelphia Flyers in 1989 against Pittsburgh in best-of-seven DF won by Philadelphia 4-3.

MOST SHORTHAND GOALS, BOTH TEAMS, ONE GAME:
  4 — **NY Islanders, NY Rangers,** April 17, 1983 at NY Rangers. NY Islanders had 3 shorthand goals, NY Rangers 1. NY Rangers won 7-6.
    — **Boston Bruins, Minnesota North Stars,** April 11, 1981, at Minnesota. Boston had 3 shorthand goals, Minnesota 1. Minnesota won 6-3.
  3 — Toronto Maple Leafs, Detroit Red Wings, April 5, 1947, at Toronto. Toronto had 2 shorthand goals, Detroit 1. Toronto won 6-1.
    — NY Rangers, Boston Bruins, April 1, 1958, at Boston. NY Rangers had 2 shorthand goals, Boston 1. NY Rangers won 5-2.
    — Minnesota North Stars, Philadelphia Flyers, May 4, 1980, at Minnesota. Minnesota had 2 shorthand goals, Philadelphia 1. Philadelphia won 5-3.
    — Edmonton Oilers, Winnipeg Jets, April 9, 1988 at Winnipeg. Winnipeg had 2 shorthand goals, Edmonton 1. Winnipeg won 6-4.
    — New Jersey Devils, NY Islanders, April 14, 1988 at New Jersey. NY Islanders had 2 shorthand goals, New Jersey 1. New Jersey won 6-5.

MOST SHORTHAND GOALS, ONE TEAM, ONE GAME:
  3 — **Boston Bruins,** April 11, 1981, at Minnesota. Minnesota won 6-3.
    — **NY Islanders,** April 17, 1983, at NY Rangers. NY Rangers won 7-6.

MOST SHORTHAND GOALS, BOTH TEAMS, ONE PERIOD:
  3 — **Toronto Maple Leafs, Detroit Red Wings,** April 5, 1947, at Toronto, first period. Toronto scored two short-hand goals; Detroit one. Toronto won 6-1.

MOST SHORTHAND GOALS ONE TEAM, ONE PERIOD:
  2 — **Toronto Maple Leafs,** April 5, 1947, at Toronto against Detroit, first period. Toronto won 6-1.
    — **Toronto Maple Leafs,** April 13, 1965, at Toronto against Montreal, first period. Montreal won 4-3.
    — **Boston Bruins,** April 20, 1969, at Boston against Montreal, first period. Boston won 3-2.
    — **Boston Bruins,** April 8, 1970, at Boston against NY Rangers, second period. Boston won 8-2.
    — **Boston Bruins,** April 30, 1972, at Boston against NY Rangers, first period. Boston won 6-5.
    — **Chicago Blackhawks,** May 3, 1973, at Chicago against Montreal, first period. Chicago won 7-4.
    — **Montreal Canadiens,** April 23, 1978, at Detroit, first period. Montreal won 8-0.
    — **NY Islanders,** April 8, 1980, at New York against Los Angeles, second period. NY Islanders won 8-1.
    — **Los Angeles Kings,** April 9, 1980, at NY Islanders, first period. Los Angeles won 6-3.
    — **Boston Bruins,** April 13, 1980, at Pittsburgh, second period. Boston won 8-3.
    — **Minnesota North Stars,** May 4, 1980, at Minnesota against Philadelphia, second period. Philadelphia won 5-3.
    — **Boston Bruins,** April 11, 1981, at Minnesota, third period. Minnesota won 6-3.
    — **NY Islanders,** May 12, 1981, at New York against Minnesota, first period. NY Islanders won 6-3.
    — **Montreal Canadiens,** April 7, 1982, at Montreal against Quebec, third period. Montreal won 5-1.
    — **Edmonton Oilers,** April 24, 1983, at Edmonton against Chicago, third period. Edmonton won 8-4.
    — **Winnipeg Jets,** April 14, 1985, at Calgary, second period. Winnipeg won 5-3.
    — **Boston Bruins,** April 6, 1988 at Boston against Buffalo, first period. Boston won 7-3.
    — **NY Islanders,** April 14, 1988 at New Jersey, third period. New Jersey won 6-5.

MOST THREE-OR-MORE GOAL GAMES BY ALL TEAMS, ONE PLAYOFF YEAR:
  12 — **1983** in 66 games.
    — **1988** in 83 games.
  11 — 1985 in 70 games.

MOST THREE-OR-MORE GOAL GAMES, ONE TEAM, ONE PLAYOFF YEAR:
  6 — **Edmonton Oilers** in 16 games, 1983.
    — **Edmonton Oilers** in 18 games, 1985.

FASTEST TWO GOALS, BOTH TEAMS:
5 Seconds — **Pittsburgh Penguins, Buffalo Sabres** at Buffalo, April 14, 1979. Gilbert Perreault scored for Buffalo at 12:59 and Jim Hamilton for Pittsburgh at 13:04 of first period. Pittsburgh won 4-3 and best-of-three PR 2-1.
8 seconds — Minnesota North Stars, St. Louis Blues at Minnesota, April 9, 1989. Bernie Federko scored for St. Louis at 2:28 of third period and Perry Berezan at 2:36 for Minnesota. Minnesota won 5-4. St. Louis won best-of-seven DSF 4-1.
9 seconds — NY Islanders, Washington Capitals at Washington, April 10, 1986. Bryan Trottier scored for New York at 18:26 of second period and Scott Stevens at 18:35 for Washington. Washington won 5-2, and won best-of-five DSF 3-0.
10 Seconds — Washington Capitals, New Jersey Devils at New Jersey, April 5, 1990. Pat Conacher scored for New Jersey at 8:02 of second period and Dale Hunter at 8:12 for Washington. Washington won 5-4, and won best-of-seven DSF 4-2.
    — Calgary Flames, Edmonton Oilers at Edmonton, April 8, 1991. Joe Nieuwendyk scored for Calgary at 2:03 of first period and Esa Tikkanen at 2:13 for Edmonton. Edmonton won 4-3, and won best-of-seven DSF 4-3.

FASTEST TWO GOALS, ONE TEAM:
5 Seconds — **Detroit Red Wings** at Detroit, April 11, 1965, against Chicago. Norm Ullman scored at 17:35 and 17:40, 2nd period. Detroit won 4-2. Chicago won best-of-seven SF 4-3.

FASTEST THREE GOALS, BOTH TEAMS:
21 Seconds — **Edmonton Oilers, Chicago Blackhawks** at Edmonton, May 7, 1985. Behn Wilson scored for Chicago at 19:22 of third period, Jari Kurri at 19:36 and Glenn Anderson at 19:43 for Edmonton. Edmonton won 7-3 and best-of-seven CF 4-2.
31 Seconds — Edmonton Oilers, Philadelphia Flyers at Edmonton, May 25, 1985. Wayne Gretzky scored for Edmonton at 1:10 and 1:25 of first period, Derrick Smith for Philadelphia at 1:41. Edmonton won 4-3 and best-of-seven F 4-1.
36 Seconds — Los Angeles Kings, Edmonton Oilers at Edmonton, April 7, 1982. Steve Bozek of Los Angeles scored at 6:00 of first period, Tom Roulston of Edmonton scored at 6:16 and Risto Siltanen of Edmonton scored at 6:36. Los Angeles won 10-8 and best-of-five DSF 3-2.
    — Montreal Canadiens, Buffalo Sabres at Buffalo, April 9, 1991. Eric Desjardins scored at 5:23 of first period, Stephane Richer at 5:31 for Montreal, and Benoit Hogue score at 5:59 for Buffalo. Buffalo won 6-4. Montreal won best-of-seven DSF 4-2.

FASTEST THREE GOALS, ONE TEAM:
23 Seconds — **Toronto Maple Leafs** at Toronto, April 12, 1979, against Atlanta Flames. Darryl Sittler scored at 4:04 of first period and again at 4:16 and Ron Ellis at 4:27. Leafs won 7-4 and best-of-three PR 2-0.
38 Seconds — NY Rangers at New York, April 12, 1986. Jim Wiemer scored at 12:29 of third period, Bob Brooke at 12:43 and Ron Grescher at 13:07. NY Rangers won 5-2 and best-of-five DSF 3-2.
56 Seconds — Montreal Canadiens at Detroit, April 6, 1954. Dickie Moore scored at 15:03 of first period, Maurice Richard at 15:28 and again at 15:59. Montreal won 3-1. Detroit won best-of-seven F 4-3.

FASTEST FOUR GOALS, BOTH TEAMS:
1 Minute, 33 Seconds — **Philadelphia Flyers, Toronto Maple Leafs** at Philadelphia, April 20, 1976. Don Saleski of Philadelphia scored at 10:04 of second period; Bob Neely, Toronto, 10:42; Gary Dornhoefer, Philadelphia, 11:24; and Don Saleski, 11:37. Philadelphia won 7-1 and best-of-seven QF series 4-3.
1 minute, 34 seconds — Montreal Canadiens, Calgary Flames at Montreal, May 20, 1986. Joel Otto of Calgary scored at 17:59 of first period; Bobby Smith, Montreal, 18:25; Mats Naslund, Montreal, 19:17; and Bob Gainey, Montreal, 19:33. Montreal won 5-3 and best-of-seven F series 4-1.
1 Minute, 38 Seconds — Boston Bruins, Philadelphia Flyers at Philadelphia, April 26, 1977. Gregg Sheppard of Boston scored at 14:01 of second period; Mike Milbury, Boston, 15:01; Gary Dornhoefer, Philadelphia, 15:16; and Jean Ratelle, Boston, 15:39. Boston won 5-4 and best-of-seven SF series 4-0.

FASTEST FOUR GOALS, ONE TEAM:
2 Minutes, 35 Seconds — **Montreal Canadiens** at Montreal, March 30, 1944, against Toronto. Toe Blake scored at 7:58 of third period and again at 8:37; Maurice Richard, 9:17; Ray Getliffe, 10:33. Montreal won 11-0 and best-of-seven SF 4-0.

FASTEST FIVE GOALS, BOTH TEAMS:
3 Minutes, 6 Seconds — **Chicago Blackhawks, Minnesota North Stars,** at Chicago April 21, 1985. Keith Brown scored for Chicago at 1:12, second period; Ken Yaremchuk, Chicago, 1:27; Dino Ciccarelli, Minnesota, 2:48; Tony McKegney, Minnesota, 4:07; and Curt Fraser, Chicago, 4:18. Chicago won 6-2 and best-of-seven DF 4-2.
3 Minutes, 20 Seconds — Minnesota North Stars, Philadelphia Flyers, at Philadelphia, April 29, 1980. Paul Shmyr scored for Minnesota at 13:20, first period; Steve Christoff, Minnesota, 13:59; Ken Linseman, Philadelphia, 14:54; Tom Gorence, Philadelphia, 15:36; and Linseman, 16:40. Minnesota won 6-5. Philadelphia won best-of-seven SF 4-1.
4 Minutes, 19 Seconds — Toronto Maple Leafs, NY Rangers at Toronto, April 9, 1932. Ace Bailey scored for Toronto at 15:07, third period; Fred Cook, NY Rangers, 16:32; Bob Gracie, Toronto, 17:36; Frank Boucher, NY Rangers, 18:26 and again at 19:26. Toronto won 6-4 and best-of-five F 3-0.

FASTEST FIVE GOALS, ONE TEAM:
3 Minutes, 36 Seconds — **Montreal Canadiens** at Montreal, March 30, 1944, against Toronto. Toe Blake scored at 7:58 of third period and again at 8:37; Maurice Richard, 9:17; Ray Getliffe, 10:33; and Buddy O'Connor, 11:34. Canadiens won 11-0 and best-of-seven SF 4-0.

Individual Records

Career

MOST YEARS IN PLAYOFFS:
20 — Gordie Howe, Detroit, Hartford (1947-58 incl.; 60-61; 63-66 incl.; 70 & 80)
19 — Red Kelly, Detroit, Toronto
— Larry Robinson, Montreal, Los Angeles
18 — Stan Mikita, Chicago
— Henri Richard, Montreal

MOST CONSECUTIVE YEARS IN PLAYOFFS:
19 — Larry Robinson, Montreal, Los Angeles (1973-1991, inclusive).
17 — Brad Park, NY Rangers, Boston, Detroit (1969-1985, inclusive).
16 — Jean Beliveau, Montreal (1954-69, inclusive).

MOST PLAYOFF GAMES:
225 — Larry Robinson, Montreal, Los Angeles
198 — Bryan Trottier, NY Islanders
185 — Denis Potvin, NY Islanders
182 — Bob Gainey, Montreal
180 — Henri Richard, Montreal

MOST POINTS IN PLAYOFFS (CAREER):
299 — Wayne Gretzky, Edmonton, Los Angeles, 93G, 206A
215 — Mark Messier, Edmonton, 80G, 135A
202 — Jari Kurri, Edmonton, 92G, 110A
183 — Glenn Anderson, Edmonton, 81G, 102A
177 — Bryan Trottier, NY Islanders, Pittsburgh 67G, 110A
176 — Jean Beliveau, Montreal, 79G, 97A

MOST GOALS IN PLAYOFFS (CAREER):
93 — Wayne Gretzky, Edmonton, Los Angeles
92 — Jari Kurri, Edmonton
85 — Mike Bossy, NY Islanders
82 — Maurice Richard, Montreal
81 — Glenn Anderson, Edmonton
80 — Mark Messier, Edmonton

MOST GAME-WINNING GOALS IN PLAYOFFS (CAREER):
18 — Maurice Richard, Montreal
— **Wayne Gretzky, Edmonton, Los Angeles**
17 — Mike Bossy, NY Islanders
15 — Jean Beliveau, Montreal
— Yvan Cournoyer, Montreal

MOST OVERTIME GOALS IN PLAYOFFS (CAREER):
6 — Maurice Richard, Montreal (1 in 1946; 3 in 1951; 1 in 1957; 1 in 1958.)
4 — Bob Nystrom, NY Islanders
— Dale Hunter, Quebec, Washington
3 — Mel Hill, Boston
— Rene Robert, Buffalo
— Danny Gare, Buffalo
— Jacques Lemaire, Montreal
— Bobby Clarke, Philadelphia
— Terry O'Reilly, Boston
— Mike Bossy, NY Islanders
— Steve Payne, Minnesota
— Ken Morrow, NY Islanders
— Lanny McDonald, Toronto, Calgary
— Glenn Anderson, Edmonton
— Peter Stastny, Quebec
— Dino Ciccarelli, Minnesota, Washington
— Wayne Gretzky, Edmonton, Los Angeles

MOST POWER-PLAY GOALS IN PLAYOFFS (CAREER):
35 — Mike Bossy, NY Islanders
27 — Denis Potvin, NY Islanders
26 — Jean Beliveau, Montreal
25 — Wayne Gretzky, Edmonton, Los Angeles
23 — Bobby Smith, Minnesota, Montreal
— Glenn Anderson, Edmonton
— Brian Propp, Philadelphia, Boston, Minnesota
— Cam Neely, Vancouver, Boston

MOST SHORTHAND GOALS IN PLAYOFFS (CAREER):
11 — Mark Messier, Edmonton
10 — Wayne Gretzky, Edmonton, Los Angeles
8 — Ed Westfall, Boston, NY Islanders
— Hakan Loob, Calgary
7 — Jari Kurri, Edmonton

MOST THREE-OR-MORE-GOAL GAMES IN PLAYOFFS (CAREER):
7 — Maurice Richard, Montreal. Four three-goal games; two four-goal games; one five-goal game.
— **Wayne Gretzky, Edmonton.** Two four-goal games; five three-goal games.
— **Jari Kurri, Edmonton.** One four-goal game; six three-goal games.
5 — Mike Bossy, NY Islanders. Four three-goal games; one four-goal game.

MOST ASSISTS IN PLAYOFFS (CAREER):
206 — Wayne Gretzky, Edmonton, Los Angeles
135 — Mark Messier, Edmonton
116 — Larry Robinson, Montreal, Los Angeles
110 — Jari Kurri, Edmonton
— Bryan Trottier, NY Islanders, Pittsburgh
108 — Denis Potvin, NY Islanders

Billy Smith has played more minutes in the post-season than any other NHL goaltender.

MOST PENALTY MINUTES IN PLAYOFFS (CAREER):
548 — Dale Hunter, Quebec, Washington
526 — Chris Nilan, Montreal, NY Rangers, Boston
466 — Willi Plett, Atlanta, Calgary, Minnesota, Boston
455 — Dave Williams, Toronto, Vancouver, Los Angeles
412 — Dave Schultz, Philadelphia, Los Angeles, Buffalo

MOST SHUTOUTS IN PLAYOFFS (CAREER):
15 — Clint Benedict, Ottawa, Mtl. Maroons
14 — Jacques Plante, Montreal, St. Louis
13 — Turk Broda, Toronto
12 — Terry Sawchuk, Detroit, Toronto, Los Angeles

MOST PLAYOFF GAMES APPEARED IN BY A GOALTENDER (CAREER):
132 — Bill Smith, NY Islanders
115 — Glenn Hall, Detroit, Chicago, St. Louis
112 — Jacques Plante, Montreal, St. Louis, Toronto, Boston
— Ken Dryden, Montreal
111 — Grant Fuhr, Edmonton
106 — Terry Sawchuk, Detroit, Toronto, Los Angeles, NY Rangers

MOST MINUTES PLAYED BY A GOALTENDER (CAREER):
7,645 — Billy Smith, NY Islanders
6,899 — Glenn Hall, Detroit, Chicago, St. Louis
6,846 — Ken Dryden, Montreal
6,651 — Jacques Plante, Montreal, St. Louis, Toronto, Boston

Single Playoff Year

MOST POINTS, ONE PLAYOFF YEAR:
47 — Wayne Gretzky, Edmonton, in 1985. 17 goals, 30 assists in 18 games.
44 — Mario Lemieux, Pittsburgh, in 1991. 16 goals, 28 assists in 23 games.
43 — Wayne Gretzky, Edmonton, in 1988. 12 goals, 31 assists in 19 games.
38 — Wayne Gretzky, Edmonton, in 1983. 12 goals, 26 assists in 16 games.
37 — Paul Coffey, Edmonton, in 1985. 12 goals, 25 assists in 18 games.
35 — Mike Bossy, NY Islanders, in 1981. 17 goals, 18 assists in 18 games.
— Wayne Gretzky, Edmonton, in 1984. 13 goals, 22 assists in 19 games.
— Mark Messier, Edmonton, in 1988. 11 goals, 23 assists in 19 games.
34 — Wayne Gretzky, Edmonton, in 1987. 5 goals, 29 assists in 21 games.
— Mark Reechi, Pittsburgh, in 1991. 10 goals, 24 assists in 24 games.
33 — Rick Middleton Boston, in 1983. 11 goals, 22 assists in 17 games.
— Kevin Stevens, Pittsburgh, in 1991. 17 goals, 16 assists in 24 games.
32 — Barry Pederson, Boston, in 1983. 14 goals, 18 assists in 17 games.

MOST POINTS BY A DEFENSEMAN, ONE PLAYOFF YEAR:
37 — Paul Coffey, Edmonton, in 1985. 12 goals, 25 assists in 18 games.
31 — Al MacInnis, Calgary, in 1989. 7 goals, 24 assists in 18 games.
25 — Denis Potvin, NY Islanders, in 1981. 8 goals, 17 assists in 18 games.
— Ray Bourque, Boston, in 1991. 7 goals, 18 assists in 19 games.
24 — Bobby Orr, Boston, in 1972. 5 goals, 19 assists in 15 games.

MOST POINTS BY A ROOKIE, ONE PLAYOFF YEAR:
21 — **Dino Ciccarelli, Minnesota,** in 1981. 14 goals, 7 assists in 19 games.
20 — Don Maloney, NY Rangers, in 1979. 7 goals, 13 assists in 18 games.

LONGEST CONSECUTIVE POINT-SCORING STREAK, ONE PLAYOFF YEAR:
18 games — Bryan Trottier, NY Islanders, 1981. 11 goals, 18 assists, 29 points.
17 games — Wayne Gretzky, Edmonton, 1988. 12 goals, 29 assists, 41 points.
— Al MacInnis, Calgary, 1989. 7 goals, 19 assists, 24 points.

LONGEST CONSECUTIVE POINT-SCORING STREAK, MORE THAN ONE PLAYOFF YEAR:
27 games — Bryan Trottier, NY Islanders, 1980, 1981 and 1982. 7 games in 1980 (3 G, 5 A, 8 PTS), 18 games in 1981 (11 G, 18 A, 29 PTS), and two games in 1982 (2 G, 3 A, 5 PTS). Total points, 42.
19 games — Wayne Gretzky, Edmonton, Los Angeles 1988 and 1989. 17 games in 1988 (12 G, 29 A, 41 PTS with Edmonton), 2 games in 1989 (1 G, 2 A, 3 PTS with Los Angeles). Total points, 44.
18 games — Phil Esposito, Boston, 1970 and 1971. 13 G, 20 A, 33 PTS.

MOST GOALS, ONE PLAYOFF YEAR:
19 — **Reggie Leach, Philadelphia,** 1976. 16 games.
— **Jari Kurri, Edmonton,** 1985. 18 games.
17 — Newsy Lalonde, Montreal, 1919. 10 games.
— Mike Bossy, NY Islanders, 1981. 18 games.
— Steve Payne, Minnesota, 1981. 19 games.
— Mike Bossy, NY Islanders, 1982. 19 games.
— Mike Bossy, NY Islanders, 1983. 19 games.
— Wayne Gretzky, Edmonton, 1985. 18 games.
— Kevin Stevens, Pittsburgh, 1991. 24 games.

MOST GOALS BY A DEFENSEMAN, ONE PLAYOFF YEAR:
12 — **Paul Coffey, Edmonton,** 1985. 18 games.
9 — Bobby Orr, Boston, 1970. 14 games.
— Brad Park, Boston, 1978. 15 games.
8 — Denis Potvin, NY Islanders, 1981. 18 games.
— Raymond Bourque, Boston, 1983. 17 games.
— Denis Potvin, NY Islanders, 1983. 20 games.
— Paul Coffey, Edmonton, 1984. 19 games

MOST GOALS BY A ROOKIE, ONE PLAYOFF YEAR:
14 — **Dino Ciccarelli, Minnesota,** 1981. 19 games.
11 — Jeremy Roenick, Chicago, 1990. 20 games.
10 — Claude Lemieux, Montreal, 1986. 20 games.
9 — Pat Flatley, NY Islanders, 1984. 21 games.
8 — Steve Christoff, Minnesota, 1980. 14 games.
— Brad Palmer, Minnesota, 1981. 19 games.
— Mike Krushelnyski, Boston, 1983. 17 games.
— Bob Joyce, Boston, 1988. 23 games.

MOST GAME-WINNING GOALS, ONE PLAYOFF YEAR:
5 — **Mike Bossy, NY Islanders,** 1983. 19 games.
— **Jari Kurri, Edmonton,** 1987. 21 games.
— **Bobby Smith, Minnesota,** 1991. 23 games.

MOST OVERTIME GOALS, ONE PLAYOFF YEAR:
3 — **Mel Hill, Boston,** 1939. All against NY Rangers in best-of-seven SF, won by Boston 4-3.
— **Maurice Richard, Montreal,** 1951. 2 against Detroit in best-of-seven SF, won by Montreal 4-2; 1 against Toronto best-of-seven F, won by Toronto 4-1.

MOST POWER-PLAY GOALS, ONE PLAYOFF YEAR:
9 — **Mike Bossy, NY Islanders,** 1981. 18 games against Toronto, Edmonton, NY Rangers and Minnesota.
— **Cam Neely, Boston,** 1991. 19 games against Hartford, Montreal, Pittsburgh.
8 — Tim Kerr, Philadelphia, 1989. 19 games.
— John Druce, Washington, 1990. 15 games.
— Brian Propp, Minnesota, 1991. 23 games.
7 — Michel Goulet, Quebec, 1985. 17 games.
— Mark Messier, Edmonton, 1988. 19 games.
— Mario Lemieux, Pittsburgh, 1991. 11 games.
— Brett Hull, St. Louis, 1990. 12 games.
— Kevin Stevens, Pittsburgh, 1991. 24 games.

MOST SHORTHAND GOALS, ONE PLAYOFF YEAR:
3 — **Derek Sanderson, Boston,** 1969. 1 against Toronto in QF, won by Boston 4-0; 2 against Montreal in SF, won by Montreal, 4-2.
— **Bill Barber, Philadelphia,** 1980. All against Minnesota in SF, won by Philadelphia 4-1.
— **Lorne Henning, NY Islanders,** 1980. 1 against Boston in QF won by NY Islanders 4-1; 1 against Buffalo in SF, won by NY Islanders 4-2, 1 against Philadelphia in F, won by NY Islanders 4-2.
— **Wayne Gretzky, Edmonton,** 1983. 2 against Winnipeg in DSF won by Edmonton 3-0; 1 against Calgary in DF won by Edmonton 4-1.
— **Wayne Presley, Chicago,** 1989. All against Detroit in DSF won by Chicago 4-2.

MOST THREE-OR-MORE GOAL GAMES, ONE PLAYOFF YEAR:
4 — **Jari Kurri, Edmonton,** 1985. 1 four-goal game, 3 three-goal games.
3 — Mark Messier, Edmonton, 1983. 3 three-goal games.
— Mike Bossy, NY Islanders, 1983. 1 four-goal game, 2 three-goal games
2 — Newsy Lalonde, Montreal, 1919. 1 five-goal game, 1 four-goal game.
— Maurice Richard, Montreal, 1944. 1 five-goal game; 1 three-goal game.
— Doug Bentley, Chicago, 1944. 2 three-goal games.
— Norm Ullman, Detroit, 1964. 2 three-goal games.
— Phil Esposito, Boston, 1970. 2 three-goal games.
— Pit Martin, Chicago, 1973. 2 three-goal games.
— Rick MacLeish, Philadelphia, 1975. 2 three-goal games.
— Lanny McDonald, Toronto, 1977. 1 three-goal game; 1 four-goal game.
— Wayne Gretzky, Edmonton, 1981. 2 three-goal games.
— Wayne Gretzky, Edmonton, 1983. 2 four-goal games.
— Wayne Gretzky, Edmonton, 1985. 2 three-goal games.
— Petr Klima, Detroit, 1988. 2 three-goal games.
— Cam Neely, Boston, 1991. 2 three-goal games.

LONGEST CONSECUTIVE GOAL-SCORING STREAK, ONE PLAYOFF YEAR:
9 Games — Reggie Leach, Philadelphia, 1976. Streak started April 17 at Toronto and ended May 9 at Montreal. He scored one goal in each of seven games; two in one game; and five in another; a total of 14 goals.

MOST ASSISTS, ONE PLAYOFF YEAR:
31 — **Wayne Gretzky, Edmonton,** 1988. 19 games.
30 — Wayne Gretzky, Edmonton, 1985. 18 games.
29 — Wayne Gretzky, Edmonton, 1987. 21 games.
28 — Mario Lemieux, Pittsburgh, 1991. 23 games.
26 — Wayne Gretzky, Edmonton, 1983. 16 games.
25 — Paul Coffey, Edmonton, 1985. 18 games.
24 — Al MacInnis, Calgary, 1989. 22 games.
— Mark Recchi, Pittsburgh, 1991. 24 games.

MOST ASSISTS BY A DEFENSEMAN, ONE PLAYOFF YEAR:
25 — **Paul Coffey, Edmonton,** 1985. 18 games.
24 — Al MacInnis, Calgary, 1989. 22 games.
19 — Bobby Orr, Boston, 1972. 15 games.
18 — Ray Bourque, Boston, 1988. 23 games.
— Ray Bourque, Boston, 1991. 19 games.
— Larry Murphy, Pittsburgh, 1991. 23 games.
17 — Larry Robinson, Montreal, 1978. 15 games.
— Denis Potvin, NY Islanders, 1981. 18 games.
— Charlie Huddy, Edmonton, 1985. 18 games.
— Larry Robinson, Montreal, 1987. 17 games.

MOST MINUTES PLAYED BY A GOALTENDER, ONE PLAYOFF YEAR:
1,540 — **Ron Hextall, Philadelphia,** 1987. 26 games.
1,401 — Bill Ranford, Edmonton, 1990. 22 games.
1,381 — Mike Vernon, Calgary, 1989. 22 games.
1,229 — Mike Vernon, Calgary, 1986. 21 games.
1,221 — Ken Dryden, Montreal, 1971. 20 games.
1,218 — Patrick Roy, Montreal, 1986. 20 games.
1,206 — Patrick Roy, Montreal, 1989. 19 games.

MOST WINS BY A GOALTENDER, ONE PLAYOFF YEAR:
16 — **Grant Fuhr, Edmonton,** 1988. 19 games.
— **Mike Vernon, Calgary,** 1989. 22 games.
— **Bill Ranford, Edmonton,** 1990. 22 games
15 — Bill Smith, NY Islanders, 1980. 20 games.
— Bill Smith, NY Islanders, 1982. 18 games.
— Grant Fuhr, Edmonton, 1985. 18 games.
— Patrick Roy, Montreal, 1986. 20 games.
— Ron Hextall, Philadelphia, 1987. 26 games.
14 — Bill Smith, NY Islanders, 1981. 17 games.
— Grant Fuhr, Edmonton, 1987. 19 games.
— Jon Casey, Minnesota, 1991. 23 games.

MOST CONSECUTIVE WINS BY A GOALTENDER, ONE PLAYOFF YEAR:
10 — **Gerry Cheevers, Boston,** 1970. 2 wins against NY Rangers in QF, won by Boston 4-2; 4 wins against Chicago in SF, won by Boston 4-0; and 4 wins against St. Louis in F, won by Boston 4-0.

MOST SHUTOUTS, ONE PLAYOFF YEAR:
4 — **Clint Benedict, Mtl. Maroons,** 1926. 8 games.
— **Clint Benedict, Mtl. Maroons,** 1928. 9 games.
— **Dave Kerr, NY Rangers,** 1937. 9 games.
— **Frank McCool, Toronto,** 1945. 13 games.
— **Terry Sawchuk, Detroit,** 1952. 8 games.
— **Bernie Parent, Philadelphia,** 1975. 17 games.
— **Ken Dryden, Montreal,** 1977. 14 games.

MOST CONSECUTIVE SHUTOUTS:
3 — **Clint Benedict, Mtl. Maroons,** 1926. Benedict shut out Ottawa 1-0, Mar. 27; he then shut out Victoria twice, 3-0, Mar. 30; 3-0, Apr. 1. Mtl. Maroons won NHL F vs. Ottawa 2 goals to 1 and won the best-of-five F vs. Victoria 3-1.
— **Frank McCool, Toronto,** 1945. McCool shut out Detroit 1-0, April 6; 2-0, April 8; 1-0, April 12. Toronto won the best-of-seven F 4-3.

LONGEST SHUTOUT SEQUENCE:
248 Minutes, 32 Seconds — Norm Smith, Detroit, 1936. In best-of-five SF, Smith shut out Mtl. Maroons 1-0, March 24, in 116:30 overtime; shut out Maroons 3-0 in second game, March 26; and was scored against at 12:02 of first period, March 29, by Gus Marker. Detroit won SF 3-0.

One-Series Records

MOST POINTS IN FINAL SERIES:
13 — Wayne Gretzky, Edmonton, in 1988, 4 games plus suspended game vs. Boston. 3 goals, 10 assists.
12 — Gordie Howe, Detroit, in 1955, 7 games vs. Montreal. 5 goals, 7 assists.
  — Yvan Cournoyer, Montreal, in 1973, 6 games vs. Chicago. 6 goals, 6 assists.
  — Jacques Lemaire, Montreal, in 1973, 6 games vs. Chicago. 3 goals, 9 assists.
  — Mario Lemieux, Pittsburgh, in 1991, 5 games vs. Minnesota. 5 goals, 7 assists.

MOST GOALS IN FINAL SERIES:
9 — Babe Dye, Toronto, in 1922, 5 games vs. Van. Millionaires.
8 — Alf Skinner, Toronto, in 1918, 5 games vs. Van. Millionaires.
7 — Jean Beliveau, Montreal, in 1956, during 5 games vs. Detroit.
  — Mike Bossy, NY Islanders, in 1982, during 4 games vs. Vancouver.
  — Wayne Gretzky, Edmonton, in 1985, during 5 games vs. Philadelphia.

MOST ASSISTS IN FINAL SERIES:
10 — Wayne Gretzky, Edmonton, in 1988, 4 games plus suspended game vs. Boston.
9 — Jacques Lemaire, Montreal, in 1973, 6 games vs. Chicago.
  — Wayne Gretzky, Edmonton, in 1987, 7 games vs. Philadelphia.
  — Larry Murphy, Pittsburgh, in 1991, 6 games vs. Minnesota.

MOST POINTS IN ONE SERIES (OTHER THAN FINAL):
19 — Rick Middleton, Boston, in 1983 DF, 7 games vs. Buffalo. 5 goals, 14 assists.
18 — Wayne Gretzky, Edmonton, in 1985 CF, 6 games vs. Chicago. 4 goals, 14 assists.
16 — Barry Pederson, Boston, in 1983 DF, 7 games vs. Buffalo. 7 goals, 9 assists.
15 — Jari Kurri, Edmonton, in 1985 CF, 6 games vs. Chicago. 12 goals, 3 assists.
  — Wayne Gretzky, Edmonton, in 1987 DSF, 5 games vs. Los Angeles. 2 goals, 13 assists.
  — Tim Kerr, Philadelphia, in 1989 DF, 7 games vs. Pittsburgh. 10 goals, 5 assists.
  — Mario Lemieux, Pittsburgh, in 1991 CF, 6 games vs. Boston. 6 goals, 9 assists.

MOST GOALS IN ONE SERIES (OTHER THAN FINAL):
12 — Jari Kurri, Edmonton, in 1985 CF, 6 games vs. Chicago.
11 — Newsy Lalonde, Montreal, in 1919 NHL F, 5 games vs. Ottawa.
10 — Tim Kerr, Philadelphia, in 1989 DF, 7 games vs. Pittsburgh.
9 — Reggie Leach, Philadelphia, in 1976 SF, 5 games vs. Boston.
  — Bill Barber, Philadelphia, in 1980 SF, 5 games vs. Minnesota.
  — Mike Bossy, NY Islanders, in 1983 CF, 6 games vs. Boston.
  — Mario Lemieux, Pittsburgh, in 1989 DF, 7 games vs. Philadelphia.

MOST ASSISTS IN ONE SERIES (OTHER THAN FINAL):
14 — Rick Middleton, Boston, in 1983 DF, 7 games vs. Buffalo.
  — **Wayne Gretzky, Edmonton,** in 1985 CF, 6 games vs. Chicago.
13 — Wayne Gretzky, Edmonton, in 1987 DSF, 5 games vs. Los Angeles.
11 — Mark Messier, Edmonton, in 1989 DSF, 7 games vs. Los Angeles.
  — Al MacInnis, Calgary, in 1984 DF, 7 games vs. Edmonton.
10 — Fleming Mackell, Boston, in 1958 SF, 6 games vs. NY Rangers.
  — Stan Mikita, Chicago, in 1962 SF, 6 games vs. Montreal.
  — Bob Bourne, NY Islanders, in 1983 DF, 6 games vs. NY Rangers.
  — Wayne Gretzky, Edmonton, in 1988 DSF, 5 games vs. Winnipeg.

MOST GAME-WINNING GOALS, ONE PLAYOFF SERIES:
4 — Mike Bossy, NY Islanders, 1983, CF vs. Boston, won by NY Islanders 4-2.

MOST OVERTIME GOALS, ONE PLAYOFF SERIES:
3 — Mel Hill, Boston, 1939, SF vs. NY Rangers, won by Boston 4-3. Hill scored at 59:25 overtime March 21 for a 2-1 win; at 8:24, March 23 for a 3-2 win; and at 48:00, April 2 for a 2-1 win.

MOST POWER-PLAY GOALS, ONE PLAYOFF SERIES:
6 — Chris Kontos, Los Angeles, 1989, DSF vs. Edmonton, won by Los Angeles 4-3.
5 — Andy Bathgate, Detroit, 1966, SF vs. Chicago, won by Detroit 4-2.
  — Denis Potvin, NY Islanders, 1981, QF vs. Edmonton, won by NY Islanders 4-2.
  — Ken Houston, Calgary, 1981, QF vs. Philadelphia, won by Calgary 4-3.
  — Rick Vaive, Chicago, 1988, DSF vs. St. Louis, won by St. Louis 4-1.
  — Tim Kerr, Philadelphia, 1989, DF vs. Pittsburgh, won by Philadelphia 4-3.
  — Mario Lemieux, Pittsburgh, 1989, DF vs. Philadelphia won by Philadelphia 4-3.
  — John Druce, Washington, 1990, DF vs. NY Rangers won by Washington 4-1.

MOST THREE-OR-MORE-GOAL GAMES, ONE PLAYOFF SERIES:
3 — Jari Kurri, Edmonton 1985, CF vs. Chicago won by Edmonton 4-2. Kurri scored 3 G May 7 at Edmonton in 7-3 win, 3 G May 14 in 10-5 win and 4 G May 16 at Chicago in 8-2 win.
2 — Doug Bentley, Chicago, 1944, SF vs. Detroit, won by Chicago 4-1. Bentley scored 3 G Mar. 28 at Chicago in 7-1 win and 3 G Mar. 30 at Detroit in 5-2 win.
  — Norm Ullman, Detroit, 1964, SF vs. Chicago, won by Detroit 4-3. Ullman scored 3 G Mar. 29 at Chicago in 7-1 win and 3 G April 7 at Detroit in 7-2 win.
  — Mark Messier, Edmonton, 1983, DF vs. Calgary won by Edmonton 4-1. Messier scored 4 G April 14 at Edmonton in 6-3 win and 3 G April 17 at Calgary in 10-2 win.
  — Mike Bossy, NY Islanders, 1983, CF vs. Boston won by NY Islanders 4-2. Bossy scored 3 G May 3 at New York in 8-3 win and 4 G on May 7 at New York in 8-4 win.

MOST SHORTHAND GOALS, ONE PLAYOFF SERIES:
3 — Bill Barber, Philadelphia, 1980, SF vs. Minnesota, won by Philadelphia 4-1.
  — **Wayne Presley, Chicago,** 1989, DSF vs. Detroit, won by Chicago 4-2.
2 — Mac Colville, NY Rangers, 1940, SF vs. Boston, won by NY Rangers 4-2.
  — Jerry Toppazzini, Boston, 1958, SF vs. NY Rangers, won by Boston 4-2.
  — Dave Keon, Toronto, 1963, F vs. Detroit, won by Toronto 4-1.
  — Bob Pulford, Toronto, 1964, F vs. Detroit, won by Toronto 4-3.
  — Serge Savard, Montreal, 1968, F vs. St. Louis, won by Montreal 4-0.
  — Derek Sanderson, Boston, 1969, SF vs. Montreal, won by Montreal 4-2.
  — Bryan Trottier, NY Islanders, 1980, PR vs. Los Angeles, won by NY Islanders 3-1.
  — Bobby Lalonde, Boston, 1981, PR vs. Minnesota, won by Minnesota 3-0.
  — Butch Goring, NY Islanders, 1981, SF vs. NY Rangers, won by NY Islanders 4-0.
  — Wayne Gretzky, Edmonton, 1983, DSF vs. Winnipeg, won by Edmonton 3-0.
  — Mark Messier, Edmonton, 1983, DF vs. Calgary, won by Edmonton 4-1.
  — Jari Kurri, Edmonton, 1983, CF vs. Chicago, won by Edmonton 4-0.
  — Wayne Gretzky, Edmonton, 1985, DF vs. Winnipeg, won by Edmonton 4-0.
  — Kevin Lowe, Edmonton, 1987, F vs. Philadelphia, won by Edmonton 4-3.
  — Bob Gould, Washington, 1988, DSF vs. Philadelphia, won by Washington 4-3.
  — Dave Poulin, Philadelphia, 1989, DF vs. Pittsburgh, won by Philadelphia 4-3.
  — Russ Courtnall, Montreal, 1991, DF vs. Boston, won by Boston 4-3.

Single Playoff Game Records

MOST POINTS, ONE GAME:
8 — Patrik Sundstrom, New Jersey, April 22, 1988 at New Jersey during 10-4 win over Washington. Sundstrom had 3 goals, 5 assists.
  — **Mario Lemieux, Pittsburgh,** April 25, 1989 at Pittsburgh during 10-7 win over Philadelphia. Lemieux had 5 goals, 3 assists.
7 — Wayne Gretzky, Edmonton, April 17, 1983 at Calgary during 10-2 win. Gretzky had 4 goals, 3 assists.
  — Wayne Gretzky, Edmonton, April 25,1985 at Winnipeg during 8-3 win. Gretzky had 3 goals, 4 assists.
  — Wayne Gretzky, Edmonton, April 9, 1987, at Edmonton during 13-3 win over Los Angeles. Gretzky had 1 goal, 6 assists.
6 — Dickie Moore, Montreal, March 25, 1954, at Montreal during 8-1 win over Boston. Moore had 2 goals, 4 assists.
  — Phil Esposito, Boston, April 2, 1969, at Boston during 10-0 win over Toronto. Esposito had 4 goals, 2 assists.
  — Darryl Sittler, Toronto, April 22, 1976, at Toronto during 8-5 win over Philadelphia. Sittler had 5 goals, 1 assist.
  — Guy Lafleur, Montreal, April 11, 1977, at Montreal during 7-2 victory vs. St. Louis. Lafleur had 3 goals, 3 assists.
  — Mikko Leinonen, NY Rangers, April 8, 1982, at New York during 7-3 win over Philadelphia. Leinonen had 6 assists.
  — Paul Coffey, Edmonton, May 14, 1985 at Edmonton during 10-5 win over Chicago. Coffey had 1 goal, 5 assists.
  — John Anderson, Hartford, April 12, 1986 at Hartford during 9-4 win over Quebec. Anderson had 2 goals, 4 assists.

MOST POINTS BY A DEFENSEMAN, ONE GAME:
6 — Paul Coffey, Edmonton, May 14, 1985 at Edmonton. 1 goal, 5 assists. Edmonton won 10-5.
5 — Eddie Bush, Detroit, April 9, 1942, at Detroit. 1 goal, 4 assists. Detroit won 5-2.
  — Bob Dailey, Philadelphia, May 1, 1980, at Philadelphia vs. Minnesota. 1 goal, 4 assists. Philadelphia won 7-0.
  — Denis Potvin, NY Islanders, April 17, 1981, at New York vs. Edmonton. 3 goals, 2 assists. NY Islanders won 6-3.
  — Risto Siltanen, Quebec, April 14, 1987 at Hartford. 5 assists. Quebec won 7-5.

MOST GOALS, ONE GAME:
5 — Newsy Lalonde, Montreal, March 1, 1919, at Montreal. Final score: Montreal 6, Ottawa 3.
  — **Maurice Richard, Montreal,** March 23, 1944, at Montreal. Final score: Montreal 5, Toronto 1.
  — **Darryl Sittler, Toronto,** April 22, 1976, at Toronto. Final score: Toronto 8, Philadelphia 5.
  — **Reggie Leach, Philadelphia,** May 6, 1976, at Philadelphia. Final score: Philadelphia 6, Boston 3.
  — **Mario Lemieux, Pittsburgh,** April 25, 1989 at Pittsburgh. Final score: Pittsburgh 10, Philadelphia 7.

MOST GOALS BY A DEFENSEMAN, ONE GAME:
3 — Bobby Orr, Boston, April 11, 1971 at Montreal. Final score: Boston 5, Montreal 2.
  — **Dick Redmond, Chicago,** April 4, 1973 at Chicago. Final score: Chicago 7, St. Louis 1.
  — **Denis Potvin, NY Islanders,** April 17, 1981 at New York. Final score: NY Islanders 6, Edmonton 3.
  — **Paul Reinhart, Calgary,** April 14, 1983 at Edmonton. Final score: Edmonton 6, Calgary 3.
  — **Paul Reinhart, Calgary,** April 8, 1984 at Vancouver. Final score: Calgary 5, Vancouver 1.
  — **Doug Halward, Vancouver,** April 7, 1984 at Vancouver. Final score: Vancouver 7, Calgary 0.

MOST POWER-PLAY GOALS, ONE GAME:
3 — **Syd Howe, Detroit,** March 23, 1939, at Detroit vs. Montreal, Detroit won 7-3.
— **Sid Smith, Toronto,** April 10, 1949, at Detroit. Toronto won 3-1.
— **Phil Esposito, Boston,** April 2, 1969, at Boston vs. Toronto. Boston won 10-0.
— **John Bucyk, Boston,** April 21, 1974, at Boston vs. Chicago. Boston won 8-6.
— **Denis Potvin, NY Islanders,** April 17, 1981, at New York vs. Edmonton. NY Islanders won 6-3.
— **Tim Kerr, Philadelphia,** April 13, 1985, at NY Rangers. Philadelphia won 6-5.
— **Jari Kurri, Edmonton,** April 9, 1987, at Edmonton vs. Los Angeles. Edmonton won 13-3.
— **Mark Johnson, New Jersey,** April 22, 1988, at New Jersey vs. Washington. New Jersey won 10-4.

MOST SHORTHAND GOALS, ONE GAME:
2 — **Dave Keon, Toronto,** April 18, 1963, at Toronto, in 3-1 win vs. Detroit.
— **Bryan Trottier, NY Islanders,** April 8, 1980 at New York, in 8-1 win vs. Los Angeles.
— **Bobby Lalonde, Boston,** April 11, 1981 at Minnesota, in 6-3 win by Minnesota.
— **Wayne Gretzky, Edmonton,** April 6, 1983 at Edmonton, in 6-3 win vs. Winnipeg.
— **Jari Kurri, Edmonton,** April 24, 1983, at Edmonton, in 8-3 win vs. Chicago.

MOST ASSISTS, ONE GAME:
6 — **Mikko Leinonen, NY Rangers,** April 8, 1982, at New York. Final score: NY Rangers 7, Philadelphia 3.
— **Wayne Gretzky, Edmonton,** April 9, 1987, at Edmonton. Final score: Edmonton 13, Los Angeles 3.
5 — **Toe Blake, Montreal,** March 23, 1944, at Montreal. Final score: Montreal 5, Toronto 1.
— **Maurice Richard, Montreal,** March 27, 1956, at Montreal. Final score: Montreal 7, NY Rangers 0.
— **Bert Olmstead, Montreal,** March 30, 1957, at Montreal. Final score: Montreal 8, NY Rangers 3.
— **Don McKenney, Boston,** April 5, 1958, at Boston. Final score: Boston 8, NY Rangers 2.
— **Stan Mikita, Chicago,** April 4, 1973, at Chicago. Final score: Chicago 7, St. Louis 1.
— **Wayne Gretzky, Edmonton,** April 8, 1981, at Montreal. Final score: Edmonton 6, Montreal 3.
— **Paul Coffey, Edmonton,** May 14, 1985, at Edmonton. Final score: Edmonton 10, Chicago 5.
— **Doug Gilmour, St. Louis,** April 15, 1986, at Minnesota. Final score: St. Louis 6, Minnesota 3.
— **Risto Siltanen, Quebec,** April 14, 1987 at Hartford. Final score: Quebec 7, Hartford 5.
— **Patrik Sundstrom, New Jersey,** April 22, 1988, at New Jersey. Final score: New Jersey 10, Washington 4.

New Jersey's Patrik Sundstrom, right, recorded eight points in a single game in the 1988 playoffs.

MOST PENALTY MINUTES, ONE GAME:
42 — **Dave Schultz, Philadelphia,** April 22, 1976, at Toronto. One minor, 2 majors, 1 10-minute misconduct and 2 game-misconducts. Final score: Toronto 8, Philadelphia 5.

MOST PENALTIES, ONE GAME:
8 — **Forbes Kennedy, Toronto,** April 2, 1969, at Boston. Four minors, 2 majors, 1 10-minute misconduct, 1 game misconduct. Final score: Boston 10, Toronto 0.
— **Kim Clackson, Pittsburgh,** April 14, 1980, at Boston. Five minors, 2 majors, 1 10-minute misconduct. Final score: Boston 6, Pittsburgh 2

MOST POINTS, ONE PERIOD:
4 — **Maurice Richard, Montreal,** March 29, 1945, at Montreal vs. Toronto. Third period, 3 goals, 1 assist. Final score: Montreal 10, Toronto 3.
— **Dickie Moore, Montreal,** March 25, 1954, at Montreal vs. Boston. First period, 2 goals, 2 assists. Final score: Montreal 8, Boston 1.
— **Barry Pederson, Boston,** April 8, 1982, at Boston vs. Buffalo. Second period, 3 goals, 1 assist. Final score: Boston 7, Buffalo 3.
— **Peter McNab, Boston,** April 11, 1982, at Buffalo. Second period, 1 goal, 3 assists. Final score: Boston 5, Buffalo 2.
— **Tim Kerr, Philadelphia,** April 13, 1985 at New York. Second period, 4 goals. Final score: Philadelphia 6, Rangers 5.
— **Ken Linseman, Boston,** April 14, 1985 at Boston vs. Montreal. Second period, 2 goals, 2 assists. Final score: Boston 7, Montreal 6.
— **Wayne Gretzky, Edmonton,** April 12, 1987, at Los Angeles. Third period, 1 goal, 3 assists. Final score: Edmonton 6, Los Angeles 3.
— **Glenn Anderson, Edmonton,** April 6, 1988, at Edmonton vs. Winnipeg. Third period, 3 goals, 1 assist. Final score: Edmonton 7, Winnipeg 4.
— **Mario Lemieux, Pittsburgh,** April 25, 1989, at Pittsburgh vs. Philadelphia. First period, 4 goals. Final score: Pittsburgh 10, Philadelphia 7.
— **Dave Gagner, Minnesota,** April 8, 1991, at Minnesota vs. Chicago. First period, 2 goals, 2 assists. Final score: Chicago 6, Minnesota 5.

MOST GOALS, ONE PERIOD:
4 — **Tim Kerr, Philadelphia,** April 13, 1985, at New York vs. NY Rangers, second period. Final score: Philadelphia 6, NY Rangers 5.
— **Mario Lemieux, Pittsburgh,** April 25, 1989, at Pittsburgh vs. Philadelphia, first period. Final score: Pittsburgh 10, Philadelphia 7.
3 — **Harvey (Busher) Jackson, Toronto,** April 5, 1932, at New York vs. NY Rangers, second period. Final score: Toronto 6, NY Rangers 4.
— **Maurice Richard, Montreal,** March 23, 1944, at Montreal vs. Toronto, second period. Final score: Montreal 5, Toronto 1.
— **Maurice Richard, Montreal,** March 29, 1945, at Montreal vs. Toronto, third period. Final score: Montreal 10, Toronto 3.
— **Maurice Richard, Montreal,** April 6, 1957 at Montreal vs. Boston, second period. Final score: Montreal 5, Boston 1.
— **Ted Lindsay, Detroit,** April 5, 1955, at Detroit vs. Montreal, second period. Final score: Detroit 7, Montreal 1.
— **Red Berenson, St. Louis,** April 15, 1969, at St. Louis vs. Los Angeles, second period. Final score: St. Louis 4, Los Angeles 0.
— **Jacques Lemaire, Montreal,** April 20, 1971, at Montreal vs. Minnesota, second period. Final score: Montreal 7, Minnesota 2.
— **Rick MacLeish, Philadelphia,** April 11, 1974, at Philadelphia vs. Atlanta, second period. Final score: Philadelphia 5, Atlanta 1.
— **Tom Williams, Los Angeles,** April 14, 1974, at Los Angeles vs. Chicago, third period. Final score: Los Angeles 5, Chicago 1.
— **Darryl Sittler, Toronto,** April 22, 1976, at Toronto vs. Philadelphia, second period. Final score: Toronto 8, Philadelphia 5.
— **Reggie Leach, Philadelphia,** May 6, 1976, at Philadelphia vs. Boston, second period. Final score: Philadelphia 6, Boston 3.
— **Bobby Schmautz, Boston,** April 11, 1977, at Boston vs. Los Angeles, first period. Final score: Boston 8, Los Angeles 3.
— **George Ferguson, Toronto,** April 11, 1978, at Toronto vs. Los Angeles, third period. Final score: Toronto 7, Los Angeles 3.
— **Barry Pederson, Boston,** April 8, 1982, at Boston vs. Buffalo, second period. Final score: Boston 7, Buffalo 3.
— **Peter Stastny, Quebec,** April 5, 1983, at Boston, first period. Final score: Boston 4, Quebec 3.
— **Wayne Gretzky, Edmonton,** April 6, 1983 at Edmonton, second period. Final score: Edmonton 6, Winnipeg 3.
— **Mike Bossy, NY Islanders,** May 7, 1983 at New York, second period. Final score: NY Islanders 8, Boston 4.
— **Dave Andreychuk, Buffalo,** April 14, 1985, at Buffalo vs. Quebec, third period. Final score: Buffalo 7, Quebec 4.
— **Wayne Gretzky, Edmonton,** May 25, 1985, at Edmonton vs. Philadelphia, first period. Final score: Edmonton 4, Philadelphia 3.
— **Glenn Anderson, Edmonton,** April 6, 1988, at Edmonton vs. Winnipeg, third period. Final score: Edmonton 7, Winnipeg 4.
— **Tim Kerr, Philadelphia,** April 19, 1989, at Pittsburgh vs. Penguins, first period. Final score: Philadelphia 4, Pittsburgh 2.
— **Petr Klima, Edmonton,** May 4, 1991, at Edmonton vs. Minnesota, first period. Final score: Edmonton 7, Minnesota 2.

MOST POWER PLAY GOALS, ONE PERIOD:
3 — **Tim Kerr, Philadelphia,** April 13, 1985 at New York, second period in 6-5 win vs. NY Rangers.
2 — Two power-play goals have been scored by one player in one period on 37 occasions. Charlie Conacher of Toronto was the first to score two power-play goals in one period, setting the mark on Mar. 26, 1936. Brian Glynn of Minnesota is the most recent to equal this mark with two power-play goals in the second period at Minnesota, April 24, 1991. Final score: Minnesota 8, St. Louis 4.

MOST SHORTHAND GOALS, ONE PERIOD:
2 — **Bryan Trottier, NY Islanders,** April 8, 1980, second period at New York in 8-1 win vs. Los Angeles.
— **Bobby Lalonde, Boston,** April 11, 1981, third period at Minnesota in 6-3 win by Minnesota.
— **Jari Kurri, Edmonton,** April 24, 1983, third period at Edmonton in 8-4 win vs. Chicago.

MOST ASSISTS, ONE PERIOD:
3 — Three assists by one player in one period of a playoff game have been recorded on **54** occasions. Larry Murphy of Pittsburgh is the most recent to equal this mark with 3 assists in the first period at Pittsburgh, May 23, 1991. Final score: Pittsburgh 6, Minnesota 4.

Wayne Gretzky has had 3 assists in one period 5 times; Ray Bourque, 3 times; Toe Blake, Jean Beliveau, Doug Harvey and Bobby Orr, twice.

Nick Metz of Toronto was the first player to be credited with 3 assists in one period of a playoff game Mar. 21, 1941 at Toronto vs. Boston.

MOST PENALTIES, ONE PERIOD AND MOST PENALTY MINUTES, ONE PERIOD:
6 Penalties; 39 Minutes — Ed Hospodar, NY Rangers, April 9, 1981, at Los Angeles, first period. Two minors, 1 major, 1 10-minute misconduct, 2 game misconducts. Final score: Los Angeles 5, NY Rangers 4.

FASTEST TWO GOALS:
5 Seconds — Norm Ullman, Detroit, at Detroit, April 11, 1965, vs. Chicago and goaltender Glenn Hall. Ullman scored at 17:35 and 17:40 of second period. Detroit won 4-2.

FASTEST GOAL FROM START OF GAME:
6 Seconds — Don Kozak, Los Angeles, April 17, 1977, at Los Angeles vs. Boston and goaltender Gerry Cheevers. Los Angeles won 7-4.
7 Seconds — Bob Gainey, Montreal, May 5, 1977, at New York vs. NY Islanders and goaltender Glenn Resch. Montreal won 2-1.
 — Terry Murray, Philadelphia, April 12, 1981, at Quebec vs. goaltender Dan Bouchard. Quebec won 4-3 in overtime.
8 Seconds — Stan Smyl, Vancouver, April 7, 1982, at Vancouver vs. Calgary and goaltender Pat Riggin. Vancouver won 5-3.

FASTEST TWO GOALS FROM START OF GAME:
1 Minute, 8 Seconds — Dick Duff, Toronto, April 9, 1963 at Toronto vs. Detroit and goaltender Terry Sawchuk. Duff scored at 49 seconds and 1:08. Final score: Toronto 4, Detroit 2.

FASTEST TWO GOALS FROM START OF PERIOD:
35 Seconds — Pat LaFontaine, NY Islanders, May 19, 1984 at Edmonton vs. goaltender Andy Moog. LaFontaine scored at 13 and 35 seconds of third period. Final score: Edmonton 5, NY Islanders 2.

FASTEST GOAL FROM START OF PERIOD (OTHER THAN FIRST):
6 Seconds — Pelle Eklund, Philadelphia, April 25, 1989, at Pittsburgh vs. goaltender Tom Barrasso, second period. Pittsburgh won 10-7.
9 Seconds — Bill Collins, Minnesota, April 9, 1968, at Minnesota vs. Los Angeles and goaltender Wayne Rutledge, third period. Minnesota won 7-5.
 — Dave Balon, Minnesota, April 25, 1968, at St. Louis vs. goaltender Glenn Hall, third period. Minnesota won 5-1.
 — Murray Oliver, Minnesota, April 8, 1971, at St. Louis vs. goaltender Ernie Wakely, third period. St. Louis won 4-2.
 — Clark Gillies, NY Islanders, April 15, 1977, at Buffalo vs. goaltender Don Edwards, third period. NY Islanders won 4-3.
 — Eric Vail, Atlanta, April 11, 1978, at Atlanta vs. Detroit and goaltender Ron Low, third period. Detroit won 5-3.
 — Stan Smyl, Vancouver, April 10, 1979, at Philadelphia vs. goaltender Wayne Stephenson, third period. Vancouver won 3-2.
 — Wayne Gretzky, Edmonton, April 6, 1983, at Edmonton vs. Winnipeg and goaltender Brian Hayward, second period. Edmonton won 6-3.
 — Mark Messier, Edmonton, April 16, 1984, at Calgary vs. goaltender Don Edwards, third period. Edmonton won 5-3.
 — Brian Skrudland, Montreal, May 18, 1986 at Calgary vs. Calgary and goaltender Mike Vernon, overtime. Montreal won 3-2.

Early Playoff Records

1893-1918
Team Records

MOST GOALS, BOTH TEAMS, ONE GAME:
25 — Ottawa Silver Seven, Dawson City at Ottawa, Jan. 16, 1905. Ottawa 23, Dawson City 2. Ottawa won best-of-three series 2-0.

MOST GOALS, ONE TEAM, ONE GAME:
23 — Ottawa Silver Seven at Ottawa, Jan. 16, 1905. Ottawa defeated Dawson City 23-2.

MOST GOALS, BOTH TEAMS, BEST-OF-THREE SERIES:
42 — Ottawa Silver Seven, Queen's University at Ottawa, 1906. Ottawa defeated Queen's 16-7, Feb. 27, and 12-7, Feb. 28.

MOST GOALS, ONE TEAM, BEST-OF-THREE SERIES:
32 — Ottawa Silver Seven in 1905 at Ottawa. Defeated Dawson City 9-2, Jan. 13, and 23-2, Jan. 16.

MOST GOALS, BOTH TEAMS, BEST-OF-FIVE SERIES:
39 — Toronto Arenas, Vancouver Millionaires at Toronto, 1918. Toronto won 5-3, Mar. 20; 6-3, Mar. 26; 2-1, Mar. 30. Vancouver won 6-4, Mar. 23, and 8-1, Mar. 28. Toronto scored 18 goals; Vancouver 21.

MOST GOALS, ONE TEAM, BEST-OF-FIVE SERIES:
26 — Vancouver Millionaires in 1915 at Vancouver. Defeated Ottawa Senators 6-2, Mar. 22; 8-3, Mar. 24; and 12-3, Mar. 26.

Individual Records

MOST GOALS IN PLAYOFFS:
63 — Frank McGee, Ottawa Silver Seven, in 22 playoff games. Seven goals in four games, 1903; 21 goals in eight games, 1904; 18 goals in four games, 1905; 17 goals in six games, 1906.

MOST GOALS, ONE PLAYOFF SERIES:
15 — Frank McGee, Ottawa Silver Seven, in two games in 1905 at Ottawa. Scored one goal, Jan. 13, in 9-2 victory over Dawson City and 14 goals, Jan. 16, in 23-2 victory.

MOST GOALS, ONE PLAYOFF GAME:
14 — Frank McGee, Ottawa Silver Seven, Jan. 16, 1905 at Ottawa in 23-2 victory over Dawson City.

FASTEST THREE GOALS:
40 Seconds — Marty Walsh, Ottawa Senators, at Ottawa, March 16, 1911, at 3:00, 3:10, and 3:40 of third period. Ottawa defeated Port Arthur 13-4.

Fred "Cyclone" Taylor scored six goals in three games in the 1915 Stanley Cup playoffs.

Jari Kurri ranks in the top five in all-time playoff goals, assists and points.

Stanley Cup Standings
1918-91

Team	Yrs.	Series	Won	Lost	Games	Won	Lost	Tied	GF	GA	Cup Wins	Winning %
Montreal	66	123*	79	43	579	351	220	8	1806	1413	22**	.606
Toronto	54	82	43	39	427	177	194	3	961	1024	13	.477
Boston	52	90	43	47	434	212	216	6	1293	1274	5	.488
Chicago	46	77	34	43	346	156	185	5	983	1112	3	.451
NY Rangers	43	73	33	40	314	143	163	8	858	905	3	.455
Detroit	40	68	35	33	326	158	167	1	874	888	7	.485
St. Louis	21	37	16	21	189	84	105	0	552	633	0	.444
Philadelphia	20	43	25	18	223	116	107	0	715	688	2	.520
Calgary***	17	28	12	16	132	61	71	0	439	475	1	.462
Los Angeles	17	24	7	17	112	40	72	0	348	454	0	.357
Minnesota	16	30	14	16	159	77	82	0	534	556	0	.484
Buffalo	16	25	9	16	116	51	65	0	366	401	0	.440
NY Islanders	15	39	28	11	196	119	77	0	687	563	4	.607
Edmonton	12	34	27	7	164	112	52	0	721	525	5	.683
Pittsburgh	11	18	8	10	86	44	42	0	273	285	1	.512
Vancouver	11	14	3	11	58	21	37	0	161	221	0	.362
Washington	9	15	6	9	79	37	42	0	257	259	0	.468
Winnipeg	8	10	2	8	43	12	31	0	133	183	0	.279
Quebec	7	13	6	7	68	31	37	0	212	242	0	.456
Hartford	7	8	1	7	42	15	27	0	125	156	0	.357
New Jersey****	4	6	2	4	35	16	19	0	109	119	0	.457

* 1919 final incomplete due to influenza epidemic.
** Montreal also won the Stanley Cup in 1916.
*** Includes totals of Atlanta 1972-80.
**** Includes totals of Colorado 1976-82.

All-Time Playoff Goal Leaders *since 1918*
(40 or more goals)

Player	Teams	Yrs.	GP	G
*Wayne Gretzky	Edm., L.A.	12	150	93
*Jari Kurri	Edmonton	10	146	92
Mike Bossy	NY Islanders	10	129	85
Maurice Richard	Montreal	15	133	82
*Mark Messier	Edmonton	11	164	81
*Glenn Anderson	Edmonton	11	162	80
Jean Beliveau	Montreal	17	162	79
Gordie Howe	Det., Hfd.	20	157	68
*Bryan Trottier	NY, Pit.	15	198	67
*Brian Propp	Phi., Bos., Min.	13	159	64
Yvan Cournoyer	Montreal	12	147	64
*Bobby Smith	Min., Mtl.	12	177	63
Bobby Hull	Chi., Hfd.	14	119	62
Phil Esposito	Chi., Bos., NYR	15	130	61
Jacques Lemaire	Montreal	11	145	61
Stan Mikita	Chicago	18	155	59
Guy Lafleur	Mtl., NYR	14	128	58
Bernie Geoffrion	Mtl., NYR	16	131	58
Denis Potvin	NY Islanders	14	185	56
*Denis Savard	Chicago, Mtl.	11	112	55
Rick MacLeish	Phi., Pit., Det.	11	114	54
Bill Barber	Philadelphia	11	129	53
*Joe Mullen	St.L., Cgy., Pit.	9	103	52
*Cam Neely	Bos.	6	84	51
Frank Mahovlich	Tor., Det., Mtl.	14	137	51
Steve Shutt	Mtl., L.A.	10	96	50
Henri Richard	Montreal	18	180	49
Reggie Leach	Philadelphia	8	96	47
Ted Lindsay	Det., Chi.	16	133	47
Clark Gillies	NYI, Buf.	13	164	47
*Esa Tikkanen	Edm.	7	98	46
Dickie Moore	Mtl., Tor., St. L.	14	135	46
Rick Middleton	NYR, Bos.	12	114	45
*Dino Ciccarelli	Min., Wsh.	9	87	44
Lanny McDonald	Tor., Cgy.	13	117	44
*Ken Linseman	Phi., Edm., Bos.	11	113	43
Bobby Clarke	Philadelphia	13	136	42
John Bucyk	Det., Bos.	14	124	41
Peter McNab	Bos., Van.	10	107	40
*Paul Coffey	Edm., Pit.	9	117	40
Bob Bourne	NYI, L.A.	13	139	40
*John Tonelli	NYI, Cgy., L.A.	13	172	40

* — Active player.

All-Time Playoff Assist Leaders *since 1918*
(60 or more assists)

Player	Teams	Yrs.	GP	A
*Wayne Gretzky	Edm., L.A.	12	150	206
*Mark Messier	Edmonton	12	166	135
*Larry Robinson	Mtl., L.A.	19	225	116
*Jari Kurri	Edmonton	10	146	110
*Bryan Trottier	NY, Pit.	15	198	110
Denis Potvin	NY Islanders	14	185	108
*Glenn Anderson	Edmonton	11	164	102
Jean Beliveau	Montreal	17	162	97
Gordie Howe	Det., Hfd.	20	157	92
*Bobby Smith	Min., Mtl.	12	177	92
Stan Mikita	Chicago	18	155	91
Brad Park	NYR, Bos., Det.	16	159	90
*Paul Coffey	Edm., Pit.	9	117	89
*Ray Bourque	Boston	12	123	89
*Brian Propp	Phi., Bos., Min.	12	159	84
*Denis Savard	Chicago, Mtl.	11	112	80
Henri Richard	Montreal	18	180	80
Jacques Lemaire	Montreal	11	145	78
*Ken Linseman	Phi., Edm., Bos.	11	113	77
Bobby Clarke	Philadelphia	13	136	77
Guy Lafleur	Mtl., NYR	14	128	76
Phil Esposito	Chi., Bos., NYR	15	130	76
Mike Bossy	NY Islanders	10	129	75
*John Tonelli	NYI, Cgy., L.A.	13	172	75
Gilbert Perreault	Buffalo	11	85	70
Alex Delvecchio	Detroit	14	121	69
Bobby Hull	Chi., Hfd.	14	119	67
Frank Mahovlich	Tor., Det., Mtl.	14	137	67
Bobby Orr	Boston	8	74	66
Bernie Federko	St. Louis	11	91	66
Jean Ratelle	NYR, Bos.	14	120	66
*Al MacInnis	Calgary	8	82	65
Dickie Moore	Mtl., Tor., St. L.	14	135	64
Doug Harvey	Mtl., NYR, St. L.	15	137	64
*Peter Stastny	Que., N.J.	9	77	63
Yvan Cournoyer	Montreal	12	147	63
John Bucyk	Det., Bos.	14	124	62
*Doug Wilson	Chicago	12	95	61
*Charlie Huddy	Edmonton	10	138	61

* — Active player.

All-Time Playoff Point Leaders *since 1918*
(100 or more points)

Player	Teams	Yrs.	GP	G	A	Pts.
*Wayne Gretzky	Edm., L.A.	12	150	93	206	299
*Mark Messier	Edmonton	12	166	80	135	215
*Jari Kurri	Edmonton	10	146	92	110	202
*Glenn Anderson	Edmonton	11	164	81	102	183
*Bryan Trottier	NY, Pit.	15	198	67	110	177
Jean Beliveau	Montreal	17	162	79	97	176
Denis Potvin	NY Islanders	14	185	56	108	164
Mike Bossy	NY Islanders	10	129	85	75	160
Gordie Howe	Det., Hfd.	20	157	68	92	160
*Bobby Smith	Min., Mtl.	12	177	63	92	155
Stan Mikita	Chicago	18	155	59	91	150
*Brian Propp	Phi., Bos., Min.	13	159	64	84	148
*Larry Robinson	Mtl., L.A.	19	225	28	116	144
Jacques Lemaire	Montreal	11	145	61	78	139
Phil Esposito	Chi., Bos., NYR	15	130	61	76	137
*Denis Savard	Chicago, Mtl.	11	112	55	80	135
Guy Lafleur	Mtl., NYR	14	128	58	76	134
Bobby Hull	Chi., Hfd.	14	119	62	67	129
Henri Richard	Montreal	18	180	49	80	129
*Paul Coffey	Edm., Pit.	9	117	40	89	129
Yvan Cournoyer	Montreal	12	147	64	63	127
Maurice Richard	Montreal	15	133	82	44	126
Brad Park	NYR, Bos., Det.	17	162	35	90	125
*Ken Linseman	Phi., Edm., Bos.	11	113	43	77	119
Bobby Clarke	Philadelphia	13	136	42	77	119
Bernie Geoffrion	Mtl., NYR	16	131	58	60	118
Frank Mahovlich	Tor., Det., Mtl.	14	137	51	67	118
*Ray Bourque	Boston	12	123	27	89	116
*John Tonelli	NYI, Cgy., L.A.	13	172	40	75	115
Dickie Moore	Mtl., Tor., St. L.	14	135	46	64	110
Bill Barber	Philadelphia	11	129	53	55	108
Rick MacLeish	Phi., Pit., Det.	11	114	54	53	107
Alex Delvecchio	Detroit	14	121	35	69	104
John Bucyk	Det., Bos.	14	124	41	62	103
Gilbert Perreault	Buffalo	14	90	33	70	103
Bernie Federko	St. Louis	11	91	35	66	101
Rick Middleton	NYR, Bos.	12	114	45	55	100

* — Active player.

Three-or-more-Goal Games, Playoffs 1918 – 1991

Player	Team	Date	City	Total Goals	Opposing Goaltender	Score	
Maurice Richard (7)	Mtl.	Mar.23/44	Mtl.	5	Paul Bibeault	Mtl. 5	Tor. 1
		Apr. 7/44	Chi.	3	Mike Karakas	Mtl. 3	Chi. 1
		Mar.29/45	Mtl.	4	Frank McCool	Mtl. 10	Tor. 3
		Apr. 14/53	Bos.	3	Gord Henry	Mtl. 7	Bos. 3
		Mar.20/56	Mtl.	3	Lorne Worsley	Mtl. 7	NYR 1
		Apr. 6/57	Mtl.	4	Don Simmons	Mtl. 5	Bos. 1
		Apr. 1/58	Mtl.	3	Terry Sawchuk	Mtl. 4	Det. 3
Wayne Gretzky (7)	Edm.	Apr. 11/81	Edm.	3	Richard Sevigny	Edm. 6	Mtl. 2
		Apr. 19/81	Edm.	3	Billy Smith	Edm. 5	NYI 2
		Apr. 6/83	Edm.	3	Brian Hayward	Edm. 6	Wpg. 3
		Apr. 17/83	Cgy.	4	Rejean Lemelin	Edm. 10	Cgy. 2
		Apr. 25/85	Wpg.	3	Bryan Hayward (2) / Marc Behrend (1)	Edm. 8	Wpg. 3
		May 25/85	Edm.	3	Pelle Lindbergh	Edm. 4	Phi. 3
		Apr. 24/86	Cgy.	3	Mike Vernon	Edm. 7	Cgy. 4
		Apr. 4/84	Edm.	3	Doug Soetaert (1) / Mike Veisor (2)	Edm. 9	Wpg. 2
Jari Kurri (7)	Edm.	Apr. 25/85	Wpg.	3	Bryan Hayward (2) / Marc Behrend (1)	Edm. 8	Wpg. 3
		May 7/85	Edm.	3	Murray Bannerman	Edm. 7	Chi. 3
		May 14/85	Edm.	3	Murray Bannerman	Edm. 10	Chi. 5
		May 16/85	Chi.	4	Murray Bannerman	Edm. 8	Chi. 2
		Apr. 9/87	Edm.	4	Roland Melanson (2) / Daren Eliot (2)	Edm. 13	L.A. 3
		May 18/90	Bos.	3	Andy Moog (2) / Rejean Lemelin (1)	Edm. 7	Bos. 2
Mike Bossy (5)	NYI	Apr. 16/79	NYI	3	Tony Esposito	NYI 6	Chi. 2
		May 8/82	NYI	3	Richard Brodeur	NYI 6	Van. 5
		Apr. 10/83	Wsh.	3	Al Jensen	NYI 6	Wsh. 3
		May 3/83	NYI	3	Pete Peeters	NYI 8	Bos. 3
		May 7/83	NYI	4	Pete Peeters	NYI 8	Bos. 4
Phil Esposito (4)	Bos.	Apr. 2/69	Bos.	3	Bruce Gamble	Bos. 10	Tor. 0
		Apr. 8/70	Bos.	3	Ed Giacomin	Bos. 8	NYR 2
		Apr. 19/70	Chi.	3	Tony Esposito	Bos. 6	Chi. 3
		Apr. 8/75	Bos.	3	Tony Esposito (2) / Michel Dumas (1)	Bos. 8	Chi. 2
Bernie Geoffrion (3)	Mtl.	Mar.27/52	Mtl.	3	Jim Henry	Mtl. 4	Bos. 0
		Apr. 7/55	Mtl.	3	Terry Sawchuk	Mtl. 4	Det. 2
		Mar.30/57	Mtl.	3	Lorne Worsley	Mtl. 8	NYR 3
Norm Ullman (3)	Det.	Mar.29/64	Det.	3	Glenn Hall	Det. 5	Chi. 4
		Apr. 7/64	Det.	3	Glenn Hall (2) / Denis DeJordy (1)	Det. 7	Chi. 2
		Apr. 11/65	Det.	3	Glenn Hall	Det. 4	Chi. 2
John Bucyk (3)	Bos.	May 3/70	St. L.	3	Jacques Plante (1) / Ernie Wakely (2)	Bos. 6	St.L. 1
		Apr. 20/72	Bos.	3	Jacques Caron (1) / Ernie Wakely (2)	Bos. 10	St.L. 2
		Apr. 21/74	Bos.	3	Tony Esposito	Bos. 8	Chi. 6
Rick MacLeish (3)	Phil	Apr. 11/74	Phil	3	Phil Myre	Phi. 5	Atl. 1
		Apr. 13/75	Phil	3	Gord McRae	Phi. 6	Tor. 3
		May 13/75	Phil	3	Glenn Resch	Phi. 4	NYI 1
Dino Ciccarelli (3)	Min.	May 5/81	Min.	3	Pat Riggin	Min. 7	Cgy. 4
		Apr. 10/82	Min.	3	Murray Bannerman	Min. 7	Chi. 1
	Wsh.	Apr. 5/90	N.J.	3	Sean Burke	Wsh. 5	N.J. 4
Denis Savard (3)	Chi.	Apr. 19/82	Chi.	3	Mike Liut	Chi. 7	StL. 4
		Apr. 10/86	Chi.	4	Ken Wregget	Tor. 6	Chi. 4
		Apr. 9/88	St.L.	3	Greg Millen	Chi. 6	St.L. 3
Mark Messier (3)	Edm.	Apr. 14/83	Edm.	4	Rejean Lemelin	Edm. 6	Cgy. 3
		Apr. 17/83	Cgy.	3	Rejean Lemelin (1) / Don Edwards (2)	Edm. 10	Cgy. 2
		Apr. 26/83	Edm.	3	Murray Bannerman	Edm. 8	Chi. 2
Tim Kerr (3)	Phi.	Apr. 13/85	NYR	4	Glen Hanlon	Phi. 6	NYR 5
		Apr. 20/87	Phi.	3	Kelly Hrudey	Phi. 4	NYI 2
		Apr. 19/89	Pit.	3	Tom Barrasso	Phi. 4	Pit. 2
Cam Neely (3)	Bos.	Apr. 9/87	Mtl.	3	Patrick Roy	Mtl. 4	Bos. 3
	Bos.	Apr. 5/91	Bos.	3	Peter Sidorkiewicz	Bos. 4	Hfd. 3
	Bos.	Apr. 25/91	Bos.	3	Patrick Roy	Bos. 4	Mtl. 1
Petr Klima (3)	Det.	Apr. 7/88	Tor.	3	Alan Bester (2) / Ken Wregett (1)	Det. 6	Tor. 2
		Apr. 21/88	St.L.	3	Greg Millen	Det. 6	St.L. 0
	Edm.	May 4/91	Edm.	3	Jon Casey	Edm. 3	Min. 2
Newsy Lalonde (2)	Mtl.	Mar. 1/19	Mtl.	5	Clint Benedict	Mtl. 6	Ott. 3
	Mtl.	Mar.22/19	Sea.	4	Harry Holmes	Mtl. 4	Sea. 2
Howie Morenz (2)	Mtl.	Mar.22/24	Mtl.	3	Charles Reid	Mtl. 6	Cgy.T. 1
	Mtl.	Mar.27/25	Mtl.	3	Harry Holmes	Mtl. 4	Vic. 2
Toe Blake (2)	Mtl.	Mar.22/38	Mtl.	3	Mike Karakas	Mtl. 6	Chi. 4
		Mar.26/46	Chi.	3	Mike Karakas	Mtl. 7	Chi. 2
Doug Bentley (2)	Chi.	Mar.28/44	Chi.	3	Connie Dion	Chi. 7	Det. 1
		Mar.30/44	Det.	3	Connie Dion	Chi. 5	Det. 2
Ted Kennedy (2)	Tor.	Apr. 14/45	Tor.	3	Harry Lumley	Det. 5	Tor. 3
		Mar.27/48	Tor.	4	Frank Brimsek	Tor. 5	Bos. 3
Bobby Hull (2)	Chi.	Apr. 7/63	Det.	3	Terry Sawchuk	Det. 7	Chi. 4
		Apr. 9/72	Pitt	3	Jim Rutherford	Chi. 6	Pit. 5
F. St. Marseille (2)	St.L.	Apr. 28/70	St.L	3	Al Smith	St.L. 5	Pit. 0
		Apr. 6/72	Min.	3	Cesare Maniago	Min. 6	St.L. 1
Pit Martin (2)	Chi.	Apr. 4/73	Chi.	3	W. Stephenson	Chi. 7	St.L. 1
		May 10/73	Mtl.	3	Ken Dryden	Mtl. 6	Chi. 4
Yvan Cournoyer (2)	Mtl.	May 5/73	Mtl.	3	Dave Dryden	Mtl. 7	Buf. 3
		Apr. 11/74	Mtl.	3	Ed Giacomin	Mtl. 4	NYR 1
Guy Lafleur (2)	Mtl.	May 1/75	Mtl.	3	Roger Crozier (1) / Gerry Desjardins (2)	Mtl. 5	Buf. 2
		Apr. 11/77	Mtl.	3	Ed Staniowski	Mtl. 7	St.L. 2
Lanny McDonald (2)	Tor.	Apr. 9/77	Pitt	3	Denis Herron	Tor. 5	Pit. 2
		Apr. 17/77	Tor.	4	W. Stephenson	Phi. 6	Tor. 5

Frank Nighbor tied for the lead among playoff scorers during the 1919-20 post-season.

Player	Team	Date	City	Total Goals	Opposing Goaltender	Score	
Butch Goring (2)	L.A.	Apr. 9/77	L.A.	3	Phil Myre	L.A. 4	Atl. 2
	NYI	May 17/81	Min.	3	Gilles Meloche	NYI 7	Min. 5
Bryan Trottier (2)	NYI	Apr. 8/80	NYI	3	Doug Keans	NYI 8	L.A. 1
		Apr. 9/81	NYI	3	Michel Larocque	NYI 5	Tor. 1
Bill Barber (2)	Phil	May 4/80	Min.	4	Gilles Meloche	Phi. 5	Min. 3
		Apr. 9/81	Phil	3	Dan Bouchard	Phi. 8	Que. 5
Brian Propp (2)	Phi.	Apr. 22/81	Phi.	3	Pat Riggin	Phi. 9	Cgy. 4
		Apr. 21/85	Phi.	3	Billy Smith	Phi. 4	NYI 2
Paul Reinhart (2)	Cgy	Apr. 14/83	Edm.	3	Andy Moog	Edm. 6	Cgy. 3
		Apr. 8/84	Van	3	Richard Brodeur	Cgy. 5	Van. 1
Peter Stastny (2)	Que.	Apr. 5/83	Bos.	3	Pete Peeters	Bos. 4	Que. 3
		Apr. 11/87	Que.	3	Mike Liut (2) / Steve Weeks (1)	Que. 5	Hfd. 3
Glenn Anderson (2)	Edm.	Apr. 26/83	Edm.	4	Murray Bannerman	Edm. 8	Chi. 2
		Apr. 6/88	Wpg.	3	Daniel Berthiaume	Edm. 7	Wpg. 4
Michel Goulet (2)	Que.	Apr. 23/85	Que.	3	Steve Penney	Que. 4	Mtl. 6
		Apr. 12/87	Que.	3	Mike Liut	Que. 4	Hfd. 1
Peter Zezel (2)	Phi.	Apr. 13/86	NYR	3	J. Vanbiesbrouck	Phi. 7	NYR 1
	St. L.	Apr. 11/89	St. L.	3	Jon Casey (2) / Kari Takko (1)	St.L. 6	Min. 1
Steve Yzerman (2)	Det.	Apr. 6/89	Det.	3	Alain Chevrier	Chi. 5	Det. 4
	Det.	Apr. 4/91	St.L.	3	Vincent Riendeau (2) / Pat Jablonski (1)	Det. 6	St. L. 3
Esa Tikkanen (2)	Edm.	May 22/88	Edm.	3	Rejean Lemelin	Edm. 6	Bos. 3
	Edm.	Apr. 16/91	Edm.	3	Mike Vernon	Edm. 5	Cgy. 2
Harry Meeking	Tor.	Mar. 11/18	Tor.	3	Georges Vezina	Tor. 7	Mtl. 1
Alf Skinner	Tor.	Mar.23/18	Tor.	3	Hugh Lehman	Van.M. 6	Tor. 4
Joe Malone	Mtl.	Feb. 23/19	Mtl.	3	Clint Benedict	Mtl. 8	Ott. 4
Odie Cleghorn	Mtl.	Feb. 27/19	Ott.	3	Clint Benedict	Mtl. 5	Ott. 2
Jack Darragh	Ott.	Apr. 1/20	Tor.	3	Harry Holmes	Ott. 6	Sea. 1
George Boucher	Ott.	Mar.10/21	Ott.	3	Jake Forbes	Ott. 5	Tor. 0
Babe Dye	Tor.	Mar.28/22	Tor.	4	Hugh Lehman	Tor. 5	Van.M. 1
Perk Galbraith	Bos.	Mar.31/27	Bos.	3	Hugh Lehman	Bos. 4	Chi. 4
Busher Jackson	Tor.	Apr. 5/32	NYR	3	John Ross Roach	Tor. 6	NYR 4
Frank Boucher	NYR	Apr. 9/32	Tor.	3	Lorne Chabot	NYR 4	Tor. 4
Charlie Conacher	Tor.	Mar.26/36	Tor.	3	Tiny Thompson	Tor. 8	Bos. 3
Syd Howe	Det.	Mar.23/39	Det.	3	Claude Bourque	Det. 7	Mtl. 3
Bryan Hextall	NYR	Apr. 3/40	NYR	3	Turk Broda	NYR 6	Tor. 2
Joe Benoit	Mtl.	Mar.22/41	Mtl.	3	Sam LoPresti	Mtl. 4	Chi. 3
Syl Apps	Tor.	Mar.25/41	Tor.	3	Frank Brimsek	Tor. 7	Bos. 2

Leading Playoff Scorers, 1918 – 1991

Player	Team	Date	City	Total Goals	Opposing Goaltender	Score	
Jack McGill	Bos.	Mar.29/42	Bos.	3	Johnny Mowers	Det. 6	Bos. 4
Don Metz	Tor.	Apr. 14/42	Tor.	3	Johnny Mowers	Tor. 9	Det. 3
Mud Bruneteau	Det.	Apr. 1/43	Det.	3	Frank Brimsek	Det. 6	Bos. 2
Don Grosso	Det.	Apr. 7/43	Bos.	3	Frank Brimsek	Det. 4	Bos. 0
Carl Liscombe	Det.	Apr. 3/45	Det.	4	Paul Bibeault	Det. 5	Bos. 3
Billy Reay	Mtl.	Apr. 1/47	Bos.	3	Frank Brimsek	Mtl. 5	Bos. 1
Gerry Plamondon	Mtl.	Mar.24/49	Det.	3	Harry Lumley	Mtl. 4	Det. 3
Sid Smith	Tor.	Apr. 10/49	Det.	3	Harry Lumley	Tor. 3	Det. 1
Pentti Lund	NYR	Apr. 2/50	NYR	3	Bill Durnan	NYR 4	Mtl. 1
Ted Lindsay	Det.	Apr. 5/55	Det.	4	Charlie Hodge (1) Jacques Plante (3)	Det. 7	Mtl. 1
Gordie Howe	Det.	Apr. 10/55	Det.	3	Jacques Plante	Det. 5	Mtl. 1
Phil Goyette	Mtl.	Mar.25/58	Mtl.	3	Terry Sawchuk	Mtl. 8	Det. 1
Jerry Toppazzini	Bos.	Apr. 5/58	Bos.	3	Lorne Worsley	Bos. 8	NYR 2
Bob Pulford	Tor.	Apr. 19/62	Tor.	3	Glenn Hall	Tor. 8	Chi. 4
Dave Keon	Tor.	Apr. 9/64	Mtl.	3	Charlie Hodge	Tor. 3	Mtl. 1
Henri Richard	Mtl.	Apr. 20/67	Mtl.	3	Terry Sawchuk (2) Johnny Bower (1)	Mtl. 6	Tor. 2
Rosaire Paiement	Phi.	Apr. 13/68	Phi.	3	Glenn Hall (1) Seth Martin (2)	Phi. 6	St. L. 1
Jean Beliveau	Mtl.	Apr. 20/68	Mtl.	3	Denis DeJordy	Mtl. 4	Chi. 1
Red Berenson	St. L.	Apr. 15/69	St. L.	3	Gerry Desjardins	St. L. 4	L.A. 0
Ken Schinkel	Pit.	Apr. 11/70	Oak.	3	Gary Smith	Pit. 5	Oak. 2
Jim Pappin	Chi.	Apr. 11/71	Phi.	3	Bruce Gamble	Chi. 6	Phi. 2
Bobby Orr	Bos.	Apr. 11/71	Mtl.	3	Ken Dryden	Bos. 5	Mtl. 2
Jacques Lemaire	Mtl.	Apr. 20/71	Mtl.	3	Lorne Worsley	Mtl. 7	Min. 2
Vic Hadfield	NYR	Apr. 22/71	NYR	3	Tony Esposito	NYR 4	Chi. 1
Fred Stanfield	Bos.	Apr. 18/72	Bos.	3	Jacques Caron	Bos. 6	St. L. 1
Ken Hodge	Bos.	Apr. 30/72	Bos.	3	Ed Giacomin	Bos. 6	NYR 5
Steve Vickers	NYR	Apr. 10/73	Bos.	3	Ross Brooks (2) Ed Johnston (1)	NYR 6	Bos. 3
Dick Redmond	Chi.	Apr. 4/73	Chi.	3	Wayne Stephenson	Chi. 7	St. L. 1
Tom Williams	L.A.	Apr. 14/74	L.A.	3	Mike Veisor	L.A. 5	Chi. 1
Marcel Dionne	L.A.	Apr. 15/76	L.A.	3	Gilles Gilbert	L.A. 6	Bos. 4
Don Saleski	Phi.	Apr. 20/76	Phil	3	Wayne Thomas	Phi. 7	Tor. 1
Darryl Sittler	Tor.	Apr. 22/76	Tor.	5	Bernie Parent	Tor. 8	Phi. 5
Reggie Leach	Phi.	May 6/76	Phi.	5	Gilles Gilbert	Phi. 6	Bos. 3
Jim Lorentz	Buf.	Apr. 7/77	Min.	3	Pete LoPresti (2) Gary Smith (1)	Buf. 7	Min. 1
Bobby Schmautz	Bos.	Apr. 11/77	Bos.	3	Rogatien Vachon	Bos. 8	L.A. 3
Billy Harris	NYI	Apr. 23/77	Mtl.	3	Ken Dryden	Mtl. 4	NYI 3
George Ferguson	Tor.	Apr. 11/78	Tor.	3	Rogatien Vachon	Tor. 7	L.A. 3
Jean Ratelle	Bos.	May 3/79	Bos.	3	Ken Dryden	Bos. 4	Mtl. 3
Stan Jonathan	Bos.	May 8/79	Bos.	3	Ken Dryden	Bos. 5	Mtl. 2
Ron Duguay	NYR	Apr. 20/80	NYR	3	Pete Peeters	NYR 4	Phi. 2
Steve Shutt	Mtl.	Apr. 22/80	Mtl.	3	Gilles Meloche	Mtl. 6	Min. 2
Gilbert Perreault	Buf.	May 6/80	NYI	3	Billy Smith (2) ENG (1)	Buf. 7	NYI 4
Paul Holmgren	Phi.	May 15/80	Phil	3	Billy Smith	Phi. 8	NYI 3
Steve Payne	Min.	Apr. 8/81	Bos.	3	Rogatien Vachon	Min. 5	Bos. 4
Denis Potvin	NYI	Apr. 17/81	NYI	3	Andy Moog	NYI 6	Edm. 3
Barry Pederson	Bos.	Apr. 8/82	Bos.	3	Don Edwards	Bos. 7	Buf. 3
Duane Sutter	NYI	Apr. 15/83	NYI	3	Glen Hanlon	NYI 5	NYR 0
Doug Halward	Van.	Apr. 7/84	Van.	3	Rejean Lemelin (2) Don Edwards (1)	Van. 7	Cgy. 4
Jorgen Pettersson	St. L.	Apr. 8/84	Det.	3	Ed Mio	St. L. 3	Det. 2
Clark Gillies	NYI	May 12/84	NYI	3	Grant Fuhr	NYI 6	Edm. 1
Ken Linseman	Bos.	Apr. 14/85	Bos.	3	Steve Penney	Bos. 7	Mtl. 6
Dave Andreychuk	Buf.	Apr. 14/85	Buf.	3	Dan Bouchard	Que. 4	Buf. 7
Greg Paslawski	StL.	Apr. 15/86	Min.	3	Don Beaupre	St. L. 6	Min. 3
Doug Risebrough	Cgy.	May 4/86	Cgy.	3	Rick Wamsley	Cgy. 8	St.L. 2
Mike McPhee	Mtl.	Apr. 11/87	Bos.	3	Doug Keans	Mtl. 5	Bos. 4
John Ogrodnick	Que.	Apr. 14/87	Hfd.	3	Mike Liut	Que. 7	Hfd. 5
Pelle-Erik Eklund	Phi.	May 10/87	Mtl.	3	Patrick Roy (1) Bryan Hayward (2)	Phi. 6	Mtl. 3
John Tucker	Buf.	Apr. 9/88	Bos.	4	Andy Moog	Buf. 6	Bos. 2
Tony Hrkac	St.L.	Apr. 10/88	St.L.	4	Darren Pang	St.L. 6	Chi. 5
Hakan Loob	Cgy.	Apr. 10/88	Cgy.	3	Glenn Healy	Cgy. 7	L.A. 3
Ed Olczyk	Tor.	Apr. 12/88	Tor.	3	Greg Stefan (2) Glen Hanlon (1)	Tor. 6	Det. 5
Aaron Broten	N.J.	Apr. 20/88	N.J.	3	Pete Peeters	N.J. 5	Wsh. 2
Mark Johnson	N.J.	Apr. 22/88	Wsh.	4	Pete Peeters	N.J. 10	Wsh. 4
Patrik Sundstrom	N.J.	Apr. 22/88	Wsh.	3	Pete Peeters (2) Clint Malarchuk (1)	N.J. 10	Wsh. 4
Bob Brooke	Min.	Apr. 5/89	St. L.	3	Greg Millen	St. L. 4	Min. 3
Chris Kontos	L.A.	Apr. 6/89	L.A.	3	Grant Fuhr	L.A. 5	Edm. 2
Mario Lemieux	Pit.	Apr. 25/89	Pit.	5	Ron Hextall	Pit. 10	Phi. 7
Wayne Presley	Chi.	Apr. 13/89	Chi.	3	Greg Stefan (1) Glen Hanlon (2)	Chi. 7	Det. 1
Tony Granato	L.A.	Apr. 10/90	L.A.	3	Mike Vernon (1) Rick Wamsley (2)	L.A. 12	Cgy. 4
Tomas Sandstrom	L.A.	Apr. 10/90	L.A.	3	Mike Vernon (1) Rick Wamsley (2)	L.A. 12	Cgy. 4
Dave Taylor	L.A.	Apr. 10/90	L.A.	3	Mike Vernon (1) Rick Wamsley (2)	L.A. 12	Cgy. 4
Mike Gartner	NYR	Apr. 13/90	NYR	3	Mark Fitzpatrick (2) Glenn Healy (1)	NYR 6	NYI 5
Bernie Nicholls	NYR	Apr. 19/90	NYR	3	Mike Liut	NYR 7	Wsh. 3
John Druce	Wsh.	Apr. 21/90	NYR	3	John Vanbiesbrouck	Wsh. 6	NYR 3
Geoff Courtnall	Van.	Apr. 4/91	L.A.	3	Kelly Hrudey	Van. 6	L.A. 5
Adam Oates	St. L.	Apr. 12/91	St. L.	3	Tim Chevaldae	St. L. 6	Det. 1
Luc Robitaille	L.A.	Apr. 26/91	L.A.	3	Grant Fuhr	L.A. 5	Edm. 2

Season	Player and Club	Games Played	Goals	Assists	Points
1990-91	Mario Lemieux, Pittsburgh	23	16	28	44
1989-90	Craig Simpson, Edmonton	22	16	15	31
	Mark Messier, Edmonton	22	9	22	31
1988-89	Al MacInnis, Calgary	22	7	24	31
1987-88	Wayne Gretzky, Edmonton	19	12	31	43
1986-87	Wayne Gretzky, Edmonton	21	5	29	34
1985-86	Doug Gilmour, St. Louis	19	9	12	21
	Bernie Federko, St. Louis	19	7	14	21
1984-85	Wayne Gretzky, Edmonton	18	17	30	47
1983-84	Wayne Gretzky, Edmonton	19	13	22	35
1982-83	Wayne Gretzky, Edmonton	16	12	26	38
1981-82	Bryan Trottier, NY Islanders	19	6	23	29
1980-81	Mike Bossy, NY Islanders	18	17	18	35
1979-80	Bryan Trottier, NY Islanders	21	12	17	29
1978-79	Jacques Lemaire, Montreal	16	11	12	23
	Guy Lafleur, Montreal	16	10	13	23
1977-78	Guy Lafleur, Montreal	15	10	11	21
	Larry Robinson, Montreal	15	4	17	21
1976-77	Guy Lafleur, Montreal	14	9	17	26
1975-76	Reggie Leach, Philadelphia	16	19	5	24
1974-75	Rick MacLeish, Philadelphia	17	11	9	20
1973-74	Rick MacLeish, Philadelphia	17	13	9	22
1972-73	Yvan Cournoyer, Montreal	17	15	10	25
1971-72	Phil Esposito, Boston	15	9	15	24
	Bobby Orr, Boston	15	5	19	24
1970-71	Frank Mahovlich, Montreal	20	14	13	27
1969-70	Phil Esposito, Boston	14	13	14	27
1968-69	Phil Esposito, Boston	10	8	10	18
1967-68	Bill Goldsworthy, Minnesota	14	8	7	15
1966-67	Jim Pappin, Toronto	12	7	8	15
1965-66	Norm Ullman, Detroit	12	6	9	15
1964-65	Bobby Hull, Chicago	14	10	7	17
1963-64	Gordie Howe, Detroit	14	9	10	19
1962-63	Gordie Howe, Detroit	11	7	9	16
	Norm Ullman, Detroit	11	4	12	16
1961-62	Stan Mikita, Chicago	12	6	15	21
1960-61	Gordie Howe, Detroit	11	4	11	15
	Pierre Pilote, Chicago	12	3	12	15
1959-60	Henri Richard, Montreal	8	3	9	12
	Bernie Geoffrion, Montreal	8	2	10	12
1958-59	Dickie Moore, Montreal	11	5	12	17
1957-58	Fleming Mackell, Boston	12	5	14	19
1956-57	Bernie Geoffrion, Montreal	11	11	7	18
1955-56	Jean Beliveau, Montreal	10	12	7	19
1954-55	Gordie Howe, Detroit	11	9	11	20
1953-54	Dickie Moore, Detroit	11	5	8	13
1952-53	Ed Sanford, Boston	11	8	3	11
1951-52	Ted Lindsay, Detroit	8	5	2	7
	Floyd Curry, Montreal	11	4	3	7
	Metro Prystai, Detroit	8	2	5	7
	Gordie Howe, Detroit	8	2	5	7
1950-51	Maurice Richard, Montreal	11	9	4	13
	Max Bentley, Toronto	11	2	11	13
1949-50	Pentti Lund, NY Rangers	12	6	5	11
1948-49	Gordie Howe, Detroit	11	8	3	11
1947-48	Ted Kennedy, Toronto	9	8	6	14
1946-47	Maurice Richard, Montreal	10	6	5	11
1945-46	Elmer Lach, Montreal	9	5	12	17
1944-45	Joe Carveth, Detroit	14	5	6	11
1943-44	Toe Blake, Montreal	9	7	11	18
1942-43	Carl Liscombe, Detroit	10	6	8	14
1941-42	Don Grosso, Detroit	12	8	6	14
1940-41	Milt Schmidt, Boston	11	5	6	11
1939-40	Phil Watson, NY Rangers	12	3	6	9
	Neil Colville, NY Rangers	12	2	7	9
1938-39	Bill Cowley, Boston	12	3	11	14
1937-38	Johnny Gottselig, Chicago	10	5	3	8
1936-37	Marty Barry, Detroit	10	4	7	11
1935-36	Buzz Boll, Toronto	9	7	3	10
1934-35	Baldy Northcott, Mtl. Maroons	7	4	1	5
	Harvey Jackson, Toronto	7	3	2	5
	Marvin Wentworth, Mtl. Maroons	7	3	2	5
1933-34	Larry Aurie, Detroit	9	3	7	10
1932-33	Cecil Dillon, NY Rangers	8	8	2	10
1931-32	Frank Boucher, NY Rangers	7	3	6	9
1930-31	Cooney Weiland, Boston	5	3	3	6
1929-30	Marty Barry, Boston	6	3	3	6
	Cooney Weiland, Boston	6	1	5	6
1928-29	Andy Blair, Toronto	4	3	0	3
	Butch Keeling, NY Rangers	6	3	0	3
	Ace Bailey, Toronto	4	1	2	3
1927-28	Frank Boucher, NY Rangers	9	7	3	10
1926-27	Harry Oliver, Boston	8	4	2	6
	Perk Galbraith, Boston	8	3	3	6
	Frank Fredrickson, Boston	8	2	4	6
1925-26	Nels Stewart, Mtl. Maroons	8	6	3	9
1924-25	Howie Morenz, Montreal	6	7	1	8
1923-24	Howie Morenz, Montreal	6	7	1	8
1922-23	Punch Broadbent, Ottawa	8	6	1	7
1921-22	Babe Dye, Toronto	7	11	2	13
1920-21	Cy Denneny, Ottawa	7	4	3	7
1919-20	Frank Nighbor, Ottawa	5	6	1	7
	Jack Darragh, Ottawa	5	5	2	7
1918-19	Newsy Lalonde, Montreal	10	17	1	18
1917-18	Alf Skinner, Toronto	7	8	1	9

Overtime Games since 1918

Abbreviations: Teams/Cities: — **Atl.** - Atlanta; **Bos.** - Boston; **Buf.** - Buffalo; **Cgy.** - Calgary; **Cgy. T.** - Calgary Tigers (Western Canada Hockey League); **Chi.** - Chicago; **Col.** - Colorado; **Det.** - Detroit; **Edm.** - Edmonton; **Edm. E.** - Edmonton Eskimos (WCHL); **Hfd.** - Hartford; **K.C.** - Kansas City; **L.A.** - Los Angeles; **Min.** - Minnesota; **Mtl.** - Montreal; **Mtl.M.** - Montreal Maroons; **N.J.** - New Jersey; **NY** - New York; **NYA** - NY Americans; **NYI** - New York Islanders; **NYR** - New York Rangers; **Oak.** - Oakland; **Ott.** - Ottawa; **Phi.** - Philadelphia; **Pit.** - Pittsburgh; **Que.** - Quebec; **St.L.** - St. Louis; **Sea.** - Seattle Metropolitans (Pacific Coast Hockey Association); **Tor.** - Toronto; **Van.** - Vancouver; **Van. M** - Vancouver Millionaires (PCHA); **Vic.** - Victoria Cougars (WCHL); **Wpg.** - Winnipeg; **Wsh.** - Washington.

SERIES — **CF** - conference final; **DF** - division final; **DSF** - division semi-final; **F** - final; **PR** - preliminary round; **QF** - quarter final; **SF** - semi-final.

Date	City	Series	Score		Scorer	Overtime	Series Winner
Mar. 26/19	Sea.	F	Mtl. 0	Sea. 0	no scorer	20:00	
Mar. 29/19	Sea.	F	Mtl. 4	Sea. 3	Odie Cleghorn	15:57	
Mar. 21/22	Tor.	F	Tor 2	Van.M. 1	Babe Dye	4:50	Tor.
Mar. 29/23	Van.	F	Ott. 2	Edm.E. 1	Cy Denneny	2:08	Ott.
Mar. 31/27	Mtl.	QF	Mtl. 1	Mtl. M. 0	Howie Morenz	12:05	Mtl.
Apr. 7/27	Bos.	F	Ott. 0	Bos. 0	no scorer	20:00	Ott.
Apr. 11/27	Ott.	F	Bos. 1	Ott. 1	no scorer	20:00	Ott.
Apr. 3/28	Mtl.	QF	Mtl. M. 1	Mtl. 0	Russ Oatman	8:20	Mtl. M.
Apr. 7/28	Mtl.	F	NYR 2	Mtl. M. 1	Frank Boucher	7:05	NYR
Mar. 21/29	NY	QF	NYR 1	NYA 0	Butch Keeling	29:50	NYR
Mar. 26/29	Tor.	SF	NYR 2	Tor. 1	Frank Boucher	2:03	NYR
Mar. 20/30	Mtl.	SF	Bos. 2	Mtl. M. 1	Harry Oliver	45:35	Bos.
Mar. 25/30	Bos.	SF	Mtl. M. 1	Bos. 0	Archie Wilcox	26:27	Bos.
Mar. 26/30	Mtl.	QF	Chi. 2	Mtl. 2	Howie Morenz (Mtl.)	51:43	Mtl.
Mar. 28/30	Mtl.	SF	Mtl. 2	NYR 1	Gus Rivers	68:52	Mtl.
Mar. 24/31	Bos.	SF	Bos. 5	Mtl. 4	Cooney Weiland	18:56	Mtl.
Mar. 26/31	Chi.	QF	Chi. 2	Tor. 1	Steward Adams	19:20	Chi.
Mar. 28/31	Mtl.	SF	Mtl. 4	Bos. 3	Georges Mantha	5:10	Mtl.
Apr. 1/31	Mtl.	SF	Mtl. 3	Bos. 2	Wildor Larochelle	19:00	Mtl.
Apr. 5/31	Chi.	F	Chi. 2	Mtl. 1	Johnny Gottselig	24:50	Mtl.
Apr. 9/31	Mtl.	F	Chi. 3	Mtl. 2	Cy Wentworth	53:50	Mtl.
Mar. 26/32	Mtl.	SF	NYR 4	Mtl. 3	Fred Cook	59:32	NYR
Apr. 2/32	Tor.	SF	Tor. 3	Mtl. M. 2	Bob Gracie	17:59	Tor.
Mar. 25/33	Bos.	SF	Bos. 2	Tor. 1	Marty Barry	14:14	Tor.
Mar. 28/33	Bos.	SF	Tor. 1	Bos. 0	Busher Jackson	15:03	Tor.
Mar. 30/33	Tor.	SF	Bos. 2	Tor. 1	Eddie Shore	4:23	Tor.
Apr. 3/33	Tor.	SF	Tor. 1	Bos. 0	Ken Doraty	104:46	Tor.
Apr. 13/33	Tor.	F	NYR 1	Tor. 0	Bill Cook	7:33	NYR
Mar. 22/34	Tor.	SF	Det. 2	Tor. 1	Herbie Lewis	1:33	Det.
Mar. 25/34	Chi.	QF	Chi. 1	Mtl. 1	Mush March (Chi)	11:05	Chi.
Apr. 3/34	Det.	F	Chi. 2	Det. 1	Paul Thompson	21:05	Chi.
Apr. 10/34	Chi.	F	Chi. 1	Det. 0	Mush March	30.05	Chi.
Mar. 23/35	Bos.	SF	Bos. 1	Tor. 0	Dit Clapper	33:26	Tor.
Mar. 26/35	Chi.	QF	Mtl. M. 1	Chi. 0	Baldy Northcott	4:02	Mtl. M.
Mar. 30/35	Tor.	SF	Tor. 2	Bos. 1	Pep Kelly	1:36	Tor.
Apr. 4/35	Tor.	F	Mtl. M. 3	Tor. 2	Dave Trottier	5:20	Mtl. M.
Mar. 24/36	Mtl.	SF	Det. 1	Mtl. M. 0	Mud Bruneteau	116:30	Det.
Apr. 9/36	Tor.	F	Tor. 4	Det. 3	Buzz Boll	0:31	Det.
Mar. 25/37	NY	QF	NYR 2	Tor. 1	Babe Pratt	13:05	NYR
Apr. 1/37	Mtl.	SF	Det. 2	Mtl. 1	Hec Kilrea	51:49	Det.
Mar. 22/38	NY	QF	NYA 2	NYR 1	Johnny Sorrell	21:25	NYA
Mar. 25/38	Tor.	SF	Tor. 1	Bos. 0	George Parsons	21:31	Tor.
Mar. 26/38	Mtl.	QF	Chi. 3	Mtl. 2	Paul Thompson	11:49	Chi.
Mar. 27/38	NY	QF	NYA 3	NYR 2	Lorne Carr	60:40	NYA
Mar. 29/38	Bos.	SF	Tor. 3	Bos. 2	Gord Drillon	10:04	Tor.
Mar. 31/38	Chi.	SF	Chi. 1	NYA 0	Cully Dahlstrom	33:01	Chi.
Mar. 21/39	NY	SF	Bos. 2	NYR 1	Mel Hill	59:25	Bos.
Mar. 23/39	Bos.	SF	Bos. 3	NYR 2	Mel Hill	8:24	Bos.
Mar. 26/39	Det.	QF	Det. 1	Mtl. 0	Marty Barry	7:47	Det.
Mar. 30/39	Bos.	SF	NYR 2	Bos. 1	Snuffy Smith	17:19	Bos.
Apr. 1/39	Tor.	SF	Tor. 5	Det. 4	Gord Drillon	5:42	Tor.
Apr. 2/39	Bos.	SF	Bos. 2	NYR 1	Mel Hill	48:00	Bos.
Apr. 9/39	Bos.	F	Tor. 3	Bos. 2	Doc Romnes	10:38	Bos.
Mar. 19/40	Det.	QF	Det. 2	NYA 1	Syd Howe	0:25	Det.
Mar. 19/40	Tor.	QF	Tor. 3	Chi. 2	Syl Apps	6:35	Tor.
Apr. 2/40	NY	F	NYR 2	Tor. 1	Alf Pike	15:30	NYR
Apr. 11/40	Tor.	F	NYR 2	Tor. 1	Muzz Patrick	31:43	NYR
Apr. 13/40	Tor.	F	NYR 3	Tor. 2	Bryan Hextall	2:07	NYR
Mar. 20/41	Det.	QF	Det. 2	NYR 1	Gus Giesebrecht	12:01	Det.
Mar. 22/41	Mtl.	QF	Mtl. 4	Chi. 3	Charlie Sands	34:04	Chi.
Mar. 29/41	Bos.	SF	Tor. 2	Bos. 1	Pete Langelle	17:31	Bos.
Mar. 30/41	Chi.	SF	Det. 2	Chi. 1	Gus Giesebrecht	9:15	Det.
Mar. 22/42	Chi.	QF	Bos. 2	Chi. 1	Des Smith	9:51	Bos.
Mar. 21/43	Bos.	SF	Bos. 5	Mtl. 4	Don Gallinger	12:30	Bos.
Mar. 23/43	Det.	SF	Tor. 3	Det. 2	Jack McLean	70:18	Det.
Mar. 25/43	Mtl.	SF	Bos. 3	Mtl. 2	Harvey Jackson	3:20	Bos.
Mar. 30/43	Tor.	SF	Det. 3	Tor. 2	Adam Brown	9:21	Det.
Mar. 30/43	Bos.	SF	Bos. 5	Mtl. 4	Ab DeMarco	3:41	Bos.
Apr. 13/44	Mtl.	F	Mtl. 5	Chi. 4	Toe Blake	9:12	Mtl.
Mar. 27/45	Tor.	SF	Tor. 4	Mtl. 3	Gus Bodnar	12:36	Tor.
Mar. 29/45	Det.	SF	Det. 3	Bos. 2	Mud Bruneteau	17:12	Det.
Apr. 21/45	Tor.	F	Det. 1	Tor. 0	Ed Bruneteau	14:16	Tor.
Mar. 28/46	Bos.	SF	Bos. 4	Det. 3	Don Gallinger	9:51	Bos.
Mar. 30/46	Mtl.	F	Mtl. 4	Bos. 3	Maurice Richard	9:08	Mtl.
Apr. 2/46	Mtl.	F	Mtl. 3	Bos. 2	Jim Peters	16:55	Mtl.
Apr. 7/46	Bos.	F	Bos. 3	Mtl. 2	Terry Reardon	15:13	Mtl.
Mar. 26/47	Tor.	SF	Tor. 3	Det. 2	Howie Meeker	3:05	Tor.
Mar. 27/47	Mtl.	SF	Mtl. 2	Bos. 1	Ken Mosdell	5:38	Mtl.
Apr. 3/47	Mtl.	SF	Mtl. 4	Bos. 3	John Quilty	36:40	Mtl.
Apr. 15/47	Tor.	F	Tor. 2	Mtl. 1	Syl Apps	16:36	Tor.
Mar. 24/48	Tor.	SF	Tor. 5	Bos. 4	Nick Metz	17:03	Tor.
Mar. 22/49	Det.	SF	Det. 2	Mtl. 1	Max McNab	44:52	Det.
Mar. 24/49	Det.	SF	Mtl. 4	Det. 3	Gerry Plamondon	2:59	Det.
Mar. 26/49	Tor.	SF	Bos. 5	Tor. 4	Woody Dumart	16:14	Tor.
Apr. 8/49	Det.	F	Tor. 3	Det. 2	Joe Klukay	17:31	Tor.
Apr. 4/50	Tor.	SF	Det. 2	Tor. 1	Leo Reise	20:38	Det.
Apr. 4/50	Mtl.	SF	Mtl. 3	NYR 2	Elmer Lach	15:19	Mtl.
Apr. 9/50	Det.	SF	Det. 1	Tor. 0	Leo Reise	8:39	Det.
Apr. 18/50	Det.	F	NYR 4	Det. 3	Don Raleigh	8:34	Det.
Apr. 20/50	Det.	F	NYR 2	Det. 1	Don Raleigh	1:38	Det.
Apr. 23/50	Det.	F	Det. 4	NYR 3	Pete Babando	28:31	Det.
Mar. 27/51	Det.	SF	Mtl. 3	Det. 2	Maurice Richard	61:09	Mtl.
Mar. 29/51	Det.	SF	Mtl. 1	Det. 0	Maurice Richard	42:20	Mtl.
Mar. 31/51	Tor.	SF	Bos. 1	Tor. 1	no scorer	20:00	Tor.
Apr. 11/51	Tor.	F	Tor. 3	Mtl. 2	Sid Smith	5:51	Tor.
Apr. 14/51	Tor.	F	Mtl. 3	Tor. 2	Maurice Richard	2:55	Tor.
Apr. 17/51	Mtl.	F	Tor. 2	Mtl. 1	Ted Kennedy	4:47	Tor.
Apr. 19/51	Mtl.	F	Tor. 3	Mtl. 2	Harry Watson	5:15	Tor.
Apr. 21/51	Tor.	F	Tor. 3	Mtl. 2	Bill Barilko	2:53	Tor.
Apr. 6/52	Bos.	SF	Mtl. 3	Bos. 2	Paul Masnick	27:49	Mtl.
Mar. 29/53	Bos.	SF	Bos. 2	Det. 1	Jack McIntyre	12:29	Bos.
Mar. 29/53	Chi.	SF	Chi. 2	Mtl. 1	Al Dewsbury	5:18	Mtl.
Apr. 16/53	Mtl.	F	Mtl. 1	Bos. 0	Elmer Lach	1:22	Mtl.
Apr. 1/54	Det.	SF	Det. 4	Tor. 3	Ted Lindsay	21:01	Det.
Apr. 11/54	Det.	F	Mtl. 1	Det. 0	Ken Mosdell	5:45	Det.
Apr. 16/54	Det.	F	Det. 2	Mtl. 1	Tony Leswick	4:29	Det.
Mar. 29/55	Bos.	SF	Mtl. 4	Bos. 3	Don Marshall	3:05	Mtl.
Mar. 24/56	Tor.	SF	Det. 5	Tor. 4	Ted Lindsay	4:22	Det.
Mar. 28/57	NY	SF	NYR 4	Mtl. 3	Andy Hebenton	13:38	Mtl.
Apr. 4/57	Mtl.	SF	Mtl. 4	NYR 3	Maurice Richard	1:11	Mtl.
Mar. 27/58	NY	SF	Bos. 4	NYR 3	Jerry Toppazzini	4:46	Bos.
Mar. 30/58	Det.	SF	Mtl. 2	Det. 1	Andre Pronovost	11:52	Mtl.
Apr. 17/58	Mtl.	F	Mtl. 3	Bos. 2	Maurice Richard	5:45	Mtl.
Mar. 28/59	Tor.	SF	Tor. 3	Bos. 2	Gerry Ehman	5:02	Tor.
Mar. 31/59	Tor.	SF	Tor. 3	Bos. 2	Frank Mahovlich	11:21	Tor.
Apr. 14/59	Tor.	F	Tor. 3	Mtl. 2	Dick Duff	10:06	Mtl.
Mar. 26/60	Mtl.	SF	Mtl. 4	Chi. 3	Doug Harvey	8:38	Mtl.
Mar. 27/60	Det.	SF	Tor. 5	Det. 4	Frank Mahovlich	43:00	Tor.
Mar. 29/60	Det.	SF	Det. 2	Tor. 1	Gerry Melnyk	1:54	Tor.
Mar. 22/61	Tor.	SF	Tor. 3	Det. 2	George Armstrong	24:51	Det.
Mar. 26/61	Chi.	SF	Chi. 2	Mtl. 1	Murray Balfour	52:12	Chi.
Apr. 5/62	Tor.	SF	Tor. 3	NYR 2	Red Kelly	24:23	Tor.
Apr. 2/64	Det.	SF	Chi. 3	Det. 2	Murray Balfour	8:21	Det.
Apr. 14/64	Tor.	F	Det. 3	Tor. 2	Larry Jeffrey	7:52	Tor.
Apr. 23/64	Det.	F	Tor. 4	Det. 3	Bobby Baun	1:43	Tor.
Apr. 6/65	Tor.	SF	Tor. 3	Mtl. 2	Dave Keon	4:17	Mtl.
Apr. 13/65	Tor.	SF	Mtl. 4	Tor. 3	Claude Provost	16:33	Mtl.
May 5/66	Det.	F	Mtl. 3	Det. 2	Henri Richard	2:20	Mtl.
Apr. 13/67	NY	SF	Mtl. 2	NYR 1	John Ferguson	6:28	Mtl.
Apr. 25/67	Tor.	F	Tor. 3	Mtl. 2	Bob Pulford	28:26	Tor.
Apr. 10/68	St. L.	QF	St. L. 3	Phi. 2	Larry Keenan	24:10	St. L.
Apr. 16/68	St. L.	QF	Phi. 2	St. L. 1	Don Blackburn	31:38	St. L.
Apr. 16/68	Min.	QF	Min. 4	L.A. 3	Milan Marcetta	9:11	Min.
Apr. 22/68	Min.	SF	Min. 3	St. L. 2	Parker MacDonald	3:41	St. L.
Apr. 27/68	St. L.	SF	St. L. 4	Min. 3	Gary Sabourin	1:32	St. L.
Apr. 28/68	Mtl.	SF	Mtl. 4	Chi. 3	Jacques Lemaire	2:14	Mtl.
Apr. 29/68	St. L.	SF	St. L. 3	Min. 2	Bill McCreary	17:27	St. L.
May 3/68	St. L.	SF	St. L. 2	Min. 1	Ron Schock	22:50	St. L.
May 5/68	St. L.	F	Mtl. 3	St. L. 2	Jacques Lemaire	1:41	Mtl.
May 9/68	Mtl.	F	Mtl. 4	St. L. 3	Bobby Rousseau	1:13	Mtl.
Apr. 2/69	Oak.	QF	L.A. 5	Oak. 4	Ted Irvine	0:19	L.A.
Apr. 10/69	Mtl.	SF	Mtl. 3	Bos. 2	Ralph Backstrom	0:42	Mtl.
Apr. 13/69	Mtl.	SF	Mtl. 4	Bos. 3	Mickey Redmond	4:55	Mtl.
Apr. 24/69	Bos.	SF	Mtl. 2	Bos. 1	Jean Beliveau	31:28	Mtl.
Apr. 12/70	Oak.	QF	Pit. 3	Oak. 2	Michel Briere	8:28	Pit.
May 10/70	Bos.	F	Bos. 4	St. L. 3	Bobby Orr	0:40	Bos.
Apr. 15/71	Tor.	QF	NYR 2	Tor. 1	Bob Nevin	9:07	NYR
Apr. 18/71	Chi.	SF	NYR 2	Chi. 1	Pete Stemkowski	1:37	Chi.
Apr. 27/71	Chi.	SF	Chi. 3	NYR 2	Bobby Hull	6:35	Chi.
Apr. 29/71	NY	SF	NYR 3	Chi. 2	Pete Stemkowski	41:29	Chi.
May 4/71	Chi.	F	Chi. 2	Mtl. 1	Jim Pappin	21:11	Mtl.
Apr. 6/72	Bos.	OF	Tor. 4	Bos. 3	Jim Harrison	2:58	Bos.
Apr. 6/72	Min.	QF	Min. 6	St. L. 5	Bill Goldsworthy	1:36	St. L.
Apr. 9/72	Pit.	QF	Chi. 6	Pit. 5	Pit Martin	0:12	Chi.
Apr. 16/72	Min.	QF	St. L. 2	Min. 1	Kevin O'Shea	10:07	St. L.
Apr. 01/73	Mtl.	QF	Buf. 3	Mtl. 2	Reńe Robert	9:18	Mtl.
Apr. 10/73	Phi.	QF	Phi. 3	Min. 2	Gary Dornhoefer	8:35	Phi.
Apr. 14/73	Mtl.	SF	Phi. 5	Mtl. 4	Rick MacLeish	2:56	Mtl.
Apr. 17/73	Mtl.	SF	Mtl. 4	Phi. 3	Larry Robinson	6:45	Mtl.
Apr. 14/74	Tor.	QF	Bos. 4	Tor. 3	Ken Hodge	1:27	Bos.
Apr. 14/74	Atl.	QF	Phi. 4	Atl. 3	Dave Schultz	5:40	Phi.
Apr. 16/74	Mtl.	QF	NYR 3	Mtl. 2	Ron Harris	4:07	NYR
Apr. 23/74	Chi.	SF	Chi. 4	Bos. 3	Jim Pappin	3:48	Bos.
Apr. 28/74	NY	SF	NYR 2	Phi. 1	Rod Gilbert	4:20	Phi.
May 9/74	Bos.	F	Phi. 3	Bos. 2	Bobby Clarke	12:01	Phi.
Apr. 8/75	L.A.	PR	L.A. 3	Tor. 2	Mike Murphy	8:53	Tor.
Apr. 10/75	Tor.	PR	Tor. 3	L.A. 2	Blaine Stoughton	10:19	Tor.
Apr. 10/75	Chi.	PR	Chi. 4	Bos. 3	Ivan Boldirev	7:33	Chi.
Apr. 11/75	NY	PR	NYI 4	NYR 3	Jean-Paul Parise	0:11	NYI
Apr. 19/75	Tor.	QF	Phi. 4	Tor. 3	Andre Dupont	1:45	Phi.
Apr. 17/75	Chi.	QF	Chi. 5	Buf. 4	Stan Mikita	2:31	Buf.
Apr. 22/75	Mtl.	QF	Mtl. 5	Van. 4	Guy Lafleur	17:06	Mtl.
May 1/75	Phi.	SF	Phi. 5	NYI 4	Bobby Clarke	2:56	Phi.
May 7/75	NYI	SF	NYI 4	Phi. 3	Jude Drouin	1:53	Phi.
Apr. 27/75	Buf.	SF	Buf. 6	Mtl. 5	Danny Gare	4:42	Buf.
May 6/75	Buf.	SF	Buf. 5	Mtl. 4	Rene Robert	5:56	Buf.
May 20/75	Buf.	F	Buf. 5	Phi. 4	Rene Robert	18:29	Phi.
Apr. 8/76	Buf.	PR	Buf. 3	St. L. 2	Danny Gare	11:43	Buf.
Apr. 9/76	Buf.	PR	Buf. 2	St. L. 1	Don Luce	14:27	Buf.
Apr. 13/76	Bos.	QF	L.A. 3	Bos. 2	Butch Goring	0:27	Bos.
Apr. 13/76	Buf.	QF	Buf. 3	NYI 2	Danny Gare	14:04	NYI
Apr. 22/76	L.A.	QF	L.A. 4	Bos. 3	Butch Goring	18:28	Bos.

Date	City	Series	Score		Scorer	Overtime	Series Winner
Apr. 29/76	Phi.	SF	Phi. 2	Bos. 1	Reggie Leach	13:38	Phi.
Apr. 15/77	Tor.	QF	Phi. 4	Tor. 3	Rick MacLeish	2:55	Phi.
Apr. 17/77	Tor.	QF	Phi. 6	Tor. 5	Reggie Leach	19:10	Phi.
Apr. 24/77	Phi.	SF	Bos. 4	Phi. 3	Rick Middleton	2:57	Bos.
Apr. 26/77	Phi.	SF	Bos. 5	Phi. 4	Terry O'Reilly	30:07	Bos.
May 3/77	Mtl.	SF	NYI 4	Mtl. 3	Billy Harris	3:58	Mtl.
May 14/77	Bos.	F	Mtl. 2	Bos. 1	Jacques Lemaire	4:32	Mtl.
Apr. 11/78	Phi.	PR	Phi. 3	Col. 2	Mel Bridgman	0:23	Phi.
Apr. 13/78	NY	PR	NYR 4	Buf. 3	Don Murdoch	1:37	Buf.
Apr. 19/78	Bos.	QF	Bos. 4	Chi. 3	Terry O'Reilly	1:50	Bos.
Apr. 19/78	NYI	QF	NYI 3	Tor. 2	Mike Bossy	2:50	Tor.
Apr. 21/78	Chi.	QF	Bos. 4	Chi. 3	Peter McNab	10:17	Bos.
Apr. 25/78	NYI	QF	NYI 2	Tor. 1	Bob Nystrom	8:02	Tor.
Apr. 29/78	NYI	QF	Tor. 2	NYI 1	Lanny McDonald	4:13	Tor.
May 2/78	Bos.	SF	Bos. 3	Phi. 2	Rick Middleton	1:43	Bos.
May 16/78	Mtl.	F	Mtl. 3	Bos. 2	Guy Lafleur	13:09	Mtl.
May 21/78	Bos.	F	Bos. 4	Mtl. 3	Bobby Schmautz	6:22	Mtl.
Apr. 12/79	L.A.	PR	NYR 2	L.A. 1	Phil Esposito	6:11	NYR
Apr. 14/79	Buf.	PR	Pit. 4	Buf. 3	George Ferguson	0:47	Pit.
Apr. 16/79	Phi.	QF	Phi. 3	NYR 2	Ken Linseman	0:44	NYR
Apr. 18/79	NYI	QF	NYI 1	Chi. 0	Mike Bossy	2:31	NYI
Apr. 21/79	Tor.	QF	Mtl. 4	Tor. 3	Cam Connor	25:25	Mtl.
Apr. 22/79	Tor.	QF	Mtl. 5	Tor. 4	Larry Robinson	4:14	Mtl.
Apr. 28/79	NYI	SF	NYI 4	NYR 3	Denis Potvin	8:02	NYR
May 3/79	NY	SF	NYI 3	NYR 2	Bob Nystrom	3:40	NYR
May 3/79	Bos.	SF	Bos. 4	Mtl. 3	Jean Ratelle	3:46	Mtl.
May 10/79	Mtl.	SF	Mtl. 5	Bos. 4	Yvon Lambert	9:33	Mtl.
May 19/79	NY	F	Mtl. 4	NYR 3	Serge Savard	7:25	Mtl.
Apr. 8/80	NY	PR	NYR 2	Atl. 1	Steve Vickers	0:33	NYR
Apr. 8/80	Phi.	PR	Phi. 4	Edm. 3	Bobby Clarke	8:06	Phi.
Apr. 8/80	Chi.	PR	Chi. 3	St. L. 2	Doug Lecuyer	12:34	Chi.
Apr. 11/80	Hfd.	PR	Mtl. 4	Hfd. 3	Yvon Lambert	0:29	Mtl.
Apr. 11/80	Tor.	PR	Min. 4	Tor. 3	Al MacAdam	0:32	Min.
Apr. 11/80	L.A.	PR	NYI 4	L.A. 3	Ken Morrow	6:55	NYI
Apr. 11/80	Edm.	PR	Phi. 3	Edm. 2	Ken Linseman	23:56	Phi.
Apr. 16/80	Bos.	QF	NYI 2	Bos. 1	Clark Gillies	1:02	NYI
Apr. 17/80	Bos.	QF	NYI 5	Bos. 4	Bob Bourne	1:24	NYI
Apr. 21/80	NYI	QF	Bos. 4	NYI 3	Terry O'Reilly	17:13	NYI
May 1/80	Buf.	SF	NYI 2	Buf. 1	Bob Nystrom	21:20	NYI
May 13/80	Phi.	F	NYI 4	Phi. 3	Denis Potvin	4:07	NYI
May 24/80	NYI	F	NYI 5	Phi. 4	Bob Nystrom	7:11	NYI
Apr. 8/81	Buf.	PR	Buf. 3	Van. 2	Alan Haworth	5:00	Buf.
Apr. 8/81	Bos.	PR	Min. 5	Bos. 4	Steve Payne	3:34	Min.
Apr. 11/81	Chi.	PR	Cgy. 5	Chi. 4	Willi Plett	35:17	Cgy.
Apr. 12/81	Que.	PR	Que. 4	Phi. 3	Dale Hunter	:37	Phi.
Apr. 14/81	St. L.	PR	St. L. 4	Pit. 3	Mike Crombeen	25:16	St. L.
Apr. 16/81	Buf.	QF	Min. 4	Buf. 3	Steve Payne	0:22	Min.
Apr. 20/81	Min.	QF	Buf. 5	Min. 4	Craig Ramsay	16:32	Min.
Apr. 20/81	Edm.	QF	NYI 5	Edm. 4	Ken Morrow	5:41	NYI
Apr. 7/82	Min.	DSF	Chi. 3	Min. 2	Greg Fox	3:34	Chi.
Apr. 8/82	Edm.	DSF	Edm. 3	L.A. 2	Wayne Gretzky	6:20	L.A.
Apr. 8/82	Van.	DSF	Van. 2	Cgy. 1	Dave Williams	14:20	Van.
Apr. 10/82	Pit.	DSF	Pit. 2	NYI 1	Rick Kehoe	4:14	NYI
Apr. 10/82	L.A.	DSF	L.A. 6	Edm. 5	Daryl Evans	2:35	L.A.
Apr. 13/82	Mtl.	DSF	Que. 3	Mtl. 2	Dale Hunter	0:22	Que.
Apr. 13/82	NY	DSF	NYI 4	Pit. 3	John Tonelli	6:19	NYI
Apr. 16/82	Van.	DF	L.A. 3	Van. 2	Steve Bozek	4:33	Van.
Apr. 18/82	Que.	DF	Que. 3	Bos. 2	Wilf Paiement	11:44	Que.
Apr. 18/82	NY	DF	NYI 4	NYR 3	Bryan Trottier	3:00	NYI
Apr. 18/82	L.A.	DF	Van. 4	L.A. 3	Colin Campbell	1:23	Van.
Apr. 21/82	St. L.	DF	St. L. 3	Chi. 2	Bernie Federko	3:28	Chi.
Apr. 23/82	Que.	DF	Bos. 6	Que. 5	Peter McNab	10:54	Que.
Apr. 27/82	Chi.	CF	Van. 2	Chi. 1	Jim Nill	28:58	Van.
May 1/82	Que.	CF	NYI 5	Que. 4	Wayne Merrick	16:52	NYI
May 8/82	NYI	F	NYI 6	Van. 5	Mike Bossy	19:58	NYI
Apr. 5/83	Bos.	DSF	Bos. 4	Que. 3	Barry Pederson	1:46	Bos.
Apr. 6/83	Cgy.	DSF	Cgy. 4	Van. 3	Eddy Beers	12:27	Cgy.
Apr. 7/83	Min.	DSF	Min. 5	Tor. 4	Bobby Smith	5:03	Min.
Apr. 10/83	Tor.	DSF	Min. 5	Tor. 4	Dino Ciccarelli	8:05	Min.
Apr. 10/83	Van.	DSF	Cgy. 4	Van. 3	Greg Meredith	1:06	Cgy.
Apr. 18/83	Min.	DF	Chi. 4	Min. 3	Rich Preston	10:34	Chi.
Apr. 24/83	Bos.	DF	Bos. 3	Buf. 2	Brad Park	1:52	Bos.
Apr. 5/84	Edm.	DSF	Edm. 5	Wpg. 4	Randy Gregg	0:21	Edm.
Apr. 7/84	Det.	DSF	St. L. 4	Det. 3	Mark Reeds	37:07	St. L.
Apr. 8/84	Det.	DSF	St. L. 3	Det. 2	Jorgen Pettersson	2:42	St. L.
Apr. 10/84	NYI	DSF	NYI 3	NYR 2	Ken Morrow	8:56	NYI
Apr. 13/84	Min.	DF	St. L. 4	Min. 3	Doug Gilmour	16:16	Min.
Apr. 13/84	Edm.	DF	Cgy. 6	Edm. 5	Carey Wilson	3:42	Edm.
Apr. 13/84	NYI	DF	NYI 5	Wsh. 4	Anders Kallur	7:35	NYI
Apr. 16/84	Mtl.	DF	Que. 4	Mtl. 3	Bo Berglund	3:00	Mtl.
Apr. 20/84	Cgy.	DF	Cgy. 5	Edm. 4	Lanny McDonald	1:04	Edm.
Apr. 22/84	Min.	DF	Min. 4	St. L. 3	Steve Payne	6:00	Min.
Apr. 10/85	Phi.	DSF	Phi. 5	NYR 4	Mark Howe	8:01	Phi.
Apr. 10/85	Wsh.	DSF	Wsh. 4	NYI 3	Alan Haworth	2:28	NYI
Apr. 10/85	Edm.	DSF	Edm. 3	L.A. 2	Lee Fogolin	3:01	Edm.
Apr. 10/85	Wpg.	DSF	Wpg. 5	Cgy. 4	Brian Mullen	7:56	Wpg.
Apr. 11/85	Wsh.	DSF	Wsh. 2	NYI 1	Mike Gartner	21:23	NYI
Apr. 13/85	L.A.	DSF	Edm. 4	L.A. 3	Glenn Anderson	0:46	Edm.
Apr. 18/85	Mtl.	DF	Que. 2	Mtl. 1	Mark Kumpel	12:23	Que.
Apr. 23/85	Que.	DF	Que. 7	Mtl. 6	Dale Hunter	18:36	Que.
May 2/85	Mtl.	DF	Que. 3	Mtl. 2	Peter Stastny	2:22	Que.
Apr. 25/85	Min.	DF	Chi. 7	Min. 6	Darryl Sutter	21:57	Chi.
Apr. 28/85	Chi.	DF	Min. 5	Chi. 4	Dennis Maruk	1:14	Chi.
Apr. 30/85	Min.	DF	Chi. 6	Min. 5	Darryl Sutter	15:41	Chi.
May 5/85	Que.	CF	Que. 2	Phi. 1	Peter Stastny	6:20	Phi.
Apr. 9/86	Que.	DSF	Hfd. 3	Que. 2	Sylvain Turgeon	2:36	Hfd.
Apr. 12/86	Wpg.	DSF	Cgy. 4	Wpg. 3	Lanny McDonald	8:25	Cgy.
Apr. 17/86	Wsh.	DF	NYR 4	Wsh. 3	Brian MacLellan	1:16	NYR
Apr. 20/86	Edm.	DF	Edm. 6	Cgy. 5	Glenn Anderson	1:04	Cgy.
Apr. 23/86	Hfd.	DF	Hfd. 2	Mtl. 1	Kevin Dineen	1:07	Mtl.
Apr. 23/86	NYR	DF	NYR 6	Wsh. 5	Bob Brooke	2:40	NYR
Apr. 26/86	St L.	DF	St L. 4	Tor. 3	Mark Reeds	7:11	St L.
Apr. 29/86	Mtl.	DF	Mtl. 2	Hfd. 1	Claude Lemieux	5:55	Mtl.
May 5/86	NYR	CF	Mtl. 4	NYR 3	Claude Lemieux	9:41	Mtl.
May 12/86	St L.	CF	St L. 6	Cgy. 5	Doug Wickenheiser	7:30	Cgy.
May 18/86	Cgy.	F	Mtl. 3	Cgy. 2	Brian Skrudland	0:09	Mtl.
Apr. 8/87	Hfd.	DSF	Hfd. 3	Que. 2	Paul MacDermid	2:20	Que.
Apr. 9/87	Mtl.	DSF	Mtl. 4	Bos. 3	Mats Naslund	2:38	Mtl.
Apr. 9/87	St. L.	DSF	Tor. 3	St. L. 2	Rick Lanz	10:17	Tor.
Apr. 11/87	Wpg.	DSF	Cgy. 3	Wpg. 2	Mike Bullard	3:53	Wpg.
Apr. 11/87	Chi.	DSF	Det. 4	Chi. 3	Shawn Burr	4:51	Det.
Apr. 16/87	Que.	DSF	Que. 5	Hfd. 4	Peter Stastny	6:05	Que.
Apr. 18/87	Wsh.	DSF	NYI 3	Wsh. 2	Pat LaFontaine	68:47	NYI
Apr. 21/87	Edm.	DF	Edm. 3	Wpg. 2	Glenn Anderson	0:36	Edm.
Apr. 26/87	Que.	DF	Mtl. 3	Que. 2	Mats Naslund	5:30	Mtl.
Apr. 27/87	Tor.	DF	Tor. 3	Det. 2	Mike Allison	9:31	Det.
May 4/87	Phi.	CF	Phi. 4	Mtl. 3	Ilkka Sinislao	9:11	Phi.
May 20/87	Edm.	F	Edm. 3	Phi. 2	Jari Kurri	6:50	Edm.
Apr. 6/88	NYI	DSF	NYI 4	N.J. 3	Pat LaFontaine	6:11	N.J.
Apr. 10/88	Phi.	DSF	Phi. 5	Wsh. 4	Murray Craven	1:18	Wsh.
Apr. 10/88	N.J.	DSF	NYI 5	N.J. 4	Brent Sutter	15:07	N.J.
Apr. 10/88	Buf.	DSF	Buf. 6	Bos. 5	John Tucker	5:32	Bos.
Apr. 12/88	Det.	DSF	Tor. 6	Det. 5	Ed Olczyk	0:34	Det.
Apr. 16/88	Wsh.	DSF	Wsh. 5	Phi. 4	Dale Hunter	5:57	Wsh.
Apr. 21/88	Cgy.	DF	Edm. 5	Cgy. 4	Wayne Gretzky	7:54	Edm.
May 4/88	Bos.	CF	N.J. 3	Bos. 2	Doug Brown	17:46	Bos.
May 9/88	Det.	CF	Edm. 4	Det. 3	Jari Kurri	11:02	Edm.
Apr. 5/89	St. L.	DSF	St. L. 4	Min. 3	Brett Hull	11:55	St. L.
Apr. 5/89	Cgy.	DSF	Van. 4	Cgy. 3	Paul Reinhart	2:47	Cgy.
Apr. 6/89	St. L.	DSF	St. L. 4	Min. 3	Rick Meagher	5:30	St. L.
Apr. 6/89	Det.	DSF	Chi. 5	Det. 4	Duane Sutter	14:36	Chi.
Apr. 8/89	Hfd.	DSF	Mtl. 5	Hfd. 4	Stephane Richer	5:01	Mtl.
Apr. 8/89	Phi.	DSF	Wsh. 4	Phi. 3	Kelly Miller	0:51	Phi.
Apr. 9/89	Hfd.	DSF	Mtl. 4	Hfd. 3	Russ Courtnall	15:12	Mtl.
Apr. 15/89	Cgy.	DSF	Cgy. 4	Van. 3	Joel Otto	19:21	Cgy.
Apr. 18/89	Cgy.	DF	Cgy. 4	L.A. 3	Doug Gilmour	7:47	Cgy.
Apr. 19/89	Mtl.	DF	Mtl. 3	Bos. 2	Bobby Smith	12:24	Mtl.
Apr. 20/89	St. L.	DF	St. L. 5	Chi. 4	Tony Hrkac	33:49	Chi.
Apr. 21/89	Phi.	DF	Pit. 4	Phi. 3	Phil Bourque	12:08	Phi.
May 8/89	Chi.	CF	Cgy. 2	Chi. 1	Al MacInnis	15:05	Cgy.
May 9/89	Mtl.	CF	Phi. 2	Mtl. 1	Dave Poulin	5:02	Mtl.
May 19/89	Mtl.	F	Mtl. 4	Cgy. 3	Ryan Walter	38:08	Cgy.
Apr. 5/90	N.J.	DSF	Wsh. 5	N.J. 4	Dino Ciccarelli	5:34	Wsh.
Apr. 6/90	Edm.	DSF	Edm. 3	Wpg. 2	Mark Lamb	4:21	Edm.
Apr. 8/90	Tor.	DSF	St. L. 6	Tor. 5	Sergio Momesso	6:04	St. L.
Apr. 8/90	L.A.	DSF	L.A. 2	Cgy. 1	Tony Granato	8:37	L.A.
Apr. 9/90	Mtl.	DSF	Mtl. 2	Buf. 1	Brian Skrudland	12:35	Mtl.
Apr. 9/90	NYI	DSF	NYI 4	NYR 3	Brent Sutter	20:59	NYR
Apr. 10/90	Wpg.	DSF	Wpg. 4	Edm. 3	Dave Ellett	21:08	Edm.
Apr. 14/90	L.A.	DSF	L.A. 4	Cgy. 3	Mike Krushelnyski	23:14	L.A.
Apr. 15/90	Hfd.	DSF	Hfd. 3	Bos. 2	Kevin Dineen	12:30	Bos.
Apr. 21/90	Bos.	DF	Bos. 5	Mtl. 4	Garry Galley	3:42	Bos.
Apr. 24/90	L.A.	DF	Edm. 6	L.A. 5	Joe Murphy	4:42	Edm.
Apr. 25/90	Wsh.	DF	Wsh. 4	NYR 3	Rod Langway	0:34	Wsh.
Apr. 27/90	NYR	DF	Wsh. 2	NYR 1	John Druce	6:48	Wsh.
May 15/90	Bos.	F	Edm. 3	Bos. 2	Petr Klima	55:13	Edm.
Apr. 4/91	Chi.	DSF	Min. 4	Chi. 3	Brian Propp	4:14	Min.
Apr. 5/91	Pit.	DSF	Pit. 5	N.J. 4	Jaromir Jagr	8:52	Pit.
Apr. 6/91	L.A.	DSF	L.A. 3	Van. 2	Wayne Gretzky	11:08	L.A.
Apr. 8/91	Van.	DSF	Van. 2	L.A. 1	Cliff Ronning	3:12	L.A.
Apr. 11/91	NYR	DSF	Wsh. 5	NYR 4	Dino Ciccarelli	6:44	Wsh.
Apr. 11/91	Mtl.	DSF	Mtl. 4	Buf. 3	Russ Courtnall	5:56	Mtl.
Apr. 14/91	Edm.	DSF	Cgy. 2	Edm. 1	Theo Fleury	4:40	Edm.
Apr. 16/91	Cgy.	DSF	Edm. 5	Cgy. 4	Esa Tikkanen	6:58	Edm.
Apr. 18/91	L.A.	DF	L.A. 4	Edm. 3	Luc Robitaille	2:13	Edm.
Apr. 19/91	Bos.	DF	Mtl. 4	Bos. 3	Stephane Richer	0:27	Bos.
Apr. 19/91	Pit.	DF	Pit. 7	Wsh. 6	Kevin Stevens	8:10	Pit.
Apr. 20/91	L.A.	DF	Edm. 4	L.A. 3	Petr Klima	24:48	Edm.
Apr. 22/91	Edm.	DF	Edm. 4	L.A. 3	Esa Tikkanen	20:48	Edm.
Apr. 27/91	Mtl.	DF	Mtl. 3	Bos. 2	Shayne Corson	17:47	Bos.
Apr. 28/91	Edm.	DF	Edm. 4	L.A. 3	Craig MacTavish	16:57	Edm.
May 3/91	Bos.	CF	Bos. 5	Pit. 4	Vladimir Ruzicka	8:14	Pit.

Ten Longest Overtime Games

Date	City	Series	Score		Scorer	Overtime	Series Winner
Mar. 24/36	Mtl.	SF	Det. 1	Mtl. M. 0	Mud Bruneteau	116:30	Det.
Apr. 3/33	Tor.	SF	Tor. 1	Bos. 0	Ken Doraty	104:46	Tor.
Mar. 23/43	Det.	SF	Tor. 3	Det. 2	Jack McLean	70:18	Det.
Mar. 28/30	Mtl.	SF	Mtl. 2	NYR 1	Gus Rivers	68:52	Mtl.
Apr. 18/87	Wsh.	DSF	NYI 3	Wsh. 2	Pat LaFontaine	68:47	NYI
Mar. 27/51	Det.	SF	Mtl. 3	Det. 2	Maurice Richard	61:09	Mtl.
Mar. 26/32	Mtl.	SF	NYR 4	Mtl. 3	Fred Cook	59:32	NYR
Mar. 21/39	NY	SF	Bos. 2	NYR 1	Mel Hill	59:25	Bos.
May 15/90	Bos.	F	Edm. 3	Bos. 2	Petr Klima	55:13	Edm.
Apr. 9/31	Mtl.	F	Chi. 3	Mtl. 2	Cy Wentworth	53:50	Mtl.

Stanley Cup Coaching Records

Coaches listed in order of total games coached in playoffs. Minimum: 65 games.

Coach	Team	Years	Series	W	L	G	W	L	T	Cups	%
Irvin, Dick	Chicago	1	3	2	1	9	5	3	1	0	.611
	Toronto	9	20	12	8	66	33	32	1	1	.508
	Montreal	14	22	11	11	115	62	53	0	3	.539
	TOTALS	24	45	25	20	190	100	88	2	4	.532
Arbour, Al	St. Louis	1	2	1	1	11	4	7	0	0	.364
	NY Islanders	13	36	27	9	176	110	66	0	4	.625
	TOTALS	14	38	28	10	187	114	73	0	4	.610
Bowman, Scott	St. Louis	4	10	6	4	52	26	26	0	0	.500
	Montreal	8	19	16	3	98	70	28	0	5	.714
	Buffalo	5	8	3	5	36	18	18	0	0	.500
	TOTALS	17	37	25	12	186	114	72	0	5	.612
Sather, Glen	Edmonton	10	27	21	6	*126	89	37	0	4	.706
Blake, Toe	Montreal	13	23	18	5	119	82	37	0	8	.689
Reay, Billy	Chicago	12	22	10	12	117	57	60	0	0	.487
Shero, Fred	Philadelphia	6	16	12	4	83	48	35	0	2	.578
	NY Rangers	2	5	3	2	25	13	12	0	0	.520
	TOTALS	8	21	15	6	108	61	47	0	2	.565
Adams, Jack	Detroit	15	27	15	12	105	52	52	1	3	.500
Francis, Emile	NY Rangers	9	14	5	9	75	34	41	0	0	.453
	St. Louis	3	4	1	3	18	6	12	0	0	.333
	TOTALS	12	18	6	12	93	40	53	0	0	.430
Keenan, Mike	Philadelphia	4	10	6	4	57	32	25	0	0	.561
	Chicago	3	7	4	3	42	21	21	0	0	.500
	TOTALS	7	17	10	7	99	53	46	0	0	.535
Imlach, Punch	Toronto	11	17	10	7	92	44	48	0	4	.478
Day, Hap	Toronto	9	14	10	4	80	49	31	0	5	.613
Johnson, Bob	Calgary	5	10	5	5	52	25	27	0	0	.481
	Pittsburgh	1	4	4	0	24	16	8	0	1	.666
	TOTALS	6	14	9	5	76	41	35	0	1	.539
Abel, Sid	Chicago	1	1	0	1	7	3	4	0	0	.429
	Detroit	8	12	4	8	69	29	40	0	0	.420
	TOTALS	9	13	4	9	76	32	44	0	0	.421
Demers, Jacques	St. Louis	3	6	3	3	33	16	17	0	0	.485
	Detroit	3	7	4	3	38	20	18	0	0	.526
	TOTALS	6	13	7	6	71	36	35	0	0	.507
Ross, Art	Boston	12	19	9	10	70	32	33	5	2	.493
Bergeron, Michel	Quebec	7	13	6	7	68	31	37	0	0	.456
Ivan, Tommy	Detroit	7	12	8	4	67	36	31	0	3	.537
Pulford, Bob	Los Angeles	4	6	2	4	26	11	15	0	0	.423
	Chicago	5	9	4	5	41	17	24	0	0	.415
	TOTALS	9	15	6	9	67	28	39	0	0	.418
Patrick, Lester	NY Rangers	12	24	14	10	65	31	26	8	2	.538

* Does not include suspended game, May 24, 1988.

Overtime Record of Current Teams

(Listed by number of OT games played)

Team	Overall GP	W	L	T	Home GP	W	L	T	Last OT Game	Road GP	W	L	T	Last OT Game
Montreal	100	54	44	2	47	30	16	1	Apr. 27/91	53	24	28	1	Apr. 19/91
Boston	83	32	48	3	39	19	19	1	May 3/91	44	13	29	2	Apr. 27/91
Toronto	75	36	38	1	48	22	25	1	Apr. 8/90	27	14	13	0	Apr. 12/88
NY Rangers	50	23	27	0	21	9	12	0	Apr. 11/91	29	14	15	0	Apr. 25/90
Detroit	47	20	27	0	29	10	19	0	Apr. 6/89	18	10	8	0	Apr. 27/87
Chicago	44	21	21	2	23	12	10	1	Apr. 4/91	21	9	11	1	Apr. 20/89
Philadelphia	34	18	16	0	13	8	5	0	Apr. 21/89	21	10	11	0	May 9/89
NY Islanders	32	25	7	0	14	12	2	0	Apr. 9/90	18	13	5	0	Apr. 10/88
St. Louis	27	16	11	0	13	11	2	0	Apr. 20/89	14	5	9	0	Apr. 8/90
Edmonton	25	16	9	0	13	9	4	0	Apr. 28/91	12	7	5	0	Apr. 20/91
Minnesota	24	11	13	0	12	5	7	0	Apr. 30/85	12	6	6	0	Apr. 4/91
*Calgary	24	11	13	0	9	4	5	0	Apr. 16/91	15	7	8	0	Apr. 14/91
Los Angeles	24	10	14	0	13	7	6	0	Apr. 20/91	11	3	8	0	Apr. 28/91
Buffalo	18	10	8	0	11	8	3	0	Apr. 10/88	7	2	5	0	Apr. 11/91
Quebec	15	9	6	0	9	5	4	0	Apr. 26/87	6	4	2	0	Apr. 8/87
Washington	14	8	6	0	6	4	2	0	Apr. 25/90	8	4	4	0	Apr. 19/91
Vancouver	13	5	8	0	4	2	2	0	Apr. 8/91	9	3	6	0	Apr. 6/91
Pittsburgh	10	6	4	0	4	3	1	0	Apr. 19/91	6	3	3	0	May 3/91
Hartford	9	4	5	0	6	3	3	0	Apr. 15/90	3	1	2	0	Apr. 16/87
Winnipeg	7	3	4	0	4	2	2	0	Apr. 10/90	3	1	2	0	Apr. 6/90
**New Jersey	6	1	5	0	2	0	2	0	Apr. 5/90	4	1	3	0	Apr. 5/91

* Totals include those of Atlanta 1974-80.
** Totals include those of Kansas City and Colorado 1975-82.

Penalty Shots in Stanley Cup Playoff Games

Date	Player	Goaltender	Scored
Mar. 25/37	Lionel Conacher, Mtl. Maroons	Tiny Thompson, Boston	No
Apr. 15/37	Alex Shibicky, NY Rangers	Earl Robertson, Detroit	No
Apr. 13/44	Virgil Johnson, Chicago	Bill Durnan, Montreal	No
Apr. 9/68	Wayne Connelly, Minnesota	Terry Sawchuk, Los Angeles	Yes
Apr. 27/68	Jim Roberts, St. Louis	Cesare Maniago, Minnesota	No
May 16/71	Frank Mahovlich, Montreal	Tony Esposito, Chicago	No
May 7/75	Bill Barber, Philadelphia	Glenn Resch, NY Islanders	No
Apr. 20/79	Mike Walton, Chicago	Glenn Resch, NY Islanders	No
Apr. 9/81	Peter McNab, Boston	Don Beaupre, Minnesota	No
Apr. 17/81	Anders Hedberg, NY Rangers	Mike Liut, St. Louis	Yes
Apr. 9/83	Denis Potvin, NY Islanders	Pat Riggin, Washington	No
Apr. 28/84	Wayne Gretzky, Edmonton	Don Beaupre, Minnesota	Yes
May 1/84	Mats Naslund, Montreal	Bill Smith, NY Islanders	No
Apr. 14/85	Bob Carpenter, Washington	Bill Smith, NY Islanders	No
May 28/85	Ron Sutter, Philadelphia	Grant Fuhr, Edmonton	No
May 30/85	Dave Poulin, Philadelphia	Grant Fuhr, Edmonton	No
Apr. 9/88	John Tucker, Buffalo	Andy Moog, Boston	Yes
Apr. 9/88	Petr Klima, Detroit	Allan Bester, Toronto	Yes
Apr. 8/89	Neal Broten, Minnesota	Greg Millen, St. Louis	No
Apr. 4/90	Al MacInnis, Calgary	Kelly Hrudey, Los Angeles	Yes
Apr. 5/90	Randy Wood, NY Islanders	Mike Richter, NY Rangers	No
May 3/90	Kelly Miller, Washington	Andy Moog, Boston	No
May 18/90	Petr Klima, Edmonton	Rejean Lemelin, Boston	No
Apr. 6/91	Basil McRae, Minnesota	Ed Belfour, Chicago	Yes
Apr. 10/91	Steve Duchesne, Los Angeles	Kirk McLean, Vancouver	Yes

* Game was decided in overtime, but shot taken during regulation time.

Mike Keenan, who has been behind the bench for 56 playoff games, has never missed post-season play as an NHL coach.

1991-92 Player Register

Note: The 1991-1992 Player Register lists forwards and defensemen only. Goaltenders are listed separately. The Player Register lists every skater who appeared in an NHL game in the 1990-91 season, every skater drafted in the first three rounds of the 1990 and 1991 Entry Drafts and other players on NHL Reserve Lists. Trades and roster changes are current as of August 15, 1991.

Abbreviations: A – assists; **G** – goals; **GP** – games played; **Lea** – league; **PIM** – penalties in minutes; **TP** – total points; * – league-leading total.

Pronunciations courtesy of the NHL Broadcasters' Association

Goaltender Register begins on page 391.

LEAGUES:

ACHL	Atlantic Coast Hockey League
AHL	American Hockey League
AJHL	Alberta Junior Hockey League
AUAA	Atlantic Universities Athletic Association
BCJHL	British Columbia Junior Hockey League
CCHA	Central Collegiate Hockey Association
CHL	Central Hockey League
CIAU	Canadian Interuniversity Athletic Union
COJHL	Central Ontario Junior Hockey League
CWUAA	Canada West Universities Athletic Association
ECAC	Eastern Collegiate Athletic Association
ECHL	East Coast Hockey League
G.N.	Great Northern
GPAC	Great Plains Athletic Conference
H.E.	Hockey East
HS	High School
IHL	International Hockey League
Jr.	Junior
MJHA	(New York) Metropolitan Junior Hockey Association
MJHL	Manitoba Junior Hockey League
NAHL	North American Hockey League
NCAA	National Collegiate Athletic Association
NHL	**National Hockey League**
OHA	Ontario Hockey Association
OHL	Ontario Hockey League
OPJHL	Ontario Provincial Junior Hockey League
OUAA	Ontario Universities Athletic Association
QJHL	Quebec Junior Hockey League
QMJHL	Quebec Major Junior Hockey League
SJHL	Saskatchewan Junior Hockey League
Sr.	Senior
SOHL	Southern Ontario Hockey League
USHL	United States Hockey League
WCHA	Western Collegiate Hockey Association
WHA	World Hockey Association
WHL	Western Hockey League

AALTONEN, PETRI　　(AL-tuh-nehn)

Center. Shoots left. 5'10", 185 lbs.　Born, Tampere, Finland, May 31, 1970.
(Quebec's 4th choice, 45th overall, in 1988 Entry Draft).

				Regular Season					Playoffs			
Season	Club	Lea	GP	G	A	TP	PIM	GP	G	A	TP	PIM
1986-87	HIFK	Fin. Jr.	30	8	5	13	24	4	0	0	0	0
1987-88	HIFK	Fin. Jr.	34	37	20	57	25	....	....	....	....	....
1988-89	HIFK	Fin.	2	0	0	0	0	....	....	....	....	....
1989-90	HIFK	Fin.	3	0	0	0	0	....	....	....	....	....
1990-91	HIFK	Fin.	43	6	9	15	12	3	1	1	2	0

ACTON, KEITH EDWARD

Center. Shoots left. 5'8", 170 lbs.　Born, Stouffville, Ont., April 15, 1958.
(Montreal's 8th choice, 103rd overall, in 1978 Amateur Draft).

				Regular Season					Playoffs			
Season	Club	Lea	GP	G	A	TP	PIM	GP	G	A	TP	PIM
1976-77	Peterborough	OHA	65	52	69	121	93	4	1	4	5	6
1977-78	Peterborough	OHA	68	42	86	128	52	21	10	8	18	16
1978-79	Nova Scotia	AHL	79	15	26	41	22	10	4	2	6	4
1979-80	**Montreal**	**NHL**	**2**	**0**	**1**	**1**	**0**	....	....	....	....	....
a	Nova Scotia	AHL	75	45	53	98	38	6	1	2	3	8
1980-81	**Montreal**	**NHL**	**61**	**15**	**24**	**39**	**74**	**2**	**0**	**0**	**0**	**6**
1981-82	**Montreal**	**NHL**	**78**	**36**	**52**	**88**	**88**	**5**	**0**	**4**	**4**	**16**
1982-83	**Montreal**	**NHL**	**78**	**24**	**26**	**50**	**63**	**3**	**0**	**0**	**0**	**0**
1983-84	**Montreal**	**NHL**	**9**	**3**	**7**	**10**	**4**	....	....	....	....	....
	Minnesota	NHL	62	17	38	55	60	15	4	7	11	12
1984-85	**Minnesota**	**NHL**	**78**	**20**	**38**	**58**	**90**	**9**	**4**	**4**	**8**	**6**
1985-86	**Minnesota**	**NHL**	**79**	**26**	**32**	**58**	**100**	**5**	**0**	**3**	**6**	
1986-87	**Minnesota**	**NHL**	**78**	**16**	**29**	**45**	**56**	....	....	....	....	....
1987-88	**Minnesota**	**NHL**	**46**	**8**	**11**	**19**	**74**	....	....	....	....	....
	Edmonton	NHL	26	3	6	9	21	7	2	0	2	16
1988-89	**Edmonton**	**NHL**	**46**	**11**	**15**	**26**	**47**	....	....	....	....	....
	Philadelphia	NHL	25	3	10	13	64	16	2	3	5	18
1989-90	**Philadelphia**	**NHL**	**69**	**13**	**14**	**27**	**80**	....	....	....	....	....
1990-91	**Philadelphia**	**NHL**	**76**	**14**	**23**	**37**	**131**	....	....	....	....	....
	NHL Totals		**813**	**209**	**326**	**535**	**952**	**62**	**12**	**21**	**33**	**80**

a AHL Second All-Star Team (1980)
Played in NHL All-Star Game (1982)

Traded to **Minnesota** by **Montreal** with Mark Napier and Toronto's third round choice (Ken Hodge) in 1984 Entry Draft — Montreal's property via earlier transaction — for Bobby Smith, October 28, 1983. Traded to **Edmonton** by **Minnesota** for Moe Mantha, January 22, 1988. Traded to **Philadelphia** by **Edmonton** with Edmonton's fifth-round choice (Dimitri Yushkevich) in 1991 Entry Draft for Dave Brown, February 7, 1989. Traded to **Winnipeg** by **Philadelphia** with Pete Peeters for Shawn Cronin and Toronto's fifth round choice (Juha Ylonen) — previously acquired by Philadelphia in 1991 Entry Draft, September 28, 1989. Traded to **Philadelphia** by **Winnipeg** with Pete Peeters for future considerations, October 3, 1989.

ADAMS, GREG

Left wing. Shoots left. 6'3", 190 lbs.　Born, Nelson, B.C., August 1, 1963.

				Regular Season					Playoffs			
Season	Club	Lea	GP	G	A	TP	PIM	GP	G	A	TP	PIM
1982-83	N. Arizona	NCAA	29	14	21	35	19	....	....	....	....	....
1983-84	N. Arizona	NCAA	26	44	29	73	24	....	....	....	....	....
1984-85	**New Jersey**	**NHL**	**36**	**12**	**9**	**21**	**14**	....	....	....	....	....
	Maine	AHL	41	15	20	35	12	11	3	4	7	0
1985-86	**New Jersey**	**NHL**	**78**	**35**	**42**	**77**	**30**	....	....	....	....	....
1986-87	**New Jersey**	**NHL**	**72**	**20**	**27**	**47**	**19**	....	....	....	....	....
1987-88	**Vancouver**	**NHL**	**80**	**36**	**40**	**76**	**30**	....	....	....	....	....
1988-89	**Vancouver**	**NHL**	**61**	**19**	**14**	**33**	**24**	**7**	**2**	**3**	**5**	**2**
1989-90	**Vancouver**	**NHL**	**65**	**30**	**20**	**50**	**18**	....	....	....	....	....
1990-91	**Vancouver**	**NHL**	**55**	**21**	**24**	**45**	**10**	**5**	**0**	**0**	**0**	**2**
	NHL Totals		**447**	**173**	**176**	**349**	**145**	**12**	**2**	**3**	**5**	**4**

Played in NHL All-Star Game (1988)
Signed as a free agent by **New Jersey**, June 25, 1984. Traded to **Vancouver** by **New Jersey** with Kirk McLean for Patrik Sundstrom and Vancouver's fourth round choice (Matt Ruchty) in 1988 Entry Draft, September 10, 1987.

AGNEW, JIM

Defense. Shoots left. 6'1", 190 lbs.　Born, Hartney, Man., March 21, 1966.
(Vancouver's 10th choice, 157th overall, in 1984 Entry Draft).

				Regular Season					Playoffs			
Season	Club	Lea	GP	G	A	TP	PIM	GP	G	A	TP	PIM
1982-83	Brandon	WHL	14	1	1	2	9	....	....	....	....	....
1983-84	Brandon	WHL	71	6	17	23	107	12	0	1	1	39
1984-85	Brandon	WHL	19	3	15	18	82	....	....	....	....	....
	Portland	WHL	44	5	24	29	223	6	0	2	2	44
1985-86a	Portland	WHL	70	6	30	36	286	9	0	1	1	48
1986-87	**Vancouver**	**NHL**	**4**	**0**	**0**	**0**	**0**	....	....	....	....	....
	Fredericton	AHL	67	0	5	5	261	....	....	....	....	....
1987-88	**Vancouver**	**NHL**	**10**	**0**	**1**	**1**	**16**	....	....	....	....	....
	Fredericton	AHL	63	2	8	10	188	14	0	2	2	43
1988-89	Milwaukee	IHL	47	2	10	12	181	11	0	2	2	34
1989-90	**Vancouver**	**NHL**	**7**	**0**	**0**	**0**	**36**	....	....	....	....	....
b	Milwaukee	IHL	51	4	10	14	238	....	....	....	....	....
1990-91	**Vancouver**	**NHL**	**20**	**0**	**0**	**0**	**81**	....	....	....	....	....
	Milwaukee	IHL	3	0	0	0	33	....	....	....	....	....
	NHL Totals		**41**	**0**	**1**	**1**	**133**					

a WHL First All-Star Team, West Division (1986)
b IHL Second All-Star Team (1990)

AHOLA, PETER

Defense. Shoots left. 6'3": 205 lbs.　Born, Espoo, Finland, May 14, 1968

				Regular Season					Playoffs			
Season	Club	Lea	GP	G	A	TP	PIM	GP	G	A	TP	PIM
1989-90	Boston U.	H.E.	43	3	20	23	65	....	....	....	....	....
1990-91a	Boston U.	H.E.	39	12	24	36	88	....	....	....	....	....

Signed as a free agent by **Los Angeles**, April 5, 1991.

a NCAA East Second All-American Team (1991)

AITKEN, BRAD (ATE-kin)

Left wing. Shoots left. 6'2", 200 lbs. Born, Scarborough, Ont., October 30, 1967.
(Pittsburgh's 3rd choice, 46th overall, in 1986 Entry Draft).

			Regular Season					Playoffs				
Season	Club	Lea	GP	G	A	TP	PIM	GP	G	A	TP	PIM
1985-86	Peterborough	OHL	48	9	28	37	77	....	....	....	....	....
	S.S. Marie	OHL	20	8	19	27	11	....	....	....	....	....
1986-87	S.S. Marie	OHL	52	27	38	65	86	4	1	2	3	5
1987-88	**Pittsburgh**	**NHL**	**5**	**1**	**1**	**2**	**0**	....	....	....	....	....
	Muskegon	IHL	74	32	31	63	128	1	0	0	0	0
1988-89	Muskegon	IHL	74	35	30	65	139	13	5	5	10	75
1989-90	Muskegon	IHL	46	10	23	33	172	....	....	....	....	....
	Phoenix	IHL	8	2	1	3	18	....	....	....	....	....
	Fort Wayne	IHL	13	5	2	7	0	5	2	1	3	12
1990-91	**Pittsburgh**	**NHL**	**6**	**0**	**1**	**1**	**25**	....	....	....	....	....
	Muskegon	IHL	44	14	17	31	143	....	....	....	....	....
	Kansas City	IHL	6	4	6	10	2	....	....	....	....	....
	Edmonton	**NHL**	**3**	**0**	**1**	**1**	**0**	....	....	....	....	....
	Cape Breton	AHL	6	2	3	5	17	3	0	2	2	6
	NHL Totals		**14**	**1**	**3**	**4**	**25**	....	....	....	....	....

Traded to **Edmonton** by **Pittsburgh** for Kim Issel, March 5, 1991. Signed as a free agent by **Toronto**, July 30, 1991.

AITKEN, DAVID (ATE-kin)

Left wing. Shoots left. 6', 200 lbs. Born, St. Stephen, N.B., September 27, 1967.
(Edmonton's 1st choice, 20th overall, in 1989 Supplemental Draft).

			Regular Season					Playoffs				
Season	Club	Lea	GP	G	A	TP	PIM	GP	G	A	TP	PIM
1986-87	N. Hampshire	H.E.	37	19	9	28	10	....	....	....	....	....
1987-88	N. Hampshire	H.E.	29	7	15	22	24	....	....	....	....	....
1988-89	N. Hampshire	H.E.	34	14	17	31	30	....	....	....	....	....
1989-90	N. Hampshire	H.E.	39	12	19	31	37	....	....	....	....	....
1990-91	Richmond	ECHL	64	28	52	80	29	4	1	3	4	0

AIVAZOFF, MICAH (AY-va-zoff)

Center. Shoots left. 6', 192 lbs. Born, Powell River, B.C., May 4, 1969.
(Los Angeles' 6th choice, 109th overall, in 1988 Entry Draft).

			Regular Season					Playoffs				
Season	Club	Lea	GP	G	A	TP	PIM	GP	G	A	TP	PIM
1986-87	Victoria	WHL	72	18	39	57	112	5	1	0	1	2
1987-88	Victoria	WHL	69	26	57	83	79	8	3	4	7	14
1988-89	Victoria	WHL	70	35	65	100	136	8	5	7	12	2
1989-90	New Haven	AHL	77	20	39	59	71	....	....	....	....	....
1990-91	New Haven	AHL	79	11	29	40	84	....	....	....	....	....

AKERBLOM, MARKUS (OHK-uhr-blum)

Left wing. Shoots left. 6', 189 lbs. Born, Ostersund, Sweden, November 22, 1969.
(Winnipeg's 8th choice, 127th overall, in 1988 Entry Draft).

			Regular Season					Playoffs				
Season	Club	Lea	GP	G	A	TP	PIM	GP	G	A	TP	PIM
1986-87	Ostersund	Swe.2	32	14	18	32	....	....	....	....	....	....
1987-88	Bjorkloven	Swe.	32	6	8	14	....	....	....	....	....	....
1988-89	Bjorkloven	Swe.	21	6	10	16	....	....	....	....	....	....
1989-90	Bjorkloven	Swe.2	15	10	10	20	....	....	....	....	....	....
1990-91	Bjorkloven	Swe.2	22	7	4	11	16	....	....	....	....	....

AKERSTROM, ROGER (OHK-uhr-struhm)

Defense. Shoots left. 5'11", 189 lbs. Born, Lulea, Sweden, April 5, 1967.
(Vancouver's 8th choice, 170th overall, in 1988 Entry Draft).

			Regular Season					Playoffs				
Season	Club	Lea	GP	G	A	TP	PIM	GP	G	A	TP	PIM
1987-88	Lulea	Swe.	34	4	3	7	28	....	....	....	....	....
1988-89	Lulea	Swe.	38	6	12	18	32	....	....	....	....	....
1989-90	Lulea	Swe.	36	5	10	15	44	5	3	2	5	2
1990-91	Lulea	Swe.	38	2	10	12	38	....	....	....	....	....

ALATALO, MIKA

Left wing. Shoots left. 5'11", 185 lbs. Born, Oulu, Finland, August 11, 1971.
(Winnipeg's 11th choice, 203rd overall, in 1990 Entry Draft).

			Regular Season					Playoffs				
Season	Club	Lea	GP	G	A	TP	PIM	GP	G	A	TP	PIM
1989-90	KooKoo	Fin.	41	3	5	8	22	....	....	....	....	....
1990-91	Lukko	Fin.	39	10	1	11	10	....	....	....	....	....

ALBELIN, TOMMY (AL-buh-LEEN)

Defense. Shoots left. 6'1", 190 lbs. Born, Stockholm, Sweden, May 21, 1964.
(Quebec's 7th choice, 152nd overall, in 1983 Entry Draft).

			Regular Season					Playoffs				
Season	Club	Lea	GP	G	A	TP	PIM	GP	G	A	TP	PIM
1982-83	Djurgarden	Swe.	19	2	5	7	4	6	1	0	1	2
1983-84	Djurgarden	Swe.	30	9	5	14	26	4	0	1	1	2
1984-85	Djurgarden	Swe.	32	9	8	17	22	8	2	1	3	4
1985-86	Djurgarden	Swe.	35	4	8	12	26	....	....	....	....	....
1986-87	Djurgarden	Swe.	33	7	5	12	49	2	0	0	0	0
1987-88	**Quebec**	**NHL**	**60**	**3**	**23**	**26**	**47**	....	....	....	....	....
1988-89	**Quebec**	**NHL**	**14**	**2**	**4**	**6**	**27**	....	....	....	....	....
	Halifax	AHL	8	2	5	7	4	....	....	....	....	....
	New Jersey	**NHL**	**46**	**7**	**24**	**31**	**40**	....	....	....	....	....
1989-90	**New Jersey**	**NHL**	**68**	**6**	**23**	**29**	**63**	....	....	....	....	....
1990-91	**New Jersey**	**NHL**	**47**	**2**	**12**	**14**	**44**	**3**	**0**	**1**	**1**	**2**
	Utica	AHL	14	4	2	6	10	....	....	....	....	....
	NHL Totals		**235**	**20**	**86**	**106**	**221**	**3**	**0**	**1**	**1**	**2**

Traded to **New Jersey** by **Quebec** for New Jersey's fourth-round choice (Niclas Andersson) in 1989 Entry Draft, December 12, 1988.

ALLAIN, RICK

Defense. Shoots left. 6', 190 lbs. Born, Guelph, Ont., May 20, 1969.
(Boston's 8th choice, 164th overall, in 1989 Entry Draft).

			Regular Season					Playoffs				
Season	Club	Lea	GP	G	A	TP	PIM	GP	G	A	TP	PIM
1986-87	Kitchener	OHL	18	0	0	0	32	....	....	....	....	....
1987-88	Kitchener	OHL	45	4	9	13	267	....	....	....	....	....
1988-89	Kitchener	OHL	62	2	16	18	245	5	0	0	0	10
1989-90	Kitchener	OHL	55	5	16	21	156	17	0	4	4	46
1990-91	Maine	AHL	13	0	1	1	33	....	....	....	....	....
	Johnstown	ECHL	36	2	12	14	100	10	0	0	0	50

ALLEN, PETER

Defense. Shoots right. 6'2", 185 lbs. Born, Calgary, Alta., March 6, 1970.
(Boston's 1st choice, 24th overall, in 1991 Supplemental Draft).

			Regular Season					Playoffs				
Season	Club	Lea	GP	G	A	TP	PIM	GP	G	A	TP	PIM
1989-90	Yale	ECAC	26	2	4	6	16	....	....	....	....	....
1990-91	Yale	ECAC	17	0	6	6	14	....	....	....	....	....

ALLISON, SCOTT

Center. Shoots left. 6'4", 194 lbs. Born, St. Boniface, Man., April 22, 1972.
(Edmonton's 1st choice, 17th overall, in 1990 Entry Draft).

			Regular Season					Playoffs				
Season	Club	Lea	GP	G	A	TP	PIM	GP	G	A	TP	PIM
1988-89	Prince Albert	WHL	51	6	9	15	37	3	0	0	0	0
1989-90	Prince Albert	WHL	66	22	16	38	73	11	1	4	5	8
1990-91	Prince Albert	WHL	30	5	5	10	57	....	....	....	....	....
	Portland	WHL	44	5	17	22	105	....	....	....	....	....

AMONTE, ANTHONY (TONY)

Right wing. Shoots right. 6', 180 lbs. Born, Hingham, MA, August 2, 1970.
(NY Rangers' 3rd choice, 68th overall, in 1988 Entry Draft).

			Regular Season					Playoffs				
Season	Club	Lea	GP	G	A	TP	PIM	GP	G	A	TP	PIM
1989-90	Boston U.	H.E.	41	25	33	58	52	....	....	....	....	....
1990-91ab	Boston U.	H.E.	38	31	37	68	82	....	....	....	....	....
	NY Rangers	**NHL**	....	....	....	....	....	**2**	**0**	**2**	**2**	**2**
	NHL Totals		....	....	....	....	....	**2**	**0**	**2**	**2**	**2**

a Hockey East Second All-Star Team (1991)
b NCAA Final Four All-Tournament Team (1991)

AMUNDSON, DARRIN

Center. Shoots right. 6'2", 175 lbs. Born, Duluth, MN, November 9, 1968.
(Winnipeg's 5th choice, 100th overall, in 1987 Entry Draft).

			Regular Season					Playoffs				
Season	Club	Lea	GP	G	A	TP	PIM	GP	G	A	TP	PIM
1987-88	Minn.-Duluth	WCHA	16	0	6	6	4	....	....	....	....	....
1988-89	Minn.-Duluth	WCHA	37	5	11	16	23	....	....	....	....	....
1989-90	Minn.-Duluth	WCHA	23	5	6	11	12	....	....	....	....	....
1990-91	Minn.-Duluth	WCHA	37	11	7	18	16	....	....	....	....	....

ANDERSON, GLENN CHRIS

Right wing. Shoots left. 6'1", 190 lbs. Born, Vancouver, B.C., October 2, 1960.
(Edmonton's 3rd choice, 69th overall, in 1979 Entry Draft).

			Regular Season					Playoffs				
Season	Club	Lea	GP	G	A	TP	PIM	GP	G	A	TP	PIM
1978-79	U. of Denver	WCHA	40	26	29	55	58	....	....	....	....	....
1979-80	Seattle	WHL	7	5	5	10	4	....	....	....	....	....
	Cdn. Olympic	...	49	21	21	42	46	....	....	....	....	....
1980-81	**Edmonton**	**NHL**	**58**	**30**	**23**	**53**	**24**	**9**	**5**	**7**	**12**	**12**
1981-82	**Edmonton**	**NHL**	**80**	**38**	**67**	**105**	**71**	**5**	**2**	**5**	**7**	**8**
1982-83	**Edmonton**	**NHL**	**72**	**48**	**56**	**104**	**70**	**16**	**10**	**10**	**20**	**32**
1983-84	**Edmonton**	**NHL**	**80**	**54**	**45**	**99**	**65**	**19**	**6**	**11**	**17**	**33**
1984-85	**Edmonton**	**NHL**	**80**	**42**	**39**	**81**	**69**	**18**	**10**	**16**	**26**	**38**
1985-86	**Edmonton**	**NHL**	**72**	**54**	**48**	**102**	**90**	**10**	**8**	**3**	**11**	**14**
1986-87	**Edmonton**	**NHL**	**80**	**35**	**38**	**73**	**65**	**21**	**14**	**13**	**27**	**59**
1987-88	**Edmonton**	**NHL**	**80**	**38**	**50**	**88**	**58**	**19**	**9**	**16**	**25**	**49**
1988-89	**Edmonton**	**NHL**	**79**	**16**	**48**	**64**	**93**	**7**	**1**	**2**	**3**	**8**
1989-90	**Edmonton**	**NHL**	**73**	**34**	**38**	**72**	**107**	**22**	**10**	**12**	**22**	**20**
1990-91	**Edmonton**	**NHL**	**74**	**24**	**31**	**55**	**59**	**18**	**6**	**7**	**13**	**41**
	NHL Totals		**828**	**413**	**483**	**896**	**771**	**164**	**81**	**102**	**183**	**314**

Played in NHL All-Star Game (1984-86, 1988)

ANDERSON, JOHN MURRAY

Right wing. Shoots left. 5'11", 200 lbs. Born, Toronto, Ont., March 28, 1957.
(Toronto's 1st choice, 11th overall, in 1977 Amateur Draft).

			Regular Season					Playoffs				
Season	Club	Lea	GP	G	A	TP	PIM	GP	G	A	TP	PIM
1973-74	Toronto	OHA	38	22	22	44	6	....	....	....	....	....
1974-75	Toronto	OHA	70	49	64	113	31	22	16	14	30	14
1975-76	Toronto	OHA	39	26	25	51	19	10	7	4	11	7
1976-77a	Toronto	OHA	64	57	62	119	42	6	3	5	8	0
1977-78	**Toronto**	**NHL**	**17**	**1**	**2**	**3**	**2**	**2**	**0**	**0**	**0**	**0**
	Dallas	CHL	55	22	23	45	6	13	*11	8	*19	2
1978-79	**Toronto**	**NHL**	**71**	**15**	**11**	**26**	**10**	**6**	**0**	**2**	**2**	**0**
1979-80	**Toronto**	**NHL**	**74**	**25**	**28**	**53**	**22**	**3**	**1**	**1**	**2**	**0**
1980-81	**Toronto**	**NHL**	**75**	**17**	**26**	**43**	**31**	**2**	**0**	**0**	**0**	**0**
1981-82	**Toronto**	**NHL**	**69**	**31**	**26**	**57**	**30**	....	....	....	....	....
1982-83	**Toronto**	**NHL**	**80**	**31**	**49**	**80**	**24**	**4**	**2**	**4**	**6**	**0**
1983-84	**Toronto**	**NHL**	**73**	**37**	**31**	**68**	**22**	....	....	....	....	....
1984-85	**Toronto**	**NHL**	**75**	**32**	**31**	**63**	**27**	....	....	....	....	....
1985-86	**Quebec**	**NHL**	**65**	**21**	**28**	**49**	**26**	....	....	....	....	....
	Hartford	**NHL**	**14**	**8**	**17**	**25**	**2**	**10**	**5**	**8**	**13**	**0**
1986-87	**Hartford**	**NHL**	**76**	**31**	**44**	**75**	**19**	**6**	**1**	**2**	**3**	**0**
1987-88	**Hartford**	**NHL**	**63**	**17**	**32**	**49**	**20**	....	....	....	....	....
1988-89	**Hartford**	**NHL**	**62**	**16**	**24**	**40**	**28**	**4**	**0**	**1**	**1**	**2**
1989-90	Binghamton	AHL	3	1	1	2	0	....	....	....	....	....
	Milano	Italy	9	7	9	16	18	....	....	....	....	....
1990-91	Fort Wayne	IHL	63	40	43	83	24	1	3	0	3	0
	NHL Totals		**814**	**282**	**349**	**631**	**263**	**37**	**9**	**18**	**27**	**2**

a OHA First All-Star Team (1977)

Traded to **Quebec** by **Toronto** for Brad Maxwell, August 21, 1985. Traded to **Hartford** by **Quebec** for Risto Siltanen, March 8, 1986.

ANDERSON, PERRY LYNN

Left wing. Shoots left. 6'1", 225 lbs. Born, Barrie, Ont., October 14, 1961.
(St. Louis' 5th choice, 117th overall, in 1980 Entry Draft).

			Regular Season					Playoffs				
Season	Club	Lea	GP	G	A	TP	PIM	GP	G	A	TP	PIM
1978-79	Kingston	OHA	61	6	13	19	85	5	2	1	3	6
1979-80	Kingston	OHA	63	17	16	33	52	3	0	0	0	6
1980-81	Kingston	OHA	38	9	13	22	118	....	....	....	....	....
	Brantford	OHA	31	8	27	35	43	6	4	2	6	15
1981-82	**St. Louis**	**NHL**	**5**	**1**	**2**	**3**	**0**	**10**	**2**	**0**	**2**	**4**
	Salt Lake	CHL	71	32	32	64	117	2	1	0	1	2
1982-83	**St. Louis**	**NHL**	**18**	**5**	**2**	**7**	**14**	....	....	....	....	....
	Salt Lake	CHL	57	23	19	42	140	....	....	....	....	....
1983-84	**St. Louis**	**NHL**	**50**	**7**	**5**	**12**	**195**	**9**	**0**	**0**	**0**	**27**
	Montana	CHL	8	7	3	10	34	....	....	....	....	....
1984-85	**St. Louis**	**NHL**	**71**	**9**	**9**	**18**	**146**	**3**	**0**	**0**	**0**	**7**
1985-86	**New Jersey**	**NHL**	**51**	**7**	**12**	**19**	**91**	....	....	....	....	....
1986-87	**New Jersey**	**NHL**	**57**	**10**	**9**	**19**	**107**	....	....	....	....	....
	Maine	AHL	9	5	4	9	42	....	....	....	....	....
1987-88	**New Jersey**	**NHL**	**60**	**4**	**6**	**10**	**222**	**10**	**0**	**0**	**0**	**113**
1988-89	**New Jersey**	**NHL**	**39**	**3**	**6**	**9**	**128**	....	....	....	....	....
1989-90	Utica	AHL	71	13	17	30	128	5	0	0	0	24
1990-91	**New Jersey**	**NHL**	**1**	**0**	**0**	**0**	**5**	**4**	**0**	**1**	**1**	**10**
	Utica	AHL	68	19	14	33	245	....	....	....	....	....
	NHL Totals		**352**	**46**	**51**	**97**	**908**	**36**	**2**	**1**	**3**	**161**

Traded to **New Jersey** by **St. Louis** for Rick Meagher and New Jersey's 12th round choice (Bill Butler) in 1986 Entry Draft, August 29, 1985. Signed as a free agent by **San Jose**, July 8, 1991.

ANDERSON, SHAWN

Defense. Shoots left. 6'1", 200 lbs. Born, Montreal, Que., February 7, 1968.
(Buffalo's 1st choice, 5th overall, in 1986 Entry Draft).

			Regular Season					Playoffs				
Season	Club	Lea	GP	G	A	TP	PIM	GP	G	A	TP	PIM
1985-86	Maine	H.E.	16	5	8	13	22	....	....	....	....	....
	Cdn. Olympic	...	49	4	14	18	38	....	....	....	....	....
1986-87	**Buffalo**	**NHL**	**41**	**2**	**11**	**13**	**23**	....	....	....	....	....
	Rochester	AHL	15	2	5	7	11	....	....	....	....	....
1987-88	**Buffalo**	**NHL**	**23**	**1**	**2**	**3**	**17**	....	....	....	....	....
	Rochester	AHL	22	5	16	21	19	6	0	0	0	0
1988-89	**Buffalo**	**NHL**	**33**	**2**	**10**	**12**	**18**	**5**	**0**	**1**	**1**	**4**
	Rochester	AHL	31	5	14	19	24	....	....	....	....	....
1989-90	**Buffalo**	**NHL**	**16**	**1**	**3**	**4**	**8**	....	....	....	....	....
	Rochester	AHL	39	2	16	18	41	9	1	0	1	4
1990-91	**Quebec**	**NHL**	**31**	**3**	**10**	**13**	**21**	....	....	....	....	....
	Halifax	AHL	4	0	1	1	2	....	....	....	....	....
	NHL Totals		**144**	**9**	**36**	**45**	**87**	**5**	**0**	**1**	**1**	**4**

Traded to **Washington** by **Buffalo** for Bill Houlder, September 30, 1990. Claimed by **Quebec** in NHL Waiver Draft, October 1, 1990.

ANDERSSON, BO MIKAEL (AN-duhr-suhn)

Left wing. Shoots left. 5'11", 185 lbs. Born, Malmo, Sweden, May 10, 1966.
(Buffalo's 1st choice, 18th overall, in 1984 Entry Draft).

			Regular Season					Playoffs				
Season	Club	Lea	GP	G	A	TP	PIM	GP	G	A	TP	PIM
1982-83	V. Frolunda	Swe.	1	1	0	1	0	....	....	....	....	....
1983-84	V. Frolunda	Swe.	18	0	3	6	....	....	....	....	....	....
1984-85	V. Frolunda	Swe.	30	16	11	27	18	6	3	2	5	2
1985-86	**Buffalo**	**NHL**	**32**	**1**	**9**	**10**	**4**	....	....	....	....	....
	Rochester	AHL	20	10	4	14	6	....	....	....	....	....
1986-87	**Buffalo**	**NHL**	**16**	**0**	**3**	**3**	**0**	....	....	....	....	....
1986-87	Rochester	AHL	42	6	20	26	14	9	1	2	3	2
1987-88	**Buffalo**	**NHL**	**37**	**3**	**20**	**23**	**10**	**1**	**1**	**0**	**1**	**0**
	Rochester	AHL	35	12	24	36	16	....	....	....	....	....
1988-89	**Buffalo**	**NHL**	**14**	**0**	**1**	**1**	**4**	....	....	....	....	....
	Rochester	AHL	56	18	33	51	12	....	....	....	....	....
1989-90	**Hartford**	**NHL**	**50**	**13**	**24**	**37**	**6**	**5**	**0**	**3**	**3**	**2**
1990-91	**Hartford**	**NHL**	**41**	**4**	**7**	**11**	**8**	....	....	....	....	....
	Springfield	AHL	26	7	22	29	10	18	*10	8	18	12
	NHL Totals		**190**	**21**	**64**	**85**	**32**	**6**	**1**	**3**	**4**	**2**

Claimed by **Hartford** in NHL Waiver Draft, October 2, 1989.

ANDERSSON, ERIK

Right wing. Shoots left. 6'2", 187 lbs. Born, Stockholm, Sweden, August 19, 1971.
(Los Angeles' 5th choice, 112th overall, in 1990 Entry Draft).

			Regular Season					Playoffs				
Season	Club	Lea	GP	G	A	TP	PIM	GP	G	A	TP	PIM
1989-90	Danderyd	Swe.	30	14	5	19	16	....	....	....	....	....
1990-91	AIK	Swe.	32	1	1	2	10	....	....	....	....	....

ANDERSSON, HENRIK

Defense. Shoots left. 6'4", 187 lbs. Born, Vasteras, Sweden, January 19, 1970.
(Winnipeg's 9th choice, 161st overall, in 1990 Entry Draft).

			Regular Season					Playoffs				
Season	Club	Lea	GP	G	A	TP	PIM	GP	G	A	TP	PIM
1989-90	Vasteras	Swe.	36	2	2	4	10	....	....	....	....	....
1990-91	Vasteras	Swe.	34	2	5	7	10	....	....	....	....	....

ANDERSSON, NICLAS (AN-duhr-suhn)

Left wing. Shoots left. 5'8", 169 lbs. Born, Kungalv, Sweden, May 20, 1971.
(Quebec's 5th choice, 68th overall, in 1989 Entry Draft).

			Regular Season					Playoffs				
Season	Club	Lea	GP	G	A	TP	PIM	GP	G	A	TP	PIM
1987-88	V. Frolunda	Swe.	15	5	5	10	....	....	....	....	....	....
1988-89	V. Frolunda	Swe.	30	13	24	37	....	....	....	....	....	....
1989-90	V. Frolunda	Swe.	38	10	21	31	14	....	....	....	....	....
1990-91	V. Frolunda	Swe.	22	6	10	16	16	....	....	....	....	....

ANDISON, TRENT L.

Left wing. Shoots left. 5'10", 190 lbs. Born, Bracebridge, Ont., May 30, 1969.
(Minnesota's 9th choice, 232nd overall, in 1988 Entry Draft).

			Regular Season					Playoffs				
Season	Club	Lea	GP	G	A	TP	PIM	GP	G	A	TP	PIM
1987-88	Cornell	ECAC	27	21	17	38	22	....	....	....	....	....
1988-89	Cornell	ECAC	28	17	16	33	28	....	....	....	....	....
1989-90	Cornell	ECAC	25	8	16	24	12	....	....	....	....	....
1990-91	Cornell	ECAC	32	22	26	48	42	....	....	....	....	....

ANDREYCHUK, DAVID (DAVE)

Left wing. Shoots right. 6'3", 220 lbs. Born, Hamilton, Ont., September 29, 1963.
(Buffalo's 3rd choice, 16th overall, in 1982 Entry Draft).

			Regular Season					Playoffs				
Season	Club	Lea	GP	G	A	TP	PIM	GP	G	A	TP	PIM
1980-81	Oshawa	OHA	67	22	22	44	80	10	3	2	5	20
1981-82	Oshawa	OHL	67	57	43	100	71	3	1	4	5	16
1982-83	**Buffalo**	**NHL**	**43**	**14**	**23**	**37**	**16**	**4**	**1**	**0**	**1**	**4**
	Oshawa	OHL	14	8	24	32	6	....	....	....	....	....
1983-84	**Buffalo**	**NHL**	**78**	**38**	**42**	**80**	**42**	**2**	**0**	**1**	**1**	**2**
1984-85	**Buffalo**	**NHL**	**64**	**31**	**30**	**61**	**54**	**5**	**4**	**2**	**6**	**4**
1985-86	**Buffalo**	**NHL**	**80**	**36**	**51**	**87**	**61**	....	....	....	....	....
1986-87	**Buffalo**	**NHL**	**77**	**25**	**48**	**73**	**46**	....	....	....	....	....
1987-88	**Buffalo**	**NHL**	**80**	**30**	**48**	**78**	**112**	**6**	**2**	**4**	**6**	**0**
1988-89	**Buffalo**	**NHL**	**56**	**28**	**24**	**52**	**40**	**5**	**0**	**3**	**3**	**0**
1989-90	**Buffalo**	**NHL**	**73**	**40**	**42**	**82**	**42**	**6**	**2**	**5**	**7**	**2**
1990-91	**Buffalo**	**NHL**	**80**	**36**	**33**	**69**	**32**	**6**	**2**	**2**	**4**	**8**
	NHL Totals		**631**	**278**	**341**	**619**	**445**	**34**	**11**	**17**	**28**	**20**

Played in NHL All-Star Game (1990)

ANDRUSAK, GREG

Defense. Shoots right. 6'1", 183 lbs. Born, Cranbrook, B.C., November 14, 1969.
(Pittsburgh's 5th choice, 88th overall, in 1988 Entry Draft).

			Regular Season					Playoffs				
Season	Club	Lea	GP	G	A	TP	PIM	GP	G	A	TP	PIM
1987-88	Minn.-Duluth	WCHA	37	4	5	9	42	....	....	....	....	....
1988-89	Minn.-Duluth	WCHA	35	4	8	12	74	....	....	....	....	....
	Cdn. Olympic	...	2	0	0	0	0	....	....	....	....	....
1989-90	Minn.-Duluth	WCHA	35	5	29	34	74	....	....	....	....	....
1990-91	Cdn. National	...	53	4	11	15	34	....	....	....	....	....

ANGLEHART, SERGE

Defense. Shoots right. 6'2", 190 lbs. Born, Hull, Que., April 18, 1970.
(Detroit's 2nd choice, 38th overall, in 1988 Entry Draft).

			Regular Season					Playoffs				
Season	Club	Lea	GP	G	A	TP	PIM	GP	G	A	TP	PIM
1987-88	Drummondville	QMJHL	44	1	8	9	122	17	0	3	3	19
1988-89	Drummondville	QMJHL	39	6	15	21	89	3	0	0	0	37
	Adirondack	AHL	....	....	....	....	....	2	0	0	0	0
1989-90	Laval	QMJHL	48	2	19	21	131	10	1	6	7	69
1990-91	Adirondack	AHL	52	3	8	11	113	....	....	....	....	....

ANTOSKI, SHAWN

Left wing. Shoots left. 6'4", 235 lbs. Born, Brantford, Ont., March 25, 1970.
(Vancouver's 2nd choice, 18th overall, in 1990 Entry Draft).

			Regular Season					Playoffs				
Season	Club	Lea	GP	G	A	TP	PIM	GP	G	A	TP	PIM
1987-88	North Bay	OHL	52	3	4	7	163	....	....	....	....	....
1988-89	North Bay	OHL	57	6	21	27	201	9	5	3	8	24
1989-90	North Bay	OHL	59	25	31	56	201	5	1	2	3	17
1990-91	**Vancouver**	**NHL**	**2**	**0**	**0**	**0**	**0**	....	....	....	....	....
	Milwaukee	IHL	62	17	7	24	330	5	1	2	3	10
	NHL Totals		**2**	**0**	**0**	**0**	**0**	....	....	....	....	....

ARCHIBALD, DAVE

Center/Left wing. Shoots left. 6'1", 190 lbs. Born, Chilliwack, B.C., April 14, 1969.
(Minnesota's 1st choice, 6th overall, in 1987 Entry Draft).

			Regular Season					Playoffs				
Season	Club	Lea	GP	G	A	TP	PIM	GP	G	A	TP	PIM
1984-85	Portland	WHL	47	7	11	18	10	3	0	2	2	0
1985-86	Portland	WHL	70	29	35	64	56	15	6	7	13	11
1986-87	Portland	WHL	65	50	57	107	40	20	10	18	28	11
1987-88	**Minnesota**	**NHL**	**78**	**13**	**20**	**33**	**26**	....	....	....	....	....
1988-89	**Minnesota**	**NHL**	**72**	**14**	**19**	**33**	**14**	**5**	**0**	**1**	**1**	**0**
1989-90	**Minnesota**	**NHL**	**12**	**1**	**5**	**6**	**6**	....	....	....	....	....
	NY Rangers	**NHL**	**19**	**2**	**3**	**5**	**6**	....	....	....	....	....
	Flint	IHL	41	14	38	52	16	4	3	2	5	0
1990-91	Cdn. National	...	29	19	12	31	20	....	....	....	....	....
	NHL Totals		**181**	**30**	**47**	**77**	**52**	**5**	**0**	**1**	**1**	**0**

Traded to **NY Rangers** by **Minnesota** for Jayson More, November 1, 1989.

ARMSTRONG, BILL

Defense. Shoots left. 6'4", 215 lbs. Born, Richmond Hill, Ont., May 18, 1970.
(Philadelphia's 6th choice, 46th overall, in 1990 Entry Draft).

			Regular Season					Playoffs				
Season	Club	Lea	GP	G	A	TP	PIM	GP	G	A	TP	PIM
1987-88	Toronto	OHL	64	1	10	11	99	....	....	....	....	....
1988-89	Toronto	OHL	64	1	16	17	82	....	....	....	....	....
1989-90	Hamilton	OHL	18	0	2	2	38	....	....	....	....	....
	Niagara Falls	OHL	4	0	1	1	13	....	....	....	....	....
	Oshawa	OHL	41	2	8	10	115	17	0	7	7	39
1990-91	Hershey	AHL	56	1	9	10	117	....	....	....	....	....

ARMSTRONG, TIM

Center. Shoots right. 5'11", 170 lbs. Born, Toronto, Ont., May 12, 1967
(Toronto's 11th choice, 211th overall, in 1985 Entry Draft).

			Regular Season					Playoffs				
Season	Club	Lea	GP	G	A	TP	PIM	GP	G	A	TP	PIM
1984-85	Toronto	OHL	63	17	45	62	28	5	5	2	7	0
1985-86	Toronto	OHL	64	35	69	104	36	4	1	3	4	9
1986-87	Newmarket	AHL	5	3	0	3	2	....	....	....	....	....
	Toronto	OHL	66	29	55	84	61	....	....	....	....	....
1987-88	Newmarket	AHL	78	19	40	59	26	....	....	....	....	....
1988-89	**Toronto**	**NHL**	**11**	**1**	**0**	**1**	**6**	....	....	....	....	....
	Newmarket	AHL	37	16	24	40	38	....	....	....	....	....
1989-90	Newmarket	AHL	63	25	37	62	24	....	....	....	....	....
1990-91	Feldkirch	Aus.	5	0	2	2	....	....	....	....	....	....
	Binghamton	AHL	56	24	32	56	37	10	1	6	7	6
	NHL Totals		**11**	**1**	**0**	**1**	**6**	....	....	....	....	....

ARMSTRONG, WILLIAM (BILL)

Left wing. Shoots left. 6'2", 195 lbs. Born, London, Ont., June 25, 1966.

			Regular Season					Playoffs				
Season	Club	Lea	GP	G	A	TP	PIM	GP	G	A	TP	PIM
1986-87	W. Michigan	CCHA	43	13	20	33	86	....	....	....	....	....
1987-88	W. Michigan	CCHA	41	22	17	39	88	....	....	....	....	....
1988-89	W. Michigan	CCHA	40	23	19	42	97	....	....	....	....	....
1989-90	Hershey	AHL	58	10	6	16	99	....	....	....	....	....
1990-91	**Philadelphia**	**NHL**	**1**	**0**	**1**	**1**	**0**	....	....	....	....	....
	Hershey	AHL	70	36	27	63	150	6	2	8	10	19
	NHL Totals		**1**	**0**	**1**	**1**	**0**	....	....	....	....	....

Signed as a free agent by **Philadelphia**, May 16, 1989.

ARNIEL, SCOTT (ar-NEEL)

Left wing. Shoots left. 6'1", 188 lbs. Born, Kingston, Ont., September 17, 1962.
(Winnipeg's 2nd choice, 22nd overall, in 1981 Entry Draft).

			Regular Season					Playoffs				
Season	Club	Lea	GP	G	A	TP	PIM	GP	G	A	TP	PIM
1980-81	Cornwall	QJHL	68	52	71	123	102	19	14	19	33	24
1981-82	**Winnipeg**	**NHL**	**17**	**1**	**8**	**9**	**14**	**3**	**0**	**0**	**0**	**0**
	Cornwall	OHL	24	18	26	44	43	....	....	....	....	....
1982-83	Winnipeg	NHL	75	13	5	18	46	2	0	0	0	0
1983-84	Winnipeg	NHL	80	21	35	56	68	2	0	0	0	5
1984-85	Winnipeg	NHL	79	22	22	44	81	8	1	2	3	9
1985-86	**Winnipeg**	**NHL**	**80**	**18**	**25**	**43**	**40**	**3**	**0**	**0**	**0**	**12**
1986-87	**Buffalo**	**NHL**	**63**	**11**	**14**	**25**	**59**	....	....	....	....	....
1987-88	**Buffalo**	**NHL**	**73**	**17**	**23**	**40**	**61**	**6**	**0**	**1**	**1**	**5**
1988-89	**Buffalo**	**NHL**	**80**	**18**	**23**	**41**	**46**	**5**	**1**	**0**	**1**	**4**
1989-90	**Buffalo**	**NHL**	**79**	**18**	**14**	**32**	**77**	**5**	**1**	**0**	**1**	**4**
1990-91	**Winnipeg**	**NHL**	**75**	**5**	**17**	**22**	**87**	....	....	....	....	....
	NHL Totals		**701**	**144**	**186**	**330**	**579**	**34**	**3**	**3**	**6**	**39**

Traded to **Buffalo** by **Winnipeg** for Gilles Hamel, June 21, 1986. Traded to **Winnipeg** by **Buffalo** with Phil Housley, Jeff Parker and Buffalo's first round choice (Keith Tkachuk) in 1990 Entry Draft for Dale Hawerchuk, Winnipeg's first round choice (Brad May) in 1990 Entry Draft and future considerations, June 16, 1990.

ASHTON, BRENT KENNETH

Left wing. Shoots left. 6'1", 210 lbs. Born, Saskatoon, Sask., May 18, 1960.
(Vancouver's 2nd choice, 26th overall, in 1979 Entry Draft).

			Regular Season					Playoffs				
Season	Club	Lea	GP	G	A	TP	PIM	GP	G	A	TP	PIM
1977-78	Saskatoon	WHL	46	38	26	64	47	....	....	....	....	....
1978-79	Saskatoon	WHL	62	64	55	119	80	11	14	4	18	5
1979-80	**Vancouver**	**NHL**	**47**	**5**	**14**	**19**	**11**	**4**	**1**	**0**	**1**	**6**
1980-81	**Vancouver**	**NHL**	**77**	**18**	**11**	**29**	**57**	**3**	**0**	**0**	**0**	**0**
1981-82	**Colorado**	**NHL**	**80**	**24**	**36**	**60**	**26**	....	....	....	....	....
1982-83	**New Jersey**	**NHL**	**76**	**14**	**19**	**33**	**47**	....	....	....	....	....
1983-84	**Minnesota**	**NHL**	**68**	**7**	**10**	**17**	**54**	**12**	**1**	**2**	**3**	**22**
1984-85	**Minnesota**	**NHL**	**29**	**4**	**7**	**11**	**15**	....	....	....	....	....
	Quebec	**NHL**	**49**	**27**	**24**	**51**	**38**	**18**	**6**	**4**	**10**	**13**
1985-86	**Quebec**	**NHL**	**77**	**26**	**32**	**58**	**64**	**3**	**2**	**1**	**3**	**9**
1986-87	**Quebec**	**NHL**	**46**	**25**	**19**	**44**	**17**	....	....	....	....	....
	Detroit	**NHL**	**35**	**15**	**16**	**31**	**22**	**16**	**4**	**9**	**13**	**6**
1987-88	**Detroit**	**NHL**	**73**	**26**	**27**	**53**	**50**	**16**	**7**	**5**	**12**	**10**
1988-89	**Winnipeg**	**NHL**	**75**	**31**	**37**	**68**	**36**	....	....	....	....	....
1989-90	**Winnipeg**	**NHL**	**79**	**22**	**34**	**56**	**37**	**7**	**3**	**1**	**4**	**2**
1990-91	**Winnipeg**	**NHL**	**61**	**12**	**24**	**36**	**58**	....	....	....	....	....
	NHL Totals		**872**	**256**	**310**	**566**	**532**	**79**	**24**	**22**	**46**	**68**

Traded to **Winnipeg** by **Vancouver** with Vancouver's fourth-round choice (Tom Martin) in the 1982 Entry Draft as compensation for Vancouver's signing of Ivan Hlinka, July 15, 1981. Traded to **Colorado** by **Winnipeg** with Winnipeg's third round choice (Dave Kasper) in 1982 Entry Draft for Lucien DeBlois, July 15, 1981. Traded to **Minnesota** by **New Jersey** for Dave Lewis, October 3, 1983. Traded to **Quebec** by **Minnesota** with Brad Maxwell for Tony McKegney and Bo Berglund, December 14, 1984. Traded to **Detroit** by **Quebec** with Gilbert Delorme and Mark Kumpel for Basil McRae, John Ogrodnick and Doug Shedden, January 17, 1987. Traded to **Winnipeg** by **Detroit** for Paul MacLean, June 13, 1988.

ASTLEY, MARK

Defense. Shoots left. 5'11", 185 lbs. Born, Calgary, Alta., March 30, 1969.
(Buffalo's 9th choice, 194th overall, in 1989 Entry Draft).

			Regular Season					Playoffs				
Season	Club	Lea	GP	G	A	TP	PIM	GP	G	A	TP	PIM
1988-89	Lake Superior	CCHA	42	3	12	15	26	....	....	....	....	....
1989-90	Lake Superior	CCHA	43	7	25	32	29	....	....	....	....	....
1990-91a	Lake Superior	CCHA	45	19	27	46	50	....	....	....	....	....

a CCHA Second All-Star Team (1991)

ATCHEYNUM, BLAIR (ATCH-uh-num)

Right wing. Shoots right. 6'2", 190 lbs. Born, Estevan, Sask., April 20, 1969.
(Hartford's 2nd choice, 52nd overall, in 1989 Entry Draft).

			Regular Season					Playoffs				
Season	Club	Lea	GP	G	A	TP	PIM	GP	G	A	TP	PIM
1985-86	Saskatoon	WHL	19	1	4	5	22	....	....	....	....	....
1986-87	Saskatoon	WHL	21	0	4	4	4	....	....	....	....	....
	Swift Current	WHL	5	2	1	3	0	....	....	....	....	....
	Moose Jaw	WHL	12	3	0	3	2	....	....	....	....	....
1987-88	Moose Jaw	WHL	60	32	16	48	52	....	....	....	....	....
1988-89a	Moose Jaw	WHL	71	70	68	138	70	7	2	5	7	13
1989-90	Binghamton	AHL	78	20	21	41	45	....	....	....	....	....
1990-91	Springfield	AHL	72	25	27	52	42	13	0	6	6	6

a WHL First All-Star Team (1989)

AUDETTE, DONALD

Right wing. Shoots right. 5'8", 177 lbs. Born, Laval, Que., September 23, 1969.
(Buffalo's 8th choice, 183rd overall, in 1989 Entry Draft).

			Regular Season					Playoffs				
Season	Club	Lea	GP	G	A	TP	PIM	GP	G	A	TP	PIM
1986-87	Laval	QMJHL	66	17	22	39	36	14	2	6	8	10
1987-88	Laval	QMJHL	63	48	61	109	56	14	7	12	19	20
1988-89a	Laval	QMJHL	70	76	85	161	123	17	17	12	29	43
1989-90bc	Rochester	AHL	70	42	46	88	78	15	9	8	17	29
	Buffalo	**NHL**	....	....	....	....	....	**2**	**0**	**0**	**0**	**0**
1990-91	**Buffalo**	**NHL**	**8**	**4**	**3**	**7**	**4**	....	....	....	....	....
	Rochester	AHL	5	4	0	4	2	....	....	....	....	....
	NHL Totals		**8**	**4**	**3**	**7**	**4**	**2**	**0**	**0**	**0**	**0**

a QMJHL First All-Star Team (1989)
b AHL First All-Star Team (1990)
c Won Dudley "Red" Garret Memorial Trophy (Top Rookie-AHL) (1990)

AVERILL, WILLIAM

Defense. Shoots right. 5'11", 175 lbs. Born, Wayland, MA, December 20, 1968.
(NY Islanders' 12th choice, 244th overall, in 1987 Entry Draft).

			Regular Season					Playoffs				
Season	Club	Lea	GP	G	A	TP	PIM	GP	G	A	TP	PIM
1987-88	Northeastern	H.E.	36	2	23	25	36	....	....	....	....	....
1988-89	Northeastern	H.E.	36	4	16	20	40	....	....	....	....	....
1989-90	Northeastern	H.E.	35	6	13	19	41	....	....	....	....	....
1990-91	Northeastern	H.E.	35	6	16	22	40	....	....	....	....	....

BABCOCK, BOBBY

Defense. Shoots left. 6'1", 222 lbs. Born, Agincourt, Ont., August 3, 1968.
(Washington's 11th choice, 208th overall, in 1986 Entry Draft).

			Regular Season					Playoffs				
Season	Club	Lea	GP	G	A	TP	PIM	GP	G	A	TP	PIM
1985-86	S.S. Marie	OHL	50	1	7	8	188	....	....	....	....	....
1986-87	S.S. Marie	OHL	62	7	8	15	243	4	0	0	0	11
1987-88	S.S. Marie	OHL	8	0	2	2	30	....	....	....	....	....
	Cornwall	OHL	42	0	16	16	120	....	....	....	....	....
1988-89	Cornwall	OHL	42	0	9	9	163	18	1	3	4	29
1989-90	Baltimore	AHL	67	0	4	4	249	7	0	0	0	23
1990-91	**Washington**	**NHL**	**1**	**0**	**0**	**0**	**0**	....	....	....	....	....
	Baltimore	AHL	38	0	3	3	112	....	....	....	....	....
	NHL Totals		**1**	**0**	**0**	**0**	**0**	....	....	....	....	....

BABE, WARREN

Left wing. Shoots left. 6'3", 200 lbs. Born, Medicine Hat, Alta., September 7, 1968
(Minnesota's 1st choice, 12th overall, in 1986 Entry Draft).

			Regular Season					Playoffs				
Season	Club	Lea	GP	G	A	TP	PIM	GP	G	A	TP	PIM
1985-86	Lethbridge	WHL	63	33	24	57	125	....	....	....	....	....
1986-87	Swift Current	WHL	16	8	12	20	19	....	....	....	....	....
	Kamloops	WHL	52	28	45	73	109	11	4	6	10	8
1987-88	**Minnesota**	**NHL**	**6**	**0**	**1**	**1**	**4**	....	....	....	....	....
	Kalamazoo	IHL	6	0	0	0	7	....	....	....	....	....
	Kamloops	WHL	32	17	19	36	73	18	5	12	17	42
1988-89	**Minnesota**	**NHL**	**14**	**2**	**3**	**5**	**19**	**2**	**0**	**0**	**0**	**0**
	Kalamazoo	IHL	62	18	24	42	102	6	1	4	5	24
1989-90			DID NOT PLAY – INJURED									
1990-91	**Minnesota**	**NHL**	**1**	**0**	**1**	**1**	**0**	....	....	....	....	....
	Kalamazoo	IHL	49	15	17	32	52	....	....	....	....	....
	NHL Totals		**21**	**2**	**5**	**7**	**23**	**2**	**0**	**0**	**0**	**0**

BABYCH, DAVID MICHAEL (DAVE) (BAB-itch)

Defense. Shoots left. 6'2", 215 lbs. Born, Edmonton, Alta., May 23, 1961.
(Winnipeg's 1st choice, 2nd overall, in 1980 Entry Draft).

			Regular Season					Playoffs				
Season	Club	Lea	GP	G	A	TP	PIM	GP	G	A	TP	PIM
1978-79	Portland	WHL	67	20	59	79	63	25	7	22	29	22
1979-80ab	Portland	WHL	50	22	60	82	71	8	1	10	11	2
1980-81	**Winnipeg**	**NHL**	**69**	**6**	**38**	**44**	**90**	....	....	....	....	....
1981-82	**Winnipeg**	**NHL**	**79**	**19**	**49**	**68**	**92**	**4**	**1**	**2**	**3**	**29**
1982-83	**Winnipeg**	**NHL**	**79**	**13**	**61**	**74**	**56**	**3**	**0**	**0**	**0**	**0**
1983-84	**Winnipeg**	**NHL**	**66**	**18**	**39**	**57**	**62**	**3**	**1**	**1**	**2**	**0**
1984-85	**Winnipeg**	**NHL**	**78**	**13**	**49**	**62**	**78**	**8**	**2**	**7**	**9**	**6**
1985-86	**Winnipeg**	**NHL**	**19**	**4**	**12**	**16**	**14**	....	....	....	....	....
	Hartford	**NHL**	**62**	**10**	**43**	**53**	**36**	**8**	**1**	**3**	**4**	**14**
1986-87	**Hartford**	**NHL**	**66**	**8**	**33**	**41**	**44**	**6**	**1**	**1**	**2**	**14**
1987-88	**Hartford**	**NHL**	**71**	**14**	**36**	**50**	**54**	**6**	**3**	**2**	**5**	**2**
1988-89	**Hartford**	**NHL**	**70**	**6**	**41**	**47**	**54**	**4**	**1**	**5**	**6**	**2**
1989-90	**Hartford**	**NHL**	**72**	**6**	**37**	**43**	**62**	**7**	**1**	**2**	**3**	**0**
1990-91	**Hartford**	**NHL**	**8**	**0**	**6**	**6**	**4**	....	....	....	....	....
	NHL Totals		**739**	**117**	**444**	**561**	**646**	**49**	**11**	**23**	**34**	**67**

a WHL First All-Star Team (1980)
b Named WHL's Top Defenseman (1980)
Played in NHL All-Star Game (1983, 1984)

Traded to **Hartford** by **Winnipeg** for Ray Neufeld, November 21, 1985. Claimed by **Minnesota** from **Hartford** in Expansion Draft, May 30, 1991. Traded to **Vancouver** by **Minnesota** for Tom Kurvers, June 22, 1991.

BACA, JERGUS

Defense. Shoots left. 6'2", 211 lbs. Born, Liptovsky Mikulas, Czech., January 4, 1965.
(Hartford's 6th choice, 141st overall, in 1990 Entry Draft).

			Regular Season					Playoffs				
Season	Club	Lea	GP	G	A	TP	PIM	GP	G	A	TP	PIM
1987-88	VSZ Kosice	Czech.	40	5	5	10	32	....	....	....	....	....
1988-89a	VSZ Kosice	Czech.	42	3	10	13	46	....	....	....	....	....
	Czech. National	...	32	2	5	7	42	....	....	....	....	....
1989-90a	VSZ Kosice	Czech.	47	9	16	25	....	....	....	....	....	....
	Czech National	...	25	0	1	1	44	....	....	....	....	....
1990-91	**Hartford**	**NHL**	**9**	**0**	**2**	**2**	**14**	....	....	....	....	....
	Springfield	AHL	57	6	23	29	89	18	3	13	16	18
	NHL Totals		**9**	**0**	**2**	**2**	**14**	....	....	....	....	....

a First Team All-Star.

BADER, DARIN

Left wing. Shoots left. 6', 202 lbs. Born, Edmonton, Alta, April 1, 1971.
(Vancouver's 4th choice, 65th overall, in 1990 Entry Draft).

			Regular Season					Playoffs				
Season	Club	Lea	GP	G	A	TP	PIM	GP	G	A	TP	PIM
1989-90	Saskatoon	WHL	54	26	31	57	107	10	6	4	10	30
1990-91	Saskatoon	WHL	40	35	32	67	106	....	....	....	....	....

BAKER, JAMIE

Center. Shoots left. 6', 190 lbs. Born, Ottawa, Ont., August 31, 1966.
(Quebec's 2nd choice, 8th overall, in 1988 Supplemental Draft).

			Regular Season					Playoffs				
Season	Club	Lea	GP	G	A	TP	PIM	GP	G	A	TP	PIM
1985-86	St. Lawrence	ECAC	31	9	16	25	52	....	....	....	....	....
1986-87	St. Lawrence	ECAC	32	8	24	32	59	....	....	....	....	....
1987-88	St. Lawrence	ECAC	34	26	24	50	38	....	....	....	....	....
1988-89	St. Lawrence	ECAC	13	11	16	27	16	....	....	....	....	....
1989-90	**Quebec**	**NHL**	**1**	**0**	**0**	**0**	**0**	....	....	....	....	....
	Halifax	AHL	74	17	43	60	47	6	0	0	0	7
1990-91	**Quebec**	**NHL**	**18**	**2**	**0**	**2**	**8**	....	....	....	....	....
	Halifax	AHL	50	14	22	36	85	....	....	....	....	....
	NHL Totals		**19**	**2**	**0**	**2**	**8**	....	....	....	....	....

BAKOVIC, PETER GEORGE (BAK-oh-VIHK)

Right wing. Shoots right. 6'2", 200 lbs. Born, Thunder Bay, Ont., January 31, 1965.

			Regular Season					Playoffs				
Season	Club	Lea	GP	G	A	TP	PIM	GP	G	A	TP	PIM
1983-84	Kitchener	OHL	28	2	6	8	87	....	....	....	....	....
	Windsor	OHL	35	10	25	35	74	3	0	2	2	14
1984-85	Windsor	OHL	58	26	48	74	259	3	0	0	0	12
1985-86	Moncton	AHL	80	18	36	54	349	10	2	2	4	30
1986-87	Moncton	AHL	77	17	34	51	280	6	3	3	6	54
1987-88	**Vancouver**	**NHL**	**10**	**2**	**0**	**2**	**48**	....	....	....	....	....
	Salt Lake	IHL	39	16	27	43	221	....	....	....	....	....
1988-89	Milwaukee	IHL	40	16	14	30	211	11	4	4	8	46
1989-90	Milwaukee	IHL	56	19	30	49	230	6	4	1	5	52
1990-91	Milwaukee	IHL	69	17	45	62	220	6	0	4	4	16
	NHL Totals		**10**	**2**	**0**	**2**	**48**	....	....	....	....	....

Signed as a free agent by **Calgary**, October 10, 1985. Traded to **Vancouver** by **Calgary** with Brian Bradley and Kevin Guy for Craig Coxe, March 6, 1988.

BANCROFT, STEVE

Defense. Shoots left. 6'1", 214 lbs. Born, Toronto, Ont., October 6, 1970.
(Toronto's 3rd choice, 21st overall, in 1989 Entry Draft).

			Regular Season					Playoffs				
Season	Club	Lea	GP	G	A	TP	PIM	GP	G	A	TP	PIM
1987-88	Belleville	OHL	56	1	8	9	42	....	....	....	....	....
1988-89	Belleville	OHL	66	7	30	37	99	5	0	2	2	10
1989-90	Belleville	OHL	53	10	33	43	135	11	3	9	12	38
1990-91	Newmarket	AHL	9	0	3	3	22	....	....	....	....	....
	Maine	AHL	53	2	12	14	46	2	0	0	0	2

Traded to **Boston** by **Toronto** for Rob Cimetta, November 9, 1990.

BANKS, DARREN ALEXANDER

Left wing. Shoots left. 6'2", 215 lbs. Born, Toronto, Ont., March 18, 1966.

			Regular Season					Playoffs				
Season	Club	Lea	GP	G	A	TP	PIM	GP	G	A	TP	PIM
1986-87	Brock	OUAA	24	5	3	8	82	....	....	....	....	....
1987-88	Brock	OUAA	26	10	11	21	110	....	....	....	....	....
1988-89	Brock	OUAA	26	19	14	33	88	....	....	....	....	....
1989-90	Salt Lake	IHL	6	0	0	0	11	1	0	0	0	10
	Fort Wayne	IHL	2	0	1	1	0	....	....	....	....	....
	Knoxville	ECHL	52	25	22	47	258	....	....	....	....	....
1990-91	Salt Lake	IHL	56	9	7	16	286	3	0	1	1	6

Signed as a free agent by **Calgary**, December 12, 1990.

BANNISTER, DARIN

Defense. Shoots right. 6', 185 lbs. Born, Calgary, Alta., January 16, 1967.
(Detroit's 11th choice, 200th overall, in 1987 Entry Draft).

			Regular Season					Playoffs				
Season	Club	Lea	GP	G	A	TP	PIM	GP	G	A	TP	PIM
1986-87	Ill.-Chicago	CCHA	38	4	16	20	38	....	....	....	....	....
1987-88	Ill.-Chicago	CCHA	39	2	26	28	96	....	....	....	....	....
1988-89	Ill.-Chicago	CCHA	41	7	26	33	88	....	....	....	....	....
1989-90	Ill.-Chicago	CCHA	37	5	22	27	72	....	....	....	....	....
1990-91	San Diego	IHL	81	4	11	15	108	....	....	....	....	....

BARAHONA, RALPH J.

Center. Shoots left. 5'10", 180 lbs. Born, Long Beach, CA, November 16, 1965.

			Regular Season					Playoffs				
Season	Club	Lea	GP	G	A	TP	PIM	GP	G	A	TP	PIM
1988-89	U.Wisc.-S.Pt.	NCAA	41	33	47	80	....	....	....	....	....	....
1989-90	U.Wisc.-S.Pt.	NCAA	35	22	30	52	18	....	....	....	....	....
1990-91	**Boston**	**NHL**	**3**	**2**	**1**	**3**	**0**	....	....	....	....	....
	Maine	AHL	72	24	33	57	14	2	1	1	2	0
	NHL Totals		**3**	**2**	**1**	**3**	**0**	....	....	....	....	....

Signed as a free agent by **Boston**, September 26, 1990.

BARBE, MARIO (BARB)

Defense. Shoots left. 6'1", 204 lbs. Born, Cadillac, Que., March 17, 1967.
(Edmonton's 9th choice, 209th overall, in 1985 Entry Draft).

			Regular Season					Playoffs				
Season	Club	Lea	GP	G	A	TP	PIM	GP	G	A	TP	PIM
1984-85	Chicoutimi	QMJHL	64	2	13	15	211	14	0	2	2	36
1985-86	Granby	QMJHL	70	5	25	30	261	....	....	....	....	....
1986-87	Granby	QMJHL	65	7	25	32	356	7	1	5	6	38
1987-88	Granby	QMJHL	45	8	10	18	294	5	1	4	5	16
1988-89	Cape Breton	AHL	70	1	11	12	137	....	....	....	....	....
1989-90	Cape Breton	AHL	64	0	15	15	138	4	0	0	0	4
1990-91	Cape Breton	AHL	63	1	4	5	81	....	....	....	....	....

BARBER, DON

Right wing/Left wing. Shoots left. 6'2", 205 lbs. Born, Victoria, B.C., December 2, 1964.
(Edmonton's 5th choice, 120th over all, in 1983 Entry Draft).

			Regular Season					Playoffs				
Season	Club	Lea	GP	G	A	TP	PIM	GP	G	A	TP	PIM
1984-85	Bowling Green	CCHA	39	15	22	37	44	....	....	....	....	....
1985-86	Bowling Green	CCHA	35	21	22	43	64	....	....	....	....	....
1986-87	Bowling Green	CCHA	43	29	34	63	107	....	....	....	....	....
1987-88	Bowling Green	CCHA	38	18	47	65	62	....	....	....	....	....
1988-89	**Minnesota**	**NHL**	**23**	**8**	**5**	**13**	**8**	**4**	**1**	**1**	**2**	**2**
	Kalamazoo	IHL	39	14	17	31	23	....	....	....	....	....
1989-90	**Minnesota**	**NHL**	**44**	**15**	**19**	**34**	**32**	**7**	**3**	**3**	**6**	**8**
	Kalamazoo	IHL	10	4	4	8	38	....	....	....	....	....
1990-91	**Minnesota**	**NHL**	**7**	**0**	**0**	**0**	**4**	....	....	....	....	....
	Winnipeg	**NHL**	**16**	**1**	**2**	**3**	**14**	....	....	....	....	....
	Moncton	AHL	38	17	21	38	32	9	4	6	10	8
	NHL Totals		**90**	**24**	**26**	**50**	**58**	**11**	**4**	**4**	**8**	**10**

Traded to **Minnesota** by **Edmonton** with Marc Habscheid and Emanuel Viveiros for Gord Sherven and Don Biggs, December 20, 1985. Traded to **Winnipeg** by **Minnesota** for Doug Smail, November 7, 1990.

BARKLEY, MICHAEL

Right wing. Shoots right. 6', 185 lbs. Born, Port Alberni, B.C., April 7, 1970.
(Buffalo's 6th choice, 119th overall, in 1989 Entry Draft).

			Regular Season					Playoffs				
Season	Club	Lea	GP	G	A	TP	PIM	GP	G	A	TP	PIM
1988-89	U. of Maine	H.E.	41	12	13	25	16	....	....	....	....	....
1989-90	U. of Maine	H.E.	43	11	19	30	20	....	....	....	....	....
1990-91	U. of Maine	H.E.	23	6	8	14	6	....	....	....	....	....

BARKOVICH, RICHARD (RICK)

Center. Shoots left. 5'10", 185 lbs. Born, Kirkland Lake, Ont., April 25, 1964.

			Regular Season					Playoffs				
Season	Club	Lea	GP	G	A	TP	PIM	GP	G	A	TP	PIM
1982-83	London	OHL	65	14	14	28	40	....	....	....	....	....
1983-84	London	OHL	67	25	29	54	83	....	....	....	....	....
1984-85	London	OHL	63	41	40	81	56	....	....	....	....	....
1986-87	Brantford	Sr.	35	31	32	63	22	....	....	....	....	....
1987-88	Salt Lake	IHL	79	34	25	59	65	17	9	11	20	18
1988-89	Indianapolis	IHL	78	32	35	67	81	....	....	....	....	....
1989-90	Salt Lake	IHL	71	20	23	43	55	7	1	1	2	4
1990-91	Kansas City	IHL	75	19	20	39	72	....	....	....	....	....

Signed as a free agent by **Calgary**, October 10, 1987.

BARNES, STU

Center. Shoots right. 5'10", 175 lbs. Born, Edmonton, Alta., December 25, 1970.
(Winnipeg's 1st choice, 4th overall, in 1989 Entry Draft).

			Regular Season					Playoffs				
Season	Club	Lea	GP	G	A	TP	PIM	GP	G	A	TP	PIM
1987-88	N. Westminster	WHL	71	37	64	101	88	5	2	3	5	6
1988-89ab	Tri-Cities	WHL	70	59	82	141	117	7	6	5	11	10
1989-90	Tri-Cities	WHL	63	52	92	144	165	7	1	5	6	26
1990-91	Cdn. National	...	53	22	27	49	68	....	....	....	....	....

a WHL West Second All-Star Team (1989)
b WHL Player of the Year (1989)

BARNETT, BRETT

Left wing. Shoots left. 6'3", 185 lbs. Born, Toronto, Ont., October 12, 1967.
(NY Rangers' 11th choice, 205th overall, in 1987 Entry Draft).

			Regular Season					Playoffs				
Season	Club	Lea	GP	G	A	TP	PIM	GP	G	A	TP	PIM
1987-88	Lake Superior	CCHA	44	16	23	39	124	....	....	....	....	....
1988-89	Lake Superior	CCHA	30	15	11	26	104	....	....	....	....	....
1989-90	Kalamazoo	IHL	35	5	5	10	38	....	....	....	....	....
1990-91	Roanoke Valley	ECHL	5	3	1	4	4	....	....	....	....	....
	Cincinnati	ECHL	25	13	15	28	62	4	0	0	0	2

Rights traded to **Minnesota** by **NY Rangers** with Paul Jerrard, the rights to Mike Sullivan, and Los Angeles' third-round choice (Murray Garbutt) in 1989 Entry Draft - acquired March 10, 1987 by Minnesota - for Brian Lawton, Igor Liba and the rights to Eric Bennett, October 11, 1988.

BARON, MURRAY

Defense. Shoots left. 6'3", 210 lbs. Born, Prince George, B.C., June 1, 1967.
(Philadelphia's 7th choice, 167th overall, in 1986 Entry Draft).

			Regular Season					Playoffs				
Season	Club	Lea	GP	G	A	TP	PIM	GP	G	A	TP	PIM
1986-87	North Dakota	WCHA	41	4	10	14	62	....	....	....	....	....
1987-88	North Dakota	WCHA	41	1	10	11	95	....	....	....	....	....
1988-89	North Dakota	WCHA	40	2	6	8	92	....	....	....	....	....
	Hershey	AHL	9	0	3	3	8	....	....	....	....	....
1989-90	**Philadelphia**	**NHL**	**16**	**2**	**2**	**4**	**12**	....	....	....	....	....
	Hershey	AHL	50	0	10	10	101	....	....	....	....	....
1990-91	**Philadelphia**	**NHL**	**67**	**8**	**8**	**16**	**74**	....	....	....	....	....
	Hershey	AHL	6	2	3	5	0	....	....	....	....	....
	NHL Totals		**83**	**10**	**10**	**20**	**86**	....	....	....	....	....

BARR, DAVID (DAVE)

Right wing. Shoots right. 6'1", 195 lbs. Born, Toronto, Ont., November 30, 1960.

			Regular Season					Playoffs				
Season	Club	Lea	GP	G	A	TP	PIM	GP	G	A	TP	PIM
1979-80	Lethbridge	WHL	60	16	38	54	47	....	....	....	....	....
1980-81	Lethbridge	WHL	72	26	62	88	106	....	....	....	....	....
1981-82	**Boston**	**NHL**	**2**	**0**	**0**	**0**	**0**	**5**	**1**	**0**	**1**	**0**
	Erie	AHL	76	18	48	66	29	....	....	....	....	....
1982-83	**Boston**	**NHL**	**10**	**1**	**1**	**2**	**7**	**10**	**0**	**0**	**0**	**2**
	Baltimore	AHL	72	27	51	78	67	....	....	....	....	....
1983-84	**NY Rangers**	**NHL**	**6**	**0**	**0**	**0**	**2**	....	....	....	....	....
	Tulsa	CHL	50	28	37	65	24	....	....	....	....	....
	St. Louis	**NHL**	**1**	**0**	**0**	**0**	**0**	....	....	....	....	....
1984-85	**St. Louis**	**NHL**	**75**	**16**	**18**	**34**	**32**	**2**	**0**	**0**	**0**	**2**
1985-86	**St. Louis**	**NHL**	**72**	**13**	**38**	**51**	**70**	**11**	**1**	**1**	**2**	**14**
1986-87	**St. Louis**	**NHL**	**2**	**0**	**0**	**0**	**0**	....	....	....	....	....
	Hartford	**NHL**	**30**	**2**	**4**	**6**	**19**	....	....	....	....	....
	Detroit	**NHL**	**37**	**13**	**13**	**26**	**49**	**13**	**1**	**0**	**1**	**14**
1987-88	**Detroit**	**NHL**	**51**	**14**	**26**	**40**	**58**	**16**	**5**	**7**	**12**	**22**
1988-89	**Detroit**	**NHL**	**73**	**27**	**32**	**59**	**69**	**6**	**3**	**1**	**4**	**6**
1989-90	**Detroit**	**NHL**	**62**	**10**	**25**	**35**	**45**	....	....	....	....	....
	Adirondack	AHL	9	1	14	15	17	....	....	....	....	....
1990-91	**Detroit**	**NHL**	**70**	**18**	**22**	**40**	**55**	....	....	....	....	....
	NHL Totals		**491**	**114**	**179**	**293**	**406**	**63**	**11**	**9**	**20**	**60**

Signed as free agent by **Boston**, September 28, 1981. Traded to **NY Rangers** by **Boston** for Dave Silk, October 5, 1983. Traded to **St. Louis** by **NY Rangers** with NY Rangers' third-round choice (Alan Perry) in the 1984 Entry Draft for Larry Patey and Bob Brooke, March 5, 1984. Traded to **Hartford** by **St. Louis** for Tim Bothwell, October 21, 1986. Traded to **Detroit** by **Hartford** for Randy Ladouceur, January 12, 1987.

BARRAULT, DOUGLAS

Right wing. Shoots right. 6'2", 205 lbs. Born, Golden, B.C., April 21, 1970.
(Minnesota's 8th choice, 155th overall, in 1990 Entry Draft).

			Regular Season					Playoffs				
Season	Club	Lea	GP	G	A	TP	PIM	GP	G	A	TP	PIM
1988-89	Lethbridge	WHL	57	14	13	27	34	....	....	....	....	....
1989-90	Lethbridge	WHL	54	14	16	30	36	19	7	3	10	0
1990-91a	Lethbridge	WHL	4	2	2	4	16	....	....	....	....	....
	Seattle	WHL	61	42	42	84	69	6	5	3	8	4

a WHL West Second All-Star Team (1991)

BARRIE, LEN

Center. Shoots left. 6', 200 lbs. Born, Kimberley, B.C., June 4, 1969.
(Edmonton's 7th choice, 124th overall, in 1988 Entry Draft).

			Regular Season					Playoffs				
Season	Club	Lea	GP	G	A	TP	PIM	GP	G	A	TP	PIM
1985-86	Calgary	WHL	32	3	0	3	18	....	....	....	....	....
1986-87	Calgary	WHL	34	13	13	26	81	....	....	....	....	....
	Victoria	WHL	34	7	6	13	92	5	0	1	1	15
1987-88	Victoria	WHL	70	37	49	86	192	8	2	0	2	29
1988-89	Victoria	WHL	67	39	48	87	157	7	5	2	7	23
1989-90	**Philadelphia**	**NHL**	**1**	**0**	**0**	**0**	**0**	....	....	....	....	....
a	Kamloops	WHL	70	*85	*100	*185	108	17	*14	23	*37	24
1990-91	Hershey	AHL	63	26	32	58	60	7	4	0	4	12
	NHL Totals		**1**	**0**	**0**	**0**	**0**	....	....	....	....	....

a WHL West First All-Star Team (1990)

Signed as a free agent by **Philadelphia**, February 28, 1990.

BARTHE, CLAUDE

Defense. Shoots right. 6'2", 197 lbs. Born, St. Pierre De Sorel, Que., June 15, 1970.
(Detroit's 5th choice, 108th overall, in 1990 Entry Draft).

			Regular Season					Playoffs				
Season	Club	Lea	GP	G	A	TP	PIM	GP	G	A	TP	PIM
1989-90a	Victoriaville	QMJHL	68	20	55	75	148	16	0	9	9	44
1990-91	Trois-Rivieres	QMJHL	28	4	17	21	43	6	1	3	4	35

a QMJHL First All-Star Team (1990)

BARTLEY, WADE

Defense. Shoots right. 6', 190 lbs. Born, Killarney, Man., May 16, 1970.
(Washington's 3rd choice, 41st overall, in 1988 Entry Draft).

			Regular Season					Playoffs				
Season	Club	Lea	GP	G	A	TP	PIM	GP	G	A	TP	PIM
1988-89	North Dakota	WCHA	32	1	1	2	8	....	....	....	....	....
1989-90	Sudbury	OHL	60	23	36	59	53	7	1	4	5	10
1990-91	Sudbury	OHL	47	11	37	48	57	5	1	3	4	4
	Baltimore	AHL	2	0	0	0	0	....	....	....	....	....

BASEGGIO, DAVID (DAVE) (buh-SEE-gee-oh)

Defense. Shoots left. 6'3", 210 lbs. Born, Niagara Falls, Ont., October 28, 1967.
(Buffalo's 5th choice, 68th overall, in 1986 Entry Draft).

			Regular Season					Playoffs				
Season	Club	Lea	GP	G	A	TP	PIM	GP	G	A	TP	PIM
1985-86	Yale	ECAC	30	7	17	24	54	....	....	....	....	....
1986-87	Yale	ECAC	29	8	17	25	52	....	....	....	....	....
1987-88	Yale	ECAC	24	4	22	26	67	....	....	....	....	....
1988-89a	Yale	ECAC	28	10	23	33	41	....	....	....	....	....
1989-90	Indianapolis	IHL	10	1	7	8	2	10	2	4	6	6
	Rochester	AHL	41	13	15	18	41	....	....	....	....	....
1990-91	Rochester	AHL	35	3	13	16	32	1	0	0	0	0

a ECAC Second All-Star Team (1989)

BASSEN, BOB

Center/Left wing. Shoots left. 5'11", 170 lbs. Born, Calgary, Alta., May 6, 1965.

			Regular Season					Playoffs				
Season	Club	Lea	GP	G	A	TP	PIM	GP	G	A	TP	PIM
1982-83	Medicine Hat	WHL	4	3	2	5	0	3	0	0	0	4
1983-84	Medicine Hat	WHL	72	29	29	58	93	14	5	11	16	12
1984-85a	Medicine Hat	WHL	65	32	50	82	143	10	2	8	10	39
1985-86	**NY Islanders**	**NHL**	**11**	**2**	**1**	**3**	**6**	**3**	**0**	**1**	**1**	**0**
	Springfield	AHL	54	13	21	34	111	....	....	....	....	....
1986-87	**NY Islanders**	**NHL**	**77**	**7**	**10**	**17**	**89**	**14**	**1**	**2**	**3**	**21**
1987-88	**NY Islanders**	**NHL**	**77**	**6**	**16**	**22**	**99**	**6**	**0**	**1**	**1**	**23**
1988-89	**NY Islanders**	**NHL**	**19**	**1**	**4**	**5**	**21**	....	....	....	....	....
	Chicago	**NHL**	**49**	**4**	**12**	**16**	**62**	**10**	**1**	**1**	**2**	**34**
1989-90	**Chicago**	**NHL**	**6**	**1**	**1**	**2**	**8**	**1**	**0**	**0**	**0**	**2**
b	Indianapolis	IHL	73	22	32	54	179	12	3	8	11	33
1990-91	**St. Louis**	**NHL**	**79**	**16**	**18**	**34**	**183**	**13**	**1**	**3**	**4**	**24**
	NHL Totals		**318**	**37**	**62**	**99**	**468**	**46**	**3**	**8**	**11**	**102**

a WHL First All-Star Team (1985)
b IHL First All-Star Team (1990)

Signed as a free agent by**NY Islanders**, October 19, 1984.Traded to **Chicago** by **NY Islanders** with Steve Konroyd for Marc Bergevin and Gary Nylund, November 25, 1988. Claimed by **St. Louis** in NHL Waiver Draft, October 1, 1990.

BASSEN, MARK

Center. Shoots right. 5'10", 170 lbs. Born, Calgary, Alta., May 9, 1969.

			Regular Season					Playoffs				
Season	Club	Lea	GP	G	A	TP	PIM	GP	G	A	TP	PIM
1986-87	Calgary	WHL	4	1	1	2	4	....	....	....	....	....
1987-88	Lethbridge	WHL	70	19	28	47	48	....	....	....	....	....
1988-89	Lethbridge	WHL	7	1	4	5	12	....	....	....	....	....
	Brandon	WHL	65	31	65	96	74	....	....	....	....	....
1989-90	Hershey	AHL	57	5	9	14	128	....	....	....	....	....
1990-91	Hershey	AHL	42	3	1	4	86	....	....	....	....	....

Signed as a free agent by **Philadelphia**, October 5, 1989.

BATEMAN, ROBERTSON (ROB)

Defense. Shoots right. 6', 175 lbs. Born, LaSalle, Que., January 2, 1968.
(Winnipeg's 6th choice, 113th overall, in 1986 Entry Draft).

			Regular Season					Playoffs				
Season	Club	Lea	GP	G	A	TP	PIM	GP	G	A	TP	PIM
1986-87	U. of Vermont	ECAC	32	2	3	5	78	....	....	....	....	....
1987-88	U. of Vermont	ECAC	34	1	3	4	64	....	....	....	....	....
1988-89	U. of Vermont	ECAC	32	1	4	5	38	....	....	....	....	....
1989-90	U. of Vermont	ECAC	31	0	4	4	62	....	....	....	....	....
1990-91	Halifax	AHL	5	0	0	0	2	....	....	....	....	....
	Greensboro	ECHL	59	3	6	9	93	13	0	1	1	8

BATTERS, JEFF

Defense. Shoots right. 6'2", 215 lbs.   Born, Victoria, B.C., October 23, 1970.
(St. Louis' 7th choice, 135th overall, in 1989 Entry Draft).

			Regular Season					Playoffs				
Season	Club	Lea	GP	G	A	TP	PIM	GP	G	A	TP	PIM
1988-89	Alaska-Anch.	NCAA	33	8	14	22	123	....	....	....	....	....
1989-90	Alaska-Anch.	NCAA	34	6	9	15	102	....	....	....	....	....
1990-91	Alaska-Anch.	NCAA	39	16	14	30	90	....	....	....	....	....

BAUER, COLLIN

Defense. Shoots left. 6'1", 180 lbs.   Born, Edmonton, Alta., September 6, 1970.
(Edmonton's 4th choice, 61st overall, in 1988 Entry Draft).

			Regular Season					Playoffs				
Season	Club	Lea	GP	G	A	TP	PIM	GP	G	A	TP	PIM
1986-87	Saskatoon	WHL	61	1	25	26	37	11	0	6	6	10
1987-88	Saskatoon	WHL	70	9	53	62	66	10	2	5	7	16
1988-89a	Saskatoon	WHL	61	17	62	79	71	8	1	8	9	8
1989-90	Saskatoon	WHL	29	4	25	29	49	10	1	8	9	14
1990-91	Cape Breton	AHL	40	4	14	18	18	4	1	1	2	4

a WHL East All-Star Team (1989)

BAUMGARTNER, KEN

Defense/Center. Shoots left. 6'1", 200 lbs.   Born, Flin Flon, Man., March 11, 1966
(Buffalo's 12th choice, 245th overall, in 1985 Entry Draft).

		Lea ..	Regular Season					Playoffs				
Season	Club		GP	G	A	TP	PIM	GP	G	A	TP	PIM
1984-85	Prince Albert	WHL	60	3	9	12	252	13	1	3	4	89
1985-86	Prince Albert	WHL	70	4	23	27	277	20	3	9	12	112
1986-87	New Haven	AHL	13	0	3	3	99	6	0	0	0	60
1987-88	Los Angeles	NHL	30	2	3	5	189	5	0	1	1	28
	New Haven	AHL	48	1	5	6	181	....	....	....	....	....
1988-89	Los Angeles	NHL	49	1	3	4	288	5	0	0	0	8
	New Haven	AHL	10	1	3	4	26	....	....	....	....	....
1989-90	Los Angeles	NHL	12	1	0	1	28	....	....	....	....	....
	NY Islanders	NHL	53	0	5	5	194	4	0	0	0	27
1990-91	NY Islanders	NHL	78	1	6	7	282	....	....	....	....	....
	NHL Totals		222	5	17	22	981	14	0	1	1	63

Traded to **Los Angeles** by **Buffalo** with Sean McKenna and Larry Playfair for Brian Engblom and Doug Smith, January 29, 1986. Traded to **NY Islanders** by **Los Angeles** with Hubie McDonough for Mikko Makela, November 29, 1989.

BAVIS, MARK

Center. Shoots left. 6', 175 lbs.   Born, Roslindale, MA, March 13, 1970.
(NY Rangers' 10th choice, 181st overall, in 1989 Entry Draft).

			Regular Season					Playoffs				
Season	Club	Lea	GP	G	A	TP	PIM	GP	G	A	TP	PIM
1989-90	Boston U.	H.E.	44	6	5	11	50	....	....	....	....	....
1990-91	Boston U.	H.E.	33	7	9	16	30	....	....	....	....	....

BAVIS, MICHAEL

Right wing. Shoots right. 6', 180 lbs.   Born, Roslindale, MA, March 13, 1970.
(Buffalo's 12th choice, 245th overall, in 1989 Entry Draft).

			Regular Season					Playoffs				
Season	Club	Lea	GP	G	A	TP	PIM	GP	G	A	TP	PIM
1989-90	Boston U.	H.E.	44	2	11	13	28	....	....	....	....	....
1990-91	Boston U.	H.E.	40	5	18	23	47	....	....	....	....	....

BAWA, ROBIN

(BAH-wuh)

Right wing. Shoots right. 6'2", 214 lbs.   Born, Chemainus, B.C., March 26, 1966.

			Regular Season					Playoffs				
Season	Club	Lea	GP	G	A	TP	PIM	GP	G	A	TP	PIM
1982-83	Kamloops	WHL	66	10	24	34	17	7	1	2	3	0
1983-84	Kamloops	WHL	64	16	28	44	40	13	4	2	6	4
1984-85	Kamloops	WHL	52	6	19	25	45	15	4	9	13	14
1985-86	Kamloops	WHL	63	29	43	72	78	16	5	13	18	4
1986-87a	Kamloops	WHL	62	57	56	113	91	13	6	7	13	22
1987-88	Fort Wayne	IHL	55	12	27	39	239	6	1	3	4	24
1988-89	Baltimore	AHL	75	23	24	47	205	....	....	....	....	....
1989-90	Washington	NHL	5	1	0	1	6	....	....	....	....	....
	Baltimore	AHL	61	7	18	25	189	11	1	2	3	49
1990-91	Fort Wayne	IHL	72	21	26	47	381	18	4	4	8	87
	NHL Totals		5	1	0	1	6	....	....	....	....	....

a WHL West All-Star Team (1987)

Signed as a free agent by **Washington**, May 22, 1987. Traded to **Vancouver** by **Washington** for cash, July 31, 1991.

BEADLE, STEVE

Defense. Shoots left. 5'11", 190 lbs.   Born, Lansing, MI, May 30, 1968.
(Philadelphia's 1st choice, 4th overall, in 1990 Supplemental Draft).

			Regular Season					Playoffs				
Season	Club	Lea	GP	G	A	TP	PIM	GP	G	A	TP	PIM
1986-87	Michigan St.	CCHA	38	0	9	9	22	....	....	....	....	....
1987-88	Michigan St.	CCHA	45	7	37	44	37	....	....	....	....	....
1988-89	Michigan St.	CCHA	46	14	40	54	35	....	....	....	....	....
1989-90	Michigan St.	CCHA	45	21	36	57	50	....	....	....	....	....
1990-91	Hershey	AHL	24	1	12	13	8	....	....	....	....	....

BEAN, TIM

Left wing. Shoots left. 6'1", 190 lbs.   Born, Sault Ste. Marie, Ont., March 9, 1967.
(Toronto's 7th choice, 127th overall, in 1985 Entry Draft).

			Regular Season					Playoffs				
Season	Club	Lea	GP	G	A	TP	PIM	GP	G	A	TP	PIM
1983-84	Belleville	OHL	63	12	13	25	131	3	0	0	0	0
1984-85	Belleville	OHL	31	10	11	21	60	....	....	....	....	....
	North Bay	OHL	28	11	13	24	61	8	2	5	7	8
1985-86	North Bay	OHL	66	32	34	66	129	10	5	5	10	22
1986-87	North Bay	OHL	65	24	39	63	134	21	4	12	16	65
1987-88	Newmarket	AHL	76	12	16	28	118	....	....	....	....	....
1988-89	Newmarket	AHL	44	4	12	16	55	....	....	....	....	....
	Flint	IHL	3	1	3	4	4	....	....	....	....	....
1989-90	Newmarket	AHL	39	5	10	15	27	....	....	....	....	....
1990-91	Newmarket	AHL	14	0	3	3	34	....	....	....	....	....
	Nashville	ECHL	16	4	8	12	8	....	....	....	....	....
	Richmond	ECHL	3	1	2	3	0	....	....	....	....	....

BEAUFAIT, MARK

Center. Shoots right. 5'9", 170 lbs.   Born, Royal Oak, MI, May 13, 1970.
(San Jose's 2nd choice, 7th overall, in 1991 Supplemental Draft).

			Regular Season					Playoffs				
Season	Club	Lea	GP	G	A	TP	PIM	GP	G	A	TP	PIM
1989-90	N. Michigan	WCHA	34	10	14	24	12	....	....	....	....	....
1990-91	N. Michigan	WCHA	47	19	30	49	18	....	....	....	....	....

BEAULIEU, COREY

Defense. Shoots left. 6'1", 210 lbs.   Born, Winnipeg, Man., September 10, 1969.
(Hartford's 5th choice, 116th overall, in 1988 Entry Draft).

			Regular Season					Playoffs				
Season	Club	Lea	GP	G	A	TP	PIM	GP	G	A	TP	PIM
1985-86	Moose Jaw	WHL	68	3	1	4	111	13	1	1	2	13
1986-87	Moose Jaw	WHL	63	2	7	9	188	9	0	0	0	17
1987-88	Seattle	WHL	67	2	9	11	225	....	....	....	....	....
1988-89	Seattle	WHL	32	0	3	3	134	....	....	....	....	....
	Moose Jaw	WHL	29	3	17	20	91	7	1	2	3	16
1989-90	Binghamton	AHL	56	0	2	2	191	....	....	....	....	....
1990-91			DID NOT PLAY									

BEAULIEU, NICOLAS

(boy-YOH)

Left wing. Shoots left. 6'2", 200 lbs.   Born, Rimouski, Que., August 19, 1968.
(Edmonton's 8th choice, 168th overall, in 1986 Entry Draft).

			Regular Season					Playoffs				
Season	Club	Lea	GP	G	A	TP	PIM	GP	G	A	TP	PIM
1985-86	Drummondville	QMJHL	70	11	20	31	93	23	0	1	1	11
1986-87	Drummondville	QMJHL	69	19	34	53	198	8	0	1	1	8
1987-88	Laval	QMJHL	64	39	56	95	240	14	3	13	16	37
1988-89	Cape Breton	AHL	60	10	13	23	85	....	....	....	....	....
1989-90	Phoenix	IHL	71	26	46	72	93	....	....	....	....	....
1990-91	Albany	IHL	49	17	21	38	69	....	....	....	....	....
	Phoenix	IHL	18	3	5	8	17	4	1	0	1	6

BEERS, BOB

Defense. Shoots right. 6'2", 200 lbs.   Born, Pittsburgh, PA, May 20, 1967.
(Boston's 10th choice, 210th overall, in 1985 Entry Draft).

			Regular Season					Playoffs				
Season	Club	Lea	GP	G	A	TP	PIM	GP	G	A	TP	PIM
1985-86	N. Arizona	NCAA	28	11	39	50	96	....	....	....	....	....
1986-87	U. of Maine	H.E.	38	0	13	13	45	....	....	....	....	....
1987-88	U. of Maine	H.E.	41	3	11	14	72	....	....	....	....	....
1988-89ab	U. of Maine	H.E.	44	10	27	37	53	....	....	....	....	....
1989-90	Boston	NHL	3	0	1	1	6	14	1	1	2	18
	Maine	AHL	74	7	36	43	63	....	....	....	....	....
1990-91	Boston	NHL	16	0	1	1	10	6	0	0	0	4
	Maine	AHL	36	2	16	18	21	....	....	....	....	....
	NHL Totals		19	0	2	2	16	20	1	1	2	22

a Hockey East Second All-Star Team (1989)
b NCAA East Second All-American Team (1989)

BELANGER, HUGO

Left wing. Shoots left. 6'1", 190 lbs.   Born, St. Hubert, Que., May 28, 1970.
(Chicago's 6th choice, 163rd overall, in 1990 Entry Draft).

			Regular Season					Playoffs				
Season	Club	Lea	GP	G	A	TP	PIM	GP	G	A	TP	PIM
1989-90	Clarkson	ECAC	36	14	25	39	12	....	....	....	....	....
1990-91	Clarkson	ECAC	40	32	43	75	18	....	....	....	....	....

BELANGER, JESSE

Center. Shoots right. 6', 170 lbs.   Born, St. Georges de Beauce, Que., June 15, 1969.

			Regular Season					Playoffs				
Season	Club	Lea	GP	G	A	TP	PIM	GP	G	A	TP	PIM
1988-89	Granby	QMJHL	67	40	63	103	26	4	0	5	5	0
1989-90	Granby	QMJHL	67	53	54	107	53	....	....	....	....	....
1990-91	Fredericton	AHL	75	40	58	98	30	6	2	4	6	0

Signed as a free agent by **Montreal**, October 3, 1990.

BELL, BRUCE

Defense. Shoots left. 6'1", 190 lbs. Born, Toronto, Ont., February 15, 1965.
(Quebec's 2nd choice, 52nd overall, in 1983 Entry Draft).

			Regular Season					Playoffs				
Season	Club	Lea	GP	G	A	TP	PIM	GP	G	A	TP	PIM
1981-82	S. S. Marie	OHL	67	11	18	29	63	12	0	2	2	24
1982-83	S. S. Marie	OHL	5	0	2	2	2	....	....	....	....	....
	Windsor	OHL	61	10	35	45	39	3	0	4	4	0
1983-84a	Brantford	OHL	63	7	41	48	55	6	0	3	3	16
1984-85b	**Quebec**	**NHL**	**75**	**6**	**31**	**37**	**44**	**16**	**2**	**2**	**4**	**21**
1985-86	**St. Louis**	**NHL**	**75**	**2**	**18**	**20**	**43**	**14**	**0**	**2**	**2**	**13**
1986-87	**St. Louis**	**NHL**	**45**	**3**	**13**	**16**	**18**	**4**	**1**	**1**	**2**	**7**
1987-88	**NY Rangers**	**NHL**	**13**	**1**	**2**	**3**	**8**	....	....	....	....	....
	Colorado	IHL	65	11	34	45	107	4	2	3	5	0
1988-89	Halifax	AHL	12	0	6	6	0	2	0	1	1	2
	Adirondack	AHL	9	1	4	5	4	....	....	....	....	....
1989-90	**Edmonton**	**NHL**	**1**	**0**	**0**	**0**	**0**	....	....	....	....	....
	Cape Breton	AHL	52	8	26	34	64	6	3	4	7	2
1990-91	Cape Breton	AHL	14	2	5	7	7	....	....	....	....	....
	Kalamazoo	IHL	48	5	21	26	32	3	0	0	0	8
	NHL Totals		**209**	**12**	**64**	**76**	**113**	**34**	**3**	**5**	**8**	**41**

a OHL First All-Star Team (1984)
b NHL All-Rookie Team (1985)

Traded to **St. Louis** by **Quebec** for Gilbert Delorme, October 2, 1985. Traded to **NY Rangers** by **St. Louis** with future considerations for Tony McKegney and Rob Whistle, May 28, 1987. Traded to **Quebec** by **NY Rangers** with Jari Gronstrand, Walt Poddubny and NY Rangers' fourth round choice (Eric Dubois) in 1989 Entry Draft for Jason Lafreniere and Normand Rochefort, August 1, 1988. Claimed by **Detroit** on waivers, December 19, 1988. Signed as a free agent by **Edmonton**, February 1, 1990. Traded to **Minnesota** by **Edmonton** for Kari Takko, November 22, 1990.

BELLEFEUILLE, BRIAN

Left wing. Shoots left. 6'2", 185 lbs. Born, Natick, MA, March 21, 1967.
(Toronto's 9th choice, 174th overall, in 1986 Entry Draft).

			Regular Season					Playoffs				
Season	Club	Lea	GP	G	A	TP	PIM	GP	G	A	TP	PIM
1986-87	Ill.-Chicago	CCHA	2	0	0	0	2	....	....	....	....	....
1987-88	U. of Maine	H.E.	15	2	2	4	30	....	....	....	....	....
1988-89	U. of Maine	H.E.	36	5	10	15	32	....	....	....	....	....
1989-90	U. of Maine	H.E.	42	13	10	23	86	....	....	....	....	....
	Newmarket	AHL	3	0	0	0	0	....	....	....	....	....
1990-91	New Haven	AHL	7	1	1	2	2	....	....	....	....	....
	Roanoke Valley	ECHL	63	21	28	49	87	....	....	....	....	....

BELLOWS, BRIAN

Left wing. Shoots right. 5'11", 195 lbs. Born, St. Catharines, Ont., September 1, 1964.
(Minnesota's 1st choice, 2nd overall, in 1982 Entry Draft).

			Regular Season					Playoffs				
Season	Club	Lea	GP	G	A	TP	PIM	GP	G	A	TP	PIM
1980-81a	Kitchener	OHA	66	49	67	116	23	16	14	13	27	13
1981-82bc	Kitchener	OHL	47	45	52	97	23	15	16	13	29	11
1982-83	**Minnesota**	**NHL**	**78**	**35**	**30**	**65**	**27**	**9**	**5**	**4**	**9**	**18**
1983-84	**Minnesota**	**NHL**	**78**	**41**	**42**	**83**	**66**	**16**	**2**	**12**	**14**	**6**
1984-85	**Minnesota**	**NHL**	**78**	**26**	**36**	**62**	**72**	**9**	**2**	**4**	**6**	**9**
1985-86	**Minnesota**	**NHL**	**77**	**31**	**48**	**79**	**46**	**5**	**5**	**0**	**5**	**16**
1986-87	**Minnesota**	**NHL**	**65**	**26**	**27**	**53**	**34**	....	....	....	....	....
1987-88	**Minnesota**	**NHL**	**77**	**40**	**41**	**81**	**81**	....	....	....	....	....
1988-89	**Minnesota**	**NHL**	**60**	**23**	**27**	**50**	**55**	**5**	**2**	**3**	**5**	**8**
1989-90d	**Minnesota**	**NHL**	**80**	**55**	**44**	**99**	**72**	**7**	**4**	**3**	**7**	**10**
1990-91	**Minnesota**	**NHL**	**80**	**35**	**40**	**75**	**43**	**23**	**10**	**19**	**29**	**30**
	NHL Totals		**673**	**312**	**335**	**647**	**496**	**74**	**30**	**45**	**75**	**97**

a OHA Third All-Star Team (1981)
b OHL First All-Star Team (1982)
c Most Sportsmanlike Player, Memorial Cup Tournament (1982)
d NHL Second All-Star Team (1990)

Played in NHL All-Star Game (1984, 1988)

BELZILE, ETIENNE

Defense. Shoots left. 6'1", 179 lbs. Born, Quebec City, Que., May 2, 1972.
(Calgary's 4th choice, 41st overall, in 1990 Entry Draft)

			Regular Season					Playoffs				
Season	Club	Lea	GP	G	A	TP	PIM	GP	G	A	TP	PIM
1989-90	Cornell	ECAC	27	1	5	6	22	....	....	....	....	....
1990-91	Cornell	ECAC	32	2	3	5	40	....	....	....	....	....

BENAK, JAROSLAV (BEH-nuhk)

Defense. Shoots left. 5'11", 187 lbs. Born, Havlickuv Brod, Czechoslovakia, April 3, 1962.
(Calgary's 13th choice, 211th overall, in 1983 Entry Draft).

			Regular Season					Playoffs				
Season	Club	Lea	GP	G	A	TP	PIM	GP	G	A	TP	PIM
1986-87	Dukla Jihlava	Czech.	34	1	6	7	....	....	....	....	....	....
1987-88	Dukla Jihlava	Czech.	26	2	8	10	....	....	....	....	....	....
1988-89	Dukla Jihlava	Czech.	28	1	6	7	....	....	....	....	....	....
1989-90	Dukla Jihlava	Czech	47	6	13	19	....	....	....	....	....	....
1990-91	SaiPa	Fin.	44	13	15	28	18	....	....	....	....	....

BENNETT, ADAM

Defense. Shoots right. 6'4", 206 lbs. Born, Georgetown, Ont., March 30, 1971.
(Chicago's 1st choice, 6th overall, in 1989 Entry Draft).

			Regular Season					Playoffs				
Season	Club	Lea	GP	G	A	TP	PIM	GP	G	A	TP	PIM
1988-89	Sudbury	OHL	66	7	22	29	133	....	....	....	....	....
1989-90a	Sudbury	OHL	65	18	43	61	116	7	1	2	3	23
1990-91b	Sudbury	OHL	54	21	29	50	123	5	1	2	3	11
	Indianapolis	IHL	3	0	1	1	12	2	0	0	0	0

a OHL Third All-Star Team (1990)
b OHL Second All-Star Team (1991)

BENNETT, ERIC (RICK)

Left wing. Shoots left. 6'4", 215 lbs. Born, Springfield, MA, July 24, 1967.
(Minnesota's 4th choice, 54th overall, in 1986 Entry Draft).

			Regular Season					Playoffs				
Season	Club	Lea	GP	G	A	TP	PIM	GP	G	A	TP	PIM
1986-87	Providence	H.E.	32	15	12	27	34	....	....	....	....	....
1987-88	Providence	H.E.	33	9	16	25	70	....	....	....	....	....
1988-89a	Providence	H.E.	32	14	32	46	74	....	....	....	....	....
1988-89b	Providence	H.E.	31	12	24	36	74	....	....	....	....	....
	NY Rangers	**NHL**	**6**	**1**	**0**	**1**	**5**	....	....	....	....	....
1990-91	**NY Rangers**	**NHL**	**6**	**0**	**0**	**0**	**6**	....	....	....	....	....
	Binghamton	AHL	71	27	32	59	206	10	2	1	3	27
	NHL Totals		**12**	**1**	**0**	**1**	**11**	....	....	....	....	....

a NCAA East Second All-American Team (1989)
b Hockey East All-Star Team (1990)

Rights traded to **NY Rangers** by **Minnesota** with Brian Lawton and Igor Liba for Paul Jerrard and Mark Tinordi, the rights to Bret Barnett and Mike Sullivan, and Los Angeles' third-round choice (Murray Garbutt) in 1989 Entry Draft - acquired March 10, 1987 by Minnesota - October 11, 1988.

BENNING, BRIAN

Defense. Shoots left. 6', 195 lbs. Born, Edmonton, Alta., June 10, 1966.
(St. Louis' 1st choice, 26th overall, in 1984 Entry Draft).

			Regular Season					Playoffs				
Season	Club	Lea	GP	G	A	TP	PIM	GP	G	A	TP	PIM
1983-84	Portland	WHL	38	6	41	47	108	....	....	....	....	....
1984-85	**St. Louis**	**NHL**	**4**	**0**	**2**	**2**	**0**	....	....	....	....	....
	Kamloops	WHL	17	3	18	21	26	....	....	....	....	....
1985-86	Cdn. Olympic	...	60	6	13	19	43	....	....	....	....	....
	St. Louis	**NHL**	....	....	....	....	....	**6**	**1**	**2**	**3**	**13**
1986-87a	**St. Louis**	**NHL**	**78**	**13**	**36**	**49**	**110**	**6**	**0**	**4**	**4**	**9**
1987-88	**St. Louis**	**NHL**	**77**	**8**	**29**	**37**	**107**	**10**	**1**	**6**	**7**	**25**
1988-89	**St. Louis**	**NHL**	**66**	**8**	**26**	**34**	**102**	**7**	**1**	**1**	**2**	**11**
1989-90	**St. Louis**	**NHL**	**7**	**1**	**1**	**2**	**2**	....	....	....	....	....
	Los Angeles	**NHL**	**48**	**5**	**18**	**23**	**104**	**7**	**0**	**2**	**2**	**10**
1990-91	**Los Angeles**	**NHL**	**61**	**7**	**24**	**31**	**127**	**12**	**0**	**5**	**5**	**6**
	NHL Totals		**341**	**42**	**136**	**178**	**552**	**48**	**3**	**20**	**23**	**74**

a NHL All-Rookie Team (1987)

Traded to **Los Angeles** by **St Louis** for Los Angeles' third round choice (Kyle Reeves) in 1991 Entry Draft, November 10, 1989.

BENNING, JAMES (JIM)

Defense. Shoots left. 6', 185 lbs. Born, Edmonton, Alta., April 29, 1963.
(Toronto's 1st choice, 6th overall, in 1981 Entry Draft).

			Regular Season					Playoffs				
Season	Club	Lea	GP	G	A	TP	PIM	GP	G	A	TP	PIM
1979-80	Portland	WHL	71	11	60	71	42	8	3	9	12	6
1980-81ab	Portland	WHL	72	28	*111	139	61	9	1	5	6	16
1981-82	**Toronto**	**NHL**	**74**	**7**	**24**	**31**	**46**	....	....	....	....	....
1982-83	**Toronto**	**NHL**	**74**	**5**	**17**	**22**	**47**	**4**	**1**	**1**	**2**	**2**
1983-84	**Toronto**	**NHL**	**79**	**12**	**39**	**51**	**66**	....	....	....	....	....
1984-85	**Toronto**	**NHL**	**80**	**9**	**35**	**44**	**55**	....	....	....	....	....
1985-86	**Toronto**	**NHL**	**52**	**4**	**21**	**25**	**71**	....	....	....	....	....
1986-87	**Toronto**	**NHL**	**5**	**0**	**0**	**0**	**4**	....	....	....	....	....
	Newmarket	AHL	10	1	5	6	0	....	....	....	....	....
	Vancouver	**NHL**	**54**	**2**	**11**	**13**	**40**	....	....	....	....	....
1987-88	**Vancouver**	**NHL**	**77**	**7**	**26**	**33**	**58**	....	....	....	....	....
1988-89	**Vancouver**	**NHL**	**65**	**3**	**9**	**12**	**48**	**3**	**0**	**0**	**0**	**0**
1989-90	**Vancouver**	**NHL**	**45**	**3**	**9**	**12**	**26**	....	....	....	....	....
1990-91	Milwaukee	IHL	66	1	31	32	75	6	0	0	0	0
	NHL Totals		**605**	**52**	**191**	**243**	**461**	**7**	**1**	**1**	**2**	**2**

a WHL First All-Star Team (1981)
b Named WHL's Top Defenseman (1981)

Traded to **Vancouver** by **Toronto** with Dan Hodgson for Rick Lanz, December 2, 1986

BERALDO, PAUL

Right wing. Shoots right. 5'11", 175 lbs. Born, Hamilton, Ont., October 5, 1967.
(Boston's 6th choice, 139th overall, in 1986 Entry Draft).

			Regular Season					Playoffs				
Season	Club	Lea	GP	G	A	TP	PIM	GP	G	A	TP	PIM
1985-86	S.S. Marie	OHL	61	15	13	28	48	....	....	....	....	....
1986-87	S.S. Marie	OHL	63	39	51	90	117	4	3	2	5	6
1987-88	**Boston**	**NHL**	**3**	**0**	**0**	**0**	**0**	....	....	....	....	....
	Maine	AHL	62	22	15	37	112	2	0	0	0	19
1988-89	**Boston**	**NHL**	**7**	**0**	**0**	**0**	**4**	....	....	....	....	....
	Maine	AHL	73	25	28	53	134	....	....	....	....	....
1989-90	Cdn. National	...	9	2	8	10	20	....	....	....	....	....
	Maine	AHL	51	14	27	41	31	....	....	....	....	....
1990-91	Milano	Italy	34	34	27	61	77	10	12	12	24	13
	NHL Totals		**10**	**0**	**0**	**0**	**4**	....	....	....	....	....

BERANEK, JOSEF (beh-RAH-nehk)

Right wing. Shoots left. 6', 180 lbs. Born, Litvinov, Czechoslovakia, October 25, 1969.
(Edmonton's 3rd choice, 78th overall, in 1989 Entry Draft).

			Regular Season					Playoffs				
Season	Club	Lea	GP	G	A	TP	PIM	GP	G	A	TP	PIM
1988-89	CHZ Litvinov	Czech.	23	14	8	22	....	....	....	....	....	....
1989-90	Dukla Trencin	Czech.	49	19	23	42	....	....	....	....	....	....
1990-91	CHZ Litvinov	Czech.	50	27	27	54	98	....	....	....	....	....

BEREHOWSKY, DRAKE

Defense. Shoots right. 6'1", 211 lbs. Born, Toronto, Ont., January 3, 1972.
(Toronto's 1st choice, 10th overall, in 1990 Entry Draft).

			Regular Season					Playoffs				
Season	Club	Lea	GP	G	A	TP	PIM	GP	G	A	TP	PIM
1988-89	Kingston	OHL	63	7	39	46	85	....	....	....	....	....
1989-90	Kingston	OHL	9	3	11	14	28	....	....	....	....	....
1990-91	**Toronto**	**NHL**	**8**	**0**	**1**	**1**	**25**	....	....	....	....	....
	Kingston	OHL	13	5	13	18	28	....	....	....	....	....
	North Bay	OHL	26	7	23	30	51	10	2	7	9	21
	NHL Totals		**8**	**0**	**1**	**1**	**25**	....	....	....	....	....

BERENS, RICK

Left wing. Shoots left. 5'11", 185 lbs. Born, Palatine, IL, August 17, 1968.
(Quebec's 2nd choice, 6th overall, in 1989 Supplemental Draft).

			Regular Season					Playoffs				
Season	Club	Lea	GP	G	A	TP	PIM	GP	G	A	TP	PIM
1987-88	U. of Denver	WCHA	39	28	20	48	52	....	....	....	....	....
1988-89	U. of Denver	WCHA	40	19	19	38	26	....	....	....	....	....
1989-90	U. of Denver	WCHA	38	27	25	52	48	....	....	....	....	....
1990-91	U. of Denver	WCHA	38	20	22	42	42	....	....	....	....	....

BEREZAN, PERRY EDMUND (BAIR-ih-ZAN)

Center. Shoots right. 6'2", 190 lbs. Born, Edmonton, Alta., December 5, 1964.
(Calgary's 3rd choice, 56th overall, in 1983 Entry Draft)

			Regular Season					Playoffs				
Season	Club	Lea	GP	G	A	TP	PIM	GP	G	A	TP	PIM
1983-84	North Dakota	WCHA	44	28	24	52	29	....	....	....	....	....
1984-85a	North Dakota	WCHA	42	23	35	58	32	....	....	....	....	....
	Calgary	**NHL**	**9**	**3**	**2**	**5**	**4**	**2**	**1**	**0**	**1**	**4**
1985-86	**Calgary**	**NHL**	**55**	**12**	**21**	**33**	**39**	**8**	**1**	**1**	**2**	**6**
1986-87	**Calgary**	**NHL**	**24**	**5**	**3**	**8**	**24**	**2**	**0**	**2**	**2**	**7**
1987-88	**Calgary**	**NHL**	**29**	**7**	**12**	**19**	**66**	**8**	**0**	**2**	**2**	**13**
1988-89	**Calgary**	**NHL**	**35**	**4**	**4**	**8**	**23**	....	....	....	....	....
	Minnesota	**NHL**	**16**	**1**	**4**	**5**	**4**	**5**	**1**	**2**	**3**	**4**
—**1989-90**	**Minnesota**	**NHL**	**64**	**3**	**12**	**15**	**31**	**5**	**1**	**0**	**1**	**0**
1990-91	**Minnesota**	**NHL**	**52**	**11**	**6**	**17**	**30**	**1**	**0**	**0**	**0**	**0**
	Kalamazoo	IHL	2	0	0	0	2	....	....	....	....	....
	NHL Totals		**284**	**46**	**64**	**110**	**221**	**31**	**4**	**7**	**11**	**34**

a WCHA Second All-Star Team (1985)

Traded to **Minnesota** by **Calgary** with Shane Churla for Brian MacLellan and Minnesota's fourth-round choice (Robert Reichel) in 1989 Entry Draft, March 4, 1989.

BERG, BILL

Left wing. Shoots left. 6'1", 190 lbs. Born, St. Catharines, Ont., October 21, 1967
(NY Islanders' 3rd choice, 59th overall, in 1986 Entry Draft).

			Regular Season					Playoffs				
Season	Club	Lea	GP	G	A	TP	PIM	GP	G	A	TP	PIM
1985-86	Toronto	OHL	64	3	35	38	143	4	0	0	0	19
	Springfield	AHL	4	1	1	2	4	....	....	....	....	....
1986-87	Toronto	OHL	57	3	15	18	138	....	....	....	....	....
1987-88	Springfield	AHL	76	6	26	32	148	....	....	....	....	....
	Peoria	IHL	5	0	1	1	8	7	0	3	3	31
1988-89	**NY Islanders**	**NHL**	**7**	**1**	**2**	**3**	**10**	....	....	....	....	....
	Springfield	AHL	69	17	32	49	122	....	....	....	....	....
1989-90	Springfield	AHL	74	12	42	54	74	15	5	12	17	35
—**1990-91**	**NY Islanders**	**NHL**	**78**	**9**	**14**	**23**	**67**	....	....	....	....	....
	NHL Totals		**85**	**10**	**16**	**26**	**77**	....	....	....	....	....

BERG, BOB

Left wing. Shoots left. 6'2", 190 lbs. Born, Beamsville, Ont., July 2, 1970.
(Los Angeles' 3rd choice, 49th overall, in 1990 Entry Draft).

			Regular Season					Playoffs				
Season	Club	Lea	GP	G	A	TP	PIM	GP	G	A	TP	PIM
1987-88	Belleville	OHL	61	15	27	42	59	....	....	....	....	....
1988-89	Belleville	OHL	66	33	51	84	88	5	1	3	4	8
1989-90a	Belleville	OHL	66	48	49	97	124	8	2	2	4	14
1990-91	New Haven	AHL	19	0	1	1	8	....	....	....	....	....
	Niagara Falls	OHL	12	8	4	12	11	....	....	....	....	....
	Sudbury	OHL	23	12	15	27	34	5	2	1	3	6

a OHL First All-Star Team (1990)

BERGER, MIKE

Defense. Shoots right. 6', 200 lbs. Born, Edmonton, Alta., June 2, 1967.
(Minnesota's 2nd choice, 69th overall, in 1985 Entry Draft).

			Regular Season					Playoffs				
Season	Club	Lea	GP	G	A	TP	PIM	GP	G	A	TP	PIM
1982-83	Lethbridge	WHL	1	0	0	0	0	....	....	....	....	....
1983-84	Lethbridge	WHL	41	2	9	11	60	5	0	1	1	7
1984-85	Lethbridge	WHL	58	9	31	40	85	4	0	3	3	9
1985-86	Spokane	WHL	57	9	40	49	95	9	1	5	6	14
1986-87	Indianapolis	IHL	4	0	3	3	4	6	0	1	1	13
	Spokane	WHL	65	26	49	75	80	2	0	0	0	2
1987-88	**Minnesota**	**NHL**	**29**	**3**	**1**	**4**	**65**	....	....	....	....	....
	Kalamazoo	IHL	36	5	10	15	94	6	2	0	2	8
1988-89	**Minnesota**	**NHL**	**1**	**0**	**0**	**0**	**2**	....	....	....	....	....
	Kalamazoo	IHL	67	9	16	25	96	6	0	2	2	8
1989-90	Phoenix	IHL	51	5	12	17	75	....	....	....	....	....
	Binghamton	AHL	10	0	4	4	10	....	....	....	....	....
1990-91	Kansas City	IHL	43	6	14	20	34	....	....	....	....	....
	Knoxville	ECHL	7	1	7	8	31	....	....	....	....	....
	NHL Totals		**30**	**3**	**1**	**4**	**67**	....	....	....	....	....

Traded to **Hartford** by **Minnesota** for Kevin Sullivan, October 7, 1989.

BERGER, PHILIP (PHIL)

Left wing. Shoots left. 6', 190 lbs. Born, Dearborn, MI, December 3, 1966.
(Quebec's 1st choice, 3rd overall, in 1988 Supplemental Draft).

			Regular Season					Playoffs				
Season	Club	Lea	GP	G	A	TP	PIM	GP	G	A	TP	PIM
1985-86	N. Michigan	WCHA	21	5	2	7	20	....	....	....	....	....
1986-87	N. Michigan	WCHA	24	11	10	21	6	....	....	....	....	....
1987-88a	N. Michigan	WCHA	38	40	32	72	22	....	....	....	....	....
1988-89b	N. Michigan	WCHA	44	30	33	63	24	....	....	....	....	....
1989-90	Fort Wayne	IHL	3	2	2	4	2	....	....	....	....	....
	Greensboro	ECHL	46	38	44	82	119	10	11	3	14	32
1990-91	Halifax	AHL	4	1	0	1	0	....	....	....	....	....
	Greensboro	ECHL	44	22	34	56	112	13	11	11	22	17

a WCHA First All-Star Team (1988)
b WCHA Second All-Star Team (1989)

BERGEVIN, MARC

Defense. Shoots left. 6', 185 lbs. Born, Montreal, Que., August 11, 1965.
(Chicago's 3rd choice, 59th overall, in 1983 Entry Draft).

			Regular Season					Playoffs				
Season	Club	Lea	GP	G	A	TP	PIM	GP	G	A	TP	PIM
1982-83	Chicoutimi	QMJHL	64	3	27	30	113	....	....	....	....	....
1983-84	Chicoutimi	QMJHL	70	10	35	45	125	....	....	....	....	....
	Springfield	AHL	7	0	1	1	2	....	....	....	....	....
1984-85	**Chicago**	**NHL**	**60**	**0**	**6**	**6**	**54**	**6**	**0**	**3**	**3**	**2**
	Springfield	AHL	....	....	....	....	....	4	0	0	0	0
1985-86	**Chicago**	**NHL**	**71**	**7**	**7**	**14**	**60**	**3**	**0**	**0**	**0**	**0**
1986-87	**Chicago**	**NHL**	**66**	**4**	**10**	**14**	**66**	**3**	**1**	**0**	**1**	**2**
1987-88	**Chicago**	**NHL**	**58**	**1**	**6**	**7**	**85**	....	....	....	....	....
	Saginaw	IHL	10	2	7	9	20	....	....	....	....	....
1988-89	**Chicago**	**NHL**	**11**	**0**	**0**	**0**	**18**	....	....	....	....	....
	NY Islanders	**NHL**	**58**	**2**	**13**	**15**	**62**	....	....	....	....	....
1989-90	**NY Islanders**	**NHL**	**18**	**0**	**4**	**4**	**30**	....	....	....	....	....
	Springfield	AHL	47	7	16	23	66	17	2	11	13	16
1990-91	Capital Dist.	AHL	7	0	5	5	6	....	....	....	....	....
	Hartford	**NHL**	**4**	**0**	**0**	**0**	**4**	....	....	....	....	....
	Springfield	AHL	58	4	23	27	85	18	0	7	7	26
	NHL Totals		**346**	**14**	**46**	**60**	**379**	**12**	**1**	**3**	**4**	**4**

Traded to **NY Islanders** by **Chicago** with Gary Nylund for Steve Konroyd and Bob Bassen, November 25, 1988. Traded to **Hartford** by **NY Islanders** for future considerations, October 30, 1990.

BERGLAND, TIM

Right wing. Shoots right. 6'3", 194 lbs. Born, Crookston, MN, January 11, 1965.
(Washington's 1st choice, 75th overall, in 1983 Entry Draft).

			Regular Season					Playoffs				
Season	Club	Lea	GP	G	A	TP	PIM	GP	G	A	TP	PIM
1983-84	U. Minnesota	WCHA	24	4	11	15	4	....	....	....	....	....
1984-85	U. Minnesota	WCHA	34	5	9	14	8	....	....	....	....	....
1985-86	U. Minnesota	WCHA	48	11	16	27	26	....	....	....	....	....
1986-87	U. Minnesota	WCHA	49	18	17	35	48	....	....	....	....	....
1987-88	Fort Wayne	IHL	13	2	1	3	9	....	....	....	....	....
	Binghamton	AHL	63	21	26	47	31	4	0	0	0	0
1988-89	Baltimore	AHL	78	24	29	53	39	....	....	....	....	....
1989-90	**Washington**	**NHL**	**32**	**2**	**5**	**7**	**31**	**15**	**1**	**1**	**2**	**10**
	Baltimore	AHL	47	12	19	31	55	....	....	....	....	....
—**1990-91**	**Washington**	**NHL**	**47**	**5**	**9**	**14**	**21**	**11**	**1**	**1**	**2**	**12**
	Baltimore	AHL	15	8	9	17	16	....	....	....	....	....
	NHL Totals		**79**	**7**	**14**	**21**	**52**	**26**	**2**	**2**	**4**	**22**

BERGMAN, JAN (BURG-muhn)

Defense. Shoots left. 5'11", 194 lbs. Born, Sodertalje, Sweden, August 7, 1969.
(Vancouver's 11th choice, 248th overall, in 1989 Entry Draft).

			Regular Season					Playoffs				
Season	Club	Lea	GP	G	A	TP	PIM	GP	G	A	TP	PIM
1988-89	Sodertalje	Swe.	34	2	4	6	14	....	....	....	....	....
1989-90	Sodertalje	Swe.	31	0	4	4	10	2	1	0	1	0
1990-91	Sodertalje	Swe.	40	4	4	8	16	....	....	....	....	....

BERGQVIST, JONAS (BURG-kvihst)

Right wing. Shoots left. 6', 185 lbs. Born, Hassleholm, Sweden, September 26, 1962.
(Calgary's 6th choice, 126th overall, in 1988 Entry Draft).

			Regular Season					Playoffs				
Season	Club	Lea	GP	G	A	TP	PIM	GP	G	A	TP	PIM
1987-88	Leksand	Swe.	37	19	12	31	....	....	....	....	....	....
1988-89	Leksand	Swe.	27	15	20	35	18	1	0	0	0	0
—**1989-90**	**Calgary**	**NHL**	**22**	**2**	**5**	**7**	**10**	....	....	....	....	....
	Salt Lake	IHL	13	6	10	16	4	....	....	....	....	....
1990-91	Mannheim	Ger.	36	16	23	39	22	....	....	....	....	....
	NHL Totals		**22**	**2**	**5**	**7**	**10**	....	....	....	....	....

BERNARD, LARRY

Left wing. Shoots left. 6'2", 195 lbs. Born, Prince George, B.C., April 16, 1967.
(NY Rangers' 8th choice, 154th overall, in 1985 Entry Draft).

			Regular Season					Playoffs				
Season	Club	Lea	GP	G	A	TP	PIM	GP	G	A	TP	PIM
1984-85	Seattle	WHL	63	18	26	44	66	....	....	....	....	....
1985-86	Seattle	WHL	54	17	25	42	64	5	1	3	4	10
1986-87	Seattle	WHL	70	40	46	86	159	....	....	....	....	....
1987-88	Colorado	IHL	64	14	13	27	68	9	0	3	3	18
1988-89	Denver	IHL	21	4	5	9	44	....	....	....	....	....
	Kalamazoo	IHL	45	9	16	25	47	1	0	0	0	5
1989-90	Moncton	AHL	66	14	17	31	93	....	....	....	....	....
1990-91	Moncton	AHL	3	0	1	1	2	....	....	....	....	....

Traded to **Minnesota** by **NY Rangers** with NY Ranger's fifth-round choice (Rhys Hollyman) in 1989 Entry Draft for Mark Hardy, December 9, 1988. Signed as a free agent by **Winnipeg**, February 20, 1990.

BERRY, BRAD

Defense. Shoots left. 6'2", 190 lbs. Born, Bashaw, Alta., April 1, 1965.
(Winnipeg's 3rd choice, 29th overall, in 1983 Entry Draft).

			Regular Season					Playoffs				
Season	Club	Lea	GP	G	A	TP	PIM	GP	G	A	TP	PIM
1983-84	North Dakota	WCHA	32	2	7	9	8	....	....	....	....	....
1984-85	North Dakota	WCHA	40	4	26	30	26	....	....	....	....	....
1985-86	North Dakota	WCHA	40	6	29	35	26	....	....	....	....	....
	Winnipeg	**NHL**	**13**	**1**	**0**	**1**	**10**	**3**	**0**	**0**	**0**	**0**
1986-87	**Winnipeg**	**NHL**	**52**	**2**	**8**	**10**	**60**	**7**	**0**	**1**	**1**	**14**
1987-88	**Winnipeg**	**NHL**	**48**	**0**	**6**	**6**	**75**	....	....	....	....	....
	Moncton	AHL	10	1	3	4	14	....	....	....	....	....
1988-89	**Winnipeg**	**NHL**	**38**	**0**	**9**	**9**	**45**	....	....	....	....	....
	Moncton	AHL	38	3	16	19	39	....	....	....	....	....
1989-90	**Winnipeg**	**NHL**	**12**	**1**	**2**	**3**	**6**	**1**	**0**	**0**	**0**	**0**
	Moncton	AHL	38	1	9	10	58	....	....	....	....	....
1990-91	Brynas	Swe.	38	3	1	4	38	....	....	....	....	....
	NHL Totals		**163**	**4**	**25**	**29**	**196**	**11**	**0**	**1**	**1**	**14**

BERRY, KENNETH E. (KEN)

Left wing. Shoots left. 5'9", 175 lbs.   Born, Burnaby, B.C., June 21, 1960.
(Vancouver's 5th choice, 112th overall, in 1980 Entry Draft).

			Regular Season					Playoffs				
Season	Club	Lea	GP	G	A	TP	PIM	GP	G	A	TP	PIM
1979-80	Cdn. National	...	57	19	20	39	48	....	....	....	....	....
	Cdn. Olympic	...	6	4	1	5	8	....	....	....	....	....
1980-81	U. of Denver	WCHA	40	22	34	56	74	....	....	....	....	....
	Wichita	CHL	9	7	6	13	13	17	2	4	6	28
1981-82	**Edmonton**	**NHL**	15	2	3	5	9	....	....	....	....	....
	Wichita	CHL	58	28	29	57	70	....	....	....	....	....
1982-83	Moncton	AHL	76	24	26	50	80	....	....	....	....	....
1983-84	**Edmonton**	**NHL**	13	2	3	5	10	....	....	....	....	....
	Moncton	AHL	53	18	20	38	75	....	....	....	....	....
1984-85	Nova Scotia	AHL	71	30	27	57	40	6	2	2	4	2
1985-86	Bayreuth	W.Ger.	33	27	25	52	88	....	....	....	....	....
	Cdn. National	...	8	1	2	3	20	....	....	....	....	....
1986-87	Cdn. National	...	52	17	27	44	60	....	....	....	....	....
1987-88	Cdn. National	...	59	18	15	33	47	....	....	....	....	....
	Cdn. Olympic	...	8	2	4	6	4	....	....	....	....	....
	Vancouver	**NHL**	14	2	3	5	6	....	....	....	....	....
1988-89	**Vancouver**	**NHL**	13	2	1	3	5	....	....	....	....	....
	Milwaukee	IHL	5	4	4	8	2	....	....	....	....	....
1989-90	Munich	W.Ger.	36	24	33	57	70	....	....	....	....	....
1990-91	Munich	Ger.	47	27	18	45	76	....	....	....	....	....
	NHL Totals		**55**	**8**	**10**	**18**	**30**	....	....	....	....	....

Traded to **Edmonton** by **Vancouver** with Garry Lariviere for Blair MacDonald and Lars-Gunnar Petersson, March 10, 1981. Signed as a free agent by **Vancouver**, March 1, 1988.

BERUBE, CRAIG   (buh-ROO-bee)

Left wing. Shoots left. 6'1", 205 lbs.   Born, Calahoo, Alta., December 17, 1965.

			Regular Season					Playoffs				
Season	Club	Lea	GP	G	A	TP	PIM	GP	G	A	TP	PIM
1982-83	Kamloops	WHL	4	0	0	0	0	....	....	....	....	....
1983-84	N. Westminster	WHL	70	11	20	31	104	8	1	2	3	5
1984-85	N. Westminster	WHL	70	25	44	69	191	10	3	2	5	4
1985-86	Kamloops	WHL	32	17	14	31	119	....	....	....	....	....
	Medicine Hat	WHL	34	14	16	30	95	25	7	8	15	102
1986-87	**Philadelphia**	**NHL**	7	0	0	0	57	5	0	0	0	17
	Hershey	AHL	63	7	17	24	325	....	....	....	....	....
1987-88	**Philadelphia**	**NHL**	27	3	2	5	108	....	....	....	....	....
	Hershey	AHL	31	5	9	14	119	....	....	....	....	....
1988-89	**Philadelphia**	**NHL**	53	1	1	2	199	16	0	0	0	56
	Hershey	AHL	7	0	2	2	19	....	....	....	....	....
1989-90	**Philadelphia**	**NHL**	74	4	14	18	291	....	....	....	....	....
1990-91	**Philadelphia**	**NHL**	74	8	9	17	293	....	....	....	....	....
	NHL Totals		**235**	**16**	**26**	**42**	**948**	**21**	**0**	**0**	**0**	**73**

Signed as a free agent by **Philadelphia**, March 19, 1986. Traded to **Edmonton** by **Philadelphia** with Craig Fisher and Scott Mellanby for Dave Brown, Corey Foster and Jari Kurri, May 30, 1991.

BEUKEBOOM, JEFF   (BOO-kuh-BOOM)

Defense. Shoots right. 6'4", 215 lbs.   Born, Ajax, Ont., March 28, 1965.
(Edmonton's 1st choice, 19th overall, in 1983 Entry Draft).

			Regular Season					Playoffs				
Season	Club	Lea	GP	G	A	TP	PIM	GP	G	A	TP	PIM
1982-83	S. S. Marie	OHL	70	0	25	25	143	16	1	4	5	46
1983-84	S. S. Marie	OHL	61	6	30	36	178	16	1	7	8	43
1984-85a	S. S. Marie	OHL	37	4	20	24	85	16	4	6	10	47
1985-86	Nova Scotia	AHL	77	9	20	29	175	....	....	....	....	....
	Edmonton	**NHL**	....	....	....	....	....	1	0	0	0	4
1986-87	**Edmonton**	**NHL**	44	3	8	11	124	....	....	....	....	....
	Nova Scotia	AHL	14	1	7	8	35	....	....	....	....	....
1987-88	**Edmonton**	**NHL**	73	5	20	25	201	7	0	0	0	16
1988-89	**Edmonton**	**NHL**	36	0	5	5	94	1	0	0	0	2
	Cape Breton	AHL	8	0	4	4	36	....	....	....	....	....
1989-90	**Edmonton**	**NHL**	46	1	12	13	86	2	0	0	0	0
1990-91	**Edmonton**	**NHL**	67	3	7	10	150	18	1	3	4	28
	NHL Totals		**266**	**12**	**52**	**64**	**655**	**29**	**1**	**3**	**4**	**50**

a OHL First All-Star Team (1985)

BIGGS, DON

Center. Shoots right. 5'8", 185 lbs.   Born, Mississauga, Ont., April 7, 1965.
(Minnesota's 9th choice, 156th overall, in 1983 Entry Draft).

			Regular Season					Playoffs				
Season	Club	Lea	GP	G	A	TP	PIM	GP	G	A	TP	PIM
1982-83	Oshawa	OHL	70	22	53	75	145	16	3	6	9	17
1983-84	Oshawa	OHL	58	31	60	91	149	7	4	4	8	18
1984-85	**Minnesota**	**NHL**	1	0	0	0	0	....	....	....	....	....
	Springfield	AHL	6	0	3	3	0	2	1	0	1	0
	Oshawa	OHL	60	48	69	117	105	5	3	4	7	6
1985-86	Springfield	AHL	28	15	16	31	46	....	....	....	....	....
	Nova Scotia	AHL	47	6	23	29	36	....	....	....	....	....
1986-87	Nova Scotia	AHL	80	22	25	47	165	5	1	2	3	4
1987-88	Hershey	AHL	77	38	41	79	151	12	5	*11	*16	22
1988-89	Hershey	AHL	76	36	67	103	158	11	5	9	14	30
1989-90	**Philadelphia**	**NHL**	11	2	0	2	8	....	....	....	....	....
	Hershey	AHL	66	39	53	92	125	....	....	....	....	....
1990-91	Rochester	AHL	65	31	57	88	115	15	9	*14	*23	14
	NHL Totals		**12**	**2**	**0**	**2**	**8**	....	....	....	....	....

Traded to **Edmonton** by **Minnesota** with Gord Sherven for Marc Habscheid, Don Barber and Emanuel Viveiros, December 20, 1985. Signed as a free agent by **Philadelphia**, July 17, 1987.

BIGNELL, GREG

Defense. Shoots left. 6', 188 lbs.   Born, Kitchener, Ont., May 9, 1969.
(Detroit's 10th choice, 200th overall, in 1989 Entry Draft).

			Regular Season					Playoffs				
Season	Club	Lea	GP	G	A	TP	PIM	GP	G	A	TP	PIM
1988-89	Belleville	OHL	54	6	27	33	180	5	0	1	1	16
1989-90	Belleville	OHL	58	6	26	32	141	11	0	6	6	31
1990-91	Hampton Roads	ECHL	55	7	21	28	265	....	....	....	....	....

BILLECK, LAURIE

Defense. Shoots right. 6'3", 210 lbs.   Born, Dauphin, Man., February 2, 1971.
(Minnesota's 2nd choice, 50th overall, in 1990 Entry Draft).

			Regular Season					Playoffs				
Season	Club	Lea	GP	G	A	TP	PIM	GP	G	A	TP	PIM
1988-89	Prince Albert	WHL	60	2	4	6	65	4	1	0	1	14
1989-90	Prince Albert	WHL	67	7	28	35	135	14	2	3	5	24
1990-91	Prince Albert	WHL	35	1	10	11	60	3	0	0	0	5

BILODEAU, BRENT

Defense. Shoots left. 6'3", 220 lbs.   Born, Dallas, TX, March 27, 1973.
(Montreal's 1st choice, 17th overall, in 1991 Entry Draft).

			Regular Season					Playoffs				
Season	Club	Lea	GP	G	A	TP	PIM	GP	G	A	TP	PIM
1989-90	Seattle	WHL	68	14	29	43	170	13	3	5	8	31
1990-91	Seattle	WHL	55	7	18	25	145	6	1	0	1	12

BIONDI, JOSEPH

Center. Shoots left. 6'1", 175 lbs.   Born, Warroad, MN, June 25, 1970.
(Minnesota's 9th choice, 176th overall, in 1990 Entry Draft).

			Regular Season					Playoffs				
Season	Club	Lea	GP	G	A	TP	PIM	GP	G	A	TP	PIM
1989-90	Minn.-Duluth	WCHA	37	10	17	27	8	....	....	....	....	....
1990-91	Minn.-Duluth	WCHA	30	6	8	14	4	....	....	....	....	....

BIOTTI, CHRIS   (bee-AH-tee)

Defense. Shoots left. 6'1", 205 lbs.   Born, Waltham, MA, April 22, 1967.
(Calgary's 1st choice, 17th overall, in 1985 Entry Draft).

			Regular Season					Playoffs				
Season	Club	Lea	GP	G	A	TP	PIM	GP	G	A	TP	PIM
1985-86	Harvard	ECAC	15	3	5	8	18	....	....	....	....	....
1986-87	Harvard	ECAC	30	1	6	7	23	....	....	....	....	....
1987-88	Salt Lake	IHL	72	5	19	24	73	12	2	3	5	33
1988-89	Salt Lake	IHL	57	6	14	20	44	12	3	4	7	16
1989-90	Salt Lake	IHL	60	9	19	28	73	3	1	0	1	2
1990-91	Brunico	Italy	32	11	18	29	16	....	....	....	....	....

BISCHOFF, GRANT

Left wing. Shoots left. 5'10", 165 lbs.   Born, Anoka, MN, October 26, 1968.
(Minnesota's 8th choice, 211th overall, in 1988 Entry Draft).

			Regular Season					Playoffs				
Season	Club	Lea	GP	G	A	TP	PIM	GP	G	A	TP	PIM
1987-88	U. Minnesota	WCHA	44	15	22	37	14	....	....	....	....	....
1988-89	U. Minnesota	WCHA	47	21	16	37	14	....	....	....	....	....
1989-90	U. Minnesota	WCHA	45	21	19	40	18	....	....	....	....	....
1990-91	U. Minnesota	WCHA	44	23	24	47	36	....	....	....	....	....

BISHOP, MICHAEL

Defense. Shoots left. 6'2", 212 lbs.   Born, Sarnia, Ont., June 15, 1966.
(Montreal's 14th choice, 226th overall, in 1985 Entry Draft).

			Regular Season					Playoffs				
Season	Club	Lea	GP	G	A	TP	PIM	GP	G	A	TP	PIM
1985-86	Colgate	ECAC	17	5	6	11	47	....	....	....	....	....
1986-87	Colgate	ECAC	30	7	17	24	68	....	....	....	....	....
1987-88	Colgate	ECAC	31	8	24	32	49	....	....	....	....	....
1988-89a	Colgate	ECAC	31	8	13	21	92	....	....	....	....	....
1989-90	Fort Wayne	IHL	12	0	0	0	6	....	....	....	....	....
	Knoxville	ECHL	22	3	9	12	28	....	....	....	....	....
1990-91	Knoxville	ECHL	35	7	13	20	74	3	0	0	0	2

a ECAC Second All-Star Team (1989)

BISSETT, TOM   (BIH-siht)

Center. Shoots left. 6', 180 lbs.   Born, Seattle, WA, March 13, 1966.
(Detroit's 11th choice, 211th overall, in 1986 Entry Draft).

			Regular Season					Playoffs				
Season	Club	Lea	GP	G	A	TP	PIM	GP	G	A	TP	PIM
1985-86	Michigan Tech.	WCHA	40	12	21	33	18	....	....	....	....	....
1986-87	Michigan Tech.	WCHA	40	16	19	35	12	....	....	....	....	....
1987-88	Michigan Tech.	WCHA	41	18	26	44	20	....	....	....	....	....
1988-89	Adirondack	AHL	5	0	1	1	0	....	....	....	....	....
	Michigan Tech.	WCHA	42	19	28	47	16	....	....	....	....	....
1989-90	Adirondack	AHL	16	11	4	15	4	....	....	....	....	....
	Hampton Roads	ECHL	5	7	7	14	2	....	....	....	....	....
1990-91	**Detroit**	**NHL**	5	0	0	0	0	....	....	....	....	....
	Adirondack	AHL	73	44	38	82	12	2	0	0	0	0
	NHL Totals		**5**	**0**	**0**	**0**	**0**	....	....	....	....	....

BJUGSTAD, SCOTT (BYOOG-stad)

Right wing. Shoots left. 6'1", 185 lbs. Born, St. Paul, MN, June 2, 1961.
(Minnesota's 13th choice, 181st overall, in 1981 Entry Draft).

			Regular Season					Playoffs				
Season	**Club**	**Lea**	**GP**	**G**	**A**	**TP**	**PIM**	**GP**	**G**	**A**	**TP**	**PIM**
1979-80	U. Minnesota	WCHA	18	2	2	4	2	....	....	....	....	....
1980-81	U. Minnesota	WCHA	35	12	23	25	34	....	....	....	....	....
1981-82	U. Minnesota	WCHA	36	29	14	43	24	....	....	....	....	....
1982-83a	U. Minnesota	WCHA	26	21	35	56	12	....	....	....	....	....
1983-84	U.S. National	...	54	31	20	51	28	....	....	....	....	....
	U.S. Olympic	...	6	3	2	5	6	....	....	....	....	....
	Minnesota	**NHL**	**5**	**0**	**0**	**0**	**2**	....	....	....	....	....
	Salt Lake	CHL	15	10	8	18	6	5	3	4	7	0
1984-85	**Minnesota**	**NHL**	**72**	**11**	**4**	**15**	**32**	....	....	....	....	....
	Springfield	AHL	5	2	3	5	2	....	....	....	....	....
1985-86	**Minnesota**	**NHL**	**80**	**43**	**33**	**76**	**24**	**5**	**0**	**1**	**1**	**0**
1986-87	**Minnesota**	**NHL**	**39**	**4**	**9**	**13**	**43**	....	....	....	....	....
	Springfield	AHL	11	4	6	10	7	....	....	....	....	....
1987-88	**Minnesota**	**NHL**	**33**	**10**	**12**	**22**	**15**	....	....	....	....	....
1988-89	**Pittsburgh**	**NHL**	**24**	**3**	**0**	**3**	**4**	....	....	....	....	....
	Kalamazoo	IHL	4	5	0	5	4	....	....	....	....	....
1989-90	**Los Angeles**	**NHL**	**11**	**1**	**2**	**3**	**2**	**2**	**0**	**0**	**0**	**2**
	New Haven	AHL	47	45	21	66	40	....	....	....	....	....
—**1990-91**	**Los Angeles**	**NHL**	**31**	**2**	**4**	**6**	**12**	**2**	**0**	**0**	**0**	**0**
	Phoenix	IHL	3	7	2	9	2	....	....	....	....	....
	NHL Totals		**295**	**74**	**64**	**138**	**134**	**9**	**0**	**1**	**1**	**2**

a WCHA First All-Star Team (1983)

Traded to **Pittsburgh** by **Minnesota** with Gord Dineen for Ville Siren and Steve Gotaas, December 17, 1988. Signed as a free agent by **Los Angeles**, August 21, 1989.

BJUHR, THOMAS (BYOOR)

Right wing. Shoots left. 6'1", 216 lbs. Born, Stockholm, Sweden, August 28, 1966.
(Detroit's 7th choice, 134th overall, in 1985 Entry Draft).

			Regular Season					Playoffs				
Season	**Club**	**Lea**	**GP**	**G**	**A**	**TP**	**PIM**	**GP**	**G**	**A**	**TP**	**PIM**
1984-85	AIK	Swe. Jr.	33	38	18	56	28	....	....	....	....	....
	AIK	Swe.	3	1	0	1	0	....	....	....	....	....
1985-86	AIK	Swe.	14	0	1	1	8	....	....	....	....	....
1986-87	Portland	WHL	39	28	26	54	23	....	....	....	....	....
1987-88	Adirondack	AHL	58	4	2	6	21	....	....	....	....	....
1988-89	AIK	Swe.	34	8	9	17	40	....	....	....	....	....
1989-90	AIK	Swe.	40	19	12	31	22	3	0	1	1	4
1990-91	AIK	Swe.	39	11	7	18	51	....	....	....	....	....

BLACK, JAMES

Center. Shoots left. 5'11", 185 lbs. Born, Regina, Sask., August 15, 1969.
(Hartford's 4th choice, 94th overall, in 1989 Entry Draft).

			Regular Season					Playoffs				
Season	**Club**	**Lea**	**GP**	**G**	**A**	**TP**	**PIM**	**GP**	**G**	**A**	**TP**	**PIM**
1987-88	Portland	WHL	72	30	50	80	50	....	....	....	....	....
1988-89	Portland	WHL	71	45	51	96	57	19	13	6	19	28
1989-90	**Hartford**	**NHL**	**1**	**0**	**0**	**0**	**0**	....	....	....	....	....
	Binghamton	AHL	80	37	35	72	34	....	....	....	....	....
1990-91	**Hartford**	**NHL**	**1**	**0**	**0**	**0**	**0**	....	....	....	....	....
	Springfield	AHL	79	35	61	96	34	18	9	9	18	6
	NHL Totals		**2**	**0**	**0**	**0**	**0**	....	....	....	....	....

BLAD, BRIAN

Defense. Shoots left. 6', 185 lbs. Born, Brockville, Ont., July 22, 1967.
(Toronto's 9th choice, 175th overall, in 1987 Entry Draft).

			Regular Season					Playoffs				
Season	**Club**	**Lea**	**GP**	**G**	**A**	**TP**	**PIM**	**GP**	**G**	**A**	**TP**	**PIM**
1984-85	Windsor	OHL	56	1	7	8	126	....	....	....	....	....
1985-86	Windsor	OHL	56	2	9	11	195	....	....	....	....	....
1986-87	Windsor	OHL	15	1	1	2	30	....	....	....	....	....
	Belleville	OHL	20	1	5	6	43	....	....	....	....	....
1987-88	Milwaukee	IHL	28	1	6	7	45	....	....	....	....	....
	Newmarket	AHL	39	0	4	4	74	....	....	....	....	....
1988-89	Newmarket	AHL	59	2	4	6	149	5	0	1	1	5
1989-90	Newmarket	AHL	58	2	4	6	216	....	....	....	....	....
1990-91	Newmarket	AHL	28	0	0	0	100	....	....	....	....	....
	Milwaukee	IHL	37	1	2	3	98	6	0	2	2	8

Traded to **Vancouver** by **Toronto** for Todd Hawkins, January 22, 1991.

BLAESER, JEFFREY

Left wing. Shoots left. 6'3", 190 lbs. Born, Parma, OH, May 11, 1970.
(Pittsburgh's 7th choice, 151st overall, in 1988 Entry Draft).

			Regular Season					Playoffs				
Season	**Club**	**Lea**	**GP**	**G**	**A**	**TP**	**PIM**	**GP**	**G**	**A**	**TP**	**PIM**
1988-89	Yale	ECAC	31	8	19	27	12	....	....	....	....	....
1989-90	Yale	ECAC	29	17	14	31	16	....	....	....	....	....
1990-91	Yale	ECAC	29	12	14	26	22	....	....	....	....	....

BLAIN, JOEL

Left wing. Shoots left. 6', 194 lbs. Born, Malartic, Que., October 12, 1961.
(Edmonton's 4th choice, 67th overall, in 1990 Entry Draft).

			Regular Season					Playoffs				
Season	**Club**	**Lea**	**GP**	**G**	**A**	**TP**	**PIM**	**GP**	**G**	**A**	**TP**	**PIM**
1989-90	Hull	QMJHL	65	31	47	78	137	11	6	6	12	16
1990-91	Hull	QMJHL	61	19	31	50	95	6	4	3	7	17

BLAISDELL, MICHAEL WALTER (MIKE) (BLAZE-dell)

Right wing. Shoots right. 6'1", 195 lbs. Born, Moose Jaw, Sask., January 18, 1960.
(Detroit's 1st choice, 11th overall, in 1980 Entry Draft).

			Regular Season					Playoffs				
Season	**Club**	**Lea**	**GP**	**G**	**A**	**TP**	**PIM**	**GP**	**G**	**A**	**TP**	**PIM**
1977-78	Regina	WHL	6	5	5	10	2	13	4	7	11	0
1978-79	U. Wisconsin	WCHA	20	7	1	8	4	....	....	....	....	....
1979-80	Regina	WHL	63	71	38	109	62	18	*16	9	25	26
1980-81	**Detroit**	**NHL**	**32**	**3**	**6**	**9**	**10**	....	....	....	....	....
	Adirondack	AHL	41	10	4	14	8	12	2	2	4	5
1981-82	**Detroit**	**NHL**	**80**	**23**	**32**	**55**	**48**	....	....	....	....	....
1982-83	**Detroit**	**NHL**	**80**	**18**	**23**	**41**	**22**	....	....	....	....	....
1983-84	**NY Rangers**	**NHL**	**36**	**5**	**6**	**11**	**31**	....	....	....	....	....
	Tulsa	CHL	32	10	8	18	23	9	6	6	12	6
1984-85	**NY Rangers**	**NHL**	**12**	**1**	**0**	**1**	**11**	....	....	....	....	....
	New Haven	AHL	64	21	23	44	41	....	....	....	....	....
1985-86	**Pittsburgh**	**NHL**	**66**	**15**	**14**	**29**	**36**	....	....	....	....	....
1986-87	**Pittsburgh**	**NHL**	**10**	**1**	**1**	**2**	**2**	....	....	....	....	....
	Baltimore	AHL	43	12	12	24	47	....	....	....	....	....
1987-88	**Toronto**	**NHL**	**18**	**3**	**2**	**5**	**2**	**6**	**1**	**2**	**3**	**10**
	Newmarket	AHL	57	25	28	53	30	....	....	....	....	....
1988-89	**Toronto**	**NHL**	**9**	**1**	**0**	**1**	**4**	....	....	....	....	....
	Newmarket	AHL	40	16	7	23	48	....	....	....	....	....
1989-90	Cdn. National	...	50	12	18	30	40	....	....	....	....	....
1990-91	Albany	IHL	6	2	0	2	0	....	....	....	....	....
	NHL Totals		**343**	**70**	**84**	**154**	**166**	**6**	**1**	**2**	**3**	**10**

Traded to **NY Rangers** by **Detroit** with Willie Huber and Mark Osborne for Ron Duguay, Eddie Mio and Eddie Johnstone, June 13, 1983. Claimed by **Pittsburgh** from **NY Rangers** in NHL Waiver Draft, October 7, 1985. Signed as a free agent by **Toronto**, July 10, 1987.

BLAKE, ROBERT (ROB)

Defense. Shoots right. 6'3", 215 lbs. Born, Simcoe, Ont., December 10, 1969.
(Los Angeles' 4th choice, 70th overall, in 1988 Entry Draft).

			Regular Season					Playoffs				
Season	**Club**	**Lea**	**GP**	**G**	**A**	**TP**	**PIM**	**GP**	**G**	**A**	**TP**	**PIM**
1987-88	Bowling Green	CCHA	43	5	8	13	88	....	....	....	....	....
1988-89a	Bowling Green	CCHA	46	11	21	32	140	....	....	....	....	....
1989-90bc	Bowling Green	CCHA	42	23	36	59	140	....	....	....	....	....
	Los Angeles	**NHL**	**4**	**0**	**0**	**0**	**4**	**8**	**1**	**3**	**4**	**4**
—**1990-91d**	**Los Angeles**	**NHL**	**75**	**12**	**34**	**46**	**125**	**12**	**1**	**4**	**5**	**26**
	NHL Totals		**79**	**12**	**34**	**46**	**129**	**20**	**2**	**7**	**9**	**30**

a CCHA Second All-Star Team (1989)
b CCHA First All-Star Team (1990)
c NCAA West First All-American Team (1990)
d NHL/Upper Deck All-Rookie Team (1991)

BLESSMAN, JOHN

Defense. Shoots left. 6'3", 211 lbs. Born, Toronto, Ont., April 27, 1967.
(New Jersey's 8th choice, 170th overall, in 1987 Entry Draft).

			Regular Season					Playoffs				
Season	**Club**	**Lea**	**GP**	**G**	**A**	**TP**	**PIM**	**GP**	**G**	**A**	**TP**	**PIM**
1984-85	Toronto	OHL	25	1	3	4	42	5	0	0	0	0
1985-86	Toronto	OHL	64	2	13	15	116	4	0	0	0	11
1986-87	Toronto	OHL	61	6	24	30	130	....	....	....	....	....
1987-88	Utica	AHL	24	0	2	2	50	....	....	....	....	....
	Toronto	OHL	23	8	11	19	64	4	0	4	4	0
1988-89	Utica	AHL	26	2	3	5	46	....	....	....	....	....
	Indianapolis	IHL	31	2	5	7	60	....	....	....	....	....
1989-90	Hershey	AHL	1	0	0	0	0	....	....	....	....	....
	Winston-Salem	ECHL	17	1	6	7	108	....	....	....	....	....
	Greensboro	ECHL	19	0	7	7	81	11	3	6	9	50
1990-91	Greensboro	ECHL	29	7	14	21	131	13	1	9	10	36

BLOEMBERG, JEFF (BLOOM-buhrg)

Defense. Shoots right. 6'2", 205 lbs. Born, Listowel, Ont., January 31, 1968.
(NY Ranger's 5th choice, 93rd overall, in 1986 Entry Draft).

			Regular Season					Playoffs				
Season	**Club**	**Lea**	**GP**	**G**	**A**	**TP**	**PIM**	**GP**	**G**	**A**	**TP**	**PIM**
1985-86	North Bay	OHL	60	2	11	13	76	8	1	2	3	9
1986-87	North Bay	OHL	60	5	13	18	91	21	1	6	7	13
1987-88	Colorado	IHL	5	0	0	0	0	11	1	0	1	8
	North Bay	OHL	46	9	26	35	60	4	1	4	5	2
1988-89	**NY Rangers**	**NHL**	**9**	**0**	**0**	**0**	**0**	....	....	....	....	....
	Denver	IHL	64	7	22	29	55	1	0	0	0	0
—**1989-90**	**NY Rangers**	**NHL**	**28**	**3**	**3**	**6**	**25**	**7**	**0**	**3**	**3**	**5**
	Flint	IHL	41	7	14	21	24	....	....	....	....	....
1990-91	**NY Rangers**	**NHL**	**3**	**0**	**2**	**2**	**0**	....	....	....	....	....
a	Binghamton	AHL	77	16	46	62	28	10	0	6	6	10
	NHL Totals		**40**	**3**	**5**	**8**	**25**	**7**	**0**	**3**	**3**	**5**

a AHL Second All-Star Team (1991)

BLOMSTEN, ARTO (BLOOM-stehn)

Defense. Shoots left. 6'3", 191 lbs. Born, Vaasa, Finland, March 16, 1965.
(Winnipeg's 11th choice, 239th overall, in 1986 Entry Draft).

			Regular Season					Playoffs				
Season	**Club**	**Lea**	**GP**	**G**	**A**	**TP**	**PIM**	**GP**	**G**	**A**	**TP**	**PIM**
1986-87	Djurgarden	Swe.	29	2	4	6	28	....	....	....	....	....
1987-88	Djurgarden	Swe.	39	12	6	18	36	2	1	0	1	0
1988-89	Djurgarden	Swe.	40	10	9	19	38	....	....	....	....	....
1989-90	Djurgarden	Swe.	36	5	21	26	28	8	4	1	5	6
1990-91	Djurgarden	Swe.	38	2	9	11	42	....	....	....	....	....

BLUM, JOHN JOSEPH

Defense. Shoots right. 6'3", 205 lbs. Born, Detroit, MI, October 8, 1959.

			Regular Season					Playoffs				
Season	Club	Lea	GP	G	A	TP	PIM	GP	G	A	TP	PIM
1980-81	Michigan	WCHA	38	9	43	52	93	....	....	....	....	....
1981-82	Wichita	CHL	78	8	33	41	247	7	0	3	3	24
1982-83	**Edmonton**	**NHL**	**5**	**0**	**3**	**3**	**24**	....	....	....	....	....
	Moncton	AHL	76	10	30	40	219	....	....	....	....	....
1983-84	**Edmonton**	**NHL**	**4**	**0**	**1**	**1**	**2**	....	....	....	....	....
	Moncton	AHL	57	3	22	25	202	....	....	....	....	....
	Boston	**NHL**	**12**	**1**	**1**	**2**	**30**	**3**	**0**	**0**	**0**	**4**
1984-85	**Boston**	**NHL**	**75**	**3**	**13**	**16**	**263**	**5**	**0**	**0**	**0**	**13**
1985-86	**Boston**	**NHL**	**61**	**1**	**7**	**8**	**80**	**3**	**0**	**0**	**0**	**6**
	Moncton	AHL	12	1	5	6	37	....	....	....	....	....
1986-87	**Washington**	**NHL**	**66**	**2**	**8**	**10**	**133**	**6**	**0**	**1**	**1**	**4**
1987-88	**Boston**	**NHL**	**19**	**0**	**1**	**1**	**70**	**3**	**0**	**1**	**1**	**0**
	Maine	AHL	43	5	18	23	136	8	0	6	6	35
1988-89	**Detroit**	**NHL**	**6**	**0**	**0**	**0**	**8**	....	....	....	....	....
	Adirondack	AHL	56	1	19	20	168	12	0	1	1	18
1989-90	**Boston**	**NHL**	**2**	**0**	**0**	**0**	**0**	....	....	....	....	....
	Maine	AHL	77	1	20	21	134	....	....	....	....	....
1990-91	Maine	AHL	57	4	8	12	75	1	0	0	0	2
	NHL Totals		**250**	**7**	**34**	**41**	**610**	**20**	**0**	**2**	**2**	**27**

Signed as free agent by **Edmonton**, May 5, 1981. Traded to **Boston** by **Edmonton** for Larry Melnyk, March 6, 1984. Claimed by **Washington** from **Boston** in NHL Waiver Draft, October 6, 1986. Traded to **Boston** by **Washington** for Boston's seventh round choice (Brad Schlegal) in 1988 Entry Draft, June 1, 1987. Signed as a free agent by **Detroit**, August 12, 1988. Signed as a free agent by **Boston**, July 6, 1989.

BLUM, KENNETH

Center. Shoots left. 6'1", 185 lbs. Born, Hackensack, NJ. June 8, 1971.
(Minnesota's 10th choice, 175th overall, in 1989 Entry Draft).

			Regular Season					Playoffs				
Season	Club	Lea	GP	G	A	TP	PIM	GP	G	A	TP	PIM
1989-90	Lake Superior	CCHA	19	2	1	3	14	....	....	....	....	....
1990-91	Ottawa	OHL	13	3	4	7	4	....	....	....	....	....

BOBACK, MICHAEL

Center. Shoots right. 5'11", 180 lbs. Born, Mt. Clemens, MI, August 13, 1970.
(Washington's 12th choice, 198th overall, in 1990 Entry Draft).

			Regular Season					Playoffs				
Season	Club	Lea	GP	G	A	TP	PIM	GP	G	A	TP	PIM
1988-89	Providence	H.E.	29	19	19	38	24	....	....	....	....	....
1989-90a	Providence	H.E.	31	13	29	42	28	....	....	....	....	....
1990-91	Providence	H.E.	26	15	24	39	6	....	....	....	....	....

a Hockey East All-Star Team (1990)

BOBYCK, BRENT

Left wing. Shoots left. 5'10", 174 lbs. Born, Regina, Sask., April 26, 1968.
(Montreal's 4th choice, 78th overall, in 1986 Entry Draft).

			Regular Season					Playoffs				
Season	Club	Lea	GP	G	A	TP	PIM	GP	G	A	TP	PIM
1986-87	North Dakota	WCHA	46	8	11	19	16	....	....	....	....	....
1987-88	North Dakota	WCHA	41	10	20	30	43	....	....	....	....	....
1988-89	North Dakota	WCHA	28	11	8	19	16	....	....	....	....	....
1989-90	North Dakota	WCHA	44	16	21	37	47	....	....	....	....	....
1990-91	Fredericton	AHL	4	0	0	0	4	....	....	....	....	....
	Albany	IHL	18	0	3	3	10	....	....	....	....	....

BODAK, ROBERT PETER (BOB)

Left wing. Shoots left. 6'2", 200 lbs. Born, Thunder Bay, Ont., May 28, 1961.

			Regular Season					Playoffs				
Season	Club	Lea	GP	G	A	TP	PIM	GP	G	A	TP	PIM
1983-84	Lakehead U.	GPAC	22	23	24	47	18	....	....	....	....	....
1984-85	Springfield	AHL	79	20	25	45	52	4	1	0	1	2
1985-86	Springfield	AHL	4	0	0	0	4	....	....	....	....	....
	Moncton	AHL	58	27	15	42	114	10	3	3	6	0
1986-87	Moncton	AHL	48	11	20	31	75	6	1	1	2	18
1987-88	**Calgary**	**NHL**	**3**	**0**	**0**	**0**	**22**	....	....	....	....	....
	Salt Lake	IHL	44	12	10	22	117	18	1	3	4	74
1988-89	Binghamton	AHL	44	15	25	40	135	....	....	....	....	....
	Salt Lake	IHL	4	0	0	0	2	....	....	....	....	....
1989-90	**Hartford**	**NHL**	**1**	**0**	**0**	**0**	**7**	....	....	....	....	....
	Binghamton	AHL	79	32	25	57	59	....	....	....	....	....
1990-91	Binghamton	AHL	27	2	11	13	36	....	....	....	....	....
	San Diego	IHL	17	1	5	6	18	....	....	....	....	....
	Albany	IHL	5	1	1	2	13	....	....	....	....	....
	NHL Totals		**4**	**0**	**0**	**0**	**29**	....	....	....	....	....

Signed as a free agent by **Calgary**, January 28, 1986. Signed as a free agent by **Hartford**, May 10, 1989.

BODDEN, JAMES (JIM)

Center. Shoots right. 5'11", 180 lbs. Born, Dundas, Ont., October 26, 1967.
(Pittsburgh's 7th choice, 131st overall, in 1987 Entry Draft).

			Regular Season					Playoffs				
Season	Club	Lea	GP	G	A	TP	PIM	GP	G	A	TP	PIM
1987-88	Miami-Ohio	CCHA	38	10	14	24	30	....	....	....	....	....
1988-89	Miami-Ohio	CCHA	33	11	10	21	15	....	....	....	....	....
1989-90	Miami-Ohio	CCHA	38	14	23	37	10	....	....	....	....	....
1990-91	Miami-Ohio	CCHA	3	1	0	1	0	....	....	....	....	....

BODGER, DOUG

Defense. Shoots left. 6'2", 210 lbs. Born, Chemainus, B.C., June 18, 1966
(Pittsburgh's 2nd choice, 9th overall, in 1984 Entry Draft).

			Regular Season					Playoffs				
Season	Club	Lea	GP	G	A	TP	PIM	GP	G	A	TP	PIM
1982-83a	Kamloops	WHL	72	26	66	92	98	7	0	5	5	2
1983-84	Kamloops	WHL	70	21	77	98	90	17	2	15	17	12
1984-85	**Pittsburgh**	**NHL**	**65**	**5**	**26**	**31**	**67**	....	....	....	....	....
1985-86	**Pittsburgh**	**NHL**	**79**	**4**	**33**	**37**	**63**	....	....	....	....	....
1986-87	**Pittsburgh**	**NHL**	**76**	**11**	**38**	**49**	**52**	....	....	....	....	....
1987-88	**Pittsburgh**	**NHL**	**69**	**14**	**31**	**45**	**103**	....	....	....	....	....
1988-89	**Pittsburgh**	**NHL**	**10**	**1**	**4**	**5**	**7**	....	....	....	....	....
	Buffalo	**NHL**	**61**	**7**	**40**	**47**	**52**	**5**	**1**	**1**	**2**	**11**
1989-90	**Buffalo**	**NHL**	**71**	**12**	**36**	**48**	**64**	**6**	**1**	**5**	**6**	**6**
1990-91	**Buffalo**	**NHL**	**58**	**5**	**23**	**28**	**54**	**4**	**0**	**1**	**1**	**0**
	NHL Totals		**489**	**59**	**231**	**290**	**462**	**15**	**2**	**7**	**9**	**17**

a WHL Second All-Star Team (1983)

Traded to **Buffalo** by **Pittsburgh** with Darrin Shannon for Tom Barrasso and Buffalo's third-round choice (Joe Dziedzic) in 1990 Entry Draft, November 12, 1988.

BODNARCHUK, MICHAEL

Right wing. Shoots right. 6'1", 175 lbs. Born, Bramalea, Ont., March 26, 1970.
(New Jersey's 6th choice, 64th overall, in 1990 Entry Draft).

			Regular Season					Playoffs				
Season	Club	Lea	GP	G	A	TP	PIM	GP	G	A	TP	PIM
1987-88	Kingston	OHL	68	12	20	32	12	....	....	....	....	....
1988-89	Kingston	OHL	63	22	38	60	30	....	....	....	....	....
1989-90a	Kingston	OHL	66	41	59	100	31	7	2	4	6	4
1990-91	Utica	AHL	69	23	32	55	28	....	....	....	....	....

a OHL Second All-Star Team (1990)

BOIVIN, CLAUDE

Left wing. Shoots left. 6'2", 200 lbs. Born, Ste. Foy, Que., March 1, 1970.
(Philadelphia's 1st choice, 14th overall, in 1988 Entry Draft).

			Regular Season					Playoffs				
Season	Club	Lea	GP	G	A	TP	PIM	GP	G	A	TP	PIM
1987-88	Drummondville	QMJHL	63	23	26	49	233	17	5	3	8	74
1988-89	Drummondville	QMJHL	63	20	36	56	218	4	0	2	2	27
1989-90	Laval	QMJHL	59	24	51	75	309	13	7	13	20	59
1990-91	Hershey	AHL	65	13	32	45	159	7	1	5	6	28

BOMBARDIR, BRAD

Defense. Shoots left. 6'2", 190 lbs. Born, Powell River, B.C., May 5, 1972.
(New Jersey's 5th choice, 56th overall, in 1990 Entry Draft).

			Regular Season					Playoffs				
Season	Club	Lea	GP	G	A	TP	PIM	GP	G	A	TP	PIM
1989-90	Powell River	BCJHL	60	10	35	45	93	....	....	....	....	....
1990-91	North Dakota	WCHA	33	3	6	9	18	....	....	....	....	....

BONDRA, PETER

Right wing. Shoots left. 5'11", 180 lbs. Born, Luck, USSR, February 7, 1968.
(Washington's 9th choice, 156th overall, in 1990 Entry Draft).

			Regular Season					Playoffs				
Season	Club	Lea	GP	G	A	TP	PIM	GP	G	A	TP	PIM
1988-89	VSZ Kosice	Czech.	40	30	10	40	20	....	....	....	....	....
1989-90	VSZ Kosice	Czech.	42	29	17	46	....	....	....	....	....	....
1990-91	**Washington**	**NHL**	**54**	**12**	**16**	**28**	**47**	**4**	**0**	**1**	**1**	**2**
	NHL Totals		**54**	**12**	**16**	**28**	**47**	**4**	**0**	**1**	**1**	**2**

BONNER, JAMES

Defense. Shoots left. 6', 195 lbs. Born, Grand Rapids, MN, November 17, 1970.
(NY Islanders' 1st choice, 4th overall, in 1991 Supplemental Draft).

			Regular Season					Playoffs				
Season	Club	Lea	GP	G	A	TP	PIM	GP	G	A	TP	PIM
1989-90	Michigan Tech	WCHA	36	3	3	6	32	....	....	....	....	....
1990-91	Michigan Tech	WCHA	37	1	1	2	30	....	....	....	....	....

BORGO, RICHARD

Right wing. Shoots right. 5'11", 190 lbs. Born, Thunder Bay, Ont., September 25, 1970.
(Edmonton's 2nd choice, 36th overall, in 1989 Entry Draft).

			Regular Season					Playoffs				
Season	Club	Lea	GP	G	A	TP	PIM	GP	G	A	TP	PIM
1986-87	Kitchener	OHL	62	5	10	15	29	....	....	....	....	....
1987-88	Kitchener	OHL	64	24	22	46	81	4	0	4	4	0
1988-89	Kitchener	OHL	66	23	23	46	75	5	0	1	1	4
1989-90	Kitchener	OHL	32	13	22	35	43	17	5	5	10	10
1990-91	Kitchener	OHL	60	43	56	99	50	6	1	0	1	12

BORSATO, LUCIANO

Center. Shoots right. 5'10", 165 lbs. Born, Richmond Hill, Ont., January 7, 1966.
(Winnipeg's 6th choice, 135th overall, in 1984 Entry Draft).

			Regular Season					Playoffs				
Season	Club	Lea	GP	G	A	TP	PIM	GP	G	A	TP	PIM
1984-85	Clarkson	ECAC	33	15	17	32	37	....	....	....	....	....
1985-86	Clarkson	ECAC	28	14	17	31	44	....	....	....	....	....
1986-87	Clarkson	ECAC	31	16	41	57	55	....	....	....	....	....
1987-88ab	Clarkson	ECAC	33	15	29	44	38	....	....	....	....	....
	Moncton	AHL	3	1	1	2	0	....	....	....	....	....
1988-89	Moncton	AHL	6	2	5	7	4	....	....	....	....	....
	Tappara	Fin.	44	31	36	67	69	7	0	3	3	4
1989-90	Moncton	AHL	1	1	0	1	0	....	....	....	....	....
1990-91	**Winnipeg**	**NHL**	**1**	**0**	**1**	**1**	**2**	....	....	....	....	....
	Moncton	AHL	41	14	24	38	40	9	3	7	10	22
	NHL Totals		**1**	**0**	**1**	**1**	**2**	....	....	....	....	....

a ECAC Second All-Star Team (1988)
b NCAA East Second All-American Team (1988)

BOSCHMAN, LAURIE JOSEPH (BOSH-man)

Center. Shoots left. 6', 185 lbs. Born, Major, Sask., June 4, 1960.
(Toronto's 1st choice, 9th overall, in 1979 Entry Draft).

			Regular Season					Playoffs				
Season	Club	Lea	GP	G	A	TP	PIM	GP	G	A	TP	PIM
1976-77	Brandon	WHL	3	0	1	1	0	12	1	1	2	17
1977-78	Brandon	WHL	72	42	57	99	227	8	2	5	7	45
1978-79a	Brandon	WHL	65	66	83	149	215	22	11	23	34	56
1979-80	**Toronto**	**NHL**	**80**	**16**	**32**	**48**	**78**	**3**	**1**	**1**	**2**	**18**
1980-81	**Toronto**	**NHL**	**53**	**14**	**19**	**33**	**178**	**3**	**0**	**0**	**0**	**7**
	New Brunswick	AHL	4	4	1	5	47	....	....	....	....	....
1981-82	**Toronto**	**NHL**	**54**	**9**	**19**	**28**	**150**	....	....	....	....	....
	Edmonton	**NHL**	**11**	**2**	**3**	**5**	**37**	**3**	**0**	**1**	**1**	**4**
1982-83	**Edmonton**	**NHL**	**62**	**8**	**12**	**20**	**183**	....	....	....	....	....
	Winnipeg	**NHL**	**12**	**3**	**5**	**8**	**36**	**3**	**0**	**1**	**1**	**12**
1983-84	**Winnipeg**	**NHL**	**61**	**28**	**46**	**74**	**234**	**3**	**0**	**1**	**1**	**5**
1984-85	**Winnipeg**	**NHL**	**80**	**32**	**44**	**76**	**180**	**8**	**2**	**1**	**3**	**21**
1985-86	**Winnipeg**	**NHL**	**77**	**27**	**42**	**69**	**241**	**3**	**0**	**1**	**1**	**6**
1986-87	**Winnipeg**	**NHL**	**80**	**17**	**24**	**41**	**152**	**10**	**2**	**3**	**5**	**32**
1987-88	**Winnipeg**	**NHL**	**80**	**25**	**23**	**48**	**229**	**5**	**1**	**3**	**4**	**9**
1988-89	**Winnipeg**	**NHL**	**70**	**10**	**26**	**36**	**163**	....	....	....	....	....
1989-90	**Winnipeg**	**NHL**	**66**	**10**	**17**	**27**	**103**	**2**	**0**	**0**	**0**	**2**
1990-91	**New Jersey**	**NHL**	**78**	**11**	**9**	**20**	**79**	**7**	**1**	**1**	**2**	**16**
	NHL Totals		**864**	**212**	**321**	**533**	**2043**	**50**	**7**	**13**	**20**	**132**

a WHL First All-Star Team (1979)

Traded to **Edmonton** by **Toronto** for Walt Poddubny and Phil Drouilliard, March 8, 1982. Traded to **Winnipeg** by **Edmonton** for Willy Lindstrom, March 7, 1983. Traded to **New Jersey** by **Winnipeg** for Bob Brooke, September 6, 1990.

BOUCHER, PHILIPPE

Defense. Shoots right. 6'2", 189 lbs. Born, St. Apollinaire, Que., March 24, 1973.
(Buffalo's 1st choice, 13th overall, in 1991 Entry Draft).

			Regular Season					Playoffs				
Season	Club	Lea	GP	G	A	TP	PIM	GP	G	A	TP	PIM
1989-90	Ste. Foy	Midget	33	18	47	65	64	....	....	....	....	....
1990-91ab	Granby	QMJHL	69	21	46	67	92	....	....	....	....	....

a Canadian Major Junior Rookie of the Year (1991)
b QMJHL Second All-Star Team (1991)

BOUDREAU, BRUCE ALLAN (BOO-droh)

Center. Shoots left. 5'9", 170 lbs. Born, Toronto, Ont., January 9, 1955.
(Toronto's 3rd choice, 42nd overall, in 1975 Amateur Draft).

			Regular Season					Playoffs				
Season	Club	Lea	GP	G	A	TP	PIM	GP	G	A	TP	PIM
1973-74	Toronto	OHA	53	46	67	113	51	....	....	....	....	....
1974-75	Toronto	OHA	69	*68	97	*165	52	22	12	*28	40	26
1975-76	Minnesota	WHA	30	3	6	9	4	....	....	....	....	....
	Johnstown	NAHL	34	25	35	60	14	....	....	....	....	....
1976-77	**Toronto**	**NHL**	**15**	**2**	**5**	**7**	**4**	**3**	**0**	**0**	**0**	**0**
	Dallas	CHL	58	*37	34	71	40	1	1	1	2	0
1977-78	**Toronto**	**NHL**	**40**	**11**	**18**	**29**	**12**	....	....	....	....	....
	Dallas	CHL	22	13	9	22	11	....	....	....	....	....
1978-79	**Toronto**	**NHL**	**26**	**4**	**3**	**7**	**2**	....	....	....	....	....
	New Brunswick	AHL	49	20	38	58	20	5	1	1	2	8
1979-80	**Toronto**	**NHL**	**2**	**0**	**0**	**0**	**2**	....	....	....	....	....
	New Brunswick	AHL	75	36	54	90	47	17	6	7	13	23
1980-81	**Toronto**	**NHL**	**39**	**10**	**14**	**24**	**18**	**2**	**1**	**0**	**1**	**0**
	New Brunswick	AHL	40	17	41	58	22	8	6	5	11	14
1981-82	**Toronto**	**NHL**	**12**	**0**	**2**	**2**	**6**	....	....	....	....	....
	Cincinnati	CHL	65	42	61	103	42	4	3	1	4	8
1982-83	St. Catharines	AHL	80	50	72	122	65	....	....	....	....	....
	Toronto	**NHL**	....	....	....	....	....	**4**	**1**	**0**	**1**	**0**
1983-84	St. Catharines	AHL	80	47	62	109	44	7	0	5	5	11
1984-85	Baltimore	AHL	17	4	7	11	4	15	3	9	12	4
1985-86	**Chicago**	**NHL**	**7**	**1**	**0**	**1**	**2**	....	....	....	....	....
	Nova Scotia	AHL	65	30	36	66	36	....	....	....	....	....
1986-87	Nova Scotia	AHL	78	35	47	82	40	5	3	3	6	4
1987-88abc	Springfield	AHL	80	42	*74	*116	84	....	....	....	....	....
1988-89	Springfield	AHL	50	28	36	64	42	....	....	....	....	....
	Newmarket	AHL	20	7	16	23	12	4	0	1	1	6
1989-90	Phoenix	IHL	82	41	68	109	89	....	....	....	....	....
1990-91	Fort Wayne	IHL	81	40	*80	120	111	19	11	7	18	30
	NHL Totals		**141**	**28**	**42**	**70**	**46**	**9**	**2**	**0**	**2**	**0**

a AHL First All-Star Team (1988)
b Won Fred Hunt Award (Sportsmanship-AHL) (1988)
c Won John Sollenberger Trophy (Top Scorer-AHL) (1988)

Claimed by **Toronto** as fill in Expansion Draft, June 13, 1979. Signed as a free agent by **Chicago**, October 10, 1985.

BOUGHNER, BOB (BOOG-nuhr)

Defense. Shoots right. 5'11", 201 lbs. Born, Windsor, Ont., March 8, 1971.
(Detroit's 2nd choice, 32nd overall, in 1989 Entry Draft).

			Regular Season					Playoffs				
Season	Club	Lea	GP	G	A	TP	PIM	GP	G	A	TP	PIM
1988-89	S.S. Marie	OHL	64	6	15	21	182	....	....	....	....	....
1989-90	S.S. Marie	OHL	49	7	23	30	122	....	....	....	....	....
1990-91	S.S. Marie	OHL	64	13	33	46	156	14	2	9	11	35

BOURQUE, PHILLIPPE RICHARD (PHIL) (BOHRK)

Left wing. Shoots left. 6'1", 196 lbs. Born, Chelmsford, MA, June 8, 1962.

			Regular Season					Playoffs				
Season	Club	Lea	GP	G	A	TP	PIM	GP	G	A	TP	PIM
1980-81	Kingston	OHL	47	4	4	8	46	6	0	0	0	10
1981-82	Kingston	OHL	67	11	40	51	111	4	0	0	0	0
1982-83	Baltimore	AHL	65	1	15	16	93	....	....	....	....	....
1983-84	**Pittsburgh**	**NHL**	**5**	**0**	**1**	**1**	**12**	....	....	....	....	....
	Baltimore	AHL	58	5	17	22	96	....	....	....	....	....
1984-85	Baltimore	AHL	79	6	15	21	164	13	2	5	7	23
1985-86	**Pittsburgh**	**NHL**	**4**	**0**	**0**	**0**	**2**	....	....	....	....	....
	Baltimore	AHL	74	8	18	26	226	....	....	....	....	....
1986-87	**Pittsburgh**	**NHL**	**22**	**2**	**3**	**5**	**32**	....	....	....	....	....
	Baltimore	AHL	49	15	16	31	183	....	....	....	....	....
1987-88	**Pittsburgh**	**NHL**	**21**	**4**	**12**	**16**	**20**	....	....	....	....	....
ab	Muskegon	IHL	52	16	36	52	66	6	1	2	3	16
1988-89	**Pittsburgh**	**NHL**	**80**	**17**	**26**	**43**	**97**	**11**	**4**	**1**	**5**	**66**
1989-90	**Pittsburgh**	**NHL**	**76**	**22**	**17**	**39**	**108**	....	....	....	....	....
1990-91	**Pittsburgh**	**NHL**	**78**	**20**	**14**	**34**	**106**	**24**	**6**	**7**	**13**	**16**
	NHL Totals		**286**	**65**	**73**	**138**	**377**	**35**	**10**	**8**	**18**	**82**

a IHL First All-Star Team (1988)
b Won Governor's Trophy (Outstanding Defenseman-IHL) (1988)

Signed as free agent by **Pittsburgh**, October 4, 1982.

BOURQUE, RAYMOND JEAN (BOHRK)

Defense. Shoots left. 5'11", 210 lbs. Born, Montreal, Que., December 28, 1960.
(Boston's 1st choice, 8th overall, in 1979 Entry Draft).

			Regular Season					Playoffs				
Season	Club	Lea	GP	G	A	TP	PIM	GP	G	A	TP	PIM
1976-77	Sorel	QJHL	69	12	36	48	61	....	....	....	....	....
1977-78	Verdun	QJHL	72	22	57	79	90	4	2	1	3	0
1978-79	Verdun	QJHL	63	22	71	93	44	11	3	16	19	18
1979-80ab	**Boston**	**NHL**	**80**	**17**	**48**	**65**	**73**	**10**	**2**	**9**	**11**	**27**
1980-81c	**Boston**	**NHL**	**67**	**27**	**29**	**56**	**96**	**3**	**0**	**1**	**1**	**2**
1981-82b	**Boston**	**NHL**	**65**	**17**	**49**	**66**	**51**	**9**	**1**	**5**	**6**	**16**
1982-83c	**Boston**	**NHL**	**65**	**22**	**51**	**73**	**20**	**17**	**8**	**15**	**23**	**10**
1983-84b	**Boston**	**NHL**	**78**	**31**	**65**	**96**	**57**	**3**	**0**	**2**	**2**	**0**
1984-85b	**Boston**	**NHL**	**73**	**20**	**66**	**86**	**53**	**5**	**0**	**3**	**3**	**4**
1985-86c	**Boston**	**NHL**	**74**	**19**	**58**	**77**	**68**	**3**	**0**	**0**	**0**	**0**
1986-87bd	**Boston**	**NHL**	**78**	**23**	**72**	**95**	**36**	**4**	**1**	**2**	**3**	**0**
1987-88bd	**Boston**	**NHL**	**78**	**17**	**64**	**81**	**72**	**23**	**3**	**18**	**21**	**26**
1988-89c	**Boston**	**NHL**	**60**	**18**	**43**	**61**	**52**	**10**	**0**	**4**	**4**	**6**
1989-90bd	**Boston**	**NHL**	**76**	**19**	**65**	**84**	**50**	**17**	**5**	**12**	**17**	**16**
1990-91bd	**Boston**	**NHL**	**76**	**21**	**73**	**94**	**75**	**19**	**7**	**18**	**25**	**12**
	NHL Totals		**870**	**251**	**683**	**934**	**703**	**123**	**27**	**89**	**116**	**119**

a Won Calder Memorial Trophy (1980)
b NHL First All-Star Team (1980, 1982, 1984, 1985, 1987, 1988, 1990, 1991)
c NHL Second All-Star Team (1981, 1983, 1986, 1989)
d Won James Norris Memorial Trophy (1987, 1988, 1990, 1991)

Played in NHL All-Star Game (1981-86, 1988-91)

BOYCE, IAN

Left wing. Shoots right. 5'8", 175 lbs. Born, St. Laurent, Que., January 24, 1968.
(Buffalo's 1st choice, 19th overall, in 1989 Supplemental Draft).

			Regular Season					Playoffs				
Season	Club	Lea	GP	G	A	TP	PIM	GP	G	A	TP	PIM
1985-86	U. Vermont	ECAC	30	10	11	21	21	....	....	....	....	....
1986-87	U. Vermont	ECAC	32	8	23	31	30	....	....	....	....	....
1987-88	U. Vermont	ECAC	33	16	22	38	10	....	....	....	....	....
1988-89	U. Vermont	ECAC	31	15	27	42	28	....	....	....	....	....
1989-90		Swe.2	UNAVAILABLE									
1990-91	Rochester	AHL	12	1	2	3	2	....	....	....	....	....
	Fort Wayne	IHL	39	10	12	22	11	19	5	4	9	0

BOYKO, DARREN

Center. Shoots right. 5'9", 169 lbs. Born, Winnipeg, Man., January 16, 1964.

			Regular Season					Playoffs				
Season	Club	Lea	GP	G	A	TP	PIM	GP	G	A	TP	PIM
1981-82	Winnipeg	WHL	65	35	37	72	14	....	....	....	....	....
1982-83	Winnipeg	WHL	72	49	81	130	8	3	0	2	2	0
1983-84	U. of Toronto	OUAA	40	33	51	84	24	9	7	10	17	4
1984-85	U. of Toronto	OUAA	39	31	53	84	42	2	1	0	1	6
1985-86	HIFK	Fin.	36	18	26	44	8	....	....	....	....	....
1986-87	HIFK	Fin.	44	22	13	35	44	....	....	....	....	....
1987-88	HIFK	Fin.	44	14	40	54	16	....	....	....	....	....
1988-89	HIFK	Fin.	34	15	15	30	10	....	....	....	....	....
	Winnipeg	**NHL**	**1**	**0**	**0**	**0**	**0**	....	....	....	....	....
	Moncton	AHL	18	3	7	10	2	4	0	0	0	0
1989-90	HIFK	Fin.	42	12	20	32	36	2	1	0	1	2
1990-91	HIFK	Fin.	42	16	22	38	20	3	0	3	3	4
	NHL Totals		**1**	**0**	**0**	**0**	**0**	....	....	....	....	....

Signed as a free agent by **Winnipeg**, May 16, 1988.

BOZEK, ROMAN

Right wing. Shoots left. 6', 190 lbs. Born, Ceske Budejovice, Czech., November 9, 1963.
(Edmonton's 9th choice, 225th overall, in 1989 Entry Draft).

			Regular Season					Playoffs				
Season	Club	Lea	GP	G	A	TP	PIM	GP	G	A	TP	PIM
1988-89	Motor	Czech.	33	16	9	25	....	....	....	....	....	....
1989-90	Motor	Czech.	42	19	16	35	....	....	....	....	....	....
1990-91	Ilves	Fin.	30	22	10	32	8	....	....	....	....	....

BOZEK, STEVEN MICHAEL (STEVE)

Left wing. Shoots left. 5'11", 180 lbs. Born, Kelowna, B.C., November 26, 1960.
(Los Angeles' 5th choice, 52nd overall, in 1980 Entry Draft).

			Regular Season					Playoffs				
Season	Club	Lea	GP	G	A	TP	PIM	GP	G	A	TP	PIM
1979-80	N. Michigan	CCHA	41	42	47	89	32	....	....	....	....	....
1980-81	N. Michigan	CCHA	44	35	55	90	0	....	....	....	....	....
1981-82	**Los Angeles**	**NHL**	**71**	**33**	**23**	**56**	**68**	**10**	**4**	**1**	**5**	**6**
1982-83	**Los Angeles**	**NHL**	**53**	**13**	**13**	**26**	**14**	....	....	....	....	....
1983-84	**Calgary**	**NHL**	**46**	**10**	**10**	**20**	**16**	**10**	**3**	**1**	**4**	**15**
1984-85	**Calgary**	**NHL**	**54**	**13**	**22**	**35**	**6**	**3**	**1**	**0**	**1**	**4**
1985-86	**Calgary**	**NHL**	**64**	**21**	**22**	**43**	**24**	**14**	**2**	**6**	**8**	**32**
1986-87	**Calgary**	**NHL**	**71**	**17**	**18**	**35**	**22**	**4**	**1**	**0**	**1**	**2**
1987-88	**Calgary**	**NHL**	**26**	**3**	**7**	**10**	**12**	....	....	....	....	....
	St. Louis	**NHL**	**7**	**0**	**0**	**0**	**2**	**7**	**1**	**1**	**2**	**6**
1988-89	**Vancouver**	**NHL**	**71**	**17**	**18**	**35**	**64**	**7**	**0**	**2**	**2**	**4**
1989-90	**Vancouver**	**NHL**	**58**	**14**	**9**	**23**	**32**	....	....	....	....	....
1990-91	**Vancouver**	**NHL**	**62**	**15**	**17**	**32**	**22**	**3**	**0**	**0**	**0**	**0**
	NHL Totals		**583**	**156**	**159**	**315**	**282**	**58**	**12**	**11**	**23**	**69**

Traded to **Calgary** by **Los Angeles** for Carl Mokosak and Kevin LaVallee, June 20, 1983. Traded to **St. Louis** by **Calgary** with Brett Hull for Rob Ramage and Rick Wamsley, March 7, 1988. Traded to **Calgary** by **St. Louis** with Mark Hunter, Doug Gilmour and Michael Dark for Mike Bullard, Craig Coxe and Tim Corkery, September 6, 1988. Traded to **Vancouver** by **Calgary** with Paul Reinhart for Vancouver's third-round pick (Veli-Pekka Kautonen) in 1989 Entry Draft, September 6, 1988. Signed as a free agent by **San Jose**, August 9, 1991.

BOZIK, MOJMIR (BOH-zhehk)

Defense. Shoots right. 5'9", 183 lbs. Born, Liptovsky Mikulas, Czech., February 26, 1962.
(Edmonton's 11th choice, 231st overall, in 1986 Entry Draft).

			Regular Season					Playoffs				
Season	Club	Lea	GP	G	A	TP	PIM	GP	G	A	TP	PIM
1980-81	VSZ Kosice	Czech.	27	1	4	5	24	....	....	....	....	....
1981-82	VSZ Kosice	Czech.	42	2	7	9	73	....	....	....	....	....
1982-83	Dukla Trencin	Czech.		DID NOT PLAY								
1983-84	Dukla Trencin	Czech.	41	1	5	6	50	....	....	....	....	....
1984-85	VSZ Kosice	Czech.	41	2	10	12	32	....	....	....	....	....
1985-86	VSZ Kosice	Czech.	47	6	20	26	22	....	....	....	....	....
1986-87	VSZ Kosice	Czech.	40	7	9	16	44	....	....	....	....	....
1987-88	VSZ Kosice	Czech.	44	5	11	16	62	....	....	....	....	....
1988-89	VSZ Kosice	Czech.	43	9	7	16	56	....	....	....	....	....
1989-90	VSZ Kosice	Czech.	49	9	14	23	....	....	....	....	....	....
1990-91	Jokerit	Fin.	44	2	11	13	54	....	....	....	....	....

BRADLEY, BRIAN WALTER RICHARD

Center. Shoots right. 5'10", 170 lbs. Born, Kitchener, Ont., January 21, 1965.
(Calgary's 2nd choice, 51st overall, in 1983 Entry Draft).

			Regular Season					Playoffs				
Season	Club	Lea	GP	G	A	TP	PIM	GP	G	A	TP	PIM
1982-83	London	OHL	67	37	82	119	37	3	1	0	1	0
1983-84	London	OHL	49	40	60	100	24	4	2	4	6	0
1984-85	London	OHL	32	27	49	76	22	8	5	10	15	4
1985-86	**Calgary**	**NHL**	**5**	**0**	**1**	**1**	**0**	**1**	**0**	**0**	**0**	**0**
	Moncton	AHL	59	23	42	65	40	10	6	9	15	4
1986-87	**Calgary**	**NHL**	**40**	**10**	**18**	**28**	**16**	....	....	....	....	....
	Moncton	AHL	20	12	16	28	8	....	....	....	....	....
1987-88	Cdn. National	...	47	8	19	37	42	....	....	....	....	....
	Cdn. Olympic	...	7	0	4	4	0	....	....	....	....	....
	Vancouver	**NHL**	**11**	**3**	**5**	**8**	**6**	....	....	....	....	....
1988-89	**Vancouver**	**NHL**	**71**	**18**	**27**	**45**	**42**	**7**	**3**	**4**	**7**	**10**
1989-90	**Vancouver**	**NHL**	**67**	**19**	**29**	**48**	**65**	....	....	....	....	....
1990-91	**Vancouver**	**NHL**	**44**	**11**	**20**	**31**	**42**	....	....	....	....	....
	Toronto	**NHL**	**26**	**0**	**11**	**11**	**20**	....	....	....	....	....
	NHL Totals		**264**	**61**	**111**	**172**	**191**	**8**	**3**	**4**	**7**	**10**

Traded to **Vancouver** by **Calgary** with Peter Bakovic and Kevin Guy for Craig Coxe, March 6, 1988. Traded to **Toronto** by **Vancouver** for Tom Kurvers, January 12, 1991.

BRADY, NEIL

Center. Shoots left. 6'2", 200 lbs. Born, Montreal, Que., April 12, 1968.
(New Jersey's 1st choice, 3rd overall, in 1986 Entry Draft).

			Regular Season					Playoffs				
Season	Club	Lea	GP	G	A	TP	PIM	GP	G	A	TP	PIM
1984-85	Calgary	Midget	37	25	50	75	75	....	....	....	....	....
	Medicine Hat	WHL	....	....	....	....	....	3	0	0	0	2
1985-86a	Medicine Hat	WHL	72	21	60	81	104	21	9	11	20	23
1986-87	Medicine Hat	WHL	57	19	64	83	126	18	1	4	5	25
1987-88	Medicine Hat	WHL	61	16	35	51	110	15	0	3	3	19
1988-89	Utica	AHL	75	16	21	37	56	4	0	3	3	0
1989-90	**New Jersey**	**NHL**	**19**	**1**	**4**	**5**	**13**	....	....	....	....	....
	Utica	AHL	38	10	13	23	21	5	0	1	1	10
1990-91	**New Jersey**	**NHL**	**3**	**0**	**0**	**0**	**0**	....	....	....	....	....
	Utica	AHL	77	33	63	96	91	....	....	....	....	....
	NHL Totals		**22**	**1**	**4**	**5**	**13**	....	....	....	....	....

a WHL Rookie of the Year (1986)

BRAIT, MATTHEW

Defense. Shoots left. 6'2", 210 lbs. Born, Toronto, Ont., June 29, 1969.
(Philadelphia's 9th choice, 222nd overall, in 1989 Entry Draft).

			Regular Season					Playoffs				
Season	Club	Lea	GP	G	A	TP	PIM	GP	G	A	TP	PIM
1989-90	Kent State	NCAA	30	4	8	12	81	....	....	....	....	....
1990-91	Kent State	NCAA	24	2	3	5	92	....	....	....	....	....

BRAUER, CAM

Defense. Shoots left. 6'3", 210 lbs. Born, Calgary, Alta., January 4, 1970.
(Edmonton's 5th choice, 82nd overall, in 1988 Entry Draft).

			Regular Season					Playoffs				
Season	Club	Lea	GP	G	A	TP	PIM	GP	G	A	TP	PIM
1987-88	RPI	ECAC	18	0	1	1	4	....	....	....	....	....
1988-89	Regina	WHL	49	0	9	9	59	....	....	....	....	....
1989-90	Regina	WHL	4	0	0	0	20	....	....	....	....	....
a	Seattle	WHL	64	1	9	10	229	10	0	0	0	27
1990-91	Springfield	AHL	45	0	1	1	65	....	....	....	....	....
	Louisville	ECHL	5	0	1	1	9	....	....	....	....	....

a WHL West Second All-Star Team (1990)

Rights traded to **Hartford** by **Edmonton** for Mark Laforge, March 6, 1990.

BRAZDA, RADOMIR (BRAHZ-duh)

Defense. Shoots right. 6'2", 175 lbs. Born, Pardubice, Czechoslovakia, October 11, 1967.
(Detroit's 6th choice, 95th overall, in 1987 Entry Draft).

			Regular Season					Playoffs				
Season	Club	Lea	GP	G	A	TP	PIM	GP	G	A	TP	PIM
1986-87	Pardubice	Czech.	31	1	1	2	....	....	....	....	....	....
1987-88	Pardubice	Czech.	11	1	2	3	....	....	....	....	....	....
1988-89	Dukla Trencin	Czech.	35	1	1	2	....	....	....	....	....	....
1989-90	Pardubice	Czech	26	2	1	3	....	....	....	....	....	....
1990-91	Pardubice	Czech.	40	5	11	16	24	....	....	....	....	....

BREAULT, FRANCOIS

Right wing. Shoots left. 5'11", 185 lbs. Born, Acton Vale, Que., May 11, 1967.

			Regular Season					Playoffs				
Season	Club	Lea	GP	G	A	TP	PIM	GP	G	A	TP	PIM
1986-87	Granby	QMJHL	60	24	33	57	134	....	....	....	....	....
1987-88	Trois-Rivieres	QMJHL	28	16	19	35	108	....	....	....	....	....
1988-89	New Haven	AHL	68	21	24	45	51	....	....	....	....	....
1989-90	New Haven	AHL	37	17	21	38	33	....	....	....	....	....
1990-91	**Los Angeles**	**NHL**	**17**	**1**	**4**	**5**	**6**	....	....	....	....	....
	NHL Totals		**17**	**1**	**4**	**5**	**6**	....	....	....	....	....

Signed as a free agent by **Los Angeles**, July, 1988.

BREEN, GEORGE

Right wing. Shoots right. 6'2", 200 lbs. Born, Webster, MA, August 3, 1973.
(Edmonton's 4th choice, 56th overall, in 1991 Entry Draft).

			Regular Season					Playoffs				
Season	Club	Lea	GP	G	A	TP	PIM	GP	G	A	TP	PIM
1989-90	Cushing Aca.	HS	20	9	8	17	....	....	....	....	....	....

BRENNAN, RICHARD

Defense. Shoots right. 6'2", 200 lbs. Born, Schnectady, NY, November 26, 1972.
(Quebec's 3rd choice, 46th overall, in 1991 Entry Draft).

			Regular Season					Playoffs				
Season	Club	Lea	GP	G	A	TP	PIM	GP	G	A	TP	PIM
1989-90	Tabor Aca.	HS	33	12	14	26	68	....	....	....	....	....
1990-91	Tabor Aca.	HS	34	13	37	50	91	....	....	....	....	....

BREWER, MIKE

Center. Shoots left. 5'10", 175 lbs. Born, Chestwick, Ont., April 13, 1969.
(Washington's 1st choice, 20th overall, in 1991 Supplemental Draft).

			Regular Season					Playoffs				
Season	Club	Lea	GP	G	A	TP	PIM	GP	G	A	TP	PIM
1989-90a	Brown	ECAC	29	7	24	31	64	....	....	....	....	....
1990-91b	Brown	ECAC	21	4	18	22	44	....	....	....	....	....

a ECAC First All-Star Team (1990)
b ECAC Second All-Star Team (1991)

BRICKLEY, ANDY

Left wing/Center. Shoots left. 5'11", 200 lbs. Born, Melrose, MA, August 9, 1961.
(Philadelphia's 10th choice, 210th overall, in 1980 Entry Draft).

			Regular Season					Playoffs				
Season	Club	Lea	GP	G	A	TP	PIM	GP	G	A	TP	PIM
1979-80	N. Hampshire	ECAC	27	15	17	32	8	....	....	....	....	....
1980-81	N. Hampshire	ECAC	31	27	25	52	16	....	....	....	....	....
1981-82ab	N. Hampshire	ECAC	35	26	27	53	6	....	....	....	....	....
1982-83	**Philadelphia**	**NHL**	**3**	**1**	**1**	**2**	**0**	....	....	....	....	....
c	Maine	AHL	76	29	54	83	10	17	9	5	14	0
1983-84	Springfield	AHL	7	1	5	6	2	....	....	....	....	....
	Pittsburgh	**NHL**	**50**	**18**	**20**	**38**	**9**	....	....	....	....	....
	Baltimore	AHL	4	0	5	5	2	....	....	....	....	....
1984-85	**Pittsburgh**	**NHL**	**45**	**7**	**15**	**22**	**10**	....	....	....	....	....
	Baltimore	AHL	31	13	14	27	8	15	*10	8	18	0
1985-86	Maine	AHL	60	26	34	60	20	5	0	4	4	0
1986-87	**New Jersey**	**NHL**	**51**	**11**	**12**	**23**	**8**	....	....	....	....	....
1987-88	**New Jersey**	**NHL**	**45**	**8**	**14**	**22**	**14**	**4**	**0**	**1**	**1**	**4**
	Utica	AHL	9	5	8	13	4	....	....	....	....	....
1988-89	**Boston**	**NHL**	**71**	**13**	**22**	**35**	**20**	**10**	**0**	**2**	**2**	**0**
1989-90	**Boston**	**NHL**	**43**	**12**	**28**	**40**	**8**	**2**	**0**	**0**	**0**	**0**
1990-91	**Boston**	**NHL**	**40**	**2**	**9**	**11**	**8**	....	....	....	....	....
	Maine	AHL	17	8	17	25	2	1	0	0	0	0
	NHL Totals		**348**	**72**	**121**	**193**	**77**	**16**	**0**	**3**	**3**	**4**

a ECAC First All-Star Team (1982)
b NCAA All-American Team (1982)
c AHL Second All-Star Team (1983)

Traded to **Pittsburgh** by **Philadelphia** with Mark Taylor, Ron Flockhart, Philadelphia's first round (Roger Belanger) and third round (Mike Stevens — later transferred to Vancouver) choices in 1984 Entry Draft for Rich Sutter and Pittsburgh's second round (Greg Smyth) and third round (David McLay) choices in 1984 Entry Draft, October 23, 1983. Signed as a free agent by **New Jersey**, July 8, 1986. Claimed by **Boston** in NHL Waiver Draft, October 3, 1988,

BRIGHT, CHRIS

Center. Shoots left. 6', 185 lbs. Born, Guelph, Ont., October 14, 1970.
(Hartford's 4th choice, 78th overall, in 1990 Entry Draft).

			Regular Season					Playoffs				
Season	Club	Lea	GP	G	A	TP	PIM	GP	G	A	TP	PIM
1987-88	Moose Jaw	WHL	20	2	2	4	10	....	....	....	....	....
1988-89	Moose Jaw	WHL	71	18	27	45	61	7	2	0	0	6
1989-90	Moose Jaw	WHL	72	36	38	74	107	....	....	....	....	....
1990-91	Springfield	AHL	37	3	4	7	32	....	....	....	....	....

BRILL, JOHN

Right wing. Shoots left. 6'3", 180 lbs. Born, St. Paul, MN, December 3, 1970.
(Pittsburgh's 3rd choice, 58th overall, in 1989 Entry Draft).

			Regular Season					Playoffs				
Season	Club	Lea	GP	G	A	TP	PIM	GP	G	A	TP	PIM
1989-90	U. Minnesota	WCHA	34	2	8	10	22	....	....	....	....	....
1990-91	U. Minnesota	WCHA	44	6	13	19	36	....	....	....	....	....

BRIND'AMOUR, ROD

Center. Shoots left. 6'1", 202 lbs. Born, Ottawa, Ont., August 9, 1970.
(St. Louis' 1st choice, 9th overall, in 1988 Entry Draft).

			Regular Season					Playoffs				
Season	Club	Lea	GP	G	A	TP	PIM	GP	G	A	TP	PIM
1988-89a	Michigan State	CCHA	42	27	32	59	63	....	....	....	....	....
	St. Louis	**NHL**	....	....	....	....	....	5	2	0	2	4
1989-90b	**St. Louis**	**NHL**	79	26	35	61	46	12	5	8	13	6
1990-91	**St. Louis**	**NHL**	78	17	32	49	93	13	2	5	7	10
	NHL Totals		157	43	67	110	139	30	9	13	22	20

a CCHA Freshman of the Year (1989)
b NHL All-Rookie Team (1990)

BRISEBOIS, PATRICE

Defense. Shoots right. 6'2", 173 lbs. Born, Montreal, Que., January 27, 1971.
(Montreal's 2nd choice, 30th overall, in 1989 Entry Draft).

			Regular Season					Playoffs				
Season	Club	Lea	GP	G	A	TP	PIM	GP	G	A	TP	PIM
1987-88	Laval	QMJHL	48	10	34	44	95	6	0	2	2	2
1988-89	Laval	QMJHL	50	20	45	65	95	17	8	14	22	45
1989-90a	Laval	QMJHL	56	18	70	88	108	13	7	9	16	26
1990-91	**Montreal**	**NHL**	10	0	2	2	4	....	....	....	....	....
bcd	Drummondville	QMJHL	54	17	44	61	72	14	6	18	24	49
	NHL Totals		10	0	2	2	4	....	....	....	....	....

a QMJHL Second All-Star Team (1990)
b Canadian Major Junior Defenseman of the Year (1991)
c QMJHL First All-Star Team (1991)
d Memorial Cup All-Star Team (1991)

BROCHU, STEPHANE (broh-SHOO)

Defense. Shoots left. 6'1", 185 lbs. Born, Sherbrooke, Que., August 15, 1967.
(NY Rangers' 9th choice, 175th overall, in 1985 Entry Draft).

			Regular Season					Playoffs				
Season	Club	Lea	GP	G	A	TP	PIM	GP	G	A	TP	PIM
1984-85	Quebec	QMJHL	59	2	16	18	56	4	0	2	2	2
1985-86	St. Jean	QMJHL	63	14	27	41	121	3	1	0	1	2
1986-87	St. Jean	QMJHL	DID NOT PLAY - INJURED					8	0	2	2	11
1987-88	St. Jean	QMHL	29	4	35	39	88	....	....	....	....	....
	Colorado	IHL	52	4	10	14	70	12	3	3	6	13
1988-89	**NY Rangers**	**NHL**	1	0	0	0	0	....	....	....	....	....
	Denver	IHL	67	5	14	19	109	3	0	0	0	0
1989-90	Flint	IHL	5	0	0	0	2	....	....	....	....	....
	Fort Wayne	IHL	63	9	19	28	98	5	0	2	2	6
1990-91	Fort Wayne	IHL	73	14	29	43	49	14	1	3	4	31
	NHL Totals		1	0	0	0	0	....	....	....	....	....

BROOKE, ROBERT W. (BOB)

Center. Shoots right. 5'11", 195 lbs. Born, Melrose, MA, December 18, 1960.
(St. Louis' 3rd choice, 75th overall, in 1980 Entry Draft).

			Regular Season					Playoffs				
Season	Club	Lea	GP	G	A	TP	PIM	GP	G	A	TP	PIM
1979-80	Yale	ECAC	24	7	22	29	38	....	....	....	....	....
1980-81	Yale	ECAC	27	12	30	42	59	....	....	....	....	....
1981-82	Yale	ECAC	25	12	30	42	60	....	....	....	....	....
1982-83ab	Yale	ECAC	21	10	27	37	48	....	....	....	....	....
1983-84	U.S. National	...	54	7	18	25	75	....	....	....	....	....
	U.S. Olympic	...	6	1	2	3	10	....	....	....	....	....
	NY Rangers	**NHL**	9	1	2	3	4	5	0	0	0	7
1984-85	**NY Rangers**	**NHL**	72	7	9	16	79	3	0	0	0	8
1985-86	**NY Rangers**	**NHL**	79	24	20	44	111	16	6	9	15	28
1986-87	**NY Rangers**	**NHL**	15	3	5	8	20	....	....	....	....	....
	Minnesota	**NHL**	65	10	18	28	78	....	....	....	....	....
1987-88	**Minnesota**	**NHL**	77	5	20	25	108	....	....	....	....	....
1988-89	**Minnesota**	**NHL**	57	7	9	16	57	5	3	0	3	2
1989-90	**Minnesota**	**NHL**	38	4	4	8	33	....	....	....	....	....
	New Jersey	**NHL**	35	8	10	18	30	5	0	0	0	14
1990-91			DID NOT PLAY									
	NHL Totals		447	69	97	166	520	34	9	9	18	59

a ECAC First All-Star Team (1983)
b NCAA All-American First Team (1983)

Rights traded to **NY Rangers** by **St. Louis** with Larry Patey for Dave Barr, NY Rangers' third round choice (Alan Perry) in 1984 Entry Draft and cash, March 5, 1984. Traded to **Minnesota** by **NY Rangers** with NY Rangers' rights to Minnesota's fourth-round choice (Jeffery Stolp) in 1988 Entry Draft previously acquired by NY Rangers in Mark Pavelich deal for Curt Giles, Tony McKegney and Minnesota's second-round choice (Troy Mallette) in 1988 Entry Draft, November 13, 1986. Traded to **New Jersey** by **Minnesota** for Aaron Broten, January 5, 1990. Traded to **Winnipeg** by **New Jersey** for Laurie Boschman, September 6, 1990.

BROTEN, AARON (BRAH-tuhn)

Left wing/Center. Shoots left. 5'10", 180 lbs. Born, Roseau, MN, November 14, 1960.
(Colorado's 5th choice, 106th overall, in 1980 Entry Draft).

			Regular Season					Playoffs				
Season	Club	Lea	GP	G	A	TP	PIM	GP	G	A	TP	PIM
1979-80	U. Minnesota	WCHA	41	25	47	72	8	....	....	....	....	....
1980-81	U. Minnesota	WCHA	45	*47	*59	*106	24	....	....	....	....	....
	Colorado	**NHL**	2	0	0	0	0	....	....	....	....	....
1981-82	**Colorado**	**NHL**	58	15	24	39	6	....	....	....	....	....
	Fort Worth	CHL	19	15	21	36	11	....	....	....	....	....
1982-83	**New Jersey**	**NHL**	73	16	39	55	28	....	....	....	....	....
	Wichita	CHL	4	0	4	4	0	....	....	....	....	....
1983-84	**New Jersey**	**NHL**	80	13	23	36	36	....	....	....	....	....
1984-85	**New Jersey**	**NHL**	80	22	35	57	38	....	....	....	....	....
1985-86	**New Jersey**	**NHL**	66	18	25	43	26	....	....	....	....	....
1986-87	**New Jersey**	**NHL**	80	26	53	79	36	....	....	....	....	....
1987-88	**New Jersey**	**NHL**	80	26	57	83	80	20	5	11	16	20
1988-89	**New Jersey**	**NHL**	80	16	43	59	81	....	....	....	....	....
1989-90	**New Jersey**	**NHL**	42	10	8	18	36	....	....	....	....	....
	Minnesota	**NHL**	35	9	9	18	22	7	0	5	5	8
1990-91	**Quebec**	**NHL**	20	5	4	9	6	....	....	....	....	....
	Toronto	**NHL**	27	6	4	10	32	....	....	....	....	....
	NHL Totals		723	182	324	506	427	27	5	16	21	28

Traded to **Minnesota** by **New Jersey** for Bob Brooke, January 5, 1990. Claimed by **Quebec** in NHL Waiver Draft, October 1, 1990. Traded to **Toronto** by **Quebec** with Lucien Deblois and Michel Petit for Scott Pearson and Toronto's second round choices in 1991 (later traded to Washington — Eric Lavigne) and 1992 Entry Drafts, November 17, 1990.

BROTEN, NEAL (BRAH-tuhn)

Center. Shoots left. 5'9", 170 lbs. Born, Roseau, MN, November 29, 1959.
(Minnesota's 3rd choice, 42nd overall, in 1979 Entry Draft).

			Regular Season					Playoffs				
Season	Club	Lea	GP	G	A	TP	PIM	GP	G	A	TP	PIM
1978-79	U. Minnesota	WCHA	40	21	50	71	18	....	....	....	....	....
1979-80	U.S. National	...	55	25	30	55	20	....	....	....	....	....
	U.S. Olympic	...	7	2	1	3	2	....	....	....	....	....
1980-81ab	U. Minnesota	WCHA	36	17	54	71	56	....	....	....	....	....
	Minnesota	**NHL**	3	2	0	2	12	19	1	7	8	9
1981-82	**Minnesota**	**NHL**	73	38	60	98	42	4	0	2	2	0
1982-83	**Minnesota**	**NHL**	79	32	45	77	43	9	1	6	7	10
1983-84	**Minnesota**	**NHL**	76	28	61	89	43	16	5	5	10	4
1984-85	**Minnesota**	**NHL**	80	19	37	56	39	9	2	5	7	10
1985-86	**Minnesota**	**NHL**	80	29	76	105	47	5	3	2	5	2
1986-87	**Minnesota**	**NHL**	46	18	35	53	33	....	....	....	....	....
1987-88	**Minnesota**	**NHL**	54	9	30	39	32	....	....	....	....	....
1988-89	**Minnesota**	**NHL**	68	18	38	56	57	5	2	2	4	4
1989-90	**Minnesota**	**NHL**	80	23	62	85	45	7	2	2	4	18
1990-91	**Minnesota**	**NHL**	79	13	56	69	26	23	9	13	22	6
	NHL Totals		718	229	500	729	419	97	25	44	69	63

Played in NHL All-Star Game (1983-86)
a WCHA First All-Star Team (1981)
b Won Hobey Baker Memorial Trophy (Top U.S. College Player) (1981)

BROTEN, PAUL (BRAH-tuhn)

Right wing. Shoots right. 5'11", 190 lbs. Born, Roseau, MN, October 27, 1965.
(NY Rangers 3rd choice, 77th overall, in 1984 Entry Draft)

			Regular Season					Playoffs				
Season	Club	Lea	GP	G	A	TP	PIM	GP	G	A	TP	PIM
1984-85	U. Minnesota	WCHA	44	8	8	16	26	....	....	....	....	....
1985-86	U. Minnesota	WCHA	38	6	16	22	24	....	....	....	....	....
1986-87	U. Minnesota	WCHA	48	17	22	39	52	....	....	....	....	....
1987-88	U. Minnesota	WCHA	38	18	21	39	42	....	....	....	....	....
1988-89	Denver	IHL	77	28	31	59	133	4	0	2	2	6
1989-90	**NY Rangers**	**NHL**	32	5	3	8	26	6	1	1	2	2
	Flint	IHL	28	17	9	26	55	....	....	....	....	....
1990-91	**NY Rangers**	**NHL**	28	4	6	10	18	5	0	0	0	2
	Binghamton	AHL	8	2	2	4	4	....	....	....	....	....
	NHL Totals		60	9	9	18	44	11	1	1	2	4

BROWN, ALAN

Defense. Shoots left. 6', 180 lbs. Born, Nepean, Ont., January 26, 1971.
(Washington's 13th choice, 219th overall, in 1990 Entry Draft).

			Regular Season					Playoffs				
Season	Club	Lea	GP	G	A	TP	PIM	GP	G	A	TP	PIM
1989-90	Colgate	ECAC	33	2	3	5	22	....	....	....	....	....
1990-91	Colgate	ECAC	32	0	5	5	26	....	....	....	....	....

BROWN, CAL

Defense. Shoots left. 6', 195 lbs. Born, Calgary, Alta., January 13, 1967.
(Hartford's 10th choice, 221st overall, in 1986 Entry Draft).

			Regular Season					Playoffs				
Season	Club	Lea	GP	G	A	TP	PIM	GP	G	A	TP	PIM
1986-87	Colorado	WCHA	41	7	17	24	80	....	....	....	....	....
1987-88	Colorado	WCHA	34	7	11	18	94	....	....	....	....	....
1988-89	Colorado	WCHA	37	2	27	29	63	....	....	....	....	....
1989-90	Colorado	WCHA	39	4	21	25	74	....	....	....	....	....
1990-91	Springfield	AHL	1	0	0	0	2	....	....	....	....	....
	Fort Wayne	IHL	6	0	3	3	4	....	....	....	....	....
	Louisville	ECHL	37	12	34	46	36	6	0	2	2	6

BROWN, CAM

Left wing. Shoots left. 6'1", 205 lbs. Born, Saskatoon, Sask., May 15, 1969.

			Regular Season					Playoffs				
Season	Club	Lea	GP	G	A	TP	PIM	GP	G	A	TP	PIM
1987-88	Brandon	WHL	69	2	13	15	185	4	1	1	2	15
1988-89	Brandon	WHL	72	17	42	59	225	....	....	....	....	....
1989-90	Brandon	WHL	68	34	41	75	182	....	....	....	....	....
1990-91	**Vancouver**	**NHL**	1	0	0	0	7	....	....	....	....	....
	Milwaukee	IHL	74	11	13	24	218	3	0	0	0	0
	NHL Totals		1	0	0	0	7	....	....	....	....	....

Signed as a free agent by **Vancouver**, April 6, 1990.

BROWN, DAVID

Right wing. Shoots right. 6'5", 205 lbs. Born, Saskatoon, Sask., October 12, 1962.
(Philadelphia's 7th choice, 140th overall, in 1982 Entry Draft).

			Regular Season					Playoffs				
Season	Club	Lea	GP	G	A	TP	PIM	GP	G	A	TP	PIM
1980-81	Spokane	WHL	9	2	2	4	21	....	....	....	....	....
1981-82	Saskatoon	WHL	62	11	33	44	344	5	1	0	1	4
1982-83	Philadelphia	NHL	2	0	0	0	5	....	....	....	....	....
	Maine	AHL	71	8	6	14	*418	16	0	0	0	*107
1983-84	Philadelphia	NHL	19	1	5	6	98	2	0	0	0	12
	Springfield	AHL	59	17	14	31	150	....	....	....	....	....
1984-85	Philadelphia	NHL	57	3	6	9	165	11	0	0	0	59
1985-86	Philadelphia	NHL	76	10	7	17	277	5	0	0	0	16
1986-87	Philadelphia	NHL	62	7	3	10	274	26	1	2	3	59
1987-88	Philadelphia	NHL	47	12	5	17	114	7	1	0	1	27
1988-89	Philadelphia	NHL	50	0	3	3	100	....	....	....	....	....
	Edmonton	NHL	22	0	2	2	56	7	0	0	0	6
1989-90	Edmonton	NHL	60	0	6	6	145	3	0	0	0	0
1990-91	Edmonton	NHL	58	3	4	7	160	16	0	1	1	30
	NHL Totals		453	36	41	77	1394	77	2	3	5	209

Traded to **Edmonton** by **Philadelphia** for Keith Acton and Edmonton's fifth-round choice (Dimitri Yushkevich) in 1991 Entry Draft, February 7, 1989. Traded to **Philadelphia** by **Edmonton** with Corey Foster and Jari Kurri for Craig Fisher, Scott Mellanby and Craig Berube, May 30, 1991.

BROWN, DOUG

Right wing. Shoots right. 5'10", 180 lbs. Born, Southborough, MA, June 12, 1964.

			Regular Season					Playoffs				
Season	Club	Lea	GP	G	A	TP	PIM	GP	G	A	TP	PIM
1982-83	Boston College	ECAC	22	9	8	17	0	....	....	....	....	....
1983-84	Boston College	ECAC	38	11	10	21	6	....	....	....	....	....
1984-85	Boston College	H.E.	45	37	31	68	10	....	....	....	....	....
1985-86	Boston College	H.E.	38	16	40	56	16	....	....	....	....	....
1986-87	New Jersey	NHL	4	0	1	1	0	....	....	....	....	....
	Maine	AHL	73	24	34	58	15	....	....	....	....	....
1987-88	New Jersey	NHL	70	14	11	25	20	19	5	1	6	6
	Utica	AHL	2	0	2	2	2	....	....	....	....	....
1988-89	New Jersey	NHL	63	15	10	25	15	....	....	....	....	....
	Utica	AHL	4	1	4	5	0	....	....	....	....	....
1989-90	New Jersey	NHL	69	14	20	34	16	6	0	1	1	2
1990-91	New Jersey	NHL	58	14	16	30	4	7	2	2	4	2
	NHL Totals		264	57	58	115	55	32	7	4	11	10

Signed as a free agent by **New Jersey**, August 6, 1986.

BROWN, GREG

Defense. Shoots right. 6', 180 lbs. Born, Hartford, CT, March 7, 1968.
(Buffalo's 2nd choice, 26th overall, in 1986 Entry Draft).

			Regular Season					Playoffs				
Season	Club	Lea	GP	G	A	TP	PIM	GP	G	A	TP	PIM
1986-87	Boston College	H.E.	37	10	27	37	22	....	....	....	....	....
1987-88	U.S. National	...	55	6	29	35	22	....	....	....	....	....
	U.S. Olympic	...	6	0	4	4	2	....	....	....	....	....
1988-89abc	Boston College	H.E.	40	9	34	43	24	....	....	....	....	....
1989-90abc	Boston College	H.E.	42	5	35	40	42	....	....	....	....	....
1990-91	Buffalo	NHL	39	1	2	3	35	....	....	....	....	....
	Rochester	AHL	31	6	17	23	16	14	1	4	5	8
	NHL Totals		39	1	2	3	35	....	....	....	....	....

a Hockey East First All-Star Team (1989, 1990)
b Hockey East Player of the Year (1989, 1990)
c NCAA East First All-American Team (1989, 1990)

BROWN, JEFF

Defense. Shoots right. 6'1", 204 lbs. Born, Ottawa, Ont., April 30, 1966.
(Quebec's 2nd choice, 36th overall, in 1984 Entry Draft).

			Regular Season					Playoffs				
Season	Club	Lea	GP	G	A	TP	PIM	GP	G	A	TP	PIM
1982-83	Sudbury	OHL	65	9	37	46	39	....	....	....	....	....
1983-84	Sudbury	OHL	68	17	60	77	39	....	....	....	....	....
1984-85	Sudbury	OHL	56	16	48	64	26	....	....	....	....	....
1985-86	Quebec	NHL	8	3	2	5	6	1	0	0	0	0
a	Sudbury	OHL	45	22	28	50	24	4	0	2	2	11
	Fredericton	AHL	....	....	....	....	....	1	0	1	1	0
1986-87	Quebec	NHL	44	7	22	29	16	13	3	3	6	2
	Fredericton	AHL	26	2	14	16	16	....	....	....	....	....
1987-88	Quebec	NHL	78	16	36	52	64	....	....	....	....	....
1988-89	Quebec	NHL	78	21	47	68	62	....	....	....	....	....
1989-90	Quebec	NHL	29	6	10	16	18	....	....	....	....	....
	St. Louis	NHL	48	10	28	38	37	12	2	10	12	4
1990-91	St. Louis	NHL	67	12	47	59	39	13	3	9	12	6
	NHL Totals		352	75	192	267	242	39	8	22	30	12

a OHL First All-Star Team (1986)

Traded to **St Louis** by **Quebec** for Tony Hrkac and Greg Millen, December 13, 1989.

BROWN, KEITH JEFFREY

Defense. Shoots right. 6'1", 192 lbs. Born, Cornerbrook, Nfld., May 6, 1960.
(Chicago's 1st choice, 7th overall, in 1979 Entry Draft).

			Regular Season					Playoffs				
Season	Club	Lea	GP	G	A	TP	PIM	GP	G	A	TP	PIM
1977-78a	Portland	WHL	72	11	53	64	51	8	0	3	3	2
1978-79bc	Portland	WHL	70	11	85	96	75	25	3	*30	33	21
1979-80	Chicago	NHL	76	2	18	20	27	6	0	0	0	4
1980-81	Chicago	NHL	80	9	34	43	80	3	0	2	2	2
1981-82	Chicago	NHL	33	4	20	24	26	4	0	2	2	5
1982-83	Chicago	NHL	50	4	27	31	20	7	0	0	0	11
1983-84	Chicago	NHL	74	10	25	35	94	5	0	1	1	10
1984-85	Chicago	NHL	56	1	22	23	55	11	2	7	9	31
1985-86	Chicago	NHL	70	11	29	40	87	3	0	1	1	9
1986-87	Chicago	NHL	73	4	23	27	86	4	0	1	1	6
1987-88	Chicago	NHL	24	3	6	9	45	5	0	2	2	10
1988-89	Chicago	NHL	74	2	16	18	84	13	1	3	4	25
1989-90	Chicago	NHL	67	5	20	25	87	18	0	4	4	43
1990-91	Chicago	NHL	45	1	10	11	55	6	1	0	1	8
	NHL Totals		722	56	250	306	746	85	4	23	27	164

a Shared WHL's Rookie of the Year with John Ogrodnick (New Westminster) (1978)
b Named WHL's Top Defenseman (1979)
c WHL First All-Star Team (1979)

BROWN, ROB

Right wing. Shoots left. 5'11", 185 lbs. Born, Kingston, Ont., April 10, 1968.
(Pittsburgh's 4th choice, 67th overall, in 1986 Entry Draft).

			Regular Season					Playoffs				
Season	Club	Lea	GP	G	A	TP	PIM	GP	G	A	TP	PIM
1984-85	Kamloops	WHL	60	29	50	79	95	15	8	8	26	28
1985-86ab	Kamloops	WHL	69	58	*115	*173	171	16	*18	*28	*46	14
1986-87abc	Kamloops	WHL	63	*76	*136	*212	101	5	6	5	11	6
1987-88	Pittsburgh	NHL	51	24	20	44	56	....	....	....	....	....
1988-89	Pittsburgh	NHL	68	49	66	115	118	11	5	3	8	22
1989-90	Pittsburgh	NHL	80	33	47	80	102	....	....	....	....	....
1990-91	Pittsburgh	NHL	25	6	10	16	31	....	....	....	....	....
	Hartford	NHL	44	18	24	42	101	5	1	0	1	7
	NHL Totals		268	130	167	297	408	16	6	3	9	29

a WHL Player of the Year (1986, 1987)
b WHL First All-Star Team (1986, 1987)
c Canadian Major Junior Player of the Year (1987)

Played in NHL All-Star Game (1989)

Traded to **Hartford** by **Pittsburgh** for Scott Young, December 21, 1990.

BROWNSCHIDLE, MARK

Defense. Shoots right. 6'2", 185 lbs. Born, East Amherst, NY, October 26, 1970.
(Winnipeg's 5th choice, 64th overall, in 1989 Entry Draft).

			Regular Season					Playoffs				
Season	Club	Lea	GP	G	A	TP	PIM	GP	G	A	TP	PIM
1988-89	Boston U.	H.E.	35	0	7	7	12	....	....	....	....	....
1989-90	Boston U.	H.E.	38	1	4	5	12	....	....	....	....	....
1990-91	Boston U.	H.E.	13	0	1	1	10	....	....	....	....	....

BRUCE, DAVID

Right wing/Center. Shoots right. 5'11", 190 lbs. Born, Thunder Bay, Ont., October 7, 1964.
(Vancouver's 2nd choice, 30th overall, in 1983 Entry Draft).

			Regular Season					Playoffs				
Season	Club	Lea	GP	G	A	TP	PIM	GP	G	A	TP	PIM
1982-83	Kitchener	OHL	67	36	35	71	199	12	7	9	16	27
1983-84	Kitchener	OHL	62	52	40	92	203	10	5	8	13	20
1984-85	Fredericton	AHL	56	14	11	25	104	5	0	0	0	37
1985-86	Vancouver	NHL	12	0	1	1	14	1	0	0	0	0
	Fredericton	AHL	66	25	16	41	151	2	0	1	1	12
1986-87	Vancouver	NHL	50	9	7	16	109	....	....	....	....	....
	Fredericton	AHL	17	7	6	13	73	....	....	....	....	....
1987-88	Vancouver	NHL	28	7	3	10	57	....	....	....	....	....
	Fredericton	AHL	30	27	18	45	115	....	....	....	....	....
1988-89	Vancouver	NHL	53	7	7	14	65	....	....	....	....	....
1989-90a	Milwaukee	IHL	68	40	35	75	148	6	5	3	8	0
1990-91	St. Louis	NHL	12	1	2	3	14	2	0	0	0	2
ab	Peoria	IHL	60	*64	52	116	78	18	*18	11	*29	40
	NHL Totals		155	24	20	44	259	3	0	0	0	2

a IHL First All-Star Team (1990, 1991)
b Won James Gatschene Memorial Trophy (MVP—IHL) (1991)

Signed as a free agent by **St. Louis**, July 6, 1990. Claimed by **San Jose** from **St. Louis** in Expansion Draft, May 30, 1991.

BRUININKS, BRIAN

Defense. Shoots right. 6', 180 lbs. Born, St. Paul, MN, March 30, 1970.
(Pittsburgh's 14th choice, 236th overall, in 1990 Entry Draft).

			Regular Season					Playoffs				
Season	Club	Lea	GP	G	A	TP	PIM	GP	G	A	TP	PIM
1988-89	Colorado	WCHA	31	1	2	3	35	....	....	....	....	....
1989-90	Colorado	WCHA	30	3	7	10	8	....	....	....	....	....
1990-91	Colorado	WCHA	38	3	8	11	35	....	....	....	....	....

BRUMWELL, JAMES (MURRAY)

Defense. Shoots left. 6'2", 190 lbs. Born, Calgary, Alta., March 31, 1960.

			Regular Season					Playoffs				
Season	Club	Lea	GP	G	A	TP	PIM	GP	G	A	TP	PIM
1978-79	Billings	WHL	61	11	32	43	62	....	....	....	....	....
1979-80	Billings	WHL	67	18	54	72	50	....	....	....	....	....
1980-81	**Minnesota**	**NHL**	**1**	**0**	**0**	**0**	**0**	....	....	....	....	....
	Oklahoma City	CHL	79	12	43	55	79	3	0	0	0	4
1981-82	**Minnesota**	**NHL**	**21**	**0**	**3**	**3**	**18**	**2**	**0**	**0**	**0**	**2**
	Nashville	CHL	55	4	21	25	66	....	....	....	....	....
1982-83	**New Jersey**	**NHL**	**59**	**5**	**14**	**19**	**34**	....	....	....	....	....
	Wichita	CHL	11	4	1	5	4	....	....	....	....	....
1983-84	**New Jersey**	**NHL**	**42**	**7**	**13**	**20**	**14**	....	....	....	....	....
	Maine	AHL	35	4	25	29	16	17	1	5	6	15
1984-85	Maine	AHL	64	8	31	39	12	10	4	5	9	19
1985-86	**New Jersey**	**NHL**	**1**	**0**	**0**	**0**	**0**	....	....	....	....	....
	Maine	AHL	66	9	28	37	35	5	0	3	3	2
1986-87	**New Jersey**	**NHL**	**1**	**0**	**0**	**0**	**2**	....	....	....	....	....
	Maine	AHL	69	10	38	48	30	....	....	....	....	....
1987-88	**New Jersey**	**NHL**	**3**	**0**	**1**	**1**	**2**	....	....	....	....	....
a	Utica	AHL	77	13	53	66	44	....	....	....	....	....
1988-89	Utica	AHL	73	5	29	34	29	5	0	0	0	2
1989-90	New Haven	AHL	62	7	29	36	24	....	....	....	....	....
1990-91	New Haven	AHL	67	8	18	26	27	....	....	....	....	....
	NHL Totals		**128**	**12**	**31**	**43**	**70**	**2**	**0**	**0**	**0**	**2**

a AHL Second All-Star Team (1988)

Signed as free agent by **Minnesota**, August 7, 1980. Claimed by **New Jersey** from **Minnesota** in Waiver Draft, October 4, 1982.

BRUNET, BENOIT (broo-NAY)

Left wing. Shoots left. 5'11", 184 lbs. Born, Ste-Anne de Bellevue, Que., August 24, 1968.
(Montreal's 2nd choice, 27th overall, in 1986 Entry Draft).

			Regular Season					Playoffs				
Season	Club	Lea	GP	G	A	TP	PIM	GP	G	A	TP	PIM
1985-86	Hull	QMJHL	71	33	37	70	81	....	....	....	....	....
1986-87a	Hull	QMJHL	60	43	67	110	105	6	7	5	12	8
1987-88	Hull	QMJHL	62	54	89	143	131	10	3	10	13	11
1988-89	**Montreal**	**NHL**	**2**	**0**	**1**	**1**	**0**	....	....	....	....	....
b	Sherbrooke	AHL	73	41	76	117	95	6	2	0	2	4
1989-90	Sherbrooke	AHL	72	32	35	67	82	12	8	7	15	20
1990-91	**Montreal**	**NHL**	**17**	**1**	**3**	**4**	**0**	....	....	....	....	....
	Fredericton	AHL	24	13	18	31	16	6	5	6	11	2
	NHL Totals		**19**	**1**	**4**	**5**	**0**	....	....	....	....	....

a QMJHL Second All-Star Team (1987)
b AHL First All-Star Team (1989)

BUCHBERGER, KELLY (BUK-BUHR-GUHR)

Left wing. Shoots left. 6'2", 210 lbs. Born, Langenburg, Sask., December 2, 1966.
(Edmonton's 8th choice, 188th overall, in 1985 Entry Draft).

			Regular Season					Playoffs				
Season	Club	Lea	GP	G	A	TP	PIM	GP	G	A	TP	PIM
1984-85	Moose Jaw	WHL	51	12	17	29	114	....	....	....	....	....
1985-86	Moose Jaw	WHL	72	14	22	36	206	13	11	4	15	37
1986-87	**Edmonton**	**NHL**	....	....	....	....	....	**3**	**0**	**1**	**1**	**5**
	Nova Scotia	AHL	70	12	20	32	257	5	0	1	1	23
1987-88	**Edmonton**	**NHL**	**19**	**1**	**0**	**1**	**81**	....	....	....	....	....
	Nova Scotia	AHL	49	21	23	44	206	2	0	0	0	11
1988-89	**Edmonton**	**NHL**	**66**	**5**	**9**	**14**	**234**	....	....	....	....	....
1989-90	**Edmonton**	**NHL**	**55**	**2**	**6**	**8**	**168**	**19**	**0**	**5**	**5**	**13**
1990-91	**Edmonton**	**NHL**	**64**	**3**	**1**	**4**	**160**	**12**	**2**	**1**	**3**	**25**
	NHL Totals		**204**	**11**	**16**	**27**	**643**	**34**	**2**	**7**	**9**	**43**

BUCKLEY, DAVID

Defense. Shoots left. 6'4", 195 lbs. Born, Newton, MA, January 27, 1966.
(Toronto's 9th choice, 192nd overall, in 1984 Entry Draft).

			Regular Season					Playoffs				
Season	Club	Lea	GP	G	A	TP	PIM	GP	G	A	TP	PIM
1985-86	Boston College	H.E.	22	0	2	2	4	....	....	....	....	....
1986-87	Boston College	H.E.	34	3	5	8	9	....	....	....	....	....
1987-88	Boston College	H.E.	33	1	8	9	40	....	....	....	....	....
1988-89	Boston College	H.E.	40	3	7	10	48	....	....	....	....	....
1989-90	Baltimore	AHL	4	0	0	0	0	....	....	....	....	....
	Hampton Roads	ECHL	56	6	33	39	63	5	0	1	1	11
1990-91	Hampton Roads	ECHL	33	5	13	18	26	....	....	....	....	....

BUCKLEY, JEROME

Right wing. Shoots right. 6'2", 200 lbs. Born, Needham, MA, June 27, 1971.
(Boston's 3rd choice, 84th overall, in 1990 Entry Draft).

			Regular Season					Playoffs				
Season	Club	Lea	GP	G	A	TP	PIM	GP	G	A	TP	PIM
1989-90	Northwood Prep.	HS	37	35	33	68	....	....	....	....	....	....
1990-91	Northwood Prep.	HS	26	31	26	57	65	....	....	....	....	....

BUCYK, RANDY (BYOO-sik)

Center. Shoots left. 5'11", 185 lbs. Born, Edmonton, Alta., November 9, 1962.

			Regular Season					Playoffs				
Season	Club	Lea	GP	G	A	TP	PIM	GP	G	A	TP	PIM
1980-81	Northeastern	ECAC	31	18	17	35	0	....	....	....	....	....
1981-82	Northeastern	ECAC	33	19	17	36	10	....	....	....	....	....
1982-83	Northeastern	ECAC	28	16	20	36	16	....	....	....	....	....
1983-84	Northeastern	ECAC	29	16	13	29	11	....	....	....	....	....
1984-85	Sherbrooke	AHL	62	21	26	47	20	8	0	0	0	20
1985-86	**Montreal**	**NHL**	**17**	**4**	**2**	**6**	**8**	**2**	**0**	**0**	**0**	**0**
	Sherbrooke	AHL	43	18	33	51	22	....	....	....	....	....
1986-87	Sherbrooke	AHL	70	24	39	63	28	17	3	11	14	2
1987-88	**Calgary**	**NHL**	**2**	**0**	**0**	**0**	**0**	....	....	....	....	....
	Salt Lake	IHL	75	37	45	82	68	19	7	8	15	12
1988-89	Salt Lake	IHL	79	28	59	87	24	14	5	5	10	4
	Cdn. National	...	4	0	0	0	2	....	....	....	....	....
1989-90	Salt Lake	IHL	67	22	41	63	16	11	2	6	8	10
1990-91	Salt Lake	IHL	18	4	4	8	2	....	....	....	....	....
	NHL Totals		**19**	**4**	**2**	**6**	**8**	**2**	**0**	**0**	**0**	**0**

Signed as a free agent by **Montreal**, January 15, 1986. Signed as a free agent by **Calgary**, June 29, 1987.

BUDA, DAVID

Right wing. Shoots left. 6'4", 190 lbs. Born, Toronto, Ont., March 14, 1966.
(Boston's 9th choice, 199th overall, in 1985 Entry Draft).

			Regular Season					Playoffs				
Season	Club	Lea	GP	G	A	TP	PIM	GP	G	A	TP	PIM
1985-86	Northeastern	H.E.	39	4	4	8	39	....	....	....	....	....
1986-87	Northeastern	H.E.	37	15	15	30	32	....	....	....	....	....
1987-88	Northeastern	H.E.	37	21	16	37	66	....	....	....	....	....
1988-89a	Northeastern	H.E.	35	23	23	46	45	....	....	....	....	....
	Maine	AHL	5	3	1	4	2	....	....	....	....	....
1989-90	Maine	AHL	39	7	4	11	14	....	....	....	....	....
1990-91	Maine	AHL	6	1	3	4	11	....	....	....	....	....
	Johnstown	ECHL	54	45	31	76	41	....	....	....	....	....

a Hockey East First All-Star Team (1989)

BULLARD, MICHAEL BRIAN (MIKE) (BULL-ard)

Center. Shoots left. 6', 195 lbs. Born, Ottawa, Ont., March 10, 1961.
(Pittsburgh's 1st choice, 9th overall, in 1980 Entry Draft).

			Regular Season					Playoffs				
Season	Club	Lea	GP	G	A	TP	PIM	GP	G	A	TP	PIM
1978-79	Brantford	OHA	66	43	56	99	66	....	....	....	....	....
1979-80a	Brantford	OHA	66	66	84	150	86	11	10	6	16	29
1980-81	**Pittsburgh**	**NHL**	**15**	**1**	**2**	**3**	**19**	**4**	**3**	**3**	**6**	**0**
b	Brantford	OHA	42	47	60	107	55	6	4	5	9	10
1981-82	**Pittsburgh**	**NHL**	**75**	**36**	**27**	**63**	**91**	**5**	**1**	**1**	**2**	**4**
1982-83	**Pittsburgh**	**NHL**	**57**	**22**	**22**	**44**	**60**	....	....	....	....	....
1983-84	**Pittsburgh**	**NHL**	**76**	**51**	**41**	**92**	**57**	....	....	....	....	....
1984-85	**Pittsburgh**	**NHL**	**68**	**32**	**31**	**63**	**75**	....	....	....	....	....
1985-86	**Pittsburgh**	**NHL**	**77**	**41**	**42**	**83**	**69**	....	....	....	....	....
1986-87	**Pittsburgh**	**NHL**	**14**	**2**	**10**	**12**	**17**	....	....	....	....	....
	Calgary	**NHL**	**57**	**28**	**26**	**54**	**34**	**6**	**4**	**3**	**7**	**2**
1987-88	**Calgary**	**NHL**	**79**	**48**	**55**	**103**	**68**	**6**	**0**	**2**	**2**	**6**
1988-89	**St. Louis**	**NHL**	**20**	**4**	**12**	**16**	**46**	....	....	....	....	....
	Philadelphia	**NHL**	**54**	**23**	**26**	**49**	**60**	**19**	**3**	**9**	**12**	**32**
1989-90	**Philadelphia**	**NHL**	**70**	**27**	**37**	**64**	**67**	....	....	....	....	....
1990-91	Ambri-Piotta	Switz.	36	36	33	69	....	5	6	4	10	....
	NHL Totals		**662**	**315**	**331**	**646**	**663**	**40**	**11**	**18**	**29**	**44**

a OHA Third All-Star Team (1979)
b OHA Second All-Star Team (1980)

Traded to **Calgary** by **Pittsburgh** for Dan Quinn, November 12, 1986. Traded to **St. Louis** by **Calgary** with Craig Coxe and Tim Corkery for Mark Hunter, Doug Gilmour, Steve Bozek and Michael Dark, September 6, 1988. Traded to **Philadelphia** by **St. Louis** for Peter Zezel, November 29, 1988. Rights traded to **Toronto** by **Philadelphia** for Toronto's fourth round choice in 1992 Entry Draft or Toronto's third round choice in 1993 Entry Draft, July 29, 1991.

BURAKOVSKY, ROBERT (boo-ruh-KAHV-skee)

Right wing. Shoots right. 5'10", 178 lbs. Born, Malmo, Sweden, November 24, 1966.
(NY Rangers' 11th choice, 217th overall, in 1985 Entry Draft).

			Regular Season					Playoffs				
Season	Club	Lea	GP	G	A	TP	PIM	GP	G	A	TP	PIM
1985-86	Leksand	Swe.	19	4	3	7	4	....	....	....	....	....
1986-87	Leksand	Swe.	36	21	15	36	26	....	....	....	....	....
1987-88	Leksand	Swe.	36	10	11	21	10	....	....	....	....	....
1988-89	Leksand	Swe.	40	23	20	43	44	10	6	7	13	4
1989-90	AIK	Swe.	37	27	29	56	32	3	0	2	2	12
1990-91	AIK	Swe.	30	8	15	23	26	....	....	....	....	....

BURE, PAVEL (boo-RAI)

Right wing/Left wing. Shoots left. 5'11", 176 lbs. Born, Moscow, Soviet Union, March 31, 1971.
(Vancouver's 4th choice, 113th overall, in 1989 Entry Draft).

			Regular Season					Playoffs				
Season	Club	Lea	GP	G	A	TP	PIM	GP	G	A	TP	PIM
1987-88	CSKA	USSR	5	1	1	2	0	....	....	....	....	....
1988-89a	CSKA	USSR	32	17	9	26	8	....	....	....	....	....
1989-90	CSKA	USSR	46	14	10	24	20	....	....	....	....	....
1990-91	CSKA	USSR	44	35	11	46	24	....	....	....	....	....

a Named Soviet National League Rookie-of-the-Year (1989)

BUREAU, MARC
(BEWR-oh)

Center. Shoots right. 6', 190 lbs.   Born, Trois-Rivieres, Que., May 19, 1966.

			Regular Season					Playoffs				
Season	Club	Lea	GP	G	A	TP	PIM	GP	G	A	TP	PIM
1983-84	Chicoutimi	QMJHL	56	6	16	22	14	....	....	....	....	....
1984-85	Chicoutimi	QMJHL	41	30	25	55	15	....	....	....	....	....
	Granby	QMJHL	27	20	45	65	14	....	....	....	....	....
1985-86	Granby	QMJHL	19	6	17	23	36	....	....	....	....	....
	Chicoutimi	QMJHL	44	30	45	75	33	9	3	7	10	10
1986-87	Longueuil	QMJHL	66	54	58	112	68	20	17	20	37	12
1987-88	Salt Lake	IHL	69	7	20	27	86	7	0	3	3	8
1988-89	Salt Lake	IHL	76	28	36	64	119	14	7	5	12	31
1989-90	**Calgary**	**NHL**	**5**	**0**	**0**	**0**	**4**	....	....	....	....	....
a	Salt Lake	IHL	67	43	48	91	173	11	4	8	12	0
1990-91	**Calgary**	**NHL**	**5**	**0**	**0**	**0**	**2**	....	....	....	....	....
a	Salt Lake	IHL	54	40	48	88	101	....	....	....	....	....
	Minnesota	**NHL**	**9**	**0**	**6**	**6**	**4**	**23**	**3**	**2**	**5**	**20**
	NHL Totals		**19**	**0**	**6**	**6**	**10**	**23**	**3**	**2**	**5**	**20**

a IHL Second All-Star Team (1990, 1991)
Signed as a free agent by **Calgary**, May 19, 1987. Traded to **Minnesota** by **Calgary** for Minnesota's third round choice (Sandy McCarthy) in 1991 Entry Draft, March 5, 1991.

BURKE, DAVID

Defense. Shoots left. 6'1", 182 lbs.   Born, Detroit, MI, October 15, 1970.
(Toronto's 6th choice, 108th overall, in 1989 Entry Draft).

			Regular Season					Playoffs				
Season	Club	Lea	GP	G	A	TP	PIM	GP	G	A	TP	PIM
1988-89	Cornell	ECAC	26	0	3	3	22	....	....	....	....	....
1989-90	Cornell	ECAC	29	0	12	12	28	....	....	....	....	....
1990-91	Cornell	ECAC	32	2	8	10	43	....	....	....	....	....

BURKE, JAMES

Defense. Shoots left. 6'2", 200 lbs.   Born, Newton, MA, January 3, 1968.
(Hartford's 7th choice, 158th overall, in 1988 Entry Draft).

			Regular Season					Playoffs				
Season	Club	Lea	GP	G	A	TP	PIM	GP	G	A	TP	PIM
1986-87	U. of Maine	H.E.	23	0	0	0	18	....	....	....	....	....
1987-88	U. of Maine	H.E.	41	2	10	12	34	....	....	....	....	....
1988-89	U. of Maine	H.E.	41	1	7	8	56	....	....	....	....	....
1989-90	U. of Maine	H.E.	45	6	23	29	60	....	....	....	....	....
	Binghamton	AHL	2	0	0	0	5	....	....	....	....	....
1990-91	Springfield	AHL	10	0	0	0	8	....	....	....	....	....
	Kansas City	IHL	46	2	9	11	37	....	....	....	....	....

BURNIE, STUART

Right wing. Shoots right. 5'11", 185 lbs.   Born, Orilla, Ont., May 7, 1962.

			Regular Season					Playoffs				
Season	Club	Lea	GP	G	A	TP	PIM	GP	G	A	TP	PIM
1982-83	W. Michigan	CCHA	36	12	7	19	50	....	....	....	....	....
1983-84	W. Michigan	CCHA	42	26	13	39	73	....	....	....	....	....
1984-85	W. Michigan	CCHA	39	21	16	37	49	....	....	....	....	....
1985-86a	W. Michigan	CCHA	42	43	36	79	78	....	....	....	....	....
1986-87	Springfield	AHL	76	21	30	51	62	....	....	....	....	....
1987-88	Springfield	AHL	78	33	22	55	98	....	....	....	....	....
1988-89	Springfield	AHL	74	28	36	64	49	....	....	....	....	....
1989-90	JoKP	Fin.	37	8	1	9	36	....	....	....	....	....
1990-91	Albany	IHL	52	16	19	35	73	....	....	....	....	....
	Fort Wayne	IHL	22	3	11	14	25	12	2	1	3	12

a CCHA Second All-Star Team (1986)
Signed as a free agent by **NY Islanders**, September 5, 1986.

BURNS, TONY

Defense. Shoots left. 6'1", 195 lbs.   Born, Duluth, MN, September 18, 1971.
(Detroit's 4th choice, 87th overall, in 1990 Entry Draft).

			Regular Season					Playoffs				
Season	Club	Lea	GP	G	A	TP	PIM	GP	G	A	TP	PIM
1989-90	Duluth-Denfield	HS	25	21	23	44	....	....	....	....	....	....
1990-91	St. Cloud	WCHA	35	2	6	8	35	....	....	....	....	....

BURR, SHAWN

Left wing/Center. Shoots left. 6'1", 180 lbs.   Born, Sarnia, Ont., July 1, 1966.
(Detroit's 1st choice, 7th overall, in 1984 Entry Draft).

			Regular Season					Playoffs				
Season	Club	Lea	GP	G	A	TP	PIM	GP	G	A	TP	PIM
1983-84	Kitchener	OHL	68	41	44	85	50	16	5	12	17	22
1984-85	**Detroit**	**NHL**	**9**	**0**	**0**	**0**	**2**	....	....	....	....	....
	Adirondack	AHL	4	0	0	0	2	....	....	....	....	....
	Kitchener	OHL	48	24	42	66	50	4	3	3	6	2
1985-86	**Detroit**	**NHL**	**5**	**1**	**0**	**1**	**4**	....	....	....	....	....
	Adirondack	AHL	3	2	2	4	2	17	5	7	12	32
a	Kitchener	OHL	59	60	67	127	104	5	2	3	5	8
1986-87	**Detroit**	**NHL**	**80**	**22**	**25**	**47**	**107**	**16**	**7**	**2**	**9**	**20**
1987-88	**Detroit**	**NHL**	**78**	**17**	**23**	**40**	**97**	**9**	**3**	**1**	**4**	**14**
1988-89	**Detroit**	**NHL**	**79**	**19**	**27**	**46**	**78**	**6**	**1**	**2**	**3**	**6**
1989-90	**Detroit**	**NHL**	**76**	**24**	**32**	**56**	**82**	....	....	....	....	....
	Adirondack	AHL	3	4	2	6	2	....	....	....	....	....
1990-91	**Detroit**	**NHL**	**80**	**20**	**30**	**50**	**112**	**7**	**0**	**4**	**4**	**15**
	NHL Totals		**407**	**103**	**137**	**240**	**482**	**38**	**11**	**9**	**20**	**55**

a OHL Second All-Star Team (1986)

BURRIDGE, RANDY

Left wing. Shoots left. 5'9", 180 lbs.   Born, Fort Erie, Ont., January 7, 1966.
(Boston's 7th choice, 157th overall, in 1985 Entry Draft).

			Regular Season					Playoffs				
Season	Club	Lea	GP	G	A	TP	PIM	GP	G	A	TP	PIM
1983-84	Peterborough	OHL	55	6	7	13	44	8	3	2	5	7
1984-85	Peterborough	OHL	66	49	57	106	88	17	9	16	25	18
1985-86	**Boston**	**NHL**	**52**	**17**	**25**	**42**	**28**	**3**	**0**	**4**	**4**	**12**
	Peterborough	OHL	17	15	11	26	23	3	1	3	4	2
	Moncton	AHL	....	....	....	....	....	3	0	2	2	2
1986-87	**Boston**	**NHL**	**23**	**1**	**4**	**5**	**16**	**2**	**1**	**0**	**1**	**2**
	Moncton	AHL	47	26	41	67	139	3	1	2	3	30
1987-88	**Boston**	**NHL**	**79**	**27**	**28**	**55**	**105**	**23**	**2**	**10**	**12**	**16**
1988-89	**Boston**	**NHL**	**80**	**31**	**30**	**61**	**39**	**10**	**5**	**2**	**7**	**6**
1989-90	**Boston**	**NHL**	**63**	**17**	**15**	**32**	**47**	**21**	**4**	**11**	**15**	**14**
1990-91	**Boston**	**NHL**	**62**	**15**	**13**	**28**	**40**	**19**	**0**	**3**	**3**	**39**
	NHL Totals		**359**	**108**	**115**	**223**	**275**	**78**	**12**	**30**	**42**	**89**

Traded to **Washington** by **Boston** for Stephen Leach, June 21, 1991.

BURT, ADAM

Defense. Shoots left. 6', 190 lbs.   Born, Detroit, MI, January 15, 1969.
(Hartford's 2nd choice, 39th overall, in 1987 Entry Draft).

			Regular Season					Playoffs				
Season	Club	Lea	GP	G	A	TP	PIM	GP	G	A	TP	PIM
1985-86	North Bay	OHL	49	0	11	11	81	10	0	0	0	24
1986-87	North Bay	OHL	57	4	27	31	138	24	1	6	7	68
1987-88	Binghamton	AHL	....	....	....	....	....	2	1	1	2	0
a	North Bay	OHL	66	17	53	70	176	2	0	3	3	6
1988-89	**Hartford**	**NHL**	**5**	**0**	**0**	**0**	**6**	....	....	....	....	....
	Binghamton	AHL	5	0	2	2	13	....	....	....	....	....
	North Bay	OHL	23	4	11	15	45	12	2	12	14	12
1989-90	**Hartford**	**NHL**	**63**	**4**	**8**	**12**	**105**	**2**	**0**	**0**	**0**	**0**
1990-91	**Hartford**	**NHL**	**42**	**2**	**7**	**9**	**63**	....	....	....	....	....
	Springfield	AHL	9	1	3	4	22	....	....	....	....	....
	NHL Totals		**110**	**6**	**15**	**21**	**174**	**2**	**0**	**0**	**0**	**0**

a OHL Second All-Star Team (1988)

BUSKAS, ROD

Defense. Shoots right. 6'1", 206 lbs.   Born, Wetaskiwin, Alta., January 7, 1961.
(Pittsburgh's 5th choice, 112th overall, in 1981 Entry Draft).

			Regular Season					Playoffs				
Season	Club	Lea	GP	G	A	TP	PIM	GP	G	A	TP	PIM
1978-79	Billings	WHL	1	0	0	0	0	....	....	....	....	....
	Medicine Hat	WHL	34	1	12	13	60	....	....	....	....	....
1979-80	Medicine Hat	WHL	72	7	40	47	284	....	....	....	....	....
1980-81	Medicine Hat	WHL	72	14	46	60	164	5	1	1	2	8
1981-82	Erie	AHL	69	1	18	19	78	....	....	....	....	....
1982-83	**Pittsburgh**	**NHL**	**41**	**2**	**2**	**4**	**102**	....	....	....	....	....
	Baltimore	AHL	31	2	8	10	45	....	....	....	....	....
1983-84	**Pittsburgh**	**NHL**	**47**	**2**	**4**	**6**	**60**	....	....	....	....	....
	Baltimore	AHL	33	2	12	14	100	10	1	3	4	22
1984-85	**Pittsburgh**	**NHL**	**69**	**2**	**7**	**9**	**191**	....	....	....	....	....
1985-86	**Pittsburgh**	**NHL**	**72**	**2**	**7**	**9**	**159**	....	....	....	....	....
1986-87	**Pittsburgh**	**NHL**	**68**	**3**	**15**	**18**	**123**	....	....	....	....	....
1987-88	**Pittsburgh**	**NHL**	**76**	**4**	**8**	**12**	**206**	....	....	....	....	....
1988-89	**Pittsburgh**	**NHL**	**52**	**1**	**5**	**6**	**105**	**10**	**0**	**0**	**0**	**23**
1989-90	**Vancouver**	**NHL**	**17**	**0**	**3**	**3**	**36**	....	....	....	....	....
	Pittsburgh	**NHL**	**6**	**0**	**0**	**0**	**13**	....	....	....	....	....
1990-91	**Los Angeles**	**NHL**	**57**	**3**	**8**	**11**	**182**	**2**	**0**	**2**	**2**	**22**
	NHL Totals		**505**	**19**	**59**	**78**	**1177**	**12**	**0**	**2**	**2**	**45**

Traded to **Vancouver** by **Pittsburgh** for Vancouver's sixth round choice (Ian Moran) in 1990 Entry Draft, October 24, 1989. Traded to **Pittsburgh** by **Vancouver** with Barry Pederson and Tony Tanti for Dave Capuano, Andrew McBain and Dan Quinn, January 8, 1990. Claimed by **Los Angeles** in NHL Waiver Draft, October 1, 1990.

BUTASAYEV, VJATESLAV

Center. Shoots left. 6'2", 200 lbs.   Born, Togliatti, Soviet Union, June 13, 1970.
(Philadelphia's 10th choice, 109th overall, in 1990 Entry Draft).

			Regular Season					Playoffs				
Season	Club	Lea	GP	G	A	TP	PIM	GP	G	A	TP	PIM
1989-90	CSKA	USSR	48	13	4	17	30	....	....	....	....	....
1990-91	CSKA	USSR	46	14	9	23	32	....	....	....	....	....

BUTCHER, GARTH

Defense. Shoots right. 6', 200 lbs.   Born, Regina, Sask., January 8, 1963.
(Vancouver's 1st choice, 10th overall, in 1981 Entry Draft).

			Regular Season					Playoffs				
Season	Club	Lea	GP	G	A	TP	PIM	GP	G	A	TP	PIM
1979-80	Regina	WHL	13	0	4	4	20	....	....	....	....	....
1980-81a	Regina	WHL	69	9	77	86	230	11	5	17	22	60
1981-82	**Vancouver**	**NHL**	**5**	**0**	**0**	**0**	**9**	**1**	**0**	**0**	**0**	**0**
a	Regina	WHL	65	24	68	92	318	19	3	17	20	95
1982-83	Vancouver	NHL	55	1	13	14	104	3	1	0	1	2
1983-84	Vancouver	NHL	28	2	0	2	34	....	....	....	....	....
	Fredericton	AHL	25	4	13	17	43	6	0	2	2	19
1984-85	**Vancouver**	**NHL**	**75**	**3**	**9**	**12**	**152**	....	....	....	....	....
	Fredericton	AHL	3	1	0	1	11	....	....	....	....	....
1985-86	**Vancouver**	**NHL**	**70**	**4**	**7**	**11**	**188**	**3**	**0**	**0**	**0**	**0**
1986-87	**Vancouver**	**NHL**	**70**	**5**	**15**	**20**	**207**	....	....	....	....	....
1987-88	**Vancouver**	**NHL**	**80**	**6**	**17**	**23**	**285**	....	....	....	....	....
1988-89	**Vancouver**	**NHL**	**78**	**0**	**20**	**20**	**227**	**7**	**1**	**1**	**2**	**22**
1989-90	**Vancouver**	**NHL**	**80**	**6**	**14**	**20**	**205**	....	....	....	....	....
1990-91	**Vancouver**	**NHL**	**69**	**6**	**12**	**18**	**257**	....	....	....	....	....
	St. Louis	**NHL**	**13**	**0**	**4**	**4**	**32**	**13**	**2**	**1**	**3**	**54**
	NHL Totals		**623**	**33**	**111**	**144**	**1700**	**27**	**4**	**2**	**6**	**76**

a WHL First All-Star Team (1981, 1982)
Traded to **St. Louis** by **Vancouver** with Dan Quinn for Geoff Courtnall, Robert Dirk, Sergio Momesso, Cliff Ronning and future considerations, March 5, 1991.

BYCE, JOHN

Center. Shoots left. 6'1", 180 lbs. Born, Madison, WI, August 9, 1967.
(Boston's 11th choice, 220th overall, in 1985 Entry Draft).

			Regular Season					Playoffs				
Season	Club	Lea	GP	G	A	TP	PIM	GP	G	A	TP	PIM
1986-87	U. Wisconsin	WCHA	40	1	4	5	12	....	....	....	....	....
1987-88	U. Wisconsin	WCHA	41	22	12	34	18	....	....	....	....	....
1988-89a	U. Wisconsin	WCHA	42	27	28	55	16	....	....	....	....	....
1989-90ab	U. Wisconsin	WCHA	46	27	44	71	20	....	....	....	....	....
	Boston	**NHL**	....	....	....	....	....	**8**	**2**	**0**	**2**	**2**
1990-91	**Boston**	**NHL**	**18**	**1**	**3**	**4**	**6**	....	....	....	....	....
	Maine	AHL	53	19	29	48	20	....	....	....	....	....
	NHL Totals		**18**	**1**	**3**	**4**	**6**	**8**	**2**	**0**	**2**	**2**

a WCHA Second All-Star Team (1989, 1990)
b NCAA All-Tournament Team (1990)

BYERS, LYNDON

Right wing. Shoots right. 6'1", 200 lbs. Born, Nipawin, Sask., February 29, 1964.
(Boston's 3rd choice, 39th overall, in 1982 Entry Draft).

			Regular Season					Playoffs				
Season	Club	Lea	GP	G	A	TP	PIM	GP	G	A	TP	PIM
1981-82	Regina	WHL	57	18	25	43	169	20	5	6	11	48
1982-83	Regina	WHL	70	32	38	70	153	5	1	1	2	16
1983-84	**Boston**	**NHL**	**10**	**2**	**4**	**6**	**32**	....	....	....	....	....
	Regina	WHL	58	32	57	89	154	23	17	18	35	78
1984-85	**Boston**	**NHL**	**33**	**3**	**8**	**11**	**41**	....	....	....	..	....
	Hershey	AHL	27	4	6	10	55	....	....	....	....	....
1985-86	**Boston**	**NHL**	**5**	**0**	**2**	**2**	**9**	....	....	....	....	....
	Moncton	AHL	14	2	4	6	26	....	....	....	....	....
	Milwaukee	IHL	8	0	2	2	22	....	....	....	....	....
1986-87	**Boston**	**NHL**	**18**	**2**	**3**	**5**	**53**	**1**	**0**	**0**	**0**	**0**
	Moncton	AHL	27	5	5	10	63	....	....	....	....	....
1987-88	**Boston**	**NHL**	**53**	**10**	**14**	**24**	**236**	**11**	**1**	**2**	**3**	**62**
	Maine	AHL	2	0	1	1	18	....	....	....	....	....
1988-89	**Boston**	**NHL**	**49**	**0**	**4**	**4**	**218**	**2**	**0**	**0**	**0**	**0**
	Maine	AHL	4	1	3	4	2	....	....	....	....	....
1989-90	**Boston**	**NHL**	**43**	**4**	**4**	**8**	**159**	**17**	**1**	**0**	**1**	**12**
1990-91	**Boston**	**NHL**	**19**	**2**	**2**	**4**	**82**	**1**	**0**	**0**	**0**	**10**
	NHL Totals		**230**	**23**	**41**	**64**	**241**	**32**	**2**	**2**	**4**	**84**

BYKOV, VIACHESLAV (BIH-kahf)

Center. 5'8", 174 lbs. Born, Chelyabinsk, Soviet Union, July 24, 1960.
(Quebec's 11th choice, 169th overall, in 1989 Entry Draft).

			Regular Season					Playoffs				
Season	Club	Lea	GP	G	A	TP	PIM	GP	G	A	TP	PIM
1979-80	Chelyabinsk	USSR	3	2	0	2	0	....	....	....	....	....
1980-81	Chelyabinsk	USSR	48	26	16	42	4	....	....	....	....	....
1981-82	Chelyabinsk	USSR	44	20	16	36	14	....	....	....	....	....
1982-83	CSKA	USSR	44	22	22	44	10	....	....	....	....	....
1983-84	CSKA	USSR	44	22	11	33	12	....	....	....	....	....
1984-85	CSKA	USSR	36	21	14	35	4	....	....	....	....	....
1985-86	CSKA	USSR	36	10	10	20	6	....	....	....	....	....
1986-87	CSKA	USSR	40	18	15	33	10	....	....	....	....	....
1987-88	CSKA	USSR	47	17	30	47	26	....	....	....	....	....
1988-89	CSKA	USSR	40	16	20	36	10	....	....	....	....	....
1989-90	CSKA	USSR	48	21	16	37	16	....	....	....	....	....
1990-91	Gotteron	Switz.	36	35	49	84	....	8	8	16	23	....

BYLSMA, DAN

Left wing. Shoots left. 6'2", 205 lbs. Born, Grand Rapids, MI, September 19, 1970.
(Winnipeg's 7th choice, 109th overall, in 1989 Entry Draft).

			Regular Season					Playoffs				
Season	Club	Lea	GP	G	A	TP	PIM	GP	G	A	TP	PIM
1988-89	Bowling Green	CCHA	32	3	7	10	10	....	....	....	....	....
1989-90	Bowling Green	CCHA	44	13	17	30	30	....	....	....	....	....
1990-91	Bowling Green	CCHA	40	9	12	21	48	....	....	....	....	....

BYRAM, SHAWN

Left wing. Shoots left. 6'2", 204 lbs. Born, Neepawa, Man., September 12, 1968.
(NY Islanders' 4th choice, 80th overall, in 1986 Entry Draft).

			Regular Season					Playoffs				
Season	Club	Lea	GP	G	A	TP	PIM	GP	G	A	TP	PIM
1985-86	Regina	WHL	46	7	6	13	45	9	0	1	1	11
1986-87	Prince Albert	WHL	67	19	21	40	147	7	1	1	2	10
1987-88	Prince Albert	WHL	61	23	28	51	178	10	5	2	7	27
1988-89	Springfield	AHL	45	5	11	16	195	....	....	....	....	....
	Indianapolis	IHL	1	0	0	0	2	....	....	....	....	....
1989-90	Springfield	AHL	31	4	4	8	30	....	....	....	....	....
	Johnstown	ECHL	8	5	5	10	35	....	....	....	....	....
1990-91	**NY Islanders**	**NHL**	**4**	**0**	**0**	**0**	**14**	....	....	....	....	....
	Capital Dist.	AHL	62	28	35	63	162	....	....	....	....	....
	NHL Totals		**4**	**0**	**0**	**0**	**14**	....	....	....	....	....

BZDEL, GERALD (bayz-DEHL)

Defense. Shoots right. 6'1", 196 lbs. Born, Wynyard, Sask., March 13, 1968.
(Quebec's 5th choice, 102nd overall, in 1986 Entry Draft).

			Regular Season					Playoffs				
Season	Club	Lea	GP	G	A	TP	PIM	GP	G	A	TP	PIM
1985-86	Regina	WHL	72	2	15	17	107	10	0	3	3	14
1986-87	Regina	WHL	13	0	3	3	38	....	....	....	....	....
	Seattle	WHL	48	4	12	16	137	....	....	....	....	....
1987-88	Moose Jaw	WHL	72	4	17	21	217	....	....	....	....	....
1988-89	Halifax	AHL	36	1	3	4	46	....	....	....	....	....
1989-90	Halifax	AHL	59	2	20	22	84	6	0	1	1	24
1990-91	Halifax	AHL	74	3	11	14	99	....	....	....	....	....

CADIEUX, STEVE

Center. Shoots left. 6', 176 lbs. Born, Ste-Therese, Que., June 17, 1969.
(Montreal's 12th choice, 251st overall, in 1989 Entry Draft).

			Regular Season					Playoffs				
Season	Club	Lea	GP	G	A	TP	PIM	GP	G	A	TP	PIM
1986-87	St. Jean	QMJHL	65	28	22	50	26	8	1	7	8	4
1987-88	St. Jean	QMJHL	66	43	50	93	18	7	4	4	8	2
1988-89	St. Jean	QMJHL	17	15	24	39	8	....	....	....	....	....
	Shawinigan	QMJHL	53	65	62	127	14	10	9	12	21	12
1989-90	Shawinigan	QMJHL	67	*73	90	163	101	6	4	7	11	26
1990-91	Winston-Salem	ECHL	9	2	2	4	22	....	....	....	....	....
	Cincinnati	ECHL	53	45	52	97	66	4	3	3	6	23

CAHILL, DARCY

Center. Shoots right. 6', 191 lbs. Born, Kingston, Ont., August 19, 1970.
(Vancouver's 10th choice, 239th overall, in 1989 Entry Draft).

			Regular Season					Playoffs				
Season	Club	Lea	GP	G	A	TP	PIM	GP	G	A	TP	PIM
1986-87	North Bay	OHL	52	7	19	26	7	....	....	....	....	....
1987-88	Kingston	OHL	66	27	41	68	19	....	....	....	....	....
1988-89	Cornwall	OHL	66	35	57	92	49	13	9	8	17	4
1989-90	Cornwall	OHL	36	24	52	76	51	....	....	....	....	....
	Sudbury	OHL	22	14	19	33	22	7	1	13	14	14
1990-91	Sudbury	OHL	4	3	5	8	10	....	....	....	....	....
	Hamilton	OHL	22	20	21	41	18	....	....	....	....	....

CAIN, PAUL

Center. Shoots right. 5'10", 180 lbs. Born, Toronto, Ont., April 6, 1969.
(NY Rangers' 9th choice, 194th overall, in 1988 Entry Draft).

			Regular Season					Playoffs				
Season	Club	Lea	GP	G	A	TP	PIM	GP	G	A	TP	PIM
1985-86	Cornwall	OHL	62	11	12	23	21	....	....	....	....	....
1986-87	Cornwall	OHL	60	13	27	40	8	....	....	....	....	....
1987-88	Cornwall	OHL	21	14	9	23	41	7	0	2	2	0
1988-89	Cornwall	OHL	44	19	47	66	26	12	5	9	14	6
1989-90	Cornwall	OHL	47	28	36	64	23	6	2	4	6	2
1990-91	Richmond	ECHL	12	5	3	8	6	....	....	....	....	....

CALLAHAN, JOHN JR. (JACK)

Center. Shoots right. 6'3", 208 lbs. Born, Melrose, MA, April 21, 1971.
(Philadelphia's 5th choice, 138th overall, in 1989 Entry Draft).

			Regular Season					Playoffs				
Season	Club	Lea	GP	G	A	TP	PIM	GP	G	A	TP	PIM
1990-91	Boston College	H.E.	30	11	5	16	16	....	....	....	....	....

CALLANDER, JOHN (JOCK)

Right wing. Shoots right. 6'1", 188 lbs. Born, Regina, Sask., April 23, 1961.

			Regular Season					Playoffs				
Season	Club	Lea	GP	G	A	TP	PIM	GP	G	A	TP	PIM
1979-80	Regina	WHL	39	9	11	20	25	18	8	5	13	0
1980-81	Regina	WHL	72	67	86	153	37	11	6	7	13	14
1981-82	Regina	WHL	71	79	111	*190	59	20	13	*26	39	37
1982-83	Salt Lake	CHL	68	20	27	47	26	6	0	1	1	9
1983-84	Montana	CHL	72	27	32	59	69	....	....	....	....	....
	Toledo	IHL	2	0	0	0	0	....	....	....	....	....
1984-85	Muskegon	IHL	82	39	68	107	86	17	13	*21	*33	
1985-86a	Muskegon	IHL	82	39	72	111	121	14	*12	11	*23	12
1986-87bcd	Muskegon	IHL	82	54	82	*136	110	15	13	7	20	23
1987-88	**Pittsburgh**	**NHL**	**41**	**11**	**16**	**27**	**45**	....	....	....	....	....
	Muskegon	IHL	31	20	36	56	49	6	2	3	5	25
1988-89	**Pittsburgh**	**NHL**	**30**	**6**	**5**	**11**	**20**	**10**	**2**	**5**	**7**	**10**
	Muskegon	IHL	48	25	39	64	40	7	5	5	10	30
1989-90	**Pittsburgh**	**NHL**	**30**	**4**	**7**	**11**	**49**	....	....	....	....	....
	Muskegon	IHL	46	29	49	78	118	15	6	*14	20	54
1990-91	Muskegon	IHL	30	14	20	34	102	....	....	....	....	....
	NHL Totals		**101**	**21**	**28**	**49**	**114**	**10**	**2**	**5**	**7**	**10**

a IHL Playoff MVP (1986)
b IHL First All-Star Team (1987)
c Shared James Gatschene Memorial Trophy (MVP-IHL) with Jeff Pyle (1987)
d Shared Leo P. Lamoureux Memorial Trophy (Top Scorer-IHL) with Jeff Pyle (1987)

Signed as free agent by **St. Louis**, September 28, 1981. Signed as a free agent by **Pittsburgh**, July 31, 1987.

CAMPBELL, JIM

Center. Shoots right. 6'1", 175 lbs. Born, Worcester, MA, April 3, 1973.
(Montreal's 2nd choice, 28th overall, in 1991 Entry Draft).

			Regular Season					Playoffs				
Season	Club	Lea	GP	G	A	TP	PIM	GP	G	A	TP	PIM
1989-90	Lawrence Aca.	HS	8	14	7	21	8	....	....	....	....	....
1990-91	Northwood Prep.	HS	26	36	47	83	36	....	....	....	....	....

CAPUANO, DAVE (KAP-yew-AN-oh)

Left wing. Shoots left. 6'2", 195 lbs. Born, Warwick, RI, July 27, 1968.
(Pittsburgh's 2nd choice, 25th overall, in 1986 Entry Draft).

			Regular Season					Playoffs				
Season	Club	Lea	GP	G	A	TP	PIM	GP	G	A	TP	PIM
1986-87	U. of Maine	H.E.	38	18	41	59	14	....	....	....	....	....
1987-88abc	U. of Maine	H.E.	42	*34	*51	*85	51	....	....	....	....	....
1988-89ac	U. of Maine	H.E.	41	37	30	67	38	....	....	....	....	....
1989-90	**Pittsburgh**	**NHL**	**6**	**0**	**0**	**0**	**2**	....	....	....	....	....
	Muskegon	IHL	27	15	15	30	22	....	....	....	....	....
	Vancouver	**NHL**	**27**	**3**	**5**	**8**	**10**	....	....	....	....	....
	Milwaukee	IHL	2	0	4	4	0	6	1	5	6	0
1990-91	**Vancouver**	**NHL**	**61**	**13**	**31**	**44**	**42**	**6**	**1**	**1**	**2**	**5**
	NHL Totals		**94**	**16**	**36**	**52**	**54**	**6**	**1**	**1**	**2**	**5**

a NCAA East First All-American Team (1988, 1989)
b NCAA All-Tournament Team (1988)
c Hockey East First All-Star Team (1988, 1989)

Traded to **Vancouver** by **Pittsburgh** with Andrew McBain and Dan Quinn for Rod Buskas, Barry Pederson and Tony Tanti, January 8, 1990.

CAPUANO, DEAN

Defense. Shoots left. 6'1", 175 lbs. Born, Providence, RI, November 3, 1971.
(Boston's 9th choice, 210th overall, in 1990 Entry Draft).

			Regular Season					Playoffs				
Season	Club	Lea	GP	G	A	TP	PIM	GP	G	A	TP	PIM
1989-90	Mt. St. Charles	HS	....	5	20	25	....	....	....	....	....	....
1990-91	Providence	H.E.	19	3	5	8	6	....	....	....	....	....

CAPUANO, JACK (KAP-yew-AN-oh)

Defense. Shoots left. 6'2", 210 lbs. Born, Cranston, RI, July 7, 1966.
(Toronto's 4th choice, 67th overall, in 1984 Entry Draft).

			Regular Season					Playoffs				
Season	Club	Lea	GP	G	A	TP	PIM	GP	G	A	TP	PIM
1985-86	U. of Maine	H.E.	39	9	18	27	51	....	....	....	....	....
1986-87a	U. of Maine	H.E.	42	10	34	44	20	....	....	....	....	....
1987-88bc	U. of Maine	H.E.	43	13	37	50	87	....	....	....	....	....
1988-89	Newmarket	AHL	74	5	16	21	52	1	0	0	0	0
1989-90	Toronto	NHL	1	0	0	0	0	....	....	....	....	....
	Newmarket	AHL	8	0	2	2	7	....	....	....	....	....
	Springfield	AHL	14	0	4	4	8	....	....	....	....	....
	Milwaukee	IHL	17	3	10	13	60	6	0	1	1	12
1990-91	Vancouver	NHL	3	0	0	0	0	....	....	....	....	....
	Milwaukee	IHL	80	20	30	50	76	6	0	1	1	2
	NHL Totals		4	0	0	0	0	....	....	....	....	....

a Hockey East Second All-Star Team (1987)
b NCAA East First All-American Team (1988)
c Hockey East First All-Star Team (1988)

Traded to **NY Islanders** by **Toronto** with Paul Gagne and Derek Laxdal for Mike Stevens and Gilles Thibaudeau, December 20, 1989. Traded to **Vancouver** by **NY Islanders** for Jeff Rohlicek, March 6, 1990. Signed as a free agent by **Boston**, August 1, 1991.

CARBONNEAU, GUY (KAR-buhn-oh, GEE)

Center. Shoots right. 5'11", 180 lbs. Born, Sept-Iles, Que., March 18, 1960.
(Montreal's 4th choice, 44th overall, in 1979 Entry Draft).

			Regular Season					Playoffs				
Season	Club	Lea	GP	G	A	TP	PIM	GP	G	A	TP	PIM
1976-77	Chicoutimi	QJHL	59	9	20	29	8	4	1	0	1	0
1977-78	Chicoutimi	QJHL	70	28	55	83	60	....	....	....	....	....
1978-79	Chicoutimi	QJHL	72	62	79	141	47	4	2	1	3	4
1979-80	Chicoutimi	QJHL	72	72	110	182	66	12	9	15	24	28
	Nova Scotia	AHL	....	....	....	....	....	2	1	1	2	2
1980-81	Montreal	NHL	2	0	1	1	0	....	....	....	....	....
	Nova Scotia	AHL	78	35	53	88	87	6	1	3	4	9
1981-82	Nova Scotia	AHL	77	27	67	94	124	9	2	7	9	8
1982-83	Montreal	NHL	77	18	29	47	68	3	0	0	0	2
1983-84	Montreal	NHL	78	24	30	54	75	15	4	3	7	12
1984-85	Montreal	NHL	79	23	34	57	43	12	4	3	7	8
1985-86	Montreal	NHL	80	20	36	56	57	20	7	5	12	35
1986-87	Montreal	NHL	79	18	27	45	68	17	3	8	11	20
1987-88a	Montreal	NHL	80	17	21	38	61	11	0	4	4	2
1988-89a	Montreal	NHL	79	26	30	56	44	21	4	5	9	10
1989-90	Montreal	NHL	68	19	36	55	37	11	2	3	5	6
1990-91	Montreal	NHL	78	20	24	44	63	13	1	5	6	10
	NHL Totals		700	185	268	453	516	123	25	36	61	105

a Won Frank J. Selke Trophy (1988, 1989)

CARKNER, TERRY

Defense. Shoots left. 6'3", 212 lbs. Born, Smiths Falls, Ont., March 7, 1966.
(NY Rangers' 1st choice, 14th overall, in 1984 Entry Draft).

			Regular Season					Playoffs				
Season	Club	Lea	GP	G	A	TP	PIM	GP	G	A	TP	PIM
1983-84	Peterborough	OHL	58	4	19	23	77	8	0	6	6	13
1984-85a	Peterborough	OHL	64	14	47	61	125	17	2	10	12	11
1985-86b	Peterborough	OHL	54	12	32	44	106	16	1	7	8	17
1986-87	NY Rangers	NHL	52	2	13	15	118	1	0	0	0	0
	New Haven	AHL	12	2	6	8	56	3	1	0	1	0
1987-88	Quebec	NHL	63	3	24	27	159	....	....	....	....	....
1988-89	Philadelphia	NHL	78	11	32	43	149	19	1	5	6	28
1989-90	Philadelphia	NHL	63	4	18	22	169	....	....	....	....	....
1990-91	Philadelphia	NHL	79	7	25	32	204	....	....	....	....	....
	NHL Totals		335	27	112	139	799	20	1	5	6	28

a OHL Second All-Star Team (1985)
b OHL First All-Star Team (1986)

Traded to **Quebec** by **NY Rangers** with Jeff Jackson for John Ogrodnick and David Shaw September, 30 1987. Traded to **Philadelphia** by **Quebec** for Greg Smyth and Philadelphia's third round choice (John Tanner) in the 1989 Entry Draft, July 25, 1988.

CARLSSON, ANDERS (KAHRL-suhn)

Center. Shoots left. 5'11", 185 lbs. Born, Gavle, Sweden, November 25, 1960.
(New Jersey's 5th choice, 66th overall, in 1986 Entry Draft).

			Regular Season					Playoffs				
Season	Club	Lea	GP	G	A	TP	PIM	GP	G	A	TP	PIM
1978-79	Brynas	Swe.	1	0	0	0	2	....	....	....	....	....
1979-80	Brynas	Swe.	17	0	1	1	2	1	0	0	0	0
1980-81	Brynas	Swe.	36	8	8	16	36	....	....	....	....	....
1981-82	Brynas	Swe.	35	5	5	10	22	....	....	....	....	....
1982-83	Brynas	Swe.	35	18	13	31	26	....	....	....	....	....
1983-84	Brynas	Swe.	35	8	26	34	34	....	....	....	....	....
1984-85	Sodertalje	Swe.	36	20	14	34	18	8	0	3	3	4
1985-86	Sodertalje	Swe.	36	12	26	38	20	7	2	4	6	0
1986-87	New Jersey	NHL	48	2	18	20	14	....	....	....	....	....
	Maine	AHL	6	0	6	6	2	....	....	....	....	....
1987-88	New Jersey	NHL	9	1	0	1	0	3	1	0	1	2
	Utica	AHL	33	12	22	34	16	....	....	....	....	....
1988-89	New Jersey	NHL	47	4	8	12	20	....	....	....	....	....
	Utica	AHL	7	2	4	6	4	....	....	....	....	....
1989-90	Brynas	Swe.	40	12	31	43	29	3	0	2	2	0
1990-91	Brynas	Swe.	34	11	24	35	22	....	....	....	....	....
	NHL Totals		104	7	26	33	34	3	1	0	1	2

CARLSSON, LEIF (KAHRL-suhn)

Defense. Shoots left. 6'1", 213 lbs. Born, Ludvika, Sweden, February 18, 1965.
(Hartford's 4th choice, 61st overall, in 1983 Entry Draft).

			Regular Season					Playoffs				
Season	Club	Lea	GP	G	A	TP	PIM	GP	G	A	TP	PIM
1983-84	Farjestad	Swe.	19	3	0	3	10	....	....	....	....	....
1984-85	Farjestad	Swe.	36	4	8	12	24	3	0	0	0	0
1985-86	Farjestad	Swe.	36	7	6	13	22	7	1	3	4	4
1986-87	Farjestad	Swe.	33	9	4	13	18	7	2	2	4	10
1987-88	Farjestad	Swe.	40	10	14	24	26	9	2	1	3	4
1988-89	Farjestad	Swe.	39	6	6	12	38	....	....	....	....	....
1989-90	V. Frolunda	Swe.	37	2	10	12	24	....	....	....	....	....
1990-91	V. Frolunda	Swe.2	22	1	3	4	10	....	....	....	....	....

CARLYLE, RANDY ROBERT

Defense. Shoots left. 5'10", 200 lbs. Born, Sudbury, Ont., April 19, 1956.
(Toronto's 1st choice, 30th overall, in 1976 Amateur Draft).

			Regular Season					Playoffs				
Season	Club	Lea	GP	G	A	TP	PIM	GP	G	A	TP	PIM
1974-75	Sudbury	OHA	67	17	47	64	118	15	3	6	9	21
1975-76a	Sudbury	OHA	60	15	64	79	126	17	6	13	19	50
1976-77	Toronto	NHL	45	0	5	5	51	9	0	1	1	20
	Dallas	CHL	26	2	7	9	63	....	....	....	....	....
1977-78	Toronto	NHL	49	2	11	13	31	7	0	1	1	8
	Dallas	CHL	21	3	14	17	31	....	....	....	....	....
1978-79	Pittsburgh	NHL	70	13	34	47	78	7	0	0	0	12
1979-80	Pittsburgh	NHL	67	8	28	36	45	5	1	0	1	4
1980-81bc	Pittsburgh	NHL	76	16	67	83	136	5	4	5	9	9
1981-82	Pittsburgh	NHL	73	11	64	75	131	5	1	3	4	16
1982-83	Pittsburgh	NHL	61	15	41	56	110	....	....	....	....	....
1983-84	Pittsburgh	NHL	50	3	23	26	82	....	....	....	....	....
	Winnipeg	NHL	5	0	3	3	2	3	0	2	2	4
1984-85	Winnipeg	NHL	71	13	38	51	98	8	1	5	6	13
1985-86	Winnipeg	NHL	68	16	33	49	93	....	....	....	....	....
1986-87	Winnipeg	NHL	71	16	26	42	93	10	1	5	6	18
1987-88	Winnipeg	NHL	78	15	44	59	210	5	0	2	2	10
1988-89	Winnipeg	NHL	78	6	38	44	78	....	....	....	....	....
1989-90	Winnipeg	NHL	53	3	15	18	50	....	....	....	....	....
1990-91	Winnipeg	NHL	52	9	19	28	44	....	....	....	....	....
	NHL Totals		967	146	489	635	1332	64	8	24	32	114

a OHA Second All-Star Team (1976)
b Won James Norris Memorial Trophy (1981)
c NHL First All-Star Team (1981)

Played in NHL All-Star Game (1981-83, 1985)

Traded to **Pittsburgh** by **Toronto** with George Ferguson for Dave Burrows, June 14, 1978. Traded to **Winnipeg** by **Pittsburgh** for Winnipeg's first round choice (Doug Bodger) in 1984 Entry Draft and future considerations (Moe Mantha), March 5, 1984.

CARNBACK, PATRIK (KAHRN-buhk)

Left wing. Shoots left. 6', 189 lbs. Born, Goteborg, Sweden, February 1, 1968.
(Montreal's 7th choice, 125th overall, in 1988 Entry Draft).

			Regular Season					Playoffs				
Season	Club	Lea	GP	G	A	TP	PIM	GP	G	A	TP	PIM
1986-87	V. Frolunda	Swe.2	28	3	1	4	4	....	....	....	....	....
1987-88	V. Frolunda	Swe.2	33	16	19	35	10	....	....	....	....	....
1988-89	V. Frolunda	Swe.2	53	39	36	75	52	....	....	....	....	....
1989-90	V. Frolunda	Swe.	40	26	27	53	34	....	....	....	....	....
1990-91	V. Frolunda	Swe.2	22	10	9	19	46	....	....	....	....	....

CARNEY, KEITH E.

Defense. Shoots left. 6'1", 199 lbs. Born, Pawtucket, RI, February 3, 1970.
(Buffalo's 3rd choice, 76th overall, in 1988 Entry Draft).

			Regular Season					Playoffs				
Season	Club	Lea	GP	G	A	TP	PIM	GP	G	A	TP	PIM
1988-89	U. of Maine	H.E.	40	4	22	26	24	....	....	....	....	....
1989-90ab	U. of Maine	H.E.	41	3	41	44	43	....	....	....	....	....
1990-91cd	U. of Maine	H.E.	40	7	49	56	38	....	....	....	....	....

a Hockey East Second All-Star Team (1990)
b NCAA East Second All-American Team (1990)
c Hockey East First All-Star Team (1991)
d NCAA East First All-American Team (1991)

CARPENTER, ROBERT (BOB)

Center/Left wing. Shoots left. 6', 190 lbs. Born, Beverly, MA, July 13, 1963.
(Washington's 1st choice, 3rd overall, in 1981 Entry Draft).

			Regular Season					Playoffs				
Season	Club	Lea	GP	G	A	TP	PIM	GP	G	A	TP	PIM
1980-81	St. John's	HS	18	14	24	38	....	....	....	....	....	....
1981-82	Washington	NHL	80	32	35	67	69	....	....	....	....	....
1982-83	Washington	NHL	80	32	37	69	64	4	1	0	1	2
1983-84	Washington	NHL	80	28	40	68	51	8	2	1	3	25
1984-85	Washington	NHL	80	53	42	95	87	5	1	4	5	8
1985-86	Washington	NHL	80	27	29	56	105	9	5	4	9	12
1986-87	Washington	NHL	22	5	7	12	21	....	....	....	....	....
	NY Rangers	NHL	28	2	8	10	20	....	....	....	....	....
	Los Angeles	NHL	10	2	3	5	6	5	1	2	3	2
1987-88	Los Angeles	NHL	71	19	33	52	84	5	1	1	2	0
1988-89	Los Angeles	NHL	39	11	15	26	16	....	....	....	....	....
	Boston	NHL	18	5	9	14	10	8	1	1	2	4
1989-90	Boston	NHL	80	25	31	56	97	21	4	6	10	39
1990-91	Boston	NHL	29	8	8	16	22	1	0	1	1	2
	NHL Totals		697	249	297	546	652	66	16	20	36	94

Played in NHL All-Star Game (1985)

Traded to **NY Rangers** by **Washington** with Washington's second-round choice (Jason Prosofsky) in 1989 Entry Draft for Bob Crawford, Kelly Miller and Mike Ridley, January 1, 1987. Traded to **Los Angeles** by **NY Rangers** with Tom Laidlaw for Jeff Crossman, Marcel Dionne and Los Angeles' third-round choice in 1989 Entry Draft (Draft choice acquired by **Minnesota,** October 12, 1988. **Minnesota** selected Murray Garbutt.) Traded to **Boston** by **Los Angeles** for Steve Kasper, January 23, 1989.

CARSON, JIMMY

Center. Shoots right. 6'1", 200 lbs. Born, Southfield, MI, July 20, 1968.
(Los Angeles' 1st choice, 2nd overall, in 1986 Entry Draft).

			Regular Season					Playoffs				
Season	Club	Lea	GP	G	A	TP	PIM	GP	G	A	TP	PIM
1984-85	Verdun	QMJHL	68	44	72	116	12	14	9	17	26	12
1985-86a	Verdun	QMJHL	69	70	83	153	46	5	2	6	8	0
1986-87b	Los Angeles	NHL	80	37	42	79	22	5	1	2	3	6
1987-88	Los Angeles	NHL	80	55	52	107	45	5	5	3	8	4
1988-89	Edmonton	NHL	80	49	51	100	36	7	2	1	3	6
1989-90	Edmonton	NHL	4	1	2	3	0	....	....	....	....	....
	Detroit	NHL	44	20	16	36	8	....	....	....	....	....
1990-91	Detroit	NHL	64	21	25	46	28	7	2	1	3	4
	NHL Totals		352	183	188	371	139	24	10	7	17	20

a QMJHL Second All-Star Team (1986)
b Named to NHL All-Rookie Team (1987)

Played in NHL All-Star Game (1989)

Traded to **Edmonton** by **Los Angeles** with Martin Gelinas, Los Angeles' first round choices in 1989 (acquired by New Jersey, June 17, 1989. New Jersey selected Jason Miller), 1991 (Martin Rucinsky) and 1993 Entry Drafts and cash for Wayne Gretzky, Mike Krushelnyski and Marty McSorley, August 9, 1988. Traded to **Detroit** by **Edmonton** with Kevin McClelland and Edmonton's fifth round choice (later traded to Montreal for Rick Green. Montreal selected Brad Layzell) in 1991 Entry Draft for Petr Klima, Joe Murphy, Adam Graves and Jeff Sharples, November 2, 1989.

CARTER, JOHN

Left wing. Shoots left. 5'10", 175 lbs. Born, Winchester, MA, May 3, 1963.

			Regular Season					Playoffs				
Season	Club	Lea	GP	G	A	TP	PIM	GP	G	A	TP	PIM
1982-83	RPI	ECAC	29	16	22	38	33	....	....	....	....	....
1983-84	RPI	ECAC	38	35	39	74	52	....	....	....	....	....
1984-85	RPI	ECAC	37	43	29	72	52	....	....	....	....	....
1985-86	RPI	ECAC	27	23	18	41	68	....	....	....	....	....
	Boston	NHL	3	0	0	0	0	....	....	....	....	....
1986-87	Boston	NHL	8	0	1	1	0	....	....	....	....	....
	Moncton	AHL	58	25	30	55	60	6	2	3	5	5
1987-88	Boston	NHL	4	0	1	1	2	....	....	....	....	....
	Maine	AHL	76	38	38	76	145	10	4	4	8	44
1988-89	Boston	NHL	44	12	10	22	24	10	1	2	3	6
	Maine	AHL	24	13	6	19	12	....	....	....	....	....
1989-90	Boston	NHL	76	17	22	39	26	21	6	3	9	45
	Maine	AHL	2	2	2	4	2	....	....	....	....	....
1990-91	Boston	NHL	50	4	7	11	68	....	....	....	....	....
	Maine	AHL	16	5	9	14	16	1	0	0	0	10
	NHL Totals		185	33	41	74	120	31	7	5	12	51

Signed as a free agent by **Boston**, May 3, 1986. Signed as a free agent by **San Jose**, August 22, 1991.

CARUSO, BRIAN

Left wing. Shoots left. 6'2", 225 lbs. Born, Thunder Bay, Ont., September 20, 1972.
(Calgary's 4th choice, 63rd overall, in 1991 Entry Draft).

			Regular Season					Playoffs				
Season	Club	Lea	GP	G	A	TP	PIM	GP	G	A	TP	PIM
1989-90	Thunder Bay	USHL	56	30	46	76	79	....	....	....	....	....
1990-91	Minn.-Duluth	WCHA	31	5	6	11	24	....	....	....	....	....

CARVEL, GREG

Center. Shoots left. 5'11", 180 lbs. Born, Canton, NY, August 17, 1970.
(Pittsburgh's 1st choice, 22nd overall, in 1991 Supplemental Draft).

			Regular Season					Playoffs				
Season	Club	Lea	GP	G	A	TP	PIM	GP	G	A	TP	PIM
1989-90	St. Lawrence	ECAC	30	5	16	21	18	....	....	....	....	....
1990-91	St. Lawrence	ECAC	34	7	15	22	18	....	....	....	....	....

CASSELMAN, MIKE

Center. Shoots left. 5'11", 180 lbs. Born, Morrisburg, Ont., September 23, 1968.
(Detroit's 1st choice, 3rd overall, in 1990 Supplemental Draft).

			Regular Season					Playoffs				
Season	Club	Lea	GP	G	A	TP	PIM	GP	G	A	TP	PIM
1987-88	Clarkson	ECAC	24	4	1	5	....	....	....	....	....	....
1988-89	Clarkson	ECAC	31	3	14	17	....	....	....	....	....	....
1989-90	Clarkson	ECAC	34	22	21	43	69	....	....	....	....	....
1990-91	Clarkson	ECAC	40	19	35	54	44	....	....	....	....	....

CASSELS, ANDREW (CASTLES)

Center. Shoots left. 6', 192 lbs. Born, Bramalea, Ont., July 23, 1969.
(Montreal's 1st choice, 17th overall, in 1987 Entry Draft).

			Regular Season					Playoffs				
Season	Club	Lea	GP	G	A	TP	PIM	GP	G	A	TP	PIM
1986-87a	Ottawa	OHL	66	26	66	92	28	11	5	9	14	7
1987-88bc	Ottawa	OHL	61	48	*103	*151	39	16	8	*24	*32	13
1988-89c	Ottawa	OHL	56	37	97	134	66	12	5	10	15	10
1989-90	Montreal	NHL	6	2	0	2	2	....	....	....	....	....
	Sherbrooke	AHL	55	22	45	67	25	12	2	11	13	6
1990-91	Montreal	NHL	54	6	19	25	20	8	0	2	2	2
	NHL Totals		60	8	19	27	22	8	0	2	2	2

a OHL Rookie of the Year (1987)
b OHL Player of the Year (1988)
c OHL First All-Star Team (1988,1989)

CASSIDY, BRUCE

Defense. Shoots left. 5'11", 176 lbs. Born, Ottawa, Ont., May 20, 1965.
(Chicago's 1st choice, 18th overall, in 1983 Entry Draft).

			Regular Season					Playoffs				
Season	Club	Lea	GP	G	A	TP	PIM	GP	G	A	TP	PIM
1982-83	Ottawa	OHL	70	25	86	111	33	9	3	9	12	10
1983-84	Chicago	NHL	1	0	0	0	0	....	....	....	....	....
a	Ottawa	OHL	67	27	68	95	58	13	6	16	22	6
1984-85	Ottawa	OHL	28	13	27	40	15	....	....	....	....	....
1985-86	Chicago	NHL	1	0	0	0	0	....	....	....	....	....
	Nova Scotia	AHL	4	0	0	0	0	....	....	....	....	....
1986-87	Chicago	NHL	2	0	0	0	0	....	....	....	....	....
	Nova Scotia	AHL	19	2	8	10	4	....	....	....	....	....
	Cdn. Olympic	...	12	3	6	9	4	....	....	....	....	....
	Saginaw	IHL	10	2	13	15	6	2	1	1	2	0
1987-88	Chicago	NHL	21	3	10	13	6	....	....	....	....	....
	Saginaw	IHL	60	9	37	46	59	10	2	3	5	19
1988-89	Chicago	NHL	9	0	2	2	4	1	0	0	0	0
b	Saginaw	IHL	72	16	64	80	80	6	0	2	2	6
1989-90	Chicago	NHL	2	1	1	2	0	....	....	....	....	....
b	Indianapolis	IHL	75	11	46	57	56	14	1	10	11	20
1990-91	Alleghe	Italy	36	23	52	75	20	10	7	8	15	2
	NHL Totals		36	4	13	17	10	1	0	0	0	0

a OHL Second All-Star Team (1984)
b IHL First All-Star Team (1989, 1990)

CAUFIELD, JAY

Right wing. Shoots right. 6'4", 237 lbs. Born, Philadelphia, PA, July 17, 1960.

			Regular Season					Playoffs				
Season	Club	Lea	GP	G	A	TP	PIM	GP	G	A	TP	PIM
1984-85	North Dakota	WCHA	1	0	0	0	0	....	....	....	....	....
1985-86	Toledo	IHL	30	5	4	9	54	....	....	....	....	....
	New Haven	AHL	40	2	3	5	40	1	0	0	0	0
1986-87	NY Rangers	NHL	13	2	1	3	45	3	0	0	0	12
	Flint	IHL	12	4	3	7	59	....	....	....	....	....
	New Haven	AHL	13	0	0	0	43	....	....	....	....	....
1987-88	Minnesota	NHL	1	0	0	0	0	....	....	....	....	....
	Kalamazoo	IHL	65	5	10	15	273	6	0	1	1	47
1988-89	Pittsburgh	NHL	58	1	4	5	285	9	0	0	0	28
1989-90	Pittsburgh	NHL	37	1	2	3	123	....	....	....	....	....
1990-91	Pittsburgh	NHL	23	1	1	2	71	....	....	....	....	....
	Muskegon	IHL	3	1	0	1	18	....	....	....	....	....
	NHL Totals		132	5	8	13	524	12	0	0	0	40

Signed as a free agent by **NY Rangers**, October 8, 1985. Traded to **Minnesota** by **NY Rangers** with Dave Gagne for Jari Gronstrand and Paul Boutilier, October 8, 1987. Claimed by **Pittsburgh** in NHL Waiver Draft, October 3, 1988.

CAVALLINI, GINO JOHN

Left wing. Shoots left. 6'1", 215 lbs. Born, Toronto, Ont., November 24, 1962.

			Regular Season					Playoffs				
Season	Club	Lea	GP	G	A	TP	PIM	GP	G	A	TP	PIM
1982-83	Bowling Green	CCHA	40	8	16	24	52	....	....	....	....	....
1983-84	Bowling Green	CCHA	43	25	23	48	16	....	....	....	....	....
1984-85	Calgary	NHL	27	6	10	16	14	3	0	0	0	4
	Moncton	AHL	51	29	19	48	28	....	....	....	....	....
1985-86	Calgary	NHL	27	7	7	14	26	....	....	....	....	....
	Moncton	AHL	4	3	2	5	7	....	....	....	....	....
	St. Louis	NHL	30	6	5	11	36	17	4	5	9	10
1986-87	St. Louis	NHL	80	18	26	44	54	6	3	1	4	2
1987-88	St. Louis	NHL	64	15	17	32	62	10	5	5	10	19
1988-89	St. Louis	NHL	74	20	23	43	79	9	0	2	2	17
1989-90	St. Louis	NHL	80	15	15	30	77	12	1	3	4	12
1990-91	St. Louis	NHL	78	8	27	35	81	13	1	3	4	2
	NHL Totals		460	95	130	225	429	70	14	19	33	66

Signed as a free agent by **Calgary**, May 16, 1984. Traded to **St. Louis** by **Calgary** with Eddy Beers and Charles Bourgeois for Joe Mullen, Terry Johnson and Rik Wilson, February 1, 1986.

CAVALLINI, PAUL

Defense. Shoots left. 6'1", 210 lbs. Born, Toronto, Ont., October 13, 1965.
(Washington's 9th choice, 205th overall, in 1984 Entry Draft).

			Regular Season					Playoffs				
Season	Club	Lea	GP	G	A	TP	PIM	GP	G	A	TP	PIM
1984-85	Providence	H.E.	37	4	10	14	52	....	....	....	....	....
1985-86	Cdn. Olympic	...	52	1	11	12	95	....	....	....	....	....
	Binghamton	AHL	15	3	4	7	20	6	0	2	2	56
1986-87	Washington	NHL	6	0	2	2	8	....	....	....	....	....
	Binghamton	AHL	66	12	24	36	188	13	2	7	9	35
1987-88	Washington	NHL	24	2	3	5	66	....	....	....	....	....
	St. Louis	NHL	48	4	7	11	86	10	1	6	7	26
1988-89	St. Louis	NHL	65	4	20	24	128	10	2	2	4	14
1989-90a	St. Louis	NHL	80	8	39	47	106	12	2	3	5	20
1990-91	St. Louis	NHL	67	10	25	35	89	13	2	3	5	20
	NHL Totals		290	28	96	124	483	45	7	14	21	80

a Won Alka-Seltzer Plus Award (NHL plus/minus leader) (1990)

Played in NHL All-Star Game (1990)

Traded to **St. Louis** by **Washington** for Montreal's second round choice (Wade Bartley) in 1988 Entry Draft — St. Louis' property via earlier deal — December 11, 1987.

CERNICH, KORD

Defense, Shoots left. 5'11", 195 lbs. Born, Ketchikan, AK, October 20, 1966.

			Regular Season					Playoffs				
Season	Club	Lea	GP	G	A	TP	PIM	GP	G	A	TP	PIM
1986-87	Lake Superior	CCHA	39	4	18	22	32	....	....	....	....	....
1987-88a	Lake Superior	CCHA	46	17	22	39	78	....	....	....	....	....
1988-89b	Lake Superior	CCHA	46	7	31	38	74	....	....	....	....	....
1989-90bc	Lake Superior	CCHA	46	11	25	36	59	....	....	....	....	....
1990-91	Binghamton	AHL	52	5	10	15	36	....	....	....	....	....

a CCHA Second All-Star Team (1988)
b CCHA First All-Star Team (1989, 1990)
c NCAA West Second All-American Team (1990)

Signed as a free agent by **NY Rangers**, July 19, 1990.

CESARSKI, ANDREW

Defense. Shoots left. 6'2", 190 lbs. Born, Ft. Monmouth, NJ, September 21, 1968.
(St. Louis' 11th choice, 207th overall, in 1987 Entry Draft).

			Regular Season					Playoffs				
Season	Club	Lea	GP	G	A	TP	PIM	GP	G	A	TP	PIM
1987-88	Princeton	ECAC	28	2	3	5	34	....	....	....	....	....
1988-89	Princeton	ECAC	26	6	10	16	34	....	....	....	....	....
1989-90	Princeton	ECAC	27	1	9	10	22	....	....	....	....	....
1990-91	Princeton	ECAC	27	4	10	14	38	....	....	....	....	....

CHABOT, JOHN DAVID (shah-BAHT)

Center. Shoots left. 6'2", 200 lbs. Born, Summerside, P.E.I., May 18, 1962.
(Montreal's 3rd choice, 40th overall, in 1980 Entry Draft).

			Regular Season					Playoffs				
Season	Club	Lea	GP	G	A	TP	PIM	GP	G	A	TP	PIM
1979-80	Hull	QMJHL	68	26	57	83	28	4	1	2	3	0
1980-81	Hull	QMJHL	70	27	62	89	24	....	....	....	....	....
	Nova Scotia	AHL	1	0	0	0	0	2	0	0	0	0
1981-82ab	Sherbrooke	QMJHL	62	34	*109	143	42	19	6	26	32	6
1982-83	Nova Scotia	AHL	76	16	73	89	19	7	1	3	4	0
1983-84	**Montreal**	**NHL**	**56**	**18**	**25**	**43**	**13**	**11**	**1**	**4**	**5**	**0**
1984-85	**Montreal**	**NHL**	**10**	**1**	**6**	**7**	**2**	....	....	....	....	....
	Pittsburgh	**NHL**	**67**	**8**	**45**	**53**	**12**	....	....	....	....	....
1985-86	**Pittsburgh**	**NHL**	**77**	**14**	**31**	**45**	**6**	....	....	....	....	....
1986-87	**Pittsburgh**	**NHL**	**72**	**14**	**22**	**36**	**8**	....	....	....	....	....
1987-88	**Detroit**	**NHL**	**78**	**13**	**44**	**57**	**10**	**16**	**4**	**15**	**19**	**2**
1988-89	**Detroit**	**NHL**	**52**	**2**	**10**	**12**	**6**	**6**	**1**	**1**	**2**	**0**
	Adirondack	AHL	8	3	12	15	0	....	....	....	....	....
1989-90	**Detroit**	**NHL**	**69**	**9**	**40**	**49**	**24**	....	....	....	....	....
1990-91	**Detroit**	**NHL**	**27**	**5**	**5**	**10**	**4**	....	....	....	....	....
	Adirondack	AHL	27	11	30	41	4	2	0	1	1	0
	NHL Totals		**508**	**84**	**228**	**312**	**85**	**33**	**6**	**20**	**26**	**2**

a QMJHL First All-Star Team (1982)
b QMJHL Most Valuable Player (1982)

Traded to **Pittsburgh** by **Montreal** for Ron Flockhart, November 9, 1984. Signed as a free agent by **Detroit**, June 25, 1987.

CHALIFOUX, DENIS

Center. Shoots right. 5'8", 165lbs. Born, Laval, Que., February 28, 1971.
(Hartford's 11th choice, 246th overall, in 1990 Entry Draft).

			Regular Season					Playoffs				
Season	Club	Lea	GP	G	A	TP	PIM	GP	G	A	TP	PIM
1989-90	Laval	QMJHL	70	41	68	109	32	14	*14	14	*28	14
1990-91a	Laval	QMJHL	67	38	79	117	77	4	1	1	2	4

a QMJHL Second All-Star Team (1991)

CHAMBERS, SHAWN

Defense. Shoots left. 6'2", 200 lbs. Born, Royal Oaks, MI, October 11, 1966.
(Minnesota's 1st choice, 4th overall, in 1987 Supplemental Draft).

			Regular Season					Playoffs				
Season	Club	Lea	GP	G	A	TP	PIM	GP	G	A	TP	PIM
1986-87	Alaska-Fair.	G.N.	28	8	29	37	84	....	....	....	....	....
	Seattle	WHL	28	8	25	33	58	....	....	....	....	....
	Ft. Wayne	IHL	12	2	6	8	0	10	1	4	5	5
1987-88	**Minnesota**	**NHL**	**19**	**1**	**7**	**8**	**21**	....	....	....	....	....
	Kalamazoo	IHL	19	1	6	7	22	....	....	....	....	....
1988-89	**Minnesota**	**NHL**	**72**	**5**	**19**	**24**	**80**	**3**	**0**	**2**	**2**	**0**
1989-90	**Minnesota**	**NHL**	**78**	**8**	**18**	**26**	**81**	**7**	**2**	**1**	**3**	**10**
1990-91	**Minnesota**	**NHL**	**29**	**1**	**3**	**4**	**24**	**23**	**0**	**7**	**7**	**16**
	Kalamazoo	IHL	3	1	1	2	0	....	....	....	....	....
	NHL Totals		**198**	**15**	**47**	**62**	**206**	**33**	**2**	**10**	**12**	**26**

Traded to **Washington** by **Minnesota** for Steve Maltais and Trent Klatt, June 21, 1991.

CHAPDELAINE, RENE (SHAP-duh-LAYN)

Defense. Shoots right. 6'1", 195 lbs. Born, Weyburn, Sask., September 27, 1966.
(Los Angeles' 7th choice, 149th overall, in 1986 Entry Draft).

			Regular Season					Playoffs				
Season	Club	Lea	GP	G	A	TP	PIM	GP	G	A	TP	PIM
1985-86	Lake Superior	CCHA	32	1	4	5	47	....	....	....	....	....
1986-87	Lake Superior	CCHA	28	1	5	6	51	....	....	....	....	....
1987-88	Lake Superior	CCHA	35	1	9	10	44	....	....	....	....	....
1988-89	Lake Superior	CCHA	46	4	9	13	62	....	....	....	....	....
1989-90	New Haven	AHL	41	0	1	1	35	....	....	....	....	....
1990-91	**Los Angeles**	**NHL**	**3**	**0**	**1**	**1**	**10**	....	....	....	....	....
	New Haven	AHL	65	3	11	14	49	....	....	....	....	....
	Phoenix	IHL	17	0	2	2	10	11	0	0	0	8
	NHL Totals		**3**	**0**	**1**	**1**	**10**	....	....	....	....	....

CHAPMAN, BRIAN

Defense. Shoots left. 6', 195 lbs. Born, Brockville, Ont., February 10, 1968.
(Hartford's 3rd choice, 74th overall, in 1986 Entry Draft).

			Regular Season					Playoffs				
Season	Club	Lea	GP	G	A	TP	PIM	GP	G	A	TP	PIM
1985-86	Belleville	OHL	66	6	31	37	168	24	2	6	8	54
1986-87	Belleville	OHL	54	4	32	36	142	6	1	1	2	10
1987-88	Belleville	OHL	63	11	57	68	180	6	1	4	5	13
1988-89	Binghamton	AHL	71	5	25	30	216	....	....	....	....	....
1989-90	Binghamton	AHL	68	2	15	17	180	....	....	....	....	....
1990-91	**Hartford**	**NHL**	**3**	**0**	**0**	**0**	**29**	....	....	....	....	....
	Springfield	AHL	60	4	23	27	200	18	1	4	5	62
	NHL Totals		**3**	**0**	**0**	**0**	**29**	....	....	....	....	....

CHARBONNEAU, JOSE (JOE) (SHAHR-buh-NOH)

Right wing. Shoots right. 6', 195 lbs. Born, Ferme-Neuve, Que., November 21, 1966.
(Montreal's 1st choice, 12th overall, in 1985 Entry Draft).

			Regular Season					Playoffs				
Season	Club	Lea	GP	G	A	TP	PIM	GP	G	A	TP	PIM
1983-84	Drummondville	QMJHL	65	31	59	90	110	....	....	....	....	....
1984-85	Drummondville	QMJHL	46	34	40	74	91	12	5	10	15	20
1985-86	Drummondville	QMJHL	57	44	45	89	158	23	16	20	36	40
1986-87	Sherbrooke	AHL	72	14	27	41	94	16	5	12	17	17
1987-88	**Montreal**	**NHL**	**16**	**0**	**2**	**2**	**6**	**8**	**0**	**0**	**0**	**4**
	Sherbrooke	AHL	55	30	35	65	108	....	....	....	....	....
1988-89	**Montreal**	**NHL**	**9**	**1**	**3**	**4**	**6**	....	....	....	....	....
	Sherbrooke	AHL	33	13	15	28	95	....	....	....	....	....
	Vancouver	**NHL**	**13**	**0**	**1**	**1**	**6**	....	....	....	....	....
	Milwaukee	IHL	13	8	5	13	46	10	3	2	5	23
1989-90	Milwaukee	IHL	65	23	38	61	137	5	0	1	1	8
1990-91	Cdn. National	...	56	22	29	51	54	....	....	....	....	....
	NHL Totals		**38**	**1**	**6**	**7**	**18**	**8**	**0**	**0**	**0**	**4**

Traded to **Vancouver** by **Montreal** for Dan Woodley, January 25, 1989.

CHARLESWORTH, TODD

Defense. Shoots left. 6'1", 190 lbs. Born, Calgary, Alta., March 22, 1965.
(Pittsburgh's 2nd choice, 22nd overall, in 1983 Entry Draft).

			Regular Season					Playoffs				
Season	Club	Lea	GP	G	A	TP	PIM	GP	G	A	TP	PIM
1982-83	Oshawa	OHL	70	6	23	29	55	17	0	4	4	20
1983-84	**Pittsburgh**	**NHL**	**10**	**0**	**0**	**0**	**8**	....	....	....	....	....
	Oshawa	OHL	57	11	35	46	54	7	0	4	4	4
1984-85	**Pittsburgh**	**NHL**	**67**	**1**	**8**	**9**	**31**	....	....	....	....	....
1985-86	**Pittsburgh**	**NHL**	**2**	**0**	**1**	**1**	**0**	....	....	....	....	....
	Baltimore	AHL	19	1	3	4	10	....	....	....	....	....
	Muskegon	IHL	51	9	27	36	78	14	3	8	11	14
1986-87	**Pittsburgh**	**NHL**	**1**	**0**	**0**	**0**	**0**	....	....	....	....	....
	Baltimore	AHL	75	5	21	26	64	....	....	....	....	....
1987-88	**Pittsburgh**	**NHL**	**6**	**2**	**0**	**2**	**2**	....	....	....	....	....
	Muskegon	IHL	64	9	31	40	49	5	0	0	0	18
1988-89a	Muskegon	IHL	74	10	53	63	85	14	2	13	15	8
1989-90	**NY Rangers**	**NHL**	**7**	**0**	**0**	**0**	**6**	....	....	....	....	....
	Flint	IHL	26	3	6	9	12	....	....	....	....	....
	Cape Breton	AHL	32	0	9	9	13	....	....	....	....	....
1990-91	Binghamton	AHL	11	0	3	3	2	....	....	....	....	....
	Muskegon	IHL	62	5	32	37	46	5	1	3	4	2
	NHL Totals		**93**	**3**	**9**	**12**	**47**	....	....	....	....	....

a IHL Second All-Star Team (1989)

Signed as a free agent by **Edmonton**, June 21, 1989. Traded to **NY Rangers** by **Edmonton** for future considerations, January 18, 1990.

CHARRON, CRAIG M.

Center. Shoots left. 5'10", 175 lbs. Born, North Easton, MA, November 15, 1967.
(Montreal's 1st choice, 25th overall, in 1989 Supplemental Draft).

			Regular Season					Playoffs				
Season	Club	Lea	GP	G	A	TP	PIM	GP	G	A	TP	PIM
1986-87	U. of Lowell	H.E.	36	11	16	27	48	....	....	....	....	....
1987-88	U. of Lowell	H.E.	39	22	18	40	32	....	....	....	....	....
1988-89	U. of Lowell	H.E.	32	14	21	35	32	....	....	....	....	....
1989-90	U. of Lowell	H.E.	35	17	29	46	10	....	....	....	....	....
1990-91	Albany	IHL	5	0	2	2	0	....	....	....	....	....
	Winston-Salem	ECHL	30	11	16	27	10	....	....	....	....	....
	Fredericton	AHL	24	2	5	7	4	5	0	3	3	0

CHARRON, ERIC

Defense. Shoots left. 6'3", 191 lbs. Born, Verdun, Que., January 14, 1970.
(Montreal's 1st choice, 20th overall, in 1988 Entry Draft).

			Regular Season					Playoffs				
Season	Club	Lea	GP	G	A	TP	PIM	GP	G	A	TP	PIM
1987-88	Trois Rivieres	QMJHL	67	3	13	16	135	....	....	....	....	....
1988-89	Trois Rivieres	QMJHL	38	2	16	18	111	....	....	....	....	....
	Verdun	QMJHL	28	2	15	17	66	....	....	....	....	....
	Sherbrooke	AHL	1	0	0	0	0	....	....	....	....	....
1989-90	Trois-Rivieres	QMJHL	68	13	38	51	152	11	3	4	7	67
	Sherbrooke	AHL	....	....	....	....	....	2	0	0	0	0
1990-91	Fredericton	AHL	71	1	11	12	108	2	1	0	1	29

CHASE, KELLY WAYNE

Right wing. Shoots right. 5'11", 195 lbs. Born, Porcupine Plain, Sask., October 25, 1967.

			Regular Season					Playoffs				
Season	Club	Lea	GP	G	A	TP	PIM	GP	G	A	TP	PIM
1985-86	Saskatoon	WHL	57	7	18	25	172	10	3	4	7	37
1986-87	Saskatoon	WHL	68	17	29	46	285	11	2	8	10	37
1987-88	Saskatoon	WHL	70	21	34	55	*343	9	3	5	8	32
1988-89	Peoria	IHL	38	14	7	21	278	....	....	....	....	....
1989-90	**St. Louis**	**NHL**	**43**	**1**	**3**	**4**	**244**	**9**	**1**	**0**	**1**	**8**
	Peoria	IHL	10	1	2	3	76	....	....	....	....	....
1990-91	**St. Louis**	**NHL**	**2**	**1**	**0**	**1**	**15**	**6**	**0**	**0**	**0**	**18**
	Peoria	IHL	61	20	34	54	406	10	4	3	7	61
	NHL Totals		**45**	**2**	**3**	**5**	**259**	**15**	**1**	**0**	**1**	**26**

Signed as a free agent by **St. Louis**, February 23, 1988.

CHASE, TIMOTHY

Center. Shoots left. 6'2", 180 lbs. Born, Gaithersburg, MD, March 23, 1970.
(Montreal's 8th choice, 146th overall, in 1988 Entry Draft).

			Regular Season					Playoffs				
Season	Club	Lea	GP	G	A	TP	PIM	GP	G	A	TP	PIM
1989-90	Brown	ECAC	8	0	0	0	0	....	....	....	....	....
1990-91	Brown	ECAC	19	5	8	13	18	....	....	....	....	....

CHEBATOR, ROB

Defense. Shoots left. 6', 170 lbs. Born, Arlington, MA, December 1, 1970.
(Toronto's 9th choice, 199th overall, in 1990 Entry Draft).

			Regular Season					Playoffs				
Season	Club	Lea	GP	G	A	TP	PIM	GP	G	A	TP	PIM
1989-90	Arlington	HS	20	16	32	48	18	....	....	....	....	....
1990-91	N. Hampshire	H.E.	33	4	2	6	14	....	....	....	....	....

CHELIOS, CHRIS (CHELL-EE-ohs)

Defense. Shoots right. 6'1", 186 lbs. Born, Chicago, IL, January 25, 1962.
(Montreal's 5th choice, 40th overall, in 1981 Entry Draft).

			Regular Season					Playoffs				
Season	Club	Lea	GP	G	A	TP	PIM	GP	G	A	TP	PIM
1981-82	U. Wisconsin	WCHA	43	6	43	49	50	....	....	....	....	....
1982-83ab	U. Wisconsin	WCHA	26	9	17	26	50	....	....	....	....	....
1983-84	U.S. National	...	60	14	35	49	58	....	....	....	....	....
	U.S. Olympic	...	6	0	4	4	8	....	....	....	....	....
	Montreal	**NHL**	**12**	**0**	**2**	**2**	**12**	**15**	**1**	**9**	**10**	**17**
1984-85c	**Montreal**	**NHL**	**74**	**9**	**55**	**64**	**87**	**9**	**2**	**8**	**10**	**17**
1985-86	**Montreal**	**NHL**	**41**	**8**	**26**	**34**	**67**	**20**	**2**	**9**	**11**	**49**
1986-87	**Montreal**	**NHL**	**71**	**11**	**33**	**44**	**124**	**17**	**4**	**9**	**13**	**38**
1987-88	**Montreal**	**NHL**	**71**	**20**	**41**	**61**	**172**	**11**	**3**	**1**	**4**	**29**
1988-89de	**Montreal**	**NHL**	**80**	**15**	**58**	**73**	**185**	**21**	**4**	**15**	**19**	**28**
1989-90	**Montreal**	**NHL**	**53**	**9**	**22**	**31**	**136**	**5**	**0**	**1**	**1**	**8**
1990-91f	**Chicago**	**NHL**	**77**	**12**	**52**	**64**	**192**	**6**	**1**	**7**	**8**	**46**
	NHL Totals		**479**	**84**	**289**	**373**	**975**	**104**	**17**	**59**	**76**	**232**

a WCHA Second All-Star Team (1983)
b NCAA All-Tournament Team (1983)
c NHL All-Rookie Team (1985)
d NHL First All-Star Team (1989)
e Won Norris Trophy (1989)
f NHL Second All-Star Team (1991)

Played in NHL All-Star Game (1985, 1990, 1991)

Traded to **Chicago** by **Montreal** with Montreal's second round choice (Michael Pomichter) in 1991 Entry Draft for Denis Savard, June 29, 1990.

CHERNOMAZ, RICHARD (RICH) (CHUR-noh-maz)

Right wing. Shoots right. 5'8", 185 lbs. Born, Selkirk, Man., September 1, 1963.
(Colorado's 2nd choice, 26th overall, in 1981 Entry Draft).

			Regular Season					Playoffs				
Season	Club	Lea	GP	G	A	TP	PIM	GP	G	A	TP	PIM
1980-81	Victoria	WHL	72	49	64	113	92	15	11	15	26	38
1981-82	**Colorado**	**NHL**	**2**	**0**	**0**	**0**	**0**	....	....	....	....	....
	Victoria	WHL	49	36	62	98	69	4	1	2	3	13
1982-83a	Victoria	WHL	64	71	53	124	113	12	10	5	15	18
1983-84	**New Jersey**	**NHL**	**7**	**2**	**1**	**3**	**2**	....	....	....	....	....
	Maine	AHL	69	17	29	46	39	2	0	1	1	0
1984-85	**New Jersey**	**NHL**	**3**	**0**	**2**	**2**	**2**	....	....	....	....	....
	Maine	AHL	64	17	34	51	64	10	2	2	4	4
1985-86	Maine	AHL	78	21	28	49	82	5	0	0	0	2
1986-87	**New Jersey**	**NHL**	**25**	**6**	**4**	**10**	**8**	....	....	....	....	....
	Maine	AHL	58	35	27	62	65	....	....	....	....	....
1987-88	**Calgary**	**NHL**	**2**	**1**	**0**	**1**	**0**	....	....	....	....	....
b	Salt Lake	IHL	73	48	47	95	122	18	4	14	18	30
1988-89	**Calgary**	**NHL**	**1**	**0**	**0**	**0**	**0**	....	....	....	....	....
	Salt Lake	IHL	81	33	68	101	122	14	7	5	12	47
1989-90	Salt Lake	IHL	65	39	35	74	170	11	6	6	12	32
1990-91b	Salt Lake	IHL	81	39	58	97	213	4	3	1	4	8
	NHL Totals		**40**	**9**	**7**	**16**	**12**	....	....	....	....	....

a WHL First All-Star Team (1983)
b IHL Second All-Star Team (1988, 1991)

Signed as a free agent by **Calgary**, August 4, 1987.

CHEVELDAYOFF, KEVIN (sheh-vehl-DAY-ahf)

Defense. Shoots right. 6', 202 lbs. Born, Saskatoon, Sask., February 4, 1970.
(New York Islanders' 1st choice, 16th overall, in 1988 Entry Draft).

			Regular Season					Playoffs				
Season	Club	Lea	GP	G	A	TP	PIM	GP	G	A	TP	PIM
1986-87	Brandon	WHL	70	0	16	16	259	....	....	....	....	....
1987-88	Brandon	WHL	71	3	29	32	265	4	0	2	2	20
1988-89	Brandon	WHL	40	4	12	16	135	....	....	....	....	....
1989-90	Brandon	WHL	33	5	12	17	56	....	....	....	....	....
	Springfield	AHL	4	0	0	0	0	....	....	....	....	....
1990-91	Capital Dist.	AHL	76	0	14	14	203	....	....	....	....	....

CHIASSON, STEVE (CHAY-sahn)

Defense. Shoots left. 6', 205 lbs. Born, Barrie, Ont., April 14, 1967.
(Detroit's 3rd choice, 50th over all, in 1985 Entry Draft).

			Regular Season					Playoffs				
Season	Club	Lea	GP	G	A	TP	PIM	GP	G	A	TP	PIM
1984-85	Guelph	OHL	61	8	22	30	139	....	....	....	....	....
1985-86	Guelph	OHL	54	12	30	42	126	18	10	10	20	37
1986-87	**Detroit**	**NHL**	**45**	**1**	**4**	**5**	**73**	**2**	**0**	**0**	**0**	**19**
1987-88	**Detroit**	**NHL**	**29**	**2**	**9**	**11**	**57**	**9**	**2**	**2**	**4**	**31**
	Adirondack	AHL	23	6	11	17	58	....	....	....	....	....
1988-89	**Detroit**	**NHL**	**65**	**12**	**35**	**47**	**149**	**5**	**2**	**1**	**3**	**6**
1989-90	**Detroit**	**NHL**	**67**	**14**	**28**	**42**	**114**	....	....	....	....	....
1990-91	**Detroit**	**NHL**	**42**	**3**	**17**	**20**	**80**	**5**	**3**	**1**	**4**	**19**
	NHL Totals		**248**	**32**	**93**	**125**	**473**	**21**	**7**	**4**	**11**	**75**

CHITARONI, MARIO BRIAN

Center. Shoots right. 5'8", 170 lbs. Born, Haileybury, Ont., March 11, 1966.

			Regular Season					Playoffs				
Season	Club	Lea	GP	G	A	TP	PIM	GP	G	A	TP	PIM
1987-88	Flint	IHL	80	49	47	96	156	12	9	8	17	60
1988-89	Flint	IHL	21	10	11	21	59	....	....	....	....	....
	New Haven	AHL	54	12	24	36	97	16	2	7	9	57
1989-90	Alleghe/Sile	Italy	36	39	35	74	87	10	14	11	25	29
1990-91	Alleghe/Sile	Italy	31	37	48	85	73	10	12	9	21	10

Signed as a free agent by **Los Angeles**, July 1, 1988.

CHORSKE, TOM

Right wing/Left wing. Shoots right. 6'1", 204 lbs. Born, Minneapolis, MN, September 18, 1966.
(Montreal's 2nd choice, 16th overall, in 1985 Entry Draft).

			Regular Season					Playoffs				
Season	Club	Lea	GP	G	A	TP	PIM	GP	G	A	TP	PIM
1985-86	U. Minnesota	WCHA	39	6	4	10	16	....	....	....	....	....
1986-87	U. Minnesota	WCHA	47	20	22	42	20	....	....	....	....	....
1987-88	U.S. National	...	36	9	16	25	24	....	....	....	....	....
1988-89a	U. Minnesota	WCHA	37	25	24	49	28	....	....	....	....	....
1989-90	**Montreal**	**NHL**	**14**	**3**	**1**	**4**	**2**	....	....	....	....	....
	Sherbrooke	AHL	59	22	24	46	54	12	4	4	8	8
1990-91	**Montreal**	**NHL**	**57**	**9**	**11**	**20**	**32**	....	....	....	....	....
	NHL Totals		**71**	**12**	**12**	**24**	**34**	....	....	....	....	....

a WCHA First All-Star Team (1989)

CHRISTIAN, DAVID (DAVE)

Right wing. Shoots right. 5'11", 195 lbs. Born, Warroad, MN, May 12, 1959.
(Winnipeg's 2nd choice, 40th overall, in 1979 Entry Draft).

			Regular Season					Playoffs				
Season	Club	Lea	GP	G	A	TP	PIM	GP	G	A	TP	PIM
1977-78	North Dakota	WCHA	38	8	16	24	14	....	....	....	....	....
1978-79	North Dakota	WCHA	40	22	24	46	22	....	....	....	....	....
1979-80	U.S. National	...	59	10	20	30	26	....	....	....	....	....
	U.S. Olympic	...	7	0	8	8	6	....	....	....	....	....
	Winnipeg	**NHL**	**15**	**8**	**10**	**18**	**2**	....	....	....	....	....
1980-81	**Winnipeg**	**NHL**	**80**	**28**	**43**	**71**	**22**	....	....	....	....	....
1981-82	**Winnipeg**	**NHL**	**80**	**25**	**51**	**76**	**28**	**4**	**0**	**1**	**1**	**2**
1982-83	**Winnipeg**	**NHL**	**55**	**18**	**26**	**44**	**23**	**3**	**0**	**0**	**0**	**0**
1983-84	**Washington**	**NHL**	**80**	**29**	**52**	**81**	**28**	**8**	**5**	**4**	**9**	**5**
1984-85	**Washington**	**NHL**	**80**	**26**	**43**	**69**	**14**	**5**	**1**	**1**	**2**	**0**
1985-86	**Washington**	**NHL**	**80**	**41**	**42**	**83**	**15**	**9**	**4**	**4**	**8**	**0**
1986-87	**Washington**	**NHL**	**76**	**23**	**27**	**50**	**8**	**7**	**1**	**3**	**4**	**6**
1987-88	**Washington**	**NHL**	**80**	**37**	**21**	**58**	**26**	**14**	**5**	**6**	**11**	**6**
1988-89	**Washington**	**NHL**	**80**	**34**	**31**	**65**	**12**	**6**	**1**	**1**	**2**	**0**
1989-90	**Washington**	**NHL**	**28**	**3**	**8**	**11**	**4**	....	....	....	....	....
	Boston	**NHL**	**50**	**12**	**17**	**29**	**8**	**21**	**4**	**1**	**5**	**4**
1990-91	**Boston**	**NHL**	**78**	**32**	**21**	**53**	**41**	**19**	**8**	**4**	**12**	**4**
	NHL Totals		**862**	**316**	**392**	**708**	**231**	**96**	**29**	**25**	**54**	**27**

Played in NHL All-Star Game (1991)

Traded to **Washington** by **Winnipeg** for Washington's first round choice (Bob Dollas) in the 1983 Entry Draft, June 8, 1983. Traded to **Boston** by **Washington** for Bob Joyce, December 13, 1989. Acquired by **St. Louis** from **Boston** with Boston's third round choice in 1992 Entry Draft and either Boston's seventh round choice in 1992 Entry Draft or sixth round choice in 1993 Entry Draft as compensation for Boston's free agent signings of Glen Featherstone and Dave Thomlinson, July 30, 1991.

CHRISTIAN, JEFF

Left wing. Shoots left. 6'1", 195 lbs. Born, Burlington, Ont., July 30, 1970.
(New Jersey's 2nd choice, 23rd overall, in 1988 Entry Draft).

			Regular Season					Playoffs				
Season	Club	Lea	GP	G	A	TP	PIM	GP	G	A	TP	PIM
1987-88	London	OHL	64	15	29	44	154	9	1	5	6	27
1988-89	London	OHL	64	27	30	57	221	20	3	4	7	56
1989-90	London	OHL	18	14	7	21	64	....	....	....	....	....
	Owen Sound	OHL	55	33	33	66	209	10	6	7	13	43
1990-91	Utica	AHL	80	24	42	66	165	....	....	....	....	....

CHURLA, SHANE

Right wing. Shoots right. 6'1", 200 lbs. Born, Fernie, B.C., June 24, 1965.
(Hartford's 4th choice, 110th overall, in 1985 Entry Draft).

			Regular Season					Playoffs				
Season	Club	Lea	GP	G	A	TP	PIM	GP	G	A	TP	PIM
1983-84	Medicine Hat	WHL	48	3	7	10	115	14	1	5	6	41
1984-85	Medicine Hat	WHL	70	14	20	34	370	9	1	0	1	55
1985-86	Binghamton	AHL	52	4	10	14	306	3	0	0	0	22
1986-87	**Hartford**	**NHL**	**20**	**0**	**1**	**1**	**78**	**2**	**0**	**0**	**0**	**42**
	Binghamton	AHL	24	1	5	6	249	....	....	....	....	....
1987-88	**Hartford**	**NHL**	**2**	**0**	**0**	**0**	**14**	....	....	....	....	....
	Binghamton	AHL	25	5	8	13	168	....	....	....	....	....
	Calgary	**NHL**	**29**	**1**	**5**	**6**	**132**	**7**	**0**	**1**	**1**	**17**
1988-89	**Calgary**	**NHL**	**5**	**0**	**0**	**0**	**25**	....	....	....	....	....
	Salt Lake	IHL	32	3	13	16	278	....	....	....	....	....
	Minnesota	**NHL**	**13**	**1**	**0**	**1**	**54**	....	....	....	....	....
1989-90	**Minnesota**	**NHL**	**53**	**2**	**3**	**5**	**292**	**7**	**0**	**0**	**0**	**44**
1990-91	**Minnesota**	**NHL**	**40**	**2**	**2**	**4**	**286**	**22**	**2**	**1**	**3**	**90**
	NHL Totals		**162**	**6**	**11**	**17**	**881**	**38**	**2**	**2**	**4**	**193**

Traded to **Calgary** by **Hartford** with Dana Murzyn for Neil Sheehy, Carey Wilson, and the rights to Lane MacDonald, January 3, 1988. Traded to **Minnesota** by **Calgary** with Perry Berezan for Brian MacLellan and Minnesota's fourth-round choice (Robert Reichel) in 1989 Entry Draft, March 4, 1989. Claimed by **San Jose** from **Minnesota** in Dispersal Draft, May 30, 1991. Traded to **Minnesota** by **San Jose** for Kelly Kisio, June 3, 1991.

CHYCHRUN, JEFF (CHIHK-rihn)

Defense. Shoots right. 6'4", 215 lbs. Born, LaSalle, Que., May 3, 1966.
(Philadelphia's 3rd choice, 37th overall, in 1984 Entry Draft).

			Regular Season					Playoffs				
Season	Club	Lea	GP	G	A	TP	PIM	GP	G	A	TP	PIM
1983-84	Kingston	OHL	63	1	13	14	137	....	....	....	....	....
1984-85	Kingston	OHL	58	4	10	14	206	....	....	....	....	....
1985-86	Kingston	OHL	61	4	21	25	127	10	2	1	3	17
	Hershey	AHL	....	....	....	....	....	4	0	1	1	9
	Kalamazoo	IHL	....	....	....	....	....	3	1	0	1	0
1986-87	**Philadelphia**	**NHL**	**1**	**0**	**0**	**0**	**4**	....	....	....	....	....
	Hershey	AHL	74	1	17	18	239	4	0	0	0	10
1987-88	**Philadelphia**	**NHL**	**3**	**0**	**0**	**0**	**4**	....	....	....	....	....
	Hershey	AHL	55	0	5	5	210	12	0	2	2	44
1988-89	**Philadelphia**	**NHL**	**80**	**1**	**4**	**5**	**245**	**19**	**0**	**2**	**2**	**65**
1989-90	**Philadelphia**	**NHL**	**79**	**2**	**7**	**9**	**250**	....	....	....	....	....
1990-91	**Philadelphia**	**NHL**	**36**	**0**	**6**	**6**	**105**	....	....	....	....	....
	NHL Totals		**199**	**3**	**17**	**20**	**608**	**19**	**0**	**2**	**2**	**65**

Traded to **Los Angeles** by **Philadelphia** with Jari Kurri for Steve Duchesne, Steve Kasper and Los Angeles' fourth round choice (Aris Brimanis) in 1991 Entry Draft, May 30, 1991.

CHYNOWETH, DEAN (shih-NOWTH)

Defense. Shoots right. 6'2", 190 lbs. Born, Calgary, Alta., October 30, 1968.
(NY Islanders' 1st choice, 13th overall, in 1987 Entry Draft).

			Regular Season					Playoffs				
Season	Club	Lea	GP	G	A	TP	PIM	GP	G	A	TP	PIM
1985-86	Medicine Hat	WHL	69	3	12	15	208	17	3	2	5	52
1986-87	Medicine Hat	WHL	67	3	18	21	285	13	4	2	6	28
1987-88	Medicine Hat	WHL	64	1	21	22	274	16	0	6	6	*87
1988-89	**NY Islanders**	**NHL**	**6**	**0**	**0**	**0**	**48**	....	....	....	....	....
1989-90	**NY Islanders**	**NHL**	**20**	**0**	**2**	**2**	**39**	....	....	....	....	....
	Springfield	AHL	40	0	7	7	98	17	0	4	4	36
1990-91	**NY Islanders**	**NHL**	**25**	**1**	**1**	**2**	**59**	....	....	....	....	....
	Capital Dist.	AHL	44	1	5	6	176	....	....	....	....	....
	NHL Totals		**51**	**1**	**3**	**4**	**146**	....	....	....	....	....

CHYZOWSKI, BARRY (chih-ZOW-skee)

Center. Shoots right. 6', 170 lbs. Born, Edmonton, Alta., May 25, 1968.
(NY Rangers' 8th choice, 156th overall, in 1986 Entry Draft).

			Regular Season					Playoffs				
Season	Club	Lea	GP	G	A	TP	PIM	GP	G	A	TP	PIM
1986-87	Minn.-Duluth	WCHA	39	5	11	16	16	....	....	....	....	....
1987-88	Minn.-Duluth	WCHA	41	22	34	56	14	....	....	....	....	....
1988-89	Denver	IHL	69	12	21	33	48	3	0	0	0	4
1989-90	Flint	IHL	30	3	8	11	6	1	0	0	0	0
	Erie	ECHL	16	9	15	24	19	5	1	4	5	0
1990-91	Erie	ECHL	31	29	40	69	12	....	....	....	....	....

CHYZOWSKI, DAVID (chih-ZOW-skee)

Left wing. Shoots left. 6'1", 190 lbs. Born, Edmonton, Alta., July 11, 1971.
(NY Islanders' 1st choice, 2nd overall, in 1989 Entry Draft).

			Regular Season					Playoffs				
Season	Club	Lea	GP	G	A	TP	PIM	GP	G	A	TP	PIM
1987-88	Kamloops	WHL	66	16	17	33	117	18	2	4	6	26
1988-89a	Kamloops	WHL	68	56	48	104	139	16	15	13	28	32
1989-90	**NY Islanders**	**NHL**	**34**	**8**	**6**	**14**	**45**	....	....	....	....	....
	Springfield	AHL	4	0	0	0	7	....	....	....	....	....
	Kamloops	WHL	4	5	2	7	17	17	11	6	17	46
1990-91	**NY Islanders**	**NHL**	**56**	**5**	**9**	**14**	**61**	....	....	....	....	....
	Capital Dist.	AHL	7	3	6	9	22	....	....	....	....	....
	NHL Totals		**90**	**13**	**15**	**28**	**106**	....	....	....	....	....

a WHL West All-Star Team (1989)

CIAVAGLIA, PETER

Center. Shoots left. 5'10", 175 lbs. Born, Albany, NY, July 15, 1969.
(Calgary's 8th choice, 145th overall, in 1987 Entry Draft).

			Regular Season					Playoffs				
Season	Club	Lea	GP	G	A	TP	PIM	GP	G	A	TP	PIM
1987-88	Harvard	ECAC	30	10	23	33	16	....	....	....	....	....
1988-89a	Harvard	ECAC	34	15	48	63	36	....	....	....	....	....
1989-90	Harvard	ECAC	28	17	18	35	22	....	....	....	....	....
1990-91abc	Harvard	ECAC	27	24	*38	*62	2	....	....	....	....	....

a ECAC Second All-Star Team (1989, 1991)
b ECAC Player of the Year (1991)
c NCAA East Second All-American Team (1991)

CICCARELLI, DINO (sih-sih-REHL-ee)

Right wing. Shoots right. 5'10", 175 lbs. Born, Sarnia, Ont., February 8, 1960.

			Regular Season					Playoffs				
Season	Club	Lea	GP	G	A	TP	PIM	GP	G	A	TP	PIM
1977-78a	London	OHA	68	72	70	142	49	9	6	10	16	6
1978-79	London	OHA	30	8	11	19	35	7	3	5	8	0
1979-80	London	OHA	62	50	53	103	72	5	2	6	8	15
1980-81	**Minnesota**	**NHL**	**32**	**18**	**12**	**30**	**29**	**19**	**14**	**7**	**21**	**25**
	Oklahoma City	CHL	48	32	25	57	45	....	....	....	....	....
1981-82	Minnesota	NHL	76	55	51	106	138	4	3	1	4	2
1982-83	Minnesota	NHL	77	37	38	75	94	9	4	6	10	11
1983-84	Minnesota	NHL	79	38	33	71	58	16	4	5	9	27
1984-85	Minnesota	NHL	51	15	17	32	41	9	3	3	6	8
1985-86	**Minnesota**	**NHL**	**75**	**44**	**45**	**89**	**51**	**5**	**0**	**1**	**1**	**6**
1986-87	**Minnesota**	**NHL**	**80**	**52**	**51**	**103**	**88**	....	....	....	....	....
1987-88	**Minnesota**	**NHL**	**67**	**41**	**45**	**86**	**79**	....	....	....	....	....
1988-89	**Minnesota**	**NHL**	**65**	**32**	**27**	**59**	**64**	....	....	....	....	....
	Washington	**NHL**	**11**	**12**	**3**	**15**	**12**	**6**	**3**	**3**	**6**	**12**
1989-90	**Washington**	**NHL**	**80**	**41**	**38**	**79**	**122**	**8**	**8**	**3**	**11**	**6**
1990-91	**Washington**	**NHL**	**54**	**21**	**18**	**39**	**66**	**11**	**5**	**4**	**9**	**22**
	NHL Totals		**747**	**406**	**378**	**784**	**842**	**87**	**44**	**33**	**77**	**119**

a OHA Second All-Star Team (1978)

Played in NHL All-Star Game (1982, 1983,1989)

Signed as free agent by **Minnesota**, September 28, 1979. Traded to **Washington** by **Minnesota** with Bob Rouse for Mike Gartner and Larry Murphy, March 7, 1989.

CICCONE, ENRICO

Defense. Shoots left. 6'4", 200 lbs. Born, Montreal, Que., April 10, 1970.
(Minnesota's 5th choice, 92nd overall, in 1990 Entry Draft).

			Regular Season					Playoffs				
Season	Club	Lea	GP	G	A	TP	PIM	GP	G	A	TP	PIM
1987-88	Shawinigan	QMJHL	61	2	12	14	324	....	....	....	....	....
1988-89	Shawinigan	QMJHL	34	7	11	18	132	....	....	....	....	....
	Trois-Rivières	QMJHL	24	0	7	7	153	....	....	....	....	....
1989-90	Trois-Rivières	QMJHL	40	4	24	28	227	3	0	0	0	15
1990-91	Kalamazoo	IHL	57	4	9	13	384	4	0	1	1	32

CICHOCKI, CHRIS (chih-HAH-kee)

Right wing. Shoots right. 5'11", 185 lbs. Born, Detroit, MI, September 17, 1963.

			Regular Season					Playoffs				
Season	Club	Lea	GP	G	A	TP	PIM	GP	G	A	TP	PIM
1982-83	Michigan Tech	CCHA	36	12	10	22	10	....	....	....	....	....
1983-84	Michigan Tech	CCHA	40	25	20	45	36	....	....	....	....	....
1984-85	Michigan Tech	CCHA	40	30	24	54	14	....	....	....	....	....
1985-86	**Detroit**	**NHL**	**59**	**10**	**11**	**21**	**21**	....	....	....	....	....
	Adirondack	AHL	9	4	4	8	6	....	....	....	....	....
1986-87	**Detroit**	**NHL**	**2**	**0**	**0**	**0**	**2**	....	....	....	....	....
	Adirondack	AHL	55	31	34	65	27	....	....	....	....	....
	Maine	AHL	7	2	2	4	0	....	....	....	....	....
1987-88	**New Jersey**	**NHL**	**5**	**1**	**0**	**1**	**2**	....	....	....	....	....
	Utica	AHL	69	36	30	66	66	....	....	....	....	....
1988-89	**New Jersey**	**NHL**	**2**	**0**	**1**	**1**	**2**	....	....	....	....	....
	Utica	AHL	59	32	31	63	50	5	0	1	1	2
1989-90	Utica	AHL	11	3	1	4	10	....	....	....	....	....
	Binghamton	AHL	60	21	26	47	22	....	....	....	....	....
1990-91	Binghamton	AHL	80	35	30	65	70	9	0	4	4	2
	NHL Totals		**68**	**11**	**12**	**23**	**27**	....	....	....	....	....

Signed as a free agent by **Detroit**, June 28, 1985. Traded to **New Jersey** by **Detroit** with Detroit's third-round choice (later transferred to Buffalo - Andrew MacVicar) in 1987 Entry Draft for Mel Bridgman, March 9, 1987. Traded to **Hartford** by **New Jersey** for Jim Thomson, October 31, 1989.

CIGER, ZDENO (SEE-gur)

Left wing. Shoots left. 6'1", 190 lbs. Born, Martin, Czech., October 19, 1969.
(New Jersey's 3rd choice, 54th overall, in 1988 Entry Draft).

			Regular Season					Playoffs				
Season	Club	Lea	GP	G	A	TP	PIM	GP	G	A	TP	PIM
1988-89	Dukla Trencin	Czech.	32	15	21	36	18	....	....	....	....	....
1989-90	Dukla Trencin	Czech.	53	18	28	46	....	....	....	....	....	....
1990-91	**New Jersey**	**NHL**	**45**	**8**	**17**	**25**	**8**	**6**	**0**	**2**	**2**	**4**
	Utica	AHL	8	5	4	9	2	....	....	....	....	....
	NHL Totals		**45**	**8**	**17**	**25**	**8**	**6**	**0**	**2**	**2**	**4**

CIMETTA, ROBERT

Left wing/Right wing. Shoots left. 6', 190 lbs. Born, Toronto, Ont., February 15, 1970.
(Boston's 1st choice, 18th overall, in 1988 Entry Draft).

			Regular Season					Playoffs				
Season	Club	Lea	GP	G	A	TP	PIM	GP	G	A	TP	PIM
1986-87	Toronto	OHL	66	21	35	56	65	....	....	....	....	....
1987-88	Toronto	OHL	64	34	42	76	90	4	2	2	4	7
1988-89	**Boston**	**NHL**	**7**	**2**	**0**	**2**	**0**	**1**	**0**	**0**	**0**	**15**
a	Toronto	OHL	58	*55	47	102	89	6	3	3	6	0
1989-90	**Boston**	**NHL**	**47**	**8**	**9**	**17**	**33**	....	....	....	....	....
	Maine	AHL	9	3	2	5	13	....	....	....	....	....
1990-91	**Toronto**	**NHL**	**25**	**2**	**4**	**6**	**21**	....	....	....	....	....
	Newmarket	AHL	29	16	18	34	24	....	....	....	....	....
	NHL Totals		**79**	**12**	**13**	**25**	**54**	**1**	**0**	**0**	**0**	**15**

a OHL First All-Star Team (1989)

Traded to **Toronto** by **Boston** for Steve Bancroft, November 9, 1990.

CIPRIANO, MARK

Right wing. Shoots right. 5'9", 191 lbs. Born, Delta, B.C., June 1, 1971.
(Vancouver's 8th choice, 170th overall, in 1990 Entry Draft).

			Regular Season					Playoffs				
Season	Club	Lea	GP	G	A	TP	PIM	GP	G	A	TP	PIM
1989-90	Victoria	WHL	66	15	27	42	264	....	....	....	....	....
1990-91	Victoria	WHL	51	15	22	37	235	....	....	....	....	....

CIRELLA, JOE (suh-REHL-uh)

Defense. Shoots right. 6'3", 210 lbs. Born, Hamilton, Ont., May 9, 1963.
(Colorado's 1st choice, 5th overall, in 1981 Entry Draft).

			Regular Season					Playoffs				
Season	Club	Lea	GP	G	A	TP	PIM	GP	G	A	TP	PIM
1980-81	Oshawa	OHA	56	5	31	36	220	11	0	2	2	41
1981-82	**Colorado**	**NHL**	**65**	**7**	**12**	**19**	**52**	....	....	....	....	....
	Oshawa	OHL	3	0	1	1	0	11	7	10	17	32
1982-83	**New Jersey**	**NHL**	**2**	**0**	**1**	**1**	**4**	....	....	....	....	....
a	Oshawa	OHL	56	13	55	68	110	17	4	16	20	37
1983-84	**New Jersey**	**NHL**	**79**	**11**	**33**	**44**	**137**	....	....	....	....	....
1984-85	**New Jersey**	**NHL**	**66**	**6**	**18**	**24**	**141**	....	....	....	....	....
1985-86	**New Jersey**	**NHL**	**66**	**6**	**23**	**29**	**147**	....	....	....	....	....
1986-87	**New Jersey**	**NHL**	**65**	**9**	**22**	**31**	**111**	....	....	....	....	....
1987-88	**New Jersey**	**NHL**	**80**	**8**	**31**	**39**	**191**	**19**	**0**	**7**	**7**	**49**
1988-89	**New Jersey**	**NHL**	**80**	**3**	**19**	**22**	**155**	....	....	....	....	....
1989-90	**Quebec**	**NHL**	**56**	**4**	**14**	**18**	**67**	....	....	....	....	....
1990-91	**Quebec**	**NHL**	**39**	**2**	**10**	**12**	**59**	....	....	....	....	....
	NY Rangers	**NHL**	**19**	**1**	**0**	**1**	**52**	**6**	**0**	**2**	**2**	**26**
	NHL Totals		**617**	**57**	**183**	**240**	**1116**	**25**	**0**	**9**	**9**	**75**

a OHL First All-Star Team (1983)

Played in NHL All-Star Game (1984)

Traded to **Quebec** by **New Jersey** with Claude Loiselle and New Jersey's eighth round choice (Alexander Karpovtsev) in 1990 Entry Draft for Walt Poddubny and Quebec's fourth round choice (Mike Bodnarchuk) in 1990 Entry Draft, June 17, 1989. Traded to **NY Rangers** by **Quebec** for Aaron Miller and NY Ranger's fifth round choice (Bill Lindsay) in 1991 Entry Draft, January 17, 1991

CIRONE, JASON

Center. Shoots left. 5'9", 185 lbs. Born, Toronto, Ont., February 21, 1971.
(Winnipeg's 3rd choice, 46th overall, in 1989 Entry Draft).

			Regular Season					Playoffs				
Season	Club	Lea	GP	G	A	TP	PIM	GP	G	A	TP	PIM
1987-88	Cornwall	OHL	53	12	11	23	41	11	1	2	3	4
1988-89	Cornwall	OHL	64	39	44	83	67	17	19	8	27	14
1989-90	Cornwall	OHL	32	22	41	63	56	6	4	2	6	14
1990-91	Cornwall	OHL	40	31	29	60	66	....	....	....	....	....
a	Windsor	OHL	23	27	23	50	31	11	9	8	17	14

a OHL Third All-Star Team (1991)

CLARK, KERRY

Right wing. Shoots right. 6'1", 190 lbs. Born, Kelvington, Sask., August 21, 1968.
(NY Islanders' 12th choice, 206th overall, in 1986 Entry Draft).

			Regular Season					Playoffs				
Season	Club	Lea	GP	G	A	TP	PIM	GP	G	A	TP	PIM
1985-86	Regina	WHL	23	4	4	8	58	....	....	....	....	....
	Saskatoon	WHL	39	5	8	13	104	13	2	2	4	33
1986-87	Saskatoon	WHL	54	12	10	22	229	8	0	1	1	23
1987-88	Saskatoon	WHL	67	15	11	26	241	10	2	2	4	16
1988-89	Springfield	AHL	63	7	7	14	264	....	....	....	....	....
	Indianapolis	IHL	3	0	1	1	12	....	....	....	....	....
1989-90	Springfield	AHL	21	0	1	1	73	....	....	....	....	....
	Phoenix	IHL	38	4	8	12	262	....	....	....	....	....
1990-91	Salt Lake	IHL	62	14	14	28	372	4	1	1	2	12

Signed as a free agent by **Calgary**, July 23, 1990.

CLARK, WENDEL

Left wing. Shoots left. 5'11", 194 lbs. Born, Kelvington, Sask., October 25, 1966.
(Toronto's 1st choice, 1st overall, in 1985 Entry Draft).

			Regular Season					Playoffs				
Season	Club	Lea	GP	G	A	TP	PIM	GP	G	A	TP	PIM
1983-84	Saskatoon	WHL	72	23	45	68	225	....	....	....	....	....
1984-85a	Saskatoon	WHL	64	32	55	87	253	3	3	3	6	7
1985-86b	**Toronto**	**NHL**	**66**	**34**	**11**	**45**	**227**	**10**	**5**	**1**	**6**	**47**
1986-87	**Toronto**	**NHL**	**80**	**37**	**23**	**60**	**271**	**13**	**6**	**5**	**11**	**38**
1987-88	**Toronto**	**NHL**	**28**	**12**	**11**	**23**	**80**	....	....	....	....	....
1988-89	**Toronto**	**NHL**	**15**	**7**	**4**	**11**	**66**	....	....	....	....	....
1989-90	**Toronto**	**NHL**	**38**	**18**	**8**	**26**	**116**	**5**	**1**	**1**	**2**	**19**
1990-91	**Toronto**	**NHL**	**63**	**18**	**16**	**34**	**152**	....	....	....	....	....
	NHL Totals		**290**	**126**	**73**	**199**	**912**	**28**	**12**	**7**	**19**	**104**

a WHL First All-Star Team, East Division (1985)
b NHL All-Rookie Team (1986)

Played in NHL All-Star Game (1986)

CLARKE, CHRISTOPHER

Defense. Shoots left. 6', 185 lbs. Born, Arnprior, Ont., August 6, 1967.
(Washington's 8th choice, 204th overall, in 1987 Entry Draft).

			Regular Season					Playoffs				
Season	Club	Lea	GP	G	A	TP	PIM	GP	G	A	TP	PIM
1987-88	W. Michigan	CCHA	42	7	32	39	64	....	....	....	....	....
1988-89	W. Michigan	CCHA	38	3	21	24	65	....	....	....	....	....
1989-90	W. Michigan	CCHA	39	2	21	23	55	....	....	....	....	....
1990-91	W. Michigan	CCHA	42	4	23	27	68	....	....	....	....	....

CLAUSS, KARL

Defense. Shoots left. 6'2", 200 lbs. Born, Williamsville, NY, May 31, 1967.
(Washington's 1st choice, 24th overall, in 1989 Supplemental Draft).

			Regular Season					Playoffs				
Season	Club	Lea	GP	G	A	TP	PIM	GP	G	A	TP	PIM
1986-87	Colgate	ECAC	12	1	1	2	0	....	....	....	....	....
1987-88	Colgate	ECAC	32	2	6	8	32	....	....	....	....	....
1988-89	Colgate	ECAC	31	1	5	6	38	....	....	....	....	....
1989-90	Colgate	ECAC	38	2	8	10	34	....	....	....	....	....
1990-91	Osby	Swe.2	32	4	4	8	28	....	....	....	....	....

CLEARY, JOSEPH

Defense. Shoots right. 5'11", 186 lbs. Born, Buffalo, NY, January 17, 1970.
(Chicago's 4th choice, 92nd overall, in 1988 Entry Draft).

			Regular Season					Playoffs				
Season	Club	Lea	GP	G	A	TP	PIM	GP	G	A	TP	PIM
1988-89	Boston College	H.E.	38	5	7	12	36	....	....	....	....	....
1989-90	Boston College	H.E.	42	5	21	26	56	....	....	....	....	....
1990-91	Boston College	H.E.	36	4	19	23	34	....	....	....	....	....

CLOUSTON, SHAUN

Left wing. Shoots left. 6'1", 205 lbs. Born, Viking, Alta., February 21, 1968.
(NY Rangers' 3rd choice, 53rd overall, in 1986 Entry Draft).

			Regular Season					Playoffs				
Season	Club	Lea	GP	G	A	TP	PIM	GP	G	A	TP	PIM
1985-86	U. of Alberta	CWUAA	53	18	21	39	75	....	....	....	....	....
1986-87	Portland	WHL	70	6	25	31	93	19	0	5	5	45
1987-88	Portland	WHL	68	29	50	79	144	....	....	....	....	....
1988-89	Portland	WHL	72	45	47	92	150	19	7	10	17	28
1989-90	Milwaukee	IHL	54	6	16	22	61	....	....	....	....	....
	Virginia	ECHL	5	3	2	5	14	2	0	0	0	2
1990-91	Milwaukee	IHL	78	13	27	40	93	6	2	0	2	8

Signed as a free agent by **Vancouver**, May 27, 1989.

COFFEY, PAUL DOUGLAS

Defense. Shoots left. 6', 200 lbs. Born, Weston, Ont., June 1, 1961.
(Edmonton's 1st choice, 6th overall, in the 1980 Entry Draft).

			Regular Season					Playoffs				
Season	Club	Lea	GP	G	A	TP	PIM	GP	G	A	TP	PIM
1978-79a	S. S. Marie	OHA	68	17	72	89	103	....	....	....	....	....
1979-80b	S. S. Marie	OHA	23	10	21	31	63	....	....	....	....	....
	Kitchener	OHA	52	19	52	71	130	....	....	....	....	....
1980-81	**Edmonton**	**NHL**	**74**	**9**	**23**	**32**	**130**	**9**	**4**	**3**	**7**	**22**
1981-82c	**Edmonton**	**NHL**	**80**	**29**	**60**	**89**	**106**	**5**	**1**	**1**	**2**	**6**
1982-83c	**Edmonton**	**NHL**	**80**	**29**	**67**	**96**	**87**	**16**	**7**	**7**	**14**	**14**
1983-84c	**Edmonton**	**NHL**	**80**	**40**	**86**	**126**	**104**	**19**	**8**	**14**	**22**	**21**
1984-85de	**Edmonton**	**NHL**	**80**	**37**	**84**	**121**	**97**	**18**	**12**	**25**	**37**	**44**
1985-86de	**Edmonton**	**NHL**	**79**	**48**	**90**	**138**	**120**	**10**	**1**	**9**	**10**	**30**
1986-87	**Edmonton**	**NHL**	**59**	**17**	**50**	**67**	**49**	**17**	**3**	**8**	**11**	**30**
1987-88	**Pittsburgh**	**NHL**	**46**	**15**	**52**	**67**	**93**	....	....	....	....	....
1988-89e	**Pittsburgh**	**NHL**	**75**	**30**	**83**	**113**	**195**	**11**	**2**	**13**	**15**	**31**
1989-90c	**Pittsburgh**	**NHL**	**80**	**29**	**74**	**103**	**95**	....	....	....	....	....
1990-91	**Pittsburgh**	**NHL**	**76**	**24**	**69**	**93**	**128**	**12**	**2**	**9**	**11**	**6**
	NHL Totals		**809**	**307**	**738**	**1045**	**1204**	**117**	**40**	**89**	**129**	**204**

a OHA Third All-Star Team (1979)
b OHA Second All-Star Team (1980)
c NHL Second All-Star Team (1982, 1983, 1984, 1990)
d Won James Norris Memorial Trophy (1985, 1986)
e NHL First All-Star Team (1985, 1986, 1989)

Played in NHL All-Star Game (1982-86, 1988-91)

Traded to **Pittsburgh** by **Edmonton** with Dave Hunter and Wayne Van Dorp for Craig Simpson, Dave Hannan, Moe Mantha and Chris Joseph, November 24, 1987.

COLE, DANTON

Center/Right wing. Shoots right. 5'11", 189 lbs. Born, Pontiac, MI, January 10, 1967.
(Winnipeg's 6th choice, 123rd overall, in 1985 Entry Draft).

			Regular Season					Playoffs				
Season	Club	Lea	GP	G	A	TP	PIM	GP	G	A	TP	PIM
1985-86	Michigan State	CCHA	43	11	10	21	22	....	....	....	....	....
1986-87	Michigan State	CCHA	44	9	15	24	16	....	....	....	....	....
1987-88	Michigan State	CCHA	46	20	36	56	38	....	....	....	....	....
1988-89	Michigan State	CCHA	47	29	33	62	46	....	....	....	....	....
1989-90	**Winnipeg**	**NHL**	**2**	**1**	**1**	**2**	**0**	....	....	....	....	....
	Moncton	AHL	80	31	42	73	18	....	....	....	....	....
1990-91	**Winnipeg**	**NHL**	**66**	**13**	**11**	**24**	**24**	....	....	....	....	....
	Moncton	AHL	3	1	1	2	0	....	....	....	....	....
	NHL Totals		**68**	**14**	**12**	**26**	**24**	....	....	....	....	....

COLES, BRUCE

Left wing. Shoots left. 5'9", 183 lbs. Born, Montreal, Que., January 12, 1968.
(Montreal's 1st choice, 23rd overall, in 1990 Supplemental Draft).

			Regular Season					Playoffs				
Season	Club	Lea	GP	G	A	TP	PIM	GP	G	A	TP	PIM
1987-88	RPI	ECAC	32	16	23	39	48	....	....	....	....	....
1988-89	RPI	ECAC	27	8	14	22	66	....	....	....	....	....
1989-90	RPI	ECAC	34	*28	24	52	142	....	....	....	....	....
1990-91	RPI	ECAC	31	23	29	52	145	....	....	....	....	....

CONACHER, PATRICK JOHN (PAT) (KAH-nuh-kuhr)

Left wing. Shoots left. 5'8", 190 lbs. Born, Edmonton, Alta., May 1, 1959.
(NY Rangers' 3rd choice, 76th overall, in 1979 Entry Draft).

			Regular Season					Playoffs				
Season	Club	Lea	GP	G	A	TP	PIM	GP	G	A	TP	PIM
1977-78	Billings	WHL	72	31	44	75	105	20	15	14	29	22
1978-79	Billings	WHL	39	25	37	62	50	....	....	....	....	....
	Saskatoon	WHL	33	15	32	47	37	....	....	....	....	....
1979-80	**NY Rangers**	**NHL**	**17**	**0**	**5**	**5**	**4**	**3**	**0**	**1**	**1**	**2**
	New Haven	AHL	53	11	14	25	43	7	1	1	2	4
1980-81			DID NOT PLAY									
1981-82	Springfield	AHL	77	23	22	45	38	....	....	....	....	....
1982-83	**NY Rangers**	**NHL**	**5**	**0**	**1**	**1**	**4**	....	....	....	....	....
	Tulsa	CHL	63	29	28	57	44	....	....	....	....	....
1983-84	**Edmonton**	**NHL**	**45**	**2**	**8**	**10**	**31**	**3**	**1**	**0**	**1**	**2**
	Moncton	AHL	28	7	16	23	30	....	....	....	....	....
1984-85	Nova Scotia	AHL	68	20	45	65	44	6	3	2	5	0
1985-86	**New Jersey**	**NHL**	**2**	**0**	**2**	**2**	**2**	....	....	....	....	....
	Maine	AHL	69	15	30	45	83	5	1	1	2	11
1986-87	Maine	AHL	56	12	14	26	47	....	....	....	....	....
1987-88	**New Jersey**	**NHL**	**24**	**2**	**5**	**7**	**12**	**17**	**2**	**2**	**4**	**14**
	Utica	AHL	47	14	33	47	32	....	....	....	....	....
1988-89	**New Jersey**	**NHL**	**55**	**7**	**5**	**12**	**14**	....	....	....	....	....
1989-90	**New Jersey**	**NHL**	**19**	**3**	**3**	**6**	**4**	**5**	**1**	**0**	**1**	**10**
	Utica	AHL	57	13	36	49	53	....	....	....	....	....
1990-91	**New Jersey**	**NHL**	**49**	**5**	**11**	**16**	**27**	**7**	**0**	**2**	**2**	**2**
	Utica	AHL	4	0	1	1	6	....	....	....	....	....
	NHL Totals		**216**	**19**	**40**	**59**	**98**	**35**	**4**	**5**	**9**	**30**

Signed as free agent by **Edmonton**, October 4, 1983. Signed as a free agent by **New Jersey**, August 14, 1985.

CONLAN, WAYNE

Center. Shoots right. 5'10", 170 lbs. Born, Minneapolis, MN, January 9, 1972.
(St. Louis' 5th choice, 138th overall, in 1990 Entry Draft).

			Regular Season					Playoffs				
Season	Club	Lea	GP	G	A	TP	PIM	GP	G	A	TP	PIM
1989-90	Trinity-Pawling	HS	....	23	22	45	....	....	....	....	....	....
1990-91	Trinity-Pawling	HS	23	31	33	64	....	....	....	....	....	....

CONROY, CRAIG

Center. Shoots right. 6'1", 181 lbs. Born, Potsdam, NY, September 4, 1971.
(Montreal's 7th choice, 123rd overall, in 1990 Entry Draft).

			Regular Season					Playoffs				
Season	Club	Lea	GP	G	A	TP	PIM	GP	G	A	TP	PIM
1989-90	Northwood Prep.	HS	31	33	43	76	....	....	....	....	....	....
1990-91	Clarkson	ECAC	39	8	22	30	24	....	....	....	....	....

CONSTANTIN, PAUL

Center. Shoots left. 6', 180 lbs. Born, Burlington, Ont., May 16, 1968.
(Vancouver's 9th choice, 191st overall, in 1988 Entry Draft).

			Regular Season					Playoffs				
Season	Club	Lea	GP	G	A	TP	PIM	GP	G	A	TP	PIM
1988-89	Lake Superior	CCHA	28	5	5	10	0	....	....	....	....	....
1989-90	Lake Superior	CCHA	29	6	2	8	10	....	....	....	....	....
1990-91	Lake Superior	CCHA	32	9	9	18	4	....	....	....	....	....

COOKE, JAMES (JAMIE)

Right wing. Shoots right. 6'1", 195 lbs. Born, Bramalea, Ont., November 5, 1968.
(Philadelphia's 8th choice, 140th overall, in 1988 Entry Draft).

			Regular Season					Playoffs				
Season	Club	Lea	GP	G	A	TP	PIM	GP	G	A	TP	PIM
1988-89	Colgate	ECAC	28	13	11	24	26	....	....	....	....	....
1989-90	Colgate	ECAC	38	16	20	36	24	....	....	....	....	....
1990-91	Colgate	ECAC	32	29	26	55	22	....	....	....	....	....

COPELAND, TODD

Defense. Shoots left. 6'2", 210 lbs. Born, Ridgewood, NJ, May 18, 1967.
(New Jersey's 2nd choice, 24th overall, in 1986 Entry Draft).

			Regular Season					Playoffs				
Season	Club	Lea	GP	G	A	TP	PIM	GP	G	A	TP	PIM
1986-87	U. of Michigan	CCHA	34	2	11	13	59	....	....	....	....	....
1987-88	U. of Michigan	CCHA	41	3	10	13	58	....	....	....	....	....
1988-89	U. of Michigan	CCHA	39	5	14	19	102	....	....	....	....	....
1989-90	U. of Michigan	CCHA	34	6	16	22	62	....	....	....	....	....
1990-91	Utica	AHL	79	6	24	30	53	....	....	....	....	....

CORBET, RENE

Left wing. Shoots left. 6', 176 lbs. Born, Victoriaville, Que., June 25, 1973.
(Quebec's 2nd choice, 24th overall, in 1991 Entry Draft).

			Regular Season					Playoffs				
Season	Club	Lea	GP	G	A	TP	PIM	GP	G	A	TP	PIM
1989-90	Richelieu	Midget	34	44	53	97	34	....	....	....	....	....
1990-91	Drummondville	QMJHL	45	25	40	65	34	14	11	6	16	15

CORKERY, TIM

Defense. Shoots right. 6'4", 210 lbs. Born, Ponoka, Alta., February 17, 1967.
(Calgary's 6th choice, 103rd overall, in 1987 Entry Draft).

			Regular Season					Playoffs				
Season	Club	Lea	GP	G	A	TP	PIM	GP	G	A	TP	PIM
1986-87	Ferris State	CCHA	40	3	7	10	120	....	....	....	....	....
1987-88	Ferris State	CCHA	40	0	6	6	108	....	....	....	....	....
1988-89	Ferris State	CCHA	23	2	5	7	53	....	....	....	....	....
1989-90	Ferris State	CCHA	32	0	6	6	64	....	....	....	....	....
1990-91	Nashville	ECHL	59	1	25	26	94	....	....	....	....	....

Traded to **St. Louis** by **Calgary** with Mike Bullard and Craig Coxe for Mark Hunter, Doug Gilmour, Steve Bozek and Michael Dark, September 6, 1988.

CORKUM, BOB

Right wing. Shoots right. 6'2", 215 lbs. Born, Salisbury, MA, December 18, 1967.
(Buffalo's 3rd choice, 47th overall, in 1986 Entry Draft).

			Regular Season					Playoffs				
Season	Club	Lea	GP	G	A	TP	PIM	GP	G	A	TP	PIM
1985-86	U. of Maine	H.E.	39	7	26	33	53	....	....	....	....	....
1986-87	U. of Maine	H.E.	35	18	11	29	24	....	....	....	....	....
1987-88	U. of Maine	H.E.	40	14	18	32	64	....	....	....	....	....
1988-89	U. of Maine	H.E.	45	17	31	48	64	....	....	....	....	....
1989-90	**Buffalo**	**NHL**	**8**	**2**	**0**	**2**	**2**	**5**	**1**	**0**	**1**	**4**
	Rochester	AHL	43	8	11	19	45	12	2	5	7	16
1990-91	Rochester	AHL	69	13	21	34	77	15	4	4	8	4
	NHL Totals		**8**	**2**	**0**	**2**	**2**	**5**	**1**	**0**	**1**	**4**

CORRIVEAU, RICK

Defense. Shoots left. 6', 208 lbs. Born, Welland, Ont., January 6, 1971.
(Washington's 8th choice, 168th overall, in 1991 Entry Draft).

			Regular Season					Playoffs				
Season	Club	Lea	GP	G	A	TP	PIM	GP	G	A	TP	PIM
1987-88a	London	OHL	62	19	47	66	51	12	4	10	14	18
1988-89	London	OHL	12	4	10	14	21	1	0	0	0	0
1989-90b	London	OHL	63	22	55	77	63	6	4	3	7	12
1990-91	London	OHL	64	27	60	87	83	7	3	7	10	16

a OHL Rookie of the Year (1988)
b OHL Third All-Star Team (1990)
Previously drafted 31st overall by **St. Louis** in 1989 Entry Draft.

CORRIVEAU, YVON

Left wing. Shoots left. 6'1", 195 lbs. Born, Welland, Ont., February 8, 1967.
(Washington's 1st choice, 19th overall, in 1985 Entry Draft).

			Regular Season					Playoffs				
Season	Club	Lea	GP	G	A	TP	PIM	GP	G	A	TP	PIM
1984-85	Toronto	OHL	59	23	28	51	65	3	0	0	0	5
1985-86	**Washington**	**NHL**	**2**	**0**	**0**	**0**	**0**	**4**	**0**	**3**	**3**	**2**
	Toronto	OHL	59	54	36	90	75	4	1	1	2	0
1986-87	**Washington**	**NHL**	**17**	**1**	**1**	**2**	**24**	....	....	....	....	....
	Toronto	OHL	23	14	19	33	23	....	....	....	....	....
	Binghamton	AHL	7	0	0	0	2	8	0	1	1	0
1987-88	**Washington**	**NHL**	**44**	**10**	**9**	**19**	**84**	**13**	**1**	**2**	**3**	**30**
	Binghamton	AHL	35	15	14	29	64	....	....	....	....	....
1988-89	**Washington**	**NHL**	**33**	**3**	**2**	**5**	**62**	**1**	**0**	**0**	**0**	**0**
	Baltimore	AHL	33	16	23	39	65	....	....	....	....	....
1989-90	**Washington**	**NHL**	**50**	**9**	**6**	**15**	**50**	....	....	....	....	....
	Hartford	**NHL**	**13**	**4**	**1**	**5**	**22**	**4**	**1**	**0**	**1**	**0**
1990-91	**Hartford**	**NHL**	**23**	**1**	**1**	**2**	**18**	....	....	....	....	....
	Springfield	AHL	44	17	25	42	10	18	*10	6	16	31
	NHL Totals		**182**	**28**	**20**	**48**	**260**	**22**	**2**	**5**	**7**	**32**

Traded to **Hartford** by **Washington** for Mike Liut, March 6, 1990.

CORSON, SHAYNE

Left wing. Shoots left. 6', 201 lbs. Born, Barrie, Ont., August 13, 1966.
(Montreal's 2nd choice, 8th overall, in 1984 Entry Draft).

			Regular Season					Playoffs				
Season	Club	Lea	GP	G	A	TP	PIM	GP	G	A	TP	PIM
1983-84	Brantford	OHL	66	25	46	71	165	6	4	1	5	26
1984-85	Hamilton	OHL	54	27	63	90	154	11	3	7	10	19
1985-86	**Montreal**	**NHL**	**3**	**0**	**0**	**0**	**2**	....	....	....	....	....
	Hamilton	OHL	47	41	57	98	153	....	....	....	....	....
1986-87	**Montreal**	**NHL**	**55**	**12**	**11**	**23**	**144**	**17**	**6**	**5**	**11**	**30**
1987-88	**Montreal**	**NHL**	**71**	**12**	**27**	**39**	**152**	**3**	**1**	**0**	**1**	**12**
1988-89	**Montreal**	**NHL**	**80**	**26**	**24**	**50**	**193**	**21**	**4**	**5**	**9**	**65**
1989-90	**Montreal**	**NHL**	**76**	**31**	**44**	**75**	**144**	**11**	**2**	**8**	**10**	**20**
1990-91	**Montreal**	**NHL**	**71**	**23**	**24**	**47**	**138**	**13**	**9**	**6**	**15**	**36**
	NHL Totals		**356**	**104**	**130**	**234**	**773**	**65**	**22**	**24**	**46**	**163**

Played in NHL All-Star Game (1990)

COTE, ALAIN GABRIEL (koh-TAY)

Defense. Shoots right. 6', 200 lbs. Born, Montmagny, Que., April 14, 1967.
(Boston's 1st choice, 31st overall, in 1985 Entry Draft).

			Regular Season					Playoffs				
Season	Club	Lea	GP	G	A	TP	PIM	GP	G	A	TP	PIM
1983-84	Quebec	QMJHL	60	3	17	20	40	5	1	3	4	8
1984-85	Quebec	QMJHL	68	9	25	34	173	4	0	1	1	12
1985-86	**Boston**	**NHL**	**32**	**0**	**6**	**6**	**14**	....	....	....	....	....
	Granby	QMJHL	22	4	12	16	48	....	....	....	....	....
1986-87	**Boston**	**NHL**	**3**	**0**	**0**	**0**	**0**	....	....	....	....	....
	Granby	QMJHL	43	7	24	31	185	4	0	3	3	2
1987-88	**Boston**	**NHL**	**2**	**0**	**0**	**0**	**0**	....	....	....	....	....
	Maine	AHL	69	9	34	43	108	9	2	4	6	19
1988-89	**Boston**	**NHL**	**31**	**2**	**3**	**5**	**51**	....	....	....	....	....
	Maine	AHL	37	5	16	21	111	....	....	....	....	....
1989-90	**Washington**	**NHL**	**2**	**0**	**0**	**0**	**2**	....	....	....	....	....
	Baltimore	AHL	57	5	19	24	161	3	0	0	0	9
1990-91	**Montreal**	**NHL**	**28**	**0**	**6**	**6**	**26**	**11**	**0**	**2**	**2**	**26**
	Fredericton	AHL	49	8	19	27	110	....	....	....	....	....
	NHL Totals		**98**	**2**	**15**	**17**	**93**	**11**	**0**	**2**	**2**	**26**

Traded to **Washington** by **Boston** for Bob Gould, September 28, 1989. Traded to **Montreal** by **Washington** for Marc Deschamps, June 22, 1990.

COTE, SYLVAIN (COH--tay)

Defense. Shoots right. 5'11", 185 lbs. Born, Duberger, Que., January 19, 1966.
(Hartford's 1st choice, 11th overall, in 1984 Entry Draft).

			Regular Season					Playoffs				
Season	Club	Lea	GP	G	A	TP	PIM	GP	G	A	TP	PIM
1982-83	Quebec	QMJHL	66	10	24	34	50	....	....	....	....	....
1983-84	Quebec	QMJHL	66	15	50	65	89	5	1	1	2	0
1984-85	**Hartford**	**NHL**	**67**	**3**	**9**	**12**	**17**	....	....	....	....	....
1985-86	**Hartford**	**NHL**	**2**	**0**	**0**	**0**	**0**	....	....	....	....	....
a	Hull	QMJHL	26	10	33	43	14	13	6	*28	34	22
	Binghamton	AHL	12	2	4	6	0	....	....	....	....	....
1986-87	**Hartford**	**NHL**	**67**	**2**	**8**	**10**	**20**	**2**	**0**	**2**	**2**	**2**
1987-88	**Hartford**	**NHL**	**67**	**7**	**21**	**28**	**30**	**6**	**1**	**1**	**2**	**4**
1988-89	**Hartford**	**NHL**	**78**	**8**	**9**	**17**	**49**	**3**	**0**	**1**	**1**	**4**
1989-90	**Hartford**	**NHL**	**28**	**4**	**2**	**6**	**14**	....	....	....	....	....
1990-91	**Hartford**	**NHL**	**73**	**7**	**12**	**19**	**17**	**6**	**0**	**2**	**2**	**2**
	NHL Totals		**382**	**31**	**61**	**92**	**147**	**17**	**1**	**6**	**7**	**12**

a QMJHL First All-Star Team (1986).

COURTNALL, GEOFF

Left wing. Shoots left. 6'1", 190 lbs. Born, Victoria, B.C., August 18, 1962.

			Regular Season					Playoffs				
Season	Club	Lea	GP	G	A	TP	PIM	GP	G	A	TP	PIM
1980-81	Victoria	WHL	11	3	4	7	6	15	2	1	3	7
1981-82	Victoria	WHL	72	35	57	90	100	4	1	0	1	2
1982-83	Victoria	WHL	71	41	73	114	186	12	6	7	13	42
1983-84	**Boston**	**NHL**	**4**	**0**	**0**	**0**	**0**	....	....	....	....	....
	Hershey	AHL	74	14	12	26	51	....	....	....	....	....
1984-85	**Boston**	**NHL**	**64**	**12**	**16**	**28**	**82**	**5**	**0**	**2**	**2**	**7**
	Hershey	AHL	9	8	4	12	4	....	....	....	....	....
1985-86	**Boston**	**NHL**	**64**	**21**	**16**	**37**	**61**	**3**	**0**	**0**	**0**	**2**
	Moncton	AHL	12	8	8	16	6	....	....	....	....	....
1986-87	**Boston**	**NHL**	**65**	**13**	**23**	**36**	**117**	**1**	**0**	**0**	**0**	**0**
1987-88	**Boston**	**NHL**	**62**	**32**	**26**	**58**	**108**	....	....	....	....	....
	Edmonton	**NHL**	**12**	**4**	**4**	**8**	**15**	**19**	**0**	**3**	**3**	**23**
1988-89	**Washington**	**NHL**	**79**	**42**	**38**	**80**	**112**	**6**	**2**	**5**	**7**	**12**
1989-90	**Washington**	**NHL**	**80**	**35**	**39**	**74**	**104**	**15**	**4**	**9**	**13**	**32**
1990-91	**St. Louis**	**NHL**	**66**	**27**	**30**	**57**	**56**	....	....	....	....	....
	Vancouver	**NHL**	**11**	**6**	**2**	**8**	**8**	**6**	**3**	**5**	**8**	**4**
	NHL Totals		**507**	**192**	**194**	**386**	**663**	**54**	**9**	**24**	**33**	**80**

Signed as free agent by **Boston**, July 6, 1983. Traded to **Edmonton** by **Boston** with Bill Ranford and future considerations for Andy Moog, March 8, 1988. Rights traded to **Washington** by **Edmonton** for Greg C. Adams, July 22, 1988. Traded to **St. Louis** by **Washington** for Peter Zezel and Mike Lalor, July 13, 1990. Traded to **Vancouver** by **St. Louis** with Robert Dirk, Sergio Momesso, Cliff Ronning and future considerations for Dan Quinn and Garth Butcher, March 5, 1991.

COURTNALL, RUSSELL (RUSS)

Center/Right wing. Shoots right. 5'11", 183 lbs.   Born, Duncan, B.C., June 2, 1965.
(Toronto's 1st choice, 7th overall, in 1983 Entry Draft).

			Regular Season					Playoffs				
Season	Club	Lea	GP	G	A	TP	PIM	GP	G	A	TP	PIM
1982-83	Victoria	WHL	60	36	61	97	33	12	11	7	18	6
1983-84	Victoria	WHL	32	29	37	66	63	....	....	....	....	....
	Cdn. Olympic	....	16	4	7	11	10	....	....	....	....	....
	Toronto	NHL	14	3	9	12	6	....	....	....	....	....
1984-85	Toronto	NHL	69	12	10	22	44	....	....	....	....	....
1985-86	Toronto	NHL	73	22	38	60	52	10	3	6	9	8
1986-87	Toronto	NHL	79	29	44	73	90	13	3	4	7	11
1987-88	Toronto	NHL	65	23	26	49	47	6	2	1	3	0
1988-89	Toronto	NHL	9	1	1	2	4	....	....	....	....	....
	Montreal	NHL	64	22	17	39	15	21	8	5	13	18
1989-90	Montreal	NHL	80	27	32	59	27	11	5	1	6	10
1990-91	Montreal	NHL	79	26	50	76	29	13	8	3	11	7
	NHL Totals		532	165	227	392	314	74	29	20	49	54

Traded to **Montreal** by **Toronto** for John Kordic and Montreal's sixth-round choice (Michael Doers) in 1989 Entry Draft, November 7, 1988.

COURTENAY, EDWARD

Right wing. Shoots right. 6'4", 200 lbs.   Born, Verdun, Que., February 2, 1968.

			Regular Season					Playoffs				
Season	Club	Lea	GP	G	A	TP	PIM	GP	G	A	TP	PIM
1987-88	Granby	QMJHL	54	37	34	71	19	5	1	1	2	2
1988-89	Granby	QMJHL	68	59	55	114	68	4	1	1	2	22
1989-90	Kalamazoo	IHL	57	25	28	53	16	....	....	....	....	....
1990-91	Kalamazoo	IHL	76	35	36	71	37	....	....	....	....	....

Acquired by **San Jose** in Minnesota-San Jose player exchange, May 30, 1991.

COUTURIER, SYLVAIN   (SIHL-vay koo-TOOR-ee-yah)

Center. Shoots left. 6'2", 205 lbs.   Born, Greenfield Park, Que., April 23, 1968.
(Los Angeles' 3rd choice, 65th overall, in 1986 Entry Draft).

			Regular Season					Playoffs				
Season	Club	Lea	GP	G	A	TP	PIM	GP	G	A	TP	PIM
1985-86	Laval	QMJHL	68	21	37	58	64	14	1	7	8	28
1986-87	Laval	QMJHL	67	39	51	90	77	13	12	14	26	19
1987-88a	Laval	QMJHL	67	70	67	137	115	....	....	....	....	....
1988-89	**Los Angeles**	NHL	16	1	3	4	2	....	....	....	....	....
	New Haven	AHL	44	18	20	38	33	10	2	2	4	11
1989-90	New Haven	AHL	50	9	8	17	47	....	....	....	....	....
1990-91	**Los Angeles**	NHL	3	0	1	1	0	....	....	....	....	....
	Phoenix	IHL	66	50	37	87	49	10	8	2	10	10
	NHL Totals		19	1	4	5	2	....	....	....	....	....

a QMJHL Third All-Star Team (1988)

COXE, CRAIG

Left wing. Shoots left. 6'4", 220 lbs.   Born, Chula Vista, CA, January 21, 1964.
(Detroit's 4th choice, 66th overall, in 1982 Entry Draft)

			Regular Season					Playoffs				
Season	Club	Lea	GP	G	A	TP	PIM	GP	G	A	TP	PIM
1982-83	Belleville	OHL	64	14	27	41	102	4	1	2	3	2
1983-84	Belleville	OHL	45	17	28	45	90	3	2	0	2	4
1984-85	**Vancouver**	NHL	9	0	0	0	49	....	....	....	....	....
	Fredericton	AHL	62	8	7	15	242	4	2	1	3	16
1985-86	Vancouver	NHL	57	3	5	8	176	3	0	0	0	2
1986-87	Vancouver	NHL	15	1	0	1	31	....	....	....	....	....
	Fredericton	AHL	46	1	12	13	168	....	....	....	....	....
1987-88	Vancouver	NHL	64	5	12	17	186	....	....	....	....	....
	Calgary	NHL	7	2	3	5	32	2	1	0	1	16
1988-89	St. Louis	NHL	41	0	7	7	127	....	....	....	....	....
	Peoria	IHL	8	2	7	9	38	....	....	....	....	....
1989-90	Vancouver	NHL	25	1	4	5	66	....	....	....	....	....
	Milwaukee	IHL	5	0	5	5	4	....	....	....	....	....
1990-91	Vancouver	NHL	7	0	0	0	27	....	....	....	....	....
	Milwaukee	IHL	36	9	21	30	116	6	3	2	5	22
	NHL Totals		225	12	31	43	694	5	1	0	1	18

Signed as a free agent by **Vancouver**, June 26, 1984. Traded to **Calgary** by **Vancouver** for Brian Bradley and Peter Bakovic, March 6, 1988. Traded to **St. Louis** by **Calgary** with Mike Bullard and Tim Corkery for Mark Hunter, Doug Gilmour, Steve Bozek and Michael Dark, September 6, 1988. Traded to **Chicago** by **St. Louis** for Rik Wilson, September 27, 1989. Claimed by **Vancouver** in NHL Waiver Draft, October 2, 1989. Claimed by **San Jose** from **Vancouver** in Expansion Draft, May 30, 1991.

CRAIG, MIKE

Right wing. Shoots right. 6'1", 180 lbs.   Born St. Mary's, Ont., June 6, 1971.
(Minnesota's 2nd choice, 28th overall, in 1989 Entry Draft).

			Regular Season					Playoffs				
Season	Club	Lea	GP	G	A	TP	PIM	GP	G	A	TP	PIM
1987-88	Oshawa	OHL	61	6	10	16	39	7	7	0	1	11
1988-89	Oshawa	OHL	63	36	36	72	34	6	3	1	4	6
1989-90	Oshawa	OHL	43	36	40	76	85	17	10	16	26	46
1990-91	**Minnesota**	NHL	39	8	4	12	32	10	1	1	2	20
	NHL Totals		39	8	4	12	32	10	1	1	2	20

CRAIGWELL, DALE

Center. Shoots left. 5'10", 178 lbs.   Born, Toronto, Ont., April 24, 1971.
(San Jose's 11th choice, 199th overall, in 1991 Entry Draft).

			Regular Season					Playoffs				
Season	Club	Lea	GP	G	A	TP	PIM	GP	G	A	TP	PIM
1988-89	Oshawa	OHL	55	9	14	23	15	....	....	....	....	....
1989-90	Oshawa	OHL	64	22	41	63	39	17	7	7	14	11
1990-91	Oshawa	OHL	56	27	68	95	34	16	7	16	23	9

CRAVEN, MURRAY

Left wing. Shoots left. 6'2", 185 lbs.   Born, Medicine Hat, Alta., July 20, 1964.
(Detroit's 1st choice, 17th overall, in 1982 Entry Draft).

			Regular Season					Playoffs				
Season	Club	Lea	GP	G	A	TP	PIM	GP	G	A	TP	PIM
1980-81	Medicine Hat	WHL	69	5	10	15	18	5	0	0	0	2
1981-82	Medicine Hat	WHL	72	35	46	81	49	....	....	....	....	....
1982-83	**Detroit**	NHL	31	4	7	11	6	....	....	....	....	....
	Medicine Hat	WHL	28	17	29	46	35	....	....	....	....	....
1983-84	**Detroit**	NHL	15	0	4	4	6	....	....	....	....	....
	Medicine Hat	WHL	48	38	56	94	53	4	5	3	8	4
1984-85	Philadelphia	NHL	80	26	35	61	30	19	4	6	10	11
1985-86	Philadelphia	NHL	78	21	33	54	34	5	0	3	3	4
1986-87	Philadelphia	NHL	77	19	30	49	38	12	3	1	4	9
1987-88	Philadelphia	NHL	72	30	46	76	58	7	2	5	7	4
1988-89	Philadelphia	NHL	51	9	28	37	52	1	0	0	0	0
1989-90	Philadelphia	NHL	76	25	50	75	42	....	....	....	....	....
1990-91	Philadelphia	NHL	77	19	47	66	53	....	....	....	....	....
	NHL Totals		557	153	280	433	319	44	9	15	24	28

Traded to **Philadelphia** by **Detroit** with Joe Paterson for Darryl Sittler, October 10, 1984.

CRAWFORD, LOUIS (LOU)

Left wing. Shoots left. 6', 185 lbs.   Born, Belleville, Ont., November 5, 1962.

			Regular Season					Playoffs				
Season	Club	Lea	GP	G	A	TP	PIM	GP	G	A	TP	PIM
1980-81	Kitchener	OHA	53	2	7	9	134	....	....	....	....	....
1981-82	Kitchener	OHL	64	11	17	28	243	15	3	4	7	71
1982-83	Rochester	AHL	64	5	11	16	142	13	1	1	2	7
1983-84	Rochester	AHL	76	7	6	13	234	17	2	4	6	87
1984-85	Rochester	AHL	70	8	7	15	213	1	0	0	0	10
1985-86	Nova Scotia	AHL	78	8	11	19	214	....	....	....	....	....
1986-87	Nova Scotia	AHL	35	3	4	7	48	....	....	....	....	....
1987-88	Nova Scotia	AHL	65	15	15	30	170	4	1	2	3	9
1988-89	Adirondack	AHL	74	23	23	46	179	9	0	6	6	32
1989-90	**Boston**	NHL	7	0	0	0	20	....	....	....	....	....
	Maine	AHL	62	15	13	28	162	....	....	....	....	....
1990-91	Maine	AHL	80	18	17	35	215	2	0	0	0	5
	NHL Totals		7	0	0	0	20	....	....	....	....	....

Signed as free agent by **Buffalo**, August 23, 1984. Signed as a free agent by **Detroit**, August 11, 1988. Signed as a free agent by **Boston**, July 6, 1989.

CREAGH, BRENDAN

Defense. Shoots left. 6', 195 lbs.   Born, Hartford, CT, February 1, 1970.
(Los Angeles' 1st choice, 26th overall, in 1991 Supplemental Draft).

			Regular Season					Playoffs				
Season	Club	Lea	GP	G	A	TP	PIM	GP	G	A	TP	PIM
1989-90	U. of Vermont	ECAC	30	4	7	11	12	....	....	....	....	....
1990-91	U. of Vermont	ECAC	31	3	7	10	26	....	....	....	....	....

CREIGHTON, ADAM   (KRAY-ton)

Center. Shoots left. 6'5", 210 lbs.   Born, Burlington, Ont., June 2, 1965.
(Buffalo's 3rd choice, 11th overall, in 1983 Entry Draft).

			Regular Season					Playoffs				
Season	Club	Lea	GP	G	A	TP	PIM	GP	G	A	TP	PIM
1981-82	Ottawa	OHL	60	15	27	42	73	17	7	1	8	40
1982-83	Ottawa	OHL	68	44	46	90	88	9	0	2	2	12
1983-84	**Buffalo**	NHL	7	2	2	4	4	....	....	....	....	....
	Ottawa	OHL	56	42	49	91	79	13	16	11	27	28
1984-85	**Buffalo**	NHL	30	2	8	10	33	....	....	....	....	....
	Rochester	AHL	6	5	3	8	2	5	2	1	3	20
	Ottawa	OHL	10	4	14	18	23	5	6	2	8	11
1985-86	Buffalo	NHL	19	1	1	2	2	....	....	....	....	....
	Rochester	AHL	32	17	21	38	27	....	....	....	....	....
1986-87	Buffalo	NHL	56	18	22	40	26	....	....	....	....	....
1987-88	Buffalo	NHL	36	10	17	27	87	....	....	....	....	....
1988-89	Buffalo	NHL	24	7	10	17	44	....	....	....	....	....
	Chicago	NHL	43	15	14	29	92	15	5	6	11	44
1989-90	Chicago	NHL	80	34	36	70	224	20	3	6	9	59
1990-91	Chicago	NHL	72	22	29	51	135	6	0	1	1	10
	NHL Totals		367	111	139	250	647	41	8	13	21	113

Traded to **Chicago** by **Buffalo** for Rick Vaive, December 26, 1988.

CRISTOFOLI, ED

Right wing. Shoots left. 6'2", 203 lbs.   Born, Trail, B.C., May 14, 1967.
(Montreal's 9th choice, 142nd overall, in 1985 Entry Draft).

			Regular Season					Playoffs				
Season	Club	Lea	GP	G	A	TP	PIM	GP	G	A	TP	PIM
1985-86	U. of Denver	WCHA	46	10	9	19	32	....	....	....	....	....
1986-87	U. of Denver	WCHA	40	14	15	29	52	....	....	....	....	....
1987-88	U. of Denver	WCHA	38	12	27	39	64	....	....	....	....	....
1988-89	U. of Denver	WCHA	43	20	19	39	50	....	....	....	....	....
1989-90	**Montreal**	NHL	9	0	1	1	4	....	....	....	....	....
	Sherbrooke	AHL	57	16	19	35	31	12	2	4	6	14
1990-91	Fredericton	AHL	34	7	16	23	24	....	....	....	....	....
	Kansas City	IHL	22	3	1	4	6	....	....	....	....	....
	NHL Totals		9	0	1	1	4	....	....	....	....	....

CRONIN, SHAWN

Defense. Shoots left. 6'2", 210 lbs. Born, Flushing, MI, August 20, 1963.

			Regular Season					Playoffs				
Season	Club	Lea	GP	G	A	TP	PIM	GP	G	A	TP	PIM
1983-84	Ill-Chicago	CCHA	32	0	4	4	41	....	....	....	....	....
1984-85	Ill-Chicago	CCHA	31	2	6	8	52	....	....	....	....	....
1985-86	Ill-Chicago	CCHA	35	3	8	11	70	....	....	....	....	....
1986-87	Salt Lake	IHL	53	8	16	24	118	....	....	....	....	....
	Binghamton	AHL	12	0	1	1	60	10	0	0	0	41
1987-88	Binghamton	AHL	65	3	8	11	212	4	0	0	0	15
1988-89	**Washington**	**NHL**	**1**	**0**	**0**	**0**	**0**	....	....	....	....	....
	Baltimore	AHL	75	3	9	12	267	....	....	....	....	....
1989-90	**Winnipeg**	**NHL**	**61**	**0**	**4**	**4**	**243**	**5**	**0**	**0**	**0**	**7**
1990-91	**Winnipeg**	**NHL**	**67**	**1**	**5**	**6**	**189**	....	....	....	....	....
	NHL Totals		**129**	**1**	**9**	**10**	**432**	**5**	**0**	**0**	**0**	**7**

Signed as a free agent by **Hartford**, March, 1986. Signed as a free agent by **Washington**, June 6, 1988. Signed as a free agent by **Philadelphia**, June 12, 1989. Traded to **Winnipeg** by **Philadelphia** for future considerations, July 21, 1989.

CROSSMAN, DOUGLAS (DOUG)

Defense. Shoots left. 6'2", 190 lbs. Born, Peterborough, Ont., June 30, 1960.
(Chicago's 6th choice, 112th overall, in 1979 Entry Draft).

			Regular Season					Playoffs				
Season	Club	Lea	GP	G	A	TP	PIM	GP	G	A	TP	PIM
1977-78	Ottawa	OHA	65	4	17	21	17	....	....	....	....	....
1978-79	Ottawa	OHA	67	12	51	63	65	4	1	3	4	0
1979-80	Ottawa	OHA	66	20	96	116	48	11	7	6	13	19
1980-81	**Chicago**	**NHL**	**9**	**0**	**2**	**2**	**2**	....	....	....	....	....
	New Brunswick	AHL	70	13	43	56	90	13	5	6	11	36
1981-82	**Chicago**	**NHL**	**70**	**12**	**28**	**40**	**24**	**11**	**0**	**3**	**3**	**4**
1982-83	**Chicago**	**NHL**	**80**	**13**	**40**	**53**	**46**	**13**	**3**	**7**	**10**	**6**
1983-84	**Philadelphia**	**NHL**	**78**	**7**	**28**	**35**	**63**	**3**	**0**	**0**	**0**	**0**
1984-85	**Philadelphia**	**NHL**	**80**	**4**	**33**	**37**	**65**	**19**	**4**	**6**	**10**	**38**
1985-86	**Philadelphia**	**NHL**	**80**	**6**	**37**	**43**	**55**	**5**	**0**	**1**	**1**	**4**
1986-87	**Philadelphia**	**NHL**	**78**	**9**	**31**	**40**	**29**	**26**	**4**	**14**	**18**	**31**
1987-88	**Philadelphia**	**NHL**	**76**	**9**	**29**	**38**	**43**	**7**	**1**	**1**	**2**	**8**
1988-89	**Los Angeles**	**NHL**	**74**	**10**	**15**	**25**	**53**	**2**	**0**	**1**	**1**	**2**
	New Haven	AHL	3	0	0	0	0	....	....	....	....	....
1989-90	**NY Islanders**	**NHL**	**80**	**15**	**44**	**59**	**54**	**5**	**0**	**1**	**1**	**6**
1990-91	**NY Islanders**	**NHL**	**16**	**1**	**6**	**7**	**12**	....	....	....	....	....
	Hartford	**NHL**	**41**	**4**	**19**	**23**	**19**	....	....	....	....	....
	Detroit	**NHL**	**17**	**3**	**4**	**7**	**17**	**6**	**0**	**5**	**5**	**6**
	NHL Totals		**779**	**93**	**316**	**409**	**482**	**97**	**12**	**39**	**51**	**105**

Traded to **Philadelphia** by **Chicago** with Chicago's second round choice (Scott Mellanby) in the 1984 Entry Draft for Behn Wilson, June 8, 1983. Traded to **Los Angeles** by **Philadelphia** for Jay Wells, September 29, 1988. Traded to **NY Islanders** by **Los Angeles** to complete February 22, 1989, transaction in which Mark Fitzpatrick and Wayne McBean were traded to **NY Islanders** by **Los Angeles** for Kelly Hrudey, May 23, 1989. Traded to **Hartford** by **NY Islanders** for Ray Ferraro, November 13, 1990. Traded to **Detroit** by **Hartford** for Doug Houda, February 20, 1991.

CROWDER, TROY

Right wing. Shoots right. 6'4", 215 lbs. Born, Sudbury, Ont., May 3, 1968.
(New Jersey's 6th choice, 108th overall, in 1986 Entry Draft).

			Regular Season					Playoffs				
Season	Club	Lea	GP	G	A	TP	PIM	GP	G	A	TP	PIM
1985-86	Hamilton	OHL	56	4	4	8	178	....	....	....	....	....
1986-87	Belleville	OHL	21	5	5	10	52	....	....	....	....	....
	North Bay	OHL	35	6	11	17	90	23	3	9	12	99
1987-88	North Bay	OHL	9	1	2	3	44	....	....	....	....	....
	Belleville	OHL	46	12	27	39	103	6	2	3	5	24
	Utica	AHL	3	0	0	0	36	....	....	....	....	....
	New Jersey	**NHL**	....	....	....	....	....	**1**	**0**	**0**	**0**	**12**
1988-89	Utica	AHL	62	6	4	10	152	2	0	0	0	25
1989-90	**New Jersey**	**NHL**	**10**	**0**	**0**	**0**	**23**	**2**	**0**	**0**	**0**	**10**
	Nashville	ECHL	3	0	0	0	15	....	....	....	....	....
1990-91	**New Jersey**	**NHL**	**59**	**6**	**3**	**9**	**182**	....	....	....	....	....
	NHL Totals		**69**	**6**	**3**	**9**	**205**	**3**	**0**	**0**	**0**	**22**

CROWLEY, EDWARD (TED)

Defense. Shoots right. 6'2", 188 lbs. Born, Concord, MA, May 3, 1970.
(Toronto's 4th choice, 69th overall, in 1988 Entry Draft).

			Regular Season					Playoffs				
Season	Club	Lea	GP	G	A	TP	PIM	GP	G	A	TP	PIM
1989-90	Boston College	H.E.	39	7	24	31	34	....	....	....	....	....
1990-91ab	Boston College	H.E.	39	12	24	36	61	....	....	....	....	....

a Hockey East First All-Star Team (1991)
b NCAA East Second All-American Team (1991)

CROWLEY, JOE

Left wing. Shoots left. 6'2", 190 lbs. Born, Concord, MA, February 29, 1972.
(Edmonton's 3rd choice, 59th overall, in 1990 Entry Draft).

			Regular Season					Playoffs				
Season	Club	Lea	GP	G	A	TP	PIM	GP	G	A	TP	PIM
1989-90	Lawrence Aca.	HS	10	8	5	13	....	....	....	....	....	....
1990-91	Boston College	H.E.	17	3	0	3	14	....	....	....	....	....

CULHANE, JIM

Defense. Shoots left. 6', 195 lbs. Born, Haileybury, Ont., March 13, 1965.
(Hartford's 6th choice, 215th overall, in 1984 Entry Draft).

			Regular Season					Playoffs				
Season	Club	Lea	GP	G	A	TP	PIM	GP	G	A	TP	PIM
1983-84	W. Michigan	CCHA	42	1	14	15	88	....	....	....	....	....
1984-85	W. Michigan	CCHA	37	2	8	10	84	....	....	....	....	....
1985-86	W. Michigan	CCHA	40	1	21	22	61	....	....	....	....	....
1986-87	W. Michigan	CCHA	43	9	24	33	163	....	....	....	....	....
1987-88	Binghamton	AHL	76	5	17	22	169	4	0	0	0	8
1988-89	Binghamton	AHL	72	6	11	17	200	....	....	....	....	....
1989-90	**Hartford**	**NHL**	**6**	**0**	**1**	**1**	**4**	....	....	....	....	....
	Binghamton	AHL	73	6	11	17	69	....	....	....	....	....
1990-91	Capital Dist.	AHL	15	0	0	0	14	....	....	....	....	....
	Kansas City	IHL	59	1	8	9	50	....	....	....	....	....
	NHL Totals		**6**	**0**	**1**	**1**	**4**	....	....	....	....	....

CULLEN, JOHN

Center. Shoots right. 5'10", 187 lbs. Born, Puslinch, Ont., August 2, 1964.
(Buffalo's 2nd choice, 10th overall, in 1986 Supplemental Draft).

			Regular Season					Playoffs				
Season	Club	Lea	GP	G	A	TP	PIM	GP	G	A	TP	PIM
1983-84a	Boston U.	ECAC	40	23	33	56	28	....	....	....	....	....
1984-85b	Boston U.	H.E.	41	27	32	59	46	....	....	....	....	....
1985-86bc	Boston U.	H.E.	43	25	49	74	54	....	....	....	....	....
1986-87d	Boston U.	H.E.	36	23	29	52	35	....	....	....	....	....
1987-88efgh	Flint	IHL	81	48	*109	*157	113	16	11	*15	26	16
1988-89	**Pittsburgh**	**NHL**	**79**	**12**	**37**	**49**	**112**	**11**	**3**	**6**	**9**	**28**
1989-90	**Pittsburgh**	**NHL**	**72**	**32**	**60**	**92**	**138**	....	....	....	....	....
1990-91	**Pittsburgh**	**NHL**	**65**	**31**	**63**	**94**	**83**	....	....	....	....	....
	Hartford	**NHL**	**13**	**8**	**8**	**16**	**18**	**6**	**2**	**7**	**9**	**10**
	NHL Totals		**229**	**83**	**168**	**251**	**351**	**17**	**5**	**13**	**18**	**38**

a ECAC Rookie of the Year (1984)
b Hockey East First All-Star Team (1985, 1986)
c NCAA East Second All-American Team (1986)
d Hockey East Second All-Star Team (1987)
e IHL First All-Star Team (1988)
f Won James Gatschene Memorial Trophy (MVP-IHL) (1988)
g Shared Garry F. Longman Memorial Trophy (Top Rookie-IHL) with Ed Belfour (1988)
h Won Leo P. Lamoureux Memorial Trophy (Top Scorer-IHL) (1988)

Played in NHL All-Star Game (1991)

Signed as a free agent by **Pittsburgh** June 21, 1988. Traded to **Hartford** by **Pittsburgh** with Jeff Parker and Zarley Zalapski for Ron Francis, Grant Jennings and Ulf Samuelsson, March 4, 1991.

CULLIMORE, JASSEN

Defense. Shoots left. 6'4", 219 lbs. Born, Simcoe, Ont., December 4, 1972.
(Vancouver's 2nd choice, 29th overall, in 1991 Entry Draft).

			Regular Season					Playoffs				
Season	Club	Lea	GP	G	A	TP	PIM	GP	G	A	TP	PIM
1989-90	Peterborough	OHL	59	2	6	8	61	11	0	2	2	8
1990-91	Peterborough	OHL	62	8	16	24	74	4	1	0	1	7

CUMMINS, JIM

Right wing. Shoots right. 6'2", 203 lbs. Born, Dearborn, MI, May 17, 1970.
(NY Rangers' 5th choice, 67th overall, in 1989 Entry Draft).

			Regular Season					Playoffs				
Season	Club	Lea	GP	G	A	TP	PIM	GP	G	A	TP	PIM
1988-89	Michigan State	CCHA	30	3	8	11	98	....	....	....	....	....
1989-90	Michigan State	CCHA	41	8	7	15	94	....	....	....	....	....
1990-91	Michigan State	CCHA	34	9	6	15	110	....	....	....	....	....

Traded to **Detroit** by **NY Rangers** with Kevin Miller and Dennis Vial for Joey Kocur and Per Djoos, March 5, 1991.

CUNNEYWORTH, RANDY WILLIAM

Left wing. Shoots left. 6', 180 lbs. Born, Etobicoke, Ont., May 10, 1961.
(Buffalo's 9th choice, 167th overall, in 1980 Entry Draft).

			Regular Season					Playoffs				
Season	Club	Lea	GP	G	A	TP	PIM	GP	G	A	TP	PIM
1979-80	Ottawa	OHA	63	16	25	41	145	11	0	1	1	13
1980-81	**Buffalo**	**NHL**	**1**	**0**	**0**	**0**	**2**	....	....	....	....	....
	Rochester	AHL	1	0	1	1	2	....	....	....	....	....
	Ottawa	OHA	67	54	74	128	240	15	5	8	13	35
1981-82	**Buffalo**	**NHL**	**20**	**2**	**4**	**6**	**47**	....	....	....	....	....
	Rochester	AHL	57	12	15	27	86	9	4	0	4	30
1982-83	Rochester	AHL	78	23	33	56	111	16	4	4	8	35
1983-84	Rochester	AHL	54	18	17	35	85	17	5	5	10	55
1984-85	Rochester	AHL	72	30	38	68	148	5	2	1	3	16
1985-86	**Pittsburgh**	**NHL**	**75**	**15**	**30**	**45**	**74**	....	....	....	....	....
1986-87	**Pittsburgh**	**NHL**	**79**	**26**	**27**	**53**	**142**	....	....	....	....	....
1987-88	**Pittsburgh**	**NHL**	**71**	**35**	**39**	**74**	**141**	....	....	....	....	....
1988-89	**Pittsburgh**	**NHL**	**70**	**25**	**19**	**44**	**156**	**11**	**3**	**5**	**8**	**26**
1989-90	**Winnipeg**	**NHL**	**28**	**5**	**6**	**11**	**34**	....	....	....	....	....
	Hartford	**NHL**	**43**	**9**	**9**	**18**	**41**	**4**	**0**	**0**	**0**	**2**
1990-91	**Hartford**	**NHL**	**32**	**9**	**5**	**14**	**49**	**1**	**0**	**0**	**0**	**0**
	Springfield	AHL	2	0	0	0	5	....	....	....	....	....
	NHL Totals		**419**	**126**	**139**	**265**	**686**	**16**	**3**	**5**	**8**	**28**

Traded to **Pittsburgh** by **Buffalo** with Mike Moller for Pat Hughes, October 4, 1985. Traded to **Winnipeg** by **Pittsburgh** with Rick Tabaracci and Dave McLlwain for Jim Kyte, Andrew McBain and Randy Gilhen, June 17, 1989. Traded to **Hartford** by **Winnipeg** for Paul MacDermid, December 13, 1989.

CURRAN, BRIAN

Defense. Shoots left. 6'5", 220 lbs. Born, Toronto, Ont., November 5, 1963.
(Boston's 2nd choice, 22nd overall, in 1982 Entry Draft).

			Regular Season					Playoffs				
Season	Club	Lea	GP	G	A	TP	PIM	GP	G	A	TP	PIM
1980-81	Portland	WHL	59	2	28	30	275	7	0	1	1	13
1981-82	Portland	WHL	51	2	16	18	132	14	1	7	8	63
1982-83	Portland	WHL	56	1	30	31	187	14	1	3	4	57
1983-84	**Boston**	**NHL**	**16**	**1**	**1**	**2**	**57**	**3**	**0**	**0**	**0**	**7**
	Hershey	AHL	23	0	2	2	94	....	....	....	....	....
1984-85	**Boston**	**NHL**	**56**	**0**	**1**	**1**	**158**	....	....	....	....	....
	Hershey	AHL	4	0	0	0	19	....	....	....	....	....
1985-86	**Boston**	**NHL**	**43**	**2**	**5**	**7**	**192**	**2**	**0**	**0**	**0**	**4**
1986-87	**NY Islanders**	**NHL**	**68**	**0**	**10**	**10**	**356**	**8**	**0**	**0**	**0**	**51**
1987-88	**NY Islanders**	**NHL**	**22**	**0**	**1**	**1**	**68**	....	....	....	....	....
	Springfield	AHL	8	1	0	1	43	....	....	....	....	....
	Toronto	**NHL**	**7**	**0**	**1**	**1**	**19**	**6**	**0**	**0**	**0**	**41**
1988-89	**Toronto**	**NHL**	**47**	**1**	**4**	**5**	**185**	....	....	....	....	....
1989-90	**Toronto**	**NHL**	**72**	**2**	**9**	**11**	**301**	**5**	**0**	**1**	**1**	**19**
1990-91	**Toronto**	**NHL**	**4**	**0**	**0**	**0**	**7**	....	....	....	....	....
	Newmarket	AHL	6	0	1	1	32	....	....	....	....	....
	Buffalo	**NHL**	**17**	**0**	**1**	**1**	**43**	....	....	....	....	....
	Rochester	AHL	10	0	0	0	36	....	....	....	....	....
	NHL Totals		**352**	**6**	**33**	**39**	**1386**	**24**	**0**	**1**	**1**	**122**

Signed as a free agent by **NY Islanders**, August 29, 1987. Traded to **Toronto** by **NY Islanders** for Toronto's sixth round choice (Pavel Gross) in 1988 Entry Draft, March 8, 1988. Traded to **Buffalo** by **Toronto** with Lou Franceschetti for Mike Foligno and Buffalo's eighth round choice (Thomas Kucharcik) in 1991 Entry Draft, December 17, 1990.

CURRIE, DAN

Left wing. Shoots left. 6'2", 195 lbs. Born, Burlington, Ont., March 15, 1968.
(Edmonton's 4th choice, 84th overall, in 1986 Entry Draft).

			Regular Season					Playoffs				
Season	**Club**	**Lea**	**GP**	**G**	**A**	**TP**	**PIM**	**GP**	**G**	**A**	**TP**	**PIM**
1985-86	S.S. Marie	OHL	66	21	24	45	37	....	....	....	....	....
1986-87	S.S. Marie	OHL	66	31	52	83	53	4	2	1	3	2
1987-88	Nova Scotia	AHL	3	4	2	6	0	5	4	3	7	0
	S.S. Marie	OHL	57	50	59	109	53	6	3	9	12	4
1988-89	Cape Breton	AHL	77	29	36	65	29	....	....	....	....	....
1989-90	Cape Breton	AHL	77	36	40	76	28	....	....	....	....	....
1990-91	**Edmonton**	**NHL**	**5**	**0**	**0**	**0**	**0**	....	....	....	....	....
	Cape Breton	AHL	71	47	45	92	51	4	3	1	4	8
	NHL Totals		**5**	**0**	**0**	**0**	**0**	....	....	....	....	....

CYR, PAUL

Left wing. Shoots left. 5'10", 180 lbs. Born, Port Alberni, B.C., October 31, 1963.
(Buffalo's 2nd choice, 9th overall, in 1982 Entry Draft).

			Regular Season					Playoffs				
Season	**Club**	**Lea**	**GP**	**G**	**A**	**TP**	**PIM**	**GP**	**G**	**A**	**TP**	**PIM**
1980-81	Victoria	WHL	64	36	22	58	85	14	6	5	11	46
1981-82a	Victoria	WHL	58	52	56	108	167	4	3	2	5	12
1982-83	Victoria	WHL	20	21	22	43	61	....	....	....	....	....
	Buffalo	**NHL**	**36**	**15**	**12**	**27**	**59**	**10**	**1**	**3**	**4**	**6**
1983-84	**Buffalo**	**NHL**	**71**	**16**	**27**	**43**	**52**	**3**	**0**	**1**	**1**	**0**
1984-85	**Buffalo**	**NHL**	**71**	**22**	**24**	**46**	**63**	**5**	**2**	**2**	**4**	**15**
1985-86	**Buffalo**	**NHL**	**71**	**20**	**31**	**51**	**120**	....	....	....	....	....
1986-87	**Buffalo**	**NHL**	**73**	**11**	**16**	**27**	**122**	....	....	....	....	....
1987-88	**Buffalo**	**NHL**	**20**	**1**	**1**	**2**	**38**	....	....	....	....	....
	NY Rangers	**NHL**	**40**	**4**	**13**	**17**	**41**	....	....	....	....	....
1988-89	**NY Rangers**	**NHL**	**1**	**0**	**0**	**0**	**2**	....	....	....	....	....
1989-90	**NY Rangers**	**NHL**	DID NOT PLAY - INJURED									
1990-91	**Hartford**	**NHL**	**70**	**12**	**13**	**25**	**107**	**6**	**1**	**0**	**1**	**10**
	NHL Totals		**453**	**101**	**137**	**238**	**604**	**24**	**4**	**6**	**10**	**31**

a WHL Second All-Star Team (1982).

Traded to **New York Rangers** by **Buffalo** with Buffalo's 10th round choice (Eric Fenton) in 1988 Entry Draft for Mike Donnelly and NY Ranger's fifth round choice (Alexander Mogilny) in 1988 Entry Draft, December 31, 1987. Signed as a free agent by **Hartford**, September 30, 1990.

DAGENAIS, MIKE

Defense. Shoots left. 6'3", 198 lbs. Born, Gloucester, Ont., July 22, 1969.
(Chicago's 4th choice, 60th overall, in 1987 Entry Draft).

			Regular Season					Playoffs				
Season	**Club**	**Lea**	**GP**	**G**	**A**	**TP**	**PIM**	**GP**	**G**	**A**	**TP**	**PIM**
1985-86	Peterborough	OHL	45	1	3	4	40	....	....	....	....	....
1986-87	Peterborough	OHL	56	1	17	18	66	12	4	1	5	20
1987-88	Peterborough	OHL	66	11	23	34	125	12	1	1	2	31
1988-89	Peterborough	OHL	62	14	23	37	122	13	3	3	6	12
1989-90	Peterborough	OHL	44	14	26	40	74	12	4	1	5	18
1990-91	Indianapolis	IHL	76	13	14	27	115	4	0	0	0	4

DAHL, KEVIN

Defense. Shoots right. 5'11", 190 lbs. Born, Regina, Sask., December 30, 1968.
(Montreal's 12th choice, 230th overall, in 1988 Entry Draft).

			Regular Season					Playoffs				
Season	**Club**	**Lea**	**GP**	**G**	**A**	**TP**	**PIM**	**GP**	**G**	**A**	**TP**	**PIM**
1987-88	Bowling Green	CCHA	44	2	23	25	78	....	....	....	....	....
1988-89	Bowling Green	CCHA	46	9	26	35	51	....	....	....	....	....
1989-90	Bowling Green	CCHA	43	8	22	30	74	....	....	....	....	....
1990-91	Fredericton	AHL	32	1	15	16	45	9	0	1	1	11
	Winston-Salem	ECHL	36	7	17	24	58	....	....	....	....	....

DAHLEN, ULF (DAH-lehn)

Right wing. Shoots left. 6'2", 195 lbs. Born, Ostersund, Sweden, January 12, 1967.
(NY Rangers' 1st choice, 7th overall, in 1985 Entry Draft).

			Regular Season					Playoffs				
Season	**Club**	**Lea**	**GP**	**G**	**A**	**TP**	**PIM**	**GP**	**G**	**A**	**TP**	**PIM**
1983-84	Ostersund	Swe.2	36	15	11	26	10	....	....	....	....	....
1984-85	Ostersund	Swe.2	36	33	26	59	20	....	....	....	....	....
1985-86	Bjorkloven	Swe.	21	4	3	7	8	....	....	....	....	....
1986-87	Bjorkloven	Swe.	31	9	12	21	20	6	6	2	8	4
1987-88	**NY Rangers**	**NHL**	**70**	**29**	**23**	**52**	**26**	....	....	....	....	....
	Colorado	IHL	2	2	2	4	0	....	....	....	....	....
1988-89	**NY Rangers**	**NHL**	**56**	**24**	**19**	**43**	**50**	**4**	**0**	**0**	**0**	**0**
1989-90	**NY Rangers**	**NHL**	**63**	**18**	**18**	**36**	**30**	....	....	....	....	....
	Minnesota	**NHL**	**13**	**2**	**4**	**6**	**0**	**7**	**1**	**4**	**5**	**2**
1990-91	**Minnesota**	**NHL**	**66**	**21**	**18**	**39**	**6**	**15**	**2**	**6**	**8**	**4**
	NHL Totals		**268**	**94**	**82**	**176**	**112**	**26**	**3**	**10**	**13**	**6**

Traded to **Minnesota** by **NY Rangers** with Los Angeles' fourth round choice (Cal McGowan) – previously acquired by NY Rangers – in 1990 Entry Draft and future considerations, March 6, 1990.

DAHLQUIST, CHRIS

Defense. Shoots left. 6'1", 196 lbs. Born, Fridley, MN, December 14, 1962.

			Regular Season					Playoffs				
Season	**Club**	**Lea**	**GP**	**G**	**A**	**TP**	**PIM**	**GP**	**G**	**A**	**TP**	**PIM**
1981-82	Lake Superior	CCHA	39	4	10	14	62	....	....	....	....	....
1982-83	Lake Superior	CCHA	35	0	12	12	63	....	....	....	....	....
1983-84	Lake Superior	CCHA	40	4	19	23	76	....	....	....	....	....
1984-85	Lake Superior	CCHA	32	4	10	14	18	....	....	....	....	....
1985-86	**Pittsburgh**	**NHL**	**5**	**1**	**2**	**3**	**2**	....	....	....	....	....
	Baltimore	AHL	65	4	21	25	64	....	....	....	....	....
1986-87	**Pittsburgh**	**NHL**	**19**	**0**	**1**	**1**	**20**	....	....	....	....	....
	Baltimore	AHL	51	1	16	17	50	....	....	....	....	....
1987-88	**Pittsburgh**	**NHL**	**44**	**3**	**6**	**9**	**69**	....	....	....	....	....
1988-89	**Pittsburgh**	**NHL**	**43**	**1**	**5**	**6**	**42**	**2**	**0**	**0**	**0**	**0**
	Muskegon	IHL	10	3	6	9	14	....	....	....	....	....
1989-90	**Pittsburgh**	**NHL**	**62**	**4**	**10**	**14**	**56**	....	....	....	....	....
	Muskegon	IHL	6	1	1	2	8	....	....	....	....	....
1990-91	**Pittsburgh**	**NHL**	**22**	**1**	**2**	**3**	**30**	....	....	....	....	....
	Minnesota	**NHL**	**42**	**2**	**6**	**8**	**33**	**23**	**1**	**6**	**7**	**20**
	NHL Totals		**237**	**12**	**32**	**44**	**252**	**25**	**1**	**6**	**7**	**20**

Signed as a free agent by **Pittsburgh**, May 7, 1985. Traded to **Minnesota** by **Pittsburgh** with Jim Johnson for Larry Murphy and Peter Taglianetti, December 11, 1990.

DAIGNEAULT, JEAN-JACQUES (DAYN-yoh)

Defense. Shoots left. 5'11", 185 lbs. Born, Montreal, Que., October 12, 1965.
(Vancouver's 1st choice, 10th overall, in 1984 Entry Draft).

			Regular Season					Playoffs				
Season	**Club**	**Lea**	**GP**	**G**	**A**	**TP**	**PIM**	**GP**	**G**	**A**	**TP**	**PIM**
1981-82	Laval	QMJHL	64	4	25	29	41	18	1	3	4	2
1982-83ab	Longueuil	QMJHL	70	26	58	84	58	15	4	11	15	35
1983-84	Cdn. Olympic	...	62	6	15	21	40	....	....	....	....	....
	Longueuil	QMJHL	10	2	11	13	6	14	3	13	16	30
1984-85	**Vancouver**	**NHL**	**67**	**4**	**23**	**27**	**69**	....	....	....	....	....
1985-86	**Vancouver**	**NHL**	**64**	**5**	**23**	**28**	**45**	**3**	**0**	**2**	**2**	**0**
1986-87	**Philadelphia**	**NHL**	**77**	**6**	**16**	**22**	**56**	**9**	**1**	**0**	**1**	**0**
1987-88	**Philadelphia**	**NHL**	**28**	**2**	**2**	**4**	**12**	....	....	....	....	....
	Hershey	AHL	10	1	5	6	8	....	....	....	....	....
1988-89	Hershey	AHL	12	0	10	10	13	....	....	....	....	....
	Sherbrooke	AHL	63	10	33	43	48	6	1	3	4	2
1989-90	**Montreal**	**NHL**	**36**	**2**	**10**	**12**	**14**	**9**	**0**	**0**	**0**	**2**
	Sherbrooke	AHL	28	8	19	27	18	....	....	....	....	....
1990-91	**Montreal**	**NHL**	**51**	**3**	**16**	**19**	**31**	**5**	**0**	**1**	**1**	**0**
	NHL Totals		**323**	**22**	**90**	**112**	**227**	**26**	**1**	**3**	**4**	**2**

a QMJHL First All-Star Team (1983)
b Named QMJHL's Top Defenseman (1983)

Traded to **Philadelphia** by **Vancouver** with Vancouver's second-round choice (Kent Hawley) in 1986 Entry Draft for Dave Richter, Rich Sutter and Vancouver's third-round choice (Don Gibson) — acquired earlier — in 1986 Entry Draft, June 6, 1986. Traded to **Montreal** by **Philadelphia** for Scott Sandelin, November 7, 1988.

DALGARNO, BRAD

Right wing. Shoots right. 6'3", 215 lbs. Born, Vancouver, B.C., August 11, 1967.
(NY Islanders' 1st choice, 6th overall, in 1985 Entry Draft).

			Regular Season					Playoffs				
Season	**Club**	**Lea**	**GP**	**G**	**A**	**TP**	**PIM**	**GP**	**G**	**A**	**TP**	**PIM**
1984-85	Hamilton	OHA	66	23	30	53	86	....	....	....	....	....
1985-86	**NY Islanders**	**NHL**	**2**	**1**	**0**	**1**	**0**	....	....	....	....	....
	Hamilton	OHL	54	22	43	65	79	....	....	....	....	....
1986-87	Hamilton	OHL	60	27	32	59	100	....	....	....	....	....
1987-88	**NY Islanders**	**NHL**	**38**	**2**	**8**	**10**	**58**	....	....	....	....	....
	Springfield	AHL	39	13	11	24	76	....	....	....	....	....
1988-89	**NY Islanders**	**NHL**	**55**	**11**	**10**	**21**	**86**	....	....	....	....	....
1989-90			DID NOT PLAY - INJURED									
1990-91	**NY Islanders**	**NHL**	**41**	**3**	**12**	**15**	**24**	....	....	....	....	....
	Capital District	AHL	27	6	14	20	26	....	....	....	....	....
	NHL Totals		**136**	**17**	**30**	**47**	**168**	....	....	....	....	....

DALLMAN, ROD

Left wing. Shoots left. 5'11", 185 lbs. Born, Prince Albert, Sask., January 26, 1967.
(NY Islanders' 8th choice, 118th overall, in 1985 Entry Draft).

			Regular Season					Playoffs				
Season	**Club**	**Lea**	**GP**	**G**	**A**	**TP**	**PIM**	**GP**	**G**	**A**	**TP**	**PIM**
1984-85	Prince Albert	WHL	40	8	11	19	133	12	3	4	7	51
1985-86	Prince Albert	WHL	59	20	21	41	198	....	....	....	....	....
1986-87	Prince Albert	WHL	47	13	21	34	240	5	0	1	1	32
1987-88	**NY Islanders**	**NHL**	**3**	**1**	**0**	**1**	**6**	....	....	....	....	....
	Springfield	AHL	59	9	17	26	355	....	....	....	....	....
	Peoria	IHL	8	3	4	7	18	7	0	2	2	65
1988-89	**NY Islanders**	**NHL**	**1**	**0**	**0**	**0**	**15**	....	....	....	....	....
	Springfield	AHL	67	12	12	24	360	....	....	....	....	....
1989-90	**NY Islanders**	**NHL**	....	....	....	....	....	**1**	**0**	**1**	**1**	**0**
	Springfield	AHL	43	10	20	30	129	15	5	5	10	59
1990-91	Hershey	AHL	2	0	0	0	0	....	....	....	....	....
	San Diego	IHL	15	3	5	8	85	....	....	....	....	....
	NHL Totals		**4**	**1**	**0**	**1**	**21**	**1**	**0**	**1**	**1**	**0**

Signed as a free agent by **Philadelphia**, July 31, 1990.

DAM, TREVOR

Right wing. Shoots right. 5'10", 208 lbs. Born, Scarborough, Ont., April 20, 1970.
(Chicago's 2nd choice, 50th overall, in 1988 Entry Draft).

			Regular Season					Playoffs				
Season	**Club**	**Lea**	**GP**	**G**	**A**	**TP**	**PIM**	**GP**	**G**	**A**	**TP**	**PIM**
1986-87	London	OHL	64	6	17	23	88	....	....	....	....	....
1987-88	London	OHL	66	25	38	63	169	12	0	3	3	19
1988-89	London	OHL	66	33	59	92	111	21	9	11	20	39
1989-90	London	OHL	56	20	54	74	91	6	2	5	7	15
1990-91	Indianapolis	IHL	50	9	10	19	28	1	0	0	0	2

DAMPHOUSSE, VINCENT (DAM-fooz)

Left wing. Shoots left. 6'1", 185 lbs. Born, Montreal, Que., December 17, 1967.
(Toronto's 1st choice, 6th overall, in 1986 Entry Draft).

			Regular Season					Playoffs				
Season	Club	Lea	GP	G	A	TP	PIM	GP	G	A	TP	PIM
1983-84	Laval	QMJHL	66	29	36	65	25	....	....	....	....	....
1984-85	Laval	QMJHL	68	35	68	103	62	....	....	....	....	....
1985-86a	Laval	QMJHL	69	45	110	155	70	14	9	27	36	12
1986-87	**Toronto**	**NHL**	**80**	**21**	**25**	**46**	**26**	**12**	**1**	**5**	**6**	**8**
1987-88	**Toronto**	**NHL**	**75**	**12**	**36**	**48**	**40**	**6**	**0**	**1**	**1**	**10**
1988-89	**Toronto**	**NHL**	**80**	**26**	**42**	**68**	**75**	....	....	....	....	....
1989-90	**Toronto**	**NHL**	**80**	**33**	**61**	**94**	**56**	**5**	**0**	**2**	**2**	**2**
1990-91	**Toronto**	**NHL**	**79**	**26**	**47**	**73**	**65**	....	....	....	....	....
	NHL Totals		**394**	**118**	**211**	**329**	**262**	**23**	**1**	**8**	**9**	**20**

a QMJHL Second All-Star Team (1986)
Played in NHL All-Star Game (1991)

DANEYKO, KENNETH (KEN) (DAN-ee-koh)

Defense. Shoots left. 6', 210 lbs. Born, Windsor, Ont., April 17, 1964.
(New Jersey's 2nd choice, 18th overall, in 1982 Entry Draft).

			Regular Season					Playoffs				
Season	Club	Lea	GP	G	A	TP	PIM	GP	G	A	TP	PIM
1980-81	Spokane	WHL	62	6	13	19	40	4	0	0	0	6
1981-82	Spokane	WHL	26	1	11	12	147	....	....	....	....	....
	Seattle	WHL	38	1	22	23	151	14	1	9	10	49
1982-83	Seattle	WHL	69	17	43	60	150	4	1	3	4	14
1983-84	**New Jersey**	**NHL**	**11**	**1**	**4**	**5**	**17**	....	....	....	....	....
	Kamloops	WHL	19	6	28	34	52	17	4	9	13	28
1984-85	**New Jersey**	**NHL**	**1**	**0**	**0**	**0**	**10**	....	....	....	....	....
	Maine	AHL	80	4	9	13	206	11	1	3	4	36
1985-86	**New Jersey**	**NHL**	**44**	**0**	**10**	**10**	**100**	....	....	....	....	....
	Maine	AHL	21	3	2	5	75	....	....	....	....	....
1986-87	**New Jersey**	**NHL**	**79**	**2**	**12**	**14**	**183**	....	....	....	....	....
1987-88	**New Jersey**	**NHL**	**80**	**5**	**7**	**12**	**239**	**20**	**1**	**6**	**7**	**83**
1988-89	**New Jersey**	**NHL**	**80**	**5**	**5**	**10**	**283**	....	....	....	....	....
1989-90	**New Jersey**	**NHL**	**74**	**6**	**15**	**21**	**216**	**6**	**2**	**0**	**2**	**21**
1990-91	**New Jersey**	**NHL**	**80**	**4**	**16**	**20**	**249**	**7**	**0**	**1**	**1**	**10**
	NHL Totals		**449**	**23**	**69**	**92**	**1297**	**33**	**3**	**7**	**10**	**114**

DANIELS, JEFF

Left wing. Shoots left. 6'1", 200 lbs. Born, Oshawa, Ont., June 24, 1968.
(Pittsburgh's 6th choice, 109th overall, in 1986 Entry Draft).

			Regular Season					Playoffs				
Season	Club	Lea	GP	G	A	TP	PIM	GP	G	A	TP	PIM
1984-85	Oshawa	OHL	59	7	11	18	16	....	....	....	....	....
1985-86	Oshawa	OHL	62	13	19	32	23	6	0	1	1	0
1986-87	Oshawa	OHL	54	14	9	23	22	15	3	2	5	5
1987-88	Oshawa	OHL	64	29	39	68	59	4	2	3	5	0
1988-89	Muskegon	IHL	58	21	21	42	58	11	3	5	8	11
1989-90	Muskegon	IHL	80	30	47	77	39	6	1	1	2	7
1990-91	**Pittsburgh**	**NHL**	**11**	**0**	**2**	**2**	**2**	....	....	....	....	....
	Muskegon	IHL	62	23	29	52	18	5	1	3	4	2
	NHL Totals		**11**	**0**	**2**	**2**	**2**	....	....	....	....	....

DANIELS, KIMBI

Center. Shoots right. 5'10", 175 lbs. Born, Brandon, Man., January 19, 1972.
(Philadelphia's 5th choice, 44th overall, in 1990 Entry Draft).

			Regular Season					Playoffs				
Season	Club	Lea	GP	G	A	TP	PIM	GP	G	A	TP	PIM
1988-89	Swift Current	WHL	68	30	31	61	48	12	6	6	12	12
1989-90	Swift Current	WHL	69	43	51	94	84	4	1	3	4	10
1990-91	**Philadelphia**	**NHL**	**2**	**0**	**1**	**1**	**0**	....	....	....	....	....
	Swift Current	WHL	69	54	64	118	68	3	4	2	6	6
	NHL Totals		**2**	**0**	**1**	**1**	**0**	....	....	....	....	....

DANIELS, SCOTT

Left wing. Shoots left. 6'3", 200 lbs. Born, Prince Albert, Sask., September 19, 1969.
(Hartford's 6th choice, 136th overall, in 1989 Entry Draft).

			Regular Season					Playoffs				
Season	Club	Lea	GP	G	A	TP	PIM	GP	G	A	TP	PIM
1986-87	Kamloops	WHL	43	6	4	10	68	....	....	....	....	....
	N. Westminster	WHL	19	4	7	11	30	....	....	....	....	....
1987-88	N. Westminster	WHL	37	6	11	17	157	....	....	....	....	....
	Regina	WHL	19	2	3	5	83	....	....	....	....	....
1988-89	Regina	WHL	64	21	26	47	241	....	....	....	....	....
1989-90	Regina	WHL	52	28	31	59	171	....	....	....	....	....
1990-91	Springfield	AHL	40	2	6	8	121	....	....	....	....	....
	Louisville	ECHL	9	5	3	8	34	1	0	2	2	0

DARBY, CRAIG

Center. Shoots right. 6'3", 180 lbs. Born, Oneida, NY, September 26, 1972.
(Montreal's 3rd choice, 43rd overall, in 1991 Entry Draft).

			Regular Season					Playoffs				
Season	Club	Lea	GP	G	A	TP	PIM	GP	G	A	TP	PIM
1990-91	Albany Aca.	HS	....	33	61	94	....	....	....	....	....	....

DARVEAU, GUY

Defense. Shoots left. 6'1", 207 lbs. Born, Montreal, Que., April 7, 1968.
(Calgary's 10th choice, 210th overall, in 1988 Entry Draft).

			Regular Season					Playoffs				
Season	Club	Lea	GP	G	A	TP	PIM	GP	G	A	TP	PIM
1985-86	Longueuil	QMJHL	55	0	8	8	139	....	....	....	....	....
1986-87	Longueuil	QMJHL	64	9	24	33	175	15	1	7	8	23
1987-88	Victoriaville	QMJHL	57	19	16	35	274	5	0	2	2	17
1988-89	Verdun	QMJHL	20	1	10	11	40	....	....	....	....	....
1989-90	Sherbrooke	AHL	38	2	2	4	120	2	0	0	0	2
1990-91	Fredericton	AHL	17	0	1	1	46	....	....	....	....	....

Signed as a free agent by **Montreal**, October 2, 1989.

DAVIDSON, LEE

Center/Left wing. Shoots left. 5'10", 165 lbs. Born, Winnipeg, Man., June 30, 1968.
(Washington's 9th choice, 166th overall, in 1986 Entry Draft).

			Regular Season					Playoffs				
Season	Club	Lea	GP	G	A	TP	PIM	GP	G	A	TP	PIM
1986-87	North Dakota	WCHA	41	16	12	28	65	....	....	....	....	....
1987-88	North Dakota	WCHA	40	22	24	46	74	....	....	....	....	....
1988-89	North Dakota	WCHA	41	16	37	53	60	....	....	....	....	....
1989-90ab	North Dakota	WCHA	45	26	*49	75	0	....	....	....	....	....
1990-91	Moncton	AHL	69	15	17	32	24	....	....	....	....	....

a WCHA Second All-Star Team (1990)
b NCAA West Second All-American Team (1990)

DAVIES, CLARK

Defense. Shoots left. 6', 185 lbs. Born, Yorkton, Sask., June 20, 1967.
(Buffalo's 1st choice, 18th overall, in 1988 Supplemental Draft).

			Regular Season					Playoffs				
Season	Club	Lea	GP	G	A	TP	PIM	GP	G	A	TP	PIM
1986-87	Ferris State	CCHA	42	5	20	25	42	....	....	....	....	....
1987-88	Ferris State	CCHA	40	4	15	19	65	....	....	....	....	....
1988-89	Ferris State	CCHA	32	3	10	13	59	....	....	....	....	....
1989-90	Ferris State	CCHA	36	4	9	13	38	....	....	....	....	....
1990-91	Erie	ECHL	59	13	55	68	78	5	0	4	4	14

DAVYDOV, EVGENY (dah-VEE-dahf)

Left wing. Shoots right. 6', 183 lbs. Born, Chelyabinsk, Soviet Union, May 27, 1967.
(Winnipeg's 14th choice, 235th overall, in 1989 Entry Draft).

			Regular Season					Playoffs				
Season	Club	Lea	GP	G	A	TP	PIM	GP	G	A	TP	PIM
1984-85	Chelyabinsk	USSR	5	1	0	1	2	....	....	....	....	....
1985-86	Chelyabinsk	USSR	39	11	5	16	22	....	....	....	....	....
1986-87	CSKA	USSR	32	11	2	13	8	....	....	....	....	....
1987-88	CSKA	USSR	44	16	7	23	18	....	....	....	....	....
1988-89	CSKA	USSR	35	9	7	16	4	....	....	....	....	....
1989-90	CSKA	USSR	44	17	6	23	16	....	....	....	....	....
1990-91	CSKA	USSR	44	10	10	20	26	....	....	....	....	....

DAWE, JASON

Left wing. Shoots left. 5'10", 189 lbs. Born, North York, Ont., March 29, 1973.
(Buffalo's 2nd choice, 35th overall, in 1991 Entry Draft).

			Regular Season					Playoffs				
Season	Club	Lea	GP	G	A	TP	PIM	GP	G	A	TP	PIM
1989-90	Peterborough	OHL	50	15	18	33	19	12	4	7	11	4
1990-91	Peterborough	OHL	66	43	27	70	43	4	3	1	4	0

DAY, JOSEPH (JOE)

Left wing. Shoots left. 5'11", 180 lbs. Born, Chicago, IL, May 11, 1968.
(Hartford's 8th choice, 186th overall, in 1987 Entry Draft).

			Regular Season					Playoffs				
Season	Club	Lea	GP	G	A	TP	PIM	GP	G	A	TP	PIM
1986-87	St. Lawrence	ECAC	33	9	11	20	25	....	....	....	....	....
1987-88	St. Lawrence	ECAC	30	21	16	37	36	....	....	....	....	....
1988-89	St. Lawrence	ECAC	36	21	27	48	44	....	....	....	....	....
1989-90a	St. Lawrence	ECAC	32	19	26	45	30	....	....	....	....	....
1990-91	Springfield	AHL	75	24	29	53	82	18	5	5	10	27

a ECAC Second All-Star Team (1990)

DEAN, KEVIN

Defense. Shoots left. 6'2", 190 lbs. Born, Madison, WI, April 1, 1969.
(New Jersey's 4th choice, 86th overall, in 1987 Entry Draft).

			Regular Season					Playoffs				
Season	Club	Lea	GP	G	A	TP	PIM	GP	G	A	TP	PIM
1987-88	N. Hampshire	H.E.	27	1	6	7	34	....	....	....	....	....
1988-89	N. Hampshire	H.E.	34	1	12	13	28	....	....	....	....	....
1989-90	N. Hampshire	H.E.	39	2	6	8	42	....	....	....	....	....
1990-91	N. Hampshire	H.E.	31	10	12	22	22	....	....	....	....	....
	Utica	AHL	7	0	1	1	2	....	....	....	....	....

DEASLEY, BRYAN

Left wing. Shoots left. 6'3", 205 lbs. Born, Toronto, Ont., November 26, 1968.
(Calgary's 1st choice, 19th overall, in 1987 Entry Draft).

			Regular Season					Playoffs				
Season	Club	Lea	GP	G	A	TP	PIM	GP	G	A	TP	PIM
1986-87	U. of Michigan	CCHA	38	13	11	24	74	....	....	....	....	....
1987-88	U. of Michigan	CCHA	27	18	4	22	38	....	....	....	....	....
1988-89	Cdn. National	...	54	19	19	38	32	....	....	....	....	....
	Salt Lake	IHL	....	....	....	....	....	7	3	3	6	25
1989-90	Salt Lake	IHL	71	16	11	27	46	11	4	0	4	8
1990-91	Salt Lake	IHL	75	24	21	45	63	....	....	....	....	....

DeBLOIS, LUCIEN (DEHB-loh-wah)

Center. Shoots right. 5'11", 200 lbs. Born, Joliette, Que., June 21, 1957.
(NY Rangers' 1st choice, 8th overall, in 1977 Amateur Draft).

			Regular Season					Playoffs				
Season	Club	Lea	GP	G	A	TP	PIM	GP	G	A	TP	PIM
1975-76	Sorel	QJHL	70	56	55	111	112	5	1	1	2	32
1976-77	Sorel	QJHL	72	56	78	134	131	....	....	....	....	....
1977-78	**NY Rangers**	**NHL**	**71**	**22**	**8**	**30**	**27**	**3**	**0**	**0**	**0**	**2**
1978-79	**NY Rangers**	**NHL**	**62**	**11**	**17**	**28**	**26**	**9**	**2**	**0**	**2**	**4**
	New Haven	AHL	7	4	6	10	6	....	....	....	....	....
1979-80	**NY Rangers**	**NHL**	**6**	**3**	**1**	**4**	**7**	....	....	....	....	....
	Colorado	**NHL**	**70**	**24**	**19**	**43**	**36**	....	....	....	....	....
1980-81	**Colorado**	**NHL**	**74**	**26**	**16**	**42**	**78**	....	....	....	....	....
1981-82	**Winnipeg**	**NHL**	**65**	**25**	**27**	**52**	**87**	**4**	**2**	**1**	**3**	**4**
1982-83	**Winnipeg**	**NHL**	**79**	**27**	**27**	**54**	**69**	**3**	**0**	**0**	**0**	**5**
1983-84	**Winnipeg**	**NHL**	**80**	**34**	**45**	**79**	**50**	**3**	**0**	**1**	**1**	**4**
1984-85	**Montreal**	**NHL**	**51**	**12**	**11**	**23**	**20**	**8**	**2**	**4**	**6**	**4**
1985-86	**Montreal**	**NHL**	**61**	**14**	**17**	**31**	**48**	**11**	**0**	**0**	**0**	**7**
1986-87	**NY Rangers**	**NHL**	**40**	**3**	**8**	**11**	**27**	**2**	**0**	**0**	**0**	**2**
1987-88	**NY Rangers**	**NHL**	**74**	**9**	**21**	**30**	**103**	....	....	....	....	....
1988-89	**NY Rangers**	**NHL**	**73**	**9**	**24**	**33**	**107**	**4**	**0**	**0**	**0**	**4**
1989-90	**Quebec**	**NHL**	**70**	**9**	**8**	**17**	**45**	....	....	....	....	....
1990-91	**Quebec**	**NHL**	**14**	**2**	**2**	**4**	**13**	....	....	....	....	....
	Toronto	**NHL**	**38**	**10**	**12**	**22**	**30**	....	....	....	....	....
	NHL Totals		**928**	**240**	**263**	**503**	**773**	**47**	**6**	**6**	**12**	**36**

Traded to **Colorado** by **NY Rangers** with Pat Hickey, Mike McEwen, Dean Turner and future consideration (Bobby Crawford) for Barry Beck, November 2, 1979. Traded to **Winnipeg** by **Colorado** for Brent Ashton and Winnipeg's third-round choice (Dave Kasper) in the 1982 Entry Draft, July 15, 1981. Traded to **Montreal** by **Winnipeg** for Perry Turnbull, June 13, 1984. Signed as a free agent by **NY Rangers**, September 8, 1986. Signed as a free agent by **Quebec**, August 2, 1989. Traded to **Toronto** by **Quebec** with Aaron Broten and Michel Petit for Scott Pearson and Toronto's second round choices in 1991 (later traded to Washington — Eric Lavigne) and 1992 Entry Drafts, November 17, 1990.

DeBOER, HEATH

Defense. Shoots left. 6'4", 210 lbs. Born, Minneapolis, MN, December 4, 1969.
(St. Louis' 11th choice, 219th overall, in 1988 Entry Draft).

			Regular Season					Playoffs				
Season	Club	Lea	GP	G	A	TP	PIM	GP	G	A	TP	PIM
1989-90	North Iowa	USHL	42	1	10	11	47	....	....	....	....	....
1990-91	Wisc.-Superior	NCAA		UNAVAILABLE								

DeBOER, PETER

Center/right wing. Shoots right. 6'1", 195 lbs. Born, Dunnville, Ont., June 13, 1968.
(Toronto's 11th choice, 237th overall, in 1988 Entry Draft).

			Regular Season					Playoffs				
Season	Club	Lea	GP	G	A	TP	PIM	GP	G	A	TP	PIM
1987-88	Windsor	OHL	54	23	18	41	41	12	4	4	8	14
1988-89	Windsor	OHL	65	45	46	91	80	4	2	3	5	0
	Milwaukee	IHL	2	0	1	1	0	1	0	2	2	2
1989-90	Milwaukee	IHL	67	21	19	40	16	6	0	3	3	4
1990-91	Milwaukee	IHL	82	27	34	61	34	6	1	3	4	0

Traded to **Vancouver** by **Toronto** for Paul Lawless, February 27, 1989.

DeBRUSK, LOUIE (dah-BRUHSK)

Left wing. Shoots left. 6'1", 225 lbs. Born, Cambridge, Ont., March 19, 1971.
(NY Rangers' 4th choice, 49th overall, in 1989 Entry Draft).

			Regular Season					Playoffs				
Season	Club	Lea	GP	G	A	TP	PIM	GP	G	A	TP	PIM
1988-89	London	OHL	59	11	11	22	149	19	1	1	2	43
1989-90	London	OHL	61	21	19	40	198	6	2	2	4	24
1990-91	London	OHL	61	31	33	64	*223	7	2	2	4	14
	Binghamton	AHL	2	0	0	0	7	2	0	0	0	9

de CARLE, MIKE

Left wing. Shoots left. 6', 200 lbs. Born, Covina, CA, August 20, 1966.
(Buffalo's 2nd choice, 6th overall, in 1987 Supplemental Draft).

			Regular Season					Playoffs				
Season	Club	Lea	GP	G	A	TP	PIM	GP	G	A	TP	PIM
1985-86	Lake Superior	CCHA	36	12	21	33	40	....	....	....	....	....
1986-87	Lake Superior	CCHA	38	34	18	52	122	....	....	....	....	....
1987-88ab	Lake Superior	CCHA	43	27	39	66	83	....	....	....	....	....
1988-89	Lake Superior	CCHA	38	20	24	44	76	....	....	....	....	....
1989-90	Phoenix	IHL	24	5	4	9	44	....	....	....	....	....
	Fort Wayne	IHL	12	4	5	9	7	5	2	6	8	15
1990-91	Erie	ECHL	51	15	31	46	180	5	1	1	2	6

a NCAA All-Tournament Team (1988)
b CCHA Second All-Star Team (1988)

DEFREITAS, RICHARD (RICH)

Defense. Shoots left. 6'2", 195 lbs. Born, Manchester, NH, January 28, 1969.
(Washington's 5th choice, 120th overall, in 1987 Entry Draft).

			Regular Season					Playoffs				
Season	Club	Lea	GP	G	A	TP	PIM	GP	G	A	TP	PIM
1988-89	Harvard	ECAC	5	0	2	2	6	....	....	....	....	....
1989-90	Harvard	ECAC	28	0	1	1	18	....	....	....	....	....
1990-91	Harvard	ECAC	21	0	7	7	20					

DEGRAY, DALE EDWARD

Defense. Shoots right. 6', 200 lbs. Born, Oshawa, Ont., September 1, 1963.
(Calgary's 7th choice, 162nd overall, in 1981 Entry Draft).

			Regular Season					Playoffs				
Season	Club	Lea	GP	G	A	TP	PIM	GP	G	A	TP	PIM
1980-81	Oshawa	OHA	61	11	10	21	93	8	1	1	2	19
1981-82	Oshawa	OHL	66	11	23	34	162	12	3	4	7	49
1982-83	Oshawa	OHL	69	20	30	50	149	17	7	7	14	36
1983-84	Colorado	CHL	67	16	14	30	67	6	1	1	2	2
1984-85a	Moncton	AHL	77	24	37	61	63	....	....	....	....	....
1985-86	**Calgary**	**NHL**	**1**	**0**	**0**	**0**	**0**	....	....	....	....	....
	Moncton	AHL	76	10	31	41	128	6	0	1	1	0
1986-87	**Calgary**	**NHL**	**27**	**6**	**7**	**13**	**29**	....	....	....	....	....
	Moncton	AHL	45	10	22	32	57	5	2	1	3	19
1987-88	**Toronto**	**NHL**	**56**	**6**	**18**	**24**	**63**	**5**	**0**	**1**	**1**	**16**
	Newmarket	AHL	8	2	10	12	8	....	....	....	....	....
1988-89	**Los Angeles**	**NHL**	**63**	**6**	**22**	**28**	**97**	**8**	**1**	**2**	**3**	**12**
1989-90	New Haven	AHL	16	2	10	12	38	....	....	....	....	....
	Buffalo	**NHL**	**6**	**0**	**0**	**0**	**6**	....	....	....	....	....
	Rochester	AHL	50	6	25	31	118	17	5	6	11	59
1990-91	Rochester	AHL	64	9	25	34	121	15	3	4	7	*76
	NHL Totals		**153**	**18**	**47**	**65**	**195**	**13**	**1**	**3**	**4**	**28**

a AHL Second All-Star Team (1985)

Traded to **Toronto** by **Calgary** for Toronto's fifth round choice (Scott Matusovich) in 1988 Entry Draft, September 17, 1987. Claimed by **Los Angeles** in NHL Waiver Draft, October 3, 1988. Traded to **Buffalo** by **Los Angeles** with future considerations for Bob Halkidis and future considerations, November 24, 1989.

DELAY, MICHAEL

Defense. Shoots left. 6', 190 lbs. Born, Boston, MA, August 31, 1969.
(Toronto's 8th choice, 174th overall, in 1988 Entry Draft).

			Regular Season					Playoffs				
Season	Club	Lea	GP	G	A	TP	PIM	GP	G	A	TP	PIM
1988-89	Boston College	H.E.	1	1	0	1	0	....	....	....	....	....
1989-90	Boston College	H.E.	7	0	0	0	0	....	....	....	....	....
1990-91	Boston College	H.E.	6	0	0	0	2	....	....	....	....	....

DELORME, GILBERT (duh-LOHRM)

Defense. Shoots right. 6'1", 199 lbs. Born, Boucherville, Que., November 25, 1962.
(Montreal's 2nd choice, 18th overall, in 1981 Entry Draft).

			Regular Season					Playoffs				
Season	Club	Lea	GP	G	A	TP	PIM	GP	G	A	TP	PIM
1979-80	Chicoutimi	QJHL	71	25	86	111	68	12	2	10	12	26
1980-81	Chicoutimi	QJHL	70	27	79	106	77	12	10	12	22	16
1981-82	**Montreal**	**NHL**	**60**	**3**	**8**	**11**	**55**	....	....	....	....	....
1982-83	**Montreal**	**NHL**	**78**	**12**	**21**	**33**	**89**	**3**	**0**	**0**	**0**	**2**
1983-84	**Montreal**	**NHL**	**27**	**2**	**7**	**9**	**8**	....	....	....	....	....
	St. Louis	**NHL**	**44**	**0**	**5**	**5**	**41**	**11**	**1**	**3**	**4**	**11**
1984-85	**St. Louis**	**NHL**	**74**	**2**	**12**	**14**	**53**	**3**	**0**	**0**	**0**	**0**
1985-86	**Quebec**	**NHL**	**64**	**2**	**18**	**20**	**51**	**2**	**0**	**0**	**0**	**5**
1986-87	**Quebec**	**NHL**	**19**	**2**	**0**	**2**	**14**	....	....	....	....	....
	Detroit	**NHL**	**24**	**2**	**3**	**5**	**33**	**16**	**0**	**2**	**2**	**14**
1987-88	**Detroit**	**NHL**	**55**	**2**	**8**	**10**	**81**	**15**	**0**	**3**	**3**	**22**
1988-89	**Detroit**	**NHL**	**42**	**1**	**3**	**4**	**51**	**6**	**0**	**1**	**1**	**2**
1989-90	**Pittsburgh**	**NHL**	**54**	**3**	**7**	**10**	**44**	....	....	....	....	....
1990-91			DID NOT PLAY									
	NHL Totals		**541**	**31**	**92**	**123**	**520**	**56**	**1**	**9**	**10**	**56**

Traded to **St. Louis** by **Montreal** with Greg Paslawski and Doug Wickenheiser for Perry Turnbull, December 21, 1983. Traded to **Quebec** by **St. Louis** for Bruce Bell, October 2, 1985. Traded to **Detroit** by **Quebec** with Brent Ashton and Mark Kumpel for Basil McRae, John Ogrodnick and Doug Shedden, January 17, 1987. Signed as a free agent by **Pittsburgh**, June 28, 1989.

DePALMA, LARRY

Left wing. Shoots left. 6', 200 lbs. Born, Trenton, MI, October 27, 1965.

			Regular Season					Playoffs				
Season	Club	Lea	GP	G	A	TP	PIM	GP	G	A	TP	PIM
1984-85	N. Westminster	WHL	65	14	16	30	87	10	1	1	2	25
1985-86	**Minnesota**	**NHL**	**1**	**0**	**0**	**0**	**0**	....	....	....	....	....
	Saskatoon	WHL	65	61	51	112	232	13	7	9	16	58
1986-87	**Minnesota**	**NHL**	**56**	**9**	**6**	**15**	**219**	....	....	....	....	....
	Springfield	AHL	9	2	2	4	82	....	....	....	....	....
1987-88	**Minnesota**	**NHL**	**7**	**1**	**1**	**2**	**15**	....	....	....	....	....
	Baltimore	AHL	16	8	10	18	121	....	....	....	....	....
	Kalamazoo	IHL	22	6	11	17	215	....	....	....	....	....
1988-89	**Minnesota**	**NHL**	**43**	**5**	**7**	**12**	**102**	**2**	**0**	**0**	**0**	**6**
1989-90	Kalamazoo	IHL	36	7	14	21	218	4	1	1	2	32
1990-91	**Minnesota**	**NHL**	**14**	**3**	**0**	**3**	**26**	....	....	....	....	....
	Kalamazoo	IHL	55	27	32	59	160	11	5	4	9	25
	NHL Totals		**121**	**18**	**14**	**32**	**362**	**2**	**0**	**0**	**0**	**6**

a QMJHL Second All-Star Team (1987)
b QMJHL First All-Star Team (1988)
c QMJHL Top Defenseman (1988)

DePOURCQ, JOHN

Center. Shoots left. 5'9", 180 lbs. Born, Penticton, B.C., February 6, 1968.
(Pittsburgh's 1st choice, 21st overall, in 1989 Supplemental Draft).

			Regular Season					Playoffs				
Season	Club	Lea	GP	G	A	TP	PIM	GP	G	A	TP	PIM
1987-88	Ferris State	CCHA	40	26	27	53	22	....	....	....	....	....
1988-89	Ferris State	CCHA	23	9	19	28	4	....	....	....	....	....
1989-90	Ferris State	CCHA	38	22	35	57	12	....	....	....	....	....
1990-91	Ferris State	CCHA	40	14	47	61	12	....	....	....	....	....

DERKATCH, DALE

Center. Shoots right. 5'5", 150 lbs. Born, Preeceville, Sask., October 17, 1964.
(Edmonton's 6th choice, 140th overall, in 1983 Entry Draft).

			Regular Season					Playoffs				
Season	Club	Lea	GP	G	A	TP	PIM	GP	G	A	TP	PIM
1981-82	Regina	WHL	71	62	80	142	92	19	11	23	34	38
1982-83a	Regina	WHL	67	*84	95	*179	62	....	....	....	....	....
1983-84	Regina	WHL	62	72	87	159	92	23	12	*41	*53	54
1984-85	Regina	WHL	4	4	7	11	0	7	2	5	7	10
1985-86	Asiago	Italy	28	41	59	100	18	8	10	16	26	12
1986-87	Ilves	Fin.	44	24	31	55	57	....	....	....	....	....
1987-88	Ilves	Fin.	41	28	24	52	24	....	....	....	....	....
1988-89	Ilves	Fin.	44	36	30	66	49	5	2	1	3	4
1989-90	Munich	W.Ger.	28	27	31	58	30	....	....	....	....	....
1990-91	Munich	Ger.	55	48	66	114	48	....	....	....	....	....

a WHL First All-Star Team (1983)

DESCHAMPS, MARC

Defense. Shoots right. 6'3", 210 lbs. Born, Kapuskasing, Ont., September 29, 1970.
(Montreal's 6th choice, 104th overall, in 1989 Entry Draft).

			Regular Season					Playoffs				
Season	Club	Lea	GP	G	A	TP	PIM	GP	G	A	TP	PIM
1988-89	Cornell	ECAC	26	0	7	7	26	....	....	....	....	....
1989-90	Cornell	ECAC	13	0	2	2	10	....	....	....	....	....
1990-91	Cornell	ECAC	7	0	1	1	0	....	....	....	....	....

Traded to **Washington** by **Montreal** for Alain Cote, June 22, 1990.

DESJARDINS, ERIC (day-jar-DAN)

Defense. Shoots right. 6'1", 200 lbs. Born, Rouyn, Que., June 14, 1969.
(Montreal's 3rd choice, 38th overall, in 1987 Entry Draft).

			Regular Season					Playoffs				
Season	Club	Lea	GP	G	A	TP	PIM	GP	G	A	TP	PIM
1986-87a	Granby	QMJHL	66	14	24	38	178	8	3	2	5	10
1987-88	Sherbrooke	AHL	3	0	0	0	6	4	0	2	2	2
bc	Granby	QMJHL	62	18	49	67	138	5	0	3	3	10
1988-89	**Montreal**	**NHL**	**36**	**2**	**12**	**14**	**26**	**14**	**1**	**1**	**2**	**6**
1989-90	**Montreal**	**NHL**	**55**	**3**	**13**	**16**	**51**	**6**	**0**	**0**	**0**	**10**
1990-91	**Montreal**	**NHL**	**62**	**7**	**18**	**25**	**27**	**13**	**1**	**4**	**5**	**8**
	NHL Totals		**153**	**12**	**43**	**55**	**104**	**33**	**2**	**5**	**7**	**24**

a QMJHL Second All-Star Team (1987)
b QMJHL First All-Star Team (1988)
c QMJHL Top Defenseman (1988)

DESJARDINS, MARTIN (day-jar-DAN)

Center. Shoots left. 5'11", 179 lbs. Born, Ste-Rose, Que., January 28, 1967.
(Montreal's 5th choice, 75th overall, in 1985 Entry Draft).

			Regular Season					Playoffs				
Season	Club	Lea	GP	G	A	TP	PIM	GP	G	A	TP	PIM
1984-85	Trois Rivieres	QMJHL	66	29	34	63	76	7	4	6	10	6
1985-86	Trois Rivieres	QMJHL	71	49	69	118	103	4	2	4	6	4
1986-87	Trois Rivieres	QMJHL	52	32	52	84	77	....	....	....	....	....
	Longueuil	QMJHL	17	7	10	17	12	19	8	10	18	18
1987-88	Sherbrooke	AHL	75	34	36	70	117	5	1	1	2	8
1988-89	Sherbrooke	AHL	70	17	27	44	104	6	2	7	9	21
1989-90	**Montreal**	**NHL**	**8**	**0**	**2**	**2**	**2**	....	....	....	....	....
	Sherbrooke	AHL	65	21	26	47	72	12	4	*13	17	28
1990-91	Fredericton	AHL	2	0	1	1	6	....	....	....	....	....
	Indianapolis	IHL	71	15	42	57	110	7	2	1	3	8
	NHL Totals		**8**	**0**	**2**	**2**	**2**	....	....	....	....	....

Traded to **Chicago** by **Montreal** for future considerations, October 10, 1990.

DESJARDINS, NORMAN

Right wing. Shoots right. 5'10", 180 lbs. Born, Montreal, Que., March 25, 1968.

			Regular Season					Playoffs				
Season	Club	Lea	GP	G	A	TP	PIM	GP	G	A	TP	PIM
1986-87	Granby	QMJHL	52	19	22	41	61	....	....	....	....	....
	Verdun	QMJHL	14	3	5	8	45	....	....	....	....	....
1987-88	Verdun	QMJHL	69	31	44	75	95	....	....	....	....	....
1988-89	Longueuil	QMJHL	63	26	61	87	72	....	....	....	....	....
1989-90	Sherbrooke	AHL	58	13	19	32	91	12	4	3	7	15
1990-91	Fredericton	AHL	74	11	13	24	110	9	2	2	4	6

Signed as a free agent by **Montreal**, November 27, 1989.

DEVEREAUX, JOHN

Center. Shoots right. 6', 175 lbs. Born, Scituate, MA, June 8, 1965.
(Hartford's 4th choice, 173rd overall, in 1984 Entry Draft).

			Regular Season					Playoffs				
Season	Club	Lea	GP	G	A	TP	PIM	GP	G	A	TP	PIM
1984-85	Boston College	H.E.	19	3	3	6	6	....	....	....	....	....
1985-86	Boston College	H.E.	41	8	6	14	24	....	....	....	....	....
1986-87	Boston College	H.E.	39	14	20	34	16	....	....	....	....	....
1987-88	Boston College	H.E.	34	14	24	38	48	....	....	....	....	....
1988-89	Flint	IHL	11	3	1	4	11	....	....	....	....	....
1989-90	Winston-Salem	ECHL	58	22	48	70	110	8	1	2	3	11
1990-91	Winston-Salem	ECHL	57	20	37	57	47	....	....	....	....	....

DIDUCK, GERALD (DID-uck)

Defense. Shoots right. 6'2", 207 lbs. Born, Edmonton, Alta., April 6, 1965.
(NY Islanders' 2nd choice, 16th overall, in 1983 Entry Draft).

			Regular Season					Playoffs				
Season	Club	Lea	GP	G	A	TP	PIM	GP	G	A	TP	PIM
1981-82	Lethbridge	WHL	71	1	15	16	81	12	0	3	3	27
1982-83	Lethbridge	WHL	67	8	16	24	151	20	3	12	15	49
1983-84	Lethbridge	WHL	65	10	24	34	133	5	1	4	5	27
	Indianapolis	IHL	....	....	....	....	....	10	1	6	7	19
1984-85	**NY Islanders**	**NHL**	**65**	**2**	**8**	**10**	**80**	....	....	....	....	....
1985-86	**NY Islanders**	**NHL**	**10**	**1**	**2**	**3**	**2**	....	....	....	....	....
	Springfield	AHL	61	6	14	20	173	....	....	....	....	....
1986-87	**NY Islanders**	**NHL**	**30**	**2**	**3**	**5**	**67**	**14**	**0**	**1**	**1**	**35**
	Springfield	AHL	45	6	8	14	120	....	....	....	....	....
1987-88	**NY Islanders**	**NHL**	**68**	**7**	**12**	**19**	**113**	**6**	**1**	**0**	**1**	**42**
1988-89	**NY Islanders**	**NHL**	**65**	**11**	**21**	**32**	**155**	....	....	....	....	....
1989-90	**NY Islanders**	**NHL**	**76**	**3**	**17**	**20**	**163**	**5**	**0**	**0**	**0**	**12**
1990-91	**Montreal**	**NHL**	**32**	**1**	**2**	**3**	**39**	....	....	....	....	....
	Vancouver	**NHL**	**31**	**3**	**7**	**10**	**66**	**6**	**1**	**0**	**1**	**11**
	NHL Totals		**377**	**30**	**72**	**102**	**685**	**31**	**2**	**1**	**3**	**100**

Traded to **Montreal** by **NY Islanders** for Craig Ludwig, September 4, 1990. Traded to **Vancouver** by **Montreal** for Vancouver's fourth round choice (Vladimir Vujtek) in 1991 Entry Draft, January 12, 1991.

DiMAIO, ROBERT (ROB) (duh-MIGH-oh)

Center. Shoots right. 5'8", 175 lbs. Born, Calgary, Alta., February 19, 1968.
(NY Islanders' 6th choice, 118th overall, in 1987 Entry Draft).

			Regular Season					Playoffs				
Season	Club	Lea	GP	G	A	TP	PIM	GP	G	A	TP	PIM
1986-87	Medicine Hat	WHL	70	27	43	70	130	20	7	11	18	46
1987-88	Medicine Hat	WHL	54	47	43	90	120	14	12	19	*31	59
1988-89	**NY Islanders**	**NHL**	**16**	**1**	**0**	**1**	**30**	....	....	....	....	....
	Springfield	AHL	40	13	18	31	67	....	....	....	....	....
1989-90	**NY Islanders**	**NHL**	**7**	**0**	**0**	**0**	**2**	**1**	**1**	**0**	**1**	**4**
	Springfield	AHL	54	25	27	52	69	16	4	7	11	45
1990-91	**NY Islanders**	**NHL**	**1**	**0**	**0**	**0**	**0**	....	....	....	....	....
	Capital Dist.	AHL	12	3	4	7	22	....	....	....	....	....
	NHL Totals		**24**	**1**	**0**	**1**	**32**	**1**	**1**	**0**	**1**	**4**

DiMUZIO, FRANK

Left wing. Shoots right. 6', 195 lbs. Born, Toronto, Ont., August 12, 1967.
(Washington's 13th choice, 250th overall, in 1985 Entry Draft).

			Regular Season					Playoffs				
Season	Club	Lea	GP	G	A	TP	PIM	GP	G	A	TP	PIM
1984-85	Belleville	OHL	68	28	22	50	40	12	4	2	6	8
1985-86	Ottawa	OHL	63	29	26	55	105	....	....	....	....	....
1986-87a	Ottawa	OHL	61	*59	30	89	57	7	5	1	6	21
1987-88	Ottawa	OHL	48	51	44	95	96	16	9	11	20	34
1988-89	Baltimore	AHL	33	5	3	8	30	....	....	....	....	....
1989-90	Fiemme	Italy	28	13	8	21	21	10	8	4	12	6
1990-91	Fiemme	Italy	34	19	19	38	58	6	5	10	15	0

a OHL Third All-Star Team (1987)

DINEEN, GORDON (GORD)

Defense. Shoots right. 6', 195 lbs. Born, Quebec City, Que., September 21, 1962.
(NY Islanders' 2nd choice, 42nd overall, in 1981 Entry Draft).

			Regular Season					Playoffs				
Season	Club	Lea	GP	G	A	TP	PIM	GP	G	A	TP	PIM
1980-81	S. S. Marie	OHA	68	4	26	30	158	19	1	7	8	58
1981-82	S. S. Marie	OHL	68	9	45	54	185	13	1	2	3	52
1982-83	**NY Islanders**	**NHL**	**2**	**0**	**0**	**0**	**4**	....	....	....	....	....
abc	Indianapolis	CHL	73	10	47	57	78	13	2	10	12	29
1983-84	**NY Islanders**	**NHL**	**43**	**1**	**11**	**12**	**32**	**9**	**1**	**1**	**2**	**28**
	Indianapolis	CHL	26	4	13	17	63	....	....	....	....	....
1984-85	**NY Islanders**	**NHL**	**48**	**1**	**12**	**13**	**89**	**10**	**0**	**0**	**0**	**26**
	Springfield	AHL	25	1	8	9	46	....	....	....	....	....
1985-86	**NY Islanders**	**NHL**	**57**	**1**	**8**	**9**	**81**	**3**	**0**	**0**	**0**	**2**
	Springfield	AHL	11	2	3	5	20	....	....	....	....	....
1986-87	**NY Islanders**	**NHL**	**71**	**4**	**10**	**14**	**110**	**7**	**0**	**4**	**4**	**4**
1987-88	**NY Islanders**	**NHL**	**57**	**4**	**12**	**16**	**62**	....	....	....	....	....
	Minnesota	**NHL**	**13**	**1**	**1**	**2**	**21**	....	....	....	....	....
1988-89	**Minnesota**	**NHL**	**2**	**0**	**1**	**1**	**2**	....	....	....	....	....
	Kalamazoo	IHL	25	2	6	8	49	....	....	....	....	....
	Pittsburgh	**NHL**	**38**	**1**	**2**	**3**	**42**	**11**	**0**	**2**	**2**	**8**
1989-90	**Pittsburgh**	**NHL**	**69**	**1**	**8**	**9**	**125**	....	....	....	....	....
1990-91	**Pittsburgh**	**NHL**	**9**	**0**	**0**	**0**	**4**	....	....	....	....	....
	Muskegon	IHL	40	1	14	15	57	5	0	2	2	0
	NHL Totals		**409**	**14**	**65**	**79**	**572**	**40**	**1**	**7**	**8**	**68**

a CHL First All-Star Team (1983)
b Won Bob Gassoff Trophy (CHL's Most Improved Defenseman) (1983)
c Won Bobby Orr Trophy (CHL's Top Defenseman) (1983)

Traded to **Minnesota** by **NY Islanders** for Chris Pryor and future considerations, March 8, 1988. Traded to **Pittsburgh** by **Minnesota** with Scott Bjugstad for Ville Siren and Steve Gotaas, December 17, 1988.

DINEEN, KEVIN

Right wing. Shoots right. 5'11", 190 lbs. Born, Quebec City, Que., October 28, 1963.
(Hartford's 3rd choice, 56th overall, in 1982 Entry Draft).

			Regular Season					Playoffs				
Season	Club	Lea	GP	G	A	TP	PIM	GP	G	A	TP	PIM
1981-82	U. of Denver	WCHA	26	10	10	20	70	....	....	....	....	....
1982-83	U. of Denver	WCHA	36	16	13	29	108	....	....	....	....	....
1983-84	Cdn. Olympic	...	52	5	11	16	2	....	....	....	....	....
1984-85	**Hartford**	**NHL**	**57**	**25**	**16**	**41**	**120**	....	....	....	....	....
	Binghamton	AHL	25	15	8	23	41	....	....	....	....	....
1985-86	**Hartford**	**NHL**	**57**	**33**	**35**	**68**	**124**	**10**	**6**	**7**	**13**	**18**
1986-87	**Hartford**	**NHL**	**78**	**40**	**39**	**79**	**110**	**6**	**2**	**1**	**3**	**31**
1987-88	**Hartford**	**NHL**	**74**	**25**	**25**	**50**	**217**	**6**	**4**	**4**	**8**	**8**
1988-89	**Hartford**	**NHL**	**79**	**45**	**44**	**89**	**167**	**4**	**1**	**0**	**1**	**10**
1989-90	**Hartford**	**NHL**	**67**	**25**	**41**	**66**	**164**	**6**	**3**	**2**	**5**	**18**
1990-91a	**Hartford**	**NHL**	**61**	**17**	**30**	**47**	**104**	**6**	**1**	**0**	**1**	**16**
	NHL Totals		**473**	**210**	**230**	**440**	**1006**	**38**	**17**	**14**	**31**	**101**

a Won Bud Light/NHL Man of the Year Award (1991)

Played in NHL All-Star Game (1988, 1989)

DINEEN, PETER KEVIN

Defense. Shoots right. 5'11", 180 lbs. Born, Kingston, Ont., November 19, 1960.
(Philadelphia's 9th choice, 189th overall, in 1980 Entry Draft).

			Regular Season					Playoffs				
Season	Club	Lea	GP	G	A	TP	PIM	GP	G	A	TP	PIM
1977-78	Seattle	WHL	....	....	....	....	....	2	0	0	0	0
1978-79	Kingston	OHA	60	7	14	21	70	11	2	6	8	28
1979-80	Kingston	OHA	32	4	10	14	54	3	0	0	0	13
1980-81	Maine	AHL	41	6	7	13	100	16	1	2	3	82
1981-82	Maine	AHL	71	6	14	20	156	3	0	0	0	2
1982-83	Maine	AHL	2	0	0	0	0	....	....	....	....	....
	Moncton	AHL	57	0	10	10	76	....	....	....	....	....
1983-84	Moncton	AHL	63	0	10	10	120	....	....	....	....	....
	Hershey	AHL	12	0	1	1	32	....	....	....	....	....
1984-85	Hershey	AHL	79	4	19	23	144	....	....	....	....	....
1985-86	Binghamton	AHL	11	0	1	1	35	....	....	....	....	....
	Moncton	AHL	55	5	13	18	136	9	1	0	1	9
1986-87	**Los Angeles**	**NHL**	**11**	**0**	**2**	**2**	**8**	....	....	....	....	....
	New Haven	AHL	59	2	17	19	140	7	0	1	1	27
1987-88	Adirondack	AHL	76	8	26	34	137	11	0	2	2	20
1988-89	Adirondack	AHL	32	2	12	14	61	17	2	5	7	22
1989-90	**Detroit**	**NHL**	**2**	**0**	**0**	**0**	**5**	....	....	....	....	....
	Adirondack	AHL	27	3	6	9	28	6	0	1	1	10
1990-91	San Diego	IHL	24	0	1	1	17	....	....	....	....	....
	NHL Totals		**13**	**0**	**2**	**2**	**13**	....	....	....	....	....

Traded to **Edmonton** by **Philadelphia** for Bob Hoffmeyer, October 22, 1982. Signed as a free agent by **Boston**, July 16, 1984. Signed as a free agent by **Los Angeles**, July 30, 1986. Signed as a free agent by **Detroit**, September 16, 1987.

DIONNE, GILBERT

Left wing. Shoots left. 6', 194 lbs. Born, Drummondville, Que., September 19, 1970.
(Montreal's 5th choice, 81st overall, in 1990 Entry Draft).

			Regular Season					Playoffs				
Season	Club	Lea	GP	G	A	TP	PIM	GP	G	A	TP	PIM
1988-89	Kitchener	OHL	66	11	33	44	13	5	1	1	2	4
1989-90a	Kitchener	OHL	64	48	57	105	85	17	13	10	23	22
1990-91	**Montreal**	**NHL**	**2**	**0**	**0**	**0**	**0**	....	....	....	....	....
	Fredericton	AHL	77	40	47	87	62	9	6	5	11	8
	NHL Totals		**2**	**0**	**0**	**0**	**0**	....	....	....	....	....

a OHL Third All-Star Team (1990)

DI PIETRO, PAUL

Center. Shoots right. 5'9", 181 lbs. Born, Sault Ste-Marie, Ont., September 8, 1970.
(Montreal's 6th choice, 102nd overall, in 1990 Entry Draft).

			Regular Season					Playoffs				
Season	Club	Lea	GP	G	A	TP	PIM	GP	G	A	TP	PIM
1986-87	Sudbury	OHL	49	5	11	16	13	....	....	....	....	....
1987-88	Sudbury	OHL	63	25	42	67	27	....	....	....	....	....
1988-89	Sudbury	OHL	57	31	48	79	27	....	....	....	....	....
1989-90a	Sudbury	OHL	66	56	63	119	57	7	3	6	9	7
1990-91	Fredericton	AHL	78	39	31	70	38	9	5	6	11	2

a OHL Third All-Star Team (1990)

DIRK, ROBERT

Defense. Shoots left. 6'4", 218 lbs. Born, Regina, Sask., August 20, 1966.
(St. Louis' 4th choice, 53rd overall, in 1984 Entry Draft).

			Regular Season					Playoffs				
Season	Club	Lea	GP	G	A	TP	PIM	GP	G	A	TP	PIM
1982-83	Regina	WHL	1	0	0	0	0	....	....	....	....	....
1983-84	Regina	WHL	62	2	10	12	64	23	1	12	13	24
1984-85	Regina	WHL	69	10	34	44	97	8	0	0	0	4
1985-86	Regina	WHL	72	19	60	79	140	10	3	5	8	8
1986-87	Peoria	IHL	76	5	17	22	155	....	....	....	....	....
1987-88	**St. Louis**	**NHL**	**7**	**0**	**1**	**1**	**16**	**6**	**0**	**1**	**1**	**2**
	Peoria	IHL	54	4	21	25	126	....	....	....	....	....
1988-89	**St. Louis**	**NHL**	**9**	**0**	**1**	**1**	**11**	....	....	....	....	....
	Peoria	IHL	22	0	2	2	54	....	....	....	....	....
1989-90	**St. Louis**	**NHL**	**37**	**1**	**1**	**2**	**128**	**3**	**0**	**0**	**0**	**0**
	Peoria	IHL	24	1	2	3	79	....	....	....	....	....
1990-91	**St. Louis**	**NHL**	**41**	**1**	**3**	**4**	**100**	....	....	....	....	....
	Peoria	IHL	3	0	0	0	2	....	....	....	....	....
	Vancouver	**NHL**	**11**	**1**	**0**	**1**	**20**	**6**	**0**	**0**	**0**	**13**
	NHL Totals		**105**	**3**	**6**	**9**	**375**	**15**	**0**	**1**	**1**	**15**

Traded to **Vancouver** by **St. Louis** with Geoff Courtnall, Sergio Momesso, Cliff Ronning and future considerations for Dan Quinn and Garth Butcher, March 5, 1991.

DI VITA, DAVID

Defense. Shoots left. 6'2", 205 lbs. Born, St. Clair Shores, MI, February 3, 1969.
(Buffalo's 6th choice, 106th overall, in 1988 Entry Draft).

			Regular Season					Playoffs				
Season	Club	Lea	GP	G	A	TP	PIM	GP	G	A	TP	PIM
1987-88	Lake Superior	CCHA	26	1	0	1	20	....	....	....	....	....
1988-89	Lake Superior	CCHA	25	1	4	5	28	....	....	....	....	....
1989-90	Lake Superior	CCHA	46	4	12	16	58	....	....	....	....	....
1990-91	Lake Superior	CCHA	43	3	5	8	63	....	....	....	....	....

DJOOS, PER (JUICE)

Defense. Shoots right. 5'11", 176 lbs. Born, Mora, Sweden, May 11, 1968.
(Detroit's 7th choice, 127th overall, in 1986 Entry Draft).

			Regular Season					Playoffs				
Season	Club	Lea	GP	G	A	TP	PIM	GP	G	A	TP	PIM
1986-87	Brynas	Swe.	23	1	2	3	16	....	....	....	....	....
1987-88	Brynas	Swe.	34	4	11	15	18	....	....	....	....	....
1988-89	Brynas	Swe.	40	1	17	18	44	....	....	....	....	....
1989-90	Brynas	Swe.	37	5	13	18	34	5	1	3	4	6
1990-91	**Detroit**	**NHL**	**26**	**0**	**12**	**12**	**16**	....	....	....	....	....
	Adirondack	AHL	20	2	9	11	6	....	....	....	....	....
	Binghamton	AHL	14	1	8	9	10	9	2	2	4	4
	NHL Totals		**26**	**0**	**12**	**12**	**16**	....	....	....	....	....

Traded to **NY Rangers** by **Detroit** with Joey Kocur for Kevin Miller, Jim Cummins and Dennis Vial, March 5, 1991.

DOBBIN, BRIAN

Right wing. Shoots right. 5'11", 205 lbs. Born, Petrolia, Ont., August 18, 1966.
(Philadelphia's 7th choice, 100th overall, in 1984 Entry Draft).

			Regular Season					Playoffs				
Season	Club	Lea	GP	G	A	TP	PIM	GP	G	A	TP	PIM
1982-83	Kingston	OHL	69	16	39	55	35	....	....	....	....	....
1983-84	London	OHL	70	30	40	70	70	....	....	....	....	....
1984-85	London	OHL	53	42	57	99	63	8	7	4	11	2
1985-86	London	OHL	59	38	55	93	113	5	2	1	3	9
	Hershey	AHL	2	1	0	1	0	18	5	5	10	21
1986-87	**Philadelphia**	**NHL**	**12**	**2**	**1**	**3**	**14**	....	....	....	....	....
	Hershey	AHL	52	26	35	61	66	5	4	2	6	15
1987-88	**Philadelphia**	**NHL**	**21**	**3**	**5**	**8**	**6**	....	....	....	....	....
	Hershey	AHL	54	36	47	83	58	12	7	8	15	15
1988-89	**Philadelphia**	**NHL**	**14**	**0**	**1**	**1**	**8**	**2**	**0**	**0**	**0**	**17**
a	Hershey	AHL	59	43	48	91	61	11	7	6	13	12
1989-90	**Philadelphia**	**NHL**	**9**	**1**	**1**	**2**	**11**	....	....	....	....	....
b	Hershey	AHL	68	38	47	85	58	....	....	....	....	....
1990-91	Hershey	AHL	80	35	43	78	82	7	1	2	3	7
	NHL Totals		**56**	**6**	**8**	**14**	**39**	**2**	**0**	**0**	**0**	**17**

a AHL First All-Star Team (1989)
b AHL Second All-Star Team (1990)

DOLLAS, BOBBY

Defense. Shoots left. 6'2", 212 lbs. Born, Montreal, Que., January 31, 1965.
(Winnipeg's 2nd choice, 14th overall, in 1983 Entry Draft).

			Regular Season					Playoffs				
Season	Club	Lea	GP	G	A	TP	PIM	GP	G	A	TP	PIM
1982-83a	Laval	QMJHL	63	16	45	61	144	11	5	5	10	23
1983-84	**Winnipeg**	**NHL**	**1**	**0**	**0**	**0**	**0**	....	....	....	....	....
	Laval	QMJHL	54	12	33	45	80	14	1	8	9	23
1984-85	**Winnipeg**	**NHL**	**9**	**0**	**0**	**0**	**0**	....	....	....	....	....
	Sherbrooke	AHL	8	1	3	4	4	17	3	6	9	17
1985-86	**Winnipeg**	**NHL**	**46**	**0**	**5**	**5**	**66**	**3**	**0**	**0**	**0**	**2**
	Sherbrooke	AHL	25	4	7	11	29	....	....	....	....	....
1986-87	Sherbrooke	AHL	75	6	18	24	87	16	2	4	6	13
1987-88	**Quebec**	**NHL**	**9**	**0**	**0**	**0**	**2**	....	....	....	....	....
	Moncton	AHL	26	4	10	14	20	....	....	....	....	....
	Fredericton	AHL	33	4	8	12	27	15	2	2	4	24
1988-89	**Quebec**	**NHL**	**16**	**0**	**3**	**3**	**16**	....	....	....	....	....
	Halifax	AHL	57	5	19	24	65	4	1	0	1	14
1989-90	Cdn. National	...	68	8	29	37	60	....	....	....	....	....
1990-91	**Detroit**	**NHL**	**56**	**3**	**5**	**8**	**20**	**7**	**1**	**0**	**1**	**13**
	NHL Totals		**137**	**3**	**13**	**16**	**104**	**10**	**1**	**0**	**1**	**15**

a QMJHL Second All-Star Team (1983).

Traded to **Quebec** by **Winnipeg** for Stu Kulak, December 17, 1987. Signed as a free agent by **Detroit**, October 18, 1990.

DOMI, TAHIR (TIE) (DOH-mee)

Right wing. Shoots right. 5'10", 200 lbs. Born, Windsor, Ont., November 1, 1969.
(Toronto's 2nd choice, 27th overall, in 1988 Entry Draft).

			Regular Season					Playoffs				
Season	Club	Lea	GP	G	A	TP	PIM	GP	G	A	TP	PIM
1986-87	Peterborough	OHL	18	1	1	2	79	....	....	....	....	....
1987-88	Peterborough	OHL	60	22	21	43	292	12	3	9	12	24
1988-89	Peterborough	OHL	43	14	16	30	175	17	10	9	19	70
1989-90	**Toronto**	**NHL**	**2**	**0**	**0**	**0**	**42**	....	....	....	....	....
	Newmarket	AHL	57	14	11	25	285	....	....	....	....	....
1990-91	**NY Rangers**	**NHL**	**28**	**1**	**0**	**1**	**185**	....	....	....	....	....
	Binghamton	AHL	25	11	6	17	219	7	3	2	5	16
	NHL Totals		**30**	**1**	**0**	**1**	**227**	....	....	....	....	....

Traded to **NY Rangers** by **Toronto** with Mark Laforest for Greg Johnston, June 28, 1990.

DONATELLI, CLARK

Left wing. Shoots left. 5'10", 180 lbs. Born, Providence, RI, November 22, 1967.
(NY Rangers' 4th choice, 98th overall, in 1984 Entry Draft).

			Regular Season					Playoffs				
Season	Club	Lea	GP	G	A	TP	PIM	GP	G	A	TP	PIM
1984-85	Boston U.	H.E.	40	17	18	35	46	....	....	....	....	....
1985-86ab	Boston U.	H.E.	43	28	34	62	30	....	....	....	....	....
1986-87	Boston U.	H.E.	37	15	23	38	46	....	....	....	....	....
1987-88	U.S. National	....	50	11	27	38	26	....	....	....	....	....
	U.S. Olympic		6	2	1	3	5					
1988-89			DID NOT PLAY									
1989-90	**Minnesota**	**NHL**	**25**	**3**	**3**	**6**	**17**	....	....	....	....	....
	Kalamazoo	IHL	27	8	9	17	47	4	0	2	2	12
1990-91	San Diego	IHL	46	17	10	27	45	....	....	....	....	....
	NHL Totals		**25**	**3**	**3**	**6**	**17**	....	....	....	....	....

a NCAA East Second All-American Team (1986)
b Hockey East Second All-Star Team (1986)

Traded to **Edmonton** by **NY Rangers** with Ville Kentala, Reijo Ruotsalainen and Jim Wiemer for Mike Golden, Don Jackson and Miloslav Horava, October 2, 1986. Signed as a free agent by **Minnesota**, June 20, 1989.

DONATO, TED

Center. Shoots left. 5'10", 170 lbs. Born, Dedham, MA, April 28, 1968.
(Boston's 6th choice, 98th overall, in 1987 Entry Draft).

			Regular Season					Playoffs				
Season	Club	Lea	GP	G	A	TP	PIM	GP	G	A	TP	PIM
1987-88	Harvard	ECAC	28	12	14	26	24	....	....	....	....	....
1988-89	Harvard	ECAC	34	14	37	51	30	....	....	....	....	....
1989-90	Harvard	ECAC	16	5	6	11	34	....	....	....	....	....
1990-91a	Harvard	ECAC	27	19	*37	56	26	....	....	....	....	....

a ECAC First All-Star Team (1991)

DONNELLY, GORDON (GORD)

Defense. Shoots right. 6'1", 202 lbs. Born, Montreal, Que., April 5, 1962.
(St. Louis' 3rd choice, 62nd overall, in 1981 Entry Draft).

			Regular Season					Playoffs				
Season	Club	Lea	GP	G	A	TP	PIM	GP	G	A	TP	PIM
1980-81	Sherbrooke	QMJHL	67	15	23	38	252	14	1	2	3	35
1981-82	Sherbrooke	QMJHL	60	8	41	49	250	22	2	7	9	106
1982-83	Salt Lake	CHL	67	3	12	15	222	6	1	1	2	8
1983-84	**Quebec**	**NHL**	**38**	**0**	**5**	**5**	**60**	....	....	....	....	....
	Fredericton	AHL	30	2	3	5	146	7	1	1	2	43
1984-85	**Quebec**	**NHL**	**22**	**0**	**0**	**0**	**33**	....	....	....	....	....
	Fredericton	AHL	42	1	5	6	134	6	0	1	1	25
1985-86	**Quebec**	**NHL**	**36**	**2**	**2**	**4**	**85**	**1**	**0**	**0**	**0**	**0**
	Fredericton	AHL	38	3	5	8	103	5	0	0	0	33
1986-87	**Quebec**	**NHL**	**38**	**0**	**2**	**2**	**143**	**13**	**0**	**0**	**0**	**53**
1987-88	**Quebec**	**NHL**	**63**	**4**	**3**	**7**	**301**	....	....	....	....	....
1988-89	**Quebec**	**NHL**	**16**	**4**	**0**	**4**	**46**	....	....	....	....	....
	Winnipeg	**NHL**	**57**	**6**	**10**	**16**	**228**	....	....	....	....	....
1989-90	**Winnipeg**	**NHL**	**55**	**3**	**3**	**6**	**222**	**6**	**0**	**1**	**1**	**8**
1990-91	**Winnipeg**	**NHL**	**57**	**3**	**4**	**7**	**265**	....	....	....	....	....
	NHL Totals		**382**	**22**	**29**	**51**	**1383**	**20**	**0**	**1**	**1**	**61**

Rights transferred to **Quebec** by **St. Louis** with rights to Claude Julien when St. Louis signed Jacques Demers as coach, August 19, 1983. Traded to **Winnipeg** by **Quebec** for Mario Marois, December 6, 1988.

DONNELLY, MIKE

Left wing. Shoots left. 5'11", 185 lbs. Born, Detroit, MI, October 10, 1963.

			Regular Season					Playoffs				
Season	Club	Lea	GP	G	A	TP	PIM	GP	G	A	TP	PIM
1982-83	Michigan State	CCHA	24	7	13	20	8	....	....	....	....	....
1983-84	Michigan State	CCHA	44	18	14	32	40	....	....	....	....	....
1984-85	Michigan State	CCHA	44	26	21	47	48	....	....	....	....	....
1985-86ab	Michigan State	CCHA	44	59	38	97	65	....	....	....	....	....
1986-87	**NY Rangers**	**NHL**	**5**	**1**	**1**	**2**	**0**	....	....	....	....	....
	New Haven	AHL	58	27	34	61	52	7	2	0	2	9
1987-88	**NY Rangers**	**NHL**	**17**	**2**	**2**	**4**	**8**	....	....	....	....	....
	Colorado	IHL	8	7	11	18	15	....	....	....	....	....
	Buffalo	**NHL**	**40**	**6**	**8**	**14**	**44**	....	....	....	....	....
1988-89	**Buffalo**	**NHL**	**22**	**4**	**6**	**10**	**10**	....	....	....	....	....
	Rochester	AHL	53	32	37	69	53	....	....	....	....	....
1989-90	**Buffalo**	**NHL**	**12**	**1**	**2**	**3**	**8**	....	....	....	....	....
	Rochester	AHL	68	43	55	98	71	16	*12	7	19	9
1990-91	**Los Angeles**	**NHL**	**53**	**7**	**5**	**12**	**41**	**12**	**5**	**4**	**9**	**6**
	New Haven	AHL	18	10	6	16	2	....	....	....	....	....
	NHL Totals		**149**	**21**	**24**	**45**	**111**	**12**	**5**	**4**	**9**	**6**

a CCHA First All-Star Team (1986)
b NCAA West First All-American Team (1986)

Signed as a free agent by **NY Rangers**, August 15, 1986. Traded to **Buffalo** by **NY Rangers** with Rangers' fifth round choice (Alexander Mogilny) in 1988 Entry Draft for Paul Cyr and Buffalo's tenth round choice (Eric Fenton) in 1988 Entry Draft, December 31, 1987. Traded to **Los Angeles** by **Buffalo** for Mikko Makela, September 30, 1990.

DOOLEY, SEAN

Defense. Shoots left. 6'3", 215 lbs. Born, Ipswich, MA, March 22, 1969.
(Buffalo's 8th choice, 148th overall, in 1987 Entry Draft).

			Regular Season					Playoffs				
Season	Club	Lea	GP	G	A	TP	PIM	GP	G	A	TP	PIM
1987-88	Merrimack	NCAA	3	0	0	0	0	....	....	....	....	....
1988-89	Merrimack	NCAA	19	2	8	10	10	....	....	....	....	....
1989-90	Merrimack	H.E.	22	1	2	3	31	....	....	....	....	....
1990-91	Merrimack	H.E.	7	0	3	3	12	....	....	....	....	....

DORE, DANIEL

Right wing. Shoots right. 6'3", 202 lbs. Born, Ferme-Neuve, Que., April 9, 1970.
(Quebec's 2nd choice, 5th overall, in 1988 Entry Draft).

			Regular Season					Playoffs				
Season	Club	Lea	GP	G	A	TP	PIM	GP	G	A	TP	PIM
1986-87	Drummondville	QMJHL	68	23	41	64	229	8	0	1	1	18
1987-88	Drummondville	QMJHL	64	24	39	63	218	17	7	11	18	42
1988-89	Drummondville	QMJHL	62	33	58	91	236	4	2	3	5	14
1989-90	**Quebec**	**NHL**	**16**	**2**	**3**	**5**	**59**	....	....	....	....	....
	Chicoutimi	QMJHL	24	6	23	29	112	6	0	3	3	27
1990-91	**Quebec**	**NHL**	**1**	**0**	**0**	**0**	**0**	....	....	....	....	....
	Halifax	AHL	50	7	10	17	139	....	....	....	....	....
	NHL Totals		**17**	**2**	**3**	**5**	**59**	....	....	....	....	....

DORION, DAN

Right wing. Shoots right. 5'9", 180 lbs. Born, Astoria, NY, March 2, 1963.
(New Jersey's 13th choice, 232nd overall, in 1982 Entry Draft).

			Regular Season					Playoffs				
Season	Club	Lea	GP	G	A	TP	PIM	GP	G	A	TP	PIM
1982-83	W. Michigan	CCHA	34	11	20	31	23	....	....	....	....	....
1983-84	W. Michigan	CCHA	42	41	50	91	42	....	....	....	....	....
1984-85	W. Michigan	CCHA	39	21	46	67	28	....	....	....	....	....
1985-86abc	W. Michigan	CCHA	42	42	62	104	48	....	....	....	....	....
	New Jersey	**NHL**	**3**	**1**	**1**	**2**	**0**	....	....	....	....	....
	Maine	AHL	....	....	....	....	....	5	2	2	4	0
1986-87	Maine	AHL	70	16	22	38	47	....	....	....	....	....
1987-88	**New Jersey**	**NHL**	**1**	**0**	**0**	**0**	**2**	....	....	....	....	....
	Utica	AHL	65	30	35	65	98	....	....	....	....	....
1988-89	Maine	AHL	16	2	3	5	13	....	....	....	....	....
	Utica	AHL	15	7	4	11	19	....	....	....	....	....
1989-90	Fiemme	Italy	29	37	32	69	66	1	1	0	1	0
1990-91			UNAVAILABLE									
	NHL Totals		**4**	**1**	**1**	**2**	**2**	....	....	....	....	....

a NCAA West First All-American Team (1986)
b CCHA First All-Star Team (1986)
c CCHA Player of the Year (1986)

Traded to **Boston** by **New Jersey** for Jean-Marc Lanthier, December 9, 1988.

D'ORSONNENS, MARTIN

Defense. Shoots left. 5'11", 185 lbs. Born, Repentigny, Que., February 11, 1972.
(Hartford's 7th choice, 162nd overall, in 1990 Entry Draft).

			Regular Season					Playoffs				
Season	Club	Lea	GP	G	A	TP	PIM	GP	G	A	TP	PIM
1989-90	Clarkson	ECAC	35	5	8	13	81	....	....	....	....	....
1990-91	Clarkson	ECAC	39	2	8	10	84	....	....	....	....	....

DOUCET, WAYNE

Left wing. Shoots left. 6'2", 203 lbs. Born, Etobicoke, Ont., June 19, 1970.
(NY Islanders' 2nd choice, 29th overall, in 1988 Entry Draft).

			Regular Season					Playoffs				
Season	Club	Lea	GP	G	A	TP	PIM	GP	G	A	TP	PIM
1986-87	Sudbury	OHL	64	20	28	48	85	....	....	....	....	....
1987-88	Sudbury	OHL	23	9	4	13	53	....	....	....	....	....
	Hamilton	OHL	37	11	14	25	74	1	0	0	0	8
1988-89	Springfield	AHL	6	2	2	4	4	....	....	....	....	....
	Niagara Falls	OHL	11	3	2	5	58	....	....	....	....	....
	Kingston	OHL	53	22	29	51	193	....	....	....	....	....
1989-90	Kingston	OHL	66	32	47	79	127	7	2	5	7	18
1990-91	Capital Dist.	AHL	21	11	6	17	93	....	....	....	....	....

DOURIS, PETER

Right wing. Shoots right. 6'1", 195 lbs. Born, Toronto, Ont., February 19, 1966.
(Winnipeg's 1st choice, 30th overall, in 1984 Entry Draft).

			Regular Season					Playoffs				
Season	Club	Lea	GP	G	A	TP	PIM	GP	G	A	TP	PIM
1983-84	N. Hampshire	ECAC	37	19	15	34	14	....	....	....	....	....
1984-85	N. Hampshire	H.E.	42	27	24	51	34	....	....	....	....	....
1985-86	**Winnipeg**	**NHL**	**11**	**0**	**0**	**0**	**0**	....	....	....	....	....
	Cdn. Olympic	...	33	16	7	23	18	....	....	....	....	....
1986-87	**Winnipeg**	**NHL**	**6**	**0**	**0**	**0**	**0**	....	....	....	....	....
	Sherbrooke	AHL	62	14	28	42	24	17	7	*15	*22	16
1987-88	**Winnipeg**	**NHL**	**4**	**0**	**2**	**2**	**0**	**1**	**0**	**0**	**0**	**0**
	Moncton	AHL	73	42	37	79	53	....	....	....	....	....
1988-89	Peoria	IHL	81	28	41	69	32	4	1	2	3	0
1989-90	**Boston**	**NHL**	**36**	**5**	**6**	**11**	**15**	**8**	**0**	**1**	**1**	**8**
	Maine	AHL	38	17	20	37	14	....	....	....	....	....
1990-91	**Boston**	**NHL**	**39**	**5**	**2**	**7**	**9**	**7**	**0**	**1**	**1**	**6**
	Maine	AHL	35	16	15	31	9	2	3	0	3	2
	NHL Totals		**96**	**10**	**10**	**20**	**24**	**16**	**0**	**2**	**2**	**14**

Traded to **St. Louis** by **Winnipeg** for Kent Carlson and St. Louis' twelfth-round choice (Sergei Kharin) in 1989 Entry Draft and St. Louis' fourth-round choice (Scott Levins) in 1990 Entry Draft, September 29, 1988. Signed as a free agent by **Boston**, June 27, 1989.

DOWD, JAMES (JIM)

Right wing. Shoots right. 6'1", 185 lbs. Born, Brick, NJ, December 25, 1968.
(New Jersey's 7th choice, 149th overall, in 1987 Entry Draft).

			Regular Season					Playoffs				
Season	Club	Lea	GP	G	A	TP	PIM	GP	G	A	TP	PIM
1987-88	Lake Superior	CCHA	45	18	27	45	16	....	....	....	....	....
1988-89	Lake Superior	CCHA	46	24	35	59	40	....	....	....	....	....
1989-90ab	Lake Superior	CCHA	46	25	*67	92	30	....	....	....	....	....
1990-91cde	Lake Superior	CCHA	44	24	*54	*78	53	....	....	....	....	....

a CCHA Second All-Star Team (1990)
b NCAA West Second All-American Team (1990)
c CCHA Player of the Year (1991)
d CCHA First All-Star Team (1991)
e NCAA West First All-American Team (1991)

DOYON, MARIO (doh-YAWN)

Defense. Shoots right. 6', 174 lbs. Born, Quebec City, Que., August 27, 1968.
(Chicago's 5th choice, 119th overall, in 1986 Entry Draft).

			Regular Season					Playoffs				
Season	Club	Lea	GP	G	A	TP	PIM	GP	G	A	TP	PIM
1985-86	Drummondville	QMJHL	71	5	14	19	129	23	5	4	9	32
1986-87	Drummondville	QMJHL	65	18	47	65	150	8	1	3	4	30
1987-88	Drummondville	QMJHL	68	23	54	77	233	17	3	14	17	46
1988-89	**Chicago**	**NHL**	**7**	**1**	**1**	**2**	**6**	....	....	....	....	....
	Saginaw	IHL	71	16	32	48	69	6	0	0	0	8
1989-90	Indianapolis	IHL	66	9	25	34	50	....	....	....	....	....
	Quebec	**NHL**	**9**	**2**	**3**	**5**	**6**	....	....	....	....	....
	Halifax	AHL	5	1	2	3	0	6	1	3	4	2
1990-91	**Quebec**	**NHL**	**12**	**0**	**0**	**0**	**4**	....	....	....	....	....
	Halifax	AHL	59	14	23	37	58	....	....	....	....	....
	NHL Totals		**28**	**3**	**4**	**7**	**16**	....	....	....	....	....

Traded to **Quebec** by **Chicago** with Everett Sanipass and Dan Vincelette for Greg Millen, Michel Goulet and Quebec's sixth round choice (Kevin St. Jacques) in 1991 Entry Draft, March 5, 1990.

DRAGON, JOE

Right wing. Shoots right. 5'11", 180 lbs.　Born, Fort Smith, N.W.T., February 20, 1969.
(Pittsburgh's 1st choice, 5th overall, in 1990 Supplemental Draft).

				Regular Season					Playoffs			
Season	Club	Lea	GP	G	A	TP	PIM	GP	G	A	TP	PIM
1988-89	Cornell	ECAC	3	1	1	2	2	.....	.....	.....	.....	.....
1989-90	Cornell	ECAC	29	15	24	39	26	.....	.....	.....	.....	.....
1990-91	Cornell	ECAC	32	8	18	26	46	.....	.....	.....	.....	.....

DRAKE, DALLAS

Center. Shoots left. 6', 163 lbs.　Born, Trail, B.C., February 4, 1969.
(Detroit's 6th choice, 116th overall, in 1989 Entry Draft).

				Regular Season					Playoffs			
Season	Club	Lea	GP	G	A	TP	PIM	GP	G	A	TP	PIM
1988-89	N. Michigan	WCHA	38	17	22	39	22	.....	.....	.....	.....	.....
1989-90	N. Michigan	WCHA	46	13	24	37	42	.....	.....	.....	.....	.....
1990-91	N. Michigan	WCHA	44	22	36	58	89	.....	.....	.....	.....	.....

DRAPER, KRIS

Center. Shoots left. 5'11", 190 lbs.　Born, Toronto, Ont., May 24, 1971.
(Winnipeg's 4th choice, 62nd overall, in 1989 Entry Draft).

				Regular Season					Playoffs			
Season	Club	Lea	GP	G	A	TP	PIM	GP	G	A	TP	PIM
1988-89	Cdn. National	...	60	11	15	26	16	.....	.....	.....	.....	.....
1989-90	Cdn. National	...	61	12	22	34	44	.....	.....	.....	.....	.....
1990-91	**Winnipeg**	**NHL**	3	1	0	1	5	.....	.....	.....	.....	.....
	Ottawa	OHL	39	19	42	61	35	17	8	11	19	20
	Moncton	AHL	7	2	1	3	2	.....	.....	.....	.....	.....
	NHL Totals		3	1	0	1	5	.....	.....	.....	.....	.....

DRIVER, BRUCE

Defense. Shoots left. 6', 185 lbs.　Born, Toronto, Ont., April 29, 1962.
(Colorado's 6th choice, 108th overall, in 1981 Entry Draft).

				Regular Season					Playoffs			
Season	Club	Lea	GP	G	A	TP	PIM	GP	G	A	TP	PIM
1980-81	U. Wisconsin	WCHA	42	5	15	20	42	.....	.....	.....	.....	.....
1981-82ab	U. Wisconsin	WCHA	46	7	37	44	84	.....	.....	.....	.....	.....
1982-83	U. Wisconsin	WCHA	49	19	42	61	100	.....	.....	.....	.....	.....
1983-84	Cdn. Olympic	...	61	11	17	28	44	.....	.....	.....	.....	.....
	New Jersey	**NHL**	4	0	2	2	0	.....	.....	.....	.....	.....
	Maine	AHL	12	2	6	8	15	16	0	10	10	8
1984-85	**New Jersey**	**NHL**	67	9	23	32	36	.....	.....	.....	.....	.....
1985-86	**New Jersey**	**NHL**	40	3	15	18	32	.....	.....	.....	.....	.....
	Maine	AHL	15	4	7	11	16	.....	.....	.....	.....	.....
1986-87	**New Jersey**	**NHL**	74	6	28	34	36	.....	.....	.....	.....	.....
1987-88	**New Jersey**	**NHL**	74	15	40	55	68	20	3	7	10	14
1988-89	**New Jersey**	**NHL**	27	1	15	16	24	.....	.....	.....	.....	.....
1989-90	**New Jersey**	**NHL**	75	7	46	53	63	6	1	5	6	6
1990-91	**New Jersey**	**NHL**	73	9	36	45	62	7	1	2	3	12
	NHL Totals		434	50	205	255	321	33	5	14	19	32

a WCHA First All-Team (1982)
b NCAA All-Tournament Team (1982)

DROPPA, IVAN

Defense. Shoots left. 6'2", 209 lbs.　Born, Liptovsky, Mikulas, Czech., February 1, 1972.
(Chicago's 2nd choice, 37th overall, in 1990 Entry Draft).

				Regular Season					Playoffs			
Season	Club	Lea	GP	G	A	TP	PIM	GP	G	A	TP	PIM
1990-91	VSZ Kosice	Czech.	49	1	7	8	12	.....	.....	.....	.....	.....

DRUCE, JOHN

Right wing. Shoots right. 6'1", 200 lbs.　Born, Peterborough, Ont., February 23, 1966.
(Washington's 2nd choice, 40th overall, in 1985 Entry Draft).

				Regular Season					Playoffs			
Season	Club	Lea	GP	G	A	TP	PIM	GP	G	A	TP	PIM
1984-85	Peterborough	OHL	54	12	14	26	90	17	6	2	8	21
1985-86	Peterborough	OHL	49	22	24	46	84	16	0	5	5	34
1986-87	Binghamton	AHL	77	13	9	22	131	12	0	3	3	28
1987-88	Binghamton	AHL	68	32	29	61	82	1	0	0	0	0
1988-89	**Washington**	**NHL**	48	8	7	15	62	1	0	0	0	0
	Baltimore	AHL	16	2	11	13	10	.....	.....	.....	.....	.....
1989-90	**Washington**	**NHL**	45	8	3	11	52	15	14	3	17	23
	Baltimore	AHL	26	15	16	31	38	.....	.....	.....	.....	.....
1990-91	**Washington**	**NHL**	80	22	36	58	46	11	1	1	2	7
	NHL Totals		173	38	46	84	160	27	15	4	19	30

DRULIA, STAN

Right wing. Shoots right. 5'11", 190 lbs.　Born, Elmira, NY, January 5, 1968.
(Pittsburgh's 11th choice, 214th overall, in 1986 Entry Draft).

				Regular Season					Playoffs			
Season	Club	Lea	GP	G	A	TP	PIM	GP	G	A	TP	PIM
1985-86	Belleville	OHL	66	43	36	79	73	.....	.....	.....	.....	.....
1986-87	Hamilton	OHL	55	27	51	78	26	.....	.....	.....	.....	.....
1987-88a	Hamilton	OHL	65	52	69	121	44	14	8	16	24	12
1988-89	Maine	AHL	3	1	1	2	0	.....	.....	.....	.....	.....
b	Niagara Falls	OHL	47	52	93	145	59	17	11	*26	37	18
1989-90	Phoenix	IHL	16	6	3	9	2	.....	.....	.....	.....	.....
	Cape Breton	AHL	31	5	7	12	2	.....	.....	.....	.....	.....
1990-91cd	Knoxville	ECHL	64	*63	77	*140	39	3	3	2	5	4

a OHL Third All-Star Team (1988)
b OHL First All-Star Team (1989)
c MVP — ECHL (1991)
d ECHL First All-Star Team (1991)

Signed as a free agent by **Edmonton**, February 24, 1989.

DRURY, TED

Center. Shoots left. 6', 185 lbs.　Born, Boston, MA, September 13, 1971.
(Calgary's 2nd choice, 42nd overall, in 1989 Entry Draft).

				Regular Season					Playoffs			
Season	Club	Lea	GP	G	A	TP	PIM	GP	G	A	TP	PIM
1989-90	Harvard	ECAC	17	9	13	22	10	.....	.....	.....	.....	.....
1990-91	Harvard	ECAC	25	18	18	36	22	.....	.....	.....	.....	.....

DUBERMAN, JUSTIN

Right wing. Shoots right. 6', 185 lbs.　Born, New Haven, CT, March 23, 1970.
(Montreal's 11th choice, 230th overall, in 1989 Entry Draft).

				Regular Season					Playoffs			
Season	Club	Lea	GP	G	A	TP	PIM	GP	G	A	TP	PIM
1988-89	North Dakota	WCHA	33	3	1	4	30	.....	.....	.....	.....	.....
1989-90	North Dakota	WCHA	42	10	9	19	50	.....	.....	.....	.....	.....
1990-91	North Dakota	WCHA	42	19	18	37	68	.....	.....	.....	.....	.....

DUBINSKY, STEVE

Center. Shoots left. 6', 180 lbs.　Born, Montreal, Que., July 9, 1970.
(Chicago's 9th choice, 226th overall, in 1990 Entry Draft).

				Regular Season					Playoffs			
Season	Club	Lea	GP	G	A	TP	PIM	GP	G	A	TP	PIM
1989-90	Clarkson	ECAC	35	7	10	17	24	.....	.....	.....	.....	.....
1990-91	Clarkson	ECAC	39	13	23	36	26	.....	.....	.....	.....	.....

DUBOIS, ERIC

Defense. Shoots right. 6', 193 lbs.　Born, Montreal, Que., May 9, 1970.
(Quebec's 6th choice, 76th overall, in 1989 Entry Draft).

				Regular Season					Playoffs			
Season	Club	Lea	GP	G	A	TP	PIM	GP	G	A	TP	PIM
1986-87	Laval	QMJHL	61	1	17	18	29	.....	.....	.....	.....	.....
1987-88	Laval	QMJHL	69	8	32	40	132	14	1	7	8	12
1988-89	Laval	QMJHL	68	15	44	59	126	17	1	11	12	55
1989-90	Laval	QMJHL	66	9	36	45	153	13	3	8	11	29
1990-91	Laval	QMJHL	57	15	45	60	122	13	3	5	8	29

DUCHESNE, GAETAN　(doo SHAYN)

Left wing. Shoots left. 5'11", 200 lbs.　Born, Les Saulles, Que., July 11, 1962.
(Washington's 8th choice, 152nd overall, in 1981 Entry Draft).

				Regular Season					Playoffs			
Season	Club	Lea	GP	G	A	TP	PIM	GP	G	A	TP	PIM
1979-80	Quebec	QJHL	46	9	28	37	22	5	0	2	2	9
1980-81	Quebec	QJHL	72	27	45	72	63	7	1	4	5	6
1981-82	**Washington**	**NHL**	74	9	14	23	46	.....	.....	.....	.....	.....
1982-83	**Washington**	**NHL**	77	18	19	37	52	4	1	1	2	4
	Hershey	AHL	1	1	0	1	0	.....	.....	.....	.....	.....
1983-84	**Washington**	**NHL**	79	17	19	36	29	8	2	1	3	2
1984-85	**Washington**	**NHL**	67	15	23	38	32	5	0	1	1	7
1985-86	**Washington**	**NHL**	80	11	28	39	39	9	4	3	7	12
1986-87	**Washington**	**NHL**	74	17	35	52	53	7	3	0	3	14
1987-88	**Quebec**	**NHL**	80	24	23	47	83	.....	.....	.....	.....	.....
1988-89	**Quebec**	**NHL**	70	8	21	29	56	.....	.....	.....	.....	.....
1989-90	**Minnesota**	**NHL**	72	12	8	20	33	7	0	0	0	6
1990-91	**Minnesota**	**NHL**	68	9	9	18	18	23	2	3	5	34
	NHL Totals		741	140	199	339	441	63	12	9	21	79

Traded to **Quebec** by **Washington** with Alan Haworth and Washington's first-round choice (Joe Sakic) in 1987 Entry Draft for Clint Malarchuk and Dale Hunter, June 13, 1987. Traded to **Minnesota** by **Quebec** for Kevin Kaminski, June 19, 1989.

DUCHESNE, STEVE

Defense. Shoots left. 5'11", 195 lbs.　Born, Sept-Iles, Que., June 30, 1965.

				Regular Season					Playoffs			
Season	Club	Lea	GP	G	A	TP	PIM	GP	G	A	TP	PIM
1983-84	Drummondville	QMJHL	67	1	34	35	79	.....	.....	.....	.....	.....
1984-85a	Drummondville	QMJHL	65	22	54	76	94	5	4	7	11	8
1985-86	New Haven	AHL	75	14	35	49	76	5	0	2	2	9
1986-87b	**Los Angeles**	**NHL**	75	13	25	38	74	5	2	2	4	4
1987-88	**Los Angeles**	**NHL**	71	16	39	55	109	5	1	3	4	14
1988-89	**Los Angeles**	**NHL**	79	25	50	75	92	11	4	4	8	12
1989-90	**Los Angeles**	**NHL**	79	20	42	62	36	10	2	9	11	6
1990-91	**Los Angeles**	**NHL**	78	21	41	62	66	12	4	8	12	8
	NHL Totals		382	95	197	292	377	43	13	26	39	44

a QMJHL First All-Star Team (1985)
b NHL All-Rookie Team (1987)
Played in NHL All-Star Game (1989, 1990)

Signed as a free agent by **Los Angeles**, October 1, 1984. Traded to **Philadelphia** by **Los Angeles** with Steve Kasper and Los Angeles' fourth round choice (Aris Brimanis) in 1991 Entry Draft for Jari Kurri and Jeff Chychrun, May 30, 1991.

DUFFY, JACK

Defense. Shoots right. 6'1", 195 lbs.　Born, Northford, CT, September 25, 1970.
(NY Islanders' 2nd choice, 10th overall, in 1991 Supplemental Draft).

				Regular Season					Playoffs			
Season	Club	Lea	GP	G	A	TP	PIM	GP	G	A	TP	PIM
1989-90	Yale	ECAC	26	1	6	7	48	.....	.....	.....	.....	.....
1990-91	Yale	ECAC	29	4	8	12	48	.....	.....	.....	.....	.....

DUFRESNE, DONALD (DOO-FRAYN)

Defense. Shoots right. 6'1", 206 lbs.   Born, Quebec City, Que., April 10, 1967.
(Montreal's 8th choice, 117th overall, in 1985 Entry Draft).

			Regular Season					Playoffs				
Season	Club	Lea	GP	G	A	TP	PIM	GP	G	A	TP	PIM
1983-84	Trois Rivieres	QMJHL	67	7	12	19	97	....	....	....	....	....
1984-85	Trois Rivieres	QMJHL	65	5	30	35	112	7	1	3	4	12
1985-86a	Trois Rivieres	QMJHL	63	8	32	40	160	1	0	0	0	0
1986-87a	Trois Rivieres	QMJHL	51	5	21	26	79	....	....	....	....	....
	Longueuil	QMJHL	16	0	8	8	18	20	1	8	9	38
1987-88	Sherbrooke	AHL	47	1	8	9	107	6	1	0	1	34
1988-89	**Montreal**	**NHL**	13	0	1	1	43	6	1	1	2	4
	Sherbrooke	AHL	47	0	12	12	170	....	....	....	....	....
1989-90	**Montreal**	**NHL**	18	0	4	4	23	10	0	1	1	18
	Sherbrooke	AHL	38	2	11	13	104	....	....	....	....	....
1990-91	**Montreal**	**NHL**	53	2	13	15	55	10	0	1	1	21
	Fredericton	AHL	10	1	4	5	35	1	0	0	0	0
	NHL Totals		**84**	**2**	**18**	**20**	**121**	**26**	**1**	**3**	**4**	**43**

a QMJHL Second All-Star Team (1986, 1987)

DUGUAY, RONALD (RON) (doo-GAY)

Center/Right wing. Shoots right. 6'2", 200 lbs.   Born, Sudbury, Ont., July 6, 1957.
(NY Rangers' 2nd choice, 13th overall, in 1977 Amateur Draft).

			Regular Season					Playoffs				
Season	Club	Lea	GP	G	A	TP	PIM	GP	G	A	TP	PIM
1975-76a	Sudbury	OHA	61	42	92	134	101	17	11	9	20	37
1976-77	Sudbury	OHA	61	43	66	109	109	6	3	7	5	5
1977-78	**NY Rangers**	**NHL**	71	20	20	40	43	3	1	1	2	2
1978-79	**NY Rangers**	**NHL**	79	27	36	63	35	18	5	4	9	11
1979-80	**NY Rangers**	**NHL**	73	28	22	50	37	9	5	2	7	11
1980-81	**NY Rangers**	**NHL**	50	17	21	38	83	14	8	9	17	16
1981-82	**NY Rangers**	**NHL**	72	40	36	76	82	10	5	1	6	31
1982-83	**NY Rangers**	**NHL**	72	19	25	44	58	9	2	2	4	28
1983-84	**Detroit**	**NHL**	80	33	47	80	34	4	2	3	5	2
1984-85	**Detroit**	**NHL**	80	38	51	89	51	3	1	0	1	7
1985-86	**Detroit**	**NHL**	67	19	29	48	26	....	....	....	....	....
	Pittsburgh	**NHL**	13	6	7	13	6	....	....	....	....	....
1986-87	**Pittsburgh**	**NHL**	40	5	13	18	30	....	....	....	....	....
	NY Rangers	**NHL**	34	9	12	21	9	6	2	0	2	4
1987-88	**NY Rangers**	**NHL**	48	4	4	8	23	....	....	....	....	....
	Colorado	IHL	2	0	0	0	0	....	....	....	....	....
	Los Angeles	**NHL**	15	2	6	8	17	2	0	0	0	0
1988-89	**Los Angeles**	**NHL**	70	7	17	24	48	11	0	0	0	6
1989-90	Mannheimer	W.Ger.	22	11	7	18	38	....	....	....	....	....
1990-91	San Diego	IHL	51	15	24	39	87	....	....	....	....	....
	NHL Totals		**864**	**274**	**346**	**620**	**582**	**89**	**31**	**22**	**53**	**118**

a OHA Third All-Star Team (1976)
Played in NHL All-Star Game (1982)
Traded to **Detroit** by **NY Rangers** with Eddie Mio and Eddie Johnstone for Willie Huber, Mark Osborne and Mike Blaisdell, June 13, 1983. Traded to **Pittsburgh** by **Detroit** for Doug Shedden, March 11, 1986. Traded to **NY Rangers** by **Pittsburgh** for Chris Kontos, January 21, 1987. Traded to **Los Angeles** by **NY Rangers** for Mark Hardy, February 23, 1988.

DUKOVAC, PAUL C.

Defense. Shoots right. 6'1", 185 lbs.   Born, New Liskeard, Ont., January 18, 1969.
(Vancouver's 1st choice, 2nd overall, in 1990 Supplemental Draft).

			Regular Season					Playoffs				
Season	Club	Lea	GP	G	A	TP	PIM	GP	G	A	TP	PIM
1988-89	Cornell	ECAC	14	1	4	5	8	....	....	....	....	....
1989-90	Cornell	ECAC	29	1	8	9	34	....	....	....	....	....
1990-91	Cornell	ECAC	32	0	7	7	36	....	....	....	....	....

DUNCAN, IAIN

Left wing. Shoots left. 6'1", 200 lbs.   Born, Weston, Ont., August 4, 1963.
(Winnipeg's 8th choice, 129th overall, in 1983 Entry Draft).

			Regular Season					Playoffs				
Season	Club	Lea	GP	G	A	TP	PIM	GP	G	A	TP	PIM
1983-84	Bowling Green	CCHA	44	11	20	31	65	....	....	....	....	....
1984-85	Bowling Green	CCHA	37	9	21	30	105	....	....	....	....	....
1985-86	Bowling Green	CCHA	41	26	26	52	124	....	....	....	....	....
1986-87a	Bowling Green	CCHA	39	28	40	68	141	....	....	....	....	....
	Winnipeg	**NHL**	6	1	2	3	0	7	0	2	2	6
1987-88b	**Winnipeg**	**NHL**	62	19	23	42	73	4	0	1	1	0
	Moncton	AHL	8	1	3	4	26	....	....	....	....	....
1988-89	**Winnipeg**	**NHL**	57	14	30	44	74	....	....	....	....	....
1989-90	Moncton	AHL	49	16	25	41	81	....	....	....	....	....
1990-91	**Winnipeg**	**NHL**	2	0	0	0	2	....	....	....	....	....
	Moncton	AHL	66	19	45	64	105	8	3	4	7	40
	NHL Totals		**127**	**34**	**55**	**89**	**149**	**11**	**0**	**3**	**3**	**6**

a CCHA First All-Star Team (1987)
b NHL All-Rookie Team (1988)

DUNCANSON, CRAIG

Left wing. Shoots left. 6', 190 lbs.   Born, Sudbury, Ont., March 17, 1967.
(Los Angeles' 1st choice, 9th overall, in 1985 Entry Draft).

			Regular Season					Playoffs				
Season	Club	Lea	GP	G	A	TP	PIM	GP	G	A	TP	PIM
1983-84	Sudbury	OHL	62	38	38	76	176	....	....	....	....	....
1984-85a	Sudbury	OHL	53	35	28	63	129	....	....	....	....	....
1985-86	**Los Angeles**	**NHL**	2	0	1	1	0	....	....	....	....	....
	Sudbury	OHL	21	12	17	29	55	....	....	....	....	....
	Cornwall	OHL	40	31	50	81	135	6	4	7	11	2
	New Haven	AHL	....	....	....	....	....	2	0	0	0	5
1986-87	**Los Angeles**	**NHL**	2	0	0	0	24	....	....	....	....	....
	Cornwall	OHL	52	22	45	67	88	5	4	3	7	20
1987-88	**Los Angeles**	**NHL**	9	0	0	0	12	....	....	....	....	....
	New Haven	AHL	57	15	25	40	170	....	....	....	....	....
1988-89	**Los Angeles**	**NHL**	5	0	0	0	0	....	....	....	....	....
	New Haven	AHL	69	25	39	64	200	17	4	8	12	60
1989-90	**Los Angeles**	**NHL**	10	3	2	5	9	....	....	....	....	....
	New Haven	AHL	51	17	30	47	152	....	....	....	....	....
1990-91	**Winnipeg**	**NHL**	7	2	0	2	16	....	....	....	....	....
	Moncton	AHL	58	16	34	50	107	9	3	11	14	31
	NHL Totals		**35**	**5**	**3**	**8**	**61**					

a OHL Third All-Star Team (1985)
Traded to **Minnesota** by **Los Angeles** for Daniel Berthiaume, September 6, 1990. Traded to **Washington** by **Winnipeg** with Brent Hughes and Simon Wheeldon for Bob Joyce, Tyler Larter and Kent Paynter, May 21, 1991.

DUPRE, YANIC

Left wing. Shoots left. 6', 189 lbs.   Born, Montreal, Que., November 20, 1972.
(Philadelphia's 2nd choice, 50th overall, in 1991 Entry Draft).

			Regular Season					Playoffs				
Season	Club	Lea	GP	G	A	TP	PIM	GP	G	A	TP	PIM
1989-90	Drummondville	QMJHL	53	15	19	34	69	....	....	....	....	....
1990-91	Drummondville	QMJHL	58	29	38	67	87	11	8	5	13	33

DUPUIS, GUY (dew-PWEE)

Defense. Shoots right. 6'2", 200 lbs.   Born, Moncton, N.B., May 10, 1970.
(Detroit's 3rd choice, 47th overall, in 1988 Entry Draft).

			Regular Season					Playoffs				
Season	Club	Lea	GP	G	A	TP	PIM	GP	G	A	TP	PIM
1986-87	Hull	QMJHL	69	5	10	15	35	8	1	2	3	2
1987-88	Hull	QMJHL	69	14	34	48	72	19	3	8	11	29
1988-89a	Hull	QMJHL	70	15	56	71	89	9	3	3	6	8
1989-90	Hull	QMJHL	70	8	41	49	96	11	1	3	4	8
1990-91	Adirondack	AHL	57	4	10	14	73	....	....	....	....	....

a QMJHL Second All-Star Team (1989)

DUUS, JESPER (DOO-uhs)

Defense. Shoots right. 5'11", 176 lbs.   Born, Rodovre, Denmark, November 24, 1967.
(Edmonton's 12th choice. 241st overall, in 1987 Entry Draft).

			Regular Season					Playoffs				
Season	Club	Lea	GP	G	A	TP	PIM	GP	G	A	TP	PIM
1985-86	Rodovre	Den.	24	3	5	8	28	6	1	2	3	4
1986-87	Rodovre	Den.	24	6	14	20	14	6	1	3	4	6
1987-88	Farjestad	Swe.	26	2	5	7	8	....	....	....	....	....
1988-89	Farjestad	Swe.	36	4	4	8	10	....	....	....	....	....
1989-90	Farjestad	Swe.	41	4	9	13	28	10	1	0	1	4
1990-91	Farjestad	Swe.	40	1	7	8	20	....	....	....	....	....

DUVAL, MURRAY

Defense. Shoots left. 6'1", 203 lbs.   Born, Thompson, Man., January 22, 1970.
(New York Rangers' 2nd choice, 26th overall, in 1988 Entry Draft).

			Regular Season					Playoffs				
Season	Club	Lea	GP	G	A	TP	PIM	GP	G	A	TP	PIM
1986-87	Spokane	WHL	27	2	6	8	21	....	....	....	....	....
1987-88	Spokane	WHL	70	26	37	63	104	15	5	2	7	22
1988-89	Tri-Cities	WHL	71	14	28	42	144	....	....	....	....	....
1989-90	Tri-Cities	WHL	7	4	4	8	10	....	....	....	....	....
	Kamloops	WHL	56	14	36	50	94	17	8	7	15	29
1990-91a	Kamloops	WHL	67	47	66	113	187	12	8	5	13	30

a WHL West Second All-Star Team (1991)

DYKHUIS, KARL

Defense. Shoots left. 6'2", 184 lbs.   Born, Sept-Iles, Que., July 8, 1972.
(Chicago's 1st choice, 16th overall, in 1990 Entry Draft).

			Regular Season					Playoffs				
Season	Club	Lea	GP	G	A	TP	PIM	GP	G	A	TP	PIM
1988-89	Hull	QMJHL	63	2	29	31	59	9	1	9	10	6
1989-90a	Hull	QMJHL	69	10	46	56	119	11	2	5	7	2
1990-91	Cdn. National	....	37	2	9	11	16	....	....	....	....	....
	Longueuil	QMJHL	3	1	4	4	6	8	2	5	7	6

a QMJHL First All-Star Team (1990)

DYKSTRA, STEVEN (DIKES-trah)

Defense. Shoots left. 6'2", 190 lbs. Born, Edmonton, Alta., December 1, 1962.

			Regular Season					Playoffs				
Season	Club	Lea	GP	G	A	TP	PIM	GP	G	A	TP	PIM
1981-82	Seattle	WHL	57	8	26	34	139	10	3	1	4	42
1982-83	Rochester	AHL	70	2	16	18	100	15	0	5	5	27
1983-84	Rochester	AHL	63	3	19	22	141	6	0	0	0	46
1984-85	Flint	IHL	15	1	7	8	36	....	....	....	....	....
	Rochester	AHL	51	9	23	32	113	2	0	1	1	10
1985-86	**Buffalo**	**NHL**	**64**	**4**	**21**	**25**	**108**	....	....	....	....	....
1986-87	**Buffalo**	**NHL**	**37**	**0**	**1**	**1**	**179**	....	....	....	....	....
	Rochester	AHL	18	0	0	0	77	....	....	....	....	....
1987-88	**Buffalo**	**NHL**	**27**	**1**	**1**	**2**	**91**	....	....	....	....	....
	Rochester	AHL	7	0	1	1	33	....	....	....	....	....
	Edmonton	**NHL**	**15**	**2**	**3**	**5**	**39**	....	....	....	....	....
1988-89	**Pittsburgh**	**NHL**	**65**	**1**	**6**	**7**	**126**	**1**	**0**	**0**	**0**	**2**
1989-90	**Hartford**	**NHL**	**9**	**0**	**0**	**0**	**2**	....	....	....	....	....
	Binghamton	AHL	53	5	17	22	55	....	....	....	....	....
	Maine	AHL	16	0	4	4	20	....	....	....	....	....
1990-91	San Diego	IHL	72	6	18	24	141	....	....	....	....	....
	NHL Totals		**217**	**8**	**32**	**40**	**545**	**1**	**0**	**0**	**0**	**2**

Signed as a free agent by **Buffalo**, December 10, 1982. Traded to **Edmonton** by **Buffalo** with Buffalo's seventh round choice (David Payne) in 1989 Entry Draft for Scott Metcalfe and Edmonton's ninth round choice (Donald Audette) in 1989 Entry Draft, February 11, 1988. Claimed by **Pittsburgh** in NHL Waiver Draft, October 3, 1988. Signed as a free agent by **Hartford**, October 9, 1989. Traded to **Boston** by **Hartford** for Jeff Sirkka, March 3, 1990.

DZIEDZIC, JOE

Left wing. Shoots left. 6'3", 200 lbs. Born, Minneapolis, MN, December 18, 1971.
(Pittsburgh's 2nd choice, 61st overall, in 1990 Entry Draft).

			Regular Season					Playoffs				
Season	Club	Lea	GP	G	A	TP	PIM	GP	G	A	TP	PIM
1989-90	Edison	HS	17	29	19	48	....	....	....	....	....	....
1990-91	U. Minnesota	WCHA	20	6	4	10	26	....	....	....	....	....

EAGLES, MICHAEL (MIKE)

Center/Left wing. Shoots left. 5'10", 187 lbs. Born, Sussex, N.B., March 7, 1963.
(Quebec's 5th choice, 116th overall, in 1981 Entry Draft).

			Regular Season					Playoffs				
Season	Club	Lea	GP	G	A	TP	PIM	GP	G	A	TP	PIM
1980-81	Kitchener	OHA	56	11	27	38	64	18	4	2	6	36
1981-82	Kitchener	OHL	62	26	40	66	148	15	3	11	14	27
1982-83	**Quebec**	**NHL**	**2**	**0**	**0**	**0**	**2**	....	....	....	....	....
	Kitchener	OHL	58	26	36	62	133	12	5	7	12	27
1983-84	Fredericton	AHL	68	13	29	42	85	4	0	0	0	5
1984-85	Fredericton	AHL	36	4	20	24	80	3	0	0	0	2
1985-86	**Quebec**	**NHL**	**73**	**11**	**12**	**23**	**49**	**3**	**0**	**0**	**0**	**2**
1986-87	**Quebec**	**NHL**	**73**	**13**	**19**	**32**	**55**	**4**	**1**	**0**	**1**	**10**
1987-88	**Quebec**	**NHL**	**76**	**10**	**10**	**20**	**74**	....	....	....	....	....
1988-89	**Chicago**	**NHL**	**47**	**5**	**11**	**16**	**44**	....	....	....	....	....
1989-90	**Chicago**	**NHL**	**23**	**1**	**2**	**3**	**34**	....	....	....	....	....
	Indianapolis	IHL	24	11	13	24	47	13	*10	10	20	34
1990-91	**Winnipeg**	**NHL**	**44**	**0**	**9**	**9**	**79**	....	....	....	....	....
	Indianapolis	IHL	25	15	14	29	47	....	....	....	....	....
	NHL Totals		**338**	**40**	**63**	**103**	**337**	**7**	**1**	**0**	**1**	**12**

Traded to **Chicago** by **Quebec** for Bob Mason, July 5, 1988. Traded to **Winnipeg** by **Chicago** for Winnipeg's fourth round choice (Igor Kravchuk) in 1991 Entry Draft, December 14, 1990.

EAKINS, DALLAS

Defense. Shoots left. 6'2", 195 lbs. Born, Dade City, FL, February 27, 1967.
(Washington's 11th choice, 208th overall, in 1985 Entry Draft).

			Regular Season					Playoffs				
Season	Club	Lea	GP	G	A	TP	PIM	GP	G	A	TP	PIM
1984-85	Peterborough	OHL	48	0	8	8	96	7	0	0	0	18
1985-86	Peterborough	OHL	60	6	16	22	134	16	0	1	1	30
1986-87	Peterborough	OHL	54	3	11	14	145	12	1	4	5	37
1987-88	Peterborough	OHL	64	11	27	38	129	12	3	12	15	16
1988-89	Baltimore	AHL	62	0	10	10	139	....	....	....	....	....
1989-90	Moncton	AHL	75	2	11	13	189	....	....	....	....	....
1990-91	Moncton	AHL	75	1	12	13	132	0	0	1	1	44

Signed as a free agent by **Winnipeg**, October 17, 1989.

EASTWOOD, MICHAEL

Center. Shoots right. 6'2", 190 lbs. Born, Ottawa, Ont., July 1, 1967.
(Toronto's 5th choice, 91st overall, in 1987 Entry Draft).

			Regular Season					Playoffs				
Season	Club	Lea	GP	G	A	TP	PIM	GP	G	A	TP	PIM
1987-88	W. Michigan	CCHA	42	5	8	13	14	....	....	....	....	....
1988-89	W. Michigan	CCHA	40	10	13	23	87	....	....	....	....	....
1989-90	W. Michigan	CCHA	40	25	27	52	36	....	....	....	....	....
1990-91a	W. Michigan	CCHA	42	29	32	61	84	....	....	....	....	....

a CCHA Second All-Star Team (1991)

EAVES, MURRAY

Center. Shoots right. 5'10", 185 lbs. Born, Calgary, Alta., May 10, 1960.
(Winnipeg's 3rd choice, 44th overall, in 1980 Entry Draft).

			Regular Season					Playoffs				
Season	Club	Lea	GP	G	A	TP	PIM	GP	G	A	TP	PIM
1978-79	U. of Michigan	WCHA	23	12	22	34	14	....	....	....	....	....
1979-80	U. of Michigan	WCHA	33	36	49	85	34	....	....	....	....	....
1980-81	**Winnipeg**	**NHL**	**12**	**1**	**2**	**3**	**5**	....	....	....	....	....
	Tulsa	CHL	59	24	34	58	59	8	5	5	10	13
1981-82	**Winnipeg**	**NHL**	**2**	**0**	**0**	**0**	**0**	....	....	....	....	....
	Tulsa	CHL	68	30	49	79	33	3	0	2	2	0
1982-83	**Winnipeg**	**NHL**	**26**	**2**	**7**	**9**	**2**	....	....	....	....	....
	Sherbrooke	AHL	40	25	34	59	16	....	....	....	....	....
1983-84	**Winnipeg**	**NHL**	**2**	**0**	**0**	**0**	**0**	**2**	**0**	**0**	**0**	**2**
	Sherbrooke	AHL	78	47	68	115	40	....	....	....	....	....
1984-85	**Winnipeg**	**NHL**	**3**	**0**	**3**	**3**	**0**	**2**	**0**	**1**	**1**	**0**
	Sherbrooke	AHL	47	26	42	68	28	15	5	13	18	35
1985-86	**Winnipeg**	**NHL**	**4**	**1**	**0**	**1**	**0**	....	....	....	....	....
	Sherbrooke	AHL	68	22	51	73	26	....	....	....	....	....
1986-87	Nova Scotia	AHL	76	26	38	64	46	4	1	1	2	2
1987-88	**Detroit**	**NHL**	**7**	**0**	**1**	**1**	**2**	....	....	....	....	....
	Adirondack	AHL	65	39	54	93	65	11	3	*11	14	8
1988-89ab	Adirondack	AHL	80	46	*72	118	11	16	*13	12	25	10
1989-90	**Detroit**	**NHL**	**1**	**0**	**0**	**0**	**0**	....	....	....	....	....
b	Adirondack	AHL	78	40	49	89	35	6	2	3	5	2
1990-91	Varese	Italy	32	22	37	59	23	10	9	9	18	4
	NHL Totals		**57**	**4**	**13**	**17**	**9**	**4**	**0**	**1**	**1**	**2**

a AHL Second All-Star Team (1989)
b Won Fred Hunt Award (Sportsmanship-AHL) (1989, 1990)

Traded to **Edmonton** by **Winnipeg** for future considerations, July 3, 1986. Signed as a free agent by **Detroit**, July 12, 1987.

EDGERLY, DEREK

Center. Shoots left. 6'1", 190 lbs. Born, Malden, MA, April 3, 1971.
(Chicago's 5th choice, 124th overall, in 1990 Entry Draft).

			Regular Season					Playoffs				
Season	Club	Lea	GP	G	A	TP	PIM	GP	G	A	TP	PIM
1989-90	Stoneham	HS	....	28	23	51	....	....	....	....	....	....
1990-91	Northeastern	H.E.	34	3	11	14	12	....	....	....	....	....

EDLUND, PAR (EHD-luhnd, PEHR)

Left wing. Shoots right. 5'11", 196 lbs. Born, Sodertalje, Sweden, April 9, 1967.
(Los Angeles' 3rd choice, 30th overall, in 1985 Entry Draft).

			Regular Season					Playoffs				
Season	Club	Lea	GP	G	A	TP	PIM	GP	G	A	TP	PIM
1986-87	Bjorkloven	Swe.	4	0	0	0	0	....	....	....	....	....
1987-88	Bjorkloven	Swe.	37	6	4	10	14	7	1	0	1	2
1988-89	Bjorkloven	Swe.	18	9	10	19	....	....	....	....	....	....
1989-90	Bjorkloven	Swe.2	18	13	9	22	0	....	....	....	....	....
1990-91	V. Frolunda	Swe.2	15	5	4	9	10	....	....	....	....	....

EGELAND, TRACY

Left wing. Shoots right. 6'1", 180 lbs. Born, Lethbridge, Alta., August 20, 1970.
(Chicago's 5th choice, 132nd overall, in 1989 Entry Draft).

			Regular Season					Playoffs				
Season	Club	Lea	GP	G	A	TP	PIM	GP	G	A	TP	PIM
1986-87	Swift Current	WHL	48	3	2	5	20	....	....	....	....	....
1987-88	Swift Current	WHL	63	10	22	32	34	....	....	....	....	....
1988-89	Medicine Hat	WHL	42	11	12	23	64	....	....	....	....	....
	Prince Albert	WHL	24	17	10	27	24	4	0	1	1	13
1989-90	Prince Albert	WHL	61	39	26	65	160	13	7	10	17	26
1990-91	Indianapolis	IHL	79	17	22	39	205	7	2	1	3	21

EISENHUT, NEIL

Center. Shoots left. 6'1", 190 lbs. Born, Oliver, B.C., January 9, 1967.
(Vancouver's 11th choice, 238th overall, in 1987 Entry Draft).

			Regular Season					Playoffs				
Season	Club	Lea	GP	G	A	TP	PIM	GP	G	A	TP	PIM
1987-88	North Dakota	WCHA	42	12	20	32	14	....	....	....	....	....
1988-89	North Dakota	WCHA	41	22	16	38	20	....	....	....	....	....
1989-90	North Dakota	WCHA	45	22	32	54	46	....	....	....	....	....
1990-91	North Dakota	WCHA	20	9	15	24	10	....	....	....	....	....

EKLUND, PER-ERIK (PELLE) (EHK-luhnd)

Center. Shoots left. 5'10", 175 lbs. Born, Stockholm, Sweden, March 22, 1963.
(Philadelphia's 7th choice, 161st overall, in 1983 Entry Draft).

			Regular Season					Playoffs				
Season	Club	Lea	GP	G	A	TP	PIM	GP	G	A	TP	PIM
1981-82	AIK	Swe.	23	2	3	5	2	....	....	....	....	....
1982-83	AIK	Swe.	34	13	17	30	14	3	1	4	5	2
1983-84	AIK	Swe.	35	9	18	27	24	6	6	7	13	2
1984-85	AIK	Swe.	35	16	33	49	10	....	....	....	....	....
1985-86	**Philadelphia**	**NHL**	**70**	**15**	**51**	**66**	**12**	**5**	**0**	**2**	**2**	**0**
1986-87	**Philadelphia**	**NHL**	**72**	**14**	**41**	**55**	**2**	**26**	**7**	**20**	**27**	**2**
1987-88	**Philadelphia**	**NHL**	**71**	**10**	**32**	**42**	**12**	**7**	**0**	**3**	**3**	**0**
1988-89	**Philadelphia**	**NHL**	**79**	**18**	**51**	**69**	**23**	**19**	**3**	**8**	**11**	**2**
1989-90	**Philadelphia**	**NHL**	**70**	**23**	**39**	**62**	**16**	....	....	....	....	....
1990-91	**Philadelphia**	**NHL**	**73**	**19**	**50**	**69**	**14**	....	....	....	....	....
	NHL Totals		**435**	**99**	**264**	**363**	**79**	**57**	**10**	**33**	**43**	**4**

ELIK, TODD   (EL-ik)

Center. Shoots left. 6'2", 190 lbs.   Born, Brampton, Ont., April 15, 1966.

				Regular Season					Playoffs			
Season	Club	Lea	GP	G	A	TP	PIM	GP	G	A	TP	PIM
1984-85	Kingston	OHL	34	14	11	25	6	....	....	....	....	....
	North Bay	OHL	23	4	6	10	2	4	2	0	2	0
1985-86	North Bay	OHL	40	12	34	46	20	10	7	6	13	0
1986-87	U. of Regina	CWUAA	27	26	34	60	137	....	....	....	....	....
1987-88	Colorado	IHL	81	44	56	100	83	12	8	12	20	9
1988-89	Denver	IHL	28	20	15	35	22	....	....	....	....	....
	New Haven	AHL	43	11	25	36	31	17	10	12	22	44
1989-90	**Los Angeles**	**NHL**	**48**	**10**	**23**	**33**	**4**	10	3	9	12	10
	New Haven	AHL	32	20	23	43	42	....	....	....	....	....
1990-91	**Los Angeles**	**NHL**	**74**	**21**	**37**	**58**	**58**	12	2	7	9	6
	NHL Totals		**122**	**31**	**60**	**91**	**62**	**22**	**5**	**16**	**21**	**16**

Signed as a free agent by **NY Rangers**, February 26, 1988. Traded to **Los Angeles** by **NY Rangers** with Igor Liba, Michael Boyce and future considerations for Dean Kennedy and Denis Larocque, December 12, 1988. Traded to **Minnesota** by **Los Angeles** for Randy Gilhen, Charlie Huddy, Jim Thomson and NY Rangers' fourth round choice (previously acquired by Minnesota — Alexei Zhitnik) in 1991 Entry Draft, June 22, 1991.

ELLETT, DAVID

Defense. Shoots left. 6'1", 200 lbs.   Born, Cleveland, OH, March 30, 1964.
(Winnipeg's 3rd choice, 75th overall, in 1982 Entry Draft).

				Regular Season					Playoffs			
Season	Club	Lea	GP	G	A	TP	PIM	GP	G	A	TP	PIM
1982-83	Bowling Green	CCHA	40	4	13	17	34	....	....	....	....	....
1983-84ab	Bowling Green	CCHA	43	15	39	54	96	....	....	....	....	....
1984-85	**Winnipeg**	**NHL**	**80**	**11**	**27**	**38**	**85**	8	1	5	6	4
1985-86	**Winnipeg**	**NHL**	**80**	**15**	**31**	**46**	**96**	3	0	1	1	0
1986-87	**Winnipeg**	**NHL**	**78**	**13**	**31**	**44**	**53**	10	0	8	8	2
1987-88	**Winnipeg**	**NHL**	**68**	**13**	**45**	**58**	**106**	5	1	2	3	10
1988-89	**Winnipeg**	**NHL**	**75**	**22**	**34**	**56**	**62**	....	....	....	....	....
1989-90	**Winnipeg**	**NHL**	**77**	**17**	**29**	**46**	**96**	7	2	0	2	6
1990-91	**Winnipeg**	**NHL**	**17**	**4**	**7**	**11**	**6**	....	....	....	....	....
	Toronto	**NHL**	**60**	**8**	**30**	**38**	**69**	....	....	....	....	....
	NHL Totals		**535**	**103**	**234**	**337**	**573**	**33**	**4**	**16**	**20**	**22**

a CCHA Second All-Star Team (1984).
b Named to NCAA All-Tournament Team (1984).
Played in NHL All-Star Game (1989)
Traded to **Toronto** by **Winnipeg** with Paul Fenton for Ed Olczyk and Mark Osborne, November 10, 1990.

ELVENAS, ROGER

Center. Shoots left. 6'1", 183 lbs.   Born, Lund, Sweden, May 29, 1968.
(Toronto's 7th choice, 153rd overall, in 1988 Entry Draft).

				Regular Season					Playoffs			
Season	Club	Lea	GP	G	A	TP	PIM	GP	G	A	TP	PIM
1987-88	Rogle	Swe.	35	21	18	39	....	....	....	....	....	....
1988-89	Rogle	Swe.	36	24	40	64	....	....	....	....	....	....
1989-90	Rogle	Swe.	35	16	25	41	24	....	....	....	....	....
1990-91	Rogle	Swe.	32	17	26	43	12	....	....	....	....	....

ELVENES, STEFAN

Right wing. Shoots left. 6'1", 183 lbs.   Born, Lund, Sweden, March 30, 1970.
(Chicago's 3rd choice, 71st overall, in 1988 Entry Draft).

				Regular Season					Playoffs			
Season	Club	Lea	GP	G	A	TP	PIM	GP	G	A	TP	PIM
1989-90	Rogle	Swe.	35	18	25	43	56	....	....	....	....	....
1990-91	Rogle	Swe.	18	14	6	20	10	....	....	....	....	....

ELYNUIK, PAT

Right wing. Shoots right. 6', 185 lbs.   Born, Foam Lake, Sask., October 30, 1967.
(Winnipeg's 1st choice, 8th overall, in 1986 Entry Draft).

				Regular Season					Playoffs			
Season	Club	Lea	GP	G	A	TP	PIM	GP	G	A	TP	PIM
1984-85	Prince Albert	WHL	70	23	20	43	54	13	9	3	12	7
1985-86a	Prince Albert	WHL	68	53	53	106	62	20	7	9	16	17
1986-87a	Prince Albert	WHL	64	51	62	113	40	8	5	5	10	12
1987-88	**Winnipeg**	**NHL**	**13**	**1**	**3**	**4**	**12**	....	....	....	....	....
	Moncton	AHL	30	11	18	29	35	....	....	....	....	....
1988-89	**Winnipeg**	**NHL**	**56**	**26**	**25**	**51**	**29**	....	....	....	....	....
	Moncton	AHL	7	8	2	10	2	....	....	....	....	....
1989-90	**Winnipeg**	**NHL**	**80**	**32**	**42**	**74**	**83**	7	2	4	6	2
1990-91	**Winnipeg**	**NHL**	**80**	**31**	**34**	**65**	**73**	....	....	....	....	....
	NHL Totals		**229**	**90**	**104**	**194**	**197**	**7**	**2**	**4**	**6**	**2**

a WHL East All-Star Team (1986, 1987).

EMERSON, NELSON

Center. Shoots right. 5'11", 165 lbs.   Born, Hamilton, Ont., August 17, 1967.
(St. Louis' 2nd choice, 44th overall, in 1985 Entry Draft).

				Regular Season					Playoffs			
Season	Club	Lea	GP	G	A	TP	PIM	GP	G	A	TP	PIM
1986-87a	Bowling Green	CCHA	45	26	35	61	28	....	....	....	....	....
1987-88bc	Bowling Green	CCHA	45	34	49	83	54	....	....	....	....	....
1988-89d	Bowling Green	CCHA	44	22	46	68	46	....	....	....	....	....
1989-90ce	Bowling Green	CCHA	44	30	52	82	42	....	....	....	....	....
	Peoria	IHL	3	1	1	2	0	....	....	....	....	....
1990-91	**St. Louis**	**NHL**	**4**	**0**	**3**	**3**	**2**	....	....	....	....	....
fg	Peoria	IHL	73	36	79	115	91	17	9	12	21	16
	NHL Totals		**4**	**0**	**3**	**3**	**2**	....	....	....	....	....

a CCHA Freshman of the Year (1987)
b NCAA West Second All-American Team (1988)
c CCHA First All-Star Team (1988, 1990)
d CCHA Second All-Star Team (1989)
e NCAA West First All-American Team (1990)
f IHL First All-Star Team (1991)
g Won Garry F. Longman Memorial Trophy (Top Rookie — IHL) (1991)

EMMA, DAVID

Center. Shoots left. 5'11", 180 lbs.   Born, Cranston, RI, January 14, 1969.
(New Jersey's 6th choice, 110th overall, in 1989 Entry Draft).

				Regular Season					Playoffs			
Season	Club	Lea	GP	G	A	TP	PIM	GP	G	A	TP	PIM
1987-88	Boston College	H.E.	30	19	16	35	30	....	....	....	....	....
1988-89	Boston College	H.E.	36	20	31	51	36	....	....	....	....	....
1989-90ab	Boston College	H.E.	42	38	34	*72	46	....	....	....	....	....
1990-91abcd	Boston College	H.E.	39	*35	46	*81	44	....	....	....	....	....

a Hockey East First All-Star Team (1990, 1991)
b NCAA East First All-American Team (1990, 1991)
c Hockey East Player of the Year (1991)
d Won Hobey Baker Award (Top U.S. Collegiate Player) (1991)

ENEBAK, JAKE

Left wing. Shoots left. 6'2", 200 lbs.   Born, Northfield, MN, December 10, 1968.
(Quebec's 8th choice, 156th overall, in 1987 Entry Draft).

				Regular Season					Playoffs			
Season	Club	Lea	GP	G	A	TP	PIM	GP	G	A	TP	PIM
1987-88	U. Minnesota	WCHA	9	1	1	2	15	....	....	....	....	....
1988-89	U. Minnesota	WCHA	15	1	2	3	26	....	....	....	....	....
1989-90	U. Minnesota	WCHA	20	0	3	3	26	....	....	....	....	....
1990-91	U. Minnesota	WCHA	20	1	2	3	23	....	....	....	....	....

ENGA, RICHARD

Center. Shoots right. 5'10", 156 lbs.   Born, Bitburg, Germany, February 15, 1972.
(NY Islanders' 9th choice, 195th overall, in 1990 Entry Draft).

				Regular Season					Playoffs			
Season	Club	Lea	GP	G	A	TP	PIM	GP	G	A	TP	PIM
1989-90	Culver Aca.	HS	37	43	56	99	16	....	....	....	....	....
1990-91	Culver Aca.	HS	37	41	48	89	13	....	....	....	....	....

ENGEVIK, GLEN

Right wing. Shoots right. 6'1", 205 lbs.   Born, Surrey, B.C., October 13, 1965.
(New Jersey's 1st choice, 3rd overall, in 1986 Supplemental Draft).

				Regular Season					Playoffs			
Season	Club	Lea	GP	G	A	TP	PIM	GP	G	A	TP	PIM
1986-87	U. of Denver	WCHA	40	10	8	18	32	....	....	....	....	....
1987-88	U. of Denver	WCHA	38	13	7	20	18	....	....	....	....	....
1988-89	U. of Denver	WCHA	42	12	12	24	33	....	....	....	....	....
1989-90	Nashville	ECHL	53	45	39	84	74	5	3	2	5	27
1990-91	Newmarket	AHL	2	0	0	0	0	....	....	....	....	....
	Nashville	ECHL	54	45	39	84	61	....	....	....	....	....

ENGLUND, PATRIK

Left wing. Shoots left. 6', 172 lbs.   Born, Stockholm, Sweden, June 3, 1970.
(Philadelphia's 11th choice, 151st overall, in 1990 Entry Draft).

				Regular Season					Playoffs			
Season	Club	Lea	GP	G	A	TP	PIM	GP	G	A	TP	PIM
1989-90	AIK	Swe.	31	11	7	18	....	....	....	....	....	....
1990-91	AIK	Swe.	40	9	7	16	4	....	....	....	....	....

ENS, KELLY

Center. Shoots left. 6'2", 195 lbs.   Born, Saskatoon, Sask., June 15, 1969.
(NY Islanders' 13th choice, 212th overall, in 1989 Entry Draft).

				Regular Season					Playoffs			
Season	Club	Lea	GP	G	A	TP	PIM	GP	G	A	TP	PIM
1989-90a	Lethbridge	WHL	72	62	58	120	139	19	14	14	28	36
1990-91	Springfield	AHL	21	4	2	6	13	....	....	....	....	....
	Louisville	ECHL	8	2	2	4	21	....	....	....	....	....

Signed as a free agent by **Hartford**, July 5, 1990.

a WHL East Second All-Star Team (1990)

ERICKSON, BRYAN

Right wing. Shoots right. 5'9", 170 lbs. Born, Roseau, MN, March 7, 1960.

			Regular Season					Playoffs				
Season	Club	Lea	GP	G	A	TP	PIM	GP	G	A	TP	PIM
1981-82	U. Minnesota	WCHA	35	25	20	45	20	....	....	....	....	....
1982-83	U. Minnesota	WCHA	42	35	47	82	34	....	....	....	....	....
	Hershey	AHL	1	0	1	1	0	3	3	0	3	0
1983-84	Washington	NHL	45	12	17	29	16	8	2	3	5	7
	Hershey	AHL	31	16	12	28	11	....	....	....	....	....
1984-85	Washington	NHL	57	15	13	28	23	....	....	....	....	....
	Binghamton	AHL	13	6	11	17	8	....	....	....	....	....
1985-86	Los Angeles	NHL	55	20	23	43	36	....	....	....	....	....
	Binghamton	AHL	7	5	3	8	2	....	....	....	....	....
	New Haven	AHL	14	8	3	11	11	....	....	....	....	....
1986-87	Los Angeles	NHL	68	20	30	50	26	3	1	1	2	0
1987-88	Los Angeles	NHL	42	6	15	21	20	....	....	....	....	....
	New Haven	AHL	3	0	0	0	0	....	....	....	....	....
	Pittsburgh	NHL	11	1	4	5	0	....	....	....	....	....
1988-89			DID NOT PLAY									
1989-90	Moncton	AHL	13	4	7	11	4	....	....	....	....	....
1990-91	Winnipeg	NHL	6	0	7	7	0	....	....	....	....	....
	Moncton	AHL	36	18	14	32	16	....	....	....	....	....
	NHL Totals		284	74	109	183	121	11	3	4	7	7

Signed as a free agent by **Washington**, April 5, 1983. Traded to **Los Angeles** by **Washington** for Bruce Shoebottom, October 31, 1985. Traded to **Pittsburgh** by **Los Angeles** for Chris Kontos and Pittsburgh's sixth round draft choice in 1988 Entry Draft (Micah Aivazoff), February 5, 1988. Signed as a free agent by **Winnipeg**, March 2, 1990.

ERICKSON, MICHAEL

Defense. Shoots left. 5'11", 175 lbs. Born, Worcester, MA, March 11, 1969.
(NY Islanders' 11th choice, 223rd overall, in 1987 Entry Draft).

			Regular Season					Playoffs				
Season	Club	Lea	GP	G	A	TP	PIM	GP	G	A	TP	PIM
1987-88	U. of Lowell	H.E.	31	2	4	6	22	....	....	....	....	....
1988-89	U. of Lowell	H.E.	33	4	2	6	50	....	....	....	....	....
1989-90	U. of Lowell	H.E.	32	1	3	4	42	....	....	....	....	....
1990-91	U. of Lowell	H.E.	31	0	9	9	37	....	....	....	....	....

ERICKSON, PATRIK (AIR-ihk-suhn)

Right wing. Shoots left. 5'11", 183 lbs. Born, Gavle, Sweden, March 13, 1969.
(Winnipeg's 2nd choice, 37th overall, in 1987 Entry Draft).

			Regular Season					Playoffs				
Season	Club	Lea	GP	G	A	TP	PIM	GP	G	A	TP	PIM
1986-87	Brynas	Swe.	25	10	5	15	8	....	....	....	....	....
1987-88	Brynas	Swe.	35	14	9	23	6	....	....	....	....	....
1988-89	Brynas	Swe.	33	6	10	16	14	....	....	....	....	....
1989-90	Brynas	Swe.	40	16	17	33	18	5	3	2	3	4
1990-91	Brynas	Swe.	33	9	14	23	36	....	....	....	....	....

ERICKSSON, TOMMY

Left wing. Shoots right. 5'11", 183 lbs. Born, Umea, Sweden, May 3, 1966.
(Chicago's 3rd choice, 66th overall, in 1984 Entry Draft).

			Regular Season					Playoffs				
Season	Club	Lea	GP	G	A	TP	PIM	GP	G	A	TP	PIM
1987-88	Djurgarden	Swe.	39	13	17	30	36	....	....	....	....	....
1988-89	Djurgarden	Swe.	4	0	0	0	0	....	....	....	....	....
1989-90	Djurgarden	Swe.	39	11	12	23	106	....	....	....	....	....
1990-91	Djurgarden	Swe.	39	16	11	27	64	....	....	....	....	....

ERIKSSON, NIKLAS (AIR-ihk-suhn)

Center. Shoots left. 5'11", 180 lbs. Born, Vastervik, Sweden, February 17, 1969.
(Philadelphia's 4th choice, 117th overall, in 1989 Entry Draft).

			Regular Season					Playoffs				
Season	Club	Lea	GP	G	A	TP	PIM	GP	G	A	TP	PIM
1988-89	Leksand	Swe.	33	18	12	30	22	....	....	....	....	....
1989-90	Leksand	Swe.	40	18	16	34	16	3	0	2	2	2
1990-91	Leksand	Swe.2	8	2	2	4	2	....	....	....	....	....

ERIKSSON, PETER (KESSLER) (AIR-ihk-suhn)

Left wing. Shoots right. 6'4", 218 lbs. Born, Kramfors, Sweden, July 12, 1965.
(Edmonton's 4th choice, 64th overall, in 1987 Entry Draft).

			Regular Season					Playoffs				
Season	Club	Lea	GP	G	A	TP	PIM	GP	G	A	TP	PIM
1985-86	HV-71	Swe.	30	7	8	15	18	1	0	0	0	0
1986-87	HV-71	Swe.	36	14	5	19	16	....	....	....	....	....
1987-88	HV-71	Swe.	37	14	9	23	20	2	1	0	1	0
1988-89	HV-71	Swe.	40	10	27	37	48	....	....	....	....	....
1989-90	Edmonton	NHL	20	3	3	6	24	....	....	....	....	....
	Cape Breton	AHL	21	5	12	17	36	5	2	2	4	2
1990-91	HV-71	Swe.	35	15	7	22	58	....	....	....	....	....
	NHL Totals		20	3	3	6	24	....	....	....	....	....

ERIKSSON, TOMAZ (AIR-ihk-suhn)

Left wing. Shoots left. 6', 194 lbs. Born, Stockholm, Sweden, March 23, 1967.
(Philadelphia's 4th choice, 83rd overall, in 1987 Entry Draft).

			Regular Season					Playoffs				
Season	Club	Lea	GP	G	A	TP	PIM	GP	G	A	TP	PIM
1986-87	Djurgarden	Swe.	20	7	4	11	14	2	2	0	2	0
1987-88	Djurgarden	Swe.	26	4	5	9	16	....	....	....	....	....
1988-89	Sodertalje	Swe.	38	6	13	19	50	....	....	....	....	....
1989-90	Sodertalje	Swe.	39	14	10	24	26	....	....	....	....	....
1990-91	Sodertalje	Swe.	26	12	14	26	26	....	....	....	....	....

ERIXON, JAN (AIR-ihk-suhn)

Left wing. Shoots left. 6', 196 lbs. Born, Skelleftea, Sweden, July 8, 1962.
(NY Rangers' 2nd choice, 30th overall, in 1981 Entry Draft).

			Regular Season					Playoffs				
Season	Club	Lea	GP	G	A	TP	PIM	GP	G	A	TP	PIM
1979-80	Skelleftea	Swe.	15	1	0	1	2	....	....	....	....	....
1980-81	Skelleftea	Swe.	32	6	6	12	4	3	1	0	1	0
1981-82	Skelleftea	Swe.	30	7	7	14	26	....	....	....	....	....
1982-83	Skelleftea	Swe.	36	10	19	29	32	....	....	....	....	....
1983-84	NY Rangers	NHL	75	5	25	30	16	5	2	0	2	4
1984-85	NY Rangers	NHL	66	7	22	29	33	2	0	0	0	2
1985-86	NY Rangers	NHL	31	2	17	19	4	12	0	1	1	4
1986-87	NY Rangers	NHL	68	8	18	26	24	6	1	0	1	0
1987-88	NY Rangers	NHL	70	7	19	26	33	....	....	....	....	....
1988-89	NY Rangers	NHL	44	4	11	15	27	4	0	1	1	2
1989-90	NY Rangers	NHL	58	4	9	13	8	10	1	0	1	2
1990-91	NY Rangers	NHL	53	7	18	25	8	6	1	2	3	0
	NHL Totals		465	44	139	183	153	45	5	4	9	14

ERREY, BOB (AIRY)

Left wing. Shoots left. 5'10", 183 lbs. Born, Montreal, Que., September 21, 1964.
(Pittsburgh's 1st choice, 15th overall, in 1983 Entry Draft).

			Regular Season					Playoffs				
Season	Club	Lea	GP	G	A	TP	PIM	GP	G	A	TP	PIM
1981-82	Peterborough	OHL	68	29	31	60	39	9	3	1	4	9
1982-83a	Peterborough	OHL	67	53	47	100	74	4	1	3	4	7
1983-84	Pittsburgh	NHL	65	9	13	22	29	....	....	....	....	....
1984-85	Pittsburgh	NHL	16	0	2	2	7	....	....	....	....	....
	Baltimore	AHL	59	17	24	41	14	8	3	4	7	11
1985-86	Pittsburgh	NHL	37	11	6	17	8	....	....	....	....	....
	Baltimore	AHL	18	8	7	15	28	....	....	....	....	....
1986-87	Pittsburgh	NHL	72	16	18	34	46	....	....	....	....	....
1987-88	Pittsburgh	NHL	17	3	6	9	18	....	....	....	....	....
1988-89	Pittsburgh	NHL	76	26	32	58	124	11	1	2	3	12
1989-90	Pittsburgh	NHL	78	20	19	39	109	....	....	....	....	....
1990-91	Pittsburgh	NHL	79	20	22	42	115	24	5	2	7	29
	NHL Totals		440	105	118	223	456	35	6	4	10	41

a OHL First All-Star Team (1983)

ESAU, LEONARD

Defense. Shoots right. 6'3", 190 lbs. Born, Meadow Lake, Sask., June 3, 1968.
(Toronto's 5th choice, 86th overall, in 1988 Entry Draft).

			Regular Season					Playoffs				
Season	Club	Lea	GP	G	A	TP	PIM	GP	G	A	TP	PIM
1988-89	St. Cloud	NCAA	35	12	27	39	69	....	....	....	....	....
1989-90	St. Cloud	NCAA	29	8	11	19	83	....	....	....	....	....
1990-91	Newmarket	AHL	75	4	14	18	28	....	....	....	....	....

ESPE, DAVID (ES-pee)

Defense. Shoots left. 6', 185 lbs. Born, St. Paul, MN, November 3, 1966.
(Quebec's 5th choice, 78th overall, in 1985 Entry Draft).

			Regular Season					Playoffs				
Season	Club	Lea	GP	G	A	TP	PIM	GP	G	A	TP	PIM
1985-86	U. Minnesota	WCHA	27	0	6	6	18	....	....	....	....	....
1986-87	U. Minnesota	WCHA	45	4	8	12	28	....	....	....	....	....
1987-88	U. Minnesota	WCHA	43	4	10	14	68	....	....	....	....	....
1988-89	U. Minnesota	WCHA	47	0	11	11	61	....	....	....	....	....
1989-90	Halifax	AHL	48	2	16	18	26	1	0	0	0	4
1990-91	Halifax	AHL	49	5	16	21	51	....	....	....	....	....

EVANS, DOUG

Left wing. Shoots left. 5'9", 185 lbs. Born, Peterborough, Ont., June 2, 1963.

			Regular Season					Playoffs				
Season	Club	Lea	GP	G	A	TP	PIM	GP	G	A	TP	PIM
1981-82	Peterborough	OHL	56	17	49	66	176	9	0	2	2	41
1982-83	Peterborough	OHL	65	31	55	86	165	4	0	3	3	23
1983-84	Peterborough	OHL	61	45	79	124	98	8	4	12	16	26
1984-85	Peoria	IHL	81	36	61	97	189	20	18	14	32	*88
1985-86	St. Louis	NHL	13	1	0	1	2	....	....	....	....	....
a	Peoria	IHL	60	46	51	97	179	10	4	6	10	32
1986-87	St. Louis	NHL	53	3	13	16	91	5	0	0	0	10
	Peoria	IHL	18	10	15	25	39	....	....	....	....	....
1987-88	St. Louis	NHL	41	5	7	12	49	2	0	0	0	0
	Peoria	IHL	11	4	16	20	64	....	....	....	....	....
1988-89	St. Louis	NHL	53	7	12	19	81	7	1	2	3	16
1989-90	St. Louis	NHL	3	0	0	0	0	....	....	....	....	....
	Peoria	IHL	42	19	28	47	128	....	....	....	....	....
	Winnipeg	NHL	27	10	8	18	33	7	2	2	4	10
1990-91	Winnipeg	NHL	70	7	27	34	108	....	....	....	....	....
	NHL Totals		260	33	67	100	364	21	3	4	7	36

a IHL First All-Star Team (1986)

Signed as a free agent by **St. Louis**, June 10, 1985. Traded to **Winnipeg** by **St. Louis** for Ron Wilson, January 22, 1990.

EVANS, DOUGLAS B.

Defense. Shoots right. 6', 200 lbs. Born, San Jose, CA, July 12, 1971.
(Winnipeg's 9th choice, 131st overall, in 1989 Entry Draft).

			Regular Season					Playoffs				
Season	Club	Lea	GP	G	A	TP	PIM	GP	G	A	TP	PIM
1988-89	U. of Michigan	CCHA	38	0	8	8	41	....	....	....	....	....
1989-90	U. of Michigan	CCHA	31	2	3	5	24	....	....	....	....	....
1990-91	U. of Michigan	CCHA	42	0	9	9	47	....	....	....	....	....

EVANS, KEVIN ROBERT

Left wing. Shoots left. 5'9", 185 lbs. Born, Peterborough, Ont., July 10, 1965.

			Regular Season					Playoffs				
Season	**Club**	**Lea**	**GP**	**G**	**A**	**TP**	**PIM**	**GP**	**G**	**A**	**TP**	**PIM**
1984-85	London	OHL	52	3	7	10	148	....	....	....	....	....
1985-86	Victoria	WHL	66	16	39	55	441	....	....	....	....	....
	Kalamazoo	IHL	11	3	5	8	97	6	3	0	3	56
1986-87	Kalamazoo	IHL	73	19	31	50	648	....	....	....	....	....
1987-88	Kalamazoo	IHL	54	9	28	37	404	5	1	1	2	46
1988-89	Kalamazoo	IHL	50	22	34	56	326	....	....	....	....	....
1989-90	Kalamazoo	IHL	76	30	54	84	346	....	....	....	....	....
1990-91	**Minnesota**	**NHL**	**4**	**0**	**0**	**0**	**19**	....	....	....	....	....
	Kalamazoo	IHL	16	10	12	22	70	....	....	....	....	....
	NHL Totals		**4**	**0**	**0**	**0**	**19**	....	....	....	....	....

Signed as a free agent by **Minnesota**, August 8, 1988. Claimed by **San Jose** from **Minnesota** in Dispersal Draft, May 30, 1991.

EVANS, SHAWN

Defense. Shoots left. 6'3", 195 lbs. Born, Kingston, Ont., September 7, 1965.
(New Jersey's 2nd choice, 24th overall, in 1983 Entry Draft).

			Regular Season					Playoffs				
Season	**Club**	**Lea**	**GP**	**G**	**A**	**TP**	**PIM**	**GP**	**G**	**A**	**TP**	**PIM**
1982-83	Peterborough	OHL	58	7	41	48	116	4	2	0	2	12
1983-84a	Peterborough	OHL	67	21	88	109	116	8	1	16	17	8
1984-85b	Peterborough	OHL	66	16	83	99	78	16	6	18	24	6
1985-86	**St. Louis**	**NHL**	**7**	**0**	**0**	**0**	**2**	....	....	....	....	....
	Peoria	IHL	55	8	26	34	36	....	....	....	....	....
1986-87	Nova Scotia	AHL	55	7	28	35	29	5	0	4	4	6
1987-88	Nova Scotia	AHL	79	8	62	70	109	5	1	1	2	40
1988-89	Springfield	AHL	68	9	50	59	125	....	....	....	....	....
1989-90	**NY Islanders**	**NHL**	**2**	**1**	**0**	**1**	**0**	....	....	....	....	....
	Springfield	AHL	63	6	35	41	102	18	6	11	17	35
1990-91	Maine	AHL	51	9	37	46	44	2	0	1	1	0
	NHL Totals		**9**	**1**	**0**	**1**	**2**	....	....	....	....	....

a OHL Second All-Star Team (1984)
b OHL Third All-Star Team (1985)

Traded to **St. Louis** by **New Jersey** with New Jersey's fifth-round choice (Michael Wolak) in 1986 Entry Draft for Mark Johnson, September 19, 1985. Traded to **Edmonton** by **St. Louis** for Todd Ewen, October 15, 1986. Signed as a free agent by **NY Islanders**, June 20, 1988. Signed as a free agent by **Hartford**, August 14, 1991.

EVASON, DEAN

Center. Shoots right. 5'10", 180 lbs. Born, Flin Flon, Man., August 22, 1964.
(Washington's 3rd choice, 89th overall, in 1982 Entry Draft).

			Regular Season					Playoffs				
Season	**Club**	**Lea**	**GP**	**G**	**A**	**TP**	**PIM**	**GP**	**G**	**A**	**TP**	**PIM**
1980-81	Spokane	WHL	3	1	1	2	0	....	....	....	....	....
1981-82	Spokane	WHL	26	8	14	22	65	....	....	....	....	....
	Kamloops	WHL	44	21	55	76	47	4	2	1	3	0
1982-83	Kamloops	WHL	70	71	93	164	102	7	5	7	12	18
1983-84	**Washington**	**NHL**	**2**	**0**	**0**	**0**	**2**	....	....	....	....	....
a	Kamloops	WHL	57	49	88	137	89	17	*21	20	41	33
1984-85	**Washington**	**NHL**	**15**	**3**	**4**	**7**	**2**	....	....	....	....	....
	Hartford	**NHL**	**2**	**0**	**0**	**0**	**0**	....	....	....	....	....
	Binghamton	AHL	65	27	49	76	38	8	3	5	8	9
1985-86	**Hartford**	**NHL**	**55**	**20**	**28**	**48**	**65**	**10**	**1**	**4**	**5**	**10**
	Binghamton	AHL	26	9	17	26	29	....	....	....	....	....
1986-87	**Hartford**	**NHL**	**80**	**22**	**37**	**59**	**67**	**5**	**3**	**2**	**5**	**35**
1987-88	**Hartford**	**NHL**	**77**	**10**	**18**	**28**	**115**	**6**	**1**	**1**	**2**	**2**
1988-89	**Hartford**	**NHL**	**67**	**11**	**17**	**28**	**60**	**4**	**1**	**2**	**3**	**10**
1989-90	**Hartford**	**NHL**	**78**	**18**	**25**	**43**	**138**	**7**	**2**	**2**	**4**	**22**
1990-91	**Hartford**	**NHL**	**75**	**6**	**23**	**29**	**170**	**6**	**0**	**4**	**4**	**29**
	NHL Totals		**451**	**90**	**152**	**242**	**619**	**38**	**8**	**15**	**23**	**108**

a WHL First All-Star Team, West Division (1984)

Traded to **Hartford** by **Washington** with Peter Sidorkiewicz for David Jensen, March 12, 1985.

EVO, MATTHEW (MATT)

Left wing. Shoots left. 6', 185 lbs. Born, Royal Oak, MI, December 31, 1968.
(Vancouver's 12th choice, 234th overall, in 1987 Entry Draft).

			Regular Season					Playoffs				
Season	**Club**	**Lea**	**GP**	**G**	**A**	**TP**	**PIM**	**GP**	**G**	**A**	**TP**	**PIM**
1987-88	Ferris State	CCHA	40	7	8	15	46	....	....	....	....	....
1988-89	Ferris State	CCHA	26	3	4	7	38	....	....	....	....	....
1989-90	Ferris State	CCHA	15	2	0	2	22	....	....	....	....	....
1990-91	Ferris State	CCHA	39	4	3	7	65	....	....	....	....	....

EWEN, TODD

Right wing. Shoots right. 6'2", 220 lbs. Born, Saskatoon, Sask., March 22, 1966.
(Edmonton's 9th choice, 168th overall, in 1984 Entry Draft).

			Regular Season					Playoffs				
Season	**Club**	**Lea**	**GP**	**G**	**A**	**TP**	**PIM**	**GP**	**G**	**A**	**TP**	**PIM**
1982-83	Kamloops	WHL	3	0	0	0	2	2	0	0	0	0
1983-84	N. Westminster	WHL	68	11	13	24	176	7	2	1	3	15
1984-85	N. Westminster	WHL	56	11	20	31	304	10	1	8	9	60
1985-86	N. Westminster	WHL	60	28	24	52	289	....	....	....	....	....
	Maine	AHL	....	....	....	....	....	3	0	0	0	7
1986-87	**St. Louis**	**NHL**	**23**	**2**	**0**	**2**	**84**	**4**	**0**	**0**	**0**	**23**
	Peoria	IHL	16	3	3	6	110	....	....	....	....	....
1987-88	**St. Louis**	**NHL**	**64**	**4**	**2**	**6**	**227**	**6**	**0**	**0**	**0**	**21**
1988-89	**St. Louis**	**NHL**	**34**	**4**	**5**	**9**	**171**	**2**	**0**	**0**	**0**	**21**
1989-90	**St. Louis**	**NHL**	**3**	**0**	**0**	**0**	**11**	....	....	....	....	....
	Peoria	IHL	2	0	0	0	12	....	....	....	....	....
	Montreal	**NHL**	**41**	**4**	**6**	**10**	**158**	**10**	**0**	**0**	**0**	**4**
1990-91	**Montreal**	**NHL**	**28**	**3**	**2**	**5**	**128**	....	....	....	....	....
	NHL Totals		**193**	**17**	**15**	**32**	**779**	**22**	**0**	**0**	**0**	**69**

Traded to **St. Louis** by **Edmonton** for Shawn Evans, October 15, 1986. Traded to **Montreal** by **St. Louis** for future considerations, December 12, 1989.

FABIAN, SEAN

Defense. Shoots right. 6'1", 200 lbs. Born, Minneapolis, MN, May 11, 1969.
(Vancouver's 4th choice, 87th overall, in 1987 Entry Draft).

			Regular Season					Playoffs				
Season	**Club**	**Lea**	**GP**	**G**	**A**	**TP**	**PIM**	**GP**	**G**	**A**	**TP**	**PIM**
1987-88	U. Minnesota	WCHA	10	0	1	1	11	....	....	....	....	....
1988-89	U. Minnesota	WCHA		DID NOT PLAY								
1989-90	U. Minnesota	WCHA	40	0	10	10	74	....	....	....	....	....
1990-91	U. Minnesota	WCHA	41	0	7	7	23	....	....	....	....	....

FALLOON, PAT

Right wing. Shoots right. 5'10", 192 lbs. Born, Birtle, Man., September 22, 1972.
(San Jose's 1st choice, 2nd overall, in 1991 Entry Draft).

			Regular Season					Playoffs				
Season	**Club**	**Lea**	**GP**	**G**	**A**	**TP**	**PIM**	**GP**	**G**	**A**	**TP**	**PIM**
1988-89	Spokane	WHL	72	22	56	78	41	....	....	....	....	....
1989-90	Spokane	WHL	71	60	64	124	48	6	5	8	13	4
1990-91abcd	Spokane	WHL	61	64	74	138	33	15	10	14	24	10

a WHL West First All-Star Team (1991)
b Canadian Major Junior Most Sportsmanlike Player of the Year (1991)
c Memorial Cup All-Star Team (1991)
d Won Stafford Smythe Memorial Trophy (Memorial Cup MVP) (1991)

FARRELL, BRIAN

Center. Shoots left. 5'11", 182 lbs. Born, West Hartford, CT, April 16, 1972.
(Pittsburgh's 4th choice, 89th overall, in 1990 Entry Draft).

			Regular Season					Playoffs				
Season	**Club**	**Lea**	**GP**	**G**	**A**	**TP**	**PIM**	**GP**	**G**	**A**	**TP**	**PIM**
1989-90	Avon Old Farms	HS	24	22	23	45	....	....	....	....	....	....
1990-91	Harvard	ECAC	28	3	8	11	16	....	....	....	....	....

FAUST, ANDRE

Center. Shoots left. 6'1", 180 lbs. Born, Joliette, Que., October 7, 1969.
(New Jersey's 8th choice, 173rd overall, in 1989 Entry Draft).

			Regular Season					Playoffs				
Season	**Club**	**Lea**	**GP**	**G**	**A**	**TP**	**PIM**	**GP**	**G**	**A**	**TP**	**PIM**
1988-89	Princeton	ECAC	27	15	24	39	28	....	....	....	....	....
1989-90a	Princeton	ECAC	22	9	28	37	20	....	....	....	....	....
1990-91	Princeton	ECAC	26	15	22	37	51	....	....	....	....	....

a ECAC Second All-Star Team (1990)

FEATHERSTONE, GLEN

Defense. Shoots left. 6'4", 216 lbs. Born, Toronto, Ont., July 8, 1968.
(St. Louis' 4th choice, 73rd overall, in 1986 Entry Draft).

			Regular Season					Playoffs				
Season	**Club**	**Lea**	**GP**	**G**	**A**	**TP**	**PIM**	**GP**	**G**	**A**	**TP**	**PIM**
1985-86	Windsor	OHL	49	0	6	6	135	14	1	1	2	23
1986-87	Windsor	OHL	47	6	11	17	154	14	2	6	8	19
1987-88	Windsor	OHL	53	7	27	34	201	12	6	9	15	47
1988-89	**St. Louis**	**NHL**	**18**	**0**	**2**	**2**	**22**	**6**	**0**	**0**	**0**	**0**
	Peoria	IHL	37	5	19	24	97	....	....	....	....	....
1989-90	**St. Louis**	**NHL**	**58**	**0**	**12**	**12**	**145**	**12**	**0**	**2**	**2**	**47**
	Peoria	IHL	15	1	4	5	43	....	....	....	....	....
1990-91	**St. Louis**	**NHL**	**68**	**5**	**15**	**20**	**204**	**9**	**0**	**0**	**0**	**31**
	NHL Totals		**144**	**5**	**29**	**34**	**371**	**27**	**0**	**2**	**2**	**78**

Signed as a free agent by **Boston**, July 25, 1991.

FEDOROV, SERGEI (FE-duh-rahf)

Center. Shoots left. 6'1", 191 lbs. Born, Pskov, Soviet Union, December 13, 1969.
(Detroit's 4th choice, 74th overall, in 1989 Entry Draft).

			Regular Season					Playoffs				
Season	**Club**	**Lea**	**GP**	**G**	**A**	**TP**	**PIM**	**GP**	**G**	**A**	**TP**	**PIM**
1985-86	CSKA	USSR	15	6	1	7	10	....	....	....	....	....
1986-87	CSKA	USSR	29	6	6	12	12	....	....	....	....	....
1987-88	CSKA	USSR	48	7	9	16	20	....	....	....	....	....
1988-89	CSKA	USSR	44	9	8	17	35	....	....	....	....	....
1989-90	CSKA	USSR	48	19	10	29	22	....	....	....	....	....
1990-91a	**Detroit**	**NHL**	**77**	**31**	**48**	**79**	**66**	**7**	**1**	**5**	**6**	**4**
	NHL Totals		**77**	**31**	**48**	**79**	**66**	**7**	**1**	**5**	**6**	**4**

a NHL/Upper Deck All-Rookie Team (1991)

FEDYK, BRENT (FEH-dihk)

Right wing. Shoots right. 6' 195 lbs. Born, Yorkton, Sask., March 8, 1967.
(Detroit's 1st choice, 8th overall, in 1985 Entry Draft).

			Regular Season					Playoffs				
Season	**Club**	**Lea**	**GP**	**G**	**A**	**TP**	**PIM**	**GP**	**G**	**A**	**TP**	**PIM**
1983-84	Regina	WHL	63	15	28	43	30	23	8	7	15	6
1984-85	Regina	WHL	66	35	35	70	48	8	5	4	9	0
1985-86	Regina	WHL	50	43	34	77	47	5	0	1	1	0
1986-87	Regina	WHL	12	9	6	15	9	....	....	....	....	....
	Seattle	WHL	13	5	11	16	9	....	....	....	....	....
	Portland	WHL	11	5	4	9	6	14	5	6	11	0
1987-88	**Detroit**	**NHL**	**2**	**0**	**1**	**1**	**2**	....	....	....	....	....
	Adirondack	AHL	34	9	11	20	22	5	0	2	2	6
1988-89	**Detroit**	**NHL**	**5**	**2**	**0**	**2**	**0**	....	....	....	....	....
	Adirondack	AHL	66	40	28	68	33	15	7	8	15	23
1989-90	**Detroit**	**NHL**	**27**	**1**	**4**	**5**	**24**	....	....	....	....	....
	Adirondack	AHL	33	14	15	29	24	6	2	1	3	4
1990-91	**Detroit**	**NHL**	**67**	**16**	**19**	**35**	**38**	**6**	**1**	**0**	**1**	**2**
	NHL Totals		**101**	**19**	**24**	**43**	**46**	**6**	**1**	**0**	**1**	**2**

FELIX, CHRIS

Defense. Shoots right. 5'10", 190 lbs. Born, Bramalea, Ont., May 27, 1964.

Season	Club	Lea	GP	G	A	TP	PIM	GP	G	A	TP	PIM
			Regular Season					Playoffs				
1982-83	S.S. Marie	OHL	68	16	57	73	39	16	2	12	14	10
1983-84	S.S. Marie	OHL	70	32	61	93	75	16	3	20	23	16
1984-85	S.S. Marie	OHL	66	29	72	101	89	16	7	*21	28	20
1985-86	Cdn. Olympic	...	73	7	33	40	33	....	....	....	....	....
1986-87	Cdn. Olympic	...	78	14	38	52	36	....	....	....	....	....
1987-88	Cdn. National	...	62	6	25	31	66	....	....	....	....	....
	Cdn. Olympic	...	6	1	2	3	2	....	....	....	....	....
	Fort Wayne	IHL	19	5	17	22	24	6	4	4	8	0
	Washington	NHL	....	....	....	....	....	1	0	0	0	0
1988-89	Washington	NHL	21	0	8	8	8	1	0	1	1	0
	Baltimore	AHL	50	8	29	37	44	....	....	....	....	....
1989-90	Washington	NHL	6	1	0	1	2	....	....	....	....	....
	Baltimore	AHL	73	19	42	61	115	12	0	11	11	18
1990-91	Washington	NHL	8	0	4	4	0	....	....	....	....	....
	Baltimore	AHL	27	4	24	28	26	6	1	4	5	6
	NHL Totals		35	1	12	13	10	8	1	5	6	6

Signed as a free agent by **Washington**, March 1, 1987.

FELSNER, DENNY

Left wing. Shoots left. 6', 185 lbs. Born, Warren, MI, April 29, 1970.
(St. Louis' 3rd choice, 55th overall, in 1989 Entry Draft).

Season	Club	Lea	GP	G	A	TP	PIM	GP	G	A	TP	PIM
			Regular Season					Playoffs				
1988-89	U. of Michigan	CCHA	39	30	19	49	22	....	....	....	....	....
1989-90	U. of Michigan	CCHA	33	27	16	43	24	....	....	....	....	....
1990-91ab	U. of Michigan	CCHA	46	*40	35	75	58	....	....	....	....	....

a CCHA First All-Star Team (1991)
b NCAA West Second All-American Team (1991)

FENTON, ERIC

Center. Shoots right. 6'2", 190 lbs. Born, Troy, NY, July 17, 1969.
(NY Rangers' 10th choice, 202nd overall, in 1988 Entry Draft).

Season	Club	Lea	GP	G	A	TP	PIM	GP	G	A	TP	PIM
			Regular Season					Playoffs				
1988-89	U. of Maine	H.E.		DID NOT PLAY								
1989-90	U. of Maine	H.E.	7	2	2	4	2	....	....	....	....	....
1990-91	U. of Maine	H.E.	10	0	1	1	16	....	....	....	....	....

FENTON, PAUL JOHN

Left wing. Shoots left. 5'11", 180 lbs. Born, Springfield, MA, December 22, 1959.

Season	Club	Lea	GP	G	A	TP	PIM	GP	G	A	TP	PIM
			Regular Season					Playoffs				
1979-80	Boston U.	ECAC	24	8	17	25	14	....	....	....	....	....
1980-81	Boston U.	ECAC	5	3	2	5	0	....	....	....	....	....
1981-82	Boston U.	ECAC	28	20	13	33	20	....	....	....	....	....
1982-83a	Peoria	IHL	82	60	51	111	53	....	....	....	....	....
	Colorado	CHL	1	0	1	1	0	3	2	0	2	2
1983-84	Binghamton	AHL	78	41	24	65	67	....	....	....	....	....
1984-85	Hartford	NHL	33	7	5	12	10	....	....	....	....	....
	Binghamton	AHL	45	26	21	47	18	....	....	....	....	....
1985-86	Hartford	NHL	1	0	0	0	0	....	....	....	....	....
b	Binghamton	AHL	75	53	35	88	87	6	2	0	2	2
1986-87	NY Rangers	NHL	8	0	0	0	2	....	....	....	....	....
c	New Haven	AHL	70	37	38	75	45	7	6	4	10	6
1987-88	Los Angeles	NHL	71	20	23	43	46	5	2	1	3	2
	New Haven	AHL	5	11	5	16	9	....	....	....	....	....
1988-89	Los Angeles	NHL	21	2	3	5	6	....	....	....	....	....
	Winnipeg	NHL	59	14	9	23	33	....	....	....	....	....
1989-90	Winnipeg	NHL	80	32	18	50	40	7	2	0	2	23
1990-91	Winnipeg	NHL	17	4	4	8	18	....	....	....	....	....
	Toronto	NHL	30	5	10	15	0	....	....	....	....	....
	Calgary	NHL	31	5	7	12	10	5	0	0	0	2
	NHL Totals		351	89	79	168	165	17	4	1	5	27

a IHL First All-Star Team (1983)
b AHL First All-Star Team (1986)
c AHL Second All-Star Team (1987)

Signed as free agent by **Hartford**, October 6, 1983. Claimed by **Los Angeles** in NHL Waiver Draft, October 5, 1987. Traded to **Winnipeg** by **Los Angeles** for Gilles Hamel, November 25, 1988. Traded to **Toronto** by **Winnipeg** with Dave Ellett for Ed Olczyk and Mark Osborne, November 10, 1990. Traded to **Washington** by **Toronto** with John Kordic for Washington's fifth round choice (Alexei Kudashov) in 1991 Entry Draft, January 24, 1991. Traded to **Calgary** by **Washington** for Ken Sabourin, January 24, 1991. Traded to **Hartford** by **Calgary** for future considerations, August 26, 1991.

FENYVES, DAVID (FEHN-vehs)

Defense. Shoots left. 5'11", 192 lbs. Born, Dunnville, Ont., April 29, 1960.

Season	Club	Lea	GP	G	A	TP	PIM	GP	G	A	TP	PIM
			Regular Season					Playoffs				
1978-79	Peterborough	OHA	66	2	23	25	122	19	0	5	5	18
1979-80a	Peterborough	OHA	66	9	36	45	92	14	0	3	3	14
1980-81	Rochester	AHL	77	6	16	22	146	....	....	....	....	....
1981-82	Rochester	AHL	73	3	14	17	68	5	0	1	1	4
1982-83	Buffalo	NHL	24	0	8	8	14	4	0	0	0	0
	Rochester	AHL	51	2	19	21	45	....	....	....	....	....
1983-84	Buffalo	NHL	10	0	4	4	9	2	0	0	0	7
	Rochester	AHL	70	3	16	19	55	16	1	4	5	22
1984-85	Buffalo	NHL	60	1	8	9	27	5	0	0	0	2
	Rochester	AHL	9	0	3	3	8	....	....	....	....	....
1985-86	Buffalo	NHL	47	0	7	7	37	....	....	....	....	....
1986-87	Buffalo	NHL	7	1	0	1	0	....	....	....	....	....
bc	Rochester	AHL	71	6	16	22	57	18	3	12	15	10
1987-88	Philadelphia	NHL	5	0	0	0	0	....	....	....	....	....
de	Hershey	AHL	75	11	40	51	47	12	1	8	9	10
1988-89	Philadelphia	NHL	1	0	1	1	0	....	....	....	....	....
de	Hershey	AHL	79	15	51	66	41	12	2	6	8	6
1989-90	Philadelphia	NHL	12	0	0	0	4	....	....	....	....	....
	Hershey	AHL	66	6	37	43	57	....	....	....	....	....
1990-91	Philadelphia	NHL	40	1	4	5	28	....	....	....	....	....
	Hershey	AHL	29	4	11	15	13	7	0	3	3	6
	NHL Totals		206	3	32	35	119	11	0	0	0	9

a OHA Second All-Star Team (1980)
b AHL Second All-Star Team (1987)
c Named AHL Playoff MVP (1987)
d AHL First All-Star Team, (1988, 1989)
e Won Eddie Shore Plaque (Outstanding Defenseman-AHL) (1988, 1989)

Signed as free agent by **Buffalo**, October 31, 1979. Claimed by **Philadelphia** in NHL Waiver Draft, October 5, 1987.

FERGUS, THOMAS JOSEPH (TOM)

Center. Shoots left. 6'3", 210 lbs. Born, Chicago, IL, June 16, 1962.
(Boston's 2nd choice, 60th overall, in 1980 Entry Draft).

Season	Club	Lea	GP	G	A	TP	PIM	GP	G	A	TP	PIM
			Regular Season					Playoffs				
1979-80	Peterborough	OHA	63	8	6	14	14	14	1	5	6	6
1980-81	Peterborough	OHA	63	43	45	88	33	5	1	4	5	2
1981-82	Boston	NHL	61	15	24	39	12	6	3	0	3	0
1982-83	Boston	NHL	80	28	35	63	39	15	2	2	4	15
1983-84	Boston	NHL	69	25	36	61	12	3	2	0	2	9
1984-85	Boston	NHL	79	30	43	73	75	5	0	0	0	4
1985-86	Toronto	NHL	78	31	42	73	64	10	5	7	12	6
1986-87	Toronto	NHL	57	21	28	49	57	2	0	1	1	2
	Newmarket	AHL	1	0	1	1	0	....	....	....	....	....
1987-88	Toronto	NHL	63	19	31	50	81	6	2	3	5	2
1988-89	Toronto	NHL	80	22	45	67	48	....	....	....	....	....
1989-90	Toronto	NHL	54	19	26	45	62	5	2	1	3	4
1990-91	Toronto	NHL	14	5	4	9	8	....	....	....	....	....
	NHL Totals		635	215	314	529	458	52	16	14	30	42

Traded to **Toronto** by **Boston** for Bill Derlago, October 11, 1985.

FERGUSON, CRAIG

Right Wing. Shoots left. 6', 185 lbs. Born, Castro Valley, CA, April 8, 1970.
(Montreal's 7th choice, 146th overall, in 1989 Entry Draft).

Season	Club	Lea	GP	G	A	TP	PIM	GP	G	A	TP	PIM
			Regular Season					Playoffs				
1988-89	Yale	ECAC	24	11	6	17	20	....	....	....	....	....
1989-90	Yale	ECAC	35	6	15	21	38	....	....	....	....	....
1990-91	Yale	ECAC	29	11	10	21	34	....	....	....	....	....

FERGUSON, JOHN Jr.

Left wing. Shoots left. 6', 192 lbs. Born, Winnipeg, Man., July 7, 1967.
(Montreal's 15th choice, 247th overall, in 1985 Entry Draft).

Season	Club	Lea	GP	G	A	TP	PIM	GP	G	A	TP	PIM
			Regular Season					Playoffs				
1985-86	Providence	H.E.	18	1	2	3	2	....	....	....	....	....
1986-87	Providence	H.E.	23	0	0	0	6	....	....	....	....	....
1987-88	Providence	H.E.	34	0	5	5	31	....	....	....	....	....
1988-89	Providence	H.E.	40	14	15	29	61	....	....	....	....	....
1989-90	Sherbrooke	AHL	17	4	3	7	8	1	0	0	0	0
	Peoria	IHL	18	1	8	9	14	3	0	0	0	2
1990-91	Fredericton	AHL	73	14	8	22	96	9	3	3	6	21

FERNER, MARK

Defense. Shoots left. 6', 193 lbs. Born, Regina, Sask., September 5, 1965.
(Buffalo's 12th choice, 194th overall, in 1983 Entry Draft).

Season	Club	Lea	GP	G	A	TP	PIM	GP	G	A	TP	PIM
			Regular Season					Playoffs				
1982-83	Kamloops	WHL	69	6	15	21	81	7	0	0	0	7
1983-84	Kamloops	WHL	72	9	30	39	169	14	1	8	9	20
1984-85a	Kamloops	WHL	69	15	39	54	91	15	4	9	13	21
1985-86	Rochester	AHL	63	3	14	17	87	....	....	....	....	....
1986-87	Buffalo	NHL	13	0	3	3	9	....	....	....	....	....
	Rochester	AHL	54	0	12	12	157	....	....	....	....	....
1987-88	Rochester	AHL	69	1	25	26	165	7	1	4	5	31
1988-89	Buffalo	NHL	2	0	0	0	2	....	....	....	....	....
	Rochester	AHL	55	0	18	18	97	....	....	....	....	....
1989-90	Washington	NHL	2	0	0	0	0	....	....	....	....	....
	Baltimore	AHL	74	7	28	35	76	11	1	2	3	21
1990-91	Washington	NHL	7	0	1	1	4	....	....	....	....	....
a	Baltimore	AHL	61	14	40	54	38	6	1	4	5	24
	NHL Totals		24	0	4	4	15	....	....	....	....	....

a WHL First All-Star Team, West Division (1985)
a AHL Second All-Star Team (1991)

Traded to **Washington** by **Buffalo** for Scott McCrory, June 1, 1989.

FERNHOLZ, JAMES (JIM)

Right wing. Shoots right. 6'2", 200 lbs. Born, Minneapolis, MN, March 16, 1969.
(Winnipeg's 9th choice, 184th overall, in 1987 Entry Draft).

			Regular Season					Playoffs				
Season	Club	Lea	GP	G	A	TP	PIM	GP	G	A	TP	PIM
1987-88	U. of Vermont	ECAC	23	3	5	8	12	....	....	....	....	....
1988-89	U. of Vermont	ECAC	28	3	11	14	16	....	....	....	....	....
1989-90	U. of Vermont	ECAC	31	3	6	9	22	....	....	....	....	....
1990-91	U. of Vermont	ECAC	33	6	8	14	22	....	....	....	....	....

FERRARO, RAY

Center. Shoots left. 5'10", 185 lbs. Born, Trail, B.C., August 23, 1964.
(Hartford's 5th choice, 88th overall, in 1982 Entry Draft).

			Regular Season					Playoffs				
Season	Club	Lea	GP	G	A	TP	PIM	GP	G	A	TP	PIM
1982-83	Portland	WHL	50	41	49	90	39	14	14	10	24	13
1983-84a	Brandon	WHL	72	*108	84	*192	84	11	13	15	28	20
1984-85	**Hartford**	**NHL**	**44**	**11**	**17**	**28**	**40**	....	....	....	....	....
	Binghamton	AHL	37	20	13	33	29	....	....	....	....	....
1985-86	**Hartford**	**NHL**	**76**	**30**	**47**	**77**	**57**	**10**	**3**	**6**	**9**	**4**
1986-87	**Hartford**	**NHL**	**80**	**27**	**32**	**59**	**42**	**6**	**1**	**1**	**2**	**8**
1987-88	**Hartford**	**NHL**	**68**	**21**	**29**	**50**	**81**	**6**	**1**	**1**	**2**	**6**
1988-89	**Hartford**	**NHL**	**80**	**41**	**35**	**76**	**86**	**4**	**2**	**0**	**2**	**4**
1989-90	**Hartford**	**NHL**	**79**	**25**	**29**	**54**	**109**	**7**	**0**	**3**	**3**	**2**
1990-91	**Hartford**	**NHL**	**15**	**2**	**5**	**7**	**18**	....	....	....	....	....
	NY Islanders	**NHL**	**61**	**19**	**16**	**35**	**52**	....	....	....	....	....
	NHL Totals		**503**	**176**	**210**	**386**	**485**	**33**	**7**	**11**	**18**	**24**

a WHL First All-Star Team (1984)

Traded to **NY Islanders** by **Hartford** for Doug Crossman, November 13, 1990.

FERREIRA, BRIAN

Right wing. Shoots right. 6', 175 lbs. Born, Falmouth, MA, January 2, 1968.
(Boston's 7th choice, 160th overall, in 1986 Entry Draft).

			Regular Season					Playoffs				
Season	Club	Lea	GP	G	A	TP	PIM	GP	G	A	TP	PIM
1986-87	RPI	ECAC	30	17	15	32	22	....	....	....	....	....
1987-88	RPI	ECAC	32	18	19	37	48	....	....	....	....	....
1988-89	RPI	ECAC	15	3	13	16	28	....	....	....	....	....
1989-90	RPI	ECAC	34	10	35	45	36	....	....	....	....	....
1990-91	Maine	AHL	5	0	1	1	2	....	....	....	....	....
	Johnstown	ECHL	38	25	22	47	47	8	9	2	11	14

FETISOV, VIACHESLAV (SLAVA) (feh-TEE-sahf)

Defense. Shoots left. 6'1", 220 lbs. Born, Moscow, Soviet Union, May 20, 1958.
(New Jersey's 6th choice, 150th overall, in 1983 Entry Draft).

			Regular Season					Playoffs				
Season	Club	Lea	GP	G	A	TP	PIM	GP	G	A	TP	PIM
1974-75	CSKA	USSR	1	0	0	0	0	....	....	....	....	....
1976-77	CSKA	USSR	27	3	4	7	14	....	....	....	....	....
1977-78a	CSKA	USSR	35	9	18	27	46	....	....	....	....	....
1978-79	CSKA	USSR	29	10	19	29	40	....	....	....	....	....
1979-80	CSKA	USSR	37	10	14	24	46	....	....	....	....	....
1980-81	CSKA	USSR	48	13	16	29	44	....	....	....	....	....
1981-82ac	CSKA	USSR	46	15	26	41	20	....	....	....	....	....
1982-83a	CSKA	USSR	43	6	17	23	46	....	....	....	....	....
1983-84ab	CSKA	USSR	44	19	30	49	38	....	....	....	....	....
1984-85a	CSKA	USSR	20	13	12	25	6	....	....	....	....	....
1985-86abc	CSKA	USSR	40	15	19	34	12	....	....	....	....	....
1986-87ab	CSKA	USSR	39	13	20	33	18	....	....	....	....	....
1987-88ab	CSKA	USSR	46	18	17	35	26	....	....	....	....	....
1988-89	CSKA	USSR	23	9	9	18	18	....	....	....	....	....
1989-90	**New Jersey**	**NHL**	**72**	**8**	**34**	**42**	**52**	**6**	**0**	**2**	**2**	**10**
1990-91	**New Jersey**	**NHL**	**67**	**3**	**16**	**19**	**62**	**7**	**0**	**0**	**0**	**15**
	Utica	AHL	1	1	1	2	0	....	....	....	....	....
	NHL Totals		**139**	**11**	**50**	**61**	**114**	**13**	**0**	**2**	**2**	**25**

a Soviet National League All-Star Team (1978, 1982-88)
b Leningradskaya-Pravda Trophy-Top Scoring Defenseman (1984, 1986-88)
c Soviet Player of the Year (1982, 1986)

FILIMONOV, DIMITRI

Defense. Shoots right. 6'4", 207 lbs. Born, Perm, USSR, October 14, 1971.
(Winnipeg's 2nd choice, 49th overall, in 1991 Entry Draft).

			Regular Season					Playoffs				
Season	Club	Lea	GP	G	A	TP	PIM	GP	G	A	TP	PIM
1990-91	Moscow D'amo	USSR	45	4	6	10	12	....	....	....	....	....

FILIPEK, DARYL

Defense. Shoots left. 6'1", 185 lbs. Born, Hay River, NWT, November 30, 1970.
(Vancouver's 6th choice, 128th overall, in 1990 Entry Draft).

			Regular Season					Playoffs				
Season	Club	Lea	GP	G	A	TP	PIM	GP	G	A	TP	PIM
1989-90	Ferris State	CCHA	38	4	20	24	44	....	....	....	....	....
1990-91	Ferris State	CCHA	39	6	11	17	68	....	....	....	....	....

FINGERHUT, TIMOTHY

Left wing. Shoots left. 6', 175 lbs. Born, Camden, NJ, May 20, 1971.
(Pittsburgh's 12th choice, 194th overall, in 1990 Entry Draft).

			Regular Season					Playoffs				
Season	Club	Lea	GP	G	A	TP	PIM	GP	G	A	TP	PIM
1989-90	Canterbury	HS	29	20	30	50	0	....	....	....	....	....
1990-91	U. of Vermont	ECAC	23	6	7	13	19	....	....	....	....	....

FINLEY, JEFF

Defense. Shoots left. 6'2", 185 lbs. Born, Edmonton, Alta., April 14, 1967.
(NY Islanders' 4th choice, 55th overall, in 1985 Entry Draft).

			Regular Season					Playoffs				
Season	Club	Lea	GP	G	A	TP	PIM	GP	G	A	TP	PIM
1983-84	Portland	WHL	5	0	0	0	5	5	0	1	1	4
1984-85	Portland	WHL	69	6	44	50	57	6	1	2	3	2
1985-86	Portland	WHL	70	11	59	70	83	15	1	7	8	16
1986-87	Portland	WHL	72	13	53	66	113	20	1	*21	22	27
1987-88	**NY Islanders**	**NHL**	**10**	**0**	**5**	**5**	**15**	**1**	**0**	**0**	**0**	**2**
	Springfield	AHL	52	5	18	23	50	....	....	....	....	....
1988-89	**NY Islanders**	**NHL**	**4**	**0**	**0**	**0**	**6**	....	....	....	....	....
	Springfield	AHL	65	3	16	19	55	....	....	....	....	....
1989-90	**NY Islanders**	**NHL**	**11**	**0**	**1**	**1**	**0**	**5**	**0**	**2**	**2**	**2**
	Springfield	AHL	57	1	15	16	41	13	1	4	5	23
1990-91	**NY Islanders**	**NHL**	**11**	**0**	**0**	**0**	**4**	....	....	....	....	....
	Capital Dist.	AHL	67	10	34	44	34	....	....	....	....	....
	NHL Totals		**36**	**0**	**6**	**6**	**25**	**6**	**0**	**2**	**2**	**4**

FINN, STEVEN

Defense. Shoots left. 6', 198 lbs. Born, Laval, Que., August 20, 1966.
(Quebec's 3rd choice, 57th overall, in 1984 Entry Draft).

			Regular Season					Playoffs				
Season	Club	Lea	GP	G	A	TP	PIM	GP	G	A	TP	PIM
1982-83	Laval	QMJHL	69	7	30	37	108	6	0	2	2	6
1983-84	Laval	QMJHL	68	7	39	46	159	14	1	6	7	27
1984-85a	Laval	QMJHL	61	20	33	53	169	....	....	....	....	....
	Fredericton	AHL	4	0	0	0	14	6	1	1	2	4
1985-86	**Quebec**	**NHL**	**17**	**0**	**1**	**1**	**28**	....	....	....	....	....
	Laval	QMJHL	29	4	15	19	111	14	6	16	22	57
1986-87	**Quebec**	**NHL**	**36**	**2**	**5**	**7**	**40**	**13**	**0**	**2**	**2**	**29**
	Fredericton	AHL	38	7	19	26	73	....	....	....	....	....
1987-88	**Quebec**	**NHL**	**75**	**3**	**7**	**10**	**198**	....	....	....	....	....
1988-89	**Quebec**	**NHL**	**77**	**2**	**6**	**8**	**235**	....	....	....	....	....
1989-90	**Quebec**	**NHL**	**64**	**3**	**9**	**12**	**208**	....	....	....	....	....
1990-91	**Quebec**	**NHL**	**71**	**6**	**13**	**19**	**228**	....	....	....	....	....
	NHL Totals		**340**	**16**	**41**	**57**	**937**	**13**	**0**	**2**	**2**	**29**

a QMJHL Second All-Star Team (1985).

FIORENTINO, PETER

Defense. Shoots right. 6'1", 200 lbs. Born, Niagara Falls, Ont., December 22, 1968.
(NY Rangers' 11th choice, 215th overall, in 1988 Entry Draft).

			Regular Season					Playoffs				
Season	Club	Lea	GP	G	A	TP	PIM	GP	G	A	TP	PIM
1985-86	S.S. Marie	OHL	58	1	6	7	87	....	....	....	....	....
1986-87	S.S. Marie	OHL	64	1	12	13	187	....	....	....	....	....
1987-88	S.S. Marie	OHL	65	5	27	32	252	6	2	2	4	21
1988-89	S.S. Marie	OHL	55	5	24	29	220	....	....	....	....	....
	Denver	IHL	10	0	0	0	39	4	0	0	0	24
1989-90	Flint	IHL	64	2	7	9	302	....	....	....	....	....
1990-91	Binghamton	AHL	55	2	11	13	361	1	0	0	0	0

FISHER, CRAIG

Center. Shoots left. 6'3", 180 lbs. Born, Oshawa, Ont., June 30, 1970.
(Philadelphia's 3rd choice, 56th overall, in 1988 Entry Draft).

			Regular Season					Playoffs				
Season	Club	Lea	GP	G	A	TP	PIM	GP	G	A	TP	PIM
1988-89	Miami-Ohio	CCHA	37	22	20	42	37	....	....	....	....	....
1989-90a	Miami-Ohio	CCHA	39	37	29	66	38	....	....	....	....	....
	Philadelphia	**NHL**	**2**	**0**	**0**	**0**	**0**	....	....	....	....	....
1990-91	**Philadelphia**	**NHL**	**2**	**0**	**0**	**0**	**0**	....	....	....	....	....
	Hershey	AHL	77	43	36	79	46	7	5	3	8	2
	NHL Totals		**4**	**0**	**0**	**0**	**0**	....	....	....	....	....

a CCHA First All-Star Team (1990)

Traded to **Edmonton** by **Philadelphia** with Scott Mellanby and Craig Berube for Dave Brown, Corey Foster and Jari Kurri, May 30, 1991.

FITZGERALD, RUSTY

Center. Shoots left. 6'1", 186 lbs. Born, Minneapolis, MN, October 4, 1972.
(Pittsburgh's 2nd choice, 38th overall, in 1991 Entry Draft).

			Regular Season					Playoffs				
Season	Club	Lea	GP	G	A	TP	PIM	GP	G	A	TP	PIM
1990-91	Silverbay	HS	21	25	27	52	24	....	....	....	....	....

FITZGERALD, TOM

Right wing/Center. Shoots right. 6'1", 195 lbs. Born, Melrose, MA, August 28, 1968.
(NY Islanders' 1st choice, 17th overall, in 1986 Entry Draft).

			Regular Season					Playoffs				
Season	Club	Lea	GP	G	A	TP	PIM	GP	G	A	TP	PIM
1986-87	Providence	H.E.	27	8	14	22	22	....	....	....	....	....
1987-88	Providence	H.E.	36	19	15	34	50	....	....	....	....	....
1988-89	**NY Islanders**	**NHL**	**23**	**3**	**5**	**8**	**10**	....	....	....	....	....
	Springfield	AHL	61	24	18	42	43	....	....	....	....	....
1989-90	**NY Islanders**	**NHL**	**19**	**2**	**5**	**7**	**4**	**4**	**1**	**0**	**1**	**4**
	Springfield	AHL	53	30	23	53	32	14	2	9	11	13
1990-91	**NY Islanders**	**NHL**	**41**	**5**	**5**	**10**	**24**	....	....	....	....	....
	Capital Dist.	AHL	27	7	7	14	50	....	....	....	....	....
	NHL Totals		**83**	**10**	**15**	**25**	**38**	**4**	**1**	**0**	**1**	**4**

FITZPATRICK, ROSS

Left wing. Shoots left. 6', 195 lbs. Born, Penticton, B.C., October 7, 1960.
(Philadelphia's 7th choice, 147th overall, in 1980 Entry Draft).

			Regular Season					Playoffs				
Season	Club	Lea	GP	G	A	TP	PIM	GP	G	A	TP	PIM
1978-79	W. Michigan	CCHA	35	16	21	37	31	....	....	....	....	....
1979-80	W. Michigan	CCHA	34	26	33	59	22	....	....	....	....	....
1980-81a	W. Michigan	CCHA	36	28	43	71	22	....	....	....	....	....
1981-82	W. Michigan	CCHA	33	30	28	58	34	....	....	....	....	....
1982-83	**Philadelphia**	**NHL**	**1**	**0**	**0**	**0**	**0**	....	....	....	....	....
	Maine	AHL	66	29	28	57	32	12	5	1	6	12
1983-84	**Philadelphia**	**NHL**	**12**	**4**	**2**	**6**	**0**	....	....	....	....	....
	Springfield	AHL	45	33	30	63	28	4	3	2	5	2
1984-85	**Philadelphia**	**NHL**	**5**	**1**	**0**	**1**	**0**	....	....	....	....	....
	Hershey	AHL	35	26	15	41	8	....	....	....	....	....
1985-86	**Philadelphia**	**NHL**	**2**	**0**	**0**	**0**	**0**	....	....	....	....	....
b	Hershey	AHL	77	50	47	97	28	17	9	7	16	10
1986-87	Hershey	AHL	66	45	40	85	34	5	1	4	5	10
1987-88	Hershey	AHL	35	14	17	31	12	12	*11	4	15	8
1988-89	Hershey	AHL	11	6	9	15	4	9	2	2	4	4
1989-90b	Hershey	AHL	74	45	*58	103	26	....	....	....	....	....
1990-91	Binghamton	AHL	69	26	29	55	26	10	3	1	4	4
	NHL Totals		**20**	**5**	**2**	**7**	**0**	....	....	....	....	....

a CCHA First All-Star Team (1981)
b AHL Second All-Star Team (1986, 1990)

FLANAGAN, JOSEPH

Center. Shoots right. 6', 180 lbs. Born, Arlington, MA, March 5, 1969.
(Los Angeles' 13th choice, 238th overall, in 1988 Entry Draft).

			Regular Season					Playoffs				
Season	Club	Lea	GP	G	A	TP	PIM	GP	G	A	TP	PIM
1988-89	N. Hampshire	H.E.	23	11	34	45	4	....	....	....	....	....
1989-90	N. Hampshire	H.E.	34	12	24	36	6	....	....	....	....	....
1990-91	N. Hampshire	H.E.	35	24	20	44	18	....	....	....	....	....

FLANAGAN, PAUL

Defense. Shoots left. 6'2", 205 lbs. Born, Acton, MA, May 17, 1969.
(Buffalo's 7th choice, 127th overall, in 1987 Entry Draft).

			Regular Season					Playoffs				
Season	Club	Lea	GP	G	A	TP	PIM	GP	G	A	TP	PIM
1988-89	Northeastern	H.E.	25	1	4	5	....	....	....	....	....	....
1989-90	Northeastern	H.E.	30	0	1	1	32	....	....	....	....	....
1990-91	Northeastern	H.E.	34	1	7	8	58	....	....	....	....	....

FLATLEY, PATRICK (FLAT-lee)

Right wing. Shoots right. 6'2", 197 lbs. Born, Toronto, Ont., October 3, 1963.
(NY Islanders' 1st choice, 21st overall, in 1982 Entry Draft).

			Regular Season					Playoffs				
Season	Club	Lea	GP	G	A	TP	PIM	GP	G	A	TP	PIM
1981-82	U. Wisconsin	WCHA	17	10	9	19	40	....	....	....	....	....
1982-83ab	U. Wisconsin	WCHA	26	17	24	41	48	....	....	....	....	....
1983-84	Cdn. Olympic	...	57	33	17	50	136	....	....	....	....	....
	NY Islanders	**NHL**	**16**	**2**	**7**	**9**	**6**	**21**	**9**	**6**	**15**	**14**
1984-85	**NY Islanders**	**NHL**	**78**	**20**	**31**	**51**	**106**	**4**	**1**	**0**	**1**	**6**
1985-86	**NY Islanders**	**NHL**	**73**	**18**	**34**	**52**	**66**	**3**	**0**	**0**	**0**	**21**
1986-87	**NY Islanders**	**NHL**	**63**	**16**	**35**	**51**	**81**	**11**	**3**	**2**	**5**	**6**
1987-88	**NY Islanders**	**NHL**	**40**	**9**	**15**	**24**	**28**	....	....	....	....	....
1988-89	**NY Islanders**	**NHL**	**41**	**10**	**15**	**25**	**31**	....	....	....	....	....
	Springfield	AHL	2	1	1	2	2	....	....	....	....	....
1989-90	**NY Islanders**	**NHL**	**62**	**17**	**32**	**49**	**101**	**5**	**3**	**0**	**3**	**2**
1990-91	**NY Islanders**	**NHL**	**56**	**20**	**25**	**45**	**74**	....	....	....	....	....
	NHL Totals		**429**	**112**	**194**	**306**	**493**	**44**	**16**	**8**	**24**	**49**

a WCHA First All-Star Team (1983)
b Named to NCAA All-Tournament Team (1983)

FLEETWOOD, BRENT

Left wing. Shoots left. 6'1", 180 lbs. Born, Edmonton, Alta., June 4, 1970.
(Montreal's 9th choice, 165th overall, in 1990 Entry Draft).

			Regular Season					Playoffs				
Season	Club	Lea	GP	G	A	TP	PIM	GP	G	A	TP	PIM
1987-88	Portland	WHL	28	7	6	13	20	....	....	....	....	....
1988-89	Portland	WHL	70	20	31	51	87	19	5	2	7	22
1989-90	Portland	WHL	72	41	43	84	114	....	....	....	....	....
1990-91	Fredericton	AHL	5	0	1	1	2	....	....	....	....	....
	Winston-Salem	ECHL	61	28	32	60	75	....	....	....	....	....

FLEMING, JOE

Defense. Shoots right. 6'4", 220 lbs. Born, Newton, MA, December 5, 1971.
(St. Louis' 9th choice, 243rd overall, in 1990 Entry Draft).

			Regular Season					Playoffs				
Season	Club	Lea	GP	G	A	TP	PIM	GP	G	A	TP	PIM
1989-90	Xaverian	HS	....	2	5	7	0	....	....	....	....	....
1990-91	N. Hampshire	H.E.	DID NOT PLAY									

FLETCHER, STEVEN

Left wing/Defense. Shoots left. 6'2", 180 lbs. Born, Montreal, Que., March 31, 1962.
(Calgary's 11th choice, 202nd overall, in 1980 Entry Draft).

			Regular Season					Playoffs				
Season	Club	Lea	GP	G	A	TP	PIM	GP	G	A	TP	PIM
1981-82	Hull	QMJHL	60	4	20	24	230	....	....	....	....	....
1982-83	Sherbrooke	AHL	36	0	1	1	119	....	....	....	....	....
	Fort Wayne	IHL	34	1	9	10	115	....	....	....	....	....
1983-84	Sherbrooke	AHL	77	3	7	10	208	....	....	....	....	....
1984-85	Sherbrooke	AHL	50	2	4	6	192	13	0	0	0	48
1985-86	Sherbrooke	AHL	64	2	12	14	293	....	....	....	....	....
1986-87	Sherbrooke	AHL	70	15	11	26	261	17	5	5	10	*82
1987-88	**Montreal**	**NHL**	....	....	....	....	....	**1**	**0**	**0**	**0**	**5**
	Sherbrooke	AHL	76	8	21	29	338	6	2	1	3	28
1988-89	**Winnipeg**	**NHL**	**3**	**0**	**0**	**0**	**5**	....	....	....	....	....
	Halifax	AHL	29	5	8	13	91	....	....	....	....	....
	Moncton	AHL	23	1	1	2	89	....	....	....	....	....
1989-90	Hershey	AHL	28	1	1	2	132	....	....	....	....	....
1990-91	Fort Wayne	IHL	66	7	9	16	289	15	2	0	2	70
	NHL Totals		**3**	**0**	**0**	**0**	**5**	**1**	**0**	**0**	**0**	**5**

Signed as a free agent by **Montreal**, August 21, 1984. Traded to **Philadelphia** by **Winnipeg** for future considerations, December 12, 1988.

FLEURY, THEOREN

Center/Right wing. Shoots right. 5'6", 160 lbs. Born, Oxbow, Sask., June 29, 1968.
(Calgary's 9th choice, 166th overall, in 1987 Entry Draft).

			Regular Season					Playoffs				
Season	Club	Lea	GP	G	A	TP	PIM	GP	G	A	TP	PIM
1984-85	Moose Jaw	WHL	71	29	46	75	82	....	....	....	....	....
1985-86	Moose Jaw	WHL	72	43	65	108	124	....	....	....	....	....
1986-87	Moose Jaw	WHL	66	61	68	129	110	9	7	9	16	34
1987-88	Moose Jaw	WHL	65	68	92	*160	235	....	....	....	....	....
	Salt Lake	IHL	2	3	4	7	7	8	11	5	16	16
1988-89	**Calgary**	**NHL**	**36**	**14**	**20**	**34**	**46**	**22**	**5**	**6**	**11**	**24**
	Salt Lake	IHL	40	37	37	74	81	....	....	....	....	....
1989-90	**Calgary**	**NHL**	**80**	**31**	**35**	**66**	**157**	**6**	**2**	**3**	**5**	**10**
1990-91	**Calgary**	**NHL**	**79**	**51**	**53**	**104**	**136**	**7**	**2**	**5**	**7**	**14**
	NHL Totals		**195**	**96**	**108**	**204**	**339**	**35**	**9**	**14**	**23**	**48**

Played in NHL All-Star Game (1991)

FLICHEL, TODD (FLIH-kehl)

Defense. Shoots right. 6'3", 195 lbs. Born, Osgoode, Ont., September 14, 1964.
(Winnipeg's 10th choice, 169th overall, in 1983 Entry Draft).

			Regular Season					Playoffs				
Season	Club	Lea	GP	G	A	TP	PIM	GP	G	A	TP	PIM
1983-84	Bowling Green	CCHA	44	1	3	4	12	....	....	....	....	....
1984-85	Bowling Green	CCHA	42	5	7	12	62	....	....	....	....	....
1985-86	Bowling Green	CCHA	42	3	10	13	84	....	....	....	....	....
1986-87	Bowling Green	CCHA	42	4	15	19	77	....	....	....	....	....
1987-88	**Winnipeg**	**NHL**	**2**	**0**	**0**	**0**	**2**	....	....	....	....	....
	Moncton	AHL	65	5	12	17	102	....	....	....	....	....
1988-89	**Winnipeg**	**NHL**	**1**	**0**	**0**	**0**	**0**	....	....	....	....	....
	Moncton	AHL	74	2	29	31	81	10	1	4	5	25
1989-90	**Winnipeg**	**NHL**	**3**	**0**	**1**	**1**	**2**	....	....	....	....	....
	Moncton	AHL	65	7	14	21	74	....	....	....	....	....
1990-91	Moncton	AHL	75	8	21	29	44	9	0	0	0	8
	NHL Totals		**6**	**0**	**1**	**1**	**4**	....	....	....	....	....

FLOCKHART, RONALD (RON)

Center/Left wing. Shoots left. 5'11", 190 lbs. Born, Smithers, B.C., October 10, 1960.

			Regular Season					Playoffs				
Season	Club	Lea	GP	G	A	TP	PIM	GP	G	A	TP	PIM
1979-80	Regina	WHL	65	54	76	130	63	17	11	23	34	18
1980-81	**Philadelphia**	**NHL**	**14**	**3**	**7**	**10**	**11**	**3**	**1**	**0**	**1**	**2**
	Maine	AHL	59	33	33	66	26	....	....	....	....	....
1981-82	**Philadelphia**	**NHL**	**72**	**33**	**39**	**72**	**44**	**4**	**0**	**1**	**1**	**2**
1982-83	**Philadelphia**	**NHL**	**73**	**29**	**31**	**60**	**49**	**2**	**1**	**1**	**2**	**2**
1983-84	**Philadelphia**	**NHL**	**8**	**0**	**3**	**3**	**4**	....	....	....	....	....
	Pittsburgh	**NHL**	**68**	**27**	**18**	**45**	**40**	....	....	....	....	....
1984-85	**Pittsburgh**	**NHL**	**12**	**0**	**5**	**5**	**4**	....	....	....	....	....
	Montreal	**NHL**	**42**	**10**	**12**	**22**	**14**	**2**	**1**	**1**	**2**	**2**
1985-86	**St. Louis**	**NHL**	**79**	**22**	**45**	**67**	**26**	**8**	**1**	**3**	**4**	**6**
1986-87	**St. Louis**	**NHL**	**60**	**16**	**19**	**35**	**12**	....	....	....	....	....
1987-88	**St. Louis**	**NHL**	**21**	**5**	**4**	**9**	**4**	....	....	....	....	....
1988-89	Peoria	IHL	2	0	2	2	2	....	....	....	....	....
	Boston	**NHL**	**4**	**0**	**0**	**0**	**0**	....	....	....	....	....
	Maine	AHL	9	5	6	11	0	....	....	....	....	....
1989-90	Bolzano	Italy	36	48	85	133	15	9	5	9	14	0
1990-91	Bolzano	Italy	33	35	44	79	32	10	7	12	19	2
	NHL Totals		**453**	**145**	**183**	**328**	**208**	**29**	**11**	**18**	**29**	**16**

Signed as free agent by **Philadelphia**, July 2, 1980. Traded to **Pittsburgh** by **Philadelphia** with Andy Brickley, Mark Taylor and Philadelphia's first round (Roger Belanger) and third round (Mike Stevens - later transferred to Vancouver) choices in 1984 Entry Draft for Rich Sutter and Pittsburgh's second round (Greg Smyth) and third round (David McLay) choices in 1984 Entry Draft, October 23, 1983. Traded to **Montreal** by **Pittsburgh** for John Chabot, November 9, 1984. Traded to **St. Louis** by **Montreal** for Perry Ganchar, August 26, 1985. Traded to **Boston** by **St. Louis** for future considerations, February 13, 1989.

FLOYD, LARRY DAVID

Center. Shoots left. 5'8", 180 lbs. Born, Peterborough, Ont., May 1, 1961.

			Regular Season					Playoffs				
Season	Club	Lea	GP	G	A	TP	PIM	GP	G	A	TP	PIM
1979-80	Peterborough	OHA	66	21	37	58	54	14	6	9	15	10
1980-81	Peterborough	OHA	44	26	37	63	43	5	2	2	4	0
1981-82	Peterborough	OHL	39	32	37	69	26	9	9	6	15	20
	Rochester	AHL	1	0	2	2	0	7	1	1	2	0
1982-83	New Jersey	NHL	5	1	0	1	2	....	....	....	....	....
a	Wichita	CHL	75	40	43	83	16	....	....	....	....	....
1983-84	New Jersey	NHL	7	1	3	4	7	....	....	....	....	....
	Maine	AHL	74	37	49	86	40	16	9	8	17	4
1984-85	Maine	AHL	72	30	51	81	24	3	0	1	1	2
1985-86	Maine	AHL	80	29	58	87	25	5	3	3	6	0
1986-87	Maine	AHL	77	30	44	74	50	....	....	....	....	....
1987-88	Utica	AHL	28	21	21	42	14	....	....	....	....	....
1988-89	Cape Breton	AHL	70	16	33	49	40	....	....	....	....	....
1989-90	Phoenix	IHL	76	39	40	79	50	....	....	....	....	....
1990-91	San Diego	IHL	73	24	54	78	34	....	....	....	....	....
	NHL Totals		12	2	3	5	9	....	....	....	....	....

a Won Ken McKenzie Trophy (CHL's Rookie of the Year) (1983)

Signed as free agent by **New Jersey**, September 16, 1982.

FOGARTY, BRYAN

Defense. Shoots left. 6'2", 198 lbs. Born, Brantford, Ont., June 11, 1969.
(Quebec's 1st choice, 9th overall, in 1987 Entry Draft).

			Regular Season					Playoffs				
Season	Club	Lea	GP	G	A	TP	PIM	GP	G	A	TP	PIM
1985-86	Kingston	OHL	47	2	19	21	14	10	1	3	4	4
1986-87a	Kingston	OHL	56	20	50	70	46	12	2	3	5	5
1987-88	Kingston	OHL	48	11	36	47	50	....	....	....	....	....
1988-89abc	Niagara Falls	OHL	60	47	*108	*155	88	17	10	22	32	36
1989-90	Quebec	NHL	45	4	10	14	31	....	....	....	....	....
	Halifax	AHL	22	5	14	19	6	6	2	4	6	0
1990-91	Quebec	NHL	45	9	22	31	24	....	....	....	....	....
	Halifax	AHL	5	0	2	2	0	....	....	....	....	....
	NHL Totals		90	13	32	45	55	....	....	....	....	....

a OHL First All-Star Team (1987, 1989)
b OHL Player of the Year (1989)
c Canadian Major Junior Player of the Year (1989)

FOLIGNO, MIKE ANTHONY (foh-LEE-noh)

Right wing. Shoots right. 6'2", 195 lbs. Born, Sudbury, Ont., January 29, 1959.
(Detroit's 1st choice, 3rd overall, in 1979 Entry Draft).

			Regular Season					Playoffs				
Season	Club	Lea	GP	G	A	TP	PIM	GP	G	A	TP	PIM
1975-76	Sudbury	OHA	57	22	14	36	45	....	....	....	....	....
1976-77	Sudbury	OHA	66	31	44	75	62	....	....	....	....	....
1977-78	Sudbury	OHA	67	47	39	86	112	....	....	....	....	....
1978-79a	Sudbury	OHA	68	65	85	*150	98	10	5	5	10	14
1979-80	Detroit	NHL	80	36	35	71	109	....	....	....	....	....
1980-81	Detroit	NHL	80	28	35	63	210	....	....	....	....	....
1981-82	Detroit	NHL	26	13	13	26	28	....	....	....	....	....
	Buffalo	NHL	56	20	31	51	149	4	2	0	2	9
1982-83	Buffalo	NHL	66	22	25	47	135	10	2	3	5	39
1983-84	Buffalo	NHL	70	32	31	63	151	3	2	1	3	19
1984-85	Buffalo	NHL	77	27	29	56	154	5	1	3	4	12
1985-86	Buffalo	NHL	79	41	39	80	168	....	....	....	....	....
1986-87	Buffalo	NHL	75	30	29	59	176	....	....	....	....	....
1987-88	Buffalo	NHL	74	29	28	57	220	6	3	2	5	31
1988-89	Buffalo	NHL	75	27	22	49	156	5	3	1	4	21
1989-90	Buffalo	NHL	61	15	25	40	99	6	0	1	1	12
1990-91	Buffalo	NHL	31	4	5	9	42	....	....	....	....	....
	Toronto	NHL	37	8	7	15	65	....	....	....	....	....
	NHL Totals		887	332	354	686	1862	39	13	11	24	143

a OHL First All-Star Team (1979)

Traded to **Buffalo** by **Detroit** with Dale McCourt and Brent Peterson for Danny Gare, Jim Schoenfeld and Derek Smith, December 2, 1981. Traded to **Toronto** by **Buffalo** with Buffalo's eighth round choice (Thomas Kucharcik) in 1991 Entry Draft for Brian Curran and Lou Franceschetti, December 17, 1990.

FOOTE, ADAM

Defense. Shoots right. 6'1", 180 lbs. Born, Toronto, Ont., July 10, 1971.
(Quebec's 2nd choice, 22nd overall, in 1989 Entry Draft).

			Regular Season					Playoffs				
Season	Club	Lea	GP	G	A	TP	PIM	GP	G	A	TP	PIM
1988-89	S.S. Marie	OHL	66	7	32	39	120	....	....	....	....	....
1989-90	S.S. Marie	OHL	61	12	43	55	199	....	....	....	....	....
1990-91a	S.S. Marie	OHL	59	18	51	69	93	14	5	12	17	28

a OHL First All-Star Team (1991)

FORSBERG, PETER

Center. Shoots left. 5'11", 167 lbs. Born, Ornskoldsvik, Sweden, July 20, 1973.
(Philadelphia's 1st choice, 6th overall, in 1991 Entry Draft).

			Regular Season					Playoffs				
Season	Club	Lea	GP	G	A	TP	PIM	GP	G	A	TP	PIM
1989-90	MoDo	Swe.	30	15	12	27	42	....	....	....	....	....
1990-91	MoDo	Swe.	23	7	10	14	22	....	....	....	....	....

FORSLUND, THOMAS (FOHRS-luhnd)

Right wing. Shoots left. 5'11", 200 lbs. Born, Falun, Sweden, November 24, 1968.
(Calgary's 4th choice, 85th overall, in 1988 Entry Draft).

			Regular Season					Playoffs				
Season	Club	Lea	GP	G	A	TP	PIM	GP	G	A	TP	PIM
1986-87	Leksand	Swe.	23	3	5	8	....	....	....	....	....	
1987-88	Leksand	Swe.	37	9	10	19	....	....	....	....	....	
1988-89	Leksand	Swe.	39	14	16	30	56	....	....	....	....	....
1989-90	Leksand	Swe.	38	14	21	35	48	3	0	1	1	2
1990-91	Leksand	Swe.2	23	5	10	15	10	....	....	....	....	....

FORTIER, MARC

Center. Shoots right. 6', 192 lbs. Born, Windsor, Que., February 26, 1966.

			Regular Season					Playoffs				
Season	Club	Lea	GP	G	A	TP	PIM	GP	G	A	TP	PIM
1983-84	Chicoutimi	QMJHL	67	16	30	46	51	....	....	....	....	....
1984-85	Chicoutimi	QMJHL	68	35	63	98	114	14	8	4	12	16
1985-86	Chicoutimi	QMJHL	71	47	86	133	49	9	2	14	16	12
1986-87	Chicoutimi	QMJHL	65	66	135	201	39	19	11	40	51	20
1987-88	Quebec	NHL	27	4	10	14	12	....	....	....	....	....
	Fredericton	AHL	50	26	36	62	48	....	....	....	....	....
1988-89	Quebec	NHL	57	20	19	39	45	....	....	....	....	....
	Halifax	AHL	16	11	11	22	14	....	....	....	....	....
1989-90	Quebec	NHL	59	13	17	30	28	....	....	....	....	....
	Halifax	AHL	15	5	6	11	6	....	....	....	....	....
1990-91	Quebec	NHL	14	0	4	4	6	....	....	....	....	....
	Halifax	AHL	58	24	32	56	85	....	....	....	....	....
	NHL Totals		157	37	50	87	91	....	....	....	....	....

Signed as a free agent by **Quebec**, February 3, 1987.

FOSTER, COREY

Defense. Shoots left. 6'3", 200 lbs. Born, Ottawa, Ont., October 27, 1969.
(New Jersey's 1st choice, 12th overall, in 1988 Entry Draft).

			Regular Season					Playoffs				
Season	Club	Lea	GP	G	A	TP	PIM	GP	G	A	TP	PIM
1986-87	Peterborough	OHL	30	3	4	7	4	1	0	0	0	0
1987-88	Peterborough	OHL	66	13	31	44	58	11	5	9	14	13
1988-89	New Jersey	NHL	2	0	0	0	0	....	....	....	....	....
a	Peterborough	OHL	55	14	42	56	42	17	1	17	18	12
1989-90	Cape Breton	AHL	54	7	17	24	32	1	0	0	0	0
1990-91	Cape Breton	AHL	67	14	11	25	51	4	2	4	6	4
	NHL Totals		2	0	0	0	0	....	....	....	....	....

a OHL Third All-Star Team (1989)

Traded to **Edmonton** by **New Jersey** for Edmonton's first-round choice (Jason Millar) in 1989 Entry Draft, June 17, 1989. Traded to **Philadelphia** by **Edmonton** with Dave Brown and Jari Kurri for Craig Fisher, Scott Mellanby and Craig Berube, May 30, 1991.

FOSTER, STEPHEN

Defense. Shoots right. 6'3", 210 lbs. Born, Brockton, MA, March 21, 1971.
(Boston's 6th choice, 122nd overall, in 1989 Entry Draft).

			Regular Season					Playoffs				
Season	Club	Lea	GP	G	A	TP	PIM	GP	G	A	TP	PIM
1989-90	Boston U.	H.E.	28	0	8	8	26	....	....	....	....	....
1990-91	Boston U.	H.E.	DID NOT PLAY									

FRANCESCHETTI, LOU (FRAN-sihs-KEH-tee)

Right/Left wing. Shoots left. 6', 190 lbs. Born, Toronto, Ont., March 28, 1958.
(Washington's 8th choice, 71st overall, in 1978 Amateur Draft).

			Regular Season					Playoffs				
Season	Club	Lea	GP	G	A	TP	PIM	GP	G	A	TP	PIM
1976-77	Niagara Falls	OHA	61	23	30	53	80	....	....	....	....	....
1977-78	Niagara Falls	OHA	62	40	50	90	46	....	....	....	....	....
1978-79	Saginaw	IHL	2	1	1	2	0	....	....	....	....	....
	Port Huron	IHL	76	45	58	103	131	....	....	....	....	....
1979-80	Port Huron	IHL	15	3	8	11	31	....	....	....	....	....
	Hershey	AHL	65	27	29	56	58	14	6	9	15	32
1980-81	Hershey	AHL	79	32	36	68	173	10	3	7	10	30
1981-82	Hershey	AHL	50	22	33	55	89	....	....	....	....	....
	Washington	NHL	30	2	10	12	23	....	....	....	....	....
1982-83	Hershey	AHL	80	31	44	75	176	5	1	2	3	16
1983-84	Washington	NHL	2	0	0	0	0	3	0	0	0	8
	Hershey	AHL	73	26	34	60	130	....	....	....	....	....
1984-85	Washington	NHL	22	4	7	11	45	5	1	1	2	15
	Binghamton	AHL	52	29	43	72	75	....	....	....	....	....
1985-86	Washington	NHL	76	7	14	21	131	8	0	0	0	15
1986-87	Washington	NHL	75	12	9	21	127	7	0	0	0	23
1987-88	Washington	NHL	59	4	8	12	113	4	0	0	0	14
	Binghamton	AHL	6	2	4	6	4	....	....	....	....	....
1988-89	Washington	NHL	63	7	10	17	123	6	1	0	1	8
	Baltimore	AHL	10	8	7	15	30	....	....	....	....	....
1989-90	Toronto	NHL	80	21	15	36	127	5	0	1	1	26
1990-91	Toronto	NHL	16	1	1	2	30	....	....	....	....	....
	Buffalo	NHL	35	1	7	8	28	6	1	0	1	2
	NHL Totals		458	59	81	140	747	44	3	2	5	111

Traded to **Toronto** by **Washington** for Toronto's fifth round choice (Mark Ouimet) in 1990 Entry Draft, June 29, 1989. Traded to **Buffalo** by **Toronto** with Brian Curran for Mike Foligno and Buffalo's eighth round choice (Thomas Kucharcik) in 1991 Entry Draft, December 17, 1990.

FRANCIS, RONALD (RON)

Center. Shoots left. 6'2", 200 lbs. Born, Sault Ste. Marie, Ont., March 1, 1963.
(Hartford's 1st choice, 4th overall, in 1981 Entry Draft).

			Regular Season					Playoffs				
Season	Club	Lea	GP	G	A	TP	PIM	GP	G	A	TP	PIM
1980-81	S. S. Marie	OHA	64	26	43	69	33	19	7	8	15	34
1981-82	Hartford	NHL	59	25	43	68	51	....	....	....	....	....
	S. S. Marie	OHL	25	18	30	48	46	....	....	....	....	....
1982-83	Hartford	NHL	79	31	59	90	60	....	....	....	....	....
1983-84	Hartford	NHL	72	23	60	83	45	....	....	....	....	....
1984-85	Hartford	NHL	80	24	57	81	66	....	....	....	....	....
1985-86	Hartford	NHL	53	24	53	77	24	10	1	2	3	4
1986-87	Hartford	NHL	75	30	63	93	45	6	2	2	4	6
1987-88	Hartford	NHL	80	25	50	75	87	6	2	5	7	2
1988-89	Hartford	NHL	69	29	48	77	36	4	0	2	2	0
1989-90	Hartford	NHL	80	32	69	101	73	7	3	3	6	8
1990-91	Hartford	NHL	67	21	55	76	51	....	....	....	....	....
	Pittsburgh	NHL	14	2	9	11	21	24	7	10	17	24
	NHL Totals		728	266	566	832	559	57	15	24	39	44

Played in NHL All-Star Game (1983, 1985, 1990)

Traded to **Pittsburgh** by **Hartford** with Grant Jennings and Ulf Samuelsson for John Cullen, Jeff Parker and Zarley Zalapski, March 4, 1991.

FRANTTI, GORDON

Center. Shoots left. 6'6", 228 lbs. Born, Laurium, MI, July 17, 1970.
(Philadelphia's 7th choice, 119th overall, in 1988 Entry Draft).

			Regular Season					Playoffs				
Season	Club	Lea	GP	G	A	TP	PIM	GP	G	A	TP	PIM
1989-90	W. Michigan	CCHA	30	7	4	11	16	....	....	....	....	....
1990-91	W. Michigan	CCHA	3	0	1	1	7	....	....	....	....	....

FRANZOSA, DAVID

Left wing. Shoots left. 5'11", 175 lbs. Born, Reading, MA, November 20, 1970.
(Boston's 11th choice, 227th overall, in 1989 Entry Draft)

			Regular Season					Playoffs				
Season	Club	Lea	GP	G	A	TP	PIM	GP	G	A	TP	PIM
1988-89	Boston College	H.E.	16	2	1	3	0	....	....	....	....	....
1989-90	Boston College	H.E.	42	8	20	28	20	....	....	....	....	....
1990-91	Boston College	H.E.	39	14	19	33	14	....	....	....	....	....

FRASER, IAIN

Center. Shoots left. 5'10", 175 lbs. Born, Scarborough, Ont., August 10, 1969.
(NY Islanders' 12th choice, 233rd overall, in 1989 Entry Draft).

			Regular Season					Playoffs				
Season	Club	Lea	GP	G	A	TP	PIM	GP	G	A	TP	PIM
1986-87	Oshawa	OHL	5	1	2	3	0	....	....	....	....	....
1987-88	Oshawa	OHL	16	4	4	8	22	6	2	3	5	2
1988-89	Oshawa	OHL	62	33	57	90	87	6	2	8	10	12
1989-90a	Oshawa	OHL	56	40	65	105	75	17	10	*22	32	8
1990-91	Capital Dist.	AHL	32	5	13	18	16	....	....	....	....	....
	Richmond	ECHL	3	1	1	2	0	....	....	....	....	....

a Memorial Cup All-Star Team, Tournament MVP (1990)

FRAWLEY, WILLIAM DANIEL (DAN)

Right wing. Shoots right. 6'1", 195 lbs. Born, Sturgeon Falls, Ont., June 2, 1962.
(Chicago's 15th choice, 204th overall, in 1980 Entry Draft).

			Regular Season					Playoffs				
Season	Club	Lea	GP	G	A	TP	PIM	GP	G	A	TP	PIM
1979-80	Sudbury	OHA	63	21	26	47	67	8	0	1	1	2
1980-81	Cornwall	QMJHL	28	10	14	28	76	18	5	12	17	37
1981-82	Cornwall	OHL	64	27	50	77	239	5	3	8	11	19
1982-83	Springfield	AHL	80	30	27	57	107	....	....	....	....	....
1983-84	**Chicago**	**NHL**	**3**	**0**	**0**	**0**	**0**	....	....	....	....	....
	Springfield	AHL	69	22	34	56	137	4	0	1	1	12
1984-85	**Chicago**	**NHL**	**30**	**4**	**3**	**7**	**64**	**1**	**0**	**0**	**0**	**0**
	Milwaukee	IHL	26	11	12	23	125	....	....	....	....	....
1985-86	**Pittsburgh**	**NHL**	**69**	**10**	**11**	**21**	**174**	....	....	....	....	....
1986-87	**Pittsburgh**	**NHL**	**78**	**14**	**14**	**28**	**218**	....	....	....	....	....
1987-88	**Pittsburgh**	**NHL**	**47**	**6**	**8**	**14**	**152**	....	....	....	....	....
1988-89	**Pittsburgh**	**NHL**	**46**	**3**	**4**	**7**	**66**	....	....	....	....	....
	Muskegon	IHL	24	12	16	28	35	14	6	4	10	31
1989-90	Muskegon	IHL	82	31	47	78	165	15	9	12	21	51
1990-91	Rochester	AHL	74	15	31	46	152	14	4	7	11	34
	NHL Totals		**273**	**37**	**40**	**77**	**674**	**1**	**0**	**0**	**0**	**0**

Claimed by **Pittsburgh** from **Chicago** in NHL Waiver Draft, October 7, 1985.

FREDERICK, JOSEPH

Right wing. Shoots right. 6'1", 190 lbs. Born, St. Hubert, Que., August 6, 1969.
(Detroit's 13th choice, 242nd overall, in 1989 Entry Draft).

			Regular Season					Playoffs				
Season	Club	Lea	GP	G	A	TP	PIM	GP	G	A	TP	PIM
1988-89	Madison	USHL	48	47	47	94	215	....	....	....	....	....
1989-90			DID NOT PLAY									
1990-91	N. Michigan	WCHA	40	9	11	20	77					

FREER, MARK (FRIHR)

Center. Shoots left. 5'10", 180 lbs. Born, Peterborough, Ont., July 14, 1968.

			Regular Season					Playoffs				
Season	Club	Lea	GP	G	A	TP	PIM	GP	G	A	TP	PIM
1985-86	Peterborough	OHL	65	16	28	44	24	14	3	4	7	13
1986-87	**Philadelphia**	**NHL**	**1**	**0**	**1**	**1**	**0**	....	....	....	....	....
	Peterborough	OHL	65	39	43	82	44	12	2	6	8	5
1987-88	**Philadelphia**	**NHL**	**1**	**0**	**0**	**0**	**0**	....	....	....	....	....
	Peterborough	OHL	63	38	70	108	63	12	5	12	17	4
1988-89	**Philadelphia**	**NHL**	**5**	**0**	**1**	**1**	**0**	....	....	....	....	....
	Hershey	AHL	75	30	49	79	77	12	4	6	10	2
1989-90	**Philadelphia**	**NHL**	**2**	**0**	**0**	**0**	**0**	....	....	....	....	....
	Hershey	AHL	65	28	36	64	31	....	....	....	....	....
1990-91	Hershey	AHL	77	18	44	62	45	7	1	3	4	17
	NHL Totals		**9**	**0**	**2**	**2**	**0**	....	....	....	....	....

Signed as a free agent by **Philadelphia**, October 7, 1986.

FRENETTE, DEREK

Left wing/Defense. Shoots left. 6'1", 175 lbs. Born, Montreal, Que., July 13, 1971.
(St. Louis' 6th choice, 124th overall, in 1989 Entry Draft).

			Regular Season					Playoffs				
Season	Club	Lea	GP	G	A	TP	PIM	GP	G	A	TP	PIM
1988-89	Ferris State	CCHA	25	3	4	7	17	....	....	....	....	....
1989-90	Ferris State	CCHA	28	1	4	5	48	....	....	....	....	....
1990-91	Hull	QMJHL	66	27	42	69	72	6	4	3	7	12
	Peoria	IHL	....	....	....	....	....	6	0	0	0	0

FROLOV, DIMITRI

Defense. Shoots left. 6'3", 213 lbs. Born, Moscow, USSR, August 22, 1966.
(Calgary's 8th choice, 146th overall, in 1990 Entry Draft).

			Regular Season					Playoffs				
Season	Club	Lea	GP	G	A	TP	PIM	GP	G	A	TP	PIM
1988-89	Moscow D'amo	USSR	45	2	9	11	18	....	....	....	....	....
1990-91	Moscow D'amo	USSR	46	5	7	12	26	....	....	....	....	....

FRYCER, MIROSLAV (FREE-chuhr)

Right wing. Shoots left. 6', 200 lbs. Born, Ostrava, Czechoslovakia, September 27, 1959.

			Regular Season					Playoffs				
Season	Club	Lea	GP	G	A	TP	PIM	GP	G	A	TP	PIM
1979-80	TJ Vitkovice	Czech.	44	31	15	46	....	....	....	....	....	....
1980-81	TJ Vitkovice	Czech.	34	33	24	57	....	....	....	....	....	....
1981-82	**Quebec**	**NHL**	**49**	**20**	**17**	**37**	**47**	....	....	....	....	....
	Fredericton	AHL	11	9	5	14	16	....	....	....	....	....
	Toronto	**NHL**	**10**	**4**	**6**	**10**	**31**	....	....	....	....	....
1982-83	**Toronto**	**NHL**	**67**	**25**	**30**	**55**	**90**	**4**	**2**	**5**	**7**	**0**
1983-84	**Toronto**	**NHL**	**47**	**10**	**16**	**26**	**55**	....	....	....	....	....
1984-85	**Toronto**	**NHL**	**65**	**25**	**30**	**55**	**55**	....	....	....	....	....
1985-86	**Toronto**	**NHL**	**73**	**32**	**43**	**75**	**74**	**10**	**1**	**3**	**4**	**10**
1986-87	**Toronto**	**NHL**	**29**	**7**	**8**	**15**	**28**	....	....	....	....	....
1987-88	**Toronto**	**NHL**	**38**	**12**	**20**	**32**	**41**	**3**	**0**	**0**	**0**	**6**
1988-89	**Detroit**	**NHL**	**23**	**7**	**8**	**15**	**47**	....	....	....	....	....
	Edmonton	**NHL**	**14**	**5**	**5**	**10**	**18**	....	....	....	....	....
1989-90	Freiburg	W.Ger.	11	4	13	17	18	....	....	....	....	....
1990-91	Freiburg	Ger.	37	20	27	47	60	....	....	....	....	....
	NHL Totals		**415**	**147**	**183**	**330**	**486**	**17**	**3**	**8**	**11**	**16**

Played in NHL All-Star Game (1985)

Signed as free agent by **Quebec**, April 21, 1980. Traded to **Toronto** by **Quebec** with Quebec's seventh round choice (Jeff Triano) in 1982 Entry Draft for Wilf Paiement, March 9, 1982. Traded to **Detroit** by **Toronto** for Darren Veitch, June 10, 1988. Traded to **Edmonton** by **Detroit** for Edmonton's tenth-round choice (Rick Judson) in the 1989 Entry Draft, January 3, 1989.

GAETZ, LINK (GAYTZ)

Defense. Shoots left. 6'4", 210 lbs. Born, Vancouver, B.C., October 2, 1968.
(Minnesota's 2nd choice, 40th overall, in 1988 Entry Draft).

			Regular Season					Playoffs				
Season	Club	Lea	GP	G	A	TP	PIM	GP	G	A	TP	PIM
1986-87	N. Westminster	WHL	44	2	7	9	52	....	....	....	....	....
1987-88	Spokane	WHL	59	9	20	29	313	10	2	2	4	70
1988-89	**Minnesota**	**NHL**	**12**	**0**	**2**	**2**	**53**	....	....	....	....	....
	Kalamazoo	IHL	37	3	4	7	192	5	0	0	0	56
1989-90	**Minnesota**	**NHL**	**5**	**0**	**0**	**0**	**33**	....	....	....	....	....
	Kalamazoo	IHL	61	5	16	21	318	9	2	2	4	59
1990-91	Kalamazoo	IHL	9	0	1	1	44	....	....	....	....	....
	Kansas City	IHL	18	1	10	11	178	....	....	....	....	....
	NHL Totals		**17**	**0**	**2**	**2**	**86**	....	....	....	....	....

Claimed by **San Jose** from **Minnesota** in Dispersal Draft, May 30, 1991.

GAGE, JOSEPH WILLIAM (JODY)

Right wing. Shoots right. 6', 190 lbs. Born, Toronto, Ont., November 29, 1959.
(Detroit's 2nd choice, 45th overall, in 1979 Entry Draft).

			Regular Season					Playoffs				
Season	Club	Lea	GP	G	A	TP	PIM	GP	G	A	TP	PIM
1977-78	Hamilton	OHA	32	15	18	33	19	....	....	....	....	....
	Kitchener	OHA	36	17	27	44	21	9	4	3	7	4
1978-79	Kitchener	OHA	58	46	43	89	40	10	1	2	3	6
1979-80	Adirondack	AHL	63	25	21	46	15	5	2	1	3	0
1980-81	**Detroit**	**NHL**	**16**	**2**	**2**	**4**	**22**	....	....	....	....	....
	Adirondack	AHL	59	17	31	48	44	17	9	6	15	12
1981-82	**Detroit**	**NHL**	**31**	**9**	**10**	**19**	**2**	....	....	....	....	....
	Adirondack	AHL	47	21	20	41	21	....	....	....	....	....
1982-83	Adirondack	AHL	65	23	30	53	33	6	1	5	6	8
1983-84	**Detroit**	**NHL**	**3**	**0**	**0**	**0**	**0**	....	....	....	....	....
	Adirondack	AHL	73	40	32	72	32	6	3	4	7	2
1984-85	Adirondack	AHL	78	27	33	60	55	....	....	....	....	....
1985-86	**Buffalo**	**NHL**	**7**	**3**	**2**	**5**	**0**	....	....	....	....	....
a	Rochester	AHL	73	42	57	99	56	....	....	....	....	....
1986-87	Rochester	AHL	70	26	39	65	60	17	*14	5	19	24
1987-88	**Buffalo**	**NHL**	**2**	**0**	**0**	**0**	**0**	....	....	....	....	....
ab	Rochester	AHL	76	*60	44	104	46	5	2	5	7	10
1988-89	Rochester	AHL	65	31	38	69	60	....	....	....	....	....
1989-90	Rochester	AHL	75	45	38	83	42	17	4	6	10	12
1990-91a	Rochester	AHL	73	42	43	85	34	15	6	10	16	14
	NHL Totals		**59**	**14**	**14**	**28**	**24**	....	....	....	....	....

a AHL First All-Star Team (1986, 1988, 1991)
b Won Les Cunningham Trophy (MVP-AHL) (1988)

Signed as a free agent by **Buffalo**, July 31, 1985

GAGNE, PAUL (GAHN-yay)

Left wing. Shoots left. 5' 10", 180 lbs. Born, Iroquois Falls, Ont., February 6, 1962.
(Colorado's 1st choice, 19th overall, in 1980 Entry Draft).

			Regular Season					Playoffs				
Season	Club	Lea	GP	G	A	TP	PIM	GP	G	A	TP	PIM
1978-79	Windsor	OHA	87	24	18	42	64	7	1	1	2	2
1979-80a	Windsor	OHA	65	48	53	101	87	13	7	8	15	19
1980-81	**Colorado**	**NHL**	**61**	**25**	**16**	**41**	**12**	....	....	....	....	....
1981-82	**Colorado**	**NHL**	**59**	**10**	**12**	**22**	**17**	....	....	....	....	....
1982-83	**New Jersey**	**NHL**	**63**	**14**	**15**	**29**	**13**	....	....	....	....	....
	Wichita	CHL	16	1	9	10	9	....	....	....	....	....
1983-84	**New Jersey**	**NHL**	**66**	**14**	**18**	**32**	**33**	....	....	....	....	....
1984-85	**New Jersey**	**NHL**	**79**	**24**	**19**	**43**	**28**	....	....	....	....	....
1985-86	**New Jersey**	**NHL**	**47**	**19**	**19**	**38**	**14**	....	....	....	....	....
1986-87			DID NOT PLAY – INJURED					....	....	....	....	....
1987-88			DID NOT PLAY – INJURED					....	....	....	....	....
1988-89	**Toronto**	**NHL**	**16**	**3**	**2**	**5**	**6**	....	....	....	....	....
	Newmarket	AHL	56	33	41	74	29	5	4	4	8	5
1989-90	Newmarket	AHL	28	13	14	27	11	....	....	....	....	....
	NY Islanders	**NHL**	**9**	**1**	**0**	**1**	**4**	....	....	....	....	....
	Springfield	AHL	36	18	29	47	6	13	10	6	16	2
1990-91	Landshut	Ger.	49	44	37	81	41	....	....	....	....	....
	NHL Totals		**400**	**11**	**101**	**211**	**127**	....	....	....	....	....

a OHA Second All-Star Team (1980)

Signed as a free agent by **Toronto**, July 28, 1988. Traded to **NY Islanders** by **Toronto** with Jack Capuano and Derek Laxdal for Mike Stevens and Gilles Thibaudeau, December 20, 1989.

GAGNER, DAVE

Center. Shoots left. 5'10", 180 lbs. Born, Chatham, Ont., December 11, 1964.
(NY Rangers' 1st choice, 12th overall, in 1983 Entry Draft).

			Regular Season					Playoffs				
Season	Club	Lea	GP	G	A	TP	PIM	GP	G	A	TP	PIM
1981-82	Brantford	OHL	68	30	46	76	31	11	3	6	9	6
1982-83a	Brantford	OHL	70	55	66	121	57	8	5	5	10	4
1983-84	Cdn. Olympic	...	50	19	18	37	26	....	....	....	....	....
	Brantford	OHL	12	7	13	20	4	6	0	4	4	6
1984-85	**NY Rangers**	**NHL**	**38**	**6**	**6**	**12**	**16**	....	....	....	....	....
	New Haven	AHL	38	13	20	33	23	....	....	....	....	....
1985-86	**NY Rangers**	**NHL**	**32**	**4**	**6**	**10**	**19**	....	....	....	....	....
	New Haven	AHL	16	10	11	21	11	4	1	2	3	2
1986-87	**NY Rangers**	**NHL**	**10**	**1**	**4**	**5**	**12**	....	....	....	....	....
	New Haven	AHL	56	22	41	63	50	7	1	5	6	18
1987-88	**Minnesota**	**NHL**	**51**	**8**	**11**	**19**	**55**	....	....	....	....	....
	Kalamazoo	IHL	14	16	10	26	26	....	....	....	....	....
1988-89	**Minnesota**	**NHL**	**75**	**35**	**43**	**78**	**104**	....	....	....	....	....
	Kalamazoo	IHL	1	0	1	1	4	....	....	....	....	....
1989-90	**Minnesota**	**NHL**	**79**	**40**	**38**	**78**	**54**	**7**	**2**	**3**	**5**	**16**
1990-91	**Minnesota**	**NHL**	**73**	**40**	**42**	**82**	**114**	**23**	**12**	**15**	**27**	**28**
	NHL Totals		**358**	**134**	**150**	**284**	**374**	**30**	**14**	**18**	**32**	**44**

a OHL Second All-Star Team (1983)

Played in NHL All-Star Game (1991)

Traded to **Minnesota** by **NY Rangers** with Jay Caulfield for Jari Gronstrand and Paul Boutilier, October 8, 1987.

GALL, WILLIAM (BILL)

Right wing. Shoots right. 6'2", 175 lbs. Born, Bryn Mawr, PA, May 14, 1968.
(Philadelphia's 5th choice, 104th overall, in 1987 Entry Draft).

			Regular Season					Playoffs				
Season	Club	Lea	GP	G	A	TP	PIM	GP	G	A	TP	PIM
1987-88	RIT	NCAA	23	8	8	16	4	....	....	....	....	....
1988-89	RIT	NCAA	37	8	19	27	46	....	....	....	....	....
1989-90	RIT	NCAA	27	9	21	30	30	....	....	....	....	....
1990-91	RIT	NCAA	28	14	31	45	80	....	....	....	....	....

GALLANT, GERARD (guh-LAHNT)

Left wing. Shoots left. 5'10", 185 lbs. Born, Summerside, P.E.I., September 2, 1963.
(Detroit's 4th choice, 107th overall, in 1981 Entry Draft).

			Regular Season					Playoffs				
Season	Club	Lea	GP	G	A	TP	PIM	GP	G	A	TP	PIM
1980-81	Sherbrooke	QMJHL	68	41	59	100	265	14	6	13	19	46
1981-82	Sherbrooke	QMJHL	58	34	58	92	260	22	14	24	38	84
1982-83	St. Jean	QMJHL	33	28	25	53	139	....	....	....	....	....
	Verdun	QMJHL	29	26	49	75	105	15	14	19	33	84
1983-84	Adirondack	AHL	77	31	33	64	195	7	1	3	4	34
1984-85	**Detroit**	**NHL**	**32**	**6**	**12**	**18**	**66**	**3**	**0**	**0**	**0**	**11**
	Adirondack	AHL	46	18	29	47	131	....	....	....	....	....
1985-86	**Detroit**	**NHL**	**52**	**20**	**19**	**39**	**106**	....	....	....	....	....
1986-87	**Detroit**	**NHL**	**80**	**38**	**34**	**72**	**216**	**16**	**8**	**6**	**14**	**43**
1987-88	**Detroit**	**NHL**	**73**	**34**	**39**	**73**	**242**	**16**	**6**	**9**	**15**	**55**
1988-89a	**Detroit**	**NHL**	**76**	**39**	**54**	**93**	**230**	**6**	**1**	**2**	**3**	**40**
1989-90	**Detroit**	**NHL**	**69**	**36**	**44**	**80**	**254**	....	....	....	....	....
1990-91	**Detroit**	**NHL**	**45**	**10**	**16**	**26**	**111**	....	....	....	....	....
	NHL Totals		**427**	**183**	**218**	**401**	**1225**	**41**	**15**	**17**	**32**	**149**

a NHL Second All-Star Team (1989)

GALLEY, GARRY

Defense. Shoots left. 6', 190 lbs. Born, Montreal, Que., April 16, 1963.
(Los Angeles' 4th choice, 100th overall, in 1983 Entry Draft).

			Regular Season					Playoffs				
Season	Club	Lea	GP	G	A	TP	PIM	GP	G	A	TP	PIM
1981-82	Bowling Green	CCHA	42	3	36	39	48	....	....	....	....	....
1982-83	Bowling Green	CCHA	40	17	29	46	40	....	....	....	....	....
1983-84ab	Bowling Green	CCHA	44	15	52	67	61	....	....	....	....	....
1984-85	**Los Angeles**	**NHL**	**78**	**8**	**30**	**38**	**82**	**3**	**1**	**0**	**1**	**2**
1985-86	**Los Angeles**	**NHL**	**49**	**9**	**13**	**22**	**46**	....	....	....	....	....
	New Haven	AHL	4	2	6	8	6	....	....	....	....	....
1986-87	**Los Angeles**	**NHL**	**30**	**5**	**11**	**16**	**57**	....	....	....	....	....
	Washington	**NHL**	**18**	**1**	**10**	**11**	**10**	**2**	**0**	**0**	**0**	**0**
1987-88	**Washington**	**NHL**	**58**	**7**	**23**	**30**	**44**	**13**	**2**	**4**	**6**	**13**
1988-89	**Boston**	**NHL**	**78**	**8**	**21**	**29**	**80**	**9**	**0**	**1**	**1**	**33**
1989-90	**Boston**	**NHL**	**71**	**8**	**27**	**35**	**75**	**21**	**3**	**3**	**6**	**34**
1990-91	**Boston**	**NHL**	**70**	**6**	**21**	**27**	**84**	**16**	**1**	**5**	**6**	**17**
	NHL Totals		**452**	**52**	**156**	**208**	**478**	**64**	**7**	**13**	**20**	**109**

a CCHA First All-Star Team (1984)
b NCAA All-American (1984)

Played in NHL All-Star Game (1991)

Traded to **Washington** by **Los Angeles** for Al Jensen, February 14, 1987. Signed as a free agent by **Boston**, July 8, 1988.

GANCHAR, PERRY

Right wing. Shoots right. 5'9", 180 lbs. Born, Saskatoon, Sask., October 28, 1963.
(St. Louis' 3rd choice, 113th overall, in 1982 Entry Draft).

			Regular Season					Playoffs				
Season	Club	Lea	GP	G	A	TP	PIM	GP	G	A	TP	PIM
1979-80	Saskatoon	WHL	27	9	14	23	60	....	....	....	....	....
1980-81	Saskatoon	WHL	72	26	53	79	117	....	....	....	....	....
1981-82	Saskatoon	WHL	53	38	52	90	82	5	3	3	6	17
1982-83	Saskatoon	WHL	68	68	48	116	105	6	1	4	5	24
	Salt Lake	CHL	....	....	....	....	....	1	0	1	1	0
1983-84	**St. Louis**	**NHL**	**1**	**0**	**0**	**0**	**0**	**7**	**3**	**1**	**4**	**0**
	Montana	CHL	59	23	22	45	77	....	....	....	....	....
1984-85	**St. Louis**	**NHL**	**7**	**0**	**2**	**2**	**0**	....	....	....	....	....
a	Peoria	IHL	63	41	29	70	114	20	4	11	15	49
1985-86	Sherbrooke	AHL	75	25	29	54	42	....	....	....	....	....
1986-87	Sherbrooke	AHL	68	22	29	51	64	17	9	8	17	37
1987-88	**Montreal**	**NHL**	**1**	**1**	**0**	**1**	**0**	....	....	....	....	....
	Sherbrooke	AHL	28	12	18	30	61	....	....	....	....	....
	Pittsburgh	**NHL**	**30**	**2**	**5**	**7**	**36**	....	....	....	....	....
1988-89	**Pittsburgh**	**NHL**	**3**	**0**	**0**	**0**	**0**	....	....	....	....	....
	Muskegon	IHL	70	39	34	73	114	14	7	8	15	6
1989-90	Muskegon	IHL	79	40	45	85	111	14	3	5	8	27
1990-91	Muskegon	IHL	80	37	38	75	87	5	2	1	3	0
	NHL Totals		**42**	**3**	**7**	**10**	**36**	**7**	**3**	**1**	**4**	**0**

a IHL Second All-Star Team (1985)

Traded to **Montreal** by **St. Louis** for Ron Flockhart, August 26, 1985. Traded to **Pittsburgh** by **Montreal** for future considerations, December 17, 1987.

GARBUTT, MURRAY

Center. Shoots left. 6'1", 205 lbs. Born, Hanna, Alta., June 29, 1971.
(Minnesota's 3rd choice, 60th overall, in 1989 Entry Draft).

			Regular Season					Playoffs				
Season	Club	Lea	GP	G	A	TP	PIM	GP	G	A	TP	PIM
1987-88	Medicine Hat	WHL	9	2	1	3	15	16	0	1	1	15
1988-89	Medicine Hat	WHL	64	14	24	38	145	3	1	0	1	6
1989-90	Medicine Hat	WHL	72	38	27	65	221	3	1	0	1	21
1990-91	Medicine Hat	WHL	30	15	26	41	97	....	....	....	....	....
	Spokane	WHL	31	17	19	36	90	15	4	8	12	44

Claimed by **San Jose** from **Minnesota** in Dispersal Draft, May 30, 1991.

GARDNER, JOEL

Center. Shoots left. 6', 175 lbs. Born, Petrolia, Ont., September 16, 1967.
(Boston's 11th choice, 244th overall, in 1986 Entry Draft).

			Regular Season					Playoffs				
Season	Club	Lea	GP	G	A	TP	PIM	GP	G	A	TP	PIM
1986-87	Colgate	ECAC	31	10	20	30	20	....	....	....	....	....
1987-88	Colgate	ECAC	31	14	32	46	24	....	....	....	....	....
1988-89	Colgate	ECAC	30	21	25	46	38	....	....	....	....	....
1989-90abc	Colgate	ECAC	38	26	36	62	62	....	....	....	....	....
1990-91	Muskegon	IHL	49	9	13	22	30	2	0	1	1	0

a ECAC First All-Star Team (1990)
b NCAA East Second All-American Team (1990)
c NCAA All-Tournament Team (1990)

Signed as a free agent by **Pittsburgh**, September 11, 1990.

GARPENLOV, JOHAN (GAHR-puhn-luhv)

Left wing. Shoots left. 5'11", 183 lbs. Born, Stockholm, Sweden, March 21, 1968.
(Detroit's 5th choice, 85th overall, in 1986 Entry Draft).

			Regular Season					Playoffs				
Season	Club	Lea	GP	G	A	TP	PIM	GP	G	A	TP	PIM
1986-87	Djurgarden	Swe.	29	5	8	13	20	....	....	....	....	....
1987-88	Djurgarden	Swe.	30	7	10	17	12	....	....	....	....	....
1988-89	Djurgarden	Swe.	36	12	19	31	20	....	....	....	....	....
1989-90	Djurgarden	Swe.	39	20	13	33	35	8	2	4	6	4
1990-91	**Detroit**	**NHL**	**71**	**18**	**22**	**40**	**18**	**6**	**0**	**1**	**1**	**4**
	NHL Totals		**71**	**18**	**22**	**40**	**18**	**6**	**0**	**1**	**1**	**4**

GARTNER, MICHAEL ALFRED (MIKE)

Right wing. Shoots right. 6', 190 lbs. Born, Ottawa, Ont., October 29, 1959.
(Washington's 1st choice, 4th overall, in 1979 Entry Draft).

			Regular Season					Playoffs				
Season	Club	Lea	GP	G	A	TP	PIM	GP	G	A	TP	PIM
1976-77	Niagara Falls	OHA	62	33	42	75	125	....	....	....	....	....
1977-78a	Niagara Falls	OHA	64	41	49	90	56	....	....	....	....	....
1978-79	Cincinnati	WHA	78	27	25	52	123	3	0	2	2	2
1979-80	**Washington**	**NHL**	**77**	**36**	**32**	**68**	**66**	....	....	....	....	....
1980-81	**Washington**	**NHL**	**80**	**48**	**46**	**94**	**100**	....	....	....	....	....
1981-82	**Washington**	**NHL**	**80**	**35**	**45**	**80**	**121**	....	....	....	....	....
1982-83	**Washington**	**NHL**	**73**	**38**	**38**	**76**	**54**	**4**	**0**	**0**	**0**	**4**
1983-84	**Washington**	**NHL**	**80**	**40**	**45**	**85**	**90**	**8**	**3**	**7**	**10**	**16**
1984-85	**Washington**	**NHL**	**80**	**50**	**52**	**102**	**71**	**5**	**4**	**3**	**7**	**9**
1985-86	**Washington**	**NHL**	**74**	**35**	**40**	**75**	**63**	**9**	**2**	**10**	**12**	**4**
1986-87	**Washington**	**NHL**	**78**	**41**	**32**	**73**	**61**	**7**	**4**	**3**	**7**	**14**
1987-88	**Washington**	**NHL**	**80**	**48**	**33**	**81**	**73**	**14**	**3**	**4**	**7**	**14**
1988-89	**Washington**	**NHL**	**56**	**26**	**29**	**55**	**71**	....	....	....	....	....
	Minnesota	**NHL**	**13**	**7**	**7**	**14**	**2**	**5**	**0**	**0**	**0**	**6**
1989-90	**Minnesota**	**NHL**	**67**	**34**	**36**	**70**	**32**	....	....	....	....	....
	NY Rangers	**NHL**	**12**	**11**	**5**	**16**	**6**	**10**	**5**	**3**	**8**	**12**
1990-91	**NY Rangers**	**NHL**	**79**	**49**	**20**	**69**	**53**	**6**	**1**	**1**	**2**	**0**
	NHL Totals		**929**	**498**	**460**	**958**	**863**	**68**	**22**	**31**	**53**	**79**

a OHA First All-Star Team (1978)

Played in NHL All-Star Game (1980, 1985, 1986, 1988, 1990)

Traded to **Minnesota** by **Washington** with Larry Murphy for Dino Ciccarelli and Bob Rouse, March 7, 1989. Traded to **NY Rangers** by **Minnesota** for Ulf Dahlen, Los Angeles' fourth round choice (Cal McGowan) – previously acquired by NY Rangers – in 1990 Entry Draft and future considerations, March 6, 1990.

GAUDREAU, ROBERT (ROB)

Right wing. Shoots right. 5'11", 185 lbs. Born, Lincoln, RI, January 20, 1970.
(Pittsburgh's 8th choice, 172nd overall, in 1988 Entry Draft).

			Regular Season					Playoffs				
Season	Club	Lea	GP	G	A	TP	PIM	GP	G	A	TP	PIM
1988-89a	Providence	H.E.	42	28	29	57	32	....	....	....	....	....
1989-90	Providence	H.E.	32	20	18	38	12	....	....	....	....	....
1990-91b	Providence	H.E.	36	34	27	61	20	....	....	....	....	....

a Co-winner Hockey East Rookie of the Year (1989)
b Hockey East Second All-Star Team (1991)

Rights traded to **Minnesota** by **Pittsburgh** for Richard Zemlak, November 1, 1988. Claimed by **San Jose** from **Minnesota** in Dispersal Draft, May 30, 1991.

GAUME, DALLAS (GAHM)

Center. Shoots left. 5'10", 185 lbs. Born, Innisfal, Alta., August 27, 1963.

			Regular Season					Playoffs				
Season	Club	Lea	GP	G	A	TP	PIM	GP	G	A	TP	PIM
1982-83	Denver	WCHA	37	19	47	66	12	....	....	....	....	....
1983-84	Denver	WCHA	32	12	25	37	22	....	....	....	....	..
1984-85	Denver	WCHA	39	15	48	63	28	....	....	....	....	....
1985-86	Denver	WCHA	47	32	67	99	18	....	....	....	....	....
1986-87	Binghamton	AHL	77	18	39	57	31	12	1	1	2	7
1987-88	Binghamton	AHL	63	24	49	73	39	4	1	2	3	0
1988-89	**Hartford**	**NHL**	**4**	**1**	**1**	**2**	**0**	....	....	....	....	....
	Binghamton	AHL	57	23	43	66	16	....	....	....	....	....
1989-90	Binghamton	AHL	76	26	39	65	43	....	....	....	....	....
1990-91	Trondheim	Nor.	8	5	6	11	6	....	....	....	....	....
	NHL Totals		**4**	**1**	**1**	**2**	**0**	....	....	....	....	....

Signed as a free agent by **Hartford**, July 10, 1986.

GAUTHIER, DANIEL

Left wing. Shoots left. 6'1", 190 lbs. Born, Charlemagne, Que., May 17, 1970.
(Pittsburgh's 3rd choice, 62nd overall, in 1988 Entry Draft).

			Regular Season					Playoffs				
Season	Club	Lea	GP	G	A	TP	PIM	GP	G	A	TP	PIM
1986-87	Longueuil	QMJHL	64	23	22	45	23	18	4	5	9	15
1987-88	Victoriaville	QMJHL	66	43	47	90	53	5	2	1	3	0
1988-89	Victoriaville	QMJHL	64	41	75	116	84	16	12	17	29	30
1989-90	Victoriaville	QMJHL	62	45	69	114	32	16	8	*19	27	16
1990-91	Albany	IHL	1	1	0	1	0	....	....	....	....	....
ab	Knoxville	ECHL	61	41	*93	134	40	2	0	4	4	4

a ECHL First All-Star Team (1991)
b Top Rookie — ECHL (1991)

GAUTHIER, LUC (GOH-chay)

Defense. Shoots right. 5'9", 205 lbs. Born, Longueuil, Que., April 19, 1964.

			Regular Season					Playoffs				
Season	Club	Lea	GP	G	A	TP	PIM	GP	G	A	TP	PIM
1984-85	Longueuil	QMJHL	60	13	47	60	111	....	....	....	....	....
1985-86	Saginaw	IHL	66	9	29	38	160	....	....	....	....	....
1986-87	Sherbrooke	AHL	78	5	17	22	8	17	2	4	6	31
1987-88	Sherbrooke	AHL	61	4	10	14	105	6	0	0	0	18
1988-89	Sherbrooke	AHL	77	8	20	28	178	6	0	0	0	10
1989-90	Sherbrooke	AHL	79	3	23	26	139	12	0	4	4	35
1990-91	**Montreal**	**NHL**	**3**	**0**	**0**	**0**	**2**	....	....	....	....	....
	Fredericton	AHL	69	7	20	27	238	9	1	1	2	10
	NHL Totals		**3**	**0**	**0**	**0**	**2**	....	....	....	....	....

Signed as a free agent by **Montreal**, October 7, 1986.

GAUVIN, STEPHANE

Left wing. Shoots left. 6'0", 175 lbs. Born, Vancouver, B.C., April 16, 1970.
(Winnipeg's 11th choice, 172nd overall, in 1989 Entry Draft).

			Regular Season					Playoffs				
Season	Club	Lea	GP	G	A	TP	PIM	GP	G	A	TP	PIM
1988-89	Cornell	ECAC	30	2	5	7	24	....	....	....	....	....
1989-90	Cornell	ECAC	29	2	2	4	34	....	....	....	....	....
1990-91	Cornell	ECAC	32	3	5	8	24	....	....	....	....	....

GAVIN, ROBERT (STEWART)

Left wing/Right wing. Shoots left. 6', 190 lbs. Born, Ottawa, Ont., March 15, 1960.
(Toronto's 4th choice, 74th overall, in 1980 Entry Draft).

			Regular Season					Playoffs				
Season	Club	Lea	GP	G	A	TP	PIM	GP	G	A	TP	PIM
1978-79	Toronto	OHA	61	24	25	49	83	3	1	0	1	0
1979-80	Toronto	OHA	68	27	30	57	52	4	1	1	2	2
1980-81	**Toronto**	**NHL**	**14**	**1**	**2**	**3**	**13**	....	....	....	....	....
	New Brunswick	AHL	46	7	12	19	42	13	1	0	1	2
1981-82	**Toronto**	**NHL**	**38**	**5**	**6**	**11**	**29**	....	....	....	....	....
1982-83	**Toronto**	**NHL**	**63**	**6**	**5**	**11**	**44**	**4**	**0**	**0**	**0**	**0**
	St. Catherines	AHL	6	2	4	6	17	....	....	....	....	....
1983-84	**Toronto**	**NHL**	**80**	**10**	**22**	**32**	**90**	....	....	....	....	....
1984-85	**Toronto**	**NHL**	**73**	**12**	**13**	**25**	**38**	....	....	....	....	....
1985-86	**Hartford**	**NHL**	**76**	**26**	**29**	**55**	**51**	**10**	**4**	**1**	**5**	**13**
1986-87	**Hartford**	**NHL**	**79**	**20**	**21**	**41**	**28**	**6**	**2**	**4**	**6**	**10**
1987-88	**Hartford**	**NHL**	**56**	**11**	**10**	**21**	**59**	**6**	**2**	**2**	**4**	**4**
1988-89	**Minnesota**	**NHL**	**73**	**8**	**18**	**26**	**34**	**5**	**3**	**1**	**4**	**10**
1989-90	**Minnesota**	**NHL**	**80**	**12**	**13**	**25**	**76**	**7**	**0**	**2**	**2**	**12**
1990-91	**Minnesota**	**NHL**	**38**	**4**	**4**	**8**	**36**	**21**	**3**	**10**	**13**	**20**
	NHL Totals		**670**	**115**	**143**	**258**	**498**	**59**	**14**	**20**	**34**	**69**

Traded to **Hartford** by **Toronto** for Chris Kotsopoulos, October 7, 1985. Claimed by **Minnesota** in NHL Waiver Draft, October 3, 1988.

GEARY, DEREK

Right wing. Shoots right. 6'3", 180 lbs. Born, Gloucester, MA, February 18, 1970.
(Boston's 5th choice, 123rd overall, in 1988 Entry Draft).

			Regular Season					Playoffs				
Season	Club	Lea	GP	G	A	TP	PIM	GP	G	A	TP	PIM
1988-89	Andover Aca.	HS	3	1	2	3	0	....	....	....	....	....
1989-90	Boston U.	H.E.	DID NOT PLAY									
1990-91	Boston U.	H.E.	DID NOT PLAY									

GELINAS, MARTIN (JEL-in-uh)

Left wing. Shoots left. 5'11", 195 lbs. Born, Shawinigan, Que., June 5, 1970.
(Los Angeles' 1st choice, 7th overall, in 1988 Entry Draft).

			Regular Season					Playoffs				
Season	Club	Lea	GP	G	A	TP	PIM	GP	G	A	TP	PIM
1987-88	Hull	QMJHL	65	63	68	131	74	17	15	18	33	32
1988-89	**Edmonton**	**NHL**	**6**	**1**	**2**	**3**	**0**	....	....	....	....	....
	Hull	QMJHL	41	38	39	77	31	9	5	4	9	14
1989-90	**Edmonton**	**NHL**	**46**	**17**	**8**	**25**	**30**	**20**	**2**	**3**	**5**	**6**
1990-91	**Edmonton**	**NHL**	**73**	**20**	**20**	**40**	**34**	**18**	**3**	**6**	**9**	**25**
	NHL Totals		**125**	**38**	**30**	**68**	**64**	**38**	**5**	**9**	**14**	**31**

Traded to **Edmonton** by **Los Angeles** with Jimmy Carson and Los Angeles' first round choices in 1989, (acquired by New Jersey, June 17, 1989. New Jersey selected Jason Miller), 1991 (Martin Rucinsky) and 1993 Entry Drafts and cash for Wayne Gretzky, Mike Krushelnyski and Marty McSorley, August 9, 1988.

GERMAIN, ERIC

Defense. Shoots left. 6'1", 195 lbs. Born, Quebec City, Que., June 26, 1966.

			Regular Season					Playoffs				
Season	Club	Lea	GP	G	A	TP	PIM	GP	G	A	TP	PIM
1983-84	St. Jean	QMJHL	57	2	15	17	60	4	1	0	1	6
1984-85	St. Jean	QMJHL	66	10	31	41	243	5	4	0	4	14
1985-86	St. Jean	QMJHL	66	5	38	43	183	10	0	6	6	56
1986-87	Flint	IHL	21	0	2	2	23	....	....	....	....	....
	Fredericton	AHL	44	2	8	10	28	....	....	....	....	....
1987-88	**Los Angeles**	**NHL**	**4**	**0**	**1**	**1**	**13**	**1**	**0**	**0**	**0**	**4**
	New Haven	AHL	69	0	10	10	0	....	....	....	....	....
1988-89	New Haven	AHL	55	0	9	9	93	17	0	3	3	23
1989-90	New Haven	AHL	59	3	12	15	112	....	....	....	....	....
1990-91	Binghamton	AHL	60	4	10	14	144	10	0	1	1	14
	NHL Totals		**4**	**0**	**1**	**1**	**13**	**1**	**0**	**0**	**0**	**4**

Signed as a free agent by **Los Angeles**, July 1, 1986. Signed as a free agent by **NY Rangers**, July 11, 1990.

GERNANDER, KEN

Center. Shoots left. 5'10", 175 lbs. Born, Coleraine, MN, June 30, 1969.
(Winnipeg's 4th choice, 96th overall, in 1987 Entry Draft).

			Regular Season					Playoffs				
Season	Club	Lea	GP	G	A	TP	PIM	GP	G	A	TP	PIM
1987-88	U. Minnesota	WCHA	44	14	14	28	14	....	....	....	....	....
1988-89	U. Minnesota	WCHA	44	9	11	20	2	....	....	....	....	....
1989-90	U. Minnesota	WCHA	44	32	17	49	24	....	....	....	....	....
1990-91	U. Minnesota	WCHA	44	23	20	43	24	....	....	....	....	....

GERVAIS, VICTOR (JUR-vay)

Right wing. Shoots left. 5'9", 172 lbs. Born, Prince George, B.C., March 13, 1969.
(Washington's 8th choice, 187th overall, in 1989 Entry Draft).

			Regular Season					Playoffs				
Season	Club	Lea	GP	G	A	TP	PIM	GP	G	A	TP	PIM
1986-87	Seattle	WHL	66	13	30	43	58	....	....	....	....	....
1987-88	Seattle	WHL	69	30	46	76	134	....	....	....	....	....
1988-89	Seattle	WHL	72	54	65	119	158	....	....	....	....	....
1989-90	Seattle	WHL	69	64	96	160	180	13	8	9	17	30
	Baltimore	AHL	....	....	....	....	....	3	0	0	0	0
1990-91	Baltimore	AHL	28	2	13	15	28	....	....	....	....	....

GIACIN, JIM

Left wing. Shoots left. 6'1", 200 lbs. Born, St. Louis, MO, January 6, 1971.
(Los Angeles' 8th choice, 182nd overall, in 1989 Entry Draft).

			Regular Season					Playoffs				
Season	Club	Lea	GP	G	A	TP	PIM	GP	G	A	TP	PIM
1989-90	St. Lawrence	ECAC	28	4	2	6	32	....	....	....	....	....
1990-91	St. Lawrence	ECAC	35	3	5	8	22	....	....	....	....	....

GIBSON, DON

Defense. Shoots right. 6'1", 210 lbs. Born, Deloraine, Man., December 29, 1967.
(Vancouver's 2nd choice, 49th overall, in 1986 Entry Draft).

			Regular Season					Playoffs				
Season	Club	Lea	GP	G	A	TP	PIM	GP	G	A	TP	PIM
1986-87	Michigan State	CCHA	43	3	3	6	74	....	....	....	....	....
1987-88	Michigan State	CCHA	43	7	12	19	118	....	....	....	....	....
1988-89	Michigan State	CCHA	39	7	10	17	107	....	....	....	....	....
1989-90a	Michigan State	CCHA	44	5	22	27	167	....	....	....	....	....
	Milwaukee	IHL	1	0	0	0	4	5	0	1	1	41
1990-91	**Vancouver**	**NHL**	**14**	**0**	**3**	**3**	**20**	....	....	....	....	....
	Milwaukee	IHL	21	4	3	7	76	....	....	....	....	....
	NHL Totals		**14**	**0**	**3**	**3**	**20**	....	....	....	....	....

a CCHA Second All-Star Team (1990)

GIFFIN, LEE

Right wing. Shoots right. 6', 188 lbs. Born, Chatham, Ont., April 1, 1967.
(Pittsburgh's 2nd choice, 23rd overall, in 1985 Entry Draft)

			Regular Season					Playoffs				
Season	Club	Lea	GP	G	A	TP	PIM	GP	G	A	TP	PIM
1983-84	Oshawa	OHL	70	23	27	50	88	7	1	4	5	12
1984-85	Oshawa	OHL	62	36	42	78	78	5	1	2	3	2
1985-86	Oshawa	OHL	54	29	37	66	28	6	0	5	5	8
1986-87	**Pittsburgh**	**NHL**	**8**	**1**	**1**	**2**	**0**	....	....	....	....	....
a	Oshawa	OHL	48	31	69	100	46	23	*17	19	36	14
1987-88	**Pittsburgh**	**NHL**	**19**	**0**	**2**	**2**	**9**	....	....	....	....	....
	Muskegon	IHL	48	26	37	63	61	6	1	3	4	2
1988-89	Muskegon	IHL	63	30	44	74	93	12	5	7	12	8
1989-90	Flint	IHL	73	30	44	74	68	4	1	2	3	0
1990-91	Kansas City	IHL	60	25	43	68	48	....	....	....	....	....
	NHL Totals		**27**	**1**	**3**	**4**	**9**	....	....	....	....	....

a OHL First All-Star Team (1987)

Traded to **NY Rangers** by **Pittsburgh** for future considerations, September 14, 1989.

GILBERT, GREGORY SCOTT (GREG)

Left wing. Shoots left. 6'1", 191 lbs. Born, Mississauga, Ont., January 22, 1962.
(NY Islanders' 5th choice, 80th overall, in 1980 Entry Draft).

			Regular Season					Playoffs				
Season	Club	Lea	GP	G	A	TP	PIM	GP	G	A	TP	PIM
1979-80	Toronto	OHA	68	10	11	21	35	....	....	....	....	....
1980-81	Toronto	OHA	64	30	37	67	73	5	2	6	8	16
1981-82	**NY Islanders**	**NHL**	1	1	0	1	0	4	1	1	2	2
a	Toronto	OHL	65	41	67	108	119	10	4	12	16	23
1982-83	**NY Islanders**	**NHL**	45	8	11	19	30	10	1	0	1	14
	Indianapolis	CHL	24	11	16	27	23	....	....	....	....	....
1983-84	**NY Islanders**	**NHL**	79	31	35	66	59	21	5	7	12	39
1984-85	**NY Islanders**	**NHL**	58	13	25	38	36	....	....	....	....	....
1985-86	**NY Islanders**	**NHL**	60	9	19	28	82	2	0	0	0	9
	Springfield	AHL	2	0	0	0	2	....	....	....	....	....
1986-87	**NY Islanders**	**NHL**	51	6	7	13	26	10	2	2	4	6
1987-88	**NY Islanders**	**NHL**	76	17	28	45	46	4	0	0	0	6
1988-89	**NY Islanders**	**NHL**	55	8	13	21	45	....	....	....	....	....
	Chicago	**NHL**	4	0	0	0	0	15	1	5	6	20
1989-90	**Chicago**	**NHL**	70	12	25	37	54	19	5	8	13	34
1990-91	**Chicago**	**NHL**	72	10	15	25	58	5	0	1	1	2
	NHL Totals		571	115	178	293	436	90	15	24	39	132

a OHL Third All-Star Team (1982)

Traded to **Chicago** by **NY Islanders** for Chicago's fifth-round choice (Steve Young) in 1989 Entry Draft, March 7, 1989.

GILCHRIST, BRENT

Left wing. Shoots left. 5'11", 181 lbs. Born, Moose Jaw, Sask., April 3, 1967.
(Montreal's 6th choice, 79th overall, in 1985 Entry Draft).

			Regular Season					Playoffs				
Season	Club	Lea	GP	G	A	TP	PIM	GP	G	A	TP	PIM
1983-84	Kelowna	WHL	69	16	11	27	16	....	....	....	....	....
1984-85	Kelowna	WHL	51	35	38	73	58	6	5	2	7	8
1985-86	Spokane	WHL	52	45	45	90	57	9	6	7	13	19
1986-87	Spokane	WHL	46	45	55	100	71	5	2	7	9	6
	Sherbrooke	AHL	....	....	....	....	....	10	2	7	9	2
1987-88	Sherbrooke	AHL	77	26	48	74	83	6	1	3	4	6
1988-89	**Montreal**	**NHL**	49	8	16	24	16	9	1	1	2	10
	Sherbrooke	AHL	7	6	5	11	7	....	....	....	....	....
1989-90	**Montreal**	**NHL**	57	9	15	24	28	8	2	0	2	2
1990-91	**Montreal**	**NHL**	51	6	9	15	10	13	5	3	8	6
	NHL Totals		157	23	40	63	54	30	8	4	12	18

GILES, CURT (JIGHLS)

Defense. Shoots left. 5'8", 175 lbs. Born, The Pas, Man., November 30, 1958.
(Minnesota's 4th choice, 54th overall, in 1978 Amateur Draft).

			Regular Season					Playoffs				
Season	Club	Lea	GP	G	A	TP	PIM	GP	G	A	TP	PIM
1977-78	Minn.-Duluth	WCHA	34	11	36	47	62	....	....	....	....	....
1978-79	Minn.-Duluth	WCHA	30	3	38	41	38	....	....	....	....	....
1979-80	Oklahoma City	CHL	42	4	24	28	35	....	....	....	....	....
	Minnesota	**NHL**	37	2	7	9	31	12	2	4	6	10
1980-81	**Minnesota**	**NHL**	67	5	22	27	56	19	1	4	5	14
1981-82	**Minnesota**	**NHL**	74	3	12	15	87	4	0	0	0	2
1982-83	**Minnesota**	**NHL**	76	2	21	23	70	5	0	2	2	6
1983-84	**Minnesota**	**NHL**	70	6	22	28	59	16	1	3	4	25
1984-85	**Minnesota**	**NHL**	77	5	25	30	49	9	0	0	0	17
1985-86	**Minnesota**	**NHL**	69	6	21	27	30	5	0	1	1	10
1986-87	**Minnesota**	**NHL**	11	0	3	3	4	....	....	....	....	....
	NY Rangers	**NHL**	61	2	17	19	50	5	0	0	0	6
1987-88	**NY Rangers**	**NHL**	13	0	0	0	10	....	....	....	....	....
	Minnesota	**NHL**	59	1	12	13	66	....	....	....	....	....
1988-89	**Minnesota**	**NHL**	76	5	10	15	77	5	0	0	0	4
1989-90	**Minnesota**	**NHL**	74	1	12	13	48	7	0	1	1	6
1990-91	**Minnesota**	**NHL**	70	4	10	14	48	10	1	0	1	16
	NHL Totals		834	42	194	236	685	97	5	15	20	116

Traded to **NY Rangers** by **Minnesota** with Tony McKegney and Minnesota's second-round choice (Troy Mallette) in 1988 Entry Draft for Bob Brooke and NY Rangers' rights to Minnesota's fourth-round choice in (Jeffery Stolp) 1988 Entry Draft previously acquired by NY Rangers in Mark Pavelich deal, November 13, 1986. Traded to **Minnesota** by **NY Rangers** for Byron Lomow and future considerations, November 20, 1987.

GILHEN, RANDY

Center. Shoots left. 6', 190 lbs. Born, Zweibrucken, West Germany, June 13, 1963.
(Hartford's 6th choice, 109th overall, in 1982 Entry Draft).

			Regular Season					Playoffs				
Season	Club	Lea	GP	G	A	TP	PIM	GP	G	A	TP	PIM
1980-81	Saskatoon	WHL	68	10	5	15	154	....	....	....	....	....
1981-82	Saskatoon	WHL	25	15	9	24	45	....	....	....	....	....
	Winnipeg	WHL	36	26	28	54	42	....	....	....	....	....
1982-83	**Hartford**	**NHL**	2	0	1	1	0	....	....	....	....	....
	Winnipeg	WHL	71	57	44	101	84	3	2	2	4	0
1983-84	Binghamton	AHL	73	8	12	20	72	....	....	....	....	....
1984-85	Salt Lake	IHL	57	20	20	40	28	....	....	....	....	....
	Binghamton	AHL	18	3	3	6	9	8	4	1	5	16
1985-86	Fort Wayne	IHL	82	44	40	84	48	15	10	8	18	6
1986-87	**Winnipeg**	**NHL**	2	0	0	0	0	....	....	....	....	....
	Sherbrooke	AHL	75	36	29	65	44	17	7	13	20	10
1987-88	**Winnipeg**	**NHL**	13	3	2	5	15	4	1	0	1	10
	Moncton	AHL	68	40	47	87	51	....	....	....	....	....
1988-89	**Winnipeg**	**NHL**	64	5	3	8	38	....	....	....	....	....
1989-90	**Pittsburgh**	**NHL**	61	5	11	16	54	....	....	....	....	....
1990-91	**Pittsburgh**	**NHL**	72	15	10	25	51	16	1	0	1	14
	NHL Totals		214	28	27	55	158	20	2	0	2	24

Traded to **Pittsburgh** by **Winnipeg** with Jim Kyte and Andrew McBain for Randy Cunnyworth, Rick Tabaracci and Dave McLlwain, June 17, 1989. Claimed by **Minnesota** from **Pittsburgh** in Expansion Draft, May 30, 1991. Traded to **Los Angeles** by **Minnesota** with Charlie Huddy, Jim Thomson and NY Rangers' fourth round choice (previously acquired by Minnesota — Alexei Zhitnik) in 1991 Entry Draft for Todd Elik, June 22, 1991.

GILL, TODD

Defense. Shoots left. 6', 185 lbs. Born, Brockville, Ont., November 9, 1965.
(Toronto's 2nd choice, 25th overall, in 1984 Entry Draft).

			Regular Season					Playoffs				
Season	Club	Lea	GP	G	A	TP	PIM	GP	G	A	TP	PIM
1982-83	Windsor	OHL	70	12	24	36	108	3	0	0	0	11
1983-84	Windsor	OHL	68	9	48	57	184	3	1	1	2	10
1984-85	**Toronto**	**NHL**	10	1	0	1	13	....	....	....	....	....
a	Windsor	OHL	53	17	40	57	148	4	0	1	1	14
1985-86	**Toronto**	**NHL**	15	1	2	3	28	1	0	0	0	0
	St. Catharines	AHL	58	8	25	33	90	10	1	6	7	17
1986-87	**Toronto**	**NHL**	61	4	27	31	92	13	2	2	4	42
	Newmarket	AHL	11	1	8	9	33	....	....	....	....	....
1987-88	**Toronto**	**NHL**	65	8	17	25	131	6	1	3	4	20
	Newmarket	AHL	2	0	1	1	2	....	....	....	....	....
1988-89	**Toronto**	**NHL**	59	11	14	25	72	....	....	....	....	....
1989-90	**Toronto**	**NHL**	48	1	14	15	92	5	0	3	3	16
1990-91	**Toronto**	**NHL**	72	2	22	24	113	....	....	....	....	....
	NHL Totals		330	28	96	124	541	25	3	8	11	78

a OHL Third All-Star Team (1985)

GILLIS, PAUL

Center. Shoots left. 5'11", 198 lbs. Born, Toronto, Ont., December 31, 1963.
(Quebec's 2nd choice, 34th overall, in 1982 Entry Draft).

			Regular Season					Playoffs				
Season	Club	Lea	GP	G	A	TP	PIM	GP	G	A	TP	PIM
1980-81	Niagara Falls	OHA	59	14	19	33	165	....	....	....	....	....
1981-82	Niagara Falls	OHL	65	27	62	89	247	5	1	5	6	26
1982-83	**Quebec**	**NHL**	7	0	2	2	2	....	....	....	....	....
	North Bay	OHL	61	34	52	86	151	6	1	3	4	26
1983-84	**Quebec**	**NHL**	57	8	9	17	59	1	0	0	0	2
	Fredericton	AHL	18	7	8	15	47	....	....	....	....	....
1984-85	**Quebec**	**NHL**	77	14	28	42	168	18	1	7	8	73
1985-86	**Quebec**	**NHL**	80	19	24	43	203	3	0	2	2	14
1986-87	**Quebec**	**NHL**	76	13	26	39	267	13	2	4	6	65
1987-88	**Quebec**	**NHL**	80	7	10	17	164	....	....	....	....	....
1988-89	**Quebec**	**NHL**	79	15	25	40	163	....	....	....	....	....
1989-90	**Quebec**	**NHL**	71	8	14	22	234	....	....	....	....	....
1990-91	**Quebec**	**NHL**	49	3	8	11	91	....	....	....	....	....
	Chicago	**NHL**	13	0	5	5	53	2	0	0	0	2
	NHL Totals		589	87	151	238	1404	37	3	13	16	156

Traded to **Chicago** by **Quebec** with Dan Vincelette for Ryan McGill and Mike McNeil, March 5, 1991.

GILMOUR, DOUGLAS (DOUG)

Center. Shoots left. 5'11", 170 lbs. Born, Kingston, Ont., June 25, 1963.
(St. Louis' 4th choice, 134th overall, in 1982 Entry Draft).

			Regular Season					Playoffs				
Season	Club	Lea	GP	G	A	TP	PIM	GP	G	A	TP	PIM
1981-82	Cornwall	OHL	67	46	73	119	42	5	6	9	15	2
1982-83ab	Cornwall	OHL	68	70	*107	*177	62	8	8	10	18	16
1983-84	**St. Louis**	**NHL**	80	25	28	53	57	11	2	9	11	10
1984-85	**St. Louis**	**NHL**	78	21	36	57	49	3	1	1	2	2
1985-86	**St. Louis**	**NHL**	74	25	28	53	41	19	9	12	*21	25
1986-87	**St. Louis**	**NHL**	80	42	63	105	58	6	2	2	4	16
1987-88	**St. Louis**	**NHL**	72	36	50	86	59	10	3	14	17	18
1988-89	**Calgary**	**NHL**	72	26	59	85	44	22	11	11	22	20
1989-90	**Calgary**	**NHL**	78	24	67	91	54	6	3	1	4	8
1990-91	**Calgary**	**NHL**	78	20	61	81	144	7	1	1	2	0
	NHL Totals		612	219	392	611	506	86	32	51	83	99

a OHL First All-Star Team (1983)
b Named OHL's Most Outstanding Player (1983)

Traded to **Calgary** by **St. Louis** with Mark Hunter, Steve Bozek and Michael Dark for Mike Bullard, Craig Coxe and Tim Corkery, September 6, 1988.

GLENNON, MATTHEW (MATT)

Left wing. Shoots left. 6', 185 lbs. Born, Hull, MA, September 20, 1968.
(Boston's 7th choice, 119th overall, in 1987 Entry Draft).

			Regular Season					Playoffs				
Season	Club	Lea	GP	G	A	TP	PIM	GP	G	A	TP	PIM
1987-88	Boston College	H.E.	16	3	3	6	16	....	....	....	....	....
1988-89	Boston College	H.E.	16	1	6	7	4	....	....	....	....	....
1989-90	Boston College	H.E.	31	7	11	18	16	....	....	....	....	....
1990-91	Boston College	H.E.	33	6	9	15	36	....	....	....	....	....

GLYNN, BRIAN

Defense. Shoots left. 6'4", 215 lbs. Born, Iserlohn, West Germany, November 23, 1967.
(Calgary's 2nd choice, 37th overall, in 1986 Entry Draft).

			Regular Season					Playoffs				
Season	Club	Lea	GP	G	A	TP	PIM	GP	G	A	TP	PIM
1984-85	Saskatoon	WHL	12	1	0	1	2	3	0	0	0	0
1985-86	Saskatoon	WHL	66	7	25	32	131	13	0	3	3	30
1986-87	Saskatoon	WHL	44	2	26	28	163	11	1	3	4	19
1987-88	**Calgary**	**NHL**	67	5	14	19	87	1	0	0	0	0
1988-89	**Calgary**	**NHL**	9	0	1	1	19	....	....	....	....	....
	Salt Lake	IHL	31	3	10	13	105	14	3	7	10	31
1989-90	**Calgary**	**NHL**	1	0	0	0	0	....	....	....	....	....
ab	Salt Lake	IHL	80	17	44	61	164	....	....	....	....	....
1990-91	Salt Lake	IHL	8	1	3	4	18	....	....	....	....	....
	Minnesota	**NHL**	66	8	11	19	83	23	2	6	8	18
	NHL Totals		143	13	26	39	189	24	2	6	8	18

a IHL First All-Star Team (1990)
b Won Governors' Trophy (Outstanding Defenseman-IHL) (1990)

Traded to **Minnesota** by **Calgary** for Frantisek Musil, October 26, 1990.

GOBER, MICHAEL

Left wing. Shoots left. 6', 192 lbs. Born, St. Louis, MO, April 10, 1967.
(Detroit's 8th choice, 137th overall, in 1987 Entry Draft).

			Regular Season					Playoffs				
Season	Club	Lea	GP	G	A	TP	PIM	GP	G	A	TP	PIM
1987-88	Trois-Rivieres	QMJHL	19	5	10	15	96	....	....	....	....	....
1988-89	Adirondack	AHL	41	15	7	22	55	2	0	0	0	4
1989-90	Adirondack	AHL	44	14	12	26	85	....	....	....	....	....
1990-91	Kansas City	IHL	26	4	7	11	87	....	....	....	....	....
	San Diego	IHL	22	8	11	19	148	....	....	....	....	....

GODYNUK, ALEXANDER

Defense. Shoots left. 6', 207 lbs. Born, Kiev, Soviet Union, January 27, 1970.
(Toronto's 5th choice, 115th overall, in 1990 Entry Draft).

			Regular Season					Playoffs				
Season	Club	Lea	GP	G	A	TP	PIM	GP	G	A	TP	PIM
1989-90	Sokol Kiev	USSR	38	3	2	5	31	....	....	....	....	....
1990-91	Sokol Kiev	USSR	19	3	1	4	20	....	....	....	....	....
	Toronto	**NHL**	**18**	**0**	**3**	**3**	**16**	....	....	....	....	....
	Newmarket	AHL	11	0	1	1	29	....	....	....	....	....
	NHL Totals		**18**	**0**	**3**	**3**	**16**	....	....	....	....	....

GOERTZ, DAVE

Defense. Shoots right. 5'11", 199 lbs. Born, Edmonton, Alta., March 28, 1965.
(Pittsburgh's 10th choice, 223rd overall, in 1983 Entry Draft).

			Regular Season					Playoffs				
Season	Club	Lea	GP	G	A	TP	PIM	GP	G	A	TP	PIM
1981-82	Regina	WHL	67	5	19	24	181	19	1	2	3	61
1982-83	Regina	WHL	69	4	22	26	132	5	0	2	2	9
1983-84	Prince Albert	WHL	60	13	47	60	111	5	2	3	5	0
	Baltimore	AHL	1	0	0	0	2	6	0	0	0	0
1984-85	Prince Albert	WHL	48	3	48	51	62	13	4	14	18	29
1985-86	Baltimore	AHL	74	1	15	16	76	....	....	....	....	....
1986-87	Baltimore	AHL	16	0	3	3	8	....	....	....	....	....
	Muskegon	IHL	44	3	17	20	44	15	0	4	4	14
1987-88	**Pittsburgh**	**NHL**	**2**	**0**	**0**	**0**	**2**	....	....	....	....	....
	Muskegon	IHL	73	8	36	44	87	6	0	4	4	14
1988-89	Muskegon	IHL	74	1	32	33	102	14	0	4	4	10
1989-90	Muskegon	IHL	51	3	18	21	64	....	....	....	....	....
	NHL Totals		**2**	**0**	**0**	**0**	**2**	....	....	....	....	....

GOLDEN, MIKE

Center. Shoots right. 6'1", 195 lbs. Born, Boston, MA, June 14, 1965.
(Edmonton's 2nd choice, 40th overall, in 1983 Entry Draft).

			Regular Season					Playoffs				
Season	Club	Lea	GP	G	A	TP	PIM	GP	G	A	TP	PIM
1985-86	U. of Maine	H.E.	24	3	16	29	10	....	....	....	....	....
1986-87	U. of Maine	H.E.	36	19	23	42	37	....	....	....	....	....
1987-88ab	U. of Maine	H.E.	44	31	44	75	46	....	....	....	....	....
1988-89	Denver	IHL	36	12	10	22	21	3	3	1	4	0
1989-90	Flint	IHL	68	13	33	46	30	4	0	0	0	2
1990-91	Binghamton	AHL	8	2	0	2	0	....	....	....	....	....
	Albany	IHL	6	3	1	4	0	....	....	....	....	....
	Milwaukee	IHL	36	2	12	14	12	4	0	0	0	0

a NCAA East Second All-American Team (1988)
b Hockey East Second All-Star Team (1988)

Traded to **NY Rangers** by **Edmonton** with Miloslav Horava and Don Jackson for Reijo Ruotsalainen, Ville Kentala, Clark Donatelli and Jim Wiemer, October 2, 1986.

GOODALL, GLEN

Center. Shoots right. 5'8", 170 lbs. Born, Fort Nelson, B.C., January 22, 1970.
(Detroit's 9th choice, 206th overall, in 1988 Entry Draft).

			Regular Season					Playoffs				
Season	Club	Lea	GP	G	A	TP	PIM	GP	G	A	TP	PIM
1984-85	Seattle	WHL	59	5	21	26	6	....	....	....	....	....
1985-86	Seattle	WHL	65	13	28	41	53	4	1	1	2	0
1986-87	Seattle	WHL	68	63	49	112	64	....	....	....	....	....
1987-88	Seattle	WHL	70	53	64	117	88	....	....	....	....	....
1988-89	Seattle	WHL	70	52	62	114	58	....	....	....	....	....
	Flint	IHL	9	5	4	9	4	....	....	....	....	....
1989-90ab	Seattle	WHL	67	76	87	163	83	10	7	7	14	2
1990-91	Adirondack	AHL	69	18	23	41	49	2	0	0	0	2

a WHL West Second All-Star Team (1990)
b WHL Player of the Year (1990)

GORDIJUK, VIKTOR

Right wing. Shoots right. 5'10", 176 lbs. Born, Moscow, Soviet Union, April 11, 1970.
(Buffalo's 6th choice, 142nd overall, in 1990 Entry Draft).

			Regular Season					Playoffs				
Season	Club	Lea	GP	G	A	TP	PIM	GP	G	A	TP	PIM
1989-90	Soviet Wings	USSR	48	11	4	15	24	....	....	....	....	....
1990-91	Soviet Wings	USSR	46	12	10	22	22	....	....	....	....	....

GORMAN, SEAN

Defense. Shoots left. 6'3", 180 lbs. Born, Cambridge, MA, February 1, 1969.
(Boston's 13th choice, 245th overall, in 1987 Entry Draft).

			Regular Season					Playoffs				
Season	Club	Lea	GP	G	A	TP	PIM	GP	G	A	TP	PIM
1987-88	Princeton	ECAC	28	0	3	3	6	....	....	....	....	....
1988-89	Princeton	ECAC	17	0	2	2	20	....	....	....	....	....
1989-90	Princeton	ECAC	27	2	4	6	8	....	....	....	....	....
1990-91	Princeton	ECAC	27	3	9	12	34	....	....	....	....	....

GOSSELIN, GUY

Defense. Shoots right. 5'10", 185 lbs. Born, Rochester, MN, January 6, 1964.
(Winnipeg's 6th choice, 159th overall, in 1982 Entry Draft).

			Regular Season					Playoffs				
Season	Club	Lea	GP	G	A	TP	PIM	GP	G	A	TP	PIM
1982-83	Minn.-Duluth	WCHA	4	0	0	0	0	....	....	....	....	....
1983-84	Minn.-Duluth	WCHA	37	3	3	6	26	....	....	....	....	....
1984-85	Minn.-Duluth	WCHA	47	3	7	10	25	....	....	....	....	....
1985-86	Minn.-Duluth	WCHA	39	2	16	18	53	....	....	....	....	....
1986-87a	Minn.-Duluth	WCHA	33	7	8	15	66	....	....	....	....	....
1987-88	U.S. National	...	50	3	19	22	82	....	....	....	....	....
	U.S. Olympic	...	6	0	3	3	2	....	....	....	....	....
	Winnipeg	**NHL**	**5**	**0**	**0**	**0**	**6**	....	....	....	....	....
1988-89	Moncton	AHL	58	2	8	10	56	10	1	1	2	2
1989-90	Moncton	AHL	70	2	10	12	37	....	....	....	....	....
1990-91	Skelleftea	Swe.2	16	0	1	1	8	....	....	....	....	....
	NHL Totals		**5**	**0**	**0**	**0**	**6**	....	....	....	....	....

a WCHA Second All-Star Team (1987)

GOTAAS, STEVE (GAH-tihs)

Center. Shoots right. 5'10", 180 lbs. Born, Camrose, Alta., May 10, 1967.
(Pittsburgh's 4th choice, 86th overall, in 1985 Entry Draft).

			Regular Season					Playoffs				
Season	Club	Lea	GP	G	A	TP	PIM	GP	G	A	TP	PIM
1983-84	Prince Albert	WHL	65	10	22	32	47	5	0	1	1	0
1984-85	Prince Albert	WHL	72	32	41	73	66	13	3	6	9	17
1985-86	Prince Albert	WHL	61	40	61	101	31	....	....	....	....	....
1986-87	Prince Albert	WHL	68	53	55	108	94	8	5	6	11	16
1987-88	**Pittsburgh**	**NHL**	**36**	**5**	**6**	**11**	**45**	....	....	....	....	....
	Muskegon	IHL	34	16	22	38	4	....	....	....	....	....
1988-89	**Minnesota**	**NHL**	**12**	**1**	**3**	**4**	**6**	**3**	**0**	**1**	**1**	**5**
	Muskegon	IHL	19	9	16	25	34	....	....	....	....	....
	Kalamazoo	IHL	30	24	22	46	12	5	2	3	5	2
1989-90	Kalamazoo	IHL	1	1	0	1	0	2	0	0	0	2
1990-91	**Minnesota**	**NHL**	**1**	**0**	**0**	**0**	**2**	....	....	....	....	....
	Kalamazoo	IHL	78	30	49	79	88	7	3	5	8	4
	NHL Totals		**49**	**6**	**9**	**15**	**53**	**3**	**0**	**1**	**1**	**5**

Traded to **Minnesota** by **Pittsburgh** with Ville Siren for Gord Dineen and Scott Bjugstad, December 17, 1988.

GOTZIAMAN, CHRIS

Right wing. Shoots right. 6'3", 200 lbs. Born, Roseau, MN, November 29, 1971.
(New Jersey's 3rd choice, 29th overall, in 1990 Entry Draft).

			Regular Season					Playoffs				
Season	Club	Lea	GP	G	A	TP	PIM	GP	G	A	TP	PIM
1989-90	Roseau	HS	28	34	31	65	....	....	....	....	....	....
1990-91	North Dakota	WCHA	40	11	8	19	26	....	....	....	....	....

GOULD, ROBERT (BOBBY)

Right wing/Center. Shoots right. 6', 195 lbs. Born, Petrolia, Ont., September 2, 1957.
(Atlanta's 7th choice, 118th overall, in 1977 Amateur Draft).

			Regular Season					Playoffs				
Season	Club	Lea	GP	G	A	TP	PIM	GP	G	A	TP	PIM
1978-79a	N. Hampshire	ECAC	25	24	17	41	....	....	....	....	....	....
	Tulsa	CHL	5	2	0	2	4	....	....	....	....	....
1979-80	**Atlanta**	**NHL**	**1**	**0**	**0**	**0**	**0**	....	....	....	....	....
	Birmingham	CHL	79	27	33	60	73	4	2	4	6	0
1980-81	**Calgary**	**NHL**	**3**	**0**	**0**	**0**	**0**	**11**	**3**	**1**	**4**	**4**
	Birmingham	CHL	58	25	25	50	43	....	....	....	....	....
	Fort Worth	CHL	18	8	6	14	6	5	5	2	7	10
1981-82	**Calgary**	**NHL**	**16**	**3**	**0**	**3**	**4**	....	....	....	....	....
	Oklahoma City	CHL	1	0	1	1	0	....	....	....	....	....
	Washington	**NHL**	**60**	**18**	**13**	**31**	**69**	....	....	....	....	....
1982-83	**Washington**	**NHL**	**80**	**22**	**18**	**40**	**43**	**4**	**5**	**0**	**5**	**4**
1983-84	**Washington**	**NHL**	**78**	**21**	**19**	**40**	**74**	**5**	**0**	**2**	**2**	**4**
1984-85	**Washington**	**NHL**	**78**	**14**	**19**	**33**	**69**	**5**	**0**	**1**	**1**	**2**
1985-86	**Washington**	**NHL**	**79**	**19**	**19**	**38**	**26**	**9**	**4**	**3**	**7**	**11**
1986-87	**Washington**	**NHL**	**78**	**23**	**27**	**50**	**74**	**7**	**0**	**3**	**3**	**8**
1987-88	**Washington**	**NHL**	**72**	**12**	**14**	**26**	**56**	**14**	**3**	**1**	**4**	**21**
1988-89	**Washington**	**NHL**	**75**	**5**	**13**	**18**	**65**	**6**	**0**	**2**	**2**	**0**
1989-90	**Boston**	**NHL**	**77**	**8**	**17**	**25**	**92**	**17**	**0**	**0**	**0**	**4**
1990-91	Maine	AHL	71	10	15	25	30	2	0	0	0	0
	NHL Totals		**697**	**145**	**159**	**304**	**572**	**78**	**15**	**13**	**28**	**58**

a ECAC Second All-Star Team (1979)

Traded to **Washington** by **Calgary** with Randy Holt for Pat Ribble and Washington's second round choice (Todd Francis — later transferred to Montreal in Doug Risebrough deal) in 1983 Entry Draft, November 25, 1981. Traded to **Boston** by **Washington** for Alain Cote, September 28, 1989.

GOULET, MICHEL (goo-LAY)

Left wing. Shoots left. 6'1", 195 lbs. Born, Peribonka, Que., April 21, 1960.
(Quebec's 1st choice, 20th overall, in 1979 Entry Draft).

			Regular Season					Playoffs				
Season	Club	Lea	GP	G	A	TP	PIM	GP	G	A	TP	PIM
1976-77	Quebec	QJHL	37	17	18	35	9	14	3	8	11	19
1977-78	Quebec	QJHL	72	73	62	135	109	1	0	1	1	0
1978-79	Birmingham	WHA	78	28	30	58	65	....	....	....	....	....
1979-80	**Quebec**	**NHL**	**77**	**22**	**32**	**54**	**48**	....	....	....	....	....
1980-81	**Quebec**	**NHL**	**76**	**32**	**39**	**71**	**45**	**4**	**3**	**4**	**7**	**7**
1981-82	**Quebec**	**NHL**	**80**	**42**	**42**	**84**	**48**	**16**	**8**	**5**	**13**	**6**
1982-83a	**Quebec**	**NHL**	**80**	**57**	**48**	**105**	**51**	**4**	**0**	**0**	**0**	**6**
1983-84b	**Quebec**	**NHL**	**75**	**56**	**65**	**121**	**76**	**9**	**2**	**4**	**6**	**17**
1984-85	**Quebec**	**NHL**	**69**	**55**	**40**	**95**	**55**	**17**	**11**	**10**	**21**	**17**
1985-86b	**Quebec**	**NHL**	**75**	**53**	**51**	**104**	**64**	**3**	**1**	**2**	**3**	**10**
1986-87b	**Quebec**	**NHL**	**75**	**49**	**47**	**96**	**61**	**13**	**9**	**5**	**14**	**35**
1987-88a	**Quebec**	**NHL**	**80**	**48**	**58**	**106**	**56**	....	....	....	....	....
1988-89	**Quebec**	**NHL**	**69**	**26**	**38**	**64**	**67**	....	....	....	....	....
1989-90	**Quebec**	**NHL**	**57**	**16**	**29**	**45**	**42**	....	....	....	....	....
	Chicago	**NHL**	**8**	**4**	**1**	**5**	**9**	**14**	**2**	**4**	**6**	**6**
1990-91	**Chicago**	**NHL**	**74**	**27**	**38**	**65**	**65**	....	....	....	....	....
	NHL Totals		**895**	**487**	**528**	**1015**	**687**	**80**	**36**	**34**	**70**	**104**

a NHL Second All-Star Team (1983, 1988)
b NHL First All-Star Team (1984, 1986, 1987)

Played in NHL All-Star Game (1983-86, 1988)

Traded to **Chicago** by **Quebec** with Greg Millen and Quebec's sixth round choice (Kevin St. Jacques) in 1991 Entry Draft for Mario Doyon, Everett Sanipass and Dan Vincelette, March 5, 1990.

GOVEDARIS, CHRIS (goh-va-DARE-us)

Left wing. Shoots left. 6', 200 lbs. Born, Toronto, Ont., February 2, 1970.
(Hartford's 1st choice, 11th overall, in 1988 Entry Draft).

			Regular Season					Playoffs				
Season	Club	Lea	GP	G	A	TP	PIM	GP	G	A	TP	PIM
1986-87	Toronto	OHL	64	36	28	64	148	....	....	....	....	....
1987-88	Toronto	OHL	62	42	38	80	118	4	2	1	3	10
1988-89	Toronto	OHL	49	41	38	79	117	6	2	3	5	0
1989-90	**Hartford**	**NHL**	**12**	**0**	**1**	**1**	**6**	**2**	**0**	**0**	**0**	**2**
	Binghamton	AHL	14	3	3	6	4	....	....	....	....	....
	Hamilton	OHL	23	11	21	32	53	....	....	....	....	....
1990-91	**Hartford**	**NHL**	**14**	**1**	**3**	**4**	**4**	....	....	....	....	....
	Springfield	AHL	56	26	36	62	133	9	2	5	7	36
	NHL Totals		**26**	**1**	**4**	**5**	**10**	**2**	**0**	**0**	**0**	**2**

GRAHAM, DIRK MILTON

Left/Right wing. Shoots right. 5'11", 198 lbs. Born, Regina, Sask., July 29, 1959.
(Vancouver's 5th choice, 89th overall, in 1979 Entry Draft).

			Regular Season					Playoffs				
Season	Club	Lea	GP	G	A	TP	PIM	GP	G	A	TP	PIM
1975-76	Regina	WCHL	2	0	0	0	0	6	1	1	2	5
1976-77	Regina	WCHL	65	37	28	65	66	....	....	....	....	....
1977-78	Regina	WCHL	72	49	61	110	87	13	15	19	34	37
1978-79	Regina	WHL	71	48	60	108	252	....	....	....	....	....
1979-80	Dallas	CHL	62	17	15	32	96	....	....	....	....	....
1980-81	Fort Wayne	IHL	6	1	2	3	12	....	....	....	....	....
a	Toledo	IHL	61	40	45	85	88	....	....	....	....	....
1981-82	Toledo	IHL	72	49	56	105	68	13	10	11	*21	8
1982-83b	Toledo	IHL	78	70	55	125	88	11	13	7	*20	30
1983-84	**Minnesota**	**NHL**	**6**	**1**	**1**	**2**	**0**	**1**	**0**	**0**	**0**	**2**
c	Salt Lake	CHL	57	37	57	94	72	5	3	8	11	2
1984-85	**Minnesota**	**NHL**	**36**	**12**	**11**	**23**	**23**	**9**	**0**	**4**	**4**	**7**
	Springfield	AHL	37	20	28	48	41	....	....	....	....	....
1985-86	**Minnesota**	**NHL**	**80**	**22**	**33**	**55**	**87**	**5**	**3**	**1**	**4**	**2**
1986-87	**Minnesota**	**NHL**	**76**	**25**	**29**	**54**	**142**	....	....	....	....	....
1987-88	**Minnesota**	**NHL**	**28**	**7**	**5**	**12**	**39**	....	....	....	....	....
	Chicago	**NHL**	**42**	**17**	**19**	**36**	**32**	**4**	**1**	**2**	**3**	**4**
1988-89	**Chicago**	**NHL**	**80**	**33**	**45**	**78**	**89**	**16**	**2**	**4**	**6**	**38**
1989-90	**Chicago**	**NHL**	**73**	**22**	**32**	**54**	**102**	**5**	**1**	**5**	**6**	**2**
1990-91d	**Chicago**	**NHL**	**80**	**24**	**21**	**45**	**88**	**6**	**1**	**2**	**3**	**17**
	NHL Totals		**501**	**163**	**196**	**359**	**602**	**46**	**8**	**18**	**26**	**72**

a IHL Second All-Star Team (1981)
b IHL First All-Star Team (1983)
c CHL First All-Star Team (1984)
d Won Frank J. Selke Trophy (1991)

Signed as free agent by **Minnesota**, August 17, 1983. Traded to **Chicago** by **Minnesota** for Curt Fraser, January 4, 1988.

GRANATO, TONY

Left wing. Shoots right. 5'10", 185 lbs. Born, Downers Grove, IL, July 25, 1964.
(NY Rangers' 5th choice, 120th overall, in 1982 Entry Draft).

			Regular Season					Playoffs				
Season	Club	Lea	GP	G	A	TP	PIM	GP	G	A	TP	PIM
1983-84	U. Wisconsin	WCHA	35	14	17	31	48	....	....	....	....	....
1984-85	U. Wisconsin	WCHA	42	33	34	67	94	....	....	....	....	....
1985-86	U. Wisconsin	WCHA	33	25	24	49	36	....	....	....	....	....
1986-87ab	U. Wisconsin	WCHA	42	28	45	73	64	....	....	....	....	....
1987-88	U.S. National	...	49	40	31	71	55	....	....	....	....	....
	U.S. Olympic	...	6	1	7	8	4	....	....	....	....	....
	Colorado	IHL	22	13	14	27	36	8	9	4	13	16
1988-89c	**NY Rangers**	**NHL**	**78**	**36**	**27**	**63**	**140**	**4**	**1**	**1**	**2**	**21**
1989-90	**NY Rangers**	**NHL**	**37**	**7**	**18**	**25**	**77**	....	....	....	....	....
	Los Angeles	**NHL**	**19**	**5**	**6**	**11**	**45**	**10**	**5**	**4**	**9**	**12**
1990-91	**Los Angeles**	**NHL**	**68**	**30**	**34**	**64**	**154**	**12**	**1**	**4**	**5**	**28**
	NHL Totals		**202**	**78**	**85**	**163**	**416**	**26**	**7**	**9**	**16**	**61**

a WCHA Second All-Star Team (1987)
b NCAA West Second All-American Team (1987)
c NHL All-Rookie Team (1989)

Traded to **Los Angeles** by **NY Rangers** with Tomas Sandstrom for Bernie Nicholls, January 20, 1990.

GRANT, KEVIN

Defense. Shoots right. 6'3", 210 lbs. Born, Toronto, Ont., January 9, 1969.
(Calgary's 3rd choice, 40th overall, in 1987 Entry Draft).

			Regular Season					Playoffs				
Season	Club	Lea	GP	G	A	TP	PIM	GP	G	A	TP	PIM
1985-86	Kitchener	OHL	63	2	15	17	204	5	0	1	1	11
1986-87	Kitchener	OHL	52	5	18	23	125	4	0	1	1	16
1987-88	Kitchener	OHL	48	3	20	23	138	4	0	1	1	4
1988-89	Salt Lake	IHL	3	0	1	1	5	3	0	0	0	12
	Sudbury	OHL	60	9	41	50	186	....	....	....	....	....
1989-90	Salt Lake	IHL	78	7	17	24	117	11	0	2	2	22
1990-91	Salt Lake	IHL	63	6	19	25	200	3	0	0	0	8

GRATTON, DAN

Center. Shoots left. 6', 185 lbs. Born, Brantford, Ont., December 7, 1966.
(Los Angeles' 2nd choice, 10th overall, in 1985 Entry Draft)

			Regular Season					Playoffs				
Season	Club	Lea	GP	G	A	TP	PIM	GP	G	A	TP	PIM
1983-84	Oshawa	OHL	65	40	34	74	55	7	2	5	7	15
1984-85	Oshawa	OHL	56	24	48	72	67	5	3	3	6	0
1985-86	Oshawa	OHL	10	3	5	8	15	....	....	....	....	....
	Ottawa	OHL	25	18	18	36	19	....	....	....	....	....
	Belleville	OHL	20	12	14	26	11	24	*20	9	29	16
1986-87	New Haven	AHL	49	6	10	16	45	2	0	0	0	0
1987-88	**Los Angeles**	**NHL**	**7**	**1**	**0**	**1**	**5**	....	....	....	....	....
	New Haven	AHL	57	18	28	46	77	....	....	....	....	....
1988-89	New Haven	AHL	29	5	13	18	41	....	....	....	....	....
	Flint	IHL	20	5	9	14	8	....	....	....	....	....
1989-90	Cdn. National	...	68	29	37	66	40	....	....	....	....	....
1990-91	Kalamazoo	IHL	44	9	11	20	32	6	0	1	1	14
	NHL Totals		**7**	**1**	**0**	**1**	**5**	....	....	....	....	....

GRAVELLE, DAN

Center. Shoots left. 5'11", 190 lbs. Born, Montreal, Que., March 10, 1970.
(Chicago's 1st choice, 28th overall, in 1991 Supplemental Draft).

			Regular Season					Playoffs				
Season	Club	Lea	GP	G	A	TP	PIM	GP	G	A	TP	PIM
1989-90	Merrimack	H.E.	10	2	1	3	13	....	....	....	....	....
1990-91	Merrimack	H.E.	32	18	21	39	22	....	....	....	....	....

GRAVES, ADAM

Center. Shoots left. 5'11", 185 lbs. Born, Toronto, Ont., April 12, 1968.
(Detroit's 2nd choice, 22nd overall, in 1986 Entry Draft).

			Regular Season					Playoffs				
Season	Club	Lea	GP	G	A	TP	PIM	GP	G	A	TP	PIM
1985-86	Windsor	OHL	62	27	37	64	35	16	5	11	16	10
1986-87	Windsor	OHL	66	45	55	100	70	14	9	8	17	32
	Adirondack	AHL	....	....	....	....	....	5	0	1	1	0
1987-88	**Detroit**	**NHL**	**9**	**0**	**1**	**1**	**8**	....	....	....	....	....
	Windsor	OHL	37	28	32	60	107	12	14	18	*32	16
1988-89	**Detroit**	**NHL**	**56**	**7**	**5**	**12**	**60**	**5**	**0**	**0**	**0**	**4**
	Adirondack	AHL	14	10	11	21	28	14	11	7	18	17
1989-90	**Detroit**	**NHL**	**13**	**0**	**1**	**1**	**13**	....	....	....	....	....
	Edmonton	**NHL**	**63**	**9**	**12**	**21**	**123**	**22**	**5**	**6**	**11**	**17**
1990-91	**Edmonton**	**NHL**	**76**	**7**	**18**	**25**	**127**	**18**	**2**	**4**	**6**	**22**
	NHL Totals		**217**	**23**	**37**	**60**	**331**	**45**	**7**	**10**	**17**	**43**

Traded to **Edmonton** by **Detroit** with Petr Klima, Joe Murphy and Jeff Sharples for Jimmy Carson, Kevin McClelland and Edmonton's fifth round choice (later traded to Montreal for Rick Green. Montreal selected Brad Layzell) in 1991 Entry Draft, November 2, 1989.

GRAVES, STEVE

Left wing. Shoots left. 5'10", 175 lbs. Born, Trenton, Ont., April 7, 1964.
(Edmonton's 2nd choice, 41st overall, in 1982 Entry Draft).

			Regular Season					Playoffs				
Season	Club	Lea	GP	G	A	TP	PIM	GP	G	A	TP	PIM
1981-82	S. S. Marie	OHL	66	12	15	27	49	13	8	5	13	14
1982-83	S. S. Marie	OHL	60	21	20	41	48	5	0	0	0	4
1983-84	**Edmonton**	**NHL**	**2**	**0**	**0**	**0**	**0**	....	....	....	....	....
a	S. S. Marie	OHL	67	41	48	89	47	16	6	8	14	8
1984-85	Nova Scotia	AHL	80	17	15	32	20	6	0	1	1	4
1985-86	Nova Scotia	AHL	78	19	18	37	22	....	....	....	....	....
1986-87	**Edmonton**	**NHL**	**12**	**2**	**0**	**2**	**0**	....	....	....	....	....
	Nova Scotia	AHL	59	18	10	28	22	5	1	1	2	2
1987-88	**Edmonton**	**NHL**	**21**	**3**	**4**	**7**	**10**	....	....	....	....	....
	Nova Scotia	AHL	11	6	2	8	4	....	....	....	....	....
1988-89	Cdn. National	...	3	5	1	6	2	....	....	....	....	....
	TPS	Fin.	43	16	12	28	48	10	2	8	10	12
1989-90	Cdn. National	...	53	24	19	43	50	....	....	....	....	....
1990-91	New Haven	AHL	3	0	1	1	2	....	....	....	....	....
	Phoenix	IHL	56	11	20	31	64	5	1	3	4	2
	NHL Totals		**35**	**5**	**4**	**9**	**10**	....	....	....	....	....

a OHL Third All-Star Team (1984)

Signed as a free agent by **Los Angeles**, July 16, 1990.

GREEN, MARK

Center. Shoots right. 6'4", 200 lbs. Born, Watertown, NY, December 26, 1967.
(Winnipeg's 8th choice, 176th overall, in 1986 Entry Draft).

			Regular Season					Playoffs				
Season	Club	Lea	GP	G	A	TP	PIM	GP	G	A	TP	PIM
1987-88	Clarkson	ECAC	18	3	6	9	18	....	....	....	....	....
1988-89	Clarkson	ECAC	30	16	11	27	42	....	....	....	....	....
1989-90	Clarkson	ECAC	32	18	17	35	42	....	....	....	....	....
1990-91	Clarkson	ECAC	38	21	24	45	32	....	....	....	....	....

GREEN, RICHARD DOUGLAS (RICK)

Defense. Shoots left. 6'3", 220 lbs. Born, Belleville, Ont., February 20, 1956.
(Washington's 1st choice and 1st overall in 1976 Amateur Draft).

			Regular Season					Playoffs				
Season	Club	Lea	GP	G	A	TP	PIM	GP	G	A	TP	PIM
1974-75	London	OHA	65	8	45	53	68	....	....	....	....	....
1975-76ab	London	OHA	61	13	47	60	69	5	1	0	1	4
1976-77	Washington	NHL	45	3	12	15	16	....	....	....	....	....
1977-78	Washington	NHL	60	5	14	19	67	....	....	....	....	....
1978-79	Washington	NHL	71	8	33	41	62	....	....	....	....	....
1979-80	Washington	NHL	71	4	20	24	52	....	....	....	....	....
1980-81	Washington	NHL	65	8	23	31	91	....	....	....	....	....
1981-82	Washington	NHL	65	3	25	28	93	....	....	....	....	....
1982-83	Montreal	NHL	66	2	24	26	58	3	0	0	0	2
1983-84	Montreal	NHL	7	0	1	1	7	15	1	2	3	33
1984-85	Montreal	NHL	77	1	18	19	30	12	0	3	3	14
1985-86	Montreal	NHL	46	3	2	5	20	18	1	4	5	8
1986-87	Montreal	NHL	72	1	9	10	10	17	0	4	4	8
1987-88	Montreal	NHL	59	2	11	13	33	11	0	2	2	2
1988-89	Montreal	NHL	72	1	14	15	25	21	1	1	2	6
1989-90	Meran	Italy	9	2	6	8	2	10	3	6	9	4
1990-91	Detroit	NHL	65	2	14	16	24	3	0	0	0	0
	NHL Totals		841	43	220	263	588	100	3	16	19	73

a OHA First All-Star Team (1976)
b OHA Outstanding Defenseman (1976)

Traded to **Montreal** by **Washington** with Ryan Walter for Brian Engblom, Rod Langway, Doug Jarvis and Craig Laughlin, September 9, 1982. Traded to **Detroit** by **Montreal** for Edmonton's fifth round choice (Brad Layzell – previously acquired by Detroit) in 1991 Entry Draft, June 15, 1990. Traded to **NY Islanders** by **Detroit** for Alan Kerr and future considerations, May 26, 1991.

GREEN, TRAVIS

Center. Shoots right. 6', 195 lbs. Born, Creston, B.C., December 20, 1970.
(NY Islanders' 2nd choice, 23rd overall, in 1989 Entry Draft).

			Regular Season					Playoffs				
Season	Club	Lea	GP	G	A	TP	PIM	GP	G	A	TP	PIM
1986-87	Spokane	WHL	64	8	17	25	27	3	0	0	0	0
1987-88	Spokane	WHL	72	33	54	87	42	15	10	10	20	13
1988-89	Spokane	WHL	75	51	51	102	79	....	....	....	....	....
1989-90	Spokane	WHL	50	45	44	89	80	....	....	....	....	....
	Medicine Hat	WHL	25	15	24	39	19	3	0	0	0	2
1990-91	Capital Dist.	AHL	73	21	34	55	26	....	....	....	....	....

GREENLAW, JEFF

Left wing. Shoots left. 6'1", 230 lbs. Born, Toronto, Ont., February 28, 1968.
(Washington's 1st choice, 19th overall, in 1986 Entry Draft).

			Regular Season					Playoffs				
Season	Club	Lea	GP	G	A	TP	PIM	GP	G	A	TP	PIM
1985-86	Cdn. Olympic	...	57	3	16	19	81	....	....	....	....	....
1986-87	Washington	NHL	22	0	3	3	44	....	....	....	....	....
	Binghamton	AHL	4	0	2	2	0	....	....	....	....	....
1987-88	Binghamton	AHL	56	8	7	15	142	1	0	0	0	2
	Washington	NHL	...	...	....	....	....	1	0	0	0	19
1988-89	Baltimore	AHL	55	12	15	27	115	....	....	....	....	....
1989-90	Baltimore	AHL	10	3	2	5	26	7	1	0	1	13
1990-91	Washington	NHL	10	2	0	2	10	1	0	0	0	2
	Baltimore	AHL	50	17	17	34	93	3	1	1	2	2
	NHL Totals		32	2	3	5	54	2	0	0	0	21

GREGG, RANDALL JOHN (RANDY)

Defense. Shoots left. 6'4", 215 lbs. Born, Edmonton, Alta., February 19, 1956.

			Regular Season					Playoffs				
Season	Club	Lea	GP	G	A	TP	PIM	GP	G	A	TP	PIM
1977-78	U. of Alberta	CWUAA	24	7	23	30	37	....	....	....	....	....
1978-79a	U. of Alberta	CWUAA	24	5	16	21	47	....	....	....	....	....
1979-80	Cdn. National	...	56	7	17	24	36	....	....	....	....	....
	Cdn. Olympic	...	6	1	1	2	2	....	....	....	....	....
1980-81	Kokuda	Japan	35	12	18	30	30	....	....	....	....	....
1981-82	Kokuda	Japan	36	12	20	32	25	....	....	....	....	....
	Edmonton	NHL	....	....	....	....	....	4	0	0	0	0
1982-83	Edmonton	NHL	80	6	22	28	54	16	2	4	6	13
1983-84	Edmonton	NHL	80	13	27	40	56	19	3	7	10	21
1984-85	Edmonton	NHL	57	3	20	23	32	17	0	6	6	12
1985-86	Edmonton	NHL	64	2	26	28	47	10	1	0	1	12
1986-87	Edmonton	NHL	52	8	16	24	42	18	3	6	9	17
1987-88	Cdn. National	...	37	2	6	8	37	....	....	....	....	....
	Cdn. Olympic	...	8	1	2	3	8	....	....	....	....	....
	Edmonton	NHL	15	1	2	3	8	19	1	8	9	24
1988-89	Edmonton	NHL	57	3	15	18	28	7	1	0	1	4
1989-90	Edmonton	NHL	48	4	20	24	42	20	2	6	8	16
1990-91			DID NOT PLAY									
	NHL Totals		453	40	148	188	309	130	13	37	50	119

a CIAU Player of the Year (1979)

Signed as a free agent by **Edmonton**, October 18, 1982. Claimed by **Vancouver** in NHL Waiver Draft, October 1, 1990.

GREIG, MARK (GREG)

Right wing. Shoots right. 5'11", 190 lbs. Born, High River, Alta., January 25, 1970.
(Hartford's 1st choice, 15th overall, in 1990 Entry Draft).

			Regular Season					Playoffs				
Season	Club	Lea	GP	G	A	TP	PIM	GP	G	A	TP	PIM
1987-88	Lethbridge	WHL	65	9	18	27	38	....	....	....	....	....
1988-89	Lethbridge	WHL	71	36	72	108	113	8	5	5	10	16
1989-90a	Lethbridge	WHL	65	55	80	135	149	18	11	21	32	35
1990-91	Hartford	NHL	4	0	0	0	0	....	....	....	....	....
	Springfield	AHL	73	32	55	87	73	17	2	6	8	22
	NHL Totals		4	0	0	0	0	....	....	....	....	....

a WHL East First All-Star Team (1990)

GRETZKY, WAYNE (GRETZ-kee)

Center. Shoots left. 6', 170 lbs. Born, Brantford, Ont., January 26, 1961.

			Regular Season					Playoffs				
Season	Club	Lea	GP	G	A	TP	PIM	GP	G	A	TP	PIM
1976-77	Peterborough	OHA	3	0	3	3	0	....	....	....	....	....
1977-78ab	S. S. Marie	OHA	64	70	112	182	14	13	6	20	26	0
1978-79	Indianapolis	WHA	8	3	3	6	0	....	....	....	....	....
cd	Edmonton	WHA	72	43	61	104	19	13	*10	10	*20	2
1979-80efg	Edmonton	NHL	79	51	*86	*137	21	3	2	1	3	0
1980-81ehijk	Edmonton	NHL	80	55	*109	*164	28	9	7	14	21	4
1981-82 ehijklmq	Edmonton	NHL	80	*92	*120	*212	26	5	5	7	12	8
1982-83 ehijmnoq	Edmonton	NHL	80	*71	*125	*196	59	16	12	*26	*38	4
1983-84 ehimq	Edmonton	NHL	74	*87	*118	*205	39	19	13	*22	*35	12
1984-85 ehijmnopqr	Edmonton	NHL	80	*73	*135	*208	52	18	17	*30	*47	4
1985-86 ehijkr	Edmonton	NHL	80	52	*163	*215	46	10	8	11	19	2
1986-87 ehimqr	Edmonton	NHL	79	*62	*121	*183	28	21	5	*29	*34	6
1987-88gnp	Edmonton	NHL	64	40	*109	149	24	19	12	*31	*43	16
1988-89egs	Los Angeles	NHL	78	54	*114	168	26	11	5	17	22	0
1989-90gi	Los Angeles	NHL	73	40	*102	*142	42	7	3	7	10	0
1990-91fhi	Los Angeles	NHL	78	41	*122	*163	16	12	4	11	15	2
	NHL Totals		925	718	*1424	*2142	407	150	*93	*206	*299	58

a OHA Second All-Star Team (1978)
b Named OHA's Rookie of the Year (1978)
c WHA Second All-Star Team (1979)
d Named WHA's Rookie of the Year (1979)
e Won Hart Trophy (1980, 1981, 1982, 1983, 1984, 1985, 1986, 1987, 1989)
f Won Lady Byng Trophy (1980, 1991)
g NHL Second All-Star Team (1980, 1988, 1989, 1990)
h NHL First All-Star Team (1981, 1982, 1983, 1984, 1985, 1986, 1987, 1991)
i Won Art Ross Trophy (1981, 1982, 1983, 1984, 1985, 1986, 1987, 1990, 1991)
j NHL record for assists in regular season (1981, 1982, 1983, 1985, 1986)
k NHL record for points in regular season (1981, 1982, 1986)
l NHL record for goals in regular season (1982)
m Won Lester B. Pearson Award (1982, 1983, 1984, 1985, 1987)
n NHL record for assists in one playoff year (1983, 1985, 1988)
o NHL record for points in one playoff year (1983, 1985)
p Won Conn Smythe Trophy (1985, 1988)
q NHL Plus/Minus Leader (1982, 1983, 1984, 1985, 1987)
r Selected Chrysler-Dodge/NHL Performer of the Year (1985, 1986, 1987)
s Won Dodge Performance of the Year Award (1989)

Played in NHL All-Star Game (1980-1986, 1988-91)

Reclaimed by **Edmonton** as an under-age junior prior to Expansion Draft, June 9, 1979. Claimed as priority selection by **Edmonton**, June 9, 1979. Traded to **Los Angeles** by **Edmonton** with Mike Krushelnyski and Marty McSorley for Jimmy Carson, Martin Gelinas, Los Angeles' first round choices in 1989 (acquired by New Jersey, June 17, 1989. New Jersey selected Jason Miller), 1991 (Martin Rucinsky) and 1993 Entry Drafts and cash, August 9, 1988.

GREYERBIEHL, JASON

Left wing. Shoots left. 6', 175 lbs. Born, Bramalea, Ont., March 24, 1970.
(Chicago's 7th choice, 174th overall, in 1989 Entry Draft).

			Regular Season					Playoffs				
Season	Club	Lea	GP	G	A	TP	PIM	GP	G	A	TP	PIM
1988-89	Colgate	ECAC	31	6	9	15	15	....	....	....	....	....
1989-90	Colgate	ECAC	38	12	20	32	20	....	....	....	....	....
1990-91	Colgate	ECAC	30	7	14	21	12	....	....	....	....	....

GRIEVE, BRENT

Left wing. Shoots left. 6'1", 202 lbs. Born, Oshawa, Ont., May 9, 1969.
(NY Islanders' 4th choice, 65th overall, in 1989 Entry Draft).

			Regular Season					Playoffs				
Season	Club	Lea	GP	G	A	TP	PIM	GP	G	A	TP	PIM
1986-87	Oshawa	OHL	60	9	19	28	102	24	3	8	11	22
1987-88	Oshawa	OHL	55	19	20	39	122	7	0	1	1	8
1988-89	Oshawa	OHL	49	34	33	67	105	6	4	3	7	4
1989-90	Oshawa	OHL	62	46	47	93	125	17	10	10	20	26
1990-91	Capital Dist.	AHL	61	14	13	27	80	....	....	....	....	....
	Kansas City	IHL	5	2	2	4	2	....	....	....	....	....

GRILLO, DEAN

Right wing. Shoots right. 6'2", 210 lbs. Born, Bemidji, MN, December 8, 1972.
(San Jose's 9th choice, 155th overall, in 1991 Entry Draft).

			Regular Season					Playoffs				
Season	Club	Lea	GP	G	A	TP	PIM	GP	G	A	TP	PIM
1990-91	Warroad	HS	24	20	15	35	0	....	....	....	....	....

GRIMSON, STU

Left wing. Shoots left. 6'5", 220 lbs. Born, Kamloops, B.C., May 20, 1965.
(Calgary's 8th choice, 143rd overall, in 1985 Entry Draft).

			Regular Season					Playoffs				
Season	Club	Lea	GP	G	A	TP	PIM	GP	G	A	TP	PIM
1982-83	Regina	WHL	48	0	1	1	105	5	0	0	0	14
1983-84	Regina	WHL	63	8	8	16	131	21	0	1	1	29
1984-85	Regina	WHL	71	24	32	56	248	8	1	2	3	14
1985-86	U. Manitoba	CWUAA	12	7	4	11	113	3	1	1	2	20
1986-87	U. Manitoba	CWUAA	29	8	8	16	67	14	4	2	6	28
1987-88	Salt Lake	IHL	38	9	5	14	268	....	....	....	....	....
1988-89	Calgary	NHL	1	0	0	0	5	....	....	....	....	....
	Salt Lake	IHL	72	9	18	27	397	14	2	3	5	86
1989-90	Calgary	NHL	3	0	0	0	17	....	....	....	....	....
	Salt Lake	IHL	62	8	8	16	319	4	0	0	0	8
1990-91	Chicago	NHL	35	0	1	1	183	5	0	0	0	46
	NHL Totals		39	0	1	1	205	5	0	0	0	46

Claimed by **Chicago** on conditional waivers, October 1, 1990.

GROLEAU, FRANCOIS

Defense. Shoots left. 6', 193 lbs. Born, Longueuil, Que., January 23, 1973.
(Calgary's 2nd choice, 41st overall, in 1991 Entry Draft).

			Regular Season					Playoffs				
Season	Club	Lea	GP	G	A	TP	PIM	GP	G	A	TP	PIM
1989-90ab	Shawinigan	QMJHL	65	11	54	65	80	6	0	1	1	12
1990-91	Shawinigan	QMJHL	70	9	60	69	70	6	0	3	3	2

a QMJHL Defensive Rookie of the Year (1990)
b QMJHL Second All-Star Team (1990)

GRONSTRAND, JARI (GRUHN-strahnd)

Defense. Shoots left. 6'3", 195 lbs. Born, Tampere, Finland, November 14, 1962.
(Minnesota's 8th choice, 96th overall, in 1986 Entry Draft).

			Regular Season					Playoffs				
Season	Club	Lea	GP	G	A	TP	PIM	GP	G	A	TP	PIM
1982-83	Tappara	Fin.	35	2	2	4	18	8	0	0	0	4
1983-84	Tappara	Fin.	32	2	4	6	14	9	0	2	2	4
1984-85	Tappara	Fin.	36	1	9	10	27	....	....	....	....	....
1985-86	Tappara	Fin.	36	9	5	14	26	8	1	2	3	4
1986-87	**Minnesota**	**NHL**	**47**	**1**	**6**	**7**	**27**	....	....	....	....	....
1987-88	**NY Rangers**	**NHL**	**62**	**3**	**11**	**14**	**63**	....	....	....	....	....
	Colorado	IHL	3	1	3	4	0	....	....	....	....	....
1988-89	**Quebec**	**NHL**	**25**	**1**	**3**	**4**	**14**	....	....	....	....	....
	Halifax	AHL	8	0	1	1	5	....	....	....	....	....
1989-90	**Quebec**	**NHL**	**7**	**0**	**1**	**1**	**2**	....	....	....	....	....
	Halifax	AHL	2	0	0	0	0	....	....	....	....	....
	NY Islanders	**NHL**	**41**	**3**	**4**	**7**	**27**	**3**	**0**	**0**	**0**	**4**
	Springfield	AHL	1	0	1	1	0	....	....	....	....	....
1990-91	**NY Islanders**	**NHL**	**3**	**0**	**1**	**1**	**2**	....	....	....	....	....
	Capital Dist.	AHL	63	13	22	35	40	....	....	....	....	....
	NHL Totals		**185**	**8**	**26**	**34**	**135**	**3**	**0**	**0**	**0**	**4**

Traded to **NY Rangers** by **Minnesota** with Paul Boutilier for Jay Caufield and Dave Gagne, October 8, 1987. Traded to **Quebec** by **NY Rangers** with Bruce Bell, Walt Poddubny and NY Rangers' fourth round choice (Eric Dubois) in 1989 Entry Draft for Jason Lafreniere and Normand Rochefort, August 1, 1988. Claimed on waivers by **NY Islanders**, November 21, 1989.

GROSS, PAVEL (GROHSS)

Right wing. Shoots right. 6'3", 195 lbs. Born, Ustin Ogroh, Czechoslovakia, May 11, 1968.
(NY Islanders' 7th choice, 111th overall, in 1988 Entry Draft).

			Regular Season					Playoffs				
Season	Club	Lea	GP	G	A	TP	PIM	GP	G	A	TP	PIM
1987-88	Sparta Praha	Czech.	24	3	4	7	0	....	....	....	....	....
1988-89	Sparta Praha	Czech.	27	12	13	25	....					
1989-90	Sparta Praha	Czech.	36	10	9	19		....	....	....	....	....
1990-91	Freiburg	Ger.	32	11	24	35	66	....	....	....	....	....

GROSSI, DINO

Right wing. Shoots right. 6', 190 lbs. Born, Toronto, Ont., June 25, 1970.
(Chicago's 10th choice, 247th overall, in 1990 Entry Draft).

			Regular Season					Playoffs				
Season	Club	Lea	GP	G	A	TP	PIM	GP	G	A	TP	PIM
1989-90	Northeastern	H.E.	31	6	9	15	43	....	....	....	....	....
1990-91	Northeastern	H.E.	34	11	11	22	70	....	....	....	....	....

GRUBA, ANTHONY

Right wing. Shoots right. 6', 205 lbs. Born, St. Paul, MN, August 23, 1972.
(Detroit's 8th choice, 171st overall, in 1990 Entry Draft).

			Regular Season					Playoffs				
Season	Club	Lea	GP	G	A	TP	PIM	GP	G	A	TP	PIM
1989-90	Hill-Murray	HS	24	24	21	45	....	....	....	....	....	....
1990-91	St. Cloud	WCHA	29	1	5	6	34	....	....	....	....	....

GRUDEN, JOHN

Defense. Shoots left. 6', 180 lbs. Born, Hastings, MN, April 6, 1970.
(Boston's 7th choice, 168th overall, in 1990 Entry Draft).

			Regular Season					Playoffs				
Season	Club	Lea	GP	G	A	TP	PIM	GP	G	A	TP	PIM
1989-90	Waterloo	USHL	47	7	39	46	35	....	....	....	....	....
1990-91	Ferris State	CCHA	37	4	11	15	27	....	....	....	....	....

GRUHL, SCOTT KENNETH (GROOL)

Left wing. Shoots left. 5'11", 185 lbs. Born, Port Colborne, Ont., September 13, 1959.

			Regular Season					Playoffs				
Season	Club	Lea	GP	G	A	TP	PIM	GP	G	A	TP	PIM
1978-79	Sudbury	OHA	68	35	49	94	78	10	5	7	12	15
1979-80	Binghamton	AHL	4	1	0	1	0	....	....	....	....	....
a	Saginaw	IHL	75	53	40	93	100	7	2	6	8	16
1980-81	Houston	CHL	4	0	0	0	0	....	....	....	....	....
	Saginaw	IHL	77	56	34	90	87	13	*11	8	*19	12
1981-82	**Los Angeles**	**NHL**	**7**	**2**	**1**	**3**	**2**	....	....	....	....	....
	New Haven	AHL	73	28	41	69	107	4	0	4	4	2
1982-83	**Los Angeles**	**NHL**	**7**	**0**	**2**	**2**	**4**	....	....	....	....	....
	New Haven	AHL	68	25	38	63	114	12	3	3	6	22
1983-84b	Muskegon	IHL	56	40	56	96	46	....	....	....	....	....
1984-85bc	Muskegon	IHL	82	62	64	126	102	17	7	16	23	25
1985-86a	Muskegon	IHL	82	*59	50	109	178	14	7	*13	20	22
1986-87	Muskegon	IHL	67	34	39	73	157	15	5	7	12	54
1987-88	**Pittsburgh**	**NHL**	**6**	**1**	**0**	**1**	**0**	....	....	....	....	....
	Muskegon	IHL	55	28	47	75	115	6	5	1	6	12
1988-89	Muskegon	IHL	79	37	55	92	163	14	8	11	19	37
1989-90	Muskegon	IHL	80	41	51	92	206	15	8	6	14	26
1990-91	Fort Wayne	IHL	59	23	47	70	109	19	4	6	10	39
	NHL Totals		**20**	**3**	**3**	**6**	**6**	....	....	....	....	....

a IHL Second All-Star Team (1980, 1986)
b IHL First All-Star Team (1984, 1985)
c Won James Gatschene Memorial Trophy (MVP-IHL) (1985)

Signed as a free agent by **Los Angeles**, October 11, 1979. Signed as a free agent by **Pittsburgh**, December 14, 1987.

GUAY, FRANCOIS (GAY)

Center. Shoots left. 6', 190 lbs. Born, Gatineau, Que., June 8, 1968.
(Buffalo's 9th choice, 152nd overall, in 1986 Entry Draft).

			Regular Season					Playoffs				
Season	Club	Lea	GP	G	A	TP	PIM	GP	G	A	TP	PIM
1985-86	Laval	QMJHL	71	19	55	74	46	14	5	6	11	15
1986-87	Laval	QMJHL	63	52	77	129	67	14	5	13	18	18
1987-88	Laval	QMJHL	66	60	84	144	142	14	10	15	25	10
1988-89	Rochester	AHL	45	6	20	26	34	....	....	....	....	....
1989-90	**Buffalo**	**NHL**	**1**	**0**	**0**	**0**	**0**	....	....	....	....	....
	Rochester	AHL	69	28	35	63	39	16	4	8	12	12
1990-91	Rochester	AHL	61	24	39	63	38	15	5	5	10	8
	NHL Totals		**1**	**0**	**0**	**0**	**0**	....	....	....	....	....

GUAY, PAUL (GAY)

Right wing. Shoots right. 5'11", 185 lbs. Born, Providence, RI, September 2, 1963.
(Minnesota's 10th choice, 118th overall, in 1981 Entry Draft).

			Regular Season					Playoffs				
Season	Club	Lea	GP	G	A	TP	PIM	GP	G	A	TP	PIM
1981-82	Providence	ECAC	33	23	17	40	38	....	....	....	....	....
1982-83a	Providence	ECAC	42	34	31	65	83	....	....	....	....	....
1983-84	U.S. National	...	62	20	18	38	44	....	....	....	....	....
	U.S. Olympic	...	6	1	0	1	8	....	....	....	....	....
	Philadelphia	**NHL**	**14**	**2**	**6**	**8**	**14**	**3**	**0**	**0**	**0**	**4**
1984-85	**Philadelphia**	**NHL**	**2**	**0**	**1**	**1**	**0**	....	....	....	....	....
	Hershey	AHL	74	23	30	53	123	....	....	....	....	....
1985-86	**Los Angeles**	**NHL**	**23**	**3**	**3**	**6**	**18**	....	....	....	....	....
	New Haven	AHL	57	15	36	51	101	5	3	0	3	11
1986-87	**Los Angeles**	**NHL**	**35**	**2**	**5**	**7**	**16**	**2**	**0**	**0**	**0**	**0**
	New Haven	AHL	6	1	3	4	11	....	....	....	....	....
1987-88	**Los Angeles**	**NHL**	**33**	**4**	**4**	**8**	**40**	**4**	**0**	**1**	**1**	**8**
	New Haven	AHL	42	21	26	47	53	....	....	....	....	....
1988-89	**Los Angeles**	**NHL**	**2**	**0**	**0**	**0**	**2**	....	....	....	....	....
	New Haven	AHL	4	4	6	10	20	....	....	....	....	....
	Boston	**NHL**	**5**	**0**	**2**	**2**	**0**	....	....	....	....	....
	Maine	AHL	61	15	29	44	77	....	....	....	....	....
1989-90	Utica	AHL	75	25	30	55	103	5	2	2	4	13
1990-91	**NY Islanders**	**NHL**	**3**	**0**	**2**	**2**	**2**	....	....	....	....	....
	Capital Dist.	AHL	74	26	35	61	81	....	....	....	....	....
	NHL Totals		**117**	**11**	**23**	**34**	**92**	**9**	**0**	**1**	**1**	**12**

a ECAC Second All-Star Team (1983)

Rights traded to **Philadelphia** by **Minnesota** with Minnesota's third round choice in 1985 Entry Draft for Paul Holmgren, February 23, 1984. Traded to **Los Angeles** by **Philadelphia** with Philadelphia's fourth-round choice (Sylvain Couturier) in 1986 Entry Draft for Steve Seguin and Los Angeles' second-round choice (Jukka Seppo) in 1986 Entry Draft, October 11, 1985. Traded to **Boston** by **Los Angeles** for the rights to Dave Pasin, November 3, 1988. Signed as a free agent by **New Jersey**, August 14, 1989. Signed as a free agent by **NY Islanders**, August 13, 1990.

GUERARD, STEPHANE

Defense. Shoots left. 6'2", 198 lbs. Born, Ste. Elizabeth, Que., April 12, 1968.
(Quebec's 3rd choice, 41st overall, in 1986 Entry Draft).

			Regular Season					Playoffs				
Season	Club	Lea	GP	G	A	TP	PIM	GP	G	A	TP	PIM
1985-86	Shawinigan	QMJHL	59	4	18	22	167	3	1	1	2	0
1986-87	Shawinigan	QMJHL	31	5	16	21	57	12	2	9	11	36
1987-88	**Quebec**	**NHL**	**30**	**0**	**0**	**0**	**34**	....	....	....	....	....
1988-89	Halifax	AHL	37	1	9	10	140	4	0	0	0	8
1989-90	**Quebec**	**NHL**	**4**	**0**	**0**	**0**	**6**	....	....	....	....	....
	Halifax	AHL	1	0	0	0	5	....	....	....	....	....
1990-91	Halifax	AHL	DID NOT PLAY									
	NHL Totals		**34**	**0**	**0**	**0**	**40**	....	....	....	....	....

Traded to **NY Rangers** by **Quebec** for Miloslav Horava, May 25, 1991.

GUERIN, BILL (GAIR-ihn)

Center/Right wing. Shoots right. 6'2", 190 lbs. Born, Wilbraham, MA, November 9, 1970.
(New Jersey's 1st choice, 5th overall, in 1989 Entry Draft).

			Regular Season					Playoffs				
Season	Club	Lea	GP	G	A	TP	PIM	GP	G	A	TP	PIM
1987-88	Springfield	USHL	38	31	44	75	146	....	....	....	....	....
1988-89	Springfield	USHL	31	32	35	67	90	....	....	....	....	....
1989-90	Boston College	H.E.	39	14	11	25	54	....	....	....	....	....
1990-91	Boston College	H.E.	38	26	19	45	102	....	....	....	....	....

GUIDOTTI, VINCE

Left wing. Shoots left. 6', 180 lbs. Born, Sacramento, CA, April 29, 1967.
(St. Louis' 9th choice, 201st overall, in 1985 Entry Draft).

			Regular Season					Playoffs				
Season	Club	Lea	GP	G	A	TP	PIM	GP	G	A	TP	PIM
1985-86	U. of Maine	H.E.	16	0	0	0	8	....	....	....	....	....
1986-87	U. of Maine	H.E.	39	1	3	4	40	....	....	....	....	....
1987-88	U. of Maine	H.E.	44	7	19	26	69	....	....	....	....	....
1988-89	U. of Maine	H.E.	42	7	23	30	76	....	....	....	....	....
1989-90	Maine	AHL	2	0	0	0	0	....	....	....	....	....
	Johnstown	ECHL	46	5	17	22	61	....	....	....	....	....
1990-91	Nashville	ECHL	20	5	11	16	25	....	....	....	....	....

GUILBERT, MICHAEL

Defense. Shoots left. 6'2", 195 lbs. Born, Manchester, NH, December 11, 1971.
(NY Islanders' 6th choice, 132nd overall, in 1990 Entry Draft).

			Regular Season					Playoffs				
Season	Club	Lea	GP	G	A	TP	PIM	GP	G	A	TP	PIM
1989-90	Gov. Dummer	HS	....	5	9	14	0	....	....	....	....	....
1990-91			UNAVAILABLE									

GUILLET, ROBERT

Right wing. Shoots right. 5'11", 189 lbs. Born, Montreal, Que., February 22, 1972.
(Montreal's 4th choice, 60th overall, in 1990 Entry Draft).

			Regular Season					Playoffs				
Season	Club	Lea	GP	G	A	TP	PIM	GP	G	A	TP	PIM
1989-90a	Longueuil	QMJHL	69	32	40	72	132	7	2	1	3	16
1990-91b	Longueuil	QMJHL	69	55	32	87	96	8	4	7	11	27

a QMJHL Third All-Star Team (1990)
b QMJHL First All-Star Team (1991)

GUSAROV, ALEXEI (goo-SAH-rahf)

Defense. Shoots left. 6'2", 183 lbs. Born, Leningrad, Soviet Union, July 8, 1964.
(Quebec's 11th choice, 213th overall, in 1988 Entry Draft).

			Regular Season					Playoffs				
Season	Club	Lea	GP	G	A	TP	PIM	GP	G	A	TP	PIM
1981-82	SKA Leningrad	USSR	20	1	2	3	16	....	....	....	....	....
1982-83	SKA Leningrad	USSR	42	2	1	3	32	....	....	....	....	....
1983-84	SKA Leningrad	USSR	43	2	3	5	32	....	....	....	....	....
1984-85	CSKA	USSR	36	3	2	5	26	....	....	....	....	....
1985-86	CSKA	USSR	40	3	5	8	30	....	....	....	....	....
1986-87	CSKA	USSR	38	4	7	11	24	....	....	....	....	....
1987-88	CSKA	USSR	39	3	2	5	28	....	....	....	....	....
1988-89	CSKA	USSR	42	5	4	9	37	....	....	....	....	....
1989-90	CSKA	USSR	42	4	7	11	42	....	....	....	....	....
1990-91	CSKA	USSR	15	0	0	0	12	....	....	....	....	....
	Quebec	**NHL**	**36**	**3**	**9**	**12**	**12**	....	....	....	....	....
	Halifax	AHL	2	0	3	3	2	....	....	....	....	....
	NHL Totals		**36**	**3**	**9**	**12**	**12**	....	....	....	....	....

GUSTAFSSON, BENGT-AKE (GUS-tuhf-suhn)

Center. Shoots left. 5'11", 198 lbs. Born, Karlskoga, Sweden, March 23, 1958.
(Washington's 7th choice, 55th overall, in 1978 Amateur Draft).

			Regular Season					Playoffs				
Season	Club	Lea	GP	G	A	TP	PIM	GP	G	A	TP	PIM
1977-78	Farjestad	Swe.	32	15	10	25	10	....	....	....	....	....
1978-79	Farjestad	Swe.	32	13	12	25	10	3	2	0	2	4
	Edmonton	WHA	....	....	....	....	....	2	1	2	3	0
1979-80	**Washington**	**NHL**	**80**	**22**	**38**	**60**	**17**	....	....	....	....	....
1980-81	**Washington**	**NHL**	**72**	**21**	**34**	**55**	**26**	....	....	....	....	....
1981-82	**Washington**	**NHL**	**70**	**26**	**34**	**60**	**40**	....	....	....	....	....
1982-83	**Washington**	**NHL**	**67**	**22**	**42**	**64**	**16**	**4**	**0**	**1**	**1**	**4**
1983-84	**Washington**	**NHL**	**69**	**32**	**43**	**75**	**16**	**5**	**2**	**3**	**5**	**0**
1984-85	**Washington**	**NHL**	**51**	**14**	**29**	**43**	**8**	**5**	**1**	**3**	**4**	**0**
1985-86	**Washington**	**NHL**	**70**	**23**	**52**	**75**	**26**	....	....	....	....	....
1986-87	Bofors IK	Swe.2	28	16	26	42	22	....	....	....	....	....
	Swe. National	...	10	3	8	11	....	....	....	....	....	....
1987-88	**Washington**	**NHL**	**78**	**18**	**36**	**54**	**29**	**14**	**4**	**9**	**13**	**6**
1988-89	**Washington**	**NHL**	**72**	**18**	**51**	**69**	**18**	**4**	**2**	**3**	**5**	**6**
1989-90	Farjestad	Swe.	37	22	24	46	14	10	4	10	14	18
1990-91	Farjestad	Swe.	37	9	21	30	6	....	....	....	....	....
	NHL Totals		**629**	**196**	**359**	**555**	**196**	**32**	**9**	**19**	**28**	**16**

Reclaimed by **Washington** from **Edmonton** prior to Expansion Draft, June 9, 1979. Claimed by **Detroit** in NHL Waiver Draft, October 1, 1990. Claimed by **San Jose** from **Detroit** in Expansion Draft, May 30,1991.

GUY, KEVAN (GIGH)

Defense. Shoots right. 6'3", 202 lbs. Born, Edmonton, Alta., July 16, 1965.
(Calgary's 5th choice, 71st overall, in 1983 Entry Draft).

			Regular Season					Playoffs				
Season	Club	Lea	GP	G	A	TP	PIM	GP	G	A	TP	PIM
1982-83	Medicine Hat	WHL	69	7	20	27	89	5	0	3	3	16
1983-84	Medicine Hat	WHL	72	15	42	57	117	14	3	4	7	14
1984-85	Medicine Hat	WHL	31	7	17	24	46	10	1	2	3	2
1985-86	Moncton	AHL	73	4	20	24	56	10	0	2	2	6
1986-87	**Calgary**	**NHL**	**24**	**0**	**4**	**4**	**19**	**4**	**0**	**1**	**1**	**23**
	Moncton	AHL	46	2	10	12	38	....	....	....	....	....
1987-88	**Calgary**	**NHL**	**11**	**0**	**3**	**3**	**8**	....	....	....	....	....
	Salt Lake	IHL	61	6	30	36	51	19	1	6	7	26
1988-89	**Vancouver**	**NHL**	**45**	**2**	**2**	**4**	**34**	**1**	**0**	**0**	**0**	**0**
1989-90	**Vancouver**	**NHL**	**30**	**2**	**5**	**7**	**32**	....	....	....	....	....
	Milwaukee	IHL	29	2	11	13	33	....	....	....	....	....
1990-91	**Vancouver**	**NHL**	**39**	**1**	**6**	**7**	**39**	....	....	....	....	....
	Calgary	**NHL**	**4**	**0**	**0**	**0**	**4**	....	....	....	....	....
	NHL Totals		**153**	**5**	**20**	**25**	**136**	**5**	**0**	**1**	**1**	**23**

Traded to **Vancouver** by **Calgary** with Brian Bradley and Peter Bakovic for Craig Coxe, March 6, 1988. Traded to **Calgary** to **Vancouver** with Ron Stern and future considerations, March 5, 1991.

HAANPAA, ARI (HAHN-puh)

Right wing. Shoots left. 6'1", 190 lbs. Born, Nokia, Finland, November 29, 1965.
(NY Islanders' 5th choice, 83rd overall, in 1984 Entry Draft).

			Regular Season					Playoffs				
Season	Club	Lea	GP	G	A	TP	PIM	GP	G	A	TP	PIM
1983-84	Ilves	Fin.	27	0	1	1	8	2	0	0	0	2
1984-85	Ilves	Fin.	13	5	0	5	2	9	3	1	4	0
1985-86	**NY Islanders**	**NHL**	**18**	**0**	**7**	**7**	**20**	....	....	....	....	....
	Springfield	AHL	20	3	1	4	13	....	....	....	....	....
1986-87	**NY Islanders**	**NHL**	**41**	**6**	**4**	**10**	**17**	**6**	**0**	**0**	**0**	**10**
1987-88	**NY Islanders**	**NHL**	**1**	**0**	**0**	**0**	**0**	....	....	....	....	....
	Springfield	AHL	61	14	19	33	34	....	....	....	....	....
1988-89	Lukko	Fin.	42	28	19	47	36	....	....	....	....	....
1989-90	Lukko	Fin.	24	17	9	26	59	....	....	....	....	....
1990-91	JyP	Fin.	32	28	17	45	100	5	3	1	4	8
	NHL Totals		**60**	**6**	**11**	**17**	**37**	**11**	**3**	**1**	**4**	**18**

HAAPAKOSKI, MIKKO (HAH-puh-koh-skee)

Defense. Shoots left. 5'9", 172 lbs. Born, Oulu, Finland, January 19, 1967.
(Detroit's 10th choice, 179th overall, in 1987 Entry Draft).

			Regular Season					Playoffs				
Season	Club	Lea	GP	G	A	TP	PIM	GP	G	A	TP	PIM
1985-86	Karpat	Fin.	17	0	4	4	0	5	1	0	1	6
1986-87	Karpat	Fin.	41	13	15	28	18	9	1	1	2	4
1987-88	Karpat	Fin.	43	7	7	14	40	....	....	....	....	....
1988-89	Karpat	Fin.	40	7	18	25	20	5	1	1	2	2
1989-90	TPS	Fin.	44	4	10	14	14	9	0	1	1	16
1990-91	TPS	Fin.	40	9	12	21	10	9	1	4	5	4

HAAS, DAVID

Left wing. Shoots left. 6'2", 196 lbs. Born, Toronto, Ont., June 23, 1968.
(Edmonton's 5th choice, 105th overall, in 1986 Entry Draft).

			Regular Season					Playoffs				
Season	Club	Lea	GP	G	A	TP	PIM	GP	G	A	TP	PIM
1985-86	London	OHL	62	4	13	17	91	5	0	1	1	0
1986-87	London	OHL	5	1	0	1	5	....	....	....	....	....
	Kitchener	OHL	4	0	1	1	4	....	....	....	....	....
	Belleville	OHL	55	10	13	23	86	6	3	0	3	13
1987-88a	Windsor	OHL	63	60	47	107	246	11	9	11	20	50
1988-89	Cape Breton	AHL	61	9	9	18	325	....	....	....	....	....
1989-90	Cape Breton	AHL	53	6	12	18	230	4	2	2	4	15
1990-91	**Edmonton**	**NHL**	**5**	**1**	**0**	**1**	**0**	....	....	....	....	....
	Cape Breton	AHL	60	24	23	47	137	3	0	2	2	12
	NHL Totals		**5**	**1**	**0**	**1**	**0**	....	....	....	....	....

a OHL Second All-Star Team (1988)

HABSCHEID, MARC JOSEPH (HAB-shide)

Right wing/Center. Shoots right. 6', 185 lbs. Born, Swift Current, Sask., March 1, 1963.
(Edmonton's 6th choice, 113th overall, in 1981 Entry Draft).

			Regular Season					Playoffs				
Season	Club	Lea	GP	G	A	TP	PIM	GP	G	A	TP	PIM
1980-81	Saskatoon	WHL	72	34	63	97	50	....	....	....	....	....
1981-82	**Edmonton**	**NHL**	**7**	**1**	**3**	**4**	**2**	....	....	....	....	....
a	Saskatoon	WHL	55	64	87	151	74	5	3	4	7	4
	Wichita	CHL	....	....	....	....	....	3	0	0	0	0
1982-83	Kamloops	WHL	6	7	16	23	8	....	....	....	....	....
	Edmonton	**NHL**	**32**	**3**	**10**	**13**	**14**	....	....	....	....	....
1983-84	**Edmonton**	**NHL**	**9**	**1**	**0**	**1**	**6**	....	....	....	....	....
	Moncton	AHL	71	19	37	56	32	....	....	....	....	....
1984-85	**Edmonton**	**NHL**	**26**	**5**	**3**	**8**	**4**	....	....	....	....	....
	Nova Scotia	AHL	48	29	29	58	65	6	4	3	7	9
1985-86	**Minnesota**	**NHL**	**6**	**2**	**3**	**5**	**0**	**2**	**0**	**0**	**0**	**0**
	Springfield	AHL	41	18	32	50	21	....	....	....	....	....
1986-87	**Minnesota**	**NHL**	**15**	**2**	**0**	**2**	**2**	....	....	....	....	....
	Cdn. Olympic	...	51	29	32	61	70	....	....	....	....	....
1987-88	Cdn. National	...	61	19	34	53	42	....	....	....	....	....
	Cdn. Olympic	...	8	5	3	8	6	....	....	....	....	....
	Minnesota	**NHL**	**16**	**4**	**11**	**15**	**6**	....	....	....	....	....
1988-89	**Minnesota**	**NHL**	**76**	**23**	**31**	**54**	**40**	**5**	**1**	**3**	**4**	**13**
1989-90	**Detroit**	**NHL**	**66**	**15**	**11**	**26**	**33**	....	....	....	....	....
1990-91	**Detroit**	**NHL**	**46**	**9**	**8**	**17**	**22**	**5**	**0**	**0**	**0**	**0**
	NHL Totals		**299**	**65**	**80**	**145**	**129**	**12**	**1**	**3**	**4**	**13**

a WHL Second All-Star Team (1982)

Traded to **Minnesota** by **Edmonton** with Don Barber and Emanuel Viveiros for Gord Sherven and Don Biggs, December 20, 1985. Signed as a free agent by **Detroit**, June 9, 1989. Traded to **Calgary** by **Detroit** for Brian MacLellan, June 11, 1991.

HAGEN, GREG

Right wing. Shoots right. 5'11", 175 lbs. Born, St. Paul, MN, July 10, 1971.
(Pittsburgh's 11th choice, 205th overall, in 1989 Entry Draft).

			Regular Season					Playoffs				
Season	Club	Lea	GP	G	A	TP	PIM	GP	G	A	TP	PIM
1988-89	Hill-Murray	HS	25	28	32	60	....	....	....	....	....	....
1989-90			DID NOT PLAY									
1990-91	St. Cloud	WCHA	23	4	4	8	2	....	....	....	....	....

HAJDU, RICHARD (HI-doo)

Left wing. Shoots left. 6'1", 185 lbs. Born, Victoria, B.C., May 10, 1965.
(Buffalo's 5th choice, 34th overall, in 1983 Entry Draft).

			Regular Season					Playoffs				
Season	Club	Lea	GP	G	A	TP	PIM	GP	G	A	TP	PIM
1981-82	Kamloops	WHL	64	19	21	40	50	4	0	0	0	0
1982-83	Kamloops	WHL	70	22	36	58	101	5	0	0	0	4
1983-84	Victoria	WHL	42	17	10	27	106	....	....	....	....	....
1984-85	Victoria	WHL	24	12	16	28	33	....	....	....	....	....
	Rochester	AHL	2	0	2	2	0	....	....	....	....	....
1985-86	**Buffalo**	**NHL**	**3**	**0**	**0**	**0**	**4**	....	....	....	....	....
	Rochester	AHL	54	10	27	37	95	....	....	....	....	....
1986-87	**Buffalo**	**NHL**	**2**	**0**	**0**	**0**	**0**	....	....	....	....	....
	Rochester	AHL	58	7	15	22	90	11	1	1	2	9
1987-88	Rochester	AHL	37	7	11	18	24	1	0	0	0	0
	Flint	IHL	17	4	6	10	30	....	....	....	....	....
1988-89	Cdn. National	...	50	14	11	25	22	....	....	....	....	....
1989-90	Cdn. National	...	42	6	10	16	8	....	....	....	....	....
1990-91	Gosser Ev	Aus.	19	10	7	17	....	....	....	....	....	....
	Cdn. National	...	27	5	6	11	10	....	....	....	....	....
	NHL Totals		**5**	**0**	**0**	**0**	**4**	....	....	....	....	....

HALKIDIS, BOB (hal-KEE-dihs)

Defense. Shoots left. 5'11", 200 lbs. Born, Toronto, Ont., March 5, 1966.
(Buffalo's 4th choice, 81st overall, in 1984 Entry Draft).

			Regular Season					Playoffs				
Season	Club	Lea	GP	G	A	TP	PIM	GP	G	A	TP	PIM
1983-84	London	OHL	51	9	22	31	123	8	0	2	2	27
1984-85ab	London	OHL	62	14	50	64	154	8	3	6	9	22
	Buffalo	**NHL**	....	....	....	....	....	**4**	**0**	**0**	**0**	**19**
1985-86	**Buffalo**	**NHL**	**37**	**1**	**9**	**10**	**115**	....	....	....	....	....
1986-87	**Buffalo**	**NHL**	**6**	**1**	**1**	**2**	**19**	....	....	....	....	....
	Rochester	AHL	59	1	8	9	144	8	0	0	0	43
1987-88	**Buffalo**	**NHL**	**30**	**0**	**3**	**3**	**115**	**4**	**0**	**0**	**0**	**22**
	Rochester	AHL	15	2	5	7	50	....	....	....	....	....
1988-89	**Buffalo**	**NHL**	**16**	**0**	**1**	**1**	**66**	....	....	....	....	....
	Rochester	AHL	16	0	6	6	64	....	....	....	....	....
1989-90	Rochester	AHL	18	1	13	14	70	....	....	....	....	....
	Los Angeles	**NHL**	**20**	**0**	**4**	**4**	**56**	....	....	....	....	....
	New Haven	AHL	30	3	17	20	67	....	....	....	....	....
1990-91	**Los Angeles**	**NHL**	**34**	**1**	**3**	**4**	**133**	**3**	**0**	**0**	**0**	**0**
	New Haven	AHL	7	1	3	4	10	....	....	....	....	....
	Phoenix	IHL	4	1	5	6	6	....	....	....	....	....
	NHL Totals		**143**	**3**	**21**	**24**	**504**	**11**	**0**	**0**	**0**	**41**

a Named Outstanding Defenseman in OHL (1985)
b OHL First All-Star Team (1985)

Traded to **Los Angeles** by **Buffalo** with future considerations for Dale DeGray and future considerations, November 24, 1989. Signed as a free agent by **Toronto**, July 24, 1991.

HALL, DEAN

Center. Shoots left. 6'1", 175 lbs. Born, Winnipeg, Man., January 14, 1968.
(Boston's 3rd choice, 76th overall, in 1986 Entry Draft).

			Regular Season					Playoffs				
Season	Club	Lea	GP	G	A	TP	PIM	GP	G	A	TP	PIM
1986-87	N. Michigan	WCHA	20	4	5	9	16	....	....	....	....	....
1987-88	N. Michigan	WCHA	31	5	6	11	22	....	....	....	....	....
1988-89	N. Michigan	WCHA	2	0	0	0	0	....	....	....	....	....
	Seattle	WHL	33	18	19	37	8	....	....	....	....	....
1989-90	Johnstown	ECHL	38	11	22	33	27	....	....	....	....	....
1990-91	Nashville	ECHL	14	2	4	6	6	....	....	....	....	....

HALL, TAYLOR

Left wing. Shoots left. 5'11", 180 lbs. Born, Regina, Sask., February 20, 1964.
(Vancouver's 4th choice, 116th overall, in 1982 Entry Draft).

			Regular Season					Playoffs				
Season	Club	Lea	GP	G	A	TP	PIM	GP	G	A	TP	PIM
1981-82	Regina	WHL	48	14	15	29	43	11	2	3	5	14
1982-83	Regina	WHL	72	37	57	94	78	5	0	3	3	12
1983-84	**Vancouver**	**NHL**	**4**	**1**	**0**	**1**	**0**	....	....	....	....	....
a	Regina	WHL	69	63	79	142	42	23	*21	20	41	26
1984-85	**Vancouver**	**NHL**	**7**	**1**	**4**	**5**	**19**	....	....	....	....	....
1985-86	**Vancouver**	**NHL**	**19**	**5**	**5**	**10**	**6**	....	....	....	....	....
	Fredericton	AHL	45	21	14	35	28	1	0	0	0	0
1986-87	**Vancouver**	**NHL**	**4**	**0**	**0**	**0**	**0**	....	....	....	....	....
	Fredericton	AHL	36	21	20	41	23	....	....	....	....	....
1987-88	**Boston**	**NHL**	**7**	**0**	**0**	**0**	**4**	....	....	....	....	....
	Maine	AHL	71	33	41	74	58	10	1	4	5	21
1988-89	Maine	AHL	8	0	1	1	7	....	....	....	....	....
	Newmarket	AHL	9	5	5	10	14	....	....	....	....	....
1989-90	New Haven	AHL	51	14	23	37	10	....	....	....	....	....
1990-91	San Diego	IHL	44	13	16	29	28	....	....	....	....	....
	NHL Totals		**41**	**7**	**9**	**16**	**29**	....	....	....	....	....

a WHL First All-Star Team, East Division (1984)

Signed as a free agent by **Boston**, July 20, 1987.

HALL, TODD

Defense. Shoots left. 6'1", 212 lbs. Born, Hamden, CT, January 22, 1973.
(Hartford's 3rd choice, 53rd overall, in 1991 Entry Draft).

			Regular Season					Playoffs				
Season	Club	Lea	GP	G	A	TP	PIM	GP	G	A	TP	PIM
1989-90	Hamden	HS	17	10	22	32	6	....	....	....	....	....
1990-91	Hamden	HS	23	10	15	25	12	....	....	....	....	....

HALLER, KEVIN

Defense. Shoots left. 6'2", 183 lbs. Born, Trochu, Alta., December 5, 1970.
(Buffalo's 1st choice, 14th overall, in 1989 Entry Draft).

			Regular Season					Playoffs				
Season	Club	Lea	GP	G	A	TP	PIM	GP	G	A	TP	PIM
1988-89	Regina	WHL	72	10	31	41	99	....	....	....	....	....
1989-90	**Buffalo**	**NHL**	**2**	**0**	**0**	**0**	**0**	....	....	....	....	....
a	Regina	WHL	58	16	37	53	93	11	2	9	11	16
1990-91	**Buffalo**	**NHL**	**21**	**1**	**8**	**9**	**20**	**6**	**1**	**4**	**5**	**10**
	Rochester	AHL	52	2	8	10	53	10	2	1	3	6
	NHL Totals		**23**	**1**	**8**	**9**	**20**	**6**	**1**	**4**	**5**	**10**

a WHL East First All-Star Team (1990)

HALVERSON, TREVOR

Left wing. Shoots left. 6', 194 lbs. Born, White River, Ont., April 6, 1971.
(Washington's 2nd choice, 21st overall, in 1991 Entry Draft).

			Regular Season					Playoffs				
Season	Club	Lea	GP	G	A	TP	PIM	GP	G	A	TP	PIM
1989-90	North Bay	OHL	54	22	20	42	172	2	2	1	3	2
1990-91a	North Bay	OHL	64	59	36	95	128	10	3	6	9	4

a OHL First All-Star Team (1991)

HAMALAINEN, ERIK (HAH-muhl-ahy-nehn)

Defense. Shoots left. 6'1", 198 lbs. Born, Rauma, Finland, April 20, 1965.
(Detroit's 10th choice, 197th overall, in 1985 Entry Draft).

			Regular Season					Playoffs				
Season	Club	Lea	GP	G	A	TP	PIM	GP	G	A	TP	PIM
1985-86	Lukko	Fin.	31	13	6	19	32	....	....	....	....	....
1986-87	Lukko	Fin.	44	8	8	16	49	....	....	....	....	....
1987-88	Lukko	Fin.	44	8	4	12	52	8	0	3	3	2
1988-89	KalPa	Fin.	43	7	4	11	14	2	0	0	0	2
1989-90	KalPa	Fin.	44	9	20	29	32	....	....	....	....	....
1990-91	KalPa	Fin.	44	14	14	28	34	8	3	4	7	4

HAMMOND, KEN

Defense. Shoots left. 6'1", 190 lbs. Born, Port Credit, Ont., August 22, 1963.
(Los Angeles' 8th choice, 152nd overall, in 1983 Entry Draft).

			Regular Season					Playoffs				
Season	Club	Lea	GP	G	A	TP	PIM	GP	G	A	TP	PIM
1982-83	RPI	ECAC	28	17	26	43	8	....	....	....	....	....
1983-84	RPI	ECAC	34	5	11	16	72	....	....	....	....	....
1984-85	**Los Angeles**	**NHL**	**3**	**1**	**0**	**1**	**0**	**3**	**0**	**0**	**0**	**4**
ab	RPI	ECAC	38	11	28	39	90	....	....	....	....	....
1985-86	**Los Angeles**	**NHL**	**3**	**0**	**1**	**1**	**2**	....	....	....	....	....
	New Haven	AHL	67	4	12	16	96	4	0	0	0	7
1986-87	**Los Angeles**	**NHL**	**10**	**0**	**2**	**2**	**11**	....	....	....	....	....
	New Haven	AHL	66	1	15	16	76	6	0	1	1	21
1987-88	**Los Angeles**	**NHL**	**46**	**7**	**9**	**16**	**69**	**2**	**0**	**0**	**0**	**4**
	New Haven	AHL	26	3	8	11	27	....	....	....	....	....
1988-89	**Edmonton**	**NHL**	**5**	**0**	**1**	**1**	**8**	....	....	....	....	....
	NY Rangers	**NHL**	**3**	**0**	**0**	**0**	**0**	....	....	....	....	....
	Denver	IHL	38	5	18	23	24	....	....	....	....	....
	Toronto	**NHL**	**14**	**0**	**2**	**2**	**12**	....	....	....	....	....
1989-90	Newmarket	AHL	75	9	45	54	106	....	....	....	....	....
1990-91	**Boston**	**NHL**	**1**	**1**	**0**	**1**	**2**	**8**	**0**	**0**	**0**	**10**
	Maine	AHL	80	10	41	51	159	2	0	1	1	16
	NHL Totals		**85**	**9**	**15**	**24**	**104**	**13**	**0**	**0**	**0**	**18**

a ECAC First All-Star Team (1985)
b Named to NCAA All-American Team (1985)

Claimed by **Edmonton** in NHL Waiver Draft, October 3, 1988. Claimed by **NY Rangers** on waivers from **Edmonton**, November 1, 1988. Traded to **Toronto** by **NY Rangers** for Chris McRae, February 21, 1989. Traded to **Boston** by **Toronto** for cash, August 20, 1990. Signed as a free agent by **San Jose**, August 9, 1991.

HAMRLIK, MARTIN

Defense. Shoots right. 5'11", 176 lbs. Born, Zlin, Czechoslovakia, May 6, 1973.
(Hartford's 2nd choice, 31st overall, in 1991 Entry Draft).

			Regular Season					Playoffs				
Season	Club	Lea	GP	G	A	TP	PIM	GP	G	A	TP	PIM
1989-90	TJ Zlin	Czech.	12	2	0	2	....	....	....	....	....	....
1990-91	TJ Zlin	Czech.	50	8	14	22	44	....	....	....	....	....

HANDY, RONALD (RON)

Left wing. Shoots left. 5'11", 175 lbs. Born, Toronto, Ont., January 5, 1963.
(NY Islanders' 3rd choice, 57th overall, in 1981 Entry Draft).

			Regular Season					Playoffs				
Season	Club	Lea	GP	G	A	TP	PIM	GP	G	A	TP	PIM
1980-81	S. S. Marie	OHA	66	43	43	86	45	18	3	5	8	25
1981-82	S. S. Marie	OHL	20	15	10	25	20	....	....	....	....	....
	Kingston	OHL	44	35	38	73	23	4	1	1	2	16
1982-83	Kingston	OHL	67	52	96	148	64	....	....	....	....	....
	Indianapolis	CHL	9	2	7	9	0	10	3	8	11	18
1983-84a	Indianapolis	CHL	66	29	46	75	40	10	2	5	7	0
1984-85	**NY Islanders**	**NHL**	**10**	**0**	**2**	**2**	**0**	....	....	....	....	....
b	Springfield	AHL	69	29	35	64	38	3	2	2	4	0
1985-86	Springfield	AHL	79	31	30	61	66	....	....	....	....	....
1986-87	Indianapolis	IHL	82	*55	80	135	57	6	4	3	7	2
1987-88	**St. Louis**	**NHL**	**4**	**0**	**1**	**1**	**0**	....	....	....	....	....
b	Peoria	IHL	78	53	63	116	61	7	2	3	5	4
1988-89	Peoria	IHL	81	43	57	100	24	....	....	....	....	....
1989-90	Peoria	IHL	82	36	39	75	52	5	3	1	4	0
1990-91	Kansas City	IHL	64	42	39	81	41	....	....	....	....	....
	NHL Totals		**14**	**0**	**3**	**3**	**0**	....	....	....	....	....

a CHL Second All-Star Team (1984)
b IHL Second All-Star Team (1985, 1988)

Signed as a free agent by **St. Louis**, September 24, 1987.

HANKINSON, BEN

Center. Shoots right. 6'2", 180 lbs. Born, Edina, MN, January 5, 1969.
(New Jersey's 5th choice, 107th overall, in 1987 Entry Draft).

			Regular Season					Playoffs				
Season	Club	Lea	GP	G	A	TP	PIM	GP	G	A	TP	PIM
1987-88	U. Minnesota	WCHA	24	4	7	11	36	....	....	....	....	....
1988-89	U. Minnesota	WCHA	43	7	11	18	115	....	....	....	....	....
1989-90a	U. Minnesota	WCHA	46	25	41	66	34	....	....	....	....	....
1990-91	U. Minnesota	WCHA	43	19	21	40	133	....	....	....	....	....

a WCHA First All-Star Team (1990)

HANKINSON, PETER

Right wing. Shoots right. 5'9", 175 lbs. Born, Edina, MN, November 24, 1967.
(Winnipeg's 1st choice, 4th overall, in 1989 Supplemental Draft).

			Regular Season					Playoffs				
Season	Club	Lea	GP	G	A	TP	PIM	GP	G	A	TP	PIM
1986-87	U. Minnesota	WCHA	43	16	12	28	10	....	....	....	....	....
1987-88	U. Minnesota	WCHA	39	25	20	45	32	....	....	....	....	....
1988-89	U. Minnesota	WCHA	48	16	27	43	42	....	....	....	....	....
1989-90	U. Minnesota	WCHA	45	19	12	31	116	....	....	....	....	....
1990-91	Fort Wayne	IHL	10	1	2	3	4	....	....	....	....	....
	Moncton	AHL	47	2	14	16	10	4	0	0	0	0

HANNAN, DAVID (DAVE)

Center. Shoots left. 5'10", 185 lbs. Born, Sudbury, Ont., November 26, 1961.
(Pittsburgh's 9th choice, 196th overall, in 1981 Entry Draft).

			Regular Season					Playoffs				
Season	Club	Lea	GP	G	A	TP	PIM	GP	G	A	TP	PIM
1979-80	S.S. Marie	OHA	28	11	10	21	31	....	....	....	....	....
	Brantford	OHA	25	5	10	15	26	....	....	....	....	....
1980-81	Brantford	OHA	56	46	35	81	155	6	2	4	6	20
1981-82	**Pittsburgh**	**NHL**	**1**	**0**	**0**	**0**	**0**	....	....	....	....	....
	Erie	AHL	76	33	37	70	129	....	....	....	....	....
1982-83	**Pittsburgh**	**NHL**	**74**	**11**	**22**	**33**	**127**	....	....	....	....	....
	Baltimore	AHL	5	2	2	4	13	....	....	....	....	....
1983-84	**Pittsburgh**	**NHL**	**24**	**2**	**3**	**5**	**33**	....	....	....	....	....
	Baltimore	AHL	47	18	24	42	98	10	2	6	8	27
1984-85	**Pittsburgh**	**NHL**	**30**	**6**	**7**	**13**	**43**	....	....	....	....	....
	Baltimore	AHL	49	20	25	45	91	....	....	....	....	....
1985-86	**Pittsburgh**	**NHL**	**75**	**17**	**18**	**35**	**91**	....	....	....	....	....
1986-87	**Pittsburgh**	**NHL**	**58**	**10**	**15**	**25**	**56**	....	....	....	....	....
1987-88	**Pittsburgh**	**NHL**	**21**	**4**	**3**	**7**	**23**	....	....	....	....	....
	Edmonton	**NHL**	**51**	**9**	**11**	**20**	**43**	**12**	**1**	**1**	**2**	**8**
1988-89	**Pittsburgh**	**NHL**	**72**	**10**	**20**	**30**	**157**	**8**	**0**	**1**	**1**	**4**
1989-90	**Toronto**	**NHL**	**39**	**6**	**9**	**15**	**55**	**3**	**1**	**0**	**1**	**4**
1990-91	**Toronto**	**NHL**	**74**	**11**	**23**	**34**	**82**	....	....	....	....	....
	NHL Totals		**519**	**86**	**131**	**217**	**710**	**23**	**2**	**2**	**4**	**16**

Traded to **Edmonton** by **Pittsburgh** with Craig Simpson, Moe Mantha and Chris Joseph for Paul Coffey, Dave Hunter and Wayne Van Dorp, November 24, 1987. Claimed by **Pittsburgh** in NHL Waiver Draft, October 3, 1988. Claimed by **Toronto** in NHL Waiver Draft, October 2, 1989.

HANSON, GREG

Defense. Shoots left. 6'3", 215 lbs. Born, Bloomington, MN, September 4, 1971.
(Philadelphia's 13th choice, 193rd overall, in 1990 Entry Draft).

			Regular Season					Playoffs				
Season	Club	Lea	GP	G	A	TP	PIM	GP	G	A	TP	PIM
1989-90	Kennedy	HS	28	4	28	32	....	....	....	....	....	....
1990-91	Dubuque	USHL	39	4	21	25	69	8	1	5	6	4

HANUS, TIM

Left wing. Shoots left. 6'1", 185 lbs. Born, Minneapolis, MN, May 12, 1969.
(Quebec's 7th choice, 135th overall, in 1987 Entry Draft).

			Regular Season					Playoffs				
Season	Club	Lea	GP	G	A	TP	PIM	GP	G	A	TP	PIM
1988-89	St. Cloud	NCAA	33	13	22	35	31	....	....	....	....	....
1989-90	St. Cloud	NCAA	34	22	24	46	54	....	....	....	....	....
1990-91	St. Cloud	WCHA	40	21	26	47	26	....	....	....	....	....

HARDING, JEFF

Right wing. Shoots right. 6'3", 220 lbs. Born, Toronto, Ont., April 6, 1969.
(Philadelphia's 2nd choice, 30th overall, in 1987 Entry Draft).

			Regular Season					Playoffs				
Season	Club	Lea	GP	G	A	TP	PIM	GP	G	A	TP	PIM
1987-88	Michigan State	CCHA	43	17	10	27	129	....	....	....	....	....
1988-89	**Philadelphia**	**NHL**	**6**	**0**	**0**	**0**	**29**	....	....	....	....	....
	Hershey	AHL	34	13	5	18	64	8	1	1	2	33
1989-90	**Philadelphia**	**NHL**	**9**	**0**	**0**	**0**	**18**	....	....	....	....	....
	Cdn. National	...	21	5	6	11	50	....	....	....	....	....
	Hershey	AHL	6	0	2	2	2	....	....	....	....	....
1990-91	Cape Breton	AHL	4	1	0	1	2	....	....	....	....	....
	Fort Wayne	IHL	11	3	4	7	10	....	....	....	....	....
	NHL Totals		**15**	**0**	**0**	**0**	**47**	....	....	....	....	....

HARDY, MARK LEA

Defense. Shoots left. 5'11", 195 lbs. Born, Semaden, Switzerland, February 1, 1959.
(Los Angeles' 3rd choice, 30th overall, in 1979 Entry Draft).

			Regular Season					Playoffs				
Season	Club	Lea	GP	G	A	TP	PIM	GP	G	A	TP	PIM
1977-78	Montreal	QJHL	72	25	57	82	150	13	3	10	13	22
1978-79	Montreal	QJHL	67	18	52	70	117	11	5	8	13	40
1979-80	Binghamton	AHL	56	3	13	16	32	....	....	....	....	....
	Los Angeles	**NHL**	**15**	**0**	**1**	**1**	**10**	**4**	**1**	**1**	**2**	**9**
1980-81	**Los Angeles**	**NHL**	**77**	**5**	**20**	**25**	**77**	**4**	**1**	**2**	**3**	**4**
1981-82	**Los Angeles**	**NHL**	**77**	**6**	**39**	**45**	**130**	**10**	**1**	**2**	**3**	**9**
1982-83	**Los Angeles**	**NHL**	**74**	**5**	**34**	**39**	**101**	....	....	....	....	....
1983-84	**Los Angeles**	**NHL**	**79**	**8**	**41**	**49**	**122**	....	....	....	....	....
1984-85	**Los Angeles**	**NHL**	**78**	**14**	**39**	**53**	**97**	**3**	**0**	**1**	**1**	**2**
1985-86	**Los Angeles**	**NHL**	**55**	**6**	**21**	**27**	**71**	....	....	....	....	....
1986-87	**Los Angeles**	**NHL**	**73**	**3**	**27**	**30**	**120**	**5**	**1**	**2**	**3**	**10**
1987-88	**Los Angeles**	**NHL**	**61**	**6**	**22**	**28**	**99**	....	....	....	....	....
	NY Rangers	**NHL**	**19**	**2**	**2**	**4**	**31**	....	....	....	....	....
1988-89	**Minnesota**	**NHL**	**15**	**2**	**4**	**6**	**26**	....	....	....	....	....
	NY Rangers	**NHL**	**45**	**2**	**12**	**14**	**45**	**4**	**0**	**1**	**1**	**31**
1989-90	**NY Rangers**	**NHL**	**54**	**0**	**15**	**15**	**94**	**3**	**0**	**1**	**1**	**2**
1990-91	**NY Rangers**	**NHL**	**70**	**1**	**5**	**6**	**89**	**6**	**0**	**1**	**1**	**30**
	NHL Totals		**792**	**60**	**282**	**342**	**1112**	**39**	**4**	**11**	**15**	**97**

Traded to **NY Rangers** by **Los Angeles** for Ron Duguay, February 23, 1988. Traded to **Minnesota** by **NY Rangers** for future considerations (Louie Debrusk) June 13, 1988. Traded to **NY Rangers** by **Minnesota** for Larry Bernard and NY Rangers fifth-round choice (Rhys Hollyman) in 1989 Entry Draft, December 9, 1988.

HARKINS, BRETT

Left wing. Shoots left. 6'1", 170 lbs. Born, North Ridgeville, OH, July 2, 1970.
(NY Islanders' 9th choice, 133rd overall, in 1989 Entry Draft).

			Regular Season					Playoffs				
Season	Club	Lea	GP	G	A	TP	PIM	GP	G	A	TP	PIM
1989-90	Bowling Green	CCHA	41	11	43	54	45	....	....	....	....	....
1990-91	Bowling Green	CCHA	40	22	38	60	30	....	....	....	....	....

HARKINS, TODD

Center. Shoots right. 6'3", 210 lbs. Born, Cleveland, OH, October 8, 1968.
(Calgary's 2nd choice, 42nd overall, in 1988 Entry Draft).

			Regular Season					Playoffs				
Season	Club	Lea	GP	G	A	TP	PIM	GP	G	A	TP	PIM
1987-88	Miami-Ohio	CCHA	34	9	7	16	133	....	....	....	....	....
1988-89	Miami-Ohio	CCHA	36	8	7	15	77	....	....	....	....	....
1989-90	Miami-Ohio	CCHA	40	27	17	44	78	....	....	....	....	....
1990-91	Salt Lake	IHL	79	15	27	42	113	3	0	0	0	0

HARLOCK, DAVID

Defense. Shoots left. 6'2", 195 lbs. Born, Toronto, Ont., March 16, 1971.
(New Jersey's 2nd choice, 24th overall, in 1990 Entry Draft).

			Regular Season					Playoffs				
Season	Club	Lea	GP	G	A	TP	PIM	GP	G	A	TP	PIM
1989-90	U. of Michigan	CCHA	42	2	13	15	44	....	....	....	....	....
1990-91	U. of Michigan	CCHA	39	2	8	10	70	....	....	....	....	....

HARLOW, SCOTT

Left wing. Shoots left. 6'1", 185 lbs. Born, East Bridgewater, MA, October 11, 1963.
(Montreal's 6th choice, 61st overall, in 1982 Entry Draft).

			Regular Season					Playoffs				
Season	Club	Lea	GP	G	A	TP	PIM	GP	G	A	TP	PIM
1982-83	Boston College	ECAC	24	6	19	25	19	....	....	....	....	....
1983-84	Boston College	ECAC	39	27	20	47	17	....	....	....	....	....
1984-85a	Boston College	ECAC	44	34	38	72	45	....	....	....	....	....
1985-86bcd	Boston College	H.E.	42	38	41	79	48	....	....	....	....	....
1986-87	Sherbrooke	AHL	66	22	26	48	6	15	5	6	11	6
1987-88	Sherbrooke	AHL	18	6	12	18	8	....	....	....	....	....
	St. Louis	**NHL**	**1**	**0**	**1**	**1**	**0**	....	....	....	....	....
	Baltimore	AHL	29	24	27	51	21	....	....	....	....	....
	Peoria	IHL	39	30	25	55	46	....	....	....	....	....
1988-89	Peoria	IHL	45	16	26	42	22	....	....	....	....	....
	Maine	AHL	30	16	17	33	8	....	....	....	....	....
1989-90	Maine	AHL	80	31	32	63	68	....	....	....	....	....
1990-91	New Haven	AHL	73	28	28	56	92	....	....	....	....	....
	NHL Totals		**1**	**0**	**1**	**1**	**0**	....	....	....	....	....

a Hockey East Second All-Star Team
b NCAA East First All-American Team (1986)
c Hockey East First All-Star Team (1986)
d Hockey East Player of the Year (1986)

Traded to **St. Louis** by **Montreal** for future considerations, January 21, 1988. Traded to **Boston** by **St. Louis** for Phil DeGaetano, February 3, 1989.

HARRIS, TIM

Right wing. Shoots right. 6'2", 190 lbs. Born, Uxbridge, Ont., October 16, 1967.
(Calgary's 5th choice, 70th overall, in 1987 Entry Draft).

			Regular Season					Playoffs				
Season	Club	Lea	GP	G	A	TP	PIM	GP	G	A	TP	PIM
1987-88	Lake Superior	CCHA	43	8	10	18	79	....	....	....	....	....
1988-89	Lake Superior	CCHA	29	1	5	6	78	....	....	....	....	....
1989-90	Lake Superior	CCHA	39	6	17	23	71	....	....	....	....	....
1990-91	Lake Superior	CCHA	45	17	22	39	122	....	....	....	....	....

HARTJE, TODD

Center. Shoots left. 6'1", 180 lbs. Born, Anoka, MN, February 27, 1968.
(Winnipeg's 7th choice, 142nd overall, in 1987 Entry Draft).

			Regular Season					Playoffs				
Season	Club	Lea	GP	G	A	TP	PIM	GP	G	A	TP	PIM
1986-87	Harvard	ECAC	32	3	9	12	36	....	....	....	....	....
1987-88	Harvard	ECAC	32	5	17	22	40	....	....	....	....	....
1988-89	Harvard	ECAC	33	4	17	21	40	....	....	....	....	....
1989-90	Harvard	ECAC	28	6	10	16	29	....	....	....	....	....
1990-91	Sokol Kiev	USSR	32	2	4	6	18	....	....	....	....	....
	Fort Wayne	IHL	1	1	0	1	2	....	....	....	....	....

HARTMAN, MIKE

Left wing. Shoots left. 6', 190 lbs. Born, Detroit, MI, February 7, 1967.
(Buffalo's 8th choice, 131st overall, in 1986 Entry Draft).

			Regular Season					Playoffs				
Season	Club	Lea	GP	G	A	TP	PIM	GP	G	A	TP	PIM
1984-85	Belleville	OHL	49	13	12	25	119	....	....	....	....	....
1985-86	Belleville	OHL	4	2	1	3	5	....	....	....	....	....
	North Bay	OHL	53	19	16	35	205	10	2	4	6	34
1986-87	**Buffalo**	**NHL**	**17**	**3**	**3**	**6**	**69**	....	....	....	....	....
	North Bay	OHL	32	15	24	39	144	19	7	8	15	88
1987-88	**Buffalo**	**NHL**	**18**	**3**	**1**	**4**	**90**	**6**	**0**	**0**	**0**	**35**
	Rochester	AHL	57	13	14	27	283	4	1	0	1	22
1988-89	**Buffalo**	**NHL**	**70**	**8**	**9**	**17**	**316**	**5**	**0**	**0**	**0**	**34**
1989-90	**Buffalo**	**NHL**	**60**	**11**	**10**	**21**	**211**	**6**	**0**	**0**	**0**	**18**
1990-91	**Buffalo**	**NHL**	**60**	**9**	**3**	**12**	**204**	**2**	**0**	**0**	**0**	**17**
	NHL Totals		**225**	**34**	**26**	**60**	**890**	**19**	**0**	**0**	**0**	**104**

HARWELL, JOE

Defense. Shoots right. 6'3", 195 lbs. Born, Minneapolis, MN, November 21, 1968.
(Winnipeg's 6th choice, 121st overall, in 1987 Entry Draft).

			Regular Season					Playoffs				
Season	Club	Lea	GP	G	A	TP	PIM	GP	G	A	TP	PIM
1989-90	U. Wisconsin	WCHA	10	0	0	0	2	....	....	....	....	....
1990-91	U. Wisconsin	WCHA	42	3	5	8	44	....	....	....	....	....

HASSELBLAD, PETER

Defense. Shoots left. 6'4", 195 lbs. Born, Orebro, Sweden, April 20, 1966.
(Calgary's 12th choice, 229th overall, in 1987 Entry Draft).

			Regular Season					Playoffs				
Season	Club	Lea	GP	G	A	TP	PIM	GP	G	A	TP	PIM
1989-90	Farjestad	Swe.	56	3	6	9	51	10	1	2	3	12
1990-91	Farjestad	Swe.	40	0	7	7	56	....	....	....	....	....

HATCHER, DERIAN

Defense. Shoots left. 6'5", 205 lbs. Born, Sterling Heights, MI, June 4, 1972.
(Minnesota's 1st choice, 8th overall, in 1990 Entry Draft).

			Regular Season					Playoffs				
Season	Club	Lea	GP	G	A	TP	PIM	GP	G	A	TP	PIM
1989-90	North Bay	OHL	64	14	38	52	81	5	2	3	5	8
1990-91a	North Bay	OHL	64	13	50	63	163	10	2	10	12	28

a OHL Third All-Star Team (1991)

HATCHER, KEVIN

Defense. Shoots right. 6'4", 225 lbs. Born, Detroit, MI, September 9, 1966.
(Washington's 1st choice, 17th overall, in 1984 Entry Draft).

			Regular Season					Playoffs				
Season	Club	Lea	GP	G	A	TP	PIM	GP	G	A	TP	PIM
1983-84	North Bay	OHL	67	10	39	49	61	4	2	2	4	11
1984-85	**Washington**	**NHL**	**2**	**1**	**0**	**1**	**0**	**1**	**0**	**0**	**0**	**0**
a	North Bay	OHL	58	26	37	63	75	8	3	8	11	9
1985-86	**Washington**	**NHL**	**79**	**9**	**10**	**19**	**119**	**9**	**1**	**1**	**2**	**19**
1986-87	**Washington**	**NHL**	**78**	**8**	**16**	**24**	**144**	**7**	**1**	**0**	**1**	**20**
1987-88	**Washington**	**NHL**	**71**	**14**	**27**	**41**	**137**	**14**	**5**	**7**	**12**	**55**
1988-89	**Washington**	**NHL**	**62**	**13**	**27**	**40**	**101**	**6**	**1**	**4**	**5**	**20**
1989-90	**Washington**	**NHL**	**80**	**13**	**41**	**54**	**102**	**11**	**0**	**8**	**8**	**32**
1990-91	**Washington**	**NHL**	**79**	**24**	**50**	**74**	**69**	**11**	**3**	**3**	**6**	**8**
	NHL Totals		**451**	**82**	**171**	**253**	**672**	**59**	**11**	**23**	**34**	**154**

a OHL Second All-Star Team (1985)

Played in NHL All-Star Game (1990, 1991)

HAUER, BRETT

Defense. Shoots right. 6'2", 180 lbs. Born, Edina, MN, July 11, 1971.
(Vancouver's 3rd choice, 71st overall, in 1989 Entry Draft).

			Regular Season					Playoffs				
Season	Club	Lea	GP	G	A	TP	PIM	GP	G	A	TP	PIM
1989-90	Minn.-Duluth	WCHA	37	2	6	8	44	....	....	....	....	....
1990-91	Minn.-Duluth	WCHA	30	1	7	8	54	....	....	....	....	....

HAWERCHUK, DALE (HOW-uhr-CHUHK)

Center. Shoots left. 5'11", 185 lbs. Born, Toronto, Ont., April 4, 1963.
(Winnipeg's 1st choice and 1st overall in 1981 Entry Draft).

			Regular Season					Playoffs				
Season	Club	Lea	GP	G	A	TP	PIM	GP	G	A	TP	PIM
1979-80	Cornwall	QJHL	72	37	66	103	21	18	20	25	45	0
1980-81abc	Cornwall	QJHL	72	81	102	183	69	19	15	20	35	8
1981-82d	**Winnipeg**	**NHL**	**80**	**45**	**58**	**103**	**47**	**4**	**1**	**7**	**8**	**5**
1982-83	**Winnipeg**	**NHL**	**79**	**40**	**51**	**91**	**31**	**3**	**1**	**4**	**5**	**8**
1983-84	**Winnipeg**	**NHL**	**80**	**37**	**65**	**102**	**73**	**3**	**1**	**1**	**2**	**0**
1984-85e	**Winnipeg**	**NHL**	**80**	**53**	**77**	**130**	**74**	**3**	**2**	**1**	**3**	**4**
1985-86	**Winnipeg**	**NHL**	**80**	**46**	**59**	**105**	**44**	**3**	**0**	**3**	**3**	**0**
1986-87	**Winnipeg**	**NHL**	**80**	**47**	**53**	**100**	**52**	**10**	**5**	**8**	**13**	**4**
1987-88	**Winnipeg**	**NHL**	**80**	**44**	**77**	**121**	**59**	**5**	**3**	**4**	**7**	**16**
1988-89	**Winnipeg**	**NHL**	**75**	**41**	**55**	**96**	**28**	....	....	....	....	....
1989-90	**Winnipeg**	**NHL**	**79**	**26**	**55**	**81**	**60**	**7**	**3**	**5**	**8**	**2**
1990-91	**Buffalo**	**NHL**	**80**	**31**	**58**	**89**	**32**	**6**	**2**	**4**	**6**	**10**
	NHL Totals		**793**	**410**	**608**	**1018**	**500**	**44**	**18**	**37**	**55**	**49**

a QMJHL First All-Star Team (1981)
b QMJHL Player of the Year (1981)
c Canadian Major Junior Player of the Year (1981)
d Won Calder Memorial Trophy (1982)
e NHL Second All-Star Team (1985)

Played in NHL All-Star Game (1982, 1985, 1986, 1988)

Traded to **Buffalo** by **Winnipeg** with Winnipeg's first round choice (Brad May) in 1990 Entry Draft and future considerations for Phil Housley, Scott Arniel, Jeff Parker and Buffalo's first round choice (Keith Tkachuk) in 1990 Entry Draft, June 16, 1990.

HAWGOOD, GREG

Left wing/Defense. Shoots left. 5'8", 175 lbs. Born, Edmonton, Alta., August 10, 1968.
(Boston's 9th choice, 202nd overall, in 1986 Entry Draft).

			Regular Season					Playoffs				
Season	Club	Lea	GP	G	A	TP	PIM	GP	G	A	TP	PIM
1983-84	Kamloops	WHL	49	10	23	33	39	....	....	....	....	....
1984-85	Kamloops	WHL	66	25	40	65	72	....	....	....	....	....
1985-86	Kamloops	WHL	71	34	85	119	86	16	9	22	31	16
1986-87a	Kamloops	WHL	61	30	93	123	139	....	....	....	....	....
1987-88	**Boston**	**NHL**	**1**	**0**	**0**	**0**	**0**	**3**	**1**	**0**	**1**	**0**
a	Kamloops	WHL	63	48	85	133	142	16	10	16	26	33
1988-89	**Boston**	**NHL**	**56**	**16**	**24**	**40**	**84**	**10**	**0**	**2**	**2**	**2**
	Maine	AHL	21	2	9	11	41	....	....	....	....	....
1989-90	**Boston**	**NHL**	**77**	**11**	**27**	**38**	**76**	**15**	**1**	**3**	**4**	**12**
1990-91	Asiago	Italy	2	3	0	3	9	....	....	....	....	....
	Boston	**NHL**	**6**	**0**	**1**	**1**	**6**	....	....	....	....	....
	Maine	AHL	5	0	1	1	13	....	....	....	....	....
	Cape Breton	AHL	55	10	32	42	73	4	0	3	3	23
	NHL Totals		**140**	**27**	**52**	**79**	**166**	**28**	**2**	**5**	**7**	**16**

a WHL West All-Star Team (1986, 1987, 1988)

Traded to **Edmonton** by **Boston** for Vladimir Ruzicka, October 22, 1990.

HAWKINS, TODD

Left wing/Right wing. Shoots right. 6'1", 195 lbs. Born, Kingston, Ont., August 2, 1966.
(Vancouver's 10th choice, 217th overall, in 1986 Entry Draft).

			Regular Season					Playoffs				
Season	Club	Lea	GP	G	A	TP	PIM	GP	G	A	TP	PIM
1984-85	Belleville	OHL	58	7	16	23	117	12	1	0	1	10
1985-86	Belleville	OHL	60	14	13	27	172	24	9	7	16	60
1986-87	Belleville	OHL	60	47	40	87	187	6	3	5	8	16
1987-88	Flint	IHL	50	13	13	26	337	16	3	5	8	*174
	Fredericton	AHL	2	0	4	4	11	....	....	....	....	....
1988-89	**Vancouver**	**NHL**	**4**	**0**	**0**	**0**	**9**	....	....	....	....	....
	Milwaukee	IHL	63	12	14	26	307	9	1	0	1	33
1989-90	**Vancouver**	**NHL**	**4**	**0**	**0**	**0**	**6**	....	....	....	....	....
	Milwaukee	IHL	61	23	17	40	273	5	4	1	5	19
1990-91	Newmarket	AHL	22	2	5	7	66	....	....	....	....	....
	Milwaukee	IHL	39	9	11	20	134	....	....	....	....	....
	NHL Totals		**8**	**0**	**0**	**0**	**15**	....	....	....	....	....

Traded to **Toronto** by **Vancouver** for Brian Blad, January 22, 1991.

HAWLEY, JOE

Right wing. Shoots right. 5'10", 186 lbs. Born, Peterborough, Ont., March 13, 1971.
(St. Louis' 8th choice, 222nd overall, in 1990 Entry Draft).

			Regular Season					Playoffs				
Season	Club	Lea	GP	G	A	TP	PIM	GP	G	A	TP	PIM
1989-90	Peterborough	OHL	66	8	40	48	59	12	2	3	5	26
1990-91	Peterborough	OHL	63	17	47	64	70	4	2	3	5	11

HAWLEY, KENT

Center. Shoots left. 6'4", 215 lbs. Born, Kingston, Ont., February 20, 1968.
(Philadelphia's 3rd choice, 28th overall, in 1986 Entry Draft).

			Regular Season					Playoffs				
Season	Club	Lea	GP	G	A	TP	PIM	GP	G	A	TP	PIM
1985-86	Ottawa	OHL	64	21	30	51	96	....	....	....	....	....
1986-87	Ottawa	OHL	64	29	53	82	86	11	0	5	5	43
1987-88	Ottawa	OHL	55	29	48	77	84	16	7	6	13	20
1988-89	Hershey	AHL	54	9	17	26	47	....	....	....	....	....
1989-90	Hershey	AHL	24	6	4	10	28	....	....	....	....	....
	Hampton Roads	ECHL	13	5	6	11	12	5	2	3	5	17
1990-91	Hershey	AHL	6	1	1	2	4	....	....	....	....	....
	Hampton Roads	ECHL	43	17	28	45	95	14	5	9	14	32

HAWORTH, ALAN JOSEPH GORDON (HAW-worth)

Center. Shoots right. 5'10", 190 lbs. Born, Drummondville, Que., September 1, 1960.
(Buffalo's 6th choice, 95th overall, in 1979 Entry Draft).

			Regular Season					Playoffs				
Season	Club	Lea	GP	G	A	TP	PIM	GP	G	A	TP	PIM
1976-77	Chicoutimi	QJHL	68	11	18	29	15	....	....	....	....	....
1977-78	Chicoutimi	QJHL	59	17	33	50	40	....	....	....	....	....
1978-79	Sherbrooke	QJHL	70	50	70	120	63	12	6	10	16	8
1979-80	Sherbrooke	QJHL	45	28	36	64	50	15	11	16	27	4
1980-81	**Buffalo**	**NHL**	**49**	**16**	**20**	**36**	**34**	**7**	**4**	**4**	**8**	**2**
	Rochester	AHL	21	14	18	32	19	....	....	....	....	....
1981-82	**Buffalo**	**NHL**	**57**	**21**	**18**	**39**	**30**	**3**	**0**	**1**	**1**	**2**
	Rochester	AHL	14	5	12	17	10	....	....	....	....	....
1982-83	**Washington**	**NHL**	**74**	**23**	**27**	**50**	**34**	**4**	**0**	**0**	**0**	**2**
1983-84	**Washington**	**NHL**	**75**	**24**	**31**	**55**	**52**	**8**	**3**	**2**	**5**	**4**
1984-85	**Washington**	**NHL**	**76**	**23**	**26**	**49**	**48**	**5**	**1**	**0**	**1**	**0**
1985-86	**Washington**	**NHL**	**71**	**34**	**39**	**73**	**72**	**9**	**4**	**6**	**10**	**11**
1986-87	**Washington**	**NHL**	**50**	**25**	**16**	**41**	**43**	**6**	**0**	**3**	**3**	**7**
1987-88	**Quebec**	**NHL**	**72**	**23**	**34**	**57**	**112**	....	....	....	....	....
1988-89	Bern	Switz.	36	24	29	53	....	....	....	....	....	....
1989-90	Bern	Switz.	36	31	30	61	....	....	....	....	....	....
1990-91	Bern	Switz.	36	27	15	42	....	10	2	5	7	....
	NHL Totals		**524**	**189**	**211**	**400**	**425**	**42**	**12**	**16**	**28**	**0**

Traded to **Washington** by **Buffalo** with Buffalo's third round choice (Milan Novy) in 1982 Entry Draft for Washington's second round choice (Mike Anderson) and fourth round choice (Timo Jutila) in 1982 Entry Draft, June 9, 1982. Traded to **Quebec** by **Washington** with Gaetan Duchesne and Washington's first-round choice (Joe Sakic) in 1987 Entry Draft for Clint Malarchuk and Dale Hunter, June 13, 1987. Traded to **Minnesota** by **Quebec** for Guy Lafleur, May 31, 1991.

HAYES, MATTHEW (MATT)

Defense. Shoots left. 6'2", 195 lbs. Born, North Andover, MA, November 7, 1969.
(St. Louis' 7th choice, 135th overall, in 1988 Entry Draft).

			Regular Season					Playoffs				
Season	Club	Lea	GP	G	A	TP	PIM	GP	G	A	TP	PIM
1988-89	U. of Lowell	H.E.	30	0	4	4	30	....	....	....	....	....
1989-90	U. of Lowell	H.E.	14	0	1	1	10	....	....	....	....	....
1990-91	U. of Lowell	H.E.		DID NOT PLAY								

HAYWARD, RICK

Defense. Shoots left. 6.', 180 lbs. Born, Toledo, OH, February 25, 1966.
(Montreal's 9th choice, 162nd overall, in 1986 Entry Draft).

			Regular Season					Playoffs				
Season	Club	Lea	GP	G	A	TP	PIM	GP	G	A	TP	PIM
1984-85	Hull	QMJHL	56	7	27	34	367	....	....	....	....	....
1985-86	Hull	QMJHL	59	3	40	43	354	15	2	11	13	98
1986-87	Sherbrooke	AHL	46	2	3	5	153	3	0	1	1	15
1987-88	Saginaw	IHL	24	3	4	7	129					
	Salt Lake	IHL	17	1	3	4	124	13	0	1	1	120
1988-89	Salt Lake	IHL	72	4	20	24	313	10	4	3	7	42
1989-90	Salt Lake	IHL	58	5	13	18	419	....	....	....	....	....
1990-91	**Los Angeles**	**NHL**	**4**	**0**	**0**	**0**	**5**	....	....	....	....	....
	Phoenix	IHL	60	9	13	22	369	7	1	2	3	44
	NHL Totals		**4**	**0**	**0**	**0**	**5**	....	....	....	....	....

Traded to **Calgary** by **Montreal** for Martin Nicoletti, February 20, 1988.

HEAPHY, SHAWN

Center. Shoots left. 5'8", 175 lbs.   Born, Sudbury, Ont., November 27, 1968.
(Calgary's 1st choice, 26th overall, in 1989 Supplemental Draft).

			Regular Season					Playoffs				
Season	Club	Lea	GP	G	A	TP	PIM	GP	G	A	TP	PIM
1987-88	Michigan State	CCHA	44	19	24	43	48	.....	.....	....	....	....
1988-89	Michigan State	CCHA	47	26	17	43	80	.....	.....	....	....	....
1989-90	Michigan State	CCHA	45	28	31	59	54	.....	.....	....	....	....
1990-91	Michigan State	CCHA	39	30	19	49	57	.....	.....	....	....	....
	Salt Lake	IHL	.....	.....	....	....	....	1	0	0	0	0

HEDICAN, BRETT

Left wing. Shoots left. 6'2", 188 lbs.   Born, St. Paul, MN, August 10, 1970.
(St. Louis' 10th choice, 198th overall, in 1988 Entry Draft).

			Regular Season					Playoffs				
Season	Club	Lea	GP	G	A	TP	PIM	GP	G	A	TP	PIM
1988-89	St. Cloud	NCAA	28	5	3	8	28	.....	.....	....	....	....
1989-90	St. Cloud	NCAA	36	4	17	21	37	.....	.....	....	....	....
1990-91a	St. Cloud	WCHA	41	21	26	47	26	.....	.....	....	....	....

a WCHA First All-Star Team (1991)

HEDLUND, TODD

Right wing. Shoots right. 6'1", 177 lbs.   Born, Roseau, MN, August 20, 1971.
(NY Rangers' 10th choice, 160th overall, in 1990 Entry Draft).

			Regular Season					Playoffs				
Season	Club	Lea	GP	G	A	TP	PIM	GP	G	A	TP	PIM
1988-89	Roseau	HS	24	8	11	19	....	.....	.....	....	....	....
1989-90	Roseau	HS	28	16	12	28	....	.....	.....	....	....	....
1990-91	U. Wisconsin	WCHA	DID NOT PLAY									

HEED, JONAS   (HAD)

Defense. Shoots left. 6', 174 lbs.   Born, Sodertalje, Sweden, January 3, 1967.
(Chicago's 6th choice, 116th overall, in 1985 Entry Draft).

			Regular Season					Playoffs				
Season	Club	Lea	GP	G	A	TP	PIM	GP	G	A	TP	PIM
1984-85	Sodertalje	Swe.	8	0	0	0	0	.....	.....	....	....	....
1985-86	Sodertalje	Swe.	17	3	2	5	6	.....	.....	....	....	....
1986-87	Sodertalje	Swe.	24	0	3	3	12	2	0	0	0	0
1987-88	Sodertalje	Swe.	26	1	4	5	12	.....	.....	....	....	....
1988-89	Sodertalje	Swe.	38	4	9	13	22	.....	.....	....	....	....
1989-90	Sodertalje	Swe.	36	7	4	11	28	2	0	0	0	0
1990-91	V. Frolunda	Swe.2	21	1	1	2	14	.....	.....	....	....	....

HEINZE, STEPHEN

Center. Shoots right. 5'11", 180 lbs.   Born, Lawrence, MA, January 30, 1970.
(Boston's 2nd choice, 60th overall, in 1988 Entry Draft).

			Regular Season					Playoffs				
Season	Club	Lea	GP	G	A	TP	PIM	GP	G	A	TP	PIM
1988-89	Boston College	H.E.	36	26	23	49	26	.....	.....	....	....	....
1989-90ab	Boston College	H.E.	40	27	36	63	41	.....	.....	....	....	....
1990-91	Boston College	H.E.	35	21	26	47	35	.....	.....	....	....	....

a Hockey East First All-Star Team (1990)
b NCAA East First All-American Team (1990)

HEJNA, TONY

Left wing. Shoots left. 6', 190 lbs.   Born, Buffalo, NY, January 8, 1968.
(St. Louis' 3rd choice, 52nd overall, in 1986 Entry Draft).

			Regular Season					Playoffs				
Season	Club	Lea	GP	G	A	TP	PIM	GP	G	A	TP	PIM
1986-87	RPI	ECAC	31	12	18	30	18	.....	.....	....	....	....
1987-88	RPI	ECAC	32	17	19	36	48	.....	.....	....	....	....
1988-89	RPI	ECAC	29	12	9	21	14	.....	.....	....	....	....
1989-90	RPI	ECAC	26	20	16	36	22	.....	.....	....	....	....
1990-91	Peoria	IHL	54	7	5	12	19	.....	.....	....	....	....

HELBER, MICHAEL

Center. Shoots right. 5'11", 175 lbs.   Born, Ann Arbor, MI, June 23, 1970.
(Winnipeg's 11th choice, 178th overall, in 1988 Entry Draft).

			Regular Season					Playoffs				
Season	Club	Lea	GP	G	A	TP	PIM	GP	G	A	TP	PIM
1988-89	U. of Michigan	CCHA	35	8	10	18	15	.....	.....	....	....	....
1989-90	U. of Michigan	CCHA	20	3	2	5	8	.....	.....	....	....	....
1990-91	U. of Michigan	CCHA	37	15	22	37	45	.....	.....	....	....	....

HELGESON, JON

Center. Shoots left. 6'4", 210 lbs.   Born, Roseau, MN, August 15, 1968.
(Vancouver's 6th choice, 133rd overall, in 1986 Entry Draft).

			Regular Season					Playoffs				
Season	Club	Lea	GP	G	A	TP	PIM	GP	G	A	TP	PIM
1987-88	U. Wisconsin	WCHA	5	0	2	2	2	.....	.....	....	....	....
1988-89	U. Wisconsin	WCHA	36	7	1	8	28	.....	.....	....	....	....
1989-90	U. Wisconsin	WCHA	18	2	2	4	12	.....	.....	....	....	....
1990-91	U. Wisconsin	WCHA	19	3	1	4	18	.....	.....	....	....	....

HENDRICKSON, DARBY

Center. Shoots left. 6', 175 lbs.   Born, Richfield, MN, August 28, 1972.
(Toronto's 3rd choice, 73rd overall, in 1990 Entry Draft).

			Regular Season					Playoffs				
Season	Club	Lea	GP	G	A	TP	PIM	GP	G	A	TP	PIM
1989-90	Richfield	HS	22	23	27	50	30	.....	.....	....	....	....
1990-91	Richfield	HS	27	32	29	61	....	.....	.....	....	....	....

HENDRY, JOHN

Left wing. Shoots left. 6'1", 180 lbs.   Born, Mississauga, Ont., May 15, 1970.
(Detroit's 11th choice, 234th overall, in 1990 Entry Draft).

			Regular Season					Playoffs				
Season	Club	Lea	GP	G	A	TP	PIM	GP	G	A	TP	PIM
1989-90	Lake Superior	CCHA	41	4	7	11	30	.....	.....	....	....	....
1990-91	Lake Superior	CCHA	44	7	10	17	42	.....	.....	....	....	....

HENRICH, ED

Defense. Shoots left. 6'1", 192 lbs.   Born, Buffalo, NY, February 4, 1971.
(Montreal's 10th choice, 209th overall, in 1989 Entry Draft).

			Regular Season					Playoffs				
Season	Club	Lea	GP	G	A	TP	PIM	GP	G	A	TP	PIM
1989-90	Nichols	HS	29	3	32	35	28	.....	.....	....	....	....
1990-91	Clarkson	ECAC	37	4	23	27	22	.....	.....	....	....	....

HENRY, DALE

Left wing. Shoots left. 6', 205 lbs.   Born, Prince Albert, Sask., September 24, 1964.
(New York Islanders' 10th choice, 163rd overall, in 1983 Entry Draft).

			Regular Season					Playoffs				
Season	Club	Lea	GP	G	A	TP	PIM	GP	G	A	TP	PIM
1981-82	Saskatoon	WHL	32	5	4	9	50	5	0	0	0	0
1982-83	Saskatoon	WHL	63	21	19	40	213	3	0	0	0	12
1983-84	Saskatoon	WHL	71	41	36	77	162	.....	.....	....	....	....
1984-85	**NY Islanders**	**NHL**	16	2	1	3	19	.....	.....	....	....	....
	Springfield	AHL	67	11	20	31	133	4	0	0	0	13
1985-86	**NY Islanders**	**NHL**	7	1	3	4	15	.....	.....	....	....	....
	Springfield	AHL	64	14	26	40	162	.....	.....	....	....	....
1986-87	**NY Islanders**	**NHL**	19	3	3	6	46	8	0	0	0	2
	Springfield	AHL	23	9	14	23	49	.....	.....	....	....	....
1987-88	**NY Islanders**	**NHL**	48	5	15	20	115	6	1	0	1	17
	Springfield	AHL	24	9	12	21	103	.....	.....	....	....	....
1988-89	**NY Islanders**	**NHL**	22	2	2	4	66	.....	.....	....	....	....
	Springfield	AHL	50	13	21	34	83	.....	.....	....	....	....
1989-90	**NY Islanders**	**NHL**	20	0	2	2	2	.....	.....	....	....	....
	Springfield	AHL	43	17	14	31	68	18	3	5	8	33
1990-91	Albany	IHL	55	16	22	38	87	.....	.....	....	....	....
	Springfield	AHL	20	5	9	14	31	18	2	7	9	24
	NHL Totals		**132**	**13**	**26**	**39**	**263**	**14**	**1**	**0**	**1**	**19**

HENTGES, MATHEW

Defense. Shoots left. 6'5", 197 lbs.   Born, St. Paul, MN, December 19, 1969.
(Chicago's 8th choice, 176th overall, in 1988 Entry Draft).

			Regular Season					Playoffs				
Season	Club	Lea	GP	G	A	TP	PIM	GP	G	A	TP	PIM
1988-89	Merrimack	NCAA	33	0	16	16	22	.....	.....	....	....	....
1989-90	Merrimack	H.E.	33	1	2	3	40	.....	.....	....	....	....
1990-91	Merrimack	H.E.	32	0	7	7	24	.....	.....	....	....	....

HEPPLE, ALAN

Defense. Shoots left. 5'9", 200 lbs.   Born, Blaydon-on-Tyne, England, August 16, 1963.
(New Jersey's 9th choice, 169th overall, in 1982 Entry Draft).

			Regular Season					Playoffs				
Season	Club	Lea	GP	G	A	TP	PIM	GP	G	A	TP	PIM
1980-81	Ottawa	OHL	64	3	13	16	110	6	0	1	1	2
1981-82	Ottawa	OHL	66	6	22	28	160	17	2	10	12	84
1982-83	Ottawa	OHL	64	10	26	36	168	9	2	1	3	24
1983-84	**New Jersey**	**NHL**	1	0	0	0	7	.....	.....	....	....	....
	Maine	AHL	64	4	23	27	117	.....	.....	....	....	....
1984-85	**New Jersey**	**NHL**	1	0	0	0	0	.....	.....	....	....	....
	Maine	AHL	80	7	17	24	125	11	0	3	3	30
1985-86	**New Jersey**	**NHL**	1	0	0	0	0	.....	.....	....	....	....
	Maine	AHL	69	4	21	25	104	5	0	0	0	11
1986-87	Maine	AHL	74	6	19	25	137	.....	.....	....	....	....
1987-88	Utica	AHL	78	3	16	19	213	.....	.....	....	....	....
1988-89	Newmarket	AHL	72	5	29	34	122	5	0	1	1	23
1989-90	Newmarket	AHL	72	6	20	26	90	.....	.....	....	....	....
1990-91	Newmarket	AHL	76	0	18	18	126	.....	.....	....	....	....
	NHL Totals		**3**	**0**	**0**	**0**	**7**	.....	.....	....	....	....

Signed as a free agent by **Toronto**, June 24, 1988.

HERNIMAN, STEVE

Defense. Shoots left. 6'4", 210 lbs.   Born, Windsor, Ont., June 9, 1968.
(Vancouver's 5th choice, 112th overall, in 1986 Entry Draft).

			Regular Season					Playoffs				
Season	Club	Lea	GP	G	A	TP	PIM	GP	G	A	TP	PIM
1985-86	Cornwall	OHL	55	3	12	15	128	6	0	0	0	2
1986-87	Cornwall	OHL	64	2	8	10	121	3	0	0	0	0
1987-88	Cornwall	OHL	5	1	0	1	8	.....	.....	....	....	....
	S.S. Marie	OHL	52	3	14	17	111	6	0	1	1	18
1988-89	Kitchener	OHL	61	3	16	19	112	5	0	0	0	4
1989-90	Milwaukee	IHL	15	0	0	0	102	.....	.....	....	....	....
	Virginia	ECHL	31	2	4	6	238	3	0	0	0	29
1990-91	Milwaukee	IHL	38	0	0	0	86	.....	.....	....	....	....
	Albany	IHL	7	0	1	1	36	.....	.....	....	....	....

HEROUX, YVES   (ay-ROO, EEV)

Right wing. Shoots right. 5'11", 185 lbs.   Born, Terrebonne, Que., April 27, 1965.
(Quebec's 1st choice, 32nd overall, in 1983 Entry Draft).

			Regular Season					Playoffs				
Season	Club	Lea	GP	G	A	TP	PIM	GP	G	A	TP	PIM
1982-83	Chicoutimi	QMJHL	70	41	40	81	44	5	0	4	4	8
1983-84	Chicoutimi	QMJHL	56	28	25	53	67	.....	.....	....	....	....
	Fredericton	AHL	4	0	0	0	0	.....	.....	....	....	....
1984-85	Chicoutimi	QMJHL	66	42	54	96	123	14	5	8	13	16
1985-86	Fredericton	AHL	31	12	10	22	42	2	0	1	1	7
	Muskegon	IHL	42	14	8	22	41	.....	.....	....	....	....
1986-87	**Quebec**	**NHL**	1	0	0	0	0	.....	.....	....	....	....
	Fredericton	AHL	37	8	6	14	13	.....	.....	....	....	....
	Muskegon	IHL	25	6	8	14	31	2	0	0	0	0
1987-88	Baltimore	AHL	5	0	2	2	2	.....	.....	....	....	....
1988-89	Flint	IHL	82	43	42	85	98	.....	.....	....	....	....
1989-90	Peoria	IHL	14	3	2	5	42	5	2	2	4	0
1990-91	Albany	IHL	45	22	18	40	46	.....	.....	....	....	....
	Peoria	IHL	33	16	8	24	26	17	4	4	8	16
	NHL Totals		**1**	**0**	**0**	**0**	**0**	.....	.....	....	....	....

Signed as a free agent by **St. Louis**, March 13, 1990.

HERTER, JASON

Defense. Shoots right. 6'1", 182 lbs. Born, Hafford, Sask., October 2, 1970.
(Vancouver's 1st choice, 8th overall, in 1989 Entry Draft).

			Regular Season					Playoffs				
Season	**Club**	**Lea**	**GP**	**G**	**A**	**TP**	**PIM**	**GP**	**G**	**A**	**TP**	**PIM**
1988-89	North Dakota	WCHA	41	8	24	32	62	....	....	....	....	....
1989-90a	North Dakota	WCHA	38	11	39	50	40	....	....	....	....	....
1990-91a	North Dakota	WCHA	39	11	26	37	52	....	....	....	....	....

a WCHA Second All-Star Team (1990, 1991)

HERVEY, MATT

Defense. Shoots right. 5'11", 205 lbs. Born, Whittier, CA, May 16, 1966.

			Regular Season					Playoffs				
Season	**Club**	**Lea**	**GP**	**G**	**A**	**TP**	**PIM**	**GP**	**G**	**A**	**TP**	**PIM**
1983-84	Victoria	WHL	67	4	19	23	89	....	....	....	....	....
1984-85	Victoria	WHL	14	1	3	4	17	....	....	....	....	....
	Lethbridge	WHL	54	3	9	12	88	....	....	....	....	....
1985-86	Lethbridge	WHL	60	9	17	26	110	....	....	....	....	....
1986-87	Seattle	WHL	66	4	5	9	59	....	....	....	....	....
1987-88	Moncton	AHL	69	9	20	29	265	....	....	....	....	....
1988-89	**Winnipeg**	**NHL**	**2**	**0**	**0**	**0**	**4**	....	....	....	....	....
	Moncton	AHL	73	8	28	36	295	10	1	2	3	42
1989-90	Moncton	AHL	47	3	13	16	168	....	....	....	....	....
1990-91	Moncton	AHL	71	4	28	32	132	7	0	1	1	23
	NHL Totals		**2**	**0**	**0**	**0**	**4**	....	....	....	....	....

Signed as a free agent by **Winnipeg**, September 27, 1988.

HEWARD, JAMIE

Right wing. Shoots right. 6'2", 183 lbs. Born, Regina, Sask., March 30, 1971.
(Pittsburgh's 1st choice, 16th overall, in 1989 Entry Draft).

			Regular Season					Playoffs				
Season	**Club**	**Lea**	**GP**	**G**	**A**	**TP**	**PIM**	**GP**	**G**	**A**	**TP**	**PIM**
1987-88	Regina	WHL	68	10	17	27	17	4	1	1	2	2
1988-89	Regina	WHL	52	31	28	59	29	....	....	....	....	....
1989-90	Regina	WHL	72	14	44	58	42	11	2	2	4	10
1990-91a	Regina	WHL	71	23	61	84	41	8	2	9	11	6

a WHL East First All-Star Team (1991)

HEXTALL, DONEVAN

Left wing. Shoots left. 6'2", 192 lbs. Born, Wolseley, Sask., February 24, 1972.
(New Jersey's 3rd choice, 33rd overall, in 1991 Entry Draft).

			Regular Season					Playoffs				
Season	**Club**	**Lea**	**GP**	**G**	**A**	**TP**	**PIM**	**GP**	**G**	**A**	**TP**	**PIM**
1989-90	Weyburn	SJHL	63	23	45	68	127	....	....	....	....	....
1990-91	Prince Albert	WHL	70	30	59	89	55	3	1	3	4	0

HILDITCH, TODD

Defense. Shoots right. 6'1", 200 lbs. Born, Vancouver, B.C., March 13, 1968.
(Washington's 9th choice, 162nd overall, in 1988 Entry Draft).

			Regular Season					Playoffs				
Season	**Club**	**Lea**	**GP**	**G**	**A**	**TP**	**PIM**	**GP**	**G**	**A**	**TP**	**PIM**
1988-89	RPI	ECAC	29	1	1	2	56	....	....	....	....	....
1989-90	RPI	ECAC	33	1	3	4	48	....	....	....	....	....
1990-91	RPI	ECAC	32	3	10	13	77	....	....	....	....	....

HILL, SEAN

Defense. Shoots right. 6', 195 lbs. Born, Duluth, MN, February 14, 1970.
(Montreal's 9th choice, 167th overall, in 1988 Entry Draft).

			Regular Season					Playoffs				
Season	**Club**	**Lea**	**GP**	**G**	**A**	**TP**	**PIM**	**GP**	**G**	**A**	**TP**	**PIM**
1988-89	U. Wisconsin	WCHA	45	2	23	25	69	....	....	....	....	....
1989-90a	U. Wisconsin	WCHA	42	14	39	53	78	....	....	....	....	....
1990-91ab	U. Wisconsin	WCHA	37	19	32	51	122	....	....	....	....	....
	Montreal	**NHL**	....	....	....	....	....	**1**	**0**	**0**	**0**	**0**
	Fredericton	AHL	....	....	....	....	....	3	0	2	2	2
	NHL Totals		....	....	....	....	....	**1**	**0**	**0**	**0**	**0**

a WCHA Second All-Star Team (1990, 1991)
b NCAA West Second All-American Team (1991)

HILLER, JIM

Right wing. Shoots right. 6', 190 lbs. Born, Port Alberni, B.C., May 15, 1969.
(Los Angeles' 10th choice, 207th overall, in 1989 Entry Draft).

			Regular Season					Playoffs				
Season	**Club**	**Lea**	**GP**	**G**	**A**	**TP**	**PIM**	**GP**	**G**	**A**	**TP**	**PIM**
1989-90	N. Michigan	WCHA	39	23	33	56	52	....	....	....	....	....
1990-91	N. Michigan	WCHA	43	22	41	63	59	....	....	....	....	....

HILLIER, RANDY GEORGE (HIHL-yuhr)

Defense. Shoots right. 6'1", 192 lbs. Born, Toronto, Ont., March 30, 1960.
(Boston's 4th choice, 102nd overall, in 1980 Entry Draft).

			Regular Season					Playoffs				
Season	**Club**	**Lea**	**GP**	**G**	**A**	**TP**	**PIM**	**GP**	**G**	**A**	**TP**	**PIM**
1978-79	Sudbury	OHA	61	8	25	33	173	10	2	5	7	21
1979-80	Sudbury	OHA	60	16	49	65	143	9	3	6	9	14
1980-81	Springfield	AHL	64	3	17	20	105	6	0	2	2	36
1981-82	Erie	AHL	35	6	13	19	52	....	....	....	....	....
	Boston	**NHL**	**25**	**0**	**8**	**8**	**29**	**8**	**0**	**1**	**1**	**16**
1982-83	**Boston**	**NHL**	**70**	**0**	**10**	**10**	**99**	**3**	**0**	**0**	**0**	**4**
1983-84	**Boston**	**NHL**	**69**	**3**	**12**	**15**	**125**	....	....	....	....	....
1984-85	**Pittsburgh**	**NHL**	**45**	**2**	**19**	**21**	**56**	....	....	....	....	....
1985-86	**Pittsburgh**	**NHL**	**28**	**0**	**3**	**3**	**53**	....	....	....	....	....
	Baltimore	AHL	8	0	5	5	14	....	....	....	....	....
1986-87	**Pittsburgh**	**NHL**	**55**	**4**	**8**	**12**	**97**	....	....	....	....	....
1987-88	**Pittsburgh**	**NHL**	**55**	**1**	**12**	**13**	**144**	....	....	....	....	....
1988-89	**Pittsburgh**	**NHL**	**68**	**1**	**23**	**24**	**141**	**9**	**0**	**1**	**1**	**49**
1989-90	**Pittsburgh**	**NHL**	**61**	**3**	**12**	**15**	**71**	....	....	....	....	....
1990-91	**Pittsburgh**	**NHL**	**31**	**2**	**2**	**4**	**32**	**8**	**0**	**0**	**0**	**24**
	NHL Totals		**507**	**16**	**109**	**125**	**847**	**28**	**0**	**2**	**2**	**93**

Traded to **Pittsburgh** by **Boston** for Pittsburgh's fourth round choice in 1985 Entry Draft (later traded to Quebec), October 15, 1984. Signed as a free agent by **NY Islanders**, June 30, 1991.

HLUSHKO, TODD

Left wing. Shoots left. 5'11", 180 lbs. Born, Toronto, Ont., February 7, 1970.
(Washington's 14th choice, 240th overall, in 1989 Entry Draft).

			Regular Season					Playoffs				
Season	**Club**	**Lea**	**GP**	**G**	**A**	**TP**	**PIM**	**GP**	**G**	**A**	**TP**	**PIM**
1988-89	Guelph	OHL	66	28	18	46	71	7	5	3	8	18
1989-90	London	OHL	65	36	34	70	70	6	2	4	6	10
1990-91	Baltimore	AHL	66	9	14	23	55	....	....	....	....	....

HODGE, KENNETH (KEN)

Center/Right wing. Shoots left. 6'1", 200 lbs. Born, Windsor, Ont., April 13, 1966.
(Minnesota's 2nd choice, 46th overall, in 1984 Entry Draft).

			Regular Season					Playoffs				
Season	**Club**	**Lea**	**GP**	**G**	**A**	**TP**	**PIM**	**GP**	**G**	**A**	**TP**	**PIM**
1984-85	Boston College	H.E.	41	20	44	64	28	....	....	....	....	....
1985-86	Boston College	H.E.	21	11	17	28	16	....	....	....	....	....
1986-87	Boston College	H.E.	37	29	33	62	30	....	....	....	....	....
1987-88	Kalamazoo	IHL	70	15	35	50	24	....	....	....	....	....
1988-89	**Minnesota**	**NHL**	**5**	**1**	**1**	**2**	**0**	....	....	....	....	....
	Kalamazoo	IHL	72	26	45	71	34	6	1	5	6	16
1989-90	Kalamazoo	IHL	68	33	53	86	19	10	5	13	18	2
1990-91a	**Boston**	**NHL**	**70**	**30**	**29**	**59**	**20**	**15**	**4**	**6**	**10**	**6**
	Maine	AHL	8	7	10	17	2	....	....	....	....	....
	NHL Totals		**75**	**31**	**30**	**61**	**20**	**15**	**4**	**6**	**10**	**6**

a NHL/Upper Deck All-Rookie Team (1991)

Traded to **Boston** by **Minnesota** for future considerations, August 21, 1990.

HODGSON, DANIEL (DAN)

Center. Shoots right. 5'10", 165 lbs. Born, Fort Vermillion, Alta., August 29, 1965.
(Toronto's 4th choice, 83rd overall, in 1983 Entry Draft).

			Regular Season					Playoffs				
Season	**Club**	**Lea**	**GP**	**G**	**A**	**TP**	**PIM**	**GP**	**G**	**A**	**TP**	**PIM**
1982-83a	Prince Albert	WHL	72	56	74	130	66	....	....	....	....	....
1983-84b	Prince Albert	WHL	66	62	*119	181	65	5	5	3	8	7
1984-85cde	Prince Albert	WHL	64	70	*112	182	86	13	10	*26	*36	32
1985-86	**Toronto**	**NHL**	**40**	**13**	**12**	**25**	**12**	....	....	....	....	....
	St. Catharines	AHL	22	13	16	29	15	13	3	9	12	14
1986-87	Newmarket	AHL	20	7	12	19	16	....	....	....	....	....
	Vancouver	**NHL**	**43**	**9**	**13**	**22**	**25**	....	....	....	....	....
1987-88	**Vancouver**	**NHL**	**8**	**3**	**7**	**10**	**2**	....	....	....	....	....
	Fredericton	AHL	13	8	18	26	16	....	....	....	....	....
1988-89	**Vancouver**	**NHL**	**23**	**4**	**13**	**17**	**25**	....	....	....	....	....
	Milwaukee	IHL	47	27	55	82	47	11	6	7	13	10
1989-90	Gotteron	Switz.	36	17	22	39	....	....	....	....	....	....
1990-91	Munich	Ger.	26	11	17	28	23	....	....	....	....	....
	NHL Totals		**114**	**29**	**45**	**74**	**64**	....	....	....	....	....

a WHL Rookie of the Year (1983)
b WHL Second Team All-Star (1984)
c WHL First Team All-Star (1985)
d Named WHL Player of the Year (1985)
e Canadian Major Junior Player of the Year (1985)

Traded to **Vancouver** by **Toronto** with Jim Benning for Rick Lanz, December 2, 1986.

HOGUE, BENOIT (HOHG)

Center. Shoots left. 5'10", 190 lbs. Born, Repentigny, Que., October 28, 1966.
(Buffalo's 2nd choice, 35th overall, in 1985 Entry Draft).

			Regular Season					Playoffs				
Season	**Club**	**Lea**	**GP**	**G**	**A**	**TP**	**PIM**	**GP**	**G**	**A**	**TP**	**PIM**
1983-84	St. Jean	QMJHL	59	14	11	25	42	....	....	....	....	....
1984-85	St. Jean	QMJHL	63	46	44	90	92	....	....	....	....	....
1985-86	St. Jean	QMJHL	65	54	54	108	115	9	6	4	10	26
1986-87	Rochester	AHL	52	14	20	34	52	12	5	4	9	8
1987-88	**Buffalo**	**NHL**	**3**	**1**	**1**	**2**	**0**	....	....	....	....	....
	Rochester	AHL	62	24	31	55	141	7	6	1	7	46
1988-89	**Buffalo**	**NHL**	**69**	**14**	**30**	**44**	**120**	**5**	**0**	**0**	**0**	**17**
1989-90	**Buffalo**	**NHL**	**45**	**11**	**7**	**18**	**79**	**3**	**0**	**0**	**0**	**10**
1990-91	**Buffalo**	**NHL**	**76**	**19**	**28**	**47**	**76**	**5**	**3**	**1**	**4**	**10**
	NHL Totals		**193**	**45**	**66**	**111**	**275**	**13**	**3**	**1**	**4**	**37**

HOHENBERGER, HERBERT

Defense. Shoots right. 5'11", 184 lbs.   Born, Villach, Austria, February 8, 1969.

			Regular Season					Playoffs			
Season	Club	Lea	GP	G	A	TP	PIM	GP	G	A	TP	PIM
1986-87	Hull	QMJHL	68	20	23	43	105	8	3	3	6	12
1987-88	Hull	QMJHL	60	21	39	60	94	19	5	11	16	34
1988-89	Villach	Aus.	40	20	23	43	120	6	4	3	7	20
1989-90	Hull	QMJHL	65	16	50	66	125	11	3	7	10	10
	Sherbrooke	AHL	....	....	....	....	....	4	1	0	1	6
1990-91	Fredericton	AHL	38	4	11	15	47	....	....	....	....	....
	Peoria	IHL	27	2	7	9	17	10	0	1	1	6

Signed as a free agent by **Montreal**, June 18, 1990.

HOLDEMAN, TOM

Right wing. Shoots right. 6'2", 205 lbs.   Born, Columbus, IN, November 8, 1970.
(Edmonton's 1st choice, 18th overall, in 1991 Supplemental Draft).

			Regular Season					Playoffs			
Season	Club	Lea	GP	G	A	TP	PIM	GP	G	A	TP	PIM
1989-90	Miami-Ohio	CCHA	28	3	1	4	8	....	....	....	....	....
1990-91	Miami-Ohio	CCHA	28	2	2	4	42	....	....	....	....	....

HOLDEN, PAUL

Defense. Shoots left. 6'3", 210 lbs.   Born, Kitchener, Ont., March 15, 1970.
(Los Angeles' 2nd choice, 28th overall, in 1988 Entry Draft).

			Regular Season					Playoffs			
Season	Club	Lea	GP	G	A	TP	PIM	GP	G	A	TP	PIM
1987-88	London	OHL	65	8	12	20	87	12	1	1	2	10
1988-89	London	OHL	54	11	21	32	90	20	1	3	4	17
1989-90a	London	OHL	61	11	31	42	78	6	1	1	2	7
	New Haven	AHL	2	1	1	2	2	....	....	....	....	....
1990-91	New Haven	AHL	59	2	8	10	23	....	....	....	....	....

a OHL Second All-Star Team (1990)

HOLIK, ROBERT (BOBBY)   (HOH-leek)

Left Wing. Shoots right. 6'3", 210 lbs.   Born, Jihlava, Czechoslovakia, January 1, 1971.
(Hartford's 1st choice, 10th overall, in 1989 Entry Draft).

			Regular Season					Playoffs			
Season	Club	Lea	GP	G	A	TP	PIM	GP	G	A	TP	PIM
1987-88	Dukla Jihlava	Czech.	31	5	9	14	....	....	....	....	....	....
1988-89	Dukla Jihlava	Czech.	24	7	10	17	....	....	....	....	....	....
1989-90	Dukla Jihlava	Czech.	42	15	26	41	....	....	....	....	....	....
1990-91	Hartford	NHL	78	21	22	43	113	6	0	0	0	7
	NHL Totals		**78**	**21**	**22**	**43**	**113**	**6**	**0**	**0**	**0**	**7**

HOLLAND, DENNIS

Center. Shoots left. 5'10", 165 lbs.   Born, Vernon, B.C., January 30, 1969.
(Detroit's 4th choice, 52nd overall, in 1987 Entry Draft).

			Regular Season					Playoffs			
Season	Club	Lea	GP	G	A	TP	PIM	GP	G	A	TP	PIM
1986-87a	Portland	WHL	72	36	77	113	96	20	7	14	21	20
1987-88b	Portland	WHL	67	58	86	144	115	....	....	....	....	....
1988-89bc	Portland	WHL	69	*82	85	*167	120	19	15	*22	*37	18
1989-90	Adirondack	AHL	78	19	34	53	53	6	1	1	2	10
1990-91	San Diego	IHL	45	25	30	55	129	....	....	....	....	....
	Adirondack	AHL	28	8	7	15	31	2	0	0	0	4

a WHL Rookie of the Year (1987)
b WHL West All-Star Team (1988, 1989)
c WHL Player of the Year (1989)

HOLLYMAN, RHYS

Defense. Shoots right. 6'3", 210 lbs.   Born, Toronto, Ont., January 30, 1970.
(Minnesota's 7th choice, 97th overall, in 1989 Entry Draft).

			Regular Season					Playoffs			
Season	Club	Lea	GP	G	A	TP	PIM	GP	G	A	TP	PIM
1988-89	Miami-Ohio	CCHA	33	8	5	13	60	....	....	....	....	....
1989-90	Miami-Ohio	CCHA	37	2	8	10	54	....	....	....	....	....
1990-91	Miami-Ohio	CCHA	24	7	10	17	39	....	....	....	....	....

HOOVER, RON

Center. Shoots left. 6'1", 185 lbs.   Born, Oakville, Ont., October 28, 1966.
(Hartford's 7th choice, 158th overall, in 1986 Entry Draft).

			Regular Season					Playoffs			
Season	Club	Lea	GP	G	A	TP	PIM	GP	G	A	TP	PIM
1985-86	W. Michigan	CCHA	43	10	23	33	36	....	....	....	....	....
1986-87	W. Michigan	CCHA	34	7	10	17	22	....	....	....	....	....
1987-88a	W. Michigan	CCHA	42	39	23	62	40	....	....	....	....	....
1988-89	W. Michigan	CCHA	42	32	27	59	66	....	....	....	....	....
1989-90	Boston	NHL	2	0	0	0	0	....	....	....	....	....
	Maine	AHL	75	28	26	54	57	....	....	....	....	....
1990-91	Boston	NHL	15	4	0	4	31	8	0	0	0	18
	Maine	AHL	62	28	16	44	40	....	....	....	....	....
	NHL Totals		**17**	**4**	**0**	**4**	**31**	**8**	**0**	**0**	**0**	**18**

a CCHA Second All-Star Team (1988)
Signed as a free agent by **Boston**, September 1, 1989.

HOPKINS, DEAN ROBERT

Right wing. Shoots right. 6'1", 210 lbs.   Born, Cobourg, Ont., June 6, 1959.
(Los Angeles' 2nd choice, 29th overall, in 1979 Entry Draft).

			Regular Season					Playoffs			
Season	Club	Lea	GP	G	A	TP	PIM	GP	G	A	TP	PIM
1977-78	London	OHA	67	19	34	53	70	11	1	5	6	24
1978-79	London	OHA	65	37	55	92	149	7	6	0	6	27
1979-80	Los Angeles	NHL	60	8	6	14	39	4	0	1	1	5
1980-81	Los Angeles	NHL	67	8	18	26	118	4	0	1	1	9
1981-82	Los Angeles	NHL	41	2	13	15	102	10	0	4	4	15
1982-83	Los Angeles	NHL	49	5	12	17	43	....	....	....	....	....
	New Haven	AHL	20	9	8	17	58	....	....	....	....	....
1983-84	New Haven	AHL	79	35	47	82	162	....	....	....	....	....
1984-85	New Haven	AHL	20	7	10	17	38	....	....	....	....	....
	Nova Scotia	AHL	49	13	17	30	93	6	1	2	3	20
1985-86	Edmonton	NHL	1	0	0	0	0	....	....	....	....	....
	Nova Scotia	AHL	60	23	32	55	131	....	....	....	....	....
1986-87	Nova Scotia	AHL	59	20	25	45	84	1	0	0	0	5
1987-88	Nova Scotia	AHL	44	20	22	42	122	5	2	5	7	16
1988-89	Quebec	NHL	5	0	2	2	4	....	....	....	....	....
	Halifax	AHL	53	18	31	49	116	3	0	1	1	6
1989-90	Halifax	AHL	54	23	32	55	167	6	1	4	5	8
1990-91	Halifax	AHL	....	....	....	....	....	....	....	....	....	....
	NHL Totals		**223**	**23**	**51**	**74**	**306**	**18**	**1**	**5**	**6**	**29**

Traded to **Edmonton** by **Los Angeles** for cash, November 27, 1984. Traded to **Los Angeles** by **Edmonton** for future considerations, May 31, 1985. Signed as a free agent by **Edmonton**, September 27, 1985. Signed as a free agent by **Quebec**, July 15, 1988.

HORACEK, TONY   (HOHR-uh-chehk)

Left wing. Shoots left. 6'4", 210 lbs.   Born, Vancouver, B.C., February 3, 1967.
(Philadelphia's 8th choice, 147th overall, in 1985 Entry Draft).

			Regular Season					Playoffs			
Season	Club	Lea	GP	G	A	TP	PIM	GP	G	A	TP	PIM
1984-85	Kelowna	WHL	67	9	18	27	114	6	0	1	1	11
1985-86	Spokane	WHL	64	19	28	47	129	9	4	5	9	29
1986-87	Spokane	WHL	64	23	37	60	177	5	1	3	4	18
	Hershey	AHL	....	....	....	....	....	1	0	0	0	0
1987-88	Hershey	AHL	1	0	0	0	0	....	....	....	....	....
	Spokane	WHL	24	17	23	40	63	....	....	....	....	....
	Kamloops	WHL	26	14	17	31	51	18	6	4	10	73
1988-89	Hershey	AHL	10	0	0	0	38	....	....	....	....	....
	Indianapolis	IHL	43	11	13	24	138	....	....	....	....	....
1989-90	Philadelphia	NHL	48	5	5	10	117	....	....	....	....	....
	Hershey	AHL	12	0	5	5	25	....	....	....	....	....
1990-91	Philadelphia	NHL	34	3	6	9	49	....	....	....	....	....
	Hershey	AHL	19	5	3	8	35	4	2	0	2	14
	NHL Totals		**82**	**8**	**11**	**19**	**166**					

HORAVA, MILOSLAV   (HOHR-shuh-vuh)

Defense. Shoots left. 6', 193 lbs.   Born, Kladno, Czechoslovakia, August 14, 1961.
(Edmonton's 8th choice, 176th overall, in 1981 Entry Draft).

			Regular Season					Playoffs			
Season	Club	Lea	GP	G	A	TP	PIM	GP	G	A	TP	PIM
1986-87	Kladno	Czech.2	38	17	26	43	....	....	....	....	....	....
1987-88	Kladno	Czech.	29	7	11	18	....	....	....	....	....	....
1988-89	Kladno	Czech.	37	10	15	25	....	....	....	....	....	....
	NY Rangers	NHL	6	0	1	1	0	....	....	....	....	....
1989-90	NY Rangers	NHL	45	4	10	14	26	2	0	1	1	0
1990-91	NY Rangers	NHL	29	1	6	7	12	....	....	....	....	....
	NHL Totals		**80**	**5**	**17**	**22**	**38**	**2**	**0**	**1**	**1**	**0**

Traded to **NY Rangers** by **Edmonton** with Don Jackson, Mike Golden and future considerations for Reijo Ruotsalainen, Ville Kentala, Clark Donatelli and Jim Wiemer, October 23, 1986. Traded to **Quebec** by **NY Rangers** for Stephane Guerard, May 25, 1991.

HOSTAK, MARTIN   (HOHS-tahk)

Center. Shoots left. 6'3", 198 lbs.   Born, Hradec Kralove, Czech., November 11, 1967.
(Philadelphia's 3rd choice, 62nd overall, in 1987 Entry Draft).

			Regular Season					Playoffs			
Season	Club	Lea	GP	G	A	TP	PIM	GP	G	A	TP	PIM
1986-87	Sparta Praha	Czech.	34	6	2	8	....	....	....	....	....	....
1987-88	Sparta Praha	Czech.	26	8	9	17	....	....	....	....	....	....
1988-89	Sparta Praha	Czech.	35	11	15	26	....	....	....	....	....	....
1989-90	Sparta Praha	Czech.	44	26	27	53	....	11	4	7	11	....
1990-91	Philadelphia	NHL	50	3	10	13	22	....	....	....	....	....
	Hershey	AHL	11	6	2	8	2	3	1	0	1	0
	NHL Totals		**50**	**3**	**10**	**13**	**22**					

HOUDA, DOUG   (HOO-duh)

Defense. Shoots right. 6'2", 190 lbs.   Born, Blairmore, Alta., June 3, 1966.
(Detroit's 2nd choice, 28th overall, in 1984 Entry Draft).

			Regular Season					Playoffs			
Season	Club	Lea	GP	G	A	TP	PIM	GP	G	A	TP	PIM
1982-83	Calgary	WHL	71	5	23	28	99	16	1	3	4	44
1983-84	Calgary	WHL	69	6	30	36	195	4	0	0	0	7
1984-85a	Calgary	WHL	65	20	54	74	182	8	3	4	7	29
1985-86	Detroit	NHL	6	0	0	0	4	....	....	....	....	....
	Calgary	WHL	16	4	10	14	60	....	....	....	....	....
	Medicine Hat	WHL	35	9	23	32	80	25	4	19	23	64
1986-87	Adirondack	AHL	77	6	23	29	142	11	1	8	9	50
1987-88	Detroit	NHL	11	1	1	2	10	....	....	....	....	....
b	Adirondack	AHL	71	10	32	42	169	11	0	3	3	44
1988-89	Detroit	NHL	57	2	11	13	67	6	0	1	1	0
	Adirondack	AHL	7	0	3	3	8	....	....	....	....	....
1989-90	Detroit	NHL	73	2	9	11	127	....	....	....	....	....
1990-91	Detroit	NHL	22	0	4	4	43	....	....	....	....	....
	Adirondack	AHL	38	9	17	26	67	....	....	....	....	....
	Hartford	NHL	19	1	2	3	41	6	0	0	0	8
	NHL Totals		**188**	**6**	**27**	**33**	**292**	**12**	**0**	**1**	**1**	**8**

a WHL Second All-Star Team, East Division (1985)
b AHL First All-Star Team (1988)
Traded to **Hartford** by **Detroit** for Doug Crossman, February 20, 1991.

HOUGH, MIKE (HUHF)

Left wing. Shoots left. 6'1", 192 lbs. Born, Montreal, Que., February 6, 1963.
(Quebec's 7th choice, 181st overall, in 1982 Entry Draft).

			Regular Season					Playoffs				
Season	Club	Lea	GP	G	A	TP	PIM	GP	G	A	TP	PIM
1981-82	Kitchener	OHL	58	14	14	28	172	14	4	1	5	16
1982-83	Kitchener	OHL	61	17	27	44	156	12	5	4	9	30
1983-84	Fredericton	AHL	69	11	16	27	142	1	0	0	0	7
1984-85	Fredericton	AHL	76	21	27	48	49	6	1	1	2	2
1985-86	Fredericton	AHL	74	21	33	54	68	6	0	3	3	8
1986-87	**Quebec**	**NHL**	**56**	**6**	**8**	**14**	**79**	**9**	**0**	**3**	**3**	**26**
	Fredericton	AHL	10	1	3	4	20	....	....	....	....	....
1987-88	**Quebec**	**NHL**	**17**	**3**	**2**	**5**	**2**	....	....	....	....	....
	Fredericton	AHL	46	16	25	41	133	15	4	8	12	55
1988-89	**Quebec**	**NHL**	**46**	**9**	**10**	**19**	**39**	....	....	....	....	....
	Halifax	AHL	22	11	10	21	87	....	....	....	....	....
1989-90	**Quebec**	**NHL**	**43**	**13**	**13**	**26**	**84**	....	....	....	....	....
1990-91	**Quebec**	**NHL**	**63**	**13**	**20**	**33**	**111**	....	....	....	....	....
	NHL Totals		**225**	**44**	**53**	**97**	**315**	**9**	**0**	**3**	**3**	**26**

HOULDER, BILL

Defense. Shoots left. 6'2", 212 lbs. Born, Thunder Bay, Ont., March 11, 1967.
(Washington's 4th choice, 82nd overall, in 1985 Entry Draft).

			Regular Season					Playoffs				
Season	Club	Lea	GP	G	A	TP	PIM	GP	G	A	TP	PIM
1984-85	North Bay	OHL	66	4	20	24	37	8	0	0	0	2
1985-86	North Bay	OHL	59	5	30	35	97	10	1	6	7	12
1986-87a	North Bay	OHL	62	17	51	68	68	22	4	19	23	20
1987-88	**Washington**	**NHL**	**30**	**1**	**2**	**3**	**10**	....	....	....	....	....
	Fort Wayne	IHL	43	10	14	24	32	....	....	....	....	....
1988-89	**Washington**	**NHL**	**8**	**0**	**3**	**3**	**4**	....	....	....	....	....
	Baltimore	AHL	65	10	36	46	50	....	....	....	....	....
1989-90	**Washington**	**NHL**	**41**	**1**	**11**	**12**	**28**	....	....	....	....	....
	Baltimore	AHL	26	3	7	10	12	7	0	2	2	2
1990-91	**Buffalo**	**NHL**	**7**	**0**	**2**	**2**	**4**	....	....	....	....	....
a	Rochester	AHL	69	13	53	66	28	15	5	13	18	4
	NHL Totals		**86**	**2**	**18**	**20**	**46**	....	....	....	....	....

a OHL Third All-Star Team (1987)
a AHL First All-Star Team (1991)

Traded to **Buffalo** by **Washington** for Shawn Anderdon, September 30, 1990.

HOUSE, BOBBY

Right wing. Shoots right. 6'1", 200 lbs. Born, Whitehorse, Yukon, January 7, 1973.
(Chicago's 4th choice, 66th overall, in 1991 Entry Draft).

			Regular Season					Playoffs				
Season	Club	Lea	GP	G	A	TP	PIM	GP	G	A	TP	PIM
1989-90	Spokane	WHL	64	18	16	34	74	5	0	0	0	6
1990-91	Spokane	WHL	38	11	19	30	63	....	....	....	....	....
	Brandon	WHL	23	18	7	25	14	....	....	....	....	....

HOUSE, KEN

Center. Shoots left. 6'1", 200 lbs. Born, Scarborough, Ont., November 3, 1969.
(Washington's 12th choice, 250th overall, in 1989 Entry Draft).

			Regular Season					Playoffs				
Season	Club	Lea	GP	G	A	TP	PIM	GP	G	A	TP	PIM
1988-89	Miami-Ohio	CCHA	38	19	14	33	18	....	....	....	....	....
1989-90	Miami-Ohio	CCHA	37	10	5	15	32	....	....	....	....	....
1990-91	Miami-Ohio	CCHA	34	13	11	24	20	....	....	....	....	....

HOUSLEY, PHIL (HOWZ-lee)

Defense. Shoots left. 5'10", 179 lbs. Born, St. Paul, MN, March 9, 1964.
(Buffalo's 1st choice, 6th overall, in 1982 Entry Draft).

			Regular Season					Playoffs				
Season	Club	Lea	GP	G	A	TP	PIM	GP	G	A	TP	PIM
1981-82	South St. Paul	HS	22	31	34	65	18	....	....	....	....	....
1982-83a	**Buffalo**	**NHL**	**77**	**19**	**47**	**66**	**39**	**10**	**3**	**4**	**7**	**2**
1983-84	**Buffalo**	**NHL**	**75**	**31**	**46**	**77**	**33**	**3**	**0**	**0**	**0**	**6**
1984-85	**Buffalo**	**NHL**	**73**	**16**	**53**	**69**	**28**	**5**	**3**	**2**	**5**	**2**
1985-86	**Buffalo**	**NHL**	**79**	**15**	**47**	**62**	**54**	....	....	....	....	....
1986-87	**Buffalo**	**NHL**	**78**	**21**	**46**	**67**	**57**	....	....	....	....	....
1987-88	**Buffalo**	**NHL**	**74**	**29**	**37**	**66**	**96**	**6**	**2**	**4**	**6**	**6**
1988-89	**Buffalo**	**NHL**	**72**	**26**	**44**	**70**	**47**	**5**	**1**	**3**	**4**	**2**
1989-90	**Buffalo**	**NHL**	**80**	**21**	**60**	**81**	**32**	**6**	**1**	**4**	**5**	**4**
1990-91	**Winnipeg**	**NHL**	**78**	**23**	**53**	**76**	**24**	....	....	....	....	....
	NHL Totals		**686**	**201**	**433**	**634**	**410**	**35**	**10**	**17**	**27**	**22**

a NHL All-Rookie Team (1983)

Played in NHL All-Star Game (1984, 1989-91)

Traded to **Winnipeg** by **Buffalo** with Scott Arniel, Jeff Parker and Buffalo's first round choice (Keith Tkachuk) in 1990 Entry Draft for Dale Hawerchuk, Winnipeg's first round choice (Brad May) in 1990 Entry Draft and future considerations, June 16, 1990.

HOWARD, SHAWN

Center. Shoots left. 6', 180 lbs. Born, Anchorage, AK, March 20, 1968.
(NY Islanders' 9th choice, 181st overall, in 1987 Entry Draft).

			Regular Season					Playoffs				
Season	Club	Lea	GP	G	A	TP	PIM	GP	G	A	TP	PIM
1987-88	Minn.-Duluth	WCHA	37	13	8	21	42	....	....	....	....	....
1988-89	Minn.-Duluth	WCHA	39	7	9	16	31	....	....	....	....	....
1989-90	Minn.-Duluth	WCHA	40	19	19	38	58	....	....	....	....	....
1990-91	Minn.-Duluth	WCHA	35	11	9	20	39	....	....	....	....	....

HOWE, MARK STEVEN

Defence. Shoots left. 5'11", 185 lbs. Born, Detroit, Mich., May 28, 1955.
(Boston's 2nd choice, 25th overall, in 1974 Amateur Draft).

			Regular Season					Playoffs				
Season	Club	Lea	GP	G	A	TP	PIM	GP	G	A	TP	PIM
1972-73	Toronto	OHA	60	38	66	104	27	....	....	....	....	....
1973-74ab	Houston	WHA	76	38	41	79	20	14	9	10	19	4
1974-75	Houston	WHA	74	36	40	76	30	13	*10	12	*22	0
1975-76	Houston	WHA	72	39	37	76	38	17	6	10	16	18
1976-77a	Houston	WHA	57	23	52	75	46	10	4	10	14	2
1977-78	New England	WHA	70	30	61	91	32	14	8	7	15	18
1978-79c	New England	WHA	77	42	65	107	32	6	4	2	6	6
1979-80	**Hartford**	**NHL**	**74**	**24**	**56**	**80**	**20**	**3**	**1**	**2**	**3**	**2**
1980-81	**Hartford**	**NHL**	**63**	**19**	**46**	**65**	**54**	....	....	....	....	....
1981-82	**Hartford**	**NHL**	**76**	**8**	**45**	**53**	**18**	....	....	....	....	....
1982-83d	**Philadelphia**	**NHL**	**76**	**20**	**47**	**67**	**18**	**3**	**0**	**2**	**2**	**4**
1983-84	**Philadelphia**	**NHL**	**71**	**19**	**34**	**53**	**44**	**3**	**0**	**0**	**0**	**2**
1984-85	**Philadelphia**	**NHL**	**73**	**18**	**39**	**57**	**31**	**19**	**3**	**8**	**11**	**6**
1985-86de	**Philadelphia**	**NHL**	**77**	**24**	**58**	**82**	**36**	**5**	**0**	**4**	**4**	**0**
1986-87d	**Philadelphia**	**NHL**	**69**	**15**	**43**	**58**	**37**	**26**	**2**	**10**	**12**	**4**
1987-88	**Philadelphia**	**NHL**	**75**	**19**	**43**	**62**	**62**	**7**	**3**	**6**	**9**	**4**
1988-89	**Philadelphia**	**NHL**	**52**	**9**	**29**	**38**	**45**	**19**	**0**	**15**	**15**	**10**
1989-90	**Philadelphia**	**NHL**	**40**	**7**	**21**	**28**	**24**	....	....	....	....	....
1990-91	**Philadelphia**	**NHL**	**19**	**0**	**10**	**10**	**8**	....	....	....	....	....
	NHL Totals		**765**	**182**	**471**	**653**	**397**	**85**	**9**	**47**	**56**	**32**

a WHA Second All-Star Team (1974, 1977)
b Named WHA's Rookie of the Year (1974)
c WHA First All-Star Team (1979)
d NHL First All-Star Team (1983, 1986, 1987)
e NHL Plus/Minus Leader (1986)

Played in NHL All-Star Game (1981, 1983, 1986, 1988)

Reclaimed by **Boston** from **Hartford** prior to Expansion Draft, June 9, 1979. Claimed as priority selection by **Hartford**, June 9, 1979. Traded to **Philadelphia** by **Hartford** with Hartford's third round choice (Derrick Smith) in 1983 Entry Draft for Ken Linseman, Greg Adams and Philadelphia's first (David Jensen) and third round choices (Leif Karlsson) in the 1983 Entry Draft, August 19, 1982.

HRBEK, PETR (huhr-BEHK)

Right wing. Shoots right. 5'11", 180 lbs. Born, Prague, Czechoslovakia, April 3, 1969.
(Detroit's 4th choice, 59th overall, in 1988 Entry Draft).

			Regular Season					Playoffs				
Season	Club	Lea	GP	G	A	TP	PIM	GP	G	A	TP	PIM
1986-87	Sparta Praha	Czech.	11	2	0	2	....	....	....	....	....	....
1987-88	Sparta Praha	Czech.	31	13	9	22	....	....	....	....	....	....
1988-89	Sparta Praha	Czech.	41	10	13	23	....	....	....	....	....	....
1989-90	Dukla Jihlava	Czech.	32	12	7	19	....	....	....	....	....	....
1990-91	Sparta Praha	Czech.	39	20	17	37	14	....	....	....	....	....

HRDINA, JIRI (huhr-DEE-nuh)

Center. Shoots left. 6', 195 lbs. Born, Prague, Czech., January 5, 1958.
(Calgary's 8th choice, 159th overall, in 1984 Entry Draft).

			Regular Season					Playoffs				
Season	Club	Lea	GP	G	A	TP	PIM	GP	G	A	TP	PIM
1985-86	Sparta Praha	Czech.	44	18	19	37	30	....	....	....	....	....
1986-87	Sparta Praha	Czech.	31	18	18	36	24	....	....	....	....	....
1987-88	Sparta Praha	Czech.	22	7	15	22	0	....	....	....	....	....
	Czech Olympic	...	8	2	5	7	4	....	....	....	....	....
	Calgary	**NHL**	**9**	**2**	**5**	**7**	**2**	**1**	**0**	**0**	**0**	**0**
1988-89	**Calgary**	**NHL**	**70**	**22**	**32**	**54**	**26**	**4**	**0**	**0**	**0**	**0**
1989-90	**Calgary**	**NHL**	**64**	**12**	**18**	**30**	**31**	**6**	**0**	**1**	**1**	**2**
1990-91	**Calgary**	**NHL**	**14**	**0**	**3**	**3**	**4**	....	....	....	....	....
	Pittsburgh	**NHL**	**37**	**6**	**14**	**20**	**13**	**14**	**2**	**2**	**4**	**6**
	NHL Totals		**194**	**42**	**72**	**114**	**76**	**25**	**2**	**3**	**5**	**8**

Traded to **Pittsburgh** by **Calgary** for Jim Kyte, December 13, 1990.

HRKAC, ANTHONY (TONY) (HUHR-kuhz)

Center. Shoots left. 5'11", 170 lbs. Born, Thunder Bay, Ont., July 7, 1966.
(St. Louis' 2nd choice, 32nd overall, in 1984 Entry Draft).

			Regular Season					Playoffs				
Season	Club	Lea	GP	G	A	TP	PIM	GP	G	A	TP	PIM
1984-85	North Dakota	WCHA	36	18	36	54	16	....	....	....	....	....
1985-86	Cdn. Olympic	....	62	19	30	49	36	....	....	....	....	....
1986-87abcd	North Dakota	WCHA	48	46	79	125	48	....	....	....	....	....
	St. Louis	**NHL**	....	....	....	....	....	**3**	**0**	**0**	**0**	**0**
1987-88	**St. Louis**	**NHL**	**67**	**11**	**37**	**48**	**22**	**10**	**6**	**1**	**7**	**4**
1988-89	**St. Louis**	**NHL**	**70**	**17**	**28**	**45**	**8**	**4**	**1**	**1**	**2**	**0**
1989-90	**St. Louis**	**NHL**	**28**	**5**	**12**	**17**	**8**	....	....	....	....	....
	Quebec	**NHL**	**22**	**4**	**8**	**12**	**2**	....	....	....	....	....
	Halifax	AHL	20	12	21	33	4	6	5	9	14	4
1990-91	**Quebec**	**NHL**	**70**	**16**	**32**	**48**	**16**	....	....	....	....	....
	Halifax	AHL	3	4	1	5	2	....	....	....	....	....
	NHL Totals		**257**	**53**	**117**	**170**	**56**	**14**	**7**	**2**	**9**	**4**

a WCHA First All-Star Team, Player of the Year (1987)
b NCAA West First All-American Team (1987)
c NCAA All-Tournament Team, Tournament MVP (1987)
d Winner of the 1987 Hobey Baker Memorial Trophy (Top U.S. Collegiate Player) (1987)

Traded to **Quebec** by **St. Louis** with Greg Millen for Jeff Brown, December 13, 1989. Traded to **San Jose** by **Quebec** for Greg Paslawski, May 31, 1991.

HRSTKA, MARTIN (hurst-KAH)

Left wing. Shoots left. 6', 180 lbs. Born, Brno, Czechoslovakia, January 26, 1967.
(Vancouver's 6th choice, 109th overall, in 1985 Entry Draft).

			Regular Season					Playoffs				
Season	Club	Lea	GP	G	A	TP	PIM	GP	G	A	TP	PIM
1986-87	Dukla Trencin	Czech.	26	2	4	6	....	....	....	....	....	....
1987-88	Dukla Trencin	Czech.	22	5	6	11	....	....	....	....	....	....
1988-89	TJ Gottwaldov	Czech.	25	4	9	13	....	....	....	....	....	....
1989-90	TJ Gottwaldov	Czech.	39	8	7	15	....	....	....	....	....	....
1990-91	TJ Zlin	Czech.	41	11	19	30	20	....	....	....	....	....

HUBER, PHIL

Center. Shoots left. 5'10", 194 lbs. Born, Calgary, Alta., January 10, 1969.
(NY Islanders' 8th choice, 149th overall, in 1989 Entry Draft).

			Regular Season					Playoffs				
Season	Club	Lea	GP	G	A	TP	PIM	GP	G	A	TP	PIM
1987-88	Kamloops	WHL	63	19	30	49	54	18	3	9	12	23
1988-89	Kamloops	WHL	72	54	68	122	103	16	18	13	31	48
1989-90a	Kamloops	WHL	72	63	89	152	176	17	12	11	23	44
1990-91	Capital Dist.	AHL	5	1	1	2	0	....	....	....	....	....
	Richmond	ECHL	56	32	40	72	87	4	1	3	4	4

a WHL West First All-Star Team (1990)

HUDDY, CHARLES WILLIAM (CHARLIE)

Defense. Shoots left. 6', 210 lbs. Born, Oshawa, Ont., June 2, 1959.

			Regular Season					Playoffs				
Season	Club	Lea	GP	G	A	TP	PIM	GP	G	A	TP	PIM
1977-78	Oshawa	OHA	59	17	18	35	81	6	2	1	3	10
1978-79	Oshawa	OHA	64	20	38	58	108	5	3	4	7	12
1979-80	Houston	CHL	79	14	34	48	46	6	1	0	1	2
1980-81	Edmonton	NHL	12	2	5	7	6	....	....	....	....	....
	Wichita	CHL	47	8	36	44	71	17	3	11	14	10
1981-82	Edmonton	NHL	41	4	11	15	46	5	1	2	3	14
	Wichita	CHL	32	7	19	26	51	....	....	....	....	....
1982-83a	Edmonton	NHL	76	20	37	57	58	15	1	6	7	10
1983-84	Edmonton	NHL	75	8	34	42	43	12	1	9	10	8
1984-85	Edmonton	NHL	80	7	44	51	46	18	3	17	20	17
1985-86	Edmonton	NHL	76	6	35	41	55	7	0	2	2	0
1986-87	Edmonton	NHL	58	4	15	19	35	21	1	7	8	21
1987-88	Edmonton	NHL	77	13	28	41	71	13	4	5	9	10
1988-89	Edmonton	NHL	76	11	33	44	52	7	2	0	2	4
1989-90	Edmonton	NHL	70	1	23	24	56	22	0	6	6	11
1990-91	Edmonton	NHL	53	5	22	27	32	18	3	7	10	10
	NHL Totals		694	81	287	368	500	138	16	61	77	105

a NHL Plus/Minus Leader (1983)

Signed as a free agent by **Edmonton**, September 14, 1979. Claimed by **Minnesota** from **Edmonton** in Expansion Draft, May 30, 1991. Traded to **Los Angeles** by **Minnesota** with Randy Gilhen, Jim Thomson and NY Rangers' fourth round choice (previously acquired by Minnesota – Alexei Zhitnik) in 1991 Entry Draft for Todd Elik, June 22, 1991.

HUDSON, MIKE

Center/Left wing. Shoots left. 6'1", 201 lbs. Born, Guelph, Ont., February 6, 1967.
(Chicago's 6th choice, 140th overall, in 1986 Entry Draft).

			Regular Season					Playoffs				
Season	Club	Lea	GP	G	A	TP	PIM	GP	G	A	TP	PIM
1984-85	Hamilton	OHL	50	10	12	22	13	....	....	....	....	....
1985-86	Hamilton	OHL	7	3	2	5	4	....	....	....	....	....
	Sudbury	OHL	59	35	42	77	20	4	2	5	7	7
1986-87	Sudbury	OHL	63	40	57	97	18	....	....	....	....	....
1987-88	Saginaw	IHL	75	18	30	48	44	10	2	3	5	20
1988-89	Chicago	NHL	41	7	16	23	20	10	1	2	3	18
	Saginaw	IHL	30	15	17	32	10	....	....	....	....	....
1989-90	Chicago	NHL	49	9	12	21	56	4	0	0	0	2
1990-91	Chicago	NHL	55	7	9	16	62	6	0	2	2	8
	Indianapolis	IHL	3	1	2	3	0	....	....	....	....	....
	NHL Totals		145	23	37	60	138	20	1	4	5	28

HUFFMAN, KERRY

Defense. Shoots left. 6'2", 200 lbs. Born, Peterborough, Ont., January 3, 1968.
(Philadelphia's 1st choice, 20th overall, in 1986 Entry Draft).

			Regular Season					Playoffs				
Season	Club	Lea	GP	G	A	TP	PIM	GP	G	A	TP	PIM
1985-86	Guelph	OHL	56	3	24	27	35	20	1	10	11	10
1986-87	Philadelphia	NHL	9	0	0	0	2	....	....	....	....	....
	Hershey	AHL	3	0	1	1	0	4	0	0	0	0
a	Guelph	OHL	44	4	31	35	20	5	0	2	2	8
1987-88	Philadelphia	NHL	52	6	17	23	34	2	0	0	0	0
1988-89	Philadelphia	NHL	29	0	11	11	31	....	....	....	....	....
	Hershey	AHL	29	2	13	15	16	....	....	....	....	....
1989-90	Philadelphia	NHL	43	1	12	13	34	....	....	....	....	....
1990-91	Philadelphia	NHL	10	1	2	3	10	....	....	....	....	....
	Hershey	AHL	45	5	29	34	20	7	1	2	3	0
	NHL Totals		143	8	42	50	111	2	0	0	0	0

a OHL First All-Star Team (1987)

HUGHES, BRENT ALLEN

Left wing. Shoots left. 5'11", 185 lbs. Born, New Westminster, B.C., April 5, 1966.

			Regular Season					Playoffs				
Season	Club	Lea	GP	G	A	TP	PIM	GP	G	A	TP	PIM
1983-84	N. Westminster	WHL	67	21	18	39	133	9	2	2	4	27
1984-85	N. Westminster	WHL	64	25	32	57	135	11	2	1	3	37
1985-86	N. Westminster	WHL	71	28	52	80	180	....	....	....	....	....
1986-87	N. Westminster	WHL	8	5	4	9	22	....	....	....	....	....
	Victoria	WHL	61	38	61	99	146	5	4	1	5	8
1987-88	Moncton	AHL	73	13	19	32	206	....	....	....	....	....
1988-89	Winnipeg	NHL	28	3	2	5	82	....	....	....	....	....
	Moncton	AHL	54	34	34	68	286	10	9	4	13	40
1989-90	Winnipeg	NHL	11	1	2	3	33	....	....	....	....	....
	Moncton	AHL	65	31	29	60	277	....	....	....	....	....
1990-91	Moncton	AHL	63	21	22	43	144	3	0	0	0	7
	NHL Totals		39	4	4	8	115	....	....	....	....	....

Signed as a free agent by **Winnipeg**, June 13, 1988. Traded to **Washington** by **Winnipeg** with Craig Duncanson and Simon Wheeldon for Bob Joyce, Tyler Larter and Kent Paynter, May 21, 1991.

HUGHES, RYAN

Center. Shoots left. 6'1", 180 lbs. Born, Montreal, Que., January 17, 1972.
(Quebec's 2nd choice, 22nd overall, in 1990 Entry Draft).

			Regular Season					Playoffs				
Season	Club	Lea	GP	G	A	TP	PIM	GP	G	A	TP	PIM
1989-90	Cornell	ECAC	27	7	16	23	35	....	....	....	....	....
1990-91	Cornell	ECAC	32	18	34	52	28	....	....	....	....	....

HULETT, DEAN

Right wing. Shoots right. 6'6", 210 lbs. Born, San Juan, Puerto Rico, July 25, 1971.
(Los Angeles' 7th choice, 154th overall, in 1990 Entry Draft).

			Regular Season					Playoffs				
Season	Club	Lea	GP	G	A	TP	PIM	GP	G	A	TP	PIM
1989-90	Lake Superior	CCHA	13	1	4	5	18	....	....	....	....	....
1990-91	Lake Superior	CCHA	36	5	8	13	52	....	....	....	....	....

HULL, BRETT

Right wing. Shoots right. 5'10", 201 lbs. Born, Belleville, Ont., August 9, 1964.
(Calgary's 6th choice, 117th overall, in 1984 Entry Draft).

			Regular Season					Playoffs				
Season	Club	Lea	GP	G	A	TP	PIM	GP	G	A	TP	PIM
1984-85	Minn.-Duluth	WCHA	48	32	28	60	24	....	....	....	....	....
1985-86a	Minn.-Duluth	WCHA	42	52	32	84	46	....	....	....	....	....
	Calgary	NHL	....	....	....	....	....	2	0	0	0	0
1986-87	Calgary	NHL	5	1	0	1	0	4	2	1	3	0
bc	Moncton	AHL	67	50	42	92	16	3	2	2	4	2
1987-88	Calgary	NHL	52	26	24	50	12	....	....	....	....	....
	St. Louis	NHL	13	6	8	14	4	10	7	2	9	4
1988-89	St. Louis	NHL	78	41	43	84	33	10	5	5	10	6
1989-90def	St. Louis	NHL	80	*72	41	113	24	12	13	8	21	17
1990-91dfghi	St. Louis	NHL	78	*86	45	131	22	13	11	8	19	4
	NHL Totals		306	232	161	393	95	51	38	24	62	31

a WCHA First All-Star Team (1986)
b AHL First All-Star Team (1987)
c Won Dudley "Red" Garrett Memorial Trophy (AHL's Top Rookie) (1987)
d NHL First All-Star Team (1990, 1991)
e Won Lady Byng Trophy (1990)
f Won Dodge Ram Tough Award (1990, 1991)
g Won Hart Memorial Trophy (1991)
h Won Lester B. Pearson Award (1991)
i Won ProSet/NHL Player of the Year Award

Played in NHL All-Star Game (1989, 1990)

Traded to **St. Louis** by **Calgary** with Steve Bozek for Rob Ramage and Rick Wamsley, March 7, 1988.

HULL, JODY

Right wing. Shoots right. 6'2", 200 lbs. Born, Cambridge, Ont., February 2, 1969.
(Hartford's 1st choice, 18th overall, in 1987 Entry Draft).

			Regular Season					Playoffs				
Season	Club	Lea	GP	G	A	TP	PIM	GP	G	A	TP	PIM
1985-86	Peterborough	OHL	61	20	22	42	29	16	1	5	6	4
1986-87	Peterborough	OHL	49	18	34	52	22	12	4	9	13	14
1987-88a	Peterborough	OHL	60	50	44	94	33	12	10	8	18	8
1988-89	Hartford	NHL	60	16	18	34	10	1	0	0	0	2
1989-90	Hartford	NHL	38	7	10	17	21	5	0	1	1	2
	Binghamton	AHL	21	7	10	17	6	....	....	....	....	....
1990-91	NY Rangers	NHL	47	5	8	13	10	....	....	....	....	....
	NHL Totals		145	28	36	64	41	6	0	1	1	4

a OHL Second All-Star Team (1988)

Traded to **NY Rangers** by **Hartford** for Carey Wilson and NY Rangers' third-round choice (Mikael Nylander) in the 1991 Entry Draft), July 9, 1990.

HULST, KENT

Center. Shoots left. 6', 180 lbs. Born, St. Thomas, Ont., April 8, 1968.
(Toronto's 4th choice, 69th overall, in 1986 Entry Draft).

			Regular Season					Playoffs				
Season	Club	Lea	GP	G	A	TP	PIM	GP	G	A	TP	PIM
1985-86	Belleville	OHL	43	6	17	23	20	....	....	....	....	....
	Windsor	OHL	17	6	10	16	9	....	....	....	....	....
1986-87	Windsor	OHL	37	18	20	38	49	....	....	....	....	....
	Belleville	OHL	27	13	10	23	17	6	1	1	2	0
1987-88	Belleville	OHL	66	42	43	85	48	6	3	1	4	7
1988-89	Belleville	OHL	45	21	41	62	43	....	....	....	....	....
	Flint	IHL	7	0	1	1	4	....	....	....	....	....
	Newmarket	AHL	....	....	....	....	....	2	1	1	2	2
1989-90	Newmarket	AHL	80	26	34	60	29	....	....	....	....	....
1990-91	Newmarket	AHL	79	28	37	65	57	....	....	....	....	....

HUMENIUK, SCOTT

Defense. Shoots right. 6', 190 lbs. Born, Saskatoon, Sask., September 10, 1969.

			Regular Season					Playoffs				
Season	Club	Lea	GP	G	A	TP	PIM	GP	G	A	TP	PIM
1986-87	Spokane	WHL	10	0	2	2	2	1	0	0	0	0
1987-88	Spokane	WHL	58	6	20	26	154	8	1	0	1	19
1988-89	Moose Jaw	WHL	56	18	39	57	159	7	5	0	5	32
1989-90	Moose Jaw	WHL	71	23	47	70	141	....	....	....	....	....
	Binghamton	AHL	4	0	1	1	11	....	....	....	....	....
1990-91	Springfield	AHL	57	6	17	23	69	14	2	2	4	18

Signed as a free agent by **Hartford**, March, 1990.

HUNT, CURTIS

Defense. Shoots left. 6', 195 lbs. Born, North Battleford, Sask., January 28, 1967.
(Vancouver's 9th choice, 172nd overall, in 1985 Entry Draft).

			Regular Season					Playoffs				
Season	Club	Lea	GP	G	A	TP	PIM	GP	G	A	TP	PIM
1984-85	Prince Albert	WHL	64	2	13	15	61	13	0	3	3	24
1985-86	Prince Albert	WHL	72	5	29	34	108	18	2	8	10	28
1986-87	Prince Albert	WHL	47	6	31	37	101	8	1	3	4	4
1987-88	Flint	IHL	76	4	17	21	181	2	0	0	0	16
	Fredericton	AHL	1	0	0	0	2	....	....	....	....	....
1988-89	Milwaukee	IHL	65	3	17	20	226	11	1	2	3	43
1989-90	Milwaukee	IHL	69	8	25	33	237	3	0	1	1	4
1990-91	Albany	IHL	45	2	12	14	122	....	....	....	....	....
	Milwaukee	IHL	27	1	5	6	85	6	0	1	1	10

Signed as a free agent by **Toronto**, July 19, 1991.

HUNTER, DALE ROBERT

Center. Shoots left. 5'10", 198 lbs. Born, Petrolia, Ont., July 31, 1960.
(Quebec's 2nd choice, 41st overall, in 1979 Entry Draft).

			Regular Season					Playoffs				
Season	Club	Lea	GP	G	A	TP	PIM	GP	G	A	TP	PIM
1977-78	Kitchener	OHA	68	22	42	64	115	....	....	....	....	....
1978-79	Sudbury	OHA	59	42	68	110	188	10	4	12	16	47
1979-80	Sudbury	OHA	61	34	51	85	189	9	6	9	15	45
1980-81	Quebec	NHL	80	19	44	63	226	5	4	2	6	34
1981-82	Quebec	NHL	80	22	50	72	272	16	3	7	10	52
1982-83	Quebec	NHL	80	17	46	63	206	4	2	1	3	24
1983-84	Quebec	NHL	77	24	55	79	232	9	2	3	5	41
1984-85	Quebec	NHL	80	20	52	72	209	17	4	6	10	*97
1985-86	Quebec	NHL	80	28	42	70	265	3	0	0	0	15
1986-87	Quebec	NHL	46	10	29	39	135	13	1	7	8	56
1987-88	Washington	NHL	79	22	37	59	240	14	7	5	12	98
1988-89	Washington	NHL	80	20	37	57	219	6	0	4	4	29
1989-90	Washington	NHL	80	23	39	62	233	15	4	8	12	61
1990-91	Washington	NHL	76	16	30	46	234	11	1	9	10	41
	NHL Totals		838	221	461	682	2471	113	28	52	80	548

Traded to **Washington** by **Quebec** with Clint Malarchuk for Gaetan Duchesne, Alan Haworth, and Washington's first-round choice (Joe Sakic) in 1987 Entry Draft, June 13, 1987.

HUNTER, MARK

Right wing. Shoots right. 6', 200 lbs. Born, Petrolia, Ont., November 12, 1962.
(Montreal's 1st choice, 7th overall, in 1981 Entry Draft).

			Regular Season					Playoffs				
Season	Club	Lea	GP	G	A	TP	PIM	GP	G	A	TP	PIM
1979-80	Brantford	OHA	66	34	56	90	171	11	2	8	10	27
1980-81	Brantford	OHA	53	39	40	79	157	6	3	3	6	27
1981-82	Montreal	NHL	71	18	11	29	143	5	0	0	0	20
1982-83	Montreal	NHL	31	8	8	16	73	....	....	....	....	....
1983-84	Montreal	NHL	22	6	4	10	42	14	2	1	3	69
1984-85	Montreal	NHL	72	21	12	33	123	11	0	3	3	13
1985-86	St. Louis	NHL	78	44	30	74	171	19	7	7	14	48
1986-87	St. Louis	NHL	74	36	33	69	167	5	0	3	3	10
1987-88	St. Louis	NHL	66	32	31	63	136	5	2	3	5	24
1988-89	Calgary	NHL	66	22	8	30	194	10	2	2	4	23
1989-90	Calgary	NHL	10	2	3	5	39	....	....	....	....	....
1990-91	Calgary	NHL	57	10	15	25	125	....	....	....	....	....
	Hartford	NHL	11	4	3	7	40	6	5	1	6	17
	NHL Totals		558	203	158	361	1253	75	18	20	38	224

Played in NHL All-Star Game (1986)

Traded to **St. Louis** by **Montreal** with Michael Dark and Montreal's second (Herb Raglan); third (Nelson Emerson); fifth (Dan Brooks); and sixth (Rick Burchill) round choices in 1985 Entry Draft, for St. Louis' first (Jose Charbonneau); second (Todd Richard); fourth (Martin Desjardins); fifth (Tom Sagissor); and sixth (Don Dufresne) round choices in 1985 Entry Draft, June 15, 1985. Traded to **Calgary** by **St. Louis** with Doug Gilmour, Steve Bozek and Michael Dark for Mike Bullard, Craig Coxe and Tim Corkery, September 6, 1988. Traded to **Hartford** by **Calgary** for Carey Wilson, March 5, 1991.

HUNTER, TIMOTHY ROBERT (TIM)

Right wing. Shoots right. 6'2", 202 lbs. Born, Calgary, Alta., September 10, 1960.
(Atlanta's 4th choice, 54th overall, in 1979 Entry Draft).

			Regular Season					Playoffs				
Season	Club	Lea	GP	G	A	TP	PIM	GP	G	A	TP	PIM
1979-80	Seattle	WHL	72	14	53	67	311	12	1	2	3	41
1980-81	Birmingham	CHL	58	3	5	8	*236	....	....	....	....	....
	Nova Scotia	AHL	17	0	0	0	62	6	0	1	1	45
1981-82	Calgary	NHL	2	0	0	0	9	....	....	....	....	....
	Oklahoma City	CHL	55	4	12	16	222	....	....	....	....	....
1982-83	Calgary	NHL	16	1	0	1	54	9	1	0	1	*70
	Colorado	CHL	46	5	12	17	225	....	....	....	....	....
1983-84	Calgary	NHL	43	4	4	8	130	7	0	0	0	21
1984-85	Calgary	NHL	71	11	11	22	259	4	0	0	0	24
1985-86	Calgary	NHL	66	8	7	15	291	19	0	3	3	108
1986-87	Calgary	NHL	73	6	15	21	*361	6	0	0	0	51
1987-88	Calgary	NHL	68	8	5	13	337	9	4	0	4	32
1988-89	Calgary	NHL	75	3	9	12	*375	19	0	4	4	32
1989-90	Calgary	NHL	67	2	3	5	279	6	0	0	0	4
1990-91	Calgary	NHL	34	5	2	7	143	7	0	0	0	10
	NHL Totals		515	48	56	104	2238	86	5	7	12	352

HURD, KELLY

Right wing. Shoots right. 5'11", 185 lbs. Born, Castlegar, B.C., May 13, 1968.
(Detroit's 6th choice, 143rd overall, in 1988 Entry Draft).

			Regular Season					Playoffs				
Season	Club	Lea	GP	G	A	TP	PIM	GP	G	A	TP	PIM
1987-88	Michigan Tech	WCHA	41	18	22	40	34	....	....	....	....	....
1988-89	Michigan Tech	WCHA	42	18	14	32	36	....	....	....	....	....
1989-90	Michigan Tech	WCHA	37	12	13	25	50	....	....	....	....	....
1990-91a	Michigan Tech	WCHA	35	29	22	51	44	....	....	....	....	....

a WCHA Second All-Star Team (1991)

HURLBUT, MICHAEL (MIKE)

Defense. Shoots left. 6'2", 195 lbs. Born, Massena, NY, October 7, 1966.
(NY Rangers' 1st choice, 5th overall, in 1988 Supplemental Draft).

			Regular Season					Playoffs				
Season	Club	Lea	GP	G	A	TP	PIM	GP	G	A	TP	PIM
1985-86	St. Lawrence	ECAC	25	2	10	12	40	....	....	....	....	....
1986-87	St. Lawrence	ECAC	35	8	15	23	44	....	....	....	....	....
1987-88	St. Lawrence	ECAC	38	6	12	18	18	....	....	....	....	....
1988-89a	St. Lawrence	ECAC	36	8	25	33	30	....	....	....	....	....
	Denver	IHL	8	0	2	2	13	4	1	2	3	2
1989-90	Flint	IHL	74	3	34	37	38	3	0	1	1	2
1990-91	San Diego	IHL	2	1	0	1	0	....	....	....	....	....
	Binghamton	AHL	33	2	11	13	27	3	0	1	1	0

a ECAC First All-Star Team (1989)

HUSCROFT, JAMIE

Defense. Shoots right. 6'2", 200 lbs. Born, Creston, B.C., January 9, 1967.
(New Jersey's 9th choice, 171st overall, in 1985 Entry Draft).

			Regular Season					Playoffs				
Season	Club	Lea	GP	G	A	TP	PIM	GP	G	A	TP	PIM
1983-84	Seattle	WHL	63	0	12	12	77	5	0	0	0	15
1984-85	Seattle	WHL	69	3	13	16	273	....	....	....	....	....
1985-86	Seattle	WHL	66	6	20	26	394	5	0	1	1	18
1986-87	Seattle	WHL	21	1	18	19	99	....	....	....	....	....
	Medicine Hat	WHL	35	4	21	25	170	20	0	3	3	*125
1987-88	Utica	AHL	71	5	7	12	316	....	....	....	....	....
	Flint	IHL	3	1	0	1	2	16	0	1	1	110
1988-89	New Jersey	NHL	15	0	2	2	51	....	....	....	....	....
	Utica	AHL	41	2	10	12	215	5	0	0	0	40
1989-90	New Jersey	NHL	42	2	3	5	149	5	0	0	0	16
	Utica	AHL	22	3	6	9	122	....	....	....	....	....
1990-91	New Jersey	NHL	8	0	1	1	27	3	0	0	0	6
	Utica	AHL	59	3	15	18	339	....	....	....	....	....
	NHL Totals		65	2	6	8	227	8	0	0	0	22

HUSS, ANDERS (HUHS)

Center. Shoots right. 5'10", 183 lbs. Born, Gavle, Sweden, April 6, 1964.
(Washington's 8th choice, 225th overall, in 1983 Entry Draft).

			Regular Season					Playoffs				
Season	Club	Lea	GP	G	A	TP	PIM	GP	G	A	TP	PIM
1985-86	Brynas	Swe.	36	20	7	27	36	3	0	0	0	0
1986-87	Brynas	Swe.	33	12	13	25	40	....	....	....	....	....
1987-88	Brynas	Swe.	40	14	12	26	28	....	....	....	....	....
1988-89	Brynas	Swe.	40	22	17	39	26	....	....	....	....	....
1989-90	Brynas	Swe.	36	19	18	37	32	5	3	2	5	0
1990-91	Brynas	Swe.	35	9	5	14	30	....	....	....	....	....

HYNES, GORD

Defense. Shoots left. 6'1", 170 lbs. Born, Montreal, Que., July 22, 1966.
(Boston's 5th choice, 115th overall, in 1985 Entry Draft).

			Regular Season					Playoffs				
Season	Club	Lea	GP	G	A	TP	PIM	GP	G	A	TP	PIM
1983-84	Medicine Hat	WHL	72	5	14	19	39	14	0	0	0	0
1984-85	Medicine Hat	WHL	70	18	45	63	61	10	6	9	15	17
1985-86	Medicine Hat	WHL	58	22	39	61	45	25	8	15	23	32
1986-87	Moncton	AHL	69	2	19	21	21	4	0	0	0	2
1987-88	Maine	AHL	69	5	30	35	65	7	1	3	4	4
1988-89	Cdn. National	...	61	8	38	46	44	....	....	....	....	....
1989-90	Cdn. National	...	12	3	1	4	4	....	....	....	....	....
	Varese	Italy	29	13	36	49	16	3	3	3	6	0
1990-91	Cdn. National	...	57	12	30	42	62	....	....	....	....	....

HYNNES, CHRIS

Defense. Shoots left. 6', 185 lbs. Born, Thunder Bay, Ont., December 8, 1970.
(Quebec's 2nd choice, 8th overall, in 1991 Supplemental Draft).

			Regular Season					Playoffs				
Season	Club	Lea	GP	G	A	TP	PIM	GP	G	A	TP	PIM
1989-90	Colorado	WCHA	17	0	3	3	10	....	....	....	....	....
1990-91	Colorado	WCHA	40	8	18	26	64	....	....	....	....	....

IAFRATE, AL (IGH-uh-FRAY-tee)

Defense. Shoots left. 6'3", 220 lbs. Born, Dearborn, Mich., March 21, 1966.
(Toronto's 1st choice, 4th overall, in 1984 Entry Draft).

			Regular Season					Playoffs				
Season	Club	Lea	GP	G	A	TP	PIM	GP	G	A	TP	PIM
1983-84	U.S. National	...	55	4	17	21	26	....	....	....	....	....
	U.S. Olympic	...	6	0	0	0	2	....	....	....	....	....
	Belleville	OHL	10	2	4	6	2	3	0	1	1	5
1984-85	Toronto	NHL	68	5	16	21	51	....	....	....	....	....
1985-86	Toronto	NHL	65	8	25	33	40	10	0	3	3	4
1986-87	Toronto	NHL	80	9	21	30	55	13	1	3	4	11
1987-88	Toronto	NHL	77	22	30	52	80	6	3	4	7	6
1988-89	Toronto	NHL	65	13	20	33	72	....	....	....	....	....
1989-90	Toronto	NHL	75	21	42	63	135	....	....	....	....	....
1990-91	Toronto	NHL	42	3	15	18	113	....	....	....	....	....
	Washington	NHL	30	6	8	14	124	10	1	3	4	22
	NHL Totals		502	87	177	264	670	39	5	13	18	43

Played in NHL All-Star Game (1988, 1990)

Traded to **Washington** by **Toronto** for Peter Zezel and Bob Rouse, January 16, 1991.

IHNACAK, MIROSLAV (IH-nuh-chehk)

Left wing. Shoots left. 5'11", 175 lbs. Born, Poprad, Czechoslovakia, November 19, 1962.
(Toronto's 12th choice, 171st overall, in 1982 Entry Draft).

			Regular Season					Playoffs				
Season	Club	Lea	GP	G	A	TP	PIM	GP	G	A	TP	PIM
1984-85	VSZ Kosice	Czech.	43	35	31	66	68	....	....	....	....	....
1985-86	VSZ Kosice	Czech.	21	16	16	32	....	....	....	....	....	....
	Toronto	NHL	21	2	4	6	27	....	....	....	....	....
	St. Catharines	AHL	13	4	4	8	2	13	8	3	11	10
1986-87	Toronto	NHL	34	6	5	11	12	1	0	0	0	0
	Newmarket	AHL	32	11	17	28	6	....	....	....	....	....
1987-88	Newmarket	AHL	51	11	17	28	24	....	....	....	....	....
1988-89	Detroit	NHL	1	0	0	0	0	....	....	....	....	....
	Adirondack	AHL	62	34	37	71	32	13	4	3	7	16
1989-90	Halifax	AHL	57	33	37	70	43	5	1	4	5	6
1990-91	Halifax	AHL	77	38	57	95	42	....	....	....	....	....
	NHL Totals		56	8	9	17	39	1	0	0	0	0

Signed as a free agent by **Detroit**, November 18, 1988.

IHNACAK, PETER   (IH-nuh-chehk)

Center. Shoots right. 5'11", 180 lbs.   Born, Poprad, Czechoslovakia, May 3, 1957.
(Toronto's 3rd choice, 25th overall, in 1982 Entry Draft).

				Regular Season					Playoffs			
Season	Club	Lea	GP	G	A	TP	PIM	GP	G	A	TP	PIM
1979-80	Sparta Praha	Czech.	44	22	12	34	....	....	....	....	....	....
1980-81	Sparta Praha	Czech.	44	23	22	45	....	....	....	....	....	....
1981-82	Sparta Praha	Czech.	39	16	22	38	30	....	....	....	....	....
1982-83	**Toronto**	NHL	80	28	38	66	44	....	....	....	....	....
1983-84	**Toronto**	NHL	47	10	13	23	24	....	....	....	....	....
1984-85	**Toronto**	NHL	70	22	22	44	24	....	....	....	....	....
1985-86	**Toronto**	NHL	63	18	27	45	16	10	2	3	5	12
1986-87	**Toronto**	NHL	58	12	27	39	16	13	2	4	6	9
	Newmarket	AHL	8	2	6	8	0	....	....	....	....	....
1987-88	**Toronto**	NHL	68	10	20	30	41	5	0	3	3	4
1988-89	**Toronto**	NHL	26	2	16	18	10	....	....	....	....	....
	Newmarket	AHL	38	14	16	30	8	....	....	....	....	....
1989-90	**Toronto**	NHL	5	0	2	2	0	....	....	....	....	....
	Newmarket	AHL	72	26	47	73	40	....	....	....	....	....
1990-91	Freiburg	Ger.	35	12	37	39	39	....	....	....	....	....
	NHL Totals		417	102	165	267	175	28	4	10	14	25

ILJINA, TIMO   (EEL-eenah)

Center. Shoots left. 5'11", 175 lbs.   Born, Oulu, Finland, June 6, 1966.
(Washington's 6th choice, 143rd overall, in 1984 Entry Draft).

				Regular Season					Playoffs			
Season	Club	Lea	GP	G	A	TP	PIM	GP	G	A	TP	PIM
1986-87	Karpat	Fin.	28	5	4	9	8	3	0	0	0	0
1987-88	Karpat	Fin.	44	17	15	32	14	....	....	....	....	....
1988-89	Karpat	Fin.	43	8	22	30	20	....	....	....	....	....
1989-90	JoKP	Fin.	44	2	19	21	23	....	....	....	....	....
1990-91	JoKP	Fin.	41	15	29	44	16	....	....	....	....	....

INGMAN, JAN   (EENG-mahn)

Left wing. Shoots left. 6'3", 194 lbs.   Born, Grums, Sweden, November 25, 1961.
(Montreal's 3rd choice, 19th overall, in 1981 Entry Draft).

				Regular Season					Playoffs			
Season	Club	Lea	GP	G	A	TP	PIM	GP	G	A	TP	PIM
1985-86	Farjestad	Swe.	33	19	12	31	20	7	4	1	5	4
1986-87	Farjestad	Swe.	28	9	11	20	14	....	....	....	....	....
1987-88	Farjestad	Swe.	28	6	7	13	14	9	5	3	8	2
1988-89	Farjestad	Swe.	32	15	19	34	24	2	1	1	2	6
1989-90	Farjestad	Swe.	32	15	13	28	16	10	5	3	8	2
1990-91	Farjestad	Swe.	27	3	2	5	14	....	....	....	....	....

Rights traded to **Winnipeg** by **Montreal** with Steve Penney for Brian Hayward, August 19, 1986.

ISSEL, KIM   (IH-sehl)

Right wing. Shoots right. 6'4", 196 lbs.   Born, Regina, Sask., September 25, 1967.
(Edmonton's 1st choice, 21st overall, in 1986 Entry Draft).

				Regular Season					Playoffs			
Season	Club	Lea	GP	G	A	TP	PIM	GP	G	A	TP	PIM
1983-84	Prince Albert	WHL	31	9	9	18	24	....	....	....	....	....
1984-85	Prince Albert	WHL	44	8	15	23	24	....	....	....	....	....
1985-86	Prince Albert	WHL	68	29	39	68	41	19	6	7	13	6
1986-87	Prince Albert	WHL	70	31	44	75	55	6	1	2	3	17
1987-88	Nova Scotia	AHL	68	2	25	27	31	2	1	0	1	10
1988-89	**Edmonton**	NHL	4	0	0	0	0	....	....	....	....	....
	Cape Breton	AHL	65	34	28	62	4	....	....	....	....	....
1989-90	Cape Breton	AHL	62	36	32	68	46	6	1	3	4	10
1990-91	Cape Breton	AHL	24	6	4	10	28	....	....	....	....	....
	Kansas City	IHL	13	7	2	9	2	....	....	....	....	....
	NHL Totals		4	0	0	0	0	....	....	....	....	....

Traded to **Pittsburgh** by **Edmonton** for Brad Aitken, March 5, 1991.

JABLONSKI, JEFF

Left wing. Shoots left. 6', 185 lbs.   Born, Toledo, OH, June 20, 1967.
(NY Islanders' 11th choice, 185th overall, in 1986 Entry Draft).

				Regular Season					Playoffs			
Season	Club	Lea	GP	G	A	TP	PIM	GP	G	A	TP	PIM
1986-87	Lake Superior	CCHA	40	17	10	27	42	....	....	....	....	....
1987-88	Lake Superior	CCHA	46	13	12	25	54	....	....	....	....	....
1988-89	Lake Superior	CCHA	45	11	12	23	48	....	....	....	....	....
1989-90	Lake Superior	CCHA	46	38	33	71	82	....	....	....	....	....
1990-91	Capital Dist.	AHL	44	6	6	12	4	....	....	....	....	....
	Kansas City	IHL	10	3	4	7	4	....	....	....	....	....

JACKSON, DANE

Right wing. Shoots right. 6'1", 190 lbs.   Born, Winnipeg, Man., May 17, 1970.
(Vancouver's 3rd choice, 44th overall, in 1988 Entry Draft).

				Regular Season					Playoffs			
Season	Club	Lea	GP	G	A	TP	PIM	GP	G	A	TP	PIM
1988-89	North Dakota	WCHA	30	4	5	9	33	....	....	....	....	....
1989-90	North Dakota	WCHA	44	15	11	26	56	....	....	....	....	....
1990-91	North Dakota	WCHA	37	17	9	26	79	....	....	....	....	....

JACKSON, JEFF

Left wing. Shoots left. 6'1", 195 lbs.   Born, Dresden, Ont., April 24, 1965.
(Toronto's 2nd choice, 28th overall, in 1983 Entry Draft).

				Regular Season					Playoffs			
Season	Club	Lea	GP	G	A	TP	PIM	GP	G	A	TP	PIM
1982-83	Brantford	OHL	64	18	25	43	63	8	1	1	2	27
1983-84	Brantford	OHL	58	27	42	69	78	2	0	1	1	0
1984-85	**Toronto**	NHL	17	0	1	1	24	....	....	....	....	....
	Hamilton	OHL	20	13	14	27	51	17	8	12	20	26
1985-86	**Toronto**	NHL	5	1	2	3	2	....	....	....	....	....
	St. Catharines	AHL	74	17	28	45	122	13	5	2	7	30
1986-87	**Toronto**	NHL	55	8	7	15	64	....	....	....	....	....
	Newmarket	AHL	7	3	6	9	13	....	....	....	....	....
	NY Rangers	NHL	9	5	1	6	15	6	1	1	2	16
1987-88	**Quebec**	NHL	68	9	18	27	103	....	....	....	....	....
1988-89	**Quebec**	NHL	33	4	6	10	28	....	....	....	....	....
1989-90	**Quebec**	NHL	65	8	12	20	71	....	....	....	....	....
1990-91	**Quebec**	NHL	10	3	1	4	4	....	....	....	....	....
	Halifax	AHL	25	8	17	25	45	....	....	....	....	....
	NHL Totals		262	38	48	86	311	6	1	1	2	16

Traded to **NY Rangers** by **Toronto** with Toronto's third-round choice (Rob Zamuner) in 1989 Entry Draft for Mark Osborne, March 5, 1987. Traded to **Quebec** by **NY Rangers** with Terry Carkner for John Ogrodnick and David Shaw, September, 30, 1987.

JACKSON, MICHAEL

Right wing. Shoots right. 6', 190 lbs.   Born, Mississauga, Ont., February 4, 1969.
(Toronto's 12th choice, 213th overall, in 1989 Entry Draft).

				Regular Season					Playoffs			
Season	Club	Lea	GP	G	A	TP	PIM	GP	G	A	TP	PIM
1988-89	Toronto	OHL	55	16	51	67	180	6	2	6	8	2
1989-90	Cornwall	OHL	26	15	29	44	59	....	....	....	....	....
	Hamilton	OHL	15	8	13	21	41	6	2	4	6	33
1990-91	Newmarket	AHL	48	5	9	14	126	....	....	....	....	....

JAGR, JAROMIR   (YA-guhr)

Right wing. Shoots left. 6'2", 208 lbs.   Born, Kladno, Czechoslovakia, February 15, 1972.
(Pittsburgh's 1st choice, 5th overall, in 1990 Entry Draft).

				Regular Season					Playoffs			
Season	Club	Lea	GP	G	A	TP	PIM	GP	G	A	TP	PIM
1988-89	Kladno	Czech.	39	8	10	18	....	....	....	....	....	....
1989-90	Kladno	Czech.	51	30	30	60	....	....	....	....	....	....
1990-91a	**Pittsburgh**	NHL	80	27	30	57	42	24	3	10	13	6
	NHL Totals		80	27	30	57	42	24	3	10	13	6

a NHL/Upper Deck All-Rookie Team (1991)

JANNEY, CRAIG

Center. Shoots left. 6'1", 190 lbs.   Born, Hartford, CT, September 26, 1967.
(Boston's 1st choice, 13th overall, in 1986 Entry Draft).

				Regular Season					Playoffs			
Season	Club	Lea	GP	G	A	TP	PIM	GP	G	A	TP	PIM
1985-86	Boston College	H.E.	34	13	14	27	8	....	....	....	....	....
1986-87ab	Boston College	H.E.	37	26	55	81	6	....	....	....	....	....
1987-88	U.S. National	...	52	26	44	70	6	....	....	....	....	....
	U.S. Olympic	...	5	3	1	4	2	....	....	....	....	....
	Boston	NHL	15	7	9	16	0	23	6	10	16	11
1988-89	**Boston**	NHL	62	16	46	62	12	10	4	9	13	21
1989-90	**Boston**	NHL	55	24	38	62	4	18	3	19	22	2
1990-91	**Boston**	NHL	77	26	66	92	8	18	4	18	22	11
	NHL Totals		209	73	159	232	24	69	17	56	73	45

a Hockey East First All-Star Team (1987)
b NCAA East First All-American Team (1987)

JANSSENS, MARK

Center. Shoots left. 6'3", 216 lbs.   Born, Surrey, B.C., May 19, 1968.
(NY Rangers' 4th choice, 72nd overall, in 1986 Entry Draft).

				Regular Season					Playoffs			
Season	Club	Lea	GP	G	A	TP	PIM	GP	G	A	TP	PIM
1984-85	Regina	WHL	70	8	22	30	51	....	....	....	....	....
1985-86	Regina	WHL	71	25	38	63	146	9	0	2	2	17
1986-87	Regina	WHL	68	24	38	62	209	3	0	1	1	14
1987-88	**NY Rangers**	NHL	1	0	0	0	0	....	....	....	....	....
	Colorado	IHL	6	2	2	4	24	12	3	2	5	20
	Regina	WHL	71	39	51	90	202	4	3	4	7	6
1988-89	**NY Rangers**	NHL	5	0	0	0	0	....	....	....	....	....
	Denver	IHL	38	19	19	38	104	4	3	0	3	18
1989-90	**NY Rangers**	NHL	80	5	8	13	161	9	2	1	3	10
1990-91	**NY Rangers**	NHL	67	9	7	16	172	6	3	0	3	6
	NHL Totals		153	14	15	29	333	15	5	1	6	16

JAQUES, STEVE

Defense. Shoots left. 5'11", 180 lbs.   Born, Burnaby, B.C., February 21, 1969.
(Los Angeles' 11th choice, 228th overall, in 1989 Entry Draft).

				Regular Season					Playoffs			
Season	Club	Lea	GP	G	A	TP	PIM	GP	G	A	TP	PIM
1987-88	N. Westminster	WHL	69	15	31	46	336	5	0	4	4	31
1988-89	Tri-Cities	WHL	61	18	34	52	233	2	0	0	0	9
1989-90a	Tri-Cities	WHL	64	20	64	84	185	6	1	2	3	55
1990-91	Phoenix	IHL	58	10	24	34	227	9	2	6	8	21

a WHL West Second All-Star Team (1990)

JARDEMYR, DANIEL

Defense. Shoots left. 6'2", 183 lbs.   Born, Uppsala, Sweden, May 28, 1971.
(Winnipeg's 7th choice, 119th overall, in 1990 Entry Draft).

				Regular Season					Playoffs			
Season	Club	Lea	GP	G	A	TP	PIM	GP	G	A	TP	PIM
1989-90	Uppsala	Swe.	27	5	9	14	32	....	....	....	....	....
1990-91	AIK	Swe.	27	1	2	3	41	....	....	....	....	....

JARVENPAA, HANNU (YAHR-vehn-pah)

Right wing. Shoots left. 6', 194 lbs. Born, Ii, Finland, May 19, 1963.
(Winnipeg's 4th choice, 71st overall, in 1986 Entry Draft).

			Regular Season					Playoffs				
Season	Club	Lea	GP	G	A	TP	PIM	GP	G	A	TP	PIM
1984-85	Karpat	Fin.	34	12	12	24	45	7	2	2	4	2
1985-86	Karpat	Fin.	36	26	9	35	48	5	5	2	7	12
1986-87	**Winnipeg**	**NHL**	**20**	**1**	**8**	**9**	**8**	....	....	....	....	....
1987-88	**Winnipeg**	**NHL**	**41**	**6**	**11**	**17**	**34**	....	....	....	....	....
	Moncton	AHL	5	3	1	4	2	....	....	....	....	....
1988-89	**Winnipeg**	**NHL**	**53**	**4**	**7**	**11**	**41**	....	....	....	....	....
	Moncton	AHL	4	1	0	1	0	....	....	....	....	....
1989-90	Lukko	Fin.	38	12	15	27	48	....	....	....	....	....
1990-91	Lukko	Fin.	43	27	18	45	54	....	....	....	....	....
	NHL Totals		**114**	**11**	**26**	**37**	**83**	....	....	....	....	....

JARVI, IIRO (YAHR-vee)

Left wing. Shoots left. 6'1", 198 lbs. Born, Helsinki, Finland, March 23, 1965.
(Quebec's 3rd choice, 54th overall, in 1983 Entry Draft).

			Regular Season					Playoffs				
Season	Club	Lea	GP	G	A	TP	PIM	GP	G	A	TP	PIM
1985-86	HIFK	Fin.	29	7	6	13	19	10	4	6	10	2
1986-87	HIFK	Fin.	43	23	30	53	82	5	1	5	6	9
1987-88	HIFK	Fin.	44	21	20	41	68	5	2	1	3	7
1988-89	**Quebec**	**NHL**	**75**	**11**	**30**	**41**	**40**	....	....	....	....	....
1989-90	**Quebec**	**NHL**	**41**	**7**	**13**	**20**	**18**	....	....	....	....	....
	Halifax	AHL	26	4	13	17	4	....	....	....	....	....
1990-91	Winterthur	Aus.	26	12	21	33	....	....	....	....	....	....
	Halifax	AHL	5	0	2	2	2	....	....	....	....	....
	NHL Totals		**116**	**18**	**43**	**61**	**58**	....	....	....	....	....

JENNINGS, GRANT

Defense. Shoots left. 6'3", 200 lbs. Born, Hudson Bay, Sask., May 5, 1965.

			Regular Season					Playoffs				
Season	Club	Lea	GP	G	A	TP	PIM	GP	G	A	TP	PIM
1983-84	Saskatoon	WHL	64	5	13	18	102	....	....	....	....	....
1984-85	Saskatoon	WHL	47	10	24	34	134	2	1	0	1	2
1985-86	Binghamton	AHL	51	0	4	4	109	....	....	....	....	....
1986-87	Fort Wayne	IHL	3	0	0	0	0	....	....	....	....	....
	Binghamton	AHL	47	1	5	6	125	13	0	2	2	17
1987-88	**Washington**	**NHL**	....	....	....	....	....	**1**	**0**	**0**	**0**	**0**
	Binghamton	AHL	56	2	12	14	195	3	1	0	1	15
1988-89	**Hartford**	**NHL**	**55**	**3**	**10**	**13**	**159**	**4**	**1**	**0**	**1**	**17**
	Binghamton	AHL	2	0	0	0	2	....	....	....	....	....
1989-90	**Hartford**	**NHL**	**64**	**3**	**6**	**9**	**171**	**7**	**0**	**0**	**0**	**13**
1990-91	**Hartford**	**NHL**	**44**	**1**	**4**	**5**	**82**	....	....	....	....	....
	Pittsburgh	**NHL**	**13**	**1**	**3**	**4**	**26**	**13**	**1**	**1**	**2**	**16**
	NHL Totals		**176**	**8**	**23**	**31**	**438**	**25**	**2**	**1**	**3**	**46**

Signed as a free agent by **Washington**, June 25, 1985. Traded to **Hartford** by **Washington** with Ed Kastelic for Mike Millar and Neil Sheehy, July 6, 1988. Traded to **Pittsburgh** by **Hartford** with Ron Francis and Ulf Samuelsson for John Cullen, Jeff Parker and Zarley Zalapski, March 4, 1991.

JENSEN, CHRIS

Right wing. Shoots right. 5'11", 170 lbs. Born, Fort St. John, B.C., October 28, 1963.
(NY Rangers' 4th choice, 78th overall, in 1982 Entry Draft).

			Regular Season					Playoffs				
Season	Club	Lea	GP	G	A	TP	PIM	GP	G	A	TP	PIM
1982-83	North Dakota	WCHA	13	3	3	6	28	....	....	....	....	....
1983-84	North Dakota	WCHA	44	24	25	49	100	....	....	....	....	....
1984-85	North Dakota	WCHA	40	25	27	52	80	....	....	....	....	....
1985-86	North Dakota	WCHA	34	25	40	65	53	....	....	....	....	....
	NY Rangers	**NHL**	**9**	**1**	**3**	**4**	**0**	....	....	....	....	....
1986-87	**NY Rangers**	**NHL**	**37**	**6**	**7**	**13**	**21**	....	....	....	....	....
	New Haven	AHL	14	4	9	13	41	....	....	....	....	....
1987-88	**NY Rangers**	**NHL**	**7**	**0**	**1**	**1**	**2**	....	....	....	....	....
	Colorado	IHL	43	10	23	33	68	10	3	7	10	8
1988-89	Hershey	AHL	45	27	31	58	66	10	4	5	9	29
1989-90	**Philadelphia**	**NHL**	**1**	**0**	**0**	**0**	**0**	....	....	....	....	....
	Hershey	AHL	43	16	26	42	101	....	....	....	....	....
1990-91	**Philadelphia**	**NHL**	**18**	**2**	**1**	**3**	**2**	....	....	....	....	....
	Hershey	AHL	50	26	20	46	83	6	2	2	4	10
	NHL Totals		**72**	**9**	**12**	**21**	**25**	....	....	....	....	....

Traded to **Philadelphia** by **NY Rangers** for Michael Boyce, September 28, 1988.

JENSEN, CHRISTOPHER

Defense. Shoots right. 6'2", 190 lbs. Born, Wilmette, IL, June 29, 1968.
(Toronto's 8th choice, 154th overall, in 1987 Entry Draft).

			Regular Season					Playoffs				
Season	Club	Lea	GP	G	A	TP	PIM	GP	G	A	TP	PIM
1989-90	N. Hampshire	H.E.	DID NOT PLAY									
1990-91	N. Hampshire	H.E.	5	0	3	3	2	....	....	....	....	....

JENSEN, DAVID A.

Center. Shoots left. 6'1", 195 lbs. Born, Newton, MA, August 19, 1965.
(Hartford's 2nd choice, 20th overall, in 1983 Entry Draft).

			Regular Season					Playoffs				
Season	Club	Lea	GP	G	A	TP	PIM	GP	G	A	TP	PIM
1983-84	U.S. National	...	61	22	56	78	6	....	....	....	....	....
	U.S. Olympic	...	6	2	7	9	0	....	....	....	....	....
1984-85	**Hartford**	**NHL**	**13**	**0**	**4**	**4**	**6**	....	....	....	....	....
	Binghamton	AHL	40	8	9	17	2	....	....	....	....	....
1985-86	**Washington**	**NHL**	**5**	**1**	**0**	**1**	**0**	**4**	**0**	**0**	**0**	**0**
	Binghamton	AHL	41	17	14	31	4	4	2	4	6	0
1986-87	**Washington**	**NHL**	**46**	**8**	**8**	**16**	**12**	**7**	**0**	**0**	**0**	**2**
	Binghamton	AHL	6	2	5	7	0	....	....	....	....	....
1987-88	**Washington**	**NHL**	**5**	**0**	**1**	**1**	**4**	....	....	....	....	....
	Binghamton	AHL	9	5	2	7	2	....	....	....	....	....
	Fort Wayne	IHL	32	10	13	23	8	5	1	1	2	0
1988-89	Maine	AHL	18	12	8	20	2	....	....	....	....	....
1989-90	Maine	AHL	4	0	2	2	0	....	....	....	....	....
1990-91	Cortina	Italy	35	27	18	45	8	6	7	7	14	4
	NHL Totals		**69**	**9**	**13**	**22**	**22**	**11**	**0**	**0**	**0**	**2**

Traded to **Washington** by **Hartford** for Dean Evason and Peter Sidorkiewicz, March 12, 1985. Signed as a free agent by **Boston**, August 1, 1988.

JERRARD, PAUL

Right wing. Shoots right. 5'10", 185 lbs. Born, Winnipeg, Man., April 20, 1965.
(NY Rangers' 10th choice, 173rd overall, in 1983 Entry Draft).

			Regular Season					Playoffs				
Season	Club	Lea	GP	G	A	TP	PIM	GP	G	A	TP	PIM
1983-84	Lake Superior	CCHA	40	8	18	26	48	....	....	....	....	....
1984-85	Lake Superior	CCHA	43	9	25	34	61	....	....	..	....	....
1985-86	Lake Superior	CCHA	38	13	11	24	34	....	....	....	....	....
1986-87	Lake Superior	CCHA	35	10	19	29	56	....	....	....	....	....
1987-88	Colorado	IHL	77	20	28	48	182	11	2	4	6	40
1988-89	Denver	IHL	2	1	1	2	21	....	....	....	....	....
	Minnesota	**NHL**	**5**	**0**	**0**	**0**	**4**	....	....	....	....	....
	Kalamazoo	IHL	68	15	25	40	195	6	2	1	3	37
1989-90	Kalamazoo	IHL	60	9	18	27	134	7	1	1	2	11
1990-91	Albany	IHL	7	0	3	3	30	....	....	....	....	....
	Kalamazoo	IHL	62	10	23	33	111	7	0	0	0	13
	NHL Totals		**5**	**0**	**0**	**0**	**4**	....	....	....	....	....

Traded to **Minnesota** by **N.Y. Rangers** with Mark Tinordi, the rights to Bret Barnett and Mike Sullivan, and Los Angeles' third-round choice (Murray Garbutt) in 1989 Entry Draft – acquired March 10, 1987 by Minnesota – for Brian Lawton, Igor Liba and the rights to Eric Bennett, October 11, 1988.

JESTADT, JEFF

Left wing. Shoots left. 6'1", 195 lbs. Born, Hinsdale, IL, September 6, 1970.
(Winnipeg's 2nd choice, 11th overall, in 1991 Supplemental Draft).

			Regular Season					Playoffs				
Season	Club	Lea	GP	G	A	TP	PIM	GP	G	A	TP	PIM
1989-90	Ferris St.	CCHA	35	7	2	9	52	....	....	....	....	....
1990-91	Ferris St.	CCHA	33	8	8	16	31	....	....	....	....	....

JIRANEK, MARTIN

Center. Shoots left. 5'11", 170 lbs. Born, Bashaw, Alta., October 3, 1969.
(Washington's 1st choice, 14th overall, in 1990 Supplemental Draft).

			Regular Season					Playoffs				
Season	Club	Lea	GP	G	A	TP	PIM	GP	G	A	TP	PIM
1988-89	Bowling Green	CCHA	41	9	18	27	36	....	....	....	....	....
1989-90	Bowling Green	CCHA	41	13	21	34	38	....	....	....	....	....
1990-91	Bowling Green	CCHA	39	31	23	54	33	....	....	....	....	....

JOBE, TREVOR (JOHB)

Left wing. Shoots left. 6'1", 190 lbs. Born, Lethbridge, Alta., May 14, 1967.
(Toronto's 7th choice, 133rd overall, in 1987 Entry Draft).

			Regular Season					Playoffs				
Season	Club	Lea	GP	G	A	TP	PIM	GP	G	A	TP	PIM
1984-85	Calgary	WHL	66	5	19	24	23	8	0	0	0	0
1985-86	Calgary	WHL	7	0	2	2	2	....	....	....	....	....
	Lethbridge	WHL	5	1	0	1	0	....	....	....	....	....
	Spokane	WHL	11	1	4	5	0	....	....	....	....	....
1986-87	Moose Jaw	WHL	58	54	33	87	53	9	4	2	6	4
1987-88	Moose Jaw	WHL	36	36	35	71	63	....	....	....	....	....
	Prince Albert	WHL	36	33	28	61	48	9	6	6	12	41
1988-89	Newmarket	AHL	75	23	24	47	90	5	0	1	1	12
1989-90	Newmarket	AHL	1	0	1	1	2	....	....	....	....	....
	Hampton Roads	ECHL	51	48	23	71	143	5	5	5	10	30
1990-91	Nashville	ECHL	59	49	60	109	229	....	....	....	....	....
	Newmarket	AHL	2	0	1	1	0	....	....	....	....	....

JOHANNSON, JAMES (JIM)

Center. Shoots right. 6'2", 200 lbs. Born, Rochester, MN, March 10, 1964.

			Regular Season					Playoffs				
Season	Club	Lea	GP	G	A	TP	PIM	GP	G	A	TP	PIM
1982-83	U. Wisconsin	WCHA	43	12	9	21	16	....	....	....	....	....
1983-84	U. Wisconsin	WCHA	35	17	21	38	52	....	....	....	....	....
1984-85	U. Wisconsin	WCHA	40	16	24	40	54	....	....	....	....	....
1985-86	U. Wisconsin	WCHA	30	18	13	31	44	....	....	....	....	....
1986-87	Landsberg	W.Ger.	57	46	56	102	90	....	....	....	....	....
1987-88	U.S. National	...	47	16	14	30	64	....	....	....	....	....
	U.S. Olympic	...	4	0	1	1	4	....	....	....	....	....
	Salt Lake	IHL	18	14	7	21	50	19	8	*15	23	55
1988-89	Salt Lake	IHL	82	35	40	75	87	13	2	5	7	13
1989-90	Indianapolis	IHL	82	22	41	63	74	14	1	4	5	6
1990-91	Indianapolis	IHL	82	28	41	69	116	7	1	2	3	8

Signed as a free agent by **Calgary**, February 25, 1988. Signed as a free agent by **Chicago**, July 6, 1989.

JOHANSSON, CALLE   (yo-HAHN-suhn)

Defense. Shoots left. 5'11", 205 lbs.   Born, Goteborg, Sweden, February 14, 1967.
(Buffalo's 1st choice, 14th overall, in 1985 Entry Draft).

			Regular Season					Playoffs				
Season	Club	Lea	GP	G	A	TP	PIM	GP	G	A	TP	PIM
1983-84	V. Frolunda	Swe.	28	4	4	8	10	....	....	....	....	....
1984-85	V. Frolunda	Swe.2	25	8	13	21	16	6	1	2	3	4
1985-86	Bjorkloven	Swe.	17	1	2	3	4	....	....	....	....	....
1986-87	Bjorkloven	Swe.	30	2	13	15	20	6	1	3	4	6
1987-88a	**Buffalo**	**NHL**	71	4	38	42	37	6	0	1	1	0
1988-89	**Buffalo**	**NHL**	47	2	11	13	33	....	....	....	....	....
	Washington	**NHL**	12	1	7	8	4	6	1	2	3	0
1989-90	**Washington**	**NHL**	70	8	31	39	25	15	1	6	7	4
1990-91	**Washington**	**NHL**	80	11	41	52	23	10	2	7	9	8
	NHL Totals		280	26	128	154	122	37	4	16	20	12

a Named to NHL All-Rookie Team (1988)

Traded to **Washington** by **Buffalo** with Buffalo's second-round choice (Byron Dafoe) in 1989 Entry Draft for Clint Malarchuk, Grant Ledyard and Washington's sixth-round choice (Brian Holzinger) in 1991 Entry Draft, March 7, 1989.

JOHANSSON, ROGER   (yo-HAHN-suhn)

Defense. Shoots left. 6'1", 185 lbs.   Born, Ljungby, Sweden, April 17, 1967.
(Calgary's 5th choice, 80th overall, in 1985 Entry Draft).

			Regular Season					Playoffs				
Season	Club	Lea	GP	G	A	TP	PIM	GP	G	A	TP	PIM
1986-87	Farjestad	Swe.	31	6	11	17	20	7	1	1	2	8
1987-88	Farjestad	Swe.	24	3	11	14	20	....	....	....	....	....
1988-89	Farjestad	Swe.	40	5	15	20	36	....	....	....	....	....
1989-90	**Calgary**	**NHL**	35	0	5	5	48	....	....	....	....	....
1990-91	**Calgary**	**NHL**	38	4	13	17	47	....	....	....	....	....
	NHL Totals		73	4	18	22	95	....	....	....	....	....

JOHNSON, CHAD

Center. Shoots left. 6', 175 lbs.   Born, Grand Forks, ND, January 10, 1970.
(New Jersey's 7th choice, 117th overall, in 1988 Entry Draft).

			Regular Season					Playoffs				
Season	Club	Lea	GP	G	A	TP	PIM	GP	G	A	TP	PIM
1989-90	Minot	SJHL	54	33	43	76	89	....	....	....	....	....
1990-91	North Dakota	WCHL	37	2	5	7	30	....	....	....	....	....

JOHNSON, CRAIG

Left wing/Center. Shoots left. 6'2", 185 lbs.   Born, St. Paul, MN, March 18, 1972.
(St. Louis' 1st choice, 33rd overall, in 1990 Entry Draft).

			Regular Season					Playoffs				
Season	Club	Lea	GP	G	A	TP	PIM	GP	G	A	TP	PIM
1989-90	Hill-Murray	HS	23	15	36	51	....	....	....	....	....	....
1990-91	U. Minnesota	WCHA	33	13	18	31	34	....	....	....	....	....

JOHNSON, GREG

Center. Shoots left. 5'10", 173 lbs.   Born, Thunder Bay, Ont., March 16, 1971.
(Philadelphia's 1st choice, 33rd overall, in 1989 Entry Draft).

			Regular Season					Playoffs				
Season	Club	Lea	GP	G	A	TP	PIM	GP	G	A	TP	PIM
1988-89abc	Thunder Bay	USHL	47	32	64	96	4	12	5	13	18	....
1989-90	North Dakota	WCHA	44	17	38	55	11	....	....	....	....	....
1990-91de	North Dakota	WCHA	38	18	*61	79	6	....	....	....	....	....

a Canadian Junior A Player of the Year (1989)
b USHL First All-Star Team (1989)
c Centennial Cup First All-Star Team (1989)
d WCHA First All-Star Team (1991)
e NCAA West First All-American Team (1991)

JOHNSON, JIM

Defense. Shoots left. 6'1", 190 lbs.   Born, New Hope, MN, August 9, 1962.

			Regular Season					Playoffs				
Season	Club	Lea	GP	G	A	TP	PIM	GP	G	A	TP	PIM
1981-82	Minn.-Duluth	WCHA	40	0	10	10	62	....	....	....	....	....
1982-83	Minn.-Duluth	WCHA	44	3	18	21	118	....	....	....	....	....
1983-84	Minn.-Duluth	WCHA	43	3	13	16	116	....	....	....	....	....
1984-85	Minn.-Duluth	WCHA	47	7	29	36	49	....	....	....	....	....
1985-86	**Pittsburgh**	**NHL**	80	3	26	29	115	....	....	....	....	....
1986-87	**Pittsburgh**	**NHL**	80	5	25	30	116	....	....	....	....	....
1987-88	**Pittsburgh**	**NHL**	55	1	12	13	87	....	....	....	....	....
1988-89	**Pittsburgh**	**NHL**	76	2	14	16	163	11	0	5	5	44
1989-90	**Pittsburgh**	**NHL**	75	3	13	16	154	....	....	....	....	....
1990-91	**Pittsburgh**	**NHL**	24	0	5	5	23	....	....	....	....	....
	Minnesota	**NHL**	44	1	9	10	100	14	0	1	1	52
	NHL Totals		434	15	104	119	758	25	0	6	6	96

Signed as a free agent by **Pittsburgh**, June 9, 1985. Traded to **Minnesota** by **Pittsburgh** with Chris Dahlquist for Larry Murphy and Peter Taglianetti, December 11, 1990.

JOHNSON, MARK

Center. Shoots left. 5'9", 170 lbs.   Born, Madison, WI, September 22, 1957.
(Pittsburgh's 3rd choice, 66th overall, in 1977 Amateur Draft).

			Regular Season					Playoffs				
Season	Club	Lea	GP	G	A	TP	PIM	GP	G	A	TP	PIM
1977-78a	U. Wisconsin	WCHA	42	*48	38	86	24	....	....	....	....	....
1978-79ab	U. Wisconsin	WCHA	40	*41	49	*90	34	....	....	....	....	....
1979-80	U.S. National	...	53	33	48	81	25	....	....	....	....	....
	U.S. Olympic	...	7	5	6	11	6	....	....	....	....	....
	Pittsburgh	**NHL**	17	3	5	8	4	5	2	2	4	0
1980-81	**Pittsburgh**	**NHL**	73	10	23	33	50	5	2	1	3	6
1981-82	**Pittsburgh**	**NHL**	46	10	11	21	30	....	....	....	....	....
	Minnesota	**NHL**	10	2	2	4	10	4	2	0	2	0
1982-83	**Hartford**	**NHL**	73	31	38	69	28	....	....	....	....	....
1983-84	**Hartford**	**NHL**	79	35	52	87	27	....	....	....	....	....
1984-85	**Hartford**	**NHL**	49	19	28	47	21	....	....	....	....	....
	St. Louis	**NHL**	17	4	6	10	2	3	0	1	1	0
1985-86	**New Jersey**	**NHL**	80	21	41	62	16	....	....	....	....	....
1986-87	**New Jersey**	**NHL**	68	25	26	51	22	....	....	....	....	....
1987-88	**New Jersey**	**NHL**	54	14	19	33	14	18	10	8	18	4
1988-89	**New Jersey**	**NHL**	40	13	25	38	24	....	....	....	....	....
1989-90	**New Jersey**	**NHL**	63	16	29	45	12	2	0	0	0	0
1990-91	Milano	Italy	36	32	45	77	15	10	7	16	23	6
	NHL Totals		669	203	305	508	260	37	16	12	28	10

a WCHA First All-Star Team (1978, 1979)
b WCHA Player of the Year (1979)

Played in NHL All-Star Game (1984)

Traded to **Minnesota** by **Pittsburgh** for Minnesota's second round choice (Tim Hrynewich) in 1982 Entry Draft, March 2, 1982. Traded to **Hartford** by **Minnesota** with Kent-Erik Andersson for Jordy Douglas and Hartford's fifth round choice (Jiri Poner) in the 1984 Entry Draft, October 1, 1982. Traded to **St. Louis** by **Hartford** with Greg Millen for Mike Liut and Jorgen Pettersson, February 21, 1985. Traded to **New Jersey** by **St. Louis** for Shawn Evans and New Jersey's fifth-round choice (Michael Wolak) in 1986 Entry Draft, September 19, 1985.

JOHNSON, ROSS

Center. Shoots right. 6', 180 lbs.   Born, Green Bay, WI, August 5, 1967.
(Minnesota's 6th choice, 153rd overall, in 1985 Entry Draft).

			Regular Season					Playoffs				
Season	Club	Lea	GP	G	A	TP	PIM	GP	G	A	TP	PIM
1988-89	North Dakota	WCHA	19	5	7	12	6	....	....	....	....	....
1989-90	North Dakota	WCHA	43	6	9	15	22	....	....	....	....	....
1990-91	North Dakota	WCHA	10	0	0	0	6	....	....	....	....	....

JOHNSTON, GREG

Right wing. Shoots right. 6'1", 205 lbs.   Born, Barrie, Ont., January 14, 1965.
(Boston's 2nd choice, 42nd overall, in 1983 Entry Draft).

			Regular Season					Playoffs				
Season	Club	Lea	GP	G	A	TP	PIM	GP	G	A	TP	PIM
1982-83	Toronto	OHL	58	18	19	37	58	4	1	0	1	4
1983-84	**Boston**	**NHL**	15	2	1	3	2	....	....	....	....	....
	Toronto	OHL	57	38	35	73	67	9	4	2	6	13
1984-85	**Boston**	**NHL**	6	0	0	0	0	....	....	....	....	....
	Hershey	AHL	3	1	0	1	0	....	....	....	....	....
	Toronto	OHL	42	22	28	50	55	5	1	3	4	4
1985-86	**Boston**	**NHL**	20	0	2	2	0	....	....	....	....	....
	Moncton	AHL	60	19	26	45	56	10	4	6	10	4
1986-87	**Boston**	**NHL**	76	12	15	27	79	4	0	0	0	0
1987-88	Maine	AHL	75	21	32	53	106	10	6	4	10	23
	Boston	**NHL**	....	....	....	....	....	3	0	1	1	2
1988-89	**Boston**	**NHL**	57	11	10	21	32	10	1	0	1	6
	Maine	AHL	15	5	7	12	31	....	....	....	....	....
1989-90	**Boston**	**NHL**	9	1	1	2	6	5	1	0	1	4
	Maine	AHL	52	16	26	42	45	....	....	....	....	....
1990-91	**Toronto**	**NHL**	1	0	0	0	0	....	....	....	....	....
	Newmarket	AHL	73	32	50	82	54	....	....	....	....	....
	NHL Totals		184	26	29	55	119	22	2	1	3	12

Traded to **NY Rangers** by **Boston** with future considerations for Chris Nilan, June 28, 1990. Traded to **Toronto** by **NY Rangers** for Tie Domi and Mark Laforest, June 28, 1990.

JONES, BRAD

Left wing. Shoots left. 6', 195 lbs.   Born, Sterling Heights, MI, June 26, 1965.
(Winnipeg's 7th choice, 156th overall, in 1984 Entry Draft).

			Regular Season					Playoffs				
Season	Club	Lea	GP	G	A	TP	PIM	GP	G	A	TP	PIM
1983-84	U. of Michigan	CCHA	37	8	26	34	32	....	....	....	....	....
1984-85	U. of Michigan	CCHA	34	21	27	48	66	....	....	....	....	....
1985-86a	U. of Michigan	CCHA	36	28	39	67	40	....	....	....	....	....
1986-87bc	U. of Michigan	CCHA	40	32	46	78	64	....	....	....	....	....
	Winnipeg	**NHL**	4	1	0	1	0	....	....	....	....	....
1987-88	**Winnipeg**	**NHL**	19	2	5	7	15	1	0	0	0	0
	U.S. National	...	50	27	23	50	59	....	....	....	....	....
1988-89	**Winnipeg**	**NHL**	22	6	5	11	6	....	....	....	....	....
	Moncton	AHL	44	20	19	39	62	7	0	1	1	22
1989-90	**Winnipeg**	**NHL**	2	0	0	0	0	....	....	....	....	....
	Moncton	AHL	15	5	6	11	47	....	....	....	....	....
	New Haven	AHL	36	8	11	19	71	....	....	....	....	....
1990-91	**Los Angeles**	**NHL**	53	9	11	20	57	8	1	1	2	2
	NHL Totals		100	18	21	39	78	9	1	1	2	2

a CCHA Second All-Star Team (1986)
b CCHA First All-Star Team (1987)
c NCAA West Second All-American Team (1987)

Traded to **Los Angeles** by **Winnipeg** for Phil Sykes, December 1, 1989. Signed as a free agent by **Philadelphia**, August 6, 1991.

JONES, DOUGLAS

Defense. Shoots right. 5'11", 175 lbs.   Born, Powell River, B.C., May 25, 1969.
(Boston's 9th choice, 249th overall, in 1988 Entry Draft).

			Regular Season					Playoffs				
Season	Club	Lea	GP	G	A	TP	PIM	GP	G	A	TP	PIM
1987-88	Kitchener	OHL	54	7	42	49	65	....	....	....	....	....
1988-89	Western Ont.	OUAA	35	12	39	51	71	....	....	....	....	....
1989-90	Western Ont.	OUAA	28	7	20	27	47	....	....	....	....	....
1990-91	Western Ont.	OUAA	33	12	14	26	55	....	....	....	....	....

JONES, KEITH

Right wing. Shoots right. 6'2", 190 lbs. Born, Brantford, Ont., November 8, 1968.
(Washington's 7th choice, 141st overall, in 1988 Entry Draft).

			Regular Season					Playoffs				
Season	Club	Lea	GP	G	A	TP	PIM	GP	G	A	TP	PIM
1988-89	W. Michigan	CCHA	37	9	12	21	51	....	....	....	....	....
1989-90	W. Michigan	CCHA	40	19	18	37	82	....	....	....	....	....
1990-91	W. Michigan	CCHA	41	30	19	49	106	....	....	....	....	....

JONSSON, STEFAN (YAHN-suhn)

Defense. Shoots left. 6'1", 194 lbs. Born, Sodertalje, Sweden, June 13, 1965.
(Calgary's 11th choice, 221st overall, in 1984 Entry Draft).

			Regular Season					Playoffs				
Season	Club	Lea	GP	G	A	TP	PIM	GP	G	A	TP	PIM
1987-88	Sodertalje	Swe.	36	4	6	10	24	2	0	0	0	8
1988-89	Sodertalje	Swe.	37	4	2	6	44	....	....	....	....	....
1989-90	Sodertalje	Swe.	37	5	10	15	62	2	0	1	1	0
1990-91	Sodertalje	Swe.	37	5	6	11	42	....	....	....	....	....

JONSSON, TOMAS (YAHN-suhn)

Defense. Shoots left. 5'11", 183 lbs. Born, Falun, Sweden, April 12, 1960.
(NY Islanders' 2nd choice, 25th overall, in 1979 Entry Draft).

			Regular Season					Playoffs				
Season	Club	Lea	GP	G	A	TP	PIM	GP	G	A	TP	PIM
1978-79	MoDo	Swe.	34	11	10	21	77	5	1	2	3	13
	Swe. National	...	15	2	3	5	16	....	....	....	....	....
1979-80	MoDo	Swe.	36	3	12	15	42	....	....	....	....	....
	Swe. National	...	18	2	4	6	24	....	....	....	....	....
1980-81	MoDo	Swe.	35	8	12	20	58	....	....	....	....	....
	Swe. National	...	19	0	2	2	2	....	....	....	....	....
1981-82	**NY Islanders**	**NHL**	**70**	**9**	**25**	**34**	**51**	**10**	**0**	**2**	**2**	**21**
1982-83	**NY Islanders**	**NHL**	**72**	**13**	**35**	**48**	**50**	**20**	**2**	**10**	**12**	**18**
1983-84	**NY Islanders**	**NHL**	**72**	**11**	**36**	**47**	**54**	**21**	**3**	**5**	**8**	**22**
1984-85	**NY Islanders**	**NHL**	**69**	**16**	**34**	**50**	**58**	**7**	**1**	**2**	**3**	**10**
1985-86	**NY Islanders**	**NHL**	**77**	**14**	**30**	**44**	**62**	**3**	**0**	**1**	**1**	**4**
1986-87	**NY Islanders**	**NHL**	**47**	**6**	**25**	**31**	**36**	**10**	**1**	**4**	**5**	**6**
1987-88	**NY Islanders**	**NHL**	**72**	**6**	**41**	**47**	**115**	**5**	**2**	**2**	**4**	**10**
1988-89	**NY Islanders**	**NHL**	**53**	**9**	**23**	**32**	**34**	....	....	....	....	....
	Edmonton	**NHL**	**20**	**1**	**10**	**11**	**22**	**4**	**2**	**0**	**2**	**6**
1989-90	Leksand	Swe.	40	11	15	26	54	3	1	1	2	4
1990-91	Leksand	Swe.2	22	7	7	14	16	....	....	....	....	....
	NHL Totals		**552**	**85**	**259**	**344**	**482**	**80**	**11**	**26**	**37**	**97**

Traded to **Edmonton** by **NY Islanders** for future considerations, February 15, 1989.

JOSEPH, ANTHONY

Right wing. Shoots right. 6'4", 203 lbs. Born, Cornwall, Ont., March 1, 1969.
(Winnipeg's 5th choice, 94th overall, in 1988 Entry Draft).

			Regular Season					Playoffs				
Season	Club	Lea	GP	G	A	TP	PIM	GP	G	A	TP	PIM
1985-86	Oshawa	OHL	41	3	1	4	28	....	....	....	....	....
1986-87	Oshawa	OHL	44	2	5	7	93	....	....	....	....	....
1987-88	Oshawa	OHL	49	9	18	27	126	7	0	0	0	9
1988-89	**Winnipeg**	**NHL**	**2**	**1**	**0**	**1**	**0**	....	....	....	....	....
	Oshawa	OHL	52	20	16	36	105	6	4	2	6	22
1989-90	Moncton	AHL	61	9	9	18	74	....	....	....	....	....
1990-91	Moncton	AHL	16	4	2	6	79	8	0	1	1	31
	NHL Totals		**2**	**1**	**0**	**1**	**0**	....	....	....	....	....

JOSEPH, CHRIS

Defense. Shoots right. 6'2", 210 lbs. Born, Burnaby, B.C., September 10, 1969.
(Pittsburgh's 1st choice, 5th overall, in 1987 Entry Draft).

			Regular Season					Playoffs				
Season	Club	Lea	GP	G	A	TP	PIM	GP	G	A	TP	PIM
1985-86	Seattle	WHL	72	4	8	12	50	5	0	3	3	12
1986-87	Seattle	WHL	67	13	45	58	155	....	....	....	....	....
1987-88	**Pittsburgh**	**NHL**	**17**	**0**	**4**	**4**	**12**	....	....	....	....	....
	Seattle	WHL	23	5	14	19	49	....	....	....	....	....
	Edmonton	**NHL**	**7**	**0**	**4**	**4**	**6**	....	....	....	....	....
	Nova Scotia	AHL	8	0	2	2	8	4	0	0	0	9
1988-89	**Edmonton**	**NHL**	**44**	**4**	**5**	**9**	**54**	....	....	....	....	....
	Cape Breton	AHL	5	1	1	2	18	....	....	....	....	....
1989-90	**Edmonton**	**NHL**	**4**	**0**	**2**	**2**	**2**	....	....	....	....	....
	Cape Breton	AHL	61	10	20	30	69	6	2	1	3	4
1990-91	**Edmonton**	**NHL**	**49**	**5**	**17**	**22**	**59**	....	....	....	....	....
	NHL Totals		**121**	**9**	**32**	**41**	**133**	....	....	....	....	....

Traded to **Edmonton** by **Pittsburgh** with Craig Simpson, Dave Hannan and Moe Mantha for Paul Coffey, Dave Hunter, and Wayne Van Dorp, November 24, 1987.

JOSEPH, FABIAN

Center. Shoots left. 5'8", 170 lbs. Born, Sydney, N.S., December 5, 1965.
(Toronto's 5th choice, 109th overall, in 1984 Entry Draft).

			Regular Season					Playoffs				
Season	Club	Lea	GP	G	A	TP	PIM	GP	G	A	TP	PIM
1982-83	Victoria	WHL	69	42	48	90	50	12	4	7	11	9
1983-84	Victoria	WHL	72	52	75	127	27	....	....	....	....	....
1984-85	Toronto	OHL	60	32	43	75	16	5	2	4	6	14
1985-86	Cdn. Olympic	...	71	26	18	44	51	....	....	....	....	....
1986-87	Cdn. Olympic	...	74	15	30	45	26	....	....	....	....	....
1987-88	Nova Scotia	AHL	77	31	39	70	20	5	0	3	3	8
1988-89	Cape Breton	AHL	70	32	34	66	30	....	....	....	....	....
1989-90	Cape Breton	AHL	77	33	53	86	46	6	0	3	3	4
1990-91	Brunico	Italy	36	30	54	84	10	6	7	11	18	2

JOYCE, JOHN

Center. Shoots right. 6'3", 185 lbs. Born, Wilbraham, MA, November 23, 1970.
(NY Islanders' 8th choice, 174th overall, in 1990 Entry Draft).

			Regular Season					Playoffs				
Season	Club	Lea	GP	G	A	TP	PIM	GP	G	A	TP	PIM
1989-90	Avon Old Farms	HS	22	16	28	44	0	....	....	....	....	....
1990-91	Boston College	H.E.	18	1	4	5	6	....	....	....	....	....

JOYCE, ROBERT THOMAS (BOB)

Left wing. Shoots left. 6'1", 195 lbs. Born, St. John, N.B., July 11, 1966.
(Boston's 4th choice, 82nd overall, in 1984 Entry Draft).

			Regular Season					Playoffs				
Season	Club	Lea	GP	G	A	TP	PIM	GP	G	A	TP	PIM
1984-85	North Dakota	WCHA	41	18	16	34	10	....	....	....	....	....
1985-86	North Dakota	WCHA	38	31	28	59	40	....	....	....	....	....
1986-87abc	North Dakota	WCHA	48	52	37	89	42	....	....	....	....	....
1987-88	Cdn. National	...	46	12	10	22	28	....	....	....	....	....
	Cdn. Olympic	...	4	1	0	1	0	....	....	....	....	....
	Boston	**NHL**	**15**	**7**	**5**	**12**	**10**	**23**	**8**	**6**	**14**	**18**
1988-89	**Boston**	**NHL**	**77**	**18**	**31**	**49**	**46**	**9**	**5**	**2**	**7**	**2**
1989-90	**Boston**	**NHL**	**23**	**1**	**2**	**3**	**22**	....	....	....	....	....
	Washington	**NHL**	**24**	**5**	**8**	**13**	**4**	**14**	**2**	**1**	**3**	**9**
1990-91	**Washington**	**NHL**	**17**	**3**	**3**	**6**	**8**	....	....	....	....	....
	Baltimore	AHL	36	10	8	18	14	6	1	0	1	4
	NHL Totals		**156**	**34**	**49**	**83**	**90**	**46**	**15**	**9**	**24**	**29**

a WCHA First All-Star Team (1987)
b NCAA West First All-American Team (1987)
c Named to NCAA All-Tournament Team (1987)

Traded to **Washington** by **Boston** for Dave Christian, December 13, 1989. Traded to **Winnipeg** by **Washington** with Tyler Larter and Kent Paynter for Craig Duncanson, Brent Hughes and Simon Wheeldon, May 21, 1991.

JUDSON, RICK

Left wing. Shoots left. 5'11", 180 lbs. Born, Toledo, OH, August 13, 1969.
(Detroit's 11th choice, 204th overall, in 1989 Entry Draft).

			Regular Season					Playoffs				
Season	Club	Lea	GP	G	A	TP	PIM	GP	G	A	TP	PIM
1988-89	Ill.-Chicago	CCHA	42	14	20	34	20	....	....	....	....	....
1989-90	Ill.-Chicago	CCHA	38	19	22	41	18	....	....	....	....	....
1990-91	Ill.-Chicago	CCHA	38	24	26	50	12	....	....	....	....	....

JUHLIN, PATRIK (ew-LEEN)

Left wing. Shoots left. 6'0", 187 lbs. Born, Huddinge, Sweden, April 24, 1970.
(Philadelphia's 2nd choice, 34th overall, in 1989 Entry Draft).

			Regular Season					Playoffs				
Season	Club	Lea	GP	G	A	TP	PIM	GP	G	A	TP	PIM
1987-88	Vasteras	Swe.	28	25	10	35	....	....	....	....	....	....
1988-89	Vasteras	Swe.	30	29	13	42	....	....	....	....	....	....
1989-90	Vasteras	Swe.	35	10	13	23	18	2	0	0	0	0
1990-91	Vasteras	Swe.	40	13	9	22	24	....	....	....	....	....

JULIEN, CLAUDE

Defense. Shoots right. 6', 198 lbs. Born, Blind River, Ont., April 23, 1960.

			Regular Season					Playoffs				
Season	Club	Lea	GP	G	A	TP	PIM	GP	G	A	TP	PIM
1979-80	Windsor	OHA	68	14	37	51	148	16	5	11	16	23
1980-81	Windsor	OHA	3	1	1	2	21	....	....	....	....	....
	Port Huron	IHL	77	15	40	55	153	4	1	1	2	4
1981-82	Salt Lake	CHL	70	4	18	22	134	5	1	4	5	0
1982-83	Salt Lake	CHL	76	14	47	61	176	6	3	3	6	16
1983-84	Milwaukee	IHL	5	0	3	3	2	....	....	....	....	....
	Fredericton	AHL	57	7	22	29	58	7	0	4	4	6
1984-85	**Quebec**	**NHL**	**1**	**0**	**0**	**0**	**0**	....	....	....	....	....
	Fredericton	AHL	77	6	28	34	97	6	2	4	6	13
1985-86	**Quebec**	**NHL**	**13**	**0**	**1**	**1**	**25**	....	....	....	....	....
	Fredericton	AHL	49	3	18	21	74	6	1	4	5	19
1986-87	Fredericton	AHL	17	1	6	7	22	....	....	....	....	....
	France	....	36	15	50	65	....	....	....	....	....	....
1987-88	Baltimore	AHL	30	6	14	20	22	....	....	....	....	....
	Fredericton	AHL	35	1	14	15	52	13	1	3	4	30
1988-89a	Halifax	AHL	79	8	52	60	72	4	0	2	2	4
1989-90	Halifax	AHL	77	6	37	43	65	4	0	1	1	7
1990-91	Kansas City	IHL	54	7	16	23	43	....	....	....	....	....
	NHL Totals		**14**	**0**	**1**	**1**	**25**	....	....	....	....	....

a AHL Second All-Star Team (1989)

Signed as free agent by **St. Louis**, September 28, 1981. Rights transfered to **Quebec** by **St. Louis** with rights to Gord Donnelly when St. Louis signed Jacques Demers as coach, August 19, 1983.

JUNEAU, JOSEPH (JOE)

Center. Shoots right. 6'0", 175 lbs. Born, Pont-Rouge, Que., January 5, 1968.
(Boston's 3rd choice, 81st overall, in 1988 Entry Draft).

			Regular Season					Playoffs				
Season	Club	Lea	GP	G	A	TP	PIM	GP	G	A	TP	PIM
1987-88	RPI	ECAC	31	16	29	45	18	....	....	....	....	....
1988-89	RPI	ECAC	30	12	23	35	40	....	....	....	....	....
1989-90a	RPI	ECAC	34	18	*52	*70	31	....	....	....	....	....
1990-91bc	RPI	ECAC	29	23	40	63	68	....	....	....	....	....
	Cdn. National	...	7	2	3	5	0	....	....	....	....	....

a NCAA East First All-American Team (1990)
b ECAC Second All-Star Team (1991)
c NCAA East Second All-American Team (1991)

KACHOWSKI, MARK EDWARD

Left wing. Shoots left. 5'11", 200 lbs. Born, Edmonton, Alta., February 20, 1965.

			Regular Season					Playoffs				
Season	Club	Lea	GP	G	A	TP	PIM	GP	G	A	TP	PIM
1983-84	Kamloops	WHL	57	6	9	15	156	....	....	....	....	....
1984-85	Kamloops	WHL	68	22	15	37	185	....	....	....	....	....
1985-86	Kamloops	WHL	61	21	31	52	182	....	....	....	....	....
1986-87	Flint	IHL	75	18	13	31	273	6	1	1	2	21
1987-88	**Pittsburgh**	**NHL**	**38**	**5**	**3**	**8**	**126**	....	....	....	....	....
	Muskegon	IHL	25	3	6	9	72	5	0	2	2	11
1988-89	**Pittsburgh**	**NHL**	**12**	**1**	**1**	**2**	**43**	....	....	....	....	....
	Muskegon	IHL	57	8	8	16	167	8	1	2	3	17
1989-90	**Pittsburgh**	**NHL**	**14**	**0**	**1**	**1**	**40**	....	....	....	....	....
	Muskegon	IHL	61	23	8	31	129	12	2	4	6	21
1990-91	Muskegon	IHL	80	19	21	40	108	5	1	1	2	9
	NHL Totals		**64**	**6**	**5**	**11**	**209**	....	....	....	....	....

Signed as a free agent by **Pittsburgh**, August 31, 1987.

KADLEC, ARNOLD (KAHD-lehts)
Defense. Shoots right. 6'1", 211 lbs.   Born, Most, Czechoslovakia, January 8, 1959.
(Minnesota's 10th choice, 206th overall, in 1982 Entry Draft).

Season	Club	Lea	GP	G	A	TP	PIM	GP	G	A	TP	PIM
1986-87	CHZ Litvinov	Czech.	32	9	16	25	....					
1987-88	CHZ Litvinov	Czech.	29	0	13	13	....					
1988-89	CHZ Litvinov	Czech.	34	11	11	22	....					
1989-90	Lukko	Fin	29	4	11	15	36					
1990-91	Brunico	Italy	21	5	17	22	12					

KADLEC, DRAHOMIR (KAHD-lehts)
Defense. Shoots left. 5'11", 187 lbs.   Born, Pribram, Czechoslovakia, November 29, 1965.
(Philadelphia's 13th choice, 245th overall, in 1988 Entry Draft).

Season	Club	Lea	GP	G	A	TP	PIM	GP	G	A	TP	PIM
1987-88	Dukla Jihlava	Czech.	29	3	7	10	....					
1988-89	Kladno	Czech.	....	7	14	21	....					
1989-90	Kladno	Czech.	49	8	21	29	....					
1990-91	HIFK	Fin.	42	3	11	14	36	3	1	1	2	24

KAISER, KEVIN
Left wing. Shoots left. 6', 185 lbs.   Born, Winnipeg, Man., July 26, 1970.
(Quebec's 7th choice, 85th overall, in 1989 Entry Draft).

Season	Club	Lea	GP	G	A	TP	PIM	GP	G	A	TP	PIM
1988-89	Minn.-Duluth	WCHA	40	2	5	7	26					
1989-90	Minn.-Duluth	WCHA	39	9	11	20	24					
1990-91	Minn.-Duluth	WCHA	39	15	17	32	57					

KAMENSKY, VALERI (kah-MEHN-skee)
Left wing. Shoots right. 6'2", 198 lbs.   Born, Voskresensk, Soviet Union, April 18, 1966.
(Quebec's 8th choice, 129th overall, in 1988 Entry Draft).

Season	Club	Lea	GP	G	A	TP	PIM	GP	G	A	TP	PIM
1982-83	Khimik	USSR	5	0	0	0	0					
1983-84	Khimik	USSR	20	2	2	4	6					
1984-85	Khimik	USSR	45	9	3	12	24					
1985-86	CSKA	USSR	40	15	9	24	8					
1986-87	CSKA	USSR	37	13	8	21	16					
1987-88	CSKA	USSR	51	26	20	46	40					
1988-89	CSKA	USSR	40	18	10	28	30					
1989-90	CSKA	USSR	45	19	18	37	40					
1990-91	CSKA	USSR	46	20	26	46	66					

KAMES, VLADIMIR (KAH-mehsh)
Center. Shoots left. 5'11", 189 lbs.   Born, Kladno, Czechoslovakia, September 28, 1964.
(New Jersey's 8th choice, 149th overall, in 1984 Entry Draft).

Season	Club	Lea	GP	G	A	TP	PIM	GP	G	A	TP	PIM
1988-89	Kladno	Czech.	34	11	22	33	28					
1989-90	Kladno	Czech.	42	17	27	44	....					
1990-91	Karpat	Fin.	44	26	35	61	32					

KAMINSKI, KEVIN
Center. Shoots left. 5'9", 170 lbs.   Born, Churchbridge, Sask., March 13, 1969.
(Minnesota's 3rd choice, 48th overall, in 1987 Entry Draft).

Season	Club	Lea	GP	G	A	TP	PIM	GP	G	A	TP	PIM
1986-87	Saskatoon	WHL	67	26	44	70	325	11	5	6	11	45
1987-88	Saskatoon	WHL	55	38	61	99	247	10	5	7	12	37
1988-89	**Minnesota**	**NHL**	1	0	0	0	0	....				
	Saskatoon	WHL	52	25	43	68	199	8	4	9	13	25
1989-90	**Quebec**	**NHL**	1	0	0	0	0	....				
	Halifax	AHL	19	3	4	7	128	2	0	0	0	5
1990-91	Halifax	AHL	7	1	0	1	44	....				
	Fort Wayne	IHL	56	9	15	24	*455	19	4	2	6	*169
	NHL Totals		2	0	0	0	0					

Traded to **Quebec** by **Minnesota** for Gaetan Duchesne, June 19, 1989.

KAMPERSAL, JEFFREY
Defense. Shoots right. 6'2", 190 lbs.   Born, Beverly, MA, January 27, 1970.
(NY Islanders' 12th choice, 205th overall, in 1988 Entry Draft).

Season	Club	Lea	GP	G	A	TP	PIM	GP	G	A	TP	PIM
1988-89	Princeton	ECAC	26	0	3	3	32					
1989-90	Princeton	ECAC	27	3	7	10	26					
1990-91	Princeton	ECAC	27	5	7	12	14					

KANE, SHAUN
Defense. Shoots left. 6'3", 195 lbs.   Born, Holyoke, MA, February 24, 1970.
(Minnesota's 3rd choice, 43rd overall, in 1988 Entry Draft).

Season	Club	Lea	GP	G	A	TP	PIM	GP	G	A	TP	PIM
1988-89	Providence	H.E.	37	2	9	11	54					
1989-90	Providence	H.E.	31	9	8	17	46					
1990-91a	Providence	H.E.	36	5	20	25	86					

a Hockey East Second All-Star Team (1991)
Claimed by **San Jose** from **Minnesota** in Dispersal Draft, May 30, 1991.

KAPUSTA, THOMAS
Center. Shoots left. 6', 187 lbs.   Born, Zlin, Czechoslovakia, February 23, 1967.
(Edmonton's 4th choice, 104th overall, in 1985 Entry Draft).

Season	Club	Lea	GP	G	A	TP	PIM	GP	G	A	TP	PIM
1988-89	Dukla Trencin	Czech.	44	8	25	33	....					
1989-90	TJ Zlin	Czech.	16	9	5	14	....					
	Cape Breton	AHL	55	12	37	49	56	6	2	7	9	4
1990-91	Cape Breton	AHL	73	21	46	67	47	4	0	2	2	21

KARABIN, LADISLAV
Left wing. Shoots left. 6'1", 189 lbs.   Born, Bratislava, Czechoslovakia, February 16, 1970.
(Pittsburgh's 11th choice, 173rd overall, in 1990 Entry Draft).

Season	Club	Lea	GP	G	A	TP	PIM	GP	G	A	TP	PIM
1990-91	Bratislava	Czech.	49	21	7	28	57					

KARALIS, TOM (kuh-RAL-ihz)
Defense. Shoots left. 6'1", 205 lbs.   Born, Montreal, Que., May 24, 1964.

Season	Club	Lea	GP	G	A	TP	PIM	GP	G	A	TP	PIM
1981-82	Shawinigan	QMJHL	42	0	5	5	107	14	2	8	10	29
1982-83	Drummondville	QMJHL	64	6	11	17	218					
1983-84	Drummondville	QMJHL	67	16	37	53	316	10	2	6	8	28
1984-85	Drummondville	QMJHL	64	21	59	80	184	9	0	7	7	12
1985-86	Fredericton	AHL	51	4	8	12	106					
	Muskegon	IHL	21	5	8	13	81	11	1	3	4	32
1986-87	Fredericton	AHL	37	0	3	3	64					
	Muskegon	IHL	28	3	9	12	94	15	2	12	14	28
1987-88	Baltimore	AHL	17	0	2	2	87					
	Flint	IHL	65	5	26	31	268	2	0	0	0	2
1988-89	New Haven	AHL	11	2	3	5	8					
	Flint	IHL	38	1	6	7	170					
	Indianapolis	IHL	26	0	8	8	132					
1989-90	New Haven	AHL	2	0	0	0	0					
	Phoenix	IHL	17	1	3	4	35					
	Peoria	IHL	48	2	8	10	182	5	0	2	2	48
1990-91	Fort Wayne	IHL	79	5	21	26	239	8	1	2	3	21

Signed as a free agent by **Quebec**, June 6, 1985.

KARJALAINEN, KYOSTI (kahr-ya-LAY-nehn)
Right wing. Shoots left. 6'1", 190 lbs.   Born, Gavle, Sweden, June 19, 1967.
(Los Angeles' 6th choice, 132nd overall, in 1987 Entry Draft).

Season	Club	Lea	GP	G	A	TP	PIM	GP	G	A	TP	PIM
1986-87	Brynas	Swe.	11	3	2	5	0					
1987-88	Brynas	Swe.	20	2	1	3	10					
1988-89	Brynas	Swe.	39	20	17	37	16					
1989-90	Brynas	Swe.	38	17	15	32	16	5	0	3	3	0
1990-91	Phoenix	IHL	70	14	35	49	10	6	2	3	5	6

KARLSSON, LARS (KAHRL-suhn)
Left wing. Shoots left. 6'3", 194 lbs.   Born, Karlstad, Sweden, August 18, 1966.
(Detroit's 7th choice, 152nd overall, in 1984 Entry Draft).

Season	Club	Lea	GP	G	A	TP	PIM	GP	G	A	TP	PIM
1986-87	Bjorkloven	Swe.	35	10	24	34	18					
1987-88	Farjestad	Swe.	39	6	13	19	42					
1988-89	Farjestad	Swe.	40	9	9	18	32	2	0	1	1	6
1989-90	Farjestad	Swe.	27	8	5	13	12	10	3	2	5	8
1990-91	Farjestad	Swe.	36	10	6	16	46					

KARPOVTSEV, ALEXANDER
Defense. Shoots left. 6'2", 189 lbs.   Born, Moscow, Soviet Union, April 7, 1970.
(Quebec's 7th choice, 158th overall, in 1990 Entry Draft).

Season	Club	Lea	GP	G	A	TP	PIM	GP	G	A	TP	PIM
1989-90	Moscow D'amo	USSR	35	1	1	2	27					
1990-91	Moscow D'amo	USSR	40	0	5	5	15					

KASATONOV, ALEXEI (kah-sah-TOH-nahf)
Defense. Shoots left. 6'1", 215 lbs.   Born, Leningrad, Soviet Union, October 14, 1959.
(New Jersey's 10th choice, 234th overall, in 1983 Entry Draft).

Season	Club	Lea	GP	G	A	TP	PIM	GP	G	A	TP	PIM
1976-77	SKA Leningrad	USSR	7	0	0	0	0					
1977-78	SKA Leningrad	USSR	35	4	7	11	15					
1978-79	CSKA	USSR	40	5	14	19	30					
1979-80a	CSKA	USSR	37	5	8	13	26					
1980-81a	CSKA	USSR	47	10	12	22	38					
1981-82a	CSKA	USSR	46	12	27	39	45					
1982-83a	CSKA	USSR	44	12	19	31	37					
1983-84a	CSKA	USSR	39	12	24	36	20					
1984-85a	CSKA	USSR	40	18	18	36	26					
1985-86a	CSKA	USSR	40	6	17	23	27					
1986-87a	CSKA	USSR	40	13	17	30	16					
1987-88a	CSKA	USSR	43	8	12	20	8					
1988-89	CSKA	USSR	41	8	14	22	8					
1989-90	CSKA	USSR	30	6	7	13	16					
	New Jersey	**NHL**	39	6	15	21	16	6	0	3	3	14
	Utica	AHL	3	0	2	2	7					
1990-91	**New Jersey**	**NHL**	78	10	31	41	76	7	1	3	4	10
	NHL Totals		117	16	46	62	92	13	1	6	7	24

a Soviet National League All-Star Team (1980-88)

KASPER, STEPHEN NEIL (STEVE)

Center. Shoots left. 5'8", 175 lbs. Born, Montreal, Que., September 28, 1961.
(Boston's 3rd choice, 81st overall, in 1980 Entry Draft).

			Regular Season					Playoffs				
Season	**Club**	**Lea**	**GP**	**G**	**A**	**TP**	**PIM**	**GP**	**G**	**A**	**TP**	**PIM**
1978-79	Verdun	QJHL	67	37	67	104	53	11	7	6	13	22
1979-80	Sorel	QJHL	70	57	65	122	117	....	....	....	....	....
1980-81	**Boston**	**NHL**	**76**	**21**	**35**	**56**	**94**	**3**	**0**	**1**	**1**	**0**
1981-82a	**Boston**	**NHL**	**73**	**20**	**31**	**51**	**72**	**11**	**3**	**6**	**9**	**22**
1982-83	**Boston**	**NHL**	**24**	**2**	**6**	**8**	**24**	**12**	**2**	**1**	**3**	**10**
1983-84	**Boston**	**NHL**	**27**	**3**	**11**	**14**	**19**	**3**	**0**	**0**	**0**	**7**
1984-85	**Boston**	**NHL**	**77**	**16**	**24**	**40**	**33**	**5**	**1**	**0**	**1**	**9**
1985-86	**Boston**	**NHL**	**80**	**17**	**23**	**40**	**73**	**3**	**1**	**0**	**1**	**4**
1986-87	**Boston**	**NHL**	**79**	**20**	**30**	**50**	**51**	**3**	**0**	**2**	**2**	**0**
1987-88	**Boston**	**NHL**	**79**	**26**	**44**	**70**	**35**	**23**	**7**	**6**	**13**	**10**
1988-89	**Boston**	**NHL**	**49**	**10**	**16**	**26**	**49**	....	....	....	....	....
	Los Angeles	**NHL**	**29**	**9**	**15**	**24**	**14**	**11**	**1**	**5**	**6**	**10**
1989-90	**Los Angeles**	**NHL**	**77**	**17**	**28**	**45**	**27**	**10**	**1**	**1**	**2**	**2**
1990-91	**Los Angeles**	**NHL**	**67**	**9**	**19**	**28**	**33**	**10**	**4**	**6**	**10**	**8**
	NHL Totals		**737**	**170**	**282**	**452**	**524**	**94**	**20**	**28**	**48**	**82**

a Won Frank J. Selke Trophy (1982)

Traded to **Los Angeles** by **Boston** for Bobby Carpenter, January 23, 1989. Traded to **Philadelphia** by **Los Angeles** with Steve Duchesne and Los Angeles' fourth round choice (Aris Brimanis) in 1991 Entry Draft for Jari Kurri and Jeff Chychrun, May 30, 1991.

KASTELIC, EDWARD (ED) (KAS-tuh-lihk)

Right wing/Left wing. Shoots right. 6'4", 215 lbs. Born, Toronto, Ont., January 29, 1964.
(Washington's 4th choice, 110th overall, in 1982 Entry Draft).

			Regular Season					Playoffs				
Season	**Club**	**Lea**	**GP**	**G**	**A**	**TP**	**PIM**	**GP**	**G**	**A**	**TP**	**PIM**
1981-82	London	OHL	68	5	18	23	63	4	0	1	1	4
1982-83	London	OHL	68	12	11	23	96	3	0	0	0	5
1983-84	London	OHL	68	17	16	33	218	8	0	2	2	41
1984-85	Moncton	AHL	62	5	11	16	187	....	....	....	....	....
	Binghamton	AHL	4	0	0	0	7	....	....	....	....	....
	Fort Wayne	IHL	5	1	0	1	37	....	....	....	....	....
1985-86	**Washington**	**NHL**	**15**	**0**	**0**	**0**	**73**	....	....	....	....	....
	Binghamton	AHL	23	7	9	16	76	....	....	....	....	....
1986-87	**Washington**	**NHL**	**23**	**1**	**1**	**2**	**83**	**5**	**1**	**0**	**1**	**13**
	Binghamton	AHL	48	17	11	28	124	....	....	....	....	....
1987-88	**Washington**	**NHL**	**35**	**1**	**0**	**1**	**78**	**1**	**0**	**0**	**0**	**19**
	Binghamton	AHL	6	4	1	5	6	....	....	....	....	....
1988-89	**Hartford**	**NHL**	**10**	**0**	**2**	**2**	**15**	....	....	....	....	....
	Binghamton	AHL	35	9	6	15	124	....	....	....	....	....
1989-90	**Hartford**	**NHL**	**67**	**6**	**2**	**8**	**198**	**2**	**0**	**0**	**0**	**0**
1990-91	**Hartford**	**NHL**	**45**	**2**	**2**	**4**	**211**	....	....	....	....	....
	NHL Totals		**195**	**10**	**7**	**17**	**658**	**8**	**1**	**0**	**1**	**32**

Traded to **Hartford** by **Washington** with Grant Jennings for Mike Millar and Neil Sheehy, July 6, 1988.

KAUTONEN, VELI-PEKKA (KAH-uh-toh-nehn)

Defense. Shoots right. 6'2", 200 lbs. Born, Helsinki, Finland, May 9, 1970.
(Calgary's 3rd choice, 50th overall, in 1989 Entry Draft).

			Regular Season					Playoffs				
Season	**Club**	**Lea**	**GP**	**G**	**A**	**TP**	**PIM**	**GP**	**G**	**A**	**TP**	**PIM**
1987-88	HIFK	Fin.	35	9	11	20	....	....	....	....	....	....
1988-89	HIFK	Fin.	36	4	5	9	....	....	....	....	....	....
1989-90	HIFK	Fin.	36	2	1	3	10	2	0	0	0	0
1990-91	SaiPa	Fin.	43	12	19	31	36	....	....	....	....	....

KEANE, MIKE

Right wing. Shoots right. 5'10", 178 lbs. Born, Winnipeg, Man., May 29, 1967.

			Regular Season					Playoffs				
Season	**Club**	**Lea**	**GP**	**G**	**A**	**TP**	**PIM**	**GP**	**G**	**A**	**TP**	**PIM**
1984-85	Moose Jaw	WHL	65	17	26	43	141	....	....	....	....	....
1985-86	Moose Jaw	WHL	67	34	49	83	162	13	6	8	14	9
1986-87	Moose Jaw	WHL	53	25	45	70	107	9	3	9	12	11
	Sherbrooke	AHL	....	....	....	....	....	9	2	2	4	16
1987-88	Sherbrooke	AHL	78	25	43	68	70	6	1	1	2	18
1988-89	**Montreal**	**NHL**	**69**	**16**	**19**	**35**	**69**	**21**	**4**	**3**	**7**	**17**
1989-90	**Montreal**	**NHL**	**74**	**9**	**15**	**24**	**78**	**11**	**0**	**1**	**1**	**8**
1990-91	**Montreal**	**NHL**	**73**	**13**	**23**	**36**	**50**	**12**	**3**	**2**	**5**	**6**
	NHL Totals		**216**	**38**	**57**	**95**	**197**	**44**	**7**	**6**	**13**	**31**

Signed as a free agent by **Montreal**, September 25, 1985.

KEARNEY, FRANCIS (TOBY)

Left wing. Shoots left. 6'2", 185 lbs. Born, Newburyport, MA, September 2, 1970.
(Calgary's 7th choice, 105th overall, in 1989 Entry Draft).

			Regular Season					Playoffs				
Season	**Club**	**Lea**	**GP**	**G**	**A**	**TP**	**PIM**	**GP**	**G**	**A**	**TP**	**PIM**
1989-90	U. of Vermont	ECAC	25	2	3	5	24	....	....	....	....	....
1990-91	U. of Vermont	ECAC	33	8	11	19	16	....	....	....	....	....

KECZMER, DAN

Defense. Shoots left. 6'1", 190 lbs. Born, Mt. Clemens, MI, May 25, 1968.
(Minnesota's 11th choice, 201st overall, in 1986 Entry Draft).

			Regular Season					Playoffs				
Season	**Club**	**Lea**	**GP**	**G**	**A**	**TP**	**PIM**	**GP**	**G**	**A**	**TP**	**PIM**
1986-87	Lake Superior	CCHA	38	3	5	8	26	....	....	....	....	....
1987-88	Lake Superior	CCHA	41	2	15	17	34	....	....	....	....	....
1988-89	Lake Superior	CCHA	46	3	26	29	68	....	....	....	....	....
1989-90a	Lake Superior	CCHA	43	13	23	36	48	....	....	....	....	....
1990-91	**Minnesota**	**NHL**	**9**	**0**	**1**	**1**	**6**	....	....	....	....	....
	Kalamazoo	IHL	60	4	20	24	60	9	1	2	3	10
	NHL Totals		**9**	**0**	**1**	**1**	**6**	....	....	....	....	....

a CCHA Second All-Star Team (1990)

Claimed by **San Jose** from **Minnesota** in Dispersal Draft, May 30, 1991.

KEENAN, CORY

Defense. Shoots left. 6'1", 182 lbs. Born, St. Louis, MO, March 19, 1970.
(Hartford's 5th choice, 120th overall, in 1990 Entry Draft).

			Regular Season					Playoffs				
Season	**Club**	**Lea**	**GP**	**G**	**A**	**TP**	**PIM**	**GP**	**G**	**A**	**TP**	**PIM**
1989-90	Kitchener	OHL	66	13	35	48	88	17	2	11	13	14
1990-91	U. of Waterloo	OUAA	41	8	14	22	77	....	....	....	....	....

KEKALAINEN, JARMO (kee kuh LAY nehn, YAHR moh)

Left wing. Shoots right. 6', 190 lbs. Born, Tampere, Finland, July 3, 1966.

			Regular Season					Playoffs				
Season	**Club**	**Lea**	**GP**	**G**	**A**	**TP**	**PIM**	**GP**	**G**	**A**	**TP**	**PIM**
1987-88	Clarkson	ECAC	32	7	11	18	38	....	....	....	....	....
1988-89	Clarkson	ECAC	31	19	25	44	47	....	....	....	....	....
1989-90	**Boston**	**NHL**	**11**	**2**	**2**	**4**	**8**	....	....	....	....	....
	Maine	AHL	18	5	11	16	6	....	....	....	....	....
1990-91	**Boston**	**NHL**	**16**	**2**	**1**	**3**	**6**	....	....	....	....	....
	Maine	AHL	11	2	4	6	4	1	0	1	1	0
	NHL Totals		**27**	**4**	**3**	**7**	**14**	....	....	....	....	....

Signed as free agent by **Boston**, May 3, 1989.

KELFER, MICHAEL (MIKE)

Center. Shoots right. 5'10", 180 lbs. Born, Peabody, MA, January 2, 1967.
(Minnesota's 5th choice, 132nd overall, in 1985 Entry Draft).

			Regular Season					Playoffs				
Season	**Club**	**Lea**	**GP**	**G**	**A**	**TP**	**PIM**	**GP**	**G**	**A**	**TP**	**PIM**
1985-86	Boston U.	H.E.	39	13	14	27	40	....	....	....	....	....
1986-87	Boston U.	H.E.	33	21	19	40	20	....	....	....	....	....
1987-88a	Boston U.	H.E.	36	36	27	63	33	....	....	....	....	....
1988-89a	Boston U.	H.E.	33	23	29	52	22	....	....	....	....	....
1989-90	Springfield	AHL	57	24	18	42	10	....	....	....	....	....
1990-91	Capital Dist.	AHL	1	0	1	1	0	....	....	....	....	....
	Kansas City	IHL	54	18	18	36	20	....	....	....	....	....

a Hockey East Second All-Star Team (1988, 1989)

Traded to **NY Islanders** by **Minnesota** to complete March 7, 1989 deal for Reed Larson, May 12, 1989.

KELLEY, ROBERT

Left wing. Shoots left. 6'1", 185 lbs. Born, Cambridge, MA, February 10, 1969.
(Montreal's 9th choice, 143rd overall, in 1987 Entry Draft).

			Regular Season					Playoffs				
Season	**Club**	**Lea**	**GP**	**G**	**A**	**TP**	**PIM**	**GP**	**G**	**A**	**TP**	**PIM**
1990-91	Merrimack	H.E.	7	1	1	2	12	....	....	....	....	....

KELLOGG, BOB

Defense. Shoots left. 6'4", 200 lbs. Born, Springfield, MA, February 16, 1971.
(Chicago's 3rd choice, 48th overall, in 1989 Entry Draft).

			Regular Season					Playoffs				
Season	**Club**	**Lea**	**GP**	**G**	**A**	**TP**	**PIM**	**GP**	**G**	**A**	**TP**	**PIM**
1989-90	Northeastern	H.E.	36	3	12	15	30	....	....	....	....	....
1990-91	Northeastern	H.E.	2	0	0	0	6	....	....	....	....	....

KELLY, PAUL

Right wing. Shoots left. 6', 180 lbs. Born, Hamilton, Ont., April 17, 1967.
(Los Angeles' 9th choice, 191st overall, in 1986 Entry Draft).

			Regular Season					Playoffs				
Season	**Club**	**Lea**	**GP**	**G**	**A**	**TP**	**PIM**	**GP**	**G**	**A**	**TP**	**PIM**
1984-85	Guelph	OHL	64	15	27	42	50	....	....	....	....	....
1985-86	Guelph	OHL	59	26	32	58	95	20	10	7	17	19
1986-87	Guelph	OHL	61	27	48	75	67	5	2	4	6	0
1987-88	New Haven	AHL	60	14	25	39	23	....	....	....	....	....
1988-89	New Haven	AHL	12	4	5	9	22	....	....	....	....	....
	Utica	AHL	34	6	8	14	25	3	0	0	0	6
	Flint	IHL	4	0	1	1	0	....	....	....	....	....
1989-90	New Haven	AHL	38	5	15	20	43	....	....	....	....	....
	Phoenix	IHL	8	3	0	3	11	....	....	....	....	....
1990-91	San Diego	IHL	3	0	2	2	2	....	....	....	....	....
	Moncton	AHL	42	10	7	17	34	5	0	3	3	6

KENNEDY, EDWARD (DEAN)

Defense. Shoots right. 6'2", 205 lbs. Born, Redver, Sask., January 18, 1963.
(Los Angeles' 2nd choice, 39th overall, in 1981 Entry Draft).

			Regular Season					Playoffs				
Season	**Club**	**Lea**	**GP**	**G**	**A**	**TP**	**PIM**	**GP**	**G**	**A**	**TP**	**PIM**
1980-81	Brandon	WHL	71	3	29	32	157	5	0	2	2	7
1981-82	Brandon	WHL	49	5	38	43	103	....	....	....	....	....
1982-83	**Los Angeles**	**NHL**	**55**	**0**	**12**	**12**	**97**	....	....	....	....	....
	Brandon	WHL	14	2	15	17	22	....	....	....	....	....
	Saskatoon	WHL	....	....	....	....	....	4	0	3	3	0
1983-84	**Los Angeles**	**NHL**	**37**	**1**	**5**	**6**	**50**	....	....	....	....	....
	New Haven	AHL	26	1	7	8	23	....	....	....	....	....
1984-85	New Haven	AHL	76	3	14	17	104	....	....	....	....	....
1985-86	**Los Angeles**	**NHL**	**78**	**2**	**10**	**12**	**132**	....	....	....	....	....
1986-87	**Los Angeles**	**NHL**	**66**	**6**	**14**	**20**	**91**	**5**	**0**	**2**	**2**	**10**
1987-88	**Los Angeles**	**NHL**	**58**	**1**	**11**	**12**	**158**	**4**	**0**	**1**	**1**	**10**
1988-89	**NY Rangers**	**NHL**	**16**	**0**	**1**	**1**	**40**	....	....	....	....	....
	Los Angeles	**NHL**	**51**	**3**	**10**	**13**	**63**	**11**	**0**	**2**	**2**	**8**
1989-90	**Buffalo**	**NHL**	**80**	**2**	**12**	**14**	**53**	**6**	**1**	**1**	**2**	**12**
1990-91	**Buffalo**	**NHL**	**64**	**4**	**8**	**12**	**119**	**2**	**0**	**1**	**1**	**17**
	NHL Totals		**505**	**19**	**83**	**102**	**803**	**28**	**1**	**7**	**8**	**57**

Traded to **NY Rangers** by **Los Angeles** with Denis Larocque for Igor Liba, Michael Boyce, Todd Elik and future considerations, December 12, 1988. Traded to **Los Angeles** by **NY Rangers** for Los Angeles' fourth-round choice – later traded to Minnesota (Cal McGowan) – in 1990 Entry Draft, February 3, 1989. Traded to **Buffalo** by **Los Angeles** for Buffalo's fourth round choice (Keith Redmond) in 1991 Entry Draft, October 4, 1989.

KENNEDY, SHELDON

Right wing. Shoots right. 5'11", 170 lbs. Born, Brandon, Man., June 15, 1969.
(Detroit's 5th choice, 80th overall, in 1988 Entry Draft).

			Regular Season					Playoffs				
Season	Club	Lea	GP	G	A	TP	PIM	GP	G	A	TP	PIM
1986-87	Swift Current	WHL	49	23	41	64	43	4	0	3	3	4
1987-88	Swift Current	WHL	59	53	64	117	45	10	8	9	17	12
1988-89	Swift Current	WHL	51	58	48	106	92	12	9	15	24	22
1989-90	**Detroit**	**NHL**	**20**	**2**	**7**	**9**	**10**	....	....	....	....	....
	Adirondack	AHL	26	11	15	26	35	....	....	....	....	....
1990-91	**Detroit**	**NHL**	**7**	**1**	**0**	**1**	**12**	....	....	....	....	....
	Adirondack	AHL	11	1	3	4	8	....	....	....	....	....
	NHL Totals		**27**	**3**	**7**	**10**	**22**	....	....	....	....	....

KENNHOLT, KENNETH

Defense. Shoots right. 6'3", 191 lbs. Born, Stockholm, Sweden, January 13, 1965.
(Calgary's 13th choice, 252nd overall, in 1989 Entry Draft).

			Regular Season					Playoffs				
Season	Club	Lea	GP	G	A	TP	PIM	GP	G	A	TP	PIM
1988-89	Djurgarden	Swe.	34	6	10	16	30	....	....	....	....	....
1989-90	Djurgarden	Swe.	38	7	10	17	30	7	2	2	4	2
1990-91	Djurgarden	Swe.	39	9	13	22	30	....	....	....	....	....

KENTALA, VILLE

Left wing. Shoots left. 5'11", 180 lbs. Born, Alajarvi, Finland, February 21, 1966.
(NY Rangers' 8th choice, 182nd overall, in 1984 Entry Draft).

			Regular Season					Playoffs				
Season	Club	Lea	GP	G	A	TP	PIM	GP	G	A	TP	PIM
1985-86	Karmu-Kissat	Fin.2	37	19	16	35	28	....	....	....	....	....
1986-87	Boston U.	H.E.	35	4	11	15	24	....	....	....	....	....
1987-88	Boston U.	H.E.	32	16	19	35	34	....	....	....	....	....
1988-89	Boston U.	H.E.	34	5	7	12	46	....	....	....	....	....
1989-90	HIFK	Fin.	43	5	4	9	6	2	0	0	0	0
1990-91	HIFK	Fin.	41	3	7	10	10	2	0	0	0	0

Traded to **Edmonton** by **NY Rangers** with Reijo Ruotsalainen, Clark Donatelli and Jim Wiemer for Don Jackson, Mike Golden, Miloslav Horava and future considerations, October 23, 1986.

KERR, ALAN

Right wing. Shoots right. 5'11", 195 lbs. Born, Hazelton, B.C., March 28, 1964.
(NY Islanders' 4th choice, 84th overall, in 1982 Entry Draft).

			Regular Season					Playoffs				
Season	Club	Lea	GP	G	A	TP	PIM	GP	G	A	TP	PIM
1981-82	Seattle	WHL	68	15	18	33	107	10	6	6	12	32
1982-83	Seattle	WHL	71	38	53	91	183	4	2	3	5	0
1983-84a	Seattle	WHL	66	46	66	112	141	5	1	4	5	12
1984-85	**NY Islanders**	**NHL**	**19**	**3**	**1**	**4**	**24**	**4**	**1**	**0**	**1**	**4**
	Springfield	AHL	62	32	27	59	140	4	1	2	3	2
1985-86	**NY Islanders**	**NHL**	**7**	**0**	**1**	**1**	**16**	**1**	**0**	**0**	**0**	**0**
	Springfield	AHL	71	35	36	71	127	....	....	....	....	....
1986-87	**NY Islanders**	**NHL**	**72**	**7**	**10**	**17**	**175**	**14**	**1**	**4**	**5**	**25**
1987-88	**NY Islanders**	**NHL**	**80**	**24**	**34**	**58**	**198**	**6**	**1**	**0**	**1**	**14**
1988-89	**NY Islanders**	**NHL**	**71**	**20**	**18**	**38**	**144**	....	....	....	....	....
1989-90	**NY Islanders**	**NHL**	**75**	**15**	**21**	**36**	**129**	**4**	**0**	**0**	**0**	**10**
1990-91	**NY Islanders**	**NHL**	**2**	**0**	**0**	**0**	**5**	....	....	....	....	....
	Capital Dist.	AHL	43	11	21	32	131	....	....	....	....	....
	NHL Totals		**326**	**69**	**85**	**154**	**691**	**29**	**3**	**4**	**7**	**53**

a WHL First All-Star Team, West Division (1984)

Traded to **Detroit** by **NY Islanders** with future considerations for Rick Green, May 26, 1991.

KERR, KEVIN

Right wing. Shoots right. 5'10", 190 lbs. Born, North Bay, Ont., September 18, 1967.
(Buffalo's 4th choice, 56th overall, in 1986 Entry Draft).

			Regular Season					Playoffs				
Season	Club	Lea	GP	G	A	TP	PIM	GP	G	A	TP	PIM
1985-86	Windsor	OHL	59	21	51	72	266	16	6	8	14	55
1986-87	Windsor	OHL	63	27	41	68	264	14	3	8	11	45
1987-88	Rochester	AHL	72	18	11	29	352	5	1	3	4	42
1988-89	Rochester	AHL	66	20	18	38	306	....	....	....	....	....
1989-90	Rochester	AHL	8	0	1	1	22	....	....	....	....	....
	Phoenix	IHL	6	0	0	0	25	....	....	....	....	....
	Fort Wayne	IHL	43	11	16	27	219	5	0	1	1	3
1990-91	Fort Wayne	IHL	13	1	6	7	32	....	....	....	....	....
	Cincinnati	ECHL	36	25	34	59	228	4	0	6	6	23

KERR, TIM

Center/Right wing. Shoots right. 6'3", 230 lbs. Born, Windsor, Ont., January 5, 1960.

			Regular Season					Playoffs				
Season	Club	Lea	GP	G	A	TP	PIM	GP	G	A	TP	PIM
1978-79	Kingston	OHA	57	17	25	42	27	6	1	1	2	2
1979-80	Kingston	OHA	63	40	33	73	39	3	0	1	1	16
	Maine	AHL	7	2	4	6	2	....	....	....	....	....
1980-81	**Philadelphia**	**NHL**	**68**	**22**	**23**	**45**	**84**	**10**	**1**	**3**	**4**	**2**
1981-82	**Philadelphia**	**NHL**	**61**	**21**	**30**	**51**	**138**	**4**	**0**	**2**	**2**	**2**
1982-83	**Philadelphia**	**NHL**	**24**	**11**	**8**	**19**	**6**	**2**	**2**	**0**	**2**	**0**
1983-84	**Philadelphia**	**NHL**	**79**	**54**	**39**	**93**	**29**	**3**	**0**	**0**	**0**	**0**
1984-85	**Philadelphia**	**NHL**	**74**	**54**	**44**	**98**	**57**	**12**	**10**	**4**	**14**	**13**
1985-86	**Philadelphia**	**NHL**	**76**	**58**	**26**	**84**	**79**	**5**	**3**	**3**	**6**	**8**
1986-87a	**Philadelphia**	**NHL**	**75**	**58**	**37**	**95**	**57**	**12**	**8**	**5**	**13**	**2**
1987-88	**Philadelphia**	**NHL**	**8**	**3**	**2**	**5**	**12**	**6**	**1**	**3**	**4**	**4**
1988-89b	**Philadelphia**	**NHL**	**69**	**48**	**40**	**88**	**73**	**19**	**14**	**11**	**25**	**27**
1989-90	**Philadelphia**	**NHL**	**40**	**24**	**24**	**48**	**34**	....	....	....	....	....
1990-91	**Philadelphia**	**NHL**	**27**	**10**	**14**	**24**	**8**	....	....	....	....	....
	NHL Totals		**601**	**363**	**287**	**650**	**577**	**73**	**39**	**31**	**70**	**58**

a NHL Second All-Star Team (1987)
b Won Bill Masterton Award (1989)

Played in NHL All-Star Game (1984-86)

Signed as free agent by **Philadelphia**, October 25, 1979. Claimed by **San Jose** from **Philadelphia** in Expansion Draft, May 30, 1991. Traded to **NY Rangers** by **San Jose** for Brian Mullen and future considerations, May 30, 1991.

KESKINEN, ESA (KEHS-kee-nehn)

Center. Shoots right. 5'9", 191 lbs. Born, Ylojarvi, Finland, February 3, 1965.
(Calgary's 6th choice, 101st overall, in 1985 Entry Draft).

			Regular Season					Playoffs				
Season	Club	Lea	GP	G	A	TP	PIM	GP	G	A	TP	PIM
1986-87	TPS	Fin.	46	25	36	61	4	5	1	1	2	0
1987-88	TPS	Fin.	44	14	55	69	14	....	....	....	....	....
1988-89	Lukko	Fin.	41	24	46	70	12	....	....	....	....	....
1989-90	Lukko	Fin.	44	25	26	51	16	....	....	....	....	....
1990-91	Lukko	Fin.	44	17	51	68	14	....	....	....	....	....

KETTELHUT, MARK

Defense. Shoots left. 6', 195 lbs. Born, Duluth, MN, November 2, 1971.
(Montreal's 11th choice, 207th overall, in 1990 Entry Draft).

			Regular Season					Playoffs				
Season	Club	Lea	GP	G	A	TP	PIM	GP	G	A	TP	PIM
1989-90	Duluth East	HS	24	10	19	29	....	....	....	....	....	....
1990-91			DID NOT PLAY									

KHARIN, SERGEI (HAH-reen)

Right wing. Shoots left. 5'11", 180 lbs. Born, Odintsovo, Soviet Union, February 20, 1963.
(Winnipeg's 15th choice, 240th overall, in 1989 Entry Draft).

			Regular Season					Playoffs				
Season	Club	Lea	GP	G	A	TP	PIM	GP	G	A	TP	PIM
1980-81	Soviet Wings	USSR	2	0	0	0	0	....	....	....	....	....
1981-82	Soviet Wings	USSR	34	4	3	7	10	....	....	....	....	....
1982-83	Soviet Wings	USSR	49	5	5	10	20	....	....	....	....	....
1983-84	Soviet Wings	USSR	33	5	3	8	18	....	....	....	....	....
1984-85	Soviet Wings	USSR	34	12	8	20	6	....	....	....	....	....
1985-86	Soviet Wings	USSR	38	15	14	29	19	....	....	....	....	....
1986-87	Soviet Wings	USSR	40	16	11	27	14	....	....	....	....	....
1987-88	Soviet Wings	USSR	45	17	13	30	20	....	....	....	....	....
1988-89	Soviet Wings	USSR	44	15	9	24	14	....	....	....	....	....
1989-90	Soviet Wings	USSR	47	12	5	17	28	....	....	....	....	....
1990-91	**Winnipeg**	**NHL**	**7**	**2**	**3**	**5**	**2**	....	....	....	....	....
	Moncton	AHL	66	22	18	40	38	5	1	0	1	2
	NHL Totals		**7**	**2**	**3**	**5**	**2**	....	....	....	....	....

KHOMUTOV, ANDREI (hoh-moo-TAHF)

Right wing. Shoots left. 5'9", 180 lbs. Born, Yaroslavl, Soviet Union, April 21, 1961.
(Quebec's 12th choice, 190th overall, in 1989 Entry Draft).

			Regular Season					Playoffs				
Season	Club	Lea	GP	G	A	TP	PIM	GP	G	A	TP	PIM
1979-80	CSKA	USSR	4	0	0	0	0	....	....	....	....	....
1980-81	CSKA	USSR	43	23	18	41	4	....	....	....	....	....
1981-82	CSKA	USSR	44	17	13	30	12	....	....	....	....	....
1982-83	CSKA	USSR	44	21	17	38	6	....	....	....	....	....
1983-84	CSKA	USSR	39	17	9	26	14	....	....	....	....	....
1984-85	CSKA	USSR	37	21	13	34	18	....	....	....	....	....
1985-86	CSKA	USSR	38	14	15	29	10	....	....	....	....	....
1986-87	CSKA	USSR	33	15	18	33	22	....	....	....	....	....
1987-88	CSKA	USSR	48	29	14	43	22	....	....	....	....	....
1988-89	CSKA	USSR	44	19	16	35	14	....	....	....	....	....
1989-90a	CSKA	USSR	47	21	14	35	16	....	....	....	....	....
1990-91	Gotteron	Switz.	36	39	43	82	....	....	13	12	25	....

a Soviet Player of the Year (1990)

KHRISTICH, DMITRI

Left wing/Center. Shoots right. 6'1", 187 lbs. Born, Kiev, Soviet Union, July 23, 1969.
(Washington's 6th choice, 120th overall, in 1988 Entry Draft).

			Regular Season					Playoffs				
Season	Club	Lea	GP	G	A	TP	PIM	GP	G	A	TP	PIM
1987-88	Sokol Kiev	USSR	37	9	1	10	18	....	....	....	....	....
1988-89	Sokol Kiev	USSR	42	17	10	27	15	....	....	....	....	....
1989-90	Sokol Kiev	USSR	47	14	22	36	32	....	....	....	....	....
1990-91	Sokol Kiev	USSR	28	10	12	22	20	....	....	....	....	....
	Washington	**NHL**	**40**	**13**	**14**	**27**	**21**	**11**	**1**	**3**	**4**	**6**
	Baltimore	AHL	3	0	0	0	0	....	....	....	....	....
	NHL Totals		**40**	**13**	**14**	**27**	**21**	**11**	**1**	**3**	**4**	**6**

KIDD, IAN

Defense. Shoots right. 5'11", 195 lbs. Born, Gresham, OR, May 11, 1964.

			Regular Season					Playoffs				
Season	Club	Lea	GP	G	A	TP	PIM	GP	G	A	TP	PIM
1985-86	North Dakota	WCHA	37	6	16	22	65	....	....	....	....	....
1986-87	North Dakota	WCHA	47	13	47	60	58	....	....	....	....	....
1987-88	**Vancouver**	**NHL**	**19**	**4**	**7**	**11**	**25**	....	....	....	....	....
	Fredericton	AHL	53	1	21	22	70	12	0	4	4	22
1988-89	**Vancouver**	**NHL**	**1**	**0**	**0**	**0**	**0**	....	....	....	....	....
	Milwaukee	IHL	76	13	40	53	124	4	0	2	2	7
1989-90	Milwaukee	IHL	65	11	36	47	86	6	2	5	7	0
1990-91	Milwaukee	IHL	72	5	26	31	41	6	0	1	1	2
	NHL Totals		**20**	**4**	**7**	**11**	**25**	....	....	....	....	....

Signed as a free agent by **Vancouver**, July 30, 1987.

KIENE, CHRIS (KEEN)

Defense. Shoots left. 6'5", 220 lbs. Born, So. Windsor, CT, March 6, 1966.
(New Jersey's 12th choice, 231st overall, in 1984 Entry Draft).

			Regular Season					Playoffs				
Season	Club	Lea	GP	G	A	TP	PIM	GP	G	A	TP	PIM
1987-88	Merrimack	NCAA	40	6	34	40	72	....	....	....	....	....
1988-89	Merrimack	NCAA	32	3	25	28	76	....	....	....	....	....
1989-90	Utica	AHL	67	5	17	22	60	1	0	0	0	2
1990-91	Johnstown	ECHL	3	0	0	0	0	....	....	....	....	....

KILSTROM, MATS
(CHEEL-struhm)

Defense. Shoots right. 6'2", 198 lbs.   Born, Ludvika, Sweden, January 3, 1964.
(Calgary's 8th choice, 118th overall, in 1982 Entry Draft).

			Regular Season					Playoffs			
Season	Club	Lea	GP	G	A	TP	PIM	GP	G	A	TP	PIM
1981-82	Sodertalje	Swe.	25	2	3	5	20	....	....	....	....	....
1982-83	Sodertalje	Swe.	17	5	0	5	35	11	1	3	4	12
1983-84	Sodertalje	Swe.	25	4	3	7	25	3	1	0	1	0
1984-85	Brynas	Swe.	35	4	9	13	14	....	....	....	....	....
1985-86	Brynas	Swe.	35	3	8	11	48	3	1	0	1	4
1986-87	Sodertalje	Swe.	32	2	4	6	28	....	....	....	....	....
1987-88	Sodertalje	Swe.	37	5	7	12	36	2	0	2	2	0
1988-89	Sodertalje	Swe.	39	3	19	22	45	....	....	....	....	....
1989-90	Sodertalje	Swe.	37	7	16	23	26	2	0	1	1	5
1990-91	Sodertalje	Swe.	29	4	10	14	40	....	....	....	....	....

KIMBLE, DARIN

Right wing. Shoots right. 6'2", 205 lbs.   Born, Lucky Lake, Sask., November 22, 1968.
(Quebec's 5th choice, 66th overall, in 1988 Entry Draft).

			Regular Season					Playoffs			
Season	Club	Lea	GP	G	A	TP	PIM	GP	G	A	TP	PIM
1985-86	Calgary	WHL	37	14	8	22	93	....	....	....	....	....
	N. Westminster	WHL	11	1	1	2	22	....	....	....	....	....
	Brandon	WHL	15	1	6	7	39	....	....	....	....	....
1986-87	Prince Albert	WHL	68	17	13	30	190	....	....	....	....	....
1987-88	Prince Albert	WHL	67	35	36	71	307	10	3	2	5	4
1988-89	Quebec	NHL	26	3	1	4	154	....	....	....	....	....
	Halifax	AHL	39	8	6	14	188	....	....	....	....	....
1989-90	Quebec	NHL	44	5	5	10	185	....	....	....	....	....
	Halifax	AHL	18	6	6	12	37	6	1	1	2	61
1990-91	Quebec	NHL	35	2	5	7	114	....	....	....	....	....
	Halifax	AHL	7	1	4	5	20	....	....	....	....	....
	St. Louis	NHL	26	1	1	2	128	13	0	0	0	38
	NHL Totals		131	11	12	23	581	13	0	0	0	38

Traded to **St. Louis** by **Quebec** for Herb Raglan, Tony Twist and Andy Rymsha, February 4, 1991.

KING, DEREK

Left wing. Shoots left. 6'1", 203 lbs.   Born, Hamilton, Ont., February 11, 1967.
(NY Islanders' 2nd choice, 13th overall, in 1985 Entry Draft).

			Regular Season					Playoffs			
Season	Club	Lea	GP	G	A	TP	PIM	GP	G	A	TP	PIM
1984-85a	S.S. Marie	OHL	63	35	38	73	106	16	3	13	16	11
1985-86	S.S. Marie	OHL	25	12	17	29	33	....	....	....	....	....
	Oshawa	OHL	19	8	13	21	15	6	3	2	5	13
1986-87	NY Islanders	NHL	2	0	0	0	0	....	....	....	....	....
b	Oshawa	OHL	57	53	53	106	74	17	14	10	24	40
1987-88	NY Islanders	NHL	55	12	24	36	30	5	0	2	2	2
	Springfield	AHL	10	7	6	13	6	....	....	....	....	....
1988-89	NY Islanders	NHL	60	14	29	43	14	....	....	....	....	....
	Springfield	AHL	4	4	0	4	0	....	....	....	....	....
1989-90	NY Islanders	NHL	46	13	27	40	20	4	0	0	0	4
	Springfield	AHL	21	11	12	23	33	....	....	....	....	....
1990-91	NY Islanders	NHL	66	19	26	45	44	....	....	....	....	....
	NHL Totals		229	58	106	164	108	9	0	2	2	6

a OHL Rookie of the Year (1985)
b OHL First All-Star Team (1987)

KING, KRIS

Left wing. Shoots left, 5'11". 210 lbs.   Born, Bracebridge, Ont., February 18, 1966.
(Washington's 4th choice, 80th overall, in 1984 Entry Draft).

			Regular Season					Playoffs			
Season	Club	Lea	GP	G	A	TP	PIM	GP	G	A	TP	PIM
1983-84	Peterborough	OHL	62	13	18	31	168	8	3	3	6	14
1984-85	Peterborough	OHL	61	18	35	53	222	16	2	8	10	28
1985-86	Peterborough	OHL	58	19	40	59	254	8	4	0	4	21
1986-87	Binghamton	AHL	7	0	0	0	18	....	....	....	....	....
	Peterborough	OHL	46	23	33	56	160	12	5	8	13	41
1987-88	Detroit	NHL	3	1	0	1	2	....	....	....	....	....
	Adirondack	AHL	76	21	32	53	337	10	4	4	8	53
1988-89	Detroit	NHL	55	2	3	5	168	2	0	0	0	2
1989-90	NY Rangers	NHL	68	6	7	13	286	10	0	1	1	38
1990-91	NY Rangers	NHL	72	11	14	25	154	6	2	0	2	36
	NHL Totals		198	20	24	44	610	18	2	1	3	76

Signed as a free agent by **Detroit**, March 23, 1987. Traded to **NY Rangers** by **Detroit** for Chris McRae and Detroit's fifth round choice (Tony Burns) in 1990 Entry Draft which was previously acquired by NY Rangers, September 7, 1989.

KING, STEVE

Right wing. Shoots right. 6', 190 lbs.   Born, Greenwich, RI, July 22, 1969.
(NY Rangers' 1st choice, 21st overall, in 1991 Supplemental Draft).

			Regular Season					Playoffs			
Season	Club	Lea	GP	G	A	TP	PIM	GP	G	A	TP	PIM
1989-90	Brown	ECAC	27	19	8	27	53	....	....	....	....	....
1990-91	Brown	ECAC	27	19	15	34	76	....	....	....	....	....

KINISKY, AL

Left wing. Shoots left. 6'4", 220 lbs.   Born, Port Coquitlam, B.C., May 31, 1972.
(Philadelphia's 8th choice, 52nd overall, in 1990 Entry Draft).

			Regular Season					Playoffs			
Season	Club	Lea	GP	G	A	TP	PIM	GP	G	A	TP	PIM
1989-90	Seattle	WHL	72	9	29	38	103	13	2	3	5	13
1990-91	Seattle	WHL	70	16	26	42	128	....	....	....	....	....

KISIO, KELLY

Center. Shoots right. 5'9", 183 lbs.   Born, Peace River, Alta., September 18, 1959.

			Regular Season					Playoffs			
Season	Club	Lea	GP	G	A	TP	PIM	GP	G	A	TP	PIM
1978-79	Calgary	WHL	70	60	61	121	73	....	....	....	....	....
1979-80	Calgary	WHL	71	65	73	138	64	....	....	....	....	....
1980-81	Adirondack	AHL	41	10	14	24	43	....	....	....	....	....
	Kalamazoo	IHL	31	27	16	43	48	8	7	7	14	13
1981-82	Dallas	CHL	78	*62	39	101	59	16	*12	*17	*29	38
1982-83	Davos	Swit.	40	49	38	87	....	....	....	....	....	....
	Detroit	NHL	15	4	3	7	0	....	....	....	....	....
1983-84	Detroit	NHL	70	23	37	60	34	4	1	0	1	4
1984-85	Detroit	NHL	75	20	41	61	56	3	0	2	2	2
1985-86	Detroit	NHL	76	21	48	69	85	....	....	....	....	....
1986-87	NY Rangers	NHL	70	24	40	64	73	4	0	1	1	2
1987-88	NY Rangers	NHL	77	23	55	78	88	....	....	....	....	....
1988-89	NY Rangers	NHL	70	26	36	62	91	4	0	0	0	9
1989-90	NY Rangers	NHL	68	22	44	66	105	10	2	8	10	8
1990-91	NY Rangers	NHL	51	15	20	35	58	....	....	....	....	....
	NHL Totals		572	178	324	502	590	25	3	11	14	25

Signed as a free agent by **Detroit**, May 2, 1983. Traded to **NY Rangers** by **Detroit** with Lane Lambert and Jim Leavins for Glen Hanlon and New York's third-round choices in 1987 (Dennis Holland) and 1988 (Guy Dupuis) Entry Drafts, July 29, 1986. Claimed by **Minnesota** from **NY Rangers** in Expansion Draft, May 30, 1991. Traded to **San Jose** by **Minnesota** for Shane Churla, June 3, 1991.

KIVELA, TEPPO
(KEE-veh-lah)

Center. Shoots left. 5'11", 178 lbs.   Born, Espoo, Finland, October 8, 1967.
(Minnesota's 5th choice, 88th overall, in 1987 Entry Draft).

			Regular Season					Playoffs			
Season	Club	Lea	GP	G	A	TP	PIM	GP	G	A	TP	PIM
1986-87	HPK	Fin.	41	26	38	64	64	6	4	7	11	4
1987-88	HPK	Fin.	36	31	39	70	20	....	....	....	....	....
1988-89	HPK	Fin.	39	20	38	58	54	....	....	....	....	....
1989-90	HPK	Fin.	44	27	34	61	44	....	....	....	....	....
1990-91	HPK	Fin.	44	23	50	73	32	8	5	7	12	12

KIVI, KARRI

Defense. Shoots left. 6', 172 lbs.   Born, Turku, Finland, January 31, 1970.
(Vancouver's 11th choice, 233rd overall, in 1990 Entry Draft).

			Regular Season					Playoffs			
Season	Club	Lea	GP	G	A	TP	PIM	GP	G	A	TP	PIM
1989-90	Ilves	Fin.	43	6	15	21	14	....	....	....	....	....
1990-91	Ilves	Fin.	43	2	9	11	18	....	....	....	....	....

KJELLBERG, PATRIK
(CHEHL-buhrg)

Left wing. Shoots left. 6'2", 196 lbs.   Born, Falun, Sweden, June 17, 1969.
(Montreal's 4th choice, 83rd overall, in 1988 Entry Draft).

			Regular Season					Playoffs			
Season	Club	Lea	GP	G	A	TP	PIM	GP	G	A	TP	PIM
1986-87	Falun	Swe.2	27	11	13	24	14	....	....	....	....	....
1987-88	Falun	Swe.2	29	15	10	25	18	....	....	....	....	....
1988-89	AIK	Swe.	25	7	9	16	8	....	....	....	....	....
1989-90	AIK	Swe.	33	8	16	24	6	3	1	0	1	0
1990-91	AIK	Swe.	38	4	11	15	18	....	....	....	....	....

KLATT, TRENT

Center. Shoots right. 6'1", 208 lbs.   Born, Robbinsdale, MN, January 30, 1971.
(Washington's 5th choice, 82nd overall, in 1989 Entry Draft).

			Regular Season					Playoffs			
Season	Club	Lea	GP	G	A	TP	PIM	GP	G	A	TP	PIM
1989-90	U. Minnesota	WCHA	38	22	14	36	16	....	....	....	....	....
1990-91	U. Minnesota	WCHA	39	16	28	44	58	....	....	....	....	....

Traded to **Minnesota** by **Washington** with Steve Maltais for Shawn Chambers, June 21, 1991.

KLEE, KEN

Defense. Shoots right. 6'1", 200 lbs.   Born, Indianapolis, IN, April 24, 1971.
(Washington's 11th choice, 177th overall, in 1990 Entry Draft).

			Regular Season					Playoffs			
Season	Club	Lea	GP	G	A	TP	PIM	GP	G	A	TP	PIM
1989-90	Bowling Green	CCHA	39	0	5	5	52	....	....	....	....	....
1990-91	Bowling Green	CCHA	37	7	28	35	50	....	....	....	....	....

KLIMA, PETR
(KLEE-muh)

Left wing. Shoots right. 6', 190 lbs.   Born, Chomutov, Czech., December 23, 1964.
(Detroit's 5th choice, 86th overall, in 1983 Entry Draft).

			Regular Season					Playoffs			
Season	Club	Lea	GP	G	A	TP	PIM	GP	G	A	TP	PIM
1982-83	Czech. Jrs.	....	44	19	17	36	74	....	....	....	....	....
1983-84	Dukla Jihlava	Czech.	41	20	16	36	46	....	....	....	....	....
	Czech. Jrs.	....	7	6	5	11		....	....	....	....	....
1984-85	Dukla Jihlava	Czech.	35	23	22	45		....	....	....	....	....
	Czech. Nat'l	....	5	2	1	3	0	....	....	....	....	....
1985-86	Detroit	NHL	74	32	24	56	16	....	....	....	....	....
1986-87	Detroit	NHL	77	30	23	53	42	13	1	2	3	4
1987-88	Detroit	NHL	78	37	25	62	46	12	10	8	18	10
1988-89	Detroit	NHL	51	25	16	41	44	6	2	4	6	19
	Adirondack	AHL	5	5	1	6	4	....	....	....	....	....
1989-90	Detroit	NHL	13	5	5	10	6	....	....	....	....	....
	Edmonton	NHL	63	25	28	53	66	21	5	0	5	8
1990-91	Edmonton	NHL	70	40	28	68	113	18	7	6	13	16
	NHL Totals		426	194	149	343	333	70	25	20	45	57

Traded to **Edmonton** by **Detroit** with Joe Murphy, Adam Graves and Jeff Sharples for Jimmy Carson, Kevin McClelland and Edmonton's fifth round choice (later traded to Montreal for Rick Green. Montreal selected Brad Layzell) in 1991 Entry Draft, November 2, 1989.

KLIPPENSTEIN, WADE

Left wing. Shoots left. 6'3", 219 lbs. Born, Boissevain, Man., May 9, 1970.
(Quebec's 11th choice, 232nd overall, in 1990 Entry Draft).

			Regular Season					Playoffs				
Season	Club	Lea	GP	G	A	TP	PIM	GP	G	A	TP	PIM
1989-90	Alaska-Fair.	G.N.	37	17	14	31	....	....	....	....	....	....
1990-91	Alaska-Fair.	G.N.	35	22	11	33	32	....	....	....	....	....

KLUZAK, GORDON (GORD) (KLOO-zak)

Defense. Shoots left. 6'4", 215 lbs. Born, Climax, Sask., March 4, 1964.
(Boston's 1st choice, 1st overall, in 1982 Entry Draft).

			Regular Season					Playoffs				
Season	Club	Lea	GP	G	A	TP	PIM	GP	G	A	TP	PIM
1980-81	Billings	WHL	68	4	34	38	160	5	0	1	1	4
1981-82a	Billings	WHL	38	9	24	33	110	....	....	....	....	....
1982-83	**Boston**	**NHL**	**70**	**1**	**6**	**7**	**105**	**17**	**1**	**4**	**5**	**54**
1983-84	**Boston**	**NHL**	**80**	**10**	**27**	**37**	**135**	**3**	**0**	**0**	**0**	**0**
1984-85			DID NOT PLAY – INJURED									
1985-86	**Boston**	**NHL**	**70**	**8**	**31**	**39**	**155**	**3**	**1**	**1**	**2**	**16**
1986-87			DID NOT PLAY – INJURED									
1987-88	**Boston**	**NHL**	**66**	**6**	**31**	**37**	**135**	**23**	**4**	**8**	**12**	**59**
1988-89	**Boston**	**NHL**	**3**	**0**	**1**	**1**	**2**	....	....	....	....	....
1989-90b	**Boston**	**NHL**	**8**	**0**	**2**	**2**	**11**	....	....	....	....	....
1990-91	**Boston**	**NHL**	**2**	**0**	**0**	**0**	**0**	....	....	....	....	....
	NHL Totals		**299**	**25**	**98**	**123**	**543**	**46**	**6**	**13**	**19**	**129**

a WHL Second All-Star Team (1982)
b Won Bill Masterton Award (1990)

KNUTSEN, ESPEN

Center. Shoots left. 5'11", 172 lbs. Born, Oslo, Norway, January 12, 1972.
(Hartford's 9th choice, 204th overall, in 1990 Entry Draft).

			Regular Season					Playoffs				
Season	Club	Lea	GP	G	A	TP	PIM	GP	G	A	TP	PIM
1989-90	Valerengen	Nor.	34	22	26	48	....	....	....	....	....	....
1990-91	Valerengen	Nor.	31	30	24	54	42	5	3	4	7	....

KOCUR, JOEY (KOH-suhr)

Right wing. Shoots right. 6', 195 lbs. Born, Calgary, Alta., December 21, 1964.
(Detroit's 6th choice, 88th overall, in 1983 Entry Draft).

			Regular Season					Playoffs				
Season	Club	Lea	GP	G	A	TP	PIM	GP	G	A	TP	PIM
1982-83	Saskatoon	WHL	62	23	17	40	289	6	2	3	5	25
1983-84	Saskatoon	WHL	69	40	41	81	258	....	....	....	....	....
	Adirondack	AHL	....	....	....	....	....	5	0	0	0	20
1984-85	**Detroit**	**NHL**	**17**	**1**	**0**	**1**	**64**	**3**	**1**	**0**	**1**	**5**
	Adirondack	AHL	47	12	7	19	171	....	....	....	....	....
1985-86	**Detroit**	**NHL**	**59**	**9**	**6**	**15**	***377**	....	....	....	....	....
	Adirondack	AHL	9	6	2	8	34	....	....	....	....	....
1986-87	**Detroit**	**NHL**	**77**	**9**	**9**	**18**	**276**	**16**	**2**	**3**	**5**	**71**
1987-88	**Detroit**	**NHL**	**63**	**7**	**7**	**14**	**263**	**10**	**0**	**1**	**1**	**13**
1988-89	**Detroit**	**NHL**	**60**	**9**	**9**	**18**	**213**	**3**	**0**	**1**	**1**	**6**
1989-90	**Detroit**	**NHL**	**71**	**16**	**20**	**36**	**268**	....	....	....	....	....
1990-91	**Detroit**	**NHL**	**52**	**5**	**4**	**9**	**253**	....	....	....	....	....
	NY Rangers	**NHL**	**5**	**0**	**0**	**0**	**36**	**6**	**0**	**2**	**2**	**21**
	NHL Totals		**404**	**56**	**55**	**111**	**1750**	**38**	**3**	**7**	**10**	**116**

Traded to **NY Rangers** by **Detroit** with Per Djoos for Kevin Miller, Jim Cummins and Dennis Vial, March 5, 1991.

KOCUR, KORY

Right wing. Shoots right. 5'11", 188 lbs. Born, Kelvington, Sask., March 6, 1969.
(Detroit's 1st choice, 17th overall, in 1988 Entry Draft).

			Regular Season					Playoffs				
Season	Club	Lea	GP	G	A	TP	PIM	GP	G	A	TP	PIM
1986-87	Saskatoon	WHL	62	13	17	30	98	4	0	0	0	7
1987-88	Saskatoon	WHL	69	34	37	71	95	10	5	4	9	18
1988-89	Saskatoon	WHL	66	45	57	102	111	8	7	11	18	15
1989-90	Adirondack	AHL	79	18	37	55	36	6	1	2	3	2
1990-91	Adirondack	AHL	65	8	13	21	83	2	0	0	0	12

KOIVUNEN, PETRO

Right wing. Shoots right. 6', 180 lbs. Born, Espoo, Finland, May 30, 1970.
(Edmonton's 2nd choice, 39th overall, in 1988 Entry Draft).

			Regular Season					Playoffs				
Season	Club	Lea	GP	G	A	TP	PIM	GP	G	A	TP	PIM
1986-87	Espoo	Fin.	30	22	14	36	26	....	....	....	....	....
1987-88	Espoo	Fin.	31	27	31	58	38	....	....	....	....	....
1988-89	Espoo	Fin.	39	22	37	59	42	....	....	....	....	....
1989-90	Espoo	Fin.	39	24	35	59	28	....	....	....	....	....
1990-91	HIFK	Fin.	39	8	15	23	20	3	0	1	1	4

KOLNIK, LUBOMIR (KOHL-neek)

Right wing. Shoots left. 5'11", 178 lbs. Born, Nitra, Czechoslovakia, January 23, 1968.
(New Jersey's 9th choice, 116th overall, in 1990 Entry Draft).

			Regular Season					Playoffs				
Season	Club	Lea	GP	G	A	TP	PIM	GP	G	A	TP	PIM
1989-90	Dukla Trencin	Czech.	53	37	25	62	....	....	....	....	....	....
1990-91	Dukla Trencin	Czech.	52	38	37	75	12	....	....	....	....	....

KOLSTAD, DEAN

Defense. Shoots left. 6'6", 210 lbs. Born, Edmonton, Alta., June 16, 1968.
(Minnesota's 3rd choice, 33rd overall, in 1986 Entry Draft).

			Regular Season					Playoffs				
Season	Club	Lea	GP	G	A	TP	PIM	GP	G	A	TP	PIM
1985-86	N. Westminster	WHL	13	0	0	0	16	....	....	....	....	....
	Prince Albert	WHL	54	2	15	17	80	20	5	3	8	26
1986-87	Prince Albert	WHL	72	17	37	54	112	8	1	5	6	8
1987-88	Prince Albert	WHL	72	14	37	51	121	10	0	9	9	20
1988-89	**Minnesota**	**NHL**	**25**	**1**	**5**	**6**	**42**	....	....	....	....	....
	Kalamazoo	IHL	51	10	23	33	91	6	1	0	1	23
1989-90a	Kalamazoo	IHL	77	10	40	50	172	10	3	4	7	14
1990-91	**Minnesota**	**NHL**	**5**	**0**	**0**	**0**	**15**	....	....	....	....	....
	Kalamazoo	IHL	33	4	8	12	50	9	1	6	7	4
	NHL Totals		**30**	**1**	**5**	**6**	**57**	....	....	....	....	....

a IHL Second All-Star Team (1990)

Claimed by **San Jose** from **Minnesota** in Dispersal Draft, May 30, 1991.

KONOWALCHUK, STEVE

Center. Shoots left. 6', 175 lbs. Born, Salt Lake City, UT, November 11, 1972.
(Washington's 5th choice, 58th overall, in 1991 Entry Draft).

			Regular Season					Playoffs				
Season	Club	Lea	GP	G	A	TP	PIM	GP	G	A	TP	PIM
1989-90	Prince Albert	Midget	36	30	28	58	22	....	....	....	....	....
1990-91	Portland	WHL	72	43	49	92	78	....	....	....	....	....

KONROYD, STEPHEN MARK (STEVE) (KON-royd)

Defense. Shoots left. 6'1", 195 lbs. Born, Scarborough, Ont., February 10, 1961.
(Atlanta's 4th choice, 39th overall, in 1980 Entry Draft).

			Regular Season					Playoffs				
Season	Club	Lea	GP	G	A	TP	PIM	GP	G	A	TP	PIM
1979-80	Oshawa	OHA	62	11	23	34	133	7	0	2	2	14
1980-81	**Calgary**	**NHL**	**4**	**0**	**0**	**0**	**4**	....	....	....	....	....
a	Oshawa	OHA	59	19	47	68	232	11	3	11	14	35
1981-82	**Calgary**	**NHL**	**63**	**3**	**14**	**17**	**78**	**3**	**0**	**0**	**0**	**12**
	Oklahoma City	CHL	14	2	3	5	15	....	....	....	....	....
1982-83	Calgary	NHL	79	4	13	17	73	9	2	1	3	18
1983-84	Calgary	NHL	80	1	13	14	94	8	1	2	3	8
1984-85	Calgary	NHL	64	3	23	26	73	4	1	4	5	2
1985-86	**Calgary**	**NHL**	**59**	**7**	**20**	**27**	**64**	....	....	....	....	....
	NY Islanders	**NHL**	**14**	**0**	**5**	**5**	**16**	**3**	**0**	**0**	**0**	**6**
1986-87	**NY Islanders**	**NHL**	**72**	**5**	**16**	**21**	**70**	**14**	**1**	**4**	**5**	**10**
1987-88	**NY Islanders**	**NHL**	**62**	**2**	**15**	**17**	**99**	**6**	**1**	**0**	**1**	**4**
1988-89	**NY Islanders**	**NHL**	**21**	**1**	**5**	**6**	**2**	....	....	....	....	....
	Chicago	**NHL**	**57**	**5**	**7**	**12**	**40**	**16**	**2**	**0**	**2**	**10**
1989-90	**Chicago**	**NHL**	**75**	**3**	**14**	**17**	**34**	**20**	**1**	**3**	**4**	**19**
1990-91	**Chicago**	**NHL**	**70**	**0**	**12**	**12**	**40**	**6**	**1**	**0**	**1**	**8**
	NHL Totals		**720**	**34**	**157**	**191**	**687**	**89**	**10**	**14**	**24**	**97**

a OHA Second All-Star Team (1981)

Traded to **NY Islanders** by **Calgary** with Richard Kromm for John Tonelli, March 11, 1986.
Traded to **Chicago** by **NY Islanders** with Bob Bassen for Marc Bergevin and Gary Nylund, November 25, 1988.

KONSTANTINOV, VLADIMIR (kohn-stahn-TEE-nahf)

Defense. Shoots right. 5'11", 176 lbs. Born, Murmansk, Soviet Union, March 19, 1967.
(Detroit's 12th choice, 221st overall, in 1989 Entry Draft).

			Regular Season					Playoffs				
Season	Club	Lea	GP	G	A	TP	PIM	GP	G	A	TP	PIM
1984-85	CSKA	USSR	40	1	4	5	10	....	....	....	....	....
1985-86	CSKA	USSR	26	4	3	7	12	....	....	....	....	....
1986-87	CSKA	USSR	35	2	2	4	19	....	....	....	....	....
1987-88	CSKA	USSR	50	3	6	9	32	....	....	....	....	....
1988-89	CSKA	USSR	37	7	8	15	20	....	....	....	....	....
1989-90	CSKA	USSR	47	14	13	27	44	....	....	....	....	....
1990-91	CSKA	USSR	45	5	12	17	42	....	....	....	....	....

KONTOS, CHRISTOPHER (CHRIS) (KONN-tohs)

Left wing/Center. Shoots left. 6'1", 195 lbs. Born, Toronto, Ont., December 10, 1963.
(NY Rangers' 1st choice, 15th overall, in 1982 Entry Draft).

			Regular Season					Playoffs				
Season	Club	Lea	GP	G	A	TP	PIM	GP	G	A	TP	PIM
1980-81	Sudbury	OHA	57	17	27	44	36	....	....	....	....	....
1981-82	Sudbury	OHL	12	6	6	12	18	....	....	....	....	....
	Toronto	OHL	59	36	56	92	68	10	7	9	16	2
1982-83	**NY Rangers**	**NHL**	**44**	**8**	**7**	**15**	**33**	....	....	....	....	....
	Toronto	OHL	28	21	33	54	23	....	....	....	....	....
1983-84	NY Rangers	NHL	6	0	1	1	8	....	....	....	....	....
	Tulsa	CHL	21	5	13	18	8	....	....	....	....	....
1984-85	**NY Rangers**	**NHL**	**28**	**4**	**8**	**12**	**24**	....	....	....	....	....
	New Haven	AHL	48	19	24	43	30	....	....	....	....	....
1985-86	Ilves	Fin.	36	16	15	31	30	....	....	....	....	....
	New Haven	AHL	21	8	15	23	12	5	4	2	6	4
1986-87	**Pittsburgh**	**NHL**	**31**	**8**	**9**	**17**	**6**	....	....	....	....	....
	New Haven	AHL	36	14	17	31	29	....	....	....	....	....
1987-88	**Pittsburgh**	**NHL**	**36**	**1**	**7**	**8**	**12**	....	....	....	....	....
	Muskegon	IHL	10	3	6	9	8	....	....	....	....	....
	Los Angeles	**NHL**	**6**	**2**	**10**	**12**	**2**	**4**	**1**	**0**	**1**	**4**
	New Haven	AHL	16	8	16	24	4	....	....	....	....	....
1988-89	Ilves	Fin.	36	16	15	31	30	....	....	....	....	....
	Los Angeles	**NHL**	**7**	**2**	**1**	**3**	**2**	**11**	**9**	**0**	**9**	**8**
1989-90	**Los Angeles**	**NHL**	**6**	**2**	**2**	**4**	**4**	**5**	**1**	**0**	**1**	**0**
	New Haven	AHL	42	10	20	30	25	....	....	....	....	....
1990-91	Phoenix	IHL	69	26	36	62	19	11	9	12	21	0
	NHL Totals		**164**	**27**	**45**	**72**	**91**	**20**	**11**	**0**	**11**	**12**

Traded to **Pittsburgh** by **NY Rangers** for Ron Duguay, January 21, 1987. Traded to **Los Angeles** by **Pittsburgh** with Pittsburgh's sixth round choice in 1988 Entry Draft (Micah Aivazoff) for Bryan Erickson, February 5, 1988.

KONTSEK, ROMAN

Right wing. Shoots right. 5'11", 183 lbs. Born, Prague, Czechoslovakia, June 11, 1970.
(Washington's 8th choice, 135th overall, in 1990 Entry Draft).

			Regular Season					Playoffs				
Season	Club	Lea	GP	G	A	TP	PIM	GP	G	A	TP	PIM
1988-89	Dukla Trencin	Czech.	21	4	8	12	....	....	....	....	....	....
1989-90	Dukla Trencin	Czech.	21	8	7	15	....	....	....	....	....	....
1990-91	Dukla Trencin	Czech.	48	13	18	31	24	....	....	....	....	....

KORDIC, DAN

Defense. Shoots left. 6'5", 220 lbs. Born, Edmonton, Alta., April 18, 1971.
(Philadelphia's 9th choice, 88th overall, in 1990 Entry Draft).

			Regular Season					Playoffs				
Season	Club	Lea	GP	G	A	TP	PIM	GP	G	A	TP	PIM
1989-90	Medicine Hat	WHL	59	4	12	16	182	3	0	0	0	9
1990-91	Medicine Hat	WHL	67	8	15	23	150	12	2	6	8	42

KORDIC, JOHN

Right wing. Shoots right. 6'2", 210 lbs. Born, Edmonton, Alta., March 22, 1965.
(Montreal's 6th choice, 78th overall, in 1983 Entry Draft).

			Regular Season					Playoffs				
Season	Club	Lea	GP	G	A	TP	PIM	GP	G	A	TP	PIM
1982-83	Portland	WHL	72	3	22	25	235	14	1	6	7	30
1983-84	Portland	WHL	67	9	50	59	232	14	0	13	13	56
1984-85a	Seattle	WHL	46	17	36	53	154	....	....	....	....	....
	Portland	WHL	25	6	22	28	73	....	....	....	....	....
	Sherbrooke	AHL	4	0	0	0	4	4	0	0	0	11
1985-86	**Montreal**	**NHL**	**5**	**0**	**1**	**1**	**12**	**18**	**0**	**0**	**0**	**53**
	Sherbrooke	AHL	68	3	14	17	238	....	....	....	....	....
1986-87	**Montreal**	**NHL**	**44**	**5**	**3**	**8**	**151**	**11**	**2**	**0**	**2**	**19**
	Sherbrooke	AHL	10	4	4	8	49	....	....	....	....	....
1987-88	**Montreal**	**NHL**	**60**	**2**	**6**	**8**	**159**	**7**	**2**	**2**	**4**	**26**
1988-89	**Montreal**	**NHL**	**6**	**0**	**0**	**0**	**13**	....	....	....	....	....
	Toronto	**NHL**	**46**	**1**	**2**	**3**	**185**	....	....	....	....	....
1989-90	**Toronto**	**NHL**	**55**	**9**	**4**	**13**	**252**	**5**	**0**	**1**	**1**	**33**
1990-91	**Toronto**	**NHL**	**3**	**0**	**0**	**0**	**9**	....	....	....	....	....
	Newmarket	AHL	8	1	1	2	79	....	....	....	....	....
	Washington	**NHL**	**7**	**0**	**0**	**0**	**101**	....	....	....	....	....
	NHL Totals		**226**	**17**	**16**	**33**	**882**	**41**	**4**	**3**	**7**	**131**

a WHL Second All-Star Team, West Division (1985).

Traded to **Toronto** by **Montreal** with Montreal's sixth-round choice (Michael Doers) in 1989 Entry Draft for Russ Courtnall, November 7, 1988. Traded to **Washington** by **Toronto** with Paul Fenton for Washington's fifth round choice (Alexei Kudashov) in 1991 Entry Draft, January 24, 1991.

KOROL, DAVID

Defense. Shoots right. 6'1", 185 lbs. Born, Winnipeg, Man., March 1, 1965.
(Detroit's 4th choice, 70th overall, in 1983 Entry Draft).

			Regular Season					Playoffs				
Season	Club	Lea	GP	G	A	TP	PIM	GP	G	A	TP	PIM
1981-82	Winnipeg	WHL	64	4	22	26	55	....	....	....	....	....
1982-83	Winnipeg	WHL	72	14	32	57	90	3	0	1	1	0
1983-84	Winnipeg	WHL	57	15	48	63	49	....	....	....	....	....
	Adirondack	AHL	2	0	4	4	0	3	0	0	0	0
1984-85	Regina	WHL	48	4	30	34	61	3	0	0	0	0
1985-86	Adirondack	AHL	74	3	9	12	56	3	0	1	1	4
1986-87	Adirondack	AHL	48	1	4	5	67	11	2	2	4	21
1987-88	Adirondack	AHL	53	2	17	19	61	10	0	4	4	7
1988-89	Adirondack	AHL	73	3	24	27	57	17	1	2	3	8
1989-90	Phoenix	IHL	62	1	12	13	45	....	....	....	....	....
1990-91	San Diego	IHL	58	1	7	8	51	....	....	....	....	....

KOSKIMAKI, PETTERI

Center. Shoots left. 6'1", 180 lbs. Born, Helsinki, Finland, May 5, 1971.
(Pittsburgh's 10th choice, 152nd overall, in 1990 Entry Draft).

			Regular Season					Playoffs				
Season	Club	Lea	GP	G	A	TP	PIM	GP	G	A	TP	PIM
1988-89	HIFK	Fin.	31	11	17	28	2	....	....	....	....	....
1989-90	Boston U.	H.E.	44	12	12	24	15	....	....	....	....	....
1990-91	Boston U.	H.E.	37	16	22	38	12	....	....	....	....	....

KOSTICHKIN, PAVEL (kohs-TEECH-keen)

Center. Shoots left. 6', 189 lbs. Born, Moscow, Soviet Union, November 9, 1968.
(Winnipeg's 12th choice, 199th overall, in 1988 Entry Draft).

			Regular Season					Playoffs				
Season	Club	Lea	GP	G	A	TP	PIM	GP	G	A	TP	PIM
1985-86	CSKA	USSR	16	5	4	9	12	....	....	....	....	....
1986-87	CSKA	USSR	13	0	3	3	4	....	....	....	....	....
1987-88	CSKA	USSR	40	8	0	8	20	....	....	....	....	....
1988-89	CSKA	USSR	31	4	2	6	16	....	....	....	....	....
1989-90	CSKA	USSR	25	3	4	7	14	....	....	....	....	....
1990-91	CSKA	USSR	26	4	4	8	10	....	....	....	....	....

KOVACS, FRANK

Left wing. Shoots left. 6'2", 205 lbs. Born, Regina, Sask., June 6, 1971.
(Minnesota's 4th choice, 71st overall, in 1990 Entry Draft).

			Regular Season					Playoffs				
Season	Club	Lea	GP	G	A	TP	PIM	GP	G	A	TP	PIM
1987-88	Regina	WHL	70	10	8	18	48	4	0	1	1	4
1988-89	Regina	WHL	70	16	27	43	90	....	....	....	....	....
1989-90	Regina	WHL	70	26	32	58	165	11	4	4	8	10
1990-91	Regina	WHL	72	50	51	101	148	8	10	3	13	15

KOVALENKO, ANDREI

Right wing. Shoots left. 5'9", 161 lbs. Born, Gorky, Soviet Union, June 7, 1970.
(Quebec's 6th choice, 148th overall, in 1990 Entry Draft).

			Regular Season					Playoffs				
Season	Club	Lea	GP	G	A	TP	PIM	GP	G	A	TP	PIM
1989-90	CSKA	USSR	48	8	5	13	18	....	....	....	....	....
1990-91	CSKA	USSR	45	13	8	21	26	....	....	....	....	....

KOVALEV, ALEXEI

Right wing. Shoots left. 6'1", 189 lbs. Born, Moscow, Soviet Union, February 24, 1973.
(NY Rangers' 1st choice, 15th overall, in 1991 Entry Draft).

			Regular Season					Playoffs				
Season	Club	Lea	GP	G	A	TP	PIM	GP	G	A	TP	PIM
1989-90	Moscow D'amo	USSR	1	0	0	0	0	....	....	....	....	....
1990-91	Moscow D'amo	USSR	16	1	2	3	4	....	....	....	....	....

KOVALEV, ANDREI

Right wing. Shoots right. 5'11", 189 lbs. Born, Minsk, Soviet Union, April 2, 1966.
(Washington's 7th choice, 114th overall, in 1990 Entry Draft).

			Regular Season					Playoffs				
Season	Club	Lea	GP	G	A	TP	PIM	GP	G	A	TP	PIM
1989-90	Moscow D'amo	USSR	41	10	8	18	8	....	....	....	....	....
1990-91	Moscow D'amo	USSR	43	17	8	25	18	....	....	....	....	....

KOZAK, MICHAEL

Right wing. Shoots right. 6'2", 195 lbs. Born, Toronto, Ont., March 14, 1969.
(Chicago's 9th choice, 216th overall, in 1989 Entry Draft).

			Regular Season					Playoffs				
Season	Club	Lea	GP	G	A	TP	PIM	GP	G	A	TP	PIM
1987-88	Clarkson	ECAC	21	3	2	5	....	....	....	....	....	....
1988-89	Clarkson	ECAC	25	10	9	19	20	....	....	....	....	....
1989-90	Clarkson	ECAC	32	8	14	22	38	....	....	....	....	....
1990-91	Clarkson	ECAC	40	13	15	28	45	....	....	....	....	....

KOZLOV, VIACHESLAV

Center. Shoots left. 5'10", 172 lbs. Born, Voskresensk, Soviet Union, May 3, 1972.
(Detroit's 2nd choice, 45th overall, in 1990 Entry Draft).

			Regular Season					Playoffs				
Season	Club	Lea	GP	G	A	TP	PIM	GP	G	A	TP	PIM
1989-90	Khimik	USSR	45	14	12	26	38	....	....	....	....	....
1990-91	Khimik	USSR	45	11	13	24	46	....	....	....	....	....

KRAMER, TED

Right wing. Shoots right. 6', 190 lbs. Born, Findlay, OH, October 29, 1969.
(Los Angeles 6th choice, 144th overall, in 1989 Entry Draft).

			Regular Season					Playoffs				
Season	Club	Lea	GP	G	A	TP	PIM	GP	G	A	TP	PIM
1988-89	U. of Michigan	CCHA	37	16	14	30	70	....	....	....	....	....
1989-90	U. of Michigan	CCHA	42	21	24	45	111	....	....	....	....	....
1990-91	U. of Michigan	CCHA	47	15	17	32	107	....	....	....	....	....

KRAUSS, ROBERT

Defense. Shoots left. 6'2", 210 lbs. Born, Grand Prairie, Alta., October 28, 1969.
(Washington's 5th choice, 78th overall, in 1988 Entry Draft).

			Regular Season					Playoffs				
Season	Club	Lea	GP	G	A	TP	PIM	GP	G	A	TP	PIM
1986-87	Calgary	WHL	70	3	17	20	130	....	....	....	....	....
1987-88	Lethbridge	WHL	69	6	21	27	245	....	....	....	....	....
1988-89	Tri-Cities	WHL	66	4	23	27	257	7	1	2	3	19
1989-90	Tri-Cities	WHL	33	5	19	24	107	....	....	....	....	....
	Portland	WHL	31	4	24	28	95	....	....	....	....	....
	Hampton Roads	ECHL	....	....	....	....	....	5	0	4	4	23
1990-91	Fort Wayne	IHL	1	0	0	0	7	....	....	....	....	....
	Adirondack	AHL	8	0	3	3	39	2	0	1	1	11
	Cincinnati	ECHL	57	4	26	30	299	4	1	1	2	6

KREICK, BRAD

Defense. Shoots right. 6'3", 193 lbs. Born, Nashua, NH, May 6, 1968.
(Detroit's 1st choice, 16th overall, in 1989 Supplemental Draft).

			Regular Season					Playoffs				
Season	Club	Lea	GP	G	A	TP	PIM	GP	G	A	TP	PIM
1989-90	Brown	ECAC	29	1	8	9	37	....	....	....	....	....
1990-91	Brown	ECAC	26	2	11	13	16	....	....	....	....	....

KRENTZ, DALE

Left wing. Shoots left. 5'11", 190 lbs. Born, Steinbach, Man., December 19, 1961.

			Regular Season					Playoffs				
Season	Club	Lea	GP	G	A	TP	PIM	GP	G	A	TP	PIM
1982-83	Michigan State	CCHA	42	11	24	35	50	....	....	....	....	....
1983-84	Michigan State	CCHA	44	12	20	32	34	....	....	....	....	....
1984-85	Michigan State	CCHA	44	24	30	54	26	....	....	....	....	....
1985-86	Adirondack	AHL	79	19	27	46	27	13	2	6	8	9
1986-87	**Detroit**	**NHL**	**8**	**0**	**0**	**0**	**0**	....	....	....	....	....
	Adirondack	AHL	71	32	39	71	68	11	3	4	7	10
1987-88	**Detroit**	**NHL**	**6**	**2**	**0**	**2**	**5**	**2**	**0**	**0**	**0**	**0**
a	Adirondack	AHL	67	39	43	82	65	8	*11	4	15	8
1988-89	**Detroit**	**NHL**	**16**	**3**	**3**	**6**	**4**	....	....	....	....	....
	Adirondack	AHL	36	21	20	41	30	....	....	....	....	....
1989-90	Adirondack	AHL	74	38	50	88	36	6	2	3	5	11
1990-91	Mannheimer	Ger.	47	29	29	58	26	....	....	....	....	....
	NHL Totals		**30**	**5**	**3**	**8**	**9**	**2**	**0**	**0**	**0**	**0**

a AHL Second All-Star Team (1988)

Signed as a free agent by **Detroit**, June 5, 1985.

KRISS, AARON

Defense. Shoots left. 6'2", 185 lbs. Born, Parma, OH, September 17, 1972.
(San Jose's 12th choice, 221st overall, in 1991 Entry Draft).

			Regular Season					Playoffs				
Season	Club	Lea	GP	G	A	TP	PIM	GP	G	A	TP	PIM
1990-91	Cranbrook	HS	24	14	21	35	95	....	....	....	....	....

KRIVOKHIZHA, YURI (kree-voh-HEE-zhah)

Defense. Shoots left. 6'2", 198 lbs. Born, Minsk, Soviet Union, March 30, 1968.
(Montreal's 11th choice, 209th overall, in 1988 Entry Draft).

			Regular Season					Playoffs				
Season	Club	Lea	GP	G	A	TP	PIM	GP	G	A	TP	PIM
1988-89	Dynamo Minsk	USSR	25	2	7	9	22	....	....	....	....	....
1989-90	Dynamo Minsk	USSR	47	4	2	6	50	....	....	....	....	....
1990-91	Dynamo Minsk	USSR	23	0	2	2	20	....	....	....	....	....

KROMM, RICHARD GORDON (RICH)

Left wing. Shoots left. 5'11", 180 lbs. Born, Trail, B.C., March 29, 1964.
(Calgary's 2nd choice, 37th overall, in 1982 Entry Draft).

			Regular Season					Playoffs				
Season	Club	Lea	GP	G	A	TP	PIM	GP	G	A	TP	PIM
1981-82	Portland	WHL	60	16	38	54	30	14	0	3	3	17
1982-83	Portland	WHL	72	35	68	103	64	14	7	13	20	12
1983-84	**Calgary**	**NHL**	**53**	**11**	**12**	**23**	**27**	**11**	**1**	**1**	**2**	**9**
	Portland	WHL	10	10	4	14	13	....	....	....	....	....
1984-85	**Calgary**	**NHL**	**73**	**20**	**32**	**52**	**32**	**3**	**0**	**1**	**1**	**4**
1985-86	**Calgary**	**NHL**	**63**	**12**	**17**	**29**	**31**	....	....	....	....	....
	NY Islanders	**NHL**	**14**	**7**	**7**	**14**	**4**	**3**	**0**	**1**	**1**	**0**
1986-87	**NY Islanders**	**NHL**	**70**	**12**	**17**	**29**	**20**	**14**	**1**	**3**	**4**	**4**
1987-88	**NY Islanders**	**NHL**	**71**	**5**	**10**	**15**	**20**	**5**	**0**	**0**	**0**	**5**
1988-89	**NY Islanders**	**NHL**	**20**	**1**	**6**	**7**	**4**	....	....	....	....	....
	Springfield	AHL	48	21	26	47	15	....	....	....	....	....
1989-90	Leksand	Swe.	40	8	16	24	28	3	3	1	4	0
	Springfield	AHL	9	3	4	7	4	16	1	5	6	4
1990-91	**NY Islanders**	**NHL**	**6**	**1**	**0**	**1**	**0**	....	....	....	....	....
	Capital Dist.	AHL	76	19	36	55	18	....	....	....	....	....
	NHL Totals		**370**	**69**	**101**	**170**	**138**	**36**	**2**	**6**	**8**	**22**

Traded to **NY Islanders** by **Calgary** with Steve Konroyd for John Tonelli, March 11, 1986.

KRON, ROBERT (KROHN)

Left wing. Shoots left. 5'10", 174 lbs. Born, Brno Czech., February 27, 1967.
(Vancouver's 5th choice, 88th overall, in 1985 Entry Draft).

			Regular Season					Playoffs				
Season	Club	Lea	GP	G	A	TP	PIM	GP	G	A	TP	PIM
1986-87	Zetor Brno	Czech.	28	14	11	25	....	....	....	....	....	....
1987-88	Zetor Brno	Czech.	32	12	6	18	....	....	....	....	....	....
1988-89	Zetor Brno	Czech.	43	28	19	47	....	....	....	....	....	....
1989-90	Dukla Trencin	Czech.	39	22	22	44	....	....	....	....	....	....
1990-91	**Vancouver**	**NHL**	**76**	**12**	**20**	**32**	**21**	....	....	....	....	....
	NHL Totals		**76**	**12**	**20**	**32**	**21**	....	....	....	....	....

KRUMPSCHMID, NORM

Center. Shoots left. 5'11", 185 lbs. Born, Sudbury, Ont., December 13, 1969.
(Vancouver's 2nd choice, 7th overall, in 1990 Supplemental Draft).

			Regular Season					Playoffs				
Season	Club	Lea	GP	G	A	TP	PIM	GP	G	A	TP	PIM
1988-89	Ferris State	CCHA	35	5	7	12	40	....	....	....	....	....
1989-90	Ferris State	CCHA	36	6	14	20	22	....	....	....	....	....
1990-91	Ferris State	CCHA	38	7	22	29	16	....	....	....	....	....

KRUPP, UWE (OO-VAY KROOP)

Defense. Shoots right. 6'6", 235 lbs. Born, Cologne, West Germany, June 24, 1965.
(Buffalo's 13th choice, 214th overall, in 1983 Entry Draft).

			Regular Season					Playoffs				
Season	Club	Lea	GP	G	A	TP	PIM	GP	G	A	TP	PIM
1983-84	KEC	W.Ger.	40	0	4	4	22	....	....	....	....	....
1984-85	KEC	W.Ger.	39	11	8	19	36	....	....	....	....	....
1985-86	KEC	W.Ger.	45	10	21	31	83	....	....	....	....	....
1986-87	**Buffalo**	**NHL**	**26**	**1**	**4**	**5**	**23**	....	....	....	....	....
	Rochester	AHL	42	3	19	22	50	17	1	11	12	16
1987-88	**Buffalo**	**NHL**	**75**	**2**	**9**	**11**	**151**	**6**	**0**	**0**	**0**	**15**
1988-89	**Buffalo**	**NHL**	**70**	**5**	**13**	**18**	**55**	**5**	**0**	**1**	**1**	**4**
1989-90	**Buffalo**	**NHL**	**74**	**3**	**20**	**23**	**85**	**6**	**0**	**0**	**0**	**4**
1990-91	**Buffalo**	**NHL**	**74**	**12**	**32**	**44**	**66**	**6**	**1**	**1**	**2**	**6**
	NHL Totals		**319**	**23**	**78**	**101**	**380**	**23**	**1**	**2**	**3**	**29**

Played in NHL All-Star Game (1991)

KRUPPKE, GORD (KRUP-kee)

Defense. Shoots right. 6'1", 200 lbs. Born, Slave Lake, Alta., April 2, 1969.
(Detroit's 2nd choice, 32nd overall, in 1987 Entry Draft).

			Regular Season					Playoffs				
Season	Club	Lea	GP	G	A	TP	PIM	GP	G	A	TP	PIM
1985-87	Prince Albert	WHL	62	1	8	9	81	20	4	4	8	22
1986-87	Prince Albert	WHL	49	2	10	12	129	8	0	0	0	9
1987-88	Prince Albert	WHL	54	8	8	16	113	10	0	0	0	46
1988-89	Prince Albert	WHL	62	6	26	32	254	3	0	0	0	11
1989-90	Adirondack	AHL	59	2	12	14	103	....	....	....	....	....
1990-91	**Detroit**	**NHL**	**4**	**0**	**0**	**0**	**0**	....	....	....	....	....
	Adirondack	AHL	45	1	8	9	153	....	....	....	....	....
	NHL Totals		**4**	**0**	**0**	**0**	**0**	....	....	....	....	....

KRUSE, PAUL

Left wing. Shoots left. 6', 202 lbs. Born, Merritt, B.C., March 15, 1970.
(Calgary's 6th choice, 83rd overall, in 1990 Entry Draft).

			Regular Season					Playoffs				
Season	Club	Lea	GP	G	A	TP	PIM	GP	G	A	TP	PIM
1988-89	Kamloops	WHL	68	8	15	23	209	....	....	....	....	....
1989-90	Kamloops	WHL	67	22	23	45	291	17	3	5	8	79
1990-91	**Calgary**	**NHL**	**1**	**0**	**0**	**0**	**7**	....	....	....	....	....
	Salt Lake	IHL	83	24	20	44	313	4	1	1	2	4

KRUSHELNYSKI, MICHAEL (MIKE) (KROO-shuhl-NIH-skee)

Left wing/Center. Shoots left. 6'2", 200 lbs. Born, Montreal, Que., April 27, 1960.
(Boston's 7th choice, 120th overall, in 1979 Entry Draft).

			Regular Season					Playoffs				
Season	Club	Lea	GP	G	A	TP	PIM	GP	G	A	TP	PIM
1978-79	Montreal	QJHL	46	15	29	44	42	11	3	4	7	8
1979-80	Montreal	QJHL	72	39	60	99	78	6	2	3	5	2
1980-81	Springfield	AHL	80	25	28	53	47	7	1	1	2	29
1981-82	**Boston**	**NHL**	**17**	**3**	**3**	**6**	**2**	**1**	**0**	**0**	**0**	**2**
	Erie	AHL	62	31	52	83	44	....	....	....	....	....
1982-83	Boston	NHL	79	23	42	65	43	17	8	6	14	12
1983-84	Boston	NHL	66	25	20	45	55	2	0	0	0	0
1984-85	Edmonton	NHL	80	43	45	88	60	18	5	8	13	22
1985-86	**Edmonton**	**NHL**	**54**	**16**	**24**	**40**	**22**	**10**	**4**	**5**	**9**	**16**
1986-87	**Edmonton**	**NHL**	**80**	**16**	**35**	**51**	**67**	**21**	**3**	**4**	**7**	**18**
1987-88	**Edmonton**	**NHL**	**76**	**20**	**27**	**47**	**64**	**19**	**4**	**6**	**10**	**12**
1988-89	**Los Angeles**	**NHL**	**78**	**26**	**36**	**62**	**110**	**11**	**1**	**4**	**5**	**4**
1989-90	**Los Angeles**	**NHL**	**63**	**16**	**25**	**41**	**50**	**10**	**1**	**3**	**4**	**12**
1990-91	**Los Angeles**	**NHL**	**15**	**1**	**5**	**6**	**10**	....	....	....	....	....
	Toronto	**NHL**	**59**	**17**	**22**	**39**	**48**	....	....	....	....	....
	NHL Totals		**667**	**206**	**284**	**490**	**531**	**109**	**26**	**36**	**62**	**98**

Played in NHL All-Star Game (1985)

Traded to **Edmonton** by **Boston** for Ken Linseman, June 21, 1984. Traded to **Los Angeles** by **Edmonton** with Wayne Gretzky and Marty McSorley for Jimmy Carson, Martin Gelinas, Los Angeles' first round choices in 1989 (acquired by New Jersey, June 17, 1989. New Jersey selected Jason Miller), 1991 (Martin Rucinsky) and 1993 Entry Drafts and cash, August 9, 1988. Traded to **Toronto** by **Los Angeles** for John McIntyre, November 9, 1990.

KRYGIER, TODD (KREE-guhr)

Left wing. Shoots left. 5'11", 180 lbs. Born, Northville, MI, October 12, 1965.
(Hartford's 1st choice, 16th overall, in 1988 Supplemental Draft).

			Regular Season					Playoffs				
Season	Club	Lea	GP	G	A	TP	PIM	GP	G	A	TP	PIM
1984-85	U. Connecticut	NCAA	14	14	11	25	12	....	....	....	....	....
1985-86	U. Connecticut	NCAA	32	29	27	56	46	....	....	....	....	....
1986-87	U. Connecticut	NCAA	28	24	24	48	44	....	....	....	....	....
1987-88	U. Connecticut	NCAA	27	32	39	71	28	....	....	....	....	....
	New Haven	AHL	13	1	5	6	34	....	....	....	....	....
1988-89	Binghamton	AHL	76	26	42	68	77	....	....	....	....	....
1989-90	**Hartford**	**NHL**	**58**	**18**	**12**	**30**	**52**	**7**	**2**	**1**	**3**	**4**
	Binghamton	AHL	12	1	9	10	16	....	....	....	....	....
1990-91	**Hartford**	**NHL**	**72**	**13**	**17**	**30**	**95**	**6**	**0**	**2**	**2**	**0**
	NHL Totals		**130**	**31**	**29**	**60**	**147**	**13**	**2**	**3**	**5**	**4**

KRYS, MARK

Defense. Shoots right. 6', 185 lbs. Born, Timmins, Ont., May 29, 1969.
(Boston's 6th choice, 165th overall, in 1988 Entry Draft).

			Regular Season					Playoffs				
Season	Club	Lea	GP	G	A	TP	PIM	GP	G	A	TP	PIM
1987-88	Boston U.	H.E.	34	0	6	6	40	....	....	....	....	....
1988-89	Boston U.	H.E.	35	0	7	7	54	....	....	....	....	....
1989-90	Boston U.	H.E.	30	0	4	4	34	....	....	....	....	....
1990-91	Boston U.	H.E.	36	1	9	10	18	....	....	....	....	....

KUCERA, FRANTISEK (kuh-CHEH-rah)

Defense. Shoots right. 6'2", 205 lbs. Born, Prague, Czechoslovakia, February 3, 1968.
(Chicago's 3rd choice, 77th overall, in 1986 Entry Draft).

			Regular Season					Playoffs				
Season	Club	Lea	GP	G	A	TP	PIM	GP	G	A	TP	PIM
1986-87	Sparta Praha	Czech.	33	7	2	9	....	....	....	....	....	....
1987-88	Sparta Praha	Czech.	34	4	2	6	....	....	....	....	....	....
1988-89	Dukla Jihlava	Czech.	45	10	9	19	....	....	....	....	....	....
1989-90	Dukla Jihlava	Czech.	43	9	10	19	....	....	....	....	....	....
1990-91	**Chicago**	**NHL**	**40**	**2**	**12**	**14**	**32**	....	....	....	....	....
	Indianapolis	IHL	35	8	19	27	23	7	0	1	1	15
	NHL Totals		**40**	**2**	**12**	**14**	**32**	....	....	....	....	....

KUCERA, JIRI

Center. Shoots left. 5'11", 180 lbs. Born, Plzen, Czechoslovakia, March 28, 1966.
(Pittsburgh's 8th choice, 152th overall, in 1987 Entry Draft).

			Regular Season					Playoffs				
Season	Club	Lea	GP	G	A	TP	PIM	GP	G	A	TP	PIM
1987-88	Skoda Plzen	Czech.	32	19	11	30	....	....	....	....	....	....
1988-89	Skoda Plzen	Czech.	32	16	13	29	....	....	....	....	....	....
1989-90	Skoda Plzen	Czech.	47	10	24	34	....	....	....	....	....	....
1990-91	Tappara	Fin.	44	23	34	57	26	3	0	2	2	4

KUCHYNA, PETER (kuh-HEE-nah)

Defense. Shoots right. 6'3", 180 lbs. Born, Jihlava, Czechoslovakia, January 14, 1970.
(New Jersey's 5th choice, 104th overall, in 1990 Entry Draft).

			Regular Season					Playoffs				
Season	Club	Lea	GP	G	A	TP	PIM	GP	G	A	TP	PIM
1989-90	Dukla Jihlava	Czech.	32	2	2	4	....	....	....	....	....	....
1990-91	Dukla Jihlava	Czech.	47	4	5	9	35	....	....	....	....	....

KUDELSKI, BOB

Right wing. Shoots right. 6'1", 200 lbs. Born, Springfield, MA, March 3, 1964.
(Los Angeles' 1st choice, 2nd overall, in 1986 Supplemental Draft).

			Regular Season					Playoffs				
Season	Club	Lea	GP	G	A	TP	PIM	GP	G	A	TP	PIM
1983-84	Yale	ECAC	21	14	12	26	12	....	....	....	....	....
1984-85	Yale	ECAC	32	21	23	44	38	....	....	....	....	....
1985-86	Yale	ECAC	31	18	23	41	48	....	....	....	....	....
1986-87a	Yale	ECAC	30	25	22	47	34	....	....	....	....	....
1987-88	Los Angeles	NHL	26	0	1	1	8	....	....	....	....	....
	New Haven	AHL	50	15	19	34	41	....	....	....	....	....
1988-89	Los Angeles	NHL	14	1	3	4	17	....	....	....	....	....
	New Haven	AHL	60	32	19	51	43	17	8	5	13	12
1989-90	Los Angeles	NHL	62	23	13	36	49	8	1	2	3	2
1990-91	Los Angeles	NHL	72	23	13	36	46	8	3	2	5	2
	NHL Totals		174	47	30	77	120	16	4	4	8	4

a ECAC First All-Star Team (1987)

KULAK, STUART (STU)

Right wing. Shoots right. 5'10", 180 lbs. Born, Edmonton, Alta., March 10, 1963.
(Vancouver's 5th choice, 115th overall, in 1981 Entry Draft).

			Regular Season					Playoffs				
Season	Club	Lea	GP	G	A	TP	PIM	GP	G	A	TP	PIM
1979-80	Sherwood Park	AJHL	53	30	23	53	111	....	....	....	....	....
	Victoria	WHL	3	0	0	0	0	....	....	....	....	....
1980-81	Victoria	WHL	72	23	24	47	44	15	3	5	8	19
1981-82	Victoria	WHL	71	38	50	88	92	4	1	2	3	43
1982-83	Vancouver	NHL	4	1	1	2	0	....	....	....	....	....
	Victoria	WHL	50	29	33	62	130	10	10	9	19	29
1983-84	Fredericton	AHL	52	12	16	28	55	5	0	0	0	59
1984-85			DID NOT PLAY — INJURED									
1985-86	Fredericton	AHL	3	1	0	1	0	6	2	1	3	0
	Kalamazoo	IHL	30	14	8	22	38	2	2	0	2	0
1986-87	Vancouver	NHL	28	1	1	2	37	....	....	....	....	....
	Edmonton	NHL	23	3	1	4	41	....	....	....	....	....
	NY Rangers	NHL	3	0	0	0	0	3	0	0	0	2
1987-88	Quebec	NHL	14	1	1	2	28	....	....	....	....	....
	Moncton	AHL	37	9	12	21	58	....	....	....	....	....
1988-89	Winnipeg	NHL	18	2	0	2	24	....	....	....	....	....
	Moncton	AHL	51	30	29	59	98	10	5	6	11	16
1989-90	Moncton	AHL	36	14	23	37	72	....	....	....	....	....
1990-91	Kansas City	IHL	47	13	28	41	20	....	....	....	....	....
	NHL Totals		90	8	4	12	130	3	0	0	0	2

Sold to **Edmonton** by **Vancouver**, December 11, 1986. Acquired by **NY Rangers** from **Edmonton** to complete Reijo Ruotsalanien trade, March 10, 1987. Claimed by **Quebec** in NHL Waiver Draft, October 5, 1987. Traded to **Winnipeg** by **Quebec** for Bob Dollas, December 17, 1987.

KULONEN, TIMO (KOO-loh-nehn)

Defense. Shoots right. 6'5", 220 lbs. Born, Forssa, Finland, November 1, 1967.
(Minnesota's 7th choice, 130th overall, in 1987 Entry Draft).

			Regular Season					Playoffs				
Season	Club	Lea	GP	G	A	TP	PIM	GP	G	A	TP	PIM
1986-87	KalPa	Fin.	39	2	8	10	20	....	....	....	....	....
1987-88	KalPa	Fin.	44	7	15	22	32	....	....	....	....	....
1988-89	KalPa	Fin.	40	9	16	25	18	2	0	1	1	0
1989-90	KalPa	Fin.	44	5	20	25	34	6	0	0	0	
1990-91	KalPa	Fin.	42	1	10	11	16	8	0	2	2	4

KUMMU, AL

Defense. Shoots right. 6'4", 195 lbs. Born, Kitchener, Ont., January 21, 1969.
(Philadelphia's 8th choice, 201st overall, in 1989 Entry Draft).

			Regular Season					Playoffs				
Season	Club	Lea	GP	G	A	TP	PIM	GP	G	A	TP	PIM
1989-90	RPI	ECAC	33	9	13	22	50	....	....	....	....	....
1990-91	RPI	ECAC	29	6	8	14	86	....	....	....	....	....

KUMMU, RYAN

Defense. Shoots left. 6'3", 205 lbs. Born, Kitchener, Ont., June 5, 1967.
(Washington's 11th choice, 246th overall, in 1987 Entry Draft).

			Regular Season					Playoffs				
Season	Club	Lea	GP	G	A	TP	PIM	GP	G	A	TP	PIM
1986-87	RPI	ECAC	28	0	2	2	32	....	....	....	....	....
1987-88	RPI	ECAC	29	5	10	15	40	....	....	....	....	....
1988-89	RPI	ECAC	29	2	5	7	28	....	....	....	....	....
1989-90	Maine	AHL	8	0	0	0	11	....	....	....	....	....
	Erie	ECHL	45	5	30	35	71	7	0	8	8	10
1990-91	Capital Dist.	AHL	6	0	0	0	14	....	....	....	....	....
a	Erie	ECHL	56	24	50	74	194	4	1	3	4	12

a ECHL Second All-Star Team (1991)

KUMPEL, MARK

Right wing. Shoots right. 6', 190 lbs. Born, Wakefield, MA, March 7, 1961.
(Quebec's 4th choice, 108th overall, in 1980 Entry Draft).

			Regular Season					Playoffs				
Season	Club	Lea	GP	G	A	TP	PIM	GP	G	A	TP	PIM
1979-80	U. of Lowell	ECAC	30	18	18	36	12	....	....	....	....	....
1980-81	U. of Lowell	ECAC	1	2	0	2	0	....	....	....	....	....
1981-82	U. of Lowell	ECAC	35	17	13	30	23	....	....	....	....	....
1982-83	U. of Lowell	ECAC	7	8	5	13	0	....	....	....	....	....
	U.S. National	...	30	14	18	32	6	....	....	....	....	....
1983-84	U.S. National	...	61	14	19	33	19	....	....	....	....	....
	U.S. Olympic	...	6	1	0	1	2	....	....	....	....	....
	Fredericton	AHL	16	1	1	2	5	3	0	0	0	15
1984-85	Quebec	NHL	42	8	7	15	26	18	3	4	7	4
	Fredericton	AHL	18	9	6	15	17	....	....	....	....	....
1985-86	Quebec	NHL	47	10	12	22	17	2	1	0	1	0
	Fredericton	AHL	7	4	2	6	4	....	....	....	....	....
1986-87	Quebec	NHL	40	1	8	9	16	....	....	....	....	....
	Detroit	NHL	5	0	1	1	0	8	0	0	0	4
	Adirondack	AHL	7	2	3	5	0	1	1	0	1	0
1987-88	Detroit	NHL	13	0	2	2	4	....	....	....	....	....
	Adirondack	AHL	4	5	0	5	2	....	....	....	....	....
	Winnipeg	NHL	32	4	4	8	19	4	0	0	0	4
1988-89	Moncton	AHL	53	22	23	45	25	10	3	4	7	0
1989-90	Winnipeg	NHL	56	8	9	17	21	7	2	0	2	2
1990-91	Winnipeg	NHL	53	7	3	10	10	....	....	....	....	....
	NHL Totals		288	38	46	84	113	39	6	4	10	14

Traded to **Detroit** by **Quebec** with Brent Ashton and Gilbert Delorme for Basil McRae, John Ogrodnick and Doug Shedden, January 17, 1987. Traded to **Winnipeg** by **Detroit** for Jim Nill, January 11, 1988.

KURRI, JARI (KUHR-ree, YAH-ree)

Right wing. Shoots right. 6'1", 195 lbs. Born, Helsinki, Finland, May 18, 1960.
(Edmonton's 3rd choice, 69th overall, in 1980 Entry Draft).

			Regular Season					Playoffs				
Season	Club	Lea	GP	G	A	TP	PIM	GP	G	A	TP	PIM
1977-78	Jokerit	Fin.	29	2	9	11	12	....	....	....	....	....
1978-79	Jokerit	Fin.	33	16	14	30	12	....	....	....	....	....
1979-80	Jokerit	Fin.	33	23	16	39	22	6	7	2	9	13
1980-81	Edmonton	NHL	75	32	43	75	40	9	5	7	12	4
1981-82	Edmonton	NHL	71	32	54	86	32	5	2	5	7	10
1982-83	Edmonton	NHL	80	45	59	104	22	16	8	15	23	8
1983-84a	Edmonton	NHL	64	52	61	113	14	19	*14	14	28	13
1984-85bc	Edmonton	NHL	73	71	64	135	30	18	*19	12	31	6
1985-86a	Edmonton	NHL	78	*68	63	131	22	10	2	10	12	4
1986-87c	Edmonton	NHL	79	54	54	108	41	21	*15	10	25	20
1987-88	Edmonton	NHL	80	43	53	96	30	19	*14	17	31	12
1988-89d	Edmonton	NHL	76	44	58	102	69	7	3	5	8	6
1989-90	Edmonton	NHL	78	33	60	93	48	22	10	15	25	18
1990-91	Milan	Italy	30	27	48	75	6	10	10	12	22	2
	NHL Totals		754	474	569	1043	348	146	92	110	202	101

a NHL Second All-Star Team (1984, 1986)
b Won Lady Byng Memorial Trophy (1985)
c NHL First All-Star Team (1985, 1987)
d NHL Second All-Star Team (1989)

Played in NHL All-Star Game (1983, 1985, 1986, 1988-90)

Traded to **Philadelphia** by **Edmonton** with Dave Brown and Corey Foster for Craig Fisher, Scott Mellanby and Craig Berube, May 30, 1991. Traded to **Los Angeles** by **Philadelphia** with Jeff Chychrun for Steve Duchesne, Steve Kasper and Los Angeles' fourth round choice (Aris Brimanis) in 1991 Entry Draft, May 30, 1991.

KURVERS, TOM

Defense. Shoots left. 6'2", 195 lbs. Born, Minneapolis, MN, September 14, 1962.
(Montreal's 10th choice, 145th overall, in 1981 Entry Draft).

			Regular Season					Playoffs				
Season	Club	Lea	GP	G	A	TP	PIM	GP	G	A	TP	PIM
1980-81	Minn.-Duluth	WCHA	39	6	24	30	48	....	....	....	....	....
1981-82	Minn.-Duluth	WCHA	37	11	31	42	18	....	....	....	....	....
1982-83	Minn.-Duluth	WCHA	26	4	23	27	24	....	....	....	....	....
1983-84ab	Minn.-Duluth	WCHA	43	18	58	76	46	....	....	....	....	....
1984-85	Montreal	NHL	75	10	35	45	30	12	0	6	6	6
1985-86	Montreal	NHL	62	7	23	30	36	....	....	....	....	....
1986-87	Montreal	NHL	1	0	0	0	0	....	....	....	....	....
	Buffalo	NHL	55	6	17	23	22	....	....	....	....	....
1987-88	New Jersey	NHL	56	5	29	34	46	19	6	9	15	38
1988-89	New Jersey	NHL	74	16	50	66	38	....	....	....	....	....
1989-90	New Jersey	NHL	1	0	0	0	0	....	....	....	....	....
	Toronto	NHL	70	15	37	52	29	5	0	3	3	4
1990-91	Toronto	NHL	19	0	3	3	8	....	....	....	....	....
	Vancouver	NHL	32	4	23	27	20	6	2	2	4	12
	NHL Totals		445	63	217	280	229	42	8	20	28	60

a WCHA First All-Star Team (1984)
b Won Hobey Baker Memorial Trophy (1984)

Traded to **Buffalo** by **Montreal** for Buffalo's second-round choice (Martin St. Amour) in 1988 Entry Draft, November 18, 1986. Traded to **New Jersey** by **Buffalo** for the rights to Detroit's third-round choice (Andrew MacVicar) in 1987 Entry Draft previously acquired by New Jersey in Mel Bridgman deal, June 13, 1987. Traded to **Toronto** by **New Jersey** for Toronto's first round choice (Scott Niedermayer) in 1991 Entry Draft, October 16, 1989. Traded to **Vancouver** by **Toronto** for Brian Bradley, January 12, 1991. Traded to **Minnesota** by **Vancouver** for Dave Babych, June 22, 1991. Traded to **NY Islanders** by **Minnesota** for Craig Ludwig, June 22, 1991.

KUSHNER, DALE

Left wing. Shoots left. 6'1", 195 lbs. Born, Terrace, B.C., June 13, 1966.

			Regular Season					Playoffs				
Season	Club	Lea	GP	G	A	TP	PIM	GP	G	A	TP	PIM
1983-84	Prince Albert	WHL	1	2	0	2	5	....	....	....	....	....
1984-85	Prince Albert	WHL	2	0	0	0	2	....	....	....	....	....
	Moose Jaw	WHL	17	5	2	7	23	....	....	....	....	....
	Medicine Hat	WHL	48	23	17	40	173	10	3	3	6	18
1985-86	Medicine Hat	WHL	66	25	19	44	218	25	0	5	5	114
1986-87	Medicine Hat	WHL	63	34	34	68	250	20	8	13	21	57
1987-88	Springfield	AHL	68	13	23	36	201	....	....	....	....	....
1988-89	Springfield	AHL	45	5	8	13	132	....	....	....	....	....
1989-90	**NY Islanders**	**NHL**	**2**	**0**	**0**	**0**	**2**	....	....	....	....	....
	Springfield	AHL	45	14	11	25	163	7	2	3	5	61
1990-91	**Philadelphia**	**NHL**	**63**	**7**	**11**	**18**	**195**	....	....	....	....	....
	Hershey	AHL	5	3	4	7	14	....	....	....	....	....
	NHL Totals		**65**	**7**	**11**	**18**	**197**	....	....	....	....	....

Signed as a free agent by **NY Islanders**, April 7, 1987. Signed as a free agent by **Philadelphia**, July 31, 1990.

KUWABARA, RYAN

Right wing. Shoots right. 6', 205 lbs. Born, Hamilton, Ont., March 23, 1972.
(Montreal's 2nd choice, 39th overall, in 1990 Entry Draft).

			Regular Season					Playoffs				
Season	Club	Lea	GP	G	A	TP	PIM	GP	G	A	TP	PIM
1989-90	Ottawa	OHL	66	30	38	68	62	4	0	0	0	0
1990-91	Ottawa	OHL	64	34	38	72	67	17	12	15	27	25

KYLLONEN, MARKKU (KOOL-loh-nehn)

Left wing. Shoots left. 5'11", 187 lbs. Born, Joensuu, Finland, February 15, 1962.
(Winnipeg's 8th choice, 163rd overall, in 1987 Entry Draft).

			Regular Season					Playoffs				
Season	Club	Lea	GP	G	A	TP	PIM	GP	G	A	TP	PIM
1984-85	JoKP	Fin.2	43	28	27	55	22	....	....	....	....	....
1985-86	JoKP	Fin.2	34	12	12	24	14	....	....	....	....	....
1986-87	Karpat	Fin.	43	24	16	40	14	9	3	2	5	4
1987-88	Karpat	Fin.	43	8	24	32	32	....	....	....	....	....
1988-89	**Winnipeg**	**NHL**	**9**	**0**	**2**	**2**	**2**	....	....	....	....	....
	Moncton	AHL	60	14	20	34	16	5	1	0	1	0
1989-90	JoKP	Fin.	42	16	12	28	22	....	....	....	....	....
1990-91	JoKP	Fin.	44	42	37	79	22	....	....	....	....	....
	NHL Totals		**9**	**0**	**2**	**2**	**2**	....	....	....	....	....

KYPREOS, NICHOLAS (NICK) (KIH-pree-ohz)

Left wing. Shoots left. 6', 195 lbs. Born, Toronto, Ont., June 4, 1966.

			Regular Season					Playoffs				
Season	Club	Lea	GP	G	A	TP	PIM	GP	G	A	TP	PIM
1983-84	North Bay	OHL	51	12	11	23	36	4	3	2	5	9
1984-85	North Bay	OHL	64	41	36	77	71	8	2	2	4	15
1985-86a	North Bay	OHL	64	62	35	97	112	....	....	....	....	....
1986-87	Hershey	AHL	10	0	1	1	4	....	....	....	....	....
b	North Bay	OHL	46	49	41	90	54	24	11	5	16	78
1987-88	Hershey	AHL	71	24	20	44	101	12	0	2	2	17
1988-89	Hershey	AHL	28	12	15	27	19	12	4	5	9	11
1989-90	**Washington**	**NHL**	**31**	**5**	**4**	**9**	**82**	**7**	**1**	**0**	**1**	**15**
	Baltimore	AHL	14	6	5	11	6	7	4	1	5	17
1990-91	**Washington**	**NHL**	**79**	**9**	**9**	**18**	**196**	**9**	**0**	**1**	**1**	**38**
	NHL Totals		**110**	**14**	**13**	**27**	**278**	**16**	**1**	**1**	**2**	**53**

a OHL First All-Star Team (1986)
b OHL Second All-Star Team (1987)

Signed as a free agent by **Philadelphia,** September 30, 1984. Claimed by **Washington** in NHL Waiver Draft, October 2, 1989.

KYTE, JAMES (JIM) (KITE)

Defense. Shoots left. 6'5", 210 lbs. Born, Ottawa, Ont., March 21, 1964.
(Winnipeg's 1st choice, 12th overall, in 1982 Entry Draft).

			Regular Season					Playoffs				
Season	Club	Lea	GP	G	A	TP	PIM	GP	G	A	TP	PIM
1981-82	Cornwall	OHL	52	4	13	17	148	5	0	0	0	10
1982-83	**Winnipeg**	**NHL**	**2**	**0**	**0**	**0**	**0**	....	....	....	....	....
	Cornwall	OHL	65	6	30	36	195	8	0	2	2	24
1983-84	**Winnipeg**	**NHL**	**58**	**1**	**2**	**3**	**55**	**3**	**0**	**0**	**0**	**11**
1984-85	**Winnipeg**	**NHL**	**71**	**0**	**3**	**3**	**111**	**8**	**0**	**0**	**0**	**14**
1985-86	**Winnipeg**	**NHL**	**71**	**1**	**3**	**4**	**126**	**3**	**0**	**0**	**0**	**12**
1986-87	**Winnipeg**	**NHL**	**72**	**5**	**5**	**10**	**162**	**10**	**0**	**4**	**4**	**36**
1987-88	**Winnipeg**	**NHL**	**51**	**1**	**3**	**4**	**128**	....	....	....	....	....
1988-89	**Winnipeg**	**NHL**	**74**	**3**	**9**	**12**	**190**	....	....	....	....	....
1989-90	**Pittsburgh**	**NHL**	**56**	**3**	**1**	**4**	**125**	....	....	....	....	....
1990-91	**Pittsburgh**	**NHL**	**1**	**0**	**0**	**0**	**2**	....	....	....	....	....
	Muskegon	IHL	25	2	5	7	157	....	....	....	....	....
	Calgary	**NHL**	**42**	**0**	**9**	**9**	**153**	**7**	**0**	**0**	**0**	**7**
	NHL Totals		**498**	**14**	**35**	**49**	**1052**	**31**	**0**	**0**	**0**	**80**

Traded to **Pittsburgh** by **Winnipeg** with Andrew McBain and Randy Gilhen for Randy Cunnyworth, Rick Tabaracci and Dave McLlwain, June 17, 1989. Traded to **Calgary** by **Pittsburgh** for Jiri Hrdina, December 13, 1990.

LACHANCE, SCOTT

Defense. Shoots left. 6'1", 197 lbs. Born, Charlottesville, VA, October 22, 1972.
(NY Islanders' 1st choice, 4th overall, in 1991 Entry Draft).

			Regular Season					Playoffs				
Season	Club	Lea	GP	G	A	TP	PIM	GP	G	A	TP	PIM
1989-90	Springfield	USHL	34	25	41	66	62	....	....	....	....	....
1990-91	Boston U.	H.E.	31	5	19	24	48	....	....	....	....	....

LABELLE, MARC

Left Wing. Shoots left. 6'1", 215 lbs. Born, Maniwaki, Que., Dec. 20, 1969.

			Regular Season					Playoffs				
Season	Club	Lea	GP	G	A	TP	PIM	GP	G	A	TP	PIM
1987-88	Victoriaville	QMJHL	63	11	14	25	236	5	2	4	6	20
1988-89	Victoriaville	QMJHL	62	9	26	35	202	5	6	3	9	30
1989-90	Victoriaville	QMJHL	56	18	21	39	192	6	4	8	12	42
1990-91	Fredericton	AHL	25	1	4	5	95	4	0	2	2	25

Signed as a free agent by **Montreal**, January 21, 1991.

LACKTEN, KURT

Right wing. Shoots right. 6', 177 lbs. Born, Kamsack, Sask., May 20, 1967.
(NY Islanders' 9th choice, 139th overall, in 1985 Entry Draft).

			Regular Season					Playoffs				
Season	Club	Lea	GP	G	A	TP	PIM	GP	G	A	TP	PIM
1984-85	Moose Jaw	WHL	66	18	13	31	141	....	....	....	....	....
1985-86	Calgary	WHL	61	5	20	25	112	....	....	....	....	....
1986-87	Swift Current	WHL	65	20	20	40	97	3	0	1	1	4
1987-88	Springfield	AHL	37	1	4	5	64	....	....	....	....	....
	Peoria	IHL	19	0	5	5	20	....	....	....	....	....
1988-89	Indianapolis	IHL	9	1	2	3	11	....	....	....	....	....
1989-90	Virginia	ECHL	8	0	4	4	7	....	....	....	....	....
1990-91	Johnstown	ECHL	12	2	7	9	18	....	....	....	....	....

LACOMBE, NORMAND

Right wing. Shoots right. 6', 210 lbs. Born, Pierrefonds, Que., October 18, 1964.
(Buffalo's 2nd choice, 10th overall, in 1983 Entry Draft).

			Regular Season					Playoffs				
Season	Club	Lea	GP	G	A	TP	PIM	GP	G	A	TP	PIM
1981-82	N. Hampshire	ECAC	35	18	16	34	38	....	....	....	....	....
1982-83	N. Hampshire	ECAC	35	18	25	43	48	....	....	....	....	....
1983-84	Rochester	AHL	44	10	16	26	45	....	....	....	....	....
1984-85	**Buffalo**	**NHL**	**30**	**2**	**4**	**6**	**25**	....	....	....	....	....
	Rochester	AHL	33	13	16	29	33	5	3	1	4	4
1985-86	**Buffalo**	**NHL**	**25**	**6**	**7**	**13**	**13**	....	....	....	....	....
	Rochester	AHL	32	10	13	23	56	....	....	....	....	....
1986-87	**Buffalo**	**NHL**	**39**	**4**	**7**	**11**	**8**	....	....	....	....	....
	Rochester	AHL	13	6	5	11	4	....	....	....	....	....
	Edmonton	**NHL**	**1**	**0**	**0**	**0**	**2**	....	....	....	....	....
	Nova Scotia	AHL	10	3	5	8	4	5	1	1	2	6
1987-88	**Edmonton**	**NHL**	**53**	**8**	**9**	**17**	**36**	**19**	**3**	**0**	**3**	**28**
1988-89	**Edmonton**	**NHL**	**64**	**17**	**11**	**28**	**57**	**7**	**2**	**1**	**3**	**21**
1989-90	**Edmonton**	**NHL**	**15**	**5**	**2**	**7**	**21**	....	....	....	....	....
	Philadelphia	**NHL**	**18**	**0**	**2**	**2**	**7**	....	....	....	....	....
1990-91	**Philadelphia**	**NHL**	**74**	**11**	**20**	**31**	**27**	....	....	....	....	....
	NHL Totals		**319**	**53**	**62**	**115**	**196**	**26**	**5**	**1**	**6**	**49**

Traded to **Edmonton** by **Buffalo** with Wayne Van Dorp and future considerations for Lee Fogolin and Mark Napier, March 6, 1987. Traded to **Philadelphia** by **Edmonton** for Philadelphia's fourth-round choice (Joel Blain) in 1990 Entry Draft, January 5, 1990.

LACOUTURE, BILL

Right wing. Shoots right. 6'2", 192 lbs. Born, Framingham, MA, May 28, 1968.
(Chicago's 11th choice, 218th overall, in 1987 Entry Draft).

			Regular Season					Playoffs				
Season	Club	Lea	GP	G	A	TP	PIM	GP	G	A	TP	PIM
1987-88	N. Hampshire	H.E.	13	1	3	4	2	....	....	....	....	....
1988-89	N. Hampshire	H.E.	20	0	1	1	2	....	....	....	....	....
1989-90	N. Hampshire	H.E.	2	0	0	0	0	....	....	....	....	....
1990-91	N. Hampshire	H.E.	2	0	0	0	0	....	....	....	....	....

LACOUTURE, DAVID

Right wing. Shoots right. 6'3", 205 lbs. Born, Framingham, MA, December 30, 1969.
(St. Louis' 5th choice, 105th overall, in 1988 Entry Draft).

			Regular Season					Playoffs				
Season	Club	Lea	GP	G	A	TP	PIM	GP	G	A	TP	PIM
1989-90	U. of Maine	H.E.	9	0	2	2	6	....	....	....	....	....
1990-91	U. of Maine	H.E.	40	7	9	16	33	....	....	....	....	....

LACROIX, DANIEL (la-QUAH)

Left wing. Shoots left. 6'2", 188 lbs. Born, Montreal, Que., March 11, 1969.
(NY Rangers' 2nd choice, 31st overall, in 1987 Entry Draft).

			Regular Season					Playoffs				
Season	Club	Lea	GP	G	A	TP	PIM	GP	G	A	TP	PIM
1986-87	Granby	QMJHL	54	9	16	25	311	8	1	2	3	22
1987-88	Granby	QMJHL	58	24	50	74	468	5	0	4	4	12
1988-89	Granby	QMJHL	70	45	49	94	320	4	1	1	2	57
	Denver	IHL	2	0	1	1	0	2	0	1	1	0
1989-90	Flint	IHL	61	12	16	28	128	4	2	0	2	24
1990-91	Binghamton	AHL	54	7	12	19	237	5	1	0	4	24

LACROIX, ERIC

Left wing. Shoots left. 6'1", 200 lbs. Born, Montreal, Que., July 15, 1971.
(Toronto's 6th choice, 136th overall, in 1990 Entry Draft).

			Regular Season					Playoffs				
Season	Club	Lea	GP	G	A	TP	PIM	GP	G	A	TP	PIM
1989-90	Gov. Dummer	HS	....	23	18	41	....	....	....	....	....	....
1990-91	St. Lawrence	ECAC	35	13	11	24	35	....	....	....	....	....

LACROIX, MARTIN

Right wing. Shoots right. 5'11", 155 lbs. Born, Rosemere, Que., January 4, 1970.
(NY Islanders' 10th choice, 216th overall, in 1990 Entry Draft).

			Regular Season					Playoffs				
Season	Club	Lea	GP	G	A	TP	PIM	GP	G	A	TP	PIM
1989-90	St. Lawrence	ECAC	32	11	8	19	14	....	....	....	....	....
1990-91	St. Lawrence	ECAC	35	16	26	42	46	....	....	....	....	....

LADOUCEUR, RANDY   (LAD-uh-SOOR)

Defense. Shoots left. 6'2", 220 lbs.   Born, Brockville, Ont., June 30, 1960.

			Regular Season					Playoffs				
Season	Club	Lea	GP	G	A	TP	PIM	GP	G	A	TP	PIM
1978-79	Brantford	OHA	64	3	17	20	141	.....	...	...	...	...
1979-80	Brantford	OHA	37	6	15	21	125	8	0	5	5	18
1980-81	Kalamazoo	IHL	80	7	30	37	52	8	1	3	4	10
1981-82	Adirondack	AHL	78	4	28	32	78	5	1	1	2	6
1982-83	**Detroit**	**NHL**	27	0	4	4	16	.....	...	...	...	...
	Adirondack	AHL	48	11	21	32	54	.....	...	...	...	...
1983-84	**Detroit**	**NHL**	71	3	17	20	58	4	1	0	1	6
	Adirondack	AHL	11	3	5	8	12	.....	...	...	...	...
1984-85	**Detroit**	**NHL**	80	3	27	30	108	3	1	0	1	0
1985-86	**Detroit**	**NHL**	78	5	13	18	196	.....	...	...	...	...
1986-87	**Detroit**	**NHL**	34	3	6	9	70	.....	...	...	...	...
	Hartford	**NHL**	36	2	3	5	51	6	0	2	2	12
1987-88	**Hartford**	**NHL**	67	1	7	8	91	6	1	1	2	4
1988-89	**Hartford**	**NHL**	75	2	5	7	95	1	0	0	0	10
1989-90	**Hartford**	**NHL**	71	3	12	15	126	7	1	0	1	10
1990-91	**Hartford**	**NHL**	67	1	3	4	118	6	1	4	5	6
	NHL Totals		**606**	**23**	**97**	**120**	**929**	**33**	**5**	**7**	**12**	**48**

Signed as a free agent by **Detroit**, November 1, 1979. Traded to **Hartford** by **Detroit** for Dave Barr, January 12, 1987.

LAFAYETTE, JUSTIN

Left wing. Shoots left. 6'6", 200 lbs.   Born, Vancouver, B.C., January 23, 1970.
(Chicago's 5th choice, 113th overall, in 1988 Entry Draft).

			Regular Season					Playoffs				
Season	Club	Lea	GP	G	A	TP	PIM	GP	G	A	TP	PIM
1987-88	Ferris State	CCHA	34	1	2	3	20	.....	...	...	...	...
1988-89	Ferris State	CCHA	36	3	4	7	59	.....	...	...	...	...
1989-90	Ferris State	CCHA	34	4	5	9	38	.....	...	...	...	...
1990-91	Ferris State	CCHA	39	11	9	20	74	.....	...	...	...	...

LAFAYETTE, NATHAN

Center. Shoots right. 6'1", 194 lbs.   Born, New Westminster, B.C., February 17, 1973.
(St. Louis' 3rd choice, 65th overall, in 1991 Entry Draft).

			Regular Season					Playoffs				
Season	Club	Lea	GP	G	A	TP	PIM	GP	G	A	TP	PIM
1989-90	Kingston	OHL	53	6	8	14	14	7	0	1	1	0
1990-91	Kingston	OHL	35	13	13	26	10	.....	...	...	...	...
	Cornwall	OHL	28	16	22	38	25	.....	...	...	...	...

LAFLEUR, GUY DAMIEN

Right wing. Shoots right. 6', 185 lbs.   Born, Thurso, Que., September 20, 1951.
(Montreal's 1st choice and 1st overall in 1971 Amateur Draft)

			Regular Season					Playoffs				
Season	Club	Lea	GP	G	A	TP	PIM	GP	G	A	TP	PIM
1969-70	Quebec	QJHL	56	*103	67	170	89	15	*25	18	*43	24
1970-71	Quebec	QJHL	62	*130	79	*209	135	14	*22	*21	*43	24
1971-72	**Montreal**	**NHL**	73	29	35	64	48	6	1	4	5	2
1972-73	**Montreal**	**NHL**	69	28	27	55	51	17	3	5	8	9
1973-74	**Montreal**	**NHL**	73	21	35	56	29	6	0	1	1	4
1974-75a	**Montreal**	**NHL**	70	53	66	119	37	11	*12	7	19	15
1975-76ab	**Montreal**	**NHL**	80	56	69	*125	36	13	7	10	17	2
1976-77abcde	**Montreal**	**NHL**	80	56	*80	*135	20	14	9	*17	26	6
1977-78abdf	**Montreal**	**NHL**	78	*60	72	*132	26	15	*10	*11	*21	16
1978-79a	**Montreal**	**NHL**	80	52	77	129	28	16	10	*13	*23	0
1979-80a	**Montreal**	**NHL**	74	50	75	125	12	3	3	1	4	0
1980-81	**Montreal**	**NHL**	51	27	43	70	29	3	0	1	1	2
1981-82	**Montreal**	**NHL**	66	27	57	84	24	5	2	1	3	4
1982-83	**Montreal**	**NHL**	68	27	49	76	12	3	0	2	2	2
1983-84	**Montreal**	**NHL**	80	30	40	70	19	12	0	3	3	5
1984-85	**Montreal**	**NHL**	19	2	3	5	10	.....	...	...	...	...
1985-86			DID NOT PLAY									
1986-87			DID NOT PLAY									
1987-88g			DID NOT PLAY									
1988-89	**NY Rangers**	**NHL**	67	18	27	45	12	4	1	0	1	0
1989-90	**Quebec**	**NHL**	39	12	22	34	4	.....	...	...	...	...
1990-91	**Quebec**	**NHL**	59	12	16	28	2	.....	...	...	...	...
	NHL Totals		**1126**	**560**	**793**	**1353**	**399**	**128**	**58**	**76**	**134**	**67**

a NHL First All-Star Team (1975, 1976, 1977, 1978, 1979, 1980)
b Won Art Ross Trophy (1976, 1977, 1978)
c Won Lester B. Pearson Award (1977)
d Won Hart Trophy (1977, 1978)
e Won Conn Smythe Trophy (1977)
f NHL Plus/Minus Leader (1978)
g Inducted into Hockey Hall of Fame (1988)
Played in NHL All-Star Game (1975-78, 1980, 1991)

Signed as a free agent by **NY Rangers**, September 26, 1988. Signed as a free agent by, **Quebec**, July 14, 1989. **NY Rangers** received **Quebec**'s fifth round choice (Sergei Zubov) in 1990 Entry Draft as compensation, June 16, 1990. Claimed by **Minnesota** from **Quebec** in Expansion Draft, May 30, 1991. Traded to **Quebec** by **Minnesota** for Alan Haworth, May 31, 1991.

LaFONTAINE, PAT

Center. Shoots right. 5'10", 177 lbs.   Born, St. Louis, MO, February 22, 1965.
(NY Islanders' 1st choice, 3rd overall, in 1983 Entry Draft).

			Regular Season					Playoffs				
Season	Club	Lea	GP	G	A	TP	PIM	GP	G	A	TP	PIM
1982-83abcd	Verdun	QMJHL	70	*104	*130	*234	10	15	11	*24	*35	4
1983-84	U.S. National	...	58	56	55	111	22	.....	...	...	...	...
	U.S. Olympic	...	6	5	5	10	0	.....	...	...	...	...
	NY Islanders	**NHL**	15	13	6	19	6	16	3	6	9	8
1984-85	**NY Islanders**	**NHL**	67	19	35	54	32	9	1	2	3	4
1985-86	**NY Islanders**	**NHL**	65	30	23	53	43	3	1	0	1	0
1986-87	**NY Islanders**	**NHL**	80	38	32	70	70	14	5	7	12	10
1987-88	**NY Islanders**	**NHL**	75	47	45	92	52	6	4	5	9	8
1988-89	**NY Islanders**	**NHL**	79	45	43	88	26	.....	...	...	...	...
1989-90e	**NY Islanders**	**NHL**	74	54	51	105	38	2	0	1	1	0
1990-91	**NY Islanders**	**NHL**	75	41	44	85	42	.....	...	...	...	...
	NHL Totals		**530**	**287**	**279**	**566**	**309**	**50**	**14**	**21**	**35**	**30**

a QMJHL First All-Star Team (1983).
b QMJHL Most Valuable Player (1983).
c QMJHL Most Valuable Player in Playoffs (1983).
d Canadian Major Junior Player of the Year (1983).
e Won Dodge Performer of the Year Award (1990)
Played in NHL All-Star Game (1988-91)

LaFORGE, MARC

Left wing. Shoots left. 6'2", 210 lbs.   Born, Sudbury, Ont., January 3, 1968.
(Hartford's 2nd choice, 32nd overall, in 1986 Entry Draft).

			Regular Season					Playoffs				
Season	Club	Lea	GP	G	A	TP	PIM	GP	G	A	TP	PIM
1984-85	Kingston	OHL	57	1	5	6	214	.....	...	...	...	...
1985-86	Kingston	OHL	60	1	13	14	248	10	0	1	1	30
1986-87	Binghamton	AHL						4	0	0	0	7
	Kingston	OHL	53	2	10	12	224	12	1	0	1	79
1987-88	Sudbury	OHL	14	0	2	2	68	.....	...	...	...	...
1988-89	Binghamton	AHL	38	2	2	4	179	.....	...	...	...	...
	Indianapolis	IHL	14	0	2	2	138	.....	...	...	...	...
1989-90	**Hartford**	**NHL**	9	0	0	0	43	.....	...	...	...	...
	Binghamton	AHL	25	2	6	8	111	.....	...	...	...	...
	Cape Breton	AHL	3	0	1	1	24	3	0	0	0	27
1990-91	Cape Breton	AHL	49	1	7	8	217	.....	...	...	...	...
	NHL Totals		**9**	**0**	**0**	**0**	**43**					

Traded to **Edmonton** by **Hartford** for the rights to Cam Brauer, March 6, 1990.

LAFRENIERE, JASON   (LAH-frehn-YAIR)

Center. Shoots right. 5'11", 185 lbs.   Born, St. Catharines, Ont., December 6, 1966.
(Quebec's 2nd choice, 36th overall, in 1985 Entry Draft).

			Regular Season					Playoffs				
Season	Club	Lea	GP	G	A	TP	PIM	GP	G	A	TP	PIM
1983-84	Brantford	OHL	70	24	57	81	4	6	2	4	6	2
1984-85	Hamilton	OHL	59	26	69	95	10	17	12	16	28	0
1985-86a	Hamilton	OHL	14	12	10	22	2	.....	...	...	...	...
a	Belleville	OHL	48	37	73	110	2	23	10	*22	*32	6
1986-87	**Quebec**	**NHL**	56	13	15	28	8	12	1	5	6	2
	Fredericton	AHL	11	3	11	14	0	.....	...	...	...	...
1987-88	**Quebec**	**NHL**	40	10	19	29	4	.....	...	...	...	...
	Fredericton	AHL	32	12	19	31	38	.....	...	...	...	...
1988-89	**NY Rangers**	**NHL**	38	8	16	24	6	3	0	0	0	17
	Denver	IHL	24	10	19	29	17	.....	...	...	...	...
1989-90	Flint	IHL	41	9	25	34	34	.....	...	...	...	...
	Phoenix	IHL	14	4	9	13	0	.....	...	...	...	...
1990-91	Cdn. National	...	59	26	33	59	50	.....	...	...	...	...
	NHL Totals		**134**	**31**	**50**	**81**	**18**	**15**	**1**	**5**	**6**	**19**

a OHL First All-Star Team (1986)

Traded to **NY Rangers** by **Quebec** with Normand Rochefort for Bruce Bell, Jari Gronstrand, Walt Poddubny and NY Rangers' fourth round choice (Eric Dubois) in 1989 Entry Draft, August 1, 1988.

LAIDLAW, THOMAS (TOM)

Defense. Shoots left. 6'1", 205 lbs.   Born, Brampton, Ont., April 15, 1958.
(NY Rangers' 7th choice, 93rd overall, in 1978 Amateur Draft)

			Regular Season					Playoffs				
Season	Club	Lea	GP	G	A	TP	PIM	GP	G	A	TP	PIM
1978-79a	N. Michigan	CCHA	29	10	20	30	137	.....	...	...	...	...
1979-80ab	N. Michigan	CCHA	39	8	30	38	83	.....	...	...	...	...
	New Haven	AHL	1	0	0	0	0	10	1	6	7	27
1980-81	**NY Rangers**	**NHL**	80	6	23	29	100	14	1	4	5	18
1981-82	**NY Rangers**	**NHL**	79	3	18	21	104	10	0	3	3	14
1982-83	**NY Rangers**	**NHL**	80	0	10	10	75	9	1	1	2	10
1983-84	**NY Rangers**	**NHL**	79	3	15	18	62	5	0	0	0	8
1984-85	**NY Rangers**	**NHL**	61	1	11	12	52	3	0	2	2	4
1985-86	**NY Rangers**	**NHL**	68	6	12	18	103	7	0	2	2	12
1986-87	**NY Rangers**	**NHL**	63	1	10	11	65	.....	...	...	...	...
	Los Angeles	**NHL**	11	0	3	3	4	5	0	0	0	2
1987-88	**Los Angeles**	**NHL**	57	1	12	13	47	5	0	2	2	4
1988-89	**Los Angeles**	**NHL**	70	3	17	20	63	11	2	3	5	6
1989-90	**Los Angeles**	**NHL**	57	1	8	9	42	.....	...	...	...	...
1990-91	Phoenix	IHL	4	0	1	1	2	.....	...	...	...	...
	NHL Totals		**705**	**25**	**139**	**164**	**717**	**69**	**4**	**17**	**21**	**78**

a CCHA First All-Star Team (1979, 1980)
b NCAA All-Tournament Team (1980)

Traded to **Los Angeles** by **NY Rangers** with Bob Carpenter for Jeff Crossman, Marcel Dionne and Los Angeles' third-round choice (Draft choice acquired by Minnesota, June 17, 1989 October 12, 1988. Minnesota selected Murray Garbut.) in 1989 Entry Draft, March 10, 1987.

LAKSO, BOB

Left wing. Shoots left. 6', 185 lbs. Born, Baltimore, MD, April 13, 1962.
(Minnesota's 9th choice, 184th overall, in 1980 Entry Draft).

			Regular Season					Playoffs				
Season	Club	Lea	GP	G	A	TP	PIM	GP	G	A	TP	PIM
1980-81	Minn.-Duluth	WCHA	25	5	3	8	2	....	....	....	....	....
1981-82	Minn.-Duluth	WCHA	22	8	10	18	6	....	....	....	....	....
1982-83	Minn.-Duluth	WCHA	26	11	17	28	4	....	....	....	....	....
1983-84	Minn.-Duluth	WCHA	26	20	18	38	8	....	....	....	....	....
1984-85	Springfield	AHL	8	2	1	3	0	....	....	....	....	....
	Indianapolis	IHL	76	26	32	58	4	6	3	2	5	2
1985-86	Springfield	AHL	17	3	6	9	2	....	....	....	....	....
	Indianapolis	IHL	58	41	35	76	4	5	4	2	6	0
1986-87	Indianapolis	IHL	79	39	55	94	6	6	2	2	4	0
1987-88	Milwaukee	IHL	80	43	28	71	10	....	....	....	....	....
1988-89	Indianapolis	IHL	82	38	34	72	10	....	....	....	....	....
1989-90a	Fort Wayne	IHL	82	42	58	100	6	5	3	3	6	0
1990-91	Fort Wayne	IHL	66	31	31	62	8	19	6	12	18	2

a Won Iron Man Award (hardest worker-IHL) (1990)

LALA, JIRI (LAH-lah)

Right wing. Shoots right. 5'10", 181 lbs. Born, Tabor, Czech., August 21, 1959.
(Quebec's 4th choice, 76th overall, in 1982 Entry Draft).

			Regular Season					Playoffs				
Season	Club	Lea	GP	G	A	TP	PIM	GP	G	A	TP	PIM
1986-87	Motor	Czech.	31	14	17	31	....	....	....	....	....	....
1987-88	Motor	Czech.	28	20	28	48	....	....	....	....	....	....
1988-89	Motor	Czech.	45	27	39	66	....	....	....	....	....	....
1989-90	Frankfurt	W.Ger.	35	36	39	75	12	....	....	....	....	....
1990-91	Frankfurt	Ger.	47	47	60	107	30	....	....	....	....	....

LALONDE, CHRISTIAN

Left wing. Shoots left. 6'1", 210 lbs. Born, La Salle, Que., May 3, 1966.

			Regular Season					Playoffs				
Season	Club	Lea	GP	G	A	TP	PIM	GP	G	A	TP	PIM
1986-87	U. of Maine	H.E.	40	8	8	16	49	....	....	....	....	....
1987-88	U. of Maine	H.E.	44	20	31	51	40	....	....	....	....	....
1988-89	U. of Maine	H.E.	39	10	29	39	41	....	....	....	....	....
1989-90	U. of Maine	H.E.	41	2	13	15	44	....	....	....	....	....
	Newmarket	AHL	3	0	0	0	0	....	....	....	....	....
1990-91	Muskegon	IHL	33	1	4	5	25	....	....	....	....	....
	Knoxville	ECHL	20	3	12	15	37	3	0	0	0	2

Signed as a free agent by **Pittsburgh**, September 4, 1990.

LALONDE, TODD

Left wing. Shoots left. 6', 190 lbs. Born, Sudbury, Ont., August 4, 1969.
(Boston's 3rd choice, 56th overall, in 1987 Entry Draft).

			Regular Season					Playoffs				
Season	Club	Lea	GP	G	A	TP	PIM	GP	G	A	TP	PIM
1985-86	Sudbury	OHL	57	17	30	47	43	4	0	1	1	8
1986-87	Sudbury	OHL	29	5	11	16	71	....	....	....	....	....
1987-88	Sudbury	OHL	59	27	43	70	79	....	....	....	....	....
1988-89	Sudbury	OHL	52	32	44	76	57	....	....	....	....	....
1989-90	Maine	AHL	5	2	0	2	6	....	....	....	....	....
	Johnstown	ECHL	1	1	0	1	2	....	....	....	....	....
1990-91	Maine	AHL	6	0	0	0	17	....	....	....	....	....

LALOR, MIKE

Defense. Shoots left. 6', 200 lbs. Born, Buffalo, NY, March 8, 1963.

			Regular Season					Playoffs				
Season	Club	Lea	GP	G	A	TP	PIM	GP	G	A	TP	PIM
1981-82	Brantford	OHL	64	3	13	16	114	11	0	6	6	11
1982-83	Brantford	OHL	65	10	30	40	113	8	1	3	4	20
1983-84	Nova Scotia	AHL	67	5	11	16	80	12	0	2	2	13
1984-85	Sherbrooke	AHL	79	9	23	32	114	17	3	5	8	36
1985-86	**Montreal**	**NHL**	**62**	**3**	**5**	**8**	**56**	**17**	**1**	**2**	**3**	**29**
1986-87	**Montreal**	**NHL**	**57**	**0**	**10**	**10**	**47**	**13**	**2**	**1**	**3**	**29**
1987-88	**Montreal**	**NHL**	**66**	**1**	**10**	**11**	**113**	**11**	**0**	**0**	**0**	**11**
1988-89	**Montreal**	**NHL**	**12**	**1**	**4**	**5**	**15**	....	....	....	....	....
	St. Louis	**NHL**	**36**	**1**	**14**	**15**	**54**	**10**	**1**	**1**	**2**	**14**
1989-90	**St. Louis**	**NHL**	**78**	**0**	**16**	**16**	**81**	**12**	**0**	**2**	**2**	**31**
1990-91	**Washington**	**NHL**	**68**	**1**	**5**	**6**	**61**	**10**	**1**	**2**	**3**	**22**
	NHL Totals		**379**	**7**	**64**	**71**	**427**	**73**	**5**	**8**	**13**	**136**

Signed as a free agent by **Montreal**, September, 1983. Traded to **St. Louis** by **Montreal** for the option (exercised by Montreal) to switch first-round picks in 1990 Entry Draft and St. Louis' third-round choice in the 1991 Entry Draft, January 16, 1989. Traded to **Washington** by **St. Louis** with Peter Zezel for Geoff Courtnall, July 13, 1990.

LAMB, MARK

Center. Shoots left. 5'9", 180 lbs. Born, Ponteix, Sask., August 3, 1964.
(Calgary's 5th choice, 72nd overall, in 1982 Entry Draft).

			Regular Season					Playoffs				
Season	Club	Lea	GP	G	A	TP	PIM	GP	G	A	TP	PIM
1981-82	Billings	WHL	72	45	56	101	46	5	4	6	10	4
1982-83	Nanaimo	WHL	30	14	37	51	16	....	....	....	....	....
	Medicine Hat	WHL	46	22	43	65	33	5	3	2	5	4
	Colorado	CHL	....	....	....	....	....	6	0	2	2	0
1983-84a	Medicine Hat	WHL	72	59	77	136	30	14	12	11	23	6
1984-85	Moncton	AHL	80	23	49	72	53	....	....	....	....	....
1985-86	**Calgary**	**NHL**	**1**	**0**	**0**	**0**	**0**	....	....	....	....	....
	Moncton	AHL	79	26	50	76	51	10	2	6	8	17
1986-87	**Detroit**	**NHL**	**22**	**2**	**1**	**3**	**8**	**11**	**0**	**0**	**0**	**11**
	Adirondack	AHL	49	14	36	50	45	....	....	....	....	....
1987-88	**Edmonton**	**NHL**	**2**	**0**	**0**	**0**	**0**	....	....	....	....	....
	Nova Scotia	AHL	69	27	61	88	45	5	0	5	5	6
1988-89	**Edmonton**	**NHL**	**20**	**2**	**8**	**10**	**14**	**6**	**0**	**2**	**2**	**8**
	Cape Breton	AHL	54	33	49	82	29	....	....	....	....	....
1989-90	**Edmonton**	**NHL**	**58**	**12**	**16**	**28**	**42**	**22**	**6**	**11**	**17**	**2**
1990-91	**Edmonton**	**NHL**	**37**	**4**	**8**	**12**	**25**	**15**	**0**	**5**	**5**	**20**
	NHL Totals		**140**	**20**	**33**	**53**	**89**	**54**	**6**	**18**	**24**	**41**

a WHL First All-Star Team, East Division (1984)

Signed as a free agent by **Detroit**, July 28, 1986. Claimed by **Edmonton** in NHL Waiver Draft, October 5, 1987.

LAMBERT, DAN

Defense. Shoots left. 5'8", 177 lbs. Born, St. Boniface, Man., January 12, 1970.
(Quebec's 8th choice, 106th overall, in 1989 Entry Draft).

			Regular Season					Playoffs				
Season	Club	Lea	GP	G	A	TP	PIM	GP	G	A	TP	PIM
1986-87	Swift Current	WHL	68	13	53	66	95	4	1	1	2	9
1987-88	Swift Current	WHL	69	20	63	83	120	10	2	10	12	45
1988-89ab	Swift Current	WHL	57	25	77	102	158	12	9	19	28	12
1989-90a	Swift Current	WHL	50	17	51	68	119	4	2	3	5	12
1990-91	**Quebec**	**NHL**	**1**	**0**	**0**	**0**	**0**	....	....	....	....	....
	Halifax	AHL	30	7	13	20	20	....	....	....	....	....
	Fort Wayne	IHL	49	10	27	37	65	19	4	10	14	20
	NHL Totals		**1**	**0**	**0**	**0**	**0**	....	....	....	....	....

a WHL East First All-Star Team (1989, 1990)
b WHL Best Defenseman (1989)

LAMBERT, LANE (LAM-buhrt)

Right wing. Shoots right. 6', 185 lbs. Born, Melfort, Sask., November 18, 1964.
(Detroit's 2nd choice, 25th overall, in 1983 Entry Draft).

			Regular Season					Playoffs				
Season	Club	Lea	GP	G	A	TP	PIM	GP	G	A	TP	PIM
1981-82	Saskatoon	WHL	72	45	69	114	111	5	1	1	2	25
1982-83a	Saskatoon	WHL	64	59	60	119	126	6	4	3	7	7
1983-84	**Detroit**	**NHL**	**73**	**20**	**15**	**35**	**115**	**4**	**0**	**0**	**0**	**10**
1984-85	**Detroit**	**NHL**	**69**	**14**	**11**	**25**	**104**	....	....	....	....	....
1985-86	**Detroit**	**NHL**	**34**	**2**	**3**	**5**	**130**	....	....	....	....	....
	Adirondack	AHL	45	16	25	41	69	16	5	5	10	9
1986-87	**NY Rangers**	**NHL**	**18**	**2**	**2**	**4**	**33**	....	....	....	....	....
	New Haven	AHL	11	3	3	6	19	....	....	....	....	....
	Quebec	**NHL**	**15**	**5**	**5**	**10**	**18**	**13**	**2**	**4**	**6**	**30**
1987-88	**Quebec**	**NHL**	**61**	**13**	**28**	**41**	**98**	....	....	....	....	....
1988-89	**Quebec**	**NHL**	**13**	**2**	**2**	**4**	**23**	....	....	....	....	....
	Halifax	AHL	59	25	35	60	162	4	0	2	2	2
1989-90	Cdn. National	...	54	28	36	64	48	....	....	....	....	....
1990-91	Ajoie	Switz.	36	26	24	50	....	....	....	....	....	....
	NHL Totals		**283**	**58**	**66**	**124**	**521**	**17**	**2**	**4**	**6**	**40**

a WHL Second All-Star Team (1983)

Traded to **NY Rangers** by **Detroit** with Kelly Kisio and Jim Leavins for Glen Hanlon and New York's third round choices in 1987 (Dennis Holland) and 1988 (Guy Dupuis) Entry Drafts, July 29, 1986. Traded to **Quebec** by **NY Rangers** for Pat Price, March 5, 1987.

LAMMENS, HANK

Defense. Shoots left. 6'2", 210 lbs. Born, Brockville, Ont., February 21, 1966.
(NY Islanders' 10th choice, 160th overall, in 1985 Entry Draft).

			Regular Season					Playoffs				
Season	Club	Lea	GP	G	A	TP	PIM	GP	G	A	TP	PIM
1984-85	St. Lawrence	ECAC	21	17	9	26	16	....	....	....	....	....
1985-86	St. Lawrence	ECAC	30	3	14	17	60	....	....	....	....	....
1986-87ab	St. Lawrence	ECAC	35	6	13	19	92	....	....	....	....	....
1987-88a	St. Lawrence	ECAC	32	3	6	9	64	....	....	....	....	....
1988-89	Springfield	AHL	69	1	13	14	55	....	....	....	....	....
1989-90	Springfield	AHL	43	0	6	6	27	7	0	0	0	14
1990-91	Capital Dist.	AHL	32	0	5	5	14	....	....	....	....	....
	Kansas City	IHL	17	0	1	1	27	....	....	....	....	....

a ECAC Second All-Star Team (1987, 1988)
b NCAA East Second All-American Team (1987)

LANG, ROBERT

Center. Shoots right. 6'2", 180 lbs. Born, Most, Czechoslovakia, December 19, 1970.
(Los Angeles' 6th choice, 133rd overall, in 1990 Entry Draft).

			Regular Season					Playoffs				
Season	Club	Lea	GP	G	A	TP	PIM	GP	G	A	TP	PIM
1989-90	CHZ Litvinov	Czech.	39	11	10	21	....	....	....	....	....	....
1990-91	CHZ Litvinov	Czech.	48	24	22	46	38	....	....	....	....	....

LANGILLE, DEREK

Defense. Shoots left. 6', 184 lbs. Born, Toronto, Ont., June 25, 1969.
(Toronto's 9th choice, 150th overall, in 1989 Entry Draft).

			Regular Season					Playoffs				
Season	Club	Lea	GP	G	A	TP	PIM	GP	G	A	TP	PIM
1986-87	Belleville	OHL	42	0	2	2	27	6	0	0	0	0
1987-88	Belleville	OHL	36	3	7	10	45	....	....	....	....	....
	Kingston	OHL	32	4	7	11	66	....	....	....	....	....
1988-89	North Bay	OHL	60	20	38	58	128	12	1	6	7	22
1989-90	Newmarket	AHL	64	5	12	17	75	....	....	....	....	....
1990-91	Newmarket	AHL	67	4	11	15	102	....	....	....	....	....

LANGWAY, ROD CORRY

Defense. Shoots left. 6'3", 218 lbs. Born, Formosa, Taiwan, May 3, 1957.
(Montreal's 3rd choice, 36th overall, in 1977 Amateur Draft).

			Regular Season					Playoffs				
Season	Club	Lea	GP	G	A	TP	PIM	GP	G	A	TP	PIM
1976-77	N. Hampshire	ECAC	34	10	43	53	52	....	....	....	....	....
1977-78	Hampton	AHL	30	6	16	22	50	....	....	....	....	....
	Birmingham	WHA	52	3	18	21	52	4	0	0	0	9
1978-79	**Montreal**	**NHL**	**45**	**3**	**4**	**7**	**30**	**8**	**0**	**0**	**0**	**16**
	Nova Scotia	AHL	18	6	13	19	29	....	....	....	....	....
1979-80	**Montreal**	**NHL**	**77**	**7**	**29**	**36**	**81**	**10**	**3**	**3**	**6**	**2**
1980-81	**Montreal**	**NHL**	**80**	**11**	**34**	**45**	**120**	**3**	**0**	**0**	**0**	**6**
1981-82	**Montreal**	**NHL**	**66**	**5**	**34**	**39**	**116**	**5**	**0**	**3**	**3**	**18**
1982-83ab	**Washington**	**NHL**	**80**	**3**	**29**	**32**	**75**	**4**	**0**	**0**	**0**	**0**
1983-84ab	**Washington**	**NHL**	**80**	**9**	**24**	**33**	**61**	**8**	**0**	**5**	**5**	**7**
1984-85c	**Washington**	**NHL**	**79**	**4**	**22**	**26**	**54**	**5**	**0**	**1**	**1**	**6**
1985-86	**Washington**	**NHL**	**71**	**1**	**17**	**18**	**61**	**9**	**1**	**2**	**3**	**6**
1986-87	**Washington**	**NHL**	**78**	**2**	**25**	**27**	**53**	**7**	**0**	**1**	**1**	**2**
1987-88	**Washington**	**NHL**	**63**	**3**	**13**	**16**	**28**	**6**	**0**	**0**	**0**	**8**
1988-89	**Washington**	**NHL**	**76**	**2**	**19**	**21**	**65**	**6**	**0**	**0**	**0**	**6**
1989-90	**Washington**	**NHL**	**58**	**0**	**8**	**8**	**39**	**15**	**1**	**4**	**5**	**12**
1990-91	**Washington**	**NHL**	**56**	**1**	**7**	**8**	**24**	**11**	**0**	**2**	**2**	**6**
	NHL Totals		**909**	**51**	**265**	**316**	**807**	**97**	**5**	**21**	**26**	**94**

a Won James Norris Memorial Trophy (1983, 1984)
b NHL First All-Star Team (1983, 1984)
c NHL Second All-Star Team (1985)

Played in NHL All-Star Game (1981-86)

Claimed by **Montreal** as fill in Expansion Draft, June 13, 1979. Traded to **Washington** by **Montreal** with Doug Jarvis, Craig Laughlin and Brian Engblom for Ryan Walter and Rick Green, September 9, 1982.

LANIEL, MARC (lan-YELL)

Defense. Shoots left. 6'1", 195 lbs. Born, Oshawa, Ont., January 16, 1968.
(New Jersey's 4th choice, 62nd overall, in 1986 Entry Draft).

			Regular Season					Playoffs				
Season	Club	Lea	GP	G	A	TP	PIM	GP	G	A	TP	PIM
1985-86	Oshawa	OHL	66	9	25	34	27	6	2	3	5	6
1986-87	Oshawa	OHL	63	14	31	45	42	26	3	13	16	20
1987-88	Utica	AHL	2	0	0	0	0	....	....	....	....	....
a	Oshawa	OHL	41	8	32	40	56	7	2	2	4	4
1988-89	Utica	AHL	80	6	28	34	43	5	0	1	1	2
1989-90	Utica	AHL	20	0	0	0	25	....	....	....	....	....
	Phoenix	IHL	26	3	15	18	10	....	....	....	....	....
1990-91	Utica	AHL	57	6	9	15	45	....	....	....	....	....

a OHL Third All-Star Team (1988)

LANZ, RICK ROMAN

Defense. Shoots right. 6'2", 203 lbs. Born, Karlouy Vary, Czech., September 16, 1961.
(Vancouver's 1st choice, 7th overall, in 1980 Entry Draft).

			Regular Season					Playoffs				
Season	Club	Lea	GP	G	A	TP	PIM	GP	G	A	TP	PIM
1978-79	Oshawa	OHA	65	12	47	59	88	5	1	3	4	14
1979-80a	Oshawa	OHA	52	18	38	56	51	7	2	3	5	6
1980-81	**Vancouver**	**NHL**	**76**	**7**	**22**	**29**	**40**	**3**	**0**	**0**	**0**	**4**
1981-82	**Vancouver**	**NHL**	**39**	**3**	**11**	**14**	**48**	....	....	....	....	....
1982-83	**Vancouver**	**NHL**	**74**	**10**	**38**	**48**	**46**	**4**	**2**	**1**	**3**	**0**
1983-84	**Vancouver**	**NHL**	**79**	**18**	**39**	**57**	**45**	**4**	**0**	**4**	**4**	**2**
1984-85	**Vancouver**	**NHL**	**57**	**2**	**17**	**19**	**69**	....	....	....	....	....
1985-86	**Vancouver**	**NHL**	**75**	**15**	**38**	**53**	**73**	**3**	**0**	**0**	**0**	**0**
1986-87	**Vancouver**	**NHL**	**17**	**1**	**6**	**7**	**10**	....	....	....	....	....
	Toronto	**NHL**	**44**	**2**	**19**	**21**	**32**	**13**	**1**	**3**	**4**	**27**
1987-88	**Toronto**	**NHL**	**75**	**6**	**22**	**28**	**65**	**1**	**0**	**0**	**0**	**2**
1988-89	**Toronto**	**NHL**	**32**	**1**	**9**	**10**	**18**	....	....	....	....	....
1989-90	Ambri	Switz.	36	4	14	18	....	....	....	....	....	....
1990-91	Indianapolis	IHL	8	0	5	5	18	....	....	....	....	....
	NHL Totals		**568**	**65**	**221**	**286**	**446**	**28**	**3**	**8**	**11**	**35**

a OHA Third All-Star Team (1980).

Traded to **Toronto** by **Vancouver** for Jim Benning and Dan Hodgson, December 2, 1986. Signed as a free agent by **Chicago**, August 13, 1990.

LAPERRIERE, DANIEL

Defense. Shoots left. 6'1", 180 lbs., Born, Laval, Que., March 28, 1969.
(St. Louis' 4th choice, 93rd overall, in 1989 Entry Draft).

			Regular Season					Playoffs				
Season	Club	Lea	GP	G	A	TP	PIM	GP	G	A	TP	PIM
1988-89	St. Lawrence	ECAC	28	0	7	7	10	....	....	....	....	....
1989-90	St. Lawrence	ECAC	31	6	19	25	16	....	....	....	....	....
1990-91a	St. Lawrence	ECAC	34	7	31	38	18	....	....	....	....	....

a ECAC Second All-Star Team (1991)

LAPOINTE, CLAUDE

Center. Shoots left. 5'9", 173 lbs. Born, Lachine, Que., October 11, 1968.
(Quebec's 12th choice, 234th overall, in 1989 Entry Draft).

			Regular Season					Playoffs				
Season	Club	Lea	GP	G	A	TP	PIM	GP	G	A	TP	PIM
1986-87	Trois-Rivieres	QMJHL	70	47	57	104	123	....	....	....	....	....
1987-88	Laval	QMJHL	69	37	83	120	143	13	2	17	19	53
1988-89	Laval	QMJHL	63	32	72	104	158	17	5	14	19	66
1989-90	Halifax	AHL	63	18	19	37	51	6	1	1	2	34
1990-91	**Quebec**	**NHL**	**13**	**2**	**2**	**4**	**4**	....	....	....	....	....
	Halifax	AHL	43	17	17	34	46	....	....	....	....	....
	NHL Totals		**13**	**2**	**2**	**4**	**4**	....	....	....	....	....

LAPOINTE, MARTIN

Right wing. Shoots right. 5'11", 197 lbs. Born, Lachine, Que., September 12, 1973.
(Detroit's 1st choice, 10th overall, in 1991 Entry Draft).

			Regular Season					Playoffs				
Season	Club	Lea	GP	G	A	TP	PIM	GP	G	A	TP	PIM
1989-90ab	Laval	QMJHL	65	42	54	96	77	14	8	17	25	54
1990-91c	Laval	QMJHL	64	44	54	98	66	13	7	14	21	26

a QMJHL First All-Star Team (1990)
b QMJHL Offensive Rookie of the Year (1990)
c QMJHL Second All-Star Team (1991)

LAPPIN, MICHAEL

Center. Shoots left. 5'10", 175 lbs. Born, Chicago, IL, January 1, 1969.
(Chicago's 12th choice, 239th overall, in 1987 Entry Draft).

			Regular Season					Playoffs				
Season	Club	Lea	GP	G	A	TP	PIM	GP	G	A	TP	PIM
1990-91	St. Lawrence	ECAC	35	27	42	69	36	....	....	....	....	....

LAPPIN, PETER

Right wing. Shoots right. 5'11", 180 lbs. Born, St. Charles, IL., December 31, 1965.
(Calgary's 1st choice, 24th overall, in 1987 Supplemental Draft).

			Regular Season					Playoffs				
Season	Club	Lea	GP	G	A	TP	PIM	GP	G	A	TP	PIM
1984-85	St. Lawrence	ECAC	32	10	12	22	22	....	....	....	....	....
1985-86	St. Lawrence	ECAC	30	20	26	46	64	....	....	....	....	....
1986-87ab	St. Lawrence	ECAC	35	34	24	58	32	....	....	....	....	....
1987-88cdef	St. Lawrence	ECAC	30	16	36	52	26	....	....	....	....	....
g	Salt Lake	IHL	3	1	1	2	0	17	*16	12	*28	11
1988-89	Salt Lake	IHL	81	48	42	90	50	14	*9	9	18	4
1989-90	**Minnesota**	**NHL**	**6**	**0**	**0**	**0**	**2**	....	....	....	....	....
h	Kalamazoo	IHL	74	45	35	80	42	8	5	2	7	4
1990-91	Kalamazoo	IHL	73	20	47	67	74	11	5	4	9	8
	NHL Totals		**6**	**0**	**0**	**0**	**2**	....	....	....	....	....

a NCAA East Second All-American Team (1987)
b ECAC Second All-Star Team (1987)
c NCAA East First All-American Team (1988)
d NCAA All-Tournament Team (1988)
e ECAC Player of the Year (1988)
f ECAC First All-Star Team (1988)
g IHL Playoff MVP (1988)
h IHL Second All-Star Team (1990)

Traded to **Minnesota** by **Calgary** for Minnesota's second round choice in 1990 Entry Draft which was later transferred to New Jersey (Chris Gotziaman), September 5, 1989. Claimed by **San Jose** from **Minnesota** in Dispersal Draft, May 30, 1991.

LAPRADE, DOUGLAS

Right wing. Shoots right. 6', 185 lbs. Born, Port Arthur, Ont., October 9, 1968.
(Los Angeles' 12th choice, 217th overall, in 1988 Entry Draft).

			Regular Season					Playoffs				
Season	Club	Lea	GP	G	A	TP	PIM	GP	G	A	TP	PIM
1987-88	Lake Superior	CCHA	30	4	2	6	30	....	....	....	....	....
1988-89	Lake Superior	CCHA	45	4	6	10	48	....	....	....	....	....
1989-90	Lake Superior	CCHA	42	4	3	7	51	....	....	....	....	....
1990-91	Lake Superior	CCHA	13	4	3	7	18	....	....	....	....	....

LARIONOV, IGOR (LAIR-ee-AH-nahf)

Center. Shoots left. 5'9", 165 lbs. Born, Voskresensk, Soviet Union, December 3, 1960.
(Vancouver's 11th choice, 214th overall, in 1985 Entry Draft).

			Regular Season					Playoffs				
Season	Club	Lea	GP	G	A	TP	PIM	GP	G	A	TP	PIM
1977-78	Khimik	USSR	6	3	0	3	4	....	....	....	....	....
1978-79	Khimik	USSR	32	3	4	7	12	....	....	....	....	....
1979-80	Khimik	USSR	42	11	7	18	24	....	....	....	....	....
1980-81	Khimik	USSR	43	22	23	45	36	....	....	....	....	....
1981-82	CSKA	USSR	46	31	22	53	6	....	....	....	....	....
1982-83a	CSKA	USSR	44	20	19	39	20	....	....	....	....	....
1983-84	CSKA	USSR	43	15	26	41	30	....	....	....	....	....
1984-85	CSKA	USSR	40	18	28	46	20	....	....	....	....	....
1985-86a	CSKA	USSR	40	21	31	52	33	....	....	....	....	....
1986-87a	CSKA	USSR	39	20	26	46	34	....	....	....	....	....
1987-88ab	CSKA	USSR	51	25	32	57	54	....	....	....	....	....
1988-89	CSKA	USSR	31	15	12	27	22	....	....	....	....	....
1989-90	**Vancouver**	**NHL**	**74**	**17**	**27**	**44**	**20**	....	....	....	....	....
1990-91	**Vancouver**	**NHL**	**64**	**13**	**21**	**34**	**14**	**6**	**1**	**0**	**1**	**6**
	NHL Totals		**138**	**30**	**48**	**78**	**34**	**6**	**1**	**0**	**1**	**6**

a Soviet National League All-Star (1983, 1985-88)
b Soviet Player of the Year (1988)

LARKIN, JAMES

Left wing. Shoots left. 6', 165 lbs. Born, Wallingford, VT, April 15, 1970.
(Los Angeles' 10th choice, 175th overall, in 1988 Entry Draft).

			Regular Season					Playoffs				
Season	Club	Lea	GP	G	A	TP	PIM	GP	G	A	TP	PIM
1988-89	U. of Vermont	ECAC	34	16	19	35	8	....	....	....	....	....
1989-90	U. of Vermont	ECAC	28	20	15	35	14	....	....	....	....	....
1990-91	U. of Vermont	ECAC	26	6	21	27	22	....	....	....	....	....

LARMER, STEVE DONALD

Right wing. Shoots left. 5'11", 189 lbs. Born, Peterborough, Ont., June 16, 1961.
(Chicago's 11th choice, 120th overall, in 1980 Entry Draft).

			Regular Season					Playoffs				
Season	Club	Lea	GP	G	A	TP	PIM	GP	G	A	TP	PIM
1977-78	Peterborough	OHA	62	24	17	41	51	18	5	7	12	27
1978-79	Niagara Falls	OHA	66	37	47	84	108	....	....	....	....	....
1979-80	Niagara Falls	OHA	67	45	69	114	71	10	5	9	14	15
1980-81	**Chicago**	**NHL**	**4**	**0**	**1**	**1**	**0**	....	....	....	....	....
a	Niagara Falls	OHA	61	55	78	133	73	12	13	8	21	24
1981-82	**Chicago**	**NHL**	**3**	**0**	**0**	**0**	**0**	....	....	....	....	....
b	New Brunswick	AHL	74	38	44	82	46	15	6	6	12	0
1982-83cd	**Chicago**	**NHL**	**80**	**43**	**47**	**90**	**28**	**11**	**5**	**7**	**12**	**8**
1983-84	**Chicago**	**NHL**	**80**	**35**	**40**	**75**	**34**	**5**	**2**	**2**	**4**	**7**
1984-85	**Chicago**	**NHL**	**80**	**46**	**40**	**86**	**16**	**15**	**9**	**13**	**22**	**14**
1985-86	**Chicago**	**NHL**	**80**	**31**	**45**	**76**	**47**	**3**	**0**	**3**	**3**	**4**
1986-87	**Chicago**	**NHL**	**80**	**28**	**56**	**84**	**22**	**4**	**0**	**0**	**0**	**2**
1987-88	**Chicago**	**NHL**	**80**	**41**	**48**	**89**	**42**	**5**	**1**	**6**	**7**	**0**
1988-89	**Chicago**	**NHL**	**80**	**43**	**44**	**87**	**54**	**16**	**8**	**9**	**17**	**22**
1989-90	**Chicago**	**NHL**	**80**	**31**	**59**	**90**	**40**	**20**	**7**	**15**	**22**	**2**
1990-91	**Chicago**	**NHL**	**80**	**44**	**57**	**101**	**79**	**6**	**5**	**1**	**6**	**4**
	NHL Totals		**727**	**342**	**437**	**779**	**362**	**85**	**37**	**56**	**93**	**63**

a OHA Second All-Star Team (1981)
b AHL Second All-Star Team (1982)
c Won Calder Trophy (1983)
d NHL All-Rookie Team (1983)

Played in NHL All-Star Game (1990, 1991)

LAROCQUE, DENIS (lah-RAHK)

Defense. Shoots left. 6'1", 205 lbs. Born, Hawkesbury, Ont., October 5, 1967.
(Los Angeles' 2nd choice, 44th overall, in 1986 Entry Draft).

			Regular Season					Playoffs				
Season	Club	Lea	GP	G	A	TP	PIM	GP	G	A	TP	PIM
1984-85	Guelph	OHL	62	1	15	16	67	....	....	....	....	....
1985-86	Guelph	OHL	66	2	17	19	144	....	....	....	....	....
1986-87	Guelph	OHL	45	4	10	14	82	5	0	2	2	9
1987-88	**Los Angeles**	**NHL**	**8**	**0**	**1**	**1**	**18**	....	....	....	....	....
	New Haven	AHL	58	4	10	14	154	....	....	....	....	....
1988-89	New Haven	AHL	15	2	2	4	51	....	....	....	....	....
	Denver	IHL	30	2	8	10	39	4	0	2	2	10
1989-90	Cape Breton	AHL	26	2	4	6	39	6	0	1	1	2
	Flint	IHL	31	1	2	3	66	....	....	....	....	....
1990-91	Moncton	AHL	68	2	9	11	92	1	0	0	0	2
	NHL Totals		**8**	**0**	**1**	**1**	**18**	....	....	....	....	....

Traded to **NY Rangers** by **Los Angeles** with Dean Kennedy for Igor Liba, Michael Boyce, Todd Elik and future considerations, December 12, 1988.

LAROSE, GUY

Center. Shoots left. 5'9", 175 lbs. Born, Hull, Que., August 31, 1967.
(Buffalo's 11th choice, 224th overall, in 1985 Entry Draft).

			Regular Season					Playoffs				
Season	Club	Lea	GP	G	A	TP	PIM	GP	G	A	TP	PIM
1984-85	Guelph	OHL	58	30	30	60	63	....	....	....	....	....
1985-86	Guelph	OHL	37	12	36	48	55	....	....	....	....	....
	Ottawa	OHL	28	19	25	44	63	....	....	....	....	....
1986-87	Ottawa	OHL	66	28	49	77	77	11	2	8	10	27
1987-88	Moncton	AHL	77	22	31	53	127	....	....	....	....	....
1988-89	**Winnipeg**	**NHL**	**3**	**0**	**1**	**1**	**6**	....	....	....	....	....
	Moncton	AHL	72	32	27	59	176	10	4	4	8	37
1989-90	Moncton	AHL	79	44	26	70	232	....	....	....	....	....
1990-91	**Winnipeg**	**NHL**	**7**	**0**	**0**	**0**	**8**	....	....	....	....	....
	Moncton	AHL	35	14	10	24	60	....	....	....	....	....
	Binghamton	AHL	34	21	15	36	48	10	8	5	13	37
	NHL Totals		**10**	**0**	**1**	**1**	**14**	....	....	....	....	....

Signed as a free agent by **Winnipeg**, July 16, 1987. Traded to **NY Rangers** by **Winnipeg** for Rudy Poeschek, January 22, 1991.

LAROUCHE, STEVE

Center. Shoots right. 5'11", 180 lbs. Born, Rouyn, Que., April 14, 1971.
(Montreal's 3rd choice, 41st overall, in 1989 Entry Draft).

			Regular Season					Playoffs				
Season	Club	Lea	GP	G	A	TP	PIM	GP	G	A	TP	PIM
1987-88	Trois-Rivieres	QMJHL	66	11	29	40	25	....	....	....	....	....
1988-89	Trois-Rivieres	QMJHL	70	51	102	153	53	4	4	2	6	6
1989-90a	Trois-Rivieres	QMJHL	60	55	90	145	40	7	3	5	8	8
1990-91	Chicoutimi	QMJHL	45	35	41	76	64	17	*13	*20	*33	20

a QMJHL Second All-Star Team (1990)

LARSON, DEAN

Center. Shoots left. 5'7", 160 lbs. Born, Calgary, Alta., June 4, 1969.
(Calgary's 1st choice, 25th overall, in 1991 Supplemental Draft).

			Regular Season					Playoffs				
Season	Club	Lea	GP	G	A	TP	PIM	GP	G	A	TP	PIM
1990-91	Alaska-Anch.	NCAA	33	13	30	43	14	....	....	....	....	....

LARSON, JON

Defense. Shoots left. 6'1", 190 lbs. Born, Roseau, MN, April 12, 1971.
(NY Islanders' 7th choice, 128th overall, in 1989 Entry Draft).

			Regular Season					Playoffs				
Season	Club	Lea	GP	G	A	TP	PIM	GP	G	A	TP	PIM
1989-90	North Dakota	WCHA	18	0	1	1	10	....	....	....	....	....
1990-91	North Dakota	WCHA	13	0	0	0	4	....	....	....	....	....

LARSON, JOSEPH

Center. Shoots left. 6'1", 165 lbs. Born, Minnetonka, MN, August 17, 1970.
(Winnipeg's 12th choice, 193rd overall, in 1989 Entry Draft).

			Regular Season					Playoffs				
Season	Club	Lea	GP	G	A	TP	PIM	GP	G	A	TP	PIM
1989-90	St. Cloud St.	NCAA	5	0	1	1	6	....	....	....	....	....
1990-91	St. Cloud St.	WCHA	DID NOT PLAY									

LARSON, REED DAVID

Defense. Shoots right. 6', 195 lbs. Born, Minneapolis, MN, July 30, 1956.
(Detroit's 2nd choice, 22nd overall, in 1976 Amateur Draft).

			Regular Season					Playoffs				
Season	Club	Lea	GP	G	A	TP	PIM	GP	G	A	TP	PIM
1975-76	U. Minnesota	WCHA	42	13	29	42	94	....	....	....	....	....
1976-77	U. Minnesota	WCHA	21	10	15	25	30	....	....	....	....	....
	Detroit	**NHL**	**14**	**0**	**1**	**1**	**23**	....	....	....	....	....
1977-78	**Detroit**	**NHL**	**75**	**19**	**41**	**60**	**95**	**7**	**0**	**2**	**2**	**4**
1978-79	**Detroit**	**NHL**	**79**	**18**	**49**	**67**	**169**	....	....	....	....	....
1979-80	**Detroit**	**NHL**	**80**	**22**	**44**	**66**	**101**	....	....	....	....	....
1980-81	**Detroit**	**NHL**	**78**	**27**	**31**	**58**	**153**	....	....	....	....	....
1981-82	**Detroit**	**NHL**	**80**	**21**	**39**	**60**	**112**	....	....	....	....	....
1982-83	**Detroit**	**NHL**	**80**	**22**	**52**	**74**	**104**	....	....	....	....	....
1983-84	**Detroit**	**NHL**	**78**	**23**	**39**	**62**	**122**	**4**	**2**	**0**	**2**	**21**
1984-85	**Detroit**	**NHL**	**77**	**17**	**45**	**62**	**139**	**3**	**1**	**2**	**3**	**20**
1985-86	**Detroit**	**NHL**	**67**	**19**	**41**	**60**	**109**	....	....	....	....	....
	Boston	**NHL**	**13**	**3**	**4**	**7**	**8**	**3**	**1**	**0**	**1**	**6**
1986-87	**Boston**	**NHL**	**66**	**12**	**24**	**36**	**95**	**4**	**0**	**2**	**2**	**2**
1987-88	**Boston**	**NHL**	**62**	**10**	**24**	**34**	**93**	**8**	**0**	**1**	**1**	**6**
	Maine	AHL	2	2	0	2	4	....	....	....	....	....
1988-89	**Edmonton**	**NHL**	**10**	**2**	**7**	**9**	**15**	....	....	....	....	....
	NY Islanders	**NHL**	**33**	**7**	**13**	**20**	**35**	....	....	....	....	....
	Minnesota	**NHL**	**11**	**0**	**9**	**9**	**18**	**3**	**0**	**0**	**0**	**4**
1989-90	Alleghe/Sile	Italy	34	17	32	49	49	9	7	18	25	2
	Buffalo	**NHL**	**1**	**0**	**0**	**0**	**0**	....	....	....	....	....
1990-91	Alleghe/Sile	Italy	36	13	38	51	24	7	3	7	10	6
	NHL Totals		**904**	**222**	**463**	**685**	**1391**	**32**	**4**	**7**	**11**	**63**

Played in NHL All-Star Game (1978, 1980, 1981)

Traded to **Boston** by **Detroit** for Mike O'Connell, March 10, 1986. Traded to **NY Islanders** by **Edmonton** for future considerations, December 6, 1988. Traded to **Minnesota** by **NY Islanders** for future considerations (Mike Kelfer), March 7, 1989. Signed as a free agent by **Buffalo**, March 6, 1990.

LARSSON, PETER (LAHR-suhn)

Center. Shoots left. 5'8", 176 lbs. Born, Sodertalje, Sweden, April 9, 1968.
(New Jersey's 10th choice, 236th overall, in 1989 Entry Draft).

			Regular Season					Playoffs				
Season	Club	Lea	GP	G	A	TP	PIM	GP	G	A	TP	PIM
1985-86	Sodertalje	Swe.	10	0	1	1	2	....	....	....	....	....
1986-87	Sodertalje	Swe.	26	3	4	7	8	....	....	....	....	....
1987-88	Sodertalje	Swe.	34	14	15	29	22	....	....	....	....	....
1988-89	Sodertalje	Swe.	40	20	17	37	26	....	....	....	....	....
1989-90	Sodertalje	Swe.	33	13	14	27	28	2	2	0	2	2
1990-91	Brynas	Swe.	40	13	12	25	12	....	....	....	....	....

LARTER, TYLER

Center. Shoots left. 5'10", 185 lbs. Born, Charlottetown, P.E.I., March 12, 1968.
(Washington's 3rd choice, 78th overall, in 1987 Entry Draft).

			Regular Season					Playoffs				
Season	Club	Lea	GP	G	A	TP	PIM	GP	G	A	TP	PIM
1985-86	S.S. Marie	OHL	60	15	40	55	137	....	....	....	....	....
1986-87	S.S. Marie	OHL	59	34	59	93	122	4	0	2	2	8
1987-88	S.S. Marie	OHL	65	44	65	109	155	4	3	9	12	8
1988-89	Baltimore	AHL	71	9	19	28	189	....	....	....	....	....
1989-90	**Washington**	**NHL**	**1**	**0**	**0**	**0**	**0**	....	....	....	....	....
	Baltimore	AHL	79	31	36	67	104	12	5	6	11	57
1990-91	Baltimore	AHL	62	21	21	42	84	6	1	0	1	13
	NHL Totals		**1**	**0**	**0**	**0**	**0**	....	....	....	....	....

Traded to **Winnipeg** by **Washington** with Bob Joyce and Kent Paynter for Craig Duncanson, Brent Hughes and Simon Wheeldon, May 21, 1991. Claimed by **Minnesota** from **Winnipeg** in Expansion Draft, May 30, 1991.

LATAL, JIRI (LAH-tuhl)

Defense. Shoots left. 6', 190 lbs. Born, Olomouc, Czechoslovakia, February 2, 1967.
(Toronto's 6th choice, 106th overall, in 1985 Entry Draft).

			Regular Season					Playoffs				
Season	Club	Lea	GP	G	A	TP	PIM	GP	G	A	TP	PIM
1984-85	Sparta Praha	Czech.	28	2	2	4	10	....	....	....	....	....
1985-86	Sparta Praha	Czech.	27	3	2	5	....	....	....	....	....	....
1986-87	Sparta Praha	Czech.	12	1	2	3	....	....	....	....	....	....
1987-88	Dukla Trencin	Czech.	46	8	15	23	27	....	....	....	....	....
1988-89	Dukla Trencin	Czech.	48	6	22	28	....	....	....	....	....	....
1989-90	**Philadelphia**	**NHL**	**32**	**6**	**13**	**19**	**6**	....	....	....	....	....
	Hershey	AHL	22	10	18	28	10	....	....	....	....	....
1990-91	**Philadelphia**	**NHL**	**50**	**5**	**21**	**26**	**14**	....	....	....	....	....
	NHL Totals		**82**	**11**	**34**	**45**	**20**	....	....	....	....	....

Traded to **Philadelphia** by **Toronto** for Philadelphia's seventh round choice in 1991 Entry Draft, August 22, 1989.

LATOS, JAMES (LA-toz)

Right wing. Shoots right. 6'1", 200 lbs. Born, Wakaw, Sask., January 4, 1966.

			Regular Season					Playoffs				
Season	Club	Lea	GP	G	A	TP	PIM	GP	G	A	TP	PIM
1986-87	Portland	WHL	69	27	18	45	210	20	5	3	8	56
1987-88	Colorado	IHL	38	11	12	23	98	....	....	....	....	....
1988-89	**NY Rangers**	**NHL**	**1**	**0**	**0**	**0**	**0**	....	....	....	....	....
	Denver	IHL	37	7	5	12	157	4	0	0	0	17
1989-90	Flint	IHL	71	12	15	27	244	4	0	0	0	0
1990-91	Kansas City	IHL	61	14	14	28	187	....	....	....	....	....
	NHL Totals		**1**	**0**	**0**	**0**	**0**	....	....	....	....	....

Signed as a free agent by **NY Rangers**, June 5, 1987.

LATTA, DAVID (LA-tuh)

Left wing. Shoots left. 6'1", 190 lbs. Born, Thunder Bay, Ont., January 3, 1967.
(Quebec's 1st choice, 15th overall, in 1985 Entry Draft).

			Regular Season					Playoffs				
Season	Club	Lea	GP	G	A	TP	PIM	GP	G	A	TP	PIM
1983-84	Kitchener	OHL	66	17	26	43	54	16	3	6	9	9
1984-85	Kitchener	OHL	52	38	27	65	26	4	2	4	6	4
1985-86	**Quebec**	**NHL**	**1**	**0**	**0**	**0**	**0**	....	....	....	....	..
	Fredericton	AHL	3	1	0	1	0	5	0	3	3	0
	Kitchener	OHL	55	36	34	70	60	5	7	1	8	15
1986-87a	Kitchener	OHL	50	32	46	78	46	4	0	3	3	2
1987-88	**Quebec**	**NHL**	**10**	**0**	**0**	**0**	**0**	....	....	....	....	....
	Fredericton	AHL	34	11	21	32	28	15	9	4	13	24
1988-89	**Quebec**	**NHL**	**24**	**4**	**8**	**12**	**4**	....	....	....	....	....
	Halifax	AHL	42	20	26	46	36	4	0	2	2	2
1989-90	Halifax	AHL	34	11	5	16	45	....	....	....	....	....
1990-91	**Quebec**	**NHL**	**1**	**0**	**0**	**0**	**0**	....	....	....	....	....
	Halifax	AHL	22	4	7	11	12	....	....	....	....	....
	Cdn. National	...	30	5	14	19	24	....	....	....	....	....
	NHL Totals		**36**	**4**	**8**	**12**	**4**	....	....	....	....	....

a OHL Third All-Star Team (1987)

LAUER, BRAD (LAU-er)

Left wing. Shoots left. 6', 195 lbs. Born, Humboldt, Sask., October 27, 1966.
(NY Islanders' 3rd choice, 34th overall, in 1985 Entry Draft).

			Regular Season					Playoffs				
Season	Club	Lea	GP	G	A	TP	PIM	GP	G	A	TP	PIM
1983-84	Regina	WHL	60	5	7	12	51	16	0	1	1	24
1984-85	Regina	WHL	72	33	46	79	57	8	6	6	12	9
1985-86	Regina	WHL	57	36	38	74	69	10	4	5	9	2
1986-87	**NY Islanders**	**NHL**	**61**	**7**	**14**	**21**	**65**	**6**	**2**	**0**	**2**	**4**
1987-88	**NY Islanders**	**NHL**	**69**	**17**	**18**	**35**	**67**	**5**	**3**	**1**	**4**	**4**
1988-89	**NY Islanders**	**NHL**	**14**	**3**	**2**	**5**	**2**	....	....	....	....	....
	Springfield	AHL	8	1	5	6	0	....	....	....	....	....
1989-90	**NY Islanders**	**NHL**	**63**	**6**	**18**	**24**	**19**	**4**	**0**	**2**	**2**	**10**
	Springfield	AHL	7	4	2	6	0	....	....	....	....	....
1990-91	**NY Islanders**	**NHL**	**44**	**4**	**8**	**12**	**45**	....	....	....	....	....
	Capital Dist.	AHL	11	5	11	16	14	....	....	....	....	....
	NHL Totals		**251**	**37**	**60**	**97**	**198**	**15**	**5**	**3**	**8**	**18**

LAUS, PAUL

Defense. Shoots right. 6'1", 212 lbs. Born, Beamsville, Ont., September 26, 1970.
(Pittsburgh's 2nd choice, 37th overall, in 1989 Entry Draft).

			Regular Season					Playoffs				
Season	Club	Lea	GP	G	A	TP	PIM	GP	G	A	TP	PIM
1987-88	Hamilton	OHL	56	1	9	10	171	14	0	0	0	28
1988-89	Niagara Falls	OHL	49	1	10	11	225	15	0	5	5	56
1989-90	Niagara Falls	OHL	60	13	35	48	231	16	6	16	22	71
1990-91	Albany	IHL	7	0	0	0	7	....	....	....	....	....
	Muskegon	IHL	35	3	4	7	103	4	0	0	0	13

LAVIGNE, ERIC

Defense. Shoots left. 6'2", 207 lbs. Born, Victoriaville, Que., November 4, 1972.
(Washington's 3rd choice, 25th overall, in 1991 Entry Draft).

			Regular Season					Playoffs				
Season	Club	Lea	GP	G	A	TP	PIM	GP	G	A	TP	PIM
1989-90a	Hull	QMJHL	69	7	11	18	203	11	0	0	0	32
1990-91	Hull	QMJHL	66	11	11	22	153	4	0	1	1	16

a QMJHL Third All-Star Team (1990)

LAVIOLETTE, PETER (LAH-vee-oh-LEHT)

Defense. Shoots left. 6'2", 200 lbs. Born, Norwood, MA, December 7, 1964.

			Regular Season					Playoffs				
Season	Club	Lea	GP	G	A	TP	PIM	GP	G	A	TP	PIM
1985-86	Westfield State	NCAA	19	12	8	20	44	....	....	....	....	....
1986-87	Indianapolis	IHL	72	10	20	30	146	....	....	....	....	....
1987-88	U.S. National	...	54	4	20	24	82	....	....	....	....	....
	U.S. Olympic	...	5	0	2	2	4	....	....	....	....	....
	Colorado	IHL	19	2	5	7	27	9	3	5	8	7
1988-89	**NY Rangers**	**NHL**	**12**	**0**	**0**	**0**	**6**	....	....	....	....	....
	Denver	IHL	57	6	19	25	120	3	0	0	0	4
1989-90	Flint	IHL	62	6	18	24	82	4	0	0	0	4
1990-91	Binghamton	AHL	65	12	24	36	72	10	2	7	9	30
	NHL Totals		**12**	**0**	**0**	**0**	**6**	....	....	....	....	....

Signed as a free agent by **NY Rangers**, August 12, 1987.

LAVISH, JAMES

Right wing. Shoots right. 5'11", 175 lbs. Born, Albany, NY, October 13, 1970.
(Boston's 9th choice, 185th overall, in 1989 Entry Draft).

			Regular Season					Playoffs				
Season	Club	Lea	GP	G	A	TP	PIM	GP	G	A	TP	PIM
1989-90	Yale	ECAC	27	6	11	17	40	....	....	....	....	....
1990-91	Yale	ECAC	29	13	7	20	42	....	....	....	....	....

LAVOIE, DOMINIC

Defense. Shoots right. 6'2", 205 lbs. Born, Montreal, Que., November 21, 1967.

			Regular Season					Playoffs				
Season	Club	Lea	GP	G	A	TP	PIM	GP	G	A	TP	PIM
1985-86	St. Jean	QMJHL	70	12	37	49	99	10	2	3	5	20
1986-87	St. Jean	QMJHL	64	12	42	54	97	8	2	7	9	2
1987-88	Peoria	IHL	65	7	26	33	54	7	2	2	4	8
1988-89	**St. Louis**	**NHL**	**1**	**0**	**0**	**0**	**0**	....	....	....	....	....
	Peoria	IHL	69	11	31	42	98	4	0	0	0	4
1989-90	**St. Louis**	**NHL**	**13**	**1**	**1**	**2**	**16**	....	....	....	....	....
	Peoria	IHL	58	19	23	42	32	5	2	2	4	16
1990-91	**St. Louis**	**NHL**	**6**	**1**	**2**	**3**	**2**	....	....	....	....	....
a	Peoria	IHL	46	15	25	40	72	16	5	7	12	22
	NHL Totals		**20**	**2**	**3**	**5**	**18**	....	....	....	....	....

a IHL First All-Star Team (1991)

Signed as a free agent by **St. Louis**, September 22, 1986.

LAWLESS, PAUL

Left wing. Shoots left. 5'11", 185 lbs. Born, Scarborough, Ont., July 2, 1964.
(Hartford's 1st choice, 14th overall, in 1982 Entry Draft).

			Regular Season					Playoffs				
Season	Club	Lea	GP	G	A	TP	PIM	GP	G	A	TP	PIM
1981-82	Windsor	OHL	68	24	25	49	47	9	1	1	2	4
1982-83	Windsor	OHL	33	15	20	35	25	....	....	....	....	....
	Hartford	**NHL**	**47**	**6**	**9**	**15**	**4**	....	....	....	....	....
1983-84	**Hartford**	**NHL**	**6**	**0**	**3**	**3**	**0**	....	....	....	....	....
a	Windsor	OHL	55	31	49	80	26	2	0	1	1	0
1984-85	Binghamton	AHL	8	1	1	2	0	....	....	....	....	....
	Salt Lake	IHL	72	49	48	97	14	7	5	3	8	20
1985-86	**Hartford**	**NHL**	**64**	**17**	**21**	**38**	**20**	**1**	**0**	**0**	**0**	**0**
1986-87	**Hartford**	**NHL**	**60**	**22**	**32**	**54**	**14**	**2**	**0**	**2**	**2**	**2**
1987-88	**Hartford**	**NHL**	**28**	**4**	**5**	**9**	**16**	....	....	....	....	....
	Philadelphia	**NHL**	**8**	**0**	**5**	**5**	**0**	....	....	....	....	....
	Vancouver	**NHL**	**13**	**0**	**1**	**1**	**0**	....	....	....	....	....
1988-89	Milwaukee	IHL	53	30	35	65	58	....	....	....	....	....
	Toronto	**NHL**	**7**	**0**	**0**	**0**	**0**	....	....	....	....	....
1989-90	**Toronto**	**NHL**	**6**	**0**	**1**	**1**	**0**	....	....	....	....	....
	Newmarket	AHL	3	1	0	1	0	....	....	....	....	....
1990-91	Lausanne	Switz.	36	26	29	55	....	....	....	....	....	....
	NHL Totals		**239**	**49**	**77**	**126**	**54**	**3**	**0**	**2**	**2**	**2**

a OHL Second All-Star Team (1984)

Traded to **Philadelphia** by **Hartford** for Lindsay Carson, January 22, 1988. Traded to **Vancouver** by **Philadelphia** with Vancouver's fifth round draft choice (acquired March 7, 1989 by Edmonton, who selected Peter White) in1989 Entry Draft — acquired earlier by Philadelphia — for Willie Huber, March 1, 1988. Traded to **Toronto** by **Vancouver** for the rights to Peter Deboer, February 27, 1989.

LAWTON, BRIAN

Left wing. Shoots left. 6', 190 lbs. Born, New Brunswick, NJ, June 29, 1965.
(Minnesota's 1st choice and 1st overall in 1983 Entry Draft).

			Regular Season					Playoffs				
Season	Club	Lea	GP	G	A	TP	PIM	GP	G	A	TP	PIM
1982-83	Mt. St. Charles	HS	23	40	43	83	....	....	....	....	....	....
1983-84	**Minnesota**	**NHL**	**58**	**10**	**21**	**31**	**33**	**5**	**0**	**0**	**0**	**10**
1984-85	**Minnesota**	**NHL**	**40**	**5**	**6**	**11**	**24**	....	....	....	....	....
	Springfield	AHL	42	14	28	42	37	4	1	1	2	2
1985-86	**Minnesota**	**NHL**	**65**	**18**	**17**	**35**	**36**	**3**	**0**	**1**	**1**	**2**
1986-87	**Minnesota**	**NHL**	**66**	**21**	**23**	**44**	**86**	....	....	....	....	....
1987-88	**Minnesota**	**NHL**	**74**	**17**	**24**	**41**	**71**	....	....	....	....	....
1988-89	**NY Rangers**	**NHL**	**30**	**7**	**10**	**17**	**39**	....	....	....	....	....
	Hartford	**NHL**	**35**	**10**	**16**	**26**	**28**	**3**	**1**	**0**	**1**	**0**
1989-90	**Hartford**	**NHL**	**13**	**2**	**1**	**3**	**6**	....	....	....	....	....
	Quebec	**NHL**	**14**	**5**	**6**	**11**	**10**	....	....	....	....	....
	Boston	**NHL**	**8**	**0**	**0**	**0**	**14**	....	....	....	....	....
	Maine	AHL	5	0	0	0	14	....	....	....	....	....
1990-91	Phoenix	IHL	63	26	40	66	108	11	4	9	13	40
	NHL Totals		**403**	**95**	**124**	**219**	**347**	**11**	**1**	**1**	**2**	**12**

Traded to **NY Rangers** by **Minnesota** with Igor Liba, and the rights to Eric Bennett for Paul Jerrard and Mark Tinordi, the rights to Bret Barnett and Mike Sullivan, and Los Angeles' third-round choice (Murray Garbutt) in 1989 Entry Draft — acquired March 10, 1987 by Minnesota — October 11, 1988. Traded to **Hartford** by **NY Rangers** with Norm MacIver and Don Maloney for Carey Wilson and Hartford's fifth-round choice (Lubos Rob) in 1990 Entry Draft, December 26, 1988. Claimed on waivers by **Quebec** from **Hartford**, December 1, 1989. Signed as a free agent by **Boston**, February 7, 1990. Signed as a free agent by **Los Angeles**, July 27, 1990. Signed as a free agent by **San Jose**, August 9, 1991.

LAXDAL, DEREK

Right wing. Shoots right. 6'1", 175 lbs. Born, St. Boniface, Man., February 21, 1966.
(Toronto's 7th choice, 151st overall, in 1984 Entry Draft).

			Regular Season					Playoffs				
Season	Club	Lea	GP	G	A	TP	PIM	GP	G	A	TP	PIM
1982-83	Portland	WHL	39	4	9	13	27	14	0	2	2	2
1983-84	Brandon	WHL	70	23	20	43	86	12	0	4	4	10
1984-85	**Toronto**	**NHL**	**3**	**0**	**0**	**0**	**6**	....	....	....	....	....
	Brandon	WHL	69	61	41	102	74	....	....	....	....	....
	St. Catharines	AHL	5	3	2	5	2	....	....	....	....	....
1985-86	Brandon	WHL	42	34	35	69	62	....	....	....	....	....
	N. Westminster	WHL	18	9	6	15	14	....	....	....	....	....
	St. Catharines	AHL	7	0	1	1	15	12	1	1	2	24
1986-87	**Toronto**	**NHL**	**2**	**0**	**0**	**0**	**7**	....	....	....	....	....
	Newmarket	AHL	78	24	20	44	69	....	....	....	....	....
1987-88	**Toronto**	**NHL**	**5**	**0**	**0**	**0**	**6**	....	....	....	....	....
	Newmarket	AHL	67	18	25	43	81	....	....	....	....	....
1988-89	**Toronto**	**NHL**	**41**	**9**	**6**	**15**	**65**	....	....	....	....	....
	Newmarket	AHL	34	22	22	44	53	2	0	2	2	5
1989-90	Newmarket	AHL	23	7	8	15	52	....	....	....	....	....
	NY Islanders	**NHL**	**12**	**3**	**1**	**4**	**6**	**1**	**0**	**2**	**2**	**2**
	Springfield	AHL	28	13	12	25	42	13	8	6	14	47
1990-91	**NY Islanders**	**NHL**	**4**	**0**	**0**	**0**	**0**	....	....	....	....	....
	Capital Dist.	AHL	65	14	25	39	75	....	....	....	....	....
	NHL Totals		**67**	**12**	**7**	**19**	**90**	**1**	**0**	**2**	**2**	**2**

Traded to **NY Islanders** by **Toronto** with Jack Capuano and Paul Gagne for Mike Stevens and Gilles Thibaudeau, December 20, 1989.

LAYLIN, CORY

Left wing. Shoots left. 5'10", 170 lbs. Born, Minneapolis, MN, January 24, 1970.
(Pittsburgh's 10th choice, 214th overall, in 1988 Entry Draft).

			Regular Season					Playoffs				
Season	Club	Lea	GP	G	A	TP	PIM	GP	G	A	TP	PIM
1988-89	U. Minnesota	WCHA	47	14	10	24	24	....	....	....	....	....
1989-90	U. Minnesota	WCHA	39	13	14	27	31	....	....	....	....	....
1990-91	U. Minnesota	WCHA	40	12	13	25	24	....	....	....	....	....

LAZARO, JEFF

Left wing. Shoots left. 5'10", 180 lbs. Born, Waltham, MA, March 21, 1968.

			Regular Season					Playoffs				
Season	Club	Lea	GP	G	A	TP	PIM	GP	G	A	TP	PIM
1986-87	N. Hampshire	H.E.	38	7	14	21	38	....	....	....	....	....
1987-88	N. Hampshire	H.E.	30	4	13	17	48	....	....	....	....	....
1988-89	N. Hampshire	H.E.	31	8	14	22	38	....	....	....	....	....
1989-90	N. Hampshire	H.E.	39	16	19	35	34	....	....	....	....	....
1990-91	**Boston**	**NHL**	**49**	**5**	**13**	**18**	**67**	**19**	**3**	**2**	**5**	**30**
	Maine	AHL	26	8	11	19	18	....	....	....	....	....
	NHL Totals		**49**	**5**	**13**	**18**	**67**	**19**	**3**	**2**	**5**	**30**

Signed as a free agent by **Boston**, September 26, 1990.

LEACH, JAMIE

Right wing. Shoots right. 6'1", 198 lbs. Born, Winnipeg, Man., August 25, 1969.
(Pittsburgh's 3rd choice, 47th overall, in 1987 Entry Draft).

			Regular Season					Playoffs				
Season	Club	Lea	GP	G	A	TP	PIM	GP	G	A	TP	PIM
1985-86	N. Westminster	WHL	58	8	7	15	20	....	....	....	....	....
1986-87	Hamilton	OHL	64	12	19	31	67	....	....	....	....	....
1987-88	Hamilton	OHL	64	24	19	43	79	14	6	7	13	12
1988-89a	Niagara Falls	OHL	58	45	62	107	47	17	9	11	20	25
1989-90	**Pittsburgh**	**NHL**	**10**	**0**	**3**	**3**	**0**	....	....	....	....	....
	Muskegon	IHL	72	22	36	58	39	15	9	4	13	14
1990-91	**Pittsburgh**	**NHL**	**7**	**2**	**0**	**2**	**0**	....	....	....	....	....
	Muskegon	IHL	43	33	22	55	26	....	....	....	....	....
	NHL Totals		**17**	**2**	**3**	**5**	**0**	....	....	....	....	....

a OHL Third All-Star Team (1989)

LEACH, STEPHEN

Right Wing. Shoots right. 5'11", 180 lbs. Born, Cambridge, MA, January 16, 1966.
(Washington's 2nd choice, 34th overall, in 1984 Entry Draft).

			Regular Season					Playoffs				
Season	Club	Lea	GP	G	A	TP	PIM	GP	G	A	TP	PIM
1984-85	N. Hampshire	H.E.	41	12	25	37	53	....	....	....	....	....
1985-86	**Washington**	**NHL**	**11**	**1**	**1**	**2**	**2**	**6**	**0**	**1**	**1**	**0**
	N. Hampshire	H.E.	25	22	6	28	30	....	....	....	....	....
1986-87	**Washington**	**NHL**	**15**	**1**	**0**	**1**	**6**	....	....	....	....	....
	Binghamton	AHL	54	18	21	39	39	13	3	1	4	6
1987-88	**Washington**	**NHL**	**8**	**1**	**1**	**2**	**17**	**9**	**2**	**1**	**3**	**0**
	U.S. National	...	49	26	20	46	30	....	....	....	....	....
	U.S. Olympic	...	6	1	2	3	0	....	....	....	....	....
1988-89	**Washington**	**NHL**	**74**	**11**	**19**	**30**	**94**	**6**	**1**	**0**	**1**	**12**
1989-90	**Washington**	**NHL**	**70**	**18**	**14**	**32**	**104**	**14**	**2**	**2**	**4**	**8**
1990-91	**Washington**	**NHL**	**68**	**11**	**19**	**30**	**99**	**9**	**1**	**2**	**3**	**8**
	NHL Totals		**246**	**43**	**54**	**97**	**322**	**44**	**6**	**6**	**12**	**28**

Traded to **Boston** by **Washington** for Randy Burridge, June 21, 1991.

LEAHY, GREG

Center. Shoots left. 6'3", 187 lbs. Born, North Bay, Ont., February 19, 1970.
(NY Rangers' 8th choice, 139th overall, in 1989 Entry Draft).

			Regular Season					Playoffs				
Season	Club	Lea	GP	G	A	TP	PIM	GP	G	A	TP	PIM
1986-87	Calgary	WHL	64	6	16	22	170	....	....	....	....	....
1987-88	Lethbridge	WHL	56	18	24	42	161	....	....	....	....	....
1988-89	Portland	WHL	66	28	49	77	128	19	16	13	29	33
1989-90	Portland	WHL	50	20	43	63	131	....	....	....	....	....
1990-91	Saskatoon	WHL	71	27	39	66	148	....	....	....	....	....

LEAVINS, JIM (LEH vihns)

Defense. Shoots left. 5'11", 185 lbs. Born, Dinsmore, Sask., July 28, 1960.

			Regular Season					Playoffs				
Season	Club	Lea	GP	G	A	TP	PIM	GP	G	A	TP	PIM
1981-82	Denver	WCHA	41	8	34	42	56	....	....	....	....	....
1982-83	Denver	WCHA	33	16	24	40	20	....	....	....	....	....
1983-84	Denver	WCHA	39	13	26	39	38	....	....	....	..	..
1984-85	Fort Wayne	IHL	76	5	20	25	57	13	3	8	11	10
1985-86	**Detroit**	**NHL**	**37**	**2**	**11**	**13**	**26**	....	....	....	....	....
	Adirondack	AHL	36	4	21	25	19	....	....	....	....	....
1986-87	**NY Rangers**	**NHL**	**4**	**0**	**1**	**1**	**4**	....	....	....	....	....
	New Haven	AHL	54	7	21	28	16	7	0	4	4	2
1987-88	New Haven	AHL	11	2	5	7	8	....	....	....	....	....
a	Salt Lake	IHL	68	12	45	57	45	16	5	5	10	8
1988-89	Salt Lake	IHL	25	8	13	21	14	14	2	11	13	6
	KooKoo	Fin.	42	12	11	23	39	....	....	....	....	....
1989-90	Salt Lake	IHL	11	0	6	6	2	....	....	....	....	....
	KooKoo	Fin.	44	7	24	31	36	....	....	....	....	....
1990-91	Farjestad	Swe.	40	9	8	17	24	....	....	....	....	....
	NHL Totals		**41**	**2**	**12**	**14**	**30**	....	....	....	....	....

a IHL Second All-Star Team (1988)

Signed as a free agent by **Detroit**, November 9, 1985. Traded to **NY Rangers** by **Detroit** with Kelly Kisio and Lane Lambert for Glen Hanlon and **New York's** third-round choices in 1987 (Dennis Holland) and 1988 Entry Drafts, July 29, 1986. Traded to **Calgary** by **NY Rangers** for Don Mercier, November 6, 1987.

LEBEAU, BENOIT (luh-BOH)

Left wing. Shoots left. 6'1", 190 lbs. Born, Montreal, Que., June 4, 1968.
(Winnipeg's 6th choice, 101st overall, in 1988 Entry Draft).

			Regular Season					Playoffs				
Season	Club	Lea	GP	G	A	TP	PIM	GP	G	A	TP	PIM
1987-88	Merrimack	NCAA	40	35	38	73	52	....	....	....	....	....
1988-89	Merrimack	NCAA	32	18	20	38	46	....	....	....	....	....
1989-90	Merrimack	H.E.	32	9	6	15	46	....	....	....	....	....
1990-91	Merrimack	H.E.	21	3	4	7	12	....	....	....	....	....

LEBEAU, PATRICK

Left wing. Shoots left. 5'10", 172 lbs. Born, St. Jerome, Que., March 17, 1970.
(Montreal's 8th choice, 167th overall, in 1989 Entry Draft).

			Regular Season					Playoffs				
Season	Club	Lea	GP	G	A	TP	PIM	GP	G	A	TP	PIM
1986-87	Shawinigan	QMJHL	66	26	52	78	90	13	2	6	8	17
1987-88	Shawinigan	QMJHL	53	43	56	99	116	11	3	9	12	16
1988-89	St. Jean	QMJHL	49	43	70	113	71	4	4	3	7	6
1989-90a	Victoriaville	QMJHL	72	68	*106	*174	109	16	7	15	22	12
1990-91	**Montreal**	**NHL**	**2**	**1**	**1**	**2**	**0**	....	....	....	....	....
bc	Fredericton	AHL	69	50	51	101	32	9	4	7	11	8
	NHL Totals		**2**	**1**	**1**	**2**	**0**	....	....	....	....	....

a QMJHL First All-Star Team (1990)
b AHL Second All-Star Team (1991)
c Won Dudley "Red" Garrett Memorial Trophy (Top Rookie – AHL) (1991)

LEBEAU, STEPHAN (leh-BOH)

Center. Shoots right. 5'10", 172 lbs. Born, St. Jerome, Que., February 28, 1968.

			Regular Season					Playoffs				
Season	Club	Lea	GP	G	A	TP	PIM	GP	G	A	TP	PIM
1984-85	Shawinigan	QMJHL	66	41	38	79	18	9	4	5	9	4
1985-86	Shawinigan	QMJHL	72	69	77	146	22	5	4	2	6	4
1986-87a	Shawinigan	QMJHL	65	77	90	167	60	14	9	20	29	20
1987-88a	Shawinigan	QMJHL	67	*94	94	188	66	11	17	9	26	10
	Sherbrooke	AHL	...	...	...	...	...	1	0	1	1	0
1988-89	**Montreal**	**NHL**	**1**	**0**	**1**	**1**	**2**	....	....	....	....	....
bcde	Sherbrooke	AHL	78	*70	64	*134	47	6	1	4	5	8
1989-90	**Montreal**	**NHL**	**57**	**15**	**20**	**35**	**11**	**2**	**3**	**0**	**3**	**0**
1990-91	**Montreal**	**NHL**	**73**	**22**	**31**	**53**	**24**	**7**	**2**	**1**	**3**	**2**
	NHL Totals		**131**	**37**	**52**	**89**	**37**	**9**	**5**	**1**	**6**	**2**

a QMJHL Second All-Star Team (1987, 1988)
b AHL First All-Star Team (1989)
c Won Dudley "Red" Garrett Memorial Trophy (Top Rookie-AHL) (1989)
d Won John B. Sollenberger Trophy (Top Scorer-AHL) 1989)
e Won Les Cunningham Trophy (MVP-AHL) (1989)

Signed as a free agent by **Montreal**, September 27, 1986.

LeBLANC, JOHN GLENN

Left wing. Shoots left. 6'1", 190 lbs. Born, Campbellton, N.B., January 21, 1964.

			Regular Season					Playoffs				
Season	Club	Lea	GP	G	A	TP	PIM	GP	G	A	TP	PIM
1983-84	Hull	QMJHL	69	39	35	74	32	....	....	....	....	....
1984-85	New Brunswick	AUAA	24	25	34	59	32	....	....	....	....	....
1985-86a	New Brunswick	AUAA	24	38	28	66	35	....	....	....	....	....
1986-87	**Vancouver**	**NHL**	**2**	**1**	**0**	**1**	**0**	....	....	....	....	....
	Fredericton	AHL	75	40	30	70	27	....	....	....	....	....
1987-88	**Vancouver**	**NHL**	**41**	**12**	**10**	**22**	**18**	....	....	....	....	....
	Fredericton	AHL	35	26	25	51	54	15	6	7	13	34
1988-89	**Milwaukee**	**IHL**	**61**	**39**	**31**	**70**	**42**	....	....	....	....	....
	Edmonton	NHL	2	1	0	1	0	1	0	0	0	0
	Cape Breton	AHL	3	4	0	4	0	....	....	....	....	....
1989-90	Cape Breton	AHL	77	*54	34	88	50	6	4	0	4	4
1990-91	Cape Breton	AHL	DID NOT PLAY									
	NHL Totals		**45**	**14**	**10**	**24**	**18**	**1**	**0**	**0**	**0**	**0**

a Canadian University Player of the Year (1986)

Signed as a free agent by **Vancouver**, April 12, 1986. Traded to **Edmonton** by **Vancouver** with Vancouver's fifth-round choice (Peter White) in 1989 Entry Draft for Doug Smith and Gregory C. Adams, March 7, 1989. Traded to **Winnipeg** by **Edmonton** with Edmonton's tenth round choice in 1992 Entry Draft for Winnipeg's fifth round choice (Ryan Haggerty) in 1991 Entry Draft, June 12, 1991.

LeBRUN, SEAN (luh-BRUN)

Left wing. Shoots left. 6'2", 200 lbs. Born, Prince George, B.C., May 2, 1969.
(New York Islanders' 3rd choice, 37th overall, in 1988 Entry Draft).

			Regular Season					Playoffs				
Season	Club	Lea	GP	G	A	TP	PIM	GP	G	A	TP	PIM
1985-86	Spokane	WHL	70	6	11	17	41	....	....	....	....	....
1986-87	Spokane	WHL	6	2	5	7	9	....	....	....	....	....
	N. Westminster	WHL	55	21	32	53	47	....	....	....	....	....
1987-88a	N. Westminster	WHL	72	36	53	89	59	5	1	3	4	2
1988-89	Tri-Cities	WHL	71	52	73	125	92	5	0	4	4	13
1989-90	Springfield	AHL	63	9	33	42	20	....	....	....	....	....
1990-91	Capital Dist.	AHL	56	14	26	40	35	....	....	....	....	....

a WHL West Division Second All-Star Team (1988)

LeCLAIR, JOHN

Left Wing. Shoots left. 6'2", 215 lbs. Born, St. Albans, VT, July 5, 1969.
(Montreal's 2nd choice, 33rd overall, in 1987 Entry Draft).

			Regular Season					Playoffs				
Season	Club	Lea	GP	G	A	TP	PIM	GP	G	A	TP	PIM
1987-88	U. of Vermont	ECAC	31	12	22	34	62	....	....	....	....	....
1988-89	U. of Vermont	ECAC	18	9	12	21	40	....	....	....	....	....
1989-90	U. of Vermont	ECAC	10	10	6	16	38	....	....	....	....	....
1990-91a	U. of Vermont	ECAC	33	25	20	45	58	....	....	....	....	....
	Montreal	**NHL**	**10**	**2**	**5**	**7**	**2**	**3**	**0**	**0**	**0**	**0**
	NHL Totals		**10**	**2**	**5**	**7**	**2**	**3**	**0**	**0**	**0**	**2**

a ECAC Second All-Star Team (1991)

LEDYARD, GRANT

Defense. Shoots left. 6'2", 200 lbs.   Born, Winnipeg, Man., November 19, 1961.

Season	Club	Lea	Regular Season					Playoffs				
			GP	G	A	TP	PIM	GP	G	A	TP	PIM
1980-81	Saskatoon	WHL	71	9	28	37	148	....	....	....	....	....
1981-82	Fort Garry	MJHL	63	25	45	70	150	....	....	....	....	....
1982-83	Tulsa	CHL	80	13	29	42	115	....	....	....	....	....
1983-84a	Tulsa	CHL	58	9	17	26	71	9	5	4	9	10
1984-85	NY Rangers	NHL	42	8	12	20	53	3	0	2	2	4
	New Haven	AHL	36	6	20	26	18	....	....	....	....	....
1985-86	NY Rangers	NHL	27	2	9	11	20	....	....	....	....	....
	Los Angeles	NHL	52	7	18	25	78	....	....	....	....	....
1986-87	Los Angeles	NHL	67	14	23	37	93	5	0	0	0	10
1987-88	Los Angeles	NHL	23	1	7	8	52	....	....	....	....	....
	New Haven	AHL	3	2	1	3	4	....	....	....	....	....
	Washington	NHL	21	4	3	7	14	14	1	0	1	30
1988-89	Washington	NHL	61	3	11	14	43	....	....	....	....	....
	Buffalo	NHL	13	1	5	6	8	5	1	2	3	2
1989-90	Buffalo	NHL	67	2	13	15	37	....	....	....	....	....
1990-91	Buffalo	NHL	60	2	23	31	46	6	3	3	6	10
	NHL Totals		433	50	124	174	444	33	5	7	12	56

a Won Bob Gassoff Trophy (CHL's Most Improved Defenseman) (1984)
Signed as a free agent by **NY Rangers**, July 7, 1982. Traded to **Los Angeles** by **NY Rangers** with Roland Melanson for Los Angeles' fourth-round choice in 1987 Entry Draft (Michael Sullivan) and Brian MacLellan, December 7, 1985. Traded to **Washington** by **Los Angeles** for Craig Laughlin, February 9, 1988. Traded to **Buffalo** by **Washington** with Clint Malarchuk and Washington's sixth-round choice (Brian Holzinger) in 1991 Entry Draft for Calle Johansson and Buffalo's second-round choice (Byron Dafoe) in 1989 Entry Draft, March 7, 1989.

LEEMAN, GARY

Right wing. Shoots right. 5'11", 175 lbs.   Born, Toronto, Ont., February 19, 1964.
(Toronto's 2nd choice, 24th overall, in 1982 Entry Draft).

Season	Club	Lea	Regular Season					Playoffs				
			GP	G	A	TP	PIM	GP	G	A	TP	PIM
1981-82	Regina	WHL	72	19	41	60	112	3	2	2	4	0
1982-83ab	Regina	WHL	63	24	62	86	88	5	1	5	6	4
	Toronto	NHL	....	....	....	....	....	2	0	0	0	0
1983-84	Toronto	NHL	52	4	8	12	31	....	....	....	....	....
1984-85	Toronto	NHL	53	5	26	31	72	....	....	....	....	....
	St. Catharines	AHL	7	2	2	4	11	....	....	....	....	....
1985-86	Toronto	NHL	53	9	23	32	20	10	2	10	12	2
	St. Catharines	AHL	25	15	13	28	6	....	....	....	....	....
1986-87	Toronto	NHL	80	21	31	52	66	5	0	1	1	14
1987-88	Toronto	NHL	80	30	31	61	62	2	2	0	2	2
1988-89	Toronto	NHL	61	32	43	75	66	....	....	....	....	....
1989-90	Toronto	NHL	80	51	44	95	63	5	3	3	6	16
1990-91	Toronto	NHL	52	17	12	29	39	....	....	....	....	....
	NHL Totals		511	169	218	387	419	24	7	14	21	34

a WHL First All-Star Team (1983)
b Named WHL's Top Defenseman (1983)
Played in NHL All-Star Game (1989)

LEETCH, BRIAN

Defense. Shoots left. 5'11", 185 lbs.   Born, Corpus Christi, TX, March 3, 1968.
(NY Rangers' 1st choice, 9th overall, in 1986 Entry Draft).

Season	Club	Lea	Regular Season					Playoffs				
			GP	G	A	TP	PIM	GP	G	A	TP	PIM
1986-87abcd	Boston College	H.E.	37	9	38	47	10	....	....	....	....	....
1987-88	U.S. National	...	50	13	61	74	38	....	....	....	....	....
	U.S. Olympic	...	6	1	5	6	4	....	....	....	....	....
	NY Rangers	NHL	17	2	12	14	0	....	....	....	....	....
1988-89ef	NY Rangers	NHL	68	23	48	71	50	4	3	2	5	2
1989-90	NY Rangers	NHL	72	11	45	56	26	....	....	....	....	....
1990-91g	NY Rangers	NHL	80	16	72	88	42	6	1	3	4	0
	NHL Totals		237	52	177	229	118	10	4	5	9	2

a Hockey East Player of the Year (1987)
b Hockey East Rookie of the Year (1987)
c Hockey East First All-Star Team (1987)
d NCAA East First All-American Team (1987)
e NHL All-Rookie Team (1989)
f Won Calder Memorial Trophy (1989)
g NHL Second All-Star Team (1991)
Played in NHL All-Star Game (1990, 1991)

LEFEBVRE, SYLVAIN

Defense. Shoots left. 6'2", 204 lbs.   Born, Richmond, Que., October 14, 1967.

Season	Club	Lea	Regular Season					Playoffs				
			GP	G	A	TP	PIM	GP	G	A	TP	PIM
1984-85	Laval	QMJHL	66	7	5	12	31	....	....	....	....	....
1985-86	Laval	QMJHL	71	8	17	25	48	14	1	0	1	25
1986-87	Laval	QMJHL	70	10	36	46	44	15	1	6	7	12
1987-88	Sherbrooke	AHL	79	3	24	27	73	6	2	3	5	4
1988-89a	Sherbrooke	AHL	77	15	32	47	119	6	1	3	4	4
1989-90	Montreal	NHL	68	3	10	13	61	6	0	0	0	2
1990-91	Montreal	NHL	63	5	18	23	30	11	1	0	1	6
	NHL Totals		131	8	28	36	91	17	1	0	1	8

a AHL Second All-Star Team (1989)
Signed as a free agent by **Montreal**, September 24, 1986.

LEGAULT, ALEXANDRE

Defense. Shoots right. 6'1", 205 lbs.   Born, Chicoutimi, Que., December 27, 1971.
(Edmonton's 2nd choice, 38th overall, in 1990 Entry Draft).

Season	Club	Lea	Regular Season					Playoffs				
			GP	G	A	TP	PIM	GP	G	A	TP	PIM
1989-90	Boston U.	H.E.	43	9	21	30	54	....	....	....	....	....
1990-91	Boston U.	H.E.	19	2	9	11	30	....	....	....	....	....

LEHMANN, TOMMY   (LEH-mahn)

Center. Shoots left. 6'1", 185 lbs.   Born, Solna, Sweden, February 3, 1964.
(Boston's 11th choice, 228th overall, in 1982 Entry Draft).

Season	Club	Lea	Regular Season					Playoffs				
			GP	G	A	TP	PIM	GP	G	A	TP	PIM
1982-83	AIK	Swe.	28	1	5	6	2	3	0	0	0	0
1983-84	AIK	Swe.	23	4	5	9	6	6	2	2	4	0
1984-85	AIK	Swe.	34	13	13	26	6	....	....	....	....	....
1985-86	AIK	Swe.	35	11	13	24	12	....	....	....	....	....
1986-87	AIK	Swe.	31	25	15	40	12	....	....	....	....	....
1987-88	Boston	NHL	9	1	3	4	6	....	....	....	....	....
	Maine	AHL	11	3	5	8	2	....	....	....	....	....
1988-89	Boston	NHL	26	4	2	6	10	....	....	....	....	....
	Maine	AHL	26	1	13	14	12	....	....	....	....	....
1989-90	AIK	Swe.	22	7	9	16	12	3	1	1	2	0
	Edmonton	NHL	1	0	0	0	0	....	....	....	....	....
	Cape Breton	AHL	19	6	11	17	7	6	2	2	4	0
1990-91	AIK	Swe.	37	11	15	26	40	....	....	....	....	....
	NHL Totals		36	5	5	10	16					

Traded to **Edmonton** by **Boston** for Edmonton's third-round choice (Wes Walz) in 1989 Entry Draft, June 17, 1989.

LEHTO, JONI

Defense. Shoots left. 6', 175 lbs.   Born, Turku, Finland, July 15, 1970.
(NY Islanders' 5th choice, 111th overall, in 1990 Entry Draft).

Season	Club	Lea	Regular Season					Playoffs				
			GP	G	A	TP	PIM	GP	G	A	TP	PIM
1989-90a	Ottawa	OHL	60	17	55	72	58	....	....	....	....	....
1990-91	Ottawa	OHL	8	2	10	12	8	....	....	....	....	....

a OHL Second All-Star Team (1990)

LEMIEUX, CLAUDE   (lehm-YOO)

Right wing. Shoots right. 6'1", 215 lbs.   Born, Buckingham, Que., July 16, 1965.
(Montreal's 2nd choice, 26th overall, in 1983 Entry Draft).

Season	Club	Lea	Regular Season					Playoffs				
			GP	G	A	TP	PIM	GP	G	A	TP	PIM
1982-83	Trois Rivières	QMJHL	62	28	38	66	187	4	1	0	1	30
1983-84	Montreal	NHL	8	1	1	2	12	....	....	....	....	....
	Verdun	QMJHL	51	41	45	86	225	9	8	12	20	63
	Nova Scotia	AHL	....	....	....	....	....	2	1	0	1	0
1984-85	Montreal	NHL	1	0	1	1	7	....	....	....	....	....
ab	Verdun	QMJHL	52	58	66	124	152	14	23	17	40	38
1985-86	Montreal	NHL	10	1	2	3	22	20	10	6	16	68
	Sherbrooke	AHL	58	21	32	53	145	....	....	....	....	....
1986-87	Montreal	NHL	76	27	26	53	156	17	4	9	13	41
1987-88	Montreal	NHL	78	31	30	61	137	11	3	2	5	20
1988-89	Montreal	NHL	69	29	22	51	136	18	4	3	7	58
1989-90	Montreal	NHL	39	8	10	18	106	11	1	3	4	38
1990-91	New Jersey	NHL	78	30	17	47	105	7	4	0	4	34
	NHL Totals		359	127	109	236	681	84	26	23	49	259

a Named Most Valuable Player in QMJHL Playoffs (1985).
b QMJHL First All-Star Team (1985).
Traded to **New Jersey** by **Montreal** for Sylvain Turgeon, September 4, 1990.

LEMIEUX, JOCELYN   (lehm-YOO)

Right wing. Shoots left. 5'10", 200 lbs.   Born, Mont-Laurier, Que., November 18, 1967.
(St. Louis' 1st choice, 10th overall, in 1986 Entry Draft).

Season	Club	Lea	Regular Season					Playoffs				
			GP	G	A	TP	PIM	GP	G	A	TP	PIM
1984-85	Laval	QMJHL	68	13	19	32	92	....	....	....	....	....
1985-86a	Laval	QMJHL	71	57	68	125	131	14	9	15	24	37
1986-87	St. Louis	NHL	53	10	8	18	94	5	0	1	1	6
1987-88	St. Louis	NHL	23	1	0	1	42	5	0	0	0	15
	Peoria	IHL	8	0	5	5	35	....	....	....	....	....
1988-89	Montreal	NHL	1	0	1	1	0	....	....	....	....	....
	Sherbrooke	AHL	73	25	28	53	134	4	3	1	4	6
1989-90	Montreal	NHL	34	4	2	6	61	....	....	....	....	....
	Chicago	NHL	39	10	11	21	47	18	1	8	9	28
1990-91	Chicago	NHL	67	6	7	13	119	4	0	0	0	0
	NHL Totals		217	31	29	60	363	32	1	9	10	49

a QMJHL First All-Star Team (1986).
Traded to **Montreal** by **St. Louis** with Darrell May and St. Louis' second round choice (Patrice Brisebois) in the 1989 Entry Draft for Sergio Momesso and Vincent Riendeau, August 9, 1988. Traded to **Chicago** by **Montreal** for Chicago's third round choice (Charles Poulin) in 1990 Entry Draft, January 5, 1990.

LEMIEUX, MARIO (lehm-YOO)

Center. Shoots right. 6'4", 210 lbs. Born, Montreal, Que., October 5, 1965.
(Pittsburgh's 1st choice and 1st overall in 1984 Entry Draft).

				Regular Season					Playoffs			
Season	Club	Lea	GP	G	A	TP	PIM	GP	G	A	TP	PIM
1981-82	Laval	QMJHL	64	30	66	96	22	18	5	9	14	31
1982-83a	Laval	QMJHL	66	84	100	184	76	12	14	18	32	18
1983-84bcd	Laval	QMJHL	70	*133	*149	*282	92	14	*29	*23	*52	29
1984-85ef	Pittsburgh	NHL	73	43	57	100	54	....	....	....	....	....
1985-86gh	Pittsburgh	NHL	79	48	93	141	43	....	....	....	....	....
1986-87g	Pittsburgh	NHL	63	54	53	107	57	....	....	....	....	....
1987-88 hijklm	Pittsburgh	NHL	77	*70	98	*168	92	....	....	....	....	....
1988-89jkmn	Pittsburgh	NHL	76	*85	*114	*199	100	11	12	7	19	16
1989-90	Pittsburgh	NHL	59	45	78	123	78	....	....	....	....	....
1990-91o	Pittsburgh	NHL	26	19	26	45	30	23	16	*28	*44	16
	NHL Totals		453	364	519	883	454	34	28	35	63	32

a QMJHL Second All-Star Team (1983)
b QMJHL First All-Star Team (1984)
c QMJHL Most Valuable Player (1984)
d Canadian Major Junior Player of the Year (1984)
e Won Calder Memorial Trophy (1985)
f NHL All-Rookie Team (1985)
g NHL Second All-Star Team (1986, 1987)
h Won Lester B. Pearson Award (1986, 1988)
i Won Hart Trophy (1988)
j Won Art Ross Trophy (1988, 1989)
k NHL First All-Star Team (1988, 1989)
l Won Dodge Performance of the Year Award (1988)
m Won Dodge Ram Tough Award (1989)
n Won Dodge Performer of the Year Award (1988, 1989)
o Won Conn Smythe Trophy (1991)

Played in NHL All-Star Game (1985, 1986, 1988-90)

LENARDON, TIM

Center/Left wing. Shoots left. 6'2", 185 lbs. Born, Trail, B.C., May 11, 1962.

				Regular Season					Playoffs			
Season	Club	Lea	GP	G	A	TP	PIM	GP	G	A	TP	PIM
1983-84	Brandon U.	CWUAA	24	22	21	43	....	....	....	....	....	....
1984-85	Brandon U.	CWUAA	24	21	39	60	....	....	....	....	....	....
1985-86a	Brandon U.	CWUAA	26	26	40	66	33	....	....	....	....	....
1986-87	New Jersey	NHL	7	1	1	2	0	....	....	....	....	....
	Maine	AHL	61	28	35	63	30	....	....	....	....	....
1987-88	Utica	AHL	79	38	53	91	72	....	....	....	....	....
1988-89	Utica	AHL	63	28	27	55	48	....	....	....	....	....
	Milwaukee	IHL	15	6	5	11	27	10	2	3	5	25
1989-90	Vancouver	NHL	8	1	0	1	4	....	....	....	....	....
	Milwaukee	IHL	66	32	36	68	134	6	1	1	2	4
1990-91	Fiemme	Italy	36	45	73	118	4	10	8	18	26	0
	NHL Totals		15	2	1	3	4	....	....	....	....	....

a Canadian University Player of the Year (1986)

Signed as a free agent by **New Jersey**, August 6, 1986. Traded to **Vancouver** by **New Jersey** for Claude Vilgrain, March 7, 1989.

LEROUX, FRANCOIS

Defense. Shoots left. 6'6", 221 lbs. Born, Ste.-Adele, Que., April 18, 1970.
(Edmonton's 1st choice, 19th overall, in 1988 Entry Draft).

				Regular Season					Playoffs			
Season	Club	Lea	GP	G	A	TP	PIM	GP	G	A	TP	PIM
1987-88	St. Jean	QMJHL	58	3	8	11	143	7	2	0	2	21
1988-89	Edmonton	NHL	2	0	0	0	0	....	....	....	....	....
	St. Jean	QMJHL	57	8	34	42	185	....	....	....	....	....
1989-90	Edmonton	NHL	3	0	1	1	0	....	....	....	....	....
	Victoriaville	QMJHL	54	4	33	37	169	....	....	....	....	....
1990-91	Edmonton	NHL	1	0	2	2	0	....	....	....	....	....
	Cape Breton	AHL	71	2	7	9	124	4	0	1	1	19
	NHL Totals		6	0	3	3	0	....	....	....	....	....

LESCHYSHYN, CURTIS

Defense. Shoots left. 6'1", 205 lbs. Born, Thompson, Man., September 21, 1969.
(Quebec's 1st choice, 3rd overall, in 1988 Entry Draft).

				Regular Season					Playoffs			
Season	Club	Lea	GP	G	A	TP	PIM	GP	G	A	TP	PIM
1986-87	Saskatoon	WHL	70	14	26	40	107	11	1	5	6	14
1987-88	Saskatoon	WHL	56	14	41	55	86	10	2	5	7	16
1988-89	Quebec	NHL	71	4	9	13	71	....	....	....	....	....
1989-90	Quebec	NHL	68	2	6	8	44	....	....	....	....	....
1990-91	Quebec	NHL	55	3	7	10	49	....	....	....	....	....
	NHL Totals		194	9	22	31	164	....	....	....	....	....

LESSARD, OWEN

Left wing. Shoots left. 6'1", 196 lbs. Born, Sudbury, Ont., January 11, 1970.
(Chicago's 7th choice, 184th overall, in 1990 Entry Draft).

				Regular Season					Playoffs			
Season	Club	Lea	GP	G	A	TP	PIM	GP	G	A	TP	PIM
1989-90	Owen Sound	OHL	46	22	33	55	77	12	5	2	7	26
1990-91	Indianapolis	IHL	73	8	14	22	52	1	0	0	0	0

LESSARD, RICK

Defense. Shoots left. 6'2", 200 lbs. Born, Timmins, Ont., January 9, 1968.
(Calgary's 6th choice, 142nd overall, in 1986 Entry Draft).

				Regular Season					Playoffs			
Season	Club	Lea	GP	G	A	TP	PIM	GP	G	A	TP	PIM
1985-86	Ottawa	OHL	64	1	20	21	231	....	....	....	....	....
1986-87	Ottawa	OHL	66	5	36	41	188	11	1	7	8	30
1987-88	Ottawa	OHL	58	5	34	39	210	16	1	0	1	31
1988-89	Calgary	NHL	6	0	1	1	2	....	....	....	....	....
a	Salt Lake	IHL	76	10	42	52	239	14	1	6	7	35
1989-90	Salt Lake	IHL	66	3	18	21	169	10	1	2	3	64
1990-91	Calgary	NHL	1	0	1	1	0	....	....	....	....	....
	Salt Lake	IHL	80	8	27	35	272	4	0	1	1	12
	NHL Totals		7	0	2	2	2	....	....	....	....	....

a IHL First All-Star Team (1989)

Claimed by **San Jose** from **Calgary** in Expansion Draft, May 30, 1991.

LEVEQUE, GUY

Center. Shoots right. 5'11", 166 lbs. Born, Kingston, Ont., December 28, 1972.
(Los Angeles' 1st choice, 42th overall, in 1991 Entry Draft).

				Regular Season					Playoffs			
Season	Club	Lea	GP	G	A	TP	PIM	GP	G	A	TP	PIM
1989-90	Cornwall	OHL	62	10	15	25	30	3	0	0	0	4
1990-91	Cornwall	OHL	66	41	56	97	34	....	....	....	....	....

LEVINS, SCOTT

Center. Shoots right. 6'4", 210 lbs. Born, Spokane, WA, January 30, 1970.
(Winnipeg's 4th choice, 75th overall, in 1990 Entry Draft).

				Regular Season					Playoffs			
Season	Club	Lea	GP	G	A	TP	PIM	GP	G	A	TP	PIM
1989-90a	Tri-City	WHL	71	25	37	62	132	6	2	3	5	18
1990-91	Moncton	AHL	74	12	26	38	133	4	0	0	0	4

a WHL West Second All-Star Team (1990)

LIBA, IGOR (LEE-bah)

Left wing. Shoots right. 6', 192 lbs. Born, Kosice, Czechoslovakia, November 4, 1960.
(Calgary's 7th choice, 91st overall, in 1983 Entry Draft).

				Regular Season					Playoffs			
Season	Club	Lea	GP	G	A	TP	PIM	GP	G	A	TP	PIM
1986-87	VSZ Kosice	Czech.	39	14	26	40	....	....	....	....	....	....
1987-88	VSZ Kosice	Czech.	31	13	16	29	....	....	....	....	....	....
1988-89	NY Rangers	NHL	10	2	5	7	15	....	....	....	....	....
	Los Angeles	NHL	27	5	13	18	21	2	0	0	0	2
1989-90	VSZ Kosice	Czech.	44	17	20	37	....	....	....	....	....	....
1990-91	VSZ Kosice	Czech.	2	0	1	1	0	....	....	....	....	....
	NHL Totals		37	7	18	25	36	2	0	0	0	2

Traded to **Minnesota** by **Calgary** for Minnesota's fifth round draft choice in 1988 Entry Draft (Thomas Forslund), May 20, 1988. Traded to **NY Rangers** by **Minnesota** with Brian Lawton and the rights to Eric Bennett for Paul Jerrard and Mark Tinordi, the rights to Bret Barnett and Mike Sullivan, and Los Angeles' third-round choice (Murray Garbutt) in 1989 Entry Draft — acquired March 10, 1987 by Minnesota — October 11, 1988. Traded to **Los Angeles** by **NY Rangers** with Michael Boyce, Todd Elik and future considerations for Dean Kennedy and Denis Larocque, December 12, 1988.

LIDSTER, DOUG

Defense. Shoots right. 6'1", 200 lbs. Born, Kamloops, B.C., October 18, 1960.
(Vancouver's 6th choice, 133rd overall, in 1980 Entry Draft).

				Regular Season					Playoffs			
Season	Club	Lea	GP	G	A	TP	PIM	GP	G	A	TP	PIM
1977-78	Seattle	WHL	2	0	0	0	0	....	....	....	....	....
1979-80	Colorado	WCHA	39	18	25	43	52	....	....	....	....	....
1980-81	Colorado	WCHA	36	10	30	40	54	....	....	....	....	....
1981-82	Colorado	WCHA	36	13	22	35	32	....	....	....	....	....
1982-83	Colorado	WCHA	34	15	41	56	30	....	....	....	....	....
1983-84	Cdn. Olympic	...	59	6	20	26	28	....	....	....	....	....
	Vancouver	NHL	8	0	0	0	4	2	0	1	1	0
1984-85	Vancouver	NHL	78	6	24	30	55	....	....	....	....	....
1985-86	Vancouver	NHL	78	12	16	28	56	3	0	1	1	2
1986-87	Vancouver	NHL	80	12	51	63	40	....	....	....	....	....
1987-88	Vancouver	NHL	64	4	32	36	105	....	....	....	....	....
1988-89	Vancouver	NHL	63	5	17	22	78	7	1	1	2	9
1989-90	Vancouver	NHL	80	8	28	36	36	....	....	....	....	....
1990-91	Vancouver	NHL	78	6	32	38	77	6	0	2	2	6
	NHL Totals		529	53	200	253	451	18	1	5	6	17

LIDSTROM, NICKLAS (LEED-struhm)

Defense. Shoots left. 6'1", 176 lbs. Born, Vasteras, Sweden, April 28, 1970.
(Detroit's 3rd choice, 53rd overall, in 1989 Entry Draft).

				Regular Season					Playoffs			
Season	Club	Lea	GP	G	A	TP	PIM	GP	G	A	TP	PIM
1988-89	Vasteras	Swe.	19	0	2	2	4	....	....	....	....	....
1989-90	Vasteras	Swe.	39	8	8	16	14	2	0	1	1	2
1990-91	Vasteras	Swe.	38	4	19	23	2	....	....	....	....	....

LIEVERS, BRETT

Center. Shoots right. 6', 170 lbs. Born, Syracuse, NY, June 18, 1971.
(NY Rangers' 13th choice, 223rd overall, in 1990 Entry Draft).

				Regular Season					Playoffs			
Season	Club	Lea	GP	G	A	TP	PIM	GP	G	A	TP	PIM
1989-90	Wayzata	HS	....	26	26	52	....	....	....	....	....	....
1990-91	St. Cloud	WCHA	40	14	18	32	4	....	....	....	....	....

LILLEY, JOHN

Center. Shoots right. 5'9", 170 lbs. Born, Wakefield, MA, August 3, 1972.
(Winnipeg's 8th choice, 140th overall, in 1990 Entry Draft).

				Regular Season					Playoffs			
Season	Club	Lea	GP	G	A	TP	PIM	GP	G	A	TP	PIM
1989-90	Cushing Aca.	HS	20	22	30	52	....	....	....	....	....	....
1990-91	Cushing Aca.	HS	25	29	42	71	....	....	....	....	....	....

LILLIE, SHAWN

Left wing. Shoots left. 6', 180 lbs. Born, Sault Ste. Marie, Ont., August 13, 1967.
(Pittsburgh's 2nd choice, 9th overall, in 1988 Supplemental Draft).

			Regular Season					Playoffs				
Season	Club	Lea	GP	G	A	TP	PIM	GP	G	A	TP	PIM
1986-87	Colgate	ECAC	30	11	10	21	4	....	....	....	....	....
1987-88	Colgate	ECAC	32	12	22	34	12	....	....	....	....	....
1988-89	Colgate	ECAC	31	16	38	54	12	....	....	....	....	....
1989-90	Colgate	ECAC	38	17	22	39	32	....	....	....	....	....
1990-91	Richmond	ECHL	31	12	20	32	13	....	....	....	....	....
	Cincinnati	ECHL	14	2	7	9	2	3	1	0	1	0

LINDBERG, CHRIS

Left wing. Shoots left. 6'1", 190 lbs. Born, Fort Frances, Ont., April 16, 1967.

			Regular Season					Playoffs				
Season	Club	Lea	GP	G	A	TP	PIM	GP	G	A	TP	PIM
1987-88	Minn.-Duluth	WCHA	35	12	10	22	36	....	....	....	....	....
1988-89	Minn.-Duluth	WCHA	36	15	18	33	51	....	....	....	....	....
1989-90	Binghamton	AHL	32	4	4	8	36	....	....	....	....	....
1990-91	Cdn. National	...	55	25	31	56	53	....	....	....	....	....
	Springfield	AHL	1	0	0	0	2	1	0	0	0	0

Signed as a free agent by **Hartford**, March 17, 1989.

LINDEN, TREVOR

Center/Right wing. Shoots right. 6'4", 205 lbs. Born, Medicine Hat, Alta., April 11, 1970.
(Vancouver's 1st choice, 2nd overall, in 1988 Entry Draft).

			Regular Season					Playoffs				
Season	Club	Lea	GP	G	A	TP	PIM	GP	G	A	TP	PIM
1986-87	Medicine Hat	WHL	72	14	22	36	59	20	5	4	9	17
1987-88	Medicine Hat	WHL	67	46	64	110	76	16	*13	12	25	19
1988-89a	**Vancouver**	**NHL**	**80**	**30**	**29**	**59**	**41**	**7**	**3**	**4**	**7**	**8**
1989-90	**Vancouver**	**NHL**	**73**	**21**	**30**	**51**	**43**	....	....	....	....	....
1990-91	**Vancouver**	**NHL**	**80**	**33**	**37**	**70**	**65**	**6**	**0**	**7**	**7**	**2**
	NHL Totals		**233**	**84**	**96**	**180**	**149**	**13**	**3**	**11**	**14**	**10**

a NHL All-Rookie Team (1989)
Played in NHL All-Star Game (1991)

LINDHOLM, MIKAEL (LIHND-hohlm)

Center. Shoots left. 6'1", 194 lbs. Born, Gavle, Sweden, December 19, 1964.
(Los Angeles' 10th choice, 237th overall, in 1987 Entry Draft).

			Regular Season					Playoffs				
Season	Club	Lea	GP	G	A	TP	PIM	GP	G	A	TP	PIM
1986-87	Brynas	Swe.	36	8	9	17	46	....	....	....	....	....
1987-88	Brynas	Swe.	38	9	8	17	56	....	....	....	....	....
1988-89	Brynas	Swe.	40	9	17	26	98	....	....	....	....	....
1989-90	**Los Angeles**	**NHL**	**18**	**2**	**2**	**4**	**2**	....	....	....	....	....
	New Haven	AHL	28	4	6	10	24	....	....	....	....	....
1990-91	Phoenix	IHL	70	16	45	61	92	11	0	12	12	14
	NHL Totals		**18**	**2**	**2**	**4**	**2**	....	....	....	....	....

LINDMAN, MIKAEL (LIHND-mahn)

Defense. Shoots left. 6'1", 194 lbs. Born, Bolsaf, Sweden, May 15, 1967.
(Detroit's 12th choice, 239th overall, in 1985 Entry Draft).

			Regular Season					Playoffs				
Season	Club	Lea	GP	G	A	TP	PIM	GP	G	A	TP	PIM
1988-89	Skelleftea	Swe.	38	7	7	14	20	....	....	....	....	....
1989-90	Skelleftea	Swe.	28	2	5	7	8	5	0	0	0	0
1990-91	Brynas	Swe.	40	3	4	7	14	....	....	....	....	....

LINDQUIST, FREDRIK

Center. Shoots left. 5'11", 167 lbs. Born, Sadertalje, Sweden, June 21, 1973.
(New Jersey's 4th choice, 55th overall, in 1991 Entry Draft).

			Regular Season					Playoffs				
Season	Club	Lea	GP	G	A	TP	PIM	GP	G	A	TP	PIM
1989-90	Huddinge	Swe.	2	0	0	0	0	....	....	....	....	....
1990-91	Djurgarden	Swe.	28	6	4	10	0	....	....	....	....	....

LINDROS, ERIC

Center. Shoots right. 6'4", 225 lbs. Born, London, Ont., February 28, 1973.
(Quebec's 1st choice, 1st overall, in 1991 Entry Draft).

			Regular Season					Playoffs				
Season	Club	Lea	GP	G	A	TP	PIM	GP	G	A	TP	PIM
1989-90	Det. Compuware	USHL	14	23	29	52	123	....	....	....	....	....
a	Oshawa	OHL	25	17	19	36	61	17	18	18	36	76
1990-91bc	Oshawa	OHL	57	*71	78	*149	189	16	*18	20	*38	*93

a Memorial Cup All-Star Team (1990)
b OHL First All-Star Team (1991)
c Canadian Major Junior Player of the Year (1991)

LINK, ANTHONY (TONY)

Defense. Shoots right. 6'2", 205 lbs. Born, Anchorage, AK, April 3, 1969.
(Philadelphia's 6th choice, 125th overall, in 1987 Entry Draft).

			Regular Season					Playoffs				
Season	Club	Lea	GP	G	A	TP	PIM	GP	G	A	TP	PIM
1988-89	U. of Maine	H.E.	22	0	3	3	12	....	....	....	....	....
1989-90	U. of Maine	H.E.	15	0	3	3	6	....	....	....	....	....
1990-91	U. of Maine	H.E.	40	0	5	5	30	....	....	....	....	....

LINSEMAN, KEN (LIHNS-muhn)

Center. Shoots left. 5'11", 180 lbs. Born, Kingston, Ont., August 11, 1958.
(Philadelphia's 2nd choice, 7th overall, in 1978 Amateur Draft).

			Regular Season					Playoffs				
Season	Club	Lea	GP	G	A	TP	PIM	GP	G	A	TP	PIM
1975-76	Kingston	OHA	65	61	51	112	92	7	5	0	5	18
1976-77a	Kingston	OHA	63	53	74	127	210	10	9	12	21	54
1977-78	Birmingham	WHA	71	38	38	76	126	5	2	2	4	15
1978-79	**Philadelphia**	**NHL**	**30**	**5**	**20**	**25**	**23**	**8**	**2**	**6**	**8**	**22**
	Maine	AHL	38	17	22	39	106	....	....	....	....	....
1979-80	**Philadelphia**	**NHL**	**80**	**22**	**57**	**79**	**107**	**17**	**4**	***18**	**22**	**40**
1980-81	**Philadelphia**	**NHL**	**51**	**17**	**30**	**47**	**150**	**12**	**4**	**16**	**20**	**67**
1981-82	**Philadelphia**	**NHL**	**79**	**24**	**68**	**92**	**275**	**4**	**1**	**2**	**3**	**6**
1982-83	**Edmonton**	**NHL**	**72**	**33**	**42**	**75**	**181**	**16**	**6**	**8**	**14**	**22**
1983-84	**Edmonton**	**NHL**	**72**	**18**	**49**	**67**	**119**	**19**	**10**	**4**	**14**	**65**
1984-85	**Boston**	**NHL**	**74**	**25**	**49**	**74**	**126**	**5**	**4**	**6**	**10**	**8**
1985-86	**Boston**	**NHL**	**64**	**23**	**58**	**81**	**97**	**3**	**0**	**1**	**1**	**17**
1986-87	**Boston**	**NHL**	**64**	**15**	**34**	**49**	**126**	**4**	**1**	**1**	**2**	**22**
1987-88	**Boston**	**NHL**	**77**	**29**	**45**	**74**	**167**	**23**	**11**	**14**	**25**	**56**
1988-89	**Boston**	**NHL**	**78**	**27**	**45**	**72**	**164**	....	....	....	....	....
1989-90	**Boston**	**NHL**	**32**	**6**	**16**	**22**	**66**	....	....	....	....	....
	Philadelphia	**NHL**	**29**	**5**	**9**	**14**	**30**	....	....	....	....	....
1990-91	**Edmonton**	**NHL**	**56**	**7**	**29**	**36**	**94**	**2**	**0**	**1**	**1**	**0**
	NHL Totals		**858**	**256**	**551**	**807**	**1725**	**113**	**43**	**77**	**120**	**325**

a OHA Second All-Star Team (1977).

Traded to **Hartford** by **Philadelphia** with Greg Adams and Philadelphia's first (David Jensen) and third round choices (Leif Karlsson) in 1983 Entry Draft for Mark Howe and Hartford's third round choice (Derrick Smith) in the 1983 Entry Draft, August 19, 1982. Traded to **Edmonton** by **Hartford** with Don Nachbaur for Risto Siltanen and Brent Loney, August 19, 1982. Traded to **Boston** by **Edmonton** for Mike Krushelnyski, June 21, 1984. Traded to **Philadelphia** by **Boston** for Dave Poulin, January 16, 1990.

LOACH, LONNIE

Left wing. Shoots left. 5'10", 181 lbs. Born, New Liskeard, Ont., April 14, 1968.
(Chicago's 4th choice, 98th overall, in 1986 Entry Draft).

			Regular Season					Playoffs				
Season	Club	Lea	GP	G	A	TP	PIM	GP	G	A	TP	PIM
1985-86a	Guelph	OHL	65	41	42	83	63	20	7	8	15	16
1986-87	Guelph	OHL	56	31	24	55	42	5	2	1	3	2
1987-88	Guelph	OHL	66	43	49	92	75	....	....	....	....	....
1988-89	Flint	IHL	41	22	26	48	30	....	....	....	....	....
	Saginaw	IHL	32	7	6	13	27	....	....	....	....	....
1989-90	Indianapolis	IHL	3	0	0	0	0	....	....	....	....	....
	Fort Wayne	IHL	54	15	33	48	40	5	4	2	6	15
1990-91bc	Fort Wayne	IHL	81	55	76	*131	45	19	5	11	16	13

a OHL Rookie of the Year (1986).
b IHL Second All-Star Team (1991)
c Won Leo P. Lamoureux Trophy (Leading Scorer – IHL) (1991)

LOCKE, BRENDAN

Right wing. Shoots right. 6'4", 180 lbs. Born, Nahant, MA, May 31, 1970.
(Philadelphia's 2nd choice, 12th overall, in 1991 Supplemental Draft).

			Regular Season					Playoffs				
Season	Club	Lea	GP	G	A	TP	PIM	GP	G	A	TP	PIM
1989-90	Merrimack	H.E.	31	1	7	8	8	....	....	....	....	....
1990-91	Merrimack	H.E.	32	4	9	13	6	....	....	....	....	....

LOEWEN, DARCY

Left wing. Shoots left. 5'10", 185 lbs. Born, Calgary, Alta., February 26, 1969.
(Buffalo's 2nd choice, 55th overall, in 1988 Entry Draft).

			Regular Season					Playoffs				
Season	Club	Lea	GP	G	A	TP	PIM	GP	G	A	TP	PIM
1986-87	Spokane	WHL	68	15	25	40	129	5	0	0	0	16
1987-88	Spokane	WHL	72	30	44	74	231	15	7	5	12	54
1988-89	Spokane	WHL	60	31	27	58	194	....	....	....	....	....
	Cdn. National	...	2	0	0	0	0	....	....	....	....	....
1989-90	**Buffalo**	**NHL**	**4**	**0**	**0**	**0**	**4**	....	....	....	....	....
	Rochester	AHL	50	7	11	18	193	5	1	0	1	6
1990-91	**Buffalo**	**NHL**	**6**	**0**	**0**	**0**	**8**	....	....	....	....	....
	Rochester	AHL	71	13	15	28	130	15	1	5	6	14
	NHL Totals		**10**	**0**	**0**	**0**	**12**	....	....	....	....	....

LOISELLE, CLAUDE (LWAH-ZEHL)

Center. Shoots left. 5'11", 195 lbs. Born, Ottawa, Ont., May 29, 1963.
(Detroit's 1st choice, 23rd overall, in 1981 Entry Draft).

			Regular Season					Playoffs				
Season	Club	Lea	GP	G	A	TP	PIM	GP	G	A	TP	PIM
1980-81	Windsor	OHA	68	38	56	94	103	11	3	3	6	40
1981-82	**Detroit**	**NHL**	**4**	**1**	**0**	**1**	**2**	....	....	....	....	....
	Windsor	OHL	68	36	73	109	192	9	2	10	12	42
1982-83	**Detroit**	**NHL**	**18**	**2**	**0**	**2**	**15**	....	....	....	....	....
	Adirondack	AHL	6	1	7	8	0	6	2	4	6	0
1983-84	**Detroit**	**NHL**	**28**	**4**	**6**	**10**	**32**	....	....	....	....	....
	Adirondack	AHL	29	13	16	29	59	....	....	....	....	....
1984-85	**Detroit**	**NHL**	**30**	**8**	**1**	**9**	**45**	**3**	**0**	**2**	**2**	**0**
	Adirondack	AHL	47	22	29	51	24	....	....	....	....	....
1985-86	**Detroit**	**NHL**	**48**	**7**	**15**	**22**	**142**	....	....	....	....	....
	Adirondack	AHL	21	15	11	26	32	16	5	10	15	38
1986-87	**New Jersey**	**NHL**	**75**	**16**	**24**	**40**	**137**	....	....	....	....	....
1987-88	**New Jersey**	**NHL**	**68**	**17**	**18**	**35**	**121**	**20**	**4**	**6**	**10**	**50**
1988-89	**New Jersey**	**NHL**	**74**	**7**	**14**	**21**	**209**	....	....	....	....	....
1989-90	**Quebec**	**NHL**	**72**	**11**	**14**	**25**	**104**	....	....	....	....	....
1990-91	**Quebec**	**NHL**	**59**	**5**	**10**	**15**	**86**	....	....	....	....	....
	Toronto	**NHL**	**7**	**1**	**1**	**2**	**2**	....	....	....	....	....
	NHL Totals		**483**	**79**	**103**	**182**	**895**	**20**	**4**	**8**	**12**	**50**

Traded to **New Jersey** by **Detroit** for Tim Higgins, June 25, 1986. Traded to **Quebec** by **New Jersey** with Joe Cirella and New Jersey's eighth round choice (Alexander Karpovtsev) in 1990 Entry Draft for Walt Poddubny and Quebec's fourth round choice (Mike Bodnarchuk) in 1990 Entry Draft, June 17, 1989. Claimed on waivers by **Toronto**, March 5, 1991.

LOMOW, BYRON

Center. Shoots right. 5'10", 175 lbs. Born, Sherwood Park, Alta., April 27, 1965.

			Regular Season					Playoffs				
Season	Club	Lea	GP	G	A	TP	PIM	GP	G	A	TP	PIM
1982-83	Brandon	OHA	62	19	26	45	21	....	....	....	....	....
1983-84	Brandon	WHL	71	44	57	101	44	12	1	5	6	16
1984-85	Brandon	WHL	71	42	70	112	90	....	....	....	....	....
1985-86	Brandon	WHL	72	52	67	119	77	....	....	....	....	....
	Indianapolis	IHL	9	8	3	11	10	5	2	11	3	2
1986-87	Indianapolis	IHL	81	28	43	71	225	6	3	5	8	21
1987-88	Baltimore	AHL	71	14	26	40	77	....	....	....	....	....
	Colorado	IHL	10	2	10	12	7	....	....	....	....	....
1988-89	Fort Wayne	IHL	81	22	35	57	207	11	3	3	6	68
1989-90	Fort Wayne	IHL	79	29	24	53	230	5	3	2	5	25
1990-91	San Diego	IHL	13	3	4	7	41	....	....	....	....	....
	Albany	IHL	40	12	9	21	177	....	....	....	....	....
	Kalamazoo	IHL	7	1	3	4	23	4	0	0	0	19

Signed as a free agent by **Minnesota**, April 21, 1986. Traded to **NY Rangers** by **Minnesota** with future considerations for Curt Giles, November 20, 1987.

LONEY, TROY

Left wing. Shoots left. 6'3", 209 lbs. Born, Bow Island, Alta., September 21, 1963.
(Pittsburgh's 3rd choice, 52nd overall, in 1982 Entry Draft).

			Regular Season					Playoffs				
Season	Club	Lea	GP	G	A	TP	PIM	GP	G	A	TP	PIM
1980-81	Lethbridge	WHL	71	18	13	31	100	9	2	2	5	14
1981-82	Lethbridge	WHL	71	26	33	59	152	12	3	3	6	10
1982-83	Lethbridge	WHL	72	33	34	67	156	20	10	7	17	43
1983-84	**Pittsburgh**	**NHL**	**13**	**0**	**0**	**0**	**9**	....	....	....	....	....
	Baltimore	AHL	63	18	13	31	147	10	0	2	2	19
1984-85	**Pittsburgh**	**NHL**	**46**	**10**	**8**	**18**	**59**	....	....	....	....	....
	Baltimore	AHL	15	4	2	6	25	....	....	....	....	....
1985-86	**Pittsburgh**	**NHL**	**47**	**3**	**9**	**12**	**95**	....	....	....	....	....
	Baltimore	AHL	33	12	11	23	84	....	....	....	....	....
1986-87	**Pittsburgh**	**NHL**	**23**	**8**	**7**	**15**	**22**	....	....	....	....	....
	Baltimore	AHL	40	13	14	27	134	....	....	....	....	....
1987-88	**Pittsburgh**	**NHL**	**65**	**5**	**13**	**18**	**151**	....	....	....	....	....
1988-89	**Pittsburgh**	**NHL**	**69**	**10**	**6**	**16**	**165**	**11**	**1**	**3**	**4**	**24**
1989-90	**Pittsburgh**	**NHL**	**67**	**11**	**16**	**27**	**168**	....	....	....	....	....
1990-91	**Pittsburgh**	**NHL**	**44**	**7**	**9**	**16**	**85**	**24**	**2**	**2**	**4**	**41**
	Muskegon	IHL	2	0	0	0	5	....	....	....	....	....
	NHL Totals		**374**	**54**	**68**	**122**	**754**	**35**	**3**	**5**	**8**	**65**

LONGO, CHRIS

Right wing. Shoots right. 5'10", 180 lbs. Born, Belleville, Ont., January 5, 1972.
(Washington's 3rd choice, 51st overall, in 1990 Entry Draft).

			Regular Season					Playoffs				
Season	Club	Lea	GP	G	A	TP	PIM	GP	G	A	TP	PIM
1989-90a	Peterborough	OHL	66	33	41	74	48	11	2	3	5	14
1990-91	Peterborough	OHL	64	30	38	68	68	4	1	0	1	0

a OHL Rookie of the Year (1990)

LOOB, HAKAN (LOOB, HOH-kuhn)

Right wing. Shoots right. 5'10", 174 lbs. Born, Visby, Sweden, July 3, 1960.
(Calgary's 10th choice, 181st overall, in 1980 Entry Draft).

			Regular Season					Playoffs				
Season	Club	Lea	GP	G	A	TP	PIM	GP	G	A	TP	PIM
1979-80	Farjestad	Swe.	36	15	4	19	20	....	....	....	....	....
1980-81	Farjestad	Swe.	36	23	6	29	14	7	5	3	8	6
	Swe. National	...	6	0	1	1	0	....	....	....	....	....
1981-82	Farjestad	Swe.	36	26	15	41	28	2	1	0	1	0
	Swe. National	...	21	8	3	11	8	....	....	....	....	....
1982-83	Farjestad	Swe.	36	42	34	76	29	8	10	4	14	6
	Swe. National	...	11	2	2	4	8	....	....	....	....	....
1983-84a	**Calgary**	**NHL**	**77**	**30**	**25**	**55**	**22**	**11**	**2**	**3**	**5**	**2**
1984-85	**Calgary**	**NHL**	**78**	**37**	**35**	**72**	**14**	**4**	**3**	**3**	**6**	**0**
1985-86	**Calgary**	**NHL**	**68**	**31**	**36**	**67**	**36**	**22**	**4**	**10**	**14**	**6**
1986-87	**Calgary**	**NHL**	**68**	**18**	**26**	**44**	**26**	**5**	**1**	**2**	**3**	**0**
1987-88b	**Calgary**	**NHL**	**80**	**50**	**56**	**106**	**47**	**9**	**8**	**1**	**9**	**4**
1988-89	**Calgary**	**NHL**	**79**	**27**	**58**	**85**	**44**	**22**	**8**	**9**	**17**	**4**
1989-90	Farjestad	Swe.	40	22	31	53	24	10	9	4	13	2
1990-91	Farjestad	Swe.	40	33	25	58	16	....	....	....	....	....
	NHL Totals		**450**	**193**	**236**	**429**	**189**	**73**	**26**	**28**	**54**	**16**

a NHL All-Rookie Team (1984)
b NHL First All-Star Team (1988)

LOVSIN, KEN

Defense. Shoots right. 6', 195 lbs. Born, Peace River, Alta., December 3, 1966.
(Hartford's 1st choice, 22nd overall, in 1987 Supplemental Draft).

			Regular Season					Playoffs				
Season	Club	Lea	GP	G	A	TP	PIM	GP	G	A	TP	PIM
1986-87	Saskatchewan	CWUAA	28	3	13	16	14	....	....	....	....	....
1987-88	Saskatchewan	CWUAA	28	14	24	38	20	....	....	....	....	....
1988-89	Cdn. National	...	59	0	10	10	59	....	....	....	....	....
1989-90	Cdn. National	...	66	7	15	22	80	....	....	....	....	....
1990-91	**Washington**	**NHL**	**1**	**0**	**0**	**0**	**0**	....	....	....	....	....
	Baltimore	AHL	79	8	28	36	54	6	1	1	2	2
	NHL Totals		**1**	**0**	**0**	**0**	**0**	....	....	....	....	....

Signed as a free agent by **Washington**, July 3, 1990.

LOWE, KEVIN HUGH (LOH)

Defense. Shoots left. 6'2", 195 lbs. Born, Lachute, Que., April 15, 1959.
(Edmonton's 1st choice, 21st overall, in 1979 Entry Draft).

			Regular Season					Playoffs				
Season	Club	Lea	GP	G	A	TP	PIM	GP	G	A	TP	PIM
1977-78	Quebec	QJHL	64	13	52	65	86	4	1	2	3	6
1978-79a	Quebec	QJHL	68	26	60	86	120	6	1	7	8	36
1979-80	**Edmonton**	**NHL**	**64**	**2**	**19**	**21**	**70**	**3**	**0**	**1**	**1**	**0**
1980-81	**Edmonton**	**NHL**	**79**	**10**	**24**	**34**	**94**	**9**	**0**	**2**	**2**	**11**
1981-82	**Edmonton**	**NHL**	**80**	**9**	**31**	**40**	**63**	**5**	**0**	**3**	**3**	**0**
1982-83	**Edmonton**	**NHL**	**80**	**6**	**34**	**40**	**43**	**16**	**1**	**8**	**9**	**10**
1983-84	**Edmonton**	**NHL**	**80**	**4**	**42**	**46**	**59**	**19**	**3**	**7**	**10**	**16**
1984-85	**Edmonton**	**NHL**	**80**	**4**	**21**	**25**	**104**	**16**	**0**	**5**	**5**	**8**
1985-86	**Edmonton**	**NHL**	**74**	**2**	**16**	**18**	**90**	**10**	**1**	**3**	**4**	**15**
1986-87	**Edmonton**	**NHL**	**77**	**8**	**29**	**37**	**94**	**21**	**2**	**4**	**6**	**22**
1987-88	**Edmonton**	**NHL**	**70**	**9**	**15**	**24**	**89**	**19**	**0**	**2**	**2**	**26**
1988-89	**Edmonton**	**NHL**	**76**	**7**	**18**	**25**	**98**	**7**	**1**	**2**	**3**	**4**
1989-90bc	**Edmonton**	**NHL**	**78**	**7**	**26**	**33**	**140**	**20**	**0**	**2**	**2**	**10**
1990-91	**Edmonton**	**NHL**	**73**	**3**	**13**	**16**	**113**	**14**	**1**	**1**	**2**	**14**
	NHL Totals		**911**	**71**	**288**	**359**	**1057**	**159**	**9**	**40**	**49**	**136**

a QMJHL Second All-Star Team (1979)
b Won Bud Man of the Year Award (1990)
c Won King Clancy Memorial Trophy (1990)

Played in NHL All-Star Game (1984-86, 1988-90)

LOWRY, DAVE

Left wing. Shoots left. 6'1", 195 lbs. Born, Sudbury, Ont., February 14, 1965.
(Vancouver's 6th choice, 110th overall, in 1983 Entry Draft).

			Regular Season					Playoffs				
Season	Club	Lea	GP	G	A	TP	PIM	GP	G	A	TP	PIM
1982-83	London	OHL	42	11	16	27	48	3	0	0	0	14
1983-84	London	OHL	66	29	47	76	125	8	6	6	12	41
1984-85a	London	OHL	61	60	60	120	94	8	6	5	11	10
1985-86	**Vancouver**	**NHL**	**73**	**10**	**8**	**18**	**143**	**3**	**0**	**0**	**0**	**0**
1986-87	**Vancouver**	**NHL**	**70**	**8**	**10**	**18**	**176**	....	....	....	....	....
1987-88	**Vancouver**	**NHL**	**22**	**1**	**3**	**4**	**38**	....	....	....	....	....
	Fredericton	AHL	46	18	27	45	59	14	7	3	10	72
1988-89	**St. Louis**	**NHL**	**21**	**3**	**3**	**6**	**11**	**10**	**0**	**5**	**5**	**4**
	Peoria	IHL	58	31	35	66	45	....	....	....	....	....
1989-90	**St. Louis**	**NHL**	**78**	**19**	**6**	**25**	**75**	**12**	**2**	**1**	**3**	**39**
1990-91	**St. Louis**	**NHL**	**79**	**19**	**21**	**40**	**168**	**13**	**1**	**4**	**5**	**35**
	NHL Totals		**343**	**60**	**51**	**111**	**611**	**38**	**3**	**10**	**13**	**78**

a OHL First All-Star Team (1985)

Traded to **St. Louis** by **Vancouver** for Ernie Vargas, September 29, 1988.

LUBINA, LADISLAV (loo-BEE-nah)

Left wing. Shoots left. 5'11", 182 lbs. Born, Dvur Kralove, Czech., February 11, 1967.
(Minnesota's 9th choice, 216th overall, in 1985 Entry Draft).

			Regular Season					Playoffs				
Season	Club	Lea	GP	G	A	TP	PIM	GP	G	A	TP	PIM
1986-87	Dukla Jihlava	Czech.	34	9	7	16	....	....	....	....	....	....
1987-88	Dukla Jihlava	Czech.	34	12	9	21	....	....	....	....	....	....
1988-89	Dukla Jihlava	Czech.	44	22	16	38	....	....	....	....	....	....
1989-90	Dukla Jihlava	Czech.	44	19	15	34	....	....	....	....	....	....
1990-91	Dukla Jihlava	Czech.	50	41	20	61	56	....	....	....	....	....

LUDWIG, CRAIG LEE

Defense. Shoots left. 6'3", 222 lbs. Born, Rhinelander, WI, March 15, 1961.
(Montreal's 5th choice, 61st overall, in 1980 Entry Draft).

			Regular Season					Playoffs				
Season	Club	Lea	GP	G	A	TP	PIM	GP	G	A	TP	PIM
1979-80	North Dakota	WCHA	33	1	8	9	32	....	....	....	....	....
1980-81	North Dakota	WCHA	34	4	8	12	48	....	....	....	....	....
1981-82	North Dakota	WCHA	37	4	17	21	42	....	....	....	....	....
1982-83	**Montreal**	**NHL**	**80**	**0**	**25**	**25**	**59**	**3**	**0**	**0**	**0**	**2**
1983-84	**Montreal**	**NHL**	**80**	**7**	**18**	**25**	**52**	**15**	**0**	**3**	**3**	**23**
1984-85	**Montreal**	**NHL**	**72**	**5**	**14**	**19**	**90**	**12**	**0**	**2**	**2**	**6**
1985-86	**Montreal**	**NHL**	**69**	**2**	**4**	**6**	**63**	**20**	**0**	**1**	**1**	**48**
1986-87	**Montreal**	**NHL**	**75**	**4**	**12**	**16**	**105**	**17**	**2**	**3**	**5**	**30**
1987-88	**Montreal**	**NHL**	**74**	**4**	**10**	**14**	**69**	**11**	**1**	**1**	**2**	**6**
1988-89	**Montreal**	**NHL**	**74**	**3**	**13**	**16**	**73**	**21**	**0**	**2**	**2**	**24**
1989-90	**Montreal**	**NHL**	**73**	**1**	**15**	**16**	**108**	**11**	**0**	**1**	**1**	**16**
1990-91	**NY Islanders**	**NHL**	**75**	**1**	**8**	**9**	**77**	....	....	....	....	....
	NHL Totals		**672**	**27**	**119**	**146**	**696**	**110**	**3**	**13**	**16**	**155**

Traded to **NY Islanders** by **Montreal** for Gerald Diduck, September 4, 1990. Traded to **Minnesota** by **NY Islanders** for Tom Kurvers, June 22, 1991.

LUDZIK, STEVE

Center. Shoots left. 5'11", 185 lbs. Born, Toronto, Ont., April 3, 1962.
(Chicago's 3rd choice, 28th overall, in 1980 Entry Draft).

			Regular Season					Playoffs				
Season	Club	Lea	GP	G	A	TP	PIM	GP	G	A	TP	PIM
1979-80	Niagara Falls	OHA	67	43	76	119	102	10	6	6	12	16
1980-81	Niagara Falls	OHA	58	50	92	142	108	12	5	9	14	40
1981-82	**Chicago**	**NHL**	**8**	**2**	**1**	**3**	**2**	....	....	....	....	....
	New Brunswick	AHL	73	21	41	62	142	15	3	7	10	6
1982-83	**Chicago**	**NHL**	**66**	**6**	**19**	**25**	**63**	**13**	**3**	**5**	**8**	**20**
1983-84	**Chicago**	**NHL**	**80**	**9**	**20**	**29**	**73**	**4**	**0**	**1**	**1**	**9**
1984-85	**Chicago**	**NHL**	**79**	**11**	**20**	**31**	**86**	**15**	**1**	**1**	**2**	**16**
1985-86	**Chicago**	**NHL**	**49**	**6**	**5**	**11**	**21**	**3**	**0**	**0**	**0**	**12**
1986-87	**Chicago**	**NHL**	**52**	**5**	**12**	**17**	**34**	**4**	**0**	**0**	**0**	**0**
1987-88	**Chicago**	**NHL**	**73**	**6**	**15**	**21**	**40**	**5**	**0**	**1**	**1**	**13**
1988-89	**Chicago**	**NHL**	**6**	**1**	**0**	**1**	**8**	....	....	....	....	....
	Saginaw	IHL	65	21	57	78	129	6	0	1	1	17
1989-90	**Buffalo**	**NHL**	**11**	**0**	**1**	**1**	**6**	....	....	....	....	....
	Rochester	AHL	54	25	29	54	71	16	5	6	11	57
1990-91	Rochester	AHL	65	22	29	51	137	8	3	5	8	6
	NHL Totals		**424**	**46**	**93**	**139**	**333**	**44**	**4**	**8**	**12**	**70**

Traded to **Buffalo** by **Chicago** with sixth round choice (Derek Edgerly) to complete earlier deal for Jacques Cloutier, September 28, 1989.

LUIK, JAAN

Defense. Shoots left. 6'1", 210 lbs.   Born, Scarborough, Ont., January 15, 1970.
(St. Louis' 4th choice, 72nd overall, in 1988 Entry Draft).

				Regular Season					Playoffs			
Season	Club	Lea	GP	G	A	TP	PIM	GP	G	A	TP	PIM
1987-88	Miami-Ohio	CCHA	35	2	5	7	93	.....	....	....	....	....
1988-89	Miami-Ohio	CCHA	33	1	8	9	43	.....	....	....	....	....
1989-90	Miami-Ohio	CCHA	35	1	11	12	64	.....	....	....	....	....
1990-91	Miami-Ohio	CCHA	35	0	8	8	70	.....	....	....	....	....

LUIK, SCOTT

Right wing. Shoots left. 6'1", 210 lbs.   Born, Scarborough, Ont., January 15, 1970.
(New Jersey's 5th choice, 75th overall, in 1988 Entry Draft).

				Regular Season					Playoffs			
Season	Club	Lea	GP	G	A	TP	PIM	GP	G	A	TP	PIM
1987-88	Miami-Ohio	CCHA	34	4	10	14	47	.....	....	....	....	....
1988-89	Miami-Ohio	CCHA	36	13	13	26	92	.....	....	....	....	....
1989-90	Miami-Ohio	CCHA	16	4	7	11	32	.....	....	....	....	....
	Oshawa	OHL	34	15	14	29	20	17	4	5	9	20
1990-91	Oshawa	OHL	56	26	51	77	74	16	6	11	17	25

LUMME, JYRKI   (LOOM-meh)

Defense. Shoots left. 6'1", 190 lbs.   Born, Tampere, Finland, July 16, 1966.
(Montreal's 3rd choice, 57th overall, in 1986 Entry Draft).

				Regular Season					Playoffs			
Season	Club	Lea	GP	G	A	TP	PIM	GP	G	A	TP	PIM
1984-85	KooVee	Fin.3	30	6	4	10	44	.....	....	....	....	....
1985-86	Ilves	Fin.	31	1	4	5	4	.....	....	....	....	....
1986-87	Ilves	Fin.	43	12	12	24	52	4	0	1	2	....
1987-88	Ilves	Fin.	43	8	22	30	75	.....	....	....	....	....
1988-89	Montreal	NHL	21	1	3	4	10	.....	....	....	....	....
	Sherbrooke	AHL	26	4	11	15	10	6	1	3	4	4
1989-90	Montreal	NHL	54	1	19	20	41	.....	....	....	....	....
	Vancouver	NHL	11	3	7	10	8	.....	....	....	....	....
1990-91	Vancouver	NHL	80	5	27	32	59	6	2	3	5	0
	NHL Totals		166	10	56	66	118	.....	....	....	....	....

Traded to **Vancouver** by **Montreal** for St. Louis' second round choice (Craig Darby) in 1991 Entry Draft (previously acquired by Vancouver), March 6, 1990.

LUND, WILLIAM

Center. Shoots left. 5'9", 165 lbs.   Born, Roseau, MN, December 16, 1971.
(Philadelphia's 15th choice, 235th overall, in 1990 Entry Draft).

				Regular Season					Playoffs			
Season	Club	Lea	GP	G	A	TP	PIM	GP	G	A	TP	PIM
1989-90	Roseau	HS	28	36	50	86		.....	....	....	....	....
1990-91	Minn.-Duluth	WCHA	20	0	2	2	8	.....	....	....	....	....

LUONGO, CHRISTOPHER (CHRIS)   (loo-ON-go)

Defense. Shoots right. 6', 180 lbs.   Born, Detroit, MI, March 17, 1967.
(Detroit's 5th choice, 92nd overall, in 1985 Entry Draft).

				Regular Season					Playoffs			
Season	Club	Lea	GP	G	A	TP	PIM	GP	G	A	TP	PIM
1985-86	Michigan State	CCHA	38	1	5	6	29	.....	....	....	....	....
1986-87a	Michigan State	CCHA	27	4	16	20	38	.....	....	....	....	....
1987-88	Michigan State	CCHA	45	3	15	18	49	.....	....	....	....	....
1988-89b	Michigan State	CCHA	47	4	21	25	42	.....	....	....	....	....
1989-90	Adirondack	AHL	53	9	14	23	37	3	0	0	0	0
	Phoenix	IHL	23	5	9	14	41	.....	....	....	....	....
1990-91	Detroit	NHL	4	0	1	1	4	.....	....	....	....	....
	Adirondack	AHL	76	14	25	39	71	2	0	0	0	7
	NHL Totals		4	0	1	1	4	.....	....	....	....	....

a Named to NCAA All-Tournament Team (1987)
b CCHA Second All-Star Team (1989)

LYONS, COREY

Right wing. Shoots left. 5'10", 186 lbs.   Born, Calgary, Alta., June 13, 1970.
(Calgary's 4th choice, 63rd overall, in 1989 Entry Draft).

				Regular Season					Playoffs			
Season	Club	Lea	GP	G	A	TP	PIM	GP	G	A	TP	PIM
1987-88	Lethbridge	WHL	2	0	0	0	0	.....	....	....	....	....
1988-89	Lethbridge	WHL	71	53	59	112	36	8	4	9	13	7
1989-90	Lethbridge	WHL	72	63	79	142	26	19	11	15	26	4
	Salt Lake	IHL	....	....	....	....	....	1	0	0	0	0
1990-91	Salt Lake	IHL	51	15	12	27	22	3	0	2	2	0

MacARTHUR, KENNETH

Defense. Shoots left. 6'2", 185 lbs.   Born, Rossland, B.C., March 15, 1968.
(Minnesota's 5th choice, 148th overall, in 1988 Entry Draft).

				Regular Season					Playoffs			
Season	Club	Lea	GP	G	A	TP	PIM	GP	G	A	TP	PIM
1987-88	U. of Denver	WCHA	38	6	16	22	69	.....	....	....	....	....
1988-89	U. of Denver	WCHA	42	11	19	30	77	.....	....	....	....	....
1989-90	U. of Denver	WCHA	38	12	29	41	96	.....	....	....	....	....
	Cdn. National	...	13	2	1	3	14	.....	....	....	....	....
1990-91	Cdn. National	...	59	4	11	15	34	.....	....	....	....	....

MacDERMID, PAUL

Right wing. Shoots right. 6'1", 205 lbs.   Born, Chesley, Ont., April 14, 1963.
(Hartford's 2nd choice, 61st overall, in 1981 Entry Draft).

				Regular Season					Playoffs			
Season	Club	Lea	GP	G	A	TP	PIM	GP	G	A	TP	PIM
1980-81	Windsor	OHA	68	15	17	32	106	.....	....	....	....	....
1981-82	Hartford	NHL	3	1	0	1	2	.....	....	....	....	....
	Windsor	OHL	65	26	45	71	179	9	6	4	10	17
1982-83	Hartford	NHL	7	0	0	0	2	.....	....	....	....	....
	Windsor	OHL	42	35	45	80	9	.....	....	....	....	....
1983-84	Hartford	NHL	3	0	1	1	0	.....	....	....	....	....
	Binghamton	AHL	70	31	30	61	130	.....	....	....	....	....
1984-85	Hartford	NHL	31	4	7	11	29	.....	....	....	....	....
	Binghamton	AHL	48	9	31	40	87	.....	....	....	....	....
1985-86	Hartford	NHL	74	13	10	23	160	10	2	1	3	20
1986-87	Hartford	NHL	72	7	11	18	202	6	2	1	3	34
1987-88	Hartford	NHL	80	20	15	35	139	6	0	5	5	14
1988-89	Hartford	NHL	74	17	27	44	141	4	1	1	2	16
1989-90	Hartford	NHL	29	6	12	18	69	.....	....	....	....	....
	Winnipeg	NHL	44	7	10	17	100	7	0	2	2	8
1990-91	Winnipeg	NHL	69	15	21	36	128	.....	....	....	....	....
	NHL Totals		486	90	114	204	972	33	5	10	15	92

Traded to **Winnipeg** by **Hartford** for Randy Cunneyworth, December 13, 1989.

MacDONALD, BRUCE

Defense. Shoots left. 6'1", 195 lbs.   Born, Plaistow, NH, December 16, 1967.
(Philadelphia's 9th choice, 188th overall, in 1987 Entry Draft).

				Regular Season					Playoffs			
Season	Club	Lea	GP	G	A	TP	PIM	GP	G	A	TP	PIM
1987-88	N. Hampshire	H.E.	12	0	1	1	8	.....	....	....	....	....
1988-89	N. Hampshire	H.E.	21	1	3	4	8	.....	....	....	....	....
1989-90	N. Hampshire	H.E.	35	2	3	5	16	.....	....	....	....	....
1990-91	N. Hampshire	H.E.	25	2	4	6	14	.....	....	....	....	....

MacDONALD, DARIN

Left wing. Shoots left. 6', 180 lbs.   Born, Calgary, Alta., January 30, 1970.
(Edmonton's 12th choice, 229th overall, in 1988 Entry Draft).

				Regular Season					Playoffs			
Season	Club	Lea	GP	G	A	TP	PIM	GP	G	A	TP	PIM
1987-88	Boston U.	H.E.	12	2	1	3	0	.....	....	....	....	....
1988-89	Boston U.	H.E.	35	6	6	12	10	.....	....	....	....	....
1989-90	Boston U.	H.E.	38	4	3	7	29	.....	....	....	....	....
1990-91	Boston U.	H.E.	22	2	4	6	20	.....	....	....	....	....

MacDONALD, DOUG

Center. Shoots left. 6', 192 lbs.   Born, Port Moody, B.C., February 8, 1969.
(Buffalo's 3rd choice, 77th overall, in 1989 Entry Draft).

				Regular Season					Playoffs			
Season	Club	Lea	GP	G	A	TP	PIM	GP	G	A	TP	PIM
1988-89	U. Wisconsin	WCHA	44	23	25	48	50	.....	....	....	....	....
1989-90	U. Wisconsin	WCHA	44	16	35	51	52	.....	....	....	....	....
1990-91	U. Wisconsin	WCHA	31	20	26	46	50	.....	....	....	....	....

MacFARLANE, SHANE

Center. Shoots left. 5'10", 165 lbs.   Born, Warroad, MN, September 4, 1968.
(Buffalo's 1st choice, 24th overall, in 1990 Supplemental Draft).

				Regular Season					Playoffs			
Season	Club	Lea	GP	G	A	TP	PIM	GP	G	A	TP	PIM
1987-88	North Dakota	WCHA	27	0	1	1	8	.....	....	....	....	....
1988-89	North Dakota	WCHA	30	1	4	5	8	.....	....	....	....	....
1989-90	North Dakota	WCHA	22	3	2	5	10	.....	....	....	....	....
1990-91	North Dakota	WCHA	1	0	0	0	2	.....	....	....	....	....

MacINNIS, ALLAN (AL)

Defense. Shoots right. 6'2", 196 lbs.   Born, Inverness, N.S., July 11, 1963.
(Calgary's 1st choice, 15th overall, in 1981 Entry Draft).

				Regular Season					Playoffs			
Season	Club	Lea	GP	G	A	TP	PIM	GP	G	A	TP	PIM
1980-81	Kitchener	OHA	47	11	28	39	59	18	4	12	16	20
1981-82	Calgary	NHL	2	0	0	0	0	.....	....	....	....	....
a	Kitchener	OHL	59	25	50	75	145	15	5	10	15	44
1982-83	Calgary	NHL	14	1	3	4	9	.....	....	....	....	....
a	Kitchener	OHL	51	38	46	84	67	8	3	8	11	9
1983-84	Calgary	NHL	51	11	34	45	42	11	2	12	14	13
	Colorado	CHL	19	5	14	19	22	.....	....	....	....	....
1984-85	Calgary	NHL	67	14	52	66	75	4	1	2	3	8
1985-86	Calgary	NHL	77	11	57	68	76	21	4	*15	19	30
1986-87b	Calgary	NHL	79	20	56	76	97	4	1	0	1	0
1987-88	Calgary	NHL	80	25	58	83	114	7	3	6	9	18
1988-89bc	Calgary	NHL	79	16	58	74	126	22	7	*24	*31	46
1989-90d	Calgary	NHL	79	28	62	90	82	6	2	3	5	8
1990-91d	Calgary	NHL	78	28	75	103	90	7	2	3	5	8
	NHL Totals		606	154	455	609	711	82	22	65	87	131

a OHL First All-Star Team (1982, 1983)
b NHL Second All-Star Team (1987, 1989)
c Won Conn Smythe Trophy (1989)
d NHL First All-Star Team (1990, 1991)
Played in NHL All-Star Game (1985, 1988, 1990, 1991)

MACIVER, NORM (mac-IGH-ver)

Defense. Shoots left. 5'11", 180 lbs. Born, Thunder Bay, Ont., September 8, 1964.

			Regular Season					Playoffs				
Season	Club	Lea	GP	G	A	TP	PIM	GP	G	A	TP	PIM
1982-83	Minn.-Duluth	WCHA	45	1	26	27	40	6	0	2	2	2
1983-84a	Minn.-Duluth	WCHA	31	13	28	41	28	8	1	10	11	8
1984-85bc	Minn.-Duluth	WCHA	47	14	47	61	63	10	3	3	6	6
1985-86bc	Minn.-Duluth	WCHA	42	11	51	62	36	4	2	3	5	2
1986-87	**NY Rangers**	**NHL**	**3**	**0**	**1**	**1**	**0**	....	....	....	....	....
	New Haven	AHL	71	6	30	36	73	7	0	0	0	9
1987-88	**NY Rangers**	**NHL**	**37**	**9**	**15**	**24**	**14**	....	....	....	....	....
	Colorado	IHL	27	6	20	26	22	....	....	....	....	....
1988-89	**NY Rangers**	**NHL**	**26**	**0**	**10**	**10**	**14**	....	....	....	....	....
	Hartford	**NHL**	**37**	**1**	**22**	**23**	**24**	**1**	**0**	**0**	**0**	**2**
1989-90	Binghamton	AHL	2	0	0	0	0	....	....	....	....	....
	Edmonton	**NHL**	**1**	**0**	**0**	**0**	**0**	....	....	....	....	....
	Cape Breton	AHL	68	13	37	50	55	6	0	7	7	10
1990-91	**Edmonton**	**NHL**	**21**	**2**	**5**	**7**	**14**	**18**	**0**	**4**	**4**	**8**
de	Cape Breton	AHL	56	13	46	59	60	....	....	....	....	....
	NHL Totals		**125**	**12**	**53**	**65**	**66**	**18**	**0**	**4**	**4**	**8**

a WCHA Second All-Star Team (1984)
b WCHA First All-Star Team (1985, 1986)
c NCAA West First All-Star Team (1985, 1986)
d AHL First All-Star Team (1991)
e Won Eddie Shore Plaque (Top Defenseman – AHL) (1991)

Signed as a free agent by **NY Rangers**, September 8, 1986. Traded to **Hartford** by **NY Rangers** with Brian Lawton and Don Maloney for Carey Wilson and Hartford's fifth-round choice (Lubos Rob) in 1990 Entry Draft, December 26, 1988. Traded to **Edmonton** by **Hartford** for Jim Ennis, October 10, 1989.

MACKEY, DAVID

Left wing. Shoots left. 6'4", 200 lbs. Born, Richmond, B.C., July 24, 1966.
(Chicago's 12th choice, 224th overall, in 1984 Entry Draft).

			Regular Season					Playoffs				
Season	Club	Lea	GP	G	A	TP	PIM	GP	G	A	TP	PIM
1982-83	Victoria	WHL	69	16	16	32	53	12	11	1	2	4
1983-84	Victoria	WHL	69	15	15	30	97	....	....	....	....	....
1984-85	Victoria	WHL	16	5	6	11	45	....	....	....	....	....
	Portland	WHL	56	28	32	60	122	6	2	1	3	13
1985-86	Kamloops	WHL	9	3	4	7	13	....	....	....	....	....
	Medicine Hat	WHL	60	25	32	57	167	25	6	3	9	72
1986-87	Saginaw	IHL	81	26	49	75	173	10	5	6	11	22
1987-88	**Chicago**	**NHL**	**23**	**1**	**3**	**4**	**71**	....	....	....	....	....
	Saginaw	IHL	62	29	22	51	211	10	3	7	10	44
1988-89	**Chicago**	**NHL**	**23**	**1**	**2**	**3**	**78**	....	....	....	....	....
	Saginaw	IHL	57	22	23	45	223	....	....	....	....	....
1989-90	**Minnesota**	**NHL**	**16**	**2**	**0**	**2**	**28**	....	....	....	....	....
1990-91	Kalamazoo	IHL	82	28	30	58	226	6	7	2	9	6
	NHL Totals		**62**	**4**	**5**	**9**	**177**	....	....	....	....	....

Claimed by **Minnesota** in NHL Waiver Draft, October 2, 1989. Traded to **Vancouver** by **Minnesota** for future considerations, September 7, 1990.

MACKEY, JAMES

Defense. Shoots right. 6'4", 225 lbs. Born, Saratoga Springs, NY, January 20, 1972.
(Boston's 6th choice, 147th overall, in 1990 Entry Draft).

			Regular Season					Playoffs				
Season	Club	Lea	GP	G	A	TP	PIM	GP	G	A	TP	PIM
1989-90	Hotchkiss	HS	25	3	7	10		....	....	....	....	....
1990-91	Yale	ECAC	18	0	1	1	12	....	....	....	....	....

MacLEAN, JOHN

Right wing. Shoots right. 6', 200 lbs. Born, Oshawa, Ont., November 20, 1964.
(New Jersey's 1st choice, 6th overall, in 1983 Entry Draft).

			Regular Season					Playoffs				
Season	Club	Lea	GP	G	A	TP	PIM	GP	G	A	TP	PIM
1981-82	Oshawa	OHL	67	17	22	39	197	12	3	6	9	63
1982-83	Oshawa	OHL	66	47	51	98	138	17	*18	20	*38	35
1983-84	**New Jersey**	**NHL**	**23**	**1**	**0**	**1**	**10**	....	....	....	....	....
	Oshawa	OHL	30	23	36	59	58	7	2	5	7	18
1984-85	**New Jersey**	**NHL**	**61**	**13**	**20**	**33**	**44**	....	....	....	....	....
1985-86	**New Jersey**	**NHL**	**74**	**21**	**36**	**57**	**112**	....	....	....	....	....
1986-87	**New Jersey**	**NHL**	**80**	**31**	**36**	**67**	**120**	....	....	....	....	....
1987-88	**New Jersey**	**NHL**	**76**	**23**	**16**	**39**	**147**	**20**	**7**	**11**	**18**	**60**
1988-89	**New Jersey**	**NHL**	**74**	**42**	**45**	**87**	**127**	....	....	....	....	....
1989-90	**New Jersey**	**NHL**	**80**	**41**	**38**	**79**	**80**	**6**	**4**	**1**	**5**	**12**
1990-91	**New Jersey**	**NHL**	**78**	**45**	**33**	**78**	**150**	**7**	**5**	**3**	**8**	**20**
	NHL Totals		**546**	**217**	**224**	**441**	**790**	**33**	**16**	**15**	**31**	**92**

Played in NHL All-Star Game (1989, 1991)

MacLEAN, PAUL (muh KLAYN)

Right wing. Shoots right. 6'2", 218 lbs. Born, Grostenquin, France, March 9, 1958.
(St. Louis' 6th choice, 109th overall, in 1978 Amateur Draft).

			Regular Season					Playoffs				
Season	Club	Lea	GP	G	A	TP	PIM	GP	G	A	TP	PIM
1977-78	Hull	QJHL	66	38	33	71	125	....	....	....	....	....
1978-79	Dalhousie	AUAA	....	....	....	....	....	....	....	....	....	....
1979-80	Cdn. National	...	50	21	11	32	90	....	....	....	....	....
	Cdn. Olympic	...	6	2	3	5	6	....	....	....	....	....
1980-81	**St. Louis**	**NHL**	**1**	**0**	**0**	**0**	**0**	....	....	....	....	....
	Salt Lake	CHL	80	36	42	78	160	17	11	5	16	47
1981-82	**Winnipeg**	**NHL**	**74**	**36**	**25**	**61**	**106**	**4**	**3**	**2**	**5**	**20**
1982-83	**Winnipeg**	**NHL**	**80**	**32**	**44**	**76**	**121**	**3**	**1**	**2**	**3**	**6**
1983-84	**Winnipeg**	**NHL**	**76**	**40**	**31**	**71**	**155**	**3**	**1**	**0**	**1**	**0**
1984-85	**Winnipeg**	**NHL**	**79**	**41**	**60**	**101**	**119**	**8**	**3**	**4**	**7**	**4**
1985-86	**Winnipeg**	**NHL**	**69**	**27**	**29**	**56**	**74**	**2**	**1**	**0**	**1**	**7**
1986-87	**Winnipeg**	**NHL**	**72**	**32**	**42**	**74**	**75**	**10**	**5**	**2**	**7**	**16**
1987-88	**Winnipeg**	**NHL**	**77**	**40**	**39**	**79**	**76**	**5**	**2**	**0**	**2**	**23**
1988-89	**Detroit**	**NHL**	**76**	**36**	**35**	**71**	**118**	**5**	**1**	**1**	**2**	**8**
1989-90	**St. Louis**	**NHL**	**78**	**34**	**33**	**67**	**100**	**12**	**4**	**3**	**7**	**20**
1990-91	**St. Louis**	**NHL**	**37**	**6**	**11**	**17**	**24**	....	....	....	....	....
	NHL Totals		**719**	**324**	**349**	**673**	**968**	**52**	**21**	**14**	**35**	**104**

Played in NHL All-Star Game (1985)

Traded to **Winnipeg** by **St. Louis** with Bryan Maxwell and Ed Staniowski for Scott Campbell and John Markell, July 3, 1981. Traded to **Detroit** by **Winnipeg** for Brent Ashton, June 13, 1988. Traded to **St. Louis** by **Detroit** with Adam Oates for Bernie Federko and Tony McKegney, June 15, 1989.

MacLELLAN, BRIAN

Left wing. Shoots left. 6'3", 215 lbs. Born, Guelph, Ont., October 27, 1958.

			Regular Season					Playoffs				
Season	Club	Lea	GP	G	A	TP	PIM	GP	G	A	TP	PIM
1978-79	Bowling Green	CCHA	44	34	29	63	94	....	....	....	....	....
1979-80	Bowling Green	CCHA	38	8	15	23	46	....	....	....	....	....
1980-81	Bowling Green	CCHA	37	11	14	25	96	....	....	....	....	....
1981-82	Bowling Green	CCHA	41	11	21	32	109	....	....	....	....	....
1982-83	**Los Angeles**	**NHL**	**8**	**0**	**3**	**3**	**7**	....	....	....	....	....
	New Haven	AHL	71	11	15	26	40	12	5	3	8	4
1983-84	**Los Angeles**	**NHL**	**72**	**25**	**29**	**54**	**45**	....	....	....	....	....
	New Haven	AHL	2	0	2	2	0	....	....	....	....	....
1984-85	**Los Angeles**	**NHL**	**80**	**31**	**54**	**85**	**53**	**3**	**0**	**1**	**1**	**0**
1985-86	**Los Angeles**	**NHL**	**27**	**5**	**8**	**13**	**19**	....	....	....	....	....
	NY Rangers	**NHL**	**51**	**11**	**21**	**32**	**47**	**16**	**2**	**4**	**6**	**15**
1986-87	**Minnesota**	**NHL**	**76**	**32**	**31**	**63**	**69**	....	....	....	....	....
1987-88	**Minnesota**	**NHL**	**75**	**16**	**32**	**48**	**74**	....	....	....	....	....
1988-89	**Minnesota**	**NHL**	**60**	**16**	**23**	**39**	**104**	....	....	....	....	....
	Calgary	**NHL**	**12**	**2**	**3**	**5**	**14**	**21**	**3**	**2**	**5**	**19**
1989-90	**Calgary**	**NHL**	**65**	**20**	**18**	**38**	**26**	**6**	**0**	**2**	**2**	**8**
1990-91	**Calgary**	**NHL**	**57**	**13**	**14**	**27**	**55**	**1**	**0**	**0**	**0**	**0**
	NHL Totals		**583**	**171**	**236**	**407**	**513**	**47**	**5**	**9**	**14**	**42**

Signed as a free agent by **Los Angeles**, May 12, 1982. Traded to **NY Rangers** by **Los Angeles** with Los Angeles' fourth-round draft choice in 1987 (Michael Sullivan) for Roland Melanson and Grant Ledyard, December 9, 1985. Traded to **Minnesota** by **NY Rangers** for Minnesota's third-round choice (Simon Gagne) in 1987 Entry Draft, September 8, 1986. Traded to **Calgary** by **Minnesota** with Minnesota's fourth-round choice (Robert Reichel) in 1989 Entry Draft for Shane Churla and Perry Berezan, March 4, 1989. Traded to **Detroit** by **Calgary** for Marc Habscheid, June 11, 1991.

MacLEOD, PAT

Defense. Shoots left. 5'11", 190 lbs. Born, Melfort, Sask., June 15, 1969.
(Minnesota's 5th choice, 87th overall, in 1989 Entry Draft).

			Regular Season					Playoffs				
Season	Club	Lea	GP	G	A	TP	PIM	GP	G	A	TP	PIM
1987-88	Kamloops	WHL	50	13	33	46	27	18	2	7	9	6
1988-89	Kamloops	WHL	37	11	34	45	14	15	7	18	25	24
1989-90	Kalamazoo	IHL	82	9	38	47	27	10	1	6	7	2
1990-91	**Minnesota**	**NHL**	**1**	**0**	**1**	**1**	**0**	....	....	....	....	....
	Kalamazoo	IHL	59	10	30	40	16	11	1	2	3	5
	NHL Totals		**1**	**0**	**1**	**1**	**0**	....	....	....	....	....

Claimed by **San Jose** from **Minnesota** in Dispersal Draft, May 30, 1991.

MACOUN, JAMIE (muh-KOW-uhn)

Defense. Shoots left. 6'2", 197 lbs. Born, Newmarket, Ont., August 17, 1961.

			Regular Season					Playoffs				
Season	Club	Lea	GP	G	A	TP	PIM	GP	G	A	TP	PIM
1980-81	Ohio State	CCHA	38	9	20	29	83	....	....	....	....	....
1981-82	Ohio State	CCHA	25	2	18	20	89	....	....	....	....	....
1982-83	Ohio State	CCHA	19	6	21	27	54	....	....	....	....	....
	Calgary	**NHL**	**22**	**1**	**4**	**5**	**25**	**9**	**0**	**2**	**2**	**8**
1983-84a	**Calgary**	**NHL**	**72**	**9**	**23**	**32**	**97**	**11**	**1**	**0**	**1**	**0**
1984-85	**Calgary**	**NHL**	**70**	**9**	**30**	**39**	**67**	**4**	**1**	**0**	**1**	**4**
1985-86	**Calgary**	**NHL**	**77**	**11**	**21**	**32**	**81**	**22**	**1**	**6**	**7**	**23**
1986-87	**Calgary**	**NHL**	**79**	**7**	**33**	**40**	**111**	**3**	**0**	**1**	**1**	**8**
1987-88			DID NOT PLAY – INJURED									
1988-89	**Calgary**	**NHL**	**72**	**8**	**19**	**27**	**76**	**22**	**3**	**6**	**9**	**30**
1989-90	**Calgary**	**NHL**	**78**	**8**	**27**	**35**	**70**	**6**	**0**	**3**	**3**	**10**
1990-91	**Calgary**	**NHL**	**79**	**7**	**15**	**22**	**84**	**7**	**0**	**1**	**1**	**4**
	NHL Totals		**549**	**60**	**172**	**232**	**611**	**84**	**6**	**19**	**25**	**87**

a NHL All-Rookie Team (1984).

Signed as free agent by **Calgary**, January 30, 1983.

MacTAVISH, CRAIG

Center. Shoots left. 6'1", 195 lbs. Born, London, Ont., August 15, 1958.
(Boston's 9th choice, 153rd overall, in 1978 Amateur Draft).

			Regular Season					Playoffs				
Season	Club	Lea	GP	G	A	TP	PIM	GP	G	A	TP	PIM
1978-79	U. of Lowell	ECAC	....	36	52	*88	....					
1979-80	**Boston**	**NHL**	**46**	**11**	**17**	**28**	**8**	**10**	**2**	**3**	**5**	**7**
	Binghamton	AHL	34	17	15	32	29	....	....	....	....	....
1980-81	**Boston**	**NHL**	**24**	**3**	**5**	**8**	**13**	....	....	....	....	....
	Springfield	AHL	53	19	24	43	81	7	5	4	9	8
1981-82	**Boston**	**NHL**	**2**	**0**	**1**	**1**	**0**	....	....	....	....	....
	Erie	AHL	72	23	32	55	37	....	....	....	....	....
1982-83	**Boston**	**NHL**	**75**	**10**	**20**	**30**	**18**	**17**	**3**	**1**	**4**	**18**
1983-84	**Boston**	**NHL**	**70**	**20**	**23**	**43**	**35**	**1**	**0**	**0**	**0**	**0**
1984-85			DID NOT PLAY									
1985-86	**Edmonton**	**NHL**	**74**	**23**	**24**	**47**	**70**	**10**	**4**	**4**	**8**	**11**
1986-87	**Edmonton**	**NHL**	**79**	**20**	**19**	**39**	**55**	**21**	**1**	**9**	**10**	**16**
1987-88	**Edmonton**	**NHL**	**80**	**15**	**17**	**32**	**47**	**19**	**0**	**1**	**1**	**31**
1988-89	**Edmonton**	**NHL**	**80**	**21**	**31**	**52**	**55**	**7**	**0**	**1**	**1**	**8**
1989-90	**Edmonton**	**NHL**	**80**	**21**	**22**	**43**	**89**	**22**	**2**	**6**	**8**	**29**
1990-91	**Edmonton**	**NHL**	**80**	**17**	**15**	**32**	**76**	**18**	**3**	**3**	**6**	**20**
	NHL Totals		**690**	**161**	**194**	**355**	**466**	**125**	**15**	**28**	**43**	**140**

Signed as a free agent by **Edmonton**, February 1, 1985.

MacVICAR, ANDREW

Left wing. Shoots left. 6'1", 210 lbs. Born, Dartmouth, N. S., March 12, 1969.
(Buffalo's 3rd choice, 53rd overall, in 1987 Entry Draft).

			Regular Season					Playoffs				
Season	Club	Lea	GP	G	A	TP	PIM	GP	G	A	TP	PIM
1986-87	Peterborough	OHL	64	6	13	19	33	11	2	1	3	7
1987-88	Peterborough	OHL	62	30	51	81	45	12	2	10	12	8
1988-89	Peterborough	OHL	66	25	29	54	56	17	5	6	11	30
1989-90	Sudbury	OHL	41	12	16	28	47	7	2	5	7	18
	Phoenix	IHL	1	0	0	0	0	....	....	....	....	....
1990-91	Johnstown	ECHL	55	27	34	61	72	10	2	6	8	18

MADILL, JEFF (muh-DILL)

Right wing. Shoots left. 5'11", 195 lbs. Born, Oshawa, Ont., June 21, 1965.
(New Jersey's 2nd choice, 7th overall, in 1987 Supplemental Draft).

			Regular Season					Playoffs				
Season	Club	Lea	GP	G	A	TP	PIM	GP	G	A	TP	PIM
1984-85	Ohio State	CCHA	12	5	6	11	18	....	....	....	....	....
1985-86	Ohio State	CCHA	41	32	25	57	65	....	....	....	....	....
1986-87	Ohio State	CCHA	43	38	32	70	139	....	....	....	....	....
1987-88	Utica	AHL	58	18	15	33	127	....	....	....	....	....
1988-89	Utica	AHL	69	23	25	48	225	4	1	0	1	35
1989-90	Utica	AHL	74	43	26	69	233	4	1	2	3	33
1990-91	**New Jersey**	**NHL**	**14**	**4**	**0**	**4**	**46**	**7**	**0**	**2**	**2**	**8**
a	Utica	AHL	54	42	35	77	151	....	....	....	....	....
	NHL Totals		**14**	**4**	**0**	**4**	**46**	**7**	**0**	**2**	**2**	**8**

a AHL Second All-Star Team (1991)

Claimed by **San Jose** from **New Jersey** in Expansion Draft, May 30, 1991.

MAGUIRE, DEREK

Defense. Shoots right. 6', 185 lbs. Born, Delbarton, NJ, December 9, 1971.
(Montreal's 10th choice, 186th overall, in 1990 Entry Draft).

			Regular Season					Playoffs				
Season	Club	Lea	GP	G	A	TP	PIM	GP	G	A	TP	PIM
1989-90	Delbarton	HS	28	38	40	78	....	....	....	....	....	....
1990-91	Harvard	ECAC	24	3	14	17	12	....	....	....	....	....

MAGUIRE, KEVIN

Right Wing. Shoots right. 6'2", 200 lbs. Born, Toronto, Ont., January 5, 1963.

			Regular Season					Playoffs				
Season	Club	Lea	GP	G	A	TP	PIM	GP	G	A	TP	PIM
1983-84	Orilla	OPJHL	....	35	42	77	....	....	....	....	....	....
1984-85	St. Catharines	AHL	76	10	15	25	112	....	....	....	....	....
1985-86	St. Catharines	AHL	61	6	9	15	161	1	0	0	0	0
1986-87	**Toronto**	**NHL**	**17**	**0**	**0**	**0**	**74**	**1**	**0**	**0**	**0**	**0**
	Newmarket	AHL	51	4	2	6	131	....	....	....	....	....
1987-88	**Buffalo**	**NHL**	**46**	**4**	**6**	**10**	**162**	**5**	**0**	**0**	**0**	**50**
1988-89	**Buffalo**	**NHL**	**60**	**8**	**10**	**18**	**241**	**5**	**0**	**0**	**0**	**36**
1989-90	**Buffalo**	**NHL**	**61**	**6**	**9**	**15**	**115**	....	....	....	....	....
	Philadelphia	**NHL**	**5**	**1**	**0**	**1**	**6**	....	....	....	....	....
1990-91	**Toronto**	**NHL**	**63**	**9**	**5**	**14**	**180**	....	....	....	....	....
	NHL Totals		**252**	**28**	**30**	**58**	**778**	**11**	**0**	**0**	**0**	**6**

Signed as a free agent by**Toronto**, October 10, 1984. Claimed by **Buffalo** in NHL Waiver Draft, October, 5, 1987. Traded to **Philadelphia** by **Buffalo** with Buffalo's second round choice (Mikael Renberg) in 1990 Entry Draft for Jay Wells and Philadelphia's fourth round choice (Peter Ambroziak) in 1991 Entry Draft, March 5, 1990. Traded to **Toronto** by **Philadelphia** with Philadelphia's eighth round choice (Dimitri Mironov) in 1991 Entry Draft for Toronto's third round choice (Al Kinisky) in 1990 Entry Draft, June 16, 1990.

MAHER, JIM

Defense. Shoots left. 6'1", 210 lbs. Born, Warren, MI, June 30, 1970.
(Los Angeles' 2nd choice, 81st overall, in 1989 Entry Draft).

			Regular Season					Playoffs				
Season	Club	Lea	GP	G	A	TP	PIM	GP	G	A	TP	PIM
1988-89	Ill.-Chicago	CCHA	31	1	5	6	40	....	....	....	....	....
1989-90	Ill.-Chicago	CCHA	38	4	12	16	64	....	....	....	....	....
1990-91	Ill.-Chicago	CCHA	37	6	8	14	49	....	....	....	....	....

MAILHOT, JACQUES (may-OH)

Left wing. Shoots left. 6'2", 208 lbs. Born, Shawinigan, Que., December 5, 1961.

			Regular Season					Playoffs				
Season	Club	Lea	GP	G	A	TP	PIM	GP	G	A	TP	PIM
1987-88	Baltimore	AHL	15	2	0	2	167	....	....	....	....	....
	Fredericton	AHL	28	2	6	8	137	8	0	0	0	18
1988-89	**Quebec**	**NHL**	**5**	**0**	**0**	**0**	**33**	....	....	....	....	....
	Halifax	AHL	35	4	1	5	259	1	0	0	0	5
1989-90	Moncton	AHL	6	0	0	0	20	....	....	....	....	....
	Cape Breton	AHL	6	0	1	1	12	....	....	....	....	....
	Hampton Roads	ECHL	5	0	2	2	62	....	....	....	....	....
1990-91	Moncton	AHL	13	0	0	0	43	....	....	....	....	....
	San Diego	IHL	1	0	0	0	2	....	....	....	....	....
	Johnstown	ECHL	2	0	0	0	21	9	1	3	4	46
	NHL Totals		**5**	**0**	**0**	**0**	**33**	....	....	....	....	....

Signed as a free agent by **Quebec**, August 15, 1988.

MAILLET, CLAUDE

Defense. Shoots right. 6'2", 200 lbs. Born, Memramcook, N.B., May 22, 1969.
(Chicago's 1st choice, 21st overall, in 1990 Supplemental Draft).

			Regular Season					Playoffs				
Season	Club	Lea	GP	G	A	TP	PIM	GP	G	A	TP	PIM
1988-89	Merrimack	NCAA	30	1	27	28	30	....	....	....	....	....
1989-90	Merrimack	H.E.	32	8	15	23	55	....	....	....	....	....
1990-91	Merrimack	H.E.	33	3	9	12	45	....	....	....	....	....

MAJOR, BRUCE

Center. Shoots left. 6'3", 180 lbs. Born, Vernon, B.C., January 3, 1967.
(Quebec's 6th choice, 99th overall, in 1985 Entry Draft).

			Regular Season					Playoffs				
Season	Club	Lea	GP	G	A	TP	PIM	GP	G	A	TP	PIM
1985-86	U. of Maine	H.E.	38	14	14	28	39	....	....	....	....	....
1986-87	U. of Maine	H.E.	37	14	10	24	12	....	....	....	....	....
1987-88	U. of Maine	H.E.	26	0	5	5	14	....	....	....	....	....
1988-89	U. of Maine	H.E.	42	13	11	24	22	....	....	....	....	....
1989-90	Halifax	AHL	32	5	6	11	23	....	....	....	....	....
	Greensboro	ECHL	12	4	3	7	6	10	2	2	4	12
1990-91	**Quebec**	**NHL**	**4**	**0**	**0**	**0**	**0**	....	....	....	....	....
	Halifax	AHL	9	2	0	2	9	....	....	....	....	....
	Fort Wayne	IHL	62	11	25	36	48	18	1	3	4	6
	NHL Totals		**4**	**0**	**0**	**0**	**0**	....	....	....	....	....

MAJOR, MARK

Left wing. Shoots left. 6'3", 223 lbs. Born, Toronto, Ont., March 20, 1970.
(Pittsburgh's 2nd choice, 25th overall, in 1988 Entry Draft).

			Regular Season					Playoffs				
Season	Club	Lea	GP	G	A	TP	PIM	GP	G	A	TP	PIM
1987-88	North Bay	OHL	57	16	17	33	272	4	0	2	2	8
1988-89	North Bay	OHL	11	3	2	5	58	....	....	....	....	....
	Kingston	OHL	53	22	29	51	193	....	....	....	....	....
1989-90	Kingston	OHL	62	29	32	61	168	6	3	3	6	12
1990-91	Muskegon	IHL	60	8	10	18	160	5	0	0	0	0

MAKAROV, SERGEI (mah-KAH-rahf)

Right wing. Shoots left. 5'11", 185 lbs. Born, Chelyabinsk, Soviet Union, June 19, 1958.
(Calgary's 14th choice, 231st overall, in 1983 Entry Draft).

			Regular Season					Playoffs				
Season	Club	Lea	GP	G	A	TP	PIM	GP	G	A	TP	PIM
1976-77	Traktor	USSR	11	1	0	1	4	....	....	....	....	....
1977-78	Traktor	USSR	36	18	13	31	10	....	....	....	....	....
1978-79a	CSKA	USSR	44	18	21	39	12	....	....	....	....	....
1979-80bc	CSKA	USSR	44	29	39	68	16	....	....	....	....	....
1980-81ab	CSKA	USSR	49	42	37	79	22	....	....	....	....	....
1981-82ab	CSKA	USSR	46	32	43	75	18	....	....	....	....	....
1982-83a	CSKA	USSR	30	25	17	42	6	....	....	....	....	....
1983-84ab	CSKA	USSR	44	36	37	73	28	....	....	....	....	....
1984-85abc	CSKA	USSR	40	26	39	65	28	....	....	....	....	....
1985-86ab	CSKA	USSR	40	30	32	62	28	....	....	....	....	....
1986-87ab	CSKA	USSR	40	21	32	53	26	....	....	....	....	....
1987-88ab	CSKA	USSR	51	23	45	68	50	....	....	....	....	....
1988-89bc	CSKA	USSR	44	21	33	54	42	....	....	....	....	....
1989-90de	**Calgary**	**NHL**	**80**	**24**	**62**	**86**	**55**	**6**	**0**	**6**	**6**	**0**
1990-91	**Calgary**	**NHL**	**78**	**30**	**49**	**79**	**44**	**3**	**1**	**0**	**1**	**0**
	NHL Totals		**158**	**54**	**111**	**165**	**99**	**9**	**1**	**6**	**7**	**0**

a Soviet National League All-Star (1981-88)
b Izvestia trophy-leading scorer (1980-82, 1984-89)
c Soviet Player of the Year (1980, 1985, 1989)
d NHL All-Rookie Team (1990)
e Won Calder Memorial Trophy (1990)

MAKELA, MIKKO (MAK-uh-luh, MEE-koh)

Left wing. Shoots left. 6'2", 200 lbs. Born, Tampere, Finland, February 28, 1965.
(NY Islanders' 5th choice, 65th overall, in 1983 Entry Draft).

			Regular Season					Playoffs				
Season	Club	Lea	GP	G	A	TP	PIM	GP	G	A	TP	PIM
1983-84	Ilves	Fin.	35	17	11	28	26	2	0	1	1	0
1984-85a	Ilves	Fin.	36	34	25	59	24	9	4	7	11	10
1985-86	**NY Islanders**	**NHL**	**58**	**16**	**20**	**36**	**28**	....	....	....	....	....
	Springfield	AHL	2	1	1	2	0	....	....	....	....	....
1986-87	**NY Islanders**	**NHL**	**80**	**24**	**33**	**57**	**24**	**11**	**2**	**4**	**6**	**8**
1987-88	**NY Islanders**	**NHL**	**73**	**36**	**40**	**76**	**22**	**6**	**1**	**4**	**5**	**6**
1988-89	**NY Islanders**	**NHL**	**76**	**17**	**28**	**45**	**22**	....	....	....	....	....
1989-90	**NY Islanders**	**NHL**	**20**	**2**	**3**	**5**	**2**	....	....	....	....	....
	Los Angeles	**NHL**	**45**	**7**	**14**	**21**	**16**	**1**	**0**	**0**	**0**	**0**
1990-91	**Buffalo**	**NHL**	**60**	**15**	**7**	**22**	**25**	....	....	....	....	....
	NHL Totals		**412**	**117**	**145**	**262**	**139**	**18**	**3**	**8**	**11**	**14**

a Finnish League First All-Star Team (1985)

Traded to **Los Angeles** by **NY Islanders** for Ken Baumgartner and Hubie McDonough, November 29, 1989. Traded to **Buffalo** by **Los Angeles** for Mike Donnelly, September 30, 1990.

MALAKHOV, VLADIMIR (mah-LAH-hahf)

Defense. 6'2", 207 lbs. Born, Sverdlovsk, Soviet Union, August 30, 1968.
(NY Islanders' 12th choice, 191st overall, in 1989 Entry Draft).

			Regular Season					Playoffs				
Season	Club	Lea	GP	G	A	TP	PIM	GP	G	A	TP	PIM
1986-87	Spartak	USSR	22	0	1	1	12	....	....	....	....	....
1987-88	Spartak	USSR	28	2	2	4	26	....	....	....	....	....
1988-89	CSKA	USSR	34	6	2	8	16	....	....	....	....	....
1989-90	CSKA	USSR	48	2	10	12	34	....	....	....	....	....
1990-91	CSKA	USSR	46	5	13	18	22	....	....	....	....	....

MALKOC, DEAN

Defense. Shoots right. 6'3", 200 lbs. Born, Vancouver, B.C., January 26, 1970.
(New Jersey's 7th choice, 95th overall, in 1990 Entry Draft).

			Regular Season					Playoffs				
Season	Club	Lea	GP	G	A	TP	PIM	GP	G	A	TP	PIM
1989-90	Kamloops	WHL	48	3	18	21	209	17	0	3	3	56
1990-91	Kamloops	WHL	8	1	4	5	47	....	....	....	....	....
	Swift Current	WHL	56	10	23	33	248	3	0	2	2	5
	Utica	AHL	1	0	0	0	0	....	....	....	....	....

MALEY, DAVID

Left wing. Shoots left. 6'2", 195 lbs. Born, Beaver Dam, WI, April 24, 1963.
(Montreal's 4th choice, 33rd overall, in 1982 Entry Draft).

			Regular Season					Playoffs				
Season	Club	Lea	GP	G	A	TP	PIM	GP	G	A	TP	PIM
1982-83	U. Wisconsin	WCHA	47	17	23	40	24	....	....	....	....	....
1983-84	U. Wisconsin	WCHA	38	10	28	38	56	....	....	....	....	....
1984-85	U. Wisconsin	WCHA	38	19	9	28	86	....	....	....	....	....
1985-86	U. Wisconsin	WCHA	42	20	40	60	135	....	....	....	....	....
	Montreal	**NHL**	**3**	**0**	**0**	**0**	**0**	**7**	**1**	**3**	**4**	**2**
1986-87	**Montreal**	**NHL**	**48**	**6**	**12**	**18**	**55**	....	....	....	....	....
	Sherbrooke	AHL	11	1	5	6	25	12	7	7	14	10
1987-88	**New Jersey**	**NHL**	**44**	**4**	**2**	**6**	**65**	**20**	**3**	**1**	**4**	**80**
	Utica	AHL	9	5	3	8	40	....	....	....	....	....
1988-89	**New Jersey**	**NHL**	**68**	**5**	**6**	**11**	**249**	....	....	....	....	....
1989-90	**New Jersey**	**NHL**	**67**	**8**	**17**	**25**	**160**	**6**	**0**	**0**	**0**	**25**
1990-91	**New Jersey**	**NHL**	**64**	**8**	**14**	**22**	**151**	....	....	....	....	....
	NHL Totals		**294**	**31**	**51**	**82**	**680**	**33**	**4**	**4**	**8**	**107**

Traded to **New Jersey** by **Montreal** for New Jersey's third-round choice (Mathieu Schneider) in 1987 Entry Draft, June 13, 1987.

MALLETTE, TROY

Left wing. Shoots left. 6'2", 210 lbs. Born, Sudbury, Ont., February 25, 1970.
(New York Rangers' 1st choice, 22nd overall, in 1988 Entry Draft).

			Regular Season					Playoffs				
Season	Club	Lea	GP	G	A	TP	PIM	GP	G	A	TP	PIM
1986-87	S.S. Marie	OHL	65	20	25	45	157	4	0	2	2	12
1987-88	S.S. Marie	OHL	62	18	30	48	186	6	1	3	4	12
1988-89	S.S. Marie	OHL	64	39	37	76	172	0	0	0	0	0
1989-90	**NY Rangers**	**NHL**	**79**	**13**	**16**	**29**	**305**	**10**	**2**	**2**	**4**	**81**
1990-91	**NY Rangers**	**NHL**	**71**	**12**	**10**	**22**	**252**	**5**	**0**	**0**	**0**	**18**
	NHL Totals		**150**	**25**	**26**	**51**	**557**	**15**	**2**	**2**	**4**	**99**

MALLGRAVE, MATTHEW

Right wing. Shoots right. 6', 180 lbs. Born, Washington, D.C., May 3, 1970.
(Toronto's 6th choice, 132nd overall, in 1988 Entry Draft).

			Regular Season					Playoffs				
Season	Club	Lea	GP	G	A	TP	PIM	GP	G	A	TP	PIM
1989-90	Harvard	ECAC	26	3	3	6	33	....	....	....	....	....
1990-91	Harvard	ECAC	25	5	14	19	14	....	....	....	....	....

MALONE, SCOTT

Defense. Shoots left. 6', 180 lbs. Born, Boston, MA, January 16, 1971.
(Toronto's 10th choice, 220th overall, in 1990 Entry Draft).

			Regular Season					Playoffs				
Season	Club	Lea	GP	G	A	TP	PIM	GP	G	A	TP	PIM
1989-90	Northfield	HS	18	10	25	35	....	....	....	....	....	....
1990-91	N. Hampshire	H.E.	DID NOT PLAY									

MALONEY, DONALD MICHAEL (DON) (ma-LOAN-ee)

Left wing. Shoots left. 6'1", 190 lbs. Born, Lindsay, Ont., September 5, 1958.
(NY Rangers' 1st choice, 26th overall, in 1978 Amateur Draft).

			Regular Season					Playoffs				
Season	Club	Lea	GP	G	A	TP	PIM	GP	G	A	TP	PIM
1976-77	Kitchener	OHA	38	22	34	56	126	....	....	....	....	....
1977-78	Kitchener	OHA	62	30	74	104	143	9	4	9	13	40
1978-79	**NY Rangers**	**NHL**	**28**	**9**	**17**	**26**	**39**	**18**	**7**	***13**	**20**	**19**
	New Haven	AHL	38	18	26	44	62	....	....	....	....	....
1979-80	**NY Rangers**	**NHL**	**79**	**25**	**48**	**73**	**97**	**9**	**0**	**4**	**4**	**10**
1980-81	**NY Rangers**	**NHL**	**61**	**29**	**23**	**52**	**99**	**13**	**1**	**6**	**7**	**13**
1981-82	**NY Rangers**	**NHL**	**54**	**22**	**36**	**58**	**73**	**10**	**5**	**5**	**10**	**10**
1982-83	**NY Rangers**	**NHL**	**78**	**29**	**40**	**69**	**88**	**5**	**0**	**1**	**1**	**0**
1983-84	**NY Rangers**	**NHL**	**79**	**24**	**42**	**66**	**62**	**5**	**1**	**4**	**5**	**0**
1984-85	**NY Rangers**	**NHL**	**37**	**11**	**16**	**27**	**32**	**3**	**4**	**0**	**4**	**2**
1985-86	**NY Rangers**	**NHL**	**68**	**11**	**17**	**28**	**56**	**16**	**2**	**1**	**3**	**31**
1986-87	**NY Rangers**	**NHL**	**72**	**19**	**38**	**57**	**117**	**6**	**2**	**1**	**3**	**6**
1987-88	**NY Rangers**	**NHL**	**66**	**12**	**21**	**33**	**60**	....	....	....	....	....
1988-89	**NY Rangers**	**NHL**	**31**	**4**	**9**	**13**	**16**	....	....	....	....	....
	Hartford	**NHL**	**21**	**3**	**11**	**14**	**23**	**4**	**0**	**0**	**0**	**8**
1989-90	**NY Islanders**	**NHL**	**79**	**16**	**27**	**43**	**47**	**5**	**0**	**0**	**0**	**2**
1990-91	**NY Islanders**	**NHL**	**12**	**0**	**5**	**5**	**6**	....	....	....	....	....
	NHL Totals		**765**	**214**	**350**	**564**	**815**	**94**	**22**	**35**	**57**	**101**

Played in NHL All-Star Game (1983, 1984)

Traded to **Hartford** by **NY Rangers** with Brian Lawton and Norm MacIver for Carey Wilson and Hartford's fifth-round choice (Lubos Rob) in 1990 Entry Draft, December 26, 1988. Signed as a free agent by **NY Islanders**, August 25, 1989.

MALTAIS, STEVE (MAHL-tayz)

Left wing. Shoots left. 6'2", 210 lbs. Born, Arvida, Que., January 25, 1969.
(Washington's 2nd choice, 57th overall, in 1987 Entry Draft).

			Regular Season					Playoffs				
Season	Club	Lea	GP	G	A	TP	PIM	GP	G	A	TP	PIM
1986-87	Cornwall	OHL	65	32	12	44	29	5	0	0	0	2
1987-88	Cornwall	OHL	59	39	46	85	30	11	9	6	15	33
1988-89	Cornwall	OHL	58	53	70	123	67	18	14	16	30	16
	Fort Wayne	IHL	....	....	....	....	....	4	2	1	3	0
1989-90	**Washington**	**NHL**	**8**	**0**	**0**	**0**	**2**	**1**	**0**	**0**	**0**	**0**
	Baltimore	AHL	67	29	37	66	54	12	6	10	16	6
1990-91	**Washington**	**NHL**	**7**	**0**	**0**	**0**	**2**	....	....	....	....	....
	Baltimore	AHL	73	36	43	79	97	6	1	4	5	10
	NHL Totals		**15**	**0**	**0**	**0**	**4**	**1**	**0**	**0**	**0**	**0**

Traded to **Minnesota** by **Washington** with Trent Klatt for Shawn Chambers, June 21, 1991.

MANDERVILLE, KENT

Left wing. Shoots left. 6'3", 200 lbs. Born, Edmonton, Alta., April 12, 1971.
(Calgary's 1st choice, 24th overall, in 1989 Entry Draft).

			Regular Season					Playoffs				
Season	Club	Lea	GP	G	A	TP	PIM	GP	G	A	TP	PIM
1989-90a	Cornell	ECAC	26	11	15	26	28	....	....	....	....	....
1990-91	Cornell	ECAC	28	17	14	31	60	....	....	....	....	....
	Cdn. National	...	3	1	2	3	0	....	....	....	....	....

a ECAC Rookie of the Year (1990)

MANSON, DAVE

Defense. Shoots left. 6'2", 202 lbs. Born, Prince Albert, Sask., January 27, 1967.
(Chicago's 1st choice, 11th overall, in 1985 Entry Draft).

			Regular Season					Playoffs				
Season	Club	Lea	GP	G	A	TP	PIM	GP	G	A	TP	PIM
1983-84	Prince Albert	WHL	70	2	7	9	233	5	0	0	0	4
1984-85	Prince Albert	WHL	72	8	30	38	247	13	1	0	1	34
1985-86	Prince Albert	WHL	70	14	34	48	177	20	1	8	9	63
1986-87	**Chicago**	**NHL**	**63**	**1**	**8**	**9**	**146**	**3**	**0**	**0**	**0**	**10**
1987-88	**Chicago**	**NHL**	**54**	**1**	**6**	**7**	**185**	**5**	**0**	**0**	**0**	**27**
	Saginaw	IHL	6	0	3	3	37	....	....	....	....	....
1988-89	**Chicago**	**NHL**	**79**	**18**	**36**	**54**	**352**	**16**	**0**	**8**	**8**	**84**
1989-90	**Chicago**	**NHL**	**59**	**5**	**23**	**28**	**301**	**20**	**2**	**4**	**6**	**46**
1990-91	**Chicago**	**NHL**	**75**	**14**	**15**	**29**	**191**	**6**	**0**	**1**	**1**	**36**
	NHL Totals		**330**	**39**	**88**	**127**	**1175**	**50**	**2**	**13**	**15**	**203**

Played in NHL All-Star Game (1989)

MANTHA, MAURICE WILLIAM (MOE) (MAN-tha)

Defense. Shoots right. 6'2", 210 lbs. Born, Lakewood, OH, January 21, 1961.
(Winnipeg's 2nd choice, 23rd overall, in 1980 Entry Draft).

			Regular Season					Playoffs				
Season	Club	Lea	GP	G	A	TP	PIM	GP	G	A	TP	PIM
1978-79	Toronto	OHA	68	10	38	48	57	4	0	2	2	11
1979-80	Toronto	OHA	58	8	38	46	86	....	....	....	....	....
1980-81	**Winnipeg**	**NHL**	**58**	**2**	**23**	**25**	**35**	....	....	....	....	....
1981-82	**Winnipeg**	**NHL**	**25**	**0**	**12**	**12**	**28**	**4**	**1**	**3**	**4**	**16**
	Tulsa	CHL	33	8	15	23	56	....	....	....	....	....
1982-83	**Winnipeg**	**NHL**	**21**	**2**	**7**	**9**	**6**	**2**	**2**	**2**	**4**	**0**
	Sherbrooke	AHL	13	1	4	5	13	....	....	....	....	....
1983-84	**Winnipeg**	**NHL**	**72**	**16**	**38**	**54**	**67**	**3**	**1**	**0**	**1**	**0**
	Sherbrooke	AHL	7	1	1	2	10	....	....	....	....	....
1984-85	**Pittsburgh**	**NHL**	**71**	**11**	**40**	**51**	**54**	....	....	....	....	....
1985-86	**Pittsburgh**	**NHL**	**78**	**15**	**52**	**67**	**102**	....	....	....	....	....
1986-87	**Pittsburgh**	**NHL**	**62**	**9**	**31**	**40**	**44**	....	....	....	....	....
1987-88	**Pittsburgh**	**NHL**	**21**	**2**	**8**	**10**	**23**	....	....	....	....	....
	Edmonton	**NHL**	**25**	**0**	**6**	**6**	**26**	....	....	....	....	....
	Minnesota	**NHL**	**30**	**9**	**13**	**22**	**4**	....	....	....	....	....
1988-89	**Minnesota**	**NHL**	**16**	**1**	**6**	**7**	**10**	....	....	....	....	....
	Philadelphia	**NHL**	**30**	**3**	**8**	**11**	**33**	**1**	**0**	**0**	**0**	**0**
1989-90	**Winnipeg**	**NHL**	**73**	**2**	**26**	**28**	**28**	**7**	**1**	**5**	**6**	**2**
1990-91	**Winnipeg**	**NHL**	**57**	**9**	**15**	**24**	**33**	....	....	....	....	....
	NHL Totals		**639**	**81**	**285**	**366**	**493**	**17**	**5**	**10**	**15**	**18**

Traded to **Pittsburgh** by **Winnipeg**, May 1, 1984 to complete deal of March 6, 1984 when Pittsburgh traded Randy Carlyle to Winnipeg. Traded to **Edmonton** by **Pittsburgh** with Craig Simpson, Dave Hannan, and Chris Joseph for Paul Coffey, Dave Hunter, and Wayne Van Dorp, November 24, 1987. Traded to **Minnesota** by **Edmonton** for Keith Acton, January 22, 1988. Traded to **Philadelphia** by **Minnesota** for Toronto's fifth-round choice (Pat MacLeod) in 1989 Entry Draft, December 8, 1988. Claimed by **Winnipeg** in NHL Waiver Draft, October 2, 1989.

MARCHMENT, BRYAN

Defense. Shoots left. 6'1", 198 lbs. Born, Scarborough, Ont., May 1, 1969.
(Winnipeg's 1st choice, 16th overall, in 1987 Entry Draft).

			Regular Season					Playoffs				
Season	Club	Lea	GP	G	A	TP	PIM	GP	G	A	TP	PIM
1985-86	Belleville	OHL	57	5	15	20	225	21	0	7	7	83
1986-87	Belleville	OHL	52	6	38	44	238	6	0	4	4	17
1987-88	Belleville	OHL	56	7	51	58	200	6	1	3	4	19
1988-89	**Winnipeg**	**NHL**	**2**	**0**	**0**	**0**	**2**	....	....	....	....	....
a	Belleville	OHL	43	14	36	50	118	5	0	1	1	12
1989-90	**Winnipeg**	**NHL**	**7**	**0**	**2**	**2**	**28**	....	....	....	....	....
	Moncton	AHL	56	4	19	23	217	....	....	....	....	....
1990-91	**Winnipeg**	**NHL**	**28**	**2**	**2**	**4**	**91**	....	....	....	....	....
	Moncton	AHL	33	2	11	13	101	....	....	....	....	....
	NHL Totals		**37**	**2**	**4**	**6**	**121**	....	....	....	....	....

a OHL Second All-Star Team (1989)

Traded to **Chicago** by **Winnipeg** with Chris Norton for Troy Murray and Warren Rychel, July 22, 1991.

MARCIANO, LANCE

Defense. Shoots right. 6'2", 200 lbs.   Born, Mt. Vernon, NY, December 12, 1969.
(NY Rangers' 12th choice, 220th overall, in 1987 Entry Draft).

				Regular Season					Playoffs			
Season	Club	Lea	GP	G	A	TP	PIM	GP	G	A	TP	PIM
1987-88	Yale	ECAC	18	0	2	2	16	....	....	....	....	....
1988-89	Yale	ECAC	24	1	0	1	26	....	....	....	....	....
1989-90	Yale	ECAC	27	0	9	9	34	....	....	....	....	....
1990-91	Yale	ECAC	28	3	5	8	38	....	....	....	....	....

MARCINYSHYN, DAVID   (MAIR-sih-NIH-shuhn)

Defense. Shoots left. 6'3", 210 lbs.   Born, Edmonton, Alta., February 4, 1967.

				Regular Season					Playoffs			
Season	Club	Lea	GP	G	A	TP	PIM	GP	G	A	TP	PIM
1985-86	Kamloops	WHL	57	2	7	9	111	16	1	3	4	12
1986-87	Kamloops	WHL	68	5	27	32	106	13	0	3	3	35
1987-88	Utica	AHL	73	2	7	9	179	....	....	....	....	....
	Flint	IHL	3	0	0	0	4	16	0	2	2	31
1988-89	Utica	AHL	74	4	14	18	101	5	0	0	0	13
1989-90	Utica	AHL	74	6	18	24	164	5	0	2	2	21
1990-91	**New Jersey**	**NHL**	**9**	**0**	**1**	**1**	**21**	....	....	....	....	....
	Utica	AHL	52	4	9	13	81	....	....	....	....	....
	NHL Totals		**9**	**0**	**1**	**1**	**21**					

Signed as a free agent by **New Jersey**, September 26, 1986. Traded to **Quebec** by **New Jersey** for Brent Severyn, June 3, 1991.

MARKOVICH, MICHAEL

Defense. Shoots left. 6'3", 200 lbs.   Born, Grand Forks, ND, April 25, 1969.
(Pittsburgh's 6th choice, 121st overall, in 1989 Entry Draft).

				Regular Season					Playoffs			
Season	Club	Lea	GP	G	A	TP	PIM	GP	G	A	TP	PIM
1988-89	U. of Denver	WCHA	30	2	12	14	24	....	....	....	....	....
1989-90	U. of Denver	WCHA	42	4	17	21	34	....	....	....	....	....
1990-91	U. of Denver	WCHA	37	5	15	20	41	....	....	....	....	....

MARKWART, NEVIN

Left wing. Shoots left. 5'10", 180 lbs.   Born, Toronto, Ont., December 9, 1964.
(Boston's 1st choice, 21st overall, in 1983 Entry Draft).

				Regular Season					Playoffs			
Season	Club	Lea	GP	G	A	TP	PIM	GP	G	A	TP	PIM
1981-82	Regina	WHL	25	2	12	14	56	20	2	2	4	82
1982-83	Regina	WHL	43	27	39	66	91	1	0	0	0	0
1983-84	**Boston**	**NHL**	**70**	**14**	**16**	**30**	**121**	....	....	....	....	....
1984-85	**Boston**	**NHL**	**26**	**0**	**4**	**4**	**36**	**1**	**0**	**0**	**0**	**0**
	Hershey	AHL	38	13	18	31	79	....	....	....	....	....
1985-86	**Boston**	**NHL**	**65**	**7**	**15**	**22**	**207**	....	....	....	....	....
1986-87	**Boston**	**NHL**	**64**	**10**	**9**	**19**	**225**	**4**	**0**	**0**	**0**	**9**
	Moncton	AHL	3	3	3	6	11	....	....	....	....	....
1987-88	**Boston**	**NHL**	**25**	**1**	**12**	**13**	**85**	**2**	**0**	**0**	**0**	**2**
1988-89	Maine	AHL	1	0	1	1	0	....	....	....	....	....
1989-90	**Boston**	**NHL**	**8**	**1**	**2**	**3**	**15**	....	....	....	....	....
1990-91	**Boston**	**NHL**	**23**	**3**	**3**	**6**	**36**	**2**	**1**	**0**	**1**	**22**
	Maine	AHL	21	5	5	10	22	....	....	....	....	....
	NHL Totals		**281**	**36**	**61**	**97**	**725**	**9**	**1**	**0**	**1**	**33**

MARINUCCI, CHRIS

Center. Shoots left. 6', 175 lbs.   Born, Grand Rapids, MN, December 29, 1971.
(NY Islanders' 4th choice, 90th overall, in 1990 Entry Draft).

				Regular Season					Playoffs			
Season	Club	Lea	GP	G	A	TP	PIM	GP	G	A	TP	PIM
1989-90	Grand Rapids	HS	28	24	39	63	0	....	....	....	....	....
1990-91	U. Minnesota	WCHA	36	6	10	16	20	....	....	....	....	....

MAROIS, DANIEL

Right wing. Shoots right. 6', 190 lbs.   Born, Montreal, Que., October 3, 1968.
(Toronto's 2nd choice, 28th overall, in 1987 Entry Draft).

				Regular Season					Playoffs			
Season	Club	Lea	GP	G	A	TP	PIM	GP	G	A	TP	PIM
1985-86	Verdun	QMJHL	58	42	35	77	110	5	4	2	6	6
1986-87	Chicoutimi	QMJHL	40	22	26	48	143	16	7	14	21	25
1987-88	Verdun	QMJHL	67	52	36	88	153	....	....	....	....	....
	Newmarket	AHL	8	4	4	8	4	....	....	....	....	....
	Toronto	**NHL**	....	....	....	....	....	**3**	**1**	**0**	**1**	**0**
1988-89	**Toronto**	**NHL**	**76**	**31**	**23**	**54**	**76**	....	....	....	....	....
1989-90	**Toronto**	**NHL**	**68**	**39**	**37**	**76**	**82**	**5**	**2**	**2**	**4**	**12**
1990-91	**Toronto**	**NHL**	**78**	**21**	**9**	**30**	**112**	....	....	....	....	....
	NHL Totals		**222**	**91**	**69**	**160**	**270**	**8**	**3**	**2**	**5**	**12**

MAROIS, MARIO   (MAIR-wah)

Defense. Shoots right. 5'11", 190 lbs.   Born, Quebec City, Que., December 15, 1957.
(NY Rangers' 5th choice, 62nd overall, in 1977 Amateur Draft).

				Regular Season					Playoffs			
Season	Club	Lea	GP	G	A	TP	PIM	GP	G	A	TP	PIM
1975-76	Quebec	QJHL	67	11	42	53	270	15	2	3	5	86
1976-77	Quebec	QJHL	72	17	67	84	239	14	1	17	18	75
1977-78	**NY Rangers**	**NHL**	**8**	**1**	**1**	**2**	**15**	**1**	**0**	**0**	**0**	**5**
	New Haven	AHL	52	8	23	31	147	12	5	3	8	31
1978-79	**NY Rangers**	**NHL**	**71**	**5**	**26**	**31**	**153**	**18**	**0**	**6**	**6**	**29**
1979-80	**NY Rangers**	**NHL**	**79**	**8**	**23**	**31**	**142**	**9**	**0**	**2**	**2**	**8**
1980-81	**NY Rangers**	**NHL**	**8**	**1**	**2**	**3**	**46**	....	....	....	....	....
	Vancouver	**NHL**	**50**	**4**	**12**	**16**	**115**	....	....	....	....	....
	Quebec	**NHL**	**11**	**0**	**7**	**7**	**20**	**5**	**0**	**1**	**1**	**6**
1981-82	**Quebec**	**NHL**	**71**	**11**	**32**	**43**	**161**	**13**	**1**	**2**	**3**	**44**
1982-83	**Quebec**	**NHL**	**36**	**2**	**12**	**14**	**108**	....	....	....	....	....
1983-84	**Quebec**	**NHL**	**80**	**13**	**36**	**49**	**151**	**9**	**1**	**4**	**5**	**6**
1984-85	**Quebec**	**NHL**	**76**	**6**	**37**	**43**	**91**	**18**	**0**	**8**	**8**	**12**
1985-86	**Quebec**	**NHL**	**20**	**1**	**12**	**13**	**42**	....	....	....	....	....
	Winnipeg	**NHL**	**56**	**4**	**28**	**32**	**110**	**3**	**1**	**4**	**5**	**6**
1986-87	**Winnipeg**	**NHL**	**79**	**4**	**40**	**44**	**106**	**10**	**1**	**3**	**4**	**23**
1987-88	**Winnipeg**	**NHL**	**79**	**7**	**44**	**51**	**111**	**5**	**0**	**4**	**4**	**6**
1988-89	**Winnipeg**	**NHL**	**7**	**1**	**1**	**2**	**17**	....	....	....	....	....
	Quebec	**NHL**	**42**	**2**	**11**	**13**	**101**	....	....	....	....	....
1989-90	**Quebec**	**NHL**	**67**	**3**	**15**	**18**	**104**	....	....	....	....	....
1990-91	**St. Louis**	**NHL**	**64**	**2**	**14**	**16**	**81**	**9**	**0**	**0**	**0**	**37**
	NHL Totals		**904**	**75**	**353**	**428**	**1674**	**100**	**4**	**34**	**38**	**182**

Traded to **Vancouver** by **NY Rangers** with Jim Mayer for Jere Gillis and Jeff Bandura, November 11, 1980. Traded to **Quebec** by **Vancouver** for Garry Lariviere, March 10, 1981. Traded to **Winnipeg** by **Quebec** for Robert Picard, November 27, 1985. Traded to **Quebec** by **Winnipeg** for Gord Donnelly, December 6, 1988. Claimed by **St. Louis** in NHL Waiver Draft, October 1, 1990.

MARSH, CHARLES BRADLEY (BRAD)

Defense. Shoots left. 6'3", 220 lbs.   Born, London, Ont., March 31, 1958.
(Atlanta's 1st choice, 11th overall, in 1978 Amateur Draft).

				Regular Season					Playoffs			
Season	Club	Lea	GP	G	A	TP	PIM	GP	G	A	TP	PIM
1976-77a	London	OHA	63	7	33	40	121	20	3	5	8	47
1977-78b	London	OHA	62	8	55	63	192	11	2	10	12	21
1978-79	**Atlanta**	**NHL**	**80**	**0**	**19**	**19**	**101**	**2**	**0**	**0**	**0**	**17**
1979-80	**Atlanta**	**NHL**	**80**	**2**	**9**	**11**	**119**	**4**	**0**	**1**	**1**	**2**
1980-81	**Calgary**	**NHL**	**80**	**1**	**12**	**13**	**87**	**16**	**0**	**5**	**5**	**8**
1981-82	**Calgary**	**NHL**	**17**	**0**	**1**	**1**	**10**	....	....	....	....	....
	Philadelphia	**NHL**	**66**	**2**	**22**	**24**	**106**	**4**	**0**	**0**	**0**	**2**
1982-83	**Philadelphia**	**NHL**	**68**	**2**	**11**	**13**	**52**	**2**	**0**	**1**	**1**	**0**
1983-84	**Philadelphia**	**NHL**	**77**	**3**	**14**	**17**	**83**	**3**	**1**	**1**	**2**	**2**
1984-85	**Philadelphia**	**NHL**	**77**	**2**	**18**	**20**	**91**	**19**	**0**	**6**	**6**	**65**
1985-86	**Philadelphia**	**NHL**	**79**	**0**	**13**	**13**	**123**	**5**	**0**	**0**	**0**	**2**
1986-87	**Philadelphia**	**NHL**	**77**	**2**	**9**	**11**	**124**	**26**	**3**	**4**	**7**	**16**
1987-88	**Philadelphia**	**NHL**	**70**	**3**	**9**	**12**	**57**	**7**	**1**	**0**	**1**	**8**
1988-89	**Toronto**	**NHL**	**80**	**1**	**15**	**16**	**79**	....	....	....	....	....
1989-90	**Toronto**	**NHL**	**79**	**1**	**13**	**14**	**95**	**5**	**1**	**0**	**1**	**2**
1990-91	**Toronto**	**NHL**	**22**	**0**	**0**	**0**	**15**	....	....	....	....	....
	Detroit	**NHL**	**20**	**1**	**3**	**4**	**16**	**1**	**0**	**0**	**0**	**0**
	NHL Totals		**972**	**20**	**168**	**188**	**1158**	**94**	**6**	**18**	**24**	**124**

a OHA Third All-Star Team (1977)
b OHA First All-Star Team (1978)

Claimed by **Atlanta** as fill in Expansion Draft, June 13, 1979. Traded to **Philadelphia** by **Calgary** for Mel Bridgman, November 11, 1981. Claimed by **Toronto** in NHL Waiver Draft, October 3, 1988. Traded to **Detroit** by **Toronto** for Detroit's eighth round choice (Robb McIntyre) in 1991 Entry Draft, February 4, 1991.

MARSHALL, CHRIS

Left wing. Shoots left. 5'10", 170 lbs.   Born, Quincy, MA, December 12, 1968.
(Buffalo's 6th choice, 106th overall, in 1987 Entry Draft).

				Regular Season					Playoffs			
Season	Club	Lea	GP	G	A	TP	PIM	GP	G	A	TP	PIM
1987-88	Michigan State	CCHA	29	0	2	2	27	....	....	....	....	....
1988-89	Michigan State	CCHA	7	0	1	1	11	....	....	....	....	....
1989-90	Michigan State	CCHA	17	0	1	1	40	....	....	....	....	....
1990-91	Cincinnati	ECHL	54	33	47	80	65	4	3	0	3	26
	Knoxville	ECHL	6	2	2	4	11	....	....	....	....	....

MARSHALL, JASON

Defense. Shoots right. 6'2", 185 lbs.   Born, Cranbrook, B.C., February 22, 1971.
(St. Louis' 1st choice, 9th overall, in 1989 Entry Draft).

				Regular Season					Playoffs			
Season	Club	Lea	GP	G	A	TP	PIM	GP	G	A	TP	PIM
1989-90	Cdn. National	...	72	1	11	12	57	....	....	....	....	....
1990-91	Tri-City	WHL	59	10	34	44	236	7	1	2	3	20
	Peoria	IHL	....	....	....	....	....	18	0	1	1	48

MARSHALL, PAUL STEVEN

Defense. Shoots left. 6'2", 185 lbs.   Born, Quincy, MA, October 22, 1966.
(Philadelphia's 5th choice, 84th overall, in 1985 Entry Draft).

				Regular Season					Playoffs			
Season	Club	Lea	GP	G	A	TP	PIM	GP	G	A	TP	PIM
1990-91	San Diego	IHL	12	1	1	2	6	....	....	....	....	....
	Albany	AHL	22	4	10	14	6	....	....	....	....	....

Signed as a free agent by **Minnesota**, July 20, 1990.

MARTELL, STEVE

Right wing. Shoots right. 5'10", 185 lbs.   Born, Sydney, N.S., March 3, 1970.
(Washington's 10th choice, 159th overall, in 1990 Entry Draft).

				Regular Season					Playoffs			
Season	Club	Lea	GP	G	A	TP	PIM	GP	G	A	TP	PIM
1988-89	London	OHL	65	9	17	26	59	21	2	5	7	18
1989-90	London	OHL	63	19	24	43	91	6	1	1	2	10
1990-91a	London	OHL	63	32	40	72	105	7	3	1	4	8

a OHL Third All-Star Team (1991)

MARTIN, CRAIG

Right wing. Shoots right. 6'2", 219 lbs. Born, Amherst, N.S., January 21, 1971.
(Winnipeg's 6th choice, 98th overall, in 1990 Entry Draft).

					Regular Season					Playoffs		
Season	**Club**	**Lea**	**GP**	**G**	**A**	**TP**	**PIM**	**GP**	**G**	**A**	**TP**	**PIM**
1989-90	Hull	QMJHL	66	14	31	45	299	11	2	1	3	65
1990-91	Hull	QMJHL	18	5	6	11	87	....	....	....	....	....
	St. Hyacinthe	QMJHL	36	8	9	17	166	....	....	....	....	....

MARTIN, DONALD

Left wing. Shoots left. 6', 200 lbs. Born, London, Ont., March 29, 1968.
(Edmonton's 6th choice, 103rd overall, in 1988 Entry Draft).

					Regular Season					Playoffs		
Season	**Club**	**Lea**	**GP**	**G**	**A**	**TP**	**PIM**	**GP**	**G**	**A**	**TP**	**PIM**
1985-86	North Bay	OHL	7	0	0	0	21	....	....	....	....	....
	London	OHL	55	7	6	13	112	5	1	0	1	14
1986-87	London	OHL	63	19	38	57	127	....	....	....	....	....
1987-88	London	OHL	57	30	32	62	190	11	6	8	14	50
1988-89	Cape Breton	AHL	3	0	0	0	2	....	....	....	....	....
	Fort Wayne	IHL	40	11	5	16	123	....	....	....	....	....
1989-90	Phoenix	IHL	8	1	0	1	10	....	....	....	....	....
1990-91	Winston-Salem	ECHL	14	7	6	13	24	....	....	....	....	....
	Richmond	ECHL	14	4	5	9	125	....	....	....	....	....

MARTIN, MATT

Defense. Shoots left. 6'3", 190 lbs. Born, Hamden, CT, April 30, 1971.
(Toronto's 4th choice, 66th overall, in 1989 Entry Draft).

					Regular Season					Playoffs		
Season	**Club**	**Lea**	**GP**	**G**	**A**	**TP**	**PIM**	**GP**	**G**	**A**	**TP**	**PIM**
1988-89	Avon Old Farms	HS	....	9	23	32	....	....	....	....	....	....
1989-90			DID NOT PLAY									
1990-91	U. of Maine	H.E.	35	3	12	15	48	....	....	....	....	....

MARTIN, TOM

Left wing. Shoots left. 6'2", 200 lbs. Born, Kelowna, B.C., May 11, 1965.
(Winnipeg's 2nd choice, 74th overall, in 1982 Entry Draft).

					Regular Season					Playoffs		
Season	**Club**	**Lea**	**GP**	**G**	**A**	**TP**	**PIM**	**GP**	**G**	**A**	**TP**	**PIM**
1982-83	U. of Denver	WCHA	37	8	18	26	128	....	....	....	....	....
1983-84	Victoria	WHL	60	30	45	75	261	....	....	....	....	....
	Sherbrooke	AHL	5	0	0	0	16	....	....	....	....	....
1984-85	**Winnipeg**	**NHL**	**8**	**1**	**0**	**1**	**42**	**3**	**0**	**0**	**0**	**2**
	Sherbrooke	AHL	58	4	15	19	212	12	1	1	2	72
1985-86	**Winnipeg**	**NHL**	**5**	**0**	**0**	**0**	**0**	....	....	....	....	....
	Sherbrooke	AHL	69	11	18	29	227	....	....	....	....	....
1986-87	**Winnipeg**	**NHL**	**11**	**1**	**0**	**1**	**49**	....	....	....	....	....
	Adirondack	AHL	18	5	6	11	57	....	....	....	....	....
1987-88	**Hartford**	**NHL**	**5**	**1**	**2**	**3**	**14**	....	....	....	....	....
a	Binghamton	AHL	71	28	61	89	344	3	0	0	0	18
1988-89	**Minnesota**	**NHL**	**4**	**1**	**1**	**2**	**4**	....	....	....	....	....
	Hartford	**NHL**	**38**	**7**	**6**	**13**	**113**	**1**	**0**	**0**	**0**	**4**
1989-90	**Hartford**	**NHL**	**21**	**1**	**2**	**3**	**27**	....	....	....	....	....
	Binghamton	AHL	24	4	10	14	113	....	....	....	....	....
1990-91	New Haven	AHL	22	11	7	18	88	....	....	....	....	....
	NHL Totals		**92**	**12**	**11**	**23**	**249**	**4**	**0**	**0**	**0**	**6**

a AHL First All-Star Team (1988)

Signed as a free agent by **Hartford**, July 29, 1987. Claimed by **Minnesota** in NHL Waiver Draft, October 3, 1988. Claimed by **Hartford** on waivers from **Minnesota**, December 1988. Signed as a free agent by **Los Angeles**, July, 1990.

MARTINI, DARCY

Defense. Shoots left. 6'4", 220 lbs. Born, Castlegar, B.C., January 30, 1969.
(Edmonton's 8th choice, 162nd overall, in 1989 Entry Draft).

					Regular Season					Playoffs		
Season	**Club**	**Lea**	**GP**	**G**	**A**	**TP**	**PIM**	**GP**	**G**	**A**	**TP**	**PIM**
1988-89	Michigan Tech	WCHA	35	1	2	3	103	....	....	....	....	....
1989-90	Michigan Tech	WCHA	36	3	6	9	151	....	....	....	....	....
1990-91	Michigan Tech	WCHA	38	4	7	11	52	....	....	....	....	....

MARTINSON, STEVEN

Left wing. Shoots left. 6'1", 205 lbs. Born, Minnetonka, MN, June 21, 1959.

					Regular Season					Playoffs		
Season	**Club**	**Lea**	**GP**	**G**	**A**	**TP**	**PIM**	**GP**	**G**	**A**	**TP**	**PIM**
1982-83	Toledo	IHL	32	9	10	19	111	....	....	....	....	....
	Birmingham	CHL	43	4	5	9	184	13	1	2	3	*80
1983-84	Tulsa	CHL	42	3	6	9	240	6	0	0	0	43
1984-85	Toledo	IHL	54	4	10	14	300	2	0	0	0	21
1985-86	Hershey	AHL	69	3	6	9	*432	3	0	0	0	56
1986-87	Hershey	AHL	17	0	3	3	85	....	....	....	....	....
	Adirondack	AHL	14	1	1	2	78	11	2	0	2	108
1987-88	**Detroit**	**NHL**	**10**	**1**	**1**	**2**	**84**	....	....	....	....	....
	Adirondack	AHL	32	6	8	14	146	6	1	2	3	66
1988-89	**Montreal**	**NHL**	**25**	**1**	**0**	**1**	**87**	**1**	**0**	**0**	**0**	**10**
	Sherbrooke	AHL	10	5	7	12	61	....	....	....	....	....
1989-90	**Montreal**	**NHL**	**13**	**0**	**0**	**0**	**64**	....	....	....	....	....
	Sherbrooke	AHL	37	6	20	26	113	....	....	....	....	....
1990-91	San Diego	IHL	53	16	24	40	268	....	....	....	....	....
	NHL Totals		**48**	**2**	**1**	**3**	**235**	**1**	**0**	**0**	**0**	**10**

Signed as a free agent by **Philadelphia**, September 30, 1985. Signed as a free agent by **Detroit**, October 3, 1987. Signed as a free agent by **Montreal**, August 2, 1988.

MARTINYUK, SERGEI

Right wing. Shoots left. 6', 178 lbs. Born, Rybynsk, USSR, January 30, 1971.
(Montreal's 13th choice, 249th overall, in 1990 Entry Draft).

					Regular Season					Playoffs		
Season	**Club**	**Lea**	**GP**	**G**	**A**	**TP**	**PIM**	**GP**	**G**	**A**	**TP**	**PIM**
1989-90	Torp. Jaroslav	USSR	40	5	1	6	8	....	....	....	....	....
1990-91	Torp. Jaroslav	USSR	37	7	11	18	52	....	....	....	....	....

MARTTILA, JUKKA (MAHR-tee-lah)

Defense. Shoots left. 6'1", 187 lbs. Born, Tampere, Finland, April 15, 1968.
(Winnipeg's 9th choice, 136th overall, in 1988 Entry Draft).

					Regular Season					Playoffs		
Season	**Club**	**Lea**	**GP**	**G**	**A**	**TP**	**PIM**	**GP**	**G**	**A**	**TP**	**PIM**
1986-87	Tappara	Fin.	33	4	1	5	18	....	....	....	....	....
1987-88	Tappara	Fin.	39	5	7	12	16	....	....	....	....	....
1988-89	Tappara	Fin.	43	11	20	31	32	....	....	....	....	....
1989-90	Tappara	Fin.	44	12	14	26	14	7	2	2	4	4
1990-91	Tappara	Fin.	42	10	21	31	32	3	0	0	0	0

MARVIN, DAVID

Defense. Shoots right. 6'1", 165 lbs. Born, Warroad, MN, March 10, 1968.
(St. Louis' 10th choice, 201st overall, in 1987 Entry Draft).

					Regular Season					Playoffs		
Season	**Club**	**Lea**	**GP**	**G**	**A**	**TP**	**PIM**	**GP**	**G**	**A**	**TP**	**PIM**
1987-88	North Dakota	WCHA	35	4	17	21	12	....	....	....	....	....
1988-89	North Dakota	WCHA	38	4	6	10	24	....	....	....	....	....
1989-90	North Dakota	WCHA	45	3	23	26	70	....	....	....	....	....
1990-91	North Dakota	WCHA	41	1	19	20	60	....	....	....	....	....

MASKARINEC, MARTIN (mahsh-KAH-ree-nehts)

Defense. Shoots left. 6'1", 185 lbs. Born, Prague, Czechoslovakia, February 3, 1969.
(Los Angeles' 9th choice, 186th overall, in 1989 Entry Draft).

					Regular Season					Playoffs		
Season	**Club**	**Lea**	**GP**	**G**	**A**	**TP**	**PIM**	**GP**	**G**	**A**	**TP**	**PIM**
1988-89	Sparta Praha	Czech.	31	3	1	4	....	....	....	....	....	....
1989-90	Sparta Praha	Czech.	46	3	11	14	....	....	....	....	....	....
1990-91	Dukla Trencin	Czech.	51	0	12	12	93	....	....	....	....	....

MATHIESON, JIM

Defense. Shoots left. 6'1", 209 lbs. Born, Kindersley, Sask., January 24, 1970.
(Washington's 3rd choice, 59th overall, in 1989 Entry Draft).

					Regular Season					Playoffs		
Season	**Club**	**Lea**	**GP**	**G**	**A**	**TP**	**PIM**	**GP**	**G**	**A**	**TP**	**PIM**
1986-87	Regina	WHL	40	0	9	9	40	3	0	1	1	2
1987-88	Regina	WHL	72	3	12	15	115	4	0	2	2	4
1988-89	Regina	WHL	62	5	22	27	151	....	....	....	....	....
1989-90	**Washington**	**NHL**	**2**	**0**	**0**	**0**	**4**	....	....	....	....	....
	Regina	WHL	67	1	26	27	158	11	0	7	7	16
	Baltimore	AHL	....	....	....	....	....	3	0	0	0	4
1990-91	Baltimore	AHL	65	3	5	8	168	4	1	0	1	6
	NHL Totals		**2**	**0**	**0**	**0**	**4**	....	....	....	....	....

MATIKAINEN, PETRI (mah-tee-KAY-nehn)

Defense. Shoots left. 6', 189 lbs. Born, Savonlinna, Finland, January 7, 1967.
(Buffalo's 7th choice, 140th overall, in 1985 Entry Draft).

					Regular Season					Playoffs		
Season	**Club**	**Lea**	**GP**	**G**	**A**	**TP**	**PIM**	**GP**	**G**	**A**	**TP**	**PIM**
1984-85	SapKo	Fin.2	24	0	4	4	34	....	....	....	....	....
1985-86	Oshawa	OHL	53	14	42	56	27	....	....	....	....	....
1986-87	Oshawa	OHL	50	8	34	42	53	21	2	12	14	36
1987-88	Tappara	Fin.	41	5	1	6	58	1	0	2	2	4
1988-89	Tappara	Fin.	44	4	13	17	32	8	0	0	0	10
1989-90	JoKP	Fin.	44	6	8	14	34	....	....	....	....	....
1990-91	JoKP	Fin.	43	16	25	41	35	....	....	....	....	....

MATILAINEN, ARI (mah-tee-LAY-nehn)

Left wing. Shoots left. 6'2", 198 lbs. Born, Pieksomaki, Finland, January 22, 1966.
(Minnesota's 7th choice, 190th overall, in 1988 Entry Draft).

					Regular Season					Playoffs		
Season	**Club**	**Lea**	**GP**	**G**	**A**	**TP**	**PIM**	**GP**	**G**	**A**	**TP**	**PIM**
1987-88	Assat	Fin.	44	15	23	38	40	....	....	....	....	....
1988-89	Karpat	Fin.	36	11	10	21	28	....	....	....	....	....
1989-90	Tappara	Fin.	28	8	7	15	30	7	1	4	5	22
1990-91	Tappara	Fin.	41	6	11	17	26	3	0	1	1	4

MATTEAU, STEPHANE (mah-TOH)

Left wing. Shoots left. 6'3", 195 lbs. Born, Rouyn-Noranda, Que., September 2, 1969.
(Calgary's 2nd choice, 25th overall, in 1987 Entry Draft).

					Regular Season					Playoffs		
Season	**Club**	**Lea**	**GP**	**G**	**A**	**TP**	**PIM**	**GP**	**G**	**A**	**TP**	**PIM**
1985-86	Hull	QMJHL	60	6	8	14	19	4	0	0	0	0
1986-87	Hull	QMJHL	69	27	48	75	113	8	3	7	10	8
1987-88	Hull	QMJHL	57	17	40	57	179	18	5	14	19	94
1988-89	Hull	QMJHL	59	44	45	89	202	9	8	6	14	30
	Salt Lake	IHL	....	....	....	....	....	9	0	4	4	13
1989-90	Salt Lake	IHL	81	23	35	58	130	10	6	3	9	38
1990-91	Salt Lake	IHL	78	15	19	34	93	....	....	....	....	....
	Calgary	**NHL**	....	....	....	....	....	**5**	**0**	**1**	**1**	**0**
	NHL Totals		....	....	....	....	....	**5**	**0**	**1**	**1**	**0**

MATTHEWS, JAMIE

Center. Shoots right. 6'1", 188 lbs. Born, Amherst, N.S., May 25, 1973.
(Chicago's 3rd choice, 44th overall, in 1991 Entry Draft).

					Regular Season					Playoffs		
Season	**Club**	**Lea**	**GP**	**G**	**A**	**TP**	**PIM**	**GP**	**G**	**A**	**TP**	**PIM**
1989-90	Sudbury	OHL	60	16	17	33	25	7	1	0	1	4
1990-91	Sudbury	OHL	66	14	38	52	41	5	3	5	8	8

MATULIK, IVAN (muh-TOO-lihk)

Right wing. Shoots left. 6'1", 200 lbs. Born, Nitra, Czechoslovakia, June 17, 1968.
(Edmonton's 7th choice, 147th overall, in 1986 Entry Draft).

					Regular Season					Playoffs		
Season	**Club**	**Lea**	**GP**	**G**	**A**	**TP**	**PIM**	**GP**	**G**	**A**	**TP**	**PIM**
1986-87	Bratislava	Czech.	25	1	3	4	....	....	....	....	....	....
1987-88	Nova Scotia	AHL	46	13	10	23	29	....	....	....	....	....
1988-89	Cape Breton	AHL	1	0	0	0	0	....	....	....	....	....
1989-90	Cape Breton	AHL	32	2	6	8	44	....	....	....	....	....
	Phoenix	IHL	29	3	5	8	46	....	....	....	....	....
1990-91	Halifax	AHL	2	0	0	0	0	....	....	....	....	....

MATUSOVICH, SCOTT

Defense. Shoots left. 6'2", 205 lbs.　　Born, Southbury, CT, October 31, 1969.
(Calgary's 5th choice, 90th overall, in 1988 Entry Draft).

			Regular Season					Playoffs			
Season	Club	Lea	GP	G	A	TP	PIM	GP	G	A	TP	PIM
1988-89	Yale	ECAC	25	3	11	14	40	....	....	....	....	....
1989-90	Yale	ECAC	28	1	15	16	55	....	....	....	....	....
1990-91	Yale	ECAC	29	3	8	11	48	....	....	....	....	....

MATVICHUK, RICHARD

Defense. Shoots left. 6'2", 190 lbs.　　Born, Edmonton, Alta., February 5, 1973.
(Minnesota's 1st choice, 8th overall, in 1991 Entry Draft).

			Regular Season					Playoffs			
Season	Club	Lea	GP	G	A	TP	PIM	GP	G	A	TP	PIM
1989-90	Saskatoon	WHL	56	8	24	32	126	10	2	8	10	16
1990-91	Saskatoon	WHL	68	13	36	49	117	....	....	....	....	....

MAY, ALAN

Right wing. Shoots right. 6'1", 200 lbs.　　Born, Barrhead, Alta., January 14, 1965.

			Regular Season					Playoffs			
Season	Club	Lea	GP	G	A	TP	PIM	GP	G	A	TP	PIM
1985-86	Medicine Hat	WHL	6	1	0	1	25	....	....	....	....	....
	N. Westminster	WHL	32	8	9	17	81	....	....	....	....	....
1986-87	Springfield	AHL	4	0	2	2	11	....	....	....	....	....
	Carolina	ACHL	42	23	14	37	310	5	2	2	4	57
1987-88	Boston	NHL	3	0	0	0	15	....	....	....	....	....
	Maine	AHL	61	14	11	25	257	....	....	....	....	....
	Nova Scotia	AHL	13	4	1	5	54	4	0	0	0	51
1988-89	Edmonton	NHL	3	1	0	1	7	....	....	....	....	....
	Cape Breton	AHL	50	12	13	25	214	....	....	....	....	....
	New Haven	AHL	12	2	8	10	99	16	6	3	9	*105
1989-90	Washington	NHL	77	7	10	17	339	15	0	0	0	37
1990-91	Washington	NHL	67	4	6	10	264	11	1	1	2	37
	NHL Totals		150	12	16	28	625	26	1	1	2	74

Signed as a free agent by Boston, October 30, 1987. Traded to Edmonton by Boston for Moe Lemay, March 8, 1988. Traded to Los Angeles by Edmonton with Jim Wiemer for Brian Wilks and John English, March 7, 1989. Traded to Washington by Los Angeles for Washington's fifth-round choice (Thomas Newman) in 1989 Entry Draft, June 17, 1989.

MAY, BRAD

Left wing. Shoots left. 6', 200 lbs.　　Born, Toronto, Ont., November 29, 1971.
(Buffalo's 1st choice, 14th overall, in 1990 Entry Draft).

			Regular Season					Playoffs			
Season	Club	Lea	GP	G	A	TP	PIM	GP	G	A	TP	PIM
1988-89	Niagara Falls	OHL	65	8	14	22	304	17	0	1	1	55
1989-90a	Niagara Falls	OHL	61	32	58	90	223	16	9	13	22	64
1990-91a	Niagara Falls	OHL	34	37	32	69	93	14	11	14	25	53

a OHL Second All-Star Team (1990, 1991)

MAYER, DEREK

Defense. Shoots right. 6', 185 lbs.　　Born, Rossland, B.C., May 21, 1967.
(Detroit's 3rd choice, 43rd overall, in 1986 Entry Draft).

			Regular Season					Playoffs			
Season	Club	Lea	GP	G	A	TP	PIM	GP	G	A	TP	PIM
1985-86	Denver	WCHA	44	2	7	9	42	....	....	....	....	....
1986-87	Denver	WCHA	38	5	17	22	87	....	....	....	....	....
1987-88	Denver	WCHA	34	5	16	21	82	....	....	....	....	....
1988-89	Cdn. National	...	58	3	13	16	81	....	....	....	....	....
1989-90	Adirondack	AHL	62	4	26	30	56	5	0	6	6	4
1990-91	San Diego	IHL	31	9	24	33	31	....	....	....	....	....
	Adirondack	AHL	21	4	9	13	20	2	0	1	1	0

MAZUR, JAY

Center/Right wing. Shoots right. 6'2", 205 lbs.　　Born, Hamilton, Ont., January 22, 1965.
(Vancouver's 12th choice, 230th overall, in 1983 Entry Draft).

			Regular Season					Playoffs			
Season	Club	Lea	GP	G	A	TP	PIM	GP	G	A	TP	PIM
1983-84	Maine	H.E.	34	14	9	23	14	....	....	....	....	....
1984-85	Maine	H.E.	31	0	6	6	20	....	....	....	....	....
1985-86	Maine	H.E.	5	7	12	18	....	....	....	....	....	....
1986-87	Maine	H.E.	39	16	10	26	61	....	....	....	....	....
1987-88	Flint	IHL	39	17	11	28	28	....	....	....	....	....
	Fredericton	AHL	31	14	6	20	28	15	4	2	6	38
1988-89	Vancouver	NHL	1	0	0	0	0	....	....	....	....	....
	Milwaukee	IHL	73	33	31	64	86	11	6	5	11	2
1989-90	Vancouver	NHL	5	0	0	0	4	....	....	....	....	....
	Milwaukee	IHL	70	20	27	47	63	6	3	0	3	6
1990-91	Vancouver	NHL	36	11	7	18	14	6	0	1	1	8
	Milwaukee	IHL	7	2	3	5	21	....	....	....	....	....
	NHL Totals		42	11	7	18	18	6	0	1	1	8

McALPINE, CHRIS

Defense. Shoots right. 6', 190 lbs.　　Born, Roseville, MN, December 1, 1971.
(New Jersey's 10th choice, 137th overall, in 1990 Entry Draft).

			Regular Season					Playoffs			
Season	Club	Lea	GP	G	A	TP	PIM	GP	G	A	TP	PIM
1989-90	Roseville	HS	25	15	13	28	....	....	....	....	....	....
1990-91	U. of Minnesota	WCHA	38	7	9	16	112	....	....	....	....	....

McAMMOND, DEAN

Center. Shoots left. 5'11", 185 lbs.　　Born, Grand Cache, B.C., June 15, 1973.
(Chicago's 1st choice, 22nd overall, in 1991 Entry Draft).

			Regular Season					Playoffs			
Season	Club	Lea	GP	G	A	TP	PIM	GP	G	A	TP	PIM
1989-90	Prince Albert	WHL	53	11	11	22	49	14	2	3	5	18
1990-91	Prince Albert	WHL	71	33	35	68	108	2	0	1	1	6

McBAIN, ANDREW

Right wing. Shoots right. 6'1", 205 lbs.　　Born, Scarborough, Ont., January 18, 1965.
(Winnipeg's 1st choice, 8th overall, in 1983 Entry Draft).

			Regular Season					Playoffs			
Season	Club	Lea	GP	G	A	TP	PIM	GP	G	A	TP	PIM
1981-82	Niagara Falls	OHL	68	19	25	44	35	5	0	3	3	4
1982-83a	North Bay	OHL	67	33	87	120	61	8	2	6	8	17
1983-84	Winnipeg	NHL	78	11	19	30	37	3	2	0	2	0
1984-85	Winnipeg	NHL	77	7	15	22	45	7	1	0	1	0
1985-86	Winnipeg	NHL	28	3	3	6	17	....	....	....	....	....
1986-87	Winnipeg	NHL	71	11	21	32	106	9	0	2	2	10
1987-88	Winnipeg	NHL	74	32	31	63	145	5	2	5	7	29
1988-89	Winnipeg	NHL	80	37	40	77	71	....	....	....	....	....
1989-90	Pittsburgh	NHL	41	5	9	14	51	....	....	....	....	....
	Vancouver	NHL	26	4	5	9	22	....	....	....	....	....
1990-91	Vancouver	NHL	13	0	5	5	32	....	....	....	....	....
	Milwaukee	IHL	47	27	24	51	69	6	2	5	7	12
	NHL Totals		488	110	148	258	526	24	5	7	12	39

a OHL Second All-Star Team (1983).

Traded to Pittsburgh by Winnipeg with Jim Kyte and Randy Gilhen for Randy Cunnyworth, Rick Tabaracci and Dave McLlwain, June 17, 1989. Traded to Vancouver by Pittsburgh with Dave Capuano and Dan Quinn for Rod Buskas, Barry Pederson and Tony Tanti, January 8, 1990.

McBEAN, WAYNE

Defense. Shoots left. 6'2", 190 lbs.　　Born, Calgary, Alta., February 21, 1969.
(Los Angeles' 1st choice, 4th overall, in 1987 Entry Draft).

			Regular Season					Playoffs			
Season	Club	Lea	GP	G	A	TP	PIM	GP	G	A	TP	PIM
1985-86	Medicine Hat	WHL	67	1	14	15	73	25	1	5	6	36
1986-87a	Medicine Hat	WHL	71	12	41	53	163	20	2	8	10	40
1987-88	Los Angeles	NHL	27	0	1	1	26	....	....	....	....	....
	Medicine Hat	WHL	30	15	30	45	48	16	6	17	23	50
1988-89	Los Angeles	NHL	33	0	5	5	23	....	....	....	....	....
	New Haven	AHL	7	1	1	2	2	....	....	....	....	....
	NY Islanders	NHL	19	0	1	1	12	....	....	....	....	....
1989-90	NY Islanders	NHL	5	0	1	1	2	2	1	1	2	0
	Springfield	AHL	58	6	33	39	48	17	4	11	15	31
1990-91	NY Islanders	NHL	52	5	14	19	47	....	....	....	....	....
	Capital Dist.	AHL	22	9	9	18	19	....	....	....	....	....
	NHL Totals		136	5	22	27	110	2	1	1	2	0

a WHL East All-Star Team (1987)

Traded to NY Islanders by Los Angeles with Mark Fitzpatrick and future considerations (Doug Crossman acquired May 23, 1989) for Kelly Hrudey, February 22, 1989.

McBRIDE, DARYN

Center. Shoots right. 5'9", 180 lbs.　　Born, Ft. Saskatchewan, Alta., March 29, 1968.
(Pittsburgh's 10th choice, 194th overall, in 1987 Entry Draft).

			Regular Season					Playoffs			
Season	Club	Lea	GP	G	A	TP	PIM	GP	G	A	TP	PIM
1986-87	U. of Denver	WCHA	38	19	13	32	54	....	....	....	....	....
1987-88a	U. of Denver	WCHA	39	30	28	58	122	....	....	....	....	....
1988-89b	U. of Denver	WCHA	42	19	32	51	74	....	....	....	....	....
	Can. National	...	15	3	7	10	6	....	....	....	....	....
1989-90	Cdn. National	...	51	15	32	47	49	....	....	....	....	....
1990-91	Phoenix	IHL	61	9	32	41	26	....	....	....	....	....
	New Haven	AHL	6	0	1	1	17	....	....	....	....	....

a WCHA Second All-Star Team (1988)
b WCHA First All-Star Team (1989)

McCARTHY, BRIAN

Center. Shoots left. 6'2", 190 lbs.　　Born, Salem, MA, December 6, 1971.
(Buffalo's 2nd choice, 82nd overall, in 1990 Entry Draft).

			Regular Season					Playoffs			
Season	Club	Lea	GP	G	A	TP	PIM	GP	G	A	TP	PIM
1989-90	Pingree	HS	....	25	40	65	....	....	....	....	....	....
1990-91	Providence	H.E.	33	7	6	13	33	....	....	....	....	....

McCARTHY, JOE

Defense. Shoots left. 6'1", 200 lbs.　　Born, Bangor, ME, November 17, 1970.
(Toronto's 2nd choice, 9th overall, in 1991 Supplemental Draft).

			Regular Season					Playoffs			
Season	Club	Lea	GP	G	A	TP	PIM	GP	G	A	TP	PIM
1989-90	U. of Vermont	ECAC	31	2	1	3	21	....	....	....	....	....
1990-91	U. of Vermont	ECAC	33	3	7	10	16	....	....	....	....	....

McCARTHY, SANDY

Right wing. Shoots right. 6'3", 224 lbs.　　Born, Toronto, Ont., June 15, 1972.
(Calgary's 3rd choice, 52nd overall, in 1991 Entry Draft).

			Regular Season					Playoffs			
Season	Club	Lea	GP	G	A	TP	PIM	GP	G	A	TP	PIM
1990-91	Laval	QMJHL	68	21	19	40	297	....	....	....	....	....

McCAULEY, WES

Defense. Shoots left. 6', 175 lbs.　　Born, Toronto, Ont., January 11, 1972.
(Detroit's 7th choice, 150th overall, in 1990 Entry Draft).

			Regular Season					Playoffs			
Season	Club	Lea	GP	G	A	TP	PIM	GP	G	A	TP	PIM
1989-90	Michigan State	CCHA	42	2	7	9	15	....	....	....	....	....
1990-91	Michigan State	CCHA	28	1	2	3	9	....	....	....	....	....

McCLELLAND, KEVIN WILLIAM

Right wing. Shoots right. 6'2", 205 lbs.   Born, Oshawa, Ont., July 4, 1962.
(Hartford's 4th choice, 71st overall, in 1980 Entry Draft).

				Regular Season					Playoffs			
Season	Club	Lea	GP	G	A	TP	PIM	GP	G	A	TP	PIM
1980-81	Niagara Falls	OHA	68	36	72	108	186	12	8	13	21	42
1981-82	**Pittsburgh**	**NHL**	**10**	**1**	**4**	**5**	**4**	**5**	**1**	**1**	**2**	**5**
	Niagara Falls	OHL	46	36	47	83	184	....	....	....	....	....
1982-83	**Pittsburgh**	**NHL**	**38**	**5**	**4**	**9**	**73**	....	....	....	....	....
1983-84	**Pittsburgh**	**NHL**	**24**	**2**	**4**	**6**	**62**	....	....	....	....	....
	Baltimore	AHL	3	1	1	2	0	....	....	....	....	....
	Edmonton	NHL	52	8	20	28	127	18	4	6	10	42
1984-85	**Edmonton**	**NHL**	**62**	**8**	**15**	**23**	**205**	**18**	**1**	**3**	**4**	**75**
1985-86	**Edmonton**	**NHL**	**79**	**11**	**25**	**36**	**266**	**10**	**1**	**0**	**1**	**32**
1986-87	**Edmonton**	**NHL**	**72**	**12**	**13**	**25**	**238**	**21**	**2**	**3**	**5**	**43**
1987-88	**Edmonton**	**NHL**	**74**	**10**	**6**	**16**	**281**	**19**	**2**	**3**	**5**	**68**
1988-89	**Edmonton**	**NHL**	**79**	**6**	**14**	**20**	**161**	**7**	**0**	**2**	**2**	**16**
1989-90	**Edmonton**	**NHL**	**10**	**1**	**1**	**2**	**13**	....	....	....	....	....
	Detroit	**NHL**	**61**	**4**	**5**	**9**	**183**	....	....	....	....	....
1990-91	**Detroit**	**NHL**	**3**	**0**	**0**	**0**	**7**	....	....	....	....	....
	Adirondack	AHL	27	5	14	19	125	....	....	....	....	....
	NHL Totals		**564**	**68**	**111**	**179**	**1620**	**98**	**11**	**18**	**29**	**281**

Traded to **Pittsburgh** by **Hartford** with Pat Boutette as compensation for Hartford's signing of free agent goaltender Greg Millen, June 29, 1981. Traded to **Edmonton** by **Pittsburgh** with Pittsburgh's sixth round choice (Emanuel Viveiros) in 1984 Entry Draft for Tom Roulston, December 5, 1983. Traded to **Detroit** by **Edmonton** with Jimmy Carson and Edmonton's fifth round choice (later traded to Montreal for Rick Green. Montreal selected Brad Layzell) in 1991 Entry Draft for Petr Klima, Joe Murphy, Adam Graves and Jeff Sharples, November 2, 1989.

McCORMACK, BRIAN

Defense. Shoots right. 5'10", 170 lbs.   Born, Bloomington, MN, November 11, 1969.
(Detroit's 7th choice, 164th overall, in 1988 Entry Draft).

				Regular Season					Playoffs			
Season	Club	Lea	GP	G	A	TP	PIM	GP	G	A	TP	PIM
1988-89	Harvard	ECAC	31	0	8	8	16	....	....	....	....	....
1989-90	Harvard	ECAC	27	2	3	5	36	....	....	....	....	....
1990-91	Harvard	ECAC	28	0	8	8	37	....	....	....	....	....

McCORMICK, MICHAEL

Left wing. Shoots left. 6'2", 220 lbs.   Born, St. Boniface, Man., May 14, 1968.
(Chicago's 6th choice, 113th overall, in 1987 Entry Draft).

				Regular Season					Playoffs			
Season	Club	Lea	GP	G	A	TP	PIM	GP	G	A	TP	PIM
1987-88	North Dakota	WCHA	41	4	0	4	28	....	....	....	....	....
1988-89	North Dakota	WCHA	29	1	4	5	22	....	....	....	....	....
1989-90	North Dakota	WCHA	2	0	1	1	4	....	....	....	....	....
1990-91	Greensboro	ECHL	50	18	19	37	90	....	....	....	....	....

McCOSH, SHAWN

Center. Shoots right. 6', 188 lbs.   Born, Oshawa, Ont., June 5, 1969.
(Detroit's 5th choice, 95th overall, in 1989 Entry Draft).

				Regular Season					Playoffs			
Season	Club	Lea	GP	G	A	TP	PIM	GP	G	A	TP	PIM
1986-87	Hamilton	OHL	50	11	17	28	49	6	1	0	1	2
1987-88	Hamilton	OHL	64	17	36	53	96	14	6	8	14	14
1988-89	Niagara Falls	OHL	56	41	62	103	75	14	4	13	17	23
1989-90	Niagara Falls	OHL	9	6	10	16	24	....	....	....	....	....
	Hamilton	OHL	39	24	28	52	65	....	....	....	....	....
1990-91	New Haven	AHL	66	16	21	37	104	....	....	....	....	....

Traded to **Los Angeles** by **Detroit** for future considerations, August 15, 1990.

McCRADY, SCOTT

Defense. Shoots right. 6'1", 195 lbs.   Born, Calgary, Alta., October 30, 1968.
(Minnesota's 2nd choice, 35th overall, in 1987 Entry Draft).

				Regular Season					Playoffs			
Season	Club	Lea	GP	G	A	TP	PIM	GP	G	A	TP	PIM
1985-86	Medicine Hat	WHL	65	8	25	33	114	25	0	7	7	67
1986-87	Medicine Hat	WHL	70	10	66	76	157	20	2	*21	23	30
1987-88a	Medicine Hat	WHL	65	7	70	77	132	16	2	17	19	34
1988-89	Kalamazoo	IHL	73	8	29	37	169	6	0	4	4	24
1989-90	Kalamazoo	IHL	3	0	0	0	11	4	0	0	0	19
1990-91	Salt Lake	IHL	58	4	49	53	133	3	0	1	1	17

a WHL East All-Star Team (1988)

Signed as a free agent by **Calgary**, August, 1990.

McCRIMMON, BYRON (BRAD)

Defense. Shoots left. 5'11", 197 lbs.   Born, Dodsland, Sask., March 29, 1959.
(Boston's 2nd choice, 15th overall, in 1979 Entry Draft).

				Regular Season					Playoffs			
Season	Club	Lea	GP	G	A	TP	PIM	GP	G	A	TP	PIM
1977-78ab	Brandon	WHL	65	19	78	97	245	8	2	11	13	20
1978-79a	Brandon	WHL	66	24	74	98	139	22	9	19	28	34
1979-80	**Boston**	**NHL**	**72**	**5**	**11**	**16**	**94**	**10**	**1**	**1**	**2**	**28**
1980-81	**Boston**	**NHL**	**78**	**11**	**18**	**29**	**148**	**3**	**0**	**1**	**1**	**2**
1981-82	**Boston**	**NHL**	**78**	**1**	**8**	**9**	**83**	**2**	**0**	**0**	**0**	**2**
1982-83	**Philadelphia**	**NHL**	**79**	**4**	**21**	**25**	**61**	**3**	**0**	**0**	**0**	**4**
1983-84	**Philadelphia**	**NHL**	**71**	**0**	**24**	**24**	**76**	**1**	**0**	**0**	**0**	**4**
1984-85	**Philadelphia**	**NHL**	**66**	**8**	**35**	**43**	**81**	**11**	**2**	**1**	**3**	**15**
1985-86	**Philadelphia**	**NHL**	**80**	**13**	**43**	**56**	**85**	**5**	**2**	**0**	**2**	**2**
1986-87	**Philadelphia**	**NHL**	**71**	**10**	**29**	**39**	**52**	**26**	**3**	**5**	**8**	**30**
1987-88cd	**Calgary**	**NHL**	**80**	**7**	**35**	**42**	**98**	**9**	**2**	**3**	**5**	**22**
1988-89	**Calgary**	**NHL**	**72**	**5**	**17**	**22**	**96**	**22**	**0**	**3**	**3**	**30**
1989-90	**Calgary**	**NHL**	**79**	**4**	**15**	**19**	**78**	**6**	**0**	**2**	**2**	**8**
1990-91	**Detroit**	**NHL**	**64**	**0**	**13**	**13**	**81**	**7**	**1**	**1**	**2**	**21**
	NHL Totals		**890**	**68**	**269**	**337**	**1033**	**105**	**11**	**17**	**28**	**168**

a WHL First All-Star Team (1978, 1979)
b Named WHL's Top Defenseman (1978)
c NHL Second All-Star Team (1988)
d NHL Plus/Minus Leader (1988)
Played in NHL All-Star Game (1988)

Traded to **Philadelphia** by **Boston** for Pete Peeters, June 9, 1982. Traded to **Calgary** by **Philadelphia** for Calgary's third round pick in 1988 Entry Draft (Dominic Roussel) and first round pick — acquired March 6, 1988 by Toronto — in 1989 Entry Draft, August 26, 1987. Toronto acquired Calgary's first round pick in 1989 Entry Draft from Philadelphia in deal for Ken Wregget, March 6, 1988. Toronto selected Steve Bancroft. Traded to **Detroit** by **Calgary** for Detroit's second round choice – later traded to New Jersey (David Harlock) – in 1990 Entry Draft, June 15, 1990.

McCRORY, SCOTT

Center. Shoots right. 5'10", 185 lbs.   Born, Sudbury, Ont., February 27, 1967.
(Washington's 13th choice, 250th overall, in 1986 Entry Draft).

				Regular Season					Playoffs			
Season	Club	Lea	GP	G	A	TP	PIM	GP	G	A	TP	PIM
1984-85	Oshawa	OHL	64	9	24	33	28	....	....	....	....	....
1985-86	Oshawa	OHL	66	52	80	132	40	6	5	8	13	0
1986-87ab	Oshawa	OHL	66	51	*99	*150	35	24	15	*22	*37	20
1987-88	Binghamton	AHL	72	18	33	51	29	4	0	1	1	2
1988-89	Baltimore	AHL	80	38	51	89	25	....	....	....	....	....
1989-90	Rochester	AHL	51	14	41	55	46	13	3	6	9	2
1990-91	Rochester	AHL	58	27	25	52	39	2	0	0	0	0

a OHL Player of the Year (1987)
b OHL First Team All-Star (1987)
Traded to **Buffalo** by **Washington** for Mark Ferner, June 1, 1989.

McDONOUGH, HUBIE

Center. Shoots left 5'9", 180 lbs.   Born, Manchester, NH, July 8, 1963.

				Regular Season					Playoffs			
Season	Club	Lea	GP	G	A	TP	PIM	GP	G	A	TP	PIM
1986-87	Flint	IHL	82	27	52	79	59	6	3	2	5	0
1987-88	New Haven	AHL	78	30	29	59	43	....	....	....	....	....
1988-89	**Los Angeles**	**NHL**	**4**	**0**	**1**	**1**	**0**	....	....	....	....	....
	New Haven	AHL	74	37	55	92	41	17	10	*21	*31	6
1989-90	**Los Angeles**	**NHL**	**22**	**3**	**4**	**7**	**10**	....	....	....	....	....
	NY Islanders	**NHL**	**54**	**18**	**11**	**29**	**26**	**5**	**1**	**0**	**1**	**4**
1990-91	**NY Islanders**	**NHL**	**52**	**6**	**6**	**12**	**10**	....	....	....	....	....
	Capital Dist.	AHL	17	9	9	18	4	....	....	....	....	....
	NHL Totals		**132**	**27**	**22**	**49**	**46**	**5**	**1**	**0**	**1**	**4**

Signed as a free agent by **Los Angeles**, April 18, 1988. Traded to **NY Islanders** by **Los Angeles** with Ken Baumgartner for Mikko Makela, November 29, 1989.

McDOUGALL, WILLIAM HENRY

Center. Shoots right. 6', 185 lbs.   Born, Mississauga, Ont., August 10, 1966.

				Regular Season					Playoffs			
Season	Club	Lea	GP	G	A	TP	PIM	GP	G	A	TP	PIM
1988-89	Pt. Basques	Sr.	26	20	41	61	129	....	....	....	....	....
1989-90abc	Erie	ECHL	57	80	68	148	226	7	5	5	10	20
	Adirondack	AHL	11	10	7	17	4	2	1	1	2	2
1990-91	**Detroit**	**NHL**	**2**	**0**	**1**	**1**	**0**	**1**	**0**	**0**	**0**	**0**
	Adirondack	AHL	71	47	52	99	192	2	1	2	3	2
	NHL Totals		**2**	**0**	**1**	**1**	**0**	**1**	**0**	**0**	**0**	**0**

a Named ECHL Most Valuable Player (1990)
b Named ECHL Rookie of the Year (1990)
c ECHL First Team All-Star (1990)
Signed as a free agent by **Detroit**, January 9, 1990.

McEACHERN, SHAWN

Center. Shoots left. 6'1", 180 lbs.   Born, Waltham, MA, February 28, 1969.
(Pittsburgh's 6th choice, 110th overall, in 1987 Entry Draft).

				Regular Season					Playoffs			
Season	Club	Lea	GP	G	A	TP	PIM	GP	G	A	TP	PIM
1988-89	Boston U.	H.E.	36	20	28	48	32	....	....	....	....	....
1989-90a	Boston U.	H.E.	43	25	31	56	78	....	....	....	....	....
1990-91bc	Boston U.	H.E.	41	34	48	82	43	....	....	....	....	....

a Hockey East Second All-Star Team (1990)
b Hockey East First All-Star Team (1991)
c NCAA East First All-American Team (1991)

McFARLANE, SHANE

Center. Shoots left. 5'11", 180 lbs.   Born, Warroad, MN, September 4, 1968.
(Buffalo's 1st choice, 24th overall, in 1990 Supplemental Draft).

				Regular Season					Playoffs			
Season	Club	Lea	GP	G	A	TP	PIM	GP	G	A	TP	PIM
1989-90	North Dakota	WCHA	23	3	2	5	10	....	....	....	....	....
1990-91	North Dakota	WCHA	1	0	0	0	2	....	....	....	....	....

McGEE, CHRIS

Center. Shoots right. 6'2", 175 lbs. Born, Pearl River, NY, April 18, 1970.
(St. Louis' 1st choice, 27th overall, in 1991 Supplemental Draft).

			Regular Season					Playoffs				
Season	Club	Lea	GP	G	A	TP	PIM	GP	G	A	TP	PIM
1989-90	Babson	NCAA	31	20	12	32	10	....	....	....	....	....
1990-91	Babson	NCAA	28	22	23	45	6	....	....	....	....	....

McGILL, ROBERT PAUL (BOB)

Defense. Shoot right. 6'1", 193 lbs. Born, Edmonton, Alta., April 27, 1962.
(Toronto's 2nd choice, 26th overall, in 1980 Entry Draft).

			Regular Season					Playoffs				
Season	Club	Lea	GP	G	A	TP	PIM	GP	G	A	TP	PIM
1979-80	Victoria	WHL	70	3	18	21	230	15	0	5	5	64
1980-81	Victoria	WHL	66	5	36	41	295	11	1	5	6	67
1981-82	**Toronto**	**NHL**	**68**	**1**	**10**	**11**	**263**	....	....	....	....	....
1982-83	**Toronto**	**NHL**	**30**	**0**	**0**	**0**	**146**	....	....	....	....	....
	St. Catharines	AHL	32	2	5	7	95	....	....	....	....	....
1983-84	**Toronto**	**NHL**	**11**	**0**	**2**	**2**	**51**	....	....	....	....	....
	St. Catharines	AHL	55	1	15	16	217	6	0	0	0	26
1984-85	**Toronto**	**NHL**	**72**	**0**	**5**	**5**	**250**	....	....	....	....	....
1985-86	**Toronto**	**NHL**	**61**	**1**	**4**	**5**	**141**	**9**	**0**	**0**	**0**	**35**
1986-87	**Toronto**	**NHL**	**56**	**1**	**4**	**5**	**103**	**3**	**0**	**0**	**0**	**0**
1987-88	**Chicago**	**NHL**	**67**	**4**	**7**	**11**	**131**	**3**	**0**	**0**	**0**	**2**
1988-89	**Chicago**	**NHL**	**68**	**0**	**4**	**4**	**155**	**16**	**0**	**0**	**0**	**33**
1989-90	**Chicago**	**NHL**	**69**	**2**	**10**	**12**	**204**	**5**	**0**	**0**	**0**	**2**
1990-91	**Chicago**	**NHL**	**77**	**4**	**5**	**9**	**151**	**5**	**0**	**0**	**0**	**2**
	NHL Totals		**579**	**13**	**51**	**64**	**1595**	**41**	**0**	**0**	**0**	**74**

Traded to **Chicago** by **Toronto** with Steve Thomas and Rick Vaive for Al Secord and Ed Olczyk, September 3, 1987. Claimed by **San Jose** from **Chicago** in Expansion Draft, May 30, 1991.

McGILL, RYAN

Defense. Shoots right. 6'2", 197 lbs. Born, Sherwood Park, Alta., February 28, 1969.
(Chicago's 2nd choice, 29th overall, in 1987 Entry Draft).

			Regular Season					Playoffs				
Season	Club	Lea	GP	G	A	TP	PIM	GP	G	A	TP	PIM
1985-86	Lethbridge	WHL	64	5	10	15	171	10	0	1	1	9
1986-87	Swift Current	WHL	72	12	36	48	226	4	1	0	1	9
1987-88	Medicine Hat	WHL	67	5	30	35	224	15	7	3	10	47
1988-89	Saginaw	IHL	8	2	0	2	12	6	0	0	0	42
	Medicine Hat	WHL	57	26	45	71	172	3	0	2	2	15
1989-90	Indianapolis	IHL	77	11	17	28	215	14	2	2	4	29
1990-91	Halifax	AHL	7	0	4	4	6	....	....	....	....	....
a	Indianapolis	IHL	63	11	40	51	200	....	....	....	....	....

a IHL Second All-Star Team (1991)

Traded to **Quebec** by **Chicago** with Mike McNeil for Paul Gillis and Dan Vincelette, March 5, 1991.

McGOWAN, CAL

Center. Shoots left. 6'1", 185 lbs. Born, Sydny, NB, June 19, 1970.
(Minnesota's 3rd choice, 70th overall, in 1990 Entry Draft).

			Regular Season					Playoffs				
Season	Club	Lea	GP	G	A	TP	PIM	GP	G	A	TP	PIM
1988-89	Kamloops	WHL	72	21	31	52	44	....	....	....	....	....
1989-90	Kamloops	WHL	71	33	45	78	76	17	4	5	9	42
1990-91a	Kamloops	WHL	71	58	81	139	147	12	7	7	14	24

a WHL West First All-Star Team (1991)

McHUGH, MICHAEL (MIKE)

Left wing. Shoots left. 5'10", 190 lbs. Born, Bowdoin, MA, August 16, 1965.
(Minnesota's 1st choice, 1st overall, in 1988 Supplemental Draft).

			Regular Season					Playoffs				
Season	Club	Lea	GP	G	A	TP	PIM	GP	G	A	TP	PIM
1984-85	U. of Maine	H.E.	25	9	8	17	9	....	....	....	....	....
1985-86	U. of Maine	H.E.	38	9	10	19	24	....	....	....	....	....
1986-87	U. of Maine	H.E.	42	21	29	50	40	....	....	....	....	....
1987-88	U. of Maine	H.E.	44	29	37	66	90	....	....	....	....	....
1988-89	**Minnesota**	**NHL**	**3**	**0**	**0**	**0**	**2**	....	....	....	....	....
	Kalamazoo	IHL	70	17	29	46	89	6	3	1	4	17
1989-90	**Minnesota**	**NHL**	**3**	**0**	**0**	**0**	**0**	....	....	....	....	....
	Kalamazoo	IHL	73	14	17	31	96	10	0	6	6	16
1990-91	**Minnesota**	**NHL**	**6**	**0**	**0**	**0**	**0**	....	....	....	....	....
	Kalamazoo	IHL	69	27	38	65	82	11	3	8	11	6
	NHL Totals		**12**	**0**	**0**	**0**	**2**	....	....	....	....	....

Claimed by **San Jose** from **Minnesota** in Dispersal Draft, May 30, 1991.

McINNIS, MARTY

Center. Shoots right. 5'10", 165 lbs. Born, Hingman, MA, June 2, 1970.
(NY Islanders' 10th choice, 163rd overall, in 1988 Entry Draft).

			Regular Season					Playoffs				
Season	Club	Lea	GP	G	A	TP	PIM	GP	G	A	TP	PIM
1988-89	Boston College	H.E.	39	13	19	32	8	....	....	....	....	....
1989-90	Boston College	H.E.	41	24	29	53	43	....	....	....	....	....
1990-91	Boston College	H.E.	38	21	36	57	40	....	....	....	....	....

McINTYRE, JOHN

Center. Shoots left. 6'1", 180 lbs. Born, Ravenswood, Ont., April 29, 1969.
(Toronto's 3rd choice, 49th overall, in 1987 Entry Draft).

			Regular Season					Playoffs				
Season	Club	Lea	GP	G	A	TP	PIM	GP	G	A	TP	PIM
1985-86	Guelph	OHL	30	4	6	10	25	20	1	5	6	31
1986-87	Guelph	OHL	47	8	22	30	95	....	....	....	....	....
1987-88	Guelph	OHL	39	24	18	42	109	....	....	....	....	....
1988-89	Guelph	OHL	52	30	26	56	129	7	5	4	9	25
	Newmarket	AHL	3	0	2	2	7	5	1	1	2	20
1989-90	**Toronto**	**NHL**	**59**	**5**	**12**	**17**	**117**	**2**	**0**	**0**	**0**	**2**
	Newmarket	AHL	6	2	2	4	12	....	....	....	....	....
1990-91	**Toronto**	**NHL**	**13**	**0**	**3**	**3**	**25**	....	....	....	....	....
	Los Angeles	**NHL**	**56**	**8**	**5**	**13**	**115**	**12**	**0**	**1**	**1**	**24**
	NHL Totals		**128**	**13**	**20**	**33**	**257**	**14**	**0**	**1**	**1**	**26**

Traded to **Los Angeles** by **Toronto** for Mike Krushelnyski, November 9, 1990.

McKAY, RANDY

Right wing. Shoots right. 6'1", 185 lbs. Born, Montreal, Que., January 25, 1967.
(Detroit's 6th choice, 113th overall, in 1985 Entry Draft).

			Regular Season					Playoffs				
Season	Club	Lea	GP	G	A	TP	PIM	GP	G	A	TP	PIM
1984-85	Michigan Tech	WCHA	25	4	5	9	32	....	....	....	....	....
1985-86	Michigan Tech	WCHA	40	12	22	34	46	....	....	....	....	....
1986-87	Michigan Tech	WCHA	39	5	11	16	46	....	....	....	....	....
1987-88	Michigan Tech	WCHA	41	17	24	41	70	....	....	....	....	....
	Adirondack	AHL	10	0	3	3	12	6	0	4	4	0
1988-89	**Detroit**	**NHL**	**3**	**0**	**0**	**0**	**0**	**2**	**0**	**0**	**0**	**2**
	Adirondack	AHL	58	29	34	63	170	14	4	7	11	60
1989-90	**Detroit**	**NHL**	**33**	**3**	**6**	**9**	**51**	....	....	....	....	....
	Adirondack	AHL	36	16	23	39	99	6	3	0	3	35
1990-91	**Detroit**	**NHL**	**47**	**1**	**7**	**8**	**183**	**5**	**0**	**1**	**1**	**41**
	NHL Totals		**83**	**4**	**13**	**17**	**234**	**7**	**0**	**1**	**1**	**43**

McKEE, MIKE

Defense. Shoots right. 6'3", 190 lbs. Born, Toronto, Ont., June 18, 1969.
(Quebec's 1st choice, 1st overall, in 1990 Supplemental Draft).

			Regular Season					Playoffs				
Season	Club	Lea	GP	G	A	TP	PIM	GP	G	A	TP	PIM
1988-89	Princeton	ECAC	16	2	1	3	14	....	....	....	....	....
1989-90a	Princeton	ECAC	26	7	18	25	18	....	....	....	....	....
1990-91	Princeton	ECAC	15	1	4	5	16	....	....	....	....	....

a ECAC Second All-Star Team (1990)

McKEGNEY, ANTHONY SYIIYD (TONY) (ma-KEG-nee)

Left wing. Shoots left. 6'1", 200 lbs. Born, Montreal, Que., February 15, 1958.
(Buffalo's 2nd choice, 32nd overall, in 1978 Amateur Draft).

			Regular Season					Playoffs				
Season	Club	Lea	GP	G	A	TP	PIM	GP	G	A	TP	PIM
1974-75	Kingston	OHA	52	27	48	75	36	....	....	....	....	....
1975-76	Kingston	OHA	65	24	56	80	20	....	....	....	....	....
1976-77a	Kingston	OHA	66	58	77	135	30	14	13	10	23	14
1977-78b	Kingston	OHA	55	43	49	92	19	5	3	3	6	0
1978-79	**Buffalo**	**NHL**	**52**	**8**	**14**	**22**	**10**	**2**	**0**	**1**	**1**	**0**
	Hershey	AHL	24	21	18	39	4	1	0	0	0	0
1979-80	**Buffalo**	**NHL**	**80**	**23**	**29**	**52**	**24**	**14**	**3**	**4**	**7**	**2**
1980-81	**Buffalo**	**NHL**	**80**	**37**	**32**	**69**	**24**	**8**	**5**	**3**	**8**	**2**
1981-82	**Buffalo**	**NHL**	**73**	**23**	**29**	**52**	**41**	**4**	**0**	**0**	**0**	**2**
1982-83	**Buffalo**	**NHL**	**78**	**36**	**37**	**73**	**18**	**10**	**3**	**1**	**4**	**4**
1983-84	**Quebec**	**NHL**	**75**	**24**	**27**	**51**	**23**	**7**	**0**	**0**	**0**	**0**
1984-85	**Quebec**	**NHL**	**30**	**12**	**9**	**21**	**12**	....	....	....	....	....
	Minnesota	**NHL**	**27**	**11**	**13**	**24**	**4**	**9**	**8**	**6**	**14**	**0**
1985-86	**Minnesota**	**NHL**	**70**	**15**	**25**	**40**	**48**	**5**	**2**	**1**	**3**	**22**
1986-87	**Minnesota**	**NHL**	**11**	**2**	**3**	**5**	**16**	....	....	....	....	....
	NY Rangers	**NHL**	**64**	**29**	**17**	**46**	**56**	**6**	**0**	**0**	**0**	**12**
1987-88	**St. Louis**	**NHL**	**80**	**40**	**38**	**78**	**82**	**9**	**3**	**6**	**9**	**8**
1988-89	**St. Louis**	**NHL**	**71**	**25**	**17**	**42**	**58**	**3**	**0**	**1**	**1**	**0**
1989-90	**Detroit**	**NHL**	**14**	**2**	**1**	**3**	**8**	....	....	....	....	....
	Quebec	**NHL**	**48**	**16**	**11**	**27**	**45**	....	....	....	....	....
1990-91	**Quebec**	**NHL**	**50**	**17**	**16**	**33**	**44**	....	....	....	....	....
	Chicago	**NHL**	**9**	**0**	**1**	**1**	**4**	**2**	**0**	**0**	**0**	**4**
	NHL Totals		**912**	**320**	**319**	**639**	**517**	**79**	**24**	**23**	**47**	**56**

a OHA First All-Star Team (1977).
b OHA Second All-Star Team (1978).

Traded to **Quebec** by **Buffalo** with Andre Savard, J.F. Sauve and Buffalo's third round choice (Iirvo Jarvi) in 1983 Entry Draft for Real Cloutier and Quebec's first round choice (Adam Creighton) in 1983 Entry Draft, June 8, 1983. Traded to **Minnesota** by **Quebec** with Bo Berglund for Brent Ashton and Brad Maxwell, December 14, 1984. Traded to **NY Rangers** by **Minnesota** with Curt Giles and Minnesota's second round (Troy Mallette) choice in 1988 Entry Draft for Bob Brooke and NY Rangers' rights to Minnesota's fourth round choice (Jeffery Stolp) in 1988 Entry Draft previously acquired by NY Rangers in Mark Pavelich deal, November 13, 1986. Traded to **St. Louis** by **NY Rangers** with Rob Whistle for Bruce Bell and future considerations, May 28, 1987. Traded to **Detroit** by **St. Louis**, with Bernie Federko for Adam Oates and Paul MacLean, June 15, 1989. Traded to **Quebec** by **Detroit** for Robert Picard and Greg C. Adams, December 4, 1989. Traded to **Chicago** by **Quebec** for Jacques Cloutier, January 29, 1991.

McKENZIE, JIM

Left wing/Defense. Shoots left. 6'3", 205 lbs. Born, Gull Lake, Sask., November 3, 1969.
(Hartford's 3rd choice, 73rd overall, in 1989 Entry Draft)

			Regular Season					Playoffs				
Season	Club	Lea	GP	G	A	TP	PIM	GP	G	A	TP	PIM
1985-86	Moose Jaw	WHL	3	0	2	2	0	....	....	....	....	....
1986-87	Moose Jaw	WHL	65	5	3	8	125	9	0	0	0	7
1987-88	Moose Jaw	WHL	62	1	17	18	134	....	....	....	....	....
1988-89	Victoria	WHL	67	15	27	42	176	8	1	4	5	30
1989-90	**Hartford**	**NHL**	**5**	**0**	**0**	**0**	**4**	....	....	....	....	....
	Binghamton	AHL	56	4	12	16	149	....	....	....	....	....
1990-91	**Hartford**	**NHL**	**41**	**4**	**3**	**7**	**108**	**6**	**0**	**0**	**0**	**8**
	Springfield	AHL	24	3	4	7	102	....	....	....	....	....
	NHL Totals		**46**	**4**	**3**	**7**	**112**	**6**	**0**	**0**	**0**	**8**

McKIM, ANDREW HARRY

Center. Shoots right. 5'8", 175 lbs. Born, St. John, N.B., July 6, 1970.

			Regular Season					Playoffs				
Season	Club	Lea	GP	G	A	TP	PIM	GP	G	A	TP	PIM
1989-90ab	Hull	QMJHL	70	66	84	130	44	11	8	10	18	8
1990-91	Salt Lake	IHL	74	30	30	60	48	4	0	2	2	6

a QMJHL First All-Star Team (1990)
b QMJHL Player of the Year (1990)

Signed as a free agent by **Calgary**, October 5, 1990.

McLAUGHLIN, MICHAEL

Left wing. Shoots right. 6'1", 175 lbs. Born, Longmeadow, MA, March 29, 1970.
(Buffalo's 7th choice, 118th overall, in 1988 Entry Draft).

			Regular Season					Playoffs				
Season	Club	Lea	GP	G	A	TP	PIM	GP	G	A	TP	PIM
1988-89	U. of Vermont	ECAC	32	5	6	11	12	....	....	....	....	....
1989-90	U. of Vermont	ECAC	29	11	12	23	37	....	....	....	....	....
1990-91	U. of Vermont	ECAC	32	12	14	26	34	....	....	....	....	....

McLEAN, JEFF

Center. Shoots left. 5'10", 185 lbs. Born, Port Moody, B.C., October 6, 1969.
(San Jose's 1st choice, 1st overall, in 1991 Supplemental Draft).

			Regular Season					Playoffs				
Season	Club	Lea	GP	G	A	TP	PIM	GP	G	A	TP	PIM
1989-90	North Dakota	WCHA	45	10	16	26	42	....	....	....	....	....
1990-91	North Dakota	WCHA	42	19	26	45	22	....	....	....	....	....

McLENNAN, DONALD (DON)

Defense. Shoots left. 6'3", 210 lbs. Born, Winnipeg, Man., October 4, 1968.
(Winnipeg's 3rd choice, 79th overall, in 1987 Entry Draft).

			Regular Season					Playoffs				
Season	Club	Lea	GP	G	A	TP	PIM	GP	G	A	TP	PIM
1986-87	U. of Denver	WCHA	35	2	2	4	38	....	....	....	....	....
1987-88	U. of Denver	WCHA	29	0	3	3	24	....	....	....	....	....
1988-89	U. of Denver	WCHA	26	1	3	4	28	....	....	....	....	....
1989-90	U. of Denver	WCHA	42	0	6	6	41	....	....	....	....	....
1990-91	Cape Breton	AHL	12	0	0	0	30	....	....	....	....	....
	Knoxville	ECHL	47	6	16	22	152	....	....	....	....	....

McLLWAIN, DAVE (MA-kuhl-WAYN)

Center/Right wing. Shoots left. 6', 190 lbs. Born, Seaforth, Ont., January 9, 1967.
(Pittsburgh's 9th choice, 172nd overall, in 1986 Entry Draft).

			Regular Season					Playoffs				
Season	Club	Lea	GP	G	A	TP	PIM	GP	G	A	TP	PIM
1984-85	Kitchener	OHL	61	13	21	34	29	....	....	....	....	....
1985-86	Kitchener	OHL	13	7	7	14	12	....	....	....	....	....
	North Bay	OHL	51	30	28	58	25	10	4	4	8	2
1986-87a	North Bay	OHL	60	46	73	119	35	24	7	18	25	40
1987-88	**Pittsburgh**	**NHL**	**66**	**11**	**8**	**19**	**40**	....	....	....	....	....
	Muskegon	IHL	9	4	6	10	23	6	2	3	5	8
1988-89	**Pittsburgh**	**NHL**	**24**	**1**	**2**	**3**	**4**	**3**	**0**	**1**	**1**	**0**
	Muskegon	IHL	46	37	35	72	51	7	8	2	10	6
1989-90	**Winnipeg**	**NHL**	**80**	**25**	**26**	**51**	**60**	**7**	**0**	**1**	**1**	**2**
1990-91	**Winnipeg**	**NHL**	**60**	**14**	**11**	**25**	**46**	....	....	....	....	....
	NHL Totals		**230**	**51**	**47**	**98**	**150**	**10**	**0**	**2**	**2**	**2**

a OHL Second Team All-Star (1987)

Traded to **Winnipeg** by **Pittsburgh** with Randy Cunnyworth and Rick Tabaracci for Jim Kyte, Andrew McBain and Randy Gilhen, June 17, 1989.

McNEILL, MICHAEL

Left wing. Shoots left. 6', 195 lbs. Born, Winona, MN, July 22, 1966.
(St. Louis' 1st choice, 14th overall, in 1988 Supplemental Draft).

			Regular Season					Playoffs				
Season	Club	Lea	GP	G	A	TP	PIM	GP	G	A	TP	PIM
1984-85	Notre Dame	NCAA	28	16	26	42	12	....	....	....	....	....
1985-86	Notre Dame	NCAA	34	18	29	47	32	....	....	....	....	....
1986-87	Notre Dame	NCAA	30	21	16	37	24	....	....	....	....	....
1987-88	Notre Dame	NCAA	32	28	44	72	12	....	....	....	....	....
1988-89	Moncton	AHL	1	0	0	0	0	....	....	....	....	....
	Fort Wayne	IHL	75	27	35	62	12	11	1	5	6	2
1989-90a	Indianapolis	IHL	74	17	24	41	10	14	6	4	10	21
1990-91	**Chicago**	**NHL**	**23**	**2**	**2**	**4**	**6**	....	....	....	....	....
	Indianapolis	IHL	33	16	9	25	19	....	....	....	....	....
	Quebec	**NHL**	**14**	**2**	**5**	**7**	**4**	....	....	....	....	....
	NHL Totals		**37**	**4**	**7**	**11**	**10**	....	....	....	....	....

a Won N.R. Poile Trophy (Playoff MVP–IHL) (1990)

Signed as a free agent by **Chicago**, September, 1989. Traded to **Quebec** by **Chicago** with Ryan McGill for Paul Gillis and Dan Vincelette, March 5, 1991.

McPHEE, MICHAEL JOSEPH (MIKE)

Left wing. Shoots left. 6'1", 203 lbs. Born, Sydney, N.S., July 14, 1960.
(Montreal's 8th choice, 124th overall, in 1980 Entry Draft).

			Regular Season					Playoffs				
Season	Club	Lea	GP	G	A	TP	PIM	GP	G	A	TP	PIM
1980-81	RPI	ECAC	29	28	18	46	22	....	....	....	....	....
1981-82	RPI	ECAC	6	0	3	3	4	....	....	....	....	....
1982-83	Nova Scotia	AHL	42	10	15	25	29	7	1	1	2	14
1983-84	**Montreal**	**NHL**	**14**	**5**	**2**	**7**	**41**	**15**	**1**	**0**	**1**	**31**
	Nova Scotia	AHL	67	22	33	55	101	....	....	....	....	....
1984-85	**Montreal**	**NHL**	**70**	**17**	**22**	**39**	**120**	**12**	**4**	**1**	**5**	**32**
1985-86	**Montreal**	**NHL**	**70**	**19**	**21**	**40**	**69**	**20**	**3**	**4**	**7**	**45**
1986-87	**Montreal**	**NHL**	**79**	**18**	**21**	**39**	**58**	**17**	**7**	**2**	**9**	**13**
1987-88	**Montreal**	**NHL**	**77**	**23**	**20**	**43**	**53**	**11**	**4**	**3**	**7**	**8**
1988-89	**Montreal**	**NHL**	**73**	**19**	**22**	**41**	**74**	**20**	**4**	**7**	**11**	**30**
1989-90	**Montreal**	**NHL**	**56**	**23**	**18**	**41**	**47**	**9**	**1**	**1**	**2**	**16**
1990-91	**Montreal**	**NHL**	**64**	**22**	**21**	**43**	**56**	**13**	**1**	**7**	**8**	**12**
	NHL Totals		**503**	**146**	**147**	**293**	**518**	**117**	**25**	**25**	**50**	**187**

Played in NHL All-Star Game (1989)

McPHERSON, DARWIN

Left wing. Shoots left. 6'2", 210 lbs. Born, Flin Flon, Man., May 16, 1968.
(Boston's 4th choice, 67th overall, in 1987 Entry Draft).

			Regular Season					Playoffs				
Season	Club	Lea	GP	G	A	TP	PIM	GP	G	A	TP	PIM
1984-85	Brandon	WHL	39	2	0	2	36	....	....	....	....	....
1985-86	N. Westminster	WHL	63	2	8	10	149	....	....	....	....	....
1986-87	N. Westminster	WHL	65	10	22	32	242	....	....	....	....	....
1987-88	N. Westminster	WHL	47	1	17	18	192	5	0	0	0	16
1988-89	Saskatoon	WHL	59	4	13	17	256	8	0	1	1	27
1989-90	Peoria	IHL	18	1	0	1	94	....	....	....	....	....
1990-91	Peoria	IHL	1	0	0	0	0	....	....	....	....	....

Signed as a free agent by **St. Louis**, August 4, 1989.

McRAE, BASIL PAUL

Left wing. Shoots left. 6'2", 205 lbs. Born, Beaverton, Ont., January 5, 1961.
(Quebec's 3rd choice, 87th overall, in 1980 Entry Draft).

			Regular Season					Playoffs				
Season	Club	Lea	GP	G	A	TP	PIM	GP	G	A	TP	PIM
1979-80	London	OHA	67	24	36	60	116	5	0	0	0	18
1980-81	London	OHA	65	29	23	52	266	....	....	....	....	....
1981-82	**Quebec**	**NHL**	**20**	**4**	**3**	**7**	**69**	**9**	**1**	**0**	**1**	**34**
	Fredericton	AHL	47	11	15	26	175	....	....	....	....	....
1982-83	**Quebec**	**NHL**	**22**	**1**	**1**	**2**	**59**	....	....	....	....	....
	Fredericton	AHL	53	22	19	41	146	12	1	5	6	75
1983-84	**Toronto**	**NHL**	**3**	**0**	**0**	**0**	**19**	....	....	....	....	....
	St. Catharines	AHL	78	14	25	39	187	6	0	0	0	40
1984-85	**Toronto**	**NHL**	**1**	**0**	**0**	**0**	**0**	....	....	....	....	....
	St. Catharines	AHL	72	30	25	55	186	....	....	....	....	....
1985-86	**Detroit**	**NHL**	**4**	**0**	**0**	**0**	**5**	....	....	....	....	....
	Adirondack	AHL	69	22	30	52	259	17	5	4	9	101
1986-87	**Detroit**	**NHL**	**36**	**2**	**2**	**4**	**193**	....	....	....	....	....
	Quebec	**NHL**	**33**	**9**	**5**	**14**	**149**	**13**	**3**	**1**	**4**	***99**
1987-88	**Minnesota**	**NHL**	**80**	**5**	**11**	**16**	**382**	....	....	....	....	....
1988-89	**Minnesota**	**NHL**	**78**	**12**	**19**	**31**	**365**	**5**	**0**	**0**	**0**	**58**
1989-90	**Minnesota**	**NHL**	**66**	**9**	**17**	**26**	***351**	**7**	**1**	**0**	**1**	**24**
1990-91	**Minnesota**	**NHL**	**40**	**1**	**3**	**4**	**224**	**22**	**1**	**1**	**2**	***94**
	NHL Totals		**383**	**43**	**61**	**104**	**1816**	**56**	**6**	**2**	**8**	**309**

Traded to **Toronto** by **Quebec** for Richard Turmel, August 12, 1983. Signed as a free agent by **Detroit**, July 17, 1985. Traded to **Quebec** by **Detroit** with John Ogrodnick and Doug Shedden for Brent Ashton, Gilbert Delorme and Mark Kumpel, January 17, 1987. Signed as a free agent by **Minnesota**, June 29, 1987.

McRAE, CHRIS

Left wing. Shoots left. 6', 200 lbs. Born, Beaverton, Ont., August 26, 1965.

			Regular Season					Playoffs				
Season	Club	Lea	GP	G	A	TP	PIM	GP	G	A	TP	PIM
1983-84	Belleville	OHL	9	0	0	0	19	....	....	....	....	....
	Sudbury	OHL	53	14	31	45	120	....	....	....	....	....
1984-85	Sudbury	OHL	6	0	2	2	10	....	....	....	....	....
	Oshawa	OHL	43	8	7	15	118	5	0	1	1	2
	St. Catharines	AHL	6	4	3	7	24	....	....	....	....	....
1985-86	St. Catharines	AHL	59	1	1	2	233	11	0	1	1	65
1986-87	Newmarket	AHL	51	3	6	9	193	....	....	....	....	....
1987-88	**Toronto**	**NHL**	**11**	**0**	**0**	**0**	**65**	....	....	....	....	....
	Newmarket	AHL	34	7	6	13	165	....	....	....	....	....
1988-89	**Toronto**	**NHL**	**3**	**0**	**0**	**0**	**12**	....	....	....	....	....
	Newmarket	AHL	18	3	1	4	85	....	....	....	....	....
	Denver	IHL	23	1	4	5	121	2	0	0	0	20
1989-90	**Detroit**	**NHL**	**7**	**1**	**0**	**1**	**45**	....	....	....	....	....
	Adirondack	AHL	46	9	10	19	290	....	....	....	....	....
1990-91	Adirondack	AHL	23	2	3	5	109	2	0	0	0	11
	NHL Totals		**21**	**1**	**0**	**1**	**122**	....	....	....	....	....

Signed as a free agent by **Toronto**, October 16, 1985. Traded to **NY Rangers** by **Toronto** for Ken Hammond, February 21, 1989. Traded to **Detroit** by **NY Rangers** with Detroit's fifth round choice (Tony Burns) in 1990 Entry Draft which was previously acquired by NY Rangers for Kris King, September 7, 1989.

McRAE, KEN

Center. Shoots right. 6'1", 195 lbs. Born, Winchester, Ont., April 23, 1968.
(Quebec's 1st choice, 18th overall, in 1986 Entry Draft).

			Regular Season					Playoffs				
Season	Club	Lea	GP	G	A	TP	PIM	GP	G	A	TP	PIM
1985-86	Sudbury	OHL	66	25	49	74	127	4	2	1	3	12
1986-87	Sudbury	OHL	21	12	15	27	40	....	....	....	....	....
	Hamilton	OHL	20	7	12	19	25	7	1	1	2	12
1987-88	**Quebec**	**NHL**	**1**	**0**	**0**	**0**	**0**	....	....	....	....	....
	Hamilton	OHL	62	30	55	85	158	14	13	9	22	35
	Fredericton	AHL	...	...	...	...	...	3	0	0	0	8
1988-89	**Quebec**	**NHL**	**37**	**6**	**11**	**17**	**68**	....	....	....	....	....
	Halifax	AHL	41	20	21	41	87	....	....	....	....	....
1989-90	**Quebec**	**NHL**	**66**	**7**	**8**	**15**	**191**	....	....	....	....	....
1990-91	**Quebec**	**NHL**	**12**	**0**	**0**	**0**	**36**	....	....	....	....	....
	Halifax	AHL	60	10	36	46	193	....	....	....	....	....
	NHL Totals		**116**	**13**	**19**	**32**	**295**	....	....	....	....	....

McREYNOLDS, BRIAN

Center. Shoots left. 6'1", 192 lbs. Born, Penetanguishene, Ont., January 5, 1965.
(NY Rangers' 6th choice, 112th overall, in 1985 Entry Draft).

			Regular Season					Playoffs				
Season	Club	Lea	GP	G	A	TP	PIM	GP	G	A	TP	PIM
1985-86	Michigan State	CCHA	45	14	24	38	78	....	....	....	....	....
1986-87	Michigan State	CCHA	45	16	24	40	68	....	....	....	....	....
1987-88	Michigan State	CCHA	43	10	24	34	50	....	....	....	....	....
1988-89	Cdn. National		58	5	25	30	59	....	....	....	....	....
1989-90	**Winnipeg**	**NHL**	**9**	**0**	**2**	**2**	**4**	....	....	....	....	....
	Moncton	AHL	72	18	41	59	87	....	....	....	....	....
1990-91	**NY Rangers**	**NHL**	**1**	**0**	**0**	**0**	**0**	....	....	....	....	....
	Binghamton	AHL	77	30	42	72	74	10	0	4	4	6
	NHL Totals		**10**	**0**	**2**	**2**	**4**	....	....	....	....	....

Signed as a free agent by **Winnipeg**, June 20, 1989. Traded to **NY Rangers** by **Winnipeg** for Simon Wheeldon, July 10, 1990.

McSORLEY, MARTIN J. (MARTY)

Defense. Shoots right. 6'1", 235 lbs. Born, Hamilton, Ont., May 18, 1963.

			Regular Season					Playoffs				
Season	Club	Lea	GP	G	A	TP	PIM	GP	G	A	TP	PIM
1981-82	Belleville	OHL	58	6	13	19	234	....	....	....	....	....
1982-83	Belleville	OHL	70	10	41	51	183	4	0	0	0	7
	Baltimore	AHL	2	0	0	0	22	....	....	....	....	....
1983-84	**Pittsburgh**	**NHL**	**72**	**2**	**7**	**9**	**224**	....	....	....	....	....
1984-85	**Pittsburgh**	**NHL**	**15**	**0**	**0**	**0**	**15**	....	....	....	....	....
	Baltimore	AHL	58	6	24	30	154	14	0	7	7	47
1985-86	**Edmonton**	**NHL**	**59**	**11**	**12**	**23**	**265**	**8**	**0**	**2**	**2**	**50**
	Nova Scotia	AHL	9	2	4	6	34	....	....	....	....	....
1986-87	**Edmonton**	**NHL**	**41**	**2**	**4**	**6**	**159**	**21**	**4**	**3**	**7**	**65**
	Nova Scotia	AHL	7	2	2	4	48	....	....	....	....	....
1987-88	**Edmonton**	**NHL**	**60**	**9**	**17**	**26**	**223**	**16**	**0**	**3**	**3**	**67**
1988-89	**Los Angeles**	**NHL**	**66**	**10**	**17**	**27**	**350**	**11**	**0**	**2**	**2**	**33**
1989-90	**Los Angeles**	**NHL**	**75**	**15**	**21**	**36**	**322**	**10**	**1**	**3**	**4**	**18**
1990-91	**Los Angeles**	**NHL**	**61**	**7**	**32**	**39**	**221**	**12**	**0**	**0**	**0**	**58**
	NHL Totals		**449**	**56**	**110**	**166**	**1779**	**78**	**5**	**13**	**18**	**291**

Signed as free agent by **Pittsburgh**, July 30, 1982. Traded to **Edmonton** by **Pittsburgh** with Tim Hrynewich for Gilles Meloche, September, 12, 1985. Traded to **Los Angeles** by **Edmonton** with Wayne Gretzky and Mike Krushelnyski for Jimmy Carson, Martin Gelinas, Los Angeles' first round choices in 1989 (acquired by New Jersey, June 17, 1989. New Jersey selected Jason Miller), 1991 (Martin Rucinsky) and 1993 Entry Drafts and cash, August 9, 1988.

McSWEEN, DON

Defense; Shoots left. 5'11", 195 lbs. Born, Detroit, MI, June 9, 1964.
(Buffalo's 10th choice, 154th overall, in 1983 Entry Draft).

			Regular Season					Playoffs				
Season	Club	Lea	GP	G	A	TP	PIM	GP	G	A	TP	PIM
1983-84	Michigan State	CCHA	46	10	26	36	30	....	....	....	....	....
1984-85	Michigan State	CCHA	44	2	23	25	52	....	....	....	....	....
1985-86a	Michigan State	CCHA	45	9	29	38	18	....	....	....	....	....
1986-87abc	Michigan State	CCHA	45	7	23	30	34	....	....	....	....	....
1987-88	**Buffalo**	**NHL**	**5**	**0**	**1**	**1**	**6**	....	....	....	....	....
	Rochester	AHL	63	9	29	38	108	6	0	1	1	15
1988-89	Rochester	AHL	66	7	22	29	45	....	....	....	....	....
1989-90	**Buffalo**	**NHL**	**4**	**0**	**0**	**0**	**6**	....	....	....	....	....
d	Rochester	AHL	70	16	43	59	43	17	3	10	13	12
1990-91	Rochester	AHL	74	7	44	51	57	15	2	5	7	8
	NHL Totals		**9**	**0**	**1**	**1**	**12**	....	....	....	....	....

a CCHA First All-Star Team (1986, 1987)
b NCAA West Second All-American Team (1987)
c Named to NCAA All-Tournament Team (1987)
d AHL First All-Star Team (1990)

MEAGHER, RICHARD (RICK) (muh-HAHR)

Center. Shoots left. 5'8", 192 lbs. Born, Belleville, Ont., November 2, 1953.

			Regular Season					Playoffs				
Season	Club	Lea	GP	G	A	TP	PIM	GP	G	A	TP	PIM
1975-76	Boston U.	ECAC	28	12	25	37	22	....	....	....	....	....
1976-77	Boston U.	ECAC	34	34	46	80	42	....	....	....	....	....
1977-78	Nova Scotia	AHL	57	20	27	47	33	11	5	3	8	11
1978-79	Nova Scotia	AHL	79	35	46	81	57	10	1	6	7	11
1979-80	**Montreal**	**NHL**	**2**	**0**	**0**	**0**	**0**	....	....	....	....	....
	Nova Scotia	AHL	64	32	44	76	53	6	3	4	7	2
1980-81	**Hartford**	**NHL**	**27**	**7**	**10**	**17**	**19**	....	....	....	....	....
	Binghamton	AHL	50	23	35	58	54	....	....	....	....	....
1981-82	**Hartford**	**NHL**	**65**	**24**	**19**	**43**	**51**	....	....	....	....	....
1982-83	**Hartford**	**NHL**	**4**	**0**	**0**	**0**	**0**	....	....	....	....	....
	New Jersey	**NHL**	**57**	**15**	**14**	**29**	**11**	....	....	....	....	....
1983-84	**New Jersey**	**NHL**	**52**	**14**	**14**	**28**	**16**	....	....	....	....	....
	Maine	AHL	10	6	4	10	2	....	....	....	....	....
1984-85	**New Jersey**	**NHL**	**71**	**11**	**20**	**31**	**22**	....	....	....	....	....
1985-86	**St. Louis**	**NHL**	**79**	**11**	**19**	**30**	**28**	**19**	**4**	**4**	**8**	**12**
1986-87	**St. Louis**	**NHL**	**80**	**18**	**21**	**39**	**54**	**6**	**0**	**0**	**0**	**11**
1987-88	**St. Louis**	**NHL**	**76**	**18**	**16**	**34**	**76**	**10**	**0**	**0**	**0**	**8**
1988-89	**St. Louis**	**NHL**	**78**	**15**	**14**	**29**	**53**	**10**	**3**	**2**	**5**	**6**
1989-90a	**St. Louis**	**NHL**	**76**	**8**	**17**	**25**	**47**	**8**	**1**	**0**	**1**	**2**
1990-91	**St. Louis**	**NHL**	**24**	**3**	**1**	**4**	**6**	**9**	**0**	**1**	**1**	**2**
	NHL Totals		**691**	**144**	**165**	**309**	**383**	**62**	**8**	**7**	**15**	**41**

a Won Frank J. Selke Trophy (1990)

Signed as a free agent by **Montreal**, June 27, 1977. Traded to **Hartford** by **Montreal** with Montreal's third round (Paul MacDermid) and fifth round (Dan Bourbonnais) choices in 1981 Entry Draft for Hartford's third round (Dieter Hegen) and fifth round (Steve Rooney) choices in 1981 Entry Draft, June 5, 1980. Traded to **New Jersey** by **Hartford** with the rights to Garry Howatt for Merlin Malinowski and the rights to Scott Fusco, October 15, 1982. Traded to **St. Louis** by **New Jersey** with New Jersey's 12th round choice (Bill Butler) in 1986 Entry Draft for Perry Anderson, August 29, 1985.

MEARS, GLEN

Defense. Shoots right. 6'3", 215 lbs. Born, Anchorage, AK, July 14, 1972.
(Calgary's 5th choice, 62nd overall, in 1990 Entry Draft).

			Regular Season					Playoffs				
Season	Club	Lea	GP	G	A	TP	PIM	GP	G	A	TP	PIM
1989-90	Rochester	USHL	46	5	20	25	95	....	....	....	....	....
1990-91	Bowling Green	CCHA	40	0	7	7	54	....	....	....	....	....

MEASURES, ALLAN

Defense. Shoots left. 5'11", 165 lbs. Born, Barrhead, Alta., May 8, 1965.
(Vancouver's 9th choice, 170th overall, in 1983 Entry Draft).

			Regular Season					Playoffs				
Season	Club	Lea	GP	G	A	TP	PIM	GP	G	A	TP	PIM
1982-83	Calgary	WHL	63	5	23	28	43	16	0	5	5	12
1983-84	Calgary	WHL	69	17	36	53	96	4	3	4	7	0
1984-85	Calgary	WHL	65	25	58	83	84	8	2	4	6	11
1985-86	Calgary	WHL	46	23	34	57	50	....	....	....	....	....
1986-87	Fredericton	AHL	29	3	8	11	12	....	....	....	....	....
	Kalamazoo	IHL	37	11	15	26	26	5	1	1	2	0
1987-88	Lukko	Fin.	44	3	13	16	72	....	....	....	....	....
1988-89	Lukko	Fin.	43	3	26	29	46	....	....	....	....	....
1989-90	Lukko	Fin.	40	10	10	20	36	....	....	....	....	....
1990-91	Lukko	Fin.	42	11	20	31	44	....	....	....	....	....

MEEHAN, SCOTT

Defense. Shoots left. 6'1", 185 lbs. Born, Walpole, MA, November 27, 1970.
(Vancouver's 1st choice, 13th overall, in 1991 Supplemental Draft).

			Regular Season					Playoffs				
Season	Club	Lea	GP	G	A	TP	PIM	GP	G	A	TP	PIM
1989-90	U. of Lowell	H.E.	24	0	0	0	16	....	....	....	....	....
1990-91	U. of Lowell	H.E.	27	1	2	3	20	....	....	....	....	....

MEJZLIK, ROMAN

Left wing/center. Shoots left. 6'2", 198 lbs. Born, Trebic, Czechoslovakia, October 31, 1967.
(Edmonton's 8th choice, 164th overall, in 1990 Entry Draft).

			Regular Season					Playoffs				
Season	Club	Lea	GP	G	A	TP	PIM	GP	G	A	TP	PIM
1987-88	Dukla Jihlava	Czech.	39	12	10	22	30	....	....	....	....	....
1988-89	Dukla Jihlava	Czech.	43	4	14	18	24	....	....	....	....	....
1989-90	Dukla Jihlava	Czech.	44	3	11	14	....	7	4	5	9	....
1990-91	Dukla Jihlava	Czech.	48	9	9	18	30	7	1	4	5	....

MELLANBY, SCOTT

Right wing. Shoots right. 6'1", 205 lbs. Born, Montreal, Que., June 11, 1966.
(Philadelphia's 2nd choice, 27th overall, in 1984 Entry Draft).

			Regular Season					Playoffs				
Season	Club	Lea	GP	G	A	TP	PIM	GP	G	A	TP	PIM
1984-85	U. Wisconsin	WCHA	40	14	24	38	60	....	....	....	....	....
1985-86	U. Wisconsin	WCHA	32	21	23	44	89	....	....	....	....	....
	Philadelphia	**NHL**	**2**	**0**	**0**	**0**	**0**	....	....	....	....	....
1986-87	**Philadelphia**	**NHL**	**71**	**11**	**21**	**32**	**94**	**24**	**5**	**5**	**10**	**46**
1987-88	**Philadelphia**	**NHL**	**75**	**25**	**26**	**51**	**185**	**7**	**0**	**1**	**1**	**16**
1988-89	**Philadelphia**	**NHL**	**76**	**21**	**29**	**50**	**183**	**19**	**4**	**5**	**9**	**28**
1989-90	**Philadelphia**	**NHL**	**57**	**6**	**17**	**23**	**77**	....	....	....	....	....
1990-91	**Philadelphia**	**NHL**	**74**	**20**	**21**	**41**	**155**	....	....	....	....	....
	NHL Totals		**355**	**83**	**114**	**197**	**694**	**50**	**9**	**11**	**20**	**90**

Traded to **Edmonton** by **Philadelphia** with Craig Fisher and Craig Berube for Dave Brown, Corey Foster and Jari Kurri, May 30, 1991.

MELNYK, DOUGLAS

Defense. Shoots left. 6', 185 lbs. Born, London, Ont., August 9, 1967.
(NY Islanders' 1st choice, 21st overall, in 1988 Supplemental Draft).

			Regular Season					Playoffs				
Season	Club	Lea	GP	G	A	TP	PIM	GP	G	A	TP	PIM
1986-87	W. Michigan	CCHA	43	2	7	9	40	....	....	....	....	....
1987-88	W. Michigan	CCHA	42	2	16	18	22	....	....	....	....	....
1988-89	W. Michigan	CCHA	30	2	4	6	28	....	....	....	....	....
1989-90	W. Michigan	CCHA	33	2	10	12	26	....	....	....	....	....
1990-91	Cincinnati	ECHL	63	4	23	27	59	4	0	0	0	6

MELROSE, KEVAN

Defense. Shoots left. 5'10", 185 lbs. Born, Calgary, Alta., March 28, 1966.
(Calgary's 7th choice, 138th overall in 1984 Entry Draft).

			Regular Season					Playoffs				
Season	Club	Lea	GP	G	A	TP	PIM	GP	G	A	TP	PIM
1986-87	Cdn. Olympic	....	8	1	0	1	4	....	....	....	....	....
	Red Deer	AJHL	29	15	15	30	171	19	8	16	24	60
1987-88	Harvard	ECAC	31	4	6	10	50	....	....	....	....	....
1988-89	Harvard	ECAC	32	2	13	15	126	....	....	....	....	....
1989-90	Harvard	ECAC	16	1	6	7	124	....	....	....	....	....
1990-91	Salt Lake	IHL	60	6	14	20	82	4	1	2	3	10

MELUZIN, ROMAN

Right wing. Shoots right. 6', 174 lbs. Born, Brno, Czechoslovakia, June 17, 1972.
(Winnipeg's 3rd choice, 74th overall, in 1990 Entry Draft).

			Regular Season					Playoffs				
Season	Club	Lea	GP	G	A	TP	PIM	GP	G	A	TP	PIM
1989-90	Zetor Brno	Czech.	34	4	6	10	....	....	....	....	....	....
1990-91	Zetor Brno	Czech.	30	14	8	22	8	....	....	....	....	....

MENDEL, ROBERT (ROB)

Defense. Shoots left. 6'1", 195 lbs. Born, Los Angeles, CA, September 19, 1968.
(Quebec's 5th choice, 93rd overall, in 1987 Entry Draft).

			Regular Season					Playoffs				
Season	Club	Lea	GP	G	A	TP	PIM	GP	G	A	TP	PIM
1986-87	U. Wisconsin	WCHA	42	1	7	8	26	....	....	....	....	....
1987-88	U. Wisconsin	WCHA	40	0	7	7	22	....	....	....	....	....
1988-89	U. Wisconsin	WCHA	44	1	14	15	37	....	....	....	....	....
1989-90	U. Wisconsin	WCHA	44	1	13	14	30	....	....	....	....	....
1990-91	Baltimore	AHL	43	0	7	7	20	....	....	....	....	....
	Newmarket	AHL	13	1	0	1	6	....	....	....	....	....
	Hampton Roads	ECHL	2	0	2	2	0	....	....	....	....	....

Signed as a free agent by **Washington**, May 24, 1990. Traded to **Toronto** by **Washington** for Bobby Reynolds, March 5, 1991.

MERKLER, KEITH

Left wing. Shoots left. 6'2", 205 lbs. Born, Syosset, NY, April 23, 1971.
(Toronto's 8th choice, 129th overall, in 1989 Entry Draft).

			Regular Season					Playoffs				
Season	Club	Lea	GP	G	A	TP	PIM	GP	G	A	TP	PIM
1989-90	Princeton	ECAC	8	0	0	0	4	....	....	....	....	....
1990-91	Princeton	ECAC	22	4	4	8	20	....	....	....	....	....

MERKOSKY, GLENN (muhr-KAH-skee)

Center. Shoots left. 5'10", 175 lbs. Born, Edmonton, Alta., April 8, 1959.

			Regular Season					Playoffs				
Season	**Club**	**Lea**	**GP**	**G**	**A**	**TP**	**PIM**	**GP**	**G**	**A**	**TP**	**PIM**
1979-80	Calgary	WHL	72	49	40	89	95	7	4	6	10	14
1980-81	Binghamton	AHL	80	26	35	61	61	5	0	2	2	2
1981-82	**Hartford**	**NHL**	**7**	**0**	**0**	**0**	**2**	....	....	....	....	....
	Binghamton	AHL	72	29	40	69	83	10	0	2	2	2
1982-83	**New Jersey**	**NHL**	**34**	**4**	**10**	**14**	**20**	....	....	....	....	....
	Wichita	CHL	45	26	23	49	15	....	....	....	....	....
1983-84	**New Jersey**	**NHL**	**5**	**1**	**0**	**1**	**0**	....	....	....	....	....
	Maine	AHL	75	28	28	56	56	17	11	10	21	20
1984-85a	Maine	AHL	80	38	38	76	19	11	2	3	5	13
1985-86	**Detroit**	**NHL**	**17**	**0**	**2**	**2**	**0**	....	....	....	....	....
	Adirondack	AHL	59	24	33	57	22	17	5	7	12	15
1986-87bc	Adirondack	AHL	77	*54	31	85	66	11	6	8	14	7
1987-88	Adirondack	AHL	66	34	42	76	34	11	4	6	10	4
1988-89	Adirondack	AHL	76	31	46	77	13	17	8	11	19	10
1989-90	**Detroit**	**NHL**	**3**	**0**	**0**	**0**	**0**	....	....	....	....	....
	Adirondack	AHL	75	33	31	64	29	6	2	1	3	6
1990-91	Adirondack	AHL	77	28	39	57	37	2	1	1	2	0
	NHL Totals		**66**	**5**	**12**	**17**	**22**	....	....	....	....	....

a AHL Second All-Star Team (1985)
b AHL First All-Star Team (1987)
c Won Fred T. Hunt Memorial Trophy (Sportsmanship-AHL 1987)

Signed as a free agent by **Hartford**, August 10, 1980. Signed as a free agent by **New Jersey**, September 14, 1982. Signed as a free agent by **Detroit**, July 15, 1985.

MERSCH, MIKE

Defense. Shoots left. 6'2", 210 lbs. Born, Skokie, IL, September 29, 1964.

			Regular Season					Playoffs				
Season	**Club**	**Lea**	**GP**	**G**	**A**	**TP**	**PIM**	**GP**	**G**	**A**	**TP**	**PIM**
1983-84	Ill.-Chicago	CCHA	29	0	5	5	18	....	....	....	....	....
1984-85	Ill.-Chicago	CCHA	35	1	14	15	36	....	....	....	....	....
1985-86	Ill.-Chicago	CCHA	36	4	19	23	30	....	....	....	....	....
1986-87	Salt Lake	IHL	43	3	12	15	101	17	0	10	10	14
1987-88	Salt Lake	IHL	1	0	0	0	2	....	....	....	....	....
	Flint	IHL	58	1	14	15	118	16	3	4	7	18
1988-89	New Haven	AHL	1	0	0	0	4	....	....	....	....	....
	Flint	IHL	55	5	20	25	101	....	....	....	....	....
	Muskegon	IHL	16	0	2	2	26	13	0	6	6	38
1989-90	Muskegon	IHL	82	10	38	48	161	15	1	4	5	41
1990-91	Muskegon	IHL	73	4	23	27	105	5	0	0	0	6

Signed as a free agent by **Calgary**, April 22, 1986. Signed as a free agent by **Pittsburgh**, August 3, 1989.

MESSIER, JOBY

Defense. Shoots right. 6', 193 lbs. Born, Regina, Sask., March 2, 1970.
(NY Rangers' 7th choice, 118th overall, in 1989 Entry Draft).

			Regular Season					Playoffs				
Season	**Club**	**Lea**	**GP**	**G**	**A**	**TP**	**PIM**	**GP**	**G**	**A**	**TP**	**PIM**
1988-89	Michigan State	CCHA	39	2	10	12	66	....	....	....	....	....
1989-90	Michigan State	CCHA	42	1	11	12	58	....	....	....	....	....
1990-91	Michigan State	CCHA	39	5	11	16	71	....	....	....	....	....

MESSIER, MARK DOUGLAS (MEHZ-yay)

Center. Shoots left. 6'1", 210 lbs. Born, Edmonton, Alta., January 18, 1961.
(Edmonton's 2nd choice, 48th overall, in 1979 Entry Draft).

			Regular Season					Playoffs				
Season	**Club**	**Lea**	**GP**	**G**	**A**	**TP**	**PIM**	**GP**	**G**	**A**	**TP**	**PIM**
1977-78	Portland	WHL	....	....	....	....	....	7	4	1	5.	2
1978-79	Indianapolis	WHA	5	0	0	0	0	....	....	....	....	....
	Cincinnati	WHA	47	1	10	11	58	....	....	....	....	....
1979-80	**Edmonton**	**NHL**	**75**	**12**	**21**	**33**	**120**	**3**	**1**	**2**	**3**	**2**
	Houston	CHL	4	0	3	3	4	....	....	....	....	....
1980-81	**Edmonton**	**NHL**	**72**	**23**	**40**	**63**	**102**	**9**	**2**	**5**	**7**	**13**
1981-82a	**Edmonton**	**NHL**	**78**	**50**	**38**	**88**	**119**	**5**	**1**	**2**	**3**	**8**
1982-83a	**Edmonton**	**NHL**	**77**	**48**	**58**	**106**	**72**	**15**	**15**	**6**	**21**	**14**
1983-84bc	**Edmonton**	**NHL**	**73**	**37**	**64**	**101**	**165**	**19**	**8**	**18**	**26**	**19**
1984-85	**Edmonton**	**NHL**	**55**	**23**	**31**	**54**	**57**	**18**	**12**	**13**	**25**	**12**
1985-86	**Edmonton**	**NHL**	**63**	**35**	**49**	**84**	**68**	**10**	**4**	**6**	**10**	**18**
1986-87	**Edmonton**	**NHL**	**77**	**37**	**70**	**107**	**73**	**21**	**12**	**16**	**28**	**16**
1987-88	**Edmonton**	**NHL**	**77**	**37**	**74**	**111**	**103**	**19**	**11**	**23**	**34**	**29**
1988-89	**Edmonton**	**NHL**	**72**	**33**	**61**	**94**	**130**	**7**	**1**	**11**	**12**	**8**
1989-90ade	**Edmonton**	**NHL**	**79**	**45**	**84**	**129**	**79**	**22**	**9**	***22**	**31**	**20**
1990-91	**Edmonton**	**NHL**	**53**	**12**	**52**	**64**	**34**	**18**	**4**	**11**	**15**	**16**
	NHL Totals		**851**	**392**	**642**	**1034**	**1122**	**166**	**80**	**135**	**215**	**175**

a NHL First All-Star Team (1982, 1983, 1990)
b NHL Second All-Star Team (1984)
c Won Conn Smythe Trophy (1984)
d Won Hart Trophy (1990)
e Won Lester B. Pearson Award (1990)

Played in NHL All-Star Game (1982-86, 1988-91)

MESSIER, MITCH

Center. Shoots right. 6'2", 200 lbs. Born, Regina, Sask., August 21, 1965.
(Minnesota's 4th choice, 56th overall, in 1983 Entry Draft).

			Regular Season					Playoffs				
Season	**Club**	**Lea**	**GP**	**G**	**A**	**TP**	**PIM**	**GP**	**G**	**A**	**TP**	**PIM**
1983-84	Michigan State	CCHA	37	6	15	21	22	....	....	....	....	....
1984-85	Michigan State	CCHA	42	12	21	33	46	....	....	....	....	....
1985-86	Michigan State	CCHA	38	24	40	64	36	....	....	....	....	....
1986-87ab	Michigan State	CCHA	45	44	48	92	89	....	....	....	....	....
1987-88	**Minnesota**	**NHL**	**13**	**0**	**1**	**1**	**11**	....	....	....	....	....
	Kalamazoo	IHL	69	29	37	66	42	4	2	1	3	0
1988-89	**Minnesota**	**NHL**	**3**	**0**	**1**	**1**	**0**	....	....	....	....	....
	Kalamazoo	IHL	67	34	46	80	71	6	4	3	7	0
1989-90	**Minnesota**	**NHL**	**2**	**0**	**0**	**0**	**0**	....	....	....	....	....
	Kalamazoo	IHL	65	26	58	84	56	8	4	3	7	25
1990-91	**Minnesota**	**NHL**	**2**	**0**	**0**	**0**	**0**	....	....	....	....	....
	Kalamazoo	IHL	73	30	46	76	34	11	4	8	12	2
	NHL Totals		**20**	**0**	**2**	**2**	**11**	....	....	....	....	....

a CCHA First All-Star Team (1987)
b NCAA West First All-American Team (1987)

METCALFE, SCOTT (MET-kaff)

Left wing. Shoots left. 6', 200 lbs. Born, Toronto, Ont., January 6, 1967.
(Edmonton's 1st choice, 20th overall, in 1985 Entry Draft).

			Regular Season					Playoffs				
Season	**Club**	**Lea**	**GP**	**G**	**A**	**TP**	**PIM**	**GP**	**G**	**A**	**TP**	**PIM**
1983-84	Kingston	OHL	68	25	49	74	154	....	....	....	....	....
1984-85	Kingston	OHL	58	27	33	60	100	....	....	....	....	....
1985-86	Kingston	OHL	66	36	43	79	213	10	3	6	9	21
1986-87	Kingston	OHL	39	15	45	60	14	....	....	....	....	....
	Windsor	OHL	18	10	12	22	52	13	5	5	10	27
1987-88	**Edmonton**	**NHL**	**2**	**0**	**0**	**0**	**0**	....	....	....	....	....
	Nova Scotia	AHL	43	9	19	28	87	....	....	....	....	....
	Buffalo	**NHL**	**1**	**0**	**1**	**1**	**0**	....	....	....	....	....
	Rochester	AHL	22	2	13	15	56	7	1	3	4	24
1988-89	**Buffalo**	**NHL**	**9**	**1**	**1**	**2**	**13**	....	....	....	....	....
	Rochester	AHL	60	20	31	51	241	....	....	....	....	....
1989-90	**Buffalo**	**NHL**	**7**	**0**	**0**	**0**	**5**	....	....	....	....	....
	Rochester	AHL	43	12	17	29	93	2	0	1	1	0
1990-91	Rochester	AHL	69	17	22	39	177	14	4	1	5	27
	NHL Totals		**19**	**1**	**2**	**3**	**18**	....	....	....	....	....

Traded to **Buffalo** by **Edmonton** with Edmonton's ninth round choice (Donald Audette) in 1989 Entry Draft for Steve Dykstra and Buffalo's seventh round choice (David Payne) in 1989 Entry Draft, February 11, 1988.

MEWS, HAROLD RANDALL (HARRY)

Center. Shoots left. 5'10", 175 lbs. Born, Nepean, Ont., February 9, 1967.
(Washington's 1st choice, 20th overall, in 1988 Supplemental Draft).

			Regular Season					Playoffs				
Season	**Club**	**Lea**	**GP**	**G**	**A**	**TP**	**PIM**	**GP**	**G**	**A**	**TP**	**PIM**
1986-87	Northeastern	H.E.	29	10	15	25	70	....	....	....	....	....
1987-88	Northeastern	H.E.	37	16	23	39	82	....	....	....	....	....
1988-89a	Northeastern	H.E.	31	18	24	42	103	....	....	....	....	....
1989-90a	Northeastern	H.E.	36	20	*39	59	82	....	....	....	....	....
1990-91	Baltimore	AHL	5	0	1	1	2	....	....	....	....	....
	Hampton Roads	ECHL	55	30	43	73	150	14	5	*18	23	47

a Hockey East Second All-Star Team (1989, 1990)

MICHAYLUK, DAVID (DAVE) (muh-KIGH-luhk)

Left wing. Shoots left. 5'10", 189 lbs. Born, Wakaw, Sask., May 18, 1962.
(Philadelphia's 5th choice, 65th overall, in 1981 Entry Draft).

			Regular Season					Playoffs				
Season	**Club**	**Lea**	**GP**	**G**	**A**	**TP**	**PIM**	**GP**	**G**	**A**	**TP**	**PIM**
1980-81	Regina	WHL	72	62	71	133	39	11	5	12	17	8
1981-82	**Philadelphia**	**NHL**	**1**	**0**	**0**	**0**	**0**	....	....	....	....	....
a	Regina	WHL	72	62	111	172	128	12	16	24	*40	23
1982-83	**Philadelphia**	**NHL**	**13**	**2**	**6**	**8**	**8**	....	....	....	....	....
	Maine	AHL	69	32	40	72	16	8	0	2	2	0
1983-84	Springfield	AHL	79	18	44	62	37	4	0	0	0	2
1984-85	Hershey	AHL	3	0	2	2	2	....	....	....	....	....
b	Kalamazoo	IHL	82	*66	33	99	49	11	7	7	14	0
1985-86	Nova Scotia	AHL	3	0	1	1	0	....	....	....	....	....
	Muskegon	IHL	77	52	52	104	73	14	6	9	15	12
1986-87c	Muskegon	IHL	82	47	53	100	29	15	2	14	16	8
1987-88c	Muskegon	IHL	81	*56	81	137	46	6	2	0	2	18
1988-89cdef	Muskegon	IHL	80	50	72	*122	84	13	*9	12	*21	24
1989-90c	Muskegon	IHL	79	*51	51	102	80	15	8	*14	22	10
1990-91	Muskegon	IHL	83	40	62	102	116	5	2	2	4	4
	NHL Totals		**14**	**2**	**6**	**8**	**8**	....	....	....	....	....

a WHL Second All-Star Team (1982)
b IHL Second All-Star Team (1985)
c IHL First All-Star Team (1987, 1988, 1989, 1990)
d IHL Playoff MVP (1989)
e Won James Gatschene Memorial Trophy (MVP-IHL) (1989)
f Won Leo P. Lamoureux Memorial Trophy (Top Scorer-IHL) (1989)

Signed as a free agent by **Pittsburgh**, May 24, 1989.

MICK, TROY

Left wing. Shoots left. 5'11", 192 lbs. Born, Burnaby, B.C., March 30, 1969.
(Pittsburgh's 6th choice, 130th overall, in 1988 Entry Draft).

			Regular Season					Playoffs				
Season	**Club**	**Lea**	**GP**	**G**	**A**	**TP**	**PIM**	**GP**	**G**	**A**	**TP**	**PIM**
1986-87	Portland	WHL	57	30	33	63	60	20	8	2	10	40
1987-88a	Portland	WHL	72	63	84	147	78	....	....	....	....	....
1988-89	Portland	WHL	66	49	*87	136	70	19	15	19	34	17
1989-90b	Regina	WHL	66	60	53	113	67	11	7	10	17	17
1990-91c	Knoxville	ECHL	38	35	48	83	24	....	....	....	....	....
	Albany	IHL	1	0	0	0	2	....	....	....	....	....

a WHL West All-Star Team (1988)
b WHL East First All-Star Team (1990)
c ECHL Second All-Star Team (1991)

MIDDENDORF, MAX

Right wing. Shoots right. 6'4", 210 lbs. Born, Syracuse, NY, August 18, 1967.
(Quebec's 3rd choice, 57th overall, in 1985 Entry Draft).

			Regular Season					Playoffs				
Season	Club	Lea	GP	G	A	TP	PIM	GP	G	A	TP	PIM
1984-85	Sudbury	OHL	63	16	28	44	106	....	....	....	....	....
1985-86	Sudbury	OHL	61	40	42	82	71	4	4	2	6	11
1986-87	**Quebec**	**NHL**	**6**	**1**	**4**	**5**	**4**	....	....	....	....	....
	Sudbury	OHL	31	31	29	60	7	....	....	....	....	....
	Kitchener	OHL	17	7	15	22	6	4	2	5	7	5
1987-88	**Quebec**	**NHL**	**1**	**0**	**0**	**0**	**0**	....	....	....	....	....
	Fredericton	AHL	38	11	13	24	57	12	4	4	8	18
1988-89	Halifax	AHL	72	41	39	80	85	4	1	2	3	6
1989-90	**Quebec**	**NHL**	**3**	**0**	**0**	**0**	**0**	....	....	....	....	....
	Halifax	AHL	48	20	17	37	60	....	....	....	....	....
1990-91	**Edmonton**	**NHL**	**3**	**1**	**0**	**1**	**2**	....	....	....	....	....
	Fort Wayne	IHL	15	9	11	20	12	....	....	....	....	....
	Cape Breton	AHL	44	14	21	35	82	4	0	1	1	6
	NHL Totals		**13**	**2**	**4**	**6**	**6**	....	....	....	....	....

Traded to **Edmonton** by **Quebec** for Edmonton's ninth round choice (Brent Brekke) in 1991 Entry Draft, November 10, 1990.

MIEHM, KEVIN (MEE-yuhm)

Centre. Shoots left. 6'2", 197 lbs. Born, Kitchener, Ont., September 10, 1969.
(St. Louis' 2nd choice, 54th overall, in 1987 Entry Draft).

			Regular Season					Playoffs				
Season	Club	Lea	GP	G	A	TP	PIM	GP	G	A	TP	PIM
1986-87	Oshawa	OHL	61	12	27	39	19	26	1	8	9	12
1987-88	Oshawa	OHL	52	16	36	52	30	7	2	5	7	0
1988-89a	Oshawa	OHL	63	43	79	122	19	6	6	6	12	0
	Peoria	IHL	3	1	1	2	0	4	0	2	2	0
1989-90	Peoria	IHL	76	23	38	61	20	3	0	0	0	4
1990-91	Peoria	IHL	73	25	39	64	14	16	5	7	12	2

a OHL Third All-Star Team (1989)

MILLAR, MIKE (MILLER)

Right wing. Shoots left. 5'10", 170 lbs. Born, St. Catharines, Ont., April 28, 1965.
(Hartford's 2nd choice, 110th overall, in 1984 Entry Draft).

			Regular Season					Playoffs				
Season	Club	Lea	GP	G	A	TP	PIM	GP	G	A	TP	PIM
1982-83	Brantford	OHL	53	20	29	49	10	8	0	5	5	2
1983-84	Brantford	OHL	69	50	45	95	48	6	4	0	4	2
1984-85	Hamilton	OHL	63	*66	60	126	54	17	9	10	19	14
1985-86	Cdn. Olympic	...	69	50	38	88	74	....	....	....	....	....
1986-87	**Hartford**	**NHL**	**10**	**2**	**2**	**4**	**0**	....	....	....	....	....
	Binghamton	AHL	61	45	32	77	38	13	7	4	11	27
1987-88	**Hartford**	**NHL**	**28**	**7**	**7**	**14**	**6**	....	....	....	....	....
	Binghamton	AHL	31	32	17	49	42	....	....	....	....	....
1988-89	**Washington**	**NHL**	**18**	**6**	**3**	**9**	**4**	....	....	....	....	....
a	Baltimore	AHL	53	47	35	82	58	....	....	....	....	....
1989-90	**Boston**	**NHL**	**15**	**1**	**4**	**5**	**0**	....	....	....	....	....
	Maine	AHL	60	40	33	73	77	....	....	....	....	....
1990-91	**Toronto**	**NHL**	**7**	**2**	**2**	**4**	**2**	....	....	....	....	....
	Newmarket	AHL	62	33	29	62	63	....	....	....	....	....
	NHL Totals		**78**	**18**	**18**	**36**	**12**	....	....	....	....	....

a AHL Second All-Star Team (1989)

Traded to **Washington** by **Hartford** with Neil Sheehy for Grant Jennings and Ed Kastelic, July 6, 1988. Traded to **Boston** by **Washington** for Alfie Turcotte, October 2, 1989. Signed as a free agent by **Toronto**, July 19, 1990.

MILLEN, COREY

Center. Shoots right. 5'7", 168 lbs. Born, Cloquet, MN, April 29, 1964.
(NY Rangers' 3rd choice, 57th overall, in 1982 Entry Draft).

			Regular Season					Playoffs				
Season	Club	Lea	GP	G	A	TP	PIM	GP	G	A	TP	PIM
1982-83	U. Minnesota	WCHA	21	14	15	29	18	....	....	....	....	....
1983-84	U.S. Olympic	...	45	15	11	26	10	....	....	....	....	....
1984-85	U. Minnesota	WCHA	38	28	36	64	60	....	....	....	....	....
1985-86ab	U. Minnesota	WCHA	48	41	42	83	64	....	....	....	....	....
1986-87bc	U. Minnesota	WCHA	42	36	29	65	62	....	....	....	....	....
1987-88	U.S. National	...	47	41	43	84	26	....	....	....	....	....
	U.S. Olympic	...	6	6	5	11	4	....	....	....	....	....
1988-89	Ambri	Switz.	36	32	22	54	18	6	4	3	7	0
1989-90	**NY Rangers**	**NHL**	**4**	**0**	**0**	**0**	**2**	....	....	....	....	....
	Flint	IHL	11	4	5	9	2	....	....	....	....	....
1990-91	**NY Rangers**	**NHL**	**4**	**3**	**1**	**4**	**0**	**6**	**1**	**2**	**3**	**0**
	Binghamton	AHL	40	19	37	56	68	6	0	7	7	6
	NHL Totals		**8**	**3**	**1**	**4**	**2**	**6**	**1**	**2**	**3**	**0**

a NCAA West Second All-American Team (1986)
b WCHA Second All-Star Team (1986, 1987)
c Named to NCAA All-Tournament Team (1987)

MILLER, AARON

Defense. Shoots right. 6'3", 175 lbs. Born, Buffalo, NY, August 11, 1971.
(NY Rangers' 6th choice, 88th overall, in 1989 Entry Draft).

			Regular Season					Playoffs				
Season	Club	Lea	GP	G	A	TP	PIM	GP	G	A	TP	PIM
1989-90	U. of Vermont	ECAC	31	1	15	16	24	....	....	....	....	....
1990-91	U. of Vermont	ECAC	30	3	7	10	22	....	....	....	....	....

Traded to **Quebec** by **NY Rangers** with NY Ranger's fifth round choice (Bill Lindsay) in 1991 Entry Draft for Joe Cirella, January 17, 1991.

MILLER, BRAD

Defense. Shoots left. 6'4", 220 lbs. Born, Edmonton, Alta., July 23, 1969.
(Buffalo's 2nd choice, 22nd overall, in 1987 Entry Draft).

			Regular Season					Playoffs				
Season	Club	Lea	GP	G	A	TP	PIM	GP	G	A	TP	PIM
1985-86	Regina	WHL	71	2	14	16	99	10	1	1	2	4
1986-87	Regina	WHL	67	10	38	48	154	3	0	0	0	6
1987-88	Rochester	AHL	3	0	0	0	4	2	0	0	0	2
	Regina	WHL	61	9	34	43	148	4	1	1	2	12
1988-89	**Buffalo**	**NHL**	**7**	**0**	**0**	**0**	**6**	....	....	....	....	....
	Regina	WHL	34	8	18	26	95	....	....	....	....	....
	Rochester	AHL	3	0	0	0	4	....	....	....	....	....
1989-90	**Buffalo**	**NHL**	**1**	**0**	**0**	**0**	**0**	....	....	....	....	....
	Rochester	AHL	60	2	10	12	273	8	1	0	1	52
1990-91	**Buffalo**	**NHL**	**13**	**0**	**0**	**0**	**67**	....	....	....	....	....
	Rochester	AHL	49	0	9	9	248	12	0	4	4	67
	NHL Totals		**21**	**0**	**0**	**0**	**73**	....	....	....	....	....

MILLER, JASON

Center. Shoots left. 6'1", 190 lbs. Born, Edmonton, Alta., March 1, 1971.
(New Jersey's 2nd choice, 18th overall, in 1989 Entry Draft).

			Regular Season					Playoffs				
Season	Club	Lea	GP	G	A	TP	PIM	GP	G	A	TP	PIM
1987-88	Medicine Hat	WHL	71	11	18	29	28	15	0	1	1	2
1988-89	Medicine Hat	WHL	72	51	55	106	44	3	1	2	3	2
1989-90	Medicine Hat	WHL	66	43	56	99	40	3	3	2	5	0
1990-91	**New Jersey**	**NHL**	**1**	**0**	**0**	**0**	**0**	....	....	....	....	....
a	Medicine Hat	WHL	66	60	76	136	31	12	9	10	19	8
	NHL Totals		**1**	**0**	**0**	**0**	**0**	....	....	....	....	....

a WHL East Second All-Star Team (1991)

MILLER, JAY

Left wing. Shoots left. 6'2", 210 lbs. Born, Wellesley, MA, July 16, 1960.
(Quebec's 2nd choice, 66th overall, in 1980 Entry Draft).

			Regular Season					Playoffs				
Season	Club	Lea	GP	G	A	TP	PIM	GP	G	A	TP	PIM
1981-82	N. Hampshire	ECAC	24	6	4	10	34	....	....	....	....	....
1982-83	N. Hampshire	ECAC	28	6	4	10	28	....	....	....	....	....
1983-84	Toledo	IHL	2	0	0	0	2	....	....	....	....	....
	Maine	AHL	15	1	1	2	27	....	....	....	....	....
1984-85	Muskegon	IHL	56	5	29	34	177	17	1	1	2	56
1985-86	**Boston**	**NHL**	**46**	**3**	**0**	**3**	**178**	**2**	**0**	**0**	**0**	**17**
	Moncton	AHL	18	4	6	10	113	....	....	....	....	....
1986-87	**Boston**	**NHL**	**55**	**1**	**4**	**5**	**208**	....	....	....	....	....
1987-88	**Boston**	**NHL**	**78**	**7**	**12**	**19**	**304**	**12**	**0**	**0**	**0**	**124**
1988-89	**Boston**	**NHL**	**37**	**2**	**4**	**6**	**168**	....	....	....	....	....
	Los Angeles	**NHL**	**29**	**5**	**3**	**8**	**133**	**11**	**0**	**1**	**1**	**63**
1989-90	**Los Angeles**	**NHL**	**68**	**10**	**2**	**12**	**224**	**10**	**1**	**1**	**2**	**10**
1990-91	**Los Angeles**	**NHL**	**66**	**8**	**12**	**20**	**259**	**8**	**0**	**0**	**0**	**17**
	NHL Totals		**379**	**36**	**37**	**73**	**1474**	**43**	**1**	**2**	**3**	**231**

Signed as a free agent by **Boston**, October 1, 1985. Traded to **Los Angeles** by **Boston** for future considerations, January 22, 1989.

MILLER, KEITH

Left wing. Shoots left. 6'2", 215 lbs. Born, Toronto, Ont., March 18, 1967.
(Quebec's 10th choice, 165th overall, in 1986 Entry Draft).

			Regular Season					Playoffs				
Season	Club	Lea	GP	G	A	TP	PIM	GP	G	A	TP	PIM
1985-86	Guelph	OHL	61	32	17	49	30	20	8	16	24	6
1986-87	Guelph	OHL	66	50	31	81	44	5	6	2	8	0
1987-88	Baltimore	AHL	21	6	5	11	12	....	....	....	....	....
1988-89	Halifax	AHL	12	6	3	9	6	....	....	....	....	....
	Fort Wayne	IHL	54	35	25	60	13	10	4	3	7	9
1989-90	Fort Wayne	IHL	51	26	19	45	10	....	....	....	....	....
1990-91	Fort Wayne	IHL	8	1	2	3	2	....	....	....	....	....
	Indianapolis	IHL	30	3	2	5	2	....	....	....	....	....
	Kansas City	IHL	20	4	10	14	2	....	....	....	....	....
	Louisville	ECHL	9	8	3	11	2	....	....	....	....	....

MILLER, KELLY

Left wing. Shoots left. 5'11", 196 lbs. Born, Lansing, MI, March 3, 1963.
(NY Rangers' 9th choice, 183rd overall, in 1982 Entry Draft).

			Regular Season					Playoffs				
Season	Club	Lea	GP	G	A	TP	PIM	GP	G	A	TP	PIM
1981-82	Michigan State	CCHA	38	11	18	29	17	....	....	....	....	....
1982-83	Michigan State	CCHA	36	16	19	35	12	....	....	....	....	....
1983-84	Michigan State	CCHA	46	28	21	49	12	....	....	....	....	....
1984-85ab	Michigan State	CCHA	43	27	23	50	21	....	....	....	....	....
	NY Rangers	**NHL**	**5**	**0**	**2**	**2**	**2**	**3**	**0**	**0**	**0**	**2**
1985-86	**NY Rangers**	**NHL**	**74**	**13**	**20**	**33**	**52**	**16**	**3**	**4**	**7**	**4**
1986-87	**NY Rangers**	**NHL**	**38**	**6**	**14**	**20**	**22**	....	....	....	....	....
	Washington	**NHL**	**39**	**10**	**12**	**22**	**26**	**7**	**2**	**2**	**4**	**0**
1987-88	**Washington**	**NHL**	**80**	**9**	**23**	**32**	**35**	**14**	**4**	**4**	**8**	**10**
1988-89	**Washington**	**NHL**	**78**	**19**	**21**	**40**	**45**	**6**	**1**	**0**	**1**	**2**
1989-90	**Washington**	**NHL**	**80**	**18**	**22**	**40**	**49**	**15**	**3**	**5**	**8**	**23**
1990-91	**Washington**	**NHL**	**80**	**24**	**26**	**50**	**29**	**11**	**4**	**2**	**6**	**6**
	NHL Totals		**474**	**99**	**140**	**239**	**260**	**72**	**17**	**17**	**34**	**47**

a CCHA First All-Star Team (1985)
b Named to NCAA All-American Team (1985)

Traded to **Washington** by **NY Rangers** with Bob Crawford and Mike Ridley for Bob Carpenter and, Washington's second-round choice (Jason Prosofsky) in 1989 Entry Draft, January 1, 1987.

MILLER, KEVIN

Center. Shoots right. 5'10", 191 lbs.   Born, Lansing, MI, September 9, 1965.
(NY Rangers' 10th choice, 202nd overall, in 1984 Entry Draft).

			Regular Season					Playoffs				
Season	Club	Lea	GP	G	A	TP	PIM	GP	G	A	TP	PIM
1984-85	Michigan State	CCHA	44	11	29	40	84	....	....	....	....	....
1985-86	Michigan State	CCHA	45	19	52	71	112	....	....	....	....	....
1986-87	Michigan State	CCHA	42	25	56	81	63	....	....	....	....	....
1987-88	U.S. National	...	48	31	32	63	33	....	....	....	....	....
	U.S. Olympic	...	5	1	3	4	4	....	....	....	....	....
	Michigan State	CCHA	9	6	3	9	18	....	....	....	....	....
1988-89	NY Rangers	NHL	24	3	5	8	2	....	....	....	....	....
	Denver	IHL	55	29	47	76	19	4	2	1	3	2
1989-90	NY Rangers	NHL	16	0	5	5	2	1	0	0	0	0
	Flint	IHL	48	19	23	42	41	....	....	....	....	....
1990-91	NY Rangers	NHL	63	17	27	44	63	....	....	....	....	....
	Detroit	NHL	11	5	2	7	4	7	3	2	5	20
	NHL Totals		114	25	39	64	71	8	3	2	5	20

Traded to **Detroit** by **NY Rangers** with Jim Cummins and Dennis Vial for Joey Kocur and Per Djoos, March 5, 1991.

MILLER, KIP

Center. Shoots left. 5'10", 160 lbs.   Born, Lansing, MI, June 11, 1969.
(Quebec's 4th choice, 72nd overall, in 1987 Entry Draft).

			Regular Season					Playoffs				
Season	Club	Lea	GP	G	A	TP	PIM	GP	G	A	TP	PIM
1986-87	Michigan State	CCHA	41	20	19	39	92	....	....	....	....	....
1987-88	Michigan State	CCHA	39	16	25	41	51	....	....	....	....	....
1988-89ab	Michigan State	CCHA	47	32	45	77	94	....	....	....	....	....
1989-90abcd	Michigan State	CCHA	45	*48	53	*101	60	....	....	....	....	....
1990-91	Quebec	NHL	13	4	3	7	7	....	....	....	....	....
	Halifax	AHL	66	36	33	69	40	....	....	....	....	....
	NHL Totals		13	4	3	7	7					

a CCHA First All-Star Team (1989, 1990)
b NCAA West First All-American Team (1989, 1990)
c CCHA Player of the Year (1990)
d Won Hobey Baker Memorial Award (Top U.S. Collegiate Player) (1990)

MILLER, KRIS

Defense. Shoots left. 6', 200 lbs.   Born, Bemidji, MN, March 30, 1969.
(Montreal's 6th choice, 80th overall, in 1987 Entry Draft).

			Regular Season					Playoffs				
Season	Club	Lea	GP	G	A	TP	PIM	GP	G	A	TP	PIM
1987-88	Minn.-Duluth	WCHA	32	1	6	7	30	....	....	....	....	....
1988-89	Minn.-Duluth	WCHA	39	2	10	12	37	....	....	....	....	....
1989-90	Minn.-Duluth	WCHA	39	2	11	13	59	....	....	....	....	....
1990-91	Minn.-Duluth	WCHA	40	6	22	28	24	....	....	....	....	....

MILLER, KURTIS

Left wing. Shoots left. 5'11", 180 lbs.   Born, Bemidji, MN, June 1, 1970.
(St. Louis' 4th choice, 117th overall, in 1990 Entry Draft).

			Regular Season					Playoffs				
Season	Club	Lea	GP	G	A	TP	PIM	GP	G	A	TP	PIM
1989-90	Rochester	USHL	48	50	39	89	56	....	....	....	....	....
1990-91	Lake Superior	CCHA	45	10	12	22	48	....	....	....	....	....

MINER, JOHN

Defense. Shoots right. 5'10", 180 lbs.   Born, Moose Jaw, Sask., August 28, 1965.
(Edmonton's 10th choice, 229th overall, in 1983 Entry Draft).

			Regular Season					Playoffs				
Season	Club	Lea	GP	G	A	TP	PIM	GP	G	A	TP	PIM
1982-83	Regina	WHL	71	11	23	34	126	5	1	1	2	20
1983-84	Regina	WHL	70	27	42	69	132	23	9	25	34	54
1984-85	Regina	WHL	66	30	54	84	128	8	4	10	14	12
1985-86	Nova Scotia	AHL	79	10	33	43	90	....	....	....	....	....
1986-87	Nova Scotia	AHL	45	5	28	33	38	5	0	3	3	4
1987-88	Edmonton	NHL	14	2	3	5	16	....	....	....	....	....
	Nova Scotia	AHL	61	8	26	34	61	....	....	....	....	....
1988-89	New Haven	AHL	7	2	3	5	4	17	3	12	15	40
1989-90	Lausanne	Switz.	36	19	32	51	....	....	....	....	....	....
	New Haven	AHL	7	1	6	7	2	....	....	....	....	....
1990-91	Lausanne	Switz2	36	12	24	36	....	....	....	....	....	....
	NHL Totals		14	2	3	5	16	....	....	....	....	....

Traded to **Los Angeles** by **Edmonton** for Craig Redmond, August 10, 1988

MISKOLCZI, TED

Right wing. Shoots right. 6'3", 180 lbs.   Born, Port Colborne, Ont., August 5, 1970.
(Boston's 11th choice, 252nd overall, in 1990 Entry Draft).

			Regular Season					Playoffs				
Season	Club	Lea	GP	G	A	TP	PIM	GP	G	A	TP	PIM
1989-90	Belleville	OHL	68	34	27	61	89	11	4	4	8	26
1990-91	Belleville	OHL	14	6	11	17	19	....	....	....	....	....
	Owen Sound	OHL	53	44	35	79	70	....	....	....	....	....

MITCHELL, ROY

Defense. Shoots right. 6'1", 199 lbs.   Born, Edmonton, Alta., March 14, 1969.
(Montreal's 9th choice, 188th overall, in 1989 Entry Draft).

			Regular Season					Playoffs				
Season	Club	Lea	GP	G	A	TP	PIM	GP	G	A	TP	PIM
1986-87	Portland	WHL	68	7	32	39	103	20	0	3	3	23
1987-88	Portland	WHL	72	5	42	47	219	....	....	....	....	....
1988-89	Portland	WHL	72	9	34	43	177	19	1	8	9	38
1989-90	Sherbrooke	AHL	77	5	12	17	98	12	0	2	2	31
1990-91	Fredericton	AHL	71	2	15	17	137	9	0	1	1	11

MITROVIC, SAVO

Right wing. Shoots right. 5'11", 190 lbs.   Born, Toronto, Ont., February 4, 1969.
(Pittsburgh's 2nd choice, 10th overall, in 1990 Supplemental Draft).

			Regular Season					Playoffs				
Season	Club	Lea	GP	G	A	TP	PIM	GP	G	A	TP	PIM
1988-89	N. Hampshire	H.E.	34	2	8	10	22	....	....	....	....	....
1989-90	N. Hampshire	H.E.	37	30	21	51	40	....	....	....	....	....
1990-91	N. Hampshire	H.E.	35	13	18	31	55	....	....	....	....	....

MODANO, MICHAEL (MIKE)

Center. Shoots left. 6'3", 190 lbs.   Born, Livonia, MI, June 7, 1970.
(Minnesota's 1st choice, 1st overall, in 1988 Entry Draft).

			Regular Season					Playoffs				
Season	Club	Lea	GP	G	A	TP	PIM	GP	G	A	TP	PIM
1986-87	Prince Albert	WHL	70	32	30	62	96	8	1	4	5	4
1987-88	Prince Albert	WHL	65	47	80	127	80	9	7	11	18	18
1988-89a	Prince Albert	WHL	41	39	66	105	74	....	....	....	....	....
	Minnesota	NHL	....	....	....	....	....	2	0	0	0	0
1989-90b	Minnesota	NHL	80	29	46	75	63	7	1	1	2	12
1990-91	Minnesota	NHL	79	28	36	64	61	23	8	12	20	16
	NHL Totals		159	57	82	139	124	32	9	13	22	28

a WHL East All-Star Team (1989)
b NHL All-Rookie Team (1990)

MODRY, JAROSLAV   (MOHD-ree)

Defense. Shoots left. 6'2", 195 lbs.   Born, Ceske-Budejovice, Czechoslovakia, Feb. 27, 1971.
(New Jersey's 11th choice, 179th overall, in 1990 Entry Draft).

			Regular Season					Playoffs				
Season	Club	Lea	GP	G	A	TP	PIM	GP	G	A	TP	PIM
1988-89	Budejovice	Czech.	28	0	1	1	....	....	....	....	....	....
1989-90	Budejovice	Czech.	41	2	2	4	....	....	....	....	....	....
1990-91	Dukla Trencin	Czech.	33	1	9	10	6	....	....	....	....	....

MOES, MICHAEL   (MOOSE)

Center. Shoots left. 5'11", 185 lbs.   Born, Burlington, Ont., March 30, 1967.
(Toronto's 2nd choice, 6th overall, in 1989 Supplemental Draft).

			Regular Season					Playoffs				
Season	Club	Lea	GP	G	A	TP	PIM	GP	G	A	TP	PIM
1986-87	U. of Michigan	CCHA	39	11	15	26	16	....	....	....	....	....
1987-88	U. of Michigan	CCHA	40	5	27	32	23	....	....	....	....	....
1988-89	U. of Michigan	CCHA	41	14	24	38	22	....	....	....	....	....
1989-90	U. of Michigan	CCHA	42	19	29	48	10	....	....	....	....	....
	Newmarket	AHL	8	2	1	3	2	....	....	....	....	....
1990-91	Newmarket	AHL	63	7	22	29	6	....	....	....	....	....

MOGER, SANDY

Right wing. Shoots right. 6'2", 187 lbs.   Born, 100 Mile House, B.C., March 21, 1969.
(Vancouver's 7th choice, 176th overall, in 1989 Entry Draft).

			Regular Season					Playoffs				
Season	Club	Lea	GP	G	A	TP	PIM	GP	G	A	TP	PIM
1988-89	Lake Superior	CCHA	21	3	5	8	26	....	....	....	....	....
1989-90	Lake Superior	CCHA	46	17	15	32	76	....	....	....	....	....
1990-91	Lake Superior	CCHA	45	27	21	48	*172	....	....	....	....	....

MOGILNY, ALEXANDER   (moh-GIHL-nee)

Left wing. Shoots left. 5'11", 195 lbs.   Born, Khabarovsk, Soviet Union, February 18, 1969.
(Buffalo's 4th choice, 89th overall, in 1988 Entry Draft).

			Regular Season					Playoffs				
Season	Club	Lea	GP	G	A	TP	PIM	GP	G	A	TP	PIM
1986-87	CSKA	USSR	28	15	1	16	4	....	....	....	....	....
1987-88	CSKA	USSR	29	12	8	20	14	....	....	....	....	....
1988-89	CSKA	USSR	31	11	11	22	24	....	....	....	....	....
1989-90	Buffalo	NHL	65	15	28	43	16	4	0	1	1	2
1990-91	Buffalo	NHL	62	30	34	64	16	6	0	6	6	2
	NHL Totals		127	45	62	107	32	10	0	7	7	4

MOHNS, TROY

Defense. Shoots right. 6', 185 lbs.   Born, Pembroke, Ont., April 20, 1971.
(Los Angeles' 11th choice, 238th overall, in 1990 Entry Draft).

			Regular Season					Playoffs				
Season	Club	Lea	GP	G	A	TP	PIM	GP	G	A	TP	PIM
1989-90	Colgate	ECAC	34	2	11	13	36	....	....	....	....	....
1990-91	Colgate	ECAC	21	0	0	0	10	....	....	....	....	....

MOKOSAK, CARL (MOH-ka-sak)

Left wing. Shoots left. 6'1", 200 lbs. Born, Fort Saskatchewan, Alta., September 22, 1962.

			Regular Season					Playoffs				
Season	Club	Lea	GP	G	A	TP	PIM	GP	G	A	TP	PIM
1979-80	Brandon	WHL	61	12	21	33	226	11	0	4	4	66
1980-81	Brandon	WHL	70	28	44	72	363	5	1	3	4	12
1981-82	**Calgary**	**NHL**	**1**	**0**	**1**	**1**	**0**	....	....	....	....	....
	Brandon	WHL	69	46	61	107	363	4	0	1	1	11
	Oklahoma City	CHL	2	1	1	2	2	4	1	1	2	0
1982-83	**Calgary**	**NHL**	**41**	**7**	**6**	**13**	**87**	....	....	....	....	....
	Colorado	CHL	28	10	12	22	106	5	1	0	1	12
1983-84	New Haven	AHL	80	18	21	39	206	....	....	....	....	....
1984-85	**Los Angeles**	**NHL**	**30**	**4**	**8**	**12**	**43**	....	....	....	....	....
	New Haven	AHL	11	6	6	12	26	....	....	....	....	....
1985-86	**Philadelphia**	**NHL**	**1**	**0**	**0**	**0**	**5**	....	....	....	....	....
	Hershey	AHL	79	30	42	72	312	16	0	4	4	111
1986-87	**Pittsburgh**	**NHL**	**3**	**0**	**0**	**0**	**4**	....	....	....	....	....
	Baltimore	AHL	67	23	27	50	228	....	....	....	....	....
1987-88	Muskegon	IHL	81	29	37	66	308	6	3	2	5	60
1988-89	**Boston**	**NHL**	**7**	**0**	**0**	**0**	**31**	**1**	**0**	**0**	**0**	**0**
	Maine	AHL	53	20	18	38	337	....	....	....	....	....
1989-90	Fort Wayne	IHL	55	12	21	33	315	....	....	....	....	....
	Phoenix	IHL	15	6	6	12	48	....	....	....	....	....
1990-91	Indianapolis	IHL	70	12	26	38	205	5	0	0	0	2
	San Diego	IHL	5	0	0	0	30	....	....	....	....	....
	NHL Totals		**83**	**11**	**15**	**26**	**170**	**1**	**0**	**0**	**0**	**0**

Signed as free agent by **Calgary**, July 21, 1981. Traded to **Los Angeles** by **Calgary** with Kevin LaVallee for Steve Bozek, June 20, 1983. Signed as a free agent by **Philadelphia**, July 23, 1985. Signed as a free agent by **Pittsburgh**, July 23, 1986.

MOKOSAK, JOHN (MOH-ka-sak)

Defense. Shoots left. 5'11", 200 lbs. Born, Edmonton, Alta., September 7, 1963.
(Hartford's 6th choice, 130th overall, in 1981 Entry Draft).

			Regular Season					Playoffs				
Season	Club	Lea	GP	G	A	TP	PIM	GP	G	A	TP	PIM
1980-81	Victoria	WHL	71	2	18	20	59	15	0	3	3	53
1981-82	Victoria	WHL	69	6	45	51	102	4	1	1	2	0
1982-83	Victoria	WHL	70	10	33	43	102	12	0	0	0	8
1983-84	Binghamton	AHL	79	3	21	24	80	....	....	....	....	....
1984-85	Binghamton	AHL	54	1	13	14	109	7	0	0	0	12
	Salt Lake	IHL	22	1	10	11	41	....	....	....	....	....
1985-86	Binghamton	AHL	64	0	9	9	196	6	0	0	0	6
1986-87	Binghamton	AHL	72	2	15	17	187	9	0	2	2	42
1987-88	Springfield	AHL	77	1	16	17	178	....	....	....	....	....
1988-89	**Detroit**	**NHL**	**8**	**0**	**1**	**1**	**14**	....	....	....	....	....
	Adirondack	AHL	65	4	31	35	195	17	0	5	5	49
1989-90	**Detroit**	**NHL**	**33**	**0**	**1**	**1**	**82**	....	....	....	....	....
	Adirondack	AHL	29	2	6	8	80	6	1	3	4	13
1990-91	Maine	AHL	68	1	12	13	194	2	0	1	1	4
	NHL Totals		**41**	**0**	**2**	**2**	**96**	....	....	....	....	....

Signed as a free agent by **Detroit,** August 29, 1988. Signed as a free agent by **Boston,** July 16, 1990.

MOLLER, RANDY

Defense. Shoots right. 6'2", 207 lbs. Born, Red Deer, Alta., August 23, 1963.
(Quebec's 1st choice, 11th overall, in 1981 Entry Draft).

			Regular Season					Playoffs				
Season	Club	Lea	GP	G	A	TP	PIM	GP	G	A	TP	PIM
1980-81	Lethbridge	WHL	46	4	21	25	176	9	0	4	4	24
1981-82 a	Lethbridge	WHL	60	20	55	75	249	12	4	6	10	65
	Quebec	**NHL**	....	....	....	....	....	**1**	**0**	**0**	**0**	**0**
1982-83	**Quebec**	**NHL**	**75**	**2**	**12**	**14**	**145**	**4**	**1**	**0**	**1**	**4**
1983-84	**Quebec**	**NHL**	**74**	**4**	**14**	**18**	**147**	**9**	**1**	**0**	**1**	**45**
1984-85	**Quebec**	**NHL**	**79**	**7**	**22**	**29**	**120**	**18**	**2**	**2**	**4**	**40**
1985-86	**Quebec**	**NHL**	**69**	**5**	**18**	**23**	**141**	**3**	**0**	**0**	**0**	**26**
1986-87	**Quebec**	**NHL**	**71**	**5**	**9**	**14**	**144**	**13**	**1**	**4**	**5**	**23**
1987-88	**Quebec**	**NHL**	**66**	**3**	**22**	**25**	**169**	....	....	....	....	....
1988-89	**Quebec**	**NHL**	**74**	**7**	**22**	**29**	**136**	....	....	....	....	....
1989-90	**NY Rangers**	**NHL**	**60**	**1**	**12**	**13**	**139**	**10**	**1**	**6**	**7**	**32**
1990-91	**NY Rangers**	**NHL**	**61**	**4**	**19**	**23**	**161**	**6**	**0**	**2**	**2**	**11**
	NHL Totals		**629**	**38**	**150**	**188**	**1302**	**64**	**6**	**14**	**20**	**181**

a WHL Second All-Star Team (1982)

Traded to **NY Rangers** by **Quebec** for Michel Petit, October 5, 1989.

MOLLOY, MITCHELL DENNIS (MITCH)

Left wing. Shoots left. 6'3", 212 lbs. Born, Red Lake, Ont., October 10, 1966.

			Regular Season					Playoffs				
Season	Club	Lea	GP	G	A	TP	PIM	GP	G	A	TP	PIM
1987-88	Virginia	AAHL	43	26	45	71	196	8	5	4	9	63
1988-89	Maine	AHL	47	1	8	9	177	....	....	....	....	....
1989-90	**Buffalo**	**NHL**	**2**	**0**	**0**	**0**	**10**	....	....	....	....	....
	Rochester	AHL	15	1	1	2	43	....	....	....	....	....
	Johnstown	ECHL	18	10	10	20	102	....	....	....	....	....
1990-91	Rochester	AHL	25	1	0	1	127	....	....	....	....	....
	NHL Totals		**2**	**0**	**0**	**0**	**10**	....	....	....	....	....

Signed as a free agent by **Buffalo**, February, 1990.

MOMESSO, SERGIO (moh-MESS-oh)

Left wing. Shoots left. 6'3", 215 lbs. Born, Montreal, Que., September 4, 1965.
(Montreal's 3rd choice, 27th overall, in 1983 Entry Draft).

			Regular Season					Playoffs				
Season	Club	Lea	GP	G	A	TP	PIM	GP	G	A	TP	PIM
1982-83	Shawinigan	QMJHL	70	27	42	69	93	10	5	4	9	55
1983-84	**Montreal**	**NHL**	**1**	**0**	**0**	**0**	**0**	....	....	....	....	....
	Shawinigan	QMJHL	68	42	88	130	235	6	4	4	8	13
	Nova Scotia	AHL	....	....	....	....	....	8	0	2	2	4
1984-85a	Shawinigan	QMJHL	64	56	90	146	216	8	7	8	15	17
1985-86	**Montreal**	**NHL**	**24**	**8**	**7**	**15**	**46**	....	....	....	....	....
1986-87	**Montreal**	**NHL**	**59**	**14**	**17**	**31**	**96**	**11**	**1**	**3**	**4**	**31**
	Sherbrooke	AHL	6	1	6	7	10	....	....	....	....	....
1987-88	**Montreal**	**NHL**	**53**	**7**	**14**	**21**	**101**	**6**	**0**	**2**	**2**	**16**
1988-89	**St. Louis**	**NHL**	**53**	**9**	**17**	**26**	**139**	**10**	**2**	**5**	**7**	**24**
1989-90	**St. Louis**	**NHL**	**79**	**24**	**32**	**56**	**199**	**12**	**3**	**2**	**5**	**63**
1990-91	**St. Louis**	**NHL**	**59**	**10**	**18**	**28**	**131**	....	....	....	....	....
	Vancouver	**NHL**	**11**	**6**	**2**	**8**	**43**	**6**	**0**	**3**	**3**	**25**
	NHL Totals		**339**	**78**	**107**	**185**	**755**	**45**	**6**	**15**	**21**	**159**

a QMJHL First All-Star Team (1985)

Traded to **St. Louis** by **Montreal** with Vincent Riendeau for Jocelyn Lemieux, Darrell May and St. Louis' second round choice (Patrice Brisebois) in the 1989 Entry Draft, August 9, 1988. Traded to **Vancouver** by **St. Louis** with Geoff Courtnall, Robert Dirk, Cliff Ronning and future considerations for Dan Quinn and Garth Butcher, March 5, 1991.

MONGEAU, MICHEL

Center. Shoots left. 5'9", 190 lbs. Born, Nun's Island, Que., February 9, 1965.

			Regular Season					Playoffs				
Season	Club	Lea	GP	G	A	TP	PIM	GP	G	A	TP	PIM
1983-84	Laval	QMJHL	60	45	49	94	30	....	....	....	....	....
1984-85	Laval	QMJHL	67	60	84	144	56	....	....	....	....	....
1985-86	Laval	QMJHL	72	71	109	180	45	....	....	....	....	....
1986-87	Saginaw	IHL	76	42	53	95	34	10	3	6	9	6
1987-88	France	....	30	31	21	52	....	....	....	....	....	....
1988-89	Flint	IHL	82	41	76	117	57	....	....	....	....	....
1989-90	**St. Louis**	**NHL**	**7**	**1**	**5**	**6**	**2**	**2**	**0**	**1**	**1**	**0**
abc	Peoria	IHL	73	39	*78	*117	53	5	3	4	7	6
1990-91	**St. Louis**	**NHL**	**7**	**1**	**1**	**2**	**0**	....	....	....	....	....
de	Peoria	IHL	73	41	65	106	114	19	10	*16	26	32
	NHL Totals		**14**	**2**	**6**	**8**	**2**	**2**	**0**	**1**	**1**	**0**

a IHL First All-Star Team (1990)
b Won James Gatschene Memorial Trophy (MVP-IHL) (1990)
c Won Leo P. Lamoureux Memorial Trophy (Top Scorer-IHL) (1990)
d IHL Second All-Star Team (1991)
e Won N.R. Poile Trophy (MVP in Playoffs–IHL) (1991)

Signed as a free agent by **St. Louis,** August 21, 1989.

MONTANARI, MARK

Center. Shoots left. 5'9", 185 lbs. Born, Toronto, Ont., June 3, 1969.
(Boston's 5th choice, 101st overall, in 1989 Entry Draft).

			Regular Season					Playoffs				
Season	Club	Lea	GP	G	A	TP	PIM	GP	G	A	TP	PIM
1986-87	Kitchener	OHL	63	9	7	16	112	....	....	....	....	....
1987-88	Kitchener	OHL	63	25	31	56	146	4	1	1	2	10
1988-89	Kitchener	OHL	64	33	69	102	172	5	2	2	4	13
1989-90	Kitchener	OHL	33	15	36	51	71	16	9	16	25	54
	Maine	AHL	17	0	7	7	90	....	....	....	....	....
1990-91	Maine	AHL	8	0	1	1	17	....	....	....	....	....
	Johnstown	ECHL	1	0	1	1	2	....	....	....	....	....

MORE, JAYSON

Defense. Shoots right. 6'1", 190 lbs. Born, Souris, Man., January 12, 1969.
(NY Rangers' 1st choice, 10th overall, in 1987 Entry Draft).

			Regular Season					Playoffs				
Season	Club	Lea	GP	G	A	TP	PIM	GP	G	A	TP	PIM
1984-85	Lethbridge	WHL	71	3	9	12	101	4	1	0	1	7
1985-86	Lethbridge	WHL	61	7	18	25	155	9	0	2	2	36
1986-87	Brandon	WHL	21	4	6	10	62	....	....	....	....	....
	N. Westminster	WHL	43	4	23	27	155	....	....	....	....	....
1987-88a	N. Westminster	WHL	70	13	47	60	270	5	0	2	2	26
1988-89	**NY Rangers**	**NHL**	**1**	**0**	**0**	**0**	**0**	....	....	....	....	....
	Denver	IHL	62	7	15	22	138	3	0	1	1	26
1989-90	Flint	IHL	9	1	5	6	41	....	....	....	....	....
	Minnesota	**NHL**	**5**	**0**	**0**	**0**	**16**	....	....	....	....	....
	Kalamazoo	IHL	64	9	25	34	316	10	0	3	3	13
1990-91	Kalamazoo	IHL	10	0	5	5	46	....	....	....	....	....
	Fredericton	AHL	57	7	17	24	152	9	1	1	2	34
	NHL Totals		**6**	**0**	**0**	**0**	**16**	....	....	....	....	....

a WHL All-Star Team (1988)

Traded to **Minnesota** by **NY Rangers** for Dave Archibald, November 1, 1989. Traded to **Montreal** by **Minnesota** for Brian Hayward, November 7, 1990. Claimed by **San Jose** from **Montreal** in Expansion Draft, May 30, 1991.

MORIN, STEPHANE (mohr-AY)

Center. Shoots left. 6', 174 lbs. Born, Montreal, Que., March 27, 1969.
(Quebec's 3rd choice, 43rd overall, in 1989 Entry Draft).

			Regular Season					Playoffs				
Season	Club	Lea	GP	G	A	TP	PIM	GP	G	A	TP	PIM
1986-87	Shawinigan	QMJHL	65	9	14	23	28	....	....	....	....	....
1987-88	Chicoutimi	QMJHL	68	38	45	83	18	6	3	8	11	2
1988-89ab	Chicoutimi	QMJHL	70	77	*109	*186	71	....	....	....	....	....
1989-90	**Quebec**	**NHL**	**6**	**0**	**2**	**2**	**2**	....	....	....	....	....
	Halifax	AHL	65	28	32	60	60	6	3	4	7	6
1990-91	**Quebec**	**NHL**	**48**	**13**	**27**	**40**	**30**	....	....	....	....	....
	Halifax	AHL	17	8	14	22	18	....	....	....	....	....
	NHL Totals		**54**	**13**	**29**	**42**	**32**	....	....	....	....	....

a QMJHL First All-Star Team (1989)
b QMJHL Player of the Year (1989)

MORRIS, JON

Center. Shoots right. 6', 175 lbs. Born, Lowell, MA, May 6, 1966.
(New Jersey's 5th choice, 86th overall, in 1984 Entry Draft).

			Regular Season					Playoffs				
Season	Club	Lea	GP	G	A	TP	PIM	GP	G	A	TP	PIM
1984-85	Lowell	H.E.	42	29	31	60	16	....	....	....	....	....
1985-86	Lowell	H.E.	39	25	31	56	52	....	....	....	....	....
1986-87ab	Lowell	H.E.	35	28	33	61	48	....	....	....	....	....
1987-88	Lowell	H.E.	37	15	39	54	39	....	....	....	....	....
1988-89	**New Jersey**	**NHL**	**4**	**0**	**2**	**2**	**0**	....	....	....	....	....
1989-90	**New Jersey**	**NHL**	**20**	**6**	**7**	**13**	**8**	**6**	**1**	**3**	**4**	**23**
	Utica	AHL	49	27	37	64	6	....	....	....	....	....
1990-91	**New Jersey**	**NHL**	**53**	**9**	**19**	**28**	**27**	**5**	**0**	**4**	**4**	**2**
	Utica	AHL	6	4	2	6	5	....	....	....	....	....
	NHL Totals		**77**	**15**	**28**	**43**	**35**	**11**	**1**	**7**	**8**	**25**

a Hockey East First All-Star Team (1987)
b NCAA East Second All-American Team (1987)

MORRIS, KEITH

Center. Shoots left. 6'1", 185 lbs. Born, Winnipeg, Man., April 24, 1971.
(Winnipeg's 13th choice, 245th overall, in 1990 Entry Draft).

			Regular Season					Playoffs				
Season	Club	Lea	GP	G	A	TP	PIM	GP	G	A	TP	PIM
1989-90	Alaska-Anch.	NCAA	28	10	18	28	14	....	....	....	....	....
1990-91	Alaska-Anch.	NCAA	25	11	11	22	36	....	....	....	....	....

MORROW, SCOTT

Left wing. Shoots left. 6'1", 181 lbs. Born, Chicago, IL, June 18, 1969.
(Hartford's 4th choice, 95th overall, in 1988 Entry Draft).

			Regular Season					Playoffs				
Season	Club	Lea	GP	G	A	TP	PIM	GP	G	A	TP	PIM
1988-89	N. Hampshire	H.E.	19	6	7	13	14	....	....	....	....	....
1989-90	N. Hampshire	H.E.	29	10	11	21	35	....	....	....	....	....
1990-91	N. Hampshire	H.E.	31	11	11	22	52	....	....	....	....	....

MORROW, STEVEN

Defense. Shoots left. 6'2", 212 lbs. Born, Plano, TX, April 3, 1968.
(Philadelphia's 10th choice, 209th overall, in 1987 Entry Draft).

			Regular Season					Playoffs				
Season	Club	Lea	GP	G	A	TP	PIM	GP	G	A	TP	PIM
1988-89	N. Hampshire	H.E.	30	0	0	0	28	....	....	....	....	....
1989-90	N. Hampshire	H.E.	35	2	7	9	40	....	....	....	....	....
1990-91	N. Hampshire	H.E.	33	2	14	16	58	....	....	....	....	....

MORTON, DEAN

Defense. Shoots right. 6'1", 196 lbs. Born, Peterborough, Ont., February 27, 1968.
(Detroit's 8th choice, 148th overall, in 1986 Entry Draft).

			Regular Season					Playoffs				
Season	Club	Lea	GP	G	A	TP	PIM	GP	G	A	TP	PIM
1985-86	Oshawa	OHL	63	5	6	11	117	5	0	0	0	9
1986-87	Oshawa	OHL	62	1	11	12	165	23	3	6	9	112
1987-88	Oshawa	OHL	57	6	19	25	187	7	0	0	0	18
1988-89	Adirondack	AHL	66	2	15	17	186	8	0	1	1	13
1989-90	**Detroit**	**NHL**	**1**	**1**	**0**	**1**	**2**	....	....	....	....	....
	Adirondack	AHL	75	1	15	16	183	6	0	0	0	30
1990-91	Adirondack	AHL	1	0	0	0	0	....	....	....	....	....
	San Diego	IHL	47	0	6	6	124	....	....	....	....	....
	NHL Totals		**1**	**1**	**0**	**1**	**2**	....	....	....	....	....

MOYLAN, DAVE

Defense. Shoots left. 6'1", 195 lbs. Born, Tillsonburg, Ont., August 13, 1967.
(Buffalo's 4th choice, 77th overall, in 1985 Entry Draft).

			Regular Season					Playoffs				
Season	Club	Lea	GP	G	A	TP	PIM	GP	G	A	TP	PIM
1984-85	Sudbury	OHL	66	1	15	16	108	....	....	....	....	....
1985-86	Sudbury	OHL	52	10	25	35	87	4	0	0	0	15
1986-87	Sudbury	OHL	13	5	6	11	41	....	....	....	....	....
	Kitchener	OHL	38	1	7	8	57	3	2	0	2	11
1987-88	Baltimore	AHL	20	4	5	9	35	....	....	....	....	....
	Rochester	AHL	26	0	0	0	2	....	....	....	....	....
	Flint	IHL	9	0	2	2	10	....	....	....	....	....
1988-89	Rochester	AHL	20	0	2	2	15	....	....	....	....	....
	Jokerit	Fin.	15	4	4	8	38	5	0	0	0	2
1989-90	Jokerit	Fin.	42	3	8	11	107	....	....	....	....	....
1990-91	New Haven	AHL	8	0	2	2	23	....	....	....	....	....
	Phoenix	IHL	15	1	2	3	8	....	....	....	....	....
	Kalamazoo	IHL	15	1	3	4	8	11	0	0	0	7

MULLEN, BRIAN

Right wing. Shoots left. 5'10", 185 lbs. Born, New York, NY, March 16, 1962.
(Winnipeg's 7th choice, 128th overall, in 1980 Entry Draft).

			Regular Season					Playoffs				
Season	Club	Lea	GP	G	A	TP	PIM	GP	G	A	TP	PIM
1980-81	U. Wisconsin	WCHA	38	11	13	24	28	....	....	....	....	....
1981-82	U. Wisconsin	WCHA	33	20	17	37	10	....	....	....	....	....
1982-83	**Winnipeg**	**NHL**	**80**	**24**	**26**	**50**	**14**	**3**	**1**	**0**	**1**	**0**
1983-84	**Winnipeg**	**NHL**	**75**	**21**	**41**	**62**	**28**	**3**	**0**	**3**	**3**	**6**
1984-85	**Winnipeg**	**NHL**	**69**	**32**	**39**	**71**	**32**	**8**	**1**	**2**	**3**	**4**
1985-86	**Winnipeg**	**NHL**	**79**	**28**	**34**	**62**	**38**	**3**	**1**	**2**	**3**	**6**
1986-87	**Winnipeg**	**NHL**	**69**	**19**	**32**	**51**	**20**	**9**	**4**	**2**	**6**	**0**
1987-88	**NY Rangers**	**NHL**	**74**	**25**	**29**	**54**	**42**	....	....	....	....	....
1988-89	**NY Rangers**	**NHL**	**78**	**29**	**35**	**64**	**60**	**3**	**0**	**1**	**1**	**4**
1989-90	**NY Rangers**	**NHL**	**76**	**27**	**41**	**68**	**42**	**10**	**2**	**2**	**4**	**8**
1990-91	**NY Rangers**	**NHL**	**79**	**19**	**43**	**62**	**44**	**5**	**0**	**2**	**2**	**0**
	NHL Totals		**679**	**224**	**320**	**544**	**320**	**44**	**9**	**14**	**23**	**28**

Played in NHL All-Star Game (1989)

Traded to **NY Rangers** by **Winnipeg** with Winnipeg's tenth-round draft choice (Brett Barnett) in 1987 Entry Draft for NY Rangers' fifth-round choice in 1988 Entry Draft (Benoit Lebeau) – acquired earlier by NY Rangers – and NY Rangers' third round choice – later traded to St. Louis (Denny Felsner) – in 1989 Entry Draft, June 8, 1987. Traded to **San Jose** by **NY Rangers** with future considerations for Tim Kerr, May 30, 1991.

MULLEN, JOE

Right wing. Shoots right. 5'9", 180 lbs. Born, New York, NY, February 26, 1957.

			Regular Season					Playoffs				
Season	Club	Lea	GP	G	A	TP	PIM	GP	G	A	TP	PIM
1977-78a	Boston College	ECAC	34	34	34	68	12	....	....	....	....	....
1978-79a	Boston College	ECAC	25	32	24	56	8	....	....	....	....	....
1979-80bc	Salt Lake	CHL	75	40	32	72	21	13	*9	11	20	0
	St. Louis	**NHL**	....	....	....	....	....	**1**	**0**	**0**	**0**	**0**
1980-81de	Salt Lake	CHL	80	59	58	*117	8	17	11	9	20	0
1981-82	**St. Louis**	**NHL**	**45**	**25**	**34**	**59**	**4**	**10**	**7**	**11**	**18**	**4**
	Salt Lake	CHL	27	21	27	48	12	....	....	....	....	....
1982-83	**St. Louis**	**NHL**	**49**	**17**	**30**	**47**	**6**	....	....	....	....	....
1983-84	**St. Louis**	**NHL**	**80**	**41**	**44**	**85**	**19**	**6**	**2**	**0**	**2**	**0**
1984-85	**St. Louis**	**NHL**	**79**	**40**	**52**	**92**	**6**	**3**	**0**	**0**	**0**	**0**
1985-86	**St. Louis**	**NHL**	**48**	**28**	**24**	**52**	**10**	....	....	....	....	....
	Calgary	**NHL**	**29**	**16**	**22**	**38**	**11**	**21**	***12**	**7**	**19**	**4**
1986-87f	**Calgary**	**NHL**	**79**	**47**	**40**	**87**	**14**	**6**	**2**	**1**	**3**	**0**
1987-88	**Calgary**	**NHL**	**80**	**40**	**44**	**84**	**30**	**7**	**2**	**4**	**6**	**10**
1988-89fgh	**Calgary**	**NHL**	**79**	**51**	**59**	**110**	**16**	**21**	***16**	**8**	**24**	**4**
1989-90	**Calgary**	**NHL**	**78**	**36**	**33**	**69**	**24**	**6**	**3**	**0**	**3**	**0**
1990-91	**Pittsburgh**	**NHL**	**47**	**17**	**22**	**39**	**6**	**22**	**8**	**9**	**17**	**4**
	NHL Totals		**693**	**358**	**404**	**762**	**146**	**103**	**52**	**40**	**92**	**26**

a ECAC First All-Star Team (1978, 1979)
b CHL Second All-Star Team (1980)
c Won Ken McKenzie Trophy (CHL's Top Rookie) (1980)
d CHL First All-Star Team (1981)
e Won Tommy Ivan Trophy (CHL's Most Valuable Player) (1981)
f Won Lady Byng Trophy (1987, 1989)
g NHL First All-Star Team (1989)
h NHL Plus/Minus Leader (1989)

Played in NHL All-Star Game (1989, 1990)

Signed as a free agent by **St. Louis**, August 16, 1979. Traded to **Calgary** by **St. Louis** with Terry Johnson and Rik Wilson for Ed Beers, Charles Bourgeois and Gino Cavallini, February 1, 1986. Traded to **Pittsburgh** by **Calgary** for Pittsburgh's second round choice (Nicolas Perreault) in 1990 Entry Draft, June 16, 1990.

MULLER, KIRK

Left wing. Shoots left. 6', 205 lbs. Born, Kingston, Ont., February 8, 1966.
(New Jersey's 1st choice, 2nd overall, in 1984 Entry Draft).

			Regular Season					Playoffs				
Season	Club	Lea	GP	G	A	TP	PIM	GP	G	A	TP	PIM
1981-82	Kingston	OHL	67	12	39	51	27	4	5	1	6	4
1982-83ab	Guelph	OHL	66	52	60	112	41	....	....	....	....	....
1983-84b	Cdn. Olympic	...	21	4	3	7	6	....	....	....	....	....
	Guelph	OHL	49	31	63	94	27	....	....	....	....	....
1984-85	**New Jersey**	**NHL**	**80**	**17**	**37**	**54**	**69**	....	....	....	....	....
1985-86	**New Jersey**	**NHL**	**77**	**25**	**41**	**66**	**45**	....	....	....	....	....
1986-87	**New Jersey**	**NHL**	**79**	**26**	**50**	**76**	**75**	....	....	....	....	....
1987-88	**New Jersey**	**NHL**	**80**	**37**	**57**	**94**	**114**	**20**	**4**	**8**	**12**	**37**
1988-89	**New Jersey**	**NHL**	**80**	**31**	**43**	**74**	**119**	....	....	....	....	....
1989-90	**New Jersey**	**NHL**	**80**	**30**	**56**	**86**	**74**	**6**	**1**	**3**	**4**	**11**
1990-91	**New Jersey**	**NHL**	**80**	**19**	**51**	**70**	**76**	**7**	**0**	**2**	**2**	**10**
	NHL Totals		**556**	**185**	**335**	**520**	**572**	**33**	**5**	**13**	**18**	**58**

a OHL's Most Gentlemanly Player (1983)
b OHL Third All-Star Team (1983, 1984)

Played in NHL All-Star Game (1985, 1986, 1988, 1990)

MULLER, MIKE

Defense. Shoots left. 6'2", 205 lbs. Born, Fairview, MN, September 18, 1971.
(Winnipeg's 2nd choice, 35th overall, in 1990 Entry Draft).

			Regular Season					Playoffs				
Season	Club	Lea	GP	G	A	TP	PIM	GP	G	A	TP	PIM
1989-90	Wayzata	HS	23	11	15	26	....	....	....	....	....	....
1990-91	U. of Minnesota	WCHA	33	4	4	8	44	....	....	....	....	....

MULVENNA, GLENN

Center. Shoots left. 5'11", 187 lbs. Born, Calgary, Alta., February 18, 1967.

			Regular Season					Playoffs				
Season	Club	Lea	GP	G	A	TP	PIM	GP	G	A	TP	PIM
1986-87	N. Westminster	WHL	53	24	44	68	43	....	....	....	....	....
	Kamloops	WHL	18	13	8	21	18	13	4	6	10	10
1987-88	Kamloops	WHL	38	21	38	59	35	....	....	....	....	....
1988-89	Flint	IHL	32	9	14	23	12	....	....	....	....	....
	Muskegon	IHL	11	3	2	5	0	....	....	....	....	....
1989-90	Muskegon	IHL	52	14	21	35	17	11	2	3	5	0
	Fort Wayne	IHL	6	2	5	7	2	....	....	....	....	....
1990-91	Muskegon	IHL	48	9	27	36	25	5	1	1	2	0

Signed as a free agent by **Pittsburgh**, December 3, 1987.

MUNI, CRAIG DOUGLAS (MYEW-nee)

Defense. Shoots left. 6'3", 200 lbs. Born, Toronto, Ont., July 19, 1962.
(Toronto's 1st choice, 25th overall, in 1980 Entry Draft).

			Regular Season					Playoffs				
Season	Club	Lea	GP	G	A	TP	PIM	GP	G	A	TP	PIM
1980-81	Kingston	OHA	38	2	14	16	65	....	....	....	....	....
	Windsor	OHA	25	5	11	16	41	11	1	4	5	14
	New Brunswick	AHL	....	....	....	....	....	2	0	1	1	10
1981-82	Toronto	NHL	3	0	0	0	2	....	....	....	....	....
	Windsor	OHL	49	5	32	37	92	9	2	3	5	16
	Cincinnati	CHL	....	....	....	....	....	3	0	2	2	2
1982-83	Toronto	NHL	2	0	1	1	0	....	....	....	....	....
	St. Catharines	AHL	64	6	32	38	52	....	....	....	....	....
1983-84	St. Catharines	AHL	64	4	16	20	79	7	0	1	1	0
1984-85	Toronto	NHL	8	0	0	0	0	....	....	....	....	....
	St. Catharines	AHL	68	7	17	24	54	....	....	....	....	....
1985-86	Toronto	NHL	6	0	1	1	4	....	....	....	....	....
	St. Catharines	AHL	73	3	34	37	91	13	0	5	5	16
1986-87	Edmonton	NHL	79	7	22	29	85	14	0	2	2	17
1987-88	Edmonton	NHL	72	4	15	19	77	19	0	4	4	31
1988-89	Edmonton	NHL	69	5	13	18	71	7	0	3	3	8
1989-90	Edmonton	NHL	71	5	12	17	81	22	0	3	3	16
1990-91	Edmonton	NHL	76	1	9	10	77	18	0	3	3	20
	NHL Totals		386	22	73	95	397	80	0	15	15	92

Signed as a free agent by **Edmonton**, August 18, 1986. Sold to **Buffalo** by **Edmonton**, October 2, 1986. Traded to **Pittsburgh** by **Buffalo** for future considerations, October 3, 1986. Acquired by **Edmonton** from **Pittsburgh** to complete earlier trade for Gilles Meloche, October 6, 1986.

MURANO, ERIC

Center. Shoots right. 6', 190 lbs. Born, Montreal, Que., May 4, 1967.
(Vancouver's 4th choice, 91st overall, in 1986 Entry Draft).

			Regular Season					Playoffs				
Season	Club	Lea	GP	G	A	TP	PIM	GP	G	A	TP	PIM
1986-87	U. of Denver	WCHA	31	5	7	12	12	....	....	....	....	....
1987-88	U. of Denver	WCHA	37	8	13	21	26	....	....	....	....	....
1988-89	U. of Denver	WCHA	42	13	16	29	52	....	....	....	....	....
1989-90a	U. of Denver	WCHA	42	33	35	68	52	....	....	....	....	....
	Cdn. Olympic	...	6	1	0	1	4	....	....	....	....	....
1990-91	Milwaukee	IHL	63	32	35	67	63	3	0	1	1	4

a WCHA Second All-Star Team (1990)

MURPHY, DANIEL

Defense. Shoots left. 6'1", 185 lbs. Born, Needham, MA, May 13, 1970.
(Boston's 5th choice, 102nd overall, in 1988 Entry Draft).

			Regular Season					Playoffs				
Season	Club	Lea	GP	G	A	TP	PIM	GP	G	A	TP	PIM
1989-90	U. of Maine	H.E.	42	1	9	10	26	....	....	....	....	....
1990-91	U. of Maine	H.E.	42	1	5	6	26	....	....	....	....	....

MURPHY, GORDON (GORD)

Defense. Shoots right. 6'2", 195 lbs. Born, Willowdale, Ont., March 23, 1967.
(Philadelphia's 10th choice, 189th overall, in 1985 Entry Draft).

			Regular Season					Playoffs				
Season	Club	Lea	GP	G	A	TP	PIM	GP	G	A	TP	PIM
1984-85	Oshawa	OHL	59	3	12	15	25	....	....	....	....	....
1985-86	Oshawa	OHL	64	7	15	22	56	6	1	1	2	6
1986-87	Oshawa	OHL	56	7	30	37	95	24	6	16	22	22
1987-88	Hershey	AHL	62	8	20	28	44	12	0	8	8	12
1988-89	Philadelphia	NHL	75	4	31	35	68	19	2	7	9	13
1989-90	Philadelphia	NHL	75	14	27	41	95	....	....	....	....	....
1990-91	Philadelphia	NHL	80	11	31	42	58	....	....	....	....	....
	NHL Totals		230	29	89	118	221	19	2	7	9	13

MURPHY, JOE

Right wing. Shoots left. 6'1", 190 lbs. Born, London, Ont., October 16, 1967.
(Detroit's 1st choice, 1st overall, in 1986 Entry Draft).

			Regular Season					Playoffs				
Season	Club	Lea	GP	G	A	TP	PIM	GP	G	A	TP	PIM
1985-86	Cdn. Olympic	...	8	3	3	6	2	....	....	....	....	....
a	Michigan State	CCHA	35	24	37	61	50	....	....	....	....	....
1986-87	Detroit	NHL	5	0	1	1	2	....	....	....	....	....
	Adirondack	AHL	71	21	38	59	61	10	2	1	3	33
1987-88	Detroit	NHL	50	10	9	19	37	8	0	1	1	6
	Adirondack	AHL	6	5	6	11	4	....	....	....	....	....
1988-89	Detroit	NHL	26	1	7	8	28	....	....	....	....	....
	Adirondack	AHL	47	31	35	66	66	16	6	11	17	17
1989-90	Detroit	NHL	9	3	1	4	4	....	....	....	....	....
	Edmonton	NHL	62	7	18	25	56	22	6	8	14	16
1990-91	Edmonton	NHL	80	27	35	62	35	15	2	5	7	14
	NHL Totals		232	48	71	119	162	45	8	14	22	36

a CCHA Rookie of the Year (1986)

Traded to **Edmonton** by **Detroit** with Petr Klima, Adam Graves and Jeff Sharples for Jimmy Carson, Kevin McClelland and Edmonton's fifth round choice (later traded to Montreal for Rick Green. Montreal selected Brad Layzell) in 1991 Entry Draft, November 2, 1989.

MURPHY, LAWRENCE THOMAS (LARRY)

Defense. Shoots right. 6'2", 210 lbs. Born, Scarborough, Ont., March 8, 1961.
(Los Angeles' 1st choice, 4th overall, in 1980 Entry Draft).

			Regular Season					Playoffs				
Season	Club	Lea	GP	G	A	TP	PIM	GP	G	A	TP	PIM
1978-79	Peterborough	OHA	66	6	21	27	82	19	1	9	10	42
1979-80a	Peterborough	OHA	68	21	68	89	88	14	4	13	17	20
1980-81	Los Angeles	NHL	80	16	60	76	79	4	3	0	3	2
1981-82	Los Angeles	NHL	79	22	44	66	95	10	2	8	10	12
1982-83	Los Angeles	NHL	77	14	48	62	81	....	....	....	....	....
1983-84	Los Angeles	NHL	6	0	3	3	0	....	....	....	....	....
	Washington	NHL	72	13	33	46	50	8	0	3	3	6
1984-85	Washington	NHL	79	13	42	55	51	5	2	3	5	0
1985-86	Washington	NHL	78	21	44	65	50	9	1	5	6	6
1986-87b	Washington	NHL	80	23	58	81	39	7	2	2	4	6
1987-88	Washington	NHL	79	8	53	61	72	13	4	4	8	33
1988-89	Washington	NHL	65	7	29	36	70	....	....	....	....	....
	Minnesota	NHL	13	4	6	10	12	5	0	2	2	8
1989-90	Minnesota	NHL	77	10	58	68	44	7	1	2	3	31
1990-91	Minnesota	NHL	31	4	11	15	38	....	....	....	....	....
	Pittsburgh	NHL	44	5	23	28	30	23	5	18	23	44
	NHL Totals		860	160	512	672	711	91	20	47	67	148

a OHA First All-Star Team (1980)
b NHL Second All-Star Team (1987)

Traded to **Washington** by **Los Angeles** for Ken Houston and Brian Engblom, October 18, 1983. Traded to **Minnesota** by **Washington** with Mike Gartner for Dino Ciccarelli and Bob Rouse, March 7, 1989. Traded to **Pittsburgh** by **Minnesota** with Peter Taglianetti for Chris Dahlquist and Jim Johnson, December 11, 1990.

MURPHY, ROB

Left wing/Center. Shoots left. 6'3", 205 lbs. Born, Hull, Que., April 7, 1969.
(Vancouver's 1st choice, 24th overall, in 1987 Entry Draft).

			Regular Season					Playoffs				
Season	Club	Lea	GP	G	A	TP	PIM	GP	G	A	TP	PIM
1986-87	Laval	QMJHL	70	35	54	89	86	14	3	4	7	15
1987-88	Vancouver	NHL	5	0	0	0	2	....	....	....	....	....
	Laval	QMJHL	26	11	25	36	82	....	....	....	....	....
	Drummondville	QMJHL	33	16	28	44	41	17	4	15	19	45
1988-89	Vancouver	NHL	8	0	1	1	2	....	....	....	....	....
	Milwaukee	IHL	8	4	2	6	4	11	3	5	8	34
	Drummondville	QMJHL	26	13	25	38	16	4	1	3	4	20
1989-90	Vancouver	NHL	12	1	1	2	0	....	....	....	....	....
a	Milwaukee	IHL	64	24	47	71	87	6	2	6	8	12
1990-91	Vancouver	NHL	42	5	1	6	90	4	0	0	0	2
	Milwaukee	IHL	23	1	7	8	48	....	....	....	....	....
	NHL Totals		67	6	3	9	94	4	0	0	0	2

a Won Garry F. Longman Memorial Trophy (Top Rookie-IHL) (1990)

MURRAY, GLEN

Right wing. Shoots right. 6'2", 200 lbs. Born, Halifax, N.S., November 1, 1972.
(Boston's 1st choice, 18th overall, in 1991 Entry Draft).

			Regular Season					Playoffs				
Season	Club	Lea	GP	G	A	TP	PIM	GP	G	A	TP	PIM
1989-90	Sudbury	OHL	62	8	28	36	17	7	0	0	0	4
1990-91	Sudbury	OHL	66	27	38	65	82	5	8	4	12	10

MURRAY, MICHAEL

Right wing. Shoots right. 6'1", 185 lbs. Born, Cumberland, RI, April 18, 1971.
(Calgary's 10th choice, 188th overall, in 1990 Entry Draft).

			Regular Season					Playoffs				
Season	Club	Lea	GP	G	A	TP	PIM	GP	G	A	TP	PIM
1989-90	Cushing Aca.	HS	....	18	23	41	....	....	....	....	....	....
1990-91	Lowell	H.E.	30	5	8	13	18	....	....	....	....	....

MURRAY, PAT

Left wing. Shoots left. 6'2", 185 lbs. Born, Stratford, Ont., August 20, 1969.
(Philadelphia's 2nd choice, 35th overall, in 1988 Entry Draft).

			Regular Season					Playoffs				
Season	Club	Lea	GP	G	A	TP	PIM	GP	G	A	TP	PIM
1987-88	Michigan State	CCHA	42	14	21	35	26	....	....	....	....	....
1988-89	Michigan State	CCHA	46	21	41	62	65	....	....	....	....	....
1989-90a	Michigan State	CCHA	45	24	60	84	36	....	....	....	....	....
1990-91	Philadelphia	NHL	16	2	1	3	15	....	....	....	....	....
	Hershey	AHL	57	15	38	53	8	7	5	2	7	0
	NHL Totals		16	2	1	3	15	....	....	....	....	....

a CCHA Second All-Star Team (1990)

MURRAY, ROB

Center. Shoots right. 6', 185 lbs. Born, Toronto, Ont., April 4, 1967.
(Washington's 3rd choice, 61st overall, in 1985 Entry Draft).

			Regular Season					Playoffs				
Season	Club	Lea	GP	G	A	TP	PIM	GP	G	A	TP	PIM
1984-85	Peterborough	OHL	63	12	9	21	155	17	2	7	9	45
1985-86	Peterborough	OHL	52	14	18	32	125	16	1	2	3	50
1986-87	Peterborough	OHL	62	17	37	54	204	3	1	4	5	8
1987-88	Fort Wayne	IHL	80	12	21	33	139	6	0	2	2	16
1988-89	Baltimore	AHL	80	11	23	34	235	....	....	....	....	....
1989-90	Washington	NHL	41	2	7	9	58	9	0	0	0	18
	Baltimore	AHL	23	5	4	9	63	....	....	....	....	....
1990-91	Washington	NHL	17	0	3	3	19	....	....	....	....	....
	Baltimore	AHL	48	6	20	26	177	4	0	0	0	12
	NHL Totals		58	2	10	12	77	9	0	0	0	18

Claimed by **Minnesota** from **Washington** in Expansion Draft, May 30, 1991. Traded to **Winnipeg** by **Minnesota** with future considerations for Winnipeg's seventh round choice (Geoff Finch) in 1991 Entry Draft and future considerations, May 31, 1991.

MURRAY, TROY NORMAN

Center. Shoots right. 6'1", 195 lbs.   Born, Calgary, Alta., July 31, 1962.
(Chicago's 6th choice, 57th overall, in 1980 Entry Draft).

Season	Club	Lea	GP	G	A	TP	PIM	GP	G	A	TP	PIM
1980-81ab	North Dakota	WCHA	38	33	45	78	28					
1981-82b	North Dakota	WCHA	26	13	17	30	62					
	Chicago	NHL	1	0	0	0	0	7	1	0	1	5
1982-83	Chicago	NHL	54	8	8	16	27	2	0	0	0	0
1983-84	Chicago	NHL	61	15	15	30	45	5	1	0	1	7
1984-85	Chicago	NHL	80	26	40	66	82	15	5	14	19	24
1985-86c	Chicago	NHL	80	45	54	99	94	2	0	0	0	2
1986-87	Chicago	NHL	77	28	43	71	59	4	0	0	0	5
1987-88	Chicago	NHL	79	22	36	58	96	5	1	0	1	8
1988-89	Chicago	NHL	79	21	30	51	113	16	3	6	9	25
1989-90	Chicago	NHL	68	17	38	55	86	20	4	4	8	2
1990-91	Chicago	NHL	75	14	23	37	74	6	0	1	1	12
	NHL Totals		654	196	287	483	676	82	15	25	40	90

a WCHA Rookie of the Year (1981)
b WCHA Second All-Star Team (1981, 1982)
c Won Frank J. Selke Memorial Trophy (1986).
Traded to **Winnipeg** by **Chicago** with Warren Rychel for Bryan Marchment and Chris Norton, July 22, 1991.

MURZYN, DANA (MUR-zihn)

Defense. Shoots left. 6'2", 200 lbs.   Born, Calgary, Alta., December 9, 1966.
(Hartford's 1st choice, 5th overall, in 1985 Entry Draft).

Season	Club	Lea	GP	G	A	TP	PIM	GP	G	A	TP	PIM
1983-84	Calgary	WHL	65	11	20	31	135	2	0	0	0	10
1984-85a	Calgary	WHL	72	32	60	92	233	8	1	11	12	16
1985-86b	Hartford	NHL	78	3	23	26	125	4	0	0	0	10
1986-87	Hartford	NHL	74	9	19	28	95	6	2	1	3	29
1987-88	Hartford	NHL	33	1	6	7	45					
	Calgary	NHL	41	6	5	11	94	5	2	0	2	13
1988-89	Calgary	NHL	63	3	19	22	142	21	0	3	3	20
1989-90	Calgary	NHL	78	7	13	20	140	6	2	2	4	2
1990-91	Calgary	NHL	19	0	2	2	30					
	Vancouver	NHL	10	1	0	1	8	6	0	1	1	8
	NHL Totals		396	30	87	117	679	48	6	7	13	82

a WHL First All-Star Team, East Division (1985).
b NHL All-Rookie Team (1986)
Traded to **Calgary** by **Hartford** with Shane Churla for Neil Sheehy, Carey Wilson and the rights to Lane MacDonald, January 3, 1988. Traded to **Vancouver** by **Calgary** for Ron Stern, Kevan Guy and future considerations, March 5, 1991.

MUSIL, FRANTISEK (moo-SIHL)

Defense. Shoots left. 6'3", 205 lbs.   Born, Pardubice, Czech., December 17, 1964.
(Minnesota's 3rd choice, 38th overall, in 1983 Entry Draft).

Season	Club	Lea	GP	G	A	TP	PIM	GP	G	A	TP	PIM
1985-86	Dukla Jihlava	Czech.	35	3	7	10	42					
1986-87	Minnesota	NHL	72	2	9	11	148					
1987-88	Minnesota	NHL	80	9	8	17	213					
1988-89	Minnesota	NHL	55	1	19	20	54	5	1	1	2	4
1989-90	Minnesota	NHL	56	2	8	10	109	4	0	0	0	14
1990-91	Minnesota	NHL	8	0	2	2	23					
	Calgary	NHL	67	7	14	21	160	7	0	0	0	10
	NHL Totals		338	21	60	81	707	16	1	1	2	28

Traded to **Calgary** by **Minnesota** for Brian Glynn, October 26, 1990.

NANNE, MARTY

Right wing. Shoots right. 6', 180 lbs.   Born, Edina, MN, July 21, 1967.
(Chicago's 7th choice, 161st overall, in 1986 Entry Draft).

Season	Club	Lea	GP	G	A	TP	PIM	GP	G	A	TP	PIM
1985-86	U. Minnesota	WCHA	19	5	5	10	29					
1986-87	U. Minnesota	WCHA	31	3	4	7	41					
1987-88	U. Minnesota	WCHA	17	1	3	4	16					
1988-89	Saginaw	IHL	36	4	10	14	47					
1989-90	Indianapolis	IHL	50	3	3	6	36					
1990-91	Indianapolis	IHL	23	3	9	12	28	6	0	0	0	8

NAPIER, ROBERT MARK (NAY-pyeer) (MARK)

Right wing. Shoots left. 5'10", 183 lbs.   Born, Toronto, Ont., January 28, 1957.
(Montreal's 1st choice, 10th overall, in 1977 Amateur Draft).

Season	Club	Lea	GP	G	A	TP	PIM	GP	G	A	TP	PIM
1973-74	Toronto	OHA	70	47	46	93	63					
1974-75a	Toronto	OHA	61	66	64	130	106	23	*24	24	*48	13
1975-76b	Toronto	WHA	78	43	50	93	20					
1976-77	Birmingham	WHA	80	60	36	96	24					
1977-78	Birmingham	WHA	79	33	32	65	9	5	0	2	2	14
1978-79	Montreal	NHL	54	11	20	31	11	12	3	2	5	2
1979-80	Montreal	NHL	76	16	33	49	7	10	2	6	8	0
1980-81	Montreal	NHL	79	35	36	71	24	3	0	0	0	2
1981-82	Montreal	NHL	80	40	41	81	14	5	3	2	5	0
1982-83	Montreal	NHL	73	40	27	67	6	3	0	0	0	0
1983-84	Montreal	NHL	5	3	2	5	0					
	Minnesota	NHL	58	13	28	41	17	12	3	2	5	0
1984-85	Minnesota	NHL	39	10	18	28	2					
	Edmonton	NHL	33	9	26	35	19	18	5	5	10	7
1985-86	Edmonton	NHL	80	24	32	56	14	10	1	4	5	0
1986-87	Edmonton	NHL	62	8	13	21	2					
	Buffalo	NHL	15	5	5	10	0					
1987-88	Buffalo	NHL	47	10	8	18	8	6	0	3	3	0
1988-89	Buffalo	NHL	66	11	17	28	33	3	1	0	1	0
1989-90	Bolzano	Italy	36	68	72	140	6	6	8	6	14	2
1990-91	Varese	Italy	36	45	73	118	4	10	8	18	26	0
	NHL Totals		767	235	306	541	157	82	18	24	42	11

a OHA First All-Star Team (1975)
b Named WHA Rookie of the Year (1976)
Traded to **Minnesota** by **Montreal** with Keith Acton and Toronto's third round choice (Ken Hodge) — Montreal's property via earlier deal — for Bobby Smith, October 28, 1983. Traded to **Edmonton** by **Minnesota** for Gord Sherven and Terry Martin, January 24, 1985. Traded to **Buffalo** by **Edmonton** with Lee Fogolin for Normand Lacombe, Wayne Van Dorp and future considerations, March 6, 1987.

NAPIERALA, JEFF

Right wing. Shoots right. 6'1", 195 lbs.   Born, Muskegon, MI, February 27, 1968.
(Vancouver's 1st choice, 3rd overall, in 1989 Supplemental Draft).

Season	Club	Lea	GP	G	A	TP	PIM	GP	G	A	TP	PIM
1987-88	Lake Superior	CCHA	7	0	0	0	0					
1988-89	Lake Superior	CCHA	43	17	9	26	22					
1989-90	Lake Superior	CCHA	44	33	26	59	32					
1990-91	Lake Superior	CCHA	45	30	27	57	70					

NASLUND, MARKUS

Right wing. Shoots left. 5'11", 174 lbs.   Born, Harnosand, Sweden, July 30, 1973.
(Pittsburgh's 1st choice, 16th overall, in 1991 Entry Draft).

Season	Club	Lea	GP	G	A	TP	PIM	GP	G	A	TP	PIM
1989-90	MoDo	Swe.Jr.	33	43	35	78	20					
1990-91	MoDo	Swe.	32	10	9	19	14					

NASLUND, MATS (NAZZ-luhnd)

Left wing. Shoots left. 5'7", 160 lbs.   Born, Timra, Sweden, October 31, 1959.
(Montreal's 2nd choice, 37th overall, in 1979 Entry Draft).

Season	Club	Lea	GP	G	A	TP	PIM	GP	G	A	TP	PIM
1977-78	Timra	Swe.	35	13	6	19	14					
1978-79	Brynas	Swe.	36	12	12	24	19					
	Swe. National		13	8	3	11	12					
1979-80	Brynas	Swe.	36	18	19	37	34	7	2	2	4	4
	Swe. Olympic	...	7	3	7	10	6					
	Swe. National		21	3	11	14	10					
1980-81	Brynas	Swe.	36	17	*25	*42	34					
	Swe. National		25	4	6	10	20					
1981-82	Brynas	Swe.	36	24	18	42	16					
	Swe. National		24	6	9	15	40					
1982-83a	Montreal	NHL	74	26	45	71	10	3	1	0	1	0
1983-84	Montreal	NHL	77	29	35	64	4	15	6	8	14	4
1984-85	Montreal	NHL	80	42	37	79	14	12	7	4	11	6
1985-86b	Montreal	NHL	80	43	67	110	16	20	8	11	19	4
1986-87	Montreal	NHL	79	25	55	80	16	17	7	15	22	7
1987-88c	Montreal	NHL	78	24	59	83	14	6	0	7	7	2
1988-89	Montreal	NHL	77	33	51	84	14	21	4	11	15	6
1989-90	Montreal	NHL	72	21	20	41	19	3	1	1	2	0
1990-91	Lugano	Switz.	36	24	33	69		11	4	9	13	
	NHL Totals		617	243	369	612	107	97	34	57	91	33

a Named to NHL All-Rookie Team (1983)
b NHL Second All-Star Team (1986)
c Won Lady Byng Memorial Trophy (1988)
Played in NHL All-Star Game (1984, 1986, 1988)

NATTRESS, ERIC (RIC)

Defense. Shoots right. 6'2", 210 lbs.   Born, Hamilton, Ont., May 25, 1962.
(Montreal's 2nd choice, 27th overall, in 1980 Entry Draft).

			Regular Season					Playoffs				
Season	Club	Lea	GP	G	A	TP	PIM	GP	G	A	TP	PIM
1979-80	Brantford	OHA	65	3	21	24	94	11	1	6	7	38
1980-81	Brantford	OHA	51	8	34	42	106	6	1	4	5	19
1981-82	Brantford	OHL	59	11	50	61	126	11	3	7	10	17
	Nova Scotia	AHL	....	....	....	....	....	5	0	1	1	7
1982-83	**Montreal**	**NHL**	40	1	3	4	19	3	0	0	0	10
	Nova Scotia	AHL	9	0	4	4	16	....	....	....	....	....
1983-84	**Montreal**	**NHL**	34	0	12	12	15	....	....	....	....	....
1984-85	**Montreal**	**NHL**	5	0	1	1	2	2	0	0	0	2
	Sherbrooke	AHL	72	8	40	48	37	16	4	13	17	20
1985-86	**St. Louis**	**NHL**	78	4	20	24	52	18	1	4	5	24
1986-87	**St. Louis**	**NHL**	73	6	22	28	24	6	0	0	0	2
1987-88	**Calgary**	**NHL**	63	2	13	15	37	6	1	3	4	0
1988-89	**Calgary**	**NHL**	38	1	8	9	47	19	0	3	3	20
1989-90	**Calgary**	**NHL**	49	1	14	15	26	6	2	0	2	0
1990-91	**Calgary**	**NHL**	58	5	13	18	63	7	1	0	1	2
	NHL Totals		438	20	106	126	285	67	5	10	15	60

Rights sold to **St. Louis** by **Montreal**, October 7, 1985. Traded to **Calgary** by **St. Louis** for Calgary's fourth-round choice (Andy Rymsha) in 1987 Entry Draft and fifth-round choice (Dave Lacouture) in 1988 Entry Draft, June 13, 1987.

NAUSS, DARREN

Right wing. Shoots right. 5'11", 180 lbs.   Born, Vancouver, B.C., March 19, 1967.
(Quebec's 11th choice, 198th overall, in 1987 Entry Draft).

			Regular Season					Playoffs				
Season	Club	Lea	GP	G	A	TP	PIM	GP	G	A	TP	PIM
1987-88	Minn.-Duluth	WCHA	41	8	13	21	24	....	....	....	....	....
1988-89	Minn.-Duluth	WCHA	40	10	4	14	40	....	....	....	....	....
1989-90	Minn.-Duluth	WCHA	37	21	17	38	24	....	....	....	....	....
1990-91	Minn.-Duluth	WCHA	39	7	13	20	43	....	....	....	....	....
	Halifax	AHL	4	0	0	0	0	....	....	....	....	....

NEATON, PAT

Defense. Shoots left. 6', 180 lbs.   Born, Redford, MI, May 21, 1971.
(Pittsburgh's 9th choice, 145th overall, in 1990 Entry Draft).

			Regular Season					Playoffs				
Season	Club	Lea	GP	G	A	TP	PIM	GP	G	A	TP	PIM
1989-90	U. of Michigan	CCHA	42	3	23	26	36	....	....	....	....	....
1990-91a	U. of Michigan	CCHA	44	15	28	43	78	....	....	....	....	....

a CCHA Second All-Star Team (1991)

NEDVED, PETR

Center. Shoots left. 6'3", 178 lbs.   Born, Liberec, Czechoslovakia, December 9, 1971.
(Vancouver's 1st choice, 2nd overall, in 1990 Entry Draft).

			Regular Season					Playoffs				
Season	Club	Lea	GP	G	A	TP	PIM	GP	G	A	TP	PIM
1988-89	CHZ Litvinov	Czech.	20	32	19	51	12	....	....	....	....	....
1989-90a	Seattle	WHL	71	65	80	145	80	11	4	9	13	2
1990-91	**Vancouver**	**NHL**	61	10	6	16	20	6	0	1	1	0
	NHL Totals		61	10	6	16	20	6	0	1	1	0

a WHL and CHL Rookie of the Year

NEEDHAM, MICHAEL

Right wing. Shoots right. 5'10", 185 lbs.   Born, Calgary, Alta., April 4, 1970.
(Pittsburgh's 7th choice, 126th overall, in 1989 Entry Draft).

			Regular Season					Playoffs				
Season	Club	Lea	GP	G	A	TP	PIM	GP	G	A	TP	PIM
1986-87	Kamloops	WHL	3	1	2	3	0	11	2	1	3	5
1987-88	Kamloops	WHL	64	31	33	64	93	5	0	1	1	5
1988-89	Kamloops	WHL	49	24	27	51	55	16	2	9	11	13
1989-90a	Kamloops	WHL	60	59	66	125	75	17	11	13	24	10
1990-91	Muskegon	IHL	65	14	31	45	17	5	2	2	4	5

a WHL West First All-Star Team (1990)

NEELY, CAM

Right wing. Shoots right. 6'1", 210 lbs.   Born, Comox, B.C., June 6, 1965.
(Vancouver's 1st choice, 9th overall, in 1983 Entry Draft).

			Regular Season					Playoffs				
Season	Club	Lea	GP	G	A	TP	PIM	GP	G	A	TP	PIM
1982-83	Portland	WHL	72	56	64	120	130	14	9	11	20	17
1983-84	**Vancouver**	**NHL**	56	16	15	31	57	4	2	0	2	2
	Portland	WHL	19	8	18	26	29	....	....	....	....	....
1984-85	**Vancouver**	**NHL**	72	21	18	39	137	....	....	....	....	....
1985-86	**Vancouver**	**NHL**	73	14	20	34	126	3	0	0	0	6
1986-87	**Boston**	**NHL**	75	36	36	72	143	4	5	1	6	8
1987-88a	**Boston**	**NHL**	69	42	27	69	175	23	9	8	17	51
1988-89	**Boston**	**NHL**	74	37	38	75	190	10	7	2	9	8
1989-90a	**Boston**	**NHL**	76	55	37	92	117	21	12	16	28	51
1990-91a	**Boston**	**NHL**	69	51	40	91	98	19	16	4	20	36
	NHL Totals		564	272	231	503	1043	84	51	31	82	162

a NHL Second All-Star Team (1988, 1990, 1991)
Played in NHL All-Star Game (1988-91)

Traded to **Boston** by **Vancouver** with Vancouver's first-round choice in 1987 Entry Draft (Glen Wesley) for Barry Pederson, June 6, 1986.

NELSON, CHRISTOPHER

Defense. Shoots right. 6'2", 190 lbs.   Born, Philadelphia, PA, February 12, 1969.
(New Jersey's 6th choice, 96th overall, in 1988 Entry Draft).

			Regular Season					Playoffs				
Season	Club	Lea	GP	G	A	TP	PIM	GP	G	A	TP	PIM
1988-89	U. Wisconsin	WCHA	21	1	4	5	24	....	....	....	....	....
1989-90	U. Wisconsin	WCHA	34	1	3	4	38	....	....	....	....	....
1990-91	U. Wisconsin	WCHA	42	5	12	17	48	....	....	....	....	....

NELSON, JEFF

Center. Shoots left. 5'11", 182 lbs.   Born, Prince Albert, Sask., December 18, 1972.
(Washington's 4th choice, 36th overall, in 1991 Entry Draft).

			Regular Season					Playoffs				
Season	Club	Lea	GP	G	A	TP	PIM	GP	G	A	TP	PIM
1989-90	Prince Albert	WHL	72	28	69	97	79	14	2	11	13	10
1990-91a	Prince Albert	WHL	72	46	74	120	58	3	1	1	2	4

a WHL East Second All-Star Team (1991)

NELSON, TODD

Defense. Shoots left. 6', 201 lbs.   Born, Prince Albert, Sask., May 15, 1969.
(Pittsburgh's 4th choice, 79th overall, in 1989 Entry Draft).

			Regular Season					Playoffs				
Season	Club	Lea	GP	G	A	TP	PIM	GP	G	A	TP	PIM
1985-86	Prince Albert	WHL	4	0	0	0	0	....	....	....	....	....
1986-87	Prince Albert	WHL	35	1	6	7	10	4	0	0	0	0
1987-88	Prince Albert	WHL	72	3	21	24	59	10	3	2	5	4
1988-89a	Prince Albert	WHL	72	14	45	59	72	4	1	3	4	4
1989-90a	Prince Albert	WHL	69	13	42	55	88	14	3	12	15	12
1990-91	Muskegon	IHL	79	4	20	24	32	3	0	0	0	4

a WHL East Second All-Star Team (1989, 1990)

NEMCHINOV, SERGEI

Center. Shoots left. 6', 183 lbs.   Born, Moscow, USSR, January 14, 1964.
(NY Rangers' 14th choice, 244th overall, in 1990 Entry Draft).

			Regular Season					Playoffs				
Season	Club	Lea	GP	G	A	TP	PIM	GP	G	A	TP	PIM
1981-82	Soviet Wings	USSR	15	1	0	1	0	....	....	....	....	....
1982-83	CSKA	USSR	11	0	0	0	2	....	....	....	....	....
1983-84	CSKA	USSR	20	6	5	11	4	....	....	....	....	....
1984-85	CSKA	USSR	31	2	4	6	4	....	....	....	....	....
1985-86	Soviet Wings	USSR	39	7	12	19	28	....	....	....	....	....
1986-87	Soviet Wings	USSR	40	13	9	22	24	....	....	....	....	....
1987-88	Soviet Wings	USSR	48	17	11	28	26	....	....	....	....	....
1988-89	Soviet Wings	USSR	43	15	14	29	28	....	....	....	....	....
1989-90	Soviet Wings	USSR	48	17	16	33	34	....	....	....	....	....
1990-91	Soviet Wings	USSR	46	21	24	45	30	....	....	....	....	....

NESICH, JIM

Center. Shoots right. 5'11", 183 lbs.   Born, Dearborn, MI, February 22, 1966.
(Montreal's 8th choice, 116th overall, in 1984 Entry Draft).

			Regular Season					Playoffs				
Season	Club	Lea	GP	G	A	TP	PIM	GP	G	A	TP	PIM
1983-84	Verdun	QMJHL	70	22	24	46	35	10	11	5	16	2
1984-85	Verdun	QMJHL	65	19	33	52	72	14	1	6	7	25
1985-86	Verdun	QMJHL	71	26	55	81	114	5	0	0	0	8
	Sherbrooke	AHL	4	0	1	1	0	....	....	....	....	....
1986-87	Verdun	QMJHL	62	20	50	70	133	....	....	....	....	....
1987-88	Sherbrooke	AHL	53	4	10	14	51	4	1	2	3	20
1988-89	Sherbrooke	AHL	74	12	34	46	112	6	1	2	3	10
1989-90	Sherbrooke	AHL	62	21	31	52	79	12	2	*13	15	18
1990-91	Fredericton	AHL	72	13	30	43	79	9	0	4	4	36

Traded to **Minnesota** by **Montreal** for future considerations, August 9, 1991.

NEUMEIER, TROY

Defense. Shoots left. 6'2", 187 lbs.   Born, Langenburg, Sask., September 3, 1970.
(Vancouver's 9th choice, 191st overall, in 1990 Entry Draft).

			Regular Season					Playoffs				
Season	Club	Lea	GP	G	A	TP	PIM	GP	G	A	TP	PIM
1989-90	Prince Albert	WHL	72	8	26	34	73	14	3	5	8	12
1990-91a	Prince Albert	WHL	72	6	27	33	56	3	0	0	0	0

a WHL East First All-Star Team (1991)

NEURURER, PHILLIP

Defense. Shoots left. 6'2", 194 lbs.   Born, Robbinsdale, MA, March 21, 1970.
(NY Islanders' 13th choice, 226th overall, in 1988 Entry Draft).

			Regular Season					Playoffs				
Season	Club	Lea	GP	G	A	TP	PIM	GP	G	A	TP	PIM
1988-89	N. Michigan	WCHA	23	0	1	1	12	....	....	....	....	....
1989-90	N. Michigan	WCHA	27	1	5	6	28	....	....	....	....	....
1990-91	N. Michigan	WCHA	11	1	2	3	6	....	....	....	....	....

NEVERS, TOM

Center. Shoots right. 6'1", 175 lbs.   Born, Edina, MN, September 13, 1971.
(Pittsburgh's 5th choice, 100th overall, in 1989 Entry Draft).

			Regular Season					Playoffs				
Season	Club	Lea	GP	G	A	TP	PIM	GP	G	A	TP	PIM
1989-90	Edina	HS	23	21	25	46	....	....	....	....	....	....
1990-91			DID NOT PLAY									

NEZIOL, THOMAS (TOM)

Left wing. Shoots left. 6'1", 190 lbs.   Born, Burlington, Ont., August 7, 1967.
(New Jersey's 6th choice, 128th overall, in 1987 Entry Draft).

			Regular Season					Playoffs				
Season	Club	Lea	GP	G	A	TP	PIM	GP	G	A	TP	PIM
1986-87	Miami-Ohio	CCHA	39	11	18	29	80	....	....	....	....	....
1987-88	Miami-Ohio	CCHA	34	13	13	26	52	....	....	....	....	....
1988-89	Miami-Ohio	CCHA	12	5	4	9	14	....	....	....	....	....
1989-90	Miami-Ohio	CCHA	31	11	4	15	14	....	....	....	....	....
1990-91	Fort Wayne	IHL	1	0	0	0	0	....	....	....	....	....
	Cincinnati	ECHL	58	37	25	62	61	4	1	2	3	7

NICHOLLS, BERNIE IRVINE (NICK-els)

Center. Shoots right. 6', 185 lbs. Born, Haliburton, Ont., June 24, 1961.
(Los Angeles' 6th choice, 73rd overall, in 1980 Entry Draft).

			Regular Season					Playoffs				
Season	Club	Lea	GP	G	A	TP	PIM	GP	G	A	TP	PIM
1979-80	Kingston	OHA	68	36	43	79	85	3	1	0	1	10
1980-81	Kingston	OHA	65	63	89	152	109	14	8	10	18	17
1981-82	**Los Angeles**	**NHL**	**22**	**14**	**18**	**32**	**27**	**10**	**4**	**0**	**4**	**23**
	New Haven	AHL	55	41	30	71	31	....	....	....	....	....
1982-83	**Los Angeles**	**NHL**	**71**	**28**	**22**	**50**	**124**	....	....	....	....	....
1983-84	**Los Angeles**	**NHL**	**78**	**41**	**54**	**95**	**83**	....	....	....	....	....
1984-85	**Los Angeles**	**NHL**	**80**	**46**	**54**	**100**	**76**	**3**	**1**	**1**	**2**	**9**
1985-86	**Los Angeles**	**NHL**	**80**	**36**	**61**	**97**	**78**	....	....	....	....	....
1986-87	**Los Angeles**	**NHL**	**80**	**33**	**48**	**81**	**101**	**5**	**2**	**5**	**7**	**6**
1987-88	**Los Angeles**	**NHL**	**65**	**32**	**46**	**78**	**114**	**5**	**2**	**6**	**8**	**11**
1988-89a	**Los Angeles**	**NHL**	**79**	**70**	**80**	**150**	**96**	**11**	**7**	**9**	**16**	**12**
1989-90	**Los Angeles**	**NHL**	**47**	**27**	**48**	**75**	**66**	....	....	....	....	....
	NY Rangers	**NHL**	**32**	**12**	**25**	**37**	**20**	**10**	**7**	**5**	**12**	**16**
1990-91	**NY Rangers**	**NHL**	**71**	**25**	**48**	**73**	**96**	**5**	**4**	**3**	**7**	**8**
	NHL Totals		**705**	**364**	**504**	**868**	**881**	**49**	**27**	**29**	**56**	**85**

a NHL Second All-Star Team (1989)

Played in NHL All-Star Game (1984, 1989, 1990)

Traded to **NY Rangers** by **Los Angeles** for Tomas Sandstrom and Tony Granato, January 20, 1990.

NIEDERMAYER, SCOTT

Defense. Shoots left. 6', 195 lbs. Born, Edmonton, Alta., August 31, 1973.
(New Jersey's 1st choice, 3rd overall, in 1991 Entry Draft).

			Regular Season					Playoffs				
Season	Club	Lea	GP	G	A	TP	PIM	GP	G	A	TP	PIM
1989-90	Kamloops	WHL	64	14	55	69	64	17	2	14	16	35
1990-91ab	Kamloops	WHL	57	26	56	82	52	....	....	....	....	....

a WHL West First All-Star Team (1991)
b Canadian Major Junior Scholastic Player of the Year (1991)

NIELSON, JEFF

Right wing. Shoots right. 6', 170 lbs. Born, Grand Rapids, MN, September 20, 1971.
(NY Rangers' 4th choice, 69th overall, in 1990 Entry Draft).

			Regular Season					Playoffs				
Season	Club	Lea	GP	G	A	TP	PIM	GP	G	A	TP	PIM
1989-90	Grand Rapids	HS	28	32	25	57	....	....	....	....	....	....
1990-91	U. Minnesota	WCHA	45	11	14	25	50	....	....	....	....	....

NIEMAN, THOMAS

Right wing. Shoots right. 6', 183 lbs. Born, Winnetka, IL, January 22, 1970.
(Buffalo's 11th choice, 223rd overall, in 1988 Entry Draft).

			Regular Season					Playoffs				
Season	Club	Lea	GP	G	A	TP	PIM	GP	G	A	TP	PIM
1988-89	Dartmouth	ECAC	26	7	11	18	38	....	....	....	....	....
1989-90	Dartmouth	ECAC	26	6	3	9	16	....	....	....	....	....
1990-91	Dartmouth	ECAC	25	2	5	7	27	....	....	....	....	....

NIEUWENDYK, JOE (NOO-ihn-DIGHK)

Center. Shoots left. 6'1", 195 lbs. Born, Oshawa, Ont., September 10, 1966.
(Calgary's 2nd choice, 27th overall, in 1985 Entry Draft).

			Regular Season					Playoffs				
Season	Club	Lea	GP	G	A	TP	PIM	GP	G	A	TP	PIM
1984-85a	Cornell	ECAC	23	18	21	39	20	....	....	....	....	....
1985-86bc	Cornell	ECAC	21	21	21	42	45	....	....	....	....	....
1986-87bcd	Cornell	ECAC	23	26	26	52	26	....	....	....	....	....
	Calgary	**NHL**	**9**	**5**	**1**	**6**	**0**	**6**	**2**	**2**	**4**	**0**
1987-88efg	**Calgary**	**NHL**	**75**	**51**	**41**	**92**	**23**	**8**	**3**	**4**	**7**	**2**
1988-89	**Calgary**	**NHL**	**77**	**51**	**31**	**82**	**40**	**22**	**10**	**4**	**14**	**10**
1989-90	**Calgary**	**NHL**	**79**	**45**	**50**	**95**	**40**	**6**	**4**	**6**	**10**	**4**
1990-91	**Calgary**	**NHL**	**79**	**45**	**40**	**85**	**36**	**7**	**4**	**1**	**5**	**10**
	NHL Totals		**319**	**197**	**163**	**360**	**139**	**49**	**23**	**17**	**40**	**26**

a ECAC Rookie of the Year (1985).
b NCAA East First All-American Team (1986, 1987)
c ECAC First All-Star Team (1986, 1987)
d ECAC Player of the Year (1987)
e Won Calder Memorial Trophy (1988)
f NHL All-Rookie Team (1988)
g Won Dodge Ram Tough Award (1988)

Played in NHL All-Star Game (1988-90)

NIKOLIC, ALEX

Left wing. Shoots left. 6'1", 200 lbs. Born, Sudbury, Ont., March 1, 1970.
(Calgary's 8th choice, 147th overall, in 1989 Entry Draft).

			Regular Season					Playoffs				
Season	Club	Lea	GP	G	A	TP	PIM	GP	G	A	TP	PIM
1988-89	Cornell	ECAC	13	0	3	3	31	....	....	....	....	....
1989-90	Cornell	ECAC	28	6	9	15	54	....	....	....	....	....
1990-91	Cornell	ECAC	15	4	3	7	16	....	....	....	....	....

NILAN, CHRISTOPHER JOHN (CHRIS) (NIGH-luhn)

Right wing. Shoots right. 6', 205 lbs. Born, Boston, MA, February 9, 1958.
(Montreal's 21st choice, 231st overall, in 1978 Amateur Draft).

			Regular Season					Playoffs				
Season	Club	Lea	GP	G	A	TP	PIM	GP	G	A	TP	PIM
1978-79	Northeastern	ECAC	32	9	17	26	....	....	....	....	....	....
1979-80	**Montreal**	**NHL**	**15**	**0**	**2**	**2**	**50**	**5**	**0**	**0**	**0**	**2**
	Nova Scotia	AHL	49	15	10	25	*304	....	....	....	....	....
1980-81	**Montreal**	**NHL**	**57**	**7**	**8**	**15**	**262**	**2**	**0**	**0**	**0**	**0**
1981-82	**Montreal**	**NHL**	**49**	**7**	**4**	**11**	**204**	**5**	**1**	**1**	**2**	**22**
1982-83	**Montreal**	**NHL**	**66**	**6**	**8**	**14**	**213**	**3**	**0**	**0**	**0**	**5**
1983-84	**Montreal**	**NHL**	**76**	**16**	**10**	**26**	***338**	**15**	**1**	**0**	**1**	***81**
1984-85	**Montreal**	**NHL**	**77**	**21**	**16**	**37**	***358**	**12**	**2**	**1**	**3**	**81**
1985-86	**Montreal**	**NHL**	**72**	**19**	**15**	**34**	**274**	**18**	**1**	**2**	**3**	***141**
1986-87	**Montreal**	**NHL**	**44**	**4**	**16**	**20**	**266**	**17**	**3**	**0**	**3**	**75**
1987-88	**Montreal**	**NHL**	**50**	**7**	**5**	**12**	**209**	....	....	....	....	....
	NY Rangers	**NHL**	**22**	**3**	**5**	**8**	**96**	....	....	....	....	....
1988-89	**NY Rangers**	**NHL**	**38**	**7**	**7**	**14**	**177**	**4**	**0**	**1**	**1**	**38**
1989-90	**NY Rangers**	**NHL**	**25**	**1**	**2**	**3**	**59**	**4**	**0**	**1**	**1**	**19**
1990-91	**Boston**	**NHL**	**41**	**6**	**9**	**15**	**277**	**19**	**0**	**2**	**2**	**62**
	NHL Totals		**632**	**104**	**107**	**211**	**2783**	**104**	**8**	**8**	**16**	**526**

Traded to **NY Rangers** by **Montreal** for a switch of first round choices in 1989 Entry Draft, January 27, 1988. Traded to **Boston** by **NY Rangers** for Greg Johnston and future considerations, June 28, 1990.

NILL, JAMES EDWARD (JIM)

Right wing. Shoots right. 6', 185 lbs. Born, Hanna, Alta., April 11, 1958.
(St. Louis' 4th choice, 89th overall, in 1978 Amateur Draft).

			Regular Season					Playoffs				
Season	Club	Lea	GP	G	A	TP	PIM	GP	G	A	TP	PIM
1975-76	Medicine Hat	WHL	62	5	11	16	69	9	1	1	2	20
1976-77	Medicine Hat	WHL	71	23	24	47	140	4	2	2	4	4
1977-78	Medicine Hat	WHL	72	47	46	93	252	12	8	7	15	37
1978-79	U. of Calgary	CWUAA	20	9	8	17	42	....	....	....	....	....
1979-80	Cdn. National	...	45	13	19	32	54	....	....	....	....	....
	Cdn. Olympic	...	6	1	2	3	4	....	....	....	....	....
1980-81	Salt Lake	CHL	79	28	34	62	222	16	9	8	17	38
1981-82	**St. Louis**	**NHL**	**61**	**9**	**12**	**21**	**127**	....	....	....	....	....
	Vancouver	**NHL**	**8**	**1**	**2**	**3**	**5**	**16**	**4**	**3**	**7**	**67**
1982-83	**Vancouver**	**NHL**	**65**	**7**	**15**	**22**	**136**	**4**	**0**	**0**	**0**	**6**
1983-84	**Vancouver**	**NHL**	**51**	**9**	**6**	**15**	**78**	....	....	....	....	....
	Boston	**NHL**	**27**	**3**	**2**	**5**	**81**	**3**	**0**	**0**	**0**	**4**
1984-85	**Boston**	**NHL**	**49**	**1**	**9**	**10**	**62**	....	....	....	....	....
	Winnipeg	**NHL**	**20**	**8**	**8**	**16**	**38**	**8**	**0**	**1**	**1**	**28**
1985-86	**Winnipeg**	**NHL**	**61**	**6**	**8**	**14**	**75**	**3**	**0**	**0**	**0**	**4**
1986-87	**Winnipeg**	**NHL**	**36**	**3**	**4**	**7**	**52**	**3**	**0**	**0**	**0**	**7**
1987-88	**Winnipeg**	**NHL**	**24**	**0**	**1**	**1**	**44**	....	....	....	....	....
	Moncton	AHL	3	0	0	0	6	....	....	....	....	....
	Detroit	**NHL**	**36**	**3**	**11**	**14**	**55**	**16**	**6**	**1**	**7**	**62**
1988-89	**Detroit**	**NHL**	**71**	**8**	**7**	**15**	**83**	**6**	**0**	**0**	**0**	**25**
1989-90	**Detroit**	**NHL**	**15**	**0**	**2**	**2**	**18**	....	....	....	....	....
	Adirondack	AHL	20	10	8	18	24	....	....	....	....	....
1990-91	Adirondack	AHL	32	3	10	13	74	2	0	0	0	2
	NHL Totals		**524**	**58**	**87**	**145**	**854**	**59**	**10**	**5**	**15**	**203**

Traded to **Vancouver** by **St. Louis** with Tony Currie, Rick Heinz and St. Louis' fourth round choice (Shawn Kilroy) in 1982 Entry Draft for Glen Hanlon, March 9, 1982. Traded to **Boston** by **Vancouver** for Peter McNab, February 3, 1984. Traded to **Winnipeg** by **Boston** for Morris Lukowich, February 14, 1985. Traded to **Detroit** by **Winnipeg** for Mark Kumpel, January 11, 1988.

NILSSON, FREDRIK NEEL-suhn)

Center. Shoots left. 6'1", 180 lbs. Born, Vasteras, Sweden, April 16, 1971.
(San Jose's 7th choice, 111th overall, in 1991 Entry Draft).

			Regular Season					Playoffs				
Season	Club	Lea	GP	G	A	TP	PIM	GP	G	A	TP	PIM
1989-90	Vasteras	Swe.	23	1	1	2	4	1	0	0	0	0
1990-91	Vasteras	Swe.	35	13	7	20	20	....	....	....	....	....

NILSSON, STEFAN

Center. Shoots right. 5'11", 185 lbs. Born, Lulea, Sweden, April 5, 1968.
(Washington's 7th choice, 124th overall, in 1986 Entry Draft).

			Regular Season					Playoffs				
Season	Club	Lea	GP	G	A	TP	PIM	GP	G	A	TP	PIM
1985-86	Lulea	Swe.	4	0	0	0	0	....	....	....	....	....
1986-87	Lulea	Swe.	23	3	9	12	14	....	....	....	....	....
1987-88	Lulea	Swe.	31	10	10	20	24	....	....	....	....	....
1988-89	Lulea	Swe.	40	9	22	31	24	....	....	....	....	....
1989-90	Lulea	Swe.	38	11	26	37	32	5	0	0	0	4
1990-91	Lulea	Swe.	38	7	39	46	64	....	....	....	....	....

NOLAN, OWEN

Right wing. Shoots right. 6'1", 194 lbs. Born, Belfast, Northern Ireland, February 12, 1972
(Quebec's 1st choice, 1st overall, in 1990 Entry Draft).

			Regular Season					Playoffs				
Season	Club	Lea	GP	G	A	TP	PIM	GP	G	A	TP	PIM
1988-89a	Cornwall	OHL	62	34	25	59	213	18	5	11	16	41
1989-90b	Cornwall	OHL	58	51	59	110	240	6	7	5	12	26
1990-91	**Quebec**	**NHL**	**59**	**3**	**10**	**13**	**109**	....	....	....	....	....
	Halifax	AHL	6	4	4	8	11	....	....	....	....	....
	NHL Totals		**59**	**3**	**10**	**13**	**109**	....	....	....	....	....

a OHL Rookie of the Year (1989)
b OHL First All-Star Team (1990)

NOONAN, BRIAN

Right wing. Shoots right. 6'1", 192 lbs. Born, Boston, MA, May 29, 1965.
(Chicago's 10th choice, 179th overall, in 1983 Entry Draft).

			Regular Season					Playoffs				
Season	Club	Lea	GP	G	A	TP	PIM	GP	G	A	TP	PIM
1984-85	N. Westminster	WHL	72	50	66	116	76	11	8	7	15	4
1985-86	Nova Scotia	AHL	2	0	0	0	0	....	....	....	....	....
	Saginaw	IHL	76	39	39	78	69	11	6	3	9	6
1986-87	Nova Scotia	AHL	70	25	26	51	30	5	3	1	4	4
1987-88	**Chicago**	**NHL**	**77**	**10**	**20**	**30**	**44**	**3**	**0**	**0**	**0**	**4**
1988-89	**Chicago**	**NHL**	**45**	**4**	**12**	**16**	**28**	**1**	**0**	**0**	**0**	**0**
	Saginaw	IHL	19	18	13	31	36	1	0	0	0	0
1989-90	**Chicago**	**NHL**	**8**	**0**	**2**	**2**	**6**	....	....	....	....	....
a	Indianapolis	IHL	56	40	36	76	85	14	6	9	15	20
1990-91	**Chicago**	**NHL**	**7**	**0**	**4**	**4**	**2**	....	....	....	....	....
b	Indianapolis	IHL	59	38	53	91	67	7	6	4	10	18
	NHL Totals		**137**	**14**	**38**	**52**	**80**	**4**	**0**	**0**	**0**	**4**

a IHL Second All-Star Team (1990)
b IHL First All-Star Team (1991)

NORDMARK, ROBERT (NOORD-mahrk)

Defense. Shoots right. 6'1", 200 lbs. Born, Lulea, Sweden, August 20, 1962.
(St. Louis' 3rd choice, 59th overall, in 1987 Entry Draft).

			Regular Season					Playoffs				
Season	Club	Lea	GP	G	A	TP	PIM	GP	G	A	TP	PIM
1984-85	Lulea	Swe.	33	3	9	12	30	....	....	....	....	....
1985-86	Lulea	Swe.	35	9	15	24	48	....	....	....	....	....
1986-87	Lulea	Swe.	32	7	8	15	46	3	0	3	3	4
1987-88	**St. Louis**	**NHL**	**67**	**3**	**18**	**21**	**60**	....	....	....	....	....
1988-89	**Vancouver**	**NHL**	**80**	**6**	**35**	**41**	**97**	**7**	**3**	**2**	**5**	**8**
1989-90	**Vancouver**	**NHL**	**44**	**2**	**11**	**13**	**34**	....	....	....	....	....
1990-91	**Vancouver**	**NHL**	**45**	**2**	**6**	**8**	**63**	....	....	....	....	....
	NHL Totals		**236**	**13**	**70**	**83**	**254**	**7**	**3**	**2**	**5**	**8**

Traded to **Vancouver** by **St. Louis** for Dave Richter and Vancouver's second-round choice in 1990 Entry Draft, September 6, 1988.

NOREN, DARRYL

Center. Shoots left. 5'10", 180 lbs. Born, Livonia, MI, August 7, 1968.
(Quebecs's 2nd choice, 6th overall, in 1990 Supplemental Draft).

			Regular Season					Playoffs				
Season	Club	Lea	GP	G	A	TP	PIM	GP	G	A	TP	PIM
1988-89	Ill-Chicago	CCHA	38	16	17	33	54	....	....	....	....	....
1989-90	Ill-Chicago	CCHA	38	29	37	66	84	....	....	....	....	....
1990-91	Albany	IHL	7	0	0	0	2	....	....	....	....	....
	Greensboro	ECHL	43	27	23	50	29	13	2	5	7	18

NORRIS, DWAYNE

Right wing. Shoots right. 5'10", 175 lbs. Born, St. John's, Nfld., January 8, 1970.
(Quebec's 5th choice, 127th overall, in 1990 Entry Draft).

			Regular Season					Playoffs				
Season	Club	Lea	GP	G	A	TP	PIM	GP	G	A	TP	PIM
1988-89	Michigan State	CCHA	40	16	21	37	32	....	....	....	....	....
1989-90	Michigan State	CCHA	33	18	25	43	30	....	....	....	....	....
1990-91	Michigan State	CCHA	40	26	25	51	60	....	....	....	....	....

NORTON, CHRIS

Defense. Shoots right. 6'2", 200 lbs. Born, Oakville, Ont., March 11, 1965.
(Winnipeg's 11th choice, 228th overall, in 1985 Entry Draft).

			Regular Season					Playoffs				
Season	Club	Lea	GP	G	A	TP	PIM	GP	G	A	TP	PIM
1984-85	Cornell	ECAC	29	4	19	23	34	....	....	....	....	..
1985-86a	Cornell	ECAC	21	8	15	23	56	....	....	....	....	....
1986-87	Cornell	ECAC	24	10	21	31	79	....	....	....	....	....
1987-88a	Cornell	ECAC	27	9	25	34	53	....	....	....	....	....
1988-89	Moncton	AHL	60	1	21	22	49	10	3	2	5	15
1989-90	Moncton	AHL	62	9	20	29	49	....	....	....	....	....
1990-91	Moncton	AHL	72	8	28	36	45	9	1	3	4	12

a ECAC Second All-Star Team (1986, 1988).

Traded to **Chicago** by **Winnipeg** with Bryan Marchment for Troy Murray and Warren Rychel, July 22, 1991.

NORTON, DARCY

Left wing. Shoots left. 6'1", 190 lbs. Born, Camrose, Alta., May 2, 1967.
(Minnesota's 6th choice, 109th overall, in 1987 Entry Draft).

			Regular Season					Playoffs				
Season	Club	Lea	GP	G	A	TP	PIM	GP	G	A	TP	PIM
1984-85	Lethbridge	WHL	50	4	11	15	49	4	0	0	0	21
1985-86	Lethbridge	WHL	69	19	25	44	69	10	2	7	9	0
1986-87	Kamloops	WHL	71	45	57	102	66	13	7	9	16	15
1987-88	Kamloops	WHL	68	64	43	107	82	18	9	13	22	20
1988-89	Kalamazoo	IHL	75	39	38	77	79	6	2	3	5	15
1989-90	Kalamazoo	IHL	66	22	25	47	55	6	3	6	9	6
1990-91	San Diego	IHL	74	22	23	45	83	....	....	....	....	....

NORTON, JEFF

Defense. Shoots left. 6'2", 195 lbs. Born, Acton, MA, November 25, 1965.
(NY Islanders' 3rd choice, 62nd overall, in 1984 Entry Draft).

			Regular Season					Playoffs				
Season	Club	Lea	GP	G	A	TP	PIM	GP	G	A	TP	PIM
1984-85	U. of Michigan	CCHA	37	8	16	24	103	....	....	....	....	....
1985-86	U. of Michigan	CCHA	37	15	30	45	99	....	....	....	....	....
1986-87a	U. of Michigan	CCHA	39	12	36	48	92	....	....	....	....	....
1987-88	U.S. National	...	54	7	22	29	52	....	....	....	....	....
	U.S. Olympic	...	6	0	4	4	4	....	....	....	....	....
	NY Islanders	**NHL**	**15**	**1**	**6**	**7**	**14**	**3**	**0**	**2**	**2**	**13**
1988-89	**NY Islanders**	**NHL**	**69**	**1**	**30**	**31**	**74**	....	....	....	....	....
1989-90	**NY Islanders**	**NHL**	**60**	**4**	**49**	**53**	**65**	**4**	**1**	**3**	**4**	**17**
1990-91	**NY Islanders**	**NHL**	**44**	**3**	**25**	**28**	**16**	....	....	....	....	....
	NHL Totals		**188**	**9**	**110**	**119**	**169**	**7**	**1**	**5**	**6**	**30**

a CCHA Second All-Star Team (1987)

NORWOOD, LEE CHARLES

Defense. Shoots left. 6'1", 198 lbs. Born, Oakland, CA, February 2, 1960.
(Quebec's 3rd choice, 62nd overall, in 1979 Entry Draft).

			Regular Season					Playoffs				
Season	Club	Lea	GP	G	A	TP	PIM	GP	G	A	TP	PIM
1978-79	Oshawa	OHA	61	23	38	61	171	5	2	2	4	17
1979-80	Oshawa	OHA	60	13	39	52	143	6	2	7	9	15
1980-81	**Quebec**	**NHL**	**11**	**1**	**1**	**2**	**9**	**3**	**0**	**0**	**0**	**2**
	Hershey	AHL	52	11	32	43	78	8	0	4	4	14
1981-82	**Quebec**	**NHL**	**2**	**0**	**0**	**0**	**2**	....	....	....	....	....
	Fredericton	AHL	29	6	13	19	74	....	....	....	....	....
	Washington	**NHL**	**26**	**7**	**10**	**17**	**125**	....	....	....	....	....
1982-83	**Washington**	**NHL**	**8**	**0**	**1**	**1**	**14**	....	....	....	....	....
	Hershey	AHL	67	12	36	48	90	5	0	1	1	2
1983-84	St. Catharines	AHL	75	13	46	59	91	7	0	5	5	31
1984-85ab	Peoria	IHL	80	17	60	77	229	18	1	11	12	62
1985-86	**St. Louis**	**NHL**	**71**	**5**	**24**	**29**	**134**	**19**	**2**	**7**	**9**	**64**
1986-87	**Detroit**	**NHL**	**57**	**6**	**21**	**27**	**163**	**16**	**1**	**6**	**7**	**31**
	Adirondack	AHL	3	0	3	3	0	....	....	....	....	....
1987-88	**Detroit**	**NHL**	**51**	**9**	**22**	**31**	**131**	**16**	**2**	**6**	**8**	**40**
1988-89	**Detroit**	**NHL**	**66**	**10**	**32**	**42**	**100**	**6**	**1**	**2**	**3**	**16**
1989-90	**Detroit**	**NHL**	**64**	**8**	**14**	**22**	**95**	....	....	....	....	....
1990-91	**Detroit**	**NHL**	**21**	**3**	**7**	**10**	**50**	....	....	....	....	....
	New Jersey	**NHL**	**28**	**3**	**2**	**5**	**87**	**4**	**0**	**0**	**0**	**18**
	NHL Totals		**405**	**52**	**134**	**186**	**910**	**64**	**6**	**21**	**27**	**171**

a Won Governors' Trophy (IHL's Top Defenseman) 1985
b IHL First All-Star Team (1985)

Traded to **Washington** by **Quebec** for Tim Tookey and Washington's seventh round choice (Daniel Poudrier) in 1982 Entry Draft, February 1, 1982. Traded to **Toronto** by **Washington** for Dave Shand, October 6, 1983. Signed as a free agent by **St. Louis**, August 13, 1985. Traded to **Detroit** by **St. Louis** for Larry Trader, August 7, 1986. Traded to **New Jersey** by **Detroit** with future considerations for Paul Ysebaert, November 27, 1990.

NUMMINEN, TEPPO (NOO-mih-nehn)

Defense. Shoots right. 6'1", 190 lbs. Born, Tampere, Finland, July 3, 1968.
(Winnipeg's 2nd choice, 29th overall, in 1986 Entry Draft).

			Regular Season					Playoffs				
Season	Club	Lea	GP	G	A	TP	PIM	GP	G	A	TP	PIM
1985-86	Tappara	Fin.	31	2	4	6	6	8	0	0	0	0
1986-87	Tappara	Fin.	44	9	9	18	16	9	4	1	5	4
1987-88	Tappara	Fin.	40	10	10	20	29	10	6	6	12	6
1988-89	**Winnipeg**	**NHL**	**69**	**1**	**14**	**15**	**36**	....	....	....	....	....
1989-90	**Winnipeg**	**NHL**	**79**	**11**	**32**	**43**	**20**	**7**	**1**	**2**	**3**	**10**
1990-91	**Winnipeg**	**NHL**	**80**	**8**	**25**	**33**	**28**	....	....	....	....	....
	NHL Totals		**228**	**20**	**71**	**91**	**84**	**7**	**1**	**2**	**3**	**10**

NUUTINEN, SAMI

Defense. Shoots left. 6', 178 lbs. Born, Espoo, Finland, June 11, 1971.
(Edmonton's 11th choice, 248th overall, in 1990 Entry Draft).

			Regular Season					Playoffs				
Season	Club	Lea	GP	G	A	TP	PIM	GP	G	A	TP	PIM
1988-89	Espoo	Fin.	39	18	10	28	46	....	....	....	....	....
1989-90	Espoo	Fin.	40	8	15	23	....	....	....	....	....	....
1990-91	K-Kissat	Fin.	3	1	0	1	0	....	....	....	....	....
	HIFK	Fin.	27	1	3	4	6	3	0	0	0	0

NYLUND, GARY (NIGH-lund)

Defense. Shoots left. 6'4", 210 lbs. Born, Surrey, B.C., October 28, 1963.
(Toronto's 1st choice, 3rd overall, in 1982 Entry Draft).

			Regular Season					Playoffs				
Season	Club	Lea	GP	G	A	TP	PIM	GP	G	A	TP	PIM
1979-80	Portland	WHL	72	5	21	26	59	8	0	1	1	2
1980-81a	Portland	WHL	70	6	40	46	186	9	1	7	8	17
1981-82bc	Portland	WHL	65	7	59	66	267	15	3	16	19	74
1982-83	**Toronto**	**NHL**	**16**	**0**	**3**	**3**	**16**	....	....	....	....	....
1983-84	**Toronto**	**NHL**	**47**	**2**	**14**	**16**	**103**	....	....	....	....	....
1984-85	**Toronto**	**NHL**	**76**	**3**	**17**	**20**	**99**	....	....	....	....	....
1985-86	**Toronto**	**NHL**	**79**	**2**	**16**	**18**	**180**	**10**	**0**	**2**	**2**	**25**
1986-87	**Chicago**	**NHL**	**80**	**7**	**20**	**27**	**190**	**4**	**0**	**2**	**2**	**11**
1987-88	**Chicago**	**NHL**	**76**	**4**	**15**	**19**	**208**	**5**	**0**	**0**	**0**	**10**
1988-89	**Chicago**	**NHL**	**23**	**3**	**2**	**5**	**63**	....	....	....	....	....
	NY Islanders	**NHL**	**46**	**4**	**8**	**12**	**74**	....	....	....	....	....
1989-90	**NY Islanders**	**NHL**	**64**	**4**	**21**	**25**	**144**	**5**	**0**	**2**	**2**	**17**
1990-91	**NY Islanders**	**NHL**	**72**	**2**	**21**	**23**	**105**	....	....	....	....	....
	NHL Totals		**579**	**31**	**137**	**168**	**1182**	**24**	**0**	**6**	**6**	**63**

a WHL Second All-Star Team (1981)
b WHL First All-Star Team (1982)
c Named WHL's Top Defenseman (1982)

Signed as a free agent by **Chicago**, August 27, 1986. Traded to **NY Islanders** by **Chicago** with Marc Bergevin for Steve Konroyd and Bob Bassen, November 25, 1988.

NYLANDER, MIKAEL

Center. Shoots left. 5'11", 176 lbs. Born, Stockholm, Sweden, October 3, 1972.
(Hartford's 4th choice, 59th overall, in 1991 Entry Draft).

			Regular Season					Playoffs				
Season	Club	Lea	GP	G	A	TP	PIM	GP	G	A	TP	PIM
1989-90	Huddinge	Swe.	31	7	15	22	4	....	....	....	....	....
1990-91	Huddinge	Swe.	33	14	20	34	10	....	....	....	....	....

OATES, ADAM

Center. Shoots right. 5'11", 189 lbs. Born, Weston, Ont., August 27, 1962.

			Regular Season					Playoffs				
Season	Club	Lea	GP	G	A	TP	PIM	GP	G	A	TP	PIM
1982-83	RPI	ECAC	22	9	33	42	8	....	....	....	....	....
1983-84	RPI	ECAC	38	26	57	83	15	....	....	....	....	....
1984-85ab	RPI	ECAC	38	31	60	91	29	....	....	....	....	....
1985-86	**Detroit**	**NHL**	**38**	**9**	**11**	**20**	**10**	....	....	....	....	....
	Adirondack	AHL	34	18	28	46	4	17	7	14	21	4
1986-87	**Detroit**	**NHL**	**76**	**15**	**32**	**47**	**21**	**16**	**4**	**7**	**11**	**6**
1987-88	**Detroit**	**NHL**	**63**	**14**	**40**	**54**	**20**	**16**	**8**	**12**	**20**	**6**
1988-89	**Detroit**	**NHL**	**69**	**16**	**62**	**78**	**14**	**6**	**0**	**8**	**8**	**2**
1989-90	**St. Louis**	**NHL**	**80**	**23**	**79**	**102**	**30**	**12**	**2**	**12**	**14**	**4**
1990-91c	**St. Louis**	**NHL**	**61**	**25**	**90**	**115**	**29**	**13**	**7**	**13**	**20**	**10**
	NHL Totals		**387**	**102**	**314**	**416**	**124**	**63**	**21**	**52**	**73**	**28**

a ECAC First All-Star Team (1985)
b Named to NCAA All-American Team (1985)
c NHL Second All-Star Team (1991)

Played in NHL All-Star Game (1991)

Signed as a free agent by **Detroit,** June 28, 1985. Traded to **St. Louis** by **Detroit** with Paul MacLean for Bernie Federko and Tony McKegney, June 15, 1989.

O'BRIEN, DAVID

Right wing. Shoots right. 6'1", 188 lbs. Born, Brighton, MA, September 13, 1966.
(St. Louis' 13th choice, 241st overall, in 1986 Entry Draft).

			Regular Season					Playoffs				
Season	Club	Lea	GP	G	A	TP	PIM	GP	G	A	TP	PIM
1985-86	Northeastern	H.E.	39	23	16	39	18	....	....	....	....	....
1986-87	Northeastern	H.E.	35	16	24	40	12	....	....	....	....	....
1987-88a	Northeastern	H.E.	37	18	29	47	18	....	....	....	....	....
1988-89	Binghamton	AHL	53	3	12	15	11	....	....	....	....	....
1989-90	Peoria	AHL	57	9	14	23	21	1	0	0	0	0
1990-91	Peoria	IHL	58	19	18	37	13	14	1	4	5	8

a Hockey East First All-Star Team (1988)

O'CONNOR, MYLES

Defense. Shoots left. 5'11", 165 lbs. Born, Calgary, Alta., April 2, 1967.
(New Jersey's 4th choice, 45th overall, in 1985 Entry Draft).

			Regular Season					Playoffs				
Season	Club	Lea	GP	G	A	TP	PIM	GP	G	A	TP	PIM
1985-86	U. of Michigan	CCHA	37	6	19	25	73	....	....	....	....	....
1986-87	U. of Michigan	CCHA	39	15	39	54	111	....	....	....	....	....
1987-88	U. of Michigan	CCHA	40	9	25	34	78	....	....	....	....	....
1988-89ab	U. of Michigan	CCHA	40	3	31	34	91	....	....	....	....	....
	Utica	AHL	1	0	0	0	0	....	....	....	....	....
1989-90	Utica	AHL	76	14	33	47	124	5	1	2	3	26
1990-91	**New Jersey**	**NHL**	**22**	**3**	**1**	**4**	**41**	....	....	....	....	....
	Utica	AHL	33	6	17	23	62	....	....	....	....	....
	NHL Totals		**22**	**3**	**1**	**4**	**41**	....	....	....	....	....

a CCHA First All-Star Team (1989)
b NCAA West First All-American Team (1989)

ODELEIN, LYLE (Ah-duh-LEEN)

Defense. Shoots left. 6'1", 206 lbs. Born, Quill Lake, Sask., July 21, 1968.
(Montreal's 8th choice, 141st overall, in 1986 Entry Draft).

			Regular Season					Playoffs				
Season	Club	Lea	GP	G	A	TP	PIM	GP	G	A	TP	PIM
1985-86	Moose Jaw	WHL	67	9	37	46	117	13	1	6	7	34
1986-87	Moose Jaw	WHL	59	9	50	59	70	9	2	5	7	26
1987-88	Moose Jaw	WHL	63	15	43	58	166	....	....	....	....	....
1988-89	Sherbrooke	AHL	33	3	4	7	120	3	0	2	2	5
	Peoria	IHL	36	2	8	10	116	....	....	....	....	....
1989-90	**Montreal**	**NHL**	**8**	**0**	**2**	**2**	**33**	....	....	....	....	....
	Sherbrooke	AHL	68	7	24	31	265	12	6	5	11	79
1990-91	**Montreal**	**NHL**	**52**	**0**	**2**	**2**	**259**	**12**	**0**	**0**	**0**	**54**
	NHL Totals		**60**	**0**	**4**	**4**	**292**	**12**	**0**	**0**	**0**	**54**

ODELEIN, SELMAR (AH-duh-LEEN)

Defense. Shoots right. 6', 205 lbs. Born, Quill Lake, Sask., April 11, 1966.
(Edmonton's 1st choice, 21st overall, in 1984 Entry Draft).

			Regular Season					Playoffs				
Season	Club	Lea	GP	G	A	TP	PIM	GP	G	A	TP	PIM
1983-84	Regina	WHL	71	9	42	51	45	23	4	11	15	45
1984-85	Regina	WHL	64	24	35	59	121	8	2	2	4	13
1985-86	**Edmonton**	**NHL**	**4**	**0**	**0**	**0**	**0**	....	....	....	....	....
	Regina	WHL	36	13	28	41	57	8	5	2	7	24
1986-87	Nova Scotia	AHL	2	0	1	1	2	....	....	....	....	....
1987-88	**Edmonton**	**NHL**	**12**	**0**	**2**	**2**	**33**	....	....	....	....	....
	Nova Scotia	AHL	43	9	14	23	75	5	0	1	1	31
1988-89	**Edmonton**	**NHL**	**2**	**0**	**0**	**0**	**2**	....	....	....	....	....
	Cape Breton	AHL	63	8	21	29	150	....	....	....	....	....
1989-90	Cdn. National	...	72	7	29	36	69					
1990-91	Gosser Ev	Aus.	38	9	21	30	....					
	NHL Totals		**18**	**0**	**2**	**2**	**35**	....	....	....	....	....

ODJIK, GINO

Left wing. Shoots left. 6'2", 220 lbs. Born, Maniwaki, Que., September 7, 1970.
(Vancouver's 5th choice, 86th overall, in 1990 Entry Draft).

			Regular Season					Playoffs				
Season	Club	Lea	GP	G	A	TP	PIM	GP	G	A	TP	PIM
1989-90	Laval	QMJHL	51	12	26	38	280	....	....	....	....	....
1990-91	**Vancouver**	**NHL**	**45**	**7**	**1**	**8**	**296**	....	....	....	....	....
	Milwaukee	IHL	17	7	3	10	102	....	....	....	....	....
	NHL Totals		**45**	**7**	**1**	**8**	**296**	....	....	....	....	....

O'DWYER, BILL

Center. Shoots left. 6', 190 lbs. Born, Boston, MA, January 25, 1960.
(Los Angeles' 10th choice, 157th overall, in 1980 Entry Draft).

			Regular Season					Playoffs				
Season	Club	Lea	GP	G	A	TP	PIM	GP	G	A	TP	PIM
1978-79	Boston College	ECAC	30	9	30	39	14	....	....	....	....	....
1979-80	Boston College	ECAC	33	20	22	42	22	....	....	....	....	....
1980-81	Boston College	ECAC	31	20	20	40	6	....	....	....	....	....
1981-82	Boston College	ECAC	30	15	26	41	10	....	....	....	....	....
1982-83	New Haven	AHL	77	24	23	47	29	11	3	4	7	9
1983-84	**Los Angeles**	**NHL**	**5**	**0**	**0**	**0**	**0**	....	....	....	....	....
	New Haven	AHL	58	15	42	57	39	....	....	....	....	....
1984-85	**Los Angeles**	**NHL**	**13**	**1**	**0**	**1**	**15**	....	....	....	....	....
	New Haven	AHL	46	19	24	43	27	....	....	....	....	....
1985-86	New Haven	AHL	41	10	15	25	41	5	0	1	1	2
1986-87	New Haven	AHL	65	22	42	64	74	3	0	0	0	14
1987-88	**Boston**	**NHL**	**77**	**7**	**10**	**17**	**83**	**9**	**0**	**0**	**0**	**0**
1988-89	**Boston**	**NHL**	**19**	**1**	**2**	**3**	**8**	....	....	....	....	....
1989-90	**Boston**	**NHL**	**6**	**0**	**1**	**1**	**7**	**1**	**0**	**0**	**0**	**2**
	Maine	AHL	71	26	45	71	56	....	....	....	....	....
1990-91	New Haven	AHL	6	2	1	3	2	....	....	....	....	....
	Phoenix	IHL	25	3	9	12	12	11	7	6	13	0
	NHL Totals		**126**	**11**	**14**	**25**	**115**	**10**	**0**	**0**	**0**	**2**

Signed as a free agent by **NY Rangers,** July 13, 1985. Signed as a free agent by **Boston,** August 13, 1987. Signed as a free agent by **Los Angeles,** July 11, 1990.

OGRODNICK, JOHN ALEXANDER (oh-GRAHD-nik)

Left wing. Shoots left. 6', 204 lbs. Born, Ottawa, Ont., June 20, 1959.
(Detroit's 4th choice, 66th overall, in 1979 Entry Draft).

			Regular Season					Playoffs				
Season	Club	Lea	GP	G	A	TP	PIM	GP	G	A	TP	PIM
1977-78a	N. Westminster	WHL	72	59	29	88	47	21	14	7	21	14
1978-79	N. Westminster	WHL	72	48	36	84	38	6	2	0	2	4
1979-80	**Detroit**	**NHL**	**41**	**8**	**24**	**32**	**8**	....	....	....	....	....
	Adirondack	AHL	39	13	20	33	21	....	....	....	....	....
1980-81	**Detroit**	**NHL**	**80**	**35**	**35**	**70**	**14**	....	....	....	....	....
1981-82	**Detroit**	**NHL**	**80**	**28**	**26**	**54**	**28**	....	....	....	....	....
1982-83	**Detroit**	**NHL**	**80**	**41**	**44**	**85**	**30**	....	....	....	....	....
1983-84	**Detroit**	**NHL**	**64**	**42**	**36**	**78**	**14**	**4**	**0**	**0**	**0**	**0**
1984-85b	**Detroit**	**NHL**	**79**	**55**	**50**	**105**	**30**	**3**	**1**	**1**	**2**	**0**
1985-86	**Detroit**	**NHL**	**76**	**38**	**32**	**70**	**18**	....	....	....	....	....
1986-87	**Detroit**	**NHL**	**39**	**12**	**28**	**40**	**6**	....	....	....	....	....
	Quebec	**NHL**	**32**	**11**	**16**	**27**	**4**	**13**	**9**	**4**	**13**	**6**
1987-88	**NY Rangers**	**NHL**	**64**	**22**	**32**	**54**	**16**	....	....	....	....	....
1988-89	**NY Rangers**	**NHL**	**60**	**13**	**29**	**42**	**14**	**3**	**2**	**0**	**2**	**0**
	Denver	IHL	3	2	0	2	0	....	....	....	....	....
1989-90	**NY Rangers**	**NHL**	**80**	**43**	**31**	**74**	**44**	**10**	**6**	**3**	**9**	**0**
1990-91	**NY Rangers**	**NHL**	**79**	**31**	**23**	**54**	**10**	**4**	**0**	**0**	**0**	**0**
	NHL Totals		**854**	**379**	**406**	**785**	**236**	**37**	**18**	**8**	**26**	**6**

a Shared WHL Rookie of the Year Award with Keith Brown (Portland) (1978)
b NHL First All-Star Team (1985)

Played in NHL All-Star Game (1981, 1982, 1984-86)

Traded to **Quebec** by **Detroit** with Basil McRae and Doug Shedden for Brent Ashton, Gilbert Delorme and Mark Kumpel, January 17, 1987. Traded to **NY Rangers** by **Quebec** with David Shaw for Jeff Jackson and Terry Carkner, September 30, 1987.

OHMAN, ROGER (OH-mahn)

Defense. Shoots left. 6'3", 202 lbs. Born, Stockholm, Sweden, June 5, 1967.
(Winnipeg's 2nd choice, 39th overall, in 1985 Entry Draft).

			Regular Season					Playoffs				
Season	Club	Lea	GP	G	A	TP	PIM	GP	G	A	TP	PIM
1986-87	V. Frolunda	Swe.	26	4	10	14	16	2	0	1	1	0
1987-88	Moncton	AHL	67	11	17	28	38	....	....	....	....	....
1988-89	AIK	Swe.	36	11	8	19	20	....	....	....	....	....
1989-90	AIK	Swe.	39	8	17	25	22	3	0	0	0	0
1990-91	Malmo	Swe.	40	11	7	18	26	....	....	....	....	....

OJANEN, JANNE (OY-uh-nehn YAHN-ee)

Center. Shoots left. 6'2", 200 lbs. Born, Tampere, Finland, April 9, 1968.
(New Jersey's 3rd choice, 45th overall, in 1986 Entry Draft).

			Regular Season					Playoffs				
Season	Club	Lea	GP	G	A	TP	PIM	GP	G	A	TP	PIM
1985-86	Tappara	Fin.Jr.	14	5	17	22	14	5	2	3	5	8
	Tappara	Fin.	3	0	0	0	2	....	....	....	....	....
1986-87	Tappara	Fin.	40	18	13	31	16	9	4	6	10	2
1987-88	Tappara	Fin.	44	21	31	52	30	10	4	4	8	12
1988-89	**New Jersey**	**NHL**	**3**	**0**	**1**	**1**	**2**	....	....	....	....	....
	Utica	AHL	72	23	37	60	10	5	0	3	3	0
1989-90	**New Jersey**	**NHL**	**64**	**17**	**13**	**30**	**12**	....	....	....	....	....
1990-91	Tappara	Fin.	44	15	33	48	36	3	1	2	3	6
	NHL Totals		**67**	**17**	**14**	**31**	**14**	....	....	....	....	....

OKSYUTA, ROMAN (ohk-SEW-tah)

Right wing. Shoots left. 6'2", 213 lbs. Born, Voskresensk, Soviet Union, August 21, 1970.
(NY Rangers' 11th choice, 202nd overall, in 1989 Entry Draft).

			Regular Season					Playoffs				
Season	Club	Lea	GP	G	A	TP	PIM	GP	G	A	TP	PIM
1987-88	Khimik	USSR	11	1	0	1	4	....	....	....	....	....
1988-89	Khimik	USSR	34	13	3	16	14	....	....	....	....	....
1989-90	Khimik	USSR	37	13	6	19	16	....	....	....	....	....
1990-91	Khimik	USSR	41	12	8	20	24	....	....	....	....	....

OLAUSSON, FREDRIK (OHL-AH-SUHN)

Defense. Shoots right. 6'2", 200 lbs. Born, Vaxsjo, Sweden, October 5, 1966.
(Winnipeg's 4th choice, 81st overall, in 1985 Entry Draft).

			Regular Season					Playoffs				
Season	Club	Lea	GP	G	A	TP	PIM	GP	G	A	TP	PIM
1984-85	Farjestad	Swe.	29	5	12	17	22	3	1	0	1	0
1985-86	Farjestad	Swe.	33	4	12	16	22	8	3	2	5	6
1986-87	Winnipeg	NHL	72	7	29	36	24	10	2	3	5	4
1987-88	Winnipeg	NHL	38	5	10	15	18	5	1	1	2	0
1988-89	Winnipeg	NHL	75	15	47	62	32	....	....	....	....	....
1989-90	Winnipeg	NHL	77	9	46	55	32	7	0	2	2	2
1990-91	Winnipeg	NHL	71	12	29	41	24	....	....	....	....	....
	NHL Totals		333	48	161	209	130	22	3	6	9	6

OLCZYK, ED (OHL-chehk)

Center. Shoots left. 6'1", 200 lbs. Born, Chicago, IL, August 16, 1966.
(Chicago's 1st choice, 3rd overall, in 1984 Entry Draft).

			Regular Season					Playoffs				
Season	Club	Lea	GP	G	A	TP	PIM	GP	G	A	TP	PIM
1983-84	U.S. Olympic	...	62	21	47	68	36	....	....	....	....	....
1984-85	Chicago	NHL	70	20	30	50	67	15	6	5	11	11
1985-86	Chicago	NHL	79	29	50	79	47	3	0	0	0	0
1986-87	Chicago	NHL	79	16	35	51	119	4	1	1	2	4
1987-88	Toronto	NHL	80	42	33	75	55	6	5	4	9	2
1988-89	Toronto	NHL	80	38	52	90	75	....	....	....	....	....
1989-90	Toronto	NHL	79	32	56	88	78	5	1	2	3	14
1990-91	Toronto	NHL	18	4	10	14	13	....	....	....	....	....
	Winnipeg	NHL	61	26	31	57	69	....	....	....	....	....
	NHL Totals		546	207	297	504	523	33	13	12	25	31

Traded to **Toronto** by **Chicago** with Al Secord for Rick Vaive, Steve Thomas and Bob McGill, September 3, 1987. Traded to **Winipeg** by **Toronto** with Mark Osborne for Dave Ellett and Paul Fenton, November 10, 1990.

O'LEARY, RYAN

Center. Shoots left. 6'1", 205 lbs. Born, Duluth, MN, June 8, 1971.
(Calgary's 6th choice, 84th overall, in 1989 Entry Draft).

			Regular Season					Playoffs				
Season	Club	Lea	GP	G	A	TP	PIM	GP	G	A	TP	PIM
1989-90	Denver U.	WCHA	39	4	6	10	30	....	....	....	....	....
1990-91	Denver U.	WCHA	38	3	6	9	40	....	....	....	....	....

OLIMB, LAWRENCE

Defense. Shoots left. 5'10", 165 lbs. Born, Warroad, MN, August 11, 1969.
(Minnesota's 10th choice, 193rd overall, in 1987 Entry Draft).

			Regular Season					Playoffs				
Season	Club	Lea	GP	G	A	TP	PIM	GP	G	A	TP	PIM
1988-89	U. Minnesota	WCHA	47	10	29	39	50	....	....	....	....	....
1989-90	U. Minnesota	WCHA	46	6	36	42	44	....	....	....	....	....
1990-91a	U. Minnesota	WCHA	45	19	38	57	52	....	....	....	....	....

a WCHA Second All-Star Team (1991)

Claimed by **San Jose** from **Minnesota** in Dispersal Draft, May 30, 1991.

OLIVER, DON

Right wing. Shoots left. 5'11", 175 lbs. Born, London, Ont., November 9, 1969.
(Detroit's 2nd choice, 8th overall, in 1990 Supplemental Draft).

			Regular Season					Playoffs				
Season	Club	Lea	GP	G	A	TP	PIM	GP	G	A	TP	PIM
1987-88	Ohio State	CCHA	34	5	13	18	81	....	....	....	....	....
1988-89	Ohio State	CCHA	39	15	14	29	29	....	....	....	....	....
1989-90	Ohio State	CCHA	40	19	26	45	27	....	....	....	....	....
1990-91	Ohio State	CCHA	37	5	20	25	32	....	....	....	....	....

OLSEN, DARRYL

Defense. Shoots left. 6', 180 lbs. Born, Calgary, Alta., October 7, 1966.
(Calgary's 10th choice, 185th overall in 1985 Entry Draft).

			Regular Season					Playoffs				
Season	Club	Lea	GP	G	A	TP	PIM	GP	G	A	TP	PIM
1985-86	N. Michigan	WCHA	37	5	20	25	46	....	....	....	....	....
1986-87	N. Michigan	WCHA	37	5	20	25	96	....	....	....	....	....
1987-88	N. Michigan	WCHA	35	11	20	31	59	....	....	....	....	....
1988-89	Cdn. National	...	3	1	0	1	4	....	....	....	....	....
ab	N. Michigan	WCHA	45	16	26	42	88	....	....	....	....	....
1989-90	Salt Lake	IHL	72	16	50	66	90	11	3	6	9	2
1990-91	Salt Lake	IHL	76	15	40	55	89	4	1	5	6	2

a NCAA West Second All-American Team (1989)
b WCHA First All-Star Team (1989)

O'REAR, HAYDEN

Defense. Shoots left. 6'1", 185 lbs. Born, Fairbanks, AK, October 8, 1970.
(Vancouver's 9th choice, 218th overall, in 1989 Entry Draft).

			Regular Season					Playoffs				
Season	Club	Lea	GP	G	A	TP	PIM	GP	G	A	TP	PIM
1989-90	Alaska-Anch.	NCAA	23	0	2	2	38	....	....	....	....	....
1990-91	Alaska-Anch.	NCAA	36	1	6	7	8	....	....	....	....	....

OSBORNE, KEITH

Right wing. Shoots right. 6'1", 188 lbs. Born, Toronto, Ont., April 2, 1969.
(St. Louis' 1st choice, 12th overall, in 1987 Entry Draft).

			Regular Season					Playoffs				
Season	Club	Lea	GP	G	A	TP	PIM	GP	G	A	TP	PIM
1986-87	North Bay	OHL	61	34	55	89	31	24	11	11	22	25
1987-88	North Bay	OHL	30	14	22	36	20	4	1	5	6	8
1988-89	North Bay	OHL	15	11	15	26	12					
	Niagara Falls	OHL	50	34	49	83	45	17	12	12	25	36
1989-90	St. Louis	NHL	5	0	2	2	8	....	....	....	....	....
	Peoria	IHL	56	23	24	47	58	....	....	....	....	....
1990-91	Peoria	IHL	54	10	20	30	79	....	....	....	....	....
	Newmarket	AHL	12	0	3	3	6	....	....	....	....	....
	NHL Totals		5	0	2	2	8					

Traded to **Toronto** by **St. Louis** for Darren Veitch and future considerations, March 5, 1991.

OSBORNE, MARK ANATOLE (AWS-born)

Left wing. Shoots left. 6'2", 205 lbs. Born, Toronto, Ont., August 13, 1961.
(Detroit's 2nd choice, 46th overall, in 1980 Entry Draft).

			Regular Season					Playoffs				
Season	Club	Lea	GP	G	A	TP	PIM	GP	G	A	TP	PIM
1979-80	Niagara Falls	OHA	52	10	33	43	104	10	2	1	3	23
1980-81	Niagara Falls	OHA	54	39	41	80	140	12	11	10	21	20
	Adirondack	AHL	....	....	....	....	....	13	2	3	5	2
1981-82	Detroit	NHL	80	26	41	67	61	....	....	....	....	....
1982-83	Detroit	NHL	80	19	24	43	83	....	....	....	....	....
1983-84	NY Rangers	NHL	73	23	28	51	88	5	0	1	1	7
1984-85	NY Rangers	NHL	23	4	4	8	33	3	0	0	0	4
1985-86	NY Rangers	NHL	62	16	24	40	80	15	2	3	5	26
1986-87	NY Rangers	NHL	58	17	15	32	101	....	....	....	....	....
	Toronto	NHL	16	5	10	15	12	9	1	3	4	6
1987-88	Toronto	NHL	79	23	37	60	102	6	1	3	4	16
1988-89	Toronto	NHL	75	16	30	46	112	....	....	....	....	....
1989-90	Toronto	NHL	78	23	50	73	91	5	2	3	5	12
1990-91	Toronto	NHL	18	3	3	6	4	....	....	....	....	....
	Winnipeg	NHL	37	8	8	16	59	....	....	....	....	....
	NHL Totals		679	183	274	457	826	43	6	13	19	71

Traded to **NY Rangers** by **Detroit** with Willie Huber and Mike Blaisdell for Ron Duguay, Eddie Mio and Eddie Johnstone, June 13, 1983. Traded to **Toronto** by **NY Rangers** for Jeff Jackson and Toronto's third-round choice (Rod Zamuner) in 1989 Entry Draft, March 5, 1987. Traded to **Winnipeg** by **Toronto** with Ed Olcyk for Dave Ellett and Paul Fenton, November 10, 1990.

O'SHEA, DAN

Right wing. Shoots right. 6'1", 175 lbs. Born, St. Cloud, MN, September 4, 1970.
(Minnesota's 1st choice, 14th overall, in 1991 Supplemental Draft).

			Regular Season					Playoffs				
Season	Club	Lea	GP	G	A	TP	PIM	GP	G	A	TP	PIM
1990-91	St. Cloud	WCHA	31	4	9	13	60	....	....	....	....	....

OSIECKI, MARK

Defense. Shoots right. 6'2", 200 lbs. Born, St. Paul, MN, July 23, 1968.
(Calgary's 10th choice, 187th overall, in 1987 Entry Draft).

			Regular Season					Playoffs				
Season	Club	Lea	GP	G	A	TP	PIM	GP	G	A	TP	PIM
1986-87	U. Wisconsin	WCHA	8	0	1	1	4	....	....	....	....	....
1987-88	U. Wisconsin	WCHA	18	0	1	1	22	....	....	....	....	....
1988-89	U. Wisconsin	WCHA	44	1	3	4	56	....	....	....	....	....
1989-90a	U. Wisconsin	WCHA	46	5	38	43	78	....	....	....	....	....
1990-91	Salt Lake	IHL	75	1	24	25	36	4	2	0	2	2

a NCAA All-Tournament Team (1990)

OSMAK, COREY

Center. Shoots left. 6'1", 180 lbs. Born, Edmonton, Alta., August 20, 1970.
(Hartford's 8th choice, 183rd overall, in 1990 Entry Draft).

			Regular Season					Playoffs				
Season	Club	Lea	GP	G	A	TP	PIM	GP	G	A	TP	PIM
1989-90	Nipawin	SJHL	61	27	42	69	103	....	....	....	....	....
1990-91	Minn.-Duluth	WCHA	22	3	0	3	34	....	....	....	....	....

O'SULLIVAN, KEVIN

Defense. Shoots left. 6', 180 lbs. Born, Dorchester, MA, November 13, 1970.
(NY Islanders' 7th choice, 99th overall, in 1989 Entry Draft).

			Regular Season					Playoffs				
Season	Club	Lea	GP	G	A	TP	PIM	GP	G	A	TP	PIM
1989-90	Boston U.	H.E.	43	0	6	6	42	....	....	....	....	....
1990-91	Boston U.	H.E.	37	4	7	11	50	....	....	....	....	....

OTEVREL, JAROSLAV

Left wing. Shoots left. 6'2", 185 lbs. Born, Gottwaldov, Czechoslovakia, Sept. 16, 1968.
(San Jose's 8th choice, 133rd overall, in 1991 Entry Draft).

			Regular Season					Playoffs				
Season	Club	Lea	GP	G	A	TP	PIM	GP	G	A	TP	PIM
1987-88	TJ Gottwaldov	Czech.	32	4	7	11	18	....	....	....	....	....
1988-89	TJ Zlin	Czech.	40	14	6	20	37	....	....	....	....	....
1989-90	Dukla Trencin	Czech.	43	7	10	17	20	....	....	....	....	....
1990-91	TJ Zlin	Czech.	49	24	26	50	105	....	....	....	....	....

OTTO . . . PASIN · 321

OTTO, JOEL STUART

Center. Shoots right. 6'4", 220 lbs.   Born, Elk River, MN, October 29, 1961.

				Regular Season					Playoffs			
Season	Club	Lea	GP	G	A	TP	PIM	GP	G	A	TP	PIM
1980-81	Bemidji State	NCAA	23	5	11	16	10	....	....	....	....	....
1981-82	Bemidji State	NCAA	31	19	33	52	24	....	....	....	....	....
1982-83	Bemidji State	NCAA	37	33	28	61	68	....	....	....	....	....
1983-84	Bemidji State	NCAA	31	32	43	75	32	....	....	....	....	....
1984-85	Calgary	NHL	17	4	8	12	30	3	2	1	3	10
	Moncton	AHL	56	27	36	63	89	....	....	....	....	....
1985-86	Calgary	NHL	79	25	34	59	188	22	5	10	15	80
1986-87	Calgary	NHL	68	19	31	50	185	2	0	2	2	6
1987-88	Calgary	NHL	62	13	39	52	194	9	3	2	5	26
1988-89	Calgary	NHL	72	23	30	53	213	22	6	13	19	46
1989-90	Calgary	NHL	75	13	20	33	116	6	2	2	4	2
1990-91	Calgary	NHL	76	19	20	39	183	7	1	2	3	8
	NHL Totals		449	116	182	298	1109	71	19	32	51	178

Signed as a free agent by **Calgary**, September 11, 1984.

OUIMET, MARK

Center. Shoots left. 5'10", 165 lbs.   Born, Poplar Hill, Ont., October 2, 1971.
(Washington's 6th choice, 94th overall, in 1990 Entry Draft).

				Regular Season					Playoffs			
Season	Club	Lea	GP	G	A	TP	PIM	GP	G	A	TP	PIM
1989-90	U. of Michigan	CCHA	38	15	32	47	14	....	....	....	....	....
1990-91	U. of Michigan	CCHA	46	18	32	50	22	....	....	....	....	....

OZOLNICH, SANDIS

Defense. Shoots left. 6'1", 189 lbs.   Born, Riga, Soviet Union, August 3, 1972.
(San Jose's 3rd choice, 30th overall, in 1991 Entry Draft).

				Regular Season					Playoffs			
Season	Club	Lea	GP	G	A	TP	PIM	GP	G	A	TP	PIM
1990-91	Dynamo Riga	USSR	44	0	3	3	49	....	....	....	....	....

PADDOCK, GORDON

Defense. Shoots right. 6', 190 lbs.   Born, Hamiota, Man., February 15, 1964.
(NY Islanders' 9th choice, 189th overall, in 1982 Entry Draft).

				Regular Season					Playoffs			
Season	Club	Lea	GP	G	A	TP	PIM	GP	G	A	TP	PIM
1981-82	Saskatoon	WHL	59	8	21	29	232	3	0	0	0	17
1982-83	Saskatoon	WHL	67	4	25	29	158	6	0	2	2	16
1983-84	Brandon	WHL	72	14	37	51	151	12	1	5	6	23
1984-85	Springfield	AHL	12	0	2	2	24	3	0	0	0	6
	Indianapolis	IHL	65	10	21	31	92	7	2	1	3	23
1985-86	Springfield	AHL	20	1	1	2	52	....	....	....	....	....
	Indianapolis	IHL	11	1	1	2	11	....	....	....	....	....
	Muskegon	IHL	47	1	20	21	87	....	....	....	....	....
1986-87	Springfield	AHL	78	6	11	17	127	....	....	....	....	....
1987-88	Springfield	AHL	74	8	26	34	127	....	....	....	....	....
1988-89	Hershey	AHL	75	6	36	42	105	12	0	1	1	17
1989-90	Hershey	AHL	65	4	19	23	60	....	....	....	....	....
1990-91	Albany	IHL	53	3	16	19	49	....	....	....	....	....
	Binghamton	AHL	21	2	8	10	37	10	0	3	3	12

Signed as a free agent by **Philadelphia**, August 29, 1988.

PAEK, JIM   (PAYK)

Defense. Shoots left. 6'1", 194 lbs.   Born, Seoul, Korea, April 7, 1967.
(Pittsburgh's 9th choice, 170th overall, in 1985 Entry Draft).

				Regular Season					Playoffs			
Season	Club	Lea	GP	G	A	TP	PIM	GP	G	A	TP	PIM
1984-85	Oshawa	OHL	54	2	13	15	57	5	1	0	1	9
1985-86	Oshawa	OHL	64	5	21	26	122	6	0	1	1	9
1986-87	Oshawa	OHL	57	5	17	22	75	26	1	14	15	43
1987-88	Muskegon	IHL	82	7	52	59	141	6	0	0	0	29
1988-89	Muskegon	IHL	80	3	54	57	96	14	1	10	11	24
1989-90	Muskegon	IHL	81	9	41	50	115	....	....	....	....	....
1990-91	Cdn. National	...	48	2	12	14	24	....	....	....	....	....
	Pittsburgh	NHL	3	0	0	0	9	8	1	0	1	2
	NHL Totals		3	0	0	0	9	8	1	0	1	2

PALFFY, ZIGMUND

Left wing. Shoots left. 5'10", 169 lbs.   Born, Skalica, Czechoslovakia, May 5, 1972.
(NY Islanders' 2nd choice, 26th overall, in 1991 Entry Draft).

				Regular Season					Playoffs			
Season	Club	Lea	GP	G	A	TP	PIM	GP	G	A	TP	PIM
1990-91	Nitra	Czech.	50	34	16	50	18	....	....	....	....	....

PARKER, JEFF

Right wing. Shoots right. 6'3", 194 lbs.   Born, St. Paul, MN, September 7, 1964.
(Buffalo's 9th choice, 111th overalll, in 1982 Entry Draft).

				Regular Season					Playoffs			
Season	Club	Lea	GP	G	A	TP	PIM	GP	G	A	TP	PIM
1983-84	Michigan State	CCHA	44	8	13	21	82	....	....	....	....	....
1984-85	Michigan State	CCHA	42	10	12	22	89	....	....	....	....	....
1985-86	Michigan State	CCHA	41	15	20	35	88	....	....	....	....	....
1986-87	**Buffalo**	NHL	15	3	3	6	7	....	....	....	....	....
	Rochester	AHL	54	14	8	22	75	14	1	3	4	19
1987-88	**Buffalo**	NHL	4	0	2	2	2	....	....	....	....	....
	Rochester	AHL	34	13	31	44	69	2	1	1	2	0
1988-89	**Buffalo**	NHL	57	9	9	18	82	5	0	0	0	26
	Rochester	AHL	6	2	4	6	9	....	....	....	....	....
1989-90	**Buffalo**	NHL	61	4	5	9	70	....	....	....	....	....
1990-91	Muskegon	IHL	11	1	7	8	13	....	....	....	....	....
	Hartford	NHL	4	0	0	0	2	....	....	....	....	....
	NHL Totals		141	16	19	35	163	5	0	0	0	26

Traded to **Winnipeg** by **Buffalo** with Phil Housley, Scott Arniel and Buffalo's first round choice (Keith Tkachuk) in 1990 Entry Draft for Dale Hawerchuk, Winnipeg's first round choice (Brad May) in 1990 Entry Draft and future considerations, June 16, 1990. Signed as a free agent by **Pittsburgh**, February 5, 1991. Traded to **Hartford** by **Pittsburgh** with John Cullen and Zarley Zalapski for Ron Francis, Grant Jennings and Ulf Samuelsson, March 4, 1991.

PARKER, JOHN

Center. Shoots right. 6'1", 180 lbs.   Born, St. Paul, MN, March 5, 1968.
(Calgary's 5th choice, 121st overall, in 1986 Entry Draft).

				Regular Season					Playoffs			
Season	Club	Lea	GP	G	A	TP	PIM	GP	G	A	TP	PIM
1986-87	U. Wisconsin	WCHA	8	0	1	1	4	....	....	....	....	....
1987-88	U. Wisconsin	WCHA	4	0	0	0	6	....	....	....	....	....
1988-89	U. Wisconsin	WCHA	20	1	7	8	16	....	....	....	....	....
1989-90	U. Wisconsin	WCHA	35	11	9	20	22	....	....	....	....	....
1990-91	U. Wisconsin	WCHA	40	6	5	11	40	....	....	....	....	....

PARKS, GREG

Center. Shoots right. 5'9", 180 lbs.   Born, Edmonton, Alta., March 25, 1967.

				Regular Season					Playoffs			
Season	Club	Lea	GP	G	A	TP	PIM	GP	G	A	TP	PIM
1989-90	Springfield	AHL	49	22	32	54	30	....	....	....	....	....
	Johnstown	ECHL	8	5	9	14	7	....	....	....	....	....
1990-91	**NY Islanders**	NHL	20	1	2	3	4	....	....	....	....	....
	Capital District	AHL	48	32	43	75	67	....	....	....	....	....
	NHL Totals		20	1	2	3	4					

Signed as a free agent by **NY Islanders**, August 13, 1990.

PARROTT, JEFF

Defense. Shoots right. 6'1", 195 lbs.   Born, The Pas, Man., April 6, 1971.
(Quebec's 4th choice, 106th overall, in 1990 Entry Draft).

				Regular Season					Playoffs			
Season	Club	Lea	GP	G	A	TP	PIM	GP	G	A	TP	PIM
1989-90	Minn.-Duluth	WCHA	35	1	5	6	60	....	....	....	....	....
1990-91	Minn.-Duluth	WCHA	39	2	8	10	65	....	....	....	....	....

PASCALL, BRAD

Defense. Shoots left. 6'2", 192 lbs.   Born, Coquitlam, B.C., July 29, 1970.
(Buffalo's 5th choice, 103rd overall, in 1990 Entry Draft).

				Regular Season					Playoffs			
Season	Club	Lea	GP	G	A	TP	PIM	GP	G	A	TP	PIM
1989-90	North Dakota	WCHA	45	1	9	10	98	....	....	....	....	....
1990-91	North Dakota	WCHA	38	1	4	5	81	....	....	....	....	....

PASCUCCI, RONALD

Defense. Shoots left. 6'1", 180 lbs.   Born, North Andover, MA, June 9, 1970.
(Washington's 14th choice, 246th overall, in 1988 Entry Draft).

				Regular Season					Playoffs			
Season	Club	Lea	GP	G	A	TP	PIM	GP	G	A	TP	PIM
1989-90	Boston College	H.E.	37	0	6	6	12	....	....	....	....	....
1990-91	Boston College	H.E.	37	1	13	14	30	....	....	....	....	....

PASEK, DUSAN   (PAH-shehk, do-SHAHN)

Center. Shoots left. 6'1", 200 lbs.   Born, Bratislava, Czechoslovakia, September 7, 1960.
(Minnesota's 4th choice, 81st overall, in 1982 Entry Draft).

				Regular Season					Playoffs			
Season	Club	Lea	GP	G	A	TP	PIM	GP	G	A	TP	PIM
1986-87	Bratislava	Czech.	32	18	27	45	....	....	....	....	....	....
1987-88	Bratislava	Czech.	28	13	10	23	....	....	....	....	....	....
1988-89	**Minnesota**	NHL	48	4	10	14	30	2	1	0	1	0
1989-90	Kalamazoo	IHL	20	10	14	24	16	....	....	....	....	....
1990-91	Bratislava	Czech.	11	11	5	16	20	....	....	....	....	....
	Asiago	Italy	34	35	41	76	22	3	5	1	6	0
	NHL Totals		48	4	10	14	30	2	1	0	1	0

PASIN, DAVE   (puh-SEEN)

Right wing. Shoots right. 6'1", 205 lbs.   Born, Edmonton, Alta., July 8, 1966.
(Boston's 1st choice, 19th overall, in 1984 Entry Draft).

				Regular Season					Playoffs			
Season	Club	Lea	GP	G	A	TP	PIM	GP	G	A	TP	PIM
1982-83	Prince Albert	WHL	62	40	42	82	48	....	....	....	....	....
1983-84	Prince Albert	WHL	71	68	54	122	68	5	1	4	5	0
1984-85a	Prince Albert	WHL	65	64	52	116	88	10	10	11	21	10
1985-86	**Boston**	NHL	71	18	19	37	50	3	0	1	1	0
1986-87	Moncton	AHL	66	27	25	52	47	6	1	1	2	14
1987-88	Maine	AHL	30	8	14	22	39	8	4	3	7	13
1988-89	Maine	AHL	11	2	5	7	6	....	....	....	....	....
	Los Angeles	NHL	5	0	0	0	0	....	....	....	....	....
	New Haven	AHL	48	25	23	48	42	17	8	8	16	47
1989-90	New Haven	AHL	7	7	4	11	14	....	....	....	....	....
	Springfield	AHL	11	2	3	5	2	3	1	2	3	2
1990-91	New Haven	AHL	39	13	25	38	57	....	....	....	....	....
	Phoenix	IHL	13	4	3	7	24	9	3	4	7	8
	NHL Totals		76	18	19	37	50	3	0	1	1	0

a WHL Second All-Star Team, East Division (1985).

Rights traded to **Los Angeles** by **Boston** for Paul Guay, November 3, 1988. Claimed on waivers by **NY Islanders** from **Los Angeles**, March 6, 1990.

PASLAWSKI, GREGORY STEPHEN (GREG) (pas-LAW-skee)

Right wing. Shoots right. 5'11", 190 lbs. Born, Kindersley, Sask., August 25, 1961.

			Regular Season					Playoffs				
Season	Club	Lea	GP	G	A	TP	PIM	GP	G	A	TP	PIM
1981-82	Nova Scotia	AHL	43	15	11	26	31	....	....	....	....	....
1982-83	Nova Scotia	AHL	75	46	42	88	32	6	1	3	4	8
1983-84	Montreal	NHL	26	1	4	5	4	....	....	....	....	....
	St. Louis	NHL	34	8	6	14	17	9	1	0	1	2
1984-85	St. Louis	NHL	72	22	20	42	21	3	0	0	0	2
1985-86	St. Louis	NHL	56	22	11	33	18	17	10	7	17	13
1986-87	St. Louis	NHL	76	29	35	64	27	6	1	1	2	4
1987-88	St. Louis	NHL	17	2	1	3	4	3	1	1	2	2
1988-89	St. Louis	NHL	75	26	26	52	18	9	2	1	3	2
1989-90	Winnipeg	NHL	71	18	30	48	14	7	1	3	4	0
1990-91	Winnipeg	NHL	43	9	10	19	10	....	....	....	....	....
	Buffalo	NHL	12	2	1	3	4	....	....	....	....	....
	NHL Totals		482	139	144	283	137	54	16	13	29	25

Signed as free agent by **Montreal**, October 5, 1981. Traded to **St. Louis** by **Montreal** with Gilbert Delorme and Doug Wickenheiser for Perry Turnbull, December 21, 1983. Traded to **Winnipeg** by **St. Louis** with St. Louis' third round choice (Kris Draper) in 1989 Entry Draft for Winnipeg's third round choice (Denny Felsner) in 1989 Entry Draft and second round choice (Steve Staios) in 1991 Entry Draft, June 17, 1989. Traded to **Buffalo** by **Winnipeg** for future considerations, February 4, 1991. Claimed by **San Jose** from **Buffalo** in Expansion Draft, May 30, 1991. Traded to **Quebec** by **San Jose** for Tony Hrkac, May 31, 1991.

PASMA, ROD

Defense. Shoots left. 6'4", 207 lbs. Born, Brampton, Ont., February 26, 1972.
(Washington's 2nd choice, 30th overall, in 1990 Entry Draft).

			Regular Season					Playoffs				
Season	Club	Lea	GP	G	A	TP	PIM	GP	G	A	TP	PIM
1989-90	Cornwall	OHL	64	3	16	19	142	6	0	2	2	15
1990-91	Cornwall	OHL	33	3	9	12	64	....	....	....	....	....
	Kingston	OHL	31	1	9	10	39	....	....	....	....	....

PATERSON, JOSEPH (JOE)

Left wing. Shoots left. 6'2", 207 lbs. Born, Toronto, Ont., June 25, 1960.
(Detroit's 5th choice, 87th overall, in 1979 Entry Draft).

			Regular Season					Playoffs				
Season	Club	Lea	GP	G	A	TP	PIM	GP	G	A	TP	PIM
1978-79	London	OHA	59	22	19	41	158	7	2	3	5	13
1979-80	London	OHA	62	21	50	71	156	....	....	....	....	....
	Kalamazoo	IHL	4	1	2	3	2	3	2	1	3	11
1980-81	Detroit	NHL	38	2	5	7	53	....	....	....	....	....
	Adirondack	AHL	39	9	16	25	68	....	....	....	....	....
1981-82	Detroit	NHL	3	0	0	0	0	....	....	....	....	....
	Adirondack	AHL	74	22	28	50	132	5	1	4	5	6
1982-83	Detroit	NHL	33	2	1	3	14	....	....	....	....	....
	Adirondack	AHL	36	11	10	21	85	6	1	2	3	21
1983-84	Detroit	NHL	41	2	5	7	148	3	0	0	0	7
	Adirondack	AHL	20	10	15	25	43	....	....	....	....	....
1984-85	Philadelphia	NHL	6	0	0	0	31	17	3	4	7	70
	Hershey	AHL	67	26	27	53	173	....	....	....	....	....
1985-86	Philadelphia	NHL	5	0	0	0	12	....	....	....	....	....
	Hershey	AHL	20	5	10	15	68	....	....	....	....	....
	Los Angeles	NHL	47	9	18	27	153	....	....	....	....	....
1986-87	Los Angeles	NHL	45	2	1	3	158	2	0	0	0	0
1987-88	Los Angeles	NHL	32	1	3	4	113	....	....	....	....	....
	NY Rangers	NHL	21	1	3	4	63	....	....	....	....	....
1988-89	NY Rangers	NHL	20	0	1	1	84	....	....	....	....	....
	Denver	IHL	9	5	4	9	31	....	....	....	....	....
1989-90	Flint	IHL	69	21	26	47	198	4	0	1	1	2
1990-91	Binghamton	AHL	80	16	35	51	221	10	5	3	8	25
	NHL Totals		291	19	37	56	829	22	3	4	7	77

Traded to **Philadelphia** by **Detroit** with Murray Craven for Darryl Sittler, October 19, 1984. Traded to **Los Angeles** by **Philadelphia** for Philadelphia's fourth-round choice (Mark Bar) — acquired earlier — in 1986 Entry Draft, December 18, 1985. Traded to **NY Rangers** by **Los Angeles** for Gordon Walker and Mike Siltala, January 21, 1988.

PATRICK, JAMES

Defense. Shoots right. 6'2", 204 lbs. Born, Winnipeg, Man., June 14, 1963.
(NY Rangers' 1st choice, 9th overall, in 1981 Entry Draft).

			Regular Season					Playoffs				
Season	Club	Lea	GP	G	A	TP	PIM	GP	G	A	TP	PIM
1981-82cde	North Dakota	WCHA	42	5	24	29	26	....	....	....	....	....
1982-83fg	North Dakota	WCHA	36	12	36	48	29	....	....	....	....	....
1983-84	Cdn. Olympic	...	63	7	24	31	52	....	....	....	....	....
	NY Rangers	NHL	12	1	7	8	2	5	0	3	3	2
1984-85	NY Rangers	NHL	75	8	28	36	71	3	0	0	0	4
1985-86	NY Rangers	NHL	75	14	29	43	88	16	1	5	6	34
1986-87	NY Rangers	NHL	78	10	45	55	62	6	1	2	3	2
1987-88	NY Rangers	NHL	70	17	45	62	52	....	....	....	....	....
1988-89	NY Rangers	NHL	68	11	36	47	41	4	0	1	1	2
1989-90	NY Rangers	NHL	73	14	43	57	50	10	3	8	11	0
1990-91	NY Rangers	NHL	74	10	49	59	58	6	0	0	0	6
	NHL Totals		525	85	282	367	424	50	5	19	24	50

a Most Valuable Player, 1981 Centennial Cup Tournament.
b First All-Star Team, 1981 Centennial Cup Tournament.
c WCHA Rookie of the Year (1982)
d WCHA Second All-Star Team (1982)
e Named to NCAA All-Tournament Team (1982)
f WCHA First All-Star Team (1983)
g NCAA All American (West) (1983)

PATTERSON, COLIN

Right wing/Left wing. Shoots right. 6'2", 195 lbs. Born, Rexdale, Ont., May 11, 1960.

			Regular Season					Playoffs				
Season	Club	Lea	GP	G	A	TP	PIM	GP	G	A	TP	PIM
1980-81	Clarkson	ECAC	34	20	31	51	8	....	....	....	....	....
1981-82	Clarkson	ECAC	34	21	31	52	32	....	....	....	....	....
1982-83	Clarkson	ECAC	31	23	29	52	30	....	....	....	....	....
	Colorado	CHL	7	1	1	2	0	3	0	0	0	15
1983-84	Calgary	NHL	56	13	14	27	15	11	1	1	2	6
	Colorado	CHL	6	2	3	5	9	....	....	....	....	....
1984-85	Calgary	NHL	57	22	21	43	5	4	0	0	0	5
1985-86	Calgary	NHL	61	14	13	27	22	19	6	3	9	10
1986-87	Calgary	NHL	68	13	13	26	41	6	0	2	2	2
1987-88	Calgary	NHL	39	7	11	18	28	9	1	0	1	8
1988-89	Calgary	NHL	74	14	24	38	56	22	3	10	13	24
1989-90	Calgary	NHL	61	5	3	8	20	....	....	....	....	....
1990-91	Calgary	NHL	....	....	....	....	....	1	0	0	0	0
	NHL Totals		416	88	99	187	187	72	11	16	27	55

Signed as a free agent by **Calgary** March 24, 1983.

PAVLAS, PETR (PAHV-lahs)

Defense. Shoots left. 5'10", 172 lbs. Born, Olomouc, Czechoslovakia, February 4, 1968.
(Washington's 10th choice, 183rd overall, in 1988 Entry Draft).

			Regular Season					Playoffs				
Season	Club	Lea	GP	G	A	TP	PIM	GP	G	A	TP	PIM
1987-88	Dukla Trencin	Czech.	20	4	7	11	....	....	....	....	....	....
1988-89	Dukla Trencin	Czech.	31	14	15	29	....	....	....	....	....	....
1989-90	TJ Zlin	Czech.	51	13	15	28	....	....	....	....	....	....
1990-91	TJ Zlin	Czech.	48	14	20	34	16	....	....	....	....	....

PAYNE, DAVIS

Left wing. Shoots left. 6'1", 190 lbs. Born, King City, Ont., October 24, 1970.
(Edmonton's 6th choice, 140th overall, in 1989 Entry Draft).

			Regular Season					Playoffs				
Season	Club	Lea	GP	G	A	TP	PIM	GP	G	A	TP	PIM
1988-89	Michigan Tech	WCHA	33	5	3	8	39	....	....	....	....	....
1989-90	Michigan Tech	WCHA	36	11	10	21	81	....	....	....	....	....
1990-91	Michigan Tech	WCHA	41	15	20	35	82	....	....	....	....	....

PAYNTER, KENT

Defense. Shoots left. 6', 183 lbs. Born, Summerside, PEI, April 17, 1965.
(Chicago's 9th choice, 159th overall, in 1983 Entry Draft).

			Regular Season					Playoffs				
Season	Club	Lea	GP	G	A	TP	PIM	GP	G	A	TP	PIM
1982-83	Kitchener	OHL	65	4	11	15	97	12	1	0	1	20
1983-84	Kitchener	OHL	65	9	27	36	94	16	4	9	13	18
1984-85	Kitchener	OHL	58	7	28	35	93	4	2	1	3	4
1985-86	Nova Scotia	AHL	23	1	2	3	36	....	....	....	....	....
	Saginaw	IHL	4	0	1	1	2	....	....	....	....	....
1986-87	Nova Scotia	AHL	66	2	6	8	57	2	0	0	0	0
1987-88	Chicago	NHL	2	0	0	0	2	....	....	....	....	....
	Saginaw	IHL	74	8	20	28	141	10	0	1	1	30
1988-89	Chicago	NHL	1	0	0	0	2	....	....	....	....	....
	Saginaw	IHL	69	12	14	26	148	6	2	2	4	17
1989-90	Washington	NHL	13	1	2	3	18	3	0	0	0	10
	Baltimore	AHL	60	7	20	27	110	11	5	6	11	34
1990-91	Washington	NHL	1	0	0	0	15	1	0	0	0	0
	Baltimore	AHL	43	10	17	27	64	6	2	1	3	8
	NHL Totals		17	1	2	3	37	4	0	0	0	10

Signed as a free agent by **Washington**, August 21, 1989. Traded to **Winnipeg** by **Washington** with Tyler Larter and Bob Joyce for Craig Duncanson, Brent Hughes and Simon Wheeldon, May 21, 1991.

PEACOCK, SHANE

Defense. Shoots right. 5'9", 198 lbs. Born, Edmonton, Alta., July 7, 1973.
(Pittsburg's 3rd choice, 60th overall, in 1991 Entry Draft).

			Regular Season					Playoffs				
Season	Club	Lea	GP	G	A	TP	PIM	GP	G	A	TP	PIM
1989-90	Lethbridge	WHL	65	7	23	30	60	19	2	8	10	42
1990-91	Lethbridge	WHL	69	12	50	62	102	16	1	14	15	26

PEAKE, PAT

Defense. Shoots right. 6', 185 lbs. Born, Detroit, MI, May 28, 1973.
(Washington's 1st choice, 14th overall, in 1991 Entry Draft).

			Regular Season					Playoffs				
Season	Club	Lea	GP	G	A	TP	PIM	GP	G	A	TP	PIM
1989-90	Detroit Comp.	USHL	34	33	44	77	48	....	....	....	....	....
1990-91	Detroit	OHL	63	39	51	90	54	....	....	....	....	....

PEARCE, RANDY

Left wing. Shoots left. 5'11", 203 lbs. Born, Kitchener, Ont., February 23, 1970.
(Washington's 4th choice, 72nd overall, in 1990 Entry Draft).

			Regular Season					Playoffs				
Season	Club	Lea	GP	G	A	TP	PIM	GP	G	A	TP	PIM
1988-89	Kitchener	OHL	64	23	21	44	87	5	0	1	1	6
1989-90	Kitchener	OHL	62	31	34	65	139	17	8	15	23	42
1990-91			DID NOT PLAY - INJURED									

PEARSON, ROB

Right wing. Shoots right. 6'1", 185 lbs. Born, Oshawa, Ont., August 3, 1971.
(Toronto's 2nd choice, 12th overall, in 1989 Entry Draft).

			Regular Season					Playoffs				
Season	Club	Lea	GP	G	A	TP	PIM	GP	G	A	TP	PIM
1988-89	Belleville	OHL	26	8	12	20	51	....	....	....	....	....
1989-90	Belleville	OHL	58	48	40	88	174	11	5	5	10	26
1990-91	Belleville	OHL	10	6	3	9	27	....	....	....	....	....
a	Oshawa	OHL	41	57	52	109	76	16	16	17	33	39
	Newmarket	AHL	3	0	0	0	29	....	....	....	....	....

a OHL First All-Star Team (1991)

PEARSON, SCOTT

Left wing. Shoots left. 6'1", 205 lbs.   Born, Cornwall, Ont., December 19, 1969.
(Toronto's 1st choice, 6th overall, in 1988 Entry Draft).

			Regular Season					Playoffs				
Season	Club	Lea	GP	G	A	TP	PIM	GP	G	A	TP	PIM
1986-87	Kingston	OHL	62	30	24	54	101	9	3	3	6	42
1987-88	Kingston	OHL	46	26	32	58	117	....	....	....	....	....
1988-89	**Toronto**	**NHL**	**9**	**0**	**1**	**1**	**2**	....	....	....	....	....
	Kingston	OHL	13	9	8	17	34	....	....	....	....	....
	Niagara Falls	OHL	32	26	34	60	90	17	14	10	24	53
1989-90	**Toronto**	**NHL**	**41**	**5**	**10**	**15**	**90**	**2**	**2**	**0**	**2**	**10**
	Newmarket	AHL	18	12	11	23	64	....	....	....	....	....
1990-91	**Toronto**	**NHL**	**12**	**0**	**0**	**0**	**20**	....	....	....	....	....
	Quebec	**NHL**	**35**	**11**	**4**	**15**	**86**	....	....	....	....	....
	Halifax	AHL	24	12	15	27	44	....	....	....	....	....
	NHL Totals		**97**	**16**	**15**	**31**	**198**	**2**	**2**	**0**	**2**	**10**

Traded to **Quebec** by **Toronto** with Toronto's second round choices in 1991 (later traded to Washington - Eric Lavigne) and 1992 Entry Drafts for Aaron Broten, Lucien Deblois and Michel Petit, November 17, 1990.

PEDERSEN, ALLEN

Defense. Shoots left. 6'3", 210 lbs.   Born, Fort Saskatchewan, Alta., January 13, 1965.
(Boston's 5th choice, 105th overall, in 1983 Entry Draft).

			Regular Season					Playoffs				
Season	Club	Lea	GP	G	A	TP	PIM	GP	G	A	TP	PIM
1982-83	Medicine Hat	WHL	63	3	10	13	49	5	0	0	0	7
1983-84	Medicine Hat	WHL	44	0	11	11	47	14	0	2	2	24
1984-85	Medicine Hat	WHL	72	6	16	22	66	10	0	0	0	9
1985-86	Moncton	AHL	59	1	8	9	39	3	0	0	0	0
1986-87	**Boston**	**NHL**	**79**	**1**	**11**	**12**	**71**	**4**	**0**	**0**	**0**	**4**
1987-88	**Boston**	**NHL**	**78**	**0**	**6**	**6**	**90**	**21**	**0**	**0**	**0**	**34**
1988-89	**Boston**	**NHL**	**51**	**0**	**6**	**6**	**69**	**10**	**0**	**0**	**0**	**2**
1989-90	**Boston**	**NHL**	**68**	**1**	**2**	**3**	**71**	**21**	**0**	**0**	**0**	**41**
1990-91	**Boston**	**NHL**	**57**	**2**	**6**	**8**	**107**	**8**	**0**	**0**	**0**	**10**
	Maine	AHL	15	0	6	6	18	2	0	1	1	2
	NHL Totals		**333**	**4**	**31**	**35**	**408**	**64**	**0**	**0**	**0**	**91**

Claimed by **Minnesota** from **Boston** in Expansion Draft, May 30, 1991.

PEDERSON, BARRY ALAN   (PEE-duhr-suhn)

Center. Shoots right. 5'11", 185 lbs.   Born, Big River, Sask., March 13, 1961.
(Boston's 1st choice, 18th overall, in 1980 Entry Draft).

			Regular Season					Playoffs				
Season	Club	Lea	GP	G	A	TP	PIM	GP	G	A	TP	PIM
1978-79	Victoria	WHL	72	31	53	84	41	....	....	....	....	....
1979-80	Victoria	WHL	72	52	88	140	50	16	13	14	27	31
1980-81	**Boston**	**NHL**	**9**	**1**	**4**	**5**	**6**	....	....	....	....	....
a	Victoria	WHL	55	65	82	147	65	15	15	21	36	10
1981-82	Boston	NHL	80	44	48	92	53	11	7	11	18	2
1982-83	Boston	NHL	77	46	61	107	47	17	14	18	32	21
1983-84	Boston	NHL	80	39	77	116	64	3	0	1	1	2
1984-85	Boston	NHL	22	4	8	12	10	....	....	....	....	....
1985-86	Boston	NHL	79	29	47	76	60	3	1	0	1	0
1986-87	Vancouver	NHL	79	24	52	76	50	....	....	....	....	....
1987-88	Vancouver	NHL	76	19	52	71	92	....	....	....	....	....
1988-89	Vancouver	NHL	62	15	26	41	22	....	....	....	....	....
1989-90	Vancouver	NHL	16	2	7	9	10	....	....	....	....	....
	Pittsburgh	NHL	38	4	18	22	29	....	....	....	....	....
1990-91	Pittsburgh	NHL	46	6	8	14	21	....	....	....	....	....
	NHL Totals		**664**	**233**	**408**	**641**	**464**	**34**	**22**	**30**	**52**	**25**

a WHL First All-Star Team (1981)
Played in NHL All-Star Game (1983, 1984)
Traded to **Vancouver** by **Boston** for Cam Neely and Vancouver's first-round choice in 1987 Entry Draft (Glen Wesley), June 6, 1986. Traded to **Pittsburgh** by **Vancouver** with Rod Buskas and Tony Tanti for Dave Capuano, Andrew McBain and Dan Quinn, January 8, 1990.

PEDERSON, MARK

Left wing. Shoots left. 6'2", 196 lbs.   Born, Prelate, Sask., January 14, 1968.
(Montreal's 1st choice, 15th overall, in 1986 Entry Draft).

			Regular Season					Playoffs				
Season	Club	Lea	GP	G	A	TP	PIM	GP	G	A	TP	PIM
1984-85	Medicine Hat	WHL	71	42	40	82	63	10	3	2	5	0
1985-86	Medicine Hat	WHL	72	46	60	106	46	25	12	6	18	25
1986-87a	Medicine Hat	WHL	69	56	46	102	58	20	*19	7	26	14
1987-88	Medicine Hat	WHL	62	53	58	111	55	16	*13	6	19	16
1988-89	Sherbrooke	AHL	75	43	38	81	53	6	7	5	12	4
1989-90	**Montreal**	**NHL**	**9**	**0**	**2**	**2**	**2**	**2**	**0**	**0**	**0**	**0**
b	Sherbrooke	AHL	72	53	42	95	60	11	10	8	18	19
1990-91	**Montreal**	**NHL**	**47**	**8**	**15**	**23**	**18**	....	....	....	....	....
	Philadelphia	**NHL**	**12**	**2**	**1**	**3**	**5**	....	....	....	....	....
	NHL Totals		**68**	**10**	**18**	**28**	**25**	**2**	**0**	**0**	**0**	**0**

a WHL East All-Star Team (1987)
b AHL First All-Star Team (1990)
Traded to **Philadelphia** by **Montreal** for Philadelphia's second round choice (Jim Campbell) in 1991 Entry Draft, March 5, 1991.

PEDERSON, THOMAS

Defense. Shoots right. 5'9", 165 lbs.   Born, Bloomington, MN, January 14, 1970.
(Minnesota's 12th choice, 217th overall, in 1989 Entry Draft).

			Regular Season					Playoffs				
Season	Club	Lea	GP	G	A	TP	PIM	GP	G	A	TP	PIM
1988-89	U. Minnesota	WCHA	36	4	20	24	40	....	....	....	....	....
1989-90	U. Minnesota	WCHA	43	8	30	38	58	....	....	....	....	....
1990-91	U. Minnesota	WCHA	36	12	20	32	46	....	....	....	....	....

Claimed by **San Jose** from **Minnesota** in Dispersal Draft, May 30, 1991.

PELLERIN, BRIAN

Right wing. Shoots right. 5'10", 175 lbs.   Born, Hinton, Alta., February 20, 1970.

			Regular Season					Playoffs				
Season	Club	Lea	GP	G	A	TP	PIM	GP	G	A	TP	PIM
1987-88	Prince Albert	WHL	62	6	2	8	113	10	0	0	0	17
1988-89	Prince Albert	WHL	60	17	16	33	216	3	0	1	1	27
1989-90	Prince Albert	WHL	53	6	15	21	175	10	1	3	4	26
1990-91a	Prince Albert	WHL	68	46	42	88	223	3	0	0	0	12

Signed as a free agent by **St. Louis**, May 31, 1991.
a WHL East First All-Star Team (1991)

PELLERIN, SCOTT

Left wing. Shoots left. 5'11", 180 lbs.   Born, Shediac, N.B., January 9, 1970.
(New Jersey's 4th choice, 47th overall, in 1989 Entry Draft).

			Regular Season					Playoffs				
Season	Club	Lea	GP	G	A	TP	PIM	GP	G	A	TP	PIM
1988-89a	U. of Maine	H.E.	45	29	33	62	92	....	....	....	....	....
1989-90	U. of Maine	H.E.	42	22	34	56	68	....	....	....	....	....
1990-91	U. of Maine	H.E.	43	23	25	48	60	....	....	....	....	....

a Co-winner Hockey East Rookie of the Year (1989)

PELTOLA, PEKKA   (PEHL-TUH-lah)

Right wing. Shoots left. 6'2" 194 lbs.   Born, Helsinki, Finland, April 24, 1965.
(Winnipeg's 8th choice, 130th overall, in 1989 Entry Draft).

			Regular Season					Playoffs				
Season	Club	Lea	GP	G	A	TP	PIM	GP	G	A	TP	PIM
1988-89	HPK	Fin.	43	28	30	58	62	....	....	....	....	....
1989-90	HPK	Fin.	45	25	24	49	42	....	....	....	....	....
1990-91	HPK	Fin.	41	23	18	41	66	8	3	2	5	10

PELTOMAA, TIMO   (PEHL-TUH-mah)

Right wing. Shoots right. 6'1", 194 lbs.   Born, Tampere, Finland, July 26, 1968.
(Los Angeles' 9th choice, 154th overall, in 1988 Entry Draft).

			Regular Season					Playoffs				
Season	Club	Lea	GP	G	A	TP	PIM	GP	G	A	TP	PIM
1987-88	Ilves	Fin.	20	0	1	1	32	....	....	....	....	....
1988-89	Ilves	Fin.	23	4	0	4	16	....	....	....	....	....
1989-90	Ilves	Fin.	43	7	3	10	28	....	....	....	....	....
1990-91	Ilves	Fin.	44	8	16	24	63	....	....	....	....	....

PELUSO, MIKE

Left wing/Defense. Shoots left. 6'4", 200 lbs.   Born, Pengilly, MN, November 8, 1965.
(New Jersey's 10th choice, 190th overall, in 1984 Entry Draft).

			Regular Season					Playoffs				
Season	Club	Lea	GP	G	A	TP	PIM	GP	G	A	TP	PIM
1985-86	Alaska-Anch.	NCAA	32	2	11	13	59	....	....	....	....	....
1986-87	Alaska-Anch.	NCAA	30	5	21	26	68	....	....	....	....	....
1987-88	Alaska-Anch.	NCAA	35	4	33	37	76	....	....	....	....	....
1988-89	Alaska-Anch.	NCAA	33	10	27	37	75	....	....	....	....	....
1989-90	**Chicago**	**NHL**	**2**	**0**	**0**	**0**	**0**	....	....	....	....	....
	Indianapolis	IHL	75	7	10	17	279	14	0	1	1	58
1990-91	**Chicago**	**NHL**	**53**	**6**	**1**	**7**	**320**	**3**	**0**	**0**	**0**	**2**
	Indianapolis	IHL	6	2	1	3	21	5	0	2	2	40
	NHL Totals		**55**	**6**	**1**	**7**	**320**	**3**	**0**	**0**	**0**	**2**

Signed as a free agent by **Chicago**, September 7, 1989.

PENNEY, JACKSON

Center. Shoots left. 5'10", 180 lbs.   Born, Edmonton, Alta., February 5, 1969.
(Boston's 4th choice, 80th overall, in 1989 Entry Draft).

			Regular Season					Playoffs				
Season	Club	Lea	GP	G	A	TP	PIM	GP	G	A	TP	PIM
1987-88	Victoria	WHL	53	22	36	58	31	8	3	2	5	14
1988-89a	Victoria	WHL	63	41	49	90	78	8	6	3	9	12
1989-90	Victoria	WHL	3	0	1	1	4	....	....	....	....	....
b	Prince Albert	WHL	55	53	32	85	91	12	11	4	15	28
1990-91	Kalamazoo	IHL	56	17	11	28	18	....	....	....	....	....

a WHL East First All-Star Team (1989)
b WHL East Second All-Star Team (1990)

PERGOLA, DAVID

Right wing. Shoots right. 6'1", 185 lbs.   Born, Waltham, MA, March 4, 1969.
(Buffalo's 5th choice, 85th overall, in 1987 Entry Draft).

			Regular Season					Playoffs				
Season	Club	Lea	GP	G	A	TP	PIM	GP	G	A	TP	PIM
1987-88	Boston College	H.E.	33	5	7	12	22	....	....	....	....	....
1988-89	Boston College	H.E.	39	12	9	21	16	....	....	....	....	....
1989-90	Boston College	H.E.	39	6	4	10	22	....	....	....	....	....
1990-91	Boston College	H.E.	35	8	12	20	24	....	....	....	....	....

PERREAULT, NICOLAS P.

Defense. Shoots left. 6'3", 200 lbs.   Born, Loretteville, Que., April 24, 1972.
(Calgary's 2nd choice, 26th overall, in 1990 Entry Draft).

			Regular Season					Playoffs				
Season	Club	Lea	GP	G	A	TP	PIM	GP	G	A	TP	PIM
1989-90	Hawkesbury	COJHL	46	22	34	56	188	....	....	....	....	....
1990-91	Michigan State	CCHA	34	1	7	8	32	....	....	....	....	....

PERREAULT, YANIC

Center. Shoots left. 5'11", 182 lbs.   Born, Sherbrooke, Que., April 4, 1971.
(Toronto's 1st choice, 47th overall, in 1991 Entry Draft).

			Regular Season					Playoffs				
Season	Club	Lea	GP	G	A	TP	PIM	GP	G	A	TP	PIM
1988-89	Trois-Rivières	QMJHL	70	53	55	108	48	....	....	....	....	....
1989-90	Trois-Rivières	QMJHL	63	51	63	114	75	7	6	5	11	19
1990-91a	Trois-Rivières	QMJHL	67	*87	98	*185	103	6	4	7	11	6

a QMJHL First All-Star Team (1991)

PERSSON, JOAKIM (PEHR-suhn)

Left wing. Shoots left. 5'8", 169 lbs. Born, Gavle, Sweden, May 15, 1966.
(Chicago's 10th choice, 195th overall, in 1984 Entry Draft).

			Regular Season					Playoffs				
Season	Club	Lea	GP	G	A	TP	PIM	GP	G	A	TP	PIM
1985-86	Stromsbro	Swe.	35	8	8	13	2	2	0	0	0	0
1986-87	Brynas	Swe.	34	9	8	17	10	....	....	....	....	....
1987-88	Stromsbro	Swe.	37	10	11	21	12	....	....	....	....	....
1988-89	Brynas	Swe.	39	7	10	17	22	....	....	....	....	....
1989-90	Brynas	Swe.	39	12	8	20	8	5	1	2	3	8
1990-91	Brynas	Swe.	40	3	4	7	18	....	....	....	....	....

PETERSON, BRETT

Defense. Shoots right. 6'2", 195 lbs. Born, St. Paul, MN, February 1, 1969.
(Calgary's 9th choice, 189th overall, in 1988 Entry Draft).

			Regular Season					Playoffs				
Season	Club	Lea	GP	G	A	TP	PIM	GP	G	A	TP	PIM
1988-89	U. of Denver	WCHA	19	0	3	3	4	....	....	....	....	....
1989-90	U. of Denver	WCHA	34	3	6	9	23	....	....	....	....	....
1990-91	U. of Denver	WCHA	37	2	9	11	28	....	....	....	....	....

PETERSON, ERIK

Center. Shoots left. 6', 185 lbs. Born, Boston, MA, March 31, 1972.
(Chicago's 8th choice, 205th overall, in 1990 Entry Draft).

			Regular Season					Playoffs				
Season	Club	Lea	GP	G	A	TP	PIM	GP	G	A	TP	PIM
1989-90	Brockton	HS	....	31	24	55	0	....	....	....	....	....
1990-91	Providence	H.E.	34	8	4	12	12	....	....	....	....	....

PETIT, MICHEL (puh-TEE)

Defense. Shoots right. 6'1", 205 lbs. Born, St. Malo, Que., February 12, 1964.
(Vancouver's 1st choice, 11th overall, in 1982 Entry Draft).

			Regular Season					Playoffs				
Season	Club	Lea	GP	G	A	TP	PIM	GP	G	A	TP	PIM
1981-82a	Sherbrooke	QMJHL	63	10	39	49	106	22	5	20	25	24
1982-83	**Vancouver**	**NHL**	**2**	**0**	**0**	**0**	**0**	....	....	....	....	....
a	St. Jean	QMJHL	62	19	67	86	196	3	0	0	0	35
1983-84	Cdn. Olympic	...	19	3	10	13	58	....	....	....	....	....
	Vancouver	**NHL**	**44**	**6**	**9**	**15**	**53**	**1**	**0**	**0**	**0**	**0**
1984-85	**Vancouver**	**NHL**	**69**	**5**	**26**	**31**	**127**	....	....	....	....	....
1985-86	**Vancouver**	**NHL**	**32**	**1**	**6**	**7**	**27**	....	....	....	....	....
	Fredericton	AHL	25	0	13	13	79	....	....	....	....	....
1986-87	**Vancouver**	**NHL**	**69**	**12**	**13**	**25**	**131**	....	....	....	....	....
1987-88	**Vancouver**	**NHL**	**10**	**0**	**3**	**3**	**35**	....	....	....	....	....
	NY Rangers	**NHL**	**64**	**9**	**24**	**33**	**223**	....	....	....	....	....
1988-89	**NY Rangers**	**NHL**	**69**	**8**	**25**	**33**	**154**	**4**	**0**	**2**	**2**	**27**
1989-90	**Quebec**	**NHL**	**63**	**12**	**24**	**36**	**215**	....	....	....	....	....
1990-91	**Quebec**	**NHL**	**19**	**4**	**7**	**11**	**47**	....	....	....	....	....
	Toronto	**NHL**	**54**	**9**	**19**	**28**	**132**	....	....	....	....	....
	NHL Totals		**495**	**66**	**156**	**222**	**1144**	**5**	**0**	**2**	**2**	**27**

a QMJHL First All-Star Team (1982, 1983)

Traded to **NY Rangers** by **Vancouver** for Willie Huber and Larry Melnyk, November 4, 1987. Traded to **Quebec** by **NY Rangers** for Randy Moller, October 5, 1989. Traded to **Toronto** by **Quebec** with Aaron Broten and Lucien Deblois for Scott Pearson and Toronto's second round choices in 1991 (later traded to Washington - Eric Lavigne) and 1992 Entry Drafts, November 17, 1990.

PHILLIPS, GUY

Right wing. Shoots right. 6', 178 lbs. Born, Brooks, Alta., February 13, 1966.

			Regular Season					Playoffs				
Season	Club	Lea	GP	G	A	TP	PIM	GP	G	A	TP	PIM
1984-85	Medicine Hat	WHL	67	16	18	34	46	6	3	3	6	4
1985-86	Medicine Hat	WHL	72	38	55	93	66	25	10	13	23	7
1986-87	Medicine Hat	WHL	44	27	32	59	36	20	10	12	22	16
1987-88	Saginaw	IHL	73	16	30	46	14	8	2	1	3	0
1988-89	Saginaw	IHL	62	20	17	37	31	5	0	0	0	0
1989-90	Indianapolis	IHL	33	4	4	8	24	2	0	0	0	0
	Nashville	ECHL	3	3	4	7	2	....	....	....	....	....
1990-91	Hershey	AHL	60	12	13	25	17	4	0	0	0	0

Signed as a free agent by **Chicago**, December 30, 1987.

PICARD, MICHEL

Left wing. Shoots left. 5'11", 190 lbs. Born, Beauport, Que., November 7, 1969.
(Hartford's 8th choice, 178th overall, in 1989 Entry Draft).

			Regular Season					Playoffs				
Season	Club	Lea	GP	G	A	TP	PIM	GP	G	A	TP	PIM
1986-87	Trois-Rivieres	QMJHL	66	33	35	68	53	....	....	....	....	....
1987-88	Trois-Rivieres	QMJHL	69	40	55	95	71	....	....	....	....	....
1988-89	Trois-Rivieres	QMJHL	66	59	81	140	170	4	1	3	4	2
1989-90	Binghamton	AHL	67	16	24	40	98	....	....	....	....	....
1990-91	**Hartford**	**NHL**	**5**	**1**	**0**	**1**	**2**	....	....	....	....	....
a	Springfield	AHL	77	*56	40	96	61	18	8	13	21	18
	NHL Totals		**5**	**1**	**0**	**1**	**2**	....	....	....	....	....

a AHL First All-Star Team (1991)

PIIPARINEN, JARKKO (pee-PAH-ree-nehn)

Left wing. Shoots left. 6'2", 202 lbs. Born, Lahti, Finland, April 18, 1966.
(New Jersey's 11th choice, 211th overall, in 1984 Entry Draft).

			Regular Season					Playoffs				
Season	Club	Lea	GP	G	A	TP	PIM	GP	G	A	TP	PIM
1988-89	Reipas	Fin.	18	5	9	14	22	....	....	....	....	....
1989-90	Reipas	Fin.	44	10	30	40	20	....	....	....	....	....
1990-91	Reipas	Fin.	40	7	5	12	22	....	....	....	....	....

PILON, RICHARD

Defense. Shoots left. 6', 202 lbs. Born, Saskatoon, Sask., April 30, 1968.
(NY Islanders' 9th choice, 143rd overall, in 1986 Entry Draft).

			Regular Season					Playoffs				
Season	Club	Lea	GP	G	A	TP	PIM	GP	G	A	TP	PIM
1986-87	Prince Albert	WHL	68	4	21	25	192	7	1	6	7	17
1987-88	Prince Albert	WHL	65	13	34	47	177	9	0	6	6	38
1988-89	**NY Islanders**	**NHL**	**62**	**0**	**14**	**14**	**242**	....	....	....	....	....
1989-90	**NY Islanders**	**NHL**	**14**	**0**	**2**	**2**	**31**	....	....	....	....	....
1990-91	**NY Islanders**	**NHL**	**60**	**1**	**4**	**5**	**126**	....	....	....	....	....
	NHL Totals		**136**	**1**	**20**	**21**	**399**	....	....	....	....	....

PION, RICHARD

Right wing. Shoots right. 5'10", 180 lbs. Born, Montreal, Que., July 20, 1965.

			Regular Season					Playoffs				
Season	Club	Lea	GP	G	A	TP	PIM	GP	G	A	TP	PIM
1985-86	Merrimack	NCAA	14	9	13	22	10	....	....	....	....	....
1986-87	Merrimack	NCAA	37	31	33	64	46	....	....	....	....	....
1987-88	Merrimack	NCAA	40	35	40	75	58	4	3	3	6	....
1988-89	Merrimack	NCAA	34	28	42	70	34	....	....	....	....	....
1989-90	Peoria	IHL	69	10	21	31	58	5	0	0	0	0
1990-91	Peoria	IHL	76	14	24	38	113	17	3	5	8	36

Signed as a free agent by **St. Louis**, August 21, 1989.

PITLICK, LANCE

Defense. Shoots right. 6', 185 lbs. Born, Minneapolis, MN, November 5, 1967.
(Minnesota's 10th choice, 180th overall, in 1986 Entry Draft).

			Regular Season					Playoffs				
Season	Club	Lea	GP	G	A	TP	PIM	GP	G	A	TP	PIM
1986-87	U. Minnesota	WCHA	45	0	9	9	88	....	....	....	....	....
1987-88	U. Minnesota	WCHA	38	3	9	12	76	....	....	....	....	....
1988-89	U. Minnesota	WCHA	47	4	9	13	95	....	....	....	....	....
1989-90	U. Minnesota	WCHA	14	3	2	5	26	....	....	....	....	....
1990-91	Hershey	AHL	64	6	15	21	75	3	0	0	0	9

PIVONKA, MICHAL (pih-VAHN-kuh)

Left wing. Shoots left. 6'2", 198 lbs. Born, Kladno, Czechoslovakia, January 28, 1966.
(Washington's 3rd choice, 59th overall, in 1984 Entry Draft).

			Regular Season					Playoffs				
Season	Club	Lea	GP	G	A	TP	PIM	GP	G	A	TP	PIM
1985-86	Dukla Jihlava	Czech.	UNAVAILABLE									
1986-87	**Washington**	**NHL**	**73**	**18**	**25**	**43**	**41**	**7**	**1**	**1**	**2**	**2**
1987-88	**Washington**	**NHL**	**71**	**11**	**23**	**34**	**28**	**14**	**4**	**9**	**13**	**4**
1988-89	**Washington**	**NHL**	**52**	**8**	**19**	**27**	**30**	**6**	**3**	**1**	**4**	**10**
	Baltimore	AHL	31	12	24	36	19	....	....	....	....	....
1989-90	**Washington**	**NHL**	**77**	**25**	**39**	**64**	**54**	**11**	**0**	**2**	**2**	**6**
1990-91	**Washington**	**NHL**	**79**	**20**	**50**	**70**	**34**	**11**	**2**	**3**	**5**	**8**
	NHL Totals		**352**	**82**	**156**	**238**	**187**	**49**	**10**	**16**	**26**	**30**

PLAGER, KEVIN

Right wing. Shoots right. 5'11", 180 lbs. Born, St. Louis, MO, April 25, 1971.
(St. Louis' 8th choice, 156th overall, in 1989 Entry Draft).

			Regular Season					Playoffs				
Season	Club	Lea	GP	G	A	TP	PIM	GP	G	A	TP	PIM
1990-91	Kalamazoo	USHL	38	14	20	34	155	....	....	....	....	....

PLANTE, DAN

Right wing. Shoots right. 5'11", 198 lbs. Born, St. Louis, MO, October 5, 1971.
(NY Islanders' 3rd choice, 48th overall, in 1990 Entry Draft).

			Regular Season					Playoffs				
Season	Club	Lea	GP	G	A	TP	PIM	GP	G	A	TP	PIM
1989-90	Edina	HS	24	8	18	26	....	....	....	....	....	....
1990-91	U. Wisconsin	WCHA	33	1	2	3	54	....	....	....	....	....

PLANTE, DEREK

Center. Shoots left. 5'11", 160 lbs. Born, Duluth, MN, January 17, 1971.
(Buffalo's 7th choice, 161st overall, in 1989 Entry Draft).

			Regular Season					Playoffs				
Season	Club	Lea	GP	G	A	TP	PIM	GP	G	A	TP	PIM
1989-90	Minn.-Duluth	WCHA	28	10	11	21	12	....	....	....	....	....
1990-91	Minn.-Duluth	WCHA	36	23	20	43	6	....	....	....	....	....

PLAQUIN, KEN

Defense. Shoots left. 6'2", 190 lbs. Born, Calgary, Alta., February 22, 1970.
(Pittsburgh's 8th choice, 131st overall, in 1990 Entry Draft).

			Regular Season					Playoffs				
Season	Club	Lea	GP	G	A	TP	PIM	GP	G	A	TP	PIM
1989-90	Michigan Tech	WCHA	33	2	13	15	20	....	....	....	....	....
1990-91	Michigan Tech	WCHA	37	3	6	9	8	....	....	....	....	....

PLAVSIC, ADRIEN

Defense. Shoots left. 6'1", 190 lbs. Born, Montreal, Que., January 13, 1970.
(St. Louis' 2nd choice, 30th overall, in 1988 Entry Draft).

			Regular Season					Playoffs				
Season	Club	Lea	GP	G	A	TP	PIM	GP	G	A	TP	PIM
1987-88	N. Hampshire	H.E.	30	5	6	11	45	....	....	....	....	....
1988-89	Cdn. National	...	62	5	10	15	25	....	....	....	....	....
1989-90	**St. Louis**	**NHL**	**4**	**0**	**1**	**1**	**2**	....	....	....	....	....
	Peoria	IHL	51	7	14	21	87	....	....	....	....	....
	Vancouver	**NHL**	**11**	**3**	**2**	**5**	**8**	....	....	....	....	....
	Milwaukee	IHL	3	1	2	3	14	6	1	3	4	6
1990-91	**Vancouver**	**NHL**	**48**	**2**	**10**	**12**	**62**	....	....	....	....	....
	NHL Totals		**63**	**5**	**13**	**18**	**72**	....	....	....	....	....

Traded to **Vancouver** by **St. Louis** with Montreal's first round choice (Shawn Antoski) – previously acquired by St. Louis – in 1990 Entry Draft and St. Louis' second round choice in 1991 Entry Draft for Rich Sutter, Harold Snepsts and St. Louis' second round choice (Craig Johnson) – previously acquired by Vancouver – in 1990 Entry Draft, March 6, 1990.

PLAYFAIR, JAMES (JIM)

Defense. Shoots left. 6'4", 200 lbs. Born, Fort St. James, B.C., May 22, 1964.
(Edmonton's 1st choice, 20th overall, in 1982 Entry Draft).

			Regular Season					Playoffs				
Season	Club	Lea	GP	G	A	TP	PIM	GP	G	A	TP	PIM
1981-82	Portland	WHL	70	4	13	17	121	15	1	2	3	21
1982-83	Portland	WHL	63	8	27	35	218	14	0	5	5	16
1983-84	**Edmonton**	**NHL**	**2**	**1**	**1**	**2**	**2**	....	....	....	....	....
	Portland	WHL	16	5	6	11	38	....	....	....	....	....
	Calgary	WHL	60	11	15	26	134	4	0	1	1	2
1984-85	Nova Scotia	AHL	41	0	4	4	107	....	....	....	....	....
1985-86	Nova Scotia	AHL	73	2	12	14	160	....	....	....	....	....
1986-87	Nova Scotia	AHL	60	1	21	22	82	....	....	....	....	....
1987-88	**Chicago**	**NHL**	**12**	**1**	**3**	**4**	**21**	....	....	....	....	....
	Saginaw	IHL	50	5	21	26	133	....	....	....	....	....
1988-89	**Chicago**	**NHL**	**7**	**0**	**0**	**0**	**28**	....	....	....	....	....
	Saginaw	IHL	23	3	6	9	73	6	0	2	2	20
1989-90	Indianapolis	IHL	67	7	24	31	137	14	1	5	6	24
1990-91	Indianapolis	IHL	23	3	4	7	31	....	....	....	....	....
	NHL Totals		**21**	**2**	**4**	**6**	**51**	....	....	....	....	....

Signed as a free agent by **Chicago**, July 31, 1987.

POCHIPINSKI, TREVOR

Defense. Shoots right. 6'2", 190 lbs. Born, Prince Albert, Sask., July 8, 1968.
(Los Angeles' 9th choice, 170th overall, in 1986 Entry Draft).

			Regular Season					Playoffs				
Season	Club	Lea	GP	G	A	TP	PIM	GP	G	A	TP	PIM
1987-88	Colorado	WCHA	37	2	6	8	91	....	....	....	....	....
1988-89	Colorado	WCHA	40	4	10	14	74	....	....	....	....	....
1989-90	Colorado	WCHA	40	5	13	18	54	....	....	....	....	....
1990-91	Colorado	WCHA	40	6	8	14	52	....	....	....	....	....
	New Haven	AHL	10	0	2	2	2	....	....	....	....	....

PODDUBNY, WALTER MICHAEL (WALT) (puh-DUHB-nee)

Left wing. Shoots left. 6'1", 210 lbs. Born, Thunder Bay, Ont., February 14, 1960.
(Edmonton's 4th choice, 90th overall, in 1980 Entry Draft).

			Regular Season					Playoffs				
Season	Club	Lea	GP	G	A	TP	PIM	GP	G	A	TP	PIM
1979-80	Kitchener	OHA	19	3	9	12	35	....	....	....	....	....
	Kingston	OHA	43	30	17	47	36	3	0	2	2	0
1980-81	Milwaukee	IHL	5	4	2	6	4	....	....	....	....	....
	Wichita	CHL	70	21	29	50	207	11	1	6	7	26
1981-82	**Edmonton**	**NHL**	**4**	**0**	**0**	**0**	**0**	....	....	....	....	....
	Wichita	CHL	60	35	46	81	79	....	....	....	....	....
	Toronto	**NHL**	**11**	**3**	**4**	**7**	**8**	....	....	....	....	....
1982-83	**Toronto**	**NHL**	**72**	**28**	**31**	**59**	**71**	**4**	**3**	**1**	**4**	**0**
1983-84	**Toronto**	**NHL**	**38**	**11**	**14**	**25**	**48**	....	....	....	....	....
1984-85	**Toronto**	**NHL**	**32**	**5**	**15**	**20**	**26**	....	....	....	....	....
	St. Catharines	AHL	8	5	7	12	10	....	....	....	....	....
1985-86	**Toronto**	**NHL**	**33**	**12**	**22**	**34**	**25**	**9**	**4**	**1**	**5**	**4**
	St. Catharines	AHL	37	28	27	55	52	....	....	....	....	....
1986-87	**NY Rangers**	**NHL**	**75**	**40**	**47**	**87**	**49**	**6**	**0**	**0**	**0**	**8**
1987-88	**NY Rangers**	**NHL**	**77**	**38**	**50**	**88**	**76**	....	....	....	....	....
1988-89	**Quebec**	**NHL**	**72**	**38**	**37**	**75**	**107**	....	....	....	....	....
1989-90	**New Jersey**	**NHL**	**33**	**4**	**10**	**14**	**28**	....	....	....	....	....
	Utica	AHL	2	1	2	3	0	....	....	....	....	....
1990-91	**New Jersey**	**NHL**	**14**	**4**	**6**	**10**	**10**	....	....	....	....	....
	NHL Totals		**461**	**183**	**236**	**419**	**448**	**19**	**7**	**2**	**9**	**12**

Played in NHL All-Star Game (1989)

Traded to **Toronto** by **Edmonton** with Phil Drouilliard for Laurie Boschman, March 28, 1982. Traded to **NY Rangers** by **Toronto** for Mike Allison, August 18, 1986. Traded to **Quebec** by **NY Rangers** with Bruce Bell, Jari Gronstrand and NY Rangers' fourth round choice (Eric Dubois) in 1989 Entry Draft for Jason Lafreniere and Normand Rochefort, August 1, 1988. Traded to **New Jersey** by **Quebec** with Quebec's fourth round choice (Mike Bodnarchuk) in 1990 Entry Draft for Joe Cirella, Claude Loiselle and New Jersey's eighth round choice (Alexander Karpovtsev) in 1990 Entry Draft, June 17, 1989.

PODEIN, SHJON

Center. Shoots left. 6'2", 200 lbs. Born, Rochester, MN, March 5, 1968.
(Edmonton's 9th choice, 166th overall, in 1988 Entry Draft).

			Regular Season					Playoffs				
Season	Club	Lea	GP	G	A	TP	PIM	GP	G	A	TP	PIM
1987-88	Minn.-Duluth	WCHA	30	4	4	8	48	....	....	....	....	....
1988-89	Minn.-Duluth	WCHA	36	7	5	12	46	....	....	....	....	....
1989-90	Minn.-Duluth	WCHA	35	21	18	39	36	....	....	....	....	....
1990-91	Cape Breton	AHL	63	14	15	29	65	4	0	0	0	5

PODIAK, BRADLEY

Center. Shoots left. 6'1", 190 lbs. Born, Plymouth, MN., March 26, 1971.
(Winnipeg's 13th choice, 214th overall, in 1989 Entry Draft).

			Regular Season					Playoffs				
Season	Club	Lea	GP	G	A	TP	PIM	GP	G	A	TP	PIM
1989-90	U. of Denver	WCHA	40	4	1	5	33	....	....	....	....	....
1990-91	U. of Denver	WCHA	37	1	2	3	28	....	....	....	....	....

PODLOSKI, RAY

Center. Shoots left. 6'2", 210 lbs. Born, Edmonton, Alta., January 5, 1966.
(Boston's 2nd choice, 40th overall, in 1984 Entry Draft).

			Regular Season					Playoffs				
Season	Club	Lea	GP	G	A	TP	PIM	GP	G	A	TP	PIM
1983-84	Portland	WHL	66	46	50	96	44	14	8	14	22	14
1984-85	Portland	WHL	67	63	75	138	41	6	3	1	4	7
1985-86	Portland	WHL	66	59	75	134	68	7	1	9	10	8
1986-87	Moncton	AHL	70	23	27	50	12	3	0	0	0	15
1987-88	Maine	AHL	36	12	20	32	12	5	1	2	3	19
1988-89	**Boston**	**NHL**	**8**	**0**	**1**	**1**	**22**	....	....	....	....	....
	Maine	AHL	71	20	34	54	70	....	....	....	....	....
1989-90	Cdn. National	...	58	18	16	34	38	....	....	....	....	....
1990-91	Nurnberg	Ger.	52	59	65	124	58	....	....	....	....	....
	NHL Totals		**8**	**0**	**1**	**1**	**2**	....	....	....	....	....

POESCHEK, RUDY (POH-shehk)

Right wing/Defense. Shoots right. 6'2", 210 lbs. Born, Kamloops, B.C., September 29, 1966.
(NY Rangers' 12th choice, 238th overall, in 1985 Entry Draft).

			Regular Season					Playoffs				
Season	Club	Lea	GP	G	A	TP	PIM	GP	G	A	TP	PIM
1983-84	Kamloops	WHL	47	3	9	12	93	8	0	2	2	7
1984-85	Kamloops	WHL	34	6	7	13	100	15	0	3	3	56
1985-86	Kamloops	WHL	32	3	13	16	92	16	3	7	10	40
1986-87	Kamloops	WHL	54	13	18	31	153	15	2	4	6	37
1987-88	**NY Rangers**	**NHL**	**1**	**0**	**0**	**0**	**2**	....	....	....	....	....
	Colorado	IHL	82	7	31	38	210	12	2	2	4	31
1988-89	**NY Rangers**	**NHL**	**52**	**0**	**2**	**2**	**199**	....	....	....	....	....
	Colorado	IHL	2	0	0	0	6	....	....	....	....	....
1989-90	**NY Rangers**	**NHL**	**15**	**0**	**0**	**0**	**55**	....	....	....	....	....
	Flint	IHL	38	8	13	21	109	4	0	0	0	16
1990-91	Binghamton	AHL	38	1	3	4	162	....	....	....	....	....
	Winnipeg	**NHL**	**1**	**0**	**0**	**0**	**5**	....	....	....	....	....
	Moncton	AHL	23	2	4	6	67	9	1	1	2	41
	NHL Totals		**69**	**0**	**2**	**2**	**261**	....	....	....	....	....

Traded to **Winnipeg** by **NY Rangers** for Guy Larose, January 22, 1991.

POHL, MICHAEL (POHL)

Center. Shoots left. 6'1", 163 lbs. Born, Rosenheim, West Germany, January 25, 1968.
(New Jersey's 14th choice, 243rd overall, in 1988 Entry Draft).

			Regular Season					Playoffs				
Season	Club	Lea	GP	G	A	TP	PIM	GP	G	A	TP	PIM
1987-88	Rosenheim	W.Ger.	44	7	9	16	32	....	....	....	....	....
1988-89	Rosenheim	W.Ger.	44	8	14	22	38	....	....	....	....	....
1989-90	Rosenheim	W.Ger.	38	10	11	21	28	....	....	....	....	....
1990-91	Rosenheim	Ger.	51	11	10	21	36	....	....	....	....	....

POLILLO, PAUL

Center. Shoots left. 5'11", 175 lbs. Born, Brantford, Ont., April 24, 1967.
(Pittsburgh's 1st choice, 4th overall, in 1988 Supplemental Draft).

			Regular Season					Playoffs				
Season	Club	Lea	GP	G	A	TP	PIM	GP	G	A	TP	PIM
1986-87	W. Michigan	CCHA	42	18	48	66	35	....	....	....	....	....
1987-88a	W. Michigan	CCHA	42	25	60	85	34	....	....	....	....	....
1988-89	W. Michigan	CCHA	41	20	46	66	32	....	....	....	....	....
1989-90	W. Michigan	CCHA	40	19	35	54	34	....	....	....	....	....
1990-91	Bolzano	Italy		UNAVAILABLE								

a CCHA First All-Star Team (1988)

POMICHTER, MICHAEL

Center. Shoots left. 6'1", 198 lbs. Born, New Haven, CT, September 10, 1973.
(Chicago's 2nd choice, 39th overall, in 1991 Entry Draft).

			Regular Season					Playoffs				
Season	Club	Lea	GP	G	A	TP	PIM	GP	G	A	TP	PIM
1989-90	Springfield	USHL	39	37	31	68	8	....	....	....	....	....
1990-91	Springfield	USHL	38	61	64	125	22	....	....	....	....	....

POPOVIC, PETER

Defense. Shoots right. 6'5", 224 lbs. Born, Koping, Sweden, February 10, 1968.
(Montreal's 5th choice, 93rd overall, in 1988 Entry Draft).

			Regular Season					Playoffs				
Season	Club	Lea	GP	G	A	TP	PIM	GP	G	A	TP	PIM
1986-87	Vasteras	Swe.2	24	1	2	3	10	....	....	....	....	....
1987-88	Vasteras	Swe.2	28	3	17	20	....	....	....	....	....	....
1988-89	Vasteras	Swe.	44	3	8	11	68	....	....	....	....	....
1989-90	Vasteras	Swe.	30	2	10	12	24	2	0	1	1	2
1990-91	Vasteras	Swe.	40	3	2	5	54	....	....	....	....	....

PORKKA, TONI

Defense. Shoots right. 6'2", 190 lbs. Born, Rauma, Finland, February 4, 1970.
(Philadelphia's 12th choice, 172nd overall, in 1990 Entry Draft).

			Regular Season					Playoffs				
Season	Club	Lea	GP	G	A	TP	PIM	GP	G	A	TP	PIM
1989-90	Lukko	Fin.	41	0	3	3	18	....	....	....	....	....
1990-91	Lukko	Fin.	34	2	2	4	8	....	....	....	....	....

POSMA, MIKE (PAHS-muh)

Defense. Shoots right. 6'1", 195 lbs. Born, Utica, NY, December 16, 1967.
(St. Louis' 2nd choice, 31st overall, in 1986 Entry Draft).

			Regular Season					Playoffs				
Season	Club	Lea	GP	G	A	TP	PIM	GP	G	A	TP	PIM
1986-87	W. Michigan	CCHA	35	12	31	43	42	....	....	....	....	....
1987-88a	W. Michigan	CCHA	42	16	38	54	30	....	....	....	....	....
1988-89	W. Michigan	CCHA	43	7	34	41	58	....	....	....	....	....
1989-90	W. Michigan	CCHA	39	8	28	36	28	....	....	....	....	....
1990-91	Utica	AHL	78	19	30	49	35	....	....	....	....	....

a CCHA Second All-Star Team (1988)

POTVIN, MARC (POT-vahn)

Right wing. Shoots right. 6'1", 185 lbs. Born, Ottawa, Ont., January 29, 1967.
(Detroit's 9th choice, 169th overall, in 1986 Entry Draft).

			Regular Season					Playoffs				
Season	Club	Lea	GP	G	A	TP	PIM	GP	G	A	TP	PIM
1986-87	Bowling Green	CCHA	43	5	15	20	74	....	....	....	....	....
1987-88	Bowling Green	CCHA	45	15	21	36	80	....	....	....	....	....
1988-89	Bowling Green	CCHA	46	23	12	35	63	....	....	....	....	....
1989-90	Bowling Green	CCHA	40	19	17	36	72	....	....	....	....	....
	Adirondack	AHL	5	2	1	3	9	4	0	1	1	23
1990-91	**Detroit**	**NHL**	**9**	**0**	**0**	**0**	**55**	**6**	**0**	**0**	**0**	**32**
	Adirondack	AHL	63	9	13	22	365	....	....	....	....	....
	NHL Totals		**9**	**0**	**0**	**0**	**55**	**6**	**0**	**0**	**0**	**32**

POULIN, CHARLES

Center. Shoots left. 6', 172 lbs.   Born, St. Jean d'Iberville, Que., July 27, 1972.
(Montreal's 3rd choice, 58th overall, in 1990 Entry Draft).

			Regular Season					Playoffs				
Season	Club	Lea	GP	G	A	TP	PIM	GP	G	A	TP	PIM
1989-90a	St. Hyacinthe	QMJHL	65	39	45	84	132	11	5	8	13	47
1990-91	St. Hyacinthe	QMJHL	64	25	46	71	166	4	0	2	2	23

a QMJHL Third All-Star Team (1990)

POULIN, DAVID JAMES (DAVE)   (POO-lihn)

Center. Shoots left. 5'11", 190 lbs.   Born, Timmins, Ont., December 17, 1958.

			Regular Season					Playoffs				
Season	Club	Lea	GP	G	A	TP	PIM	GP	G	A	TP	PIM
1978-79	Notre Dame	WCHA	37	28	31	59	32	....	....	....	....	....
1979-80	Notre Dame	WCHA	24	19	24	43	46	....	....	....	....	....
1980-81	Notre Dame	WCHA	35	13	22	35	53	....	....	....	....	....
1981-82a	Notre Dame	CCHA	39	29	30	59	44	....	....	....	....	....
1982-83	Rogle	Swe.	32	35	27	62	64	....	....	....	....	....
	Philadelphia	NHL	2	2	0	2	2	3	1	3	4	9
	Maine	AHL	16	7	9	16	2	....	....	....	....	....
1983-84	Philadelphia	NHL	73	31	45	76	47	3	0	0	0	2
1984-85	Philadelphia	NHL	73	30	44	74	59	11	3	5	8	6
1985-86	Philadelphia	NHL	79	27	42	69	49	5	2	0	2	2
1986-87b	Philadelphia	NHL	75	25	45	70	53	15	3	3	6	14
1987-88	Philadelphia	NHL	68	19	32	51	32	7	2	6	8	4
1988-89	Philadelphia	NHL	69	18	17	35	49	19	6	5	11	16
1989-90	Philadelphia	NHL	28	9	8	17	12	....	....	....	....	....
	Boston	NHL	32	6	19	25	12	18	8	5	13	8
1990-91	Boston	NHL	31	8	12	20	25	16	0	9	9	20
	NHL Totals		530	175	264	439	340	97	25	36	61	81

a CCHA Second All-Star Team (1982).
b Won Frank J. Selke Trophy (1987).
Played in NHL All-Star Game (1986, 1988)
Signed as free agent by **Philadelphia**, March 8, 1983. Traded to **Boston** by **Philadelphia** for Ken Linseman, January 16, 1990.

POULIN, PATRICK

Left wing. Shoots left. 6'1", 208 lbs.   Born, Vanier, Que., April 23, 1973.
(Hartford's 1st choice, 9th overall, in 1991 Entry Draft).

			Regular Season					Playoffs				
Season	Club	Lea	GP	G	A	TP	PIM	GP	G	A	TP	PIM
1989-90a	St. Hyacinthe	QMJHL	60	25	26	51	55	12	1	9	10	5
1990-91	St. Hyacinthe	QMJHL	56	32	38	70	82	4	0	2	2	23

a QMJHL Third All-Star Team (1990)

PRAJSLER, PETR   (PRAYS-luhr)

Defense. Shoots left. 6'2", 200 lbs.   Born, Hradec Kralove, Czech., September 21, 1965.
(Los Angeles' 5th choice, 93rd overall, in 1985 Entry Draft).

			Regular Season					Playoffs				
Season	Club	Lea	GP	G	A	TP	PIM	GP	G	A	TP	PIM
1986-87	Pardubice	Czech.	41	3	4	7	....	....	....	....	....	....
1987-88	**Los Angeles**	**NHL**	7	0	0	0	2	....	....	....	....	....
	New Haven	AHL	41	3	8	11	58	....	....	....	....	....
1988-89	**Los Angeles**	**NHL**	2	0	3	3	0	1	0	0	0	0
	New Haven	AHL	43	4	6	10	96	16	3	3	6	34
1989-90	**Los Angeles**	**NHL**	34	3	7	10	47	3	0	0	0	0
	New Haven	AHL	6	1	7	8	2	....	....	....	....	....
1990-91	Phoenix	IHL	77	13	34	47	140	9	1	9	10	18
	NHL Totals		43	3	10	13	49	4	0	0	0	0

Signed as a free agent by **Boston**, August 1, 1991.

PRATT, JONATHAN

Center. Shoots left. 6'1", 195 lbs.   Born, Danvers, MA, September 25, 1970.
(Minnesota's 9th choice, 154th overall, in 1989 Entry Draft).

			Regular Season					Playoffs				
Season	Club	Lea	GP	G	A	TP	PIM	GP	G	A	TP	PIM
1989-90	Boston U.	H.E.				DID NOT PLAY		....	....	....	....	....
1990-91	Boston U.	H.E.	16	3	1	4	26	....	....	....	....	....

PRAZNIK, JODY

Defense. Shoots right. 6'1", 180 lbs.   Born, Winnipeg, Man., June 28, 1969.
(Detroit's 8th choice, 185th overall, in 1988 Entry Draft).

			Regular Season					Playoffs				
Season	Club	Lea	GP	G	A	TP	PIM	GP	G	A	TP	PIM
1987-88	Colorado	WCHA	37	5	10	15	46	....	....	....	....	....
1988-89	Saskatoon	WHL	28	2	9	11	28	8	0	2	2	2
1989-90	Hampton Roads	ECHL	55	7	35	42	40	5	0	4	4	0
1990-91	Hampton Roads	ECHL	64	15	39	54	30	11	0	2	2	10

PRESLEY, WAYNE

Right wing. Shoots right. 5'11", 180 lbs.   Born, Detroit, MI, March 23, 1965.
(Chicago's 2nd choice, 39th overall, in 1983 Entry Draft).

			Regular Season					Playoffs				
Season	Club	Lea	GP	G	A	TP	PIM	GP	G	A	TP	PIM
1982-83	Kitchener	OHL	70	39	48	87	99	12	1	4	5	9
1983-84a	Kitchener	OHL	70	63	76	139	156	16	12	16	28	38
1984-85	**Chicago**	**NHL**	3	0	1	1	0	....	....	....	....	....
	Kitchener	OHL	31	25	21	46	77	....	....	....	....	....
	S.S. Marie	OHL	11	5	9	14	14	16	13	9	22	13
1985-86	**Chicago**	**NHL**	38	7	8	15	38	3	0	0	0	0
	Nova Scotia	AHL	29	6	9	15	22	....	....	....	....	....
1986-87	**Chicago**	**NHL**	80	32	29	61	114	4	1	0	1	9
1987-88	**Chicago**	**NHL**	42	12	10	22	52	5	0	0	0	4
1988-89	**Chicago**	**NHL**	72	21	19	40	100	14	7	5	12	18
1989-90	**Chicago**	**NHL**	49	6	7	13	69	19	9	6	15	29
1990-91	**Chicago**	**NHL**	71	15	19	34	122	6	0	1	1	38
	NHL Totals		355	93	93	186	495	51	17	12	29	98

a OHL First All-Star Team (1984)

PRIAKHIN, SERGEI   (pree-YAH-ihn)

Right wing. Shoots left. 6'3", 210 lbs.   Born, Moscow, Soviet Union, December 7, 1963.
(Calgary's 12th choice, 252nd overall, in 1988 Entry Draft).

			Regular Season					Playoffs				
Season	Club	Lea	GP	G	A	TP	PIM	GP	G	A	TP	PIM
1987-88	Soviet Wings	USSR	44	10	15	25	16	....	....	....	....	....
1988-89	Soviet Wings	USSR	44	11	15	26	23	....	....	....	....	....
	Calgary	**NHL**	2	0	0	0	2	1	0	0	0	0
1989-90	**Calgary**	**NHL**	20	2	2	4	0	....	....	....	....	....
	Salt Lake	IHL	3	1	0	1	0	....	....	....	....	....
1990-91	**Calgary**	**NHL**	24	1	6	7	0	....	....	....	....	....
	Salt Lake	IHL	18	5	12	17	2	....	....	....	....	....
	NHL Totals		46	3	8	11	2	1	0	0	0	0

PRIESTLAY, KEN

Center. Shoots left. 5'10", 190 lbs.   Born, Richmond, B.C., August 24, 1967.
(Buffalo's 5th choice, 98th overall, in 1985 Entry Draft).

			Regular Season					Playoffs				
Season	Club	Lea	GP	G	A	TP	PIM	GP	G	A	TP	PIM
1983-84	Victoria	WHL	55	10	18	28	31	....	....	....	....	....
1984-85	Victoria	WHL	50	25	37	62	48	....	....	....	....	....
1985-86	Victoria	WHL	72	73	72	145	45	....	....	....	....	....
	Rochester	AHL	4	0	2	2	0	....	....	....	....	....
1986-87	**Buffalo**	**NHL**	34	11	6	17	8	....	....	....	....	....
	Victoria	WHL	33	43	39	82	37	....	....	....	....	....
	Rochester	AHL						8	3	2	5	4
1987-88	**Buffalo**	**NHL**	33	5	12	17	35	6	0	0	0	11
	Rochester	AHL	43	27	24	51	47	....	....	....	....	....
1988-89	**Buffalo**	**NHL**	15	2	0	2	2	3	0	0	0	2
	Rochester	AHL	64	56	37	93	60	....	....	....	....	....
1989-90	**Buffalo**	**NHL**	35	7	7	14	14	5	0	0	0	8
	Rochester	AHL	40	19	39	58	46	....	....	....	....	....
1990-91	Cdn. National	...	40	20	26	46	34	....	....	....	....	....
	Pittsburgh	**NHL**	2	0	1	1	0	....	....	....	....	....
	NHL Totals		119	25	26	51	59	14	0	0	0	21

Traded to **Pittsburgh** by **Buffalo** for Tony Tanti, March 5, 1991.

PRIMEAU, KEITH

Center. Shoots left. 6'4", 220 lbs.   Born, Toronto, Ont., November 24, 1971.
(Detroit's 1st choice, 3rd overall, in 1990 Entry Draft).

			Regular Season					Playoffs				
Season	Club	Lea	GP	G	A	TP	PIM	GP	G	A	TP	PIM
1987-88	Hamilton	OHL	47	6	6	12	69	....	....	....	....	....
1988-89	Niagara Falls	OHL	48	20	35	55	56	17	9	16	25	12
1989-90a	Niagara Falls	OHL	65	*57	70	*127	97	16	*16	17	*33	49
1990-91	**Detroit**	**NHL**	58	3	12	15	106	5	1	1	2	25
	Adirondack	AHL	6	3	5	8	8	....	....	....	....	....
	NHL Totals		58	3	12	15	106	5	1	1	2	25

a OHL Second All-Star Team (1990)

PROBERT, BOB   (PROH buhrt)

Left wing. Shoots left. 6'3", 215 lbs.   Born, Windsor, Ont., June 5, 1965.
(Detroit's 3rd choice, 46th overall, in 1983 Entry Draft).

			Regular Season					Playoffs				
Season	Club	Lea	GP	G	A	TP	PIM	GP	G	A	TP	PIM
1982-83	Brantford	OHL	51	12	16	28	133	8	2	2	4	23
1983-84	Brantford	OHL	65	35	38	73	189	6	0	3	3	16
1984-85	S.S. Marie	OHL	44	20	52	72	172	....	....	....	....	....
	Hamilton	OHL	4	0	1	1	21	....	....	....	....	....
1985-86	**Detroit**	**NHL**	44	8	13	21	186	....	....	....	....	....
	Adirondack	AHL	32	12	15	27	152	10	2	3	5	68
1986-87	**Detroit**	**NHL**	63	13	11	24	221	16	3	4	7	63
	Adirondack	AHL	7	1	4	5	15	....	....	....	....	....
1987-88	**Detroit**	**NHL**	74	29	33	62	*398	16	8	13	21	51
1988-89	**Detroit**	**NHL**	25	4	2	6	106	....	....	....	....	....
1989-90	**Detroit**	**NHL**	4	3	0	3	21	....	....	....	....	....
1990-91	**Detroit**	**NHL**	55	16	23	39	315	6	1	2	3	50
	NHL Totals		265	73	82	155	1247	38	12	19	31	164

Played in NHL All-Star Game (1988)

PRONGER, SEAN

Center. Shoots left. 6'3", 195 lbs.   Born, Thunder Bay, Ont., November 30, 1972.
(Vancouver's 3rd choice, 51st overall, in 1991 Entry Draft).

			Regular Season					Playoffs				
Season	Club	Lea	GP	G	A	TP	PIM	GP	G	A	TP	PIM
1989-90	Thunder Bay	USHL	48	18	34	52	61	....	....	....	....	....
1990-91	Bowling Green	CCHA	40	3	7	10	30	....	....	....	....	....

PROPP, BRIAN PHILIP

Left wing. Shoots left. 5'10", 195 lbs. Born, Lanigan, Sask., February 15, 1959.
(Philadelphia's 1st choice, 14th overall, in 1979 Entry Draft).

			Regular Season					Playoffs				
Season	Club	Lea	GP	G	A	TP	PIM	GP	G	A	TP	PIM
1976-77	Brandon	WHL	72	55	80	135	47	16	*14	12	26	5
1977-78a	Brandon	WHL	70	70	*112	*182	200	8	7	6	13	12
1978-79ab	Brandon	WHL	71	*94	*100	*194	127	22	15	23	*38	40
1979-80	**Philadelphia**	**NHL**	**80**	**34**	**41**	**75**	**54**	**19**	**5**	**10**	**15**	**29**
1980-81	**Philadelphia**	**NHL**	**79**	**26**	**40**	**66**	**110**	**12**	**6**	**6**	**12**	**32**
1981-82	**Philadelphia**	**NHL**	**80**	**44**	**47**	**91**	**117**	**4**	**2**	**2**	**4**	**4**
1982-83	**Philadelphia**	**NHL**	**80**	**40**	**42**	**82**	**72**	**3**	**1**	**2**	**3**	**8**
1983-84	**Philadelphia**	**NHL**	**79**	**39**	**53**	**92**	**37**	**3**	**0**	**1**	**1**	**6**
1984-85	**Philadelphia**	**NHL**	**76**	**43**	**53**	**96**	**43**	**19**	**8**	**10**	**18**	**6**
1985-86	**Philadelphia**	**NHL**	**72**	**40**	**57**	**97**	**47**	**5**	**0**	**2**	**2**	**4**
1986-87	**Philadelphia**	**NHL**	**53**	**31**	**36**	**67**	**45**	**26**	**12**	**16**	**28**	**10**
1987-88	**Philadelphia**	**NHL**	**74**	**27**	**49**	**76**	**76**	**7**	**4**	**2**	**6**	**8**
1988-89	**Philadelphia**	**NHL**	**77**	**32**	**46**	**78**	**37**	**18**	**14**	**9**	**23**	**14**
1989-90	**Philadelphia**	**NHL**	**40**	**13**	**15**	**28**	**31**	....	....	....	....	....
	Boston	**NHL**	**14**	**3**	**9**	**12**	**10**	**20**	**4**	**9**	**13**	**2**
1990-91	**Minnesota**	**NHL**	**79**	**26**	**47**	**73**	**58**	**23**	**8**	**15**	**23**	**28**
	NHL Totals		**883**	**398**	**535**	**933**	**737**	**159**	**64**	**84**	**148**	**151**

a WHL First All-Star Team (1978, 1979)
b WHL Player of the Year (1979)

Played in NHL All-Star Game (1980, 1982, 1984, 1986, 1990)

Traded to **Boston** by **Philadelphia** for Boston's second round choice (Terran Sandwith) in 1990 Entry Draft, March 2, 1990. Signed as a free agent by **Minnesota**, July 25, 1990.

PROSOFSKY, JASON

Right wing. Shoots right. 6'4", 220 lbs. Born, Medicine Hat, Alta., May 4, 1971.
(NY Rangers' 2nd choice, 40th overall, in 1989 Entry Draft).

			Regular Season					Playoffs				
Season	Club	Lea	GP	G	A	TP	PIM	GP	G	A	TP	PIM
1987-88	Medicine Hat	WHL	47	6	1	7	94	14	0	0	0	20
1988-89	Medicine Hat	WHL	67	7	16	23	170	3	1	0	1	6
1989-90	Medicine Hat	WHL	71	12	13	25	153	3	0	0	0	8
1990-91	Medicine Hat	WHL	72	15	15	30	195	12	6	8	14	33

PRYOR, CHRIS

Defense. Shoots right. 5'11", 210 lbs. Born, St. Paul, MN, January 23, 1961.

			Regular Season					Playoffs				
Season	Club	Lea	GP	G	A	TP	PIM	GP	G	A	TP	PIM
1979-80	N. Hampshire	ECAC	27	9	13	22	27	....	....	....	....	....
1980-81	N. Hampshire	ECAC	33	10	27	37	36	....	....	....	....	....
1981-82	N. Hampshire	ECAC	35	3	16	19	36	....	....	....	....	....
1982-83	N. Hampshire	ECAC	34	4	9	13	23	....	....	....	....	....
1983-84	Salt Lake	CHL	72	7	21	28	215	5	1	2	3	11
1984-85	**Minnesota**	**NHL**	**4**	**0**	**0**	**0**	**16**	....	....	....	....	....
	Springfield	AHL	77	3	21	24	158	....	....	....	....	....
1985-86	**Minnesota**	**NHL**	**7**	**0**	**1**	**1**	**0**	....	....	....	....	....
	Springfield	AHL	55	4	16	20	104	....	....	....	....	....
1986-87	**Minnesota**	**NHL**	**50**	**1**	**3**	**4**	**49**	....	....	....	....	....
	Springfield	AHL	5	0	2	2	17	....	....	....	....	....
1987-88	**Minnesota**	**NHL**	**3**	**0**	**0**	**0**	**6**	....	....	....	....	....
	Kalamazoo	IHL	56	4	16	20	171	....	....	....	....	....
	NY Islanders	**NHL**	**1**	**0**	**0**	**0**	**2**	....	....	....	....	....
1988-89	**NY Islanders**	**NHL**	**7**	**0**	**0**	**0**	**25**	....	....	....	....	....
	Springfield	AHL	54	3	6	9	205	....	....	....	....	....
1989-90	**NY Islanders**	**NHL**	**10**	**0**	**0**	**0**	**24**	....	....	....	....	....
	Springfield	AHL	60	3	7	10	105	18	1	3	4	12
1990-91	Capital Dist.	AHL	41	1	8	9	94	....	....	....	....	....
	NHL Totals		**82**	**1**	**4**	**5**	**122**	....	....	....	....	....

Signed as a free agent by **Minnesota**, January 10, 1985. Traded to **NY Islanders** by **Minnesota** with future considerations for Gord Dineen, March 8, 1988.

PULLOLA, TOMMI (PUHL-loh-lah)

Center. Shoots left. 6'5", 207 lbs. Born, Vaasa, Finland, May 18, 1971.
(Chicago's 4th choice, 111th overall, in 1989 Entry Draft).

			Regular Season					Playoffs				
Season	Club	Lea	GP	G	A	TP	PIM	GP	G	A	TP	PIM
1988-89	Sport	Fin.	40	11	13	24	....	....	....	....	....	....
1989-90	Lukko	Fin.	40	7	9	16	8	....	....	....	....	....
1990-91	Lukko	Fin.	42	17	17	34	40	....	....	....	....	....

PURVES, JOHN (PUR-vihs)

Right wing. Shoots right. 6'1", 201 lbs. Born, Toronto, Ont., February 12, 1968.
(Washington's 6th choice, 103rd overall, in 1986 Entry Draft).

			Regular Season					Playoffs				
Season	Club	Lea	GP	G	A	TP	PIM	GP	G	A	TP	PIM
1985-86	Belleville	OHL	16	3	9	12	6	....	....	....	....	....
	Hamilton	OHL	36	13	28	41	36	....	....	....	....	....
1986-87	Hamilton	OHL	28	12	11	23	37	9	2	0	2	12
1987-88	Hamilton	OHL	64	39	44	83	65	14	7	18	25	4
1988-89a	Niagara Falls	OHL	5	5	11	16	2	....	....	....	....	....
	North Bay	OHL	42	34	52	86	38	12	14	12	26	16
1989-90	Baltimore	AHL	75	29	35	64	12	9	5	7	12	4
1990-91	**Washington**	**NHL**	**7**	**1**	**0**	**1**	**0**	....	....	....	....	....
	Baltimore	AHL	53	22	29	51	27	6	2	3	5	0
	NHL Totals		**7**	**1**	**0**	**1**	**0**	....	....	....	....	....

a OHL Second All-Star Team (1989)

PUSHOR, JAMIE

Defense. Shoots right. 6'3", 192 lbs. Born, Lethbridge, Alta., February 11, 1973.
(Detroit's 2nd choice, 32nd overall, in 1991 Entry Draft).

			Regular Season					Playoffs				
Season	Club	Lea	GP	G	A	TP	PIM	GP	G	A	TP	PIM
1989-90	Lethbridge	WHL	10	0	2	2	2	....	....	....	....	....
1990-91	Lethbridge	WHL	71	1	13	14	193	....	....	....	....	....

QUENNEVILLE, JOEL NORMAN (KWEHN vihl)

Defense. Shoots left. 6'1", 200 lbs. Born, Windsor, Ont., September 15, 1958.
(Toronto's 1st choice, 21st overall, in 1978 Amateur Draft).

			Regular Season					Playoffs				
Season	Club	Lea	GP	G	A	TP	PIM	GP	G	A	TP	PIM
1975-76	Windsor	OHA	66	15	33	48	61	....	....	....	....	....
1976-77	Windsor	OHA	65	19	59	78	169	9	6	5	11	112
1977-78a	Windsor	OHA	66	27	76	103	114	6	2	3	5	17
1978-79	**Toronto**	**NHL**	**61**	**2**	**9**	**11**	**60**	**6**	**0**	**1**	**1**	**4**
	New Brunswick	AHL	16	1	10	11	10	....	....	....	....	....
1979-80	**Toronto**	**NHL**	**32**	**1**	**4**	**5**	**24**	....	....	....	....	....
	Colorado	**NHL**	**35**	**5**	**7**	**12**	**26**	....	....	....	....	....
1980-81	**Colorado**	**NHL**	**71**	**10**	**24**	**34**	**86**	....	....	....	....	....
1981-82	**Colorado**	**NHL**	**64**	**5**	**10**	**15**	**55**	....	....	....	....	....
1982-83	**New Jersey**	**NHL**	**74**	**5**	**12**	**17**	**46**	....	....	....	....	....
1983-84	**Hartford**	**NHL**	**80**	**5**	**8**	**13**	**95**	....	....	....	....	....
1984-85	**Hartford**	**NHL**	**79**	**6**	**16**	**22**	**96**	....	....	....	....	....
1985-86	**Hartford**	**NHL**	**71**	**5**	**20**	**25**	**83**	**10**	**0**	**2**	**2**	**12**
1986-87	**Hartford**	**NHL**	**37**	**3**	**7**	**10**	**24**	**6**	**0**	**0**	**0**	**0**
1987-88	**Hartford**	**NHL**	**77**	**1**	**8**	**9**	**44**	**6**	**0**	**2**	**2**	**2**
1988-89	**Hartford**	**NHL**	**69**	**4**	**7**	**11**	**32**	**4**	**0**	**3**	**3**	**4**
1989-90	**Hartford**	**NHL**	**44**	**1**	**4**	**5**	**34**	....	....	....	....	....
1990-91	**Washington**	**NHL**	**9**	**1**	**0**	**1**	**0**	....	....	....	....	....
	Baltimore	AHL	59	6	13	19	58	6	1	1	2	6
	NHL Totals		**803**	**54**	**136**	**190**	**705**	**26**	**0**	**8**	**8**	**22**

a OHA Second All-Star Team (1978)

Traded to **Colorado** by **Toronto** with Lanny McDonald for Pat Hickey and Wilf Paiement, December 29, 1979. Traded to **Calgary** by **New Jersey** with Steve Tambellini for Phil Russell and Mel Bridgman, June 20, 1983. Traded to **Hartford** by **Calgary** with Richie Dunn for Mickey Volcan, July 5, 1983. Traded to **Washington** by **Hartford** for cash, October 3, 1990.

QUINN, DAN

Center. Shoots left. 5'11", 182 lbs. Born, Ottawa, Ont., June 1, 1965.
(Calgary's 1st choice, 13th overall, in 1983 Entry Draft).

			Regular Season					Playoffs				
Season	Club	Lea	GP	G	A	TP	PIM	GP	G	A	TP	PIM
1981-82	Belleville	OHL	67	19	32	51	41	....	....	....	....	....
1982-83	Belleville	OHL	70	59	88	147	27	4	2	6	8	2
1983-84	**Calgary**	**NHL**	**54**	**19**	**33**	**52**	**20**	**8**	**3**	**5**	**8**	**4**
	Belleville	OHL	24	23	36	59	12	....	....	....	....	....
1984-85	**Calgary**	**NHL**	**74**	**20**	**38**	**58**	**22**	**3**	**0**	**0**	**0**	**0**
1985-86	**Calgary**	**NHL**	**78**	**30**	**42**	**72**	**44**	**18**	**8**	**7**	**15**	**10**
1986-87	**Calgary**	**NHL**	**16**	**3**	**6**	**9**	**14**	....	....	....	....	....
	Pittsburgh	**NHL**	**64**	**28**	**43**	**71**	**40**	....	....	....	....	....
1987-88	**Pittsburgh**	**NHL**	**70**	**40**	**39**	**79**	**50**	....	....	....	....	....
1988-89	**Pittsburgh**	**NHL**	**79**	**34**	**60**	**94**	**102**	**11**	**6**	**3**	**9**	**10**
1989-90	**Pittsburgh**	**NHL**	**41**	**9**	**20**	**29**	**22**	....	....	....	....	....
	Vancouver	**NHL**	**37**	**16**	**18**	**34**	**27**	....	....	....	....	....
1990-91	**Vancouver**	**NHL**	**64**	**18**	**31**	**49**	**46**	....	....	....	....	....
	St. Louis	**NHL**	**14**	**4**	**7**	**11**	**20**	**13**	**4**	**7**	**11**	**32**
	NHL Totals		**591**	**221**	**337**	**558**	**407**	**53**	**21**	**22**	**43**	**56**

Traded to **Pittsburgh** by **Calgary** for Mike Bullard, November 12, 1986. Traded to **Vancouver** by **Pittsburgh** with Dave Capuano and Andrew McBain for Rod Buskas, Barry Pederson and Tony Tanti, January 8, 1990. Traded to **St. Louis** by **Vancouver** with Garth Butcher for Geoff Courtnall, Robert Dirk, Sergio Momesso, Cliff Ronning and future considerations, March 5, 1991.

QUINN, JOE

Right wing. Shoots right. 5'11", 185 lbs. Born, Calgary, Alta., February 10, 1967.
(Hartford's 5th choice, 116th overall, in 1986 Entry Draft).

			Regular Season					Playoffs				
Season	Club	Lea	GP	G	A	TP	PIM	GP	G	A	TP	PIM
1986-87	Bowling Green	CCHA	39	4	13	17	22	....	....	....	....	....
1987-88	Bowling Green	CCHA	39	14	13	27	24	....	....	....	....	....
1988-89	Cdn. National	...	4	0	1	1	2	....	....	....	....	....
	Bowling Green	CCHA	47	21	20	41	36	....	....	....	....	....
1989-90	Bowling Green	CCHA	42	11	18	29	43	....	....	....	....	....
1990-91	Richmond	ECHL	12	4	8	12	2	....	....	....	....	....

QUINNEY, KEN (KWIH-nee)

Right wing. Shoots right. 5'10", 186 lbs. Born, New Westminster, B.C., May 23, 1965.
(Quebec's 9th choice, 203th overall, in 1984 Entry Draft).

			Regular Season					Playoffs				
Season	Club	Lea	GP	G	A	TP	PIM	GP	G	A	TP	PIM
1981-82	Calgary	WHL	63	11	17	28	55	2	0	0	0	15
1982-83	Calgary	WHL	71	26	25	51	71	16	6	1	7	46
1983-84	Calgary	WHL	71	64	54	118	38	4	5	2	7	0
1984-85a	Calgary	WHL	56	47	67	114	65	7	6	4	10	15
1985-86	Fredericton	AHL	61	11	26	37	34	6	2	2	4	9
1986-87	**Quebec**	**NHL**	**25**	**2**	**7**	**9**	**16**	....	....	....	....	....
	Fredericton	AHL	48	14	27	41	20	....	....	....	....	....
1987-88	**Quebec**	**NHL**	**15**	**2**	**2**	**4**	**5**	....	....	....	....	....
b	Fredericton	AHL	58	37	39	76	39	13	3	5	8	35
1988-89	Halifax	AHL	72	41	49	90	65	4	3	0	3	0
1989-90	Halifax	AHL	44	9	16	25	63	2	0	0	0	2
1990-91	**Quebec**	**NHL**	**19**	**3**	**4**	**7**	**2**	....	....	....	....	....
	Halifax	AHL	44	20	20	40	76	....	....	....	....	....
	NHL Totals		**59**	**7**	**13**	**20**	**23**	....	....	....	....	....

a WHL First All-Star Team, East Division (1985)
b Won Tim Horton Award (Most Three-Star Points-AHL) (1988)

QUINTAL, STEPHANE (kihn-TAHL)

Defense. Shoots right. 6'3", 215 lbs. Born, Boucherville, Que., October 22, 1968.
(Boston's 2nd choice, 14th overall, in 1987 Entry Draft).

			Regular Season					Playoffs				
Season	Club	Lea	GP	G	A	TP	PIM	GP	G	A	TP	PIM
1985-86	Granby	QMJHL	67	2	17	19	144	....	....	....	....	....
1986-87a	Granby	QMJHL	67	13	41	54	178	8	0	9	9	10
1987-88	Hull	QMJHL	38	13	23	36	138	19	7	12	19	30
1988-89	**Boston**	**NHL**	**26**	**0**	**1**	**1**	**29**	....	....	....	....	....
	Maine	AHL	16	4	10	14	28	....	....	....	....	....
1989-90	**Boston**	**NHL**	**38**	**2**	**2**	**4**	**22**	....	....	....	....	....
	Maine	AHL	37	4	16	20	27	....	....	....	....	....
1990-91	**Boston**	**NHL**	**45**	**2**	**6**	**8**	**89**	**3**	**0**	**1**	**1**	**7**
	Maine	AHL	23	1	5	6	30	....	....	....	....	....
	NHL Totals		**109**	**4**	**9**	**13**	**140**	**3**	**0**	**1**	**1**	**7**

a QMJHL First All-Star Team (1987)

QUINTIN, JEAN-FRANCOIS

Center. Shoots left. 6'1", 180 lbs. Born, St. Jean, Que., May 28, 1969.
(Minnesota's 4th choice, 75th overall, in 1989 Entry Draft).

			Regular Season					Playoffs				
Season	Club	Lea	GP	G	A	TP	PIM	GP	G	A	TP	PIM
1987-88	Shawinigan	QMJHL	70	28	70	98	143	11	5	8	13	26
1988-89	Shawinigan	QMJHL	69	52	100	152	105	10	9	15	24	16
1989-90	Kalamazoo	IHL	68	20	18	38	38	10	8	4	12	14
1990-91	Kalamazoo	IHL	78	31	43	74	64	9	1	5	6	11

Claimed by **San Jose** from **Minnesota** in Dispersal Draft, May 30, 1991.

RACINE, YVES

Defense. Shoots left. 6', 185 lbs. Born, Matane, Que., February 7, 1969.
(Detroit's 1st choice, 11th overall, in 1987 Entry Draft).

			Regular Season					Playoffs				
Season	Club	Lea	GP	G	A	TP	PIM	GP	G	A	TP	PIM
1986-87	Longueuil	QMJHL	70	7	43	50	50	20	3	11	14	14
1987-88	Adirondack	AHL	....	....	....	....	....	9	4	2	6	2
a	Victoriaville	QMJHL	69	10	84	94	150	5	0	0	0	13
1988-89a	Victoriaville	QMJHL	63	23	85	108	95	16	3	*30	*33	41
	Adirondack	AHL	....	....	....	....	....	2	1	1	2	0
1989-90	**Detroit**	**NHL**	**28**	**4**	**9**	**13**	**23**	....	....	....	....	....
	Adirondack	AHL	46	8	27	35	31	....	....	....	....	....
1990-91	**Detroit**	**NHL**	**62**	**7**	**40**	**47**	**33**	**7**	**2**	**0**	**2**	**0**
	Adirondack	AHL	16	3	9	12	10	....	....	....	....	....
	NHL Totals		**90**	**11**	**49**	**60**	**56**	**7**	**2**	**0**	**2**	**0**

a QMJHL First-All Star Team (1988, 1989)

RAGLAN, HERB

Right wing. Shoots right. 6', 205 lbs. Born, Peterborough, Ont., August 5, 1967.
(St. Louis' 1st choice, 37th overall, in 1985 Entry Draft).

			Regular Season					Playoffs				
Season	Club	Lea	GP	G	A	TP	PIM	GP	G	A	TP	PIM
1984-85	Peterborough	OHL	58	20	22	42	166	....	....	....	....	....
1985-86	**St. Louis**	**NHL**	**7**	**0**	**0**	**0**	**5**	**10**	**1**	**1**	**2**	**24**
	Kingston	OHL	28	10	9	19	88	10	5	2	7	30
1986-87	**St. Louis**	**NHL**	**62**	**6**	**10**	**16**	**159**	**4**	**0**	**0**	**0**	**2**
1987-88	**St. Louis**	**NHL**	**73**	**10**	**15**	**25**	**190**	**10**	**1**	**3**	**4**	**11**
1988-89	**St. Louis**	**NHL**	**50**	**7**	**10**	**17**	**144**	**8**	**1**	**2**	**3**	**13**
1989-90	**St. Louis**	**NHL**	**11**	**0**	**1**	**1**	**21**	....	....	....	....	....
1990-91	**St. Louis**	**NHL**	**32**	**3**	**3**	**6**	**52**	....	....	....	....	....
	Quebec	**NHL**	**15**	**1**	**3**	**4**	**30**	....	....	....	....	....
	NHL Totals		**250**	**27**	**42**	**69**	**601**	**32**	**3**	**6**	**9**	**50**

Traded to **Quebec** by **St. Louis** with Tony Twist and Andy Rymsha for Darin Kimble, February 4, 1991.

RAHN, NOEL

Center. Shoots left. 6', 155 lbs. Born, Edina, MN, February 6, 1971.
(Quebec's 14th choice, 232nd overall, in 1989 Entry Draft).

			Regular Season					Playoffs				
Season	Club	Lea	GP	G	A	TP	PIM	GP	G	A	TP	PIM
1989-90	U. Wisconsin	WCHA	4	0	0	0	0	....	....	....	....	....
1990-91	U. Wisconsin	WCHA	DID NOT PLAY									

RAITANEN, RAULI

Center. Shoots left. 6'2", 183 lbs. Born, Pori, Finland, January 14, 1970.
(Winnipeg's 10th choice, 182nd overall, in 1990 Entry Draft).

			Regular Season					Playoffs				
Season	Club	Lea	GP	G	A	TP	PIM	GP	G	A	TP	PIM
1989-90	Assat	Fin.	41	17	44	61	20	....	....	....	....	....
1990-91	Assat	Fin.	43	6	16	22	14	....	....	....	....	....

RAMAGE, GEORGE (ROB) (RAM-ihj)

Defense. Shoots right. 6'2", 200 lbs. Born, Byron, Ont., January 11, 1959.
(Colorado's 1st choice and 1st overall 1979 Entry Draft).

			Regular Season					Playoffs				
Season	Club	Lea	GP	G	A	TP	PIM	GP	G	A	TP	PIM
1975-76	London	OHA	65	12	31	43	113	5	0	1	1	11
1976-77a	London	OHA	65	15	58	73	177	20	3	11	14	55
1977-78b	London	OHA	59	17	48	65	162	11	4	5	9	29
1978-79	Birmingham	WHA	80	12	36	48	165	....	....	....	....	....
1979-80	**Colorado**	**NHL**	**75**	**8**	**20**	**28**	**135**	....	....	....	....	....
1980-81	**Colorado**	**NHL**	**79**	**20**	**42**	**62**	**193**	....	....	....	....	....
1981-82	**Colorado**	**NHL**	**80**	**13**	**29**	**42**	**201**	....	....	....	....	....
1982-83	**St. Louis**	**NHL**	**78**	**16**	**35**	**51**	**193**	**4**	**0**	**3**	**3**	**22**
1983-84	**St. Louis**	**NHL**	**80**	**15**	**45**	**60**	**121**	**11**	**1**	**8**	**9**	**32**
1984-85	**St. Louis**	**NHL**	**80**	**7**	**31**	**38**	**178**	**3**	**1**	**3**	**4**	**6**
1985-86	**St. Louis**	**NHL**	**77**	**10**	**56**	**66**	**171**	**19**	**1**	**10**	**11**	**66**
1986-87	**St. Louis**	**NHL**	**59**	**11**	**28**	**39**	**108**	**6**	**2**	**2**	**4**	**21**
1987-88	**St. Louis**	**NHL**	**67**	**8**	**34**	**42**	**127**	....	....	....	....	....
	Calgary	**NHL**	**12**	**1**	**6**	**7**	**37**	**9**	**1**	**3**	**4**	**21**
1988-89	**Calgary**	**NHL**	**68**	**3**	**13**	**16**	**156**	**20**	**1**	**11**	**12**	**26**
1989-90	**Toronto**	**NHL**	**80**	**8**	**41**	**49**	**202**	**5**	**1**	**2**	**3**	**20**
1990-91	**Toronto**	**NHL**	**80**	**10**	**25**	**35**	**173**	....	....	....	....	....
	NHL Totals		**915**	**130**	**405**	**535**	**1995**	**77**	**8**	**42**	**50**	**214**

a OHA Third All-Star Team (1977)
b OHA First All-Star Team (1978)

Played in NHL All-Star Game (1981, 1984, 1986, 1988)

Traded to **St. Louis** by **New Jersey** for St. Louis' first round choice (Rocky Trottier) in 1982 Entry Draft and first round choice (John MacLean) in 1983 Entry Draft, June 9, 1982. Traded to **Calgary** by **St. Louis** with Rick Wamsley for Brett Hull and Steve Bozek, March 7, 1988. Traded to **Toronto** by **Calgary** for Toronto's second-round choice (Kent Manderville) in 1989 Entry Draft, June 16, 1989. Claimed by **Minnesota** from **Toronto** in Expansion Draft, May 30, 1991.

RAMSEY, MICHAEL ALLEN (MIKE)

Defense. Shoots left. 6'3", 195 lbs. Born, Minneapolis, MN, December 3, 1960.
(Buffalo's 1st choice, 11th overall, in 1979 Entry Draft).

			Regular Season					Playoffs				
Season	Club	Lea	GP	G	A	TP	PIM	GP	G	A	TP	PIM
1978-79	U. Minnesota	WCHA	26	6	11	17	30	....	....	....	....	....
1979-80	U.S. National	...	56	11	22	33	55	....	....	....	....	....
	U.S. Olympic	...	7	0	2	2	8	....	....	....	....	....
	Buffalo	**NHL**	**13**	**1**	**6**	**7**	**6**	**13**	**1**	**2**	**3**	**12**
1980-81	**Buffalo**	**NHL**	**72**	**3**	**14**	**17**	**56**	**8**	**0**	**3**	**3**	**20**
1981-82	**Buffalo**	**NHL**	**80**	**7**	**23**	**30**	**56**	**4**	**1**	**1**	**2**	**14**
1982-83	**Buffalo**	**NHL**	**77**	**8**	**30**	**38**	**55**	**10**	**4**	**4**	**8**	**15**
1983-84	**Buffalo**	**NHL**	**72**	**9**	**22**	**31**	**82**	**3**	**0**	**1**	**1**	**6**
1984-85	**Buffalo**	**NHL**	**79**	**8**	**22**	**30**	**102**	**5**	**0**	**1**	**1**	**23**
1985-86	**Buffalo**	**NHL**	**76**	**7**	**21**	**28**	**117**	....	....	....	....	....
1986-87	**Buffalo**	**NHL**	**80**	**8**	**31**	**39**	**109**	....	....	....	....	....
1987-88	**Buffalo**	**NHL**	**63**	**5**	**16**	**21**	**77**	**6**	**0**	**3**	**3**	**29**
1988-89	**Buffalo**	**NHL**	**56**	**2**	**14**	**16**	**84**	**5**	**1**	**0**	**1**	**11**
1989-90	**Buffalo**	**NHL**	**73**	**4**	**21**	**25**	**47**	**6**	**0**	**1**	**1**	**8**
1990-91	**Buffalo**	**NHL**	**71**	**6**	**14**	**20**	**46**	**5**	**1**	**0**	**1**	**12**
	NHL Totals		**812**	**68**	**234**	**302**	**837**	**65**	**8**	**16**	**24**	**150**

Played in NHL All-Star Game (1982, 1983, 1985, 1986)

RANHEIM, PAUL

Left wing. Shoots right. 6', 195 lbs. Born, St. Louis, MO, January 25, 1966.
(Calgary's 3rd choice, 38th overall, in 1984 Entry Draft).

			Regular Season					Playoffs				
Season	Club	Lea	GP	G	A	TP	PIM	GP	G	A	TP	PIM
1984-85	U. Wisconsin	WCHA	42	11	11	22	40	....	....	....	....	....
1985-86	U. Wisconsin	WCHA	33	17	17	34	34	....	....	....	....	....
1986-87a	U. Wisconsin	WCHA	42	24	35	59	54	....	....	....	....	....
1987-88bc	U. Wisconsin	WCHA	44	36	26	62	63	....	....	....	....	....
1988-89	**Calgary**	**NHL**	**5**	**0**	**0**	**0**	**0**	....	....	....	....	....
def	Salt Lake	IHL	75	*68	29	97	16	14	5	5	10	8
1989-90	**Calgary**	**NHL**	**80**	**26**	**28**	**54**	**23**	**6**	**1**	**3**	**4**	**2**
1990-91	**Calgary**	**NHL**	**39**	**14**	**16**	**30**	**4**	**7**	**2**	**2**	**4**	**0**
	NHL Totals		**124**	**40**	**44**	**84**	**27**	**13**	**3**	**5**	**8**	**2**

a WCHA Second All-Star Team (1987)
b NCAA West First All-American Team (1988)
c WCHA First All-Star Team (1988)
d IHL Second All-Star Team (1989)
e Won Garry F. Longman Memorial Trophy (Top Rookie-IHL) (1989)
f Won Ken McKenzie Trophy (Outstanding U.S.-born Rookie-IHL) (1989)

RATHBONE, JASON

Right wing. Shoots right. 6'0", 210 lbs. Born, Brookline, MA, April 13, 1970.
(NY Islanders' 8th choice, 121st overall, in 1988 Entry Draft).

			Regular Season					Playoffs				
Season	Club	Lea	GP	G	A	TP	PIM	GP	G	A	TP	PIM
1988-89	Boston College	H.E.	21	0	3	3	10	....	....	....	....	....
1989-90	Boston College	H.E.	37	4	7	11	20	....	....	....	....	....
1990-91	Boston College	H.E.	31	0	1	1	16	....	....	....	....	....

RATUSHNY, DAN

Defense. Shoots right. 6'1", 185 lbs. Born, Nepean, Ont., October 29, 1970.
(Winnipeg's 2nd choice, 25th overall, in 1989 Entry Draft).

			Regular Season					Playoffs				
Season	Club	Lea	GP	G	A	TP	PIM	GP	G	A	TP	PIM
1988-89	Cornell	ECAC	28	2	13	15	50	....	....	....	....	....
1989-90ab	Cornell	ECAC	26	5	14	19	54	....	....	....	....	....
1990-91ac	Cornell	ECAC	26	7	24	31	52	....	....	....	....	....
	Cdn. National	...	12	0	1	1	6	....	....	....	....	....

a ECAC First All-Star Team (1990, 1991)
b NCAA East Second All-American Team (1990)
c NCAA East First All-American Team (1991)

RAY, ROBERT

Left wing. Shoots left. 6'0", 210 lbs. Born, Stirling, Ont., June 8, 1968.
(Buffalo's 5th choice, 97th overall, in 1988 Entry Draft).

			Regular Season					Playoffs				
Season	Club	Lea	GP	G	A	TP	PIM	GP	G	A	TP	PIM
1985-86	Cornwall	OHL	53	6	13	19	253	6	0	0	0	26
1986-87	Cornwall	OHL	46	17	20	37	158	5	1	1	2	16
1987-88	Cornwall	OHL	61	11	41	52	179	11	2	3	5	33
1988-89	Rochester	AHL	74	11	18	29	*446	....	....	....	....	....
1989-90	**Buffalo**	**NHL**	**27**	**2**	**1**	**3**	**99**	....	....	....	....	....
	Rochester	AHL	43	2	13	15	335	17	1	3	4	115
1990-91	**Buffalo**	**NHL**	**66**	**8**	**8**	**16**	***350**	**6**	**1**	**1**	**2**	**56**
	Rochester	AHL	8	1	1	2	15	....	....	....	....	....
	NHL Totals		**93**	**10**	**9**	**19**	**449**	**6**	**1**	**1**	**2**	**56**

RECCHI, MARK

Right wing. Shoots left. 5'10", 185 lbs. Born, Kamloops, B.C., February 1, 1968.
(Pittsburgh's 4th choice, 67th overall, in 1988 Entry Draft).

			Regular Season					Playoffs				
Season	Club	Lea	GP	G	A	TP	PIM	GP	G	A	TP	PIM
1985-86	N. Westminster	WHL	72	21	40	61	55	....	....	....	....	....
1986-87	Kamloops	WHL	40	26	50	76	63	13	3	16	19	17
1987-88a	Kamloops	WHL	62	61	*93	154	75	17	10	*21	*31	18
1988-89	**Pittsburgh**	**NHL**	**15**	**1**	**1**	**2**	**0**	....	....	....	....	....
b	Muskegon	IHL	63	50	49	99	86	14	7	*14	*21	28
1989-90	**Pittsburgh**	**NHL**	**74**	**30**	**37**	**67**	**44**	....	....	....	....	....
	Muskegon	IHL	4	7	4	11	2	....	....	....	....	....
1990-91	**Pittsburgh**	**NHL**	**78**	**40**	**73**	**113**	**48**	**24**	**10**	**24**	**34**	**33**
	NHL Totals		**167**	**71**	**111**	**182**	**92**	**24**	**10**	**24**	**34**	**33**

a WHL West All-Star Team (1988)
b IHL Second All-Star Team (1989)

Played in NHL All-Star Game (1991)

REED, JACE

Defense. Shoots left. 6'3", 210 lbs. Born, Grand Rapids, MN, March 22, 1971.
(NY Islanders' 5th choice, 86th overall, in 1989 Entry Draft).

			Regular Season					Playoffs				
Season	Club	Lea	GP	G	A	TP	PIM	GP	G	A	TP	PIM
1989-90	North Dakota	WCHA	10	0	0	0	0	....	....	....	....	....
1990-91	North Dakota	WCHA	13	0	0	0	4	....	....	....	....	....

REEKIE, JOE

Defense. Shoots left. 6'3", 215 lbs. Born, Victoria, B.C., February 22, 1965.
(Buffalo's 6th choice, 119th overall, in 1985 Entry Draft)

			Regular Season					Playoffs				
Season	Club	Lea	GP	G	A	TP	PIM	GP	G	A	TP	PIM
1982-83	North Bay	OHL	59	2	9	11	49	8	0	1	1	11
1983-84	North Bay	OHL	9	1	0	1	18	....	....	....	....	....
	Cornwall	OHL	53	6	27	33	166	3	0	0	0	4
1984-85	Cornwall	OHL	65	19	63	82	134	9	4	13	17	18
1985-86	**Buffalo**	**NHL**	**3**	**0**	**0**	**0**	**14**	....	....	....	....	....
	Rochester	AHL	77	3	25	28	178	....	....	....	....	....
1986-87	**Buffalo**	**NHL**	**56**	**1**	**8**	**9**	**82**	....	....	....	....	....
	Rochester	AHL	22	0	6	6	52	....	....	....	....	....
1987-88	**Buffalo**	**NHL**	**30**	**1**	**4**	**5**	**68**	**2**	**0**	**0**	**0**	**4**
1988-89	**Buffalo**	**NHL**	**15**	**1**	**3**	**4**	**26**	....	....	....	....	....
	Rochester	AHL	21	1	2	3	56	....	....	....	....	....
1989-90	**NY Islanders**	**NHL**	**31**	**1**	**8**	**9**	**43**	....	....	....	....	....
	Springfield	AHL	15	1	4	5	24	....	....	....	....	....
1990-91	**NY Islanders**	**NHL**	**66**	**3**	**16**	**19**	**96**	....	....	....	....	....
	Capital Dist.	AHL	2	1	0	1	0	....	....	....	....	....
	NHL Totals		**201**	**7**	**39**	**46**	**329**	**2**	**0**	**0**	**0**	**4**

Traded to **NY Islanders** by **Buffalo** for NY Islanders' sixth round choice (Bill Pye) in 1989 Entry Draft, June 17, 1989.

REEVES, KYLE

Right wing. Shoots right. 5'11", 190 lbs. Born, Stonewall, Man., May 12, 1971.
(St. Louis' 2nd choice, 64th overall, in 1991 Entry Draft).

			Regular Season					Playoffs				
Season	Club	Lea	GP	G	A	TP	PIM	GP	G	A	TP	PIM
1989-90	Tri-City	WHL	67	67	36	103	94	7	2	1	3	8
1990-91a	Tri-City	WHL	63	*89	40	129	146	3	1	3	4	10

a WHL West Second All-Star Team (1991)

REICHEL, ROBERT (RAY-hahl)

Center. Shoots left. 5'11", 180 lbs. Born, Litvinov, Czechoslovakia, June 25, 1971.
(Calgary's 5th choice, 70th overall, in 1989 Entry Draft).

			Regular Season					Playoffs				
Season	Club	Lea	GP	G	A	TP	PIM	GP	G	A	TP	PIM
1988-89	Litvinov	Czech.	....	20	31	51	....	....	....	....	....	....
1989-90	Litvinov	Czech.	52	49	34	83	....	....	....	....	....	....
1990-91	**Calgary**	**NHL**	**66**	**19**	**22**	**41**	**22**	**6**	**1**	**1**	**2**	**0**
	NHL Totals		**66**	**19**	**22**	**41**	**22**	**6**	**1**	**1**	**2**	**0**

REID, DAVID

Left wing. Shoots left. 6'1", 205 lbs. Born, Toronto, Ont., May 15, 1964.
(Boston's 4th choice, 60th overall, in 1982 Entry Draft).

			Regular Season					Playoffs				
Season	Club	Lea	GP	G	A	TP	PIM	GP	G	A	TP	PIM
1981-82	Peterborough	OHL	68	10	32	42	41	9	2	3	5	11
1982-83	Peterborough	OHL	70	23	34	57	33	4	3	1	4	0
1983-84	**Boston**	**NHL**	**8**	**1**	**0**	**1**	**2**	....	....	....	....	....
	Peterborough	OHL	60	33	64	97	12	....	....	....	....	....
1984-85	**Boston**	**NHL**	**35**	**14**	**13**	**27**	**27**	**5**	**1**	**0**	**1**	**0**
	Hershey	AHL	43	10	14	24	6	....	....	....	....	....
1985-86	**Boston**	**NHL**	**37**	**10**	**10**	**20**	**10**	....	....	....	....	....
	Moncton	AHL	26	14	18	32	4	....	....	....	....	....
1986-87	**Boston**	**NHL**	**12**	**3**	**3**	**6**	**0**	**2**	**0**	**0**	**0**	**0**
	Moncton	AHL	40	12	22	34	23	5	0	1	1	0
1987-88	**Boston**	**NHL**	**3**	**0**	**0**	**0**	**0**	....	....	....	....	....
	Maine	AHL	63	21	37	58	40	10	6	7	13	0
1988-89	**Toronto**	**NHL**	**77**	**9**	**21**	**30**	**22**	....	....	....	....	....
1989-90	**Toronto**	**NHL**	**70**	**9**	**19**	**28**	**9**	**3**	**0**	**0**	**0**	**0**
1990-91	**Toronto**	**NHL**	**69**	**15**	**13**	**28**	**18**	....	....	....	....	....
	NHL Totals		**311**	**61**	**79**	**140**	**88**	**10**	**1**	**0**	**1**	**0**

Signed as a free agent by **Toronto**, June 23, 1988.

REIERSON, DAVID (DAVE)

Defense. Shoots right. 6', 185 lbs. Born, Bashaw, Alta., August 30, 1964.
(Calgary's 1st choice, 29th overall, in 1982 Entry Draft).

			Regular Season					Playoffs				
Season	Club	Lea	GP	G	A	TP	PIM	GP	G	A	TP	PIM
1982-83	Michigan Tech	CCHA	38	2	14	16	52	....	....	....	....	....
1983-84	Michigan Tech	CCHA	38	4	15	19	63	....	....	....	....	....
1984-85	Michigan Tech	CCHA	36	5	27	32	76	....	....	....	....	....
1985-86	Michigan Tech	WCHA	39	7	16	23	51	....	....	....	....	....
1986-87	Moncton	AHL	....	....	....	....	....	6	0	1	1	12
	Cdn. Olympic	...	61	1	17	18	36	....	....	....	....	....
1987-88	Salt Lake	IHL	48	10	19	29	42	16	2	14	16	30
	Cdn. Olympic	...	32	2	8	10	18	....	....	....	....	....
1988-89	**Calgary**	**NHL**	**2**	**0**	**0**	**0**	**2**	....	....	....	....	....
	Salt Lake	IHL	76	7	46	53	70	13	1	8	9	12
1989-90	Tappara	Fin.	32	7	5	12	28	7	0	2	2	12
1990-91	Tappara	Fin.	41	1	8	9	18	3	0	0	0	2
	Cdn. National	...	8	0	1	1	6	....	....	....	....	....
	NHL Totals		**2**	**0**	**0**	**0**	**2**	....	....	....	....	....

REILLY, JOHN

Left wing. Shoots left. 6'3", 188 lbs. Born, Lawrence, MA, January 5, 1968.
(Chicago's 8th choice, 155th overall, in 1987 Entry Draft).

			Regular Season					Playoffs				
Season	Club	Lea	GP	G	A	TP	PIM	GP	G	A	TP	PIM
1987-88	Boston College	H.E.	8	0	0	0	0	....	....	....	....	....
1988-89	Boston College	H.E.	DID NOT PLAY									
1989-90	Boston College	H.E.	9	1	2	3	0	....	....	....	....	....
1990-91	Boston College	H.E.	13	0	0	0	4	....	....	....	....	....

REIRDEN, TODD

Defense. Shoots left. 6'4", 175 lbs. Born, Arlington Heights, IL, June 25, 1971.
(New Jersey's 14th choice, 242nd overall, in 1990 Entry Draft).

			Regular Season					Playoffs				
Season	Club	Lea	GP	G	A	TP	PIM	GP	G	A	TP	PIM
1989-90	Tabor	HS	....	10	28	38	....	....	....	....	....	....
1990-91	Bowling Green	CCHA	28	1	5	6	22	....	....	....	....	....

REISMAN, ERIC

Defense. Shoots left. 6'2", 220 lbs. Born, New York, NY, May 19, 1968.
(Boston's 8th choice, 228th overall, in 1988 Entry Draft).

			Regular Season					Playoffs				
Season	Club	Lea	GP	G	A	TP	PIM	GP	G	A	TP	PIM
1987-88	Ohio State	CCHA	29	0	3	3	45	....	....	....	....	....
1988-89	Ohio State	CCHA	38	4	6	10	56	....	....	....	....	....
1989-90	Ohio State	CCHA	39	1	2	3	91	....	....	....	....	....
1990-91	Ohio State	CCHA	40	2	8	10	105	....	....	....	....	....

RENBERG, MIKAEL (REHN-buhrg)

Left wing. Shoots left. 6'2", 185 lbs. Born, Pitea, Sweden, May 5, 1972.
(Philadelphia's 3rd choice, 40th overall, in 1990 Entry Draft).

			Regular Season					Playoffs				
Season	Club	Lea	GP	G	A	TP	PIM	GP	G	A	TP	PIM
1988-89	Pitea	Swe.2	12	6	3	9	....	....	....	....	....	....
1989-90	Pitea	Swe.2	29	15	19	34	....	....	....	....	....	....
1990-91	Lulea	Swe.	29	11	6	17	12	....	....	....	....	....

REVENBERG, JAMES

Right wing. Shoots right. 6'1", 199 lbs. Born, Windsor, Ont., July 23, 1969.
(Vancouver's 5th choice, 134th overall, in 1989 Entry Draft).

			Regular Season					Playoffs				
Season	Club	Lea	GP	G	A	TP	PIM	GP	G	A	TP	PIM
1987-88	Windsor	OHL	66	1	6	7	206	12	0	0	0	41
1988-89	Windsor	OHL	58	9	15	24	292	3	2	0	2	32
1989-90	Milwaukee	IHL	56	1	6	7	314	4	0	0	0	45
1990-91	Milwaukee	IHL	7	0	2	2	71	....	....	....	....	....

REYNOLDS, BOBBY

Left wing. Shoots left. 5'11", 175 lbs.   Born, Flint, MI, July 14, 1967.
(Toronto's 10th choice, 190th overall, in 1985 Entry Draft).

				Regular Season					Playoffs			
Season	Club	Lea	GP	G	A	TP	PIM	GP	G	A	TP	PIM
1985-86	Michigan State	CCHA	45	9	10	19	26	.....	....	....	....	....
1986-87	Michigan State	CCHA	40	20	13	33	40	.....	....	....	....	....
1987-88a	Michigan State	CCHA	46	42	25	67	52	.....	....	....	....	....
1988-89ab	Michigan State	CCHA	47	36	41	77	78	.....	....	....	....	....
1989-90	**Toronto**	**NHL**	**7**	**1**	**1**	**2**	**0**	.....	....	....	....	....
	Newmarket	AHL	66	22	28	50	55	.....	....	....	....	....
1990-91	Newmarket	AHL	65	24	22	46	59	.....	....	....	....	....
	Baltimore	AHL	14	4	9	13	8	6	2	2	4	10
	NHL Totals		**7**	**1**	**1**	**2**	**0**	.....	....	....	....	....

a CCHA Second All-Star Team (1988, 1989)
b NCAA West First All-American Team (1989)
Traded to **Washington** by **Toronto** for Rob Mendel, March 5, 1991.

RICARD, ERIC

Defense. Shoots left. 6'4", 220 lbs.   Born, St. Cesaire, Que., February 16, 1969.
(Los Angeles' 3rd choice, 102nd overall, in 1989 Entry Draft).

				Regular Season					Playoffs			
Season	Club	Lea	GP	G	A	TP	PIM	GP	G	A	TP	PIM
1988-89	Granby	QMJHL	68	5	31	36	213	4	1	1	2	21
1989-90	New Haven	AHL	28	1	1	2	55	.....	....	....	....	....
1990-91	New Haven	AHL	35	1	4	5	65	.....	....	....	....	....
	Phoenix	IHL	16	1	3	4	24	.....	....	....	....	....

RICCI, MIKE   (RICK-ee)

Center. Shoots left. 6', 190 lbs.   Born, Scarborough, Ont., October 27, 1971.
(Philadelphia's 1st choice, 4th overall, in 1990 Entry Draft).

				Regular Season					Playoffs			
Season	Club	Lea	GP	G	A	TP	PIM	GP	G	A	TP	PIM
1987-88	Peterborough	OHL	41	24	37	61	20	.....	....	....	....	....
1988-89a	Peterborough	OHL	60	54	52	106	43	17	19	16	35	18
1989-90bcd	Peterborough	OHL	60	52	64	116	39	12	5	7	12	26
1990-91	**Philadelphia**	**NHL**	**68**	**21**	**20**	**41**	**64**	.....	....	....	....	....
	NHL Totals		**68**	**21**	**20**	**41**	**64**	.....	....	....	....	....

a OHL Second All-Star Team (1989)
b Canadian Major Junior Player of the Year (1990)
c OHL First All-Star Team (1990)
d OHL Player of the Year (1990)

RICE, STEVEN

Right wing. Shoots right. 6', 215 lbs.   Born, Kitchener, Ont., May 26, 1971.
(NY Rangers' 1st choice, 20th overall, in 1989 Entry Draft).

				Regular Season					Playoffs			
Season	Club	Lea	GP	G	A	TP	PIM	GP	G	A	TP	PIM
1987-88	Kitchener	OHL	59	11	14	25	43	4	0	1	1	0
1988-89	Kitchener	OHL	64	36	30	66	42	5	2	1	3	8
1989-90ab	Kitchener	OHL	58	39	37	76	102	16	4	8	12	24
1990-91	**NY Rangers**	**NHL**	**11**	**1**	**1**	**2**	**4**	**2**	**2**	**1**	**3**	**6**
	Binghamton	AHL	8	4	1	5	12	5	2	0	2	2
c	Kitchener	OHL	29	30	30	60	43	6	5	6	11	2
	NHL Totals		**11**	**1**	**1**	**2**	**4**	**2**	**2**	**1**	**3**	**6**

a OHL Third All-Star Team (1990)
b Memorial Cup All-Star Team (1990)
c OHL Second All-Star Team (1991)

RICHARD, JEAN-MARC

Defense. Shoots left. 5'11", 178 lbs.   Born, St.-Raymond, Que., October 8, 1966.

				Regular Season					Playoffs			
Season	Club	Lea	GP	G	A	TP	PIM	GP	G	A	TP	PIM
1985-86a	Chicoutimi	QMJHL	72	20	87	107	111	9	3	5	8	14
1986-87a	Chicoutimi	QMJHL	67	21	81	102	105	16	6	25	31	28
1987-88	**Quebec**	**NHL**	**4**	**2**	**1**	**3**	**2**	.....	....	....	....	....
	Fredericton	AHL	68	14	42	56	52	7	2	1	3	4
1988-89	Halifax	AHL	57	8	25	33	38	4	1	0	1	4
1989-90	**Quebec**	**NHL**	**1**	**0**	**0**	**0**	**0**	.....	....	....	....	....
	Halifax	AHL	40	1	24	25	38	.....	....	....	....	....
1990-91	Halifax	AHL	80	7	41	48	76	.....	....	....	....	....
	Fort Wayne	IHL	1	0	0	0	0	19	3	9	12	8
	NHL Totals		**5**	**2**	**1**	**3**	**2**	.....	....	....	....	....

a QMJHL First All-Star Team (1986, 1987)
Signed as a free agent by **Quebec**, April 13, 1987.

RICHARD, MICHAEL (MIKE)

Center. Shoots left. 5'10", 190 lbs.   Born, Scarborough, Ont., July 9, 1966.

				Regular Season					Playoffs			
Season	Club	Lea	GP	G	A	TP	PIM	GP	G	A	TP	PIM
1983-84	Toronto	OHL	66	19	17	36	12	9	2	1	3	0
1984-85	Toronto	OHL	66	31	41	72	15	5	0	0	0	11
1985-86	Toronto	OHL	63	32	48	80	28	4	1	1	2	2
1986-87	Toronto	OHL	66	57	50	107	38	.....	....	....	....	....
1987-88	**Washington**	**NHL**	**4**	**0**	**0**	**0**	**0**	.....	....	....	....	....
a	Binghamton	AHL	72	46	48	94	23	4	0	3	3	4
1988-89	Baltimore	AHL	80	44	63	107	51	.....	....	....	....	....
1989-90	**Washington**	**NHL**	**3**	**0**	**2**	**2**	**0**	.....	....	....	....	....
b	Baltimore	AHL	53	41	42	83	14	11	4	*13	17	6
1990-91	Zurich	Switz.	36	28	23	51	...	....	1	3	4	...
	NHL Totals		**7**	**0**	**2**	**2**	**0**	.....	....	....	....	....

a Won Dudley "Red" Garrett Memorial Trophy (Top Rookie - AHL) (1988).
b AHL Second All-Star Team (1990)
Signed as a free agent by **Washington**, October 9, 1987.

RICHARDS, TODD

Defense. Shoots right. 6', 194 lbs.   Born, Robindale, MN, October, 20, 1966.
(Montreal's 3rd choice, 33rd overall, in 1985 Entry Draft).

				Regular Season					Playoffs			
Season	Club	Lea	GP	G	A	TP	PIM	GP	G	A	TP	PIM
1985-86	U. Minnesota	WCHA	38	6	23	29	38	.....	....	....	....	....
1986-87	U. Minnesota	WCHA	49	8	43	51	70	.....	....	....	....	....
1987-88a	U. Minnesota	WCHA	34	10	30	40	26	.....	....	....	....	....
1988-89abc	U. Minnesota	WCHA	46	6	32	38	60	.....	....	....	....	....
1989-90	Sherbrooke	AHL	71	6	18	24	73	5	1	2	3	6
1990-91	Fredericton	AHL	3	0	1	1	2	.....	....	....	....	....
	Hartford	**NHL**	**2**	**0**	**4**	**4**	**2**	**6**	**0**	**0**	**0**	**2**
	Springfield	AHL	71	10	41	51	62	14	2	8	10	2
	NHL Totals		**2**	**0**	**4**	**4**	**2**	**6**	**0**	**0**	**0**	**2**

a WCHA Second All-Star Team (1988, 1989)
b NCAA West Second All-American Team (1989)
c NCAA All-Tournament Team (1989)
Traded to **Hartford** by **Montreal** for future considerations, October 11, 1990.

RICHARDS, TRAVIS

Defense. Shoots left. 6'1", 185 lbs.   Born, Crystal, MN, March 22, 1970.
(Minnesota's 6th choice, 169th overall, in 1988 Entry Draft).

				Regular Season					Playoffs			
Season	Club	Lea	GP	G	A	TP	PIM	GP	G	A	TP	PIM
1988-89	U. Minnesota	WCHA		DID NOT PLAY								
1989-90	U. Minnesota	WCHA	45	4	24	28	38	.....	....	....	....	....
1990-91	U. Minnesota	WCHA	45	9	25	34	28	.....	....	....	....	....

RICHARDSON, LUKE

Defense. Shoots left. 6'3", 215 lbs.   Born, Ottawa, Ont., March 26, 1969.
(Toronto's 1st choice, 7th overall, in 1987 Entry Draft).

				Regular Season					Playoffs			
Season	Club	Lea	GP	G	A	TP	PIM	GP	G	A	TP	PIM
1985-86	Peterborough	OHL	63	6	18	24	57	16	2	1	3	50
1986-87	Peterborough	OHL	59	13	32	45	70	12	0	5	5	24
1987-88	**Toronto**	**NHL**	**78**	**4**	**6**	**10**	**90**	**2**	**0**	**0**	**0**	**0**
1988-89	**Toronto**	**NHL**	**55**	**2**	**7**	**9**	**106**	.....	....	....	....	....
1989-90	**Toronto**	**NHL**	**67**	**4**	**14**	**18**	**122**	**5**	**0**	**0**	**0**	**22**
1990-91	**Toronto**	**NHL**	**78**	**1**	**9**	**10**	**238**	.....	....	....	....	....
	NHL Totals		**278**	**11**	**36**	**47**	**556**	**7**	**0**	**0**	**0**	**22**

RICHER, STEPHANE J. G.   (REE-shay)

Defense. Shoots right. 5'11", 200 lbs.   Born, Hull, Que., April 28, 1966.

				Regular Season					Playoffs			
Season	Club	Lea	GP	G	A	TP	PIM	GP	G	A	TP	PIM
1986-87	Hull	QMJHL	33	6	22	28	74	8	3	4	7	17
1987-88	Baltimore	AHL	22	0	3	3	6	.....	....	....	....	....
	Sherbrooke	AHL	41	4	7	11	46	5	1	0	1	10
1988-89	Sherbrooke	AHL	70	7	26	33	158	6	1	2	3	18
1989-90	Sherbrooke	AHL	60	10	12	22	85	12	4	9	13	16
1990-91	New Haven	AHL	3	0	1	1	0	.....	....	....	....	....
	Phoenix	IHL	67	11	38	49	48	11	4	6	10	6

Signed as a free agent by **Montreal**, January 9, 1988. Signed as a free agent by **Los Angeles**, July 11, 1990.

RICHER, STEPHANE J. J.   (REE-shay)

Right wing. Shoots right. 6'2", 200 lbs.   Born, Ripon, Que., June 7, 1966.
(Montreal's 3rd choice, 29th overall, in 1984 Entry Draft).

				Regular Season					Playoffs			
Season	Club	Lea	GP	G	A	TP	PIM	GP	G	A	TP	PIM
1983-84a	Granby	QMJHL	67	39	37	76	58	3	1	1	2	4
1984-85	Granby	QMJHL	30	30	27	57	31	.....	....	....	....	....
b	Chicoutimi	QMJHL	27	31	32	63	40	12	13	13	26	25
	Montreal	**NHL**	**1**	**0**	**0**	**0**	**0**	.....	....	....	....	....
	Sherbrooke	AHL	.....	....	....	....	....	9	6	3	9	10
1985-86	**Montreal**	**NHL**	**65**	**21**	**16**	**37**	**50**	**16**	**4**	**1**	**5**	**23**
1986-87	**Montreal**	**NHL**	**57**	**20**	**19**	**39**	**80**	**5**	**3**	**2**	**5**	**0**
	Sherbrooke	AHL	12	10	4	14	11	.....	....	....	....	....
1987-88	**Montreal**	**NHL**	**72**	**50**	**28**	**78**	**72**	**8**	**7**	**5**	**12**	**6**
1988-89	**Montreal**	**NHL**	**68**	**25**	**35**	**60**	**61**	**21**	**6**	**5**	**11**	**14**
1989-90	**Montreal**	**NHL**	**75**	**51**	**40**	**91**	**46**	**9**	**7**	**3**	**10**	**2**
1990-91	**Montreal**	**NHL**	**75**	**31**	**30**	**61**	**53**	**13**	**9**	**5**	**14**	**6**
	NHL Totals		**413**	**198**	**168**	**366**	**362**	**72**	**36**	**21**	**57**	**51**

a QMJHL Rookie of the Year (1984)
b QMJHL Second All-Star Team (1985)
Played in NHL All-Star Game (1990)

RICHISON, GRANT DAVID

Defense. Shoots left. 6'2", 205 lbs.   Born, Detroit, MI, May 5, 1967.

				Regular Season					Playoffs			
Season	Club	Lea	GP	G	A	TP	PIM	GP	G	A	TP	PIM
1988-89	U. of Calgary	CWUAA	16	2	12	14	59	.....	....	....	....	....
1989-90	Moncton	AHL	50	2	10	12	28	.....	....	....	....	....
1990-91	Moncton	AHL	49	4	10	14	57	.....	....	....	....	....

Signed as a free agent by **Winnipeg**, October 18, 1989.

RICHMOND, STEVE

Defense. Shoots left. 6'1", 205 lbs. Born, Chicago, IL, December 11, 1959.

			Regular Season					Playoffs				
Season	Club	Lea	GP	G	A	TP	PIM	GP	G	A	TP	PIM
1978-79	U. of Michigan	CCHA	34	2	5	7	38	....	....	....	....	....
1979-80	U. of Michigan	CCHA	38	10	19	29	26	....	....	....	....	....
1980-81	U. of Michigan	CCHA	39	22	32	54	56	....	....	....	....	....
1981-82a	U. of Michigan	CCHA	38	6	30	36	68	....	....	....	....	....
1982-83	Tulsa	CHL	68	5	13	18	187	....	....	....	....	....
1983-84	**NY Rangers**	**NHL**	**26**	**2**	**5**	**7**	**110**	**4**	**0**	**0**	**0**	**12**
	Tulsa	CHL	38	1	17	18	114	....	....	....	....	....
1984-85	**NY Rangers**	**NHL**	**34**	**0**	**5**	**5**	**90**	....	....	....	....	....
	New Haven	AHL	37	3	10	13	122	....	....	....	....	....
1985-86	**NY Rangers**	**NHL**	**17**	**0**	**2**	**2**	**63**	....	....	....	....	....
	New Haven	AHL	11	2	6	8	32	....	....	....	....	....
	Detroit	**NHL**	**29**	**1**	**2**	**3**	**82**	....	....	....	....	....
	Adirondack	AHL	20	1	7	8	23	17	2	9	11	34
1986-87	**New Jersey**	**NHL**	**44**	**1**	**7**	**8**	**143**	....	....	....	....	....
1987-88	Utica	AHL	79	6	27	33	141	....	....	....	....	....
1988-89	**Los Angeles**	**NHL**	**9**	**0**	**2**	**2**	**26**	....	....	....	....	....
	New Haven	AHL	49	6	35	41	114	17	3	10	13	84
1989-90	Flint	IHL	10	1	3	4	19	4	0	1	1	16
1990-91	San Diego	IHL	12	3	7	10	19	....	....	....	....	....
	NHL Totals		**159**	**4**	**23**	**27**	**514**	**4**	**0**	**0**	**0**	**12**

a CCHA Second All-Star Team (1982)

Signed as a free agent by **NY Rangers**, June 22, 1982. Traded to **Detroit** by **NY Rangers** for Mike McEwen, December 26, 1985. Traded to **New Jersey** by **Detroit** for Sam St. Laurent, August 18, 1986. Signed as a free agent by **Los Angeles**, July 7, 1988.

RICHTER, BARRY

Defense. Shoots left. 6'2", 185 lbs. Born, Madison, WI, September 11, 1970.
(Hartford's 2nd choice, 32nd overall, in 1988 Entry Draft).

			Regular Season					Playoffs				
Season	Club	Lea	GP	G	A	TP	PIM	GP	G	A	TP	PIM
1989-90	U. Wisconsin	WCHA	42	13	23	36	36	....	....	....	....	....
1990-91	U. Wisconsin	WCHA	43	15	20	35	42	....	....	....	....	....

RICHTER, DAVE (RIHK-tuhr)

Defense. Shoots right. 6'5", 225 lbs. Born, St. Boniface, Man., April 8, 1960.
(Minnesota's 10th choice, 205th overall, in 1980 Entry Draft).

			Regular Season					Playoffs				
Season	Club	Lea	GP	G	A	TP	PIM	GP	G	A	TP	PIM
1980-81	U. of Michigan	WCHA	36	2	13	15	56	....	....	....	....	....
1981-82	U. of Michigan	WCHA	36	9	12	21	78	....	....	....	....	....
	Minnesota	**NHL**	**3**	**0**	**0**	**0**	**11**	....	....	....	....	....
	Nashville	CHL	2	0	1	1	0	....	....	....	....	....
1982-83	**Minnesota**	**NHL**	**6**	**0**	**0**	**0**	**4**	....	....	....	....	....
	Birmingham	CHL	69	6	17	23	211	13	3	1	4	36
1983-84	**Minnesota**	**NHL**	**42**	**2**	**3**	**5**	**132**	**8**	**0**	**0**	**0**	**20**
	Salt Lake	CHL	10	1	4	5	39	....	....	....	....	....
1984-85	**Minnesota**	**NHL**	**55**	**2**	**8**	**10**	**221**	**9**	**1**	**0**	**1**	**39**
	Springfield	AHL	3	0	0	0	2	....	....	....	....	....
1985-86	**Minnesota**	**NHL**	**14**	**0**	**3**	**3**	**29**	....	....	....	....	....
	Philadelphia	**NHL**	**50**	**0**	**2**	**2**	**138**	**5**	**0**	**0**	**0**	**21**
1986-87	**Vancouver**	**NHL**	**78**	**2**	**15**	**17**	**172**	....	....	....	....	....
1987-88	**Vancouver**	**NHL**	**49**	**2**	**4**	**6**	**224**	....	....	....	....	....
1988-89	**St. Louis**	**NHL**	**66**	**1**	**5**	**6**	**99**	....	....	....	....	....
1989-90	**St. Louis**	**NHL**	**2**	**0**	**0**	**0**	**0**	....	....	....	....	....
	Peoria	IHL	9	1	4	5	30	....	....	....	....	....
	Phoenix	IHL	20	0	5	5	49	....	....	....	....	....
	Baltimore	AHL	13	0	1	1	13	....	....	....	....	....
1990-91	Albany	IHL	41	0	1	1	128	....	....	....	....	....
	Capital Dist.	AHL	3	0	1	1	0	....	....	....	....	....
	NHL Totals		**365**	**9**	**40**	**49**	**1030**	**22**	**1**	**0**	**1**	**80**

Traded to **Philadelphia** by **Minnesota** with Bo Berglund for Ed Hospodar and Todd Bergen, November 29, 1985. Traded to **Vancouver** by **Philadelphia** with Rich Sutter and Vancouver's third-round choice (Don Gibson) — acquired earlier — in 1986 Entry Draft fror J.J. Daigneault and Vancouver's second-round choice (Kent Hawley) in 1986 Entry Draft, June 6, 1986. Traded to **St. Louis** by **Vancouver** with Vancouver's second-round choice in 1990 Entry Draft for Robert Nordmark, September 6, 1988.

RIDLEY, MIKE

Center. Shoots left. 6'1", 200 lbs. Born, Winnipeg, Man., July 8, 1963.

			Regular Season					Playoffs				
Season	Club	Lea	GP	G	A	TP	PIM	GP	G	A	TP	PIM
1983-84a	U. of Manitoba	GPAC	46	39	41	80	...	....	....	....	....	....
1984-85b	U. of Manitoba	GPAC	30	29	38	67	48	....	....	....	....	....
1985-86c	**NY Rangers**	**NHL**	**80**	**22**	**43**	**65**	**69**	**16**	**6**	**8**	**14**	**26**
1986-87	**NY Rangers**	**NHL**	**38**	**16**	**20**	**36**	**20**	....	....	....	....	....
	Washington	**NHL**	**40**	**15**	**19**	**34**	**20**	**7**	**2**	**1**	**3**	**6**
1987-88	**Washington**	**NHL**	**70**	**28**	**31**	**59**	**22**	**14**	**6**	**5**	**11**	**10**
1988-89	**Washington**	**NHL**	**80**	**41**	**48**	**89**	**49**	**6**	**0**	**5**	**5**	**2**
1989-90	**Washington**	**NHL**	**74**	**30**	**43**	**73**	**27**	**14**	**3**	**4**	**7**	**8**
1990-91	**Washington**	**NHL**	**79**	**23**	**48**	**71**	**26**	**11**	**3**	**4**	**7**	**8**
	NHL Totals		**461**	**175**	**252**	**427**	**233**	**68**	**20**	**27**	**47**	**60**

a Canadian University Player of the Year; CIAU All-Canadian, GPAC MVP and First All-Star Team (1984)
b CIAU All-Canadian, GPAC First All-Star Team (1985)
c NHL All-Rookie Team (1986)

Played in NHL All-Star Game (1989)

Signed as a free agent by **NY Rangers**, September 26, 1985. Traded to **Washington** by **NY Rangers** with Bob Crawford and Kelly Miller for Bob Carpenter and, Washington's second-round choice (Jason Prosofsky) in 1989 Entry Draft, January 1, 1987.

RIIHIJARVI, HEIKKI (ree-hee-YAHR-vee)

Defense. Shoots left. 6'4", 222 lbs. Born, Salla, Finland, June 4, 1966.
(Edmonton's 8th choice, 147th overall, in 1984 Entry Draft).

			Regular Season					Playoffs				
Season	Club	Lea	GP	G	A	TP	PIM	GP	G	A	TP	PIM
1985-86	TPS	Fin.Jr.	25	6	8	14	12	....	....	....	....	....
1986-87	Karpat	Fin.	36	4	4	8	10	....	....	....	....	....
1987-88	Karpat	Fin.	21	0	5	5	0	....	....	....	....	....
1988-89	Karpat	Fin.	43	8	11	19	14	5	0	2	2	4
1989-90	Jokerit	Fin.	44	3	10	13	16	....	....	....	....	....
1990-91	Jokerit	Fin.	36	4	4	8	12	....	....	....	....	....

ROBERGE, MARIO

Left wing. Shoots left. 5'11", 185 lbs. Born, Quebec City, Que., January 23, 1964.

			Regular Season					Playoffs				
Season	Club	Lea	GP	G	A	TP	PIM	GP	G	A	TP	PIM
1987-88	Pt. Basques	Sr.	35	25	64	89	152	....	....	....	....	....
1988-89	Sherbrooke	AHL	58	4	9	13	249	6	0	2	2	8
1989-90	Sherbrooke	AHL	73	13	27	40	247	12	5	2	7	53
1990-91	**Montreal**	**NHL**	**5**	**0**	**0**	**0**	**21**	**12**	**0**	**0**	**0**	**24**
	Fredericton	AHL	68	12	27	39	*365	2	0	2	2	5
	NHL Totals		**5**	**0**	**0**	**0**	**21**	**12**	**0**	**0**	**0**	**24**

Signed as a free agent by **Montreal**, October 5, 1988.

ROBERGE, SERGE

Right wing. Shoots right. 6'1", 195 lbs. Born, Quebec City, Que., March 31, 1965.

			Regular Season					Playoffs				
Season	Club	Lea	GP	G	A	TP	PIM	GP	G	A	TP	PIM
1984-85	Drummondville	QMJHL	45	8	19	27	299	....	....	....	....	....
1985-86	DID NOT PLAY											
1986-87	Virginia	ACHL	47	9	15	24	346	....	....	....	....	....
1987-88	Sherbrooke	AHL	30	0	1	1	130	5	0	0	0	21
1988-89	Sherbrooke	AHL	65	5	7	12	352	6	0	1	1	10
1989-90	Sherbrooke	AHL	66	8	5	13	343	12	2	0	2	44
1990-91	**Quebec**	**NHL**	**9**	**0**	**0**	**0**	**24**	....	....	....	....	....
	Halifax	AHL	52	0	5	5	152	....	....	....	....	....
	NHL Totals		**9**	**0**	**0**	**0**	**24**	....	....	....	....	....

Signed as a free agent by **Montreal**, January 25, 1988. Signed as a free agent by **Quebec**, December 28, 1990.

ROBERTS, ALEX

Defense. Shoots left. 6'1", 185 lbs. Born, Bloomfield Hills, MI, January 11, 1968.
(Chicago's 1st choice, 11th overall, in 1989 Supplemental Draft).

			Regular Season					Playoffs				
Season	Club	Lea	GP	G	A	TP	PIM	GP	G	A	TP	PIM
1986-87	U. of Michigan	CCHA	37	1	7	8	117	....	....	....	....	....
1987-88	U. of Michigan	CCHA	39	4	9	13	77	....	....	....	....	....
1988-89	U. of Michigan	CCHA	41	5	19	24	116	....	....	....	....	....
1989-90	U. of Michigan	CCHA	41	14	21	35	105	....	....	....	....	....
1990-91	Indianapolis	IHL	79	11	18	29	89	7	0	3	3	10

ROBERTS, DAVID

Left wing. Shoots left. 6', 185 lbs. Born, Alameda, CA, May 28, 1970.
(St. Louis' 5th choice, 114th overall, in 1989 Entry Draft).

			Regular Season					Playoffs				
Season	Club	Lea	GP	G	A	TP	PIM	GP	G	A	TP	PIM
1989-90a	U. of Michigan	CCHA	42	21	32	53	46	....	....	....	....	....
1990-91bc	U. of Michigan	CCHA	43	40	35	75	58	....	....	....	....	....

a CCHA Rookie of the Year (1990)
b CCHA Second All-Star Team (1991)
c NCAA West Second All-American Team (1991)

ROBERTS, GARY

Left wing. Shoots left. 6'1", 190 lbs. Born, North York, Ont., May 23, 1966.
(Calgary's 1st choice, 12th overall, in 1984 Entry Draft).

			Regular Season					Playoffs				
Season	Club	Lea	GP	G	A	TP	PIM	GP	G	A	TP	PIM
1982-83	Ottawa	OHL	53	12	8	20	83	5	1	0	1	19
1983-84	Ottawa	OHL	48	27	30	57	144	13	10	7	17	62
1984-85	Moncton	AHL	7	4	2	6	7	....	....	....	....	....
a	Ottawa	OHL	59	44	62	106	186	5	2	8	10	10
1985-86a	Ottawa	OHL	24	26	25	51	83	....	....	....	....	....
a	Guelph	OHL	23	18	15	33	65	20	18	13	31	43
1986-87	**Calgary**	**NHL**	**32**	**5**	**10**	**15**	**85**	**2**	**0**	**0**	**0**	**4**
	Moncton	AHL	38	20	18	38	72	....	....	....	....	....
1987-88	**Calgary**	**NHL**	**74**	**13**	**15**	**28**	**282**	**9**	**2**	**3**	**5**	**29**
1988-89	**Calgary**	**NHL**	**71**	**22**	**16**	**38**	**250**	**22**	**5**	**7**	**12**	**57**
1989-90	**Calgary**	**NHL**	**78**	**39**	**33**	**72**	**222**	**6**	**2**	**5**	**7**	**41**
1990-91	**Calgary**	**NHL**	**80**	**22**	**31**	**53**	**252**	**7**	**1**	**3**	**4**	**18**
	NHL Totals		**335**	**101**	**105**	**206**	**1091**	**46**	**10**	**18**	**28**	**149**

a OHL Second All-Star Team (1985, 1986)

ROBERTS, GORDON (GORDIE)

Defense. Shoots left. 6', 190 lbs.   Born, Detroit, MI, October 2, 1957.
(Montreal's 7th choice, 54th overall, in 1977 Amateur Draft).

Season	Club	Lea	GP	G	A	TP	PIM	GP	G	A	TP	PIM
1974-75	Victoria	WHL	53	19	45	64	145	12	1	9	10	42
1975-76	New England	WHA	77	3	19	22	102	17	2	9	11	36
1976-77	New England	WHA	77	13	33	46	169	5	2	2	4	6
1977-78	New England	WHA	78	15	46	61	118	14	0	5	5	29
1978-79	New England	WHA	79	11	46	57	113	10	0	4	4	10
1979-80	**Hartford**	NHL	80	8	28	36	89	3	1	1	2	2
1980-81	**Hartford**	NHL	27	2	11	13	81	....	....	....	....	....
	Minnesota	NHL	50	6	31	37	94	19	1	5	6	17
1981-82	**Minnesota**	NHL	79	4	30	34	119	4	0	3	3	27
1982-83	**Minnesota**	NHL	80	3	41	44	103	9	1	5	6	14
1983-84	**Minnesota**	NHL	77	8	45	53	132	15	3	7	10	23
1984-85	**Minnesota**	NHL	78	6	36	42	112	9	1	6	7	6
1985-86	**Minnesota**	NHL	76	2	21	23	101	5	0	4	4	8
1986-87	**Minnesota**	NHL	67	3	10	13	98	....	....	....	....	....
1987-88	**Minnesota**	NHL	48	1	10	11	103	....	....	....	....	....
	Philadelphia	NHL	11	1	2	3	15	....	....	....	....	....
	St. Louis	NHL	11	1	3	4	25	10	1	2	3	33
1988-89	**St. Louis**	NHL	77	2	24	26	90	10	1	7	8	8
1989-90	**St. Louis**	NHL	75	3	14	17	140	10	0	2	2	26
1990-91	**St. Louis**	NHL	3	0	1	1	8	....	....	....	....	....
	Peoria	IHL	6	0	8	8	4	....	....	....	....	....
	Pittsburgh	NHL	61	3	12	15	70	24	1	2	3	63
	NHL Totals		900	53	319	372	1350	118	10	44	54	227

Claimed by **Hartford** from **Montreal** in 1979 Expansion Draft, June 22, 1979. Traded to **Minnesota** by **Hartford** for Mike Fidler, December 16, 1980. Traded to **Philadelphia** by **Minnesota** for future considerations, February 8, 1988. Traded to **St. Louis** by **Philadelphia** for future considerations, March 8, 1988. Traded to **Pittsburgh** by **St. Louis** for future considerations, October 27, 1990.

ROBERTS, TIMOTHY

Center. Shoots left. 6'2", 180 lbs.   Born, Boston, MA, March 6, 1969.
(Buffalo's 9th choice, 153rd overall, in 1987 Entry Draft).

Season	Club	Lea	GP	G	A	TP	PIM	GP	G	A	TP	PIM
1987-88	RPI	ECAC	28	5	9	14	40	....	....	....	....	....
1988-89	RPI	ECAC	27	4	11	15	50	....	....	....	....	....
1989-90	RPI	ECAC	26	2	10	12	31	....	....	....	....	....
1990-91	RPI	ECAC	32	5	19	24	57	....	....	....	....	....

ROBERTSON, TORRIE ANDREW

Left wing. Shoots left. 5'11", 200 lbs.   Born, Victoria, B.C., August 2, 1961.
(Washington's 3rd choice, 55th overall, in 1980 Entry Draft).

Season	Club	Lea	GP	G	A	TP	PIM	GP	G	A	TP	PIM
1978-79	Victoria	WHL	69	18	23	41	141	15	1	2	3	29
1979-80	Victoria	WHL	72	23	24	47	298	17	5	7	12	117
1980-81	**Washington**	NHL	3	0	0	0	0	....	....	....	....	....
	Victoria	WHL	59	45	66	111	274	15	10	13	23	55
1981-82	**Washington**	NHL	54	8	13	21	204	....	....	....	....	....
	Hershey	AHL	21	5	3	8	60	....	....	....	....	....
1982-83	**Washington**	NHL	5	2	0	2	4	....	....	....	....	....
	Hershey	AHL	69	21	33	54	187	5	1	2	3	8
1983-84	**Hartford**	NHL	66	7	13	20	198	....	....	....	....	....
1984-85	**Hartford**	NHL	74	11	30	41	337	....	....	....	....	....
1985-86	**Hartford**	NHL	76	13	24	37	358	10	1	0	1	67
1986-87	**Hartford**	NHL	20	1	0	1	98	....	....	....	....	....
1987-88	**Hartford**	NHL	63	2	8	10	293	6	0	1	1	6
1988-89	**Hartford**	NHL	27	2	4	6	84	....	....	....	....	....
	Detroit	NHL	12	2	2	4	63	6	1	0	1	17
1989-90	**Detroit**	NHL	42	1	5	6	112	....	....	....	....	....
	Adirondack	IHL	27	3	13	16	47	6	1	1	2	33
1990-91	Rochester	AHL	1	0	1	1	0	....	....	....	....	....
	Albany	IHL	1	0	0	0	0	....	....	....	....	....
	NHL Totals		442	49	99	148	1751	22	2	1	3	90

Traded to **Hartford** by **Washington** for Greg Adams, October 3, 1983. Traded to **Detroit** by **Hartford** for Jim Pavese, March 7, 1989.

ROBINSON, LARRY CLARK

Defense. Shoots left. 6'4", 225 lbs.   Born, Winchester, Ont., June 2, 1951.
(Montreal's 4th choice, 20th overall, in 1971 Amateur Draft).

Season	Club	Lea	GP	G	A	TP	PIM	GP	G	A	TP	PIM
1969-70	Brockville	OHA	40	22	29	51	74	....	....	....	....	....
1970-71	Kitchener	OHA	61	12	39	51	65	....	....	....	....	....
1971-72	Nova Scotia	AHL	74	10	14	24	54	15	2	10	12	31
1972-73	**Montreal**	NHL	36	2	4	6	20	11	1	4	5	9
	Nova Scotia	AHL	38	6	33	39	33	....	....	....	....	....
1973-74	**Montreal**	NHL	78	6	20	26	66	6	0	1	1	26
1974-75	**Montreal**	NHL	80	14	47	61	76	11	0	4	4	27
1975-76	**Montreal**	NHL	80	10	30	40	59	13	3	3	6	10
1976-77abc	**Montreal**	NHL	77	19	66	85	45	14	2	10	12	12
1977-78de	**Montreal**	NHL	80	13	52	65	39	15	4	*17	*21	6
1978-79b	**Montreal**	NHL	67	16	45	61	33	16	6	9	15	8
1979-80ab	**Montreal**	NHL	72	14	61	75	39	10	0	4	4	2
1980-81e	**Montreal**	NHL	65	12	38	50	37	3	0	1	1	2
1981-82	**Montreal**	NHL	71	12	47	59	41	5	0	1	1	8
1982-83	**Montreal**	NHL	71	14	49	63	33	3	0	0	0	2
1983-84	**Montreal**	NHL	74	9	34	43	39	15	0	5	5	22
1984-85	**Montreal**	NHL	76	14	33	47	44	12	3	8	11	8
1985-86e	**Montreal**	NHL	78	19	63	82	39	20	0	13	13	22
1986-87	**Montreal**	NHL	70	13	37	50	44	17	3	17	20	6
1987-88	**Montreal**	NHL	53	6	34	40	30	11	1	4	5	4
1988-89	**Montreal**	NHL	74	4	26	30	22	21	2	8	10	12
1989-90	**Los Angeles**	NHL	64	7	32	39	34	10	2	3	5	10
1990-91	**Los Angeles**	NHL	62	1	22	23	16	12	1	4	5	15
	NHL Totals		1328	205	740	945	756	225	28	116	144	211

a Won James Norris Memorial Trophy (1977, 1980)
b NHL First All-Star Team (1977, 1979, 1980)
c NHL Plus/Minus Leader (1977)
d Won Conn Smythe Trophy (1978)
e NHL Second All-Star Team (1978, 1981, 1986)
Played in NHL All-Star Game (1974, 1976-78, 1980, 1982, 1986, 1988, 1989)
Signed as a free agent by **Los Angeles**, July 26, 1989.

ROBINSON, ROBERT (ROB)

Defense. Shoots left. 6'1", 214 lbs.   Born, St. Catharines, Ont., April 19, 1967.
(St. Louis' 6th choice, 117th overall, in 1987 Entry Draft).

Season	Club	Lea	GP	G	A	TP	PIM	GP	G	A	TP	PIM
1985-86	Miami-Ohio	CCHA	38	1	9	10	24	....	....	....	....	....
1986-87	Miami-Ohio	CCHA	33	3	5	8	32	....	....	....	....	....
1987-88	Miami-Ohio	CCHA	35	1	3	4	56	....	....	....	....	....
1988-89	Miami-Ohio	CCHA	30	3	4	7	42	....	....	....	....	....
	Peoria	IHL	11	2	0	2	6	....	....	....	....	....
1989-90	Peoria	IHL	60	2	11	13	72	5	0	1	1	10
1990-91a	Peoria	IHL	79	2	21	23	42	19	0	6	6	8

a IHL Second All-Star Team (1991)

ROBISON, JEFF

Defense. Shoots left. 6'1", 175 lbs.   Born, Wrentham, MA, June 3, 1970.
(Los Angeles' 5th choice, 91st overall, in 1988 Entry Draft).

Season	Club	Lea	GP	G	A	TP	PIM	GP	G	A	TP	PIM
1988-89	Providence	H.E.	41	0	5	5	36	....	....	....	....	....
1989-90	Providence	H.E.	35	2	8	10	16	....	....	....	....	....
1990-91	Providence	H.E.	36	3	8	11	34	....	....	....	....	....

ROBITAILLE, LUC   (ROH-buh-tigh)

Left wing. Shoots left. 6'1", 190 lbs.   Born, Montreal, Que., February 17, 1966.
(Los Angeles' 9th choice, 171st overall, in 1984 Entry Draft).

Season	Club	Lea	GP	G	A	TP	PIM	GP	G	A	TP	PIM
1983-84	Hull	QMJHL	70	32	53	85	48	....	....	....	....	....
1984-85a	Hull	QMJHL	64	55	94	149	115	5	4	2	6	27
1985-86bcd	Hull	QMJHL	63	68	123	191	91	15	17	27	44	28
1986-87ef	**Los Angeles**	NHL	79	45	39	84	28	5	1	4	5	2
1987-88g	**Los Angeles**	NHL	80	53	58	111	82	5	2	5	7	18
1988-89g	**Los Angeles**	NHL	78	46	52	98	65	11	2	6	8	10
1989-90g	**Los Angeles**	NHL	80	52	49	101	38	10	5	5	10	10
1990-91g	**Los Angeles**	NHL	76	45	46	91	68	12	12	4	16	22
	NHL Totals		393	241	244	485	281	43	22	24	46	62

a QMJHL Second All-Star Team (1985)
b QMJHL First All-Star Team (1986)
c QMJHL Player of the Year (1986)
d Canadian Major Junior Player of the Year (1986)
e Won Calder Memorial Trophy (1987)
f NHL Second All-Star Team (1987)
g NHL First All-Star Team (1988, 1989, 1990, 1991)
Played in NHL All-Star Game (1988-91)

ROBITAILLE, MARTIN

Center. Shoots right. 5'10", 165 lbs.   Born, St. Romuald, Que., March 17, 1969.
(Toronto's 1st choice, 15th overall, in 1990 Supplemental Draft).

Season	Club	Lea	GP	G	A	TP	PIM	GP	G	A	TP	PIM
1988-89	U. of Maine	H.E.	45	17	31	48	10	....	....	....	....	....
1989-90	U. of Maine	H.E.	46	24	28	52	24	....	....	....	....	....
1990-91	U. of Maine	H.E.	43	23	25	48	28	....	....	....	....	....

ROCHEFORT, NORMAND (ROHSH-fohr)

Defense. Shoots left. 6'1", 214 lbs. Born, Trois Rivieres, Que., January 28, 1961.
(Quebec's 1st choice, 24th overall, in 1980 Entry Draft).

			Regular Season					Playoffs				
Season	Club	Lea	GP	G	A	TP	PIM	GP	G	A	TP	PIM
1978-79	Trois Rivieres	QJHL	72	17	57	74	30	13	3	11	14	17
1979-80	Trois Rivieres	QJHL	20	5	25	30	22	....	....	....	....	....
a	Quebec	QJHL	52	8	39	47	68	5	1	3	4	8
1980-81	Quebec	NHL	56	3	7	10	51	5	0	0	0	4
	Quebec	QJHL	9	2	6	8	14	....	....	....	....	....
1981-82	Quebec	NHL	72	4	14	18	115	16	0	2	2	10
1982-83	Quebec	NHL	62	6	17	23	40	1	0	0	0	2
1983-84	Quebec	NHL	75	2	22	24	47	6	1	0	1	6
1984-85	Quebec	NHL	73	3	21	24	74	18	2	1	3	8
1985-86	Quebec	NHL	26	5	4	9	30	....	....	....	....	....
1986-87	Quebec	NHL	70	6	9	15	46	13	2	1	3	26
1987-88	Quebec	NHL	46	3	10	13	49	....	....	....	....	....
1988-89	NY Rangers	NHL	11	1	5	6	18	....	....	....	....	....
1989-90	NY Rangers	NHL	31	3	1	4	24	10	2	1	3	26
	Flint	IHL	7	3	2	5	4	....	....	....	....	....
1990-91	NY Rangers	NHL	44	3	7	10	35	....	....	....	....	....
	NHL Totals		566	39	117	156	529	69	7	5	12	82

a QMJHL Second All-Star Team (1980)

Traded to **NY Rangers** by **Quebec** with Jason Lafreniere for Bruce Bell, Jari Gronstrand, Walt Poddubny and NY Rangers' fourth round choice (Eric Dubois) in 1989 Entry Draft, August 1, 1988.

RODERICK, JOHN

Defense. Shoots left. 6'2", 190 lbs. Born, Cambridge, MA, February 25, 1971.
(St. Louis' 9th choice, 177th overall, in 1989 Entry Draft).

			Regular Season					Playoffs				
Season	Club	Lea	GP	G	A	TP	PIM	GP	G	A	TP	PIM
1989-90	St. Lawrence	ECAC	16	0	1	1	20	....	....	....	....	....
1990-91	St. Lawrence	ECAC	21	0	2	2	20	....	....	....	....	....

ROENICK, JEREMY (ROH-nihk)

Center. Shoots right. 6', 170 lbs. Born, Boston, MA, January 17, 1970.
(Chicago's 1st choice, 8th overall, in 1988 Entry Draft).

			Regular Season					Playoffs				
Season	Club	Lea	GP	G	A	TP	PIM	GP	G	A	TP	PIM
1988-89a	Hull	QMJHL	28	34	36	70	14	....	....	....	....	....
	U.S. Jr. Nat'l.	....	11	8	8	16	0	....	....	....	....	....
	Chicago	NHL	20	9	9	18	4	10	1	3	4	7
1989-90	Chicago	NHL	78	26	40	66	54	20	11	7	18	8
1990-91	Chicago	NHL	79	41	53	94	80	6	3	5	8	4
	NHL Totals		177	76	102	178	138	36	15	15	30	19

a QMJHL Second All-Star Team (1989)

Played in NHL All-Star Game (1991)

ROHLICEK, JEFF (ROHL-ih-chehk)

Center. Shoots left. 6', 180 lbs. Born, Park Ridge, IL, January 27, 1966.
(Vancouver's 2nd choice, 31st overall, in 1984 Entry Draft).

			Regular Season					Playoffs				
Season	Club	Lea	GP	G	A	TP	PIM	GP	G	A	TP	PIM
1983-84	Portland	WHL	71	44	53	97	22	14	13	8	21	10
1984-85a	Kelowna	WHL	65	39	52	91	26	6	3	6	9	2
	Portland	WHL	16	5	13	18	2	....	....	....	....	....
1985-86	Spokane	WHL	57	50	52	102	39	9	6	2	8	16
1986-87	Fredericton	AHL	70	19	37	56	22	....	....	....	....	....
1987-88	Vancouver	NHL	7	0	0	0	4	....	....	....	....	....
	Fredericton	AHL	65	26	31	57	50	....	....	....	....	....
1988-89	Vancouver	NHL	2	0	0	0	4	....	....	....	....	....
b	Milwaukee	IHL	78	47	63	110	106	11	6	6	12	8
1989-90	Springfield	AHL	12	1	2	3	4	7	3	2	5	6
	Milwaukee	IHL	53	22	26	48	37	....	....	....	....	....
1990-91	New Haven	AHL	4	1	1	2	6	....	....	....	....	....
	Phoenix	IHL	74	29	31	60	67	10	7	6	13	12
	NHL Totals		9	0	0	0	8	....	....	....	....	....

a WHL Second All-Star Team, West Division (1985)
b IHL First All-Star Team (1989)

Traded to **NY Islanders** by **Vancouver** for Jack Capuano, March 6, 1990.

ROHLIN, LEIF (roh-LEEN)

Defense. Shoots left. 6'1", 198 lbs. Born, Vasteras, Sweden, February 26, 1968.
(Vancouver's 2nd choice, 33rd overall, in 1988 Entry Draft).

			Regular Season					Playoffs				
Season	Club	Lea	GP	G	A	TP	PIM	GP	G	A	TP	PIM
1987-88	Vasteras	Swe.2	30	2	15	17	46	10	6	6	12	8
1988-89	Vasteras	Swe.	22	3	7	10	18	....	....	....	....	....
1989-90	Vasteras	Swe.	32	3	6	9	40	....	....	....	....	....
1990-91	Vasteras	Swe.	40	4	10	14	48	....	....	....	....	....

ROHLOFF, JON

Defense. Shoots right. 5'11", 200 lbs. Born, Mankato, MN, October 3, 1969.
(Boston's 7th choice, 186th overall, in 1988 Entry Draft).

			Regular Season					Playoffs				
Season	Club	Lea	GP	G	A	TP	PIM	GP	G	A	TP	PIM
1988-89	Minn.-Duluth	WCHA	39	1	2	3	44	....	....	....	....	....
1989-90	Minn.-Duluth	WCHA	5	0	1	1	6	2	0	0	0	2
1990-91	Minn.-Duluth	WCHA	32	6	11	17	38	....	....	....	....	....

ROHR, STEPHEN

Center. Shoots right. 6'2", 180 lbs. Born, Flint, MI, March 22, 1972.
(Montreal's 8th choice, 144th overall, in 1990 Entry Draft).

			Regular Season					Playoffs				
Season	Club	Lea	GP	G	A	TP	PIM	GP	G	A	TP	PIM
1989-90	Culver Aca.	HS	32	27	29	56	69	....	....	....	....	....
1990-91	Miami-Ohio	CCHA	26	6	6	12	8	....	....	....	....	....

ROLFE, DANIEL

Defense. Shoots left. 6'4", 200 lbs. Born, Inglewood, CA, December 25, 1967.
(St. Louis' 12th choice, 222nd overall, in 1987 Entry Draft).

			Regular Season					Playoffs				
Season	Club	Lea	GP	G	A	TP	PIM	GP	G	A	TP	PIM
1987-88	Ferris State	CCHA	13	1	1	2	36	....	....	....	....	....
1988-89	Ferris State	CCHA	28	0	2	2	54	....	....	....	....	....
1989-90	Ferris State	CCHA	31	0	6	6	48	....	....	....	....	....
1990-91	Ferris State	CCHA	31	1	1	2	36	....	....	....	....	....

ROLSTON, BRIAN

Center. Shoots left. 6'1", 175 lbs. Born, Flint, MI, February 21, 1973.
(New Jersey's 2nd choice, 11th overall, in 1991 Entry Draft).

			Regular Season					Playoffs				
Season	Club	Lea	GP	G	A	TP	PIM	GP	G	A	TP	PIM
1989-90	Detroit Jr. A	USHL	40	36	37	73	57	....	....	....	....	....
1990-91	Detroit Jr. A	USHL	36	49	46	95	14	....	....	....	....	....

ROMANIUK, RUSSELL

Left wing. Shoots left. 6', 185 lbs. Born, Winnipeg, Man., June 9, 1970.
(Winnipeg's 2nd choice, 31st overall, in 1988 Entry Draft).

			Regular Season					Playoffs				
Season	Club	Lea	GP	G	A	TP	PIM	GP	G	A	TP	PIM
1988-89	North Dakota	WCHA	39	17	14	31	32	....	....	....	....	....
	Cdn. National	...	3	1	0	1	0	....	....	....	....	....
1989-90	North Dakota	WCHA	45	36	15	51	54	....	....	....	....	....
1990-91a	North Dakota	WCHA	39	40	28	68	30	....	....	....	....	....

a WCHA First All-Star Team (1991)

RONAN, EDWARD (ED)

Right wing. Shoots right. 5'11", 170 lbs. Born, Quincy, MA, March 21, 1968.
(Montreal's 13th choice, 227th overall, in 1987 Entry Draft).

			Regular Season					Playoffs				
Season	Club	Lea	GP	G	A	TP	PIM	GP	G	A	TP	PIM
1987-88	Boston U.	H.E.	31	2	5	7	20	....	....	....	....	....
1988-89	Boston U.	H.E.	36	4	11	15	34	....	....	....	....	....
1989-90	Boston U.	H.E.	44	17	23	40	50	....	....	....	....	....
1990-91	Boston U.	H.E.	41	16	19	35	38	....	....	....	....	....

RONNING, CLIFF

Center. Shoots left. 5'8", 175 lbs. Born, Vancouver, B.C., October 1, 1965.
(St. Louis' 9th choice, 134th overall, in 1984 Entry Draft)

			Regular Season					Playoffs				
Season	Club	Lea	GP	G	A	TP	PIM	GP	G	A	TP	PIM
1983-84a	N. Westminster	WHL	71	69	67	136	10	9	8	13	21	10
1984-85bc	N. Westminster	WHL	70	*89	108	*197	20	11	10	14	24	4
1985-86	Cdn. Olympic	...	71	55	63	118	53	....	....	....	....	....
	St. Louis	NHL	....	....	....	....	....	5	1	1	2	2
1986-87	St. Louis	NHL	42	11	14	25	6	4	0	1	1	0
	Cdn. Olympic	...	26	16	16	32	12	....	....	....	....	....
1987-88	St. Louis	NHL	26	5	8	13	12	....	....	....	....	....
1988-89	St. Louis	NHL	64	24	31	55	18	7	1	3	4	0
	Peoria	IHL	12	11	20	31	8	....	....	....	....	....
1989-90	Asiago	Italy	36	67	49	116	25	6	7	12	19	4
1990-91	St. Louis	NHL	48	14	18	32	10	....	....	....	....	....
	Vancouver	NHL	11	6	6	12	0	6	6	3	9	12
	NHL Totals		191	60	77	137	46	22	8	8	16	14

a WHL Rookie of the Year (1984)
b WHL First All-Star Team (1985)
c WHL Most Valuable Player (1985)

Traded to **Vancouver** by **St. Louis** with Geoff Courtnall, Robert Dirk, Sergio Momesso and future considerations for Dan Quinn and Garth Butcher, March 5, 1991.

ROONEY, LARRY

Defense. Shoots left. 5'11", 165 lbs. Born, Boston, MA, January 30, 1968.
(Buffalo's 6th choice, 89th overall, in 1986 Entry Draft).

			Regular Season					Playoffs				
Season	Club	Lea	GP	G	A	TP	PIM	GP	G	A	TP	PIM
1987-88	Providence	H.E.	33	1	9	10	34	....	....	....	....	....
1988-89	Providence	H.E	10	0	4	4	18	....	....	....	....	....
1989-90	Providence	H.E	33	7	12	19	34	....	....	....	....	....
1990-91	Providence	H.E	35	8	18	26	24	....	....	....	....	....

ROONEY, STEVE

Left wing. Shoots left. 6'2", 195 lbs. Born, Canton, MA, June 28, 1962.
(Montreal's 8th choice, 88th overall, in 1981 Entry Draft)

			Regular Season					Playoffs				
Season	Club	Lea	GP	G	A	TP	PIM	GP	G	A	TP	PIM
1981-82	Providence	ECAC	31	7	10	17	41	....	....	....	....	....
1982-83	Providence	ECAC	42	10	20	30	31	....	....	....	....	....
1983-84	Providence	ECAC	33	11	16	27	46	....	....	....	....	....
1984-85	Montreal	NHL	3	1	0	1	7	11	2	2	4	19
	Providence	H.E.	31	7	10	17	41	....	....	....	....	....
1985-86	Montreal	NHL	38	2	3	5	114	1	0	0	0	0
1986-87	Montreal	NHL	2	0	0	0	22	....	....	....	....	....
	Sherbrooke	AHL	22	4	11	15	66	....	....	....	....	....
	Winnipeg	NHL	30	2	3	5	57	8	0	0	0	34
1987-88	Winnipeg	NHL	56	7	6	13	217	5	1	0	1	33
1988-89	New Jersey	NHL	25	3	1	4	79	....	....	....	....	....
1989-90	Utica	AHL	57	9	16	25	134	....	....	....	....	....
1990-91	New Haven	AHL	44	14	17	31	141	....	....	....	....	....
	Phoenix	IHL	11	2	5	7	76	....	....	....	....	....
	NHL Totals		154	15	13	28	496	25	3	2	5	86

Traded to **Winnipeg** by **Montreal** for Winnipeg's third-round choice (Francois Gravel) in 1987 Entry Draft, January 8, 1987. Traded to **New Jersey** by **Winnipeg** with Winnipeg's third round choice (Brad Bombardir) in 1990 Entry Draft for Alain Chevrier and New Jersey's seventh round choice (Doug Evans) in 1989 Entry Draft, July 19, 1988.

ROOT, WILLIAM JOHN (BILL)

Defense. Shoots right. 6', 210 lbs. Born, Toronto, Ont., September 6, 1959.

			Regular Season					Playoffs				
Season	**Club**	**Lea**	**GP**	**G**	**A**	**TP**	**PIM**	**GP**	**G**	**A**	**TP**	**PIM**
1977-78	Niagara Falls	OHA	67	6	11	17	61	....	....	....	....	....
1978-79	Niagara Falls	OHA	67	4	31	35	119	20	4	7	11	42
1979-80	Nova Scotia	AHL	55	4	15	19	57	6	1	1	2	2
1980-81	Nova Scotia	AHL	63	3	12	15	76	6	0	1	1	2
1981-82	Nova Scotia	AHL	77	6	25	31	105	9	1	0	1	4
1982-83	**Montreal**	**NHL**	**46**	**2**	**3**	**5**	**24**	....	....	....	....	....
	Nova Scotia	AHL	24	0	7	7	29	....	....	....	....	....
1983-84	**Montreal**	**NHL**	**72**	**4**	**13**	**17**	**45**	....	....	....	....	....
1984-85	**Toronto**	**NHL**	**35**	**1**	**1**	**2**	**23**	....	....	....	....	....
	St. Catharines	AHL	28	5	9	14	10	....	....	....	....	....
1985-86	**Toronto**	**NHL**	**27**	**0**	**1**	**1**	**29**	**7**	**0**	**2**	**2**	**13**
	St. Catharines	AHL	14	7	4	11	11	....	....	....	....	....
1986-87	**Toronto**	**NHL**	**34**	**3**	**3**	**6**	**37**	**13**	**1**	**0**	**1**	**12**
	Newmarket	AHL	32	4	11	15	23	....	....	....	....	....
1987-88	**St. Louis**	**NHL**	**9**	**0**	**0**	**0**	**6**	....	....	....	....	....
	Philadelphia	**NHL**	**24**	**1**	**2**	**3**	**16**	**2**	**0**	**0**	**0**	**0**
1988-89	Newmarket	AHL	66	10	22	32	39	5	0	0	0	18
1989-90	Newmarket	AHL	47	8	7	15	20	....	....	....	....	....
1990-91	Newmarket	AHL	36	2	4	6	39	....	....	....	....	....
	NHL Totals		**247**	**11**	**23**	**34**	**180**	**22**	**1**	**2**	**3**	**25**

Signed as free agent by **Montreal**, October 4, 1979. Traded to **Toronto** by **Montreal** for option of **Toronto** 's fourth round choice in 1985 or 1986 Entry Draft (choice was later traded back to **Toronto**), August 21, 1984. Traded to **Hartford** by **Toronto** for Dave Semenko, September 8, 1987. Claimed by **St. Louis** in NHL Waiver Draft, October 5, 1987. Claimed on waivers by **Philadelphia** form **St. Louis**, November 26, 1987. Traded to **Toronto** by **Philadelphia** for Mike Stothers, June 21, 1988.

ROSENBLATT, HOWARD DAVID

Defense. Shoots right. 6', 195 lbs. Born, Pawtucket, RI, January 3, 1969.
(Boston's 1st choice, 26th overall, in 1990 Supplemental Draft).

			Regular Season					Playoffs				
Season	**Club**	**Lea**	**GP**	**G**	**A**	**TP**	**PIM**	**GP**	**G**	**A**	**TP**	**PIM**
1987-88	Merrimack	NCAA	3	1	0	1	0	....	....	....	....	....
1988-89	Merrimack	NCAA	7	1	1	2	8	....	....	....	....	....
1989-90	Merrimack	H.E.	29	10	14	24	36	....	....	....	....	....
1990-91	Merrimack	H.E.	31	19	16	35	*118	....	....	....	....	....

ROSS, PATRICK

Right wing. Shoots left. 6'1", 185 lbs. Born, Jonkoping, Sweden, February 27, 1970.
(Los Angeles' 9th choice, 196th overall, in 1990 Entry Draft).

			Regular Season					Playoffs				
Season	**Club**	**Lea**	**GP**	**G**	**A**	**TP**	**PIM**	**GP**	**G**	**A**	**TP**	**PIM**
1989-90	HV 71	Swe.	37	14	7	21	0	....	....	....	....	....
1990-91	HV 71	Swe.	21	4	1	5	0	....	....	....	....	....

ROUPE, MAGNUS (roo-PAY)

Left wing. Shoots left. 6', 189 lbs. Born, Gislaved, Sweden, March 23, 1963.
(Philadelphia's 9th choice, 182nd overall, in 1982 Entry Draft).

			Regular Season					Playoffs				
Season	**Club**	**Lea**	**GP**	**G**	**A**	**TP**	**PIM**	**GP**	**G**	**A**	**TP**	**PIM**
1981-82	Farjestad	Swe.	24	5	3	8	8	2	0	0	0	0
1982-83	Farjestad	Swe.	29	7	4	11	16	6	1	1	2	8
1983-84	Farjestad	Swe.	36	2	3	5	38	....	....	....	....	....
1984-85	Farjestad	Swe.	31	9	6	15	16	3	1	0	1	0
1985-86	Farjestad	Swe.	35	11	10	21	38	8	3	2	5	18
1986-87	Farjestad	Swe.	31	11	6	17	64	7	0	2	2	10
1987-88	**Philadelphia**	**NHL**	**33**	**2**	**4**	**6**	**32**	....	....	....	....	....
	Hershey	AHL	23	6	16	22	10	11	3	4	7	31
1988-89	**Philadelphia**	**NHL**	**7**	**1**	**1**	**2**	**10**	....	....	....	....	....
	Hershey	AHL	12	2	6	8	17	....	....	....	....	....
	Farjestad	Swe.	18	9	4	13	58	2	0	1	1	6
1989-90	Farjestad	Swe.	39	19	17	36	64	9	1	2	3	14
1990-91	Farjestad	Swe.	39	9	11	20	54	....	....	....	....	....
	NHL Totals		**40**	**3**	**5**	**8**	**42**	....	....	....	....	....

ROUSE, ROBERT (BOB)

Defense. Shoots right. 6'1", 210 lbs. Born, Surrey, B.C., June 18, 1964.
(Minnesota's 3rd choice, 80th overall, in 1982 Entry Draft).

			Regular Season					Playoffs				
Season	**Club**	**Lea**	**GP**	**G**	**A**	**TP**	**PIM**	**GP**	**G**	**A**	**TP**	**PIM**
1980-81	Billings	WHL	70	0	13	13	116	5	0	0	0	2
1981-82	Billings	WHL	71	7	22	29	209	5	0	2	2	10
1982-83	Nanaimo	WHL	29	7	20	27	86	....	....	....	....	....
	Lethbridge	WHL	42	8	30	38	82	20	2	13	15	55
1983-84	**Minnesota**	**NHL**	**1**	**0**	**0**	**0**	**0**	....	....	....	....	....
a	Lethbridge	WHL	71	18	42	60	101	5	0	1	1	28
1984-85	**Minnesota**	**NHL**	**63**	**2**	**9**	**11**	**113**	....	....	....	....	....
	Springfield	AHL	8	0	3	3	6	....	....	....	....	....
1985-86	**Minnesota**	**NHL**	**75**	**1**	**14**	**15**	**151**	**3**	**0**	**0**	**0**	**0**
1986-87	**Minnesota**	**NHL**	**72**	**2**	**10**	**12**	**179**	....	....	....	....	....
1987-88	**Minnesota**	**NHL**	**74**	**0**	**12**	**12**	**168**	....	....	....	....	....
1988-89	**Minnesota**	**NHL**	**66**	**4**	**13**	**17**	**124**	....	....	....	....	....
	Washington	**NHL**	**13**	**0**	**2**	**2**	**36**	**6**	**2**	**0**	**2**	**4**
1989-90	**Washington**	**NHL**	**70**	**4**	**16**	**20**	**123**	**15**	**2**	**3**	**5**	**47**
1990-91	**Washington**	**NHL**	**47**	**5**	**15**	**20**	**65**	....	....	....	....	....
	Toronto	**NHL**	**13**	**2**	**4**	**6**	**10**	....	....	....	....	....
	NHL Totals		**494**	**20**	**95**	**115**	**969**	**24**	**4**	**3**	**7**	**53**

a WHL First All-Star Team, East Division (1984)

Traded to **Washington** by **Minnesota** with Dino Ciccarelli for Mike Gartner and Larry Murphy, March 7, 1989. Traded to **Toronto** by **Washington** with Peter Zezel for Al Iafrate, January 16, 1991.

ROUTA, ANTONIN

Right wing. Shoots right. 6'2", 170 lbs. Born, Okro, Czechoslovakia, March 2, 1968.
(Montreal's 13th choice, 227th overall, in 1987 Entry Draft).

			Regular Season					Playoffs				
Season	**Club**	**Lea**	**GP**	**G**	**A**	**TP**	**PIM**	**GP**	**G**	**A**	**TP**	**PIM**
1989-90	Tabor	USSR	40	17	23	40	50	....	....	....	....	....
1990-91	Fredericton	AHL	28	1	5	6	4	4	1	3	4	0

RUBACHUK, BRAD

Center. Shoots left. 5'11", 173 lbs. Born, Winnipeg, Man., June 11, 1970.
(Buffalo's 11th choice, 250th overall, in 1990 Entry Draft).

			Regular Season					Playoffs				
Season	**Club**	**Lea**	**GP**	**G**	**A**	**TP**	**PIM**	**GP**	**G**	**A**	**TP**	**PIM**
1989-90	Lethbridge	WHL	67	37	36	73	179	16	3	7	10	51
1990-91	Lethbridge	WHL	70	64	68	132	237	16	*14	14	28	55

RUCHTY, MATTHEW

Left wing. Shoots left. 6'1", 210 lbs. Born, Kitchener, Ont., November 27, 1969.
(New Jersey's 4th choice, 65th overall, in 1988 Entry Draft).

			Regular Season					Playoffs				
Season	**Club**	**Lea**	**GP**	**G**	**A**	**TP**	**PIM**	**GP**	**G**	**A**	**TP**	**PIM**
1987-88	Bowling Green	CCHA	41	6	15	21	78	....	....	....	....	....
1988-89	Bowling Green	CCHA	43	11	21	32	110	....	....	....	....	....
1989-90	Bowling Green	CCHA	42	28	21	49	135	....	....	....	....	....
1990-91	Bowling Green	CCHA	38	13	18	31	147	....	....	....	....	....

RUCINSKY, MARTIN

Left wing. Shoots left. 5'11", 178 lbs. Born, Most, Czechoslovakia, March 11, 1971.
(Edmonton's 2nd choice, 20th overall, in 1991 Entry Draft).

			Regular Season					Playoffs				
Season	**Club**	**Lea**	**GP**	**G**	**A**	**TP**	**PIM**	**GP**	**G**	**A**	**TP**	**PIM**
1989-90	CHZ Litvinov	Czech.	47	12	6	18	....	....	....	....	....	....
1990-91	CHZ Litvinov	Czech.	49	23	18	41	69	....	....	....	....	....

RUFF, JASON

Left wing. Shoots left. 6'2", 192 lbs. Born, Kelowna, B.C., January 27, 1970.
(St Louis' 3rd choice, 96th overall, in 1990 Entry Draft).

			Regular Season					Playoffs				
Season	**Club**	**Lea**	**GP**	**G**	**A**	**TP**	**PIM**	**GP**	**G**	**A**	**TP**	**PIM**
1989-90	Lethbridge	WHL	72	55	64	119	114	19	9	10	19	18
1990-91a	Lethbridge	WHL	66	61	75	136	154	16	12	17	29	18

a WHL East First All-Star Team (1991)

RUFF, LINDY CAMERON

Defense/Left wing. Shoots left. 6'2", 201 lbs. Born, Warburg, Alta., February 17, 1960.
(Buffalo's 2nd choice, 32nd overall, in 1979 Entry Draft).

			Regular Season					Playoffs				
Season	**Club**	**Lea**	**GP**	**G**	**A**	**TP**	**PIM**	**GP**	**G**	**A**	**TP**	**PIM**
1977-78	Lethbridge	WHL	66	9	24	33	219	8	2	8	10	4
1978-79	Lethbridge	WHL	24	9	18	27	108	6	0	1	1	0
1979-80	**Buffalo**	**NHL**	**63**	**5**	**14**	**19**	**38**	**8**	**1**	**1**	**2**	**19**
1980-81	**Buffalo**	**NHL**	**65**	**8**	**18**	**26**	**121**	**6**	**3**	**1**	**4**	**23**
1981-82	**Buffalo**	**NHL**	**79**	**16**	**32**	**48**	**194**	**4**	**0**	**0**	**0**	**28**
1982-83	**Buffalo**	**NHL**	**60**	**12**	**17**	**29**	**130**	**10**	**4**	**2**	**6**	**47**
1983-84	**Buffalo**	**NHL**	**58**	**14**	**31**	**45**	**101**	**3**	**1**	**0**	**1**	**9**
1984-85	**Buffalo**	**NHL**	**39**	**13**	**11**	**24**	**45**	**5**	**2**	**4**	**6**	**15**
1985-86	**Buffalo**	**NHL**	**54**	**20**	**12**	**32**	**158**	....	....	....	....	....
1986-87	**Buffalo**	**NHL**	**50**	**6**	**14**	**20**	**74**	....	....	....	....	....
1987-88	**Buffalo**	**NHL**	**77**	**2**	**23**	**25**	**179**	**6**	**0**	**2**	**2**	**23**
1988-89	**Buffalo**	**NHL**	**63**	**6**	**11**	**17**	**86**	....	....	....	....	....
	NY Rangers	**NHL**	**13**	**0**	**5**	**5**	**31**	**2**	**0**	**0**	**0**	**17**
1989-90	**NY Rangers**	**NHL**	**56**	**3**	**6**	**9**	**80**	**8**	**0**	**3**	**3**	**12**
1990-91	**NY Rangers**	**NHL**	**14**	**0**	**1**	**1**	**27**	....	....	....	....	....
	NHL Totals		**691**	**105**	**195**	**300**	**1264**	**52**	**11**	**13**	**24**	**193**

Traded to **NY Rangers** by **Buffalo** for NY Rangers' fifth-round choice (Richard Smehlik) in 1990 Entry Draft, March 7, 1989.

RUMBLE, DARREN

Defense. Shoots left. 6'1", 200 lbs. Born, Barrie, Ont., January 23, 1969.
(Philadelphia's 1st choice, 20th overall, in 1987 Entry Draft).

			Regular Season					Playoffs				
Season	**Club**	**Lea**	**GP**	**G**	**A**	**TP**	**PIM**	**GP**	**G**	**A**	**TP**	**PIM**
1986-87	Kitchener	OHL	64	11	32	43	44	4	0	1	1	9
1987-88	Kitchener	OHL	55	15	50	65	64	....	....	....	....	....
1988-89	Kitchener	OHL	46	11	28	39	25	5	1	0	1	2
1989-90	Hershey	AHL	57	2	13	15	31	....	....	....	....	....
1990-91	**Philadelphia**	**NHL**	**3**	**1**	**0**	**1**	**0**	....	....	....	....	....
	Hershey	AHL	73	6	35	41	48	3	0	5	5	2
	NHL Totals		**3**	**1**	**0**	**1**	**0**	....	....	....	....	....

RUOHO, DANIEL

Defense. Shoots left. 6'3", 220 lbs. Born, Madison, WI, June 22, 1970.
(Buffalo's 9th choice, 160th overall, in 1988 Entry Draft).

			Regular Season					Playoffs				
Season	**Club**	**Lea**	**GP**	**G**	**A**	**TP**	**PIM**	**GP**	**G**	**A**	**TP**	**PIM**
1989-90	N. Michigan	WCHA	18	2	4	6	26	....	....	....	....	....
1990-91	N. Michigan	WCHA	6	0	1	1	9	....	....	....	....	....

RUOTSALAINEN, REIJO (ROOTS-a-LAY-nen)

Defense. Shoots right. 5'8", 170 lbs. Born, Oulu, Finland, April 1, 1960.
(NY Rangers' 5th choice, 119th overall, in 1980 Entry Draft).

			Regular Season					Playoffs				
Season	Club	Lea	GP	G	A	TP	PIM	GP	G	A	TP	PIM
1977-78	Karpat	Fin.	30	9	14	23	4	....	....	....	....	....
1978-79	Karpat	Fin.	36	14	8	22	47	....	....	....	....	....
1979-80a	Karpat	Fin.	30	15	13	28	31	6	5	2	7	0
1980-81a	Karpat	Fin.	36	28	23	51	28	12	7	4	11	6
1981-82	NY Rangers	NHL	78	18	38	56	27	10	4	5	9	2
1982-83	NY Rangers	NHL	77	16	53	69	22	9	4	2	6	6
1983-84	NY Rangers	NHL	74	20	39	59	26	5	1	1	2	2
1984-85	NY Rangers	NHL	80	28	45	73	32	3	2	0	2	6
1985-86	NY Rangers	NHL	80	17	42	59	47	16	0	8	8	6
1986-87	Edmonton	NHL	16	5	8	13	6	21	2	5	7	10
	Bern	Switz.	36	26	28	54	....	....	....	....	....	....
1987-88	HV71	Swe.	39	10	22	32	26	....	....	....	....	....
1988-89	Bern	Switz.	36	17	30	47	....	9	4	7	11	....
1989-90	New Jersey	NHL	31	2	5	7	14	....	....	....	....	....
	Edmonton	NHL	10	1	7	8	6	22	2	11	13	12
1990-91	Bern	Switz.	36	13	25	38	....	10	5	9	14	....
	NHL Totals		446	107	237	344	180	86	15	32	47	44

a Named to Finnish League All-Star Team (1980, 1981)

Played in NHL All-Star Game (1986)

Traded to **Edmonton** by **NY Rangers** with Clark Donatelli, Ville Kentala and Jim Wiemer for Mike Golden, Don Jackson and Miloslav Horava, October 2, 1986. Claimed by **New Jersey** in NHL Waiver Draft, October 5, 1987. Traded to **Edmonton** by **New Jersey** for Jeff Sharples, March 6, 1990.

RUSNAK, DARIUS (RUHS-nahk)

Center. Shoots right. 6'1", 185 lbs. Born, Ruzomberok, Czechoslovakia, December 2, 1959.
(Philadelphia's 11th choice, 230th overall, in 1987 Entry Draft).

			Regular Season					Playoffs				
Season	Club	Lea	GP	G	A	TP	PIM	GP	G	A	TP	PIM
1986-87	Bratislava	Czech.	32	15	13	28	....	....	....	....	....	....
1987-88	Dukla Jihlava	Czech.	31	14	23	37	....	....	....	....	....	....
1988-89	Bratislava	Czech.	31	16	15	31	....	....	....	....	....	....
1989-90	KalPa	Fin.	44	29	24	53	77	1	0	1	1	0
1990-91	KalPa	Fin.	44	22	38	60	58	8	3	3	6	8

RUSSELL, CAM

Defense. Shoots left. 6'4", 174 lbs. Born, Halifax, N.S., January 12, 1969.
(Chicago's 3rd choice, 50th overall, in 1987 Entry Draft).

			Regular Season					Playoffs				
Season	Club	Lea	GP	G	A	TP	PIM	GP	G	A	TP	PIM
1985-86	Hull	QMJHL	56	3	4	7	24	15	0	2	2	4
1986-87	Hull	QMJHL	66	3	16	19	119	8	0	1	1	16
1987-88a	Hull	QMJHL	53	9	18	27	141	19	2	5	7	39
1988-89	Hull	QMJHL	66	8	32	40	109	9	2	6	8	6
1989-90	Chicago	NHL	19	0	1	1	27	1	0	0	0	0
	Indianapolis	IHL	46	3	15	18	114	9	0	1	1	24
1990-91	Chicago	NHL	3	0	0	0	5	1	0	0	0	0
	Indianapolis	IHL	53	5	9	14	125	6	0	2	2	30
	NHL Totals		22	0	1	1	32	2	0	0	0	0

a QMJHL Third All-Star Team (1988)

RUSSELL, KERRY

Right wing. Shoots right. 5'11", 164 lbs. Born, Kamloops, B.C., June 23, 1969.
(Hartford's 6th choice, 137th overall, in 1988 Entry Draft).

			Regular Season					Playoffs				
Season	Club	Lea	GP	G	A	TP	PIM	GP	G	A	TP	PIM
1987-88	Michigan State	CCHA	46	16	23	39	50	....	....	....	....	....
1988-89	Michigan State	CCHA	46	5	23	28	50	....	....	....	....	....
1989-90	Michigan State	CCHA	45	15	12	27	62	....	....	....	....	....
1990-91	Michigan State	CCHA	39	20	28	48	36	....	....	....	....	....

RUTHERFORD, PAUL

Center. Shoots left. 6', 190 lbs. Born, Sudbury, Ont., January 1, 1969.
(NY Islanders' 6th choice, 100th overall, in 1988 Entry Draft).

			Regular Season					Playoffs				
Season	Club	Lea	GP	G	A	TP	PIM	GP	G	A	TP	PIM
1987-88	Ohio State	CCHA	40	18	23	41	40	....	....	....	....	....
1988-89	Ohio State	CCHA	39	16	27	43	52	....	....	....	....	....
1989-90	Ohio State	CCHA	40	15	16	31	40	....	....	....	....	....
1990-91	Ohio State	CCHA	40	24	17	41	34	....	....	....	....	....
	Capital Dist.	AHL	4	0	0	0	0					

RUUTTU, CHRISTIAN (ROO-TOO)

Center. Shoots left. 5'11", 194 lbs. Born, Lappeenranta, Finland, February 20, 1964.
(Buffalo's 9th choice, 134th overall, in 1983 Entry Draft).

			Regular Season					Playoffs				
Season	Club	Lea	GP	G	A	TP	PIM	GP	G	A	TP	PIM
1982-83	Assat	Fin.	36	15	18	33	34	....	....	....	....	....
1983-84	Assat	Fin.	37	18	42	60	72	9	2	5	7	12
1984-85	Assat	Fin.	32	14	32	46	34	8	1	6	7	8
1985-86	HIFK	Fin.	36	16	38	54	47	10	3	6	9	8
1986-87	Buffalo	NHL	76	22	43	65	62	....	....	....	....	....
1987-88	Buffalo	NHL	73	26	45	71	85	6	2	5	7	4
1988-89	Buffalo	NHL	67	14	46	60	98	2	0	0	0	2
1989-90	Buffalo	NHL	75	19	41	60	66	6	0	0	0	4
1990-91	Buffalo	NHL	77	16	34	50	96	6	1	3	4	29
	NHL Totals		368	97	209	306	407	20	3	8	11	39

Played in NHL All-Star Game (1988)

RUZICKA, VLADIMIR (ROO-zheech-kah)

Center. Shoots left. 6'3", 212 lbs. Born, Most, Czechoslovakia, June 6, 1963.
(Toronto's 5th choice, 73rd overall, in 1982 Entry Draft).

			Regular Season					Playoffs				
Season	Club	Lea	GP	G	A	TP	PIM	GP	G	A	TP	PIM
1986-87	CHZ Litvinov	Czech.	32	24	15	39	....	....	....	....	....	....
1987-88	Dukla Trencin	Czech.	34	32	21	53	....	....	....	....	....	....
1988-89	Dukla Trencin	Czech.	45	46	38	84	....	....	....	....	....	....
1989-90	CHZ Litvinov	Czech.	32	21	23	44	....	....	....	....	....	....
	Edmonton	NHL	25	11	6	17	10	....	....	....	....	....
1990-91	Boston	NHL	29	8	8	16	19	17	2	11	13	0
	NHL Totals		54	19	14	33	29	17	2	11	13	0

Traded to **Edmonton** by **Toronto** for Edmonton's fourth round choice (Greg Walters) in 1990 Entry Draft, December 21, 1989. Traded to **Boston** by **Edmonton** for Greg Hawgood, October 22, 1990.

RYCHEL, WARREN (RIGH-chuhl)

Left wing. Shoots left. 6', 190 lbs. Born, Tecumseh, Ont., May 12, 1967.

			Regular Season					Playoffs				
Season	Club	Lea	GP	G	A	TP	PIM	GP	G	A	TP	PIM
1984-85	Sudbury	OHL	35	5	8	13	74	....	....	....	....	....
	Guelph	OHL	29	1	3	4	48	....	....	....	....	....
1985-86	Guelph	OHL	38	14	5	19	119	....	....	....	....	....
	Ottawa	OHL	29	11	18	29	54	....	....	....	....	....
1986-87	Ottawa	OHL	28	11	7	18	57	....	....	....	....	....
	Kitchener	OHL	21	5	5	10	39	4	0	0	0	9
1987-88	Peoria	IHL	7	2	1	3	7	....	....	....	....	....
	Saginaw	IHL	51	2	7	9	113	1	0	0	0	0
1988-89	Chicago	NHL	2	0	0	0	17	....	....	....	....	....
	Saginaw	IHL	50	15	14	29	226	6	0	0	0	51
1989-90	Indianapolis	IHL	77	23	16	39	374	14	1	3	4	64
1990-91	Indianapolis	IHL	68	33	30	63	338	5	2	1	3	30
	Chicago	NHL	....	....	....	....	....	3	1	3	4	2
	NHL Totals		2	0	0	0	17	3	1	3	4	2

Signed as a free agent by **Chicago**, September 19, 1986. Traded to **Winnipeg** by **Chicago** with Troy Murray for Bryan Marchment and Chris Norton, July 22, 1991.

RYDMARK, DANIEL (REWD-mahrk)

Center. Shoots left. 5'10", 169 lbs. Born, Vasteras, Sweden, February 23, 1970.
(Los Angeles' 5th choice, 123rd overall, in 1989 Entry Draft).

			Regular Season					Playoffs				
Season	Club	Lea	GP	G	A	TP	PIM	GP	G	A	TP	PIM
1989-90	Farjestad	Swe.	35	9	12	21	20	5	0	0	0	4
1990-91	Malmo	Swe.	39	14	14	28	34	....	....	....	....	....

RYMSHA, ANDREW (ANDY)

Defense. Shoots left. 6'3", 210 lbs. Born, St. Catharines, Ont., December 10, 1968.
(St. Louis' 5th choice, 82nd overall, in 1987 Entry Draft).

			Regular Season					Playoffs				
Season	Club	Lea	GP	G	A	TP	PIM	GP	G	A	TP	PIM
1986-87	W. Michigan	CCHA	41	7	12	19	60	....	....	....	....	....
1987-88	W. Michigan	CCHA	42	5	6	11	114	....	....	....	....	....
1988-89	W. Michigan	CCHA	35	3	4	7	139	....	....	....	....	....
1989-90	W. Michigan	CCHA	37	1	10	11	108	....	....	....	....	....
1990-91	Halifax	AHL	12	1	2	3	22	....	....	....	....	....
	Peoria	IHL	45	2	9	11	64	....	....	....	....	....

Traded to **Quebec** by **St. Louis** with Herb Raglan and Tony Twist for Darin Kimble, February 4, 1991.

SABOL, SHAUN (SAY-buhl)

Defense. Shoots left. 6'3", 230 lbs. Born, Minneapolis, MN, July 13, 1966.
(Philadelphia's 9th choice, 209th overall, in 1986 Entry Draft).

			Regular Season					Playoffs				
Season	Club	Lea	GP	G	A	TP	PIM	GP	G	A	TP	PIM
1986-87	U. Wisconsin	WCHA	40	7	16	23	98	....	....	....	....	....
1987-88	U. Wisconsin	WCHA	8	4	3	7	10	....	....	....	....	....
	Hershey	AHL	51	1	9	10	66	2	0	0	0	5
1988-89	Hershey	AHL	58	7	11	18	134	12	0	2	2	35
1989-90	Philadelphia	NHL	2	0	0	0	0	....	....	....	....	....
	Hershey	AHL	46	6	16	22	49	....	....	....	....	....
1990-91	Hershey	AHL	59	6	13	19	136	7	0	1	1	34
	NHL Totals		2	0	0	0	0	....	....	....	....	....

Traded to **NY Rangers** by **Philadelpia** for future considerations, August 5, 1991.

SABOURIN, KEN

Defense. Shoots left. 6'3", 205 lbs. Born, Scarborough, Ont. April 28, 1966.
(Calgary's 2nd choice, 33rd overall, in 1984 Entry Draft).

			Regular Season					Playoffs				
Season	Club	Lea	GP	G	A	TP	PIM	GP	G	A	TP	PIM
1982-83	S.S. Marie	OHL	58	0	8	8	90	10	0	0	0	14
1983-84	S.S. Marie	OHL	63	7	14	21	157	9	0	1	1	25
1984-85	S.S. Marie	OHL	63	5	19	24	139	16	1	4	5	10
1985-86	Moncton	AHL	3	0	0	0	0	6	0	1	1	2
	S.S. Marie	OHL	25	1	5	6	77	....	....	....	....	....
	Cornwall	OHL	37	3	12	15	94	6	1	2	3	6
1986-87	Moncton	AHL	75	1	10	11	166	6	0	1	1	27
1987-88	Salt Lake	IHL	71	2	8	10	186	16	1	6	7	57
1988-89	Calgary	NHL	6	0	1	1	26	1	0	0	0	0
	Salt Lake	IHL	74	2	18	20	197	11	0	1	1	26
1989-90	Calgary	NHL	5	0	0	0	10	....	....	....	....	....
	Salt Lake	IHL	76	5	19	24	336	11	0	2	2	40
1990-91	Calgary	NHL	16	1	3	4	36	....	....	....	....	....
	Salt Lake	IHL	28	2	15	17	77	....	....	....	....	....
	Washington	NHL	28	1	4	5	81	11	0	0	0	34
	NHL Totals		55	2	8	10	153	12	0	0	0	34

Traded to **Wasington** by **Calgary** for Paul Fenton, January 24, 1991.

SACCO, DAVID

Defense. Shoots right. 6'11", 190 lbs. Born, Malden, MA, July 31, 1970.
(Toronto's 9th choice, 195th overall, in 1988 Entry Draft).

			Regular Season					Playoffs				
Season	Club	Lea	GP	G	A	TP	PIM	GP	G	A	TP	PIM
1988-89	Boston U.	H.E.	35	14	29	43	40	....	....	....	....	....
1989-90	Boston U.	H.E.	3	0	4	4	2	....	....	....	....	....
1990-91	Boston U.	H.E.	40	21	40	61	24	....	....	....	....	....

SACCO, JOSEPH (JOE)

Left wing. Shoots right. 6'1", 180 lbs. Born, Medford, MA, February 4, 1969.
(Toronto's 4th choice, 71st overall, in 1987 Entry Draft).

			Regular Season					Playoffs				
Season	Club	Lea	GP	G	A	TP	PIM	GP	G	A	TP	PIM
1987-88	Boston U.	H.E.	34	16	20	36	40	....	....	....	....	....
1988-89	Boston U.	H.E.	33	21	19	40	66	....	....	....	....	....
1989-90	Boston U.	H.E.	44	28	24	52	70	....	....	....	....	....
1990-91	**Toronto**	**NHL**	**20**	**0**	**5**	**5**	**2**	....	....	....	....	....
	Newmarket	AHL	49	18	17	35	24	....	....	....	....	....
	NHL Totals		**20**	**0**	**5**	**5**	**2**	....	....	....	....	....

SAGISSOR, THOMAS (TOM)

Right wing. Shoots right. 5'11", 202 lbs. Born, Hastings, MN, September 12, 1967.
(Montreal's 7th choice, 96th overall, in 1985 Entry Draft).

			Regular Season					Playoffs				
Season	Club	Lea	GP	G	A	TP	PIM	GP	G	A	TP	PIM
1986-87	U. Wisconsin	WCHA	41	1	4	5	32	....	....	....	....	....
1987-88	U. Wisconsin	WCHA	38	4	5	9	65					
1988-89	U. Wisconsin	WCHA	40	7	11	18	119	....	....	....	....	....
1989-90	U. Wisconsin	WCHA	43	19	28	47	122	....	....	....	....	....
1990-91	Fredericton	AHL	52	8	13	21	99	....	....	....	....	....

SAILYNOJA, KEIJO

Right wing. Shoots right. 6'2", 187 lbs. Born, Vantaa, Finland, February 17, 1970.
(Edmonton's 6th choice, 122nd overall, in 1990 Entry Draft).

			Regular Season					Playoffs				
Season	Club	Lea	GP	G	A	TP	PIM	GP	G	A	TP	PIM
1989-90	Jokerit	Fin.	41	15	13	28	8	....	....	....	....	....
1990-91	Jokerit	Fin.	44	21	25	46	14	....	....	....	....	....

ST. AMOUR, MARTIN

Left wing. Shoots left. 6'3", 194 lbs. Born, Montreal, Que., January 30, 1970.
(Montreal's 2nd choice, 34th overall, in 1988 Entry Draft).

			Regular Season					Playoffs				
Season	Club	Lea	GP	G	A	TP	PIM	GP	G	A	TP	PIM
1987-88	Verdun	QMJHL	61	20	50	70	111	....	....	....	....	....
1988-89	Verdun	QMJHL	28	19	17	36	87	....	....	....	....	....
	Trois-Rivieres	QMJHL	26	8	21	29	69	4	1	2	3	0
1989-90	Trois-Rivieres	QMJHL	60	57	79	136	162	7	7	9	16	19
	Sherbrooke	AHL	....	....	....	....	....	1	0	0	0	0
1990-91	Fredericton	AHL	45	13	16	29	51	1	0	0	0	0

ST. CYR, JEFF

Defense. Shoots right. 6'4", 200 lbs. Born, New Liskeard, Ont., February 16, 1967.
(Hartford's 5th choice, 123rd overall, in 1987 Entry Draft).

			Regular Season					Playoffs				
Season	Club	Lea	GP	G	A	TP	PIM	GP	G	A	TP	PIM
1986-87	Michigan Tech.	WCHA	38	0	2	2	82	....	....	....	....	....
1987-88	Michigan Tech.	WCHA	40	0	7	7	98	....	....	....	....	....
1988-89	Michigan Tech.	WCHA	41	0	7	7	79	....	....	....	....	....
1989-90	Michigan Tech.	WCHA	36	2	7	9	81	....	....	....	....	....
1990-91	Winston-Salem	ECHL	21	3	5	8	45	....	....	....	....	....

ST. LAURENT, JEFFREY

Right wing. Shoots right. 6'2", 175 lbs. Born, Sanford, ME, May 16, 1971.
(Toronto's 10th choice, 171st overall, in 1989 Entry Draft).

			Regular Season					Playoffs				
Season	Club	Lea	GP	G	A	TP	PIM	GP	G	A	TP	PIM
1989-90	N. Hampshire	H.E.	DID NOT PLAY									
1990-91	N. Hampshire	H.E.	5	0	1	1	4	....	....	....	....	....

SAKIC, JOE (SAY-kick)

Center. Shoots left. 5'11", 185 lbs. Born, Burnaby, B.C., July 7, 1969.
(Quebec's 2nd choice, 15th overall, in 1987 Entry Draft).

			Regular Season					Playoffs				
Season	Club	Lea	GP	G	A	TP	PIM	GP	G	A	TP	PIM
1986-87ab	Swift Current	WHL	72	60	73	133	31	4	0	1	1	0
1987-88acd	Swift Current	WHL	64	*78	82	*160	64	10	11	13	24	12
1988-89	**Quebec**	**NHL**	**70**	**23**	**39**	**62**	**24**	....	....	....	....	....
1989-90	**Quebec**	**NHL**	**80**	**39**	**63**	**102**	**27**	....	....	....	....	....
1990-91	**Quebec**	**NHL**	**80**	**48**	**61**	**109**	**24**	....	....	....	....	....
	NHL Totals		**230**	**110**	**163**	**273**	**75**	....	....	....	....	....

a WHL Player of the Year (1987, 1988)
b WHL Rookie of the Year (1987)
c Canadian Major Junior Player of the Year (1988)
d WHL East All-Star Team (1988)

Played in NHL All-Star Game (1990, 1991)

SALLE, JOHAN

Defense. Shoots left. 6'1", 187 lbs. Born, Orebro, Sweden, February 21, 1967.
(Philadelphia's 9th choice, 161st overall, in 1988 Entry Draft).

			Regular Season					Playoffs				
Season	Club	Lea	GP	G	A	TP	PIM	GP	G	A	TP	PIM
1987-88	Malmo	Swe.	36	9	4	13	48	....	....	....	....	....
1988-89	Malmo	Swe.	18	6	10	16	32	....	....	....	....	....
1989-90	Malmo	Swe.	32	12	16	28	98	....	....	....	....	....
1990-91	Malmo	Swe.	38	4	5	9	34	....	....	....	....	....

SALMING, ANDERS BORJE (SAHL-mihng, BOHR-yuh)

Defense. Shoots left. 6'1", 193 lbs. Born, Kiruna, Sweden, April 17, 1951.

			Regular Season					Playoffs				
Season	Club	Lea	GP	G	A	TP	PIM	GP	G	A	TP	PIM
1970-71	Brynas	Swe.	27	2	6	8	22	....	....	....	....	....
1971-72	Brynas	Swe.	28	1	5	6	50	....	....	....	....	....
1972-73	Brynas	Swe.	26	5	4	9	34	....	....	....	....	....
1973-74	**Toronto**	**NHL**	**76**	**5**	**34**	**39**	**48**	**4**	**0**	**1**	**1**	**4**
1974-75a	**Toronto**	**NHL**	**60**	**12**	**25**	**37**	**34**	**7**	**0**	**4**	**4**	**6**
1975-76a	**Toronto**	**NHL**	**78**	**16**	**41**	**57**	**70**	**10**	**3**	**4**	**7**	**9**
1976-77b	**Toronto**	**NHL**	**76**	**12**	**66**	**78**	**46**	**9**	**3**	**6**	**9**	**6**
1977-78a	**Toronto**	**NHL**	**80**	**16**	**60**	**76**	**70**	**6**	**2**	**2**	**4**	**6**
1978-79a	**Toronto**	**NHL**	**78**	**17**	**56**	**73**	**76**	**6**	**0**	**1**	**1**	**8**
1979-80a	**Toronto**	**NHL**	**74**	**19**	**52**	**71**	**94**	**3**	**1**	**1**	**2**	**2**
1980-81	**Toronto**	**NHL**	**72**	**5**	**61**	**66**	**154**	**3**	**0**	**2**	**2**	**4**
1981-82	**Toronto**	**NHL**	**69**	**12**	**44**	**56**	**170**	....	....	....	....	....
1982-83	**Toronto**	**NHL**	**69**	**7**	**38**	**45**	**104**	**4**	**1**	**4**	**5**	**10**
1983-84	**Toronto**	**NHL**	**68**	**5**	**38**	**43**	**92**	....	....	....	....	....
1984-85	**Toronto**	**NHL**	**73**	**6**	**33**	**39**	**76**	....	....	....	....	....
1985-86	**Toronto**	**NHL**	**41**	**7**	**15**	**22**	**48**	**10**	**1**	**6**	**7**	**14**
1986-87	**Toronto**	**NHL**	**56**	**4**	**16**	**20**	**42**	**13**	**0**	**3**	**3**	**14**
1987-88	**Toronto**	**NHL**	**66**	**2**	**24**	**26**	**82**	**6**	**1**	**3**	**4**	**8**
1988-89	**Toronto**	**NHL**	**63**	**3**	**17**	**20**	**86**	....	....	....	....	....
1989-90	**Detroit**	**NHL**	**49**	**2**	**17**	**19**	**52**	....	....	....	....	....
1990-91	AIK	Swe.	36	4	8	12	46	....	....	....	....	....
	NHL Totals		**1148**	**150**	**637**	**787**	**1344**	**81**	**12**	**37**	**49**	**91**

a NHL Second All-Star Team (1975, 1976, 1978, 1979, 1980)
b NHL First All-Star Team (1977)

Played in NHL All-Star Game (1976-78)

Signed as free agent by **Toronto**, May 12, 1973. Signed as a free agent by **Detroit**, June 12, 1989.

SALO, VESA (SAH-loh)

Defense. Shoots left. 6'3", 198 lbs. Born, Rauma, Finland, April 17, 1965.
(NY Rangers' 3rd choice, 49th overall, in 1983 Entry Draft).

			Regular Season					Playoffs				
Season	Club	Lea	GP	G	A	TP	PIM	GP	G	A	TP	PIM
1986-87	Lukko	Fin.	44	4	22	26	34	....	....	....	....	....
1987-88	Ilves	Fin.	43	8	15	23	42	4	0	1	1	4
1988-89	Tappara	Fin.	42	7	14	21	46	8	0	2	2	8
1989-90	Tappara	Fin.	35	2	12	14	22	7	0	2	2	4
1990-91	Tappara	Fin.	44	9	16	25	32	3	0	3	3	6

SAMUELSSON, KJELL (suh-MOO-ehl-suhn, SHELL)

Defense. Shoots right. 6'6", 235 lbs. Born, Tyngsryd, Sweden, October 18, 1958.
(NY Rangers' 5th choice, 119th overall, in 1984 Entry Draft).

			Regular Season					Playoffs				
Season	Club	Lea	GP	G	A	TP	PIM	GP	G	A	TP	PIM
1982-83	Tyngsryd	Swe.2	32	11	6	17	57	....	....	....	....	....
1983-84	Leksand	Swe.	36	6	7	13	59	....	....	....	....	....
1984-85	Leksand	Swe.	35	9	5	14	34	....	....	....	....	....
1985-86	**NY Rangers**	**NHL**	**9**	**0**	**0**	**0**	**10**	**9**	**0**	**1**	**1**	**8**
	New Haven	AHL	56	6	21	27	87	3	0	0	0	10
1986-87	**NY Rangers**	**NHL**	**30**	**2**	**6**	**8**	**50**	....	....	....	....	....
	Philadelphia	**NHL**	**46**	**1**	**6**	**7**	**86**	**26**	**0**	**4**	**4**	**25**
1987-88	**Philadelphia**	**NHL**	**74**	**6**	**24**	**30**	**184**	**7**	**2**	**5**	**7**	**23**
1988-89	**Philadelphia**	**NHL**	**69**	**3**	**14**	**17**	**140**	**19**	**1**	**3**	**4**	**24**
1989-90	**Philadelphia**	**NHL**	**66**	**5**	**17**	**22**	**91**	....	....	....	....	....
1990-91	**Philadelphia**	**NHL**	**78**	**9**	**19**	**28**	**82**	....	....	....	....	....
	NHL Totals		**372**	**26**	**86**	**112**	**643**	**61**	**3**	**13**	**16**	**80**

Played in NHL All-Star Game (1988)

Traded to **Philadelphia** by **NY Rangers** with NY Rangers' second-round choice (Patrik Juhlin) in 1989 Entry Draft for Bob Froese, December 18, 1986.

SAMUELSSON, MORGAN (suh-MOO-ehl-suhn)

Left wing. Shoots left. 5'9", 169 lbs. Born, Boden, Sweden, April 6, 1968.
(Quebec's 7th choice, 123rd overall, in 1986 Entry Draft).

			Regular Season					Playoffs				
Season	Club	Lea	GP	G	A	TP	PIM	GP	G	A	TP	PIM
1988-89	Lulea	Swe.	36	14	19	33	14	....	....	....	....	....
1989-90	Lulea	Swe.	29	4	10	14	30	5	1	0	1	4
1990-91	Sodertalje	Swe.	40	23	15	38	14	....	....	....	....	....

SAMUELSSON, ULF (suh-MOO-ehl-suhn)

Defense. Shoots left. 6'1", 195 lbs. Born, Fagersta, Sweden, March 26, 1964.
(Hartford's 4th choice, 67th overall, in 1982 Entry Draft).

			Regular Season					Playoffs				
Season	Club	Lea	GP	G	A	TP	PIM	GP	G	A	TP	PIM
1981-82	Leksand	Swe.	31	3	1	4	40	....	....	....	....	....
1982-83	Leksand	Swe.	33	9	6	15	72	....	....	....	....	....
1983-84	Leksand	Swe.	36	5	11	16	53	....	....	....	....	....
1984-85	**Hartford**	**NHL**	**41**	**2**	**6**	**8**	**83**	....	....	....	....	....
	Binghamton	AHL	36	5	11	16	92	....	....	....	....	....
1985-86	**Hartford**	**NHL**	**80**	**5**	**19**	**24**	**174**	**10**	**1**	**2**	**3**	**38**
1986-87	**Hartford**	**NHL**	**78**	**2**	**31**	**33**	**162**	**5**	**0**	**1**	**1**	**41**
1987-88	**Hartford**	**NHL**	**76**	**8**	**33**	**41**	**159**	**5**	**0**	**0**	**0**	**8**
1988-89	**Hartford**	**NHL**	**71**	**9**	**26**	**35**	**181**	**4**	**0**	**2**	**2**	**4**
1989-90	**Hartford**	**NHL**	**55**	**2**	**11**	**13**	**177**	**7**	**1**	**0**	**1**	**2**
1990-91	**Hartford**	**NHL**	**62**	**3**	**18**	**21**	**174**	....	....	....	....	....
	Pittsburgh	**NHL**	**14**	**1**	**4**	**5**	**37**	**20**	**3**	**2**	**5**	**34**
	NHL Totals		**477**	**32**	**148**	**180**	**1147**	**51**	**5**	**7**	**12**	**127**

Traded to **Pittsburgh** by **Hartford** with Ron Francis and Grant Jennings for John Cullen, Jeff Parker and Zarley Zalapski, March 4, 1991.

SANDELIN, SCOTT (SAN-duh-lin)

Defense. Shoots right. 6′, 200 lbs.   Born, Hibbing, MN, August 8, 1964.
(Montreal's 5th choice, 40th overall, in 1982 Entry Draft).

			Regular Season					Playoffs			
Season	Club	Lea	GP	G	A	TP	PIM	GP	G	A	TP	PIM
1982-83	North Dakota	WCHA	21	0	4	4	10	....	....	....	....	....
1983-84	North Dakota	WCHA	41	4	23	27	24	....	....	....	....	....
1984-85	North Dakota	WCHA	38	4	17	21	30	....	....	....	....	....
1985-86ab	North Dakota	WCHA	40	7	31	38	38	....	....	....	....	....
	Sherbrooke	AHL	6	0	2	2	2	....	....	....	....	....
1986-87 ·	**Montreal**	**NHL**	**1**	**0**	**0**	**0**	**0**	....	....	....	....	....
	Sherbrooke	AHL	74	7	22	29	35	16	2	4	6	2
1987-88	**Montreal**	**NHL**	**8**	**0**	**1**	**1**	**2**	....	....	....	....	....
	Sherbrooke	AHL	58	8	14	22	35	4	0	2	2	0
1988-89	Sherbrooke	AHL	12	0	9	9	8	....	....	....	....	....
	Hershey	AHL	39	6	9	15	38	8	2	1	3	4
1989-90	Hershey	AHL	70	4	27	31	38	....	....	....	....	....
1990-91	**Philadelphia**	**NHL**	**15**	**0**	**3**	**3**	**0**	....	....	....	....	....
	Hershey	AHL	39	3	10	13	21	7	1	2	3	0
	NHL Totals		**24**	**0**	**4**	**4**	**2**	....	....	....	....	....

a NCAA West Second All-Star Team (1986)
b WCHA First All-Star Team (1986).
Traded to **Philadelphia** by **Montreal** for the rights to J.J. Daigneault, November 7, 1988.
Signed as a free agent by **Minnesota**, August 12, 1991.

SANDERSON, GEOFF

Center. Shoots left. 6′, 185 lbs.   Born, Hay River, N.W.T, February 1, 1972.
(Hartford's 2nd choice, 36th overall, in 1990 Entry Draft).

			Regular Season					Playoffs			
Season	Club	Lea	GP	G	A	TP	PIM	GP	G	A	TP	PIM
1988-89	Swift Current	WHL	58	17	11	28	16	12	3	5	8	6
1989-90	Swift Current	WHL	70	32	62	94	56	4	1	4	5	8
1990-91	**Hartford**	**NHL**	**2**	**1**	**0**	**1**	**0**	**3**	**0**	**0**	**0**	**0**
	Swift Current	WHL	70	62	50	112	57	3	1	2	3	4
	Springfield	AHL	....	....	....	....	....	1	0	0	0	2
	NHL Totals		**2**	**1**	**0**	**1**	**0**	**3**	**0**	**0**	**0**	**0**

SANDLAK, JIM

Right wing. Shoots right. 6′4″, 219 lbs.   Born, Kitchener, Ont., December 12, 1966.
(Vancouver's 1st choice, 4th overall, in 1985 Entry Draft)

			Regular Season					Playoffs			
Season	Club	Lea	GP	G	A	TP	PIM	GP	G	A	TP	PIM
1983-84	London	OHL	68	23	18	41	143	8	1	11	12	13
1984-85a	London	OHL	58	40	24	64	128	8	3	2	5	14
1985-86	**Vancouver**	**NHL**	**23**	**1**	**3**	**4**	**10**	**3**	**0**	**1**	**1**	**0**
	London	OHL	16	8	14	22	38	5	2	3	5	24
1986-87b	**Vancouver**	**NHL**	**78**	**15**	**21**	**36**	**66**	....	....	....	....	....
1987-88	**Vancouver**	**NHL**	**49**	**16**	**15**	**31**	**81**	....	....	....	....	....
	Fredericton	AHL	24	10	15	25	47	....	....	....	....	....
1988-89	**Vancouver**	**NHL**	**72**	**20**	**20**	**40**	**99**	**6**	**1**	**1**	**2**	**2**
1989-90	**Vancouver**	**NHL**	**70**	**15**	**8**	**23**	**104**	....	....	....	....	....
1990-91	**Vancouver**	**NHL**	**59**	**7**	**6**	**13**	**125**	....	....	....	....	....
	NHL Totals		**351**	**74**	**73**	**147**	**485**	**9**	**1**	**2**	**3**	**2**

a OHL Third All-Star Team (1985)
b NHL All-Rookie Team (1987)

SANDSTROM, TOMAS (SAND-struhm)

Right wing. Shoots left. 6′2″, 200 lbs.   Born, Jakobstad, Finland, September 4, 1964.
(NY Rangers' 2nd choice, 36th overall, in 1982 Entry Draft).

			Regular Season					Playoffs			
Season	Club	Lea	GP	G	A	TP	PIM	GP	G	A	TP	PIM
1983-84	Brynas	Swe.	34	19	16	29	81	....	....	....	....	....
1982-83	Brynas	Swe.	36	22	14	36	36	....	....	....	....	....
1983-84	Brynas	Swe.	43	20	10	30	81	....	....	....	....	....
1984-85a	**NY Rangers**	**NHL**	**74**	**29**	**29**	**58**	**51**	**3**	**0**	**2**	**2**	**0**
1985-86	**NY Rangers**	**NHL**	**73**	**25**	**29**	**54**	**109**	**16**	**4**	**6**	**10**	**20**
1986-87	**NY Rangers**	**NHL**	**64**	**40**	**34**	**74**	**60**	**6**	**1**	**2**	**3**	**20**
1987-88	**NY Rangers**	**NHL**	**69**	**28**	**40**	**68**	**95**	....	....	....	....	....
1988-89	**NY Rangers**	**NHL**	**79**	**32**	**56**	**88**	**148**	**4**	**3**	**2**	**5**	**12**
1989-90	**NY Rangers**	**NHL**	**48**	**19**	**19**	**38**	**100**	....	....	....	....	....
	Los Angeles	**NHL**	**28**	**13**	**20**	**33**	**28**	**10**	**5**	**4**	**9**	**19**
1990-91	**Los Angeles**	**NHL**	**68**	**45**	**44**	**89**	**106**	**10**	**4**	**4**	**8**	**14**
	NHL Totals		**503**	**231**	**271**	**502**	**697**	**49**	**17**	**20**	**37**	**85**

a NHL All-Rookie Team (1985)
Played in NHL All-Star Game (1988, 1991)
Traded to **Los Angeles** by **NY Rangers** with Tony Granato for Bernie Nicholls, January 20, 1990.

SANDSTROM, ULF (SAND-struhm)

Right wing. Shoots right. 5′11″, 178 lbs.   Born, Fagersta, Sweden, April 24, 1967.
(Chicago's 5th choice, 92nd overall, in 1987 Entry Draft).

			Regular Season					Playoffs			
Season	Club	Lea	GP	G	A	TP	PIM	GP	G	A	TP	PIM
1986-87	MoDo	Swe.	25	2	4	6	14	6	3	0	3	0
1987-88	MoDo	Swe.	38	26	9	35	12	....	....	....	....	....
1988-89	MoDo	Swe.	39	19	14	33	16	....	....	....	....	....
1989-90	MoDo	Swe.	18	6	4	10	2	....	....	....	....	....
1990-91	Lulea	Swe.	37	4	5	9	4	....	....	....	....	....

SANDWITH, TERRAN

Defense. Shoots left. 6′4″, 210 lbs.   Born, Stoney Plain, Alta., April 17, 1972.
(Philadelphia's 4th choice, 42nd overall, in 1990 Entry Draft).

			Regular Season					Playoffs			
Season	Club	Lea	GP	G	A	TP	PIM	GP	G	A	TP	PIM
1988-89	Tri-Cities	WHL	31	0	0	0	29	6	0	0	0	4
1989-90	Tri-Cities	WHL	70	4	14	18	92	7	0	2	2	14
1990-91	Tri-Cities	WHL	46	5	17	22	132	7	1	0	1	14

SANGSTER, ROBERT (ROB)

Left wing. Shoots left. 6′2″, 200 lbs. Born, Kitchener, Ont., May 2, 1969.
(Vancouver's 6th choice, 155th overall, in 1989 Entry Draft).

			Regular Season					Playoffs			
Season	Club	Lea	GP	G	A	TP	PIM	GP	G	A	TP	PIM
1987-88	Kitchener	OHL	58	2	7	9	196	4	0	1	1	12
1988-89	Kitchener	OHL	64	10	25	35	337	5	1	0	1	12
1989-90	Milwaukee	IHL	1	0	0	0	4	....	....	....	....	....
	Kitchener	OHL	24	6	18	24	151	....	....	....	....	....
	Ottawa	OHL	21	2	8	10	100	1	0	0	0	7
1990-91	Roanoke Valley	ECHL	38	2	6	8	331	....	....	....	....	....

SANIPASS, EVERETT

Left wing. Shoots left. 6′2″, 204 lbs.   Born, Big Cove, N.B., February 13, 1968.
(Chicago's 1st choice, 14th overall, in 1986 Entry Draft).

			Regular Season					Playoffs			
Season	Club	Lea	GP	G	A	TP	PIM	GP	G	A	TP	PIM
1985-86	Verdun	QMJHL	67	23	66	89	320	5	0	2	2	16
1986-87	**Chicago**	**NHL**	**7**	**1**	**3**	**4**	**2**	....	....	....	....	....
a	Granby	QMJHL	35	34	48	82	220	8	6	4	10	48
1987-88	**Chicago**	**NHL**	**57**	**8**	**12**	**20**	**126**	**2**	**2**	**0**	**2**	**2**
1988-89	**Chicago**	**NHL**	**50**	**6**	**9**	**15**	**164**	**3**	**0**	**0**	**0**	**2**
	Saginaw	IHL	23	9	12	21	76	....	....	....	....	....
1989-90	**Chicago**	**NHL**	**12**	**2**	**2**	**4**	**17**	....	....	....	....	....
	Indianapolis	IHL	33	15	13	28	121	....	....	....	....	....
	Quebec	**NHL**	**9**	**3**	**3**	**6**	**8**	....	....	....	....	....
1990-91	**Quebec**	**NHL**	**29**	**5**	**5**	**10**	**41**	....	....	....	....	....
	Halifax	AHL	14	11	7	18	41	....	....	....	....	....
	NHL Totals		**164**	**25**	**34**	**59**	**358**	**5**	**2**	**0**	**2**	**4**

a QMJHL First All-Star Team (1987)
Traded to **Quebec** by **Chicago** with Mario Doyon and Dan Vincelette for Greg Millen, Michel Goulet and Quebec's sixth round choice (Kevin St. Jacques) in 1991 Entry Draft, March 5, 1990.

SAPERGIA, BRENT (suh-PUHR-juh)

Right wing. Shoots right. 5′10″, 195 lbs.   Born, Moose Jaw, Sask. November 16, 1962.

			Regular Season					Playoffs			
Season	Club	Lea	GP	G	A	TP	PIM	GP	G	A	TP	PIM
1984-85a	Salt Lake	IHL	76	47	47	94	36	7	2	7	9	15
1985-86b	Salt Lake	IHL	80	58	65	123	127	1	0	1	1	2
1986-87	KalPa	Fin.	33	25	13	38	117	....	....	....	....	....
	New Haven	AHL	2	0	1	1	0	....	....	....	....	....
1987-88	Salt Lake	IHL	22	10	6	16	22	9	0	1	1	9
1988-89	Indianapolis	IHL	52	43	33	76	246	....	....	....	....	....
1989-90	Phoenix	IHL	43	19	13	32	159	....	....	....	....	....
1990-91	San Diego	IHL	26	15	12	27	64	....	....	....	....	....

a IHL Second All-Star Team (1985)
b IHL First All-Star Team (1986)
Signed as a free agent by **NY Rangers**, March 6, 1987. Signed as a free agent by **New Jersey**, September 1, 1989.

SARAULT, YVES

Left wing. Shoots left. 6′1″, 170 lbs.   Born, Valleyfield, Que., December 23, 1972.
(Montreal's 3rd choice, 61st overall, in 1991 Entry Draft).

			Regular Season					Playoffs			
Season	Club	Lea	GP	G	A	TP	PIM	GP	G	A	TP	PIM
1989-90	Victoriaville	QMJHL	70	12	28	40	140	16	0	3	3	26
1990-91	St. Jean	QMJHL	56	22	24	46	113	....	....	....	....	....

SATARDALEN, JEFF

Right wing. Shoots right. 6′1″, 180 lbs.   Born, Superior, WI, July 8, 1969.
(NY Islanders' 8th choice, 160th overall, in 1987 Entry Draft).

			Regular Season					Playoffs			
Season	Club	Lea	GP	G	A	TP	PIM	GP	G	A	TP	PIM
1988-89	St. Cloud	NCAA	35	17	19	36	22	....	....	....	....	....
1989-90	St. Cloud	NCAA	38	24	33	57	34	....	....	....	....	....
1990-91	St. Cloud	WCHA	38	21	20	41	24	....	....	....	....	....

SAUNDERS, MATTHEW (MATT)

Left wing. Shoots left. 6′, 180 lbs.   Born, Ottawa, Ont., July 17, 1970.
(Chicago's 8th choice, 195th overall, in 1989 Entry Draft).

			Regular Season					Playoffs			
Season	Club	Lea	GP	G	A	TP	PIM	GP	G	A	TP	PIM
1988-89	Northeastern	H.E	26	8	9	17	14	....	....	....	....	....
1989-90	Northeastern	H.E	35	19	21	40	51	....	....	....	....	....
1990-91	Northeastern	H.E.	29	13	12	25	36	....	....	....	....	....

SAVAGE, JOEL

Right wing. Shoots right. 5′11″, 205 lbs.   Born, Surrey, B.C., December 25, 1969.
(Buffalo's 1st choice, 13th overall, in 1988 Entry Draft).

			Regular Season					Playoffs			
Season	Club	Lea	GP	G	A	TP	PIM	GP	G	A	TP	PIM
1986-87	Victoria	WHL	68	14	13	27	48	5	2	0	2	0
1987-88	Victoria	WHL	69	37	32	69	73	....	....	....	....	....
1988-89	Victoria	WHL	60	17	30	47	95	6	1	1	2	8
1989-90	Rochester	AHL	43	6	7	13	39	5	0	1	1	4
1990-91	**Buffalo**	**NHL**	**3**	**0**	**1**	**1**	**0**	....	....	....	....	....
	Rochester	AHL	61	25	19	44	45	15	3	3	6	8
	NHL Totals		**3**	**0**	**1**	**1**	**0**	....	....	....	....	....

SAVAGE, REGINALD (REGGIE)

Center. Shoots left. 5′10″, 187 lbs.   Born, Montreal, Que., May 1, 1970.
(Washington's 1st choice, 15th overall, in 1988 Entry Draft).

			Regular Season					Playoffs			
Season	Club	Lea	GP	G	A	TP	PIM	GP	G	A	TP	PIM
1987-88	Victoriaville	QMJHL	68	68	54	122	77	5	2	3	5	8
1988-89	Victoriaville	QMJHL	54	58	55	113	178	16	15	13	28	52
1989-90	Victoriaville	QMJHL	63	51	43	94	79	16	13	10	23	40
1990-91	**Washington**	**NHL**	**1**	**0**	**0**	**0**	**0**	....	....	....	....	....
	Baltimore	AHL	62	32	29	61	10	6	1	1	2	6
	NHL Totals		**1**	**0**	**0**	**0**	**0**	....	....	....	....	....

SAVARD, DENIS JOSEPH (sa-VARH, den-NY)

Center. Shoots right. 5'10", 175 lbs.   Born, Pointe Gatineau, Que., February 4, 1961.
(Chicago's 1st choice, 3rd overall, in 1980 Entry Draft).

				Regular Season					Playoffs			
Season	Club	Lea	GP	G	A	TP	PIM	GP	G	A	TP	PIM
1978-79	Montreal	QJHL	70	46	*112	158	88	11	5	6	11	46
1979-80ab	Montreal	QJHL	72	63	118	181	93	10	7	16	23	8
1980-81	Chicago	NHL	76	28	47	75	47	3	0	0	0	0
1981-82	Chicago	NHL	80	32	87	119	82	15	11	7	18	52
1982-83c	Chicago	NHL	78	35	86	121	99	13	8	9	17	22
1983-84	Chicago	NHL	75	37	57	94	71	5	1	3	4	9
1984-85	Chicago	NHL	79	38	67	105	56	15	9	20	29	20
1985-86	Chicago	NHL	80	47	69	116	111	3	4	1	5	6
1986-87	Chicago	NHL	70	40	50	90	108	4	1	0	1	12
1987-88	Chicago	NHL	80	44	87	131	95	5	4	3	7	17
1988-89	Chicago	NHL	58	23	59	82	110	16	8	11	19	10
1989-90	Chicago	NHL	60	27	53	80	56	20	7	15	22	41
1990-91	Montreal	NHL	70	28	31	59	52	13	2	11	13	35
	NHL Totals		806	379	693	1072	887	112	55	80	135	224

a QMJHL First All-Star Team (1980).
b Named QMJHL's Most Valuable Player (1980).
c NHL Second All-Star Team (1983).
Played in NHL All-Star Game (1982-84, 1986, 1988, 1991)
Traded to **Montreal** by **Chicago** for Chris Chelios and Montreal's second round choice (Michael Pomichter) in 1991 Entry Draft, June 29, 1990.

SAWYER, DAN

Defense. Shoots left. 6'1", 210 lbs.   Born, Denville, NJ, October 28, 1970.
(Calgary's 11th choice, 210th overall, in 1989 Entry Draft).

				Regular Season					Playoffs			
Season	Club	Lea	GP	G	A	TP	PIM	GP	G	A	TP	PIM
1989-90	Notre Dame	SJHL	33	12	10	22	68	....	....	....	....	....
1990-91				UNAVAILABLE								

SCHAFHAUSER, PATRICK (PAT)

Defense. Shoots left. 6'1", 195 lbs. Born, St. Paul, MN, July 27, 1971.
(Pittsburgh's 8th choice, 142nd overall, in 1989 Entry Draft).

				Regular Season					Playoffs			
Season	Club	Lea	GP	G	A	TP	PIM	GP	G	A	TP	PIM
1989-90	Boston College	H.E.	39	1	6	7	30	....	....	....	....	....
1990-91	Boston College	H.E.	18	1	2	3	8	....	....	....	....	....

SCHEIFELE, STEVE (SHIGH-ful-ee)

Right wing. Shoots right. 6', 190 lbs.   Born, Alexandria, VA, April 18, 1968.
(Philadelphia's 5th choice, 125th overall, in 1986 Entry Draft).

				Regular Season					Playoffs			
Season	Club	Lea	GP	G	A	TP	PIM	GP	G	A	TP	PIM
1986-87	Boston College	H.E.	38	13	13	26	14	....	....	....	....	....
1987-88	Boston College	H.E.	30	11	16	27	22	....	....	....	....	....
1988-89	Boston College	H.E.	40	24	14	38	30	....	....	....	....	....
1989-90	Boston College	H.E.	12	7	0	7	2	....	....	....	....	....
	Hershey	AHL	35	2	3	5	6	....	....	....	....	....
1990-91	Hershey	AHL	24	6	6	12	12	....	....	....	....	....
	Richmond	ECHL	23	18	10	28	8	4	1	0	1	9

SCHENA, ROB

Defense. Shoots left. 6'1", 190 lbs.   Born, Saugess, MA, February 5, 1967.
(Detroit's 9th choice, 176th overall, in 1985 Entry Draft).

				Regular Season					Playoffs			
Season	Club	Lea	GP	G	A	TP	PIM	GP	G	A	TP	PIM
1986-87	RPI	ECAC	30	1	9	10	32	....	....	....	....	....
1987-88	RPI	ECAC	30	5	9	14	56	....	....	....	....	....
1988-89	RPI	ECAC	32	7	5	12	64	....	....	....	....	....
	Adirondack	AHL	9	1	1	2	2	....	....	....	....	....
1989-90	Adirondack	AHL	43	5	8	13	36	....	....	....	....	....
1990-91	San Diego	IHL	1	0	0	0	0	....	....	....	....	....

SCHLEGEL, BRAD

Defense. Shoots right. 5'10", 181 lbs.   Born, Kitchener, Ont., July 22, 1968.
(Washington's 8th choice, 144th overall, in 1988 Entry Draft).

				Regular Season					Playoffs			
Season	Club	Lea	GP	G	A	TP	PIM	GP	G	A	TP	PIM
1986-87	London	OHL	65	4	23	27	24	....	....	....	....	....
1987-88a	London	OHL	66	13	63	76	49	12	8	17	25	6
1988-89	Cdn. National	...	60	2	22	24	30	....	....	....	....	....
1989-90	Cdn. National	...	72	7	25	32	44	....	....	....	....	....
1990-91	Cdn. National	...	59	8	20	28	64	....	....	....	....	....

a OHL Second All-Star Team (1988)

SCHNEIDER, MATHIEU

Defense. Shoots left. 5'11", 189 lbs.   Born, New York, NY, June 12, 1969.
(Montreal's 4th choice, 44th overall, in 1987 Entry Draft).

				Regular Season					Playoffs			
Season	Club	Lea	GP	G	A	TP	PIM	GP	G	A	TP	PIM
1986-87	Cornwall	OHL	63	7	29	36	75	5	0	0	0	22
1987-88	Montreal	NHL	4	0	0	0	2	....	....	....	....	....
a	Cornwall	OHL	48	21	40	61	83	11	2	6	8	14
	Sherbrooke	AHL	....	....	....	....	....	3	0	3	3	12
1988-89	Cornwall	OHL	59	16	57	73	96	18	7	20	27	30
1989-90	Montreal	NHL	44	7	14	21	25	9	1	3	4	31
	Sherbrooke	AHL	28	6	13	19	20	....	....	....	....	....
1990-91	Montreal	NHL	69	10	20	30	63	13	2	7	9	18
	NHL Totals		117	17	34	51	90	22	3	10	13	49

a OHL First All-Star Team (1988)

SCHNEIDER, SCOTT

Center. Shoots right. 6'1", 175 lbs.   Born, Rochester, MN, May 18, 1965.
(Winnipeg's 4th choice, 93rd overall, in 1984 Entry Draft).

				Regular Season					Playoffs			
Season	Club	Lea	GP	G	A	TP	PIM	GP	G	A	TP	PIM
1983-84	Colorado	WCHA	35	19	14	33	24	....	....	....	....	....
1984-85	Colorado	WCHA	33	16	13	29	60	....	....	....	....	....
1985-86	Colorado	WCHA	40	16	22	38	32	....	....	....	....	....
1986-87	Colorado	WCHA	42	21	22	43	36	....	....	....	....	....
1987-88	Moncton	AHL	68	12	23	35	28	....	....	....	....	....
1988-89	Moncton	AHL	64	29	36	65	51	6	2	6	8	4
1989-90	Moncton	AHL	61	17	23	40	57	....	....	....	....	....
1990-91	Moncton	AHL	61	21	21	42	22	7	0	2	2	6

SCISSONS, SCOTT

Center. Shoots left. 6'1", 201 lbs.   Born, Saskatoon, Sask., October 29, 1971.
(NY Islanders' 1st choice, 6th overall, in 1990 Entry Draft).

				Regular Season					Playoffs			
Season	Club	Lea	GP	G	A	TP	PIM	GP	G	A	TP	PIM
1988-89	Saskatoon	WHL	71	30	56	86	65	7	0	4	4	16
1989-90	Saskatoon	WHL	61	40	47	87	81	10	3	8	11	6
1990-91	NY Islanders	NHL	1	0	0	0	0	....	....	....	....	....
	Saskatoon	WHL	57	24	53	77	61	....	....	....	....	....
	NHL Totals		1	0	0	0	0	....	....	....	....	....

SCOTT, KEVIN

Center. Shoots left. 5'10", 170 lbs.   Born, Vernon, B.C., November 3, 1967.
(Detroit's 9th choice, 158th overall, in 1987 Entry Draft).

				Regular Season					Playoffs			
Season	Club	Lea	GP	G	A	TP	PIM	GP	G	A	TP	PIM
1987-88	N. Michigan	WCHA	36	9	12	21	42	....	....	....	....	....
1988-89	N. Michigan	WCHA	40	11	14	25	36	....	....	....	....	....
1989-90	N. Michigan	WCHA	34	20	14	34	46	....	....	....	....	....
1990-91	N. Michigan	WCHA	47	27	30	57	42	....	....	....	....	....

SCREMIN, CLAUDIO

Defense. Shoots right. 6'2", 205 lbs.   Born, Burnaby, B.C., May 28, 1968.
(Washington's 12th choice, 204th overall, in 1988 Entry Draft).

				Regular Season					Playoffs			
Season	Club	Lea	GP	G	A	TP	PIM	GP	G	A	TP	PIM
1986-87	U. of Maine	H.E.	15	0	1	1	2	....	....	....	....	....
1987-88	U. of Maine	H.E.	44	6	18	24	22	....	....	....	....	....
1988-89	U. of Maine	H.E.	45	5	24	29	42	....	....	....	....	....
1989-90	U. of Maine	H.E.	45	4	26	30	14	....	....	....	....	....
1990-91	Kansas City	IHL	77	7	14	21	60	....	....	....	....	....

Traded to **Minnesota** by **Washington** for Don Beaupre, November 1, 1988.

SEARS, SVERRE

Defense. Shoots left. 6'2", 185 lbs.   Born, Boston, MA, October 17, 1970.
(Philadelphia's 6th choice, 159th overall, in 1989 Entry Draft).

				Regular Season					Playoffs			
Season	Club	Lea	GP	G	A	TP	PIM	GP	G	A	TP	PIM
1989-90	Princeton	ECAC	3	0	1	1	14	....	....	....	....	....
1990-91	Princeton	ECAC	27	2	9	11	56	....	....	....	....	....

SEFTEL, STEVE (SEFF-tuhl)

Left wing. Shoots left. 6'3", 200 lbs.   Born, Kitchener, Ont., May 14, 1968.
(Washington's 2nd choice, 40th overall, in 1986 Entry Draft).

				Regular Season					Playoffs			
Season	Club	Lea	GP	G	A	TP	PIM	GP	G	A	TP	PIM
1985-86	Kingston	OHL	42	11	16	27	53	....	....	....	....	....
1986-87	Kingston	OHL	54	21	43	64	55	12	1	4	5	9
1987-88	Binghamton	AHL	3	0	0	0	2	....	....	....	....	....
	Kingston	OHL	66	32	43	75	51	....	....	....	....	....
1988-89	Baltimore	AHL	58	12	15	27	70	....	....	....	....	....
1989-90	Baltimore	AHL	74	10	19	29	52	12	4	3	7	10
1990-91	Washington	NHL	4	0	0	0	2	....	....	....	....	....
	Baltimore	AHL	66	22	22	44	46	6	0	0	0	14
	NHL Totals		4	0	0	0	2	....	....	....	....	....

SEJBA, JIRI (SHAY-bah)

Left wing. Shoots left. 5'10", 185 lbs.   Born, Pardubice, Czech., July 22, 1962.
(Buffalo's 9th choice, 182nd overall, in 1985 Entry Draft).

				Regular Season					Playoffs			
Season	Club	Lea	GP	G	A	TP	PIM	GP	G	A	TP	PIM
1986-87	Pardubice	Czech.	34	23	11	34	....	....	....	....	....	....
1987-88	Pardubice	Czech.	23	10	15	25	....	....	....	....	....	....
1988-89	Pardubice	Czech.	44	38	21	59	68	....	....	....	....	....
1989-90	Pardubice	Czech.	26	11	14	25	....	....	....	....	....	....
1990-91	Buffalo	NHL	11	0	2	2	8	....	....	....	....	....
	Rochester	AHL	31	15	13	28	54	14	6	7	13	29
	NHL Totals		11	0	2	2	8	....	....	....	....	....

SELANNE, TEEMU (SEH-lahn-nay)

Right wing. Shoots right. 6', 181 lbs.   Born, Helsinki, Finland, July 3, 1970.
(Winnipeg's 1st choice, 10th overall, in 1988 Entry Draft).

				Regular Season					Playoffs			
Season	Club	Lea	GP	G	A	TP	PIM	GP	G	A	TP	PIM
1987-88	Jokerit	Fin.Jr.	33	43	23	66	18	5	4	3	7	2
	Jokerit	Fin.2	5	1	1	2	0	....	....	....	....	....
1988-89	Jokerit	Fin.	34	35	33	68	12	5	7	3	10	4
1989-90	Jokerit	Fin.	11	4	8	12	0	....	....	....	....	....
1990-91	Jokerit	Fin.	42	33	25	58	12	....	....	....	....	....

SELYANIN, SERGEI

Defense. Shoots right. 6'2", 198 lbs. Born, Novosibirsk, USSR, September 20, 1966.
(Winnipeg's 12th choice, 224th overall, in 1990 Entry Draft).

			Regular Season					Playoffs				
Season	Club	Lea	GP	G	A	TP	PIM	GP	G	A	TP	PIM
1985-86	CSKA	USSR	8	0	0	0	6	....	....	....	....	....
1986-87	CSKA	USSR	34	0	0	0	28	....	....	....	....	....
1987-88	CSKA	USSR	21	2	0	2	16	....	....	....	....	....
	Khimik	USSR	11	2	2	4	8	....	....	....	....	....
1988-89	Khimik	USSR	44	6	4	10	42	....	....	....	....	....
1989-90	Khimik	USSR	33	2	4	6	....	....	....	....	....	....
1990-91	Khimik	USSR	43	4	7	11	56	....	....	....	....	....

SEMAK, ALEXANDER (seh-MAHK)

Center. Shoots right. 5'10", 185 lbs. Born, Ufa, Soviet Union, February 11, 1966.
(New Jersey's 12th choice, 207th overall, in 1988 Entry Draft).

			Regular Season					Playoffs				
Season	Club	Lea	GP	G	A	TP	PIM	GP	G	A	TP	PIM
1987-88	Moscow D'amo	USSR	47	21	14	35	40	....	....	....	....	....
1988-89	Moscow D'amo	USSR	44	18	10	28	22	....	....	....	....	....
1989-90	Moscow D'amo	USSR	43	23	11	34	33	....	....	....	....	....
1990-91	Moscow D'amo	USSR	46	17	21	38	48	....	....	....	....	....

SEMCHUK, THOMAS (BRANDY)

Right wing. Shoots right. 6'1", 185 lbs. Born, Calgary, Alta., September 22, 1971.
(Los Angeles' 2nd choice, 28th overall, in 1990 Entry Draft)

			Regular Season					Playoffs				
Season	Club	Lea	GP	G	A	TP	PIM	GP	G	A	TP	PIM
1988-89	Cdn. National	...	42	11	11	22	60	....	....	....	....	....
1989-90	Cdn. National	...	55	10	15	25	40	....	....	....	....	....
1990-91	Lethbridge	WHL	14	9	8	17	10	15	8	5	13	18
	New Haven	AHL	21	1	4	5	6	....	....	....	....	....

SEMENOV, ANATOLI (seh-MEH-nahf)

Center/left wing. Shoots left. 6'2", 190 lbs. Born, Moscow, Soviet Union, March 5, 1962.
(Edmonton's 5th choice, 120th overall, in 1989 Entry Draft).

			Regular Season					Playoffs				
Season	Club	Lea	GP	G	A	TP	PIM	GP	G	A	TP	PIM
1979-80	Moscow D'amo	USSR	8	3	0	3	2	....	....	....	....	....
1980-81	Moscow D'amo	USSR	47	18	14	32	18	....	....	....	....	....
1981-82	Moscow D'amo	USSR	44	12	14	26	28	....	....	....	....	....
1982-83	Moscow D'amo	USSR	44	22	18	40	26	....	....	....	....	....
1983-84	Moscow D'amo	USSR	19	10	5	15	14	....	....	....	....	....
1984-85	Moscow D'amo	USSR	30	17	12	29	32	....	....	....	....	....
1985-86	Moscow D'amo	USSR	32	18	17	35	19	....	....	....	....	....
1986-87	Moscow D'amo	USSR	40	15	29	44	32	....	....	....	....	....
1987-88	Moscow D'amo	USSR	32	17	8	25	22	....	....	....	....	....
1988-89	Moscow D'amo	USSR	31	9	12	21	24	....	....	....	....	....
1989-90	Moscow D'amo	USSR	48	13	20	33	16	....	....	....	....	....
	Edmonton	**NHL**	**....**	**....**	**....**	**....**	**....**	**2**	**0**	**0**	**0**	**0**
1990-91	**Edmonton**	**NHL**	**57**	**15**	**16**	**31**	**26**	**12**	**5**	**5**	**10**	**6**
	NHL Totals		**57**	**15**	**16**	**31**	**26**	**14**	**5**	**5**	**10**	**6**

SENTNER, PETER G.

Defense. Shoots left. 6'1", 200 lbs. Born, Boston, MA, June 13, 1969.
(Los Angeles' 1st choice, 12th overall, in 1990 Supplemental Draft).

			Regular Season					Playoffs				
Season	Club	Lea	GP	G	A	TP	PIM	GP	G	A	TP	PIM
1987-88	U. of Lowell	ECAC	21	0	0	0	14	....	....	....	....	....
1988-89	U. of Lowell	ECAC	34	6	20	26	46	....	....	....	....	....
1989-90	U. of Lowell	ECAC	25	1	6	7	6	....	....	....	....	....
1990-91	New Haven	AHL	2	0	0	0	0	....	....	....	....	....
	Phoenix	IHL	8	0	0	0	0	....	....	....	....	....
	Roanoke Valley	ECHL	49	3	13	16	39	....	....	....	....	....

SEPPO, JUKKA PEKKA (SEHP-poh)

Center. Shoots left. 6'2", 198 lbs. Born, Vaasa, Finland, January 22, 1968.
(Philadelphia's 2nd choice, 23rd overall, in 1986 Entry Draft).

			Regular Season					Playoffs				
Season	Club	Lea	GP	G	A	TP	PIM	GP	G	A	TP	PIM
1986-87	Tappara	Fin.	39	11	16	27	50	....	....	....	....	....
1987-88	Sport	Fin.2	42	28	37	65	78	....	....	....	....	....
1988-89	HIFK	Fin.	35	7	13	20	28	....	....	....	....	....
1989-90	HIFK	Fin.	39	15	27	42	50	....	....	....	....	....
1990-91	HIFK	Fin.	35	17	22	39	81	3	1	0	1	2

SEROWIK, JEFF (sir-OH-ik)

Defense. Shoots right. 6', 190 lbs. Born, Manchester, NH, October 1, 1967.
(Toronto's 5th choice, 85th overall, in 1985 Entry Draft).

			Regular Season					Playoffs				
Season	Club	Lea	GP	G	A	TP	PIM	GP	G	A	TP	PIM
1986-87	Providence	H.E.	33	3	8	11	22	....	....	....	....	....
1987-88	Providence	H.E.	33	3	9	12	44	....	....	....	....	....
1988-89	Providence	H.E.	35	3	14	17	48	....	....	....	....	....
1989-90a	Providence	H.E.	35	6	19	25	34	....	....	....	....	....
1990-91	**Toronto**	**NHL**	**1**	**0**	**0**	**0**	**0**	....	....	....	....	....
	Newmarket	AHL	60	8	15	23	45	....	....	....	....	....
	NHL Totals		**1**	**0**	**0**	**0**	**0**	....	....	....	....	....

a Hockey East Second All-Star Team (1990)

SEVCIK, JAROSLAV (SEHV-chihk, YAR-o-slav)

Left wing. Shoots right. 5'9", 170 lbs. Born, Brno, Czechoslovakia, May 15, 1965.
(Quebec's 9th choice, 177th overall, in 1987 Entry Draft).

			Regular Season					Playoffs				
Season	Club	Lea	GP	G	A	TP	PIM	GP	G	A	TP	PIM
1986-87	Zetor Brno	Czech.	34	12	5	17	....	....	....	....	....	....
1987-88	Fredericton	AHL	32	9	7	16	6	....	....	....	....	....
1988-89	Halifax	AHL	78	17	41	58	17	4	1	1	2	2
1989-90	**Quebec**	**NHL**	**13**	**0**	**2**	**2**	**2**	....	....	....	....	....
	Halifax	AHL	50	17	17	34	36	3	0	1	1	0
1990-91	Halifax	AHL	66	16	26	42	22	....	....	....	....	....
	NHL Totals		**13**	**0**	**2**	**2**	**2**	....	....	....	....	....

SEVERYN, BRENT

Left wing. Shoots left. 6'2", 210 lbs. Born, Vegreville, Alta., February 22, 1966.

			Regular Season					Playoffs				
Season	Club	Lea	GP	G	A	TP	PIM	GP	G	A	TP	PIM
1983-84	Seattle	WHL	72	14	22	36	49	....	....	....	....	....
1984-85	Seattle	WHL	38	8	32	40	54	....	....	....	....	....
	Brandon	WHL	26	7	16	23	57	....	....	....	....	....
1985-86	Seattle	WHL	33	11	20	31	164	....	....	....	....	....
	Saskatoon	WHL	9	1	4	5	38	....	....	....	....	....
1986-87	U. of Alberta	CWUAA	....	....	....	....	....	....	....	....	....	....
1987-88	U. of Alberta	CWUAA	46	21	29	50	178	....	....	....	....	....
1988-89	Halifax	AHL	47	2	12	14	141	....	....	....	....	....
1989-90	**Quebec**	**NHL**	**35**	**0**	**2**	**2**	**42**	....	....	....	....	....
	Halifax	AHL	43	6	9	15	105	6	1	2	3	49
1990-91	Halifax	AHL	50	7	26	33	202	....	....	....	....	....
	NHL Totals		**35**	**0**	**2**	**2**	**42**	....	....	....	....	....

Signed as a free agent by **Quebec**, July 15, 1988. Traded to **New Jersey** by **Quebec** for Dave Marcinyshyn, June 3, 1991.

SEVIGNY, PIERRE

Left wing. Shoots left. 6', 189 lbs. Born, Trois-Rivieres, Que., September 8, 1971.
(Montreal's 4th choice, 51st overall, in 1989 Entry Draft).

			Regular Season					Playoffs				
Season	Club	Lea	GP	G	A	TP	PIM	GP	G	A	TP	PIM
1988-89	Verdun	QMJHL	67	27	43	70	88	....	....	....	....	....
1989-90a	St-Hyacinthe	QMJHL	67	47	72	119	205	12	8	8	16	42
1990-91a	St-Hyacinthe	QMJHL	60	36	46	82	203	....	....	....	....	....

a QMJHL Second All-Star Team (1990, 1991)

SHANAHAN, BRENDAN

Right wing. Shoots right. 6'3", 210 lbs. Born, Mimico, Ont., January 23, 1969.
(New Jersey's 1st choice, 2nd overall, in 1987 Entry Draft).

			Regular Season					Playoffs				
Season	Club	Lea	GP	G	A	TP	PIM	GP	G	A	TP	PIM
1985-86	London	OHL	59	28	34	62	70	5	5	5	10	5
1986-87	London	OHL	56	39	53	92	92	....	....	....	....	....
1987-88	**New Jersey**	**NHL**	**65**	**7**	**19**	**26**	**131**	**12**	**2**	**1**	**3**	**44**
1988-89	**New Jersey**	**NHL**	**68**	**22**	**28**	**50**	**115**	....	....	....	....	....
1989-90	**New Jersey**	**NHL**	**73**	**30**	**42**	**72**	**137**	**6**	**3**	**3**	**6**	**20**
1990-91	**New Jersey**	**NHL**	**75**	**29**	**37**	**66**	**141**	**7**	**3**	**5**	**8**	**12**
	NHL Totals		**281**	**88**	**126**	**214**	**524**	**25**	**8**	**9**	**17**	**76**

Signed as a free agent by **St. Louis**, July 25, 1991.

SHANK, DANIEL

Right wing. Shoots right. 5'10", 190 lbs. Born, Montreal, Que., May 12, 1967.

			Regular Season					Playoffs				
Season	Club	Lea	GP	G	A	TP	PIM	GP	G	A	TP	PIM
1985-86	Shawinigan	QMJHL	51	34	38	72	184	....	....	....	....	....
1986-87	Hull	QMJHL	46	26	43	69	325	....	....	....	....	....
1987-88	Hull	QMJHL	42	23	34	57	274	5	3	2	5	16
1988-89	Adirondack	AHL	42	5	20	25	113	17	11	8	19	102
1989-90	**Detroit**	**NHL**	**57**	**11**	**13**	**24**	**143**	....	....	....	....	....
	Adirondack	AHL	14	8	8	16	36	....	....	....	....	....
1990-91	**Detroit**	**NHL**	**7**	**0**	**1**	**1**	**14**	....	....	....	....	....
	Adirondack	AHL	60	26	49	75	278	....	....	....	....	....
	NHL Totals		**64**	**11**	**14**	**25**	**157**	....	....	....	....	....

Signed as a free agent by **Detroit**, May 26, 1989.

SHANNON, DARRIN

Left wing. Shoots left. 6'2", 200 lbs. Born, Barrie, Ont., December 8, 1969.
(Pittsburgh's 1st choice, 4th overall, in 1988 Entry Draft).

			Regular Season					Playoffs				
Season	Club	Lea	GP	G	A	TP	PIM	GP	G	A	TP	PIM
1986-87	Windsor	OHL	60	16	67	83	116	14	4	6	10	8
1987-88	Windsor	OHL	43	33	41	74	49	12	6	12	18	9
1988-89	**Buffalo**	**NHL**	**3**	**0**	**0**	**0**	**0**	**2**	**0**	**0**	**0**	**0**
	Windsor	OHL	54	33	48	81	47	4	1	6	7	2
1989-90	**Buffalo**	**NHL**	**17**	**2**	**7**	**9**	**4**	**6**	**0**	**1**	**1**	**4**
	Rochester	AHL	50	20	23	43	25	9	4	1	5	2
1990-91	**Buffalo**	**NHL**	**34**	**8**	**6**	**14**	**12**	**6**	**1**	**2**	**3**	**4**
	Rochester	AHL	49	26	34	60	56	10	3	5	8	22
	NHL Totals		**54**	**10**	**13**	**23**	**16**	**14**	**1**	**3**	**4**	**8**

Traded to **Buffalo** by **Pittsburgh** with Doug Bodger for Tom Barrasso and Buffalo's third-round choice (Joe Dziedzic) in 1990 Entry Draft, November 12, 1988.

SHANNON, DARRYL

Defense. Shoots left. 6'2", 195 lbs. Born, Barrie, Ont., June 21, 1968.
(Toronto's 2nd choice, 36th overall, in 1986 Entry Draft).

			Regular Season					Playoffs				
Season	Club	Lea	GP	G	A	TP	PIM	GP	G	A	TP	PIM
1985-86	Windsor	OHL	57	6	21	27	52	16	5	6	11	22
1986-87a	Windsor	OHL	64	23	27	50	83	14	4	8	12	18
1987-88b	Windsor	OHL	60	16	67	83	116	12	3	8	11	17
1988-89	**Toronto**	**NHL**	**14**	**1**	**3**	**4**	**6**	....	....	....	....	....
	Newmarket	AHL	61	5	24	29	37	5	0	3	3	10
1989-90	**Toronto**	**NHL**	**10**	**0**	**1**	**1**	**12**	....	....	....	....	....
	Newmarket	AHL	47	4	15	19	58	....	....	....	....	....
1990-91	**Toronto**	**NHL**	**10**	**0**	**1**	**1**	**0**	....	....	....	....	....
	Newmarket	AHL	47	2	14	16	51	....	....	....	....	....
	NHL Totals		**34**	**1**	**5**	**6**	**18**	....	....	....	....	....

a OHL Second All-Star Team
b OHL First All-Star Team (1988)

SHARPLES, JEFF

Defense. Shoots left. 6'1", 195 lbs. Born, Terrace, B.C., July 28, 1967.
(Detroit's 2nd choice, 29th overall, in 1985 Entry Draft)

			Regular Season					Playoffs				
Season	Club	Lea	GP	G	A	TP	PIM	GP	G	A	TP	PIM
1983-84	Kelowna	WHL	72	9	24	33	51	....	....	....	....	....
1984-85a	Kelowna	WHL	72	12	41	53	90	6	0	1	1	6
1985-86	Spokane	WHL	3	0	0	0	4	....	....	....	....	....
	Portland	WHL	19	2	6	8	44	15	2	6	8	6
1986-87	**Detroit**	**NHL**	**3**	**0**	**1**	**1**	**2**	**2**	**0**	**0**	**0**	**2**
	Portland	WHL	44	25	35	60	92	20	7	15	22	23
1987-88	**Detroit**	**NHL**	**56**	**10**	**25**	**35**	**42**	**4**	**0**	**3**	**3**	**4**
	Adirondack	AHL	4	2	1	3	4	....	....	....	....	....
1988-89	**Detroit**	**NHL**	**46**	**4**	**9**	**13**	**26**	**1**	**0**	**0**	**0**	**0**
	Adirondack	AHL	10	0	4	4	8	....	....	....	....	....
1989-90	Adirondack	AHL	9	2	5	7	6	....	....	....	....	....
1989-90	Cape Breton	AHL	38	4	13	17	28	....	....	....	....	....
	Utica	AHL	13	2	5	7	19	5	1	2	3	15
1990-91	Utica	AHL	64	16	29	45	42	....	....	....	....	....
	NHL Totals		**105**	**14**	**35**	**49**	**70**	**7**	**0**	**3**	**3**	**6**

a WHL Second All-Star Team, West Division (1985)

Traded to **Edmonton** by **Detroit** with Petr Klima, Joe Murphy and Adam Graves for Jimmy Carson, Kevin McClelland and Edmonton's fifth round choice (later traded to Montreal for Rick Green. Montreal selected Brad Layzell) in 1991 Entry Draft, November 2, 1989. Traded to **New Jersey** by **Edmonton** for Reijo Ruotsalainen, March 6, 1990.

SHAUNESSY, SCOTT

Defense/Left wing. Shoots left. 6'4", 220 lbs. Born, Newport, RI, January 22, 1964.
(Quebec's 9th choice, 192nd overall, in 1983 Entry Draft).

			Regular Season					Playoffs				
Season	Club	Lea	GP	G	A	TP	PIM	GP	G	A	TP	PIM
1983-84	Boston U.	ECAC	40	6	22	28	48	....	....	....	....	....
1984-85a	Boston U.	H.E.	42	7	15	22	87	....	....	....	....	....
1985-86b	Boston U.	H.E.	38	6	13	19	31	....	....	....	....	....
1986-87	**Quebec**	**NHL**	**3**	**0**	**0**	**0**	**7**	....	....	....	....	....
	Boston U.	H.E.	32	2	13	15	71	....	....	....	....	....
1987-88	Fredericton	AHL	60	0	9	9	257	1	0	0	0	2
1988-89	**Quebec**	**NHL**	**4**	**0**	**0**	**0**	**16**	....	....	....	....	....
	Halifax	AHL	41	3	10	13	106	....	....	....	....	....
1989-90	Halifax	AHL	26	3	5	8	107	....	....	....	....	....
	Fort Wayne	IHL	45	3	9	12	267	5	0	1	1	31
1990-91	Albany	IHL	34	3	9	12	126	....	....	....	....	....
	Muskegon	IHL	23	1	4	5	104	5	0	0	0	21
	NHL Totals		**7**	**0**	**0**	**0**	**23**	....	....	....	....	....

a Hockey East Second All-Star Team (1985)
b Hockey East First All-Star Team (1986)

SHAW, BRAD

Defense. Shoots right. 6', 190 lbs. Born, Cambridge, Ont., April 28, 1964.
(Detroit's 5th choice, 86th overall, in 1982 Entry Draft).

			Regular Season					Playoffs				
Season	Club	Lea	GP	G	A	TP	PIM	GP	G	A	TP	PIM
1981-82	Ottawa	OHL	68	13	59	72	24	15	1	13	14	4
1982-83	Ottawa	OHL	63	12	66	78	24	9	2	9	11	4
1983-84a	Ottawa	OHL	68	11	71	82	75	13	2	*27	29	9
1984-85	Binghamton	AHL	24	1	10	11	4	8	1	8	9	6
	Salt Lake	IHL	44	3	29	32	25	....	....	....	....	....
1985-86	**Hartford**	**NHL**	**8**	**0**	**2**	**2**	**4**	....	....	....	....	....
	Binghamton	AHL	64	10	44	54	33	5	0	2	2	6
1986-87	**Hartford**	**NHL**	**2**	**0**	**0**	**0**	**0**	....	....	....	....	....
bc	Binghamton	AHL	77	9	30	39	43	12	1	8	9	2
1987-88	**Hartford**	**NHL**	**1**	**0**	**0**	**0**	**0**	....	....	....	....	....
b	Binghamton	AHL	73	12	50	62	50	4	0	5	5	4
1988-89	Verese	Italy	35	10	30	40	44	11	4	8	12	13
	Cdn. National	...	4	1	0	1	2	....	....	....	....	....
	Hartford	**NHL**	**3**	**1**	**0**	**1**	**0**	**3**	**1**	**0**	**1**	**0**
1989-90d	**Hartford**	**NHL**	**64**	**3**	**32**	**35**	**30**	**7**	**2**	**5**	**7**	**0**
1990-91	**Hartford**	**NHL**	**72**	**4**	**28**	**32**	**29**	**6**	**1**	**2**	**3**	**2**
	NHL Totals		**150**	**8**	**62**	**70**	**63**	**16**	**4**	**7**	**11**	**2**

a OHL First All-Star Team (1984)
b AHL First All-Star Team (1987, 1988)
c Won Eddie Shore Plaque (AHL Outstanding Defenseman) (1987)
d NHL All-Rookie Team (1990)

Rights traded to **Hartford** by **Detroit** for Hartford's eighth round choice (Urban Nordin) in 1984 Entry Draft, May 29, 1984.

SHAW, DAVID

Defense. Shoots right. 6'2", 204 lbs. Born, St. Thomas, Ont., May 25, 1964.
(Quebec's 1st choice, 13th overall, in 1982 Entry Draft).

			Regular Season					Playoffs				
Season	Club	Lea	GP	G	A	TP	PIM	GP	G	A	TP	PIM
1981-82	Kitchener	OHL	68	6	25	31	94	15	2	2	4	51
1982-83	**Quebec**	**NHL**	**2**	**0**	**0**	**0**	**0**	....	....	....	....	....
	Kitchener	OHL	57	18	56	74	78	12	2	10	12	18
1983-84	**Quebec**	**NHL**	**3**	**0**	**0**	**0**	**0**	....	....	....	....	....
a	Kitchener	OHL	58	14	34	48	73	16	4	9	13	12
1984-85	**Quebec**	**NHL**	**14**	**0**	**0**	**0**	**11**	....	....	....	....	
	Fredericton	AHL	48	7	6	13	73	2	0	0	0	7
1985-86	**Quebec**	**NHL**	**73**	**7**	**19**	**26**	**78**	....	....	....	....	....
1986-87	**Quebec**	**NHL**	**75**	**0**	**19**	**19**	**69**	....	....	....	....	....
1987-88	**NY Rangers**	**NHL**	**68**	**7**	**25**	**32**	**100**	....	....	....	....	....
1988-89	**NY Rangers**	**NHL**	**63**	**6**	**11**	**17**	**88**	**4**	**0**	**2**	**2**	**30**
1989-90	**NY Rangers**	**NHL**	**22**	**2**	**10**	**12**	**22**	....	....	....	....	....
1990-91	**NY Rangers**	**NHL**	**77**	**2**	**10**	**12**	**89**	**6**	**0**	**0**	**0**	**11**
	NHL Totals		**397**	**24**	**94**	**118**	**457**	**10**	**0**	**2**	**2**	**41**

a OHL First All-Star Team (1984).

Traded to **NY Rangers** by **Quebec** with John Ogrodnick for Jeff Jackson and Terry Carkner, September 30, 1987.

SHEDDEN, DOUGLAS ARTHUR (DOUG)

Center. Shoots right. 6', 185 lbs. Born, Wallaceburg, Ont., April 29, 1961.
(Pittsburgh's 4th choice, 93rd overall, in 1980 Entry Draft).

			Regular Season					Playoffs				
Season	Club	Lea	GP	G	A	TP	PIM	GP	G	A	TP	PIM
1979-80	Kitchener	OHA	16	10	16	26	26	....	....	....	....	....
	S. S. Marie	OHA	45	30	44	74	59	....	....	....	....	....
1980-81	S. S. Marie	OHA	66	51	72	123	114	19	16	22	38	10
1981-82	**Pittsburgh**	**NHL**	**38**	**10**	**15**	**25**	**12**	....	....	....	....	....
	Erie	AHL	17	4	6	10	14	....	....	....	....	....
1982-83	**Pittsburgh**	**NHL**	**80**	**24**	**43**	**67**	**54**	....	....	....	....	....
1983-84	**Pittsburgh**	**NHL**	**67**	**22**	**35**	**57**	**20**	....	....	....	....	....
1984-85	**Pittsburgh**	**NHL**	**80**	**35**	**32**	**67**	**30**	....	....	....	....	....
1985-86	**Pittsburgh**	**NHL**	**67**	**32**	**34**	**66**	**32**	....	....	....	....	....
	Detroit	**NHL**	**11**	**2**	**3**	**5**	**2**	....	....	....	....	....
1986-87	**Detroit**	**NHL**	**33**	**6**	**12**	**18**	**6**	....	....	....	....	....
	Adirondack	AHL	5	2	2	4	4	....	....	....	....	....
	Quebec	**NHL**	**16**	**0**	**2**	**2**	**8**	....	....	....	....	....
	Fredericton	AHL	15	12	6	18	0	....	....	....	....	....
1987-88	Baltimore	AHL	80	37	51	88	32	....	....	....	....	....
1988-89	**Toronto**	**NHL**	**1**	**0**	**0**	**0**	**2**	....	....	....	....	....
	Newmarket	AHL	29	14	26	40	6	....	....	....	....	....
1989-90	Newmarket	AHL	47	26	33	59	12	....	....	....	....	....
1990-91	**Toronto**	**NHL**	**23**	**8**	**10**	**18**	**10**	....	....	....	....	....
	Newmarket	AHL	47	15	34	49	16	....	....	....	....	....
	NHL Totals		**416**	**139**	**186**	**325**	**176**	....	....	....	....	....

Traded to **Detroit** by **Pittsburgh** for Ron Duguay, March 11, 1986. Traded to **Quebec** by **Detroit** with Basil McRae and John Ogrodnick for Brent Ashton, Gilbert Delorme and Mark Kumpel, January 17, 1987. Signed as a free agent by **Toronto**, August 4, 1988.

SHEEHY, NEIL

Defense. Shoots right. 6'2", 214 lbs. Born, International Falls, MN, February 9, 1960.

			Regular Season					Playoffs				
Season	Club	Lea	GP	G	A	TP	PIM	GP	G	A	TP	PIM
1979-80	Harvard	ECAC	13	0	0	0	10	....	....	....	....	....
1980-81	Harvard	ECAC	26	4	8	12	22	....	....	....	....	....
1981-82	Harvard	ECAC	30	7	11	18	46	....	....	....	....	....
1982-83	Harvard	ECAC	34	5	13	18	48	....	....	....	....	....
1983-84	**Calgary**	**NHL**	**1**	**1**	**0**	**1**	**2**	**4**	**0**	**0**	**0**	**4**
	Colorado	CHL	74	5	18	23	151	....	....	....	....	....
1984-85	**Calgary**	**NHL**	**31**	**3**	**4**	**7**	**109**	....	....	....	....	....
	Moncton	AHL	34	6	9	15	101	....	....	....	....	....
1985-86	**Calgary**	**NHL**	**65**	**2**	**16**	**18**	**271**	**22**	**0**	**2**	**2**	**79**
	Moncton	AHL	4	1	1	2	21	....	....	....	....	....
1986-87	**Calgary**	**NHL**	**54**	**4**	**6**	**10**	**151**	**6**	**0**	**0**	**0**	**21**
1987-88	**Calgary**	**NHL**	**36**	**2**	**6**	**8**	**73**	....	....	....	....	....
	Hartford	**NHL**	**26**	**1**	**4**	**5**	**116**	**1**	**0**	**0**	**0**	**7**
1988-89	**Washington**	**NHL**	**72**	**3**	**4**	**7**	**179**	**6**	**0**	**0**	**0**	**19**
1989-90	**Washington**	**NHL**	**59**	**1**	**5**	**6**	**291**	**13**	**0**	**1**	**1**	**92**
1990-91	**Washington**	**NHL**	....	....	....	....	....	**2**	**0**	**0**	**0**	**19**
	NHL Totals		**344**	**17**	**45**	**62**	**1192**	**54**	**0**	**3**	**3**	**241**

Signed as free agent by **Calgary**, August 16, 1983. Traded to **Hartford** by **Calgary** with Carey Wilson and the rights to Lane MacDonald for Dana Murzyn and Shane Churla, January 3, 1988. Traded to **Washington** by **Hartford** with Mike Millar for Grant Jennings and Ed Kastelic, July 6, 1988.

SHEPPARD, RAY

Right wing. Shoots right. 6'1", 182 lbs. Born, Pembroke, Ont., May 27, 1966.
(Buffalo's 3rd choice, 60th overall, in 1984 Entry Draft).

			Regular Season					Playoffs				
Season	Club	Lea	GP	G	A	TP	PIM	GP	G	A	TP	PIM
1983-84	Cornwall	OHL	68	44	36	80	69	....	....	....	....	....
1984-85	Cornwall	OHL	49	25	33	58	51	9	2	12	14	4
1985-86ab	Cornwall	OHL	63	*81	61	*142	25	6	7	4	11	0
1986-87	Rochester	AHL	55	18	13	31	11	15	12	3	15	2
1987-88c	**Buffalo**	**NHL**	**74**	**38**	**27**	**65**	**14**	**6**	**1**	**1**	**2**	**2**
1988-89	**Buffalo**	**NHL**	**67**	**22**	**21**	**43**	**15**	**1**	**0**	**1**	**1**	**0**
1989-90	**Buffalo**	**NHL**	**18**	**4**	**2**	**6**	**0**	....	....	....	....	....
	Rochester	AHL	5	3	5	8	2	17	8	7	15	9
1990-91	**NY Rangers**	**NHL**	**59**	**24**	**23**	**47**	**21**	....	....	....	....	....
	NHL Totals		**218**	**88**	**73**	**161**	**50**	**7**	**1**	**2**	**3**	**2**

a OHL Player of the Year (1986)
b OHL First All-Star Team (1986)
c NHL All-Rookie Team (1988)

Traded to **NY Rangers** by **Buffalo** for cash and future considerations, July 9, 1990. Signed as a free agent by **Detroit**, August 5, 1991.

SHIER, ANDREW

Center. Shoots right. 5'11", 165 lbs. Born, Lansing, MI, August 15, 1971.
(NY Islanders' 11th choice, 237th overall, in 1990 Entry Draft).

			Regular Season					Playoffs				
Season	Club	Lea	GP	G	A	TP	PIM	GP	G	A	TP	PIM
1989-90	Detroit Comp.	USHL	42	28	54	82	71	....	....	....	....	....
1990-91	U. Wisconsin	WCHA	20	4	9	13	28	....	....	....	....	....

SHOEBOTTOM, BRUCE

Defense. Shoots left. 6'2", 200 lbs. Born, Windsor, Ont., August 20, 1965.
(Los Angeles' 1st choice, 47th overall, in 1983 Entry Draft).

			Regular Season					Playoffs				
Season	Club	Lea	GP	G	A	TP	PIM	GP	G	A	TP	PIM
1982-83	Peterborough	OHL	34	2	10	12	106	....	....	....	....	....
1983-84	Peterborough	OHL	16	0	5	5	73	....	....	....	....	....
1984-85	Perterborough	OHL	60	2	15	17	143	17	0	4	4	26
1985-86	New Haven	AHL	6	2	0	2	12	....	....	....	....	....
	Binghamton	AHL	62	7	5	12	249	....	....	....	....	....
1986-87	Fort Wayne	IHL	75	2	10	12	309	10	0	0	0	31
1987-88	**Boston**	**NHL**	**3**	**0**	**1**	**1**	**0**	**4**	**1**	**0**	**1**	**42**
	Maine	AHL	70	2	12	14	338	....	....	....	....	....
1988-89	**Boston**	**NHL**	**29**	**1**	**3**	**4**	**44**	**10**	**0**	**2**	**2**	**35**
	Maine	AHL	44	0	8	8	265	....	....	....	....	....
1989-90	**Boston**	**NHL**	**2**	**0**	**0**	**0**	**4**	....	....	....	....	....
	Maine	AHL	66	3	11	14	228	....	....	....	....	....
1990-91	**Boston**	**NHL**	**1**	**0**	**0**	**0**	**5**	....	....	....	....	....
	Maine	AHL	71	2	8	10	238	1	0	0	0	14
	NHL Totals		**35**	**1**	**4**	**5**	**53**	**14**	**1**	**2**	**3**	**77**

Traded to **Washington** by **Los Angeles** for Bryan Erickson, October 31, 1985. Signed as a free agent by **Boston**, July 20, 1987.

SHUCHUK, GARY (SHOO-chuk)

Right wing. Shoots right. 5'10", 185 lbs. Born, Edmonton, Alta., February 17, 1967.
(Detroit's 1st choice, 22nd overall, in 1988 Supplemental Draft).

			Regular Season					Playoffs				
Season	Club	Lea	GP	G	A	TP	PIM	GP	G	A	TP	PIM
1986-87	U. Wisconsin	WCHA	42	19	11	30	72	....	....	....	....	....
1987-88	U. Wisconsin	WCHA	44	7	22	29	70	....	....	....	....	....
1988-89	U. Wisconsin	WCHA	46	18	19	37	102	....	....	....	....	....
1989-90abc	U. Wisconsin	WCHA	45	*41	39	*80	70	....	....	....	....	....
1990-91	**Detroit**	**NHL**	**6**	**1**	**2**	**3**	**6**	**3**	**0**	**0**	**0**	**0**
	Adirondack	AHL	59	23	24	47	32	....	....	....	....	....
	NHL Totals		**6**	**1**	**2**	**3**	**6**	**3**	**0**	**0**	**0**	**0**

a WCHA First All-Star Team (1990)
b WCHA Player of the Year (1990)
c NCAA West First All-American Team (1990)

SHUTE, DAVID

Center. Shoots left. 5'11", 185 lbs. Born, Carlisle, PA, February 10, 1971.
(Pittsburgh's 9th choice, 163rd overall, in 1989 Entry Draft).

			Regular Season					Playoffs				
Season	Club	Lea	GP	G	A	TP	PIM	GP	G	A	TP	PIM
1988-89	Victoria	WHL	69	5	11	16	26	8	0	1	1	10
1989-90	Victoria	WHL	14	4	5	9	25	....	....	....	....	....
	Medicine Hat	WHL	48	13	15	28	56	....	....	....	....	....
1990-91	Victoria	WHL	72	31	28	59	91	11	6	2	8	9

SIDOROV, ANDREI (SEE-duh-rahf)

Left wing. Shoots right. 5'11", 174 lbs. Born, Kiev, Soviet Union, May 15, 1969.
(Washington's 10th choice, 229th overall, in 1989 Entry Draft).

			Regular Season					Playoffs				
Season	Club	Lea	GP	G	A	TP	PIM	GP	G	A	TP	PIM
1989-90	Dynamo Harkov	USSR	29	6	5	11	14	....	....	....	....	....
1990-91	Sokol Kiev	USSR	42	7	1	8	10	....	....	....	....	....

SILLINGER, MIKE

Center. Shoots right. 5'10", 191 lbs. Born, Regina, Sask., June 29, 1971.
(Detroit's 1st choice, 11th overall, in 1989 Entry Draft).

			Regular Season					Playoffs				
Season	Club	Lea	GP	G	A	TP	PIM	GP	G	A	TP	PIM
1987-88	Regina	WHL	67	18	25	43	17	4	2	2	4	0
1988-89	Regina	WHL	72	53	78	131	52	....	....	....	....	....
1989-90a	Regina	WHL	70	57	72	129	41	11	12	10	22	2
	Adirondack	AHL	....	....	....	....	....	1	0	0	0	0
1990-91	**Detroit**	**NHL**	**3**	**0**	**1**	**1**	**0**	**3**	**0**	**1**	**1**	**0**
b	Regina	WHL	57	50	66	116	42	8	6	9	15	4
	NHL Totals		**3**	**0**	**1**	**1**	**0**	**3**	**0**	**1**	**1**	**0**

a WHL East Second All-Star Team (1990)
b WHL East First All-Star Team (1991)

SILVERMAN, ANDREW

Defense. Shoots left. 6'3", 210 lbs. Born, Beverly, MA, August 23, 1972.
(NY Rangers' 11th choice, 181st overall, in 1990 Entry Draft).

			Regular Season					Playoffs				
Season	Club	Lea	GP	G	A	TP	PIM	GP	G	A	TP	PIM
1989-90	Beverly	HS	24	8	20	28	....	....	....	....	....	....
1990-91	Cushing Aca.	HS	25	8	26	34	84	....	....	....	....	....

SIM, TREVOR

Right wing. Shoots left. 6'2", 192 lbs. Born, Calgary, Alta., June 9, 1970.
(Edmonton's 3rd choice, 53rd overall, in 1988 Entry Draft).

			Regular Season					Playoffs				
Season	Club	Lea	GP	G	A	TP	PIM	GP	G	A	TP	PIM
1987-88	Seattle	WHL	67	17	18	35	87	....	....	....	....	....
1988-89	Regina	WHL	21	4	8	12	48	....	....	....	....	....
	Swift Current	WHL	42	16	19	35	69	11	10	6	16	20
1989-90	**Edmonton**	**NHL**	**3**	**0**	**1**	**1**	**2**	....	....	....	....	....
	Swift Current	WHL	6	3	2	5	21	....	....	....	....	....
	Kamloops	WHL	43	27	35	62	53	17	3	13	16	28
1990-91	Cape Breton	AHL	62	20	9	29	39	2	0	0	0	0
	NHL Totals		**3**	**0**	**1**	**1**	**2**	....	....	....	....	....

SIMARD, MARTIN

Right wing. Shoots right. 6'3", 215 lbs. Born, Montreal, Que., June 25, 1966.

			Regular Season					Playoffs				
Season	Club	Lea	GP	G	A	TP	PIM	GP	G	A	TP	PIM
1984-85	Granby	QMJHL	58	22	31	53	78	8	3	7	10	21
1985-86	Granby	QMJHL	54	32	28	60	129	....	....	....	....	....
	Hull	QMJHL	14	8	8	16	55	14	8	19	27	19
1986-87	Granby	QMJHL	41	30	47	77	105	8	3	7	10	21
1987-88	Salt Lake	IHL	82	8	23	31	281	19	6	3	9	100
1988-89	Salt Lake	IHL	71	13	15	28	221	14	4	0	4	45
1989-90	Salt Lake	IHL	59	22	23	45	151	11	5	8	13	12
1990-91	**Calgary**	**NHL**	**16**	**0**	**2**	**2**	**53**	....	....	....	....	....
	Salt Lake	IHL	54	24	25	49	113	4	3	0	3	20
	NHL Totals		**16**	**0**	**2**	**2**	**53**	....	....	....	....	....

Signed as a free agent by **Calgary**, May 19, 1987.

SIMON, CHRIS

Left wing. Shoots left. 6'3", 220 lbs. Born, Wawa, Ont., January 30, 1972.
(Philadelphia's 2nd choice, 25th overall, in 1990 Entry Draft).

			Regular Season					Playoffs				
Season	Club	Lea	GP	G	A	TP	PIM	GP	G	A	TP	PIM
1987-88	S.S. Marie	OHL	55	42	36	78	172	....	....	....	....	....
1988-89	Ottawa	OHL	36	4	2	6	31	....	....	....	....	....
1989-90	Ottawa	OHL	57	36	38	74	146	3	2	1	3	4
1990-91	Ottawa	OHL	20	16	6	22	69	17	5	9	14	59

SIMON, DARCY

Defense. Shoots right. 6'1", 200 lbs. Born, North Battleford, Sask., January 21, 1970.

			Regular Season					Playoffs				
Season	Club	Lea	GP	G	A	TP	PIM	GP	G	A	TP	PIM
1987-88	Seattle	WHL	67	5	9	14	226	....	....	....	....	....
1988-89	Seattle	WHL	62	3	15	18	208	....	....	....	....	....
1989-90	Seattle	WHL	63	5	13	18	285	13	1	2	3	79
1990-91	Fredericton	AHL	29	0	3	3	183	9	2	0	2	45

Signed as a free agent by **Montreal**, October 3, 1991.

SIMON, JASON

Left wing. Shoots left. 6'1", 190 lbs. Born, Sarnia, Ont., March 21, 1969.
(New Jersey's 9th choice, 215th overall, in 1989 Entry Draft).

			Regular Season					Playoffs				
Season	Club	Lea	GP	G	A	TP	PIM	GP	G	A	TP	PIM
1986-87	London	OHL	33	1	2	3	33	....	....	....	....	....
	Sudbury	OHL	26	2	3	5	50	....	....	....	....	....
1987-88	Sudbury	OHL	26	5	7	12	35	....	....	....	....	....
	Hamilton	OHL	29	5	13	18	124	11	0	2	2	15
1988-89	Windsor	OHL	62	23	39	62	193	4	1	4	5	13
1989-90	Utica	AHL	16	3	4	7	28	2	0	0	0	12
	Nashville	ECHL	13	4	3	7	81	5	1	3	4	17
1990-91	Utica	AHL	50	2	12	14	189	....	....	....	....	....
	Johnstown	ECHL	22	11	9	20	55	....	....	....	....	....

SIMPSON, CRAIG

Left wing. Shoots right. 6'2", 195 lbs. Born, London, Ont., February 15, 1967.
(Pittsburgh's 1st choice, 2nd overall, in 1985 Entry Draft)

			Regular Season					Playoffs				
Season	Club	Lea	GP	G	A	TP	PIM	GP	G	A	TP	PIM
1983-84	Michigan State	CCHA	46	14	43	57	38	....	....	....	....	....
1984-85ab	Michigan State	CCHA	42	31	53	84	33	....	....	....	....	....
1985-86	**Pittsburgh**	**NHL**	**76**	**11**	**17**	**28**	**49**	....	....	....	....	....
1986-87	**Pittsburgh**	**NHL**	**72**	**26**	**25**	**51**	**57**	....	....	....	....	....
1987-88	**Pittsburgh**	**NHL**	**21**	**13**	**13**	**26**	**34**	....	....	....	....	....
	Edmonton	**NHL**	**59**	**43**	**21**	**64**	**43**	**19**	**13**	**6**	**19**	**26**
1988-89	**Edmonton**	**NHL**	**66**	**35**	**41**	**76**	**80**	**7**	**2**	**0**	**2**	**10**
1989-90	**Edmonton**	**NHL**	**80**	**29**	**32**	**61**	**180**	**22**	***16**	**15**	***31**	**8**
1990-91	**Edmonton**	**NHL**	**75**	**30**	**27**	**57**	**66**	**18**	**5**	**11**	**16**	**12**
	NHL Totals		**449**	**187**	**176**	**363**	**509**	**66**	**36**	**32**	**68**	**56**

a CCHA First All-Star Team (1985)
b NCAA All-American (1985)

Traded to **Edmonton** by **Pittsburgh** with Dave Hannan, Moe Mantha and Chris Joseph for Paul Coffey, Dave Hunter and Wayne Van Dorp, November 24, 1987.

SIMPSON, GEOFF

Defense. Shoots right. 6'1", 180 lbs. Born, Victoria, B.C., March 6, 1969.
(Boston's 10th choice, 206th overall, in 1989 Entry Draft).

			Regular Season					Playoffs				
Season	Club	Lea	GP	G	A	TP	PIM	GP	G	A	TP	PIM
1989-90	N. Michigan	WCHA	39	4	19	23	40	....	....	....	....	....
1990-91	N. Michigan	WCHA	44	2	15	17	27	....	....	....	....	....

SIMPSON, REID

Left wing. Shoots left. 6'1", 211 lbs. Born, Flin Flon, Man., May 21, 1969.
(Philadelphia's 3rd choice, 72nd overall, in 1989 Entry Draft).

			Regular Season					Playoffs				
Season	Club	Lea	GP	G	A	TP	PIM	GP	G	A	TP	PIM
1987-88	Prince Albert	WHL	72	13	14	27	164	10	1	0	1	43
1988-89	Prince Albert	WHL	59	26	29	55	264	4	2	1	3	30
1989-90	Prince Albert	WHL	29	15	17	32	121	14	4	7	11	34
	Hershey	AHL	28	2	2	4	175	....	....	....	....	....
1990-91	Hershey	AHL	54	9	15	24	183	1	0	0	0	0

SINISALO, ILKKA (sin-i-SAL-oh)

Right wing. Shoots left. 6', 200 lbs. Born, Valeakoski, Finland, July 10, 1958.

			Regular Season					Playoffs				
Season	Club	Lea	GP	G	A	TP	PIM	GP	G	A	TP	PIM
1977-78	HIFK	Fin.	36	9	3	12	18	....	....	....	....	....
1978-79	HIFK	Fin.	30	6	4	10	16	6	0	5	5	25
1979-80	HIFK	Fin.	35	16	9	25	16	7	1	3	4	12
1980-81	HIFK	Fin.	36	27	17	44	14	6	5	3	8	4
1981-82	**Philadelphia**	**NHL**	**66**	**15**	**22**	**37**	**22**	**4**	**0**	**2**	**2**	**0**
1982-83	**Philadelphia**	**NHL**	**61**	**21**	**29**	**50**	**16**	**3**	**1**	**1**	**2**	**0**
1983-84	**Philadelphia**	**NHL**	**73**	**29**	**17**	**46**	**29**	**2**	**2**	**0**	**2**	**0**
1984-85	**Philadelphia**	**NHL**	**70**	**36**	**37**	**73**	**16**	**19**	**6**	**1**	**7**	**0**
1985-86	**Philadelphia**	**NHL**	**74**	**39**	**37**	**76**	**31**	**5**	**2**	**2**	**4**	**2**
1986-87	**Philadelphia**	**NHL**	**42**	**10**	**21**	**31**	**8**	**18**	**5**	**1**	**6**	**4**
1987-88	**Philadelphia**	**NHL**	**68**	**25**	**17**	**42**	**30**	**7**	**4**	**2**	**6**	**0**
1988-89	**Philadelphia**	**NHL**	**13**	**1**	**6**	**7**	**2**	**8**	**1**	**1**	**2**	**0**
1989-90	**Philadelphia**	**NHL**	**59**	**23**	**23**	**46**	**26**	....	....	....	....	....
1990-91	**Minnesota**	**NHL**	**46**	**5**	**12**	**17**	**24**	....	....	....	....	....
	Los Angeles	**NHL**	**7**	**0**	**0**	**0**	**2**	**2**	**0**	**1**	**1**	**0**
	NHL Totals		**579**	**204**	**221**	**425**	**206**	**68**	**21**	**11**	**32**	**6**

Signed as free agent by **Philadelphia**, February 14, 1981. Signed as a free agent by **Minnesota**, July 3, 1990. Traded to **Los Angeles** by **Minnesota** for Los Angeles' eighth round choice (Michael Burkett) in 1991 Entry Draft, March 5, 1991.

SIREN, VILLE (SIH-rihn)

Defense. Shoots left. 6'2", 191 lbs. Born, Tampere, Finland, February 11, 1964.
(Hartford's 3rd choice, 23rd overall, in 1983 Entry Draft).

			Regular Season					Playoffs				
Season	Club	Lea	GP	G	A	TP	PIM	GP	G	A	TP	PIM
1982-83	Ilves	Fin.	29	3	2	5	42	8	1	3	4	8
1983-84	Ilves	Fin.	36	1	10	11	40	2	0	0	0	2
	Fin. Olympic	...	2	0	0	0	0	....	....	....	....	....
1984-85	Ilves	Fin	36	11	13	24	24	9	0	2	2	10
1985-86	**Pittsburgh**	**NHL**	**60**	**4**	**8**	**12**	**32**	....	....	....	....	....
1986-87	**Pittsburgh**	**NHL**	**69**	**5**	**17**	**22**	**50**	....	....	....	....	....
1987-88	**Pittsburgh**	**NHL**	**58**	**1**	**20**	**21**	**62**	....	....	....	....	....
1988-89	**Pittsburgh**	**NHL**	**12**	**1**	**0**	**1**	**14**	....	....	....	....	....
	Minnesota	**NHL**	**38**	**2**	**10**	**12**	**58**	**4**	**0**	**0**	**0**	**4**
1989-90	**Minnesota**	**NHL**	**53**	**1**	**13**	**14**	**60**	**3**	**0**	**0**	**0**	**2**
1990-91	HPK	Fin.	44	4	9	13	90	8	1	1	2	37
	NHL Totals		**290**	**14**	**68**	**82**	**276**	**15**	**1**	**1**	**2**	**43**

Traded to **Pittsburgh** by **Hartford** for Pat Boutette, November 16, 1984. Traded to **Minnesota** by **Pittsburgh** with Steve Gotaas for Gord Dineen and Scott Bjugstad, December 17, 1988.

SIRKKA, JEFFREY

Defense. Shoots left. 6'1", 200 lbs. Born, Sudbury, Ont., June 17, 1968.

			Regular Season					Playoffs				
Season	Club	Lea	GP	G	A	TP	PIM	GP	G	A	TP	PIM
1986-87	Kingston	OHL	64	0	5	5	156	....	....	....	....	....
1987-88	Kingston	OHL	59	1	16	17	114	....	....	....	....	....
1989-90	Maine	AHL	56	0	9	9	110	....	....	....	....	....
1990-91	Indianapolis	IHL	69	6	12	18	203	6	0	0	0	6

Tradede to **Hartford** by **Boston** for Steve Dykstra, March 3, 1990. Signed as a free agent by **Chicago**, September 20, 1990.

SJODIN, TOMMY (SHOH-deen)

Defense. Shoots right. 5'11", 190 lbs. Born, Sundsvall, Sweden, August 13, 1965.
(Minnesota's 10th choice, 237th overall, in 1985 Entry Draft).

			Regular Season					Playoffs				
Season	Club	Lea	GP	G	A	TP	PIM	GP	G	A	TP	PIM
1987-88	Brynas	Swe.	40	6	9	15	28	....	....	....	....	....
1988-89	Brynas	Swe.	40	8	11	19	54	....	....	....	....	....
1989-90	Brynas	Swe.	40	14	14	28	46	5	0	0	0	2
1990-91	Brynas	Swe.	38	12	17	29	79	....	....	....	....	....

SJOGREN, THOMAS (SHOH-gruhn)

Right wing. Shoots right. 5'9", 185 lbs. Born, Umea, Sweden, June 8, 1968.
(Washington's 7th choice, 162nd overall, in 1987 Entry Draft).

			Regular Season					Playoffs				
Season	Club	Lea	GP	G	A	TP	PIM	GP	G	A	TP	PIM
1987-88	V. Frolunda	Swe.2	36	36	27	63	42	10	6	6	12	8
1988-89	Sodertalje	Swe.	40	23	19	42	22	....	....	....	....	....
1989-90	Sodertalje	Swe.	33	7	8	15	14	2	0	1	1	0
1990-91	Baltimore	AHL	72	29	24	53	34	2	0	1	1	0

SKALDE, JARROD

Center. Shoots left. 6', 170 lbs. Born, Niagara Falls, Ont., February 26, 1971.
(New Jersey's 3rd choice, 26th overall, in 1989 Entry Draft).

			Regular Season					Playoffs				
Season	Club	Lea	GP	G	A	TP	PIM	GP	G	A	TP	PIM
1987-88	Oshawa	OHL	60	12	16	28	24	7	2	1	3	2
1988-89	Oshawa	OHL	65	38	38	76	36	6	1	5	6	2
1989-90	Oshawa	OHL	62	40	52	92	66	17	10	7	17	6
1990-91	**New Jersey**	**NHL**	**1**	**0**	**1**	**1**	**0**	....	....	....	....	....
	Utica	AHL	3	3	2	5	0	....	....	....	....	....
	Oshawa	OHL	15	8	14	22	14	....	....	....	....	....
a	Belleville	OHL	40	30	52	82	21	6	9	6	15	10
	NHL Totals		**1**	**0**	**1**	**1**	**0**	....	....	....	....	....

a OHL Second All-Star Team (1991)

SKARDA, RANDY

Defense. Shoots right. 6'1", 205 lbs. Born, St. Paul, MN, May 5, 1968.
(St. Louis' 8th choice, 157th overall, in 1986 Entry Draft).

			Regular Season					Playoffs				
Season	Club	Lea	GP	G	A	TP	PIM	GP	G	A	TP	PIM
1986-87	U. Minnesota	WCHA	43	3	10	13	77	....	....	....	....	....
1987-88ab	U. Minnesota	WCHA	42	19	26	45	102	....	....	....	....	....
1988-89	U. Minnesota	WCHA	43	6	24	30	91	....	....	....	....	....
1989-90	**St. Louis**	**NHL**	**25**	**0**	**5**	**5**	**11**	....	....	....	....	....
	Peoria	IHL	38	7	17	24	40	4	0	0	0	0
1990-91	Peoria	IHL	78	8	34	42	126	19	3	5	8	22
	NHL Totals		**25**	**0**	**5**	**5**	**11**	....	....	....	....	....

a NCAA West Second All-American Team (1988)
b WCHA First All-Star Team (1988)

SKRIKO, PETRI (SKREE-koh)

Left wing. Shoots left. 5'10", 175 lbs. Born, Lappeenranta, Finland, March 12, 1962.
(Vancouver's 7th choice, 157th overall, in 1981 Entry Draft)

			Regular Season					Playoffs				
Season	Club	Lea	GP	G	A	TP	PIM	GP	G	A	TP	PIM
1981-82	SaiPa	Fin.	33	19	27	46	24	....	....	....	....	....
1982-83	SaiPa	Fin.	36	23	12	35	12	....	....	....	....	....
1983-84	SaiPa	Fin.	32	25	26	51	13	....	....	....	....	....
	Fin. Olympic	...	7	1	1	2	0	....	....	....	....	....
1984-85	**Vancouver**	**NHL**	**72**	**21**	**14**	**35**	**10**	....	....	....	....	....
1985-86	**Vancouver**	**NHL**	**80**	**38**	**40**	**78**	**34**	**3**	**0**	**0**	**0**	**0**
1986-87	**Vancouver**	**NHL**	**76**	**33**	**41**	**74**	**44**	....	....	....	....	....
1987-88	**Vancouver**	**NHL**	**73**	**30**	**34**	**64**	**32**	....	....	....	....	....
1988-89	**Vancouver**	**NHL**	**74**	**30**	**36**	**66**	**57**	**7**	**1**	**5**	**6**	**0**
1989-90	**Vancouver**	**NHL**	**77**	**15**	**33**	**48**	**36**	....	....	....	....	....
1990-91	**Vancouver**	**NHL**	**20**	**4**	**4**	**8**	**8**	....	....	....	....	....
	Boston	**NHL**	**28**	**5**	**14**	**19**	**9**	**18**	**4**	**4**	**8**	**4**
	NHL Totals		**500**	**176**	**216**	**392**	**230**	**28**	**5**	**9**	**14**	**4**

Traded to **Boston** by **Vancouver** for Boston's second round choice in the 1992 Entry Draft, January 16, 1991.

SKRUDLAND, BRIAN (SKROOD-luhnd)

Center. Shoots left. 6', 196 lbs. Born, Peace River, Alta., July 31, 1963.

			Regular Season					Playoffs				
Season	Club	Lea	GP	G	A	TP	PIM	GP	G	A	TP	PIM
1980-81	Saskatoon	WHL	66	15	27	42	97	....	....	....	....	....
1981-82	Saskatoon	WHL	71	27	29	56	135	5	0	1	1	2
1982-83	Saskatoon	WHL	71	35	59	94	42	6	1	3	4	19
1983-84	Nova Scotia	AHL	56	13	12	25	55	12	2	8	10	14
1984-85	Sherbrooke	AHL	70	22	28	50	109	17	9	8	17	23
1985-86	**Montreal**	**NHL**	**65**	**9**	**13**	**22**	**57**	**20**	**2**	**4**	**6**	**76**
1986-87	**Montreal**	**NHL**	**79**	**11**	**17**	**28**	**107**	**14**	**1**	**5**	**6**	**29**
1987-88	**Montreal**	**NHL**	**79**	**12**	**24**	**36**	**112**	**11**	**1**	**5**	**6**	**24**
1988-89	**Montreal**	**NHL**	**71**	**12**	**29**	**41**	**84**	**21**	**3**	**7**	**10**	**40**
1989-90	**Montreal**	**NHL**	**59**	**11**	**31**	**42**	**56**	**11**	**3**	**5**	**8**	**30**
1990-91	**Montreal**	**NHL**	**57**	**15**	**19**	**34**	**85**	**13**	**3**	**10**	**13**	**42**
	NHL Totals		**410**	**70**	**133**	**203**	**501**	**90**	**13**	**36**	**49**	**241**

Signed as a free agent by **Montreal**, September 13, 1983.

SLANEY, JOHN

Defense. Shoots left. 5'11", 186 lbs. Born, St. John's, Nfld., February 7, 1972.
(Washington's 1st choice, 9th overall, in 1990 Entry Draft).

			Regular Season					Playoffs				
Season	Club	Lea	GP	G	A	TP	PIM	GP	G	A	TP	PIM
1988-89	Cornwall	OHL	66	16	43	59	23	18	8	16	24	10
1989-90a	Cornwall	OHL	64	38	59	97	68	6	0	8	8	11
1990-91b	Cornwall	OHL	34	21	25	46	28	....	....	....	....	....

a OHL First All-Star Team (1990)
b OHL Second All-Star Team (1991)

SLANINA, PETER (slah-NEE-nah)

Defense. Shoots right. 6'1", 211 lbs. Born, Banska Bystrica, Czechoslovakia, Dec. 16, 1959.
(Toronto's 11th choice, 233rd overall, in 1984 Entry Draft).

			Regular Season					Playoffs				
Season	Club	Lea	GP	G	A	TP	PIM	GP	G	A	TP	PIM
1986-87	VSZ Kosice	Czech.	33	11	7	18	....	....	....	....	....	....
1987-88	VSZ Kosice	Czech.	34	7	15	22	....	....	....	....	....	....
1988-89	VSZ Kosice	Czech.	42	12	24	36	....	....	....	....	....	....
1989-90	KalPa	Fin.	39	12	17	29	45	6	0	0	0	4
1990-91	KalPa	Fin.	44	10	27	37	46	8	1	4	5	51

SLEGR, JIRI (SHLEHGR)

Defense. Shoots left. 5'11", 183 lbs. Born, Litvinov, Czechoslovakia, May 30, 1971.
(Vancouver's 3rd choice, 23rd overall, in 1990 Entry Draft).

			Regular Season					Playoffs				
Season	Club	Lea	GP	G	A	TP	PIM	GP	G	A	TP	PIM
1988-89	CHZ Litvinov	Czech.	8	0	0	0	....	....	....	....	....	....
1989-90	CHZ Litvinov	Czech.	51	4	15	19	....	....	....	....	....	....
1990-91	CHZ Litvinov	Czech.	39	10	33	43	26					

SMAIL, DOUGLAS (DOUG)

Left wing. Shoots left. 5'9", 175 lbs. Born, Moose Jaw, Sask., September 2, 1957.

			Regular Season					Playoffs				
Season	Club	Lea	GP	G	A	TP	PIM	GP	G	A	TP	PIM
1978-79	North Dakota	WCHA	35	24	34	58	46	....	....	....	....	....
1979-80ab	North Dakota	WCHA	40	43	44	87	70	....	....	....	....	....
1980-81	Winnipeg	NHL	30	10	8	18	45	....	....	....	....	....
1981-82	Winnipeg	NHL	72	17	18	35	55	4	0	0	0	0
1982-83	Winnipeg	NHL	80	15	29	44	32	3	0	0	0	6
1983-84	Winnipeg	NHL	66	20	17	37	62	3	0	1	1	7
1984-85	Winnipeg	NHL	80	31	35	66	45	8	2	1	3	4
1985-86	Winnipeg	NHL	73	16	26	42	32	3	1	0	1	0
1986-87	Winnipeg	NHL	78	25	18	43	36	10	4	0	4	10
1987-88	Winnipeg	NHL	71	15	16	31	34	5	1	0	1	22
1988-89	Winnipeg	NHL	47	14	15	29	52	....	....	....	....	....
1989-90	Winnipeg	NHL	79	25	24	49	63	5	1	0	1	0
1990-91	Winnipeg	NHL	15	1	2	3	10	....	....	....	....	....
	Minnesota	NHL	57	7	13	20	38	1	0	0	0	0
	NHL Totals		748	196	221	417	504	42	9	2	11	49

a WCHA Second All-Star Team (1980).
b Most Valuable Player, NCAA Tournament (1980).

Played in NHL All-Star Game (1990)

Signed as free agent by **Winnipeg**, May 22, 1980. Traded to **Minnesota** by **Winnipeg** for Don Barber, November 7, 1990.

SMART, JASON

Center. Shoots left. 6'4", 212 lbs. Born, Prince George, B.C., January 23, 1970.
(Pittsburgh's 13th choice, 247th overall, in 1989 Entry Draft).

			Regular Season					Playoffs				
Season	Club	Lea	GP	G	A	TP	PIM	GP	G	A	TP	PIM
1986-87	Prince Albert	WHL	57	9	22	31	62	8	3	3	6	8
1987-88	Prince Albert	WHL	72	16	29	45	77	10	1	2	3	11
1988-89	Prince Albert	WHL	12	1	3	4	31	....	....	....	....	....
	Saskatoon	WHL	36	6	17	23	33	8	1	6	7	16
1989-90	Saskatoon	WHL	66	27	48	75	187	10	1	5	6	19
1990-91	Albany	IHL	15	4	2	6	28	....	....	....	....	....
	Muskegon	IHL	36	12	27	39	55	5	0	3	3	11

SMEHLIK, RICHARD

Defense. Shoots left. 6'3", 208 lbs. Born, Ostrava, Czechoslovakia, January 23, 1970.
(Buffalo's 3rd choice, 97th overall, in 1990 Entry Draft).

			Regular Season					Playoffs				
Season	Club	Lea	GP	G	A	TP	PIM	GP	G	A	TP	PIM
1989-90	Vitkovice	Czech.	43	4	3	7	....	....	....	....	....	....
1990-91	Dukla Jihlava	Czech.	51	4	2	6	22	....	....	....	....	....

SMITH, DARIN

Left wing. Shoots left. 6'2", 205 lbs. Born, Vineland Station, Ont., February 20, 1967.
(St. Louis' 4th choice, 75th overall, in 1987 Entry Draft).

			Regular Season					Playoffs				
Season	Club	Lea	GP	G	A	TP	PIM	GP	G	A	TP	PIM
1986-87	North Bay	OHL	59	22	25	47	142	23	3	8	11	84
1987-88	Peoria	IHL	81	21	23	44	144	7	1	2	3	16
1988-89	Peoria	IHL	62	13	17	30	127	4	1	0	1	7
1989-90	Peoria	IHL	76	16	13	29	147	5	1	0	1	2
1990-91	Kansas City	IHL	78	22	38	60	161	....	....	....	....	....

SMITH, DENNIS

Defense. Shoots left. 5'11", 190 lbs. Born, Detroit, MI, July 27, 1964.

			Regular Season					Playoffs				
Season	Club	Lea	GP	G	A	TP	PIM	GP	G	A	TP	PIM
1981-82	Kingston	OHL	48	2	24	26	84	4	0	2	2	0
1982-83	Kingston	OHL	58	6	30	36	100	....	....	....	....	....
1983-84	Kingston	OHL	62	10	41	51	165	....	....	....	....	....
1984-85	Osby	Swe.	30	15	15	30	74	....	....	....	....	....
1985-86	Peoria	IHL	70	5	15	20	102	10	0	2	2	18
1986-87	Adirondack	AHL	64	4	24	28	120	6	0	0	0	8
1987-88	Adirondack	AHL	75	6	24	30	213	11	2	2	4	47
1988-89	Adirondack	AHL	75	5	35	40	176	17	1	6	7	47
1989-90	Washington	NHL	4	0	0	0	0	....	....	....	....	....
a	Baltimore	AHL	74	8	25	33	103	12	0	3	3	65
1990-91	Los Angeles	NHL	4	0	0	0	4	....	....	....	....	....
	New Haven	AHL	61	7	25	32	148	....	....	....	....	....
	NHL Totals		8	0	0	0	4	....	....	....	....	....

a AHL Second All-Star Team (1990)

Signed as a free agent by **Detroit**, December 2, 1986. Signed as a free agent by **Washington**, July 25, 1989. Signed as a free agent by **Los Angeles**, September 28, 1990. Signed as a free agent by **Boston**, August 2, 1991.

SMITH, DERRICK

Left wing. Shoots left. 6'2", 215 lbs. Born, Scarborough, Ont., January 22, 1965.
(Philadelphia's 2nd choice, 44th overall, in 1983 Entry Draft).

			Regular Season					Playoffs				
Season	Club	Lea	GP	G	A	TP	PIM	GP	G	A	TP	PIM
1982-83	Peterborough	OHL	70	16	19	35	47	....	....	....	....	....
1983-84	Peterborough	OHL	70	30	36	66	31	8	4	4	8	7
1984-85	Philadelphia	NHL	77	17	22	39	31	19	2	5	7	16
1985-86	Philadelphia	NHL	69	6	6	12	57	4	0	0	0	10
1986-87	Philadelphia	NHL	71	11	21	32	34	26	6	4	10	26
1987-88	Philadelphia	NHL	76	16	8	24	104	7	0	0	0	6
1988-89	Philadelphia	NHL	74	16	14	30	43	19	5	2	7	12
1989-90	Philadelphia	NHL	55	3	6	9	32	....	....	....	....	....
1990-91	Philadelphia	NHL	72	11	10	21	37	....	....	....	....	....
	NHL Totals		494	80	87	167	338	75	13	11	24	70

SMITH, DOUGLAS ERIC (DOUG)

Center. Shoots right. 5'11", 186 lbs. Born, Ottawa, Ont., May 17, 1963.
(Los Angeles' 1st choice, 2nd overall, in 1981 Entry Draft).

			Regular Season					Playoffs				
Season	Club	Lea	GP	G	A	TP	PIM	GP	G	A	TP	PIM
1979-80	Ottawa	OHA	64	23	34	57	45	11	2	0	2	33
1980-81	Ottawa	OHA	54	45	56	101	61	7	5	6	11	13
1981-82	Los Angeles	NHL	80	16	14	30	64	10	3	2	5	11
1982-83	Los Angeles	NHL	42	11	11	22	12	....	....	....	....	....
1983-84	Los Angeles	NHL	72	16	20	36	28	....	....	....	....	....
1984-85	Los Angeles	NHL	62	21	20	41	58	3	1	0	1	4
1985-86	Los Angeles	NHL	48	8	9	17	56	....	....	....	....	....
	Buffalo	NHL	30	10	11	21	73	....	....	....	....	....
1986-87	Buffalo	NHL	62	16	24	40	106	....	....	....	....	....
	Rochester	AHL	15	5	6	11	35	....	....	....	....	....
1987-88	Buffalo	NHL	70	9	19	28	117	1	0	0	0	0
1988-89	Edmonton	NHL	19	1	1	2	9	....	....	....	....	....
	Cape Breton	AHL	24	11	11	22	69	....	....	....	....	....
	Vancouver	NHL	10	3	4	7	4	4	0	0	0	6
1989-90	Vancouver	NHL	30	3	4	7	72	....	....	....	....	....
1989-90	Pittsburgh	NHL	10	1	1	2	25	....	....	....	....	....
1990-91	Graz	Aus.	42	33	36	69	....	....	....	....	....	....
	NHL Totals		535	115	138	253	624	18	4	2	6	21

Traded to **Buffalo** by **Los Angeles** with Brian Engblom for Sean McKenna, Larry Playfair and Ken Baumgartner, January 30, 1986. Claimed by **Edmonton** in NHL Waiver Draft, October 3, 1988. Traded to **Vancouver** by **Edmonton** with Gregory C. Adams for Jean LeBlanc and Vancouver's fifth round choice (Peter White) in 1989 Entry Draft, March 7, 1989. Traded to **Pittsburgh** by **Vancouver** for cash, February 26, 1990.

SMITH, GEOFF

Defense. Shoots left. 6'3", 200 lbs. Born, Edmonton, Alta., March 7, 1969.
(Edmonton's 3rd choice, 63rd overall, in 1987 Entry Draft).

			Regular Season					Playoffs				
Season	Club	Lea	GP	G	A	TP	PIM	GP	G	A	TP	PIM
1987-88	North Dakota	WCHA	42	4	12	16	34	....	....	....	....	....
1988-89	North Dakota	WCHA	9	0	1	1	8	....	....	....	....	....
	Kamloops	WHL	32	4	31	35	29	6	1	3	4	12
1989-90a	Edmonton	NHL	74	4	11	15	52	3	0	0	0	0
1990-91	Edmonton	NHL	59	1	12	13	55	4	0	0	0	0
	NHL Totals		133	5	23	28	107	7	0	0	0	0

a NHL All-Rookie Team (1990)

SMITH, JAMES STEPHEN (STEVE)

Defense. Shoots left. 6'4", 215 lbs. Born, Glasgow, Scotland, April 30, 1963.
(Edmonton's 5th choice, 111th overall, in 1981 Entry Draft).

			Regular Season					Playoffs				
Season	Club	Lea	GP	G	A	TP	PIM	GP	G	A	TP	PIM
1980-81	London	OHA	62	4	12	16	141	....	....	....	....	....
1981-82	London	OHL	58	10	36	46	207	4	1	2	3	13
1982-83	Moncton	AHL	2	0	0	0	0	....	....	....	....	....
	London	OHL	50	6	35	41	133	3	1	0	1	10
1983-84	Moncton	AHL	64	1	8	9	176	....	....	....	....	....
1984-85	Edmonton	NHL	2	0	0	0	2	....	....	....	....	....
	Nova Scotia	AHL	68	2	28	30	161	5	0	3	3	40
1985-86	Edmonton	NHL	55	4	20	24	166	6	0	1	1	14
	Nova Scotia	AHL	4	0	2	2	11	....	....	....	....	....
1986-87	Edmonton	NHL	62	7	15	22	165	15	1	3	4	45
1987-88	Edmonton	NHL	79	12	43	55	286	19	1	11	12	55
1988-89	Edmonton	NHL	35	3	19	22	97	7	2	2	4	20
1989-90	Edmonton	NHL	75	7	34	41	171	22	5	10	15	37
1990-91	Edmonton	NHL	77	13	41	54	193	18	1	2	3	45
	NHL Totals		385	46	172	218	1080	87	10	29	39	216

Played in NHL All-Star Game (1991)

SMITH, RANDY

Center. Shoots left. 6'4", 200 lbs. Born, Saskatoon, Sask., July 7, 1965.

			Regular Season					Playoffs				
Season	Club	Lea	GP	G	A	TP	PIM	GP	G	A	TP	PIM
1983-84	Saskatoon	WHL	69	19	21	40	53	....	....	....	....	....
1984-85	Saskatoon	WHL	71	34	51	85	26	8	4	3	7	0
1985-86	Minnesota	NHL	1	0	0	0	0	....	....	....	....	....
	Saskatoon	WHL	70	60	86	146	44	9	4	9	13	4
1986-87	Minnesota	NHL	2	0	0	0	0	....	....	....	....	....
	Springfield	AHL	75	20	44	64	24	....	....	....	....	....
1987-88	Kalamazoo	IHL	77	13	43	56	54	6	0	8	8	2
1988-89	Maine	AHL	33	9	16	25	34	....	....	....	....	....
	Kalamazoo	IHL	23	4	9	13	2	....	....	....	....	....
1989-90	Kalamazoo	IHL	8	1	2	3	12	....	....	....	....	....
	Salt Lake	IHL	30	5	6	11	10	3	0	0	0	0
1990-91	Cdn. National	...	58	17	39	56	42	....	....	....	....	....
	NHL Totals		3	0	0	0	0	....	....	....	....	....

Signed as a free agent by **Minnesota**, May 12, 1986.

SMITH, ROBERT DAVID (BOBBY)

Center. Shoots left. 6'4", 210 lbs. Born, North Sydney, N.S., February 12, 1958.
(Minnesota's 1st choice and 1st overall in 1978 Amateur Draft).

			Regular Season					Playoffs				
Season	**Club**	**Lea**	**GP**	**G**	**A**	**TP**	**PIM**	**GP**	**G**	**A**	**TP**	**PIM**
1976-77a	Ottawa	OHA	64	*65	70	135	52	19	16	16	32	29
1977-78bc	Ottawa	OHA	61	69	*123	*192	44	16	15	15	30	10
1978-79d	**Minnesota**	**NHL**	**80**	**30**	**44**	**74**	**39**	....	....	....	....	....
1979-80	**Minnesota**	**NHL**	**61**	**27**	**56**	**83**	**24**	**15**	**1**	**13**	**14**	**9**
1980-81	**Minnesota**	**NHL**	**78**	**29**	**64**	**93**	**73**	**19**	**8**	**17**	**25**	**13**
1981-82	**Minnesota**	**NHL**	**80**	**43**	**71**	**114**	**82**	**4**	**2**	**4**	**6**	**5**
1982-83	**Minnesota**	**NHL**	**77**	**24**	**53**	**77**	**81**	**9**	**6**	**4**	**10**	**17**
1983-84	**Minnesota**	**NHL**	**10**	**3**	**6**	**9**	**9**	....	....	....	....	....
	Montreal	**NHL**	**70**	**26**	**37**	**63**	**62**	**15**	**2**	**7**	**9**	**8**
1984-85	**Montreal**	**NHL**	**65**	**16**	**40**	**56**	**59**	**12**	**5**	**6**	**11**	**30**
1985-86	**Montreal**	**NHL**	**79**	**31**	**55**	**86**	**55**	**20**	**7**	**8**	**15**	**22**
1986-87	**Montreal**	**NHL**	**80**	**28**	**47**	**75**	**72**	**17**	**9**	**9**	**18**	**19**
1987-88	**Montreal**	**NHL**	**78**	**27**	**66**	**93**	**78**	**11**	**3**	**4**	**7**	**8**
1988-89	**Montreal**	**NHL**	**80**	**32**	**51**	**83**	**69**	**21**	**11**	**8**	**19**	**46**
1989-90	**Montreal**	**NHL**	**53**	**12**	**14**	**26**	**35**	**11**	**1**	**4**	**5**	**6**
1990-91	**Minnesota**	**NHL**	**73**	**15**	**31**	**46**	**60**	**23**	**8**	**8**	**16**	**56**
	NHL Totals		**964**	**343**	**635**	**978**	**798**	**177**	**63**	**92**	**155**	**239**

a OHA Second All-Star Team (1977)
b OHA First All-Star Team (1978)
c Named Canadian Major Junior Player of the Year (1978)
d Won Calder Memorial Trophy (1979)

Played in NHL All-Star Game (1981, 1982, 1989, 1991)

Traded to **Montreal** by **Minnesota** for Keith Acton, Mark Napier and Toronto's third round choice (Ken Hodge) in 1984 Entry Draft — Montreal's property via earlier deal — October 28, 1983. Traded to **Minnesota** by **Montreal** for Minnesota's fourth round choice in the 1992 Entry Draft, August 7, 1990.

SMITH, SANDY

Right wing. Shoots right. 5'11", 200 lbs. Born, Brainerd, MN, October 23, 1967.
(Pittsburgh's 5th choice, 88th overall, in 1986 Entry Draft).

			Regular Season					Playoffs				
Season	**Club**	**Lea**	**GP**	**G**	**A**	**TP**	**PIM**	**GP**	**G**	**A**	**TP**	**PIM**
1986-87	Minn.-Duluth	WCHA	35	3	3	6	26	....	....	....	....	....
1987-88	Minn.-Duluth	WCHA	41	22	9	31	47	....	....	....	....	....
1988-89	Minn.-Duluth	WCHA	40	6	16	22	75	....	....	....	....	....
1989-90	Minn.-Duluth	WCHA	39	15	16	31	53	....	....	....	....	....
	Muskegon	IHL	3	1	0	1	0	....	....	....	....	....
1990-91	Muskegon	IHL	82	25	29	54	51	5	1	1	2	6

SMITH, STEVE

Defense. Shoots left. 5'9", 215 lbs. Born, Trenton, Ont., April 4, 1963.
(Philadelphia's 1st choice, 16th overall, in 1981 Entry Draft).

			Regular Season					Playoffs				
Season	**Club**	**Lea**	**GP**	**G**	**A**	**TP**	**PIM**	**GP**	**G**	**A**	**TP**	**PIM**
1980-81a	S. S. Marie	OHA	61	3	37	40	143	19	0	6	6	60
1981-82	**Philadelphia**	**NHL**	**8**	**0**	**1**	**1**	**0**	....	....	....	....	....
b	S. S. Marie	OHL	50	7	20	27	179	12	0	2	2	23
1982-83b	S. S. Marie	OHL	55	11	33	44	139	16	0	8	8	28
1983-84	Springfield	AHL	70	4	25	29	77	4	0	0	0	0
1984-85	**Philadelphia**	**NHL**	**2**	**0**	**0**	**0**	**7**	....	....	....	....	....
	Hershey	AHL	65	10	20	30	83	....	....	....	....	....
1985-86	**Philadelphia**	**NHL**	**2**	**0**	**0**	**0**	**2**	....	....	....	....	....
	Hershey	AHL	49	1	11	12	96	16	2	4	6	43
1986-87	**Philadelphia**	**NHL**	**2**	**0**	**0**	**0**	**6**	....	....	....	....	....
	Hershey	AHL	66	11	26	37	191	5	0	2	2	8
1987-88	**Philadelphia**	**NHL**	**1**	**0**	**0**	**0**	**0**	....	....	....	....	....
	Hershey	AHL	66	10	19	29	132	12	2	10	12	35
1988-89	**Buffalo**	**NHL**	**3**	**0**	**0**	**0**	**0**	....	....	....	....	....
	Rochester	AHL	48	2	12	14	79	....	....	....	....	....
1989-90	Rochester	AHL	42	3	15	18	107	17	0	5	5	27
1990-91	Rochester	AHL	37	2	4	6	74	5	0	0	0	4
	NHL Totals		**18**	**0**	**1**	**1**	**15**	....	....	....	....	....

a OHA Second All-Star Team (1981).
b OHL Second All-Star Team (1982, 1983).

Claimed by **Buffalo** in NHL Waiver Draft, October 3, 1988.

SMITH, VERN

Defense. Shoots left. 6'1", 190 lbs. Born, Winnipeg, Man., May 30, 1964.
(NY Islanders' 2nd choice, 42nd overall, in 1982 Entry Draft).

			Regular Season					Playoffs				
Season	**Club**	**Lea**	**GP**	**G**	**A**	**TP**	**PIM**	**GP**	**G**	**A**	**TP**	**PIM**
1981-82	Lethbridge	WHL	72	5	38	43	73	12	0	2	2	8
1982-83	Lethbridge	WHL	30	2	10	12	54	....	....	....	....	....
	Nanaimo	WHL	42	6	21	27	62	....	....	....	....	....
1983-84	N. Westminster	WHL	69	13	44	57	94	9	6	6	12	12
1984-85	**NY Islanders**	**NHL**	**1**	**0**	**0**	**0**	**0**	....	....	....	....	....
	Springfield	AHL	76	6	20	26	115	4	0	2	2	9
1985-86	Springfield	AHL	55	3	11	14	83	....	....	....	....	....
1986-87	Springfield	AHL	41	1	10	11	58	....	....	....	....	....
1987-88	Springfield	AHL	64	5	22	27	78	....	....	....	....	....
1988-89	Springfield	AHL	80	3	26	29	121	....	....	....	....	....
1989-90	Phoenix	IHL	48	4	19	23	37	....	....	....	....	....
	Binghamton	AHL	17	3	2	5	14	....	....	....	....	....
1990-91	New Haven	AHL	9	0	1	1	2	....	....	....	....	....
	Albany	IHL	46	5	15	20	48	....	....	....	....	....
	NHL Totals		**1**	**0**	**0**	**0**	**0**	....	....	....	....	....

SMOLINSKI, BRYAN

Center. Shoots right. 6'1", 195 lbs. Born, Toledo, OH, December 27, 1971.
(Boston's 1st choice, 21st overall, in 1990 Entry Draft).

			Regular Season					Playoffs				
Season	**Club**	**Lea**	**GP**	**G**	**A**	**TP**	**PIM**	**GP**	**G**	**A**	**TP**	**PIM**
1989-90	Michigan St.	CCHA	35	9	13	22	34	....	....	....	....	....
1990-91	Michigan St.	CCHA	35	9	12	21	24	....	....	....	....	....

SMYL, STANLEY PHILLIP (STAN) (SMEEL)

Right wing. Shoots right. 5'8", 185 lbs. Born, Glendon, Alta., January 28, 1958.
(Vancouver's 3rd choice, 40th overall, in 1978 Amateur Draft).

			Regular Season					Playoffs				
Season	**Club**	**Lea**	**GP**	**G**	**A**	**TP**	**PIM**	**GP**	**G**	**A**	**TP**	**PIM**
1975-76	N. Westminster	WHL	72	32	42	74	169	19	8	6	14	58
1976-77	N. Westminster	WHL	72	36	31	66	200	13	6	7	13	51
1977-78	N. Westminster	WHL	53	29	47	76	211	20	14	21	35	43
1978-79	**Vancouver**	**NHL**	**62**	**14**	**24**	**38**	**89**	**2**	**1**	**1**	**2**	**0**
	Dallas	CHL	3	1	1	2	9	....	....	....	....	....
1979-80	**Vancouver**	**NHL**	**77**	**31**	**47**	**78**	**204**	**4**	**0**	**2**	**2**	**14**
1980-81	**Vancouver**	**NHL**	**80**	**25**	**38**	**63**	**171**	**3**	**1**	**2**	**3**	**0**
1981-82	**Vancouver**	**NHL**	**80**	**34**	**44**	**78**	**144**	**17**	**9**	**9**	**18**	**25**
1982-83	**Vancouver**	**NHL**	**74**	**38**	**50**	**88**	**114**	**4**	**3**	**2**	**5**	**12**
1983-84	**Vancouver**	**NHL**	**80**	**24**	**43**	**67**	**136**	**4**	**2**	**1**	**3**	**4**
1984-85	**Vancouver**	**NHL**	**80**	**27**	**37**	**64**	**100**	....	....	....	....	....
1985-86	**Vancouver**	**NHL**	**73**	**27**	**35**	**62**	**144**	....	....	....	....	....
1986-87	**Vancouver**	**NHL**	**66**	**20**	**23**	**43**	**84**	....	....	....	....	....
1987-88	**Vancouver**	**NHL**	**57**	**12**	**25**	**37**	**110**	....	....	....	....	....
1988-89	**Vancouver**	**NHL**	**75**	**7**	**18**	**25**	**102**	**7**	**0**	**0**	**0**	**9**
1989-90	**Vancouver**	**NHL**	**47**	**1**	**15**	**16**	**71**	....	....	....	....	....
1990-91	**Vancouver**	**NHL**	**45**	**2**	**12**	**14**	**87**	....	....	....	....	....
	NHL Totals		**896**	**262**	**411**	**673**	**1556**	**41**	**16**	**17**	**33**	**64**

SMYTH, GREG (SMIHTH)

Defense. Shoots right. 6'3", 212 lbs. Born, Oakville, Ont., April 23, 1966.
(Philadelphia's 1st choice, 22nd overall, in 1984 Entry Draft).

			Regular Season					Playoffs				
Season	**Club**	**Lea**	**GP**	**G**	**A**	**TP**	**PIM**	**GP**	**G**	**A**	**TP**	**PIM**
1983-84	London	OHL	64	4	21	25	252	6	1	0	1	24
1984-85	London	OHL	47	7	16	23	188	8	2	2	4	27
1985-86	Hershey	AHL	2	0	1	1	5	8	0	0	0	60
a	London	OHL	46	12	42	54	199	4	1	2	3	28
1986-87	**Philadelphia**	**NHL**	**1**	**0**	**0**	**0**	**0**	**1**	**0**	**0**	**0**	**2**
	Hershey	AHL	35	0	2	2	158	2	0	0	0	19
1987-88	**Philadelphia**	**NHL**	**48**	**1**	**6**	**7**	**192**	**5**	**0**	**0**	**0**	**38**
	Hershey	AHL	21	0	10	10	102	....	....	....	....	....
1988-89	**Quebec**	**NHL**	**10**	**0**	**1**	**1**	**70**	....	....	....	....	....
	Halifax	AHL	43	3	9	12	310	4	0	1	1	35
1989-90	**Quebec**	**NHL**	**13**	**0**	**0**	**0**	**57**	....	....	....	....	....
	Halifax	AHL	49	5	14	19	235	6	1	0	1	52
1990-91	**Quebec**	**NHL**	**1**	**0**	**0**	**0**	**0**	....	....	....	....	....
	Halifax	AHL	56	6	23	29	340	....	....	....	....	....
	NHL Totals		**73**	**1**	**7**	**8**	**319**	....	....	....	....	....

a OHL Second All-Star Team (1986).

Traded to **Quebec** by **Philadelphia** with Philadelphia's third round choice (John Tanner) in the 1989 Entry Draft for Terry Carkner, July 25, 1988.

SNEDDON, KEVIN

Defense. Shoots left. 5'11", 170 lbs. Born, St. Catharines, Ont., April 23, 1970.
(Los Angeles' 12th choice, 249th overall, in 1989 Entry Draft).

			Regular Season					Playoffs				
Season	**Club**	**Lea**	**GP**	**G**	**A**	**TP**	**PIM**	**GP**	**G**	**A**	**TP**	**PIM**
1988-89	Harvard	ECAC	24	0	5	5	16	....	....	....	....	....
1989-90	Harvard	ECAC	26	0	8	8	18	....	....	....	....	....
1990-91	Harvard	ECAC	17	0	4	4	26	....	....	....	....	....

SNEPSTS, HAROLD JOHN (SNEHPS)

Defense. Shoots left. 6'3", 210 lbs. Born, Edmonton, Alta., October 24, 1954.
(Vancouver's 3rd choice, 59th overall, in 1974 Amateur Draft).

			Regular Season					Playoffs				
Season	**Club**	**Lea**	**GP**	**G**	**A**	**TP**	**PIM**	**GP**	**G**	**A**	**TP**	**PIM**
1972-73	Edmonton	WHL	68	2	24	26	155	11	0	1	1	54
1973-74	Edmonton	WHL	68	8	41	49	239	....	....	....	....	....
1974-75	**Vancouver**	**NHL**	**27**	**1**	**2**	**3**	**30**	....	....	....	....	....
	Seattle	CHL	19	1	6	7	58	....	....	....	....	....
1975-76	**Vancouver**	**NHL**	**78**	**3**	**15**	**18**	**125**	**2**	**0**	**0**	**0**	**4**
1976-77	**Vancouver**	**NHL**	**79**	**4**	**18**	**22**	**149**	....	....	....	....	....
1977-78	**Vancouver**	**NHL**	**75**	**4**	**16**	**20**	**118**	....	....	....	....	....
1978-79	**Vancouver**	**NHL**	**76**	**7**	**24**	**31**	**130**	**3**	**0**	**0**	**0**	**0**
1979-80	**Vancouver**	**NHL**	**79**	**3**	**20**	**23**	**202**	**4**	**0**	**2**	**2**	**8**
1980-81	**Vancouver**	**NHL**	**76**	**3**	**16**	**19**	**212**	**3**	**0**	**0**	**0**	**8**
1981-82	**Vancouver**	**NHL**	**68**	**3**	**14**	**17**	**153**	**17**	**0**	**4**	**4**	**50**
1982-83	**Vancouver**	**NHL**	**46**	**2**	**8**	**10**	**80**	**4**	**1**	**1**	**2**	**8**
1983-84	**Vancouver**	**NHL**	**79**	**4**	**16**	**20**	**152**	**4**	**0**	**1**	**1**	**15**
1984-85	**Minnesota**	**NHL**	**71**	**0**	**7**	**7**	**232**	**9**	**0**	**0**	**0**	**24**
1985-86	**Detroit**	**NHL**	**35**	**0**	**6**	**6**	**75**	....	....	....	....	....
1986-87	**Detroit**	**NHL**	**54**	**1**	**13**	**14**	**129**	**11**	**0**	**2**	**2**	**18**
1987-88	**Detroit**	**NHL**	**31**	**1**	**4**	**5**	**67**	**10**	**0**	**0**	**0**	**40**
	Adirondack	AHL	3	0	2	2	14	....	....	....	....	....
1988-89	**Vancouver**	**NHL**	**59**	**0**	**8**	**8**	**69**	**7**	**0**	**1**	**1**	**6**
1989-90	**Vancouver**	**NHL**	**39**	**1**	**3**	**4**	**26**	....	....	....	....	....
	St. Louis	**NHL**	**7**	**0**	**1**	**1**	**10**	**11**	**0**	**3**	**3**	**38**
1990-91	**St. Louis**	**NHL**	**54**	**1**	**4**	**5**	**50**	**8**	**0**	**0**	**0**	**12**
	NHL Totals		**1033**	**38**	**195**	**233**	**2009**	**93**	**1**	**14**	**15**	**231**

Played in NHL All-Star Game (1977, 1982)

Traded to **Minnesota** by **Vancouver** for Al MacAdam, June 21, 1984. Signed as a free agent by **Detroit**, July 31, 1985. Signed as a free agent by **Vancouver**, October 6, 1988. Traded to **St. Louis** by **Vancouver** with Rich Sutter and St. Louis' second round choice (Craig Johnson) – previously acquired by Vancouver – in 1990 Entry Draft for Adrien Plavsic, Montreal's first round choice (Shawn Antoski) – previously acquired by St. Louis – in 1990 Entry Draft and St. Louis' second round choice in 1991 Entry Draft, March 6, 1990.

SNUGGERUD, DAVE

Right wing. Shoots left. 6', 190 lbs. Born, Minnetonka, MN. June 20, 1966.
(Buffalo's 1st choice, 1st overall, in 1987 Supplemental Draft).

			Regular Season					Playoffs				
Season	Club	Lea	GP	G	A	TP	PIM	GP	G	A	TP	PIM
1985-86	U. Minnesota	WCHA	42	14	18	32	47	....	....	....	....	....
1986-87	U. Minnesota	WCHA	39	30	29	59	38	....	....	....	....	....
1987-88	U.S. National	...	51	14	21	35	26	....	....	....	....	....
	U.S. Olympic	...	6	3	2	5	4	....	....	....	....	....
1988-89ab	U. Minnesota	WCHA	45	29	20	49	39	....	....	....	....	....
1989-90	**Buffalo**	**NHL**	**80**	**14**	**16**	**30**	**41**	**6**	**0**	**0**	**0**	**2**
1990-91	**Buffalo**	**NHL**	**80**	**9**	**15**	**24**	**32**	**6**	**1**	**3**	**4**	**4**
	NHL Totals		**160**	**23**	**31**	**54**	**73**	**12**	**1**	**3**	**4**	**6**

a WCHA Second All-Star Team (1989)
b NCAA West Second All-American Team (1989)

SOBERLAK, PETER (SOH-buhr-lak)

Left wing. Shoots left. 6'2", 195 lbs. Born, Kamloops, B.C., May 12, 1969.
(Edmonton's 1st choice, 21st overall, in 1987 Entry Draft).

			Regular Season					Playoffs				
Season	Club	Lea	GP	G	A	TP	PIM	GP	G	A	TP	PIM
1985-86	Kamloops	WHL	55	10	11	21	46	3	1	1	2	9
1986-87	Kamloops	WHL	16	2	7	9	26	....	....	....	....	....
	Swift Current	WHL	52	31	35	66	19	....	....	....	....	....
1987-88	Swift Current	WHL	67	43	56	99	47	10	5	7	12	14
1988-89	Swift Current	WHL	37	25	33	58	21	12	5	11	16	11
1989-90	Cape Breton	AHL	60	15	8	23	22	....	....	....	....	....
1990-91	Cape Breton	AHL	70	18	18	36	17	....	....	....	....	....

SOCHA, GARY

Center. Shots left. 6'4", 185 lbs. Born, North Attleboro, MA, December 30, 1969.
(Calgary's 3rd choice, 84th overall, in 1988 Entry Draft).

			Regular Season					Playoffs				
Season	Club	Lea	GP	G	A	TP	PIM	GP	G	A	TP	PIM
1989-90	Providence	H.E.	25	2	2	4	8	....	....	....	....	....
1990-91	Providence	H.E.	35	15	13	28	20	....	....	....	....	....

SOLLY, JIM

Center. Shoots left. 6'1", 180 lbs. Born, St. Catharines, Ont., March 19, 1970.
(Winnipeg's 10th choice, 151st overall, in 1989 Entry Draft).

			Regular Season					Playoffs				
Season	Club	Lea	GP	G	A	TP	PIM	GP	G	A	TP	PIM
1988-89	Bowling Green	CCHA	40	4	9	13	14	....	....	....	....	....
1989-90	Bowling Green	CCHA	44	9	11	20	14	....	....	....	....	....
1990-91	Bowling Green	CCHA	31	1	2	3	14	....	....	....	....	....

SORENSEN, KELLY

Right wing. Shoots right. 5'11", 170 lbs. Born, Newmarket, Ont., June 11, 1970.
(Detroit's 1st choice, 16th overall, in 1991 Supplemental Draft).

			Regular Season					Playoffs				
Season	Club	Lea	GP	G	A	TP	PIM	GP	G	A	TP	PIM
1989-90	Ferris State	CCHA	37	7	12	19	48	....	....	....	....	....
1990-91	Ferris State	CCHA	37	8	15	23	42	....	....	....	....	....

SORENSEN, MARK

Defense. Shoots left. 6', 180 lbs. Born Newmarket, Ont. March 27, 1969.
(Washington's 11th choice, 192nd overall, in 1988 Entry Draft).

			Regular Season					Playoffs				
Season	Club	Lea	GP	G	A	TP	PIM	GP	G	A	TP	PIM
1987-88	U. of Michigan	CCHA	39	3	9	12	77	....	....	....	....	....
1988-89	U. of Michigan	CCHA	33	1	5	6	33	....	....	....	....	....
1989-90	U. of Michigan	CCHA	40	3	5	8	42	....	....	....	....	....
1990-91	U. of Michigan	CCHA	47	1	12	13	86	....	....	....	....	....

SOULES, JASON

Defense. Shoots left. 6'2", 212 lbs. Born, Hamilton, Ont., March 14, 1971.
(Edmonton's 1st choice, 15th overall, in 1989 Entry Draft).

			Regular Season					Playoffs				
Season	Club	Lea	GP	G	A	TP	PIM	GP	G	A	TP	PIM
1987-88	Hamilton	OHL	19	1	1	2	56	4	0	0	0	13
1988-89	Niagara Falls	OHL	57	3	8	11	187	....	....	....	....	....
1989-90	Niagara Falls	OHL	9	2	8	10	20	....	....	....	....	....
	Hamilton	OHL	18	0	2	2	42	....	....	....	....	....
1990-91	Hamilton	OHL	25	3	16	19	50	....	....	....	....	....
	Belleville	OHL	37	5	26	31	94	6	1	2	3	4
	Cape Breton	AHL	1	0	0	0	0	....	....	....	....	....

SPANGLER, KEN

Defense. Shoots right. 5'11", 190 lbs. Born, Edmonton, Alta., May 2, 1967.
(Toronto's 2nd choice, 22nd overall, in 1985 Entry Draft).

			Regular Season					Playoffs				
Season	Club	Lea	GP	G	A	TP	PIM	GP	G	A	TP	PIM
1983-84	Calgary	WHL	71	1	12	13	119	4	0	0	0	6
1984-85	Calgary	WHL	71	5	30	35	251	8	6	2	8	18
1985-86a	Calgary	WHL	66	19	36	55	237	....	....	....	....	....
	St. Catharines	AHL	7	0	0	0	16	2	0	0	0	15
1986-87	Calgary	WHL	49	12	24	36	185	....	....	....	....	....
1987-88	Newmarket	AHL	64	3	6	9	128	....	....	....	....	....
1988-89	Baltimore	AHL	12	0	3	3	33	....	....	....	....	....
	Flint	IHL	37	4	15	19	97	....	....	....	....	....
1989-90	Phoenix	IHL	58	3	16	19	156	....	....	....	....	....
1990-91	Nashville	ECHL	45	9	25	34	226	....	....	....	....	....

a WHL East All-Star Team (1986)

SPEER, MICHAEL

Defense. Shoots left. 6'2", 202 lbs. Born, Toronto, Ont., March 26, 1971.
(Chicago's 2nd choice, 27th overall, in 1989 Entry Draft).

			Regular Season					Playoffs				
Season	Club	Lea	GP	G	A	TP	PIM	GP	G	A	TP	PIM
1987-88	Guelph	OHL	53	4	10	14	60	....	....	....	....	....
1988-89	Guelph	OHL	65	9	31	40	185	7	2	4	6	23
1989-90	Owen Sound	OHL	61	18	39	57	176	12	3	7	10	21
1990-91	Owen Sound	OHL	32	13	19	32	86	....	....	....	....	....
	Windsor	IHL	25	8	28	36	40	11	2	7	9	15
	Indianapolis	IHL	1	0	1	1	0	1	0	0	0	5

SPENRATH, GREG

Left wing. Shoots left. 6'1", 212 lbs. Born, Edmonton, Alta., September 27, 1969.
(NY Rangers' 9th choice, 160th overall, in 1989 Entry Draft).

			Regular Season					Playoffs				
Season	Club	Lea	GP	G	A	TP	PIM	GP	G	A	TP	PIM
1987-88	N.Westminster	WHL	72	18	24	42	210	5	0	4	4	16
1988-89	Tri-Cities	WHL	64	26	35	61	213	7	4	2	6	23
1989-90	Tri-Cities	WHL	67	36	32	68	256	7	1	0	1	15
1990-91	Binghampton	AHL	2	0	0	0	14	....	....	....	....	....
	Erie	ECHL	61	29	36	65	*407	4	1	2	3	46

SPROTT, JIM

Defense. Shoots left. 6'1", 200 lbs. Born, Oakville, Ont., April 11, 1969.
(Quebec's 3rd choice, 51st overall, in 1987 Entry Draft).

			Regular Season					Playoffs				
Season	Club	Lea	GP	G	A	TP	PIM	GP	G	A	TP	PIM
1986-87	London	OHL	66	8	30	38	153	....	....	....	....	....
1987-88	London	OHL	65	8	23	31	211	12	1	6	7	8
1988-89a	London	OHL	64	15	42	57	236	21	4	17	21	68
1989-90	Halifax	AHL	22	2	1	3	103	....	....	....	....	....
1990-91	Halifax	AHL	9	0	2	2	17	....	....	....	....	....
	Fort Wayne	IHL	19	0	1	1	67	....	....	....	....	....
	Peoria	IHL	31	2	5	7	92	....	....	....	....	....
	Greensboro	ECHL	3	0	0	0	31	....	....	....	....	....

a OHL Second All-Star Team (1989)

SRSEN, TOMAS (suhz-SHEHN)

Left wing. Shoots left. 5'11", 180 lbs. Born, Olomouc, Czechoslovakia, August 25, 1966.
(Edmonton's 7th choice, 147th overall, in 1987 Entry Draft).

			Regular Season					Playoffs				
Season	Club	Lea	GP	G	A	TP	PIM	GP	G	A	TP	PIM
1987-88	Zetor Brno	Czech.	34	14	5	19	....	....	....	....	....	....
1988-89	Zetor Brno	Czech.2	42	19	11	30	....	....	....	....	....	....
1989-90	Zetor Brno	Czech.	30	7	15	22	....	....	....	....	....	....
1990-91	**Edmonton**	**NHL**	**2**	**0**	**0**	**0**	**0**	....	....	....	....	....
	Cape Breton	AHL	72	32	26	58	100	4	3	1	4	6
	NHL Totals		**2**	**0**	**0**	**0**	**0**	....	....	....	....	....

STAIOS, STEVE

Defense. Shoots right. 6', 183 lbs. Born, Hamilton, Ont., July 28, 1973.
(St. Louis' 1st choice, 27th overall, in 1991 Entry Draft).

			Regular Season					Playoffs				
Season	Club	Lea	GP	G	A	TP	PIM	GP	G	A	TP	PIM
1989-90	Hamilton	OPJHL	40	9	27	36	66	....	....	....	....	....
1990-91	Niagara Falls	OHL	66	17	29	46	115	12	2	3	5	10

STANTON, PAUL

Defense. Shoots right. 6', 193 lbs. Born, Boston, MA, June 22, 1967.
(Pittsburgh's 8th choice, 149th overall, in 1985 Entry Draft).

			Regular Season					Playoffs				
Season	Club	Lea	GP	G	A	TP	PIM	GP	G	A	TP	PIM
1985-86	U. Wisconsin	WCHA	36	4	6	10	16	....	....	....	....	....
1986-87	U. Wisconsin	WCHA	41	5	17	22	70	....	....	....	....	....
1987-88ab	U. Wisconsin	WCHA	45	9	38	47	98	....	....	....	....	....
1988-89c	U. Wisconsin	WCHA	45	7	29	36	126	....	....	....	....	....
1989-90	Muskegon	IHL	77	5	27	32	61	15	2	4	6	21
1990-91	**Pittsburgh**	**NHL**	**75**	**5**	**18**	**23**	**40**	**22**	**1**	**2**	**3**	**24**
	NHL Totals		**75**	**5**	**18**	**23**	**40**	**22**	**1**	**2**	**3**	**24**

a NCAA West First All-American Team (1988)
b WCHA Second All-Star Team (1988)
c WCHA First All-Star Team (1989)

STAPLETON, MIKE

Center. Shoots right. 5'10", 183 lbs. Born, Sarnia, Ont., May 5, 1966.
(Chicago's 7th choice, 132nd overall, in 1984 Entry Draft).

			Regular Season					Playoffs				
Season	Club	Lea	GP	G	A	TP	PIM	GP	G	A	TP	PIM
1983-84	Cornwall	OHL	70	24	45	69	94	3	1	2	3	4
1984-85	Cornwall	OHL	56	41	44	85	68	9	2	4	6	23
1985-86	Cornwall	OHL	56	39	64	103	74	6	2	3	5	2
1986-87	**Chicago**	**NHL**	**39**	**3**	**6**	**9**	**6**	**4**	**0**	**0**	**0**	**2**
	Cdn. Olympic	...	21	2	4	6	4	....	....	....	....	....
1987-88	**Chicago**	**NHL**	**53**	**2**	**9**	**11**	**59**	....	....	....	....	....
	Saginaw	IHL	31	11	19	30	52	10	5	6	11	10
1988-89	**Chicago**	**NHL**	**7**	**0**	**1**	**1**	**7**	....	....	....	....	....
	Saginaw	IHL	69	21	47	68	162	6	1	3	4	4
1989-90	Indianapolis	IHL	16	5	10	15	6	13	9	10	19	38
1990-91	**Chicago**	**NHL**	**7**	**0**	**1**	**1**	**2**	....	....	....	....	....
	Indianapolis	IHL	75	29	52	81	76	7	1	4	5	0
	NHL Totals		**106**	**5**	**17**	**22**	**74**	**4**	**0**	**0**	**0**	**2**

STARIKOV, SERGEI (STAIR-in-kahf)

Defense. Shoots left. 5'10", 225 lbs. Born, Chelyabinsk, Soviet Union, December 4, 1958.
(New Jersey's 7th choice, 152nd overall, in 1989 Entry Draft).

			Regular Season					Playoffs				
Season	Club	Lea	GP	G	A	TP	PIM	GP	G	A	TP	PIM
1976-77	Traktor	USSR	35	2	4	6	28	....	....	....	....	....
1977-78	Traktor	USSR	36	3	5	8	26	....	....	....	....	....
1978-79	Traktor	USSR	44	6	8	14	34	....	....	....	....	....
1979-80	CSKA	USSR	39	10	8	18	14	....	....	....	....	....
1980-81	CSKA	USSR	49	4	8	12	26	....	....	....	....	....
1981-82	CSKA	USSR	40	1	4	5	14	....	....	....	....	....
1982-83	CSKA	USSR	44	6	14	20	14	....	....	....	....	....
1983-84	CSKA	USSR	44	11	7	18	20	....	....	....	....	....
1984-85	CSKA	USSR	40	3	10	13	12	....	....	....	....	....
1985-86	CSKA	USSR	37	3	2	5	6	....	....	....	....	....
1986-87	CSKA	USSR	34	4	2	6	8	....	....	....	....	....
1987-88	CSKA	USSR	38	2	11	13	12	....	....	....	....	....
1988-89	CSKA	USSR	30	3	3	6	4	....	....	....	....	....
1989-90	**New Jersey**	**NHL**	**16**	**0**	**1**	**1**	**8**	....	....	....	....	....
	Utica	AHL	43	8	11	19	14	4	0	3	3	0
1990-91	Utica	AHL	51	2	7	9	26	....	....	....	....	....
	NHL Totals		**16**	**0**	**1**	**1**	**8**	....	....	....	....	....

STASTNY, ANTON (STAHST-nee)

Left wing. Shoots left. 6', 188 lbs. Born, Bratislava, Czechoslovakia, August 5, 1959.
(Quebec's 4th choice, 83rd overall, in 1979 Entry Draft).

			Regular Season					Playoffs				
Season	Club	Lea	GP	G	A	TP	PIM	GP	G	A	TP	PIM
1978-79	Slovan	Czech.	44	32	19	51	....	....	....	....	....	....
1979-80	Slovan	Czech.	40	30	30	60	....	....	....	....	....	....
	Czech. Olympic	...	6	4	4	8	2	....	....	....	....	....
1980-81	**Quebec**	**NHL**	**80**	**39**	**46**	**85**	**12**	**5**	**4**	**3**	**7**	**2**
1981-82	**Quebec**	**NHL**	**68**	**26**	**46**	**72**	**16**	**16**	**5**	**10**	**15**	**10**
1982-83	**Quebec**	**NHL**	**79**	**32**	**60**	**92**	**25**	**4**	**2**	**2**	**4**	**0**
1983-84	**Quebec**	**NHL**	**69**	**25**	**37**	**62**	**14**	**9**	**2**	**5**	**7**	**7**
1984-85	**Quebec**	**NHL**	**79**	**38**	**42**	**80**	**30**	**16**	**3**	**3**	**6**	**6**
1985-86	**Quebec**	**NHL**	**74**	**31**	**43**	**74**	**19**	**3**	**1**	**1**	**2**	**0**
1986-87	**Quebec**	**NHL**	**77**	**27**	**35**	**62**	**8**	**13**	**3**	**8**	**11**	**6**
1987-88	**Quebec**	**NHL**	**69**	**27**	**45**	**72**	**14**	....	....	....	....	....
1988-89	**Quebec**	**NHL**	**55**	**7**	**30**	**37**	**12**	....	....	....	....	....
	Halifax	AHL	16	9	5	14	4	....	....	....	....	....
1989-90	Gotteron	Switz.	36	25	22	47	....	....	....	....	....	....
1990-91	Olten	Switz.	36	26	14	40	....	....	....	....	....	....
	NHL Totals		**650**	**252**	**384**	**636**	**150**	**66**	**20**	**32**	**52**	**31**

STASTNY, PETER (STAHST-nee)

Center. Shoots left. 6'1", 200 lbs. Born, Bratislava, Czechoslovakia, September 18, 1956.

			Regular Season					Playoffs				
Season	Club	Lea	GP	G	A	TP	PIM	GP	G	A	TP	PIM
1978-79	Slovan	Czech.	44	32	23	55	....	....	....	....	....	....
1979-80a	Slovan	Czech.	40	30	30	60	....	....	....	....	....	....
	Czech. Olympic	...	16	7	7	14	6	....	....	....	....	....
1980-81bcd	**Quebec**	**NHL**	**77**	**39**	**70**	**109**	**37**	**5**	**2**	**8**	**10**	**7**
1981-82	**Quebec**	**NHL**	**80**	**46**	**93**	**139**	**91**	**12**	**7**	**11**	**18**	**10**
1982-83	**Quebec**	**NHL**	**75**	**47**	**77**	**124**	**78**	**4**	**3**	**2**	**5**	**10**
1983-84	**Quebec**	**NHL**	**80**	**46**	**73**	**119**	**73**	**9**	**2**	**7**	**9**	**31**
1984-85	**Quebec**	**NHL**	**75**	**32**	**68**	**100**	**95**	**18**	**4**	**19**	**23**	**24**
1985-86	**Quebec**	**NHL**	**76**	**41**	**81**	**122**	**60**	**3**	**0**	**1**	**1**	**2**
1986-87	**Quebec**	**NHL**	**64**	**24**	**53**	**77**	**43**	**13**	**6**	**9**	**15**	**12**
1987-88	**Quebec**	**NHL**	**76**	**46**	**65**	**111**	**69**	....	....	....	....	....
1988-89	**Quebec**	**NHL**	**72**	**35**	**50**	**85**	**117**	....	....	....	....	....
1989-90	**Quebec**	**NHL**	**62**	**24**	**38**	**62**	**24**	....	....	....	....	....
	New Jersey	**NHL**	**12**	**5**	**6**	**11**	**16**	**6**	**3**	**2**	**5**	**2**
1990-91	**New Jersey**	**NHL**	**77**	**18**	**42**	**60**	**53**	**7**	**3**	**4**	**7**	**2**
	NHL Totals		**826**	**403**	**716**	**1119**	**756**	**77**	**30**	**63**	**93**	**100**

a Czechoslovakian League Player of the Year (1980)
b Won Calder Memorial Trophy (1981)
c NHL record for assists by a rookie (1981)
d NHL record for points by a rookie (1981)

Played in NHL All-Star Game (1981, 1982-84, 1986, 1988)

Signed as free agent by **Quebec**, August 26, 1980. Traded to **New Jersey** by **Quebec** for Craig Wolanin and future considerations (Randy Velischek), March 6, 1990.

STAUBER, PETE

Left wing. Shoots left. 5'11", 185 lbs. Born, Duluth, MN, May 10, 1966.

			Regular Season					Playoffs				
Season	Club	Lea	GP	G	A	TP	PIM	GP	G	A	TP	PIM
1986-87	Lake Superior	CCHA	40	22	13	35	80	....	....	....	....	....
1987-88	Lake Superior	CCHA	45	25	33	58	103	....	....	....	....	....
1988-89	Lake Superior	CCHA	46	25	13	38	115	....	....	....	....	....
1989-90	Lake Superior	CCHA	46	25	31	56	90	....	....	....	....	....
1990-91	Adirondack	AHL	26	7	11	18	2	....	....	....	....	....

Signed as a free agent by **Detroit**, June 21, 1990.

STAVJANA, ANTONIN (stahv-YAH-nah)

Defense. Shoots left. 6', 187 lbs. Born, Gottwaldov, Czechoslovakia, February 10, 1963.
(Calgary's 11th choice, 247th overall, in 1986 Entry Draft).

			Regular Season					Playoffs				
Season	Club	Lea	GP	G	A	TP	PIM	GP	G	A	TP	PIM
1986-87	TJ Gottwaldov	Czech.	33	11	7	18	....	....	....	....	....	....
1987-88	TJ Gottwaldov	Czech.	28	5	11	16	....	....	....	....	....	....
1988-89	TJ Gottwaldov	Czech.	43	11	12	23	....	....	....	....	....	....
1989-90	TJ Zlin	Czech.	46	7	14	21	....	....	....	....	....	....
1990-91	JoKP	Fin.	42	13	35	48	10	....	....	....	....	....

STEEN, THOMAS (STEEN)

Center. Shoots left. 5'10", 195 lbs. Born, Grums, Sweden, June 8, 1960.
(Winnipeg's 5th choice, 103rd overall, in 1979 Entry Draft).

			Regular Season					Playoffs				
Season	Club	Lea	GP	G	A	TP	PIM	GP	G	A	TP	PIM
1976-77	Leksand	Swe.	2	1	1	2	2	....	....	....	....	....
1977-78	Leksand	Swe.	35	5	6	11	30	....	....	....	....	....
1978-79	Leksand	Swe.	23	13	4	17	35	2	0	0	0	0
	Swe. National	...	2	0	0	0	0	....	....	....	....	....
1979-80	Leksand	Swe.	18	7	7	14	14	2	0	0	0	6
1980-81	Farjestad	Swe.	32	16	23	39	30	7	4	2	6	8
	Swe. National	...	19	2	5	7	12	....	....	....	....	....
1981-82	**Winnipeg**	**NHL**	**73**	**15**	**29**	**44**	**42**	**4**	**0**	**4**	**4**	**2**
1982-83	**Winnipeg**	**NHL**	**75**	**26**	**33**	**59**	**60**	**3**	**0**	**2**	**2**	**0**
1983-84	**Winnipeg**	**NHL**	**78**	**20**	**45**	**65**	**69**	**3**	**0**	**1**	**1**	**9**
1984-85	**Winnipeg**	**NHL**	**79**	**30**	**54**	**84**	**80**	**8**	**2**	**3**	**5**	**17**
1985-86	**Winnipeg**	**NHL**	**78**	**17**	**47**	**64**	**76**	**3**	**1**	**1**	**2**	**4**
1986-87	**Winnipeg**	**NHL**	**75**	**17**	**33**	**50**	**59**	**10**	**3**	**4**	**7**	**8**
1987-88	**Winnipeg**	**NHL**	**76**	**16**	**38**	**54**	**53**	**5**	**1**	**5**	**6**	**2**
1988-89	**Winnipeg**	**NHL**	**80**	**27**	**61**	**88**	**80**	....	....	....	....	....
1989-90	**Winnipeg**	**NHL**	**53**	**18**	**48**	**66**	**35**	**7**	**2**	**5**	**7**	**16**
1990-91	**Winnipeg**	**NHL**	**58**	**19**	**48**	**67**	**49**	....	....	....	....	....
	NHL Totals		**725**	**205**	**436**	**641**	**603**	**43**	**9**	**25**	**34**	**58**

STEER, JAMIE

Right wing. Shoots right. 5'11", 180 lbs. Born, Calgary, Alta., February 24, 1969.
(Buffalo's 1st choice, 19th overall, in 1991 Supplemental Draft).

			Regular Season					Playoffs				
Season	Club	Lea	GP	G	A	TP	PIM	GP	G	A	TP	PIM
1989-90	Michigan Tech	WCHA	40	21	21	42	26	....	....	....	....	....
1990-91	Michigan Tech	WCHA	39	14	14	28	20	....	....	....	....	....

STERN, RONALD (RONNIE)

Right wing. Shoots right. 6', 195 lbs. Born, Ste. Agathe, Que., January 11, 1967.
(Vancouver's 3rd choice, 70th overall, in 1986 Entry Draft).

			Regular Season					Playoffs				
Season	Club	Lea	GP	G	A	TP	PIM	GP	G	A	TP	PIM
1984-85	Longueuil	QMJHL	67	6	14	20	176	....	....	....	....	....
1985-86	Longueuil	QMJHL	70	39	33	72	317	....	....	....	....	....
1986-87	Longueuil	QMJHL	56	32	39	71	266	19	11	9	20	55
1987-88	**Vancouver**	**NHL**	**15**	**0**	**0**	**0**	**52**	....	....	....	....	....
	Fredericton	AHL	2	1	0	1	4	....	....	....	....	....
	Flint	IHL	55	14	19	33	294	16	8	8	16	94
1988-89	**Vancouver**	**NHL**	**17**	**1**	**0**	**1**	**49**	**3**	**0**	**1**	**1**	**17**
	Milwaukee	IHL	45	19	23	42	280	5	1	0	1	11
1989-90	**Vancouver**	**NHL**	**34**	**2**	**3**	**5**	**208**	....	....	....	....	....
	Milwaukee	IHL	26	8	9	17	165	....	....	....	....	....
1990-91	**Vancouver**	**NHL**	**31**	**2**	**3**	**5**	**171**	....	....	....	....	....
	Milwaukee	IHL	7	2	2	4	81	....	....	....	....	....
	Calgary	**NHL**	**13**	**1**	**3**	**4**	**69**	**7**	**1**	**3**	**4**	**14**
	NHL Totals		**110**	**6**	**9**	**15**	**549**	**10**	**1**	**4**	**5**	**31**

Traded to **Calgary** by **Vancouver** with Kevan Guy and future considerations, March 5, 1991.

STEVENS, JOHN

Defense. Shoots left. 6'1", 195 lbs. Born, Campbelton, N.B., May 4, 1966.
(Philadelphia's 5th choice, 47th overall, in 1984 Entry Draft).

			Regular Season					Playoffs				
Season	Club	Lea	GP	G	A	TP	PIM	GP	G	A	TP	PIM
1983-84	Oshawa	OHL	70	1	10	11	71	7	0	1	1	6
1984-85	Oshawa	OHL	44	2	10	12	61	5	0	2	2	4
	Hershey	AHL	3	0	0	0	0	....	....	....	....	....
1985-86	Kalamazoo	IHL	6	0	1	1	8	6	0	3	3	9
	Oshawa	OHL	65	1	7	8	146	6	0	2	2	14
1986-87	**Philadelphia**	**NHL**	**6**	**0**	**2**	**2**	**14**	....	....	....	....	....
	Hershey	AHL	63	1	15	16	131	3	0	0	0	7
1987-88	**Philadelphia**	**NHL**	**3**	**0**	**0**	**0**	**0**	....	....	....	....	....
	Hershey	AHL	59	1	15	16	108	....	....	....	....	....
1988-89	Hershey	AHL	78	3	13	16	129	12	1	1	2	29
1989-90	Hershey	AHL	79	3	10	13	193	....	....	....	....	....
1990-91	**Hartford**	**NHL**	**14**	**0**	**1**	**1**	**11**	....	....	....	....	....
	Springfield	AHL	65	0	12	12	139	18	0	6	6	35
	NHL Totals		**23**	**0**	**3**	**3**	**25**	....	....	....	....	....

Signed as a free agent by **Hartford**, July 30, 1990.

STEVENS, KEVIN

Left wing. Shoots left. 6'3", 217 lbs. Born, Brockton, MA, April 15, 1965.
(Los Angeles' 6th choice, 108th overall, in 1983 Entry Draft).

			Regular Season					Playoffs				
Season	Club	Lea	GP	G	A	TP	PIM	GP	G	A	TP	PIM
1983-84	Boston College	ECAC	37	6	14	20	36	....	....	....	....	....
1984-85	Boston College	H.E.	40	13	23	36	36	....	....	....	....	....
1985-86	Boston College	H.E.	42	17	27	44	56	....	....	....	....	....
1986-87ab	Boston College	H.E.	39	35	35	70	54	....	....	....	....	....
1987-88	U.S. National	...	44	22	23	45	52	....	....	....	....	....
	U.S. Olympic	...	5	1	3	4	2	....	....	....	....	....
	Pittsburgh	**NHL**	**16**	**5**	**2**	**7**	**8**	....	....	....	....	....
1988-89	**Pittsburgh**	**NHL**	**24**	**12**	**3**	**15**	**19**	**11**	**3**	**7**	**10**	**16**
	Muskegon	IHL	45	24	41	65	113	....	....	....	....	....
1989-90	**Pittsburgh**	**NHL**	**76**	**29**	**41**	**70**	**171**	....	....	....	....	....
1990-91c	**Pittsburgh**	**NHL**	**80**	**40**	**46**	**86**	**133**	**24**	***17**	**16**	**33**	**53**
	NHL Totals		**196**	**86**	**92**	**178**	**331**	**35**	**20**	**23**	**43**	**69**

a Hockey East First All-Star Team (1987)
b NCAA East Second All-American Team (1987)
c NHL Second All-Star Team (1991)

Played in NHL All-Star Game (1991)

Rights traded to **Pittsburgh** by **Los Angeles** for Anders Hakansson, September 9, 1983.

STEVENS, MIKE

Left wing. Shoots left. 5'11", 195 lbs. Born, Kitchener, Ont., December 30, 1965.
(Vancouver's 5th choice, 58th overall, in 1984 Entry Draft).

			Regular Season					Playoffs				
Season	Club	Lea	GP	G	A	TP	PIM	GP	G	A	TP	PIM
1982-83	Kitchener	OHL	13	0	4	4	16	12	0	1	1	9
1983-84	Kitchener	OHL	66	19	21	40	109	16	10	7	17	40
1984-85	**Vancouver**	**NHL**	**6**	**0**	**3**	**3**	**6**	....	....	....	....	....
	Kitchener	OHL	37	17	18	35	121	4	1	1	2	8
1985-86	Fredericton	AHL	79	12	19	31	208	6	1	1	2	35
1986-87	Fredericton	AHL	71	7	18	25	258	....	....	....	....	....
1987-88	**Boston**	**NHL**	**7**	**0**	**1**	**1**	**9**	....	....	....	....	....
	Maine	AHL	63	30	25	55	265	7	1	2	3	37
1988-89	**NY Islanders**	**NHL**	**9**	**1**	**0**	**1**	**14**	....	....	....	....	....
	Springfield	AHL	42	17	13	30	120	....	....	....	....	....
1989-90	Springfield	AHL	28	12	10	22	75	....	....	....	....	....
	Toronto	**NHL**	**1**	**0**	**0**	**0**	**0**	....	....	....	....	....
	Newmarket	AHL	46	16	28	44	86	....	....	....	....	....
1990-91	Newmarket	AHL	68	24	23	47	229	....	....	....	....	....
	NHL Totals		**23**	**1**	**4**	**5**	**29**	....	....	....	....	....

Traded to **Boston** by **Vancouver** for cash, October 6, 1987. Signed as a free agent by **NY Islanders**, August 20, 1988. Traded to **Toronto** by **NY Islanders** with Gilles Thibaudeau for Jack Capuano, Paul Gagne and Derek Laxdal, December 20, 1989.

STEVENS, SCOTT

Defense. Shoots left. 6'2", 215 lbs. Born, Kitchener, Ont., April 1, 1964.
(Washington's 1st choice, 5th overall, in 1982 Entry Draft).

			Regular Season					Playoffs				
Season	Club	Lea	GP	G	A	TP	PIM	GP	G	A	TP	PIM
1980-81	Kitchener	OPJHL	39	7	33	40	82	....	....	....	....	....
	Kitchener	OHA	1	0	0	0	0	....	....	....	....	....
1981-82	Kitchener	OHL	68	6	36	42	158	15	1	10	11	71
1982-83a	**Washington**	**NHL**	**77**	**9**	**16**	**25**	**195**	**4**	**1**	**0**	**1**	**26**
1983-84	**Washington**	**NHL**	**78**	**13**	**32**	**45**	**201**	**8**	**1**	**8**	**9**	**21**
1984-85	**Washington**	**NHL**	**80**	**21**	**44**	**65**	**221**	**5**	**0**	**1**	**1**	**20**
1985-86	**Washington**	**NHL**	**73**	**15**	**38**	**53**	**165**	**9**	**3**	**8**	**11**	**12**
1986-87	**Washington**	**NHL**	**77**	**10**	**51**	**61**	**283**	**7**	**0**	**5**	**5**	**19**
1987-88b	**Washington**	**NHL**	**80**	**12**	**60**	**72**	**184**	**13**	**1**	**11**	**12**	**46**
1988-89	**Washington**	**NHL**	**80**	**7**	**61**	**68**	**225**	**6**	**1**	**4**	**5**	**11**
1989-90	**Washington**	**NHL**	**56**	**11**	**29**	**40**	**154**	**15**	**2**	**7**	**9**	**25**
1990-91	**St. Louis**	**NHL**	**78**	**5**	**44**	**49**	**150**	**13**	**0**	**3**	**3**	**36**
	NHL Totals		**679**	**103**	**375**	**478**	**1778**	**80**	**9**	**47**	**56**	**216**

a NHL All-Rookie Team (1983)
b NHL First All-Star Team (1988)

Played in NHL All-Star Game (1985, 1989, 1991)

Signed as a free agent by **St. Louis**, July 16, 1990.

STEVENSON, SHAYNE

Right wing. Shoots right. 6'1", 190 lbs. Born, Newmarket, Ont., October 26, 1970.
(Boston's 1st choice, 17th overall, in 1989 Entry Draft).

			Regular Season					Playoffs				
Season	Club	Lea	GP	G	A	TP	PIM	GP	G	A	TP	PIM
1986-87	London	OHL	61	7	15	22	56	....	....	....	....	....
1987-88	London	OHL	36	14	25	39	56	....	....	....	....	....
	London	OHL	30	10	25	35	48	4	1	1	2	4
1988-89	Kitchener	OHL	56	25	50	75	86	5	2	3	5	4
1989-90	Kitchener	OHL	56	28	61	89	225	17	16	21	37	31
1990-91	**Boston**	**NHL**	**14**	**0**	**0**	**0**	**26**	....	....	....	....	....
	Maine	AHL	58	22	28	50	112	....	....	....	....	....
	NHL Totals		**14**	**0**	**0**	**0**	**26**	....	....	....	....	....

STEVENSON, TURNER

Right wing. Shoots right. 6'3", 215 lbs. Born, Prince George, B.C., May 18, 1972.
(Montreal's 1st choice, 12th overall, in 1990 Entry Draft).

			Regular Season					Playoffs				
Season	Club	Lea	GP	G	A	TP	PIM	GP	G	A	TP	PIM
1988-89	Seattle	WHL	69	15	12	27	84	....	....	....	....	....
1989-90	Seattle	WHL	62	29	32	61	276	13	3	2	5	35
1990-91	Seattle	WHL	57	36	27	63	222	6	1	5	6	15
	Fredericton	AHL	....	....	....	....	....	4	0	0	0	5

STEWART, ALLAN

Left wing. Shoots left. 6', 195 lbs. Born, Fort St. John, B.C., January 31, 1964.
(New Jersey's 9th choice, 213th overall, in 1983 Entry Draft).

			Regular Season					Playoffs				
Season	Club	Lea	GP	G	A	TP	PIM	GP	G	A	TP	PIM
1982-83	Prince Albert	WHL	70	25	34	59	272	....	....	....	....	....
1983-84	Prince Albert	WHL	67	44	39	83	216	5	1	2	3	29
	Maine	AHL	....	....	....	....	....	3	0	0	0	0
1984-85	Maine	AHL	75	8	11	19	241	11	1	2	3	58
1985-86	**New Jersey**	**NHL**	**4**	**0**	**0**	**0**	**21**	....	....	....	....	....
	Maine	AHL	58	7	12	19	181	....	....	....	....	....
1986-87	**New Jersey**	**NHL**	**7**	**1**	**0**	**1**	**26**	....	....	....	....	....
	Maine	AHL	74	14	24	38	143	....	....	....	....	....
1987-88	**New Jersey**	**NHL**	**1**	**0**	**0**	**0**	**0**	....	....	....	....	....
	Utica	AHL	49	8	17	25	129	....	....	....	....	....
1988-89	**New Jersey**	**NHL**	**6**	**0**	**2**	**2**	**15**	....	....	....	....	....
	Utica	AHL	72	9	23	32	110	5	1	0	1	4
1989-90	Utica	AHL	....	....	....	....	....	1	0	0	0	11
1990-91	**New Jersey**	**NHL**	**41**	**5**	**2**	**7**	**159**	....	....	....	....	....
	Utica	AHL	9	2	0	2	9	....	....	....	....	....
	NHL Totals		**59**	**6**	**4**	**10**	**221**	....	....	....	....	....

STEWART, CAMERON

Center. Shoots left. 5'11", 190 lbs. Born, Kitchener, Ont., September 18, 1971.
(Boston's 2nd choice, 63rd overall, in 1990 Entry Draft).

			Regular Season					Playoffs				
Season	Club	Lea	GP	G	A	TP	PIM	GP	G	A	TP	PIM
1989-90	Elmira	Jr.B	46	44	95	139	172	....	....	....	....	....
1990-91	U. of Michigan	CCHA	44	8	24	32	122	....	....	....	....	....

STEWART, MICHAEL

Defense. Shoots left. 6'3", 210 lbs. Born, Calgary, Alta., May 30, 1972.
(NY Rangers' 1st choice, 13th overall, in 1990 Entry Draft).

			Regular Season					Playoffs				
Season	Club	Lea	GP	G	A	TP	PIM	GP	G	A	TP	PIM
1989-90	Michigan State	CCHA	40	2	6	8	39	....	....	....	....	....
1990-91	Michigan State	CCHA	37	3	12	15	58	....	....	....	....	....

STIENBURG, TREVOR

Right wing. Shoots right. 6'1", 200 lbs. Born, Kingston, Ont., May 13, 1966.
(Quebec's 1st choice, 15th overall, in 1984 Entry Draft).

			Regular Season					Playoffs				
Season	Club	Lea	GP	G	A	TP	PIM	GP	G	A	TP	PIM
1983-84	Guelph	OHL	65	33	18	51	104	....	....	....	....	....
1984-85	Guelph	OHL	18	7	12	19	38	....	....	....	....	....
	London	OHL	22	9	11	20	45	8	1	3	4	22
1985-86	**Quebec**	**NHL**	**2**	**1**	**0**	**1**	**0**	**1**	**0**	**0**	**0**	**0**
	London	OHL	31	12	18	30	88	5	0	0	0	20
1986-87	**Quebec**	**NHL**	**6**	**1**	**0**	**1**	**12**	....	....	....	....	....
	Fredericton	AHL	48	14	12	26	123	....	....	....	....	....
1987-88	**Quebec**	**NHL**	**8**	**0**	**1**	**1**	**24**	....	....	....	....	....
	Fredericton	AHL	55	12	24	36	279	13	3	3	6	115
1988-89	**Quebec**	**NHL**	**55**	**6**	**3**	**9**	**125**	....	....	....	....	....
1989-90	Halifax	AHL	11	3	3	6	36	....	....	....	....	....
1990-91	Halifax	AHL	41	16	7	23	190	....	....	....	....	....
	NHL Totals		**71**	**8**	**4**	**12**	**161**	**1**	**0**	**0**	**0**	**0**

STIVER, DAN

Right wing. Shoots right. 6', 185 lbs. Born, Chicoutimi, Que., September 14, 1971.
(Toronto's 7th choice, 157th overall, in 1990 Entry Draft).

			Regular Season					Playoffs				
Season	Club	Lea	GP	G	A	TP	PIM	GP	G	A	TP	PIM
1989-90	U. of Michigan	CCHA	40	9	10	19	6	....	....	....	....	....
1990-91	U. of Michigan	CCHA	41	14	15	29	26	....	....	....	....	....

STOJANOV, ALEX

Right wing. Shoots left. 6'4", 220 lbs. Born, Windsor, Ont., April 25, 1973.
(Vancouver's 1st choice, 7th overall, in 1991 Entry Draft).

			Regular Season					Playoffs				
Season	Club	Lea	GP	G	A	TP	PIM	GP	G	A	TP	PIM
1989-90	Hamilton	OHL	37	4	4	8	91	....	....	....	....	....
1990-91	Hamilton	OHL	62	25	20	45	181	4	1	1	2	14

STOLK, DARREN

Defense. Shoots left. 6'4", 210 lbs. Born, Taber, Alta., July 22, 1968.
(Pittsburgh's 11th choice, 235th overall, in 1988 Entry Draft).

			Regular Season					Playoffs				
Season	Club	Lea	GP	G	A	TP	PIM	GP	G	A	TP	PIM
1986-87	Brandon	WHL	71	3	9	12	60	....	....	....	....	....
1987-88	Lethbridge	WHL	60	3	10	13	79	....	....	....	....	....
1988-89	Medicine Hat	WHL	65	8	31	39	141	3	0	0	0	2
1989-90	Muskegon	IHL	65	3	3	6	59	6	1	0	1	2
1990-91	Kansas City	IHL	23	2	10	12	36	....	....	....	....	....
	Muskegon	IHL	47	2	8	10	40	....	....	....	....	....

STONE, DONALD

Center. Shoots left. 5'11", 165 lbs. Born, Detroit, MI, May 6, 1969.
(Detroit's 11th choice, 248th overall, in 1988 Entry Draft).

			Regular Season					Playoffs				
Season	Club	Lea	GP	G	A	TP	PIM	GP	G	A	TP	PIM
1987-88	U. of Michigan	CCHA	38	18	19	37	22	....	....	....	....	....
1988-89	U. of Michigan	CCHA	40	24	17	41	19	....	....	....	....	....
1989-90	U. of Michigan	CCHA	42	20	24	44	12	....	....	....	....	....
1990-91	U. of Michigan	CCHA	47	21	27	48	20	....	....	....	....	....

STOTHERS, MICHAEL PATRICK (MIKE)

Defense. Shoots left. 6'4", 212 lbs. Born, Toronto, Ont., February 22, 1962.
(Philadelphia's 1st choice, 21st overall, in 1980 Entry Draft).

			Regular Season					Playoffs				
Season	Club	Lea	GP	G	A	TP	PIM	GP	G	A	TP	PIM
1979-80	Kingston	OHA	66	4	23	27	137	....	....	....	....	....
1980-81	Kingston	OHA	66	4	22	26	237	14	0	3	3	27
1981-82	Kingston	OHL	61	1	20	21	203	4	0	1	1	8
	Maine	AHL	5	0	0	0	4	1	0	0	0	0
1982-83	Maine	AHL	80	2	16	18	139	12	0	0	0	21
1983-84	Maine	AHL	61	2	10	12	109	17	0	1	1	34
1984-85	**Philadelphia**	**NHL**	**1**	**0**	**0**	**0**	**0**	....	....	....	....	....
	Hershey	AHL	60	8	18	26	142	....	....	....	....	....
1985-86	**Philiadelphia**	**NHL**	**6**	**0**	**1**	**1**	**6**	**3**	**0**	**0**	**0**	**4**
	Hershey	AHL	66	4	9	13	221	13	0	3	3	88
1986-87	**Philadelphia**	**NHL**	**2**	**0**	**0**	**0**	**4**	**2**	**0**	**0**	**0**	**7**
	Hershey	AHL	75	5	11	16	283	5	0	0	0	10
1987-88	**Philadelphia**	**NHL**	**3**	**0**	**0**	**0**	**13**	....	....	....	....	....
	Hershey	AHL	13	3	2	5	55	....	....	....	....	....
	Toronto	**NHL**	**18**	**0**	**1**	**1**	**42**	....	....	....	....	....
	Newmarket	AHL	38	1	9	10	69	....	....	....	....	....
1988-89	Hershey	AHL	76	4	11	15	262	9	0	2	2	29
1989-90	Hershey	AHL	56	1	6	7	170	....	....	....	....	....
1990-91	Hershey	AHL	72	5	6	11	234	7	0	1	1	9
	NHL Totals		**30**	**0**	**2**	**2**	**65**	**5**	**0**	**0**	**0**	**11**

Traded to **Toronto** by **Philadelphia** for future considerations, December 4, 1987. Traded to **Philadelphia** by **Toronto** for Bill Root, June 21, 1988.

STROMBERG, MIKA

Defense. Shoots left. 5'11", 178 lbs. Born, Helsinki, Finland, February 28, 1970.
(Quebec's 10th choice, 211th overall, in 1990 Entry Draft).

			Regular Season					Playoffs				
Season	Club	Lea	GP	G	A	TP	PIM	GP	G	A	TP	PIM
1988-89	Jokerit	Fin.	39	6	12	18	....	....	....	....	....	....
1989-90	Jokerit	Fin.	42	2	15	17	....	....	....	....	....	....
1990-91	Jokerit	Fin.	44	4	16	20	38	....	....	....	....	....

STUMPEL, JOZEF

Right wing. Shoots right. 6'1", 187 lbs. Born, Nitra, Czechoslovakia, June 20, 1972.
(Boston's 2nd choice, 40th overall, in 1991 Entry Draft).

			Regular Season					Playoffs				
Season	Club	Lea	GP	G	A	TP	PIM	GP	G	A	TP	PIM
1989-90	Nitra	Czech.	38	12	11	23	....	....	....	....	....	....
1990-91	Nitra	Czech.	49	23	22	45	14	....	....	....	....	....

SUHY, ANDY

Defense. Shoots left. 6'1", 190 lbs. Born, Detroit, MI, March 9, 1970.
(Detroit's 8th choice, 158th overall, in 1989 Entry Draft).

			Regular Season					Playoffs				
Season	Club	Lea	GP	G	A	TP	PIM	GP	G	A	TP	PIM
1988-89	W. Michigan	CCHA	42	0	4	4	74	....	....	....	....	....
1989-90	W. Michigan	CCHA	34	3	5	8	52	....	....	....	....	....
1990-91	W. Michigan	CCHA	42	4	7	11	84	....	....	....	....	....

SULLIVAN, BRIAN

Right wing. Shoots right. 6'4", 195 lbs. Born, South Windsor, CT, April 23, 1969.
(New Jersey's 3rd choice, 65th overall, in 1987 Entry Draft).

			Regular Season					Playoffs				
Season	Club	Lea	GP	G	A	TP	PIM	GP	G	A	TP	PIM
1987-88	Northeastern	H.E.	37	20	12	32	18	....	....	....	....	....
1988-89	Northeastern	H.E.	34	13	14	27	65	....	....	....	....	....
1989-90	Northeastern	H.E.	34	24	21	45	54	....	....	....	....	....
1990-91	Northeastern	H.E.	32	17	23	40	75	....	....	....	....	....

SULLIVAN, KEVIN

Right wing. Shoots right. 6'2", 180 lbs. Born, Hartford, CT, May 16, 1968.
(Hartford's 9th choice, 228th overall, in 1987 Entry Draft).

			Regular Season					Playoffs				
Season	Club	Lea	GP	G	A	TP	PIM	GP	G	A	TP	PIM
1986-87	Princeton	ECAC	25	1	0	1	10	....	....	....	....	....
1987-88	Princeton	ECAC	22	0	3	3	8	....	....	....	....	....
1988-89	Princeton	ECAC	26	7	7	14	58	....	....	....	....	....
1989-90	Princeton	ECAC	27	12	13	25	28	....	....	....	....	....
1990-91	Kansas City	IHL	24	0	4	4	15	....	....	....	....	....
	Nashville	ECHL	33	14	14	28	29	....	....	....	....	....

Traded to **Minnesota** by **Hartford** for Mike Berger, October 7, 1989.

SULLIVAN, MICHAEL

Center. Shoots left. 6'2", 185 lbs. Born, Marshfield, MA, February 27, 1968.
(NY Rangers' 4th choice, 69th overall, in 1987 Entry Draft).

			Regular Season					Playoffs				
Season	Club	Lea	GP	G	A	TP	PIM	GP	G	A	TP	PIM
1986-87	Boston U.	H.E.	37	13	18	31	18	....	....	....	....	....
1987-88	Boston U.	H.E.	30	18	22	40	30	....	....	....	....	....
1988-89	Boston U.	H.E.	36	19	17	36	30	....	....	....	....	....
1989-90	Boston U.	H.E.	38	11	20	31	26	....	....	....	....	....
1990-91	San Diego	IHL	74	12	23	35	27	....	....	....	....	....

Rights traded to **Minnesota** by **NY Rangers** with Paul Jerrard, the rights to Bret Barnett, and Los Angeles' third-round choice (Murray Garbutt) in 1989 Entry Draft — acquired March 10, 1987 by Minnesota — for Brian Lawton, Igor Liba and the rights to Eric Bennett, October 11, 1988. Signed as a free agent by **San Jose**, August 9, 1991.

SUMMANEN, RAIMO (SOO-ma-nen, RYE-moh)

Left wing. Shoots left. 5'11", 191 lbs. Born, Jyvaskyla, Finland, March 2, 1962.
(Edmonton's 6th choice, 125th overall, in 1982 Entry Draft).

			Regular Season					Playoffs				
Season	Club	Lea	GP	G	A	TP	PIM	GP	G	A	TP	PIM
1981-82	Reipas	Fin.	36	15	6	21	17	2	2	0	2	0
1982-83	Ilves	Fin.	36	45	15	60	36	8	7	3	10	2
1983-84	Ilves	Fin.	37	28	19	47	26	....	....	....	....	....
	Edmonton	NHL	2	1	4	5	2	5	1	4	5	0
1984-85	Edmonton	NHL	9	0	4	4	0	....	....	....	....	....
	Nova Scotia	AHL	66	20	33	53	2	5	1	2	3	0
1985-86	Edmonton	NHL	73	19	18	37	16	5	1	1	2	0
1986-87	Edmonton	NHL	48	10	7	17	15	....	....	....	....	....
	Vancouver	NHL	10	4	4	8	0	....	....	....	....	....
1987-88	Vancouver	NHL	9	2	3	5	2	....	....	....	....	....
	Fredericton	AHL	20	7	15	22	38	....	....	....	....	....
	Flint	IHL	7	1	1	2	0	....	....	....	....	....
1988-89	Ilves	Fin.	44	35	46	81	22	5	4	3	7	6
1989-90	Ilves	Fin.	40	39	31	70	42	9	3	4	7	8
1990-91	Ilves	Fin.	39	25	30	55	67	8	6	2	8	20
	NHL Totals		151	36	40	76	35	10	2	5	7	0

Traded to **Vancouver** by **Edmonton** for Moe Lemay, March 10, 1987.

SUNDBLAD, NIKLAS

Right wing. Shoots right. 6'1", 196 lbs. Born, Stockholm, Sweden, January 3, 1973.
(Calgary's 1st choice, 19th overall, in 1991 Entry Draft).

			Regular Season					Playoffs				
Season	Club	Lea	GP	G	A	TP	PIM	GP	G	A	TP	PIM
1990-91	AIK	Swe.	39	1	3	4	14	....	....	....	....	....

SUNDIN, MATS (sahn-DEEN)

Center/Right wing. Shoots right. 6'2", 189 lbs. Born, Sollentuna, Sweden, February 13, 1971.
(Quebec's 1st choice, 1st overall, in 1989 Entry Draft).

			Regular Season					Playoffs				
Season	Club	Lea	GP	G	A	TP	PIM	GP	G	A	TP	PIM
1988-89	Nacka	Swe.	25	10	8	18	18	....	....	....	....	....
1989-90	Djurgarden	Swe.	34	10	8	18	16	8	7	0	7	4
1990-91	Quebec	NHL	80	23	36	59	58	....	....	....	....	....
	NHL Totals		80	23	36	59	58	....	....	....	....	....

SUNDSTROM, PATRIK (SAHND-struhm)

Center. Shoots left. 6'1", 200 lbs. Born, Skelleftea, Sweden, December 14, 1961.
(Vancouver's 8th choice, 175th overall, in 1980 Entry Draft).

			Regular Season					Playoffs				
Season	Club	Lea	GP	G	A	TP	PIM	GP	G	A	TP	PIM
1979-80	Bjorkloven	Swe.	26	5	7	12	20	3	1	0	1	4
1980-81	Bjorkloven	Swe.	36	10	18	28	30	3	1	0	1	4
	Swe. National	...	15	4	2	6	6	....	....	....	....	....
1981-82	Bjorkloven	Swe.	36	22	13	35	38	7	3	4	7	6
	Swe. National	...	36	17	7	24	24	....	....	....	....	....
1982-83	Vancouver	NHL	74	23	23	46	30	4	0	0	0	2
1983-84	Vancouver	NHL	78	38	53	91	37	4	0	1	1	7
1984-85	Vancouver	NHL	71	25	43	68	46	....	....	....	....	....
1985-86	Vancouver	NHL	79	18	48	66	28	3	1	0	1	0
1986-87	Vancouver	NHL	72	29	42	71	40	....	....	....	....	....
1987-88	New Jersey	NHL	78	15	36	51	42	18	7	13	20	14
1988-89	New Jersey	NHL	65	28	41	69	36	....	....	....	....	....
1989-90	New Jersey	NHL	74	27	49	76	34	6	1	3	4	2
1990-91	New Jersey	NHL	71	15	31	46	48	2	0	0	0	0
	NHL Totals		662	218	366	584	341	37	9	17	26	25

Traded to **New Jersey** by **Vancouver** with Vancouver's fourth round choice (Matt Ruchty) in 1988 Entry Draft for Kirk McLean and Greg Adams, September 15, 1987.

SUNDSTROM, PETER (SAHND-struhm)

Left wing. Shoots left. 6', 180 lbs. Born, Skelleftea, Sweden, December 14, 1961.
(New York Rangers' 3rd choice, 50th overall, in 1981 Entry Draft).

			Regular Season					Playoffs				
Season	Club	Lea	GP	G	A	TP	PIM	GP	G	A	TP	PIM
1980-81	Bjorkloven	Swe.	29	7	2	9	8	....	....	....	....	....
1981-82	Bjorkloven	Swe.	35	10	14	24	18	7	2	1	3	0
1982-83	Bjorkloven	Swe.	33	14	11	25	3	2	0	2	0	4
1983-84	NY Rangers	NHL	77	22	22	44	24	5	1	3	4	0
1984-85	NY Rangers	NHL	76	18	25	43	34	3	0	0	0	0
1985-86	NY Rangers	NHL	53	8	15	23	12	1	0	0	0	2
	New Haven	AHL	8	3	6	9	4	....	....	....	....	....
1986-87	Bjorkloven	Swe.	36	22	16	38	44	6	2	5	7	8
1987-88	Washington	NHL	76	8	17	25	34	14	2	0	2	6
1988-89	Washington	NHL	35	4	2	6	12	....	....	....	....	....
1989-90	New Jersey	NHL	21	1	2	3	4	....	....	....	....	....
	Utica	AHL	31	11	18	29	6	5	4	1	5	0
1990-91	Malmo	Swe.	40	12	18	30	50	....	....	....	....	....
	NHL Totals		338	61	83	144	120	23	3	3	6	8

Traded by **NY Rangers** to **Washington** for Washington's fifth round selection in the 1988 Entry Draft, August 27, 1987. Traded to **Washington** by **NY Rangers** for Washington's fifth round choice (Martin Bergeron) in 1988 Entry Draft, August 28, 1987. Traded to **New Jersey** by **Washington** for New Jersey's 10th round choice (Rob Leask) in 1991 Entry Draft, June 19, 1989.

SUTER, GARY

Defense. Shoots left. 6', 190 lbs. Born, Madison, WI, June 24, 1964.
(Calgary's 9th choice, 180th overall, in 1984 Entry Draft).

			Regular Season					Playoffs				
Season	Club	Lea	GP	G	A	TP	PIM	GP	G	A	TP	PIM
1983-84	U. Wisconsin	WCHA	35	4	18	22	32	....	....	....	....	....
1984-85	U. Wisconsin	WCHA	39	12	39	51	110	....	....	....	....	....
1985-86ab	Calgary	NHL	80	18	50	68	141	10	2	8	10	8
1986-87	Calgary	NHL	68	9	40	49	70	6	0	3	3	10
1987-88c	Calgary	NHL	75	21	70	91	124	9	1	9	10	6
1988-89	Calgary	NHL	63	13	49	62	78	5	0	3	3	10
1989-90	Calgary	NHL	76	16	60	76	97	6	0	1	1	14
1990-91	Calgary	NHL	79	12	58	70	102	7	1	6	7	12
	NHL Totals		441	89	327	416	612	43	4	30	34	54

a Won Calder Memorial Trophy (1986)
b NHL All-Rookie Team (1986)
c NHL Second All-Star Team (1988)

Played in NHL All-Star Game (1986, 1988, 1989, 1991)

SUTTER, BRENT COLIN (SUH-tuhr)

Center. Shoots right. 5'11", 180 lbs. Born, Viking, Alta., June 10, 1962.
(NY Islanders' 1st choice, 17th overall, in 1980 Entry Draft).

			Regular Season					Playoffs				
Season	Club	Lea	GP	G	A	TP	PIM	GP	G	A	TP	PIM
1979-80	Red Deer	AJHL	59	70	101	171	....	....	....	....	....	....
	Lethbridge	WHL	5	1	0	1	2	....	....	....	....	....
1980-81	NY Islanders	NHL	3	2	2	4	0	....	....	....	....	....
	Lethbridge	WHL	68	54	54	108	116	9	6	4	10	51
1981-82	NY Islanders	NHL	43	21	22	43	114	19	2	6	8	36
	Lethbridge	WHL	34	46	33	79	162	....	....	....	....	....
1982-83	NY Islanders	NHL	80	21	19	40	128	20	10	11	21	26
1983-84	NY Islanders	NHL	69	34	15	49	69	20	4	10	14	18
1984-85	NY Islanders	NHL	72	42	60	102	51	10	3	3	6	14
1985-86	NY Islanders	NHL	61	24	31	55	74	3	0	1	1	2
1986-87	NY Islanders	NHL	69	27	36	63	73	5	1	0	1	4
1987-88	NY Islanders	NHL	70	29	31	60	55	6	2	1	3	18
1988-89	NY Islanders	NHL	77	29	34	63	77	....	....	....	....	....
1989-90	NY Islanders	NHL	67	33	35	68	65	5	2	3	5	2
1990-91	NY Islanders	NHL	75	21	32	53	49	....	....	....	....	....
	NHL Totals		686	283	317	600	755	88	24	35	59	120

Played in NHL All-Star Game (1985)

SUTTER, RICHARD (RICH) (SUH-tuhr)

Right wing. Shoots right. 5'11", 188 lbs. Born, Viking, Alta., December 2, 1963.
(Pittsburgh's 1st choice, 10th overall, in 1982 Entry Draft).

			Regular Season					Playoffs				
Season	Club	Lea	GP	G	A	TP	PIM	GP	G	A	TP	PIM
1980-81	Lethbridge	WHL	72	23	18	41	255	9	3	1	4	35
1981-82	Lethbridge	WHL	57	38	31	69	263	12	3	3	6	55
1982-83	Pittsburgh	NHL	4	0	0	0	0	....	....	....	....	....
	Lethbridge	WHL	64	37	30	67	200	17	14	9	23	43
1983-84	Pittsburgh	NHL	5	0	0	0	0	....	....	....	....	....
	Baltimore	AHL	2	0	1	1	0	....	....	....	....	....
	Philadelphia	NHL	70	16	12	28	93	3	0	0	0	15
1984-85	Philadelphia	NHL	56	6	10	16	89	11	3	0	3	10
	Hershey	AHL	13	3	7	10	14	....	....	....	....	....
1985-86	Philadelphia	NHL	78	14	25	39	199	5	2	0	2	19
1986-87	Vancouver	NHL	74	20	22	42	113	....	....	....	....	....
1987-88	Vancouver	NHL	80	15	15	30	165	....	....	....	....	....
1988-89	Vancouver	NHL	75	17	15	32	122	7	2	1	3	12
1989-90	Vancouver	NHL	62	9	9	18	133	....	....	....	....	....
	St. Louis	NHL	12	2	0	2	22	12	2	1	3	39
1990-91	St. Louis	NHL	77	16	11	27	122	13	4	2	6	16
	NHL Totals		593	115	119	234	1058	51	13	4	17	111

Traded to **Philadelphia** by **Pittsburgh** with Pittsburgh's second round (Greg Smyth) and third round (David McLay) choices in 1984 Entry Draft for Andy Brickley, Mark Taylor, Ron Flockhart, Philadelphia's first round (Roger Belanger) and third round (Mike Stevens — later transferred to Vancouver) choices in 1984 Entry Draft, October 23, 1983. Traded to **Vancouver** by **Philadelphia**, with Dave Richter and Vancouver's third-round choice (Don Gibson) in 1986 Entry Draft — acquired earlier — for J.J. Daigneault and Vancouver's second-round choice (Kent Hawley) in 1986 Entry Draft, June 6, 1986. Traded to **St Louis** by **Vancouver** with Harold Snepsts and St. Louis' second round choice (Craig Johnson) - previously acquired by Vancouver - in 1990 Entry Draft for Adrien Plavsic, Montreal's first round choice (Shawn Antoski) - previously acquired by St. Louis - in 1990 Entry Draft and St. Louis' second round choice in 1991 Entry Draft, March 6, 1990.

SUTTER, RONALD (RON) (SUH-tuhr)

Center. Shoots right. 6', 180 lbs. Born, Viking, Alta., December 2, 1963.
(Philadelphia's 1st choice, 4th overall, in 1982 Entry Draft).

			Regular Season					Playoffs				
Season	Club	Lea	GP	G	A	TP	PIM	GP	G	A	TP	PIM
1980-81	Lethbridge	WHL	72	13	32	45	152	9	2	5	7	29
1981-82	Lethbridge	WHL	59	38	54	92	207	12	6	5	11	28
1982-83	Philadelphia	NHL	10	1	1	2	9	....	....	....	....	....
	Lethbridge	WHL	58	35	48	83	98	20	*22	*19	*41	45
1983-84	Philadelphia	NHL	79	19	32	51	101	3	0	0	0	22
1984-85	Philadelphia	NHL	73	16	29	45	94	19	4	8	12	28
1985-86	Philadelphia	NHL	75	18	42	60	159	5	0	2	2	10
1986-87	Philadelphia	NHL	39	10	17	27	69	16	1	7	8	12
1987-88	Philadelphia	NHL	69	8	25	33	146	7	0	1	1	26
1988-89	Philadelphia	NHL	55	26	22	48	80	19	1	9	10	51
1989-90	Philadelphia	NHL	75	22	26	48	104	....	....	....	....	....
1990-91	Philadelphia	NHL	80	17	28	45	92	....	....	....	....	....
	NHL Totals		555	137	222	359	854	69	6	27	33	149

SUTTON, BOYD

Center/Left wing. Shoots left. 5'10", 175 lbs. Born, Anchorage, AK, December 6, 1966.
(Buffalo's 10th choice, 203rd overall, in 1985 Entry Draft).

			Regular Season					Playoffs				
Season	Club	Lea	GP	G	A	TP	PIM	GP	G	A	TP	PIM
1985-86	Miami-Ohio	CCHA	33	8	13	21	24	....	....	....	....	....
1986-87	Miami-Ohio	CCHA	39	19	18	37	44	....	....	....	....	....
1987-88	Miami-Ohio	CCHA	37	17	16	33	34	....	....	....	....	....
1988-89	Miami-Ohio	CCHA	37	16	23	39	24	....	....	....	....	....
1989-90	Greensboro	ECHL	60	32	26	58	25	10	2	9	11	26
1990-91	Greensboro	ECHL	60	28	41	69	75	13	1	9	10	36

SUTTON, KENNETH

Defense. Shoots left. 6', 195 lbs. Born, Edmonton, Alta., May 11, 1969.
(Buffalo's 4th choice, 98th overall, in 1989 Entry Draft).

			Regular Season					Playoffs				
Season	Club	Lea	GP	G	A	TP	PIM	GP	G	A	TP	PIM
1988-89	Saskatoon	WHL	71	22	31	53	104	8	2	5	7	12
1989-90	Rochester	AHL	57	5	14	19	83	11	1	6	7	15
1990-91	Buffalo	NHL	15	3	6	9	13	6	0	1	1	2
	Rochester	AHL	62	7	24	31	65	3	1	1	2	14
	NHL Totals		15	3	6	9	13	6	0	1	1	2

SVENSSON, MAGNUS (SVEHN-suhn)

Defense. Shoots left. 5'11", 180 lbs. Born, Leksand, Sweden, March 1, 1963.
(Calgary's 13th choice, 250th overall, in 1987 Entry Draft).

			Regular Season					Playoffs				
Season	Club	Lea	GP	G	A	TP	PIM	GP	G	A	TP	PIM
1983-84	Leksand	Swe.	35	3	8	11	20	....	....	....	....	....
1984-85	Leksand	Swe.	35	8	7	15	22	....	....	....	....	....
1985-86	Leksand	Swe.	36	6	9	15	62	....	....	....	....	....
1986-87	Leksand	Swe.	33	8	16	24	42	....	....	....	....	....
1987-88	Leksand	Swe.	40	12	11	23	20	....	....	....	....	....
1988-89	Leksand	Swe.	39	15	22	37	40	10	3	5	8	8
1989-90	Leksand	Swe.	26	11	12	23	60	1	0	0	0	0
1990-91	Lugano	Switz.	36	16	20	36	....	11	3	2	5	....

SVETLOV, SERGEI (sveht-LAHF)

Right wing. Shoots left. 6'1", 194 lbs. Born, Penza, Soviet Union, January 17, 1961.
(New Jersey's 10th choice, 180th overall, in 1988 Entry Draft).

			Regular Season					Playoffs				
Season	Club	Lea	GP	G	A	TP	PIM	GP	G	A	TP	PIM
1987-88	Moscow D'amo	USSR	35	12	18	30	14	....	....	....	....	....
1988-89	Moscow D'amo	USSR	31	12	10	22	21	....	....	....	....	....
1989-90	Moscow D'amo	USSR	15	3	4	7	8	....	....	....	....	....
1990-91	Ratingen	Ger.	30	30	31	61	57	....	....	....	....	....

SVITEK, VLADIMIR (SVEE-tehk)

Right wing. Shoots right. 6'1", 200 lbs. Born, Banska Bystrica, Czech., October 19, 1962.
(Philadelphia's 9th choice, 137th overall, in 1981 Entry Draft).

			Regular Season					Playoffs				
Season	Club	Lea	GP	G	A	TP	PIM	GP	G	A	TP	PIM
1986-87	VSZ Kosice	Czech.	22	4	8	12	....	....	....	....	....	....
1987-88	VSZ Kosice	Czech.	21	13	8	21	....	....	....	....	....	....
1988-89	VSZ Kosice	Czech.	45	13	24	37	....	....	....	....	....	....
1989-90	VSZ Kosice	Czech.	50	16	27	43	....	....	....	....	....	....
1990-91	HPK	Fin.	42	9	11	20	20	8	1	3	4	6

SVOBODA, PETR (svah-BOH-duh)

Defense. Shoots left. 6'1", 174 lbs. Born, Most, Czechoslovakia, February 14, 1966.
(Montreal's 1st choice, 5th overall, in 1984 Entry Draft).

			Regular Season					Playoffs				
Season	Club	Lea	GP	G	A	TP	PIM	GP	G	A	TP	PIM
1983-84	Czech. Jrs.	...	40	15	21	36	14	....	....	....	....	....
1984-85	Montreal	NHL	73	4	27	31	65	7	1	1	2	12
1985-86	Montreal	NHL	73	1	18	19	93	8	0	0	0	21
1986-87	Montreal	NHL	70	5	17	22	63	14	0	5	5	10
1987-88	Montreal	NHL	69	7	22	29	149	10	0	5	5	12
1988-89	Montreal	NHL	71	8	37	45	147	21	1	11	12	16
1989-90	Montreal	NHL	60	5	31	36	98	10	0	5	5	7
1990-91	Montreal	NHL	60	4	22	26	52	2	0	1	1	2
	NHL Totals		476	34	174	208	667	72	2	28	30	80

SWEENEY, DON

Defense. Shoots left. 5'11", 170 lbs. Born, St. Stephen, N.B., August 17, 1966.
(Boston's 8th choice, 166th overall, in 1984 Entry Draft).

			Regular Season					Playoffs				
Season	Club	Lea	GP	G	A	TP	PIM	GP	G	A	TP	PIM
1984-85	Harvard	ECAC	29	3	7	10	30	....	....	....	....	....
1985-86	Harvard	ECAC	31	4	5	9	12	....	....	....	....	....
1986-87	Harvard	ECAC	34	7	4	11	22	....	....	....	....	....
1987-88ab	Harvard	ECAC	30	6	23	29	37	....	....	....	....	....
	Maine	AHL	....	....	....	....	....	6	1	3	4	0
1988-89	Boston	NHL	36	3	5	8	20	....	....	....	....	....
	Maine	AHL	42	8	17	25	24	....	....	....	....	....
1989-90	Boston	NHL	58	3	5	8	58	21	1	5	6	18
	Maine	AHL	11	0	8	8	8	....	....	....	....	....
1990-91	Boston	NHL	77	8	13	21	67	19	3	0	3	25
	NHL Totals		171	14	23	37	145	40	4	5	9	43

a NCAA East All-American Team (1988)
b ECAC First All-Star Team (1988)

SWEENEY, ROBERT (BOB)

Center/Right wing. Shoots right. 6'3", 200 lbs. Born, Concord, MA, January 25, 1964.
(Boston's 6th choice, 123rd overall, in 1982 Entry Draft).

			Regular Season					Playoffs				
Season	Club	Lea	GP	G	A	TP	PIM	GP	G	A	TP	PIM
1982-83	Boston College	ECAC	30	17	11	28	10	....	....	....	....	....
1983-84	Boston College	ECAC	23	14	7	21	10	....	....	....	....	....
1984-85a	Boston College	ECAC	44	32	32	64	43	....	....	....	....	....
1985-86	Boston College	H.E.	41	15	24	39	52	....	....	....	....	....
1986-87	Boston	NHL	14	2	4	6	21	3	0	0	0	0
	Moncton	AHL	58	29	26	55	81	4	0	2	2	13
1987-88	Boston	NHL	80	22	23	45	73	23	6	8	14	66
1988-89	Boston	NHL	75	14	14	28	99	10	2	4	6	19
1989-90	Boston	NHL	70	22	24	46	93	20	0	2	2	30
1990-91	Boston	NHL	80	15	33	48	115	17	4	2	6	45
	NHL Totals		319	75	98	173	401	73	12	16	28	160

a ECAC Second Team All-Star (1985)

SWEENEY, TIM

Left wing. Shoots left. 5'11", 180 lbs. Born, Boston. MA, April 12, 1967.
(Calgary's 7th choice, 122nd overall, in 1985 Entry Draft).

			Regular Season					Playoffs				
Season	Club	Lea	GP	G	A	TP	PIM	GP	G	A	TP	PIM
1985-86	Boston College	H.E.	32	8	4	12	8	....	....	....	....	....
1986-87	Boston College	H.E.	38	31	18	49	28	....	....	....	....	....
1987-88	Boston College	H.E.	18	9	11	20	18	....	....	....	....	....
1988-89ab	Boston College	H.E.	39	29	44	73	26	....	....	....	....	....
1989-90cd	Salt Lake	IHL	81	46	51	97	32	11	5	4	9	4
1990-91	Calgary	NHL	42	7	9	16	8	....	....	....	....	....
	Salt Lake	IHL	31	19	16	35	8	4	3	3	6	0
	NHL Totals		42	7	9	16	8	....	....	....	....	....

a Hockey East First All-Star Team (1989)
b NCAA East Second All-American Team (1989)
c IHL Second All-Star Team (1990)
d Won Ken McKenzie Trophy (Outstanding U.S.-born rookie—IHL) (1990)

SYDOR, DARRYL (CEE-der)

Defense. Shoots left. 6', 200 lbs. Born, Edmonton, Alta., May 13, 1972.
(Los Angeles' 1st choice, 7th overall, in 1990 Entry Draft).

			Regular Season					Playoffs				
Season	Club	Lea	GP	G	A	TP	PIM	GP	G	A	TP	PIM
1988-89	Kamloops	WHL	65	12	14	26	86	15	1	4	5	19
1989-90a	Kamloops	WHL	67	29	66	95	129	17	2	9	11	28
1990-91a	Kamloops	WHL	66	27	78	105	88	12	3	*22	25	10

a WHL West First All-Star Team (1990)

SYKES, PHIL

Left wing. Shoots left. 6', 175 lbs. Born, Dawson Creek, B.C., March 18, 1959.

			Regular Season					Playoffs				
Season	Club	Lea	GP	G	A	TP	PIM	GP	G	A	TP	PIM
1979-80	North Dakota	WCHA	37	22	27	49	34	....	....	....	....	....
1980-81	North Dakota	WCHA	38	28	34	62	22	....	....	....	....	....
1981-82abc	North Dakota	WCHA	37	22	27	49	34	....	....	....	....	....
1982-83	**Los Angeles**	**NHL**	**7**	**2**	**0**	**2**	**2**	....	....	....	....	....
	New Haven	AHL	71	19	26	45	111	12	2	2	4	21
1983-84	**Los Angeles**	**NHL**	**3**	**0**	**0**	**0**	**2**	....	....	....	....	....
	New Haven	AHL	77	29	37	66	101	....	....	....	....	....
1984-85	**Los Angeles**	**NHL**	**79**	**17**	**15**	**32**	**38**	**3**	**0**	**1**	**1**	**4**
1985-86	**Los Angeles**	**NHL**	**76**	**20**	**24**	**44**	**97**	....	....	....	....	....
1986-87	**Los Angeles**	**NHL**	**58**	**6**	**15**	**21**	**133**	**5**	**0**	**1**	**1**	**8**
1987-88	**Los Angeles**	**NHL**	**40**	**9**	**12**	**21**	**82**	**4**	**0**	**0**	**0**	**0**
1988-89	**Los Angeles**	**NHL**	**23**	**0**	**1**	**1**	**8**	**3**	**0**	**0**	**0**	**8**
	New Haven	AHL	34	9	17	26	23	....	....	....	....	....
1989-90	New Haven	AHL	25	3	12	15	32	....	....	....	....	....
	Winnipeg	**NHL**	**48**	**9**	**6**	**15**	**26**	**4**	**0**	**0**	**0**	**0**
	Moncton	AHL	5	0	1	1	20	....	....	....	....	....
1990-91	**Winnipeg**	**NHL**	**70**	**12**	**10**	**22**	**59**	....	....	....	....	....
	NHL Totals		**404**	**75**	**83**	**158**	**447**	**19**	**0**	**2**	**2**	**20**

a WCHA First All-Star Team (1982)
b Named WCHA Player of the Year (1982)
c Named Most Valuable Player, NCAA Tournament (1982)

Signed as a free agent by **Los Angeles**, April 5, 1982. Traded to **Winnipeg** by **Los Angeles** for Brad Jones, December 1, 1989.

TAGLIANETTI, PETER

Defense. Shoots left. 6'2", 200 lbs. Born, Framingham, MA, August 15, 1963.
(Winnipeg's 4th choice, 43rd overall, in 1983 Entry Draft).

			Regular Season					Playoffs				
Season	Club	Lea	GP	G	A	TP	PIM	GP	G	A	TP	PIM
1981-82	Providence	ECAC	2	0	0	0	2	....	....	....	....	....
1982-83	Providence	ECAC	43	4	17	21	68	....	....	....	....	....
1983-84	Providence	ECAC	30	4	25	29	68	....	....	....	....	....
1984-85	**Winnipeg**	**NHL**	**1**	**0**	**0**	**0**	**0**	**1**	**0**	**0**	**0**	**0**
a	Providence	H.E.	35	6	18	24	32	....	....	....	....	....
1985-86	**Winnipeg**	**NHL**	**18**	**0**	**0**	**0**	**48**	**3**	**0**	**0**	**0**	**2**
	Sherbrooke	AHL	24	1	18	9	75	....	....	....	....	....
1986-87	**Winnipeg**	**NHL**	**3**	**0**	**0**	**0**	**12**	....	....	....	....	....
	Sherbrooke	AHL	54	5	14	19	104	10	2	5	7	25
1987-88	**Winnipeg**	**NHL**	**70**	**6**	**17**	**23**	**182**	**5**	**1**	**1**	**2**	**12**
1988-89	**Winnipeg**	**NHL**	**66**	**1**	**14**	**15**	**226**	....	....	....	....	....
1989-90	**Winnipeg**	**NHL**	**49**	**3**	**6**	**9**	**136**	**5**	**0**	**0**	**0**	**6**
	Moncton	AHL	3	0	2	2	2	....	....	....	....	....
1990-91	**Minnesota**	**NHL**	**16**	**0**	**1**	**1**	**14**	....	....	....	....	....
	Pittsburgh	**NHL**	**39**	**3**	**8**	**11**	**93**	**19**	**0**	**3**	**3**	**49**
	NHL Totals		**262**	**13**	**46**	**59**	**711**	**33**	**1**	**4**	**5**	**69**

a Hockey East First All-Star Team (1985).

Traded to **Minnesota** by **Winnipeg** for future considerations, September 30, 1990. Traded to **Pittsburgh** by **Minnesota** with Larry Murphy for Chris Dahlquist and Jim Johnson, December 11, 1990.

TAMER, CHRIS

Defense. Shoots left. 6'2", 185 lbs. Born, Dearborn, MI, November 17, 1970.
(Pittsburgh's 3rd choice, 68th overall, in 1990 Entry Draft).

			Regular Season					Playoffs				
Season	Club	Lea	GP	G	A	TP	PIM	GP	G	A	TP	PIM
1989-90	U. of Michigan	CCHA	42	2	7	9	147	....	....	....	....	....
1990-91	U. of Michigan	CCHA	45	8	19	27	130	....	....	....	....	....

TANCILL, CHRIS (TAN-sihl)

Center. Shoots left. 5'10", 185 lbs. Born, Livonia, MI, February 7, 1968.
(Hartford's 1st choice, 15th overall, in 1989 Supplemental Draft).

			Regular Season					Playoffs				
Season	Club	Lea	GP	G	A	TP	PIM	GP	G	A	TP	PIM
1986-87	U. Wisconsin	WCHA	40	9	23	32	26	....	....	....	....	....
1987-88	U. Wisconsin	WCHA	44	13	14	27	48	....	....	....	....	....
1988-89	U. Wisconsin	WCHA	44	20	23	43	50	....	....	....	....	....
1989-90a	U. Wisconsin	WCHA	45	39	32	71	44	....	....	....	....	....
1990-91	**Hartford**	**NHL**	**9**	**1**	**1**	**2**	**4**	....	....	....	....	....
	Springfield	AHL	72	37	35	72	46	17	8	4	12	32
	NHL Totals		**9**	**1**	**1**	**2**	**4**	....	....	....	....	....

a NCAA All-Tournament Team, Tournament MVP (1990)

TANTI, TONY (TAN-tee)

Right wing. Shoots left. 5'9", 184 lbs. Born, Toronto, Ont., September 7, 1963.
(Chicago's 1st choice, 12th overall, in 1981 Entry Draft).

			Regular Season					Playoffs				
Season	Club	Lea	GP	G	A	TP	PIM	GP	G	A	TP	PIM
1980-81a	Oshawa	OHA	67	81	69	150	197	11	7	8	15	41
1981-82	**Chicago**	**NHL**	**2**	**0**	**0**	**0**	**0**	....	....	....	....	....
b	Oshawa	OHL	57	62	64	126	138	12	14	12	26	15
1982-83	**Chicago**	**NHL**	**1**	**1**	**0**	**1**	**0**	....	....	....	....	....
	Oshawa	OHL	30	34	28	62	35	....	....	....	....	....
	Vancouver	**NHL**	**39**	**8**	**8**	**16**	**16**	**4**	**0**	**1**	**1**	**0**
1983-84	**Vancouver**	**NHL**	**79**	**45**	**41**	**86**	**50**	**4**	**1**	**2**	**3**	**0**
1984-85	**Vancouver**	**NHL**	**68**	**39**	**20**	**59**	**45**	....	....	....	....	....
1985-86	**Vancouver**	**NHL**	**77**	**39**	**33**	**72**	**85**	**3**	**0**	**1**	**1**	**11**
1986-87	**Vancouver**	**NHL**	**77**	**41**	**38**	**79**	**84**	....	....	....	....	....
1987-88	**Vancouver**	**NHL**	**73**	**40**	**37**	**77**	**90**	....	....	....	....	....
1988-89	**Vancouver**	**NHL**	**77**	**24**	**25**	**49**	**69**	**7**	**0**	**5**	**5**	**4**
1989-90	**Vancouver**	**NHL**	**41**	**14**	**18**	**32**	**50**	....	....	....	....	....
	Pittsburgh	**NHL**	**37**	**14**	**18**	**32**	**22**	....	....	....	....	....
1990-91	**Pittsburgh**	**NHL**	**46**	**6**	**12**	**18**	**44**	....	....	....	....	....
	Buffalo	**NHL**	**10**	**1**	**7**	**8**	**6**	**5**	**2**	**0**	**2**	**8**
	NHL Totals		**627**	**272**	**257**	**529**	**561**	**23**	**3**	**9**	**12**	**23**

a OHA First All-Star Team (1981)
b OHL Second All-Star Team (1982)

Played in NHL All-Star Game (1986)

Traded to **Vancouver** by **Chicago** for Curt Fraser, January 6, 1983. Traded to **Pittsburgh** by **Vancouver** with Rod Buskas and Barry Pederson for Dave Capuano, Andrew McBain and Dan Quinn, January 8, 1990. Traded to **Buffalo** by **Pittsburgh** for Ken Priestlay, March 5, 1991.

TARDIF, PATRICE

Center. Shoots left. 6'2", 175 lbs. Born, Thetford Mines, Que., October 30, 1970.
(St. Louis' 2nd choice, 54th overall, in 1990 Entry Draft).

			Regular Season					Playoffs				
Season	Club	Lea	GP	G	A	TP	PIM	GP	G	A	TP	PIM
1989-90	Lennoxville	CEGEP	27	58	36	94	36	....	....	....	....	....
1990-91	U. of Maine	H.E.	36	13	12	25	18	....	....	....	....	....

TATARINOV, MIKHAIL (tah-TAH-ree-nahf)

Defense. Shoots left. 5'10", 195 lbs. Born, Angarsk, Soviet Union, July 16, 1966.
(Washington's 10th choice, 225th overall, in 1984 Entry Draft).

			Regular Season					Playoffs				
Season	Club	Lea	GP	G	A	TP	PIM	GP	G	A	TP	PIM
1983-84	Sokol Kiev	USSR	38	7	3	10	46	....	....	....	....	....
1984-85	Sokol Kiev	USSR	34	3	6	9	54	....	....	....	....	....
1985-86	Sokol Kiev	USSR	37	7	5	12	41	....	....	....	....	....
1986-87	Moscow D'amo	USSR	40	10	8	18	43	....	....	....	....	....
1987-88	Moscow D'amo	USSR	30	2	2	4	8	....	....	....	....	....
1988-89	Moscow D'amo	USSR	4	1	0	1	2	....	....	....	....	....
1989-90	Moscow D'amo	USSR	44	11	10	21	34	....	....	....	....	....
1990-91	Moscow D'amo	USSR	11	5	4	9	6	....	....	....	....	....
	Washington	**NHL**	**65**	**8**	**15**	**23**	**82**	....	....	....	....	....
	NHL Totals		**65**	**8**	**15**	**23**	**82**	....	....	....	....	....

Traded to **Quebec** by **Washington** for Toronto's second round choice (previously acquired by Quebec – Eric Lavigne) in 1991 Entry Draft, June 22, 1991.

TAYLOR, CHRIS

Center. Shoots left. 6', 185 lbs. Born, Stratford, Ont., March 6, 1972.
(NY Islanders' 2nd choice, 27th overall, in 1990 Entry Draft).

			Regular Season					Playoffs				
Season	Club	Lea	GP	G	A	TP	PIM	GP	G	A	TP	PIM
1988-89	London	OHL	62	7	16	23	52	15	0	2	2	15
1989-90	London	OHL	66	45	60	105	60	6	3	2	5	6
1990-91a	London	OHL	65	50	78	128	50	7	4	8	12	6

a OHL Third All-Star Team (1991)

TAYLOR, DAVID ANDREW (DAVE)

Right wing. Shoots right. 6', 190 lbs. Born, Levack, Ont., December 4, 1955.
(Los Angeles' 14th choice, 210th overall, in 1975 Amateur Draft).

			Regular Season					Playoffs				
Season	Club	Lea	GP	G	A	TP	PIM	GP	G	A	TP	PIM
1976-77	Clarkson	ECAC	34	41	67	108	....	....	....	....	....	....
	Fort Worth	CHL	7	2	4	6	6	....	....	....	....	....
1977-78	**Los Angeles**	**NHL**	**64**	**22**	**21**	**43**	**47**	**2**	**0**	**0**	**0**	**5**
1978-79	**Los Angeles**	**NHL**	**78**	**43**	**48**	**91**	**124**	**2**	**0**	**0**	**0**	**2**
1979-80	**Los Angeles**	**NHL**	**61**	**37**	**53**	**90**	**72**	**4**	**2**	**1**	**3**	**4**
1980-81a	**Los Angeles**	**NHL**	**72**	**47**	**65**	**112**	**130**	**4**	**2**	**2**	**4**	**10**
1981-82	**Los Angeles**	**NHL**	**78**	**39**	**67**	**106**	**130**	**10**	**4**	**6**	**10**	**20**
1982-83	**Los Angeles**	**NHL**	**46**	**21**	**37**	**58**	**76**	....	....	....	....	....
1983-84	**Los Angeles**	**NHL**	**63**	**20**	**49**	**69**	**91**	....	....	....	....	....
1984-85	**Los Angeles**	**NHL**	**79**	**41**	**51**	**92**	**132**	**3**	**2**	**2**	**4**	**8**
1985-86	**Los Angeles**	**NHL**	**76**	**33**	**38**	**71**	**110**	....	....	....	....	....
1986-87	**Los Angeles**	**NHL**	**67**	**18**	**44**	**62**	**84**	**5**	**2**	**3**	**5**	**6**
1987-88	**Los Angeles**	**NHL**	**68**	**26**	**41**	**67**	**129**	**5**	**3**	**3**	**6**	**6**
1988-89	**Los Angeles**	**NHL**	**70**	**26**	**37**	**63**	**80**	**11**	**1**	**5**	**6**	**19**
1989-90	**Los Angeles**	**NHL**	**58**	**15**	**26**	**41**	**96**	**6**	**4**	**4**	**8**	**2**
1990-91bc	**Los Angeles**	**NHL**	**73**	**23**	**30**	**53**	**148**	**12**	**2**	**1**	**3**	**12**
	NHL Totals		**953**	**411**	**607**	**1018**	**1449**	**64**	**22**	**27**	**49**	**94**

a NHL Second All-Star Team (1981)
b Won Bill Masterton Memorial Trophy (1991)
c Won King Clancy Memorial Trophy (1991)

Played in NHL All-Star Game (1981, 1982, 1986)

TAYLOR, TIM

Center. Shoots left. 6', 180 lbs. Born, Stratford, Ont., February 6, 1969.
(Washington's 2nd choice, 36th overall, in 1988 Entry Draft).

			Regular Season					Playoffs				
Season	Club	Lea	GP	G	A	TP	PIM	GP	G	A	TP	PIM
1986-87	London	OHL	34	7	9	16	11	....	....	....	....	....
1987-88	London	OHL	64	46	50	96	66	12	9	9	18	26
1988-89	London	OHL	61	34	80	114	93	21	*21	25	*46	58
1989-90	Baltimore	AHL	79	31	36	67	124	9	2	2	4	13
1990-91	Baltimore	AHL	79	25	42	67	75	5	0	1	1	4

TEPPER, STEPHEN

Right wing. Shoots right. 6'4", 225 lbs. Born, Santa Ana, CA, March 10, 1969.
(Chicago's 7th choice, 134th overall, in 1987 Entry Draft).

			Regular Season					Playoffs				
Season	Club	Lea	GP	G	A	TP	PIM	GP	G	A	TP	PIM
1988-89	U. of Maine	H.E.	26	3	9	12	32	....	....	....	....	....
1989-90	U. of Maine	H.E.	41	10	6	16	68	....	....	....	....	....
1990-91	U. of Maine	H.E.	38	6	11	17	58	....	....	....	....	....

THERIEN, CHRIS

Defense. Shoots left. 6'3", 205 lbs. Born, Ottawa, Ont., December 14, 1971.
(Philadelphia's 7th choice, 47th overall, in 1990 Entry Draft).

			Regular Season					Playoffs				
Season	Club	Lea	GP	G	A	TP	PIM	GP	G	A	TP	PIM
1989-90	Northwood Prep	HS	31	35	37	72	54	....	....	....	....	....
1990-91	Providence	H.E.	36	4	18	22	36	....	....	....	....	....

THIBAUDEAU, GILLES (TIB-ah-doh)

Center. Shoots left. 5'10", 165 lbs. Born, Montreal, Que., March 4, 1963.

			Regular Season					Playoffs				
Season	Club	Lea	GP	G	A	TP	PIM	GP	G	A	TP	PIM
1983-84	St. Antoine	Jr. B	38	63	77	140	146	....	....	....	....	....
1984-85	Sherbrooke	AHL	7	2	4	6	0	....	....	....	....	....
a	Flint	IHL	71	52	45	97	81	....	....	....	....	....
1985-86	Sherbrooke	AHL	61	15	23	38	20	....	....	....	....	....
1986-87	**Montreal**	**NHL**	**9**	**1**	**3**	**4**	**0**	....	....	....	....	....
	Sherbrooke	AHL	62	27	40	67	26	....	....	....	....	....
1987-88	**Montreal**	**NHL**	**17**	**5**	**6**	**11**	**0**	**8**	**3**	**3**	**6**	**2**
	Sherbrooke	AHL	59	39	57	96	45	....	....	....	....	....
1988-89	**Montreal**	**NHL**	**32**	**6**	**6**	**12**	**6**	....	....	....	....	....
1989-90	**NY Islanders**	**NHL**	**20**	**4**	**4**	**8**	**17**	....	....	....	....	....
	Springfield	AHL	6	5	8	13	0	....	....	....	....	....
	Toronto	**NHL**	**21**	**7**	**11**	**18**	**13**	....	....	....	....	....
	Newmarket	AHL	10	7	13	20	4	....	....	....	....	....
1990-91	**Toronto**	**NHL**	**20**	**2**	**7**	**9**	**4**	....	....	....	....	....
	Newmarket	AHL	60	34	37	71	28	....	....	....	....	....
	NHL Totals		**119**	**25**	**37**	**62**	**40**	**8**	**3**	**3**	**6**	**2**

a IHL Second All-Star Team (1985)

Signed as a free agent by **Montreal**, October 9, 1984. Traded to **Toronto** by **NY Islanders** with Mike Stevens for Jack Capuano, Paul Gagne and Derek Laxdal, December 20, 1989.

THOMAS, JOHN (SCOTT)

Right wing. Shoots right. 6'2", 195 lbs. Born, Buffalo, NY, January 18, 1970.
(Buffalo's 2nd choice, 56th overall, in 1989 Entry Draft).

			Regular Season					Playoffs				
Season	Club	Lea	GP	G	A	TP	PIM	GP	G	A	TP	PIM
1989-90	Clarkson	ECAC	34	19	13	32	95	....	....	....	....	....
1990-91	Clarkson	ECAC	40	28	14	42	89	....	....	....	....	....

THOMAS, STEVE

Left wing. Shoots left. 5'11", 185 lbs. Born, Stockport, England, July 15, 1963.

			Regular Season					Playoffs				
Season	Club	Lea	GP	G	A	TP	PIM	GP	G	A	TP	PIM
1983-84	Toronto	OHL	70	51	54	105	77	....	....	....	....	....
1984-85	**Toronto**	**NHL**	**18**	**1**	**1**	**2**	**2**	....	....	....	....	....
ab	St. Catharines	AHL	64	42	48	90	56	....	....	....	....	....
1985-86	**Toronto**	**NHL**	**65**	**20**	**37**	**57**	**36**	**10**	**6**	**8**	**14**	**9**
	St. Catharines	AHL	19	18	14	32	35	....	....	....	....	....
1986-87	**Toronto**	**NHL**	**78**	**35**	**27**	**62**	**114**	**13**	**2**	**3**	**5**	**13**
1987-88	**Chicago**	**NHL**	**30**	**13**	**13**	**26**	**40**	**3**	**1**	**2**	**3**	**6**
1988-89	**Chicago**	**NHL**	**45**	**21**	**19**	**40**	**69**	**12**	**3**	**5**	**8**	**10**
1989-90	**Chicago**	**NHL**	**76**	**40**	**30**	**70**	**91**	**20**	**7**	**6**	**13**	**33**
1990-91	**Chicago**	**NHL**	**69**	**19**	**35**	**54**	**129**	**6**	**1**	**2**	**3**	**15**
	NHL Totals		**381**	**149**	**162**	**311**	**481**	**64**	**20**	**26**	**46**	**86**

a Won AHL Rookie of the Year (1985)
b AHL First All-Star Team (1985)

Signed as a free agent by **Toronto**, May 12, 1984. Traded to **Chicago** by **Toronto** with Rick Vaive and Bob McGill for Al Secord and Ed Olczyk, September 3, 1987.

THOMLINSON, DAVE

Left wing. Shoots left. 6'1", 196 lbs. Born, Edmonton, Alta., October 22, 1966.
(Toronto's 3rd choice, 43rd overall, in 1985 Entry Draft).

			Regular Season					Playoffs				
Season	Club	Lea	GP	G	A	TP	PIM	GP	G	A	TP	PIM
1984-85	Brandon	WHL	26	13	14	27	70	....	....	....	....	....
1985-86	Brandon	WHL	53	25	20	45	116	....	....	....	....	....
1986-87	Brandon	WHL	2	0	1	1	9	....	....	....	....	....
	Moose Jaw	WHL	70	44	36	80	117	9	7	3	10	19
1987-88	Peoria	IHL	74	27	30	57	56	7	4	3	7	11
1988-89	Peoria	IHL	64	27	29	56	154	3	0	1	1	8
1989-90	**St. Louis**	**NHL**	**19**	**1**	**2**	**3**	**12**	....	....	....	....	....
	Peoria	IHL	59	27	40	67	87	5	1	1	2	15
1990-91	**St. Louis**	**NHL**	**3**	**0**	**0**	**0**	**0**	**9**	**3**	**1**	**4**	**4**
	Peoria	IHL	80	53	54	107	107	11	6	7	13	28
	NHL Totals		**22**	**1**	**2**	**3**	**12**	....	....	....	....	....

Signed as a free agent by **St. Louis**, June 4, 1987. Signed as a free agent by **Boston**, July 30, 1991

THOMPSON, BRENT

Defense. Shoots left. 6'2", 175 lbs. Born, Calgary, Alta., January 9, 1971.
(Los Angeles' 1st choice, 39th overall, in 1989 Entry Draft).

			Regular Season					Playoffs				
Season	Club	Lea	GP	G	A	TP	PIM	GP	G	A	TP	PIM
1988-89	Medicine Hat	WHL	72	3	10	13	160	3	0	0	0	2
1989-90	Medicine Hat	WHL	68	10	35	45	167	3	0	1	1	14
1990-91a	Medicine Hat	WHL	51	5	40	45	87	12	1	7	8	16
	Phoenix	IHL	....	....	....	....	....	4	0	1	1	6

a WHL East Second All-Star Team (1991)

THOMPSON, MICHAEL

Right wing. Shoots right. 6', 202 lbs. Born, Montreal, Que., February 1, 1971.
(Pittsburg's 13th choice, 215th overall, in 1990 Entry Draft).

			Regular Season					Playoffs				
Season	Club	Lea	GP	G	A	TP	PIM	GP	G	A	TP	PIM
1989-90	Michigan State	CCHA	17	4	4	8	4	....	....	....	....	....
1990-91	Michigan State	CCHA	15	1	3	4	8	....	....	....	....	....

THOMSON, JIM

Right wing. Shoots right. 6'1", 205 lbs. Born, Edmonton, Alta., December 30, 1965.
(Washington's 18th choice, 185th overall, in 1984 Entry Draft).

			Regular Season					Playoffs				
Season	Club	Lea	GP	G	A	TP	PIM	GP	G	A	TP	PIM
1983-84	Toronto	OHL	60	10	18	28	68	9	1	0	1	26
1984-85	Toronto	OHL	63	23	28	51	122	5	3	1	4	25
	Binghamton	AHL	4	0	0	0	2	....	....	....	....	....
1985-86	Binghamton	AHL	59	15	9	24	195	....	....	....	....	....
1986-87	**Washington**	**NHL**	**10**	**0**	**0**	**0**	**35**	....	....	....	....	....
	Binghamton	AHL	57	13	10	23	360	10	0	1	1	40
1987-88	Binghamton	AHL	25	8	9	17	64	4	1	2	3	7
1988-89	**Washington**	**NHL**	**14**	**2**	**0**	**2**	**53**	....	....	....	....	....
	Baltimore	AHL	41	25	16	41	129	....	....	....	....	....
	Hartford	**NHL**	**5**	**0**	**0**	**0**	**14**	....	....	....	....	....
1989-90	Binghamton	AHL	8	1	2	3	30	....	....	....	....	....
	New Jersey	**NHL**	**3**	**0**	**0**	**0**	**31**	....	....	....	....	....
	Utica	AHL	60	20	23	43	124	4	1	0	1	19
1990-91	**Los Angeles**	**NHL**	**8**	**1**	**0**	**1**	**19**	....	....	....	....	....
	New Haven	AHL	27	5	8	13	121	....	....	....	....	....
	NHL Totals		**40**	**3**	**0**	**3**	**152**	....	....	....	....	....

Traded to **Hartford** by **Washington** for Scot Kleinendorst, March 6, 1989. Traded to **New Jersey** by **Hartford** for Chris Cichocki, October 31, 1989. Signed as a free agent by **Los Angeles**, July 2, 1990. Claimed by **Minnesota** from **Los Angeles** in Expansion Draft, May 30, 1991. Traded to **Los Angeles** by **Minnesota** with Randy Gilhen, Charlie Huddy and NY Rangers' fourth round choice (previously acquired by Minnesota - Alexei Zhitnik) in 1991 Entry Draft for Todd Elik, June 22, 1991.

THORNTON, SCOTT

Center. Shoots left. 6'2", 200 lbs. Born, London, Ont., January 9, 1971.
(Toronto's 1st choice, 3rd overall, in 1989 Entry Draft).

			Regular Season					Playoffs				
Season	Club	Lea	GP	G	A	TP	PIM	GP	G	A	TP	PIM
1987-88	Belleville	OHL	62	11	19	30	54	6	0	1	1	2
1988-89	Belleville	OHL	59	28	34	62	103	5	1	1	2	6
1989-90	Belleville	OHL	47	21	28	49	91	11	2	10	12	15
1990-91	**Toronto**	**NHL**	**33**	**1**	**3**	**4**	**30**	....	....	....	....	....
	Newmarket	AHL	5	1	0	1	4	....	....	....	....	....
	Belleville	OHL	3	2	1	3	2	6	0	7	7	14
	NHL Totals		**33**	**1**	**3**	**4**	**30**	....	....	....	....	....

THYER, MARIO

Center. Shoots left. 5'11", 170 lbs. Born, Montreal, Que., September 29, 1966.

			Regular Season					Playoffs				
Season	Club	Lea	GP	G	A	TP	PIM	GP	G	A	TP	PIM
1987-88	U. of Maine	H.E.	44	24	42	66	4	....	....	....	....	....
1988-89	U. of Maine	H.E.	9	9	7	16	0	....	....	....	....	....
1989-90	**Minnesota**	**NHL**	**5**	**0**	**0**	**0**	**0**	**1**	**0**	**0**	**0**	**2**
	Kalamazoo	IHL	68	19	42	61	12	10	2	6	8	4
1990-91	Kalamazoo	IHL	75	15	51	66	15	10	4	5	9	2
	NHL Totals		**5**	**0**	**0**	**0**	**0**	**1**	**0**	**0**	**0**	**2**

Signed as a free agent by **Minnesota**, July 12, 1989.

TICHY, MILAN (TEE-hee)

Defense. Shoots left. 6'3", 194 lbs. Born, Plzen, Czechoslovakia, September 22, 1969.
(Chicago's 6th choice, 153rd overall, in 1989 Entry Draft).

			Regular Season					Playoffs				
Season	Club	Lea	GP	G	A	TP	PIM	GP	G	A	TP	PIM
1988-89	Skoda Plzen	Czech.	36	1	12	13	44	....	....	....	....	....
1989-90	Dukla Trencin	Czech.	51	14	8	22	....	....	....	....	....	....
1990-91	Dukla Trencin	Czech.	39	9	11	20	72	....	....	....	....	....

TIKKANEN, ESA (TEE-kuh-nehn)

Left wing. Shoots left. 6'1", 200 lbs. Born, Helsinki, Finland, January 25, 1965.
(Edmonton's 4th choice, 80th overall, in 1983 Entry Draft).

			Regular Season					Playoffs				
Season	Club	Lea	GP	G	A	TP	PIM	GP	G	A	TP	PIM
1981-82	Regina	WHL	2	0	0	0	0	....	....	....	....	....
1982-83	HIFK	Fin.Jr.	30	34	31	65	104	4	4	3	7	10
	HIFK	Fin.	....	....	....	....	....	1	0	0	0	2
1983-84	HIFK	Fin.Jr.	6	5	9	14	13	4	4	3	7	8
	HIFK	Fin.	36	19	11	30	30	2	0	0	0	0
1984-85	HIFK	Fin.	36	21	33	54	42	....	....	....	....	....
	Edmonton	**NHL**	....	....	....	....	....	**3**	**0**	**0**	**0**	**2**
1985-86	**Edmonton**	**NHL**	**35**	**7**	**6**	**13**	**28**	**8**	**3**	**2**	**5**	**7**
	Nova Scotia	AHL	15	4	8	12	17	....	....	....	....	....
1986-87	**Edmonton**	**NHL**	**76**	**34**	**44**	**78**	**120**	**21**	**7**	**2**	**9**	**22**
1987-88	**Edmonton**	**NHL**	**80**	**23**	**51**	**74**	**153**	**19**	**10**	**17**	**27**	**72**
1988-89	**Edmonton**	**NHL**	**67**	**31**	**47**	**78**	**92**	**7**	**1**	**3**	**4**	**12**
1989-90	**Edmonton**	**NHL**	**79**	**30**	**33**	**63**	**161**	**22**	**13**	**11**	**24**	**26**
1990-91	**Edmonton**	**NHL**	**79**	**27**	**42**	**69**	**85**	**18**	**12**	**8**	**20**	**24**
	NHL Totals		**416**	**152**	**223**	**375**	**639**	**98**	**46**	**43**	**89**	**165**

TILLEY, TOM

Defense. Shoots right. 6', 189 lbs.   Born, Trenton, Ont., March 28, 1965.
(St. Louis' 13th choice, 196th overall, in 1984 Entry Draft).

			Regular Season					Playoffs				
Season	Club	Lea	GP	G	A	TP	PIM	GP	G	A	TP	PIM
1984-85	Michigan State	CCHA	37	1	5	6	58	....	....	....	....	....
1985-86	Michigan State	CCHA	42	9	25	34	48	....	....	....	....	....
1986-87	Michigan State	CCHA	42	7	14	21	48	....	....	....	....	....
1987-88a	Michigan State	CCHA	46	8	18	26	44	....	....	....	....	....
1988-89	**St. Louis**	**NHL**	70	1	22	23	47	10	1	2	3	17
1989-90	St. Louis	NHL	34	0	5	5	6	....	....	....	....	....
	Peoria	IHL	22	1	8	9	13	....	....	....	....	....
1990-91	**St. Louis**	**NHL**	22	2	4	6	4	....	....	....	....	....
b	Peoria	IHL	48	7	38	45	53	13	2	9	11	25
	NHL Totals		126	3	31	34	57	10	1	2	3	17

a CCHA First All-Star Team (1988)
b IHL Second All-Star Team (1991)

TINORDI, MARK

Defense. Shoots left. 6'4", 205 lbs.   Born, Red Deer, Alta., May 9, 1966.

			Regular Season					Playoffs				
Season	Club	Lea	GP	G	A	TP	PIM	GP	G	A	TP	PIM
1982-83	Lethbridge	WHL	64	0	4	4	50	20	1	1	2	6
1983-84	Lethbridge	WHL	72	5	14	19	53	5	0	1	1	7
1984-85	Lethbridge	WHL	58	10	15	25	134	4	0	2	2	12
1985-86	Lethbridge	WHL	58	8	30	38	139	8	1	3	4	15
1986-87	Calgary	WHL	61	29	37	66	148	....	....	....	....	....
	New Haven	AHL	2	0	0	0	2	2	0	0	0	0
1987-88	**NY Rangers**	**NHL**	24	1	2	3	50	....	....	....	....	....
	Colorado	IHL	41	8	19	27	150	11	1	5	6	31
1988-89	**Minnesota**	**NHL**	47	2	3	5	107	5	0	0	0	0
	Kalamazoo	IHL	10	0	0	0	35	....	....	....	....	....
1989-90	**Minnesota**	**NHL**	66	3	7	10	240	7	0	1	1	16
1990-91	**Minnesota**	**NHL**	69	5	27	32	189	23	5	6	11	78
	NHL Totals		206	11	39	50	586	35	5	7	12	94

Signed as a free agent by **NY Rangers**, January 4, 1987.
Traded to **Minnesota** by **NY Rangers** with Paul Jerrard, the rights to Bret Barnett and Mike Sullivan, and Los Angeles' third-round choice (Murray Garbutt) in 1989 Entry Draft — acquired March 10, 1987 by Minnesota — for Brian Lawton, Igor Liba and the rights to Eric Bennett, October 11, 1988.

TIPPETT, DAVE   (TIP-it)

Left wing. Shoots left. 5'10", 180 lbs.   Born, Moosomin, Sask., August 25, 1961.

			Regular Season					Playoffs				
Season	Club	Lea	GP	G	A	TP	PIM	GP	G	A	TP	PIM
1981-82	North Dakota	WCHA	43	13	28	41	20	....	....	....	....	....
1982-83	North Dakota	WCHA	36	15	31	46	24	....	....	....	....	....
1983-84	Cdn. Olympic	...	66	14	19	33	24	....	....	....	....	....
	Hartford	NHL	17	4	2	6	2	....	....	....	....	....
1984-85	**Hartford**	**NHL**	80	7	12	19	12	....	....	....	....	....
1985-86	**Hartford**	**NHL**	80	14	20	34	18	10	2	2	4	4
1986-87	**Hartford**	**NHL**	80	9	22	31	42	6	0	2	2	4
1987-88	**Hartford**	**NHL**	80	16	21	37	32	6	0	0	0	2
1988-89	**Hartford**	**NHL**	80	17	24	41	45	4	0	1	1	0
1989-90	Hartford	NHL	66	8	19	27	32	7	1	3	4	2
1990-91	**Washington**	**NHL**	61	6	9	15	24	10	2	3	5	8
	NHL Totals		544	81	129	210	207	43	5	11	16	20

Signed as free agent by **Hartford**, February 29, 1984. Traded to **Washington** by **Hartford** for future considerations, September 30, 1990.

TIRKKONEN, PEKKA   (TEER-kuh-nehn)

Center. Shoots left. 6'1", 194 lbs.   Born, Savonlinna, Finland, July 17, 1968.
(Boston's 2nd choice, 34th overall, in 1986 Entry Draft).

			Regular Season					Playoffs				
Season	Club	Lea	GP	G	A	TP	PIM	GP	G	A	TP	PIM
1987-88	TPS	Fin.	44	11	12	23	4	....	....	....	....	....
1988-89	TPS	Fin.	42	11	15	26	8	10	1	2	3	0
1989-90	TPS	Fin.	41	17	11	28	0	9	3	4	7	0
1990-91	TPS	Fin.	44	9	23	32	10	9	4	2	6	0

TISDALE, TIMOTHY

Center. Shoots left. 6'1", 186 lbs.   Born, Shaunavon, Sask., May 28, 1968.
(Edmonton's 13th choice, 250th overall, in 1988 Entry Draft).

			Regular Season					Playoffs				
Season	Club	Lea	GP	G	A	TP	PIM	GP	G	A	TP	PIM
1986-87	Swift Current	WHL	66	20	29	49	25	....	....	....	....	....
1987-88	Swift Current	WHL	32	11	15	26	45	....	....	....	....	....
1988-89	Swift Current	WHL	68	57	82	139	89	12	17	15	32	22
1989-90	Cape Breton	AHL	66	15	21	36	24	3	0	0	0	0
1990-91	Cape Breton	AHL	64	10	18	28	42	1	0	0	0	0

TKACHUK, KEITH   (kuh-CHUK)

Left wing. Shoots left. 6'2", 200 lbs.   Born, Melrose, MA, March 28, 1972.
(Winnipeg's 1st choice, 19th overall, in 1990 Entry Draft).

			Regular Season					Playoffs				
Season	Club	Lea	GP	G	A	TP	PIM	GP	G	A	TP	PIM
1989-90	Malden Catholic	HS	6	12	14	26	....	....	....	....	....	....
1990-91	Boston U.	H.E.	36	17	23	40	70	....	....	....	....	....

TOCCHET, RICK   (TAHK-iht)

Right wing. Shoots right. 6', 205 lbs.   Born, Scarborough, Ont., April 9, 1964.
(Philadelphia's 5th choice, 121st overall, in 1983 Entry Draft).

			Regular Season					Playoffs				
Season	Club	Lea	GP	G	A	TP	PIM	GP	G	A	TP	PIM
1981-82	S. S. Marie	OHL	59	7	15	22	184	11	1	1	2	28
1982-83	S. S. Marie	OHL	66	32	34	66	146	16	4	13	17	67
1983-84	S. S. Marie	OHL	64	44	64	108	209	16	*22	14	*36	41
1984-85	**Philadelphia**	**NHL**	75	14	25	39	181	19	3	4	7	72
1985-86	**Philadelphia**	**NHL**	69	14	21	35	284	5	1	2	3	26
1986-87	**Philadelphia**	**NHL**	69	21	26	47	288	26	11	10	21	72
1987-88	**Philadelphia**	**NHL**	65	31	33	64	301	5	1	4	5	55
1988-89	**Philadelphia**	**NHL**	66	45	36	81	183	16	6	6	12	69
1989-90	Philadelphia	NHL	75	37	59	96	196	....	....	....	....	....
1990-91	**Philadelphia**	**NHL**	70	40	31	71	150	....	....	....	....	....
	NHL Totals		489	202	231	433	1583	71	22	26	48	294

Played in NHL All-Star Game (1989-91)

TODD, KEVIN

Center. Shoots left. 5'10", 175 lbs.   Born, Winnipeg, Man., May 4, 1968.
(New Jersey's 7th choice, 129th overall, in 1986 Entry Draft).

			Regular Season					Playoffs				
Season	Club	Lea	GP	G	A	TP	PIM	GP	G	A	TP	PIM
1985-86	Prince Albert	WHL	55	14	25	39	19	20	7	6	13	29
1986-87	Prince Albert	WHL	71	39	46	85	92	8	2	5	7	17
1987-88	Prince Albert	WHL	72	49	72	121	83	10	8	11	19	27
1988-89	**New Jersey**	**NHL**	1	0	0	0	0	....	....	....	....	....
	Utica	AHL	78	26	45	71	62	4	2	0	2	6
1989-90	Utica	AHL	71	18	36	54	72	5	2	4	6	2
1990-91	**New Jersey**	**NHL**	1	0	0	0	0	1	0	0	0	6
abc	Utica	AHL	75	37	*81	*118	75	....	....	....	....	....
	NHL Totals		2	0	0	0	0	1	0	0	0	6

a AHL First All-Star Team (1991)
b Won Les Cunningham Plaque (MVP - AHL) (1991)
c Won John B. Sollenberger Trophy (Leading Scorer - AHL) (1991)

TOIVOLA, TERO   (TOHI-voh-lah)

Right wing. Shoots left. 5'10", 191 lbs.   Born, Tampere, Finland, July 22, 1968.
(Washington's 10th choice, 187th overall, in 1986 Entry Draft).

			Regular Season					Playoffs				
Season	Club	Lea	GP	G	A	TP	PIM	GP	G	A	TP	PIM
1987-88	Tappara	Fin.	31	6	8	14	18	7	0	1	1	12
1988-89	Tappara	Fin.	32	7	14	21	16	5	2	1	3	4
1989-90	KooKoo	Fin.	42	14	32	46	41	....	....	....	....	....
1990-91	SaiPa	Fin.	44	12	11	23	28	....	....	....	....	....

TOMBERLIN, JUSTIN

Center. Shoots left. 6', 191 lbs.   Born, Grand Rapids, MN, November 15, 1970.
(Toronto's 11th choice, 192nd overall, in 1989 Entry Draft).

			Regular Season					Playoffs				
Season	Club	Lea	GP	G	A	TP	PIM	GP	G	A	TP	PIM
1989-90	U. of Maine	H.E.	35	10	7	17	6	....	....	....	....	....
1990-91	U. of Maine	H.E.	26	8	5	13	10	....	....	....	....	....

TOMLAK, MIKE

Center/Left wing. Shoots left. 6'3", 205 lbs.   Born, Thunder Bay, Ont., October 17, 1964.
(Toronto's 10th choice, 208th overall, in 1983 Entry Draft).

			Regular Season					Playoffs				
Season	Club	Lea	GP	G	A	TP	PIM	GP	G	A	TP	PIM
1982-83	Cornwall	OHL	70	18	49	67	26	....	....	....	....	....
1983-84	Cornwall	OHL	64	24	64	88	21	....	....	....	....	....
1984-85	Cornwall	OHL	66	30	70	100	9	....	....	....	....	....
1985-86	Western Ont.	OUAA	38	28	20	48	45	....	....	....	....	....
1986-87	Western Ont.	OUAA	38	16	30	46	10	....	....	....	....	....
1987-88	Western Ont.	OUAA	39	24	52	76		....	....	....	....	....
1988-89	Western Ont.	OUAA	35	16	34	50		....	....	....	....	....
1989-90	Hartford	NHL	70	7	14	21	48	7	0	1	1	2
1990-91	**Hartford**	**NHL**	64	8	8	16	55	3	0	0	0	2
	Springfield	AHL	15	4	9	13	15	....	....	....	....	....
	NHL Totals		134	15	22	37	103	10	0	1	1	4

Signed as a free agent by **Hartford**, June, 1989.

TOMLINSON, DAVE

Center. Shoots left. 5'11", 177 lbs.   Born, North Vancouver, B.C., May 8, 1969.
(Toronto's 1st choice, 3rd overall, in 1989 Supplemental Draft).

			Regular Season					Playoffs				
Season	Club	Lea	GP	G	A	TP	PIM	GP	G	A	TP	PIM
1987-88	Boston U.	H.E.	34	16	20	36	28	....	....	....	....	....
1988-89	Boston U.	H.E.	34	16	30	46	40	....	....	....	....	....
1989-90	Boston U.	H.E.	43	15	22	37	53	....	....	....	....	....
1990-91	Boston U.	H.E.	41	30	30	60	55	....	....	....	....	....

TONELLI, JOHN   (tah-NEL-ee)

Left wing. Shoots left. 6'1", 200 lbs.   Born, Milton, Ont., March 23, 1957.
(NY Islanders' 2nd choice, 33rd overall, in 1977 Amateur Draft).

Season	Club	Lea	GP	G	A	TP	PIM	GP	G	A	TP	PIM
1973-74	Toronto	OHA	69	18	37	55	62	....	....	....	....	....
1974-75a	Toronto	OHA	70	49	86	135	85	....	....	....	....	....
1975-76	Houston	WHA	79	17	14	31	66	17	7	7	14	18
1976-77	Houston	WHA	80	24	31	55	109	11	3	4	7	12
1977-78	Houston	WHA	65	23	41	64	103	6	1	3	4	8
1978-79	NY Islanders	NHL	73	17	39	56	44	10	1	6	7	0
1979-80	NY Islanders	NHL	77	14	30	44	49	21	7	9	16	18
1980-81	NY Islanders	NHL	70	20	32	52	57	16	5	8	13	16
1981-82b	NY Islanders	NHL	80	35	58	93	57	19	6	10	16	18
1982-83	NY Islanders	NHL	76	31	40	71	55	20	7	11	18	20
1983-84	NY Islanders	NHL	73	27	40	67	66	17	1	3	4	31
1984-85b	NY Islanders	NHL	80	42	58	100	95	10	1	8	9	10
1985-86	NY Islanders	NHL	65	20	41	61	50	....	....	....	....	....
	Calgary	NHL	9	3	4	7	10	22	7	9	16	49
1986-87	Calgary	NHL	78	20	31	51	72	3	0	0	0	4
1987-88	Calgary	NHL	74	17	41	58	84	6	2	5	7	8
1988-89	Los Angeles	NHL	77	31	33	64	110	6	0	0	0	4
1989-90	Los Angeles	NHL	73	31	37	68	62	10	1	2	3	6
1990-91	Los Angeles	NHL	71	14	16	30	49	12	2	4	6	12
	NHL Totals		976	322	500	822	860	172	40	75	115	200

a OHA First All-Star Team (1975)
b NHL Second Team All-Star (1982, 1985)
Played in NHL All-Star Game (1982, 1985)
Traded to **Calgary** by **NY Islanders** for Richard Kromm and Steve Konroyd, March 11, 1986. Signed as a free agent by **Los Angeles**, June 29, 1988. Signed as a free agent by **Chicago**, June 30, 1991.

TOOKEY, TIMOTHY RAYMOND (TIM)

Center. Shoots left. 5'11", 185 lbs.   Born, Edmonton, Alta., August 29, 1960.
(Washington's 4th choice, 88th overall, in 1979 Entry Draft).

Season	Club	Lea	GP	G	A	TP	PIM	GP	G	A	TP	PIM
1977-78	Portland	WHL	72	16	15	31	55	8	2	2	4	5
1978-79	Portland	WHL	56	33	47	80	55	25	6	14	20	6
1979-80	Portland	WHL	70	58	83	141	55	8	2	5	7	4
1980-81	Washington	NHL	29	10	13	23	18	....	....	....	....	....
	Hershey	AHL	47	20	38	58	129	....	....	....	....	....
1981-82	Washington	NHL	28	8	8	16	35	....	....	....	....	....
	Hershey	AHL	14	4	9	13	10	....	....	....	....	....
	Fredericton	AHL	16	6	10	16	16	....	....	....	....	....
1982-83	Quebec	NHL	12	1	6	7	4	....	....	....	....	....
	Fredericton	AHL	53	24	43	67	24	9	5	4	9	0
1983-84	Pittsburgh	NHL	8	0	2	2	2	....	....	....	....	....
	Baltimore	AHL	58	16	28	44	25	8	1	1	2	2
1984-85	Baltimore	AHL	74	25	43	68	74	15	8	10	18	13
1985-86ab	Hershey	AHL	69	35	*62	97	66	18	*11	8	19	10
1986-87	Philadelphia	NHL	2	0	0	0	0	10	1	3	4	2
cde	Hershey	AHL	80	51	*73	*124	45	5	5	4	9	0
1987-88	Los Angeles	NHL	20	1	6	7	8	....	....	....	....	....
	New Haven	AHL	11	6	7	13	2	....	....	....	....	....
1988-89	Los Angeles	NHL	7	2	1	3	4	....	....	....	....	....
	New Haven	AHL	33	11	18	29	30	....	....	....	....	....
	Muskegon	IHL	18	7	14	21	7	8	2	9	11	4
1989-90	Hershey	AHL	42	18	22	40	28	....	....	....	....	....
1990-91	Hershey	AHL	51	17	42	59	43	5	0	5	5	0
	NHL Totals		106	22	36	58	71	10	1	3	4	2

a AHL Second All-Star Team (1986)
b AHL Playoff MVP (1986)
c AHL First All-Star Team (1987)
d Won Les Cunningham Plaque (MVP-AHL 1987)
e Won John B. Sollenberger Trophy (Top Scorer–AHL 1987)
Traded to **Quebec** by **Washington** with Washington's seventh round choice (Daniel Poudrier) in 1982 Entry Draft for Lee Norwood and Quebec's sixth round choice (Mats Kihlstron) —later transferred to Calgary— in 1982 Entry Draft, February 1, 1982. Signed as free agent by **Pittsburgh**, September 12, 1983. Signed as a free agent by **Philadelphia**, July 23, 1985. Claimed by **Los Angeles** in NHL Waiver Draft, October 5, 1987. Traded to **Pittsburgh** by **Los Angeles** for Patrick Mayer, March 7, 1989. Signed as a free agent by **Philadelphia**, June 30, 1989.

TOPOROWSKI, KERRY

Defense. Shoots right. 6'2", 213 lbs.   Born, Paddockwood, Sask., April 9, 1971.
(San Jose's 5th choice, 67th overall, in 1991 Entry Draft).

Season	Club	Lea	GP	G	A	TP	PIM	GP	G	A	TP	PIM
1989-90	Spokane	WHL	65	1	13	14	384	6	0	0	0	37
1990-91	Spokane	WHL	65	11	16	27	*505	15	2	2	4	*108

TORKKI, JARI   (TOHR-kee)

Left wing. Shoots left. 5'11", 185 lbs.   Born, Rauma, Finland, August 11, 1965.
(Chicago's 6th choice, 115th overall, in 1983 Entry Draft).

Season	Club	Lea	GP	G	A	TP	PIM	GP	G	A	TP	PIM
1985-86	Lukko	Fin.	32	22	18	40	40	....	....	....	....	....
1986-87	Lukko	Fin.	44	27	8	35	42	....	....	....	....	....
1987-88	Lukko	Fin.	43	23	24	47	54	8	4	3	7	12
1988-89	Chicago	NHL	4	1	0	1	0	....	....	....	....	....
	Saginaw	IHL	72	30	42	72	22	6	2	1	3	4
1989-90	Indianapolis	IHL	66	25	29	54	50	11	5	2	7	8
1990-91	Lukko	Fin.	44	23	26	49	52	....	....	....	....	....
	NHL Totals		4	1	0	1	0	....	....	....	....	....

TORREL, DOUGLAS

Center. Shoots right. 6'2", 175 lbs.   Born, Hibbing, MN, April 29, 1969.
(Vancouver's 3rd choice, 66th overall, in 1987 Entry Draft).

Season	Club	Lea	GP	G	A	TP	PIM	GP	G	A	TP	PIM
1988-89	Minn.-Duluth	WCHA	40	4	6	10	36	....	....	....	....	....
1989-90	Minn.-Duluth	WCHA	39	11	11	22	48	....	....	....	....	....
1990-91	Minn.-Duluth	WCHA	40	17	18	35	78	....	....	....	....	....

TORREY, JEFF

Right wing. Shoots right. 6', 190 lbs.   Born, Syracuse, NY, March 6, 1970.
(Montreal's 1st choice, 23rd overall, in 1991 Supplemental Draft).

Season	Club	Lea	GP	G	A	TP	PIM	GP	G	A	TP	PIM
1989-90	Clarkson	ECAC	26	4	8	12	24	....	....	....	....	....
1990-91	Clarkson	ECAC	40	10	21	31	36	....	....	....	....	....

TOUPAL, RADEK

Center. Shoots right. 5'11", 185 lbs.   Born, Pisek, Czechoslovakia, August 16, 1966.
(Edmonton's 6th choice, 126th overall, in 1987 Entry Draft).

Season	Club	Lea	GP	G	A	TP	PIM	GP	G	A	TP	PIM
1982-83	Motor	Czech.	3	1	0	1	0	....	....	....	....	....
1983-84	Motor	Czech.	6	0	2	2	0	....	....	....	....	....
1984-85	Motor	Czech.	40	8	10	18	16	....	....	....	....	....
1985-86	Motor	Czech.	43	21	14	35	....	....	....	....	....	....
1986-87	Motor	Czech.	35	16	14	30	20	....	....	....	....	....
1987-88	Motor	Czech.	31	16	17	33	10	....	....	....	....	....
1988-89	Motor	Czech.	43	29	29	58	10	....	....	....	....	....
1989-90	Motor	Czech.	47	23	27	50	....	....	....	....	....	....
1990-91	Motor	Czech.	8	0	0	0	0	....	....	....	....	....
	Dukla Trencin	Czech.	50	22	54	76	32	....	....	....	....	....

TOWNSHEND, GRAEME

Right wing. Shoots right. 6'2", 225 lbs. Born, Kingston, Jamaica, October 2, 1965.

Season	Club	Lea	GP	G	A	TP	PIM	GP	G	A	TP	PIM
1985-86	RPI	ECAC	29	1	7	8	52	....	....	....	....	....
1986-87	RPI	ECAC	29	6	1	7	50	....	....	....	....	....
1987-88	RPI	ECAC	32	6	14	20	64	....	....	....	....	....
1988-89	Maine	AHL	5	2	1	3	11	....	....	....	....	....
	RPI	ECAC	31	6	16	22	50	....	....	....	....	....
1989-90	Boston	NHL	4	0	0	0	7	....	....	....	....	....
	Maine	AHL	64	15	13	28	162	....	....	....	....	....
1990-91	Boston	NHL	18	2	5	7	12	....	....	....	....	....
	Maine	AHL	46	16	10	26	119	2	2	0	2	4
	NHL Totals		22	2	5	7	19	....	....	....	....	....

Signed as a free agent by **Boston**, May 12, 1989.

TRESL, LADISLAV   (TREHSHL)

Center. Shoots left. 6'1", 170 lbs.   Born, Brno, Czechoslovakia, July 30, 1961.
(Quebec's 10th choice, 183rd overall, in 1987 Entry Draft)

Season	Club	Lea	GP	G	A	TP	PIM	GP	G	A	TP	PIM
1986-87	Zetor Brno	Czech.	33	13	11	24	....	....	....	....	....	....
1987-88	Fredericton	AHL	30	6	16	22	16	....	....	....	....	....
1988-89	Halifax	AHL	67	24	35	59	28	4	0	1	1	4
1989-90	Halifax	AHL	66	35	39	74	64	6	3	2	5	6
1990-91	New Haven	AHL	77	25	42	67	59	....	....	....	....	....

TRETOWICZ, DAVID

Defense. Shoots left. 5'11", 190 lbs.   Born, Liverpool, NY, March 15, 1969.
(Calgary's 11th choice, 231st overall, in 1988 Entry Draft).

Season	Club	Lea	GP	G	A	TP	PIM	GP	G	A	TP	PIM
1987-88	Clarkson	ECAC	35	8	14	22	28	....	....	....	....	....
1988-89	Clarkson	ECAC	32	6	17	23	22	....	....	....	....	....
1989-90a	Clarkson	ECAC	35	15	24	39	34	....	....	....	....	....
1990-91b	Clarkson	ECAC	40	4	32	36	18	....	....	....	....	....

a ECAC Second All-Star Team (1990)
b ECAC First All-Star Team (1991)

TROMBLEY, DAVE

Center. Shoots left. 5'11", 175 lbs.   Born, Toronto, Ont., August 11, 1968.
(Quebec's 1st choice, 2nd overall, in 1991 Supplemental Draft).

Season	Club	Lea	GP	G	A	TP	PIM	GP	G	A	TP	PIM
1989-90	Clarkson	ECAC	34	15	27	42	44	....	....	....	....	....
1990-91	Clarkson	ECAC	36	31	38	69	42	....	....	....	....	....

TROTTIER, BRYAN JOHN (TRAH-chay)

Center. Shoots left. 5'11", 195 lbs. Born, Val Marie, Sask., July 17, 1956.
(NY Islanders' 2nd choice, 22nd overall, in 1974 Amateur Draft).

			Regular Season					Playoffs				
Season	Club	Lea	GP	G	A	TP	PIM	GP	G	A	TP	PIM
1972-73	Swift Current	WHL	67	16	29	45	10	....	....	....	....	....
1973-74	Swift Current	WHL	68	41	71	112	76	13	7	8	15	8
1974-75ab	Lethbridge	WHL	67	46	*98	144	103	6	2	5	7	14
1975-76c	NY Islanders	NHL	80	32	63	95	21	13	1	7	8	8
1976-77	NY Islanders	NHL	76	30	42	72	34	12	2	8	10	2
1977-78d	NY Islanders	NHL	77	46	*77	123	46	7	0	3	3	4
1978-79defg	NY Islanders	NHL	76	47	*87	*134	50	10	2	4	6	13
1979-80h	NY Islanders	NHL	78	42	62	104	68	21	*12	17	*29	16
1980-81	NY Islanders	NHL	73	31	72	103	74	*18	11	*18	29	34
1981-82i	NY Islanders	NHL	80	50	79	129	88	19	6	*23	*29	40
1982-83	NY Islanders	NHL	80	34	55	89	68	17	8	12	20	18
1983-84i	NY Islanders	NHL	68	40	71	111	59	21	8	6	14	49
1984-85	NY Islanders	NHL	68	28	31	59	47	10	4	2	6	8
1985-86	NY Islanders	NHL	78	37	59	96	72	3	1	1	2	2
1986-87	NY Islanders	NHL	80	23	64	87	50	14	8	5	13	12
1987-88j	NY Islanders	NHL	77	30	52	82	48	6	0	0	0	10
1988-89k	NY Islanders	NHL	73	17	28	45	44	....	....	....	....	....
1989-90	NY Islanders	NHL	59	13	11	24	29	4	1	0	1	4
1990-91	Pittsburgh	NHL	52	9	19	28	24	23	3	4	7	49
	NHL Totals		1175	509	872	1381	822	198	67	110	177	269

a WHL Most Valuable Player (1975)
b WHL First All-Star Team (1975)
c Won Calder Memorial Trophy (1976)
d NHL First All-Star Team (1978, 1979)
e Won Art Ross Trophy (1979)
f Won Hart Trophy (1979)
g NHL Plus/Minus Leader (1979)
h Won Conn Smythe Trophy (1980)
i NHL Second All-Star Team (1982, 1984)
j Named Budweiser/NHL Man of the Year (1988)
k Won King Clancy Memorial Trophy (1989)

Played in NHL All-Star Game (1976, 1978, 1980, 1982, 1983, 1985, 1986)

Signed as a free agent by **Pittsburgh**, July 20, 1990.

TRUE, SOREN

Left wing. Shoots left. 6'1", 180 lbs. Born, Aarhus, Denmark, February 9, 1968.
(NY Rangers' 12th choice, 240th overall, in 1986 Entry Draft).

			Regular Season					Playoffs				
Season	Club	Lea	GP	G	A	TP	PIM	GP	G	A	TP	PIM
1989-90	Flint	IHL	54	15	17	32	49	4	0	1	1	2
1990-91	Albany	IHL	55	15	16	31	40	....	....	....	....	....
	San Diego	IHL	19	7	4	11	18	....	....	....	....	....

TSCHUPP, CHRIS

Center. Shoots left. 6'2", 180 lbs. Born, Toms River, NJ, April 6, 1971.
(Calgary's 7th choice, 125th overall, in 1990 Entry Draft).

			Regular Season					Playoffs				
Season	Club	Lea	GP	G	A	TP	PIM	GP	G	A	TP	PIM
1990-91	Notre Dame	NCAA	33	1	6	7	26	....	....	....	....	....

TUCKER, CHRIS

Center. Shoots left. 5'11", 183 lbs. Born, White Plains, NY, February 9, 1972.
(Chicago's 3rd choice, 79th overall, in 1990 Entry Draft).

			Regular Season					Playoffs				
Season	Club	Lea	GP	G	A	TP	PIM	GP	G	A	TP	PIM
1989-90	Jefferson	HS	24	24	24	48	0	....	....	....	....	....
1990-91	U. Wisconsin	WCHA	35	5	6	11	6	....	....	....	....	....

TUCKER, JOHN

Center. Shoots right. 6', 200 lbs. Born, Windsor, Ont., September 29, 1964.
(Buffalo's 4th choice, 31st overall, in 1983 Entry Draft).

			Regular Season					Playoffs				
Season	Club	Lea	GP	G	A	TP	PIM	GP	G	A	TP	PIM
1981-82	Kitchener	OHL	67	16	32	48	32	15	2	3	5	2
1982-83	Kitchener	OHL	70	60	80	140	33	11	5	9	14	10
1983-84ab	Buffalo	NHL	21	12	4	16	4	3	1	0	1	0
	Kitchener	OHL	39	40	60	100	25	12	12	18	30	8
1984-85	Buffalo	NHL	64	22	27	49	21	5	1	5	6	0
1985-86	Buffalo	NHL	75	31	34	65	39	....	....	....	....	....
1986-87	Buffalo	NHL	54	17	34	51	21	....	....	....	....	....
1987-88	Buffalo	NHL	45	19	19	38	20	6	7	3	10	18
1988-89	Buffalo	NHL	60	13	31	44	31	3	0	3	3	0
1989-90	Buffalo	NHL	8	1	2	3	2	....	....	....	....	....
	Washington	NHL	38	9	19	28	10	12	1	7	8	4
1990-91	Buffalo	NHL	18	1	3	4	4	....	....	....	....	....
	NY Islanders	NHL	20	3	4	7	4	....	....	....	....	....
	NHL Totals		403	128	177	305	156	29	10	18	28	22

a OHL First All-Star Team (1984)
b OHL Player of the Year (1984)

Traded to **Washington** by **Buffalo** for future considerations, January 5, 1990. Traded to **Buffalo** by **Washington** for cash, July 3, 1990. Traded to **NY Islanders** by **Buffalo** for future considerations, January 21, 1991.

TUCKER, TRAVIS

Defense. Shoots right. 6'4", 205 lbs. Born, Hartford, CT., March 15, 1971.
(Detroit's 9th choice, 192nd overall, in 1990 Entry Draft).

			Regular Season					Playoffs				
Season	Club	Lea	GP	G	A	TP	PIM	GP	G	A	TP	PIM
1989-90	Avon Old Farms	HS	24	3	7	10	....	....	....	....	....	....
1990-91	U. of Lowell	H.E.	22	0	0	0	40	....	....	....	....	....

TUER, ALLAN (AL) (TOOR)

Defense. Shoots left. 6', 190 lbs. Born, North Battleford, Sask., July 19, 1963.
(Los Angeles' 8th choice, 186th overall, in 1981 Entry Draft).

			Regular Season					Playoffs				
Season	Club	Lea	GP	G	A	TP	PIM	GP	G	A	TP	PIM
1980-81	Regina	WHL	31	0	7	7	58	8	0	1	1	37
1981-82	Regina	WHL	63	2	18	20	*486	13	0	3	3	117
1982-83	Regina	WHL	71	3	27	30	229	5	0	0	0	37
1983-84	New Haven	AHL	78	0	20	20	195	....	....	....	....	....
1984-85	New Haven	AHL	56	0	7	7	241	....	....	....	....	....
1985-86	Los Angeles	NHL	45	0	1	1	150	....	....	....	....	....
	New Haven	AHL	8	1	0	1	53	....	....	....	....	....
1986-87	New Haven	AHL	69	1	14	15	273	5	0	1	1	48
1987-88	Minnesota	NHL	6	1	0	1	29	....	....	....	....	....
	Kalamazoo	IHL	68	2	15	17	303	7	0	0	0	34
1988-89	Hartford	NHL	4	0	0	0	23	....	....	....	....	....
	Binghamton	AHL	43	1	7	8	234	....	....	....	....	....
1989-90	Hartford	NHL	2	0	0	0	6	....	....	....	....	....
	Binghamton	AHL	58	3	7	10	56	....	....	....	....	....
1990-91	San Diego	IHL	60	0	5	5	305	....	....	....	....	....
	NHL Totals		57	1	1	2	208					

Signed as a free agent by **Edmonton**, August 18, 1986. Claimed by **Minnesota** in NHL Waiver Draft, October 5, 1987. Signed as a free agent by **Hartford**, July 12, 1988.

TURCOTTE, ALFIE

Center. Shoots left. 5'11", 185 lbs. Born, Gary, IN, June 5, 1965.
(Montreal's 1st choice, 17th overall, in 1983 Entry Draft).

			Regular Season					Playoffs				
Season	Club	Lea	GP	G	A	TP	PIM	GP	G	A	TP	PIM
1982-83	Nanaimo	WHL	36	23	27	50	22	....	....	....	....	....
	Portland	WHL	39	26	51	77	26	14	14	18	32	9
1983-84	Montreal	NHL	30	7	7	14	10	....	....	....	....	....
	Portland	WHL	32	22	41	63	39	....	....	....	....	....
1984-85	Montreal	NHL	53	8	16	24	35	5	0	0	0	0
1985-86	Montreal	NHL	2	0	0	0	2	....	....	....	....	....
	Sherbrooke	AHL	75	29	36	65	60	....	....	....	....	....
1986-87	Nova Scotia	AHL	70	27	41	68	37	5	2	4	6	2
1987-88	Winnipeg	NHL	3	0	0	0	0	....	....	....	....	....
a	Baltimore	AHL	33	21	33	54	42	....	....	....	....	....
	Moncton	AHL	25	12	25	37	18	....	....	....	....	....
	Sherbrooke	AHL	8	3	8	11	4	....	....	....	....	....
1988-89	Winnipeg	NHL	14	1	3	4	2	....	....	....	....	....
	Moncton	AHL	54	27	39	66	74	10	3	9	12	17
1989-90	Washington	NHL	4	0	2	2	0	....	....	....	....	....
	Baltimore	AHL	65	26	40	66	42	12	7	9	16	14
1990-91	Washington	NHL	6	1	1	2	0	....	....	....	....	....
	Baltimore	AHL	65	33	52	85	20	6	3	3	6	4
	NHL Totals		112	17	29	46	49	5	0	0	0	0

a AHL Second All-Star team (1988)

Traded to **Edmonton** by **Montreal** for future considerations, June 25, 1986. Sold to **Montreal** by **Edmonton**, May 14, 1987. Traded to **Winnipeg** by **Montreal** for future considerations, January 14, 1988. Signed as a free agent by **Boston**, June 27, 1989. Traded to **Washington** by **Boston** for Mike Millar, October 2, 1989.

TURCOTTE, DARREN

Center. Shoots left. 6', 185 lbs. Born, Boston, MA, March 2, 1968.
(NY Rangers' 6th choice, 114th overall, in 1986 Entry Draft).

			Regular Season					Playoffs				
Season	Club	Lea	GP	G	A	TP	PIM	GP	G	A	TP	PIM
1984-85	North Bay	OHL	62	33	32	65	28	....	....	....	....	....
1985-86	North Bay	OHL	62	35	37	72	35	10	3	4	7	8
1986-87	North Bay	OHL	55	30	48	78	20	18	12	8	20	6
1987-88	North Bay	OHL	32	30	33	63	16	4	3	0	3	4
	Colorado	IHL	8	4	3	7	9	6	2	6	8	8
1988-89	NY Rangers	NHL	20	7	3	10	4	1	0	0	0	0
	Denver	IHL	40	21	28	49	32	....	....	....	....	....
1989-90	NY Rangers	NHL	76	32	34	66	32	10	1	6	7	4
1990-91	NY Rangers	NHL	74	26	41	67	37	6	1	2	3	0
	NHL Totals		170	65	78	143	73	17	2	8	10	4

Played in NHL All-Star Game (1991)

TURGEON, PIERRE

Center. Shoots left. 6'1", 203 lbs. Born, Rouyn, Que., August 29, 1969.
(Buffalo's 1st choice, 1st overall, in 1987 Entry Draft).

			Regular Season					Playoffs				
Season	Club	Lea	GP	G	A	TP	PIM	GP	G	A	TP	PIM
1985-86	Granby	QMJHL	69	47	67	114	31	....	....	....	....	....
1986-87	Granby	QMJHL	58	69	85	154	8	7	9	6	15	15
1987-88	Buffalo	NHL	76	14	28	42	34	6	4	3	7	4
1988-89	Buffalo	NHL	80	34	54	88	26	5	3	5	8	2
1989-90	Buffalo	NHL	80	40	66	106	29	6	2	4	6	2
1990-91	Buffalo	NHL	78	32	47	79	26	6	3	1	4	6
	NHL Totals		314	120	195	315	115	23	12	13	25	14

Played in NHL All-Star Game (1990)

TURGEON, SYLVAIN

Left wing. Shoots left. 6', 200 lbs. Born, Noranda, Que., January 17, 1965.
(Hartford's 1st choice, 2nd overall, in 1983 Entry Draft).

			Regular Season					Playoffs				
Season	Club	Lea	GP	G	A	TP	PIM	GP	G	A	TP	PIM
1981-82	Hull	QMJHL	57	33	40	73	78	14	11	11	22	16
1982-83a	Hull	QMJHL	67	54	109	163	103	7	8	7	15	10
1983-84b	Hartford	NHL	76	40	32	72	55	....	....	....	....	....
1984-85	Hartford	NHL	64	31	31	62	67	....	....	....	....	....
1985-86	Hartford	NHL	76	45	34	79	88	9	2	3	5	4
1986-87	Hartford	NHL	41	23	13	36	45	6	1	2	3	4
1987-88	Hartford	NHL	71	23	26	49	71	6	0	0	0	4
1988-89	Hartford	NHL	42	16	14	30	40	4	0	2	2	4
1989-90	New Jersey	NHL	72	30	17	47	81	1	0	0	0	0
1990-91	Montreal	NHL	19	5	7	12	20	5	0	0	0	2
	NHL Totals		461	213	174	387	467	31	3	7	10	18

a QMJHL First All-Star Team (1983)
b NHL All-Rookie Team (1984)

Played in NHL All-Star Game (1986)

Traded to **New Jersey** by **Hartford** for Pat Verbeek, June 17, 1989. Traded to **Montreal** by **New Jersey** for Claude Lemieux, September 4, 1990.

TURNER, BRAD

Defense. Shoots right. 6'2", 205 lbs. Born, Winnipeg, Man., May 25, 1968.
(Minnesota's 6th choice, 58th overall, in 1986 Entry Draft).

			Regular Season					Playoffs				
Season	Club	Lea	GP	G	A	TP	PIM	GP	G	A	TP	PIM
1986-87	U. of Michigan	CCHA	40	3	10	13	40	....	....	....	....	....
1987-88	U. of Michigan	CCHA	39	3	11	14	52	....	....	....	....	....
1988-89	U. of Michigan	CCHA	33	3	8	11	38	....	....	....	....	....
1989-90	U. of Michigan	CCHA	32	8	9	17	34	....	....	....	....	....
1990-91	Capital Dist.	AHL	31	1	2	3	8	....	....	....	....	....
	Richmond	ECHL	40	16	25	41	31	....	....	....	....	....

TUSTIAN, ROBERT (ROB)

Right wing. Shoots right. 6'2", 220 lbs. Born, Hamilton, Ont., April 4, 1968.
(St. Louis' 1st choice, 14th overall, in 1989 Supplemental Draft).

			Regular Season					Playoffs				
Season	Club	Lea	GP	G	A	TP	PIM	GP	G	A	TP	PIM
1988-89	Michigan Tech	WCHA	37	0	3	3	51	....	....	....	....	....
1989-90	Michigan Tech	WCHA	37	6	9	15	74	....	....	....	....	....
1990-91	Michigan Tech	WCHA	38	4	7	11	52	....	....	....	....	....

TUTT, BRIAN

Defense. Shoots left. 6'1", 195 lbs. Born, Small Well, Alta., June 9, 1962.
(Philadelphia's 6th choice, 126th overall, in 1980 Entry Draft).

			Regular Season					Playoffs				
Season	Club	Lea	GP	G	A	TP	PIM	GP	G	A	TP	PIM
1979-80	Calgary	WHL	2	0	0	0	2	4	0	1	1	6
1980-81	Calgary	WHL	72	10	41	51	111	22	3	11	14	30
1981-82	Calgary	WHL	40	2	16	18	85	9	2	2	4	22
1982-83	Maine	AHL	31	0	0	0	28	....	....	....	....	....
	Toledo	IHL	23	5	10	15	26	11	1	7	8	16
1983-84	Springfield	AHL	1	0	0	0	2	....	....	....	....	....
a	Toledo	IHL	82	7	44	51	79	13	0	6	6	16
1984-85	Hershey	AHL	3	0	0	0	8	....	....	....	....	....
a	Kalamazoo	IHL	80	8	45	53	62	11	2	4	6	19
1985-86	Kalamazoo	IHL	82	11	39	50	129	6	1	6	7	11
1986-87	Maine	AHL	41	6	15	21	19	....	....	....	....	....
	Kalamazoo	IHL	19	2	7	9	10	....	....	....	....	....
1987-88	New Haven	AHL	32	1	12	13	33	....	....	....	....	....
1988-89	Baltimore	AHL	6	1	5	6	6	....	....	....	....	....
	Cdn. National	...	63	0	19	19	87	....	....	....	....	....
1989-90	Washington	NHL	7	1	0	1	2	....	....	....	....	....
	Baltimore	AHL	67	2	13	15	80	9	1	0	1	4
1990-91	Cdn. National	...	10	4	3	7	14	....	....	....	....	....
	NHL Totals		7	1	0	1	2	....	....	....	....	....

a IHL Second All-Star Team (1984, 1985)

Signed as a free agent by **Washington**, July 25, 1989.

TUTTLE, STEVE

Right wing. Shoots right. 6'1", 197 lbs. Born, Vancouver, B.C., January 5, 1966.
(St. Louis' 8th choice, 113th overall, in 1984 Entry Draft).

			Regular Season					Playoffs				
Season	Club	Lea	GP	G	A	TP	PIM	GP	G	A	TP	PIM
1984-85	U. Wisconsin	WCHA	28	3	4	7	0	....	....	....	....	....
1985-86	U. Wisconsin	WCHA	32	2	10	12	2	....	....	....	....	....
1986-87	U. Wisconsin	WCHA	42	31	21	52	14	....	....	....	....	....
1987-88ab	U. Wisconsin	WCHA	45	27	39	66	18	....	....	....	....	....
1988-89	St. Louis	NHL	53	13	12	25	6	6	1	2	3	0
1989-90	St. Louis	NHL	71	12	10	22	4	5	0	1	1	2
1990-91	St. Louis	NHL	20	3	6	9	2	6	0	3	3	0
	Peoria	IHL	42	24	32	56	8	....	....	....	....	....
	NHL Totals		144	28	28	56	12	17	1	6	7	2

a NCAA West Second All-American Team (1988)
b WCHA Second All-Star Team (1988)

TWIST, ANTHONY (TONY)

Defense. Shoots left. 6', 212 lbs. Born, Sherwood Park, Alta., May 9, 1968.
(St. Louis' 9th choice, 177th overall, in 1988 Entry Draft).

			Regular Season					Playoffs				
Season	Club	Lea	GP	G	A	TP	PIM	GP	G	A	TP	PIM
1987-88	Saskatoon	WHL	55	1	8	9	226	10	1	1	2	6
1988-89	Peoria	IHL	67	3	8	11	312	....	....	....	....	....
1989-90	St. Louis	NHL	28	0	0	0	124	....	....	....	....	....
	Peoria	IHL	36	1	5	6	200	5	0	1	1	8
1990-91	Peoria	IHL	38	2	10	12	244	....	....	....	....	....
	Quebec	NHL	24	0	0	0	104	....	....	....	....	....
	NHL Totals		52	0	0	0	228	....	....	....	....	....

Traded to **Quebec** by **St. Louis** with Herb Ragian and Andy Rymsha for Darin Kimble, February 4, 1991.

UNIAK, JOHN

Defense. Shoots right. 5'11", 210 lbs. Born, Stratford, Ont., March 29, 1971.
(Montreal's 12th choice, 228th overall, in 1990 Entry Draft).

			Regular Season					Playoffs				
Season	Club	Lea	GP	G	A	TP	PIM	GP	G	A	TP	PIM
1988-89	Sudbury	OHL	20	1	6	7	13	....	....	....	....	....
	Kitchener	OHL	45	5	13	18	32	5	0	2	2	0
1989-90	Kitchener	OHL	57	9	35	44	38	14	1	1	2	2
1990-91	Kitchener	OHL	58	12	59	71	53	6	0	3	3	8

VACHON, NICK

Center. Shoots left. 5'10", 190 lbs. Born, Montreal, Que., July 20, 1972.
(Toronto's 11th choice, 241st overall, in 1990 Entry Draft).

			Regular Season					Playoffs				
Season	Club	Lea	GP	G	A	TP	PIM	GP	G	A	TP	PIM
1989-90	Gov. Dummer	HS	22	20	22	42	....	....	....	....	....	....
1990-91	Boston U.	H.E.	8	0	1	1	4	....	....	....	....	....

VAIVE, RICHARD CLAUDE (RICK) (VIHV)

Right wing. Shoots right. 6', 200 lbs. Born, Ottawa, Ont., May 14, 1959.
(Vancouver's 1st choice, 5th overall, in 1979 Entry Draft).

			Regular Season					Playoffs				
Season	Club	Lea	GP	G	A	TP	PIM	GP	G	A	TP	PIM
1976-77	Sherbrooke	QJHL	67	51	59	110	91	18	10	13	23	78
1977-78	Sherbrooke	QJHL	68	76	79	155	199	9	8	4	12	38
1978-79	Birmingham	WHA	75	26	33	59	*248	....	....	....	....	....
1979-80	Vancouver	NHL	47	13	8	21	111	....	....	....	....	....
	Toronto	NHL	22	9	7	16	77	3	1	0	1	11
1980-81	Toronto	NHL	75	33	29	62	229	3	1	0	1	4
1981-82	Toronto	NHL	77	54	35	89	157	....	....	....	....	....
1982-83	Toronto	NHL	78	51	28	79	105	4	2	5	7	6
1983-84	Toronto	NHL	76	52	41	93	114	....	....	....	....	....
1984-85	Toronto	NHL	72	35	33	68	112	....	....	....	....	....
1985-86	Toronto	NHL	61	33	31	64	85	9	6	2	8	9
1986-87	Toronto	NHL	73	32	34	66	61	13	4	2	6	23
1987-88	Chicago	NHL	76	43	26	69	108	5	6	2	8	38
1988-89	Chicago	NHL	30	12	13	25	60	....	....	....	....	....
	Buffalo	NHL	28	19	13	32	64	5	2	1	3	8
1989-90	Buffalo	NHL	70	29	19	48	74	6	4	2	6	6
1990-91	Buffalo	NHL	71	25	27	52	74	6	1	2	3	6
	NHL Totals		856	440	344	784	1431	54	27	16	43	111

Played in NHL All-Star Game (1982-84)

Traded to **Toronto** by **Vancouver** with Bill Derlago for Dave Williams and Jerry Butler, February 18, 1980. Traded to **Chicago** by **Toronto** with Steve Thomas and Bob McGill for Al Secord and Ed Olczyk, September 3, 1987. Traded to **Buffalo** by **Chicago** for Adam Creighton, December 26, 1988.

VALILA, MIKA

Center. Shoots left. 6', 172 lbs. Born, Sodertalje, Sweden, February 20, 1970.
(Pittsburgh's 7th choice, 130th overall, in 1990 Entry Draft).

			Regular Season					Playoffs				
Season	Club	Lea	GP	G	A	TP	PIM	GP	G	A	TP	PIM
1989-90	Tappara	Fin.	44	8	16	24	16	7	2	2	4	4
1990-91	Tappara	Fin.	41	10	9	19	16	3	0	1	1	0

VALIMONT, CARL

Defense. Shoots left. 6'1", 200 lbs. Born, Southington, CT, March 1, 1966.
(Vancouver's 10th choice, 193rd overall, in 1985 Entry Draft).

			Regular Season					Playoffs				
Season	Club	Lea	GP	G	A	TP	PIM	GP	G	A	TP	PIM
1984-85	U. of Lowell	H.E.	40	4	11	15	24	....	....	....	....	....
1985-86	U. of Lowell	H.E.	26	1	9	10	12	....	....	....	....	....
1986-87	U. of Lowell	H.E.	36	8	9	17	36	....	....	....	....	....
1987-88a	U. of Lowell	H.E.	38	6	26	32	59	....	....	....	....	....
1988-89	Milwaukee	IHL	79	4	33	37	56	11	2	8	10	12
1989-90	Milwaukee	IHL	78	13	28	41	48	3	0	1	1	6
1990-91	Milwaukee	IHL	80	10	21	31	66	6	2	1	3	2

a Hockey East Second All-Star Team (1988)

VALK, GARRY

Left wing. Shoots left. 6'1", 190 lbs. Born, Edmonton, Alta., November 27, 1967.
(Vancouver's 5th choice, 108th overall, in 1987 Entry Draft).

			Regular Season					Playoffs				
Season	Club	Lea	GP	G	A	TP	PIM	GP	G	A	TP	PIM
1987-88	North Dakota	WCHA	38	23	12	35	64	....	....	....	....	....
1988-89	North Dakota	WCHA	40	14	17	31	71	....	....	....	....	....
1989-90	North Dakota	WCHA	43	22	17	39	92	....	....	....	....	....
1990-91	Vancouver	NHL	59	10	11	21	67	5	0	0	0	20
	Milwaukee	IHL	10	12	4	16	13	3	0	0	0	2
	NHL Totals		59	10	11	21	67	5	0	0	0	20

VALLIS, LINDSAY

Right wing. Shoots right. 6'3", 207 lbs. Born, Winnipeg, Man., January 12, 1971.
(Montreal's 1st choice, 13th overall, in 1989 Entry Draft).

			Regular Season					Playoffs				
Season	Club	Lea	GP	G	A	TP	PIM	GP	G	A	TP	PIM
1987-88	Seattle	WHL	68	31	45	76	65	....	....	....	....	....
1988-89	Seattle	WHL	63	21	32	53	48	....	....	....	....	....
1989-90	Seattle	WHL	65	34	43	77	68	13	6	5	11	14
1990-91	Seattle	WHL	72	41	38	79	119	6	1	3	4	17
	Fredericton	AHL	....	....	....	....	....	7	0	0	0	6

VALO, JOHN

Defense. Shoots left. 6', 210 lbs. Born, Warren, MI, April 12, 1970.
(St. Louis' 10th choice, 198th overall, in 1989 Entry Draft.)

			Regular Season					Playoffs				
Season	Club	Lea	GP	G	A	TP	PIM	GP	G	A	TP	PIM
1989-90	Hamilton	OHL	31	3	6	9	38	....	....	....	....	....
1990-91	Nashville	ECHL	8	0	0	0	12	....	....	....	....	....
	Roanoke Valley	ECHL	26	0	6	6	16	....	....	....	....	....

VAN ALLEN, SHAUN

Center. Shoots left. 6'1", 200 lbs. Born, Shaunavon, Sask., August 29, 1967.
(Edmonton's 5th choice, 105th overall, in 1987 Entry Draft).

			Regular Season					Playoffs				
Season	Club	Lea	GP	G	A	TP	PIM	GP	G	A	TP	PIM
1984-85	Swift Current	WHL	61	12	20	32	136	....	....	....	....	....
1985-86	Saskatoon	WHL	55	12	11	23	43	13	4	8	12	28
1986-87	Saskatoon	WHL	72	38	59	97	116	11	4	6	10	24
1987-88	Milwaukee	IHL	40	14	28	42	34	....	....	....	....	....
	Nova Scotia	AHL	19	4	10	14	17	4	1	1	2	4
1988-89	Cape Breton	AHL	76	32	42	74	81	....	....	....	....	....
1989-90	Cape Breton	AHL	61	25	44	69	83	4	0	2	2	8
1990-91	**Edmonton**	**NHL**	**2**	**0**	**0**	**0**	**0**	....	....	....	....	....
a	Cape Breton	AHL	76	25	75	100	182	4	0	1	1	8
	NHL Totals		**2**	**0**	**0**	**0**	**0**	....	....	....	....	....

a AHL Second All-Star Team (1991)

VANDERYDT, ROBERT

Center. Shoots left. 6'1", 177 lbs. Born, Blenheim, Ont., June 8, 1968.
(NY Islanders' 1st choice, 2nd overall, in 1989 Supplemental Draft).

			Regular Season					Playoffs				
Season	Club	Lea	GP	G	A	TP	PIM	GP	G	A	TP	PIM
1987-88	Miami-Ohio	CCHA	37	14	20	34	26	....	....	....	....	....
1988-89	Miami-Ohio	CCHA	38	12	18	30	26	....	....	....	....	....
1989-90	Miami-Ohio	CCHA	30	10	14	24	14	....	....	....	....	....
1990-91	Miami-Ohio	CCHA	34	14	8	22	20	....	....	....	....	....

VAN DORP, WAYNE

Left wing. Shoots left. 6'4", 225 lbs. Born, Vancouver, B.C., May 19, 1961.

			Regular Season					Playoffs				
Season	Club	Lea	GP	G	A	TP	PIM	GP	G	A	TP	PIM
1979-80	Seattle	WHL	68	8	13	21	195	12	3	1	4	33
1980-81	Seattle	WHL	63	22	30	52	242	5	1	0	1	10
1984-85	GIJS Groningen	Neth.	29	38	46	84	112	6	6	2	8	23
	Erie	ACHL	7	9	8	17	21	10	0	2	6	2
1985-86a	GIJS Groningen	Neth.	29	19	24	43	81	8	9	*12	21	6
1986-87	Rochester	AHL	47	7	3	10	192	....	....	....	....	....
	Edmonton	**NHL**	**3**	**0**	**0**	**0**	**25**	**3**	**0**	**0**	**0**	**2**
	Nova Scotia	AHL	11	2	3	5	37	5	0	0	0	56
1987-88	**Pittsburgh**	**NHL**	**25**	**1**	**3**	**4**	**75**	....	....	....	....	....
	Nova Scota	AHL	12	2	2	4	87	....	....	....	....	....
1988-89	Rochester	AHL	28	3	6	9	202	....	....	....	....	....
	Chicago	**NHL**	**8**	**0**	**0**	**0**	**23**	**16**	**0**	**1**	**1**	**17**
	Saginaw	IHL	11	4	3	7	60	....	....	....	....	....
1989-90	**Chicago**	**NHL**	**61**	**7**	**4**	**11**	**303**	**8**	**0**	**0**	**0**	**23**
1990-91	**Quebec**	**NHL**	**4**	**1**	**0**	**1**	**30**	....	....	....	....	....
	NHL Totals		**101**	**9**	**7**	**16**	**456**	**27**	**0**	**1**	**1**	**42**

a Named playoff MVP (1986)

Traded to **Edmonton** by **Buffalo** with Normand Lacombe and future considerations for Lee Fogolin and Mark Napier, March 6, 1987. Traded to **Pittsburgh** by **Edmonton** with Paul Coffey and Dave Hunter for Craig Simpson, Dave Hannan, Moe Mantha, and Chris Joseph, November 24, 1987. Traded to **Buffalo** by **Pittsburgh** for future considerations, September 30, 1988. Traded to **Chicago** by **Buffalo** for Chicago's seventh-round choice (Viktor Gordijuk) in 1990 Entry Draft, February 16, 1989. Claimed by **Quebec** in NHL Waiver Draft, October 1, 1990.

VAN KESSEL, JOHN

Right wing. Shoots right. 6'4", 193 lbs. Born, Bridgewater, N.S., December 19, 1969.
(Los Angeles' 3rd choice, 49th overall, in 1988 Entry Draft).

			Regular Season					Playoffs				
Season	Club	Lea	GP	G	A	TP	PIM	GP	G	A	TP	PIM
1986-87	Belleville	OHL	61	1	10	11	58	....	....	....	....	....
1987-88	North Bay	OHL	50	13	16	29	214	4	1	1	2	16
1988-89	North Bay	OHL	50	7	13	20	218	11	2	4	6	31
1989-90	New Haven	AHL	6	1	1	2	9	....	....	....	....	....
	North Bay	OHL	40	7	21	28	127	5	0	3	3	16
1990-91	Phoenix	IHL	65	15	15	30	246	3	1	1	2	16

VARY, JOHN

Defense. Shoots right. 6'1", 207 lbs. Born, Owen Sound, Ont., February 11, 1972.
(NY Rangers' 3rd choice, 55th overall, in 1990 Entry Draft).

			Regular Season					Playoffs				
Season	Club	Lea	GP	G	A	TP	PIM	GP	G	A	TP	PIM
1988-89	North Bay	OHL	45	2	7	9	38	3	0	0	0	0
1989-90	North Bay	OHL	59	7	39	46	79	5	0	2	2	8
1990-91	North Bay	OHL	39	5	21	26	108	....	....	....	....	....
	Kingston	OHL	31	5	15	20	16	....	....	....	....	....

VASKE, DENNIS (VAS-kee)

Defense. Shoots left. 6'2", 210 lbs. Born, Rockford, IL., October 11, 1967.
(NY Islanders' 2nd choice, 38th overall, in 1986 Entry Draft).

			Regular Season					Playoffs				
Season	Club	Lea	GP	G	A	TP	PIM	GP	G	A	TP	PIM
1986-87	Minn.-Duluth	WCHA	33	0	2	2	40	....	....	....	....	....
1987-88	Minn.-Duluth	WCHA	39	1	6	7	90	....	....	....	....	....
1988-89	Minn.-Duluth	WCHA	37	9	19	28	86	....	....	....	....	....
1989-90	Minn.-Duluth	WCHA	37	5	24	29	72	....	....	....	....	....
1990-91	**NY Islanders**	**NHL**	**5**	**0**	**0**	**0**	**2**	....	....	....	....	....
	Capital Dist.	AHL	67	10	10	20	65	....	....	....	....	....
	NHL Totals		**5**	**0**	**0**	**0**	**2**	....	....	....	....	....

VEILLEUX, STEVE

Defense. Shoots right. 6', 198 lbs. Born, Lachenaie, Que., March 9, 1969.
(Vancouver's 2nd choice, 45th overall, in 1987 Entry Draft).

			Regular Season					Playoffs				
Season	Club	Lea	GP	G	A	TP	PIM	GP	G	A	TP	PIM
1985-86	Trois Rivieres	QMJHL	67	1	20	21	132	5	0	0	0	13
1986-87	Trois Rivieres	QMJHL	62	6	22	28	227	....	....	....	....	....
1987-88a	Trois Rivieres	QMJHL	63	7	25	32	150	....	....	....	....	....
1988-89a	Trois Rivieres	QMJHL	49	5	28	33	149	4	0	0	0	10
	Milwaukee	IHL	1	0	0	0	0	4	0	0	0	13
1989-90	Milwaukee	IHL	76	4	12	16	195	2	0	0	0	2
1990-91	Milwaukee	IHL	58	0	9	9	152	....	....	....	....	....
	Indianapolis	IHL	11	1	3	4	30	7	0	3	3	13

a QMJHL Second All-Star Team (1988, 1989)

Signed as a free agent by **Montreal**, August 6, 1991.

VEITCH, DARREN WILLIAM (VEECH)

Defense. Shoots right. 5'11", 195 lbs. Born, Saskatoon, Sask., April 24, 1960.
(Washington's 1st choice, 5th overall, in 1980 Entry Draft).

			Regular Season					Playoffs				
Season	Club	Lea	GP	G	A	TP	PIM	GP	G	A	TP	PIM
1976-77	Regina	WHL	1	0	0	0	0	....	....	....	....	....
1977-78	Regina	WHL	71	13	32	45	135	9	0	2	2	4
1978-79	Regina	WHL	51	11	36	47	80	....	....	....	....	....
1979-80a	Regina	WHL	71	29	*93	122	118	18	13	18	31	13
1980-81	**Washington**	**NHL**	**59**	**4**	**21**	**25**	**46**	....	....	....	....	....
	Hershey	AHL	26	6	22	28	12	10	6	3	9	15
1981-82	**Washington**	**NHL**	**67**	**9**	**44**	**53**	**54**	....	....	....	....	....
	Hershey	AHL	10	5	10	15	16	....	....	....	....	....
1982-83	**Washington**	**NHL**	**10**	**0**	**8**	**8**	**0**	....	....	....	....	....
	Hershey	AHL	5	0	1	1	2	....	....	....	....	....
1983-84	**Washington**	**NHL**	**46**	**6**	**18**	**24**	**17**	**5**	**0**	**1**	**1**	**15**
	Hershey	AHL	11	1	6	7	4	....	....	....	....	....
1984-85	**Washington**	**NHL**	**75**	**3**	**18**	**21**	**37**	**5**	**0**	**1**	**1**	**4**
1985-86	**Washington**	**NHL**	**62**	**3**	**9**	**12**	**27**	....	....	....	....	....
	Detroit	**NHL**	**13**	**0**	**5**	**5**	**2**	....	....	....	....	....
1986-87	**Detroit**	**NHL**	**77**	**13**	**45**	**58**	**52**	**12**	**3**	**4**	**7**	**8**
1987-88	**Detroit**	**NHL**	**63**	**7**	**33**	**40**	**45**	**11**	**1**	**5**	**6**	**6**
1988-89	**Toronto**	**NHL**	**37**	**3**	**7**	**10**	**16**	....	....	....	....	....
	Newmarket	AHL	33	5	19	24	29	5	0	4	4	4
1989-90b	Newmarket	AHL	78	13	54	67	30	....	....	....	....	....
1990-91	**Toronto**	**NHL**	**2**	**0**	**1**	**1**	**0**	....	....	....	....	....
	Newmarket	AHL	56	7	28	35	26	....	....	....	....	....
	Peoria	IHL	18	2	14	16	10	19	4	12	16	10
	NHL Totals		**511**	**48**	**209**	**257**	**296**	**33**	**4**	**11**	**15**	**33**

a WHL First All-Star Team (1980)
b AHL Second All-Star Team (1990)

Traded to **Detroit** by **Washington** for John Barrett and Greg Smith, March 10, 1986. Traded to **Toronto** by **Detroit** for Miroslav Frycer, June 10, 1988. Traded to **St. Louis** by **Toronto** with future considerations for Keith Osborne, March 5, 1991.

VELISCHEK, RANDY (VEHL-ih-shehk)

Defense. Shoots left. 6', 200 lbs. Born, Montreal, Que., February 10, 1962.
(Minnesota's 3rd choice, 53rd overall, in 1980 Entry Draft).

			Regular Season					Playoffs				
Season	Club	Lea	GP	G	A	TP	PIM	GP	G	A	TP	PIM
1979-80	Providence	ECAC	31	5	5	10	20	....	....	....	....	....
1980-81	Providence	ECAC	33	3	12	15	26	....	....	....	....	....
1981-82a	Providence	ECAC	33	1	14	15	38	....	....	....	....	....
1982-83bc	Providence	ECAC	41	18	34	52	50	....	....	....	....	....
	Minnesota	**NHL**	**3**	**0**	**0**	**0**	**2**	**9**	**0**	**0**	**0**	**0**
1983-84	**Minnesota**	**NHL**	**33**	**2**	**2**	**4**	**10**	**1**	**0**	**0**	**0**	**0**
	Salt Lake	CHL	43	7	21	28	54	5	0	3	3	2
1984-85	**Minnesota**	**NHL**	**52**	**4**	**9**	**13**	**26**	**9**	**2**	**3**	**5**	**8**
	Springfield	AHL	26	2	7	9	22	....	....	....	....	....
1985-86	**New Jersey**	**NHL**	**47**	**2**	**7**	**9**	**39**	....	....	....	....	....
	Maine	AHL	21	0	4	4	4	....	....	....	....	....
1986-87	**New Jersey**	**NHL**	**64**	**2**	**16**	**18**	**52**	....	....	....	....	....
1987-88	**New Jersey**	**NHL**	**51**	**3**	**9**	**12**	**66**	**19**	**0**	**2**	**2**	**20**
1988-89	**New Jersey**	**NHL**	**80**	**4**	**14**	**18**	**70**	....	....	....	....	....
1989-90	**New Jersey**	**NHL**	**62**	**0**	**6**	**6**	**72**	**6**	**0**	**0**	**0**	**4**
1990-91	**Quebec**	**NHL**	**79**	**2**	**10**	**12**	**42**	....	....	....	....	....
	NHL Totals		**471**	**19**	**73**	**92**	**379**	**44**	**2**	**5**	**7**	**32**

a ECAC Second All-Star Team (1982)
b ECAC First All-Star Team (1983)
c Named ECAC Player of the Year (1983)

Claimed by **New Jersey** from **Minnesota** in NHL Waiver Draft, October 7, 1985. Traded to **Quebec** by **New Jersey** as future considerations with Craig Wolanin to complete March 6, 1990 Peter Stastny deal, August 13, 1990.

VENKUS, CHRISTOPHER (CHRIS)

Right wing. Shoots right. 5'11", 190 lbs. Born, Hinsdale, IL, April 14, 1969.
(Washington's 13th choice, 225th overall, in 1988 Entry Draft).

			Regular Season					Playoffs				
Season	Club	Lea	GP	G	A	TP	PIM	GP	G	A	TP	PIM
1987-88	W. Michigan	CCHA	42	8	9	17	76	....	....	....	....	....
1988-89	W. Michigan	CCHA	42	2	11	13	66	....	....	....	....	....
1989-90			DID NOT PLAY									
1990-91	Colorado	WCHA	5	0	1	1	2	....	....	....	....	....

VERBEEK, PATRICK (PAT)   (vuhr-BEEK)

Right wing/Left wing. Shoots right. 5'9", 190 lbs.   Born, Sarnia, Ont., May 24, 1964.
(New Jersey's 3rd choice, 43rd overall, in 1982 Entry Draft).

				Regular Season					Playoffs			
Season	Club	Lea	GP	G	A	TP	PIM	GP	G	A	TP	PIM
1981-82	Sudbury	OHL	66	37	51	88	180	....	....	....	....	....
1982-83	**New Jersey**	**NHL**	**6**	**3**	**2**	**5**	**8**	....	....	....	....	....
	Sudbury	OHL	61	40	67	107	184	....	....	....	....	....
1983-84	**New Jersey**	**NHL**	**79**	**20**	**27**	**47**	**158**	....	....	....	....	....
1984-85	**New Jersey**	**NHL**	**78**	**15**	**18**	**33**	**162**	....	....	....	....	....
1985-86	**New Jersey**	**NHL**	**76**	**25**	**28**	**53**	**79**	....	....	....	....	....
1986-87	**New Jersey**	**NHL**	**74**	**35**	**24**	**59**	**120**	....	....	....	....	....
1987-88	**New Jersey**	**NHL**	**73**	**46**	**31**	**77**	**227**	**20**	**4**	**8**	**12**	**51**
1988-89	**New Jersey**	**NHL**	**77**	**26**	**21**	**47**	**189**	....	....	....	....	....
1989-90	**Hartford**	**NHL**	**80**	**44**	**45**	**89**	**228**	**7**	**2**	**2**	**4**	**26**
1990-91	**Hartford**	**NHL**	**80**	**43**	**39**	**82**	**246**	**6**	**3**	**2**	**5**	**40**
	NHL Totals		**623**	**257**	**235**	**492**	**1417**	**33**	**9**	**12**	**21**	**117**

Played in NHL All-Star Game (1991)
Traded to **Hartford** by **New Jersey** for Sylvain Turgeon, June 17, 1989.

VERMETTE, MARK

Right wing. Shoots right. 6'1", 203 lbs.   Born, Cochenour, Ont., October 3, 1967.
(Quebec's 8th choice, 134th overall, in 1986 Entry Draft).

				Regular Season					Playoffs			
Season	Club	Lea	GP	G	A	TP	PIM	GP	G	A	TP	PIM
1985-86	Lake Superior	CCHA	32	1	4	5	7	....	....	....	....	....
1986-87	Lake Superior	CCHA	38	19	17	36	59	....	....	....	....	....
1987-88abc	Lake Superior	CCHA	46	*45	30	75	154	....	....	....	....	....
1988-89	**Quebec**	**NHL**	**12**	**0**	**4**	**4**	**7**	....	....	....	....	....
	Halifax	AHL	52	12	16	28	30	1	0	0	0	0
1989-90	**Quebec**	**NHL**	**11**	**1**	**5**	**6**	**8**	....	....	....	....	....
	Halifax	AHL	47	20	17	37	44	6	1	5	6	6
1990-91	**Quebec**	**NHL**	**34**	**3**	**4**	**7**	**10**	....	....	....	....	....
	Halifax	AHL	46	26	22	48	37	....	....	....	....	....
	NHL Totals		**57**	**4**	**13**	**17**	**25**	....	....	....	....	....

a NCAA West All-American Team (1988)
b CCHA Player of the Year (1988)
c CCHA First All-Star Team (1988)

VESEY, JIM

Center/Right wing. Shoots right. 6'1", 202 lbs..   Born, Columbus, MA, October 29, 1965.
(St. Louis' 11th choice, 155th overall, in 1984 Entry Draft).

				Regular Season					Playoffs			
Season	Club	Lea	GP	G	A	TP	PIM	GP	G	A	TP	PIM
1984-85	Merrimack	NCAA	33	19	11	30	28	....	....	....	....	....
1985-86	Merrimack	NCAA	32	29	32	61	67	....	....	....	....	....
1986-87	Merrimack	NCAA	35	22	36	58	57	....	....	....	....	....
1987-88	Merrimack	NCAA	33	33	50	83	....	....	....	....	....	....
1988-89	**St. Louis**	**NHL**	**5**	**1**	**1**	**2**	**7**	....	....	....	....	....
a	Peoria	IHL	76	47	46	93	137	4	1	2	3	6
1989-90	**St. Louis**	**NHL**	**6**	**0**	**1**	**1**	**0**	....	....	....	....	....
	Peoria	IHL	60	47	44	91	75	5	1	3	4	21
1990-91	Peoria	IHL	58	32	41	73	69	19	4	14	18	26
	NHL Totals		**11**	**1**	**2**	**3**	**7**	....	....	....	....	....

a IHL First All-Star Team (1989)

Traded to **Winnipeg** by **St. Louis** (future consideration in trade which sent Tom Draper to St. Louis on February 28, 1991) May 24, 1991. Traded to **Boston** by **Winnipeg** for future considerations, June 20, 1991.

VIAL, DENNIS   (vee-AHL)

Defense. Shoots left. 6'1", 215 lbs.   Born, Sault Ste. Marie, Ont., April 10, 1969.
(NY Rangers' 5th choice, 110th overall, in 1988 Entry Draft).

				Regular Season					Playoffs			
Season	Club	Lea	GP	G	A	TP	PIM	GP	G	A	TP	PIM
1985-86	Hamilton	OHL	31	1	1	2	66	....	....	....	....	....
1986-87	Hamilton	OHL	53	1	8	9	194	8	0	0	0	8
1987-88	Hamilton	OHL	52	3	17	20	229	13	2	2	4	49
1988-89	Niagara Falls	OHL	50	10	27	37	227	15	1	7	8	44
1989-90	Flint	IHL	79	6	29	35	351	4	0	0	0	10
1990-91	**NY Rangers**	**NHL**	**21**	**0**	**0**	**0**	**61**	....	....	....	....	....
	Binghamton	AHL	40	2	7	9	250	....	....	....	....	....
	Detroit	**NHL**	**9**	**0**	**0**	**0**	**16**	....	....	....	....	....
	NHL Totals		**30**	**0**	**0**	**0**	**77**	....	....	....	....	....

Traded to **Detroit** by **NY Rangers** with Kevin Miller and Jim Cummins for Joey Kocur and Per Djoos, March 5, 1991.

VICHOREK, MARK   (vuh-CHORE-ik)

Defense. Shoots right. 6'3", 200 lbs.   Born, Moose Lake, MN, August 11, 1966.
(Philadelphia's 12th choice, 245th overall, in 1982 Entry Draft).

				Regular Season					Playoffs			
Season	Club	Lea	GP	G	A	TP	PIM	GP	G	A	TP	PIM
1982-83	Lake Superior	CCHA	36	2	13	15	24	....	....	....	....	....
1983-84	Lake Superior	CCHA	40	3	8	11	14	....	....	....	....	....
1984-85	Lake Superior	CCHA	44	4	11	15	36	....	....	....	....	....
1985-86	Lake Superior	CCHA	41	9	11	20	40	....	....	....	....	....
1986-87	Binghamton	AHL	64	1	12	13	63	....	....	....	....	....
	Salt Lake	IHL	16	1	0	1	32	17	0	8	8	23
1987-88	Binghamton	AHL	26	0	4	4	48	....	....	....	....	....
	Milwaukee	IHL	49	4	5	9	67	....	....	....	....	....
1988-89	New Haven	AHL	23	1	5	6	26	17	2	4	6	57
	Flint	IHL	44	4	9	13	47	....	....	....	....	....
1989-90	Phoenix	IHL	29	2	8	10	57	....	....	....	....	....
	Fort Wayne	IHL	31	2	4	6	30	5	0	1	1	19
1990-91	Kansas City	IHL	10	0	1	1	4	....	....	....	....	....
	San Diego	IHL	14	1	4	5	20	....	....	....	....	....
	Nashville	ECHL	36	6	29	35	70	....	....	....	....	....

VILGRAIN, CLAUDE

Right wing. Shoots right. 6'1", 205 lbs.   Born, Port-au-Prince, Haiti, March 1, 1963.
(Detroit's 6th choice, 107th overall, in 1982 Entry Draft).

				Regular Season					Playoffs			
Season	Club	Lea	GP	G	A	TP	PIM	GP	G	A	TP	PIM
1983-84	U. of Moncton	AUAA	20	11	20	31	8	....	....	....	....	....
1984-85	U. of Moncton	AUAA	24	35	28	63	20	....	....	....	....	....
1985-86	U. of Moncton	AUAA	19	17	20	37	25	....	....	....	....	....
1986-87	Cdn. Olympic	...	78	28	42	70	38	....	....	....	....	....
1987-88	Cdn. Olympic	...	6	0	0	0	0	....	....	....	....	....
	Cdn. National	...	61	21	20	41	41	....	....	....	....	....
	Vancouver	**NHL**	**6**	**1**	**1**	**2**	**0**	....	....	....	....	....
1988-89	Milwaukee	IHL	23	9	13	22	26	....	....	....	....	....
	Utica	AHL	55	23	30	53	41	5	0	2	2	2
1989-90	**New Jersey**	**NHL**	**6**	**1**	**2**	**3**	**4**	**4**	**0**	**0**	**0**	**0**
	Utica	AHL	73	37	52	89	32	....	....	....	....	....
1990-91	Utica	AHL	59	32	46	78	26	....	....	....	....	....
	NHL Totals		**12**	**2**	**3**	**5**	**4**	**4**	**0**	**0**	**0**	**0**

Signed as a free agent by **Vancouver**, June 18, 1987. Traded to **New Jersey** by **Vancouver** for Tim Lenardon, March 7, 1989.

VINCELETTE, DANIEL

Left wing. Shoots left. 6'2", 202 lbs.   Born, Verdun, Que., August 1, 1967.
(Chicago's 3rd choice, 74th overall, in 1985 Entry Draft).

				Regular Season					Playoffs			
Season	Club	Lea	GP	G	A	TP	PIM	GP	G	A	TP	PIM
1984-85	Drummondville	QMJHL	64	11	24	35	124	12	0	1	1	11
1985-86	Drummondville	QMJHL	70	37	47	84	234	22	11	14	25	40
1986-87	Drummondville	QMJHL	50	34	35	69	288	8	6	5	11	17
	Chicago	**NHL**						**3**	**0**	**0**	**0**	**0**
1987-88	**Chicago**	**NHL**	**69**	**6**	**11**	**17**	**109**	**4**	**0**	**0**	**0**	**0**
1988-89	**Chicago**	**NHL**	**66**	**11**	**4**	**15**	**119**	**5**	**0**	**0**	**0**	**4**
	Saginaw	IHL	2	0	0	0	14	....	....	....	....	....
1989-90	**Chicago**	**NHL**	**2**	**0**	**0**	**0**	**4**	....	....	....	....	....
	Indianapolis	IHL	49	16	13	29	262	....	....	....	....	....
	Quebec	**NHL**	**11**	**0**	**1**	**1**	**25**	....	....	....	....	....
1990-91	Halifax	AHL	24	4	9	13	85	....	....	....	....	....
	Indianapolis	IHL	15	5	3	8	51	7	2	1	3	62
	NHL Totals		**148**	**17**	**16**	**33**	**257**	**12**	**0**	**0**	**0**	**4**

Traded to **Quebec** by **Chicago** with Mario Doyon and Everett Sanipass for Greg Millen, Michel Goulet and Quebec's sixth round choice (Kevin St. Jacques) in 1991 Entry Draft, March 5, 1990. Traded to **Chicago** by **Quebec** with Paul Gillis for Ryan McGill and Mike McNeil, March 5, 1991.

VIRTA, HANNU   (VIR-ta, HAN-oo)

Defense. Shoots left. 5'11", 180 lbs.   Born, Turku, Finland, March 22, 1963.
(Buffalo's 2nd choice, 38th overall, in 1981 Entry Draft).

				Regular Season					Playoffs			
Season	Club	Lea	GP	G	A	TP	PIM	GP	G	A	TP	PIM
1980-81a	TPS	Fin.	1	0	1	1	0	4	0	1	1	4
1981-82b	TPS	Fin.	36	5	12	17	6	7	1	1	2	2
	Buffalo	**NHL**	**3**	**0**	**1**	**1**	**4**	**4**	**0**	**1**	**1**	**0**
1982-83	**Buffalo**	**NHL**	**74**	**13**	**24**	**37**	**18**	**10**	**1**	**2**	**3**	**4**
1983-84	**Buffalo**	**NHL**	**70**	**6**	**30**	**36**	**12**	**3**	**0**	**0**	**0**	**2**
1984-85	**Buffalo**	**NHL**	**51**	**1**	**23**	**24**	**16**	....	....	....	....	....
1985-86	**Buffalo**	**NHL**	**47**	**5**	**23**	**28**	**16**	....	....	....	....	....
1986-87c	TPS	Fin.	41	13	30	43	20	5	0	3	3	2
1987-88	TPS	Fin.	44	10	28	38	20	....	....	....	....	....
1988-89	TPS	Fin.	43	7	25	32	30	10	1	7	8	0
1989-90	TPS	Fin.	41	7	19	26	14	9	0	6	6	10
1990-91	TPS	Fin.	43	4	16	20	40	9	4	2	6	4
	NHL Totals		**245**	**25**	**101**	**126**	**66**	**26**	**5**	**5**	**10**	**10**

a Named to All-Star Team, 1981 European Junior Championships
b Named Rookie of the Year in Finnish National League (1982)
c Finnish League First All-Star Team (1987)

VITOLINSH, HARIJS   (VEE-toh-leensh)

Center. Shoots left. 6'3", 205 lbs.   Born, Riga, Soviet Union, April 30, 1968.
(Montreal's 10th choice, 188th overall, in 1988 Entry Draft).

				Regular Season					Playoffs			
Season	Club	Lea	GP	G	A	TP	PIM	GP	G	A	TP	PIM
1987-88	Dynamo Riga	USSR	30	3	3	6	27	....	....	....	....	....
1988-89	Dynamo Riga	USSR	36	3	2	5	16	....	....	....	....	....
1989-90	Dynamo Riga	USSR	45	7	6	13	18	....	....	....	....	....
1990-91	Dynamo Riga	USSR	46	12	19	31	22	....	....	....	....	....

VIVEIROS, EMANUEL   (VEE-VEH-ROHZ)

Defense. Shoots left. 6', 175 lbs.   Born, St. Albert, Alta., January 8, 1966.
(Edmonton's 6th choice, 106th overall, in 1984 Entry Draft).

				Regular Season					Playoffs			
Season	Club	Lea	GP	G	A	TP	PIM	GP	G	A	TP	PIM
1982-83	Prince Albert	WHL	59	6	26	32	55	....	....	....	....	....
1983-84	Prince Albert	WHL	67	15	94	109	48	2	0	3	3	6
1984-85a	Prince Albert	WHL	68	17	71	88	94	13	2	9	11	14
1985-86	**Minnesota**	**NHL**	**4**	**0**	**1**	**1**	**0**	....	....	....	....	....
bc	Prince Albert	WHL	57	22	70	92	30	20	4	24	28	4
1986-87	**Minnesota**	**NHL**	**1**	**0**	**1**	**1**	**0**	....	....	....	....	....
	Springfield	AHL	76	7	35	42	38	....	....	....	....	....
1987-88	**Minnesota**	**NHL**	**24**	**1**	**9**	**10**	**6**	....	....	....	....	....
	Kalamazoo	IHL	57	15	48	63	41	....	....	....	....	....
1988-89	Kalamazoo	IHL	54	11	29	40	37	....	....	....	....	....
1989-90	Kaufberer	W.Ger.	8	2	7	9	8	....	....	....	....	....
1990-91	Springfield	AHL	48	2	22	24	29	7	0	2	2	4
	NHL Totals		**29**	**1**	**11**	**12**	**6**	....	....	....	....	....

a WHL Second All-Star Team, East Division (1985)
b WHL East All-Star Team (1986)
c WHL Player of the Year (1986)

Traded to **Minnesota** by **Edmonton** with Marc Habscheid, Don Barber for Gord Sherven and Don Biggs, December 20, 1985. Signed as a free agent by **Hartford**, February 9, 1990.

VLACH, ROSTISLAV (VLAHH)

Center/left wing. Shoots left. 6', 170 lbs.   Born, Gottwaldov, Czech., July 3, 1962.
(Los Angeles' 9th choice, 216th overall, in 1987 Entry Draft).

			Regular Season					Playoffs				
Season	Club	Lea	GP	G	A	TP	PIM	GP	G	A	TP	PIM
1987-88	TJ Gottwaldov	Czech.	30	15	14	29	4	....	....	....	....	....
1988-89	TJ Gottwaldov	Czech.	41	20	18	38	83	....	....	....	....	....
1989-90	TJ Zlin	Czech.	51	16	24	40		....	....	....	....	....
1990-91	JoKP	Fin.	44	33	48	81	83	....	....	....	....	....

VLK, PETR (VULK)

Left wing. Shoots left. 6', 180 lbs.   Born, Havlickuv Brod, Czechoslovakia, January 7, 1964.
(NY Islanders' 5th choice, 97th overall, in 1987 Entry Draft).

			Regular Season					Playoffs				
Season	Club	Lea	GP	G	A	TP	PIM	GP	G	A	TP	PIM
1987-88	Dukla Jihlava	Czech.	18	6	3	9	....					
1988-89	Dukla Jihlava	Czech.	33	11	8	19	66					
1989-90	Dukla Jihlava	Czech.	48	19	21	40	....					
1990-91	Dukla Jihlava	Czech.	50	18	24	42	48					

VOLEK, DAVID (VAH-lehk)

Left/Right wing. Shoots left. 6', 185 lbs.   Born, Prague, Czechoslovakia, June 18, 1966.
(NY Islanders' 11th choice, 208th overall, in 1984 Entry Draft).

			Regular Season					Playoffs				
Season	Club	Lea	GP	G	A	TP	PIM	GP	G	A	TP	PIM
1986-87	Sparta Praha	Czech.	39	27	25	52		....	....	....	....	....
1987-88	Sparta Praha	Czech.	30	18	12	30		....	....	....	....	....
1988-89a	NY Islanders	NHL	77	25	34	59	24	....	....	....	....	....
1989-90	NY Islanders	NHL	80	17	22	39	41	5	1	4	5	0
1990-91	NY Islanders	NHL	77	22	34	56	57	....	....	....	....	....
	NHL Totals		234	64	90	154	122	5	1	4	5	0

a NHL All-Rookie Team (1989)

VOLHOFFER, TROY

Right wing. Shoots right. 5'11", 180 lbs.   Born, Regina, Sask., February 9, 1966.

			Regular Season					Playoffs				
Season	Club	Lea	GP	G	A	TP	PIM	GP	G	A	TP	PIM
1983-84	Winnipeg	WHL	66	22	37	59	92	....	....	....	....	....
1984-85	Saskatoon	WHL	62	21	31	52	82	....	....	....	....	....
1985-86	Saskatoon	WHL	72	55	55	110	118	13	8	10	18	20
1986-87	Baltimore	AHL	67	11	25	36	90	....	....	....	....	....
1987-88	New Haven	AHL	18	2	6	8	30	....	....	....	....	....
	Muskegon	IHL	33	4	13	17	54	....	....	....	....	....
1988-89	Flint	IHL	63	6	23	29	186	....	....	....	....	....
	Muskegon	IHL	2	0	0	0	9	....	....	....	....	....
1989-90	Winston-Salem	ECHL	46	26	40	66	157	9	8	6	14	23
1990-91	Winston-Salem	ECHL	64	37	42	79	112	....	....	....	....	....

Signed as a free agent by **Pittsburgh**, December 9, 1986.

VON STEFENELLI, PHILIP

Defense. Shoots left. 6'1", 195 lbs.   Born, Vancouver, B.C., April 10, 1969.
(Vancouver's 5th choice, 122nd overall, in 1988 Entry Draft).

			Regular Season					Playoffs				
Season	Club	Lea	GP	G	A	TP	PIM	GP	G	A	TP	PIM
1987-88	Boston U.	H.E.	34	3	13	16	38	....	....	....	....	....
1988-89	Boston U.	H.E.	33	2	6	8	34	....	....	....	....	....
1989-90	Boston U.	H.E.	44	8	20	28	40	....	....	....	....	....
1990-91	Boston U.	H.E.	41	7	23	30	32	....	....	....	....	....

VUKONICH, MICHAEL

Center. Shoots left. 6'1", 190 lbs.   Born, Duluth, MN, May 11, 1968.
(Los Angeles' 4th choice, 90th overall, in 1987 Entry Draft).

			Regular Season					Playoffs				
Season	Club	Lea	GP	G	A	TP	PIM	GP	G	A	TP	PIM
1987-88	Harvard	ECAC	32	9	14	23	24	....	....	....	....	....
1988-89	Harvard	ECAC	27	11	8	19	12	....	....	....	....	....
1989-90a	Harvard	ECAC	27	22	29	51	18	....	....	....	....	....
1990-91b	Harvard	ECAC	27	31	23	54	28	....	....	....	....	....

a ECAC First All-Star Team (1990)
b ECAC Second All-Star Team (1991)

VUKOTA, MICK

Right wing. Shoots right. 6'2", 195 lbs.   Born, Saskatoon, Sask., September 14, 1966.

			Regular Season					Playoffs				
Season	Club	Lea	GP	G	A	TP	PIM	GP	G	A	TP	PIM
1983-84	Winnipeg	WHL	3	1	1	2	10	....	....	....	....	....
1984-85	Kelowna	WHL	66	10	6	16	247	....	....	....	....	....
1985-86	Spokane	WHL	64	19	14	33	369	9	6	4	10	68
1986-87	Spokane	WHL	61	25	28	53	*337	4	0	0	0	40
1987-88	NY Islanders	NHL	17	1	0	1	82	2	0	0	0	23
	Springfield	AHL	52	7	9	16	375	....	....	....	....	....
1988-89	NY Islanders	NHL	48	2	2	4	237	....	....	....	....	....
	Springfield	AHL	3	1	0	1	33	....	....	....	....	....
1989-90	NY Islanders	NHL	76	4	8	12	290	1	0	0	0	17
1990-91	NY Islanders	NHL	60	2	4	6	238	....	....	....	....	....
	Capital Dist.	AHL	2	0	0	0	9	....	....	....	....	....
	NHL Totals		201	9	14	23	847	3	0	0	0	40

Signed as a free agent by **NY Islanders**, March 2, 1987.

VYAZMIKIN, IGOR (VYAZ-MEE-kin)

Right wing/Left wing. Shoots left. 6'1", 194 lbs.   Born, Moscow, Soviet Union, Jan. 8, 1966.
(Edmonton's 13th choice, 252nd overall, in 1987 Entry Draft).

			Regular Season					Playoffs				
Season	Club	Lea	GP	G	A	TP	PIM	GP	G	A	TP	PIM
1983-84	CSKA	USSR	38	8	12	20	4	....	....	....	....	....
1984-85	CSKA	USSR	26	6	5	11	6	....	....	....	....	....
1985-86	CSKA	USSR	19	7	6	13	6	....	....	....	....	....
1986-87	CSKA	USSR	4	0	0	0	0	....	....	....	....	....
1987-88	CSKA	USSR	8	1	0	1	16	....	....	....	....	....
1988-89	CSKA	USSR	30	10	7	17	20	....	....	....	....	....
1989-90	Khimik	USSR	34	11	13	24	26	....	....	....	....	....
1990-91	Khimik	USSR	23	7	12	19	17	....	....	....	....	....
	Edmonton	NHL	4	1	0	1	0	....	....	....	....	....
	Cape Breton	AHL	33	12	19	31	21	4	3	2	5	10
	NHL Totals		4	1	0	1	0					

VYKOUKAL, JIRI (Vee-KOH-uh-kahl)

Defense. Shoots right. 5'11", 176 lbs.   Born, Olomouc, Czechoslovakia, March 11, 1971.
(Washington's 9th choice, 208th overall, in 1989 Entry Draft).

			Regular Season					Playoffs				
Season	Club	Lea	GP	G	A	TP	PIM	GP	G	A	TP	PIM
1989-90	Sparta Praha	Czech.	47	5	12	17		....	....	....	....	....
1990-91	Baltimore	AHL	60	4	22	26	41	....	....	....	....	....

WAHLSTEN, SAMI (VAHL-stuhn)

Left wing. Shoots left. 6', 185 lbs.   Born, Turku, Finland, November 25, 1967.
(Philadelphia's 6th choice, 146th overall, in 1986 Entry Draft).

			Regular Season					Playoffs				
Season	Club	Lea	GP	G	A	TP	PIM	GP	G	A	TP	PIM
1987-88	TPS	Fin.	43	11	8	19	23	....	....	....	....	....
1988-89	Jokerit	Fin.	44	27	30	57	24	5	1	1	2	0
1989-90	Jokerit	Fin.	44	21	15	36	15	....	....	....	....	....
1990-91	Jokerit	Fin.	44	10	11	21	24	....	....	....	....	....

WALKER, GORD

Right wing. Shoots left. 6', 175 lbs.   Born, Castlegar, B.C., August 12, 1965.
(New York Rangers' 4th choice, 53rd overall, in 1983 Entry Draft).

			Regular Season					Playoffs				
Season	Club	Lea	GP	G	A	TP	PIM	GP	G	A	TP	PIM
1982-83	Portland	WHL	66	24	30	54	95	14	5	8	13	12
1983-84	Portland	WHL	58	28	41	69	65	14	8	11	19	18
1984-85a	Kamloops	WHL	66	67	67	134	76	15	*13	14	27	34
1985-86	New Haven	AHL	46	11	28	39	66	....	....	....	....	....
1986-87	NY Rangers	NHL	1	1	0	1	4	....	....	....	....	....
	New Haven	AHL	59	24	20	44	58	7	3	2	5	0
1987-88	NY Rangers	NHL	18	1	4	5	17	....	....	....	....	....
	New Haven	AHL	14	10	9	19	17	....	....	....	....	....
	Colorado	IHL	16	4	9	13	4	....	....	....	....	....
1988-89	Los Angeles	NHL	11	1	0	1	2	....	....	....	....	....
	New Haven	AHL	60	21	25	46	50	17	7	8	15	23
1989-90	Los Angeles	NHL	1	0	0	0	0	....	....	....	....	....
1989-90	New Haven	AHL	24	14	7	21	8	....	....	....	....	....
1990-91	San Diego	IHL	22	3	7	10	24	....	....	....	....	....
	NHL Totals		31	3	4	7	23					

a WHL First All-Star Team (1985)

Traded to **Los Angeles** by **NY Rangers** with Mike Siltala for Joe Paterson, January 21, 1988.

WALLWORK, ROBERT

Center. Shoots left. 5'11", 180 lbs.   Born, Boston, Mass., March, 15, 1968.
(Buffalo's 12th choice, 244th overall, in 1988 Entry Draft).

			Regular Season					Playoffs				
Season	Club	Lea	GP	G	A	TP	PIM	GP	G	A	TP	PIM
1987-88	Miami-Ohio	CCHA	36	6	24	30	59	....	....	....	....	....
1988-89	Miami-Ohio	CCHA	19	1	8	9	30	....	....	....	....	....
1989-90	Miami-Ohio	CCHA	40	12	30	42	60	....	....	....	....	....
1990-91	Miami-Ohio	CCHA	20	3	7	10	30	....	....	....	....	....
	Cincinnati	ECHL	18	7	11	18	18	2	0	0	0	0

WALSH, MIKE

Left wing. Shoots right. 6'2", 195 lbs.   Born, New York, NY, April 3, 1962.

			Regular Season					Playoffs				
Season	Club	Lea	GP	G	A	TP	PIM	GP	G	A	TP	PIM
1980-81	Colgate	ECAC	35	10	15	25	62	....	....	....	....	....
1981-82	Colgate	ECAC	26	2	7	9	42	....	....	....	....	....
1982-83	Colgate	ECAC	24	9	14	23	36	....	....	....	....	....
1983-84	Colgate	ECAC	35	16	17	33	94	....	....	....	....	....
1984-85			DID NOT PLAY									
1985-86	Malmo	Swe.	42	52	27	79		....	....	....	....	....
1986-87	Springfield	AHL	67	20	26	46	32	....	....	....	....	....
1987-88	NY Islanders	NHL	1	0	0	0	0	....	....	....	....	....
	Springfield	AHL	77	27	23	50	48	....	....	....	....	....
1988-89	NY Islanders	NHL	13	2	0	2	4	....	....	....	....	....
	Springfield	AHL	68	31	34	65	73	....	....	....	....	....
1989-90	Springfield	AHL	69	34	20	54	43	8	2	2	4	10
1990-91	Cortina	Italy	36	15	21	36	49	6	7	4	11	19
	NHL Totals		14	2	0	2	4					

Signed as a free agent by **NY Islanders**, August, 1986.

WALTER, RYAN WILLIAM

Center/Left wing. Shoots left. 6', 200 lbs. Born, New Westminster, B.C., April 23, 1958.
(Washington's 1st choice, 2nd overall, in 1978 Amateur Draft).

			Regular Season					Playoffs				
Season	Club	Lea	GP	G	A	TP	PIM	GP	G	A	TP	PIM
1974-75	Kamloops	WHL	9	8	4	12	2	2	1	1	2	2
1975-76	Kamloops	WHL	72	35	49	84	96	12	3	9	12	10
1976-77	Kamloops	WHL	71	41	58	99	100	5	1	3	4	11
1977-78abc	Seattle	WHL	62	54	71	125	148	....	....	....	....	....
1978-79	**Washington**	**NHL**	**69**	**28**	**28**	**56**	**70**	....	....	....	....	....
1979-80	**Washington**	**NHL**	**80**	**24**	**42**	**66**	**106**	....	....	....	....	....
1980-81	**Washington**	**NHL**	**80**	**24**	**44**	**68**	**150**	....	....	....	....	....
1981-82	**Washington**	**NHL**	**78**	**38**	**49**	**87**	**142**	....	....	....	....	....
1982-83	**Montreal**	**NHL**	**80**	**29**	**46**	**75**	**40**	**3**	**0**	**0**	**0**	**11**
1983-84	**Montreal**	**NHL**	**73**	**20**	**29**	**49**	**83**	**15**	**2**	**1**	**3**	**4**
1984-85	**Montreal**	**NHL**	**72**	**19**	**19**	**38**	**59**	**12**	**2**	**7**	**9**	**13**
1985-86	**Montreal**	**NHL**	**69**	**15**	**34**	**49**	**45**	**5**	**0**	**1**	**1**	**2**
1986-87	**Montreal**	**NHL**	**76**	**23**	**23**	**46**	**34**	**17**	**7**	**12**	**19**	**10**
1987-88	**Montreal**	**NHL**	**61**	**13**	**23**	**36**	**39**	**11**	**2**	**4**	**6**	**6**
1988-89	**Montreal**	**NHL**	**78**	**14**	**17**	**31**	**48**	**21**	**3**	**5**	**8**	**6**
1989-90	**Montreal**	**NHL**	**70**	**8**	**16**	**24**	**59**	**11**	**0**	**2**	**2**	**0**
1990-91	**Montreal**	**NHL**	**25**	**0**	**1**	**1**	**12**	**5**	**0**	**0**	**0**	**2**
	NHL Totals		**911**	**255**	**371**	**626**	**887**	**100**	**16**	**32**	**48**	**54**

a WHL Most Valuable Player (1978)
b WHL Player of the Year (1978)
c WHL First All-Star Team (1978)

Played in NHL All-Star Game (1983)

Traded to **Montreal** by **Washington** with Rick Green for Rod Langway, Brian Engblom, Doug Jarvis and Craig Laughlin, September 9, 1982. Signed as a free agent by **Vancouver**, July 26, 1991.

WALTERS, GREG

Center. Shoots right. 6'1", 195 lbs. Born, Calgary, Alta., August 12, 1970.
(Toronto's 4th choice, 80th overall, in 1990 Entry Draft).

			Regular Season					Playoffs				
Season	Club	Lea	GP	G	A	TP	PIM	GP	G	A	TP	PIM
1989-90	Ottawa	OHL	63	36	54	90	57	....	....	....	....	....
1990-91	Newmarket	AHL	54	7	14	21	58	....	....	....	....	....

WALZ, WES

Center. Shoots right. 5'10", 180 lbs. Born, Calgary, Alta., May 15, 1970.
(Boston's 3rd choice, 57th overall, in 1989 Entry Draft).

			Regular Season					Playoffs				
Season	Club	Lea	GP	G	A	TP	PIM	GP	G	A	TP	PIM
1988-89a	Lethbridge	WHL	63	29	75	104	32	8	1	5	6	6
1989-90	**Boston**	**NHL**	**2**	**1**	**1**	**2**	**0**	....	....	....	....	....
b	Lethbridge	WHL	56	54	86	140	69	19	13	*24	*37	33
1990-91	**Boston**	**NHL**	**56**	**8**	**8**	**16**	**32**	**2**	**0**	**0**	**0**	**0**
	Maine	AHL	20	8	12	20	19	2	0	0	0	21
	NHL Totals		**58**	**9**	**9**	**18**	**32**	**2**	**0**	**0**	**0**	**0**

a WHL Rookie of the Year (1989)
b WHL East First All-Star Team (1990)

WARD, AARON

Defense. Shoots right. 6'2", 200 lbs. Born, Windsor, Ont., January 17, 1973.
(Winnipeg's 1st choice, 5th overall, in 1991 Entry Draft).

			Regular Season					Playoffs				
Season	Club	Lea	GP	G	A	TP	PIM	GP	G	A	TP	PIM
1989-90	Nepean	Midget	52	6	33	39	85	....	....	....	....	....
1990-91	U. of Michgan	CCHA	46	8	11	19	126	....	....	....	....	....

WARD, DIXON

Right wing. Shoots right. 6'0", 195 lbs. Born, Leduc, Alta., September 23, 1968.
(Vancouver's 6th choice, 128th overall, in 1988 Entry Draft).

			Regular Season					Playoffs				
Season	Club	Lea	GP	G	A	TP	PIM	GP	G	A	TP	PIM
1988-89	North Dakota	WCHA	37	8	9	17	26	....	....	....	....	....
1989-90	North Dakota	WCHA	45	35	34	69	44	....	....	....	....	....
1990-91a	North Dakota	WCHA	43	34	35	69	84	....	....	....	....	....

a WCHA Second All-Star Team (1991)

WARD, EDWARD

Right wing. Shoots right. 6'3", 190 lbs. Born, Edmonton, Alta., November 10, 1969.
(Quebec's 7th choice, 108th overall, in 1988 Entry Draft).

			Regular Season					Playoffs				
Season	Club	Lea	GP	G	A	TP	PIM	GP	G	A	TP	PIM
1987-88	N. Michigan	WCHA	25	0	2	2	40	....	....	....	....	....
1988-89	N. Michigan	WCHA	42	5	15	20	36	....	....	....	....	....
1989-90	N. Michigan	WCHA	39	5	11	16	77	....	....	....	....	....
1990-91	N. Michigan	WCHA	46	13	18	31	109	....	....	....	....	....

WARE, MICHAEL

Right wing. Shoots right. 6'5", 216 lbs. Born, York, Ont., March 22, 1967.
(Edmonton's 3rd choice, 62nd overall, in 1985 Entry Draft).

			Regular Season					Playoffs				
Season	Club	Lea	GP	G	A	TP	PIM	GP	G	A	TP	PIM
1984-85	Hamilton	OHL	57	4	14	18	225	12	0	1	1	29
1985-86	Hamilton	OHL	44	8	11	19	155	....	....	....	....	....
1986-87	Cornwall	OHL	50	5	19	24	173	5	0	1	1	10
1987-88	Nova Scotia	AHL	52	0	8	8	253	3	0	0	0	16
1988-89	**Edmonton**	**NHL**	**2**	**0**	**1**	**1**	**11**	....	....	....	....	....
	Cape Breton	AHL	48	1	11	12	317	....	....	....	....	....
1989-90	**Edmonton**	**NHL**	**3**	**0**	**0**	**0**	**4**	....	....	....	....	....
	Cape Breton	AHL	54	6	13	19	191	6	0	3	3	29
1990-91	Cape Breton	AHL	43	4	8	12	176	3	0	0	0	4
	NHL Totals		**5**	**0**	**1**	**1**	**15**	....	....	....	....	....

WATTERS, TIMOTHY J. (TIM)

Defense. Shoots left. 5'11", 185 lbs. Born, Kamloops, B.C., July 25, 1959.
(Winnipeg's 6th choice, 124th overall, in 1979 Entry Draft).

			Regular Season					Playoffs				
Season	Club	Lea	GP	G	A	TP	PIM	GP	G	A	TP	PIM
1978-79	Michigan Tech	WCHA	38	6	21	27	48	....	....	....	....	....
1979-80	Cdn. National	...	56	8	21	29	43	....	....	....	....	....
	Cdn. Olympic	...	6	1	1	2	0	....	....	....	....	....
1980-81ab	Michigan Tech	WCHA	43	12	38	50	36	....	....	....	....	....
1981-82	Tulsa	CHL	5	1	2	3	0	....	....	....	....	....
	Winnipeg	**NHL**	**69**	**2**	**22**	**24**	**97**	**4**	**0**	**1**	**1**	**8**
1982-83	**Winnipeg**	**NHL**	**77**	**5**	**18**	**23**	**98**	**3**	**0**	**0**	**0**	**2**
1983-84	**Winnipeg**	**NHL**	**74**	**3**	**20**	**23**	**169**	**3**	**1**	**0**	**1**	**2**
1984-85	**Winnipeg**	**NHL**	**63**	**2**	**20**	**22**	**74**	**8**	**0**	**1**	**1**	**16**
1985-86	**Winnipeg**	**NHL**	**56**	**6**	**8**	**14**	**97**	....	....	....	....	....
1986-87	**Winnipeg**	**NHL**	**63**	**3**	**13**	**16**	**119**	**10**	**0**	**0**	**0**	**21**
1987-88	Cdn. National	...	8	0	1	1	2	....	....	....	....	....
	Cdn. Olympic	...	2	0	2	2	0	....	....	....	....	....
	Winnipeg	**NHL**	**36**	**0**	**0**	**0**	**106**	**4**	**0**	**0**	**0**	**4**
1988-89	**Los Angeles**	**NHL**	**76**	**3**	**18**	**21**	**168**	**11**	**0**	**1**	**1**	**6**
1989-90	**Los Angeles**	**NHL**	**62**	**1**	**10**	**11**	**92**	**4**	**0**	**0**	**0**	**6**
1990-91	**Los Angeles**	**NHL**	**45**	**0**	**4**	**4**	**92**	**7**	**0**	**0**	**0**	**12**
	NHL Totals		**621**	**25**	**133**	**158**	**1112**	**54**	**1**	**3**	**4**	**77**

a WCHA First All-Star Team (1981)
b Named to NCAA All-Tournament Team (1981)

Signed as a free agent by **Los Angeles**, June 27, 1988.

WAVER, JEFF

Defense. Shoots left. 5'11", 195 lbs. Born, St. Boniface, Man., September 28, 1968.
(Pittsburgh's 5th choice, 89th overall, in 1987 Entry Draft).

			Regular Season					Playoffs				
Season	Club	Lea	GP	G	A	TP	PIM	GP	G	A	TP	PIM
1986-87	Hamilton	OHL	63	12	28	40	132	9	0	5	5	23
1987-88	Hamilton	OHL	64	27	34	61	134	14	6	7	13	24
1988-89a	Kingston	OHL	55	30	43	73	95	....	....	....	....	....
	Muskegon	IHL	3	0	1	1	0	1	0	0	0	0
1989-90	Virginia	ECHL	55	28	20	48	73	4	1	4	5	4
	Muskegon	IHL	4	0	2	2	2	....	....	....	....	....
1990-91	Albany	IHL	32	6	9	15	18	....	....	....	....	....

a OHL Third All-Star Team (1989)

WEIGHT, DOUG

Center. Shoots left. 5'11", 185 lbs. Born, Warren, MI, January 21, 1971.
(NY Rangers' 2nd choice, 34th overall, in 1990 Entry Draft).

			Regular Season					Playoffs				
Season	Club	Lea	GP	G	A	TP	PIM	GP	G	A	TP	PIM
1989-90	Lake Superior	CCHA	46	21	48	69	44	....	....	....	....	....
1990-91ab	Lake Superior	CCHA	42	29	46	75	86	....	....	....	....	....
	NY Rangers	**NHL**	....	....	....	....	....	**1**	**0**	**0**	**0**	**0**
	NHL Totals		....	....	....	....	....	**1**	**0**	**0**	**0**	**0**

a CCHA First All-Start Team (1991)
b NCAA West Second All-American Team (1991)

WEINRICH, ALEXANDER

Defense. Shoots right. 6', 180 lbs. Born, Lewiston, ME, March 12, 1969.
(Toronto's 12th choice, 238th overall, in 1987 Entry Draft).

			Regular Season					Playoffs				
Season	Club	Lea	GP	G	A	TP	PIM	GP	G	A	TP	PIM
1990-91	Merrimack	H.E.	38	2	12	14	16	....	....	....	....	....

WEINRICH, ERIC (WIGHN-rick)

Defense. Shoots left. 6'1", 210 lbs. Born, Roanoke, VA, December 19, 1966.
(New Jersey's 3rd choice, 32nd overall, in 1985 Entry Draft).

			Regular Season					Playoffs				
Season	Club	Lea	GP	G	A	TP	PIM	GP	G	A	TP	PIM
1985-86	U. of Maine	H.E.	34	0	15	15	26	....	....	....	....	....
1986-87ab	U. of Maine	H.E.	41	12	32	44	59	....	....	....	....	....
1987-88	U. of Maine	H.E.	8	4	7	11	22	....	....	....	....	....
	U.S. National	...	38	3	9	12	24	....	....	....	....	....
	U.S. Olympic	...	3	0	0	0	0	....	....	....	....	....
1988-89	**New Jersey**	**NHL**	**2**	**0**	**0**	**0**	**0**	....	....	....	....	....
	Utica	AHL	80	17	27	44	70	5	0	1	1	4
1989-90	**New Jersey**	**NHL**	**19**	**2**	**7**	**9**	**11**	**6**	**1**	**3**	**4**	**17**
cd	Utica	AHL	57	12	48	60	38	....	....	....	....	....
1990-91e	**New Jersey**	**NHL**	**76**	**4**	**34**	**38**	**48**	**7**	**1**	**2**	**3**	**6**
	NHL Totals		**97**	**6**	**41**	**47**	**59**	**13**	**2**	**5**	**7**	**23**

a Hockey East First All-Star Team (1987)
b NCAA East Second All-American Team (1987)
c AHL First All-Star Team (1990)
d Won Eddie Shore Plaque (Outstanding Defenseman-AHL) (1990)
e NHL/Upper Deck All-Rookie Team (1991)

WEINRICH, JASON

Defense. Shoots right. 6'2", 189 lbs. Born, Lewiston, ME, February 13, 1972.
(NY Rangers' 8th choice, 118th overall, in 1990 Entry Draft).

			Regular Season					Playoffs				
Season	Club	Lea	GP	G	A	TP	PIM	GP	G	A	TP	PIM
1989-90	Springfield Aca.	HS	30	7	35	42	....	....	....	....	....	....
1990-91	U. of Maine	H.E.	14	1	1	2	4	....	....	....	....	....

WEISBROD, JOHN

Right wing. Shoots right. 6'3", 210 lbs. Born, Syosset, NY, October 8, 1968.
(Minnesota's 4th choice, 73rd overall, in 1987 Entry Draft).

			Regular Season					Playoffs				
Season	Club	Lea	GP	G	A	TP	PIM	GP	G	A	TP	PIM
1987-88	Harvard	ECAC	22	8	11	19	16	....	....	....	....	....
1988-89	Harvard	ECAC	31	22	13	35	61	....	....	....	....	....
1989-90	Harvard	ECAC	27	11	21	32	62	....	....	....	....	....
1990-91	Harvard	ECAC	5	2	8	10	8	....	....	....	....	....

Claimed by **San Jose** from **Minnesota** in Dispersal Draft, May 30, 1991.

WELLS, GORDON (JAY)
Defense. Shoots left. 6'1", 210 lbs.   Born, Paris, Ont., May 18, 1959.
(Los Angeles' 1st choice, 16th overall, in 1979 Entry Draft).

				Regular Season					Playoffs			
Season	Club	Lea	GP	G	A	TP	PIM	GP	G	A	TP	PIM
1977-78	Kingston	OHA	68	9	13	22	195	5	1	2	3	6
1978-79a	Kingston	OHA	48	6	21	27	100	11	2	7	9	29
1979-80	**Los Angeles**	**NHL**	43	0	0	0	113	4	0	0	0	11
	Binghamton	AHL	28	0	6	6	48	....	....	....	....	....
1980-81	Los Angeles	NHL	72	5	13	18	155	4	0	0	0	27
1981-82	Los Angeles	NHL	60	1	8	9	145	10	1	3	4	41
1982-83	Los Angeles	NHL	69	3	12	15	167	....	....	....	....	....
1983-84	Los Angeles	NHL	69	3	18	21	141	....	....	....	....	....
1984-85	Los Angeles	NHL	77	2	9	11	185	3	0	1	1	0
1985-86	Los Angeles	NHL	79	11	31	42	226	....	....	....	....	....
1986-87	Los Angeles	NHL	77	7	29	36	155	5	1	2	3	10
1987-88	Los Angeles	NHL	58	2	23	25	159	5	1	2	3	21
1988-89	Philadelphia	NHL	67	2	19	21	184	18	0	2	2	51
1989-90	Philadelphia	NHL	59	3	16	19	129	....	....	....	....	....
	Buffalo	NHL	1	0	1	1	0	6	0	0	0	12
1990-91	Buffalo	NHL	43	1	2	3	86	1	0	1	1	0
	NHL Totals		774	40	181	221	1845	56	3	11	14	173

a OHA First All-Star Team (1979)
Traded to **Philadelphia** by **Los Angeles** for Doug Crossman, September 29, 1988. Traded to **Buffalo** by **Philadelphia** with Philadelphia's fourth round choice (Peter Ambroziak) in 1991 Entry Draft for Kevin Maguire and Buffalo's second round choice (Mikael Renberg) in 1990 Entry Draft, March 5, 1990.

WERENKA, BRAD
Defense. Shoots left. 6'2", 205 lbs.   Born, Two Hills, Alta., February 12, 1969.
(Edmonton's 2nd choice, 42nd overall, in 1987 Entry Draft).

				Regular Season					Playoffs			
Season	Club	Lea	GP	G	A	TP	PIM	GP	G	A	TP	PIM
1986-87	N. Michigan	WCHA	30	4	4	8	35	....	....	....	....	....
1987-88	N. Michigan	WCHA	34	7	23	30	26	....	....	....	....	....
1988-89	N. Michigan	WCHA	28	7	13	20	16	....	....	....	....	....
1989-90	N. Michigan	WCHA	8	2	5	7	8	....	....	....	....	....
1990-91abc	N. Michigan	WCHA	47	20	43	63	36	....	....	....	....	....

a WCHA First All-Star Team (1991)
b NCAA West First All-American Team (1991)
c NCAA Final Four All-Tournament Team (1991)

WERENKA, DARCY
Defense. Shoots right. 6'1", 210 lbs.   Born, Edmonton, Alta., May 13, 1973.
(NY Rangers' 2nd choice, 37th overall, in 1991 Entry Draft).

				Regular Season					Playoffs			
Season	Club	Lea	GP	G	A	TP	PIM	GP	G	A	TP	PIM
1989-90	Lethbridge	WHL	63	1	18	19	16	19	0	2	2	4
1990-91a	Lethbridge	WHL	72	13	37	50	39	16	1	7	8	4

a WHL East Second All-Star Team (1991)

WERNESS, LANCE
Right wing. Shoots right. 6', 175 lbs.   Born, Burnsville, MN, March 28, 1969.
(Chicago's 9th choice, 176th overall, in 1987 Entry Draft).

				Regular Season					Playoffs			
Season	Club	Lea	GP	G	A	TP	PIM	GP	G	A	TP	PIM
1987-88	U. Minnesota	WCHA	27	8	5	13	20	....	....	....	....	....
1988-89	U. Minnesota	WCHA	13	2	4	6	12	....	....	....	....	....
1989-90	U. Minnesota	WCHA	2	0	1	1	2	....	....	....	....	....
1990-91	U. Minnesota	WCHA	13	2	1	3	4	....	....	....	....	....

WESLEY, GLEN
Defense. Shoots left. 6'1", 195 lbs.   Born, Red Deer, Alta., October 2, 1968.
(Boston's 1st choice, 3rd overall, in 1987 Entry Draft).

				Regular Season					Playoffs			
Season	Club	Lea	GP	G	A	TP	PIM	GP	G	A	TP	PIM
1983-84	Portland	WHL	3	1	2	3	0	....	....	....	....	....
1984-85	Portland	WHL	67	16	52	68	76	6	1	6	7	8
1985-86a	Portland	WHL	69	16	75	91	96	15	3	11	14	29
1986-87a	Portland	WHL	63	16	46	62	72	20	8	18	26	27
1987-88b	**Boston**	**NHL**	79	7	30	37	69	23	6	8	14	22
1988-89	Boston	NHL	77	19	35	54	61	10	0	2	2	4
1989-90	Boston	NHL	78	9	27	36	48	21	2	6	8	36
1990-91	Boston	NHL	80	11	32	43	78	19	2	9	11	19
	NHL Totals		314	46	124	170	256	73	10	25	35	81

a WHL West All-Star Team (1986, 1987)
b NHL All-Rookie Team (1988)
Played in NHL All-Star Game (1989)

WETHERILL, DARREN
Defense. Shoots left. 6', 180 lbs.   Born, Regina, Sask., January 28, 1970.
(Boston's 8th choice, 189th overall, in 1990 Entry Draft).

				Regular Season					Playoffs			
Season	Club	Lea	GP	G	A	TP	PIM	GP	G	A	TP	PIM
1989-90	Minot	USHL	65	6	39	45	156	....	....	....	....	....
1990-91	Lake Superior	CCHA	26	0	6	6	14	....	....	....	....	....

WHEELDON, SIMON
Center, Shoots left. 5'11", 170 lbs.   Born, Vancouver, B.C., August 30, 1966.
(Edmonton's 11th choice, 229th overall, in 1984 Entry Draft).

				Regular Season					Playoffs			
Season	Club	Lea	GP	G	A	TP	PIM	GP	G	A	TP	PIM
1983-84	Victoria	WHL	56	14	24	38	43	....	....	....	....	....
1984-85a	Victoria	WHL	67	50	76	126	78	....	....	....	....	....
	Nova Scotia	AHL	4	0	1	1	0	1	0	0	0	0
1985-86	Victoria	WHL	70	61	96	157	85	....	....	....	....	....
1986-87	Flint	IHL	41	17	53	70	20	....	....	....	....	....
	New Haven	AHL	38	11	28	39	39	5	0	0	0	6
1987-88	**NY Rangers**	**NHL**	5	0	1	1	4	....	....	....	....	....
b	Colorado	IHL	69	45	54	99	80	13	8	11	19	12
1988-89	**NY Rangers**	**NHL**	6	0	1	1	2	....	....	....	....	....
b	Denver	IHL	74	50	56	106	77	4	0	2	2	6
1989-90	Flint	IHL	76	34	49	83	61	4	1	2	3	2
1990-91	**Winnipeg**	**NHL**	4	0	0	0	4	....	....	....	....	....
	Moncton	AHL	66	30	38	68	38	8	4	3	7	2
	NHL Totals		15	0	2	2	10	....	....	....	....	....

a WHL Second All-Star Team, West Division (1985)
b IHL Second All-Star Team (1988, 1989)
Signed as a free agent by **NY Rangers**, September 8, 1986. Traded to **Winnipeg** by **NY Rangers** for Brian McReynolds, July 9, 1990. Traded to **Washington** by **Winnipeg** with Craig Duncanson and Brent Hughes for Bob Joyce, Tyler Larter and Kent Paynter, May 21, 1991.

WHITE, PETER
Left wing. Shoots left. 5'11", 200 lbs. Born, Montreal, Que., March 15, 1969.
(Edmonton's 4th choice, 92nd overall, in 1989 Entry Draft).

				Regular Season					Playoffs			
Season	Club	Lea	GP	G	A	TP	PIM	GP	G	A	TP	PIM
1988-89	Michigan State	CCHA	46	20	33	53	17	....	....	....	....	....
1989-90	Michigan State	CCHA	45	22	40	62	6	....	....	....	....	....
1990-91	Michigan State	CCHA	37	7	31	38	28	....	....	....	....	....

WHITE, ROBERT (ROB)
Defense. Shoots right. 6'0", 190 lbs.   Born, Brockville, Ont., March 9, 1968.
(Hartford's 10th choice, 221st overall, in 1988 Entry Draft).

				Regular Season					Playoffs			
Season	Club	Lea	GP	G	A	TP	PIM	GP	G	A	TP	PIM
1986-87	St. Lawrence	ECAC	30	2	9	11	52	....	....	....	....	....
1987-88	St. Lawrence	ECAC	31	4	16	20	29	....	....	....	....	....
1988-89	St. Lawrence	ECAC	35	5	19	24	64	....	....	....	....	....
1989-90	St. Lawrence	ECAC	32	2	15	17	96	....	....	....	....	....
1990-91	Erie	ECHL	18	0	5	5	19	....	....	....	....	....

WHITNEY, RAY
Center. Shoots left. 5'9", 160 lbs.   Born, Edmonton, Alta., May 8, 1972.
(San Jose's 2nd choice, 23rd overall, in 1991 Entry Draft).

				Regular Season					Playoffs			
Season	Club	Lea	GP	G	A	TP	PIM	GP	G	A	TP	PIM
1988-89	Spokane	WHL	71	17	33	50	16	....	....	....	....	....
1989-90	Spokane	WHL	71	57	56	113	50	6	3	4	7	6
1990-91abc	Spokane	WHL	72	67	118	*185	36	15	13	18	*31	12

a WHL West First All-Star Team (1991)
b Memorial Cup All-Star Team (1991)
c Won George Parsons Trophy (Memorial Cup Most Sportsmanlike Player) (1991)

WHITTEMORE, TODD
Center. Shoots right. 6'1", 175 lbs.   Born, Taunton, MA, June 20, 1967.
(Toronto's 9th choice, 169th overall, in 1985 Entry Draft).

				Regular Season					Playoffs			
Season	Club	Lea	GP	G	A	TP	PIM	GP	G	A	TP	PIM
1986-87	Providence	H.E.	29	1	4	5	12	....	....	....	....	....
1987-88	Providence	H.E.	34	5	10	15	38	....	....	....	....	....
1988-89	Providence	H.E.	29	7	1	8	28	....	....	....	....	....
1989-90	Providence	H.E.	16	4	2	6	30	....	....	....	....	....
1990-91	Richmond	ECHL	13	0	2	2	26	....	....	....	....	....

WHYTE, SEAN
Right wing. Shoots right. 6', 198 lbs.   Born, Sudbury, Ont., May 4, 1970.
(Los Angeles' 7th choice, 165th overall, in 1989 Entry Draft).

				Regular Season					Playoffs			
Season	Club	Lea	GP	G	A	TP	PIM	GP	G	A	TP	PIM
1986-87	Guelph	OHL	41	1	3	4	13	....	....	....	....	....
1987-88	Guelph	OHL	62	6	22	28	71	....	....	....	....	....
1988-89	Guelph	OHL	53	20	44	64	57	....	....	....	....	....
1989-90	Owen Sound	OHL	54	23	30	53	90	3	0	1	1	10
1990-91	Phoenix	IHL	60	18	17	35	61	4	1	0	1	2

WICKENHEISER, DOUGLAS PETER (DOUG) (WIHK ehn HIGH zuhr)

Center. Shoots left. 6'1", 200 lbs. Born, Regina, Sask., March 30, 1961.
(Montreal's 1st choice and 1st overall in 1980 Entry Draft).

			Regular Season					Playoffs				
Season	Club	Lea	GP	G	A	TP	PIM	GP	G	A	TP	PIM
1977-78	Regina	WHL	68	37	51	88	49	13	4	5	9	4
1978-79	Regina	WHL	68	32	62	94	141	....	....	....	....	....
1979-80abc	Regina	WHL	71	*89	81	*170	99	18	14	*26	*40	20
1980-81	**Montreal**	**NHL**	**41**	**7**	**8**	**15**	**20**	....	....	....	....	....
1981-82	**Montreal**	**NHL**	**56**	**12**	**23**	**35**	**43**	....	....	....	....	....
1982-83	**Montreal**	**NHL**	**78**	**25**	**30**	**55**	**49**	....	....	....	....	....
1983-84	**Montreal**	**NHL**	**27**	**5**	**5**	**10**	**6**	....	....	....	....	....
	St. Louis	**NHL**	**46**	**7**	**21**	**28**	**19**	**11**	**2**	**2**	**4**	**2**
1984-85	**St. Louis**	**NHL**	**68**	**23**	**20**	**43**	**36**	....	....	....	....	....
1985-86	**St. Louis**	**NHL**	**36**	**8**	**11**	**19**	**16**	**19**	**2**	**5**	**7**	**12**
1986-87	**St. Louis**	**NHL**	**80**	**13**	**15**	**28**	**37**	**6**	**0**	**0**	**0**	**2**
1987-88	**Vancouver**	**NHL**	**80**	**7**	**19**	**26**	**36**	....	....	....	....	....
1988-89	**NY Rangers**	**NHL**	**1**	**1**	**0**	**1**	**0**	....	....	....	....	....
	Flint	IHL	21	9	7	16	18	....	....	....	....	....
	Cdn. National	...	26	7	15	22	40	....	....	....	....	....
	Washington	**NHL**	**16**	**2**	**5**	**7**	**4**	**5**	**0**	**0**	**0**	**2**
	Baltimore	AHL	2	0	5	5	0	....	....	....	....	....
1989-90	**Washington**	**NHL**	**27**	**1**	**8**	**9**	**20**	....	....	....	....	....
	Baltimore	AHL	35	9	19	28	22	12	2	5	7	22
1990-91	Asiago	Italy	35	25	32	57	9	....	....	....	....	....
	NHL Totals		**556**	**111**	**165**	**276**	**286**	**41**	**4**	**7**	**11**	**18**

a WHL First All-Star Team (1980)
b WHL Most Valuable Player (1980)
c Named Canadian Major Junior Player of the Year (1980)

Traded to **St. Louis** by **Montreal** with Gilbert Delorme and Greg Paslawski for Perry Turnbull, December 21, 1983. Claimed by **Hartford** in NHL Waiver Draft, October 5, 1987. Claimed by **Vancouver** in NHL Waiver Draft, October 5, 1987. Signed as a free agent by **NY Rangers**, August 12, 1988. Signed as a free agent by **Washington**, February 28, 1989.

WIDMEYER, STEVE

Right wing. Shoots right. 6'2", 200 lbs. Born, Waterloo, Ont., September 29, 1970.
(St. Louis' 7th choice, 201st overall, in 1990 Entry Draft).

			Regular Season					Playoffs				
Season	Club	Lea	GP	G	A	TP	PIM	GP	G	A	TP	PIM
1989-90	U. of Maine	H.E.	26	5	1	6	30	....	....	....	....	....
1990-91	U. of Maine	H.E.	25	4	2	6	61	....	....	....	....	....

WIEMER, JAMES DUNCAN (JIM) (WEE-muhr)

Defense. Shoots left. 6'4", 210 lbs. Born, Sudbury, Ont., January 9, 1961.
(Buffalo's 5th choice, 83rd overall, in 1980 Entry Draft).

			Regular Season					Playoffs				
Season	Club	Lea	GP	G	A	TP	PIM	GP	G	A	TP	PIM
1978-79	Peterborough	OHA	61	15	12	27	50	18	4	4	8	15
1979-80	Peterborough	OHA	53	17	32	49	63	14	6	9	15	19
1980-81	Peterborough	OHA	65	41	54	95	102	5	1	2	3	15
1981-82	Rochester	AHL	74	19	26	45	57	9	0	4	4	2
1982-83	Rochester	AHL	74	15	44	59	43	15	5	15	20	22
	Buffalo	**NHL**	....	....	....	....	....	**1**	**0**	**0**	**0**	**0**
1983-84	**Buffalo**	**NHL**	**64**	**5**	**15**	**20**	**48**	....	....	....	....	....
	Rochester	AHL	12	4	11	15	11	18	3	13	16	20
1984-85	**Buffalo**	**NHL**	**10**	**3**	**2**	**5**	**4**	....	....	....	....	....
	Rochester	AHL	13	1	9	10	24	....	....	....	....	....
	NY Rangers	**NHL**	**22**	**4**	**3**	**7**	**30**	**1**	**0**	**0**	**0**	**0**
	New Haven	AHL	33	9	27	36	39	....	....	....	....	....
1985-86	**NY Rangers**	**NHL**	**7**	**3**	**0**	**3**	**2**	**8**	**1**	**0**	**1**	**6**
ab	New Haven	AHL	73	24	49	73	108	....	....	....	....	....
1986-87	New Haven	AHL	6	0	7	7	6	....	....	....	....	....
	Nova Scotia	AHL	59	9	25	34	72	5	0	4	4	2
1987-88	**Edmonton**	**NHL**	**12**	**1**	**2**	**3**	**15**	**2**	**0**	**0**	**0**	**2**
	Nova Scotia	AHL	57	11	32	43	99	5	1	1	2	14
1988-89	Cape Breton	AHL	51	12	29	41	80	....	....	....	....	....
	Los Angeles	**NHL**	**9**	**2**	**3**	**5**	**20**	**10**	**2**	**1**	**3**	**19**
	New Haven	AHL	3	1	1	2	2	7	2	3	5	2
1989-90	**Boston**	**NHL**	**61**	**5**	**14**	**19**	**63**	**8**	**0**	**1**	**1**	**4**
	Maine	AHL	6	3	4	7	27	....	....	....	....	....
1990-91	**Boston**	**NHL**	**61**	**4**	**19**	**23**	**62**	**16**	**1**	**3**	**4**	**14**
	NHL Totals		**246**	**27**	**58**	**85**	**244**	**46**	**4**	**5**	**9**	**45**

a AHL First All-Star Team (1986)
b AHL Defenseman of the Year (1986)

Traded to **NY Rangers** by **Buffalo** with Steve Patrick for Dave Maloney and Chris Renaud, December 6, 1984. Traded to **Edmonton** by **NY Rangers** with Reijo Ruotsalainen, Clark Donatelli and Ville Kentala for Don Jackson, Mike Golden, Miloslav Horvava and future considerations, October 23, 1986. Traded to **Los Angeles** by **Edmonton** with Alan May for Brian Wilks and John English, March 7, 1989. Signed as a free agent by **Boston**, July 6, 1989.

WILDGOOSE, LYLE

Left wing. Shoots left. 6'1", 180 lbs. Born, Chelmsford, Ont., October 28, 1968.
(Calgary's 1st choice, 25th overall, in 1990 Supplemental Draft).

			Regular Season					Playoffs				
Season	Club	Lea	GP	G	A	TP	PIM	GP	G	A	TP	PIM
1987-88	Providence	H.E.	33	12	19	31	54	....	....	....	....	....
1988-89	Providence	H.E.	32	11	17	28	34	....	....	....	....	....
1989-90	Providence	H.E.	35	17	18	35	38	....	....	....	....	....
1990-91	Providence	H.E.	29	21	17	38	55	....	....	....	....	....

WILKIE, BOB

Defense. Shoots right. 6'2", 200 lbs. Born, Calgary, Alta., February 11, 1969.
(Detroit's 3rd choice, 41st overall, in 1987 Entry Draft).

			Regular Season					Playoffs				
Season	Club	Lea	GP	G	A	TP	PIM	GP	G	A	TP	PIM
1985-86	Calgary	WHL	63	8	19	27	56	....	....	....	....	....
1986-87	Swift Current	WHL	65	12	38	50	50	4	1	3	4	2
1987-88	Swift Current	WHL	67	12	68	80	124	10	4	12	16	8
1988-89	Swift Current	WHL	62	18	67	85	89	12	1	11	12	47
1989-90	Adirondack	AHL	58	5	33	38	64	6	1	4	5	2
1990-91	**Detroit**	**NHL**	**8**	**1**	**2**	**3**	**2**	....	....	....	....	....
	Adirondack	AHL	43	6	18	24	71	2	1	0	1	2
	NHL Totals		**8**	**1**	**2**	**3**	**2**	....	....	....	....	....

WILKINSON, NEIL

Defense. Shoots right. 6'3", 190 lbs. Born, Selkirk, Man., October 16, 1967.
(Minnesota's 2nd choice, 30th overall, in 1986 Entry Draft).

			Regular Season					Playoffs				
Season	Club	Lea	GP	G	A	TP	PIM	GP	G	A	TP	PIM
1986-87	Michigan State	CCHA	19	3	4	7	18	....	....	....	....	....
1987-88	Medicine Hat	WHL	55	11	21	32	157	5	1	0	1	2
1988-89	Kalamazoo	IHL	39	5	15	20	96	....	....	....	....	....
1989-90	**Minnesota**	**NHL**	**36**	**0**	**5**	**5**	**100**	**7**	**0**	**2**	**2**	**11**
	Kalamazoo	IHL	20	6	7	13	62	....	....	....	....	....
1990-91	**Minnesota**	**NHL**	**50**	**2**	**9**	**11**	**117**	**22**	**3**	**3**	**6**	**12**
	Kalamazoo	IHL	10	0	3	3	38	....	....	....	....	....
	NHL Totals		**86**	**2**	**14**	**16**	**217**	**29**	**3**	**5**	**8**	**23**

Claimed by **San Jose** from **Minnesota** in Dispersal Draft, May 30, 1991.

WILLIAMS, DARRYL

Left wing. Shoots left. 5'11", 185 lbs. Born, Mt. Pearl, Nfld., February 9, 1968.

			Regular Season					Playoffs				
Season	Club	Lea	GP	G	A	TP	PIM	GP	G	A	TP	PIM
1986-87	Belleville	OHL	58	9	10	19	108	....	....	....	....	....
1987-88	Belleville	OHL	63	29	39	68	169	....	....	....	....	....
1988-89	Belleville	AHL	46	24	21	45	137	....	....	....	....	....
1989-90	New Haven	AHL	51	9	13	22	124	....	....	....	....	....
1990-91	New Haven	AHL	57	14	11	25	278	....	....	....	....	....

Signed as a free agent by **Los Angeles**, September, 1989.

WILLIAMS, DAVID

Defense. Shoots right. 6'2", 195 lbs. Born, Plainfield, NJ, August 25, 1967.
(New Jersey's 12th choice, 234th overall, in 1985 Entry Draft).

			Regular Season					Playoffs				
Season	Club	Lea	GP	G	A	TP	PIM	GP	G	A	TP	PIM
1986-87	Dartmouth	ECAC	23	2	19	21	20	....	....	....	....	....
1987-88	Dartmouth	ECAC	25	8	14	22	30	....	....	....	....	....
1988-89ab	Dartmouth	ECAC	25	4	11	15	28	....	....	....	....	....
1989-90	Dartmouth	ECAC	26	3	12	15	32	....	....	....	....	....
1990-91	New Haven	AHL	57	14	11	25	278	....	....	....	....	....
	Muskegon	IHL	14	1	2	3	4	....	....	....	....	....

a ECAC First All-Star Team (1989)
b NCAA East Second All-American Team (1989)

Signed as a free agent by **San Jose**, August 9, 1991.

WILLIAMS, SEAN

Center. Shoots left. 6'1", 182 lbs. Born, Oshawa, Ont., January 28, 1968.
(Chicago's 11th choice, 245th overall, in 1986 Entry Draft).

			Regular Season					Playoffs				
Season	Club	Lea	GP	G	A	TP	PIM	GP	G	A	TP	PIM
1984-85	Oshawa	OHL	40	6	7	13	28	5	1	0	1	0
1985-86	Oshawa	OHL	55	15	23	38	23	6	2	3	5	4
1986-87	Oshawa	OHL	62	21	23	44	32	25	7	5	12	19
1987-88a	Oshawa	OHL	65	*58	65	123	38	7	3	3	6	6
1988-89	Saginaw	IHL	77	32	27	59	75	6	0	3	3	0
1989-90	Indianapolis	IHL	78	21	37	58	25	14	8	5	13	12
1990-91	Indianapolis	IHL	82	46	52	98	59	7	1	2	3	12

a OHL First All-Star Team (1988)

WILLIS, RICK

Left wing. Shoots left. 6', 185 lbs. Born, Lynn, MA, January 9, 1972.
(NY Rangers' 5th choice, 76th overall, in 1990 Entry Draft).

			Regular Season					Playoffs				
Season	Club	Lea	GP	G	A	TP	PIM	GP	G	A	TP	PIM
1989-90	Pingree	HS	24	17	30	47	....	....	....	....	....	....
1990-91	Northwood	HS	18	12	10	22	20	....	....	....	....	....

WILSON, CAREY

Center. Shoots right. 6'2", 195 lbs. Born, Winnipeg, Man., May 19, 1962.
(Chicago's 8th choice, 67th overall, in 1980 Entry Draft).

			Regular Season					Playoffs				
Season	Club	Lea	GP	G	A	TP	PIM	GP	G	A	TP	PIM
1979-80	Dartmouth	ECAC	31	16	22	38	20	....	....	....	....	....
1980-81	Dartmouth	ECAC	24	9	13	22	52	....	....	....	....	....
1981-82	HIFK	Fin.	29	15	17	32	58	7	1	4	5	6
1982-83	HIFK	Fin.	36	16	24	40	62	9	1	3	4	12
1983-84	Cdn. Olympic	...	56	19	24	43	34	....	....	....	....	....
	Calgary	**NHL**	**15**	**2**	**5**	**7**	**2**	**6**	**3**	**1**	**4**	**2**
1984-85	**Calgary**	**NHL**	**74**	**24**	**48**	**72**	**27**	**4**	**0**	**0**	**0**	**0**
1985-86	**Calgary**	**NHL**	**76**	**29**	**29**	**58**	**24**	**9**	**0**	**2**	**2**	**2**
1986-87	**Calgary**	**NHL**	**80**	**20**	**36**	**56**	**42**	**6**	**1**	**1**	**2**	**6**
1987-88	**Calgary**	**NHL**	**34**	**9**	**21**	**30**	**18**	....	....	....	....	....
	Hartford	**NHL**	**36**	**18**	**20**	**38**	**22**	**6**	**2**	**4**	**6**	**2**
1988-89	**Hartford**	**NHL**	**34**	**11**	**11**	**22**	**14**	....	....	....	....	....
	NY Rangers	**NHL**	**41**	**21**	**34**	**55**	**45**	**4**	**1**	**2**	**3**	**2**
1989-90	**NY Rangers**	**NHL**	**41**	**9**	**17**	**26**	**57**	**10**	**2**	**1**	**3**	**0**
1990-91	**Hartford**	**NHL**	**45**	**8**	**15**	**23**	**16**	....	....	....	....	....
	Calgary	**NHL**	**12**	**3**	**3**	**6**	**2**	**7**	**2**	**2**	**4**	**0**
	NHL Totals		**488**	**154**	**239**	**393**	**269**	**52**	**11**	**13**	**24**	**14**

Rights traded to **Calgary** by **Chicago** for Denis Cyr, November 8, 1982. Traded to **Hartford** by **Calgary** with Neil Sheehy and the rights to Lane MacDonald for Dana Murzyn and Shane Churla, January 3, 1988. Traded by **NY Rangers** by **Hartford** with Hartford's fifth-round choice (Lubos Rob) in 1990 Entry Draft for Brian Lawton, Norm MacIver and Don Maloney, December 26, 1988. Traded to **Hartford** by **NY Rangers** with NY Rangers' third-round choice (Mikael Nylander) in 1991 Entry Draft for Jody Hull, July 9, 1990. Traded to **Calgary** by **Hartford** for Mark Hunter, March 5, 1991.

WILSON, DOUGLAS, JR. (DOUG)

Defense. Shoots left. 6'1", 187 lbs. Born, Ottawa, Ont., July 5, 1957.
(Chicago's 1st choice, 6th overall, in 1977 Amateur Draft).

			Regular Season					Playoffs				
Season	Club	Lea	GP	G	A	TP	PIM	GP	G	A	TP	PIM
1975-76	Ottawa	OHA	58	26	62	88	142	12	5	10	15	24
1976-77a	Ottawa	OHA	43	25	54	79	85	19	4	20	24	34
1977-78	Chicago	NHL	77	14	20	34	72	4	0	0	0	0
1978-79	Chicago	NHL	56	5	21	26	37	....	....	....	....	....
1979-80	Chicago	NHL	73	12	49	61	70	7	2	8	10	6
1980-81	Chicago	NHL	76	12	39	51	80	3	0	3	3	2
1981-82bc	Chicago	NHL	76	39	46	85	54	15	3	10	13	32
1982-83	Chicago	NHL	74	18	51	69	58	13	4	11	15	12
1983-84	Chicago	NHL	66	13	45	58	64	5	0	3	3	2
1984-85d	Chicago	NHL	78	22	54	76	44	12	3	10	13	12
1985-86	Chicago	NHL	79	17	47	64	80	3	1	1	2	2
1986-87	Chicago	NHL	69	16	32	48	36	4	0	0	0	0
1987-88	Chicago	NHL	27	8	24	32	28	....	....	....	....	....
1988-89	Chicago	NHL	66	15	47	62	69	4	1	2	3	0
1989-90d	Chicago	NHL	70	23	50	73	40	20	3	12	15	18
1990-91	Chicago	NHL	51	11	29	40	32	5	2	1	3	2
	NHL Totals		**938**	**225**	**554**	**779**	**764**	**95**	**19**	**61**	**80**	**88**

a OHA First All-Star Team (1977)
b Won James Norris Memorial Trophy (1982)
c NHL First All-Star Team (1982)
d NHL Second All-Star Team (1985, 1990)
Played in NHL All-Star Game (1982-86, 1990)

WILSON, MITCH

Right wing. Shoots right. 5'8", 199 lbs. Born, Kelowna, B.C., February 15, 1962.

			Regular Season					Playoffs				
Season	Club	Lea	GP	G	A	TP	PIM	GP	G	A	TP	PIM
1980-81	Seattle	WHL	64	8	23	31	253	5	3	0	3	31
1981-82	Seattle	WHL	60	18	17	35	436	10	3	7	10	55
1982-83	Wichita	CHL	55	4	6	10	186	....	....	....	....	....
1983-84	Maine	AHL	71	6	8	14	349	17	3	6	9	98
1984-85	New Jersey	NHL	9	0	2	2	21	....	....	....	....	....
	Maine	AHL	51	6	3	9	220	2	0	0	0	32
1985-86	Maine	AHL	64	4	3	7	217	3	0	0	0	2
1986-87	Pittsburgh	NHL	17	2	1	3	83	....	....	....	....	....
	Baltimore	AHL	58	8	9	17	*353	....	....	....	....	....
1987-88	Muskegon	IHL	68	27	25	52	400	5	1	0	1	23
1988-89	Muskegon	IHL	61	16	34	50	*382	11	4	5	9	*83
1989-90	Muskegon	IHL	63	13	24	37	283	15	1	4	5	97
1990-91	Muskegon	IHL	78	14	19	33	387	4	1	2	3	34
	NHL Totals		**26**	**2**	**3**	**5**	**104**	**....**	**....**	**....**	**....**	**....**

Signed as a free agent by **New Jersey**, October 12, 1982. Signed as a free agent by **Pittsburgh**, July 24, 1986.

WILSON, RICHARD WILLIAM (RIK)

Defense. Shoots right. 6', 185 lbs. Born, Long Beach, CA, June 17, 1962.
(St. Louis' 1st choice, 12th overall, in 1980 Entry Draft).

			Regular Season					Playoffs				
Season	Club	Lea	GP	G	A	TP	PIM	GP	G	A	TP	PIM
1980-81a	Kingston	OHA	68	30	70	100	108	13	1	9	10	18
	Salt Lake	CHL	....	....	....	....	....	4	1	1	2	2
1981-82	St. Louis	NHL	48	3	18	21	24	9	0	3	3	14
	Kingston	OHL	16	9	10	19	38	....	....	....	....	....
1982-83	St. Louis	NHL	56	3	11	14	50	....	....	....	....	....
	Salt Lake	CHL	4	0	0	0	0	....	....	....	....	....
1983-84	St. Louis	NHL	48	7	11	18	53	11	0	0	0	9
	Montana	CHL	6	0	3	3	2	....	....	....	....	....
1984-85	St. Louis	NHL	51	8	16	24	39	2	0	1	1	0
1985-86	St. Louis	NHL	32	0	4	4	48	....	....	....	....	....
	Calgary	NHL	2	0	0	0	0	....	....	....	....	....
	Nova Scotia	AHL	13	4	5	9	11	....	....	....	....	....
	Moncton	AHL	8	3	3	6	2	....	....	....	....	....
1986-87	Nova Scotia	AHL	45	8	13	21	109	5	1	3	4	20
1987-88	Chicago	NHL	14	4	5	9	6	....	....	....	....	....
	Saginaw	IHL	33	4	5	9	105	....	....	....	....	....
1988-89	Villach	Aus.	45	17	43	60	110	....	....	....	....	....
1989-90	Peoria	IHL	15	1	4	5	34	....	....	....	....	....
1990-91	Bic	Aus.	44	13	45	58	....	....	....	....	....	....
	NHL Totals		**251**	**25**	**65**	**90**	**220**	**22**	**0**	**4**	**4**	**23**

a OHA First All-Star Team (1981)
Traded to **Calgary** by **St. Louis** with Joe Mullen and Terry Johnson for Ed Beers, Charles Bourgeois and Gino Cavallini, February 1, 1986. Traded to **Chicago** by **Calgary** for Tom McMurchy, March 11, 1986. Signed as a free agent by **St. Louis**, July 19, 1989. Traded to **St. Louis** by **Chicago** for Craig Coxe, September 27, 1989.

WILSON, RONALD LEE (RON)

Center. Shoots left. 5'9", 180 lbs. Born, Toronto, Ont., May 13, 1956.
(Montreal's 15th choice, 133rd overall, in 1976 Amateur Draft).

			Regular Season					Playoffs				
Season	Club	Lea	GP	G	A	TP	PIM	GP	G	A	TP	PIM
1974-75	Toronto	OHA	16	6	12	18	6	23	9	17	26	6
1975-76	St. Catharines	OHA	64	37	62	99	44	4	1	6	7	7
1976-77	Nova Scotia	AHL	67	15	21	36	18	6	0	0	0	0
1977-78	Nova Scotia	AHL	59	15	25	40	17	11	4	4	8	9
1978-79	Nova Scotia	AHL	77	33	42	75	91	10	5	6	11	14
1979-80	Winnipeg	NHL	79	21	36	57	28	....	....	....	....	....
1980-81	Winnipeg	NHL	77	18	33	51	55	....	....	....	....	....
1981-82	Winnipeg	NHL	39	3	13	16	49	....	....	....	....	....
	Tulsa	CHL	41	20	38	58	22	3	1	0	1	2
1982-83	Winnipeg	NHL	12	6	3	9	4	3	2	2	4	2
	Sherbrooke	AHL	65	30	55	85	71	....	....	....	....	....
1983-84	Winnipeg	NHL	51	3	12	15	12	....	....	....	....	....
	Sherbrooke	AHL	22	10	30	40	16	....	....	....	....	....
1984-85	Winnipeg	NHL	75	10	9	19	31	8	4	2	6	2
1985-86	Winnipeg	NHL	54	6	7	13	16	1	0	0	0	0
	Sherbrooke	AHL	10	9	8	17	9	....	....	....	....	....
1986-87	Winnipeg	NHL	80	3	13	16	13	10	1	2	3	0
1987-88	Winnipeg	NHL	69	5	8	13	28	1	0	0	0	2
1988-89a	Moncton	AHL	80	31	61	92	110	8	1	4	5	20
1989-90	Moncton	AHL	47	16	37	53	39	....	....	....	....	....
	St. Louis	NHL	33	3	17	20	23	12	3	5	8	18
1990-91	St. Louis	NHL	73	10	27	37	54	7	0	0	0	28
	NHL Totals		**642**	**88**	**178**	**266**	**313**	**42**	**10**	**11**	**21**	**52**

a AHL Second All-Star Team (1989)
Sold to **Winnipeg** by **Montreal**, October 4, 1979. Traded to **St. Louis** by **Winnipeg** for Doug Evans, January 22, 1990.

WILSON, ROSS

Right wing. Shoots right. 6'3", 197 lbs. Born, The Pas, Man., June 26, 1969.
(Los Angeles' 3rd choice, 43rd overall, in 1987 Entry Draft).

			Regular Season					Playoffs				
Season	Club	Lea	GP	G	A	TP	PIM	GP	G	A	TP	PIM
1986-87	Peterborough	OHL	66	28	11	39	91	12	3	5	8	16
1987-88	Peterborough	OHL	66	29	30	59	114	12	2	9	11	15
1988-89	Peterborough	OHL	64	48	41	89	90	15	10	13	23	23
1989-90	New Haven	AHL	61	19	14	33	39	....	....	....	....	....
1990-91	New Haven	AHL	68	29	17	46	28	....	....	....	....	....

WINCH, JASON

Left wing. Shoots left. 6'1", 203 lbs. Born, Listowel, Ont., May 23, 1971.
(Buffalo's 8th choice, 187th overall, in 1990 Entry Draft).

			Regular Season					Playoffs				
Season	Club	Lea	GP	G	A	TP	PIM	GP	G	A	TP	PIM
1989-90	Niagara Falls	OHL	64	31	63	94	23	16	9	12	21	4
1990-91	Niagara Falls	OHL	66	40	82	122	16	14	14	12	26	6

WINNES, CHRISTOPHER (CHRIS)

Right wing. Shoots right. 6', 170 lbs. Born, Ridgefield, CT, February 12, 1968.
(Boston's 9th choice, 161st overall, in 1987 Entry Draft).

			Regular Season					Playoffs				
Season	Club	Lea	GP	G	A	TP	PIM	GP	G	A	TP	PIM
1987-88	N. Hampshire	H.E.	30	17	19	36	28	....	....	....	....	....
1988-89	N. Hampshire	H.E.	30	11	20	31	22	....	....	....	....	....
1989-90	N. Hampshire	H.E.	24	10	13	23	12	....	....	....	....	....
1990-91	N. Hampshire	H.E.	33	15	16	31	24	....	....	....	....	....
	Maine	AHL	7	3	1	4	0	1	0	2	2	0
	Boston	NHL	....	....	....	....	....	1	0	0	0	0
	NHL Totals		**....**	**....**	**....**	**....**	**....**	**1**	**0**	**0**	**0**	**0**

WITKOWSKI, BYRON

Left wing. Shoots left. 6'3", 197 lbs. Born, Edenwold, Sask., November 20, 1969.
(Quebec's 13th choice, 211th overall, in 1989 Entry Draft).

			Regular Season					Playoffs				
Season	Club	Lea	GP	G	A	TP	PIM	GP	G	A	TP	PIM
1989-90	W. Michigan	CCHA	36	1	2	3	36	....	....	....	....	....
1990-91	W. Michigan	CCHA	31	10	4	14	66	....	....	....	....	....

WOLANIN, CHRISTOPHER

Defense. Shoots left. 6'2", 205 lbs. Born, Detroit, MI, September 12, 1968.
(Vancouver's 10th choice, 212th overall, in 1988 Entry Draft).

			Regular Season					Playoffs				
Season	Club	Lea	GP	G	A	TP	PIM	GP	G	A	TP	PIM
1987-88	Ill-Chicago	CCHA	37	1	6	7	38	....	....	....	....	....
1988-89	Ill-Chicago	CCHA	30	1	9	10	33	....	....	....	....	....
1989-90	Ill-Chicago	CCHA	34	1	6	7	116	....	....	....	....	....
1990-91	Ill-Chicago	CCHA	37	4	13	17	104	....	....	....	....	....

WOLANIN, CRAIG   (wuh-LAN-ihn)

Defense. Shoots left. 6'3", 205 lbs. Born, Grosse Pointe, MI, July 27, 1967.
(New Jersey's 1st choice, 3rd overall, in 1985 Entry Draft).

			Regular Season					Playoffs				
Season	Club	Lea	GP	G	A	TP	PIM	GP	G	A	TP	PIM
1984-85	Kitchener	OHL	60	5	16	21	95	4	1	1	2	2
1985-86	New Jersey	NHL	44	2	16	18	74	....	....	....	....	....
1986-87	New Jersey	NHL	68	4	6	10	109	....	....	....	....	....
1987-88	New Jersey	NHL	78	6	25	31	170	18	2	5	7	51
1988-89	New Jersey	NHL	56	3	8	11	69	....	....	....	....	....
1989-90	New Jersey	NHL	37	1	7	8	47	....	....	....	....	....
	Utica	AHL	6	2	4	6	2	....	....	....	....	....
	Quebec	NHL	13	0	3	3	10	....	....	....	....	....
1990-91	Quebec	NHL	80	5	13	18	89	....	....	....	....	....
	NHL Totals		**376**	**21**	**78**	**99**	**568**	**18**	**2**	**5**	**7**	**51**

Traded to **Quebec** by **New Jersey** with future considerations (Randy Velischek) for Peter Stastny, March 6, 1990.

WOLF, GREGORY (GREGG)

Defense. Shoots left. 6'1", 200 lbs. Born, Buffalo, NY, August 20, 1969.
(Hartford's 6th choice, 144th overall, in 1987 Entry Draft).

			Regular Season					Playoffs				
Season	Club	Lea	GP	G	A	TP	PIM	GP	G	A	TP	PIM
1987-88	Colgate	ECAC	32	0	7	7	66	....	....	....	....	....
1988-89	Colgate	ECAC	13	1	3	4	20	....	....	....	....	....
1989-90	Colgate	ECAC	38	1	0	1	58	....	....	....	....	....
1990-91	Colgate	ECAC	29	0	4	4	65	....	....	....	....	....

WOOD, DODY

Center. Shoots left. 5'11", 181 lbs. Born, Chetwynd, B.C., March 10, 1972.
(San Jose's 4th choice, 45th overall, in 1991 Entry Draft).

			Regular Season					Playoffs				
Season	Club	Lea	GP	G	A	TP	PIM	GP	G	A	TP	PIM
1989-90	Ft. St. John	Tier II	44	51	73	124	270	....	....	....	....	....
	Seattle	WHL	....	....	....	....	....	5	0	0	0	2
1990-91	Seattle	WHL	69	28	37	65	272	6	0	1	1	2

WOOD, RANDY

Left wing/Center. Shoots left. 6', 195 lbs. Born, Princeton, NJ, October 12, 1963.

			Regular Season					Playoffs				
Season	Club	Lea	GP	G	A	TP	PIM	GP	G	A	TP	PIM
1982-83	Yale	ECAC	26	5	14	19	10	....	....	....	....	....
1983-84	Yale	ECAC	18	7	7	14	10	....	....	....	....	....
1984-85a	Yale	ECAC	32	25	28	53	23	....	....	....	....	....
1985-86bc	Yale	ECAC	31	25	30	55	26	....	....	....	....	....
1986-87	**NY Islanders**	**NHL**	**6**	**1**	**0**	**1**	**4**	**13**	**1**	**3**	**4**	**14**
	Springfield	AHL	75	23	24	47	57	....	....	....	....	....
1987-88	**NY Islanders**	**NHL**	**75**	**22**	**16**	**38**	**80**	**5**	**1**	**0**	**1**	**6**
	Springfield	AHL	1	0	1	1	0	....	....	....	....	....
1988-89	**NY Islanders**	**NHL**	**77**	**15**	**13**	**28**	**44**	....	....	....	....	....
	Springfield	AHL	1	1	1	2	0	....	....	....	....	....
1989-90	**NY Islanders**	**NHL**	**74**	**24**	**24**	**48**	**39**	**5**	**1**	**1**	**2**	**4**
1990-91	**NY Islanders**	**NHL**	**76**	**24**	**18**	**42**	**45**	....	....	....	....	....
	NHL Totals		**308**	**86**	**71**	**157**	**212**	**23**	**3**	**4**	**7**	**24**

a ECAC Second All-Star Team (1985)
b ECAC First All-Star Team (1986)
c NCAA East Second All-Star Team (1986)

Signed as a free agent by **NY Islanders**, September 17, 1986.

WOODCROFT, CRAIG

Left wing. Shoots left. 6'1", 185 lbs. Born, Toronto, Ont., December 3, 1969.
(Chicago's 6th choice, 134th overall, in 1988 Entry Draft).

			Regular Season					Playoffs				
Season	Club	Lea	GP	G	A	TP	PIM	GP	G	A	TP	PIM
1987-88	Colgate	ECAC	29	7	10	17	28	....	....	....	....	....
1988-89	Colgate	ECAC	29	20	29	49	62	....	....	....	....	....
	Cdn. National	...	2	0	0	0	4	....	....	....	....	....
1989-90	Colgate	ECAC	37	20	26	46	108	....	....	....	....	....
1990-91	Colgate	ECAC	32	26	30	56	52	....	....	....	....	....

WOODLEY, DAN

Right wing. Shoots right. 5'11", 185 lbs. Born, Oklahoma City, OK, December 29, 1967.
(Vancouver's 1st choice, 7th overall, in 1986 Entry Draft).

			Regular Season					Playoffs				
Season	Club	Lea	GP	G	A	TP	PIM	GP	G	A	TP	PIM
1984-85	Portland	WHL	63	21	36	57	108	1	0	0	0	0
1985-86	Portland	WHL	62	45	47	92	100	12	0	8	8	31
1986-87	Portland	WHL	47	30	50	80	81	19	*19	17	*36	52
1987-88	**Vancouver**	**NHL**	**5**	**2**	**0**	**2**	**17**	....	....	....	....	....
a	Flint	IHL	69	29	37	66	104	9	1	3	4	26
1988-89	Milwaukee	IHL	30	9	12	21	48	....	....	....	....	....
	Sherbrooke	AHL	30	9	16	25	69	4	1	6	7	5
1989-90	Sherbrooke	AHL	65	18	40	58	144	10	1	6	7	58
1990-91	Fredericton	AHL	4	0	0	0	4	....	....	....	....	....
	Kansas City	IHL	20	6	4	10	30	....	....	....	....	....
	Albany	IHL	31	8	17	25	36	....	....	....	....	....
	NHL Totals		**5**	**2**	**0**	**2**	**17**	....	....	....	....	....

a Won Ken McKenzie Trophy (American Rookie of the Year-IHL) (1988)

Traded to **Montreal** by **Vancouver** for Jose Charbonneau, January 25, 1989.

WOODS, ROBERT (BOB)

Defense. Shoots left. 6'1", 195 lbs. Born, Leroy, Sask., January 24, 1968.
(New Jersey's 11th choice, 201st overall, in 1988 Entry Draft).

			Regular Season					Playoffs				
Season	Club	Lea	GP	G	A	TP	PIM	GP	G	A	TP	PIM
1987-88	Brandon	WHL	72	21	56	77	84	4	1	5	6	9
1988-89	Brandon	WHL	68	26	50	76	100	....	....	....	....	....
	Utica	AHL	11	0	1	1	2	4	0	0	0	2
1989-90	Utica	AHL	58	2	12	14	30	5	0	0	0	6
1990-91	Utica	AHL	33	4	6	10	21	....	....	....	....	....
	Johnstown	ECHL	23	12	25	37	32	....	....	....	....	....

WOODWARD, ROBERT (ROB)

Left wing. Shoots left. 6'4", 225 lbs. Born, Evanston, IL, January 15, 1971.
(Vancouver's 2nd choice, 29th overall, in 1989 Entry Draft).

			Regular Season					Playoffs				
Season	Club	Lea	GP	G	A	TP	PIM	GP	G	A	TP	PIM
1989-90	Michigan State	CCHA	37	17	9	26	8	....	....	....	....	....
1990-91	Michigan State	CCHA	32	5	13	18	16	....	....	....	....	....

WOOLF, MARK

Right wing. Shoots right. 5'11", 200 lbs. Born, Brandon, Man., September 30, 1970.
(Boston's 5th choice, 126th overall, in 1990 Entry Draft).

			Regular Season					Playoffs				
Season	Club	Lea	GP	G	A	TP	PIM	GP	G	A	TP	PIM
1989-90	Spokane	WHL	68	52	52	104	73	6	2	1	3	9
1990-91	Spokane	WHL	67	41	49	90	96	13	8	6	14	14

WOOLLEY, JASON

Defense. Shoots left. 6'0", 186 lbs. Born, Toronto, Ont., July 27, 1969.
(Washington's 4th choice, 61st overall, in 1989 Entry Draft).

			Regular Season					Playoffs				
Season	Club	Lea	GP	G	A	TP	PIM	GP	G	A	TP	PIM
1988-89	Michigan State	CCHA	47	12	25	37	26	....	....	....	....	....
1989-90	Michigan State	CCHA	45	10	38	48	26	....	....	....	....	....
1990-91ab	Michigan State	CCHA	40	15	44	59	24	....	....	....	....	....

a CCHA First All-Star Team (1991)
b NCAA West First All-American Team (1991)

WRIGHT, TYLER

Center. Shoots right. 5'11", 170 lbs. Born, Canora, Sask., April 6, 1973.
(Edmonton's 1st choice, 12th overall, in 1991 Entry Draft).

			Regular Season					Playoffs				
Season	Club	Lea	GP	G	A	TP	PIM	GP	G	A	TP	PIM
1989-90	Swift Current	WHL	67	14	18	32	139	4	0	0	0	12
1990-91	Swift Current	WHL	66	41	51	92	157	3	0	0	0	6

YAKE, TERRY

Center. Shoots right. 5'11", 185 lbs. Born, New Westminster, B.C., October 22, 1968.
(Hartford's 3rd choice, 81st overall, in 1987 Entry Draft).

			Regular Season					Playoffs				
Season	Club	Lea	GP	G	A	TP	PIM	GP	G	A	TP	PIM
1984-85	Brandon	WHL	11	1	1	2	0	....	....	....	....	....
1985-86	Brandon	WHL	72	26	26	52	49	....	....	....	....	....
1986-87	Brandon	WHL	71	44	58	102	64	....	....	....	....	....
1987-88	Brandon	WHL	72	55	85	140	59	3	4	2	6	7
1988-89	**Hartford**	**NHL**	**2**	**0**	**0**	**0**	**0**	....	....	....	....	....
	Binghamton	AHL	75	39	56	95	57	....	....	....	....	....
1989-90	**Hartford**	**NHL**	**2**	**0**	**1**	**1**	**0**	....	....	....	....	....
	Binghamton	AHL	77	13	42	55	37	....	....	....	....	....
1990-91	**Hartford**	**NHL**	**19**	**1**	**4**	**5**	**10**	**6**	**1**	**1**	**2**	**16**
	Springfield	AHL	60	35	42	77	56	15	9	9	18	10
	NHL Totals		**23**	**1**	**5**	**6**	**10**	**6**	**1**	**1**	**2**	**16**

YASHIN, SERGEI

(YA-sheen)

Left wing. Shoots left. 5'11", 200 lbs. Born, Penza, Soviet Union, March 6, 1962.
(Edmonton's 7th choice, 141st overall, in 1989 Entry Draft).

			Regular Season					Playoffs				
Season	Club	Lea	GP	G	A	TP	PIM	GP	G	A	TP	PIM
1979-80	Moscow D'amo	USSR	2	0	1	1	0	....	....	....	....	....
1980-81	Moscow D'amo	USSR	23	2	6	8	6	....	....	....	....	....
1981-82	Moscow D'amo	USSR	41	13	13	26	4	....	....	....	....	....
1982-83	Moscow D'amo	USSR	43	17	6	23	36	....	....	....	....	....
1983-84	Moscow D'amo	USSR	34	16	9	25	22	....	....	....	....	....
1984-85	Moscow D'amo	USSR	40	15	20	35	32	....	....	....	....	....
1985-86	Moscow D'amo	USSR	40	14	19	33	26	....	....	....	....	....
1986-87	Moscow D'amo	USSR	40	6	11	17	36	....	....	....	....	....
1987-88	Moscow D'amo	USSR	47	13	11	24	34	....	....	....	....	....
1988-89	Moscow D'amo	USSR	44	18	10	28	30	....	....	....	....	....
1989-90	Moscow D'amo	USSR	48	14	16	30	14	....	....	....	....	....
1990-91	Berlin Dynamo	Ger.	45	27	28	55	40	....	....	....	....	....

YAWNEY, TRENT

Defense. Shoots left. 6'3", 192 lbs. Born, Hudson Bay, Sask., September 29, 1965.
(Chicago's 2nd choice, 45th overall, in 1984 Entry Draft).

			Regular Season					Playoffs				
Season	Club	Lea	GP	G	A	TP	PIM	GP	G	A	TP	PIM
1982-83	Saskatoon	WHL	59	6	31	37	44	6	0	2	2	0
1983-84	Saskatoon	WHL	73	13	46	59	81	....	....	....	....	....
1984-85	Saskatoon	WHL	72	16	51	67	158	3	1	6	7	7
1985-86	Cdn. Olympic	...	73	6	15	21	60	....	....	....	....	....
1986-87	Cdn. Olympic	...	51	4	15	19	37	....	....	....	....	....
1987-88	Cdn. National	...	60	4	12	16	81	....	....	....	....	....
	Cdn. Olympic	...	8	1	1	2	6	....	....	....	....	....
	Chicago	**NHL**	**15**	**2**	**8**	**10**	**15**	**5**	**0**	**4**	**4**	**8**
1988-89	**Chicago**	**NHL**	**69**	**5**	**19**	**24**	**116**	**15**	**3**	**6**	**9**	**20**
1989-90	**Chicago**	**NHL**	**70**	**5**	**15**	**20**	**82**	**20**	**3**	**5**	**8**	**27**
1990-91	**Chicago**	**NHL**	**61**	**3**	**13**	**16**	**77**	**1**	**0**	**0**	**0**	**0**
	NHL Totals		**215**	**15**	**55**	**70**	**290**	**41**	**6**	**15**	**21**	**55**

YORK, JASON

Defense. Shoots right. 6'1", 192 lbs. Born, Ottawa, Ont., May 20, 1970.
(Detroit's 6th choice, 129th overall, in 1990 Entry Draft).

			Regular Season					Playoffs				
Season	Club	Lea	GP	G	A	TP	PIM	GP	G	A	TP	PIM
1989-90	Kitchener	OHL	64	20	55	75	55	17	3	19	22	10
1990-91a	Windsor	OHL	66	13	80	93	40	11	3	10	13	12

a OHL Third All-Star Team (1991)

YOUNG, C.J.

Right wing. Shoots right. 5'10", 180 lbs. Born, Waban, MA, January 1, 1968.
(New Jersey's 1st choice, 5th overall, in 1989 Supplemental Draft).

			Regular Season					Playoffs				
Season	Club	Lea	GP	G	A	TP	PIM	GP	G	A	TP	PIM
1986-87	Harvard	ECAC	34	17	12	29	30	....	....	....	....	....
1987-88	Harvard	ECAC	28	13	16	29	40	....	....	....	....	....
1988-89a	Harvard	ECAC	36	20	31	51	36	....	....	....	....	....
1989-90bc	Harvard	ECAC	28	21	28	49	32	....	....	....	....	....

a ECAC Second All-Star Team (1989)
b ECAC First All-Star Team (1990)
c NCAA East Second All-American Team (1990)

YOUNG, JASON

Left wing. Shoots left. 5'10", 182 lbs. Born, Sudbury, Ont., December 16, 1972.
(Buffalo's 3rd choice, 57th overall, in 1991 Entry Draft).

			Regular Season					Playoffs				
Season	Club	Lea	GP	G	A	TP	PIM	GP	G	A	TP	PIM
1989-90	Sudbury	OHL	62	26	47	73	64	7	3	2	5	8
1990-91	Sudbury	OHL	37	21	38	59	22	5	0	4	4	10

YOUNG, SCOTT

Right wing. Shoots right. 6', 190 lbs. Born, Clinton, MA, October 1, 1967.
(Hartford's 1st choice, 11th overall, in 1986 Entry Draft).

			Regular Season					Playoffs				
Season	Club	Lea	GP	G	A	TP	PIM	GP	G	A	TP	PIM
1985-86a	Boston U.	H.E.	38	16	13	29	31	....	....	....	....	....
1986-87	Boston U.	H.E.	33	15	21	36	24	....	....	....	....	....
1987-88	U.S. National	...	56	11	47	58	31	....	....	....	....	....
	U.S. Olympic	...	6	2	6	8	4	....	....	....	....	....
	Hartford	NHL	7	0	0	0	2	4	1	0	1	0
1988-89	Hartford	NHL	76	19	40	59	27	4	2	0	2	4
1989-90	Hartford	NHL	80	24	40	64	47	7	2	0	2	2
1990-91	Hartford	NHL	34	6	9	15	8	....	....	....	....	....
	Pittsburgh	NHL	43	11	16	27	33	17	1	6	7	2
	NHL Totals		240	60	105	165	117	32	6	6	12	8

a Hockey East Rookie of the Year (1986)

Traded to **Pittsburgh** by **Hartford** for Rob Brown, December 21, 1990.

YOUNG, SCOTT MELBOURNE

Defense. Shoots left. 6'1", 195 lbs. Born, Burlington, Ont., May 26, 1965.

			Regular Season					Playoffs				
Season	Club	Lea	GP	G	A	TP	PIM	GP	G	A	TP	PIM
1985-86	Colgate	ECAC	28	5	6	11	88	....	....	....	....	....
1986-87	Colgate	ECAC	33	13	15	28	113	....	....	....	....	....
1987-88	Colgate	ECAC	14	4	10	14	44	....	....	....	....	....
1988-89	Colgate	ECAC	31	15	22	37	150	....	....	....	....	....
	New Haven	AHL	7	1	1	2	4	6	0	0	0	2
1989-90	New Haven	AHL	58	7	11	18	62	....	....	....	....	....
1990-91	New Haven	AHL	34	5	10	15	20	....	....	....	....	....
	Phoenix	IHL	5	0	0	0	2	....	....	....	....	....
	San Diego	IHL	14	0	5	5	12	....	....	....	....	....
	Knoxville	ECHL	8	3	8	11	49	3	2	1	3	12

Signed as a free agent by **Los Angeles**, March 28, 1989.

YSEBAERT, PAUL (IGHS-BAHRT)

Center. Shoots left. 6'1", 190 lbs. Born, Sarnia, Ont., May 15, 1966.
(New Jersey's 4th choice, 74th overall, in 1984 Entry Draft).

			Regular Season					Playoffs				
Season	Club	Lea	GP	G	A	TP	PIM	GP	G	A	TP	PIM
1984-85	Bowling Green	CCHA	42	23	32	55	54	....	....	....	....	....
1985-86a	Bowling Green	CCHA	42	23	45	68	50	....	....	....	....	....
1986-87a	Bowling Green	CCHA	45	27	58	85	44	....	....	....	....	....
	Cdn. Olympic	...	5	1	0	1	4	....	....	....	....	....
1987-88	Utica	AHL	78	30	49	79	60	....	....	....	....	....
1988-89	New Jersey	NHL	5	0	4	4	0	....	....	....	....	....
	Utica	AHL	56	36	44	80	22	5	0	1	1	4
1989-90	New Jersey	NHL	5	1	2	3	0	....	....	....	....	....
bcd	Utica	AHL	74	53	52	*105	61	5	2	4	6	0
1990-91	New Jersey	NHL	11	4	3	7	6	....	....	....	....	....
	Detroit	NHL	51	15	18	33	16	2	0	2	2	0
	NHL Totals		72	20	27	47	22	2	0	2	2	0

a CCHA Second All-Star Team (1986, 1987)
b AHL First All-Star Team (1990)
c Won John B. Sollenberger Trophy (Top Scorer-AHL) (1990)
d Won Les Cunningham Trophy (MVP-AHL) (1990)

Traded to **Detroit** by **New Jersey** for Lee Norwood and future considerations, November 27, 1990.

YUDIN, ALEXANDER (EW-deen)

Defense. Shoots left. 6'1", 191 lbs. Born, Minsk, Soviet Union, April 1, 1969.
(Calgary's 12th choice, 231st overall, in 1989 Entry Draft).

			Regular Season					Playoffs				
Season	Club	Lea	GP	G	A	TP	PIM	GP	G	A	TP	PIM
1986-87	Dynamo Minsk	USSR2	35	0	4	4	36	....	....	....	....	....
1987-88	Dynamo Minsk	USSR2	33	2	7	9	28	....	....	....	....	....
1988-89	Moscow D'amo	USSR	21	2	2	4	27	....	....	....	....	....
1989-90	Moscow D'amo	USSR	36	4	5	9	36	....	....	....	....	....
1990-91	Moscow D'amo	USSR	36	1	7	8	78	....	....	....	....	....

YZERMAN, STEVE (IGH-zuhr-muhn)

Center. Shoots right. 5'11", 183 lbs. Born, Cranbrook, B.C., May 9, 1965.
(Detroit's 1st choice, 4th overall, in 1983 Entry Draft).

			Regular Season					Playoffs				
Season	Club	Lea	GP	G	A	TP	PIM	GP	G	A	TP	PIM
1981-82	Peterborough	OHL	58	21	43	64	65	6	0	1	1	16
1982-83	Peterborough	OHL	56	42	49	91	33	4	1	4	5	0
1983-84a	Detroit	NHL	80	39	48	87	33	4	3	3	6	0
1984-85	Detroit	NHL	80	30	59	89	58	3	2	1	3	2
1985-86	Detroit	NHL	51	14	28	42	16	....	....	....	....	....
1986-87	Detroit	NHL	80	31	59	90	43	16	5	13	18	8
1987-88	Detroit	NHL	64	50	52	102	44	3	1	3	4	6
1988-89b	Detroit	NHL	80	65	90	155	61	6	5	5	10	2
1989-90	Detroit	NHL	79	62	65	127	79	....	....	....	....	....
1990-91	Detroit	NHL	80	51	57	108	34	7	3	3	6	4
	NHL Totals		594	342	458	800	368	39	19	28	47	22

a NHL All-Rookie Team (1984)
b Won Lester B. Pearson Award (1989)

Played in NHL All-Star Game (1984, 1988-91)

ZALAPSKI, ZARLEY

Defense. Shoots left. 6'1", 211 lbs. Born, Edmonton, Alta., April 22, 1968.
(Pittsburgh's 1st choice, 4th overall, in 1986 Entry Draft).

			Regular Season					Playoffs				
Season	Club	Lea	GP	G	A	TP	PIM	GP	G	A	TP	PIM
1985-86	Cdn. Olympic	...	59	22	37	59	56	....	....	....	....	....
1986-87	Cdn. Olympic	...	74	11	29	40	28	....	....	....	....	....
1987-88	Cdn. National	...	47	3	13	16	32	....	....	....	....	....
	Cdn. Olympic	...	8	1	3	4	2	....	....	....	....	....
	Pittsburgh	NHL	15	3	8	11	7	....	....	....	....	....
1988-89a	Pittsburgh	NHL	58	12	33	45	57	11	1	8	9	13
1989-90	Pittsburgh	NHL	51	6	25	31	37	....	....	....	....	....
1990-91	Pittsburgh	NHL	66	12	36	48	59	....	....	....	....	....
	Hartford	NHL	11	3	3	6	6	6	1	3	4	8
	NHL Totals		201	36	105	141	166	17	2	11	13	21

a NHL All-Rookie Team (1989)

Traded to **Hartford** by **Pittsburgh** with John Cullen and Jeff Parker for Ron Francis, Grant Jennings and Ulf Samuelsson, March 4, 1991.

ZAMUNER, ROB (ZAM-un-uhr)

Center. Shoots left. 6'2", 202 lbs. Born, Oakville, Ont., September 17, 1969.
(NY Rangers' 3rd choice, 45th overall, in 1989 Entry Draft).

			Regular Season					Playoffs				
Season	Club	Lea	GP	G	A	TP	PIM	GP	G	A	TP	PIM
1986-87	Guelph	OHL	62	6	15	21	8	....	....	....	....	....
1987-88	Guelph	OHL	58	20	41	61	18	....	....	....	....	....
1988-89a	Guelph	OHL	66	46	65	111	38	7	5	5	10	9
1989-90	Flint	IHL	77	44	35	79	32	4	1	0	1	6
1990-91	Binghamton	AHL	80	25	58	83	50	9	7	6	13	35

a OHL Third All-Star Team (1989)

ZAVISHA, BRAD

Left wing. Shoots left. 6'1", 195 lbs. Born, Hines Creek, Alta., January 4, 1972.
(Quebec's 3rd choice, 43rd overall, in 1990 Entry Draft).

			Regular Season					Playoffs				
Season	Club	Lea	GP	G	A	TP	PIM	GP	G	A	TP	PIM
1988-89	Seattle	WHL	52	8	13	21	43	....	....	....	....	....
1989-90	Seattle	WHL	69	22	38	60	124	13	1	6	7	16
1990-91	Seattle	WHL	24	15	12	27	40	....	....	....	....	....
	Portland	WHL	48	25	22	47	41	....	....	....	....	....

ZELEPUKIN, VALERI (zeh-leh-POO-kin)

Right wing. Shoots left. 5'11", 180 lbs. Born, Voskresensk, Soviet Union, September 17, 1968.
(New Jersey's 13th choice, 221st overall, in 1990 Entry Draft).

			Regular Season					Playoffs				
Season	Club	Lea	GP	G	A	TP	PIM	GP	G	A	TP	PIM
1984-85	Khimik	USSR	5	0	0	0	2	....	....	....	....	....
1985-86	Khimik	USSR	33	2	2	4	10	....	....	....	....	....
1986-87	Khimik	USSR	19	1	0	1	4	....	....	....	....	....
1987-88	SKA MVO	USSR	18	18	6	24	....	....	....	....	....	....
	CSKA	USSR	19	3	1	4	8	....	....	....	....	....
1988-89	CSKA	USSR	17	2	3	5	2	....	....	....	....	....
1989-90	Khimik	USSR	46	17	14	31	26	....	....	....	....	....
1990-91	Khimik	USSR	46	12	19	31	22	....	....	....	....	....

ZEMLAK, RICHARD ANDREW

Right wing. Shoots right. 6'2", 190 lbs. Born, Wynard, Sask., March 3, 1963.
(St. Louis' 9th choice, 209th overall, in 1981 Entry Draft).

			Regular Season					Playoffs				
Season	Club	Lea	GP	G	A	TP	PIM	GP	G	A	TP	PIM
1980-81	Spokane	WHL	72	19	19	38	132	4	1	1	2	6
1981-82	Spokane	WHL	26	9	20	29	113	....	....	....	....	....
	Winnipeg	WHL	2	1	2	3	0	....	....	....	....	....
	Medicine Hat	WHL	41	11	20	31	70	....	....	....	....	....
	Salt Lake	CHL	6	0	0	0	2	1	0	0	0	0
1982-83	Medicine Hat	WHL	51	20	17	37	119	....	....	....	....	....
	Nanaimo	WHL	18	2	8	10	50	....	....	....	....	....
1983-84	Montana	CHL	14	2	2	4	17	....	....	....	....	....
	Toledo	IHL	45	8	19	27	101	....	....	....	....	....
1984-85	Muskegon	IHL	64	19	18	37	223	17	5	4	9	68
	Fredericton	AHL	16	3	4	7	59	....	....	....	....	....
1985-86	Fredericton	AHL	58	6	5	11	305	3	0	0	0	49
	Muskegon	IHL	3	1	2	3	36	....	....	....	....	....
1986-87	Quebec	NHL	20	0	2	2	47	....	....	....	....	....
	Fredericton	AHL	29	9	6	15	201	....	....	....	....	....
1987-88	Minnesota	NHL	54	1	4	5	307	....	....	....	....	....
1988-89	Minnesota	NHL	3	0	0	0	13	....	....	....	....	....
	Kalamazoo	IHL	2	1	3	4	22	....	....	....	....	....
	Pittsburgh	NHL	31	0	0	0	135	1	0	0	0	10
	Muskegon	IHL	18	5	4	9	55	8	1	1	2	35
1989-90	Pittsburgh	NHL	19	1	5	6	43	....	....	....	....	....
	Muskegon	IHL	61	17	39	56	263	14	3	4	7	105
1990-91	Salt Lake	IHL	59	14	20	34	194	3	0	1	1	14
	NHL Totals		127	2	11	13	545	1	0	0	0	10

Rights sold to **Quebec** by **St. Louis** with rights to Dan Wood and Roger Hagglund, June 22, 1984. Claimed by **Minnesota** in NHL Waiver Draft, October 5, 1987. Traded to **Pittsburgh** by **Minnesota** for the rights to Rob Gaudreau, November 1, 1988.

ZEMLICKA, RICHARD

Right wing/Left wing. Shoots left. 6'1", 189 lbs. Born, Czechoslovakia, April 13, 1964.
(Edmonton's 9th choice, 185th overall, in 1990 Entry Draft).

			Regular Season					Playoffs				
Season	Club	Lea	GP	G	A	TP	PIM	GP	G	A	TP	PIM
1987-88	Sparta Praha	Czech.	44	8	10	18	32	....	....	....	....	....
1988-89	Sparta Praha	Czech.	42	20	17	37	40	....	....	....	....	....
1989-90	Sparta Praha	Czech.	45	15	14	29		....	....	....	....	....
1990-91	Sparta Praha	Czech.	51	22	30	52	99	....	....	....	....	....

ZENT, JASON

Left wing. Shoots left. 5'11", 180 lbs.   Born, Buffalo, NY, April 15, 1971.
(NY Islanders' 3rd choice, 44th overall, in 1989 Entry Draft).

				Regular Season					Playoffs			
Season	Club	Lea	GP	G	A	TP	PIM	GP	G	A	TP	PIM
1989-90	Nichols	HS	29	49	32	81	26	....	....	....	....	....
1990-91	U. Wisconsin	WCHA	39	19	18	37	51	....	....	....	....	....

ZETTLER, ROB

Defense. Shoots left. 6'3", 190 lbs.   Born, Sept Iles, Que., March 8, 1968.
(Minnesota's 5th choice, 55th overall, in 1986 Entry Draft).

				Regular Season					Playoffs			
Season	Club	Lea	GP	G	A	TP	PIM	GP	G	A	TP	PIM
1985-86	S.S. Marie	OHL	57	5	23	28	92	....	....	....	....	....
1986-87	S.S. Marie	OHL	64	13	22	35	89	4	0	0	0	0
1987-88	Kalamazoo	IHL	2	0	1	1	0	7	0	2	2	2
	S.S. Marie	OHL	64	7	41	48	77	6	2	2	4	9
1988-89	Minnesota	NHL	2	0	0	0	0	....	....	....	....	....
	Kalamazoo	IHL	80	5	21	26	79	6	0	1	1	26
1989-90	Minnesota	NHL	31	0	8	8	45	....	....	....	....	....
	Kalamazoo	IHL	41	6	10	16	64	7	0	0	0	6
1990-91	Minnesota	NHL	47	1	4	5	119	....	....	....	....	....
	Kalamazoo	IHL	1	0	0	0	2	....	....	....	....	....
	NHL Totals		80	1	12	13	164	....	....	....	....	....

Claimed by **San Jose** from **Minnesota** in Dispersal Draft, May 30, 1991.

ZEZEL, PETER   (ZEH-zuhl)

Center. Shoots left. 5'11", 200 lbs.   Born, Toronto, Ont., April 22, 1965.
(Philadelphia's 1st choice, 41st overall, in 1983 Entry Draft).

				Regular Season					Playoffs			
Season	Club	Lea	GP	G	A	TP	PIM	GP	G	A	TP	PIM
1982-83	Toronto	OHL	66	35	39	74	28	4	2	4	6	0
1983-84	Toronto	OHL	68	47	86	133	31	9	7	5	12	4
1984-85	Philadelphia	NHL	65	15	46	61	26	19	1	8	9	28
1985-86	Philadelphia	NHL	79	17	37	54	76	5	3	1	4	4
1986-87	Philadelphia	NHL	71	33	39	72	71	25	3	10	13	10
1987-88	Philadelphia	NHL	69	22	35	57	42	7	3	2	5	7
1988-89	Philadelphia	NHL	26	4	13	17	15	....	....	....	....	....
	St. Louis	NHL	52	17	36	53	27	10	6	6	12	4
1989-90	St. Louis	NHL	73	25	47	72	30	12	1	7	8	4
1990-91	Washington	NHL	20	7	5	12	10	....	....	....	....	....
	Toronto	NHL	32	14	14	28	4	....	....	....	....	....
	NHL Totals		487	154	272	426	301	78	17	34	51	57

Traded to **St. Louis** by **Philadelphia** for Mike Bullard, November 29, 1988. Traded to **Washington** by **St. Louis** with Mike Lalor for Geoff Courtnall, July 13, 1990. Traded to **Toronto** by **Washington** with Bob Rouse for Al Iafrate, January 16, 1991.

ZHAMNOV, ALEXEI

Center. Shoots left. 6'1", 187 lbs.   Born, Moscow, USSR, October 1, 1970.
(Winnipeg's 5th choice, 77th overall, in 1990 Entry Draft).

				Regular Season					Playoffs			
Season	Club	Lea	GP	G	A	TP	PIM	GP	G	A	TP	PIM
1989-90	Moscow D'amo	USSR	43	11	6	17	21	....	....	....	....	....
1990-91	Moscow D'amo	USSR	46	16	12	28	24	....	....	....	....	....

ZMOLEK, DOUG

Defense. Shoots left. 6'1", 195 lbs.   Born, Rochester, MN, November 3, 1970.
(Minnesota's 1st choice, 7th overall, in 1989 Entry Draft).

				Regular Season					Playoffs			
Season	Club	Lea	GP	G	A	TP	PIM	GP	G	A	TP	PIM
1989-90	U. Minnesota	WCHA	40	1	10	11	52	....	....	....	....	....
1990-91	U. Minnesota	WCHA	34	11	6	17	38	....	....	....	....	....

Claimed by **San Jose** from **Minnesota** in Dispersal Draft, May 30, 1991.

ZOMBO, RICHARD (RICK)

Defense. Shoots right. 6'1", 195 lbs.   Born, Des Plaines, IL., May 8, 1963.
(Detroit's 6th choice, 149th overall, in 1981 Entry Draft).

				Regular Season					Playoffs			
Season	Club	Lea	GP	G	A	TP	PIM	GP	G	A	TP	PIM
1981-82	North Dakota	WCHA	45	1	15	16	31	....	....	....	....	....
1982-83	North Dakota	WCHA	35	5	11	16	41	....	....	....	....	....
1983-84	North Dakota	WCHA	34	7	24	31	40	....	....	....	....	....
1984-85	Detroit	NHL	1	0	0	0	0	....	....	....	....	....
	Adirondack	AHL	56	3	32	35	70	....	....	....	....	....
1985-86	Detroit	NHL	14	0	1	1	16	....	....	....	....	....
	Adirondack	AHL	69	7	34	41	94	17	0	4	4	40
1986-87	Detroit	NHL	44	1	4	5	59	7	0	1	1	9
	Adirondack	AHL	25	0	6	6	22	....	....	....	....	....
1987-88	Detroit	NHL	62	3	14	17	96	16	0	6	6	55
1988-89	Detroit	NHL	75	1	20	21	106	6	0	1	1	16
1989-90	Detroit	NHL	77	5	20	25	95	....	....	....	....	....
1990-91	Detroit	NHL	77	4	19	23	55	7	1	0	1	10
	NHL Totals		350	14	78	92	427	36	1	8	9	90

ZUBOV, SERGEI   (ZOO-bahf)

Defense. Shoots right. 6', 187 lbs. Born, Moscow, Soviet Union, July 22, 1970.
(NY Rangers' 6th choice, 85th overall, in 1990 Entry Draft).

				Regular Season					Playoffs			
Season	Club	Lea	GP	G	A	TP	PIM	GP	G	A	TP	PIM
1988-89	CSKA	USSR	29	1	4	5	10	....	....	....	....	....
1989-90	CSKA	USSR	48	6	2	8	16	....	....	....	....	....
1990-91	CSKA	USSR	41	6	5	11	12	....	....	....	....	....

ZYGULSKI, SCOTT

Defense. Shoots right. 6'1", 190 lbs.   Born, South Bend, IN, April 11, 1970.
(Detroit's 7th choice, 137th overall, in 1989 Entry Draft).

				Regular Season					Playoffs			
Season	Club	Lea	GP	G	A	TP	PIM	GP	G	A	TP	PIM
1989-90	Boston College	H.E.	14	0	1	1	6	....	....	....	....	....
1990-91	Boston College	H.E.	25	0	5	5	2	....	....	....	....	....

Late Signings and Additions to Player Register

Peter Ciavaglia signed as a free agent by Buffalo, August 30, 1991.

Troy Crowder signed as a free agent by Detroit, August 27, 1991.

Larry DePalma signed as a free agent by San Jose, August 30, 1991.

Glen Goodall signed as a free agent by NY Rangers, August 28, 1991.

Adam Graves signed as a free agent by NY Rangers, September 3, 1991.

Stephane Guerard traded to Quebec by NY Islanders for cash, September 3, 1991.

Kevin McClelland signed as a free agent by Toronto, September 2, 1991.

John Mokosak signed as a free agent by NY Rangers, August 28, 1991.

Doug Smail signed as a free agent by Quebec, August 30, 1991.

Scott Stevens acquired by New Jersey from St. Louis as compensation for signing of free agent **Brendan Shanahan**, September 3, 1991.

Graeme Townshend signed as a free agent by NY Islanders, September 3, 1991.

Doug Wilson traded to San Jose by Chicago for **Kerry Toporowski** and San Jose's second-round choice in the 1992 Entry Draft, September 6, 1991.

Dave Barr and **Randy McKay** acquired by New Jersey from Detroit as compensation for signing of free agent **Troy Crowder**, September 9, 1991.

CONN, ROB

Left wing/Right wing. Shoots right. 6'2", 200 lbs.   Born, Calgary, Alta., September 3, 1968.

				Regular Season					Playoffs			
Season	Club	Lea	GP	G	A	TP	PIM	GP	G	A	TP	PIM
1988-89	Alaska-Anch.	NCAA	33	21	17	38	46	....	....	....	....	....
1989-90	Alaska-Anch.	NCAA	34	27	21	48	46	....	....	....	....	....
1990-91	Alaska-Anch.	NCAA	43	28	32	60	53	....	....	....	....	....

Signed as a free agent by **Chicago**, July 31, 1991.

JOHNSTON, KARL

Defense. Shoots left. 6', 190 lbs.   Born, Windsor, Ont., August 11, 1967.

				Regular Season					Playoffs			
Season	Club	Lea	GP	G	A	TP	PIM	GP	G	A	TP	PIM
1987-88	Lake Superior	CCHA	42	7	13	20	38	....	....	....	....	....
1988-89	Lake Superior	CCHA	43	7	19	26	38	....	....	....	....	....
1989-90	Lake Superior	CCHA	43	12	28	40	32	....	....	....	....	....
1990-91ab	Lake Superior	CCHA	45	14	36	50	86	....	....	....	....	....

a CCHA First All-Star Team (1991)
b NCAA West Second All-American Team (1991)
Signed as a free agent by **Hartford**, August 14, 1991.

JOYCE, DUANE

Defense. Shoots right. 6'2", 203 lbs.   Born, Pembroke, MA, May 5, 1965.

				Regular Season					Playoffs			
Season	Club	Lea	GP	G	A	TP	PIM	GP	G	A	TP	PIM
1989-90	Kalamazoo	IHL	2	0	0	0	2	....	....	....	....	....
	Fort Wayne	IHL	66	10	26	36	53	....	....	....	....	....
	Muskegon	IHL	13	3	10	13	8	12	3	7	10	13
1990-91	Kalamazoo	IHL	80	12	32	44	53	11	0	3	3	6

Signed as a free agent by **San Jose**, August 13, 1991.

PAVELICH, MARK

Center. Shoots right. 5'8", 170 lbs.   Born, Eveleth, MN, February 28, 1958.
(St. Louis' 5th choice, 117th overall, in 1980 Entry Draft).

				Regular Season					Playoffs			
Season	Club	Lea	GP	G	A	TP	PIM	GP	G	A	TP	PIM
1978-79a	Minn.-Duluth	WCHA	37	31	48	79	52	....	....	....	....	....
1979-80	U.S. National	...	53	15	30	45	12	....	....	....	....	....
	U.S. Olympic	...	7	1	6	7	2	....	....	....	....	....
1980-81	Lugano	Switz.	60	24	49	73	....	....	....	....	....	....
1981-82	NY Rangers	NHL	79	33	43	76	67	6	1	5	6	0
1982-83	NY Rangers	NHL	78	37	38	75	52	9	4	5	9	12
1983-84	NY Rangers	NHL	77	29	53	82	96	5	2	4	6	0
1984-85	NY Rangers	NHL	48	14	31	45	29	3	0	3	3	2
1985-86	NY Rangers	NHL	59	20	20	40	82	....	....	....	....	....
1986-87	Minnesota	NHL	12	4	6	10	10	....	....	....	....	....
1987-88	Davos	Switz.	UNAVAILABLE									
1988-89	Dundee	Brit.	UNAVAILABLE									
1989-90			DID NOT PLAY									
1990-91			DID NOT PLAY									
	NHL Totals		353	137	191	328	336	23	7	17	24	14

a WCHA First All-Star Team (1979)
Signed as a free agent by **NY Rangers**, June 5, 1981. Traded to **Minnesota** by **NY Rangers** for Minnesota's second round choice (Troy Mallette) in 1988 Entry Draft, October 24, 1986. Signed as a free agent by **San Jose**, August 9, 1991.

Guy Lafleur concluded his remarkable 17-year NHL career at the end of the 1991-92 season. "The Flower" was the league's most electrifying superstar in the second half of the 1970s, winning a First All-Star Team berth at right wing in six consecutive seasons beginning in 1974-75. As a member of the Montreal Canadiens, he played on five Stanley Cup winners, won the Art Ross Trophy three times and the Hart Trophy twice. He also won the Conn Smythe Trophy as playoff MVP in 1977. Lafleur retired early in 1984-85, and was inducted into the Hockey Hall of Fame after he had been out of hockey for three seasons. But Lafleur felt he still had some hockey to play and, in the summer of 1988, was offered a tryout with the New York Rangers. He made the club, played one year in New York and then moved to Quebec City where he played with the Nordiques for two more seasons. At the time of his second retirement, Lafleur had 560 goals and 1,353 assists and ranked eighth on the NHL's all-time point-scoring list.

Retired NHL Player Index

Abbreviations: Teams/Cities: — **Atl.** – Atlanta, **Bos.** – Boston; **Bro.** – Brooklyn; **Buf.** – Buffalo; **Cal.** – California; **Cgy.** – Calgary; **Chi.** – Chicago; **Cle.** – Cleveland; **Col.** – Colorado; **Det.** – Detroit; **Edm.** – Edmonton; **Ham.** – Hamilton; **Hfd.** – Hartford; **K.C.** – Kansas City; **L.A.** – Los Angeles; **Min.** – Minnesota; **Mtl.** – Montreal; **Mtl.M.** – Montreal Maroons; **Mtl.W.** – Montreal Wanderers; **N.J.** – New Jersey; **NYA** – NY Americans; **NYI** – New York Islanders; **NYR** – New York Rangers; **Oak.** – Oakland; **Ott.** – Ottawa; **Phi.** – Philadelphia; **Pit.** – Pittsburgh; **Que.** – Quebec; **St.L.** – St. Louis; **Tor.** – Toronto; **Van.** – Vancouver; **Wpg.** – Winnipeg; **Wsh.** – Washington.

Total seasons are rounded off to the nearest full season. **A** – assists; **G** – goals; **GP** – games played; **PIM** – penalties in minutes; **TP** – total points. Assists not recorded during 1917-18 season.

			Regular Schedule					Playoffs							
Name	**NHL Teams**	**NHL Seasons**	**GP**	**G**	**A**	**TP**	**PIM**	**GP**	**G**	**A**	**TP**	**PIM**	**NHL Cup Wins**	**First NHL Season**	**Last NHL Season**
A															
Abbott, Reg	Mtl.	1	3	0	0	0	0	....	....	....	....	....		1952-53	1952-53
Abel, Gerry	Det.	1	1	0	0	0	0	....	....	....	....	....		1966-67	1966-67
Abel, Sid	Det., Chi.	14	613	189	283	472	376	96	28	30	58	77	3	1938-39	1953-54
Abel, Clarence	NYR, Chi.	8	333	18	18	36	359	38	1	1	2	58	2	1926-27	1933-34
Abgrall, Dennis	L.A.	1	13	0	2	2	4	....	....	....	....	....		1975-76	1975-76
Abrahamsson, Thommy	Hfd.	1	32	6	11	17	16	....	....	....	....	....		1980-81	1980-81
Achtymichuk, Gene	Mtl., Det.	4	32	3	5	8	2	....	....	....	....	....		1951-52	1958-59
Acomb, Doug	Tor.	1	2	0	1	1	0	....	....	....	....	....		1969-70	1969-70
Adam, Douglas	NYR	1	4	0	1	1	0	....	....	....	....	....		1949-50	1949-50
Adam, Russ	Tor.	1	8	1	2	3	11	....	....	....	....	....		1982-83	1982-83
Adams, Greg C.	Phi., Hfd., Wsh., Edm., Van., Que., Det.	10	545	84	143	227	1173	43	2	11	13	153		1980-81	1989-90
Adams, Jack J.	Tor., Ott.	7	173	82	29	111	307	10	3	0	3	12	2	1917-18	1926-27
Adams, Jack	Mtl.	1	42	6	12	18	11	3	0	0	0	0		1940-41	1940-41
Adams, Stewart	Chi., Tor.	4	106	9	26	35	60	11	3	3	6	14		1929-30	1932-33
Adduono, Rick	Bos., Atl.	2	4	0	0	0	2	....	....	....	....	....		1975-76	1979-80
Affleck, Bruce	St.L., Van., NYI	7	280	14	66	80	86	8	0	0	0	0		1974-75	1983-84
Ahern, Fred	Cal., Cle., Col.	4	146	31	30	61	130	2	0	1	1	2		1974-75	1977-78
Ahlin	Chi.	1	1	0	0	0	0	....	....	....	....	....		1937-38	1937-38
Ahrens, Chris	Min.	6	52	0	3	3	14	1	0	0	0	0		1973-74	1977-78
Ailsby, Lloyd	NYR	1	3	0	0	0	2	....	....	....	....	....		1951-52	1951-52
Albright, Clint	NYR	1	59	14	5	19	19	....	....	....	....	....		1948-49	1948-49
Aldcorn, Gary	Tor., Det., Bos.	5	226	41	56	97	78	6	1	2	3	4		1956-57	1960-61
Alexander, Claire	Tor., Van.	4	155	18	47	65	36	16	2	4	6	4		1974-75	1977-78
Alexandre, Art	Mtl.	2	11	0	2	2	8	4	0	0	0	0		1931-32	1932-33
Allen, George	NYR, Chi., Mtl.	8	339	82	115	197	179	41	9	10	19	32		1938-39	1946-47
Allen, Jeff	Cle.	1	4	0	0	0	2	....	....	....	....	....		1977-78	1977-78
Allen, Keith	Det.	2	28	0	4	4	8	5	0	0	0	0	1	1953-54	1954-55
Allen, Viv	NYA	1	6	0	1	1	0	....	....	....	....	....		1940-41	1940-41
Alley, Steve	Hfd.	2	15	3	3	6	11	3	0	1	1	0		1979-80	1980-81
Allison, Dave	Mtl.	1	3	0	0	0	12	....	....	....	....	....		1983-84	1983-84
Allison, Mike	NYR, Tor., L.A.	10	499	102	166	268	630	82	9	17	26	135		1980-81	1989-90
Allison, Ray	Hfd., Phi.	7	238	64	93	157	223	12	2	3	5	20		1979-80	1986-87
Allum, Bill	NYR	1	1	0	1	1	0	....	....	....	....	....		1940-41	1940-41
Amadio, Dave	Det., L.A.	3	125	5	11	16	163	16	1	2	3	18		1957-58	1968-69
Amodeo, Mike	Wpg.	1	19	0	0	0	2	....	....	....	....	....		1979-80	1979-80
Anderson, Bill	Bos.	1	....	....	....	....	....	1	0	0	0	0		1942-43	1942-43
Anderson, Dale	Det.	1	13	0	0	0	6	2	0	0	0	0		1956-57	1956-57
Anderson, Doug	Mtl.	1	....	....	....	....	....	2	0	0	0	0	1	1952-53	1952-53
Anderson, Earl	Det., Bos.	3	109	19	19	38	22	5	0	1	1	0		1974-75	1976-77
Anderson, Jim	L.A.	1	7	1	2	3	2	....	....	....	....	....		1967-68	1967-68
Anderson, Murray	Wsh.	1	40	0	1	1	68	....	....	....	....	....		1974-75	1974-75
Anderson, Ron C.	Det., L.A., St.L., Buf.	5	251	28	30	58	146	5	0	0	0	4		1967-68	1971-72
Anderson, Ron H.	Wsh.	1	28	9	7	16	8	....	....	....	....	....		1974-75	1974-75
Anderson, Russ	Pit., Hfd., L.A.	10	519	22	99	121	1086	10	0	3	3	28		1976-77	1984-85
Anderson, Tom	Det., NYA, Bro.	8	319	62	127	189	190	16	2	7	9	62		1934-35	1941-42
Andersson Kent-Erik	Min., NYR	7	456	72	103	175	78	50	4	11	15	4		1977-78	1983-84
Andersson, Peter	Wsh., Que.	3	172	10	41	51	80	7	0	2	2	2		1983-84	1985-86
Andrascik, Steve	NYR	1	....	....	....	....	....	1	0	0	0	0		1971-72	1971-72
Andrea, Paul	NYR, Pit., Cal., Buf.	4	150	31	49	80	12	....	....	....	....	....		1965-66	1970-71
Andrews, Lloyd	Tor.	4	53	8	5	13	10	7	2	0	2	5		1921-22	1924-25
Andruff, Ron	Mtl., Col.,	5	153	19	36	55	54	2	0	0	0	0		1974-75	1978-79
Angotti, Lou	NYR, Chi., Phi., Pit., St.L.	10	653	103	186	289	228	65	8	8	16	17		1964-65	1973-74
Anholt, Darrel	Chi.	1	1	0	0	0	0	....	....	....	....	....		1983-84	1983-84
Anslow, Bert	NYR	1	2	0	0	0	0	....	....	....	....	....		1947-48	1947-48
Antonovich, Mike	Min., Hfd., N.J.	5	87	10	15	25	37	....	....	....	....	....		1975-76	1983-84
Apps, Syl (Jr.)	NYR, Pit., L.A.	10	727	183	423	606	311	23	5	5	10	23		1970-71	1979-80
Apps, Syl (Sr.)	Tor.	10	423	201	231	432	56	69	25	28	53	16	3	1936-37	1947-48
Arbour, Al	Det., Chi., Tor., St.L.	14	626	12	58	70	617	86	1	8	9	92	3	1953-54	1970-71
Arbour, Amos	Mtl., Ham., Tor.	6	109	51	13	64	66	....	....	....	....	....		1918-19	1923-24
Arbour, Jack	Det., Tor.	2	47	5	1	6	56	....	....	....	....	....		1926-27	1928-29
Arbour, John	Bos., Pit., Van., St.L.	5	106	1	9	10	149	5	0	0	0	0		1965-66	1971-72
Arbour, Ty	Pit., Chi.	5	207	28	28	56	112	11	2	0	2	6		1926-27	1930-31
Archambault, Michel	Chi.	1	3	0	0	0	0	....	....	....	....	....		1976-77	1976-77
Archibald, Jim	Min.	3	16	1	2	3	45	....	....	....	....	....		1984-85	1986-87
Areshenkoff, Ronald	Edm.	1	4	0	0	0	0	....	....	....	....	....		1979-80	1979-80
Armstrong, Bob	Bos.	12	542	13	86	99	671	42	1	7	8	28		1950-51	1961-62
Armstrong, George	Tor.	21	1187	296	417	713	721	110	26	34	60	88	4	1949-50	1970-71
Armstrong, Murray	Tor., NYA, Bro., Det.	8	270	67	121	188	62	30	4	6	10	2		1937-38	1945-46
Armstrong, Red	Tor.	1	7	1	1	2	2	....	....	....	....	....		1962-63	1962-63
Arnason, Chuck	Mtl., Atl., Pit., K.C., Col., Cle., Min., Wsh.	8	401	109	90	199	122	9	2	4	6	4		1971-72	1978-79
Arthur, Fred	Hfd., Phi.	3	80	1	8	9	49	4	0	0	0	2		1980-81	1982-83
Arundel, John	Tor.	1	3	0	0	0	0	....	....	....	....	....		1949-50	1949-50
Ashbee, Barry	Bos., Phi.	5	284	15	70	85	291	17	0	4	4	22	1	1965-66	1973-74
Ashby, Don	Tor., Col., Edm.	6	188	40	56	96	40	12	1	0	1	4		1975-76	1980-81
Ashworth, Frank	Chi.	1	18	5	4	9	2	....	....	....	....	....		1946-47	1946-47
Asmundson, Oscar	NYR, Det., St.L., NYA, Mtl.	5	112	11	23	34	30	9	0	2	2	4	1	1932-33	1937-38
Atanas, Walt	NYR	1	49	13	8	21	40	....	....	....	....	....		1944-45	1944-45
Atkinson, Steve	Bos., Buf., Wsh.	6	302	60	51	111	104	1	0	0	0	0		1968-69	1974-75
Attwell, Bob	Col.	2	22	1	5	6	0	....	....	....	....	....		1979-80	1980-81
Attwell, Ron	St.L., NYR	1	21	1	7	8	8	....	....	....	....	....		1967-68	1967-68
Aubin, Norm	Tor.	2	69	18	13	31	30	1	0	0	0	0		1981-82	1982-83
Aubry, Pierre	Que., Det.	5	202	24	26	50	133	20	1	1	2	32		1980-81	1984-85
Aubuchon, Ossie	Bos., NYR	2	50	19	12	31	4	6	1	0	1	0		1942-43	1943-44
Auge, Les	Col.	1	6	0	3	3	4	....	....	....	....	....		1980-81	1980-81
Aurie, Larry	Det.	12	489	147	129	276	279	24	6	9	15	10	2	1927-28	1938-39
Awrey, Don	Bos., St.L., Mtl., Pit., NYR, Col.	16	969	31	158	189	1065	71	0	18	18	150	2	1963-64	1978-79
Ayres, Vern	NYA, Mtl.M., St.L., NYR	6	211	6	14	20	350	....	....	....	....	....		1930-31	1935-36
B															
Babando, Pete	Bos., Det., Chi., NYR	6	351	86	73	159	194	17	3	3	6	6	1	1947-48	1952-53
Babin, Mitch	St.L.	1	8	0	0	0	0	....	....	....	....	....		1975-76	1975-76
Baby, John	Cle., Min.	2	26	2	8	10	26	....	....	....	....	....		1977-78	1978-79
Babych, Wayne	St.L., Pit., Que., Hfd.	9	519	192	246	438	498	41	7	9	16	25		1978-79	1986-87
Backman, Mike	NYR	3	18	1	6	7	18	10	2	2	4	2		1981-82	1983-84
Backor, Peter	Tor.	1	36	4	5	9	6	....	....	....	....	....	1	1944-45	1944-45
Backstrom, Ralph	Mtl., L.A., Chi.	17	1032	278	361	639	386	116	27	32	59	68	6	1956-57	1972-73
Bailey, Ace (I.)	Tor.	8	314	111	82	193	472	20	3	4	7	12	1	1926-27	1933-34
Bailey, Ace (G.)	Bos., Det., St.L., Wsh.	10	568	107	171	278	633	15	2	4	6	28	1	1968-69	1977-78
Bailey, Bob	Tor., Det., Chi.	4	150	15	21	36	207	15	0	4	4	22		1953-54	1957-58
Bailey, Reid	Phi., Tor., Hfd.	4	40	1	3	4	105	16	0	2	2	25		1980-81	1983-84

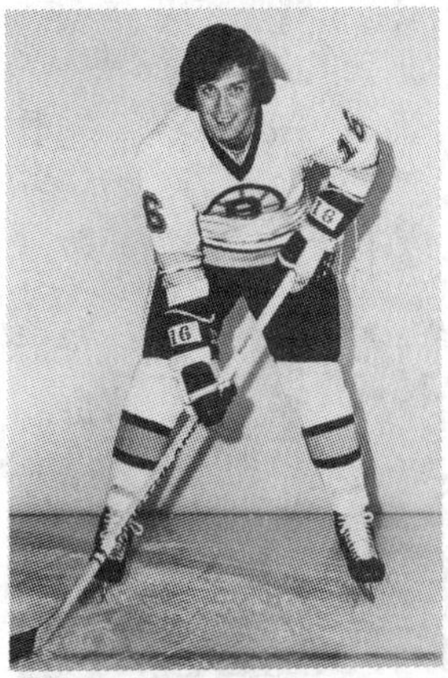

Earl Anderson

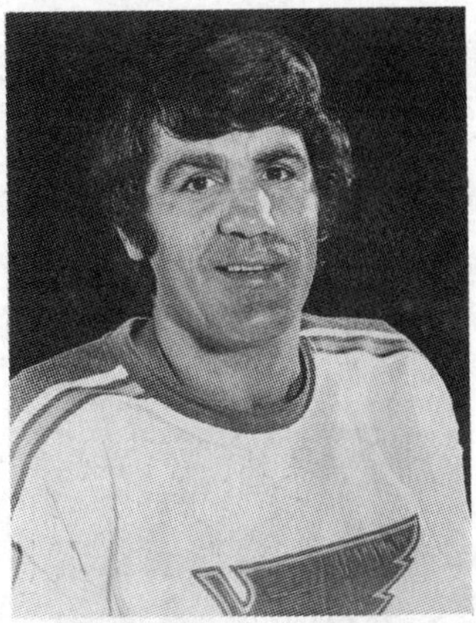

Lou Angotti

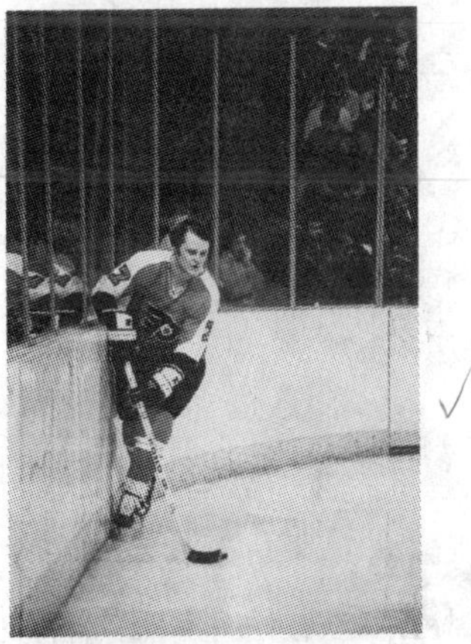

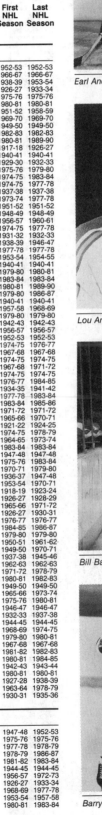

Bill Barber

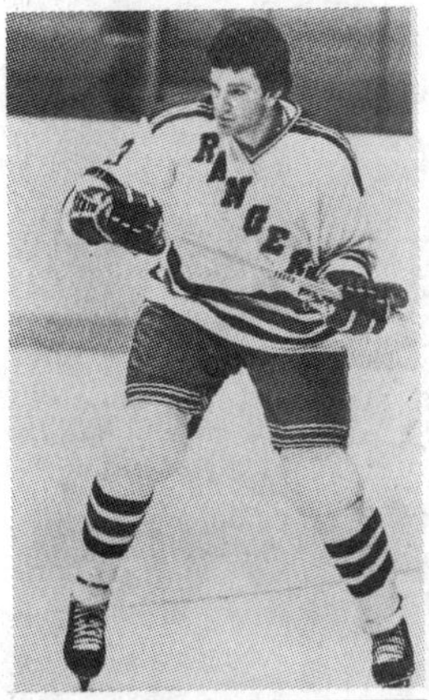

Barry Beck

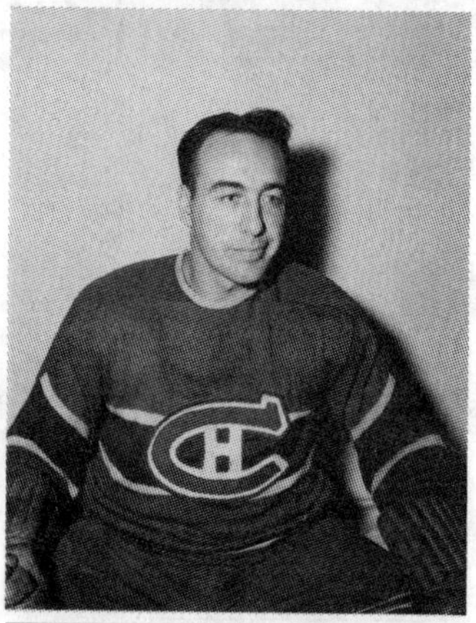

Hector "Toe" Blake

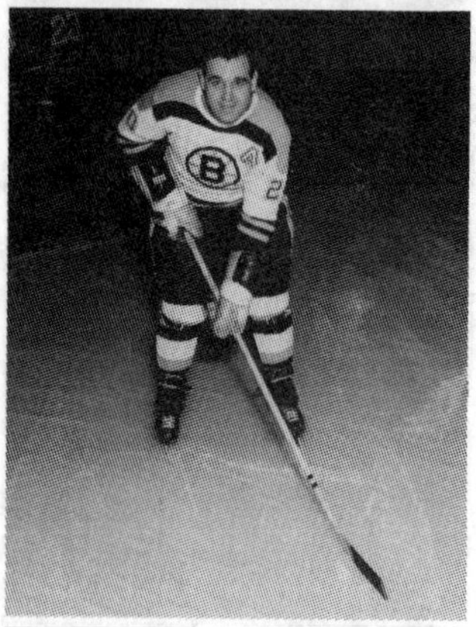

Leo Boivin

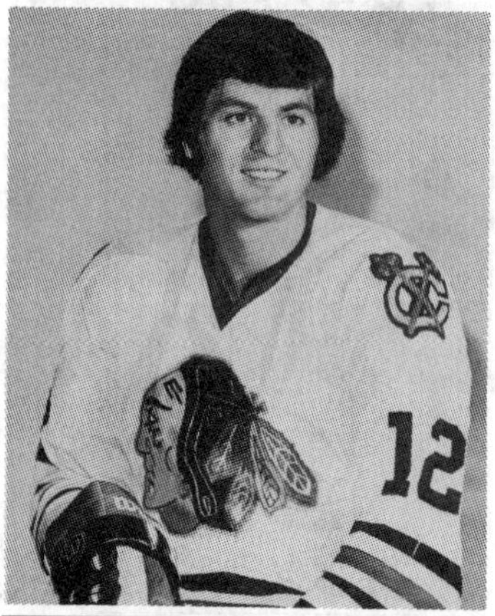

Ivan Boldirev

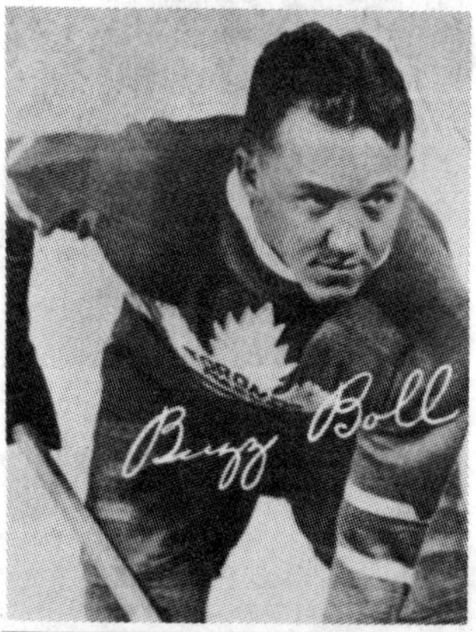

Frank "Buzz" Boll

Name	NHL Teams	NHL Seasons	Regular Schedule GP	G	A	TP	PIM	Playoffs GP	G	A	TP	PIM	NHL Cup Wins	First NHL Season	Last NHL Season
Baillargeon, Joel	Wpg., Que.	3	20	0	2	2	31	....	....	....	....	....		1986-87	1988-89
Baird, Ken	Cal.	1	10	0	2	2	15	....	....	....	....	....		1971-72	1971-72
Baker, Bill	Mtl., Col., St.L., NYR	3	143	7	25	32	175	6	0	0	0	0		1980-81	1982-83
Balderis, Helmut	Min.	1	26	3	6	9	2	....	....	....	....	....		1989-90	1989-90
Baldwin, Doug	Tor., Det., Chi.	3	24	0	1	1	8	....	....	....	....	....		1945-46	1947-48
Balfour, Earl	Tor., Chi.,	7	288	30	22	52	78	26	0	3	3	4	1	1951-52	1960-61
Balfour, Murray	Mtl., Chi., Bos.	8	306	67	90	157	393	40	9	10	19	45	1	1956-57	1964-65
Ball, Terry	Phi., Buf.	4	74	7	19	26	26	....	....	....	....	....		1967-68	1971-72
Balon, Dave	NYR, Mtl., Min., Van.	14	776	192	222	414	607	78	14	21	35	109	2	1959-60	1972-73
Baltimore, Byron	Edm.	1	2	0	0	0	4	....	....	....	....	....		1979-80	1979-80
Baluik, Stanley	Bos.	1	7	0	0	0	2	....	....	....	....	....		1959-60	1959-60
Bandura, Jeff	NYR	1	2	0	1	1	0	....	....	....	....	....		1980-81	1980-81
Barbe, Andy	Tor.	1	1	0	0	0	2	....	....	....	....	....		1950-51	1950-51
Barber, Bill	Phi.	12	903	420	463	883	623	129	53	55	108	109	2	1972-73	1984-85
Barilko, Bill	Tor.	5	252	26	36	62	456	47	5	7	12	104	4	1946-47	1950-51
Barkley, Doug	Chi., Det.	6	253	24	80	104	382	30	0	9	9	63		1957-58	1965-66
Barlow, Bob	Min.	2	77	16	17	33	10	6	2	2	4	6		1969-70	1970-71
Barnes, Blair	L.A.	1	1	0	0	0	0	....	....	....	....	....		1982-83	1982-83
Barnes, Norm	Phi., Hfd.	4	156	6	38	44	178	12	0	0	0	8		1976-77	1981-82
Bartel, Robin	Cgy., Van.	2	41	0	1	1	14	6	0	0	0	0		1985-86	1986-87
Brennan, Dan	L.A.	2	8	0	1	1	9	....	....	....	....	....		1983-84	1985-86
Baron, Normand	Mtl., St.L.	2	27	2	0	2	51	3	0	0	0	22		1983-84	1985-86
Barrett, Fred	Min., L.A.	13	745	25	123	148	671	44	0	2	2	60		1970-71	1983-84
Barrett, John	Det., Wsh., Min.	8	488	20	77	97	604	16	2	2	4	50		1980-81	1987-88
Barrie, Doug	Pit., Buf., L.A.	3	158	10	42	52	268	....	....	....	....	....		1968-69	1971-72
Barry, Ed	Bos.	1	19	1	3	4	2	....	....	....	....	....		1946-47	1946-47
Barry, Marty	NYA, Bos., Det., Mtl.	12	509	195	192	387	231	43	15	18	33	34	2	1927-28	1939-40
Barry, Ray	Bos.	1	18	1	2	3	6	....	....	....	....	....		1951-52	1951-52
Bartel, Robin	Cgy., Van.	2	41	0	1	1	14	6	0	0	0	16		1985-86	1986-87
Bartlett, Jim	Mtl., NYR, Bos.	5	191	34	23	57	273	2	0	0	0	0		1954-55	1960-61
Barton, Cliff	Pit., Phi., NYR	3	85	10	9	19	22	....	....	....	....	....		1929-30	1939-40
Bathe, Frank	Det., Phi.,	9	224	3	28	31	542	27	1	3	4	42		1974-75	1983-84
Bathgate, Andy	NYR, Tor., Det., Pit.	17	1069	349	624	973	624	54	21	14	35	76	1	1952-53	1970-71
Bathgate, Frank	NYR	1	2	0	0	0	2	....	....	....	....	....		1952-53	1952-53
Bauer, Bobby	Bos.	10	327	123	137	260	36	48	11	8	19	6	2	1935-36	1951-52
Baumgartner, Mike	K.C.	1	17	0	0	0	0	....	....	....	....	....		1974-75	1974-75
Baun, Bob	Tor., Oak., Det.	17	964	37	187	224	1493	96	3	12	15	171	4	1956-57	1972-73
Baxter, Paul	Que., Pit., Cgy.	8	472	48	121	169	1564	40	0	5	5	162		1979-80	1986-87
Beadle, Sandy	Wpg.	1	6	1	0	1	2	....	....	....	....	....		1980-81	1980-81
Beaton, Frank	NYR	2	25	1	1	2	43	....	....	....	....	....		1978-79	1979-80
Beattie, Red	Bos., Det., NYA	9	335	62	85	147	137	22	4	2	6	6		1930-31	1938-39
Beaudin, Norm	St.L., Min.	2	25	1	2	3	4	....	....	....	....	....		1967-68	1970-71
Beaudoin, Serge	Atl.	1	3	0	0	0	0	....	....	....	....	....		1979-80	1979-80
Beaudoin, Yves	Wsh.	3	11	0	0	0	5	....	....	....	....	....		1985-86	1987-88
Beck, Barry	Col., NYR, L.A.	10	615	104	251	355	1016	51	10	23	33	77		1977-78	1989-90
Beckett, Bob	Bos.	4	68	7	6	13	18	....	....	....	....	....		1956-57	1963-64
Bedard, James	Chi.	2	22	1	1	2	8	....	....	....	....	....		1949-50	1950-51
Bednarski, John	NYR, Edm.	4	100	2	18	20	114	1	0	0	0	0		1974-75	1979-80
Beers, Eddy	Cgy., St.L.	5	250	94	116	210	256	41	7	10	17	47		1981-82	1985-86
Behling, Dick	Det.	2	5	1	0	1	2	....	....	....	....	....		1940-41	1942-43
Beisler, Frank	NYA	2	2	0	0	0	0	....	....	....	....	....		1936-37	1939-40
Belanger, Alain	Tor.	1	9	0	1	1	6	....	....	....	....	....		1977-78	1977-78
Belanger, Roger	Pit.	1	44	3	5	8	32	....	....	....	....	....		1984-85	1984-85
Belisle, Danny	NYR	1	4	2	0	2	0	....	....	....	....	....		1960-61	1960-61
Beliveau, Jean	Mtl.	20	1125	507	712	1219	1029	162	79	97	176	211	10	1950-51	1970-71
Bell, Billy	Mtl.W, Mtl., Ott.	6	61	3	1	4	4	9	0	0	0	0	1	1917-18	1923-24
Bell, Harry	NYR	1	1	0	1	1	0	....	....	....	....	....		1946-47	1946-47
Bell, Joe	NYR	2	62	8	9	17	18	....	....	....	....	....		1942-43	1946-47
Belland, Neil	Van., Pit.	6	109	13	32	45	54	21	2	9	11	23		1981-82	1986-87
Bellefeuille, Pete	Tor., Det.	4	92	26	4	30	58	....	....	....	....	....		1925-26	1929-30
Bellemer, Andy	Mtl.M.	1	15	0	0	0	0	....	....	....	....	....		1932-33	1932-33
Bend, Lin	NYR	1	8	3	1	4	2	....	....	....	....	....		1942-43	1942-43
Bennett, Bill	Bos., Hfd.	2	31	4	7	11	65	....	....	....	....	....		1978-79	1979-80
Bennett, Curt	St.L., NYR, Atl.	10	580	152	182	334	347	21	1	1	2	57		1970-71	1979-80
Bennett, Frank	Det.	1	7	0	1	1	2	....	....	....	....	....		1943-44	1943-44
Bennett, Harvey	Pit., Wsh., Phi., Min., St.L.	5	268	44	46	90	347	4	0	0	0	2		1974-75	1978-79
Bennett, Max	Mtl.	1	1	0	0	0	0	....	....	....	....	....		1935-36	1935-36
Benoit, Joe	Mtl.	5	185	75	69	144	94	11	6	3	9	11	1	1940-41	1946-47
Benson, Bill	NYA, Bro.	2	67	11	25	36	35	....	....	....	....	....		1940-41	1941-42
Benson, Bobby	Bos.	1	8	0	1	1	4	....	....	....	....	....		1924-25	1924-25
Bentley, Doug	Chi., NYR	13	566	219	324	543	217	23	9	8	17	8		1939-40	1953-54
Bentley, Max	Chi., Tor., NYR	12	646	245	299	544	179	52	18	27	45	14	3	1940-41	1953-54
Bentley, Reggie	Chi.	1	11	1	2	3	2	....	....	....	....	....		1942-43	1942-43
Berenson, Red	Mtl., NYR, St.L., Det.	17	987	261	397	658	305	85	23	14	37	49	2	1961-62	1977-78
Bergdinon, Fred	Bos.	1	2	0	0	0	0	....	....	....	....	....		1925-26	1925-26
Bergen, Todd	Phi.	1	14	11	5	16	4	17	4	9	13	8		1984-85	1984-85
Bergeron, Michel	Det., NYI, Wsh.	5	229	80	58	138	165	....	....	....	....	....		1974-75	1978-79
Bergeron, Yves	Pit.	2	3	0	0	0	0	....	....	....	....	....		1974-75	1976-77
Berglund, Bo	Que., Min., Phi.	3	130	28	39	67	40	9	2	0	2	6		1983-84	1985-86
Bergloff, Bob	Min.	1	2	0	0	0	5	....	....	....	....	....		1982-83	1982-83
Bergman, Gary	Det., Min., K.C.	12	838	68	299	367	1249	21	0	5	5	20		1964-65	1975-76
Bergman, Thommie	Det.	6	246	21	44	65	243	7	0	2	2	2		1972-73	1979-80
Berlinquette, Louis	Mtl., Mtl.M., Pit.	8	193	44	29	73	111	16	1	1	2	0		1917-18	1925-26
Bernier, Serge	Phi., L.A., Que.	7	302	78	119	197	234	5	1	1	2	0		1968-69	1980-81
Berry, Bob	Mtl., L.A.	8	541	159	191	350	344	26	2	6	8	6		1968-69	1976-77
Berry, Doug	Col.	2	121	10	33	43	25	....	....	....	....	....		1979-80	1980-81
Berry, Fred	Det.	1	3	0	0	0	0	....	....	....	....	....		1976-77	1976-77
Besler, Phil	Bos., Chi., Det.	2	30	1	4	5	18	....	....	....	....	....		1935-36	1938-39
Bessone, Pete	Det.	1	6	0	1	1	6	....	....	....	....	....		1937-38	1937-38
Bethel, John	Wpg.	1	17	0	2	2	4	....	....	....	....	....		1979-80	1979-80
Bettio, Sam	Bos.	1	44	9	12	21	32	....	....	....	....	....		1949-50	1949-50
Beverley, Nick	Bos., Pit., NYR, Min., L.A., Col.	11	502	18	94	112	156	7	0	1	1	0		1966-67	1979-80
Bialowas, Dwight	Atl., Min.	4	164	11	46	57	46	....	....	....	....	....		1973-74	1976-77
Bianchin, Wayne	Pit., Edm.	7	276	68	41	109	137	3	0	1	1	6		1973-74	1979-80
Bidner, Todd	Wsh.	1	12	2	1	3	7	....	....	....	....	....		1981-82	1981-82
Biggs, Don	Min.	1	1	0	0	0	0	....	....	....	....	....		1984-85	1984-85
Bignell, Larry	Pit.	2	20	0	3	3	2	3	0	0	0	2		1973-74	1974-75
Bilodeau, Gilles	Que.	1	9	0	1	1	25	....	....	....	....	....		1979-80	1979-80
Bionda, Jack	Tor., Bos.	4	93	3	9	12	113	11	0	1	1	14		1955-56	1958-59
Black, Stephen	Det., Chi.	2	113	11	20	31	77	13	0	0	0	13	1	1949-50	1950-51
Blackburn, Bob	NYR., Pit.	3	135	8	12	20	105	6	0	0	0	4		1968-69	1970-71
Blackburn, Don	Bos., Phi., NYR, NYI, Min.	6	185	23	44	67	87	12	3	0	3	10		1962-63	1972-73
Blade, Hank	Chi.	2	24	2	3	5	2	....	....	....	....	....		1946-47	1947-48
Bladon, Tom	Phi., Pit., Edm., Wpg., Det.	9	610	73	197	270	392	86	8	29	37	70	2	1972-73	1980-81
Blaine, Gary	Mtl.	1	1	0	0	0	0	....	....	....	....	....		1954-55	1954-55
Blair, Andy	Tor., Chi.	9	402	74	86	160	323	38	6	6	12	32	1	1928-29	1936-37
Blair, Chuck	Tor.	2	3	0	0	0	0	....	....	....	....	....		1948-49	1950-51
Blair, George	Tor.	1	2	0	0	0	0	....	....	....	....	....		1950-51	1950-51
Blake, Mickey	St.L., Bos., Tor.	2	16	1	1	2	4	....	....	....	....	....		1934-35	1935-36
Blake, Toe	Mtl.M., Mtl.	15	578	235	292	527	272	57	25	37	62	23	3	1932-33	1947-48
Blight, Rick	Van., L.A.	7	326	96	125	221	170	5	0	5	5	2		1975-76	1982-83
Blinco, Russ	Mtl.M, Chi.	6	268	59	66	125	24	19	3	3	6	4	1	1933-34	1938-39
Block, Ken	Van.	1	1	0	0	0	0	....	....	....	....	....		1970-71	1970-71
Blomqvist, Timo	Wsh., N.J.	5	243	4	53	57	293	13	0	0	0	24		1981-82	1986-87
Bloom, Mike	Wsh., Det.	3	201	30	47	77	215	....	....	....	....	....		1974-75	1976-77
Boddy, Gregg	Van.	5	273	23	44	67	263	3	0	0	0	0		1971-72	1975-76
Bodnar, Gus	Tor., Chi., Bos.	12	667	142	254	396	207	32	4	3	7	10	2	1943-44	1954-55
Boehm, Ron	Oak.	1	16	2	1	3	10	....	....	....	....	....		1967-68	1967-68
Boesch, Garth	Tor.	4	197	9	28	37	205	34	2	5	7	18	3	1946-47	1949-50
Boh, Rick	Min.	1	8	2	1	3	4	....	....	....	....	....		1987-88	1987-88
Boileau, Marc	Det.	1	54	5	6	11	8	....	....	....	....	....		1961-62	1961-62
Boileau, Rene	NYA	1	7	0	0	0	0	....	....	....	....	....		1925-26	1925-26
Boimistruck, Fred	Tor.	2	83	4	14	18	45	....	....	....	....	....		1981-82	1982-83

Name	NHL Teams	NHL Seasons	Regular Schedule					Playoffs					NHL Cup Wins	First NHL Season	Last NHL Season
			GP	G	A	TP	PIM	GP	G	A	TP	PIM			
Boisvert, Serge	Tor., Mtl.	5	46	5	7	12	8	23	3	7	10	4	1	1982-83	1987-88
Boivin, Leo	Tor., Bos., Det., Pit., Min.	19	1150	72	250	322	1192	54	3	10	13	59		1951-52	1969-70
Boland, Mike A.	Phi.	1	2	0	0	0	0	....	....	....	....	....		1974-75	1974-75
Boland, Mike J.	K.C., Buf.	2	23	1	2	3	29	3	1	0	1	2		1974-75	1978-79
Boldirev, Ivan	Bos., Cal., Chi., Atl., Van., Det.	15	1052	361	505	866	507	48	13	20	33	14		1970-71	1984-85
Bolduc, Danny	Det., Cgy.	3	102	22	19	41	33	1	0	0	0	0		1978-79	1983-84
Bolduc, Michel	Que.	2	10	0	0	0	6	....	....	....	....	....		1981-82	1982-83
Boll, Buzz	Tor., NYA, Bro., Bos.	11	436	133	130	263	148	29	7	3	10	13		1933-34	1943-44
Bolonchuk, Larry	Van., Wsh.	4	74	3	9	12	97	....	....	....	....	....		1972-73	1977-78
Bolton, Hughie	Tor.	8	235	10	51	61	221	17	0	5	5	14		1949-50	1956-57
Bonar, Dan	L.A.	3	170	25	39	64	208	14	3	4	7	22		1980-81	1982-83
Bonin, Marcel	Det., Bos., Mtl.	9	454	97	175	272	336	50	11	14	25	51	4	1952-53	1961-62
Boo, Jim	Min.	1	6	0	0	0	22	....	....	....	....	....		1977-78	1977-78
Boone, Buddy	Bos.	2	34	5	3	8	28	22	2	1	3	25		1956-57	1957-58
Boothman, George	Tor.	2	58	17	19	36	18	5	2	1	3	2		1942-43	1943-44
Bordeleau, Chris.	Mtl., St.L., Chi.,	4	205	38	65	103	82	19	4	7	11	17	1	1968-69	1971-72
Bordeleau, J. P.	Chi.	10	519	97	126	223	143	48	3	6	9	12		1969-70	1979-80
Bordeleau, Paulin	Van.	3	183	33	56	89	47	5	2	1	3	0		1973-74	1975-76
Borotsik, Jack	St.L.	1	1	0	0	0	0	....	....	....	....	....		1974-75	1974-75
Bossy, Mike	NYI	10	752	573	553	1126	210	129	85	75	160	38	4	1977-78	1986-87
Bostrom, Helge	Chi.	4	96	3	3	6	58	13	0	0	0	16		1929-30	1932-33
Botell, Mark	Phi.	1	32	4	10	14	31	....	....	....	....	....		1981-82	1981-82
Bothwell, Tim	NYR, St.L., Hfd.	11	502	28	93	121	382	49	0	3	3	56		1978-79	1988-89
Botting, Cam	Atl.	1	2	0	1	1	0	....	....	....	....	....		1975-76	1975-76
Boucha, Henry	Det., Min., K.C., Col.	6	247	53	49	102	157	....	....	....	....	....		1971-72	1976-77
Bouchard, Emile (Butch)	Mtl.	15	785	49	144	193	863	113	11	21	32	121	4	1941-42	1955-56
Bouchard, Dick	NYR	1	1	0	0	0	0	....	....	....	....	....		1954-55	1954-55
Bouchard, Edmond	Mtl., Ham., NYA, Pit.	8	223	19	20	39	105	....	....	....	....	....		1921-22	1928-29
Bouchard, Pierre	Mtl., Wsh.	12	595	24	82	106	433	76	3	10	13	56	5	1970-71	1981-82
Boucher, Billy	Mtl., Bos., NYA	7	213	93	35	128	391	21	9	3	12	35	1	1921-22	1927-28
Boucher, Frank	Ott., NYR	14	557	161	262	423	119	56	16	18	34	12	2	1921-22	1943-44
Boucher, George	Ott., Mtl.M, Chi.	15	457	122	62	184	712	44	11	4	15	84	4	1917-18	1931-32
Boucher, Robert	Mtl.	1	12	0	0	0	0	....	....	....	....	....	1	1923-24	1923-24
Boudrias, Andre	Mtl., Min., Chi., St.L., Van.	12	662	151	340	491	218	34	6	10	16	12		1963-64	1975-76
Boughner, Barry	Oak., Cal.	2	20	0	0	0	11	....	....	....	....	....		1969-70	1970-71
Bourbonnais, Dan	Hfd.	2	59	3	25	28	11	....	....	....	....	....		1981-82	1983-84
Bourbonnais, Rick	St.L.	3	71	9	15	24	29	4	0	1	1	0		1975-76	1977-78
Bourcier, Conrad	Mtl.	1	6	0	0	0	0	....	....	....	....	....		1935-36	1935-36
Bourcier, Jean	Mtl.	1	9	0	1	1	0	....	....	....	....	....		1935-36	1935-36
Bourgeault, Leo	Tor. NYR, Ott., Mtl.	8	307	24	20	44	269	24	1	1	2	18	1	1926-27	1934-35
Bourgeois, Charlie	Cgy., St.L., Hfd.	7	290	16	54	70	788	40	2	3	5	194		1981-82	1987-88
Bourne, Bob	NYI, L.A.	14	964	258	324	582	605	139	40	56	96	108	4	1974-75	1987-88
Boutette, Pat	Tor., Hfd., Pit.	10	756	171	282	453	1354	46	10	14	24	109		1975-76	1984-85
Boutilier, Paul	NYI, Bos., Min., NYR, Wpg.	8	288	27	83	110	358	41	1	9	10	45		1981-82	1988-89
Bowcher, Clarence	NYA	2	47	2	2	4	110	....	....	....	....	....		1926-27	1927-28
Bowman, Kirk	Chi.	3	88	11	17	28	19	7	1	0	1	0		1976-77	1978-79
Bowman, Ralph	Ott., St.L., Det.	7	274	8	17	25	260	22	2	2	4	6	2	1933-34	1939-40
Bownass, Jack	Mtl., NYR	4	80	3	8	11	58	....	....	....	....	....		1957-58	1961-62
Bowness, Rick	Atl., Det., St. L, Wpg.	7	173	18	37	55	191	5	0	0	0	2		1975-76	1981-82
Boyd, Bill	NYR, NYA	4	138	15	7	22	72	9	0	0	0	2	1	1926-27	1929-30
Boyd, Irwin	Bos., Det.	4	97	18	19	37	51	15	0	1	1	4		1931-32	1943-44
Boyd, Randy	Pit., Chi., NYI, Van.	8	257	20	67	87	328	13	0	2	2	26		1981-82	1988-89
Boyer, Wally	Tor., Chi., Oak. Pit.	7	365	54	105	159	163	15	1	3	4	0		1965-66	1971-72
Brackenborough, John	Bos.	1	7	0	0	0	0	....	....	....	....	....		1925-26	1925-26
Brackenbury, Curt	Que., Edm., St.L.	4	141	9	17	26	226	2	0	0	0	0		1979-80	1982-83
Bradley, Barton	Bos.	1	1	0	0	0	0	....	....	....	....	....		1949-50	1949-50
Bradley, Lyle	Cal. Cle.	2	6	1	0	1	2	....	....	....	....	....		1973-74	1976-77
Bragnalo, Rick	Wsh.	4	145	15	35	50	46	....	....	....	....	....		1975-76	1978-79
Brannigan, Andy	NYA, Bro.	2	26	1	2	3	31	....	....	....	....	....		1940-41	1941-42
Brasar, Per-Olov	Min., Van.	5	348	64	142	206	33	13	1	2	3	0		1977-78	1981-82
Brayshaw, Russ	Chi.	1	43	5	9	14	24	....	....	....	....	....		1944-45	1944-45
Breitenbach, Ken	Buf.	3	68	1	13	14	49	8	0	1	1	4		1975-76	1978-79
Brennan, Doug	NYR	3	123	9	7	16	152	16	1	0	1	21	1	1931-32	1933-34
Brennan, Tom	Bos.	2	22	2	2	4	2	....	....	....	....	....		1943-44	1944-45
Brenneman, John	Chi., NYR, Tor., Det., Oak.	5	152	21	19	40	46	....	....	....	....	....		1964-65	1968-69
Bretto, Joe	Chi.	1	3	0	0	0	4	....	....	....	....	....		1944-45	1944-45
Brewer, Carl	Tor., Det., St.L.	12	604	25	198	223	1037	72	3	17	20	146	3	1957-58	1979-80
Briden, Archie	Det., Pit.	2	72	9	5	14	56	....	....	....	....	....		1926-27	1929-30
Bridgman, Mel	Phi., Cgy., N.J., Det., Van.	14	977	252	449	701	1625	125	28	39	67	298		1975-76	1988-89
Briere, Michel	Pit.	1	76	12	32	44	20	10	5	3	8	17		1969-70	1969-70
Brindley, Doug	Tor.	1	3	0	0	0	0	....	....	....	....	....		1970-71	1970-71
Brink, Milt	Chi.	1	5	0	0	0	0	....	....	....	....	....		1936-37	1936-37
Brisson, Gerry	Mtl.	1	4	0	2	2	4	....	....	....	....	....		1962-63	1962-63
Britz, Greg	Tor., Hfd.	3	8	0	0	0	4	....	....	....	....	....		1983-84	1986-87
Broadbent, Harry	Ott. Mt.M, NYA	11	302	122	45	167	553	41	13	3	16	69	4	1918-19	1928-29
Broden, Connie	Mtl.	3	6	2	1	3	2	7	0	1	1	0	2	1955-56	1957-58
Brooks, Gord	St.L., Wsh.	3	70	7	18	25	37	....	....	....	....	....		1971-72	1974-75
Brophy, Bernie	Mtl.M, Det.	3	62	4	4	8	25	2	0	0	0	2	1	1925-26	1929-30
Brossart, Willie	Phi., Tor., Wsh.	6	129	1	14	15	88	1	0	0	0	0		1970-71	1975-76
Brown, Adam	Det. Chi. Bos.	10	391	104	113	217	358	26	2	14	6	14	1	1941-42	1951-52
Brown, Arnie	Tor. NYR, Det., NYI, Atl.	12	681	44	141	185	738	22	0	6	6	23		1961-62	1973-74
Brown, Connie	Det.	5	91	15	24	39	12	14	2	3	5	0		1938-39	1942-43
Brown, Fred	Mtl.M	1	19	1	0	1	0	9	0	0	0	0		1927-28	1927-28
Brown, George	Mtl.	3	79	6	22	28	34	7	0	0	0	2		1936-37	1938-39
Brown, Gerry	Det.	2	23	4	5	9	2	12	2	1	3	4		1941-42	1945-46
Brown, Harold	NYR	1	13	2	1	3	2	....	....	....	....	....		1945-46	1945-46
Brown, Jim	L.A.	1	3	0	1	1	5	....	....	....	....	....		1982-83	1982-83
Brown, Larry	NYR, Det., Phi., L.A.	9	455	7	53	60	180	35	0	4	4	10		1969-70	1977-78
Brown, Stan	NYR, Det.	2	48	8	2	10	18	2	0	0	0	0		1926-27	1927-28
Brown, Wayne	Bos.	1	....	....	....	....	....	4	0	0	0	2		1953-54	1953-54
Browne, Cecil	Chi.	1	13	2	0	2	4	....	....	....	....	....		1927-28	1927-28
Brownschidle, Jack	St.L., Hfd.	9	494	39	162	201	151	26	0	5	5	18		1977-78	1985-86
Brownschidle, Jeff	Hfd.	2	7	0	1	1	2	....	....	....	....	....		1981-82	1982-83
Brubaker, Jeff	Hfd., Mtl., Cgy., Tor., Edm., NYR, Det.	8	178	16	9	25	512	2	0	0	0	27		1979-80	1988-89
Bruce, Gordie	Bos.	3	28	4	9	13	13	7	2	3	5	4		1940-41	1945-46
Bruce, Morley	Ott.	4	72	8	1	9	27	12	0	0	0	3	2	1917-18	1921-22
Bruneteau, Eddie	Det.	7	180	40	42	82	35	26	7	6	13	0		1940-41	1948-49
Bruneteau, Mud	Det.	11	411	139	138	277	80	77	23	14	37	22	3	1935-36	1945-46
Brydge, Bill	Tor., Det., NYA	9	368	26	52	78	506	2	0	0	0	4		1926-27	1935-36
Brydges, Paul	Buf.	1	15	2	2	4	6	....	....	....	....	....		1986-87	1986-87
Brydson, Glenn	Mtl.M, St.L., NYR, Chi.	8	299	56	79	135	203	11	0	0	0	8		1930-31	1937-38
Brydson, Gord	Tor.	1	8	2	0	2	8	....	....	....	....	....		1929-30	1929-30
Bubla, Jiri	Van.	5	256	17	101	118	202	6	0	0	0	7		1981-82	1985-86
Buchanan, Al	Tor.	2	4	0	1	1	2	....	....	....	....	....		1948-49	1949-50
Buchanan, Bucky	NYR	1	2	0	0	0	0	....	....	....	....	....		1948-49	1948-49
Buchanan, Mike	Chi.	1	1	0	0	0	0	....	....	....	....	....		1951-52	1951-52
Buchanan, Ron	Bos., St.L.	2	5	0	0	0	0	....	....	....	....	....		1966-67	1969-70
Bucyk, John	Det., Bos.,	23	1540	556	813	1369	497	124	41	64	103	42	2	1955-56	1977-78
Buhr, Doug	K.C.	1	6	0	2	2	4	....	....	....	....	....		1974-75	1974-75
Bukovich, Tony	Det.	2	44	7	3	10	6	6	0	1	1	0		1943-44	1944-45
Buller, Hy	Det., NYR	5	188	22	58	80	215	....	....	....	....	....		1943-44	1953-54
Bulley, Ted	Chi., Wsh., Pit.	8	414	101	113	214	704	29	5	5	10	24		1976-77	1983-84
Burch, Billy	Ham., NYA, Bos., Chi.	11	390	137	53	190	251	2	0	0	0	0		1922-23	1932-33
Burchell, Fred	Mtl.	2	4	0	0	0	2	....	....	....	....	....		1950-51	1953-54
Burdon, Glen	K.C.	1	11	0	2	2	0	....	....	....	....	....		1974-75	1974-75
Burega, Bill	Bos.	1	4	0	1	1	4	....	....	....	....	....		1955-56	1955-56
Burke, Eddie	Bos., NYA	4	106	29	20	49	55	....	....	....	....	....		1931-32	1934-35
Burke, Marty	Mtl., Pit., Ott., Chi.	11	494	19	47	66	560	31	2	4	6	44	2	1927-28	1937-38
Burmeister, Roy	NYA	3	67	4	3	7	2	....	....	....	....	....		1929-30	1931-32
Burnett, Kelly	NYR	1	3	1	0	1	0	....	....	....	....	....		1952-53	1952-53
Burns, Bobby	Chi.	3	20	1	0	1	8	....	....	....	....	....		1927-28	1929-30
Burns, Charlie	Det., Bos., Oak., Pit., Min.	11	749	106	198	304	252	31	5	4	9	4		1958-59	1972-73
Burns, Gary	NYR	2	11	2	2	4	18	5	0	0	0	6		1980-81	1981-82

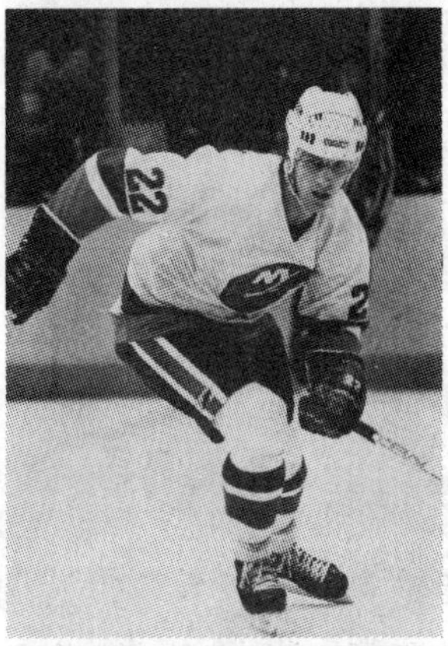

Mike Bossy

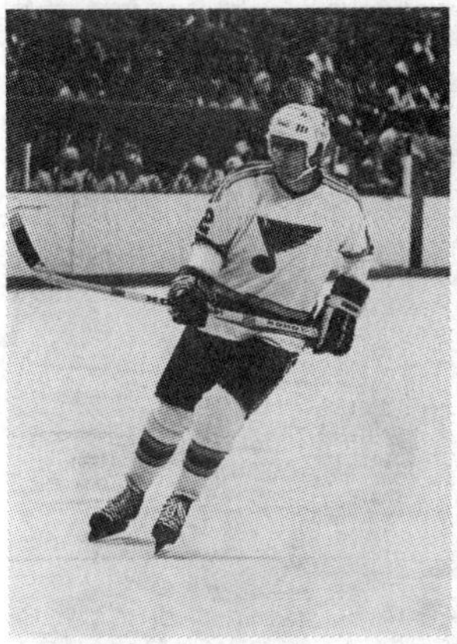

Rick Bowness

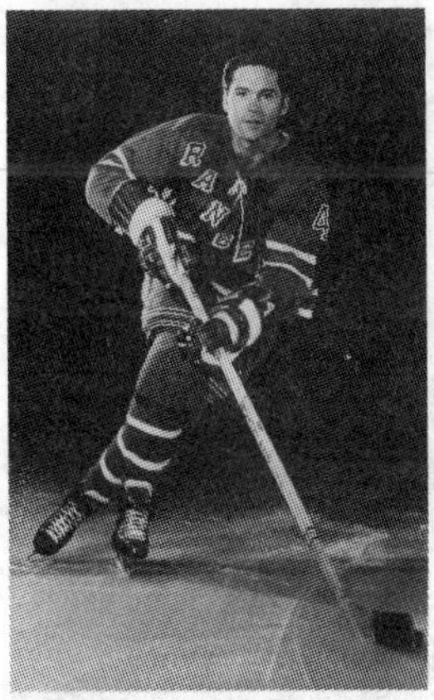

Arnie Brown

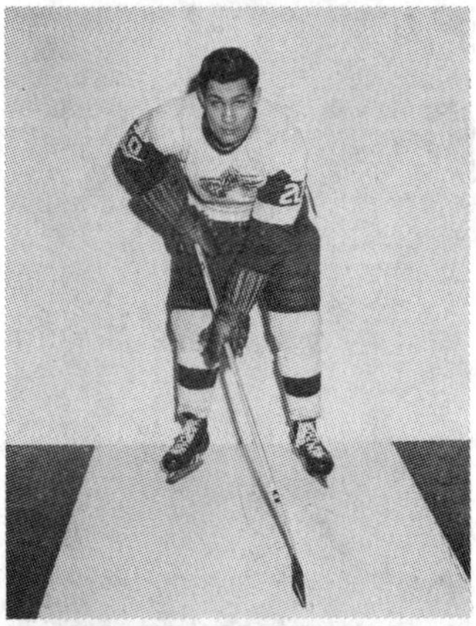

John Bucyk

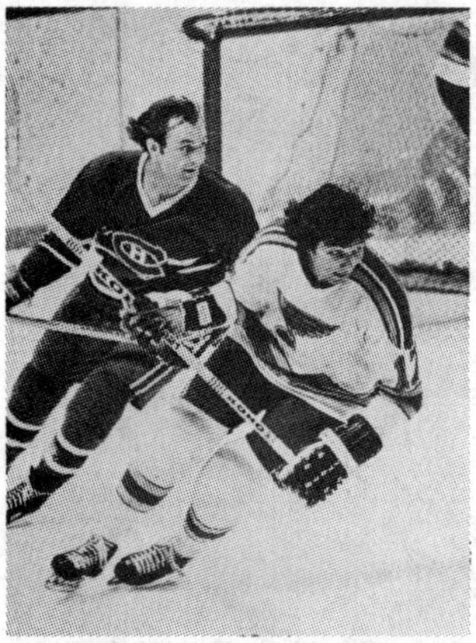

Jerry Butler

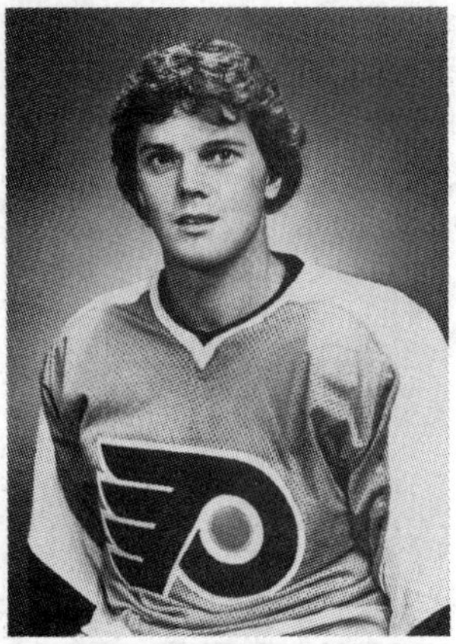

Lindsay Carson

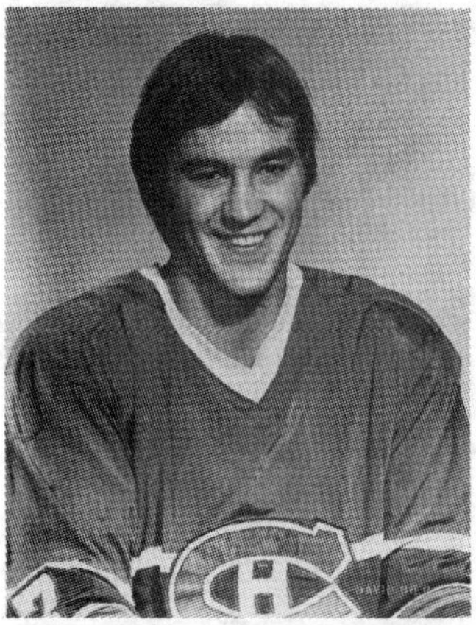

Rick Chartraw

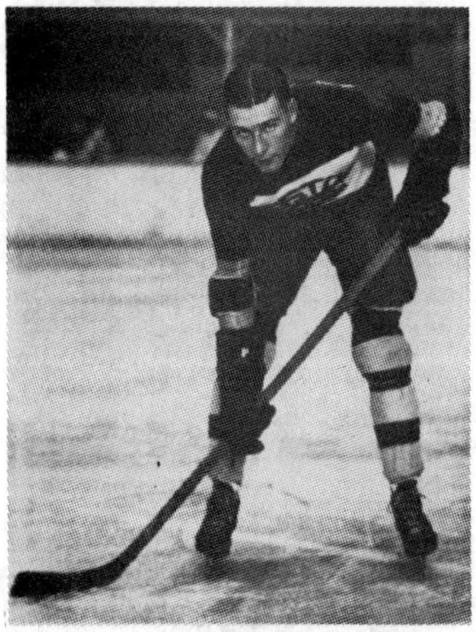

Dit Clapper

			Regular Schedule					Playoffs							
Name	NHL Teams	NHL Seasons	GP	G	A	TP	PIM	GP	G	A	TP	PIM	NHL Cup Wins	First NHL Season	Last NHL Season
Burns, Norm	NYR	1	11	0	4	4	2	....	....	....	....	....		1941-42	1941-42
Burns, Robin	Pit., K.C.	5	190	31	38	69	139	....	....	....	....	....		1970-71	1975-76
Burrows, Dave	Pit., Tor.	10	724	29	135	164	377	29	1	5	6	25		1971-72	1980-81
Burry, Bert	Ott.	1	4	0	0	0	0	....	....	....	....	....		1932-33	1932-33
Burton, Cummy	Det.	3	43	0	2	2	21	3	0	0	0	0		1955-56	1958-59
Burton, Nelson	Wsh.	2	8	1	0	1	21	....	....	....	....	....		1977-78	1978-79
Bush, Eddie	Det.	2	27	4	6	10	50	12	1	6	7	23		1938-39	1941-42
Busniuk, Mike	Phi.	2	143	3	23	26	297	25	2	5	7	34		1979-80	1980-81
Busniuk, Ron	Buf.	2	6	0	3	3	4	....	....	....	....	....		1972-73	1973-74
Buswell, Walt	Det., Mtl.	8	368	10	40	50	164	24	2	1	3	10		1932-33	1939-40
Butler, Dick	Chi.	1	7	2	0	2	0	....	....	....	....	....		1947-48	1947-48
Butler, Jerry	NYR, St.L., Tor., Van., Wpg.	11	641	99	120	219	515	48	3	3	6	79		1972-73	1982-83
Butters, Bill	Min.	2	72	1	4	5	77	....	....	....	....	....		1977-78	1978-79
Buttrey, Gord	Chi.	1	10	0	0	0	0	10	0	0	0	0		1943-44	1943-44
Buynak, Gordon	St. L	1	4	0	0	0	2	....	....	....	....	....		1974-75	1974-75
Byers, Gord	Bos.	1	1	0	1	1	0	....	....	....	....	....		1949-50	1949-50
Byers, Jerry	Min., Atl, NYR	4	43	3	4	7	10	....	....	....	....	....		1972-73	1977-78
Byers, Mike	Tor., Phi., Buf., L.A.	4	166	42	34	76	39	4	0	1	1	0		1967-68	1971-72
C															
Caffery, Jack	Tor., Bos.	3	57	3	2	5	22	10	1	0	1	4		1954-55	1957-58
Caffery, Terry	Chi., Min.	2	14	0	0	0	0	1	0	0	0	0		1969-70	1970-71
Cahan, Larry	Tor., NYR, Oak., L.A.	13	665	38	92	130	700	29	1	1	2	38		1954-55	1970-71
Cahill, Chuck	Bos.	2	32	0	1	1	4	....	....	....	....	....		1925-26	1926-27
Cain, Herbert	Mtl.M, Mtl., Bos.	13	571	206	194	400	178	64	16	13	29	13	2	1933-34	1945-46
Cain, Jim	Mtl.M, Tor.	2	61	4	0	4	35	....	....	....	....	....	1	1924-25	1925-26
Cairns, Don	K.C., Col.	2	9	0	1	1	2	....	....	....	....	....		1975-76	1976-77
Calder, Eric	Wsh.	2	2	0	0	0	0	....	....	....	....	....		1981-82	1982-83
Calladine, Norm	Bos.	3	63	19	29	48	8	....	....	....	....	....		1942-43	1944-45
Callander, Drew	Phi., Van.	4	39	6	2	8	7	....	....	....	....	....		1976-77	1979-80
Callighen, Brett	Edm.	3	160	56	89	145	132	14	4	6	10	8		1979-80	1981-82
Callighen, Patsy	NYR	1	36	0	0	0	32	9	0	0	0	0	1	1927-28	1927-28
Camazzola, James	Chi.	2	3	0	0	0	0	....	....	....	....	....		1983-84	1986-87
Camazzola, Tony	Wsh.	1	3	0	0	0	4	....	....	....	....	....		1981-82	1981-82
Cameron, Al	Det., Wpg.	6	282	11	44	55	356	7	0	1	1	2		1975-76	1980-81
Cameron, Scotty	NYR	1	35	8	11	19	0	....	....	....	....	....		1942-43	1942-43
Cameron, Billy	Mtl., NYA	2	39	0	0	0	2	6	0	0	0	0	1	1923-24	1925-26
Cameron, Craig	Det., St.L., Min., NYI	9	552	87	65	152	202	27	3	1	4	17		1966-67	1975-76
Cameron, Dave	Col., N.J.	3	168	25	28	53	238	....	....	....	....	....		1981-82	1983-84
Cameron, Harry	Tor., Ott., Mtl.	6	127	90	27	117	120	20	7	3	10	29	3	1917-18	1922-23
Campbell, Bryan	L.A., Chi.	5	260	35	71	106	74	22	3	4	7	2		1967-68	1971-72
Campbell, Colin	Pit., Col., Edm., Van., Det.	11	636	25	103	128	1292	45	4	10	14	181		1974-75	1984-85
Campbell, Dave	Mtl.	1	3	0	0	0	0	....	....	....	....	....		1920-21	1920-21
Campbell, Don	Chi.	1	17	1	3	4	8	....	....	....	....	....		1943-44	1943-44
Campbell, Scott	Wpg., St.L.	3	80	4	21	25	243	....	....	....	....	....		1979-80	1981-82
Campbell, Spiff	Ott., NYA	3	77	5	1	6	12	2	0	0	0	0		1923-24	1925-26
Campbell, Wade	Wpg., Bos.	6	213	9	27	36	305	10	0	0	0	20		1982-83	1987-88
Campeau, Tod	Mtl.	3	42	5	9	14	16	1	0	0	0	0		1943-44	1948-49
Campedelli, Dom	Mtl.	1	2	0	0	0	0	....	....	....	....	....		1985-86	1985-86
Carbol, Leo	Chi.	1	6	0	1	1	4	....	....	....	....	....		1942-43	1942-43
Cardin, Claude	St.L.	1	1	0	0	0	0	....	....	....	....	....		1967-68	1967-68
Cardwell, Steve	Pit.	3	53	9	11	20	35	4	0	0	0	2		1970-71	1972-73
Carey, George	Que, Ham., Tor.	5	72	22	8	30	14	....	....	....	....	....		1919-20	1923-24
Carleton, Wayne	Tor., Bos., Cal.	7	278	55	73	128	172	18	2	4	6	14	1	1965-66	1971-72
Carlin, Brian	L.A.	1	5	1	0	1	0	....	....	....	....	....		1971-72	1971-72
Carlson, Jack	Min., St.L.	6	236	30	15	45	417	25	1	2	3	72		1978-79	1986-87
Carlson, Kent	Mtl., St.L., Wsh.	5	113	7	11	18	148	8	0	0	0	13		1983-84	1988-89
Carlson, Steve	L.A.	1	52	9	12	21	23	4	1	1	2	7		1979-80	1979-80
Caron, Alain	Oak., Mtl.	2	60	9	13	22	18	....	....	....	....	....		1967-68	1968-69
Carpenter, Eddie	Que, Ham.	2	44	10	4	14	23	....	....	....	....	....		1919-20	1920-21
Carr, Al	Tor.	1	5	0	1	1	4	....	....	....	....	....		1943-44	1943-44
Carr, Gene	St.L., NYR, L.A., Pit., Atl.	8	465	79	136	215	365	35	5	8	13	66		1971-72	1978-79
Carr, Lorne	NYR, NYA, Tor.	13	580	204	222	426	132	53	10	9	19	13	1	1933-34	1945-46
Carriere, Larry	Buf. Atl, Van., L.A., Tor.	7	366	16	74	90	463	27	0	3	3	42		1972-73	1979-80
Carrigan, Gene	NYR, StL, Det.	3	37	2	1	3	13	4	0	0	0	0		1930-31	1934-35
Carroll, Billy	NYI, Edm., Det.	7	322	30	54	84	113	71	6	12	18	18	4	1980-81	1986-87
Carroll, George	Mtl.M, Bos.	1	15	0	0	0	9	....	....	....	....	....		1924-25	1924-25
Carroll, Greg	Wsh., Det., Hfd.	2	131	20	34	54	44	....	....	....	....	....		1978-79	1979-80
Carruthers, Dwight	Det. Phi.	2	2	0	0	0	0	....	....	....	....	....		1965-66	1967-68
Carse, Bill	NYR, Chi.	4	124	28	43	71	38	16	3	2	5	0		1938-39	1941-42
Carse, Bob	Chi., Mtl.	5	167	32	55	87	52	10	0	2	2	2		1939-40	1947-48
Carson, Bill	Tor., Bos.	4	159	54	24	78	156	11	3	0	3	14	1	1926-27	1929-30
Carson, Frank	Mtl.M., NYA, Det.	7	248	42	48	90	166	22	0	2	2	9	1	1925-26	1933-34
Carson, Gerry	Mtl., NYR, Mtl.M.	6	261	12	11	23	205	22	0	0	0	12	1	1928-29	1936-37
Carson, Lindsay	Phi., Hfd.	7	373	66	80	146	524	49	4	10	14	56		1981-82	1987-88
Carter, Billy	Mtl., Bos.	3	16	0	0	0	6	....	....	....	....	....		1957-58	1961-62
Carter, Ron	Edm.	1	2	0	0	0	0	....	....	....	....	....		1979-80	1979-80
Carveth, Joe	Det., Bos., Mtl.	11	504	150	189	339	81	69	21	16	37	28	2	1940-41	1950-51
Cashman, Wayne	Bos.	17	1027	277	516	793	1041	145	31	57	88	250	2	1964-65	1982-83
Cassidy, Tom	Pit.	1	26	3	4	7	15	....	....	....	....	....		1977-78	1977-78
Cassolato, Tony	Wsh.	3	23	1	6	7	4	....	....	....	....	....		1979-80	1981-82
Ceresino, Ray	Tor.	1	12	1	1	2	2	....	....	....	....	....		1948-49	1948-49
Cernik, Frantisek	Det.	1	49	5	4	9	13	....	....	....	....	....		1984-85	1984-85
Chad John	Chi.	3	80	15	22	37	29	10	0	1	1	2		1939-40	1945-46
Chalmers, Bill	NYR	1	1	0	0	0	0	....	....	....	....	....		1953-54	1953-54
Chalupa, Milan	Det.	1	14	0	5	5	6	....	....	....	....	....		1984-85	1984-85
Chamberlain, Murph	Tor., Mtl., Bro., Bos.	12	510	100	175	275	769	66	14	17	31	96	2	1937-38	1948-49
Champagne, Andre	Tor.	1	2	0	0	0	0	....	....	....	....	....		1962-63	1962-63
Chapman, Art	Bos., NYA	10	438	62	176	238	140	25	1	5	6	9		1930-31	1939-40
Chapman, Blair	Pit., St.L.	7	402	106	125	231	158	25	4	6	10	15		1976-77	1982-83
Charlebois, Bob	Min.	1	7	1	0	1	0	....	....	....	....	....		1967-68	1967-68
Charron, Guy	Mtl., Det., K.C., Wsh.	12	734	221	309	530	146	....	....	....	....	....		1969-70	1980-81
Chartier, Dave	Wpg.	1	1	0	0	0	0	....	....	....	....	....		1980-81	1980-81
Chartraw, Rick	Mtl., L.A., NYR, Edm.	10	420	28	64	92	399	75	7	9	16	80	4	1974-75	1983-84
Check, Lude	Det., Chi.	2	27	6	2	8	4	....	....	....	....	....		1943-44	1944-45
Chernoff, Mike	Min.	1	1	0	0	0	0	....	....	....	....	....		1968-69	1968-69
Cherry, Dick	Bos., Phi.	3	145	12	10	22	45	4	1	0	1	4		1956-57	1969-70
Cherry, Don	Bos.	1	....	....	....	....	....	1	0	0	0	0		1954-55	1954-55
Chevrefils, Real	Bos., Det.	8	387	104	97	201	185	30	5	4	9	20		1951-52	1958-59
Chicoine, Dan	Cle. Min.	3	31	1	2	3	12	1	0	0	0	0		1977-78	1979-80
Chinnick, Rick	Min.	2	4	0	2	2	0	....	....	....	....	....		1973-74	1974-75
Chipperfield, Ron	Edm., Que.,	2	83	22	24	46	34	....	....	....	....	....		1979-80	1980-81
Chisholm, Art	Bos.	1	3	0	0	0	0	....	....	....	....	....		1960-61	1960-61
Chisholm, Colin	Min.	1	1	0	0	0	0	....	....	....	....	....		1986-87	1986-87
Chisholm, Lex	Tor.	2	54	10	8	18	19	3	1	0	1	0		1939-40	1940-41
Chorney, Marc	Pit. L.A.	4	210	8	27	35	209	7	0	1	1	2		1980-81	1983-84
Chouinard, Gene	Ott.	1	8	0	0	0	0	....	....	....	....	....		1927-28	1927-28
Chouinard, Guy	Atl, Cgy., St.L.	10	578	205	370	575	120	46	9	28	37	12		1974-75	1983-84
Christie, Mike	Cal., Cle., Col., Van.	7	412	15	101	116	550	2	0	0	0	0		1974-75	1980-81
Christoff, Steve	Min. Cgy., L.A.	5	248	77	64	141	108	35	16	12	28	25		1979-80	1983-84
Chrystal, Bob	NYR	2	132	11	14	25	112	....	....	....	....	....		1953-54	1954-55
Church, Jack	Tor., Bro., Bos.	6	145	5	22	27	164	25	1	1	2	18		1938-39	1945-46
Ciesla, Hank	Chi., NYR	4	269	26	51	77	87	6	0	2	2	0		1955-56	1958-59
Clackson, Kim	Pit., Que.	2	106	0	8	8	370	8	0	0	0	70		1979-80	1980-81
Clancy, Francis (King)	Ott., Tor.	16	592	137	143	280	904	61	9	8	17	92	3	1921-22	1936-37
Clancy, Terry	Oak., Tor.	4	93	6	6	12	39	....	....	....	....	....		1967-68	1972-73
Clapper, Dit	Bos.	20	833	228	246	474	462	86	13	17	30	50	3	1927-28	1946-47
Clark, Andy	Bos.	1	5	0	0	0	0	....	....	....	....	....		1927-28	1927-28
Clark, Dan	NYR	1	4	0	1	1	6	....	....	....	....	....		1978-79	1978-79
Clark, Dean	Edm.	1	1	0	0	0	0	....	....	....	....	....		1983-84	1983-84
Clark, Gordie	Bos.	2	8	0	1	1	0	1	0	0	0	0		1974-75	1975-76

Name	NHL Teams	NHL Seasons	Regular Schedule					Playoffs					NHL Cup Wins	First NHL Season	Last NHL Season
			GP	G	A	TP	PIM	GP	G	A	TP	PIM			
Clarke, Bobby	Phi.	15	1144	358	852	1210	1453	136	42	77	119	152	2	1969-70	1983-84
Cleghorn, Odie	Mtl., Pit.	10	180	95	29	124	147	23	9	2	11	2	1	1918-19	1927-28
Cleghorn, Sprague	Ott. Tor. Mtl., Bos.	10	256	84	39	123	489	37	7	8	15	48	3	1918-19	1927-28
Clement, Bill	Phi., Wsh., Atl., Cgy.	11	719	148	208	356	383	50	5	3	8	26	2	1971-72	1981-82
Cline, Bruce	NYR	1	30	2	3	5	10	....	....	....	....	....		1956-57	1956-57
Clippingdale, Steve	L.A., Wsh.	2	19	1	2	3	9	1	0	0	0	0		1976-77	1979-80
Cloutier, Real	Que. Buf.	6	317	146	198	344	119	25	7	5	12	20		1979-80	1984-85
Cloutier, Rejean	Det.	2	5	0	2	2	2	....	....	....	....	....		1979-80	1981-82
Cloutier, Roland	Det., Que.	3	34	8	9	17	2	....	....	....	....	....		1977-78	1979-80
Clune, Wally	Mtl.	1	5	0	0	0	6	....	....	....	....	....		1955-56	1955-56
Coalter, Gary	Cal., K.C.	2	34	2	4	6	2	....	....	....	....	....		1973-74	1974-75
Coates, Steve	Det.	1	5	1	0	1	24	....	....	....	....	....		1976-77	1976-77
Cochrane, Glen	Phi., Van., Chi., Edm.	10	411	17	72	89	1556	18	1	1	2	31		1978-79	1988-89
Coflin, Hughie	Chi.	1	31	0	3	3	33	....	....	....	....	....		1950-51	1950-51
Colley, Tom	Min.	1	1	0	0	0	2	....	....	....	....	....		1974-75	1974-75
Collings, Norm	Mtl.	1	1	0	1	1	0	....	....	....	....	....		1934-35	1934-35
Collins, Bill	Min., Mtl., Det., St. L, NYR, Phi., Wsh.	11	768	157	154	311	415	18	3	5	8	12		1967-68	1977-78
Collins, Gary	Tor.	1	....	....	....	....	....	2	0	0	0	0		1958-59	1958-59
Collyard, Bob	St.L.	1	10	1	3	4	4	....	....	....	....	....		1973-74	1973-74
Colville, Mac	NYR	9	353	71	104	175	130	40	9	10	19	14	1	1935-36	1946-47
Colville, Neil	NYR	12	464	99	166	265	213	46	7	19	26	33	1	1935-36	1948-49
Colwill, Les	NYR	1	69	7	6	13	16	....	....	....	....	....		1958-59	1958-59
Comeau, Rey	Mtl., Atl, Col.	9	564	98	141	239	175	9	2	1	3	8		1971-72	1979-80
Conacher, Brian	Tor., Det.	5	154	28	28	56	84	12	3	2	5	21	1	1961-62	1971-72
Conacher, Charlie	Tor., Det., NYA	12	460	225	173	398	523	49	17	18	35	53	1	1929-30	1940-41
Conacher, Jim	Det., Chi., NYR	8	328	85	117	202	91	19	5	2	7	4		1945-46	1952-53
Conacher, Lionel	Pit., NYA, Mtl.M., Chi.	12	500	80	105	185	882	35	2	2	4	34	2	1925-26	1936-37
Conacher, Pete	Chi., NYR, Tor.	6	229	47	39	86	57	7	0	0	0	0		1951-52	1957-58
Conacher, Roy	Bos., Det., Chi.	11	490	226	200	426	90	42	15	15	30	14	2	1938-39	1951-52
Conn, Hugh	NYA	2	96	9	28	37	22	....	....	....	....	....		1933-34	1934-35
Connelly, Wayne	Mtl., Bos., Min., Det., St. L, Van.	10	543	133	174	307	156	24	11	7	18	4		1960-61	1971-72
Connolly, Bert	NYR, Chi.	3	87	13	15	28	37	14	1	0	1	0	1	1934-35	1937-38
Connor, Cam	Mtl., Edm., NYR	5	89	9	22	31	256	20	5	0	5	6	1	1978-79	1982-83
Connor, Harry	Bos., NYA, Ott.	4	134	16	5	21	139	10	0	0	0	2		1927-28	1930-31
Connors, Bobby	NYA, Det.	3	78	17	10	27	110	2	0	0	0	10		1926-27	1929-30
Contini, Joe	Col., Min.	3	68	17	21	38	34	2	0	0	0	0		1977-78	1980-81
Convey, Eddie	NYR	3	36	1	1	2	33	....	....	....	....	....		1930-31	1932-33
Cook, Bill	NYR	11	452	229	138	367	386	46	13	12	25	66	2	1926-27	1936-37
Cook, Bob	Van., Det., NYI, Min.	4	72	13	9	22	22	....	....	....	....	....		1970-71	1974-75
Cook, Bud	Bos., Ott., St.L.	3	51	5	4	9	22	....	....	....	....	....		1931-32	1934-35
Cook, Bun	NYR, Bos.	11	473	158	144	302	449	46	15	3	18	57	2	1926-27	1936-37
Cook, Lloyd	Bos.	1	4	1	0	1	0	....	....	....	....	....		1924-25	1924-25
Cook, Tom	Chi., Mtl.M.	8	311	77	98	175	184	24	2	4	6	17	1	1929-30	1937-38
Cooper, Carson	Bos., Mtl., Det.	8	278	110	57	167	111	4	0	0	0	2		1924-25	1931-32
Cooper, Ed	Col.	2	49	8	7	15	46	....	....	....	....	....		1980-81	1981-82
Cooper, Hal	NYR	1	8	0	0	0	2	....	....	....	....	....		1944-45	1944-45
Cooper, Joe	NYR, Chi.	11	420	30	66	96	442	32	3	5	8	6		1935-36	1946-47
Copp, Bob	Tor.	2	40	3	9	12	26	....	....	....	....	....		1942-43	1950-51
Corbeau, Bert	Mtl.. Ham., Tor.,	10	257	64	31	95	501	14	2	0	2	10		1917-18	1926-27
Corbett, Michael	L.A.	1	....	....	....	....	....	2	0	1	1	2		1967-68	1967-68
Corcoran, Norm	Bos., Det., Chi.	4	29	1	3	4	21	4	0	0	0	6		1949-50	1955-56
Cormier, Roger	Mtl.	1	0	0	0	0	0	....	....	....	....	....		1925-26	1925-26
Corrigan, Charlie	Tor., NYA	2	19	2	2	4	2	....	....	....	....	....		1937-38	1940-41
Corrigan, Mike	L.A., Van., Pit.	10	594	152	195	347	698	17	2	3	5	20		1967-68	1977-78
Corriveau, Andre	Mtl.	1	3	0	1	1	0	....	....	....	....	....		1953-54	1953-54
Cory, Ross	Wpg.	2	51	2	10	12	41	....	....	....	....	....		1979-80	1980-81
Cossete, Jacques	Pit.	3	64	8	6	14	29	3	0	1	1	4		1975-76	1978-79
Costello, Les	Tor.	3	15	2	3	5	11	6	2	2	4	2	1	1947-48	1949-50
Costello, Murray	Chi., Bos., Det.	4	162	13	19	32	54	5	0	0	0	2		1953-54	1956-57
Costello, Rich	Tor.	2	12	2	2	4	2	....	....	....	....	....		1983-84	1985-86
Cotch, Charlie	Ham.	1	11	1	0	1	0	....	....	....	....	....		1924-25	1924-25
Cote, Alain	Que.	10	696	103	190	293	383	67	9	15	24	44		1979-80	1988-89
Cote, Ray	Edm.	3	15	0	0	0	4	14	3	2	5	0		1982-83	1984-85
Cotton, Baldy	Pit., Tor., NYA	12	500	101	103	204	419	43	4	9	13	46	1	1925-26	1936-37
Coughlin, Jack	Tor., Que, Mtl., Ham.	3	19	2	0	2	0	....	....	....	....	....	1	1917-18	1920-21
Coulis, Tim	Wsh., Min.	4	47	4	5	9	138	3	1	0	1	2		1979-80	1985-86
Coulson, D'arcy	Phi.	1	28	0	0	0	103	....	....	....	....	....		1930-31	1930-31
Coulter, Art	Chi., NYR	11	465	30	82	112	543	49	4	5	9	61	2	1931-32	1941-42
Coulter, Neal	NYI	3	26	5	5	10	11	1	0	0	0	0		1985-86	1987-88
Coulter, Tommy	Chi.	1	2	0	0	0	0	....	....	....	....	....		1933-34	1933-34
Cournoyer, Yvan	Mtl.	16	968	428	435	863	255	147	64	63	127	47	10	1963-64	1978-79
Courteau, Yves	Cgy., Hfd.	3	22	2	5	7	4	1	0	0	0	0		1984-85	1986-87
Couture, Billy	Mtl., Ham., Bos.	10	239	33	18	51	350	32	2	0	2	42	1	1917-18	1926-27
Couture, Gerry	Det., Mtl., Chi.,	10	385	86	70	156	89	45	9	7	16	4	1	1944-45	1953-54
Couture, Rosie	Chi., Mtl.	8	304	48	56	104	184	23	1	5	6	15		1928-29	1935-36
Cowan, Tommy	Phi.	1	1	0	0	0	0	....	....	....	....	....		1930-31	1930-31
Cowick, Bruce	Phi., Wsh., St.L.	3	70	5	6	11	43	8	0	0	0	9	1	1973-74	1975-76
Cowley, Bill	St.L., Bos.	13	549	195	353	548	143	64	13	33	46	22	2	1934-35	1946-47
Cox, Danny	Tor., Ott., Det., NYR, St.L.	9	329	47	49	96	110	10	0	1	1	6		1926-27	1934-35
Crashley, Bart	Det., K.C., L.A.	6	140	7	36	43	50	....	....	....	....	....		1965-66	1975-76
Crawford, Bob	St.L., Hfd., NYR, Wsh.	7	246	71	71	142	72	11	0	1	1	8		1979-80	1986-87
Crawford, Bobby	Col., Det.	2	16	1	3	4	6	....	....	....	....	....		1980-81	1982-83
Crawford, John	Bos.	13	547	38	140	178	202	66	4	13	17	36	2	1937-38	1949-50
Crawford, Marc	Van.	6	176	19	31	50	229	20	1	2	3	44		1981-82	1986-87
Crawford, Rusty	Ott., Tor.,	2	38	10	3	13	51	2	2	1	3	0	1	1917-18	1918-19
Creighton, Dave	Bos., Chi., Tor., NYR	12	615	140	174	314	223	51	11	13	24	20		1948-49	1959-60
Creighton, Jimmy	Det.,	1	11	1	0	1	2	....	....	....	....	....		1930-31	1930-31
Cressman, Dave	Min.	2	85	6	8	14	37	....	....	....	....	....		1974-75	1975-76
Cressman, Glen	Mtl.	1	4	0	0	0	2	....	....	....	....	....		1956-57	1956-57
Crisp, Terry	Bos., St.L., Phi., NYI	11	536	67	134	201	135	110	15	28	43	40	2	1965-66	1976-77
Croghen, Maurice	Mtl.M.	1	16	0	0	0	4	....	....	....	....	....		1937-38	1937-38
Crombeen, Mike	Cle., St.L., Hfd.	8	475	55	68	123	218	27	6	2	8	32		1977-78	1984-85
Crossett, Stan	Phi.,	1	21	0	0	0	10	....	....	....	....	....		1930-31	1930-31
Croteau, Gary	L.A., Det., Cal., K.C., Col.	12	684	144	175	319	143	11	3	2	5	8		1968-69	1979-80
Crowder, Bruce	Bos., Pit.	4	243	47	51	98	156	31	8	4	12	41		1981-82	1984-85
Crowder, Keith	Bos., L.A.	10	662	223	271	494	1346	85	14	22	36	218		1980-81	1989-90
Crozier, Joe	Tor.,	1	5	0	3	3	2	....	....	....	....	....		1959-60	1959-60
Crutchfield, Nels	Mtl.	1	41	5	5	10	20	2	0	1	1	22		1934-35	1934-35
Cullen, Barry	Tor., Det.	5	219	32	52	84	111	6	0	0	0	2		1955-56	1959-60
Cullen, Brian	Tor., NYR	7	326	56	100	156	92	19	3	0	3	2		1954-55	1960-61
Cullen, Ray	NYR, Det., Min., Van.	6	313	92	123	215	120	20	3	10	13	2		1965-66	1970-71
Cummins, Barry	Cal.	1	36	1	2	3	39	....	....	....	....	....		1973-74	1973-74
Cunningham, Bob	NYR	2	4	0	1	1	0	....	....	....	....	....		1960-61	1961-62
Cunningham, Jim	Phi.	1	1	0	0	0	4	....	....	....	....	....		1977-78	1977-78
Cunningham, Les	NYA, Chi.	2	60	7	19	26	21	1	0	0	0	2		1936-37	1939-40
Cupolo, Bill	Bos.	1	47	11	13	24	10	7	1	2	3	0		1944-45	1944-45
Currie, Glen	Wsh., L.A.	8	326	39	79	118	100	12	1	3	4	4		1979-80	1987-88
Currie, Hugh	Mtl.	1	1	0	0	0	0	....	....	....	....	....		1950-51	1950-51
Currie, Tony	St.L., Hfd., Van.	8	290	92	119	211	73	16	4	12	16	14		1977-78	1984-85
Curry, Floyd	Mtl.	11	601	105	99	204	147	91	23	17	40	38	4	1947-48	1957-58
Curtale, Tony	Cgy.	1	2	0	0	0	0	....	....	....	....	....		1980-81	1980-81
Curtis, Paul	Mtl., L.A., St.L.	4	185	3	34	37	151	5	0	0	0	2		1969-70	1972-73
Cushenan, Ian	Chi., Mtl., NYR, Det.	5	129	3	11	14	134	....	....	....	....	....		1956-57	1963-64
Cusson, Jean	Oak.	1	2	0	0	0	0	....	....	....	....	....		1967-68	1967-68
Cyr, Denis	Cgy., Chi., St.L.	6	193	41	43	84	36	4	0	0	0	0		1980-81	1985-86

D

Name	NHL Teams	NHL Seasons	GP	G	A	TP	PIM	GP	G	A	TP	PIM	NHL Cup Wins	First NHL Season	Last NHL Season
Dahlin, Kjell	Mtl.	3	166	57	59	116	10	35	6	11	17	6	1	1985-86	1987-88
Dahlstrom, Cully	Chi.	8	342	88	118	206	52	29	6	8	14	4	1	1937-38	1944-45
Daigle, Alain	Chi.	6	389	56	50	106	122	17	0	1	1	0		1974-75	1979-80
Dailey, Bob	Van., Phi.	9	561	94	231	325	814	63	12	34	46	106		1973-74	1981-82

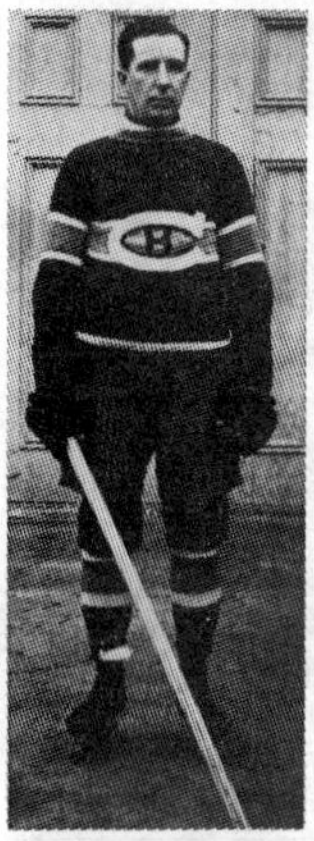

Sprague Cleghorn

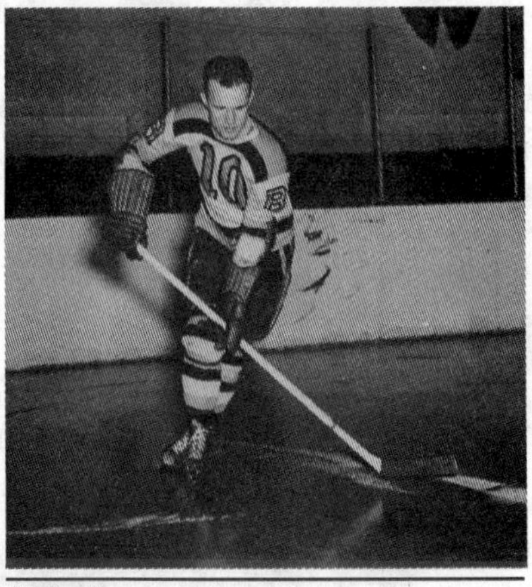

Bill Cowley

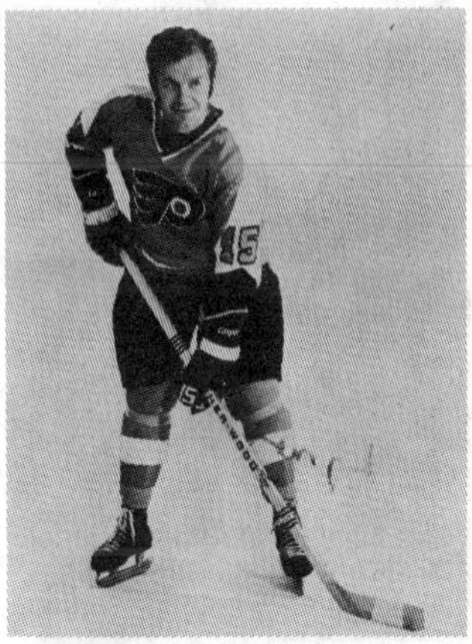

Terry Crisp

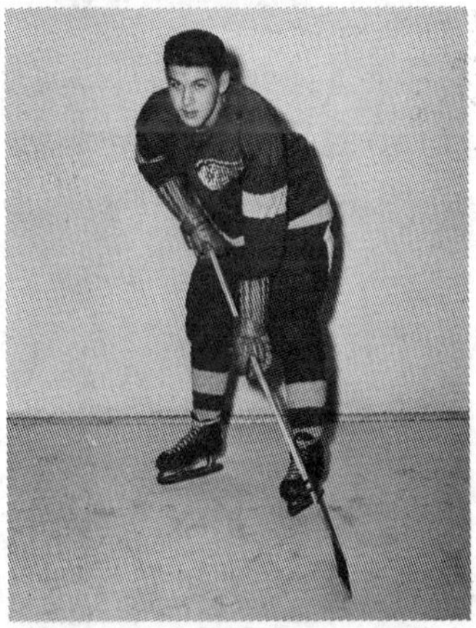

Alex Delvecchio

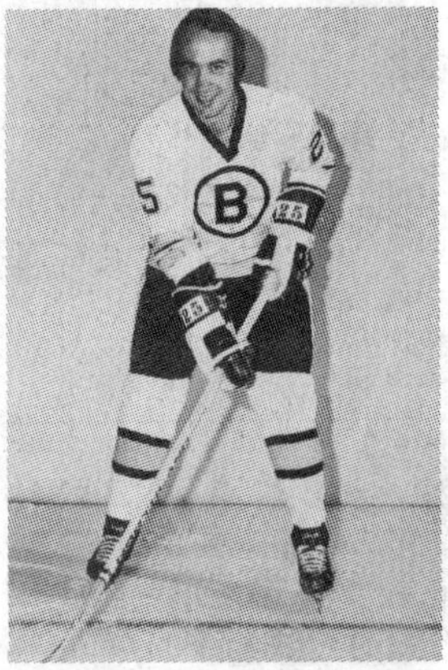

Gary Doak

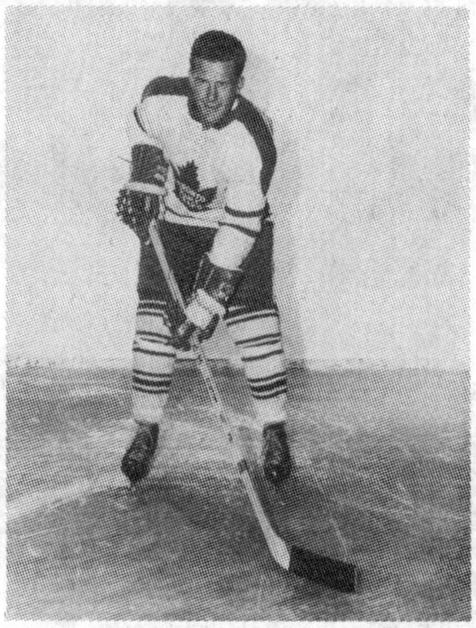

Kent Douglas

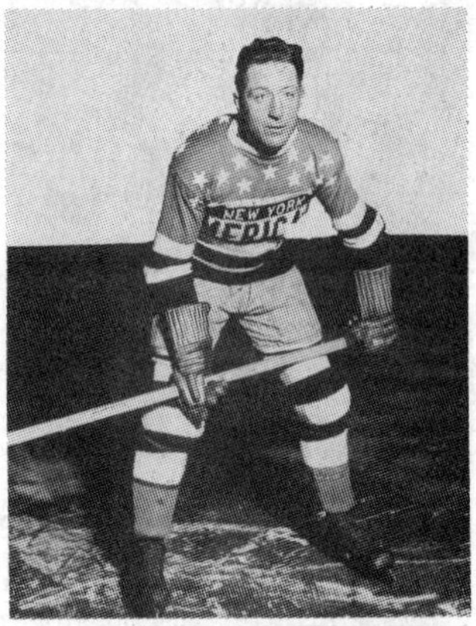

Mervyn "Red" Dutton

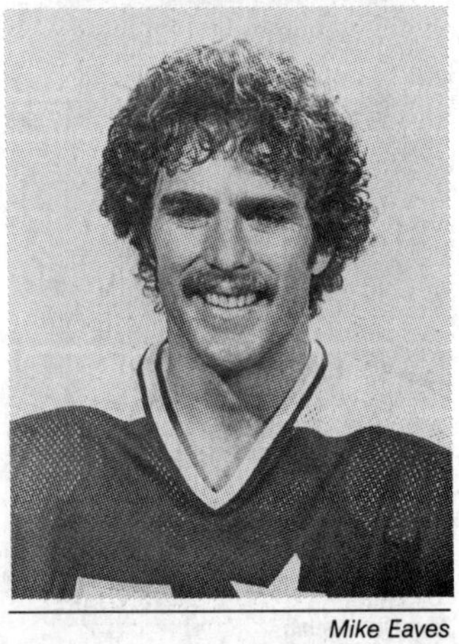

Mike Eaves

			Regular Schedule					Playoffs					NHL	First	Last
Name	NHL Teams	NHL Seasons	GP	G	A	TP	PIM	GP	G	A	TP	PIM	Cup Wins	NHL Season	NHL Season
Daley, Frank	Det.	1	5	0	0	0	0	2	0	0	0	0		1928-29	1928-29
Daley, Pat	Wpg.	2	12	1	0	1	13	....	....	....	....	....		1979-80	1980-81
Dallman, Marty	Tor.	2	6	0	1	1	0	....	....	....	....	....		1987-88	1988-89
Dame, Bunny	Mtl.	1	34	2	5	7	4	....	....	....	....	....		1941-42	1941-42
Damore, Hank	NYR	1	4	1	0	1	2	....	....	....	....	....		1943-44	1943-44
Daoust, Dan	Mtl., Tor.	8	522	87	167	254	544	32	7	5	12	83		1982-83	1989-90
Dark, Michael	St.L.	2	43	5	6	11	14	....	....	....	....	....		1986-87	1987-88
Darragh, Harry	Pit., Phi., Bos., Tor.	8	308	68	49	117	50	16	1	3	4	4	1	1925-26	1932-33
Darragh, Jack	Ott.	6	120	68	21	89	84	21	14	2	16	7	3	1917-18	1923-24
David, Richard	Que.	3	31	4	4	8	10	1	0	0	0	0		1979-80	1982-83
Davidson, Bob	Tor.,	12	491	94	160	254	398	82	5	17	22	79	2	1934-35	1945-46
Davidson, Gord	NYR	2	51	3	6	9	8	....	....	....	....	....		1942-43	1943-44
Davie, Bob	Bos.	3	41	0	1	1	25	....	....	....	....	....		1933-34	1935-36
Davies, Ken	NYR	1	....	....	....	....	....	1	0	0	0	0		1947-48	1947-48
Davis, Bob	Det.	1	3	0	0	0	0	....	....	....	....	....		1932-33	1932-33
Davis, Kim	Pit., Tor.	4	36	5	7	12	12	4	0	0	0	0		1977-78	1980-81
Davis, Lorne	Mtl., Chi., Det., Bos.	6	95	8	12	20	20	18	3	1	4	10	1	1951-52	1959-60
Davis, Mal	Det., Buf.	5	100	31	22	53	34	7	1	0	1	0		1980-81	1985-86
Davison, Murray	Bos.	1	1	0	0	0	0	....	....	....	....	....		1965-66	1965-66
Dawes, Robert	Tor., Mtl.	4	32	2	7	4	6	10	0	0	0	2	1	1946-47	1950-51
Day, Hap	Tor., NYA	14	581	86	116	202	601	53	4	7	11	56	1	1924-25	1937-38
Dea, Billy	Chi., NYR, Det., Pit.	8	397	67	54	121	44	11	2	0	2	6		1953-54	1970-71
Deacon, Don	Det.	3	30	6	4	10	6	2	2	1	3	0		1936-37	1939-40
Deadmarsh, Butch	Buf., ATL, K.C.	5	137	12	5	17	155	4	0	0	0	17		1970-71	1974-75
Dean, Barry	Col., Phi.	3	165	25	56	81	146	....	....	....	....	....		1976-77	1978-79
Debenedet, Nelson	Det., Pit.	2	46	10	4	14	13	....	....	....	....	....		1973-74	1974-75
Debol, David	Hfd.	2	92	26	26	52	4	3	0	0	0	0		1979-80	1980-81
Defazio, Dean	Pit.	1	22	0	2	2	28	....	....	....	....	....		1983-84	1983-84
Delmonte, Armand	Bos.	1	1	0	0	0	0	....	....	....	....	....		1945-46	1945-46
Delorme, Ron	Col., Van.	9	524	83	83	166	667	25	1	2	3	59		1976-77	1984-85
Delory, Valentine	NYR	1	0	0	0	0	0	....	....	....	....	....		1948-49	1948-49
Delparte, Guy	Col.	1	48	1	8	9	18	....	....	....	....	....		1976-77	1976-77
Delvecchio, Álex	Det.	24	1549	456	825	1281	383	121	35	69	104	29	3	1950-51	1973-74
DeMarco, Ab	Chi., Tor., Bos., NYR	7	209	72	93	165	53	11	3	0	3	2		1938-39	1946-47
DeMarco, Albert	NYR, St.L., Pit., Van., L.A., Bos.	9	344	44	80	124	75	25	1	2	3	17		1969-70	1978-79
DeMeres, Tony	Mtl., NYR	6	83	20	22	42	23	3	0	0	0	0		1937-38	1943-44
Denis, Johnny	NYR	2	10	0	2	2	2	....	....	....	....	....		1946-47	1949-50
Denis, Lulu	Mtl.	2	3	0	1	1	0	....	....	....	....	....		1949-50	1950-51
Denneny, Corbett	Tor., Ham., Chi.	9	175	99	29	128	130	15	7	4	11	6	2	1917-18	1927-28
Denneny, Cy	Ott., Bos.	12	326	246	69	315	176	37	18	3	21	31	5	1917-18	1928-29
Dennis, Norm	St.L.	4	12	3	0	3	11	5	0	0	0	2		1968-69	1971-72
Denoird, Gerry	Tor.	1	15	0	0	0	0	....	....	....	....	....		1922-23	1922-23
Derlago, Bill	Van., Bos., Wpg., Que., Tor.	9	555	189	227	416	247	13	5	0	5	8		1978-79	1986-87
Desaulniers, Gerard	Mtl.	3	8	0	2	2	4	....	....	....	....	....		1950-51	1953-54
Desilets, Joffre	Mtl., Chi.	5	192	37	45	82	57	7	1	0	1	7		1935-36	1939-40
Desjardins, Vic	Chi., NYR	2	87	6	15	21	27	16	0	0	0	0		1930-31	1931-32
Deslauriers, Jacques	Mtl.	1	2	0	0	0	0	....	....	....	....	....		1955-56	1955-56
Devine, Kevin	NYI	1	2	0	1	1	8	....	....	....	....	....		1982-83	1982-83
Dewar, Tom	NYR	1	9	0	2	2	4	....	....	....	....	....		1943-44	1943-44
Dewsbury, Al	Det., Chi.	9	347	30	78	108	365	14	1	5	6	60	1	1946-47	1955-56
Deziel, Michel	Buf.	1	....	....	....	....	....	1	0	0	0	0		1974-75	1974-75
Dheere, Marcel	Mtl.	1	11	1	2	3	2	5	0	0	0	6		1942-43	1942-43
Diachuk, Edward	Det.	1	12	0	0	0	19	....	....	....	....	....		1960-61	1960-61
Dick, Harry	Chi.	1	12	0	1	1	12	....	....	....	....	....		1946-47	1946-47
Dickens, Ernie	Tor., Chi.	6	278	12	44	56	48	13	0	0	0	4	1	1941-42	1950-51
Dickenson, Herb	NYR	2	48	18	17	35	10	....	....	....	....	....		1951-52	1952-53
Dietrich, Don	Chi., N.J.	2	28	0	7	7	10	....	....	....	....	....		1983-84	1985-86
Dill, Bob	NYR	2	76	15	15	30	135	....	....	....	....	....		1943-44	1944-45
Dillabough, Bob	Det., Bos., Pit., Oak.	7	283	32	54	86	76	17	3	0	3	0		1961-62	1969-70
Dillon, Cecil	NYR, Det.	10	453	167	131	298	105	43	14	9	23	14	1	1930-31	1939-40
Dillon, Gary	Col.	1	13	1	1	2	29	....	....	....	....	....		1980-81	1980-81
Dillon, Wayne	NYR, Wpg.	4	229	43	66	109	60	3	0	1	1	0		1975-76	1979-80
Dineen, Bill	Det., Chi.	5	323	51	44	95	122	37	1	1	2	18	2	1953-54	1957-58
Dineen, Gary	Min.	1	4	0	1	1	0	....	....	....	....	....		1968-69	1968-69
Dinsmore, Chuck	Mtl.M	4	100	6	2	8	44	12	1	0	1	6	1	1924-25	1929-30
Dionne, Marcel	Det., L.A., NYR	18	1348	731	1040	1771	600	49	21	24	45	17		1971-72	1988-89
Doak, Gary	Det., Bos., Van., NYR	16	789	23	107	130	908	78	2	4	6	121	1	1965-66	1980-81
Dobson, Jim	Min., Col.	3	11	0	0	0	6	....	....	....	....	....		1979-80	1981-82
Doherty, Fred	Mtl.	1	3	0	0	0	0	....	....	....	....	....		1918-19	1918-19
Donaldson, Gary	Chi.	1	1	0	0	0	0	....	....	....	....	....	2	1973-74	1973-74
Donnelly, Babe	Mtl.M.	1	34	0	1	1	14	2	0	0	0	0		1926-27	1926-27
Donnelly, Dave	Bos., Chi., Edm.	5	137	15	24	39	150	5	0	0	0	0		1983-84	1987-88
Doran, Red (I.)	Det.	1	24	3	2	5	10	....	....	....	....	....		1946-47	1946-47
Doran, Red (J.)	NYA., Det., Mtl.	5	98	5	10	15	110	3	0	0	0	0		1933-34	1939-40
Doraty, Ken	Chi., Tor., Det.	5	103	15	26	41	24	15	7	2	9	2		1926-27	1937-38
Dore, Andre	NYR, St.L., Que.	7	257	14	81	95	261	23	1	2	3	32		1978-79	1984-85
Dorey, Jim	Tor., NYR	4	232	25	74	99	553	11	0	2	2	40		1968-69	1971-72
Dornhoefer, Gary	Bos., Phi.	14	787	214	328	542	1291	80	17	19	36	203	2	1963-64	1977-78
Dorohoy, Eddie	Mtl.	1	16	0	0	0	6	....	....	....	....	....		1948-49	1948-49
Douglas, Jordy	Hfd., Min., Wpg.	6	268	76	62	138	160	6	0	0	0	4		1979-80	1984-85
Douglas, Kent	Tor., Oak., Det.	7	428	33	115	148	631	19	1	3	4	33	1	1962-63	1968-69
Douglas, Les	Det.	4	52	6	12	18	8	10	3	2	5	0	1	1940-41	1946-47
Downie, Dave	Tor.	1	11	0	1	1	2	....	....	....	....	....		1932-33	1932-33
Draper, Bruce	Tor.	1	1	0	0	0	0	....	....	....	....	....		1962-63	1962-63
Drillon, Gordie	Tor., Mtl.	7	311	155	139	294	56	50	26	15	41	10	1	1936-37	1942-43
Driscoll, Pete	Edm.	2	60	3	8	11	97	3	0	0	0	0		1979-80	1980-81
Drolet, Rene	Phi., Det.	2	2	0	0	0	0	....	....	....	....	....		1971-72	1974-75
Drouillard, Clarence	Det.	1	10	0	1	1	0	....	....	....	....	....		1937-38	1937-38
Drouin, Jude	Mtl., Min., NYI, Wpg.	12	666	151	305	456	346	72	27	41	68	33		1968-69	1980-81
Drouin, Polly	Mtl.	6	173	23	50	73	80	5	0	1	1	5		1935-36	1940-41
Drummond, John	NYR	1	2	0	0	0	0	....	....	....	....	....		1944-45	1944-45
Drury, Herb	Pit., Phi.	6	213	24	13	37	203	4	1	1	2	0		1925-26	1930-31
Dube, Gilles	Mtl.., Det.	2	12	1	2	3	2	2	0	0	0	0	1	1949-50	1953-54
Dube, Norm	K.C.	2	57	8	10	18	54	....	....	....	....	....		1974-75	1975-76
Dudley, Rick	Buf., Wpg.	6	309	75	99	174	292	25	7	2	9	69		1972-73	1980-81
Duff, Dick	Tor., NYR, Mtl., L.A., Buf.	18	1030	283	289	572	743	114	30	49	79	78	6	1954-55	1971-72
Dufour, Luc	Bos., Que., St.L.	3	167	23	21	44	199	18	1	0	1	32		1982-83	1984-85
Dufour, Marc	NYR, L.A.	3	14	1	0	1	2	....	....	....	....	....		1963-64	1968-69
Duggan, Jack	Ott.	1	27	0	0	0	0	2	0	0	0	0		1925-26	1925-26
Duggan, Ken	Min.	1	1	0	0	0	0	....	....	....	....	....		1987-88	1987-88
Duguid, Lorne	Mtl.M, Det., Bos.	6	135	9	15	24	57	2	0	0	0	4		1931-32	1936-37
Dumart, Woodie	Bos.	16	771	211	218	429	99	82	12	15	27	23	2	1935-36	1953-54
Dunbar, Dale	Van., Bos.	2	2	0	0	0	2	....	....	....	....	....		1985-86	1988-89
Duncan, Art	Det., Tor.	5	156	18	16	34	225	5	0	0	0	4		1926-27	1930-31
Dundas, Rocky	Tor.	1	5	0	0	0	14	....	....	....	....	....		1989-90	1989-90
Dunlap, Frank	Tor.	1	15	0	1	1	2	....	....	....	....	....		1943-44	1943-44
Dunlop, Blake	Min., Phi., St.L., Det.	11	550	130	274	404	172	40	4	10	14	18		1973-74	1983-84
Dunn, Dave	Van., Tor.	3	184	14	41	55	313	10	1	1	2	41		1973-74	1975-76
Dunn, Richie	Buf., Cgy., Hfd.	12	483	36	140	176	314	36	3	15	18	24		1977-78	1988-89
Dupere, Denis	Tor., Wsh., St.L., K.C., Col.	8	421	80	99	179	66	16	1	0	1	0		1970-71	1977-78
Dupont, Andre	NYR, St.L., Phi., Que.	13	810	59	185	244	1986	140	14	18	32	352	2	1970-71	1982-83
Dupont, Jerome	Chi., Tor.	6	214	7	29	36	468	20	0	2	2	56		1981-82	1986-87
Dupont, Norm	Mtl., Wpg., Hfd.	5	256	55	85	140	52	13	4	2	6	0		1979-80	1983-84
Durbano, Steve	St.L., Pit., K.C., Col.	6	220	13	60	73	1127	5	0	2	2	8		1972-73	1978-79
Duris, Vitezslav	Tor.	2	89	3	20	23	62	3	0	1	1	2		1980-81	1982-83
Dussault, Norm	Mtl.	4	206	31	62	93	47	7	3	1	4	0		1947-48	1950-51
Dutkowski, Duke	Chi., NYA, NYR	5	200	16	30	46	172	6	0	0	0	6		1926-27	1933-34
Dutton, Red	Mtl.M, NYA	10	449	29	67	96	871	18	1	0	1	33		1926-27	1935-36
Dvorak, Miroslav	Phi.	3	193	11	74	85	51	18	0	2	2	6		1982-83	1984-85
Dwyer, Mike	Col., Cgy.	4	31	2	6	8	25	1	1	0	1	0		1978-79	1981-82
Dyck, Henry	NYR	1	1	0	0	0	0	....	....	....	....	....		1943-44	1943-44
Dye, Babe	Tor., Ham., Chi., NYA	11	271	202	41	243	205	15	11	2	13	11	1	1919-20	1930-31
Dyte, John	Chi.	1	27	1	0	1	31	....	....	....	....	....		1943-44	1943-44

Name	NHL Teams	NHL Seasons	Regular Schedule GP	G	A	TP	PIM	Playoffs GP	G	A	TP	PIM	NHL Cup Wins	First NHL Season	Last NHL Season
E															
Eakin, Bruce	Cgy., Det.	4	13	2	2	4	4	....	....	....	....	....		1981-82	1985-86
Eatough, Jeff	Buf.	1	1	0	0	0	0	....	....	....	....	....		1981-82	1981-82
Eaves, Mike	Min., Cgy.	8	324	83	143	226	80	43	7	10	17	14		1978-79	1985-86
Ecclestone, Tim	St.L., Det., Tor., Atl.	11	692	126	233	359	346	48	6	11	17	76		1967-68	1977-78
Edberg, Rolf	Wsh.	3	184	45	58	103	24	....	....	....	....	....		1978-79	1980-81
Eddolls, Frank	Mtl., NYR	8	317	23	43	66	114	31	0	2	2	10	1	1944-45	1951-52
Edestrand, Darryl	St.L., Phi., Pit., Bos., L.A.	10	455	34	90	124	404	42	3	9	12	57		1967-68	1978-79
Edmundson, Garry	Mtl., Tor.	3	43	4	6	10	49	11	0	1	1	8		1951-52	1960-61
Edur, Tom	Col., Pit	2	158	17	70	87	67	....	....	....	....	....		1976-77	1977-78
Egan, Pat	Bro., Det., Bos., NYR	11	554	77	153	230	776	44	9	4	13	44		1939-40	1950-51
Egers, Jack	NYR, St.L., Wsh.	7	284	64	69	133	154	32	5	6	11	32		1969-70	1975-76
Ehman, Gerry	Bos., Det., Tor., Oak, Cal.	9	429	96	118	214	100	41	10	10	20	12	1	1957-58	1970-71
Eldebrink, Anders	Van., Que.	2	55	3	11	14	29	14	0	0	0	0		1981-82	1982-83
Elik, Boris	Det.	1	3	0	0	0	0	....	....	....	....	....		1962-63	1962-63
Elliot, Fred	Ott.	1	43	2	0	2	6	....	....	....	....	....		1928-29	1928-29
Ellis, Ron	Tor.	16	1034	332	308	640	207	70	18	8	26	20	1	1963-64	1980-81
Eloranta, Kari	Cgy., St.L.	5	267	13	103	116	155	26	1	7	8	19		1981-82	1986-87
Emberg, Eddie	Mtl.	1	....	....	....	....	....	2	1	0	1	0		1944-45	1944-45
Emms, Hap	Mtl.M, NYA, Det., Bos.	10	320	36	53	89	311	14	0	0	0	12		1926-27	1937-38
Engblom, Brian	Mtl., Wsh., L.A., Buf., Cgy.	11	659	29	177	206	599	48	3	9	12	43	3	1976-77	1986-87
Engele, Jerry	Min.	3	100	2	13	15	162	2	0	1	1	0		1975-76	1977-78
English, John	L.A.	1	3	1	3	4	4	1	0	0	0	0		1987-88	1987-88
Ennis, Jim	Edm.	1	5	1	0	1	10	....	....	....	....	....		1987-88	1987-88
Erickson, Aut	Bos., Chi., Oak., Tor.	7	227	7	84	31	182	7	0	0	0	2	1	1959-60	1969-70
Erickson, Grant	Bos., Min.	2	6	1	0	1	4	....	....	....	....	....		1968-69	1969-70
Eriksson, Rolie	Min., Van.	3	193	48	95	143	26	2	1	0	1	0		1976-77	1978-79
Eriksson, Thomas	Phi.	5	208	22	76	98	107	19	0	3	3	6		1980-81	1985-86
Esposito, Phil	Chi., Bos., NYR	18	1282	717	873	1590	910	130	61	76	137	137	2	1963-64	1980-81
Evans, Chris	Tor., Buf., St.L., Det., K.C.	5	241	19	42	61	143	12	1	1	2	8		1969-70	1974-75
Evans, Daryl	L.A., Wsh., Tor.	6	113	22	30	52	25	11	5	8	13	12		1981-82	1986-87
Evans, Jack	NYR, Chi.	14	752	19	80	99	989	56	2	2	4	97	1	1948-49	1962-63
Evans, John	Phi.	3	103	14	25	39	34	1	0	0	0	0		1978-79	1982-83
Evans, Paul	Tor.	2	11	1	1	2	21	2	0	0	0	0		1976-77	1977-78
Evans, Stewart	Det., Mtl.M., Mtl.	8	367	28	49	77	425	26	0	0	0	20	1	1930-31	1938-39
Ezinicki, Bill	Tor., Bos., NYR	9	368	79	105	184	713	40	5	8	13	87	3	1944-45	1954-55
F															
Fahey, Trevor	NYR	1	1	0	0	0	0	....	....	....	....	....		1964-65	1964-65
Fairbairn, Bill	NYR, Min. St.L.	11	658	162	261	423	173	54	13	22	35	42		1968-69	1978-79
Falkenberg, Bob	Det.	5	54	1	5	6	26	....	....	....	....	....		1966-67	1971-72
Farrant, Walt	Chi.	1	1	0	0	0	0	....	....	....	....	....		1943-44	1943-44
Farrish, Dave	NYR, Que, Tor.	7	430	17	110	127	440	14	0	2	2	24		1976-77	1983-84
Fashoway, Gordie	Chi.	1	13	3	2	5	14	....	....	....	....	....		1950-51	1950-51
Faubert, Mario	Pit.	7	231	21	90	111	292	10	2	2	4	6		1974-75	1981-82
Faulkner, Alex	Tor., Det.	3	101	15	17	32	15	12	5	0	5	2		1961-62	1963-64
Fauss, Ted	Tor.	2	28	0	2	2	15	....	....	....	....	....		1986-87	1987-88
Feamster, Dave	Chi.	4	169	13	24	37	155	33	3	5	8	61		1981-82	1984-85
Featherstone, Tony	Oak., Cal., Min.	3	130	17	21	38	65	2	0	0	0	0		1969-70	1973-74
Federko, Bernie	St.L., Det.	14	1000	369	761	1130	487	91	35	66	101	83		1976-77	1989-90
Feltrin, Tony	Pit., NYR	4	48	3	3	6	65	....	....	....	....	....		1980-81	1985-86
Ferguson	Chi.	1	1	0	0	0	0	....	....	....	....	....		1939-40	1939-40
Ferguson, George	Tor., Pit, Min	12	797	160	238	398	431	86	14	23	37	44		1972-73	1983-84
Ferguson, John	Mtl.	8	500	145	158	303	1214	85	20	18	38	260	5	1963-64	1970-71
Ferguson, Lorne	Bos., Det., Chi.	8	422	82	80	162	193	31	6	3	9	24		1949-50	1958-59
Ferguson, Norm	Oak., Cal.	4	279	73	66	139	72	10	1	4	5	7		1968-69	1971-72
Ferner, Mark	Buf.	1	13	0	3	3	9	....	....	....	....	....		1986-87	1986-87
Fidler, Mike	Cle., Min, Hfd., Chi.	7	271	84	97	181	124	....	....	....	....	....		1976-77	1982-83
Field, Wilf	Bro., Mtl., Chi.	6	218	17	25	42	151	3	0	0	0	0		1936-37	1944-45
Fielder, Guyle	Det., Chi.	4	36	0	0	0	2	6	0	0	0	2		1950-51	1957-58
Fillion, Bob	Mtl.	7	327	42	61	103	84	33	7	4	11	10	2	1943-44	1949-50
Fillion, Marcel	Bos.	1	1	0	0	0	0	....	....	....	....	....		1944-45	1944-45
Filmore, Tommy	Det., NYA, Bos.	4	116	15	12	27	33	....	....	....	....	....		1930-31	1933-34
Finkbeiner, Lloyd	NYA	1	1	0	0	0	0	....	....	....	....	....		1940-41	1940-41
Finney, Sid	Chi.	3	59	10	7	17	4	7	0	0	0	2		1951-52	1953-54
Finnigan, Ed	Bos.	1	3	0	0	0	0	....	....	....	....	....		1935-36	1935-36
Finnigan, Frank	Ott., Tor., St.L.	14	555	115	88	203	405	39	6	9	15	22	2	1923-24	1936-37
Fischer, Ron	Buf.	2	18	0	7	7	6	....	....	....	....	....		1981-82	1982-83
Fisher, Alvin	Tor.	1	9	1	0	1	4	....	....	....	....	....		1924-25	1924-25
Fisher, Dunc	NYR, Bos., Det.	7	275	45	70	115	104	21	4	4	8	14		1947-48	1958-59
Fisher, Joe	Det.	4	66	8	12	20	13	15	2	1	3	6	1	1939-40	1942-43
Fitchner, Bob	Que	2	78	12	20	32	59	3	0	0	0	10		1979-80	1980-81
Fitzpatrick, Sandy	NYR, Min.	2	22	3	6	9	8	12	0	0	0	0		1964-65	1967-68
Flaman, Fern	Bos., Tor.	17	910	34	174	208	1370	63	4	8	12	93	1	1944-45	1960-61
Fleming, Reggie	Mtl., Chi., Bos., NYR, Phi., Buf.	12	749	108	132	240	1468	50	3	6	9	106	1	1959-60	1970-71
Flesch	Ham.	1	1	0	0	0	0	....	....	....	....	....		1920-21	1920-21
Flesch, John	Min, Pit, Col.	4	124	18	23	41	117	....	....	....	....	....		1974-75	1979-80
Flett, Bill	L.A., Phi., Tor., Atl, Edm.	11	689	202	215	417	501	52	7	16	23	42	1	1967-68	1979-80
Flockhart, Rob	Van., Min	5	55	2	5	7	14	1	1	0	1	2		1976-77	1980-81
Floyd, Larry	N.J.	2	12	2	3	5	9	....	....	....	....	....		1982-83	1983-84
Fogolin, Lee	Buf., Edm.	13	924	44	195	239	1318	108	5	19	24	173	2	1974-75	1986-87
Fogolin, Lidio (Lee)	Det., Chi.	9	427	10	48	58	575	28	0	2	2	30	1	1947-48	1955-56
Folco, Peter	Van.	1	2	0	0	0	0	....	....	....	....	....		1973-74	1973-74
Foley, Gerry	Tor., NYR, L.A.	4	142	9	14	23	99	9	0	1	1	2		1954-55	1968-69
Foley, Rick	Chi., Phi., Det.	3	67	11	26	37	180	4	0	1	1	4		1970-71	1973-74
Folk, Bill	Det.	2	12	0	0	0	4	....	....	....	....	....		1951-52	1952-53
Fontaine, Len	Det.	2	46	8	11	19	10	....	....	....	....	....		1972-73	1973-74
Fontas, Jon	Min.	2	2	0	0	0	0	....	....	....	....	....		1979-80	1980-81
Fonteyne, Val	Det., NYR, Pit.	13	820	75	154	229	26	59	3	10	13	8		1959-60	1971-72
Fontinato, Louie	NYR, Mtl.	9	535	26	78	104	1247	21	0	2	2	42		1954-55	1962-63
Forbes, Dave	Bos., Wsh.	6	363	64	64	128	341	45	1	4	5	13		1973-74	1978-79
Forbes, Mike	Bos., Edm.	3	50	1	11	12	41	....	....	....	....	....		1977-78	1981-82
Forey, Connie	St.L.	1	4	0	0	0	2	....	....	....	....	....		1973-74	1973-74
Forsey, Jack	Tor.	1	19	7	9	16	10	3	0	1	1	0		1942-43	1942-43
Forslund, Gus	Ott.	1	48	4	9	13	2	....	....	....	....	....		1932-33	1932-33
Forsyth, Alex	Wsh.	1	1	0	0	0	0	....	....	....	....	....		1976-77	1976-77
Fortier, Charles	Mtl.	1	1	0	0	0	0	....	....	....	....	....	1	1923-24	1923-24
Fortier, Dave	Tor., NYI, Van.	4	205	8	21	29	335	20	0	2	2	33		1972-73	1976-77
Fortin, Ray	St.L.	3	92	2	6	8	33	6	0	0	0	8		1967-68	1969-70
Foster, Dwight	Bos., Col., N.J., Det.	10	541	111	163	274	420	35	5	12	17	4		1977-78	1986-87
Foster, Herb	NYR	2	5	1	0	1	5	....	....	....	....	....		1940-41	1947-48
Foster, Harry	NYR, Bos., Det.	4	83	3	2	5	32	....	....	....	....	....		1929-31	1934-35
Fotiu, Nick	NYR, Hfd., Cgy., Phi., Edm.	13	646	60	77	137	1362	38	0	4	4	67		1976-77	1988-89
Fowler, Jimmy	Tor.	3	135	18	29	47	39	18	0	3	3	2		1936-37	1938-39
Fowler, Tom	Chi.	1	24	0	1	1	18	....	....	....	....	....		1946-47	1946-47
Fox, Greg	Atl, Chi., Pit.	8	494	14	92	106	637	44	1	9	10	67		1977-78	1984-85
Fox, Jim	L.A.	10	578	186	293	479	143	22	4	8	12	0		1980-81	1989-90
Foyston, Frank	Det.	2	64	17	7	24	32	....	....	....	....	....		1926-27	1927-28
Frampton, Bob	Mtl.	1	2	0	0	0	0	3	0	0	0	0		1949-50	1949-50
Francis, Bobby	Det.	1	14	2	0	2	0	....	....	....	....	....		1982-83	1982-83
Fraser, Archie	NYR	1	3	0	1	1	0	....	....	....	....	....		1943-44	1943-44
Fraser, Curt	Van., Chi., Min.	12	704	193	240	433	1306	65	15	18	33	198		1978-79	1989-90
Fraser, Gord	Chi., Det., Mtl., Pit., Phi.	5	144	24	12	36	224	2	1	0	1	6		1926-27	1930-31
Fraser, Harry	Chi.	1	21	5	4	9	0	....	....	....	....	....		1944-45	1944-45
Fraser, Jack	Ham.	1	1	0	0	0	0	....	....	....	....	....		1923-24	1923-24
Frederickson, Frank	Det., Bos., Pit.	5	165	39	34	73	207	10	2	5	7	26	1	1926-27	1930-31
Frew, Irv	Mtl.M, St.L., Mtl.	3	95	2	5	7	146	4	0	0	0	6		1933-34	1935-36
Friday, Tim	Det.	1	23	0	3	3	6	....	....	....	....	....		1985-86	1985-86
Fridgen, Dan	Hfd.	2	13	2	3	5	2	....	....	....	....	....		1981-82	1982-83

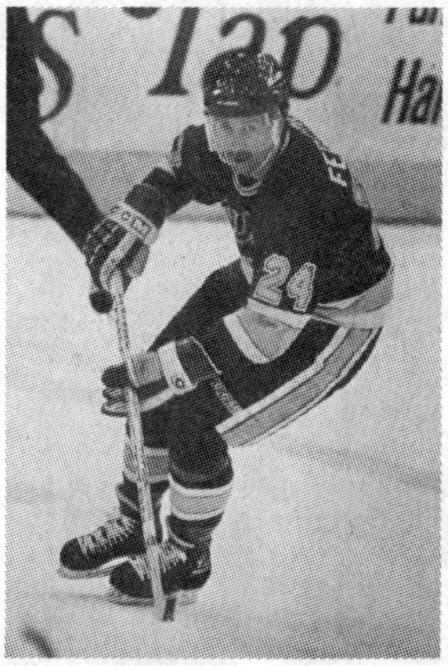

Bernie Federko

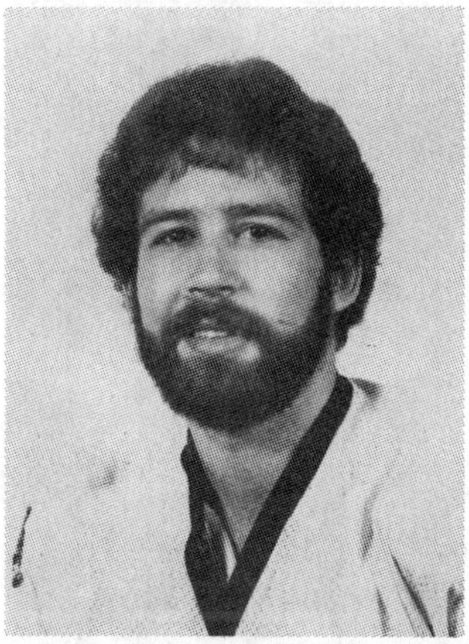

Dwight Foster

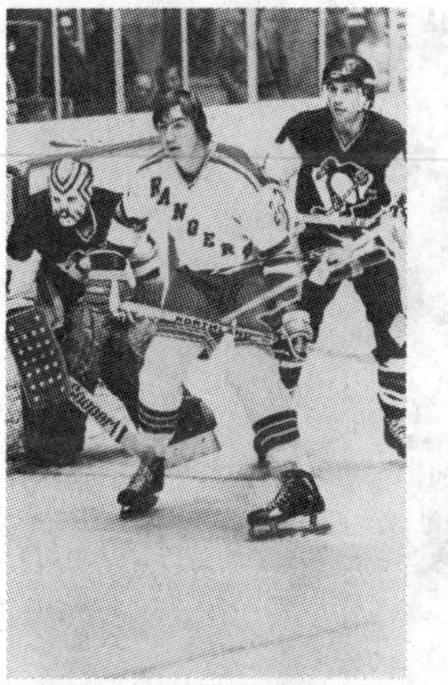

Nick Fotiu

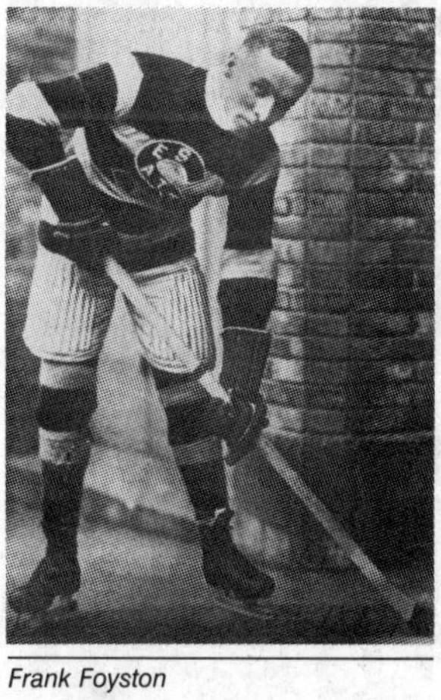

Frank Foyston

Name	NHL Teams	NHL Seasons	Regular Schedule GP	G	A	TP	PIM	Playoffs GP	G	A	TP	PIM	NHL Cup Wins	First NHL Season	Last NHL Season
Friest, Ron	Min.	3	64	7	7	14	191	6	1	0	1	7		1980-81	1982-83
Frig, Len	Chi., Cal., Cle., St.L.	7	311	13	51	64	479	14	2	1	3	0		1972-73	1979-80
Frost, Harry	Bos.	1	3	0	0	0	0	1	0	0	0	0		1938-39	1938-39
Fryday, Bob	Mtl.	2	5	1	0	1	0	....	....	....	....	....		1949-50	1951-52
Ftorek, Robbie	Det., Que, NYR	8	334	77	150	227	262	19	9	6	15	28		1972-73	1984-85
Fullan, Lawrence	Wsh.	1	4	1	0	1	0	....	....	....	....	....		1974-75	1974-75
Fusco, Mark	Hfd.	2	80	3	12	15	42	....	....	....	....	....		1983-84	1984-85

G

Name	NHL Teams	NHL Seasons	Regular Schedule GP	G	A	TP	PIM	Playoffs GP	G	A	TP	PIM	NHL Cup Wins	First NHL Season	Last NHL Season
Gadsby, Bill	Chi., NYR, Det.	20	1248	130	437	567	1539	67	4	23	27	92		1946-47	1965-66
Gagne, Art	Mtl., Bos., Ott., Det.	6	228	67	33	100	257	11	2	1	3	20		1926-27	1931-32
Gagne, Pierre	Bos.	1	2	0	0	0	0	....	....	....	....	....		1959-60	1959-60
Gagnon, Germaine	Mtl., NYI, Chi., K.C.	5	259	40	101	141	72	19	2	3	5	2		1971-72	1975-76
Gagnon, Johnny	Mtl., Bos., NYA	10	454	120	141	261	295	32	12	12	24	37	1	1930-31	1939-40
Gainey, Bob	Mtl.	16	1160	239	262	501	585	182	25	48	73	151	5	1973-74	1988-89
Gainor, Dutch	Bos., NYR, Ott., Mtl.M	7	243	51	56	107	129	25	2	1	3	14	2	1927-28	1934-35
Galarneau, Michel	Hfd.	3	78	7	10	17	34	....	....	....	....	....		1980-81	1982-83
Galbraith, Percy	Bos., Ott.	8	347	29	31	60	223	31	4	7	11	24		1926-27	1933-34
Gallagher, John	Mtl.M, Det., NYA	7	204	14	19	33	153	22	2	3	5	27	1	1930-31	1938-39
Gallimore, Jamie	Min.	1	2	0	0	0	0	....	....	....	....	....		1977-78	1977-78
Gallinger, Don	Bos.	5	222	65	88	153	89	23	5	5	10	19		1942-43	1947-48
Gamble, Dick	Mtl., Chi., Tor.	8	195	41	41	82	66	14	1	2	3	4	2	1950-51	1966-67
Gambucci, Gary	Min.	2	51	2	7	9	9	....	....	....	....	....		1971-72	1973-74
Gans, Dave	L.A.	2	6	0	0	0	2	....	....	....	....	....		1982-83	1985-86
Gardiner, Herb	Mtl., Chi.	3	101	10	9	19	52	7	0	1	1	14		1926-27	1928-29
Gardner, Bill	Chi., Hfd.	9	380	73	115	188	68	45	3	8	11	17		1980-81	1988-89
Gardner, Cal	NYR, Tor., Chi., Bos.	12	696	154	238	392	517	61	7	10	17	20	2	1945-46	1956-57
Gardner, Dave	Mtl., St.L., Cal., Cle., Phi.	7	350	75	115	190	41	....	....	....	....	....		1972-73	1979-80
Gardner, Paul	Col., Tor., Pit., Wsh., Buf.	7	447	201	201	402	207	16	2	6	8	14		1976-77	1985-86
Gare, Danny	Buf., Det., Edm.	13	827	354	331	685	1285	64	25	21	46	195		1974-75	1986-87
Gariepy, Ray	Bos., Tor.	2	36	1	6	7	43	....	....	....	....	....		1953-54	1955-56
Garland, Scott	Tor., L.A.	3	91	13	24	37	115	7	1	2	3	35		1975-76	1978-79
Garner, Bob	Pit.	1	1	0	0	0	0	....	....	....	....	....		1982-83	1982-83
Garrett, Red	NYR	1	23	1	1	2	18	....	....	....	....	....		1942-43	1942-43
Gassoff, Bob	St.L.	4	245	11	47	58	866	9	0	1	1	16		1973-74	1976-77
Gassoff, Brad	Van.	4	122	19	17	36	163	3	0	0	0	0		1975-76	1978-79
Gatzos, Steve	Pit.	4	89	15	20	35	83	1	0	0	0	0		1981-82	1984-85
Gaudreault, Armand	Bos.	1	44	15	9	24	27	7	0	2	2	8		1944-45	1944-45
Gaudreault, Leo	Mtl.	3	67	8	4	12	30	....	....	....	....	....		1927-28	1932-33
Gaulin, Jean-Marc	Que.	4	26	4	3	7	8	1	0	0	0	0		1982-83	1985-86
Gauthier, Art	Mtl.	1	13	0	0	0	0	1	0	0	0	0		1926-27	1926-27
Gauthier, Fern	NYR, Mtl., Det.	6	229	46	50	96	35	22	5	1	6	7		1943-44	1948-49
Gauthier, Jean	Mtl., Phi., Bos.	10	166	6	29	35	150	14	1	3	4	22	1	1960-61	1969-70
Gauvreau, Jocelyn	Mtl.	1	2	0	0	0	0	....	....	....	....	....		1983-84	1983-84
Geale, Bob	Pit.	1	1	0	0	0	2	....	....	....	....	....		1984-85	1984-85
Gee, George	Chi., Det.	9	551	135	183	318	345	41	6	13	19	32	1	1945-46	1953-54
Geldart, Gary	Min.	1	4	0	0	0	5	....	....	....	....	....		1970-71	1970-71
Gendron, Jean-Guy	NYR, Mtl., Bos., Phi.	14	863	182	201	383	701	42	7	4	11	47		1955-56	1971-72
Geoffrion, Bernie	Mtl., NYR	16	883	393	429	822	689	132	58	60	118	88	6	1950-51	1967-68
Geoffrion, Danny	Mtl., Wpg.	3	111	20	32	52	99	2	0	0	0	7		1979-80	1981-82
Geran, Gerry	Mtl.W., Bos.	2	37	5	1	6	6	....	....	....	....	....		1917-18	1925-26
Gerard, Eddie	Ott.	6	128	50	30	80	94	26	7	3	10	51	4	1917-18	1922-23
Getliffe, Ray	Bos., Mtl.	10	393	136	137	273	260	45	9	10	19	30	2	1935-36	1944-45
Giallonardo, Mario	Col.	2	23	0	3	3	6	....	....	....	....	....		1979-80	1980-81
Gibbs, Barry	Bos., Min., Atl., St.L., L.A.	13	797	58	224	282	945	36	4	2	6	67		1967-68	1979-80
Gibson, Doug	Bos., Wsh.	3	63	9	19	28	0	1	0	0	0	0		1973-74	1977-78
Gibson, John	L.A., Tor., Wpg.	3	48	0	2	2	120	....	....	....	....	....		1980-81	1983-84
Giesebrecht, Gus	Det.	4	135	27	51	78	13	17	2	3	5	0		1938-39	1941-42
Gilbert, Ed	K.C., Pit.	3	166	21	31	52	22	....	....	....	....	....		1974-75	1976-77
Gilbert, Jean	Bos.	2	9	0	0	0	4	....	....	....	....	....		1962-63	1964-65
Gilbert, Rod	NYR	18	1065	406	615	1021	508	79	34	33	67	43		1960-61	1977-78
Gilbertson, Stan	Cal., St.L., Wsh., Pit.	6	428	85	89	174	148	3	1	1	2	2		1971-72	1976-77
Gillen, Don	Phi., Hfd.	2	35	2	4	6	22	....	....	....	....	....		1979-80	1981-82
Gillie, Ferrand	Det.	1	1	0	0	0	0	....	....	....	....	....		1928-29	1928-29
Gillies, Clark	NYI, Buf.	14	958	319	378	697	1023	164	47	47	94	287	4	1974-75	1987-88
Gillis, Jere	Que., Buf., Phi., Van., NYR	9	386	78	95	173	230	19	4	7	11	9		1977-78	1986-87
Gillis, Mike	Col., Bos.	6	246	33	43	76	186	27	2	5	7	10		1978-79	1983-84
Gingras, Gaston	Mtl., Tor., St.L.	10	476	61	174	235	161	52	6	18	24	20	1	1979-80	1988-89
Girard, Bob	Cal., Cle., Wsh.	5	305	45	69	114	140	....	....	....	....	....		1975-76	1979-80
Girard, Kenny	Tor.	3	7	0	1	1	2	....	....	....	....	....		1956-57	1959-60
Giroux, Art	Mtl., Bos., Det.	3	54	6	4	10	14	2	0	0	0	0		1932-33	1935-36
Giroux, Larry	St.L., K.C., Det., Hfd.	7	274	15	74	89	333	5	0	0	0	4		1973-74	1979-80
Giroux, Pierre	L.A.	1	6	1	0	1	17	....	....	....	....	....		1982-83	1982-83
Gladney, Bob	L.A., Pit.	2	14	1	5	6	4	....	....	....	....	....		1982-83	1983-84
Gladu, Jean	Bos.	1	40	6	14	20	2	7	2	2	4	0		1944-45	1944-45
Glennie, Brian	Tor., L.A.	10	572	14	100	114	621	32	0	1	1	66		1969-70	1978-79
Gloeckner, Lorry	Det.	1	13	0	2	2	6	....	....	....	....	....		1978-79	1978-79
Gloor, Dan	Van.	1	2	0	0	0	0	....	....	....	....	....		1973-74	1973-74
Glover, Fred	Det., Chi.	4	92	13	11	24	62	3	0	0	0	0		1948-49	1952-53
Glover, Howie	Chi., Det., NYR, Mtl.	5	144	29	17	46	101	11	1	2	3	2		1958-59	1968-69
Godden, Ernie	Tor.	1	5	1	1	2	6	....	....	....	....	....		1981-82	1981-82
Godfrey, Warren	Bos., Det.	16	786	32	125	157	752	52	1	4	5	42		1952-53	1967-68
Godin, Eddy	Wsh.	2	27	3	6	9	12	....	....	....	....	....		1977-78	1978-79
Godin, Sammy	Ott., Mtl.	3	83	4	3	7	36	....	....	....	....	....		1927-28	1933-34
Goegan, Peter	Det., NYR, Min.	11	383	19	67	86	365	33	1	3	4	61		1957-58	1967-68
Goldham, Bob	Tor., Chi., Det.	12	650	28	143	171	400	66	3	14	17	53	4	1941-42	1955-56
Goldsworthy, Bill	Bos., Min., NYR	14	771	283	258	541	793	40	18	19	37	30		1964-65	1977-78
Goldsworthy, Leroy	NYR, Det., Chi., Mtl., Bos., NYA	9	337	66	57	123	79	22	1	0	1	4	1	1929-30	1938-39
Goldup, Glenn	Mtl., L.A.	9	291	52	67	119	303	16	4	3	7	22		1973-74	1981-82
Goldup, Hank	Tor., NYR	6	181	63	80	143	97	26	5	1	6	6	1	1939-40	1945-46
Gooden, Bill	NYR	2	53	9	11	20	15	....	....	....	....	....		1942-43	1943-44
Goodenough, Larry	Phi., Van.	6	242	22	77	99	179	22	3	15	18	10	1	1974-75	1979-80
Goodfellow, Ebbie	Det.	14	554	134	190	324	511	45	8	8	16	65	3	1929-30	1942-43
Gordon, Fred	Det., Bos.	2	77	8	7	15	68	1	0	0	0	0		1926-27	1927-28
Gordon, Jackie	NYR	3	36	3	10	13	0	9	1	1	2	7		1948-49	1950-51
Gorence, Tom	Phi., Edm.	6	303	58	53	111	89	37	9	6	15	47		1978-79	1983-84
Goring, Butch	L.A., NYI, Bos.	16	1107	375	513	888	102	134	38	50	88	32	4	1969-70	1984-85
Gorman, Dave	Atl.	1	3	0	0	0	0	....	....	....	....	....		1979-80	1979-80
Gorman, Ed	Ott., Tor.	4	111	14	5	19	108	8	0	0	0	2	1	1924-25	1927-28
Gosselin, Benoit	NYR	1	7	0	0	0	33	....	....	....	....	....		1977-78	1977-78
Gottselig, Johnny	Chi.	16	589	176	195	371	203	43	13	13	26	20	2	1928-29	1944-45
Gould, John	Buf., Van., Atl.	9	504	131	138	269	113	14	3	2	5	4		1971-72	1979-80
Gould, Larry	Van.	1	2	0	0	0	0	....	....	....	....	....		1973-74	1973-74
Goupille, Red	Mtl.	8	222	12	28	40	256	8	2	0	2	6		1935-36	1942-43
Goyer, Gerry	Chi.	1	40	1	2	3	4	3	0	0	0	2		1967-68	1967-68
Goyette, Phil	Mtl., NYR, St.L., Buf.	16	941	207	467	674	131	94	17	29	46	26	4	1956-57	1971-72
Graboski, Tony	Mtl.	3	66	6	10	16	18	2	0	0	0	0		1940-41	1942-43
Gracie, Bob	Tor., Bos., NYA, Mtl.M., Mtl., Chi.	9	378	82	109	191	204	33	4	7	11	4	2	1930-31	1938-39
Gradin, Thomas	Van., Bos.	9	677	209	384	593	298	42	17	25	42	20		1978-79	1986-87
Graham, Leth	Ott., Ham.	6	26	3	0	3	0	1	0	0	0	0	1	1920-21	1925-26
Graham, Pat	Pit., Tor.	3	103	11	17	28	136	4	0	0	0	2		1981-82	1983-84
Graham, Rod	Bos.	1	14	2	1	3	7	....	....	....	....	....		1974-75	1974-75
Graham, Ted	Chi., Mtl.M., Det., St.L., Bos., NYA	9	343	14	25	39	300	23	3	1	4	34		1927-28	1936-37
Grant, Danny	Mtl., Min., Det., L.A.	13	736	263	273	536	239	43	10	14	24	19	1	1965-66	1978-79
Gratton, Norm	NYR, Atl., Buf., Min.	5	201	39	44	83	64	6	0	1	1	2		1971-72	1975-76
Gravelle, Leo	Mtl., Det.	5	223	44	34	78	42	17	4	1	5	2		1946-47	1950-51
Graves, Hilliard	Cal., Atl., Van., Wpg.	9	556	118	163	281	209	2	0	0	0	0		1970-71	1979-80
Gray, Alex	NYR, Tor.	2	50	7	0	7	30	13	1	0	1	0	1	1927-28	1928-29
Gray, Terry	Bos., Mtl., L.A., St.L.	6	147	26	28	54	64	35	5	5	10	22		1961-62	1970-71
Green	Det.	1	2	0	0	0	0	....	....	....	....	....		1928-29	1928-29
Green, Red	Ham., NYA, Bos.	6	195	59	13	72	261	....	....	....	....	....	1	1923-24	1928-29

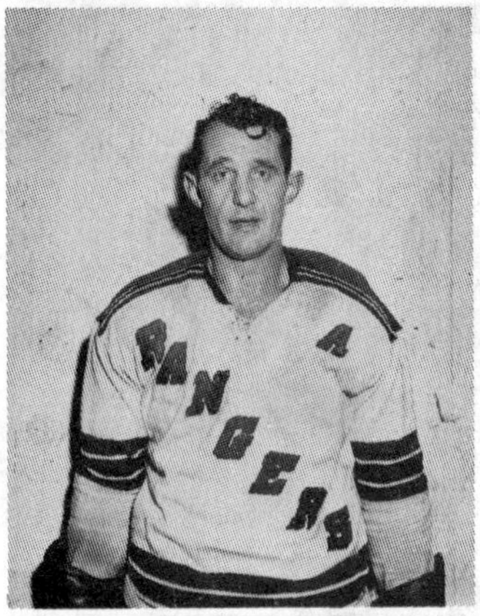
Bill Gadsby

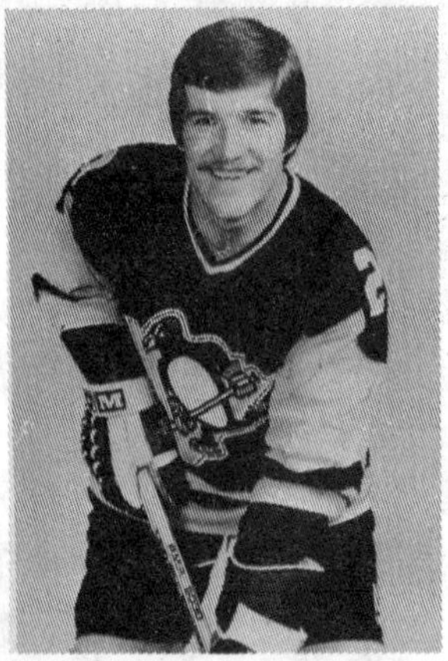
Paul Gardner

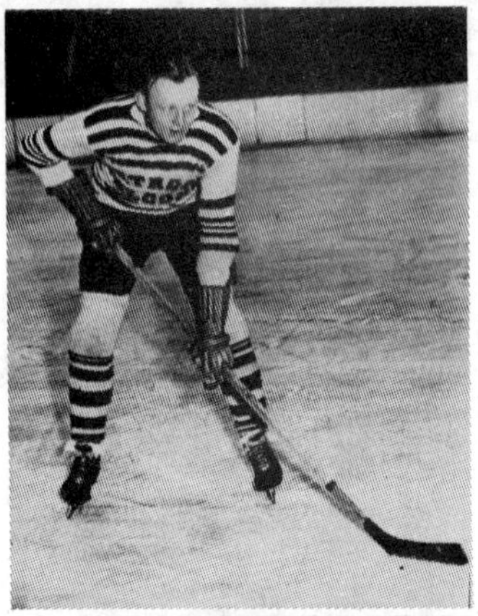
Ebbie Goodfellow

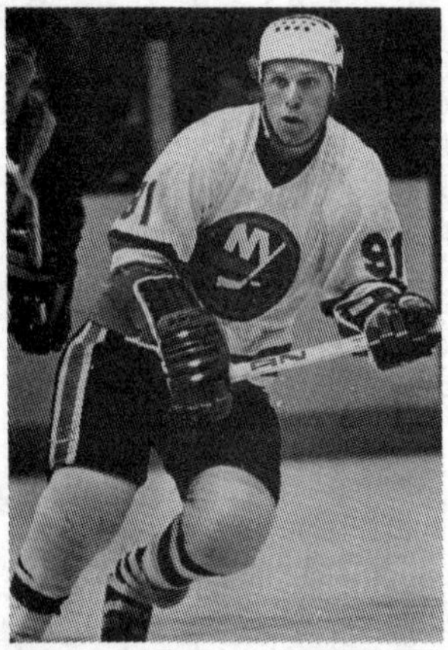
Butch Goring

Name	NHL Teams	NHL Seasons	Regular Schedule GP	G	A	TP	PIM	Playoffs GP	G	A	TP	PIM	NHL Cup Wins	First NHL Season	Last NHL Season
Green, Ted	Bos.	11	620	48	206	254	1029	31	4	8	12	54	1	1960-61	1971-72
Green, Wilf	Ham., NYA	4	103	33	8	41	151	....	....	....	....	....		1923-24	1926-27
Greig, Bruce	Cal.	2	9	0	1	1	46	....	....	....	....	....		1973-74	1974-75
Grenier, Lucien	Mtl., L.A.	4	151	14	14	28	18	2	0	0	0	0	1	1968-69	1971-72
Grenier, Richard	NYI	1	10	1	1	2	2	....	....	....	....	....		1972-73	1972-73
Greschner, Ron	NYR	16	982	179	431	610	1226	84	17	32	49	106		1974-75	1989-90
Grigor, George	Chi.	1	2	1	0	1	0	1	0	0	0	0		1943-44	1943-44
Grisdale, John	Tor., Van.	6	250	4	39	43	346	10	0	1	1	15		1972-73	1978-79
Gronsdahl, Lloyd	Bos.	1	10	1	2	3	0	....	....	....	....	....		1941-42	1941-42
Gross, Llyod	Tor., NYA, Bos., Det.	3	62	11	5	16	20	1	0	0	0	0		1926-27	1934-35
Grosso, Don	Det., Chi., Bos.	9	334	87	117	204	90	50	14	12	26	46	1	1938-39	1946-47
Grosvenar, Len	Ott., NYA, Mtl.	6	147	9	11	20	78	4	0	0	0	2		1927-28	1932-33
Groulx, Wayne	Que.	1	1	0	0	0	0	....	....	....	....	....		1984-85	1984-85
Gruen, Danny	Det., Col.	3	49	9	13	22	19	....	....	....	....	....		1972-73	1976-77
Gryp, Bob	Bos., Wsh.	3	74	11	13	24	33	....	....	....	....	....		1973-74	1975-76
Guevremont, Jocelyn	Van., Buf., NYR	9	571	84	223	307	319	40	4	17	21	18		1971-72	1979-80
Guidolin, Aldo	NYR	4	182	9	15	24	117	....	....	....	....	....		1952-53	1955-56
Guidolin, Bep	Bos., Det., Chi.	9	519	107	171	278	606	24	5	7	12	35		1942-43	1951-52
Guindon, Bobby	Wpg.	1	6	0	1	1	0	....	....	....	....	....		1979-80	1979-80
Gustavsson, Peter	Col.	1	2	0	0	0	0	....	....	....	....	....		1981-82	1981-82

H

Name	NHL Teams	NHL Seasons	Regular Schedule GP	G	A	TP	PIM	Playoffs GP	G	A	TP	PIM	NHL Cup Wins	First NHL Season	Last NHL Season
Hachborn, Len	Phi., L.A.	3	102	20	39	59	29	7	0	3	3	7		1983-84	1985-86
Haddon, Lloyd	Det.	1	8	0	0	0	2	1	0	0	0	0		1959-60	1959-60
Hadfield, Vic	NYR, Pit.	16	1002	323	389	712	1154	73	27	21	48	117		1961-62	1976-77
Haggarty, Jim	Mtl.	1	5	1	1	2	0	3	2	1	3	0		1941-42	1941-42
Hagglund, Roger	Que.	1	3	0	0	0	0	....	....	....	....	....		1984-85	1984-85
Hagman, Matti	Bos., Edm.	4	237	56	89	145	36	20	5	2	7	6		1976-77	1981-82
Haidy, Gord	Det.	1	....	....	....	....	....	1	0	0	0	0	1	1949-50	1949-50
Hajt, Bill	Buf.	14	854	42	202	244	433	80	2	16	18	70		1973-74	1986-87
Hakansson, Anders	Min., Pit., L.A.	5	330	52	46	98	141	6	0	0	0	2		1981-82	1985-86
Halderson, Slim	Det., Tor.	1	44	3	2	5	65	....	....	....	....	....	1	1926-27	1926-27
Hale, Larry	Phi.	4	196	5	37	42	90	8	0	0	0	12		1968-69	1971-72
Haley, Len	Det.	2	30	2	2	4	14	6	1	3	4	6		1959-60	1960-61
Hall, Bob	NYA	1	8	0	0	0	0	....	....	....	....	....		1925-26	1925-26
Hall, Del	Cal.	3	9	2	0	2	2	....	....	....	....	....		1971-72	1973-74
Hall, Joe	Mtl.	2	37	15	1	16	85	12	0	2	2	0		1917-18	1918-19
Hall, Murray	Chi., Det., Min., Van.	9	164	35	48	83	46	6	0	0	0	0		1961-62	1971-72
Hall, Wayne	NYR	1	4	0	0	0	0	....	....	....	....	....		1960-61	1960-61
Halliday, Milt	Ott.	3	67	1	0	1	6	6	0	0	0	0	1	1926-27	1928-29
Hallin, Mats	NYI, Min.	5	152	17	14	31	193	15	1	0	1	13	1	1982-83	1986-87
Halward, Doug	Bos., L.A., Van., Det., Edm.	14	653	69	224	293	774	47	7	10	17	113		1975-76	1988-89
Hamel, Gilles	Buf., Wpg., L.A.	9	519	127	147	274	276	27	4	5	9	10		1980-81	1988-89
Hamel, Herb	Tor.	1	2	0	0	0	14	....	....	....	....	....		1930-31	1930-31
Hamel, Jean	St.L., Det., Que., Mtl.	12	699	26	95	121	766	33	0	2	2	44		1972-73	1983-84
Hamill, Red	Bos., Chi.	12	418	128	94	222	160	13	1	2	3	12	2	1937-38	1950-51
Hamilton, Al	NYR, Buf., Edm.	7	257	10	78	88	258	7	0	0	0	2		1965-66	1979-80
Hamilton, Chuck	Mtl., St.L.	2	4	0	2	2	2	....	....	....	....	....		1961-62	1972-73
Hamilton, Jack	Tor.	3	138	31	48	79	76	11	2	1	3	0		1942-43	1945-46
Hamilton, Jim	Pit.	8	95	14	18	32	28	6	3	0	3	0		1977-78	1984-85
Hamilton, Reg	Tor., Chi.	12	387	21	87	108	412	64	6	6	12	54	2	1935-36	1946-47
Hammarstrom, Inge	Tor., St.L.	6	427	116	123	239	86	13	2	3	5	4		1973-74	1978-79
Hampson, Gord	Cgy.	1	4	0	0	0	5	....	....	....	....	....		1982-83	1982-83
Hampson, Ted	Tor., NYR, Det., Oak., Cal., Min.	12	676	108	245	353	94	35	7	10	17	2		1959-60	1971-72
Hampton, Rick	Cal., Cle., L.A.	6	337	59	113	172	147	2	0	0	0	0		1974-75	1979-80
Hamway, Mark	NYI	3	53	5	13	18	9	1	0	0	0	0		1984-85	1986-87
Hangsleben, Al	Hfd., Wsh., L.A.	3	185	21	48	69	396	....	....	....	....	....		1979-80	1981-82
Hanna, John	NYR, Mtl., Phi.	5	198	6	26	32	206	....	....	....	....	....		1958-59	1967-68
Hannigan, Gord	Tor.	4	161	29	31	60	117	9	2	0	2	8		1952-53	1955-56
Hannigan, Pat	Tor., NYR, Phi.	5	182	30	39	69	116	11	1	2	3	11		1959-60	1968-69
Hannigan, Ray	Tor.	1	3	0	0	0	2	....	....	....	....	....		1948-49	1948-49
Hansen, Ritchie	NYI, St.L.	4	20	2	8	10	6	....	....	....	....	....		1976-77	1981-82
Hanson, Dave	Det., Min.	2	33	1	1	2	65	....	....	....	....	....		1978-79	1979-80
Hanson, Emil	Det.	1	7	0	0	0	6	....	....	....	....	....		1932-33	1932-33
Hanson, Keith	Cgy.	1	25	0	2	2	77	....	....	....	....	....		1983-84	1983-84
Hanson, Ossie	Chi.	1	7	0	0	0	0	....	....	....	....	....		1937-38	1937-38
Harbaruk, Nick	Pit., St.L.	5	364	45	75	120	273	14	3	1	4	20		1969-70	1973-74
Hardy, Joe	Oak., Cal.	2	63	9	14	23	51	4	0	0	0	0		1969-70	1970-71
Hargreaves, Jim	Van.	2	66	1	7	8	105	....	....	....	....	....		1970-71	1972-73
Harmon, Glen	Mtl.	9	452	50	96	146	334	53	5	10	15	37	2	1942-43	1950-51
Harms, John	Chi.	2	44	5	5	10	21	3	3	0	3	2		1943-44	1944-45
Harnott, Happy	Bos.	1	6	0	0	0	6	....	....	....	....	....		1933-34	1933-34
Harper, Terry	Mtl., L.A., Det., St.L., Col.	19	1066	35	221	256	1362	112	4	13	17	140	5	1962-63	1980-81
Harrer, Tim	Cgy.	1	3	0	0	0	2	....	....	....	....	....		1982-83	1982-83
Harrington, Hago	Bos., Mtl.	3	72	9	3	12	15	4	1	0	1	2		1925-26	1932-33
Harris, Billy	Tor., Oak., Cal., Pit.	12	769	126	219	345	205	62	8	10	18	30	3	1955-56	1968-69
Harris, Billy	NYI, L.A., Tor.	12	897	231	327	558	394	71	19	19	38	48		1972-73	1983-84
Harris, Duke	Min., Tor.	1	26	1	4	5	4	....	....	....	....	....		1967-68	1967-68
Harris, Hugh	Buf.	1	60	12	26	38	17	3	0	0	0	0		1972-73	1972-73
Harris, Ron	Det., Oak., Atl., NYR	12	476	20	91	111	484	28	4	3	7	33		1962-63	1975-76
Harris, Smokey	Bos.	2	40	5	5	10	28	2	0	0	0	0		1924-25	1930-31
Harris, Ted	Mtl., Min., Det., St.L., Phi.	12	788	30	168	198	1000	100	1	22	23	230	5	1963-64	1974-75
Harrison, Ed	Bos., NYR	4	194	27	24	51	53	9	1	0	1	2		1947-48	1950-51
Harrison, Jim	Bos., Tor., Chi., Edm.	8	324	67	86	153	435	13	1	1	2	43		1968-69	1979-80
Hart, Gerry	Det., NYI, Que., St.L.	15	730	29	150	179	1240	78	3	12	15	175		1968-69	1982-83
Hart, Gizzy	Det., Mtl.	3	100	6	8	14	12	8	0	1	1	0	1	1926-27	1932-33
Hartsburg, Craig	Min.	10	570	98	315	413	818	61	15	27	42	70		1979-80	1988-89
Harvey, Doug	Mtl., NYR, Det., St.L.	20	1113	88	452	540	1216	137	8	64	72	152	6	1947-48	1968-69
Harvey, Fred	Min., Atl., K.C., Det.	7	407	90	118	208	131	14	0	2	2	8		1970-71	1976-77
Harvey, Hugh	K.C.	2	18	1	1	2	4	....	....	....	....	....		1974-75	1975-76
Hassard, Bob	Tor., Chi.	5	126	9	28	37	22	....	....	....	....	....		1949-50	1954-55
Hatoum, Ed	Det., Van.	3	47	3	6	9	25	....	....	....	....	....		1968-69	1970-71
Haworth, Alan	Buf., Wsh., Que.	8	524	189	211	400	425	42	12	16	28	28		1980-81	1987-88
Haworth, Gord	NYR	1	2	0	1	1	0	....	....	....	....	....		1952-53	1952-53
Hawryliw, Neil	NYI	1	1	0	0	0	0	....	....	....	....	....		1981-82	1981-82
Hay, Billy	Chi.	8	506	113	273	386	244	67	15	21	36	62		1959-60	1966-67
Hay, George	Chi., Det.	7	242	74	60	134	84	8	2	3	5	14		1926-27	1933-34
Hay, Jim	Det.	3	75	1	5	6	22	9	1	0	1	2	1	1952-53	1954-55
Hayek, Peter	Min.	1	1	0	0	0	0	....	....	....	....	....		1981-82	1981-82
Hayes, Chris	Bos.	1	....	....	....	....	....	1	0	0	0	0	1	1971-72	1971-72
Haynes, Paul	Mtl.M., Bos., Mtl.	11	390	61	134	195	164	25	2	8	10	13		1930-31	1940-41
Hazlett, Steve	Van.	1	1	0	0	0	0	....	....	....	....	....		1979-80	1979-80
Head, Galen	Det.	1	1	0	0	0	0	....	....	....	....	....		1967-68	1967-68
Headley, Fern	Bos., Mtl.	1	27	1	1	2	6	5	0	0	0	0		1924-25	1924-25
Healey, Dick	Det.	1	1	0	0	0	2	....	....	....	....	....		1960-61	1960-61
Heaslip, Mark	NYR, L.A.	3	117	10	19	29	110	5	0	0	0	2		1976-77	1978-79
Heath, Randy	NYR	2	13	2	4	6	15	....	....	....	....	....		1984-85	1985-86
Hebenton, Andy	NYR, Bos.	9	630	189	202	391	83	22	6	5	11	8		1955-56	1963-64
Hedberg, Anders	NYR	7	465	172	225	397	144	58	22	24	46	31		1978-79	1984-85
Heffernan, Frank	Tor.	1	17	0	0	0	4	....	....	....	....	....		1919-20	1919-20
Heffernan, Gerry	Mtl.	3	83	33	35	68	27	11	3	3	6	8	1	1941-42	1943-44
Heidt, Mike	L.A.	1	6	0	1	1	7	....	....	....	....	....		1983-84	1983-84
Heindl, Bill	Min., NYR	3	18	2	1	3	0	....	....	....	....	....		1970-71	1972-73
Heinrich, Lionel	Bos.	1	35	1	1	2	33	....	....	....	....	....		1955-56	1955-56
Heiskala, Earl	Phi.	3	127	13	11	24	294	....	....	....	....	....		1968-69	1970-71
Helander, Peter	L.A.	1	7	0	1	1	0	....	....	....	....	....		1982-83	1982-83
Heller, Ott.	NYR	15	647	55	176	231	465	61	6	8	14	61	2	1931-32	1945-46
Helman, Harry	Ott.	3	42	1	0	1	7	5	0	0	0	0	1	1922-23	1924-25
Helminen, Raimo	NYR, Min., NYI	3	117	13	46	59	16	2	0	0	0	0		1985-86	1988-89
Hemmerling, Tony	NYA	2	24	3	3	6	4	....	....	....	....	....		1935-36	1936-37
Henderson, Archie	Wsh., Min., Hfd.	3	23	3	1	4	92	....	....	....	....	....		1980-81	1982-83

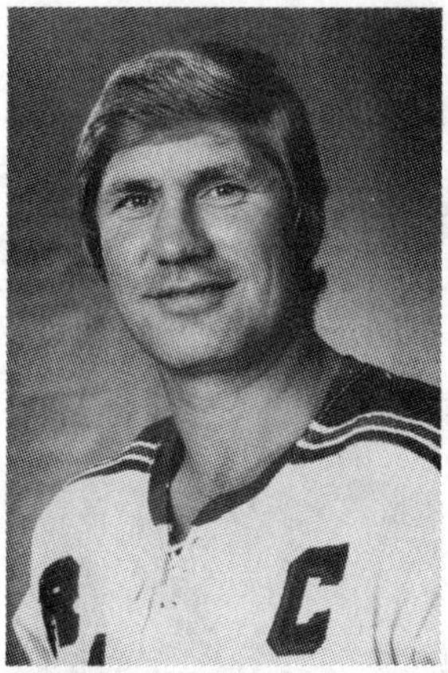

Vic Hadfield

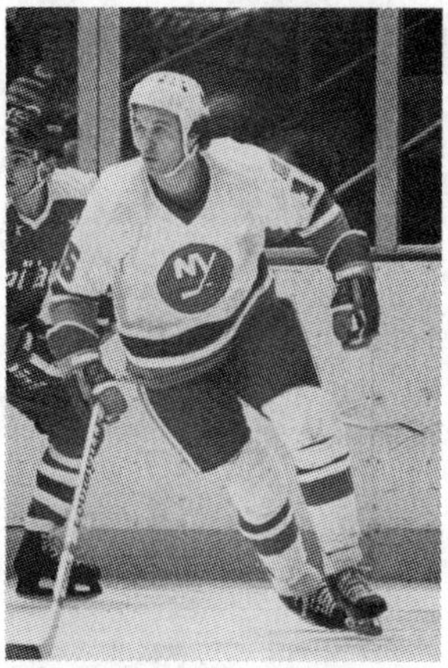

Billy Harris

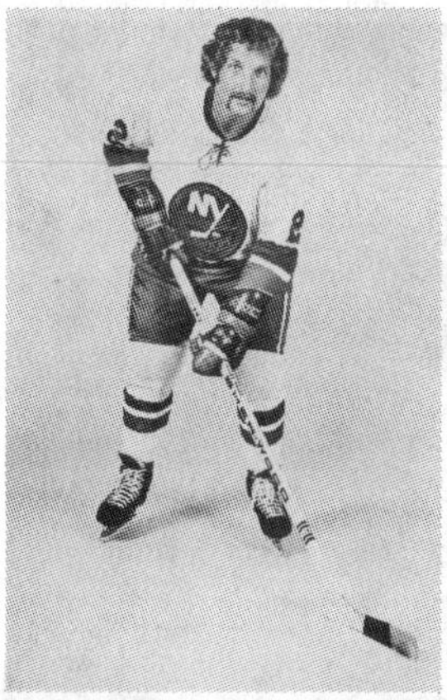

Gerry Hart

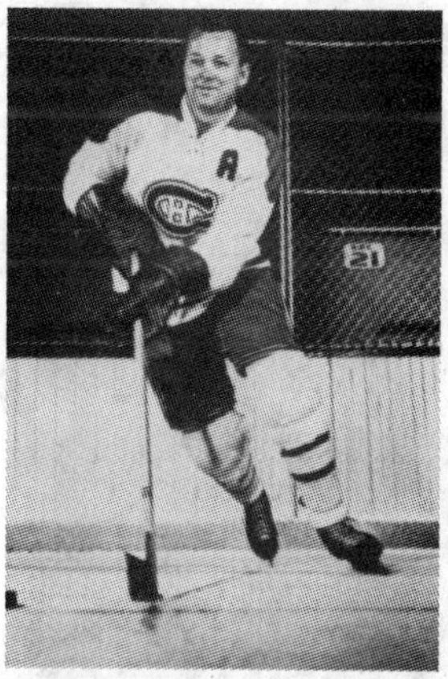

Doug Harvey

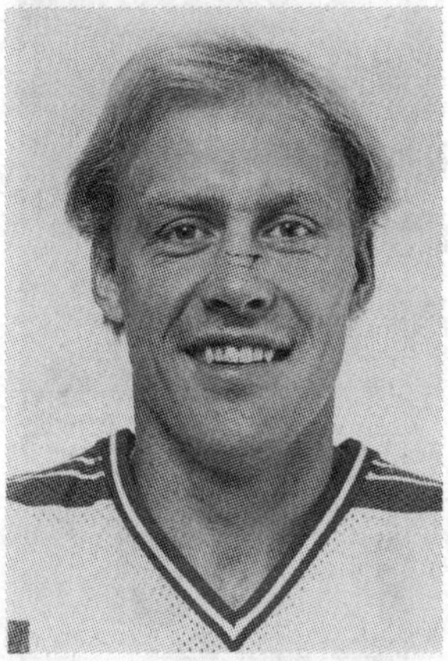

Anders Hedberg

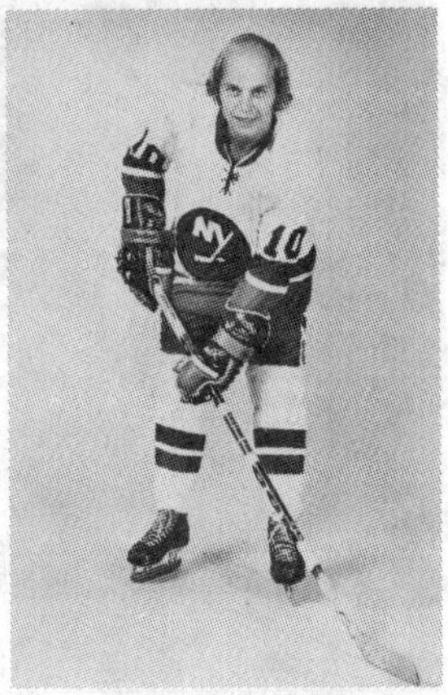

Lorne Henning

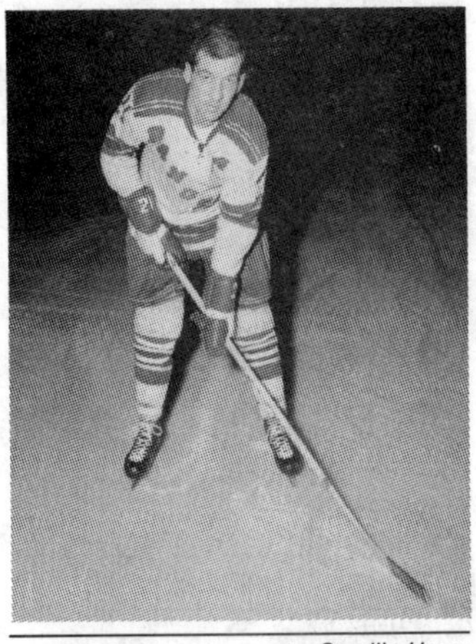

Camille Henry

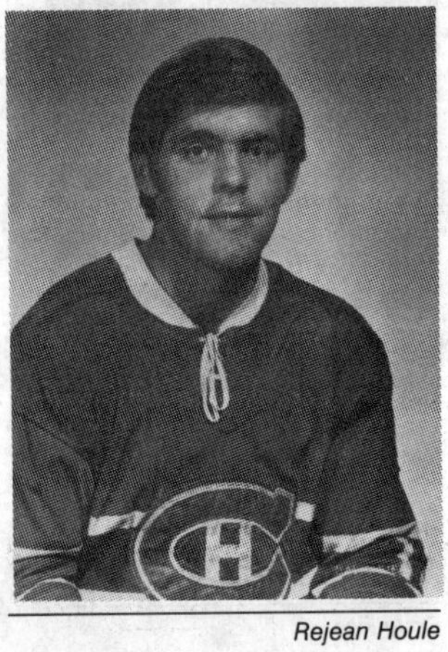

Rejean Houle

			Regular Schedule					Playoffs							
Name	NHL Teams	NHL Seasons	GP	G	A	TP	PIM	GP	G	A	TP	PIM	NHL Cup Wins	First NHL Season	Last NHL Season
Henderson, Murray	Bos.	8	405	24	62	86	305	41	2	3	5	23		1944-45	1951-52
Henderson, Paul	Det., Tor., Atl.	13	707	236	241	477	304	56	11	14	25	28		1962-63	1979-80
Hendrickson, John	Det.	3	5	0	0	0	4	....	....	....	....	....		1957-58	1961-62
Henning, Lorne	NYI	9	544	73	111	184	102	81	7	7	14	8	2	1972-73	1980-81
Henry, Camille	NYR, Chi., St.L.	14	727	279	249	528	88	47	6	12	18	7		1953-54	1969-70
Hepple, Alan	N.J.	3	3	0	0	0	7	....	....	....	....	....		1983-84	1985-86
Herberts, Jimmy	Bos., Tor., Det.	6	206	83	29	112	250	9	3	0	3	35		1924-25	1929-30
Herchenratter, Art	Det.	1	10	1	2	3	2	....	....	....	....	....		1940-41	1940-41
Hergerts, Fred	NYA	2	19	2	4	6	2	....	....	....	....	....		1934-35	1935-36
Hergesheimer, Philip	Chi., Bos.	4	125	21	41	62	19	7	0	0	0	2		1939-40	1942-43
Hergesheimer, Wally	NYR, Chi.	7	351	114	85	199	106	5	1	0	1	0		1951-52	1958-59
Heron, Red	Tor., Bro., Mtl.	4	106	21	19	40	38	16	2	2	4	55		1938-39	1941-42
Hess, Bob	St.L., Buf., Hfd.	8	329	27	95	122	178	4	1	1	2	2		1974-75	1983-84
Heximer, Orville	NYR, Bos., NYA	3	85	13	7	20	28	5	0	0	0	2		1929-30	1934-35
Hextall, Bryan Sr.	NYR	11	447	187	175	362	227	37	8	9	17	19	1	1936-37	1947-48
Hextall, Bryan Jr.	NYR, Pit., Atl., Det., Min.	8	549	99	161	260	738	18	0	4	4	59		1962-63	1975-76
Hextall, Dennis	NYR, L.A., Cal., Min., Det., Wsh.	13	681	153	350	503	1398	22	3	3	6	45		1968-69	1979-80
Heyliger, Vic	Chi.	2	34	2	3	5	2	....	....	....	....	....		1937-38	1943-44
Hicke, Bill	Mtl., NYR, Oak.	14	729	168	234	402	395	42	3	10	13	41	2	1958-59	1971-72
Hicke, Ernie	Cal., Atl., NYI, Min., L.A.	8	520	132	140	272	407	2	1	0	1	0		1970-71	1977-78
Hickey, Greg	NYR	1	1	0	0	0	0	....	....	....	....	....		1977-78	1977-78
Hickey, Pat	NYR, Col., Tor., Que., St.L.	10	646	192	212	404	351	55	5	11	16	37		1975-76	1984-85
Hicks, Doug	Min., Chi., Edm., Wsh.	9	561	37	131	168	442	....	....	....	....	....		1974-75	1982-83
Hicks, Glenn	Det.	2	108	6	12	18	127	....	....	....	....	....		1979-80	1980-81
Hicks, Hal	Mtl.M., Det.	3	110	7	2	9	72	....	....	....	....	....		1928-29	1930-31
Hicks, Wayne	Chi., Bos., Mtl., Phi., Pit.	5	115	13	23	36	22	2	0	1	1	2	1	1959-60	1967-68
Hidi, Andre	Wsh.	2	7	2	1	3	9	2	0	0	0	0		1983-84	1984-85
Hiemer, Uli	N.J.	3	143	19	54	73	176	....	....	....	....	....		1984-85	1986-87
Higgins, Paul	Tor.	2	25	0	0	0	152	1	0	0	0	0		1981-82	1982-83
Higgins, Tim	Chi., N.J., Det.	11	706	154	198	352	719	65	5	8	13	77		1978-79	1988-89
Hildebrand, Ike	NYR, Chi.	2	41	7	11	18	16	....	....	....	....	....		1953-54	1954-55
Hill, Al	Phi.	8	221	40	55	95	227	51	8	11	19	43		1976-77	1987-88
Hill, Brian	Hfd.	1	19	1	1	2	4	....	....	....	....	....		1979-80	1979-80
Hill, Mel	Bos., Bro., Tor.	9	323	89	109	198	138	43	12	7	19	18	3	1937-38	1945-46
Hiller, Dutch	NYR, Det., Bos., Mtl.	9	385	91	113	204	163	48	9	8	17	21	2	1937-38	1945-46
Hillman, Floyd	Bos.	1	6	0	0	0	10	....	....	....	....	....		1956-57	1956-57
Hillman, Larry	Det., Bos., Tor., Min., Mtl., Phi., L.A., Buf.	19	790	36	196	232	579	74	2	9	11	30	4	1954-55	1972-73
Hillman, Wayne	Chi., NYR, Min., Phi.	13	691	18	86	104	534	28	0	3	3	19	1	1960-61	1972-73
Hilworth, John	Det.	3	57	1	1	2	89	....	....	....	....	....		1977-78	1979-80
Himes, Normie	NYA	9	402	106	113	219	127	2	0	0	0	0		1926-27	1934-35
Hindmarch, Dave	Cgy.	4	99	21	17	38	25	10	0	0	0	6		1980-81	1983-84
Hinse, Andre	Tor.	1	4	0	0	0	0	....	....	....	....	....		1967-68	1967-68
Hinton, Dan	Chi.	1	14	0	0	0	16	....	....	....	....	....		1976-77	1976-77
Hirsch, Tom	Min.	3	31	1	7	8	30	12	0	0	0	6		1983-84	1987-88
Hirschfeld, Bert	Mtl.	2	33	1	4	5	2	5	1	0	1	0		1949-50	1950-51
Hislop, Jamie	Que., Cgy.	5	345	75	103	178	86	28	3	2	5	11		1979-80	1983-84
Hitchman, Lionel	Ott., Bos.	12	413	28	33	61	523	40	4	1	5	77	2	1922-23	1933-34
Hlinka, Ivan	Van.	2	137	42	81	123	28	16	3	10	13	8		1981-82	1982-83
Hodge, Ken	Chi., Bos., NYR	13	881	328	472	800	779	97	34	47	81	120		1965-66	1977-78
Hodgson, Rick	Hfd.	1	6	0	0	0	6	1	0	0	0	0		1979-80	1979-80
Hodgson, Ted	Bos.	1	4	0	0	0	0	....	....	....	....	....		1966-67	1966-67
Hoekstra, Cecil	Mtl.	1	4	0	0	0	0	....	....	....	....	....		1959-60	1959-60
Hoekstra, Ed	Phi.	1	70	15	21	36	6	7	0	1	1	0		1967-68	1967-68
Hoene, Phi.	L.A.	3	37	2	4	6	22	....	....	....	....	....		1972-73	1974-75
Hoffinger, Vic	Chi.	2	28	0	1	1	30	....	....	....	....	....		1927-28	1928-29
Hoffman, Mike	Hfd.	3	9	1	3	4	2	....	....	....	....	....		1982-83	1985-86
Hoffmeyer, Bob	Chi., Phi., N.J.	6	198	14	52	66	325	3	0	1	1	25		1977-78	1984-85
Hofford, Jim	Buf., L.A.	3	18	0	0	0	47	....	....	....	....	....		1985-86	1988-89
Hogaboam, Bill	Atl., Det., Min.	8	332	80	109	189	100	2	0	0	0	0		1972-73	1979-80
Hoganson, Dale	L.A., Mtl., Que.	7	343	13	77	90	186	11	0	3	3	12		1969-70	1981-82
Holbrook, Terry	Min.	2	43	3	6	9	4	6	0	0	0	0		1972-73	1973-74
Holland, Jerry	NYR	2	37	8	4	12	6	....	....	....	....	....		1974-75	1975-76
Hollett, Frank	Tor., Ott., Bos., Det.	13	565	132	181	313	358	79	8	26	34	38	2	1933-34	1945-46
Hollingworth, Gord	Chi., Det.	4	163	4	14	18	201	3	0	0	0	2		1954-55	1957-58
Holmes, Bill	Mtl., NYA.	2	51	6	4	10	35	....	....	....	....	....		1925-26	1929-30
Holmes, Chuck	Det.	2	23	1	3	4	10	....	....	....	....	....		1958-59	1961-62
Holmes, Lou	Chi.	2	59	1	4	5	6	2	0	0	0	2		1931-32	1932-33
Holmes, Warren	L.A.	3	45	8	18	26	7	....	....	....	....	....		1981-82	1983-84
Holmgren, Paul	Phi., Min.	10	527	144	179	323	1684	82	19	32	51	195		1975-76	1984-85
Holota, John	Det.	2	15	2	0	2	0	....	....	....	....	....		1942-43	1945-46
Holloway, Bruce	Van.	1	2	0	0	0	0	....	....	....	....	....		1984-85	1984-85
Holst, Greg	NYR	3	11	0	0	0	0	....	....	....	....	....		1975-76	1977-78
Holt, Gary	Cal., Clev., St.L.	5	101	13	11	24	183	....	....	....	....	....		1973-74	1977-78
Holt, Randy	Chi., Clev., Van., L.A., Cgy., Wsh., Phi.	10	395	4	37	41	1438	21	2	3	5	83		1974-75	1983-84
Holway, Albert	Tor., Mtl.M., Pit.	5	117	7	2	9	48	8	0	0	0	2	1	1923-24	1928-29
Homenuke, Ron	Van.	1	1	0	0	0	0	....	....	....	....	....		1972-73	1972-73
Hopkins, Dean	L.A., Edm.	5	218	23	49	72	302	18	1	5	6	29		1979-80	1985-86
Hopkins, Larry	Tor., Wpg.	4	60	13	16	29	26	6	0	0	0	2		1977-78	1982-83
Horbul, Doug	K.C.	1	4	1	0	1	2	....	....	....	....	....		1974-75	1974-75
Hordy, Mike	NYI	2	11	0	0	0	7	....	....	....	....	....		1978-79	1979-80
Horeck, Pete	Chi., Det., Bos.	8	426	106	118	224	340	34	6	8	14	43		1944-45	1951-52
Horne, George	Mtl.M, Tor.	3	54	9	3	12	34	4	0	0	0	4	1	1925-26	1928-29
Horner, Red	Tor.	12	490	42	110	152	1264	71	7	10	17	166	1	1928-29	1939-40
Hornung, Larry	St.L.	2	48	2	9	11	10	11	0	2	2	2		1970-71	1971-72
Horton, Tim	Tor., NYR, Buf., Pit.	24	1446	115	403	518	1611	126	11	39	50	183	4	1949-50	1973-74
Horvath, Bronco	NYR, Mtl., Bos., Chi., Tor., Min.	9	434	141	185	326	319	36	12	9	21	18		1955-56	1967-68
Hospodar, Ed	NYR, Hfd., Phi., Min., Buf.	9	450	17	51	68	1314	44	4	1	5	206		1979-80	1987-88
Hotham Greg	Tor., Pit.	6	230	15	74	89	139	5	0	3	3	6		1979-80	1984-85
Houck, Paul	Min.	3	16	1	2	3	2	....	....	....	....	....		1985-86	1987-88
Houde, Claude	K.C.	2	59	3	6	9	40	....	....	....	....	....		1974-75	1975-76
Houle, Rejean	Mtl.	11	635	161	247	408	395	90	14	34	48	66	5	1969-70	1982-83
Houston, Ken	Atl., Cgy., Wsh., L.A.	9	570	161	167	328	624	35	10	9	19	66		1975-76	1983-84
Howard, Frank	Tor.	1	2	0	0	0	0	....	....	....	....	....		1936-37	1936-37
Howatt, Garry	NYI, Hfd., N.J.	12	720	112	156	268	1836	87	12	14	26	289	2	1972-73	1983-84
Howe, Gordie	Det., Hfd.	26	1767	801	1049	1850	1685	157	68	92	160	220	4	1946-47	1979-80
Howe, Marty	Hfd., Bos.	6	197	2	29	31	99	15	1	2	3	9		1979-80	1984-85
Howe, Syd	Ott., Phi., Tor., St.L., Det.	17	691	237	291	528	212	70	17	27	44	10	3	1929-30	1945-46
Howe, Vic	NYR	3	33	3	4	7	10	....	....	....	....	....		1950-51	1954-55
Howell, Harry	NYR, Oak., L.A.	21	1411	94	324	418	1298	38	3	3	6	32		1952-53	1972-73
Howell, Ron	NYR	2	4	0	0	0	4	....	....	....	....	....		1954-55	1955-56
Howse, Don	L.A.	1	33	2	5	7	6	2	0	0	0	0		1979-80	1979-80
Howson, Scott	NYI	2	18	5	3	8	4	....	....	....	....	....		1984-85	1985-86
Hoyda, Dave	Phi., Wpg.	4	132	6	17	23	299	12	0	0	0	17		1977-78	1980-81
Hrechkosy, Dave	Cal., St.L.	4	140	42	24	66	41	3	1	0	1	2		1973-74	1976-77
Hrycuik, Jim	Wsh.	1	21	5	5	10	12	....	....	....	....	....		1974-75	1974-75
Hrymnak, Steve	Chi., Det.	2	18	2	1	3	4	2	0	0	0	0		1951-52	1952-53
Hrynewich, Tim	Pit.	2	55	6	8	14	82	....	....	....	....	....		1982-83	1983-84
Huard, Rolly	Tor.	1	1	1	0	1	0	....	....	....	....	....		1930-31	1930-31
Huber, Willie	Det., NYR, Van., Phi.	10	655	104	217	321	950	33	5	5	10	35		1978-79	1987-88
Hubick, Greg	Tor., Van.	2	77	6	9	15	10	....	....	....	....	....		1975-76	1979-80
Huck, Fran	Mtl., St.L.	3	94	24	30	54	38	11	3	4	7	2		1969-70	1972-73
Hucul, Fred	Chi., St.L.	5	164	11	30	41	113	6	1	0	1	10		1950-51	1967-68
Hudson, Dave	NYI, K.C., Col.	6	409	59	124	183	89	2	1	1	2	0		1972-73	1977-78
Hudson, Lex	Pit.	1	2	0	0	0	0	2	0	0	0	0		1978-79	1978-79
Hudson, Ron	Det.	2	34	5	2	7	2	....	....	....	....	....		1937-38	1939-40
Huggins, Al	Mtl.M	1	20	1	1	2	2	....	....	....	....	....		1930-31	1930-31
Hughes, Al	NYA	2	60	6	8	14	22	....	....	....	....	....		1930-31	1931-32
Hughes, Brent	L.A., Phi., St.L., Det., K.C.	8	435	15	117	132	440	22	1	3	4	53		1967-68	1974-75
Hughes, Frank	Cal.	1	5	0	0	0	0	....	....	....	....	....		1971-72	1971-72
Hughes, Howie	L.A.	3	168	25	32	57	30	14	2	0	2	2		1967-68	1969-70
Hughes, Jack	Col.	2	46	2	5	7	104	....	....	....	....	....		1980-81	1981-82
Hughes, John	Van., Edm., NYR	3	70	2	14	16	211	7	0	1	1	16		1979-80	1980-81

Name	NHL Teams	NHL Seasons	Regular Schedule GP	G	A	TP	PIM	Playoffs GP	G	A	TP	PIM	NHL Cup Wins	First NHL Season	Last NHL Season
Hughes, Pat	Mtl., Pit., Edm., Buf., St.L., Hfd.	10	573	130	128	258	646	71	8	25	33	77	3	1977-78	1986-87
Hughes, Rusty	Det.	1	40	0	1	1	48	....	....	....	....	....		1929-30	1929-30
Hull, Bobby	Chi., Wpg., Hfd.	16	1063	610	560	1170	640	119	62	67	129	102	1	1957-58	1979-80
Hull, Dennis	Chi., Det.	14	959	303	351	654	261	104	33	34	67	30		1964-65	1977-78
Hunt, Fred	NYA, NYR	2	59	15	14	29	6	....	....	....	....	....		1940-41	1944-45
Hunter, Dave	Edm., Pit., Wpg.	10	746	133	190	323	918	105	16	24	40	211	3	1979-80	1988-89
Huras, Larry	NYR	1	1	0	0	0	0	....	....	....	....	....		1976-77	1976-77
Hurlburt, Bob	Van.	1	1	0	0	0	2	....	....	....	....	....		1974-75	1974-75
Hurley, Paul	Bos.	1	1	0	1	1	0	....	....	....	....	....		1968-69	1968-69
Hurst, Ron	Tor.	2	64	9	7	16	7	3	0	2	2	4		1955-56	1956-57
Huston, Ron	Cal.	2	79	15	31	46	8	....	....	....	....	....		1973-74	1974-75
Hutchinson, Ronald	NYR	1	9	0	0	0	0	....	....	....	....	....		1960-61	1960-61
Hutchison, Dave	L.A., Tor., Chi., N.J.	10	584	19	97	116	1550	48	2	12	14	149		1974-75	1983-84
Hutton, William	Bos., Ott., Phi.	2	64	3	2	5	8	2	0	0	0	0		1929-30	1930-31
Hyland, Harry	Mtl.W, Ott.	1	16	14	0	14	0	....	....	....	....	....		1917-18	1917-18
Hynes, Dave	Bos.	2	22	4	0	4	2	....	....	....	....	....		1973-74	1974-75

I

Imlach, Brent	Tor.	2	3	0	0	0	2	....	....	....	....	....		1965-66	1966-67
Ingarfield, Earl	NYR, Pit., Oak., Cal.	13	746	179	226	405	239	21	9	8	17	10		1958-59	1970-71
Ingarfield, Earl Jr.	Atl., Cgy., Det.	2	39	4	4	8	22	2	0	1	1	0		1979-80	1980-81
Inglis, Bill	L.A., Buf.	3	36	1	3	4	4	11	1	2	3	4		1967-68	1970-71
Ingoldsby, Johnny	Tor.	2	29	5	1	6	15	....	....	....	....	....		1942-43	1943-44
Ingram, Frank	Bos., Chi.	4	102	24	16	40	69	11	0	1	1	2		1924-25	1931-32
Ingram, Ron	Chi., Det., NYR	4	114	5	15	20	81	2	0	0	0	0		1956-57	1964-65
Irvin, Dick	Chi.	3	94	29	23	52	76	2	2	0	2	4		1926-27	1928-29
Irvine, Ted	Bos., L.A., NYR, St.L.	11	724	154	177	331	657	83	16	24	40	115		1963-64	1976-77
Irwin, Ivan	Mtl., NYR	5	155	2	27	29	214	5	0	0	0	8		1952-53	1957-58
Isaksson, Ulf	L.A.	1	50	7	15	22	10	....	....	....	....	....		1982-83	1982-83

J

Jackson, Art	Bos., Tor.	11	466	123	178	301	144	51	8	12	20	27	2	1934-35	1944-45
Jackson, Harvey	Tor., Bos., NYA	15	636	241	234	475	437	71	18	12	30	53	1	1929-30	1943-44
Jackson, Don	Min., Edm., NYR	10	311	16	52	68	640	53	4	5	9	147	2	1977-78	1986-87
Jackson, Hal	Chi., Det.	8	222	17	34	51	208	31	1	2	3	33	2	1936-37	1946-47
Jackson, Jim	Cgy., Buf.	4	112	17	30	47	20	14	3	2	5	6		1982-83	1987-88
Jackson, John	Chi.	1	48	2	5	7	38	....	....	....	....	....		1946-47	1946-47
Jackson, Lloyd	NYA	1	14	1	1	2	0	....	....	....	....	....		1936-37	1936-37
Jackson, Stan	Tor., Bos., Ott.	5	84	9	4	13	74	....	....	....	....	....	1	1921-22	1926-27
Jackson, Walt	NYA	3	82	16	11	27	18	....	....	....	....	....		1932-33	1934-35
Jacobs, Paul	Tor.	1	1	0	0	0	0	....	....	....	....	....		1918-19	1918-19
Jacobs, Tim	Cal.	1	46	0	10	10	35	....	....	....	....	....		1975-76	1975-76
Jalo, Risto	Edm.	1	3	0	3	3	0	....	....	....	....	....		1985-86	1985-86
Jalonen, Kari	Cgy., Edm.	2	37	9	6	15	4	5	1	0	1	0		1982-83	1983-84
James, Gerry	Tor.	5	149	14	26	40	257	15	1	0	1	8		1954-55	1959-60
James, Val	Buf., Tor.	2	11	0	0	0	30	....	....	....	....	....		1981-82	1986-87
Jamieson, Jim	NYR	1	1	0	1	1	0	....	....	....	....	....		1943-44	1943-44
Jankowski, Lou	Det., Chi.	4	127	19	18	37	15	1	0	0	0	0		1950-51	1954-55
Jarrett, Doug	Chi., NYR	13	775	38	182	220	631	99	7	16	23	82		1964-65	1976-77
Jarrett, Gary	Tor., Det., Oak., Cal.	7	341	72	92	164	131	11	3	1	4	9		1960-61	1971-72
Jarry, Pierre	NYR, Tor., Det., Min.	7	344	88	117	205	142	5	0	1	1	0		1971-72	1977-78
Jarvis, Doug	Mtl., Wsh., Hfd.	13	964	139	264	403	263	105	14	27	41	42	4	1975-76	1987-88
Jarvis, Jim	Pit., Phi., Tor.	3	108	17	15	32	62	....	....	....	....	....		1929-30	1936-37
Jarvis, Wes	Wsh., Min., L.A., Tor.	8	237	31	55	86	98	2	0	0	0	2		1979-80	1987-88
Javanainen, Arto	Pit.	1	14	4	1	5	2	....	....	....	....	....		1984-85	1984-85
Jeffrey, Larry	Det., Tor., NYR	8	368	39	62	101	293	38	4	10	14	42	1	1961-62	1968-69
Jenkins, Dean	L.A.	1	5	0	0	0	2	....	....	....	....	....		1983-84	1983-84
Jenkins, Roger	Tor., Chi., Mtl., Bos., Mtl.M., NYA	8	328	15	39	54	279	25	1	7	8	12	2	1930-31	1938-39
Jennings, Bill	Det., Bos.	5	108	32	33	65	45	20	4	4	8	6		1940-41	1944-45
Jensen, David H.	Min.	3	18	0	2	2	11	....	....	....	....	....		1983-84	1985-86
Jensen, Steve	Min., L.A.	7	438	113	107	220	318	12	0	3	3	9		1975-76	1981-82
Jeremiah, Ed	NYA, Bos.	1	15	0	1	1	0	....	....	....	....	....		1931-32	1931-32
Jerwa, Frank	Bos.	1	28	4	5	9	12	....	....	....	....	....		1931-32	1931-32
Jerwa, Joe	NYR, Bos., St.L., NYA	9	293	36	69	105	338	17	2	3	5	20		1930-31	1938-39
Jirik, Jaroslav	St.L.	1	3	0	0	0	0	....	....	....	....	....		1969-70	1969-70
Joanette, Rosario	Mtl.	1	2	0	1	1	4	....	....	....	....	....		1944-45	1944-45
Jodzio, Rick	Col., Clev.	1	70	2	8	10	71	....	....	....	....	....		1977-78	1977-78
Johannesen, Glenn	NYI	1	2	0	0	0	0	....	....	....	....	....		1985-86	1985-86
Johansen, Trevor	Tor., Col., L.A.	5	286	11	46	57	282	13	0	3	3	21		1977-78	1981-82
Johansson, Bjorn	Clev.	2	15	1	1	2	10	....	....	....	....	....		1976-77	1977-78
Johannson, John	N.J.	1	5	0	0	0	0	....	....	....	....	....		1983-84	1983-84
Johns, Don	NYR, Mtl., Min.	6	153	2	21	23	76	....	....	....	....	....		1960-61	1967-68
Johnson, Al	Mtl., Det.	4	105	21	28	49	30	11	2	2	4	6		1956-57	1962-63
Johnson, Brian	Det.	1	3	0	0	0	5	....	....	....	....	....		1983-84	1983-84
Johnson, Ivan	NYR, NYA	12	435	38	48	86	808	60	5	2	7	161	2	1926-27	1937-38
Johnson, Danny	Tor., Van., Det.	3	121	18	19	37	24	....	....	....	....	....		1969-70	1971-72
Johnson, Earl	Det.	1	1	0	0	0	0	....	....	....	....	....		1953-54	1953-54
Johnson, Jim	NYR, Phi., L.A.	8	302	75	111	186	73	7	0	2	2	2		1964-65	1971-72
Johnson, Norm	Bos., Chi.	3	61	5	20	25	41	14	4	0	4	6		1957-58	1959-60
Johnson, Terry	Que., St.L., Cgy., Tor.	9	285	3	24	27	580	38	0	4	4	118		1979-80	1987-88
Johnson, Tom	Mtl., Bos.	17	978	51	213	264	960	111	8	15	23	109	6	1947-48	1964-65
Johnson, Virgil	Chi.	3	75	2	9	11	27	19	0	3	3	4	1	1937-38	1944-45
Johnson, William	Tor.	1	1	0	0	0	0	....	....	....	....	....		1949-50	1949-50
Johnston, Bernie	Hfd.	2	57	12	24	36	44	3	0	1	1	0		1979-80	1980-81
Johnston, George	Chi.	4	58	20	12	32	2	....	....	....	....	....		1941-42	1946-47
Johnston, Jay	Wsh.	2	8	0	0	0	13	....	....	....	....	....		1980-81	1981-82
Johnston, Joey	Min., Cal., Chi.	6	332	85	106	191	320	....	....	....	....	....		1968-69	1975-76
Johnston, Larry	L.A., Det., K.C., Col.	7	320	9	64	73	580	....	....	....	....	....		1967-68	1976-77
Johnston, Marshall	Min., Cal.	7	251	14	52	66	58	6	0	0	0	2		1967-68	1973-74
Johnston, Randy	NYI	1	4	0	0	0	4	....	....	....	....	....		1979-80	1979-80
Johnstone, Eddie	NYR, Det.	10	426	122	136	258	375	55	13	10	23	83		1975-76	1986-87
Johnstone, Ross	Tor.	2	42	5	4	9	14	3	0	0	0	0	1	1943-44	1944-45
Joliat, Aurel	Mtl.	16	654	270	190	460	757	54	14	19	33	89	3	1922-23	1937-38
Joliat, Bobby	Mtl.	1	1	0	0	0	0	....	....	....	....	....		1924-25	1924-25
Joly, Greg	Wsh., Det.	9	365	21	76	97	250	5	0	0	0	8		1974-75	1982-83
Joly, Yvan	Mtl.	3	2	0	0	0	0	10	0	0	0	0		1979-80	1982-83
Jonathon, Stan	Bos., Pit.	8	411	91	110	201	751	63	8	4	12	137		1975-76	1982-83
Jones, Bob	NYR	1	2	0	0	0	0	....	....	....	....	....		1968-69	1968-69
Jones, Buck	Det., Tor.	4	50	2	2	4	36	12	0	1	1	18		1938-39	1942-43
Jones, Jim	Cal.	1	2	0	0	0	0	....	....	....	....	....		1971-72	1971-72
Jones, Jimmy	Tor.	3	148	13	18	31	68	19	1	5	6	11		1977-78	1979-80
Jones, Ron	Bos., Pit., Wsh.	5	54	1	4	5	31	....	....	....	....	....		1971-72	1975-76
Joyal, Eddie	Det., Tor., L.A., Phi.	9	466	128	134	262	103	50	11	8	19	18		1962-63	1971-72
Juckes, Bing	NYR	2	16	2	1	3	6	....	....	....	....	....		1947-48	1949-50
Jutila, Timo	Buf.	1	10	1	5	6	13	....	....	....	....	....		1984-85	1984-85
Juzda, Bill	NYR, Tor.	9	393	14	54	68	398	42	0	3	3	46	2	1940-41	1951-52

K

Kabel, Bob	NYR	2	48	5	13	18	34	....	....	....	....	....		1959-60	1960-61
Kachur, Ed	Chi.	2	96	10	14	24	35	....	....	....	....	....		1956-57	1957-58
Kaese, Trent	Buf.	1	1	0	0	0	0	....	....	....	....	....		1988-89	1988-89
Kaiser, Vern	Mtl.	1	50	7	5	12	33	2	0	0	0	0		1950-51	1950-51
Kalbfleish, Walter	Ott., St.L., NYA, Bos.	4	36	0	4	4	32	5	0	0	0	2		1933-34	1936-37
Kaleta, Alex	Chi., NYR	7	387	92	121	213	190	17	1	6	7	2		1941-42	1950-51
Kallur, Anders	NYI	6	383	101	110	211	149	78	12	23	35	32	4	1979-80	1984-85
Kaminsky, Max	Ott., St.L., Bos., Mtl.M.	4	130	22	34	56	38	4	0	0	0	0		1933-34	1936-37
Kampman, Bingo	Tor.	5	189	14	30	44	287	47	1	4	5	38	1	1937-38	1941-42

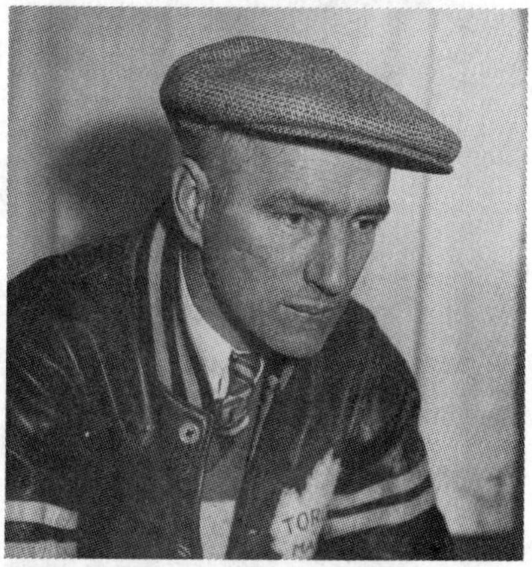
Dick Irvin

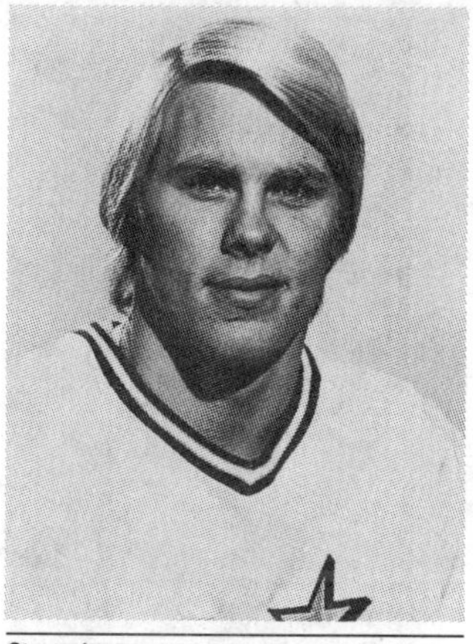
Steve Jensen

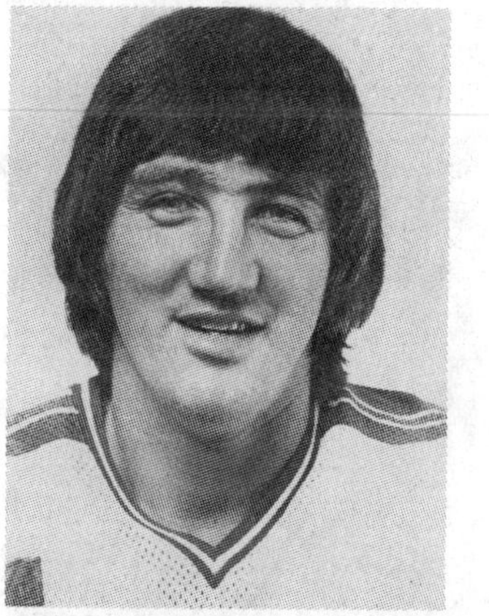
Eddie Johnstone

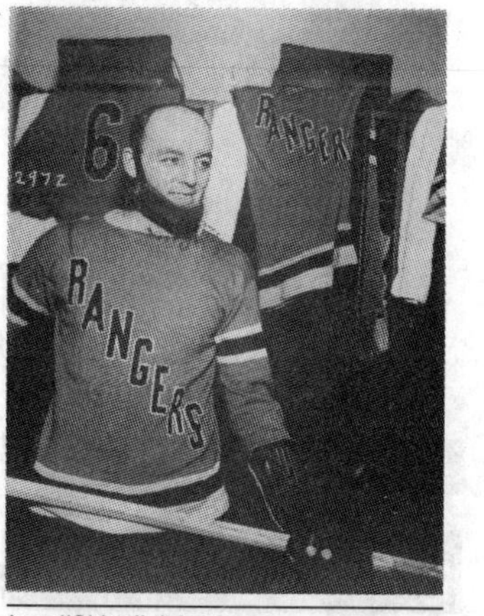

Ivan "Ching" Johnson

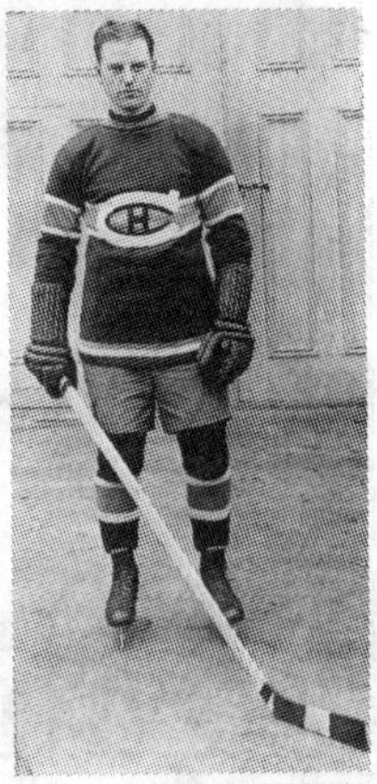

Aurel Joliet

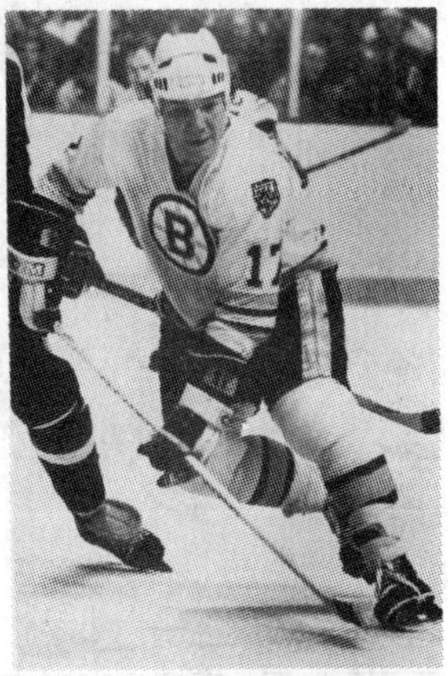

Stan Jonathan

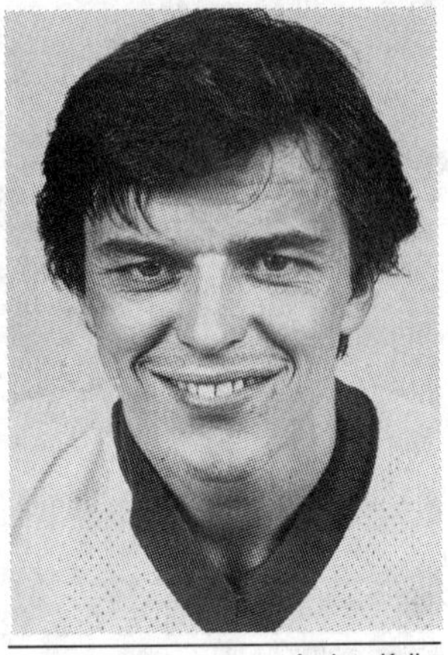

Anders Kallur

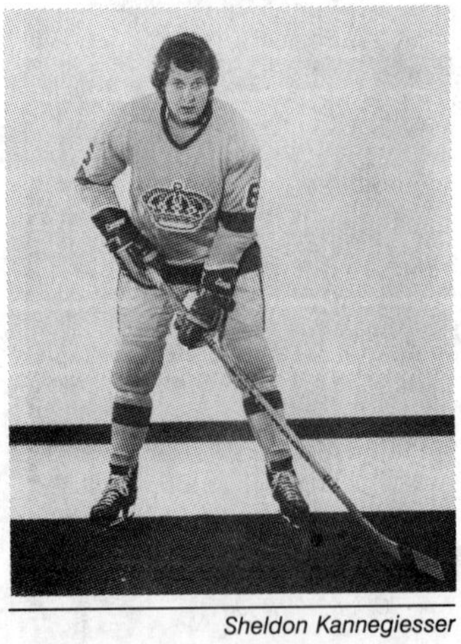

Sheldon Kannegiesser

			Regular Schedule					Playoffs					NHL	First	Last
Name	NHL Teams	NHL Seasons	GP	G	A	TP	PIM	GP	G	A	TP	PIM	Cup Wins	NHL Season	NHL Season
Kane, Frank	Det.	1	2	0	0	0	0	....	....	....	....	....		1943-44	1943-44
Kannegiesser, Gord	St.L.	2	23	0	1	1	15	....	....	....	....	....		1967-68	1971-72
Kannegiesser, Sheldon	Pit., NYR, L.A., Van.	8	366	14	67	81	292	18	0	2	2	10		1970-71	1977-78
Karlander, Al	Det.	4	212	36	56	92	70	4	0	1	1	0		1969-70	1972-73
Kaszycki, Mike	NYI, Wsh., Tor.	5	226	42	80	122	108	19	2	6	8	10		1977-78	1982-83
Kea, Ed	Atl., St.L.	10	583	30	145	175	508	32	2	4	6	39		1973-74	1982-83
Kearns, Dennis	Van.	10	677	31	290	321	386	11	1	2	3	8		1971-72	1980-81
Keating, Jack	NYA	2	35	5	5	10	17	....	....	....	....	....		1931-32	1932-33
Keating, John	Det.	2	11	2	1	3	4	....	....	....	....	....		1938-39	1939-40
Keating, Mike	NYR	1	1	0	0	0	0	....	....	....	....	....		1977-78	1977-78
Keats, Duke	Det., Chi.	3	80	3	19	49	113	....	....	....	....	....		1926-27	1928-29
Keeling, Butch	Tor., NYR	12	528	157	63	220	331	47	11	11	22	32	1	1926-27	1937-38
Keenan, Larry	Tor., St.L., Buf., Phi.	6	233	38	64	102	28	46	15	16	31	12		1961-62	1971-72
Kehoe, Rick	Tor., Pit.	14	906	371	396	767	120	39	4	17	21	4		1971-72	1984-85
Keller, Ralph	NYR	1	3	1	0	1	6	....	....	....	....	....		1962-63	1962-63
Kellgren, Christer	Col.	1	5	0	0	0	0	....	....	....	....	....		1981-82	1981-82
Kelly, Bob	St.L., Pit., Chi.	6	425	87	109	196	687	23	6	3	9	40		1973-74	1978-79
Kelly, Bob	Phi., Wsh.	12	837	154	208	362	1454	101	9	14	23	172	2	1970-71	1981-82
Kelly, Dave	Det.	1	16	2	0	2	4	....	....	....	....	....		1976-77	1976-77
Kelly, John Paul	L.A.	7	400	54	70	124	366	18	1	1	2	41		1979-80	1985-86
Kelly, Reg	Tor., Chi., Bro.	8	289	74	53	127	105	39	7	6	13	10		1934-35	1941-42
Kelly, Pete	St.L., Det., NYA, Bro.	7	180	21	38	59	68	19	3	1	4	8	2	1934-35	1941-42
Kelly, Red	Det., Tor.	20	1316	281	542	823	327	164	33	59	92	51	8	1947-48	1966-67
Kemp, Kevin	Hfd.	1	3	0	0	0	4	....	....	....	....	....		1980-81	1980-81
Kemp, Stan	Tor.	1	1	0	0	0	2	....	....	....	....	....		1948-49	1948-49
Kendall, William	Chi., Tor.	5	132	16	10	26	28	5	0	0	0	0	1	1933-34	1937-38
Kennedy, Forbes	Chi., Det., Bos., Phi., Tor.	11	603	70	108	178	988	12	2	4	6	64		1956-57	1968-69
Kennedy, Ted	Tor.	14	696	231	329	560	432	78	29	31	60	32	5	1942-43	1956-57
Kenny, Eddie	NYR, Chi.	2	11	0	0	0	18	....	....	....	....	....		1930-31	1934-35
Keon, Dave	Tor., Hfd.	18	1296	396	590	986	117	92	32	36	68	6	4	1960-61	1981-82
Kerr, Reg	Cle., Chi., Edm.	6	263	66	94	160	169	7	1	0	1	7		1977-78	1983-84
Kessell, Rick	Pit., Cal.	5	135	4	24	28	6	....	....	....	....	....		1969-70	1973-74
Ketola, Veli-Pekka	Col.	1	44	9	5	14	4	....	....	....	....	....		1981-82	1981-82
Ketter, Kerry	Atl.	1	41	0	2	2	58	....	....	....	....	....		1972-73	1972-73
Kiessling, Udo	Min.	1	1	0	0	0	2	....	....	....	....	....		1981-82	1981-82
Kilrea, Brian	Det., L.A.	2	26	3	5	8	12	....	....	....	....	....		1957-58	1967-68
Kilrea, Hec	Ott., Det., Tor.	15	633	167	129	296	438	48	8	7	15	18	3	1925-26	1939-40
Kilrea, Ken	Det.	5	88	16	23	39	8	10	2	2	4	4		1938-39	1943-44
Kilrea, Wally	Ott., Phi., NYA, Mtl.M., Det.	9	315	35	58	93	87	25	2	4	6	6		1929-30	1937-38
Kindrachuk, Orest	Phi., Pit., Wsh.	10	508	118	261	379	648	76	20	20	40	53	2	1972-73	1981-82
King, Frank	Mtl.	1	10	1	0	1	2	....	....	....	....	....		1950-51	1950-51
King, Wayne	Cal.	3	73	5	18	23	34	....	....	....	....	....		1973-74	1975-76
Kinsella, Brian	Wsh.	2	10	0	1	1	0	....	....	....	....	....		1975-76	1976-77
Kinsella, Ray	Ott.	1	14	0	0	0	0	....	....	....	....	....		1930-31	1930-31
Kirk, Bobby	NYR	1	39	4	8	12	14	....	....	....	....	....		1937-38	1937-38
Kirkpatrick, Bob	NYR	1	49	12	12	24	6	....	....	....	....	....		1942-43	1942-43
Kirton, Mark	Tor., Det., Van.	6	266	57	56	113	121	4	1	2	3	7		1979-80	1984-85
Kitchen, Bill	Mtl., Tor.	4	41	1	4	5	40	3	0	1	1	0		1981-82	1984-85
Kitchen, Hobie	Mtl.M., Det.	2	47	5	4	9	58	....	....	....	....	....		1925-26	1926-27
Kitchen, Mike	Col., N.J.	8	474	12	62	74	370	2	0	0	0	2		1976-77	1983-84
Klassen, Ralph	Cal., Clev., Col., St.L.	9	497	52	93	145	120	26	4	2	6	12		1975-76	1983-84
Klein, Jim	Bos., NYA	8	169	30	24	54	68	5	0	0	0	2	1	1928-29	1937-38
Kleinendorst, Scot	NYR, Hfd., Wsh.	8	281	12	46	58	452	26	2	7	9	40		1982-83	1989-90
Klingbeil, Ike	Chi.	1	5	1	2	3	2	....	....	....	....	....		1936-37	1936-37
Klukay, Joe	Tor., Bos.	11	566	109	127	236	189	71	13	10	23	23	4	1942-43	1955-56
Knibbs, Bill	Bos.	1	53	7	10	17	4	....	....	....	....	....		1964-65	1964-65
Knott, Nick	Bro.	1	14	3	1	4	9	....	....	....	....	....		1941-42	1941-42
Knox, Paul	Tor.	1	1	0	0	0	0	....	....	....	....	....		1954-55	1954-55
Komadoski, Neil	L.A., St.L.	8	502	16	76	92	632	23	0	2	2	47		1972-73	1979-80
Konik, George	Pit.	1	52	7	8	15	26	....	....	....	....	....		1967-68	1967-68
Kopak, Russ	Bos.	1	24	7	9	16	0	....	....	....	....	....		1943-44	1943-44
Korab, Jerry	Chi., Van., Buf., L.A.	15	975	114	341	455	1629	93	8	18	26	201		1970-71	1984-85
Korn, Jim	Det., Tor., Buf., N.J., Cgy.	10	597	66	122	188	1801	16	1	2	3	109		1979-80	1989-80
Korney, Mike	Det., NYR	4	77	9	10	19	59	....	....	....	....	....		1973-74	1978-79
Koroll, Cliff	Chi.	11	814	208	254	462	376	85	19	29	48	67		1969-70	1979-80
Kortko, Roger	NYI	2	79	7	17	24	28	10	0	3	3	17		1984-85	1985-86
Kostynski, Doug	Bos.	2	15	3	1	4	4	....	....	....	....	....		1983-84	1984-85
Kotanen, Dick	Det., NYR	2	2	0	1	1	0	....	....	....	....	....		1948-49	1950-51
Kotsopoulos, Chris	NYR, Hfd., Tor., Det.	10	479	44	109	153	827	31	1	3	4	91		1980-81	1989-90
Kowal, Joe	Buf.	2	22	0	5	5	13	2	0	0	0	0		1976-77	1977-78
Kozak, Don	L.A., Van.	7	437	96	86	182	480	29	7	2	9	69		1972-73	1978-79
Kozak, Les	Tor.	1	12	1	0	1	2	....	....	....	....	....		1961-62	1961-62
Kraftcheck, Stephen	Bos., NYR, Tor.	4	157	11	18	29	83	6	0	0	0	7		1950-51	1958-59
Krake, Skip	Bos., L.A., Buf.	7	249	23	40	63	182	10	1	0	1	17		1963-64	1970-71
Krol, Joe	NYR, Bro.	3	26	10	4	14	8	....	....	....	....	....		1936-37	1941-42
Krook, Kevin	Col.	1	3	0	0	0	2	....	....	....	....	....		1978-79	1978-79
Krulicki, Jim	NYR, Det.	1	41	0	3	3	6	....	....	....	....	....		1970-71	1970-71
Krutov, Vladimir	Van.	1	61	11	23	34	20	....	....	....	....	....		1989-90	1989-90
Kryskow, Dave	Chi., Wsh., Det., Atl.	4	231	33	56	89	174	12	2	0	2	4		1972-73	1975-76
Kryznowski, Edward	Bos., Chi.	5	237	15	22	37	65	18	0	1	1	4		1948-49	1952-53
Kuhn, Gord	NYA	1	12	1	1	2	4	....	....	....	....	....		1932-33	1932-33
Kukulowicz, Adolph	NYR	2	4	1	0	1	0	....	....	....	....	....		1952-53	1953-54
Kullman, Arnie	Bos.	2	13	0	1	1	11	....	....	....	....	....		1947-48	1949-50
Kullman, Eddie	NYR	6	343	56	70	126	298	6	1	0	1	2		1947-48	1953-54
Kuntz, Alan	NYR	2	45	10	12	22	12	6	1	0	1	2		1941-42	1945-46
Kuntz, Murray	St.L.	1	7	1	2	3	0	....	....	....	....	....		1974-75	1974-75
Kurtenbach, Orland	NYR, Bos., Tor., Van.	13	639	119	213	332	628	19	2	4	6	70		1960-61	1973-74
Kuryluk, Mervin	Chi.	1	....	....	....	....	....	2	0	0	0	0		1961-62	1961-62
Kuzyk, Ken	Clev.	2	41	5	9	14	8	....	....	....	....	....		1976-77	1977-78
Kwong, Larry	NYR	1	1	0	0	0	0	....	....	....	....	....		1947-48	1947-48
Kyle, Bill	NYR	2	3	0	3	3	0	....	....	....	....	....		1949-50	1950-51
Kyle, Gus	NYR, Bos.	3	203	6	20	26	362	14	1	2	3	34		1949-50	1951-52

L

Labadie, Mike	NYR	1	3	0	0	0	0	....	....	....	....	....		1952-53	1952-53
Labatte, Neil	St.L.	2	26	0	2	2	19	....	....	....	....	....		1978-79	1981-82
L'abbe, Moe	Chi.	1	5	0	1	1	0	....	....	....	....	....		1972-73	1972-73
Labine, Leo	Bos., Det.	11	643	128	193	321	730	60	11	12	23	82		1951-52	1961-62
Labossierre, Gord	NYR, L.A., Min.	6	215	44	62	106	75	10	2	3	5	28		1963-64	1971-72
Labovitch, Max	NYR	1	5	0	0	0	4	....	....	....	....	....		1943-44	1943-44
Labraaten, Dan	Det., Cgy.	4	268	71	73	144	47	5	1	0	1	4		1978-79	1981-82
Labre, Yvon	Pit., Wsh.	9	371	14	87	101	788	....	....	....	....	....		1970-71	1980-81
Labrie, Guy	Bos., NYR	2	42	4	9	13	16	....	....	....	....	....		1943-44	1944-45
Lach, Elmer	Mtl.	14	664	215	408	623	478	76	19	45	64	36	3	1940-41	1953-54
Lachance, Earl	Mtl.	1	1	0	0	0	0	....	....	....	....	....		1926-27	1926-27
Lachance, Michel	Col.	1	21	0	4	4	22	....	....	....	....	....		1978-79	1978-79
Lacombe, Francois	Oak., Buf., Que.	4	78	2	17	19	54	3	1	0	1	0		1968-69	1979-80
Lacroix, Andre	Phi., Chi., Hfd.	6	325	79	119	198	44	16	2	5	7	0		1967-68	1979-80
Lacroix, Pierre	Que., Hfd.	4	274	24	108	132	197	8	0	2	2	10		1979-80	1982-83
Lafleur, Rene	Mtl.	1	0	0	0	0	0	....	....	....	....	....		1924-25	1924-25
Laforce, Ernie	Mtl.	1	0	0	0	0	0	....	....	....	....	....		1942-43	1942-43
LaForest, Bob	L.A.	1	5	1	0	1	2	....	....	....	....	....		1983-84	1983-84
Laforge, Claude	Mtl., Det., Phi.	8	192	24	33	57	82	5	1	2	3	15		1957-58	1968-69
Laframboise, Pete	Cal., Wsh., Pit.	4	227	33	55	88	70	9	1	0	1	0		1971-72	1974-75
Lafrance, Adie	Mtl.	1	3	0	0	0	2	2	0	0	0	0		1933-34	1933-34
Lafrance, Leo	Mtl., Chi.	2	33	2	0	2	6	....	....	....	....	....		1926-27	1927-28
Lafreniere, Roger	Det., St.L.	2	13	0	0	0	4	....	....	....	....	....		1962-63	1972-73
Lagace, Jean-Guy	Pit., Buf., K.C.	6	187	9	39	48	251	....	....	....	....	....		1968-69	1975-76
Laird, Robbie	Min.	1	1	0	0	0	0	....	....	....	....	....		1979-80	1979-80
Lajeunesse, Serge	Det., Phi.	5	103	1	4	5	103	7	1	2	3	4		1970-71	1974-75
Lalande, Hec	Chi., Det.	4	151	21	39	60	120	....	....	....	....	....		1953-54	1957-58

Name	NHL Teams	NHL Seasons	Regular Schedule					Playoffs					NHL Cup Wins	First NHL Season	Last NHL Season
			GP	G	A	TP	PIM	GP	G	A	TP	PIM			
Lalonde, Bobby	Van., Atl., Bos., Cgy.	11	641	124	210	334	298	16	4	2	6	6		1971-72	1981-82
Lalonde, Edouard	Mtl., NYA	6	99	124	27	151	122	12	22	1	23	0	1	1917-18	1926-27
Lalonde, Ron	Pit., Wsh.	7	397	45	78	123	106	....	....	....	....	....		1972-73	1978-79
Lamb, Joe	Mtl.M., Ott., NYA, Bos., Mtl., St.L., Det.	11	444	108	101	209	601	18	1	1	2	51		1927-28	1937-38
Lambert, Yvon	Mtl., Buf.	10	683	206	273	479	340	90	27	22	49	67	4	1972-73	1981-82
Lamby, Dick	St.L.	3	22	0	5	5	22	....	....	....	....	....		1978-79	1980-81
Lamirande, Jean-Paul	NYR, Mtl.	4	49	5	5	10	26	8	0	0	0	4		1946-47	1954-55
Lamoureux, Leo	Mtl.	6	235	19	79	98	175	28	1	6	7	16	2	1941-42	1946-47
Lamoureux, Mitch	Pit., Phi.	3	73	11	9	20	59	....	....	....	....	....		1983-84	1987-88
Lampman, Mike	St.L., Van., Wsh.	4	96	17	20	37	34	....	....	....	....	....		1972-73	1976-77
Lancien, Jack	NYR	4	63	1	5	6	35	6	0	1	1	2		1946-47	1950-51
Landon, Larry	Mtl., Tor.	2	9	0	0	0	2	....	....	....	....	....		1983-84	1984-85
Lane, Gord	Wsh., NYI	10	539	19	94	113	1228	75	3	14	17	214	4	1975-76	1984-85
Lane, Myles	NYR, Bos.	3	60	4	1	5	41	10	0	0	0	0	1	1928-29	1933-34
Langdon, Steve	Bos.	3	7	0	1	1	2	4	0	0	0	2		1974-75	1977-78
Langelle, Pete	Tor.	4	137	22	51	73	11	41	5	9	14	4	1	1938-39	1941-42
Langevin, Chris	Buf.	2	22	3	1	4	22	....	....	....	....	....		1983-84	1985-86
Langevin, Dave	NYI, Min., L.A.	8	513	12	107	119	530	87	2	15	17	106	4	1979-80	1986-87
Langlais, Alain	Min.	2	25	4	4	8	10	....	....	....	....	....		1973-74	1974-75
Langlois, Al	Mtl., NYR, Det., Bos.	9	448	21	91	112	488	53	1	5	6	60	3	1957-58	1965-66
Langlois, Charlie	Ham., NYA., Pit., Mtl.	4	151	22	3	25	201	2	0	0	0	0		1924-25	1927-28
Lanthier, Jean-Marc	Van.	4	105	16	16	32	29	....	....	....	....	....		1983-84	1987-88
Lanyon, Ted	Pit.	1	5	0	0	0	4	....	....	....	....	....		1967-68	1967-68
Laperriere, Jacques	Mtl.	12	691	40	242	282	674	88	9	22	31	101	6	1962-63	1973-74
Lapointe, Guy	Mtl., St.L., Bos.	16	884	171	451	622	893	123	26	44	70	138	6	1968-69	1983-84
Lapointe, Rick	Det., Phi., St.L., Que., L.A.	11	664	44	176	220	831	46	2	7	9	64		1975-76	1985-86
Laprade, Edgar	NYR	10	501	108	172	280	42	18	4	9	13	4		1945-46	1954-55
LaPrairie, Ben	Chi.	1	7	0	0	0	0	....	....	....	....	....		1936-37	1936-37
Lariviere, Garry	Que., Edm.	4	219	6	57	63	167	14	0	5	5	8		1979-80	1982-83
Larmer, Jeff	Col., N.J., Chi.	5	158	37	51	88	57	5	1	0	1	2		1981-82	1985-86
Larochelle, Wildor	Mtl., Chi.	12	474	92	74	166	211	34	6	4	10	24	2	1925-26	1936-37
Larose, Charles	Bos.	1	6	0	0	0	0	....	....	....	....	....		1925-26	1925-26
Larose, Claude	Mtl., Min., St.L.	16	943	226	257	483	887	97	14	18	32	143	5	1962-63	1977-78
Larose, Claude	NYR	2	25	4	7	11	2	2	0	0	0	0		1979-80	1981-82
Larouche, Pierre	Pit., Mtl., Hfd., NYR	14	812	395	427	822	237	64	20	34	54	16	1	1974-75	1987-88
Larson, Norman	NYA., Bro., NYR	3	89	25	18	43	12	....	....	....	....	....		1940-41	1946-47
Latreille, Phil	NYR	1	4	0	0	0	2	....	....	....	....	....		1960-61	1960-61
Lauder, Marty	Bos.	1	3	0	0	0	2	....	....	....	....	....		1927-28	1927-28
Lauen, Mike	Wpg.	1	3	0	1	1	0	....	....	....	....	....		1983-84	1983-84
Laughlin, Craig	Mtl., Wsh., L.A., Tor.	8	549	136	205	341	364	33	6	6	12	20		1981-82	1988-89
Laughton, Mike	Oak., Cal.	4	189	39	48	87	101	11	2	4	6	0		1967-68	1970-71
Laurence, Red	Atl., St.L.	2	79	15	22	37	14	....	....	....	....	....		1978-79	1979-80
LaVallee, Kevin	Cgy., L.A., St.L., Pit.	7	366	110	125	235	85	32	5	8	13	24		1980-81	1986-87
Lavarre, Mark	Chi.	3	78	9	16	25	58	1	0	0	0	2		1985-86	1987-88
Lavender, Brian	St.L., NYI, Det., Cal.	4	184	16	26	42	174	3	0	0	0	2		1971-72	1974-75
Laviolette, Jack	Mtl.	1	18	2	0	2	0	2	0	0	0	0		1917-18	1917-18
Lawson, Danny	Det., Min., Buf.	5	219	28	29	57	61	16	0	1	1	2		1967-68	1971-72
Laycoe, Hal	NYR, Mtl., Bos.	11	531	25	77	102	292	40	2	5	7	39		1945-46	1955-56
Leach, Larry	Bos.	3	126	13	29	42	91	7	1	1	2	8		1958-59	1961-62
Leach, Reggie	Bos., Cal., Phi., Det.	13	934	381	285	666	387	94	47	22	69	22	1	1970-71	1982-83
Leavins, Jim	Det., NYR	2	41	2	12	14	30	....	....	....	....	....		1985-86	1986-87
LeBlanc, Fern	Det.	3	34	5	6	11	0	....	....	....	....	....		1976-77	1978-79
LeBlanc, J.P.	Chi., Det.	5	153	14	30	44	87	2	0	0	0	0		1968-69	1978-79
LeBrun, Al	NYR	2	6	0	2	2	4	....	....	....	....	....		1960-61	1965-66
Lecaine, Bill	Pit.	1	4	0	0	0	0	....	....	....	....	....		1968-69	1968-69
Leclair, Jackie	Mtl.,	3	160	20	40	60	56	20	6	0	7	6	1	1954-55	1956-57
Leclerc, Rene	Det.	2	87	10	11	21	105	....	....	....	....	....		1968-69	1970-71
Lecuyer, Doug	Chi., Wpg., Pit.	4	126	11	31	42	178	7	4	0	4	15		1978-79	1982-83
Ledingham, Walt	Chi., NYI	3	15	0	2	2	4	....	....	....	....	....		1972-73	1976-77
LeDuc, Albert	Mtl., Ott., NYR	10	383	57	35	92	614	31	5	6	11	32	2	1925-26	1934-35
LeDuc, Rich	Bos., Que.	4	130	28	38	66	55	5	0	0	0	9		1972-73	1980-81
Lee, Bobby	Mtl.	1	1	0	0	0	0	....	....	....	....	....		1942-43	1942-43
Lee, Edward	Que.	1	2	0	0	0	5	....	....	....	....	....		1984-85	1984-85
Lee, Peter	Pit.	6	431	114	131	245	257	19	0	8	8	4		1977-78	1982-83
Lefley, Bryan	N.Y.I., K.C., Col.	5	228	7	29	36	101	2	0	0	0	0		1972-73	1977-78
Lefley, Chuck	Mtl., St.L.	9	407	128	164	292	137	29	5	8	13	10		1970-71	1980-81
Leger, Roger	NYR, Mtl.	5	187	18	53	71	71	20	0	7	7	14		1943-44	1949-50
Legge, Barry	Que., Wpg.	3	107	1	11	12	144	....	....	....	....	....		1979-80	1981-82
Legge, Randy	NYR	1	12	0	2	2	2	....	....	....	....	....		1972-73	1972-73
Lehto, Petteri	Pit.	1	6	0	0	0	4	....	....	....	....	....		1984-85	1984-85
Lehtonen, Antero	Wsh.	1	65	9	12	21	14	....	....	....	....	....		1979-80	1979-80
Lehvonen, Henri	K.C.	1	4	0	0	0	0	....	....	....	....	....		1974-75	1974-75
Leier, Edward	Chi.	2	16	2	1	3	2	....	....	....	....	....		1949-50	1950-51
Leinonen, Mikko	NYR, Wsh.	4	162	31	78	109	71	20	2	11	13	28		1981-82	1984-85
Leiter, Bobby	Bos., Pit., Atl.	10	447	98	126	224	144	8	3	0	3	2		1962-63	1975-76
Leiter, Ken	NYI, Min.	5	143	14	36	50	62	15	0	6	6	8		1984-85	1989-90
Lemaire, Jacques	Mtl.	12	853	366	469	835	217	145	61	78	139	63	8	1967-68	1978-79
Lemay, Moe	Van., Edm., Bos., Wpg.	8	317	72	94	166	442	28	6	3	9	55	1	1981-82	1988-89
Lemelin, Roger	K.C., Col.	4	36	1	2	3	27	....	....	....	....	....		1974-75	1977-78
Lemieux, Alain	St.L., Que., Pit.	6	119	28	44	72	38	19	4	6	10	0		1981-82	1986-87
Lemieux, Bob	Oak.	1	19	0	1	1	12	....	....	....	....	....		1967-68	1967-68
Lemieux, Jacques	L.A.	2	19	0	4	4	8	1	0	0	0	0		1967-68	1969-70
Lemieux, Jean	L.A., Atl., Wsh.	6	204	23	63	86	39	3	1	1	2	0		1969-70	1977-78
Lemieux, Real	Det., L.A., NYR, Buf.	7	381	40	75	115	184	18	2	4	6	10		1966-67	1973-74
Lemieux, Richard	Van., St.L., K.C., Atl.	5	274	39	82	121	132	2	0	0	0	0		1971-72	1975-76
Lepine, Hec	Mtl.	1	33	5	2	7	2	....	....	....	....	....		1925-26	1925-26
Lepine, Pit	Mtl.	13	526	143	98	241	392	41	7	5	12	26	2	1925-26	1937-38
Leroux, Gaston	Mtl.	1	2	0	0	0	0	....	....	....	....	....		1935-36	1935-36
Lesieur, Art	Mtl., Chi.	4	100	4	2	6	50	14	0	0	0	4	1	1928-29	1935-36
Lesuk, Bill	Bos., Phi., L.A., Wsh., Wpg.	8	388	44	63	107	368	9	1	0	1	12	1	1968-69	1979-80
Leswick, Jack	Chi.	1	47	1	7	8	16	....	....	....	....	....	1	1933-34	1933-34
Leswick, Peter	NYA, Bos.	2	3	1	0	1	0	....	....	....	....	....		1936-37	1944-45
Leswick, Tony	NYR, Det., Chi.	12	740	165	159	324	900	59	13	10	23	91	3	1945-46	1957-58
Levandoski, Joseph	NYR	1	8	1	1	2	0	....	....	....	....	....		1946-47	1946-47
Leveille, Norm	Bos.	2	75	17	25	42	49	....	....	....	....	....		1981-82	1982-83
Lever, Don	Van., Atl., Cgy., Col., N.J., Buf.	15	1020	313	367	680	593	30	7	10	17	26		1972-73	1986-87
Levie, Craig	Wpg., Min., Van., St.L.	6	183	22	53	75	177	16	2	3	5	32		1981-82	1986-87
Levinsky, Alex	Tor., Chi., NYR	9	367	19	49	68	307	34	2	1	3	2	2	1930-31	1938-39
Levo, Tapio	Col., N.J.,	2	107	16	53	69	36	....	....	....	....	....		1981-82	1982-83
Lewicki, Danny	Tor., NYR, Chi.	9	461	105	135	240	177	28	0	4	4	8	1	1950-51	1958-59
Lewis, Bob	NYR	1	8	0	0	0	0	....	....	....	....	....		1975-76	1975-76
Lewis, Dave	NYI, L.A., N.J., Det.	15	1008	36	187	223	953	91	1	20	21	143		1973-74	1987-88
Lewis, Douglas	Mtl..	1	3	0	0	0	0	....	....	....	....	....		1946-47	1946-47
Lewis, Herbie	Det.	11	483	148	161	309	248	38	13	10	23	6	2	1928-29	1938-39
Ley, Rick	Tor., Hfd.	6	310	12	72	84	528	14	0	2	2	20		1968-69	1980-81
Libett, Nick	Det., K.C., Pit.	14	982	237	268	505	472	16	6	2	8	2		1967-68	1980-81
Licari, Anthony	Det.	1	9	0	1	1	0	....	....	....	....	....		1946-47	1946-47
Liddington, Bob	Tor.	1	11	0	1	1	2	....	....	....	....	....		1970-71	1970-71
Lindgren, Lars	Van., Min.	6	394	25	113	138	325	40	5	6	11	20		1978-79	1983-84
Lindsay, Ted	Det., Chi.	17	1068	379	472	851	1808	133	47	49	96	194	4	1944-45	1964-65
Lindstrom, Willy	Wpg., Edm., Pit.	8	582	161	162	323	200	57	14	18	32	24	2	1979-80	1986-87
Liscombe, Carl	Det.	9	383	137	140	277	117	59	22	19	41	20	1	1937-38	1945-46
Litzenberger, Ed	Mtl., Chi., Det., Tor.	12	618	178	238	416	283	40	5	13	18	34	4	1952-53	1963-64
Locas, Jacques	Mtl..	2	59	7	8	15	66	....	....	....	....	....		1947-48	1948-49
Lochead, Bill	NYR, Det., Col.	6	330	69	62	131	180	7	3	0	3	6		1974-75	1979-80
Locking, Norm	Chi.	2	48	2	6	8	26	1	0	0	0	0		1934-35	1935-36
Lofthouse, Mark	Wsh., Det.	6	181	42	38	80	73	....	....	....	....	....		1977-78	1982-83
Logan, Dave	Chi., Van.	6	218	5	29	34	470	12	0	0	0	10		1975-76	1980-81
Logan, Robert	Buf., L.A.	3	42	10	5	15	0	....	....	....	....	....		1986-87	1988-89
Long, Barry	L.A., Det., Wpg.	5	280	11	68	79	250	5	0	1	1	18		1972-73	1981-82
Long, Stanley	Mtl..	1	....	....	....	....	....	3	0	0	0	0		1951-52	1951-52
Lonsberry, Ross	Phi., Pit., Bos., L.A.	15	968	256	310	566	806	100	21	25	46	87	2	1966-67	1980-81
Loob, Peter	Que.	1	8	1	2	3	0	....	....	....	....	....		1984-85	1984-85

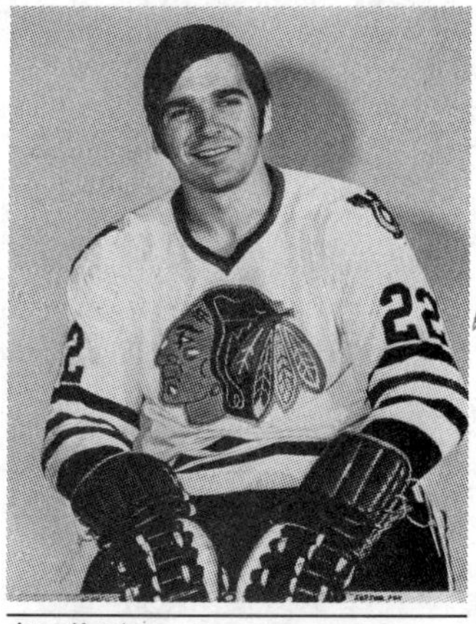

Jerry Korab

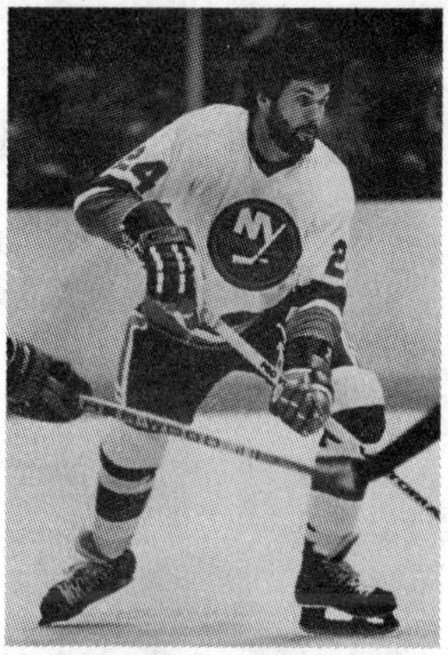

Gord Lane

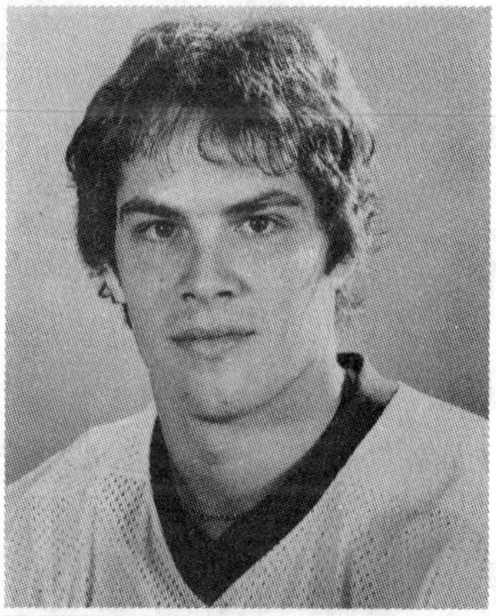

Dave Langevin

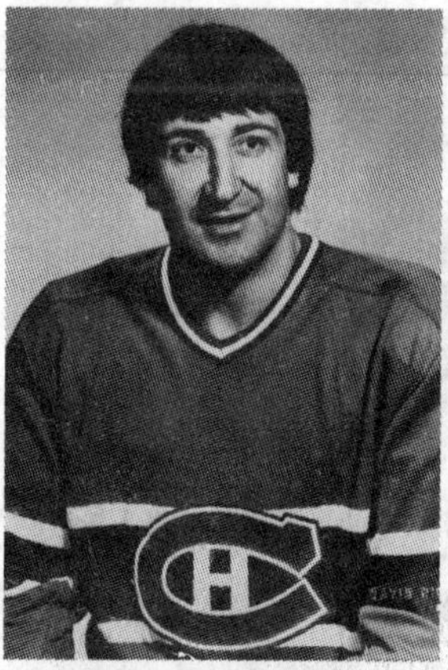

Guy Lapointe

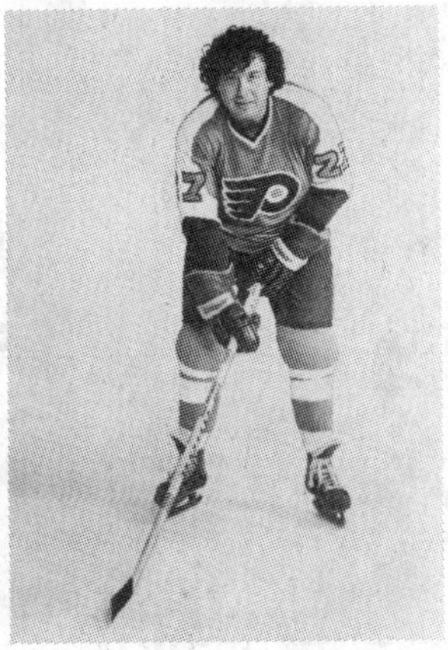

Reggie Leach

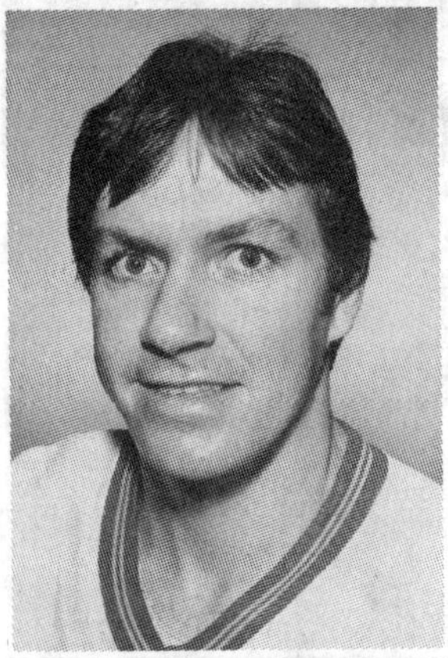

Don Lever

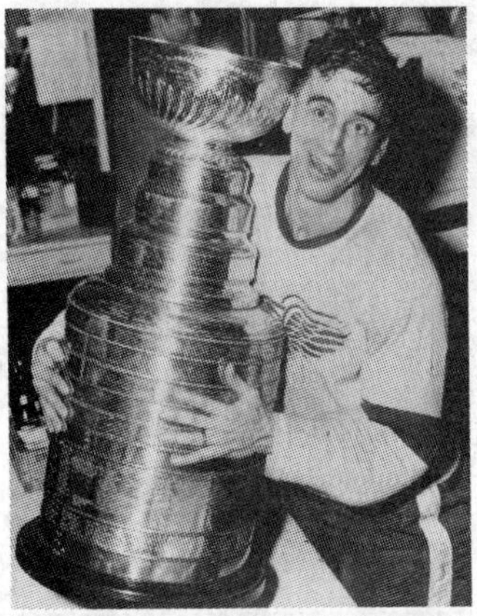

Ted Lindsay

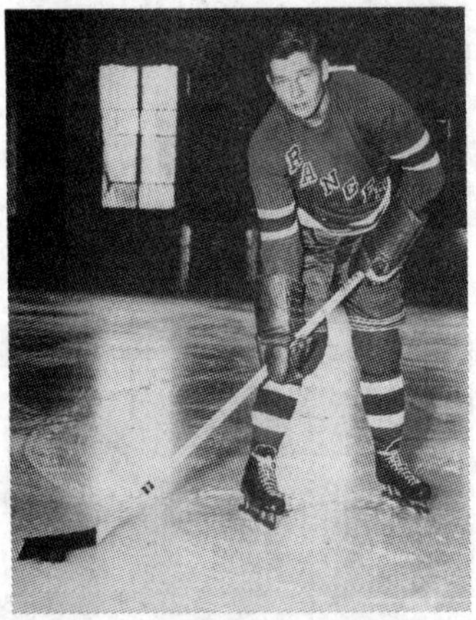

Pentti Lund

			Regular Schedule					Playoffs					NHL Cup	First NHL	Last NHL
Name	NHL Teams	NHL Seasons	GP	G	A	TP	PIM	GP	G	A	TP	PIM	Wins	Season	Season
Lorentz, Jim	NYR, Buf., Bos., St.L.	10	659	161	238	399	208	54	12	10	22	30	1	1968-69	1977-78
Lorimer, Bob	NYI, Col., N.J.	10	529	22	90	112	431	49	3	10	13	83	2	1976-77	1985-86
Lorraine, Rod	Mtl..	6	179	28	39	67	30	11	0	3	3	0		1935-36	1941-42
Loughlin, Clem	Det., Chi.	3	101	8	6	14	77	....	....	....	....	....		1926-27	1928-29
Loughlin, Wilf	Tor.	1	14	0	0	0	2	....	....	....	....	....		1923-24	1923-24
Lowdermilk, Dwayne	Wsh.	1	2	0	1	1	2	....	....	....	....	....		1980-81	1980-81
Lowe, Darren	Pit.	1	8	1	2	3	0	....	....	....	....	....		1983-84	1983-84
Lowe, Norm	NYR	2	4	1	1	2	0	....	....	....	....	....		1948-49	1949-50
Lowe, Ross	Bos., Mtl..	3	77	6	8	14	82	2	0	0	0	0		1949-50	1951-52
Lowery, Fred	Mtl.M., Pit.	2	54	1	0	1	10	2	0	0	0	6	1	1924-25	1925-26
Lowrey, Eddie	Ott., Ham.	3	24	2	0	2	3	....	....	....	....	....		1917-18	1920-21
Lowrey, Gerry	Chi., Ott., Tor., Phi., Pit.	6	209	48	48	96	168	2	1	0	1	2		1927-28	1932-33
Lucas, Danny	Phi.	1	6	1	0	1	0	....	....	....	....	....		1978-79	1978-79
Lucas, Dave	Det.	1	1	0	0	0	0	....	....	....	....	....		1962-63	1962-63
Luce, Don	NYR, Det., Buf., L.A., Tor.	13	894	225	329	554	364	71	17	22	39	52		1969-70	1981-82
Ludvig, Jan	N.J., Buf.	7	314	54	87	141	418	....	....	....	....	....		1982-83	1988-89
Lukowich, Bernie	Pit., St.L.	2	79	13	15	28	34	2	0	0	0	0		1973-74	1974-75
Lukowich, Morris	Wpg., Bos., L.A.	8	582	199	219	418	584	11	0	2	2	24		1979-80	1986-87
Luksa, Charlie	Hfd.	1	8	0	1	1	4	....	....	....	....	....		1979-80	1979-80
Lumley, Dave	Mtl., Edm., Hfd.	9	437	98	160	258	680	61	6	8	14	131	2	1978-79	1986-87
Lund, Pentti	NYR, Bos.	7	259	44	55	99	40	18	7	5	12	0		1946-47	1952-53
Lundberg, Brian	Pit.	1	1	0	0	0	2	....	....	....	....	....		1982-83	1982-83
Lunde, Len	Min., Van., Det., Chi.	8	321	39	83	122	75	20	3	2	5	2		1958-59	1970-71
Lundholm, Bengt	Wpg.	5	275	48	95	143	72	14	3	4	7	14		1981-82	1985-86
Lundrigan, Joe	Tor., Wsh.	2	52	2	8	10	22	....	....	....	....	....		1972-73	1974-75
Lundstrom, Tord	Det.	1	11	1	1	2	0	....	....	....	....	....		1973-74	1973-74
Lundy, Pat	Det. Chi.	5	150	37	32	69	31	9	1	1	2	2		1945-46	1950-51
Lupien, Gilles	Mtl., Pit., Hfd.	5	226	5	25	30	416	25	0	0	0	21	2	1977-78	1981-82
Lupul, Gary	Van.	7	293	70	75	145	243	25	4	7	11	11		1979-80	1985-86
Lyle, George	Det., Hfd.	4	99	24	38	62	51	....	....	....	....	....		1979-80	1982-83
Lynch, Jack	Pit., Det., Wsh.	7	382	24	106	130	336	....	....	....	....	....		1972-73	1978-79
Lynn, Vic	Det., Mtl., Tor., Bos., Chi.	10	326	49	76	125	274	47	7	10	17	46	3	1943-44	1953-54
Lyon, Steve	Pit.	1	3	0	0	0	2	....	....	....	....	....		1976-77	1976-77
Lyons, Ron	Bos., Phi.	1	36	2	4	6	29	5	0	0	0	0		1930-31	1930-31
Lysiak, Tom	Atl., Chi.	13	919	292	551	843	567	78	25	38	63	49		1973-74	1985-86

M

			Regular Schedule					Playoffs					NHL Cup	First NHL	Last NHL
Name	NHL Teams	NHL Seasons	GP	G	A	TP	PIM	GP	G	A	TP	PIM	Wins	Season	Season
MacAdam, Al	Phi., Cal., Cle., Min., Van.	12	864	240	351	591	509	64	20	24	44	21	1	1973-74	1984-85
MacDonald, Blair	Edm., Van.	4	219	91	100	191	65	11	0	6	6	2		1979-80	1982-83
MacDonald, Brett	Van.	1	1	0	0	0	0	....	....	....	....	....		1987-88	1987-88
MacDonald, Kilby	NYR	4	151	36	34	70	47	15	1	2	3	4	1	1939-40	1944-45
MacDonald, Lowell	Det., L.A., Pit.	13	506	180	210	390	92	30	11	11	22	12		1961-62	1977-78
MacDonald, Parker	Tor., NYR, Det., Bos., Min.	14	676	144	179	323	253	75	14	14	28	20		1952-53	1968-69
MacDougall, Kim	Min.	1	1	0	0	0	0	....	....	....	....	....		1974-75	1974-75
MacEachern, Shane	St.L.	1	1	0	0	0	0	....	....	....	....	....		1987-88	1987-88
Macey, Hubert	NYR, Mtl.	3	30	6	9	15	0	8	0	0	0	0		1941-42	1946-47
MacGregor, Bruce	Det., NYR	14	893	213	257	470	217	107	19	28	47	44		1960-61	1973-74
MacGregor, Randy	Hfd.	1	2	1	1	2	2	....	....	....	....	....		1981-82	1981-82
MacGuigan, Garth	NYI	1	2	0	0	0	0	....	....	....	....	....		1979-80	1979-80
MacIntosh, Ian	NYR	1	4	0	0	0	4	....	....	....	....	....		1952-53	1952-53
MacIver, Don	Wpg.	1	6	0	0	0	2	....	....	....	....	....		1979-80	1979-80
MacKasey, Blair	Tor.	1	1	0	0	0	2	....	....	....	....	....		1976-77	1976-77
MacKay, Calum	Det., Mtl.	8	237	50	55	105	214	38	5	13	18	20	1	1946-47	1954-55
Mackay, Dave	Chi.	1	29	3	0	3	26	5	0	1	1	2		1940-41	1940-41
MacKay, Mickey	Chi., Pit., Bos.	4	151	44	19	63	79	11	0	0	0	6	1	1926-27	1929-30
MacKay, Murdo	Mtl.	3	19	0	3	3	0	15	1	2	3	0		1945-46	1947-48
Mackell, Fleming	Tor., Bos.	13	665	149	220	369	562	80	22	41	63	75	2	1947-48	1959-60
MacKenzie, Barry	Min.	1	6	0	1	1	6	....	....	....	....	....		1968-69	1968-69
MacKenzie, Bill	Chi., Mtl.(M),Mtl., NYR	7	266	15	14	29	133	19	1	1	2	11	1	1932-33	1939-40
MacKey, Reggie	NYR	1	34	0	0	0	16	1	0	0	0	0		1926-27	1926-27
Mackie, Howie	Det.	2	20	1	0	1	4	8	0	0	0	0	1	1936-37	1937-38
MacKinnon, Paul	Wsh.	5	147	5	23	28	91	....	....	....	....	....		1979-80	1983-84
MacLeish, Rick	Phi., Hfd., Pit., Det.	14	846	349	410	759	434	114	54	53	107	38	2	1970-71	1983-84
MacMillan, Billy	Tor., Atl., NYI	7	446	74	77	151	184	53	6	6	12	40		1970-71	1976-77
MacMillan, Bob	NYR, St.L., Atl., Cgy., Col., N.J., Chi.	11	753	228	349	577	260	31	8	11	19	16		1974-75	1984-85
MacMillan, John	Tor., Det.	5	104	5	10	15	32	12	0	1	1	2	2	1960-61	1964-65
MacNeil, Al	Tor., Mtl., Chi., NYR, Pit.	11	524	17	75	92	617	37	0	4	4	67		1955-56	1967-68
MacNeil, Bernie	St.L.	1	4	0	0	0	0	....	....	....	....	....		1973-74	1973-74
Macoun, Jamie	Cgy.	5	320	37	111	148	381	49	3	9	12	43		1982-83	1986-87
MacPherson, Bud	Mtl.	7	259	5	33	38	233	29	0	3	3	21	1	1948-49	1956-57
MacSweyn, Ralph	Phi.	5	47	0	5	5	10	8	0	0	0	6		1967-68	1971-72
Madigan, Connie	St.L.	1	20	0	3	3	25	5	0	0	0	4		1972-73	1972-73
Magee, Dean	Min.	1	7	0	0	0	4	....	....	....	....	....		1977-78	1977-78
Maggs, Daryl	Chi., Cal., Tor.	3	135	14	19	33	54	4	0	0	0	0		1971-72	1979-80
Magnan, Marc	Tor.	1	4	0	1	1	5	....	....	....	....	....		1982-83	1982-83
Magnuson, Keith	Chi.	11	589	14	125	139	1442	68	3	9	12	164		1969-70	1979-80
Mahaffy, John	Mtl., NYR	3	37	11	25	36	4	1	0	1	1	0		1942-43	1944-45
Mahovlich, Frank	Tor., Det., Mtl.	18	1181	533	570	1103	1056	137	51	67	118	163	6	1956-57	1973-74
Mahovlich, Pete	Det., Mtl., Pit.	16	884	288	485	773	916	88	30	42	72	134	4	1965-66	1980-81
Mailley, Frank	Mtl.	1	1	0	0	0	0	....	....	....	....	....		1942-43	1942-43
Mair, Jim	Phi., NYI, Van.	5	76	4	15	19	49	3	1	2	3	4		1970-71	1974-75
Majeau, Fern	Mtl.	2	56	22	24	46	43	1	0	0	0	0	1	1943-44	1944-45
Maki, Chico	Chi.	15	841	143	292	435	345	113	17	36	53	43	1	1960-61	1975-76
Maki, Wayne	Chi., St.L., Van.	6	246	57	79	136	184	2	1	0	1	2		1967-68	1972-73
Makkonen, Karl	Edm.	1	9	2	2	4	0	....	....	....	....	....		1979-80	1979-80
Malinowski, Merlin	Col., N.J., Hfd.	5	282	54	111	165	121	....	....	....	....	....		1978-79	1982-83
Malone, Cliff	Mtl.	1	3	0	0	0	0	....	....	....	....	....		1951-52	1951-52
Malone, Greg	Pit., Hfd., Que.	11	704	191	310	501	661	20	3	5	8	32		1976-77	1986-87
Malone, Joe	Mtl., Que., Ham.	7	125	146	21	167	23	9	5	0	5	0	1	1917-18	1923-24
Maloney, Dan	Chi., L.A., Det., Tor.	11	737	192	259	451	1489	40	4	7	11	35		1970-71	1981-82
Maloney, Dave	NYR, Buf.	11	657	71	246	317	1154	49	7	17	24	91		1974-75	1984-85
Maloney, Phi.	Bos., Tor., Chi.	5	158	28	43	71	16	6	0	0	0	0		1949-50	1959-60
Maluta, Ray	Bos.	2	25	2	3	5	6	2	0	0	0	0		1975-76	1976-77
Manastersky, Tom	Mtl.	1	6	0	0	0	11	....	....	....	....	....		1950-51	1950-51
Mancuso, Gus	Mtl., NYR	4	42	7	9	16	17	....	....	....	....	....		1937-38	1942-43
Mandich, Dan	Min.	4	111	5	11	16	303	7	0	0	0	2		1982-83	1985-86
Manery, Kris	Van., Wpg., Clev., Min.	4	250	63	64	127	91	....	....	....	....	....		1977-78	1980-81
Manery, Randy	L.A., Det., Atl.	10	582	50	206	256	415	13	0	2	2	12		1970-71	1979-80
Mann, Jack	NYR	2	9	3	4	7	0	....	....	....	....	....		1943-44	1944-45
Mann, Jimmy	Wpg., Que., Pit.	8	293	10	20	30	895	22	0	0	0	89		1979-80	1987-88
Mann, Ken	Det.	1	1	0	0	0	0	....	....	....	....	....		1975-76	1975-76
Mann, Norm	Tor.	2	31	0	3	3	4	1	0	0	0	0		1938-39	1940-41
Manners, Rennison	Pit., Phi.	2	37	3	2	5	14	....	....	....	....	....		1929-30	1930-31
Manno, Bob	Van., Tor., Det.	8	371	41	131	172	274	17	2	4	6	12		1976-77	1984-85
Manson, Ray	Bos., NYR	2	2	0	1	1	0	....	....	....	....	....		1947-48	1948-49
Mantha, Georges	Mtl..	13	498	89	102	181	148	36	6	2	8	16	2	1928-29	1940-41
Mantha, Sylvio	Mtl., Bos.	14	543	63	72	135	667	46	5	4	9	66	3	1923-24	1936-37
Maracle, Buddy	NYR	1	11	1	3	4	4	4	0	0	0	0		1930-31	1930-31
Marcetta, Milan	Tor., Min.	3	54	7	15	22	10	17	7	7	14	4	1	1966-67	1968-69
March, Mush	Chi.	17	758	153	230	383	540	48	12	15	27	41	2	1928-29	1944-45
Marchinko, Brian	Tor., NYI	4	47	2	6	8	0	....	....	....	....	....		1970-71	1973-74
Marcon, Lou	Det.	3	70	0	4	4	42	....	....	....	....	....		1958-59	1962-63
Marcotte, Don	Bos.	15	868	230	255	485	317	132	34	27	61	81	2	1965-66	1981-82
Marini, Hector	NYI, N.J.	5	154	27	46	73	246	10	3	6	9	14	2	1978-79	1983-84
Mario, Frank	Bos.	2	53	9	19	28	24	....	....	....	....	....		1941-42	1944-45
Mariucci, John	Chi.	5	223	11	34	45	308	8	0	3	3	26		1940-41	1947-48
Mark, Gordon	N.J.	2	55	3	7	10	109	....	....	....	....	....		1986-87	1987-88
Markell, John	Wpg.	2	52	11	10	21	36	....	....	....	....	....		1979-80	1980-81
Marker, Gus	Det., Mtl.M., Tor., Bro.	10	336	64	69	133	133	45	6	8	14	36	1	1932-33	1941-42
Markham, Ray	NYR	1	14	1	1	2	21	7	1	0	1	24		1979-80	1979-80
Markle, Jack	Tor.	1	8	0	1	1	0	....	....	....	....	....		1935-36	1935-36

Name	NHL Teams	NHL Seasons	Regular Schedule GP	G	A	TP	PIM	Playoffs GP	G	A	TP	PIM	NHL Cup Wins	First NHL Season	Last NHL Season
Marks, Jack	Mtl.W, Tor., Que.	2	7	0	0	0	4	....	....	....	....	....	1	1917-18	1919-20
Marks, John	Chi.	10	657	112	163	275	330	57	5	9	14	60		1972-73	1981-82
Marotte, Gilles	Bos., Chi., L.A., NYR, St.L.	12	808	56	265	321	872	29	3	3	6	26		1965-66	1976-77
Marquess, Mark	Bos.	1	27	5	4	9	27	4	0	0	0	0		1946-47	1946-47
Marsh, Gary	Det., Tor.	2	7	1	3	4	4	....	....	....	....	....		1967-68	1968-69
Marsh, Peter	Wpg., Chi.	5	278	48	71	119	224	26	1	5	6	33		1979-80	1983-84
Marshall, Bert	Det., Oak., Cal., NYR, NYI	14	868	17	181	198	926	72	4	22	26	99		1965-66	1978-79
Marshall, Don	Mtl., NYR, Buf., Tor.	19	1176	265	324	589	127	94	8	15	23	14	5	1951-52	1971-72
Marshall, Paul	Pit., Tor., Hfd.	4	95	15	18	33	17	1	0	0	0	0		1979-80	1982-83
Marshall, Willie	Tor.	4	33	1	15	16	2	....	....	....	....	....		1952-53	1958-59
Marson, Mike	Wsh., L.A.	6	196	24	24	48	233	....	....	....	....	....		1974-75	1979-80
Martin, Clare	Bos., Det., Chi., NYR	6	237	12	28	40	78	22	0	2	2	6	1	1941-42	1951-52
Martin, Frank	Bos., Chi.	6	282	11	46	57	122	10	0	1	1	2		1952-53	1957-58
Martin, Grant	Van., Wsh.	4	44	0	4	4	55	1	1	0	1	2		1983-84	1986-87
Martin, Jack	Tor.	1	1	0	0	0	0	....	....	....	....	....		1960-61	1960-61
Martin, Pit	Det., Bos., Chi., Van.	17	1101	324	485	809	609	100	27	31	58	56		1961-62	1978-79
Martin, Rick	Buf., L.A.	11	685	384	317	701	477	63	24	29	53	74		1971-72	1981-82
Martin, Ron	NYA	2	94	13	16	29	36	....	....	....	....	....		1932-33	1933-34
Martin, Terry	Buf., Que., Tor., Edm., Min.	10	479	104	101	205	202	21	4	2	6	26		1975-76	1984-85
Martin, Tom	Tor.	1	3	1	0	1	0	....	....	....	....	....		1967-68	1967-68
Martineau, Don	Atl., Min., Det.	4	90	6	10	16	63	....	....	....	....	....		1973-74	1976-77
Maruk, Dennis	Cal., Clev., Min., Wsh.	14	888	356	522	878	761	34	14	22	36	26		1975-76	1988-89
Masnick, Paul	Mtl., Chi., Tor.	6	232	18	41	59	139	33	4	5	9	27	1	1950-51	1957-58
Mason, Charley	NYR, NYA, Det., Chi.	4	95	7	18	25	44	4	0	1	1	0		1934-35	1938-39
Massecar, George	NYA	3	100	12	11	23	46	....	....	....	....	....		1929-30	1931-32
Masters, Jamie	St.L.	3	33	1	13	14	2	2	0	0	0	0		1975-76	1978-79
Masterton, Bill	Min.	1	38	4	8	12	4	....	....	....	....	....		1967-68	1967-68
Mathers, Frank	Tor.	3	23	1	3	4	4	....	....	....	....	....		1948-49	1951-52
Mathiasen, Dwight	Pit.	3	33	1	7	8	18	....	....	....	....	....		1985-86	1987-88
Matte, Joe	Tor., Ham., Bos., Mtl.	4	64	18	14	32	43	....	....	....	....	....		1919-20	1925-26
Matte, Joe	Chi.	1	12	0	1	1	0	....	....	....	....	....		1942-43	1942-43
Matte, Roland	Det.	1	12	0	1	1	0	....	....	....	....	....		1929-30	1929-30
Mattiussi, Dick	Pit., Oak., Cal.	4	200	8	31	39	124	8	0	1	1	6		1967-68	1970-71
Matz, Johnny	Mtl.	1	30	3	2	5	0	5	0	0	0	2		1924-25	1924-25
Maxner, Wayne	Bos.	2	62	8	9	17	48	....	....	....	....	....		1964-65	1965-66
Maxwell, Brad	Min., Que., Tor., Van., NYR	10	612	98	270	368	1292	79	12	49	61	178		1977-78	1986-87
Maxwell, Bryan	Min., St.L., Wpg., Pit.	8	331	18	77	95	745	15	1	1	2	86		1977-78	1984-85
Maxwell, Kevin	Min., Col., N.J.	3	66	6	15	21	61	16	3	4	7	24		1980-81	1983-84
Maxwell, Wally	Tor.	1	2	0	0	0	0	....	....	....	....	....		1952-53	1952-53
Mayer, Jim	NYR	1	4	0	0	0	0	....	....	....	....	....		1979-80	1979-80
Mayer, Pat	Pit.	1	1	0	0	0	4	....	....	....	....	....		1987-88	1987-88
Mayer, Shep	Tor.	1	12	1	2	3	4	....	....	....	....	....		1942-43	1942-43
Mazur, Eddie	Mtl., Chi.	6	107	8	20	28	120	25	4	5	9	22	1	1950-51	1956-57
McAdam, Gary	Buf., Pit., Det., Cal., Wsh., N.J., Tor.	11	534	96	132	228	243	30	6	5	11	16		1975-76	1985-86
McAdam, Sam	NYR	1	5	0	0	0	0	....	....	....	....	....		1930-31	1930-31
McAndrew, Hazen	Bro.	1	7	0	1	1	6	....	....	....	....	....		1941-42	1941-42
McAneeley, Ted	Cal.	3	158	8	35	43	141	....	....	....	....	....		1972-73	1974-75
McAtee, Jud	Det.	3	46	15	13	28	6	14	2	1	3	0		1942-43	1944-45
McAtee, Norm	Bos.	1	13	0	1	1	0	....	....	....	....	....		1946-47	1946-47
McAvoy, George	Mtl.	1	....	....	....	....	....	4	0	0	0	0		1954-55	1954-55
McBride, Cliff	Mtl.M., Tor.	2	2	0	0	0	0	....	....	....	....	....		1928-29	1929-30
McBurney, Jim	Chi.	1	1	0	1	1	0	....	....	....	....	....		1952-53	1952-53
McCabe, Stan	Det., Mtl.M.	4	78	9	4	13	49	....	....	....	....	....		1929-30	1933-34
McCaffrey, Bert	Tor., Pit., Mtl.	7	260	42	30	72	202	8	2	1	3	12		1924-25	1930-31
McCahill, John	Col.	1	1	0	0	0	0	....	....	....	....	....		1977-78	1977-78
McCaig, Douglas	Det., Chi.	7	263	8	21	29	255	17	0	1	1	8		1941-42	1950-51
McCallum, Dunc	NYR, Pit.	5	187	14	35	49	230	10	1	2	3	12		1965-66	1970-71
McCalmon, Eddie	Chi., Phi.	2	39	5	0	5	14	....	....	....	....	....		1927-28	1930-31
McCann, Rick	Det.	6	43	1	4	5	6	....	....	....	....	....		1967-68	1974-75
McCarthy, Dan	NYR	1	5	4	0	4	4	....	....	....	....	....		1980-81	1980-81
McCarthy, Kevin	Phi., Van., Pit.	10	537	67	191	258	527	21	2	3	5	20		1977-78	1986-87
McCarthy, Tom	Det., Bos.	4	60	8	9	17	8	....	....	....	....	....		1956-57	1960-61
McCarthy, Tom	Que., Ham.	2	34	19	3	22	10	....	....	....	....	....		1919-20	1920-21
McCarthy, Tom	Min., Bos.	9	460	178	221	399	330	68	12	26	38	67		1979-80	1987-88
McCartney, Walt	Mtl.	1	2	0	0	0	0	....	....	....	....	....		1932-33	1932-33
McCaskill, Ted	Min.	1	4	0	2	2	0	....	....	....	....	....		1967-68	1967-68
McClanahan, Rob	Buf., Hfd., NYR	5	224	38	63	101	126	34	4	12	16	31		1979-80	1983-84
McCord, Bob	Bos., Det., Min., St.L.	7	316	58	68	126	262	14	2	5	7	10		1963-64	1972-73
McCord, Dennis	Van.	1	3	0	0	0	0	....	....	....	....	....		1973-74	1973-74
McCormack, John	Tor., Mtl., Chi.	8	311	25	49	74	35	22	1	1	2	0	1	1947-48	1954-55
McCourt, Dale	Det., Buf., Tor.	7	532	194	284	478	124	21	9	7	16	6		1977-78	1983-84
McCreary, Bill E.	NYR, Det., Mtl., St.L.	10	309	53	62	115	108	48	6	16	22	14		1953-54	1970-71
McCreary, Bill	Tor.	1	12	1	0	1	4	....	....	....	....	....		1980-81	1980-81
McCreary, Keith	Mtl., Pit., Atl.	10	532	131	112	243	294	16	0	4	4	6		1961-62	1974-75
McCreedy, Johnny	Tor.	2	64	17	12	29	25	21	4	3	7	16	2	1941-42	1944-45
McCrimmon, Jim	St.L.	1	2	0	0	0	0	....	....	....	....	....		1974-75	1974-75
McCulley, Bob	Mtl.	1	1	0	0	0	0	....	....	....	....	....		1934-35	1934-35
McCurry, Duke	Pit.	4	148	21	11	32	119	4	0	2	2	4		1925-26	1928-29
McCutcheon, Brian	Det.	3	37	3	1	4	7	....	....	....	....	....		1974-75	1976-77
McCutheon, Darwin	Tor.	1	1	0	0	0	0	....	....	....	....	....		1981-82	1981-82
McDill, Jeff	Chi.	1	1	0	0	0	0	....	....	....	....	....		1976-77	1976-77
McDonagh, Bill	NYR	1	4	0	0	0	2	....	....	....	....	....		1949-50	1949-50
McDonald, Ab	Mtl., Chi., Bos., Det., Pit., St.L.	15	762	182	248	430	200	84	21	29	50	42	4	1957-58	1971-72
McDonald, Brian	Chi., Buf.	2	12	0	0	0	29	8	0	0	0	2		1967-68	1970-71
McDonald, Bucko	Det., Tor., NYR	11	448	35	88	123	206	63	6	1	7	24	3	1934-35	1944-45
McDonald, Butch	Det., Chi.	2	66	8	20	28	2	5	0	2	2	10		1939-40	1944-45
McDonald, Gerry	Hfd.	1	3	0	0	0	0	....	....	....	....	....		1981-82	1981-82
McDonald, Jack	Mtl.W, Mtl., Que., Tor.	5	73	27	11	38	13	12	2	0	2	0		1917-18	1921-22
McDonald, John	NYR	1	43	10	9	19	6	....	....	....	....	....		1943-44	1943-44
McDonald, Lanny	Tor., Col., Cgy.	16	1111	500	506	1006	899	117	44	40	84	120	1	1973-74	1988-89
McDonald, Robert	NYR	1	1	0	0	0	0	....	....	....	....	....		1943-44	1943-44
McDonald, Terry	K.C.	1	8	0	1	1	6	....	....	....	....	....		1975-76	1975-76
McDonnell, Joe	Van., Pit.	3	50	2	10	12	34	....	....	....	....	....		1981-82	1985-86
McDonnell, Moylan	Ham.	1	20	1	1	2	0	....	....	....	....	....		1920-21	1920-21
McDonough, Al	L.A., Pit., Atl., Det.	5	237	73	88	161	73	8	0	1	1	2		1970-71	1977-78
McDougal, Mike	NYR, Hfd.	4	61	8	10	18	43	....	....	....	....	....		1978-79	1982-83
McElmury, Jim	Min., K.C., Col.	5	180	14	47	61	49	....	....	....	....	....		1972-73	1977-78
McEwen, Mike	NYR, Col., NYI, L.A., Wsh., Det., Hfd.	12	716	108	296	404	460	78	12	36	48	48	3	1976-77	1987-88
McFadden, Jim	Det., Chi.	7	412	100	126	226	89	49	10	9	19	30	1	1947-48	1953-54
McFadyen, Don	Chi.	4	179	12	33	45	77	12	2	2	4	5	1	1932-33	1935-36
McFall, Dan	Wpg.	2	9	0	1	1	0	....	....	....	....	....		1984-85	1985-86
McFarland, George	Chi.	1	2	0	0	0	0	....	....	....	....	....		1926-27	1926-27
McGeough, Jim	Wsh., Pit.	4	57	7	10	17	32	....	....	....	....	....		1981-82	1986-87
McGibbon, John	Mtl.	1	1	0	0	0	2	....	....	....	....	....		1942-43	1942-43
McGill, Jack	Mtl.	3	134	27	10	37	71	3	2	0	2	0		1934-35	1936-37
McGill, Jack G.	Bos.	4	97	23	36	59	42	27	7	4	11	17		1941-42	1946-47
McGregor, Sandy	NYR	1	2	0	0	0	2	....	....	....	....	....		1963-64	1963-64
McGuire, Mickey	Pit.	2	36	3	0	3	6	....	....	....	....	....		1926-27	1927-28
McIlhargey, Jack	Phi., Van., Hfd.	8	393	11	36	47	1102	27	0	3	3	68		1974-75	1981-82
McInenly, Bert	Det., NYA, Ott., Bos.	6	166	19	15	34	144	4	0	0	0	2		1930-31	1935-36
McIntosh, Bruce	Min.	1	2	0	0	0	0	....	....	....	....	....		1972-73	1972-73
McIntosh, Paul	Buf.	2	48	0	0	2	66	2	0	0	0	7		1974-75	1975-76
McIntyre, Jack	Bos., Chi., Det.	11	499	109	102	211	173	29	7	6	13	4		1949-50	1959-60
McIntyre, Larry	Tor.	2	41	0	3	3	26	....	....	....	....	....		1969-70	1972-73
McKay, Doug	Det.	1	....	....	....	....	....	1	0	0	0	0	1	1949-50	1949-50
McKay, Ray	Chi., Buf., Cal.	6	140	2	16	18	102	....	....	....	....	....		1968-69	1973-74
McKechnie, Walt	Min., Cal., Bos., Det., Wsh., Clev., Tor., Col.	16	955	214	392	606	469	15	7	5	12	9		1967-68	1982-83
McKegney, Ian	Chi.	1	3	0	0	0	2	....	....	....	....	....		1976-77	1976-77
McKell, Jack	Ott.	2	42	4	1	5	42	9	0	0	0	0	1	1919-20	1920-21
McKendry, Alex	NYI, Cgy.	4	46	3	6	9	21	6	2	2	4	0	1	1977-78	1980-81
McKenna, Sean	Buf., L.A., Tor.	9	414	82	80	162	181	15	1	2	3	2		1981-82	1989-90
McKenney, Don	Bos., NYR, Tor., Det., St.L.	13	798	237	345	582	211	58	18	29	47	10	1	1954-55	1967-68

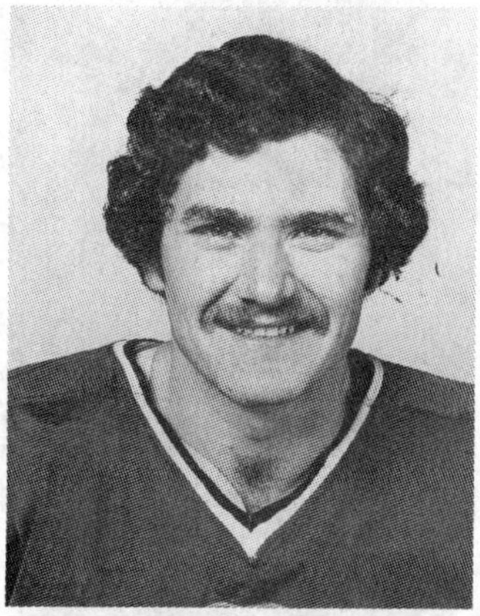

Blair Mackasey

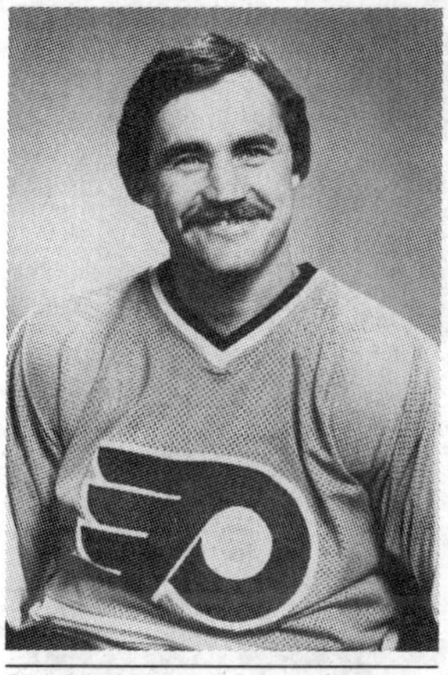

Rick MacLeish

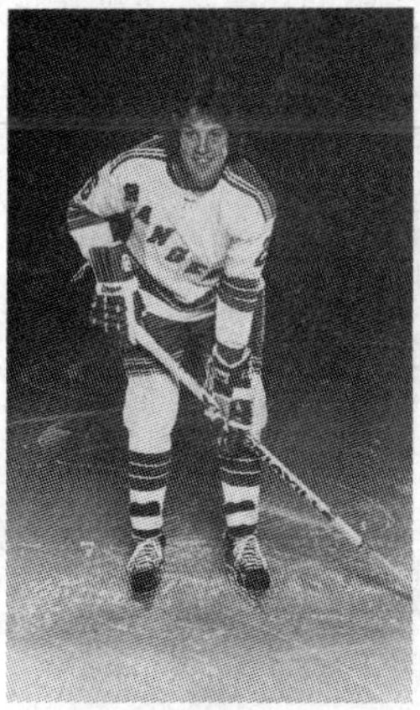

Dave Maloney

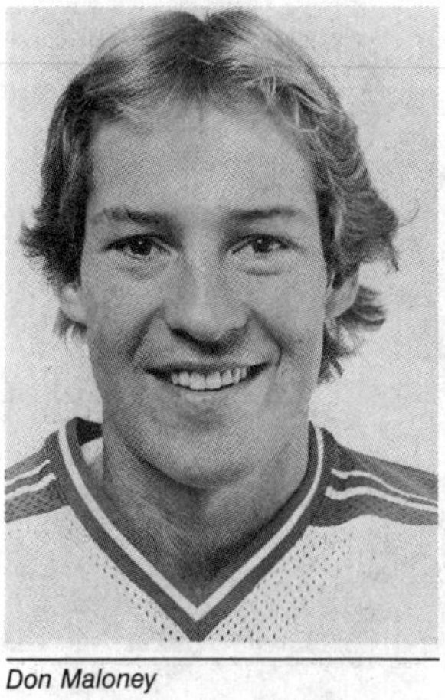

Don Maloney

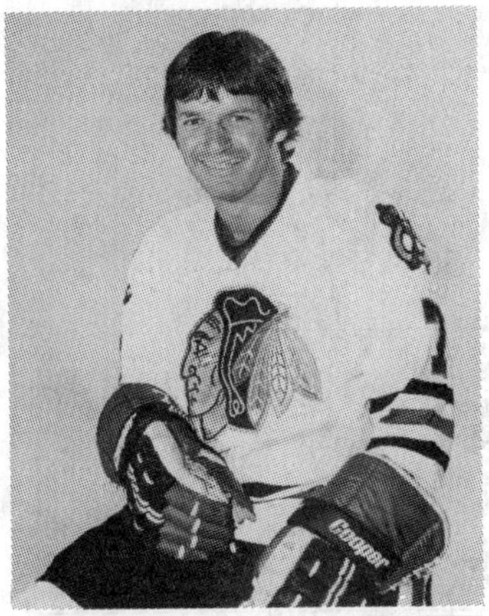

Pit Martin

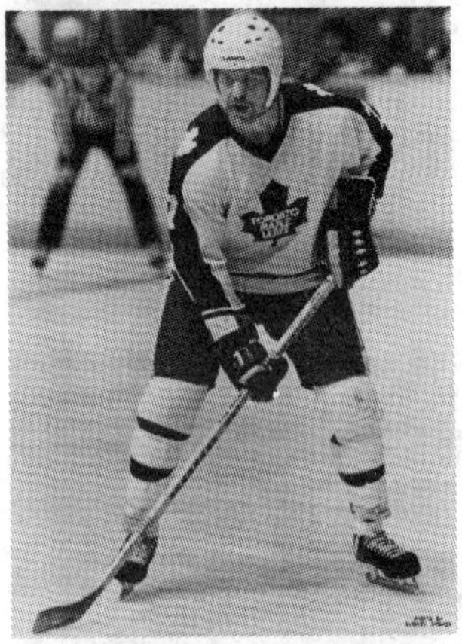

Lanny McDonald

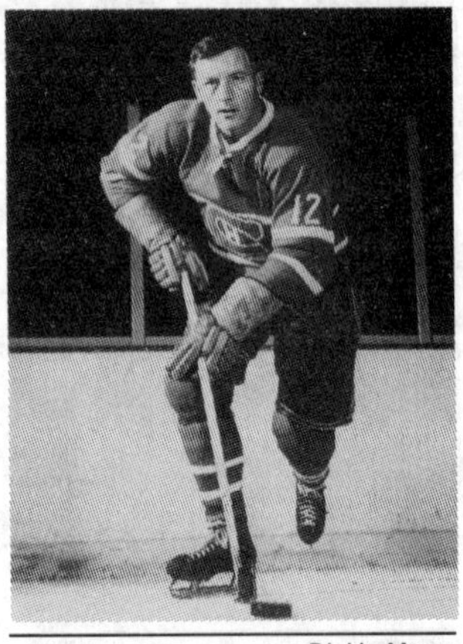

Dickie Moore

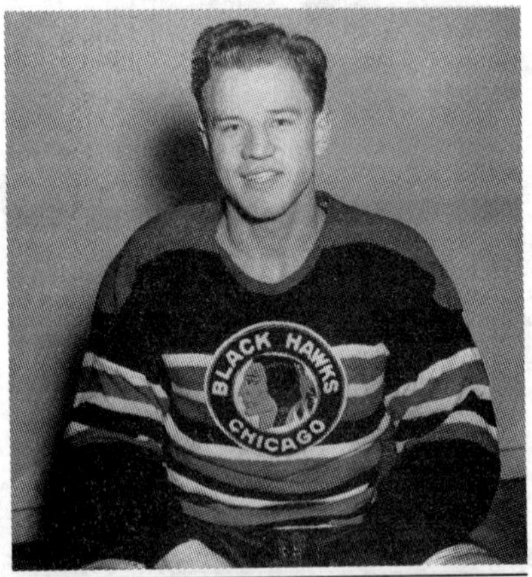

Bill Mosienko

Name	NHL Teams	NHL Seasons	Regular Schedule GP	G	A	TP	PIM	Playoffs GP	G	A	TP	PIM	NHL Cup Wins	First NHL Season	Last NHL Season
McKenny, Jim	Tor., Min.	14	604	82	247	329	294	37	7	9	16	10		1965-66	1978-79
McKenzie, Brian	Pit.	1	6	1	1	2	4	....	....	....	....	....		1971-72	1971-72
McKenzie, John	Chi., Det., NYR, Bos.	12	691	206	268	474	917	69	15	32	47	133	2	1958-59	1971-72
McKinnon, Alex	Ham., NYA, Chi.	5	194	19	10	29	235	....	....	....	....	....		1924-25	1928-29
McKinnon, Bob	Chi.	1	2	0	0	0	0	....	....	....	....	....		1928-29	1928-29
McKinnon, John	Mtl., Pit., Phi.	6	218	28	11	39	224	2	0	0	0	4		1925-26	1930-31
McLean, Don	Wsh.	1	9	0	0	0	6	....	....	....	....	....		1975-76	1975-76
McLean, Fred	Que., Ham.	2	9	0	0	0	2	....	....	....	....	....		1919-20	1920-21
McLean, Jack	Tor.	3	67	14	24	38	76	13	2	2	4	8	1	1942-43	1944-45
McLellan, John	Tor.	1	2	0	0	0	0	....	....	....	....	....		1951-52	1951-52
McLellan, Scott	Bos.	1	2	0	0	0	0	....	....	....	....	....		1982-83	1982-83
McLellan, Todd	NYI	1	5	1	1	2	0	....	....	....	....	....		1987-88	1987-88
McLenahan, Roly	Det.	1	9	2	1	3	10	2	0	0	0	0		1945-46	1945-46
McLeod, Al	Det.	1	26	2	2	4	24	....	....	....	....	....		1973-74	1973-74
McLeod, Jackie	NYR	5	106	14	23	37	12	7	0	0	0	0		1949-50	1954-55
McMahon, Mike	NYR, Min., Chi., Det., Pit., Buf.	8	224	15	68	83	171	14	3	7	10	4		1963-64	1971-72
McMahon, Mike C.	Mtl., Bos.	3	57	7	18	25	102	13	1	2	3	30	1	1942-43	1945-46
McManama, Bob	Pit.	3	99	11	25	36	28	8	0	1	1	6		1973-74	1975-76
McManus, Sammy	Mtl.M., Bos.	2	26	0	1	1	8	1	0	0	0	0	1	1934-35	1936-37
McMurchy, Tom	Chi., Edm.	4	55	8	4	12	65	....	....	....	....	....		1983-84	1987-88
McNab, Max	Det.	4	128	16	19	35	24	25	1	0	1	4	1	1947-48	1950-51
McNab, Peter	Buf., Bos., Van., N.J.	14	954	363	450	813	179	107	40	42	82	20		1973-74	1986-87
McNabney, Sid	Mtl.	1	....	....	....	....	....	5	0	1	1	2		1950-51	1950-51
McNamara, Howard	Mtl.	1	11	1	0	1	2	....	....	....	....	....		1919-20	1919-20
McNaughton, George	Que.B.	1	1	0	0	0	0	....	....	....	....	....		1919-20	1919-20
McNeill, Billy	Det.	6	257	21	46	67	142	4	1	1	2	4		1956-57	1963-64
McNeill, Stu	Det.	3	10	1	1	2	2	....	....	....	....	....		1957-58	1959-60
McPhee, George	NYR, N.J.	7	115	24	25	49	257	29	5	3	8	69		1982-83	1988-89
McReavy, Pat	Bos., Det.	4	55	5	10	15	4	20	3	3	6	9	1	1938-39	1941-42
McSheffrey, Bryan	Van., Buf.	3	90	13	7	20	44	....	....	....	....	....		1972-73	1974-75
McTaggart, Jim	Wsh.	2	71	3	10	13	205	....	....	....	....	....		1980-81	1981-82
McTavish, Gordon	St.L., Wpg.	2	11	1	3	4	2	....	....	....	....	....		1978-79	1979-80
McVeigh, Charley	Chi., NYA	9	397	84	88	172	138	4	0	0	0	2		1926-27	1934-35
McVicar, Jack	Mtl.M.	2	88	2	4	6	63	2	0	0	0	2		1930-31	1931-32
Meehan, Gerry	Tor., Phi., Buf., Van., Atl., Wsh.	10	670	180	243	423	111	10	0	1	1	0		1968-69	1978-79
Meeke, Brent	Cal., Clev.	5	75	9	22	31	8	....	....	....	....	....		1972-73	1976-77
Meeker, Howie	Tor.	8	346	83	102	185	329	42	6	9	15	50	3	1946-47	1953-54
Meeker, Mike	Pit.	1	4	0	0	0	5	....	....	....	....	....		1978-79	1978-79
Meeking, Harry	Tor., Det., Bos.	3	63	18	3	21	42	14	4	2	6	0	1	1917-18	1926-27
Meger, Paul	Mtl.	6	212	39	52	91	112	35	3	8	11	16	1	1949-50	1954-55
Meighan, Ron	Min., Pit.	2	48	3	7	10	18	....	....	....	....	....		1981-82	1982-83
Meissner, Barrie	Min.	2	6	0	1	1	4	....	....	....	....	....		1967-68	1968-69
Meissner, Dick	Bos., NYR	5	171	11	15	26	37	....	....	....	....	....		1959-60	1964-65
Melametsa, Anssi	Wpg.	1	27	0	3	3	2	....	....	....	....	....		1985-86	1985-86
Melin, Roger	Min.	2	3	0	0	0	0	....	....	....	....	....		1980-81	1981-82
Mellor, Tom	Det.	2	26	2	4	6	25	....	....	....	....	....		1973-74	1974-75
Melnyk, Gerry	Det., Chi., St.L.	6	269	39	77	116	34	53	6	6	12	6		1955-56	1967-68
Melnyk, Larry	Bos., Edm., NYR, Van.	10	432	11	63	74	686	66	2	9	11	127		1980-81	1989-90
Melrose, Barry	Wpg., Tor., Det.	6	300	10	23	33	728	7	0	2	2	38		1979-80	1985-86
Menard, Hillary	Chi.	1	1	0	0	0	0	....	....	....	....	....		1953-54	1953-54
Menard, Howie	Det., L.A., Chi., Oak.	4	151	23	42	65	87	19	3	7	10	36		1963-64	1969-70
Mercredi, Vic	Atl.	1	2	0	0	0	0	....	....	....	....	....		1974-75	1974-75
Meredith, Greg	Cgy.	2	38	6	4	10	8	5	3	1	4	4		1980-81	1982-83
Merkosky, Glenn	Hfd., N.J., Det.	4	63	5	12	17	22	....	....	....	....	....		1981-82	1985-86
Meronek, Bill	Mtl.	2	19	5	8	13	0	1	0	0	0	0		1939-40	1942-43
Merrick, Wayne	St.L., Cal., Clev., NYI	12	774	191	265	456	303	102	19	30	49	30	4	1972-73	1983-84
Merrill, Horace	Ott.	2	11	0	0	0	0	....	....	....	....	....	1	1917-18	1919-20
Messier, Paul	Col.	1	9	0	0	0	4	....	....	....	....	....		1978-79	1978-79
Metz, Don	Tor.	8	172	20	35	55	42	47	7	8	15	10	5	1939-40	1948-49
Metz, Nick	Tor.	12	518	131	119	250	149	76	19	20	39	31	4	1934-35	1947-48
Michaluk, Art	Chi.	1	5	0	0	0	0	....	....	....	....	....		1947-48	1947-48
Michaluk, John	Chi.	1	1	0	0	0	0	....	....	....	....	....		1950-51	1950-51
Michayluk, Dave	Phi.	2	14	2	6	8	8	....	....	....	....	....		1981-82	1982-83
Micheletti, Joe	St.L., Col.	3	158	11	60	71	114	11	1	11	12	10		1979-80	1981-82
Micheletii, Pat	Min.	1	12	2	0	2	8	....	....	....	....	....		1987-88	1987-88
Mickey, Larry	Chi., NYR., Tor., Mtl., L.A., Phi., Buf.	11	292	39	53	92	160	9	1	0	1	10		1964-65	1974-75
Mickoski, Nick	NYR, Chi., Det., Bos.	13	703	158	184	342	319	18	1	6	7	6		1947-48	1959-60
Middleton, Rick	NYR, Bos.	14	1005	448	540	988	157	114	45	55	100	19		1974-75	1987-88
Migay, Rudy	Tor.	10	418	59	92	151	293	15	1	0	1	20		1949-50	1959-60
Mikita, Stan	Chi.	22	1394	541	926	1467	1270	155	59	91	150	169	1	1958-59	1979-80
Mikkelson, Bill	L.A., N.Y.I., Wsh.	4	147	4	18	22	105	....	....	....	....	....		1971-72	1976-77
Mikol, Jim	Tor., NYR	2	34	1	4	5	8	....	....	....	....	....		1962-63	1964-65
Milbury, Mike	Bos.	12	754	49	189	238	1552	86	4	24	28	219		1975-76	1986-87
Milks, Hib	Pit., Phi., NYR, Ott.	8	314	87	41	128	179	10	0	0	0	2		1925-26	1932-33
Millar, Hugh	Det.	1	4	0	0	0	0	1	0	0	0	0		1946-47	1946-47
Miller, Bill	Mtl.M., Mtl.	3	95	7	3	10	16	12	0	0	0	0	1	1934-35	1936-37
Miller, Bob	Bos., Col., L.A.	6	404	75	119	194	220	36	4	7	11	27		1977-78	1984-85
Miller, Earl	Chi., Tor.	5	116	19	14	33	124	10	1	0	1	6	1	1927-28	1931-32
Miller, Jack	Chi.	2	17	0	0	0	4	....	....	....	....	....		1949-50	1950-51
Miller, Paul	Col.	1	3	0	3	3	0	....	....	....	....	....		1981-82	1981-82
Miller, Perry	Det.	4	217	10	51	61	387	....	....	....	....	....		1977-78	1980-81
Miller, Tom	Det., NYI	4	118	16	25	41	34	....	....	....	....	....		1970-71	1974-75
Miller, Warren	NYR, Hfd.	4	262	40	50	90	137	6	1	0	1	0		1979-80	1982-83
Minor, Gerry	Van.	5	140	11	21	32	173	12	1	3	4	25		1979-80	1983-84
Miszuk, John	Det., Chi., Phi., Min.	6	237	7	39	46	232	19	0	3	3	19		1963-64	1969-70
Mitchell, Bill	Det.	1	1	0	0	0	0	....	....	....	....	....		1963-64	1963-64
Mitchell, Herb	Bos.	2	53	6	0	6	38	....	....	....	....	....		1924-25	1925-26
Mitchell, Red	Chi.	3	83	4	5	9	67	....	....	....	....	....		1941-42	1944-45
Moe, Billy	NYR	5	261	11	42	53	163	1	0	0	0	0		1944-45	1948-49
Moffat, Lyle	Tor., Wpg.	3	97	12	16	28	51	....	....	....	....	....		1972-73	1979-80
Moffat, Ron	Det.	3	36	1	1	2	8	7	0	0	0	0		1932-33	1934-35
Moher, Mike	N.J.	1	9	0	1	1	28	....	....	....	....	....		1982-83	1982-83
Mohns, Doug	Bos., Chi., Min., Atl., Wsh.	22	1390	248	462	710	1250	94	14	36	50	122		1953-54	1974-75
Mohns, Lloyd	NYR	1	1	0	0	0	0	....	....	....	....	....		1943-44	1943-44
Molin, Lars	Van.	3	172	33	65	98	37	19	2	9	11	7		1981-82	1983-84
Moller, Mike	Buf., Edm.	7	134	15	28	43	41	3	0	1	1	0		1980-81	1986-87
Molyneaux, Larry	NYR	2	45	0	1	1	20	3	0	0	0	8		1937-38	1938-39
Monahan, Garry	Mtl., Det., L.A., Tor., Van.	12	748	116	169	285	484	22	3	1	4	13		1967-68	1978-79
Monahan, Hartland	Cal., NYR, Wsh., Pit., L.A., St.L.	7	334	61	80	141	163	6	0	0	0	4		1973-74	1980-81
Mondou, Armand	Mtl.	12	385	47	71	118	99	35	3	5	8	12	2	1928-29	1939-40
Mondou, Pierre	Mtl.	9	548	194	262	456	179	69	17	28	45	26	3	1976-77	1984-85
Mongrain, Bob	Buf., L.A.	6	83	13	14	27	14	11	1	2	3	2		1979-80	1985-86
Monteith, Hank	Det.	3	77	5	12	17	6	4	0	0	0	0		1968-69	1970-71
Moore, Dickie	Mtl., Tor., St.L.	14	719	261	347	608	652	135	46	64	110	122	6	1951-52	1967-68
Moran, Amby	Mtl., Chi.	2	35	1	1	2	24	....	....	....	....	....		1926-27	1927-28
Morenz, Howie	Mtl., Chi., NYR	14	550	273	197	470	563	47	21	11	32	68	3	1923-24	1936-37
Moretto, Angelo	Clev.	1	5	1	2	3	2	....	....	....	....	....		1976-77	1976-77
Morin, Pete	Mtl.	1	31	10	12	22	7	1	0	0	0	0		1941-42	1941-42
Morris, Bernie	Bos.	1	6	2	0	2	0	....	....	....	....	....		1924-25	1924-25
Morris, Elwyn	Tor., NYR	4	135	13	29	42	58	18	4	2	6	16	1	1943-44	1948-49
Morrison, Dave	L.A., Van.	4	39	3	3	6	4	....	....	....	....	....		1980-81	1984-85
Morrison, Don	Det., Chi.	3	112	18	28	46	12	3	0	1	1	0		1947-48	1950-51
Morrison, Doug	Bos.	4	23	7	3	10	15	....	....	....	....	....		1979-80	1984-85
Morrison, Gary	Phi.	3	43	1	15	16	70	5	0	1	1	2		1979-80	1981-82
Morrison, George	St.L.	2	115	17	21	38	13	3	0	0	0	0		1970-71	1971-72
Morrison, Jim	Bos., Tor., Det., NYR, Pit.	12	704	40	160	200	542	36	0	12	12	38		1951-52	1970-71
Morrison, John	NYA	1	18	0	0	0	0	....	....	....	....	....		1925-26	1925-26
Morrison, Kevin	Col.	1	41	4	11	15	23	....	....	....	....	....		1979-80	1979-80
Morrison, Lew	Phi., Atl., Wsh., Pit.	9	564	39	52	91	107	17	0	0	0	2		1969-70	1977-78
Morrison, Mark	NYR	2	10	1	1	2	0	....	....	....	....	....		1981-82	1983-84
Morrison, Roderick	Det.	1	34	8	7	15	4	3	0	0	0	0		1947-48	1947-48
Morrow, Ken	NYI	10	550	17	88	105	309	127	11	22	33	97	4	1979-80	1988-89
Mortson, Gus	Tor., Chi., Det.	13	797	46	152	198	1380	54	5	8	13	68	4	1946-47	1958-59

Name	NHL Teams	NHL Seasons	Regular Schedule GP	G	A	TP	PIM	Playoffs GP	G	A	TP	PIM	NHL Cup Wins	First NHL Season	Last NHL Season
Mosdell, Kenny	Bro., Mtl., Chi.	16	693	141	168	309	475	79	16	13	29	48	4	1941-42	1958-59
Mosienko, Bill	Chi.	14	711	258	282	540	117	22	10	4	14	15		1941-42	1954-55
Mott, Morris	Cal.	3	199	18	32	50	49	....	....	....	....	....		1972-73	1974-75
Motter, Alex	Bos., Det.	8	267	39	64	103	135	40	3	9	12	41	1	1934-35	1942-43
Moxey, Jim	Cal., Clev., L.A.	3	127	22	27	49	59	....	....	....	....	....		1974-75	1976-77
Mulhern, Richard	Atl., L.A., Tor., Wpg.	6	303	27	93	120	217	7	0	3	3	5		1975-76	1980-81
Muloin, Wayne	Det., Oak., Cal., Min.	3	147	3	21	24	93	11	0	0	0	2		1963-64	1970-71
Mulvey, Grant	Chi., N.J.	10	586	149	135	284	816	42	10	5	15	70		1974-75	1983-84
Mulvey, Paul	Wsh., Pit., L.A.	4	225	30	51	81	613	....	....	....	....	....		1978-79	1981-82
Mummery, Harry	Tor., Que., Mtl., Ham.	6	106	33	13	46	161	7	1	4	5	0		1917-18	1922-23
Munro, Dunc	Mtl.	8	239	28	18	46	170	25	3	2	5	24	1	1924-25	1931-32
Munro, Gerry	Mtl., Tor.	2	33	1	0	1	22	....	....	....	....	....		1924-25	1925-26
Murdoch, Bob L.	Cal., Clev., St.L.	4	260	72	85	157	127	....	....	....	....	....		1975-76	1978-79
Murdoch, Bob J.	Mtl., L.A., Atl., Cgy.	12	757	60	218	278	764	69	4	18	22	92	2	1970-71	1981-82
Murdoch, Don	NYR, Edm., Det.	6	320	121	117	238	155	24	10	8	18	16		1976-77	1981-82
Murdoch, Murray	NYR	11	507	84	108	192	197	55	9	12	21	28		1926-27	1936-37
Murphy, Brian	Det.	1	1	0	0	0	0	....	....	....	....	....		1974-75	1974-75
Murphy, Mike	St.L. NYR, L.A.	12	831	238	318	556	514	66	13	23	36	54		1971-72	1982-83
Murphy, Ron	NYR, Chi., Det., Bos.	18	889	205	274	479	460	53	7	8	15	26	1	1952-53	1969-70
Murray, Allan	NYA	7	277	5	9	14	163	14	0	0	0	8		1933-34	1939-40
Murray, Bob J.	Atl., Van.	4	194	6	16	22	98	9	1	1	2	15		1973-74	1976-77
Murray, Jim	L.A.	1	30	0	2	2	14	....	....	....	....	....		1967-68	1967-68
Murray, Ken	Tor., N.Y.I., Det., K.C.	5	106	1	10	11	135	....	....	....	....	....		1969-70	1975-76
Murray, Leo	Mtl.	1	6	0	0	0	2	....	....	....	....	....		1932-33	1932-33
Murray, Mike	Phi.	1	1	0	0	0	0	....	....	....	....	....		1987-88	1987-88
Murray, Randy	Tor.	1	3	0	0	0	2	....	....	....	....	....		1969-70	1969-70
Murray, Terry	Cal., Phi., Det., Wsh.	8	302	4	76	80	199	18	2	2	4	10		1972-73	1981-82
Myers, Hap	Buf.	1	13	0	0	0	6	....	....	....	....	....		1970-71	1970-71
Myles, Vic	NYR	1	45	6	9	15	57	....	....	....	....	....		1942-43	1942-43

N

Name	NHL Teams	NHL Seasons	Regular Schedule GP	G	A	TP	PIM	Playoffs GP	G	A	TP	PIM	NHL Cup Wins	First NHL Season	Last NHL Season
Nachbaur, Don	Hfd., Edm., Phi.	8	223	23	46	69	465	11	1	1	2	24		1980-81	1989-90
Nahrgang, Jim	Det.	3	57	5	12	17	34	....	....	....	....	....		1974-75	1976-77
Nanne, Lou	Min.	11	635	68	157	225	356	32	4	10	14	9		1967-68	1977-78
Nantais, Richard	Min.	3	63	5	4	9	79	....	....	....	....	....		1974-75	1976-77
Nattrass, Ralph	Chi.	4	223	18	38	56	308	....	....	....	....	....		1946-47	1949-50
Natyshak, Mike	Que.	1	4	0	0	0	0	....	....	....	....	....		1987-88	1987-88
Nechaev, Victor	L.A.	1	3	1	0	1	0	....	....	....	....	....		1982-83	1982-83
Nedomansky, Vaclav	Det., NYR, St.L.	6	421	122	156	278	88	7	3	5	8	0		1977-78	1982-83
Neely, Bob	Tor., Col.	5	283	39	59	98	266	26	5	7	12	15		1973-74	1977-78
Neilsen, Jim	NYR, Cal., Clev.	16	1023	69	299	368	904	65	1	17	18	61		1962-63	1977-78
Nelson, Gordie	Tor.	1	3	0	0	0	11	....	....	....	....	....		1969-70	1969-70
Nemeth, Steve	NYR	1	12	2	0	2	2	....	....	....	....	....		1987-88	1987-88
Nesterenko, Eric	Tor., Chi.	21	1219	250	324	574	1273	124	13	24	37	127	1	1951-52	1971-72
Nethery, Lance	NYR, Edm.	2	41	11	14	25	14	14	5	3	8	9		1980-81	1981-82
Neufeld, Ray	Hfd., Win., Bos.	11	595	157	200	357	816	28	8	6	14	55		1979-80	1989-90
Neville, Mike	Tor., NYA	4	62	6	3	9	14	2	0	0	0	0	1	1917-18	1930-31
Nevin, Bob	Tor., NYR, Min., L.A.	18	1128	307	419	726	211	84	16	18	34	24	2	1957-58	1975-76
Newberry, John	Mtl., Hfd.	4	22	0	4	4	6	2	0	0	0	0		1982-83	1985-86
Newell, Rick	Det.	2	7	0	0	0	0	....	....	....	....	....		1972-73	1973-74
Newman, Dan	NYR, Mtl., Edm.	4	126	17	24	41	63	3	0	0	0	4		1976-77	1979-80
Newman, John	Det.	1	8	1	1	2	0	....	....	....	....	....		1930-31	1930-31
Nicholson, Al	Bos.	2	19	0	1	1	4	....	....	....	....	....		1955-56	1956-57
Nicholson, Edward	Det.	1	1	0	0	0	0	....	....	....	....	....		1947-48	1947-48
Nicholson, Graeme	Bos., Col., NYR	3	52	2	7	9	60	....	....	....	....	....		1978-79	1982-83
Nicholson, John	Chi.	1	2	1	0	1	0	....	....	....	....	....		1937-38	1937-38
Nicholson, Neil	Oak., N.Y.I.	4	39	3	1	4	23	2	0	0	0	0		1969-70	1977-78
Nicholson, Paul	Wsh.	3	62	4	8	12	18	....	....	....	....	....		1974-75	1976-77
Niekamp, Jim	Det.	2	29	0	2	2	27	....	....	....	....	....		1970-71	1971-72
Nienhuis, Kraig	Bos.	3	87	20	16	36	39	2	0	0	0	14		1985-86	1987-88
Nighbor, Frank	Ott., Tor.	13	348	136	60	196	241	36	11	9	20	27	4	1917-18	1929-30
Nigro, Frank	Tor.	2	68	8	18	26	39	3	0	0	0	2		1982-83	1983-84
Nilsson, Kent	Atl., Cgy., Min., Edm.	8	547	263	422	685	116	59	11	41	52	14	1	1979-80	1986-87
Nilsson, Ulf	NYR	4	170	57	112	169	85	25	8	14	22	27		1978-79	1982-83
Nistico, Lou	Col.	1	3	0	0	0	0	....	....	....	....	....		1977-78	1977-78
Noble, Reg	Tor., Mtl.M., Det.	16	526	167	79	246	807	32	4	5	9	39	3	1917-18	1932-33
Noel, Claude	Wsh.	1	7	0	0	0	0	....	....	....	....	....		1979-80	1979-80
Nolan, Pat	Tor.	1	2	0	0	0	0	....	....	....	....	....	1	1921-22	1921-22
Nolan, Ted	Det., Pit.	3	78	6	16	22	105	....	....	....	....	....		1981-82	1985-86
Nolet, Simon	Phi., K.C., Pit., Col.	10	562	150	182	332	187	34	6	3	9	8	1	1967-68	1976-77
Noris, Joe	Pit., St.L., Buf.	3	55	2	5	7	22	....	....	....	....	....		1971-72	1973-74
Norrish, Rod	Min.	2	21	3	3	6	2	....	....	....	....	....		1973-74	1974-75
Northcott, Baldy	Mtl.M., Chi.	11	446	133	112	245	273	31	8	5	13	14	1	1928-29	1938-39
Norwich, Craig	Wpg., St.L., Col.	2	104	17	58	75	60	....	....	....	....	....		1979-80	1980-81
Novy, Milan	Wsh.	1	73	18	30	48	16	2	0	0	0	0		1982-83	1982-83
Nowak, Hank	Pit., Det., Bos.	4	180	26	29	55	161	13	1	0	1	8		1973-74	1976-77
Nykoluk, Mike	Tor.	1	32	3	1	4	20	....	....	....	....	....		1956-57	1956-57
Nyrop, Bill	Mtl., Min.	4	207	12	51	63	101	35	1	7	8	22	3	1975-76	1981-82
Nystrom, Bob	NYI	14	900	235	278	513	1248	157	39	44	83	236	4	1972-73	1985-86

O

Name	NHL Teams	NHL Seasons	Regular Schedule GP	G	A	TP	PIM	Playoffs GP	G	A	TP	PIM	NHL Cup Wins	First NHL Season	Last NHL Season
Oatman, Russell	Det., Mtl.M., NYR	3	124	20	9	29	100	17	1	0	1	18		1926-27	1928-29
O'Brien, Dennis	Min., Col., Clev., Bos.	10	592	31	91	122	1017	34	1	2	3	101		1970-71	1979-80
O'Brien, Obie	Bos.	1	2	0	0	0	0	....	....	....	....	....		1955-56	1955-56
O'Callahan, Jack	Chi., N.J.	7	389	27	104	131	541	32	4	11	15	41		1982-83	1988-89
O'Connell, Mike	Chi., Bos., Det.	13	860	105	334	439	605	82	8	24	32	64		1977-78	1989-90
O'Connor, Buddy	Mtl., NYR	10	509	140	257	397	34	53	15	21	36	6	2	1941-42	1950-51
Oddleifson, Chris	Bos., Van.	9	524	95	191	286	464	14	1	6	7	8		1972-73	1980-81
O'Donnell, Fred	Bos.	2	115	15	11	26	98	5	0	1	1	5		1972-73	1973-74
O'Donoghue, Don	Oak., Cal.	3	125	18	17	35	35	3	0	0	0	0		1969-70	1971-72
Odrowski, Gerry	Det., Oak., St.L.	6	299	12	19	31	111	30	0	1	1	16		1960-61	1971-72
O'Flaherty, Gerry	Tor., Van., Atl.	8	438	99	95	194	168	7	2	2	4	6		1971-72	1978-79
O'Flaherty, John	NYA, Bro.	2	21	5	1	6	0	....	....	....	....	....		1940-41	1941-42
Ogilvie, Brian	Chi., St.L.	6	90	15	21	36	29	....	....	....	....	....		1972-73	1978-79
O'Grady, George	Mtl.M.	1	4	0	0	0	0	....	....	....	....	....		1917-18	1917-18
Okerlund, Todd	NYI	1	4	0	0	0	2	....	....	....	....	....		1987-88	1987-88
Oliver, Harry	Bos., NYA	11	473	127	85	212	147	35	10	6	16	22	1	1926-27	1936-37
Oliver, Murray	Det., Bos., Tor., Min.	17	1127	274	454	728	319	35	9	16	25	10		1957-58	1974-75
Olmstead, Bert	Chi., Mtl., Tor.	14	848	181	421	602	884	115	16	42	58	101	5	1948-49	1961-62
Olson, Dennis	Det.	1	4	0	0	0	0	....	....	....	....	....		1957-58	1957-58
O'Neil, Paul	Van., Bos.	2	6	0	0	0	0	....	....	....	....	....		1973-74	1975-76
O'Neill, Jim	Bos., Mtl.	6	165	6	30	36	109	11	1	1	2	13		1933-34	1941-42
O'Neill, Tom	Tor.	2	66	10	12	22	53	4	0	0	0	6	1	1943-44	1944-45
O'Regan, Tom	Pit.	3	60	5	12	17	10	....	....	....	....	....		1983-84	1985-86
Orban, Bill	Chi., Min.	3	114	8	15	23	67	3	0	0	0	0		1967-68	1969-70
O'Ree, Willie	Bos.	2	45	4	10	14	26	....	....	....	....	....		1957-58	1960-61
O'Reilly, Terry	Bos.	14	891	204	402	606	2095	108	25	42	67	335		1971-72	1984-85
Orlando, Gaetano	Buf.	3	98	18	26	44	51	5	0	4	4	14		1984-85	1986-87
Orlando, Jimmy	Det.	6	200	7	24	31	375	36	0	9	9	105	1	1936-37	1942-43
Orleski, Dave	Mtl.	2	2	0	0	0	0	....	....	....	....	....		1980-81	1981-82
Orr, Bobby	Bos., Chi.	12	657	270	645	915	953	74	26	66	92	107	2	1966-67	1978-79
Osburn, Randy	Tor., Phi.	2	27	0	2	2	0	....	....	....	....	....		1972-73	1974-75
O'Shea, Danny	Min., Chi., St.L.	5	369	64	115	179	265	39	3	7	10	62		1968-69	1972-73
O'Shea, Kevin	Buf., St.L.	3	134	13	18	31	85	12	2	1	3	10		1970-71	1972-73
Ouelette, Eddie	Chi.	1	43	3	2	5	11	1	0	0	0	0		1935-36	1935-36
Ouelette, Gerry	Bos.	1	34	5	4	9	0	....	....	....	....	....		1960-61	1960-61
Owchar, Dennis	Pit., Col.	6	288	30	85	115	200	10	1	1	2	8		1974-75	1979-80
Owen, George	Bos.	5	192	44	33	77	151	21	2	5	7	25	1	1928-29	1932-33

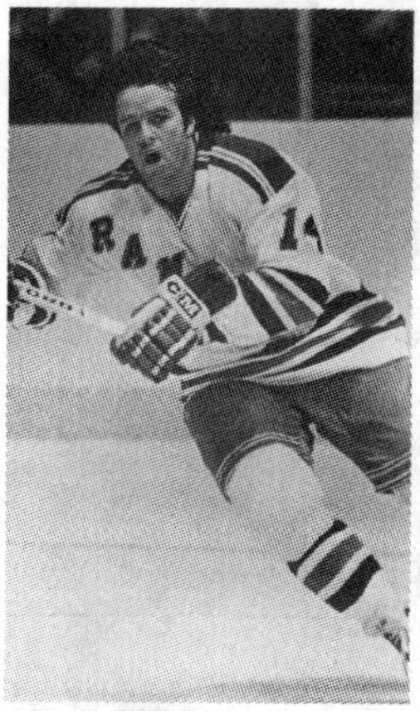

Don Murdoch

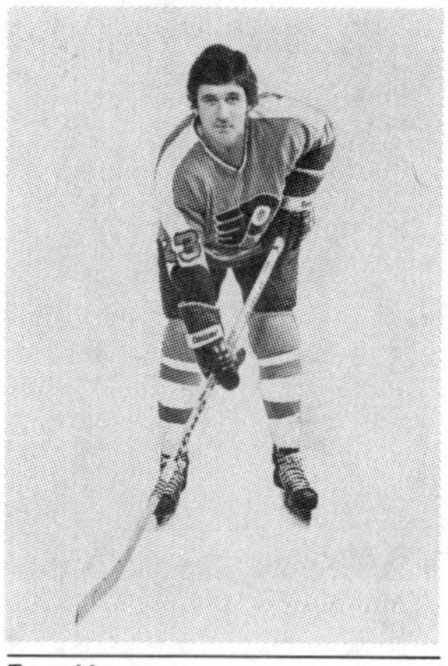

Terry Murray

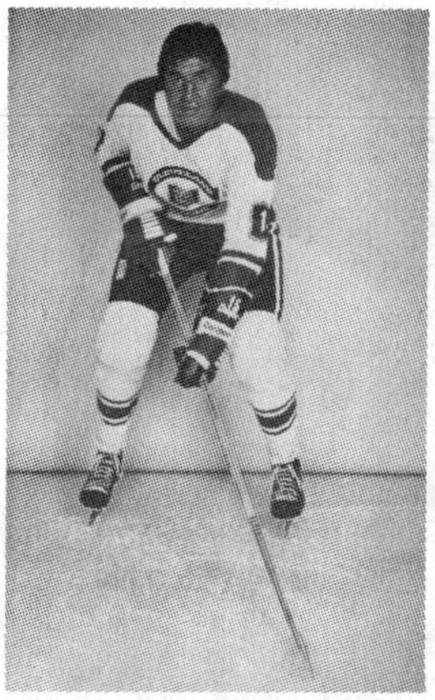

Jim Neilson

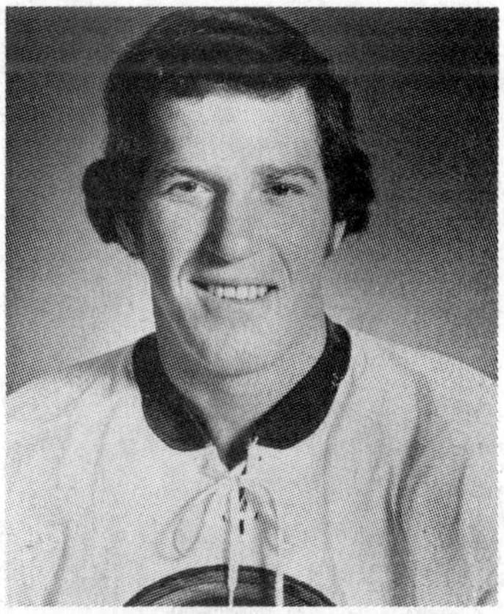

Neil Nicholson

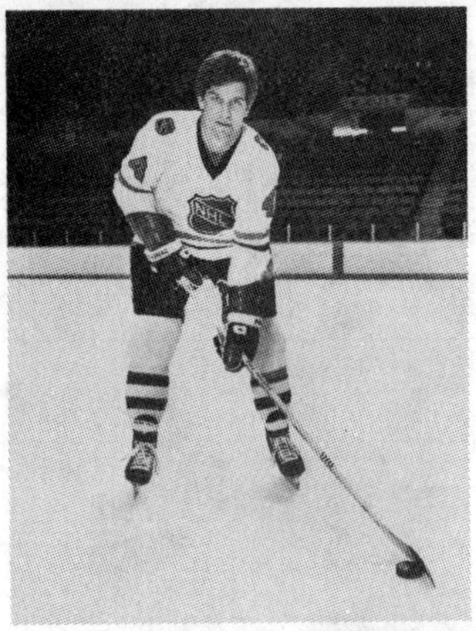

Bobby Orr

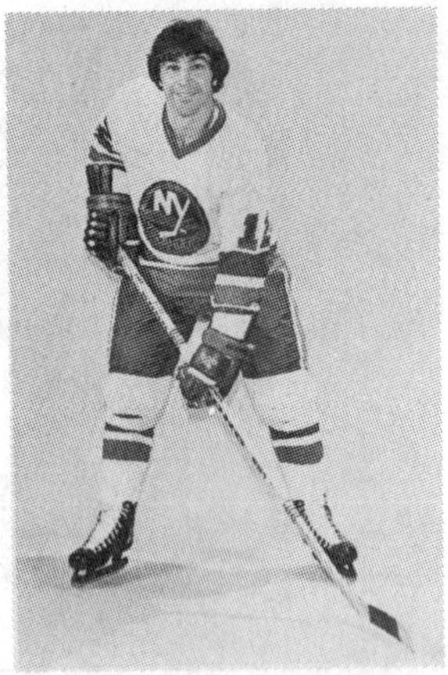

J.P. Parise

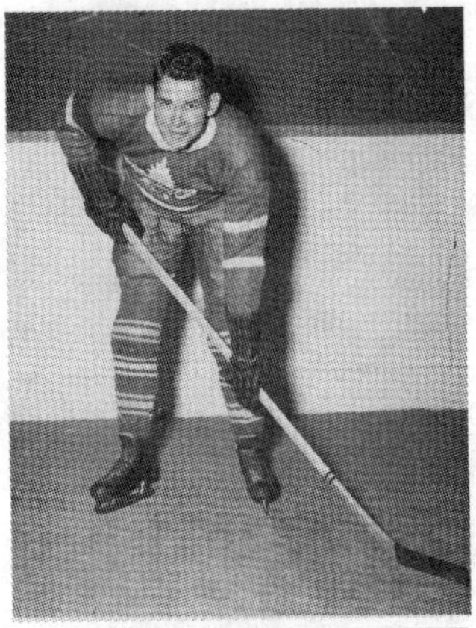

George Parsons

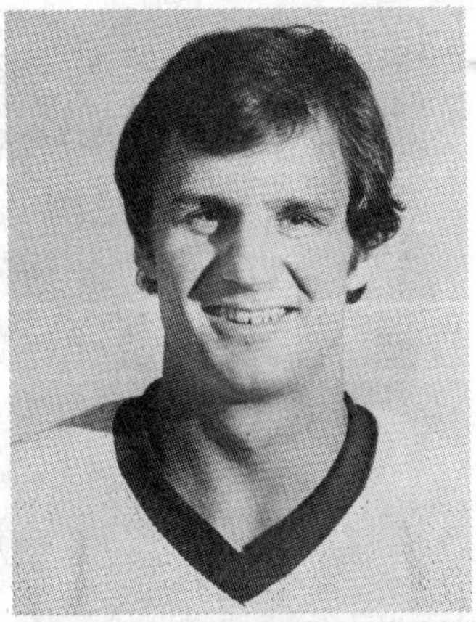

Stefan Persson

			Regular Schedule					Playoffs					NHL	First	Last
Name	NHL Teams	NHL Seasons	GP	G	A	TP	PIM	GP	G	A	TP	PIM	Cup Wins	NHL Season	NHL Season
P															
Pachal, Clayton	Bos., Col.	3	35	2	3	5	95	....	....	....	....	....		1976-77	1978-79
Paddock, John	Wsh., Phi., Que.	5	87	8	14	22	86	5	2	0	2	0		1975-76	1982-83
Paiement, Rosaire	Phi., Van.	5	190	48	52	100	343	3	3	0	3	0		1967-68	1971-72
Paiement, Wilf	K.C., Col., Tor., Que., NYR, Buf., Pit.	14	946	356	458	814	1757	69	18	17	35	185		1974-75	1987-88
Palangio, Peter	Mtl., Det., Chi.	5	71	13	10	23	28	7	0	0	0	0	1	1926-27	1937-38
Palazzari, Aldo	Bos., NYR	1	35	8	3	11	4	....	....	....	....	....		1943-44	1943-44
Palazzari, Doug	St.L.	4	108	18	20	38	23	2	0	0	0	0		1974-75	1978-79
Palmer, Brad	Min., Bos.	3	168	32	38	70	58	29	9	5	14	16		1980-81	1982-83
Palmer, Rob R.	L.A., N.J.	7	320	9	101	110	115	8	1	2	3	6		1977-78	1983-84
Palmer, Rob H.	Chi.	3	16	0	3	3	2	....	....	....	....	....		1973-74	1975-76
Panagabko, Ed	Bos.	2	29	0	3	3	38	....	....	....	....	....		1955-56	1956-57
Papike, Joe	Chi.	3	21	3	3	6	4	5	0	2	2	0		1940-41	1944-45
Pappin, Jim	Tor., Chi., Cal., Clev.	14	767	278	295	573	667	92	33	34	67	101	2	1963-64	1976-77
Paradise, Bob	Min., Atl., Pit., Wsh.	8	368	8	54	62	393	12	0	1	1	19		1971-72	1978-79
Pargeter, George	Mtl.	1	4	0	0	0	0	....	....	....	....	....		1946-47	1946-47
Parise, J.P.	Bos., Tor., Min., NYI, Clev.	14	890	238	356	594	706	86	27	31	58	87		1965-66	1978-79
Parizeau, Michel	St.L., Phi.	1	58	3	14	17	18	....	....	....	....	....		1971-72	1971-72
Park, Brad	NYR, Bos., Det.	17	1113	213	683	896	1429	161	35	90	125	217		1968-69	1984-85
Parkes, Ernie	Mtl.M.	1	17	0	0	0	2	....	....	....	....	....		1924-25	1924-25
Parsons, George	Tor.	3	64	12	13	25	17	7	3	2	5	11		1936-37	1938-39
Paterson, Mark	Hfd.	4	29	3	3	6	33	....	....	....	....	....		1982-83	1985-86
Paterson, Rick	Chi.	9	430	50	43	93	136	61	7	10	17	51		1978-79	1986-87
Patey, Doug	Wsh.	3	45	4	2	6	8	....	....	....	....	....		1976-77	1978-79
Patey, Larry	Cal., St.L., NYR	12	717	153	163	316	631	40	8	10	18	57		1973-74	1984-85
Patrick, Craig	Cal., St.L., K.C., Min., Wsh.	8	401	72	91	163	61	2	0	1	1	0		1971-72	1978-79
Patrick, Glenn	St.L., Cal., Clev.	3	38	2	3	5	72	....	....	....	....	....		1973-74	1976-77
Patrick, Lester	NYR	1	1	0	0	0	2	....	....	....	....	....		1926-27	1926-27
Patrick, Lynn	NYR	10	455	145	190	335	240	44	10	6	16	22	1	1934-35	1945-46
Patrick, Muzz	NYR	5	166	5	26	31	133	25	4	0	4	34	1	1937-38	1945-46
Patrick, Steve	Buf., NYR, Que.	6	250	40	68	108	242	12	0	1	1	12		1980-81	1985-86
Patterson, Dennis	K.C., Phi.	3	138	6	22	28	67	....	....	....	....	....		1974-75	1979-80
Patterson, George	Bos., Det., St.L., Tor., Mtl., NYA	9	289	51	27	78	218	3	0	0	0	2		1926-27	1934-35
Paul, Butch	Det.	1	3	0	0	0	0	....	....	....	....	....		1964-65	1964-65
Paulus, Rollie	Mtl.	1	33	0	0	0	0	....	....	....	....	....		1925-26	1925-26
Pavelich, Marty	Det.	10	634	93	159	252	454	91	13	15	28	74	4	1947-48	1956-57
Pavese, Jim	St.L., NYR, Det., Hfd.	8	328	13	44	57	689	34	0	6	6	81		1981-82	1988-89
Payer, Evariste	Mtl.	1	1	0	0	0	0	....	....	....	....	....		1917-18	1917-18
Payne, Steve	Min.	10	613	228	238	466	435	71	35	35	70	60		1978-79	1987-88
Pearson, Mel	NYR, Pit.	5	38	2	6	8	25	....	....	....	....	....		1949-50	1967-68
Peer, Bert	Det.	1	1	0	0	0	0	....	....	....	....	....		1939-40	1939-40
Peirson, Johnny	Bos.	11	545	153	173	326	315	49	9	17	26	26		1946-47	1957-58
Pelensky, Perry	Chi.	1	4	0	0	0	5	....	....	....	....	....		1983-84	1983-84
Pelletier, Roger	Phi.	1	1	0	0	0	0	....	....	....	....	....		1967-68	1967-68
Peloffy, Andre	Wsh.	1	9	0	0	0	2	....	....	....	....	....		1974-75	1974-75
Pelyk, Mike	Tor.	9	441	26	88	114	566	40	0	3	3	41		1967-68	1977-78
Pennington, Cliff	Mtl., Bos.	3	101	17	42	59	6	....	....	....	....	....		1960-61	1962-63
Peplinski, Jim	Cgy.	10	705	161	262	423	1456	99	15	31	46	382	1	1980-81	1989-90
Perlini, Fred	Tor.	2	8	2	3	5	0	....	....	....	....	....		1981-82	1983-84
Perreault, Fern	NYR	2	3	0	0	0	0	....	....	....	....	....		1947-48	1949-50
Perreault, Gilbert	Buf.	17	1191	512	814	1326	500	90	33	70	103	44		1970-71	1986-87
Perry, Brian	Oak., Buf.	3	96	16	29	45	24	8	1	1	2	4		1968-69	1970-71
Persson, Stefan	NYI	9	622	52	317	369	574	102	7	50	57	69	4	1977-78	1985-86
Pesut, George	Cal.	2	92	3	22	25	130	....	....	....	....	....		1974-75	1975-76
Peters, Frank	NYR	1	43	0	0	0	59	4	0	0	0	2		1930-31	1930-31
Peters, Garry	Mtl., NYR, Phi., Bos.	8	331	34	34	68	261	9	2	2	4	31	1	1964-65	1971-72
Peters, Jim	Det., Chi., Mtl., Bos.	9	574	125	150	275	186	60	5	9	14	22	3	1945-46	1953-54
Peters, Jimmy	Det., L.A.	9	309	37	36	73	48	11	0	2	2	2		1964-65	1974-75
Peters, Steve	Col.	1	2	0	1	1	0	....	....	....	....	....		1979-80	1979-80
Peterson, Brent	Det., Buf., Van., Hfd.	10	620	72	141	213	484	31	4	4	8	65		1979-80	1988-89
Pettersson, Jorgen	St.L., Hfd., Wsh.	6	435	174	192	366	117	44	15	12	27	4		1980-81	1985-86
Pettinger, Eric	Ott., Bos., Tor.	3	97	7	12	19	83	4	1	0	1	8		1928-29	1930-31
Pettinger, Gord	Det., NYR, Bos.	8	292	42	74	116	77	49	4	5	9	11	4	1932-33	1939-40
Phair, Lyle	L.A.	3	48	6	7	13	12	1	0	0	0	0		1985-86	1987-88
Phillipoff, Harold	Atl., Chi.,	3	141	26	57	83	267	6	0	2	2	9		1977-78	1979-80
Phillips, Bat	Mtl.M.	1	27	1	1	2	6	4	0	0	0	2		1929-30	1929-30
Phillips, Bill	Mtl.M., NYA.	8	302	52	31	83	232	28	6	2	8	19	1	1925-26	1932-33
Phillips, Charlie	Mtl.	1	17	0	0	0	6	....	....	....	....	....		1942-43	1942-43
Picard, Noel	Atl., Mtl., St.L.	7	335	12	63	75	616	50	2	11	13	167	1	1964-65	1972-73
Picard, Robert	Wsh. Tor., Mtl., Wpg., Que., Det.	13	899	104	319	423	1025	36	5	15	20	39		1977-78	1989-90
Picard, Roger	St.L.	1	15	2	2	4	21	....	....	....	....	....		1967-68	1967-68
Pichette, Dave	Que., St.L., N.J., NYR	7	322	41	140	181	348	28	3	7	10	54		1980-81	1987-88
Picketts, Hal	NYA.	1	48	3	1	4	32	....	....	....	....	....		1933-34	1933-34
Pidhirny, Harry	Bos.	1	2	0	0	0	0	....	....	....	....	....		1957-58	1957-58
Pierce, Randy	Col., N.J., Hfd.	8	277	62	76	138	223	2	0	0	0	0		1977-78	1984-85
Pike, Alf	NYR	6	234	42	77	119	145	21	4	2	6	12	1	1939-40	1946-47
Pilote, Pierre	Chi., Tor.	14	890	80	418	498	1251	86	8	53	61	102	1	1955-56	1968-69
Pinder, Gerry	Chi., Cal.	3	223	55	69	124	135	17	0	4	4	6		1969-70	1971-72
Pirus, Alex	Min., Det.	4	159	30	28	58	94	2	0	1	1	2		1976-77	1979-80
Pitre, Didier	Mtl.	6	127	64	17	81	50	14	2	2	4	0		1917-18	1922-23
Plager, Barclay	St.L.	10	614	44	187	231	1115	68	3	20	23	182		1967-68	1976-77
Plager, Bob	NYR, St.L.	14	644	20	126	146	802	74	2	17	19	195		1964-65	1977-78
Plager, William	Min., St.L., Atl.	9	263	4	34	38	292	31	0	2	2	26		1967-68	1975-76
Plamondon, Gerry	Mtl.	5	74	7	13	20	10	11	5	2	7	2	1	1945-46	1950-51
Plante, Cam	Tor.	1	2	0	0	0	0	....	....	....	....	....		1984-85	1984-85
Plante, Pierre	NYR, Que., Phi., St.L., Chi.	9	599	125	172	297	599	33	2	6	8	51		1971-72	1979-80
Plantery, Mark	Wpg.	1	25	1	5	6	14	....	....	....	....	....		1980-81	1980-81
Plaxton, Hugh	Mtl.M.	1	15	1	2	3	4	....	....	....	....	....		1932-33	1932-33
Playfair, Larry	Buf., L.A.	12	688	26	94	120	1812	43	0	6	6	111		1978-79	1989-90
Pleau, Larry	Mtl.	3	94	9	15	24	27	4	0	0	0	0		1969-70	1971-72
Plett, Willi	Atl., Cgy., Min., Bos.	13	834	222	215	437	2572	83	24	22	46	466		1975-76	1987-88
Plumb, Rob	Det.	1	7	2	1	3	0	....	....	....	....	....		1977-78	1977-78
Plumb, Ron	Hfd.	1	26	3	4	7	14	....	....	....	....	....		1979-80	1979-80
Pocza, Harvie	Wsh.	2	3	0	0	0	0	....	....	....	....	....		1979-80	1981-82
Podolsky, Nels	Det.	1	1	0	0	0	0	7	0	0	0	4		1948-49	1948-49
Poeta, Anthony	Chi.	1	1	0	0	0	0	....	....	....	....	....		1951-52	1951-52
Poile, Bud	NYR, Bos., Det., Tor., Chi.,	7	311	107	122	229	91	23	4	4	8	8	1	1942-43	1949-50
Poile, Don	Det.	2	66	7	9	16	12	4	0	0	0	0		1954-55	1957-58
Poirer, Gordie	Mtl.	1	10	0	1	1	0	....	....	....	....	....		1939-40	1939-40
Polanic, Tom	Min.	2	19	0	2	2	53	5	1	1	2	4		1969-70	1970-71
Polich, John	NYR	2	3	0	1	1	0	....	....	....	....	....		1939-40	1940-41
Polich, Mike	Mtl., Min.	5	226	24	29	53	57	23	2	1	3	2	1	1976-77	1980-81
Polis, Greg	Pit., St.L., NYR, Wsh.	10	615	174	169	343	391	7	0	2	2	6		1970-71	1979-80
Poliziani, Daniel	Bos.	1	1	0	0	0	0	3	0	0	0	0		1958-59	1958-59
Polonich, Dennis	Det.	8	390	59	82	141	1242	7	1	0	1	19		1974-75	1982-83
Pooley, Poul	Wpg.	2	15	0	3	3	0	....	....	....	....	....		1984-85	1985-86
Popein, Larry	NYR, Oak.	8	449	80	141	221	162	16	1	4	5	6		1954-55	1967-68
Popiel, Paul	Bos., L.A., Det., Van., Edm.	7	224	13	41	54	210	4	1	0	1	4		1965-66	1979-80
Portland, Jack	Chi., Mtl., Bos.	10	381	15	56	71	323	33	1	3	4	25	1	1933-34	1942-43
Porvari, Jukka	Col., N.J.	2	39	3	9	12	4	....	....	....	....	....		1981-82	1982-83
Posa, Victor	Chi.	1	2	0	0	0	2	....	....	....	....	....		1985-86	1985-86
Posavad, Mike	St.L.	2	8	0	0	0	0	....	....	....	....	....		1985-86	1986-87
Potvin, Denis	NYI	15	1060	310	742	1052	1356	185	56	108	164	253	4	1973-74	1987-88
Potvin, Jean	L.A., Min., Phi., NYI, Cle.	11	613	63	224	287	478	39	2	9	11	17	1	1970-71	1980-81
Poudrier, Daniel	Que.	1	25	1	5	6	10	....	....	....	....	....		1985-86	1987-88
Poulin, Dan	Min., Phi.	2	5	3	1	4	4	....	....	....	....	....		1981-82	1982-83
Pouzar, Jaroslav	Edm.	4	186	34	48	82	135	29	6	4	10	16	3	1982-83	1986-87
Powell, Ray	Chi.	1	31	7	15	22	2	....	....	....	....	....		1950-51	1950-51
Powis, Geoff	Chi.	1	2	0	0	0	0	....	....	....	....	....		1967-68	1967-68
Powis, Lynn	Chi., K.C.	2	130	19	33	52	25	1	0	0	0	0		1973-74	1974-75

			Regular Schedule					Playoffs							
Name	NHL Teams	NHL Seasons	GP	G	A	TP	PIM	GP	G	A	TP	PIM	NHL Cup Wins	First NHL Season	Last NHL Season
Pratt, Babe	Bos., NYR, Tor.	12	517	83	209	292	473	63	12	17	29	90	2	1935-36	1946-47
Pratt, Jack	Bos.	2	37	2	0	2	42	4	0	0	0	0		1930-31	1931-32
Pratt, Kelly	Pit.	1	22	0	6	6	15	....	....	....	....	....		1974-75	1974-75
Pratt, Tracy	Van., Col., Buf., Pit. Tor., Oak.	10	580	17	97	114	1026	25	0	1	1	62		1967-68	1976-77
Prentice, Dean	Pit., Min., Det., NYR, Bos.	22	1378	391	469	860	484	54	13	17	30	38		1952-53	1973-74
Prentice, Eric	Tor.	1	5	0	0	0	4	....	....	....	....	....		1943-44	1943-44
Preston, Rich	Chi., N.J.	8	580	127	164	291	348	47	4	18	22	56		1979-80	1986-87
Preston, Yves	Phi.	2	28	7	3	10	4	....	....	....	....	....		1978-79	1980-81
Price, Bob	Ott.	1	1	0	0	0	0	....	....	....	....	....		1919-20	1919-20
Price, Jack	Chi.	3	57	4	6	10	24	4	0	0	0	0		1951-52	1953-54
Price, Noel	Pit., L.A., Det., Tor., NYR, Mtl., Atl.	14	499	14	114	128	333	12	0	1	1	8	1	1957-58	1975-76
Price, Pat	NYI, Edm., Pit., Que., NYR, Min.	13	726	43	218	261	1456	74	2	10	12	195		1975-76	1987-88
Price, Tom	Cal., Clev., Pit.	5	29	0	2	2	12	....	....	....	....	....		1974-75	1978-79
Primeau, Joe	Tor.	9	310	66	177	243	105	38	5	18	23	12	1	1927-28	1935-36
Primeau, Kevin	Van.	1	2	0	0	0	4	....	....	....	....	....		1980-81	1980-81
Pringle, Ellie	NYA	1	6	0	0	0	0	....	....	....	....	....		1930-31	1930-31
Prodgers, Goldie	Tor., Ham.	6	110	63	22	85	33	....	....	....	....	....		1919-20	1924-25
Pronovost, Andre	Det., Min., Mtl., Bos.	10	556	94	104	198	408	70	11	11	22	58	4	1956-57	1967-68
Pronovost, Jean	Wsh., Pit., Atl.	14	998	391	383	774	413	35	11	9	20	14		1968-69	1981-82
Pronovost, Marcel	Det., Tor.	21	1206	88	257	345	851	134	8	23	31	104	5	1950-51	1969-70
Provost, Claude	Mtl.	15	1005	254	335	589	469	126	25	38	63	86	9	1955-56	1969-70
Prystai, Metro	Chi., Det.	11	674	151	179	330	231	43	12	14	26	8	2	1947-48	1957-58
Pudas, Al	Tor.	1	3	0	0	0	0	....	....	....	....	....		1926-27	1926-27
Pulford, Bob	Tor., L.A.	16	1079	281	362	643	792	89	25	26	51	126	4	1956-57	1971-72
Pulkkinen, Dave	NYI	1	2	0	0	0	0	....	....	....	....	....		1972-73	1972-73
Purpur, Cliff	Det., Chi., St.L.	5	144	26	34	60	46	16	1	2	3	4		1934-35	1944-45
Pusie, Jean	Mtl., NYR, Bos.	5	61	1	4	5	28	7	0	0	0	0	1	1930-31	1935-36
Pyatt, Nelson	Det., Wsh., Col.	7	296	71	63	134	69	....	....	....	....	....		1973-74	1979-80

Q

Quackenbush, Bill	Det., Bos.	14	774	62	222	284	95	79	2	19	21	8		1942-43	1955-56
Quackenbush, Max	Bos., Chi.,	2	61	4	7	11	30	6	0	0	0	4		1950-51	1951-52
Quenneville, Leo	NYR	1	25	0	3	3	10	3	0	0	0	0		1929-30	1929-30
Quilty, John	Mtl., Bos.	4	125	36	34	70	81	13	3	5	8	9		1940-41	1947-48
Quinn, Pat	Tor., Van., Atl.	9	606	18	113	131	950	11	0	1	1	21		1968-69	1976-77

R

Radley, Yip	NYA, Mtl.M.	2	18	0	1	1	13	....	....	....	....	....		1930-31	1936-37
Raglan, Clare	Det., Chi.	3	100	4	9	13	52	3	0	0	0	0		1950-51	1952-53
Raleigh, Don	NYR	10	535	101	219	320	96	18	6	5	11	6		1943-44	1955-56
Ramsay, Beattie	Tor.,	1	43	0	2	2	10	....	....	....	....	....		1927-28	1927-28
Ramsay, Craig	Buf.	14	1070	252	420	672	201	89	17	31	48	27		1971-72	1984-85
Ramsay, Wayne	Buf.	1	2	0	0	0	0	....	....	....	....	....		1977-78	1977-78
Ramsey, Les	Chi.	1	11	2	2	4	2	....	....	....	....	....		1944-45	1944-45
Randall, Ken	Tor., Ham., NYA	10	217	67	28	95	360	13	3	1	4	19	2	1917-18	1926-27
Ranieri, George	Bos.	1	2	0	0	0	0	....	....	....	....	....		1956-57	1956-57
Ratelle, Jean	NYR, Bos.	21	1281	491	776	1267	276	123	32	66	98	24		1960-61	1980-81
Rathwell, John	Bos.	1	1	0	0	0	0	....	....	....	....	....		1974-75	1974-75
Rausse, Errol	Wsh.	3	31	7	3	10	0	....	....	....	....	....		1979-80	1981-82
Rautakallio, Pekka	Atl., Cgy.	3	235	33	121	154	122	23	2	5	7	8		1979-80	1981-82
Ravlich, Matt	Bos., Chi., Det., L.A.	9	410	12	78	90	364	24	1	5	6	16		1962-63	1972-73
Raymond, Armand	Mtl.	2	22	0	2	2	10	....	....	....	....	....		1937-38	1939-40
Raymond, Paul	Mtl.	4	76	2	3	5	6	5	0	0	0	2		1932-33	1937-38
Read, Mel	NYR	1	1	0	0	0	0	....	....	....	....	....		1946-47	1946-47
Reardon, Ken	Mtl.	7	341	26	96	122	604	31	2	5	7	62	1	1940-41	1949-50
Reardon, Terry	Bos., Mtl.	7	193	47	53	100	73	30	8	10	18	12	1	1938-39	1946-47
Reaume, Marc	Tor., Det., Mtl., Van.	9	344	8	43	51	273	21	0	2	2	8		1954-55	1970-71
Reay, Billy	Det., Mtl.	10	479	105	162	267	202	63	13	16	29	43	2	1943-44	1952-53
Redahl, Gord	Bos.	1	18	0	1	1	2	....	....	....	....	....		1958-59	1958-59
Redding, George	Bos.	2	35	3	2	5	10	....	....	....	....	....		1924-25	1925-26
Redmond, Craig	L.A., Edm.	5	191	16	68	84	134	3	1	0	1	2		1984-85	1988-89
Redmond, Dick	Min., Cal., Chi., St.L., Atl., Bos.	13	771	133	312	445	504	66	9	22	31	27		1969-70	1981-82
Redmond, Mickey	Mtl., Det.	9	538	233	195	428	219	16	2	3	5	2	2	1967-68	1975-76
Reeds, Mark	St.L., Hfd.	8	365	45	114	159	135	53	8	9	17	23		1981-82	1988-89
Regan, Bill	NYR, NYA	3	67	3	2	5	67	8	0	0	0	2		1929-30	1932-33
Regan, Larry	Bos., Tor.,	5	280	41	95	136	71	42	7	14	21	18		1956-57	1960-61
Regier, Darcy	Clev., NYI	3	26	0	2	2	35	....	....	....	....	....		1977-78	1983-84
Reibel, Earl	Det., Chi., Bos.	6	409	84	161	245	75	39	6	14	20	4	2	1953-54	1958-59
Reid, Dave	Tor.	3	7	0	0	0	0	....	....	....	....	....		1952-53	1955-56
Reid, Gerry	Det.	1	....	....	....	....	....	2	0	0	0	2		1948-49	1948-49
Reid, Gordie	NYA	1	1	0	0	0	2	....	....	....	....	....		1936-37	1936-37
Reid, Reg	Tor.	2	40	2	0	2	4	2	0	0	0	0		1924-25	1925-26
Reid, Tom	Chi., Min.	11	701	17	113	130	654	42	1	13	14	49		1967-68	1977-78
Reigle, Ed	Bos.	1	17	0	2	2	25	....	....	....	....	....		1950-51	1950-51
Reinhart, Paul	Atl., Cgy., Van.	11	648	133	426	559	277	83	23	54	77	42		1979-80	1989-90
Reinikka, Ollie	NYR	1	16	0	0	0	0	....	....	....	....	....		1926-27	1926-27
Reise, Leo Jr.	Chi., Det., NYR	9	494	28	81	109	399	52	8	5	13	68	2	1945-46	1953-54
Reise, Leo Sr.	Ham., NYA, NYR	8	199	36	29	65	177	6	0	0	0	16		1920-21	1929-30
Renaud, Mark	Hfd., Buf.	5	152	6	50	56	86	....	....	....	....	....		1979-80	1983-84
Ribble, Pat	Atl., Chi., Tor., Wsh., Cgy.	8	349	19	60	79	365	8	0	1	1	12		1975-76	1982-83
Richard, Henri	Mtl.	20	1256	358	688	1046	928	180	49	80	129	181	11	1955-56	1974-75
Richard, Jacques	Alt., Buf., Que.	10	556	160	187	347	307	35	5	5	10	34		1972-73	1982-83
Richard, Maurice	Mtl.	18	978	544	421	965	1285	133	82	44	126	188	8	1942-43	1959-60
Richardson, Dave	NYR, Chi., Det.	4	45	3	2	5	27	....	....	....	....	....		1963-64	1967-68
Richardson, Glen	Van.	1	24	3	6	9	19	....	....	....	....	....		1975-76	1975-76
Richardson, Ken	St.L.	3	49	8	13	21	16	....	....	....	....	....		1974-75	1978-79
Richer, Bob	Buf.	1	3	0	0	0	0	....	....	....	....	....		1972-73	1972-73
Riley, Bill	Wsh., Wpg.	5	139	31	30	61	320	....	....	....	....	....		1974-75	1979-80
Riley, Jack	Det., Mtl., Bos.,	4	104	10	22	32	8	4	0	3	3	0		1932-33	1935-36
Riley, Jim	Det.	1	17	0	2	2	14	....	....	....	....	....		1926-27	1926-27
Riopellie, Howard	Mtl.	3	169	27	16	43	73	8	1	1	2	2		1947-48	1949-50
Rioux, Gerry	Wpg.	1	8	0	0	0	6	....	....	....	....	....		1979-80	1979-80
Rioux, Pierre	Cgy.	1	14	1	2	3	4	....	....	....	....	....		1982-83	1982-83
Ripley, Vic	Chi., Bos., NYR, St.L.	7	278	51	49	100	173	20	4	1	5	10		1928-29	1934-35
Risebrough, Doug	Mtl., Cgy.	14	740	185	286	471	1542	124	21	37	58	238	4	1974-75	1986-87
Rissling, Gary	Wsh., Pit.	7	221	23	30	53	1008	5	0	1	1	4		1978-79	1984-85
Ritchie, Bob	Phi., Det.	2	29	8	4	12	10	....	....	....	....	....		1976-77	1977-78
Ritchie, Dave	Mtl.W, Ott., Tor., Que., Mtl.	6	54	15	3	18	27	1	0	0	0	0		1917-18	1925-26
Ritson, Alex	NYR	1	1	0	0	0	0	....	....	....	....	....		1944-45	1944-45
Rittinger, Alan	Bos.	1	19	3	7	10	0	....	....	....	....	....		1943-44	1943-44
Rivard, Bob	Pit.	1	27	5	12	17	4	....	....	....	....	....		1967-68	1967-68
Rivers, Gus	Mtl.	3	88	4	5	9	12	16	2	0	2	2	2	1929-30	1931-32
Rivers, Wayne	Det., Bos., St.L., NYR	7	108	15	30	45	94	....	....	....	....	....		1961-62	1968-69
Rizzuto, Garth	Van.	1	37	3	4	7	16	....	....	....	....	....		1970-71	1970-71
Roach, Mickey	Tor., Ham., NYA	8	209	75	27	102	41	....	....	....	....	....		1919-20	1926-27
Robert, Claude	Mtl.	1	23	1	0	1	9	....	....	....	....	....		1950-51	1950-51
Robert, Rene	Tor., Pit., Buf., Col.	12	744	284	418	702	597	50	22	19	41	73		1970-71	1981-82
Robert, Sammy	Ott.	1	1	0	0	0	0	....	....	....	....	....		1917-18	1917-18
Roberto, Phil	Mtl., St.L., Det., K.C., Col., Clev.	8	385	75	106	181	464	31	9	8	17	69	1	1969-70	1976-77
Roberts, Doug	Det., Dak., Cal., Bos.	10	419	43	104	147	342	16	2	3	5	46		1965-66	1974-75
Roberts, Jim	Mtl., St.L.	15	1006	126	194	320	621	153	20	16	36	160	5	1963-64	1977-78
Roberts, Jimmy	Min.	3	106	17	23	40	33	2	0	0	0	0		1976-77	1978-79
Robertson, Fred	Tor., Det.,	2	34	1	0	1	35	7	0	0	0	0	1	1931-32	1933-34
Robertson, Geordie	Buf.	1	5	1	2	3	7	....	....	....	....	....		1982-83	1982-83
Robertson, George	Mtl.	2	31	2	5	7	6	....	....	....	....	....		1947-48	1948-49
Robidoux, Florent	Chi.	3	52	7	4	11	75	....	....	....	....	....		1980-81	1983-84
Robinson, Doug	Chi., NYR, L.A.	7	239	44	67	111	34	11	4	3	7	0		1963-64	1970-71
Robinson, Douglas	Min.	1	1	0	0	0	2	....	....	....	....	....		1989-90	1989-90
Robinson, Earl	Mtl.M., Chi., Mtl.	11	418	83	98	181	123	25	5	4	9	0	1	1928-29	1939-40

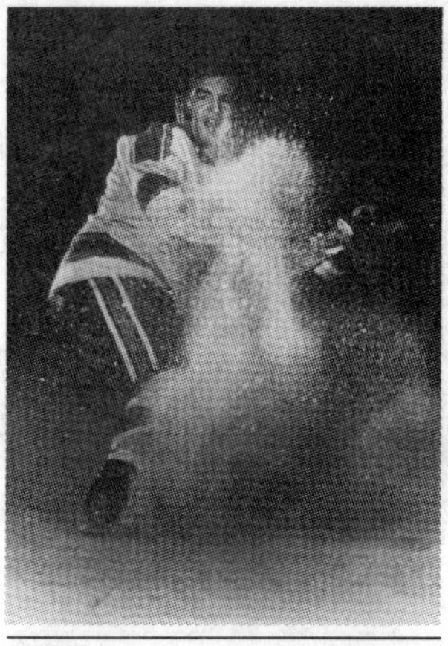

Bob Plager

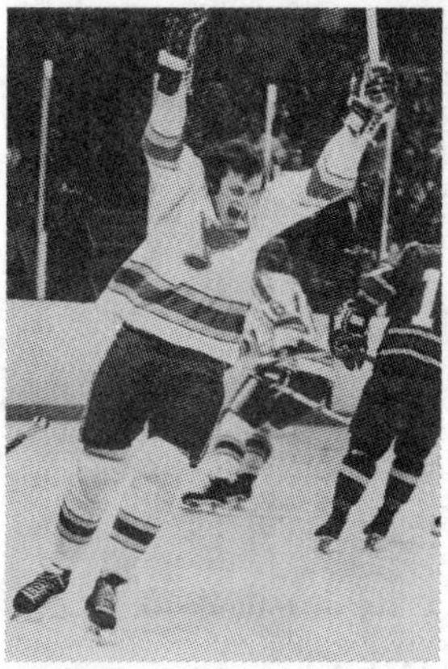

Pierre Plante

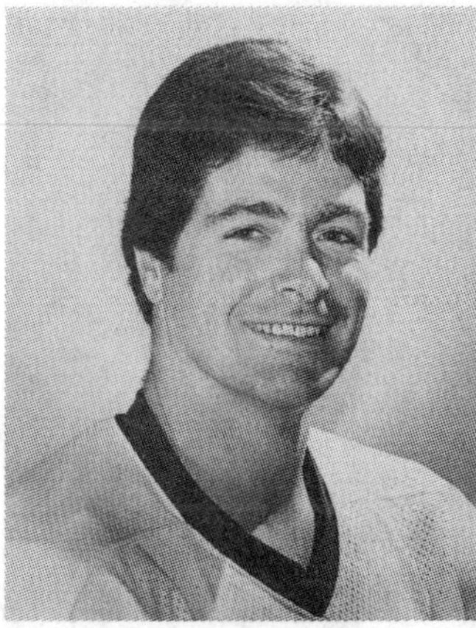

Jean Potvin

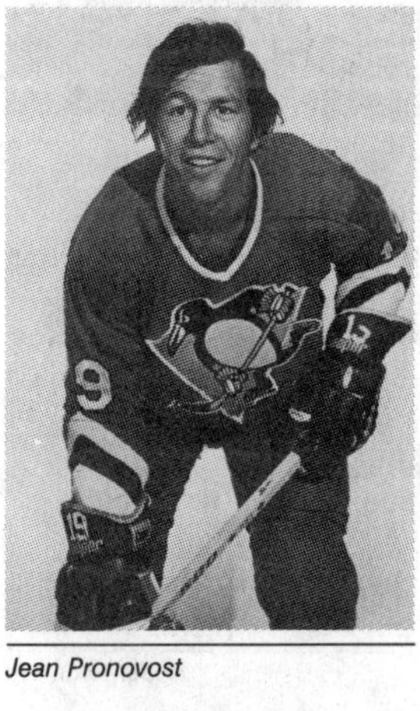

Jean Pronovost

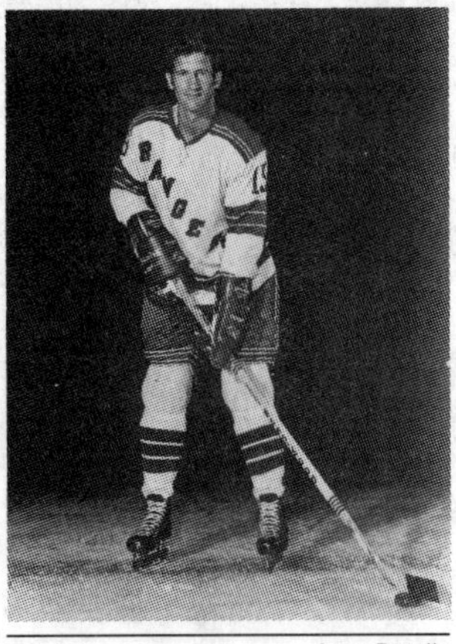

Jean Ratelle

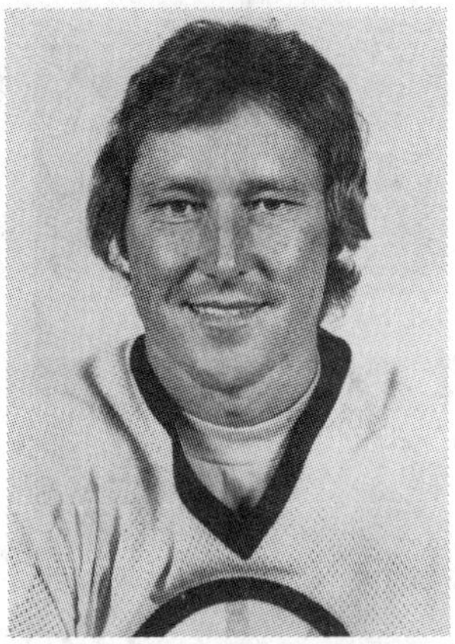

Dick Redmond

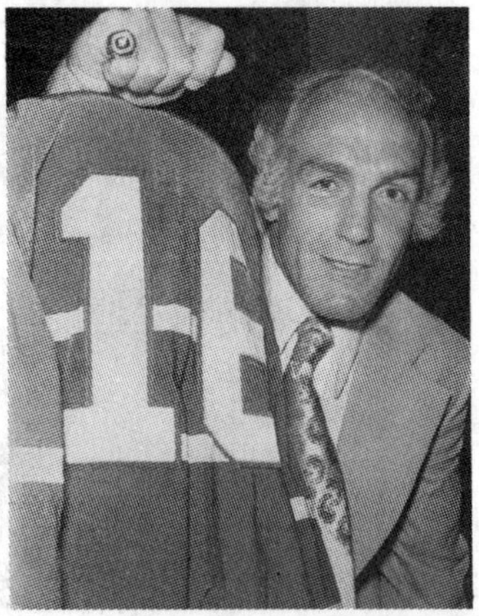

Henri Richard

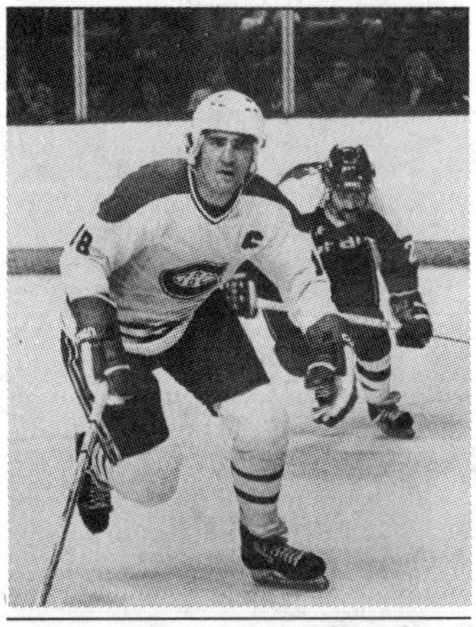

Serge Savard

Name	NHL Teams	NHL Seasons	Regular Schedule GP	G	A	TP	PIM	Playoffs GP	G	A	TP	PIM	NHL Cup Wins	First NHL Season	Last NHL Season
Robinson, Moe	Mtl.	1	1	0	0	0	0	....	....	....	....	....		1979-80	1979-80
Robitaille, Mike	NYR, Det., Buf., Van.	8	382	23	105	128	280	13	0	1	1	4		1969-70	1976-77
Roche, Michel	Mtl.M., Ott., St.L., Mtl., Det.	4	112	20	18	38	44	....	....	....	....	....		1930-31	1934-35
Roche, Earl	Mtl.M., Bos., Ott., St.L., Det.	4	146	25	27	52	48	2	0	0	0	0		1930-31	1934-35
Roche, Ernest	Mtl.	1	4	0	0	0	2	....	....	....	....	....		1950-51	1950-51
Rochefort, Dave	Det.	1	1	0	0	0	0	....	....	....	....	....		1966-67	1966-67
Rochefort, Leon	NYR, Mtl., Phi., L.A., Det., Atl., Van.	15	617	121	147	268	93	39	4	4	8	16	2	1960-61	1975-76
Rockburn, Harvey	Det., Ott.	3	94	4	2	6	254	....	....	....	....	....		1929-30	1932-33
Rodden, Eddie	Chi., Tor., Bos., NYR	4	98	6	14	20	152	2	0	1	1	0	1	1926-27	1930-31
Rogers, Alfred	Min.	2	14	2	4	6	0	....	....	....	....	....		1973-74	1974-75
Rogers, Mike	Hfd., NYR, Edm.	7	484	202	317	519	184	17	1	13	14	6		1979-80	1985-86
Rolfe, Dale	Bos., L.A., Det., NYR	9	509	25	125	150	556	71	5	24	29	89		1959-60	1974-75
Romanchych, Larry	Chi., Atl	6	298	68	97	165	102	7	2	2	4	4		1970-71	1976-77
Rombough, Doug	Buf., NYI, Min.	4	150	24	27	51	80	....	....	....	....	....		1972-73	1975-76
Romnes, Doc	Chi., Tor., NYA	10	359	68	136	204	42	43	7	18	25	4	2	1930-31	1939-40
Ronan, Skene	Ott.	1	11	0	0	0	0	....	....	....	....	....		1918-19	1918-19
Ronson, Len	NYR, Oak.	2	18	2	1	3	10	....	....	....	....	....		1960-61	1968-69
Ronty, Paul	Bos., NYR, Mtl.	8	488	101	211	312	103	21	1	7	8	6		1947-48	1954-55
Ross, Art	Mtl.W	1	3	1	0	1	0	....	....	....	....	....		1917-18	1917-18
Ross, Jim	NYR	2	62	2	11	13	29	....	....	....	....	....		1951-52	1952-53
Rossignol, Roland	Det., Mtl.	3	14	3	5	8	6	1	0	0	0	2		1943-44	1945-46
Rota, Darcy	Chi., Atl., Van.	11	794	256	239	495	973	60	14	7	21	147		1973-74	1983-84
Rota, Randy	Mtl., L.A., K.C., Col.	5	212	38	39	77	60	5	0	1	1	0		1972-73	1976-77
Rothschild, Sam	Mtl.M., NYA	4	99	8	6	14	24	10	0	0	0	0	1	1924-25	1927-28
Roulston, Rolly	Det.	3	24	0	6	6	10	....	....	....	....	....	1	1935-36	1937-38
Roulston, Tom	Edm., Pit.	6	195	47	49	96	74	21	2	2	4	2		1980-81	1985-86
Rousseau, Bobby	Mtl., Min., NYR	15	942	245	458	703	359	128	27	57	84	69	4	1960-61	1974-75
Rousseau, Guy	Mtl.	2	4	0	1	1	0	....	....	....	....	....		1954-55	1956-57
Rousseau, Roland	Mtl.	1	2	0	0	0	0	....	....	....	....	....		1952-53	1952-53
Routhier, Jean-Marc	Que.	1	8	0	0	0	9	....	....	....	....	....		1989-90	1989-90
Rowe, Bobby	Bos.	1	4	1	0	1	0	....	....	....	....	....		1924-25	1924-25
Rowe, Mike	Pit.	3	11	0	0	0	11	....	....	....	....	....		1984-85	1986-87
Rowe, Ron	NYR	1	5	1	0	1	0	....	....	....	....	....		1947-48	1947-48
Rowe, Tom	Wsh., Hfd., Det.	7	357	85	100	185	615	3	2	0	2	0		1976-77	1982-83
Roy, Stephane	Min.	1	12	1	0	1	0	....	....	....	....	....		1987-88	1987-88
Rozzini, Gino	Bos.	1	31	5	10	15	20	6	1	2	3	6		1944-45	1944-45
Rucinski, Mike	Chi.	2	1	0	0	0	0	2	0	0	0	0		1987-88	1988-89
Ruelle, Bernard	Det.	1	2	1	0	1	0	....	....	....	....	....		1943-44	1943-44
Ruhnke, Kent	Bos.	1	2	0	1	1	0	....	....	....	....	....		1975-76	1975-76
Rundqvist, Thomas	Mtl.	1	2	0	1	1	0	....	....	....	....	....		1984-85	1984-85
Runge, Paul	Bos., Mtl.M., Mtl.	7	143	18	22	40	57	7	0	0	0	6		1930-31	1937-38
Ruotsalinen, Reijo	NYR, Edm.	6	405	104	225	329	160	64	13	21	34	32	2	1981-82	1986-87
Rupp, Duane	NYR, Tor., Min., Pit.	10	374	24	93	117	220	10	2	2	4	8		1962-63	1972-73
Ruskowski, Terry	Chi., L.A., Pit., Min.	10	630	113	313	426	1354	21	1	6	7	86		1979-80	1988-89
Russell, Churchill	NYR	3	90	20	16	36	12	....	....	....	....	....		1945-46	1947-48
Russell, Phil	Chi., Atl., Cgy., N.J., Buf.	15	1016	99	325	424	2038	73	4	22	26	202		1972-73	1986-87

S

Name	NHL Teams	NHL Seasons	Regular Schedule GP	G	A	TP	PIM	Playoffs GP	G	A	TP	PIM	NHL Cup Wins	First NHL Season	Last NHL Season
Saarinen, Simo	NYR	1	8	0	0	0	0	....	....	....	....	....		1984-85	1984-85
Sabourin, Bob	Tor.	1	1	0	0	0	2	....	....	....	....	....		1951-52	1951-52
Sabourin, Gary	St.L., Tor., Cal., Clev.	10	627	169	188	357	397	62	19	11	30	58		1967-68	1976-77
Sacharuk, Larry	NYR, St.L.	5	151	29	33	62	42	2	1	1	2	2		1972-73	1976-77
Saganiuk, Rocky	Tor., Pit.	6	259	57	65	122	201	6	1	0	1	15		1978-79	1983-84
St. Laurent, Andre	NYI, Det., L.A., Pit.	11	644	129	187	316	749	59	8	12	20	48		1973-74	1983-84
St. Laurent, Dollard	Mtl., Chi.	12	652	29	133	162	496	92	2	22	24	87	5	1950-51	1961-62
St. Marseille, Frank	St.L., L.A.	10	707	140	285	425	242	88	20	25	45	18		1967-68	1976-77
St. Sauveur, Claude	Atl.	1	79	24	24	48	23	2	0	0	0	0		1975-76	1975-76
Saleski, Don	Phi., Col.	9	543	128	125	253	629	82	13	17	30	131	2	1971-72	1979-80
Salovaara, John	Det.	2	90	2	13	15	70	....	....	....	....	....		1974-75	1975-76
Salvian, Dave	NYI	1	....	0	1	1	2	1	0	1	1	2		1976-77	1976-77
Samis, Phi.	Tor.	2	2	0	0	0	0	5	0	1	1	2	1	1947-48	1949-50
Sampson, Gary	Wsh.	4	105	13	22	35	25	12	1	0	1	0		1983-84	1986-87
Sanderson, Derek	Bos., NYR, St.L., Van., Pit.	13	598	202	250	452	911	56	18	12	30	187	2	1965-66	1977-78
Sandford, Ed	Bos., Det., Chi.	9	502	106	145	251	355	42	12	11	24	27		1947-48	1955-56
Sands, Charlie	Tor., Bos., Mtl., NYR	12	432	99	109	208	58	44	6	6	12	4	1	1932-33	1943-44
Sargent, Gary	L.A., Min.	8	402	61	161	222	273	20	5	7	12	8		1975-76	1982-83
Sarner, Craig	Bos.	1	7	0	0	0	0	....	....	....	....	....		1974-75	1974-75
Sarrazin, Dick	Phi.	3	100	20	35	55	22	4	0	0	0	0		1968-69	1971-72
Saskamoose, Fred	Chi.	1	11	0	0	0	6	....	....	....	....	....		1953-54	1953-54
Sasser, Grant	Pit.	1	3	0	0	0	0	....	....	....	....	....		1983-84	1983-84
Sather, Glen	Bos., Pit., NYR, St.L., Mtl., Min.	10	658	80	113	193	724	72	1	5	6	86		1966-67	1975-76
Saunders, Bernie	Que.	2	10	0	1	1	8	....	....	....	....	....		1979-80	1980-81
Saunders, Bud	Ott.	1	19	1	3	4	4	....	....	....	....	....		1933-34	1933-34
Saunders, David	Van.	1	56	7	13	20	10	....	....	....	....	....		1987-88	1987-88
Sauve, Jenn F.	Buf., Que.	7	290	65	138	203	117	36	9	12	21	10		1980-81	1986-87
Savage, Tony	Bos., Mtl.	1	49	1	5	6	6	2	0	0	0	0		1934-35	1934-35
Savard, Andre	Bos., Buf., Que.	12	790	211	271	482	411	85	13	18	31	77		1973-74	1984-85
Savard, Jean	Chi., Hfd.	3	43	7	12	19	29	....	....	....	....	....		1977-78	1979-80
Savard, Serge	Mtl., Wpg.	17	1040	106	333	439	592	130	19	49	68	88	7	1966-67	1982-83
Scamurra, Peter	Wsh.	4	132	8	25	33	59	....	....	....	....	....		1975-76	1979-80
Sceviour, Darin	Chi.	1	1	0	0	0	0	....	....	....	....	....		1986-87	1986-87
Schaeffer, Butch	Chi.,	1	5	0	0	0	6	....	....	....	....	....		1936-37	1936-37
Schamehorn, Kevin	Det., L.A.	3	10	0	0	0	17	....	....	....	....	....		1976-77	1980-81
Schella, John	Van.	2	115	2	18	20	224	....	....	....	....	....		1970-71	1971-72
Scherza, Chuck	Bos., NYR	2	56	6	6	12	35	....	....	....	....	....		1943-44	1944-45
Schinkel, Ken	NYR, Pit.	12	636	127	198	325	163	19	7	2	9	4		1959-60	1972-73
Schliebener, Andy	Van.	3	84	2	11	13	74	6	0	0	0	0		1981-82	1984-85
Schmautz, Bobby	Chi., Bos., Edm., Col., Van.	13	764	271	286	557	988	73	28	33	61	92		1967-68	1980-81
Schmautz, Cliff	Buf., Phi.	1	56	13	19	32	33	....	....	....	....	....		1970-71	1970-71
Schmidt, Clarence	Bos.,	1	7	1	0	1	2	....	....	....	....	....		1943-44	1943-44
Schmidt, Jackie	Bos.	1	45	6	7	13	6	5	0	0	0	0		1942-43	1942-43
Schmidt, Joseph	Bos.	1	2	0	0	0	0	....	....	....	....	....		1943-44	1943-44
Schmidt, Milt	Bos.	16	778	229	346	575	466	86	24	25	49	60	2	1936-37	1954-55
Schmidt, Norm	Pit.	4	125	23	33	56	73	....	....	....	....	....		1983-84	1987-88
Schnarr, Werner	Bos.	2	25	0	0	0	0	....	....	....	....	....		1924-25	1925-26
Schock, Danny	Bos., Phi.	2	20	1	2	3	0	1	0	0	0	0	1	1969-70	1970-71
Schock, Ron	Bos., St.L., Pit., Buf.	15	909	166	351	517	260	55	4	16	20	29		1963-64	1977-78
Schoenfeld, Jim	Buf., Det., Bos.	13	719	51	204	255	1132	75	3	13	16	151		1972-73	1984-85
Schofield, Dwight	Det., Mtl., St.L., Wsh., Pit., Wpg.	7	211	8	22	30	631	9	0	0	0	55		1976-77	1987-88
Schreiber, Wally	Min.	2	41	8	10	18	12	....	....	....	....	....		1987-88	1988-89
Schriner, Sweeny	NYA, Tor.	11	484	201	204	405	148	60	18	11	29	54	2	1934-35	1945-46
Schultz, Dave	Phi., L.A., Pit., Buf.	9	535	79	121	200	2294	73	8	12	20	412	2	1971-72	1979-80
Schurman, Maynard	Hfd.	1	7	0	0	0	0	....	....	....	....	....		1979-80	1979-80
Schutt, Rod	Mtl., Pit., Tor.	8	286	77	92	169	177	22	8	6	14	26		1977-78	1985-86
Sclisizzi, Enio	Det., Chi.	6	81	12	11	23	26	13	0	0	0	6		1946-47	1952-53
Scott, Ganton	Tor., Ham., Mtl.M.	3	53	1	1	2	0	....	....	....	....	....		1922-23	1924-25
Scott, Laurie	NYA, NYR	2	62	6	3	9	28	....	....	....	....	....	1	1926-27	1927-28
Scruton, Howard	L.A.	1	4	0	4	4	9	....	....	....	....	....		1982-83	1982-83
Seabrooke, Glen	Phi.	3	19	1	6	7	4	....	....	....	....	....		1986-87	1988-89
Secord, Al	Bos., Chi., Tor, Phi.	12	766	273	222	495	2093	102	21	34	55	382		1978-79	1989-90
Sedlbauer, Ron	Van., Chi., Tor.	7	430	143	86	229	210	19	1	3	4	27		1974-75	1980-81
Seguin, Dan	Min., Van.	2	37	2	6	8	50	....	....	....	....	....		1970-71	1973-74
Seguin, Steve	L.A.	1	5	0	0	0	9	....	....	....	....	....		1984-85	1984-85
Seibert, Earl	NYR, Chi., Det.	15	652	89	187	276	768	11	8	9	19	66	2	1931-32	1945-46
Seiling, Ric	Buf., Det.	10	738	179	208	387	573	62	14	14	28	36		1977-78	1986-87
Seiling, Rod	Tor., NYR, Wsh., St.L., Atl.	17	979	62	269	331	603	77	4	8	12	55		1962-63	1978-79
Selby, Brit	Tor., Phi., St.L.	8	350	55	62	117	163	16	1	1	2	8		1964-65	1971-72
Self, Steve	Wsh.	1	3	0	0	0	0	....	....	....	....	....		1976-77	1976-77
Selwood, Brad	Tor., L.A.	3	163	7	40	47	153	6	0	0	0	4		1970-71	1979-80
Semenko, Dave	Edm., Hfd., Tor.	9	575	65	88	153	1175	73	6	6	12	208	2	1979-80	1987-88
Senick, George	NYR	1	13	2	3	5	8	....	....	....	....	....		1952-53	1952-53

			Regular Schedule					Playoffs					NHL	First	Last
Name	NHL Teams	NHL Seasons	GP	G	A	TP	PIM	GP	G	A	TP	PIM	Cup Wins	NHL Season	NHL Season
Seppa, Jyrki	Wpg.	1	13	0	2	2	6	....	....	....	....	....		1983-84	1983-84
Serafini, Ron	Cal.	1	2	0	0	0	2	....	....	....	....	....		1973-74	1973-74
Servinis, George	Min.	1	5	0	0	0	0	....	....	....	....	....		1987-88	1987-88
Shack, Eddie	NYR, Tor., Bos., L.A., Buf., Pit.	17	1047	239	226	465	1437	74	6	7	13	151	4	1958-59	1974-75
Shack, Joe	NYR	2	70	23	13	36	20	....	....	....	....	....		1942-43	1944-45
Shakes, Paul	Cal.	1	21	0	4	4	12	....	....	....	....	....		1973-74	1973-74
Shanahan, Sean	Mtl., Col., Bos.	3	40	1	3	4	47	....	....	....	....	....		1975-76	1977-78
Shand, Dave	Atl., Tor., Wsh.	8	421	19	84	103	544	26	1	2	3	83		1976-77	1984-85
Shannon, Charles	NYA	1	4	0	0	0	2	....	....	....	....	....		1939-40	1939-40
Shannon, Gerry	Ott., St.L., Bos., Mtl.M.	5	183	23	29	52	121	9	0	1	1	2		1933-34	1937-38
Sharpley, Glen	Min., Chi.	6	389	117	161	278	199	27	7	11	18	24		1976-77	1981-82
Shaunessy, Scott	Que.	1	3	0	0	0	7	....	....	....	....	....		1986-87	1986-87
Shay, Norman	Bos., Tor.	2	53	5	2	7	34	....	....	....	....	....		1924-25	1925-26
Shea, Pat	Chi.	1	14	0	1	1	0	....	....	....	....	....		1931-32	1931-32
Sheehan, Bobby	Mtl., Cal., Chi., Det., NYR, Col., L.A.	9	310	48	63	111	50	25	4	3	7	8	1	1969-70	1981-82
Sheehy, Tim	Det., Hfd.	2	27	2	1	3	0	....	....	....	....	....		1977-78	1979-80
Shelton, Doug	Chi.	1	5	0	1	1	0	....	....	....	....	....		1967-68	1967-68
Sheppard, Frank	Det.	1	8	1	1	2	0	....	....	....	....	....		1927-28	1927-28
Sheppard, Gregg	Bos., Pit.	10	657	205	293	498	243	92	32	40	72	31		1972-73	1981-82
Sheppard, Johnny	Det., NYA, Bos., Chi.	8	311	68	58	126	224	10	0	0	0	0	1	1926-27	1933-34
Sherf, John	Det.	5	19	0	0	0	8	8	0	1	1	2	1	1935-36	1943-44
Shero, Fred	NYR	3	145	6	14	20	137	13	0	2	2	8		1947-48	1949-50
Sherritt, Gordon	Det.	1	8	0	0	0	12	....	....	....	....	....		1943-44	1943-44
Sherven, Gord	Edm., Min., Hfd.	5	97	13	22	35	33	3	0	0	0	0		1983-84	1987-88
Shewchuck, Jack	Bos.	6	187	9	19	28	160	20	0	1	1	19	1	1938-39	1944-45
Shibicky, Alex	NYR	8	317	110	91	201	159	40	12	12	24	12	1	1935-36	1945-46
Shields, Al	Ott., Phi., NYA, Mtl.M., Bos.	11	460	42	46	88	637	17	0	1	1	14	1	1927-28	1937-38
Shill, Bill	Bos.	3	79	21	13	34	18	7	1	2	3	2		1942-43	1946-47
Shill, Jack	Tor., Bos., NYA, Chi.	6	163	15	20	35	70	27	1	6	7	13	1	1933-34	1938-39
Shinske, Rick	Clev., St.L.	3	63	5	16	21	10	....	....	....	....	....		1976-77	1978-79
Shires, Jim	Det., St.L., Pit.	3	56	3	6	9	32	....	....	....	....	....		1970-71	1972-73
Shmyr, Paul	Chi., Cal., Min., Hfd.	7	343	13	72	85	528	34	3	3	6	44		1968-69	1981-82
Shore, Eddie	Bos., NYA	14	553	105	179	284	1047	55	6	13	19	187	2	1926-27	1939-40
Shore, Hamby	Ott.	1	18	3	0	3	0	....	....	....	....	....		1917-18	1917-18
Shores, Aubry	Phi.	1	1	0	0	0	0	....	....	....	....	....		1930-31	1930-31
Short, Steve	L.A., Det.	2	6	0	0	0	2	....	....	....	....	....		1977-78	1978-79
Shudra, Ron	Edm.	1	10	0	5	5	6	....	....	....	....	....		1987-88	1987-88
Shutt, Steve	Mtl., L.A.	13	930	424	393	817	410	99	50	48	98	65	5	1972-73	1984-85
Siebert, Babe	Mtl.M., NYR, Bos., Mtl.	14	593	140	156	296	982	54	8	7	15	62	2	1925-26	1938-39
Silk, Dave	NYR, Bos., Wpg., Det.	7	249	54	59	113	271	13	2	4	6	13		1979-80	1985-86
Siltala, Mike	Wsh., NYR	3	7	1	0	1	2	....	....	....	....	....		1981-82	1987-88
Siltanen, Risto	Edm., Hfd., Que.	8	562	90	265	355	266	32	6	12	18	30		1979-80	1986-87
Simonetti, Frank	Bos.	4	115	5	8	13	76	12	0	1	1	8		1984-85	1987-88
Simmer, Charlie	Cal., Cle., L.A., Bos., Pit.	14	712	342	369	711	544	24	9	9	18	32		1974-75	1987-88
Simmons, Al	Cal., Bos.	3	11	0	1	1	21	1	0	0	0	0		1971-72	1975-76
Simon, Cully	Det., Chi.	3	130	4	11	15	121	14	0	1	1	6	1	1942-43	1944-45
Simon, Thain	Det.	1	3	0	0	0	0	....	....	....	....	....		1946-47	1946-47
Simpson, Bobby	Atl., St.L., Pit.	5	175	35	29	64	98	6	0	1	1	2		1976-77	1982-83
Simpson, Cliff	Det.	2	6	0	1	1	0	2	0	0	0	0		1946-47	1947-48
Simpson, Joe	NYA	6	228	21	19	40	156	2	0	0	0	0		1925-26	1930-31
Sims, Al	Bos., Hfd., L.A.	10	475	49	116	165	286	41	0	2	2	14		1973-74	1982-83
Sinclair, Reg	NYR, Det.	3	208	49	43	92	139	3	1	0	1	0		1950-51	1952-53
Singbush, Alex	Mtl.	1	32	0	5	5	15	3	0	0	0	4		1940-41	1940-41
Sirois, Bob	Phi., Wsh.	6	286	92	120	212	42	....	....	....	....	....		1974-75	1979-80
Sittler, Darryl	Tor., Phi., Det.	15	1096	484	637	1121	948	76	29	45	74	137		1970-71	1984-85
Sjoberg, Lars-Erik	Wpg.	1	79	7	27	34	48	....	....	....	....	....		1979-80	1979-80
Skaare, Bjorne	Det.	1	1	0	0	0	0	....	....	....	....	....		1978-79	1978-79
Skilton, Raymie	Mtl.W	1	1	1	0	1	0	....	....	....	....	....		1917-18	1917-18
Skinner, Alf	Tor., Bos., Mtl.M., Pit.	4	70	26	4	30	56	7	8	1	9	0	1	1917-18	1925-26
Skinner, Larry	Col.	4	47	10	12	22	8	2	0	0	0	0		1976-77	1979-80
Skov, Glen	Det., Chi., Mtl.	12	650	106	136	242	413	53	7	7	14	48	3	1949-50	1960-61
Sleaver, John	Chi.	2	24	2	0	2	6	....	....	....	....	....		1953-54	1956-57
Sleigher, Louis	Que., Bos.	6	194	46	53	99	146	17	1	1	2	64		1979-80	1985-86
Sloan, Tod	Tor., Chi.	13	745	220	262	482	781	47	9	12	21	47	2	1947-48	1960-61
Slobodzian, Peter	NYA	1	41	3	2	5	54	....	....	....	....	....		1940-41	1940-41
Slowinski, Eddie	NYR	6	291	58	74	132	63	16	2	6	8	6		1947-48	1952-53
Sly, Darryl	Tor., Min., Van.	4	79	1	2	3	20	....	....	....	....	....		1965-66	1970-71
Smart, Alec	Mtl.	1	8	2	5	7	0	....	....	....	....	....		1942-43	1942-43
Smedsmo, Dale	Tor.	1	4	0	0	0	0	....	....	....	....	....		1972-73	1972-73
Smillie, Don	Bos.	1	12	2	2	4	4	....	....	....	....	....		1933-34	1933-34
Smith, Alex	Ott., Det., Bos., NYA	11	443	41	50	91	643	19	0	2	2	40	1	1924-25	1934-35
Smith, Arthur	Tor., Ott.	4	137	15	10	25	249	4	1	1	2	8		1927-28	1930-31
Smith, Barry	Bos., Col.	3	114	7	7	14	10	....	....	....	....	....		1975-76	1980-81
Smith, Brad	Van., Atl., Cgy., Det., Tor.	9	222	28	34	62	591	20	3	3	6	49		1978-79	1986-87
Smith, Brian D.	L.A., Min.	2	67	10	10	20	33	7	0	0	0	0		1967-68	1968-69
Smith, Brian S.	Det.	3	61	2	8	10	12	5	0	0	0	0		1957-58	1960-61
Smith, Carl	Det.	1	7	1	1	2	2	....	....	....	....	....		1943-44	1943-44
Smith, Clint	NYR, Chi.	11	483	161	236	397	24	44	10	14	24	2	1	1936-37	1946-47
Smith, Dallas	Bos., NYR	16	890	55	252	307	959	86	3	29	32	128	2	1959-60	1977-78
Smith, Dalton	NYA, Det.	2	11	1	2	3	0	....	....	....	....	....		1936-37	1943-44
Smith, Derek	Buf., Det.	8	335	78	116	194	60	30	9	14	23	13		1975-76	1982-83
Smith, Des	Mtl.M., Mtl., Chi., Bos.	5	195	22	25	47	236	25	1	4	5	18	1	1937-38	1941-42
Smith, Don	Mtl.	1	10	1	0	1	4	....	....	....	....	....		1919-20	1919-20
Smith, Don A.	NYR	1	11	1	1	2	0	1	0	0	0	0		1949-50	1949-50
Smith, Floyd	Bos., NYR, Det., Tor., Buf.	13	616	129	178	307	207	48	12	11	23	16		1954-55	1971-72
Smith, George	Tor.	1	9	0	0	0	0	....	....	....	....	....		1921-22	1921-22
Smith, Glen	Chi.	1	2	0	0	0	0	....	....	....	....	....		1950-51	1950-51
Smith, Glenn	Tor.	1	9	0	0	0	0	....	....	....	....	....		1922-23	1922-23
Smith, Gord	Wsh., Wpg.	6	299	9	30	39	284	....	....	....	....	....		1974-75	1979-80
Smith, Greg	Cal., Clev., Min., Det., Wsh.	13	829	56	232	288	1110	63	4	7	11	106		1975-76	1987-88
Smith, Hooley	Ott., Mtl.M., Bos., NYA	17	715	200	215	415	1013	54	11	8	19	109	2	1924-25	1940-41
Smith, Kenny	Bos.	7	331	78	93	171	49	30	8	13	21	6		1944-45	1950-51
Smith, Randy	Min.	2	3	0	0	0	0	....	....	....	....	....		1985-86	1986-87
Smith, Rick	Bos., Cal., St.L., Det., Wsh.	11	687	52	167	219	560	78	3	23	26	73	1	1968-69	1980-81
Smith, Roger	Pit., Phi.	6	210	20	4	24	172	4	3	0	3	0		1925-26	1930-31
Smith, Ron	NYI	1	11	1	1	2	14	....	....	....	....	....		1972-73	1972-73
Smith, Sid	Tor.	12	601	186	183	369	94	44	17	10	27	2	3	1946-47	1957-58
Smith, Stan	NYR	2	9	2	1	3	0	....	....	....	....	....	1	1939-40	1940-41
Smith, Stu E.	Mtl.	2	17	2	4	6	2	....	....	....	....	....		1940-41	1941-42
Smith, Stu G.	Hfd.	4	77	2	10	12	95	....	....	....	....	....		1979-80	1982-83
Smith, Tommy	Que.B.	1	10	0	0	0	9	....	....	....	....	....		1919-20	1919-20
Smith, Wayne	Chi.	1	2	1	1	2	2	1	0	0	0	0		1966-67	1966-67
Smith, Vern	NYI	1	1	0	0	0	0	....	....	....	....	....		1984-85	1984-85
Smrke, John	St.L., Que.	3	103	11	17	28	33	....	....	....	....	....		1977-78	1979-80
Smrke, Stan	Mtl.	2	9	0	3	3	0	....	....	....	....	....		1956-57	1957-58
Smylie, Rod	Tor., Ott.	6	76	4	1	5	10	9	1	2	3	2	1	1920-21	1925-26
Snell, Ron	Pit.	2	7	3	2	5	6	....	....	....	....	....		1968-69	1969-70
Snell, Ted	Pit., K.C., Det.	2	104	7	18	25	22	....	....	....	....	....		1973-74	1974-75
Snow, Sandy	Det.	1	3	0	0	0	2	....	....	....	....	....		1968-69	1968-69
Sobchuk, Denis	Det., Que.	2	35	5	6	11	2	....	....	....	....	....		1979-80	1982-83
Sobchuk, Gene	Van.	1	1	0	0	0	0	....	....	....	....	....		1973-74	1973-74
Solheim, Ken	Chi., Min., Det., Edm.	5	135	19	20	39	34	3	1	1	2	2		1980-81	1985-86
Solinger, Bob	Tor., Det.	5	99	10	11	21	19	....	....	....	....	....		1951-52	1959-60
Somers, Art	Chi., NYR	6	222	33	56	89	189	30	1	5	6	20	1	1929-30	1934-35
Sommer, Roy	Edm.	1	3	1	0	1	7	....	....	....	....	....		1980-81	1980-81
Songin, Tom	Bos.	3	43	5	5	10	22	....	....	....	....	....		1978-79	1980-81
Sonmor, Glen	NYR	2	28	2	0	2	21	....	....	....	....	....		1953-54	1954-55
Sorrell, John	Det., NYA	11	490	127	119	246	100	42	12	15	27	10	2	1930-31	1940-41
Sparrow, Emory	Bos.	1	6	0	0	0	4	....	....	....	....	....		1924-25	1924-25
Speck, Fred	Det., Van.	3	28	1	2	3	2	....	....	....	....	....		1968-69	1971-72
Speer, Bill	Pit., Bos.	4	130	5	20	25	79	8	1	0	1	4	1	1967-68	1970-71
Speers, Ted	Det.	1	4	1	1	2	0	....	....	....	....	....		1985-86	1985-86
Spencer, Brian	Tor., NYI, Buf., Pit.	10	553	80	143	223	634	37	1	5	6	29		1969-70	1978-79

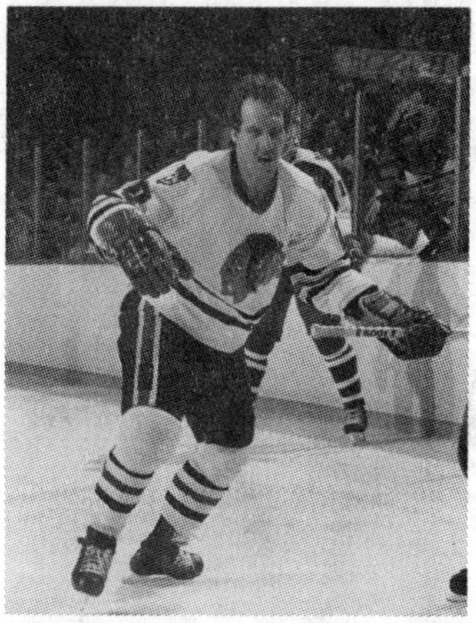
Al Secord

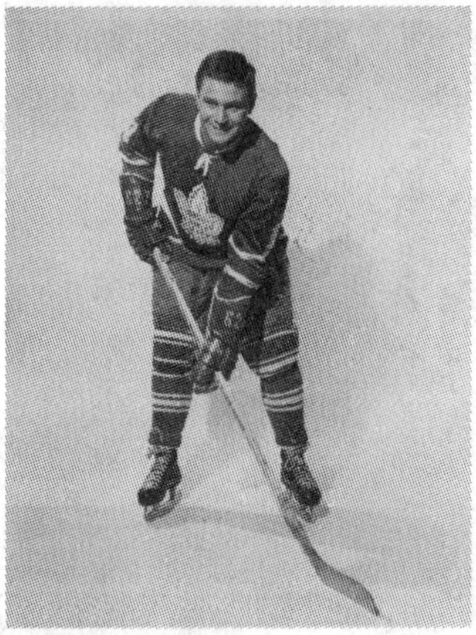
Brit Selby

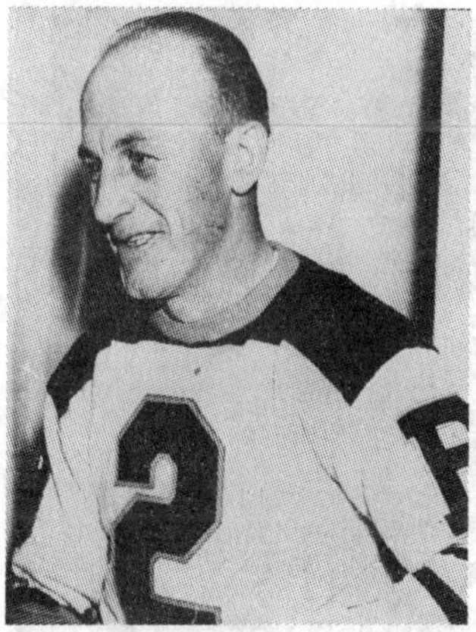
Eddie Shore

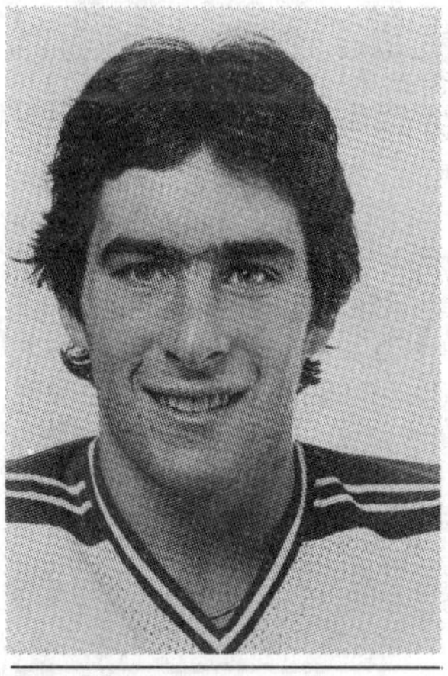
Dave Silk

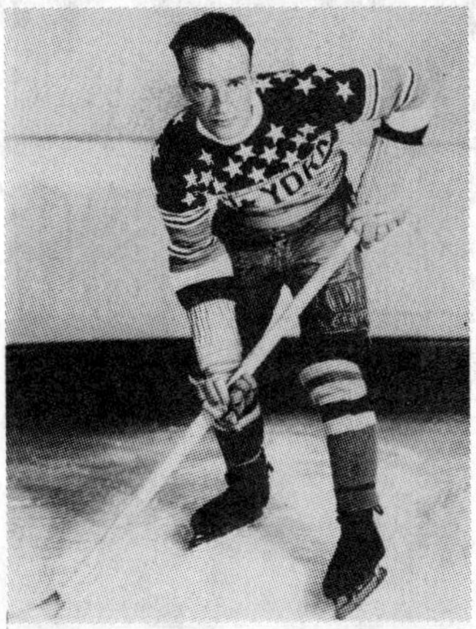
Joe Simpson

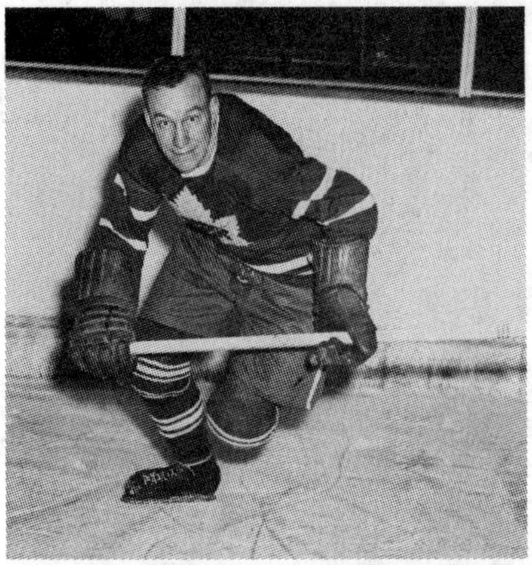
Bob Solinger

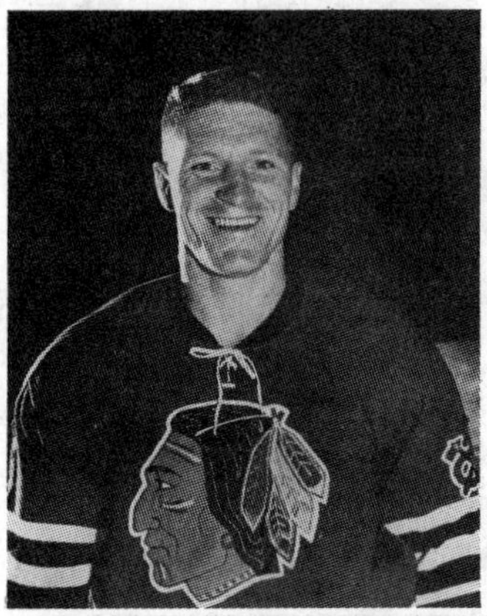
"Red" Sullivan

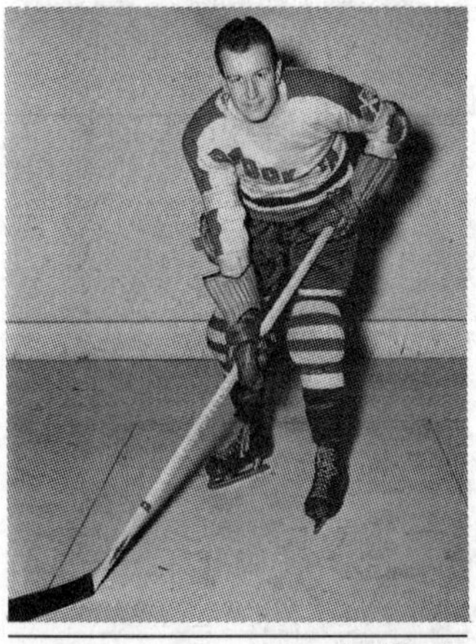
Fred Thurier

			Regular Schedule					Playoffs					NHL	First	Last
Name	NHL Teams	NHL Seasons	GP	G	A	TP	PIM	GP	G	A	TP	PIM	Cup Wins	NHL Season	NHL Season
Spencer, Irv	NYR, Bos., Det.	8	230	12	38	50	127	16	0	0	0	8		1959-60	1967-68
Speyer, Chris	Tor., NYA	3	14	0	0	0	0	....	....	....	....	....		1923-24	1933-34
Spring, Don	Wpg.	4	259	1	52	55	80	6	0	0	0	10		1980-81	1983-84
Spring, Frank	Bos., St.L., Cal., Clev.	5	61	14	20	34	12	....	....	....	....	....		1969-70	1976-77
Spring, Jesse	Ham., Pit., Tor., NYA	6	137	11	2	13	62	2	0	2	2	2		1923-24	1929-30
Spruce, Andy	Van., Col.	3	172	31	42	73	111	2	0	2	2	2		1976-77	1978-79
Stackhouse, Ron	Cal., Det., Pit.	12	889	87	372	459	824	32	5	8	13	38		1970-71	1981-82
Stackhouse, Ted	Tor.	1	12	0	0	0	2	5	0	0	0	0	1	1921-22	1921-22
Stahan, Butch	Mtl.	1	....	....	....	....	....	3	0	1	1	2		1944-45	1944-45
Staley, Al	NYR	1	1	0	1	1	0	....	....	....	....	....		1948-49	1948-49
Stamler, Lorne	L.A., Tor., Wpg.	4	116	14	11	25	16	....	....	....	....	....		1976-77	1979-80
Standing, George	Min.	1	2	0	0	0	0	....	....	....	....	....		1967-68	1967-68
Stanfield, Fred	Chi., Bos., Min., Buf.	14	914	211	405	616	134	106	21	35	56	10	2	1964-65	1977-78
Stanfield, Jack	Chi.	1	....	....	....	....	....	1	0	0	0	0		1965-66	1965-66
Stanfield, Jim	L.A.	3	7	0	1	1	0	....	....	....	....	....		1969-70	1971-72
Stankiewicz, Edward	Det.	2	6	0	0	0	2	....	....	....	....	....		1953-54	1955-56
Stankiewicz, Myron	St.L., Phi.	1	35	0	7	7	36	1	0	0	0	0		1968-69	1968-69
Stanley, Allan	NYR, Chi., Bos., Tor., Phi.	21	1244	100	333	433	792	109	7	36	43	80	4	1948-49	1968-69
Stanley, Barney	Chi.	1	1	0	0	0	0	....	....	....	....	....		1927-28	1927-28
Stanley, Daryl	Phi., Van.	6	189	8	17	25	408	17	0	0	0	30		1983-84	1989-90
Stanowski, Wally	Tor., NYR	10	428	23	88	111	160	60	3	14	17	13	4	1939-40	1950-51
Stapleton, Brian	Wsh.	1	1	0	0	0	0	....	....	....	....	....		1975-76	1975-76
Stapleton, Pat	Bos., Chi.	10	635	43	294	337	353	65	10	39	49	38		1961-62	1972-73
Starr, Harold	Ott., Mtl.M., Mtl., NYR	7	203	6	5	11	186	17	1	0	1	2		1929-30	1935-36
Starr, Wilf	NYA, Det.	4	89	8	6	14	25	7	0	2	2	2	1	1932-33	1935-36
Stasiuk, Vic	Chi., Det., Bos.	14	745	183	254	437	669	69	16	18	34	40	2	1949-50	1962-63
Stastny, Marian	Que., Tor.	5	322	121	173	294	110	32	5	17	22	7		1981-82	1985-86
Staszak, Ray	Det.	1	4	0	1	1	7	....	....	....	....	....		1985-86	1985-86
Steele, Frank	Det.	1	1	0	0	0	0	....	....	....	....	....		1930-31	1930-31
Steen, Anders	Wpg.	1	42	5	11	16	22	....	....	....	....	....		1980-81	1980-81
Stefaniw, Morris	Atl.	1	13	1	1	2	2	....	....	....	....	....		1972-73	1972-73
Stefanski, Bud	NYR	1	1	0	0	0	0	....	....	....	....	....		1977-78	1977-78
Stemkowski, Pete	Tor., Det., NYR, L.A.	15	967	206	349	555	866	83	25	29	54	136	1	1963-64	1977-78
Stenlund, Vern	Clev.	1	4	0	0	0	0	....	....	....	....	....		1976-77	1976-77
Stephens, Phil	Mtl.W, Mtl.	2	8	1	0	1	0	....	....	....	....	....		1917-18	1921-22
Stephenson, Bob	Hfd., Tor.	1	18	2	3	5	4	....	....	....	....	....		1979-80	1979-80
Sterner, Ulf	NYR	1	4	0	0	0	0	....	....	....	....	....		1964-65	1964-65
Stevens, Paul	Bos.	1	17	0	0	0	0	....	....	....	....	....		1925-26	1925-26
Stewart, Bill	Buf., St.L., Tor., Min.	8	261	7	64	71	424	13	1	3	4	11		1977-78	1985-86
Stewart, Blair	Det., Wsh., Que.	7	229	34	44	78	326	....	....	....	....	....		1973-74	1979-80
Stewart, Gaye	Tor., Chi., Det., NYR, Mtl.	11	502	185	159	344	274	25	2	9	11	16	2	1941-42	1953-54
Stewart, Jack	Det., Chi.	12	565	31	84	115	765	80	5	14	19	143	2	1938-39	1951-52
Stewart, John	Pit., Atl., Cal., Que.	6	260	58	60	118	158	4	0	0	0	10		1970-71	1979-80
Stewart, Ken	Chi.	1	6	1	1	2	2	....	....	....	....	....		1941-42	1941-42
Stewart, Nels	Mtl.M., Bos., NYA	15	651	324	191	515	953	54	15	13	28	61	1	1925-26	1939-40
Stewart, Paul	Que.	1	21	2	0	2	74	....	....	....	....	....		1979-80	1979-80
Stewart, Ralph	Van., NYI	7	252	57	73	130	28	19	4	4	8	2		1970-71	1977-78
Stewart, Robert	Bos., Cal., Clev., St.L., Pit.	9	510	27	101	128	809	5	1	1	2	2		1971-72	1979-80
Stewart, Ron	Tor., Bos., St.L., NYR, Van., NYI	21	1353	276	253	529	560	119	14	21	35	60	3	1952-53	1972-73
Stewart, Ryan	Wpg.	1	3	1	0	1	0	....	....	....	....	....		1985-86	1985-86
Stiles, Tony	Cgy.	1	30	2	7	9	20	....	....	....	....	....		1983-84	1983-84
Stoddard, Jack	NYR	2	80	16	15	31	31	....	....	....	....	....		1951-52	1952-53
Stoltz, Roland	Wsh.	1	14	2	2	4	14	....	....	....	....	....		1981-82	1981-82
Stone, Steve	Van.	1	2	0	0	0	0	....	....	....	....	....		1973-74	1973-74
Stoughton, Blaine	Pit., Tor., Hfd., NYR	8	526	258	191	449	204	8	4	2	6	2		1973-74	1983-84
Stoyanovich, Steve	Hfd.	1	23	3	5	8	11	....	....	....	....	....		1983-84	1983-84
Strain, Neil	NYR	1	52	11	13	24	12	....	....	....	....	....		1952-53	1952-53
Strate, Gord	Det.	3	61	0	0	0	34	....	....	....	....	....		1956-57	1958-59
Stratton, Art	NYR, Det., Chi., Pit., Phi.	4	95	18	33	51	24	5	0	0	0	0		1959-60	1967-68
Strobel, Art	NYR	1	7	0	0	0	0	....	....	....	....	....		1943-44	1943-44
Strong, Ken	Tor.	3	15	2	2	4	6	....	....	....	....	....		1982-83	1984-85
Strueby, Todd	Edm.	3	5	0	1	1	2	....	....	....	....	....		1981-82	1983-84
Stuart, Billy	Tor., Bos.	7	193	30	17	47	145	17	1	0	1	12	1	1920-21	1926-27
Stumpf, Robert	St.L., Pit.	1	10	1	1	2	20	....	....	....	....	....		1974-75	1974-75
Sturgeon, Peter	Col.	2	6	0	1	1	2	....	....	....	....	....		1979-80	1980-81
Suikkanen, Kai	Buf.	2	2	0	0	0	0	....	....	....	....	....		1981-82	1982-83
Sulliman, Doug	NYR, Hfd., N.J., Phi.	11	631	160	168	328	175	16	1	3	4	2		1979-80	1989-90
Sullivan, Barry	Det.	1	1	0	0	0	0	....	....	....	....	....		1947-48	1947-48
Sullivan, Bob	Hfd.	1	62	18	19	37	18	....	....	....	....	....		1982-83	1982-83
Sullivan, Frank	Tor., Chi.	4	8	0	0	0	2	....	....	....	....	....		1949-50	1955-56
Sullivan, Peter	Wpg.	2	126	28	54	82	40	....	....	....	....	....		1979-80	1980-81
Sullivan, Red	Bos., Chi., NYR	11	557	107	239	346	441	18	1	2	3	7		1949-50	1960-61
Summerhill, Bill	Mtl., Bro.	3	72	14	17	31	70	3	0	0	0	2		1938-39	1941-42
Suomi, Al	Chi.	1	5	0	0	0	0	....	....	....	....	....		1936-37	1936-37
Sutherland, Bill	Mtl., Phi., Tor., St.L., Det.	6	250	70	58	128	99	14	2	4	6	0		1962-63	1971-72
Sutherland, Ron	Bos.	1	2	0	0	0	0	....	....	....	....	....		1931-32	1931-32
Sutter, Brian	St.L.	12	779	303	333	636	1786	65	21	21	42	249		1976-77	1987-88
Sutter, Darryl	Chi.	8	406	161	118	279	288	51	24	19	43	26		1979-80	1986-87
Sutter, Duane	NYI, Chi.	11	731	139	203	342	1333	161	26	32	58	405		1979-80	1989-90
Suzor, Mark	Phi., Col.	2	64	4	16	20	60	....	....	....	....	....		1976-77	1977-78
Svensson, Leif	Wsh.	2	121	6	40	46	49	....	....	....	....	....		1978-79	1979-80
Swain, Garry	Pit.	1	9	1	1	2	0	....	....	....	....	....		1968-69	1968-69
Swarbrick, George	Oak., Pit., Phi.	4	132	17	25	42	173	....	....	....	....	....		1967-68	1970-71
Sweeny, Bill	NYR	1	4	1	0	1	0	....	....	....	....	....		1959-60	1959-60
Sykes, Bob	Tor.	1	2	0	0	0	0	....	....	....	....	....		1974-75	1974-75
Szura, Joe	Oak.	2	90	10	15	25	30	7	2	3	5	2		1967-68	1968-69

T

Taft, John	Det.	1	15	0	2	2	4	....	....	....	....	....		1978-79	1978-79
Talafous, Dean	Atl., Min., NYR	8	497	104	154	258	163	21	4	7	11	11		1974-75	1981-82
Talakoski, Ron	NYR	2	9	0	1	1	33	....	....	....	....	....		1986-87	1987-88
Talbot, Jean-Guy	Mtl., Min., Det., St.L., Buf.	17	1056	43	242	285	1006	150	4	26	30	142	7	1954-55	1970-71
Tallon, Dale	Van., Chi., Pit.	10	642	98	238	336	568	33	2	10	12	45		1970-71	1979-80
Tambellini, Steve	NYI, Col., N.J., Cgy., Van.	10	553	160	150	310	105	2	0	1	1	0	1	1978-79	1987-88
Tanguay, Chris	Que.	1	2	0	0	0	0	....	....	....	....	....		1981-82	1981-82
Tannahill, Don	Van.	2	111	30	33	63	25	....	....	....	....	....		1972-73	1973-74
Tardif, Marc	Mtl., Que.	8	517	194	207	401	443	62	13	15	28	75	2	1969-70	1982-83
Taylor, Billy	Tor., Det., Bos., NYR	7	323	87	180	267	120	33	6	18	24	13	1	1939-40	1947-48
Taylor, Billy	NYR	1	2	0	0	0	0	....	....	....	....	....		1964-65	1964-65
Taylor, Bob	Bos.	1	8	0	0	0	6	....	....	....	....	....		1929-30	1929-30
Taylor, Ted	NYR, Det., Min., Van.	6	166	23	35	58	181	....	....	....	....	....		1964-65	1971-72
Taylor, Harry	Tor., Chi.	3	66	5	10	15	30	1	0	0	0	0	1	1946-47	1951-52
Taylor, Mark	Phi., Pit., Wsh.	5	209	42	68	110	73	6	0	0	0	0		1981-82	1985-86
Taylor, Ralph	Chi., NYR	3	99	4	1	5	169	4	0	0	0	10		1927-28	1929-30
Teal, Jeff	Mtl.	1	6	0	1	1	0	....	....	....	....	....		1984-85	1984-85
Teal, Skip	Bos.	1	1	0	0	0	0	....	....	....	....	....		1954-55	1954-55
Teal, Victor	NYI	1	1	0	0	0	0	....	....	....	....	....		1973-74	1973-74
Tebbutt, Greg	Que., Pit.	2	26	0	3	3	35	....	....	....	....	....		1979-80	1983-84
Terbenche, Paul	Chi., Buf.	5	189	5	26	31	28	12	0	0	0	0		1967-68	1973-74
Terrion, Greg	L.A., Tor.	8	561	93	150	243	339	35	2	9	11	41		1980-81	1987-88
Terry, Bill	Min.	1	5	0	0	0	0	....	....	....	....	....		1987-88	1987-88
Tessier, Orval	Mtl., Bos.	3	59	5	7	12	6	....	....	....	....	....		1954-55	1960-61
Thatchell, Spence	NYR	1	1	0	0	0	0	....	....	....	....	....		1942-43	1942-43
Theberge, Greg	Wsh.	5	153	15	63	78	73	4	0	1	1	0		1979-80	1983-84
Therrien, Gaston	Que.	3	22	0	8	8	12	9	0	1	1	4		1980-81	1982-83
Thelin, Mats	Bos.	3	163	8	19	27	107	5	0	0	0	6		1984-85	1986-87
Thelven, Michael	Bos.	5	207	20	80	100	217	34	4	10	14	34		1985-86	1989-90
Thibeault, Laurence	Det., Mtl.	2	5	0	2	2	0	....	....	....	....	....		1944-45	1945-46
Thiffault, Leo	Min.	1	....	....	....	....	....	5	0	0	0	0		1967-68	1967-68
Thomas, Cy	Chi., Tor.	1	14	2	2	4	12	....	....	....	....	....		1947-48	1947-48
Thomas, Reg	Que.	1	39	9	7	16	6	....	....	....	....	....		1979-80	1979-80

Name	NHL Teams	NHL Seasons	Regular Schedule					Playoffs					NHL Cup Wins	First NHL Season	Last NHL Season
			GP	G	A	TP	PIM	GP	G	A	TP	PIM			
Thompson, Cliff	Bos.	2	13	0	1	1	2	....	....	....	....	....		1941-42	1948-49
Thompson, Errol	Tor., Det., Pit.	10	599	208	185	393	184	34	7	5	12	11		1970-71	1980-81
Thompson, Kenneth	Mtl.W	1	1	0	0	0	0	....	....	....	....	....		1917-18	1917-18
Thompson, Paul	NYR, Chi.	13	586	153	179	332	336	48	11	11	22	54	3	1926-27	1938-39
Thoms, Bill	Tor., Chi., Bos.	13	549	135	206	341	172	44	6	10	16	6		1932-33	1944-45
Thomson, Bill	Det., Chi.	2	10	2	2	4	0	2	0	0	0	0		1938-39	1943-44
Thomson, Floyd	St.L.	8	411	56	97	153	341	10	0	2	2	6		1971-72	1979-80
Thomson, Jack	NYA	3	15	1	1	2	0	2	0	0	0	0		1938-39	1940-41
Thomson, Jimmy	Tor., Chi.	13	787	19	215	234	920	63	2	13	15	135	4	1945-46	1957-58
Thomson, Rhys	Mtl., Tor.	2	25	0	2	2	38	....	....	....	....	....		1939-40	1942-43
Thornbury, Tom	Pit.	1	14	1	8	9	16	....	....	....	....	....		1983-84	1983-84
Thorsteinson, Joe	NYA	1	4	0	0	0	0	....	....	....	....	....		1932-33	1932-33
Thurier, Fred	NYA, Bro., NYR	3	80	25	27	52	18	....	....	....	....	....		1940-41	1944-45
Thurlby, Tom	Oak.	1	20	1	2	3	4	....	....	....	....	....		1967-68	1967-68
Tidey, Alex	Buf., Edm.	3	9	0	0	0	8	2	0	0	0	0		1976-77	1979-80
Timgren, Ray	Tor., Chi.	6	251	14	44	58	70	30	3	9	12	6	2	1948-49	1954-55
Titanic, Morris	Buf.	2	19	0	0	0	0	....	....	....	....	....		1974-75	1975-76
Tkaczuk, Walt	NYR	14	945	227	451	678	556	93	19	32	51	119		1967-68	1980-81
Toal, Mike	Edm.	1	3	0	0	0	0	....	....	....	....	....		1979-80	1979-80
Tomalty, Glenn	Wpg.	1	1	0	0	0	0	....	....	....	....	....		1979-80	1979-80
Tomlinson, Kirk	Min.	1	1	0	0	0	0	....	....	....	....	....		1987-88	1987-88
Toomey, Sean	Min.	1	1	0	0	0	0	....	....	....	....	....		1986-87	1986-87
Toppazzini, Jerry	Bos., Chi., Det.	12	783	163	244	407	436	40	13	9	22	13		1952-53	1963-64
Toppazzini, Zellio	Bos., NYR, Chi.	5	123	21	22	43	49	2	0	0	0	0		1948-49	1956-57
Touhey, Bill	Mtl.M., Ott., Bos.	7	280	65	40	105	107	2	1	0	1	0		1927-28	1933-34
Toupin, Jaques	Chi.	1	8	1	2	3	0	4	0	0	0	0		1943-44	1943-44
Townsend, Art	Chi.	1	5	0	0	0	0	....	....	....	....	....		1926-27	1926-27
Trader, Larry	Det., St.L., Mtl.	4	91	5	13	18	74	3	0	0	0	0		1982-83	1987-88
Trainor, Wes	NYR	1	17	1	2	3	6	....	....	....	....	....		1948-49	1948-49
Trapp, Bobby	Chi.	2	82	4	4	8	129	2	0	0	0	4		1926-27	1927-28
Trapp, Doug	Buf.	1	2	0	0	0	0	....	....	....	....	....		1986-87	1986-87
Traub, Percy	Chi., Det.	3	130	3	3	6	214	4	0	0	0	6		1926-27	1928-29
Tredway, Brock	L.A.	1	....	....	....	....	....	1	0	0	0	0		1981-82	1981-82
Tremblay, Brent	Wsh.	2	10	1	0	1	6	....	....	....	....	....		1978-79	1979-80
Tremblay, Gilles	Mtl.	9	509	168	162	330	161	48	9	14	23	4	2	1960-61	1968-69
Tremblay, J.C.	Mtl.	13	794	57	306	363	204	108	14	51	65	58	5	1959-60	1971-72
Tremblay, Marcel	Mtl.	1	10	0	2	2	0	....	....	....	....	....		1938-39	1938-39
Tremblay, Mario	Mtl.	12	852	258	326	584	1043	100	20	29	49	187	5	1974-75	1985-86
Tremblay, Nels	Mtl.	2	3	0	1	1	0	2	0	0	0	0		1944-45	1945-46
Trimper, Tim	Chi., Wpg., Min.	6	190	30	36	66	153	2	0	0	0	2		1979-80	1984-85
Trottier, Dave	Mtl.M., Det.	11	446	121	113	234	517	31	4	3	7	41	1	1928-29	1938-39
Trottier, Guy	NYR, Tor.	3	115	28	17	45	37	9	1	0	1	16		1968-69	1971-72
Trottier, Rocky	N.J.	2	38	6	4	10	2	....	....	....	....	....		1983-84	1984-85
Trudel, Louis	Chi., Mtl.	8	306	49	69	118	122	24	1	3	4	6	2	1933-34	1940-41
Trudell, Rene	NYR	3	129	24	28	52	72	5	0	0	0	2		1945-46	1947-48
Tudin, Connie	Mtl.	1	4	0	1	1	4	....	....	....	....	....		1941-42	1941-42
Tudor, Rob	Van., St.L.	3	28	4	4	8	19	3	0	0	0	0		1978-79	1982-83
Turlick, Gord	Bos.	1	2	0	0	0	2	....	....	....	....	....		1959-60	1959-60
Turnbull, Ian	Tor., L.A., Pit.	10	628	123	317	440	736	55	13	32	45	94		1973-74	1982-83
Turnbull, Perry	St.L., Mtl., Wpg.	9	608	188	163	351	1245	34	6	7	13	86		1979-80	1987-88
Turnbull, Randy	Cgy.	1	1	0	0	0	2	....	....	....	....	....		1981-82	1981-82
Turner, Bob	Mtl., Chi.	8	478	19	51	70	307	68	1	4	5	44	5	1955-56	1962-63
Turner, Dean	NYR, Col., L.A.	4	35	1	0	1	59	....	....	....	....	....		1978-79	1982-83
Tustin, Norman	NYR	1	18	2	4	6	0	....	....	....	....	....		1941-42	1941-42
Tuten, Audley	Chi.	2	39	4	8	12	48	....	....	....	....	....		1941-42	1942-43

UV

Name	NHL Teams	NHL Seasons	GP	G	A	TP	PIM	GP	G	A	TP	PIM	NHL Cup Wins	First NHL Season	Last NHL Season
Ubriaco, Gene	Pit., Oak., Chi.	3	177	39	35	74	50	11	2	0	2	4		1967-68	1969-70
Ullman, Norm	Det., Tor.	20	1410	490	739	1229	712	106	30	53	83	67		1955-56	1974-75
Unger, Garry	Tor., Det., St.L., Atl., L.A., Edm.	16	1105	413	391	804	1075	52	12	18	30	105		1967-68	1982-83
Vadnais, Carol	Mtl., Oak., Cal., Bos., NYR, N.J.	17	1087	169	418	587	1813	106	10	40	50	185	2	1966-67	1982-83
Vail, Eric	Atl, Cgy., Det.	9	591	216	260	476	281	20	5	6	11	6		1973-74	1981-82
Vail, Melville	NYR	2	50	4	1	5	18	10	0	0	0	2		1928-29	1929-30
Valentine, Chris	Wsh.	3	105	43	52	95	127	2	0	0	0	4		1981-82	1983-84
Valiquette, Jack	Tor., Col.	7	350	84	134	218	79	23	3	6	9	4		1974-75	1980-81
Van Boxmeer, John	Mtl., Col., Buf., Que.	11	588	84	274	358	465	38	5	15	20	37		1973-74	1983-84
Van Impe, Ed	Chi., Phi., Pit.	11	700	27	126	153	1025	66	1	12	13	131	2	1966-67	1976-77
Vasko, Elmer	Chi., Min.	13	786	34	166	200	719	78	2	7	9	73	1	1956-57	1969-70
Vasko, Rick	Det.	3	31	3	7	10	29	....	....	....	....	....		1977-78	1980-81
Vautour, Yvon	NYI, Col., N.J., Que.	6	204	26	33	59	401	....	....	....	....	....		1979-80	1984-85
Vaydik, Greg	Chi.	1	5	0	0	0	0	....	....	....	....	....		1976-77	1976-77
Venasky, Vic	L.A.	7	430	61	101	162	66	21	1	5	6	12		1972-73	1978-79
Veneruzzo, Gary	St.L.	2	7	1	1	2	0	9	0	2	2	2		1967-68	1971-72
Verret, Claude	Buf.	2	14	2	5	7	2	....	....	....	....	....		1983-84	1984-85
Verstraete, Leigh	Tor.	3	8	0	1	1	14	....	....	....	....	....		1982-83	1987-88
Ververgaert, Dennis	Van., Phi., Wsh.	8	583	176	216	392	247	8	1	2	3	6		1973-74	1980-81
Veysey, Sid	Van.	1	1	0	0	0	0	....	....	....	....	....		1977-78	1977-78
Vickers, Steve	NYR	10	698	246	340	586	330	68	24	25	49	58		1972-73	1981-82
Vigneault, Alain	St.L.	2	42	2	5	7	82	4	0	1	1	26		1981-82	1982-83
Vipond, Pete	Cal.	1	3	0	0	0	0	....	....	....	....	....		1972-73	1972-73
Vokes, Ed	Chi.	1	5	0	0	0	0	....	....	....	....	....		1930-31	1930-31
Volcan, Mickey	Hfd., Cgy.	4	162	8	33	41	146	....	....	....	....	....		1980-81	1983-84
Volmar, Doug	Det., L.A.	4	62	13	8	21	26	2	1	0	1	0		1969-70	1972-73
Voss, Carl	Tor., NYR, Det., Ott., St.L., Mtl.M., NYA, Chi.	8	261	34	70	104	50	24	5	3	8	0		1926-27	1937-38

W

Name	NHL Teams	NHL Seasons	GP	G	A	TP	PIM	GP	G	A	TP	PIM	NHL Cup Wins	First NHL Season	Last NHL Season
Waddell, Don	L.A.	1	1	0	0	0	0	....	....	....	....	....		1980-81	1980-81
Waite, Frank	NYR	1	17	1	3	4	4	....	....	....	....	....		1930-31	1930-31
Walker, Howard	Wsh., Cal.	3	83	2	13	15	133	....	....	....	....	....		1980-81	1982-83
Walker, Jack	Det.	2	80	5	8	13	18	....	....	....	....	....		1926-27	1927-28
Walker, Kurt	Tor.	3	71	4	5	9	152	16	0	0	0	34		1975-76	1977-78
Walker, Russ	L.A.	2	17	1	0	1	41	....	....	....	....	....		1976-77	1977-78
Wall, Bob	Det., L.A., St.L.	8	322	30	55	85	155	22	0	3	3	2		1964-65	1971-72
Wallin, Peter	NYR	2	52	3	14	17	14	14	2	6	8	6		1980-81	1981-82
Walsh, Jim	Buf.	1	4	0	1	1	4	....	....	....	....	....		1981-82	1981-82
Walton, Bobby	Mtl.	1	4	0	0	0	0	....	....	....	....	....		1943-44	1943-44
Walton, Mike	Tor., Bos., Van., Chi., St.L.	12	588	201	247	448	357	47	14	10	24	45	2	1965-66	1978-79
Wappel, Gord	Atl., Cgy.	3	20	1	1	2	10	2	0	0	0	4		1979-80	1981-82
Ward, Don	Chi., Bos.	2	34	0	1	1	16	....	....	....	....	....		1957-58	1959-60
Ward, Jimmy	Mtl.M., Mtl.	12	532	147	127	274	465	31	4	4	8	18	1	1927-28	1938-39
Ward, Joe	Col.	1	4	0	0	0	2	....	....	....	....	....		1980-81	1980-81
Ward, Ron	Tor., Van.,	2	89	2	5	7	6	....	....	....	....	....		1969-70	1971-72
Wares, Eddie	NYR, Det., Chi.	9	291	60	102	162	161	45	5	7	12	34	1	1936-37	1946-47
Warner, Bob	Tor.	2	10	1	1	2	4	4	0	0	0	0		1975-76	1976-77
Warner, Jim	Hfd.	1	32	0	3	3	10	....	....	....	....	....		1979-80	1979-80
Warwick, Bill	NYR	2	14	3	3	6	16	....	....	....	....	....		1942-43	1943-44
Warwick, Grant	NYR, Bos., Mtl.	9	395	147	142	289	220	16	2	4	6	6		1941-42	1949-50
Wasnie, Nick	Chi., Mtl., NYA, Ott., St.L.	7	248	57	34	91	176	14	6	3	9	20	2	1927-28	1934-35
Watson, Bill	Chi.	4	115	23	36	59	12	6	0	2	2	0		1985-86	1988-89
Watson, Bryan	Mtl., Oak., Pit., Det., St.L., Wsh.	16	878	17	135	152	2212	32	2	0	2	70		1963-64	1978-79
Watson, Dave	Col.	2	18	0	1	1	10	....	....	....	....	....		1979-80	1980-81
Watson, Harry	Bro., Det., Tor., Chi.	14	805	236	207	443	150	62	16	9	25	27	5	1941-42	1956-57
Watson, Jim	Det., Buf.	7	221	4	19	23	345	....	....	....	....	....		1963-64	1971-72
Watson, Jimmy	Phi.	10	613	38	148	186	492	101	5	34	39	89	2	1972-73	1981-82
Watson, Joe	Bos., Phi., Col.	14	835	38	178	216	447	84	3	12	15	82	2	1964-65	1978-79
Watson, Phil	NYR, Mtl.	13	590	144	265	409	542	45	10	25	35	67	2	1935-36	1947-48
Watts, Brian	Det.	1	4	0	0	0	0	....	....	....	....	....		1975-76	1975-76
Webster, Aubrey	Phi., Mtl.M.	2	5	0	0	0	0	....	....	....	....	....		1930-31	1934-35

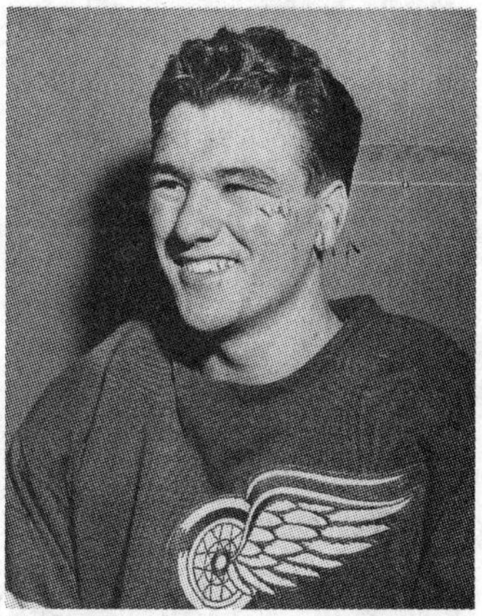

Norm Ullman

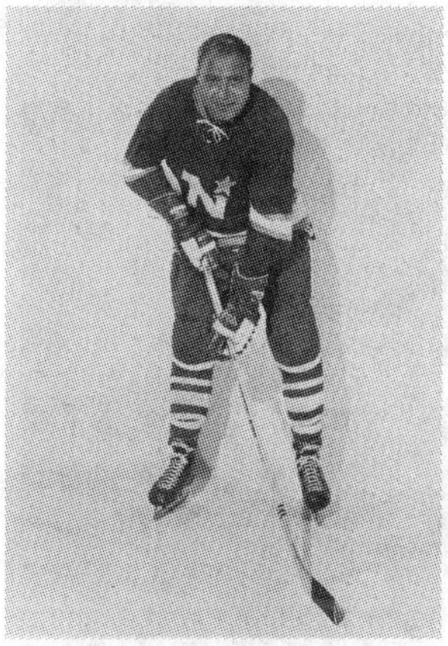

Elmer "Moose" Vasko

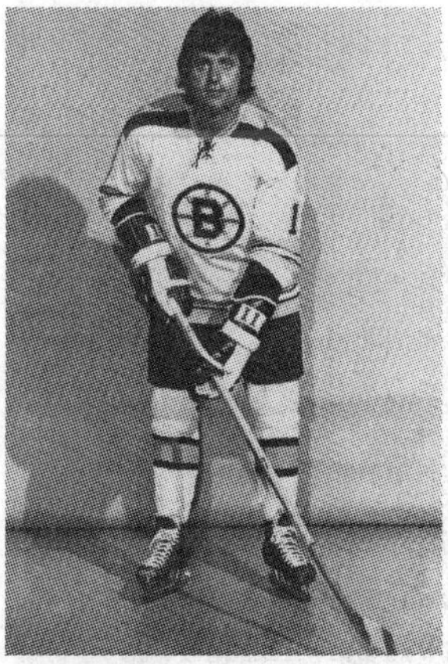

Mike Walton

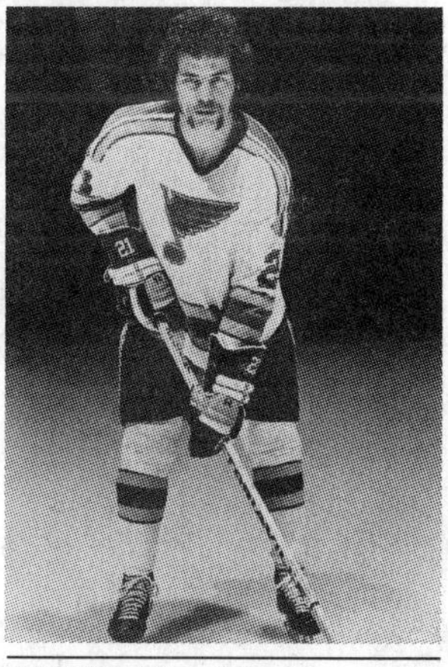

John Wensink

Murray Wilson

Howie Young

Mike Zuke

Name	NHL Teams	NHL Seasons	Regular Schedule GP	G	A	TP	PIM	Playoffs GP	G	A	TP	PIM	NHL Cup Wins	First NHL Season	Last NHL Season
Webster, Don	Tor.	1	27	7	6	13	28	5	0	0	0	12		1943-44	1943-44
Webster, John	NYR	1	14	0	0	0	4							1949-50	1949-50
Webster, Tom	Bos., Det., Cal.	5	102	33	42	75	61	1	0	0	0	0		1968-69	1979-80
Weiland, Cooney	Bos., Ott., Det.	11	508	173	160	333	147	45	12	10	22	12		1928-29	1938-39
Weir, Stan	Cal., Tor., Edm., Col., Det.	10	642	139	207	346	183	37	6	5	11	4		1972-73	1982-83
Weir, Wally	Que., Hfd., Pit.	6	320	21	45	66	625	23	0	1	1	96		1979-80	1984-85
Wellington, Duke	Que.	1	1	0	0	0	0							1919-20	1919-20
Wensink, John	Bos., Que., Col., N.J., St.L.	8	403	70	68	138	840	43	2	6	8	86		1973-74	1982-83
Wentworth, Cy	Chi., Mtl.M., Mtl.	13	578	39	68	107	355	35	5	6	11	22	1	1927-28	1939-40
Wesley, Blake	Phi., Hfd., Que., Tor.	7	298	18	46	64	486	19	2	2	4	30		1979-80	1985-86
Westfall, Ed	Bos., NYI	18	1227	231	394	625	544	95	22	37	59	41	2	1961-62	1978-79
Wharram, Kenny	Chi.	14	766	252	281	533	222	80	16	27	43	38	1	1951-52	1968-69
Wharton, Len	NYR	1	1	0	0	0	0							1944-45	1944-45
Wheldon, Donald	St.L.	1	2	0	0	0	0							1974-75	1974-75
Whelton, Bill	Wpg.	1	2	0	0	0	0							1980-81	1980-81
Whistle, Rob	NYR, St.L.	2	51	7	5	12	16	4	0	0	0	2		1985-86	1987-88
White, Bill	L.A., Chi.	9	604	50	215	265	495	91	7	32	39	76		1967-68	1975-76
White, Moe	Mtl.	1	4	0	1	1	2							1945-46	1945-46
White, Sherman	NYR	2	4	0	2	2	0							1946-47	1949-50
White, Tex	Pit., NYA, Phi.	6	203	33	12	45	141	4	0	0	0	2		1925-26	1930-31
White, Tony	Wsh., Min.	5	164	37	28	65	104							1974-75	1979-80
Whitelaw, Bob	Det.	2	32	0	2	2	2	8	0	0	0	0		1940-41	1941-42
Whitlock, Bob	Min.	1	1	0	0	0	0							1969-70	1969-70
Widing, Juha	NYR, L.A., Clev.	8	575	144	226	370	208	8	1	2	3	2		1969-70	1976-77
Wiebe, Art	Chi.	11	411	14	27	41	209	31	1	3	4	8	1	1932-33	1943-44
Wilcox, Archie	Mtl.M., Bos., St.L.	6	212	8	14	22	158	12	1	0	1	10		1929-30	1934-35
Wilcox, Barry	Van.	2	33	3	2	5	15							1972-73	1974-75
Wilder, Arch	Det.	1	18	0	2	2	2							1940-41	1940-41
Wiley, Jim	Pit., Van.	5	63	4	10	14	8							1972-73	1976-77
Wilkins, Barry	Bos., Van., Pit.	9	418	27	125	152	663	6	0	1	1	4		1966-67	1975-76
Wilkinson, John	Bos.	1	9	0	0	0	3							1943-44	1943-44
Wilks, Brian	L.A.	4	48	4	8	12	27							1984-85	1988-89
Willard, Rod	Tor.	1	1	0	0	0	0							1982-83	1982-83
Williams, Burr	Det., St.L., Bos.	3	19	0	1	1	28	2	0	0	0	8		1933-34	1936-37
Williams, Dave	Tor., Van., Det., L.A., Hfd.	14	962	241	272	513	3966	83	12	23	35	455		1974-75	1987-88
Williams, Fred	Det.	1	44	2	5	7	10							1976-77	1976-77
Williams, Gord	Phi.	2	2	0	0	0	2							1981-82	1982-83
Williams, Tom	Bos., Min., Cal., Wsh.	13	663	161	269	430	177	10	2	5	7	2		1961-62	1975-76
Williams, Tommy	NYR, L.A.	8	397	115	138	253	73	29	8	7	15	4		1971-72	1978-79
Williams, Warren	St.L., Cal.	3	108	14	35	49	131							1973-74	1975-76
Willson, Don	Mtl.	2	22	2	7	9	4	3	0	0	0	0		1937-38	1938-39
Wilson, Behn	Phi., Chi.	9	601	98	260	358	1480	67	12	29	41	190		1978-79	1987-88
Wilson, Bert	NYR, L.A., St.L., Cgy.	8	478	37	44	81	646	21	0	2	2	42		1973-74	1980-81
Wilson, Bob	Chi.	1	1	0	0	0	0							1953-54	1953-54
Wilson, Cully	Tor., Mtl., Ham., Chi.	5	125	60	23	83	232	2	1	0	1	6		1919-20	1926-27
Wilson, Gord	Bos.	1	....	....	....	....	....	2	0	0	0	0		1954-55	1954-55
Wilson, Hub	NYA	1	2	0	0	0	0							1931-32	1931-32
Wilson, Jerry	Mtl.	1	3	0	0	0	2							1956-57	1956-57
Wilson, Johnny	Det., Chi., Tor., NYR	13	688	161	171	332	190	66	14	13	27	11	4	1949-50	1961-62
Wilson, Larry	Det., Chi.	6	152	21	48	69	75	4	0	0	0	0		1949-50	1955-56
Wilson, Murray	Mtl., L.A.	7	386	94	95	189	162	53	5	14	19	32	3	1972-73	1978-79
Wilson, Rick	Mtl., St.L., Det.	4	239	6	26	32	165	3	0	0	0	0		1973-74	1976-77
Wilson, Roger	Chi.	1	7	0	2	2	6							1974-75	1974-75
Wilson, Ron	Tor., Min.	7	177	26	67	93	68	20	4	13	17	8		1977-78	1987-88
Wilson, Wally	Bos.	1	53	11	8	19	18	1	0	0	0	0		1947-48	1947-48
Wing, Murray	Det.	1	1	0	1	1	0							1973-74	1973-74
Wiseman, Eddie	Det., NYA, Bos.	10	454	115	164	279	137	45	10	10	20	16	1	1932-33	1941-42
Wiste, Jim	Chi., Van.	3	52	1	10	11	8							1968-69	1970-71
Witherspoon, Jim	L.A.	1	2	0	0	0	0							1975-76	1975-76
Witiuk, Steve	Chi.	1	33	3	8	11	14							1951-52	1951-52
Woit, Benny	Det., Chi.	7	334	7	26	33	170	41	2	6	8	18	3	1950-51	1956-57
Wojciechowski, Steven	Det.	2	54	19	20	39	17	6	0	1	1	0		1944-45	1946-47
Wolf, Bennett	Pit.	3	30	0	1	1	133							1980-81	1982-83
Wong, Mike	Det.	1	22	1	1	2	12							1975-76	1975-76
Wood, Robert	NYR	1	1	0	0	0	0							1950-51	1950-51
Woods, Paul	Det.	7	501	72	124	196	276	7	0	5	5	4		1977-78	1983-84
Woytowich, Bob	Bos., Min., Pit., L.A.	8	503	32	126	158	352	24	1	3	4	20		1964-65	1971-72
Wright, John	Van., St.L., K.C.	3	127	16	36	52	67							1972-73	1974-75
Wright, Keith	Phi.	1	1	0	0	0	0							1967-68	1967-68
Wright, Larry	Phi., Cal., Det.	5	106	4	8	12	19							1971-72	1977-78
Wycherley, Ralph	NYA, Bro.	2	28	4	7	11	6							1940-41	1941-42
Wylie, Duane	Chi.	2	14	3	3	6	2							1974-75	1976-77
Wylie, William	NYR	1	1	0	0	0	0							1950-51	1950-51
Wyrozub, Randy	Buf.	4	100	8	10	18	10							1970-71	1973-74

YZ

Name	NHL Teams	NHL Seasons	Regular Schedule GP	G	A	TP	PIM	Playoffs GP	G	A	TP	PIM	NHL Cup Wins	First NHL Season	Last NHL Season
Yackel, Ken	Bos.	1	6	0	0	0	2	2	0	0	0	0		1958-59	1958-59
Yaremchuk, Gary	Tor.	4	34	1	4	5	28							1981-82	1984-85
Yaremchuk, Ken	Chi., Tor.	6	235	36	56	92	106	31	6	8	14	49		1983-84	1988-89
Yates, Ross	Hfd.	1	7	1	1	2	4							1983-84	1983-84
Young, Brian	Chi.	1	8	0	2	2	6							1980-81	1980-81
Young, Douglas	Mtl., Det.	10	391	35	45	80	303	28	1	5	6	16	2	1931-32	1940-41
Young, Howie	Det., Chi., Van.	8	336	12	62	74	851	19	2	4	6	46		1960-61	1970-71
Young, Tim	Min., Wpg., Phi.	10	628	195	341	536	438	36	7	24	31	27		1975-76	1984-85
Young, Warren	Min., Pit., Det.	7	236	72	77	149	472							1981-82	1987-88
Younghans, Tom	Min., NYR	6	429	44	41	85	373	24	2	1	3	21		1976-77	1981-82
Zabroski, Marty	Chi.	1	1	0	0	0	0							1944-45	1944-45
Zaharko, Miles	Atl., Chi.	4	129	5	32	37	84	3	0	0	0	0		1977-78	1981-82
Zaine, Rod	Pit., Buf.	2	61	10	6	16	25							1970-71	1971-72
Zanussi, Joe	NYR, Bos., St.L.	3	87	1	13	14	46	4	0	1	1	2		1974-75	1976-77
Zanussi, Ron	Min., Tor.	5	299	52	83	135	373	17	0	4	4	17		1977-78	1981-82
Zeidel, Larry	Det., Chi., Phi.	5	158	3	16	19	198	12	0	1	1	12		1951-52	1968-69
Zeniuk, Ed	Det.	1	2	0	0	0	0							1954-55	1954-55
Zetterstrom, Lars	Van.	1	14	0	1	1	2							1978-79	1978-79
Zuke, Mike	St.L., Hfd.	8	455	86	196	282	220	26	6	6	12	12		1978-79	1985-86
Zunich, Ruby	Det.	1	2	0	0	0	2							1943-44	1943-44

1991-92 Goaltender Register

Note: The 1991-92 Goaltender Register lists every goaltender who appeared in an NHL game in the 1990-91 season, every goaltender drafted in the first three rounds of the 1990 and 1991 Entry Drafts and other goaltenders on NHL Reserve Lists.

Trades and roster changes are current as of August 15, 1991.

To calculate a goaltender's goals-against-per-game average **(Avg)**, divide goals against **(GA)** by minutes played **(Mins)** and multiply this result by **60**.

Abbreviations: A list of league names can be found at the beginning of the Player Register. **Avg** – goals against per game average; **GA** – goals against; **GP** – games played; **L** – losses; **Lea** – league; **SO** – shutouts; **T** – ties; **W** – wins.

Player Register begins on page 207.

ANDERSON, DEAN

Goaltender. Catches left. 5′10″, 175 lbs. Born, Oshawa, Ont., July 14, 1966.
(Toronto's 1st choice, 11th overall, in 1988 Supplemental Draft).

			Regular Season								Playoffs						
Season	Club	Lea	GP	W	L	T	Mins	GA	SO	Avg	GP	W	L	Mins	GA	SO	Avg
1984-85	U. Wisconsin	WCHA	36	21	13	0	2072	148	0	4.29	....	....	....	....	....	....	....
1985-86	U. Wisconsin	WCHA	20	13	6	0	1128	80	0	4.25	....	....	....	....	....	....	....
1986-87	U. Wisconsin	WCHA	9	4	2	0	409	27	0	3.96	....	....	....	....	....	....	....
1987-88a	U. Wisconsin	WCHA	45	30	13	2	2718	148	2	3.27	....	....	....	....	....	....	....
1988-89	Newmarket	AHL	2	0	1	0	38	4	0	6.32	1	0	1	30	1	0	2.00
	Flint	IHL	16	1	12	0	770	82	1	6.39	....	....	....	....	....	....	....
1989-90	Knoxville	ECHL	17	6	8	3	997	73	0	4.39	....	....	....	....	....	....	....
1990-91	Newmarket	AHL	3	1	2	0	180	16	0	5.33	....	....	....	....	....	....	....
b	Knoxville	ECHL	29	*23	3	2	1625	80	*3	*2.95	3	0	3	187	10	0	3.20

a WCHA Second All-Star Team (1988)
b ECHL First All-Star Team (1991)

BALES, MICHAEL

Goaltender. Catches left. 6′1″, 180 lbs. Born, Prince Albert, Sask., August 6, 1971.
(Boston's 4th choice, 105th overall, in 1990 Entry Draft).

			Regular Season								Playoffs						
Season	Club	Lea	GP	W	L	T	Mins	GA	SO	Avg	GP	W	L	Mins	GA	SO	Avg
1989-90	Ohio State	CCHA	21	6	13	2	1117	95	0	5.11	....	....	....	....	....	....	....
1990-91	Ohio State	CCHA	*39	11	24	3	*2180	184	0	5.06	....	....	....	....	....	....	....

BARRASSO, TOM (buh-RAH-soh)

Goaltender. Catches right. 6′3″, 211 lbs. Born, Boston, MA, March 31, 1965.
(Buffalo's 1st choice, 5th overall, in 1983 Entry Draft).

			Regular Season								Playoffs						
Season	Club	Lea	GP	W	L	T	Mins	GA	SO	Avg	GP	W	L	Mins	GA	SO	Avg
1982-83	Acton-Boxboro	HS	23	....	....	....	1035	17	10	0.73	....	....	....	....	....	....	....
1983-84abcd	Buffalo	NHL	42	26	12	3	2475	117	2	2.84	3	0	2	139	8	0	3.45
1984-85ef	Buffalo	NHL	54	25	18	10	3248	144	*5	*2.66	5	2	3	300	22	0	4.40
	Rochester	AHL	5	3	1	1	267	6	1	1.35	....	....	....	....	....	....	....
1985-86	Buffalo	NHL	60	29	24	5	3561	214	2	3.61	....	....	....	....	....	....	....
1986-87	Buffalo	NHL	46	17	23	2	2501	152	2	3.65	....	....	....	....	....	....	....
1987-88	Buffalo	NHL	54	25	18	8	3133	173	2	3.31	4	1	3	224	16	0	4.29
1988-89	Buffalo	NHL	10	2	7	0	545	45	0	4.95	....	....	....	....	....	....	....
	Pittsburgh	NHL	44	18	15	7	2406	162	0	4.04	11	7	4	631	40	0	3.80
1989-90	Pittsburgh	NHL	24	7	12	3	1294	101	0	4.68	....	....	....	....	....	....	....
1990-91	Pittsburgh	NHL	48	27	16	3	2754	165	1	3.59	20	12	7	1175	51	*1	*2.60
	NHL Totals		382	176	145	41	21917	1273	14	3.48	43	22	19	2469	137	1	3.33

a NHL First All-Star Team (1984)
b Won Vezina Trophy (1984)
c Won Calder Memorial Trophy (1984)
d NHL All-Rookie Team (1984)
e NHL Second All-Star Team (1985)
f Shared William Jennings Trophy with Bob Sauve (1985)

Played in NHL All-Star Game (1985)

Traded to **Pittsburgh** by **Buffalo** with Buffalo's third-round choice (Joe Dziedzic) in 1990 Entry Draft for Doug Bodger and Darrin Shannon, November 12, 1988.

BEAUPRE, DONALD WILLIAM (DON) (boh-PRAY)

Goaltender. Catches left. 5′9″, 165 lbs. Born, Waterloo, Ont., September 19, 1961.
(Minnesota's 2nd choice, 32nd overall, in 1980 Entry Draft).

			Regular Season								Playoffs						
Season	Club	Lea	GP	W	L	T	Mins	GA	SO	Avg	GP	W	L	Mins	GA	SO	Avg
1978-79	Sudbury	OHA	54	....	....	....	3248	260	2	4.78	10	....	....	600	44	0	4.20
1979-80a	Sudbury	OHA	59	28	29	2	3447	248	0	4.32	9	5	4	552	38	0	4.13
1980-81	Minnesota	NHL	44	18	14	11	2585	138	0	3.20	6	4	2	360	26	0	4.33
1981-82	Minnesota	NHL	29	11	8	9	1634	101	0	3.71	2	0	1	60	4	0	4.00
	Nashville	CHL	5	2	3	0	299	25	0	5.02	....	....	....	....	....	....	....
1982-83	Minnesota	NHL	36	19	10	5	2011	120	0	3.58	4	2	2	245	20	0	4.90
	Birmingham	CHL	10	8	2	0	599	31	0	3.11	....	....	....	....	....	....	....
1983-84	Minnesota	NHL	33	16	13	2	1791	123	0	4.12	13	6	7	782	40	1	3.07
	Salt Lake	CHL	7	2	5	0	419	30	0	4.30	....	....	....	....	....	....	....
1984-85	Minnesota	NHL	31	10	17	3	1770	109	1	3.69	4	1	1	184	12	0	3.91
1985-86	Minnesota	NHL	52	25	20	6	3073	182	1	3.55	5	2	3	300	17	0	3.40
1986-87	Minnesota	NHL	47	17	20	6	2622	174	1	3.98	....	....	....	....	....	....	....
1987-88	Minnesota	NHL	43	10	22	3	2288	161	0	4.22	....	....	....	....	....	....	....
1988-89	Minnesota	NHL	1	0	1	0	59	3	0	3.05	....	....	....	....	....	....	....
	Kalamazoo	IHL	3	1	2	0	179	9	1	3.02	....	....	....	....	....	....	....
	Washington	NHL	11	5	4	0	578	28	1	2.91	....	....	....	....	....	....	....
	Baltimore	AHL	30	14	12	2	1715	102	0	3.57	....	....	....	....	....	....	....
1989-90	Washington	NHL	48	23	18	5	2793	150	2	3.22	8	4	3	401	18	0	2.69
1990-91	Washington	NHL	45	20	18	3	2572	113	*5	2.64	11	5	5	624	29	*1	2.79
	Baltimore	AHL	2	2	0	0	120	3	0	1.50	....	....	....	....	....	....	....
	NHL Totals		420	174	165	53	23776	1402	11	3.54	53	24	23	2956	166	2	3.37

a OHA First All-Star Team (1980)

Played in NHL All-Star Game (1981)

Traded to **Washington** by **Minnesota** for rights to Claudio Scremin, November 1, 1988.

BEAUREGARD, STEPHANE

Goaltender. Catches right. 5′11″, 185 lbs. Born, Cowansville, Que., January 10, 1968.
(Winnipeg's 3rd choice, 52nd overall, in 1988 Entry Draft).

			Regular Season								Playoffs						
Season	Club	Lea	GP	W	L	T	Mins	GA	SO	Avg	GP	W	L	Mins	GA	SO	Avg
1986-87	St. Jean	QMJHL	13	6	7	0	785	58	0	4.43	5	1	3	260	26	0	6.00
1987-88a	St. Jean	QMJHL	66	38	20	3	3766	229	2	3.65	7	3	4	423	34	0	4.82
1988-89	Moncton	AHL	15	4	8	2	824	62	0	4.51	....	....	....	....	....	....	....
	Fort Wayne	IHL	16	9	5	0	830	43	0	3.10	9	4	4	484	21	*1	*2.60
1989-90	Winnipeg	NHL	19	7	8	3	1079	59	0	3.28	4	1	3	238	12	0	3.03
	Ft. Wayne	IHL	33	20	8	3	1949	115	0	3.54	....	....	....	....	....	....	....
1990-91	Winnipeg	NHL	16	3	10	1	836	55	0	3.95	....	....	....	....	....	....	....
	Moncton	AHL	9	3	4	1	504	20	1	2.38	1	1	0	60	1	0	1.00
	Fort Wayne	IHL	32	14	13	2	1761	109	0	3.71	*19	*10	9	*1158	57	0	2.95
	NHL Totals		35	10	18	4	1915	114	0	3.57	4	1	3	238	12	0	3.03

a QMJHL First All-Star Team (1988)

BELFOUR, ED

Goaltender. Catches left. 5′11″, 182 lbs. Born, Carman, Man., April 21, 1965.

			Regular Season								Playoffs						
Season	Club	Lea	GP	W	L	T	Mins	GA	SO	Avg	GP	W	L	Mins	GA	SO	Avg
1986-87a	North Dakota	WCHA	34	29	4	0	2049	81	3	2.43	....	....	....	....	....	....	....
1987-88bc	Saginaw	IHL	61	32	25	0	*3446	183	3	3.19	9	4	5	561	33	0	3.53
1988-89	Chicago	NHL	23	4	12	3	1148	74	0	3.87	....	....	....	....	....	....	....
	Saginaw	IHL	29	12	10	0	1760	92	0	3.10	5	2	3	298	14	0	2.82
1989-90	Cdn. National	...	33	13	12	6	1808	93	0	3.08	....	....	....	....	....	....	....
	Chicago	NHL	....	....	....	....	....	....	....	....	9	4	2	409	17	0	2.49
1990-91 defghi	Chicago	NHL	*74	*43	19	7	*4127	170	4	*2.47	6	2	4	295	20	0	4.07
	NHL Totals		97	47	31	10	5275	244	4	2.78	15	6	6	704	37	0	3.15

a WCHA First All-Star Team (1987)
b IHL First All-Star Team (1988)
c Shared Garry F. Longman Memorial Trophy (Top Rookie - IHL) (1988)
d NHL First All-Star Team (1991)
e Won Vezina Trophy (1991)
f Won Calder Memorial Trophy (1991)
g Won William M. Jennings Trophy (1991)
h Won Trico Goaltender Award (1991)
i NHL/Upper Deck All-Rookie Team (1991)

Signed as a free agent by **Chicago**, September 25, 1987.

BERGERON, JEAN-CLAUDE

Goaltender. Catches left. 6′2″, 192 lbs. Born, Hauterive, Que., October 14, 1968.
(Montreal's 6th choice, 104th overall, in 1988 Entry Draft).

			Regular Season								Playoffs						
Season	Club	Lea	GP	W	L	T	Mins	GA	SO	Avg	GP	W	L	Mins	GA	SO	Avg
1987-88	Verdun	QMJHL	49	13	31	3	2715	265	0	5.86	....	....	....	....	....	....	....
1988-89	Verdun	QMJHL	44	8	34	1	2417	199	0	4.94	....	....	....	....	....	....	....
	Sherbrooke	AHL	5	4	1	0	302	18	0	3.58	....	....	....	....	....	....	....
1989-90abc	Sherbrooke	AHL	40	21	8	7	2254	103	2	*2.74	9	6	2	497	28	0	3.38
1990-91	Montreal	NHL	18	7	6	2	941	59	0	3.76							
	Fredericton	AHL	18	12	6	0	1083	59	1	3.27	10	5	5	546	32	0	3.52
	NHL Totals		18	7	6	2	941	59	0	3.76	....	....	....	....	....	....	....

a AHL First All-Star Team (1990)
b Shared Harry "Hap" Holmes Trophy (fewest goals-against-AHL) with Andre Racicot (1990)
c Won Baz Bastien Award (Top Goaltender-AHL) (1990)

BERTHIAUME, DANIEL (bair-TYOHM)

Goaltender. Catches left. 5′9″, 150 lbs. Born, Longueuil, Que., January 26, 1966.
(Winnipeg's 3rd choice, 60th overall, in 1985 Entry Draft).

			Regular Season								Playoffs						
Season	Club	Lea	GP	W	L	T	Mins	GA	SO	Avg	GP	W	L	Mins	GA	SO	Avg
1984-85	Chicoutimi	QMJHL	59	40	11	2	2177	149	0	4.11	14	8	6	770	51	0	3.97
1985-86	Chicoutimi	QMJHL	66	34	29	3	3718	286	1	4.62	9	4	5	580	36	0	3.72
	Winnipeg	NHL	....	....	....	....	....	....	....	....	1	0	1	68	4	0	3.53
1986-87	Winnipeg	NHL	31	18	7	3	1758	93	1	3.17	8	4	4	439	21	0	2.87
	Sherbrooke	AHL	7	4	3	0	420	23	0	3.29	....	....	....	....	....	....	....
1987-88	Winnipeg	NHL	56	22	19	7	3010	176	2	3.51	5	1	4	300	25	0	5.00
1988-89	Winnipeg	NHL	9	0	8	0	443	44	0	5.96	....	....	....	....	....	....	....
	Moncton	AHL	21	6	9	2	1083	76	0	4.21	3	1	2	180	11	0	3.67
1989-90	Winnipeg	NHL	24	10	11	3	1387	86	1	3.72	....	....	....	....	....	....	....
	Minnesota	NHL	5	1	3	0	240	14	0	3.50	....	....	....	....	....	....	....
1990-91	Los Angeles	NHL	37	20	11	4	2119	117	1	3.31	....	....	....	....	....	....	....
	NHL Totals		162	71	59	17	8957	530	5	3.55	14	5	9	807	50	0	3.72

Traded to **Minnesota** by **Winnipeg** for future considerations, January 22, 1990. Traded to **Los Angeles** by **Minnesota** for Craig Duncanson, September 6, 1990.

BESTER, ALLAN J.

Goaltender. Catches left. 5'7", 155 lbs. Born, Hamilton, Ont., March 26, 1964.
(Toronto's 3rd choice, 48th overall, in 1983 Entry Draft).

			Regular Season								Playoffs						
Season	Club	Lea	GP	W	L	T	Mins	GA	SO	Avg	GP	W	L	Mins	GA	SO	Avg
1981-82	Brantford	OHL	19	4	11	0	970	68	0	4.21	....	....	....	....	....	....	....
1982-83a	Brantford	OHL	56	29	21	3	3210	188	0	3.51	8	3	3	480	20	*1	*2.50
1983-84	**Toronto**	**NHL**	**32**	**11**	**16**	**4**	**1848**	**134**	**0**	**4.35**	....	....	....	....	....	....	....
	Brantford	OHL	23	12	9	1	1271	71	1	3.35	1	0	1	60	5	0	5.00
1984-85	**Toronto**	**NHL**	**15**	**3**	**9**	**1**	**767**	**54**	**1**	**4.22**	....	....	....	....	....	....	....
	St. Catharines	AHL	30	9	18	1	1669	133	0	4.78	....	....	....	....	....	....	....
1985-86	**Toronto**	**NHL**	**1**	**0**	**0**	**0**	**20**	**2**	**0**	**6.00**	....	....	....	....	....	....	....
	St.Catharines	AHL	50	23	23	3	2855	173	1	3.64	11	7	3	637	27	0	2.54
1986-87	**Toronto**	**NHL**	**36**	**10**	**14**	**3**	**1808**	**110**	**2**	**3.65**	**1**	**0**	**0**	**39**	**1**	**0**	**1.54**
	Newmarket	AHL	3	1	0	0	190	6	0	1.89	....	....	....	....	....	....	....
1987-88	**Toronto**	**NHL**	**30**	**8**	**12**	**5**	**1607**	**102**	**2**	**3.81**	**5**	**2**	**3**	**253**	**21**	**0**	**4.98**
1988-89	**Toronto**	**NHL**	**43**	**17**	**20**	**3**	**2460**	**156**	**2**	**3.80**	....	....	....	....	....	....	....
1989-90	**Toronto**	**NHL**	**42**	**20**	**16**	**0**	**2206**	**165**	**0**	**4.49**	**4**	**0**	**3**	**196**	**14**	**0**	**4.29**
	Newmarket	AHL	5	2	1	1	264	18	0	4.09	....	....	....	....	....	....	....
1990-91	**Toronto**	**NHL**	**6**	**0**	**4**	**0**	**247**	**18**	**0**	**4.37**	....	....	....	....	....	....	....
	Newmarket	AHL	19	7	8	4	1157	58	1	3.01	....	....	....	....	....	....	....
	Detroit	**NHL**	**3**	**0**	**3**	**0**	**178**	**13**	**0**	**4.38**	**1**	**0**	**0**	**20**	**1**	**0**	**3.00**
	NHL Totals		**208**	**69**	**94**	**16**	**11141**	**754**	**7**	**4.06**	**11**	**2**	**6**	**508**	**37**	**0**	**4.37**

a OHL First All-Star Team (1983)

Traded to **Detroit** by **Toronto** for Detroit's sixth round choice (Alexander Kuzminsky) in 1991 Entry Draft, March 5, 1991.

BILLINGTON, CRAIG

Goaltender. Catches left. 5'10", 170 lbs. Born, London, Ont., September 11, 1966.
(New Jersey's 2nd choice, 23rd overall, in 1984 Entry Draft).

			Regular Season								Playoffs						
Season	Club	Lea	GP	W	L	T	Mins	GA	SO	Avg	GP	W	L	Mins	GA	SO	Avg
1983-84	Belleville	OHL	44	20	19	0	2335	162	1	4.16	1	0	0	30	3	0	6.00
1984-85a	Belleville	OHL	47	26	19	0	2544	180	1	4.25	14	7	5	761	47	1	3.71
1985-86	**New Jersey**	**NHL**	**18**	**4**	**9**	**1**	**901**	**77**	**0**	**5.13**	....	....	....	....	....	....	....
	Belleville	OHL	3	2	1	0	180	11	0	3.67	20	9	6	1133	68	0	3.60
1986-87	**New Jersey**	**NHL**	**22**	**4**	**13**	**2**	**1114**	**89**	**0**	**4.79**	....	....	....	....	....	....	....
	Maine	AHL	20	9	8	2	1151	70	0	3.65	....	....	....	....	....	....	....
1987-88	Utica	AHL	*59	22	27	8	*3404	208	1	3.67	....	....	....	....	....	....	....
1988-89	**New Jersey**	**NHL**	**3**	**1**	**1**	**0**	**140**	**11**	**0**	**4.71**	....	....	....	....	....	....	....
	Utica	AHL	41	17	18	6	2432	150	2	3.70	4	1	3	220	18	0	4.91
1989-90	Utica	AHL	38	20	13	1	2087	138	0	3.97	....	....	....	....	....	....	....
1990-91	Cdn. National	...	34	17	14	2	1879	110	2	3.51	....	....	....	....	....	....	....
	NHL Totals		**43**	**9**	**23**	**3**	**2155**	**177**	**0**	**4.93**	....	....	....	....	....	....	....

a OHL First All-Star Team (1985)

BLUE, JOHN

Goaltender. Catches left. 5'10", 190 lbs. Born, Huntington Beach, CA, February 19, 1966.
(Winnipeg's 9th choice, 197th overall, in 1986 Entry Draft).

			Regular Season								Playoffs						
Season	Club	Lea	GP	W	L	T	Mins	GA	SO	Avg	GP	W	L	Mins	GA	SO	Avg
1984-85	U. Minnesota	WCHA	34	23	10	0	1964	111	2	3.39	....	....	....	....	....	....	....
1985-86a	U. Minnesota	WCHA	29	20	6	0	1588	80	2	3.02	....	....	....	....	....	....	....
1986-87	U. Minnesota	WCHA	33	21	9	1	1889	99	3	3.14	....	....	....	....	....	....	....
1987-88	Kalamazoo	IHL	15	3	8	4	847	65	0	4.60	1	0	1	40	6		9.00
	U.S. National	...	13	3	4	1	588	33	0	3.37	....	....	....	....	....	....	....
1988-89	Kalamazoo	IHL	17	8	6	0	970	69	0	4.27	....	....	....	....	....	....	....
	Kalamazoo	IHL	4	2	1	1	232	18	0	4.65	....	....	....	....	....	....	....
1989-90	Phoenix	IHL	19	5	10	3	986	92	0	5.65	....	....	....	....	....	....	....
	Knoxville	ECHL	19	6	10	1	1000	85	0	5.15	....	....	....	....	....	....	....
1990-91	Maine	AHL	10	3	4	2	545	22	0	2.42	1	0	1	40	7	0	10.50
	Albany	IHL	19	11	6	0	1077	71	0	3.96	....	....	....	....	....	....	....
	Kalamazoo	IHL	1	1	0	0	64	2	0	1.88	....	....	....	....	....	....	....
	Peoria	IHL	4	4	0	0	240	12	0	3.00	....	....	....	....	....	....	....
	Knoxville	ECHL	3	1	1	0	149	13	0	5.23	....	....	....	....	....	....	....

a WCHA First All-Star Team (1986)

Traded to **Minnesota** by **Winnipeg** for Winnipeg's seventh round choice in 1988 Entry Draft (Markus Akerblom), March 7, 1988. Signed as a free agent by **Boston**, August 1, 1991.

BRADLEY, JOHN

Goaltender. Catches left. 6', 165 lbs. Born, Pawtucket, RI, February 6, 1968.
(Buffalo's 4th choice, 84th overall, in 1987 Entry Draft).

			Regular Season								Playoffs						
Season	Club	Lea	GP	W	L	T	Mins	GA	SO	Avg	GP	W	L	Mins	GA	SO	Avg
1987-88	Boston U.	H.E.	9	4	4	0	528	40	0	4.53	....	....	....	....	....	....	....
1988-89	Boston U.	H.E.	11	5	4	1	584	53	0	5.45	....	....	....	....	....	....	....
1989-90	Boston U.	H.E.	7	2	3	1	377	20	1	3.18	....	....	....	....	....	....	....
1990-91	Boston U.	H.E.	20	14	4	1	1177	62	*3	3.16	....	....	....	....	....	....	....

BRODEUR, MARTIN

Goaltender. Catches left. 6', 190 lbs. Born, Montreal, Que., May 6, 1972.
(New Jersey's 1st choice, 20th overall, in 1990 Entry Draft).

			Regular Season								Playoffs						
Season	Club	Lea	GP	W	L	T	Mins	GA	SO	Avg	GP	W	L	Mins	GA	SO	Avg
1989-90a	St. Hyacinthe	QMJHL	42	23	13	2	2333	156	0	4.01	12	5	7	678	46	0	4.07
1990-91	St. Hyacinthe	QMJHL	52	22	24	2	2946	162	2	3.30	4	0	4	232	16	0	4.14

a QMJHL Third All-Star Team (1990)

BROWER, SCOTT

Goaltender. Catches left. 6', 192 lbs. Born, Viking, Alta., September 26, 1964.
(NY Rangers' 12th choice, 243rd overall, in 1984 Entry Draft).

			Regular Season								Playoffs						
Season	Club	Lea	GP	W	L	T	Mins	GA	SO	Avg	GP	W	L	Mins	GA	SO	Avg
1984-85	North Dakota	WCHA	31	15	12	2	1808	99	0	3.28	....	....	....	....	....	....	....
1985-86	North Dakota	WCHA	20	11	6	0	1096	67	0	3.47	....	....	....	....	....	....	....
1986-87	North Dakota	WCHA	15	11	4	0	803	44	0	3.29	....	....	....	....	....	....	....
1987-88	North Dakota	WCHA	23	10	12	0	1450	88	1	3.64	....	....	....	....	....	....	....
1988-89	Flint	IHL	5	1	2	0	235	22	0	5.62	....	....	....	....	....	....	....
	Denver	IHL	20	3	5	0	938	82	0	5.25	1	0	0	31	1	0	1.94
1989-90	Flint	IHL	21	7	7	3	1078	80	0	4.45	....	....	....	....	....	....	....
	Phoenix	IHL	1	0	1	0	20	1	0	3.00	....	....	....	....	....	....	....
	Erie	ECHL	5	2	2	0	243	20	0	4.93	....	....	....	....	....	....	....
1990-91	San Diego	IHL	37	11	19	4	2027	139	1	4.11	....	....	....	....	....	....	....

BRUNETTA, MARIO

Goaltender. Catches left. 6'3", 180 lbs. Born, Quebec City, Que., January 25, 1967.
(Quebec's 9th choice, 162nd overall, in 1985 Entry Draft).

			Regular Season								Playoffs						
Season	Club	Lea	GP	W	L	T	Mins	GA	SO	Avg	GP	W	L	Mins	GA	SO	Avg
1984-85	Quebec	QMJHL	45	20	21	1	2255	192	0	5.11	2	0	2	120	13	0	6.50
1985-86	Laval	QMJHL	63	30	25	1	3383	279	0	4.95	14	9	5	834	60	0	4.32
1986-87	Laval	QMJHL	59	27	25	4	3469	261	1	4.51	14	8	6	820	63	0	4.61
1987-88	**Quebec**	**NHL**	**29**	**10**	**12**	**1**	**1550**	**96**	**0**	**3.72**	....	....	....	....	....	....	....
	Fredericton	AHL	5	4	1	0	300	24	0	4.80	....	....	....	....	....	....	....
1988-89	**Quebec**	**NHL**	**5**	**1**	**3**	**0**	**226**	**19**	**0**	**5.04**	....	....	....	....	....	....	....
	Halifax	AHL	36	14	14	5	1898	124	0	3.92	3	0	2	142	12	0	5.07
1989-90	**Quebec**	**NHL**	**6**	**1**	**2**	**0**	**191**	**13**	**0**	**4.08**	....	....	....	....	....	....	....
	Halifax	AHL	24	8	14	2	1444	99	0	4.11	....	....	....	....	....	....	....
1990-91	Asiago	Italy	42	....	....	....	2446	160	3	3.92	....	....	....	....	....	....	....
	NHL Totals		**40**	**12**	**17**	**1**	**1967**	**128**	**0**	**3.90**	....	....	....	....	....	....	....

BURKE, SEAN

Goaltender. Catches left. 6'4", 210 lbs. Born, Windsor, Ont., January 29, 1967.
(New Jersey's 2nd choice, 24th overall, in 1985 Entry Draft).

			Regular Season								Playoffs						
Season	Club	Lea	GP	W	L	T	Mins	GA	SO	Avg	GP	W	L	Mins	GA	SO	Avg
1984-85	Toronto	OHL	49	25	21	3	2987	211	0	4.24	5	1	3	266	25	0	5.64
1985-86	Toronto	OHL	47	16	27	3	2840	233	0	4.92	4	0	4	238	24	0	6.05
1986-87	Cdn. Olympic	...	42	27	13	2	2550	130	0	3.05	....	....	....	....	....	....	....
1987-88	Cdn. National	...	37	19	9	2	1962	92	1	2.81	....	....	....	....	....	....	....
	Cdn. Olympic	...	4	1	2	1	238	12	0	3.02	....	....	....	....	....	....	....
	New Jersey	**NHL**	**13**	**10**	**1**	**0**	**689**	**35**	**1**	**3.05**	**17**	**9**	**8**	**1001**	**57**	***1**	**3.42**
1988-89	**New Jersey**	**NHL**	**62**	**22**	**31**	**9**	**3590**	**230**	**3**	**3.84**	....	....	....	....	....	....	....
1989-90	**New Jersey**	**NHL**	**52**	**22**	**22**	**6**	**2914**	**175**	**0**	**3.60**	**2**	**0**	**2**	**125**	**8**	**0**	**3.84**
1990-91	**New Jersey**	**NHL**	**35**	**8**	**12**	**8**	**1870**	**112**	**0**	**3.59**	....	....	....	....	....	....	....
	NHL Totals		**162**	**62**	**66**	**23**	**9063**	**552**	**4**	**3.65**	**19**	**9**	**10**	**1126**	**65**	**1**	**3.46**

Played in NHL All-Star Game (1989)

CAPPRINI, JOSEPH

Goaltender. Catches left. 5'10", 165 lbs. Born, Pingree, MA, February 26, 1968.
(NY Islanders' 14th choice, 247th overall, in 1988 Entry Draft).

			Regular Season								Playoffs						
Season	Club	Lea	GP	W	L	T	Mins	GA	SO	Avg	GP	W	L	Mins	GA	SO	Avg
1987-88	Babson	NCAA	21	14	5	0	1260	53	0	2.76	....	....	....	....	....	....	....
1988-89	Babson	NCAA	28	17	10	1	1680	71	0	2.60	....	....	....	....	....	....	....
1989-90	Babson	NCAA	19	11	2	5	1140	41	0	2.27	....	....	....	....	....	....	....
1990-91	Babson	NCAA	24	15	6	0	1440	55	0	2.58	....	....	....	....	....	....	....

CASEY, DENIS

Goaltender. Catches left. 5'10", 180 lbs. Born, Kelowna, B.C., March 5, 1971.
(Pittsburgh's 6th choice, 110th overall, in 1990 Entry Draft).

			Regular Season								Playoffs						
Season	Club	Lea	GP	W	L	T	Mins	GA	SO	Avg	GP	W	L	Mins	GA	SO	Avg
1989-90	Colorado	WCHA	19	7	9	1	1059	75	1	4.15	....	....	....	....	....	....	....
1990-91	Colorado	WCHA	11	3	7	0	607	43	0	4.25	....	....	....	....	....	....	....

CASEY, JON

Goaltender. Catches left. 5'10", 155 lbs. Born, Grand Rapids, MN, March 29, 1962.

			Regular Season								Playoffs						
Season	Club	Lea	GP	W	L	T	Mins	GA	SO	Avg	GP	W	L	Mins	GA	SO	Avg
1980-81	North Dakota	WCHA	5	3	1	0	300	19	0	3.80	....	....	....	....	....	....	....
1981-82	North Dakota	WCHA	18	15	3	0	1038	48	1	2.77	....	....	....	....	....	....	....
1982-83	North Dakota	WCHA	17	9	6	2	1020	42	0	2.51	....	....	....	....	....	....	....
1983-84	North Dakota	WCHA	37	25	10	2	2180	115	2	3.13	....	....	....	....	....	....	....
	Minnesota	**NHL**	**2**	**1**	**0**	**0**	**84**	**6**	**0**	**4.29**	....	....	....	....	....	....	....
1984-85ab	Baltimore	AHL	46	30	11	4	2646	116	*4	*2.63	*13	8	3	689	38	0	3.31
1985-86	**Minnesota**	**NHL**	**26**	**11**	**11**	**1**	**1402**	**91**	**0**	**3.89**	....	....	....	....	....	....	....
	Springfield	AHL	9	4	3	1	464	30	0	3.88	....	....	....	....	....	....	....
1986-87	Springfield	AHL	13	1	8	0	770	56	0	4.36	....	....	....	....	....	....	....
	Indianapolis	IHL	31	14	15	0	1794	133	0	4.45	....	....	....	....	....	....	....
1987-88	**Minnesota**	**NHL**	**14**	**1**	**7**	**4**	**663**	**41**	**0**	**3.71**	....	....	....	....	....	....	....
	Kalamazoo	IHL	42	24	13	5	2541	154	2	3.64	7	3	3	382	26	0	4.08
1988-89	**Minnesota**	**NHL**	**55**	**18**	**17**	**12**	**2961**	**151**	**1**	**3.06**	**4**	**1**	**3**	**211**	**16**	**0**	**4.55**
1989-90	**Minnesota**	**NHL**	**61**	***31**	**22**	**4**	**3407**	**183**	**3**	**3.22**	**7**	**3**	**4**	**415**	**21**	**1**	**3.04**
1990-91	**Minnesota**	**NHL**	**55**	**21**	**20**	**11**	**3185**	**158**	**3**	**2.98**	***23**	***14**	**7**	***1205**	**61**	***1**	**3.04**
	NHL Totals		**213**	**83**	**77**	**32**	**11702**	**630**	**7**	**3.23**	**34**	**18**	**14**	**1831**	**98**	**2**	**3.21**

a Won Baz Bastien Trophy (AHL Most Valuable Goaltender) (1985)
b AHL First All-Star Team (1985)

Signed as a free agent by **Minnesota**, April 1, 1984.

CASHMAN, SCOTT

Goaltender. Catches left. 6'2", 175 lbs. Born, Ottawa, Ont., September 20, 1969.
(Minnesota's 8th choice, 112th overall, in 1989 Entry Draft).

			Regular Season								Playoffs						
Season	Club	Lea	GP	W	L	T	Mins	GA	SO	Avg	GP	W	L	Mins	GA	SO	Avg
1989-90ab	Boston U.	H.E.	*39	*23	14	1	*2277	122	*2	3.27	....	....	....	....	....	....	....
1990-91	Boston U.	H.E.	22	14	7	1	1307	79	0	3.58	....	....	....	....	....	....	....

a Hockey East Rookie of the Year (1990)
b Hockey East Second All-Star Team (1990)

Claimed by **San Jose** from **Minnesota** in Dispersal Draft, May 30, 1991.

CHABOT, FREDERIC

Goaltender. Catches right. 5'11", 177 lbs. Born, Hebertville-Station, Que., February 12, 1968.
(New Jersey's 10th choice, 192nd overall, in 1986 Entry Draft).

			Regular Season								Playoffs						
Season	Club	Lea	GP	W	L	T	Mins	GA	SO	Avg	GP	W	L	Mins	GA	SO	Avg
1986-87	Drummondville	QMJHL	62	31	29	0	3508	293	1	5.01	8	2	6	481	40	0	4.99
1987-88	Drummondville	QMJHL	58	27	24	4	3276	237	1	4.34	16	10	6	1019	56	*1	*3.30
1988-89a	Prince Albert	WHL	54	21	29	0	2957	202	2	4.10	4	1	1	199	16	0	4.82
1989-90	Sherbrooke	AHL	2	1	1	0	119	8	0	4.03	....	....	....	....	....	....	....
	Fort Wayne	IHL	23	6	13	3	1208	87	1	4.32	....	....	....	....	....	....	....
1990-91	**Montreal**	**NHL**	**3**	**0**	**0**	**1**	**108**	**6**	**0**	**3.33**	....	....	....	....	....	....	....
	Fredericton	AHL	35	9	15	5	1800	122	0	4.07	....	....	....	....	....	....	....
	NHL Totals		**3**	**0**	**0**	**1**	**108**	**6**	**0**	**3.33**	....	....	....	....	....	....	....

a WHL East All-Star Team (1989)

Signed as a free agent by **Montreal**, January 16, 1990.

CHEVELDAE, TIM (SHE-vehl-day)

Goaltender. Catches left. 5'11", 180 lbs. Born, Melville, Sask., February 15, 1968.
(Detroit's 4th choice, 64th overall, in 1986 Entry Draft).

			Regular Season								Playoffs						
Season	Club	Lea	GP	W	L	T	Mins	GA	SO	Avg	GP	W	L	Mins	GA	SO	Avg
1985-86	Saskatoon	WHL	36	21	10	3	2030	165	0	4.88	8	6	2	480	29	0	3.63
1986-87	Saskatoon	WHL	33	20	11	0	1909	133	2	4.18	5	4	1	308	20	0	3.90
1987-88a	Saskatoon	WHL	66	44	19	3	3798	235	1	3.71	6	4	2	364	27	0	4.45
1988-89	Detroit	NHL	2	0	2	0	122	9	0	4.43	....	....	....	....	....	....	....
	Adirondack	AHL	30	20	8	0	1694	98	1	3.47	2	1	0	99	9	0	5.45
1989-90	Detroit	NHL	28	10	9	8	1600	101	0	3.79	....	....	....	....	....	....	....
	Adirondack	AHL	31	17	8	6	1848	116	0	3.77	....	....	....	....	....	....	....
1990-91	Detroit	NHL	65	30	26	5	3615	214	2	3.55	7	3	4	398	22	0	3.32
	NHL Totals		95	40	37	13	5337	324	2	3.64	7	3	4	398	22	0	3.32

a WHL East All-Star Team (1988)

CHEVRIER, ALAIN

Goaltender. Catches left. 5'8", 180 lbs. Born, Cornwall Ont., April 23, 1961.

			Regular Season								Playoffs						
Season	Club	Lea	GP	W	L	T	Mins	GA	SO	Avg	GP	W	L	Mins	GA	SO	Avg
1982-83	Miami-Ohio	CCHA	33	15	16	1	1894	125	0	3.96	....	....	....	....	....	....	....
1983-84	Miami-Ohio	CCHA	32	9	19	1	1509	123	0	4.89	....	....	....	....	....	....	....
1984-85	Fort Wayne	IHL	56	26	21	7	3219	194	0	3.62	9	5	4	556	28	0	3.02
1985-86	New Jersey	NHL	37	11	18	2	1862	143	0	4.61	....	....	....	....	....	....	....
1986-87	New Jersey	NHL	58	24	26	2	3153	227	0	4.32	....	....	....	....	....	....	....
1987-88	New Jersey	NHL	45	18	19	3	2354	148	1	3.77	....	....	....	....	....	....	....
1988-89	Winnipeg	NHL	22	8	8	2	1092	78	1	4.29	....	....	....	....	....	....	....
	Chicago	NHL	27	13	11	2	1573	92	0	3.51	16	9	7	1013	44	0	2.61
1989-90	Chicago	NHL	39	16	14	3	1894	132	0	4.18	....	....	....	....	....	....	....
	Pittsburgh	NHL	3	1	2	0	166	14	0	5.06	....	....	....	....	....	....	....
1990-91	Detroit	NHL	3	0	2	0	108	11	0	6.11	....	....	....	....	....	....	....
	San Diego	IHL	32	10	16	1	1689	124	0	4.40	....	....	....	....	....	....	....
	NHL Totals		234	91	100	14	12202	845	2	4.16	16	9	7	1013	44	0	2.61

Signed as a free agent by **New Jersey**, May 31, 1985. Traded to **Winnipeg** by **New Jersey** with New Jersey's seventh round (Doug Evans) choice in 1989 Entry Draft for Steve Rooney and **Winnipeg's** third round choice (Brad Bombardir) in 1990 Entry Draft, July 19, 1988. Traded to **Chicago** by **Winnipeg** for Chicago's fourth-round choice (Allain Roy) in 1989 Entry Draft, January 19, 1989. Traded to **Pittsburgh** by **Chicago** for future considerations, March 6, 1990. Signed as a free agent by **Detroit**, July 5, 1990.

CLIFFORD, CHRIS

Goaltender. Catches left. 5'9", 167 lbs. Born, Kingston, Ont., May 26, 1966.
(Chicago's 6th choice, 111th overall, in 1984 Entry Draft).

			Regular Season								Playoffs						
Season	Club	Lea	GP	W	L	T	Mins	GA	SO	Avg	GP	W	L	Mins	GA	SO	Avg
1983-84	Kingston	OHL	50	16	28	0	2808	229	2	4.89	....	....	....	....	....	....	....
1984-85	Chicago	NHL	1	0	0	0	20	0	0	0.00	....	....	....	....	....	....	....
	Kingston	OHL	52	15	34	0	2768	241	0	5.22	....	....	....	....	....	....	....
1985-86	Kingston	OHL	50	26	21	3	2988	178	1	3.57	10	5	5	564	31	1	3.30
1986-87	Kingston	OHL	44	18	25	0	2596	191	1	4.41	12	6	6	730	42	0	3.45
1987-88	Saginaw	IHL	22	9	7	2	1146	80	0	4.19	....	....	....	....	....	....	....
1988-89	Chicago	NHL	1	0	0	0	4	0	0	0.00	....	....	....	....	....	....	....
	Saginaw	IHL	7	4	2	0	321	23	0	4.30	....	....	....	....	....	....	....
1989-90	Muskegon	IHL	23	17	4	1	1352	77	0	3.42	6	3	3	360	24	0	4.01
	Virginia	ECHL	10	7	1	0	547	16	0	1.75	....	....	....	....	....	....	....
1990-91	Muskegon	IHL	*56	24	26	4	*3247	215	1	3.97	5	1	4	299	20	0	4.01
	NHL Totals		2	0	0	0	24	0	0	0.00	....	....	....	....	....	....	....

Signed as a free agent by **Pittsburgh**, September 6, 1989.

CLOUTIER, JACQUES (clootz-YAY)

Goaltender. Catches left. 5'7", 168 lbs. Born, Noranda, Que., January 3, 1960.
(Buffalo's 4th choice, 55th overall, in 1979 Entry Draft).

			Regular Season								Playoffs						
Season	Club	Lea	GP	W	L	T	Mins	GA	SO	Avg	GP	W	L	Mins	GA	SO	Avg
1977-78	Trois Rivieres	QJHL	71	....	....	....	4134	240	*4	3.48	13	....	....	779	40	1	3.08
1978-79a	Trois Rivieres	QJHL	72	....	....	....	4168	218	*3	*3.14	13	....	....	780	36	0	*2.77
1979-80	Trois Rivieres	QJHL	55	27	20	7	3222	231	2	4.30	7	3	4	420	33	0	4.71
1980-81	Rochester	AHL	*61	27	27	6	*3478	209	1	3.61	....	....	....	....	....	....	....
1981-82	Buffalo	NHL	7	5	1	0	311	13	0	2.51	....	....	....	....	....	....	....
	Rochester	AHL	23	14	7	2	1366	64	0	2.81	....	....	....	....	....	....	....
1982-83	Buffalo	NHL	25	10	7	6	1390	81	0	3.50	....	....	....	....	....	....	....
	Rochester	AHL	13	7	3	1	634	42	0	3.97	16	12	4	992	47	0	2.84
1983-84	Rochester	AHL	*51	26	22	1	*2841	172	1	3.63	*18	9	9	*1145	68	0	3.56
1984-85	Buffalo	NHL	1	0	0	1	65	4	0	3.69	....	....	....	....	....	....	....
	Rochester	AHL	14	10	2	1	803	36	0	2.69	....	....	....	....	....	....	....
1985-86	Buffalo	NHL	15	5	9	1	872	49	1	3.37	....	....	....	....	....	....	....
	Rochester	AHL	14	10	2	2	835	38	1	2.73	....	....	....	....	....	....	....
1986-87	Buffalo	NHL	40	11	19	5	2167	137	0	3.79	....	....	....	....	....	....	....
1987-88	Buffalo	NHL	20	4	8	2	851	67	0	4.72	....	....	....	....	....	....	....
1988-89	Buffalo	NHL	36	15	14	0	1786	108	0	3.63	4	1	3	238	10	1	2.52
	Rochester	AHL	11	2	7	0	527	41	0	4.67	....	....	....	....	....	....	....
1989-90	Chicago	NHL	43	18	15	2	2178	112	2	3.09	4	0	2	175	8	0	2.74
1990-91	Chicago	NHL	10	2	3	0	403	24	0	3.57	....	....	....	....	....	....	....
	Quebec	NHL	15	3	8	2	829	61	0	4.41	....	....	....	....	....	....	....
	NHL Totals		212	73	84	19	10852	656	3	3.63	8	1	5	413	18	1	2.62

a QMJHL First All-Star Team (1979)

Traded to **Chicago** by **Buffalo** for future considerations, September 28, 1989. Traded to **Quebec** by **Chicago** for Tony McKegney, January 29, 1991.

COLE, THOMAS

Goaltender. Catches left. 6', 185 lbs. Born, Woburn, MA, February 18, 1969.
(Edmonton's 10th choice, 187th overall, in 1988 Entry Draft).

			Regular Season								Playoffs						
Season	Club	Lea	GP	W	L	T	Mins	GA	SO	Avg	GP	W	L	Mins	GA	SO	Avg
1988-89	Northeastern	H.E.	6	2	4	0	319	30	0	5.64	....	....	....	....	....	....	....
1989-90	Northeastern	H.E.	25	10	12	2	1412	106	0	4.51	....	....	....	....	....	....	....
1990-91	Northeastern	H.E.	*31	8	18	1	*1583	137	1	5.19	....	....	....	....	....	....	....

CONNELL, PAUL

Goaltender. Catches left. 5'8", 160 lbs. Born, Cranston, RI, March 19, 1967.
(Philadelphia's 1st choice, 19th overall, in 1988 Supplemental Draft).

			Regular Season								Playoffs						
Season	Club	Lea	GP	W	L	T	Mins	GA	SO	Avg	GP	W	L	Mins	GA	SO	Avg
1986-87	Bowling Green	CCHA	7	4	1	0	324	23	0	4.26	....	....	....	....	....	....	....
1987-88	Bowling Green	CCHA	39	27	10	2	2322	155	0	4.00	....	....	....	....	....	....	....
1988-89	Bowling Green	CCHA	41	21	16	3	2439	140	0	3.44	....	....	....	....	....	....	....
1989-90	Bowling Green	CCHA	18	8	6	0	943	79	0	5.03	....	....	....	....	....	....	....
1990-91	Roanoke	ECHL	1	1	0	0	65	2	0	1.84	....	....	....	....	....	....	....

COUSINEAU, MARCEL

Goaltender. Catches left. 5'9", 180 lbs. Born, Delson, Que., April 30, 1973.
(Boston's 3rd choice, 62nd overall, in 1991 Entry Draft).

			Regular Season								Playoffs						
Season	Club	Lea	GP	W	L	T	Mins	GA	SO	Avg	GP	W	L	Mins	GA	SO	Avg
1990-91	Beauport	QMJHL	49	13	29	3	2739	196	1	4.29	....	....	....	....	....	....	....

COWLEY, WAYNE

Goaltender. Catches left. 6'0", 185 lbs. Born, Scarborough, Ont., December 4, 1964.

			Regular Season								Playoffs						
Season	Club	Lea	GP	W	L	T	Mins	GA	SO	Avg	GP	W	L	Mins	GA	SO	Avg
1985-86	Colgate	ECAC	7	2	2	0	313	23	1	4.42	....	....	....	....	....	....	....
1986-87	Colgate	ECAC	31	21	8	1	1805	106	0	3.52	....	....	....	....	....	....	....
1987-88	Colgate	ECAC	20	11	7	1	1162	58	1	2.99	....	....	....	....	....	....	....
1988-89	Salt Lake	IHL	29	17	7	1	1423	94	0	3.96	2	1	0	69	6	0	5.22
1989-90	Salt Lake	IHL	36	15	12	5	2009	124	1	3.70	3	0	0	118	6	0	3.05
1990-91	Salt Lake	IHL	7	3	4	0	377	23	1	3.66	....	....	....	....	....	....	....
a	Cincinnati	ECHL	30	19	9	2	1680	108	1	3.85	4	1	3	249	13	*1	3.13

a ECHL Second All-Star Team (1991)

Signed as a free agent by **Calgary**, May 1, 1988.

CROZIER, JIM

Goaltender. Catches left. 5'8", 165 lbs. Born, North Bay, Ont., February 9, 1968.
(Hartford's 1st choice, 20th overall, in 1990 Supplemental Draft).

			Regular Season								Playoffs						
Season	Club	Lea	GP	W	L	T	Mins	GA	SO	Avg	GP	W	L	Mins	GA	SO	Avg
1987-88	Cornell	ECAC	3	2	1	0	180	11	0	3.67	....	....	....	....	....	....	....
1988-89	Cornell	ECAC	5	1	0	0	127	2	0	0.94	....	....	....	....	....	....	....
1989-90	Cornell	ECAC	16	6	7	2	866	38	0	*2.63	....	....	....	....	....	....	....
1990-91	Cornell	ECAC	15	8	3	0	739	40	0	3.25	....	....	....	....	....	....	....

DAFOE, BYRON

Goaltender. Catches left. 5'11", 175 lbs. Born, Duncan, B.C., February 25, 1971.
(Washington's 2nd choice, 35th overall, in 1989 Entry Draft).

			Regular Season								Playoffs						
Season	Club	Lea	GP	W	L	T	Mins	GA	SO	Avg	GP	W	L	Mins	GA	SO	Avg
1988-89	Portland	WHL	59	29	24	3	3279	291	1	5.32	*18	10	8	*1091	81	*1	4.45
1989-90	Portland	WHL	40	14	21	3	2265	193	0	5.11	....	....	....	....	....	....	....
1990-91	Portland	WHL	8	1	5	1	414	41	0	5.94	....	....	....	....	....	....	....
	Prince Albert	WHL	32	13	12	4	1839	124	0	4.05	....	....	....	....	....	....	....

D'ALESSIO, CORRIE

Goaltender. Catches left. 5'11", 155 lbs. Born, Cornwall, Ont., September 9, 1969.
(Vancouver's 4th choice, 107th overall, in 1988 Entry Draft).

			Regular Season								Playoffs						
Season	Club	Lea	GP	W	L	T	Mins	GA	SO	Avg	GP	W	L	Mins	GA	SO	Avg
1987-88a	Cornell	ECAC	25	17	8	0	1457	67	0	2.76	....	....	....	....	....	....	....
1988-89	Cornell	ECAC	29	15	13	1	1684	96	1	3.42	....	....	....	....	....	....	....
1989-90	Cornell	ECAC	16	6	7	2	887	50	0	3.38	....	....	....	....	....	....	....
1990-91	Cornell	ECAC	24	10	8	3	1160	67	0	3.47	....	....	....	....	....	....	....

a ECAC All-Rookie Team (1988)

D'AMOUR, MARC (dah-MOHR)

Goaltender. Catches left. 5'9", 190 lbs. Born, Sudbury, Ont., April 29, 1961.

			Regular Season								Playoffs						
Season	Club	Lea	GP	W	L	T	Mins	GA	SO	Avg	GP	W	L	Mins	GA	SO	Avg
1979-80	S. S. Marie	OHA	33	16	15	0	1429	117	0	4.91	....	....	....	....	....	....	....
1980-81	S. S. Marie	OHA	16	7	1	1	653	38	0	3.49	14	5	4	683	41	0	3.60
1981-82a	S. S. Marie	OHL	41	28	12	1	3284	130	1	*3.27	10	3	2	504	30	0	3.57
1982-83	Colorado	CHL	42	16	21	2	2373	153	1	3.87	1	....	....	59	4	0	4.08
1983-84	Colorado	CHL	36	18	12	1	1917	131	0	4.10	1	0	0	20	0	0	0.00
1984-85	Moncton	AHL	37	18	14	2	2051	115	0	3.36	....	....	....	....	....	....	....
	Salt Lake	IHL	12	7	2	2	694	33	0	2.85	....	....	....	....	....	....	....
1985-86	Calgary	NHL	15	2	4	2	560	32	0	3.43	....	....	....	....	....	....	....
	Moncton	AHL	21	6	9	3	1129	72	0	3.83	5	1	4	296	20	0	4.05
1986-87	Binghamton	AHL	8	5	3	0	461	30	0	3.90	....	....	....	....	....	....	....
	Salt Lake	IHL	10	3	6	0	523	37	0	4.24	....	....	....	....	....	....	....
	Can. Olympic	...	1	0	0	0	30	4	0	8.00	....	....	....	....	....	....	....
1987-88	Salt Lake	IHL	*62	26	19	5	3245	177	0	3.27	*19	*12	7	*1123	67		3.58
1988-89	Philadelphia	NHL	1	0	0	0	19	0	0	0.00	....	....	....	....	....	....	....
	Hershey	AHL	39	19	13	3	2174	127	0	3.51	....	....	....	....	....	....	....
	Indianapolis	IHL	6	2	3	0	324	20	0	3.70	....	....	....	....	....	....	....
1989-90	Hershey	AHL	43	15	20	6	2505	148	2	3.54	....	....	....	....	....	....	....
1990-91	Hershey	AHL	28	10	8	4	1331	80	0	3.61	2	0	1	80	5	0	3.75
	Fort Wayne	IHL	3	1	0	0	136	9	0	3.97	....	....	....	....	....	....	....
	NHL Totals		16	2	4	2	579	32	0	3.32	....	....	....	....	....	....	....

a OHL First All-Star Team (1982)

Signed as free agent by **Calgary**, June 7, 1982. Signed as a free agent by **Philadelphia**, September 30, 1988.

DelGUIDICE, MATT (del-GOO-dis)

Goaltender. Catches right. 5'9", 170 lbs. Born, West Haven, CT, March 5, 1967.
(Boston's 5th choice, 77th overall, in 1987 Entry Draft).

			Regular Season								Playoffs						
Season	Club	Lea	GP	W	L	T	Mins	GA	SO	Avg	GP	W	L	Mins	GA	SO	Avg
1987-88					DID NOT PLAY												
1988-89	U. of Maine	H.E.	20	16	4	0	1090	57	1	*3.14	....	....	....	....	....	....	....
1989-90	U. of Maine	H.E.	23	16	4	0	1257	68	0	3.25	....	....	....	....	....	....	....
1990-91	Boston	NHL	1	0	0	0	10	0	0	0.00	....	....	....	....	....	....	....
	Maine	AHL	52	23	18	9	2893	160	2	3.32	2	1	1	82	5	0	3.66
	NHL Totals		1	0	0	0	10	0	0	0.00	....	....	....	....	....	....	....

DERKSEN, DUANE

Goaltender. Catches left. 6′1″, 180 lbs. Born, St. Boniface, Man., July 7, 1968.
(Washington's 4th choice, 57th overall, in 1988 Entry Draft).

			Regular Season								Playoffs						
Season	Club	Lea	GP	W	L	T	Mins	GA	SO	Avg	GP	W	L	Mins	GA	SO	Avg
1988-89	U. Wisconsin	WCHA	11	4	5	0	561	37	1	3.96	....	....	....	....	....	....	....
1989-90ab	U. Wisconsin	WCHA	*41	*31	8	1	*2345	133	*2	*3.40	....	....	....	....	....	....	....
1990-91a	U. Wisconsin	WCHA	*42	24	15	3	*2474	133	3	3.23	....	....	....	....	....	....	....

a WCHA Second All-Star Team (1990, 1991)
b NCAA All-Tournament Team, Tournament Top Goaltender (1990).

DONEGHEY, MICHAEL

Goaltender. Catches left. 6′, 165 lbs. Born, Boston, MA, July 28, 1970.
(Chicago's 10th choice, 237th overall, in 1989 Entry Draft).

			Regular Season								Playoffs						
Season	Club	Lea	GP	W	L	T	Mins	GA	SO	Avg	GP	W	L	Mins	GA	SO	Avg
1989-90	Merrimack	H.E.	9	3	5	0	424	36	1	5.09	....	....	....	....	....	....	....
1990-91	Merrimack	H.E.	12	2	4	1	557	48	0	4.90	....	....	....	....	....	....	....

DRAPER, TOM

Goaltender. Catches left. 5′11″, 180 lbs. Born, Outremont, Que., November 20, 1966.
(Winnipeg's 8th choice, 165th overall, in 1985 Entry Draft).

			Regular Season								Playoffs						
Season	Club	Lea	GP	W	L	T	Mins	GA	SO	Avg	GP	W	L	Mins	GA	SO	Avg
1983-84	U. of Vermont	ECAC	20	8	12	0	1205	82	0	4.08	...	...	...	...	...	...	...
1984-85	U. of Vermont	ECAC	24	5	17	0	1316	90	0	4.11	...	...	...	...	...	...	...
1985-86	U. of Vermont	ECAC	29	15	12	1	1697	87	1	3.08	...	...	...	...	...	...	...
1986-87a	U. of Vermont	ECAC	29	16	13	0	1662	96	2	3.47	...	...	...	...	...	...	...
1987-88	Tappara	Fin.	28	16	3	9	1619	87	0	3.22	....	....	....	....	....	....	....
1988-89	**Winnipeg**	**NHL**	**2**	**1**	**1**	**0**	**120**	**12**	**0**	**6.00**	....	....	....	....	....	....	....
b	Moncton	AHL	*54	27	17	5	*2962	171	2	3.46	7	5	2	419	24	0	3.44
1989-90	**Winnipeg**	**NHL**	**6**	**2**	**4**	**0**	**359**	**26**	**0**	**4.35**	....	....	....	....	....	....	....
	Moncton	AHL	51	20	24	3	2844	167	1	3.52	....	....	....	....	....	....	....
1990-91	Moncton	AHL	30	15	13	2	1779	95	1	3.20	....	....	....	....	....	....	....
	Fort Wayne	IHL	10	5	3	1	564	32	0	3.40	....	....	....	....	....	....	....
	Peoria	IHL	10	6	3	1	584	36	0	3.70	4	2	1	214	10	0	2.80
	NHL Totals		**8**	**3**	**5**	**0**	**479**	**38**	**0**	**4.76**	....	....	....	....	....	....	....

a ECAC First All-Star Team (1987).
b AHL Second All-Star Team (1989)

Traded to **St. Louis** by **Winnipeg** for future considerations (Jim Vesey - May 24, 1991), February 28, 1991. Traded to **Winnipeg** by **St. Louis** for future considerations, May 24, 1991. Traded to **Buffalo** by **Winnipeg** for future considerations, June 22, 1991.

DUFFUS, PARRIS

Goaltender. Catches left. 6′2″, 192 lbs. Born, Denver, CO, January 27, 1970.
(St. Louis' 6th choice, 180th overall, in 1990 Entry Draft).

			Regular Season								Playoffs						
Season	Club	Lea	GP	W	L	T	Mins	GA	SO	Avg	GP	W	L	Mins	GA	SO	Avg
1989-90	Melfort	SJHL	51	....	....	....	2828	226	2	4.79	....	....	....	....	....	....	....
1990-91	Cornell	ECAC	4	0	0	0	37	3	0	4.86	....	....	....	....	....	....	....

DUNHAM, MICHAEL

Goaltender. Catches left. 6′2″, 170 lbs. Born, Johnson City, NY, June 1, 1972.
(New Jersey's 4th choice, 53rd overall, in 1990 Entry Draft).

			Regular Season								Playoffs						
Season	Club	Lea	GP	W	L	T	Mins	GA	SO	Avg	GP	W	L	Mins	GA	SO	Avg
1989-90	Canterbury	HS	32	....	....	....	1558	68	3	1.96	....	....	....	....	....	....	....
1990-91	U. of Maine	H.E.	23	14	5	2	1275	63	0	*2.96	....	....	....	....	....	....	....

DYCK, LARRY

Goaltender. Catches left. 5′11″, 180 lbs. Born, Winkler, Man., December 15, 1965.

			Regular Season								Playoffs						
Season	Club	Lea	GP	W	L	T	Mins	GA	SO	Avg	GP	W	L	Mins	GA	SO	Avg
1988-89	Kalamazoo	IHL	42	17	20	2	2308	168	0	4.37	....	....	....	....	....	....	....
1989-90	Kalamazoo	IHL	36	20	12	0	1959	116	0	3.55	7	2	3	353	22	0	3.74
	Knoxville	ECHL	3	1	1	1	184	12	0	3.91	....	....	....	....	....	....	....
1990-91	Kalamazoo	IHL	38	21	15	0	2182	133	1	3.66	1	0	1	60	6	0	6.00

Signed as a free agent by **Minnesota**, November 10, 1988.

ERICKSON, CHAD

Goaltender. Catches right. 5′9″, 175 lbs. Born, Minneapolis, MN, August 21, 1970.
(New Jersey's 8th choice, 138th overall, in 1988 Entry Draft).

			Regular Season								Playoffs						
Season	Club	Lea	GP	W	L	T	Mins	GA	SO	Avg	GP	W	L	Mins	GA	SO	Avg
1988-89	Minn.-Duluth	WCHA	15	5	7	1	821	49	0	3.58	....	....	....	....	....	....	....
1989-90ab	Minn.-Duluth	WCHA	39	19	19	1	2301	141	0	3.68	....	....	....	....	....	....	....
1990-91	Minn.-Duluth	WCHA	40	14	19	7	2393	159	0	3.99	....	....	....	....	....	....	....

a WCHA Second All-Star Team (1990)
b NCAA West First All-American Team (1990)

ESSENSA, BOB (EH-sehn-sah)

Goaltender. Catches left. 6′, 160 lbs. Born, Toronto, Ont., January 14, 1965.
(Winnipeg's 5th choice, 69th overall, in 1983 Entry Draft).

			Regular Season								Playoffs						
Season	Club	Lea	GP	W	L	T	Mins	GA	SO	Avg	GP	W	L	Mins	GA	SO	Avg
1983-84	Michigan State	CCHA	17	11	4	0	946	44	2	2.79	....	....	....	....	....	....	....
1984-85	Michigan State	CCHA	18	15	2	0	1059	29	2	1.64	....	....	....	....	....	....	....
1985-86a	Michigan State	CCHA	23	17	4	1	1333	74	1	3.33	....	....	....	....	....	....	....
1986-87	Michigan State	CCHA	25	19	3	1	1383	64	2	2.78	....	....	....	....	....	....	....
1987-88	Moncton	AHL	27	7	11	1	1287	100	1	4.66	....	....	....	....	....	....	....
1988-89	**Winnipeg**	**NHL**	**20**	**6**	**8**	**3**	**1102**	**68**	**1**	**3.70**	....	....	....	....	....	....	....
	Fort Wayne	IHL	22	14	7	0	1287	70	0	3.26	....	....	....	....	....	....	....
1989-90b	**Winnipeg**	**NHL**	**36**	**18**	**9**	**5**	**2035**	**107**	**1**	**3.15**	**4**	**2**	**1**	**206**	**12**	**0**	**3.50**
	Moncton	AHL	6	3	3	0	358	15	0	2.51	....	....	....	....	....	....	....
1990-91	**Winnipeg**	**NHL**	**55**	**19**	**24**	**6**	**2916**	**153**	**4**	**3.15**	....	....	....	....	....	....	....
	Moncton	AHL	2	1	0	1	125	6	0	2.88	....	....	....	....	....	....	....
	NHL Totals		**111**	**43**	**41**	**14**	**6053**	**328**	**6**	**3.25**	**4**	**2**	**1**	**206**	**12**	**0**	**3.50**

a CCHA Second All-Star Team (1986)
b NHL All-Rookie Team (1990)

EXELBY, RANDY

Goaltender. Catches left. 5′9″, 170 lbs. Born, Toronto, Ont., August 13, 1965.
(Montreal's 1st choice, 20th overall, in 1986 Supplemental Draft).

			Regular Season								Playoffs						
Season	Club	Lea	GP	W	L	T	Mins	GA	SO	Avg	GP	W	L	Mins	GA	SO	Avg
1983-84	Lake Superior	CCHA	21	6	10	0	905	75	0	4.97	...	...	...	...	...	...	...
1984-85	Lake Superior	CCHA	36	22	11	1	1999	112	0	3.36	...	...	...	...	...	...	...
1985-86	Lake Superior	CCHA	28	14	11	1	1625	98	0	3.61	...	...	...	...	...	...	...
1987-87	Lake Superior	CCHA	28	12	9	1	1357	91	0	4.02	...	...	...	...	...	...	...
1987-88	Sherbrooke	AHL	19	7	10	0	1050	49	0	2.80	4	2	2	212	13	0	3.68
1988-89	**Montreal**	**NHL**	**1**	**0**	**0**	**0**	**3**	**0**	**0**	**0.00**	....	....	....	....	....	....	....
abc	Sherbrooke	AHL	52	*31	13	6	2935	146	*6	*2.98	6	1	4	329	24	0	4.38
1989-90	**Edmonton**	**NHL**	**1**	**0**	**1**	**0**	**60**	**5**	**0**	**5.00**	....	....	....	....	....	....	....
	Phoenix	IHL	41	11	18	5	2146	163	0	4.56	....	....	....	....	....	....	....
1990-91	Springfield	AHL	4	1	2	1	245	20	0	4.90	....	....	....	....	....	....	....
	Kansas City	IHL	16	0	13	0	785	65	0	4.97	....	....	....	....	....	....	....
	Louisville	ECHL	13	6	5	1	743	60	0	4.84	....	....	....	....	....	....	....
	NHL Totals		**2**	**0**	**1**	**0**	**63**	**5**	**0**	**4.76**	....	....	....	....	....	....	....

a AHL First All-Star Team (1989)
b Shared Harry "Hap Holmes Trophy (fewest goals-against-AHL) with Francois Gravel (1989)
c Won Baz Bastien Award (Top Goaltender-AHL) (1989)

Traded to **Edmonton** by **Montreal** for future considerations, October 2, 1989.

FELICIO, MARC

Goaltender. Catches left. 5′8″, 175 lbs. Born, Smithfield, RI, December 1, 1968.
(Minnesota's 11th choice, 214th overall, in 1987 Entry Draft).

			Regular Season								Playoffs						
Season	Club	Lea	GP	W	L	T	Mins	GA	SO	Avg	GP	W	L	Mins	GA	SO	Avg
1987-88	Ferris State	CCHA	18	4	9	0	806	74	0	5.50	....	....	....	....	....	....	....
1988-89	Ferris State	CCHA	19	6	9	1	1045	85	0	4.88	....	....	....	....	....	....	....
1989-90	Ferris State	CCHA	17	2	7	0	738	59	0	4.81	....	....	....	....	....	....	....
1990-91	Ferris State	CCHA	20	10	4	4	1137	61	1	3.22	....	....	....	....	....	....	....

FISET, STEPHANE

Goaltender. Catches left. 6′, 175 lbs. Born, Montreal, Que., June 17, 1970.
(Quebec's 3rd choice, 24th overall, in 1988 Entry Draft).

			Regular Season								Playoffs						
Season	Club	Lea	GP	W	L	T	Mins	GA	SO	Avg	GP	W	L	Mins	GA	SO	Avg
1987-88	Victoriaville	QMJHL	40	15	17	4	2221	146	1	3.94	2	0	2	163	10	0	3.68
1988-89a	Victoriaville	QMJHL	43	25	14	0	2401	138	1	*3.45	12	*9	2	711	33	0	*2.78
1989-90	**Quebec**	**NHL**	**6**	**0**	**5**	**1**	**342**	**34**	**0**	**5.96**	....	....	....	....	....	....	....
	Victoriaville	QMJHL	24	14	6	3	1383	63	1	*2.73	*14	7	6	*790	49	0	3.72
1990-91	**Quebec**	**NHL**	**3**	**0**	**2**	**1**	**186**	**12**	**0**	**3.87**	....	....	....	....	....	....	....
	Halifax	AHL	36	10	15	8	1902	131	0	4.13	....	....	....	....	....	....	....
	NHL Totals		**9**	**0**	**7**	**2**	**528**	**46**	**0**	**5.23**	....	....	....	....	....	....	....

a QMJHL First All-Star Team (1989)

FITZPATRICK, MARK

Goaltender. Catches left. 6′1″, 190 lbs. Born, Toronto, Ont., November 13, 1968.
(Los Angeles' 2nd choice, 27th overall, in 1987 Entry Draft).

			Regular Season								Playoffs						
Season	Club	Lea	GP	W	L	T	Mins	GA	SO	Avg	GP	W	L	Mins	GA	SO	Avg
1985-86	Medicine Hat	WHL	41	26	6	1	2074	99	1	2.86	19	12	5	986	58	0	3.53
1986-87	Medicine Hat	WHL	50	31	11	4	2844	159	4	3.35	20	12	8	1224	71	1	3.48
1987-88	Medicine Hat	WHL	63	36	15	6	3600	194	2	3.23	16	12	4	959	52	*1	*3.25
1988-89	**Los Angeles**	**NHL**	**17**	**6**	**7**	**3**	**957**	**64**	**0**	**4.01**	....	....	....	....	....	....	....
	New Haven	AHL	18	10	5	1	980	54	1	3.31	....	....	....	....	....	....	....
	NY Islanders	**NHL**	**11**	**3**	**5**	**2**	**627**	**41**	**0**	**3.92**	....	....	....	....	....	....	....
1989-90	**NY Islanders**	**NHL**	**47**	**19**	**19**	**5**	**2653**	**150**	**3**	**3.39**	**4**	**0**	**2**	**152**	**13**	**0**	**5.13**
1990-91	**NY Islanders**	**NHL**	**2**	**1**	**1**	**0**	**120**	**6**	**0**	**3.00**	....	....	....	....	....	....	....
	Capital Dist.	AHL	12	3	7	2	734	47	0	3.84	....	....	....	....	....	....	....
	NHL Totals		**77**	**29**	**32**	**10**	**4357**	**261**	**3**	**3.59**	**4**	**0**	**2**	**152**	**13**	**0**	**5.13**

Traded to **NY Islanders** by **Los Angeles** with Wayne McBean and future considerations (Doug Crossman, acquired May 23, 1989) for Kelly Hrudey, February 22, 1989.

FLETCHER, JOHN

Goaltender. Catches right. 5′7″, 165 lbs. Born, Holden, MA, October 14, 1967.
(Vancouver's 9th choice, 192nd overall, in 1987 Entry Draft).

			Regular Season								Playoffs						
Season	Club	Lea	GP	W	L	T	Mins	GA	SO	Avg	GP	W	L	Mins	GA	SO	Avg
1986-87a	Clarkson	ECAC	23	11	8	1	1240	62	4	2.99	....	....	....	....	....	....	....
1987-88bc	Clarkson	ECAC	33	16	11	3	1820	97	1	3.19	....	....	....	....	....	....	....
1988-89	Clarkson	ECAC	23	9	8	2	1146	79	0	4.13	....	....	....	....	....	....	....
1989-90	Clarkson	ECAC	34	20	11	3	1900	89	0	3.13	....	....	....	....	....	....	....
1990-91	Winston Salem	ECHL	11	0	8	0	534	57	0	6.40	....	....	....	....	....	....	....
	Cincinnati	ECHL	14	3	8	1	783	71	0	5.44	....	....	....	....	....	....	....

a ECAC Rookie of the Year (1987)
b ECAC First All-Star Team (1988)
c NCAA East Second All-American Team (1988)

FORD, BRIAN

Goaltender. Catches left. 5′10″, 170 lbs. Born, Edmonton, Alta., September 22, 1961.

			Regular Season								Playoffs						
Season	Club	Lea	GP	W	L	T	Mins	GA	SO	Avg	GP	W	L	Mins	GA	SO	Avg
1980-81	Billings	WHL	44	14	26	0	2435	204	0	5.03	3	....	....	143	15	0	4.66
1981-82	Billings	WHL	53	19	26	1	2791	256	0	5.50	5	....	....	226	26	0	5.86
1982-83	Carolina	ACHL	4	....	....	....	203	7	0	2.07	....	....	....	....	....	....	....
	Fredericton	AHL	27	14	7	2	1443	84	0	*3.49	1	0	0	11	1	0	5.56
1983-84	**Quebec**	**NHL**	**3**	**1**	**1**	**0**	**123**	**13**	**0**	**6.34**	....	....	....	....	....	....	....
a	Fredericton	AHL	36	17	17	1	2132	105	2	*2.96	4	1	3	223	18	0	4.84
1984-85	**Pittsburgh**	**NHL**	**8**	**2**	**6**	**0**	**457**	**48**	**0**	**6.30**	....	....	....	....	....	....	....
	Baltimore	AHL	6	3	3	0	363	21	0	3.47	....	....	....	....	....	....	....
	Muskegon	IHL	22	17	5	0	1321	59	1	2.68	....	....	....	....	....	....	....
1985-86	Baltimore	AHL	39	12	20	4	2230	136	1	3.66	....	....	....	....	....	....	....
	Muskegon	IHL	9	4	4	0	513	33	0	3.06	*13	*12	1	*793	41	0	3.10
1986-87	Baltimore	AHL	32	10	11	0	1541	99	0	3.85	....	....	....	....	....	....	....
1987-88	Springfield	AHL	35	12	15	4	1898	118	0	3.73	....	....	....	....	....	....	....
1988-89	Rochester	AHL	19	12	4	1	1075	60	2	3.35	....	....	....	....	....	....	....
1989-90	Rochester	AHL	19	7	6	4	1076	69	0	3.85	....	....	....	....	....	....	....
1990-91	Moncton	AHL	1	0	1	0	60	5	0	5.00	1	0	0	1	1	0	60.00
	NHL Totals		**11**	**3**	**7**	**0**	**580**	**61**	**0**	**6.31**	....	....	....	....	....	....	....

a Won Harry (Hap) Holmes Memorial Trophy (AHL's leading goaltender) (1984)

Signed as a free agent by **Quebec**, August 1, 1982. Traded to **Pittsburgh** by **Quebec** for Tom Thornbury, December 6, 1984.

FOSTER, NORM

Goaltender. Catches left. 5'9", 175 lbs. Born, Vancouver, B.C., February 10, 1965.
(Boston's 11th choice, 222nd overall, in 1983 Entry Draft).

			Regular Season								Playoffs						
Season	**Club**	**Lea**	**GP**	**W**	**L**	**T**	**Mins**	**GA**	**SO**	**Avg**	**GP**	**W**	**L**	**Mins**	**GA**	**SO**	**Avg**
1984-85	Michigan State	CCHA	26	22	4	0	1531	67	0	2.63	....	....	....	....	....	....	....
1985-86	Michigan State	CCHA	24	17	5	1	1414	87	0	3.69	....	....	....	....	....	....	....
1986-87	Michigan State	CCHA	24	14	7	1	1383	90	1	3.90	....	....	....	....	....	....	....
1987-88	Milwaukee	IHL	38	10	22	1	2001	170	0	5.10	....	....	....	....	....	....	....
1988-89	Maine	AHL	47	16	17	6	2411	156	1	3.88	....	....	....	....	....	....	....
1989-90	Maine	AHL	*64	23	28	10	*3664	217	3	3.55	....	....	....	....	....	....	....
1990-91	**Boston**	**NHL**	**3**	**2**	**1**	**0**	**184**	**14**	**0**	**4.57**	....	....	....	....	....	....	....
	Maine	AHL	2	1	1	0	122	7	0	3.44	....	....	....	....	....	....	....
	Cape Breton	AHL	40	15	14	7	2207	135	1	3.67	2	0	2	128	8	0	3.75
	NHL Totals		**3**	**2**	**1**	**0**	**184**	**14**	**0**	**4.57**	....	....	....	....	....	....	....

FRANCIS, MICHAEL (MIKE)

Goaltender. Catches left. 6'1", 180 lbs. Born, Brunswick, MA, November 19, 1969.
(St. Louis' 12th choice, 240th overall, in 1988 Entry Draft).

			Regular Season								Playoffs						
Season	**Club**	**Lea**	**GP**	**W**	**L**	**T**	**Mins**	**GA**	**SO**	**Avg**	**GP**	**W**	**L**	**Mins**	**GA**	**SO**	**Avg**
1987-88	Harvard	ECAC	10	6	3	0	580	25	0	2.59	....	....	....	....	....	....	....
1988-89	Harvard	ECAC	3	2	0	0	140	2	0	0.86	....	....	....	....	....	....	....
1989-90	Harvard	ECAC	3	1	1	0	143	9	0	3.78	....	....	....	....	....	....	....
1990-91	Harvard	ECAC	5	1	3	1	271	14	0	2.99	....	....	....	....	....	....	....

FROESE, ROBERT GLENN (BOB) (FROHZ)

Goaltender. Catches left. 5'11", 176 lbs. Born, St. Catharines, Ont., June 30, 1958.
(St. Louis' 11th choice, 160th overall, in 1978 Amateur Draft).

			Regular Season								Playoffs						
Season	**Club**	**Lea**	**GP**	**W**	**L**	**T**	**Mins**	**GA**	**SO**	**Avg**	**GP**	**W**	**L**	**Mins**	**GA**	**SO**	**Avg**
1975-76	St. Catharines	OHA	39	....	....	....	1976	193	0	5.83	4	....	....	240	20	0	5.00
1976-77	Niagara Falls	OHA	39	....	....	....	2063	162	2	4.68	....	....	....	....	....	....	....
1977-78	Niagara Falls	OHA	52	....	....	....	3128	249	0	4.71	3	....	....	236	17	0	4.36
1978-79	Saginaw	IHL	21	....	....	....	1050	58	0	3.31	....	....	....	....	....	....	....
	Milwaukee	IHL	14	....	....	....	715	42	1	3.52	7	....	....	334	23	0	4.14
1979-80	Maine	AHL	1	0	1	0	60	5	0	5.00	....	....	....	....	....	....	....
	Saginaw	IHL	52	....	....	....	2827	178	0	3.78	4	....	....	213	13	0	3.66
1980-81	Saginaw	IHL	43	....	....	....	2298	114	3	2.98	*13	....	....	*806	29	*2	*2.16
1981-82	Maine	AHL	33	16	11	4	1900	104	2	3.28	....	....	....	....	....	....	....
1982-83	**Philadelphia**	**NHL**	**25**	**17**	**4**	**2**	**1407**	**59**	**4**	**2.52**	....	....	....	....	....	....	....
	Maine	AHL	33	18	11	3	1966	110	2	3.36	....	....	....	....	....	....	....
1983-84	**Philadelphia**	**NHL**	**48**	**28**	**13**	**7**	**2863**	**150**	**2**	**3.14**	**3**	**0**	**2**	**154**	**11**	**0**	**4.28**
1984-85	**Philadelphia**	**NHL**	**17**	**13**	**2**	**0**	**923**	**37**	**1**	**2.41**	**4**	**0**	**1**	**146**	**11**	**0**	**4.52**
	Hershey	AHL	4	1	2	1	245	15	0	3.67	....	....	....	....	....	....	....
1985-86ab	**Philadelphia**	**NHL**	**51**	***31**	**10**	**3**	**2728**	**116**	***5**	***2.55**	**5**	**2**	**3**	**293**	**15**	**0**	**3.07**
1986-87	**Philadelphia**	**NHL**	**3**	**3**	**0**	**0**	**180**	**8**	**0**	**2.67**	....	....	....	....	....	....	....
	NY Rangers	**NHL**	**28**	**14**	**11**	**0**	**1474**	**92**	**0**	**3.74**	**4**	**1**	**1**	**165**	**10**	**0**	**3.64**
1987-88	**NY Rangers**	**NHL**	**25**	**8**	**11**	**3**	**1443**	**85**	**0**	**3.53**	....	....	....	....	....	....	....
1988-89	**NY Rangers**	**NHL**	**30**	**9**	**14**	**4**	**1621**	**102**	**1**	**3.78**	**2**	**0**	**2**	**72**	**8**	**0**	**6.67**
1989-90	**NY Rangers**	**NHL**	**15**	**5**	**7**	**1**	**812**	**45**	**0**	**3.33**	....	....	....	....	....	....	....
1990-91	**NY Rangers**		DID NOT PLAY														
	NHL Totals		**242**	**128**	**72**	**20**	**13451**	**694**	**13**	**3.10**	**18**	**3**	**9**	**830**	**55**	**0**	**3.98**

a NHL Second All-Star Team (1986)
b Shared William Jennings Trophy with Darren Jensen (1986)

Played in NHL All-Star Game (1986)

Signed as a free agent by **Philadelphia**, June 18, 1981. Traded to **NY Rangers** by **Philadelphia** for Kjell Samuelsson and NY Rangers' second round choice (Patrik Juhlin) in 1989 Entry Draft, December 18, 1986.

FUHR, GRANT (FYOOR)

Goaltender. Catches right. 5'10", 186 lbs. Born, Spruce Grove, Alta., September 28, 1962.
(Edmonton's 1st choice, 8th overall, in 1981 Entry Draft).

			Regular Season								Playoffs						
Season	**Club**	**Lea**	**GP**	**W**	**L**	**T**	**Mins**	**GA**	**SO**	**Avg**	**GP**	**W**	**L**	**Mins**	**GA**	**SO**	**Avg**
1979-80ab	Victoria	WHL	43	30	12	0	2488	130	2	3.14	8	5	3	465	22	0	2.84
1980-81a	Victoria	WHL	59	48	9	1	3448	160	*4	*2.78	15	12	3	899	45	*1	*3.00
1981-82c	**Edmonton**	**NHL**	**48**	**28**	**5**	**14**	**2847**	**157**	**0**	**3.31**	**5**	**2**	**3**	**309**	**26**	**0**	**5.05**
1982-83	**Edmonton**	**NHL**	**32**	**13**	**12**	**5**	**1803**	**129**	**0**	**4.29**	**1**	**0**	**0**	**11**	**0**	**0**	**0.00**
	Moncton	AHL	10	4	5	1	604	40	0	3.98	....	....	....	....	....	....	....
1983-84	**Edmonton**	**NHL**	**45**	**30**	**10**	**4**	**2625**	**171**	**1**	**3.91**	**16**	**11**	**4**	**883**	**44**	**1**	**2.99**
1984-85	**Edmonton**	**NHL**	**46**	**26**	**8**	**7**	**2559**	**165**	**1**	**3.87**	***18**	***15**	**3**	**1064**	**55**	**0**	**3.10**
1985-86	**Edmonton**	**NHL**	**40**	**29**	**8**	**0**	**2184**	**143**	**0**	**3.93**	**9**	**5**	**4**	**541**	**28**	**0**	**3.11**
1986-87	**Edmonton**	**NHL**	**44**	**22**	**13**	**3**	**2388**	**137**	**0**	**3.44**	**19**	**14**	**5**	**1148**	**47**	**0**	**2.46**
1987-88de	**Edmonton**	**NHL**	***75**	***40**	**24**	**9**	***4304**	**246**	***4**	**3.43**	***19**	***16**	**2**	***1136**	**55**	**0**	**2.90**
1988-89	**Edmonton**	**NHL**	**59**	**23**	**26**	**6**	**3341**	**213**	**1**	**3.83**	**7**	**3**	**4**	**417**	**24**	**1**	**3.45**
1989-90	**Edmonton**	**NHL**	**21**	**9**	**7**	**3**	**1081**	**70**	**1**	**3.89**	....	....	....	....	....	....	....
	Cape Breton	AHL	2	2	0	0	120	6	0	3.01	....	....	....	....	....	....	....
1990-91	**Edmonton**	**NHL**	**13**	**6**	**4**	**3**	**778**	**39**	**1**	**3.01**	**17**	**8**	**7**	**1019**	**51**	**0**	**3.00**
	Cape Breton	AHL	4	2	2	0	240	17	0	4.25	....	....	....	....	....	....	....
	NHL Totals		**425**	**226**	**118**	**54**	**23945**	**1476**	**9**	**3.70**	**111**	**74**	**32**	**6528**	**330**	**2**	**3.03**

a WHL First All-Star Team (1980, 1981)
b WHL Rookie of the Year (1980)
c NHL Second All-Star Team (1982)
d NHL First All-Star Team (1988)
e Won Vezina Trophy (1988)

Played in NHL All-Star Game (1982, 1984-86, 1988-89)

GAGNON, DAVID

Goaltender. Catches left. 6', 185 lbs. Born, Windsor, Ont., October 31, 1967.
(Detroit's 5th choice, 85th overall, in 1986 Entry Draft).

			Regular Season								Playoffs						
Season	**Club**	**Lea**	**GP**	**W**	**L**	**T**	**Mins**	**GA**	**SO**	**Avg**	**GP**	**W**	**L**	**Mins**	**GA**	**SO**	**Avg**
1987-88	Colgate	ECAC	13	6	4	2	743	43	1	3.47	....	....	....	....	....	....	....
1988-89	Colgate	ECAC	28	17	9	2	1622	102	0	3.77	....	....	....	....	....	....	....
1989-90ab	Colgate	ECAC	33	28	3	1	1986	93	0	2.88	....	....	....	....	....	....	....
1990-91	**Detroit**	**NHL**	**2**	**0**	**1**	**0**	**35**	**6**	**0**	**10.29**	....	....	....	....	....	....	....
	Adirondack	AHL	24	8	8	5	1356	94	0	4.16	....	....	....	....	....	....	....
	c Hampton Roads	ECHL	10	7	1	2	606	26	2	2.57	11	*10	1	696	27	0	*2.32
	NHL Totals		**2**	**0**	**1**	**0**	**35**	**6**	**0**	**10.29**	....	....	....	....	....	....	....

a ECAC First All-Star Team (1990)
b ECAC Player of the Year (1990)
c MVP in Playoffs — ECHL (Shared with Dave Flanagan) (1991)

GALUPPO, SANDY

Goaltender. Catches left. 5'10", 160 lbs. Born, Farmingdale, NY, October 4, 1969.
(Edmonton's 1st choice, 22nd overall, in 1990 Supplemental Draft).

			Regular Season								Playoffs						
Season	**Club**	**Lea**	**GP**	**W**	**L**	**T**	**Mins**	**GA**	**SO**	**Avg**	**GP**	**W**	**L**	**Mins**	**GA**	**SO**	**Avg**
1987-88	Boston College	H.E.	8	2	2	1	341	30	0	5.28	....	....	....	....	....	....	....
1988-89	Boston College	H.E.	12	6	3	0	525	28	0	3.20	....	....	....	....	....	....	....
1989-90	Boston College	H.E.	22	11	9	1	1235	73	0	3.55	....	....	....	....	....	....	....
1990-91	Boston College	H.E.	23	15	4	0	1158	65	0	3.37	....	....	....	....	....	....	....

GAMBLE, TROY

Goaltender. Catches left. 5'11", 195 lbs. Born, New Glasgow, N.S., April 7, 1967.
(Vancouver's 2nd choice, 25th overall, in 1985 Entry Draft).

			Regular Season								Playoffs						
Season	**Club**	**Lea**	**GP**	**W**	**L**	**T**	**Mins**	**GA**	**SO**	**Avg**	**GP**	**W**	**L**	**Mins**	**GA**	**SO**	**Avg**
1984-85a	Medicine Hat	WHL	37	27	6	2	2095	100	3	2.86	2	1	1	120	9	0	4.50
1985-86	Medicine Hat	WHL	45	28	11	0	2264	142	0	3.76	11	5	4	530	31	0	3.51
1986-87	**Vancouver**	**NHL**	**1**	**0**	**1**	**0**	**60**	**4**	**0**	**4.00**	....	....	....	....	....	....	....
	Medicine Hat	WHL	11	7	3	0	646	46	0	4.27	....	....	....	....	....	....	....
	Spokane	WHL	38	17	17	1	2155	163	0	4.54	5	0	5	298	35	0	7.05
1987-88b	Spokane	WHL	67	36	26	1	3824	235	0	3.69	15	7	8	875	56	1	3.84
1988-89	**Vancouver**	**NHL**	**5**	**2**	**3**	**0**	**302**	**12**	**0**	**2.38**	....	....	....	....	....	....	....
	Milwaukee	IHL	42	23	9	0	2198	138	0	3.77	11	5	5	640	35	0	3.28
1989-90	Milwaukee	IHL	*56	22	21	4	2779	160	2	4.21	....	....	....	....	....	....	....
1990-91	**Vancouver**	**NHL**	**47**	**16**	**16**	**6**	**2433**	**140**	**1**	**3.45**	**4**	**1**	**3**	**249**	**16**	**0**	**3.86**
	NHL Totals		**53**	**18**	**20**	**6**	**2795**	**156**	**1**	**3.35**	**4**	**1**	**3**	**249**	**16**	**0**	**3.86**

a WHL First All-Star Team, East Division (1985)
b WHL First All-Star Team, West Division (1988)

GILMOUR, DARRYL

Goaltender. Catches left. 6', 171 lbs. Born, Winnipeg, Man., February 13, 1967.
(Philadelphia's 3rd choice, 48th overall, in 1985 Entry Draft).

			Regular Season								Playoffs						
Season	**Club**	**Lea**	**GP**	**W**	**L**	**T**	**Mins**	**GA**	**SO**	**Avg**	**GP**	**W**	**L**	**Mins**	**GA**	**SO**	**Avg**
1984-85	Moose Jaw	WHL	58	15	35	0	3004	297	0	5.93	....	....	....	....	....	....	....
1985-86a	Moose Jaw	WHL	62	19	34	3	3482	276	1	4.76	9	4	4	490	48	0	5.88
1986-87	Moose Jaw	WHL	31	14	13	2	1776	123	2	4.16	....	....	....	....	....	....	....
	Portland	WHL	24	15	7	1	1460	111	0	4.56	19	12	7	1167	83	1	4.27
1987-88	Hershey	AHL	25	14	7	0	1273	78	1	3.68	....	....	....	....	....	....	....
1988-89	Hershey	AHL	38	16	14	5	2093	144	0	4.13	....	....	....	....	....	....	....
1989-90	New Haven	AHL	23	10	11	2	1356	85	0	3.76	....	....	....	....	....	....	....
	Nashville	ECHL	10	6	3	0	529	43	0	4.87	....	....	....	....	....	....	....
1990-91	New Haven	AHL	26	5	14	3	1375	90	1	3.93	....	....	....	....	....	....	....
	Phoenix	IHL	4	2	0	0	180	13	0	4.33	....	....	....	....	....	....	....

a WHL First All-Star Team, East Division (1986).

Signed as a free agent by **Los Angeles**, December 15, 1989.

GILMORE, MIKE

Goaltender. Catches left. 5'10", 173 lbs. Born, Detroit, MI, March 11, 1968.
(NY Rangers' 1st choice, 18th overall, in 1990 Supplemental Draft).

			Regular Season								Playoffs						
Season	**Club**	**Lea**	**GP**	**W**	**L**	**T**	**Mins**	**GA**	**SO**	**Avg**	**GP**	**W**	**L**	**Mins**	**GA**	**SO**	**Avg**
1988-89	Michigan State	CCHA	3	1	0	0	74	5	0	4.04	....	....	....	....	....	....	....
1989-90	Michigan State	CCHA	12	9	1	0	638	29	0	2.73	....	....	....	....	....	....	....
1990-91a	Michigan State	CCHA	22	9	8	3	1218	54	*2	2.66	....	....	....	....	....	....	....

a CCHA Second All-Star Team (1991)

GORANELO, HANS

Goaltender. Catches left. 6'2", 202 lbs. Born, Stockholm, Sweden, June 27, 1966.
(Winnipeg's 11th choice, 247th overall, in 1987 Entry Draft).

			Regular Season								Playoffs						
Season	**Club**	**Lea**	**GP**	**W**	**L**	**T**	**Mins**	**GA**	**SO**	**Avg**	**GP**	**W**	**L**	**Mins**	**GA**	**SO**	**Avg**
1990-91	Hammarby	Swe. 2	24	....	....	....	1440	89	0	3.71	....	....	....	....	....	....	....

GORDON, SCOTT

Goaltender. Catches left. 5'10", 175 lbs. Born, Brockton, MA, February 6, 1963.

			Regular Season								Playoffs						
Season	**Club**	**Lea**	**GP**	**W**	**L**	**T**	**Mins**	**GA**	**SO**	**Avg**	**GP**	**W**	**L**	**Mins**	**GA**	**SO**	**Avg**
1982-83	Boston College	ECAC	9	3	3	0	371	15	0	2.43	...	...	...	...	...	...	...
1983-84	Boston College	ECAC	35	21	13	0	2034	127	1	3.75	...	...	...	...	...	...	...
1984-85	Boston College	H.E.	36	23	11	2	2179	131	1	3.61	...	...	...	...	...	...	...
1985-86a	Boston College	H.E.	32	17	8	1	1852	112	2	3.63	...	...	...	...	...	...	...
1986-87	Fredericton	AHL	32	9	12	2	1616	120	0	4.46	...	...	...	...	...	...	...
1987-88	Baltimore	AHL	34	7	17	3	1638	145	0	5.31	....	....	....	....	....	....	....
1988-89	Halifax	AHL	2	0	2	0	116	10	0	5.17	....	....	....	....	....	....	....
	Johnstown	ECHL	31	....	....	....	1839	117	2	3.82	....	....	....	....	....	....	....
1989-90	**Quebec**	**NHL**	**10**	**2**	**8**	**0**	**597**	**53**	**0**	**5.33**	....	....	....	....	....	....	....
	Halifax	AHL	48	28	16	3	2851	158	0	3.33	6	2	4	340	28	0	4.94
1990-91	**Quebec**	**NHL**	**13**	**0**	**8**	**0**	**485**	**48**	**0**	**5.94**	....	....	....	....	....	....	....
	Halifax	AHL	24	12	10	2	1410	87	2	3.70	....	....	....	....	....	....	....
	NHL Totals		**23**	**2**	**16**	**0**	**1082**	**101**	**0**	**5.60**	....	....	....	....	....	....	....

a Hockey East First All-Star Team (1986)

Signed as a free agent by **Quebec**, October 2, 1986.

GOSSELIN, MARIO

Goaltender. Catches left. 5'8", 160 lbs. Born, Thetford Mines, Que., June 15, 1963.
(Quebec's 3rd choice, 55th overall, in 1982 Entry Draft).

			Regular Season								Playoffs						
Season	Club	Lea	GP	W	L	T	Mins	GA	SO	Avg	GP	W	L	Mins	GA	SO	Avg
1980-81	Shawinigan	QMJHL	21	4	9	0	907	75	0	4.96	1	0	0	20	2	0	6.00
1981-82a	Shawinigan	QMJHL	60	....	....	....	3404	2496	0	4.05	14	....	....	788	58	0	4.42
1982-83	Shawinigan	QMJHL	46	32	9	1	2496	133	3	3.12	8	5	3	457	29	0	3.81
1983-84	Cdn. Olympic	...	36	....	....	....	2007	126	0	3.77	....	....	....	....	....	....	....
	Quebec	**NHL**	**3**	**2**	**0**	**0**	**148**	**3**	**1**	**1.21**	....	....	....	....	....	....	....
1984-85	**Quebec**	**NHL**	**35**	**19**	**10**	**3**	**1960**	**109**	**1**	**3.34**	**17**	**9**	**8**	**1059**	**54**	**0**	**3.06**
1985-86	**Quebec**	**NHL**	**31**	**14**	**14**	**1**	**1726**	**111**	**2**	**3.86**	**1**	**0**	**1**	**40**	**5**	**0**	**7.50**
	Fredericton	AHL	5	2	2	1	304	15	0	2.96	....	....	....	....	....	....	....
1986-87	**Quebec**	**NHL**	**30**	**13**	**11**	**1**	**1625**	**86**	**0**	**3.18**	**11**	**7**	**4**	**654**	**37**	**0**	**3.39**
1987-88	**Quebec**	**NHL**	**54**	**20**	**28**	**4**	**3002**	**189**	**2**	**3.78**	....	....	....	....	....	....	....
1988-89	**Quebec**	**NHL**	**39**	**11**	**19**	**3**	**2064**	**146**	**0**	**4.24**	....	....	....	....	....	....	....
	Halifax	AHL	3	3	0	0	183	9	0	2.95	....	....	....	....	....	....	....
1989-90	**Los Angeles**	**NHL**	**26**	**7**	**11**	**1**	**1226**	**79**	**0**	**3.87**	**3**	**0**	**2**	**63**	**3**	**0**	**2.90**
1990-91	Phoenix	IHL	46	24	15	4	2673	172	1	3.86	11	7	4	670	43	0	3.83
	NHL Totals		**218**	**86**	**93**	**13**	**11751**	**723**	**6**	**3.69**	**32**	**16**	**15**	**1815**	**99**	**0**	**3.27**

a QMJHL Second All-Star Team (1982)

Played in NHL All-Star Game (1986)

Signed as a free agent by **Los Angeles**, June 14, 1989. Signed as a free agent by **Hartford**, September 4, 1991.

GOVERDE, DAVID

Goaltender. Catches right. 6'1", 205 lbs. Born, Toronto, Ont., April 9, 1970.
(Los Angeles' 4th choice, 91st overall, in 1990 Entry Draft).

			Regular Season								Playoffs						
Season	Club	Lea	GP	W	L	T	Mins	GA	SO	Avg	GP	W	L	Mins	GA	SO	Avg
1989-90	Sudbury	OHL	52	28	12	7	2941	182	0	3.71	7	3	3	394	25	0	3.81
1990-91	Phoenix	IHL	40	11	19	5	2007	137	0	4.10	....	....	....	....	....	....	....

GRAVEL, FRANCOIS (gruh-VEHL)

Goaltender. Catches left. 6'2", 185 lbs. Born, Ste-Foy, Que., October 21, 1968.
(Montreal's 5th choice, 58th overall, in 1987 Entry Draft).

			Regular Season								Playoffs						
Season	Club	Lea	GP	W	L	T	Mins	GA	SO	Avg	GP	W	L	Mins	GA	SO	Avg
1985-86	St. Jean	QMJHL	42	13	15	2	1827	151	0	4.96	5	3	2	307	38	0	7.42
1986-87	Shawinigan	QMJHL	40	18	17	5	2415	194	0	4.82	11	8	3	678	47	0	4.16
1987-88	Shawinigan	QMJHL	44	19	20	2	2499	200	1	4.80	8	4	4	488	39	0	4.80
1988-89a	Sherbrooke	AHL	33	12	10	3	1625	95	2	3.51	1	1	0	40	3	0	4.50
1989-90	Sherbrooke	AHL	12	4	3	3	545	38	0	4.18	....	....	....	....	....	....	....
	Halifax	AHL	2	0	1	1	125	10	0	4.79	....	....	....	....	....	....	
1990-91	Moncton	AHL	3	0	2	0	122	9	0	4.43	2	1	0	54	4	0	4.44
	Rochester	AHL	3	1	2	0	159	10	0	3.77	....	....	....	....	....	....	....

a Shared Harry "Hap" Holmes Trophy (fewest goals-against-AHL) with Randy Exelby (1989)

GRAVISTIN, SHAWN

Goaltender. Catches left. 5'7", 150 lbs. Born, Calgary, Alta., November 17, 1970.
(Hartford's 1st choice, 15th overall, in 1991 Supplemental Draft).

			Regular Season								Playoffs						
Season	Club	Lea	GP	W	L	T	Mins	GA	SO	Avg	GP	W	L	Mins	GA	SO	Avg
1989-90	Alaska-Anch.	NCAA	2	1	0	0	81	3	0	2.22	....	....	....	....	....	....	....
1990-91	Alaska-Anch.	NCAA	8	1	4	2	425	20	1	2.82	....	....	....	....	....	....	....

GREENLAY, MIKE

Goaltender. Catches left. 6'3", 200 lbs. Born, Vitoria, Brazil, September 15, 1968.
(Edmonton's 9th choice, 189th overall, in 1986 Entry Draft).

			Regular Season								Playoffs						
Season	Club	Lea	GP	W	L	T	Mins	GA	SO	Avg	GP	W	L	Mins	GA	SO	Avg
1986-87	Lake Superior	CCHA	17	7	5	0	744	44	0	3.54	...	...	...	...	...	...	...
1987-88	Lake Superior	CCHA	19	10	3	3	1023	57	0	3.34	....	....	....	....	....	....	....
1988-89	Saskatoon	WHL	20	10	8	1	1128	86	0	4.57	6	2	0	174	16	0	5.52
	Lake Superior	CCHA	2	1	1	0	85	6	0	4.23	....	....	....	....	....	....	....
1989-90	**Edmonton**	**NHL**	**2**	**0**	**0**	**0**	**20**	**4**	**0**	**12.00**	....	....	....	....	....	....	....
	Cape Breton	AHL	46	19	18	5	2595	146	2	3.38	5	1	3	306	26	0	5.09
1990-91	Cape Breton	AHL	11	5	2	0	493	33	0	4.02	....	....	....	....	....	....	....
	Knoxville	ECHL	29	17	9	2	1725	108	2	3.75	....	....	....	....	....	....	....
	NHL Totals		**2**	**0**	**0**	**0**	**20**	**4**	**0**	**12.00**	....	....	....	....	....	....	....

GREGORIO, MICHAEL (MIKE)

Goaltender. Catches left. 6'3", 195 lbs. Born, Reading, MA, August 17, 1969.
(Toronto's 10th choice, 216th overall, in 1988 Entry Draft).

			Regular Season								Playoffs						
Season	Club	Lea	GP	W	L	T	Mins	GA	SO	Avg	GP	W	L	Mins	GA	SO	Avg
1989-90	Kent State	NCAA	2	0	0	0	38	2	0	3.18	....	....	....	....	....	....	....
1990-91	Salem State	NCAA	UNAVAILABLE														

GUENETTE, STEVE (guh-NEHT)

Goaltender. Catches left. 5'10", 175 lbs. Born, Gloucester Ont., November 13, 1965.

			Regular Season								Playoffs						
Season	Club	Lea	GP	W	L	T	Mins	GA	SO	Avg	GP	W	L	Mins	GA	SO	Avg
1983-84	Guelph	OHL	38	9	18	2	1808	155	0	5.14	....	....	....	....	....	....	....
1984-85	Guelph	OHL	47	16	22	4	2593	200	1	4.63	....	....	....	....	....	....	....
1985-86a	Guelph	OHL	48	26	20	1	2908	165	*3	3.40	20	15	3	1167	54	1	2.77
1986-87	**Pittsburgh**	**NHL**	**2**	**0**	**2**	**0**	**113**	**8**	**0**	**4.25**	....	....	....	....	....	....	....
	Baltimore	AHL	54	21	23	0	3035	157	5	3.10	....	....	....	....	....	....	....
1987-88	**Pittsburgh**	**NHL**	**19**	**12**	**7**	**0**	**1092**	**61**	**1**	**3.35**	....	....	....	....	....	....	....
bc	Muskegon	IHL	33	23	4	5	1943	91	*4	*2.81	....	....	....	....	....	....	....
1988-89	**Pittsburgh**	**NHL**	**11**	**5**	**6**	**0**	**574**	**41**	**0**	**4.29**	....	....	....	....	....	....	....
	Muskegon	IHL	10	6	4	0	597	39	0	*3.92	....	....	....	....	....	....	....
c	Salt Lake	IHL	30	24	5	0	1810	82	2	*2.72	*13	*8	5	*782	44	0	3.38
1989-90	**Calgary**	**NHL**	**2**	**1**	**1**	**0**	**119**	**8**	**0**	**4.03**	....	....	....	....	....	....	....
	Salt Lake	IHL	47	22	21	4	2779	160	0	3.45	*10	4	4	545	35	*1	3.85
1990-91	**Calgary**	**NHL**	**1**	**1**	**0**	**0**	**60**	**4**	**0**	**4.00**	....	....	....	....	....	....	....
	Salt Lake	IHL	43	*26	13	4	2521	137	2	3.26	2	0	1	59	9	0	9.15
	NHL Totals		**35**	**19**	**16**	**0**	**1958**	**122**	**1**	**3.74**	....	....	....	....	....	....	....

a OHL Second All-Star Team (1986)
b Won James Norris Memorial Trophy (IHL Top Goaltender) (1988, 1989)
c IHL Second All-Star Team (1988, 1989)

Signed as a free agent by **Pittsburgh**, April 6, 1985. Traded to **Calgary** by **Pittsburgh** for Calgary's sixth-round choice (Mike Needham) in 1989 Entry Draft, January 9, 1989. Traded to **Minnesota** by **Calgary** for Minnesota's seventh round choice (Matt Hoffman) in 1991 Entry Draft, May 30, 1991.

HACKETT, JEFF

Goaltender. Catches left. 6'1", 175 lbs. Born, London, Ont., June 1, 1968.
(NY Islanders's 2nd choice, 34th overall, in 1987 Entry Draft).

			Regular Season								Playoffs						
Season	Club	Lea	GP	W	L	T	Mins	GA	SO	Avg	GP	W	L	Mins	GA	SO	Avg
1986-87	Oshawa	OHL	31	18	9	2	1672	85	2	3.05	15	8	7	895	40	0	2.68
1987-88a	Oshawa	OHL	53	30	21	2	3165	205	0	3.89	7	3	4	438	31	0	4.25
1988-89	**NY Islanders**	**NHL**	**13**	**4**	**7**	**0**	**662**	**39**	**0**	**3.53**	....	....	....	....	....	....	....
	Springfield	AHL	29	12	14	2	1677	116	0	4.15	....	....	....	....	....	....	....
1989-90b	Springfield	AHL	54	24	25	3	3045	187	1	3.68	*17	*10	5	934	60	0	3.85
1990-91	**NY Islanders**	**NHL**	**30**	**5**	**18**	**1**	**1508**	**91**	**0**	**3.62**	....	....	....	....	....	....	....
	NHL Totals		**43**	**9**	**25**	**1**	**2170**	**130**	**0**	**3.59**	....	....	....	....	....	....	....

a OHL Third All-Star Team (1988)
b Won Jack Butterfield Trophy (Playoff MVP-AHL) (1990)

Claimed by **San Jose** from **NY Islanders** in Expansion Draft, May 30, 1991.

HANLON, GLEN

Goaltender. Catches right. 6', 185 lbs. Born, Brandon, Man., February 20, 1957.
(Vancouver's 3rd choice, 40th overall, in 1977 Amateur Draft).

			Regular Season								Playoffs						
Season	Club	Lea	GP	W	L	T	Mins	GA	SO	Avg	GP	W	L	Mins	GA	SO	Avg
1974-75	Brandon	WHL	43	....	....	....	2498	176	0	4.22	5	....	....	284	29	0	6.12
1975-76a	Brandon	WHL	64	....	....	....	3523	234	4	3.99	5	....	....	300	33	0	6.60
1976-77a	Brandon	WHL	65	....	....	....	3784	195	*4	*3.09	16	....	....	914	53	0	3.48
1977-78	**Vancouver**	**NHL**	**4**	**1**	**2**	**1**	**200**	**9**	**0**	**2.70**	....	....	....	....	....	....	....
bc	Tulsa	CHL	53	....	....	....	3123	160	*3	3.07	2	....	....	120	5	0	*2.50
1978-79	**Vancouver**	**NHL**	**31**	**12**	**13**	**5**	**1821**	**94**	**3**	**3.10**	....	....	....	....	....	....	....
1979-80	**Vancouver**	**NHL**	**57**	**17**	**29**	**10**	**3341**	**193**	**0**	**3.47**	**2**	**0**	**0**	**60**	**3**	**0**	**3.00**
1980-81	**Vancouver**	**NHL**	**17**	**5**	**8**	**0**	**798**	**59**	**1**	**4.44**	....	....	....	....	....	....	....
	Dallas	CHL	4	3	1	0	239	8	1	2.01	....	....	....	....	....	....	....
1981-82	**Vancouver**	**NHL**	**28**	**8**	**14**	**5**	**1610**	**106**	**1**	**3.95**	....	....	....	....	....	....	....
	St. Louis	**NHL**	**2**	**0**	**1**	**0**	**76**	**8**	**0**	**6.30**	**3**	**0**	**2**	**109**	**9**	**0**	**4.95**
1982-83	**St. Louis**	**NHL**	**14**	**3**	**8**	**1**	**671**	**50**	**0**	**4.47**	....	....	....	....	....	....	....
	NY Rangers	**NHL**	**21**	**9**	**10**	**1**	**1173**	**67**	**0**	**3.43**	**1**	**0**	**1**	**60**	**5**	**0**	**5.00**
1983-84	**NY Rangers**	**NHL**	**50**	**28**	**14**	**4**	**2837**	**166**	**1**	**3.51**	**5**	**2**	**3**	**308**	**13**	**1**	**2.53**
1984-85	**NY Rangers**	**NHL**	**44**	**14**	**20**	**7**	**2510**	**175**	**0**	**4.18**	**3**	**0**	**3**	**168**	**14**	**0**	**5.00**
1985-86	**NY Rangers**	**NHL**	**23**	**5**	**12**	**1**	**1170**	**65**	**0**	**3.33**	**3**	**0**	**0**	**75**	**6**	**0**	**4.80**
	Adirondack	AHL	10	5	4	1	605	33	0	3.27	....	....	....	....	....	....	....
	New Haven	AHL	5	3	2	0	279	22	0	4.73	....	....	....	....	....	....	....
1986-87	**Detroit**	**NHL**	**36**	**11**	**16**	**5**	**1963**	**104**	**1**	**3.18**	**8**	**5**	**2**	**467**	**13**	***2**	**1.67**
1987-88	**Detroit**	**NHL**	**47**	**22**	**17**	**5**	**2623**	**141**	***4**	**3.23**	**8**	**4**	**3**	**431**	**22**	***1**	**3.06**
1988-89	**Detroit**	**NHL**	**39**	**13**	**14**	**8**	**2092**	**124**	**1**	**3.56**	**2**	**0**	**1**	**78**	**7**	**0**	**5.38**
1989-90	**Detroit**	**NHL**	**45**	**15**	**18**	**5**	**2290**	**154**	**1**	**4.03**	....	....	....	....	....	....	....
1990-91	**Detroit**	**NHL**	**19**	**4**	**6**	**3**	**862**	**46**	**0**	**3.20**	....	....	....	....	....	....	....
	San Diego	IHL	11	6	4	0	603	39	0	3.88	....	....	....	....	....	....	....
	NHL Totals		**477**	**167**	**202**	**61**	**26037**	**1561**	**13**	**3.60**	....	....	....	....	....	....	....

a WHL First All-Star Team (1976, 1977)
b CHL Rookie of the Year (1978)
c CHL First All-Star Team (1978)

Traded to **St. Louis** by **Vancouver** for Tony Currie, Jim Nill, Rick Heinz and St. Louis' fourth round choice (Shawn Kilroy) in 1982 Entry Draft, March 9, 1982. Traded to **NY Rangers** by **St. Louis** with Vaclav Nedomansky for Andre Dore, January 4, 1983. Traded to **Detroit** by **NY Rangers** with New York's third round choices in 1987 (Dennis Holland) and 1988 (Guy Dupuis) Entry Drafts for Kelly Kisio, Lane Lambert and Jim Leavins, July 29, 1986.

HANSCH, RANDY

Goaltender. Catches right. 5'10", 165 lbs. Born, Edmonton, Alta., February 8, 1966.
(Detroit's 5th choice, 112th overall, in 1984 Entry Draft).

			Regular Season								Playoffs						
Season	Club	Lea	GP	W	L	T	Mins	GA	SO	Avg	GP	W	L	Mins	GA	SO	Avg
1983-84	Victoria	WHL	36	12	19	0	1894	144	0	4.56	....	....	....	....	....	....	....
1984-85	Victoria	WHL	52	17	28	3	3021	260	0	5.16	....	....	....	....	....	....	....
1985-86	Kamloops	WHL	31	10	21	0	1821	172	0	5.67	14	11	2	820	36	1	2.63
1986-87	Kalamazoo	IHL	16	8	7	0	926	60	2	3.88	....	....	....	....	....	....	....
	Adirondack	AHL	10	6	4	0	544	36	0	3.97	10	5	4	579	34	0	3.52
1987-88			DID NOT PLAY-INJURED														
1988-89	Cdn. National	...	29	9	12	4	1489	96	0	3.86	....	....	....	....	....	....	....
1989-90	Hampton Roads	ECHL	4	1	3	0	240	20	0	5.00	....	....	....	....	....	....	....
1990-91	Adirondack	AHL	21	11	9	1	1118	77	2	4.13	3	1	2	113	9	0	4.78

HARRIS, PETER

Goaltender. Catches left. 6'2", 210 lbs. Born, Haverhill, MA, April 22, 1968.
(NY Islanders' 8th choice, 164th overall, in 1986 Entry Draft).

			Regular Season								Playoffs						
Season	Club	Lea	GP	W	L	T	Mins	GA	SO	Avg	GP	W	L	Mins	GA	SO	Avg
1986-87	U. of Lowell	H.E.	6	1	2	1	279	22	0	4.73	....	....	....	....	....	....	....
1987-88	U. of Lowell	H.E.	DID NOT PLAY														
1988-89	U. of Lowell	H.E.	9	1	2	0	401	29	0	4.34	....	....	....	....	....	....	....
1989-90	U. of Lowell	H.E.	1	0	0	0	31	3	0	5.86	....	....	....	....	....	....	....
1990-91	Greensboro	ECHL	3	0	1	0	100	11	0	6.60	....	....	....	....	....	....	....
	Richmond	ECHL	13	3	5	3	738	61	0	4.95	....	....	....	....	....	....	....

HARVEY, CHRIS

Goaltender. Catches left. 6'1", 180 lbs. Born, Cambridge, MA, December 8, 1967.
(Boston's 1st choice, 23rd overall, in 1988 Supplemental Draft).

			Regular Season								Playoffs						
Season	Club	Lea	GP	W	L	T	Mins	GA	SO	Avg	GP	W	L	Mins	GA	SO	Avg
1986-87	Brown	ECAC	22	9	13	0	1241	88	0	4.26	....	....	....	....	....	....	....
1987-88	Brown	ECAC	21	3	17	1	1235	104	0	5.05	....	....	....	....	....	....	....
1988-89	Brown	ECAC	23	1	22	0	1327	131	0	5.92	....	....	....	....	....	....	....
1989-90ab	Brown	ECAC	28	10	15	3	1646	107	0	3.90	....	....	....	....	....	....	....
1990-91	Maine	AHL	3	1	1	0	149	8	0	3.22	....	....	....	....	....	....	....
	Johnstown	ECHL	31	11	13	2	1606	113	1	4.22	2	0	0	68	8	0	7.05

a ECAC Second All-Star Team (1990)
b NCAA East Second All-American Team (1990)

HASEK, DOMINIK (HAH-shehk)

Goaltender. Catches left. 5'11", 165 lbs. Born, Pardubice, Czechoslovakia, January 29, 1965.
(Chicago's 11th choice, 199th overall, in 1983 Entry Draft).

			Regular Season								Playoffs						
Season	Club	Lea	GP	W	L	T	Mins	GA	SO	Avg	GP	W	L	Mins	GA	SO	Avg
1981-82	Pardubice	Czech.	12	....	....	....	661	34	....	3.09	....	....	....	....	....	....	....
1982-83	Pardubice	Czech.	42	....	....	....	2358	105	....	2.67	....	....	....	....	....	....	....
1983-84	Pardubice	Czech.	40	....	....	....	2304	108	....	2.81	....	....	....	....	....	....	....
1984-85	Pardubice	Czech.	42	....	....	....	2419	131	....	3.25	....	....	....	....	....	....	....
1985-86a	Pardubice	Czech.	45	....	....	....	2689	138	....	3.08	....	....	....	....	....	....	....
1986-87ab	Pardubice	Czech.	43	....	....	....	2515	103	....	2.46	....	....	....	....	....	....	....
1987-88ac	Pardubice	Czech.	31	....	....	....	2265	98	....	2.60	....	....	....	....	....	....	....
1988-89abc	Pardubice	Czech.	42	....	....	....	2507	114	....	2.73	....	....	....	....	....	....	....
1989-90abc	Dukla Jihlava	Czech.	40	....	....	....	2251	80	....	2.13	....	....	....	....	....	....	....
1990-91	**Chicago**	**NHL**	**5**	**3**	**0**	**1**	**195**	**8**	**0**	**2.46**	**3**	**0**	**0**	**69**	**3**	**0**	**2.61**
d	Indianapolis	IHL	33	20	11	1	1903	80	*5	*2.52	1	1	0	60	3	0	3.00
	NHL Totals		**5**	**3**	**0**	**1**	**195**	**8**	**0**	**2.46**	**3**	**0**	**0**	**69**	**3**	**0**	**2.61**

a Czechoslovakian Goaltender-of-the-Year (1986, 1987, 1988, 1989, 1990).
b Czechoslovakian Player-of-the-Year (1987, 1989, 1990).
c Czechoslovakian First-Team All-Star (1988, 1989, 1990).
d IHL First All-Star Team (1991)

HAYWARD, BRIAN

Goaltender. Catches left. 5'10", 180 lbs. Born, Weston, Ont., June 25, 1960.

			Regular Season								Playoffs						
Season	Club	Lea	GP	W	L	T	Mins	GA	SO	Avg	GP	W	L	Mins	GA	SO	Avg
1978-79	Cornell	ECAC	25	18	6	0	1469	95	0	3.88	3	2	1	179	14	0	4.66
1979-80	Cornell	ECAC	12	2	7	0	508	52	0	6.02	....	....	....	....	....	....	....
1980-81	Cornell	ECAC	19	11	4	1	967	58	1	3.54	4	2	1	181	18	0	4.50
1981-82ab	Cornell	ECAC	22	11	10	1	1320	68	0	3.09	....	....	....	....	....	....	....
1982-83	**Winnipeg**	**NHL**	**24**	**10**	**12**	**2**	**1440**	**89**	**1**	**3.71**	**3**	**0**	**3**	**160**	**14**	**0**	**5.24**
	Sherbrooke	AHL	22	6	11	3	1208	89	1	4.42	....	....	....	....	....	....	....
1983-84	**Winnipeg**	**NHL**	**28**	**7**	**18**	**2**	**1530**	**124**	**0**	**4.86**	....	....	....	....	....	....	....
	Sherbrooke	AHL	15	4	8	0	781	69	0	5.30	....	....	....	....	....	....	....
1984-85	**Winnipeg**	**NHL**	**61**	**33**	**17**	**7**	**3436**	**220**	**0**	**3.84**	**6**	**2**	**4**	**309**	**23**	**0**	**4.47**
1985-86	**Winnipeg**	**NHL**	**52**	**13**	**28**	**5**	**2721**	**217**	**0**	**4.79**	**2**	**0**	**1**	**68**	**6**	**0**	**5.29**
	Sherbrooke	AHL	3	2	0	1	185	5	0	1.62	....	....	....	....	....	....	....
1986-87c	**Montreal**	**NHL**	**37**	**19**	**13**	**4**	**2178**	**102**	**1**	***2.81**	**13**	**6**	**5**	**708**	**32**	**0**	**2.71**
1987-88c	**Montreal**	**NHL**	**39**	**22**	**10**	**4**	**2247**	**107**	**2**	**2.86**	**4**	**2**	**2**	**230**	**9**	**0**	**2.35**
1988-89c	**Montreal**	**NHL**	**36**	**20**	**13**	**3**	**2091**	**101**	**1**	**2.90**	**2**	**1**	**1**	**124**	**7**	**0**	**3.39**
1989-90	**Montreal**	**NHL**	**29**	**10**	**12**	**6**	**1674**	**94**	**1**	**3.37**	**1**	**0**	**0**	**33**	**2**	**0**	**3.64**
1990-91	**Minnesota**	**NHL**	**26**	**6**	**15**	**3**	**1473**	**77**	**2**	**3.14**	**6**	**0**	**2**	**171**	**11**	**0**	**3.86**
	Kalamazoo	IHL	2	2	0	0	120	5	0	2.50	....	....	....	....	....	....	....
	NHL Totals		**332**	**140**	**138**	**36**	**18790**	**1131**	**8**	**3.61**	**37**	**11**	**18**	**1803**	**104**	**0**	**3.46**

a ECAC First All-Star Team (1982)
b NCAA All-America Team (1982)
c Shared William Jennings Trophy with Patrick Roy (1987, 1988, 1989)

Signed as a free agent by **Winnipeg**, May 5, 1982. Traded to **Montreal** by **Winnipeg** for Steve Penney and the rights to Jan Ingman, August 19, 1986. Traded to **Minnesota** by **Montreal** for Jayson More, November 7, 1990. Claimed by **San Jose** from **Minnesota** in Dispersal Draft, May 30, 1991.

HEALY, GLENN

Goaltender. Catches left. 5'10", 175 lbs. Born, Pickering, Ont., August 23, 1962.

			Regular Season								Playoffs						
Season	Club	Lea	GP	W	L	T	Mins	GA	SO	Avg	GP	W	L	Mins	GA	SO	Avg
1981-82	W. Michigan	CCHA	27	7	19	1	1569	116	0	4.44	....	....	....	....	....	....	....
1982-83	W. Michigan	CCHA	30	8	19	2	1732	116	0	4.01	....	....	....	....	....	....	....
1983-84	W. Michigan	CCHA	38	19	16	3	2241	146	0	3.90	....	....	....	....	....	....	....
1984-85	W. Michigan	CCHA	37	21	14	2	2171	118	0	3.26	....	....	....	....	....	....	....
1985-86	**Los Angeles**	**NHL**	**1**	**0**	**0**	**0**	**51**	**6**	**0**	**7.06**	....	....	....	....	....	....	....
	New Haven	AHL	43	21	15	4	2410	160	0	3.98	2	0	2	49	11	0	5.55
1986-87	New Haven	AHL	47	21	15	0	2828	173	1	3.67	7	3	4	427	19	0	2.67
1987-88	**Los Angeles**	**NHL**	**34**	**12**	**18**	**1**	**1869**	**135**	**1**	**4.33**	**4**	**1**	**3**	**240**	**20**	**0**	**5.00**
1988-89	**Los Angeles**	**NHL**	**48**	**25**	**19**	**2**	**2699**	**192**	**0**	**4.27**	**3**	**0**	**1**	**97**	**6**	**0**	**3.71**
1989-90	**NY Islanders**	**NHL**	**39**	**12**	**19**	**6**	**2197**	**128**	**2**	**3.50**	**4**	**1**	**2**	**166**	**9**	**0**	**3.25**
1990-91	**NY Islanders**	**NHL**	**53**	**18**	**24**	**9**	**2999**	**166**	**0**	**3.32**	....	....	....	....	....	....	....
	NHL Totals		**175**	**67**	**80**	**18**	**9815**	**627**	**3**	**3.83**	**8**	**2**	**5**	**406**	**29**	**0**	**4.29**

Signed as a free agent by **Los Angeles**, June 13, 1985. Signed as a free agent by **NY Islanders**, August 16, 1989.

HEBERT, GUY (HEE-buhrt, GIGH)

Goaltender. Catches left. 5'11", 180 lbs. Born, Troy, NY, January 7, 1967.
(St. Louis' 8th choice, 159th overall, in 1987 Entry Draft).

			Regular Season								Playoffs						
Season	Club	Lea	GP	W	L	T	Mins	GA	SO	Avg	GP	W	L	Mins	GA	SO	Avg
1986-87	Hamilton Col.	NCAA	18	12	5	0	1070	40	0	2.19	....	....	....	....	....	....	....
1987-88	Hamilton Col.	NCAA	8	5	3	0	450	19	0	2.53	....	....	....	....	....	....	....
1988-89	Hamilton Col.	NCAA	25	18	7	0	1453	62	0	2.56	....	....	....	....	....	....	....
1989-90	Peoria	IHL	30	7	13	7	1706	124	1	4.36	2	0	1	76	5	0	3.95
1990-91a	Peoria	IHL	36	24	10	1	2093	100	2	2.87	8	3	4	458	32	0	4.19

a IHL Second All-Star Team (1991)

HEINKE, MICHAEL

Goaltender. Catches left. 5'11", 165 lbs. Born, Denville, NY, January 11, 1971.
(New Jersey's 5th choice, 89th overall, in 1989 Entry Draft).

			Regular Season								Playoffs						
Season	Club	Lea	GP	W	L	T	Mins	GA	SO	Avg	GP	W	L	Mins	GA	SO	Avg
1989-90	Avon Old Farms	HS	23				1020	42	0	1.85	....	....	....	....	....	....	....
1990-91	Providence	H.E.	14	8	7	1	923	74	0	4.81	....	....	....	....	....	....	....

HENDERSON, TODD

Goaltender. Catches left. 6'1", 155 lbs. Born, Sault Ste. Marie, Ont., March 8, 1969.
(Buffalo's 11th choice, 224th overall, in 1989 Entry Draft).

			Regular Season								Playoffs						
Season	Club	Lea	GP	W	L	T	Mins	GA	SO	Avg	GP	W	L	Mins	GA	SO	Avg
1990-91	Alaska-Fair.	NCAA	20	10	9	1	1155	74	0	3.85	....	....	....	....	....	....	....

HEXTALL, RON

Goaltender. Catches left. 6'3", 192 lbs. Born, Brandon, Man., May 3, 1964.
(Philadelphia's 6th choice, 119th overall, in 1982 Entry Draft).

			Regular Season								Playoffs						
Season	Club	Lea	GP	W	L	T	Mins	GA	SO	Avg	GP	W	L	Mins	GA	SO	Avg
1981-82	Brandon	WHL	30	12	11	0	1398	133	0	5.71	3	0	2	103	16	0	9.32
1982-83	Brandon	WHL	44	13	30	0	2589	249	0	5.77	....	....	....	....	....	....	....
1983-84	Brandon	WHL	46	29	13	2	2670	190	0	4.27	10	5	5	592	37	0	3.75
1984-85	Hershey	AHL	11	4	6	0	555	34	0	3.68	....	....	....	....	....	....	....
	Kalamazoo	IHL	19	6	11	1	1103	80	0	4.35	....	....	....	....	....	....	....
1985-86ab	Hershey	AHL	*53	30	19	2	*3061	174	*5	3.41	13	5	7	780	42	*1	3.23
1986-87cdef	**Philadelphia**	**NHL**	***66**	**37**	**21**	**6**	***3799**	**190**	**1**	**3.00**	***26**	**15**	**11**	***1540**	**71**	***2**	**2.77**
1987-88g	**Philadelphia**	**NHL**	**62**	**30**	**22**	**7**	**3561**	**208**	**0**	**3.50**	**7**	**2**	**4**	**379**	**30**	**0**	**4.75**
1988-89h	**Philadelphia**	**NHL**	***64**	**30**	**28**	**6**	***3756**	**202**	**0**	**3.23**	**15**	**8**	**7**	**886**	**49**	**0**	**3.32**
1989-90	**Philadelphia**	**NHL**	**8**	**4**	**2**	**1**	**419**	**29**	**0**	**4.15**	....	....	....	....	....	....	....
	Hershey	AHL	1	1	0	0	49	3	0	3.67	....	....	....	....	....	....	....
1990-91	**Philadelphia**	**NHL**	**36**	**13**	**16**	**5**	**2035**	**106**	**0**	**3.13**	....	....	....	....	....	....	....
	NHL Totals		**236**	**114**	**89**	**25**	**13570**	**735**	**1**	**3.25**	**48**	**25**	**22**	**2805**	**150**	**2**	**3.21**

a AHL First All-Star Team (1986)
b AHL Rookie of the Year (1986)
c NHL First All-Star Team (1987)
d Won Vezina Trophy (1987)
e Won Conn Smythe Trophy (1987)
f NHL All-Rookie Team (1987)
g Scored a goal vs. Boston, December 8, 1987
h Scored a goal in playoffs vs. Washington, April 11, 1989

Played in NHL All-Star Game (1988)

HILLEBRANDT, JON

Goaltender. Catches left. 5'10", 160 lbs. Born, Cottage Grove, WI, December 18, 1971.
(NY Rangers' 12th choice, 202nd overall, in 1990 Entry Draft).

			Regular Season								Playoffs						
Season	Club	Lea	GP	W	L	T	Mins	GA	SO	Avg	GP	W	L	Mins	GA	SO	Avg
1989-90	Monona Grove	HS	22	14	7	1	1320	48	3	2.18	....	....	....	....	....	....	....
1990-91	Madison	USHL	28	10	14	3	1631	111	0	4.08	....	....	....	....	....	....	....

HOFFORT, BRUCE

Goaltender. Catches left. 5'10", 185 lbs. Born, North Battleford, Sask., July 30, 1966.

			Regular Season								Playoffs						
Season	Club	Lea	GP	W	L	T	Mins	GA	SO	Avg	GP	W	L	Mins	GA	SO	Avg
1987-88ab	Lake Superior	CCHA	31	23	4	3	1787	79	2	2.65	....	....	....	....	....	....	....
1988-89ac	Lake Superior	CCHA	44	27	10	5	2595	117	0	2.71	....	....	....	....	....	....	....
1989-90	**Philadelphia**	**NHL**	**7**	**3**	**0**	**2**	**329**	**19**	**0**	**3.47**	....	....	....	....	....	....	....
	Hershey	AHL	40	16	18	4	2284	139	1	3.65	....	....	....	....	....	....	....
1990-91	**Philadelphia**	**NHL**	**2**	**1**	**0**	**1**	**39**	**3**	**0**	**4.62**	....	....	....	....	....	....	....
	Hershey	AHL	18	3	12	1	913	74	0	4.86	....	....	....	....	....	....	....
	Kansas City	IHL	18	6	7	0	883	68	0	4.62	....	....	....	....	....	....	....
	NHL Totals		**9**	**4**	**0**	**3**	**368**	**22**	**0**	**3.59**	....	....	....	....	....	....	....

a CCHA First All-Star Team (1988, 1989)
b NCAA All-Tournament Team (1988)
c CCHA Player of the Year (1989)

Signed as free agent by **Philadelphia**, June 30, 1989.

HORYNA, ROBERT

Goaltender. Catches left. 5'11", 185 lbs. Born, Hradec Kralove, Czech., September 10, 1970.
(Toronto's 8th choice, 178th overall, in 1990 Entry Draft).

			Regular Season								Playoffs						
Season	Club	Lea	GP	W	L	T	Mins	GA	SO	Avg	GP	W	L	Mins	GA	SO	Avg
1989-90	Dukla Jihlava	Czech.	13	....	....	....	710	41	....	3.46	....	....	....	....	....	....	....
1990-91	Newmarket	AHL	22	8	10	2	1162	81	0	4.18	....	....	....	....	....	....	....

HOUK, ROD

Goaltender. Catches left. 5'8", 170 lbs. Born, Regina, Sask., February 2, 1968.
(Minnesota's 1st choice, 13th overall, in 1990 Supplemental Draft).

			Regular Season								Playoffs						
Season	Club	Lea	GP	W	L	T	Mins	GA	SO	Avg	GP	W	L	Mins	GA	SO	Avg
1988-89	Regina	WHL	59	20	30	6	3466	248	0	4.29	....	....	....	....	....	....	....
1989-90	U. of Regina	CWUAA	18	7	9	1	1064	58	1	3.27	....	....	....	....	....	....	....
1990-91	U. of Regina	CWUAA	28	13	14	1	1671	111	1	3.99	....	....	....	....	....	....	....

HRIVNAK, JIM

Goaltender. Catches left. 6'2", 185 lbs. Born, Montreal, Que., May 28, 1968.
(Washington's 4th choice, 61st overall, in 1986 Entry Draft).

			Regular Season								Playoffs						
Season	Club	Lea	GP	W	L	T	Mins	GA	SO	Avg	GP	W	L	Mins	GA	SO	Avg
1985-86	Merrimack	NCAA	21	12	8	0	1230	75	0	3.66	....	....	....	....	....	....	....
1986-87	Merrimack	NCAA	34	27	7	0	1618	58	3	2.14	....	....	....	....	....	....	....
1987-88	Merrimack	NCAA	37	31	6	0	2119	84	4	2.38	....	....	....	....	....	....	....
1988-89	Merrimack	NCAA	22	....	....	....	1295	52	4	2.41	....	....	....	....	....	....	....
	Baltimore	AHL	10	1	8	0	502	55	0	6.57	....	....	....	....	....	....	....
1989-90	Washington	NHL	11	5	5	0	609	36	0	3.55	....	....	....	....	....	....	....
a	Baltimore	AHL	47	24	19	2	2722	139	*4	3.06	6	4	2	360	19	0	3.17
1990-91	Washington	NHL	9	4	2	1	432	26	0	3.61	....	....	....	....	....	....	....
	Baltimore	AHL	42	20	16	6	2481	134	1	3.24	6	2	3	324	21	0	3.89
	NHL Totals		20	9	7	1	1041	62	0	3.57	....	....	....	....	....	....	....

a AHL Second All-Star Team (1990)

HRUDEY, KELLY STEPHEN (ROO-dee)

Goaltender. Catches left. 5'10", 180 lbs. Born, Edmonton, Alta., January 13, 1961.
(NY Islanders' 2nd choice, 38th overall, in 1980 Entry Draft).

			Regular Season								Playoffs						
Season	Club	Lea	GP	W	L	T	Mins	GA	SO	Avg	GP	W	L	Mins	GA	SO	Avg
1978-79	Medicine Hat	WHL	57	12	34	7	3093	318	0	6.17	....	....	....	....	....	....	....
1979-80	Medicine Hat	WHL	57	25	23	4	3049	212	1	4.17	13	6	6	638	48	0	4.51
1980-81a	Medicine Hat	WHL	55	32	19	1	3023	200	4	3.97	4	....	....	244	17	0	4.18
	Indianapolis	CHL	....	....	....	....	....	....	....	....	2	....	....	135	8	0	3.56
1981-82bc	Indianapolis	CHL	51	27	19	4	3033	149	1	*2.95	13	11	2	842	34	*1	*2.42
1982-83bcd	Indianapolis	CHL	47	*26	17	1	2744	139	2	3.04	10	*7	3	*637	28	0	*2.64
1983-84	NY Islanders	NHL	12	7	2	0	535	28	0	3.14	....	....	....	....	....	....	....
	Indianapolis	CHL	6	3	2	1	370	21	0	3.40	....	....	....	....	....	....	....
1984-85	NY Islanders	NHL	41	19	17	3	2335	141	2	3.62	5	1	3	281	8	0	1.71
1985-86	NY Islanders	NHL	45	19	15	8	2563	137	1	3.21	2	0	2	120	6	0	3.00
1986-87	NY Islanders	NHL	46	21	15	7	2634	145	0	3.30	14	7	7	842	38	0	2.71
1987-88	NY Islanders	NHL	47	22	17	5	2751	153	3	3.34	6	2	4	381	23	0	3.62
1988-89	NY Islanders	NHL	50	18	24	3	2800	183	0	3.92	....	....	....	....	....	....	....
	Los Angeles	NHL	16	10	4	2	974	47	1	2.90	10	4	6	566	35	0	3.71
1989-90	Los Angeles	NHL	52	22	21	6	2860	194	2	4.07	9	4	4	539	39	0	4.34
1990-91	Los Angeles	NHL	47	26	13	6	2730	132	3	2.90	12	6	6	798	37	0	2.78
	NHL Totals		356	164	128	40	20182	1160	12	3.45	58	24	32	3527	186	0	3.16

a WHL Second All-Star Team (1981)
b CHL First All-Star Team (1982, 1983)
c Shared Terry Sawchuk Trophy (CHL's Leading Goaltenders) with Rob Holland (1982, 1983)
d Won Tommy Ivan Trophy (CHL's Most Valuable Player) (1983)

Traded to **Los Angeles** by **NY Islanders** for Mark Fitzpatrick, Wayne McBean and future considerations (Doug Crossman, acquired May 23, 1989) February 22, 1989.

HUGHES, CHARLES

Goaltender. Catches right. 5'8", 165 lbs. Born, Quincy, MA, January 30, 1970.
(New Jersey's 13th choice, 222nd overall, in 1988 Entry Draft).

			Regular Season								Playoffs						
Season	Club	Lea	GP	W	L	T	Mins	GA	SO	Avg	GP	W	L	Mins	GA	SO	Avg
1988-89	Harvard	ECAC	17	15	1	0	990	46	1	2.79	....	....	....	....	....	....	....
1989-90	Harvard	ECAC	11	5	5	1	669	43	0	3.86	....	....	....	....	....	....	....
1990-91	Harvard	ECAC	12	5	4	1	622	39	0	3.95	....	....	....	....	....	....	....

ING, PETER

Goaltender. Catches left. 6'2", 165 lbs. Born, Toronto, Ont., April 28, 1969.
(Toronto's 3rd choice, 48th overall, in 1988 Entry Draft).

			Regular Season								Playoffs						
Season	Club	Lea	GP	W	L	T	Mins	GA	SO	Avg	GP	W	L	Mins	GA	SO	Avg
1986-87	Windsor	OHL	28	13	11	3	1615	105	0	3.90	5	4	0	161	9	0	3.35
1987-88	Windsor	OHL	43	30	7	1	2422	125	2	3.10	3	2	0	225	7	0	1.87
1988-89	Windsor	OHL	19	7	7	3	1043	76	*1	4.37	....	....	....	....	....	....	....
a	London	OHL	32	18	11	2	1848	104	*2	3.38	21	11	9	1093	82	0	4.50
1989-90	Toronto	NHL	3	0	2	1	182	18	0	5.93	....	....	....	....	....	....	....
	Newmarket	AHL	48	16	19	12	2829	184	0	3.90	....	....	....	....	....	....	....
	London	OHL	8	6	2	0	480	27	0	3.38	....	....	....	....	....	....	....
1990-91	Toronto	NHL	56	16	29	8	3126	200	1	3.84	....	....	....	....	....	....	....
	NHL Totals		59	16	31	9	3308	218	1	3.95	....	....	....	....	....	....	....

a OHL Third All-Star Team (1989)

IRBE, ARTUR (EER-bay)

Goaltender. Catches left. 5'8", 172 lbs. Born, Riga, Soviet Union, February 2, 1967.
(Minnesota's 11th choice, 196th overall, in 1989 Entry Draft).

			Regular Season								Playoffs						
Season	Club	Lea	GP	W	L	T	Mins	GA	SO	Avg	GP	W	L	Mins	GA	SO	Avg
1986-87	Dynamo Riga	USSR	2	....	....	....	27	1	0	2.22	....	....	....	....	....	....	....
1987-88a	Dynamo Riga	USSR	34	....	....	....	1870	6	4	2.69	....	....	....	....	....	....	....
1988-89	Dynamo Riga	USSR	40	....	....	....	2460	116	4	2.85	....	....	....	....	....	....	....
1989-90	Dynamo Riga	USSR	48	....	....	....	2880	115	2	2.42	....	....	....	....	....	....	....
1990-91	Dynamo Riga	USSR	46	....	....	....	2713	133	5	2.94	....	....	....	....	....	....	....

a Soviet National League Rookie-of-the-Year (1988)

Claimed by **San Jose** from **Minnesota** in Dispersal Draft, May 30, 1991.

JABLONSKI, PAT

Goaltender. Catches right. 6', 178 lbs. Born, Toledo, OH, June 20, 1967.
(St. Louis' 6th choice, 138th overall, in 1985 Entry Draft).

			Regular Season								Playoffs						
Season	Club	Lea	GP	W	L	T	Mins	GA	SO	Avg	GP	W	L	Mins	GA	SO	Avg
1985-86	Windsor	OHL	29	6	16	4	1600	119	1	4.46	6	0	3	263	20	0	4.56
1986-87	Windsor	OHL	41	22	14	2	2328	128	*3	3.30	12	8	4	710	38	0	3.21
1987-88	Peoria	IHL	5	2	2	1	285	17	0	3.58	....	....	....	....	....	....	....
	Windsor	OHL	18	14	3	0	994	48	2	*2.90	9	*8	0	537	28	0	3.13
1988-89	Peoria	IHL	35	11	20	0	2051	163	1	4.77	3	0	2	130	13	0	6.00
1989-90	St. Louis	NHL	4	0	3	0	208	17	0	4.90	....	....	....	....	....	....	....
	Peoria	IHL	36	14	17	4	2023	165	0	4.89	4	1	3	223	19	0	5.11
1990-91	St. Louis	NHL	8	2	3	3	492	25	0	3.05	3	0	0	90	5	0	3.33
	Peoria	IHL	29	23	3	2	1738	87	0	3.00	10	7	2	532	23	0	2.59
	NHL Totals		12	2	6	3	700	42	0	3.60	3	0	0	90	5	0	3.33

JOSEPH, CURTIS

Goaltender. Catches left. 5'10", 182 lbs. Born, Keswick, Ont., April 29, 1967.

			Regular Season								Playoffs						
Season	Club	Lea	GP	W	L	T	Mins	GA	SO	Avg	GP	W	L	Mins	GA	SO	Avg
1988-89abc	U. Wisconsin	WCHA	38	21	11	5	2267	94	1	2.49	....	....	....	....	....	....	....
1989-90	St. Louis	NHL	15	9	5	1	852	48	0	3.38	6	4	1	327	18	0	3.30
	Peoria	IHL	23	10	8	2	1241	80	0	3.87	....	....	....	....	....	....	....
1990-91	St. Louis	NHL	30	16	10	2	1710	89	0	3.12	....	....	....	....	....	....	....
	NHL Totals		45	25	15	3	2562	137	0	3.21	6	4	1	327	18	0	3.30

a WCHA First All-Star Team (1989)
b WCHA Player of the Year (1989)
c WCHA Rookie of the Year (1989)

Signed as a free agent by **St. Louis**, June 16, 1989.

KIDD, TREVOR

Goaltender. Catches left. 6'2", 176 lbs. Born, Dugald, Man., March 29, 1972.
(Calgary's 1st choice, 11th overall, in 1990 Entry Draft).

			Regular Season								Playoffs						
Season	Club	Lea	GP	W	L	T	Mins	GA	SO	Avg	GP	W	L	Mins	GA	SO	Avg
1988-89	Brandon	WHL	32	....	....	....	1509	102	0	4.06	....	....	....	....	....	....	....
1989-90a	Brandon	WHL	*63	24	32	2	*3676	254	2	4.15	....	....	....	....	....	....	....
1990-91	Brandon	WHL	30	10	19	1	1730	117	0	4.06	....	....	....	....	....	....	....
	Spokane	WHL	14	8	3	0	749	44	0	3.52	15	*14	1	926	32	2	*2.07

a WHL East First All-Star Team (1990)

KING, SCOTT

Goaltender. Catches left. 6'1", 170 lbs. Born, Thunder Bay, Ont., June 25, 1967.
(Detroit's 10th choice, 190th overall, in 1986 Entry Draft).

			Regular Season								Playoffs						
Season	Club	Lea	GP	W	L	T	Mins	GA	SO	Avg	GP	W	L	Mins	GA	SO	Avg
1986-87	U. of Maine	H.E.	21	11	6	1	1111	58	0	3.13	...	...	...	...	...	...	...
1987-88a	U. of Maine	H.E.	33	25	5	1	1761	91	0	3.10	....	....	....	....	....	....	....
1988-89a	U. of Maine	H.E.	27	13	8	0	1394	83	0	3.57	....	....	....	....	....	....	....
1989-90b	U. of Maine	H.E.	29	17	7	2	1526	67	1	2.63	....	....	....	....	....	....	....
1990-91	Detroit	NHL	1	0	0	0	45	2	0	2.67	....	....	....	....	....	....	....
	Adirondack	AHL	24	8	10	2	1287	91	0	4.24	1	0	0	32	4	0	7.50
	Hampton Roads	ECHL	15	8	4	1	819	57	0	4.17	....	....	....	....	....	....	....
	NHL Totals		1	0	0	0	45	2	0	2.67	....	....	....	....	....	....	....

a Hockey East Second All-Star Team (1988, 1989)
b Hockey East First All-Star Team (1990).

KNICKLE, RICHARD (RICK)

Goaltender. Catches left. 5'10", 155 lbs. Born, Chatham, N.B., February 26, 1960.
(Buffalo's 7th choice, 116th overall, in 1979 Entry Draft).

			Regular Season								Playoffs						
Season	Club	Lea	GP	W	L	T	Mins	GA	SO	Avg	GP	W	L	Mins	GA	SO	Avg
1977-78	Brandon	WHL	49	34	5	7	2806	182	0	3.89	8	....	....	450	36	0	4.82
1978-79a	Brandon	WHL	38	26	3	8	2240	118	1	*3.16	16	12	3	886	41	*1	*2.78
1979-80	Brandon	WHL	33	11	14	1	1604	125	0	4.68	....	....	....	....	....	....	....
	Muskegon	IHL	16	....	....	....	829	52	0	3.76	3	....	....	156	17	0	6.54
1980-81b	Erie	EHL	43	....	....	....	2347	125	1	*3.20	8	....	....	446	14	0	*1.88
1981-82	Rochester	AHL	31	10	12	5	1753	108	1	3.70	3	0	2	125	7	0	3.37
1982-83	Flint	IHL	27	....	....	....	1638	92	2	3.37	3	....	....	193	10	0	3.11
	Rochester	AHL	4	....	....	....	143	11	0	4.64	....	....	....	....	....	....	....
1983-84c	Flint	IHL	60	32	21	5	3518	203	3	3.46	8	8	0	480	24	0	3.00
1984-85	Sherbrooke	AHL	14	7	6	0	780	53	0	4.08	....	....	....	....	....	....	....
	Flint	IHL	36	18	11	3	2018	115	2	3.42	7	3	4	401	27	0	4.04
1985-86	Saginaw	IHL	39	16	15	0	2235	135	2	3.62	3	2	1	193	12	0	3.73
1986-87	Saginaw	IHL	26	9	13	0	1413	113	0	4.80	5	1	4	329	21	0	3.83
1987-88	Flint	IHL	1	0	1	0	60	4	0	4.00	....	....	....	....	....	....	....
	Peoria	IHL	13	2	8	1	705	58	0	4.94	6	3	3	294	20		4.08
1988-89de	Fort Wayne	IHL	47	22	16	0	2716	141	1	*3.11	4	1	2	173	15	0	5.20
1989-90	Flint	IHL	55	25	24	1	2998	210	1	4.20	2	0	2	101	13	0	7.72
1990-91	Albany	IHL	14	4	6	2	679	52	0	4.59	....	....	....	....	....	....	....
	Springfield	AHL	9	6	0	2	509	28	0	3.30	....	....	....	....	....	....	....

a WHL First All-Star Team (1979)
b EHL First All-Star Team (1981)
c IHL Second All-Star Team (1984)
d IHL First All-Star Team (1989)
e Won James Norris Memorial Trophy (Top Goaltender-IHL) (1989)

Signed as a free agent by **Montreal**, February 8, 1985.

KOLZIG, OLAF

Goaltender. Catches left. 6'3", 207 lbs. Born, Johannesburg, South Africa, April 9, 1970.
(Washington's 1st choice, 19th overall, in 1989 Entry Draft).

			Regular Season								Playoffs						
Season	Club	Lea	GP	W	L	T	Mins	GA	SO	Avg	GP	W	L	Mins	GA	SO	Avg
1987-88	N. Westminster	WHL	15	6	5	0	650	48	1	4.43	3	....	....	149	11	0	4.43
1988-89	Tri-Cities	WHL	30	16	10	2	1671	97	1	*3.48	....	....	....	....	....	....	....
1989-90	Washington	NHL	2	0	2	0	120	12	0	6.00	....	....	....	....	....	....	....
	Tri-Cities	WHL	48	27	27	3	2504	250	1	4.38	6	4	0	318	27	0	5.09
1990-91	Baltimore	AHL	26	10	12	1	1367	72	0	3.16	....	....	....	....	....	....	....
	Hampton Roads	ECHL	21	11	9	1	1248	71	2	3.41	3	1	2	180	14	0	4.66
	NHL Totals		2	0	2	0	120	12	0	6.00	....	....	....	....	....	....	....

KRAKE, PAUL

Goaltender. Catches left. 6', 175 lbs. Born, Lloydminster, Sask., March 25, 1969.
(Quebec's 10th choice, 148th overall, in 1989 Entry Draft).

			Regular Season								Playoffs						
Season	Club	Lea	GP	W	L	T	Mins	GA	SO	Avg	GP	W	L	Mins	GA	SO	Avg
1988-89	Alaska-Anch.	NCAA	19	....	....	....	1111	75	0	4.05	....	....	....	....	....	....	....
1989-90	Alaska-Anch.	NCAA	18	8	6	2	937	58	0	3.87	....	....	....	....	....	....	....
1990-91	Alaska-Anch.	NCAA	37	18	15	3	2183	123	4	3.38	....	....	....	....	....	....	....

KRUHLAK, ROB

Goaltender. Catches left. 5'11", 170 lbs. Born, Calgary, Alta., April 18, 1970.
(New Jersey's 1st choice, 17th overall, in 1991 Supplemental Draft).

			Regular Season								Playoffs						
Season	Club	Lea	GP	W	L	T	Mins	GA	SO	Avg	GP	W	L	Mins	GA	SO	Avg
1989-90	N. Michigan	WCHA	9	1	4	0	357	22	0	3.69	....	....	....	....	....	....	....
1990-91	N. Michigan	WCHA	11	5	2	0	428	18	0	*2.52	....	....	....	....	....	....	....

KUNTAR, LES

Goaltender. Catches left. 6'2", 185 lbs. Born, Elma, NY, July 28, 1969.
(Montreal's 8th choice, 122nd overall, in 1987 Entry Draft).

			Regular Season								Playoffs						
Season	Club	Lea	GP	W	L	T	Mins	GA	SO	Avg	GP	W	L	Mins	GA	SO	Avg
1987-88	St. Lawrence	ECAC	10	6	1	0	488	27	0	3.31	....	....	....	....	....	....	....
1988-89	St. Lawrence	ECAC	14	11	2	0	786	31	0	2.37	....	....	....	....	....	....	....
1989-90	St. Lawrence	ECAC	20	7	11	1	1136	80	0	4.23	....	....	....	....	....	....	....
1990-91ab	St. Lawrence	ECAC	*33	*19	11	1	*1797	97	*1	*3.24	....	....	....	....	....	....	....

a ECAC First All-Star Team (1991)
b NCAA East First All-American Team (1991)

LaFOREST, MARK ANDREW

Goaltender. Catches left. 5'11", 190 lbs. Born, Welland, Ont., July 10, 1962.

			Regular Season								Playoffs						
Season	Club	Lea	GP	W	L	T	Mins	GA	SO	Avg	GP	W	L	Mins	GA	SO	Avg
1981-82	Niagara Falls	OHL	24	10	13	1	1365	105	1	4.62	5	1	2	300	19	0	3.80
1982-83	North Bay	OHL	54	34	17	1	3140	195	0	3.73	8	4	4	474	31	0	3.92
1983-84	Adirondack	AHL	7	3	3	1	351	29	0	4.96	....	....	....	....	....	....	....
	Kalamazoo	IHL	13	4	5	2	718	48	1	4.01	....	....	....	....	....	....	....
1984-85	Adirondack	AHL	11	2	3	1	430	35	0	488	....	....	....	....	....	....	....
1985-86	**Detroit**	**NHL**	**28**	**4**	**21**	**0**	**1383**	**114**	**1**	**4.95**	....	....	....	....	....	....	....
	Adirondack	AHL	19	13	5	1	1142	57	0	2.99	*17	*12	5	*1075	58	0	3.24
1986-87	**Detroit**	**NHL**	**5**	**2**	**1**	**0**	**219**	**12**	**0**	**3.29**	....	....	....	....	....	....	....
a	Adirondack	AHL	37	23	8	0	2229	105	*3	2.83	....	....	....	....	....	....	....
1987-88	**Philadelphia**	**NHL**	**21**	**5**	**9**	**2**	**972**	**60**	**1**	**3.70**	**2**	**1**	**0**	**48**	**1**	**0**	**1.25**
	Hershey	AHL	5	2	1	2	309	13	0	2.52	....	....	....	....	....	....	....
1988-89	**Philadelphia**	**NHL**	**17**	**5**	**7**	**2**	**933**	**64**	**0**	**4.12**	....	....	....	....	....	....	....
	Hershey	AHL	3	2	0	0	185	9	0	2.92	12	7	5	744	27	1	2.18
1989-90	**Toronto**	**NHL**	**27**	**9**	**14**	**0**	**1343**	**87**	**0**	**3.89**	....	....	....	....	....	....	....
	Newmarket	AHL	10	6	4	0	604	33	1	3.28	....	....	....	....	....	....	....
1990-91ab	Binghamton	AHL	45	25	14	2	2452	129	0	3.16	9	3	4	442	28	1	3.80
	NHL Totals		**98**	**25**	**52**	**4**	**4850**	**337**	**2**	**4.17**	**2**	**1**	**0**	**48**	**1**	**0**	**1.25**

a Won Baz Bastien Trophy (Top Goalie - AHL) (1987, 1991)
b AHL Second All-Star Team (1991)

Signed as free agent by **Detroit**, April 29, 1983. Traded to **Philadelphia** by **Detroit** for Philadelphia's second-round choice (Bob Wilkie) in 1987 Entry Draft, June 13, 1987. Traded to **Toronto** by **Philadelphia** for Toronto's sixth round choice in 1991 Entry Draft and its seventh round choice in 1991 Entry Draft (previously obtained from Philadelphia), September 8, 1989. Traded to **NY Rangers** by **Toronto** with Tie Domi for Greg Johnston, June 28, 1990.

LAGRAND, SCOTT

Goaltender. Catches left. 6', 165 lbs. Born, Potsdam, NY, February 11, 1970.
(Philadelphia's 5th choice, 77th overall, in 1988 Entry Draft).

			Regular Season								Playoffs						
Season	Club	Lea	GP	W	L	T	Mins	GA	SO	Avg	GP	W	L	Mins	GA	SO	Avg
1989-90	Boston College	H.E.	24	17	4	0	1268	57	0	2.70	....	....	....	....	....	....	....
1990-91a	Boston College	H.E.	12	7	2	0	557	39	2	4.20	....	....	....	....	....	....	....

a Hockey East First All-Star Team (1991)

LAURIN, STEVE

Goaltender. Catches left. 5'10", 155 lbs. Born, Barrie, Ont., December 2, 1967.
(Hartford's 10th choice, 249th overall, in 1987 Entry Draft).

			Regular Season								Playoffs						
Season	Club	Lea	GP	W	L	T	Mins	GA	SO	Avg	GP	W	L	Mins	GA	SO	Avg
1986-87	Dartmouth	ECAC	15	0	14	0	883	75	0	5.09	....	....	....	....	....	....	....
1987-88a	Dartmouth	ECAC	16	4	9	1	874	59	1	4.05	....	....	....	....	....	....	....
1988-89	Dartmouth	ECAC	13	2	9	1	747	57	0	4.57	....	....	....	....	....	....	....
1989-90	Dartmouth	ECAC	22	4	14	4	1366	100	0	4.32	....	....	....	....	....	....	....
1990-91	Fort Wayne	IHL	19	8	9	1	975	68	0	4.18	1	0	0	13	1	0	4.62
	Cincinnati	ECHL	9	6	1	0	500	30	0	3.60	....	....	....	....	....	....	....

a ECAC Second All-Star Team (1988)

LEBLANC, RAYMOND

Goaltender. Catches right. 5'10", 170 lbs. Born, Fitchburg, MA, October 24, 1964.

			Regular Season								Playoffs						
Season	Club	Lea	GP	W	L	T	Mins	GA	SO	Avg	GP	W	L	Mins	GA	SO	Avg
1983-84	Kitchener	OHL	54	....	....	....	2965	185	1	3.74	....	....	....	....	....	....	....
1984-85	Pinebridge	ACHL	40	....	....	....	2178	150	0	4.13	....	....	....	....	....	....	....
1985-86	Carolina	ACHL	42	....	....	....	2505	133	3	3.19	....	....	....	....	....	....	....
1986-87	Flint	IHL	64	....	....	....	3417	222	0	3.90	....	....	....	....	....	....	....
1987-88	Flint	IHL	62	27	19	8	3269	239	1	4.39	16	10	6	925	55	1	3.57
1988-89	Flint	IHL	15	5	9	0	852	67	0	4.72	....	....	....	....	....	....	....
	Saginaw	IHL	29	19	7	2	1655	99	0	3.59	1	0	1	5	9	0	3.05
1989-90	Indianapolis	IHL	23	15	6	2	1334	71	2	3.19	....	....	....	....	....	....	....
	Fort Wayne	IHL	15	3	3	3	680	44	0	3.88	3	0	2	139	11	0	4.75
1990-91	Indianapolis	IHL	3	2	0	0	145	7	0	2.90	....	....	....	....	....	....	....
	Fort Wayne	IHL	21	10	8	0	1072	69	0	3.86	....	....	....	....	....	....	....

Signed as a free agent by **Chicago**, September, 1989.

LEHKONEN, TIMO (LEH-koh-nehn)

Goaltender. Catches left. 5'11", 183 lbs. Born, Helsinki, Finland, January 8, 1966.
(Chicago's 4th choice, 90th overall, in 1984 Entry Draft).

			Regular Season								Playoffs						
Season	Club	Lea	GP	W	L	T	Mins	GA	SO	Avg	GP	W	L	Mins	GA	SO	Avg
1983-84	Jokerit	Fin.	1	....	....	....	60	7	0	7.00	....	....	....	....	....	....	....
1984-85	Toronto	OHL	16	....	....	....	821	64	0	4.68	1	....	....	34	4	0	7.06
1985-86	Jokerit	Fin.	2	....	....	....	57	9	0	9.47	....	....	....	....	....	....	....
1986-87	Jokerit	Fin.	13	....	....	....	679	66	0	5.83	....	....	....	....	....	....	....
1987-88	TPS	Fin.	17	....	....	....	910	60	2	3.96	....	....	....	....	....	....	....
1988-89	TPS	Fin.	12	8	4	0	644	25	3	2.33	8	....	....	459	14	1	1.91
1989-90	HPK	Fin.	35	18	13	4	2032	123	0	3.63	....	....	....	....	....	....	....
1990-91	HPK	Fin.	37	....	....	....	....	123	....	....	8	....	....	440	26	....	3.55

LEMELIN, REJEAN (REGGIE) (LEHM-uh-lihn)

Goaltender. Catches left. 5'11", 170 lbs. Born, Quebec City, Que. November 19, 1954.
(Philadelphia's 6th choice, 125th overall, in 1974 Amateur Draft).

			Regular Season								Playoffs						
Season	Club	Lea	GP	W	L	T	Mins	GA	SO	Avg	GP	W	L	Mins	GA	SO	Avg
1972-73	Sherbrooke	QJHL	28	....	....	....	1681	146	0	5.21	2	....	....	120	12	0	6.00
1973-74	Sherbrooke	QJHL	35	....	....	....	2061	158	0	4.60	1	....	....	60	3	0	3.00
1974-75	Philadelphia	NAHL	43	....	....	....	2277	131	3	3.45	....	....	....	....	....	....	....
1975-76	Philadelphia	NAHL	29	....	....	....	1601	97	1	3.63	3	....	....	171	15	0	5.26
1976-77	Springfield	AHL	3	2	1	0	180	10	0	3.33	....	....	....	....	....	....	....
	Philadelphia	NAHL	51	26	19	1	2763	170	1	3.61	3	....	....	191	14	0	4.40
1977-78a	Philadelphia	AHL	60	31	21	7	3585	177	4	2.96	2	0	2	119	12	0	6.05
1978-79	**Atlanta**	**NHL**	**18**	**8**	**8**	**1**	**994**	**55**	**0**	**3.32**	**1**	**0**	**0**	**20**	**0**	**0**	**0.00**
	Philadelphia	AHL	13	3	9	1	780	36	0	2.77	....	....	....	....	....	....	....
1979-80	**Atlanta**	**NHL**	**3**	**0**	**2**	**0**	**150**	**15**	**0**	**6.00**	....	....	....	....	....	....	....
	Birmingham	CHL	38	13	21	2	2188	137	0	3.76	2	0	1	79	5	0	3.80
1980-81	**Calgary**	**NHL**	**29**	**14**	**6**	**7**	**1629**	**88**	**2**	**3.24**	**6**	**3**	**3**	**366**	**22**	**0**	**3.61**
	Birmingham	CHL	13	3	8	2	757	56	0	4.44	....	....	....	....	....	....	....
1981-82	**Calgary**	**NHL**	**34**	**10**	**5**	**6**	**1866**	**135**	**0**	**4.34**	....	....	....	....	....	....	....
1982-83	**Calgary**	**NHL**	**39**	**16**	**12**	**8**	**2211**	**133**	**0**	**3.61**	**7**	**3**	**3**	**327**	**27**	**0**	**4.95**
1983-84	**Calgary**	**NHL**	**51**	**21**	**12**	**9**	**2568**	**150**	**0**	**3.50**	**8**	**4**	**4**	**448**	**32**	**0**	**4.29**
1984-85	**Calgary**	**NHL**	**56**	**30**	**12**	**10**	**3176**	**183**	**1**	**3.46**	**4**	**1**	**3**	**248**	**15**	**1**	**3.63**
1985-86	**Calgary**	**NHL**	**60**	**29**	**24**	**4**	**3369**	**229**	**1**	**4.08**	**3**	**0**	**1**	**109**	**7**	**0**	**3.85**
1986-87	**Calgary**	**NHL**	**34**	**16**	**9**	**1**	**1735**	**94**	**2**	**3.25**	**2**	**0**	**1**	**101**	**6**	**0**	**3.56**
1987-88	**Boston**	**NHL**	**49**	**24**	**17**	**6**	**2828**	**138**	**3**	**2.93**	**17**	**11**	**6**	**1027**	**45**	***1**	***2.63**
1988-89	**Boston**	**NHL**	**40**	**19**	**15**	**6**	**2392**	**120**	**0**	**3.01**	**4**	**1**	**3**	**252**	**16**	**0**	**3.81**
1989-90b	**Boston**	**NHL**	**43**	**22**	**15**	**2**	**2310**	**108**	**2**	**2.81**	**3**	**0**	**1**	**135**	**13**	**0**	**5.78**
1990-91	**Boston**	**NHL**	**33**	**17**	**10**	**3**	**1829**	**111**	**1**	**3.64**	**2**	**0**	**0**	**32**	**0**	**0**	**0.00**
	NHL Totals		**489**	**226**	**147**	**63**	**27057**	**1559**	**12**	**3.46**	**57**	**23**	**25**	**3065**	**183**	**2**	**3.58**

a AHL First All-Star Team (1978)
b Shared William Jennings Trophy with Andy Moog (1990)

Played in NHL All-Star Game (1989)

Signed as free agent by **Atlanta**, August 17, 1978. Signed as a free agent by **Boston**, August 13, 1987.

LENARDUZZI, MIKE

Goaltender. Catches left. 6', 165 lbs. Born, Mississauga, Ont., September 14, 1972.
(Hartford's 3rd choice, 57th overall, in 1990 Entry Draft).

			Regular Season								Playoffs						
Season	Club	Lea	GP	W	L	T	Mins	GA	SO	Avg	GP	W	L	Mins	GA	SO	Avg
1989-90	Oshawa	OHL	12	6	3	1	444	32	0	4.32	....	....	....	....	....	....	....
1990-91a	S. S. Marie	OHL	35	19	8	3	1966	107	0	3.27	5	3	1	268	13	*1	2.91

a OHL Third All-Star Team (1991)

LETOURNEAU, RAYMOND GEORGE (RAY)

Goaltender. Catches left. 5'11", 185 lbs. Born, Penacook, NH, January 14, 1969.
(Philadelphia's 2nd choice, 9th overall, in 1990 Supplemental Draft).

			Regular Season								Playoffs						
Season	Club	Lea	GP	W	L	T	Mins	GA	SO	Avg	GP	W	L	Mins	GA	SO	Avg
1987-88	Yale	ECAC	4	0	3	0	175	24	0	8.21	....	....	....	....	....	....	....
1988-89	Yale	ECAC	7	1	5	0	378	42	0	6.66	....	....	....	....	....	....	....
1989-90	Yale	ECAC	28	8	19	1	1631	125	0	4.59	....	....	....	....	....	....	....
1990-91	Yale	ECAC	27	11	14	2	1572	106	0	4.05	....	....	....	....	....	....	....

LEVY, JEFF

Goaltender. Catches left. 5'11", 160 lbs. Born, Salt Lake City, UT, December 9, 1970.
(Minnesota's 7th choice, 134th overall, in 1990 Entry Draft).

			Regular Season								Playoffs						
Season	Club	Lea	GP	W	L	T	Mins	GA	SO	Avg	GP	W	L	Mins	GA	SO	Avg
1989-90	Rochester	USHL	32	24	7	0	1823	97	3	3.19	....	....	....	....	....	....	....
1990-91abc	N. Hampshire	H.E.	24	15	7	2	1490	80	0	3.22	....	....	....	....	....	....	....

a Hockey East Rookie of the Year (1991)
b Hockey East Second All-Star Team (1991)
c NCAA East Second All-American Team (1991)

LIBERTUCCI, ANGELO

Goaltender. Catches left. 5'10", 165 lbs. Born, Toronto, Ont., January 3, 1970.
(Philadelphia's 1st choice, 6th overall, in 1991 Supplemental Draft).

			Regular Season								Playoffs						
Season	Club	Lea	GP	W	L	T	Mins	GA	SO	Avg	GP	W	L	Mins	GA	SO	Avg
1989-90	Bowling Green	CCHA	28	16	10	1	1591	107	0	4.03	....	....	....	....	....	....	....
1990-91	Bowling Green	CCHA	29	12	15	1	1594	124	1	4.67	....	....	....	....	....	....	....

LINDFORS, SAKARI (LIHND-fohrs)

Goaltender. Catches left. 5'7", 150 lbs. Born, Helsinki, Finland, April 27, 1966.
(Quebec's 9th choice, 150th overall, in 1988 Entry Draft).

			Regular Season								Playoffs						
Season	Club	Lea	GP	W	L	T	Mins	GA	SO	Avg	GP	W	L	Mins	GA	SO	Avg
1988-89	HIFK	Fin.	24	11	11	2	1433	89	1	3.75	....	....	....	....	....	....	....
1989-90	HIFK	Fin.	42	23	15	4	2518	146	2	3.48	....	....	....	....	....	....	....
1990-91	HIFK	Fin.	41	....	....	....	....	137	....	....	3	....	....	180	14	0	4.67

LITTMAN, DAVID

Goaltender. Catches left. 6', 172 lbs. Born, Cranston, RI, June 13, 1967.
(Buffalo's 12th choice, 211th overall, in 1987 Entry Draft).

			Regular Season								Playoffs						
Season	Club	Lea	GP	W	L	T	Mins	GA	SO	Avg	GP	W	L	Mins	GA	SO	Avg
1985-86	Boston College	H.E.	7	4	0	1	312	18	0	3.46	....	....	....	....	....	....	....
1986-87	Boston College	H.E.	21	15	5	0	1182	68	0	3.45	....	....	....	....	....	....	....
1987-88a	Boston College	H.E.	30	11	16	2	1726	116	0	4.03	....	....	....	....	....	....	....
1988-89bc	Boston College	H.E.	*32	19	9	4	*1945	107	0	3.30	....	....	....	....	....	....	....
1989-90	Rochester	AHL	14	5	6	1	681	37	0	3.26	....	....	....	....	....	....	....
	Phoenix	IHL	18	8	7	2	1047	64	0	3.67	....	....	....	....	....	....	....
1990-91	**Buffalo**	**NHL**	**1**	**0**	**0**	**0**	**36**	**3**	**0**	**5.00**	....	....	....	....	....	....	....
d	Rochester	AHL	*56	*33	13	5	*3155	160	3	3.04	8	4	2	378	16	0	2.54
	NHL Totals		**1**	**0**	**0**	**0**	**36**	**3**	**0**	**5.00**	....	....	....	....	....	....	....

a Hockey East Second All-Star Team (1988)
b Hockey East First All-Star Team (1989)
c NCAA East Second All-American Team (1989)
d AHL First All-Star Team (1991)

LIUT, MICHAEL (MIKE) (lee-OOT)

Goaltender. Catches left. 6'2", 195 lbs. Born, Weston, Ont., January 7, 1956.
(St. Louis' 5th choice, 56th overall, in 1976 Amateur Draft).

			Regular Season								Playoffs						
Season	Club	Lea	GP	W	L	T	Mins	GA	SO	Avg	GP	W	L	Mins	GA	SO	Avg
1973-74	Bowling Green	CCHA	24	10	12	0	1272	88	1	4.15	....	....	....	....	....	....	....
1974-75	Bowling Green	CCHA	20	12	6	1	1174	78	0	3.99	....	....	....	....	....	....	....
1975-76	Bowling Green	CCHA	21	13	5	0	1171	50	2	2.56	....	....	....	....	....	....	....
1976-77	Bowling Green	CCHA	24	18	4	0	1346	61	2	2.72	....	....	....	....	....	....	....
1977-78	Cincinnati	WHA	27	8	12	0	1215	86	0	4.25	....	....	....	....	....	....	....
1978-79	Cincinnati	WHA	54	23	27	4	3181	184	*3	3.47	3	1	2	179	12	0	4.02
1979-80	**St. Louis**	**NHL**	**64**	**32**	**23**	**9**	**3661**	**194**	**2**	**3.18**	**3**	**0**	**3**	**193**	**12**	**0**	**3.73**
1980-81ab	**St. Louis**	**NHL**	**61**	**33**	**14**	**13**	**3570**	**199**	**1**	**3.34**	**11**	**5**	**6**	**685**	**50**	**0**	**4.38**
1981-82	**St. Louis**	**NHL**	***64**	**28**	**28**	**7**	***3691**	**250**	**2**	**4.06**	**10**	**5**	**3**	**494**	**27**	**0**	**3.28**
1982-83	**St. Louis**	**NHL**	***68**	**21**	**27**	**13**	***3794**	**235**	**1**	**3.72**	**4**	**1**	**3**	**240**	**15**	**0**	**3.75**
1983-84	**St. Louis**	**NHL**	**58**	**25**	**29**	**4**	**3425**	**197**	**3**	**3.45**	**11**	**6**	**5**	**714**	**29**	**1**	**2.44**
1984-85	**St. Louis**	**NHL**	**32**	**12**	**12**	**6**	**1869**	**119**	**1**	**3.82**	....	....	....	....	....	....	....
	Hartford	**NHL**	**12**	**4**	**7**	**1**	**731**	**36**	**1**	**2.95**	....	....	....	....	....	....	....
1985-86	**Hartford**	**NHL**	**57**	**27**	**23**	**4**	**3282**	**198**	**2**	**3.62**	**8**	**5**	**2**	**441**	**14**	***1**	***1.90**
1986-87c	**Hartford**	**NHL**	**59**	**31**	**22**	**5**	**3476**	**187**	***4**	**3.23**	**6**	**2**	**4**	**332**	**25**	**0**	**4.52**
1987-88	**Hartford**	**NHL**	**60**	**25**	**28**	**5**	**3532**	**187**	**2**	**3.18**	**3**	**1**	**1**	**160**	**11**	**0**	**4.13**
1988-89	**Hartford**	**NHL**	**35**	**13**	**19**	**1**	**2006**	**142**	**1**	**4.25**	....	....	....	....	....	....	....
1989-90	**Hartford**	**NHL**	**29**	**15**	**12**	**1**	**1683**	**74**	***3**	***2.64**	....	....	....	....	....	....	....
	Washington	**NHL**	**8**	**4**	**4**	**0**	**478**	**17**	***1**	***2.13**	**9**	**4**	**4**	**507**	**28**	**0**	**3.31**
1990-91	**Washington**	**NHL**	**35**	**13**	**16**	**3**	**1834**	**114**	**0**	**3.73**	**2**	**0**	**1**	**48**	**4**	**0**	**5.00**
	NHL Totals		**642**	**283**	**264**	**72**	**37032**	**2149**	**24**	**3.48**	**67**	**29**	**32**	**3814**	**215**	**2**	**3.38**

a NHL First All-Star Team (1981)
b Won Lester B. Pearson Award (1981)
c NHL Second All-Star Team (1987)

Played in NHL All-Star Game (1981)

Reclaimed by **St. Louis** from Cincinnati (WHA) prior to Expansion Draft, June 9, 1979. Traded to **Hartford** by **St. Louis** with Jorgen Pettersson for Mark Johnson and Greg Millen, February 21, 1985. Traded to **Washington** by **Hartford** for Yvon Corriveau, March 6, 1990.

LOEWEN, JAMIE

Goaltender. Catches left. 5'10", 165 lbs. Born, Vancouver, B.C., September 23, 1968.
(Minnesota's 1st choice, 12th overall, in 1989 Supplemental Draft).

			Regular Season								Playoffs						
Season	Club	Lea	GP	W	L	T	Mins	GA	SO	Avg	GP	W	L	Mins	GA	SO	Avg
1988-89	Alaska-Fair.	NCAA	24	....	....	....	1501	84	0	3.48	....	....	....	....	....	....	....
1989-90	Alaska-Fair.	NCAA	17	5	12	0	1023	101	0	5.94	....	....	....	....	....	....	....
1990-91	Alaska-Fair.	NCAA	15	7	7	1	938	52	1	3.33	....	....	....	....	....	....	....

LORENZ, DANNY

Goaltender. Catches left. 5'10", 170 lbs. Born, Murrayville, B.C., December 12, 1969.
(NY Islanders' 4th choice, 58th overall, in 1988 Entry Draft).

			Regular Season								Playoffs						
Season	Club	Lea	GP	W	L	T	Mins	GA	SO	Avg	GP	W	L	Mins	GA	SO	Avg
1986-87	Seattle	WHL	38	12	21	2	2103	199	0	5.68	....	....	....	....	....	....	....
1987-88	Seattle	WHL	62	20	37	2	3302	314	0	5.71	....	....	....	....	....	....	....
1988-89	Springfield	AHL	4	2	1	0	210	12	0	3.43	....	....	....	....	....	....	....
a	Seattle	WHL	*68	31	33	4	*4003	240	*3	3.60	....	....	....	....	....	....	....
1989-90a	Seattle	WHL	56	37	15	2	3226	221	0	4.11	13	6	7	751	40	0	3.21
1990-91	**NY Islanders**	**NHL**	**2**	**0**	**1**	**0**	**80**	**5**	**0**	**3.75**	....	....	....	....	....	....	....
	Capital Dist.	AHL	17	5	9	2	940	70	0	4.47	....	....	....	....	....	....	....
	Richmond	ECHL	20	6	9	2	1020	75	0	4.41	....	....	....	....	....	....	....
	NHL Totals		**2**	**0**	**1**	**0**	**80**	**5**	**0**	**3.75**	....	....	....	....	....	....	....

a WHL West First All-Star Team (1989, 1990)

LOUDER, GREG

Goaltender. Catches left. 6'1", 185 lbs. Born, Concord, MA, November 16, 1971.
(Edmonton's 5th choice, 101st overall, in 1990 Entry Draft).

			Regular Season								Playoffs						
Season	Club	Lea	GP	W	L	T	Mins	GA	SO	Avg	GP	W	L	Mins	GA	SO	Avg
1990-91	Notre Dame	NCAA	33	16	5	2	1958	134	1	4.11	....	....	....	....	....	....	....

LUKOWSKI, BRIAN

Goaltender. Catches left. 5'9", 160 lbs. Born, Buffalo, NY, January 8, 1971.
(St. Louis' 11th choice, 219th overall, in 1989 Entry Draft).

			Regular Season								Playoffs						
Season	Club	Lea	GP	W	L	T	Mins	GA	SO	Avg	GP	W	L	Mins	GA	SO	Avg
1989-90	Lake Superior	CCHA	4	1	0	0	114	8	0	4.20	....	....	....	....	....	....	....
1990-91	Lake Superior	CCHA	4	3	0	0	200	8	0	2.40	....	....	....	....	....	....	....

MALARCHUK, CLINT

Goaltender. Catches left. 6', 187 lbs. Born, Grande Prairie, Alta. May 1, 1961.
(Quebec's 3rd choice, 74th overall, in 1981 Entry Draft).

			Regular Season								Playoffs						
Season	Club	Lea	GP	W	L	T	Mins	GA	SO	Avg	GP	W	L	Mins	GA	SO	Avg
1979-80	Portland	WHL	37	21	10	0	1948	147	0	4.53	1	0	0	40	3	0	4.50
1980-81	Portland	WHL	38	28	8	0	2235	142	3	3.81	4	....	....	307	21	0	4.10
1981-82	**Quebec**	**NHL**	**2**	**0**	**1**	**1**	**120**	**14**	**0**	**7.00**	....	....	....	....	....	....	....
	Fredericton	AHL	51	15	34	2	2906	247	0	5.10	....	....	....	....	....	....	....
1982-83	**Quebec**	**NHL**	**15**	**8**	**5**	**2**	**900**	**71**	**0**	**4.73**	....	....	....	....	....	....	....
	Fredericton	AHL	25	....	....	....	1506	78	0	3.11	....	....	....	....	....	....	....
1983-84	**Quebec**	**NHL**	**23**	**10**	**9**	**2**	**1215**	**80**	**0**	**3.95**	....	....	....	....	....	....	....
	Fredericton	AHL	11	5	5	1	663	40	0	3.62	....	....	....	....	....	....	....
1984-85	Fredericton	AHL	*56	26	25	4	*3347	198	2	3.55	6	2	4	379	20	0	3.17
1985-86	**Quebec**	**NHL**	**46**	**26**	**12**	**4**	**2657**	**142**	**4**	**3.21**	**3**	**0**	**2**	**143**	**11**	**0**	**4.62**
1986-87	**Quebec**	**NHL**	**54**	**18**	**26**	**9**	**3092**	**175**	**1**	**3.40**	**3**	**0**	**2**	**140**	**8**	**0**	**3.43**
1987-88	**Washington**	**NHL**	**54**	**24**	**20**	**4**	**2926**	**154**	***4**	**3.16**	**4**	**0**	**2**	**193**	**15**	**0**	**4.66**
1988-89	**Washington**	**NHL**	**42**	**16**	**18**	**7**	**2428**	**141**	**1**	**3.48**	**1**	**0**	**1**	**59**	**5**	**0**	**5.08**
	Buffalo	**NHL**	**7**	**3**	**1**	**1**	**326**	**13**	**1**	**2.39**	....	....	....	....	....	....	....
1989-90	**Buffalo**	**NHL**	**29**	**14**	**11**	**2**	**1596**	**89**	**0**	**3.35**	....	....	....	....	....	....	....
1990-91	**Buffalo**	**NHL**	**37**	**12**	**14**	**10**	**2131**	**119**	**1**	**3.35**	**4**	**2**	**2**	**246**	**17**	**0**	**4.15**
	NHL Totals		**309**	**131**	**117**	**42**	**17391**	**998**	**12**	**3.44**	**15**	**2**	**9**	**781**	**56**	**0**	**4.30**

Traded to **Washington** by **Quebec** with Dale Hunter for Gaetan Duchesne, Alan Haworth, and Washington's first-round choice (Joe Sakic) in 1987 Entry Draft, June 13, 1987. Traded to **Buffalo** by **Washington** with Grant Ledyard and Washington's sixth-round choice (Brian Holzinger) in 1991 Entry Draft for Calle Johansson and Buffalo's second-round choice (Byron Dafoe) in 1989 Entry Draft, March 7, 1989.

MANELUK, GEORGE

Goaltender. Catches left. 5'11", 185 lbs. Born, Winnipeg, Man., July 25, 1967.
(NY Islanders' 4th choice, 76th overall, in 1987 Entry Draft).

			Regular Season								Playoffs						
Season	Club	Lea	GP	W	L	T	Mins	GA	SO	Avg	GP	W	L	Mins	GA	SO	Avg
1986-87	Brandon	WHL	58	16	35	4	3258	315	0	5.80	....	....	....	....	....	....	....
1987-88	Brandon	WHL	64	24	33	3	3651	297	0	4.88	4	1	3	271	22	0	4.87
	Springfield	AHL	2	0	1	1	125	9	0	4.32	....	....	....	....	....	....	....
	Peoria	IHL	3	1	2	0	148	14	0	5.68	1	0	1	60	5	0	5.00
1988-89	Springfield	AHL	24	7	13	0	1202	84	0	4.19	....	....	....	....	....	....	....
1989-90	Springfield	AHL	27	11	9	1	1382	94	1	4.08	4	2	1	174	9	0	3.10
	Winston-Salem	ECHL	3	2	0	0	140	11	0	4.71	....	....	....	....	....	....	....
1990-91	**NY Islanders**	**NHL**	**4**	**1**	**1**	**0**	**140**	**15**	**0**	**6.43**	....	....	....	....	....	....	....
	Capital Dist.	AHL	29	10	14	1	1524	103	1	4.06	....	....	....	....	....	....	....
	NHL Totals		**4**	**1**	**1**	**0**	**140**	**15**	**0**	**6.43**	....	....	....	....	....	....	....

MASON, BOB

Goaltender. Catches right. 6'1", 180 lbs. Born, International Falls, MN, April 22, 1961.

			Regular Season								Playoffs						
Season	Club	Lea	GP	W	L	T	Mins	GA	SO	Avg	GP	W	L	Mins	GA	SO	Avg
1981-82	Minn.-Duluth	WCHA	26	....	....	....	1401	115	0	4.45	....	....	....	....	....	....	....
1982-83	Minn.-Duluth	WCHA	43	....	....	....	2593	151	1	3.49	....	....	....	....	....	....	....
1983-84	U.S. National	...	33	....	....	....	1895	89	0	2.82	....	....	....	....	....	....	....
	U.S. Olympic	...	3	....	....	....	160	10	0	3.75	....	....	....	....	....	....	....
	Washington	**NHL**	**2**	**2**	**0**	**0**	**120**	**3**	**0**	**1.50**	....	....	....	....	....	....	....
	Hershey	AHL	5	1	4	0	282	26	0	5.53	....	....	....	....	....	....	....
1984-85	**Washington**	**NHL**	**12**	**8**	**2**	**1**	**661**	**31**	**1**	**2.81**	....	....	....	....	....	....	....
	Binghamton	AHL	20	10	6	1	1052	58	1	3.31	....	....	....	....	....	....	....
1985-86	**Washington**	**NHL**	**1**	**1**	**0**	**0**	**16**	**0**	**0**	**0.00**	....	....	....	....	....	....	....
	Binghamton	AHL	34	20	11	2	1940	126	0	3.90	3	1	1	124	9	0	4.35
1986-87	**Washington**	**NHL**	**45**	**20**	**18**	**5**	**2536**	**137**	**0**	**3.24**	**4**	**2**	**2**	**309**	**9**	**1**	**1.75**
	Binghamton	AHL	2	1	1	0	119	4	0	2.02	....	....	....	....	....	....	....
1987-88	**Chicago**	**NHL**	**41**	**13**	**18**	**8**	**2312**	**160**	**0**	**4.15**	**1**	**0**	**1**	**60**	**3**	**0**	**3.00**
1988-89	**Quebec**	**NHL**	**22**	**5**	**14**	**1**	**1168**	**92**	**0**	**4.73**	....	....	....	....	....	....	....
	Halifax	AHL	23	11	7	1	1278	73	1	3.43	2	0	2	97	9	0	5.57
1989-90	**Washington**	**NHL**	**16**	**4**	**9**	**1**	**822**	**48**	**0**	**3.50**	....	....	....	....	....	....	....
	Baltimore	AHL	13	9	2	2	770	44	0	3.43	6	2	4	373	20	0	3.22
1990-91	**Vancouver**	**NHL**	**6**	**2**	**4**	**0**	**353**	**29**	**0**	**4.93**	....	....	....	....	....	....	....
	Milwaukee	IHL	22	8	12	1	1199	82	0	4.10	....	....	....	....	....	....	....
	NHL Totals		**145**	**55**	**65**	**16**	**7988**	**500**	**1**	**3.76**	**5**	**2**	**3**	**369**	**12**	**1**	**1.95**

Signed as a free agent by **Washington**, February 21, 1984. Signed as a free agent by **Chicago**, June 12, 1987. Traded to **Quebec** by **Chicago** for Mike Eagles, July 5, 1988. Traded to **Washington** by **Quebec** for future considerations, June 17, 1989.

MAZZOLI, PAT

Goaltender. Catches left. 5'10", 172 lbs. Born, Toronto, Ont., March 16, 1970.
(Quebec's 8th choice, 169th overall, in 1990 Entry Draft).

			Regular Season								Playoffs						
Season	Club	Lea	GP	W	L	T	Mins	GA	SO	Avg	GP	W	L	Mins	GA	SO	Avg
1990-91	Ferris State	CCHA	21	13	7	1	1202	64	0	3.19	....	....	....	....	....	....	....

McKAY, ROSS LEE

Goaltender. Catches right. 5'11", 175 lbs. Born, Edmonton, Alta., March 3, 1964.

			Regular Season								Playoffs						
Season	Club	Lea	GP	W	L	T	Mins	GA	SO	Avg	GP	W	L	Mins	GA	SO	Avg
1988-89	Binghamton	AHL	19	5	9	2	938	81	1	5.18	....	....	....	....	....	....	....
	Indianapolis	IHL	5	1	3	0	187	18	0	5.78	....	....	....	....	....	....	....
1989-90	Binghamton	AHL	18	0	10	1	713	58	0	4.88	....	....	....	....	....	....	....
	Knoxville	ECHL	8	4	2	1	426	20	0	2.81	....	....	....	....	....	....	....
1990-91	**Hartford**	**NHL**	**1**	**0**	**0**	**0**	**35**	**3**	**0**	**5.14**	....	....	....	....	....	....	....
	Springfield	AHL	23	7	10	3	1275	75	0	3.53	3	1	2	191	11	0	3.46
	NHL Totals		**1**	**0**	**0**	**0**	**35**	**3**	**0**	**5.14**	....	....	....	....	....	....	....

Signed as a free agent by **Hartford**, May 2, 1988.

McKERSIE, JOHN

Goaltender. Catches left. 6', 210 lbs. Born, Madison, WI, June 23, 1972.
(Minnesota's 12th choice, 239th overall, in 1990 Entry Draft).

			Regular Season								Playoffs						
Season	Club	Lea	GP	W	L	T	Mins	GA	SO	Avg	GP	W	L	Mins	GA	SO	Avg
1990-91	Dubuque	USHL	37	13	18	0	1274	151	0	4.60	....	....	....	....	....	....	....

McKICHAN, STEVE (muh-KEE-Kan)

Goaltender. Catches left. 5'11", 180 lbs. Born, Strathroy, Ont., May 29, 1967.
(Vancouver's 2nd choice, 7th overall, in 1988 Supplemental Draft).

			Regular Season								Playoffs						
Season	Club	Lea	GP	W	L	T	Mins	GA	SO	Avg	GP	W	L	Mins	GA	SO	Avg
1986-87	Miami-Ohio	CCHA	28	3	19	0	1351	130	0	5.77	....	....	....	....	....	....	....
1987-88	Miami-Ohio	CCHA	34	12	17	1	1767	140	1	4.75	....	....	....	....	....	....	....
1988-89	Miami-Ohio	CCHA	21	4	15	0	1014	85	0	5.02	....	....	....	....	....	....	....
1989-90	Virginia	ECHL	28	16	11	2	1445	97	0	4.02	3	....	....	209	11	0	3.16
	Milwaukee	IHL	1	1	0	0	40	2	0	3.00	....	....	....	....	....	....	....
1990-91	**Vancouver**	**NHL**	**1**	**0**	**0**	**0**	**20**	**2**	**0**	**6.00**	....	....	....	....	....	....	....
	Milwaukee	IHL	30	12	10	2	1571	87	2	3.32	4	1	2	212	13	0	3.68
	NHL Totals		**1**	**0**	**0**	**0**	**20**	**2**	**0**	**6.00**	....	....	....	....	....	....	....

McLEAN, KIRK

Goaltender. Catches left. 6', 195 lbs. Born, Willowdale, Ont., June 26, 1966.
(New Jersey's 6th choice, 107th overall, in 1984 Entry Draft).

			Regular Season								Playoffs						
Season	Club	Lea	GP	W	L	T	Mins	GA	SO	Avg	GP	W	L	Mins	GA	SO	Avg
1983-84	Oshawa	OHL	17	5	9	0	940	67	0	4.28	....	....	....	....	....	....	....
1984-85	Oshawa	OHL	47	23	17	2	2581	143	1	*3.32	5	1	3	271	21	0	4.65
1985-86	**New Jersey**	**NHL**	**2**	**1**	**1**	**0**	**111**	**11**	**0**	**5.95**	....	....	....	....	....	....	....
	Oshawa	OHL	51	24	21	2	2830	169	1	3.58	4	1	2	201	18	0	5.37
1986-87	**New Jersey**	**NHL**	**4**	**1**	**1**	**0**	**160**	**10**	**0**	**3.75**	....	....	....	....	....	....	....
	Maine	AHL	45	15	23	4	2606	140	1	3.22	....	....	....	....	....	....	....
1987-88	**Vancouver**	**NHL**	**41**	**11**	**27**	**3**	**2380**	**147**	**1**	**3.71**	....	....	....	....	....	....	....
1988-89	**Vancouver**	**NHL**	**42**	**20**	**17**	**3**	**2477**	**127**	**4**	**3.08**	**5**	**2**	**3**	**302**	**18**	**0**	**3.58**
1989-90	**Vancouver**	**NHL**	***63**	**21**	**30**	**10**	***3739**	**216**	**0**	**3.47**	....	....	....	....	....	....	....
1990-91	**Vancouver**	**NHL**	**41**	**10**	**22**	**3**	**1969**	**131**	**0**	**3.99**	**2**	**1**	**1**	**123**	**7**	**0**	**3.41**
	NHL Totals		**193**	**64**	**98**	**19**	**10836**	**642**	**5**	**3.55**	**7**	**3**	**4**	**425**	**25**	**0**	**3.53**

Played in NHL All-Star Game (1990)

Traded to **Vancouver** by **New Jersey** with Greg Adams for Patrik Sundstrom and Vancouver's fourth round choice (Matt Ruchty) in 1988 Entry Draft, September 15, 1987.

McLENNAN, JAMIE

Goaltender. Catches left. 5'11", 190 lbs. Born, Edmonton, Alta., June 30, 1971.
(NY Islanders' 3rd choice, 48th overall, in 1991 Entry Draft).

			Regular Season								Playoffs						
Season	Club	Lea	GP	W	L	T	Mins	GA	SO	Avg	GP	W	L	Mins	GA	SO	Avg
1989-90	Lethbridge	WHL	34	20	4	2	1690	110	1	3.91	13	6	5	677	44	0	3.90
1990-91a	Lethbridge	WHL	56	32	18	4	3230	205	0	3.81	*16	8	8	*970	56	0	3.46

a WHL East First All-Star Team (1991)

MELANSON, ROLAND JOSEPH (ROLLIE) (mel-AWN-son)

Goaltender. Catches left. 5'10", 185 lbs. Born, Moncton, N.B., June 28, 1960.
(NY Islanders' 4th choice, 59th overall, in 1979 Entry Draft).

			Regular Season								Playoffs						
Season	Club	Lea	GP	W	L	T	Mins	GA	SO	Avg	GP	W	L	Mins	GA	SO	Avg
1978-79a	Windsor	OHA	58	....	....	....	3468	258	1	4.41	7	....	....	392	31	0	4.75
1979-80	Windsor	OHA	22	11	8	0	1099	90	0	4.91	....	....	....	....	....	....	....
	Oshawa	OHA	38	26	12	0	2240	136	3	3.64	7	3	4	420	32	0	4.57
1980-81bc	NY Islanders	NHL	11	8	1	1	620	32	0	3.10	3	1	0	92	6	0	3.91
	Indianapolis	CHL	52	31	16	3	3056	131	2	*2.57	....	....	....	....	....	....	....
1981-82	NY Islanders	NHL	36	22	7	6	2115	114	0	3.23	3	0	1	64	5	0	4.69
1982-83de	NY Islanders	NHL	44	24	12	5	2460	109	1	2.66	5	2	2	238	10	0	2.52
1983-84	NY Islanders	NHL	37	20	11	2	2019	110	0	3.27	6	0	1	87	5	0	3.45
1984-85	NY Islanders	NHL	8	3	3	0	425	35	0	4.94	....	....	....	....	....	....	....
	Minnesota	NHL	20	5	10	3	1142	78	0	4.10	....	....	....	....	....	....	....
1985-86	Minnesota	NHL	6	2	1	2	325	24	0	4.43	....	....	....	....	....	....	....
	Los Angeles	NHL	22	4	16	1	1246	87	0	4.19	....	....	....	....	....	....	....
	New Haven	AHL	3	1	2	0	179	13	0	4.36	....	....	....	....	....	....	....
1986-87	Los Angeles	NHL	46	18	21	6	2734	168	1	3.69	5	1	4	260	24	0	5.54
1987-88	Los Angeles	NHL	47	17	20	7	2676	195	2	4.37	1	0	1	60	9	0	9.00
1988-89	Los Angeles	NHL	4	1	1	0	178	19	0	6.40	....	....	....	....	....	....	....
	New Haven	AHL	29	11	15	3	1734	106	1	3.67	*17	9	8	*1019	74	1	4.36
1989-90	Utica	AHL	48	24	19	3	2737	167	1	3.66	5	1	4	298	20	0	4.03
1990-91	New Jersey	NHL	1	0	0	0	20	2	0	6.00	....	....	....	....	....	....	....
	Utica	AHL	54	23	28	1	3058	208	0	4.08	....	....	....	....	....	....	....
	NHL Totals		282	124	103	33	15960	973	4	3.66	23	4	9	801	59	0	4.42

a OHA Second All-Star Team (1979)
b CHL First All-Star Team (1981)
c Won Ken McKenzie Trophy (CHL's Rookie of the Year) (1981)
d Shared William Jennings Trophy with Billy Smith (1983)
e NHL Second All-Star Team (1983)

Traded to **Minnesota** by **NY Islanders** for Minnesota's first round choice in 1985 Entry draft (Brad Dalgarno), November 19, 1984. Traded to **NY Rangers** by **Minnesota** for New York's second round draft choice in 1986 (Neil Wilkinson) and fourth round choice in 1987 (John Weisbrod), December 9, 1985. Traded to **Los Angeles** by **NY Rangers** with Grant Ledyard for Brian MacLellan and Los Angeles' fourth round draft choice in 1987 (Michael Sullivan), December 9, 1985. Signed as a free agent by **New Jersey**, August 10, 1989.

MERTEN, MATT

Goaltender. Catches left. 6'3", 190 lbs. Born, Milford, MA, June 29, 1967.
(Vancouver's 8th choice, 175th overall, in 1986 Entry Draft).

			Regular Season								Playoffs						
Season	Club	Lea	GP	W	L	T	Mins	GA	SO	Avg	GP	W	L	Mins	GA	SO	Avg
1986-87	Providence	H.E.	24	6	14	2	1455	104	0	4.29	....	....	....	....	....	....	....
1987-88	Providence	H.E.	25	8	11	1	1328	100	0	4.52	....	....	....	....	....	....	....
1988-89	Providence	H.E.	20	7	8	1	1067	69	0	3.88	....	....	....	....	....	....	....
1989-90	Providence	H.E.	16	8	4	2	908	38	0	*2.51	....	....	....	....	....	....	....
1990-91	Greensboro	ECHL	28	12	10	1	1446	103	0	4.27	1	0	0	20	1	0	3.00

MILLEN, GREG H.

Goaltender. Catches right. 5'9", 175 lbs. Born, Toronto, Ont., June 25, 1957.
(Pittsburgh's 4th choice, 102nd overall, in 1977 Amateur Draft).

			Regular Season								Playoffs						
Season	Club	Lea	GP	W	L	T	Mins	GA	SO	Avg	GP	W	L	Mins	GA	SO	Avg
1976-77	Peterborough	OHA	59	....	....	....	3457	244	0	4.23	4	....	....	240	23	0	5.75
1977-78	Kalamazoo	IHL	3	....	....	....	180	14	0	4.67	....	....	....	....	....	....	....
	S. S. Marie	OHA	25	....	....	....	1449	105	1	4.29	13	....	....	774	61	0	4.73
1978-79	Pittsburgh	NHL	28	14	11	1	1532	86	2	3.37	....	....	....	....	....	....	....
1979-80	Pittsburgh	NHL	44	18	18	7	2586	157	2	3.64	5	2	3	300	21	0	4.20
1980-81	Pittsburgh	NHL	63	25	27	10	3721	258	0	4.16	5	2	3	325	19	0	3.51
1981-82	Hartford	NHL	55	11	30	12	3201	229	0	4.29	....	....	....	....	....	....	....
1982-83	Hartford	NHL	60	14	38	6	3520	282	1	4.81	....	....	....	....	....	....	....
1983-84	Hartford	NHL	*60	21	30	9	*3583	221	2	3.70	....	....	....	....	....	....	....
1984-85	Hartford	NHL	44	16	22	6	2659	187	1	4.22	....	....	....	....	....	....	....
	St. Louis	NHL	10	2	7	1	607	35	0	3.46	1	0	1	60	2	0	2.00
1985-86	St. Louis	NHL	36	14	16	6	2168	129	1	3.57	10	6	3	586	29	0	2.97
1986-87	St. Louis	NHL	42	15	18	9	2482	146	0	3.53	4	1	3	250	10	0	2.40
1987-88	St. Louis	NHL	48	21	19	7	2854	167	1	3.51	10	5	5	600	38	0	3.80
1988-89	St. Louis	NHL	52	22	20	7	3019	170	*6	3.38	10	5	5	649	34	0	3.14
1989-90	St. Louis	NHL	21	11	7	3	1245	61	1	2.94	....	....	....	....	....	....	....
	Quebec	NHL	18	3	14	1	1080	95	0	5.28	....	....	....	....	....	....	....
	Chicago	NHL	10	5	4	1	575	32	0	3.34	14	6	6	613	40	0	3.92
1990-91	Chicago	NHL	3	0	1	0	58	4	0	4.14	....	....	....	....	....	....	....
	NHL Totals		594	212	282	86	34890	2259	17	3.88	59	27	29	3383	193	0	3.42

Signed as free agent by **Hartford**, June 15, 1981. As compensation, **Pittsburgh** received Pat Boutette and the rights to Kevin McLelland, June 29, 1981. Traded to **St. Louis** by **Hartford** with Mark Johnson for Mike Liut and Jorgen Pettersson, February 21, 1985. Traded to **Quebec** by **St. Louis** with Tony Hrkac for Jeff Brown, December 13, 1989. Traded to **Chicago** by **Quebec** with Michel Goulet and Quebec's sixth round choice (Kevin St. Jacques) in 1991 Entry Draft for Mario Doyon, Everett Sanipass and Dan Vincelette, March 5, 1990.

MOOG, DONALD ANDREW (ANDY) (MOHG)

Goaltender. Catches left. 5'8", 170 lbs. Born, Penticton, B.C., February 18, 1960.
(Edmonton's 6th choice, 132nd overall, in 1980 Entry Draft).

			Regular Season								Playoffs						
Season	Club	Lea	GP	W	L	T	Mins	GA	SO	Avg	GP	W	L	Mins	GA	SO	Avg
1978-79	Billings	WHL	26	13	5	4	1306	90	4	4.13	5	1	3	229	21	0	5.50
1979-80a	Billings	WHL	46	23	14	1	2435	149	1	3.67	3	2	1	190	10	0	3.16
1980-81	Edmonton	NHL	7	3	3	0	313	20	0	3.83	9	5	4	526	32	0	3.65
	Wichita	CHL	29	14	13	1	1602	89	0	3.33	5	3	2	300	16	0	3.20
1981-82	Edmonton	NHL	8	3	5	0	399	32	0	4.81	....	....	....	....	....	....	....
b	Wichita	CHL	40	23	13	3	2391	119	1	2.99	7	3	4	434	23	0	3.18
1982-83	Edmonton	NHL	50	33	8	7	2833	167	1	3.54	16	11	5	949	48	0	3.03
1983-84	Edmonton	NHL	38	27	8	1	2212	139	1	3.77	7	4	0	263	12	0	2.74
1984-85	Edmonton	NHL	39	22	9	3	2019	111	1	3.30	2	0	0	20	0	0	0.00
1985-86	Edmonton	NHL	47	27	9	7	2664	164	1	3.69	1	1	0	60	1	0	1.00
1986-87	Edmonton	NHL	46	28	11	3	2461	144	0	3.51	2	2	0	120	8	0	4.00
1987-88	Cdn. National	...	27	10	7	5	1438	86	0	3.58	....	....	....	....	....	....	....
	Cdn. Olympic	...	4	4	0	0	240	9	1	2.25	....	....	....	....	....	....	....
	Boston	NHL	6	4	2	0	360	17	1	2.83	7	1	4	354	25	0	4.24
1988-89	Boston	NHL	41	18	14	8	2482	133	1	3.22	6	4	2	359	14	0	2.34
1989-90c	Boston	NHL	46	24	10	7	2536	122	3	2.89	20	13	7	1195	44	*2	*2.21
1990-91	Boston	NHL	51	25	13	9	2844	136	4	2.87	19	10	9	1133	60	0	3.18
	NHL Totals		379	214	92	45	21123	1185	13	3.37	89	51	31	4979	244	2	2.94

a WHL Second All-Star Team (1980)
b CHL Second All-Star Team (1982)
c Shared William Jennings Trophy with Rejean Lemelin (1990)

Played in NHL All-Star Game (1985, 1986, 1991)

Traded to **Boston** by **Edmonton** for Geoff Courtnall, Bill Ranford and future considerations, March 8, 1988.

MORISSETTE, ALAIN

Goaltender. Catches left. 5'9", 160 lbs. Born, Rimouski, Que., August 26, 1969.

			Regular Season								Playoffs						
Season	Club	Lea	GP	W	L	T	Mins	GA	SO	Avg	GP	W	L	Mins	GA	SO	Avg
1988-89	Trois Rivières	QMJHL	46	25	16	2	2360	167	1	4.25	4	0	4	243	18	0	4.44
1989-90	Trois Rivières	QMJHL	49	31	16	0	2674	166	1	3.72	5	2	3	297	28	0	5.66
1990-91	Fredericton	AHL	14	2	6	3	709	43	0	3.64	2	0	0	17	1	0	3.53
	Winston Salem	ECHL	23	10	13	0	1222	99	0	4.86	....	....	....	....	....	....	....

Signed as a free agent by **Montreal**, October 15, 1990.

MORSCHAUSER, GUS

Goaltender. Catches left. 5'9", 155 lbs. Born, Kitchener, Ont., March 26, 1969.
(Vancouver's 8th choice, 197th overall, in 1989 Entry Draft).

			Regular Season								Playoffs						
Season	Club	Lea	GP	W	L	T	Mins	GA	SO	Avg	GP	W	L	Mins	GA	SO	Avg
1987-88	Kitchener	OHL	36	....	....	....	1880	144	0	4.60	....	....	....	....	....	....	....
1988-89	Kitchener	OHL	41	....	....	....	2311	132	2	3.43	....	....	....	....	....	....	....
1989-90	Kitchener	OHL	6	2	2	1	345	141	0	3.83	....	....	....	....	....	....	....
	Hamilton	OHL	38	6	27	3	2110	184	0	5.23	....	....	....	....	....	....	....
	Milwaukee	IHL	3	1	1	0	119	12	0	6.05	....	....	....	....	....	....	....
1990-91	Milwaukee	IHL	3	0	2	0	163	13	0	4.79	....	....	....	....	....	....	....
	Roanoke	ECHL	20	5	7	1	832	64	0	4.61	....	....	....	....	....	....	....
	Winston Salem	ECHL	4	1	2	1	249	21	0	5.06	....	....	....	....	....	....	....

MULLAHY, BRAD

Goaltender. Catches left. 5'10", 180 lbs. Born, North Easton, MA, February 12, 1970.
(Winnipeg's 1st choice, 5th overall, in 1991 Supplemental Draft).

			Regular Season								Playoffs						
Season	Club	Lea	GP	W	L	T	Mins	GA	SO	Avg	GP	W	L	Mins	GA	SO	Avg
1989-90	Providence	H.E.	5	2	1	0	207	13	0	3.77	....	....	....	....	....	....	....
1990-91	Providence	H.E.	22	14	5	1	1257	65	0	3.10	....	....	....	....	....	....	....

MURRAY, SHAWN

Goaltender. Catches left. 5'9", 160 lbs. Born, St. Paul, MN, September 3, 1971.
(Calgary's 9th choice, 167th overall, in 1990 Entry Draft).

			Regular Season								Playoffs						
Season	Club	Lea	GP	W	L	T	Mins	GA	SO	Avg	GP	W	L	Mins	GA	SO	Avg
1990-91	Colgate	ECAC	6	2	2	0	311	21	0	4.06	....	....	....	....	....	....	....

MUZZATTI, JASON

Goaltender. Catches left. 6'1", 190 lbs. Born, Toronto, Ont., February 3, 1970.
(Calgary's 1st choice, 21st overall, in 1988 Entry Draft).

			Regular Season								Playoffs						
Season	Club	Lea	GP	W	L	T	Mins	GA	SO	Avg	GP	W	L	Mins	GA	SO	Avg
1987-88a	Michigan State	CCHA	33	19	9	3	1915	109	0	3.41	....	....	....	....	....	....	....
1988-89	Michigan State	CCHA	42	32	9	1	2515	127	3	*3.03	....	....	....	....	....	....	....
1989-90bc	Michigan State	CCHA	33	*24	6	0	1976	99	0	3.01	....	....	....	....	....	....	....
1990-91	Michigan State	CCHA	22	8	10	2	1204	75	1	3.74	....	....	....	....	....	....	....

a CCHA Second All-Star Team (1988)
b CCHA First All-Star Team (1990)
c NCAA West Second All-American Team (1990)

MYLLYS, JARMO (YAR-moh MEE-lus)

Goaltender. Catches left. 5'8", 160 lbs. Born, Savonlinna, Finland, May 29, 1965.
(Minnesota's 9th choice, 172nd overall, in 1987 Entry Draft).

			Regular Season								Playoffs						
Season	Club	Lea	GP	W	L	T	Mins	GA	SO	Avg	GP	W	L	Mins	GA	SO	Avg
1987-88	Lukko	Fin.	43	....	....	....	2580	160	....	3.72	....	....	....	....	....	....	....
1988-89	Minnesota	NHL	6	1	4	0	238	22	0	5.55	....	....	....	....	....	....	....
	Kalamazoo	IHL	28	13	8	4	1523	93	0	3.66	6	2	4	419	22	0	3.15
1989-90	Minnesota	NHL	4	0	3	0	156	16	0	6.15	....	....	....	....	....	....	....
a	Kalamazoo	IHL	49	31	9	3	2715	159	1	3.51	5	4	0	258	11	0	2.56
1990-91	Minnesota	NHL	2	0	2	0	78	8	0	6.15	....	....	....	....	....	....	....
	Kalamazoo	IHL	38	24	13	1	2278	144	1	3.79	10	6	4	600	26	0	*2.60
	NHL Totals		12	1	9	0	472	46	0	5.85	....	....	....	....	....	....	....

a IHL Second All-Star Team (1990)

Claimed by **San Jose** from **Minnesota** in Dispersal Draft, May 30, 1991.

NEWMAN, THOMAS

Goaltender. Catches left. 6'1", 190 lbs. Born, Golden Valley, MN, February 23, 1971.
(Los Angeles' 4th choice, 103rd overall, in 1989 Entry Draft).

			Regular Season								Playoffs						
Season	Club	Lea	GP	W	L	T	Mins	GA	SO	Avg	GP	W	L	Mins	GA	SO	Avg
1989-90	U. Minnesota	WCHA	35	19	13	2	1982	127	0	3.84	....	....	....	....	....	....	....
1990-91	U. Minnesota	WCHA	22	12	2	2	942	54	2	3.44	....	....	....	....	....	....	....

O'NEILL, MICHAEL (MIKE)

Goaltender. Catches left. 5'7", 155 lbs. Born, LaSalle, Que., November 3, 1967.
(Winnipeg's 1st choice, 15th overall, in 1988 Supplemental Draft).

			Regular Season								Playoffs						
Season	Club	Lea	GP	W	L	T	Mins	GA	SO	Avg	GP	W	L	Mins	GA	SO	Avg
1985-86	Yale	ECAC	6	3	1	0	389	17	0	3.53	....	....	....	....	....	....	....
1986-87a	Yale	ECAC	16	9	6	1	964	55	2	3.42	....	....	....	....	....	....	....
1987-88	Yale	ECAC	24	6	17	0	1385	101	0	4.37	....	....	....	....	....	....	....
1988-89ab	Yale	ECAC	25	10	14	1	1490	93	0	3.74	....	....	....	....	....	....	....
1989-90	Tappara	Fin.	41	23	13	5	2369	127	2	3.22	....	....	....	....	....	....	....
1990-91	Fort Wayne	IHL	8	5	2	1	490	31	0	3.80	....	....	....	....	....	....	....
	Moncton	AHL	30	13	7	6	1613	84	0	3.12	8	3	4	435	29	0	4.00

a ECAC First All-Star Team (1987, 1989)
b NCAA East First All-American Team (1989)

OSGOOD, CHRIS

Goaltender. Catches left. 5'10", 156 lbs. Born, Peace River, Alta., November 26, 1972.
(Detroit's 3rd choice, 54th overall, in 1991 Entry Draft).

			Regular Season								Playoffs						
Season	Club	Lea	GP	W	L	T	Mins	GA	SO	Avg	GP	W	L	Mins	GA	SO	Avg
1989-90	Medicine Hat	WHL	57	24	28	2	3094	228	0	4.42	3	0	3	173	17	0	5.91
1990-91a	Medicine Hat	WHL	46	23	18	3	2630	173	2	3.95	12	7	5	712	42	0	3.54

a WHL East Second All-Star Team (1991)

PARSON, MIKE

Goaltender. Catches left. 6'0", 170 lbs. Born, Listowel, Ont., March 12, 1970.
(Boston's 2nd choice, 38th overall, in 1989 Entry Draft).

			Regular Season								Playoffs						
Season	Club	Lea	GP	W	L	T	Mins	GA	SO	Avg	GP	W	L	Mins	GA	SO	Avg
1987-88	Guelph	OHL	31	9	17	2	1703	135	0	4.76	....	....	....	....	....	....	....
1988-89	Guelph	OHL	*53	25	22	5	*3047	194	0	3.82	7	3	4	421	29	0	4.13
1989-90	Owen Sound	OHL	29	21	21	4	2750	207	1	4.52	12	5	7	722	61	0	4.24
1990-91	Maine	AHL	24	6	10	1	1154	79	0	4.11	....	....	....	....	....	....	....
	Johnstown	ECHL	6	4	2	0	333	23	0	4.14	....	....	....	....	....	....	....

PEETERS, PETER (PETE)

Goaltender. Catches left. 6'1", 195 lbs. Born, Edmonton, Alta., August 17, 1957.
(Philadelphia's 9th choice, 135th overall, in 1977 Amateur Draft).

			Regular Season								Playoffs						
Season	Club	Lea	GP	W	L	T	Mins	GA	SO	Avg	GP	W	L	Mins	GA	SO	Avg
1975-76	Medicine Hat	WHL	37	....	....	....	2074	147	0	4.25	....	....	....	....	....	....	....
1976-77	Medicine Hat	WHL	62	....	....	....	3423	232	1	4.07	4	....	....	204	17	0	5.00
1977-78	Milwaukee	IHL	32	....	....	....	1698	93	1	3.29	....	....	....	....	....	....	....
	Maine	AHL	17	....	....	....	855	40	1	2.80	11	....	....	562	25	*1	2.67
1978-79	Philadelphia	NHL	5	1	2	1	280	16	0	3.43	....	....	....	....	....	....	....
ab	Maine	AHL	35	25	6	3	2067	100	*2	*2.90	6	5	0	329	15	0	2.74
1979-80	Philadelphia	NHL	40	29	5	5	2373	108	1	2.73	13	8	5	799	37	1	2.78
1980-81	Philadelphia	NHL	40	22	12	5	2333	115	2	2.96	3	2	1	180	12	0	4.00
1981-82	Philadelphia	NHL	44	23	18	3	2591	160	0	3.71	4	1	2	220	17	0	4.64
1982-83cd	Boston	NHL	62	*40	11	9	3611	142	*8	*2.36	17	9	8	*1024	61	1	3.57
1983-84	Boston	NHL	50	29	16	2	2868	151	0	3.16	3	0	3	180	10	0	3.33
1984-85	Boston	NHL	51	19	26	4	2975	172	1	3.47	1	0	1	60	4	0	4.00
1985-86	Boston	NHL	8	3	4	1	485	31	0	3.84	....	....	....	....	....	....	....
	Washington	NHL	34	19	11	3	2021	113	1	3.35	9	5	4	544	24	0	2.65
1986-87	Washington	NHL	37	17	11	4	2002	107	0	3.21	3	1	2	180	9	0	3.00
	Binghamton	AHL	4	3	0	0	245	4	1	0.98	....	....	....	....	....	....	....
1987-88	Washington	NHL	35	14	12	5	1896	88	2	*2.78	12	7	5	654	34	0	3.12
1988-89	Washington	NHL	33	20	7	3	1854	88	4	2.85	6	2	4	359	24	0	4.01
1989-90	Philadelphia	NHL	24	1	13	5	1140	72	1	3.79	....	....	....	....	....	....	....
1990-91	Philadelphia	NHL	26	9	7	1	1270	61	1	2.88	....	....	....	....	....	....	....
	Hershey	AHL	2	0	1	0	105	11	0	6.29	....	....	....	....	....	....	....
	NHL Totals		489	246	155	51	27699	1424	21	3.08	71	35	35	4200	232	2	3.31

a AHL Second All-Star Team (1979)
b Shared Harry "Hap" Holmes Memorial Trophy (AHL's Leading Goaltenders) with Robbie Moore (1979)
c NHL First All-Star Team (1983)
d Won Vezina Trophy (1983)

Played in NHL All-Star Game (1980, 1981, 1983, 1984)

Traded to **Boston** by **Philadelphia** for Brad McCrimmon, June 9, 1982. Traded to **Washington** by **Boston** for Pat Riggin, November 14, 1985. Signed as a free agent by **Philadelphia**, June 17, 1989. Traded to **Winnipeg** by **Philadelphia** with Keith Acton for future considerations, September 28, 1989. Traded to **Philadelphia** by **Winnipeg** with Keith Acton for future considerations, October 3, 1989.

PIETRANGELO, FRANK (PEE-tuhr-AN-jehl-oh)

Goaltender. Catches left. 5'10", 185 lbs. Born, Niagara Falls, Ont., December 17, 1964.
(Pittsburgh's 4th choice, 63rd overall, in 1983 Entry Draft).

			Regular Season								Playoffs						
Season	Club	Lea	GP	W	L	T	Mins	GA	SO	Avg	GP	W	L	Mins	GA	SO	Avg
1982-83	U. Minnesota	WCHA	25	15	6	1	1348	80	1	3.55	....	....	....	....	....	....	....
1983-84	U. Minnesota	WCHA	20	13	7	0	1141	66	0	3.47	....	....	....	....	....	....	....
1984-85	U. Minnesota	WCHA	17	8	3	3	912	52	0	3.42	....	....	....	....	....	....	....
1985-86	U. Minnesota	WCHA	23	15	7	0	1284	76	0	3.55	....	....	....	....	....	....	....
1986-87	Muskegon	IHL	35	23	11	0	2090	119	2	3.42	15	10	4	923	46	0	2.99
1987-88	Pittsburgh	NHL	21	9	11	0	1207	80	1	3.98	....	....	....	....	....	....	....
	Muskegon	IHL	15	11	3	1	868	43	2	2.97	....	....	....	....	....	....	....
1988-89	Pittsburgh	NHL	15	5	3	0	669	45	0	4.04	....	....	....	....	....	....	....
	Muskegon	IHL	13	10	1	0	760	38	1	3.00	9	*8	1	566	29	0	3.07
1989-90	Pittsburgh	NHL	21	8	6	2	1066	77	0	4.33	....	....	....	....	....	....	....
	Muskegon	IHL	12	9	2	1	691	38	0	3.30	....	....	....	....	....	....	....
1990-91	Pittsburgh	NHL	25	10	11	1	1311	86	0	3.94	5	4	1	288	15	*1	3.13
	NHL Totals		82	32	31	3	4253	288	1	4.06	5	4	1	288	15	1	3.13

POTVIN, FELIX

Goaltender. Catches left. 6'1", 183 lbs. Born, Anjou, Que., June 23, 1971.
(Toronto's 2nd choice, 31st overall, in 1990 Entry Draft).

			Regular Season								Playoffs						
Season	Club	Lea	GP	W	L	T	Mins	GA	SO	Avg	GP	W	L	Mins	GA	SO	Avg
1988-89	Chicoutimi	QMJHL	*65	25	31	1	*3489	271	*2	4.66	....	....	....	....	....	....	....
1989-90a	Chicoutimi	QMJHL	*62	*31	26	2	*3478	231	*2	3.99	....	....	....	....	....	....	....
1990-91bcde	Chicoutimi	QMJHL	54	33	15	4	3216	145	*6	*2.71	*16	*11	5	*992	46	0	*2.78

a QMJHL Second All-Star Team (1990)
b QMJHL First All-Star Team (1991)
c Canadian Major Junior Goaltender of the Year (1991)
d Memorial Cup All-Star Team (1991)
e Won Hap Emms Memorial Trophy (Memorial Cup Top Goalie) (1991)

POWER, MICHAEL

Goaltender. Catches left. 6'2", 190 lbs. Born, Thunder Bay, Ont., March 2, 1971.
(Edmonton's 7th choice, 143rd overall, in 1990 Entry Draft).

			Regular Season								Playoffs						
Season	Club	Lea	GP	W	L	T	Mins	GA	SO	Avg	GP	W	L	Mins	GA	SO	Avg
1989-90	W. Michigan	CCHA	24	7	14	1	1303	105	0	4.83	....	....	....	....	....	....	....
1990-91	W. Michigan	CCHA	1	0	1	0	60	5	0	5.00	....	....	....	....	....	....	....

PUPPA, DAREN (POO-puh)

Goaltender. Catches right. 6'3", 205 lbs. Born, Kirkland Lake, Ont., March 23, 1965.
(Buffalo's 6th choice, 74th overall, in 1983 Entry Draft).

			Regular Season								Playoffs						
Season	Club	Lea	GP	W	L	T	Mins	GA	SO	Avg	GP	W	L	Mins	GA	SO	Avg
1983-84	RPI	ECAC	32	24	6	0	....	....	....	2.94	....	....	....	....	....	....	....
1984-85	RPI	ECAC	32	31	1	0	1830	78	0	2.56	....	....	....	....	....	....	....
1985-86	Buffalo	NHL	7	3	4	0	401	21	1	3.14	....	....	....	....	....	....	....
	Rochester	AHL	20	8	11	0	1092	79	0	4.34	....	....	....	....	....	....	....
1986-87	Buffalo	NHL	3	0	2	1	185	13	0	4.22	....	....	....	....	....	....	....
1986-87a	Rochester	AHL	57	*33	14	0	3129	146	1	2.80	*16	*10	6	*944	48	*1	3.05
1987-88	Buffalo	NHL	17	8	6	1	874	61	0	4.19	3	1	1	142	11	0	4.65
	Rochester	AHL	26	14	8	2	1415	65	2	2.76	2	0	1	108	5	0	2.78
1988-89	Buffalo	NHL	37	17	10	6	1908	107	1	3.36	....	....	....	....	....	....	....
1989-90b	Buffalo	NHL	56	*31	16	6	3241	156	1	2.89	6	2	4	370	15	0	2.43
1990-91	Buffalo	NHL	38	15	11	6	2092	118	2	3.38	2	0	1	81	10	0	7.41
	NHL Totals		158	74	49	20	8701	476	5	3.28	11	3	6	593	36	0	3.64

a AHL First All-Star Team (1987)
b NHL Second All-Star Team (1990)

Played in NHL All-Star Game (1990)

PYE, BILL

Goaltender. Shoots left. 5'9", 170 lbs. Born, Canton, MI, April 9, 1969.
(Buffalo's 5th choice, 107th overall, in 1989 Entry Draft).

			Regular Season								Playoffs						
Season	Club	Lea	GP	W	L	T	Mins	GA	SO	Avg	GP	W	L	Mins	GA	SO	Avg
1987-88	N. Michigan	WCHA	13	....	....	....	654	49	0	4.49	....	....	....	....	....	....	....
1988-89	N. Michigan	WCHA	43	26	15	2	2533	133	1	3.15	....	....	....	....	....	....	....
1989-90	N. Michigan	WCHA	36	20	14	1	2035	149	1	4.39	....	....	....	....	....	....	....
1990-91abc	N. Michigan	WCHA	39	*32	3	4	2300	109	*4	2.84	....	....	....	....	....	....	....

a WCHA First All-Star Team (1991)
b NCAA West Second All-American Team (1991)
c NCAA Final Four All-Tournament Team (1991)

RACICOT, ANDRE

Goaltender. Catches left. 5'11", 165 lbs. Born, Rouyn-Noranda, Que., June 9, 1969.
(Montreal's 5th choice, 83rd overall, in 1989 Entry Draft).

			Regular Season								Playoffs						
Season	Club	Lea	GP	W	L	T	Mins	GA	SO	Avg	GP	W	L	Mins	GA	SO	Avg
1986-87	Granby	QMJHL	3	1	2	0	180	19	0	6.33	....	....	....	....	....	....	....
1987-88	Granby	QMJHL	30	15	11	1	1547	105	1	4.07	5	1	4	298	23	0	4.63
1988-89a	Granby	QMJHL	54	22	24	3	2944	198	0	4.04	4	0	4	218	18	0	4.95
1989-90	Montreal	NHL	1	0	0	0	13	3	0	13.85	....	....	....	....	....	....	....
b	Sherbrooke	AHL	33	19	11	2	1948	97	1	2.99	5	0	4	227	18	0	4.76
1990-91	Montreal	NHL	21	7	9	2	975	52	1	3.20	2	0	1	12	2	0	10.00
	Fredericton	AHL	22	13	8	1	1252	60	1	2.88	....	....	....	....	....	....	....
	NHL Totals		21	7	9	2	975	52	1	3.20	2	0	1	12	2	0	10.00

a QMJHL Second All-Star Team (1989)
b Shared Harry "Hap" Holmes Trophy (fewest goals-against-AHL) with J.C. Bergeron (1990)

RACINE, BRUCE

Goaltender. Catches left. 6', 178 lbs. Born, Cornwall, Ont., August 9, 1966.
(Pittsburgh's 3rd choice, 58th overall, in 1985 Entry Draft).

			Regular Season								Playoffs						
Season	Club	Lea	GP	W	L	T	Mins	GA	SO	Avg	GP	W	L	Mins	GA	SO	Avg
1984-85	Northeastern	H.E.	26	11	14	1	1615	103	1	3.83	....	....	....	....	....	....	....
1985-86	Northeastern	H.E.	32	17	14	1	1920	147	0	4.56	....	....	....	....	....	....	....
1986-87ab	Northeastern	H.E.	33	12	18	3	1966	133	0	4.06	....	....	....	....	....	....	....
1987-88b	Northeastern	H.E.	30	15	11	4	1808	108	1	3.58	....	....	....	....	....	....	....
1988-89	Muskegon	IHL	51	*37	11	0	*3039	184	*3	3.63	5	4	1	300	15	0	3.00
1989-90	Muskegon	IHL	49	29	15	4	2911	182	1	3.75	....	....	....	....	....	....	....
1990-91	Albany	IHL	29	7	18	1	1567	104	0	3.98	....	....	....	....	....	....	....
	Muskegon	IHL	9	4	4	1	516	40	0	3.90	....	....	....	....	....	....	....

a Hockey East First All-Star Team (1987)
b NCAA East First All-American Team (1987, 1988)

RANFORD, BILL

Goaltender. Catches left. 5'10", 170 lbs. Born, Brandon, Man., December 14, 1966.
(Boston's 2nd choice, 52nd overall, in 1985 Entry Draft).

			Regular Season								Playoffs						
Season	Club	Lea	GP	W	L	T	Mins	GA	SO	Avg	GP	W	L	Mins	GA	SO	Avg
1983-84	N. Westminster	WHL	27	10	14	0	1450	130	0	5.38	1	0	0	27	2	0	4.44
1984-85	N. Westminster	WHL	38	19	17	0	2034	142	0	4.19	7	2	3	309	26	0	5.05
1985-86	Boston	NHL	4	3	1	0	240	10	0	2.50	2	0	2	120	7	0	3.50
	N. Westminster	WHL	53	17	29	1	2791	225	0	4.84							
1986-87	Boston	NHL	41	16	20	2	2234	124	3	3.33	2	0	2	123	8	0	3.90
	Moncton	AHL	3	3	0	0	180	6	0	2.00							
1987-88	Maine	AHL	51	27	16	6	2856	165	1	3.47							
	Edmonton	NHL	6	3	0	2	325	16	0	2.95							
1988-89	Edmonton	NHL	29	15	8	2	1509	88	1	3.50							
1989-90a	Edmonton	NHL	56	24	16	9	3107	165	1	3.19	*22	*16	6	*1401	59	0	2.53
1990-91	Edmonton	NHL	60	27	27	3	3415	182	0	3.20	3	1	2	135	8	0	3.56
	NHL Totals		196	88	72	18	10830	585	5	3.24	29	17	12	1779	82	0	2.77

a Won Conn Smythe Trophy (1990)
Played in NHL All-Star Game (1991)
Traded to **Edmonton** by **Boston** with Geoff Courtnall and future considerations for Andy Moog, March 8, 1988.

RAYMOND, ALAIN

Goaltender. Catches left. 5'10", 180 lbs. Born, Rimouski, Que., June 24, 1965.
(Washington's 7th choice, 215th overall, in 1983 Entry Draft).

			Regular Season								Playoffs						
Season	Club	Lea	GP	W	L	T	Mins	GA	SO	Avg	GP	W	L	Mins	GA	SO	Avg
1983-84	Trois Rivieres	QMJHL	53	18	25	0	2725	223	3	4.91							
1984-85a	Trois Rivieres	QMJHL	58	29	26	1	3295	220	2	4.01	7	3	5	438	32	0	4.38
1985-86	Cdn. Olympic	...	46	25	18	3	2571	151	4	3.52							
1986-87b	Fort Wayne	IHL	45	23	16	0	2433	134	1	*3.30	6	2	3	320	23	0	4.31
1987-88	Washington	NHL	1	0	1	0	40	2	0	3.00							
	Fort Wayne	IHL	40	20	15	3	2271	142	2	3.75	2	0	1	67	7		6.27
1988-89	Baltimore	AHL	41	14	22	2	2301	162	0	4.22							
1989-90	Baltimore	AHL	11	4	5	2	612	34	0	3.33							
	Hampton-Roads	ECHL	31	17	12	1	2048	123	0	3.60							
1990-91	Peoria	IHL	5	1	3	1	304	22	0	4.34							
	Nashville	ECHL	43	21	18	3	2508	189	1	4.52							
	NHL Totals		1	0	1	0	40	2	0	3.00							

a QMJHL Second All-Star Team (1985)
b Shared James Norris Memorial Trophy (IHL's Top Goaltender) with Michel Dufour (1987)
Signed as a free agent by **St. Louis**, September 12, 1990.

REAUGH, DARYL (RAY)

Goaltender. Catches left. 5'8", 175 lbs. Born, Prince George, B.C., February 13, 1965.
(Edmonton's 2nd choice, 42nd overall, in 1984 Entry Draft).

			Regular Season								Playoffs						
Season	Club	Lea	GP	W	L	T	Mins	GA	SO	Avg	GP	W	L	Mins	GA	SO	Avg
1983-84	Kamloops	WHL	55				2748	199	1	4.34	17			972	57	0	3.52
1984-85	Edmonton	NHL	1	0	1	0	60	5	0	5.00							
a	Kamloops	WHL	49				2749	170	2	3.71	14			787	56	0	4.27
1985-86	Nova Scotia	AHL	38	15	18	4	2205	156	0	4.24							
1986-87	Nova Scotia	AHL	46	19	22	0	2637	163	1	3.71	2	0	2	120	13	0	6.50
1987-88	Edmonton	NHL	6	1	1	0	176	14	0	4.77							
	Nova Scotia	AHL	8	2	5	0	443	33	0	4.47							
	Milwaukee	IHL	9	0	8	0	493	44	0	5.35							
1988-89	Cape Breton	AHL	13	3	10	0	778	72	0	5.55							
1989-90	Binghamton	AHL	52	8	31	6	2375	192	0	4.21							
1990-91	Hartford	NHL	20	7	7	1	1010	53	1	3.15							
	Springfield	AHL	16	7	6	3	912	55	0	3.62							
	NHL Totals		27	8	9	1	1246	72	1	3.47							

a WHL First All-Star Team, West Division (1985)
Signed as a free agent by **Hartford**, October 9, 1989.

REDDICK, ELDON

Goaltender. Catches left. 5'8", 170 lbs. Born, Halifax, N.S., October 6, 1964.

			Regular Season								Playoffs						
Season	Club	Lea	GP	W	L	T	Mins	GA	SO	Avg	GP	W	L	Mins	GA	SO	Avg
1982-83	Nanaimo	WHL	66	19	38	1	3549	383	0	6.46							
1983-84	N. Westminster	WHL	50	24	22	2	2930	215	0	4.40	9	4	5	542	53	0	5.87
1984-85	Brandon	WHL	47	14	30	1	2585	243	0	5.64							
1985-86	Fort Wayne	IHL	29	15	11	0	1674	86	*3	3.00							
1986-87	Winnipeg	NHL	48	21	21	4	2762	149	0	3.24	3	0	2	166	10	0	3.61
1987-88	Winnipeg	NHL	28	9	13	3	1487	102	0	4.12							
	Moncton	AHL	9	2	6	1	545	26	0	2.86							
1988-89	Winnipeg	NHL	41	11	17	7	2109	144	0	4.10							
1989-90	Edmonton	NHL	11	5	4	2	604	31	0	3.08	1	0	0	2	0	0	0.00
	Cape Breton	AHL	15	9	4	1	821	54	0	3.95							
	Phoenix	IHL	3	2	1	0	185	7	0	2.27							
1990-91	Edmonton	NHL	2	0	2	0	120	9	0	4.50							
	Cape Breton	AHL	31	19	10	0	1673	97	2	3.48	2	0	2	124	10	0	4.84
	NHL Totals		130	46	57	16	7082	435	0	3.69	4	0	2	168	10	0	3.57

Signed as a free agent by **Winnipeg**, September 27, 1985. Traded to **Edmonton** by **Winnipeg** for future considerations, September 28, 1989.

REED, BRANDON

Goaltender. Catches left. 5'10", 160 lbs. Born, Lansing, MI, January 23, 1969.
(NY Islanders' 1st choice, 11th overall, in 1990 Supplemental Draft).

			Regular Season								Playoffs						
Season	Club	Lea	GP	W	L	T	Mins	GA	SO	Avg	GP	W	L	Mins	GA	SO	Avg
1987-88	Lake Superior	CCHA	1	0	0	0	20	3	0	9.00							
1988-89	Lake Superior	CCHA	3	1	0	1	111	3	0	1.63							
1989-90	Lake Superior	CCHA	19	11	3	2	975	61	0	3.76							
1990-91	Lake Superior	CCHA	8	4	2	1	384	21	0	3.28							

REESE, JEFF

Goaltender. Catches left. 5'9", 170 lbs. Born, Brantford, Ont., March 24, 1966.
(Toronto's 3rd choice, 67th overall, in 1984 Entry Draft).

			Regular Season								Playoffs						
Season	Club	Lea	GP	W	L	T	Mins	GA	SO	Avg	GP	W	L	Mins	GA	SO	Avg
1983-84	London	OHL	43	18	19	0	2308	173		4.50	6	3	3	327	27	0	4.95
1984-85	London	OHL	50	31	15	1	2878	186	1	3.88	8	5	2	440	20	1	2.73
1985-86	London	OHL	57	25	26	3	3281	215	0	3.93	5	0	4	299	25	0	5.02
1986-87	Newmarket	AHL	50	11	29	0	2822	193	1	4.10							
1987-88	Toronto	NHL	5	1	2	1	249	17	0	4.10							
	Newmarket	AHL	28	10	14	3	1587	103	0	3.89							
1988-89	Toronto	NHL	10	2	6	1	486	40	0	4.94							
	Newmarket	AHL	37	17	14	3	2072	132	0	3.82							
1989-90	Toronto	NHL	21	9	6	3	1101	81	0	4.41	2	1	1	108	6	0	3.33
	Newmarket	AHL	7	3	2	2	431	29	0	4.04							
1990-91	Toronto	NHL	30	6	13	3	1430	92	1	3.86							
	Newmarket	AHL	3	2	1	0	180	7	0	2.33							
	NHL Totals		66	18	27	8	3266	230	1	4.23	2	1	1	108	6	0	3.33

REID, JOHN

Goaltender. Catches right. 5'11", 202 lbs. Born, Windsor, Ont., February 18, 1967.
(Chicago's 8th choice, 158th overall, in 1985 Entry Draft).

			Regular Season								Playoffs						
Season	Club	Lea	GP	W	L	T	Mins	GA	SO	Avg	GP	W	L	Mins	GA	SO	Avg
1984-85	Belleville	OHL	31	16	6	0	1443	92	0	3.83	2	1	0	79	4	0	3.04
1985-86	North Bay	OHL	47	28	14	2	2627	164	1	3.75	10	5	4	577	37	0	3.85
1986-87	North Bay	OHL	47	*33	12	1	2737	142	1	3.11	24	14	10	1496	92	0	3.69
1987-88	Colorado	IHL	32	15	14	1	1673	117	0	4.20							
	Saginaw	IHL	5	3	1	0	260	11	0	2.54	1	0	1	58	5		5.17
1988-89	Indianapolis	IHL	5	2	2	0	244	16	0	3.93							
	Saginaw	IHL	12	6	3	0	633	37	0	3.51							
1989-90	Nashville	ECHL	36	18	17	3	2004	149	0	4.46	3			179	12	0	4.02
1990-91	Nashville	ECHL	23	7	12	1	1222	113	0	5.54							
	Kansas City	IHL	3	1	1	0	79	2	0	1.52							

REIMER, MARK (RIGH-muhr)

Goaltender. Catches left. 5'11", 170 lbs. Born, Calgary, Alta., March 23, 1967.
(Detroit's 5th choice, 74th overall, in 1987 Entry Draft).

			Regular Season								Playoffs						
Season	Club	Lea	GP	W	L	T	Mins	GA	SO	Avg	GP	W	L	Mins	GA	SO	Avg
1984-85	Saskatoon	WHL	2	2	0	0	120	7	0	3.50							
1985-86	Saskatoon	WHL	41	17	18	3	2362	192	0	4.88	5			300	25	0	5.00
1986-87	Saskatoon	WHL	42	24	15	2	2442	141	1	3.46	6			360	20	0	3.33
1987-88	Portland	WHL	38	13	23	2	2268	208	0	5.50							
	Flint	IHL	5	0	3	0	169	22	0	7.86							
	Adirondack	AHL	8	6	1	0	459	24	0	3.14	1	0	0	20	0	0	0.00
1988-89	Adirondack	AHL	18	5	6	3	900	64	0	4.27							
	Flint	IHL	17	5	8	0	1022	83	0	4.87							
1989-90	Adirondack	AHL	36	14	17	3	2092	131	0	3.76							
1990-91	Adirondack	AHL	19	6	9	2	1019	71	0	4.18							
	San Diego	IHL	14	3	6	3	688	51	0	4.45							
	Erie	ECHL									4	2	2	240	13	0	3.25

REIN, KENTON (RIGHN)

Goaltender. Catches left. 6', 195 lbs. Born, Saskatoon, Sask., September 12, 1967.
(Buffalo's 11th choice, 194th overall, in 1986 Entry Draft).

			Regular Season								Playoffs						
Season	Club	Lea	GP	W	L	T	Mins	GA	SO	Avg	GP	W	L	Mins	GA	SO	Avg
1985-86	Prince Albert	WHL	23	18	3	0	1302	71	0	3.27	6	5	0	308	4	2	0.78
1986-87a	Prince Albert	WHL	51	29	18	3	2996	159	0	3.18	8	3	5	443	31	0	4.20
1987-88	Flint	IHL	1	0	1	0	20	3	0	9.00							
1988-89	Rochester	AHL	15	5	6	2	676	39	2	3.46							
	Flint	IHL	8	1	6	0	439	29	0	3.96							
1989-90	Winston-Salem	ECHL	24	16	6	1	1353	88	0	3.90	9			570	28	0	2.95
1990-91	Winston-Salem	ECHL	31	9	18	1	1714	134	0	4.69							

a WHL First All-Star Team (1987)

RHODES, DAMIAN

Goaltender. Catches left. 6', 165 lbs. Born, St. Paul, MN, May 28, 1969.
(Toronto's 6th choice, 112th overall, in 1987 Entry Draft).

			Regular Season								Playoffs						
Season	Club	Lea	GP	W	L	T	Mins	GA	SO	Avg	GP	W	L	Mins	GA	SO	Avg
1987-88	Michigan Tech	WCHA	29	16	10	1	1625	114	0	4.20							
1988-89	Michigan Tech	WCHA	37	15	22	0	2216	163	0	4.41							
1989-90	Michigan Tech	WCHA	25	6	17	0	1358	119	0	6.26							
1990-91	Toronto	NHL	1	1	0	0	60	1	0	1.00							
	Newmarket	AHL	38	8	24	3	2154	144	1	4.01							
	NHL Totals		1	1	0	0	60	1	0	1.00							

RICHARDS, MARK A.

Goaltender. Catches left. 5'7", 180 lbs. Born, Jamison, PA, June 24, 1969.
(Winnipeg's 1st choice, 19th overall, in 1990 Supplemental Draft).

			Regular Season								Playoffs						
Season	Club	Lea	GP	W	L	T	Mins	GA	SO	Avg	GP	W	L	Mins	GA	SO	Avg
1988-89	U. of Lowell	H.E.	18	1	12	1	918	83	0	5.42							
1989-90	U. of Lowell	H.E.	32	11	19	2	1773	149	0	5.04							
1990-91	U. of Lowell	H.E.	22	5	13	1	1149	91	0	4.75							

RICHTER, MIKE

Goaltender. Catches left. 5'10", 187 lbs. Born, Abington, PA, September 22, 1966.
(NY Rangers' 2nd choice, 28th overall, in 1985 Entry Draft.)

			Regular Season								Playoffs						
Season	Club	Lea	GP	W	L	T	Mins	GA	SO	Avg	GP	W	L	Mins	GA	SO	Avg
1985-86a	U. Wisconsin	WCHA	24	14	9	0	1394	92	1	3.96							
1986-87b	U. Wisconsin	WCHA	36	19	16	1	2136	126	0	3.54							
1987-88	Colorado	IHL	22	16	5	0	1298	68	1	3.14	10	5	3	536	35		3.92
	U.S. National	...	29	17	7	2	1559	86	0	3.31							
	U.S. Olympic	...	4	2	2	0	230	15	0	3.91							
1988-89	Denver	IHL	*57	23	26	0	3031	217	1	4.30	4	0	4	210	21	0	6.00
	NY Rangers	NHL									1	1	0	58	4	0	4.14
1989-90	NY Rangers	NHL	23	12	5	5	1320	66	0	3.00	6	3	2	330	19	0	3.45
	Flint	IHL	13	7	4	2	782	49	0	3.76							
1990-91	NY Rangers	NHL	45	21	13	7	2596	135	0	3.12	6	2	4	313	14	*1	2.68
	NHL Totals		68	33	18	12	3916	201	0	3.08	13	5	7	701	37	1	3.17

a WCHA Rookie of the Year (1986)
b WCHA Second All-Star Team (1987)

RIENDEAU, VINCENT (ree-EHN-doh)

Goaltender. Catches left. 5'10", 181 lbs. Born, St. Hyacinthe, Que., April 20, 1966.

			Regular Season								Playoffs						
Season	Club	Lea	GP	W	L	T	Mins	GA	SO	Avg	GP	W	L	Mins	GA	SO	Avg
1985-86a	Drummondville	QMJHL	57	33	20	3	3336	215	2	3.87	23	10	13	1271	106	1	5.00
1986-87b	Sherbrooke	AHL	41	25	14	0	2363	114	2	2.89	13	8	5	742	47	0	3.80
1987-88	**Montreal**	**NHL**	**1**	**0**	**0**	**0**	**36**	**5**	**0**	**8.33**	....	....	....	....	....	....	....
c	Sherbrooke	AHL	44	27	13	3	2521	112	*4	*2.67	2	0	2	127	7	0	3.31
1988-89	**St. Louis**	**NHL**	**32**	**11**	**15**	**5**	**1842**	**108**	**0**	**3.52**	....	....	....	....	....	....	....
1989-90	**St. Louis**	**NHL**	**43**	**17**	**19**	**5**	**2551**	**149**	**1**	**3.50**	**8**	**3**	**4**	**397**	**24**	**0**	**3.63**
1990-91	**St. Louis**	**NHL**	**44**	**29**	**9**	**6**	**2671**	**134**	**3**	**3.01**	**13**	**6**	**7**	**687**	**35**	***1**	**3.06**
	NHL Totals		**120**	**57**	**43**	**16**	**7100**	**396**	**4**	**3.35**	**21**	**9**	**11**	**1084**	**59**	**1**	**3.27**

a QMJHL Second All-Star Team (1986)
b Won Harry "Hap" Holmes Memorial Trophy (AHL Leading Goaltender) (1987)
c Shared Harry "Hap" Holmes Memorial Trophy (AHL Leading Goaltender) with Jocelyn Perreault (1988)

Signed as a free agent by **Montreal**, October 9, 1985. Traded to **St. Louis** by **Montreal** with Sergio Momesso for Jocelyn Lemieux, Darrell May and St. Louis' second round choice (Patrice Brisebois) in 1989 Entry Draft, August 9, 1988.

ROMAINE, MARK

Goaltender. Catches left. 5'9", 160 lbs. Born, Sharon, MA, October 25, 1968.
(New Jersey's 2nd choice, 10th overall, in 1989 Supplemental Draft).

			Regular Season								Playoffs						
Season	Club	Lea	GP	W	L	T	Mins	GA	SO	Avg	GP	W	L	Mins	GA	SO	Avg
1986-87	Providence	H.E.	5	....	....	....	289	25	0	5.19	....	....	....	....	....	....	....
1987-88	Providence	H.E.	19	....	....	....	883	60	0	4.08	....	....	....	....	....	....	....
1988-89	Providence	H.E.	29	....	....	....	1536	95	1	3.71	....	....	....	....	....	....	....
1989-90	Providence	H.E.	19	12	5	1	1023	52	1	3.05	....	....	....	....	....	....	....
1990-91	Utica	AHL	35	13	14	1	1710	125	0	4.39	....	....	....	....	....	....	....

ROSATI, MICHAEL

Goaltender. Catches left. 5'10", 170 lbs. Born, Toronto, Ont., January 7, 1968.
(N Y Rangers' 6th choice, 131st overall, in 1988 Entry Draft).

			Regular Season								Playoffs						
Season	Club	Lea	GP	W	L	T	Mins	GA	SO	Avg	GP	W	L	Mins	GA	SO	Avg
1986-87	Hamilton	OHL	26	....	....	....	1334	85	1	3.82	....	....	....	....	....	....	....
1987-88	Hamilton	OHL	62	29	25	3	3468	233	1	4.03	14	8	6	833	66	0	4.75
1988-89	Niagara Falls	OHL	52	*28	15	2	2339	174	1	4.46	16	10	4	861	62	0	4.32
1989-90	Erie	ECHL	18	12	5	0	1056	73	0	4.14	....	....	....	....	....	....	....
1990-91	Bolzano	Italy	46	....	....	....	2700	212	0	4.71	....	....	....	....	....	....	....

ROUSSEL, DOMINIC (roo-SEHL)

Goaltender. Catches left. 6'1", 185 lbs. Born, Hull, Que., February 22, 1970.
(Philadelphia's 4th choice, 63rd overall, in 1988 Entry Draft).

			Regular Season								Playoffs						
Season	Club	Lea	GP	W	L	T	Mins	GA	SO	Avg	GP	W	L	Mins	GA	SO	Avg
1987-88	Trois Rivieres	QMJHL	51	18	25	4	2905	251	0	5.18	....	....	....	....	....	....	....
1988-89	Shawinigan	QMJHL	46	24	15	2	2555	171	0	4.02	10	6	4	638	36	0	3.39
1989-90	Shawinigan	QMJHL	37	20	14	1	1985	133	0	4.02	2	1	1	120	12	0	6.00
1990-91	Hershey	AHL	45	20	14	7	2507	151	1	3.61	7	3	4	366	21	0	3.44

ROY, ALAIN

Goaltender. Catches left. 5'10", 170 lbs. Born, Campbellton, N.B., February 6, 1970.
(Winnipeg's 6th choice, 69th overall, in 1989 Entry Draft).

			Regular Season								Playoffs						
Season	Club	Lea	GP	W	L	T	Mins	GA	SO	Avg	GP	W	L	Mins	GA	SO	Avg
1988-89	Harvard	ECAC	16	14	2	0	952	40	0	2.46	....	....	....	....	....	....	....
1989-90	Harvard	ECAC	15	7	8	0	867	54	1	3.74	....	....	....	....	....	....	....
1990-91	Harvard	ECAC	14	7	5	2	821	45	*1	3.29	....	....	....	....	....	....	....

ROY, PATRICK (WAH)

Goaltender. Catches left. 6', 182 lbs. Born, Quebec City, Que., October 5, 1965.
(Montreal's 4th choice, 51st overall, in 1984 Entry Draft).

			Regular Season								Playoffs						
Season	Club	Lea	GP	W	L	T	Mins	GA	SO	Avg	GP	W	L	Mins	GA	SO	Avg
1982-83	Granby	QMJHL	54	....	....	....	2808	293	0	6.26	....	....	....	....	....	....	....
1983-84	Granby	QMJHL	61	29	29	1	3585	265	0	4.44	4	0	4	244	22	0	5.41
1984-85	**Montreal**	**NHL**	**1**	**1**	**0**	**0**	**20**	**0**	**0**	**0.00**	....	....	....	....	....	....	....
	Granby	QMJHL	44	16	25	1	2463	228	0	5.55	....	....	....	....	....	....	....
	Sherbrooke	AHL	1	1	0	0	60	4	0	4.00	12	10	3	*769	37	0	*2.89
1985-86ab	**Montreal**	**NHL**	**47**	**23**	**18**	**3**	**2651**	**148**	**1**	**3.35**	**20**	***15**	**5**	**1218**	**39**	***1**	**1.92**
1986-87c	**Montreal**	**NHL**	**46**	**22**	**16**	**6**	**2686**	**131**	**1**	**2.93**	**6**	**4**	**2**	**330**	**22**	**0**	**4.00**
1987-88cd	**Montreal**	**NHL**	**45**	**23**	**12**	**9**	**2586**	**125**	**3**	**2.90**	**8**	**3**	**4**	**430**	**24**	**0**	**3.35**
1988-89cefg	**Montreal**	**NHL**	**48**	**33**	**5**	**6**	**2744**	**113**	**4**	***2.47**	**19**	**13**	**6**	**1206**	**42**	**2**	***2.09**
1989-90efg	**Montreal**	**NHL**	**54**	***31**	**16**	**5**	**3173**	**134**	**3**	***2.53**	**11**	**5**	**6**	**641**	**26**	**1**	**2.43**
1990-91d	**Montreal**	**NHL**	**48**	**25**	**15**	**6**	**2835**	**128**	**1**	**2.71**	**13**	**7**	**5**	**785**	**40**	**0**	**3.06**
	NHL Totals		**289**	**158**	**82**	**35**	**16695**	**779**	**13**	**2.80**	**77**	**47**	**28**	**4610**	**193**	**4**	**2.51**

a Won Conn Smythe Trophy (1986)
b NHL All-Rookie Team (1986)
c Shared William Jennings Trophy with Brian Hayward (1987, 1988, 1989)
d NHL Second All-Star Team (1988, 1991)
e Won Vezina Trophy (1989, 1990)
f NHL First All-Star Team (1989, 1990)
g Won Trico Goaltending Award (1989, 1990)

Played in NHL All-Star Game (1988, 1990, 1991)

ST. LAURENT, SAM (sa-luh-RAH)

Goaltender. Catches left. 5'10", 190 lbs. Born, Arvida, Que., February 16, 1959.

			Regular Season								Playoffs						
Season	Club	Lea	GP	W	L	T	Mins	GA	SO	Avg	GP	W	L	Mins	GA	SO	Avg
1977-78	Chicoutimi	QJHL	60	....	....	....	3251	351	0	6.46	....	....	....	....	....	....	....
1978-79	Chicoutimi	QJHL	70	....	....	....	3806	290	0	4.57	1	....	....	47	8	0	10.21
1979-80	Maine	AHL	5	2	1	0	229	17	0	4.45	....	....	....	....	....	....	....
	Toledo	IHL	38	....	....	....	2143	138	2	3.86	4	....	....	239	24	0	6.03
1980-81	Maine	AHL	7	3	3	0	363	28	0	4.63	....	....	....	....	....	....	....
	Toledo	IHL	30	....	....	....	1614	113	1	4.20	....	....	....	....	....	....	....
1981-82	Toledo	IHL	4	....	....	....	248	11	0	2.66	....	....	....	....	....	....	....
	Maine	AHL	25	15	7	1	1396	76	0	3.27	4	1	3	240	18	0	4.50
1982-83	Maine	AHL	30	....	....	....	1739	109	0	3.76	*17	....	....	*1012	54	0	3.20
1983-84	Maine	AHL	38	14	18	4	2158	145	0	4.03	12	9	2	708	32	*1	*2.71
1984-85a	Maine	AHL	55	26	22	7	3245	168	4	3.11	10	5	5	656	45	0	4.12
1985-86	**New Jersey**	**NHL**	**4**	**2**	**1**	**0**	**188**	**13**	**1**	**4.15**	....	....	....	....	....	....	....
	Maine	AHL	50	24	20	4	2862	161	1	3.38	....	....	....	....	....	....	....
1986-87	**Detroit**	**NHL**	**6**	**1**	**2**	**2**	**342**	**16**	**0**	**2.81**	....	....	....	....	....	....	....
	Adirondack	AHL	25	7	13	0	1397	98	1	4.21	3	0	2	105	10	0	5.71
1987-88	**Detroit**	**NHL**	**6**	**2**	**2**	**0**	**294**	**16**	**0**	**3.27**	**1**	**0**	**0**	**10**	**1**	**0**	**6.00**
	Adirondack	AHL	32	12	14	4	1826	104	2	3.42	1	0	1	59	6	0	6.10
1988-89	**Detroit**	**NHL**	**4**	**0**	**1**	**1**	**141**	**9**	**0**	**3.83**	....	....	....	....	....	....	....
b	Adirondack	AHL	34	20	11	3	2054	113	0	3.30	16	*11	5	956	47	*2	*2.95
1989-90	**Detroit**	**NHL**	**14**	**2**	**6**	**1**	**607**	**38**	**0**	**3.76**	....	....	....	....	....	....	....
	Adirondack	AHL	13	10	2	1	785	40	0	3.06	....	....	....	....	....	....	....
1990-91	Binghamton	AHL	45	19	16	4	2379	138	1	3.48	3	1	2	160	11	0	4.13
	NHL Totals		**34**	**7**	**12**	**4**	**1572**	**92**	**1**	**3.51**	**1**	**0**	**0**	**10**	**1**	**0**	**6.00**

a AHL Second All-Star Team (1985)
b Won Jack Butterfield Trophy (Playoff MVP-AHL) (1989)

Signed as a free agent by **Philadelphia**, October 10, 1979. N.S. Traded to **Detroit** by **New Jersey** for Steve Richmond, August 18, 1986. Traded to **NY Rangers** by **Detroit** for cash, June 26, 1990.

SARJENT, GEOFF

Goaltender. Catches left. 5'9", 175 lbs. Born, Newmarket, Ont., November 30, 1969.
(St. Louis' 1st choice, 17th overall, in 1990 Supplemental Draft).

			Regular Season								Playoffs						
Season	Club	Lea	GP	W	L	T	Mins	GA	SO	Avg	GP	W	L	Mins	GA	SO	Avg
1988-89	Michigan Tech	WCHA	6	0	3	2	329	22	0	4.01	....	....	....	....	....	....	....
1989-90	Michigan Tech	WCHA	19	4	13	0	1043	94	0	5.41	....	....	....	....	....	....	....
1990-91	Michigan Tech	WCHA	23	5	15	3	1540	97	0	3.78	....	....	....	....	....	....	....

SCHOEN, BRYAN

Goaltender. Catches left. 6'2", 180 lbs. Born, St. Paul, MN, September 9, 1971.
(Minnesota's 6th choice, 91st overall, in 1989 Entry Draft).

			Regular Season								Playoffs						
Season	Club	Lea	GP	W	L	T	Mins	GA	SO	Avg	GP	W	L	Mins	GA	SO	Avg
1989-90	U. of Denver	WCHA	18	8	9	0	1040	81	0	4.67	....	....	....	....	....	....	....
1990-91	U. of Denver	WCHA	19	4	13	2	1103	94	0	5.11	....	....	....	....	....	....	....

Claimed by **San Jose** from **Minnesota** in Dispersal Draft, May 30, 1991.

SCHWAB, COREY

Goaltender. Catches left. 6', 180 lbs. Born, Battleford, Sask., November 4, 1970.
(New Jersey's 12th choice, 200th overall, in 1990 Entry Draft).

			Regular Season								Playoffs						
Season	Club	Lea	GP	W	L	T	Mins	GA	SO	Avg	GP	W	L	Mins	GA	SO	Avg
1988-89	Seattle	WHL	10	2	2	0	386	31	0	4.82	....	....	....	....	....	....	....
1989-90	Seattle	WHL	27	15	2	1	1150	69	0	3.60	....	....	....	....	....	....	....
1990-91	Seattle	WHL	*58	32	18	3	*3289	224	0	4.09	6	1	5	382	25	0	3.93

SCOTT, RON

Goaltender. Catches left. 5'8", 155 lbs. Born, Guelph, Ont., July 21, 1960.

			Regular Season								Playoffs						
Season	Club	Lea	GP	W	L	T	Mins	GA	SO	Avg	GP	W	L	Mins	GA	SO	Avg
1980-81	Michigan State	WCHA	33	11	21	1	1899	123	2	3.89	....	....	....	....	....	....	....
1981-82	Michigan State	CCHA	39	24	13	1	2298	109	2	2.85	....	....	....	....	....	....	....
1982-83a	Michigan State	CCHA	40	29	9	1	2273	100	2	2.64	....	....	....	....	....	....	....
1983-84	**NY Rangers**	**NHL**	**9**	**2**	**3**	**3**	**485**	**29**	**0**	**3.59**	....	....	....	....	....	....	....
b	Tulsa	CHL	29	13	13	3	1717	109	0	3.81	5	....	....	280	20	0	4.28
1984-85	New Haven	AHL	36	13	18	4	2047	130	0	3.81	....	....	....	....	....	....	....
1985-86	**NY Rangers**	**NHL**	**4**	**0**	**3**	**0**	**156**	**11**	**0**	**4.23**	....	....	....	....	....	....	....
	New Haven	AHL	19	8	8	1	1069	66	1	3.70	2	1	1	143	8	0	3.36
1986-87	**NY Rangers**	**NHL**	**1**	**0**	**0**	**1**	**65**	**5**	**0**	**4.62**	....	....	....	....	....	....	....
	New Haven	AHL	29	16	7	0	1744	107	2	3.68	....	....	....	....	....	....	....
1987-88	**NY Rangers**	**NHL**	**2**	**1**	**1**	**0**	**90**	**6**	**0**	**4.00**	....	....	....	....	....	....	....
	New Haven	AHL	17	8	7	1	963	49	0	3.05	....	....	....	....	....	....	....
	Colorado	IHL	8	3	4	0	395	33	0	5.01	5	1	4	259	16		3.71
1988-89	Denver	IHL	18	7	11	0	990	79	0	4.79	....	....	....	....	....	....	....
1989-90	**Los Angeles**	**NHL**	**12**	**5**	**6**	**0**	**654**	**40**	**0**	**3.67**	**1**	**0**	**0**	**32**	**4**	**0**	**7.50**
	New Haven	AHL	22	8	11	1	1224	79	1	3.87	....	....	....	....	....	....	....
1990-91	New Haven	AHL	29	5	15	4	1540	104	0	4.05	....	....	....	....	....	....	....
	NHL Totals		**28**	**8**	**13**	**4**	**1450**	**91**	**0**	**3.77**	**1**	**0**	**0**	**32**	**4**	**0**	**7.50**

a CCHA First All-Star Team (1983)
b Shared Terry Sawchuk Trophy (CHL's leading goaltenders) with John Vanbiesbrouck (1984)

Signed as a free agent by **NY Rangers**, May 25, 1983. Signed as a free agent by **Los Angeles**, January 12, 1990.

SHARPLES, WARREN

Goaltender. Catches left. 6', 180 lbs. Born, Calgary, Alta., March 1, 1965.
(Calgary's 8th choice, 184th overall, in 1986 Entry Draft).

			Regular Season								Playoffs						
Season	Club	Lea	GP	W	L	T	Mins	GA	SO	Avg	GP	W	L	Mins	GA	SO	Avg
1986-87	U. of Michigan	CCHA	32	12	16	1	1720	148	1	5.14	....	....	....	....	....	....	....
1987-88	U. of Michigan	CCHA	33	18	15	0	1930	132	0	4.10	....	....	....	....	....	....	....
1988-89	U. of Michigan	CCHA	33	17	11	2	1887	116	0	3.69	....	....	....	....	....	....	....
1989-90	U. of Michigan	CCHA	*39	20	10	0	*2165	117	0	3.24	....	....	....	....	....	....	....
	Salt Lake	IHL	3	0	3	0	178	13	0	4.38	....	....	....	....	....	....	....
1990-91	Salt Lake	IHL	37	21	11	1	2097	124	2	3.55	4	0	3	188	14	0	4.47

SIDORKIEWICZ, PETER (sih-DOHR-kuh-vihch)

Goaltender. Catches left. 5'9", 180 lbs. Born, Dabrowa Bialostocka, Poland, June 29, 1963.
(Washington's 5th choice, 91st overall, in 1981 Entry Draft).

			Regular Season								Playoffs						
Season	Club	Lea	GP	W	L	T	Mins	GA	SO	Avg	GP	W	L	Mins	GA	SO	Avg
1980-81	Oshawa	OHA	7	3	3	0	308	24	0	4.68	5	2	2	266	20	0	4.52
1981-82	Oshawa	OHL	29	14	11	1	1553	123	*2	4.75	1	0	0	13	1	0	4.62
1982-83	Oshawa	OHL	60	36	20	3	3536	213	0	3.61	17	15	1	1020	60	0	3.53
1983-84a	Oshawa	OHL	52	28	21	1	2966	250	1	4.15	7	3	4	420	27	*1	3.86
1984-85	Binghamton	AHL	45	31	9	5	2691	137	3	3.05	8	4	4	481	31	0	3.87
	Fort Worth	IHL	10	4	4	2	590	43	0	4.37	....	....	....	....	....	....	....
1985-86	Binghamton	AHL	49	21	22	3	2819	150	2	*3.19	4	1	3	235	12	0	3.06
1986-87b	Binghamton	AHL	57	23	16	0	3304	161	4	2.92	13	6	7	794	36	0	*2.72
1987-88	**Hartford**	**NHL**	**1**	**0**	**1**	**0**	**60**	**6**	**0**	**6.00**	....	....	....	....	....	....	....
	Binghamton	AHL	42	19	17	3	2345	144	0	3.68	3	0	2	147	8	0	3.27
1988-89c	**Hartford**	**NHL**	**44**	**22**	**18**	**4**	**2635**	**133**	**4**	**3.03**	**2**	**0**	**2**	**124**	**8**	**0**	**3.87**
1989-90	**Hartford**	**NHL**	**46**	**19**	**19**	**7**	**2703**	**161**	**1**	**3.57**	**7**	**3**	**4**	**429**	**23**	**0**	**3.22**
1990-91	**Hartford**	**NHL**	**52**	**21**	**22**	**7**	**2953**	**164**	**1**	**3.33**	**6**	**2**	**4**	**359**	**24**	**0**	**4.01**
	NHL Totals		**143**	**62**	**60**	**18**	**8351**	**464**	**6**	**3.33**	**15**	**5**	**10**	**912**	**55**	**0**	**3.62**

a OHL Third All-Star Team (1984).
b AHL Second All-Star Team (1987)
c NHL All-Rookie Team (1989)

Traded to **Hartford** by **Washington** with Dean Evason for David Jensen, March 12, 1985.

SIMPSON, SHAWN

Goaltender. Catches left. 5'11", 183 lbs. Born, Gloucester Ont., August 10, 1968.
(Washington's 3rd choice, 60th overall, in 1986 Entry Draft).

			Regular Season								Playoffs						
Season	Club	Lea	GP	W	L	T	Mins	GA	SO	Avg	GP	W	L	Mins	GA	SO	Avg
1985-86	S.S. Marie	OHL	42	10	26	1	2213	217	1	5.88	....	....	....	....	....	....	....
1986-87a	S.S. Marie	OHL	46	20	22	2	2673	184	0	4.13	4	0	4	243	17	0	4.20
1987-88	S.S. Marie	OHL	57	26	29	1	3214	234	2	4.37	6	2	4	401	27	0	4.04
1988-89	Baltimore	AHL	1	0	1	0	60	7	0	7.00	....	....	....	....	....	....	....
	Oshawa	OHL	33	18	10	3	1818	131	0	4.32	6	2	4	368	23	1	3.75
1989-90	Baltimore	AHL	15	6	4	1	733	45	0	3.68	9	5	4	566	32	0	3.39
1990-91	Baltimore	AHL	19	7	6	0	859	73	0	5.10	1	0	1	34	1	0	1.76

a OHL Second All-Star Team (1987)

SNOW, GARTH

Goaltender. Catches left. 6'3", 200 lbs. Born, Wrentham, MA, July 28, 1969.
(Quebec's 6th choice, 114th overall, in 1986 Entry Draft).

			Regular Season								Playoffs						
Season	Club	Lea	GP	W	L	T	Mins	GA	SO	Avg	GP	W	L	Mins	GA	SO	Avg
1988-89	U. of Maine	H.E.	5	2	2	0	241	14	1	3.49	....	....	....	....	....	....	....
1989-90					DID NOT PLAY												
1990-91	U. of Maine	H.E.	25	*18	4	0	1290	64	2	2.98	....	....	....	....	....	....	....

SODERSTROM, TOMMY

Goaltender. Catches ..... 5'9", 165 lbs. Born, Stockholm, Sweden, July 17, 1969.
(Philadelphia's 14th choice, 214th overall, in 1990 Entry Draft).

			Regular Season								Playoffs						
Season	Club	Lea	GP	W	L	T	Mins	GA	SO	Avg	GP	W	L	Mins	GA	SO	Avg
1989-90	Djurgarden	Swe.	4	....	....	....	240	14	0	3.50	....	....	....	....	....	....	....
1990-91	Djurgarden	Swe.	39	....	....	....	2340	104	3	2.67	7	....	....	420	10	....	1.43

STAUBER, ROBB

Goaltender. Catches left. 6', 170 lbs. Born, Duluth, MN, November 25, 1967.
(Los Angeles' 5th choice, 107th overall, in 1986 Entry Draft).

			Regular Season								Playoffs						
Season	Club	Lea	GP	W	L	T	Mins	GA	SO	Avg	GP	W	L	Mins	GA	SO	Avg
1986-87	U. Minnesota	WCHA	20	13	5	0	1072	63	0	3.53	....	....	....	....	....	....	....
1987-88abcd	U. Minnesota	WCHA	44	34	10	0	2621	119	5	2.72	....	....	....	....	....	....	....
1988-89e	U. Minnesota	WCHA	34	26	8	0	2024	82	0	2.43	....	....	....	....	....	....	....
1989-90	**Los Angeles**	**NHL**	**2**	**0**	**1**	**0**	**83**	**11**	**0**	**7.95**	....	....	....	....	....	....	....
	New Haven	AHL	14	6	6	2	851	43	0	3.03	5	2	3	302	24	0	4.77
1990-91	New Haven	AHL	33	13	16	4	1882	115	1	3.67	....	....	....	....	....	....	....
	Phoenix	IHL	4	1	2	0	160	11	0	4.13	....	....	....	....	....	....	....
	NHL Totals		**2**	**0**	**1**	**0**	**83**	**11**	**0**	**7.95**	....	....	....	....	....	....	....

a Won Hobey Baker Memorial Award (Top U.S. Collegiate Player) (1988)
b NCAA West First All-American Team (1988)
c WCHA Player of the Year (1988)
d WCHA First All-Star Team (1988)
e WCHA Second All-Star Team (1989)

STEFAN, GREGORY STEVEN (GREG) (STEH-fihn)

Goaltender. Catches left. 5'11", 180 lbs. Born, Brantford, Ont., February 11, 1961.
(Detroit's 5th choice, 128th overall, in 1981 Entry Draft).

			Regular Season								Playoffs						
Season	Club	Lea	GP	W	L	T	Mins	GA	SO	Avg	GP	W	L	Mins	GA	SO	Avg
1979-80	Oshawa	OHA	17	8	6	0	897	58	0	3.88	....	....	....	....	....	....	....
1980-81	Oshawa	OHA	46	23	14	3	2407	174	0	4.34	6	2	3	298	20	0	4.02
1981-82	**Detroit**	**NHL**	**2**	**0**	**2**	**0**	**120**	**10**	**0**	**5.00**	....	....	....	....	....	....	....
	Adirondack	AHL	29	11	13	3	1571	99	2	3.78	1	0	0	20	0	0	0.00
1982-83	**Detroit**	**NHL**	**35**	**6**	**16**	**9**	**1847**	**139**	**0**	**4.52**	....	....	....	....	....	....	....
1983-84	**Detroit**	**NHL**	**50**	**19**	**22**	**2**	**2600**	**152**	**2**	**3.51**	**3**	**1**	**2**	**210**	**8**	**0**	**2.29**
1984-85	**Detroit**	**NHL**	**46**	**21**	**19**	**3**	**2635**	**190**	**0**	**4.33**	**3**	**0**	**3**	**138**	**17**	**0**	**7.39**
1985-86	**Detroit**	**NHL**	**37**	**10**	**20**	**5**	**2068**	**155**	**1**	**4.50**	....	....	....	....	....	....	....
1986-87	**Detroit**	**NHL**	**43**	**20**	**17**	**3**	**2351**	**135**	**1**	**3.45**	**9**	**4**	**5**	**508**	**24**	**0**	**2.83**
1987-88	**Detroit**	**NHL**	**33**	**17**	**9**	**5**	**1854**	**96**	**1**	**3.11**	**10**	**5**	**4**	**531**	**32**	**1**	**3.62**
1988-89	**Detroit**	**NHL**	**46**	**21**	**17**	**3**	**2499**	**167**	**0**	**4.01**	**5**	**2**	**3**	**294**	**18**	**0**	**3.67**
1989-90	**Detroit**	**NHL**	**7**	**1**	**5**	**0**	**359**	**24**	**0**	**4.01**	....	....	....	....	....	....	....
	Adirondack	AHL	3	1	0	1	128	7	0	3.28	....	....	....	....	....	....	....
1990-91	Adirondack	AHL	2	0	1	0	66	7	0	6.36	....	....	....	....	....	....	....
	NHL Totals		**299**	**115**	**127**	**30**	**16333**	**1068**	**5**	**3.92**	**30**	**12**	**17**	**1681**	**99**	**1**	**3.53**

STOLP, JEFFREY

Goaltender. Catches left. 6', 180 lbs. Born, Nashwauk, MN, June 20, 1970.
(Minnesota's 4th choice, 64th overall, in 1988 Entry Draft).

			Regular Season								Playoffs						
Season	Club	Lea	GP	W	L	T	Mins	GA	SO	Avg	GP	W	L	Mins	GA	SO	Avg
1988-89	U. Minnesota	WCHA	16	7	2	3	742	45	0	3.64	....	....	....	....	....	....	....
1989-90	U. Minnesota	WCHA	10	5	1	0	417	33	1	4.75	....	....	....	....	....	....	....
1990-91	U. Minnesota	WCHA	32	18	8	3	1766	82	2	2.79	....	....	....	....	....	....	....

TABARACCI, RICHARD (RICK)

Goaltender. Catches left. 5'10", 185 lbs. Born, Toronto, Ont., January 2, 1969.
(Pittsburgh's 2nd choice, 26th overall, in 1987 Entry Draft).

			Regular Season								Playoffs						
Season	Club	Lea	GP	W	L	T	Mins	GA	SO	Avg	GP	W	L	Mins	GA	SO	Avg
1986-87	Cornwall	OHL	59	23	32	3	3347	290	1	5.20	5	1	4	303	26	0	3.17
1987-88a	Cornwall	OHL	58	*33	18	6	3448	200	*3	3.48	11	5	6	642	37	0	3.46
	Muskegon	IHL	...	...	...	...	....	....	...	....	1	0	0	13	1	0	4.62
1988-89	**Pittsburgh**	**NHL**	**1**	**0**	**0**	**0**	**33**	**4**	**0**	**7.27**	....	....	....	....	....	....	....
b	Cornwall	OHL	50	24	20	5	2974	210	1	4.24	18	10	8	1080	65	*1	3.61
1989-90	Moncton	AHL	27	10	15	2	1580	107	2	4.06	....	....	....	....	....	....	....
	Fort Wayne	IHL	22	8	9	1	1064	73	0	4.12	3	1	2	159	19	0	7.17
1990-91	**Winnipeg**	**NHL**	**24**	**4**	**9**	**4**	**1093**	**71**	**1**	**3.90**	....	....	....	....	....	....	....
	Moncton	AHL	11	4	5	2	645	41	0	3.81	....	....	....	....	....	....	....
	NHL Totals		**25**	**4**	**9**	**4**	**1126**	**75**	**1**	**4.00**	....	....	....	....	....	....	....

a OHL First All-Star Team (1988)
b OHL Second All-Star Team (1989)

Traded to **Winnipeg** by **Pittsburgh** with Randy Cunnyworth and Dave McLlwain for Jim Kyte, Andrew McBain and Randy Gilhen, June 17, 1989.

TAKKO, KARI (TAH-koh)

Goaltender. Catches left. 6'2", 185 lbs. Born, Uusikaupunki, Finland, June 23, 1962.
(Minnesota's 5th choice, 97th overall, in 1984 Entry Draft).

			Regular Season								Playoffs						
Season	Club	Lea	GP	W	L	T	Mins	GA	SO	Avg	GP	W	L	Mins	GA	SO	Avg
1978-79	Assat	Fin.	2	....	....	....	....	2	....	....	....	....	....	....	....	....	....
1979-80	Assat	Fin.	2	....	....	....	....	8	....	....	....	....	....	....	....	....	....
1980-81	Assat	Fin.	4	....	....	....	....	16	....	....	....	....	....	....	....	....	....
1981-82	Assat	Fin.	14	....	....	....	....	60	....	....	....	....	....	....	....	....	....
1982-83	Assat	Fin.	21	....	....	....	....	77	0	....	....	....	....	....	....	....	....
1983-84	Assat	Fin.	32	....	....	....	....	102	3	....	9	....	....	....	37	0	....
1984-85	Assat	Fin.	35	....	....	....	....	123	3	....	8	....	....	....	32	0	....
1985-86	**Minnesota**	**NHL**	**1**	**0**	**1**	**0**	**60**	**3**	**0**	**3.00**	....	....	....	....	....	....	....
	Springfield	AHL	43	18	19	3	2286	161	1	4.05	....	....	....	....	....	....	....
1986-87	**Minnesota**	**NHL**	**38**	**13**	**18**	**4**	**2075**	**119**	**0**	**3.44**	....	....	....	....	....	....	....
	Springfield	AHL	5	3	2	0	300	16	1	3.20	....	....	....	....	....	....	....
1987-88	**Minnesota**	**NHL**	**37**	**8**	**19**	**6**	**1919**	**143**	**1**	**4.47**	....	....	....	....	....	....	....
1988-89	**Minnesota**	**NHL**	**32**	**8**	**15**	**4**	**1603**	**93**	**0**	**3.48**	**3**	**0**	**1**	**105**	**7**	**0**	**4.00**
1989-90	**Minnesota**	**NHL**	**21**	**4**	**12**	**0**	**1012**	**68**	**0**	**4.03**	**1**	**0**	**0**	**4**	**0**	**0**	**0.00**
1990-91	**Minnesota**	**NHL**	**2**	**0**	**2**	**0**	**119**	**12**	**0**	**6.05**	....	....	....	....	....	....	....
	Kalamazoo	IHL	5	4	1	0	300	10	1	2.00	....	....	....	....	....	....	....
	Edmonton	**NHL**	**11**	**4**	**4**	**0**	**529**	**37**	**0**	**4.20**	....	....	....	....	....	....	....
	NHL Totals		**142**	**37**	**71**	**14**	**7317**	**475**	**1**	**3.90**	**4**	**0**	**1**	**109**	**7**	**0**	**3.85**

Traded to **Edmonton** by **Minnesota** for Bruce Bell, November 22, 1990.

TANNER, JOHN

Goaltender. Catches left. 6'3", 182 lbs. Born, Cambridge, Ont., March 17, 1971.
(Quebec's 4th choice, 54th overall, in 1989 Entry Draft).

			Regular Season								Playoffs						
Season	Club	Lea	GP	W	L	T	Mins	GA	SO	Avg	GP	W	L	Mins	GA	SO	Avg
1987-88a	Peterborough	OHL	26	18	4	3	1532	88	0	3.45	2	1	0	98	3	0	1.84
1988-89	Peterborough	OHL	34	22	10	0	1923	107	2	*3.34	8	4	3	369	23	0	3.74
1989-90	**Quebec**	**NHL**	**1**	**0**	**1**	**0**	**60**	**3**	**0**	**3.00**	....	....	....	....	....	....	....
	Peterborough	OHL	18	6	8	2	1037	70	0	4.05	....	....	....	....	....	....	....
	London	OHL	19	12	5	1	1097	53	1	2.90	6	2	4	341	24	0	4.22
1990-91	**Quebec**	**NHL**	**6**	**1**	**3**	**1**	**228**	**16**	**0**	**4.21**	....	....	....	....	....	....	....
	London	OHL	7	3	3	1	427	29	0	4.07	....	....	....	....	....	....	....
	Sudbury	OHL	19	10	8	0	1043	60	0	3.45	5	1	4	274	21		4.60
	NHL Totals		**7**	**1**	**4**	**1**	**288**	**19**	**0**	**3.96**	....	....	....	....	....	....	....

a Won Dave Pinkney Trophy (Top Team Goaltending OHL) shared with Todd Bojcun (1989)

TERRERI, CHRIS

Goaltender. Catches left. 5'8", 155 lbs. Born, Providence, RI, November 15, 1964.
(New Jersey's 3rd choice, 87th overall, in 1983 Entry Draft).

			Regular Season								Playoffs						
Season	Club	Lea	GP	W	L	T	Mins	GA	SO	Avg	GP	W	L	Mins	GA	SO	Avg
1982-83	Providence	ECAC	11	7	1	0	528	17	2	1.93	....	....	....	....	....	....	....
1983-84	Providence	ECAC	10	4	2	0	391	20	0	3.07	....	....	....	....	....	....	....
1984-85abc	Providence	H.E.	33	15	13	5	1956	116	1	3.35	....	....	....	....	....	....	....
1985-86	Providence	H.E.	22	6	16	0	1320	84	0	3.74	....	....	....	....	....	....	....
1986-87	**New Jersey**	**NHL**	**7**	**0**	**3**	**1**	**286**	**21**	**0**	**4.41**	....	....	....	....	....	....	....
	Maine	AHL	14	4	9	1	765	57	0	4.47	....	....	....	....	....	....	....
1987-88	Utica	AHL	7	5	1	0	399	18	0	2.71	....	....	....	....	....	....	....
	U.S. National	...	26	17	7	2	1430	81	0	3.40	....	....	....	....	....	....	....
	U.S. Olympic	...	3	1	1	0	128	14	0	6.56	....	....	....	....	....	....	....
1988-89	**New Jersey**	**NHL**	**8**	**0**	**4**	**2**	**402**	**18**	**0**	**2.69**	....	....	....	....	....	....	....
	Utica	AHL	39	20	15	3	2314	132	0	3.42	2	0	1	80	6	0	4.50
1989-90	**New Jersey**	**NHL**	**35**	**15**	**12**	**3**	**1931**	**110**	**0**	**3.42**	**4**	**2**	**2**	**238**	**13**	**0**	**3.28**
1990-91	**New Jersey**	**NHL**	**53**	**24**	**21**	**7**	**2970**	**144**	**1**	**2.91**	**7**	**3**	**4**	**428**	**21**	**0**	**2.94**
	NHL Totals		**103**	**39**	**40**	**13**	**5589**	**293**	**1**	**3.15**	**11**	**5**	**6**	**666**	**34**	**0**	**3.06**

a Hockey East All-Star Team
b Hockey East Player of the Year (1985)
c NCAA All-American Team (1985)

TORCHIA, MIKE

Goaltender. Catches left. 5'11", 225 lbs. Born, Toronto, Ont., February 23, 1972.
(Minnesota's 2nd choice, 74th overall, in 1991 Entry Draft).

			Regular Season								Playoffs						
Season	Club	Lea	GP	W	L	T	Mins	GA	SO	Avg	GP	W	L	Mins	GA	SO	Avg
1988-89	Kitchener	OHL	30	14	9	4	1472	102	0	4.02	2	0	2	126	8	0	3.81
1989-90a	Kitchener	OHL	40	25	11	2	2280	136	1	3.58	*17	*11	6	*1023	60	0	3.52
1990-91	Kitchener	OHL	57	25	24	7	*3317	219	0	3.95	6	2	4	382	30	0	4.71

a Memorial Cup All-Star Team, Top Goaltender (1990)

TUGNUTT, RON

Goaltender. Catches left. 5'11", 155 lbs. Born, Scarborough, Ont., October 22, 1967.
(Quebec's 4th choice, 81st overall, in 1986 Entry Draft).

			Regular Season								Playoffs						
Season	Club	Lea	GP	W	L	T	Mins	GA	SO	Avg	GP	W	L	Mins	GA	SO	Avg
1984-85	Peterborough	OHL	18	7	4	2	938	59	0	3.77	....	....	....	....	....	....	....
1985-86	Peterborough	OHL	26	18	7	0	1543	74	1	2.88	3	2	0	133	6	0	2.71
1986-87a	Peterborough	OHL	31	21	7	2	1891	88	2	*2.79	6	3	3	374	21	1	3.37
1987-88	**Quebec**	**NHL**	**6**	**2**	**3**	**0**	**284**	**16**	**0**	**3.38**	....	....	....	....	....	....	....
	Fredericton	AHL	34	20	9	4	1964	118	1	3.60	4	1	2	204	11	0	3.24
1988-89	**Quebec**	**NHL**	**26**	**10**	**10**	**3**	**1367**	**82**	**0**	**3.60**	....	....	....	....	....	....	....
	Halifax	AHL	24	14	7	2	1368	79	1	3.46	....	....	....	....	....	....	....
1989-90	**Quebec**	**NHL**	**35**	**5**	**24**	**3**	**1978**	**152**	**0**	**4.61**	....	....	....	....	....	....	....
	Halifax	AHL	6	1	5	0	366	23	0	3.77	....	....	....	....	....	....	....
1990-91	**Quebec**	**NHL**	**56**	**12**	**29**	**10**	**3144**	**212**	**0**	**4.05**	....	....	....	....	....	....	....
	Halifax	AHL	2	0	1	0	100	8	0	4.80	....	....	....	....	....	....	....
	NHL Totals		**123**	**29**	**66**	**16**	**6773**	**462**	**0**	**4.09**	....	....	....	....	....	....	....

a OHL First All-Star Team (1987)

TUREK, ROMAN

Goaltender. Catches left. 6'3", 190 lbs. Born, Pisek, Czechoslovakia, May 21, 1970.
(Minnesota's 6th choice, 113th overall, in 1990 Entry Draft).

			Regular Season								Playoffs						
Season	Club	Lea	GP	W	L	T	Mins	GA	SO	Avg	GP	W	L	Mins	GA	SO	Avg
1989-90	VTJ Tabor	Czech.2			UNAVAILABLE												
1990-91	Motor	Czech.	21	....	....	....	1244	98	0	4.70	....	....	....	....	....	....	....

VANBIESBROUCK, JOHN (van-BEES-bruhk)

Goaltender. Catches left. 5'8", 172 lbs. Born, Detroit, MI, September 4, 1963.
(NY Rangers' 5th choice, 72nd overall, in 1981 Entry Draft).

			Regular Season								Playoffs						
Season	Club	Lea	GP	W	L	T	Mins	GA	SO	Avg	GP	W	L	Mins	GA	SO	Avg
1980-81a	S.S. Marie	OHA	56	31	16	1	2941	203	0	4.14	11	3	3	457	24	1	3.15
1981-82	**NY Rangers**	**NHL**	**1**	**1**	**0**	**0**	**60**	**1**	**0**	**1.00**	....	....	....	....	....	....	....
	S.S. Marie	OHL	31	12	12	2	1686	102	0	3.62	7	1	4	276	20	0	4.35
1982-83b	S.S. Marie	OHL	62	39	21	1	3471	209	0	3.61	16	7	6	944	56	*1	3.56
1983-84	**NY Rangers**	**NHL**	**3**	**2**	**1**	**0**	**180**	**10**	**0**	**3.33**	**1**	**0**	**0**	**1**	**0**	**0**	**0.00**
cde	Tulsa	CHL	37	20	13	2	2153	124	*3	3.46	4	4	0	240	10	0	*2.50
1984-85	**NY Rangers**	**NHL**	**42**	**12**	**24**	**3**	**2358**	**166**	**1**	**4.22**	**1**	**0**	**0**	**20**	**0**	**0**	**0.00**
1985-86fg	**NY Rangers**	**NHL**	**61**	***31**	**21**	**5**	**3326**	**184**	**3**	**3.32**	**16**	**8**	**8**	**899**	**49**	***1**	**3.27**
1986-87	**NY Rangers**	**NHL**	**50**	**18**	**20**	**5**	**2656**	**161**	**0**	**3.64**	**4**	**1**	**3**	**195**	**11**	**1**	**3.38**
1987-88	**NY Rangers**	**NHL**	**56**	**27**	**22**	**7**	**3319**	**187**	**2**	**3.38**	....	....	....	....	....	....	....
1988-89	**NY Rangers**	**NHL**	**56**	**28**	**21**	**4**	**3207**	**197**	**0**	**3.69**	**2**	**0**	**1**	**107**	**6**	**0**	**3.36**
1989-90	**NY Rangers**	**NHL**	**47**	**19**	**19**	**7**	**2734**	**154**	**1**	**3.38**	**6**	**2**	**3**	**298**	**15**	**0**	**3.02**
1990-91	**NY Rangers**	**NHL**	**40**	**15**	**18**	**6**	**2257**	**126**	**3**	**3.35**	**1**	**0**	**0**	**52**	**1**	**0**	**1.15**
	NHL Totals		**356**	**153**	**146**	**37**	**20097**	**1186**	**10**	**3.54**	**31**	**11**	**15**	**1572**	**82**	**2**	**3.13**

a OHA Third All-Star Team (1981).
b OHL Second All-Star Team (1983).
c CHL First All-Star Team (1984)
d Shared Terry Sawchuk Trophy (CHL's leading goaltenders) with Ron Scott (1984)
e Shared Tommy Ivan Trophy (CHL's Most Valuable Player) with Bruce Affleck of Indianapolis (1984)
f Won Vezina Trophy (1986)
g NHL First All-Star Team (1986)

VERNON, MICHAEL (MIKE)

Goaltender. Catches left. 5'9", 170 lbs. Born, Calgary, Alta., February 24, 1963.
(Calgary's 2nd choice, 56th overall, in 1981 Entry Draft).

			Regular Season								Playoffs						
Season	Club	Lea	GP	W	L	T	Mins	GA	SO	Avg	GP	W	L	Mins	GA	SO	Avg
1980-81	Calgary	WHL	59	33	17	1	3154	198	1	3.77	22	....	....	1271	82	1	3.87
1981-82ab	Calgary	WHL	42	22	14	2	2329	143	3	3.68	9	....	....	527	30	0	3.42
	Oklahoma City	CHL	....	....	....	....	....	....	....	....	1	0	1	70	4	0	3.43
1982-83	**Calgary**	**NHL**	**2**	**0**	**2**	**0**	**100**	**11**	**0**	**6.59**	....	....	....	....	....	....	....
ab	Calgary	WHL	50	19	18	2	2856	155	3	3.26	16	9	7	925	60	0	3.89
1983-84	**Calgary**	**NHL**	**1**	**0**	**1**	**0**	**11**	**4**	**0**	**22.22**	....	....	....	....	....	....	....
c	Colorado	CHL	46	30	13	2	2648	148	1	*3.35	6	2	4	347	21	0	3.63
1984-85	Moncton	AHL	41	10	20	4	2050	134	0	3.92	....	....	....	....	....	....	....
1985-86	**Calgary**	**NHL**	**18**	**9**	**3**	**3**	**921**	**52**	**1**	**3.39**	***21**	**12**	***9**	**1229**	**60**	**0**	**2.93**
	Moncton	AHL	6	3	1	2	374	21	0	3.37	....	....	....	....	....	....	....
	Salt Lake	IHL	10	....	....	....	600	34	1	3.40	....	....	....	....	....	....	....
1986-87	**Calgary**	**NHL**	**54**	**30**	**21**	**1**	**2957**	**178**	**1**	**3.61**	**5**	**2**	**3**	**263**	**16**	**0**	**3.65**
1987-88	**Calgary**	**NHL**	**64**	**39**	**16**	**7**	**3565**	**210**	**1**	**3.53**	**9**	**4**	**4**	**515**	**34**	**0**	**3.96**
1988-89d	**Calgary**	**NHL**	**52**	***37**	**6**	**5**	**2938**	**130**	**0**	**2.65**	***22**	***16**	**5**	***1381**	**52**	***3**	**2.26**
1989-90	**Calgary**	**NHL**	**47**	**23**	**14**	**9**	**2795**	**146**	**0**	**3.13**	**6**	**2**	**3**	**342**	**19**	**0**	**3.33**
1990-91	**Calgary**	**NHL**	**54**	**31**	**19**	**3**	**3121**	**172**	**1**	**3.31**	**7**	**3**	**4**	**427**	**21**	**0**	**2.95**
	NHL Totals		**292**	**169**	**82**	**24**	**16408**	**903**	**4**	**3.30**	**70**	**39**	**28**	**4157**	**202**	**0**	**2.92**

a WHL First All-Star Team (1982, 1983)
b WHL Most Valuable Player (1982, 1983)
c CHL Second All-Star Team (1984)
d NHL Second All-Star Team (1989)

Played in NHL All-Star Game (1988-91)

VERNER, ANDREW

Goaltender. Catches left. 6', 194 lbs. Born, Weston, Ont., November 20, 1972.
(Edmonton's 3rd choice, 34th overall, in 1991 Entry Draft).

			Regular Season								Playoffs						
Season	Club	Lea	GP	W	L	T	Mins	GA	SO	Avg	GP	W	L	Mins	GA	SO	Avg
1989-90	Peterborough	OHL	13	7	3	0	624	38	1	3.65	....	....	....	....	....	....	....
1990-91a	Peterborough	OHL	46	22	14	7	2523	148	0	3.52	3	0	3	185	15	0	4.86

a OHL Second All-Star Team (1991)

WAITE, JIMMY

Goaltender. Catches left. 6'1", 182 lbs. Born, Sherbrooke, Que., April 15, 1969.
(Chicago's 1st choice, 8th overall, in 1987 Entry Draft).

			Regular Season								Playoffs						
Season	Club	Lea	GP	W	L	T	Mins	GA	SO	Avg	GP	W	L	Mins	GA	SO	Avg
1986-87a	Chicoutimi	QMJHL	50	23	17	3	2569	209	2	4.48	11	4	6	576	54	1	5.63
1987-88	Chicoutimi	QMJHL	36	17	16	1	2000	150	0	4.50	4	1	2	222	17	0	4.59
1988-89	**Chicago**	**NHL**	**11**	**0**	**7**	**1**	**494**	**43**	**0**	**5.22**	....	....	....	....	....	....	....
	Saginaw	IHL	5	3	1	0	304	10	0	1.97	....	....	....	....	....	....	....
1989-90	**Chicago**	**NHL**	**4**	**2**	**0**	**0**	**183**	**14**	**0**	**4.59**	....	....	....	....	....	....	....
bc	Indianapolis	IHL	54	*34	14	5	*3207	135	*5	*2.53	*10	*9	1	*602	19	*1	*1.89
1990-91	**Chicago**	**NHL**	**1**	**1**	**0**	**0**	**60**	**2**	**0**	**2.00**	....	....	....	....	....	....	....
	Indianapolis	IHL	49	*26	18	4	2888	167	3	3.47	6	2	4	369	20	0	3.25
	NHL Totals		**16**	**3**	**7**	**1**	**737**	**59**	**0**	**4.80**	....	....	....	....	....	....	....

a QMJHL Second All-Star Team (1987)
b IHL First All-Star Team (1990)
c Won James Norris Memorial Trophy (Top Goaltender-IHL) (1990)

WAKALUK, DARCY (WAHK-uh-luhk)

Goaltender. Catches left. 5'11", 180 lbs. Born, Pincher Creek, Alta., March 14, 1966.
(Buffalo's 7th choice, 144th overall, in 1984 Entry Draft).

			Regular Season								Playoffs						
Season	Club	Lea	GP	W	L	T	Mins	GA	SO	Avg	GP	W	L	Mins	GA	SO	Avg
1983-84	Kelowna	WHL	31	....	....	....	1555	163	0	6.29	....	....	....	....	....	....	....
1984-85	Kelowna	WHL	54	19	30	4	3094	244	0	4.73	5	1	4	282	22	0	4.68
1985-86	Spokane	WHL	47	21	22	1	2562	224	1	5.25	7	3	4	419	37	0	5.30
1986-87	Rochester	AHL	11	2	2	0	545	26	0	2.86	5	2	0	141	11	0	4.68
1987-88	Rochester	AHL	55	27	16	3	2763	159	0	3.45	6	3	3	328	22	0	4.02
1988-89	**Buffalo**	**NHL**	**6**	**1**	**3**	**0**	**214**	**15**	**0**	**4.21**	....	....	....	....	....	....	....
	Rochester	AHL	33	11	14	0	1566	97	1	3.72	....	....	....	....	....	....	....
1989-90	Rochester	AHL	56	31	16	4	3095	173	2	3.35	*17	*10	6	*1001	50	0	*3.01
1990-91	**Buffalo**	**NHL**	**16**	**4**	**5**	**3**	**630**	**35**	**0**	**3.33**	**2**	**0**	**1**	**37**	**2**	**0**	**3.24**
	Rochester	AHL	26	10	10	3	1363	68	4	*2.99	9	6	3	544	30	0	3.31
	NHL Totals		**22**	**5**	**8**	**3**	**844**	**50**	**0**	**3.55**	**2**	**0**	**1**	**37**	**2**	**0**	**3.24**

Traded to **Minnesota** by **Buffalo** for Minnesota's eighth round choice (Jiri Kuntos) in 1991 Entry Draft, May 26, 1991.

WAMSLEY, RICHARD (RICK) (WAHMS-lee)

Goaltender. Catches left. 5'11", 185 lbs. Born, Simcoe, Ont., May 25, 1959.
(Montreal's 5th choice, 58th overall, in 1979 Entry Draft).

			Regular Season								Playoffs						
Season	Club	Lea	GP	W	L	T	Mins	GA	SO	Avg	GP	W	L	Mins	GA	SO	Avg
1977-78	Hamilton	OHA	25	....	....	....	1495	74	2	2.97	....	....	....	....	....	....	....
1978-79	Brantford	OHA	24	....	....	....	1444	128	0	5.32	....	....	....	....	....	....	....
1979-80	Nova Scotia	AHL	40	19	16	2	2305	125	2	3.25	3	1	1	143	12	0	5.03
1980-81	**Montreal**	**NHL**	**5**	**3**	**0**	**1**	**253**	**8**	**1**	**1.90**	....	....	....	....	....	....	....
	Nova Scotia	AHL	43	17	19	3	2372	155	0	3.92	4	2	1	199	6	*1	1.81
1981-82a	**Montreal**	**NHL**	**38**	**23**	**7**	**7**	**2206**	**101**	**2**	**2.75**	**5**	**2**	**3**	**300**	**11**	**0**	***2.20**
1982-83	**Montreal**	**NHL**	**46**	**27**	**12**	**5**	**2583**	**151**	**0**	**3.51**	**3**	**0**	**3**	**152**	**7**	**0**	**2.77**
1983-84	**Montreal**	**NHL**	**42**	**19**	**17**	**3**	**2333**	**144**	**2**	**3.70**	**1**	**0**	**1**	**32**	**0**	**0**	**0.00**
1984-85	**St. Louis**	**NHL**	**40**	**23**	**12**	**5**	**2319**	**126**	**0**	**3.26**	**2**	**0**	**2**	**120**	**7**	**0**	**3.50**
1985-86	**St. Louis**	**NHL**	**42**	**22**	**16**	**3**	**2517**	**144**	**1**	**3.43**	**10**	**4**	**6**	**569**	**29**	**0**	**3.06**
1986-87	**St. Louis**	**NHL**	**41**	**17**	**15**	**6**	**2410**	**142**	**0**	**3.54**	**2**	**1**	**1**	**120**	**5**	**0**	**2.50**
1987-88	**St. Louis**	**NHL**	**31**	**13**	**16**	**1**	**1818**	**103**	**2**	**3.40**	....	....	....	....	....	....	....
	Calgary	**NHL**	**2**	**1**	**0**	**0**	**73**	**5**	**0**	**4.11**	**1**	**0**	**1**	**33**	**2**	**0**	**3.64**
1988-89	**Calgary**	**NHL**	**35**	**17**	**11**	**4**	**1927**	**95**	**2**	**2.96**	**1**	**0**	**1**	**20**	**2**	**0**	**6.00**
1989-90	**Calgary**	**NHL**	**36**	**18**	**8**	**6**	**1969**	**107**	**2**	**3.26**	**1**	**0**	**1**	**49**	**9**	**0**	**11.02**
1990-91	**Calgary**	**NHL**	**29**	**14**	**7**	**5**	**1670**	**85**	**0**	**3.05**	**1**	**0**	**0**	**2**	**1**	**0**	**30.00**
	NHL Totals		**387**	**197**	**121**	**46**	**22078**	**1211**	**12**	**3.29**	**27**	**7**	**19**	**1397**	**73**	**0**	**3.14**

a Shared Williams Jennings Trophy with Denis Herron (1982)

Traded to **St. Louis** by **Montreal** with Hartford's second round choice (Brian Benning); — Montreal property via earlier deal — Montreal's second round choice (Tony Hrkac) and third round choice (Robert Dirk), all in the 1984 Entry Draft, for St. Louis' first (Shayne Corson) and second round (Stephane Richer) choices in the 1984 Entry Draft, June 9, 1984. Traded to **Calgary** by **St. Louis** with Rob Ramage for Brett Hull and Steve Bozek, March 7, 1988.

WEEKS, STEPHEN (STEVE)

Goaltender. Catches left. 5'11", 170 lbs. Born, Scarborough, Ont., June 30, 1958.
(NY Rangers' 12th choice, 176th overall, in 1978 Amateur Draft).

			Regular Season								Playoffs						
Season	Club	Lea	GP	W	L	T	Mins	GA	SO	Avg	GP	W	L	Mins	GA	SO	Avg
1977-78	N. Michigan	CCHA	19	....	....	....	1015	56	1	3.31	....	....	....	....	....	....	....
1978-79	N. Michigan	CCHA	25	....	....	....	1437	82	0	3.42	....	....	....	....	....	....	....
1979-80	N. Michigan	CCHA	36	29	6	1	2133	105	0	2.95	....	....	....	....	....	....	....
1980-81	**NY Rangers**	**NHL**	**1**	**0**	**1**	**0**	**60**	**2**	**0**	**2.00**	**1**	**0**	**0**	**14**	**1**	**0**	**4.29**
	New Haven	AHL	36	14	17	3	2065	142	1	4.04	....	....	....	....	....	....	....
1981-82	**NY Rangers**	**NHL**	**49**	**23**	**16**	**9**	**2852**	**179**	**1**	**3.77**	**4**	**1**	**2**	**127**	**9**	**0**	**4.25**
1982-83	**NY Rangers**	**NHL**	**18**	**9**	**5**	**3**	**1040**	**68**	**0**	**3.92**	....	....	....	....	....	....	....
	Tulsa	CHL	19	8	10	0	1116	60	0	3.23	....	....	....	....	....	....	....
1983-84	**NY Rangers**	**NHL**	**26**	**10**	**11**	**2**	**1361**	**90**	**0**	**3.97**	....	....	....	....	....	....	....
	Tulsa	CHL	3	3	0	0	180	7	0	2.33	....	....	....	....	....	....	....
1984-85	**Hartford**	**NHL**	**24**	**10**	**12**	**2**	**1457**	**93**	**2**	**3.82**	....	....	....	....	....	....	....
	Binghamton	AHL	5	5	0	0	303	13	0	2.57	....	....	....	....	....	....	....
1985-86	**Hartford**	**NHL**	**27**	**13**	**13**	**0**	**1544**	**99**	**1**	**3.85**	**3**	**1**	**2**	**169**	**8**	**0**	**2.84**
1986-87	**Hartford**	**NHL**	**25**	**12**	**8**	**2**	**1367**	**78**	**1**	**3.42**	**1**	**0**	**0**	**36**	**1**	**0**	**1.67**
1987-88	**Hartford**	**NHL**	**18**	**6**	**7**	**2**	**918**	**55**	**0**	**3.59**	....	....	....	....	....	....	....
	Vancouver	**NHL**	**9**	**4**	**3**	**2**	**550**	**31**	**0**	**3.38**	....	....	....	....	....	....	....
1988-89	**Vancouver**	**NHL**	**35**	**11**	**19**	**5**	**2056**	**102**	**0**	**2.98**	**3**	**1**	**1**	**140**	**8**	**0**	**3.43**
1989-90	**Vancouver**	**NHL**	**21**	**4**	**11**	**4**	**1142**	**79**	**0**	**4.15**	....	....	....	....	....	....	....
1990-91	**Vancouver**	**NHL**	**1**	**0**	**1**	**0**	**59**	**6**	**0**	**6.10**	....	....	....	....	....	....	....
	Milwaukee	IHL	37	16	19	0	2014	127	0	3.78	3	1	2	210	13	0	3.71
	NHL Totals		**254**	**102**	**107**	**33**	**14406**	**882**	**5**	**3.67**	**12**	**3**	**5**	**486**	**27**	**0**	**3.33**

Traded to **Vancouver** by **Hartford** for Richard Brodeur, March 8, 1988. Traded to **Buffalo** by **Vancouver** for future considerations, March 5, 1991.

WHITMORE, KAY

Goaltender. Catches left. 5'11", 175 lbs.   Born, Sudbury, Ont., April 10, 1967.
(Hartford's 2nd choice, 26th overall, in 1985 Entry Draft).

						Regular Season						Playoffs				
Season	Club	Lea	GP	W	L	T	Mins	GA	SO	Avg	GP	W	L	Mins	GA	SO	Avg
1983-84	Peterborough	OHL	29	17	8	0	1471	110	0	4.49	....	....	....	....	....	....	....
1984-85a	Peterborough	OHL	53	*35	16	2	3077	172	*2	3.35	17	10	4	1020	58	0	3.41
1985-86b	Peterborough	OHL	41	27	12	2	2467	114	*3	*2.77	14	8	5	837	40	0	2.87
1986-87	Peterborough	OHL	36	14	17	5	2159	118	1	3.28	7	3	3	366	17	1	2.79
1987-88	Binghamton	AHL	38	17	15	4	2137	121	*3	3.40	2	0	2	118	10	0	5.08
1988-89	**Hartford**	**NHL**	3	2	1	0	180	10	0	3.33	2	0	2	135	10	0	4.44
	Binghamton	AHL	*56	21	29	4	*3200	241	1	4.52	....	....	....	....	....	....	....
1989-90	**Hartford**	**NHL**	9	4	2	1	442	26	0	3.53	....	....	....	....	....	....	....
	Binghamton	AHL	24	3	19	2	1386	109	0	4.72	....	....	....	....	....	....	....
1990-91	**Hartford**	**NHL**	18	3	9	3	850	52	0	3.67	....	....	....	....	....	....	....
c	Springfield	AHL	33	22	9	1	1916	98	1	3.07	*15	*11	4	*926	37	0	*2.40
	NHL Totals		**30**	**9**	**13**	**5**	**1472**	**88**	**0**	**3.59**	**2**	**0**	**2**	**135**	**10**	**0**	**4.44**

a OHL Third All-Star Team (1985)
b OHL First All-Star Team (1986)
c Won Jack A. Butterfield Trophy (MVP in Playoffs - AHL) (1991)

WILLIAMS, MIKE

Goaltender. Catches left. 6', 185 lbs.   Born, Woodhaven, MI, April 16, 1967.
(Quebec's 12th choice, 219th overall, in 1987 Entry Draft).

						Regular Season						Playoffs				
Season	Club	Lea	GP	W	L	T	Mins	GA	SO	Avg	GP	W	L	Mins	GA	SO	Avg
1986-87	Ferris State	CCHA	17	4	9	0	846	65	0	4.61	....	....	....	....	....	....	....
1987-88	Ferris State	CCHA	30	11	11	5	1671	122	0	4.38	....	....	....	....	....	....	....
1988-89	Ferris State	CCHA	25	6	13	5	1394	84	0	3.62	....	....	....	....	....	....	....
1989-90	Ferris State	CCHA	31	9	16	3	1697	138	0	4.88	....	....	....	....	....	....	....
1990-91	Nashville	ECHL	3	1	1	0	121	12	0	5.95	....	....	....	....	....	....	....
	Cincinnati	ECHL	12	6	6	0	671	58	0	5.18	....	....	....	....	....	....	....

WREGGET, KEN

Goaltender. Catches left. 6'1", 195 lbs.   Born, Brandon, Man., March 25, 1964.
(Toronto's 4th choice, 45th overall, in 1982 Entry Draft).

						Regular Season						Playoffs				
Season	Club	Lea	GP	W	L	T	Mins	GA	SO	Avg	GP	W	L	Mins	GA	SO	Avg
1981-82	Lethbridge	WHL	36	19	12	0	1713	118	0	4.13	3	....	....	84	3	0	2.14
1982-83	Lethbridge	WHL	48	26	17	1	2696	157	0	3.49	20	14	5	1154	58	1	3.02
1983-84	**Toronto**	**NHL**	3	1	1	1	165	14	0	5.09	....	....	....	....	....	....	....
a	Lethbridge	WHL	53	32	20	0	*3053	161	0	*3.16	4	1	3	210	18	0	5.14
1984-85	**Toronto**	**NHL**	23	2	15	3	1278	103	0	4.84	....	....	....	....	....	....	....
	St. Catharines	AHL	12	2	8	1	688	48	0	4.19	....	....	....	....	....	....	....
1985-86	**Toronto**	**NHL**	30	9	13	4	1566	113	0	4.33	10	6	4	607	32	*1	3.16
	St. Catharines	AHL	18	8	9	0	1058	78	1	4.42	....	....	....	....	....	....	....
1986-87	**Toronto**	**NHL**	56	22	28	3	3026	200	0	3.97	13	7	6	761	29	1	2.29
1987-88	**Toronto**	**NHL**	56	12	35	4	3000	222	2	4.44	2	0	1	108	11	0	6.11
1988-89	**Toronto**	**NHL**	32	9	20	2	1888	139	0	4.42	....	....	....	....	....	....	....
	Philadelphia	**NHL**	3	1	1	0	130	13	0	6.00	5	2	2	268	10	1	2.24
1989-90	**Philadelphia**	**NHL**	51	22	24	3	2961	169	0	3.42	....	....	....	....	....	....	....
1990-91	**Philadelphia**	**NHL**	30	10	14	3	1484	88	0	3.56	....	....	....	....	....	....	....
	NHL Totals		**284**	**88**	**151**	**23**	**15498**	**1061**	**2**	**4.11**	**30**	**15**	**13**	**1744**	**82**	**3**	**2.82**

a WHL First All-Star Team, East Division (1984)

Traded to **Philadelphia** by **Toronto** for Philadelphia's first-round choice (Rob Pearson) and Calgary's first-round choice (Steve Bancroft) — acquired by Philadelphia in the Brad McCrimmon trade — in 1989 Entry Draft, March 6, 1989.

YOUNG, WENDELL

Goaltender. Catches left. 5'9", 181 lbs.   Born, Halifax, N.S., August 1, 1963.
(Vancouver's 3rd choice, 73rd overall, in 1981 Entry Draft).

						Regular Season						Playoffs				
Season	Club	Lea	GP	W	L	T	Mins	GA	SO	Avg	GP	W	L	Mins	GA	SO	Avg
1980-81	Kitchener	OHA	42	19	15	0	2215	164	1	4.44	14	9	1	800	42	*1	3.15
1981-82	Kitchener	OHL	60	38	17	2	3470	195	1	3.37	15	12	1	900	35	*1	*2.33
1982-83a	Kitchener	OHL	61	41	19	0	3611	231	1	3.84	12	6	5	720	43	0	3.58
1983-84	Fredericton	AHL	11	7	3	0	569	39	1	4.11	....	....	....	....	....	....	....
	Milwaukee	IHL	6	....	....	....	339	17	0	3.01	....	....	....	....	....	....	....
	Salt Lake	CHL	20	11	6	0	1094	80	0	4.39	4	0	2	122	11	0	5.42
1984-85	Fredericton	AHL	22	7	11	3	1242	83	0	4.01	....	....	....	....	....	....	....
1985-86	**Vancouver**	**NHL**	22	4	9	3	1023	61	0	3.58	1	0	1	60	5	0	5.00
	Fredericton	AHL	24	12	8	4	1457	78	0	3.21	....	....	....	....	....	....	....
1986-87	**Vancouver**	**NHL**	8	1	6	1	420	35	0	5.00	....	....	....	....	....	....	....
	Fredericton	AHL	30	11	16	0	1676	118	0	4.22	....	....	....	....	....	....	....
1987-88	**Philadelphia**	**NHL**	6	3	2	0	320	20	0	3.75	....	....	....	....	....	....	....
bcd	Hershey	AHL	51	*33	15	1	2922	135	1	2.77	12	*12	0	*767	28	*1	*2.19
1988-89	**Pittsburgh**	**NHL**	22	12	9	0	1150	92	0	4.80	1	0	0	39	1	0	1.54
1989-90	**Pittsburgh**	**NHL**	43	16	20	3	2318	161	0	4.17	....	....	....	....	....	....	....
1990-91	**Pittsburgh**	**NHL**	18	4	6	2	773	52	0	4.04	....	....	....	....	....	....	....
	NHL Totals		**119**	**40**	**52**	**9**	**6004**	**421**	**1**	**4.21**	**2**	**0**	**1**	**99**	**6**	**0**	**3.64**

a OHL Third All-Star Team (1983)
b AHL First All-Star Team (1988)
c Won Baz Bastien Award (AHL Most Valuable Goaltender) (1988)
d Won Jack Butterfield Trophy (AHL Playoff MVP) (1988)

Traded to **Philadelphia** by **Vancouver** with Vancouver's third round choice (Kimbi Daniels) in 1990 Entry Draft for Daryl Stanley, August 28, 1987. Traded to **Pittsburgh** by **Philadelphia** with Philadelphia's seventh-round choice (Mika Valila) in 1990 Entry Draft for Pittsburgh's third-round choice (Chris Therien) in 1990 Entry Draft, Steptember 1, 1988.

Emile "Cat" Francis

Bernie Parent

Billy Smith

Glenn Hall

Dave Reece

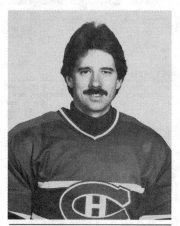

Doug Soetaert

Rick Heinz

Terry Sawchuk

Cecil "Tiny" Thompson

Phil Myre

Don Simmons

Lorne "Gump" Worsley

Retired NHL Goaltender Index

Abbreviations: Teams/Cities:—**Atl.**-Atlanta; **Bos.**-Boston; **Bro.**-Brooklyn; **Buf.**-Buffalo; **Cal.**-California; **Cgy.**-Calgary; **Chi.**-Chicago; **Cle.**-Cleveland; **Col.**-Colorado; **Det.**-Detroit; **Edm.**-Edmonton; **Ham.**-Hamilton; **Hfd.**-Hartford; **K.C.**-Kansas City; **L.A.**-Los Angeles; **Min.**-Minnesota; **Mtl.**-Montreal; **Mtl. M.**-Montreal Maroons; **Mtl. W.**-Montreal Wanderers; **N.J.**-New Jersey; **NY**-New York; **NYA**-NY Americans; **NYI**-New York Islanders; **NYR**-New York Rangers; **Oak.**-Oakland; **Ott.**-Ottawa; **Phi.**-Philadelphia; **Pit.**-Pittsburgh; **Que.**-Quebec; **St. L.**-St. Louis; **Tor.**-Toronto; **Van.**-Vancouver; **Wpg.**-Winnipeg; **Wsh.**-Washington.

Avg – goals against per 60 minutes played; **GA** – goals against; **GP** – games played; **Mins** – minutes played; **SO** – shutouts.

			Regular Schedule								Playoffs										
Name	NHL Teams	NHL Seasons	GP	W	L	T	Mins	GA	SO	Avg	GP	W	L	T	Mins	GA	SO	Avg	NHL Cup Wins	First NHL Season	Last NHL Season
Abbott, George	Bos.	1	1	0	1	0	60	7	0	7.00	....	....	....	....	....	....	....	....		1943-44	1943-44
Adams, John	Bos., Wsh.	2	22	9	10	1	1180	85	1	4.32	....	....	....	....	....	....	....	....		1972-73	1974-75
Aiken, Don	Mtl.	1	1	0	1	0	34	6	0	10.59	....	....	....	....	....	....	....	....		1957-58	1957-58
Aitkenhead, Andy	NYR	3	106	47	43	16	6570	257	11	2.35	10	6	3	1	608	15	3	1.48	1	1932-33	1934-35
Almas, Red	Det., Chi.	3	3	0	2	1	180	13	0	4.33	5	1	3	....	263	13	0	2.97		1946-47	1952-53
Anderson, Lorne	NYR	1	3	1	2	0	180	18	0	6.00	....	....	....	....	....	....	....	....		1951-52	1951-52
Astrom, Hardy	NYR, Col.	3	83	17	44	12	4456	278	0	3.74	....	....	....	....	....	....	....	....		1977-78	1980-81
Baker, Steve	NYR	4	57	20	20	11	3081	190	3	3.70	14	7	7	....	826	55	0	4.00		1979-80	1982-83
Bannerman, Murray	Van., Chi.	8	289	116	125	33	16470	1051	8	3.83	40	20	18	....	2322	165	0	4.26		1977-78	1986-87
Baron, Marco	Bos., L.A., Edm.	6	86	34	39	9	4822	292	1	3.63	1	0	1	....	20	3	0	9.00		1979-80	1984-85
Bassen, Hank	Chi., Det., Pit.	9	157	47	66	31	8829	441	5	2.99	5	1	4	....	274	11	0	2.41		1954-55	1967-68
Bastien, Baz	Tor.	1	5	0	4	1	300	20	0	4.00	....	....	....	....	....	....	....	....		1945-46	1945-46
Bauman, Gary	Mtl., Min.	3	35	6	18	6	1718	102	0	3.56	....	....	....	....	....	....	....	....		1966-67	1968-69
Bedard, Jim	Wsh.	2	73	17	40	13	4232	278	1	3.94	....	....	....	....	....	....	....	....		1977-78	1978-79
Behrend, Marc	Wpg.	3	38	12	19	3	1991	164	1	4.94	7	1	3	....	312	19	0	3.65		1983-84	1985-86
Belanger, Yves	St.L., Atl., Bos.	6	78	27	36	6	4134	259	2	3.76	....	....	....	....	....	....	....	....		1974-75	1979-80
Belhumeur, Michel	Phi., Wsh.	3	65	9	36	7	3306	254	0	4.61	1	0	0	....	10	1	0	6.00		1972-73	1975-76
Bell, Gordie	Tor., NYR	2	8	3	5	0	480	31	0	3.88	2	1	1	....	120	9	0	4.50		1945-46	1955-56
Benedict, Clint	Ott., Mtl.M.	13	362	190	43	28	22321	863	57	2.32	48	25	18	4	2907	87	15	1.80	4	1917-18	1929-30
Bennett, Harvey	Bos.	1	24	10	12	2	1470	103	0	4.20	....	....	....	....	....	....	....	....		1944-45	1944-45
Bernhardt, Tim	Cgy., Tor.	4	67	17	36	2	3748	267	0	4.27	....	....	....	....	....	....	....	....		1982-83	1986-87
Beveridge, Bill	Det., Ott., St.L., Mtl.M., NYR	9	297	87	166	42	18375	879	18	2.87	5	2	3	....	300	11	0	2.20		1929-30	1942-43
Bibeault, Paul	Mtl., Tor., Bos., Chi.	7	214	68	82	21	12890	785	10	3.65	20	6	14	....	1237	71	2	3.44		1940-41	1946-47
Binette, Andre	Mtl.	1	1	1	0	0	60	4	0	4.00	....	....	....	....	....	....	....	....		1954-55	1954-55
Binkley, Les	Pit.	5	196	58	94	34	11046	575	11	3.12	7	5	2	....	428	15	0	2.10		1967-68	1971-72
Bittner, Richard	Bos.	1	1	0	0	1	60	3	0	3.00	....	....	....	....	....	....	....	....		1949-50	1949-50
Blake, Mike	L.A.	3	40	13	5	15	2117	150	0	4.25	....	....	....	....	....	....	....	....		1981-82	1983-84
Boisvert, Gilles	Det.	1	3	0	3	0	180	9	0	3.00	....	....	....	....	....	....	....	....		1959-60	1959-60
Bouchard, Dan	Atl., Cgy., Que., Wpg.	14	655	286	232	113	37919	2061	27	3.26	43	13	30	....	2549	147	1	3.46		1972-73	1985-86
Bourque, Claude	Mtl., Det.	2	62	16	38	8	3830	192	5	3.01	3	1	2	....	188	8	1	2.55		1938-39	1939-40
Boutin, Rollie	Wsh.	3	22	7	10	1	1137	75	0	3.96	....	....	....	....	....	....	....	....		1978-79	1980-81
Bouvrette, Lionel	NYR	1	1	0	1	0	60	6	0	6.00	....	....	....	....	....	....	....	....		1942-43	1942-43
Bower, Johnny	NYR, Tor.	15	552	251	196	90	32077	1347	37	2.52	74	34	35	....	4350	184	5	2.54	4	1953-54	1969-70
Brannigan, Andy	NYA	1	1	0	0	0	7	0	0	0.00	....	....	....	....	....	....	....	....		1940-41	1940-41
Brimsek, Frank	Bos., Chi.	10	514	252	182	80	31210	1404	40	2.70	68	32	36	....	4365	186	2	2.56	2	1938-39	1949-50
Broda, Turk	Tor.	14	629	302	224	101	38173	1609	62	2.53	101	58	42	1	6389	211	13	1.98	5	1936-37	1951-52
Broderick, Ken	Min., Bos.	3	27	11	12	1	1464	74	2	3.03	....	....	....	....	....	....	....	....		1969-70	1974-75
Broderick, Len	Mtl.	1	1	1	0	0	60	2	0	2.00	....	....	....	....	....	....	....	....		1957-58	1957-58
Brodeur, Richard	NYI, Van., Hfd.	9	385	131	176	62	21968	1410	6	3.85	33	13	20	....	2009	111	1	3.32		1979-80	1987-88
Bromley, Gary	Buf., Van.	6	136	54	44	28	7427	425	7	3.43	7	2	5	....	360	25	0	4.17		1973-74	1980-81
Brooks, Arthur	Tor.	1	4	2	1	0	220	23	0	5.75	....	....	....	....	....	....	....	....		1917-18	1917-18
Brooks, Ross	Bos.	3	54	37	7	6	3047	134	4	2.64	1	0	0	....	20	3	0	9.00		1972-73	1974-75
Brophy, Frank	Que.	1	21	3	18	0	1247	148	0	7.05	....	....	....	....	....	....	....	....		1919-20	1919-20
Brown, Andy	Det., Pit.	3	62	22	26	9	3373	213	1	3.79	....	....	....	....	....	....	....	....		1971-72	1973-74
Brown, Ken	Chi.	1	1	0	0	0	18	1	0	3.33	....	....	....	....	....	....	....	....		1970-71	1970-71
Bullock, Bruce	Van.	3	16	3	9	3	927	74	0	4.79	....	....	....	....	....	....	....	....		1972-73	1976-77
Buzinski, Steve	NYR	1	9	2	6	1	560	55	0	5.89	....	....	....	....	....	....	....	....		1942-43	1942-43
Caley, Don	St.L.	1	1	0	0	0	30	3	0	6.00	....	....	....	....	....	....	....	....		1967-68	1967-68
Caprice, Frank	Van.	6	102	31	40	11	5589	391	1	4.20	....	....	....	....	....	....	....	....		1982-83	1987-88
Caron, Jacques	L.A., St.L., Van.	5	72	24	29	11	3846	211	2	3.29	12	4	7	....	639	34	0	3.19		1967-68	1973-74
Carter, Lyle	Cal.	1	15	4	7	0	721	50	0	4.16	....	....	....	....	....	....	....	....		1971-72	1971-72
Chabot, Lorne	NYR, Tor., Mtl., Chi., Mtl.M., NYA	11	411	206	140	65	25309	861	73	2.04	37	13	17	6	2558	64	5	1.50	2	1926-27	1936-37
Chadwick, Ed	Tor., Bos.	6	184	57	92	35	10980	551	14	3.01	....	....	....	....	....	....	....	....		1955-56	1961-62
Champoux, Bob	Det., Cal.	2	17	2	11	3	923	80	0	5.20	1	0	0	....	55	4	0	4.36		1963-64	1973-74
Cheevers, Gerry	Tor., Bos.	13	418	230	94	74	24394	1175	26	2.89	88	47	35	....	5396	242	8	2.69	2	1961-62	1979-80
Clancy, Frank	Tor.	1	1	0	0	0	1	0	0	0.00	....	....	....	....	....	....	....	....		1931-32	1931-32
Cleghorn, Odie	Pit.	1	1	1	0	0	60	2	0	2.00	....	....	....	....	....	....	....	....		1925-26	1925-26
Colvin, Les	Bos.	1	1	0	1	0	60	4	0	4.00	....	....	....	....	....	....	....	....		1948-49	1948-49
Conacher, Charlie	Tor., Det.	13	3	0	0	0	9	0	0	0.00	....	....	....	....	....	....	....	....		1929-30	1940-41
Connell, Alex	Ott., Det., NYA, Mtl.M.	12	417	199	155	59	26030	830	81	1.91	21	9	5	7	1309	26	4	1.19	2	1924-25	1936-37
Corsi, Jim	Edm.	1	26	8	14	3	1366	83	0	3.65	....	....	....	....	....	....	....	....		1979-80	1979-80
Courteau, Maurice	Bos.	1	6	2	4	0	360	33	0	5.50	....	....	....	....	....	....	....	....		1943-44	1943-44
Cox, Abbie	Mtl.M., Det., NYA, Mtl.	3	5	1	1	2	263	11	0	2.51	....	....	....	....	....	....	....	....		1929-30	1935-36
Craig, Jim	Atl., Bos., Min.	3	30	11	10	7	1588	100	0	3.78	....	....	....	....	....	....	....	....		1979-80	1983-84
Crha, Jiri	Tor.	2	69	28	27	11	3942	261	0	3.97	5	0	4	....	186	21	0	6.77		1979-80	1980-81
Crozier, Roger	Det., Buf., Wsh.	14	518	206	197	74	28567	1446	30	3.04	31	14	15	....	1769	82	1	2.78		1963-64	1976-77
Cude, Wilf	Phi., Bos., Chi., Det., Mtl.	10	282	100	129	49	17486	796	24	2.73	19	7	11	1	1317	51	1	2.32		1930-31	1940-41
Cutts, Don	Edm.	1	6	1	2	1	269	16	0	3.57	....	....	....	....	....	....	....	....		1979-80	1979-80
Cyr, Claude	Mtl.	1	1	0	0	0	20	1	0	3.00	....	....	....	....	....	....	....	....		1958-59	1958-59
Dadswell, Doug	Cgy.	2	27	8	8	3	1346	99	0	4.41	....	....	....	....	....	....	....			1986-87	1987-88
Daley, Joe	Pit., Buf., Det.	4	105	34	44	19	5836	326	3	3.35	....	....	....	....	....	....	....	....		1968-69	1971-72
Damore, Nick	Bos.	1	1	0	1	0	60	3	0	3.00	....	....	....	....	....	....	....	....		1941-42	1941-42
D'Amour, Mark	Cgy.	1	15	2	4	2	560	32	0	3.43	....	....	....	....	....	....	....	....		1985-86	1985-86
Daskalakis, Cleon	Bos.	3	12	3	4	1	506	41	0	4.86	....	....	....	....	....	....	....	....		1984-85	1986-87
Davidson, John	St.L., NYR	10	301	123	124	39	17109	1004	7	3.52	31	16	14	....	1862	77	1	2.48		1973-74	1982-83
Decourcy, Robert	NYR	1	1	0	1	0	29	6	0	12.41	....	....	....	....	....	....	....	....		1947-48	1947-48
Defelice, Norman	Bos.	1	10	3	5	2	600	30	0	3.00	....	....	....	....	....	....	....	....		1956-57	1956-57
DeJordy, Denis	Chi., L.A., Mtl., Det.	11	316	124	127	51	17798	929	15	3.13	18	6	9	....	946	55	0	3.49		1962-63	1973-74
Desjardins, Gerry	L.A., Chi., NYI, Buf.	10	331	122	153	44	19014	1042	12	3.29	35	15	15	....	1874	108	0	3.46		1968-69	1977-78
Dickie, Bill	Chi.	1	1	1	0	0	60	3	0	3.00	....	....	....	....	....	....	....	....		1941-42	1941-42
Dion, Connie	Det.	2	38	23	11	4	2280	119	0	3.13	5	1	4	....	300	17	0	3.40		1943-44	1944-45
Dion, Michel	Que., Wpg., Pit.	6	227	60	118	32	12695	898	2	4.24	5	2	3	....	304	22	0	4.34		1979-80	1984-85
Dolson, Clarence	Det.	3	93	35	44	13	5820	192	16	1.98	2	0	2	....	120	7	0	3.50		1928-29	1930-31
Dowie, Bruce	Tor.	1	2	0	1	0	72	4	0	3.33	....	....	....	....	....	....	....	....		1983-84	1983-84
Dryden, Dave	NYR, Chi., Buf., Edm.	9	203	48	57	24	10424	555	9	3.19	3	0	2	....	133	9	0	4.06		1961-62	1979-80
Dryden, Ken	Mtl.	8	397	258	57	74	23352	870	46	2.24	112	80	32	....	6846	274	10	2.40	6	1970-71	1978-79
Dumas, Michel	Chi.	2	8	2	1	2	362	24	0	3.98	1	0	0	....	19	1	0	3.16		1974-75	1976-77
Dupuis, Bob	Edm.	1	1	0	1	0	60	4	0	4.00	....	....	....	....	....	....	....	....		1979-80	1979-80
Durnan, Bill	Mtl.	7	383	208	112	62	22945	901	34	2.36	45	27	18	....	2851	99	2	2.08	2	1943-44	1949-50
Dyck, Ed	Van.	3	49	8	28	5	2453	178	1	4.35	....	....	....	....	....	....	....	....		1971-72	1973-74
Edwards, Don	Buf., Cgy., Tor.	10	459	208	155	77	26181	1449	16	3.32	42	16	21	....	2302	132	1	3.44		1976-77	1985-86
Edwards, Gary	St.L., L.A., Clev., Min., Edm., Pit.	13	286	88	125	43	16002	973	10	3.65	11	5	4	....	537	34	0	3.80		1968-69	1981-82
Edwards, Marv	Pit., Tor., Cal.	4	61	15	34	7	3467	218	2	3.77	....	....	....	....	....	....	....	....		1968-69	1973-74
Edwards, Roy	Det., Pit.	7	236	92	88	38	13109	637	12	2.92	4	0	3	....	206	11	0	3.20		1967-68	1973-74
Eliot, Darren	L.A., Det., Buf.	5	89	25	41	12	4931	377	1	4.59	1	0	0		40	7	0	10.50		1984-85	1988-89
Ellacott, Ken	Van.	1	12	2	3	4	555	41	0	4.43	....	....	....	....	....	....	....	....		1982-83	1982-83
Esposito, Tony	Mtl., Chi.	16	886	423	307	151	52585	2563	76	2.92	99	45	53	....	6017	308	6	3.09	1	1968-69	1983-84
Evans, Claude	Mtl., Bos.	2	5	2	2	1	280	16	0	3.43	....	....	....	....	....	....	....	....		1954-55	1957-58
Farr, Rocky	Buf.	3	19	2	6	3	722	42	0	3.49	....	....	....	....	....	....	....	....		1972-73	1974-75

Name	NHL Teams	NHL Seasons	Regular Schedule GP	W	L	T	Mins	GA	SO	Avg	Playoffs GP	W	L	T	Mins	GA	SO	Avg	NHL Cup Wins	First NHL Season	Last NHL Season
Favell, Doug	Phi., Tor., Col.	12	373	123	153	69	20771	1096	18	3.17	21	5	16	....	1270	66	1	3.12		1967-68	1978-79
Forbes, Jake	Tor., Ham., NYA, Phi.	13	210	84	114	11	12922	594	19	2.76	2	0	2	....	120	7	0	3.50		1919-20	1932-33
Ford, Brian	Que., Pit.	2	11	3	7	0	580	61	0	6.31	....	....	....	....	....	....	....	....		1983-84	1984-85
Fowler, Hec	Bos.	1	7	1	6	0	420	43	0	6.14	....	....	....	....	....	....	....	....		1924-25	1924-25
Francis, Emile	Chi., NYR	6	95	31	52	11	5660	355	1	3.76	....	....	....	....	....	....	....	....		1946-47	1951-52
Franks, Jim	Det., NYR, Bos.	4	43	12	23	7	2580	185	1	4.30	1	0	1	....	30	2	0	4.00	1	1936-37	1943-44
Frederick, Ray	Chi.	1	5	0	4	1	300	22	0	4.40	....	....	....	....	....	....	....	....		1954-55	1954-55
Friesen, Karl	N.J.	1	4	0	2	1	130	16	0	7.38	....	....	....	....	....	....	....	....		1986-87	1986-87
Gamble, Bruce	NYR, Bos., Tor., Phi.	10	327	109	139	47	18442	992	22	3.23	5	0	4	....	206	25	0	7.28		1958-59	1971-72
Gardiner, Bert	NYR, Mtl., Chi., Bos.	6	144	49	68	27	8760	554	3	3.79	9	4	5	....	647	20	0	1.85		1935-36	1943-44
Gardiner, Chuck	Chi.	7	316	112	152	52	19687	664	42	2.02	21	12	6	3	1532	35	5	1.37	1	1927-28	1933-34
Gardner, George	Det., Van.	5	66	16	30	6	3313	207	0	3.75	....	....	....	....	....	....	....	....		1965-66	1971-72
Garrett, John	Hfd., Que., Van.	6	207	68	91	37	11763	837	1	4.27	9	4	3	....	461	33	0	4.30		1979-80	1984-85
Gatherum, Dave	Det.	1	3	2	0	1	180	3	1	1.00	....	....	....	....	....	....	....	....		1953-54	1953-54
Gauthier, Paul	Mtl.	1	1	0	0	1	70	2	0	1.71	....	....	....	....	....	....	....	....		1937-38	1937-38
Gelineau, Jack	Bos., Chi.	4	143	46	64	33	8580	447	7	3.13	4	2	2	....	260	7	1	1.62		1948-49	1953-54
Giacomin, Ed	NYR, Det.	13	610	289	206	97	35693	1675	54	2.82	65	29	35	....	3834	180	1	2.82		1965-66	1977-78
Gilbert, Gilles	Min., Bos., Det.	14	416	182	148	60	23677	1290	18	3.27	32	17	15	....	1919	97	3	3.03		1969-70	1982-83
Gill, Andre	Bos.	1	5	3	2	0	270	13	1	2.89	....	....	....	....	....	....	....	....		1967-68	1967-68
Goodman, Paul	Chi.	3	52	23	20	9	3240	117	6	2.17	3	0	3	....	187	10	0	3.21	1	1937-38	1940-41
Grahame, Ron	Bos., L.A., Que.	4	114	50	43	15	6472	409	5	3.79	4	2	1	....	202	7	0	2.08		1977-78	1980-81
Grant, Ben	Tor., NYA., Bos.	6	50	17	26	4	2990	188	4	3.77	....	....	....	....	....	....	....	....		1928-29	1943-44
Grant, Doug	Det., St.L.	7	77	27	34	8	4199	280	2	4.00	....	....	....	....	....	....	....	....		1973-74	1979-80
Gratton, Gilles	St.L., NYR	2	47	13	18	9	2299	154	0	4.02	....	....	....	....	....	....	....	....		1975-76	1976-77
Gray, Gerry	Det., NYI	2	8	1	5	1	440	35	0	4.77	....	....	....	....	....	....	....	....		1970-71	1972-73
Gray, Harrison	Det.	1	1	0	0	0	40	5	0	730	....	....	....	....	....	....	....	....		1963-64	1963-64
Hainsworth, George	Mtl., Tor.	11	465	246	145	74	29415	937	94	1.91	52	21	26	5	3486	112	8	1.93	2	1926-27	1936-37
Hall, Glenn	Det., Chi., St.L.	18	906	407	327	165	53484	2239	84	2.51	115	49	65	....	6899	321	6	2.79	1	1952-53	1970-71
Hamel, Pierre	Tor., Wpg.	4	69	13	41	7	3766	276	0	4.40	....	....	....	....	....	....	....	....		1974-75	1980-81
Harrison, Paul	Min., Tor., Pit., Buf.	7	109	28	53	8	5806	408	2	4.22	4	0	1	....	157	9	0	3.44		1975-76	1981-82
Head, Don	Bos.	1	38	9	26	3	2280	161	2	4.24	....	....	....	....	....	....	....	....		1961-62	1961-62
Hebert, Sammy	Tor., Ott.	2	4	1	3	0	200	19	0	5.70	....	....	....	....	....	....	....	....	1	1917-18	1923-24
Heinz, Rick	St.L., Van.	5	49	14	19	5	2356	159	2	4.05	1	0	0	....	8	1	0	7.50		1980-81	1984-85
Henderson, John	Bos.	2	46	15	15	15	2700	113	5	2.51	2	0	2	....	120	8	0	4.00		1954-55	1955-56
Henry, Gord	Bos.	4	3	1	2	0	180	5	1	1.67	5	0	4	....	283	21	0	4.45		1948-49	1952-53
Henry, Jim	NYR, Chi., Bos.	9	404	159	178	67	24240	1166	28	2.88	29	11	18	....	1741	81	2	2.79		1941-42	1954-55
Herron, Denis	Pit., K.C., Mtl.	14	462	146	203	76	25608	1579	10	3.70	15	5	10	....	901	50	0	3.33		1972-73	1985-86
Highton, Hec	Chi.	1	24	10	14	0	1440	108	0	4.50	....	....	....	....	....	....	....	....		1943-44	1943-44
Himes, Normie	NYA	2	2	0	0	1	79	3	0	2.28	....	....	....	....	....	....	....	....		1927-28	1928-29
Hodge, Charlie	Mtl., Oak., Van.	13	358	152	124	60	20593	927	24	2.70	16	6	8	....	803	32	2	2.39	1	1954-55	1970-71
Hoganson, Paul	Pit.	1	2	0	1	0	57	7	0	7.37	....	....	....	....	....	....	....	....		1970-71	1970-71
Hogosta, Goran	NYI, Que.	2	22	5	12	3	1208	83	1	4.12	....	....	....	....	....	....	....	....		1977-78	1979-80
Holden, Mark	Mtl., Wpg.	4	8	2	2	1	372	25	0	4.03	....	....	....	....	....	....	....	....		1981-82	1984-85
Holland, Ken	Hfd.	1	1	0	1	0	60	7	0	7.00	....	....	....	....	....	....	....	....		1980-81	1980-81
Holland, Robbie	Pit.	2	44	11	22	9	2513	171	1	4.06	....	....	....	....	....	....	....	....		1979-80	1980-81
Holmes, Harry	Tor., Det.	4	105	41	54	10	6510	264	17	2.43	7	4	3	....	420	26	0	3.71		1917-18	1927-28
Horner, Red	Tor.	1	1	0	0	0	1	1	0	60.00	....	....	....	....	....	....	....	....		1932-33	1932-33
Inness, Gary	Pit., Phi., Wsh.	7	162	58	61	27	8710	494	2	3.40	9	5	4	....	540	24	0	2.67		1973-74	1980-81
Ireland, Randy	Buf.	1	2	0	0	0	30	3	0	6.00	....	....	....	....	....	....	....	....		1978-79	1978-79
Irons, Robbie	St.L.	1	1	0	0	0	3	0	0	0.00	....	....	....	....	....	....	....	....		1968-69	1968-69
Ironstone, Joe	NYA, Tor.	2	2	1	1	0	110	3	0	1.64	....	....	....	....	....	....	....	....		1925-26	1927-28
Jackson, Doug	Chi.	1	6	2	3	1	360	42	0	7.00	....	....	....	....	....	....	....	....		1947-48	1947-48
Jackson, Percy	Bos., NYA, NYR	4	7	1	3	1	392	26	0	3.98	....	....	....	....	....	....	....	....		1931-32	1935-36
Janaszak, Steve	Min., Col.	2	3	0	1	1	160	15	0	5.63	....	....	....	....	....	....	....	....		1979-80	1981-82
Janecyk, Bob	Chi., L.A.	6	110	43	47	13	6250	432	2	4.15	3	0	3	....	184	10	0	3.26		1983-84	1988-89
Jenkins, Roger	NYA	1	1	0	1	0	30	7	0	14.00	....	....	....	....	....	....	....	....		1938-39	1938-39
Jensen, Al	Det., Wsh., L.A.	7	179	95	53	18	9974	557	8	3.35	12	5	5	....	598	32	0	3.21		1980-81	1986-87
Jensen, Darren	Phi.	2	30	15	10	1	1496	95	2	3.81	....	....	....	....	....	....	....	....		1984-85	1985-86
Johnson, Bob	St.L., Pit.	2	24	9	9	1	1059	66	0	3.74	....	....	....	....	....	....	....	....		1972-73	1974-75
Johnston, Eddie	Bos., Tor., St.L., Chi.	16	592	236	256	87	34209	1855	32	3.25	18	7	10	....	1023	57	1	3.34	2	1962-63	1977-78
Junkin, Joe	Bos.	1	1	0	0	0	8	0	0	0.00	....	....	....	....	....	....	....	....		1968-69	1968-69
Kaarela, Jari	Col.	1	5	2	2	0	220	22	0	6.00	....	....	....	....	....	....	....	....		1980-81	1980-81
Kampurri, Hannu	N.J.	1	13	1	10	1	645	54	0	5.02	....	....	....	....	....	....	....	....		1984-85	1984-85
Karakas, Mike	Chi., Mtl.	8	336	114	169	53	20616	1002	28	2.92	23	11	12	....	1434	72	3	3.01	1	1935-36	1945-46
Keans, Doug	L.A., Bos.	9	210	96	64	26	11388	666	4	3.51	9	2	6		432	34	0	4.72		1979-80	1987-88
Keenan, Don	Bos.	1	1	0	1	0	60	4	0	4.00	....	....	....	....	....	....	....	....		1958-59	1958-59
Kerr, Dave	Mtl.M., NYA, NYR	11	426	203	148	75	26519	960	51	2.17	40	18	19	3	2616	76	8	1.74	1	1930-31	1940-41
Kleisinger, Terry	NYR	1	4	0	2	0	191	14	0	4.40	....	....	....	....	....	....	....	....		1985-86	1985-86
Klymkiw, Julian	NYR	1	1	0	0	0	19	2	0	6.32	....	....	....	....	....	....	....	....		1958-59	1958-59
Kurt, Gary	Cal.	1	16	1	7	5	838	60	0	4.30	....	....	....	....	....	....	....	....		1971-72	1971-72
Lacroix, Al	Mtl.	1	5	1	4	0	280	16	0	3.20	....	....	....	....	....	....	....	....		1925-26	1925-26
LaFerriere, Rick	Col.	1	1	0	0	0	20	1	0	3.00	....	....	....	....	....	....	....	....		1981-82	1981-82
Larocque, Michel	Mtl., Tor., Phi., St.L.	11	312	160	89	45	17615	978	17	3.33	14	6	6	....	759	37	1	2.92	4	1973-74	1983-84
Laskowski, Gary	L.A.	2	59	19	27	5	2942	228	0	4.65	....	....	....	....	....	....	....	....		1982-83	1983-84
Laxton, Gord	Pit.	4	17	4	9	0	800	74	0	5.55	....	....	....	....	....	....	....	....		1975-76	1978-79
LeDuc, Albert	Mtl.	1	1	0	0	0	2	1	0	30.00	....	....	....	....	....	....	....	....		1931-32	1931-32
Legris, Claude	Det.	2	4	0	1	1	91	4	0	2.64	....	....	....	....	....	....	....	....		1980-81	1981-82
Lehman, Hugh	Chi.	2	48	20	24	4	3047	136	6	2.68	2	0	1	1	120	10	0	5.00		1926-27	1927-28
Lessard, Mario	L.A.	6	240	92	97	39	13529	843	9	3.74	20	6	12	....	1136	83	0	4.38		1978-79	1983-84
Levasseur, Louis	Min.	1	1	0	1	0	60	7	0	7.00	....	....	....	....	....	....	....	....		1979-80	1979-80
Levinsky, Alex	Tor.	1	1	0	0	0	1	1	0	60.00	....	....	....	....	....	....	....	....		1932-33	1932-33
Lindbergh, Pelle	Phi.	5	157	87	49	15	9151	503	7	3.30	23	12	10	....	1214	63	3	3.11		1981-82	1985-86
Lindsay, Bert	Mtl.W., Tor.	2	20	6	14	0	2219	118	0	3.19	....	....	....	....	....	....	....	....		1917-18	1918-19
Lockett, Ken	Van.	2	55	13	15	8	2348	131	2	3.35	1	0	1	....	60	6	0	6.00		1974-75	1975-76
Lockhart, Howie	Tor., Que., Ham., Bos.	5	57	17	39	0	3371	282	1	5.02	....	....	....	....	....	....	....	....		1919-20	1924-25
LoPresti, Pete	Min., Edm.	6	175	43	102	20	9858	668	5	4.07	2	0	2	....	77	6	0	4.68		1974-75	1980-81
LoPresti, Sam	Chi.	2	74	30	38	6	4530	236	4	3.13	8	3	5	....	530	17	1	1.92		1940-41	1941-42
Loustel, Ron	Wpg.	1	1	0	1	0	60	10	0	10.00	....	....	....	....	....	....	....	....		1980-81	1980-81
Low, Ron	Tor., Wsh., Det., Que., Edm., NJ	11	382	102	203	37	20502	1463	4	4.28	7	1	6	....	452	29	0	3.85		1972-73	1984-85
Lozinski, Larry	Det.	1	30	6	11	7	1459	105	0	4.32	....	....	....	....	....	....	....	....		1980-81	1980-81
Lumley, Harry	Det., NYR, Chi., Tor., Bos.	16	804	332	324	143	48107	2210	71	2.76	76	29	47	....	4759	199	7	2.51	1	1943-44	1959-60
MacKenzie, Shawn	N.J.	1	4	0	1	0	130	15	0	6.92	....	....	....	....	....	....	....	....		1982-83	1982-83
Maniago, Cesare	Tor., Mtl., NYR, Min., Van.	15	568	189	261	96	32570	1774	30	3.27	36	15	21	....	2245	100	3	2.67		1960-61	1977-78
Marios, Jean	Tor., Chi.	2	3	1	2	0	180	15	0	5.00	....	....	....	....	....	....	....	....		1943-44	1953-54
Martin, Seth	St.L.	1	30	8	10	7	1552	67	1	2.59	2	0	0	....	73	5	0	4.11		1967-68	1967-68
Mattson, Markus	Wpg., Min., L.A.	4	92	21	46	14	5007	343	6	4.11	....	....	....	....	....	....	....	....		1979-80	1983-84
May, Darrell	St.L.	2	6	1	5	0	364	31	0	5.11	....	....	....	....	....	....	....	....		1985-86	1987-88
Mayer, Gilles	Tor.	4	9	1	7	1	540	25	0	2.78	....	....	....	....	....	....	....	....		1949-50	1955-56
McAuley, Ken	NYR	2	96	17	64	15	5740	537	1	5.61	....	....	....	....	....	....	....	....		1943-44	1944-45
McCartan, Jack	NYR	2	12	3	7	2	680	43	1	3.79	....	....	....	....	....	....	....	....		1959-60	1960-61
McCool, Frank	Tor.	2	72	34	31	7	4320	242	4	3.36	13	8	5	....	807	30	4	2.23	1	1944-45	1945-46
McDuffe, Pete	St.L., NYR, K.C., Det.	5	57	11	36	6	3207	218	0	4.08	1	0	1	....	60	7	0	7.00		1971-72	1975-76
McGrattan, Tom	Det.	1	1	0	0	0	8	0	0	0.00	....	....	....	....	....	....	....	....		1947-48	1947-48
McKenzie, Bill	Det., K.C., Col.	6	91	18	49	13	4776	326	2	4.10	....	....	....	....	....	....	....	....		1973-74	1979-80
McLachlan, Murray	Tor.	1	2	0	1	0	25	4	0	9.60	....	....	....	....	....	....	....	....		1970-71	1970-71
McLelland, Dave	Van.	1	2	1	1	0	120	10	0	5.00	....	....	....	....	....	....	....	....		1972-73	1972-73
McLeod, Don	Det., Phi.	2	18	3	10	1	879	74	0	5.05	....	....	....	....	....	....	....	....		1970-71	1971-72
McLeod, Jim	St.L.	1	16	6	6	4	880	44	0	3.00	....	....	....	....	....	....	....	....		1971-72	1971-72
McNamara, Gerry	Tor.	2	7	2	2	1	323	15	0	2.79	....	....	....	....	....	....	....	....		1960-61	1969-70
McNeil, Gerry	Mtl.	7	276	119	105	52	16535	650	28	2.36	35	17	18	....	2284	72	5	1.89	1	1947-48	1956-57
McRae, Gord	Tor.	5	71	21	32	10	3799	221	1	3.49	8	2	5	....	454	22	0	2.91		1972-73	1977-78
Meloche, Gilles	Chi., Cal., Cle., Min., Pit.	18	788	270	351	131	45401	2756	20	3.64	45	21	19	....	2464	143	2	3.48		1970-71	1987-88
Micalef, Corrado	Det.	5	1i3	26	59	15	5794	409	2	4.24	3	0	0	....	49	8	0	9.80		1981-82	1985-86

			Regular Schedule								Playoffs										
Name	NHL Teams	NHL Seasons	GP	W	L	T	Mins	GA	SO	Avg	GP	W	L	T	Mins	GA	SO	Avg	NHL Cup Wins	First NHL Season	Last NHL Season
Middlebrook, Lindsay	Wpg., Min., N.J., Edm.	4	37	3	23	6	1845	152	0	4.94	....	....	....	....	....	....	....	....		1979-80	1982-83
Millar, Joe	Bos.	1	6	1	3	2	360	25	0	4.17	....	....	....	....	....	....	....	....		1957-58	1957-58
Miller, Joe	NYA, Pit., Phi.	4	130	24	90	16	7981	386	16	2.90	3	2	1	....	180	3	1	1.00		1927-28	1930-31
Mio, Eddie	Edm., NYR, Det.	7	192	83	85	31	12299	822	6	4.01	17	9	7	....	986	63	0	3.83		1979-80	1985-86
Mitchell, Ivan	Tor.	3	21	11	9	0	1232	93	0	4.53	....	....	....	....	....	....	....	....	1	1919-20	1921-22
Moffatt, Mike	Bos.	3	19	7	7	2	979	70	0	4.29	11	6	5	....	663	38	0	3.44		1981-82	1983-84
Moore, Alfie	NYA, Det., Chi.,	4	21	7	14	0	1290	81	1	3.77	3	1	2	....	180	7	0	2.33	1	1936-37	1939-40
Moore, Robbie	Phi., Wsh.	2	6	3	1	1	257	8	2	1.87	5	3	2	....	268	18	0	4.03		1978-79	1982-83
Morisette, Jean	Mtl.	1	1	0	1	0	36	4	0	6.67	....	....	....	....	....	....	....	....		1963-64	1963-64
Mowers, Johnny	Det.	4	152	65	55	25	9350	399	15	2.56	32	19	13	....	2000	85	2	2.55	1	1940-41	1946-47
Mrazek, Jerry	Phi.	1	1	0	0	0	6	1	0	10.00	....	....	....	....	....	....	....	....		1975-76	1975-76
Mummery, Harry	Que., Ham.	2	4	2	1	0	191	20	0	6.28	....	....	....	....	....	....	....	....		1919-20	1921-22
Murphy, Hal	Mtl.	1	1	1	0	0	60	4	0	4.00	....	....	....	....	....	....	....	....		1952-53	1952-53
Murray, Tom	Mtl.	1	1	0	1	0	60	4	0	4.00	....	....	....	....	....	....	....	....		1929-30	1929-30
Mylnikov, Sergei	Que.	1	10	1	7	2	568	47	0	4.96	....	....	....	....	....	....	....	....		1989-90	1989-90
Myre, Phil	Mtl., Atl., St.L., Phi., Col., Buf.	14	439	149	198	76	25220	1482	14	3.53	12	6	5	....	747	41	1	3.29		1969-70	1982-83
Newton, Cam	Pit.	2	16	4	7	1	814	51	0	3.76	....	....	....	....	....	....	....	....		1970-71	1972-73
Norris, Jack	Bos., Chi., L.A.	4	58	19	26	4	3119	202	2	3.89	....	....	....	....	....	....	....	....		1964-65	1970-71
Oleschuk, Bill	K.C., Col.	4	55	7	28	10	2835	188	1	3.98	....	....	....	....	....	....	....	....		1975-76	1979-80
Olesevich, Dan	NYR	1	1	0	0	1	40	2	0	3.00	....	....	....	....	....	....	....	....		1961-62	1961-62
Ouimet, Ted	St.L.	1	1	0	1	0	60	2	0	2.00	....	....	....	....	....	....	....	....		1968-69	1968-69
Pageau, Paul	L.A.	1	1	0	1	0	60	8	0	8.00	....	....	....	....	....	....	....	....		1980-81	1980-81
Paille, Marcel	NYR	7	107	33	52	21	6342	362	2	3.42	....	....	....	....	....	....	....	....		1957-58	1964-65
Palmateer, Mike	Tor., Wsh.	8	356	149	138	52	20131	1183	17	3.53	29	12	17	....	1765	89	2	3.03		1976-77	1983-84
Pang, Darren	Chi.	3	81	27	35	7	4252	287	0	4.05	6	1	3	....	250	18	0	4.32		1984-85	1988-89
Parent, Bernie	Bos., Tor., Phi.	13	608	270	197	121	35136	1493	55	2.55	71	38	33	....	4302	174	6	2.43	2	1965-66	1978-79
Parent, Bob	Tor.	2	3	0	2	0	160	15	0	5.63	....	....	....	....	....	....	....	....		1981-82	1982-83
Parro, Dave	Wsh.	4	77	21	36	10	4015	274	2	4.09	....	....	....	....	....	....	....	....		1980-81	1983-84
Patrick, Lester	NYR	....	....	....	....	....	....	....	....	....	1	1	0	0	46	1	0	1.30	1	1927-28	1927-28
Pelletier, Marcel	Chi., NYR	2	8	1	6	1	395	33	0	5.01	....	....	....	....	....	....	....	....		1950-51	1962-63
Penney, Steve	Mtl., Wpg.	5	91	35	38	12	5194	313	1	3.62	27	15	12	....	1604	72	4	2.69		1983-84	1987-88
Perreault, Robert	Mtl., Det., Bos.	3	31	8	16	6	1833	106	2	3.47	....	....	....	....	....	....	....	....		1955-56	1962-63
Pettie, Jim	Bos.	3	21	9	7	2	1157	71	1	3.68	....	....	....	....	....	....	....	....		1976-77	1978-79
Plante, Jacques	Mtl., NYR, St.L., Tor., Bos.	18	837	434	246	137	49553	1965	82	2.38	112	71	37	....	6651	241	15	2.17	5	1952-53	1972-73
Plasse, Michel	St.L., Mtl., K.C., Pit., Col., Que.	11	299	92	136	54	16760	1058	2	3.79	4	1	2	....	195	9	1	2.77	1	1970-71	1981-82
Plaxton, Hugh	Mtl.M.	1	1	0	1	0	59	5	0	5.08	....	....	....	....	....	....	....	....		1932-33	1932-33
Pronovost, Claude	Bos., Mtl.	2	3	1	1	0	120	7	1	3.50	....	....	....	....	....	....	....	....		1955-56	1958-59
Pusey, Chris	Det.	1	1	0	0	0	40	3	0	4.50	....	....	....	....	....	....	....	....		1985-86	1985-86
Rayner, Chuck	NYA, Bro., NYR	10	424	138	209	77	25491	1294	25	3.05	18	9	9	....	1134	46	1	2.43		1940-41	1952-53
Redquest, Greg	Pit.	1	1	0	0	0	13	3	0	13.85	....	....	....	....	....	....	....	....		1977-78	1977-78
Reece, Dave	Bos.	1	14	7	5	2	777	43	2	3.32	....	....	....	....	....	....	....	....		1975-76	1975-76
Resch, Glenn	NYI, Col., N.J., Phi.	14	571	231	224	82	32279	1761	26	3.27	41	17	17	....	2044	85	2	2.50	1	1973-74	1986-87
Rheaume, Herb	Mtl.	1	31	10	19	1	1889	92	0	2.97	....	....	....	....	....	....	....	....		1925-26	1925-26
Ricci, Nick	Pit.	4	19	7	12	0	1087	79	0	4.36	....	....	....	....	....	....	....	....		1979-80	1982-83
Richardson, Terry	Det., St.L.	5	20	3	11	0	906	85	0	5.63	....	....	....	....	....	....	....	....		1973-74	1978-79
Ridley, Curt	NYR, Van., Tor.	6	104	27	47	16	5498	355	1	3.87	2	0	2	....	120	8	0	4.00		1974-75	1980-81
Riggin, Denis	Det.	2	18	5	10	2	985	54	1	3.29	....	....	....	....	....	....	....	....		1959-60	1962-63
Riggin, Pat	Atl., Cgy., Wsh., Bos., Pit.	9	350	153	120	52	19872	1135	11	3.43	25	8	13	....	1336	72	0	3.23		1979-80	1987-88
Ring, Bob	Bos.	1	1	0	0	0	34	4	0	7.06	....	....	....	....	....	....	....	....		1965-66	1965-66
Rivard, Fern	Min.	4	55	9	20	7	2865	190	2	3.98	....	....	....	....	....	....	....	....		1968-69	1974-75
Roach, John	Tor., NYR, Det.	14	491	218	204	69	30423	1246	58	2.46	34	15	16	3	2206	69	8	1.88	1	1921-22	1934-35
Roberts, Moe	Bos., NYA, Chi.	4	10	2	5	0	506	31	0	3.68	....	....	....	....	....	....	....	....		1925-26	1951-52
Robertson, Earl	NYA, Bro., Det.	6	190	60	95	34	11820	575	16	2.92	15	6	7	....	995	29	2	1.75	1	1936-37	1941-42
Rollins, Al	Tor., Chi., NYR	9	430	138	205	84	25717	1196	28	2.79	13	6	7	....	755	30	0	2.38	1	1949-50	1959-60
Romano, Roberto	Pit., Bos.	5	125	45	64	7	7046	474	4	4.04	....	....	....	....	....	....	....	....		1982-83	1986-87
Rupp, Pat	Det.	1	1	0	1	0	60	4	0	4.00	....	....	....	....	....	....	....	....		1963-64	1963-64
Rutherford, Jim	Det., Pit., Tor., L.A.	13	457	150	227	59	25895	1576	14	3.65	8	2	5	....	440	28	0	3.82		1970-71	1982-83
Rutledge, Wayne	L.A.	3	82	22	30	5	4325	241	2	3.34	8	2	2	....	378	20	0	3.17		1967-68	1969-70
St.Croix, Rick	Phi., Tor.	8	129	49	54	18	7275	450	2	3.71	11	4	6	....	562	29	1	3.10		1977-78	1984-85
Sands, Charlie	Mtl.	1	1	0	0	0	25	5	0	12.00	....	....	....	....	....	....	....	....		1939-40	1939-40
Sands, Mike	Min.	2	6	0	5	0	302	26	0	5.17	....	....	....	....	....	....	....	....		1984-85	1986-87
Sauve, Bob	Buf., Det., Chi., N.J.	12	405	178	149	53	22991	1321	8	3.45	34	15	16		1850	95	4	3.08		1976-77	1987-88
Sawchuk, Terry	Det., Bos., Tor., L.A., NYR	21	971	435	337	188	57205	2401	103	2.52	106	54	48	....	6291	267	12	2.64	3	1949-50	1969-70
Schaefer, Joe	NYR	2	2	0	1	0	86	8	0	5.58	....	....	....	....	....	....	....	....		1959-60	1960-61
Sevigny, Richard	Mtl., Que.	8	176	90	44	20	9485	507	5	3.21	6	0	3	....	208	13	0	3.75	1	1979-80	1986-87
Shields, Al	NYA	1	2	0	0	0	41	9	0	13.17	....	....	....	....	....	....	....	....		1931-32	1931-32
Simmons, Don	Bos., Tor., NYR	11	247	100	104	39	14436	705	20	2.93	24	13	11	....	1436	64	3	2.67	1	1956-57	1968-69
Simmons, Gary	Cal., Clev., L.A.	4	107	30	57	15	6162	366	5	3.56	1	0	0	....	20	1	0	3.00		1974-75	1977-78
Skidmore, Paul	St.L.	1	2	1	1	0	120	6	0	3.00	....	....	....	....	....	....	....	....		1981-82	1981-82
Skorodenski, Warren	Chi., Edm.	5	35	12	11	4	1732	100	2	3.46	2	0	0	....	33	6	0	10.91		1981-82	1987-88
Smith, Al	Tor., Pit., Det., Buf., Hfd., Col.	10	233	68	99	36	12752	735	10	3.46	6	1	4	....	317	21	0	3.97		1965-66	1980-81
Smith, Billy	L.A., NYI	18	680	305	233	105	38431	2031	22	3.17	132	88	36		7645	348	5	2.73	4	1971-72	1988-89
Smith, Gary	Tor., Oak., Cal., Chi., Van., Min., Wsh., Wpg.	14	532	152	237	67	29619	1675	26	3.39	20	5	13	....	1153	62	1	3.23		1965-66	1979-80
Smith, Norman	Mtl.M., Det.	8	199	81	83	35	12297	475	17	2.32	12	9	2	....	880	18	3	1.23	2	1931-32	1944-45
Sneddon, Bob	Cal.	1	5	0	2	0	225	21	0	5.60	....	....	....	....	....	....	....	....		1970-71	1970-71
Soetaert, Doug	NYR, Wpg., Mtl.	12	284	110	103	44	15583	1030	6	3.97	5	1	2	....	180	14	0	4.67	1	1975-76	1986-87
Spooner, Red	Pit.	1	1	0	1	0	60	6	0	6.00	....	....	....	....	....	....	....	....		1929-30	1929-30
Staniowski, Ed	St.L., Wpg., Hfd.	10	219	67	104	21	12075	818	2	4.06	8	1	6	....	428	28	0	3.92		1975-76	1984-85
Starr, Harold	Mtl.M.	1	1	0	0	0	3	0	0	0.00	....	....	....	....	....	....	....	....		1931-32	1931-32
Stein, Phil	Tor.	1	1	0	0	1	70	2	0	1.71	....	....	....	....	....	....	....	....		1939-40	1939-40
Stephenson, Wayne	St.L., Phi., Wsh.	10	328	146	93	46	18343	937	14	3.06	26	11	12	....	1522	79	2	3.11	1	1971-72	1980-81
Stevenson, Doug	NYR, Chi.	2	8	2	6	0	480	39	0	4.88	....	....	....	....	....	....	....	....		1944-45	1945-46
Stewart, Charles	Bos.	3	77	31	41	5	4737	194	10	2.46	....	....	....	....	....	....	....	....		1924-25	1926-27
Stewart, Jim	Bos.	1	1	0	1	0	20	5	0	15.00	....	....	....	....	....	....	....	....		1979-80	1979-80
Stuart, Herb	Det.	1	3	0	1	0	180	5	0	1.67	....	....	....	....	....	....	....	....		1926-27	1926-27
Sylvestri, Don	Bos.	1	3	0	0	2	102	6	0	3.53	....	....	....	....	....	....	....	....		1984-85	1984-85
Tataryn, Dave	NYR	1	2	1	1	0	80	10	0	7.50	....	....	....	....	....	....	....	....		1976-77	1976-77
Taylor, Bobby	Phi., Pit.	5	46	15	17	6	2268	155	0	4.10	....	....	....	....	....	....	....	....	1	1971-72	1975-76
Teno, Harvey	Det.	1	5	2	3	0	3.00	15	0	3.00	....	....	....	....	....	....	....	....		1938-39	1938-39
Thomas, Wayne	Mtl., Tor., NYR	8	243	103	93	34	13768	766	10	3.34	15	6	8	....	849	50	1	3.53		1972-73	1980-81
Thompson, Tiny	Bos., Det.	12	553	284	194	75	34174	1183	81	2.08	44	20	22	....	2970	93	7	1.88	1	1928-29	1939-40
Tremblay, Vince	Tor., Pit.	5	58	12	26	8	2785	223	1	4.80	....	....	....	....	....	....	....	....		1979-80	1983-84
Tucker, Ted	Cal.	1	5	1	1	1	177	10	0	3.39	....	....	....	....	....	....	....	....		1973-74	1973-74
Turner, Joe	Det.	1	1	0	0	1	60	3	0	3.00	....	....	....	....	....	....	....	....		1941-42	1941-42
Vachon, Rogatien	Mtl., L.A., Det., Bos.	16	795	355	291	115	46298	2310	51	2.99	48	23	23	....	2876	133	2	2.77	3	1966-67	1981-82
Veisor, Mike	Chi., Hfd., Wpg.	10	139	41	62	26	7806	532	5	4.09	4	0	2	....	180	15	0	5.00		1973-74	1983-84
Vezina, Georges	Mtl.	9	191	105	80	5	11564	633	13	3.28	26	19	6	....	1596	74	4	2.78	2	1917-18	1925-26
Villemure, Gilles	NYR, Chi.	10	205	98	65	27	11581	542	13	2.81	14	5	5	....	656	32	0	2.93		1963-64	1976-77
Wakely, Ernie	Mtl., St.L.	5	113	41	42	17	6344	290	8	2.79	10	2	6	....	509	37	1	4.36		1962-63	1971-72
Walsh, James	Mtl.M., NYA	7	108	48	43	16	6461	250	12	2.32	8	2	4	2	570	16	2	1.68		1926-27	1932-33
Watt, Jim	St.L.	1	1	0	0	0	20	2	0	6.00	....	....	....	....	....	....	....	....		1973-74	1973-74
Wetzel, Carl	Det., Min.	2	7	1	3	1	302	22	0	4.37	....	....	....	....	....	....	....	....		1964-65	1967-68
Wilson, Dunc	Phi., Van., Tor., NYR, Pit.	10	287	80	150	33	15851	988	8	3.74	....	....	....	....	....	....	....	....		1969-70	1978-79
Wilson, Lefty	Det., Tor., Bos.	3	3	0	0	1	85	1	0	0.71	....	....	....	....	....	....	....	....		1953-54	1957-58
Winkler, Hal	NYR, Bos.	2	75	35	26	14	4739	126	21	1.60	10	2	3	5	640	18	2	1.69		1926-27	1927-28
Wolfe, Bernie	Wsh.	4	120	20	61	21	6104	424	1	4.17	....	....	....	....	....	....	....	....		1975-76	1978-79
Woods, Alec	NYA	1	1	0	1	0	70	3	0	2.57	....	....	....	....	....	....	....	....		1936-37	1936-37
Worsley, Gump	NYR, Mtl., Min.	21	862	335	353	150	50232	2432	43	2.90	70	41	25	....	4081	192	5	2.82	4	1952-53	1973-74
Worters, Roy	Pit., NYA, Mtl.	12	484	171	233	68	30175	1143	66	2.27	11	3	6	2	690	24	3	2.09		1925-26	1936-37
Worthy, Chris	Oak., Cal.	3	26	5	10	4	1326	98	0	4.43	....	....	....	....	....	....	....	....		1968-69	1970-71
Young, Doug	Det.	1	1	0	0	0	21	1	0	2.86	....	....	....	....	....	....	....	....		1933-34	1933-34
Zanier, Mike	Edm.	1	3	1	1	1	185	12	0	3.89	....	....	....	....	....	....	....	....		1984-85	1984-85

THE NATIONAL HOCKEY LEAGUE IS PLEASED TO PRESENT A...

NEW COMMEMORATIVE BOOK AND VIDEO

MARKING THE 75TH ANNIVERSARY OF THE NHL.

THE OFFICIAL
National Hockey League 75th Anniversary Commemorative Book

The objective for this special book was simple: to create the most comprehensive survey and celebration of the game of hockey ever produced. The result is a deluxe, large-format, hard-cover book that makes the game and its history come to life by combining superb color and black and white photography with text, anecdotes, behind-the-scenes information, and special features written by some of the game's most respected and best-known chroniclers.

The entire scope of NHL hockey is described and depicted in this book, including the formation of the league, the evolution of rules, the growth of dynasty teams, the first superstars, the Stanley Cup, expansion, the Entry Draft, and international play. The book is packed with insights that stem from first-hand knowledge of the events described. It's a lifetime record of three-quarters of a century of NHL play

The Official National Hockey League 75th Anniversary Commemorative Book,
9½" x 11", 352 pages, hard cover. 200 color, 100 black and white photographs. $50.00 per copy.

The Official Video of the NHL's 75th Anniversary
Hockey, Heroes and History

Molstar Communications in cooperation with the NHL screened hundreds of hockey games on film and videotape in order to assemble this documentary history of the National Hockey League.

NHL Anniversary Ambassador and five hundred goal-scorer Lanny McDonald hosts the presentation as it describes the formation and growth of the league, the golden era of what has come to be known as the "original six" teams, and the emergence of today's high-tempo high-skilled hockey. Lanny is ably assisted by narrators Dick Irvin and Brian McFarlane who add *Hockey Night In Canada's* expert touch to the production.

Also featured are modern on-ice highlights and rare vintage footage that stretches back to the league's earliest days. Combined, this game action provides a rare opportunity to compare NHL play in nine different decades.

Hockey, Heroes and History videocassette. 87 minutes. VHS format. $18.99 per copy.

• RESERVATION FORM •

Send me _____ copies of the *NHL 75th Anniversary Commemorative Book.*

Canada: $50.00 plus $6.71 for postage, handling and GST   **TOTAL:** $56.71 per copy

USA: $50.00 plus $4.95 for postage and handling.   **TOTAL:** $54.95 per copy

Overseas: $50.00CDN plus $8.50 for postage and handling   **TOTAL:** $58.50CDN per copy

Send me _____ copies of the NHL videocassette *Hockey, Heroes and History.*

Canada: $18.99 plus $5.61 for postage, handling and GST   **TOTAL:** $24.60 per copy

Ontario residents please add 8% PST of $1.52   **TOTAL:** $26.12 per copy

USA: $18.99 plus $5.00 for postage and handling.   **TOTAL:** $23.99 per copy

Overseas: $18.99CDN plus $8.00 for postage and handling   **TOTAL:** $26.99CDN per copy

❏ Enclosed is my cheque or money order

Charge my   ❏ MasterCard   ❏ Visa   ❏ AmEx

CREDIT CARD # _____   EXPIRY _____

SIGNATURE _____

NAME _____

ADDRESS _____

CITY _____ PROVINCE/STATE _____ POSTAL/ZIP CODE _____

To order, mail to... 194 Dovercourt Road, Toronto, Ontario, Canada M6J 3C8
Or order by FAX with your credit card: (416) 531-3939, open 24 hours

TO ORDER BY PHONE:
1-800-563-0077
*VISA, MC, AMEX
CANADA & U.S.
OPEN 24 HOURS*

Notes

1990-91 Transactions

August, 1990

15 - **Shawn McCosh** traded from Detroit to Los Angeles for future considerations.

20 - **Ken Hammond** traded from Toronto to Boston for cash.

21 - **Ken Hodge. Jr.** traded from Minnesota to Boston for future considerations.

September

4 - **Claude Lemieux** traded from Montreal to New Jersey for **Sylvain Turgeon.**

- **Craig Ludwig** traded from Montreal to NY Islanders for **Gerald Diduck.**

6 - **Daniel Berthiaume** traded from Minnesota to Los Angeles for **Craig Duncanson.**

- **Bob Brooke** traded from New Jersey to Winnipeg for **Laurie Boschman.**

7 - **David Mackey** traded from Minnesota to Vancouver for future considerations.

30 - **Dave Tippett** traded from Hartford to Washington for future considerations.

- **Mike Donnelly** traded from Buffalo to Los Angeles for **Mikko Makela.**

- **Peter Taglianetti** traded from Winnipeg to Minnesota for future considerations.

- **Bill Houlder** traded from Washington to Buffalo for **Shawn Anderson.**

October

1 - **NHL Waiver Draft**

Player	Claimed by	From
Wayne Van Dorp	Quebec	Chicago
Bengt Gustafsson	Detroit	Washington
Shawn Anderson	Quebec	Washington
Randy Gregg	Vancouver	Edmonton
Rod Buskas	Los Angeles	Pittsburgh
Mario Marois	St. Louis	Quebec
Aaron Broten	Quebec	Minnesota
Bob Bassen	St. Louis	Chicago

3 - **Joel Quenneville** traded from Hartford to Washington for cash.

10 - **Martin Desjardins** traded from Montreal to Chicago for future considerations.

11 - **Todd Richards** traded from Montreal to Hartford for future considerations.

22 - **Vladimir Ruzicka** traded from Edmonton to Boston for **Greg Hawgood.**

26 - **Brian Glynn** traded from Calgary to Minnesota for **Frantisek Musil.**

27 - **Gordie Roberts** traded from St. Louis to Pittsburgh for future considerations.

30 - **Marc Bergevin** traded from NY Islanders to Hartford for future considerations.

November

7 - **Doug Smail** traded from Winnipeg to Minnesota for **Don Barber.**

- **Brian Hayward** traded from Montreal to Minnesota for **Jayson More.**

9 - **Steve Bancroft** traded from Toronto to Boston for **Rob Cimetta.**

- **John McIntyre** traded from Toronto to Los Angeles for **Mike Krushelnyski.**

10 - **Dave Ellett** and **Paul Fenton** traded from Winnipeg to Toronto for **Ed Olczyk** and **Mark Osborne.**

- **Max Middendorf** traded from Quebec to Edmonton for Edmontons's 9th round choice in 1991 Entry Draft (**Brent Brekke**).

13 - **Doug Crossman** traded from NY Islanders to Hartford for **Ray Ferraro.**

17 - **Scott Pearson** and Toronto's 2nd round draft choices in the 1991 Entry Draft (pick later transferred to Washington — **Éric Lavigne**) and 1992 Entry Draft traded from Toronto to Quebec for **Aaron Broten, Lucien Deblois** and **Michel Petit.**

22 - **Bruce Bell** traded from Edmonton to Minnesota for **Kari Takko.**

27 - **Lee Norwood** and future considerations traded from Detroit to New Jersey for **Paul Ysebaert.**

December

11 - **Chris Dahlquist** and **Jim Johnson** traded from Pittsburgh to Minnesota for **Larry Murphy** and **Peter Taglianetti**.

13 - **Jim Kyte** traded from Pittsburgh to Calgary for **Jiri Hrdina**.

14 - **Mike Eagles** traded from Chicago to Winnipeg for Winnipeg's 4th round choice in 1991 Entry Draft (**Igor Kravchuk**).

17 - **Brian Curran** and **Lou Franceschetti** traded from Toronto to Buffalo for **Mike Foligno** and Buffalo's 8th round choice in 1991 Entry Draft (**Thomas Kucharcik**).

21 - **Scott Young** traded from Hartford to Pittsburgh for **Rob Brown**.

January 1991

12 - **Gerald Diduck** traded from Montreal to Vancouver for Vancouver's 4th round draft choice in 1991 Entry Draft (**Vladimir Vujtek**).

- **Tom Kurvers** traded from Toronto to Vancouver for **Brian Bradley**.

16 - **Peter Zezel** and **Bob Rouse** traded from Washington to Toronto for **Al Iafrate**.

- **Petri Skriko** traded from Vancouver to Boston for Boston's 2nd round draft choice in 1992 Entry Draft.

17 - **Joe Cirella** traded from Quebec to NY Rangers for **Aaron Miller** and NY Rangers' 5th round draft choice in 1991 Entry Draft (**Bill Lindsay**).

21 - **John Tucker** traded from Buffalo to NY Islanders for future considerations.

22 - **Rudy Poeschek** traded from NY Rangers to Winnipeg for **Guy Larose**.

- **Brian Blad** traded from Toronto to Vancouver for **Todd Hawkins**.

24 - **Paul Fenton** and **John Kordic** traded from Toronto to Washington for Washington's 5th round draft choice in 1991 Entry Draft (**Alexei Kudashov**).

- **Paul Fenton** traded from Washington to Calgary for **Ken Sabourin**.

29 - **Jacques Cloutier** traded from Chicago to Quebec for **Tony McKegney**.

February

4 - **Herb Raglan**, **Tony Twist** and **Andy Rymsha** traded from St. Louis to Quebec for **Darin Kimble**.

- **Greg Paslawski** traded from Winnipeg to Buffalo for future considerations.

- **Brad Marsh** traded from Toronto to Detroit for Detroit's 8th round choice in 1991 Entry Draft (**Robb McIntyre**).

20 - **Doug Crossman** traded from Hartford to Detroit for **Doug Houda**.

27 - **Tom Draper** traded from Winnipeg to St. Louis for future considerations.

March

4 - **Ron Francis**, **Grant Jennings** and **Ulf Samuelsson** traded from Hartford to Pittsburgh for **John Cullen**, **Jeff Parker** and **Zarley Zalapski**.

5 - **Allan Bester** traded from Toronto to Detroit for Detroit's 6th round draft choice in 1991 Entry Draft (**Alexander Kuzminsky**).

- **Geoff Courtnall**, **Robert Dirk**, **Sergio Momesso**, **Cliff Ronning** and future considerations traded from St. Louis to Vancouver for **Dan Quinn** and **Garth Butcher**.

- **Mark Hunter** traded from Calgary to Hartford for **Carey Wilson**.

- **Mark Pederson** traded from Montreal to Philadelphia for Philadelphia's 2nd round draft choice in 1991 Entry Draft (**Jim Campbell**) and future considerations.

- **Keith Osborne** traded from St. Louis to Toronto for **Darren Veitch** and future considerations.

- **Ken Priestlay** traded from Buffalo to Pittsburgh for **Tony Tanti**.

- **Dana Murzyn** traded from Calgary to Vancouver for **Ron Stern**, **Kevan Guy** and future considerations.

- **Kim Issel** traded from Edmonton to Pittsburgh for **Brad Aitken**.

- **Steve Weeks** traded from Vancouver to Buffalo for future considerations and cash.

- **Marc Bureau** traded from Calgary to Minnesota for Minnesota's 3rd round choice in 1991 Entry Draft (**Sandy McCarthy**).

- **Joey Kocur** and **Per Djoos** traded from Detroit to NY Rangers for **Kevin Miller**, **Jim Cummins** and **Dennis Vial**.

- **Bobby Reynolds** traded from Toronto to Washington for **Robert Mendel**.

- **Mike McNeill** and **Ryan McGill** traded from Chicago to Quebec for **Paul Gillis** and **Daniel Vincelette**.

- **Ilkka Sinisalo** traded from Minnesota to Los Angeles for Los Angeles' 8th round choice in 1991 Entry Draft (**Michael Burkett**).

May

21 - **Bob Joyce**, **Tyler Larter** and **Kent Paynter** traded from Washington to Winnipeg for **Craig Duncanson**, **Brent Hughes** and **Simon Wheeldon**.

24 - **Jim Vesey** traded from St. Louis to Winnipeg as future consideration in Tom Draper trade, February 28, 1991.

- **Tom Draper** traded from St. Louis to Winnipeg for future considerations.

25 - **Miloslav Horava** traded from NY Rangers to Quebec for **Stephane Guerard**.

26 - **Darcy Wakaluk** traded from Buffalo to Minnesota for Minnesota's 8th round choice in 1991 Entry Draft (**Jiri Kuntos**).

- **Rick Green** traded from Detroit to NY Islanders for **Alan Kerr** and future considerations.

30 - **Craig Fisher**, **Scott Mellanby** and **Craig Berube** traded from Philadelphia to Edmonton for **Dave Brown**, **Corey Foster** and **Jari Kurri**.

- **Brian Mullen** and future considerations traded from NY Rangers to San Jose for **Tim Kerr**.

- **Jari Kurri** and **Jeff Chychrun** traded from Philadelphia to Los Angeles for **Steve Duchesne**, **Steve Kasper** and Los Angeles' 4th round choice in 1991 Entry Draft (**Aris Brimanis**).

- **Steve Guenette** traded from Calgary to Minnesota for Minnesota's 7th round choice in 1991 Entry Draft (**Matt Hoffman**).

31 - **Alan Haworth** traded from Quebec to Minnesota for **Guy Lafleur**.

- **Tony Hrkac** traded from Quebec to San Jose for **Greg Paslawski**.

- **Rob Murray** and future considerations traded from Minnesota to Winnipeg for Winnipeg's 7th round choice in 1991 Entry Draft (**Geoff Finch**) and future considerations.

June

3 - **David Marcinyshyn** traded from New Jersey to Quebec for **Brent Severyn**.

- **Shane Churla** traded from San Jose to Minnesota for **Kelly Kisio**.

11 - **Marc Habscheid** traded from Detroit to Calgary for **Brian MacLellan**.

20 - **Jim Vesey** traded from Winnipeg to Boston for future considerations.

21 - **Steve Maltais** and **Trent Klatt** traded from Washington to Minnesota for **Shawn Chambers**.

- **Randy Burridge** traded from Boston to Washington for **Stephen Leach**.

- **NHL Supplemental Draft:**

San Jose	Jeff McLean	(North Dakota)
Quebec	Dave Trombley	(Clarkson)
Toronto	Pat McGarry	(Dalhousie)
NY Islanders	James Bonner	(Michigan Tech.)
Winnipeg	Brad Mullahy	(Providence)
Philadelphia	Angelo Libertucci	(Bowling Green)
San Jose	Mark Beaufait	(Northern Michigan)
Quebec	Chris Hynnes	(Colorado College)
Toronto	Joe McCarthy	(Vermont)
NY Islanders	Jack Duffy	(Yale)
Winnipeg	Jeff Jestadt	(Ferris State)
Philadelphia	Brendan Locke	(Merrimack)
Vancouver	Scott Meehan	(Lowell)
Minnesota	Dan O'Shea	(St. Cloud)
Hartford	Shaun Gravistan	(Alaska-Anchorage)
Detroit	Kelly Sorenson	(Ferris State)
New Jersey	Rob Kruhlak	(Northern Michigan)
Edmonton	Tom Holdeman	(Miami-Ohio)
Buffalo	Jamie Steer	(Michigan Tech.)
Washington	Mike Brewer	(Brown)
NY Rangers	Steve King	(Brown)
Pittsburgh	Greg Carval	(St. Lawrence)
Montreal	Jeff Torrey	(Clarkson)
Boston	Peter Allen	(Yale)
Calgary	Dean Larson	(Alaska-Anchorage)
Los Angeles	Brenden Creagh	(Vermont)
St. Louis	Chris McKee	(Babson)
Chicago	Dan Gravelle	(Merrimack)

22 - **David Babych** traded from Minnesota to Vancouver for **Tom Kurvers**.

- **Craig Ludwig** traded from NY Islanders to Minnesota for **Tom Kurvers**.

- **Randy Gilhen**, **Charlie Huddy**, **Jim Thomson** and the NY Rangers' 4th round choice in 1991 Entry Draft (previously acquired) traded from Minnesota to Los Angeles for **Todd Elik**.

- **Mikhail Tatarinov** traded from Washington to Quebec for Quebec's 2nd round choice in 1991 Entry Draft.

- **Tom Draper** traded from Winnipeg to Buffalo for future considerations.

July

22 - **Bryan Marchment** and **Chris Norton** traded from Winnipeg to Chicago for **Troy Murray** and **Warren Rychel**.

26 - **Mike Bullard** traded from Philadelphia to Toronto for future considerations.

31 - **Robin Bawa** traded from Washington to Vancouver for cash.

August

5 - **Shaun Sabol** traded from Philadelphia to New York Rangers for future considerations.

8 - **Don Biggs** traded from Philadelphia to New York Rangers for future considerations.

9 - **Jim Nesich** traded from Montreal to Minnesota for cash.

26 - **Paul Fenton** traded from Calgary to Hartford for Hartford's 6th round pick in 1992 Entry Draft.

NHL Schedule 1991-92
continued from inside front cover

* Afternoon Game

Game #	Visitor	Home
Thur. Dec. 5		
292	Quebec	Boston
293	Montreal	NY Islanders
294	Calgary	New Jersey
295	Washington	Philadelphia
296	Pittsburgh	San Jose
297	Los Angeles	Chicago
Fri. Dec. 6		
298	NY Rangers	Detroit
299	Edmonton	Winnipeg
Sat. Dec. 7		
300	Philadelphia	Boston
301	Buffalo	Hartford
302	Calgary	Montreal
303	Los Angeles	Quebec
304	Chicago	NY Islanders
305	Detroit	New Jersey
306	Pittsburgh	St Louis
307	Washington	Minnesota
308	Vancouver	Toronto
Sun. Dec. 8		
309	Boston	NY Rangers
310	Calgary	Buffalo
311	New Jersey	Philadelphia
312	Washington	Winnipeg
313	Minnesota	Chicago
314	San Jose	Edmonton
Mon. Dec. 9		
315	Montreal	Toronto
Tues. Dec. 10		
316	Boston	Quebec
317	St Louis	NY Islanders
318	NY Rangers	Pittsburgh
319	New Jersey	Minnesota
320	Calgary	Washington
321	Chicago	Detroit
322	Winnipeg	San Jose
323	Edmonton	Vancouver
Wed. Dec. 11		
324	St Louis	Buffalo
325	NY Islanders	Toronto
Thur. Dec. 12		
326	Montreal	Boston
327	Quebec	Detroit
328	Toronto	Philadelphia
329	Minnesota	Vancouver
330	Winnipeg	Los Angeles
331	Edmonton	San Jose
Fri. Dec. 13		
332	Hartford	Buffalo
333	NY Rangers	Washington
334	Pittsburgh	New Jersey
Sat. Dec. 14		
335	Toronto	Boston
336	NY Rangers	Hartford
337	Buffalo	Montreal
338	St Louis	Quebec
339	New Jersey	NY Islanders
340	*Chicago	Philadelphia
341	Washington	Pittsburgh
342	Detroit	Calgary
343	Minnesota	San Jose
344	Vancouver	Edmonton
345	Vancouver	Los Angeles
Sun. Dec. 15		
346	Philadelphia	Chicago
347	Detroit	Edmonton
Mon. Dec. 16		
348	St Louis	Montreal
349	San Jose	NY Rangers
Tues. Dec. 17		
350	NY Islanders	Hartford
351	Quebec	Washington
352	San Jose	Pittsburgh
353	Detroit	Vancouver
354	Minnesota	Los Angeles
355	Winnipeg	Calgary
Wed. Dec. 18		
356	Washington	Buffalo
357	Philadelphia	NY Rangers
358	Edmonton	Toronto
Thur. Dec. 19		
359	Pittsburgh	Boston
360	New Jersey	Hartford
361	Montreal	Chicago
362	Quebec	Calgary
363	NY Islanders	Philadelphia
364	San Jose	St Louis
365	Winnipeg	Vancouver
Fri. Dec. 20		
366	Edmonton	Buffalo
367	Toronto	Washington
Sat. Dec. 21		
368	Edmonton	Boston
369	Hartford	Montreal
370	Buffalo	Toronto
371	Quebec	San Jose
372	NY Islanders	St Louis
373	NY Rangers	Pittsburgh
374	Chicago	New Jersey
375	Philadelphia	Minnesota
376	Detroit	Los Angeles
377	Calgary	Winnipeg
Sun. Dec. 22		
378	Boston	Montreal
379	Quebec	Vancouver
380	Washington	Philadelphia
381	St Louis	Chicago
Mon. Dec. 23		
382	Buffalo	Hartford
383	Pittsburgh	NY Islanders
384	New Jersey	NY Rangers
385	Winnipeg	Toronto
386	Calgary	Edmonton
Thur. Dec. 26		
387	Hartford	Boston
388	Montreal	Quebec
389	New Jersey	NY Islanders
390	NY Rangers	Washington
391	Toronto	Pittsburgh
392	Chicago	St Louis
393	Minnesota	Winnipeg
394	San Jose	Los Angeles
Fri. Dec. 27		
395	Boston	Buffalo
396	Philadelphia	Vancouver
397	Winnipeg	Chicago
Sat. Dec. 28		
398	Hartford	Quebec
399	Buffalo	New Jersey
400	NY Rangers	NY Islanders
401	Philadelphia	Calgary
402	Pittsburgh	Washington
403	Detroit	Toronto
404	St Louis	Minnesota
405	Los Angeles	Edmonton
406	Vancouver	San Jose
Sun. Dec. 29		
407	Boston	Winnipeg
408	NY Islanders	Hartford
409	Montreal	Edmonton
410	Pittsburgh	NY Rangers
411	Washington	New Jersey
412	Detroit	Chicago
413	Los Angeles	Calgary
Mon. Dec. 30		
414	Toronto	Quebec
Tues. Dec. 31		
415	Boston	Detroit
416	St Louis	Buffalo
417	Montreal	Calgary
418	*NY Rangers	Winnipeg
419	New Jersey	Pittsburgh
420	Chicago	Minnesota
421	Vancouver	Los Angeles
Wed. Jan. 1		
422	*NY Islanders	Washington
Thur. Jan. 2		
423	Winnipeg	Boston
424	Quebec	Hartford
425	NY Rangers	Chicago
426	Pittsburgh	New Jersey
427	Minnesota	St Louis
428	Edmonton	Los Angeles
Fri. Jan. 3		
429	NY Islanders	Buffalo
430	Philadelphia	San Jose
431	Vancouver	Washington
432	Toronto	Detroit
Sat. Jan. 4		
433	Buffalo	Boston
434	Washington	Hartford
435	Montreal	San Jose
436	Quebec	NY Islanders
437	NY Rangers	New Jersey
438	Philadelphia	Los Angeles
439	*Winnipeg	Pittsburgh
440	Chicago	Toronto
441	Detroit	St Louis
442	Vancouver	Minnesota
443	Edmonton	Calgary
Sun. Jan. 5		
444	Minnesota	Chicago
445	Calgary	Edmonton
Mon. Jan. 6		
446	Winnipeg	NY Rangers
447	St Louis	Toronto
Tues. Jan. 7		
448	Buffalo	Philadelphia
449	NY Islanders	Detroit
450	Los Angeles	Pittsburgh
451	Minnesota	Washington
452	San Jose	Vancouver
Wed. Jan. 8		
453	Boston	Montreal
454	Quebec	Buffalo
455	St Louis	NY Rangers
456	Edmonton	Winnipeg
457	San Jose	Calgary
Thur. Jan. 9		
458	Quebec	Boston
459	Hartford	NY Islanders
460	St Louis	New Jersey
461	Los Angeles	Philadelphia
462	Toronto	Chicago
463	Minnesota	Detroit
Fri. Jan. 10		
464	Edmonton	Buffalo
465	Pittsburgh	Calgary
466	Los Angeles	Washington
467	Chicago	Winnipeg
Sat. Jan. 11		
468	Philadelphia	Boston
469	Hartford	Montreal
470	NY Rangers	Quebec
471	St Louis	NY Islanders
472	Toronto	New Jersey
473	Edmonton	Detroit
474	San Jose	Minnesota
Sun. Jan. 12		
475	NY Rangers	Buffalo
476	NY Islanders	Philadelphia
477	Los Angeles	New Jersey
478	*Pittsburgh	Vancouver
479	Washington	Chicago
480	San Jose	Winnipeg
Mon. Jan. 13		
481	Calgary	Montreal
482	Edmonton	Minnesota
Tues. Jan. 14		
483	Buffalo	NY Rangers
484	Calgary	Quebec
485	Detroit	NY Islanders
486	Chicago	Philadelphia
487	Washington	St Louis
488	Vancouver	Winnipeg
489	San Jose	Los Angeles
Wed. Jan. 15		
490	Boston	Hartford
491	Buffalo	New Jersey
492	Montreal	Minnesota
493	Vancouver	Edmonton
Thur. Jan. 16		
494	Hartford	Boston
495	Montreal	St Louis
496	Philadelphia	NY Islanders
497	Calgary	NY Rangers
498	Pittsburgh	Detroit
499	Washington	Los Angeles
500	Toronto	Chicago
Sat. Jan. 18		
All-Star Game at Philadelphia		
Tues. Jan. 21		
501	Winnipeg	Hartford
502	Buffalo	St Louis
503	Vancouver	Quebec
504	Philadelphia	Detroit
505	San Jose	Edmonton
Wed. Jan. 22		
506	Boston	Toronto
507	NY Rangers	Calgary
508	Los Angeles	Minnesota
Thur. Jan. 23		
509	Montreal	Boston
510	Buffalo	Pittsburgh
511	Quebec	Chicago
512	Toronto	NY Islanders
513	NY Rangers	Edmonton
514	Winnipeg	Philadelphia
515	Vancouver	Detroit
516	Los Angeles	St Louis
Fri. Jan. 24		
517	New Jersey	Washington
518	Calgary	San Jose
Sat. Jan. 25		
519	*Boston	Hartford
520	*Buffalo	Montreal
521	*Winnipeg	Quebec
522	*Pittsburgh	NY Islanders
523	Detroit	New Jersey
524	Philadelphia	Toronto
525	*Chicago	Minnesota
526	Vancouver	St Louis
527	Calgary	Los Angeles
528	Edmonton	San Jose
Sun. Jan. 26		
529	*Hartford	Montreal
530	*Winnipeg	Buffalo
531	*Pittsburgh	Washington
Mon. Jan. 27		
532	Minnesota	Boston
533	Chicago	Calgary
Tues. Jan. 28		
534	Boston	Quebec
535	Minnesota	Hartford
536	NY Rangers	San Jose
537	Washington	Philadelphia
538	Winnipeg	Pittsburgh
539	St Louis	Los Angeles
540	Edmonton	Vancouver
Wed. Jan. 29		
541	Buffalo	Detroit
542	New Jersey	Montreal
543	Quebec	Toronto
544	Chicago	Edmonton
Thur. Jan. 30		
545	Calgary	Boston
546	NY Islanders	Pittsburgh
547	NY Rangers	Los Angeles
548	Minnesota	Philadelphia
549	Chicago	Vancouver
550	St Louis	San Jose
Fri. Jan. 31		
551	Hartford	Edmonton
552	Montreal	Buffalo
553	Quebec	Winnipeg
554	New Jersey	Detroit
Sat. Feb. 1		
555	Buffalo	Boston
556	Hartford	Vancouver
557	Detroit	Montreal
558	Philadelphia	NY Islanders
559	NY Rangers	Minnesota
560	New Jersey	Toronto
Sat. Feb. 1		
561	St Louis	Pittsburgh
562	Calgary	Washington
563	Chicago	Los Angeles
Sun. Feb. 2		
564	*Quebec	Edmonton
565	Calgary	NY Islanders
566	St Louis	Philadelphia
567	*San Jose	Winnipeg
Mon. Feb. 3		
568	Detroit	Pittsburgh
569	Toronto	Minnesota
Tues. Feb. 4		
570	Boston	Winnipeg
571	Hartford	San Jose
572	Washington	Buffalo
573	Montreal	Vancouver
574	NY Islanders	Los Angeles
575	Philadelphia	New Jersey
Wed. Feb. 5		
576	Montreal	Edmonton
577	Quebec	Calgary
578	Pittsburgh	NY Rangers
579	Washington	Detroit
580	Minnesota	Toronto
581	Chicago	San Jose
Thur. Feb. 6		
582	Boston	Philadelphia
583	Hartford	Los Angeles
584	NY Islanders	Vancouver
585	New Jersey	St Louis
Fri. Feb. 7		
586	Minnesota	Buffalo
587	NY Islanders	Edmonton
588	NY Rangers	Washington
589	Toronto	Detroit
590	Calgary	Winnipeg
Sat. Feb. 8		
591	*New Jersey	Boston
592	Montreal	Toronto
593	*Philadelphia	Quebec
594	*Los Angeles	Pittsburgh
595	Chicago	St Louis